C0000 00127 0939

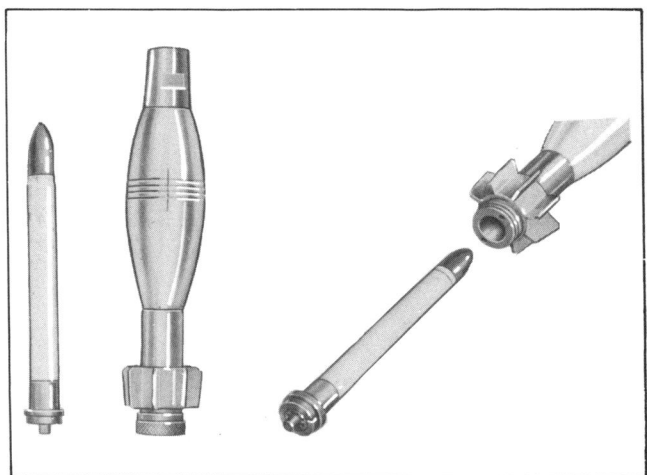
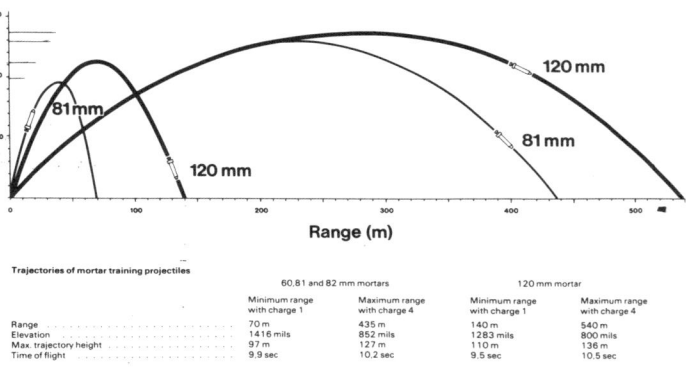

JANE'S INFANTRY WEAPONS

Edited by Denis H. R. Archer M.A.

Order of Contents

World Sales Distribution

Jane's Yearbooks
Paulton House, 8 Shepherdess Walk
London N1 7LW, England

All the World
except
United States of America and Canada:
Franklin Watts Inc
730 Fifth Avenue
New York, NY 10019

Editorial communication to:
The Editor, Jane's Infantry Weapons
Jane's Yearbooks, Paulton House, 8 Shepherdess Walk
London N1 7LW, England
Telephone 01-251 1666

Advertisement communication to:
The Advertisement Manager
Jane's Yearbooks, Paulton House, 8 Shepherdess Walk
London N1 7LW, England
Telephone 01-251 1666

*Classified List of Advertisers
The various products available from the advertisers in this edition are listed alphabetically under about sixty headings.

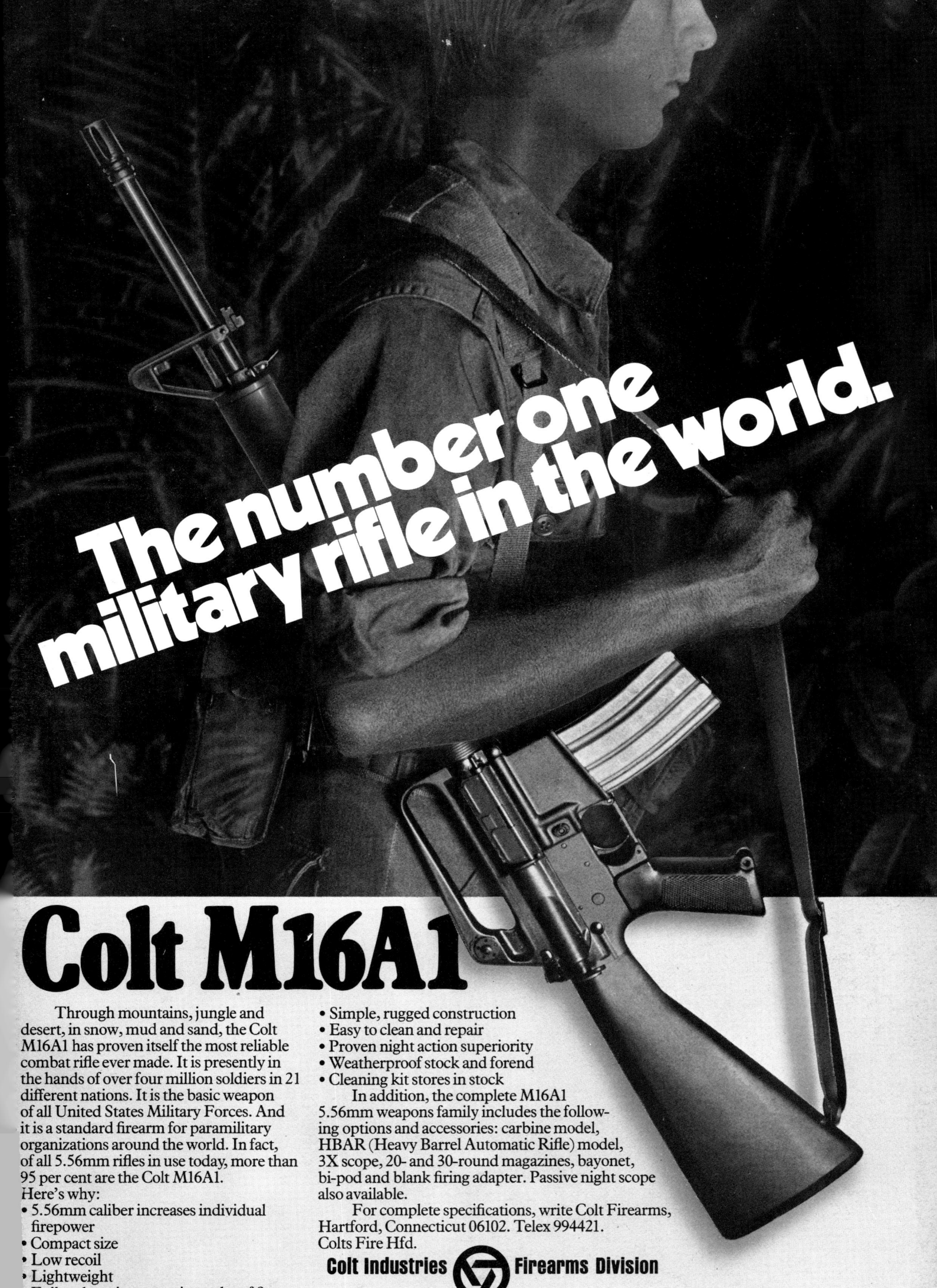

The number one military rifle in the world.

Colt M16A1

Through mountains, jungle and desert, in snow, mud and sand, the Colt M16A1 has proven itself the most reliable combat rifle ever made. It is presently in the hands of over four million soldiers in 21 different nations. It is the basic weapon of all United States Military Forces. And it is a standard firearm for paramilitary organizations around the world. In fact, of all 5.56mm rifles in use today, more than 95 per cent are the Colt M16A1.
Here's why:
- 5.56mm caliber increases individual firepower
- Compact size
- Low recoil
- Lightweight
- Full and semi-automatic modes of fire
- Simple, rugged construction
- Easy to clean and repair
- Proven night action superiority
- Weatherproof stock and forend
- Cleaning kit stores in stock

In addition, the complete M16A1 5.56mm weapons family includes the following options and accessories: carbine model, HBAR (Heavy Barrel Automatic Rifle) model, 3X scope, 20- and 30-round magazines, bayonet, bi-pod and blank firing adapter. Passive night scope also available.

For complete specifications, write Colt Firearms, Hartford, Connecticut 06102. Telex 994421.
Colts Fire Hfd.

Colt Industries ⊘ **Firearms Division**

JANE'S INFANTRY WEAPONS
ALPHABETICAL LIST OF ADVERTISERS
1977 EDITION

Detection, Observation and Aiming at Low Light Level

Thermal detection unit type WZI with image intensifier telescope type BN 21S
— designed and developed by AEG-Sondertechnik
This passive unit for detecting heat-emitting objects supplies — when combined with night viewing units — essential additional information being a decisive feature in practical applications.

Image intensifier telescope type BN 21
— designed and developed by AEG-Sondertechnik
A passive binocular viewing unit for orienting and observation purposes at low light level which is light-weight and handy, but at the same time sturdy and reliable.

Observation and aiming unit type ORION
— designed and developed by ELTRO/Zeiss
A passive image intensifier unit for observation and — in combination with infantry weapons — for aiming at low light level. This highly-efficient unit has been tested by the army, is easy to handle and reliable.

IR-observation and aiming unit type B8-V
— designed and developed by Eltro
An active image converter unit with IR-searchlight and battery for use at low light level with and without weapons. The IR-illuminated scene invisible to the human eye is made visible by the image converter tube. A unit which has been field tested and proven in military use.

Eltro GmbH, Gesellschaft für Strahlungstechnik · D-6900 Heidelberg 1 · Telex 04-61811

ALPHABETICAL LIST OF ADVERTISERS – *continued*

This helicopter is leaving on a mission,
at the end of which
it will have scattered 2,200 mines
throughout an area
50 metres wide and over 1 km long.
All this will be done in a few seconds,
creating a trap network
of third-generation mines that cannot
be crossed by men and tanks.
These mines cannot be identified on the
ground as they are specially designed
to immediately take on the appearance of the
land onto which they are dropped,
nor can they be removed in the event they
should be identified.

JANE'S INFANTRY WEAPONS
CLASSIFIED LIST OF ADVERTISERS
1977 EDITION

The companies advertising in this publication have informed us that they are involved in the fields of manufacture indicated below:

AIR DEFENCE SYSTEMS
Oerlikon-Bührle
Rheinmetall

AIRCRAFT (CANNONS)
Oerlikon-Bührle

AIRCRAFT JET ENGINES
Fabrique Nationale Herstal

AMMUNITION
Fabrique Nationale Herstal

AMMUNITION LOADING PLANTS
Alsetex
Eurometaal
Fabrique Nationale Herstal
G.I.A.T.
Israel Military Industries
PRB
Rheinmetall
Snia Viscosa

ANTI-RIOT WEAPONS
Beretta
Fabrique Nationale Herstal
Schermuly
Snia Viscosa
Wallop Industries

ARMAMENT SYSTEMS
G.I.A.T.
Israel Military Industries
MAB
Rheinmetall
Snia Viscosa
Valtec Italiana

ARMOURED FIGHTING VEHICLES
G.I.A.T.
Rheinmetall
Steyr-Daimler-Puch

ARMOURED FIGHTING VEHICLES (WEAPONS)
Oerlikon-Bührle

AUTOMATIC PISTOLS
Fabrique Nationale Herstal
SIG
Steyr-Daimler-Puch

AUTOMATIC RIFLES
Beretta
Fabrique Nationale Herstal
Israel Military Industries
Rheinmetall
SIG
Sterling Armament
Steyr-Daimler-Puch

BAYONETS
Beretta
Sterling Armament

BINOCULARS
Pilkington P.E.
Sopelem

BOMBS
Eurometaal
Israel Military Industries
PRB

CABLES, ELECTRICAL AND ELECTROMECHANICAL
Standard Telephone and Cables

CARBINES
Fabrique Nationale Herstal
Israel Military Industries
Sterling Armament

COASTGUARD EQUIPMENT
Wallop Industries

ELECTRO OPTIC SYSTEMS
Bonaventure International
Dyno Industries
Eltro
Pilkington P.E.
Rank Pullin
Singlepoint Avionics

EXPLOSIVES
Dyno Industries

FIRE CONTROL EQUIPMENT
G.I.A.T.
Oerlikon-Bührle

GUIDANCE SYSTEMS, OPTICAL
G.I.A.T.
Pilkington P.E.

GUN SYSTEMS
G.I.A.T.
Oerlikon-Bührle
Rheinmetall

GYROSCOPE
G.I.A.T.

HEAD-UP DISPLAYS (OPTICS)
Pilkington P.E.

HEATED WINDOWS
Pilkington P.E.

INFLATABLE CRAFT
RFD Group

INFLATABLE LIFE JACKETS
RFD Group

INFLATABLE LIFE RAFTS
RFD Group

INFRA-RED EQUIPMENT
Eltro
G.I.A.T.
Pilkington P.E.
Sopelem

LASER RANGEFINDERS
Eltro
Sopelem

LAW ENFORCEMENT AND RIOT CONTROL EQUIPMENT
Fabrique Nationale Herstal
Pilkington P.E.
Schermuly

LENSES
Bonaventure International
Pilkington P.E.
Rank Pullin
Singlepoint Avionics
Sopelem

MACHINE GUNS
Fabrique Nationale Herstal
Steyr-Daimler-Puch

METAL DETECTORS
Bonaventure International

MISSILES
G.I.A.T.

MORTARS
Thomson-Brandt

MOVING MAP DISPLAYS (OPTICS)
Pilkington P.E.

MUNITIONS AND ORDNANCE
Alsetex
Borletti
Eurometaal
G.I.A.T.
Israel Military Industries
Oerlikon-Bührle
PRB
Rheinmetall
Snia Viscosa
Sofremas
Thomson-Brandt
Wallop Industries

MOVING TARGET SYSTEMS (Small Arms)
A.T.A.

NAVAL DEFENCE SYSTEMS
Oerlikon-Bührle
Rheinmetall
Snia Viscosa

NIGHT VISION EQUIPMENT
Bonaventure International
Eltro
Pilkington P.E.
Rank Pullin
Sopelem

PHOTOGRAPHIC EQUIPMENT
Bonaventure International

PORTABLE ANTI-TANK WEAPONS
G.I.A.T.
Israel Military Industries
PRB
Snia Viscosa

PROPELLANTS
Dyno Industries
G.I.A.T.
Israel Military Industries
PRB
Snia Viscosa

PROTECTIVE CLOTHING
RFD Group

LIGHTWEIGHT
BODY
ARMOUR
LTD

Front

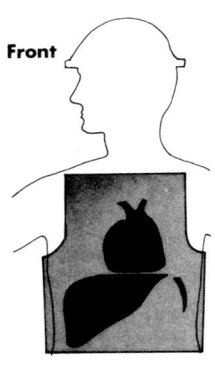

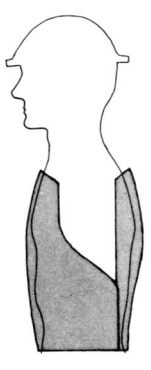

Back

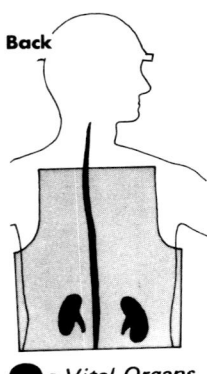

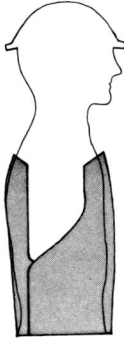

● = Vital Organs

LIGHTWEIGHT BODY ARMOUR has been designed and manufactured in England. It is particularly intended to protect against 9mm sub-machine gun.
The vests are lightweight, flexible and comfortable to wear at all times.
Backface Trauma is virtually zero against 9mm 2Z at 4 metres.
Maximum protection to vital organs.

SPECIFICATION
British made, 100% waterproof ballistic insert. Removable washable outer shell. All stitching in ballistic thread. Three models are produced. The unique design ensures that a comb nation of model 39A worn under the shirt can, by the addition of model 2Z over the shirt, be rapidly changed to mcdel 39B.

BALLISTIC RESISTANCE

MODEL	WEIGHT	COVERAGE	THICKNESS	RESISTANCE	VELOCITY	COMMENT
2Z	1.3K	.38 sq. m.	0.7cm	UK 2Z	430m/sec	Factory loaded
39A	3.0K	.38 sq. m.	1.5cm	Norma 39A	355m/sec	
39B	4.3K	.38 sq. m.	2.3cm	Norma 39B	420m/sec	Armour piercing

Sub Machine Guns 9mm — .45 cal. UZI Schmeisser MP 40 Star, Ingram, Thompson, Sterling, Beretta.
Hand Guns 9mm FMJ — .357 Magnum .45 Cal .44 Magnum.

LIGHTWEIGHT BODY ARMOUR vests are designed to sustain following bursts of 9mm sub-machine gun fire.
LIGHTWEIGHT BODY ARMOUR will stop most military and commercial ammunition. Certain rounds may cause trouble and we recommend that purchasers conduct their own tests with experimental panels.

P.O. Box 6, Banbury, Oxfordshire OX16 8LJ, England. Telephone: Banbury (0295) 58359. Telex: 837279 G.

PYROTECHNIC ILLUMINATORS AND SIGNALS
Eurometaal
Israel Military Industries
Oerlikon-Bührle
PRB
Rheinmetall
Schermuly
Wallop Industries

RADIO COMMUNICATION EQUIPMENT
G.I.A.T.

RECONNAISSANCE
G.I.A.T.
Oerlikon-Bührle
Sofremas

RECOVERY SYSTEMS, AIRCRAFT
G.I.A.T.
RFD Group

RIFLES
Beretta
Fabrique Nationale Herstal
Israel Military Industries
Sofremas
Sterling Armament
Steyr-Daimler-Puch

ROCKETS
Alsetex
G.I.A.T.
Israel Military Industries
Oerlikon-Bührle
PRB
Snia Viscosa
Thomson-Brandt
Wallop Industries

ROCKET LAUNCHERS
Israel Military Industries
Oerlikon-Bührle
PRB
Thomson-Brandt
Wallop Industries

SEA AND SUBMARINE SIGNALS
Wallop Industries

SELF-PROPELLED FIELD ARTILLERY
G.I.A.T.
Israel Military Industries
Rheinmetall
Snia Viscosa

SELF-PROPELLED ANTI-AIRCRAFT EQUIPMENT
G.I.A.T.
Oerlikon-Bührle

SHELTER, INFLATABLE, PORTABLE
G.I.A.T.
RFD Group
Steyr-Daimler-Puch

SIGHTS
Bonaventure International
Pilkington P.E.
Rank Pullin
Singlepoint Avionics
Sopelem

SILENCED WEAPONS
PRB
Sterling Armament

SIMULATORS
G.I.A.T.
Eltro
Rheinmetall
Wallop Industries

SMOKE DEVICES
Alsetex
Eurometaal
Israel Military Industries
PRB
Schermuly
Wallop Industries

SUB-CALIBRE CONVERSIONS
RFD Group

SUB-MACHINE GUNS
Israel Military Industries
Sterling Armament
Steyr-Daimler-Puch

TANKS
G.I.A.T.
Oerlikon-Bührle
Steyr-Daimler-Puch

TARGET SYSTEMS (Small Arms)
A.T.A.

TIMERS, TIMING SYSTEMS
Borletti

TRACKING EQUIPMENT
Oerlikon-Bührle
Pilkington P.E.

TRAINING AIDS
A.T.A.
Wallop Industries

UNDERWATER SYSTEMS
Rheinmetall

VEHICLE, MILITARY (TRACK & WHEEL)
G.I.A.T.
Fabrique Nationale Herstal
Steyr-Daimler-Puch

WEAPON SIMULATORS
RFD Group

WEAPON SYSTEMS
Beretta
Fabrique Nationale Herstal
G.I.A.T.
Israel Military Industries
MAB
Oerlikon-Bührle
Rheinmetall
SIG
Snia Viscosa

WEAPON TRAINING SYSTEMS
RFD Group

WEAPON TRAINING SYSTEMS (Small Arms)
A.T.A.

GIAT:
prime contractor from concept to combat~readiness

The major land weapon's industry of a nation. An instrument of French
political independence. Prime contractor for sophisticated defence
systems developed and delivered to stringent French military specifications.
As a State organisation, the GIAT makes available outside France,
a range of oustanding equipment, series-produced to the same high technical
criteria imposed by French defence agencies.
In ten nationally integrated centres for research, development and production,
the industrial capacities and technological innovations of 17,000 skilled workers,
led by 2,500 engineers and technicians, confirm the standing of GIAT
among the mechanical engineering giants of Europe.

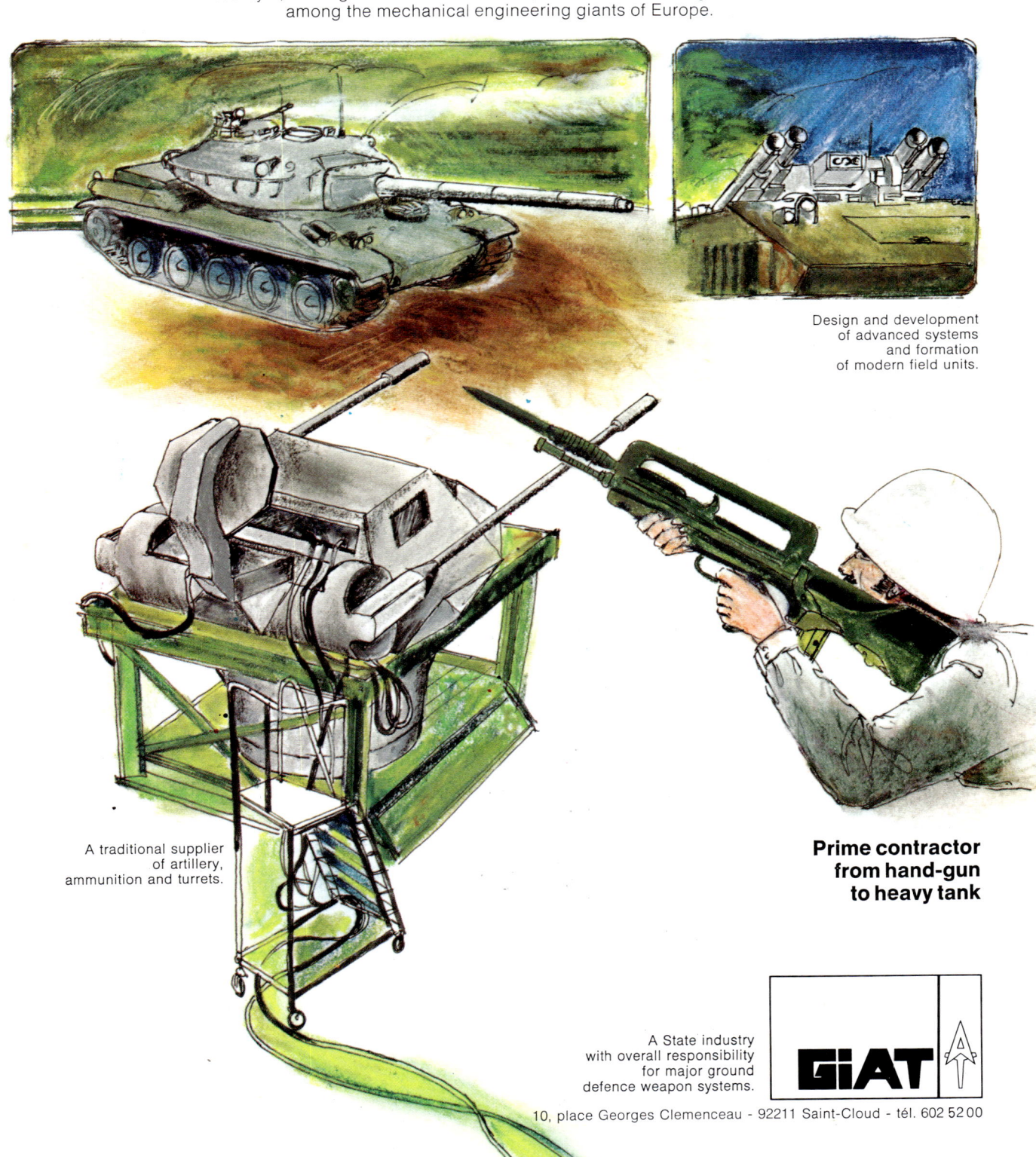

Design and development
of advanced systems
and formation
of modern field units.

A traditional supplier
of artillery,
ammunition and turrets.

**Prime contractor
from hand-gun
to heavy tank**

A State industry
with overall responsibility
for major ground
defence weapon systems.

GiAT

10, place Georges Clemenceau - 92211 Saint-Cloud - tél. 602 52 00

Plessey P6/2 Metal Detector

Description:
The P6/2 equipment consists of a waterproof electronic unit and a set of operator- interchangeable waterproof probes. The operating mode is pulsed induction. Target detection is indicated audibly by a loudspeaker or plug-in earphone(s). Switched sensitivity and response times are provided. Power is from internal batteries or an external source (via an adaptor). An in-built battery check is provided. The function switch, loudspeaker, probe and earphone sockets are located on a control panel at the top of the electronic unit. The electronic unit is carried in a slung webbing haversack for manpack operation.

Four types of probe can be provided as standard, each for a specific purpose. A connection cable terminated in a quick release plug is integral with each probe.

P6A/2 is a tubular ferrite probe suitable for searches in bushes, streams and rugged urban and rural environments.

P6E/2 Open Loop Probe is a lightweight probe, for ground search applications.

P6F/2 is a short robust probe for general searches in restricted environments.

P6G/2 is a light easy-to-use probe designed for the searching of persons.

Special probes can be designed for particular applications e.g. the P6C/2 sledge probe.

Electro-magnetic compatibility
The equipment has been designed to give the following performance over the frequency range 50 to 500MHz. When fitted with a P6A/2 or P6F/2 probe and an MDA7/2 earpiece the equipment is capable of operating within 4 metres of a 1W, hand-held radio transmitter or within 6 metres of a vehicle-mounted 10W radio transmitter without malfunctioning, blocking, or causing interference to the receiver in the radio station.

Maintenance
The equipment is designed so that it can be maintained with the aid of conventional workshop test equipment.

STATUS:
The equipment is in service use with the British Army as Detecting Set L4A1, JS Catalogue Number Z5/6665-99-965-0734. This equipment has been sold overseas.

CHARACTERISTICS:
Typical detection range for P6E/2 Probe
Approx. 220mm with 2p coin or 250mm² copper, 18 G
Approx. 400mm with pistol.

MANUFACTURER:
Plessey Radar Limited,
Station Road, Addlestone, Surrey, KT15 2PW.
Tel : (0932) 47282 Telex : 262329.

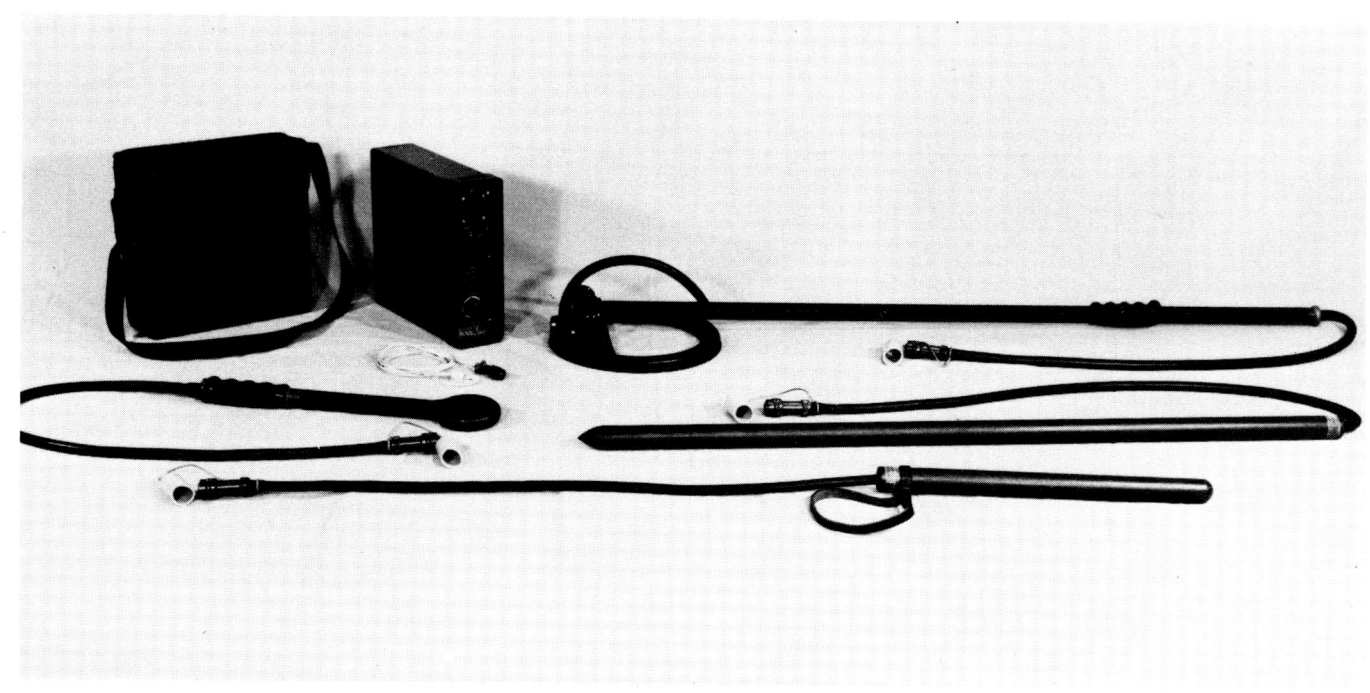

603P225

Information and security systems

An integrated capability for high technology security systems and special purpose equipments in the following fields:

Search and Detection
Intruder Alarms
Perimeter Protection
Secure Communications
Police Systems
Information Handling

 **PLESSEY**
electronic systems

PLESSEY RADAR

Addlestone Surrey
United Kingdom KT15 2PW
Telephone: Weybridge (0932) 47282

603 P228

Leadership has always been the science of seeing in the dark.

Leadership has always been the science of seeing in the dark.

These days – literally. Rank passive nightsights lead the world. So do the people who are equipped with them. In armoured vehicles, on heavy weapons, small arms, light field artillery, for night surveillance, search and reconnaissance operations and artillery and mortar fire control.

They give high resolution images and exceptional performance at low ambient light levels. No artificial lighting needed.

All Rank nightsights have automatic brightness control image intensifiers which compensate for different light intensities. And all Rank nightsights detect infra red devices as though they were white light.

All are easy to operate, and many spares are common to a range of Rank sights, making them really economic in use.

Ask Rank for details of their nightsight range. Study the facts and get a clear picture. You'll never be in the dark again.

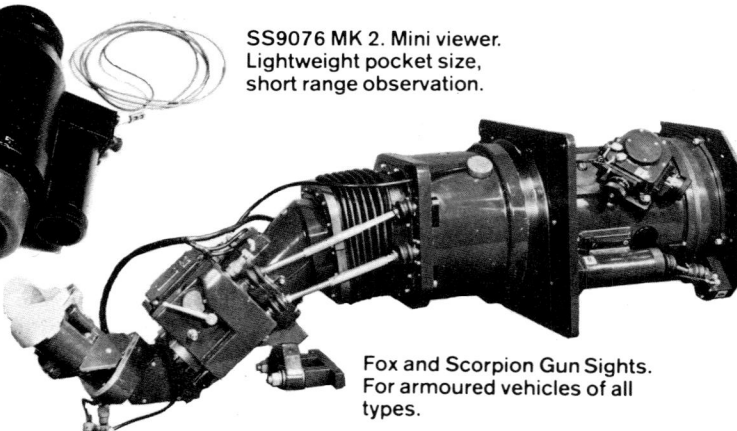

SS32 Night Viewing Device.
An artillery and mortar fire control device with a range from 20 metres to infinity.

SS30 Crew Served Weapon Sight.
For recoil-less anti-tank guns and surveillance.

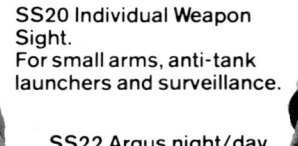

SS20 Individual Weapon Sight.
For small arms, anti-tank launchers and surveillance.

SS22 Argus night/day armoured vehicle sight. Gunner's sight or commander's viewer/ sight for wide range of armoured vehicles including main battle tanks.

SS9076 MK 2. Mini viewer. Lightweight pocket size, short range observation.

Fox and Scorpion Gun Sights. For armoured vehicles of all types.

RANK PRECISION INDUSTRIES

RANK PULLIN CONTROLS, DEBDEN
Langston Road, Loughton, Essex.
Telephone: 01-508 5522
Telex: 23855
Cables: Microptics, Loughton.

[15]

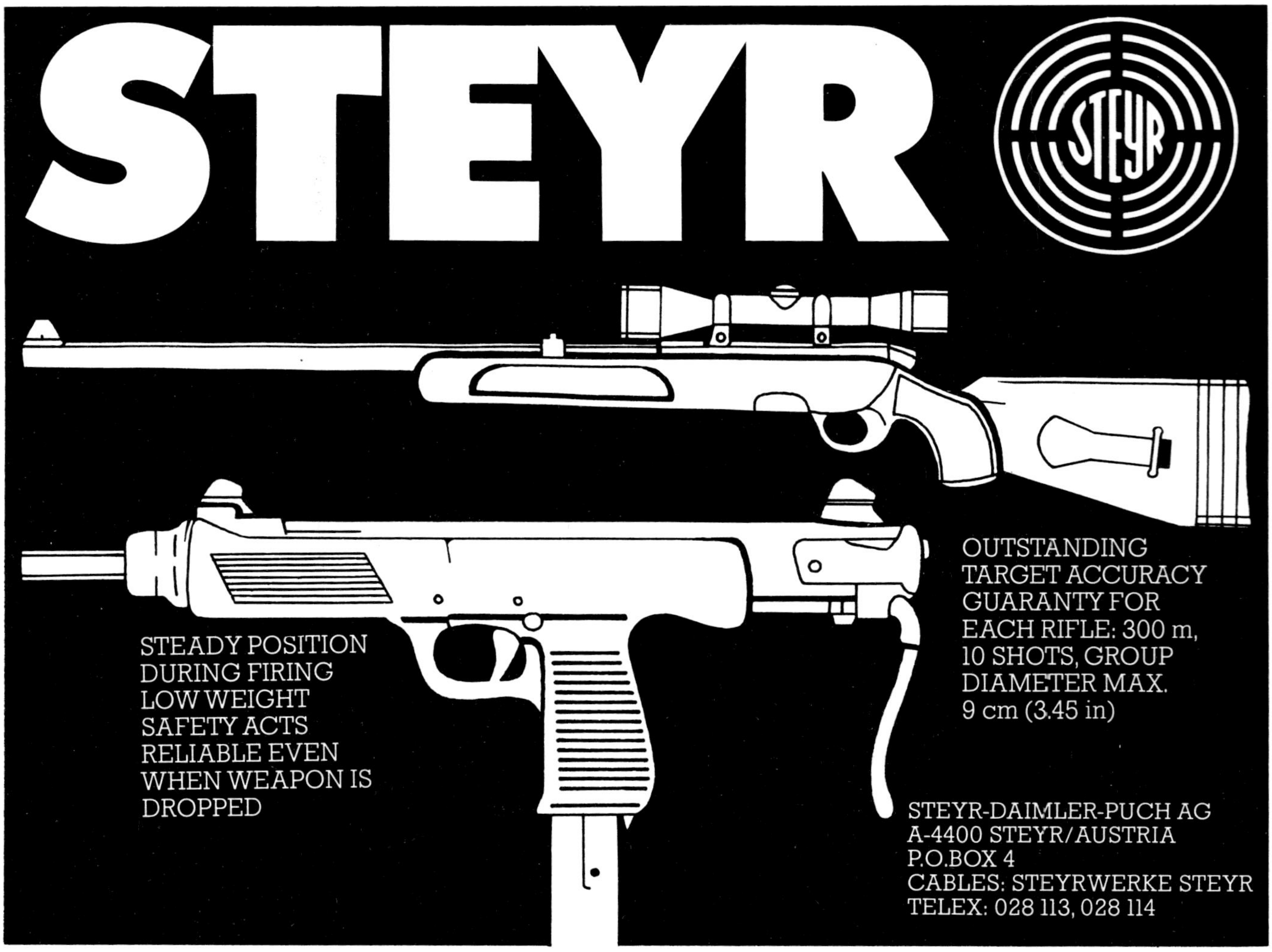

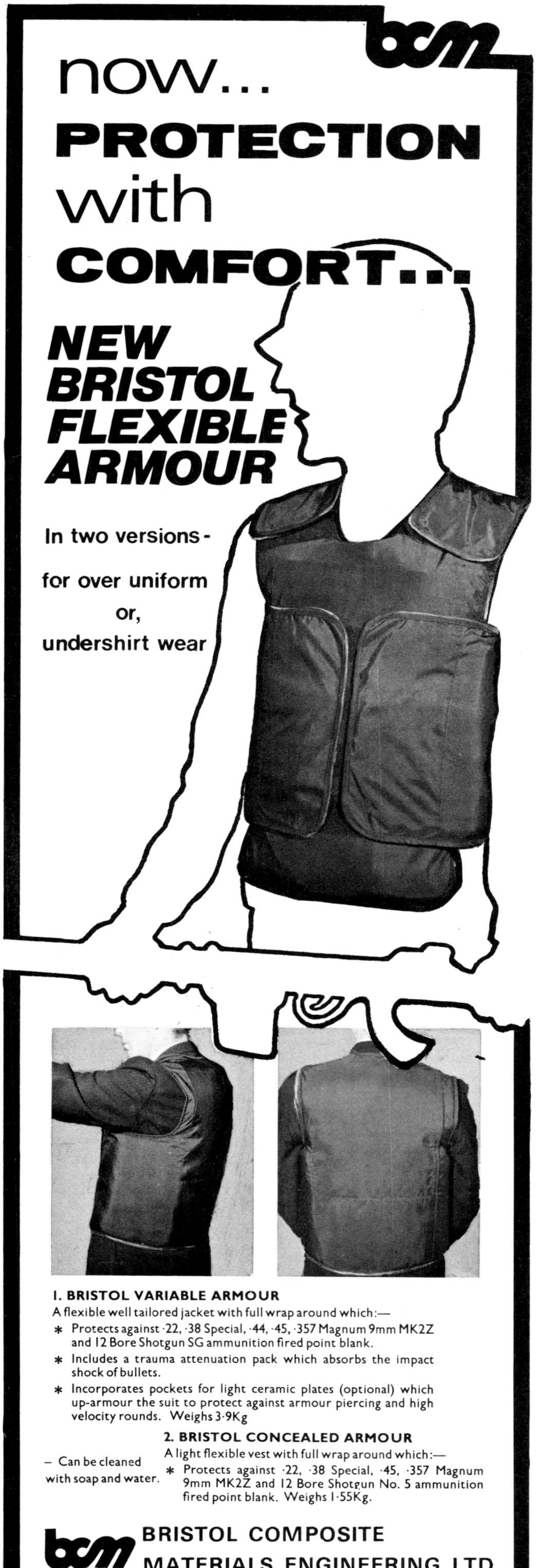

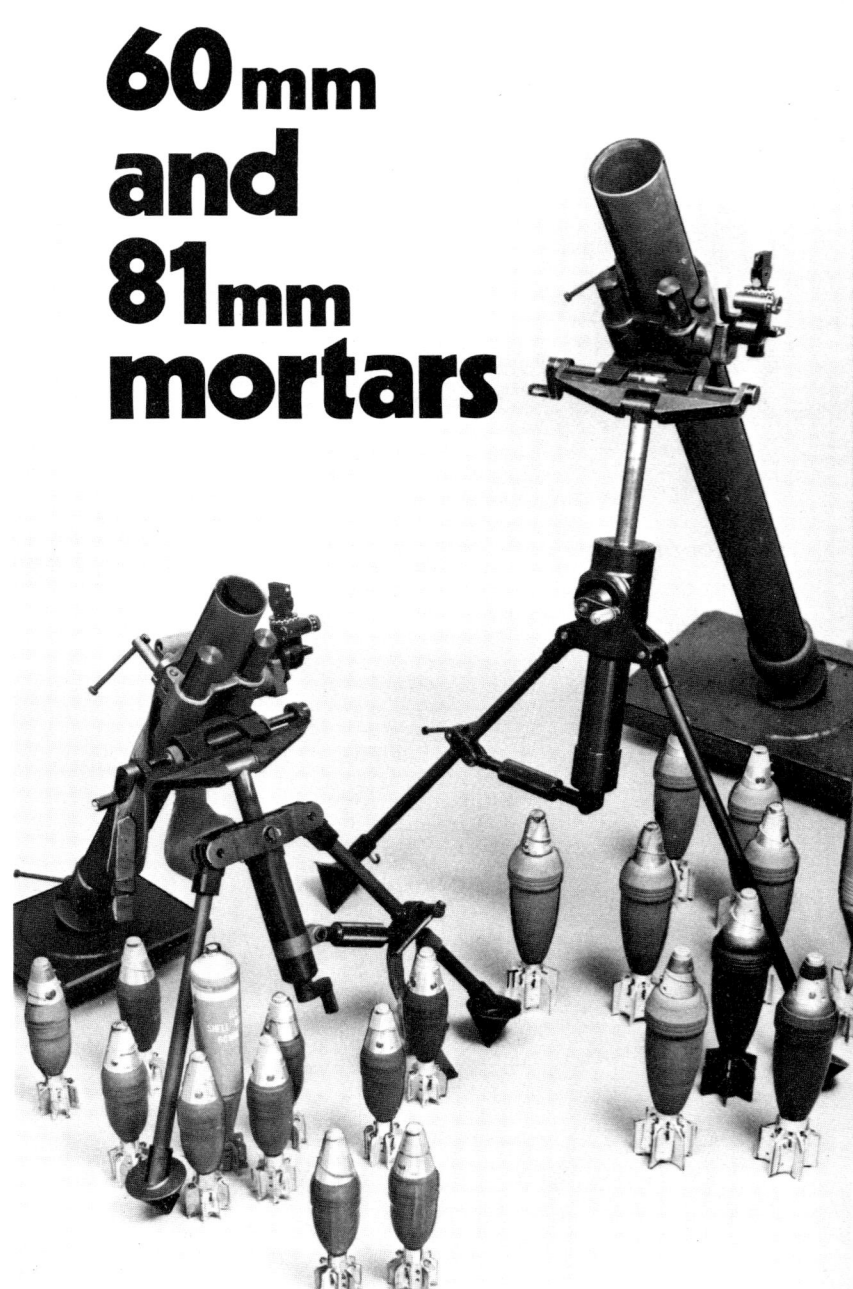

5.56mm
7.62mm
9 mm.
0.5"
20 mm.
30 mm.
52 mm.
75 mm.
81 mm.
82 mm.
90 mm.
105 mm.
* 106 mm.
* 120 mm.
155 mm.
175 mm

this is our range of calibers from the smallest to the largest-ammunition to illuminate, pierce & blast your target

All our ammunition passes a severe acceptance test and is thoroughly scrutinized. We bear responsibility for the whole range and all the components:

■ Propellants & explosives ■ Metal parts & hardware ■ Fuzes ■ Fillings (Pyrotechnic chemicals for smoke and illumination, high explosives of different types)

All are manufactured and co-ordinated under one roof: Our organization.

For further information, please apply to:
I.M.I. – Israel Military Industries, P.O.Box 7055, Tel Aviv, Israel.

★ Some calibers cover various sorts of ammunition. For example: The 120 mm. ILLUMINATING MORTAR SHELL:

Designed and manufactured by I.M.I., it is original and advanced in concept, embodying radically new factors:

● Location of the parachute assembly in the tail section, allowing the internal volume of the shell body to be devoted entirely to the illumination assembly – which thus contains a maximum amount of pyrotechnic composition.

● A unique accelerating and decelerating sequence, involving a miniature rocket motor and a small braking parachute, which prevents the main parachute from opening until the discarded tail section is well clear and collision is impossible.

● Superior **effectiveness** due to high illuminating power, long burning and slow descent: 1,200,000 candle-power during 60 seconds.

JANE'S

FOR INTERNATIONAL REFERENCE

Established over three quarters of a century, **JANE'S** is a name synonymous with accuracy and authority throughout the world. Free of bias and opinion with every fact checked and re-checked, the nine **Jane's Yearbooks** are *the* recognised reference works on Defence, Transport, Finance and Ocean Technology.

JANE'S YEARBOOKS
Paulton House
8 Shepherdess Walk, London N1
Telephone 01-251 1666
Telex 23168
Cables MACJANES LDN

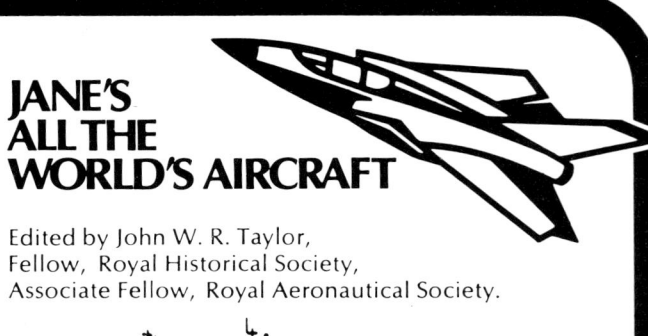

JANE'S ALL THE WORLD'S AIRCRAFT

Edited by John W. R. Taylor,
Fellow, Royal Historical Society,
Associate Fellow, Royal Aeronautical Society.

JANE'S FIGHTING SHIPS

Edited by Captain J. E. Moore, Royal Navy

JANE'S WEAPON SYSTEMS

Edited by Ronald Pretty

JANE'S INFANTRY WEAPONS

Edited by Denis H. R. Archer

JANE'S SURFACE SKIMMERS

Edited by Roy McLeavy

JANE'S OCEAN TECHNOLOGY

Edited by Robert L. Trillo

JANE'S FREIGHT CONTAINERS

Edited by Patrick Finlay

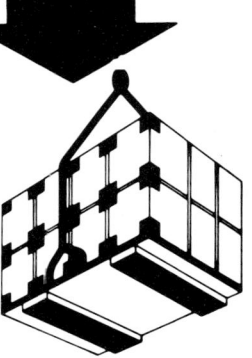

JANE'S WORLD RAILWAYS

Edited by Paul Goldsack

JANE'S MAJOR COMPANIES OF EUROPE

Edited by Jonathan Love

The AN PVS-2 System

The AN/PVS-2 system 75 is a proven and reliable AN/PVS-2 individual served weapon night vision sight (starlight scope) which has been modified to incorporate the advances which have been made in night vision since the starlight scope was originally designed for the U.S. Government. The advances have been incorporated to increase the performance and/or rated specifications of the AN/PVS-2, however, the basic parts of the AN/PVS-2 system 75 will not require drastic changes in supply, maintenance and training operations, but will result in the higher performance which can now be achieved in night vision.

The basic scope utilizes a 18mm first generation three stage image tube intensifer with an integral automatic brightness control (ABC) circuit,

a 95mm, T1.6. catadioptric objective with high efficiency anti-reflection (HEA) coatings, an integral variable illuminated projected reticle, a highly accurate azimuth and elevation boresight adjustment mechanism, and a standard AN/PVS-2 25mm EFL, monocular eyepiece, inherent in the design of the unit is the ability to use either an 18mm first generation, an 18mm second generation, or a 25mm second generation image intensifier tube. The ability to interchange existing optics (objectives and eyepieces) also increases the possibility of utilizing any night vision stock which is available. (It should be noted that the usage of objectives which were designed for scopes with external boresight sight mechanisms shall require modification to incorporate an integral projected reticle).

The AN/PVS-2 system 75 is a device which has been proven and tested under combat conditions. The modifications which have been made incorporate the higher reliability and performance components which have been developed in the subsequent developments phases of night vision equipment. The AN/PVS-2 system 75 provides a basic scope whose reliability has been proven and whose performance has been increased through the incorporation of later developments. Since standard components are utilized, modifications of the scope capability is not restricted to one type and/or one source.

18mm 1st Generation Sight (95mm Lens)

Optical		Resolution (Middle)	35 1p/mm. Min.
Magnification (System)	3.8X.	(Edge)	32 1p/mm. Min.
Field of View	10'	Light Amplification	40 – 60,000
Focus Range	4 metres to inf.	Distortion	6% measured from radius of 7mm
Objective			
Focal Length	95mm	**Electrical**	
T Number	1.6	Power Source	2.76V D.C. Mallory TR 132
Eyepiece		Normal Operating Time per battery	24 hours
Focal Length	25mm		
Eye Relief	20mm	**Mechanical**	
Diopter Range	+−4	Length	37 cm
Image Tube		Diameter	8.6cm
Type	18mm 3 stage cascade with ABC.	Weight	1.9 kilo
Photocathode	S − 20		

18mm 2nd Generation Sight (95mm Lens)

		Photocathode	S25
		Screen Phosphor	P20
		Resolution (Middle)	30 1p/mm
Optical		(Edge)	30 1p/mm
Magnification	3.8X.	Light amplification (preset)	10,000 to 50,000 or 50,000 to 100,000
Field of View	10'		
Focus Range	4 metres to inf.	Distortion	14% measured from a radius of 7mm
Objective			
Focal Length	95mm	**Electrical**	
T Number	1.6	Power Source	2.76V D.C. Mallory TR 132
Eyepiece		Normal Operating time per battery	24 hours
Focal Length	25mm		
Eye Relief	20mm	**Mechanical**	
Diopter Range	+−4	Length	25mm
Image Tube		Diameter	8.6mm
Type	18mm. MCP Inverter	Weight	1.36 kilo

18mm 2nd Generation Crew Served Sight (158mm Lens)

		Screen Phosphor	P20
		Resolution (Middle)	30 1p/mm
Optical		(Edge)	30 1p/mm
Magnification	6.32X.	Light Amplification (preset)	10,000 to 50,000 or 50,000 to 100,000
Field of View	6.7'		
Focus Range	10 metres to inf.	Distortion	14% measured from a radius of 7mm
Objective			
Focal Length	158mm	**Electrical**	
T Number	1.6	Power Source	2.76V D.C. Mallory TR 132
Eyepiece		Normal Operating time per battery	24 hours
Focal Length	25mm		
Eye Relief	20mm	**Mechanical**	
Diopter Range	+−4	Length	33cm
Image Tube		Diameter	15cm
Type	18mm. MCP. Inverter	Weight	2.7 kilo
Photocathode	S25		

ICW SYSTEMS

ICW SYSTEMS
Grellenger 35
4028 Basel, Switzerland

Telex 63972 ICW CH
Telephone 061 - 41 55 14
Cable: ICWBASLE

TIRRENA S.p.Az.

Practice rockets

Practice ammunition

Weapons and ammunition's parts

Shoulder borne and transportable flamethrowers

Studies on prototypes and special weapons

ENERGA rifle-grenade
for anti-tank
firing training (for rifle
7,62 NATO)

Head for 3.5"
practice anti-tank
rockets
(88 mm bazooka)

Flamethrower with
electronic ignition Model
T 148A (shoulderborne)

Mortar for smoke
and tear bombs
Model TIR-22 X

OFFICE: **Via del Quirinale, 22 - 00187 ROME**
Tel. 487100 - 487155 - 487823
Cable "TIRSO" Telex 68444

PLANTS: **Via Salaria, km. 13,650 - 00138 ROME**
Tel. 6919704
Via Salaria, km. 12,800 - 00138 ROME
Tel. 691988 - 6919753

FFV
Anti-Tank Programme

The FFV Anti-Tank Programme provides the capability
of deploying an effective integrated AT-defence
system for medium and short ranges.

Anti-Tank System FFV 550
84 mm RCL Carl-Gustaf
Now equipped with a rocket-assisted HEAT Shell and a
Range and Lead Finding Sight, the well proven 84 mm
Recoilless Gun Carl-Gustaf meets the tactical requirement for
maximum effect against heavily armoured targets at
combat ranges up to 700 metres.

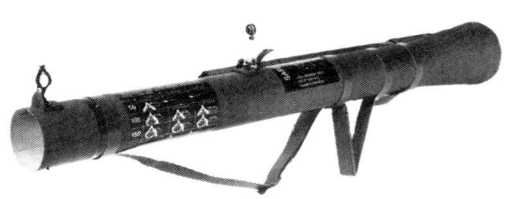

Miniman
Light Anti-Tank Weapon
MINIMAN is designed to provide all units with the capability
of repulsing massed armoured enemy attacks at ranges
up to 250 metres. Its HEAT Shell is effective against
modern fighting vehicles including those
equipped with protective devices.

Anti-Tank Mine FFV 028
With Hollow-Charge Effect
Detonation over the complete width of the tank is achieved
by the Anti-Tank Mine FFV 028 which incorporates an
influence fuze system. Featuring the hollow-charge effect,
the mine will inflict penetration of the hull of the
tank and beyond armour damage of devastating
effect inside the tank.

FFV ORDNANCE DIVISION
S - 631 87 Eskilstuna • Sweden

[22]

RFD Moving Target Training Systems

RFD MARKSMAN ADVANCED TRAINER

This trainer has been developed to overcome some of the major problems encountered when attempting to achieve realistic, cost effective substitutes for small arms field training. When used in a controlled environment with variable light conditions and sound effects, the Marksman Advanced Trainer provides a near equivalent to battle experience and presents moving targets for weapons from pistols to anti-tank guns.

Films of tactical situations with moving targets in varying surroundings are projected on to a screen at which live sub-calibre ammunition can be fired from normal weapons. When a shot is fired, an acoustic trigger stops the projector and holds the 'target' frame as a still. The shot hole is illuminated from behind to allow an immediate assessment of accuracy. After the assessment period, which can be varied by the Instructor, the film restarts ready for the next target.

A smaller version (MIT) has been designed to meet the special needs of police forces, internal security services, etc.

Up to five men can select targets and fire at the screen; infantry and anti-tank training can be combined.

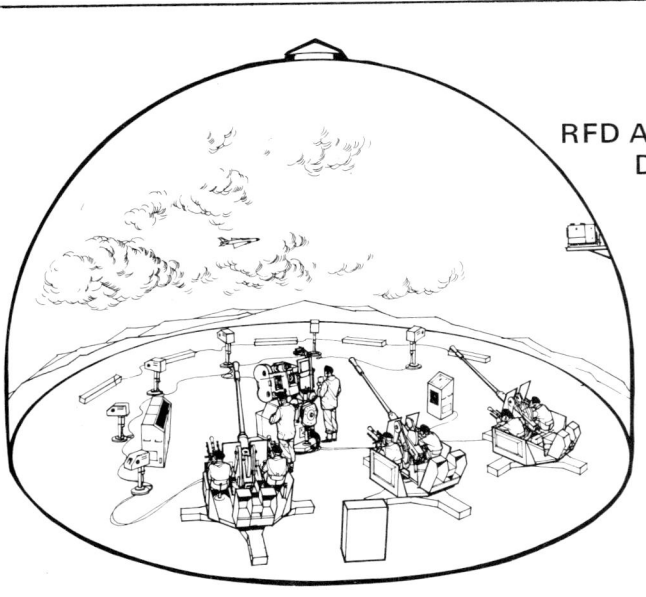

RFD ANTI-AIRCRAFT DOME TRAINER

The RFD Anti-Aircraft Dome Trainer meets the need for a training system which is cost-effective and offers the highest possible realism to troops under instruction.

The system is housed in a domed theatre and can be adapted for training with most anti-aircraft weapons. Films of aircraft, attacking from all angles at various speeds, are projected on to the interior of the dome against a scenic background while loud speakers relay sound track of aircraft and battle noises. No rounds are fired but shots and hits are electronically recorded on a control console.

For training naval gunners, a 'rolling platform' which simulates the pitch and roll of a ship, can be installed.

Designed and produced by:

RFD SYSTEMS ENGINEERING LTD., 77 CATTESHALL LANE, GODALMING, SURREY, GU7 1LH. ENGLAND

Telephone: Godalming (04868) 4122   Cables: Airships Godalming   Telex: 859233

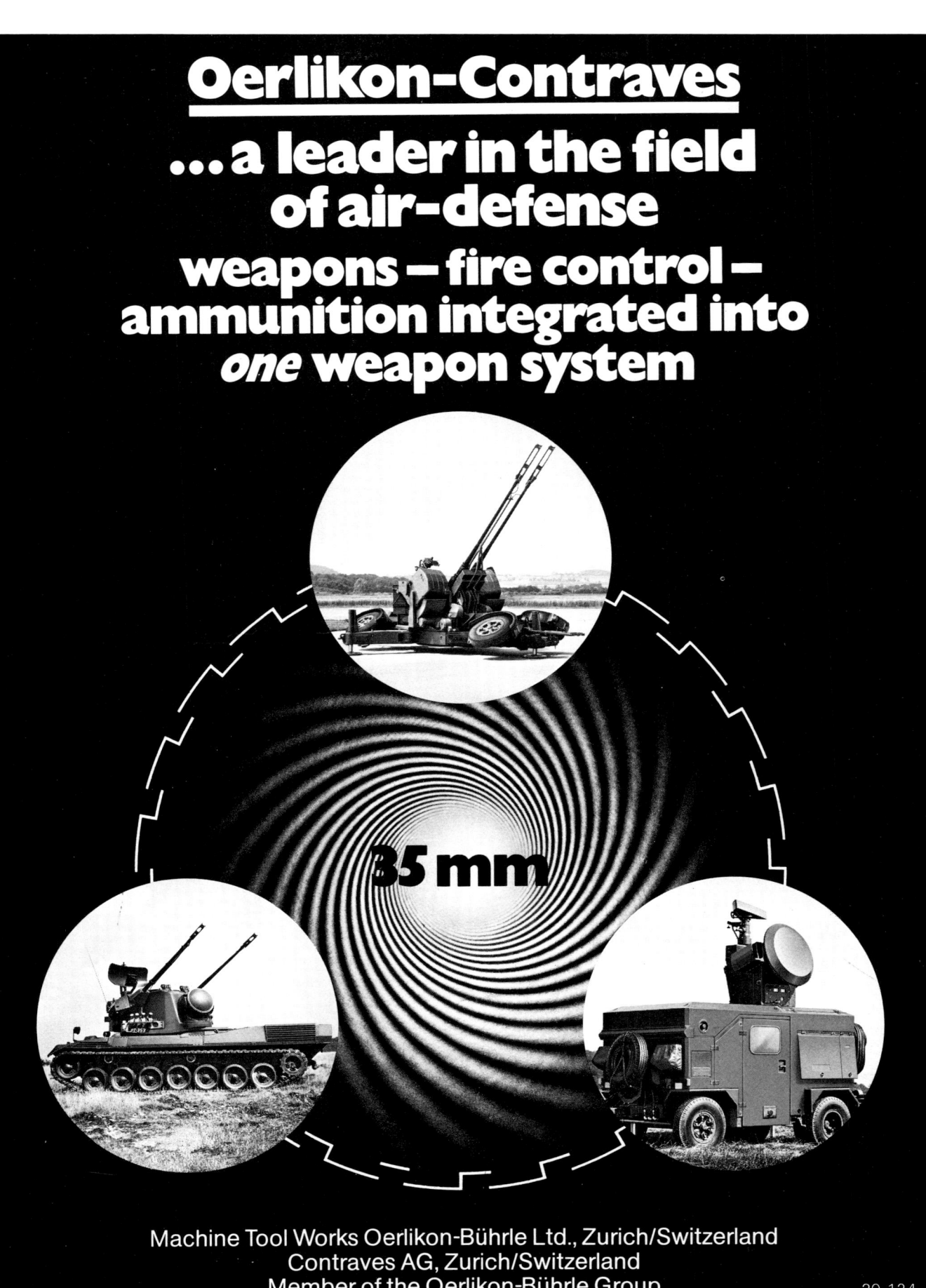

Oerlikon-Contraves

...a leader in the field of air-defense

weapons – fire control – ammunition integrated into *one* weapon system

35 mm

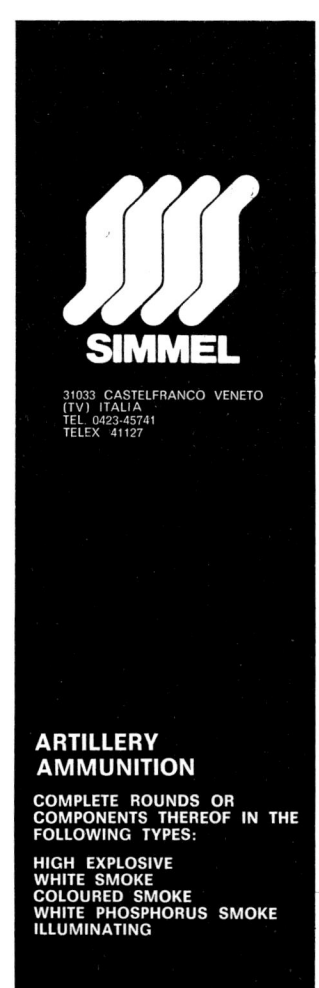

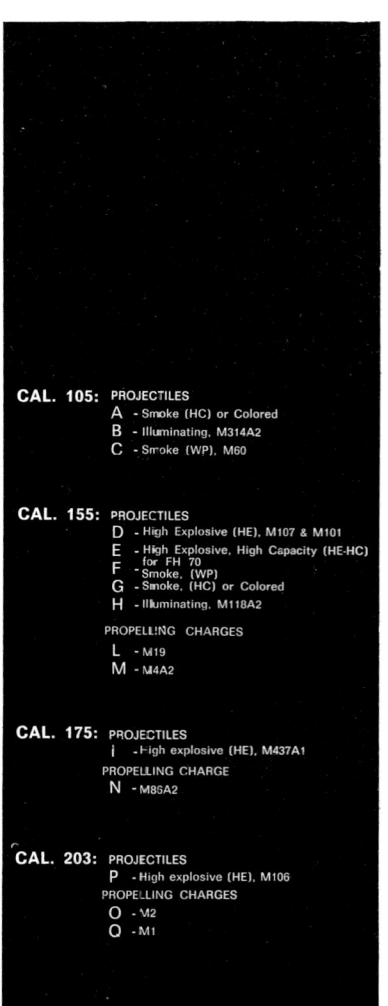

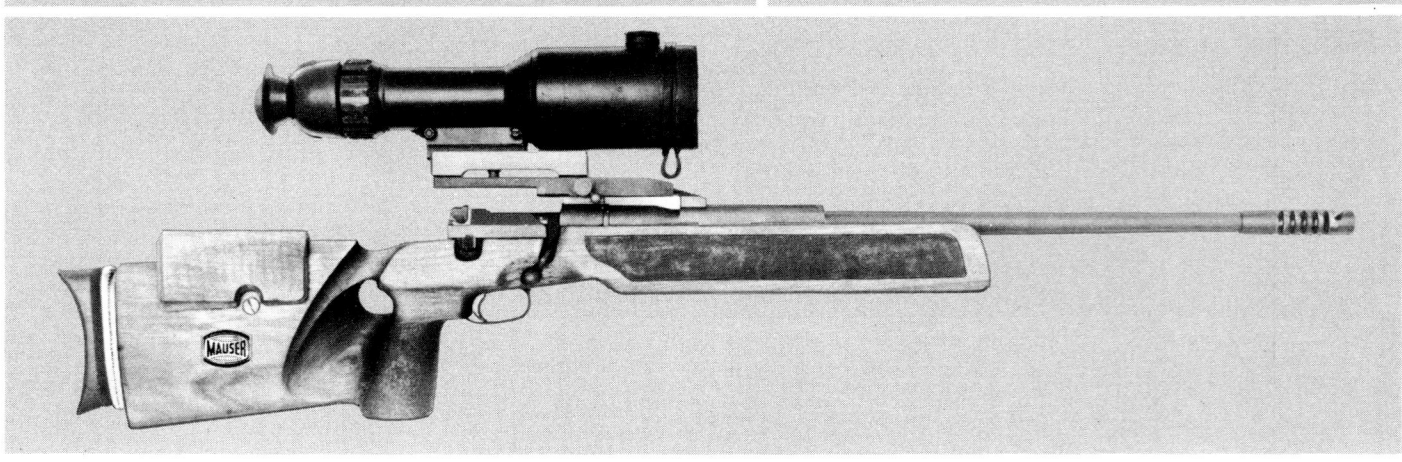

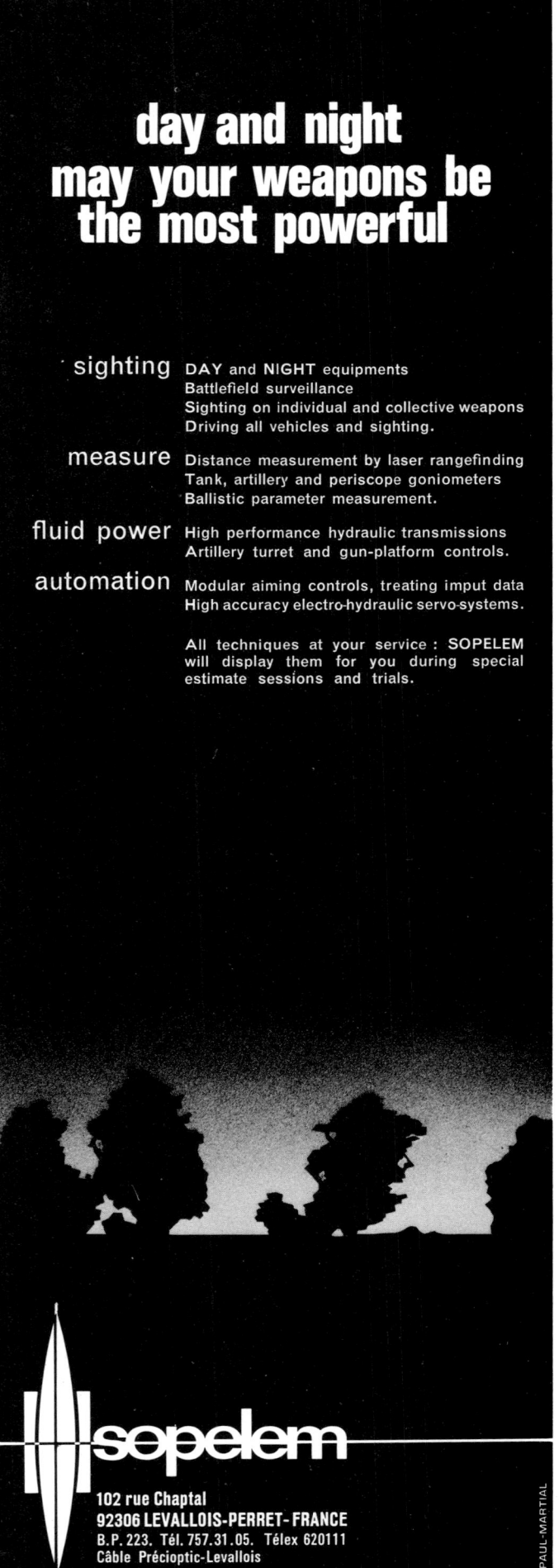

STERLING

STERLING SUB MACHINE GUN 9 mm MARK 4 (L2A3)

The standard sub machine guns with the British Forces and in service in over 80 countries in the world. Continues to function in the most adverse conditions of mud, sand, snow and ice. Exceptionally accurate and of renowned reliability. Illustrated with optional bayonet. Also available as a police carbine, i.e. semi-automatic fire only.

STERLING PATCHETT SUB MACHINE GUN 9 mm MARK 5 (L34A1)

Developed to meet a requirement for a fully silenced weapon. It retains all the other features of the Mark 4 and uses standard 9mm Parabellum ammunition. The bullet is slowed to sub-sonic speeds by the silencing arrangements giving a truly silent weapon. There is nothing to wear out in the built in silencer and thousands of rounds can be fired without attention except normal cleaning. Also available as a police carbine.

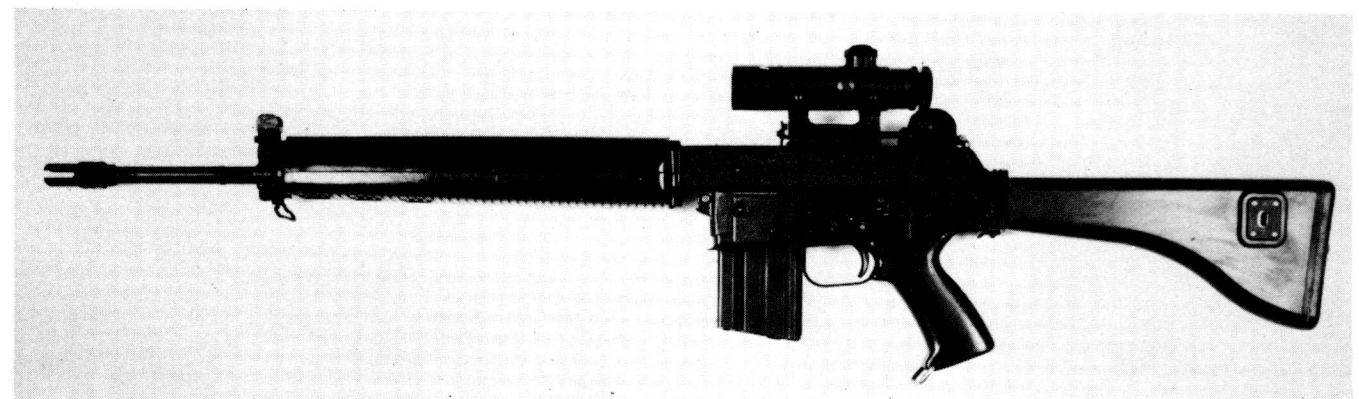

STERLING AR 18 5·56 mm COMBAT RIFLE
(Shown with immediately detachable 3x telescopic sight)

Designed by Armalite Inc. of the USA who were also responsible for the AR 15 which was re-designated the M16 and made in large quantities for the US Forces by Colts.

By improving on the best design features of the AR 15, the AR 18 gives outstanding performance and is considerably cheaper to manufacture than the M16 as extensive use is made of pressings and machine turned parts with a design requiring a minimum of close tolerances.

Armalite and Sterling have come to an agreement whereby the AR 18 is being manufactured by Sterling and is known as the Sterling AR 18. A shortened version in sub machine gun configuration, known as the Sterling AR 18S, is also available. Also available as a police carbine as the Sterling AR 180.

All weapons are fitted with folding butts.

STERLING ARMAMENT COMPANY LIMITED

Factory: Rainham Road South
Dagenham, Essex, England
Tel: 01 595 2226
Telex: FTERLN G
Telegrams: Sterling Dagenham

JANE'S
INFANTRY WEAPONS

THIRD EDITION

EDITED BY
DENIS H. R. ARCHER M.A.

1977

I.S.B.N. 0 354 00549 9

JANE'S YEARBOOKS

LONDON

Compact and reliable
The MK 20 Rh 202

High firepower, simple operation, functional reliability even under extreme conditions and low recoil forces are characteristic features of the 20 mm MK 20 gun.

Its short installed length and separate belt feed make the weapon particularly suitable for

The MK 20 Rh 202 mounting with belt feed.

incorporation in various types of mounting such as single, twin and ring mountings, and on aircraft, helicopters and ships.

The MK 20 is designed for ground combat and low-level air defense. Developed by Rheinmetall, it is now in series production.

JANE'S INFANTRY WEAPONS 1977

EDITED by DENIS H. R. ARCHER M.A.

The Editor has been assisted in the compilation of this edition as follows:

CHRISTOPHER F. FOSS
AREA WEAPONS
ARMOURED INFANTRY VEHICLES

CONTENTS

"JANE'S" is a registered trade mark

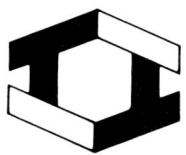

FOREWORD

This book is concerned with military hardware, with what it does, who makes it and where it is to be found, and with current and possible future trends in the development of new weapons and associated equipment. Most of it is devoted to descriptions of devices that already exist in service, in reserve or in the late stages of development. To the extent that the facts are ascertainable, therefore, these descriptions are purely factual and largely historical.

Neither the deployment of current weapons and equipment nor the future development of new devices can be sensibly discussed, however, otherwise than against the background of the global military scene; and this in turn must be considered in the context of international political developments, and particularly of the continuing change in the location and relative influence of the centres of world political power. In order to anchor this discussion to its primarily military theme, however, it will probably be helpful to set the military scene first.

WORLD MILITARY EXPENDITURE

A recent estimate [1] puts the global total of military expenditure at nearly three hundred thousand million dollars a year. So vast a figure is difficult for ordinary mortals to interpret; and even such comparisons as that between total military and state education expenditure (they are much the same) do little to clarify matters, although they may enthuse those who enjoy moralising on such subjects. Some analysis of the total, however, may be helpful: for example, well over half and possibly as much as two-thirds of the global total is accounted for – in roughly equal proportions – by the USA and the USSR and more than three-quarters can be attributed to the two giant powers and their NATO and WTO allies. In population terms this means that more than half the money is being spent by less than one-eighth of the world's population, and more than three-quarters by less than a quarter.

In the estimates for expenditure on military research and development [2] an even greater concentration of effort is apparent: somewhere between seventy and ninety per cent is accounted for by the USA and the USSR and about another ten per cent by France and the UK. In terms of human effort it has been estimated [3] that about four hundred thousand qualified scientists and engineers are engaged on military research and development projects.

To complete the picture of world military expenditure it would be helpful to add details of the international trade in arms. Unfortunately, however, the value of this trade cannot be assessed even to the degree of approximation used in compiling the other data. In terms of identifiable official contracts for major weapons and systems the recent annual value of the international trade would appear to have been around seven billion dollars, of which nearly forty per cent was imported by the industrialized countries of Europe, North America, Australasia and Japan, about thirty per cent by Middle Eastern countries and about seven per cent each by Far Eastern, North African and South American countries. These figures and proportions, however, take virtually no account of the large official trade in small arms, ammunition and explosives and they ignore altogether the substantial and increasing private traffic in arms. It would not be surprising to learn that the value of trade in these omitted categories is at least as great as that in major weapon systems. [4]

TOO HIGH?

Be that as it may, the data presented above, inaccurate though they undoubtedly are, provide a reasonable basis for some general observations on the general pattern of military spending; and the first of these must surely be that in some areas the rate of expenditure is far too high. Expenditure per head of population in the USA and USSR is about four times the average for the remaining NATO and WTO countries and probably about fifteen times the average for the rest of the world [5]. Even allowing for the dominant roles which the two big powers are playing and seeking to play in world affairs and for the widely-held view that expenditure in some other NATO countries, at least, is too low, the discrepancy in level seems excessive.

Some commentators would argue that the discrepancy is a simple consequence of the Russo-American arms race in which each country is seeking to establish a position of military dominance over the other. So far as Russia is concerned there may well be much truth in this assessment: certainly the strength of her strategic rocket forces, naval surface and subsurface forces and fixed and mobile anti-aircraft defences have increased enormously compared with those of any other nation in the past two decades; and there have been significant though less dramatic improvements in other areas of military development. In the United States, on the other hand, the accent has for some time been on qualitative improvements in weapons and systems; and although it is difficult to quantify total military strength in any way that permits clear-cut comparisons of two such enormous and diverse distributions of manpower and materials, it will probably be agreed that American military expenditure has resulted in a smaller advance in total operational capability than has that of the Russians – although the Americans are probably still justified in their claim to enjoy technological superiority.

It is probably reasonable, therefore, to regard Russian military expenditure policy over the past twenty or thirty years as having been largely determined by a desire to achieve parity with or superiority over American military power; and when it is also observed that the US authorities have from time to time found it necessary to institute emergency development or deployment programmes to redress some perceived adverse imbalance it can fairly be said, at least, that there *has been* an arms race between the two countries. During the course of this race, moreover, the Russians have moved from a position of considerable inferiority to the Americans in all military respects save that of armed manpower to one in which they could expect to compete with their rivals on fairly level terms, and have in the process greatly narrowed the technological gap between the two nations.

IS THERE STILL AN ARMS RACE?

All this, however, does not necessarily validate the view that there is a continuing arms race between the two great powers: indeed one commentator has observed that "though it is customary to speak of the arms race between the United States and the Soviet Union, it is worth considering the possibility that there is no race – just two military bureaucracies, each doing its own thing" [6]. In support of this alternative view it can be argued that much of Russia's current military budget is directed towards qualitative improvements involving the replacement rather than, as hitherto, the augmentation of older weapons and systems. There is thus a broad similarity between the programmes of the two nations: in some areas of exceptional operational capability, such as anti-submarine warfare and possibly the development of laser weapons, the competition between them could perhaps still be described as a race in that there is the theoretical possibility that a large measure of success could give one nation a sudden advantage over the other; but across the broad spectrum of their activities it is not obvious that their enormous investment is now producing any marked change in their relative – or indeed absolute – operational capabilities.

---

[1] *SIPRI Yearbook 1976* (Stockholm International Peace Research Institute) put the total for 1975 at $280 billion (p. 123). The sums included here and elsewhere for Russian expenditure are by no means universally agreed and those for the Chinese People's Republic contain a large element of guesswork.

[2] Estimated at $20-25 billion annually in *SIPRI Yearbook 1975* (p. 102). Again the Chinese element is very difficult to assess.

[3] Ibid.

[4] *SIPRI Yearbook 1976* p.16 suggests a figue of $10-12 billion annually but points out that the rate of increase since the 1973 Arab-Israeli war has been explosive and shows no sign of slackening.

[5] There are, of course, special areas in which *per capita* expenditure is exceptionally high. Israel has been at the top of the league in recent years but Saudi Arabia may well take over from her.

[6] John C. Garnett. *Some Constraints on Defence Policy Makers* in *The Management of Defence* ed. Laurence Martin (Macmillan 1976) p.45.

STC. Supreme in its field: supreme in the field.

Standard Telephones and Cables Limited is a major supplier of many types of cables and associated products to the armed forces of the world.

STC's capability includes field telephone cables, special aerial arrangements, control of wire guided missiles, fibre optics applications and connectors for field power distribution networks. And these are only some of STC's products and technology now in use in the field, whose operating ability in a wide range of environments from the Tropics to the Arctic has been well established.

Development work by STC has resulted in new equipment which combines the highest standards of electrical and mechanical efficiency with minimum weight and long-term reliability under the most arduous conditions.

Standard Telephones and Cables Limited, Hydrospace Division, Department J4, Christchurch Way, Greenwich, London SE10 0AG.

Standard Telephones and Cables Limited
A British Company of ITT

As already noted, it is extremely difficult to quantify these capabilities, but it seems evident that to whatever extent they can be measured it must be in relation to some reasonable conflict postulate; and it is certainly arguable – and has been vigorously argued [7] – that some of the more expensive developments in the American programme (and, by implication, in the Russian programme also) have little relevance to any reasonably probable future conflict. Without necessarily accepting all the critical arguments that have been deployed against US defence policies in recent years (and it is one of the great strengths of the American system that its critics can be both so well informed and at liberty to air their criticisms in public) it may nevertheless be agreed that the main thrust of US military development has been aimed at inhibiting, by a show of superior operational capability, a direct conflict with Russia in the form of all-out strategic nuclear war or of a major clash on the ground in Europe – or indeed of both.

PROBABLE AND IMPROBABLE WARS

There are certainly grounds for regarding both conflicts as unlikely to be generated deliberately in the near future, if only because it is not obvious that either side could derive any benefit from such contests, but on the other hand there are no obvious grounds for recommending a significant unilateral relaxation. So far as the possible strategic nuclear confrontation is concerned, moreover, the mere fact that the US authorities have direct access to better information regarding Russian activities and capabilities than is available to any other body of people outside Russia puts those who would criticise their strategic defence policies in a weak position.

What can be said with some confidence, however, is that the framework of international relationships and concomitant freedoms of thought and action which the USA and its allies and friends are at least ostensibly committed to preserve is threatened more severely and more immediately in many other places than it is in Europe. Currently the most obvious source of probable trouble is southern Africa, but the less-publicised recent developments in Asia and South America give little cause for comfort to those who value individual liberty.

That these threats, and particularly that in Africa, have been exacerbated by the quite astonishing ineptitude of Western foreign policy in some of the key areas is one aspect of the global pattern: of more immediate relevance here, however, is the effect which excessive concentration on the European theatre has had on the ability of Western nations to contend with problems elsewhere.

Setting aside the more recent developments in strategic nuclear weapons – such as the Trident SLBM, M-X ICBM and strategic cruise missile programmes, the B-1 bomber and the continuing work on advanced ballistic missile re-entry systems, all of which are currently absorbing much research and development expenditure but proportionately rather less in terms of procurement – much of the hardware section of the US defence budget is concerned with high-technology weapon systems appropriate to a major war against an opponent armed with weapons of comparable sophistication, and particularly to a war with Russia on the European continent and adjacent oceans. This survey is not a proper place for a detailed commentary on weapon systems that have little or nothing to do with the main contents of this book; but it is necessary to the subsequent argument to draw attention to such developments as the controversial AWACS airborne air defence warning and control system and the multiplicity of new combat aircraft costing up to twenty million dollars per copy.

DRIVING FORCES

These and many other weapons and systems are the logical results for the time being of the policy of continuous technological innovation which has been a major feature of US defence activities for many years and to which the massive aerospace and other high-technology American industries are geared. Irrespective of the undoubted merits of many of the products concerned, there are some grounds for supposing that the rate of innovation is attributable more to the combination of the capabilities and needs of the supply industries, the enthusiasms and rivalries of the customer services and the tendency towards self-perpetuation of the bureaucratic structures that unite the other elements, than it is to the real demands of the international situation.

It is quite likely, too, that *mutatis mutandis* the driving forces behind the Russian system-improvement programmes are of the same general nature; and this postulate of technological momentum as the dominant element in the superpower programmes makes credible the suggestion noted above that there may no longer be a real arms race between them. As yet there is no evidence of a similar state of affairs in China; but there was certainly a similar tendency in Britain in the 1950s and 1960s and it could well be that there is some critical combination of industrial capability and military prosperity beyond which regenerative developments of this kind tend to occur.

While this notion might form the basis of an interesting academic investigation, which might in turn lead to some valuable predictions of future developments in Asian and South American countries (India, for example, or Brazil) which are currently building up their defence industries, it is the immediate effect of the current programmes that must be considered here.

How the American people choose to spend their national wealth is very largely their own affair: the other NATO nations have good cause to be grateful for much that their big ally has done to preserve the integrity of the alliance's territory; and this thought must be much in the mind of any European who seeks to criticise any aspect of US defence policy. What is worrying, however, is that the military and economic dominance of the USA within the alliance has drawn and apparently inevitably must continue to draw the other nations into a common technological whirl in which their armed forces are equipped either with American weapons and systems (and whether they are made in Europe or America is in this context irrelevant) or with weapons and systems of European design but of comparable sophistication and thus of comparable cost.

THE NARROWING FRONT

If this argument is valid, the most probable outcome must surely be that the continuing political pressure to contain and if possible reduce European defence expenditure will cause the nations concerned to acquire the irreducible minimum of these costly goods and to trim their capabilities and commitments in other directions in order to accommodate this minimum within their budgets.

To a very large extent this has already happened. The ability of the West European nations to take any military action outside Europe has dwindled to almost negligible proportions, and without a major policy change there is no prospect of its increasing. The only credible extra-European forces currently in being are the British and French ballistic missile submarines, a few large surface vessels and some air transport, and the circumstances in which any of these could be used are severely restricted.

That the European nations should be willing and able to defend their territory is obviously sensible: what is far from obvious is that this necessary ability is also sufficient for their continuing safety and prosperity in the modern world; and it would be comforting if more attention were devoted to the implications of this question by those who are ultimately responsible for that safety and prosperity.

POLITICS AND POLICY

Lip-service is regularly paid by politicians of all kinds to the importance of trade to Europe, but few of them seem to care to examine the real meaning of the statement. Too rarely is it recognised that the whole fabric of West European civilisation has been reared not merely on trade as such but also on the ability to control the mechanics of trade and guarantee the safe passage of goods over the trade routes of the world. This control has been exercised by different nations at different times and has frequently been used by one nation to coerce another; but the interruptions have usually been short and have always been followed by a restoration of free passage.

In a few short years, however, this control has been destroyed – not lost to a superior power, but deliberately and wantonly destroyed as a political act. Naval forces have been reduced to the point where their ability even to protect European fishing interests is in doubt; overseas bases have been dismantled, independence has been granted to dozens of former colonies with little or no attempt to preserve European trading interests in those territories; the Simonstown agreement was jettisoned as a political gesture and the network of friendly relationships with the old dominions of the British Commonwealth and other countries with strong European ties has been sacrificed to the greater glory of the European Economic Community.

If trade were no more than the source of the gilt on the European gingerbread it might be possible to cobble together some sort of

[7] See, among many examples, *Current Issues in US Defense Policy* ed. David T. Johnson and Barry R. Schneider (Praeger, 1976).

defence for these policies. If, as many politicians appear to believe, oil were the only really vital import, the cautious use of the North Sea resources might offer the means of salvation until something better turned up. But oil is not the only vital import and secure trade routes and the ability to influence remote suppliers and purchasers are the foundations of European industrial society as it exists today. It is just conceivable that the nations concerned could so modify their way of life as to be able to survive without overseas trade; but the upheaval that would be required would be enormous and almost certainly beyond the control of any existing political institutions. "Export or die" has long been a popular slogan on the lips of politicians anxious to encourage industrialists to avert the economic consequences of profligate domestic policies. "Import or die" is nearer to the truth of the matter.

ARMS PROLIFERATION

It may be argued that Western Europe's inability to control its trade routes has persisted now for several years and that nothing very dreadful has happened. During this period, however, world power has in the main been exercised by other developed countries and the newly-independent nations have been much concerned to import European manufactures and technology in exchange for their traditional supplies of food and raw materials. As these countries develop their own industries, however, they will be able to afford to be more selective in their external purchases and less dependent on exporting their own products.

At the same time the developed countries have been doing a roaring trade in arms with the developing countries. This trade has been much criticised on moral grounds; but the aspect of it which has received least public attention is the extent to which arms manufacturing capabilities are being built up in countries which formerly relied largely on cheap cast-off equipment from the forces of the big powers. The arms deals that attract the greatest publicity are those involving the more spectacular weapons of the world's armouries; but the attentive reader of this book will observe the in many ways more important widespread facilities for the manufacture of humbler weapons, many of which may well be more directly relevant to the real conflicts of the coming years.

These developments in themselves cannot justifiably be criticised by the established powers: the newly-independent countries have a perfect right to develop their own industries to reduce their dependence on others. Common prudence dictates, however, that the other nations should note the possibility of the formation of what might be hostile associations of such countries and take appropriate precautions. One obvious present danger of this kind is the spread of Marxist influence in Africa and the establishment of Russian bases on the African coasts. The African countries concerned are at present too weak to take effective action to interfere with the busy trade routes round Africa, and it is most unlikely that any overt action would be taken by the Russians: nevertheless possibilities of covert interference already exist and are likely to increase.

THE ESSENTIAL PROGRAMME

These and many other dangers to Western civilisation must be faced by those who are threatened. Europe may choose to leave the business of strategic nuclear warfare to the USA but it cannot expect its great ally also to arrange for its supplies of food, oil and other raw materials and protect its world trade routes. It can, however, expect some help from that quarter and it needs urgently to re-establish the world network of friendly relationships which will enable it to count on help from many other quarters; but a large measure of self-help is also essential and provision for this must be made over and above any continuing commitment to the confrontation in Europe itself.

This does not mean that Europe has to attempt to reconstitute itself as the dominant military influence in the world. It simply means that, collectively and individually, the European nations have to demonstrate a determination to fight – though not inevitably to prevail – in defence of their interests, so that those who might seek to threaten these interests must weigh the probable consequences of the provocation. Most of the threats that are likely to arise are relatively small ones: terrorist or guerrilla activities, piracy, territorial encroachments in European, allied or friendly countries, and threats to European communities in foreign countries are all much more probable than major assaults which might lead to global war.

To meet such threats the primary need will be for conventional forces, conventionally armed and able to go anywhere and fight anyone. If, having made such provision, the West European nations and their allies and friends are able also to deal with the problem of superpower deterrence, the rest of the world will undoubtedly be much relieved; but measures to protect the sub-continent against long-familiar hazards must come first. Even if one lives in an earthquake zone there is no sense in allowing the fire and burglary insurance to lapse; and it is often forgotten that when NATO was first set up the European members were well able to protect their vital international supply lines.

It would be idle to pretend that what is proposed here will be either easily achieved or readily acceptable to those who currently govern the nations concerned. Obviously there will be a need for a fundamental reappraisal of all military priorities; but this alone will not be sufficient: diplomatic and political attitudes and ideologies will need to be re-assessed, trading and manufacturing policies and priorities reconsidered, treaties and alliances renegotiated and so on. An analysis of all the changes required is obviously beyond the scope of this survey; but it is certainly appropriate to point to the need to regard the pedestrian fighting man as the fundamental element of all land and amphibious arms of the lifeline preservation forces. On his training and on the quality and reliability of his equipment will depend – as it has always depended – the successful execution of a host of minor missions to which most of the elaborate and costly paraphernalia in the NATO military inventory are totally irrelevant.

Reference is made in the first section of this book to the infantry weapon trials which are intended to select a new generation of individual and section weapons for NATO forces in the 1980s. It is to be hoped that the European participants in these trials and in the subsequent discussions will ensure that the chosen weapons are as appropriate to the small-scale operations listed above as they would be to a military showdown with the Russians. It is also to be hoped that equal consideration will be given to ensuring that other infantry weapons, both large and small, are equally appropriate to these roles and to making the manpower and materials available for their performance, and that all this will be accorded first priority in the shopping list for European land forces.

ENVOI

If, in the middle of all this, the improbable large-scale assault from the East should occur, it is entirely possible – as it always has been – that Western Europe might not on this occasion weather the storm. Down the centuries, however, European civilisation has made enormous contributions to the well-being of the rest of the world and its achievements will probably be remembered longer than its follies. It has had a good long run; and if it must go it is surely consistent with its past vigour and dignity that it should go with a bang – rather than by default with that awful whimper.

February 1977   **Denis Archer**

CHANGES IN THIS ISSUE

In addition to the usual revision of all entries and the incorporation of additional items in existing sections of the book, a new section has been added this year and several rearrangements have been made in the hope that these will make the book easier to use. The new section deals with those armoured vehicles that have been designed primarily for infantry use and includes armoured personnel carriers, armoured infantry fighting vehicles and mechanised infantry combat vehicles; but it does not cover tanks, assault guns or other vehicles which are essentially appropriate to armoured warfare as such. Some small sub-sections covering flame throwers and various aspects of mine warfare have also been added.

A major reorganisation has been introduced in the grenade section. The number of grenades and grenade-like devices currently available is nowadays so large that the original composite section was thought to be excessively unwieldy. It has now been divided into sub-sections dealing with combat grenades, grenade launchers, riot control munitions and pyrotechnics; and while this subdivision necessarily involves some arbitrary decisions it is hoped that the rearrangement, coupled with the prefatory explanatory notes, will make this section more readily intelligible to the reader.

A smaller reorganisation has brought the descriptions of cannon out of the anti-aircraft section and into a more logical position following machine guns in the point target weapon section; and this new sub-section is now followed by the sub-section dealing with ammunition. Anti-aircraft mountings for these weapons, however, continue to be described in the anti-aircraft section.

Finally, attention is drawn to the special article which follows this foreword. It deals with the often neglected need for protecting the hearing of soldiers from the damaging effects of weapon and vehicle noise. It is perhaps worth noting that hearing damage is by far the commonest injury suffered by soldiers – even by those who have never been near a front line – and is one of the most important grounds for the payment of disability pensions. The author of this article, Mr. A.G. Gorman, is a well-known British expert in the field and has spent most of his working life in research and development activities associated with acoustic measurements and with the design and development of hearing aids and hearing protectors.

ACKNOWLEDGEMENTS

One of the most agreeable aspects of the task of editing a work of this kind is the generous and friendly way in which total strangers spring to one's aid. Following the publication of the last edition there has been a steady flow of correspondence from weapons experts and enthusiasts giving advice and making suggestions for improvement, many of which I have been glad to adopt, pointing out errors of detail and often clothing the bare bones of a weapon's development history with fascinating and often entertaining anecdote. To all these correspondents I offer my sincere thanks for taking so much trouble on our behalf.

As always, the many embassies and government departments that we have consulted have dealt courteously and helpfully with our enquiries; and I am especially grateful to the many manufacturers who have supplied information for incorporation in this edition. We had to work to a tight schedule this year and thus were unable to give as much notice as we normally do when we issue requests for information. That they processed our often unreasonable requests with so little complaint does them great credit.

Mr. Gorman's contribution on the dangers of noise and the remedies available has already been noted; but acknowledgement is also due to Mr. Christopher Foss who compiled the new section on armoured vehicles and revised the mortar section. As is his wont, he has also furnished much other information for other parts of the book. Finally, and very importantly, it is the editor's privilege to thank the home team for their efforts. Special thanks are due to Mrs. Brenda Perfect who, at no notice but with great competence, took over the vital function of co-ordinating the flow of editorial copy half-way through the book's cycle – and thus at the peak of the year's activity – but we are all dependent on the steady support of the production team under Mr. Kenneth Harris and particularly of Mr. Stuart Bannerman, whose special care this book has been, of Mrs. Christine Richards, who with her team of artists contrives to convert the editor's woolly ideas into sensible layouts, and lastly of the patient printers and platemakers for whom making silk purses out of sows' ears is pure routine.

By the time these words are read by anyone outside the publishing organisation the machinery for the production of the next edition will already be in motion and these acknowledgements will be no more than a matter of record. That is simply one of the peculiarities of the publishing business, however; and it in no way detracts from the sincerity with which the acknowledgements are made.

Denis Archer

SNIA

DEFENCE AND AEROSPACE DIVISION

COMPLETE ROUNDS FOR ARTILLERY AND MORTARS • CARTRIDGES FOR SMALL ARMS • PROPELLING POWDERS AND BURSTING EXPLOSIVES

AIR-TO-AIR AND AIR-TO-GROUND ROCKETS • FIELDS ROCKETS • WARHEADS FOR ROCKETS AND MISSILES • SOLID PROPELLANT ROCKET ENGINES FOR MILITARY AND SPACE USE • DOUBLE BASE AND COMPOSITE SOLID PROPELLANTS

RESEARCH AND DEVELOPMENT IN THE MISSILE AND SPACE FIELD

VIA SICILIA 162, 00187 ROME
TELEF 4680 • TELEX 61114

NOISE – AN ENEMY WITHIN THE RANKS

BY
A G Gorman DFH C Eng MIEE *

We live in an age of noise. Our ears are assailed from all sides by the din from the products of our technological skills. The weapons of war are no exception. They have been generating various degrees of loud noise at least since the introduction of chemical propellants. That particular innovation was some time ago. Since then size and range, firing rate and so on have continually increased and the by-product noise has been accepted as inevitable at ever increasing levels. Rarely is anything done to reduce it at source if only because fire-power might be diminished. It is not only the high power weaponry which produces significant noise levels – current types of small arms also generate very loud bangs at close quarters.

The modern soldier does not do as much marching as in the past and tends to be transported in APCs and the like. These powerful, usually tracked, vehicles have internal noise levels high enough to leave their passengers feeling somewhat stunned after any journey of more than a few minutes in length.

Of all the problems which properly have to engage the attention of military organisations today, does acoustic noise really have to be added to the list? The noise has been with us for a long time now and by and large everyone seems to have survived it. Why should any more attention be paid to it now than in the past? Why should any expenditure be allocated for noise protection against all the other priorities clamouring for financial allocation?

This article will show that today's knowledge of the various effects of noise makes it virtually impossible to ignore or dismiss the need to protect the hearing of troops from high noise levels. Progress in hearing protector design now makes it possible to specify the most cost effective and appropriate type of protection without undue difficulty. To provide the protection gives some unexpected benefits and bonuses. Not to protect from noise may cause a variety of serious and also expensive consequences. The need for protection applies equally to training, exercise and combat situations – noise is noise whatever the circumstances.

The main results of exposure to high noise levels are listed below, approximately in order of immediacy of effect and with a brief hint of the consequences of withholding protection.

1. Inability to hear airborne words of lower level than the noise, so commands not reliably understood.
2. Requirement for high power electrical input to the earphones of communications equipment. The high reproduction level of the signal may itself become an auditory hazard!
3. Premature onset of fatigue with difficulty in concentrating, so increase in performance errors, resulting in reduced efficiency and risk of serious and possibly dangerous error.
4. Temporary reduction of hearing ability, causing the same problems as 3 above, which can take several hours for complete recovery. With really high noise levels there is a subjective feeling of being partially stunned. Orientation and alertness can be seriously affected at a time when it may be most needed.
5. Permanent reduction of hearing ability, with all the consequences listed above plus a reduction in the useful active service period of the affected individual and possibility of expensive compensation claims.

In order to discuss noise and its effects in any detail some technical terms are necessary, together with some understanding of the way in which noise, hearing and hearing loss are measured. The following brief and very incomplete introduction to the subject will assist those who do not normally have to be familiar with the basic technicalities.

Characteristics and Measurement of Noise

Noise occurs in many different patterns (eg., impulsive, as from rifles, mortars and explosions generally, or continuous, as with vehicle noise) and may have its energy confined within a narrow band of frequency – the ultimate being a single tone sine wave – or may cover a wide range of frequencies as do the majority of noises.

Acoustic noise is measured with a suitable microphone whose output signal is assessed by appropriate electronic instrumentation. It is general practice to measure the root-mean-square acoustic pressure of a noise signal, this being a measure of the acoustic power level of the noise. As noise usually fluctuates, the measuring time constant is important and this is chosen from one of two internationally accepted values. Occasionally, and especially with impulsive noise, the peak height of the pulse may be measured. With more or less continuous noise the power measurement may be made through various frequency filters to establish the frequency spectrum of the noise.

The noise power level is quoted in the now generally familiar decibel (abbreviated dB). This unit is strictly a measure of the *ratio* of two quantities; but by specifying the actual noise power of some low reference noise level and calling this 0dB, all higher levels have their power adequately expressed by their decibel value. The decibel is also a logarithmic unit, being ten times the logarithm (to the base 10) of the ratio of two power levels. The logarithm of 2 is about 0.3 and ten times this is of course 3. So every time a noise power level is *doubled*, 3 dB is *added* to its decibel value.

This logarithmic unit has considerable advantages for quoting acoustic measurements. For instance, the ratio of powers between the quietest just audible sound and the noise of a moon rocket launch is no less than $10^{20}:1$. This enormous power range is covered by the figures 0–200 in the decibel system. Moreover the human ear judges relative loudness by the ratio of two sound levels rather than by their arithmetic difference, so defining sound levels in decibels fits this hearing characteristic rather nicely. The smallest detectable ratio of sound levels is about 6% by healthy ears. This is about 0.25 dB.

When assessing the subjective loudness (or danger) of sounds of various frequencies it is found that the ear is more tolerant of low frequency than of high frequency sounds and so it is standard practice to reduce the sensitivity, of sound measuring equipment, to these lower frequency sounds. Such a measuring characteristic is referred to as "A-weighting" and decibel values measured with this frequency weighting in use are described as dBA. These dBA values are an excellent indication of the subjective loudness of noise (or any sound). Even when wide-band acoustic noise is measured through filters, usually of 1-octave bandwidth, the A-weighting correction is applied to the individual octave band noise levels, to indicate the subjective significance. FIG I shows the complete A-weighted measuring characteristic.

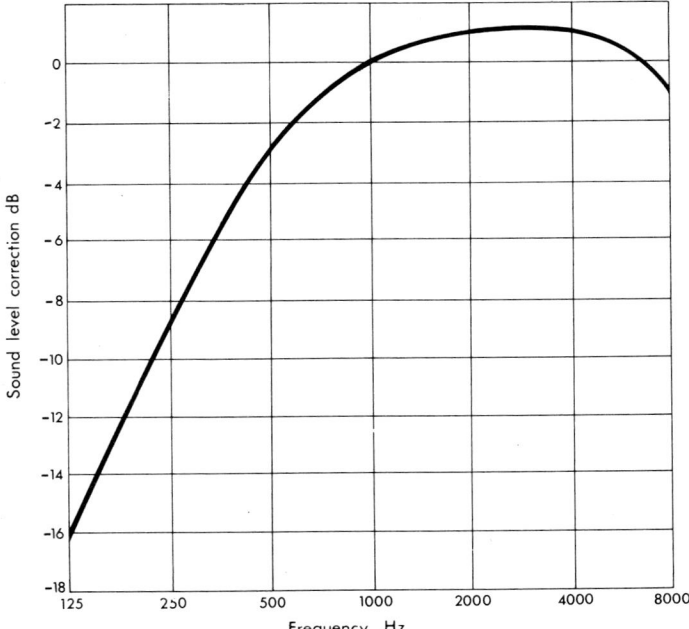

I A-weighted sound measuring characteristic showing much reduced significance of lower frequency sounds.

* Technical Director Racal-Amplivox Communications Limited

The table of approximate sound levels below puts various sounds and noises into rank order. The quietest just audible sound is taken as the 0dB reference level. This is not strictly in accordance with the facts but is very approximately true.

Approximate Sound Level dBA	Typical Source
200	Moon rocket lift-off 400 metres away.
190	ICBM launch 300 metres away.
180	Peak level of some heavy artillery at crew positions.
160	Peak level of some small arms at firer's position.
150	ABSOLUTE MAXIMUM SAFE PEAK PRESSURE AT EAR
140–150	Fighter aircraft take-off, at ground crew positions.
130	Some aircraft cockpits during take-off.
120	THRESHOLD OF PAIN FOR CONTINUOUS NOISE
110–120	Some helicopter cockpits.
110	Inside Armoured Personnel Carriers and Fighting Vehicles (tracked).
100	Heavy rubber-tyred vehicles in driving position.
90–100	Vehicle repair shops.
90	Heavy traffic passing at 7 metres.
85–90	LOWER LIMIT OF HAZARDOUS LEVELS
80	Quiet aircraft flight deck.
70	Normal speech at 1 m.
60	Average office.
50	Quiet office.
25	Open countryside. No man-made noise.
0	Threshold of hearing.

It can be seen that many of the noises afflicting the infantryman are well towards the more intense end of the sound level range.

Measurement of Hearing and Hearing Loss

Like noise, hearing sensitivity is measured in decibels and the reference level is internationally agreed as representing the quietest sounds just audible. Hearing measurements are made by presenting simple tones to the ear at accurately known levels and determining the lowest level which is audible. The test is made at a number of frequencies within the range of audio sounds.

Young people in good health should have hearing acuity near to the international threshold level although variations of about plus or minus 10 dB are quite normal. As age increases, hearing commonly deteriorates due to natural causes. FIG II shows the sort of pattern that hearing loss may follow with age. The loss of mostly higher frequency sensitivity is significant and will be further discussed in a later section.

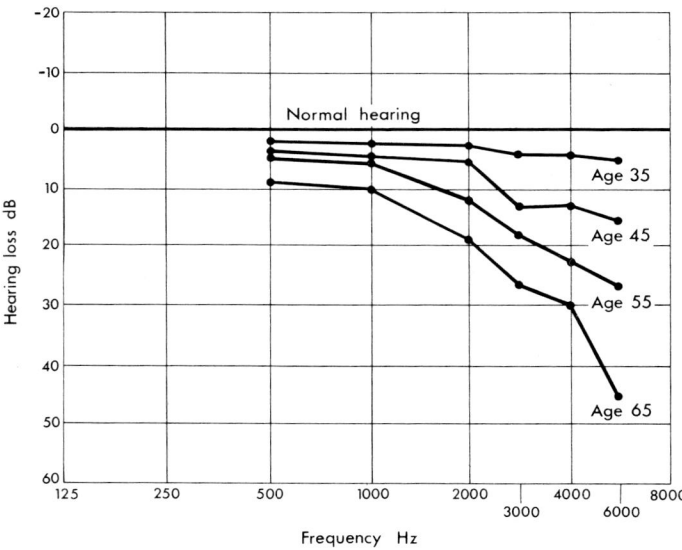

II Approximate hearing loss due to age plus social noise exposure.

Another method of measuring hearing or hearing loss is by testing the ability to understand speech clearly. Specially chosen test words are presented at accurately known sound levels and the recognition (or lack of it) of each word is noted. The total score for the complete test is a good measure of effective hearing loss.

The Effect of Noise on Hearing

As long ago as the early phases of the industrial revolution it was first observed that high noise levels seemed to cause deafness. Since about 1930 much effort has been devoted by many workers to quantifying both the cause (the noise) and the effect (the hearing loss). One of many major steps forward, about twenty years ago, was the introduction of the A-weighting into noise measurements. This recognised, as a result of much research, that the ear was more tolerant of low frequency sounds. Originally the use of the A-weighting was restricted to measurement of relatively low level sounds but subsequent research proved its value at all levels.

More recently it has been clearly established that any adverse effect of noise upon the human hearing mechanism is, for practical purposes, in proportion to the energy in the noise. Now energy is power multiplied by time. The power in the noise is given by its dBA value and this increases by 3 dBA as noise power doubles. To limit the energy to the same value, the exposure time to the noise must therefore be halved for every 3 dBA increase in the noise level. When this philosophy was first put forward it did not receive immediate and complete acceptance and there is still at least one major country only requiring a halving of exposure time (in industry) for every 5 dBA increase in noise level. However, the "Equal energy" concept will soon be universally accepted.

It is of course only when the noise is above a certain dBA level that any danger to hearing arises. Again, there are today slightly varying views as to the exact level above which noise should be regarded as potentially damaging and levels between 85 dBA and 90 dBA are quoted. Disagreement largely centres around differing opinions as to how much noise-induced hearing loss constitutes a serious disability. One thing which is certain is that there is an increasing tendency to specify lower noise levels and shorter exposure times as more knowledge of the long term effects of noise becomes available.

The foregoing remarks in this section apply most obviously to continuous or near continuous noise, the type produced by vehicles, machinery and so on. The infantryman is, on the whole, exposed to impulsive noises arising from his great variety of weaponry. For this type of noise it is not so obvious that the dBA measurement and the concept of "Equal energy" is applicable. Impulsive noises will after all have a wide variety of envelope shapes (level v. time characteristic). In addition the ratio of noise to no-noise periods will vary with the firing rate of the weapon. Until recently, the view was taken that impulsive noise assessment required a different approach involving measurements of a number of parameters of the impulse envelope. Again, the latest view held by at least some experts, is that impulsive noise can be assessed very similarly to continuous noise although special measuring (integrating) sound level metering equipment is necessary because of the intermittent nature of the noise. If however the peak pressure of the noise pulses is greater than 150 dB then the more detailed measuring methods must still

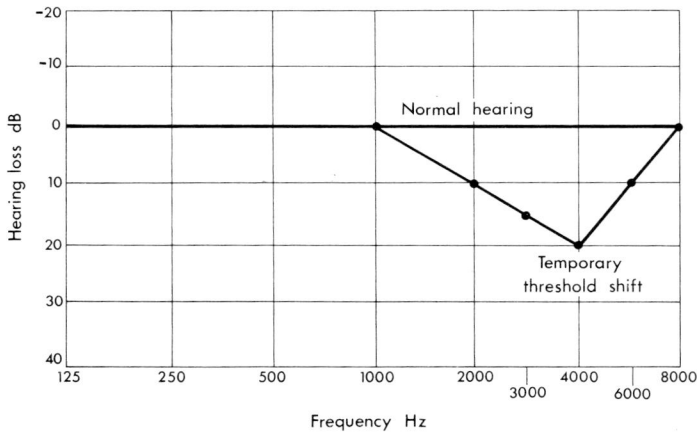

III An example of noise-induced temporary threshold shift.

be used. Instantaneous levels at the ear should never exceed 150 dB however brief the duration of the noise pulse.

Whether noise is impulsive or continuous, once the total energy in a given exposure time exceeds the safe figure then the hearing of exposed personnel will be at risk of immediate deterioration. Initially any loss of hearing is temporary and largely confined to a narrow band of frequencies around 4 kHz. FIG III shows a typical temporary threshold shift which might be produced by exposure to a 90 dBA noise level for a few hours.

This threshold shift, being temporary, will reduce to zero after some hours but in the meantime it will have caused fatigue, reduced ability to hear commands and messages, increase of reaction time and a general sensation of not being quite up to the best standard of alertness and efficiency. The symptoms are very real indeed and not in any way imaginary.

The threshold shift shown in FIG III and the symptoms noted above might equally well have been produced by 30 minutes in an armoured personnel carrier travelling at about 45 km/hr on a metalled road. The shorter exposure is balanced by the much higher noise level of, maybe, 110 dBA.

Again a marked threshold shift would be caused by a soldier firing 100 rounds from his rifle during the course of a few hours. Use of automatic weapons can build up a hazardous noise exposure in a very short space of time. The peak noise levels will quite probably be in the vicinity of 160 dB and what is not commonly realised is that adjacent personnel will be at the same risk as the firer.

Repeated exposure to noise energy levels capable of producing temporary threshold shifts carries a high risk of eventually producing permanent, irreversible hearing loss. Virtually irrespective of the nature of the offending noise, the greatest hearing loss again occurs initially around the frequency of 4 kHz. As the hearing damage progresses with continued exposure, the loss at 4 kHz increases and other frequencies become involved. FIG IV shows a possible pattern of hearing loss progression with repeated exposure to hazardous levels of noise.

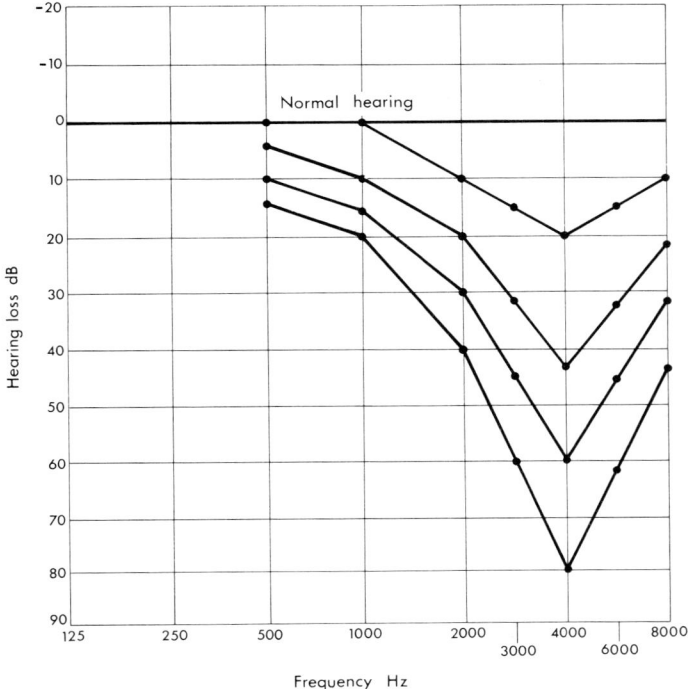

IV Progressive permanent noise-induced hearing loss.

It is obvious that after only a comparatively few years of unprotected exposure to the noise levels existing in many military situations and environments, a permanent hearing loss can be produced, equivalent to a much longer period of exposure in civilian industry. This alarming fact arises because a greater proportion of military personnel are subjected to really high noise levels than is the case in industry where the majority of workers at noise risk are in noise environments of less than 100 dBA.

It is also worth noting that there is increasing evidence of a risk of other long term health deterioration arising from noise. Increased incidence of neurological and circulatory disorders can occur as well as chronic fatigue, irritability and unsocial behaviour patterns. These physiological and psychological disturbances are typical stress reactions. Noise is thus identified as a stress producing phenomenon. Military personnel are obviously subject to many stress producing situations and environments but the results of stress are additive and cumulative. It makes good sense to reduce those stresses about which some action can be taken.

The Effects of Hearing Loss on the Man

It has already been stated and shown (FIG IV) that noise-induced hearing loss is most severe at the higher frequencies. Unfortunately it is no great consolation that the low frequency loss is smaller.

The ability to hear and comprehend the speech of our fellow men

is obviously the most important attribute of our sense of hearing. That our hearing makes us aware of the many other sounds of life is an important bonus (especially perhaps to military personnel whose very lives will sometimes depend on a keen sense of hearing) but in the final analysis it is human speech to which we most often listen and which we most need to hear and comprehend. The clarity and intelligibility of speech is very dependent on the frequency response of its reproduction (or perception). The total frequency bandwidth produced by male speech is from about 30 Hz to 10,000 Hz but the majority of the *intelligibility* is contained within the frequency band 1000–4000 Hz. This is why well-designed communications systems sound rather high pitched. Above 4000 Hz they cut-off sharply (sometimes even above 3000 Hz) and also reduce the level of sounds below 1000 Hz frequency. Quality and recognisability may suffer but the speech reproduction sounds crisp and clear. If, alternatively, the important high frequency speech sounds are reduced and the less important low frequency sounds are left at full strength then the clarity of the speech is reduced for two reasons – the first is the actual attenuation of the important frequency band and the second is that the now predominant lower frequencies produce a phenomenon known as upward masking. The high frequency sounds become submerged in the low frequency sounds. The result is that the speech with the reduced higher frequencies is even less clear than if *all* frequencies had been reduced!

Noise-induced hearing loss produces just this selective extra attenuation of the higher frequencies which so reduces the clarity and intelligibility of perceived speech. Once the total loss, as an average of the losses at several important frequencies, is more than about 20 dB then the difficulty in clearly perceiving speech will be noticeable and significant. At and above this degree of hearing handicap, then, the usefulness of the man becomes increasingly limited. Having in mind the rapidity with which this stage can be reached, it is a situation to be avoided by proper attention to noise control and protection.

Hearing Damage Risk Criteria

Against the background that a reduction in the ability to hear speech clearly is the most meaningful measure of noise-induced disability, a variety of criteria have been evolved for accurately measuring the degree of speech perception impairment. Direct measurement of speech perception (speech audiometry) is slow and difficult. Impairment is therefore normally assessed by taking an average of the hearing loss at (usually) three frequencies, as measured with simple tones (pure tone audiometry). Some minimum average hearing loss is taken as representing the onset of a significant permanent hearing handicap.

It will serve no useful purpose in this article to list the differing criteria which have been produced by various national and international organisations. What is important is that the most recent criteria are also the most stringent. For instance a recent revision of UK Standard BS 5330 *Method of estimating the risk of hearing handicap due to noise exposure* specifies an average of the 1, 2 and 3 kHz losses of 30 dB or more as indicating a hearing handicap. A hearing loss graph as shown in FIG V is one which represents a 30 dB average loss. This is one curve from the series in FIG IV.

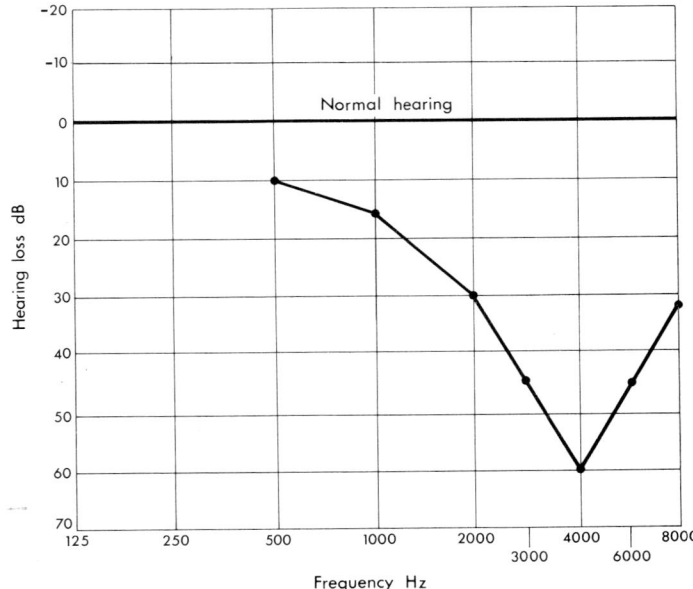

V Degree of hearing loss constituting noticeable hearing handicap in terms of speech perception.

As an example, an 18-year-old recruit, subjected to a noise level of 116 dBA for 1 hour per day, 5 days per week, 48 weeks per year for five years, would at the age of 23 have approximately a 20% chance of possessing the hearing handicap shown in FIG V. If the noise exposure continued for a further five years, then at the age of 28 this soldier would have a greater chance, of about 36%, of suffering this hearing handicap. The noise exposure suggested may seem an extreme example but almost inevitably exposures to impulse noise from small arms, mortars, missile launchers, etc., during training and exercise phases, would be additive to any exposure to continuous noise and therefore the total noise exposure might well be of the magnitude suggested – with the result stated.

Other Effects of Noise

As well as the biological effects of noise, ie., on hearing and other human systems, noise has physical effects which should not be ignored. The one of main interest in a military situation is known as signal masking. Everyone is aware, from experience, that to hear speech or to be heard in a high noise level is difficult or impossible. Shouting is no real help because it is uncomfortable for both speaker and listener, exhausting for both if continuously necessary and still not entirely reliable.

If this problem arises in an area where speaking is direct person to person it is bad enough but if communications sets are in use and without noise excluding headphones then the problem is very serious indeed in several different ways.

Speech signals as listened to from a headphone need to be at least 10 dB and preferably 20 dB louder than the local ambient acoustic noise level at the listener's ears, if reception is to be entirely distinct. If the local acoustic noise is for example, at a level of 110 dB and is only reduced to 105 dB by an unsuitable type of headphone giving little noise protection, then the signal from the earphones must be set to a level of 115 dB to achieve the 10 dB minimum signal-to-noise ratio which is essential. FIG VI shows this situation in pictorial form. There are two disadvantages; first, the speech level of 115 dB can of itself be a hearing hazard! If the speech was continuous at this level it could only safely be listened to for 10 minutes per week! Luckily, speech is a discontinuous type of signal and normally appears only in short bursts in the average communications system. The level is nevertheless too high for comfort and a maximum speech level of 110 dB should be aimed at wherever possible – with such reduction of environmental noise as is necessary to achieve a suitable signal-to-noise ratio.

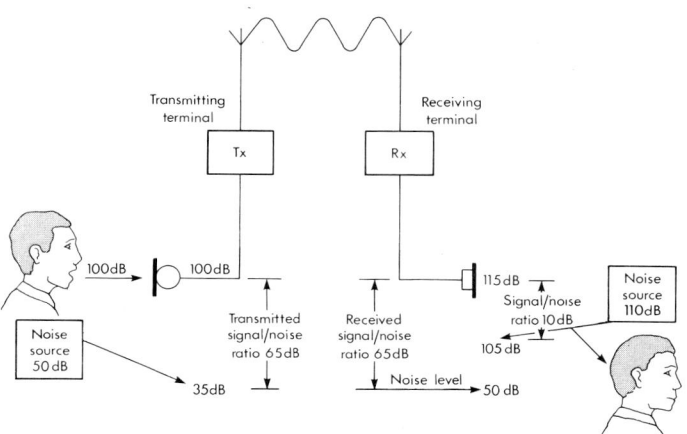

VI 110 dB noise level at a receiving terminal and without noise-reducing headphone. Signal output level has to be at 115 dB level to be audible.

The second disadvantage is that the audio power required to achieve a 115 dB level from a headphone can be fairly considerable – perhaps three Watts. This power (per headphone) is rarely available and therefore in high noise levels the required speech level cannot be achieved and intelligibility of the signal seriously suffers. Even if the power is available the headphone reproduction may be noticeably distorted when operated at this high level. Furthermore, such high audio power causes increase of cost, weight, complexity and battery drain of the equipment.

Consider the change brought about by specifying an appropriate noise-reducing headset, say with a noise attenuation of 25 dB. The situation then becomes as shown in FIG VII. The 110 dB noise level is reduced to 85 dB within the noise reducing headphone and a 10 dB signal-to-noise ratio is achieved with a headphone output level of 95 dB. Only 30 mWatts of audio power (1/100 of that previously required) is now sufficient for each headphone and the ambient noise level, within the headphones, is safe for indefinite periods of

exposure. The speech level is also no longer hazardous – several problems solved by one decision.

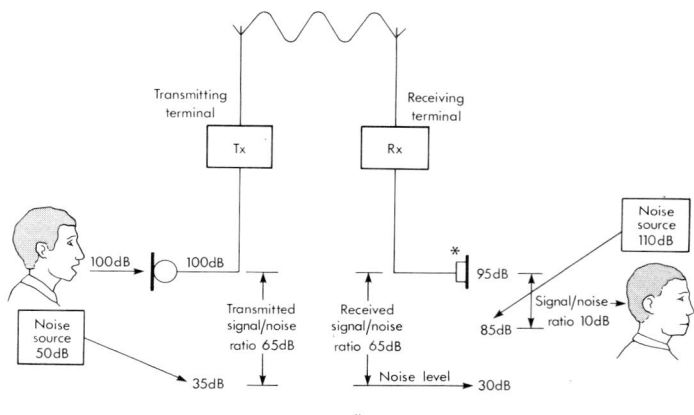

VII 110 dB noise level at a receiving terminal with noise-reducing headphone giving 25 dB attenuation. Signal output level can now be reduced to 95 dB.

The Case for Hearing Protection

The most important effects of high noise levels have now been discussed and it is possible to consider objectively whether there is now a real need to specify noise control and hearing protection.

It is obvious that there are no advantageous effects of noise. On the contrary very few would disagree today with the statement that not only are there immediate and obvious disadvantageous effects (the simple inability to hear commands and the loss of efficiency) but also proven long term effects of an entirely irreversible nature.

It is also true that, principles apart, the noise levels produced today by weaponry of almost all types and inside vehicles and aircraft, constitute real noise hazards.

So what should be done about it, if anything? Not so long ago, the decision could fairly justifiably be taken to do little or nothing. Not enough knowledge had been accumulated as to the precise levels of noise which caused particular degrees of hearing hazard and this problem had earlier been compounded by the lack of a measure of noise which directly related to its hazard. A further complication was (and is) that individuals vary in their resistance to noise and therefore in any resultant hearing handicap; it is the *risk* of hearing damage which has to be assessed.

Today the technical uncertainties have very largely disappeared and the risks to individuals exposed to varying degrees of noise are well established and on record in various national and international standards. So the decision, to protect or not, has to be taken on other grounds. On the basis for instance of concern for the welfare of one's men and concern for their immediate and continued efficiency as part of a fighting machine.

There are also possible legal considerations. In those countries where national standards, for noise exposure, exist or where an international standard is accepted these are usually legally enforceable in civilian industrial environments. Some progressive countries have also made such legislation binding on their armed forces. In at least one country, troops have the legal right to refuse duty (in peace time) in circumstances or environments exceeding the nationally specified noise limits. Even where any legislation has not been extended to include the armed forces it may in practice be impracticable or at the least inadvisable to condone in the armed forces a basic everyday hazard not tolerated in civilian industry. Where noise exposure regulations are legally enforceable, even only in civilian industry, there may well be questions of claims for compensation or disability pensions arising out of excessive and avoidable noise exposure. The degree of success of any such claims must obviously depend upon local law.

Faced with this range of problems of excessive noise the case for taking protective action is surely overwhelming. It is lucky that whatever aspect of the effects of noise is considered, be it man-efficiency, reliability and safety or the possibility or disability claims, the cure can be cost effective.

The Means of Hearing Protection

There are circumstances where the level of an offending noise can be reduced at source, so rendering hearing protection unnecessary. This is rarely easy and especially so in a military context. Some noise reduction measures are feasible on vehicles but not sufficient in themselves to avoid the need for hearing protection. It is unknown for the impulse noise of weaponry, lying in the range

160–190 dB to be reduced to tolerable levels. The responsibility for reducing noise levels therefore falls on individual hearing protection devices.

As the realization of the need for individual hearing protection has grown, increasing and widespread effort has been put into both research and design of suitable products. Perhaps a little surprisingly the method of operation of a hearing protector is not so obvious as it might seem. Some products have therefore been unnecessarily large, heavy or clumsy, relative to their performance level while other products have performed better than it would seem they should. The detailed mechanism of the noise attenuation is now well understood, at least by the major manufacturers in this field, and a product can be designed with a high degree of accuracy to a given noise attenuation specification. There are of course limits to what can be achieved, some of these being associated with the man himself, for sound can reach the sensitive inner ear by routes other than the ear canal. Within these limits however, performance is continuously being improved although the major advances have now been made and implementation of a hearing conservation policy should not be delayed in the hope of a better product "next year".

Hearing protectors fall into two rather broad categories.

First, those which directly block the ear canal, eg., preformed rubber or plastic earplugs or individually shaped plastic or glass wool materials.

Secondly, cups or shells which cover the whole ear sealing against the head around the ear. These are referred to as "Circumaural" devices. The earcups or earshells may take a variety of forms and commonly contain earphones for communication reception, the whole device thereby becoming a Hearing Protector Headphone. Again the earcups (with or without earphones) may be integrated into a helmet providing impact and ballistic protection.

Earplugs sometimes have advantages where no communications facilities are required or where space is extremely restricted. They cannot however provide the degree of noise reduction obtainable from the best circumaural protectors. In addition earplugs have the disadvantage of not being very visible, so it is not easy to check that they are being worn, and of promoting infections of the ear canal by preventing ventilation. They can also introduce dirt into the ear canal if not kept scrupulously clean.

In military use, earplugs have their greatest application on small arms firing ranges during training and practice drills. Here their lack of projection from the head prevents any interference with weapon handling and their attenuation can be sufficient to reduce the peak noise levels to a safe figure for trainee soldiers. (For full-time instructors greater protection is required!) A special type of earplug originally developed by a UK Institute of Naval Medicine research team and known commercially as Gunfender has particular advantages on firing ranges. In quiet surroundings it has only limited attenuation but has much higher attenuation, approaching that of normal earplugs, to high level noise. It thus overcomes one problem of wearing hearing protection in an environment which is normally quiet but punctuated with short bursts of noise, that is the slight difficulty in hearing normal speech. The Gunfender, because of its design, also permits some ventilation of the ear canal. A graph of the approximate overall attenuation of the Gunfender v. noise level is shown in FIG VIII with a comparative curve for a standard preformed plastic earplug. A graph of attenuation v. frequency for all noise levels and for one type of standard preformed plastic earplug is shown in FIG IX.

Circumaural hearing protectors are the most widely used type, because of the greater noise attenuation which can be achieved together with their versatility in being adapted to integration with other facilities and equipment, such as communications headphones and protective helmets. The noise attenuation can usually be designed to be adequate in spite of various constraints on shape and (to some extent) size. As increasing awareness of the damaging effect of noise has led to demands for higher attenuation from hearing protectors, it has been possible to provide this extra performance without, in many cases, any increase of size or weight by the application of the results of recent research and development.

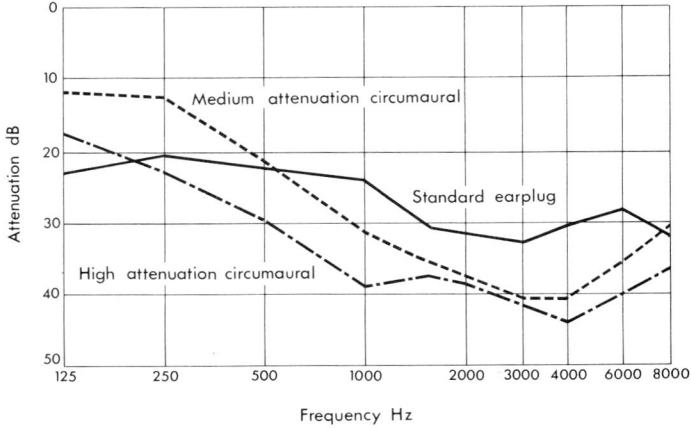

IX Noise attenuation curves for a standard earplug and two representative circumaural protectors.

FIG IX shows attenuation response curves of one type of moulded plastic earplug together with two types of circumaural protector. The lower attenuation characteristic is very applicable to continuous exposure to lesser noise levels (90–100 dBA) or to occasional exposure to higher levels. One example of a hearing protector with this performance is shown in FIG X. It is an item from the British Army Clansman range and is intended for Staff users who would not normally be in high noise environments for long periods, but who do need communications facilities and the ability to wear a steel helmet when necessary. This product is an example of a circumaural hearing protector adapted to include other facilities (the communications) and to integrate with yet others (the helmet) which it succeeds in doing while continuing to

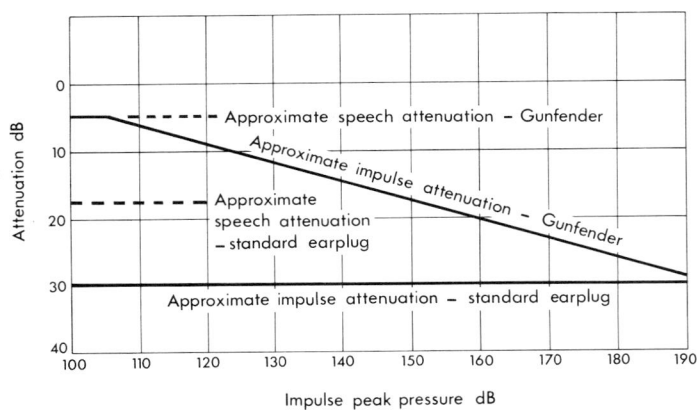

VIII Increase of attenuation of a Gunfender earplug as noise level increases. Pulse attenuation of a standard earplug is shown as is speech attenuation for both types.

X Hearing protector headset with which steel helmet can be worn and providing ample noise attenuation for occasional exposure to high noise levels.

provide the required degree of noise attenuation. This particular design also contains a unique feature which permits the attenuation to be reduced to zero by moving a small lever on each earshell. Thus when in quiet surroundings, person to person conversation can be held as normal, without having to remove the headset which would also lose the communications facility. When the so-called "Acoustic Valve" is open there is still a measure of hearing protection against explosive noises.

FIG XI shows an impact protective helmet mostly relevant to AFV crews but sometimes used by APC drivers. Again circumaural hearing protectors are incorporated and in products of this general type hearing protection can either be at a similar level to the Staff Users headphone described above or at the higher level shown in the third curve in FIG IX. Attenuation figures like this represent about the best that can be achieved today in production devices. Undoubtedly further improvements, especially in the lower frequency attenuation, will become available in the future.

It is often convenient to quote hearing protector attenuation as a single figure. This can be done by subtracting the dB or dBA noise level inside the protector shell, from the dB or dBA noise levels in the environment. One then has a single dB or dBA total attenuation figure and as noise levels are normally measured with the A-weighting, hearing protector attenuation is normally quoted in dBA. Noise levels inside the earshell are actually calculated from the attenuation curve – they cannot normally be measured.

An important fact not always realized is that the dBA attenuation figure for a normal hearing protector is *not* invariable but depends upon the spectrum of the environmental noise. The actual figure applicable to any particular environment has to be calculated using a simple method familiar to acoustics engineers.

Best Results from Hearing Protectors

Even the most efficient hearing protector cannot prevent a hearing handicap if it is not worn. This statement may sound so obvious as

XI Circumaural hearing protector integrated into protective helmet. Adequate hearing protection can be provided to safely permit long exposure times to the vehicle noise.

XII A high attenuation hearing protector whose protective capability is essential for really high noise situations.

FIG XII shows a hearing protector headset designed mainly for aircraft use and providing noise attenuation similar to the best curve in FIG IX. This particular product designed some years ago uses liquid filled earcushions to achieve its performance but modern versions use foam-filled earcushions, overcoming the slight unpopularity of the liquid-filled type.

Hearing Protector Performance Measurement

The attenuating properties are measured at a number of frequencies usually specified in a national or international standard. It is a very difficult matter to measure the attenuation accurately by purely instrumental means and all figures quoted for product selection purposes are derived from measurements on people. The precise method need not be detailed here but the outcome is a curve similar to those shown in FIG IX. The attenuation figures used for drawing the graph are normally the average results obtained from the subjective measurements. The attenuations achieved by some of the test subjects will however have been somewhat lower (as well as some being higher). For safety, a measure of the lower rather than the average attenuation may be used for product selection purposes against a known noise hazard. The actual lower figure used is chosen on a statistical basis and would often, though not always, be the so-called lower quartile.

not to be worth making. What is not however so obvious until it is explained, is that if a hearing protector is *not worn* for only 1% of the exposure duration, then even a device providing infinite attenuation would not have provided more than 20 dBA of protection in these circumstances. This sobering situation arises from the fact that the unattenuated noise heard for one-hundredth of the time (when the hearing protector is not worn) has exactly the same energy as a noise level 20 dBA lower but heard for the total time.

If it cannot be guaranteed that hearing protectors will be worn more than 90% of the total exposure time then there is no point in specifying products having more than 10 dBA attenuation. It is not seriously suggested that such a situation should be permitted. There are however some lessons to be learned from the quoted facts.

The decision to implement hearing conservation measures does not end with the supply of the best available protectors or noise reducing headphones. It is necessary to ensure on a continuing basis that the hearing protection, once supplied, is worn for the whole of the exposure time to any high noise levels.

Hearing protectors are much more likely to be worn for all of the necessary time if they are acceptably comfortable. It is unfortunately a fact that high attenuation hearing protectors tend to be less comfortable than those of more moderate performance. Hearing protection should not therefore be over-specified or the surprising end result may be less actual protection because the equipment may not be worn for a sufficient percentage of the necessary time.

The Cost of Hearing Protection

Is the provision of hearing protection a cost effective exercise? Is it cheaper to provide the necessary earplugs, circumaural protection and noise-reducing headphones or cheaper to tolerate the effects and consequences, both short and long term, of injury to hearing? Each nation and even perhaps each arm of a force will make its own decision. The author's own view, to protect in all circumstances, will no doubt have become absolutely clear to the reader. This view is based on the moderate cost of earplugs and simple circumaural protectors and on the moderate on-cost of noise-reducing headphones compared with those types providing little or no noise reduction. The benefits of hearing protection are numerous and the most important ones have been outlined in this article.

The disadvantages of ignoring the problem in terms of lower efficiency, danger from mis-heard messages and orders, shortening of useful life of expensively trained men and risk of disability compensations are serious and potentially very costly matters, all avoidable by provision of effective hearing protection.

If the need for hearing protection is considered before communications equipment is specified then there can be savings in that equipment, as previously explained, which can assist in offsetting any extra expenditure on the noise-reducing type of headphones. Even replacing existing communications headphones by noise-reducing types will provide benefits by reducing the audio power level at which communications receivers must work. Further the signal-to-noise ratio will be immediately improved and the reliability of the system thereby increased.

One armed force found also that the accuracy of firing improved noticeably when hearing protection was provided. It seemed that the men, relieved of the tension accompanying the anticipation of the high noise level produced by firing their weapons, concentrated better on aiming correctly. Every armed force should carefully investigate the costs and benefits of hearing protection from noise before deciding that it dares not to provide this protection.

Acknowledgements

This article has set out to state the danger and problem of high acoustic noise levels which can occur in military environments and to discuss the ways, means and advantages of protecting troops from the noise hazard.

To those in forces where hearing protection is not yet the order of the day perhaps this article will serve to have the matter given some consideration. On the other hand members of those enlightened forces where hearing protection is already a high priority matter will perhaps have gleaned some snippet of useful information.

The author has not set out to introduce new concepts on this occasion but to explain the present state of knowledge and the implication of that knowledge. Acknowledgement is therefore due to the many scientists, doctors, engineers and others who by their very number must go unnamed but whose work over the years has contributed to the author's ability to write an article such as this.

SECTION ONE

POINT TARGET WEAPONS

INTRODUCTION
PISTOLS AND REVOLVERS
SUB-MACHINE GUNS
RIFLES
MACHINE GUNS
CANNON
AMMUNITION

POINT TARGET WEAPONS

INTRODUCTION

For centuries, the most economical way of effectively engaging a target which is visible to the firer has involved the use of a point target weapon comprising a projectile, a propellant charge, a barrel to give direction to the projectile, and a sighting system to enable the barrel to be correctly aligned.

Modern point target weapons are more efficient than their predecessors; but their construction is more complex and, as commonly happens during the development of a specialised branch of engineering, some of the words used to describe these complex functions have acquired special meanings.

In this preliminary essay the general principles of the mechanisms of modern point target weapons are described and the vocabulary is explained.

These descriptions are appropriate to such tube weapons as rifles in which the projectile or bullet is accelerated up the barrel by gas pressure generated in a chamber at one end of the barrel, the rear end of the chamber being closed during the most important phase of the projectile's acceleration, and which depend for their accuracy mainly on the way in which they are aimed and held when fired. Recoilless weapons, tube-launched rockets and some guided missile systems, although they have much in common with closed-tube weapons, also have special characteristics which are separately described in the appropriate sections.

METHODS OF OPERATION

A modern rifle or similar tube weapon cartridge of conventional design (and there are others) consists of a metallic container which holds the propellant, the bullet and the means of igniting the propellant, in one self contained package. The cartridge is initially loaded into a container called a magazine or an ammunition belt and from there is fed into the chamber. Propellant ignition is provided by a primer or cap which is either detonated by a blow from the firing pin (or hammer) or, in heavier weapons, ignited by an electric current. The propellant charge burns inside the cartridge case and produces a large volume of gas at a very high temperature.

This combination of volume and temperature leads to a very rapid build up of pressure. The bullet is driven out of the cartridge case and is engaged by the rifling in the bore. The mouth of the cartridge case expands and seals the front end of the chamber to prevent any gas escaping back through the breech closing arrangements. This process is known as obturation.

Because the pressure is high and the gases are very hot, it is essential that the cartridge case, which may be of either brass or steel, is fully supported. The steel walls of the chamber prevent the undue expansion of the case radially but some arrangement must be made to hold the case firmly in the chamber from the rear and this may be done by having a breech block, or bolt, which is locked to the barrel, either directly into a barrel extension or to the receiver which is secured to the barrel. The distinction is drawn because, as will be seen, different methods of operation make different demands. The breech block may also be supporting the case by resting against it and relying on the mass of the block and the resulting inertia to prevent undue motion whilst the pressure in the chamber is still high.

As the bullet is accelerated up the barrel it acquires a substantial momentum (mv=mass × velocity) measured along the axis of the barrel: so also do the molecules of the gas which is propelling the bullet. The principle of conservation of momentum requires that this forward momentum be balanced by an equal and opposite momentum acquired by something moved rearwards (recoiling) by the same gas pressure. What this something is depends on the construction of the weapon: it may be the cartridge case and breech block moving away from the barrel, or the barrel chamber and breech block locked together and moving relative to the main body of the weapon, or the whole weapon moving relative to the firer, or any sequential combination of such movements. Since the mass of any of these recoiling elements is very much greater than that of the bullet, the velocity it must acquire to conserve momentum will be relatively very small.

The propellant carried in the cartridge case contains a great deal of chemical energy – of the order of 1,000 calories/gram – and this is liberated when the flash from the primer ignites the charge. The total energy release is the product of the quantity of propellant and its calorimetric equivalent, and it is found that about 20 to 30 per cent of the total energy input is used to do work on the projectile by accelerating it up the bore. This can be measured by ascertaining the kinetic energy ($\frac{1}{2}mv^2$) of the bullet at the muzzle. It will readily be appreciated that the recoiling mass also acquires kinetic energy – though very much less than the bullet since the kinetic energy is proportional to the square of the velocity but only the first power of the mass. It follows, therefore, that for a given bullet, barrel and propellant, the share of the same total energy acquired by the bullet will be greater if the recoiling mass is large than it will if the recoiling mass is small. Thus the efficiency of the gun as an internal combustion engine varies according to design, barrel length and wear from 20 to 30 per cent which is not unfavourable in comparison with a petrol engine or a diesel engine. The remaining 70 to 80 per cent of the energy input is distributed as follows:

Heat to the barrel: approx 30%
Muzzle blast: approx 40%
Rotational energy of the bullet: approx 0.2%
Work done to overcome friction: approx 3.0%
Work done on the gases moving up the bore: approx 3.0%
Recoil energy: approx 0.1%

In any point target weapon the sequence of operations which leads from the firing of one round to the firing of the next comprises, for modern weapons, a basic cycle which is common to almost all weapons and a series of associated operations which varies with the weapon type. Where this sequence of operations is wholly or partly automatic the energy required can come from only two sources – recoil energy or energy which would otherwise be wasted as muzzle blast. It should be noted that the vast amount of heat going to the barrel is the designer's greatest problem. If this could be utilised to operate a working cycle then many of the practical difficulties in gun design would be solved.

These two sources of energy lead to the three methods used today in all automatic weapons:

Blowback operation
Recoil operation
Gas operation.

The basic cycle referred to above, however, takes place regardless of method of operation and it should be noted that although only one of the three names for the operating methods contains the word 'recoil' it is in fact a recoil effect that is used in each case. In weapons other than automatic, some part of the cycle is carried out by the operator but in the automatic cycle these operations occur for every round that is fired. Starting with a fired round the characteristic cycle is:

The support of the cartridge case is removed
The breech block is retracted
The empty case is extracted from the chamber
The return spring is compressed to store energy
The empty case is ejected from the gun
The firing mechanism is cocked
The next round is fed into position
The round is chambered
The case is supported
The firing mechanism is operated.

BLOWBACK OPERATION

In this method of operation the energy required to carry out the cycle of operations is supplied to the bolt by the backward movement of the cartridge case, caused by the gas pressure.

SIMPLE BLOWBACK

This system in its simplest form allows a totally unlocked breech, and relies simply on the mass of the breech block and the strength of the return spring to prevent the cartridge case from coming back too quickly after

N.C. PROPELLANT (52 GRAINS)
CAP
CORE:- LEAD AND ANTIMONY
CONTRACTORS INITIALS OR RECOGNIZED TRADE MARK
YEAR OF MANUFACTURE
BRASS CASE SECURED TO BULLET BY CONING
ENVELOPE:- STEEL COATED WITH GILDING METAL
CALIBRE
ANNULUS - PURPLE
0·473
3·34
·30 - IN MK.4Z BALL CARTRIDGE

N.C. PROPELLANT (52 GRAINS)
PRIMING COMPOSITION
TRACER COMPOSITION
CORE:- LEAD AND ANTIMONY
ANNULUS - PURPLE
DISC
BRASS WASHER
BRASS CASE SECURED TO BULLET BY CONING
ENVELOPE:- STEEL COATED WITH GILDING METAL
BULLET TIP COLOURED RED
·30 - IN.G MK.IZ TRACER CARTRIDGE
DIMENSIONS IN INCHES

Typical cartridge construction

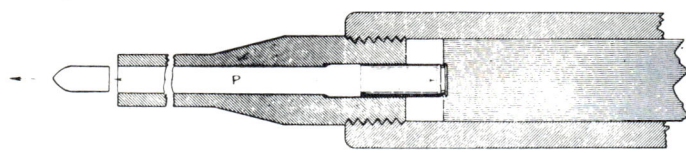

Simple blowback. The bolt is unlocked and blown to the rear by gas pressure

firing. This form of operation is suitable only where the cartridge is of low power relative to the weight of the breech block; and simple blowback actions are thus effectively restricted to pistols and sub-machine guns.

With sub-machine guns the heavy breech block usually incorporates a fixed firing pin, and during the process of stripping a round from the magazine during the forward travel of the breech block, the firing pin is positioned directly upon the primer cap of the cartridge. As the round is chambered the resistance offered to the cartridge case allows the firing pin to actuate the cap. At this point the breech block is still moving forward in the final stage of crushing up the cartridge, and the breech face is not quite home.

ADVANCED PRIMER IGNITION

More sophisticated blowback designs have been incorporated into large calibre machine guns. These take advantage of the fact that a cartridge fired before being fully chambered allows half the firing impulse to be devoted to slowing down the breech block so that only half the impulse is available to force the block back again. This in effect allows the breech block to be made lighter. In such weapons the fixed firing pin of the simple blowback design is replaced by a controlled pin which strikes the cap at the desired point in the forward travel of the cartridge.

DELAYED BLOWBACK

(Also called "retarded blowback" or "hesitation blowback.")

Here as in the previous blowback systems the breech block is not locked, but some mechanical delay is incorporated to ensure that the breech block cannot move back sufficiently rapidly to allow the unsupported case to emerge from the chamber whilst the pressure is still high. The delay may be due to the use of a lever system (see the French AA 52 GPMG) or a system of rollers, as used by Heckler and Koch in nearly all their weapons, which must be forced in from engagement with the barrel extension before the breech block can move back.

A feature of all delayed blowback systems is that the delaying force is greatest whilst the pressure is high and is reduced as the pressure drops off.

A well designed delay system such as that used in the Swiss SIG 710-3 enables the breech block weight to be reduced to 1/16 of the weight of a simple blowback block.

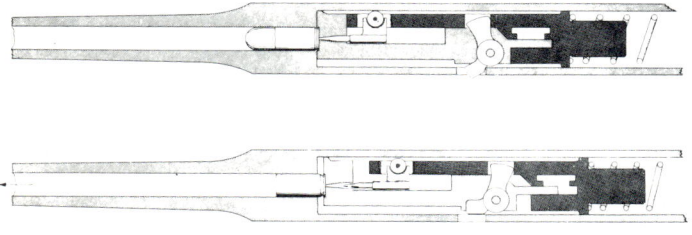

Delayed blowback. The Hungarian M39 SMG. The lever mounted in the front part of the block must be rotated before the breech face can be blown back

BLOWBACK WITH A LOCKED BREECH

Here the breech block is physically locked to the receiver of the weapon whilst the pressure is high but is unlocked in time to allow the residual pressure to blow the breech block to the rear. This method allows the lightest possible breech block with a high powered cartridge, but the timing of the breech opening is critical and the system tends to be expensive.

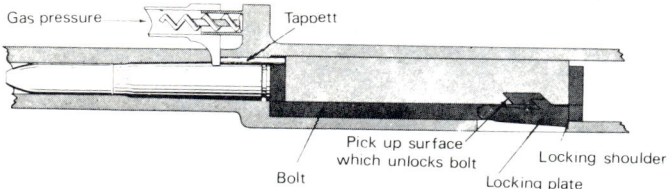

Blowback with a locked breech. The Hispano-Suiza 20mm gun. The gas tapped off drives back side plates which lift the locking plate out of the receiver

ADVANTAGES AND DISADVANTAGES OF BLOWBACK OPERATION

The method is cheap, simple and reliable. Barrel change is very good.

There is no way of adjusting the power. There is a lot of fouling in the breech. There is a release of toxic fumes from the breech which makes the system unsuitable for use in a confined space.

RECOIL OPERATION

In this method of operation the energy required to carry out the cycle of operations is supplied to the bolt by the rearward movement of the bolt and

barrel, locked together, caused by the gas pressure.

The system differs from the blowback system in having a fully locked breech and in having the barrel move back with the breech block.

LONG RECOIL

In the long recoil system the bolt and barrel both recoil a distance which is greater than the length of the unfired round. The breech block is then held to the rear whilst the barrel is driven forward by its own spring. When the barrel is fully forward it trips the catch releasing the breech block which then feeds the next round into the chamber. This method produces a very slow rate of fire but has advantages where it is important to keep down the forces exerted on the mounting, and apart from this special requirement it is very rarely met. A current military example is the British 30mm Rarden gun.

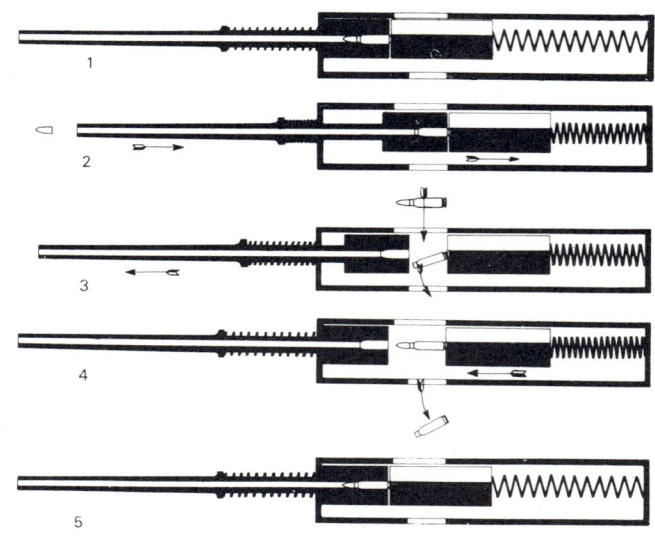

Long recoil: (1) Gun ready to fire; (2) Barrel and block recoiling; (3) Bolt held to rear; Barrel going forward; (4) Barrel fully forward; Bolt going forward; (5) Round chambered. Gun ready to fire

SHORT RECOIL

Here the breech block remains locked to the barrel only whilst the pressure is high and in practice, with a rifle calibre round, this involves a barrel travel of only a centimetre or so. The device locking the breech to the barrel is then released and the two components separate. The barrel may remain stationary and await the return of the breech block but in most modern designs the barrel has its own spring and goes forward into battery.

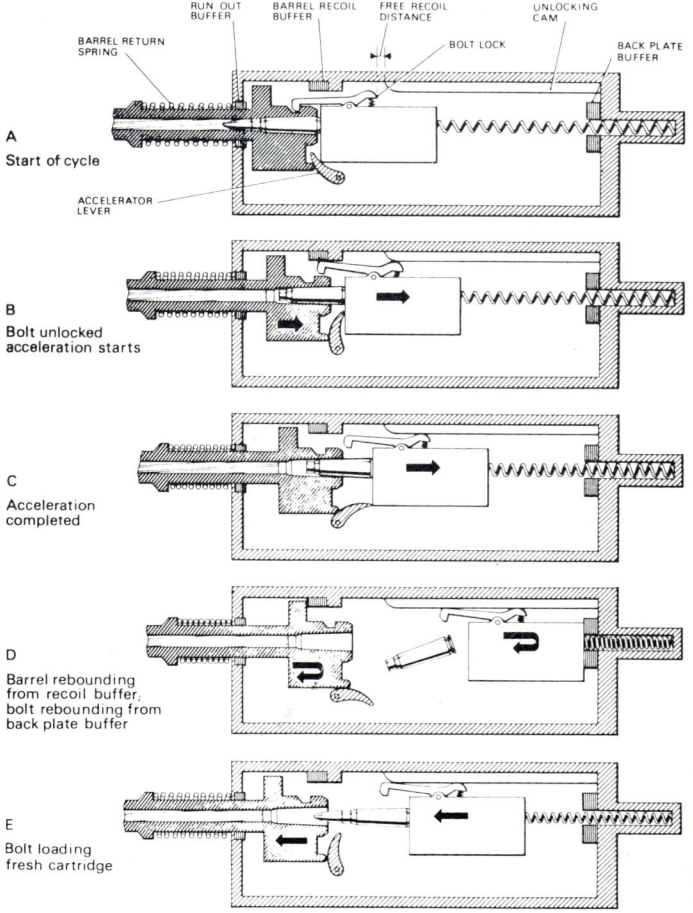

Elements of the short recoil system

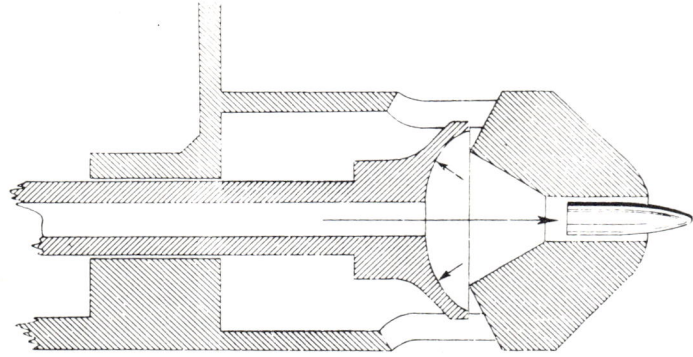

The recoil intensifier

This system has the advantage of having a locked breech which reduces the weight of the breech block compared with that required in a blowback system. In a rifle calibre weapon, however, there is a shortage of recoil energy; and the system will not work unless steps are taken both to maximise the available energy and to use it to the best advantage.

To increase the available energy a recoil intensifier can be used. This consists of a chamber located at the muzzle and attached, not to the barrel, but to the main body of the weapon, the barrel face forming a movable rear wall of the chamber. The gases following the bullet up the bore expand into this chamber and exert a backward force on the barrel face which accelerates the barrel, and the breech block locked to it, backwards.

Secondly, the energy and momentum of the barrel can be harnessed to assist the rearward movement of the breech block. This is done by a device called an accelerator which transfers energy from the barrel to the block. It may take one of several forms but the most common and certainly the easiest to understand is the lever, or claw, accelerator. This is a lever pinned to the non-recoiling receiver and having, effectively, a short and a long arm.

The shorter arm is rotated by the barrel and the longer arm bears on and accelerates the breech block to the rear. The velocity ratio works out in practice to be about 1.5 and so the breech block velocity is increased by this ratio and its energy by 2.25. The effect of the use of the locked breech, the recoil intensifier and the accelerator is to increase the rate of fire, if so required, and recoil-operated guns can produce rates of fire which can be as high as 1,800 rounds a minute: the Mauser MG 81 is fired at this rate from each of its two barrels. The current German MG 3 produces 1,200 rounds/minute.

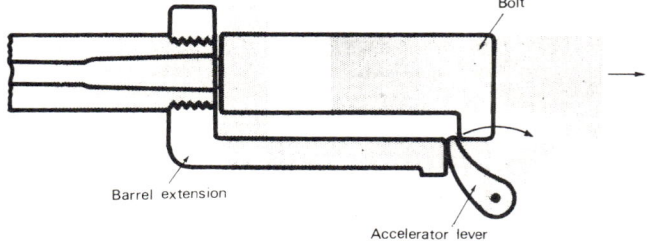

Principle of a lever accelerator

ADVANTAGES AND DISADVANTAGES OF RECOIL OPERATION

The recoil-operated machine gun is particularly suitable for use in an armoured fighting vehicle. The rate of fire can be slowed down by delaying the moment of breech opening and this has also the great advantage that the pressure has dropped to ambient and so no fumes are drawn into the crew compartment. Recoil operated guns are sturdy. The barrel change can easily be arranged to the rear. There is, however, no way of adjusting the power under adverse conditions.

GAS OPERATION

This is a system of operation in which the energy required is obtained from the pressure of gas tapped off from the barrel. The amount of gas required to operate a machine gun is not very great and the effect on the pressure in the barrel and hence on the velocity of the projectile is correspondingly small.

The gas can be tapped off anywhere between breech and muzzle and examples can be found of every conceivable gas position. There are different effects to be obtained at the different positions. Gas taken off near to the breech is very hot, and at very high pressure, but it is "clean" because

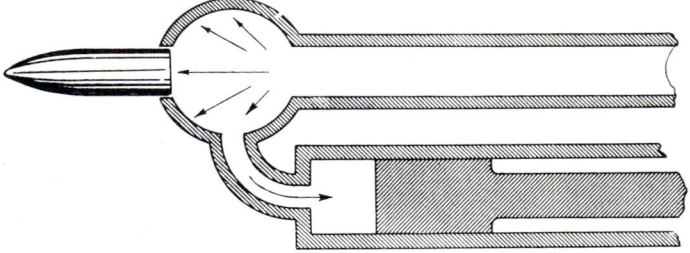

The muzzle trap

all the carbon has been sublimated and is totally gaseous. The heat and pressure tend to erode the metal around the gas vent, however, with the result that more gas is taken into the cylinder than the designer catered for and the action becomes progressively harsher.

The high pressure at the breech also requires that the piston and operating rod, or piston extension, be massive to withstand the sudden impulsive loading applied.

At the muzzle the gas is at a low pressure and is much cooler. As a result more gas must be led off to obtain the same working force. The carbon is de-sublimated and so there is a lot of fouling. The working parts can be light but since they are so far away from the breech they tend to be thin and "spidery".

Gas has been collected in a muzzle trap to operate a piston: at the other extreme a gun has been produced which had a hole in the chamber wall through which a small section of the brass cartridge case was blown to release the gas to drive back a very short tappet. In general a compromise is made, with a tap-off point somewhere about 20 to 30cm from the muzzle according to the calibre and barrel length.

The gas pressure can be used in three different ways to operate the gun. These are:

Long stroke piston operation
Short stroke piston operation
Direct gas operation.

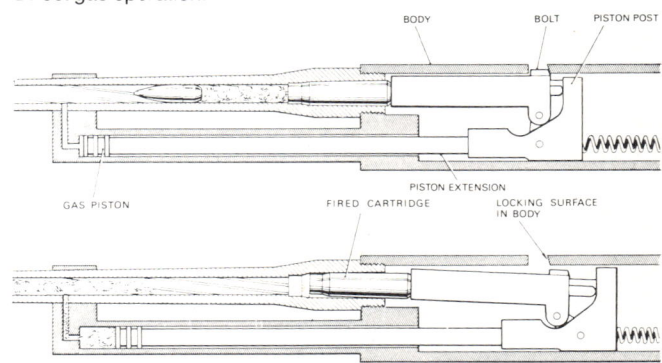

Diagrammatic representation of a gas-operated gun

LONG STROKE PISTON OPERATION

In this system the piston is connected directly to the breech block and controls the position of the block at all times. This sort of arrangement is found in by far the greatest number of modern machine guns. Typical examples are the FN MAG, the USA M 60 and the Russian PK. The piston tends to be long and heavy and the recoiling mass is considerable.

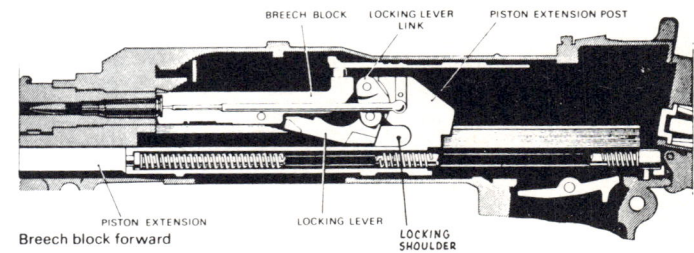

Breech block forward

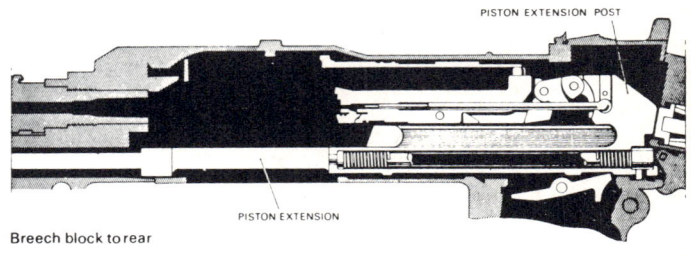

Breech block to rear

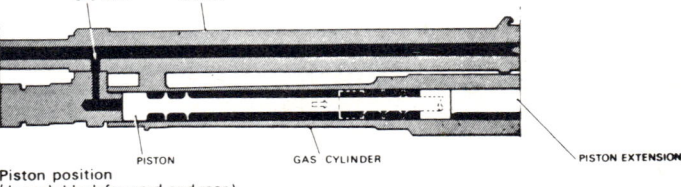

Piston position
(breech block forward and rear)

Long stroke piston – L7A1, GPMG

SHORT STROKE PISTON OPERATION

Here the piston moves back a distance that can be as short as only a millimetre or two but it imparts its energy to an operating rod which forces the breech block to the rear.

This way of arranging things is found on the great majority of gas operated rifles (a notable exception is the Russian Kalashnikov system which is a long stroke system) largely because it avoids large changes in the centre of mass of the weapon during firing and thus tends to have less effect on the firer's aim than a long stroke system. The operating rod impinges on a bolt carrier and the movement of the carrier first unlocks the bolt and then carries it to the rear. The operating rod and the bolt can be quite light and so there is not an excessive change of the centre of mass.

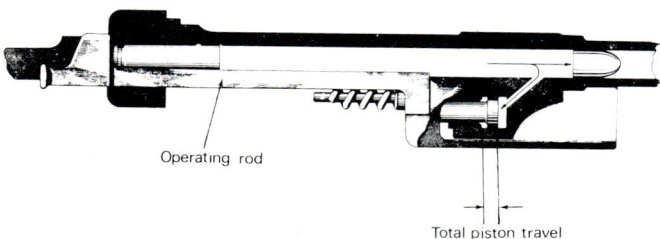

The short stroke piston

DIRECT GAS ACTION

No piston at all is used in this method. The gas is tapped off from the barrel and ducted back along a tube. It then imparts energy to the bolt carrier and again the carrier unlocks the bolt and transports it to the rear. The first use of this type of operation is credited to the Swede, Ljungman, who designed a rifle on this principle in 1942. It has since been used in the French SL rifle and also in the current US M16 rifle. The direct gas action system produces the lightest possible moving mass but can result in a lot of fouling because the gases cool in the duct and bolt carrier, depositing solid residue in a critically inaccessible area where the accummulation of carbon can lead to difficult and prolonged stoppages.

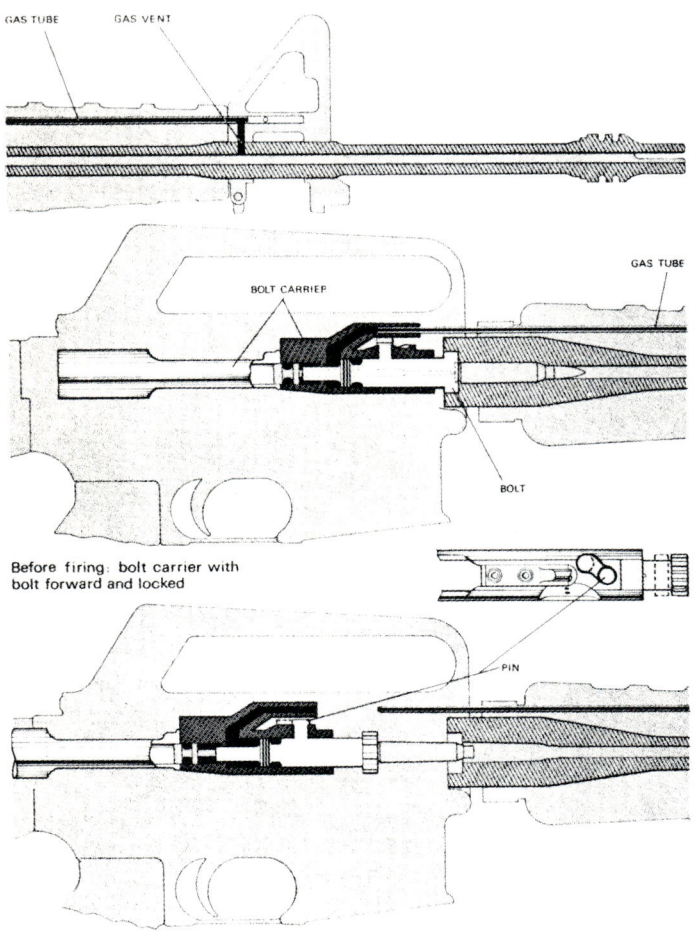

Direct gas action – M16 rifle

ADVANTAGES AND DISADVANTAGES OF GAS OPERATION

Gas operation is the only system that can genuinely regulate the power available and control it according to the needs of the moment. When the gun is dirty or there is a lot of ammunition to lift in a belt, or a prolonged period of firing has produced fouling, then the amount of gas drawn off to operate the gun can be increased by using a simple regulator.

Disadvantages include the likelihood of fouling and the emission of toxic fumes which make it, generally, unsuitable for use in an armoured fighting vehicle without special changes to alter the gas system. The barrel change, due to the mating of barrel and gas cylinder, must be on a forward direction which again is not an advantage in an armoured vehicle.

MECHANICAL SAFETY

The high pressures produced by modern propellants make it essential that the gases in the chamber are fully contained and unable to escape backwards through the breech closing arrangements. This leads to the definition of mechanical safety as "a feature of design ensuring that the round cannot be fired until it is fully supported in the chamber and that the support cannot be removed until the pressure has dropped to a safe low level".

In practice the requirement is met by making the breech closing arrangement control the firing mechanism. This applies to the bolt operated rifle where the firing pin cannot reach the cap if the bolt is not fully forward and rotated completely, and to the machine gun where the final forward movement of bolt or piston, or the final movement of bolt locking, releases a safety sear which until then holds up the firing mechanism even if the trigger mechanism has been operated.

In all guns except those operated by blowback, a locked breech is used. This is simply a mechanical arrangement securing the bolt to either the barrel or the receiver. In modern designs it is becoming more and more the practice to lock the bolt to the barrel extension and not to the receiver. The advantages of this are that the stresses are confined to the breech face and the barrel and all the rest of the weapon is relatively unstressed. This leads to a lighter and cheaper weapon as well as better control of the cartridge head space*. It is also suitable for both gas and recoil operation whereas locking into the receiver is possible only with gas operation.

The actual method of locking selected can vary a great deal. The commonest is the rotating bolt. This is used in the American 5.56mm rifles, in the Russian Kalashnikov system for both rifles and machine guns and in many machine guns in current use – the US M60 is a good example. Another frequently-used system involves tilting the bolt so that one end lifts, swings or drops into a recess in the receiver. This system is used in the FN Rifle, the Bren Gun and the Russian Goryunov machine guns. There are several other locking systems but it is sufficient to mention only one more and that is the "projecting lug". This is a blanket term which covers all the arrangements by which a lug moves out from the bolt into the receiver or, conversely, from the receiver into the bolt. Examples are the Browning Machine Gun with a single lug, the Degtyarev with a symmetrical support from two lugs and the German MG 42 where the lugs were rollers in form.

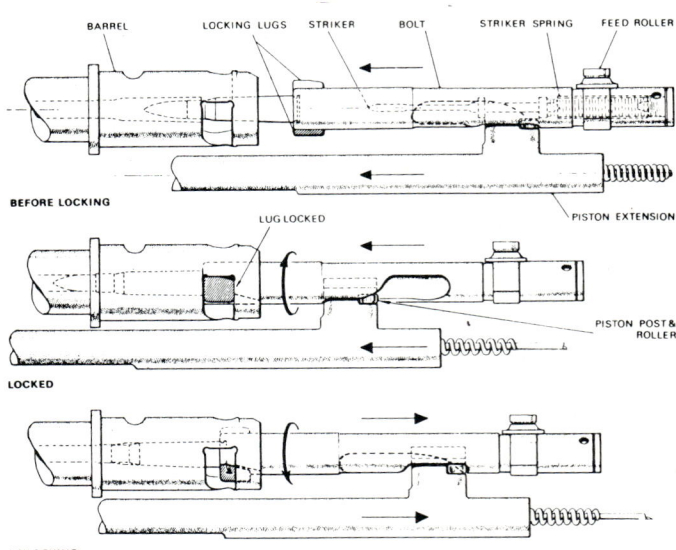

Rotating bolt application – US GPMG M60

The essential feature of the locking system is that it connects the bolt to the barrel or receiver and has sufficient mechanical strength not only to hold up the block against gas pressure but also to ensure that there is no yielding or set back of the breech face.

Finally there is the last requirement of mechanical safety that the support afforded the cartridge case in the chamber should not be removed whilst the pressure is still high. This is achieved in different ways with different methods of operation. In blowback operation, the mass of the block is critical; with delayed blowback the mass is replaced by a system producing

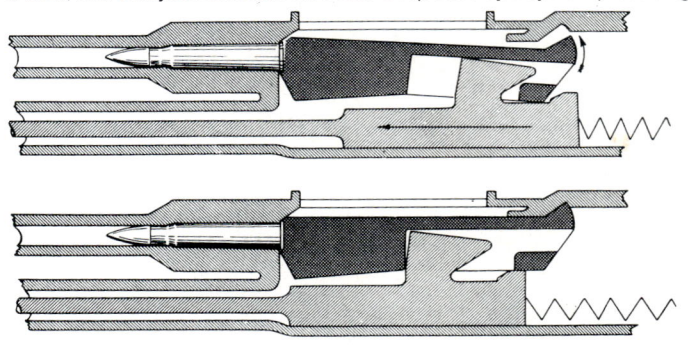

Tilting block locking system

*Defined as "the distance from the front face of the bolt to the seating surface of the cartridge in the chamber". This is the thickness of the rim in a rimmed cartridge case and in the case of a rimless round, the distance to a datum diameter selected by the designer.

a mechanical disadvantage to delay bolt movement. With recoil operation the bolt is never unlocked until the bullet is clear of the muzzle and the pressure is down; with gas operation the first movement of the mechanism is an idle so that no force is exerted to start the unlocking process until the chamber pressure is very low.

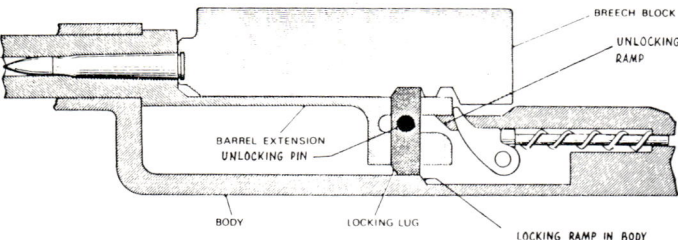

Projecting lug locking – Browning MG

FEED

The method of feed selected for a gun varies according to the tactical role. A rifle needs less ammunition than a machine gun, but when the supply is exhausted it is often a matter of urgency to effect a quick re-supply, whereas with the machine gun the enemy is further away and the urgency somewhat less. This leads to magazines for rifles and light machine guns, and belts for medium machine guns. This argument can be carried further by relating the method of supply to the mobility required of the weapon. The more mobile the weapon the smaller and more compact the ammunition supply – thus again rifles have small magazines and heavy machine guns have long belts.

The actual process of positioning the round for feeding into the chamber is critical and poor feed produces a high proportion of the failures in automatic weapons. Moving the cartridge from the belt into the chamber and then moving the belt across to position the next round for feeding can lead to quite complicated mechanisms. These must be sturdy to lift all the weight of ammunition that can be involved in the belt feeding of a fast firing machine gun.

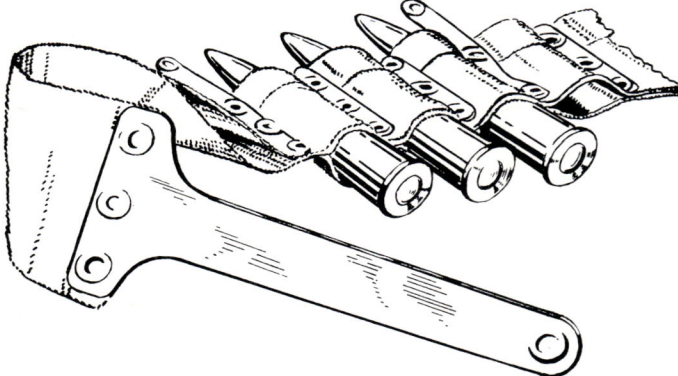

A closed-pocket belt

The earliest machine guns of the Maxim type, and later those of Browning, had complicated feed systems in which the cartridge was withdrawn from the belt at a level above that of the chamber, carried to the rear and subsequently lowered to the level of the chamber before being fed forward. This complication was not due to using a rimmed round – Browning of course never did use a rimmed round – but to the use of the closed pocket belt which completely enclosed the cartridge. This made it impossible to use the bolt to drive the round straight into the chamber, since the bolt must

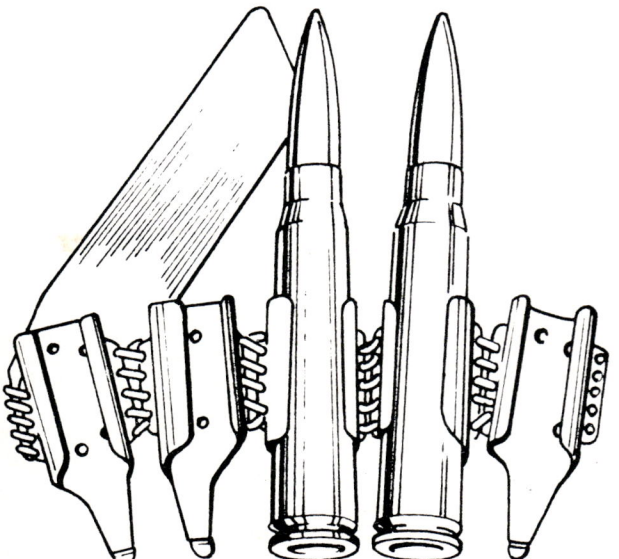

An open-pocket belt

inevitably come into contact with the belt and so cause a stoppage. This problem disappeared with the advent of the open pocket belt.

With magazine feed there are also problems. These are associated with the questions of spring strength and the entry of dirt. If the spring is too strong the first round cannot be fed forward. If it is too weak the last rounds are not held securely into the path of the bolt. Storage with the spring compressed for a long period of time also brings difficulties. The magazine must be designed to allow the dirt, sand, snow etc that must inevitably find its way into the magazine, to fall to the bottom and not jam the rounds.

The choice between the magazine and the belt is far less clear cut than it was a few years ago. It was generally accepted that Light Machine Guns would be magazine fed and Medium Machine Guns would be belt fed. This was based on the tactical roles of the weapons but in the period after the Second World War the major nations seem to have been so impressed with the concept of the General Purpose Machine Gun as exemplified by the German MG 42, that they have all gone to belt feed for all machine gun roles. There is a tendency today for the troops to prefer the magazine for weapons where prolonged, sustained fire is not required and anyone who has had a length of belt catch in undergrowth at a critical moment, could well support that view. It is significant that the Russians, who adopted the RPD, a belt fed light machine gun, after the war, have now gone back to a magazine feed in their new LMG, the RPK.

EXTRACTION

The process of removing the fired round from the chamber is not as simple as it looks. The high pressure forces the brass case outwards against the chamber walls to provide the obturation necessary to prevent gas escape. At the same time if that case is expanded beyond its elastic limit it will not return to its original dimensions when the pressure drops and the friction force will be very high when the extractor starts to move it rearward. It may be sufficiently high for the extractor to tear a segment out of the rim or head of the case.

In a recoil-operated gun, or a gas-operated gun it is possible to arrange what is called "primary extraction" where the act of removing the support of the bolt provides a slow powerful leverage which loosens the case in the chamber and frees it sufficiently to take the stress off the extractor and rim. In a blowback-operated gun this is not possible as the motive power for bolt motion can come only from the case movement and the bolt can exert no rearward force on the case. The problem with blowback operation is that if the case sticks in the chamber the friction force can exceed the ultimate tensile strength of the case which is then separated by the backward gas force and the bolt is blown back, leaving part of the case in the chamber and so preventing the feed of the next round into the chamber.

In the past it has been the practice to lubricate the cartridge case in blowback operated guns to ensure clean extraction but this has proved to be an unsatisfactory process in the field and is generally regarded as unacceptable today. Instead the process of fluting the chamber is used, whereby gas is allowed to bleed back from the neck of the case and surround the forward part of the round. The case can then be regarded as floating in a film of gas and there is no friction force preventing movement.

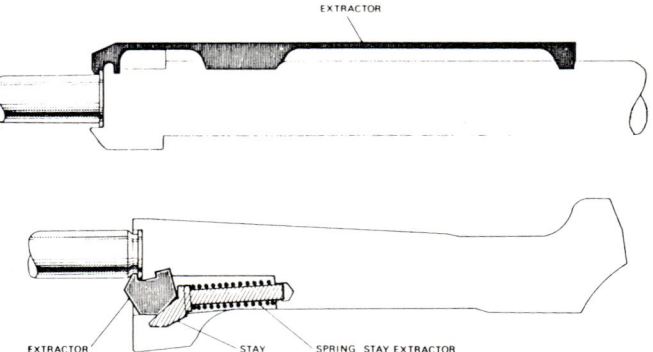

Top diagram: a one-piece extractor of the type used in a rifle bolt. Bottom diagram: the multi-piece extractor used on the Bren gun

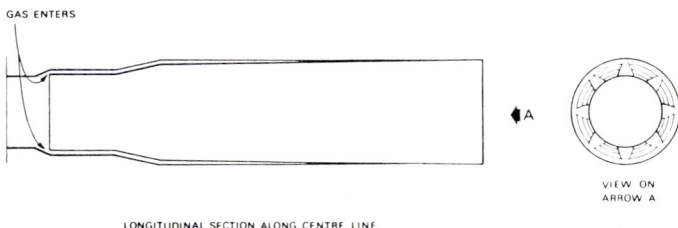

Fluted chamber

EJECTION

This is the process of removing the empty case or unfired round from the feedway. In a weapon of conventional design it is sufficient to bring the cartridge case into contact with a fixed projection which will then rotate it about the extractor and impart to it the energy required to direct it clear of the gun. This method, the earliest and simplest used, is still employed in the majority of guns. Alternatively a spring loaded plunger may be located within the face of the bolt and when the case is withdrawn clear of the

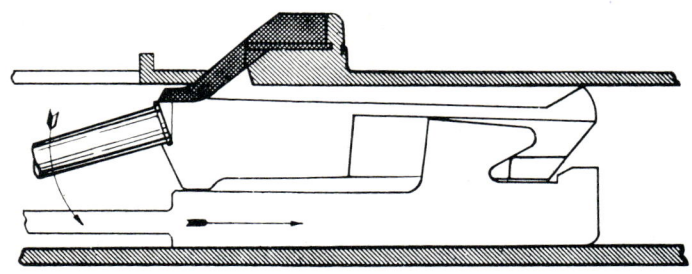

A fixed ejector

restraint imposed by the chamber, the plunger is able to emerge and rotate the case about the extractor and propel it out of the weapon.

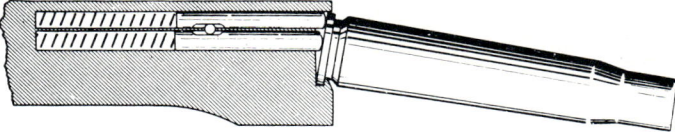

The spring loaded plunger ejector

The only real problem in ejector design is to ensure that the case goes in the right direction when it leaves the gun. The number two of the gun rarely relishes a stream of hot cases directed into his face.

REVOLVERS AND SELF-LOADING PISTOLS

INTRODUCTION

The pistol can be defined as a weapon designed to be fired using only one hand. It exists today in the form of the pistol revolver and the self-loading pistol. Of the two types the pistol revolver is the earlier and the self-loading pistol is, comparatively, a newcomer to the battlefield.

PISTOLS, REVOLVER

The pistol followed the musket in adopting various forms of ignition that were evolved, developed and subsequently discarded for some new principle or application of an existing system, which offered savings in time or increased assurance of successful functioning. The earliest pistols were single-barrel weapons; these were followed by cluster barrels – often referred to as 'pepper boxes'. The first modern revolver as the term is now understood, was probably that of E. H. Collier of Boston, Massachusetts. (There was a revolver in the time of Charles I but the state of the art of metallurgy prevented its success). Collier obtained an English patent in 1818 for a flintlock revolver which had a five-chambered cylinder. The most interesting part of the design was that the cylinder moved forward before the cock fell and the front of the chamber fitted over the cone-shaped rear end of the barrel in a manner almost identical to that used in the Belgian Nagant revolver adopted by the Russian Army in 1895. The method ensured that gas did not escape from the front of the cylinder and so dissipate energy that should have been forcing the bullet up the bore.

The development of percussion ignition simplified the design of hand guns. In 1835 Samuel Colt took out an English patent for a revolving cylinder weapon with six chambers. A ratchet with six teeth was cut round the head of the cylinder and as the firer retracted the hammer a metal 'hand' rotated the cylinder one sixth of a revolution – or 60 degrees – and it was then locked. The percussion caps were fitted over hollow nipples and a partition separated the nipples to prevent the flash from one setting off its neighbour.

After initial setbacks Colt set up a production line at Hartford, Connecticut, and from 1853 to 1857 he also manufactured single action revolvers in London.

The single action revolver requires the firer to cock the hammer by hand between shots. A pull on the trigger releases the hammer which is rotated forward by its compressed spring.

The double action pistol enables the firer first to cock the hammer and rotate the cylinder and then to release the hammer – all as a result of one long trigger pull. In most designs the weapon can also be thumb-cocked like a single action revolver. The first double action revolver of significance was produced by Beaumont in London in 1855. This could function as either a double action or single action revolver and the idea was used in the Adams revolver which became the official British Service revolver. Colt then gave up his British factory in 1857 and returned to the States. His six-chambered percussion 1860 model in .44 calibre was extensively used in the American

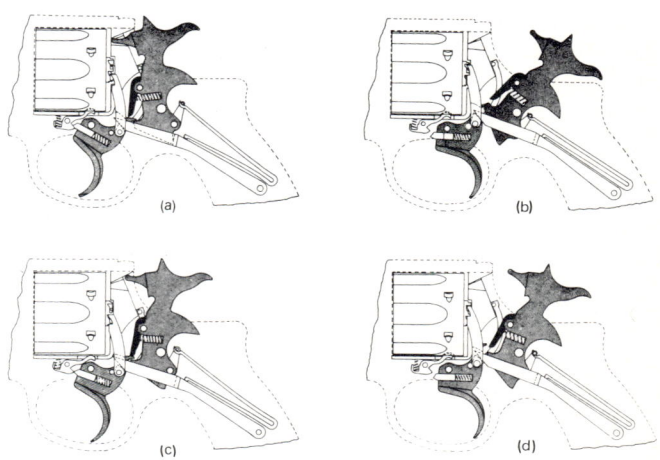

(a) Single action hammer withdrawn; *(b)* Single action, cocked position, cylinder locked; *(c)* Double action, cocking, hammer rotating cylinder; *(d)* Double action, hammer cocked

Civil War and more than 200,000 were made.

The pin-fire revolver saw a brief popularity and then the rimfire percussion cartridge was evolved by Flobert in Paris. Smith and Wesson, probably second only to Colt in the development of revolvers, bought up the patents held by Rollin White and became the only manufacturer in the USA able to drill the chamber through to allow insertion of a metal cartridge from the rear.

When their patents expired in 1869 a host of other manufacturers produced revolvers but Colt was the most successful and the solid frame pistol known as the Single Action Army was bought in large numbers from the date of its introduction in 1873. This .45 revolver, using a metallic cartridge, was a direct descendant of the Colt Model 1860. It had a top strap and spring loaded ejector.

In 1889 the US Government adopted the Colt .38 revolver which introduced the swing-out cylinder – giving the strength of the solid frame and quick loading and unloading. The British Army adopted the Webley hinged frame in 1894. This had a stirrup-shaped lock which engaged over the barrel stop to produce a very rigid frame. Development of the revolver has subsequently produced no new principles but many small innovations.

The principle of the double action revolver which can also be thumb cocked to act as a single pistol is shown in the accompanying diagram.

PISTOLS, SELF-LOADING

This type of weapon carries out all the stages of the cycle of operations, except that of firing, using energy which originates from the powder charge. The trigger must be released and then pulled for each shot fired. It is important to appreciate that many so called "automatic" pistols are in fact "self-loading" or "semi automatic". The true automatic pistol, which fires successive rounds during one continued trigger pull, is rarely met. The Russian Stechkin pistol is an example of the automatic pistol but, like all such pistols, the displacement between the line of backward force along the barrel and the position where the pistol is gripped, produces a turning movement which causes the muzzle to accelerate upwards as each successive round is fired. As a result the rounds go higher and higher and the chance of a hit gets progressively less.

The self-loading pistol became possible because of the development in ammunition. The production of a strong case, capable of producing total obturation as well as withstanding not only the powder pressure but also the stress of extraction, was the first requirement. Next came the production of propellants able to burn away completely during the first few centimetres of bullet travel and lastly the jacketed bullet, firmly crimped into a brass case, which could withstand the shock of loading.

When such a cartridge became available the self-loading (SL) pistol followed as a matter of course and the first practical example is generally taken to be the Schonberger, made by the Austrian Arms Works at Steyr. This was charger loaded through the top, like a magazine rifle, and the charger fell out of the bottom of the magazine when the last round was chambered.

The Borchardt SL pistol of 1893 was the first such pistol to be widely known and was developed into the Luger which is still made by the German

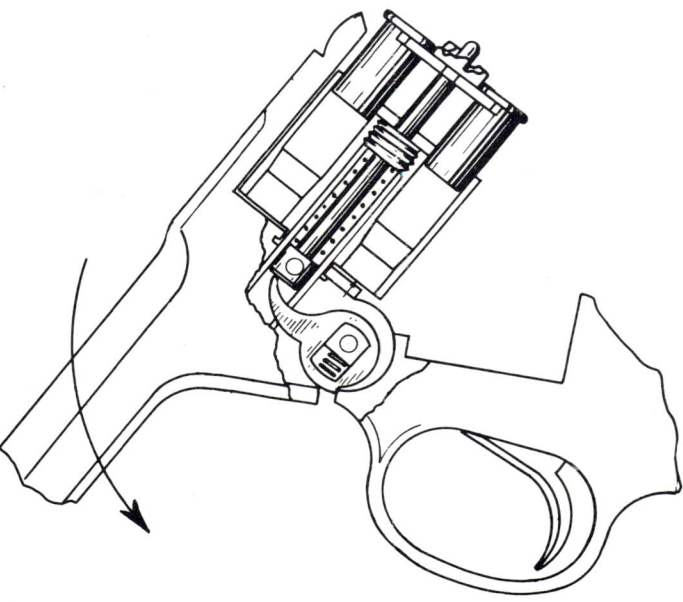

Combined extractor – ejector. As the barrel is swung down, the pawl lifts the extractor. When the barrel forces the pawl off the step, against its spring, the extractor spring closes the extractor and rotates the pawl

firm of Mauser. The cartridge Borchardt developed became the 7.63mm Mauser which is essentially the same as the 7.62mm 'P' ball used by the Russians for many years in both pistols and sub-machine guns, and still so employed by the satellite countries.

The first Browning pistol was made for Fabrique Nationale, at Herstal near Liège, and a patent granted on 21 March 1899. From this start a wide variety of Browning designs have appeared. The curent US military pistol – the Colt M1911A1 – stems directly from Browning's early designs.

The self-loading pistol is not an exceptionally complicated piece of mechanism but there are some factors which, if appreciated, make understanding easier. First comes the method of operation. The energy required to carry out the cycle of operations – moving the support from the empty case in the chamber, extracting that case, ejecting it from the gun, storing energy in a return spring, feeding a new round into the chamber and lastly supporting it there, all comes from the propellant. The last stage of the cycle of operations – 'firing' – is carried out by the user releasing the trigger and then squeezing it when he desires to discharge the weapon.

This propellant energy can be used in one of two ways. The pistol can be either blowback-operated or recoil-operated. Gas-operated pistols have never passed beyond the experimental stage.

The blowback-operated pistol will have a low powered cartridge of parallel sided shape, firing a light bullet at a comparatively low velocity. This method of operation is commonly found in .22RF pistols and will be met in pistols up to .380ACP (9mm short) calibre. The Russians use it with their 9mm × 18 pistol cartridge which is significantly lower in power than the NATO 9mm × 19 Parabellum, (9mm × 19 is the customary method of defining calibre and cartridge case length). The 9mm × 19 cartridge is not used in blowback-operated pistols.

The principle of blowback is that at the moment of firing the breech is unlocked and the cartridge is supported by the mass – or inertia – of the breech-block, and its return spring. When the propellant is ignited the resulting pressure forces the case back and this in turn drives the breech-block to the rear, compressing the return spring. The cartridge case, of course, needs no extractor but one is invariably fitted to deal with misfires, practice rounds and to position the empty case correctly for ejection. The return spring forces the breech-block forward, another round is chambered and the block closes up to support the case. The firer must release the trigger and then when it is pulled again another round is fired. The characteristics of blowback operation may be listed as:

A low powered cartridge with parallel sided case to provide obturation as it moves out of the chamber.

A heavy breech-block and powerful return spring to support the cartridge in the chamber.

A short barrel, to allow the pressure to drop off quickly, which results in a not very accurate weapon.

The powerful military pistol cartridge such as the 9mm × 19 Parabellum, the Soviet 7.62mm × 25 'P' ball, or the USA .45ACP cartridge, all demand a locked breech at the moment of firing.

This leads to recoil operation and in this method the breech-block is locked to the barrel and the gas pressure now forces back the mass of both breech-block and barrel. When the gas pressure has dropped to a safe level the breech-block is unlocked from the barrel. The breech-block continues to the rear to carry out the cycle of operations. The barrel stops and is returned to its forward position when the breech-block locks on to it again when the next round is chambered. Whereas the blowback operated pistol will inevitably be found to have a near parallel sided case, the recoil operated pistol has no such limitations and will be found in some weapons to have a bottle-necked case whilst in others a parallel sided case is employed.

REVOLVER VERSUS SELF-LOADING PISTOLS

The first essential in any discussion on the relative merits of the two types of pistol is to establish, without doubt, the purpose for which the weapon is to be employed.

The two broad categories are military use and police use and the two are quite different. The characteristics of the weapons required are equally diverse. The distinctive differences between the pistol revolver and the self-loading pistol can be listed as follows:

Pistol, Revolver	Pistol, Self-Loading
Simple mechanism	Complicated mechanism
Ammunition in chamber visible	Ammunition concealed
No applied safety needed	Applied safety essential
No misfire problems	Misfire requires hand operation to clear
Single action firing produces smooth trigger action leading to extreme accuracy	Trigger action rarely as smooth
Bulky	Can be made flat and unobtrusive
Generally limited to 6 rounds	Can take up to c. 13 rounds
Long time to reload chamber	Simple to replace magazine
Produces lower muzzle velocity	Produces high muzzle velocity

The foregoing leads to the conclusion that:

(1) The self-loading pistol produces a greater volume of fire in a given time, is less reliable, is not so safe except in expert hands, and its stoppages take a lot longer to clear. In small calibres it is easily concealed. The training time is lengthy if the user is to be capable of firing and maintaining the pistol under all conditions.

(2) The pistol revolver is safer and more reliable and training time is greatly reduced. It contains fewer rounds, fires at a lower muzzle velocity and is more bulky.

It would seem that the self-loading pistol is largely a military weapon where training of the user can be carried out by military personnel.

The pistol revolver is best suited for police work where its simplicity, reliability and short training time are advantageous. Its sole disadvantage is that of bulk.

It is worthy of note that in the United States of America where excellent pistols of both categories are available, the military employ a self-loading pistol and the police – in over 99 per cent of all cases – use a pistol revolver.

ARGENTINA

.45in MODEL 1916 PISTOL

This pistol was a copy of the USA Colt 1911 (qv). It was purchased from Colt initially and then manufactured at the Fabrica Militar de Armas Portatiles 'Domingo Matheu', an Ordnance Factory, at Rosario, Santa Fe.

The M1916 replaced a Mannlicher pistol which had been in service since before the First World War. Most of the Mannlichers were sold to the USA and are unlikely to be encountered: the M1916 was replaced by the M1927 (see below) but some may still exist.

.45in AUTOMATIC PISTOL MODEL 1927

This pistol was a copy of the Colt 1911 A1 (qv). It was also manufactured at Rosario and is still in service with some units of the Argentinian Army.

.45in BALLESTER MOLINA

The firm of Hispano Argentino Fabrica de Automoviles SA – HAFDASA – at Buenos Aires manufactured the Ballester Molina – a variation of the Colt 1911 automatic pistol – in considerable numbers during World War II. It achieved a high reputation for functioning under adverse conditions and was used by various allied undercover groups. The pistol differs from the Colt only in minor details. The trigger pivots instead of sliding, there is a trigger extension, on the right of the grip, to operate the disconnector and the hammer strut is smaller. The magazines are interchangeable.

HAFDASA no longer makes pistols.

The .45 Ballester Molina pistol (RSAF)

DATA
Cartridge: .45 Colt ACP
Method of operation: Recoil
Method of locking: Projecting lugs
Method of feed: 7-round box magazine
Method of fire: Semi-automatic
Weight: 1.02kg
Length: 216mm
Barrel: 127mm
      Rifling: 6 grooves RH
Sights: Foresight: Blade
      Rearsight: Notch
Muzzle velocity: 253 metres/sec
Muzzle energy: 49 mkp
Rate of fire: 35 rounds/min
Range, maximum effective: 50 metres
Manufacturer: Hispano Argentino Fabrica de Automoviles SA
Status: Still in service but obsolescent and no longer in production.

9mm FN GP PISTOL

This pistol is now being produced at the Government Factory at Rosario. It is similar to that produced by FN in Belgium.
Manufacturer: Fabrica Militar de Armas Portatilos 'Domingo Matheu', Rosario.
Status: In production and in service.

AUSTRIA

AUSTRIAN ARMY PISTOLS

In the early years of this century the Austrian Army was issued with the Roth Steyr Pistol M1907 made by Osterreichische Waffenfabrik at Steyr and by Femaru Fegyver in Budapest. Between the wars they changed to the 9mm Steyr M12 pistol, (see below).   Both weapons are now obsolete: the current Austrian Army pistol is the 9mm Parabellum Walther P38 (P1) manufactured by Steyr-Daimler-Puch AG (see under Germany – Federal Republic).

9mm STEYR M12 PISTOL

Although obsolete and long since replaced in Austrian military service by the Walther P38 design built by Steyr-Daimler-Puch, the M12 is worthy of note partly because it may still be encountered and partly because parts of its design have been copied elsewhere – for example in the 0.45in Mexican Obregon pistol (qv). The particular feature these copied was the rotating-barrel unlocking system in which the barrel is rotated through 60 degrees by threads engaging in recesses in the receiver. The M12 was originally designed for the 9mm Steyr cartridge, but some were converted, during the Second World War, to take the 9mm Parabellum round.
DATA
Cartridge: 9mm Steyr (some converted to 9mm × 19 Parabellum)
Method of operation: Recoil
Method of locking: Rotating barrel
Method of feed: 8-round clip into internal magazine
Method of fire: Semi-automatic
Weight: 930g
Length: 216mm
Barrel: 127mm
      Rifling: 4 grooves RH

Steyr M12 pistol (RSAF)
Sights: Foresight: Blade
      Rearsight: Notch
Muzzle velocity: 341m/sec (Steyr)
Muzzle energy: 51mkp
Rate of fire: 24 rounds/min
Effective range: 50m
Manufacturer: Steyr Waffenfabrik
Status: No longer made. Formerly used by the armed forces of Austria, Chile, Germany (wartime) and various Balkan countries but now officially obsolete in all of them

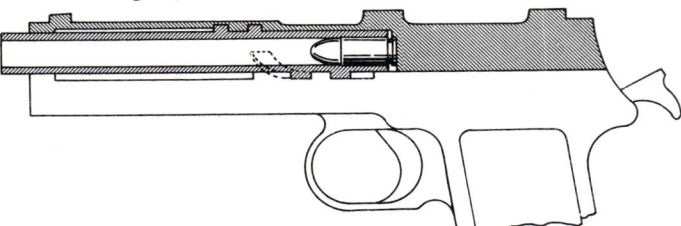

The Steyr rotating-barrel locking system (RSAF)

BELGIUM

BROWNING PISTOLS

The most famous name in Belgian pistol design is that of John Moses Browning who left his native USA and went to Herstal to work with Fabrique Nationale d'Armes de Guerre.

This partnership produced a number of designs which achieved wide use and were manufactured on a large scale. Chief among these designs were the following:
M1900: Blowback design, in 7.65mm (.32ACP) calibre;
M1903: Blowback design, in 9mm Browning long calibre;
M1910: Blowback design, in 7.65mm (.32ACP) and 9mm Short (.380ACP) calibre;
M1922: Blowback design, in 7.65mm (.32ACP) and 9mm Short (.380ACP) calibre.

Of the above self-loading pistols, only a few M1900 weapons, manufactured in North Korea, and possibly some M1903 pistols in Turkey, survive in official use.

The M1910 pistol is still in production for commercial sale; and while it is not known to be used by any official armed body it may well be in guerrilla or para-military use. It is described below.

The 9mm Browning M1910 pistol (RSAF)

The 9mm Browning M1903

7.65mm BROWNING MODEL 1910 PISTOL

This pistol was manufactured by FN using the 7.65mm (.32 ACP) cartridge and also the 9mm Short (.380 ACP). It was a striker fired, blowback operated pistol with the return spring around the barrel. It had a grip safety, a manual safety and the Browning disconnector.

Although designed in 1910 and marketed in 1912 it is still in production for sale to the USA.

The 7.65mm Browning Model 1910 (RSAF)

DATA
Cartridge: 7.65mm (.32ACP) 9mm Short (.380ACP)
Method of operation: Blowback
Method of locking: Nil
Method of feed: 7-round detachable box magazine
Method of fire: Semi-automatic
Weight: 582g
Length: 152mm
Barrel: 89mm
        Rifling: 6 grooves RH
Sights: Foresight: Blade
        Rearsight: Notch
Muzzle velocity: 299mm/sec (.32ACP)
Muzzle energy: 21mkp
Rate of fire: 35 rounds/min
Range, maximum effective: 40 metres
Manufacturer: Fabrique Nationale, Herstal
Status: Still in production for commercial sale. Not known to be in service with any regular military formation

9mm BROWNING HP PISTOL

The Browning High Power pistol was designed in 1925 by John M. Browning and granted US Patent No 1,618,510 on 22th February 1927 some three months after his death. It was produced in 1935 and in the USA it is still often referred to as the 1935 Model. When first introduced in 1935, two models were available: the "Ordinary Model" had fixed sights and the alternative, which had a tangent rear sight graduated to 500 metres and a dovetail slot in the rear of the pistol grip to take a wooden shoulder stock attached to a leather holster, was known as the "Adjustable Rear Sight Model". In Belgium the pistol is known as the GP (Grande Puissance). The High Power has been manufactured in Belgium by Fabrique Nationale (FN) at Herstal near Liège for sale in Europe. It was in service in Belgium, Denmark, Holland, Lithuania and Romania. During World War II the pistol was made in Liège for the use of the German SS Troops. It was manufactured by the John Inglis Company in Toronto during World War II and was used by Australian, British, Canadian and Chinese troops. In the USA it is distributed as a commercial model by the Browning Arms Co of St Louis. The High Power has different names in different countries and a short list of the better known names follows:
Belgium: Pistolet Automatique Browning Modèle à Grande Puissance
Canada: Pistol Browning FN 9mm HP No1, Mks 1 and 1*
Denmark: 9mm Pistol M/46
Germany: Pistole 640 (b)
Netherlands: Pistool, 9mm Browning, FN, GP
UK: Pistol, Automatic 9mm FN Browning No 2 Mk 1

CONSTRUCTION
The pistol consists of the receiver, the slide and the barrel. The receiver forms the pistol grip and extending forward is a semi-cylindrical shell for the

The 9mm Browning HP pistol. This is the current 9mm HP sold by FN as the "Vigilante"

slide and slide abutment. The barrel fits into the slide and on its underside, beneath the chamber where the barrel is strongly reinforced, is a lug into which is cut a forward and upward sloping camway. This is generally referred to in US literature as the 'barrel nose'. A cam is riveted to the receiver in such a way that when the barrel moves backward the cam enters the upward sloping cam path and pulls the rear of the barrel down. The

The 9mm Browning HP pistol. This is the current 9mm pistol sold by FN as the "Capitan". Note the tangent rear sight

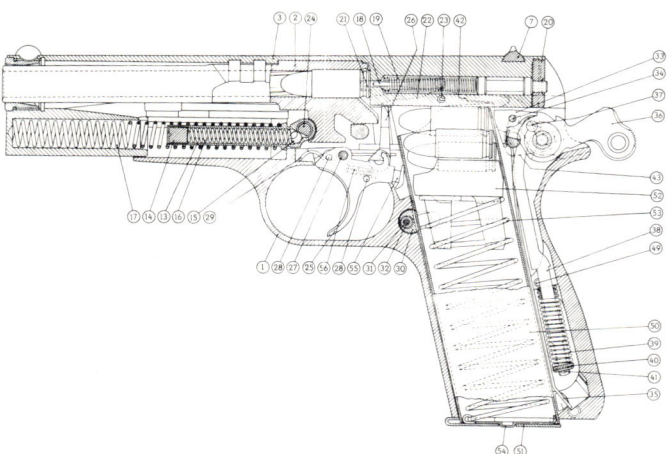

Sectioned view of the FN HP pistol. Key: (1) Frame with ring for lanyard; (2) Barrel; (3) Slide with foresight and cap; (7) Rearsight; (STA 126) Foresight; (13) Return spring guide; (14) Return spring guide cap; (15) Ball; (16) Spring of return spring guide; (17) Return spring; (18) Firing pin; (19) Firing pin spring; (20) Firing pin retaining plate; (21) Pivoting Extractor; (22) Sear lever; (23) Sear lever axis pin; (24) Slide stop; (25) Trigger; (26) Trigger lever; (27) Trigger pin; (28) Trigger and magazine safety pin (2); (29) Trigger spring; (30) Magazine stop; (31) Magazine stop spring; (33) Sear; (34) Sear pin; (35) Sear spring; (36) Hammer; (37) Hammer pin; (38) Hammer strut; (39) Hammer spring; (40) Hammer spring support; (41) Hammer strut pin; (42) Ejector; (43) Safety; (44) Safety stud; (45) Safety stud; (46) Safety spring; (47) Right hand grip; (48) Left hand grip; (49) Grip screws (2); (50) Magazine body; (51) Magazine base; (52) Magazine platform; (53) Magazine spring; (54) Magazine bottom plate catch; (55) Magazine safety; (56) Magazine safety spring; (STA 139) Extractor pin; (66) Extractor spring

receiver also has (a) a stop to arrest the slide (b) the firing mechanism and (c) the magazine well with the magazine retaining catch. The trigger mechanism consists of a trigger pivoted at its top front edge so that the rear end of the trigger assembly rises when the trigger is pulled. This forces up a short straight trigger lever which comes up under the front end of a long horizontal, centrally pivoted sear lever mounted in the slide. The lowering of the rear end of this sear lever pivots the sear out of engagement with the bent of the hammer. The safety catch, mounted on the left of the receiver behind the pistol grip, is pivoted to lock the slide and a projection on its lower side fits into the rear of the sear to prevent the release of the hammer. There is no grip safety fitted.

The slide contains the integral breech block at the rear. The front end has a single recess for the muzzle of the barrel and a solid face below in which the return spring is seated. There is therefore no bushing and plugs which form a weakness in many designs. The slide travels in the receiver and has an ejection opening on the right side. Within the top of the slide are the recesses in which the barrel locking lugs engage.

OPERATION
On firing, the gas pressure forces the breech block – which is part of the slide – rearwards and the barrel is pulled back by the slide since the barrel locking lugs are engaged in the recesses in the slide. The backward movement of the slide carries the sear lever back until the tail is no longer directly above the trigger lever. After 5mm of free travel, the cam path below the barrel rides over the cam and the rear end of the barrel is pulled down, to unlock it from the slide, and the barrel movement is terminated. The slide continues back to ride over the hammer and the extractor on the breech block pulls out the empty case which hits the ejector and is thrown out of the ejection port on the right of the slide. As the slide recoils the return spring is compressed around its guide rod. Rearward movement ceases when the slide stop hits the stop in the receiver. The slide is driven forward by the compressed return spring. The breech block feeds a round from the magazine up the bullet guide and into the chamber. The breech block forces the barrel forward and the cam forces the breech up and holds it up when the locking lugs on the barrel enter the recesses in the slide ceiling.

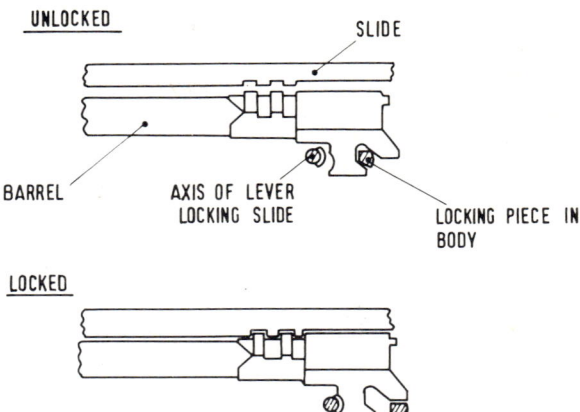

Breech locking and unlocking

The sear lever comes forward with the slide and pushes the trigger lever ahead of it. To enable the trigger lever to return to a position under the tail of the sear lever, the trigger, which at this moment is still held back, must be released. This disconnector system produces a self loading action, that is to say one shot for each trigger pull.

When the firer pulls the trigger again, the trigger lever is raised, the tail of the sear lever is forced up and the nose is forced down to contact the sear in the receiver and rotate it out of engagement with the notch of the hammer. The mainspring, lying in the rear of the pistol grip, rotates the hammer which strikes the spring retracted firing pin in the breech block and drives it forward to hit the cap and fire the cartridge.

When the ammunition is expended, the magazine follower forces up the slide stop and the slide is held to the rear. When a fresh magazine has been inserted into the pistol grip, the slide stop can be pressed down to allow the return spring to expand and force the slide forward. When the magazine is taken out a spring loaded safety lever is forced out into the magazine well and it is linked to the trigger lever and forces it forward from beneath the tail of the sear lever. Thus when the magazine is removed and a cartridge is left in the chamber, the pistol cannot be inadvertently discharged and the magazine must be replaced before firing is possible.

Should the slide not be fully forward and locking not completed, the gun cannot be fired because the sear lever is not fully forward and the trigger lever cannot be positioned under its tail.

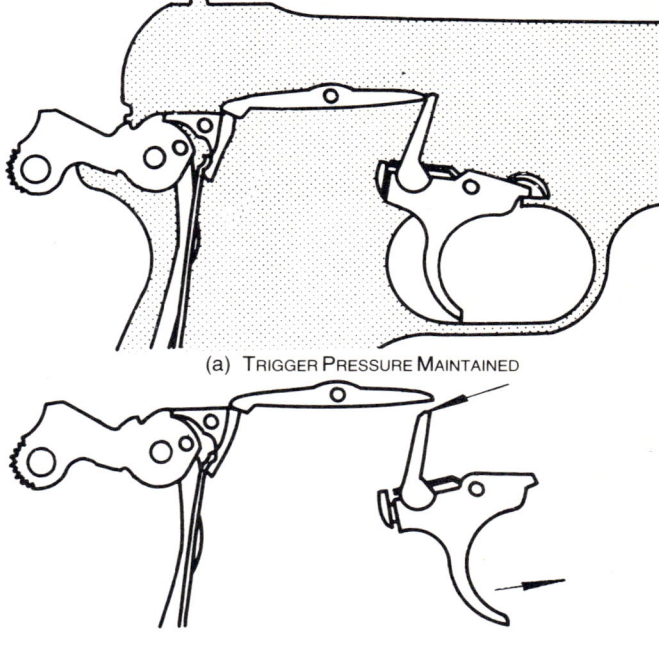

(a) TRIGGER PRESSURE MAINTAINED

(b) TRIGGER RELEASED

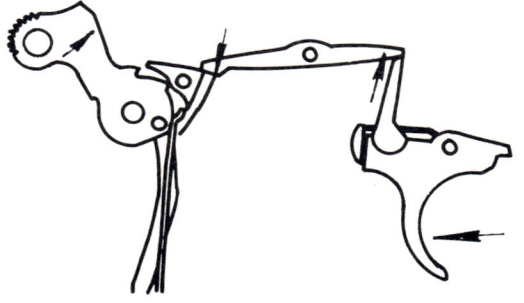

(c) TRIGGER PRESSED

The trigger mechanism of the FN HP pistol

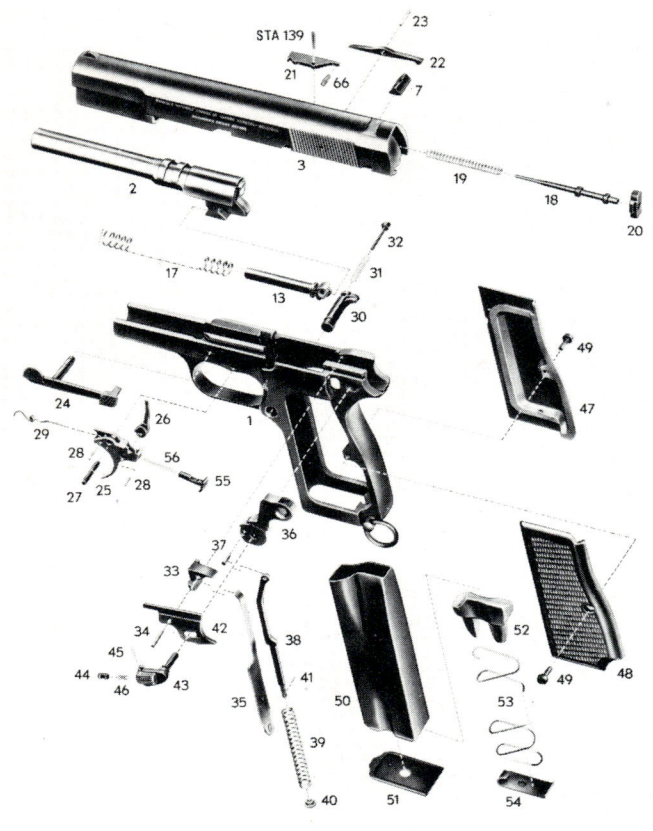

The component parts of the FN HP pistol (identification numbers correspond with those on the sectioned view)

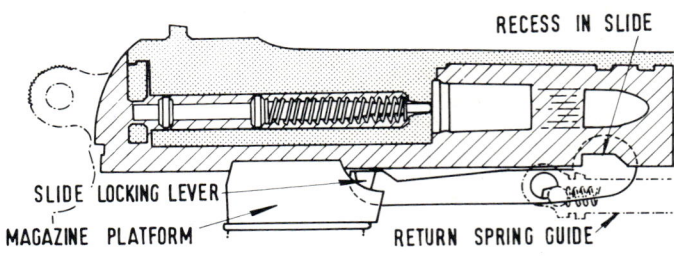

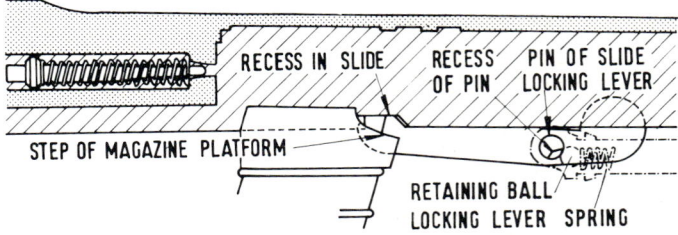

The holding open device

STRIPPING

(1) Press magazine release catch on receiver behind trigger and drop magazine out of pistol grip.
(2) Operate slide and check chamber is empty.
(3) Retract slide and push safety catch up into second notch in the slide.
(4) Press up slide stop and withdraw it on the left of the receiver.
(5) Grasp slide, press catch out of engagement and remove slide and barrel assembly from the front.
(6) Push recoil spring guide towards muzzle to release the head of the guide from the barrel, and remove it.
(7) Remove barrel from the breech end.
(8) Remove stocks.

DATA
Cartridge: 9mm Parabellum
Method of operation: Recoil
Method of locking: Projecting lug
Method of feed: 13-round box magazine
Method of fire: Semi-automatic

WEIGHTS
Pistol only: 0.88kg
Magazine empty: 85g
Magazine full: 205g
Pistol with full magazine: 1.01kg
Trigger pull: 2.28-3.64kp

LENGTHS
Pistol: 196mm
Barrel: 112mm

MECHANICAL FEATURES
Rifling: Concentric. 6 grooves. RH 1 turn in 254mm
Sights: Foresight: Barleycorn adjustable laterally
          Rearsight: Square notch integral with slide
                          159mm

FIRING CHARACTERISTICS
Muzzle velocity: 354 metres/sec
Muzzle energy: 51mkp
Chamber pressure: 2,160kg/cm²
Rate of fire: Single shot 40 rounds/min
Range, maximum effective: 45 metres
Manufacturer: Fabrique Nationale d'Armes de Guerre; Fabrica Militar de Armas Portatiles, Rosario, Argentina; John Inglis Co, Toronto, Ontario, Canada
Status: Current manufacture at FN and at Rosario, in service in Argentina, Australia, Canada, Belgium, China (Taiwan), Denmark, Holland and elsewhere.

7.65mm FN PISTOL

As at mid-1975, this self-loading pistol had reached the final stage of development, and production was likely to commence soon. Minor modifications could still be incorporated, and full details of the pistol are not therefore available.

The pistol may be fired single action or double action initially, and an unusual feature is that the safety catch may be operated from either the left or the right hand side of the slide.

Currently, Fabrique Nationale are upgrading the 7.65mm cartridge by a basic redesign of the bullet. This in its new form, will have a truncated nose and it is designed to have superior stopping characteristics, compared with the standard 7.65mm ammunition.

FN 7.65mm pistol

.38in FN REVOLVER

This revolver is FN's first venture into revolver manufacture, and the weapon is currently at a fairly advanced stage of development, although production is not likely to commence in the immediate future.

In appearance the revolver is conventional, having a five-chamber side-loading cylinder. Designed basically for the .38in Special cartridge, the weapon is intended also for the .38in Smith and Wesson, and the 9mm Parabellum cartridges. The latter requires suitably chambered cylinders able to accept the rimless cartridge case.

FN .38in Revolver

CANADA

9mm FN BROWNING HIGH POWER PISTOL

This pistol was made by John Inglis and Co. of Toronto during the 1939-1945 war. Production was originally set up to supply the Chinese Nationalists fighting the Japanese, but the weapon was issued also to airborne forces and commandos of the British Army. Although Canadian manufacture was based strictly on the pattern of the original FN pistol there were several variations, but the only version now issued to Canadian Forces is the No. 2 Mark 1*.

BROWNING FN 9mm HP No 1 Mark 1 PISTOL

This had a tangent leaf rear sight graduated from 60 to 500 metres. To make use of this range a shoulder-stock holster was used. The butt was machined to enable it to take the tenon of the holster stock.

Browning FN 9mm HP No 1 Mk 1 pistol. This particular pistol was manufactured during the war by John Inglis and Co. of Toronto for the Chinese Government (RSAF)

BROWNING FN 9mm HP No 1 Mark 1* PISTOL

This also had the shoulder-stock holster. The height of the ejector was increased and the sight – similar to that on the Mark 1 pistol – had a clearance cut to take the Mk 2 ejector. The extractor could not be interchanged with that of the Mk1.

Browning FN 9mm HP No 1 Mk 1 pistol (RSAF)*

BROWNING FN 9mm HP No 2 Mark 1 PISTOL

This version had a non-adjustable rear sight with a U notch. There was no need for a shoulder stock and the grip was not machined to take one. The small ejector and the extractor of the Mark 1 pistol were fitted.

Browning FN 9mm No 2 Mk 1 pistol (RSAF)

BROWNING FN 9mm HP No 2 Mark 1* PISTOL

This weapon is the same as the No 2 Mk 1 but uses the ejector and extractor of the No 1 Mk 1*. After the war a lightweight version was produced for tests in Canada, UK and USA. This had grooves cut in both sides of the slide to reduce weight. The Canadian 9mm FN Browning High

Power pistol, together with Belgian pistols, is used by the British Army, Canada and Australia. The necessary spare parts are still made by the Long Branch Arsenal at Ontario.

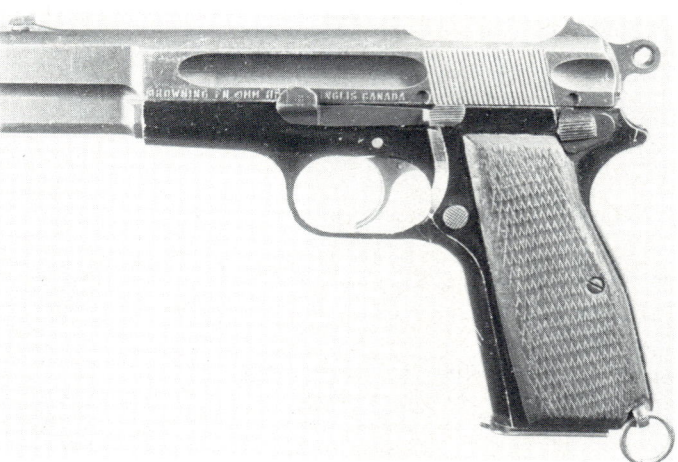

Browning FN 9mm HP No 1 Mk 1 pistol (RSAF)*

Browning FN 9mm HP No 2 Mk 1 pistol, specially lightened by using light materials and cutting away unnecessary metal (RSAF)*

CHINA (PEOPLE'S REPUBLIC)

7.62mm TYPE 51 (OR TYPE 54) PISTOL

This is a direct copy of the Soviet 7.62mm Tokarev TTM 1933 pistol and is the standard pistol in the Chinese Army. The Chinese version may be distinguished from the Russian or Polish pistols by the serrations on the slide. The Russian and Polish pistols have a series of alternate wide and narrow vertical cuts and the Chinese pistols have uniform narrow vertical serrations. The Chinese pistol can be further distinguished from the Hun-

garian 48M and Yugoslav M54 (which also have uniform narrow slots) by the markings 五一式 or 五四式 on the receiver or top of the slide. (The Yugoslav pistol carries "7.62mm M57" on the left side of the slide, and the Hungarian 48M has an emblem consisting of a star, wheatsheaf and hammer, in a wreath, on the grip.) The same pistol is also referred to by the Chinese as the Type 54 although there is no sign of a change in design or manufacture.

The 7.62mm Type 51 pistol (RSAF)

DATA
Cartridge: 7.62mm 'P' cartridge or 7.63mm Mauser
Method of operation: Recoil
Method of locking: Projecting lugs
Method of feed: 8-round box magazine
Method of fire: Semi-automatic
Weight: 854g
Length: 196mm
Barrel: 116mm
      Rifling: 4 grooves RH
Sights: Foresight: Blade
      Rearsight: Notch
Muzzle velocity: 420m/sec
Muzzle energy: 50mkp
Rate of fire: 35 rounds/min
Range, maximum effective: 50 metres
Manufacturer: State Arsenals
Status: In service

9mm TYPE 59 PISTOL

This is the designation by which the Chinese copy of the Russian 9mm Mokarov SL pistol (qv) is known. The Chinese pistols are marked '59 SHI on the receiver, otherwise details are the same as those given in the Russian entry.

DATA
Manufacturer: State factories
Status: In service

7.65mm TYPE 64 SILENCED PISTOL

This is a pistol produced solely as an assassination weapon. It is an ingenious design and may be used either as a manually operated single shot arm or as a self loader.

When the ultimate silencing effect is required the lugs of the rotating bolt in the slide engage recesses in the receiver and the weapon fires from a locked breech. After the round has been fired the slide is hand operated to unlock the bolt, retract the slide and extract the fired case. When the

7.65mm Type 64 pistol. Silenced (RMCS)

7.65mm Type 64 pistol. Silenced, breech open

The baffles, gauze and mesh make up the interior of the silencer

selector bar is pushed to the right, the locking lugs do not engage in the recesses in the receiver and the pistol functions as a blowback operated semi-automatic. This results in a more noisy method of operation as the slide reciprocates and the empty case is ejected. The cartridge is 7.65mm × 17. It is rimless and unique. No other round can be used in this pistol.

The silencing effect is obtained by placing a large bulbous attachment on the front of the receiver extending well forward of the muzzle. The gases leave the muzzle and expand into a wire mesh cylinder surrounded by an expanded metal sleeve. The bullet passes through a series of rubber discs which trap the gases. Used as a single shot manually operated pistol it is extremely quiet. Its reduced muzzle velocity greatly affects its powers of penetration.

Type 64 pistol. Silenced and stripped

DATA
Cartridge: 7.65mm × 17 rimless
Method of operation: (a) Manual or (b) Blowback
Method of locking: (a) Rotating bolt or (b) Nil
Method of feed: 8-round box magazine
Method of fire: (a) Single shot or (b) Semi-automatic
Weight: 1.27kg
Length: 330mm
Barrel: 124mm

Sights: Foresight: Blade
    Rearsight: Notch
Muzzle velocity: 274 metres/sec
Muzzle energy: 20mkp
Rate of fire: 32 rounds/min
Range, maximum effective: 35 metres
Manufacturer: State Arsenals
Status: In service

CZECHOSLOVAKIA

7.65mm Vz27 PISTOL

This self loading pistol was made in large numbers before World War II and was also adopted by the German Army as the Pistol 27 (t) which was marked Bohmische Waffenfabrik AG, Prague, and was modified slightly. When the war ended production continued and weapons manufactured in this period are marked 'Narodni Podnik'. The Vz27 is a blowback-operated pistol of conventional design, but differs from most such pistols in having a detachable barrel which can be rotated out of the receiver in a manner similar to that of the USA Colt .32 and .380 SL pistols.

DATA
Cartridge: 7.65mm (.32 ACP)
Method of operation: Blowback
Method of locking: Nil
Method of feed: 8-round detachable box magazine
Method of fire: Semi-automatic
Weight: 710g
Length: 160mm
Barrel: 99mm
    Rifling: 6 grooves. RH
Sights: Foresight: Blade
    Rearsight: Notch
Muzzle velocity: 299 metres/sec
Muzzle energy: 21mkp
Rate of fire: 30 rounds/min
Range, maximum effective: 40 metres
Manufacturer: Ceskoslovenska Zbrojovka, Prague
Status: No longer in production. Obsolescent

7.65mm Vz27 pistol (RSAF)

9mm Vz38 AND Vz38/39 PISTOLS

Vz38 is a blowback operated pistol which functions in the same way as the Model 27 but has had the trigger mechanism so modified that it will fire only at double action. It can be set at half cock by thumbing back the external hammer and if the trigger is then pulled the hammer comes back, trips, and then fires the round. The barrel is secured to a collar which is pinned to the receiver. When the slide is taken off, the barrel can be tilted from the rear for examination or cleaning.

Because the Vz38 model was found to be unsatisfactory an improved version, known as the Vz38/39 was produced.

DATA
Cartridge: 9mm Short (.380 ACP)
Method of operation: Blowback
Method of locking: Nil
Method of feed: 8-round detachable box magazine
Method of fire: Semi-automatic
Weight: 909g
Length: 198mm
Barrel: 119mm
    Rifling: 6 grooves. RH

9mm Vz38 pistol

9mm Vz38/39 pistol (RSAF)

Sights: Foresight: Blade
      Rearsight: Notch
Muzzle velocity: 296 metres/sec
Muzzle energy: 28 mkp

Rate of fire: 30 rounds/min
Range, maximum effective: 40 metres
Manufacturer: Ceskoslovenska Zbrojovka, Prague
Status: Obsolescent and no longer in production

7.65mm MODEL 50 PISTOL

This blowback pistol is generally similar to the German Walther PP and PPK. The safety catch has been located at the top of the left grip instead of the slide Model 50 is a double action pistol with an external hammer and

cannot be used in the single action mode. It is still carried by senior officers of the Czechoslovakian Army but is not on general issue. It is exported by Omnipol and export models are stamped "Vz50". Production has now ceased.

DATA
Cartridge: 7.65mm (.32ACP)
Method of operation: Blowback
Method of locking: Nil
Method of feed: 8-round detachable box magazine
Weight: 681g
Length: 173mm
Barrel: 97mm
      Rifling: 6 grooves RH
Sights: Foresight: Blade
      Rearsight: Notch
Muzzle velocity: 280 metres/sec
Muzzle energy: 19mkp
Rate of fire: 35 rounds/min
Range, maximum effective: 40 metres
Manufacturer: Ceskoslovenska Zbrojovka, Strakonice
Status: In very limited home service and no longer in production. Many exported

The 7.65mm Vz50 (RSAF)

7.62mm PISTOL MODEL 52

The Czech armament group based on Brno has produced a military, self-loading, recoil operated pistol of 7.62mm calibre which has several novel features. Normal practice in Czechoslovakia is to make each of the various factories of the group produce batches of various assemblies and parts, and to assemble these at one selected centre. This, however, can lead to difficulties where tolerances are close and it is understood that the M52 pistol is produced completely at Uherskybrod.

M52 was designed to fire the Model 48 cartridge which has the same physical dimensions as the German Mauser 7.63mm round, and the Soviet Type P pistol cartridge. The Czech round, however, has a larger propellant load than either the Soviet military round or most commercial cartridges of this type. This has probably been the reason for the use of the very unusual, but very rigid, roller locking system employed.

In 1947 and 1948, before general production started, a 9mm version was put up for the Swiss pistol trials against the SIG210 and the Waffenfabrik Bern models. This pistol differed from the production model, not only in calibre but also in detail of the hammer, safety operation and the grips. The magazine release button was on the body, above the trigger, on the 9mm version. The pistol was not chosen by the Swiss, and the Eastern Bloc at that time wanted the pistol to fire the 'P' 7.62mm Russian cartridge so the M52 was eventually manufactured for that cartridge. Later Colonel M. Hamdi of the Egyptian Army re-designed the pistol for 9mm but Omnipol in Prague decided conversion would be unduly expensive.

OPERATION

Before the weapon can be fired the slide must be fully forward and this implies that the locking process has been completed and the slide – which incorporates the breech face – is locked to the barrel. The roller locking system which is used is unique to the M52 pistol. There is a rectangular barrel lug sweated over the chamber of the barrel and in the bottom surface of this is carried a locking block and two rollers. Two slots in the barrel lug permit the rollers to move outwards. At the rear end of the locking block a tongue is formed, and a projection – the unlocking lug – reaches down and rests against a projection in the receiver. When the barrel and slide are fully

7.62mm M52 pistol (RMCS)

forward the locking block forces the two rollers outwards and they enter recesses in the slide, thus locking barrel and slide together. On firing, the gas pressure forces the breech face rearwards and the slide, which is integral with it, moves back also. The slide is locked to the barrel by the two projecting rollers and so the barrel recoils also. The unlocking lug of the locking block, reaching down into the receiver, is in contact with a fixed projection and so the locking block remains still. After 5mm of barrel recoil the rollers are carried over the narrow tongue of the locking block and are carried into their housings in the barrel lug by the edges of the recesses in the slide, thus unlocking the barrel from the slide.

The slide continues to the rear, cocking the hammer, and the barrel comes up against the barrel stop in the receiver and is arrested. One advantage of this system is that the barrel movement is purely one of reciprocation and unlike either the Colt 1911A1 or the Browning HP there is

The roller locking system of the M52 (RMCS)

no tilting of the barrel to unlock. Thus there is no need for a loose fit at the front barrel bearing, and also there is very little wear after a large number of rounds have been fired. This results in a long accuracy life for this weapon.

The extractor is fitted at three-o'clock on the breech face and the empty case is carried back against a fixed ejector on the left of the receiver which throws it out through the ejection port in the right hand side of the slide.

The backward movement of the slide terminates when the underside of the front barrel bearing in the slide comes up against the receiver and the return spring then forces the slide forward. The feed horn below the breech face picks up a round from the magazine and the breech face pushes it against the bullet guide and into the chamber. There is no loaded chamber indicator.

When the recesses in the slide come up to the rollers the latter are forced outwards by the barrel lug, along the tongue of the locking block and in the final 5mm of forward movement of both barrel and slide, the full width of the locking block holds the rollers so that they are engaging both the slide and the barrel lug. This provides a firm and rigid locking system.

The procedure is repeated for each operation of the trigger. When the ammunition in the magazine is exhausted, a holding open device controlled by the forward edge of the magazine platform pivots a lever on the left of the receiver causing it to rise and engage in a cut-out section of the slide, just in front of the locking roller recess.

TRIGGER AND FIRING MECHANISM

Connected to the trigger is a trigger bar running back along the right hand side of the receiver. When the trigger is operated this bar moves forward and rotates the sear off the trigger notch, enabling the hammer spring which is held in compression inside the pistol grip, to rotate the hammer against the firing pin. Since the arm is designed to be self loading a disconnector is fitted. This takes the form of a lug fitted halfway along the trigger bar which rises into a cut-away on the slide when the trigger is pulled. As soon as the slide recoils the lug is forced downwards and the end of the trigger bar is moved to a position below the sear. To fire another round the lug must be allowed to rise for the trigger bar to re-connect with the sear and for this to happen, first, the trigger must be released and, secondly, the slide must be fully forward to present the cut-away to the rising lug. If the slide is not fully in battery the trigger remains disconnected and the hammer cannot be released.

When the sear is rotated a small arm rises with it and comes up under the feed rib of the slide. Here it depresses a spring-loaded plunger which not only locks the firing pin by entering a slot in it but cams it back from the breech face as soon as the slide moves it back off this sear arm after firing. Thus the firing pin is locked at all times except when the trigger is deliberately operated and the sear arm releases it. This prevents any discharge of the weapon due to the inertia of the firing pin.

The safety lever is mounted on the left hand side of the receiver where it can be operated by the thumb. There are three positions. 'Fire' is at the bottom, with the safety lever pointed downwards towards the heel of the butt. The middle position – indicated by a red dot – is 'safe'. In this position the hammer can be cocked and the slide operated. The effect of this position is both to block the trigger bar and also to hold the rebound notch of the hammer, preventing the hammer from being dislodged if the arm should be dropped on a hard surface whilst set at 'safe'.

The top position of the safety lever – the third position – can only be adopted with the hammer cocked. It is designed to allow the hammer to be lowered on a loaded chamber in safety. The hammer goes forward but the rebound notch is held and the firing pin is not reached. It should be remembered that the sear arm is down so that the firing pin is still locked by its spring loaded plunger.

These safety arrangements are comprehensive and very effective.

STRIPPING

(1) Remove the magazine and check the chamber and feedway are clear.
(2) Pull down the two catches mounted one on each side above the front of the trigger guard. The return spring will then force the slide – and barrel – forward 3mm and the slide-barrel assembly can be lifted straight off.
(3) To remove the barrel from the slide, turn the assembly over and place the lug at the bottom of the magazine in the hole in the locking block. The locking block must be moved towards the muzzle and when the rollers are out of the recesses in the slide, the breech end of the barrel can be lifted with the thumb of the other hand. The return spring will then force the barrel back and free of the slide.

This process becomes comparatively easy after a little practice but the necessity for using the magazine or a punch and the need to control the barrel whilst it is under the influence of the return spring, makes stripping a less easy procedure than that with either the Colt M1911 or Browning 9mm HP which require no tools. The butt plates come off when the spring clip is removed.

The arm is not designed to be further stripped and any attention to the trigger mechanism needs an armourer's shop. The lock can be removed by driving out the transverse pin through the barrel lug and the rollers can then be replaced if cartridge head space becomes incorrect but this again is a workshop job.

To re-assemble the barrel to the slide, place the return spring over the barrel and insert the muzzle through the front bearing bush. Drop the rollers in the recesses in the slide. Use the magazine lug and push the locking block towards the muzzle carrying the rollers forward until they enter the small cut-away in the slide-bearing, ⅞in forward of the recesses. They will then drop and the return spring can be used to drive them back into the locked postion. The slide is placed over the receiver guides, pushed back 3mm and the thumb catches will then rise to retain.it.

LOADING AND FIRING

The magazine holds eight 7.62mm bottlenecked rounds and fits into the well of the pistol grip where it is retained by a catch activated by the hammer spring. The arm is loaded by retracting the slide and releasing. This can be done with the safety catch in any of the three positions. Unlike the Colt M1911 or Browning High Power, the slide is not locked when the safety catch is applied with the hammer cocked.

When the safety is set to "fire" the arm can be discharged but it should be noted that it is not a double action pistol and if the safety catch has been pressed up to the top position to lower the hammer over a loaded chamber, it must be re-cocked by hand before firing can take place.

When the magazine is empty the slide will be held to the rear. Unlike the Colt and Browning there is no external release. The magazine catch located at the heel of the butt must be pressed back, the magazine removed

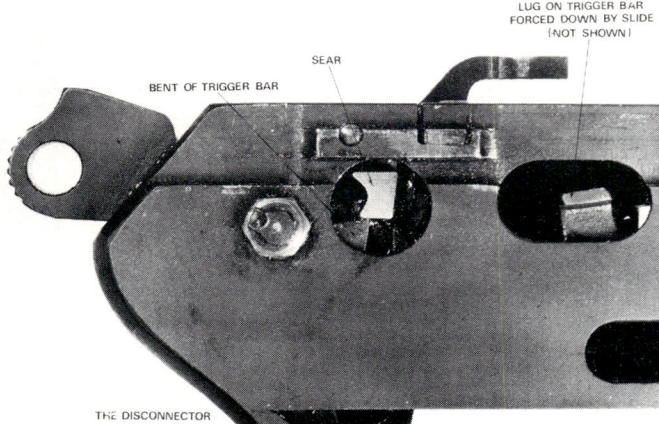

The disconnector of the M52 SL pistol

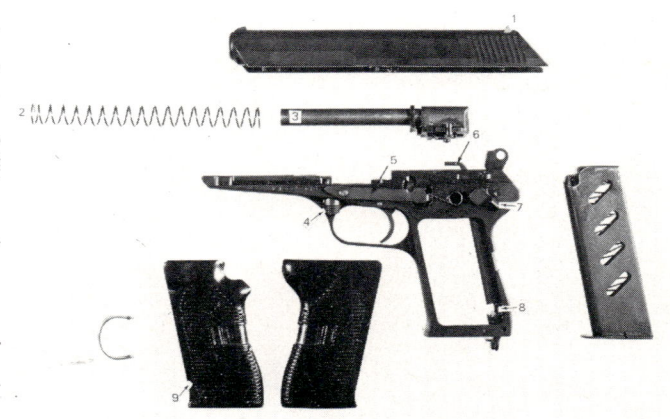

The M52 stripped

and replaced and then the slide pulled back to feed the top round to the chamber.

DATA
Cartridge: 7.62mm Bottleneck M48, 7.63mm Mauser, 7.62mm Type 'P'
Method of operation: Recoil
Method of locking: Rollers
Method of feed: 8-round box magazine
Method of fire: Self-loading. Single action

WEIGHTS
Pistol empty: 0.96kg
Pistol loaded: 1.11kg

MECHANICAL FEATURES
Barrel: Rifling 4 grooves
Sights: Foresight: Blade
    Rearsight: Square notch
    Zeroing: Elevation, change foresight blade. Rearsight is dovetailed
    Graduations: Nil

FIRING CHARACTERISTICS
Muzzle velocity: 492 metres/sec
Muzzle energy: 67.8mkp
Rate of fire: Self loading 32 rounds/min
Range, maximum effective: 63 metres
Manufacturer: Uherskybrod Ordnance Factory
Status: No longer manufactured. In service with Czech Army Reserve Units

7.65mm Vz61 PISTOL (SKORPION)

During the last few years of the 1950s, Omnipol, which controls Czech arms production, hastened the pace of weapon development and the first post-war weapons were replaced. The M52 pistol was superseded by a dual purpose pistol-SMG called the Skorpion, of unusual but effective design. Like the great majority of dual purpose weapons it carriès out neither role to perfection and is really neither a pistol nor an SMG but is best described as a "machine pistol". It fires the American .32 Colt ACP and this feature distinguishes it from all other Communist weapons. The .32 (7.65mm) cartridge with its light bullet and low muzzle velocity produces a muzzle energy which is less than that of a high velocity .22LR cartridge; and it seems likely that commercial considerations dictated the choice of a cartridge which is readily available almost everywhere. A number of African states have purchased the Skorpion. It is issued to the Czech Army and Security Forces and was clearly in evidence in European television coverage of the riots that took place in Prague in August 1969 on the first Anniversary of the Russian occupation of Czechoslovakia.

Skorpion 7.65mm Vz61 pistol, designed by Eng. Rybar. He died soon after

OPERATION

The weapon can produce either single shots or full automatic fire. The change lever is marked '1' at the rear position for single shot, '0' for safe and '20' for auto – a system comprehensible to anyone familiar with western numerals. The cartridge produces a very low recoil impulse and this enables simple blowback operation to be employed. Gas pressure drives the case back in the chamber against the resistance provided by the inertia of the bolt and its two driving springs. The block goes back, extracting the empty case which is ejected straight upwards and can hit the firer full in the face. Because the block is so light it is necessary to have a device to control the rate of fire which, otherwise, would be well over 1,000rpm. The rate reducer operates as follows. When the bolt reaches the end of its rearward stroke it strikes, and is caught by, a spring-loaded hook mounted on the back plate. At the same time it drives a light, spring-loaded plunger down into the pistol grip. The light plunger is easily accelerated and passes through a heavy weight which due to its inertia is left behind. The plunger, having compressed its spring, is driven up again and then meets the descending inertia pellet. This slows down the rising plunger which, when it reaches the top of its travel, rotates the hook, releasing the bolt which is driven forward by the compressed driving springs. This reduces the rate of fire to 840 rounds a minute. The bolt feeds a round from the 20 shot magazine, chambers it and supports the case in the chamber. Since it is a simple blowback operated system there is no bolting or delay device and the sole support to the cartridge is the inertia of the bolt and the strength of the driving springs. The magazine platform operates a plunger which retains the bolt in the rear position when the ammunition supply is exhausted.

TRIGGER AND FIRING MECHANISM

The trigger mechanism is based on that of the M1 Garand rifle with two sears on the trigger bar. The primary sear is fixed: the secondary sear is spring loaded. The hammer has two bents – a primary bent and a secondary. When the selector lever is set to 'single shot' the bolt comes back, depressing the hammer and allowing the secondary bent to engage the secondary, spring-loaded, sear. Since the trigger is fully back it must be released to fire another round. The forward movement of the trigger bar allows the hammer to rotate and the primary bent and sear are engaged. When the trigger is operated the sear releases the hammer bent and another round is fired.

When the change lever is set to '20' the spindle carries the spring loaded secondary sear rearwards out of engagement. The hammer is then controlled entirely by a safety sear which is operated by the bolt in the last part of its forward motion.

SIGHTS

The front sight is a screw threaded pillar mounted on an eccentric and all zeroing is done on this sight. The rear sight is a flip over notch with ranges of 75 and 150 metres. The sight base is 171mm.

SILENCER

This weapon has a clandestine operations role which is largely based on its silencer. This consists of a plastic cylindrical sleeve with a cap at the forward end and a milled locking nut at the rear end. The attachment goes over a threaded collar on the muzzle, which also acts as the bayonet seating, and the locking nut at the rear end is screwed up to secure it.

Adjacent to the muzzle is a small metal cone which bears up against a washer perforated to take the bullet. As the bullet passes through the washer pressure builds up and the gases come out of the holes drilled in the casing and these – in theory at least – are deflected forward by the flange of the locking cap. The bullet perforates the rubber cap at the end of the expansion cylinder which contracts to prevent gas exit.

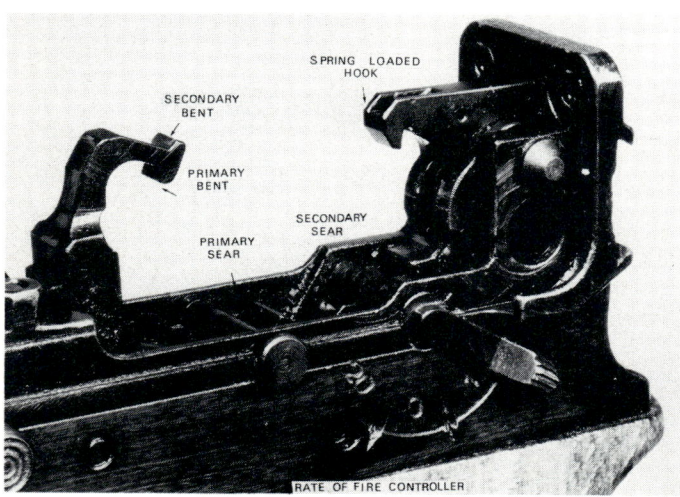

The rate of fire controller (RMCS)

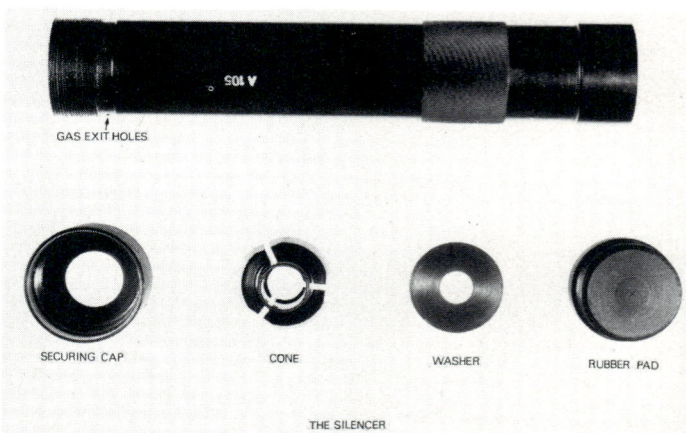

The silencer of the Skorpion (RMCS)

The Vz 61 with the silencer fitted (RMCS)

When the silencer is fitted, the normal muzzle velocity of 317m/sec is reduced to 274m/sec but there is increased dispersion or rate of fire. The silencer is readily attached and removed but produces a lot of smoke by day and its rubber cap is very soon shot out. Using the silencer reduces the effective range to about 100 metres.

STRIPPING

On the left hand side of the receiver, forward of the magazine is a takedown pin. This can be pulled out with the fingers. The receiver is forced forwards a few millimetres and then the barrel and receiver can be pivoted down. There are two small cocking knobs, one on each side, and when these are pulled back the bolt comes to the rear. The cocking knobs can then be taken out through the widened slots in the receiver. The bolt and return springs can then be removed from the receiver. This is the limit of field stripping. Further dismantling includes taking the inertia pellet out through the bottom of the butt and pulling out a single pin releases the trigger mechanism group.

The Skorpion stripped (RMCS)

DATA
Cartridge: .32 ACP (7.65mm)
Method of operation: Blowback
Method of locking: Nil
Method of feed: 10- or 20-round box magazine
Method of fire: Selective

WEIGHTS
Gun empty: 1.59kg
Magazine loaded: (20 rounds) 0.41kg
Gun loaded: 2.0kg
Silencer: 0.341kg
Trigger pull: 0.345kp

LENGTHS
Gun, butt extended: 513mm
Gun, butt retracted: 269mm
Barrel: 112mm
Silencer: 222mm
Gun with silencer fitted: (butt extended) 716mm

MECHANICAL FEATURES
Barrel: Rifling: Grooves. RH. 1 turn in 305mm
            Cooling: Air
Sights: Foresight: Cylindrical post
           Rearsight: Flip. 75 and 150 metres
           Zeroing: On foresight. Sight Radius. 171mm

FIRING CHARACTERISTICS
Muzzle velocity: 317 metres/sec
Muzzle velocity with silencer: 274 metres/sec
Muzzle energy: 20mkp
Rate of fire (normal): 840 rounds/min
Rate of fire (silenced): 950 rounds/min
Rate of fire SS: 40 rounds/min
Range, maximum effective: (stock retracted) 50 metres
                              (stock extended) 200 metres

Note: The Skorpion has been reported in 9mm × 18 calibre and also with a 3-round burst fire control.

Manufacturer: State Ordnance Factories
Status: No longer manufactured. Still in service with Czechoslovakian units

FINLAND

9mm M35 PISTOL

In 1935 the Lahti M35 replaced the 9mm Luger which had been the standard pistol in the Finnish Army since its adoption in 1923. The M35 was designed by Aimo Lahti and the weapon was manufactured by Valtion Kiväärithedas (VKT) Jyväskylä. It is a mixture of the Luger and the Bergmann-Bayard with a feature from Browning's designs. In appearance it resembles the Luger and it strips like the Luger but its action is different. The barrel is screwed to the slide and the rear end of the slide is enlarged to hold the breech-block. The breech-block travels in the slide and cocks the hammer as it recoils. It has thumb pieces by which it can be pulled back to the rear (like the Bergmann Bayard) to cock the action. When the breech-block is fully forward the locking piece is in mortices on each side of the slide as its inner surfaces are engaged in slots in the breech-block. Cam faces on the sides of the locking piece raise and lower it during rearward and forward travel. One very unusual device is the accelerator which, although a stan-dard feature on a short recoil operated machine gun, is unique in a pistol. It is similar to that on the Browning .30 calibre guns and when the barrel ceases its rearward travel the accelerator is rotated and the breech-block thrown rearwards with increased velocity. The magazine, like the Luger, has a button which relieves the weight of the spring whilst loading is carried out. The button operates a pivoted lever so the breech-block remains open when the ammunition is expended.

The Lahti M35 is extremely well sealed to keep out mud, snow and sand and is very difficult to strip without workshop facilities. It is also very reliable and this probably accounts for the retention in service of a relatively heavy pistol of rather old design.

It is also used, in a slightly modified form, in Sweden where it is known as the M40. Some of the Swedish weapons, in turn, were taken to Denmark from Sweden by Danish troops after the Second World War and were there taken on charge as the Model 40(S).

9mm M35 pistol (RSAF)

DATA
Cartridge: 9mm Parabellum
Method of operation: Short recoil
Method of locking: Dropping-block
Method of feed: 8-round detachable magazine
Method of fire: Semi-automatic
Weight: 1.22kg
Length: 246mm
Barrel: 107mm
      Rifling: 6 grooves RH
Sights: Foresight: Blade
           Rearsight: Notch
Muzzle velocity: 350 metres/sec
Muzzle energy: 50mkp
Rate of fire: 30 rounds/min
Range, maximum effective: 40 metres
Manufacturer: VKT, Jyvaskyla
Status: In service in Finland and Sweden (see text)

FRANCE

9mm MAS MODEL 1950 SL PISTOL

This pistol was designed at the French Arsenal at St. Etienne and manufactured at the Chatellerault factory. Some were also made at St. Etienne.

OPERATION

The pistol is loaded by removing the magazine, inserting nine 9mm Parabellum cartridges, and replacing the magazine in the butt.

9mm 1950 pistol

The magazine release catch is located on the left side of the receiver, behind the trigger. Pulling back on the rear end of the slide and then releasing it, positions the cartridge in the chamber. There is an indicator to the rear of the ejection slot which projects above the slide to indicate that the chamber is loaded. The safety catch is located on the left rear of the slide. When the lever is horizontal the pistol is safe. When it is below the horizontal a red dot is exposed to indicate that this is the 'fire' position. The hammer can be lowered by pulling the trigger if the pistol is set to 'safe' because the safety blocks the hammer from hitting the firing pin.

When the pistol is fired, the gas pressure forces the breech face – part of the slide – rearwards. The locking ribs on top of the barrel are fitted into the grooves on the inside of the slide and so the barrel goes back with it. The lower rear end of the barrel is attached to the receiver by a swinging link. The barrel and slide move back together for a short distance and then, since the lower portion of the link is attached to the non recoiling receiver, the link pulls the rear end of the barrel down. This separates the locking ribs of the barrel from the recesses inside the slide and when the locking system is disconnected the barrel is at rest and the slide continues to the rear under its own momentum. The empty case comes out on the breech face and stays there until it strikes the fixed ejector. It is then rotated about the extractor and flung out to the right. The hammer is cocked and the return spring compressed.

The return spring forces the slide forward and the face of the breech block carries the top cartridge in the magazine forward into the chamber. The extractor on the bolt face slips into the cannelure of the cartridge. The breech block contacts the barrel and pushes it forward. As the barrel goes forward the link raises the breech, and the ribs on the top of the barrel enter the grooves on the slide and lock the two together. Forward movement ceases when the lug on the bottom of the barrel contacts the slide stop pin.

TRIGGER AND FIRING MECHANISM

The trigger and firing mechanism on the Model 1950 is simple. With the hammer cocked, pulling the trigger causes it to rotate about its pin, located at the top, and push the trigger bar rearward. The end of the trigger bar contacts a lug on the bottom of the sear, causing the sear to rotate out of the hammer notch. The hammer spring drives the hammer against the spring retracted firing pin. As the slide moves back, the disconnector is forced down onto the trigger bar. The trigger bar is displaced down sufficiently to release the sear which returns to its original position. The slide rolls the hammer back and when the slide goes forward the hammer follows it until it is caught by the sear. The trigger is still pressed and must be released. This allows the trigger bar to move forward and then up in front of the sear. Renewed pressure on the trigger forces the trigger bar against the sear and another round is fired.

The pistol cannot be fired until the slide is fully forward. Nor can it be fired with the magazine removed. When the ammunition supply is expended the slide is held to the rear.

STRIPPING

To strip the Model 1950 the procedure is:
(1) Remove the magazine and pull the slide rearwards. Hold it back with the slide stop above the trigger, on the left of the receiver. Hold the slide and with the stop still rotated up into the slide notch, pull the slide stop out to the left. Ease the slide forward off the receiver.
(2) Invert the slide and take out the return spring and guide. Lift the rear end of the barrel up and pull it out of the slide
(3) The hammer mechanism pulls out of the receiver as an entity.

9mm MAB P15 PISTOL

The firm of MAB manufactures a number of commercial and target pistols. Amongst these is the 9mm MAB P15 which is used by the French Army. The pistol has the bulky grip required to accommodate 15 9mm Parabellum cartridges. It has a very prominent spur at the rear of the receiver and a burr type hammer.

There are several versions of this pistol. These are the standard models used by the French Army as military pistols, the P15S, and the PAP Model F1 which is a target model with target sights and a tubular slide extension.

9mm MAS Model 1950 pistol, field-stripped

DATA
Cartridge: 9mm Parabellum
Method of operation: Recoil
Method of locking: Projecting lug
Method of feed: 9-round box magazine
Method of fire: Self-loading. Single action

WEIGHTS
Pistol empty: 860kg
Magazine empty: 77g
Magazine full: 182g
Trigger pull: 3kp

LENGTHS
Pistol: 195mm
Barrel: 112mm

MECHANICAL FEATURES
Barrel: Rifling: 4 grooves. RH. 1 turn in 254mm
Sights: Foresight: Blade
    Rearsight: Notch
    Graduation: Nil
    Zeroing: Elevation. Change foresight blade.
    Rearsight slides in dovetail
Sight radius: 159mm

FIRING CHARACTERISTICS
Muzzle velocity: 354 metres/sec
Muzzle energy: 51mkp
Chamber pressure: 2,160kg/cm²
Rate of fire: Single shots, 30 rounds/min
Range, maximum effective: 50 metres
Manufacturer: Manufacture Nationale d'Armes de Chatellerault
    Manufacture Nationale d'Armes de Saint-Etienne
Status: No longer in production. Still in service with French Armed Forces and elsewhere

There is also a Model P8 which has an 8-round magazine, weighs 30g less and has a thinner grip.

OPERATION

The P15 has an unusual method of operation for a self loading pistol. It is delayed blowback action or – as some describe it – it has a "hesitation lock". The barrel seat, cut in the return spring guide, is pinned to the receiver and cannot recoil back. The barrel carries a lug which engages a cam groove on the slide and initial gas pressure is used to rotate the barrel in the slide and thus delay the rearward movement of the slide. When the chamber pressure has reached a safe level the slide is blown back, compressing the return spring, rotating the hammer and depressing the trigger bar. The empty case is held to the bolt face and is ejected to the right of the gun.

The return spring forces the slide forward. The top round in the magazine is pushed forward up the bullet guide and enters the chamber. The cam groove on the slide then causes the barrel to rotate and the extractor grips the rim of the case. The trigger bar rises into its recess when the slide is fully forward and the pistol is ready to fire another round.

TRIGGER AND FIRING MECHANISM

When the hammer is cocked it is held by the sear which is spring loaded. When the trigger is squeezed back the trigger bar mounted above the trigger fulcrum, moves forward and a hook on its rear pulls the sear forward off the hammer which goes forward onto the firing pin and the round is fired.

As the slide recoils the trigger bar is forced down and releases the sear which under the influence of its spring rotates and holds the hammer back.

When the slide runs out the hammer remains cocked, held by the sear. The trigger is still held back and the hook on the trigger bar is disengaged from the sear. When the trigger is released the trigger bar can go back and rise into its recess. In so doing the hook moves behind the sear and is correctly positioned for firing the next shot.

There is a magazine safety that prevents the hammer going forward when the magazine is out of the gun. There is also a holding open device.

STRIPPING

The magazine catch is located on the left of the grip immediately behind the trigger. When the magazine is out the slide should be retracted and the chamber and feedway checked.

With the slide held back about 6mm, the slide stop pin can be pushed to the left and then removed.

The slide can be pulled forward off the receiver. With the slide upside down the return spring guide and barrel seat can be pressed towards the muzzle. They can then be disengaged and lifted out. The barrel will lift out of the slide if it is pushed forward about 8mm.

9mm AUTOMATIC PRECISION PISTOL MODEL F1

This weapon, currently in service with the French military and police forces, is designed for competition shooting and features a long band and sight radius an adjustable trigger and a micrometer rear sight. It is designed to fire 9mm Parabeillum cartridges and has been shown to be a very accurate weapon up to a range of 50 metres. The Leclerc Cup in 1967 and the Berlin Inter-Armies Challenge in 1968 were both won with it.
DATA
Calibre: 9mm Parabeillium

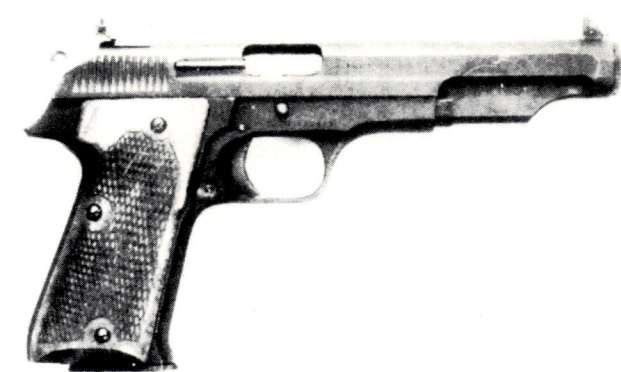

9mm MAB P15
DATA
Cartridge: 9mm Parabellum
Method of operation: Delayed blowback
Method of delay: Barrel lug rotates in cam path in slide
Method of feed: 15-round box magazine
Method of fire: Semi-automatic
Weight: 1.09kg
Length: 203mm
Barrel: 117mm
        Rifling: 4 grooves, RH
Sights: Foresight: Blade
        Rearsight: Notch
Muzzle Velocity: 350 metres/sec
Muzzle energy: 47mkp
Rate of fire: 40 rounds/min
Range, maximum effective: 50 metres
Manufacturer: Manufacture d'Armes Automatiques, Bayonne
Status: In production. In service with the French Army

Magazine: 15-round detachable box
Weight: Pistol only, 1.215kg. Empty magazine. 0.095kg
Length: 234mm
Barrel: Length: 150mm
        Rifling: 6 grooves. One turn in 310mm
Manufacturer: Manufacture d'Armes Automatiques (MAB) 64100-Bayonne
Status: In service with the French Army, Air Force and Police

MANURHIN SL PISTOLS

The French firm of Manurhin has manufactured Walther pistols for several years. They produce at present the PP in .22LR and the PPK in 7.65mm. The details of the original German pistols will be found among the entries for the Federal German Republic.

.22LR Manurhin PP pistol (RSAF)

7.65mm Manurhin PPK pistol

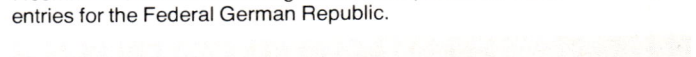

0.357in MANURHIN MR 73 REVOLVER

This compact double-action revolver is available in three different barrel lengths and can fire .38 Special ammunition as well as the .357 Magnum round. It has a 6-shot cylinder which swings sideways for reloading. For competition shooting a series of target models are also made with adjustable rear sight and a choice of four barrel lengths.

DATA
Calibre: .357 Magnum (will fire .38 Special)
Operation: Double-action or single-action
Cylinder: Side-loading 6-chamber
Weight: 2.5in barrel 860g: 3in barrel 890g: 4in barrel 950g (Combat versions)

Length: 195mm, 207mm or 233mm overall (Combat versions)
Barrel: Combat versions 2.5in (63.5mm) 3in (76.2mm) or 4in (100.8mm). Competition versions 4in, 5.25in, 6in and 8in.
Sights: Foresight: Blade
        Rearsight: Notch for combat models. Adjustable sight for competition versions
Muzzle energy: Between 27 and 116mkp
Manufacturer: Manufacture de Machines du Haut-Rhin (Manurhin) 68060 Mulhouse-Bourtzwiller, France
Status: In production. Combat versions in service with the French Army, police forces and other government and security organisations

GERMANY (FEDERAL REPUBLIC)

9mm LUGER SL PISTOL

In 1893 Hugo Borchardt invented an unusual looking pistol which was produced by Ludwig Loewe & Co of Berlin. It incorporated a magazine which loaded into the grip and was the first pistol to do so. It also used the toggle joint and was a leader too in this respect. Its success, however, was short lived and in 1899 Ludwig Loewe ceased production.

The Luger was designed by George Luger and was largely based on the Borchardt pistol. It was produced in Germany by DWM (Deutsch Waffen und Munitionsfabriken) in 7.65mm Parabellum in 1898.

The first country to adopt the Luger as a service weapon was Switzerland who in 1900 bought the pistol in 7.65mm. The pistol, the Model 1900, had a grip safety, a safety lock on the left and a 4¾in barrel. The Model 1902 was made by DWM in 9mm calibre with a 4in or 4¾in barrel. The Model 1904 was adopted by the German Navy in 9mm. It had a grip safety until 1917 after which date the safety was omitted. This version had a 6in barrel and adjustable rear sight. It also had a leather holster attached to a wooden shoulder stock.

The models 1900-06, 1902-06, 1904-06 differed only from the model 1900, 02 and 04 respectively, in having a helical coil return spring in place of a flat leaf.

The model 1908 in 9mm with a 4in barrel was made by DWM without a grip safety. It was adopted by the German Army and remained the standard military pistol until officially replaced by the P38 in 1938. Due to service needs nearly 400,000 Luger 08's were made between 1938 and 1943.

An 8in-barrelled version of the 9mm Luger 08 with an adjustable backsight, known as the Artillery model, was also issued. In addition there was a 12in-barrelled 7.65mm carbine. This used a black-cased round with about 14 per cent increased loading and was issued with a wooden shoulder stock and holster. The 8in-barrelled pistols used 32 round snail magazines.

After 1918 only the firm of Simson and Co of Suhl were permitted by the Versailles Treaty to manufacture the Luger pistol.

In 1920 DWM started producing again for export and home commercial sales. In 1934 Mauser started production of Luger pistols in 7.65mm and 9mm using machinery purchased from DWM. After 1935 only the 9mm pistol was produced. In the late 1960s Mauser started producing the Luger again for the market and now offer it in both 7.65mm and 9mm calibres.

Vickers-Armstrong manufactured 9,000 9mm Lugers for Holland in the 1920s, possibly assembling parts obtained from German stocks. These went to the Dutch East Indies and most of them were captured by the Japanese.

One thousand were produced by DWM for the USA pistol trials of 1907 and subsequently sold in the USA.

The Luger has been manufactured by: DWM, Simson, Krieghoff, Erfurt, Vickers, Waffenfabrik, Bern and Mauser. Over 2,000,000 have been produced and there are some 35 variations.

Erma produce a .22LR insert and Mauser are the only firm still producing Luger pistols for commercial sale.

OPERATION

The Luger pistol is a short recoil operated weapon using a toggle joint locking system. It fires only as a self loading pistol.

The barrel is screwed into a barrel extension which has two arms extending back to provide the mounting for the rear end of the toggle joint. The bolt runs in grooves in the inner surfaces of the two arms of the barrel extension. The toggle joint consists of two arms with a joint between them. The rear end of the rear arm is attached to the barrel extension. The front end of the front arm is attached to the rear of the bolt. When the bolt is fully forward, closing the chamber and supporting the cartridge therein, the central joint between the two arms drops below the line connecting the two end joints. Thus any force applied to the breech face tends to drive this central joint downwards against the frame of the pistol, whereas to break the joint an upward force is required.

The bolt has a flat flush extractor mounted in the top surface. When it is forced over the rim of the case the extractor becomes proud and gives a visual or tactile indication that a round is in the chamber.

The hollow interior of the bolt houses the firing pin and spring. A projection from the pin emerges through a slot in the left side of the bolt and is held back by the sear when the action is cocked by the front arm of the toggle joint.

The joint of the rear arm carries a swivel which hangs down into the handgrip and is connected via a bell crank to the helical return spring. Thus as the joint is rotated the spring is compressed.

The safety catch is pulled back for 'safe' and forward for 'fire'. If a grip safety is fitted it prevents the sear from being released from the projection extending from the firing pin, until the firmness of the firer's grip forces the safety in.

The magazine catch is located on the left of the receiver just behind the trigger. When pressed in it allows the magazine to be withdrawn. The magazine spring force can be controlled by pulling down the button on the right of the magazine and then the 8 cartridges can be placed in the magazine. The magazine slides up into the grip until retained by the catch.

To load the pistol, the central joint of the two toggle arms is grasped between the forefinger and thumb of the left hand and pulled back and upwards. The joint is broken and the bolt retracted. The claw at the bottom of the forward arm engages the spur on the firing pin and withdraws the firing pin back to be caught by the sear. The swivel compresses the return spring.

When the toggle joint is released the return spring rotates the rear joint and forces the barrel extension and bolt forward. As the bolt goes forward it strips the top round from the magazine into the chamber, the extractor rises over the rim, and the bolt is locked as the toggle joint drops down. The gun is then ready to fire.

When the trigger is pulled the firing pin strikes the cap and fires the round. The gas pressure forces the cartridge case back against the bolt face and

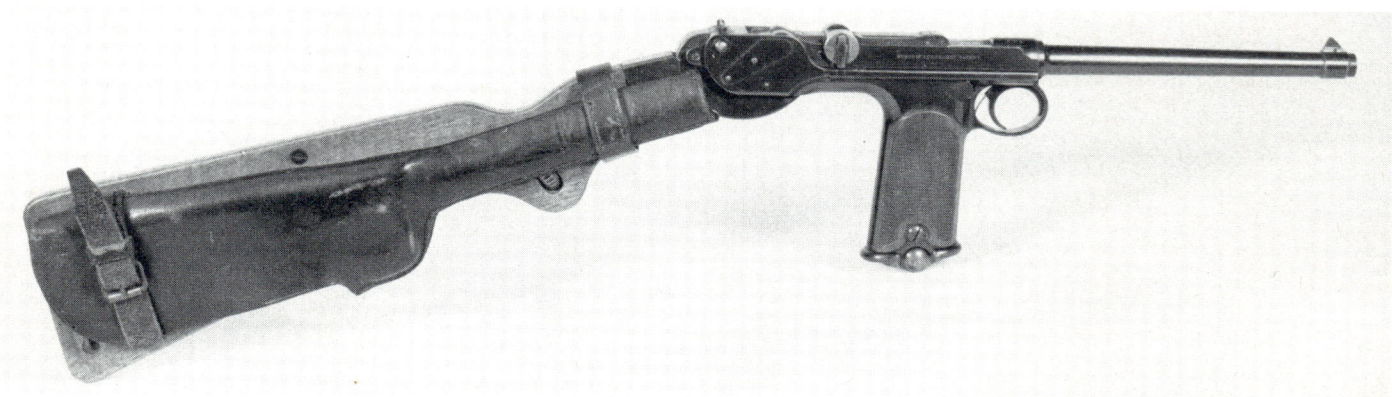

7.65mm Borchardt pistol. With the holster stock attached, the Borchardt was extremely accurate (RSAF)

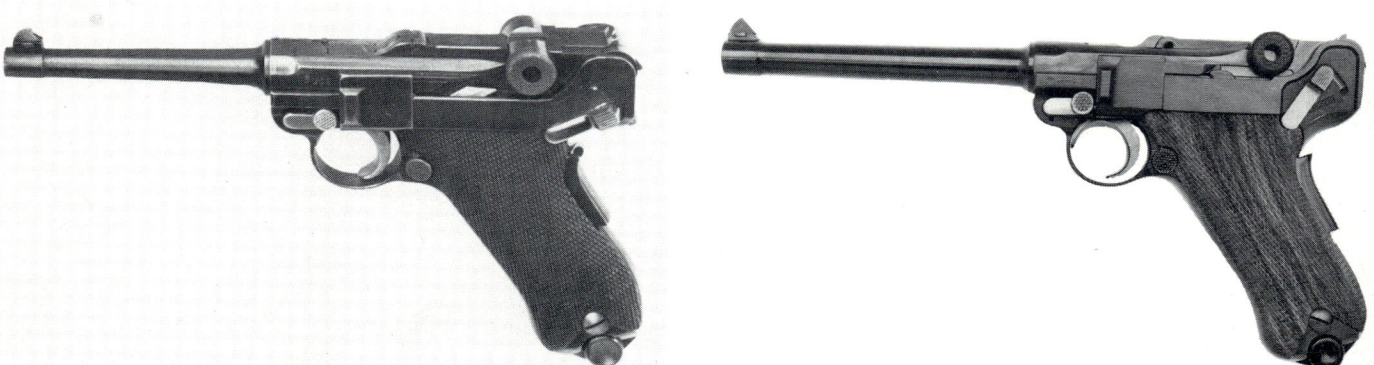

7.65mm Luger pistol Model 1906. Note the grip safety (RMCS)

9mm Parabellum model from current Mauser production

9mm Luger .08 pistol. This is the 8in Artillery model with a 32-round snail magazine (RSAF)

7.65mm Luger pistol. This model has an 11¾in barrel (RMCS)

the bolt goes back. The two arms of the toggle joint act like a strut and transmit the backward force to the rear joint which is connected to the barrel extension. The barrel extension goes back, pulling the barrel back. Thus the locked bolt and barrel recoil together for about a quarter of an inch (6mm). During this time the gas pressure in the chamber drops to atmospheric. The central joint of the toggle then strikes upward curved ramps on the receiver and as the joint is forced upwards the lock is broken and the

bolt is accelerated to the rear. The empty cartridge case is withdrawn from the chamber and, when it meets the stationary ejector, it is thrown upwards out of the pistol. The firing pin is withdrawn to the cocked position. The return spring is fully compressed and the bolt is thrown forward feeding a round into the chamber, and the toggle joint locks behind it.

When the magazine has been emptied the magazine follower rises and pivots a lever which holds the breech block to the rear with the toggle folded up. A new magazine is inserted, and when the toggle joint is pulled slightly back and then released, the compressed return spring drives the bolt forward, feeding a cartridge into the chamber.

The bolt cannot go forward with an empty magazine in place. If it is not desirable or possible to put a loaded magazine into the grip, then the magazine must be lowered sufficiently for the follower to clear the lever of the holding open device. The bolt can then be closed and the magazine pushed back up to the locked position.

TRIGGER AND FIRING MECHANISM

The firing pin and its helical coil spring are contained in the bolt. The cocking action occurs when the toggle breaks and moves up. The front end of the front arm of the toggle has a claw which catches the front of the firing pin and pulls it back until a projection on the left side of the firing pin is held by the sear. This claw on the toggle arm catches the firing pin if the sear is accidentally dislodged before the toggle joint is properly locked, and in this way provides mechanical safety before firing.

The trigger moves down at the top when it is rotated. This pulls down the arm of a horizontally pivoted bell crank and the other arm pushes in a plunger in front of the sear. The sear is pivoted at its midpoint and so the back of the sear, which is in contact with the firing pin, moves out. The firing pin is driven forward to fire the round. When the action comes forward again the trigger must be released to let the sear plunger move over the sear.

When the safety is applied, a bar comes up and prevents the sear from rotating.

The action of the Luger pistol (RMCS)

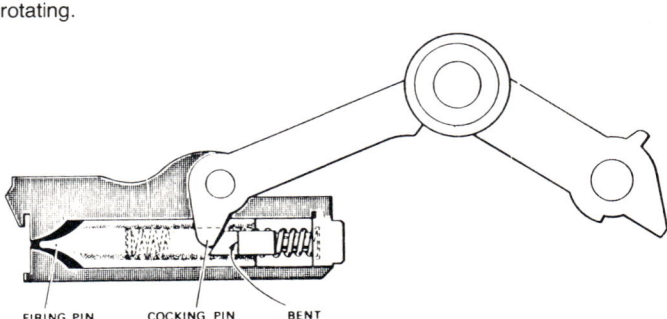

FIRING PIN   COCKING PIN   BENT

Toggle action

STRIPPING

Extract magazine, break toggle and pull back to inspect the chamber. Release the toggle.

Place muzzle on a hard surface and press down on the grip so that the barrel recoils about 13mm. Rotate the thumb catch in front of the trigger on the left of the weapon, vertically down.

Lift out the side plate on the left, above the trigger.

Slide the barrel forward, complete with toggle and barrel extension side plates.

Bend the toggle joint and push out pin connecting rear joint to barrel extension. Pull bolt and toggle back out of barrel extension.

Re-assemble in reverse order taking care to hook the stirrup, on the rear of the toggle, into the bell crank lever above the coiled return spring in the grip.

DATA (MODEL 1908)
Cartridge: 9mm Parabellum or 7.65mm Luger
Method of operation: Short recoil
Method of locking: Toggle joint
Method of feed: 8-round box magazine
Method of firing: Single action

WEIGHTS
Pistol: 0.877kg
Magazine: 63g
Trigger pull: 3.18-4kg

LENGTHS
Pistol: 222mm
Barrel: 103mm (long frame) or 100mm (short frame)

MECHANICAL FEATURES
Barrel: Rifling: 6 grooves RH. 1 turn in 254mm. 7.65mm weapon has 4 grooves
Sights: Foresight: Blade
Rearsight: U notch
Zeroing: Elevation. Change foresight. Line. Foresight slides in dovetail
Graduation: Nil
Sight radius: 197mm

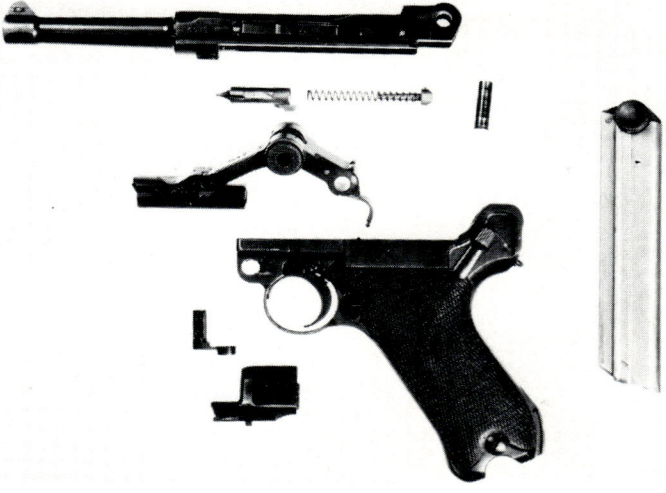

The 9mm Luger 08 pistol stripped (RMCS)

FIRING CHARACTERISTICS
Muzzle velocity: 381 metres/sec
Muzzle energy: 55mkp
Range, maximum effective: 50 metres
Maximum: 1,400 metres
Rate of fire: Single shot, 32 rounds/min
Manufacturer: Current production by Mauser-Werke GmbH, Oberndorf-Neckar, Germany. For earlier manufacturers see text
Status: Current production for commercial sale. No longer in military service with any significant military force but there are certainly still a great many Lugers about

7.63mm (or 9mm) MAUSER 1896 PISTOL

This pistol was designed by the three Feederle brothers in 1894 and patents were taken out by Mauser in 1895. In 1896 development work was completed and production began with about 100 pistols. At the end of 1896 quantity production of the weapon in 7.63mm began. The cartridge was based on the 7.65mm round developed for the Borchardt pistol. The further study of the Mauser development involves consideration of a number of relatively minor amendments such as the provision of a hammer safety and a change of hammer size to clear the sight line.

In 1916 the Mauser was produced in 9mm Parabellum and some pistols of this type have the figure 9 impressed into the grip – usually in red. A combined holster – shoulder stock was also produced.

In 1920 a short barrelled version was made to avoid the restrictions of the Versailles treaty and sold to Bolshevik Russia. These guns were called the Bolo model – presumably from Bolshevik.

In 1930 the M711 was offered with a detachable 20-round magazine. In 1931 a selective fire version was produced and is generally referred to as the Schnellfeuer or M712 and was offered with either 10-round or 20-round magazines. Pistols of this patern were sold to China in 1931 and Yugoslavia took some in 1934. They were very hard to control at automatic fire.

OPERATION

The pistol fires from a closed locked breech. The barrel and barrel extension are one piece and the bolt travels inside the barrel extension. The bolt carries the firing pin and spring and has an extractor on top.

The bolt is locked by a locking piece positioned below it. The locking block is in the receiver and it has two projections on its upper side which enter recesses in the bottom of the bolt. At the bottom rear end of the locking piece is a projection – or tongue – which extends back and down.

When the pistol is fired the gas pressure forces the breech block rearwards carrying with it the locking piece and the barrel extension and barrel. The assembly moves back about 5mm whilst the chamber pressure is falling. The tongue of the locking block then enters a recess in the receiver and the block is cammed down out of engagement with the bolt. The barrel movement is stopped when the block contacts the receiver. The bolt continues to the rear, extracts the empty case, which strikes a projection extending up from the receiver into the bolt way, and is thrown upwards out of the gun. The hammer is rotated back by the recoiling bolt and held to the rear by the sear.

The return spring drives the bolt forward, the next round is chambered and the spring force pushes the barrel and block fully forward. The tongue on the locking block is forced up the inclined plane on the top of the receiver and the locking block is swung up and the two locking lugs engage their recesses in the underside of the bolt.

There is a holding open device which is operated by a projection on the magazine follower.

7.63mm Mauser M1895 pistol. This was the first production model and was clip loaded (RSAF)

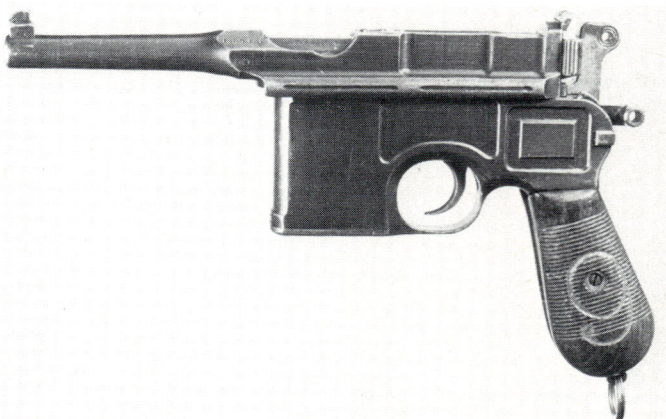

9mm Mauser 1898 pistol. This pistol was converted to 9mm during the 1939-45 war. Both sides of the grip were marked "9" (RSAF)

The safety catch is located at the left rear of the receiver and can be applied with the hammer back or forward. On models up to 1930 the safety is set by pressing the hammer down with the thumb of the hand holding the pistol and raising the safety lever with the other. On models from 1930 onwards only one hand is needed and the safety lever is operated with the thumb. When the lever is vertical the pistol is 'safe' and the letter 'S' can be seen. When ready to fire, the lever is down and the letter 'F' is visible on the lever.

DATA
Cartridge: 7.63mm Mauser (some 9mm Parabellum)
Method of operation: Short recoil
Method of locking: Swinging block
Method of feed: 10-round internal magazine
Method of fire: Semi-automatic (Models 1931 and 1932 selective)
Weight: 1.22kg
Length: 308mm
Barrel: 140mm
    Rifling: 6 grooves RH
Sights: Foresight: Blade
    Rearsight: Notch
Muzzle velocity: 433 metres/sec
Muzzle energy: 53mkp
Rate of fire: 24 rounds/min
Range, maximum effective: 50 metres

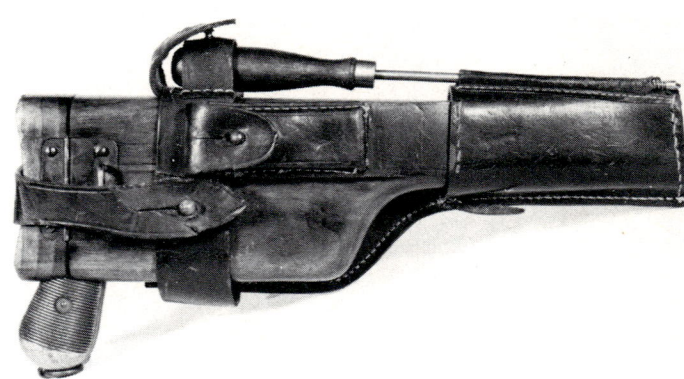

The Mauser pistol in its holster stock (RSAF)

Manufacturer: Waffenfabrik Mauser AG, Oberndorf/Neckar
Status: No longer manufactured and no longer in regular service

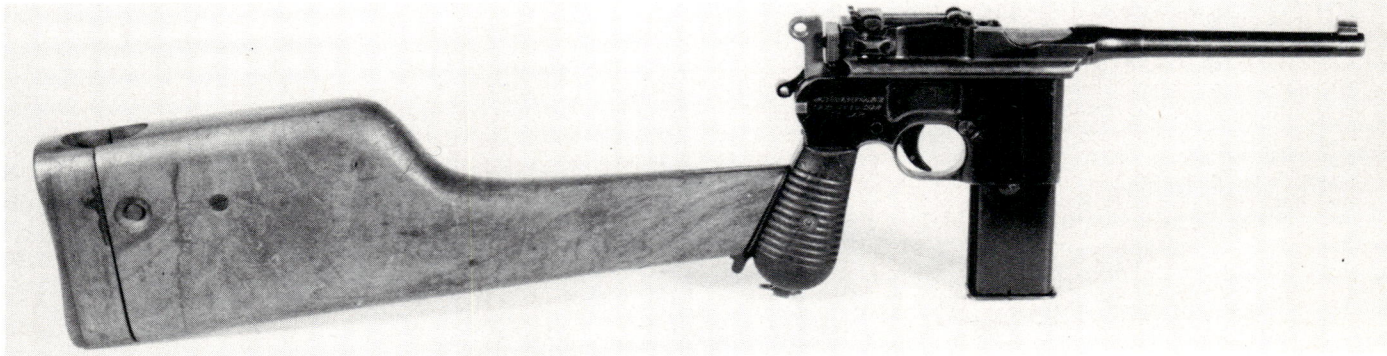

The 7.63 Mauser Model 1932 issued to Waffen SS Units (RSAF)

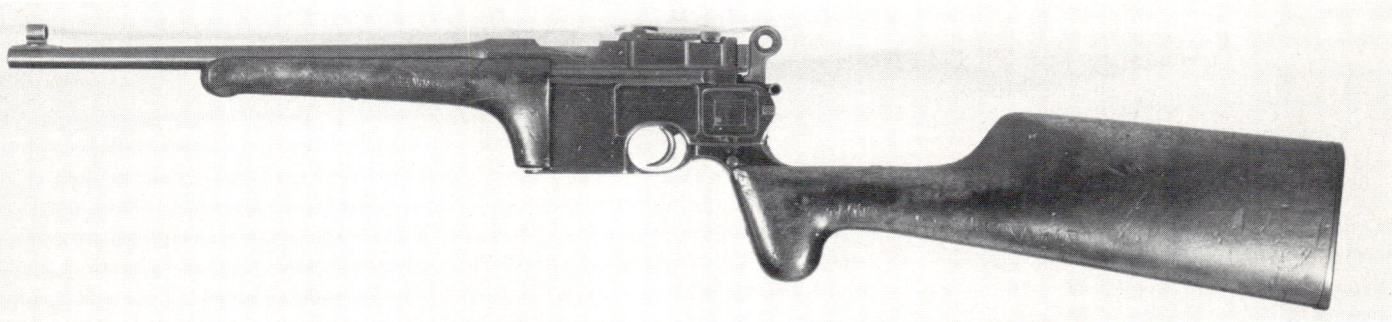

The 12in barrel Mauser (RSAF)

7.65mm MAUSER MODEL 1910 PISTOL

This was a straight blowback pistol chambered to fire either the 6.35mm cartridge or the 7.65mm round. It was a well designed pistol and made the maximum use of the cartridge it fired. It had a plunger protruding through a hole in the rear of the slide as a warning that the pistol was cocked. It also had an unusual arrangement to release the holding open device. The insertion of a magazine, either loaded or empty, caused the slide stop to release the slide and if a loaded magazine had been inserted, a cartridge was fed forward into the chamber.

The Mauser 7.65mm M1910 pistol (RSAF)

7.65mm (or 9mm) MAUSER HSc PISTOL

This pistol was introduced in 1940 and is a double action blowback pistol of very attractive shape, and of advanced design. The hammer is almost entirely concealed and just sufficient is exposed to allow the firer to use his thumb to lower it on a loaded chamber. A few pistols were made with totally enclosed hammers. The safety device on this pistol is a lever which turns to lift the head of the firing pin into a recess and out of alignment with the hammer. The action is straightforward. When the slide is retracted the hammer is cocked and the return spring, wrapped round the barrel, is compressed. The spring bears against a step formed by a strengthened section of the barrel over the chamber. When the slide is released the top round is fed into the chamber. The hammer can be lowered on the firing pin and fired with a long pull. When the ammunition is expended the slide is held open by the magazine follower. When the magazine is removed the slide will go forward as soon as a magazine – loaded or empty – is inserted. If the magazine is loaded the top round is fed into the chamber. When the magazine is out of the pistol, the hammer cannot go forward. A disconnec-

7.65mm Mauser HSc pistol with a finger spur to the magazine

7.65mm Mauser HSc pistol as currently produced

tor moves up into a recess in the slide when the latter is fully home. Until this occurs the trigger bar is not in contact with the sear.

There was a 9mm version called the HSv which was considered as the German service pistol but not adopted.

The HSc was used during World War II by the German Air Force and the Navy. After the war ended commercial production was resumed. Over the years there have been minor changes in styling as the accompanying illustrations indicate.

STRIPPING

The pistol is stripped as follows. Cock the weapon and check that the safety is applied. Remove the magazine and check the chamber is clear. Press in the catch in the trigger guard against its spring and at the same time push the slide forward and then move it back and up out of the receiver guide. The slide and barrel come out together. Push the barrel forward, compressing the return spring, and then lift up the breech and allow the spring to push the barrel back out of the slide.

DATA
Cartridge: 7.65mm (.32 ACP) or 9mm short (.380 ACP)
Method of operation: Blowback
Method of locking: Nil
Method of feed: 8-round detachable box magazine
Method of fire: Semi-automatic
Weight: 596g
Length: 165mm
Barrel: 86mm
　　　　　Rifling: 4 groove RH
Sights: Foresight: Blade
　　　　　Rearsight: Notch
Muzzle velocity: 290 metres/sec
Muzzle energy: 20.5mkp
Rate of fire: 30 rounds/min
Range, maximum effective: 40 metres
Manufacturer: Mauser-Werke AG Oberndorf/Neckar. Currently manufactured. Not in regular military service but wartime weapons may survive

7.65mm SAUER MODEL 1938(H) PISTOL

The Model H was produced for police work and as a pocket pistol in 6.35mm (.25 ACP), 7.65mm (.32 ACP) and 9mm (Short) (.380 ACP). When adopted as a German substitute standard in calibre 7.65mm, it was called the Model 1938 and throughout the war of 1939-1945 it was used by air and tank forces.

As a weapon it was superior to the earlier and now obsolete models 1913 and 1930. It was a blowback operated pistol with a double action trigger: if the hammer was forward a long trigger pull would both cock and fire the hammer. It could also be cocked to fire single action by means of a unique

system. A lever on the left of the grip projected towards the trigger. If the hammer was cocked, downward pressure on this lever lowered the hammer under control. If the hammer was forward, downward pressure rotated the concealed hammer back to the cocked position. A safety catch was fitted on the left of the slide. When rotated down it turned a cut away bolt inside the slide to push the hammer out of contact with the sear and at the same time it blocked the firing pin.

Overall it was a very advanced design which might have achieved much greater fame but for the arrival of the Second World War.

DATA
Cartridge: 7.65mm (.32 ACP). See text
Method of operation: Blowback
Method of locking: Nil
Method of feed: 8-round detachable box magazine
Method of fire: Semi-automatic
Weight: 738g
Length: 159mm
Barrel: 85mm
　　　　　Rifling: 4 grooves RH
Sights: Foresight: Blade
　　　　　Rearsight: Notch
Muzzle velocity: 328 metres/sec
Muzzle energy: 18mkp
Rate of fire: 24 rounds/min
Range, maximum effective: 30 metres
Manufacturer: J.P. Sauer & Sohn, Suhl
Status: No longer manufactured. Not in military service

7.65mm Sauer Model 38 (RSAF)

7.65mm WALTHER MODELS PP AND PPK PISTOLS

The first pistol produced by the firm of Karl Walther, then located at Zella Mehlis, was the Model 3 of 1909. This was followed in 1910 by the Model 4 which was more successful. It was a simple blowback pistol with the slide enclosing the barrel and return spring. The empty case was ejected through a port on the left of the slide across the firer's sight line.   The dimensions were:

In 1929 the 'Police Pistol' was introduced for carrying on the uniform belt and was widely adopted by police forces. Originally the pistol was made in .32 calibre but later it was constructed in .22 LR and .380 ACP (9mm Short). A small number of 6.35mm models were also made.

In 1931 a smaller pistol called the PPK appeared in the same calibres. This was intended for police use as a concealed weapon and the initials stood for "Police Criminal" (Kriminal). This differed in size and also in the construction of the handgrip. In the PP the butt was forged to shape and had simple plastic side plates but in the PPK it was rectangular with a plastic butt

providing the contour. Both pistols were blowback operated and well constructed and finished. Both used a pin, with centre fire cartridges, to indicate a loaded chamber. This protruded from the rear of the slide. The pistols made before the war were offered with some extras. Dural frames and slides were available to reduce weight; plastic magazine floor plates, with spurs to increase the length of the grip, were available for policemen with big hands. Luminous night sights could be added. The weapons were used extensively during the 1939-1945 war and often the loaded chamber indicator was omitted in wartime production. The finish in the war was often poor. After the war the pistols were copied and used by several countries including Turkey and Hungary. The French firm of Manurhin produced the pistols under licence until very recently. They are now made by Karl Walther at Ulm, Donau, in West Germany.

The PP and PPK are straight blowback pistols with external hammers, double action triggers and very adequate safety arrangements. The ham-

7.65mm Walther Model 4 (RSAF)

7.65mm Walther PPK

7.65 Walther PP

7.65mm PP sectioned

mer is prevented from reaching the firing pin until the sear movement, when the trigger is pulled, moves the block clear. The disconnector works into a recess in the slide and until the disconnector can rise, the sear cannot rotate. This only occurs when the slide is fully forward.

In spite of the criticism levelled against the PP in May 1974, when it was withdrawn as the pistol for the bodyguards of the British Royal Family, it is an excellent pistol when properly maintained.

DATA
Cartridge: 7.65mm (.32 ACP), 9mm Short (.38 ACP) .22 LR and (a few) 6.35mm (.25 ACP)
Method of operation: Blowback
Method of locking: Nil
Method of feed: Detachable box magazine. **PP** 8 rounds, **PPK** 7 rounds
Weight: PP 682g. **PPK** 568g

Length: PP 173mm. **PPK** 155mm
Barrel: PP 99mm. **PPK** 86mm
 Rifling: 6 grooves RH
Sights: Foresight: Blade
 Rearsight: Notch
Muzzle velocity (7.65mm): PP 290 metres/sec. **PPK** 280 metres/sec
Muzzle energy: PP 20mkp. **PPK** 19mkp
Rate of fire: 30 rounds/min
Range, maximum effective: 40 metres
Manufacturer: Karl Walther, Ulm, Donau, Germany. Made under licence in France by Manurhin. See also the entries under Hungary and Turkey, and the Russian Makarov pistol and copies.
Status: Current manufacture. Widely used during the Second World War and still in use (from German, French, Hungarian or Turkish production) by the armed forces or police of all four countries

9mm WALTHER MODEL P1 PISTOL

The P1 is the current version of the Walther P38 used by the German Army in World War II. It differs from the P38 in having a lightweight dural receiver and a firing pin of improved design which cannot be exchanged with that used in the P38. The difference in markings on the two weapons is small. Both have "Walther" and then "Carl Walther Waffenfabrik Ulm/Do". The Army pistol has the words "P1 Cal 9mm" and the commercial weapons "P.38 Cal 9mm".

The main parts of the pistol are the barrel, receiver, slide and the locking lug. There is a double action trigger mechanism that enables the hammer to be cocked and released by a single trigger pull. The hammer can also be cocked manually to produce a single action with a reduced trigger pull. If the weapon is set to 'safe' with the hammer cocked, the hammer will go forward but the spindle of the change lever locks the firing pin which cannot go forward.

OPERATION
The P1 pistol is a short-recoil operated weapon. When it is fired the barrel and slide are locked together; the gas pressure forces the breech face back and the slide recoils pulling the barrel with it. A locking lug holds the barrel to the slide. A plunger mounted in the barrel forging hits the receiver after about ⅜in of free travel. The plunger is driven forward and strikes an inclined face at the rear of the locking lug. The locking lug is rotated down at its rear end into a recess in the receiver and so the barrel is locked into the receiver and the slide continues to the rear under its own momentum and

9mm Model P1 pistol (RSAF)

with some blowback assistance from the cartridge case. The empty case is held to the breech face by the extractor and when it reaches the ejector it is thrown out to the left.

The return springs and guides are fitted in grooves at the top of the receiver and drive the slide forward to chamber the top cartridge in the magazine. The barrel is still locked to the receiver but recesses in the slide rib of the breech block slide come opposite the locking lug which is cammed up to release the barrel from the receiver and lock it to the slide. The slide then drives the barrel forward to the fully run out position.

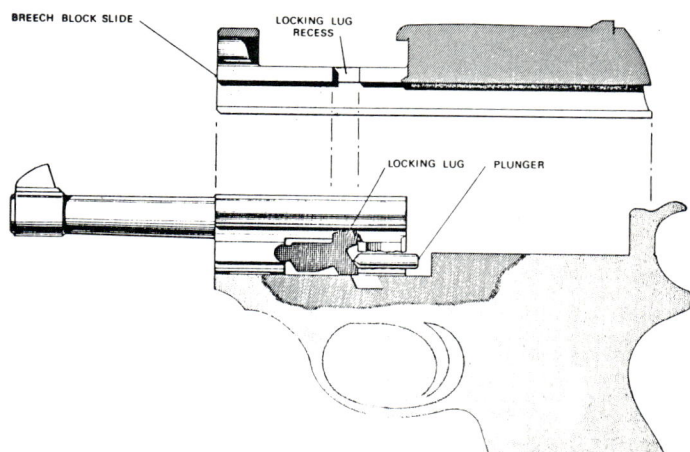

The locking action of the P1

TRIGGER AND FIRING MECHANISM

The trigger and firing mechanism of this pistol is somewhat unusual because of the choice of double or single action and the safety arrangements. Assuming the hammer to be in the forward position and action fully forward, pulling the trigger moves the trigger bar forward and a hook on its upper rear end rotates the sear upward. The rotation of the sear lifts a pawl which is attached to the hammer and rocks the hammer back, and then the sear moves enough to slip free of the pawl. The hammer spring then drives the hammer forward again to fire the cap. The disconnector action comes from the rearward movement of the slide forcing the trigger bar down and so lowering its hook out of engagement with the sear. The sear spring returns to its original position. The rearward movement of the slide pushes the hammer back. A projection at the bottom of the hammer lifts the sear which holds it, when the slide runs out, in the cocked position. Another trigger pull again moves the trigger bar forward and the hook pulls the sear out of engagement with the hammer which flies toward to the hit the firing pin.

LOADING AND FIRING

The weapon is simple and practical to operate. The magazine is removed by depressing the magazine catch in the base of the butt and eight 9mm Parabellum cartridges can be inserted. With the loaded magazine in place, retraction of the slide and subsequent release, feeds a round into the chamber and locks the barrel to the slide. A 'chamber loaded' indicator then protrudes from the back of the slide above the hammer and this pin remains proud as long as a cartridge remains in the chamber. If the thumb safety lever on the left of the slide is down to 'safe' the external hammer will not remain cocked but will travel forward with the slide. Since the firing pin is locked, this provides a secure method of loading the chamber without cocking the hammer. If the safety catch is in the horizontal position – i.e. at 'fire' – when the slide is operated, the hammer is held in the cocked position to the rear.

To fire the pistol the safety catch is placed at 'fire' and if the hammer is forward it can be cocked by hand and then released by trigger action. Alternatively a long sustained pull on the trigger will cock and then fire the pistol. This enables a second hammer blow if a misfire occurs. When the ammunition supply is expended, the slide is held to the rear. When a loaded magazine is inserted, the slide can be released either by a short rearward pull and subsequent return spring action or by operating the slide release on the left of the receiver.

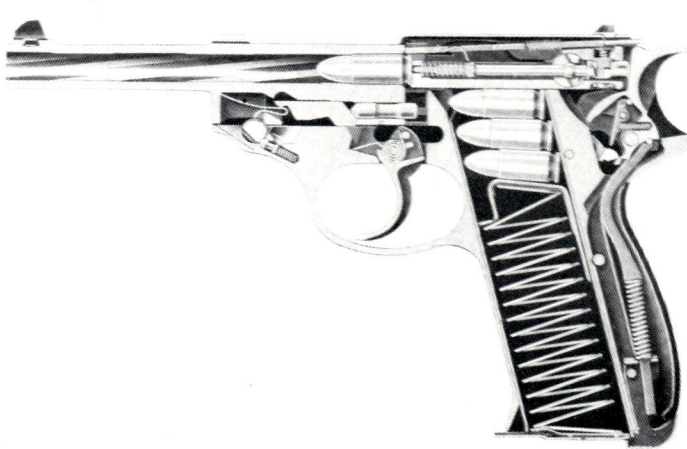

Sectional view of the P.38 pistol

STRIPPING

Stripping the P1 for cleaning or maintenance is carried out by first removing the magazine and then checking that the chamber is empty. The slide is retracted and held to the rear with the slide stop, and the take down lever located on the left side of the receiver forward of the trigger is rotated down. Ease the slide back to release the slide stop then move it forward off the receiver. The unlocking plunger behind the slide releases the barrel from the slide and the barrel can be pulled forward and clear.

The P38 pistol stripped (RMCS)

DATA
Cartridge: 9mm × 19 Parabellum
Method of operation: Short recoil
Method of locking: Hinged locking piece
Method of feed: 8-round box magazine
Method of fire: Self-loading. Double action

WEIGHTS
Pistol empty: 772g
Pistol loaded: 960g
Trigger pull: (SA) 2.28kp. (DA) 6.9kp

LENGTHS
Pistol: 218mm
Barrel: 24mm

MECHANICAL FEATURES
Barrel: Rifling: 6 grooves RH 1 turn in 10in
Sights: Foresight: Blade
    Rearsight: U notch
    Graduations: Nil
    Zeroing: Line. Foresight on dovetail. Elevation. Change front sight blade

FIRING CHARACTERISTICS
Muzzle velocity: 350 metres/sec
Muzzle energy: 46.6mkp
Rate of fire: Self-loading 32 rounds/min
Range, maximum effective: 50 metres
Manufacturer: Carl Walther Waffenfabrik, Ulm-Donau, Germany
Status: Current manufacture. In service with German Armed Forces. Exported to Chile and Norway where the P38 is made under licence.

The Pistol P38 in 22RF cartridge

HECKLER AND KOCH HK4 SL PISTOL

The Heckler and Koch HK4 pistol is a self-loading, double action pocket pistol designed for easy conversion from centre fire to rim fire – or vice versa – through a variety of calibres – 9mm Short (.380)-7.65mm (.32), 6.35mm (.25) and .22LR. The safety catch on the left side of the receiver, is down for 'safe' and up for 'fire'. A white spot indicates 'safe', a red spot 'fire'. The pistol is set to safe before unloading or loading. The magazine is removed from the pistol by pressing back the magazine catch located below the pistol grip, and loaded by placing the cartridge on the follower, in front of the lips, and pressing it down and then sliding it back, to the rear of the magazine. The magazine is slotted to show the number of rounds loaded. Loading the pistol can be done with the slide either open or closed. If the slide is open, when closed it will load a round into the chamber and the hammer will be held in the cocked position. If the slide is closed, no round will be in the chamber and the hammer will, normally, be forward. To chamber a round, the slide must be retracted, cocking the hammer, and then released. When a round is in the chamber, the extractor on the right of the slide is proud and this can be seen by day and felt with the forefinger at night. When the pistol is set to 'safe' the hammer can be uncocked by pulling the trigger. The adoption of the 'safe' position blocks the firing pin from the hammer. When the magazine is emptied the slide remains to the rear. Putting in a loaded magazine releases the slide stop and the slide goes forward to chamber a round. To unload a loaded magazine, the weapon is put to 'safe', the magazine catch pressed and the magazine removed. To ensure the weapon is 'safe', the slide must be retracted and the chamber and feedway inspected. The slide will remain at the rear and may be released by pulling the trigger. The slide will go forward leaving the hammer cocked and to release the hammer the trigger must be pulled again. It cannot be emphasised too strongly that the weapon must be set to 'safe' before these operations are carried out. To fire the weapon the safety should be raised to 'fire'. If the hammer is cocked, the trigger pressure will be light. If the hammer is forward it may be cocked using the thumb to retract the partly exposed hammer or alternatively it can be operated as a double action pistol using a single long pull.

OPERATION

The operation of the pistol is simple blowback. The gas pressure generated inside the cartridge case, will drive the bullet up the bore and force the case back. The breech-block, part of the slide, is pulled back and as it rotates the hammer and compresses the return spring wrapped around the barrel, the empty case emerges from the chamber held to the breech face by the extractor. The ejector strikes the base of the case, rotates it round the extractor, and throws it out of the pistol to the right through the ejection port. The recoil of the slide compresses the plastic buffer and the return spring then drives it forward. The top round is eased from the magazine, fed into the chamber, and the extractor grips the rim or the cannelure of the case. The trigger can then be released and operated again. Provided the slide is fully forward, another round can be fired.

TRIGGER AND FIRING MECHANISM

The trigger and firing mechanism operate as follows. The disconnector fits into a recess in the slide. As the slide recoils the disconnector is forced down, clear of the sear. The slide also cocks the hammer and as it rotates back the sear slips into the hammer notch and holds the hammer in the cocked position. Only when the slide is fully forward can the disconnector move up but with the trigger pressed another round cannot be fired. When the trigger is released the disconnector returns behind the sear and trigger operation fires the pistol again.

STRIPPING

Stripping the weapon is as follows. The safety is put down to 'safe'. The magazine is removed and the slide retracted. The chamber and feedway are inspected to ensure that no cartridge is in the weapon. The barrel catch situated in the rear surface of the trigger guard, is pushed forward. The slide is eased forward to the stop – located approximately 7mm from the fully forward position – and then lifted off the receiver. The barrel is removed from the slide by pulling it forward with the projection of the magazine floor plate. When the extractor on the breech face clears the extractor groove, the barrel can be lifted clear. Re-assembly is equally simple. The barrel is pushed forward through the front hole in the slide, compressing the return spring, until the chamber face clears the breech face plate and the extractor. The slide is then placed on the receiver so that the two front ribs are above the cut-out in the receiver, dropped and pulled back to the stop.

Heckler and Koch HK4 SL pistol

Cutaway view of the HK4

CHANGE OF CALIBRE

To change from one centre fire barrel to another of a different calibre is merely a matter of changing barrels, springs and magazines. To change from centre fire to rim fire the firing pin must also be re-aligned. This is done by removing the extractor, holding the extractor clear of the breech face plate with a pin or a nail and removing the breech face plate. When using .22LR rim fire the face plate is turned so that the side marked 'R' is showing. The firing pin protrudes from the top hole. When converting back to centre fire the plate marking 'Z' is to the front and the firing pin comes through the lower hole.

DATA (COMMON TO ALL CALIBRES)
Method of operation: Blowback
Method of locking: Nil
Method of feed: Box magazine
Method of fire: Self-loading. Double action

WEIGHTS
Pistol, empty: 480g
Magazine, empty: 40g
Trigger pull: 2.75kp

LENGTHS
Pistol: 157mm
Barrel: 85mm

MECHANICAL FEATURES
Barrel: Rifling: 6 grooves LH 1 turn in 254mm
Sights: Foresight: Blade
        Rearsight: Notch
        Graduation: Nil
        Zeroing: Elevation. Change foresight blade. Line. Move rearsight in dovetail

FIRING CHARACTERISTICS
Rate of fire: Single shots
Range, maximum effective: 27 metres

The alternative barrels for the HK4

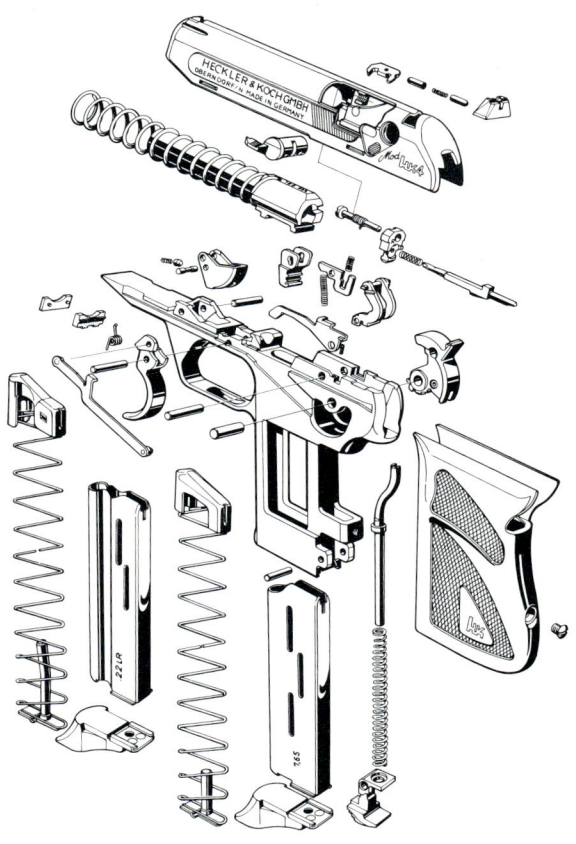

DATA VARYING WITH CALIBRE
Calibre: (a) .22LR (.22lfB)
(b) .25ACP (6.35mm)
(c) .32ACP (7.65mm)
(d) .380ACP (9mm)
Magazine capacity: (a), (b) 10
(c) 9
(d) 8
Muzzle velocity: (a) 300 metres/sec
(b) 257 metres/sec
(c) 302 metres/sec
(d) 299 metres/sec
Muzzle energy: (a) 11.2mkp
(b) 10.4mkp
(c) 21mkp
(d) 27.5mkp
Manufacturer: Heckler and Koch GmbH, Oberndorf-Neckar, Germany
Status: Current manufacture. Wide commercial and police sales. No known military sales

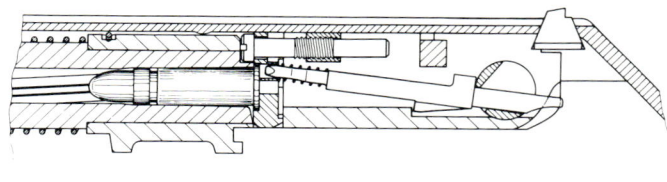

Sectioned view showing the firing pin aligned for a rim-fire cartridge

Exploded view of HK4 pistol

9mm HECKLER AND KOCH P9 AND P9S PISTOLS

The 9mm P9 and P9S SL Pistols differ only in the trigger mechanism. The P9 has a single action trigger and the P9S has a double action trigger.

The safety catch located on the rear of the left side of the slide is pressed down for 'safe'. This uncovers a white spot. When rotated clockwise up to the horizontal position the weapon is set to 'fire' and a red spot is revealed.

To remove the magazine for loading, the magazine catch, located below the pistol grip, is pushed to the rear. The magazine will then be eased out and can be withdrawn. The cartridge is placed on the magazine platform with the base in front of the magazine lips. It is pushed down and then fully rearward under the magazine lips. The magazine holds 9 cartridges. With the safety applied, the magazine can be inserted into the pistol grip until the catch engages. To place a cartridge in the chamber the slide is pulled fully back and then released. This also cocks the hammer. When the hammer is cocked, a pin protrudes from the rear of the slide when the latter is fully forward. When a cartridge is chambered the extractor stands proud. Both of these indicators can be felt at night and seen by day. When the ammunition is expended the pistol will cease firing with the slide to the rear. As soon as a loaded magazine is inserted the slide may be released by pressing down on the cocking lever located on the left side of the receiver behind the trigger or by pulling the slide back and letting the return spring drive it forward. As the slide goes forward a round is chambered and the hammer is left cocked. The cocked hammer may be released by removing the safety, pressing down the cocking lever, pulling the trigger and holding it back whilst the cocking lever is allowed to rise again, releasing the trigger and applying the safety catch. The model 9S can be fired from this postion by a long trigger pull but with the model 9 the slide must be retracted, ejecting the cartridge in the chamber. The single action gives a lighter trigger pull off.

OPERATION

The pistol is delay blowback operated. The method of connecting the slide to the barrel is to use a two-part breech-block consisting of a bolt head containing the two rollers and a heavy bolt body which by means of angled faces, forces the rollers out into barrel extensions. This method is derived from Heckler and Koch's G3 rifle and a more detailed account of the action will be found there. When the pistol fires, the gas pressure forces back the breech face but movement is severely limited because the projecting rollers are engaged in recesses in the barrel extension. The rollers must be free of these seatings before the breech face can move back significantly. The reaction of the recesses drives the rollers inwards but their inward movement is resisted by the angled faces of the bolt body and the strength of the return spring. The velocity ratio obtained by the angles of the recesses in the barrel extension and the angle of the faces of the bolt body results in the heavy bolt body having a rearward movement four times as great as the bolt face. Eventually the rollers are forced fully in, the bolt is then blown back by the residual pressure and the empty case comes out, held to the breech face by the extractor. The hammer is rotated back by the bolt body, the empty case is thrown out by the ejector and the rearward movement of the bolt ceases on contact with the plastic buffer. The return spring around the barrel expands and the slide goes forward, feeding a round into the chamber. To fire another round the trigger must be released to allow the disconnector to bear on the sear which is engaged in the hammer notch.

Heckler & Koch Model P9

Model P9S with modified trigger guard

STRIPPING

The following procedure should be followed to strip the pistol. First engage the safety, remove the magazine, and inspect the chamber and feedway to ensure no cartridge remains in the weapon. Return the slide to the forward position. Press the barrel catch located in the rear surface of the trigger guard in front of the trigger. Push the slide as far forward as it will go

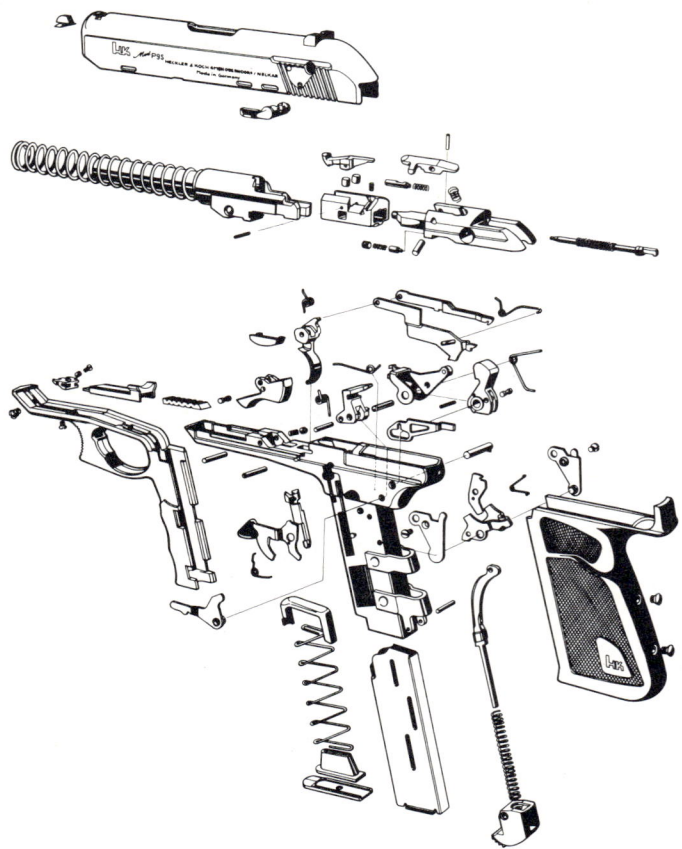

Exploded view of the P9S

Cutaway view of the P9

and lift it off. The barrel is removed by pushing it forward against the return spring until it can be removed from the slide. The bolt head can be removed by using one side of the barrel extension to press between the bolt head and the slide against the locking lever until the bolt head springs forward and the bolt then can be removed.

PERFORMANCE
The P9 and P9S Pistols have polygonal rifling. The advantages claimed for this form of rifling are that it reduces the deformation of the bullet, less work is done on the bullet by engraving and the muzzle velocity is increased. The lack of corners at the bottom of the grooves leads to less accumulation of fouling and both accuracy and ease of maintenance are improved.

The pistols can be regarded as primarily for military use but they can be used for target shooting. There is the choice of two target barrels – one five inches long and the other half an inch longer. With the longer barrel there is a barrel weight fitting over the muzzle which protrudes forward of the slide. This improves the balance for competition work. A trigger stop is located in the rear portion of the trigger guard and normally fits flush. It can be raised, by loosening the retaining screw, to limit the length of trigger pull. On the model P9S the adjustable trigger stop is longer and prevents double action functioning of the trigger by restraining its movement. Also for target shooting an adjustment device can be fitted for regulating the trigger travel between the let off point and hammer release. It consists of a screw fitment which when rotated clockwise reduces the overlap between the catch lever

and the hammer. A click sight, adjustable for elevation and windage, can be fitted. Using a small screwdriver, rotating the sight screw clockwise lowers the point of impact 1.5cm per click at 25 metres range. The windage screw is adjusted similarly, every click clockwise moving the point of impact 1cm to the left at 25 metres.

DATA
Cartridge: 9mm × 19 Parabellum
Method of operation: Delayed blowback
Method of delay: Rollers
Method of feed: 9-round box magazine
Method of fire: Self-loading. Model P9 single-action. Model P9S double-action

WEIGHTS
Pistol empty: 880g
Magazine empty: 74g
Magazine loaded: 183g
Pistol loaded: 1.065kg

LENGTHS
Pistol: 137mm
Barrel: 102mm

MECHANICAL FEATURES
Barrel: Rifling: Polygonal
Sights: Foresight: Blade
        Rearsight: Notch
        Graduation: Nil
        Zeroing: Elevation. Change rearsight. Line: Foresight moves in dovetail
        Sight radius: 5.8in

FIRING CHARACTERISTICS
Muzzle velocity: 351 metres/sec
Muzzle energy: 50mkp
Manufacturer: Heckler and Koch GmbH Oberndorf-Neckar, Germany
Status: Current manufacture for commercial sales. Used by many German police forces. No known military sales

9mm HECKLER AND KOCH VP70 AUTOMATIC PISTOL
The VP70 is an automatic pistol of original and unusual design, making considerable use of plastics. As a hand held weapon it fires only in the self loading mode but as soon as the holster stock is attached it can also fire three round bursts at a cyclic rate of 2,200 rounds a minute. To make use of this burst fire ability a large capacity magazine is needed and the VP70 magazine takes 18 rounds. The very high cyclic rate of fire makes considerable demands on the moving parts and the associated accelerations impose considerable forces. The number of moving parts has been kept to a minimum by careful design; only four operating parts are necessary and the makers claim a life of 30,000 rounds. The receiver is plastic with support for the fixed barrel moulded in.

OPERATION
The VP70, by itself, functions as a self-loading pistol. To remove the magazine from the pistol for loading, the catch at the heel of the magazine is pressed back and the magazine is then partly ejected. The 18 rounds are inserted one by one by placing each on the platform and pressing it first down and then back. The magazine is pressed home in the grip until the catch engages and retains it. To cock the weapon the slide must be pulled back as far as possible and then released. The top round is picked up and chambered and the extractor snaps into the groove. When this is done the firer is aware that the chamber is loaded because the extractor is proud.

Heckler and Koch VP70

The weapon can be carried in this condition with safety because it is not cocked.

The trigger is of unusual design. It is a double action mechanism and when pulled straight back it has a first pressure that can be plainly felt. Further pressure causes the trigger bar to slip off the spring loaded firing pin which goes forward to fire the cap.

The system of operation is pure blowback and the gas pressure generated inside the cartridge case pushes the bullet forward and the slide rearward. The inertia of the slide and the resistance of the return spring, wrapped round the barrel, control the rearward velocity of the slide. The round pushes the slide back and is then held to the breech face by the extractor until the ejector projects it out of the feedway, through the ejection port, to the right. The slide comes to rest, the compressed return spring re-asserts itself and as the slide goes forward the top round is fed into the chamber. The trigger is still held back and is disengaged from the firing pin. When it is released it moves forward and in front of the firing pin lug. Another trigger pull again pulls the firing pin back and the trigger bar slips off to allow the firing spring to drive the pin forward into the cap.

This type of trigger mechanism is very simple and allows provision of an elementary form of safety in the push through button located on the receiver behind the trigger. At 'safe' the spindle blocks the trigger bar but on pressing through to fire, a cut-out D section in the shaft provides a gap through which the trigger bar can pass. When the ammunition is expended, the slide stops in the forward position and to renew firing a fresh magazine must be inserted and the slide withdrawn to chamber a round.

STRIPPING

To strip the weapon for maintenance and cleaning, the magazine is removed, the slide pulled back and the chamber and feedway visually inspected. The slide is released. Above the trigger guard is a slide retaining catch and when this is pulled down the slide can be pulled right back, lifted up and backwards and then allowed to slide forward. The firing pin is removed by rotating the end cap in the breech through 90 deg to the right and removing it. No further stripping is required. The barrel is permanently attached to the receiver and is cleaned in situ.

SMG CONVERSION

The holster plays a very important part in the concept of this pistol. First it provides a convenient transit holder enabling the firer to carry the pistol in almost any conceivable position. This is done by having a carrying plate to which the holster is attached and a harness that enables it to be located on a waist belt, or on either thigh, or under either armpit with the butt facing either forward or rearward at will. The holster can also be attached to the pistol to convert it into a sub-machine gun. The holster carries the selector lever in this mode, allowing single shots or bursts of three rounds for each trigger operation. The lever is located on the left side of the holster/stock well forward and rotates down for single and up for multi shots. To attach the holster to the pistol the fire selector lever is set to 1 i.e. single shot fire, and the catch at the bottom of the holster is pressed back. There are two grooves at the back of the pistol and the stock is inserted into the grooves and pushed upwards until the latch engages.

VP70 with holster stock attached to convert it to a SMG

DATA (PISTOL ONLY)
Cartridge: 9mm × 19
Method of operation: Blowback
Method of locking: Nil
Method of feed: 18-round box magazine
Method of fire: Pistol only – self-loading double action

WEIGHTS
Pistol: 823g
Magazine with 18 rounds: 315g

LENGTHS
Pistol: 204mm
Barrel: 116mm

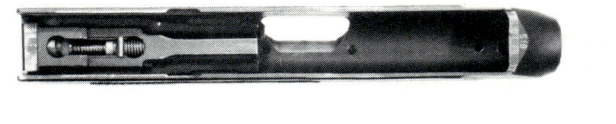

The slide removed from the VP70 to show the trigger and the spring-loaded firing pin

VP70 field-stripped

MECHANICAL FEATURES
Sights: Foresight: Blade
      Rearsight: Notch
      Graduations: Nil
      Zeroing: Elevation. Change backsight. Line. Backsight moves on dovetail
      Sight radius: 175mm

FIRING CHARACTERISTICS
Muzzle velocity: 360 metres/sec
Muzzle energy: 52mkp
Rate of fire: Self-loading 40 rounds/min
Range, maximum effective: 50 metres

DATA (PISTOL AND HOLSTER STOCK)
Method of fire: Single shot or 3-round bursts

WEIGHTS
Stock: 454g
Magazine with 18 rounds: 315g
Pistol unloaded: 820g
Total weight of loaded pistol with attached stock: 1.6kg

LENGTHS
Pistol and holder stock: 545mm

FIRING CHARACTERISTICS
Rate of fire: Cyclic: 2,200 rounds/min
      Bursts: 100 rounds/min
      Self-loading: 40 rounds/min
Range, maximum effective: 150 metres
Manufacturer: Heckler and Koch GmbH Oberndorf-Neckar, Germany
Status: Limited numbers produced. No known military sales

GERMANY (DEMOCRATIC REPUBLIC)

PISTOLE M

The East German Army is equipped with the Pistole M. This is manufactured in the country and is a copy of the Russian Makarov pistol which itself is copied from the German Walther PP. It is an eight shot, blowback operated, self-loading pistol using the 9mm × 18 cartridge which was developed for the weapon. The trigger mechanism enables the pistol to be used as a single action model by cocking the hammer manually: alternatively a single long pull can be used to cock and then fire.

There are some differences between the Pistole M and the Walther PP. The Pistole M does not have a loaded chamber indicator. The East German pistol has a leaf spring to rotate the hammer instead of a coil spring and there are differences in the trigger mechanism. The slide stop of the Walther is completely enclosed – that of the Pistole M is externally operated. Lastly, the safety catch of the East German pistol goes up for 'safe' and that of the Walther goes down.

An East German copy of the 7.65mm Walther PP known as the Modele 1001-0 (RSAF)

An East German copy of the Soviet 9mm × 18 Makarov pistol known as the Pistole M (RSAF)

DATA
Cartridge: 9mm × 18
Method of operation: Blowback
Method of locking: Nil
Method of feed: 8-round detachable box magazine
Method of fire: Self-loading
Weight: 663g
Length: 160mm

Barrel: 91mm
    Rifling: 4 grooves RH
Sights: Foresight: Blade
    Rearsight: Notch
Muzzle velocity: 315 metres/sec
Muzzle energy: 30mkp
Rate of fire: 35 rounds/min
Range, maximum effective: 50 metres
Manufacturer: State factory
Status: In service in East Germany

HUNGARY

7.65mm M1937 PISTOL

The Hungarian Army adopted this pistol in 1937. It is basically a modified Browning blowback design. An earlier version – the Model 1929 – had a bolt separate from the slide but the Model 1937 is orthodox in having the breech integral with the slide. The M1937 was also chambered for the 9mm short cartridge (.38ACP). The pistol was well made, somewhat heavy, but popular with the troops to whom it was issued. It had a grip safety, a small exposed hammer and a spur below the magazine for the man with an oversize hand. No manual safety was fitted.

The German Army took the pistol during the Second World War. The model produced for the Reich differed in having a manual safety on the left of the receiver as well as the grip safety, and of course had different markings. The German markings were P Mod 37 KAL 7.65 and the Hungarian marking was FEMARU-FEGYVER ES GEPGYAR PT 37M.

DATA
Cartridge: 7.65mm (.32ACP) and 9mm Short (.380 ACP)

Method of operation: Blowback
Method of locking: Nil
Method of feed: 7-round detachable box magazine
Method of fire: Semi-automatic
Weight: 767g
Length: 173mm
Barrel: 99mm
    Rifling: 6 grooves RH
Sights: Foresight: Blade
    Rearsight: Notch
Muzzle velocity: 290 metres/sec
Muzzle energy: 20mkp
Rate of fire: 28 rounds/min
Range, maximum effective: 40 metres
Manufacturer: Fegyvergyan, Budapest
Status: No longer manufactured and probably rare

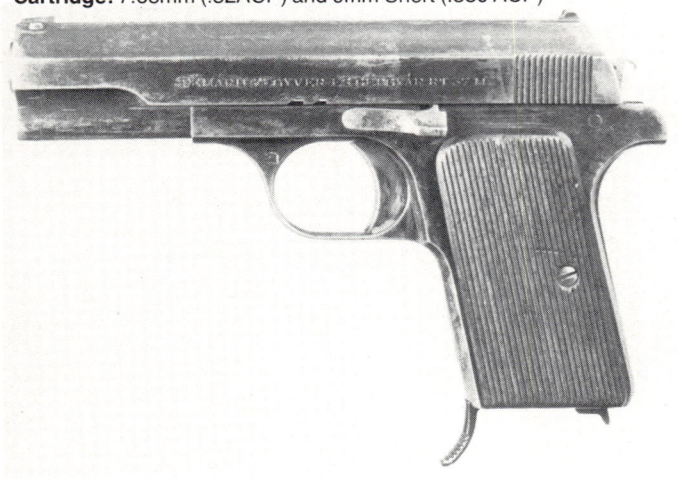

7.65mm Model 1937 pistol (RSAF)

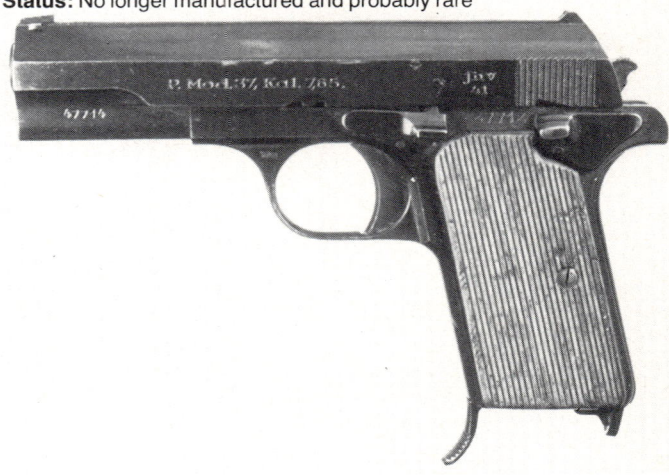

7.65mm Model 37 pistol, produced under German occupation (RSAF)

7.62mm MODEL 48 PISTOL

The Russian 7.62mm Tokarev (TT-33) was manufactured in Hungary as the Model 48. The Hungarian pistol is identified by the crest on the grip (a star, wheatsheaf and a hammer surrounded by a wreath) and the uniform narrow vertical cuts on the slide for the firer to grip whilst cocking the pistol. All other details are the same as the Russian Tokarev (TT-33). The pistol was produced by State Arsenals and is still in service.

DATA
Cartridge: 7.62mm × 25 Pistol 'P' cartridge
Method of operation: Short recoil
Method of locking: Projecting lugs
Method of feed: 8-round box magazine
Method of fire: Semi-automatic

Weight: 846g
Length: 196mm
Barrel: 116mm
     Rifling: 4 grooves RH
Sights: Foresight: Blade
         Rearsight: Notch
Muzzle velocity: 420 metres/sec
Muzzle energy: 49mkp
Rate of fire: 35 rounds/min
Range, maximum effective: 50 metres
Manufacturer: State arsenals
Status: In service

7.62mm Model 48 pistol. This is the Hungarian copy of the Soviet Tokarev TT33 (RSAF)

7.65mm MODEL 48 PISTOL

This is a copy of the German Walther PP. It differs only in that the loaded chamber indicator emerges from the left top side of the slide, over the chamber, rather than at the rear. It was used by the Hungarian police force.

9mm WALAM 48 PISTOL

This is a copy of the German Walther PP made in 9mm Short (.380ACP) calibre. It was made for sale to Egypt but only a limited number were produced and those have been sold commercially.

7.65mm Model 48 pistol. This has a loaded chamber indicator over the chamber rather than at the back of the slide as in the Walther PP (RSAF)

9mm TOKAGYPT PISTOL

This pistol was a Tokarev TT33 modified to take the 9mm × 19 Parabellum cartridge. It was made for the Egyptian Army but was then diverted to the police forces. It was, apparently, not liked there and deliveries were curtailed. The pistol has since appeared on the commercial market. It has never been used in the Hungarian Armed Forces.

The Tokagypt differs from the Tokarev TT33 in cartridge and has had some modifications. A safety catch has been added on the left rear of the receiver, a plastic grip has gone round the handle and the floor plate of the magazine has a finger spur.

Tokagypt

The Tokagypt stripped

9mm PA-63 PISTOL

Based on the German Walther PP pistol, this is a light 9mm weapon and is the latest of several such pistols to be produced for Hungarian military use. It is a double-action blowback-operated weapon, similar in appearance to the PP but somewhat less bulky.
DATA
Calibre: 9mm
Operation: Blowback
Feed: 7-round detachable box magazine
Fire: Double-action semi-automatic

Weight: 0.7kg
Length: 17.5cm
Band: 8.5cm
Sights: Foresight: blade
         Rearsight: Notch
Muzzle velocity: 315 metres/sec
Effective range: 50m
Manufacturer: State factories
Status: In limited service in the Hungarian Army

INDONESIA

9mm PINDAD PISTOL

The fluctuating tide of occupation and war in Indonesia has left behind a legacy of weapons of many kinds. The Dutch colonial troops used a variety of weapons ranging from the Revolver 9.4mm Model 1873 through the Pistol 9mm Browning Model 1903 using the Browning long cartridge, the Pistol 9mm Browning M1922 with the .380ACP round (the Model 25), the Vickers manufactured Pistol 9mm Luger (Model 1920) to some Japanese pistols – mainly the Nambu 1904 types which were left behind after World War II. The Americans supplied a quantity of Pistols .45 Colt M1911A, and

immediately prior to the confrontation with Britain in 1965 a number of Tokarev TT33 7.63mm Pistols appeared. Some Walther PP pistols were also purchased.

The Ordnance Factory at Pindad is now manufacturing the Pistol 9mm FN Browning HP which is called the 'Pindad'. It carries on the left side of the slide the marking "Fabrik Sendjata Ringan" and below that 'Pindad' followed by "P1A9mm". The backsight is a simple notch and there is no tangent ramp version in use.

The Pindad

DATA
Cartridge: 9mm × 19 Parabellum
Method of operation: Recoil
Method of locking: Projecting lug
Method of feed: 13-round detachable box magazine
Method of fire: Semi-automatic
Weight: 0.88kg
Length: 196mm
Barrel: 112mm
Rifling: 6 grooves RH
Sights: Foresight: Blade
Rearsight: Notch
Muzzle velocity: 354 metres/sec
Muzzle energy: 51mkp
Rate of fire: 39 rounds/min
Range, maximum effective: 50 metres
Manufacturer: Ordnance factory at Pindad
Status: In service with Indonesian forces

ISRAEL

ISRAELI ARMY PISTOLS

The Israeli Army started with a whole variety of pistols. Some came from British sources and were mainly .455 Webley and .38 Enfield. There were also German P38 and Luger pistols and a few pistols 9mm FN Browning High Power. The Israeli "Workers Industry for Arms" produced a 6-chamber revolver of 9mm calibre firing the Parabellum cartridge. This necessitates the use of three-round clips. The revolver is based on the Smith and Wesson .38 Military and Police revolver weighs 0.9kg, is 28cm long, has a 155mm barrel and is used by police units.

The military pistol which the Israeli Army adopted is the Italian 9mm Beretta Model 1951. This pistol is also that adopted by the Egyptian Army and the Israeli supplies were somewhat augmented after the Six Day War of 1967.

9mm Beretta M1951 currently used by the Israeli Armed Forces (RSAF)

ITALY

9mm BERETTA MODEL 1934 PISTOL

This is an improved model of the earlier 1915 pattern using the 9mm short (.380ACP) cartridge. It incorporates features from the models of 1921 and 1923 and has been a successful pistol. It is well made and simple but with one or two drawbacks. The operation is typically blowback with the slide cocking the hammer and at the same time forcing a disconnector down, disconnecting the trigger from the sear. The return spring is compressed about its guide rod which protrudes through the front of the slide, below the barrel, as the slide moves back, When it is fully forward again,

feeding a round into the chamber in the process, the disconnector rises into its notch and the sear and trigger are re-connected.

When the last round has been fired the slide is held to the rear by the magazine follower and a lot of force is required to extract the magazine. As soon as the magazine drops, the slide runs forward onto an empty chamber and so the holding open device in this form does not save time in reloading. A separate slide stop would improve the situation.

The safety catch locks the trigger but not the hammer. Thus the hammer can be cocked by hand, or catch in the pocket or equipment, and without a positive hammer lock this can be a dangerous procedure.

The model 1935 is in 7.65mm (.32ACP) and is a little lighter.

9mm Beretta M1934 pistol

DATA
Cartridge: 9mm short (.380ACP). Some 7.65mm (.32ACP) were also made
Method of operation: Blowback
Method of locking: Nil
Method of feed: 7-round detachable box magazine
Method of fire: Semi-automatic
Weight: 568g
Length: 152mm
Barrel: 90mm
Rifling: 4 grooves RH
Sights: Foresight: Blade
Rearsight: Notch
Muzzle velocity: 290 metres/sec
Muzzle energy: 26mkp
Rate of fire: 28 rounds/min
Range, maximum effective: 40 metres
Manufacturer: Pietro Beretta SpA, Gardone
Status: In production. In service with the Italian Army

9mm BERETTA MODEL 1951SL PISTOL

The Model 51 is the standard pistol of the Italian Armed Forces and is manufactured by the firm of Pietro Beretta at Valdone, Brescia. It is also used by both the Israeli and Egyptian Armies and in Nigeria.

The weapon has three main parts; the receiver, barrel and slide. The receiver holds the magazine and trigger and firing mechanism and has a forward extension to take the slide. The barrel carries a swinging locking piece pivoting from a lug on the underside, and the slide fits over the receiver, sliding in grooves.

To load the pistol the magazine release in the lower left side of the grip is pressed and the magazine removed. It takes eight 9mm Parabellum cartridges. When the magazine is in place the pistol is cocked by pulling the slide fully back and then releasing it. The safety catch is a push through type mounted at the top rear of the butt. 'Safe' comes from pushing from right to left.

When the pistol is fired, the breech block – integral with the slide – goes back and the barrel which is locked to the slide goes back with it. After a short period of free travel of about 13mm the unlocking plunger on the rear barrel lug, strikes the receiver and stops. As the barrel and slide continue back the locking piece strikes the stationary plunger and is forced down into recesses in the slide in a manner similar to that of the Walther P38. The barrel comes to rest but the slide continues rearward for a further 5cm. The hammer is rolled back and the empty cartridge case is held to the face of the breech block until it reaches the fixed ejector and is thrown out of the pistol. The slide continues to compress the return spring located below it. The return spring housing contacts the barrel lug and terminates rearward motion. Provided there is ammunition in the magazine the return spring then pushes the slide forward and the feed rib pushes the top cartridge forward into the chamber. The slide picks up the barrel and the locking piece on the barrel lug is lifted up by the receiver cam to lock the barrel to the slide. The forward motion of the slide and barrel stops when the barrel reaches the takedown lever spindle.

The hammer is held back, by the sear engaging in a notch, in the cocked position. When the trigger is pulled to fire the first shot, the trigger bar moves back and rotates the sear on its pivot to release the trigger. The hammer spring rotates the hammer on to the firing pin and the cartridge is fired. The firing pin is strongly spring loaded and rebounds against the hammer. If there is a misfire the hammer must be manually cocked before it has the energy to impel the pin forward for second blow. There is no double action. When the slide comes back a cam pushes down the disconnector lever which forces the trigger bar down off the sear. The sear, under the influence of its spring, rotates to a position where it can hold up the hammer when the latter starts forward after being rocked back by the slide. Only when the slide is fully forward can the trigger push the disconnector up to enter the notch on the slide. If the slide is not fully forward the disconnector bar remains down and there is no connection between the trigger bar and the sear. When the barrel is locked to the slide, and the slide is fully forward, releasing the trigger pulls the trigger bar forward to clear the sear. When it has cleared the sear the spring-loaded trigger bar moves up in front of the lower end of the sear where it is positioned to rotate the sear again when the trigger is operated.

The safety catch is a push-through pin, located at the top rear of the butt. When pushed from right to left the body of the pin blocks the sear movement. When pushed to the fire position a cutaway section of the spindle allows the sear to move out of the hammer notch.

STRIPPING

Stripping the M1951 pistol follows this sequence:
(1) Remove magazine and check that the chamber is empty by retracting the slide and inspecting.
(2) Hold the slide to the rear until the takedown lever is aligned with the notch of the slide. Rotate the takedown lever forward and the slide will come forward off the receiver.
(3) Disengage the return spring guide from the housing and then lift it up and back. Invert the slide, press on the unlocking plunger and then lift the rear of the barrel from the slide and pull it out backwards.

DATA

Cartridge: 9mm × 19 Parabellum
Method of operation: Short recoil
Method of locking: Swinging arm
Method of feed: 8-round box magazine
Method of fire: Self-loading. Single action

WEIGHTS

Pistol empty: 0.87kg with steel receiver
0.78kg with aluminium receiver

LENGTHS

Pistol: 203.2mm
Barrel: 114.2mm

MECHANICAL FEATURES

Barrel: Rifling: 4 grooves RH. 1 turn in 254mm
Sights: Foresight: Blade
Rearsight: Notch
Graduation: Nil
Zeroing: Elevation. Change backsight. Line. Backsight moves in dovetail
Sight radius: 140mm

9mm Beretta M1951

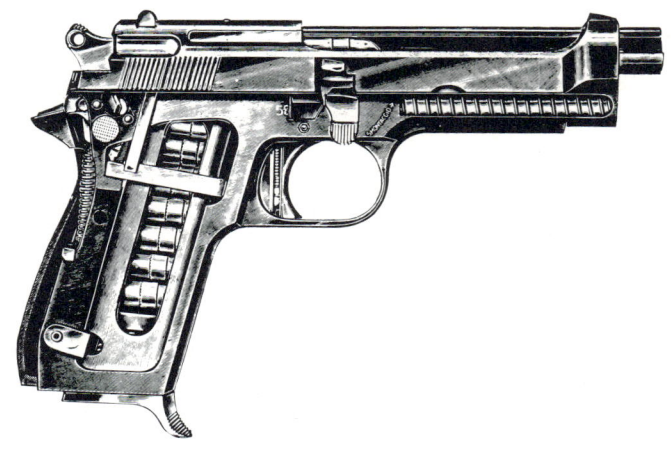

Cutaway view of the 9mm Beretta M1951

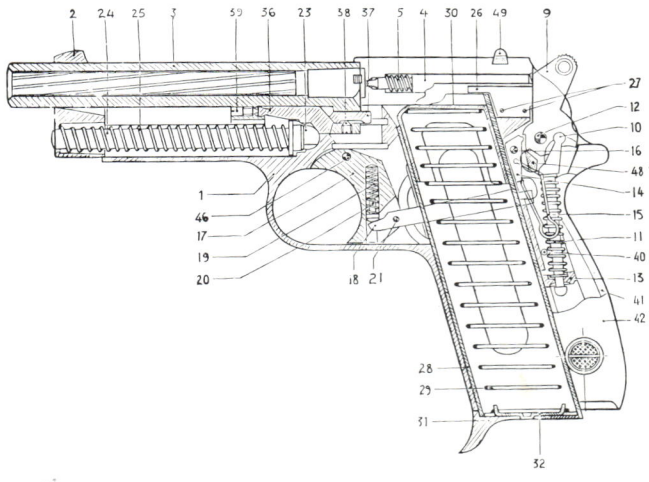

Sectioned view of the 9mm Beretta, M1951 pistol. Key: **(1)** Body; **(2)** Bolt; **(3)** Barrel; **(4)** Percussion pin; **(5)** Percussion pin spring; **(6)** Extractor; **(7)** Extractor spring; **(8)** Extractor pin; **(9)** Hammer; **(10)** Hammer spring rod; **(11)** Hammer spring; **(12)** Hammer pivot; **(13)** Hammer spring rod support; **(14)** Sear lever; **(15)** Sear lever and safety catch spring; **(16)** Sear lever pivot; **(17)** Trigger; **(18)** Trigger lever; **(19)** Trigger lever spring; **(20)** Trigger lever spring rod; **(21)** Trigger lever pivot; **(22)** Trigger lever disengaging rod; **(23)** Disassembling catch; **(24)** Recoil spring rod; **(25)** Recoil spring; **(26)** Ejector; **(27)** Ejector pin; **(28)** Magazine chamber; **(29)** Magazine spring (feeder spring); **(30)** Magazine feeder; **(31)** Magazine base; **(32)** Base plate; **(33)** Magazine catch button; **(34)** Magazine catch spring; **(35)** Magazine catch; **(36)** Locking catch; **(37)** Locking catch control pin **(38)** Control pin screw; **(39)** Catch screw; **(40)** Cheek screws; **(41)** Right cheek; **(42)** Left cheek; **(43)** Bolt catch lever; **(44)** Bolt catch lever spring screw; **(45)** Bolt catch lever spring; **(46)** Trigger pivot; **(47)** Bolt catch lever pin; **(48)** Safety catch; **(49)** Rear sight; **(50)** Locking catch spring

FIRING CHARACTERISTICS

Muzzle velocity: 350 metres/sec
Muzzle energy: 45.2mkp
Rate of fire: Self-loading, 32 rounds/min
Range, maximum effective: 50 metres
Manufacturer: Pietro Beretta SpA, Gardone Valtrompia, Brescia, Italy
Status: Still manufactured. In service with Italian Armed Forces. In use with Egyptian and Israeli troops and the Nigerian police

7.65mm DOUBLE-ACTION PISTOL MODEL 81

Model 81 is one of three Beretta pistols which entered full-scale production in 1976. The other two are the 9mm Short Model 84, which is identical with the Model 81 in most respects, and the larger Model 92 which fires the 9mm Parabellum round and operates on the short round principle whereas the two smaller weapons are operated by blowback. All three pistols have a number of design features in common, however, and while the description that follows relates primarily to Model 81 it covers points that are relevant also to the other two weapons.

7.65mm Beretta Model 81 (A right-hand view is shown in the entry for Model 84)

OPERATION

To load the weapon a loaded magazine is inserted in the butt and the slide operated manually to chamber a round. The firing pin is spring-loaded and shorter than the breech block: it thus requires a sharp blow to cause it to overcome the spring resistance and fire the cartridge so that the hammer can be safely levered under thumb restraint without firing a round. A manual safety, operable from either side of the weapon locks both the trigger mechanism and the slide in the closed position.

With the manual safety released and the hammer forward, rearward motion of the trigger pulls the trigger bar forwards and rotates the hammer rearwards against the pressure of the hammer spring until the fully cocked position is reached. Beyond this point, further trigger pressure disengages the trigger bar from the hammer and rotates the rear forwards thus releasing the hammer to deliver a sharp blow on the protruding end of the firing pin and fire the round.

When the round is fired the pressure in the chamber drives the cartridge case, together with the slide assembly, back against the combined pressure of the recoil spring and hammer spring, the case being held on the face of the breech block by the extractor until it spikes the ejector. As the slide moves rearwards it depresses the trigger bar and disengages it from the rear; so that at the limit of the slide travel, with the hammer fully cocked the rear engages the bent on the hammer and retains it in the cocked position as the slide moves forwards to chamber a fresh round.

If the magazine is empty the slide is held open. If the magazine is not empty the slide will move forward to chamber a round and when it has done so the extractor will protrude laterally, showing red, and can thus be seen and felt. The hammer will remain cocked and the next round can be fired by single action.

In the event of a misfire, there will be no blowback action and the hammer will be forward. A second attempt to fire the round can then be made by releasing the trigger and pulling it again.

Other features of the weapon include a 12-round magazine with a staggered loading arrangement, a reversible magazine release button to suit either right-handed or left-handed firers, a stripping catch arrangement, which makes stripping easy but guards against accidental disassembly, and an optional magazine safety which prevents the weapon from being fired when the magazine is removed and a cartridge remains in the chamber.

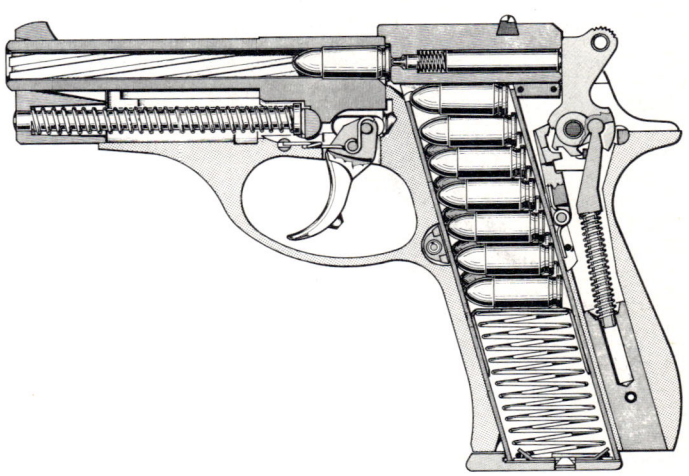

Sectional drawing of Models 81 and 84

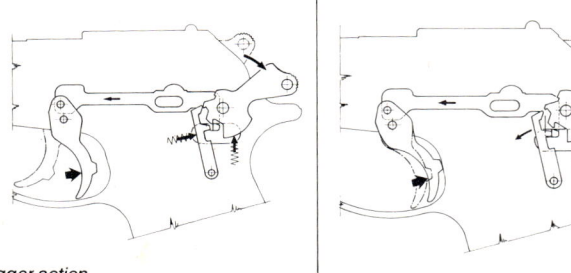

Trigger action

STRIPPING

To strip the pistol, first ensure that the chamber is empty then remove the magazine. Hold the pistol in the left hand and, with the left forefinger, press the disassembling latch release button and, with the right thumb rotate the disassembling latch (on the right of the weapon) anti-clockwise as far as it will go. Still holding the pistol in the left hand, pull forward the slide barrel group with the recoil spring and guide. Remembering that the recoil spring and guide are under compression, slightly press the spring and guide to disengage them from the barrel then allow the spring to stretch slowly. Remove the spring and guide and take the barrel out of the slide. Any further stripping should be left to an expert.

DATA

Calibre: 7.65mm
Method of Operation: Blowback
Method of feed: 12-round detachable box magazine
Method of fire: Single- or double-action
Weight: 665g with empty magazine
Length: 172mm
Barrel: 97mm
    Rifling: 6 grooves RH 250mm pitch
Sights: Foresight: Blade, integral with slide
    Rearsight: Notched bar dovetailed to slide
    Sight radius: 127mm
Muzzle velocity: 300 metres/sec minimal
Muzzle energy: 22mkp minimal

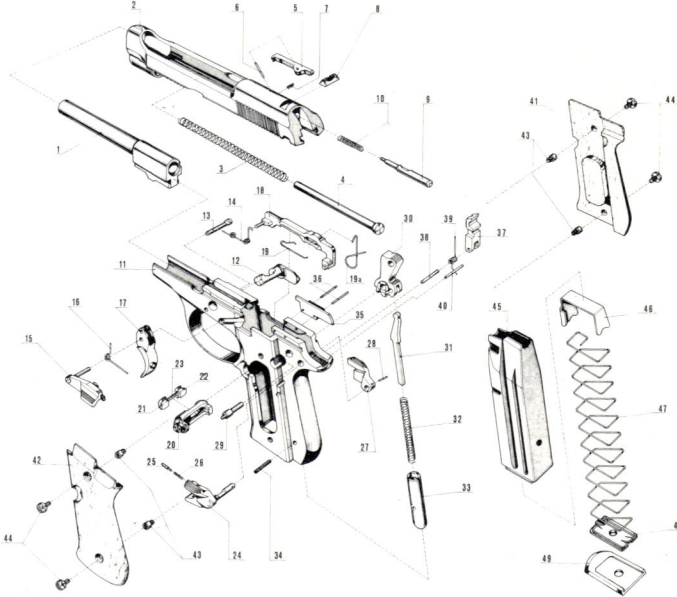

Exploded view of Models 81 and 84. Key: (1) Barrel; (2) Slide; (3) Recoil spring; (4) Recoil spring guide; (5) Extractor; (6) Extractor pin; (7) Extractor spring; (8) Rear sight; (9) Firing pin; (10) Firing pin spring; (11) Frame; (12) Disassembling latch; (13) Disassembling latch release button; (14) Trigger spring; (15) Slide catch; (16) Slide catch spring; (17) Trigger; (18) Trigger bar; (19) Trigger bar spring; (19a) Magazine safety spring; (20) Magazine release button; (21) Magazine release button bush; (22) Magazine release button spring bush; (23) Magazine release button spring; (24) Left safety; (25) Safety spring pin; (26) Safety spring; (2)7 Right safety; (28) Safety pin; (29) Hammer pin; (30) Hammer; (31) Hammer spring strut; (32) Hammer spring; (33) Hammer strut guide; (34) Hammer strut guide pin; (35) Ejector; (36) Ejector pin (2 pieces); (37) Sear; (38) Sear pin; (39) Sear spring; (40) Sear spring pin; (41) Right grip; (42) Left grip; (43) Grip bush (4 pieces); (44) Grip screw (4 pieces); (45) Magazine box; (46) Magazine follower; (47) Magazine spring; (48) Magazine plate; (49) Magazine bottom

Safety devices: Manual applied safety
    Inertia operated firing pin
    Half-cock position
    Optional magazine safety
Manufacturer: Pietro Beretta SpA, Gardone Valtrompia, Brescia, Italy
Status: Production

9MM DOUBLE-ACTION PISTOL MODEL 84

This Beretta pistol resembles the 7.65mm Model 81 described above in all respects save those that are relevant to the change of calibre to 9mm

Short. Components affected are the barrel, magazine box, magazine follower and magazine spring and it should be noted that the magazine capacity of the Model 84 is 13 rounds instead of 12. Details of the characteristics that distinguish the Model 84 from the Model 81 are given below: all other characteristics are the same and the drawings illustrating the entry for the Model 81 are relevant also to the Model 84. The accompanying photograph is of the right-hand side of the Model 84: apart from the markings this is indistinguishable from that of the Model 81 and the same is true of the left-hand illustration in the previous entry.

DATA
Calibre: 9mm Short
Method of feed: 13-round detachable box magazine
Weight: 640g with empty magazine
Muzzle velocity: 280 metres/sec nominal
Muzzle energy: 24mkp nominal
Manufacturer: Pietro Beretta
Status: Production

9mm Beretta Model 84

9mm DOUBLE-ACTION PISTOL MODEL 92

Firing the 9mm Parabellum round this third member of the family of Beretta pistols put into production in 1976 is both larger and more powerful than the Models 81 and 84: it also employs a short recoil operating system in place of the blowback system suited to the less powerful rounds of the smaller weapons.

In most general design respects, however, the Model 92 clearly resembles the other pistols. It has a double-action trigger system working on the same principles, a similar firing pin assembly and a similar arrangement for stripping. The short recoil system uses a falling locking block which is driven down to disengage the slide from the barrel and halt the rearward motion of the barrel but otherwise the extraction, cocking and loading operations are similar to those of the smaller weapons; the extractor provides the same loaded-chamber indication and the slide is held to the rear when the magazine is empty.

Beretta Model 92, left-hand view

STRIPPING
Although the method of stripping generally resembles that of the smaller

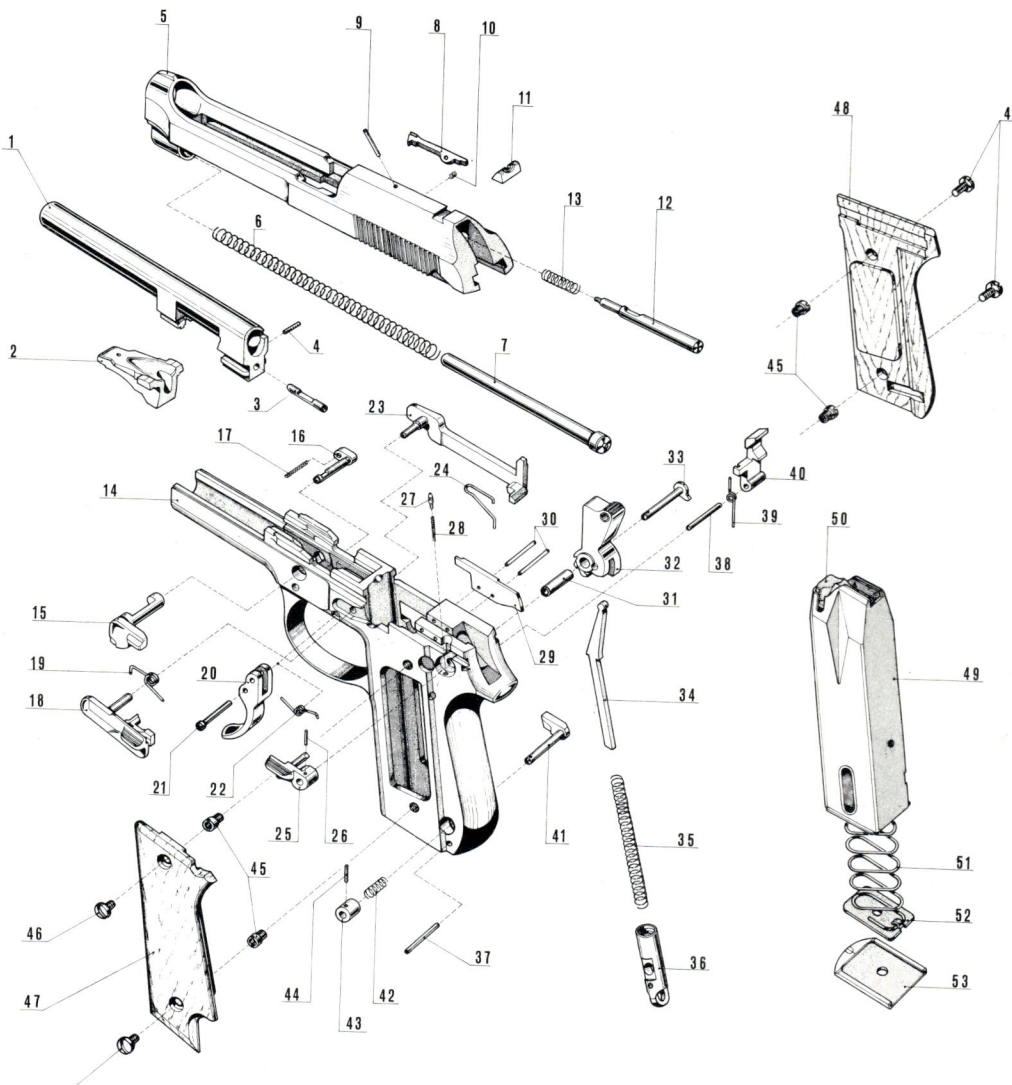

Exploded view of Model 92. Key: (1) Barrel; (2) Locking block; (3) Locking block plunger; (4) Locking block plunger pin; (5) Slide; (6) Recoil spring; (7) Recoil spring guide; (8) Extractor; (9) Extractor pin; (10) Extractor spring; (11) Rear sight; (12) Firing pin; (13) Firing pin spring; (14) Frame; (15) Disambling latch; (16) Disassembling latch release button; (17) Disassembling latch release spring; (18) Slide catch;(1)9 Slide catch spring; (20) Trigger; :21) Trigger pin; (22) Trigger spring; (23) Trigger bar; (24) Trigger bar spring; (25) Safety; (26) Safety pin; (27) Safety spring pin; (28) Safety spring; (2)9 Ejector; (30) Ejector pin (2 pieces); (31) Hammer bush; (32) Hammer; (33) Safety pin; (34) Hammer spring strut; (35) Hammer spring; (36) Hammer strut guide; (37) Hammer strut guide pin; (38) Sear pin; (39) Sear spring; (40) Sear; (41) Magazine release button; (42) Magazine release button spring; (43) Magazine release button bush; (44) Magazine release button pin; (45) Grip bush (4 pieces); (46) Grip screw (4 pieces), (47) Left grip; (48) Right grip; (49) Magazine box; (50) Magazine follower; (51) Magazine spring; (52) Magazine plate; (53) Magazine bottom

Beretta Model 92, right-hand view

weapons there are some differences of detail. First remove the magazine by pressing the magazine release button and ensure that the chamber is empty. Hold the pistol in the right hand, press the disassembling latch release button with the left forefinger and rotate the latch, with the left thumb, anti-clockwise until it stops. Pull forward the slide barrel group with the locking block, recoil spring and guide. Remembering that they are under compression, press the recoil spring and guide sufficiently to disengage them from the barrel then lift them, allowing the spring to stretch slowly. Press the locking block plunger and remove the band and locking group from the slide. Further stripping requires the services of an expert. Assemble in reverse order, and when rotating the disassembling latch ensure that the slide is aligned with the rear end of the frame.

DATA
Calibre: 9mm Parabellum
Method of operation: Short recoil
Method of locking: Falling block
Method of firing: Semi-automatic with single- or double-action
Method of feed: 15-round detachable magazine

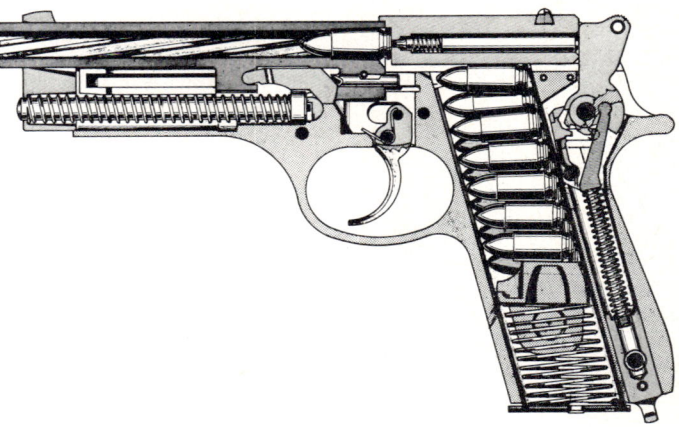

Sectional drawing of Model 92

Weight: 950g with empty magazine
Length: 217mm
Barrel: 125mm
    Rifling: 6 grooves RH 250mm pitch
Sights: Foresight: Blade integral with slide
    Rearsight: Notched bar dovetailed to slide
    Sight radius: 155mm
Muzzle velocity: 390 metres/sec nominal
Muzzle energy: 63mkp
Safety devices: Manual applied safety
    Inertia-operated firing pin
    Half-cock position
Manufacturer: Pietro Beretta
Status: Production

JAPAN

NEW NAMBU MODEL 57A AUTOMATIC PISTOL

This self-loading pistol (called automatic by the maker) is in 9mm Parabellum. It is made by Shin Chuo Kogyo of Tokyo. The weapon is of modern design and suitable for large scale production should the requirement arise.

The 9mm New Nambu Model 57A automatic pistol

The action is similar to that of the Colt M1911A1 and the stock has been built to accommodate only eight cartridges. The magazine catch is at the left side and bottom rear of the grip of the Japanese pistol. The pistol has a magazine safety and differs further from the Colt pistol in having no grip safety.

DATA
Cartridge: 9mm × 19 Parabellum
Method of operation: Recoil
Method of locking: Lug and guide
Method of feed: 8-round box magazine
Method of fire: Self-loading
Weight: 890g
Length: 198mm
Barrel: 118mm
Sights: Foresight: Fixed blade
    Rearsight: Fixed square notch
Muzzle velocity: 350 metres/sec
Muzzle energy: 49mkp
Rate of fire: 24 rounds/min
Range, maximum effective: 50 metres
Manufacturer: Shin Chuo Kogyo Co Ltd., Tokyo
Status: In limited production

NEW NAMBU MODEL 57B AUTOMATIC PISTOL

This self-loading pistol fires the .32ACP (7.65mm) cartridge. It is a simple blowback-operated pistol of straightforward design, based on Browning ideas. It has an external hammer and a loaded chamber indicator.

DATA
Cartridge: .32ACP
Method of operation: Blowback
Method of locking: Nil
Method of feed: 8-round box magazine
Method of fire: Self-loading
Weight: 600g
Length: 150mm
Barrel: 90mm
Sights: Foresight: Fixed blade
    Rearsight: Fixed square notch
Muzzle velocity: 300 metres/sec
Muzzle energy: 22mkp
Rate of fire: 24 rounds/min
Range, maximum effective: 40 metres

The 7.65mm New Nambu Model 57B automatic pistol

NEW NAMBU REVOLVER MODEL 60

This Smith and Wesson type pistol in .38 Special has been the Japanese Police pistol since 1961 and some 70,000 of them have been sold. The revolver is also issued to the Japanese Maritime Safety Guard.

DATA
Cartridge: .38 Special
Method of operation: Manual – revolver
Method of locking: NA
Method of feed: 5-chamber cylinder
Method of fire: Single action. Double action
Weight: 680g
Length: 197mm
Barrel: 77mm
Sights: Foresight: Fixed half-tapered serrated ramp
      Rearsight: Square notch
Muzzle velocity: 220 metres/sec
Muzzle energy: 25mkp
Rate of fire: 15 rounds/min
Range, maximum effective: 40 metres
Manufacturer: Shin Chuo Kogyo Co, Ltd, Tokyo.
Status: In production. Mainly Police use

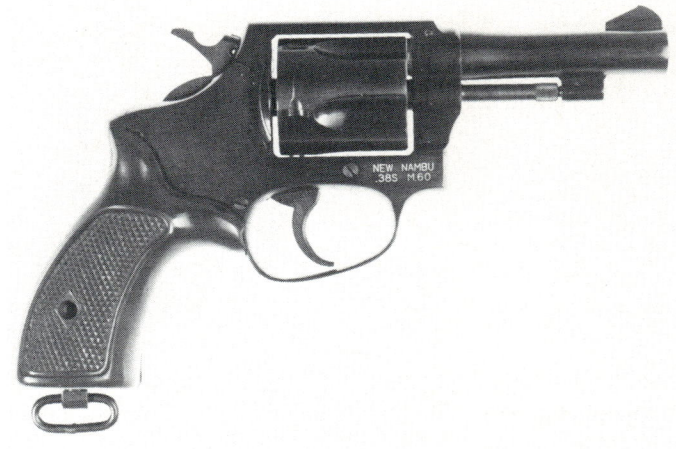

The New Nambu revolver Model 60

KOREA (NORTH)

7.65mm TYPE 64 PISTOL

The North Korean design authority has resurrected the old Browning Model 1900 pistol. A photograph of Browning's pistol is shown.

The North Korean Type 64 has the stamping "1964 7.62" on the left side but all the same it takes the 7.65mm × 17 SR cartridge which is the American Colt .32ACP. The typical "over under" appearance of the pistol is shown in the photograph of the North Korean weapon.

There is also the Type 64 silenced pistol. It has a shortened slide to allow the muzzle to protrude and the end of the barrel is threaded to take the silencer attachment.

The basic parameters of the pistol are the same as the Browning Model 1900.

North Korean Type 64 pistols. These are stamped "1964 7.62" on the left side but are actually chambered for the 7.65mm × 17 SR – .32ACP – cartridge

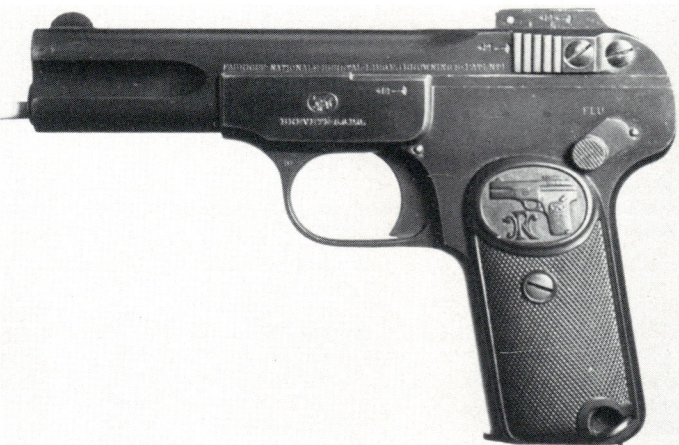

Browning Model 1900 7.65mm (RSAF)

DATA
Cartridge: 7.65mm (.32ACP)
Method of operation: Blowback
Method of locking: Nil
Method of feed: 7-round detachable box magazine
Method of fire: Semi-automatic
Weight: 624g
Length: 171mm
Barrel: 102mm
      Rifling: 6 groove RH
Sights: Foresight: Blade
      Rearsight: Notch
Muzzle velocity: About 290 metres/sec
Muzzle energy: 20mkp
Range, maximum effective: 30 metres
Status: In limited service with North Korean Forces

7.62mm TYPE 68 PISTOL

This is a much modified Tokarev TT33. It is shorter and bulkier than either the Russian TT33 or the Chinese Type 51 or Type 54. It may further be distinguished from these pistols by the serrations on the rear of the slide intended to give a grip whilst the weapon is being cocked. The variations are:
Russian TT33: Vertical, alternately wide and narrow
Chinese Type 51 or 54: Vertical, narrow
North Korean Type 68: Sloping forward, narrow

Internally the Tokarev has been re-worked considerably. The link system, used to lift and lower the barrel ribs into and out of the grooves in the slide, has been replaced by a cam cut into a lug under the chamber in a manner similar to that used in the Belgian 9mm FN Browning HP. The magazine catch has been relocated and is now at the heel of the magazine. It follows from this change that the magazine from the Tokarev TT33 will work in the Type 68 pistol but the converse is not true as the Type 68 magazine lacks the necessary cut-out for the magazine catch.

OPERATION
The magazine is removed from the grip and charged with 8 cartridges. It is replaced, and retained by the magazine catch. When the slide is drawn to the rear and then released, the top round is driven forward into the chamber and the barrel is locked to the slide.

The North Korean Type 68 pistol

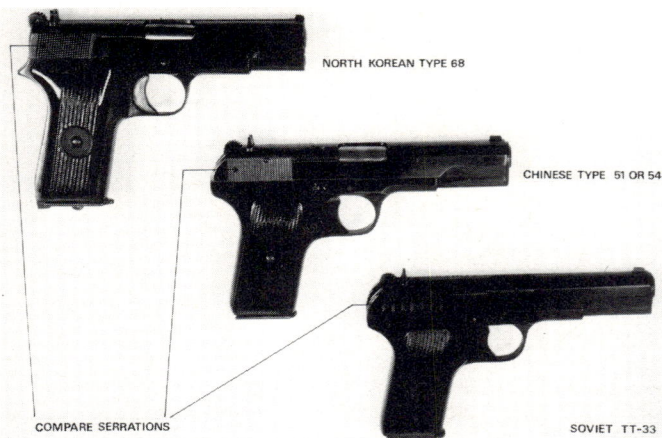

A comparison of the Russian TT33, the PRC Type 51 or 54 and the North Korean Type 68

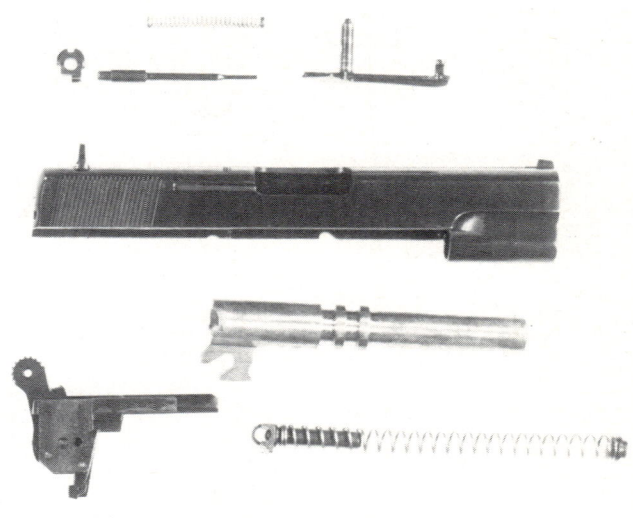

When the trigger is pulled the hammer drives the firing pin into the cap of the cartridge. The resulting gas pressure drives the breech block back. The barrel has raised ribs which enter recesses in the ceiling of the slide and so as the breech block, integral with the slide, goes back, it pulls the barrel back with it. The lug under the chamber of the barrel has a slot extending towards the muzzle and upward. A transverse pin in the receiver goes through this slot so that as the barrel recoils the pin draws the rear of the barrel down and disengages it from the slide. The slide continues rearward. The extractor holds the empty case to the breech face until the case strikes the ejector on the left extension of the hammer housing and is thrown out to the right of the pistol. The return spring is compressed and when the slide contacts the receiver and stops, the spring force drives the slide forward. The feed rib pushes the top round from the magazine into the chamber, the extractor moves over the rim of the case, and the slide pushes the barrel forward. The cam, cut in the lug under the barrel, lifts the rear end of the barrel and the lugs on the top of the barrel move into recesses in the top of the slide and lock the barrel to the slide. Forward movement of the barrel and slide stops when the lug under the barrel reaches the return spring guide.

TRIGGER AND FIRING MECHANISM

When the trigger is pulled, the trigger bar moves back and the end of that bar pushes the bottom of the sear and rotates it clear of the hammer. The hammer spring rotates the hammer forward to hit the firing pin.

At the moment of firing the disconnector reaches up into a recess in the slide. As the slide moves back the disconnector is forced down, pushing the trigger bar clear of the sear. The sear is held by its spring against the hammer and holds the hammer to the rear. When the slide goes fully forward the disconnector can rise and the trigger bar moves up under the sear. To get the trigger bar into position where it can act on the sear, the trigger must be released and the trigger bar will go forward and rise into a position where it can rotate the sear when the trigger is next pulled.

There is no safety catch on the Type 68. The hammer can be lowered, under control, to the half cock position. When in this position, a lug on the side of the sear is moved under the disconnector. This prevents the disconnector from falling and since the top of the disconnector rests in a recess in the slide, the slide is locked and cannot be retracted. At the same time the sear nose goes into the half cock notch on the hammer. This is undercut and so pulling the trigger will not disengage the sear.

STRIPPING

Remove the magazine, retract the slide and check that the chamber is empty. Withdraw the slide until the half-round notch reaches the slide stop. Press the slide stop in through from right to left. Pull out the slide stop. Pull the slide forwards off the receiver.

Lift the hammer mechanism out of the receiver.

Remove the return spring guide rod and the spring.

Lift the rear end of the barrel and draw the latter back, out of the slide. Re-assemble in logical reverse order.

The North Korean Type 68 stripped. Note the FN-Browning cam under the barrel and note how it compares with Tokarev TT33

DATA
Cartridge: 7.62mm × 25 Type P. 7.63mm Mauser
Method of operation: Short recoil
Method of locking: Projecting lug
Method of feed: 8-round box magazine
Method of fire: Self-loading, single action

WEIGHTS
Pistol empty: 795g
Magazine empty: 86g
Trigger pull: 2.73kp

LENGTHS
Pistol: 185mm
Barrel: 108mm

MECHANICAL FEATURES
Rifling: 4 grooves RH, 1 turn in 305mm
Sights: Foresight: Blade
            Rearsight: Notch
            Graduation: Nil
            Zeroing: Line. Backsight in dovetail. Elevation. Change backsight
            Sight radius: 160mm

FIRING CHARACTERISTICS
Muzzle velocity: 395 metres/sec
Muzzle energy: 45mkp
Rate of fire: 32 rounds/min
Range, maximum effective: 50 metres
Manufacturer: State factories
Status: In service with North Korean forces

MEXICO

.45in OBREGON PISTOL

The first line units of the Mexican Army use the Colt .45 M1911A1 pistol. The Obregon is the only pistol to be made in Mexico and, although it is no longer manufactured, it continues in service with second line units.

The locking system of this short recoil operated weapon is based on that of the Austrian Steyr Model 12. The barrel has locking lugs which engage in recesses in the slide. There is also a helical lug on the underside of the barrel which operates in a separate camming piece. This camming piece is held in the receiver by the pin of the combined safety and slide stops.

When the gun fires the slide is forced back carrying the barrel which has lugs engaging in recesses in the slide. As the barrel moves back there is a short period of free travel and then the helical lug on its underside engages

the cam slot in the camming piece and the barrel rotates. This disengages the locking lugs from the slide. The barrel comes to rest and the slide continues rearward. The return spring is compressed, the empty case ejected on the right of the gun and then the slide goes forward to feed the top round forward into the chamber. The slide pushes the barrel forward and the camming piece rotates the barrel locking lug into engagement with the recesses in the slide.

Until the slide is fully forward the disconnector cannot rise into its slot and the trigger and sear have no contact. Externally the pistol looks rather like the M1911A1 but the front part of the slide is rounded rather than flat.

DATA
Cartridge: .45ACP
Method of operation: Short recoil
Method of locking: Rotating barrel
Method of feed: 7-round detachable box magazine
Method of fire: Semi-automatic
Weight: 1.13kg
Length: 216mm
Barrel: 127mm
          Rifling: 6 grooves RH
Sights: Foresight: Blade
          Rearsight: Notch
Muzzle velocity: 253 metres/sec
Muzzle energy: 49mkp
Rate of fire: 32 rounds/min
Range, maximum effective: 50 metres
Manufacturer: Fabrica de Armas, Mexico City
Status: No longer in production. In service with second line units of the Mexican Army

The .45in Obregon pistol (J.E. Smith)

NORWAY

NORWEGIAN ARMY PISTOLS

From 1883 to 1914 the Belgian Nagant revolver was used by the Norwegian Army. In 1914 the Colt .45 M1911 pistol was adopted. The first 300 came from Hartford and thereafter they were manufactured by Kongsberg Vaapenfabrikk.

After World War II the Colt .45 M1911A1 was purchased and remains in service with the Norwegian Army as does the 9mm Walther M38. Copies of the M1911A1 are designated M1912 and M1914 in the Norwegian vocabulary, the first being a direct copy of the American weapon and the second having a lengthened finger-piece on the slide stop. All three weapons are made by Kongsberg.

POLAND

9mm RADOM MODEL 35 PISTOL

This pistol is also known as the 'VIS' from the initials, on the grips, of the two designers Professor Wilniewczyc and Skrzpinski but the title RADOM from the name of the manufacturing centre is more generally used. From 1935 this was the standard Polish military pistol, and was of extremely high standard with a very good finish. It carried the Polish eagle on the slide. When the Germans took over production in 1940 the finish deteriorated. The Model 35(S), made by the Germans, has German markings.

The pistol is a mixture of the design features of the Colt M1911A1 and the FN Browning HP with some ideas from the Polish designers.

It is a short recoil operated pistol with the Browning type shaped lug on the underside of the barrel to raise and lower the barrel into engagement with the slide. The holding open device, operated by a step on the magazine platform, is taken from the Colt; it forces the slide stop up into the slide notch. If the hammer is cocked it can be released and lowered by pressing on the thumb catch on the left side of the slide below the rearsight. This rotates a cutaway bolt inside the slide. The effect of this is first to retract the spring-loaded firing pin, then to interpose a bolt between the pin and the hammer, and then to move the sear off the hammer which rotates onto the bolt.

There is a grip safety but no applied safety. The lever which looks like a Colt type thumb safety is a slide lock which is required to allow the weapon to be stripped. The pistol is quite orthodox in its action and in stripping.

DATA
Cartridge: 9mm Parabellum
Method of operation: Short recoil
Method of locking: Projecting lug
Method of feed: 8-round detachable box magazine
Method of fire: Semi-automatic
Weight: 1.022kg
Length: 197mm
Barrel: 121mm
          Rifling: 6 grooves RH
Sights: Foresight: Blade
          Rearsight: Notch
Muzzle velocity: 351 metres/sec
Muzzle energy: 50mkp
Rate of fire: 32 rounds/min
Range, maximum effective: 50 metres
Manufacturer: Fabryka Broni Radom
Status: No longer in production. Still in service in Poland at least

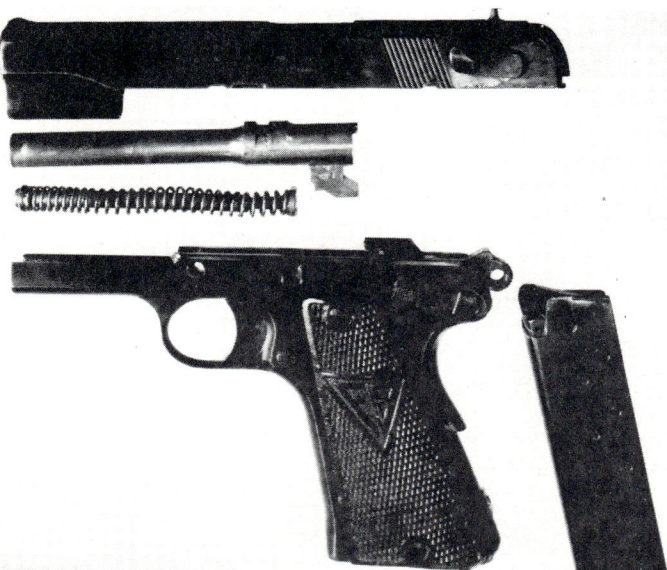

The Radom field-stripped (RMCS)

9mm Radom pistol (RMCS)

9mm MACHINE PISTOL 9mm Wz63

This weapon has a combination of the characteristics of the SL pistol and the fully automatic sub-machine gun. It has the advantage that single shots can be fired using only one hand. If fully automatic fire is needed the shoulder stock can be pulled out and the fore-end dropped to provide a steady hold – which is necessary with the 9mm × 18 cartridge.

The Wz63 fires from the open breech position which is customary for a SMG but does not produce great accuracy for the pistol role. In some aspects it compares with the Czechoslovakian Skorpion. It was designed by Professor Wilniewczyc and is now issued to parachute and some armoured units of the Polish Army. It may readily be identified by the trough-like compensator projecting forward under the barrel.

OPERATION

The magazine catch is at the heel of the pistol grip and the magazine will hold 25 or 40 cartridges. The cartridge is placed on the magazine platform and pressed down until it moves under the magazine lips and rolls to one side. The magazine is inserted and held by the catch. Since the gun fires from the open breech position, the slide must be pulled back to cock the

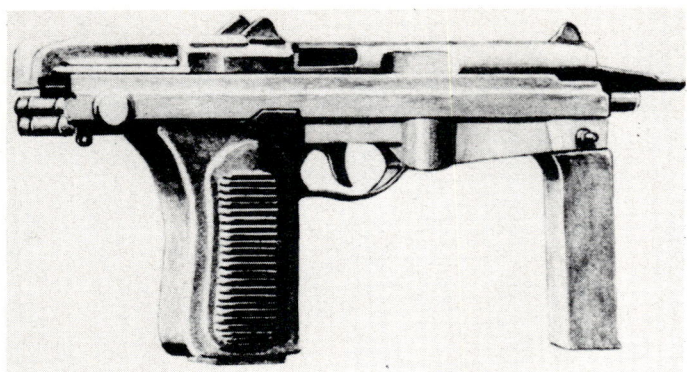

The 9mm Wz63

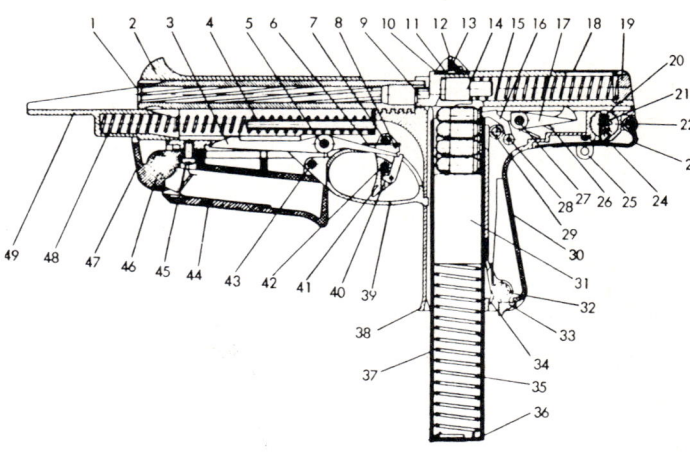

Sectioned view of the Wz 63. Key: **(1)** Barrel; **(2)** Front sight; **(3)** Trigger lever; **(4)** Recoil spring guide; **(5)** Trigger lever (axis) pin; **(6)** Trigger spring; **(7)** Trigger pin; **(8)** Trigger (axis) pin; **(9)** Firing pin; **(10)** Sight-leaf; **(11)** Sight spring; **(12)** Rear sight; **(13)** Rear sight pin; **(14)** Retarder; **(15)** Retarder spring; **(16)** Slide stop; **(17)** Retarder lever; **(18)** Bearing latch; **(19)** Bearing; **(20)** Grip mount; **(21)** Butt-latch spring; **(22)** Butt-plate axis spring; **(23)** Butt plate; **(24)** Butt latch; **(25)** Lanyard loop; **(26)** Retarder lever spring; **(27)** Retarder lever (axis) pin; **(28)** Slide-stop (axis) pin; **(29)** Safety lock; **(30)** Stock; **(31)** Magazine follower; **(32)** Magazine-catch (axis) pin; **(33)** Magazine catch; **(34)** Magazine catch spring; **(35)** Magazine spring; **(36)** Magazine cover; **(37)** Pistol body; **(38)** Pistol grip (handle); **(39)** Trigger guard; **(40)** Trigger catch lever; **(41)** Trigger catch; **(42)** Trigger catch lever spring; **(43)** Back screw of the frame; **(44)** Grip (handle); **(45)** Front screw of the frame; **(46)** Grip (handle) catch; **(47)** Frame; **(48)** Recoil spring; **(49)** Slide (compensator) (US Army photograph)

action. Alternatively, the compensator can be held against a vertical surface and the weapon pushed forward.

When the trigger is pulled the slide is released and is driven forward, feeding a round from the magazine into the chamber. As soon as the cartridge is lined up with the chamber the extractor grips the cannelure and the gun fires whilst the slide is still going forward. The firing impulse halts the slide and drives it back against the return spring. The extractor grips the empty case until the ejector pushes it through the ejection port in the right of the slide. The slide continues to the rear and the return spring, under the barrel, is fully compressed. The slide rides over a retarder lever which snaps up and holds the slide to the rear. The retarder – an inertia pellet in the rear of the slide – continues rearward under its own momentum and compresses its own spring. When the spring is fully compressed it throws the retarder forward and this pushes the retarder lever down out of engagement with the slide and, provided the trigger is still depressed and ammunition remains in the magazine, the slide goes forward to repeat the cycle. The retarder keeps the cyclic rate of fire down to 600 rounds a minute from a natural frequency of about 840.

TRIGGER AND FIRING MECHANISM

The sear is located forward of the trigger and is a long centrally pivoted lever. The front end rises to engage a notch in the underside of the slide to hold it to the rear. The rear end is in contact with the disconnector mounted on the trigger. When a light pressure is exerted on the trigger the disconnector lifts the rear of the sear and the front end drops out of the slide notch. When the slide returns after the round is fired it impinges on the disconnector which frees the sear and the front end of the sear rises to hold up the slide. To fire another round the trigger must be released to allow the disconnector to move back under the tail of the sear.

When the trigger is pulled right back automatic fire results. The trigger revolves sufficiently to carry the disconnector clear of the recoiling slide and the gun continues firing at full automatic until the trigger is released.

After the ammunition is expended the back of the magazine follower lifts the slide stop up to intercept the slide and hold it to the rear.

The safety catch is on the left side of the receiver above the pistol grip. When it is rotated to the horizontal position the shaft rotates and a cam forces the slide stop up to lock the slide. The safety is only necessary when the slide is to the rear and cannot be applied at any other time.

STRIPPING

(1) Remove the magazine, pull the slide back and check that the chamber and feedway are free. Leave the slide in the cocked position.
(2) Grip the muzzle around the serrations and rotate the barrel anti-clockwise out of the receiver. Grip the slide, press the trigger and let the slide go forward under control, off the receiver. Take the barrel out of the slide, remove the return spring and its guide from the receiver.

To re-assemble the pistol – place the return spring guide and then its spring into the receiver. Put the barrel in the slide and rotate so that the 5 lugs at the rear are in the recess in the slide. Fit the slide into the guide ribs in the receiver. Retract the slide and rotate the barrel to its locked position. The slide can then be moved forward by pulling the trigger.

DATA
Cartridge: 9mm × 18
Method of operation: Blowback
Method of locking: Nil
Method of feed: 25- or 40-round box magazine
Method of fire: Selective

WEIGHT
Pistol (with empty 25-round magazine): 1.8kg

LENGTH
Pistol stock retracted: 333mm
Barrel: 6in 152mm

MECHANICAL FEATURES
Barrel: Rifling: 6 grooves RH. 1 turn in 203mm
Sights: Foresight: Blade
　　　　Rearsight: Flip aperture
　　　　Graduation: 100 and 200 metres
　　　　Zeroing: Nil
　　　　Sight radius: 112mm

FIRING CHARACTERISTICS
Muzzle velocity: 323 metres/sec
Muzzle energy: 31mkp
Rate of fire: Cyclic: 600 rounds/min
　　　　　　Automatic: 75 rounds/min
　　　　　　Single shot: 40 rounds/min
Range, maximum effective: Stock retracted 40 metres; Stock extended 200 metres
Manufacturer: State factories
Status: No longer produced but still in service

9mm SL PISTOL P-64

The Polish armed forces were at one time equipped with the 7.62mm Pistolet TT which is identical to the Soviet Tokarev TT-33 pistol except for the handgrips. This pistol is now obsolete and has been replaced by the blowback operated P-64 which although an original Polish design looks rather like the Soviet Makarov and has some design features which originated with the German Walther PP pistol. It has the inscription "9mm P-64" on the left side of the slide.

OPERATION

To load the pistol, the magazine is removed by pressing the magazine catch at the foot of the butt, and each 9mm × 18 cartridge is placed on the follower forward of the feed lips and then pressed down and back to the rear wall of the magazine. The magazine is inserted into the well and pushed up until the catch holds it. Pulling back the slide fully to the rear and then releasing it feeds the top round into the chamber.

When the trigger is operated the hammer strikes the firing pin and drives it into the cap. The gas pressure forces the breech block back and since this is part of the slide, the slide goes back with it. The extractor holds the empty

case to the face of the breech block until the case hits the ejector, which is integral with the slide stop, and then it is thrown out of the pistol through the ejection port in the slide. The slide, as it goes back, rotates the hammer round and compresses the return spring wrapped round the stationary barrel. When the slide goes forward driven by the return spring, it picks up the top round and feeds it into the chamber.

TRIGGER AND FIRING MECHANISM

The weapon may be fired as either a single action or a double action pistol. As a single action pistol the hammer is thumbed back and held back by the sear which engages in a bent. When the trigger is operated, the trigger bar – attached to the trigger above its pivot point – goes forward. A lug on the side of the bar bears on the bottom of the sear and rotates it forward clear of the hammer which is then driven forward by its spring to hit the firing pin.

If double action is used, the trigger bar goes forward and a step on top enters a notch in the base of the hammer and pulls it forward. The long trigger pull rotates the top of the hammer back until the step on the trigger

Top: the Soviet Makarov 9mm × 18PM pistol and, bottom: the Polish P64 9mm × 18 pistol

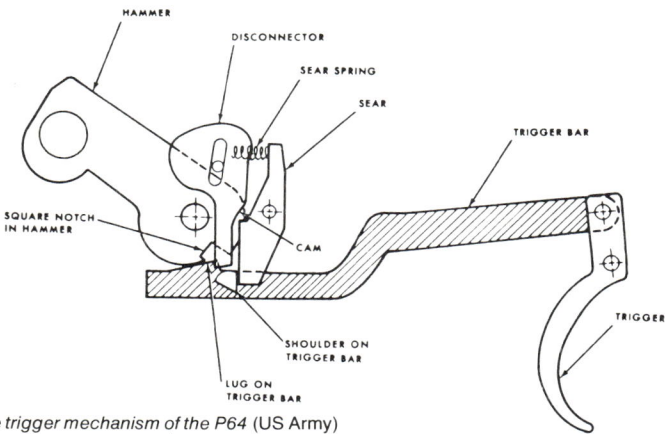

The trigger mechanism of the P64 (US Army)

The 9mm P-64 pistol

The P64 field-stripped

bar rides out of the notch of the hammer which then is rotated forward by its spring, into contact with the firing pin.

When the slide goes back it rotates the hammer to the cocked position and it pushes the disconnector down on to the trigger bar which in turn is pushed down. The lug on the side of the bar moves down off the sear which is then rotated by its spring into the hammer bent. The sear thus holds the hammer cocked. When the slide moves fully forward, and the next round is chambered, the disconnector can rise again and this puts the lug in contact with the bottom of the sear. To fire another round the trigger must be released to allow the trigger bar to move back. The lug moves behind the sear and when the trigger bar rises again, the lug is in position to rotate the bottom of the sear forward as soon as the trigger is pulled. The safety lever is located on the left of the slide at the rear. The 'fire' position is fully up and the safety is applied by pushing the lever down to cover the red dot on the slide. When this is done a pair of lugs move to protect the firing pin from the hammer. Next the shaft cams the disconnector down and this pushes the sear outwards away from the hammer which is then driven forward on the two protecting lugs. The disconnector also pushes the trigger bar down so if the trigger is pulled when the pistol is at 'safe' the step on the trigger bar moves below the hammer and does not touch it. When the safety catch is moved to 'fire' the disconnector rises; the sear moves back against the hammer and the lug on the trigger bar rises behind it. The protecting lugs swing away from the firing pin and the pistol, again, can be fired either single or double action.

When the ammunition is expended the magazine follower rises and pushes the slide stop up to hold the slide to the rear.

STRIPPING
(1) Remove the magazine and then check that the chamber and feedway are clear of live rounds.
(2) Pull down the front of the trigger guard and push it to one side and rest it against the receiver. Pull the slide back, lift the rear end out of the receiver. Move the slide forward off the weapon. The return spring can then be moved from the barrel.

To re-assemble, the hammer is cocked and the safety lever is pushed up to the 'safe' position. The trigger guard is placed in the position adopted for stripping. The return spring is placed over the barrel which is pushed through the hole in the front of the slide. The slide is pulled to the rear, dropped into the locating slots in the receiver, and forced forward by the return spring. The trigger guard is re-located and the pistol is ready for use.

DATA
Cartridge: 9mm × 18
Method of operation: Blowback
Method of locking: Nil
Method of feed: 6-round box magazine
Method of fire: Self-loading. Double action

WEIGHT
Pistol empty: 0.636kg

LENGTH
Pistol: 155mm
Barrel: 84mm

MECHANICAL FEATURES
Sights: Foresight: Blade
    Rearsight: Notch
    Graduation: Nil
    Zeroing: Elevation. Change backsight. Line. Backsight on dovetail
    Sight radius: 114mm

FIRING CHARACTERISTICS
Muzzle velocity: 314 metres/sec
Muzzle energy: 30mkp
Rate of fire: Self-loading: 30 rounds/min
Range, maximum effective: 50 metres
Manufacturer: State arsenals
Status: Still produced. In service with Polish troops

PORTUGAL

7.65mm M/908 and M/915 PISTOLS

The Portuguese Army has always obtained its pistols from abroad. There have been many suppliers. British Webley .455 revolvers, and the German 9mm Luger made up a large proportion of their hand arms. The only pistols still in use and not described elsewhere in this book are the US Savage M1907 and M1915.

The Savage M1907 was based on the 1905 patents of E.H. Searle. It was known in the Portuguese Army as the M/908. The M/915 differed only in the spur type cocking piece and a grip safety.

The Savage was a delayed blowback operated pistol. The barrel had a lug on the top resting in a slot in the ceiling of the slide. This slot had a sharp twist to the left and so the barrel was rotated until the slot straightened out. The designer claimed that the rotating bullet produced a torque that resisted this rotation of the barrel and so delayed the period of opening. It has been stated* that German spark photographs comparing this pistol with a Colt blowback show clearly that the action opens quicker than that of the Colt, both slides starting back before the bullets leave the barrel.

The M/908 had a burr-type exposed cocking piece but did not have a hammer. Lowering the striker attached to the cocking spur placed the point of the striker against the cap and made the weapon particularly dangerous.

*Pistols and Revolvers – J.E. Smith, Seventh Edition, p293.

The 7.65mm M/908 pistol (RSAF)

DATA
Cartridge: 7.65mm (.380ACP)
Method of operation: Delayed blowback
Method of delay: Rotating barrel
Method of feed: 10-round detachable box magazine
Method of fire: Semi-automatic
Weight: 568g
Length: 165mm
Barrel: 95mm
    Rifling: 4 grooves RH
Sight: **Foresight:** Blade
    Rearsight: Notch
Muzzle velocity: 290 metres/sec
Muzzle energy: 20mkp
Rate of fire: 40 rounds/min
Range, maximum effective: 40 metres
Manufacturer: Savage Arms Corporation, Chicopee Falls, Massachusetts
Status: No longer manufactured. Used by training units only

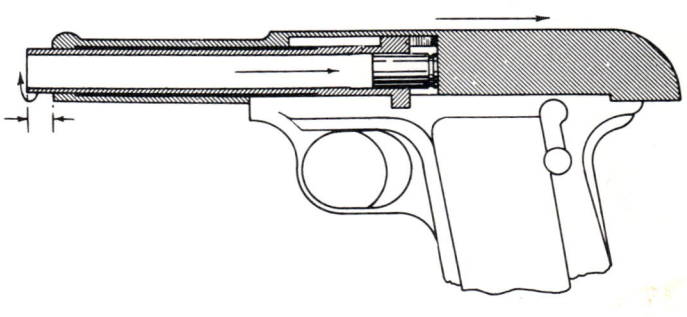

The action of the Savage pistol (RMCS)

SPAIN

9mm ASTRA PISTOLS

Of a wide variety of pistols made by the various Spanish companies whose titles are generally grouped under the name Astra, those most likely to be encountered in military or para-military use today are the Model 400 (the 'water-pistol') and its derivatives, the Model 300 (.32ACP but mainly .380ACP) and Model 400 (9mm Parabellum), both of which were supplied to the German Army.

Model 400 entered production in 1921 and was adopted as the standard weapon for the Spanish Army. It was designed primarily to use the 9mm Largo round but was supposed to be able to accept smaller 9mm rounds. This appears not to have been a satisfactory arrangement, however, and was probably the reason why the German Army specified a 9mm Parabellum version for the otherwise similar Model 600. The Model 300 was smaller and lighter.

Although the Model 400 was first conceived as a delayed blowback weapon, most were produced as simple blowback devices using heavy recoil and hammer springs to cope with the powerful cartridge. It had an 8-round magazine, was fitted with grip, slide and magazine safety devices and weighed about 1kg. The pistol was 20.5cm long and had a 13.5cm band.

The Model 300 derivative was shorter (16.5cm with a 9cm band) and lighter and in the .380ACP version (which was made in the larger quantity) the magazine held only six rounds. The magazine of the other version held seven.

None of these pistols is in official service today.

9mm SUPER STAR PISTOL

This is the standard pistol of the Spanish Army. It looks like the .45 M1911A1 but the barrel is raised and lowered in the slide by a cam under the chamber, operating – in the same way as the FN Browning – on the slide stop pin. The trigger is a pivoting type rather than the sliding trigger of the M1911A1 and there is no grip safety.

STRIPPING

Stripping is carried out by pushing down and forward on the lever on the right side of the receiver. The slide, barrel and return spring plug can then be slid forward off the receiver.

DATA
Cartridge: 9mm Largo
Method of operation: Short recoil
Method of locking: Projecting lugs
Method of feed: 9-round detachable box magazine
Method of fire: Semi-automatic
Weight: 1.02kg
Length: 204mm

The STAR 9mm "Super Star" (RSAF)

Barrel: 133mm
    Rifling: 4 grooves RH
Sights: Foresight: Blade
    Rearsight: Notch
Muzzle velocity: 366 metres/sec

Muzzle energy: 58mkp
Rate of fire: 36 rounds/min
Range, maximum effective: 50 metres
Manufacturer: Bonifacio Echeverria SA, Eibar
Status: In service with Spanish forces

SWEDEN

9mm LAHTI MODEL 40 PISTOL

This is the Swedish-made copy of the Finnish Lahti pistol, manufactured by Husqvarna Vapenfabrik AB. It is the standard pistol of the Swedish Army.

Like the Lahti it has features from the Luger and the Bergmann-Bayard, and has a Browning-type accelerator. It is in many ways an improvement on the Luger and some of the drawbacks of that design have been eliminated. The toggle joint has been replaced by a fully enclosed locking block which slides in slots in the receiver and is also in slots in the breech-block. This change has added considerably to the reliability of the pistol. The unsatisfactory side operating sear of the Luger has been replaced by a conventional sear and an internal hammer. The Lahti employs an accelerator to get all the possible energy from the recoiling barrel into the breech-block and this ensures efficient functioning under adverse conditions.

DATA
Cartridge: 9mm Parabellum
Method of operation: Short recoil
Method of locking: Dropping block
Method of feed: 8-round detachable box magazine
Method of fire: Semi-automatic
Weight: 1.11kg
Length: 271mm
Barrel: 140mm
    Rifling: 4 grooves RH
Sights: Foresight: Blade
    Rearsight: Notch

The 9mm Husqvarna M1940 pistol

Muzzle velocity: 381 metres/sec
Muzzle energy: 55mkp
Rate of fire: 32 rounds/min
Range, maximum effective: 50 metres
Manufacturer: Husqvarna Vapenfabrik AB
Status: No longer in production. In service with Swedish Army

SWITZERLAND

7.65mm MODEL 06/29 PISTOL

The Swiss Army had a double action 7.5mm revolver in 1882 and this remained in service, modified in 1929, until shortly before World War II.

In 1900 the Swiss adopted the Luger pistol in 7.65mm and had 3000 of the Model 1900 made for them in that calibre by DWM plus a further 2000 for commercial sale. Subsequently they acquired quantities of the Model 1906 in the same calibre for military and police use. In 1924 manufacture of a slightly modified copy of the M1906 was started at Waffenfabrik, Bern, and further modifications – to the grip shape and safety were made in 1929, the resultant pistol being designated Model 00-06-29. This was the first line pistol until 1949 when it was relegated to reserve units.

The Swiss version of the 9mm Luger pistol. This is known as the 06/29 pistol. The Swiss national emblem can be seen on top of the receiver

9mm SIG PISTOLS MODELS 49 and 210

The Swiss firm of S.I.G., Schweizerische Industrie-Gesellschaft, located at Neuhausen-am-Rheinfalls, took up Charles Petter's patents from S.A.C.M. – Societe Alsacienne de Construction Mechaniques – to develop and produce the improved Browning Colt pistol mentioned in the entry on French pistols. A series of weapons was produced. The 9mm Model 44/16 held 16 rounds and the 44/8 had eight rounds but these were only produced in small numbers. The Model 49 is the current Swiss military pistol and differs from the widely-used P210 only in the finish and the grips. Whereas the P210 has a highly polished finish, the Model 49 has a dull sandblast finish and plastic grips. The SIG P210 pistol is produced in four versions. The P210-1 and P210-2 are military or police pistols with 120mm barrels and the P210-5 and P210-6 are target pistols. The P210-5 has a 150mm barrel and the P210-6 a 120mm barrel but this model is no longer produced and has been replaced as a sports weapon by the Centre Fire Target Pistol SIG-Hämmerli P240 calibre .38 special.

The P210-1 and 2 are produced in either 9mm Parabellum or 7.65 Parabellum. The calibre can be changed by substituting the other barrel, of the alternative calibre, with its own return spring. Either pistol can be converted to .22LR by changing the barrel, return spring, slide and magazine, and this of course reduces training costs. The P210-1 has a polished finish and wooden butt grip plates. The P210-5 with its 6in (150mm) barrel is essentially a competition pistol. It has a micrometer rear sight, special front sight mounted on the projecting barrel and a short, adjustable pull, light trigger. The P210-6 has a 4¾in (120mm) barrel and carries its foresight on the slide but otherwise is the same as the P210-5.

OPERATION
The magazine is removed for loading by pressing rearward the magazine catch located at the heel of the pistol grip. The magazine takes eight

The SIG P210

cartridges. With the magazine in place, pulling back the slide and then releasing it, drives a cartridge into the chamber and pulling the trigger fires one round.

When the round fires, the gas pressure forces back the breech-block which is part of the slide. The barrel is locked to the slide by two raised ribs on the barrel entering recesses in the slide. Beneath the chamber is a lug into which is machined a cam groove. The shaft of the slide stop passes right through the cam groove. The barrel and slide recoil together for about 3mm and during this period the barrel recoils straight back. (Thus there is

The Swiss military pistol, Model 49

9mm P210-5 pistol

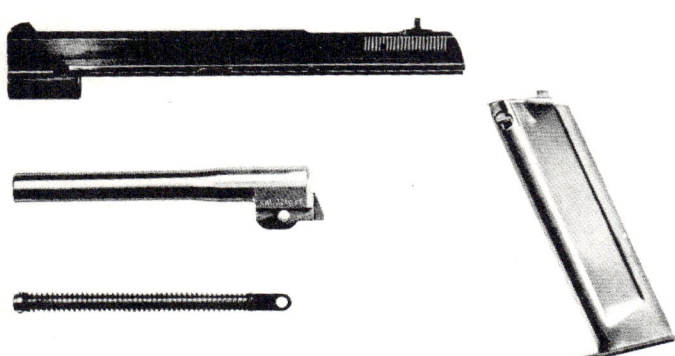

The .22LR conversion unit

9mm P210-6 pistol

no tilting of the barrel whilst the bullet is in the bore.) Then the shaft of the stationary slide stop pulls the rear of the barrel down. This disengages the locking lugs of the barrel from the recesses in the top of the slide. The barrel comes to rest and the momentum of the slide carries it to the rear. The empty case is extracted from the chamber and held in the extractor until ejected to the right of the pistol. The return spring, under the barrel, is compressed during recoil to store energy and the hammer is forced back by the slide. The slide is stopped when it reaches a shoulder in the receiver. The return spring forces the slide forward and a cartridge is fed into the chamber. The slide moves the barrel forward and the cam groove, moving across the shaft of the slide stop, forces it up until the locking lugs on the top of the barrel enter the locking recesses in the ceiling of the slide.

TRIGGER AND FIRING MECHANISM

The trigger and firing mechanism function as follows. With the hammer cocked, pulling the trigger causes it to revolve on its top mounted pin and force the trigger bar rearwards. The end of the trigger has a lug bearing on the sear and this trigger pressure causes the trigger bar to rotate the sear out of engagement with the hammer. The hammer spring, in the butt, drives the hammer against the firing pin. When the slide recoils it forces the trigger bar down and disconnects it from the sear. The sear, under its spring, rotates back against the hammer. The further movement of the slide forces the hammer back. When the slide goes forward the sear holds the hammer against the force exerted by the hammer spring. The trigger is still held to the rear and the trigger bar remains disconnected from the sear. When the trigger is released the trigger bar follows it forward and the other end is able to rise and the lug positions itself against the sear. When the trigger is squeezed the cycle is repeated.

When the ammunition is expended the slide is held to the rear by the slide stop which is forced into the notch on the slide by a lip on the magazine follower.

STRIPPING

Stripping the pistol is effected as follows. The magazine is removed and the slide pulled back about 6mm and held back in this position. The slide stop shaft can then be pressed through from right to left until the stop is clear of the slide. The slide can then be released and the slide stop pulled out. Take the slide off the receiver. Invert it and lift the rear of the return spring guide out of engagement with the barrel. Hold the cam lug and pull the barrel up and back. The hammer mechanism will lift out as a single unit.

DATA

Data below are common to 9mm, 7.65mm or .22 versions of P210-1 or P210-2 unless otherwise specified

Cartridge: 9mm P (or 7.65mm P or .22LR)
Method of operation: Short recoil
Method of locking: Projecting lug
Method of feed: 8-round box magazine
Method of fire: Self-loading

WEIGHTS
Pistol empty: 909g but 852g for .22
Magazine empty: 85g but 94g for .22
Trigger pull: 2,250 ± 250g

LENGTHS
Pistol: 216mm
Barrel: 120mm

MECHANICAL FEATURES
Barrel Rifling: Grooves – 6 RH but 4 for 7.65mm
Twists – 1 turn in 250mm
but 450mm for .22
Sights: Foresight: Blade
Rearsight: Notch
Radius: 165mm

FIRING CHARACTERISTICS
Muzzle velocity: 335 metres/sec but 385 and 330 metres/sec for 7.65mm and .22 respectively
Muzzle energy: 40mkp but 46 and 13.1mkp for 7.65mm and .22 respectively

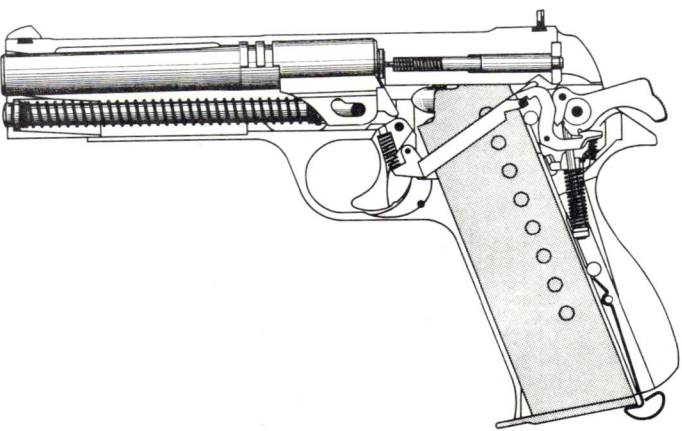

A cross section of the P210-1 or 2

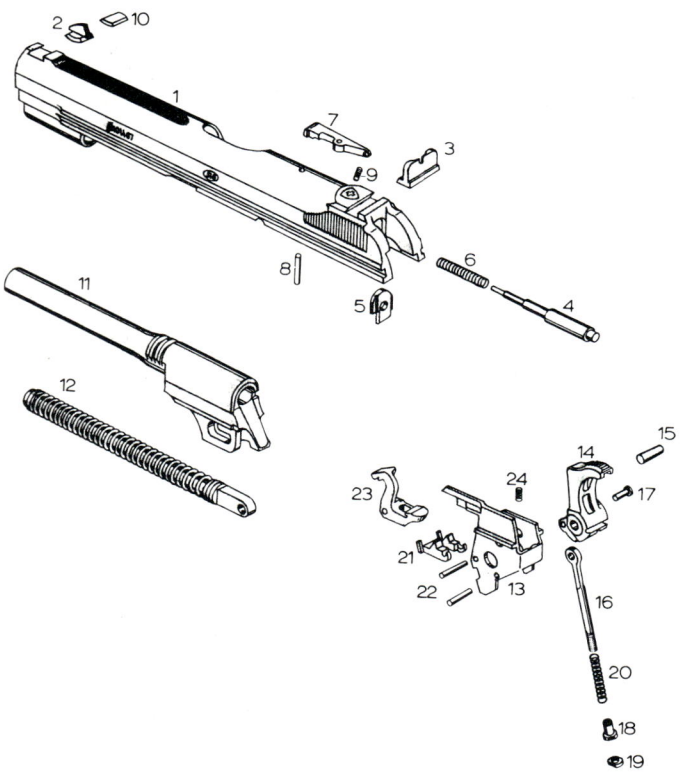

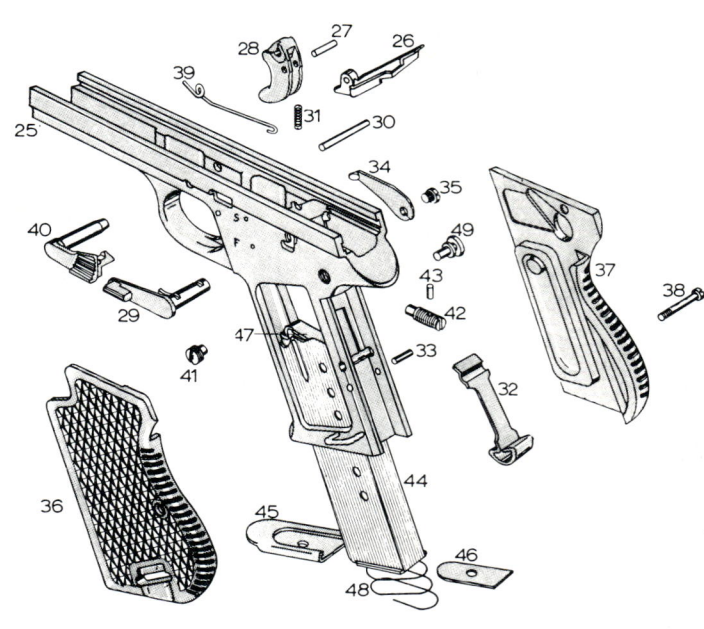

The 9mm P210 stripped

Rate of fire: SS: 32 rounds/min
Range, maximum effective: 50m
Manufacturer: Swiss Industrial Company, Neuhausen Rhinefalls, Switzerland

Status: Still in production and in military service in Switzerland and Denmark. Deliveries to the Swiss Army have ceased, however, and deliveries of the SIG-Saver P220 (Model 75) have begun instead. Commercial target pistols sold on a world-wide basis

SIG-SAUER P220 (MODEL 75) and P230 SL PISTOLS

The Swiss firm of SIG, makers of the P210 pistol, have joined with the German firm of JP Sauer & Sohn to produce two new pistols – the P220 and P230. The pistols were designed by SIG at Neuhausen am Rhinefalls and are being produced at the new Sauer works in Eckernforde. The reason for this international co-operation was the mutual benefit to be gained by both parties. The Swiss firm, although well able to produce the weapons at their factory at Neuhausen am Rhinefalls, found themselves so restricted by the very rigorous control of weapon export exercised by the Swiss Government that commercial opportunity for large scale overseas sales was virtually non-existent. JP Sauer & Sohn desired to manufacture good self-loading military and police pistols and had the capacity at their premises at Eckenforde – to which they moved from Suhl in Thuringen in 1951.

The P220 is a military pistol and the P230 is primarily a police pistol. One of the more interesting features is the wide choice of calibre available for the pistols and the facilities provided to convert the weapons from one calibre to another. The P220 will be made in .45ACP, .38 Super, 9mm Para, 7.65mm Para, and .22LR. The P230 calibre will be: 9mm Police, 9mm short (.380) 7.65mm Browning and .22LR. Conversion kits for .22LR will be available.

Both pistols have double-action mechanisms and all versions have aluminium frames except the P230 9mm Police which is steel-framed. Many of the metal parts have been designed to be produced as stampings in order to keep the cost down.

PRODUCTION
At the time of writing the production programme is:
P220 9mm: in production
    .45: in production
P230 7.65mm: in production
    9mm short: in production
    9mm Police: in production

P220 (MODEL 75)
ACTION

The magazine catch is located below the heel of the butt and the magazine is loaded in the conventional way by placing the round on the follower, pressing it down in front of the lips and then sliding it back. The magazine is pushed up into the butt and the catch clicks into place.

The slide is pulled to the rear and released to feed a round into the chamber. If it is not intended to fire the weapon immediately the cocked hammer should be lowered. This is done by pressing down on a hammer release lever located above and slightly behind the trigger on the left side of the receiver. The effect of depressing this lever is to lift the sear out of engagement with the hammer which is rotated by its spring until the safety notch is caught by the sear and it comes to rest held clear of the firing pin. The firing pin itself is locked by a pin which is forced through it by a spring and cannot move even if the pistol is dropped.

The pistol can be fired double action by a long pull on the trigger or it can be used as a single action weapon by cocking the hammer by hand and then using a shorter, lighter, trigger pull.

When the round is fired the pressure in the chamber forces the cartridge case back against the breech face which is part of the slide. The slide, and the barrel which is locked to it, recoil together for about 3mm. After this period of free travel during which the chamber pressure is dropping to a safe level, the barrel unlocks from the slide. The locking system is basically the same as that used with the breech block of the Bren gun. In this case it is the barrel which is tilted up at the rear and supported in position by resting on a steel ramp in the receiver.

The barrel is locked up in the slide and moves back with it. The locking piece under the barrel, moves over the flat surface of the ramp in the receiver for some 3mm whilst the bullet leaves the barrel and the pressure drops. The unlocking surface under the barrel then strikes the sloping front

9mm P220 pistol

face of the ramp and is forced down. This separates the barrel from the slide and stops any further barrel motion.

The slide continues rearward and extracts the empty case which remains held to the breech face until it is thrown out through the ejection slot in the top of the slide. The return spring is compressed. The hammer is cocked. The slide comes to rest when it reaches a stop in the receiver above the butt, and is then thrown forward. The top round is fed into the chamber and the extractor springs into the cannelure. The slide drives the barrel forward. The locking piece under the barrel rides up the fixed ramp in the receiver and the rear of the barrel is lifted up into a recess in the ceiling of the slide. The locking piece slides forward a further 3mm along the flat top of the ramp and the rear end of the barrel is fully supported and locked to the slide.

TRIGGER AND FIRING MECHANISM

The pistol can function in either double action or single action mode. When the hammer is forward, held in the safety notch, a long trigger pull of 13mm and a force of 4.5kg is required to fire the pistol. When the trigger is pulled, the trigger bar moves forward and the hammer is rotated back to the cocked position. As the trigger bar approaches the point where it will lift the sear from the hammer notch, it rotates the spring-loaded safety lever which rises under the firing pin and pushes the safety locking pin through the firing pin which is then free to go forward when struck by the hammer. It should be noted that the spring-loaded safety locking pin is held through the firing pin by spring pressure at all times until positively forced out by the trigger bar immediately prior to firing.

The hammer strikes the firing pin which goes forward, hits the cap, and is then returned to its retracted position by its own spring and locked in position by the safety locking pin. There is therefore no problem due to the inertia of the firing pin when the gun is carried with the hammer in either the forward or cocked position.

When the hammer is cocked the trigger pressure is lighter, 1.7kg and shorter, 4mm. Again before the trigger bar pulls the sear off the hammer, it rotates the safety lever to force the safety locking pin through the firing pin.

As a result of the incorporation of this safety device locking the firing pin, no manual safety catch is required or fitted.

When the ammunition is expended the magazine follower rises and lifts the slide stop, located on the left of the receiver above the butt, into a recess in the slide.

When a loaded magazine is inserted the slide can be released either by pressing down on the slide stop with the thumb of the right hand or by gripping the slide, pulling back slightly and then releasing it. In both cases the slide goes forward and chambers a cartridge and the hammer is cocked for immediate action.

STRIPPING

To disassemble the P220 the magazine must be removed and the chamber and feedway checked. The slide is retracted until the cutaway lines up with the take-down pin which is located on the receiver. This pin is rotated down and the slide can then move forward off the receiver. The barrel and return spring can be lifted out of the slide.

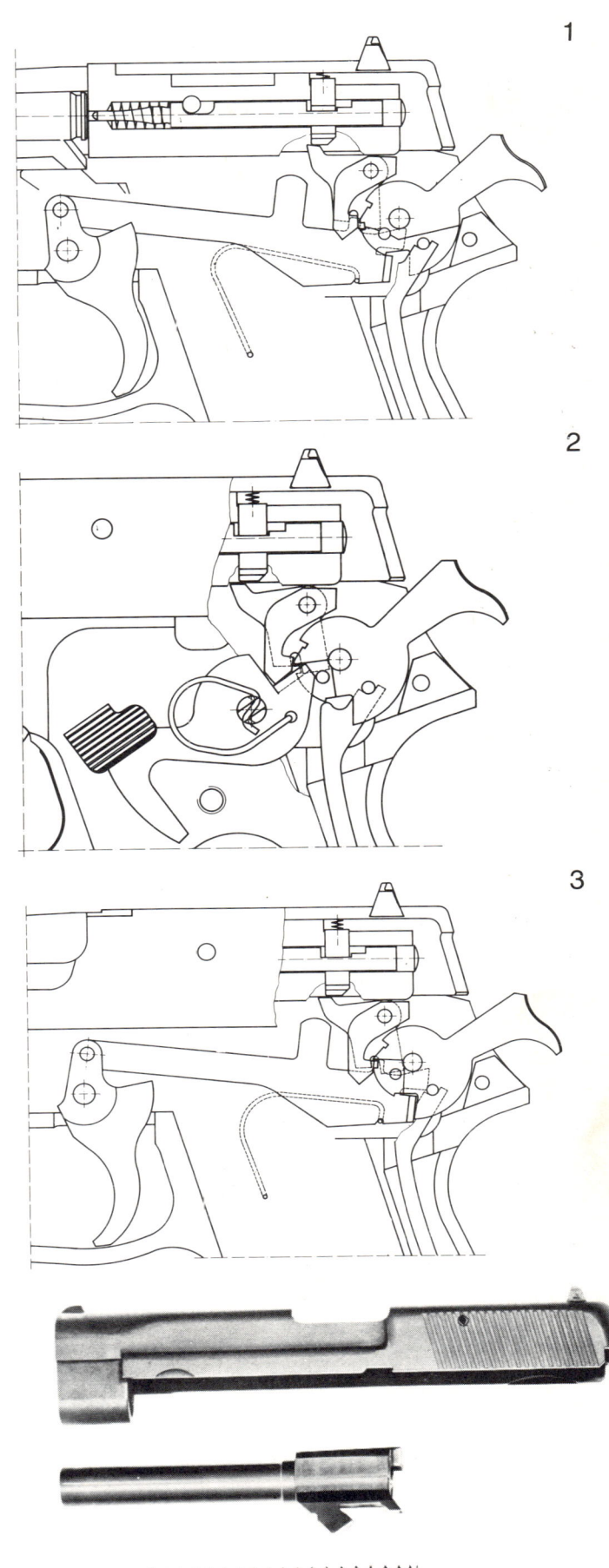

The action of the P220 (1) Double-action triggering. If the loaded weapon is not cocked, the shot can be fired directly via the trigger, by way of the double action of the latter. The trigger is squeezed, whereby the hammer is cocked via the trigger rod. In the process the safety lever is pressed against the lock pin. The sear is moved away from the hammer, and the firing pin released by the lock pin. On squeezing further, the hammer lifts out of register and fires the shot (2) De-cocking lever and hammer the hammer into the safety notch, so that the loaded weapon can be carried without danger. The safety notch is the position of rest for the hammer. The firing pin is always blocked during and after de-cocking. The weapon is therefore absolutely safe. (3) Firing pin safety catch. In order to achieve maximum safety, the firing pin is locked. Quick readiness for firing is always assured, as this safety catch is released automatically by the trigger action, without the manipulation of any lever. The catch is thus not released until the shot is about to be wilfully fired. Thanks to this style of safety device, a loaded weapon is always safe, even with the hammer cocked

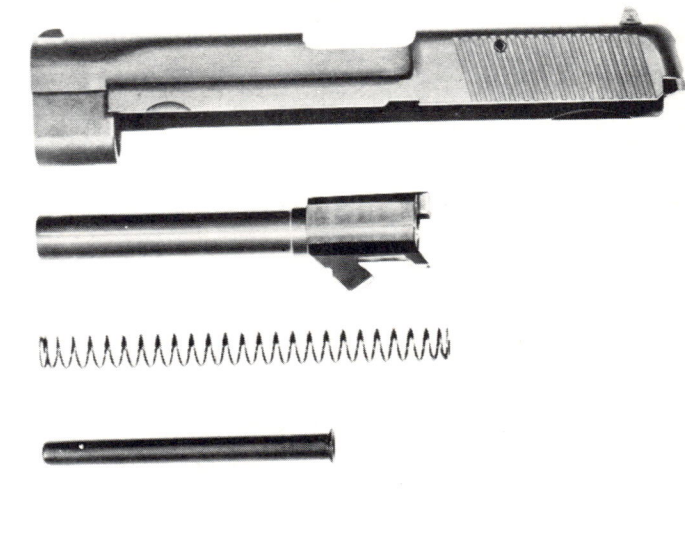

P220 stripped

DATA   (Note: Data in 9mm column is common to all versions except where the contrary is indicated)

	9mm Parabellum	7.65mm Parabellum	.45 ACP	.38 Super	.22LR
Cartridge:	9mm Parabellum	7.65mm Parabellum	.45 ACP	.38 Super	.22LR
Method of operation:	Short recoil				
Method of locking:	Projection lug				
Method of feed					
Box magazine:	9	9	7	9	10
Method of fire:	Self-loading Single-or- double action				

WEIGHTS

Pistol without magazine:	750g	764g	732g	750g	784g
Empty magazine:	80g	80g	70g	70g	95g
Trigger pull: (hammer cocked)	1.5-2.0kg				
Trigger pull: (hammer forward)	4.5kg				

LENGTHS
Pistol: 198mm
Barrel: 112mm

MECHANICAL FEATURES

Barrel Rifling:	6 grooves RH	4 grooves			
One turn in:	250mm	250mm	400mm	250mm	400mm

Sights: Foresight: Blade 3mm wide. White spot on surface
  Rearsight: Square notch 3mm wide. White spot below notch
  Graduation: Nil
  Zeroing: Lateral, rearsight moves in dovetail. Elevation. Change rearsight. 8 sizes available in steps of 0.27mm corresponding to 4.2cm at 25m or 8.4cm at 50 metres.
  Sight radius: 160mm
  (Von Stavenhagen contrast sights)

FIRING CHARACTERISTICS

Muzzle velocity:	343 metres/sec	363 metres/sec	244 metres/sec	352 metres/sec	293 metres/sec
Muzzle energy:	41mkp	56mkp	52mkp		
Rate of fire:	Single shots	40 rounds/min			

Manufacturer: SIG-Sauer. Production at JP Sauer & Sohn, Eckenforde
Status: See introductory text for general production details. An order for 10,000 of the 9mm version has been placed with SIG by the Swiss Government and deliveries of these to the Swiss Army, under the military designation Model 75, have begun

P230

The P230 is a blowback operated pocket pistol which, although designed for police work, could well be carried by military personnel, such as staff officers, for self protection.

It can be used as a single action or double action pistol and has the same facility for lowering the hammer, by depressing the hammer release lever, as the P220. Similarly the firing pin is permanently locked except when released by the trigger bar immediately before the hammer falls.

The pistol is designed to fire a range of cartridges. A new cartridge – the 9mm Police – has been developed to lie between the 9mm Parabellum, which is a military cartridge, and the 9mm short (.380) which is a much less powerful round. The pistol designed to fire the 9mm Police ammunition has the same dimensions as that for the 9mm short but has a slide which is 70 grammes heavier, to keep the recoil velocity down to the required figure, and a steel frame.

The magazine platform forces the slide stop on the left of the receiver up when the ammunition is expended. The slide stop can be pressed down with the thumb of the right hand, when a loaded magazine has been inserted, and a round fed into the chamber.

Stripping follows the same general pattern as the P220. The magazine is removed, feedway checked, and the slide retracted. The takedown pin on the left of the receiver is rotated down and the slide will then go forward off the receiver.

The P230

DATA

Cartridge:	9mm Police	9mm Short (.380ACP)	7.65 Browning (.32ACP)	.22LR
Method of operation:	Blowback			
Method of locking:	Nil			
Method of feed: (box magazine)	7	7	8	10
Method of fire:	Self loading Single or double action			

WEIGHTS

Pistol empty:	690g	464g	464g	440g
Magazine:	40g	40g	50g	40g
Trigger pull: (hammer cocked)	1.7kg			
Trigger pull: (hammer forward)	4.5kg			

LENGTHS
Pistol: 168mm
Barrel: 92mm

MECHANICAL FEATURES
Barrel, rifling: 6 grooves RH
One turn in: 250mm   250mm   250mm   400mm
Sights: Foresight: Blade
    Rearsight: Notch
    Graduation: Nil
    Zeroing: Elevation. Change backsight. Line. 5 sizes available in steps of 0.3mm corresponding to 6.2cm at 25m. Backsight moves in dovetail.
    Sight radius: 120mm
    (Von Stavenhagen contrast sights)

FIRING CHARACTERISTICS
Muzzle velocity: 312 metres/sec   300 metres/sec   300 metres/sec   299 metres/sec
Muzzle energy: 26.5mkp   20mkp   11.1mkp
Rate of fire: Self-loading
    40 rounds/min
Manufacturer: SIG-Sauer. Production at JP Sauer & Sohn, Eckenforde.
Status: See introductory text

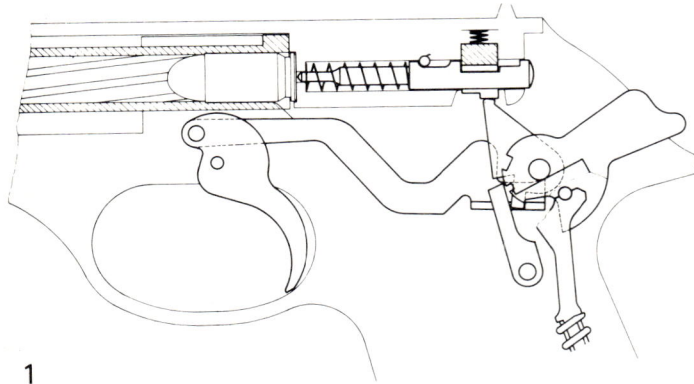

1

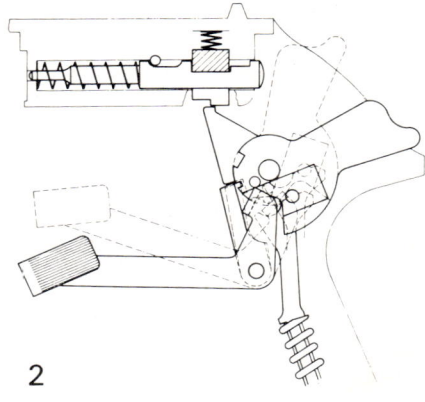

2

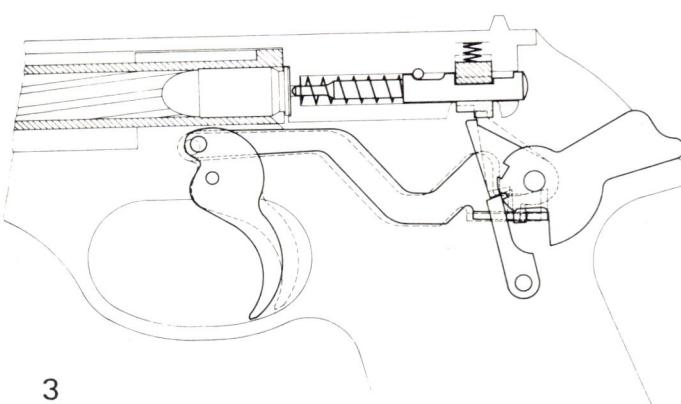

3

The action of the P230. *(1) Double-action triggering. If the loaded weapon is not cocked, the shot can be fired directly via the trigger, by way of the double action of the latter. The trigger is squeezed, whereby the hammer is cocked via the trigger rod. In the process the safety lever is pressed against the lock pin. On squeezing further, the hammer lifts out of register and fires the shot. (2) De-cocking lever and hammer safety notch. The de-cocking lever permits hazardless lowering of the hammer into the safety notch, so that the loaded weapon can be carried without danger. The safety notch is the position of rest for the hammer. The firing pin is always blocked during and after de-cocking. The weapon is therefore absolutely safe. (3) Firing pin safety catch. Thanks to the automatic firing pin safety catch, the firing pin is locked until the hammer is on the verge of release. The catch is thus not released until the shot is about to be wilfully fired; hence with this style of safety device, the weapon is always safe, even if dropped with hammer cocked*

TURKEY

9mm MKE and 7.65mm MKE PISTOLS

These pistols are made by Makina ve Kimya Endüstrisi Kurumu at Kíríkkale, Ankara. They are based on the Walther PP. The pistols are marked MKE on the grip and the slide on the right side of the pistol and marked Kíríkkale Tüfek Fb Cap 9mm on the left.

The method of operation is exactly the same as the Walther PP and there are only minor external modifications such as the shape of the magazine finger rest.

DATA
Cartridge: 9mm short (.380ACP) or 7.65mm (.32ACP)
Method of operation: Blowback
Method of locking: Nil
Method of feed: 7-round detachable box magazine
Weight: 680g empty
Length: 170mm
Barrel: 98mm
    Rifling: 6 grooves RH
Sights: Foresight: Blade
    Rearsight: Notch
Muzzle velocity: 260-280 metres/sec
Muzzle energy: 23mkp (9mm) or 18mkp (7.65mm)
Rate of fire: 35 rounds/min
Range, maximum effective: 30 metres

The 9mm MKE pistol

Manufacturer: Makina ve Kimya, Endüstrisi Kurumu, Ankara
Status: In production. In service with the Turkish Army

UNION OF SOVIET SOCIALIST REPUBLICS

7.62mm TOKAREV (TT-33) PISTOL

Although the TT-33 pistol is no longer used by the Warsaw Pact countries and has been replaced by the Makarov Pistol, it is still widely used by many Asian Communist countries and by Yugoslavia. It has been produced by Russia, Communist China, Hungary, Poland and Yugoslavia. A variant in 9mm × 19 (the 9mm Parabellum cartridge), called the Tokagypt, was produced in Hungary and exported.

The Tokarev TT-33 is prepared for firing by removing the magazine from the pistol grip. The magazine catch is located immediately behind the trigger on the side of the butt. The magazine takes eight 7.62mm × 25 Type 'P' pistol cartridges. The cartridges are inserted by being placed on the magazine follower, forward of the feed lips, and pressed down and slid to the rear, under the feed lips, up to the back of the magazine.

The magazine is inserted into the butt and the pistol is cocked by pulling the slide fully to the rear against the return spring. When released the slide is forced forward, feeding a round into the chamber. There is no safety catch on the Tokarev pistol which is usually carried in the half-cock position with a cartridge in the chamber. This position is achieved by holding the hammer back with the thumb and squeezing the trigger. As soon as the hammer is freed it is lowered fractionally and the trigger released. The hammer is carefully lowered until it is held in the half-cock position which lies midway between the fired and cocked position. When the hammer is held in this position the slide is also locked. To use the pistol necessitates returning the hammer to the cocked position. The self-loading action produces one shot each time the trigger is pulled. When the last shot is fired the slide remains to the rear. It can be released by depressing the slide stop on the left side of the receiver or alternatively by lowering the magazine and then retracting and releasing the slide.

OPERATION

The TT-33 is a recoil operated pistol: the chamber pressure developed forces back the breech-block which is part of the slide, and since the barrel is locked to the slide, the barrel recoils also. The barrel and slide go back together for a short distance while the pressure drops to a safe level; the barrel is then disconnected from the slide and comes to rest. The slide continues back and carries out the cycle of operations. The TT-33 uses a system which is attributed to John Browning and is used in the Colt Model 1911 pistol. The barrel has two ribs machined right round the outer surface which engage in recesses in the top of the inside of the slide and so barrel and slide are locked together. The lug below the chamber of the barrel is connected to the receiver by the barrel link. When the gas pressure pushes back the breech face and the slide, the barrel locked to it, moves back. The bottom of the barrel link is fixed to the receiver and the top end to the barrel. The barrel is pivoted down, when it comes to the end of its free travel, and disconnected from the slide. The slide continues rearward under its own momentum and rocks the hammer back. The empty cartridge case is pulled from the chamber and held by the extractor until the ejector on the left side of the hammer housing pivots it out of the ejection slot on the right of the slide. The return spring is compressed, and slide motion is terminated when the slide hits the driving spring guide. The breech face picks up the top cartridge from the magazine and chambers it. The link pulls the barrel up to lock to the slide.

TRIGGER AND FIRING MECHANISM

The trigger and firing mechanism function as follows. The hammer is held to the rear by the sear engaging in a notch. Pulling the trigger moves the trigger bar back, against the trigger spring, until it reaches the bottom of the sear. Further movement rotates the sear out of the hammer notch, the hammer is thrown forward by its spring and the firing pin is driven into the cap of the cartridge. The top end of the vertical disconnector fits into a cutaway in the slide. As soon as the slide recoils the cutaway moves back and the slide forces the disconnector down. The trigger bar is pushed down, away from the sear, and the sear is released. Its spring forces it against the hammer and when the hammer is rotated back the sear holds it. Only when the slide is fully forward, and the action locked, can the disconnector rise again into the cutaway. This allows the trigger bar to move up under the sear. To fire another shot the trigger is released, the trigger bar comes forward and can rise in front of the sear. When the trigger is pulled the trigger pushes the sear round and the hammer is released.

STRIPPING

The weapon is stripped as follows. The magazine is removed and the slide retracted to enable the chamber and feedway to be inspected. The recoil spring plunger, under the muzzle, is pressed in, using the nose of a cartridge, to unlock the barrel bushing. The barrel bushing is rotated and removed together with the return spring and plunger. The base of the magazine is used to move the clip retaining the slide stop, to the rear. This clip is located on the right side of the receiver above the trigger. The slide stop can then be pulled to the left out of the receiver and when the pistol is inverted the slide can be moved forward off the receiver. When the slide is removed, the barrel can be freed by lifting the chamber end and sliding forward out of the slide. The hammer mechanism comes out of the receiver as one assembly.

Tokarev TT 33

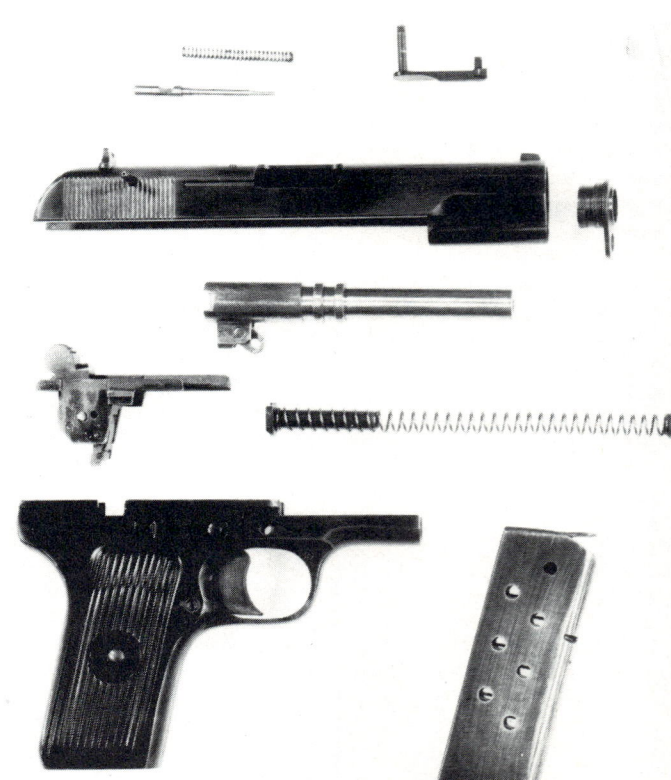

The Tokarev TT 33 stripped. Note the Colt-type link between the barrel and receiver

DATA

Cartridge: 7.62mm × 25 Type P
Method of operation: Short recoil
Method of locking: Projecting lug
Method of feed: 8-round magazine
Method of fire: Self-loading. Single action

WEIGHTS

Pistol, empty: 0.85kg
Magazine, empty: 6g
Trigger pull: 2.72kg

LENGTHS

Pistol: 196mm
Barrel: 116mm

MECHANICAL FEATURES

Barrel: Rifling: 4 grooves RH 1 turn in 305mm
Sights: Foresight: Blade
Rearsight: Notch
Graduation: Nil
Zeroing: Elevation. Change backsight
Sight radius: 155mm

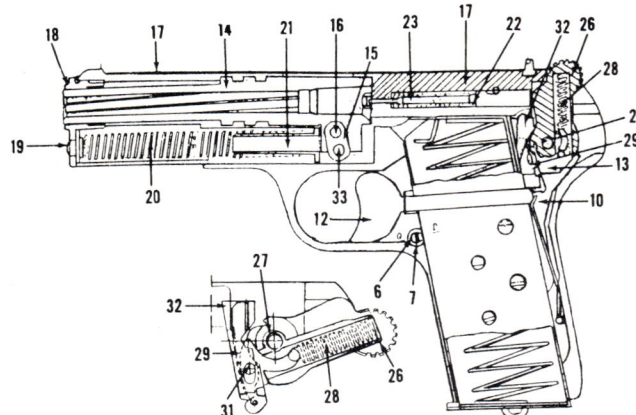

FIRING CHARACTERISTICS
Muzzle velocity: 420 metres/sec
Muzzle energy: 50mkp
Rate of fire: Single shot 32 rounds/min
Range, maximum effective: 50 metres
Manufacturer: State factories in USSR; People's Republic of China; Hungary; Poland; Yugoslavia; North Korea (Type 68)
Status: Obsolete in Warsaw Pact countries. In service in Yugoslavia and Asian Communist countries

Sectioned view of the Tokarev: (1) Receiver; (6) Magazine catch lock; (7) Magazine catch; (10) Trigger spring; (12) Trigger; (13) Hammer and sear housing; (14) Barrel; (15) Barrel link; (16) Barrel link pin; (17) Slide; (18) Barrel bushing; (19) Recoil spring plug; (20) Recoil spring; (21) Recoil spring guide; (22) Firing pin; (23) Firing pin spring; (26) Hammer; (27) Hammer pin; (28) Hammer spring; (29) Sear; (31) Sear pin; (32) Disconnector; (33) Slide stop

9mm STECHKIN AUTOMATIC PISTOL (APS)

The Stechkin is unusual in that it is a true automatic pistol which fires a continuous succession of shots for as long as the trigger is pulled and the ammunition supply lasts. Such pistols are inherently difficult to use as the muzzle rises at an ever increasing rate and if the target is not hit with the first round the chances are that it will not be struck by subsequent shots. This is due to the fact that the backward force exerted along the axis of the bore passes above the point of support which lies approximately half-way up the butt, producing a turning moment. To increase the chance of a hit the holster-stock can be attached to the butt of the pistol.

This pistol is no longer in military service with the Soviet Army but is reported still to be carried by the Security Police.

ACTION

The magazine is removed by pressing in the catch at the heel of the butt and loaded by pressing the cartridge into the magazine platform in front of the lips and then pushing it back under the lips to the rear wall of the magazine. The magazine is inserted in the butt and pushed up until the catch clicks into place. Whilst the selector barrel – on the left of the slide above the butt – is at 'safe', the slide cannot be retracted. When the selector is set to 'semi-automatic' or 'automatic' the slide is free and can be pulled back. When the slide is released, the top round is fed from the magazine into the chamber. When the trigger is operated the hammer will be released and the pistol will fire – provided that the slide is fully forward.

OPERATION

The Stechkin is a blowback operated pistol. This means that the barrel is not locked to the slide and the velocity of recoil of the slide is controlled by its mass. The gas pressure produced in the chamber forces the cartridge case

9mm Stechkin pistol (US Army photograph)

back and this pushes the breech face – part of the slide – rearward. The slide rapidly gains energy and the cartridge case very soon loses it, but the extractor holds the case to the breech face until it hits the ejector, which is

The Stechkin pistol with shoulder stock-holster attached

an extension of the slide stop, and is thrown out of the ejection slot in the top of the slide.

As the slide moves back a cam rides over the head of a delay device – or retarder – which is forced down against its spring. The effect of this is two-fold. Energy is taken from the slide – which slows it down – and transferred to the retarder. Furthermore the retarder rises after the slide has run out and provided the slide is fully forward, the retarder strikes the trigger bar which initiates the firing of the weapon, at full automatic, in a way that will be described in the next section. The slide compresses the return spring which is mounted around the barrel, cocks the hammer and is then returned to its forward position as the spring re-asserts itself. The round is fed into the chamber and fired when the hammer falls.

TRIGGER AND FIRING MECHANISM

The Stechkin pistol can be fired either at double action or single action. Attached to the trigger, above the trigger fulcrum, is the trigger bar. When the trigger is pulled the bar goes forward and a lug engages in a notch in the bottom of the hammer and rotates it to the cocked position and tensions the hammer spring. Continued movement of the trigger pulls the trigger bar out of engagement with the hammer notch and the hammer spring drives the hammer forward into the firing pin. As the trigger bar goes forward it lifts the disconnector and a lug on the disconnector lifts the sear away from the hammer. When the slide recoils after the first shot is fired the disconnector is forced down and the lug moves off the sear allowing it to drop and hold the hammer. As the disconnector moves down it depresses the trigger bar against the force of the retarder spring. At single shot the trigger must be released to allow the trigger bar to move back from under the disconnector and rise again under the force of the retarder spring. When the trigger is operated the trigger bar moves forward which lifts the disconnector, which in turn lifts the sear off the hammer and another round is fired.

At full auto the rotation of the selector shaft allows the retarder to rise sufficiently to push the trigger bar up and this lifts the disconnector which releases the sear and the hammer flies forward. Thus at automatic fire the semi automatic process is short circuited.

When the safety catch is applied, projecting lugs on the selector shaft cam the firing pin back and hold it there. The sear is also cammed off the hammer which flies forward onto the immovable firing pin and rebounds to the half-cock position.

The last action of the selector shaft is to hold the slide to the receiver so the action cannot be retracted either wilfully or accidentally.

When the ammunition is expended the magazine follower rises under the slide stop which enters a cut away in the slide and holds it to the rear. When a loaded magazine is inserted, depressing the slide stop will allow the slide to fly forward, or, alternatively, the slide may be pulled back slightly and released to go forward and chamber a round.

STRIPPING

Remove the magazine and inspect the chamber and feedway for live rounds. Pull the front of the trigger guard down. Retract the slide, lift its rear end out of the receiver and ease it forward. Take off the return spring. To re-assemble: check that the hammer is cocked, the selector is NOT at safe, and the trigger guard is pulled down.

Put the return spring over the barrel and insert into the slide. When the barrel goes through the hole in the front of the slide, pull the slide to the rear and press it down into the receiver and allow it to go forward. Press the trigger guard up into position.

The Stechkin field-stripped (US Army photograph)

DATA
Cartridge: 9mm × 18
Method of operation: Blowback
Method of locking: Nil
Method of feed: 20-round box magazine
Method of fire: Selective. Double action

WEIGHTS
Pistol empty: 1.03kg
Pistol empty with holster stock: 1.58kg

LENGTHS
Pistol: 225mm
Barrel: 127mm

FIRING CHARACTERISTICS
Muzzle velocity: 340 metres/sec
Muzzle energy: 35mkp
Rate of fire: Cyclic: 750 rounds/min
           Automatic: 80 rounds/min
           SS: 40 rounds/min
Range, maximum effective: Pistol only 50 metres, with stock attached 200 metres

Manufacturer: State Arsenals·
Status: No longer produced. No longer in service with Russian first line units. Still in service with Border Guards

9mm MAKAROV SL PISTOL (PM)

The Makarov pistol is used by the majority of the Eastern Bloc armies and those countries in Asia which are directly supplied by Russia. It is produced in Russia, East Germany and the Chinese People's Republic. The names used by each country and the identifying characteristics are as follows:

RUSSIA
Pistolet Makarov (PM)
5 pointed star on grips
Lanyard loop at heel of pistol grip

EAST GERMANY
Pistole M
No markings on grips
No lanyard loop

PEOPLE'S REPUBLIC OF CHINA
Type 59 Pistol
'59 SHI' on receiver

OPERATION

The Makarov is prepared for firing by removing the magazine from the pistol grip. The magazine catch is located at the heel of the grip, below the lanyard loop. The magazine takes 8 rounds inserted by hand in the conventional way, placed on the magazine follower and pressed down in front of the feed lips. When pressed down, and slid back, the cartridge slips rearward to the rear wall of the magazine.

The magazine is inserted in the butt and the pistol is cocked by drawing the slide back, holding the milled surfaces prepared for that purpose, and letting the return spring force it forward, feeding a round into the chamber. The safety catch is on the slide above the left hand pistol grip. When the selector is rotated upwards to the 'safe' position the red dot is covered. It

The 9mm Makarov SL pistol

should be noted that setting the safety to 'safe' with the hammer cocked, drops the hammer but the firing pin is blocked. When it is required to use the pistol the safety is pulled down by the right thumb to the 'fire' position and the trigger can be operated either as a single action by cocking the external hammer with the thumb, or at double action by a long pull which both cocks and fires the pistol. The self-loading action necessitates one round fired for each trigger pull. When the magazine is empty, the slide remains to the rear. It can be released by depressing the slide stop on the left hand side of the receiver or dropping the magazine and pulling back on the slide and then releasing it.

The Makarov pistol uses the 9mm × 18 cartridge which is a low powered round and permits utilisation of blowback action. When the trigger is pulled the cartridge is in the chamber and the slide is fully forward. When the cap is fired the gas pressure developed in the chamber forces the bullet up the bore and at the same time drives the cartridge case back against the breech face of the slide. The inertia of the slide and the resistance provided by the return spring prevent any backward motion whilst the bullet travels to the muzzle. By the time the slide has recoiled sufficiently to allow about 3mm of brass cartridge case to protrude unsupported from the chamber, the pressure has dropped to a safe low level. The extractor holds the case to the breech face until the ejector strikes it and throws it out of the ejection slot on the right of the slide. The rearward motion of the slide compresses the return spring and is stopped when the rear portion reaches the trigger guard extension. The return spring reasserts itself and as the slide goes forward the feed rib picks up the top cartridge in the magazine and feeds it into the chamber; the extractor springs into the groove at the base of the round and the slide comes to rest.

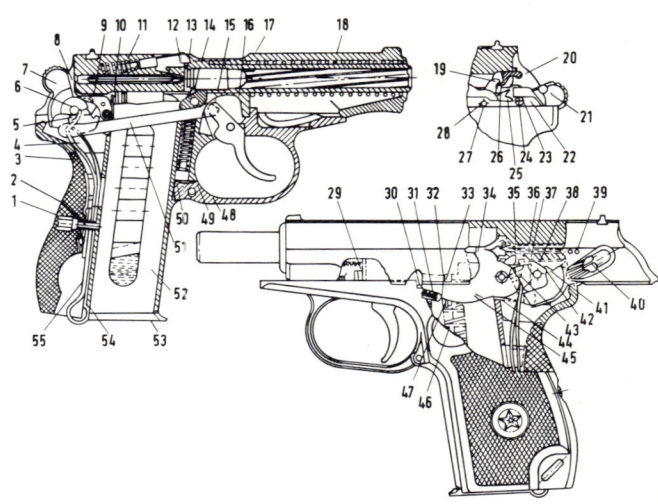

THE TRIGGER AND FIRING MECHANISM

The trigger and firing mechanism of the Makarov pistol is unusual in the way it operates. Assuming the pistol is fired at double action, the sustained pull on the trigger, pivoted about its mid-point, moves the trigger bar forward. The cocking lever is pivoted to enter a notch in the hammer and the further movement of the trigger bar forces the cocking lever round to rotate the hammer back. This movement continues until the cocking lever slips out of the notch in the hammer, taking the sear with it. The hammer is then free to go forward and drive the firing pin forward to fire the cap.

The recoiling slide forces the cocking lever sideways, clear of the sear. The sear is then impelled against the hammer by its spring; as the hammer is rocked back by the slide, the sear engages and holds the hammer notch. When the slide runs out the hammer remains held back. The slide completes its forward movement but the trigger is still pressed and must be released. When this occurs the cocking lever rotates forward and moves under the sear. When the trigger is pressed the cocking lever engages the sear and moves it out of engagement with the hammer which swings forward, under the influence of its own spring, to drive the firing pin into the cap.

When the ammunition is expended the magazine follower rises under the influence of the spring and a lug on the lower left side presses the slide stop up to enter a notch in the slide and hold it to the rear. The slide stop will release the slide if it is pressed down. If a loaded magazine is inserted. the slide will be released and load a round if it is initially pulled back and then let go.

The safety lever is moved up to the 'safe' position and interposes a block between the hammer and pin; shortly afterwards a projection meets a tooth on the sear and lifts the sear from the hammer. The hammer falls and is locked in its forward position by the safety. When the safety is applied the slide is locked.

STRIPPING

To strip the pistol, the magazine is removed, the safety set to 'fire' to release the slide which is retracted, and the chamber and feedway inspected.

If there is no cartridge in the pistol the slide is returned to the forward position. The front of the trigger guard is pulled down out of the receiver, pressed to one side and rested against the receiver. The slide is pulled fully back and the rear end lifted out of the receiver. It is then eased forward over the barrel.

DATA
Cartridge: 9mm × 18
Method of operation: Blowback

Sectioned view of the Makarov SL pistol. Key: (1) Screw; (2) Hole for screw; (3) Mainspring wide leaf; (4) Mainspring narrow leaf; (5) Recess for sear lug; (6) Curved end of mainspring wide-leaf; (7) Hammer; (8) Safety lug; (9) Sear lug; (10) Sear spring; (11) Extractor spring; (12) Extractor; (13) Extractor hook; (14) Bullet guide of barrel; (15) Trigger upper end; (16) Receiver curved slot; (17) Recoil spring turn (of less diameter); (18) Recoil spring; (19) Sear tooth; (20) Hook for locking hammer; (21) Recess on hammer head; (22) Slide guiding slot; (23) Trunnion seat for hammer trunnion; (24) Hammer trunnion; (25) Hammer rebound tooth; (26) Shoulder of safety recess; (27) Sear trunnion; (28) Trunnion seat for sear trunnion; (29) Recess on trigger guard lug; (30) Slide stop recess; (31) Slide stop catch knob; (32) Slide stop lug; (33) Slidetooth; (34) Slide stop ejector; (35) Disconnecting lug of cocking lever; (36) Sear; (37) Hammer cocking notch; (38) Slide rib; (39) Recess for safety thumb catch; (40) Safety thumb catch; (41) Lug for locking hammer; (42) Hammer safety notch; (43) Rebound lug of cocking lever; (44) Shoulder for trigger bar; (45) Slide stop; (46) Follower spring; (47) Follower claw; (48) Trigger guard; (49) Trigger guard spring; (50) Trigger guard lug; (51) Trigger bar; (52) Magazine body; (53) Follower spring bent end; (54) Lug for magazine catch; (55) Mainspring lower end (US Army)

Method of locking: Nil
Method of feed: 8-round\box magazine
Method of fire: Self-loading, Double action

WEIGHT
Pistol, empty: 663g

LENGTHS
Pistol: 160mm
Barrel: 91mm

MECHANICAL FEATURES
Barrel: Rifling: 6 groove RH
Sights: Foresight: Blade
    Rearsight: Notch
    Graduation: Nil
    Zeroing: Elevation. Change rearsight. Line. Rearsight on dovetail
    Sight radius: 130mm

FIRING CHARACTERISTICS
Muzzle velocity: 315metres/sec
Muzzle energy: 30mkp
Rate of fire: Self-loading 35 rounds/min
Range, maximum effective: 50 metres

UNITED KINGDOM

.455in WEBLEY PISTOL

The Pistol Webley .455 Mark I was introduced into service in November 1887. Subsequent marks followed as shown.

Mk 1** October 1894
Mk 2 October 1894
Mk 3 October 1897
Mk 4 July 1899
Mk 5 December 1913
Mk 1** April 1915
Mk 2* April 1915
Mk 2** April 1915

These pistols differed only in minor detail. They were all top-breaking revolvers locked by a heavy stirrup, barrel catch and all had the "birds head" grip.

All the above pistols had 4in barrels but in 1905 the practice was begun

Webley .455 pistol No 1 (RSAF)

with the Mk 3 of producing 6in barrels for officers' use and in June 1915 the Mk 1 and Mk 2 pistols undergoing repair were fitted with 6in barrels leading to:

Pistol Webley, 6in Barrel, Mk 1** June 1915.
Mark 2** June 1915
Mark 5 May 1915 "Bird's head" grip
Mark 6 May 1915 Square grip.

In 1927 the Mark 6 was re-named the Pistol Revolver .455 No 1 Mk 6 and it remained in service until declared obsolete in 1947.

DATA (Pistol Revolver – No 1 Mk 6)
Cartridge: .455 SAA Ball
Method of operation: Manual – revolver
Method of feed: 6 chambered cylinder

Method of fire: Single shots
Weight: 1.07kg
Length: 286mm
Barrel: 152mm
Rifling: 7 grooves RH
Sights: Foresight: Blade
Rearsight: Notch
Muzzle velocity: 183 metres/sec
Muzzle energy: 29mkp
Rate of fire: 24 rounds/min
Range, maximum effective: 50 metres
Manufacturer: Webley and Scott Ltd, Birmingham, Royal Small Arms Factory, Enfield
Status: No longer manufactured. No longer in British military service but still to be found in a number of former British dependencies

.38in NO 2 PISTOL REVOLVER

After World War 1 the British Army decided to adopt a smaller calibre cartridge and a lighter revolver which, it was hoped, would demand less skill from the firer. They examined the Webley and Scott Mk III commercial model using a .38 cartridge.

The Royal Small Arms Factory at Enfield took over design responsibility for the new pistol in 1926. The Webley design was modified by incorporating changes in the trigger mechanism and lock-work and introducing a hammer lock designed to increase the weapon's safety. When the design was completed the pistol was called the Pistol Revolver No 2 Mark 1. It came into service on 2 June 1932, and was declared obsolescent in June 1938.

This was followed in June 1938 with the Pistol Revolver No 2 Mark 1* which was purely a double action pistol and the comb and single action cocking notch on the hammer were removed. Although the mainspring was reduced in strength the pull was still about 12lb and as a result it was difficult to achieve a high standard of accuracy. The change was made to suit the Tank Corps which considered a single action pistol dangerous.

The Pistol Revolver No 2 Mk 1** was introduced in 1942 to save production time. The hammer safety stop was removed. This may well have saved time but it also made the revolver subject to accidental discharge when dropped and after the war the stop was restored and they were re-marked Mk 1*.

Pistol Revolver .38 No 2 Mk 1 (RSAF)

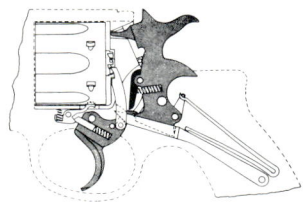
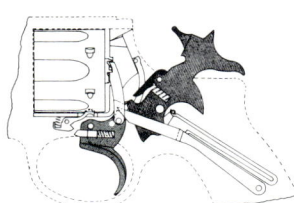
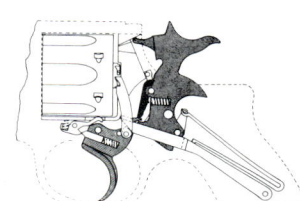
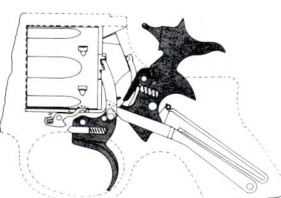

The functioning of the pistol revolver .38 No 2 Mk 1

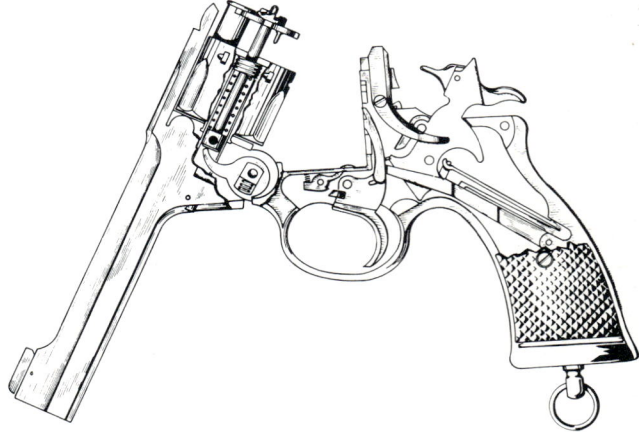

The mechanism of the revolver pistol .38 No 2 Mk 1 (RMCS)

DATA
Cartridge: .380 in SAA Ball
.380 Revolver
.38 Smith and Wesson
.38 Webley
Method of operation: Manual-revolver No. 2 Mk 1 single or double action
Mk 1* double action
Mk 1** double action
Method of feed: 6 chambered cylinder
Method of fire: Single shots
Weight: 767g
Length: 260mm
Barrel: 5in (127mm)
Rifling: 7 grooves RH
Sights: Foresight: Blade
Rearsight: Notch
Muzzle velocity: 183 metres/sec
Muzzle energy: 16mkp
Rate of fire: 24 rounds/min
Range, maximum effective: 30 metres
Manufacturer: Royal Small Arms Factory, Enfield. Albion Motors, Glasgow. Singer Sewing Machine Co., Clydebank (components only, assembled at RSAF Enfield)

.38 No 2 Mk 1 pistol revolver (RSAF)

Status: No longer manufactured. No longer in British military service but still to be found in the military and police forces in a number of former British dependencies

.38in WEBLEY MK IV PISTOL REVOLVER

This is the development of the Webley .38 pistol from which Enfield produced the Pistol Revolver No 2 Mk 1. It was issued in 1943 to supplement the standard pistols. It became obsolete in British military service in 1963. It has been available since then, and is still offered, as a commercial pistol.

DATA
Cartridge: .380in SAA Ball, .380 Revolver, .38 Smith and Wesson, .38 Webley
Method of operation: Manual – revolver
Method of locking: NA
Method of feed: 6 chambered cylinder
Method of fire: Single shots
Weight: 767g
Length: 267mm
Barrel: 5in (127mm)
 Rifling: 7 grooves RH
Sights: Foresight: Blade
  Rearsight: Notch
Muzzle velocity: 183 metres/sec
Muzzle energy: 16mkp
Rate of fire: 24 rounds/min
Range, maximum effective: 30 metres
Manufacturer: Webley & Scott Ltd, Birmingham

.38in Webley Mk IV pistol revolver (RSAF)

Status: Still manufactured. Not in official British military service but likely to be encountered in many parts of the world

SMITH AND WESSON PISTOL REVOLVER
NO 2 Cal. 380

This pistol was purchased from USA in 1940 and issued to British units. It was a six-chambered version of the Smith and Wesson Regulation Police Model and was frequently referred to as the 38/200 where the calibre and the bullet weight were used as a means of identification. The revolver was manufactured from April 1940 to 1945 and some 890,000 were produced.

It was a solid frame pistol with the cylinder mounted on a crane to swing out to the left when unlocked. It could be fired either as a single action pistol having been thumb cocked or with one long straight trigger pull. The hammer was of the rebound type, withdrawing into the frame after firing. The cylinder rotated anti-clockwise and the empty cases were ejected with an ejector rod when the cylinder was swung out.

DATA
Cartridge: .380in
Method of operation: Hand
Method of feed: 6 chambered cylinder
Method of fire: Single shots
Weight: 890g
Length: 257mm
Barrel: 5in (127mm) (some 4 and 6in barrels)
  Rifling: 5 grooves RH. 1 twist in 18¾in (476mm)
Muzzle velocity: 198 metres/sec
Muzzle energy: 24mkp
Rate of fire: 24 rounds/min
Range, maximum effective: 40 metres
Manufacturer: Smith & Wesson Arms Co, Springfield, Mass.
Status: No longer manufactured. No longer in official British military service but there are still a great many about

The Smith and Wesson Pistol Revolver No 2, cal .380 (RMCS)

UNITED STATES OF AMERICA

.45 M1911A1 AUTOMATIC PISTOL

The American tradition and experience favoured the revolver and a number of such weapons were used until 1911 when the Colt Automatic Pistol was adopted. During the last decade of the 19th century the .38 calibre pistols in use were subject to criticism and it was considered during the Philippine Campaign of 1898-1900 that the .38 Long Colt with its hollow base bullet was incapable of stopping a determined Moro and a number of .45 revolvers were obtained.

This predilection for the large bore pistol was continued and the 1907 Pistol Trials were conducted in calibre .45. The best two results came from the Savage rotating barrel pistol – subsequently adopted by Portugal, and the Browning-designed model 1905 pistol. Two hundred Colt and 200 Savage pistols were bought for troop trials and as a result of these the Colt pistol was adopted with the nomenclature US Pistol, Automatic, Calibre .45 M1911.

This weapon and its successor the M1911A1 can trace their ancestry back to 1896 when Colt purchased four designs from Browning. In 1900 Colt produced the automatic Sporting Model using the new .38 Colt Automatic Pistol Cartridge – thereafter known as the .38 ACP – which had the unprecedented high velocity of 1,260 ft/sec. The pistol was recoil operated and locked by grooves on the upperside of the barrel entering recesses in the ceiling of the slide. A link was furnished at each end of the barrel to disconnect barrel and slide after a short initial recoil. On this gun the slide was removed backwards and was held during gas pressure by a small metal slide stop.

In 1902 a modified model of the 1900 Sporting Model appeared and, more important, the .38 ACP Military Model. The weight had gone up from 35oz to 37oz, there were now 8 shots available instead of 7 and there was a holding open device when the ammunition was expended.

Following the criticisms of the .38 calibre noted above, Frankfurt Arsenal

US automatic pistol, calibre .45 M 1911 (RSAF)

developed .45 and .41 cartridges; the former being used in the 1907 pistol trials. The Colt entry for these trials was a modified version of the 1902 ACP, retaining the double link arrangement and the slide stop as the only impediment preventing the slide from blowing back into the firer's face.

Between the 1907 trials – which narrowed the choice to the Colt and Savage pistols – and the troop trials in 1911, substantial modifications were made. The modified weapon had a grip safety and an applied safety, and the slide was mounted on the receiver from the front. The double link was

US automatic Cal. .45 M 1911 A1 pistol (RSAF)

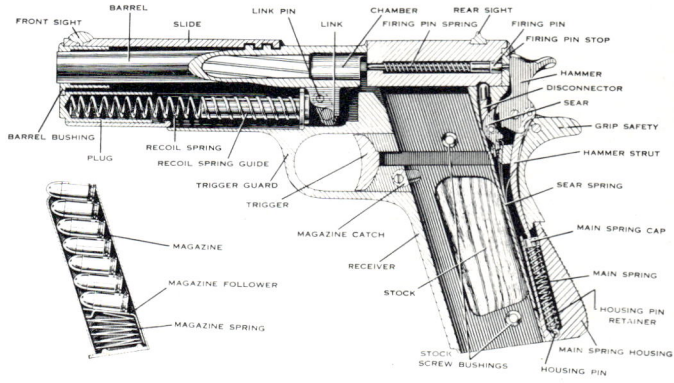

(a) NORMAL   (b) DISCONNECTOR RELEASING SEAR TO
                              ARREST HAMMER

The action of the disconnector

replaced by a single link at the rear. In effect the 1911 pistol was a new pistol. It was adopted for the US Army and remained unaltered until the introduction of a new version in 1926. This resulted from a development begun in April 1923 by the Springfield Armoury and aimed at improving both sighting and weapon control in which the shape of the back of the handgrip was altered to a more arched form and checkered, a shorter, grooved, trigger was fitted, the receiver behind the trigger was chambered to take the trigger finger, the grip safety was lengthened slightly and the hammer spur was shortened. The new version was designated the Model 1911A1.

OPERATION

The magazine is removed from the pistol by pressing the thumb release on the left side of the grip, behind the trigger. The magazine holds seven cartridges, loaded consecutively by placing the round on the front end of the magazine follower and pressing down the back. The loaded magazine is inserted into the handle and pushed in until the magazine locks. When the milled grips at the rear of the receiver are grasped in the left hand, the slide can be retracted. It comes back over the cartridge in the magazine, cocks the hammer, and when the slide is released the compressed return spring, under the barrel, drives it forward. It picks up the top round which is lifted by the magazine spring into the path of the breech block ready for chambering. The extractor, on the front face of the breech block, enters the extraction groove at the rear of the cartridge. The breech block face strikes the barrel and pushes it forward. The barrel is connected to the receiver by a single link and as the barrel goes forward the link lifts the chamber, and two ribs on the top surface of the barrel enter recesses in the ceiling of the slide. The link rotates beyond the top dead centre position and the barrel is locked into the slide. When the slide is fully forward the disconnector rises into the recess and when the trigger is pulled the hammer flies forward and hits the firing pin. The firing pin is a notable feature of Browning's design. It is shorter than the length of its hole and is spring retracted. The hammer drives it forward, it strikes the cap and is immediately withdrawn into the breech block.

The gas pressure drives the bullet up the bore. The breech face is forced back and the barrel is pulled back with it. The lower end of the link remains locked to the receiver and the top end rotates through the arc of a circle. After a short delay until the link passes top dead centre, the breech end of the barrel is rotated down and disconnected from the slide. The barrel is halted and the slide continues rearward. The empty case comes back on

the breech face and is then struck by the ejector in the receiver and thrown out through the ejection port on the right of the slide. As the slide continues back, the plug housing the return spring is forced back by the barrel bushing and the return spring is compressed. The hammer is rotated back and held by the sear. The slide goes forward and if there is ammunition in the magazine, the cycle is repeated, the round is chambered and the barrel locks to the slide. If there is no ammunition, the stop on the left side of the magazine follower will lift the slide stop catch into a slot in the slide and hold it to the rear. The barrel will go forward if the slide stop is manually depressed. If a loaded magazine is inserted, pressing down on the slide stop will enable the breech block to feed a round out of the magazine lips and chamber it.

TRIGGER AND FIRING MECHANISM

The Colt .45 M1911A has a disconnector, a grip safety and a manual safety. When the manual safety is pushed up it locks the hammer and sear and enters a recess in the slide and prevents any movement.

With the slide fully forward and the manual safety pulled down to 'fire' the operation of the trigger pushes back the trigger bar. If the grip safety is being operated by the firer the trigger bar will move back and rotate the sear off the hammer bent (or notch). The hammer spring will rotate the hammer to fire the round. If the grip safety is not operated the nose of the operating lever rests against the trigger bar and prevents trigger movement. When it is squeezed in it is rotated about its top pivot and the nose of the operating lever is rotated above the trigger bar which is then free to move back.

As the slide moves back the disconnector, which is a vertical rod resting in a recess in the underside of the slide, is forced down as the recess moves back. At the bottom of the disconnector is a flange against which the tail of the sear rests. When the disconnector moves down the flange is pushed below the sear which is rotated by its spring against the hammer which it holds back. There is now no connection between the trigger bar and the sear and the gun cannot be fired.

When the slide is fully forward the top of the disconnector is under the

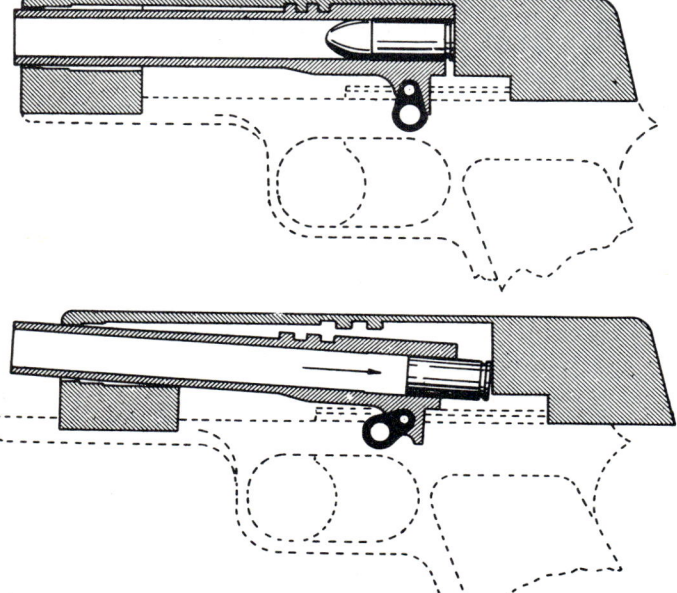

The locking system of the M 1911·A1

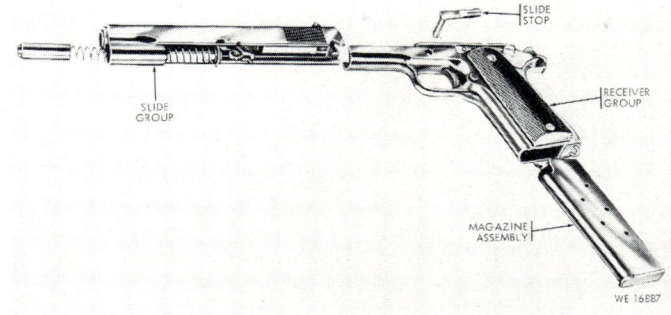

A section view of the M 1911 A1

The M 1911 A1 field-stripped (US Army)

recess again. When the trigger is released the trigger bar moves away from the bottom end of the disconnector which follows it and at the same time as the top moves up into the recess, the flange at the bottom comes between the trigger bar and the sear. When the trigger moves the trigger bar back again, the flange rotates the sear off the hammer and another round is fired.

There is a half-cock bent on the hammer which enables the pistol to be carried in safety with a round in the chamber. It also enables the sear to catch the hammer before it reaches the firing pin, if for some reason the sear slips off the main bent.

STRIPPING

(1) Remove magazine, retract slide, check chamber and feedway are clear. Allow slide to go forward under control.
(2) Press in return spring plug under the muzzle and rotate bushing clockwise. Allow plug to come out under control. Remove return spring. Remove barrel bearing.
(3) Cock hammer. Pull slide back until rear of slide stop is aligned with rear recess in centre of slide.
(4) Push slide stop out. Pull slide and barrel forward off receiver.
(5) Remove return spring guide. Rotate barrel and remove from slide.
   Re-assembly is in natural reverse order but ensure barrel link is forward and link pin is not proud before sliding receiver forward into slide assembly.

DATA
Cartridge: .45 ball M1911 (and see below)
Method of operation: Short recoil
Method of locking: Projecting lug
Method of feed: Magazine
Method of fire: Self-loading

WEIGHTS
Pistol with empty magazine: 1.13kg
Pistol with loaded magazine: 1.36kg
Trigger pull: 2.25-3.0kg

LENGTHS
Pistol: 219mm
Barrel: 127mm
Rifling: 105mm
Bore diameter: 0.45in

MECHANICAL FEATURES
Barrel: Rifling: 6 grooves LH. 1 turn in 406mm
Cooling: Air
Sights: Foresight: Fixed blade
Rearsight: U notch on dovetail slide
Zeroing: Elevation. Back sight changed. Line. Back sight moved
Sight radius: 164.6mm

FIRING CHARACTERISTICS
Muzzle velocity: 253 metres/sec
Muzzle energy: 51.1mkp
Chamber pressure: 1335kg/cm²
Rate of fire: 35 rounds/min
Effective range: 50 metres

Ammunition: .45 Ball 1911 Blank M9 Dummy M1921 Tracer M26 High Density Shot M261 (This employs 16 spheres in a sabot of shape similar to the ball round and is used against personnel.)

Manufacturer: Colt's Patent Firearms Manufacturing Co, Hartford, Connecticut. Firearms Division, Colt Industries, Hartford, Connecticut. Ithaca Gun Co, Ithaca, New York. Remington Rand Inc, Syracuse, New York. Remington Arms-Union Metallic Cartridge Co. Bridgeport, Connecticut. Springfield Armoury, Springfield, Massachusetts. Union Switch & Signal Co, Swissvale, Pennsylvania
Status: Current manufacture by Firearms Division of Colt Industries. In service with US Armed Forces and virtually all dependent countries such as South Korea, Taiwan, Philippines

9mm COLT MODEL 1971 MILITARY PISTOL

The Colt Model 1971 is a modern, double action, 9mm pistol, which has been designed to retain many of the handling characteristics of the M1911. Apart from the change of calibre other new features include the use of stainless steel alloys throughout, the main portion of a 15-shot magazine and a double-action trigger which, combined with a safety acting directly on the firing pin, makes it possible to carry the pistol safely with a round in the chamber.

DATA
Calibre: 9mm
Length overall: 202mm
Length of barrel: 114mm
Height: 136mm
Weight (with magazine): kg
Sights: Fixed
Magazine capacity: 15 rounds
Manufacturer: Colt Patent Firearms Co, Hartford, Connecticut

13mm GYROJET ROCKET PISTOL

In 1962 the Advanced Research Project Agency set up a study with MBA Associates of San Ramon, San Francisco to investigate the potentialities of a pistol firing micro-rockets. The aim was to produce a pistol with an effective range of 100 feet (30.5m), a grouping accuracy not exceeding 7 mils, and a reliability of 0.9.

The manufacturers produced a pistol which was tested and revealed faults which led to modifications of the round. The resulting tests led to no official acceptance but the weapon was placed on the market.

DESCRIPTION

The pistol is a lightweight self-loading model made of zamac – an aluminium alloy – with a steel insert in the barrel. The barrel is grooved but in itself does not impart spin to the bullet. The magazine in the butt contains six cartridges. The use of stampings gives an angular unorthodox appearance to the pistol. The maker claims certain advantages. Because the gas pressure is contained within the projectile the barrel can be of thin section and cheap to construct. Similarly the heat of combustion is carried away from the barrel in the round and since there is no heating problem the barrel does not have to be massive.

The only moving part is the feed arm: there is no recoil since the rocket is a self contained system with a net zero momentum and no vibrations induced by any locking system. All this increases the consistency of the system. There is no extraction or ejection and so the mechanism is simple, and capable of operating satisfactorily under very dirty conditions.

Lastly it is said to work satisfactorily under water.

The projectile is a deep drawn steel case with a diameter of 13mm and a length of 30mm. The hollow interior of the round is filled with propellant. The base of the bullet has four peripheral nozzles offset at 20 deg from the longitudinal axis to impart rotation to stabilise during flight. In the centre of the base is a conventional percussion primer. In 1968 each round cost $1.35.

The maker states that the bullet is rotating at 200,000 revolutions/minute when the propellant is all burnt. The velocity claimed is 1250ft/sec (385 metres/sec) at all burnt and 625ft/sec (192 metres/sec) at 350yds (322 metres). The maximum energy of 600ft lb (83mkp) is obtained when all the propellant is consumed which occurs about 16yds (15 metres) from the muzzle. This is in excess of that obtained from the Colt 1911A1 pistol with a .45 bullet weighing 230grains and with a muzzle velocity of 830ft/sec.

OPERATION

The magazine is loaded from the top by pulling down the magazine

The 13mm Gyrojet rocket pistol, Model B Mk 1 (RSAF)

follower, by its outside projection, against the light magazine spring. The gun must be loaded with the hammer uncocked and safety on. The number of rounds in the magazine can be counted through a slot on the left of the grip. A lever on the left of the receiver is pushed down to position the loading arm and tension its spring. The safety catch is located behind the grip on the left side. With the safety at 'fire', pulling the trigger releases the feed arm which presses on the nose of the top round and throws it backwards against the fixed firing pin. The blow crushes the primer cap and the propellant is ignited. The propellant is double base, high energy, with the outside surface inhibited. The pressure build up is slow and the feed arm holds back the round until there is sufficient force for the bullet to start forward and in so doing push the feed arm back to the cocked position and re-tension its spring. The bullet passes up the bore and emerges at the muzzle having burnt only about 10 per cent of the propellant. It continues to accelerate as the propellant is consumed, reaching maximum velocity of 1,250ft/sec at about 16yds (15 metres) from the muzzle.

The total burning time is about 100 millisec.

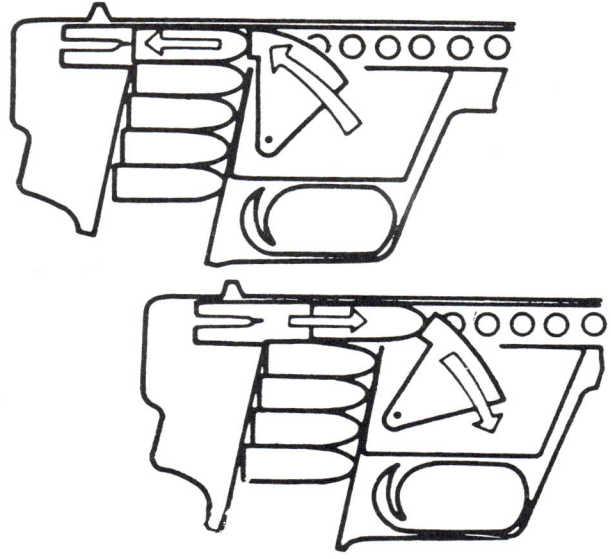

Loading and firing the Gyrojet

FIRING RESULTS

A report on the weapon* showed that its penetration at the muzzle was extremely limited. In fact it failed to penetrate one thickness of cotton sheet with a backing of corrugated card, held half an inch from the muzzle. It would seem that if such a weapon is pointed at you the best plan is to rush up to the firer. (This assumes you can recognise the weapon when you see it. A mistake could be fatal.) Other firings have produced groups of diameter of 11.2in at 10yds. This order of accuracy is not really surprising. The manufacturing problems of keeping the bullet to such close tolerances that its centre of gravity not only lies exactly on the longitudinal axis but remains there throughout the prolonged period of propellant burning, are considerable. Similarly any variation of the venturis can give a deviation in flight – even assuming the thrust is evenly distributed about the centre line. The gas swirl from the nozzle can also produce side forces.

DATA
Cartridge: 13mm Gyrojet
Method of operation: Rocket
Method of feed: 6-round box magazine
Method of fire: Self-loading

Journal of the Forensic Science Society, 1967. D.J. Dillan and J. Thornton.

WEIGHTS
Pistol empty: 0.476kg
Pistol loaded: 0.476kg
Trigger pull: 7.15kg

LENGTHS
Pistol: 276mm
Barrel: 5in (127.0mm)

MECHANICAL FEATURES
Barrel: Steel insert in alloy tube
    Rifling: None
    Cooling: Air
Sights: Foresight: Blade
    Rearsight: V notch
    Graduations: Nil
    Zeroing: Elevation. Foresight. Line. Nil
    Sight radius: 216mm

FIRING CHARACTERISTICS
Maximum velocity: 385metres/sec
Maximum energy: 90.5mkp
Recoil energy: Negligible
Rate of fire: SS: 20-rounds/min
Range, maximum effective: 50metres

The following table compares the standard 13mm gyrojet projectile with some conventional bullets.

Cartridge	Projectile weight (grains)	Muzzle Velocity (ft/s)	Energy (ft/lb) at (yds)
Gyrojet	188	1250	100
.45 ACP	230	850	440
.38 Special	158	855	305
.38 Special (Metal piercing)	110	1320	220
.357 Magnum	158	1410	440
9mm Parabellum	115	1150	205
.41 Magnum	210	1050	405
.41 Magnum (at 45 feet)	210	1500	695

There is also a 13mm Gyrojet Rocket carbine firing the same round.
Manufacturer: MBA Associates, San Ramon, California
Status: No longer manufactured. Not in military service

Gyrojet rocket carbine (RSAF)

COMMERCIALLY-PRODUCED WEAPONS

A large number of revolvers and self-loading pistols are produced commercially in the United States, mainly for sale to the public or to law enforcement agencies. They are not military pistols, and so for the greater part will never be an issue item to infantry units, or to armies generally, including para-military forces. Such arms are sometimes in the private possession of individual soldiers, or may, in exceptional circumstances be purchased officially for some particular internal security requirement in very small numbers. Listed below are typical commercially made US pistols of current design which fall within this category.

REVOLVERS

COLT'S AGENT MODEL D-4
Calibre .38 Special. 6-shot. Length 6.75in. Barrel 2in. Weight 14oz. Fixed sights with 200 grain lead bullet the muzzle velocity is 770 ft/sec with 6in test barrel.

COLT'S COBRA MODEL D-3
Calibre .38 Special. 6-shot. Length 6.75in with 2in barrel. 8.75in with 4in barrel. Weight 15oz. Fixed sights. With 200 grain bullet in 6in test barrel, velocity is 730ft/sec.

COLT'S POLICE POSITIVE SPECIAL MODEL D-2
Calibre .38 Special. 6-shot. Length 8.75in with 4in barrel, 9.75in with 5in barrel. Weight 23oz. With 200 grain bullet and 6in test barrel, velocity is 730ft/sec.

COLT'S MARK III LAWMAN
Calibre .357 Magnum. 6-shot. Length 9.25in. Barrel 2in. Fixed sights. Weight 36oz. With 158 grain bullet in 8.5in test barrel velocity is 1410ft/sec.

SMITH AND WESSON No 10 MILITARY AND POLICE MODEL
Calibre .38 S and W special. 6-shot. Length with 4in barrel is 9.5in. Weight 30.5oz. Fixed sights. (Barrel length of 2, 5, or 6in also available.)

SMITH AND WESSON No 12 MILITARY AND POLICE "AIRWEIGHT"
Calibre .38 S and W special. 6-shot. Length with 2in barrel 6.9in. Fixed sights. Weight 18oz (4in barrel also available.)

SMITH AND WESSON K-38 MASTERPIECE
Calibre Smith and Wesson .38 special. 6-shot. Length with 6in barrel 11.1in Weight 38.5oz. Fixed front sights, micrometer rear sight. (8in barrel also available.)

SMITH AND WESSON COMBAT MASTERPIECE
Calibre .38 Smith and Wesson special. 6-shot. Length with 4in barrel 9.1in. Weight 34oz. Fixed sights. (2in barrel also available.)

SMITH AND WESSON COMBAT MAGNUM
Calibre .357 Magnum. 6-shot. Length 7.5in with 2.5in barrel. Weight 31oz. Fixed front sight, micrometer rear sight.

SMITH AND WESSON .357 HIGHWAY PATROLMAN
Calibre .357 Magnum. 6-shot. Length 11.25in with 6in barrel. Weight 44oz. Fixed front sight, micrometer rear sight. (4in barrel also available.)

SMITH AND WESSON No 29 .44 MAGNUM
Calibre .44 Magnum. 6-shot. Length 11.9in with 6.5in barrel. Weight 47oz. Fixed front sight, micrometer rear sight. (4in and 8in barrels also available.)

SMITH AND WESSON .38 CHIEFS SPECIAL
Calibre Smith and Wesson .38 special. 5-shot. Length 6.5in with 2in barrel. Weight 19oz. Fixed sights. (3in barrel also available.)

SMITH AND WESSON .38 CHIEFS SPECIAL "AIRWEIGHT"
Calibre .38 Smith and Wesson special. 5-shot. Length 6.5in with 2in barrel. Weight 14oz. Fixed sights. (3in barrel also available.)

SMITH AND WESSON .38 BODYGUARD "AIRWEIGHT"
Calibre .38 Smith and Wesson special. 5-shot. Length 6.4in with 2in barrel. Weight 14.5oz. Fixed sights.

SMITH AND WESSON .38 CENTENNIAL "AIRWEIGHT"
Calibre .38 Smith and Wesson special. 5-shot. Length 6.5in with 2in barrel. Weight 13oz. Fixed sights.

LUGER SECURITY SIX
Calibre .357 Magnum or .38 Special. 6-shot. Barrel lengths 2.75in, 4in and 6in. Weight loaded with 4in barrel 34oz. Fixed sights.

SELF-LOADING PISTOLS

COLTS MODEL 0-4613 COMBAT COMMANDER
Available in calibre .45 ACP, .38 Special or 9mm Parabellum. Magazine capacities respectively 7, 9, and 9 rounds.

The .45 ACP model measures 8in overall, with 4.25in barrel, and weighs 33oz. With 230 grain bullet muzzle velocity is 850 feet per second.

SMITH AND WESSON No 39 9mm DOUBLE ACTION MODEL
4 Calibre 9mm Parabellum. 8-round magazine capacity. Overall length 7in with 4in barrel. Weight 26.5oz without magazine. Micrometer rear sight.

SMITH AND WESSON No 59 PISTOL, 9mm
Calibre 9mm Parabellum. 14-round magazine capacity. 4in barrel. Weight 27oz without magazine. Micrometer rear sight.

YUGOSLAVIA

YUGOSLAVIAN PISTOLS
The Yugoslav Armed Forces use a variety of pistols. These include the 7.62mm M57, which is the Yugoslav model of the Soviet Tokarev (TT-33) pistol and can be distinguished from the Soviet model by a crest on the grip which consists of a star, sheaf of wheat, and a hammer enclosed within a wreath. The M65 is the M57 built to accept 9mm × 19 Parabellum cartridges. Large quantities of the Italian Beretta 9mm M34 and the German 9mm P38 are still in service. The most recent Yugoslav pistol is the M-67 which is built in both 7.65mm and 9mm versions.

DATA (M67)
Cartridge: 7.65mm × 17SR or 9mm × 17

Method of operation: Blowback
Method of feed: 6-round box magazine
Method of fire: Self-loading
Length overall: 165mm
Length of barrel: 94mm
Weight loaded: .78kg
Weight with empty magazine: .7kg
Practical rate of fire: 24 rounds/min
Range, maximum effective: 50m
Manufacturer: Yugoslav State Arsenals
Status: In production and in service with Yugoslav forces

SUB-MACHINE GUNS

INTRODUCTION

The sub-machine gun can be regarded as a weapon which has the characteristics of an automatic pistol but has been developed to extend both range and fire-power. It differs from the pistol in requiring the user to employ both hands.

The ammunition used is that of the pistol and the method of operation in the vast majority of cases is blowback.

The sub-machine gun (SMG) is a comparatively recent innovation and was a product of the close quarter battles of the First World War. The first such weapon was the Italian Villar Perosa produced in 1915 but the credit for being the forerunner of the modern form of the weapon must go to the German MP 18.1 designed by Hugo Schmeisser in 1917.

The Second World War saw the use of the SMG by all the belligerents who were attracted to the concept of a weapon producing such a large volume of fire while being comparatively small and in some instances easy to make.

A significant SMG characteristic is its short effective range – rarely exceeding 200 metres – and limited accuracy and penetration resulting from the use of a low powered pistol cartridge.

Although all military powers employ the SMG today, considerable doubt must exist about its future. There can be little doubt that, before long, small, lightweight automatic rifles will be in widespread use in most armies; and since such weapons can well carry out the tasks for which the SMG has hitherto been appropriate, it seems likely that the SMG will disappear from

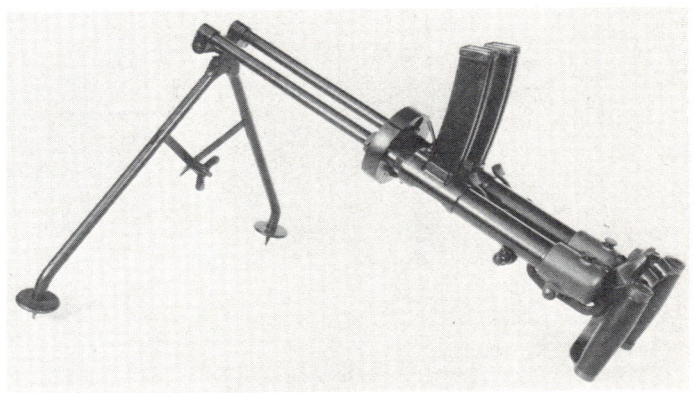

The 9mm Villar Perosa SMG

the inventories of these armies. In small regular and irregular forces, however, the more reliable and less expensive of current SMGs are likely to remain in use for many years

---

ARGENTINA

.45 HALCON SMG

The arms factory of Halcon at Buenos Aires produced a series of blowback operated sub-machine guns, starting in 1943.

MODEL 1943

This SMG was of unusual appearance. It had a large muzzle brake-compensator and a fully finned barrel which carried a bayonet lug behind the muzzle. The magazine housing was shaped to make a forward hand-grip for the 17- or 30-round magazine. The magazine release catch was on the forward part of the trigger guard and moved rearward to release the magazine. The cocking handle was on the left of the receiver and the safety also on the left over the trigger. The change button was also above the trigger.

The buffer cap, overhanging the small of the distinctively shaped butt, is rotated to allow removal of the bolt and return spring. The long bolt has a separate spring retracted firing pin and is of the reduced diameter type.

Halcon M 1943 SMG

MODEL 1946

This differed from the Model 43 in having a metal buttstock which swung forward and could be parked under the receiver. It had a separate rear pistol grip. The compensator looked like the Cutt's. The magazine housing was not shaped to make a forward grip. The weapon was lighter than the model 1943 but was substantially the same in performance.

45 Halcon Model 1946 SMG

LIGHT MODEL 57

This model was quite different from its two predecessors. The barrel had no fins, the light stamped sheet receiver was tubular with a cocking handle on the right. The magazine was curved and reached well below the rear pistol grip to accommodate 40 rounds. The metal stock pivoted vertically on the left side of the receiver.

The bolt operating system was somewhat akin to that of the earlier Thompson SMG. A pivoting hammer in the bolt was rotated when it struck a fixed block in the receiver and drove the firing pin into the cartridge cap.

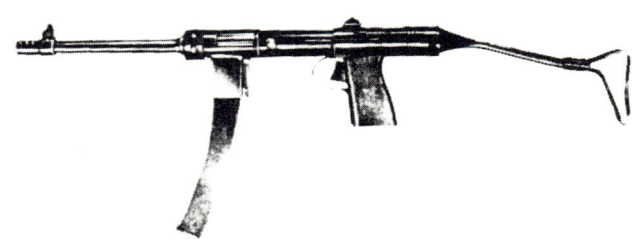

9mm Halcon Light Model 57 SMG

LIGHT MODEL 60

This was similar to the Model 57 but the fire selector was removed from the receiver and a two trigger system incorporated. The rear trigger gave full automatic fire and the front trigger single shot.

9mm Halcon Light Model 60 SMG

DATA
Cartridge: .45 ACP
Method of operation: Blowback
Method of locking: Nil
Method of feed: 17- or 30-round magazine
Method of fire: Selective
Weight (unloaded): 4.75kg
Weight (loaded): 5.68kg
Length: 878mm
Barrel: (with compensator): 292mm
    Rifling: 6 grooves RH
Sights: Foresight: Blade
    Rearsight: U notch on flip. 100 and 200 metres.
Muzzle velocity: 290metres/sec
Muzzle energy: 63mkp

Rate of fire: Cylic: 700 rounds/min
    Auto: 120 rounds/min
    SS: 40 rounds/min
Range, maximum effective: 200 metres
Manufacturer: Halcon, Buenos Aires
Status: No longer manufactured. Not in military service

The Model 1943, although originally designed with the .45 ACP cartridge for the police forces, was used by the Argentinian Army in 9mm. It was never a first line weapon and not many were supplied.

9mm PAM SMG

The two versions of the PAM SMG – PAM 1 and PAM 2 – are both modelled on the USA M3 A1 SMG. They differ from the US weapon in being shorter and lighter and in using the 9mm Parabellum Cartridge. In all other respects they are similar to the M3A1 and have the same ejection port cover safety. The main difference between the two models is the ability of the PAM 2 to provide selective fire.

9mm PAM 1 SMG

9mm PA3-DM SMG

This is the current SMG being manufactured by Fabrica Militar de Armas Portatiles, Rosario. It is a blowback operated weapon of modern design.

It is produced in two models, one with a fixed plastic butt and the other with a sliding butt modelled on the USA M3. The body of the gun is a metal pressing and there is a screw threaded cap at the front end to allow easy release of the barrel. A plastic fore-end grip is located under the receiver. The 25-round magazine fits into the pistol grip which has a grip safety at the back. There is also a safety position on the selector.

The cocking handle is on the left side of the receiver, well forward, and there is a slide which covers the cocking slot to keep dirt out.

The PA 3-DM is designed with a wrap round bolt. The bolt encloses 180mm of the barrel which itself is 290mm long. This, the manufacturers claim, leads to good control and stability in firing, as well as reducing the length.

The gun will fire at either single shot or full automatic and can be used to project grenades.

STRIPPING

The magazine is removed, the bolt retracted and the chamber checked.

The pin holding the butt in position is located at the rear of the receiver and can be pressed out with the nose of the round to allow the butt assembly to slide rearwards.

The bolt and return spring are withdrawn when the cocking handle is retracted.

The trigger group is released by pressing out the forward pin.

The barrel comes out of the receiver as soon as the front end cap is unscrewed.

DATA
Cartridge: 9mm Parabellum
Method of operation: Blowback
Method of locking: Nil
Method of feed: 25-round box magazine
Method of fire: Selective

WEIGHTS
Weight, without magazine
  fixed butt: 3.4kg
  sliding stock: 3.45kg
Magazine, empty: 190g
Magazine, loaded: 500g

LENGTHS
Weapon with fixed butt: 700mm
Weapon with sliding butt
  extended: 693mm
  retracted: 523mm
Barrel: 290mm

DATA
Cartridge: 9mm Parabellum
Method of operation: Blowback
Method of locking: Nil
Method of feed: 30-round box magazine
Method of fire: Automatic (PAM 1) Selective (PAM 2)
Weight (unloaded): 3kg
Weight (loaded): 3.64kg
Length (stock extended): 723mm
Length (stock retracted): 538mm
Barrel: 200mm
    Rifling: 6 grooves RH
Sights: Foresight: Blade
    Rearsight: U notch, flip. 100 and 200 metres
Muzzle velocity: 366metres/sec
Muzzle energy: 51mkp
Rate of fire: Cyclic: 450 rounds/min
    Auto: 210 rounds/min
Range, maximum effective: 200metres
Manufacturer: Fabrica Militar de Armas Portatiles, Domingo Matheu, Rosario, Santa Fé
Status: No longer manufactured. No longer in military service in Argentina but may exist elsewhere

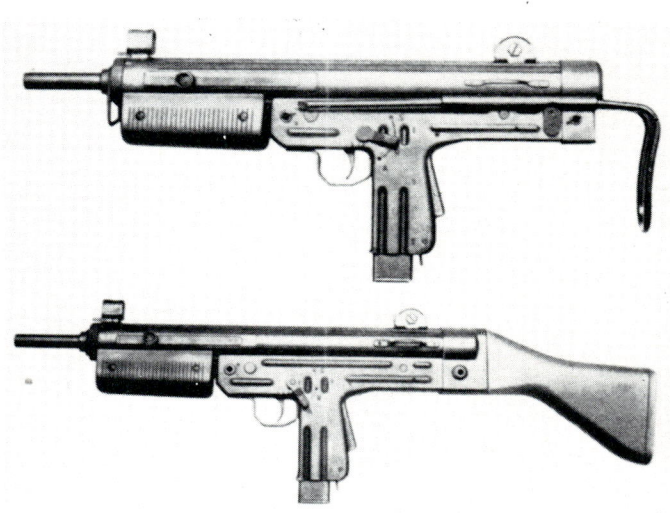

PA3 – DM SMG

MECHANICAL FEATURES
Barrel: Rifling: 6 grooves RH 1 turn in 250mm
    Cooling: Air
Sights: Foresight: Pillar
    Rearsight: Flip aperture. 50 and 100 metres
    Zeroing: Elevation. Foresight screws up and down. Line. Rearsight
    Sight radius: 320mm

FIRING CHARACTERISTICS
Muzzle velocity: 400metres/sec
Muzzle energy: 60mkp
Rate of fire: Cyclic: 650 rounds/min
    Automatic: 100 rounds/min
    SS: 50 rounds/min
Range, maximum effective: 200 metres
Manufacturer: Fabrica Militar de Armas Portatiles, Rosario, Argentina
Status: In production. In service

AUSTRALIA

9mm AUSTEN SMG

The Austen – Australian Sten – was designed in 1941 by Uarre Ridell. At this time the Australian army was very short of weapons and neither Britain nor the USA could do much to help. The Austen was a mixture of features from the Sten and the German MP40. The bolt and its telescoping return spring of Erma design, and the folding stock were taken from the MP40. The receiver, barrel, trigger housing and trigger mechanism came from the Sten Mk II. The magazine, with all its defects, was the single position feed of the Sten. About 20,000 Austens Mk I were produced between June 1942 and March 1945.

The Mark II Austen was quite different. The tubular body of the gun was enclosed in a two piece aluminium frame. The rear assembly held the

The 9mm Austen Mk I SMG (RMCS)

trigger housing and rear pistol grip and acted as the rear location of the return spring. The forward assembly fitted over the barrel and contained the magazine housing and forward pistol grip. The bolt was a Sten type with a fixed firing pin.

The Mark II was manufactured in 1944 and 1945.

9mm Austen Mk II SMG (RMCS)

DATA (AUSTEN MK I)
Cartridge: 9mm Parabellum
Method of operation: Blowback
Method of locking: Nil
Method of feed: 28-round box magazine
Method of fire: Selective
Weight (unloaded): 4kg
Weight (loaded): 4.66kg
Length butt extended: 844mm
Length butt folded: 552mm
Barrel: 198mm
Sights: Foresight: Blade
      Rearsight: Aperture – set for 100yds (98.4 metres)

Muzzle velocity: 266metres/sec
Muzzle energy: 51mkp
Rate of fire: Cyclic: 500 rounds/min
      Auto: 120 rounds/min
      SS: 40 rounds/min
Range, maximum effective: 200 metres
Manufacturer: Diecasters Ltd, Melbourne, Victoria
      W.J. Carmichael and Co, Melbourne, Victoria
Status: No longer manufactured. No longer in service in Australia but some may still be in use elsewhere

9mm OWEN SMG

The Owen SMG was designed by Lt Evelyn Owen. It was adopted on 20 Nov 1941 and manufacture was started shortly afterwards by Lysaghts at the Newcastle Works, Newcastle in New South Wales. 45,000 Owens were produced before production ended in September 1944.

The Owen is readily recognised by the forward sloping box magazine mounted on top of the receiver. It was extremely reliable and had a high reputation in the jungle of New Guinea. There were some unusual features such as a quick release finned barrel. The designer went to great pains to keep dirt out of the mechanism and the bolt carried a fibre washer to ensure that any dust etc coming into the receiver through the cocking slot at the rear did not get forward to the bolt itself. The gun was usually painted in camouflage colouring.

The first model was called the Mk I/42. The Mk I/43 was lightened by having holes cut in the frame and the fins removed from the barrel. The Mk I/44 had a bayonet. The Mk II/43 was manufactured in very limited numbers for trials (about 200) but never went into large scale production.

The Owen was a good sturdy reliable weapon, but heavy and expensive to produce.

9mm Owen Mk I/42 SMG (RMCS)

DATA (MK I/43)
Cartridge: 9mm Parabellum
Method of operation: Blowback
Method of locking: Nil
Method of feed: Top mounted 33-round box magazine
Method of fire: Selective
Weight unloaded: 4.23kg
Weight loaded: 4.86kg
Length; 813mm
Barrel: 250mm
      Rifling: 7 grooves RH
Muzzle velocity: 366 metres/sec
Muzzle energy: 51mkp
Rate of fire: Cyclic: 700 rounds/min
      Automatic: 120 rounds/min
      SS: 40 rounds/min
Range, maximum effective: 200 metres
Manufacturer: Lysaght Newcastle Works, Newcastle, NSW
Status: No longer in production. No longer in Australian Army service. May be encounted elsewhere – particularly in S.E. Asia

9mm Owen Mk I/43 SMG

9mm Owen Mk II/43 SMG (RSAF)

9mm F1 SMG

After World War II the Australian Army continued to sponsor design and development towards producing a new SMG. A questionnaire had been circulated in May 1945 to a large number of users. Over 1,500 replies were received and these were used to fix the design parameters. The resulting weapon was called the Kokoda. It had a forward grip under the muzzle and the magazine was inserted into the shaped pistol grip from below in a manner later used in the UZI SMG (qv). The butt was of steel wire and slid forward under the receiver in the fashion used in the USA M3 SMG. The barrel could be removed by rotating a knurled collar.

The Kokoda was tested and got excessively hot. It was modified and the resulting Military Carbine Experimental Model 1 was tested in England and returned to Australia for modification into the MCEM2. This in turn led to the XI in 1959 and X2 in 1960. The X3 went into production as the F1 in 1962.

The 9mm F1 SMG has a cylindrical body extended forward over the barrel and perforated for cooling. The curved 34-round magazine is mounted over the receiver. The butt is a prolongation of the barrel and receiver and so there is no turning movement which will cause the muzzle to rise at full automatic. Since the magazine is mounted above the gun the

9mm Kokoda SMG (Australian Army photograph)

sights must be offset. This feature – in common with the Owen – has the disadvantage that the magazine produces a blind area to the left front. The rearsight of the F1 is a plate which when lifted raises the aperture some three inches above the centre line of the barrel. This comes from the straight-through butt layout and the high sight line does tend to increase the exposure of the user when firing over cover.

The sling swivel at the nose of the weapon prevents the firer placing his hand or fingers over the muzzle and a handguard adjacent to the ejection port limits the rearward positioning of the hand, thereby preventing personal injury by the breech bolt.

TRIGGER AND SAFETY MECHANISM

The trigger mechanism is fitted with a change lever which renders the gun safe or ready for single shot and automatic fire.

When this safety catch is applied the sear and trigger are positively locked to prevent discharge of the gun. The safety catch may be applied with the bolt to the rear in the cocked position where it cams the bolt back from the sear; or it may be applied when the bolt is forward on an empty chamber where it securely locks the bolt, thereby preventing accidental discharge if a loaded magazine is in place and the weapon is dropped or violently shaken.

MAGAZINE

The F1 has been designed to accept the UK and Canadian 9mm 34-round magazines, thereby assuring interchangeability of magazines which are in current use and available from a number of sources.

BAYONET

The bayonet is the standard L1A2 as used on the 7.62mm L1A1 Rifle and is fitted to the right-hand side of the gun in a horizontal plan, cutting edge facing out.

COCKING HANDLE

A non-reciprocating cocking handle and cover have been fitted to the left-hand side of the tubular body. This permits cocking of the gun without removal of the hand from the pistol grip. It also duplicates the action and grip of the 7.62mm L1A1 Rifle with which most users are familiar. The cover assists in preventing ingress of dirt into the body of the gun.

The cocking handle has the added advantage of being locked into the breech bolt, if and when required, which permits manual operation both back and forward to assist in clearing dirt etc., from the body of the weapon.

COMMON COMPONENTS

A number of 7.62mm L1A1 Rifle components have been incorporated into the weapon. The pistol grip from the L1A1, complete with Arctic grip, has also been adapted to the F1.

DATA

Cartridge: 9mm Parabellum
Method of operation: Blowback
Method of locking: Nil
Method of feed: Top mounted 34-round box magazine
Method of fire: Selective
Weight unloaded: 3.27kg
Weight loaded: 4.30kg with bayonet
Length: 714mm plus 203mm with bayonet
Barrel: 213mm
    Rifling: 6 grooves RH. 1 turn in 305mm
Sights: Foresight: Blade – offset to right
    Rearsight: Hinged plate – aperture. Offset
Muzzle velocity: 366 metres/sec
Muzzle energy: 51mkp

The 9mm Military Carbine, Experimental Model 1 (RSAF)

The Military Carbine, Experimental Model 2 (RSAF)

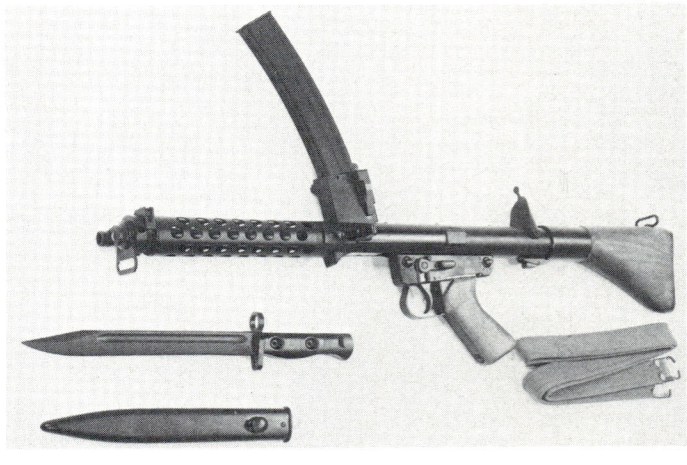

9mm F 1 SMG with bayonet and sling

Rate of fire: Cyclic: 600-640 rounds/min
    Auto: 120 rounds/min
    SS: 40 rounds/min
Range, maximum effective: 200 metres
Manufacturer: Small Arms Factory, Lithgow, New South Wales
Status: In production and in service with the Australian Army

AUSTRIA

9mm STEYR-DAIMLER-PUCH MPi 69 SMG

The Steyr SMG was designed under the direction of Mr Hugo Stowasser and it bears a strong resemblance externally to the UZI 9mm SMG. However, a closer look shows that there are considerable differences and the Steyr, generally, is a simpler weapon.

The receiver pressing is of light-gauge steel and is welded into a hollow box with two gaps on the right hand side – one in the middle for ejection of the spent case and one approximately three inches from the front to accept and insert, to take the barrel seating, barrel release catch and barrel securing nut. The cocking slide, which itself is a simple pressing, is located at the front left hand side of the receiver.

The ejector is a simple bent strip riveted in position in the middle of the base of the receiver to run in a groove in the bottom of the breech-block. Spot welded under the receiver at the back is a small bracket which provides guides for the spring steel telescoping butt and spring loaded release plungers. The strip-down catch is also located at the rear. Screwed to blocks on the top of the receiver is the Singlepoint sight. The nylon-moulded receiver cover fits under the receiver and carries the trigger mechanism, the pistol and magazine housing.

The barrel is 25cm long and is cold-forged on a rifling mandrel. This results in a cleaner groove than that obtained by the usual button rifling and both the inner and outer skins of the barrel are work-hardened. The process is also cheap.

The breech-block has a fixed firing pin on the bolt face which is half way along the bolt length. Thus the bolt 'wraps round' the barrel and has a slot cut along the right hand side for ejection. By this means the weight of the bolt which is required for blowback operation can be kept to the necessary

9mm MPi SMG (RMCS)

level without being excessively long and at the same time the telescoping of the breech-block over the barrel enables the length of the latter to be increased with a resulting increase in muzzle velocity and accuracy. However, the long barrel maintains its pressure longer and so the bolt has to be somewhat heavier than it would be with a normal barrel length of about eight inches. This ensures that the block does not blow back too rapidly and so allow the unsupported case to emerge from the chamber whilst the pressure is still high enough to destroy the relatively weak brass.

OPERATION

The weapon is operated on the advanced primer ignition system of blowback. The round is chambered from the magazine, which fits through the pistol grip, and is inclined to the axis of the bore until it has partially entered the chamber. Once it is in the bore it can fire as soon as the dimensions of the case and chamber produce sufficient friction for the primer to be crushed by the firing pin. From this it will be seen that the actual position of firing will vary. If the case is on the large limit of dimensional tolerance and the chamber is on the small limit, it will fire early. If the case is on the small limit and the chamber is on the largest permitted tolerance it will fire late. In general, firing occurs with the round and breech-block still moving forward and about 1.5mm clearance between the front face of the block and the chamber face.

If firing occurs early due to carbon build up or friction from dirt etc then the design of the bolt, which is telescoped over the breech, will ensure that no danger exists for the firer and no damage is sustained by the weapon.

In the unlikely event of a hang-fire the bolt cannot bounce back sufficiently to allow the burst resulting from the unsupported case to hurt the firer. All the proceeds from the explosion come through the ejection slot on the right hand side of the gun and the firer is protected by the bolt as well as the steel body of the receiver.

TRIGGER AND FIRING MECHANISM

The weapon fires either single shot or full auto. The choice is controlled by finger pressure on the single trigger. A slight pull gives a single shot, a long pull gives automatic fire. This is a very unusual arrangement and the mechanism to produce it, although simple, is very ingenious.

The sear is a double pronged fork pivoted through an oval bearing in the stem on a spring loaded bar which tends to force it back. The trigger is centre pivoted and the forward extension lies between the two prongs of the sear. At its end it has a cross bar. When the bolt is held up on the sear in the cocked position, the sear is forced forward and the cross bar of the trigger rests on the end of the sear between the two raised prongs.

When single shot firing is required, the trigger is pulled back slightly (allowing about 10mm movement at the tip) and the sear is depressed. The bolt goes forward and on its return stroke it strikes the sear forcing the two prongs back against their spring. They then move back under the cross bar of the trigger and rise. The bent on the bolt contacts the sear as it comes forward and the bolt is held up in the cocked position. To fire another round the trigger is released and the cross bar rises. The force exerted by the bolt pushes the sear forward under the cross bar of the trigger and another operation of the trigger fires one more round.

When automatic fire is wanted the trigger is pulled right back and the cross bar pushes the sear down and holds it down so that the bolt rides clear over the sear. Firing is continued until either the ammunition is expended or the trigger released.

The mechanism works well but there is a tendency to fire only single shots when a burst is required and if a target suddenly appears the natural reaction is to squeeze the trigger hard and fire a burst when one round is required. However, with familiarity and training, a firer would soon get the feel of the weapon and avoid this.

The applied safety is a cross bolt which is pressed through the receiver. One side is marked 'S' in white and projects when the gun is at 'Safe'. On the other end is marked 'F' in red and this projects from the receiver when the gun is set to fire. When the pin is in the middle position – ie the 'safe' button is only half way through – the gun will fire single shot only. This can be confusing and it is better to press the button marked 'F' when you wish to set the gun to safe and the end marked 'S' before firing. In the dark neither can be read so one end should be milled and the other plain or some other distinctive feel adopted such as one square and the other round. At the moment anyone picking up the gun either by day or night can be very confused about the applied safety.

The device itself has a simple cut-away in which the trigger can operate when the gun is set to 'fire'. When it is moved fully across the trigger is locked. When moved half-way across, the bar prevents the trigger dropping enough to produce automatic fire. It is not necessary to move the hand from the pistol grip or the finger from the trigger. When setting the weapon to fire, the button marked 'S' can be pressed with the side of the forefinger as it moves towards the trigger. When setting the gun to 'safe' the button marked 'F' can be operated by the thumb. The weapon can be locked when set at 'safe'.

Mechanical safety before firing comes from the basic system of advanced primer ignition and the cap on the cartridge is never lined up with the fixed striker until the round is in the correct position for firing. After firing, mechanical safety is produced by the inertia of the breech-block which holds the case in the chamber where it is supported until such time as the pressure has dropped to a safe level.

There are, however, other hazards with a sub-machine gun. The early Sten for example could be dropped on its butt and the inertia of the bolt would set it back sufficiently to feed, chamber and fire a round. Sometimes more than one round was fired. With the USA M3 it is possible to pull back the bolt with the forefinger to cock it and let the bolt slip from a sweaty finger before the bent and sear can engage. The bolt has come back far enough to pass over the next round in the magazine which is fed, chambered and fired. Neither of these failings can occur with the Steyr SMG. The breech-block has three bents.

The first bent is the front edge of the block and this engages the sear before the bolt has moved back enough to pass over the base of the round in the magazine. This is about 4cm of backward travel. The second bent

The bolt of the MPI 69 SMG showing the three bents and the fixed firing pin (RMCS)

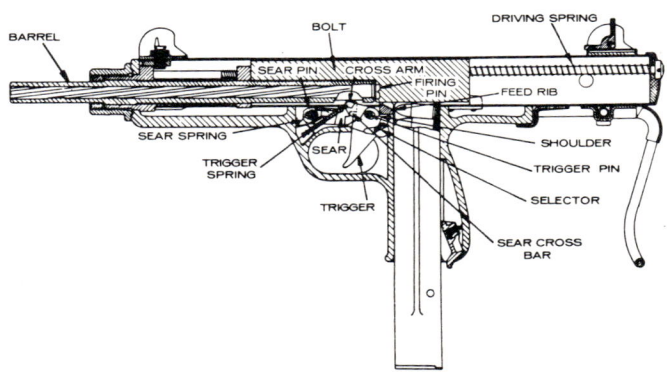

Sectioned view of the MPi 69 SMG

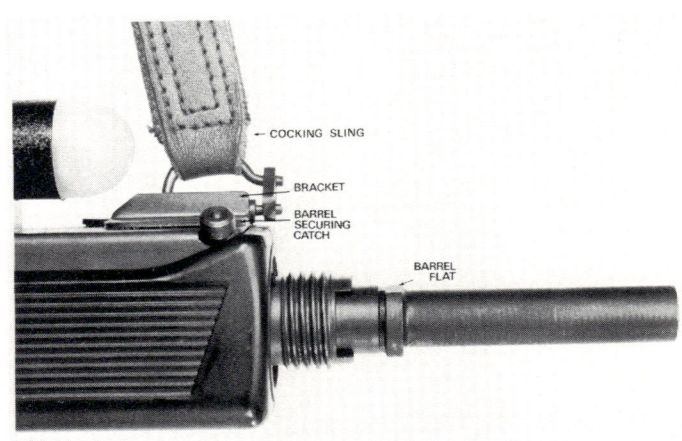

The cocking arrangements of the MPi 69 SMG (RMCS)

allows the bolt a further centimetre or so of travel and the same distance further back is the third bent. It was found to be impossible to bounce the bent off the sear in any of the three positions.

The third bent is the normal working bent and the second bent is provided to prevent a runaway gun when using 9mm ammunition of lower impulse than usual. The weapon cannot be accidentally discharged and is at least as safe as others with more complicated safety arrangements.

The trigger pull averages a little over 2kg.

The cocking lever is a pressing running in a groove at the top of the left side of the receiver at the front. The method of cocking is unusual. The sling is attached to the cocking lever and the soldier cocks the gun by pulling back on the sling. To prevent this happening unintentionally a bracket is welded to the top of the receiver which prevents movement of the cocking lever backwards unless the sling is held out at right angles to the gun.

STRIPPING

The weapon is easy to strip and re-assemble. To remove the bolt press the button at the rear of the receiver and lift the catch. The bolt can be pulled straight out by the nylon plate attached to the return spring rod.

To remove the barrel, pull back the barrel securing catch, rotate and remove the barrel housing and the barrel is free.

To remove the nylon moulding holding the trigger mechanism, extend the shoulder stock, push the moulding forward, drop the rear and push straight off over the front. All this can be done in 15 seconds.

The weapon can be reassembled, in reverse order, in 15 seconds. There is only one point to watch. The barrel has a flange with a flat on each side. These flats are not parallel so the barrel will only go into the housing in one position. Apart from this minor point there are no snags and obviously the stripping of the weapon has been carefully studied in the design stage.

SIGHTS

The weapon can be provided either with a cheap sight consisting of a rear aperture with two leaves giving 100 and 200m which is zeroed entirely on the front sight which is rotated and then locked; or with the Singlepoint ht.

DATA
Cartridge: 9mm × 19 Parabellum
Method of operation: Blowback
Method of locking: Nil
Method of feed: 25-round or 32-round box magazine
Method of fire: Selective

WEIGHTS
Gun without magazine: 2.95kg
25-round magazine-empty: 0.227kg
Gun with loaded magazine: 3.52kg
Trigger pull: 2.27kg

LENGTHS
Gun, butt extended: 673mm
Gun, butt retracted: 470mm
Barrel length: 260mm

MECHANICAL FEATURES
Barrel: Diameter across grooves: 8.76mm
          Diameter across lands: 8.76mm
          Rifling: 6 grooves RH. 1 turn in 254mm
          Cooling: Air
Sights: Zeroing: Elevation. Foresight screws up or down
          Line: Foresight on eccentric
          Sight radius: 340mm
(Alternatives of Singlepoint sight or 100/200mm flip rearsight and cylindrical post foresight)

FIRING CHARACTERISTICS
Muzzle velocity: 381metres/sec
Muzzle energy: 51mkp
Chamber pressure: 2,151kg/cm²
Rate of fire: Cyclic: 550 rounds/min
            Auto: 100 rounds/min
            SS: 50 rounds/min

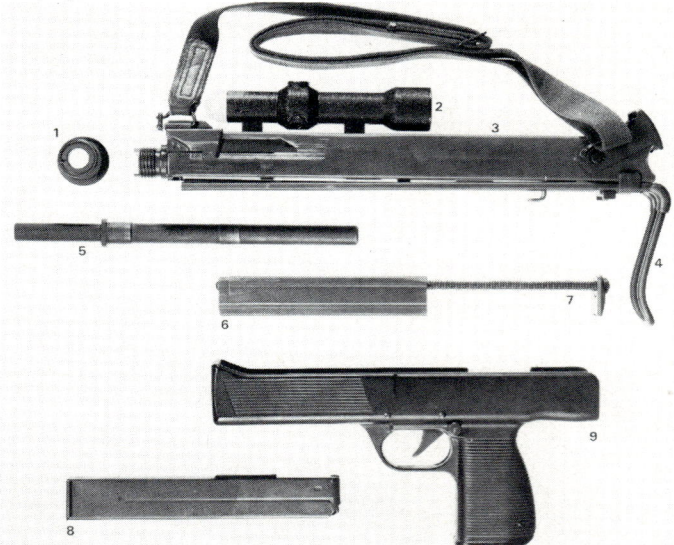

The 9mm MPi 69 SMG field stripped. Key: (1) Barrel securing nut; (2) Singlepoint sight; (3) Receiver; (4) Stock; (5) Barrel; (6) Bolt; (7) Driving spring and rod; (8) Magazine; (9) Receiver cover and pistol grip (RMCS)

Range, maximum effective: 200 metres
Manufacturer: Steyr-Daimler-Puch AG, Steyr
Status: In production. It has been tested by the Austrian Army and a trial consignment was evaluated in Saudi Arabia

.22in AM180 SMG

This light selective-fire weapon has been produced by Voere GmbH, is of simple and robust construction and is easy to operate. Blowback-operated, it fires .22 long rifle ammunition and has little recoil, muzzle blast, barrel climb or body rotation, although the cycle rate of fire is very high, and a test firing of over 50,000 rounds produced no noticeable wear or decrease in accuracy. The weapon has a detachable butt and employs a drum magazine.
DATA
Calibre: .22 LR

Operation: Blowback
Feed: 177-round drum magazine
Fire: Selective
Weight unloaded: 3.9kg
Weight loaded: 4.5kg
Length: 90cm overall or 64.5cm without butt
Rate of fire: 1680 rounds/min cyclic
Effective range: 90 metres (160 metres maximum)
Manufacturer: Voere GmbH, Kufstein, Austria

BELGIUM

9mm MITRAILLETTE VIGNERON M2 SMG

After the Second World War the Belgian Army adopted the Mitraillette Vigneron M2 in 1953. This was designed by Colonel Vigneron, a retired Belgian army officer, and manufactured by the Société Anonyme Précision Liègeoise at Herstal near Liège.

The Vigneron M2 is made from sheet metal stampings. It is a blowback operated design with a rather longer barrel than is customary in a weapon so operated. The cooling rings around the barrel and the compensator add to the cost of the barrel production without, apparently, significant improvement in performance. The stock is made of steel wire and telescopes along the receiver. There are three alternative positions. The pistol grip contains a grip safety which must be held in before the sear can release the bent of the bolt. The selector has three positions – safe, single and automatic. When the lever is set to automatic it is still possible to obtain single shots by first pressure on the trigger and full automatic when the trigger is fully in.

In addition to the Belgian armed forces the Vigneron was issued to the 'Force Publique' in the Congo and when that country became independent some of the Vignerons remained with them.

DATA
Cartridge: 9mm Parabellum
Method of operation: Blowback
Method of locking: Nil
Method of feed: 32-round box magazine
Method of fire: Selective
Weight, unloaded: 3.29kg
Weight, loaded: 3.69kg
Length, butt extended: 886mm

The 9mm Mitraillette Vigneron (RSAF)

Length, butt retracted: 706mm
Barrel: 305mm with compensator
        Rifling: 6 grooves RH
Sights: Foresight: Blade
        Rearsight: Aperture set for 50 metres
Muzzle velocity: 381 metres/sec
Muzzle energy: 55mkp
Rate of fire: Cyclic: 620 rounds/min
            Auto: 120 rounds/min
            SS: 40 rounds/min
Range, maximum effective: 200 metres
Manufacturer: Société Anonyme Précision Liègeoise, Herstal
Status: No longer in production. In service with Belgian Forces. Formerly in service in the Belgian Congo and probably still used in the area

BRAZIL

.45 INA SMG MB50 and MODEL 953

The MB 50 is a copy of the Danish Madsen Model 1946 made under licence by the Industria National de Armas SA, São Paulo, Brazil. It has the Brazilian crest on the left side of the receiver and is marked "Exercito Brasileiro". The models used by the Police are marked 'Policia Civil'.

The weapon remains a true copy of the Madsen.

The Model 953 has an enlarged magazine housing which has a wire clip around the mouth to keep the two halves together. The cocking handle has been removed from the top of the receiver to the right side.

The INA strips in the same way as the Danish Model 1946.

DATA
Cartridge: .45 ACP
Method of operation: Blowback
Method of locking: Nil
Method of feed: 30-round magazine
Method of fire: Automatic
Weight, unloaded: 3.4kg
Weight, loaded: 4.32kg
Length, stock extended: 794mm
Length, stock retracted: 546mm
Barrel: 213mm
  Rifling: 4 groove RH
Sights: Foresight: Blade
  Rearsight: Aperture 100 metres
Muzzle velocity: 280metres/sec
Muzzle energy: 63mkp
Rate of fire: Cyclic: 650 rounds/min
  Auto: 120 rounds/min
  SS: 40 rounds/min

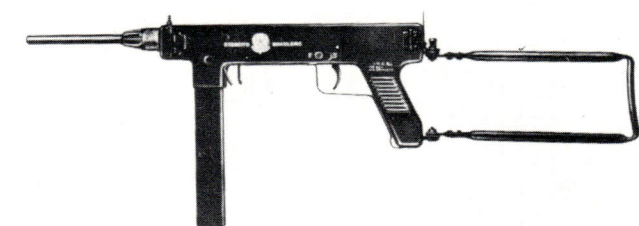

INA .45 MB 50 SMG

Range, maximum effective: 200 metres
Manufacturer: Industria National de Armas SA, São Paulo
Status: No longer in production. Still in service with reserve units

---

BURMA

9mm BA52 SMG

This blowback-operated automatic SMG is a copy of the Italian TZ45 developed during the Second World War. It is of extremely simple design and easily made. Of tubular design and fitted with a small muzzle brake, it can otherwise be recognised by the grip safety located behind the magazine housing and its telescopic stock.

DATA
Calibre: 9mm Parabellum
Operation: Blowback

Feed: 40-round detachable box magazine
Fire: Automatic only
Weight: 3.75kg loaded
Length: Stock extended 810mm: stock retracted 560mm
Sights: Foresight: Blade
  Rearsight: Fixed aperture
Rate of fire: 100-120 rounds/min automatic
Effective range: 100 metres
Status: In service

CANADA

9mm SUB-MACHINE GUN C1

When the British L2A1 SMG was developed the Canadian Army made some modifications and Canadian Arsenals Ltd have produced the C1 since 1958. The differences between the C1 and the British Sterling and L2 series are not great. The magazine has been changed both in capacity and design. It no longer holds 34 rounds but only 30. A 10-round magazine has also been produced. The design change involves the removal of the rollers and the substitution of an orthodox magazine follower. The bayonet for the C1 is that from the FAL rifle whereas the L2A3 takes the No. 5 bayonet. The components are largely interchangeable between the two guns and the C1 is said to be cheaper to manufacture. The performance of the two weapons is much the same.

The 9mm C1 SMG (RSAF)

DATA
Cartridge: 9mm Parabellum
Method of operation: Blowback
Method of locking: Nil
Method of feed: 30-round box magazine
Method of fire: Selective
Weight, unloaded: 2.95kg
Weight, loaded: 3.46kg
Length, butt extended: 686mm
Length, butt folded: 493mm
Barrel: 198mm
  Rifling: 6 grooves RH

Sights: Foresight: Blade
  Rearsight: Flip. Aperture. 100 and 200 yards
Muzzle velocity: 366 metres/sec
Muzzle energy: 51mkp
Rate of fire: Cyclic: 550 rounds/min
  Auto: 120 rounds/min
  SS: 40 rounds/min
Range, maximum effective: 200 metres
Manufacturer: Canadian Arsenals Ltd, Long Branch, Ontario
Status: No longer manufactured. In service with Canadian armed forces

---

CHINA (PEOPLE'S REPUBLIC)

7.62mm TYPES 43 and 50 SMG

The Chinese Communists turned to Russia for supplies during the Korean War and were provided with the Russian PPSh-41 SMG and the PPS-43. Both of these are described in the pages on Russian SMGs. The Chinese subsequently manufactured the PPSh-41 as the Type 50 SMG. This differs from the Russian produced gun only in the markings. The PPS-43 was manufactured in China and known as the Type 43 Copy SMG. At one time this weapon was called the Type 54 SMG in the West but this nomenclature has since been found to be incorrect. Again the only difference between the Soviet and the Chinese SMGs is the markings.

7.62mm Type 50 SMG, a copy of the Soviet PPSh-41 (RMCS)

7.62mm Type 43 copy SMG. This is the Chinese copy of the Russian PPS-43 (RMCS)

7.62mm Type 43 copy SMG. Note the position of the folded stock

7.62mm TYPE 64 SILENCED SMG

This is a Chinese designed and constructed SMG. It has a number of features taken from various European weapons and put together to make up a composite SMG. The bolt action is the same as the Type 43 Copy SMG which was taken from the Soviet PPS-43. The trigger mechanism, giving selective fire, was taken from the Bren gun, numbers of which fell into Chinese hands during the Korean War. This mechanism was itself derived from that of the Zb series of light machine guns which were purchased from Czechoslovakia by the pre-war mainland government. The weapon is blowback actuated using the 7.62mm × 25 pistol cartridge held in a curved magazine located under the receiver. The chamber contains 3 flutes each 0.1mm wide and 0.075mm deep, extending from the commencement of the small cone to just beyond the mouth of the chamber – a total length of 10mm. The suppressor is of the Maxim type. The barrel is 20cm long. The first 125mm are perfectly normal. For a distance of 60mm there are four rows of holes, each following the rifling groove, and each having 9 holes of 3mm diameter, making 36 holes in all. The tube surrounding the barrel continues forward for a further 165mm and then there is a muzzle cap. Between the end of the barrel and the cap is a stack of baffles. Each of these is dished with a central hole of 9mm diameter and two rods pass down through the baffles keeping the stack together and properly lined up. The rods can be rotated and then are free to come out through the baffles, allowing ready disassembly.

The suppressor is reasonably effective and also has the virtue of preventing any flash from either muzzle or breech. The long slim outline of the silenced SMG is readily recognised.

DATA
Cartridge: 7.62mm × 25 'P' Ball
Method of operation: Blowback
Method of locking: Nil
Method of feed: 30-round, curved box magazine
Method of fire: Selective
Weight empty: 3.4kg

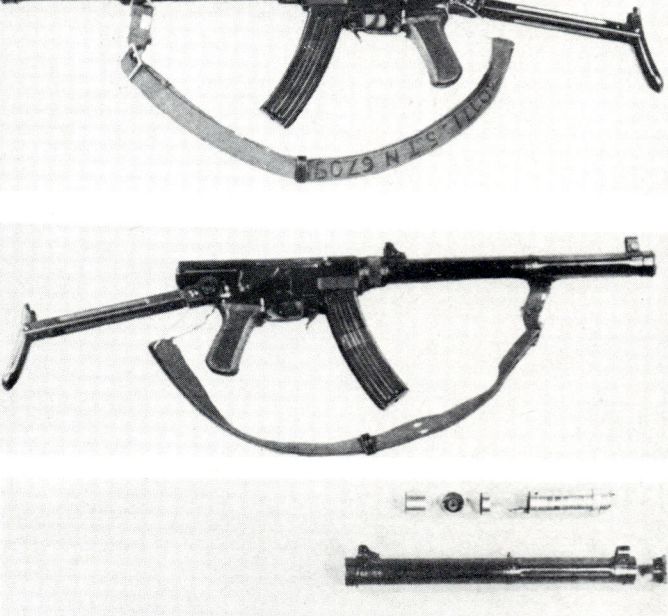

The 7.62mm Type 64 Silenced SMG. **Top:** *Right side.* **Middle:** *left side.* **Bottom:* Suppressor stripped*

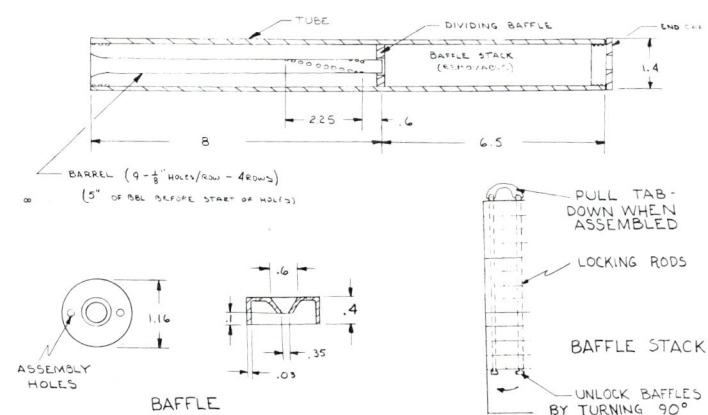

A sketch of the suppressor of the Type 64 silenced SMG

Weight of bolt: 390g
Length, stock open: 843mm
Length, stock closed: 635mm
Barrel: Length: 244mm
             Rifling: 4 grooves RH
Muzzle velocity; 513 metres/sec
Muzzle energy: 75mkp
Rate of fire: Cyclic: 1315 rounds/min
Range,maximum effective: 135 metres
Manufacturer: State factories
Status: No longer manufactured. In service with Chinese units. Used by North Vietnamese units during the Vietnam war and probably still there

CHINA (TAIWAN)

CHINESE SMG

The Chinese came to Taiwan with a very mixed collection of weapons. During the Second World War they received very large quantities of arms flown in from the United States. After the war some of these were copied in factories in mainland China and the Japanese plants in Manchuria were set to work for them. When they arrived in Taiwan they were supplied by the USA with the necessary machinery to produce their own weapons.

The Chinese not only had Thompson .45 SMGs but made the Thompson model 1921. The US wartime M3 and M3A1 SMGs were supplied to the Nationalists and they manufactured a copy of the M3A1 known as the Type 36. (It should be noted that the Nationalists use a calendar starting with the date of China's nationalist revolution which was 1911. Thus the Type 36 was made in 1947.) The Type 37 was a copy of the M3A1 made in 9mm Parabellum.

Status: The Thompson, the US M3A1 and its copy, the Type 36, are still first line weapons on Taiwan. The Type 37 is less commonly encountered. All these weapons are also to be found elsewhere in the Far East.

CZECHOSLOVAKIA

9mm ZK 383 SMG

The Czechs have produced a lot of very good sub-machine guns but not all of them have sold as well or achieved as high a reputation as they deserved.

The ZK383 was designed by Josef and Frantisek Koucky in 1933 at the Zbrojovka plant in Brno. It remained in service until 1948. It has some unusual features including a bipod and a quick change barrel. There was a choice of two rates of fire of 500 or 700 rounds/minute. This was achieved by having a removable 170gm weight in the bolt.

The ZK 383 was used by Bulgarian Troops in World War II and continued in service until 1960. It was also used by the SS. Some were sold to Venezuela, Bolivia and Brazil and although not now used by military units may be available to police forces.

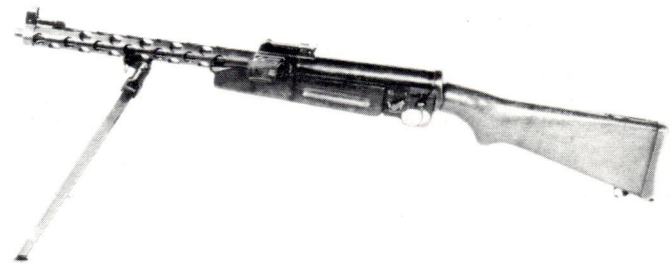

Czechoslovakian ZK 383 9mm SMG (RSAF)

9mm ZK 466 SMG

This was designed by the Koucky brothers in 1948 and produced in limited numbers by the Brno factory. This gun had a folding magazine housing which lay up under the receiver when not in use. The stock was similar to that of the USA M3 SMG. There were two safeties – a grip safety, and a position on the selector located on the left of the receiver. The weapon was only 43cm long and was advertised for airborne use.

9mm ZK 467 SMG

This was a further weapon designed by Josef and Frantisek Koucky. It was unusual in that it fired from a closed breech. The bolt in this weapon partly surrounded the barrel.

A number of other weapons were designed by the Koucky brothers (ZK 476, 480, Cz 47, Cz 247) but these were all produced in very small numbers.

VZ 23, 24, 25 and 26 SMGs

These were all designed by Vaclav Holek and were produced in 1949. They differ only in cartridge and butt-stock.

The VZ 23 fires 9mm × 19 Parabellum cartridges and has a wooden stock.

The Vz 25 fires 9mm × 19 Parabellum cartridges and has a folding metal stock.

The Vz 24 fires the 7.62mm × 25 pistol cartridge and has a wooden stock.

The Vz 26 fires the 7.62mm × 25 pistol cartridge and has a folding metal stock.

All the guns are blowback operated, selective fire weapons and use box magazines.

The 9mm capacity is 24 or 40 and the 7.62mm magazines hold 32 rounds.

The weapons offer selective fire with control exercised by trigger pull. A short pull produces single shots and a long pull produces automatic fire. The bolt is of the wrap round variety with the firing pin and breech face located well back from the front of the bolt which envelops the breech at the moment the firing pin reaches the chambered round.

All the weapons carry a magazine filler on the right side of the foregrip. The Vz 24 and Vz 26 have magazines that slope forward whereas those of the Vz 23 and Vz 25 are vertical.

The Vz 23 and Vz 25 – firing the 9mm Parabellum cartridge – were in service with the Czech army in 1951 and 1952 and were then replaced by the 7.62mm × 25 Vz 24 and Vz 26, which remained in service until 1962. This was but one example, of many, of the USSR forcing the satellites to conform and use the standard Russian cartridge.

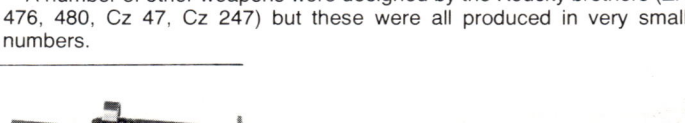

Czechoslovakian 9mm Model 23 (RSAF)

9mm Czechoslovakian Vz 25 SMG (RSAF)

DATA

Vz 23, 25
Cartridge: 9mm × 19 Parabellum
Method of operation: Blowback
Method of locking: Nil
Method of feed: 24- or 40-round box magazine
Method of fire: Selective
Weight: Vz 23: 3.27kg
           Vz 25: 3.5kg
Length (stock extended): 686mm
Length (stock folded): 445mm
Barrel: 284mm
      Rifling: 6 grooves RH
Muzzle velocity: 381 metres/sec
Muzzle energy: 55mkp
Rate of fire: Cyclic: 650 rounds/min

Range, maximum effective: 200 metres
Manufacturer: Ceskoslovenska Zbrojovka, Brno
Status: No longer manufactured. No longer in Czech military service. Many used in Nigerian Civil War. Supplied to Cuba and Syria where some are probably still in use.

Vz 24, 26
As Vz 23, 25 except
Cartridge: 7.62mm × 25 Pistol 'P'
Magazine: 32 rounds
Weight: 3.41kg
Stock: non-folding
Rifling: 4 grooves RH
Muzzle velocity: 550m/sec
Muzzle energy: 87mkp
Status: No longer made. Certainly in first-line service until 1962 and still used in Czechoslovakia.

DENMARK

9mm HOVEA M49 SMG

This weapon was designed in Sweden at the Husqvarna arms factory and competed with the Carl Gustav weapon in arms trials at which the latter weapon (the M45) was selected for Swedish use. The Hovea SMG was preferred by the Danish authorities, however, and they purchased a quantity together with a manufacturing licence; and Danish-built weapons are still in service with Danish forces.

The weapon was originally designed to take the Finnish 50-round magazine, but this was subsequently replaced by the 36-round Carl Gustav box. Fitted with a rectangular folding stock, the Hovea M49 bears a superficial resemblance to both the Carl Gustav M45 and the Madsen weapons.

DATA
Calibre: 9mm Parabellum
Operation: Blowback
Fire: Automatic only
Feed: 36-round detachable box (see text)
Weight: 3.4kg empty. 4.0kg loaded
Length: Stock extended 810mm. Stock retracted 550mm. Barrel 215mm
Sights: Foresight: Blade
    Rearsight: V-notch flip 100/200 metres
Rate of fire: 600 rounds/min cycle
Effective range: 150 metres
Manufacturer: HaerensVabenarsenalat, Kølenharn
Status: In Danish Army service

9mm MADSEN MODEL 50 SUB-MACHINE GUN

The Danish firm of Madsen has produced a series of SMGs of the same basic simple design. These are the M1946, M1950, M1953 and the Mk II. All have the same rectangular section folding stock. The M1946 had a shaped cocking handle which fitted over the receiver and down on each side; the M1950 has a small cylindrical knob on top of the receiver; the M1953 has a knurled cylindrical barrel nut that screws on to the barrel whereas the 1946 and 1950 models have a grooved nut fitting onto the receiver. The magazines of the M1946 and M1950 are 32-round, single position feed, straight flat sided types. Those of the Model 1953 and Mk II are current two position feed types also holding 32 rounds. The Mk II is the only one giving selective fire: it may have a peforated barrel jacket. A feature of these SMGs is a grip safety located behind the magazine wall. This has to be pressed forward before the weapon can be cocked or fired. It engages the bent in the bolt to hold it when the bolt is cocked and blocks the sear when the bolt is forward.

The 9mm Madsen 1953 Mk2 with jacket

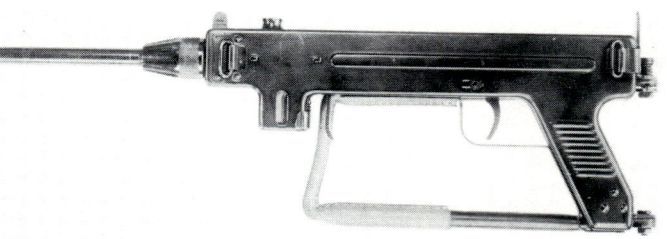

9mm Madsen Model 50 (RMCS)

OPERATION

The 32-round magazine is most easily loaded by employing a filler which is carried inside the pistol grip. To get at it means opening up the two halves of the receiver shell and so putting the gun out of action for a short while. As a result the filler is not always used and hand filling is adopted which can be difficult as the magazine spring is progressively compressed. A broad bladed screwdriver is often employed to push the cartridge down. The filler fits over the top of the magazine and has a plunger to depress the magazine follower. The base of the cartridge is slid under the lips whilst the plunger takes the weight of the spring, and pushed fully home when the plunger is released.

When the grip safety is pushed forward, and the trigger operated, the sear will release the bolt which will go forward under the action of the compressed return spring. The feed rib on the bottom of the bolt picks up the top cartridge in the magazine and feeds it up over the bullet guide into the chamber. The cartridge is chambered, the extractor snaps into the groove and the fixed firing pin on the bolt face fires the cap whilst the bolt is still moving forward. The gas pressure forces the cartridge case rearwards and the bolt movement is halted and reversed. The extractor holds the case to the bolt face until it hits the fixed ejector and is ejected to the right of the gun. The return spring is compressed. At the end of rearward travel the bolt is impelled forward again. If the trigger or grip safety has been released the bolt will be held back; otherwise the cycle is repeated until the magazine is empty.

Section of the Madsen Model 1946

STRIPPING

Basically the same procedure for stripping is used for all the Madsen SMGs. There is a slight difference for the Model 1946 where the cocking handle must be pulled up and out of the bolt after releasing the spring loaded detent.

The magazine in each case is removed and the chamber and feedway inspected to see that they are empty. The barrel nut is unscrewed and removed. With the Mk II model fitted with a barrel jacket, unscrew the jacket which carries the barrel nut. The receiver can now be opened up like a suitcase, hinged at the rear. The barrel will lift out. The return spring and its guide rod come out after the rear end of the guide rod has been eased forward to unseat it. The bolt lifts out.

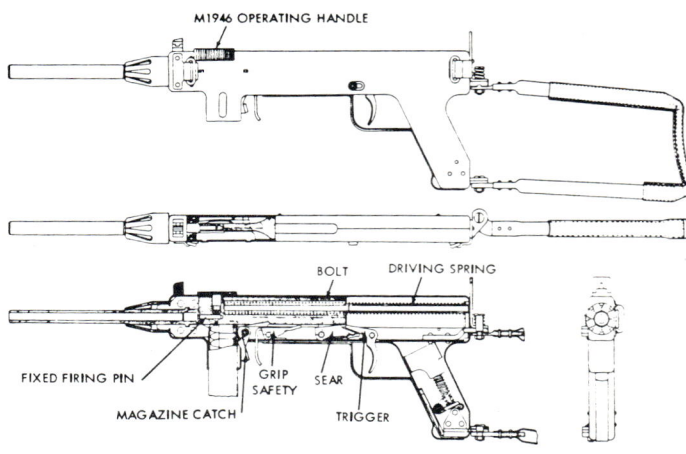

Sectioned view of the Madsen Model 50

DATA
Length, stock extended: 793.7mm
Length, stock folded: 528.3mm
Weight, empty: 3.2kg
Barrel length: 198.12mm
Magazine capacity: 32 rounds
Type of fire: Automatic
Muzzle velocity: 390 metres/sec
Practical range: 100 metres
Rate of fire: 100 rounds/min
        Cyclic: 550 rounds/min
        Selective: 40-50 rounds/min (Mk II only)
Range, maximum effective: 150 metres

Manufacturer: Dansk Industri Syndikat, Madsen, Kølnhavn
Status: In service with Danish police forces and with the armed forces of several South American countries. Also found in South East Asia. Made under licence by INA in Brazil

FINLAND

9mm M1931 SMG

Finland was a leader in Europe in the design of SMGs after the First World War. The principal designer was Aimo Johannes Lahti who produced a number of designs in the very early 1920s. His weapons were called 'Suomi' which means 'Finland'. The 1922, firing the 7.65mm Parabellum was his first model. It was not produced and was followed by the Model 1926 which was adopted by the Finnish Army in 7.65mm Parabellum. Some guns were made in 9mm Mauser and these had a large buffer housing behind the receiver. The model 1926 had some unusual features — a compressed air buffer, a quick change barrel and the first non-reciprocating cocking handle.

The Model 1931, which followed the Model 1926, was very successful. In Finland it was made by Oy Tikkakoski Ab, in Sweden by Husqvana and by Hispano-Suiza in Switzerland. It was sold also to Norway. The M1931 was very heavy – extremely well made but as it was all machined from the solid it was very expensive. The magazine was original. It consisted of two compartments separated by a central partition extending to about 4cm from the top, each with its own follower and spring. The rounds fed to a single position exit at the top.

There was a 71-round drum magazine which was later copied by the Russians in the PPD 34/38 SMG.

DATA
Cartridge: 9mm Parabellum
Method of operation: Blowback
Method of locking: Nil
Method of feed: 50-round box magazine or 71-round drum magazine
Method of fire: Selective
Weight unloaded: 4.68kg

The 9mm Suomi 31

Weight loaded with 71-round drum: 7.09kg
Length: 870mm
Barrel: 318mm
    Rifling: 4 grooves RH
Muzzle velocity; 399 metres/sec
Muzzle energy: 61mkp
Rate of fire: Cyclic: 900 rounds/min
        Automatic: 120 rounds/min
        SS: 40 rounds/min
Range, maximum effective: 200 metres
Manufacturer: Oy Tikkakoski A6, Sakava.
Status: In service in Finland. No longer made

9mm MODEL 1944 SMG

This is a copy of the Russian PPS-43 using the 9mm Parabellum cartridge. A large number were made in Finland in 1944 before the war ended and the weapon is still in service, having been modified to take the Carl Gustav 36-round magazine as well as the 71-round drum magazine.

The M44 was manufactured at Oy Tikkakoski Ab and the manager of that factory, Willi Daugs, moved to Sweden at the end of the war, on to Holland and then to Spain. He took the manufacturing drawings of the MP44 and subsequently the gun was produced at Oviedo as the Dux SMG. As this was produced by Ludwig Vorgrimmler of Mauser and later by J G Anschutz at Ulm there is mention of the Dux in the section on German weapons.

DATA
Cartridge: 9mm × 19 Parabellum
Method of operation: Blowback
Method of locking: Nil
Method of feed: 36-round box magazine or 71-round drum

Method of fire: Automatic
Weight unloaded: 2.9kg
Weight loaded: 3.6kg (36-round box magazine) 4.3kg (71-round drum)
Length stock extended: 831mm
Length stock folded: 622mm
Barrel: 249mm
    Rifling: 4 grooves RH
Sights: Foresight: Blade
    Rearsight: Notch
Muzzle velocity: 399 metres/sec
Muzzle energy: 61mkp
Rate of fire: Cyclic: 650 rounds/min
        Auto: 120 rounds/min
Range, maximum effective: 200 metres
Manufacturer: Oy Tikkakoski Ab, Sakava
Status: No longer manufactured. In service with Finnish troops

FRANCE

7.65mm MAS MODEL 38

This SMG followed the experimental model produced in 1935, the MAS 35, and used the 7.65mm Long cartridge which was a cartridge used only by France in the SMG role. The gun was manufactured by machining from the solid. It has a distinctive 'broken back' appearance because the barrel was angled to the receiver to avoid a high sight line. The breech block travels at an angle to the line of the bore and so the front face is angled back to fit flush as the round is chambered. The bolt travels well back beyond the sear and so on its forward travel has acquired a lot of kinetic energy when it strikes the sear. To prevent damage the sear is spring buffered – a feature found in no other SMG.

Efforts were made to keep out dirt by having a spring loaded plate on the magazine well which closes it off when the magazine is withdrawn.

To lock the bolt in either the forward or cocked position, the trigger is pushed forward inside the trigger guard – another unique feature.

When the gun is fully cocked the cocking handle opens the ejector port and is then disconnected from the bolt and retained to the rear, to prevent it reciprocating and at the same time to keep the ejection port open.

The MAS 38, although accurate, lacked penetration. It was produced in 1939 and production continued throughout the German occupation. It was used in the French Indo-China campaign and many fell into the hands of the Viet Cong and were used in the recent war.

DATA
Cartridge: 7.65mm Long
Method of operation: Blowback
Method of locking: Nil
Method of feed: 32-round detachable box magazine
Method of fire: Automatic

7.65mm MAS Model 38 (RMCS)

Weight unloaded: 2.87kg
Weight loaded: 3.40kg
Length: 734mm
Barrel: 224mm
    Rifling: 4 grooves RH
Sights: Foresight: Blade
    Rearsight: Notch
Muzzle velocity: 351 metres/sec
Muzzle energy: 35mkp
Rate of fire: Cyclic: 600 rounds/min
        Auto: 120 rounds/min
Range, maximum effective: 150 metres
Manufacturer: Manufacture d'Armes de St Etienne
Status: No longer manufactured. Not in military service in France but may be found elsewhere. Was in service in Vietnam

9mm MAT 49 SMG

At the conclusion of World War II the French Army was equipped with a variety of weapons of British, American and native origin. The Sten, Thompson and MAS 38 were all in use with a corresponding mixture of 9mm, .45in and 7.65mm Long cartridges.

The Section Technique de l'Arme (STA) set up a programme for future development in 1946. The experience of the war had shown the 7.65mm Long cartridge to be accurate but lacking in penetration; the .45 ACP although a powerful cartridge produced a heavy weapon. The 9mm

Parabellum, used by most Western European countries, possessed adequate range penetration and lethality, and was adopted. After a number of weapons had been designed and produced in limited numbers by the Arsenals at Chatellerault (MAC), Tulle (MAT) and St Etienne (MAS), the MAT 49 was selected for service.

The MAT 49 is a very solid, strongly made weapon making considerable use of stampings from heavy gauge steel sheet. It is of conventional blowback design, firing the 9mm × 19 cartridge, but has a number of features which, although not original, are seldom met.

The magazine housing can be pivoted forward in front of the trigger to allow the magazine to lie along the underside of the barrel jacket. A housing release is located forward of the trigger guard; when this is operated the housing – holding the 32 round magazine – can be rotated forward. When under the barrel jacket it is retained by the housing catch. When the housing catch is released the weight of a loaded magazine will swing it down into the firing position. The magazine housing is shaped to afford a firing grip for the left hand. When the housing is under the barrel it seals off the feed opening into the receiver and this, together with the spring loaded ejection port cover, makes the weapon proof against the ingress of sand, dirt etc into the working parts. When the magazine is housed under the barrel the weapon is completely safe since forward movement of the bolt, whether accidental or otherwise, cannot feed, chamber and fire a round. When the magazine is swung into the firing position, safety is provided by the grip safety which has two functions. It locks the bolt in the forward position and locks the trigger when the bolt is cocked. This ensures that if the weapon is inadvertently dropped or jarred, the bolt cannot move back from its forward position, under its own inertia, to chamber and fire a round, nor can the cocked bolt go forward. When the grip safety is operated by the act of grasping the pistol-grip, the trigger restraint is released and the lock preventing bolt movement is lowered. Since bolt movement is possible only when the grip safety is operated, no manual safety of the usual 'Fire' and 'Safe' type is required or provided.

The bolt is of interesting shape. The modern conception of design is to shorten the overall length of the SMG by using a 'wrap round' bolt, enveloping the chamber, with a fixed firing pin located towards the rear of the bolt. This puts three quarters of the barrel inside the bolt at the moment of firing. A suitable ejection slot is cut in the bolt and in many designs the bolt encloses some part of the barrel throughout its travel, to ensure the minimum displacement of the centre of mass of the bolt during firing and maximum consistency during the burst of fire. The bolt of the MAT 49 has a small, reduced section projection on the front face which enters a recess in the breech face – thus producing a wrap round barrel. The MAT 49 has a fixed firing pin and fires whilst the bolt is still moving forward; the design of the bolt face and breech ensures that shielding is provided to minimise the effects of both early firing and a hangfire.

The length of this French SMG can be adjusted by a sliding wire stock, similar to that of the USA M3 SMG. There are two indentations in which the stock latch can engage, giving the fully retracted position and an intermediate location as well as the fully extended stock required for firing from the shoulder.

OPERATION

The magazine is removed for filling. It is of the double column, single feed position type used in many early SMGs such as the Sten, and it is difficult to load without the filler even when using a screw driver or some similar improvised tool to press down the cartridges.

When the magazine is filled it is swung up and housed under the barrel if action is not imminent. When required it is dropped down into position for loading. After the weapon is cocked and provided the grip safety is pressed in, it can be fired at will. There is no safety catch as such. The bolt goes forward, the top round is chambered and the fixed firing pin crushes the cartridge cap whilst the bolt is still moving forward. The firing impulse checks the forward velocity of the bolt and then drives it back. The empty case is held to the breech face and the return spring is compressed. The case is ejected and when the compressed return spring forces the bolt forward another round is chambered.

TRIGGER MECHANISM

The trigger mechanism is extremely simple. The trigger is extended to form a ⌐. The end of the horizontal arm, (the trigger extension) lies under the front end of the sear. Rotation of the trigger raises the trigger extension and the front end of the pivotting sear. The rear of the sear falls and the bolt is freed to be driven forward by the return spring. Since the gun fires only at full auto the complication of a disconnector is avoided.

STRIPPING

Stripping is accomplished without the need of a tool. The gun is made safe by removing the magazine and checking the chamber. The magazine housing is freed from the receiver but not latched to the barrel jacket. This permits pressing in the knurled take down button under the rear end of the barrel jacket and the barrel and receiver can then be swung up off the trigger frame. The bolt and its return spring can then be withdrawn to the rear to complete field stripping. Re-assembly is carried out logically by returning the bolt and spring into the receiver. The rear of the receiver goes into the cap at the rear of the trigger frame and the front is dropped down and pressed back until the receiver and trigger frame lock together.

DATA
Cartridge: 9mm Parabellum
Method of operation: Blowback
Method of feed: 32-round box magazine

9mm MAT 49 SMG (RMCS)

The bolt of the MAT 49 SMG (RMCS)

The MAT 49 stripped (RMCS)

Method of fire: Automatic

WEIGHTS
Gun unloaded: 3.64kg
Loaded magazine: 0.64kg
Gun loaded: 4.76kg

LENGTHS
Gun, butt extended: 710mm
Gun, butt retracted: 558mm
Barrel: 228mm

MECHANICAL FEATURES
Barrel: 4 grooves LH
Sights: Foresight: Hooded blade
          Rearsight: Flip, aperture, 100 and 200 metre
          Zeroing: Foresight

FIRING CHARACTERISTICS
Muzzle velocity: 354 metres/sec
Muzzle energy: 69mkp
Rate of fire: Cyclic: 600 rounds/min
              Auto: 128 rounds/min
Range, maximum effective: 200 metres
Manufacturer: Manufacture d'Armes de Tulle, Tulle
Status: No longer in production. Standard weapon in the French Armed Forces and to be found elsewhere in former French territory

9mm GEVARM and GEVELOT SMG

This is a simple and sturdy weapon designed for satisfactory operation in a wide range of climatic conditions. It can be stripped and reassembled without tools and is fitted with a simple retractable wire stock.

DATA
Cartridge: 9mm Parabellum
Operation: Blowback
Feed: 32-round detachable box magazine
Fire: Selective

WEIGHTS
Gun unloaded: 3.2kg
Empty magazine: 318g
Full magazine: 715g

LENGTHS
Total length: (stock retracted) 500mm
Barrel length: 220mm

MECHANICAL FEATURES
Sights: Foresight: Blade
Rear sight: Flip. 50/100 metres
Sight radius: 450mm

FIRING CHARACTERISTICS
Rate of fire: 600 rounds/min
Effective range: 100 metres
Manufacturers: Société Gevarm & Gevelot, 50 rue Ampère, 75017 Paris, France
Status: Production

GERMANY (FEDERAL REPUBLIC)

9mm MP 18.1 SMG

The MP 18.1 was designed by Hugo Schmeisser and manufactured by the firm of Theodore Bergmann at Suhl. It was the first practical sub-machine gun – although the Italian Villar Perosa appeared earlier – and its sturdy configuration set a pattern that was adhered to until shortly before the 1939-45 war.

It was a blowback operated gun of simple design, using a cylindrical bolt, and fed from the snail magazine developed for the Luger pistol using an adaptor to prevent the magazine entering too far and fouling the bolt. The magazine was angled back at 45 degrees. In later models this was replaced by a housing holding a 20- or 32-round magazine on the left of the gun at right angles.

The MP 18.1 is no longer in service but it represents one of the turning points in the development of hand-held automatic weapons.

DATA
Cartridge: 9mm × 19 Parabellum
Method of operation: Blowback
Method of locking: Nil
Method of feed: Snail magazine with 32 rounds. Subsequently box magazine with 20 or 32 rounds
Method of fire: Automatic

The Schmeisser-designed MP 18.1 (RMCS)

Weight unloaded: 4.18kg
Weight loaded: 5.26kg
Length: 815mm
Barrel: 200mm
Rifling: 6 grooves RH
Sights: Foresight: Blade
Rearsight: Flip. Notch 100 and 200 metres
Muzzle velocity: 381 metres/sec
Muzzle energy: 55mkp
Rate of fire: Cyclic: 400 rounds/min
Auto: 120 rounds/min
Range, maximum effective: 200 metres

9mm ERMA SMGs

The firm of Erma-Werke at Erfurt played a significant part in SMG development. The gun designed by Heinrich Vollmer and named after him introduced some features which were retained in subsequent Erma designs.

9mm MP 38, MP 40, and MP38/40 SMGs

The MP 38 is generally referred to – with its immediate successors the MP 40 and MP 38/40 – as the 'Schmeisser'. This is a misnomer as the gun was not designed by Schmeisser but was the product of Erma-Werke. It was a great improvement on any previous SMG. It was of all metal construction with a good folding buttstock and was designed specifically for the new German concept of mobile, armoured warfare. The conventional wooden stock and fore-end were abolished, together with the perforated jacket which protected the barrel. The MP 38 was made from steel tubing with longitudinal slots machined along the receiver to reduce weight. The cover below the receiver was made of cast anodized aluminium with the foregrip and pistol grip of phenolic resin with a paper fibre filling. The double rod stock could be swung down and forward with a knurled release button above the left side of the pistol grip. The gun was costly to produce due to the high proportion of machining operations and the magazine was not ideal in its functioning. The weapon was manufactured only by Erma-Werke.
Status: No longer manufactured or in regular service in Europe. Was still in use in Asia until recently and may still be encountered

9mm MP 38 (RMCS)

9mm MP 38/40

9mm MP 40 SMG

The MP 40 was essentially an MP 38 modified for mass production in wartime. The receiver was made of stamped steel sheet, brazed and spot welded. There were no ridges along its length. The construction of the many sub-assembles was contracted out and widely dispersed.

The MP 40 was also made with a dual magazine, consisting of two 32-round magazines welded together side by side. This was introduced to counter the 71-round drum magazine used by the Russians. The magazine housing could be slid through the receiver and when the first magazine was empty, the gun could be re-cocked and the housing pushed through to

9mm MP 40 (RMCS)

move the new magazine into position. With the two magazines loaded it weighed 5.5kg. It was a heavy, cumbersome, arrangement and did not prove popular. It was known as the MP 40/2.

It was found in 1939, in Poland, that the bolt of the MP 38 would recoil when the weapon was dropped and when it went forward again a round would be fired. To combat this the two piece cocking handle of the MP 40 was used to replace that of the MP 38 and a slot was cut in the forward end of the cocking way to hold the bolt in the forward position. This gun was called the MP 38/40 and known by the Germans as the 'mixed model'.

9mm MP 40/2 (RSAF)

DATA
Cartridge: 9mm× 19 Parabellum
Method of operation: Blowback
Method of locking: Nil
Method of feed: 32-round box magazine
Method of fire: Automatic
Weight, unloaded: 4.03kg
Weight, loaded: 4.7kg
Length stock extended: 833mm
Length stock folded: 630mm
Barrel: 251mm
      Rifling: 6 grooves RH
Sights: Foresight: Blade
      Rearsight: Flip, notch 100 and 200 metres

Muzzle velocity: 381 metres/sec
Muzzle energy: 55mkp
Rate of fire: Cyclic: 500 rounds/min
      Automatic: 120 rounds/min
Range, maximum effective: 200 metres
Manufacturer: Erma-Werke, Erfurt
Status: No longer produced. No longer in regular European service but still widely used – especially in Asia

9mm ERMA 56 SMG

The Russians overran the Erma Works at Erfurt at the end of the Second World War and the workers fled west. In 1951 the factory was re-opened at Dachau in Bavaria. In the following years Erma produced a number of weapons.

The MP 56 was made from a design produced by Louis Camillis. It had a wrap round bolt and fired at full automatic. It was carried to the prototype stage and then the sponsor – one Fenner Achenbach – transferred the project to Mauser and it became the Mauser Model 57.

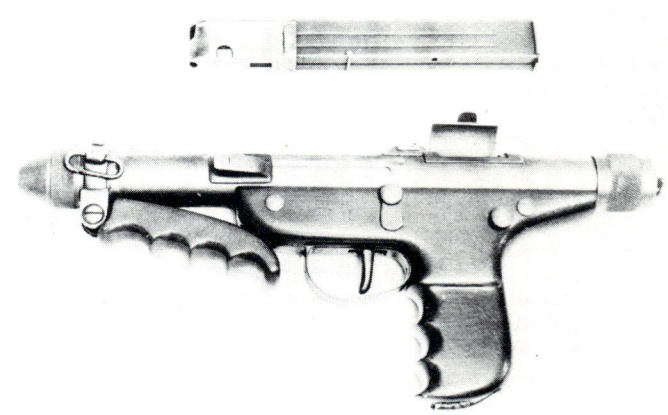

The Camillis-designed 9mm MP 56

9mm ERMA-PANZER (SMART) SMG

In 1958 the unusual Erma-Panzer was produced. This was a conventional SMG but some stress was laid on its ability to fire grenades at armour. It fired from a closed bolt and when tested at Meppen did well. It was not adopted.

The 9mm Erma-Panzer SMG

9mm ERMA MP 58 SMG

The Bundeswehr asked for a SMG to meet their requirements for a cheap SMG. The overall length was 16in, barrel 7.4in, weight 6.8lb with a cyclic rate of 650-680 rounds/min. It used the MP 40 magazine and was a blowback design employing the old Vollmer type of telescopic return spring. It was never fully developed.

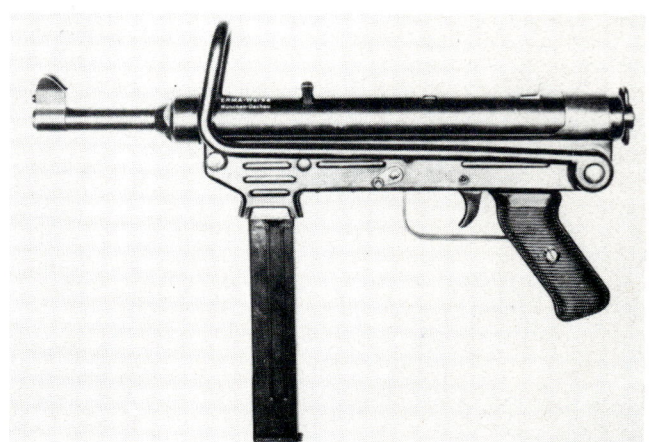

9mm Erma MP 58 SMG

9mm ERMA MP 59 SMG

The MP 59 was designed to meet the requirements of 400 to 450 rounds a minute and a hydraulic buffer was developed which functioned at a rate of 100 to 600 rounds/min. The seals did not stand up to their work and so the gun was redesigned. The barrel length was increased from 7.3 to 10.3in and given a longer body and therefore a longer bolt travel. A new magazine of double staggered column type, with alternate feed from each side , was adopted. The weapon functioned well but no order was placed.

9mm Erma MP 59 SMG

9mm ERMA MP 60 SMG

This was quite different from the traditional Erma approach. The receiver and barrel casing were stamped in one piece. The buttstock swung to the right of the gun. The bolt had two springs on rods passing through in the same way as the USA M3 SMG. The Volmer telescopic spring was not used.

The Swedish Carl Gustav magazine, with two separated compartments each with its own spring and follower, was adopted. Twenty guns were taken by the Bundeswehr for testing in September 1960 for troop trials and a further twenty models eight weeks later.

The Chief Engineer, Josef Eder, continued research and an MP 61 and finally the MP 64 were produced. After this Erma Werke gave up.

The 9mm MP 60

The 9mm MP 64. This was Erma's last SMG

9mm MAUSER MODEL 57 SMG

This was based on the design of Louis Bonnet de Camillis which had previously been used by Erma in their MP 56. It was different from the Erma in firing both single shot and full automatic. There was a pistol grip below the muzzle which folded back under the barrel. The magazine held 32 rounds and fitted into the grip behind the trigger. The double strut wire stock folded over the barrel giving a very short folded length of 43cm.

The Mauser MP 57. This 9mm SMG was based on the same design as the Erma MP 56

9mm MAUSER MODEL 60 SMG

Designed by Ludwig Vorgrimmler and Kimmick, this was Mauser's answer to the Erma-Panzer MP 58 and like that weapon it was intended to fire anti-tank grenades. There was a muzzle brake to reduce the heavy recoil produced by the grenade cartridge and also to act as a forward guide when the grenade was placed over the barrel. The bolt was locked by the selector axis as it was rotated to the grenade launching position. The weapon fired from a closed bolt using a hammer. It was an accurate gun and was impressive at its trials.

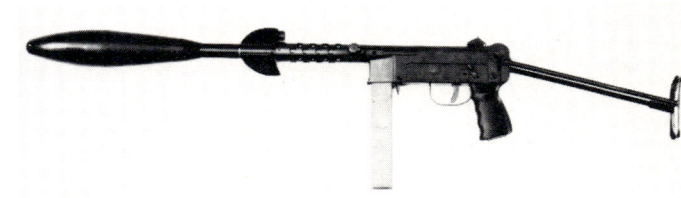

Mauser Model 60 9mm

9mm DUX SMGs

The original design for these weapons came from the Finnish MP 44. The manager of the Tikkakoski Arsenal brought the designs, eventually, to Spain and then Ludwig Vorgrimmler modified them for production at Oviedo. This model was the predecessor of the Dux 53. 1,000 models of the DUX 53 were ordered by the West German Border Guard – the Bundes Grenz Schutze – and delivered in 1954.

The Bundeswehr ordered 25 of these SMGs for evaluation and placed them with the German firms of Mauser, Anschutz, and Sauer and Sohn for modification. Eventually the design produced by Anschutz at Ulm-Donau was produced as the Dux 59. It is an improvement on and somewhat stronger than the 53 and looks less like the Soviet PPS 43.

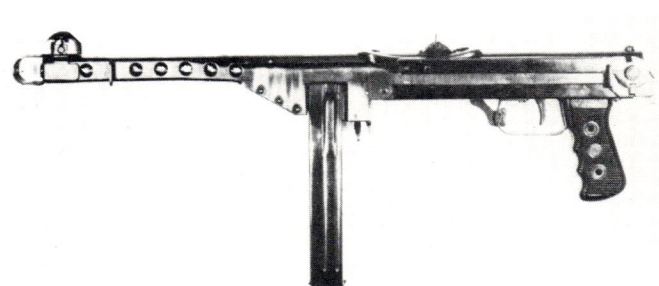

The 9mm Dux 53 SMG

DATA (DUX 53)
Cartridge: 9mm × 19 Parabellum
Method of operation: Blowback
Method of locking: Nil
Method of feed: 50-round Suomi box magazine
Method of fire: Automatic
Weight unloaded: 3.58kg
Weight loaded: 4.06kg
Length, stock extended: 826mm
Length, stock folded: 616mm
Barrel: 251mm
  Rifling: 6 grooves RH
Sights: Foresight: Blade
  Rearsight: Flip, notch 100 and 200 metres
Muzzle velocity: 381 metres/sec
Muzzle energy: 55mkp

9mm Dux 59 SMG

Rate of fire: Cyclic: 500 rounds/min
  Auto: 120 rounds/min
Range, maximum effective: 200 metres

Manufacturer: Mauser-Werke
Status: No longer manufactured. Still seen with West German Border Guards
DUX 59
As for DUX 53 except

Magazine: 32- or 40-round box
Weight, unloaded: 2.98kg
Weight, loaded: 3.58kg
Length, stock extended: 792mm
Length, stock folded: 582mm

9mm WALTHER MP-K and MP-L SUB-MACHINE GUNS

The two sub-machine guns are made by the firm of Walther at Ulm in West Germany, and differ only in the length of the barrel. The MP-L has a long barrel and the MP-K a short barrel. The weapons are not used by the armies of any major power but are used by various police and some naval forces. Both have selective fire systems and use 32-round box magazines. A silencer can be fitted.

The magazine, fitting into the magazine well below the weapon, is removed by pressing forward the magazine catch situated in front of the trigger guard. No filler is required to fill the magazine and none is issued with the weapon. The stock is of unusual design. When extended it is used in a conventional way in the firer's shoulder. When it is extended it can be swung back after pressing down on the stock release button situated above the top hinge. When folded, the shoulder piece becomes the forward grip for close quarter firing. The selector lever, located on the left of the receiver above the pistol grip, allows the choice of single shots (E), full automatic (D) and a safe position at S.

The sights are set for 100 metres and feature an unusual arrangement by which firing in poor light is accomplished using the upper open rear sight and the top of the front sight protector whilst in normal conditions the firer should use the lower aperture sight and the usual foresight. Since the gun operates from the open breech position the bolt will be held to the rear when the trigger is released.

The gun is prepared for firing by inserting the magazine, and cocking the action by pulling back the cocking handle on the right of the receiver. (Note that whereas the cocking handle does not normally travel back and forward with the bolt, it can be locked to the bolt, by pressing it inward, if it becomes necessary to work the bolt by hand when clearing a stoppage.) The selector lever is rotated to the desired mode of fire and operation of the trigger causes the sear to move down and the bolt to fly forward under the force of the compressed driving springs. The feed rib below the bolt slides the top round out of the magazine and it is guided into the chamber along the inclined bullet guide below the barrel. As soon as the cartridge is straightened up in the chamber, the extractor snaps into the groove and as the cartridge is slowed down in the chamber by friction force the fixed pin on the bolt face fires the cap. The bolt is still pushing the case forward when firing occurs and part of the firing impulse is used to overcome bolt foward momentum and the remainder to drive it back. The cartridge case acts as a piston to force the bolt back and remains held to the bolt face by the extractor until the fixed ejector flings it out through the ejection port on the right of the gun. The return spring is fully compressed and the bolt starts forward again. If the selector lever is at 'auto' the cycle is repeated, if it is at single shot the bolt is held up on the raised sear and remains to the rear.

The trigger mechanism functions as follows. The sear has a horizontally extended slot which enables it to move backward and forward on its mounting pin. The rear end is forced upwards and backwards by a spring which also forces the trigger forward. The trigger has a tripping mechanism.

When the selector lever is set to 'D' – automatic fire – the rotation of the lever spindle forces the sear forward so that the mounting pin is at the back of the elongated slot. When the trigger is pressed it rotates on its pin and the trip rises under the tail of the sear and the sear pivots on its mounting pin and the nose drops out of the notch in the bolt. The bolt goes forward and continues to reciprocate so long as the trigger is pressed and there is ammunition in the magazine. When the selector lever is set to 'E' or single shot fire, the sear is not constrained and can move forward or backward on its mounting pin according to the force applied. Initially it is forced back by the trigger spring. When the weapon is cocked the return spring forces the bolt forward and the sear also is pushed forward on its pin. When the trigger is pressed it rotates and the trip rises under the tail of the sear, depressing the nose, and the bolt goes forward. When the bolt goes forward and removes the forward force on the sear, the sear is forced back by the trigger spring and moves off the trip. The nose of the sear is then forced up and catches the bolt as it travels forward after firing only one round. The sear once more is forced forward, by the strength of the return spring, with its elongated slot sliding over the mounting pin. The sear strikes the trip and firing cannot be continued until the trigger is released to allow the trip to move back with the trigger, to a position under the tail of the sear. When the trigger is pulled, the trip lifts the tail of the sear and the nose of the sear drops and another round is fired.

When the change lever is turned to 'S', safe, a boss prevents any trigger movement. One feature of this trigger mechanism is a safety sear which catches and holds the bolt if it has been drawn back far enough to engage a round in the magazine but not far enough for the sear to hold it to the sear. This safety engages in an undercut in the bolt and so the bolt has to be pulled back to free it. This ensures the sear engaging the bent on the bolt.

Stripping the Walther MP-K or L, involves the following action. The magazine is removed and the gun cocked to inspect the bolt way and chamber. The bolt is allowed forward under control. The take down pin is located on the left of the receiver just forward of the magazine well.

The spring catch in this pin is pressed and the pin pulled out as far as it will go. Pressure under the barrel then separates the receiver into an upper and lower component. When the cocking handle is pulled back the return spring and bolt can be grasped and pulled out.

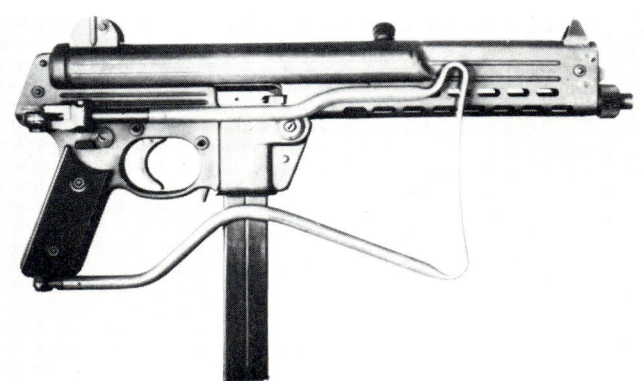

The 9mm Walther MP-L SMG

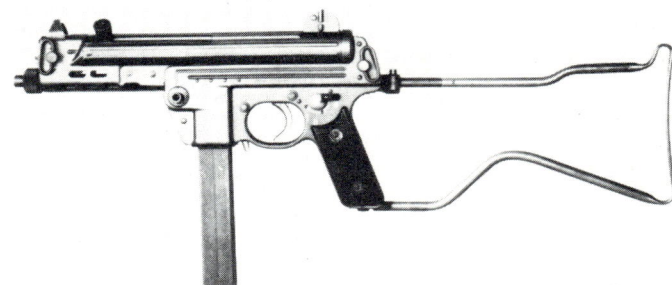

9mm Walther MP-K SMG

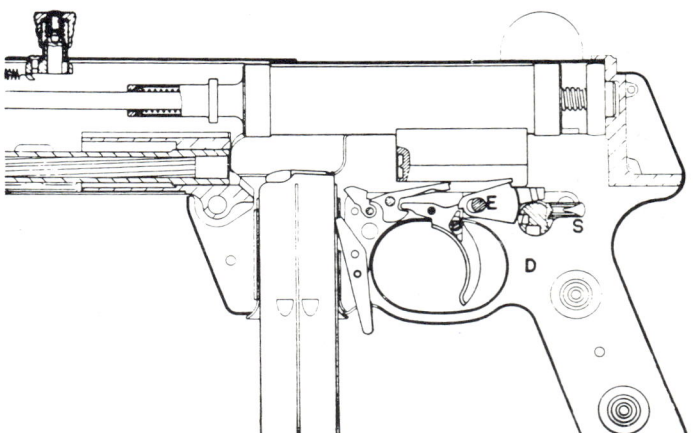

A sectioned view of the Walther MP

DATA
Cartridge: 9mm × 19
Method of operation: Blowback
Method of locking: Nil
Method of feed: 32-round box magazine
Method of fire: Selective

WEIGHTS
Gun only: 2.8kg
Magazine empty: 0.2kg
Magazine loaded (32rds): 0.625kg
Gun loaded: 3.425kg

LENGTHS
Gun, stock open: 653mm
Gun, stock closed: 368mm
Barrel: 171mm

MECHANICAL FEATURES
Barrel: Rifling: 6 grooves RH
       Cooling: Air
Sights: Foresight: Blade
       Rearsight: Notch – 75m. Aperture 125m
       Graduation: Nil
       Zeroing: Elevation. Foresight screws up and down
              Line: Foresight on eccentric
Sight radius: 270mm

FIRING CHARACTERISTICS
Muzzle velocity: 356 m/sec
Muzzle energy: 48mkp
Chamber pressure: 2,151 kg/cm²
Rate of fire: Cyclic: 550 rounds/min
                    Auto: 96 rounds/min
                      SS: 40 rounds/min
Manufacturer: Carl Walther, Ulm, Donau
Status: In use by German police forces and some naval forces

MP-L
As for MP-K except

WEIGHTS
Gun only: 3kg
Magazine loaded (32rds): 0.625kg
Gun loaded: 3.625kg

LENGTHS
Gun, stock open: 737mm
Gun, stock closed: 455mm
Barrel: 257mm
Sight radius: 357mm

FIRING CHARACTERISTICS
Muzzle velocity: 396m/sec
Muzzle energy: 60mkp

9mm HECKLER AND KOCH MP5 SMG

The MP5 SMG was developed from the G3 rifle and utilises the same method of operation. Some parts are interchangeable with those used on the rifle. The SMG was adopted in late 1966 by the Police Forces of Germany and by the Border police. It has been purchased by the military forces of several nations.

OPERATION

The magazine is removed from the gun by pushing forward the release catch. It is filled by putting a 9mm Parabellum cartridge on the magazine platform, pressing down until the cartridge is held under the magazine lips, and repeating until the magazine is full. There are 10-, 15- or 30-round magazines available. When the magazine is placed in the magazine well it is held in place by the spring loaded catch. The selector is located above the slightly behind the trigger. The weapon usually offers single shot or full automatic but a burst fire device, allowing 3-, 4- or 5-round bursts each time the trigger is operated, is offered by the manufacturers to those requiring this facility. In fact this trigger arrangement can be fitted to all automatic weapons in the Heckler and Koch series. The top position of the selector lever is 'safe' and the selector spindle lies over the trigger lug and prevents sufficient movement of the trigger to disengage the sear from the hammer notch.

The breech mechanism is of the same design as that used in the G3 rifle. It is ⌐ shaped with the long arm extended forward over the bolt head. It may be described, in brief, as a two-part bolt with rollers projecting from the bolt head. The more massive bolt body lies up against the bolt head when the weapon is ready to fire and inclined planes on the front lie between the rollers and force them out into recesses in the barrel extension. The weapon is unusual for a sub-machine gun in that it fires from a closed breech position using a hammer notch and the cap is struck. The gas pressure forces back on the bolt head which is unable to go back since the rollers are in the recesses in the barrel extension and must move in against the incline planes of the heavy bolt body. The selected-angles of the recesses and the incline on the bolt body, produce a velocity ratio of about 4:1 between the bolt body and the bolt head. Thus the bolt head only moves back about 1mm whilst the bolt body moves some 4mm. Due to the short barrel of the SMG the pressure drops quickly and there is no danger of excessive case protrusion whilst the internal pressure is high. As soon as the rollers are fully in, the two parts of the breech are driven back together. The empty case is held to the breech face by the extractor until it strikes the ejector arm and is thrown out of the ejection port to the right of the gun. The return spring is compressed during the backward movement of the bolt and drives the bolt forward. A round is fed into the chamber and the bolt face comes to rest. The bolt body continues to move forward and the inclined planes drive the rollers out again into the barrel extension recesses. The bolt body closes up to the bolt head and the weapon is ready to fire another round.

TRIGGER AND FIRING MECHANISM

If the selector is set to full auto the trigger has moved up sufficiently for the nose of the sear to be depressed so far that it does not re-engage the hammer and the next round is fired as soon as the bolt is fully closed, and the safety sear is moved out of engagement with the hammer. If the selector is located at single shot the trigger is unable to rise fully and the spring loaded sear holds the hammer until the trigger is released and re-pressed. Provided the bolt is fully closed the hammer will be released. The action is dealt with more fully in the description of the operation of the G3 rifle.

Sectioned view of the 9mm MP 5. Key: (1) Receiver with cocking lever housing; (2) Grip assembly; (3) Safety catch; (4) Rotary rear sight; (5) Sight support; (6) Sight base; (7) Butt stock; (8) Sling holder; (9) Butt plate; (10) Eyebolt; (11) Locking pin for handguard; (12) Handguard; (13) Cylindrical pin; (14) Hook; (15) Locking pin for grip assembly; (16) Magazine catch; (17) Locking pin for butt stock; (18) Front sight holder; (19) Cap; (20) Clamping sleeve for front sight; (21) Front sight; (22) Catch bolt; (23) Stop ring; (24) Rivet for catch lever; (25) Catch lever; (26) Catch spring; (27) Axle for cocking lever; (28) Cocking lever support with collar; (29) Stop pin for recoil spring; (30) Guide ring; (31) Recoil spring guide rod; (32) Clamping sleeve; (33) Bolt head carrier; (34) Firing pin with firing pin spring; (35) Release lever; (36) Elbow spring for trigger; (37) Hammer; (38) Ejector spindle; (39) Ejector; (40) Ejector pressure spring; (41) Screw socket with rivet; (42) Binding screw with locking washer; (43) Recoil spring; (44) Rivet; (45) Back plate; (46) Barrel; (47) Barrel extension; (48) Follower; (49) Follower spring; (50) Magazine tube; (51) Magazine floor plate; (52) Safety cup with guide bush; (53) Magazine catch lever with roller; (54) Transmitting piece for magazine catch; (55) Magazine release lever; (56) Elbow spring with roller; (57) Sear; (58) Trigger; (59) Safety pin; (60) Pressure shank and pressure spring; (61) Trigger housing; (62) Extractor with extractor spring; (63) Cocking lever; (64) Bolt head; (65) Locking roller; (66) Locking piece

Heckler and Koch MP 5 A2 SMG

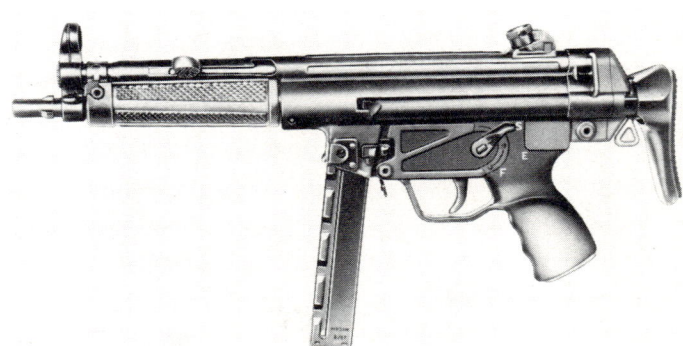

Heckler and Koch MP 5 A3

The Heckler and Koch MP 5 A2 with a telescopic sight

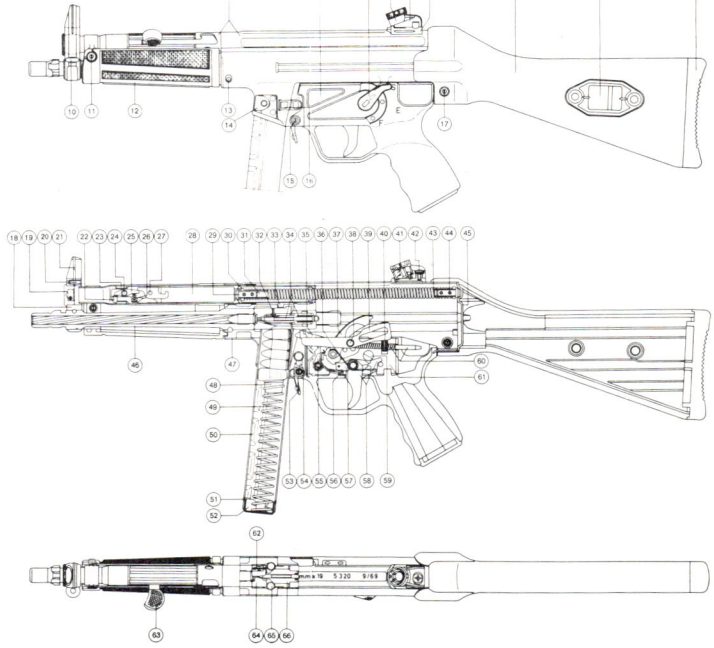

If a burst fire control is fitted a ratchet counting device in the trigger mechanism holds the sear off the hammer until the allotted number of rounds have been fired. This device ensures the correct number of cartridges are discharged in a single burst and any interruption – for example, the magazine is emptied – starts a fresh count. After the burst the trigger must be released to set the counter back to zero and another sustained pressure on the trigger fires another burst of the same duration ie 2, 3 or 4 rounds.

STRIPPING

Stripping the MP5 SMG is carried out as follows. First remove the magazine and then cock the weapon by pulling back on the cocking handle which is located well forward on the left hand side of the tube carrying the bolt extension and the return spring. After checking that the chamber and feedway are clear, the bolt may be allowed to travel forward. The single take down pin is located behind the pistol grip and when it is pulled out the buttstock and return spring can be withdrawn from the receiver and the trigger group allowed to hang down from its front securing pin. Retracting the cocking handle will pull the bolt assembly to the rear of the receiver where it can be gripped and extracted. The bolt head can be turned 90 degrees clockwise and pulled out of the bolt body. The firing pin and spring can then be taken out.

The normal MP5 has a rigid buttstock made of a nylon based plastic. The manufacturer refers to this model as the MP5 A2. The MP5 A3 has a single metal strut stock which may be slid forward to give a considerable reduction to the overall length of the SMG.

DATA (MP 5A2 or MP 5A3)
Cartridge: 9mm × 19 Parabellum
Method of operation: Delayed blowback
Method of delay: Rollers
Method of feed: 10-, 15-, or 30-round box magazine
Method of fire: Selective

WEIGHTS
Gun empty: 2.45kg or 2.55kg
Magazine empty: 0.16kg
Magazine full (30 rounds): 492g
Gun with full magazine: 2.94kg or 3.03kg

LENGTH
Length, stock open: 680mm or 660mm
Length, stock folded: 490mm
Length of barrel: 225mm

MECHANICAL FEATURES
Barrel: Rifling: 4 grooves RH
Regulator: Nil
Cooling: Air
Sights: Foresight: Fixed Post
Rearsight: Apertures for different eye relief
Zeroing: Elevation. Adjust right drum. Line. Rearsight moves across.
Sight radius: 340mm
FIRING CHARACTERISTICS
Muzzle velocity: 400 metres/sec
Muzzle energy: 65mkp
Rate of fire: Cyclic: 750 rounds/min
Auto: 100 rounds/min
Semi-auto: 40-50 rounds/min
Range, maximum effective: 200 metres
Manufacturer: Heckler & Koch GmbH, 7238 Oberndorf/Neckar
Status: In production. In service with German Police and various armed forces

BLANK FIRING ATTACHMENTS

There are two blank firing attachments available. The first is a conventional device with a restricted gas flow. It is placed on the muzzle using the bayonet attachment and is retained by a catch. It is marked with a red ring to enable the firer to identify it as a training aid. It can only be employed with 9mm × 19 blanks.

The other device has an additional bullet trap added. This will catch a live round and stop the weapon from functioning – thus preventing a recurrence. It will also digest wooden bulleted blank. With ordinary blank it functions by restricted gas flow. The unit consists of a bullet trap to hold ONE live and a helix beyond it which deals with wooden bullets, plastic training bullets and blank ammunition of the brass case plastic tip type.

SUB-CALIBRE CONVERSION UNIT

To facilitate training in limited areas and to reduce the cost of firing, a sub-calibre device was introduced. This device uses the .22 LR cartridge (5.6mm × 16). It consists of a sub-calibre tube, a bolt assembly and a magazine. It is contained in a rectangular carrying case together with two magazines and cleaning kit.

The sub-calibre tube fits into the barrel. A machined disc at the breech end has parallel planes milled to fit into the barrel extension. The bolt assembly replaces the 9mm bolt and the magazine holding 20 rounds is built into a standard magazine body. When the sub-calibre conversion is fitted complete with a loaded 20-round magazine its weight is that of the normal MP5.

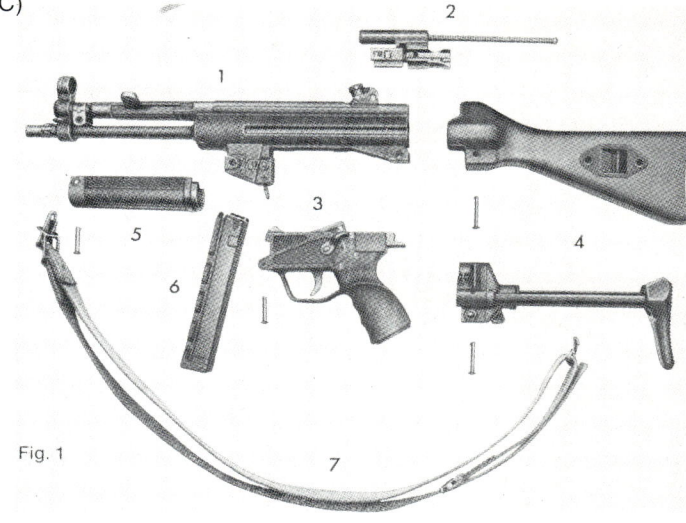

Fig. 1

HK MP5 stripped

DATA
Cartridge: .22LR (5.6mm × 16)
Method of operation: Blowback
Method of delay: Inertia
Method of feed: 20-round box magazine
Method of fire: Selective
Weight of gun with conversion kit: 2.4kg
Weight of conversion kit in storage case: 2.15kg
Muzzle velocity: 330 metres/sec
Muzzle energy: 14mkp
Rate of fire: Cyclic: 650 rounds/min
Auto: 80 rounds/min
Semi-auto: 40 rounds/min
Range, maximum effective: 45 metres
Manufacturer: Heckler and Koch GmbH, 7238 Oberndorf/Neckar
Status: In production

TYPE 1003 AIMING PROJECTOR

This is a lightweight illuminating source which is secured above the barrel, using the telescopic sight mount, and zeroed to be parallel with the bore. The purpose of the device is to produce a long range, high intensity beam of light which remains parallel and enables the firer to acquire, identify and engage a target in total darkness out to a range of 100 metres.

The equipment consists of a 100 watt halogen quartz bulb in a sturdy metal bodied lamp and a 12 volt battery with a capacity of 4.5 ampere hours. The battery is carried in a satchel and the necessary wiring connects to the lamp on top of the sub-machine gun with a switch located on the left side of the receiver under the thumb of the left hand. When the button is pressed, a parallel beam of light allows illumination up to 150 metres. If the target is facing towards the user the intensity of the light is blinding. The light from the lamp consists of an illuminated ring with a central bright spot and a projected image sighting post, and is projected from a metal reflector behind a telescopic lens. The weapon can be fired from the shoulder or from the hip and aiming consists of placing the bright spot and the projected post on the target. The tactical employment of the device in Internal Security Operations, is to use the light, dazzling the immediate target, for not more than 10 seconds during which six single, aimed, shots can be fired and then shifting position in the next few seconds before using the light again.

DATA
Weight of projector with mount: 1.15kg
Weight of battery: 2.35kp
Weight of MP5: 2.45kp
Total weight: 5.95kp

Power of halogen quartz light: 100 watts
Battery capacity: 4.5 amp hrs
Continuous lighting: 40 minutes

Heckler and Koch 1003 aiming device

9mm MP5 SD SMG

The MP5 SD is a silenced version of the MP5. Its mechanism is the same as the MP5 and it differs in having a drilled barrel surrounded with a jacket. The gas escapes from the barrel and enters a surrounding cylindrical steel jacket. This jacket contains a helix in which the gases lose their velocity and emerge eventually at a speed below that of sound. The diversion of a proportion of the gas reduces the muzzle velocity of the bullet to a subsonic velocity and so there is no mach wave as the bullet emerges. There will be a reduced muzzle energy accompanying the lower velocity.

The MP5 SD may have a rigid plastic butt, a retractable butt stock or be fitted with a receiver end cap and no stock. It may be used with iron sights, a telescopic sight, the 1003 Light Projector, or an image intensifier sight.

9mm MP 5 SD SMG

DATA
Cartridge: 9mm × 19 Parabellum
Operation: Delayed blow-back
Delay: Rollers
Feed: 10-, 15-, or 30-round box magazine
Method of fire: Selective

WEIGHTS
With rigid buttstock: 2.65kg
With retractable buttstock: 2.95kg
With receiver cap: 2.4kg
Magazine empty: 136g
Magazine full (30 rounds): 492g

9mm 5 SD field stripped

LENGTHS
With rigid buttstock: 780mm
With buttstock retracted: 610mm
With receiver cap: 550mm

MECHANICAL FEATURES
Barrel: 4 grooves RH
Sights: Iron sights – as MP5. Telescopic. 4X Telescope. 1003 Light projector. Image intensifier sight

FIRING CHARACTERISTICS
Muzzle velocity: 285 metres/sec
Muzzle energy: 38mkp
Rate of fire: Cyclic: 650 rounds/min
                  Auto: 100 rounds/min
                  SS: 40 rounds/min
Range, maximum effective: 135 metres
Manufacturer: Heckler and Koch GmbH, 7238 Oberndorf/Neckar
Status: In production

9mm MP5K SMG

For use by special police and anti-terrorist squads, Heckler and Koch have introduced an extra-short version of the MP5 design measuring only 325mm in length and weighing only 2kg. The mechanism is generally identical with that of the MP5A2/A3 models but the barrel length has been reduced to 115mm, a small handgrip has been added in front of the magazine and the butt stock has been removed, and the rear iron sights (adjustable) are open although a telescopic sight can be fitted.

DATA
Calibre: 9mm × 19 Luger
Operation: Delayed blowback
Delay: Rollers
Feed: 15- or 30-round detachable box magazine
Fire: Selective
Weight: Gun without magazine: 2kg
         15-round magazine, empty: 0.11kg
         30-round magazine, empty: 0.16kg
         30-round magazine, full: 0.52kg
Length: 325mm
Barrel: 115mm 4 grooves RH
Sights: Ring foresight and open rotary rearsight adjustable for windage or 4× telescopic
Sight radius: 260mm

The MP5K SMG

Muzzle velocity: 375m/sec
Muzzle energy: 57mkp
Rate of fire: 840 rounds/min cyclic
Manufacturer: Heckler & Koch GmbH, 7238 Oberndorf/Neckar
Status: Production

5.56mm HECKLER AND KOCH HK 53 SMG

The HK 53 SMG is a weapon in the Heckler and Koch Group II which comprises two rifles, the sub-machine and two machine guns chambered for the 5.56mm × 45 cartridge. The method of operation is similar to the other rifles and SMGs made by Heckler and Koch and utilises the system of rollers which delay the rearward movement of the breech-head until the pressure has dropped sufficiently to allow the breech-block to be blown back in safety.

In appearance it is very similar to the HK 33K and can be fitted with either a conventional plastic butt or a double strut telescoping butt stock. The HK 53 is the shortest of the 5.56mm weapons. The length, with butt retracted, is only 56cm whereas that of the HK 33K is 67cm and the HK 33 A3 is 73cm. If required the butt stock can be removed from the HK 53 and a metal cap fitted over the end of the receiver.

The HK 53 is capable of either single shots or full automatic, with a selector lever located on the left of the receiver above the pistol grip, using a 40 round magazine of aluminium alloy.

The HK 53 may be regarded as a scaled down version of the G3 rifle, which fires the NATO 7.62mm × 51 cartridge, and many of the parts of the two weapons are interchangeable with each other and the HK 33. The 9mm MP 5 SMG also has interchangeable parts with the G3 and HK 33 and it is extremely important that the bolts, or part of the bolts (particularly the 'locking' pieces), are not interchanged between weapons of different calibre and different recoil impulse.

The HK 53 does not have a bayonet.

The 5.56mm HK 53 SMG

DATA
Cartridge: 5.56mm × 45
Method of operation: Delayed blowback
Method of delay: Rollers
Method of feed: 40-round box magazine
Method of fire: Selective

WEIGHTS
Gun empty: 3.05kg
Magazine empty: 157g
Magazine full: 0.6kg
Gun with full magazine: 3.96kg

LENGTH
Gun, butt retracted: 563mm
Gun, butt extended: 755mm
Barrel: 225mm

MECHANICAL FEATURES
Barrel: Rifling: 4 grooves RH. 1 turn in 305mm
 Regulator: Nil
 Cooling: Air
 Change: Nil

Sights: Foresight: Post
 Rearsight: Apertures for 200, 300, 400 metres. V 100 metres battle sight
 Zeroing: Elevation. Adjust range drum. Line. Rearsight moves across
 Sight radius: 385mm

FIRING CHARACTERISTICS
Muzzle velocity: 750 metres/sec
Muzzle energy: 102mkp
Chamber pressure: 3622 kg/cm^2
Rate of fire: Cyclic: 700 rounds/min
 Auto: 160 rounds/min
 SS: 40 rounds/min
Range, maximum effective: 400 metres
Manufacturer: Heckler and Koch GmbH, 7238 Oberndorf/Neckar

5.56mm HECKLER AND KOCH HK 53 KL SMG

This derivative of the HK 53 was specially developed for the US Mechanized Infantry Combat Vehicle (MICV) as a Fire Port Weapon (FPW). It was designed to give close-in cover to deal with infantry getting inside the arc of depression of the machine gun. It differs from all other Heckler and Koch weapons in firing from an open breech position. The whole bolt is held to the rear in the 'ready to fire' position. This increases the lock time, which is unimportant in such a tactical role, but gives improvement in the heat dissipation properties of the barrel. The barrel is detachable.
Manufacturer: Heckler and Koch GmbH, 7238 Oberndorf/Neckar

HK 53 KL SMG

HUNGARY

7.62mm 48M SMG

This is a Hungarian copy of the Russian PPSh-41. It is well made with a good finish. Its physical characteristics and performance are identical to those of the USSR weapon.

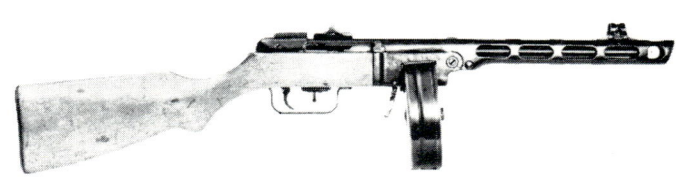

7.62mm 48M SMG (RMCS)

7.62mm AMD SMG

The Hungarian Army is alone among Warsaw Pact countries in having a sub-machine gun version of the AKM assault rifle. It has exactly the same breech action as the Russian SKM rifle and can readily be identified by its short barrel, the large muzzle brake and the forward pistol grip. It has a single strut, folding stock. The short barrel has resulted in a reduced muzzle velocity but it is still a very effective albeit slightly heavy SMG.

DATA
Cartridge: 7.62mm × 39
Method of operation: Gas
Method of locking: Rotating bolt
Method of feed: 30-round detachable box magazine
Method of fire: Selective
Weight: 3.27kg
Length, butt extended: 851mm
Length, butt folded: 648mm
Barrel – with muzzle brake: 378mm
Barrel – no muzzle brake: 318mm
Rifling: 4 groove RH
Muzzle velocity: 700 metres/sec
Muzzle energy: 186mkp

The Hungarian 7.62mm AMD SMG with butt stock extended (RSAF)

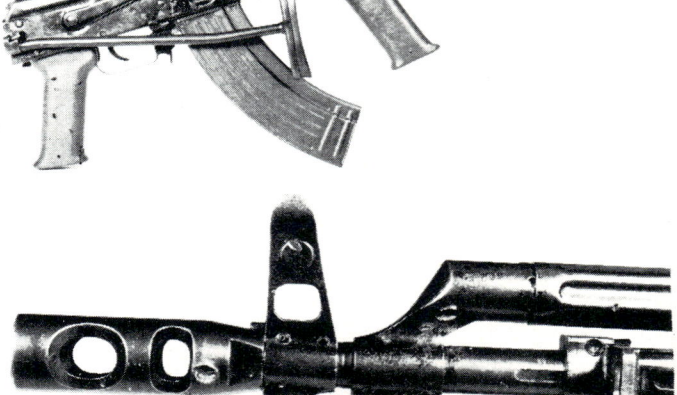

The AMD SMG with butt stock folded (RSAF)

Rate of fire: Cyclic: 600 rounds/min
 Auto: 120 rounds/min
 SS: 40 rounds/min
Range, maximum effective: 300 metres
Manufacturer: State Arsenals
Status: In production. In service

The muzzle brake of the AMD (RSAF)

INDONESIA

INDONESIAN SMG

A number of locally produced SMGs appeared during the confrontation with the UK in 1963. These were all copies of European models. The Beretta and the Spanish Star were the most common but the Carl Gustav was also seen.

9mm P.M. MODEL VII SMG

An original design produced by the Bandung Arsenal, Pabrik Sendjata Dan Mesiu, was produced in 1957. This was an orthodox blowback operated SMG. The circular receiver was made from seamless steel tubing and the bolt was machined. The slotted barrel jacket reached almost to the Beretta type compensator. The design owed some inspiration to the US M3 SMG and had the cover which locks the bolt in either position, and also the sliding wire butt stock. The magazine housing, which is also the forward grip, was longer than is usual and had a distinctive sloping entry.

DATA
Cartridge: 9mm × 19 Parabellum
Method of operation: Blowback
Method of locking: Nil
Method of feed: 33-round box magazine
Method of fire: Automatic
Weight unloaded: 3.29kg
Weight loaded: 3.92kg
Length, stock extended: 840mm
Length, stock retracted: 540mm
Barrel: 274mm (incl. compensator)

FIRING CHARACTERISTICS
Muzzle velocity: 381m/sec
Muzzle energy: 54mkp
Rate of fire: Cyclic: 600 rounds/min
          Auto: 120 rounds/min
Range, maximum effective: 200 metres
Manufacturer: Pabrik Sendjata Dan Mesiu, Bandung
Status: No longer manufactured. In limited use

An Indonesian copy of the 9mm Beretta 38/49 (RSAF)

An Indonesian copy of the Spanish 9mm Star SMG (RSAF)

The 9mm Model VIII, 1957 (RSAF)

IRAN

IRANIAN SMG

From 1943 onwards the Russian SMG, the PPSh-41, was produced at the Mosalsalsasi Factory near Teheran. This gun was called the Model 22 from the Persian year of its adoption 1322, (1943). During the Second World War production went directly to Russia.

After the war production continued but the Model 22 was then made in 9mm calibre and the Iranian Army was partly equipped with this weapon. A quantity of US M3A1 SMGs were obtained in the immediate post-war years but no effort was made to re-equip entirely with this weapon. The Uzi produced by FN at Herstal near Liège has been adopted as the standard gun and large numbers have been imported.

ISRAEL

9mm UZI SMG

During the Arab Israeli War of 1948, immediately after the British Mandate in Palestine ended, the Israelis found themselves without a reliable sub-machine gun.

In 1949 Major Uziel Gal of the Israeli Army started work on a weapon of this type intended for use by all branches of the armed services of his country. He had previously studied the Czechoslovakian pre-war sub-machine guns, particularly the 9mm models 23 and 25 and the designs produced for the Russian 7.62mm Type P cartridge which were the models 24 and 26. These weapons and the post-war ZK 476 9mm SMG provided the foundation on which the UZI was built and this weapon has retained many of the characteristics of its Czech parents. The bolt design shows this origin clearly.

OPERATION
The UZI is a blowback-operated gun using the system of advanced primer ignition in which the round is fired whilst the bolt is still travelling forward. This produces a reduced impulse to the bolt and as a result this component can be designed to weigh less than half the amount that would be required for a static firing breech-block.

For any given weapon the minimum overall length is the sum of the barrel length plus the length of the breech block behind the chamber plus the compressed return spring length. The UZI is 44.5cm long from the muzzle to the rear of the breech casing. This is a less than average length for a weapon of this type. The UZI also has a very pronounced advantage in that in its short length it achieves a 26cm barrel. This is managed by wrapping the bolt around the chamber and putting the breech face not on the front face of the bolt but 9.5cm further back. Thus at the moment of firing the bolt completely surrounds the rear end of the barrel except for a cut-out section on the right hand side which allows ejection of the fired case. A further advantage of this design is that if a round is fired early or a hang fire occurs, the soldier is protected from the effects of the bursting of the unsupported case by the wrap round bolt.

The magazine is inserted into the pistol grip. This has the advantage of making magazine changing very easy in the dark and also giving positive support to the magazine over a greater length than is usual. This makes for greater rigidity and more precise location. The gun stops firing with the bolt to the rear and when the trigger is operated the bolt goes forward, collects a round from the top of the 25-round magazine and feeds it over the bullet

The 9mm UZI SMG. This is the original version with the wooden butt made by IMI (RSAF)

9mm UZI SMG with the folding butt. This is the version manufactured by FN and used in the German Army as the MP2 (RMCS)

guide into the chamber. The cartridge is held in the magazine at an angle with the nose slightly elevated so that it does not line up with the fixed firing pin on the breech face until the cartridge case enters the chamber. At any time thereafter it can be fired when the friction force between the case and the chamber wall produces the required resistance.

TRIGGER AND FIRING MECHANISM

The change lever provides the three positions of Automatic (A), Single Shot (R), and Safe (S). Also there is a grip safety which must be fully depressed before the gun can be either cocked or fired. In addition extra safety is provided by fitting a ratchet in the cocking handle slide to prevent accidental discharge if the hand cocking the gun should slip off the handle, after the breech block has come back far enough to pass behind a round in the magazine. After the cocking handle has come back 4.75cm, it cannot go forward again until it has been withdrawn fully to the rear which is a distance of 8cm. Until the wire clip is pushed fully forward i.e. the cocking handle is fully to the rear, the catch cannot go forward and the bolt is held up.

The trigger is ⌐ shaped. It is located in the gun with the short arm as the trigger itself and the long arm inclined forward in a horizontal plan. It is pivoted at its highest point which is the junction of the two arms. Operation of the trigger therefore depresses the trigger bar. Attached to the end of the trigger bar is a pivoting disconnector.

The disconnector holds down the sear when the gun is fired. The sear is a double pronged fork and the disconnector fits between the prongs. When the change lever is set to 'Automatic' the disconnector simply moves down and pulls the sear with it. Whilst the trigger is operated the gun will continue to fire until the ammunition supply is exhausted. When the trigger is released the disconnector rises with the end of the trigger bar and the sear spring forces the sear up into the path of the forward moving breech block and the bent and the sear come into contact and the breech block is held to the rear.

When 'R' is set on the change lever the disconnector will not only be pulled down by the trigger bar but will also rotate about the change lever bar extension.

This rotation carries the disconnector through the slots in the sear and the sear rises to intercept the bent on the breech block. To fire another round it is necessary to release the trigger which will allow the disconnector to rotate back through the sear slots and re-engage the sear. This is a very neat and effective disconnector system.

The method of operation of the grip safety is as follows. The projecting lug on the right hand side of the trigger mechanism – alongside the disconnector – fits under the sear and prevents it from moving down. When the grip safety is operated the bar goes forward and the lug moving with it clears the way for the sear to drop.

METHOD OF MANUFACTURE

The UZI is very largely made from pressings, which are bent into form and welded up using either spot or running welds. A heavy gauge sheet steel is used and the body is strengthened by the formation of fullering grooves which also provide cavities to accommodate sand and mud in adverse operating conditions and so allow the breech block to reciprocate without being slowed down by undue friction.

At the front end of the body a steel tube is welded into the box section to take the barrel. This tube is 9.5cm long and so the barrel is well supported and aligned. The front end of the tube is externally screw threaded to take the barrel nut. The bullet guide is welded in front of the magazine opening and the ejector is riveted behind it. The body is given additional rigidity by the spot welding of bridges across at the front end and at the rear on which the sights are located. The fore grip is made of plastic and a small air space exists between it and the body of the gun to allow some measure of heat dissipation.

The foresight is a tapered post mounted eccentrically on a screw threaded cylindrical base. A key is used to loosen the locking screw and the post can then be adjusted for both elevation and line. Although the foresight can be adjusted for elevation without affecting the line setting, the converse is not true and it is not possible to vary the line without some effect – although small – on elevation. The rearsight is an aperture with two flip over positions marked 100 and 200.

To increase the fire capacity two 32-round magazines have been brazed together at their bases to make an L shape. When both magazines are loaded the one not in use extends forward under the muzzle and helps to keep the muzzle down at automatic fire. When one magazine has been expended the empty magazine lies back under the butt.

STRIPPING

(1) Remove the magazine, cock the action and check that the chamber is empty, return the bolt, under control, to the forward position.
(2) Depress the catch in front of the rearsight and lift the top cover plate right off.
(3) Slide the bolt back 6.5cm and lift out together with the return spring, rod and end plate.
(4) Rotate the barrel nut off and withdraw the barrel forward.
(5) Push out the transverse pin through the trigger group and drop out the trigger assembly.

DATA

Cartridge: 9mm × 19
Method of operation: Blowback
Method of locking: Nil
Method of feed: 25-, 32- and 64-round box magazines
Method of fire: Selective

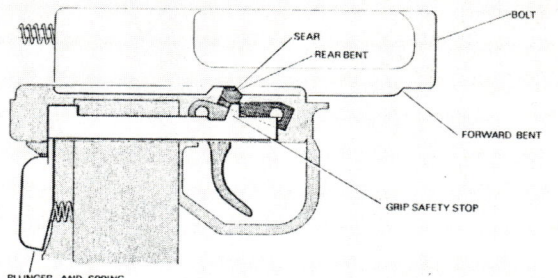

1 Sear engaged in rear bent; gun cannot be cocked until grip safety is operated as in 3

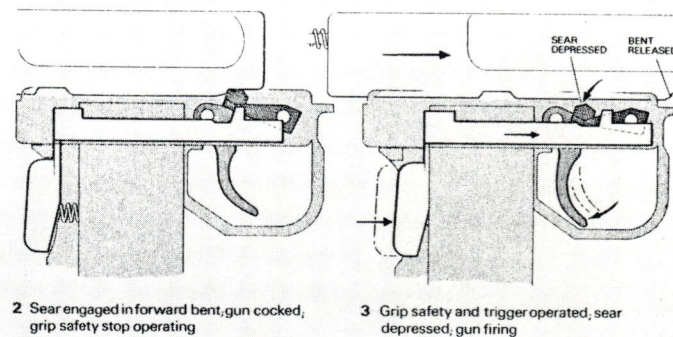

2 Sear engaged in forward bent; gun cocked; grip safety stop operating

3 Grip safety and trigger operated; sear depressed; gun firing

The trigger and firing mechanism of the UZI

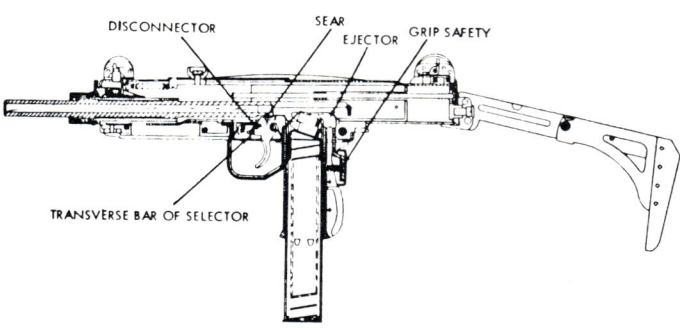

A sectioned view of the UZI 9mm SMG

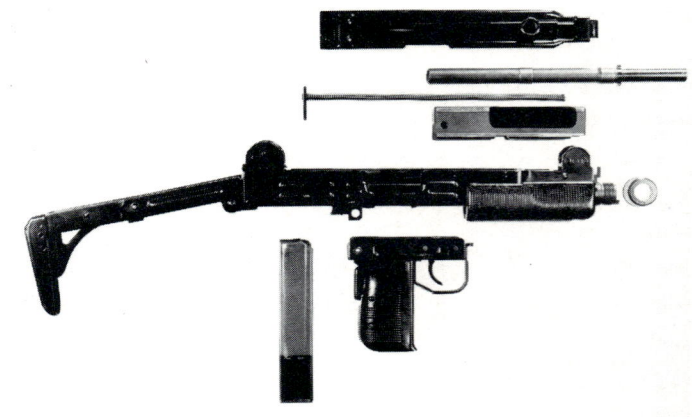

The UZI stripped

WEIGHTS

Gun empty: 3.6kg
Magazine empty: 227g
Magazine full (25 rounds): 0.5kg
Gun with loaded 25-round magazine: 4.12kg

LENGTHS

Gun, butt extended: 640mm
Gun, butt folded: 470mm
Gun, wooden stock: 640mm
Gun, with bayonet: 820mm
Barrel: 259mm

MECHANICAL FEATURES

Barrel: Rifling: 4 grooves RH 1 turn in 254mm
Cooling: Air

Sights: Foresight: Cylindrical post
  Rearsight: Flip aperture 100m and 200m
  Graduation: Nil
  Zeroing: Elevation. Front sight screws up and down
  Line. Front sight on eccentric
  Sight radius: 311mm

FIRING CHARACTERISTICS
Muzzle velocity: 400metres/sec

Muzzle energy: 61mkp
Chamber pressure: 2158kg/cm²
Rate of fire: Cyclic: 550-600 rounds/min
    Automatic: 128 rounds/min
    SS: 64 rounds/min
Manufacturers: Israel Military Industries, Tel Aviv, Israel. Fabrique Nationale d'Armes de Guerre, Herstal, Liège, Belgium
Status: In production. In service in Belgium, Iran, Israel, The Netherlands, Venezuela, West Germany, and elsewhere

ITALY

9mm BERETTA MODEL 1918-30 SMG

This was a self-loading carbine designed for police work but never produced in large numbers. It had a cocking ring at the rear end which sits back towards the firer's eye at every shot. A box magazine holding 15 rounds was underneath the weapon and a feed cover was fitted. Ejection was through the top. The back sight was adjustable for ranges of 100 to 500 metres.

There was a closed breech firing system using a hammer and a firing pin. The carbine was purchased by the Argentinian police.

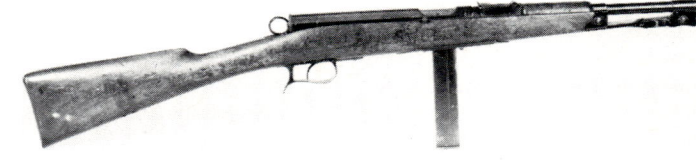

Beretta Model 1918-30

9mm BERETTA MODEL 1935 SMG

This was another police carbine with the same action as the Model 1918-30. It had a completely new receiver based largely on the successful German MP 34 with a barrel jacket with long oval perforations. Only limited production occurred.

9mm BERETTA MODEL 1938A SG

The Moschetto Automatic Beretta (MAB) 1938A was a most successful design. It went into production in 1938 and continued throughout the War. Manufacture finally ceased in 1950. It was the standard SMG in the Italian Army, was issued in quantity to German troops and largely equipped the Romanian Army.

The MAB 1938A was a blowback-operated gun but of somewhat complex design for a SMG. When the bolt was fully home a cam came into contact with the ejector stud and was revolved to drive the firing pin forward. The return spring was of narrow diameter and entered the bolt to bear on the firing pin. The other end was enclosed in a tube which fitted into a recess in the end closure cap of the receiver. The magazine opening had a sliding plate to keep out dirt when the gun had no magazine on.

There were three variants of the M1938A.

The first – produced in January 1938 – had a jacket with long cooling slots and a simple compensator with two large ports separated at the top by a central bar. A folding bayonet was fitted. There were two triggers – the forward one for semi-automatic fire and the rearward one for full automatic. The safety catch was on the left of the receiver above the trigger.

The second version had a barrel jacket with small circular perforations but the same compensator. Not only was there the safety catch but a bar was fitted in the rear of the trigger guard which, when pushed to the right, blocked the rear (automatic) trigger, enabling only single shots to be fired. This model was produced in large numbers. It usually had the Italian crest on the right side of the stock.

The third model, at the end of 1938, had no fixed bayonet. The compensator was simplified into four cuts on top of the muzzle, directing gas back. This model was mass produced from 1938 to 1944 for Italian and German forces. In 1939 it was supplied to Rumania and in 1947 it went to Argentina. This third version was modified in 1949 and 1950 by the addition of a cross bolt safety taken from a later model – the 38/49 SMG. The Model 1938A was a great success. It was heavy and rather expensive but it was reliable and effective.

In addition to the normal 9mm Parabellum round a special cartridge known as the M38 was used in the MAB 38A. It was of the same dimensions as the lower powered Glisenti 9mm cartridge but had a considerably heavier powder charge. The cartridge was identified and distinguished from the Glisenti by having a 1mm groove cut two-thirds of the way up the case; this allowed recognition by touch when loading at night. The current pistol at this time was the Beretta M34 taking the 9mm short cartridge (.380 ACP) and so the SMG and the service pistol used different ammunition. The SMG ammunition was loaded into Mannlicher type clips holding 10, 20 or 40 cartridges.

DATA
Cartridge: 9mm M1938
Method of operation: Blowback
Method of locking: Nil
Method of feed: Box magazine 10, 20, 30 and 40 rounds
Method of fire: Selective
Weight unloaded: 4.2kg
Weight loaded: 4.97kg
Length: 946mm

MECHANICAL FEATURES
Barrel: 315mm
  Rifling: 6 grooves RH
Sights: Foresight: Blade
  Rearsight: Tangent. V. 100-500 metres

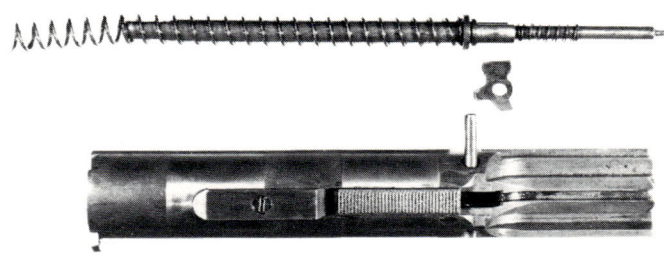

The firing arrangements of the 9mm Model 1938A SMG

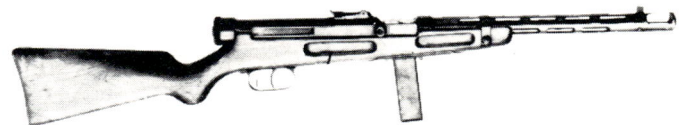

The first model of the 38A SMG. Note the shape of the compensator and the barrel jacket slots

The second model (first variant) of the 38A SMG. Note the changed shape of the cooling holes in the barrel jacket

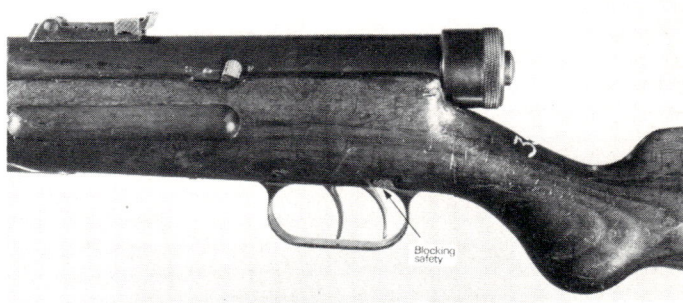

The second model had a safety which blocked trigger movement

The third model (second variant) of the 38A SMG. The compensator is now merely four slots in the top of the muzzle

FIRING CHARACTERISTICS
Muzzle velocity: 420 metres/sec
Muzzle energy: 67mkp
Rate of fire: Cyclic: 600 rounds/min
        Automatic: 120 rounds/min
        SS: 40 rounds/min

Range, maximum effective: 200 metres
Manufacturer: Pietro Beretta SpA, Gardone-val-Trompia, Brescia.
Status: No longer in production. Not in military service

9mm BERETTA MODEL 38/42 SMG

The 38/42 was issued to the Italian Army. It used stampings for the receiver and magazine housing. The bolt had a fixed firing pin and the return spring of the M1938A. The guide rod of the return spring projected to the rear of the end closure cap and provided a ready identification between this model and the 1938/44 which followed it.

The barrel jacket was removed and the barrel shortened. The prototype had a thick barrel, heavily fluted. The first production version had a fluted barrel but this was later supplanted by a barrel with a smooth exterior contour. This was often called 38/43. The compensator had two cuts above the muzzle. The cocking handle had an attached dust cover. After cocking was completed the handle was pushed forward and the cocking way sealed. The handle did not reciprocate with the bolt.

The prototype of the Model 38/42 had a thick fluted barrel

DATA
Cartridge: 9mm Parabellum
Method of operation: Blowback
Method of locking: Nil
Method of feed: 20- and 40-round box magazine
Method of fire: Selective
Weight unloaded: 3.27kg
Weight loaded: 4.03kg
Length: 800mm
Barrel: 213mm
        Rifling: 6 grooves RH
Sights: Foresight: Blade
        Rearsight: Flip. Notch. 100 and 200 metres
Muzzle velocity: 381 metres/sec
Muzzle energy: 55mkp

The production model of the 38/42 had a thinner fluted barrel

Rate of fire: Cyclic: 550 rounds/min
        Automatic: 120 rounds/min
        SS: 40 rounds/min
Range, maximum effective: 200 metres
Manufacturer: Pietro Beretta SpA, Gardone-val-Trompia, Brescia
Status: No longer in production. Not in military service in Italy but some surplus weapons may still exist elsewhere

9mm BERETTA MODEL 38/44

This was a simplified version of the 38/42. The bolt length was reduced from 7.1in to 5.9in and the narrow diameter return spring used on all of Marengoni's designs thus far, was replaced by a large spring and the end closure cap of the SMG was plain. The 38/44 went into production in February 1944 and production reached 3000 a month in December. These were sold to Syria, Iraq, Pakistan and Costa Rica.
Manufacturer: Pietro Beretta SpA, Gardone val Trompia, Brescia
Status: See text

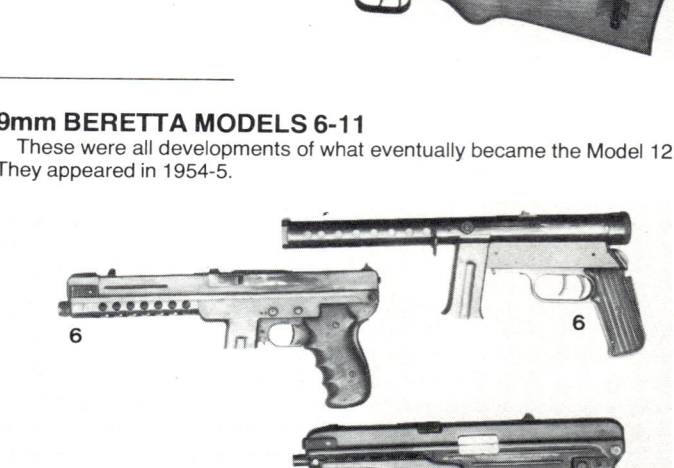

The smooth barrelled version was known as the Mod.38/43. It could be distinguished from the Mod. 38/44 which followed it by the guide rod recess in the end cap

9mm BERETTA MODEL 38/49 (The Model 4)

The 38/49 was a modified version of the Model 38/44 with a cross bolt safety located above the forward of the double trigger. It locked the bolt in either the forward or cocked position. If the cross bolt safety was in the midway position the sear was locked. In 1956 it was renamed the Model 4 and is still so designated. The Model 4 is still the standard SMG in the Italian Army. It was ordered by the West German Border Police in 1951 and again as the MP1. With a folding bayonet attached it was sold to Egypt.

The 38/49 has been a very successful SMG both mechanically and financially. It showed that Marengoni's original concept of the M1938A was sound and could be modernised as users increased their requirements. It was sold to Cost Rica, Egypt, Indonesia, Dominica, Thailand, Tunisia and in 1961 it was purchased by the Republic of the Yemen. It is still the standard SMG in the Italian Armed Forces.
Manufacturer: Pietro Beretta SpA, Gardone val Trompia, Brescia
Status: See text

9mm BERETTA MODELS 6-11

These were all developments of what eventually became the Model 12. They appeared in 1954-5.

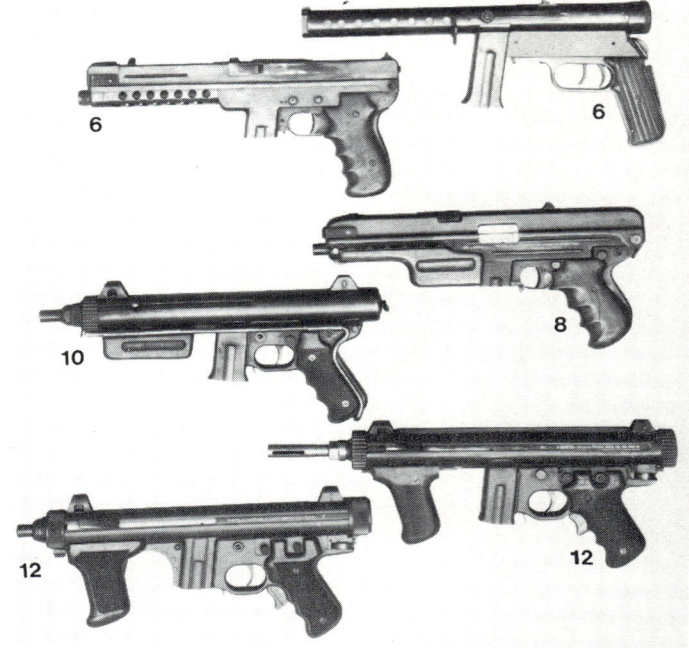

This 38/49 – the Model 4 – is still in service with the Italian Armed Forces

The varying stages in the development of the Model 12 are shown here. The final versions are on the left and the prototypes on the right.

9mm BERETTA MODEL 12

This is Beretta's latest SMG. It was produced in 1958 and went into series production in 1959. It was adopted by the Italian Army as the M12 SMG and is used by special troops. It is not the general issue SMG which remains the MAB 38/49. The Model 12 has been sold to Brazil, Gabon, Libya, Nigeria, Saudi Arabia and Venezuela. Heavy sheet metal stampings spot-welded together form the receiver and magazine housing. There are longitudinal grooves extending the full length of the receiver to ensure efficient functioning in conditions of dust, sand and snow. The receiver, forward pistol grip, magazine housing, trigger housing and pistol grip are all one unit. The breech block is of the wrap round type and envelops the barrel before firing. The fixed firing pin is located well back and, of the total barrel length of 200mm, 150mm lies inside the breech block at the moment of firing.

The principle of the wrap round bolt does help in keeping the vibrations to a minimum. The gun is very steady at automatic fire and there seems little tendency for the muzzle to rise at full automatic.

The weapon has two safety systems. There is a grip safety in the front of the pistol grip, below the trigger, which locks the bolt when released in either the forward or cocked position. It must be held in before the action can be cocked. There is also a push button safety just above the pistol grip and this locks the grip safety until pushed to the right. The selector lever is a push through type. The weapon normally has a metal stock which folds laterally to the right; it can be fitted with a quickly detachable wooden butt.

The Beretta Model 12. In current service'

The bolt wraps round the barrel of this 9mm SMG

DATA
Cartridge: 9mm Parabellum
Method of operation: Blowback
Method of locking: Nil
Method of feed: 20, 30 and 40 rounds
Method of fire: Selective
Weight unloaded: 3kg folding metal stock
    3.4kg wooden stock
    3.77kg folding metal stock
Weight loaded: 4.18kg wooden stock
Length, stock extended: 645mm
Length, stock folded: 416mm
Barrel: 200mm
    Rifling: 6 grooves RH
Sights: Foresight: Blade
    Rearsight: Flip. Notch. 100 and 200 metres

Muzzle velocity: 381 metres/sec
Muzzle energy: 55mkp
Rate of fire: Cyclic: 550 rounds/min
    Automatic: 120 rounds/min
    SS: 40 rounds/min
Range, maximum effective: 200 metres
Manufacturer: Pietro Beretta SpA, Gardone-val-Trompia, Brescia
Status: In production. In service with the Italian Army. Sold to Brazil, Gabon, Libya, Nigeria, Saudi Arabia, and Venezuela. Also manufactured by Bandung Arsenal, Indonesia

9mm MODEL LF57 SMG

This gun was produced by the firm of Luigi Franchi of Brescia. The prototype, known as the LF-56, appeared in 1956 and the production version, the LF-57, was produced in the next year. The bolt was ⌐ shaped with the long arm above the barrel and the firing pin and extractor, together with the feed horn, on the lower arm, thus raising the centre of gravity of the gun up to the thrust line of the barrel and preventing muzzle rise at full auto. The grip safety was located at the front of the pistol grip. No other applied safety was fitted. The entire gun – except barrel and bolt – was produced from stampings of heavy sheet steel.

The LF-57 was the first SMG manufactured in every respect by the Luigi Franchi Company and several thousands were taken by the Italian Army in 1962 and by some other countries.

The LF-57 had a barrel 8.1in long. In 1962 a semi-automatic version with a 16in barrel was made and exported to the United States as the Police Model 1962.

The Luigi Franchi LF 57 9mm SMG. This was sold to the Italian Army

DATA
Cartridge: 9mm × 19 Parabellum
Method of operation: Blowback
Method of fire: Automatic
Method of feed: Detachable magazine holding 20, 30 or 40 cartridges
Weight: 3.3kg
Weight of loaded 40 round magazine: 730g
Weight of breech block: 820g

Length with butt extended: 686mm
Length with butt folded: 425mm
Barrel: 205mm
    Rifling: 6 grooves RH 1 turn in 250mm
Sights: Foresight: Blade
    Rearsight: Notch
    Sightbase: 312mm
Muzzle velocity: 395-420 metres/sec
Rate of fire: 450-470 rounds/min
Range, maximum effective: 200 metres
Manufacturer: Luigi Franchi SpA, Brescia
Status: Manufactured on request. Still in service with the Italian Military Police and in Africa.

JAPAN

9mm SCK SMG MODEL 65

Post-war Japanese weapon manufacture started up in 1961 but SMGs of US manufacture equipped Japanese forces for several years. The SMGs used were the M1 (Thompson) and the M2A1.

The current 9mm SCK SMG is very much like the Carl Gustav made in Sweden. It has the same cylindrical receiver and barrel extension but the latter is not perforated. The conventional blowback system is used. There is a grip safety, operating on the same principle as that of the Danish Madsen, which holds the bolt to the rear until the firer pushes a lever forward when he grips the forward pistol grip. The magazine is inserted in the forward grip which is located at the point of balance. The rear pistol grip is placed at the very back of the receiver – rather like the Sten Mk IVA. The ejection port cover is hinged on the left side. It acts as a safety catch when it is closed and, like the US M3A1, holds the bolt stationary in either the forward or cocked position. The cocking handle is on the right side of the receiver and does not reciprocate with the bolt. There is a grip safety which must be fully depressed before the gun can be either cocked or fired; and further safety is provided by fitting latches in the cocking handle to prevent accidental discharge if, when the gun is being cocked and the breech block has been pulled back past the rounds in the magazine, the cocking handle should slip

The SCK 9mm SMG. Note the grip safety

from the firer's hand. After the cocking handle has come back 23mm it cannot go forward again until it has been drawn fully to the rear (85mm). Only then do the latches come free from the ratchet which is fixed to the main frame. The barrel casing and barrel can be removed by rotating.

There is a spring catch bearing on a knurled ring around the rear part of the barrel casing and this must be held clear before the barrel can be removed. This feature also would appear to have been derived from the US M3 SMG. The butt stock swings to the right of the receiver.

The SMG was designed and manufactured by the Shin Chuo Kogyo Co Ltd in Tokyo and was introduced in 1965.

DATA
Cartridge: 9mm × 19 Parabellum
Method of operation: Blowback
Method of locking: Nil
Method of feed: 30-round box magazine
Method of fire: Selective
Weight: 4.08kg
Length, stock extended: 762mm
Length, stock folded: 501mm
Sights: Foresight: Blade
Rearsight: Flip aperture
Muzzle velocity: 360 metres/sec
Muzzle energy: 53mkp
Rate of fire: Cyclic: 550 rounds/min

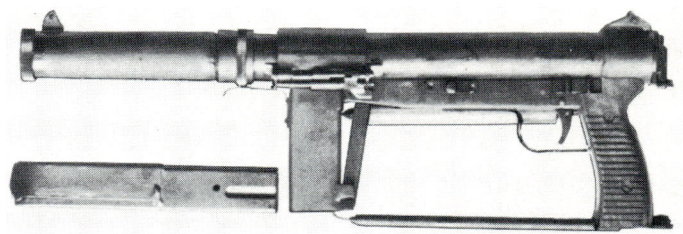

The arrangement of the two grips make this SMG easy to control with the stock folded

Automatic: 120 rounds/min
SS: 40 rounds/min
Range, maximum effective: 200 metres

Manufacturer: Shin Chuo Kogyo Co. Ltd., Tokyo
Status: Production for Japanese Self Defence Forces only

9mm SCK SMG MODEL 66

Shin Chuo Kogyo Co Ltd have produced a modification of the earlier model 65, known as the Model 66. The data for both weapons is the same except that the Model 66 has a lower rate of fire, which is only 465 rounds per minute as against the 550 rate of the model 65.

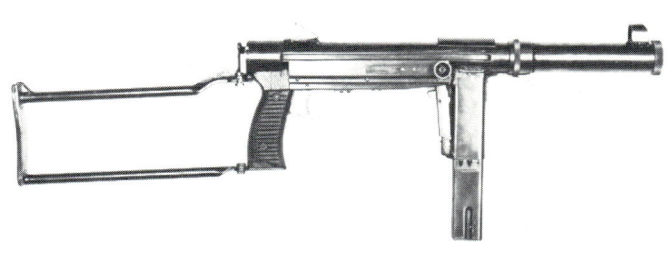

SCK Model 66

KOREA (NORTH)

7.62mm TYPE 49 SMG

This was a direct copy of the Russian PPSh-41. It was made in Pyongyang from 1949 to 1950 when the factory was captured and held for a short while by USA troops. The factory was then moved north and production was rapidly resumed. The Type 49 remained in production until the last months of 1955.

The North Korean version has the same physical parameters as the Russian PPSh-41 (qv) but may be distinguished by the receiver marking which is a star surrounded by a circle. The Type 49 also has an aperture rearsight which is an instant recognition feature.

LUXEMBOURG

9mm SOLA SMG

The Société Luxembourgeoise d'Armes SA produced the Sola Model Super in their factory at Ettelbruck in 1954. The designer, said to be named Jansen, intended the weapon to be as cheap as possible. In appearance it resembles the Belgian Vigneron and the use of such details as the small, rotating ejection cover, strengthens the connection.

The weapon functions as a conventional blowback operated weapon. It has a long receiver made from a stamping and an adjustable telescoping wire stock. There is a muzzle brake fitted to the rather long barrel. There are only 38 parts to the weapon which adds to the ease of production.

The weapon was not a great success but a few were sold in North Africa and some were reported in South America.

In an effort to improve sales the 'Light Model' was produced. The weapon had a smaller trigger mechanism, and the ejection port cover was eliminated together with the compensator. The modifications did not have the desired effects on sales and the competition forced the manufacturers out of business.

DATA 'SUPER'	'LIGHT MODEL'
Cartridge: 9mm × 19 Parabellum	
Method of operation: Blowback	
Method of locking: Nil	
Method of feed: 32-round box magazine	
Method of fire: Selective	
Weight unloaded: 2.86kg	2.72kg
Weight loaded: 3.6kg	3.43kg
Length, stock extended: 889mm	787mm
Length, stock retracted: 610mm	572mm
Barrel: 305mm	203mm
Rifling: 6 grooves RH	
Sights: Foresight: Blade	
Rearsight: Flip aperture 50 and 150 metres Notch 100 metres	
Muzzle velocity: 396 metres/sec 381 metres/sec	
Muzzle energy: 60mkp	55mkp
Rate of fire: Cyclic: 550 rounds/min	
Auto: 120 rounds/min	
SS: 40 rounds/min	

The Luxembourg 9mm Sola Model Super (RSAF)

Manufacturer: Société Luxembourgeoise d'Armes SA, Ettelbruck
Status: No longer manufactured. Not in service in Europe. Possibly exists in North Africa or South America

MEXICO

9mm MODEL HM-3 SMG

This sub-machine gun is manufactured by Productos Mendoza SA in Mexico. It is a lightweight weapon, of reduced overall length achieved by largely extending forward around the barrel. A grip safety is provided to prevent accidental discharge. The stock is fixed, not folding.

DATA
Cartridge: 9mm × 19 Parabellum
Method of operation: Blowback
Method of fire: Automatic or repetition

Method of feed: 32-round box magazine
Weight of weapon without magazine: 2.69kg
Weight of empty magazine: 275g
Weight of full magazine: 655g
Overall length: 635mm
Barrel length: 255mm
Rate of fire: approx. 600 rounds/min
Manufacturer: Productos Mendoza SA, Mexico DF
Status: Production

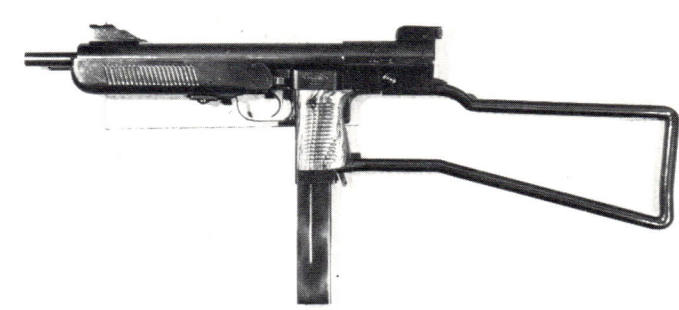

Model HM-3

POLAND

The Polish SMG known as the MORS model 1939 was designed by P. Wilniewczyca and J. Skrzypinskiego whose initials appear as 'VIS' on the Polish Radom pistol. The country was overrun by the Germans in 1939 and not more than 50 SMGs were produced. After World War II the Russian PPS-43 was produced. It differs from the Soviet gun in having a wooden stock and a slightly longer receiver but otherwise is the same as the PPS-43 (qv). The Polish gun was called the M 1943-52.

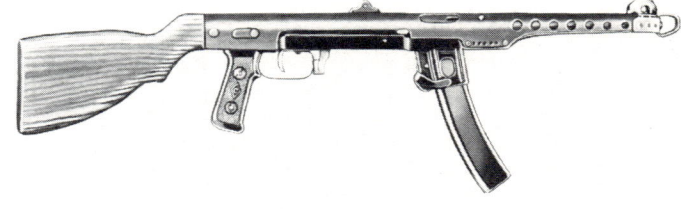

Polish 7.62mm 1943/52 SMG

PORTUGAL

9mm FBP M.48 SMG

This SMG was designed by Major Gonclaves Cardoso and was produced by Fabrica de Braco de Prata. The weapon is a collection of well tried ideas from older SMGs. The German MP-40 provides the bolt, return spring and telescopic guide. The bolt has been simplified for manufacture by only boring out sufficiently to allow a seating for the return spring. The receiver is made from stampings and is based on the US M3 SMG. The retracting wire stock comes from the same source.

In operation the weapon is a straightforward blowback design using the 9mm Parabellum cartridge.

DATA
Cartridge: 9mm × 19 Parabellum
Method of operation: Blowback
Method of locking: Nil
Method of feed: 32-round box magazine
Method of fire: Automatic
Weight unloaded: 3.75kg
Weight loaded: 4.43kg
Length, stock extended: 813mm
Length, stock retracted: 635mm
Barrel: 249mm
        Rifling: 6 grooves RH

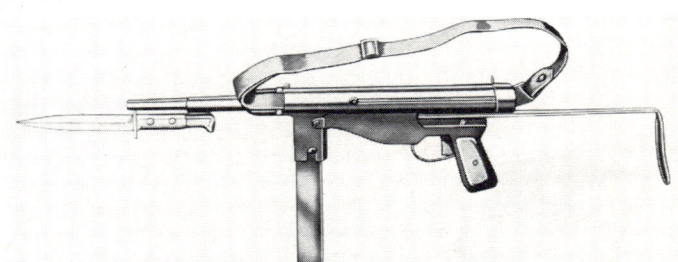

Portuguese 9mm Model 48 FBP (J. Smith)

Muzzle velocity: 381 metres/sec
Muzzle energy: 55mkp
Rate of fire: Cyclic: 500 rounds/min
           Automatic: 120 rounds/min
Range, maximum effective: 200 metres
Manufacturer: Fabrica de Braco de Prata
Status: No longer manufactured. In service with Portuguese Army and probably now to be found in former Portuguese colonies – especially Angola and Mozambique

ROMANIA

9mm ORITA M 1941 SMG

This SMG was designed by Leopold Jaska and manufactured at the Cugir Arsenal from 1941 to 1944. It was issued to Romanian troops and used in the invasion of Soviet Russia in 1941. It remained the Romanian standard SMG. When Romania became part of the Soviet bloc it re-equipped with Russian weapons and the Orita was relegated to the People's Militia and Police units. It is still in service with these forces. The Orita is much like the German MP 40 in appearance but was machined from the solid and consequently is a very robust weapon. The butt is usually of wood but a folding type – again rather like that of the MP 40 – is sometimes encountered. The magazine is straight, holding 25 rounds but it seems that a curved type holding 32 cartridges existed. The cocking handle is on the left of the receiver.

The weapon is a simple blowback operated type but it has a bolt rather like the early Thompson, in which the hammer is carried in the bolt head and rotated to fire the cap by a projection standing proud of the floor of the bolt way. There is a choice of single shots or automatic fire. The safety is a push through button in the front part of the trigger guard with the button projecting on the right for 'safe'. The change lever is located on the right of the receiver, forward of the trigger guard. When it is rotated down, the gun produces automatic fire and single shots are selected when the lever is pushed up. The rearsight is large and sufficiently noticeable to provide a recognition feature.

DATA
Cartridge: 9mm Parabellum
Method of operation: Blowback
Method of locking: Nil
Method of feed: 25-round box (a 32-round curved box was also made)

Romanian 9mm Orita M 1941 SMG (J. Smith)

The prominent back sight of the Orita aids recognition (J. Smith)

Method of fire: Selective
Weight empty: 3.46kg
Weight loaded: 4kg

Length: 894mm
Barrel: 287mm
    Rifling: 6 grooves RH
Sights: Foresight: Blade
    Rearsight: Tangent. Notch 100-500 metres
Muzzle velocity: 381metres/sec
Muzzle energy: 55mkp

Rate of fire: Cyclic: 600 rounds/min
    Automatic: 120 rounds/min
    SS: 40 rounds/min
Range, maximum effective: 200 metres
Manufacturer: Cugir Arsenal, Cugir
Status: No longer in production. In service with People's Militia and Police units

SPAIN

9mm STAR MODEL Z45 SMG

The Model Z45 is based on the German MP 40 but differs in having the cocking handle on the right. It also has a protective perforated barrel jacket and an easily removable barrel which screws out.

There is a version of the Z45 with a wooden stock and both models have selective fire.

Like the MP 40 it is blowback operated and of simple design and construction. It has a compensator to keep the muzzle down at full automatic and it is by rotating this that the barrel can be removed.

The safety arrangements have been improved by fitting an extra catch to the cocking handle which secures the bolt in the forward position. The cocking handle and the catch must be pulled together to free the bolt. The trigger provides single shots when pulled halfway back and full automatic when fully back.

The Z45 was manufactured initially for sale to Germany but production did not get under way until July, 1944. The gun was taken by the Spanish Civil Guard and then the Air Force. In June 1948 it was adopted by the Spanish Army. It has been sold to Chile, Cuba, Portugal and Saudi Arabia. The quantities involved have not been large and in no case has it become the standard SMG.

DATA
Cartridge: 9mm Bergmann Bayard (9mm Largo)

Method of operation: Blowback
Method of locking: Nil
Method of feed: 30-round box magazine
Method of fire: Selective
Weight unloaded: 3.86kg
Weight loaded: 4.54kg
Length – stock extended: 838mm
Length – stock folded: 579mm
Barrel: 198mm
    Rifling: 6 grooves RH
Sights: Foresight: Blade
    Rearsight: Flip. Notch 100 and 200 metres
Muzzle velocity: 381 metres/sec
Muzzle energy: 59mkp
Rate of fire: Cyclic: 450 rounds/min
    Automatic: 120 rounds/min
    SS: 40 rounds/min
Range, maximum effective: 200 metres
Manufacturer: Bonifacio Echeverria SA, Eibar, Spain
Status: No longer manufactured. Still in service in Spanish Army. Sold to Chile, Cuba, Portugal, and Saudi Arabia, all in small quantities. Being replaced in Spanish service by the Z62

9mm STAR MODEL Z62 SMG

The Z62 is a blowback operated weapon which is replacing the Z45 as the SMG in the Spanish Armed Forces. It is conventional design but has some features of interest. The problem of bolt set back when the weapon is dropped has always been difficult to solve and most modern weapons provide some form of bolt lock in both forward and cocked positions. However these often entail some conscious action by the user and soldiers often do not bother. The Z62 incorporates a holding device which is independent of the firer.

The firing pin is operated by the hammer in the bolt. The hammer is rotated by a rod projecting from the bolt face and driven back when the bolt closes. At the same time as the rod rotates the hammer it disengages a bolt lock which at all other times prevents hammer movement.

The trigger mechanism of the Z62 produces single shots from the lower part of the trigger and full automatic from the top half. The safety catch is a push through type in the upper part of the pistol grip. A D section normally allows the sear to move in the cut-out part of the safety but when pushed across, the full diameter of the safety locks the sear and prevents bolt movement.

The weapon uses pressings, plastics and has a folding stock based on the Czech Model 25.

DATA
Cartridge: 9mm Bergmann Bayard and 9mm Parabellum
Method of operation: Blowback
Method of locking: Nil
Method of feed: 20-, 30- or 40-round box magazine
Method of fire: Selective

The Star Model Z-62 9mm SMG

Weight empty: 2.87kg
Weight, loaded (30 rounds): 3.55kg
Length, stock extended: 701mm
Length, stock folded: 480mm
Barrel: 201mm
Sights: Foresight: Blade
    Rearsight: Flip. Aperture 100 and 200 metres
Muzzle velocity: 380 metres/sec (9mm Parabellum)
Muzzle energy: 55mkp
Rate of fire: Cyclic: 550 rounds/min
    Automatic: 120 rounds/min
    SS: 40 rounds/min
Range, maximum effective: 200 metres

Manufacturer: Bonifacio Echeverria SA, Eibar, Spain
Status: In production. In service with Spanish Forces

9mm STAR MODEL Z-70/B

The Z-70/B was introduced into the Spanish Army in 1971. It was produced because of difficulties with the trigger mechanism of the Z-62. The basic mechanism of the Z-62 remains unchanged but a new trigger mechanism has been designed. Instead of firing single shot and automatic from the two halves of the trigger, a conventional system with a selector on the left of the receiver above the pistol grip has been installed. The safety catch lies under the trigger guard and is pulled back to the safe position and pushed forward to fire. This can be seen in the photograph.

The dimensions and weights remain unchanged from those of the Z-62.

The Star Model Z-70/B 9mm SMG

9mm C2 SMG

This is a small and handy weapon which can be used with either the 9mm Largo or 9mm Parabellum round. Particular attention has been paid to the balance of the weapon which can be controlled with one hand.

Blowback-operated, the C2 differs from many weapons of similar size in not having a fixed, firing pin, the system used being similar to that of the Z62 and incorporates a bolt holding device as one of its three safeties. The bolt can also be locked forward for transport as in the Z45; and the third safety is a position on the selector lever.

Other characteristics of the weapon include a horizontal magazine holding 32 rounds in a double stack; a grooved bolt surface to reduce susceptibility to jamming by dust; a folding metal stock and a generally robust but economical construction.

DATA
Cartridge: 9mm Parabellum or 9mm Largo
Operation: Blowback
Feed: 32-round detachable magazine
Fire: Selective by lever
Weight, without magazine: 2.65kg
Weight of empty magazine: 0.22kg
Length: 72cm, with stock extended, or 50cm
Barrel: 212mm; 4 grooves RH
Sights: Foresight: Blade
    Rearsight: Flip operation 100/200 metres
    Sight radius: 400mm

Muzzle velocity: 325m/sec (Parabellum) or 340m/sec (Largo)
Rate of fire: 600 rounds/min cyclic
Effective range: 200 metres

Manufacturer: Bonifacio Echeverria SA Eibar
Status: In production and in service

SWEDEN

9mm MODEL 37-39F SMG

This was based on the Finnish Suomi Model 31 but the barrel and jacket were shortened by some 11cm. There were other changes to the trigger and cocking handle and the shape of the butt was changed to produce a straight through action. The manufacturer was Husqvarna.

The 37-39 which was also produced was also a copy of the Suomi design but retained the original dimensions.

9mm MODEL 45 SMG

This is the standard weapon of the Swedish Armed Forces. It is made by Carl Gustav and employs stampings from heavy gauge steel sheet. Originally the gun used the Suomi 50-round box magazine from the model 37-39. In 1948 Carl Gustav developed an excellent two-column magazine holding 36 rounds. This was a wedge shaped magazine which has been distinguished by its reliability. It has been copied widely and has been used – or a similar type developed – in Czechoslovakia, other Scandinavian countries and in Germany. This change of magazine led to a detachable housing to allow both types of magazine to be used. The gun incorporating this feature was known as the M45B. The current gun takes only the Carl Gustav magazine and so this led to the simultaneous use of guns with three different magazine housings.

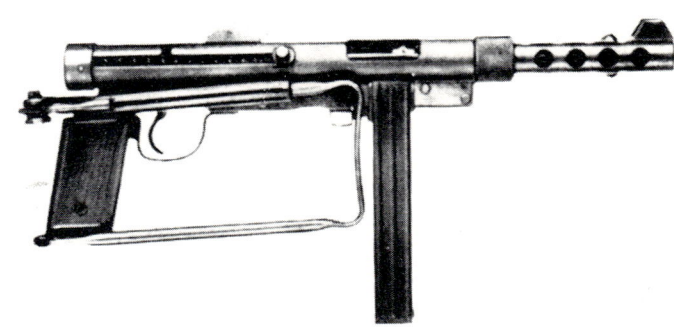

Early model of the M 45

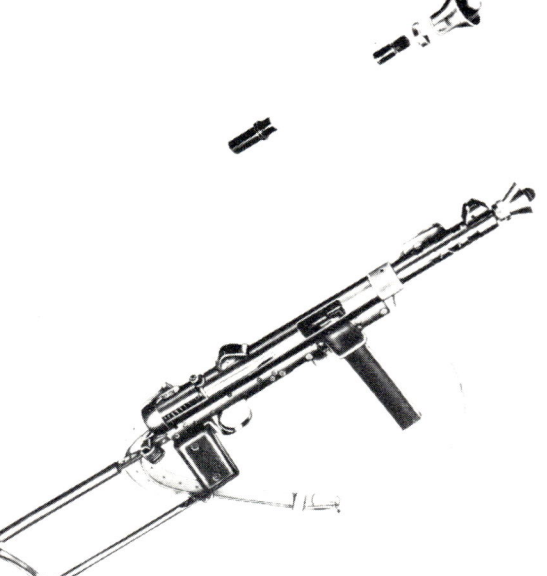

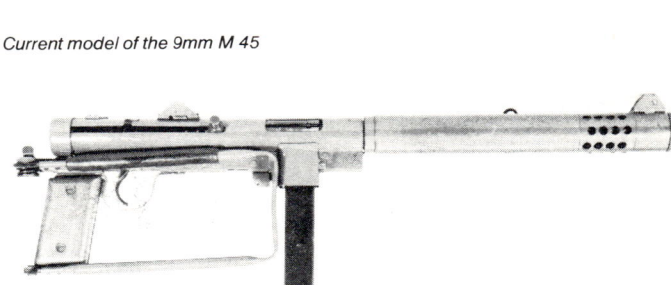

Current model of the 9mm M 45

The close range firing insert for the Model 45. This projects a plastic bullet with a steel ball at the tip for target practice up to 50 metres

DATA
Cartridge: 9mm M39B
Method of operation: Blowback
Method of locking: Nil
Method of feed: 36-round box magazine
Method of fire: Automatic
Weight: 4.2kg
Length: 808mm
Sights: Foresight: Post
       Rearsight: Flip
Muzzle velocity: 365metres/sec
Range, maximum effective: 200 metres
Manufacturer: Carl Gustav Stads Gevarsfactori, Eskilstuna
Status: No longer manufactured. Still in service in Sweden. Supplied also to Egypt and Indonesia and copied in both countries

The Model 45 fitted with a silencer designed for the CIA. Although not very effective it has been used by American Special Forces in Vietnam (RSAF)

Sectioned view of the Carl Gustav

UNION OF SOVIET SOCIALIST REPUBLICS

7.62mm PPD 1934/38 SMG

The Pistolet Pulemet – 'machine pistol' – was the name used by the Russians for a series of sub-machine guns using the 7.62mm × 25 'P' pistol cartridge, starting with the Degtyarev model of 1934. Vasily Degtyarev was one of Russia's greatest designers. His greatest success was his light machine gun which equipped the Russian infantry, armour and aircraft throughout World War II.

The PPD 1934/38 was based on the Finnish Suomi and the German MP 28 and had features from each of these weapons. The 71-round drum magazine came directly from the Suomi and the general shape of the barrel casing and the stock were from the Schmeisser. The magazine is easily identified by a vertical extension which fitted up into the receiver and is unique in the series of Russian SMGs. A curved 25-round box magazine was also made.

OPERATION

The gun fires from the open breech position. The cocking handle can be held to the rear in a slot in the cocking way, by means of a sliding latch. There is also a similar slot to hold the bolt ready for use in the forward position. The bolt is held up on the sear and released when the trigger is operated. The round is chambered, the extractor on the bolt face grips the case and the cartridge is fired by a fixed firing pin on the breech block face. The barrel and chamber were chromium plated, good quality steel was used in the body and there was a great deal of machinery involved in production. Over the years three variations were introduced. The earliest manufactured weapons had a drum with fewer feed followers and so could take 73 rounds. The change lever, fitted in front of the trigger was a flag showing either '73' or '1' when rotated. The firing pin had the Schmeisser external camming lever, the bolt was polished and the trigger guard was a one-piece fabrication. The ejection slot in front of the back sight was very narrow. The second, standard, gun had a 71-round magazine and a fixed firing pin on the bolt face and the bolt was blued. The trigger guard was in two parts riveted together and the ejection slot was much wider. The third and last version differed in having only three slots in the barrel jacket as opposed to 8.

The PPD 34/38 was used by the Russians in the Far East and also in their campaign against the Finns in 1940. Stripping involves removing the magazine, retracting the bolt and inspecting the chamber and feedway. The rear end of the receiver has a screwed cap which is rotated off after which the return spring and bolt can be withdrawn.

DATA
Cartridge: 7.62mm × 25 'P' Pistol cartridge of 7.63mm Mauser
Method of operation: Blowback
Method of locking: Nil
Method of feed: 25-round box magazine. 71-round drum magazine
Method of fire: Selective

WEIGHTS
Gun without magazine: 3.75kg
Loaded magazine (25 rounds): 0.45kg
Loaded drum (71 rounds): 1.93kg
Gun with 25-round box magazine: 4.2kg
Gun with 71-round drum magazine: 5.68kg

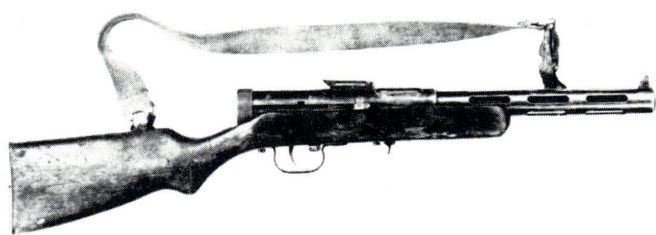

The PPD 1934/38

LENGTH
Gun, overall: 780mm
Barrel: 275mm

MECHANICAL FEATURES
Barrel: Rifling: 4 grooves RH 1 turn in 240mm
    Cooling: Air
Sights: Foresight: Blade
    Rearsight: Tangent notch
    Graduation: 50-500 metres by 50m increments
    Zeroing: Elevation. Change foresight. Zeroing. Line. Foresight on dovetail
    Sight radius: 380mm

FIRING CHARACTERISTICS
Muzzle velocity: 490metres/sec
Muzzle energy: 68mkp
Rate of fire: Cyclic: 800 rounds/min
    Automatic: 100 rounds/min
    SS: 50 rounds/min
Range, maximum effective: 200 metres
Manufacturer: Tula and Sestorets Arsenals
Status: No longer manufactured. No longer in service

7.62mm PPD 1940 SMG

The PPD – like the 1934/38 – was designed by Degtyarev and produced at Tula and Sestorets and was used in the Finnish campaign. The barrel housing is similar to that of the 34/38 but they are not interchangeable and the PPD 1940 can be distinguished from the earlier gun by the wooden fore-end in front of the magazine. The early model 1940 had a tangent rear sight like the 1934/38 but later versions had a simple V notch rearsight. The drum magazine does not have a vertical extension to fit into the gun but has a single lip fitting directly into the magazine holder in the receiver. There is also only one follower.

Although the receiver and cap, return spring, trigger mechanism and sling fittings are interchangeable with those of the 34/38, the bolt is not. This has a movable firing pin controlled by a lever on the bolt head which ensures that the bolt is fully closed before the round is fired.

PPD 40 7.62mm SMG (RMCS)

The 71-round drum magazine of the PPD 40 (RMCS)

The nearest soldier has the RPD 40 SMG. The second soldier has the PPD 34/38 SMG

DATA
Cartridge: 7.62mm × 25
Method of operation: Blowback
Method of locking: Nil
Method of feed: 71-round drum magazine
Method of fire: Selective
Weight unloaded: 3.6kg
Weight loaded: 5.5kg
Length: 790mm
Barrel: 270mm
Sights: Foresight: Blade
    Rearsight: Tangent. Notch on early models. Flip sight 100 and 200 metres on later models

Muzzle velocity: 490metres/sec
Muzzle energy: 68mkp
Rate of fire: Cyclic: 800 rounds/min
    Automatic: 100 rounds/min
    SS: 50 rounds/min
Range, maximum effective: 200 metres
Manufacturer: Soviet arsenals including Tula and Sestorets
Status: No longer manufactured. No longer in service

7.62mm PPSh-41 SMG

The PPSh-41 was designed by George S. Shpagin, hero of Socialist Labour and later Lieut. General of the Red Army, in 1941. The SMG used heavy gauge steel stampings for the receiver and barrel jacket, the bolt was simple to construct and over 5,000,000 were constructed between 1942 and the end of the war. It is now obsolete in the Soviet Army but has been sent in quantity to such areas of Soviet influence as Vietnam and the Middle East where the photographs of the Arab forces, during the October war in 1973, showed it being carried. It has been used by the East German Border Guards for many years. It was manufactured in several other countries including Communist China, Hungary, Iran, and North Korea. In China it is known as the Type 50 SMG, in Hungary as the Model 48M, and in North Korea as the Type 49 SMG. These weapons can usually be identified by the markings on the receiver but additional information can be obtained from the rearsight. The Chinese Type 50 and the North Korean Type 49 have aperture rearsights. The Russian and Iranian PPSh-41 and the Hungarian 48M have V backsights. The North Vietnam K-50 SMG has been altered extensively and is described separately.

Other versions of the PPSh-41 are the models converted by the Germans and Iranians to fire the 9 × 19mm Parabellum cartridge but these are now rare.

The PPSh-41 is a blowback-operated selective-fire weapon with a wooden butt. The barrel is chromium plated and the weapon is extremely reliable and sturdy. The earliest Russian models had a tangent leaf rearsight but in late 1942 a simple flip back sight, giving 100 and 200 metres, was introduced. The front sight is a screw which can be moved on a lateral dovetail. Early models had no foresight protectors. Later models had a simple tubular protector. The magazine is either a 71-round drum with two feed lips or a 35-round, slightly curved, box magazine. The PPSh-41 has a distinctive appearance, and is readily identified by the shape of the front and of the barrel jacket which extends beyond the barrel and is sloped back from top to bottom. It is vented on both sides and on the top and so acts both as a muzzle brake and as a compensator to keep the muzzle down. The change lever is no longer the flag used in the earlier Degtyarev SMGs but is a sliding catch enclosed within the trigger guard. Pressing forward gives full automatic fire: the rearward position operates the disconnector to produce single shots. The safety catch is a sliding latch on the cocking handle which can be moved in to engage in slots in the cocking way. These slots enable the cocking handle to be held in the forward or the cocked position.

OPERATION

To prepare the gun for firing, the magazine must be charged. The cartridge is placed on the magazine follower forward of the feed lips and pressed down. It is then slid to the rear under the feed lips to the rear wall of the magazine. As the spring becomes compressed, loading is assisted by using a screwdriver or similar aid. The Degtyarev drum cannot be used on the PPSh-41 and the special 71-round drum is loaded as follows. Press in the central button in the rear of the drum and swing down the latch on the front cover of the drum. Lift off the cover and latch. Grasp the rotor in the centre of the drum and rotate it counter-clockwise as far as possible. (This will be two revolutions.) During the first revolution (four clicks) the spiral cartridge conveyor must be held stationary. The spiral track insert should then be rotated anti-clockwise as far as possible. Place 71 cartridges in the spiral, bullets up. When all 71 have been loaded, grasp the rotor and turn it slightly anti-clockwise against its spring; simultaneously press in the central button to release the spring and ease the rotor clockwise until it stops. Replace the cover on the magazine and place the latch back in the locked position.

It should be noted that the magazine and the gun should have the same serial number and if this is not so, the combination must be fired to check functioning.

The loaded magazine is slid into the magazine well until the magazine catch engages. The gun is cocked by ensuring the safety slide on the cocking handle is fully out and then the handle can be drawn back. The safety catch is pushed inwards to engage the slot in the cocking way if the gun is not going to be used immediately. To fire the PPSh-41 the selector is placed forward for automatic fire, or slid to the rear for single shots. The safety slide on the cocking handle is moved outwards and the trigger is operated.

When the trigger is operated the sear moves from the bolt and the compressed return spring drives the bolt forward. On its forward stroke the bolt picks up a cartridge from the magazine and feeds it into the chamber. The extractor grips the rim of the case and holds it to the fixed firing pin on the bolt face. The cartridge is fired with the bolt still moving forward. The pressure produced by the burning propellant arrests the forward movement of the bolt before metal-to-metal contact occurs and then drives it back. The empty case is still held to the bolt face and comes back with it until it hits the fixed ejector and is thrown out through the very narrow opening on top of the receiver. The bolt continues back, compressing the return spring until it strikes the buffer and rebounds. If the trigger is still held back, at auto, the cycle will be repeated. If semi-automatic is set, the bolt will be held to the rear. If the ammunition is exhausted the bolt stops in the forward position.

TRIGGER MECHANISM

The sear is a pivoted bar with a step at the rear end which is depressed by a spring loaded pawl carried by the trigger. A disconnector is forced up into the bolt way when the selector is to the rear in the single shot position. When the bolt strikes the disconnector the trigger pawl is forced off the step in the sear which rises to catch the bolt. To fire another shot the trigger must be released and the trigger pawl can then rise and engage the sear again.

PPSh-41 SMG with the 71-round drum. This is an early version with the tangent rear sight (RMCS)

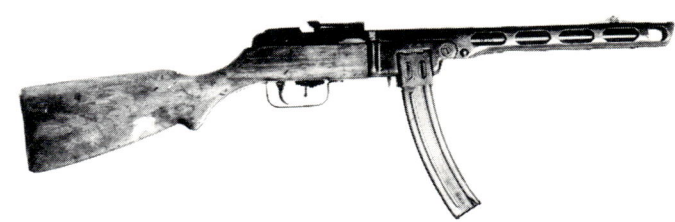

PPSh-41 with the 35-round box magazine. The change lever can be seen in front of the trigger (RMCS)

PPSh-41 with the 71-round drum magazine. The simple rear sight indicates that this is a later version of the gun

PPSh-41 (Novosti)

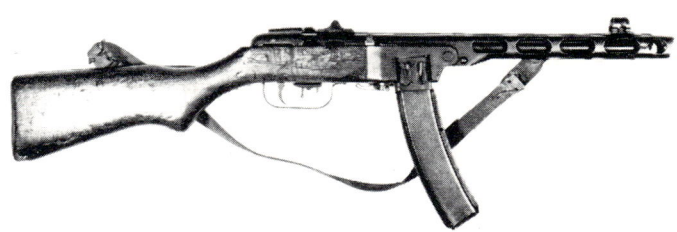

The late version of the gun with the magazine which was produced hurriedly (Lowland Brigade Depot)

STRIPPING

(1) Remove the magazine and check the chamber and feed way are clear.
(2) Press in the receiver catch at the rear of the receiver and pivot the barrel down.
(3) Pull the cocking handle back and the bolt, return spring and buffer can be removed.
(4) Pull return spring from the bolt and buffer from the return spring.

DATA

Cartridge: 7.62mm × 25 – 'P' pistol cartridge
Method of operation: Blowback
Method of locking: Nil
Method of feed: 35-round box magazine; 71-round drum magazine
Method of fire: Selective

WEIGHTS

Gun empty: 8.0lb (3.63kg)
Loaded box magazine: 1.5lb (0.68kg)
Loaded drum magazine: 4.0lb (1.81kg)

Gun with loaded box magazine: 9.5lb (4.31kg)
Gun with loaded drum magazine: 12.0lb (5.45kg)
Trigger pull: 5.0lb (2.27kg)

LENGTHS
Gun: 843mm
Barrel: 270mm

MECHANICAL FEATURES
Barrel: Rifling: 4 grooves RH 1 turn in 240mm
      Cooling: Air
Sights: Foresight: Post
      Rearsight: Early models Tangent notch. 50-500 metres Late models Flip notch. 100 and 200 metres
      Graduations: Early models 50-500 metres by 50m increments Late models Nil
      Zeroing: Elevation. Foresight screws up and down Line. Foresight on dovetail
      Sight radius: 391mm

FIRING CHARACTERISTICS
Muzzle velocity: 490metres/sec
Muzzle energy: 68mkp
Rate of fire: Cyclic: 900 rounds/min
      Automatic: 105 rounds/min
      SS: 40 rounds/min

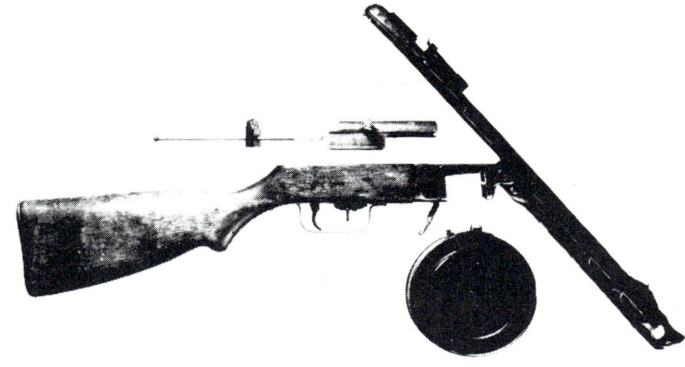

The PPSh-41 field-stripped (RMCS)

Range, maximum effective: 200 metres
Manufacturer: State factories
Status: No longer manufactured. Obsolete in the USSR but still in service in various parts of the world. It has been seen recently in service in the Middle East and with the East German Border Guards and has been manufactured in China, Hungary, Iran, and North Korea and supplied to Vietnam and neighbouring countries

7.62mm PPS-42 and PPS-43 SMGs

The PPS-42 was designed by Alexei Sudayev, an engineer who had previously worked on earth-moving machinery. It is made of sheet steel of heavy gauge stamped into shape and riveted and welded. The buttstock is of folding metal design and this made it suitable for parachute and armoured troops who found the fixed wooden butt of the PPSh-41 inconvenient. When the metal buttstock is folded the shoulder piece folds over and around the ejection port on top of the receiver. This allows a ready distinction between this gun and the amended version known as the PPS-43 where the stock was shortened and when folded located the shoulder piece behind the ejection slot.

The PPS-42 was designed for a quick production and so is extremely unsophisticated. It used only a simple 35-round box magazine, which will not fit PPSh-41 or earlier guns, and fired only at full automatic; but since the rate of fire was reduced from 900 rpm of the PPSh-41 to 650, a skilled operator can achieve single shots by dexterous trigger manipulation. A sheet metal muzzle brake and compensator of very distinctive design is attached to the front of the barrel jacket. The rear of it supports the muzzle and it is welded at the bottom of the jacket and riveted at the top. The stock is released, for rotation over the barrel, by pressing down on the plunger above the rear of the receiver.

The PPS-43 was an improvement produced by Sudayev, after the PPS-42 had been used in action against the Germans, and continued the process of simplification. The fixed ejector of the PPS-42 was removed and the return spring guide rod allowed to project in front of the bolt face, as the bolt came back, to act as an ejector. The magazine sloped forward at an increased angle, the folding stock was shorter, and in later versions the muzzle brake was not welded to the bottom of the jacket but to an additional strap to give more support to the muzzle.

The PPS-43 is now obsolete in the Russian Army but has been issued to a number of satellite countries. It has been manufactured in Poland, as the Model 43/52 SMG which differs in having a lengthened receiver and a rigid wooden butt, and in Communist China as the Type 43 Copy SMG (not the type 54 SMG as it is often erroneously called).

OPERATION

The magazine is loaded, in the usual way, by putting rounds successively on the magazine platform in front of the lips and pressing down the back; the magazine takes 35 rounds and slides up into the magazine well until caught by the magazine catch when fully home. The safety catch is located alongside the front of the trigger guard on the right hand side and is put to 'safe' by rotating it back and up. It then locks the sear in the raised position and prevents bolt movement.

When the trigger is operated the sear is lowered and the bolt is driven forward by the compressed return spring. The feed rib on the bottom face of the breech block picks up the top round from the magazine and forces it up into the chamber. The extractor slips over the rim of the case as the cartridge is aligned with the chamber and the fixed firing pin fires the round as the bolt is still moving forward. The firing impulse arrests and then blows back the bolt. The empty case is held by the extractor until the return spring rod rotates it round the extractor and out of the ejection slot on top of the receiver. The bolt continues rearward until it reaches the buffer. The return spring drives it forward and the cycle is repeated as long as ammunition remains in the magazine and the trigger is operated. When the ammunition is expended the bolt stops in the forward position.

The sear is mounted at its lower end in the bottom of the receiver and slopes back and up to enter a notch in the underside of the bolt. The trigger is pivoted to the sear at its top end. The trigger spring is a plunger which projects through a hole in the trigger and pushes it forward. When the trigger is operated it pivots its top end down and forward and the sear, to

PPS-43 7.62mm SMG (Novosti)

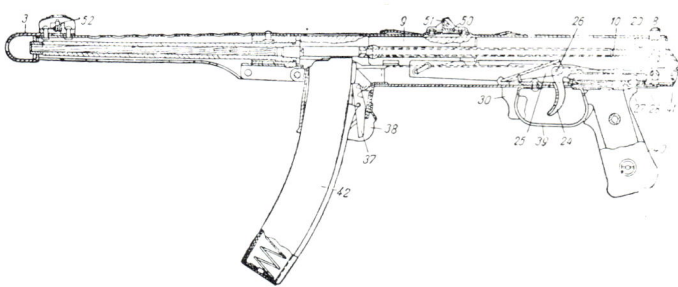

Sectioned view of the PPS-43: **(3)** *Muzzle brake* **(52)** *Sight post* **(9)** *Bolt* **(50, 51)** *Pear sight leaf* **(26)** *Trigger pin* **(10)** *Driving spring* **(20)** *Buffer* **(8)** *Stock button* **(41)** *Receiver catch* **(28)** *Locking plunger* **(27)** *Trigger spring* **(40)** *Stocks* **(24)** *Trigger* **(39)** *Trigger guard* **(25)** *Sear* **(30)** *Safety* **(38)** *Magazine guide* **(37)** *Magazine catch* **(42)** *Magazine*

The PPS-43 field-stripped (RMCS)

which it is pinned, is lowered to release the bolt. When the trigger is released the spring pushes it forward, the top end rotates and the sear is raised.

The pin connecting the trigger to the sear passes through the safety catch. When the safety is applied this pin cannot move, so the sear and the trigger are locked. When the safety is pulled back to 'safe' it rotates upwards and locks the bolt in either the forward or rearward position.

STRIPPING

The gun is stripped by removing the magazine and checking the chamber and feedway and then the lower receiver is dropped by pressing in the receiver catch at the lower rear end of the receiver. The cocking handle is retracted and the bolt swings down out of the receiver. The return spring assembly comes out sideways from the bolt.

DATA
PPS-42
Cartridge: 7.62mm × 25 'P' pistol cartridge 7.63mm Mauser
Method of operation: Blowback
Method of locking: Nil
Method of feed: 35-round box magazine
Method of fire: Automatic

WEIGHTS
Gun unloaded: 2.95kg
Loaded magazine: 0.7kg
Gun loaded: 3.65kg
Trigger pull: 2.3kg

LENGTHS
Gun, stock extended: 905mm

Gun, stock retracted: 640mm
Barrel: 273mm

FIRING CHARACTERISTICS
Muzzle velocity: 500metres/sec
Practical range S/A: 200metres
Practical range auto: 100metres
Rate of fire: S/A: 40rpm
    Auto: 100rpm
    Cyclic: 700rpm
Range, maximum effective: 200metres
Manufacturer: Russian and other state factories
Status: No longer manufactured. No longer in service with Russian or European Communist countries. In service in China with People's Militia. Used by Viet Cong and therefore presumably still in use in Vietnam

PPS-43
As PPS-42 except
WEIGHTS
Gun, unloaded: 3.36kg
Loaded magazine: 0.57kg
Gun, loaded: 3.93kg
Trigger pull: 2.25kg

LENGTHS
Gun, stock extended: 820mm
Gun, stock retracted: 615mm
Barrel: 255mm

FIRING CHARACTERISTICS
Rate of fire: Auto: 650 rounds/min

UNITED ARAB REPUBLIC

EGYPTIAN SMG

When Egypt obtained her independence a small arms industry was set up. The first weapon produced was a copy of the US Thompson. The barrels and the magazines were purchased and were originally produced by Auto Ordnance at Bridgeport. The weapon was altered in several respects. The cocking handle was removed from the top and, like that of the M1 and M1A1, placed on the side of the receiver. The rearsight was of local design and the cylindrical receiver had a screw-on end closure cap.

The weapon which was made in some quantity was the 'Port Said' which was a very close copy of the Swedish Carl Gustaf Model 45B. This weapon is still in service. The accompanying photograph shows the 'Port Said' carried by a soldier crossing the Suez Canal in the October 1973 war.

The Egyptian first line troops are entirely equipped with Russian-made AK 47 and AKM rifles which also carry out the SMG task.

The version of the Thompson .45 SMG made in Egypt (RSAF)

The 'Port Said' SMG is a copy of the Carl Gustav (RSAF)

Egyptian troops crossing the Suez Canal during the Yom Kippur War, Note the 'Port Said' SMG as well as the Russian Kalashnikovs (AP)

UNITED KINGDOM

9mm STEN SMG

In January 1941 the Design Department of the Royal Small Arms Factory at Enfield announced that it had built a prototype of a new SMG. The designer was H. J. Turpin of the RSAF and the project officer was Major R. V. Shepherd who had been recalled to the Army after retiring and working for the Birmingham Small Arms Co. The name given to the gun was STEN – taken from the initials of Shepherd and Turpin and the EN from Enfield where the design work was done. The prototype was demonstrated on 10 January 1941 and in that month fired a limited endurance trial of 5,000 rounds. It functioned well and managed to pass the sand and mud tests and was put into production.

DESCRIPTION

The Mk I gun was designed for rapid production. The cylindrical barrel casing was unperforated. It had a curved tubular metal stock, a large flash hider of semi-coned shape, and a wooden fore-end. There was a tubular

9mm Sten Mk I

wooden handgrip that could be pulled down to the vertical position.

The Mk I* was introduced at the end of 1941 to simplify production. The flash hider was removed together with the wooden fore-end and hand grip. Some 100,000 Mk I and Mk I* guns were made.

The Mk II simplified production by introducing a two groove barrel and a single strut butt with a welded T piece for the shoulder. It was also issued as a silent weapon – the Mk IIS. This was probably the most successful silenced SMG of the War and was used by most of the Special Forces groups. Over 2,000,000 Mk II Stens were made.

The Mk III Sten was produced in 1943. The body of the gun was a formed metal sheet with spot welds and riveting. The barrel was fixed.

The Mk IV Sten was produced only in limited numbers for trial. It was intended for airborne use and was made shorter and more compact with a folding butt. There were two versions – the Mk IVA and Mk IVB. They differed in the shape of the folding butt and the trigger mechanism of the Mk IVB was different from all the other Stens.

The Mk V Sten, introduced in 1944, had a wooden butt and a forward pistol grip which was subsequently removed. The trigger housing was moved forward and the bolt modified. It was a very good SMG – possibly the best produced in the war. A silenced version of it was made and was called the Mk VI.

All the Sten guns had one failing: the magazine was very poor. It was a single feed-position magazine holding 32 rounds and stamped out from sheet. The lips were easily damaged or deformed and the lip angle was critical. If dirt got in there was nowhere for it to go and consequently the magazine was very prone to feed stoppages.

All the Sten guns had basically the same working parts; the bolt was a simple solid cylinder. The front end was machined to allow feed and to take an extractor, the firing pin was a fixed pin on the bolt face and the cocking handle fitted into the bolt. On the early Stens it was possible to drop the weapon on its butt and the inertia of the bolt was enough to make it set back sufficiently to move back past the magazine and feed a round and fire it. Later models were modified so that the cocking lever could be pressed through to lock the bolt in the forward position. At the rear the pin was rotated into a slot cut above the cocking way.

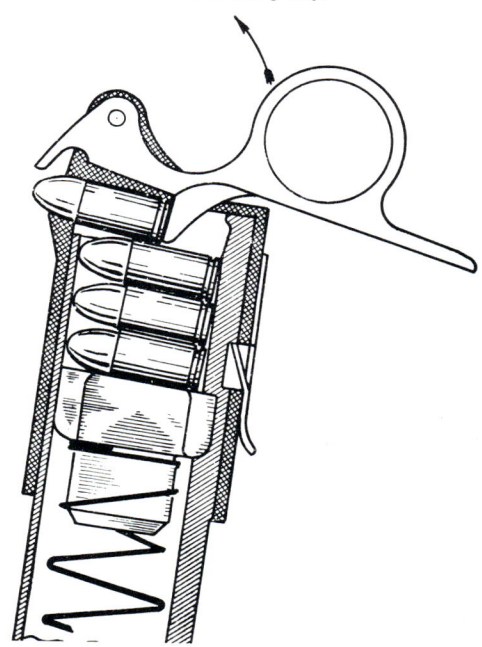

Sten magazine filler

OPERATION

The magazine is removed from its horizontal position on the left of the gun by pressing in the catch on top of the magazine housing with the thumb of the left hand, and the magazine pulled out with the fingers of the left hand.

The magazine filler is placed over the mouth of the magazine. The round is inserted and leverage to force it down comes from the filler lever.

The loaded magazine holding 32 9mm Parabellum cartridges is placed in the gun with the left hand and pushed in until the magazine catch engages.

The cocking handle on the right of the receiver is pulled back to cock the gun and the handle can be placed in the locking recess if firing is not imminent. The mode of fire is selected by pushing the selector button from left to right for single shots (the left-hand end of the selector is marked 'R' for repetition) or from right to left ('A' for automatic) for automatic fire.

With the cocking handle removed from the safety slot, the bolt is held by the sear. When the trigger is pulled the sear is lowered and the bolt is driven forward by the compressed return spring. The feed ribs feed a round from the magazine on the left and push it forward into the chamber. Until the round is in the chamber it is inclined across the feedway and the fixed firing pin on the bolt face cannot reach the cap. When the round is lined up the friction force between the cartridge case and the wall of the chamber slows the cartridge and the fixed firing pin crushes the cap and the round is fired. This system of advanced primer ignition means that the dimensions of the cartridge and the chamber as well as the amount of dirt or carboning present will produce firing at different positions in the chamber from round to round and so there will be small variations in shot travel and chamber pressure. Since the bolt has about 4.5mm to travel forward to the breech face when maximum pressure is developed in the chamber, there will never be metal to metal contact and the breech block floats. This system is sometimes referred to as 'floating firing' and is very commonly met on

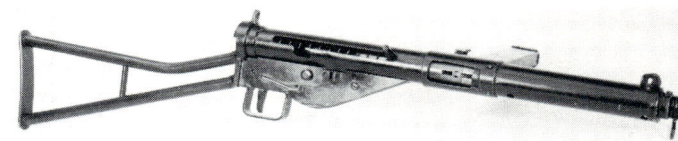

9mm Sten Mk I* (RMCS)

9mm Sten Mk II (RMCS)

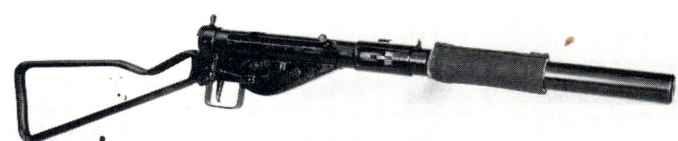

The 9mm Sten Mk IIS was probably the best of the silenced SMGs used in World War II (RMCS)

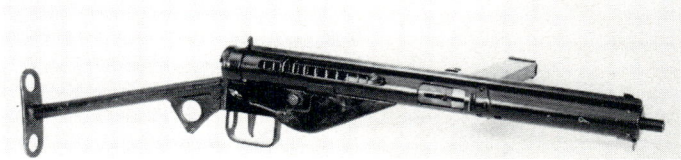

9mm Sten Mk III (RSAF)

9mm Sten Mk IVA (RSAF)

9mm Sten Mk IVB (RSAF)

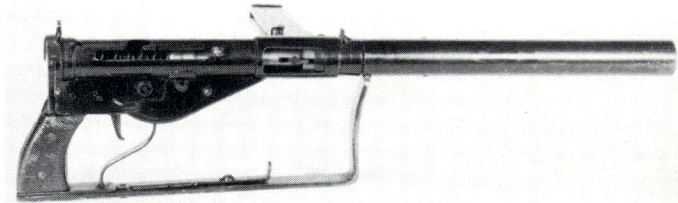

9mm Sten Mk IVA silenced (RSAF)

The 9mm Sten Mk V. This was the early model with the forward hand grip (RSAF)

SMGs of simple design with a fixed firing pin. Half the cartridge impulse is used to bring the bolt to rest and the other half is used to blow the bolt back and provide energy for the cycle of operations.

As the bolt is pushed back by the cartridge case, the return spring is compressed, the empty case is positioned by the extractor for the fixed ejector and the fired cartridge is thrown out to the right. As the bolt moves back over the magazine, the magazine spring forces the next round up ready for feeding when the bolt comes forward again.

TRIGGER AND FIRING MECHANISM

The selector is a simple transverse plunger with a cut-out section which is moved across the gun. It lies over the long tripping lever which at the rear end is attached to the trigger. The tripping lever extends forward and at its front end is swept up into the bolt way and is spring loaded upwards.

At single shot the selector moves so that the cut-out section is over the tripping lever which is free to rise into the bolt way.

When the trigger is pulled the tripping lever is pushed forward.

A stop on its top surface rotates the sear off the bent under the bolt and the bolt goes forward. It hits the top of the tripping lever and forces it down. As it goes down it drops out of contact with the sear which rotates up, under the pull of its spring, and catches the bolt as it comes forward.

At full auto the selector moves across and forces the tripping lever down. It still engages the sear but does not protrude up into the bolt way. When the trigger is pulled the tripping lever goes forward, rotates the sear and releases it from the bent of the bolt, and the bolt passes over the head of the tripping lever without contacting it. When the trigger is released the sear rotates up and catches the bent on the underside of the bolt.

There is no holding open device. When the magazine is empty the bolt stops in the forward position on an empty chamber.

STRIPPING

Remove the magazine, pull back the cocking handle and check that the chamber is empty.

Press in the stud at the rear of the return spring housing and slide the butt

9mm Sten Mk V. Standard model (RMCS)

9mm (silenced) Sten Mk VI (RSAF)

down out of the slots at the rear of the gun.

Remove return spring by rotating cap to left. Pull cocking handle back to the safety slot. Rotate and remove cocking handle. Elevate the muzzle and catch the bolt as it falls out of the rear of the gun.

DATA
Cartridge: 9mm Parabellum
Method of operation: Blowback
Method of locking: Nil
Method of feed: 32-round box magazine
Method of fire: Selective

WEIGHTS	Mk I	Mk I*	Mk II	MkIIS	MkIII	MkIVA	MkIVB	Mk V	MkVI
SMG unloaded kg	3.27	3.18	2.8	3.5	3.18	3.5	3.45	3.9	4.32
Loaded magazine kg	0.64	0.64	0.64	0.64	0.64	0.64	0.64	0.64	0.64
Trigger pull kg	2.73	2.73	2.73	2.27	2.73	2.73	2.73	2.27	2.27
LENGTHS									
SMG butt extended mm	845	794	762	857	762	699	622	762	857
SMG butt folded mm						445	445		
Barrel mm	198	198	197	91.4	197	97.8	97.8	198	95.0

MECHANICAL FEATURES
Barrel: Rifling: 6 grooves. RH. 1 turn in 254mm
(Mk II SMG has 2 grooves)
Sights: Foresight: Blade
    Rearsight: Aperture

FIRING CHARACTERISTICS
Muzzle velocity: All 366metres/sec except Mk IIS and Mk VI 305metres/sec
Muzzle energy: All 51mkp except Mk IIS and Mk VI 35.7mkp

Rate of fire: Cyclic: 540 rounds/min (Mks I, I*, II, III) 575 rounds/min (others)
    Full auto: 128 rounds/min
    SS: 40 rounds/min
Range, maximum effective: All 200metres except Mk IIS and Mk VI 150 metres
Manufacturers: Birmingham Small Arms Co Ltd at Tyseley. Royal Ordance Factory, Fazackerley. Long Branch Arsenal, Canada
Status: No longer produced. No longer in service with any major power. Used in the Nigerian Civil War. Used by various African irregular forces and may be encountered all over the world

---

9mm L2A3 SUB-MACHINE GUN (THE STERLING)

The current SMG in the British Army is the L2A3. This gun is the military version of the Sterling Mk 4 SMG manufactured by the Sterling Armament Co at Dagenham. The original SMG was designed by Mr George William Patchett in 1942. It was produced by Sterling in 1944, and the Patchett Mk II from 1944 to 1954. The gun was called the Sterling Mk 3 in 1953 and was adopted by the British Army as the L2A1. The L2A2 which featured some small modifications came into service in 1955 and the L2A3 in 1956.

The magazine fits horizontally into the left hand side of the receiver. It holds 34 9mm parabellum cartridges. The magazine of the Sten gun, Lanchester, or Canadian C1 will all fit the L2A3. The butt stock may be extended and the weapon used from the shoulder. Alternatively it may be folded under the barrel and the gun fired from the hip. The selector lever is directly above the trigger and the three positions are A (automatic) , R (repetition), S (safe).

The weapon consists of a tubular, perforated receiver, a cylindrical bolt and the stock.

OPERATION

When the weapon is in the 'ready to fire' position, the bolt is held to the rear by the sear and the ammunition is in the magazine. When the trigger is

9mm Patchett Mk 1 SMG (RSAF)

pulled, the bolt goes forward under the influence of the return spring and the first round in the magazine is fed forward into the chamber. Since the magazine is on the side of the gun the round is angled inwards towards the chamber and the cap is not aligned with the fixed firing pin on the breech-face. As the round enters the chamber it becomes lined up with the axis of the bore and as the extractor grips into the groove of the cartridge, the firing pin touches the cap of the cartridge case. The friction force between the cartridge and the chamber wall slows the cartridge and the fixed firing pin fires the cartridge whilst the bolt is still moving forward. The rapid development of the pressure quickly brings the bolt to a standstill and then reverses its direction and blows it back against the return spring. The weight and forward velocity of the bolt at the moment of cap initiation ensure that the rate of return of the bolt is not enough to allow the residual pressure to blow out the case. The cartridge case is forced back by the gas pressure and drives the bolt back. The extractor holds the case to the bolt face until the cartridge hits the fixed ejector which throws it out of the ejection port to the right. The compressed return spring drives the bolt forward and if the selector is at 'auto' the cycle continues; if the selector is at 'single shot', the bolt is held to the rear.

TRIGGER AND FIRING MECHANISM

The trigger mechanism works as follows. The sear is fitted into a spring loaded sear carrier. The disconnector is ⌐ shaped and is pivoted at the junction of the two arms to the sear carrier. The nose of the disconnector is spring loaded to bear against the step on the rear of the sear and the lower arm reaches down towards the spindle of the selector lever. The selector lever spindle has an inner arm which limits the movement of the lower end of the disconnector. The trigger is pivoted at the top and has a shoulder fitting under the sear carrier, which lifts the front of the carrier when the trigger is pulled.

When the selector is set to 'auto' the selector spindle is rotated forward so that the inner arm is not in contact with the lower end of the disconnector. When the trigger is pulled the sear carrier is rotated up at the front and the nose of the sear is lowered off the bent of the bolt which goes forward. The bolt reciprocation continues as long as the trigger is pulled and ammunition remains in the magazine.

When the selector is set to 'repetition' the inner arm is rotated upwards toward the lower end of the disconnector. When the trigger is pulled the sear comes down as before and the bolt is released. The lower arm of the ⌐ shaped disconnector hits the inner arm of the selector lever and rotates clockwise. This causes the nose to slip off the spring loaded sear which promptly rises to hold up the bolt. When the trigger is released the sear carrier rises and the top arm of the disconnector springs back over the shoulder of the sear.

When the selector is set to 'safe' the inner arm moves rearward under the lower arm of the disconnector. The disconnector is firmly held because it is pivoted on the sear carrier that also is held. Since the sear carrier does not descend the sear holds the sear notch of the bolt or, if the bolt is forward, the safety notch at the rear of the bolt.

STRIPPING

To strip the L2A3, press the magazine release catch above the magazine housing, and remove the magazine. Retract the bolt and check the feedway is clear. Allow the bolt forward under control. Press the release catch under the rear of the receiver and push the receiver cap forward and rotate anti-clockwise. The cap can then be drawn off. Pull the cocking handle back along its slot to the enlarged section where the cocking handle can be withdrawn. The return spring can then be withdrawn. If the gun is then elevated and the trigger pulled, the bolt will come out at the rear.

DATA
Cartridge: 9mm × 19
Method of operation: Blowback
Method of locking: Nil
Method of feed: 34-round box magazine
Method of fire: Selective

WEIGHTS
Gun, empty: 272kg
Magazine, empty: 0.27kg
Magazine, loaded: 0.75kg
Gun, loaded: 3.47kg
Bolt: 0.68kg
Trigger pull: 3.86kg

LENGTHS
Gun, stock extended: 710mm
Gun, stock folded: 483mm
Barrel: 198mm

MECHANICAL FEATURES
Barrel: Rifling: 6 grooves RH 1 turn in 250mm
       Cooling: Air
Sights: Foresight: Blade
       Rearsight: Flip aperture. 100 and 200yds
       Graduation: Nil
       Zeroing: Elevation. Foresight blade screws in and out. Line. Foresight on dovetail
       Sight radius: 410mm

FIRING CHARACTERISTICS
Muzzle velocity: 390metres/sec
Muzzle energy: 62mkp
Chamber pressure: 2151kg/cm²
Rate of fire: Cyclic: 550 rounds/min
       Automatic: 102 rounds/min
       SS: 40 rounds/min

9mm Patchett Mk II also known as 9mm Sterling Mk 3 and also as the 9mm SMG L2A1. Shown with a blank firing attachment (RSAF)

9mm SMG L2A2 (RMCS)

9mm SMG L2A3 (RMCS)

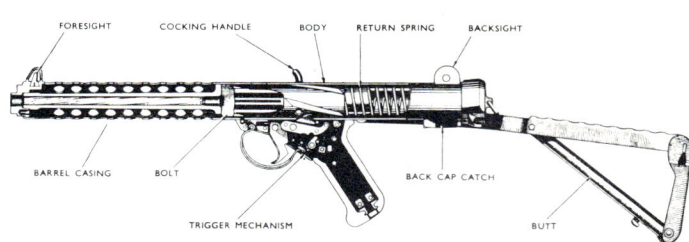

Sectioned view of the Sterling SMG

Sterling SMG on a British Army exercise (MOD photo)

The Sterling Mk 4 SMG

Range, maximum effective: 200metres
Manufacturer: See entry for the L34A1 below
Status: See L34A1 entry

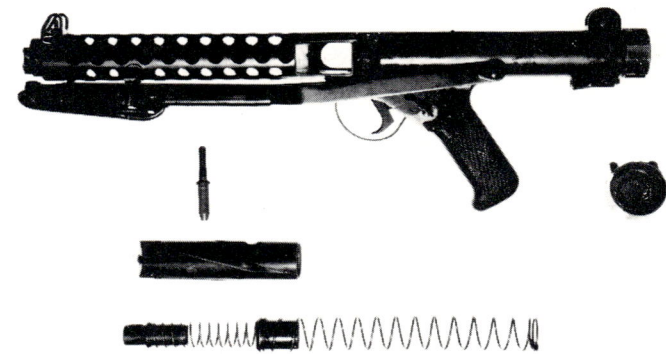

L2A3 stripped (RMCS)

9mm L34A1 SUB-MACHINE GUN

This is the silenced version of the L2A3 SMG used by Infantry Battalions in the British Army. The commercial version is the Patchett/Sterling Mk V SMG.

The bore of the barrel has seventy two radial holes drilled through it, allowing some of the propellent gas to escape and thus reduce the muzzle velocity of the bullet.

The gases which pass through the radial holes in the barrel enter a diffuser tube. This has a series of holes bored through it, and the gases pass from this and are contained in the barrel casing. Eventually they seep forward through the barrel supporting plate or return to the barrel. The silencer casing is extended forward of the barrel and contains a spiral diffuser. The bullet passes down the centre of this but the gases following behind are given a swirling action by the diffuser. The gases which follow closely behind the bullet are deflected back by the end cap and mingle with the gases coming forward through the diffuser. The result of this action is to ensure that the gas velocity on leaving the weapon is low.

As the effective pressure is reduced it is necessary to have a lightened bolt and only a single return spring to enable the blowback action to function efficiently.

9mm SMG L34A1 designed by Patchett in 1964

9mm Patchett/Sterling Mk 5 silenced SMG. This is the commercial version manufactured at Dagenham for export

DATA
Cartridge: 9mm × 19
Method of operation: Blowback
Method of locking: Nil
Method of feed: 34-round box magazine
Method of fire: Selective

WEIGHTS
Gun, empty: 3.6kg
Magazine, empty: 0.27kg
Magazine, loaded: 0.75kg
Gun, loaded: 4.31kg
Bolt: 0.51kg
Trigger pull: 3.4kg

LENGTHS
Gun, stock extended: 864mm
Gun, stock folded: 660mm
Barrel: 198mm

MECHANICAL FEATURES
Barrel: Rifling: 6 grooves. RH 1 turn in 250mm
   Cooling: Air
Sights: Foresight: Blade
   Rearsight: Flip aperture
   Graduation: Nil

Zeroing: Elevation. Foresight screws in and out
   Line. Foresight on dovetail
Sight radius: 521mm

FIRING CHARACTERISTICS
Muzzle velocity: 293-310metres/sec
Muzzle energy: 32-37mkp
Rate of fire: Cyclic: 515-565 rounds/min
   Automatic: 102 rounds/min
   SS: 45 rounds/min
Range, maximum effective: 150metres
Manufacturer: Both the L2A3 and the L34A1 were made by Sterling Armament Co at Dagenham. In addition the L2A3 was manufactured at the Royal Ordnance Factory at Fazackerley. The Sterling Mk 4 and the Patchett/Sterling Mk 5 are currently manufactured at Dagenham. The Canadian SMG, the C1, is basically the Sterling. The gun is also manufactured in India
Status: The L2A3 and the L34A1 are in current service with the British Army. The Sterling Mk 4 has been sold abroad on a considerable scale, some 78 countries having purchased the gun in varying quantities. The principal purchasers have been India – who now manufactures under licence – Malaysia, Tunisia, and Ghana. Nigeria and Libya have also purchased considerable quantities.

UNITED STATES OF AMERICA

.45in THOMPSON SMG

The Thompson SMG was designed by Brigadier-General John Taliaferro Thompson. He spent most of his military career in the Ordnance Department of the US Army. He worked on the Springfield 1903 rifle and the .30.06 rifle cartridge and played a part in the adoption of the Colt 1911 calibre pistol. He retired in 1914 and became Chief Consulting Engineer for Remington Arms Corporation. He laid out the rifle factory at Eddystone, Pennsylvania to produce rifles for the British Army and in 1916 set up the Bridgeport, Connecticut, factory to make the Mosin-Nagant rifle for Imperial Russia.

In 1914 he started designing a blowback operated rifle, in 1915 Commander John Blish USNR joined him and his delay system incorporating an H piece was used in the rifle. Thompson worked with Theodore M. Eikhoff and in 1917 a weapon was produced which Thompson called his 'Trench Broom'. It was the first American SMG. The war ended before it was accepted but Thompson had 15,000 guns made by Colt (the model 1921)

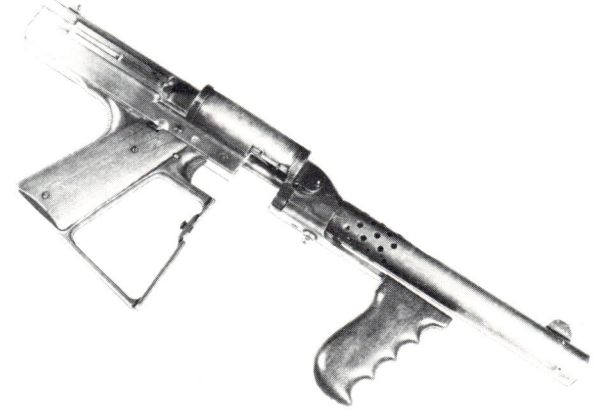

The first prototype of the Thompson SMG used with a tape feed (US Marine Corps Museum)

with parts produced by various other well known firms. The guns were tested by the US Ordnance Department in 1920 and by the US Marines in 1920 and 1921. The reports were good but in the post-war economies there was no procurement action.

The Thompson achieved notoriety during the gangster era in the USA in the 1920s. It was offered in Europe in the 1920s but with little success. In 1928 the Cutts' Compensator was adopted. This was a device which diverted some of the emergent gases upward and forced the barrel down.

In 1938 the Thompson was standardised as the .45 M1928A1 and when war broke out in Europe large quantities were supplied initially to France as well as Britain. General Thompson died on 21 June 1940. His gun was produced in very large numbers and was used by American, Canadian, British and other Commonwealth troops.

The M1928A1 was followed by the M1 and M1A1. The M1 eliminated the Blish piece and the Cutts Compensator and fitted simple sights. The M1A1 removed the hammer and had an integral firing pin. Nearly 1,400,000 Thompson SMGs of various types were made.

DESCRIPTION

The Thompson SMG Cal .45 was a blowback-operated, air-cooled, magazine-fed selective-fire weapon designed to be fired from the shoulder. The butt could be removed, in the M1928A1 only, to enable it to be fired from the hip. It produced selective fire.

The receiver was machined from the solid. It was flat sided and carried the trigger group below and the wooden butt at the rear. The barrel of the M1928A1 had radial fins and a compensator. The M1 and M1A1 had plain barrels and no compensator. The bolt was rectangular in section at the rear with a cylindrical forward extension of about 1in diameter. The bolt of the M1928A1 was lubricated by oiler pads in the receiver. The bolt of the M1928A1 and that of the M1 carried a triangular hammer which struck the receiver and was rotated on to the firing pin. The bolt of the M1A1 had no hammer but had a fixed firing pin.

In the model 1928A1 the Blish piece was used. This was made of phosphor bronze and was ⌐ shaped. The piece lay in the bolt in slots inclined forward at 70 deg. The projecting lugs engaged in 45 deg. grooves in the receiver. The cross-piece engaged in the actuator knob in a slot sloping back at 10 deg. The object of this piece was to take the force produced by the gases and due to the difference in angles it was forced upwards and only slightly back. The theory was the greater the force the more the ⌐ piece jammed. At lower pressures it moved quite freely. It was ultimately found to be unnecessary and was removed from the M1 and M1A1. The actuator carried the actuator knob which was a separate open box connected to the bolt by the ⌐ piece engaging in the actuator knob. It too disappeared on the M1 and M1A1 and was replaced by a conventional cocking handle on the right hand side of the receiver.

The rearsight of the M1928A1 was an adjustable leaf with a windage adjustment. The M1 and M1A1 had a simple fixed aperture.

In general, the M1 functioned in the same way as the M1928A1 but had no actuator, Blish piece or oiling pads. The M1A1 functioned in the same way as the M1 but had a fixed firing pin and no hammer.

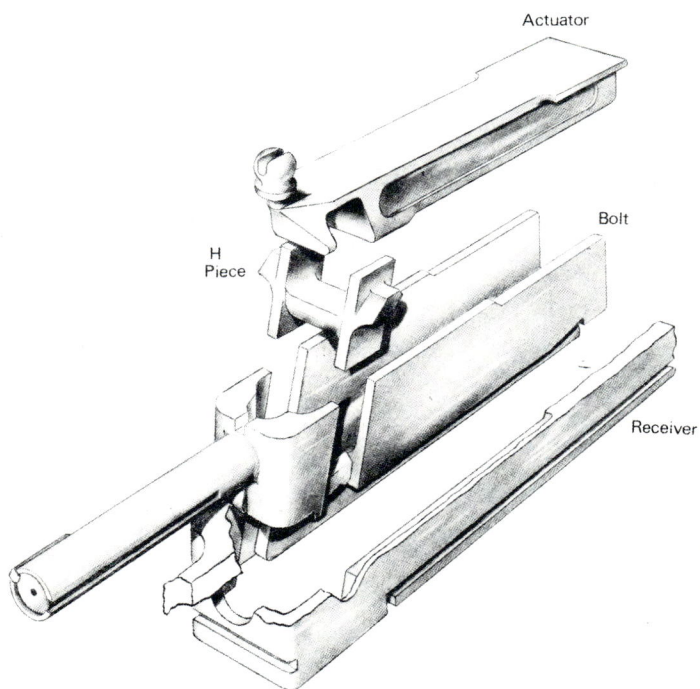

The Blish delay device

OPERATION

All three models take 20- and 30-round box magazines of conventional pattern which are loaded in the usual way by forcing individual cartridges through the feed lips. The gun must be cocked and preferably set to 'safe' before the magazine is inserted. The rib at the back of the magazine fits into a recess at the front of the trigger guard.

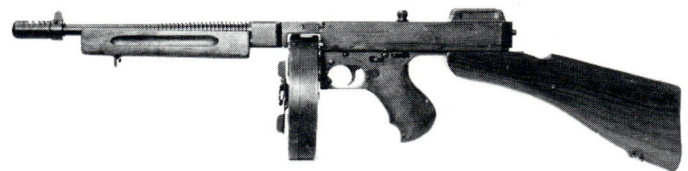

The .45 Thompson SMG Model 1928A1 (RMCS)

Thompson Model M1 (RMCS)

Thompson Model M1A1 (RMCS)

There are also 50-round and 100-round drum magazines that will fit these guns.

The procedure for loading is:
(1) Raise the flat spring to disengage the stud and slide off the key.
(2) Lift off the magazine cover.
(3) Load five rounds, base down, in each section of the spiral track, moving round the outside from right to left, starting at the feed opening.
(4) Replace cover and slide key on. Wind key clockwise 10 clicks.

Cock the gun and set to 'safe'. Insert guide ribs on magazine into grooves in the receiver, from the left, and push magazine in until catch engages.

The gun is now cocked and set to 'safe'. Select either 'single shot' or 'auto' and set the safety catch to 'fire'. When the trigger is pulled the bolt is driven forward by the compressed return spring. The cylindrical front section of the bolt drives the top cartridge from the magazine forward until the nose reaches the bullet guide. The lips of the magazine hold the cartridge in a straight line until the round has cleared the magazine. The bullet guide directs the cartridge into the chamber. The extractor snaps round the rim of the cartridge. In the M1928A1 and M1, the hammer on the underside of the bolt hits the receiver when the round is fully home. The hammer is triangular in shape and when the lower point strikes the receiver, the hammer is rotated about the hammer pin and the upper point of the hammer hits the firing pin. In the M1A1 the fixed firing pin hits the cap of the chambered cartridge. The rectangular surface of the bolt hits an abutment in the receiver to stop the forward motion.

The gas pressure forces the empty case back and drives the bolt to the rear. In the M1928A1 the Blish piece operates to slow the action. The empty case is held to the front face of the bolt. After about 5cm of rearward travel the fixed ejector running in a groove in the left of the bolt, hits the base of the case and throws it out of the gun to the right. The bolt travels back another 4.5cm and then the rear end hits the fibre disc buffer. The compressed return spring then drives the bolt forward again. If the sear is up it will catch one of the two bents on the under side of the bolt. If the sear is down the cycle will be repeated. If there is no ammunition in the magazine a small projection on the back of the magazine follower rises up under the trip of the trigger mechanism and releases the disconnector, allowing the sear to rise and catch the bolt, holding it to the rear.

TRIGGER MECHANISM

With the selector lever set to 'single' the trigger rotates and the rear end lifts the disconnector under the tail of the sear. The tail of the sear is lifted and the nose falls to release the bolt. As the bolt goes forward the point of the rocker is in the T groove under the bolt. This groove pushes the rocker forward against the disconnector and pushes it out from under the tail of the sear. The nose of the sear rises and catches the bolt. The trigger must be released to re-position the disconnector under the sear tail. With the selector lever set to 'Full Auto' the rocker is lowered and the bolt does not contact it as it goes forward, and continuous fire results.

When the safety is set to 'safe' the safety catch spindle engages in a groove in the rear of the sear and locks the sear up. The safety can be operated only when the bolt is cocked.

DATA

Cartridge: Cal .45 ACP
Method of operation: Blowback (with delay in the case of M1928A1)
Method of locking: Nil

Method of feed: 20- or 30-round box magazine
                50-round drum
Method of fire: Selective

WEIGHTS
Gun empty: 4.9kg (M1928A1)
            4.8kg (M1, M1A1)
20-round box magazine empty: 170kg
30-round box magazine empty: 228g
50-round drum magazine empty: 1.25kg
20-round box magazine full: 0.57kg
30-round box magazine full: 0.73kg
50-round drum magazine full: 2.23kg
100-round drum magazine empty: 1.82kg
100-round drum magazine full: 3.86kg
Trigger pull: 3.9kg (M1928A1)
             5.9kg (M1 & M1A1)

LENGTHS
Gun overall M1928A1: 852mm
               M1: 810mm
M1928A1 – Less butt: 635mm
Barrel: 267mm

MECHANICAL FEATURES
Barrel: Rifling: 6 grooves. RH. 1 turn in 406mm
         Cooling: Air

Sights: Foresight: Blade
       Rearsight: M1928A1 – leaf aperture
                   M1 and M1A1 – fixed aperture
       Graduation: (M1928A1 only) 0-6 by 50yds increments
       Zeroing: Windage scale (M1928A only)
                M1 & M1A1 – nil
       Sight radius: 560mm (M1928A1)
                    537mm (M1 and M1A1)

FIRING CHARACTERISTICS
Muzzle velocity: 282metres/sec
Muzzle energy: 58mkp
Recoil energy: 1.38kp
Chamber pressure: 1415kg/cm²
Rate of fire: Cyclic: 700 rounds/min
            Automatic: 120 rounds/min
            SS: 40 rounds/min
Range, maximum effective: 200metres
Maximum: 1600metres
Manufacturer: Auto Ordnance Corporation, Bridgeport, Connecticut. Savage Arms Co. Utica
Status: No longer in production. Not used by any regular military force. Still found in Ireland, Vietnam (locally made) and in Egypt (locally made) and elsewhere. Chinese copies of the early 1922 model may also occasionally be encountered

---

.45 M3 SMG

When the USA entered the Second World War it had only one sub-machine gun in production. This was the Thompson which was heavy, expensive to produce and very demanding in labour and machine tools. A new gun, designed by George Hyde and developed by the Inland Division of General Motors Corporation, and known as the Hyde-Inland, was designated US sub-machine gun calibre .45 M2 on 18 April 1942. Marlin Firearms Corporation had production capacity but had difficulties with their sub-contractors. The M2 was never produced in quantity and on 18 June 1943 was declared obsolescent.

In October 1942 work was authorised on a new SMG. The requirement called for an all-metal weapon, easily disassembled and easily converted to accept the 9mm Parabellum as well as the Cal .45 ACP cartridge. The cost and performance were to be at least comparable to the British Sten gun. The project officer was Colonel Rene Studler, the designer was George Hyde and Frederick Sampson, Chief Engineer of the Inland Division of General Motors Corporation, was responsible for production.

The first design was a selective fire, lightweight weapon, known as the Machine Pistol T15. The selective fire capacity was removed and the Machine Pistol T20 resulted. Five prototypes were tested at Aberdeen Proving Ground in the period 18-24 November 1942. There were only two malfunctions – both due to sticking magazine platforms in 5,000 rounds fired. The accuracy, at the low cyclic rate of 400 rounds per minute, was very good, and it proved reliable in mud and sand tests. The sliding metal stock was lengthened to make the distance from butt to trigger the same as the M1 rifle. On 24 December 1942 it was adopted as the Sub-machine Gun Cal .45 M3.

The M3 was manufactured by the Guide Lamp Division of General Motors Corporation at Anderson, Indiana. The bolts were made by the Buffalo Arms Co. Many difficulties were met in construction and the schedule fell back but in 1944 production was running at about 8,000 a week.

During March 1944 the Office of Strategic Services (OSS) asked for 25,000 9mm conversions of the M3 for supply in the South Pacific Area. The conversion required a magazine adapter, a new barrel and bolt and a single column magazine of the Sten type.

The last of the modified, 9mm, guns was delivered in September 1944. A silencer was made for the M3. Only about 1,000 silenced guns were made – all for the OSS. A flash hider was developed which could be added to the weapon. Over 600,000 M3 guns were made.

DESCRIPTION

The receiver group is cylindrical in shape made up of two side plate assemblies welded together. The barrel bushing is welded to the front of the side plates and has a right hand thread to receive the barrel assembly. A ratchet assembly is riveted to the front of the side plate assemblies, and bears against the serrations in the barrel assembly to prevent the barrel unscrewing. The cover assembly is hinged to the left side plate and carries the safety lock which engages the bolt when the cover is closed. If the bolt is forward the safety lock prevents it from being cocked. If the bolt is cocked the safety lock forces it back off the sear, locking the bolt and making the trigger and sear ineffective. The cover must be open before the gun can be fired.

The rod stock slides along the sides of the receiver in grooves formed in the housing and is retained by a stock catch.

The bolt is cylindrical with two longitudinal holes drilled through to take the guide rods. The return springs are round the guide rods behind the bolt. The bolt face carries a fixed firing pin and an extractor.

The housing assembly consists of a retracting lever assembly, the

The ill-fated .45 in M2 SMG was never produced in any numbers (US Army photograph)

.45 M3 SMG. Notice the cocking handle (RMCS)

The M3 modified, with magazine adaptor, to 9mm calibre (US Army photograph)

Silenced version of the .45 M3 SMG (RSAF)

retracting handle assembly, a housing with ejector assembly and the retracting lever return spring. When the retracting handle, on the right of the receiver, is rotated rearwards it rotates the retracting lever pushing the pawl against a shoulder in the bolt and so retracting the bolt to its cocked position. The top surface of the housing carries the guides for the stock and the trigger and sear mechanism is held in its lower portion.

The magazine consists of the body, magazine follower, spring and base, and is retained in the receiver by the magazine catch.

OPERATION

The box magazine is removed from the gun by depressing the magazine catch on the left of the receiver above the magazine. 30 rounds are loaded into the magazine by pushing each down and back in turn, through the magazine lips.

A hand loader is provided and this, if available, is slid down over the top of the magazine. Insert a cartridge into the magazine until its base contacts the loader. Then raise the loader until it clears the cartridge and push the cartridge to the rear of the magazine. Press the loader down on top of the first cartridge and insert a second cartridge. This procedure is continued until 30 rounds are contained in the magazine.

The magazine is inserted into the magazine opening in the underside of the receiver. The stock is pulled out – if so desired – and the cover opened fully. The cocking handle is rotated and the bolt retracted to the cocked position where it is held by the sear. The cocking handle is allowed to rotate back to its forward position.

When the trigger is pulled, the sear releases the bolt. The two compressed return springs drive the bolt forward. The bolt engages the base of the top round and pushes it forward. It is guided into the chamber and the extractor on the front face of the bolt grips the cannelure in the cartridge head. The firing pin strikes the cap of the cartridge.

The gas pressure generated drives the cartridge case back, pushing the bolt in front of it. The momentum acquired by the bolt carries it to the rear. The cartridge case is held on the front face of the bolt until it hits the ejector and is then thrown out of the ejection port on the right of the gun. The bolt continues moving towards the rear, compressing the two return springs, until the recoil energy is absorbed. After the return springs have brought the bolt to rest, they drive it forward again for the next cycle. If the trigger is released the sear engages the bolt and holds it in its cocked position.

When the ammunition is expended the bolt comes to rest in the forward position.

TRIGGER MECHANISM

Since the gun fires only at full automatic, the trigger mechanism is very simple. The trigger is pivoted on the trigger pin and the top is rotated forwards when the trigger is pulled. The trigger bar is pushed forward and as this is connected to the bottom of the sear block, the top of the sear is

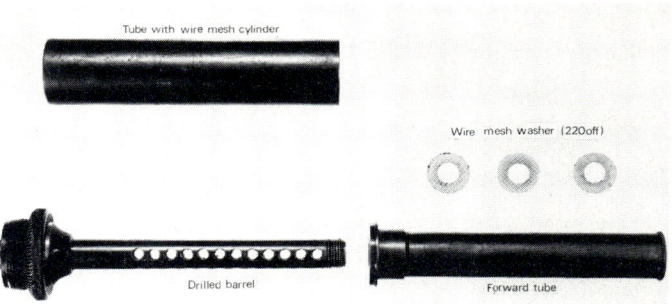

The silencing arrangements for the M3

rotated down out of engagement with the bent under the bolt.

When the trigger is released, the trigger spring, which is connected between the trigger and the trigger bar, is able to contract and pulls the trigger bar back and the trigger forward. The sear is rotated forwards and up until a shoulder hits the front portion of the trigger pin. The hardened face of the sear then holds the bolt to the rear.

STRIPPING

(1) Remove the magazine, rotate the cocking handle back and check the chamber.
(2) Push in the stock catch on the left of the receiver and withdraw the stock. Use the shoulder end of the stock as a fulcrum in the trigger guard and press the lower end of the trigger guard out of the pistol grip. Rotate the trigger guard towards the front of the gun to unhook it from the housing assembly.
(3) Remove the housing assembly by pulling down approximately 1in from the pistol grip and then pulling to the rear until it is released.
(4) Hold the ratchet clear of the barrel collar and unscrew the barrel.
(5) Open the cover and slide the bolt and guide rods forward out of the receiver.

DATA

General data for the M3 weapon are incorporated with those given in the entry for the M3A1 below.
Manufacturer: Guide Lamp Division, General Motors Corporation, Anderson, Indiana
Status: No longer made or in US Army service. May be encountered in South America or S.E. Asia

---

.45 M3A1 SMG

In January 1944 troops training with the M3 SMG reported that the cocking lever and the pawl pulling the bolt back were giving trouble. The problem was investigated and it was found that the entire cocking assembly was not essential to the gun. Instead a cavity was made in the bolt to allow the soldier to insert the forefinger of his right hand and pull the bolt to the rear.

The gun so modified was known as the M3A1. The opportunity was taken to incorporate other modifications to rectify small faults that had shown themselves in the preceding months. These changes were:

Elimination of the retracting lever assembly, retracting handle assembly, retracting lever spring and a cotter pin retaining the retracting handle assembly.

Larger port.
Finger hole in bolt.
Guard over magazine catch to prevent accidental operation.
Magazine filler and stock plate added to stock.
Barrel ratchet redesigned.

The advantages of these modifications were soon apparent. The cost of production was reduced, the gun was lightened and could now be stripped simply by removing the barrel and sliding the bolt forward without removing the housing.

In 1945, 15,469 of the M3A1 were manufactured at a cost of about $22 each. During the Korean War an order for 70,000 was placed with the Ithaca Gun Co of Ithaca, NY, of which 33,000 were completed; the contract was then cancelled.

The .45 M3A1 SMG. The cocking handle was removed and a hole in the bolt took the firer's finger. The flash hider was an optional screw-on feature (RMCS)

DATA (Common to M3 and M3A1 except where otherwise indicated)
Cartridge: .45 ACP
Method of operation: Blowback
Method of locking: Nil
Method of feed: 30-round box magazine
Method of fire: Automatic

WEIGHTS
SMG less magazine, sling, oil bottle: M1: 3.63kg. M3A1: 3.47kg
Magazine empty: .34kg
SMG with empty magazine, oil bottle and sling: M1: 4.1kg. M3A1: 3.88kg
SMG with full magazine, oil bottle and sling: M1: 4.7kg. M3A1: 4.52kg
Trigger pull: 2.3-3.2kg

LENGTHS
Gun overall, stock extended: 757mm
Gun overall, stock retracted: 579mm
Barrel: 203mm

MECHANICAL FEATURES
Barrel: Rifling: 4 grooves. RH. 1 turn in 405mm
Cooling: Air
Sights: Foresight: Blade
Rearsight: Aperture set for 100yds (92metres)
Zeroing: Nil
Sight radius: 276mm

FIRING CHARACTERISTICS
Muzzle velocity: 280metres/sec
Muzzle energy: 58mkp
Chamber pressure: 1406kg/cm^2
Rate of fire: Cyclic: 450 rounds/min
Automatic: 120 rounds/min

Range, maximum effective: 200metres
Maximum: 1,550metres
Manufacturer: Guide Lamp Division, General Motors Corp, Anderson,

Indiana. Ithaca Gun Co, Ithaca, NY. Buffalo Arms Co, Buffalo (bolts only)
Status: No longer manufactured. Used by several South American countries and Taiwan and copied by S. E. Asian insurgents

ARMALITE AR–18S 5.56mm SMG

This is a shortened version of the Armalite AR-18 5.56mm rifle (qv). It functions in exactly the same way as its parent rifle and has the same

rotating bolt locking system. The weapon is often fitted with a telescope and the makers have claimed some very accurate shooting.

The 5.56mm Armalite AR-18S

A manufacturer's photograph showing the accuracy and penetration of the AR-18S at 300 and 365yds

DATA
Cartridge: 5.56mm × 45
Method of operation: Gas
Method of locking: Rotating bolt
Method of feed: 20- and 30-round box magazines
Method of fire: Selective
Weight, unloaded: 3.1kg
Length (butt extended): 765mm
Barrel: 257mm
Sights: Foresight: Cylinder
     Rearsight: Aperture

Muzzle velocity: 780metres/sec
Muzzle energy: 111mkp
Rate of fire: Cyclic: 800 rounds/min
     Automatic: 100 rounds/min
     SS: 40 rounds/min
Range, maximum effective: 330metres
Manufacturer: Armalite Inc., Costa Mesa, California and Sterling Armament Co Ltd, Dagenham, UK
Status: Produced in limited numbers. Available for production

ATCHISSON SMGs

Maxwell Atchisson has developed a number of SMGs, rifles and an assault shotgun. He has worked for a number of American firms and his current weapons are marketed by Defence Systems International Inc of Powder Springs, Georgia.

The 9mm Model 1957 is a neat and handy SMG with the 32-round magazine fitting up into the underside of the magazine housing located immediately behind the trigger guard. The magazine makes the rear grip and a wooden fore grip is located below the barrel.

The steel wire stock can be extended in the same way as that of the M3 SMG.

The action is of the conventional blowback system with a single return spring working on a guide rod bearing on the upper half of the rear of the bolt. There is no cocking handle reciprocating with the bolt which, with the return spring, can quickly be withdrawn for maintenance. The very light weight and short length make it a very handy weapon.

Atchisson 9mm M 1957 SMG (Bennett B. Bintliff)

DATA
Cartridge: 9mm × 19 Parabellum
Method of operation: Blowback
Method of locking: Nil
Method of feed: 32-round box magazine
Method of fire: Selective
Length, butt extended: 610mm
Length, butt retracted: 387mm
Barrel: 203mm
Weight: 2.1kg
Muzzle velocity: 366metres/sec

Muzzle energy: 51mkp
Range: 200metres
Manufacturer: WAK Inc, Medway, Ohio
Status: Available

9mm ATCHISSON M16 SMGs

These are three 9mm SMGs all based on the basic configuration and making use of the essential parts of the M16A1 Rifle converted to take the 9mm Parabellum cartridge.

The first version is a short-barrelled gun with a plastic forearm and a telescoping stock. A 25-round magazine fits up into the M16 magazine well. All the general external features of the M16, such as the cocking handle, ejection slot, and bolt enclosure device are unchanged.

Atchisson 9mm 16 SMG. Note the short barrel and the telescoping stock (Bennett B. Bintliff)

The second version has a perforated metal jacket that surrounds the barrel. This reduces the weight of the gun. Otherwise there are no differences.

The third version has a suppressor. The idea of this gun was to provide closed bolt operation with the 9mm round and produce a high order of accurate single-shot fire. A hammer fires the cartridge. The suppressor reduces the velocity of gas exit to sub-sonic velocity and so reduces the noise level at the muzzle.

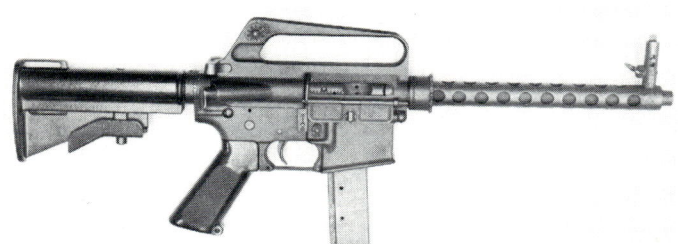

Atchisson M 16 using a perforated barrel casing (Bennett B. Bintliff)

Atchisson M 16 with a MAC type suppressor (Bennett B. Bintliff)

DATA	Plastic forearm	Perforated forearm	Suppressed
Cartridge:	9mm Parabellum	9mm Parabellum	9mm Parabellum
Method of operation:	Blowback	Blowback	Blowback
Method of locking:	Nil	Nil	Nil
Method of feed: 25-round box magazine			
Bolt position at firing:	Open	Open	Closed (Hammer operated)
Method of fire:	Automatic	Automatic	Self-loading
Weight:	2.27kg	2.16kg	2.95kg
Length, stock open:	692mm	692mm	838mm
Length, stock closed:	610mm	610mm	756mm
Barrel:	260mm	260mm	406mm
Status:	Awaiting purchaser		

5.56mm COLT COMMANDO SMG

The widespread use of the Colt manufactured M16A1 rifle in Vietnam led to the call for a shorter handier version specifically intended for the close quarter battle. Colt's Patent Firearms Corporation met this demand by producing the Colt Commando. This weapon was originally designed as a survival weapon but it served so well in the sub-machine gun role that the US Special Forces were issued with it.

The barrel has been reduced from the 508mm of the M16 to 254mm. This has produced a very large muzzle flash and a bigger flash suppressor was found necessary.

The butt is of the straight tube telescoping variety and the length is controlled by a large latch under the butt.

The mechanical features of the M16A1 remain unchanged and the weapon features selective fire and a holding-open device and is actuated by the same direct gas action.

As might be expected the shorter barrel increases dispersion of fire and increases the muzzle blast.

Details of the internal functioning of the Colt Commando are identical with those of the Armalite AR 15 and will be found under that heading. Similarly stripping is carried out in the same way.

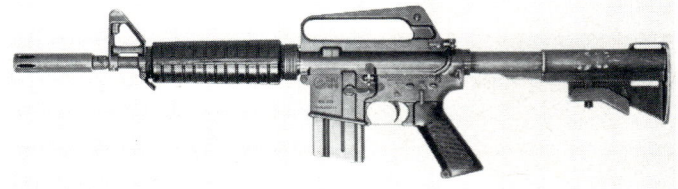

5.56mm Colt Commando (RMCS)

DATA
Cartridge: 5.56mm × 45
Method of operation: Gas
Method of locking: Rotating bolt
Method of feed: Magazine
Method of fire: Selective

WEIGHTS
Colt Commando without magazine and sling: 2.78kg
Sling M1: 0.18kg
Aluminium magazine – empty: 0.09kg
Aluminium magazine – loaded: 0.32kg
Colt Commando with sling and loaded: 3.23kg
Bayonet knife M7: 0.28kg
Scabbard M8A1: 0.14kg
Trigger pull maximum: 3.85kg
                minimum: 2.26kg

The Colt Commando field stripped (RMCS)

LENGTHS
Colt Commando – butt extended: 787mm
Colt Commando – butt telescoped: 711mm
Colt Commando with bayonet knife: 914mm
Barrel: 254mm
Barrel with flash suppressor: 305mm

MECHANICAL FEATURES
Barrel: Rifling: 6 grooves RH. 1 turn in 305mm
        Bore. Maximum: 5.6mm
        Across grooves: 5.7mm
Sights: Foresight: Cylindrical post
        Rearsight: Flip. Aperture

Graduations: 0-100. 100-200 metres
Zeroing: Elevation – foresight. Line – rearsight
Sight radius: 374mm

FIRING CHARACTERISTICS
Muzzle velocity: 924metres/sec
Muzzle energy: 247mkp
Recoil energy: 0.85mkp
Chamber pressure: 3,622kg/cm²

Rate of fire: Cyclic: 700-800 rounds/min
Automatic: 150-200 rounds/min
SS: 40-50 rounds/min
Sustained rate: 12-15 round/min
Maximum effective: 200metres
Maximum (approx): 2,320metres
Manufacturer: Colt's Military Arms Division. Colt's Industries, Hartford, Connecticut
Status: Evaluated as the sub-machine gun 5.56mm XM 177E2.

FOOTE SMGs

John P. Foote has designed several SMGs, assault rifles and an LMG.

The MP 970 9mm SMG is constructed from rectangular welded tubing making up the receiver. This material can easily be handled by firms or countries which do not have advanced manufacturing facilities. The gun is very compact and, as shown, can be handled without the butt. The bolt design is similar to that of the Luigi Franchi 57 (qv) with a fixed firing pin. The gun fires at full auto only.

DATA
Cartridge: 9mm × 19 Parabellum
Method of operation: Blowback
Method of locking: Nil
Method of feed: 32-round box magazine
Weight unloaded: 2.95kg
Length with no stock: 381mm
Length with stock: 622mm
Length of barrel: 203mm
Rate of fire: Cyclic: 650 rounds/min
Automatic: 100 rounds/min
Range, maximum effective: 200metres
Manufacturer: Prototypes only
Status: Prototype only. Available for manufacture

The 9mm Foote MP – 970 SMG (D. Thomas)

.221 IMP SMG

The current acceptance of limited effective ranges for rifles has led to the design of weapons using cartridges of such small calibres that the whole idea would have seemed bizarre only a few years ago. The passage of time and the change in tactical requirements have resulted in weapons designed specifically for one role being considered for use in a different context. An example of such a weapon is the IMP. In the mid 1960s the United States Air Force put out a specification for an aircrew survival rifle and to meet this the Technical Director of the USAF Armament Laboratory at Elgin Air Force Base, Dr Dale M. Davis, produced an unconventional weapon without a butt, using the firer's forearm to carry out the usual functions fo the stock – ie supporting the barrel and action and conveying the recoil to the firer. A wooden mock-up was handled, tried and criticised by a number of people at Elgin and a modified firing model was made using a Remington XP100 pistol taking the .221 Remington Fireball cartridge. This proved a great success and a further model was made from a Mauser 98 bolt action using the full power 7.62mm NATO rifle cartridge. The weight of only 5½lb would never have been acceptable in a conventional design but it appeared to produce little discomfort when fired at single shot.

The .221 IMP (USAF)

In early 1969 it was decided that the concept should be developed by an external contractor to show the characteristics of (a) a survival rifle and (b) a 5.56mm rifle/sub machine gun. Rather than develop a new cartridge for the survival rifle it was decided to continue to make use of the .221 Fireball round, which lay midway between the two cartridges required, and to evaluate the resulting weapon and extrapolate from the results in both directions.

The United States Air Force placed a Research and Development contract with Colt's Military Arms Division for a lightweight weapon which could be used either as a survival rifle or as a rifle/SMG. The contract called for the design and manufacture of four weapons within one year and the provision of non-firing models scaled to take the calibre .17/Frankford Arsenal SP1W round, and the 5.56mm.

The Imp is a gas-operated SMG/Rifle firing at either single shot or full auto. The cartridge is fired in a fully locked breech. The breech bolt has eight locking lugs and is rotated into and out of the locked position by the action of a pin which is rotated about the longitudinal axis of the bolt by a cam slot in the carrier. When the gun fires, some of the gases following the bullet are diverted through a gas port in the top of the barrel and force back a piston which in turn drives the operating rod rearwards. If the gas force is found to be insufficient the piston can be rotated on its rod through 180deg. to provide more gas and a slightly longer power stroke. This operation is easy to carry out and involves a simple disassembly and reassembly operation. The operating rod engages the bolt carrier and prevents the latter from rotating during bolt locking and unlocking. It also carries the return spring and cocking handle. A rectangular slot is aligned over the magazine, when the rod is fully to the rear, and the fired cases are ejected upwards through this aperture.

The carrier is driven back by the operating rod and rotates the bolt to unlock the eight lugs from the abutments in the barrel extension. The extractor on the bolt face is located above the cannelure of the cartridge and the spring loaded ejector impels it upwards through the slot in the operating rod and the ejection port in the top of the receiver.

The .221 IMP showing the ammunition and also the sights (USAF)

The biggest difference between the original project and the final weapon appears in the trigger mechanism. It was intended to have a simple mechanism in which the hammer was rotated down by the carrier and then held by the automatic sear which was released after locking, and during cam dwell, when the carrier pushed the sear release lever forward. A disconnector came in at single shot to hold the hammer until released when pressure on the trigger was relaxed; this allowed the sear to engage the hammer.

In practice it was found necessary to incorporate an inertial rate reducer to delay hammer fall and restrict the rate of fire to 500rpm.

Since there is no butt, a forearm pad is provided to locate the weapon and increase the comfort of the firer. Since the gun is intended to be used by either left or right handed firers, this pad attaches to the right side of the receiver for right handed users and to the left side for left handed users.

The adaptation to the needs of both left and right handed firers leads to an arrangement by which the pistol grip and trigger can be rotated to one of three positions. These are 38 deg. to the right for right handed firers, or 38 deg. to the left; for storage or for use as a pistol, the group can be located in the central position. There are three foresights and three rearsights. The foresights are posts threaded into the front of the gas tube – corresponding to the three positions of the pistol grip – and adjusted vertically for zeroing. The three U backsights can be adjusted laterally. The universal use of the weapon has been carried further by putting the fire selector dial under the weapon behind the magazine where it can be reached by either hand.

Stripping the IMP is quite simple and consists of the following operations carried out after the weapon has been made safe by removing the magazine, cocking the action and checking the chamber.
(1) Press the receiver latch through the body using the nose of a cartridge, and swing the lower part of the receiver down.
(2) Remove the return spring from the barrel abutment.
(3) Pull back and lift out the operating rod.
(4) Slide the bolt and carrier rod out of the rear of the receiver.
(5) Strip the carrier and bolt.

A detailed evaluation programme has been carried out and two of the weapons were tried out in Vietnam. The basic idea of a high velocity weapon without a butt seems generally to have been accepted for firing at ranges out to 100 metres. Beyond this an optical sight must be incorporated in the design. Various other small changes have been proposed such as providing single shots from a restricted trigger pull and full auto from a long trigger pull. The safety catch might well go inside the trigger guard.

The rifle has now been officially designated "Rifle, calibre .221 GUU – 4/P".

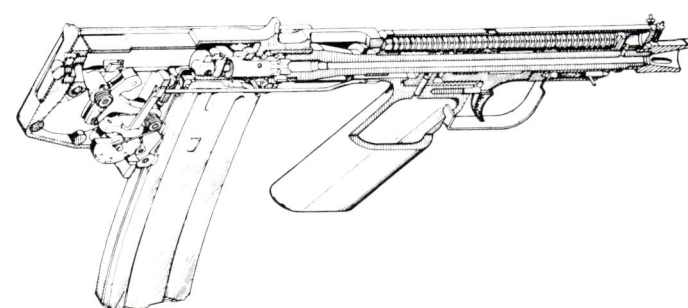

The IMP sectioned (USAF)

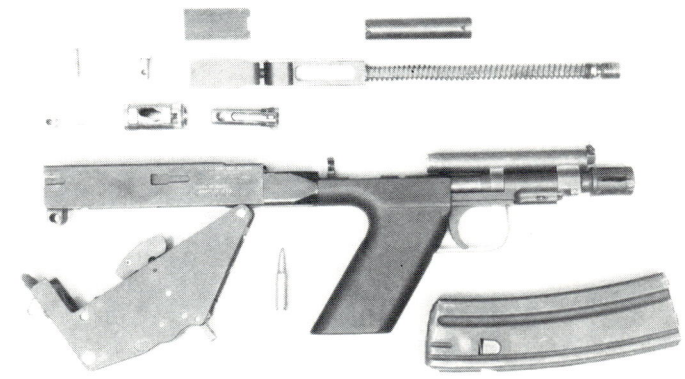

The IMP field stripped (USAF)

DATA	EVALUATION	RIFLE/SMG	SURVIVAL RIFLE
Cartridge:	.221 Fireball	.223 M 193	.17 Frankford Arsenal
Method of operation: Gas operation			
Method of locking: Rotating bolt			
Method of feed:	Box magazine	Box magazine	Box magazine
	30 rounds	30 rounds	10 rounds
Method of fire:	Selective	Selective	Self-loading
WEIGHTS			
Weapon empty:	1.81kg	1.9kg	1.13g
Bullet:	3.24g	3.56g	1.62g
LENGTHS			
Weapon:	403mm	467mm	330mm
Barrel:	254mm	305mm	203mm
MECHANICAL FEATURES			
Barrel:			
Regulator: Nil			
Rifling: 6 grooves RH 1 turn in 305m			
Cooling: Air			
Sights: Foresight: Post			
Rearsight: Notch			
FIRING CHARACTERISTICS			
Muzzle velocity:	732metres/sec	854metres/sec	915metres/sec
Muzzle energy:	119mkp	135mkp	691mkp
Rate of fire: Cyclic:	500 rounds/min	550 rounds/min	
Range, maximum effective:	300metres	300metres	300metres
Manufacturer: Colt's Patent Firearms Co. Ltd., Hartford, Connecticut			
Status: Under evaluation			

INGRAM SMGs

Gordon B. Ingram designed a series of SMGs after he returned to the USA after World War II. All his weapons have been simple designs firing at automatic. He started designing SMGs when the current American weapon was the M3. He allowed for a possible M4 and started his guns at M5. The M5 was a perfectly conventional SMG with a wooden butt, a tubular, perforated barrel casing and used the Reising 12-round magazine. Only one prototype was made. The Model 6 was a blowback model produced by the Police Ordnance Company and sold in .45 ACP to Cuba for the Navy and to Peru for the Army. About 15,000 .45 ACPs were sold in the United States and 8,000 in Peru.

Model 7 was hardly distinguishable from the Model 6 but fired from a closed bolt position.

Model 8 was an improved Model 6 and the Thai government invited Ingram to come to Bangkok to lay out a production line. This he did in 1954 but no production resulted.

Model 9 was an improved version of the Model 8 with a steel butt stock of the M3 type. A prototype appeared in 1959.

MODELS 10 AND 11

In 1969 Ingram started working for Sionics Ltd, a company based in Atlanta, Georgia, specialising in rifle suppressors. They produced a suppressor used on the 7.62mm rifle which produced good results in Vietnam. In 1970 the company was enlarged and the Military Armament Corporation was formed at Powder Springs, Georgia.

DESCRIPTION

The M10 and M11 are of the same basic design and differ in the weight and length dictated by the cartridge used. The model 10 is chambered for the .45 ACP or the 9mm Parabellum. The model 11 takes the 9mm short cartridge (.380 ACP). The weapons are very short, very compact, solidly built and made from steel pressings. The bolts are of the 'wrap round' type with the bolt face and fixed firing pin located well back to allow the greater part of the bolt to envelop the breech. This leads to a shorter weapon or alternatively the same overall length but a longer barrelled weapon. It also helps to keep the centre of gravity over the pistol grip during the firing of a short burst and thus keeps down the magnitude of the oscillations produced during the reciprocating action of the bolt. With the bolt forward all openings are closed and no dirt can get into the action.

Both Model 10 and Model 11 are externally threaded at the muzzle to take the MAC suppressor. The suppressor differs from the conventional silencer in that the bullet is allowed to reach its full velocity and therefore becomes supersonic. The suppressor is added to the muzzle and is intended to reduce the emergent gas velocity to a subsonic level. Thus the 'crack' of the bullet remains but the 'thump' is eliminated. It becomes exceedingly difficult for the target to establish where the firer is since the only sound he hears is the crack of the supersonic bullet as it passes. The suppressor consists of helical channels going forward from the muzzle of the gun which meet similar channels coming back from the front of the screwed-on tube. The meeting of the two gas streams results in a dissipation of their energy inside the suppressor. The suppressor tube is covered with Nomex-A heat-resistant material.

The cocking handle is located on top of the receiver and, like the early Thompsons, has a U notch to allow an unimpeded line of sight. When the bolt is in the closed position, rotating the cocking handle through 90 deg. locks it. The firer is, of course, warned that his bolt is locked because he can no longer use his sights. There is a second safety catch located on the right of the trigger guard, forward of the trigger. When it is pulled to the rear the bolt is locked in either the forward or cocked positions.

The shoulder stock pulls out for firing from the shoulder and pushes in when the gun is to be fired from the hip.

*Top: Ingram Model 7. **Bottom:** Model 6 (Gordon Ingram)*

OPERATION

The magazine release is located at the bottom of the pistol grip and the magazine is filled by pressing the cartridges straight into the top between the lips. The magazine goes up into the grip until the catch locks it in place.

The cocking handle is on the top and can be operated by either hand. Before the gun can be cocked it is necessary to ensure that the cocking handle itself is not rotated to lock the bolt forward and also that the safety slide in the trigger guard is forward to 'fire'. The selector lever determining whether full auto or single shots are fired, is on the left of the receiver forward of the trigger. When the bolt is cocked the sear holds the bent under the bolt.

When the trigger is operated the bolt goes forward, picks up the top round from the magazine and chambers it. The firing pin is fixed to the bolt face and the gun fires whilst the bolt is still travelling forward. The muzzle impulse halts the forward motion and drives the bolt back. The empty case adheres to the bolt face until the ejector throws it out sideways to the right. The return spring is compressed and drives the bolt forward to repeat the cycle.

When the ammunition is expended the bolt stops in the forward position and must be manually recocked.

The Ingram Model 5 (Gordon Ingram)

THE TRIGGER MECHANISM

The trigger is ⌐ shaped. When the trigger is pulled back the extension bar drops. Mounted on the front of the extension bar is a catch, spring loaded forward, which lies over the sear. When the selector is set to auto and the trigger is pressed, the catch holds the sear down and firing continues.

When the selector is set to 'semi' the shaft revolves and cams back a tripping lever which rests under the spring loaded catch. The forward end of the tripping lever (the tripping head) is lifted at the same time. When the bolt goes forward it hits the tripping head and pushes it forward and down. The end under the catch then forces the catch back off the sear and the sear rises to trap the bolt. To get the catch back over the sear it is necessary to release the trigger. When the safety catch is slid back to 'safe' it places a bar under the sear which cannot then be depressed.

STRIPPING

(1) Remove the magazine, retract the bolt and check chamber is clear.
(2) Push the locking pin located at the front of the right side of the receiver, through the gun.
(3) Lift barrel and receiver forward and up, out of the frame.
(4) Pull cocking handle fully to the rear and lift out.
(5) Slide bolt and return spring assembly out through the back of the receiver.

Re-assembly is in reverse order.

The Ingram M10 and M11 SMGs (RMCS)

The Ingram field stripped (RMCS)

DATA	Model 10	Model 10	Model 11
Cartridge:	.45 ACP	9mm Parabellum	9mm short (.380 ACP)
Method of operation:	Blowback	Blowback	Blowback
Method of feed. Box magazine:	30 rounds	32 rounds	16 or 32 rounds
Method of fire:	Selective	Selective	Selective
WEIGHTS			
Gun, empty:	2.84kg	2.84kg	1.59kg
Loaded 16-round magazine:	—	—	282g
Loaded 30-round magazine:	978g	—	—
Loaded 32-round magazine:	—	0.62kg	0.51kg
Suppressor:	0.545kg	0.545kg	0.455kg
LENGTHS			
Gun, no stock:	267mm	267mm	222mm
Gun, stock telescoped:	269mm	269mm	248mm
Gun, stock extended:	548mm	548mm	460mm
Barrel:	146mm	146mm	129mm
Suppressor, length:	291mm	291mm	224mm
Suppressor, diameter:	54mm	54mm	44.5mm
Gun, with suppressor, no stock:	517mm	517mm	413mm
Gun, with suppressor, stock telescoped:	545mm	545mm	440mm
Gun, with suppressor, stock extended:	798mm	798mm	650mm

MECHANICAL FEATURES
Barrel: .45 Rifling: 5 grooves RH. 1 turn in 508mm
9mm Rifling: 6 grooves RH. 1 turn in 305mm
.380 ACP Rifling: 6 grooves RH. 1 turn in 305mm

Sights: Foresight:	Blade	Blade	Blade
Rearsight:	Aperture	Aperture (set for 100 metres)	Aperture (set for 50 metres)
Graduation:	Nil	Nil	Nil
Zeroing:	Nil	Nil	Nil
Sight radius:	210mm	210mm	178mm

FIRING CHARACTERISTICS			
Muzzle velocity:	280metres/sec	366metres/sec	293metres/sec
Muzzle energy:	61mkp	55.3mkp	26.5mkp
Rate of fire: Cyclic:	1,145 rounds/min	1,090 rounds/min	1,200 rounds/min
Automatic:	90 rounds/min	96 rounds/min	96 rounds/min
SS:	40 rounds/min	40 rounds/min	40 rounds/min
Range, maximum effective:	100metres	100metres	100metres

Manufacturer: Military Armament Corporation, Marietta, Georgia
Status: Quantity manufactured. Sold to Chile, Yugoslavia, and trial batches to several countries. See also notes in text on deliveries of earlier models

---

L R ASSAULT SUB-MACHINE GUN

This weapon combines in part the characteristics of the sub-machine gun and the rifle, utilising the basic Ingram SMG body, pistol grip and magazine assembly etc, with carbine length barrel, chambered for pistol ammunition. As an optional extra, the telescopic stock can be replaced with a wooden stock, and further option is the ability to convert the weapon back to a sub-machine gun with a suppressor attachment capability.

DATA
Cartridge: 9mm or .45 ACP
Method of operation: Blowback
Method of feed: Box magazine (32 rounds 9mm or 30 rounds .45 ACP)
Method of fire: Semi- or full automatic
Weight of gun without magazine: 3.635kg
Weight of gun without magazine or flash hider: 3.521kg
Weight of gun and loaded 9mm magazine: 4.316kg
Length with butt folded: 640mm including flash hider
Length with butt extended: 830mm
Length of barrel: 450mm
Sights: Foresight: Hooded post
Rearsight: Adjustable 50 to 350 metres
Cyclic rate of fire: 1,090 rounds per minute
Manufacturer: Military Armament Corporation, Marietta, Georgia, USA

LR Assault SMG

STONER 63 5.56mm SMG

This is part of the Stoner system which allows the conversion of the basic parts consisting of the receiver, bolt, piston and return spring into a whole series of weapons by changing the barrel, stock and trigger mechanism as required. This system as such is described in the section dealing with American Machine Guns, but a brief account of the Carbine (SMG) follows.

The SMG is gas operated with a long stroke piston action. The bolt carries seven locking lugs which are rotated to engage into locking recesses in the barrel extension by the action of the bolt carrier moving a cam path over a cam pin attached to the bolt.

DATA
Cartridge: 5.56mm
Method of operation: Gas
Method of locking: Rotating bolt
Method of feed: 30-round box magazine

Stoner SMG, butt folded

Method of fire: Selective
Weight: 3.7kg
Length, stock extended: 903mm
Length, stock folded: 680mm
Barrel length: 400mm
Sights: Foresight: Post
Rearsight: Flip

Muzzle velocity: 915metres/sec
Muzzle energy: 151mkp
Rate of fire: 750 rounds/min
Range, maximum effective: 300metres
Manufacturer: Cadillac Gage Co
Status: Not in production. Not in service

VIETNAM

7.62mm K-50 M SMG

The Chinese Communist copy of the Russian PPSh-41 SMG is called the Type 50 SMG. The Viet Cong in Vietnam modified the Chinese weapon and named it the K-50 modified sub-machine gun (K-50 M). The major modifications are the removal of the upward folding butt and the substitution of a sliding metal buttstock of the type used in the French MAT 49 SMG. The barrel jacket has been shortened and squeezed in at the second slot. The muzzle brake-cum-compensator has been dispensed with. The lower receiver has been reshaped and a pistol grip added. The foresight has been placed on the barrel.

The weapon is loaded and operates in exactly the same way as the Russian PPSh-41 (qv).

DATA
Cartridge: 7.62mm × 25 Pistol type P
7.62mm × 25 PRC Type Pistol Cartridge
7.63mm Mauser
Method of operation: Blowback
Method of locking: Nil
Method of feed: 35-round box magazine

WEIGHTS
Gun only: 3.4kg
Loaded magazine: 0.681kg
Gun loaded: 4.09kg
Trigger pull: 2.3kg

LENGTHS
Gun, stock extended: 756mm
Gun, stock retracted: 571mm
Barrel: 269mm

The 7.62mm K-50M SMG (RSAF)

MECHANICAL FEATURES
Barrel: Rifling: 4 grooves RH. 1 turn in 241mm
Cooling: Air
Sights: Foresight: Post
Rearsight: Flip notch. 100m and 200m
Zeroing: Elevation. Foresight screws in and out
Line. Foresight on eccentric
Sight radius: 356mm

FIRING CHARACTERISTICS
Muzzle velocity: 488metres/sec
Muzzle energy: 68mkp
Rate of fire: Cyclic: 700 rounds/min
Automatic: 105 rounds/min
SS: N/A
Manufacturer: Local workshops
Status: No longer produced. Probably still in service

7.62mm MODIFIED MAT 49 SMG

The North Vietnamese had a number of French MAT 49 9mm SMGs which they captured during the French Indo-China campaign. They decided to convert these to take the Soviet 7.62mm × 25 pistol cartridge and did so by replacing the French 9mm barrel by a much longer barrel. All the typical features of the MAT 49 – the grip safety, the dust cover and the sliding rod stock – have been retained.

The North Vietnamese 7.62mm SMG. This is a modified version of the French MAT 49 9mm SMG (J. Smith)

.45 VIET CONG THOMPSON SMG

The Viet Cong showed considerable ingenuity in copying weapons of American or European origin. Among the many that they produced was this copy of the Thompson SMG. This is a simplified version of the original gun with a fixed firing pin and it incorporated nearly all the features of the original sub-machine gun.

A Viet Cong copy of the Thompson .45 SMG (US Marine Corps Museum)

YUGOSLAVIA

7.62mm M49 and M49/57 SMGs

The M49 and M49/57 SMGs are based on the Soviet PPSh-41 SMG. Although the general method of operation is the same there are several detail differences. The methods of construction are not the same. Whereas the Russians used stamped parts the Yugoslav gun is constructed from machined parts or drawn tube. The M49 and M49/57 have a large push through safety situated in the forestock in front of the trigger guard; the barrel jacket has small circular holes rather than long slots. The buffer assembly, consisting of a separate buffer spring and split rings, is located at the end of the return spring guide. It resembles that used in the Beretta M38A.

There is no fitting for the Soviet 71-round drum magazine but the Yugoslav guns will not only take their own 35-round curved box magazine but will also take the Soviet magazine from the PPSh-41 and that from the People's Republic of China Type 50 SMG.

The M49 and M49/57 SMGs differ only in non-important details.

DATA
Cartridge: 7.62mm × 25 Pistol 'P' or 7.63mm Mauser
Method of operation: Blowback
Method of locking: Nil

Method of feed: 35-round curved box magazine
Method of fire: Selective
Weight unloaded: 3.95kg
Weight loaded: 4.54kg
Length: 870mm
Barrel: 273mm
Sights: Foresight: Blade
      Rearsight: Flip. Notch. 100 and 200 metres
Muzzle velocity: 500metres/sec
Muzzle energy: 72mkp
Rate of fire: Cyclic: 700 rounds/min
      Automatic: 120 rounds/min
      SS: 40 rounds/min
Range, maximum effective: 200 metres
Manufacturer: Crvena Zastava, Kragujavac
Status: No longer in production. In service with Yugoslav army

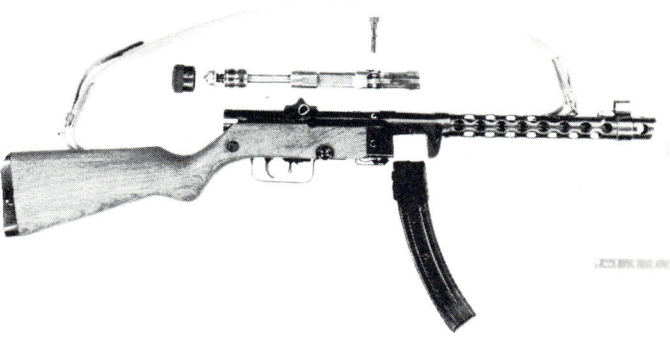

The Yugoslav 7.62mm × 25 M 49/57 SMG. The SMG is a direct copy of the Russian PPSh-41

7.62mm M56 SMG

This SMG is similar in appearance to the German MP 40. The barrel looks very long and fragile and it takes a knife pattern bayonet. The cocking handle is on the right of the receiver and there are locking slots at each end of the cocking way allowing the bolt to be secured in either the forward or cocked positions. The folding stock is of the same pattern as the MP 40.

DATA
Cartridge: 7.62mm × 25 Pistol 'P' or 7.63mm Mauser
Method of operation: Blowback
Method of locking: Nil
Method of feed: 35-round box magazine
Method of fire: Selective
Weight: 3kg
Length, stock extended: 870mm
Length, stock folded: 591mm
Barrel: 250mm
Muzzle velocity: 500metres/sec
Muzzle energy: 72mkp
Rate of fire: Cyclic: 600 rounds/min
      Automatic: 120 rounds/min
      SS: 40 rounds/min
Range, maximum effective: 200metres
Manufacturer: Crvena Zastava, Kragujavac
Status: No longer in production. In service with Yugoslav troops

Yugoslav troops with the 7.62mm M56

RIFLES

INTRODUCTION

The first record of an infantry gun appears about 1364. It was known as a cannon-lock because it was in all aspects a small cannon mounted on a stave and was carried by a single soldier. The word 'lock' refers to the means of ignition and here a burning ember, and later on a slow match, was applied to a touch-hole at the rear end in the same way as to a cannon of the time. It was not until the end of the 15th century that the matchlock appeared. With this type of weapon the iron barrel was attached to a wooden stock that rested on the firer's chest and the burning slow match was held in an S-shaped holder with the lower end acting as a trigger. Pulling the trigger lowered the smouldering match into the powder priming and this set off the main propellant charge. This type of weapon is often called the arquebus. It produced a very slow rate of fire. Before reloading the burning match had to be removed from the serpentine and the powder could then be measured out and poured into the muzzle. The over-charge wad was then inserted followed by the ball and another, retaining wad. The ram rod was then used to consolidate these elements and the priming pan replenished with gunpowder and protected, in many guns, by placing a cover over it. The match was replaced in the serpentine and all was ready for another shot. The amount of match consumed was immense.

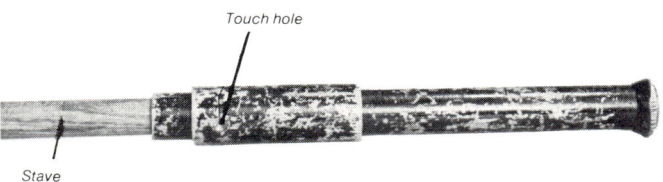

A reproduction of a cannon lock

The situation improved with the introduction of the wheel-lock in the early 16th century. This embodied a principle still used in the modern cigarette lighter. A steel wheel with a serrated periphery was released by pulling the trigger and rotated by a pre-tensioned spring to rub across a piece of iron pyrites. The resulting sparks were thrown into the priming pan full of gunpowder and this set off the main charge in the chamber. The original idea is credited to Leonardo da Vinci and the first practical weapon is attributed to Johann Kiefuss at Nürnberg in 1517. One of the immediate effects of this system of ignition was the development of a short-barrelled weapon which could be used with one hand by a horseman whilst controlling his mount with the other. Cavalry, at this time charged at the trot and when close to the enemy infantry successive ranks fired, turned to the left and filed off to the rear. The pistol was also used as a defensive weapon or in the mêlée which resulted when two bodies of horse came together, but the sword remained the principal weapon of shock in the encounter with infantry.

The wheel-lock was not popular for several reasons. The pyrites tended to crumble with use. It was necessary to use a key to tension the spring and there was no chance of a rapid remedial action after a misfire. Since the 'flash-in-the-pan' was not uncommon the weapon was viewed with distrust. The wheel-lock was expensive to manufacture and if damaged it could not be repaired by the village blacksmith but needed the attention of a gunsmith. Thus it tended to be used by the wealthy – which in those days meant the officers – whilst the troops had to rely on short matchlocks. The answer to these drawbacks came with the introduction of the flintlock at the end of the 16th century. A piece of shaped flint was held in screw-tightened jaws which were pulled back to the cocked position. This tensioned a V-spring and the cock – as it was called from its shape – was held back by the engagement of the trigger sear in a notch. Pulling the trigger released the cock which flew forward and the flint struck a steel plate. The resulting sparks ignited the powder in the flash pan. In the English pattern flintlock there was a cover over the flash pan to protect the powder from wind and rain and the flint in pushing this forward produced the required sparks. This type of ignition was still being made for the African trade in the 1930s. The art of knapping (shaping) flints, was practised at Brandon in Suffolk until 1969. In 1646 General Monk recommended the flintlock for selected marksmen in each regiment of infantry and in 1660 when he became

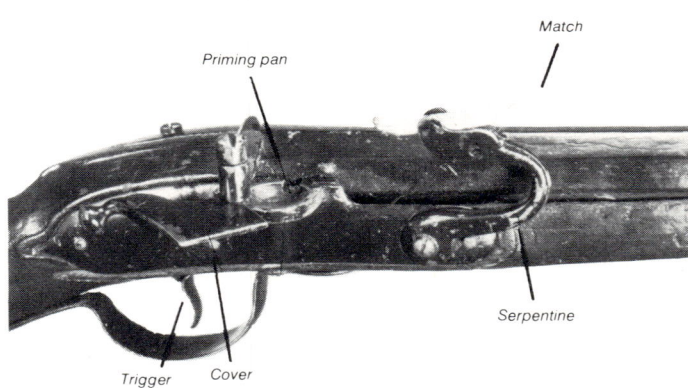

The matchlock

Commander in Chief he equipped his own regiment, the Coldstream, with the flintlock. The flintlock became the main military weapon for over two centuries. Brown Bess, the most famous of all flintlocks, came into the British Army in 1690 and remained the first line weapon until 1840 and was retained by Volunteer regiments until the Crimean War.

One of the grave disadvantages of the early firearms was the complete helplessness of the soldier during the period of reloading, particularly if attacked by the cavalry. This led to the retention of the pike for many years. In 1647 the first bayonet was devised by the Seigneur de Puysegur of Bayonne. This was a plug bayonet which was placed in the muzzle of the musket. In 1685 the Royal Fusiliers copied the French Fusilier Regiments and adopted this form of bayonet. The Battle of Killiecrankie (1689) exposed the limitations of the system. The English Infantry having fixed bayonets prematurely were unable to fire at Dundee's Highlanders, as they rushed in with the broadsword, and were put to flight. General Mackay, the English Commander at Killiecrankie produced the ring bayonet which slipped over the muzzle and allowed the soldier to fire his musket. It came into service in 1697 and remained in use until General Sir John Moore introduced the modern form of spring clip bayonet in 1805. It should be noted that after the bayonet was fixed only one effective round could be fired, unless the troops were very well trained, because the bayonet prevented proper ramming home of the ball; and without correct ramming muzzle-loaders produced extremely inaccurate fire.

So far the soldiers' arm had invariably been muzzle-loaded. In 1775 came the Ferguson Rifle. This is one of the most interesting stories in weapon development. Captain Patrick Ferguson of the 71st Regiment of

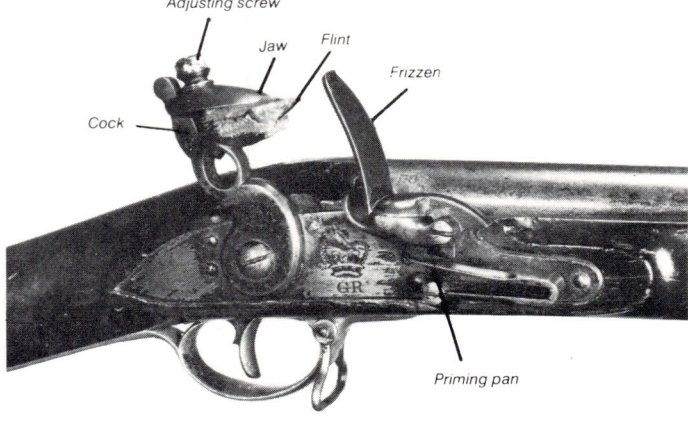

The flintlock

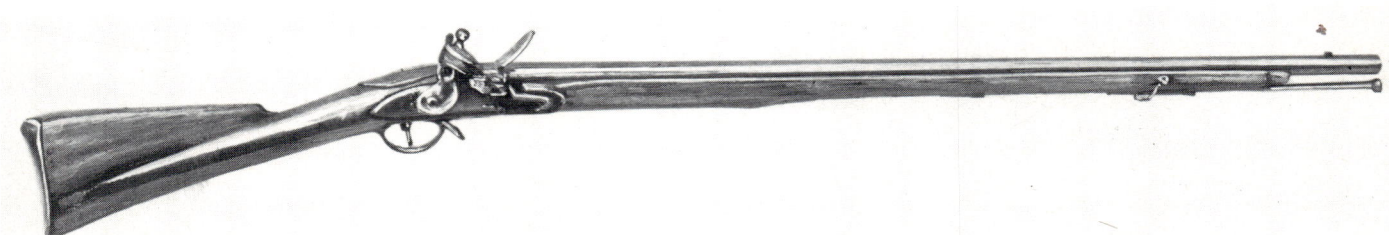

The Brown Bess remained in service from 1730 to the introduction of percussion ignition in 1836. It was of .753 calibre and was used by Marlborough and Wellington

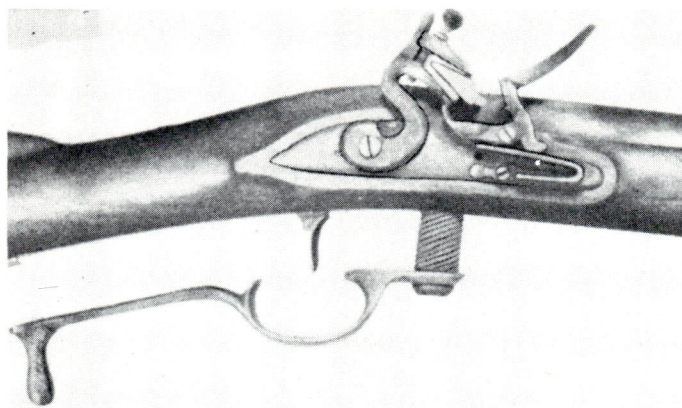

The screw breech of Ferguson's rifle

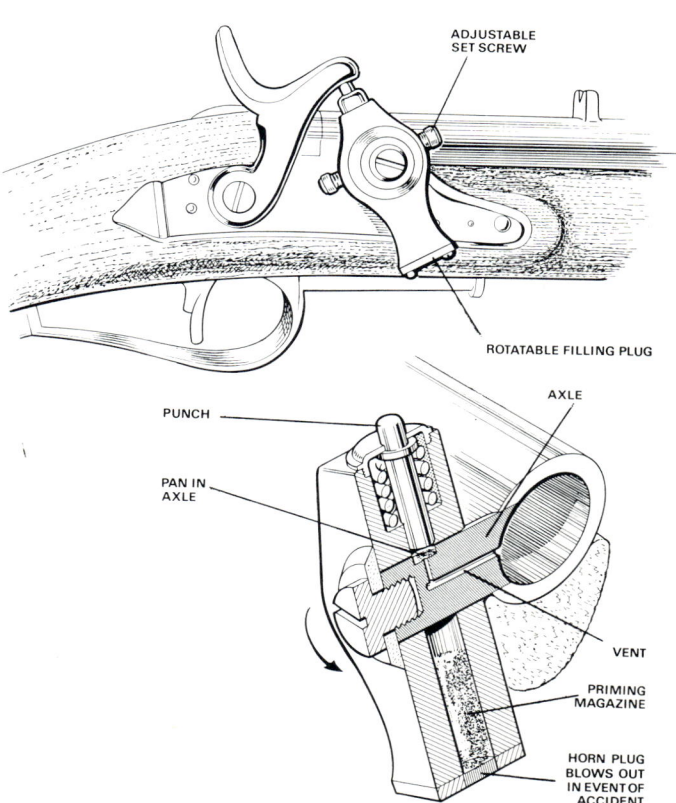

Forsyth's 'Scent Bottle' of 1807

Foot invented the first practical breech-loader. A 12-start screw-threaded plug went through the body of the rifle directly behind the chamber which the plug sealed. The trigger guard was attached to the bottom of this plug and one revolution of the guard lowered the breech closure sufficiently for a ball of 15 gauge (18mm) to be loaded into the chamber and positioned against the commencement of the rifling. The powder was poured in from a metered powder horn and the trigger guard rotated to its normal position. The flash pan was primed and subsequently was fired as a conventional flintlock. At his own expense Ferguson equipped a Company of the 71st with his rifle. In July 1776 he was able to give a demonstration on Woolwich marshes to the Commander-in-Chief and a bevy of distinguished generals. The day chosen could not have produced a more exacting test. It was raining in torrents and no conventional musket would function at all. Ferguson gave a demonstration of loading and firing and produced six shots in a minute all of which hit the target at 200 yards. He then showed that the rifle could be loaded, primed and fired on the move by advancing at a brisk walk and maintaining four rounds a minute. A round every 15 seconds was just twice as fast as the current 'rapid' rate fired from the halt. The military spectators were extremely impressed but showed themselves quite typical of the War Office hierarchy both before and later by doing absolutely nothing to adopt anything 'newfangled'.

In the autumn of 1776 the 71st were sent to North America to help quell the revolt of the settlers and with them went Ferguson's Company. The rifle was used in a number of actions with success including the battles of New York, Dobb's Ferry and Brandwine Creek in September 1777. In 1779 Ferguson's company formed part of the garrison of Stony Point. The American colonists made use of the tactics learned from the Indians and crept up during the night. Before the garrison was awake the position was captured and the rifles passed into the hands of the Americans. Lieutenant-Colonel Ferguson was killed on 7 October 1780, defending King's Mountain against 3,000 Allegheny backwoodsmen during Cornwallis' advance into North Carolina. The British Army did not have another breech-loading rifle for 80 years.

All the weapons described so far, except Ferguson's rifle, were smooth-bored. The reasons for this are obvious. It was cheap and simple. But being muzzle-loaded the ball was of smaller diameter than the bore to facilitate its passage to the breech, and therefore a proportion of the propellant gases escaped. Hard ramming could enlarge the ball and so make a gas-tight fit but such a flattened ball did not fly true. The use of a cloth patch made the ball a tighter fit but slowed loading somewhat. As early as 1500 a barrel had been made in Vienna with a straight rifling and in 1520 a gunsmith named August Kotter of Nurnberg is credited with the first spiral groove rifling. This caused the ball to rotate and so increased its accuracy. In the 16th century this increased accuracy was attributed to the rotation causing the 'devils riding on the bullet to fall off.' The process of rifling was not easy and was expensive to undertake. It was only used by the richest of the hunters in Europe. The military authorities did not take up the idea for three hundred years. The inaccuracy of the muzzle-loaded, smooth-bore was not of great significance when such weapons were used by all armies and the style of warfare relied on mass volleys from troops in close order. The first official British rifle was the muzzle-loaded Baker – issued to the Rifle Brigade in 1800. The flintlock finally gave way to the percussion lock. This was invented by James Forsyth, a Scottish clergyman who had a living at Belhelvie. He was keenly interested in shooting and this led him to experiment with mercury fulminate as a means of igniting the charge in the barrel of a shot-gun. He came to London and interested the Master General of the

Ordnance, Lord Moira, in his work. He was given facilities to continue his experiments in the Tower of London and there produced his percussion ignition system. A hollow spindle entered the barrel and mounted on this was the 'Scent Bottle'. This was so called from its shape. The 'bottle' was in two halves. One contained a punch and the other, situated below it, the mercury fulminate. When the vessel was rotated around the hollow spindle the fulminate came to the top, and some of it entered the hollow shaft. A rotation of 180 degrees brought the punch to the top. When the trigger released the hammer, the blow detonated the mercury fulminate left in the spindle. The resulting flash set off the main charge.

The next step was to produce a pill of fulminate which, being placed on a hollow nipple, produced a flash when it was crushed by the hammer; later a small tube of the compound was used, being placed in a hollow vent and crushed. The percussion cap – shaped like a top-hat and placed over the hollow nipple – is generally attributed to Joshua Shaw, an American, in 1814, although Joseph Manton, a well-known London gunsmith, is also credited with this invention. Following this, Jean Pauly, a Swiss who worked in Paris, produced the first self-contained cartridge case in which the bullet, charge and primer were all incorporated in one unit.

Pauly's apprentice, J.N. Dreyse, went back to Germany in 1827 and offered his muzzle-loaded Needle Gun to the Prussian Army. The 1838 model needle gun was a breech-loader with a bolt which had all the essential features of much later bolt rifles. It had a long thin firing pin which reached through a paper cartridge to a cap located in the middle of the propellant immediately behind the ball. It was not a very good system; the needle eroded badly and when it fired there was a large and frightening flash from the breech. Because of this it was not taken up by Britain or France but it proved to be very successful when used by the Prussians who officially adopted it in 1848. William I of Prussia had re-organised the army and Bismarck made use of it against the Austrians in 1866. The outcome was a triumph for the needle gun which in spite of all its shortcomings enabled the Prussians to achieve a notable victory. As an Austrian officer said, 'Our soldiers are demoralised not by the rapidity of your fire . . . but because you are always ready to fire'. The importance of the ability of the man armed with a breech-loader to load in the prone position was not appreciated until after this war.

In 1823 a Captain Norton of the 34th Regiment of Foot designed a cylindrical bullet with a conical nose. It had a hollow base which expanded under gas pressure to seal the bore. This idea he took from the natives of

The Dreyse rifle or Prussian Needle Gun of 1838

Southern India whose darts expanded in their blow pipes in a similar way. The British Government was not interested in this idea, nor in the improved version by Greener in 1836, yet when M. Minié introduced the idea almost unchanged in France in 1849 the British Government adopted it. They paid Minié £20,000 for his bullet and after Greener protested he was awarded £1,000. The Minié rifle came into British service in 1851.

The final development made possible by the percussion cap was the expanding brass cartridge which itself made the breech-loading rifle a safe, practical and reliable arm. In 1847 Houiller – a Paris gunsmith – invented the pin-fire cartridge. This, as its name implies, had a pin, projecting from the side of the base, which when struck ignited the charge. It was not very safe to carry about and the rim-fire cartridge, developed from an idea of Pauly's, took its place. This is still used in .22 type cartridges, but was superseded by the centre-fire cartridge, invented by Daws in 1861, in more powerful rounds. The first effective centre-fire cartridge adopted in Britain was developed by Colonel Boxer, Superintendent of the Royal Laboratory at Woolwich. This had an iron base and walls of wrapped, rolled brass sheet. It was used from 1866, but was progressively replaced in service by solid-drawn cases first introduced in Britain in 1873 for the .45in Gatling gun. This expanded under the breech pressure and sealed the breech. When the pressure died away it returned to its original dimensions which permitted easy extraction of the case.

The rifle bullet was still propelled by gunpowder. The main disadvantage of this mixture was that it burned very quickly and produced a lot of black smoke and fouling. The French chemist, P. Vielle, produced a gelatinised nitro-cellulose powder – known as Poudre B, from 'blanche' in contradistinction to black powder – in 1884. This was followed by Nobel's ballistite which was nitrated cellulose (gun cotton) gelatinised by nitro-glycerine and stabilised by the addition of mineral jelly. These 'smokeless powders' produced higher muzzle velocities and permitted a reduction in bore diameter from some 0.6in to about half this calibre. Thus a bullet of about 0.3in calibre, weighing about 175 grains and discharged at over 2,000 ft/second was common to most nations at the beginning of the 20th century. The reduction in diameter and increase in velocity led to instability and this necessitated an increase in the twist of the rifling. At these velocities lead bullets would not accept the rifling and stripped their outer surfaces. To combat this Major Rubin of the Swiss Army invented a bullet in which the lead was protected by a harder envelope – initially copper but later cupro-nickel – which allowed the rifling to grip and twist the projectile.

The most telling use of rifle fire probably came in two very different wars. At Gettysburg in the American Civil War the Southern infantry advanced with incredible bravery into the massed rifle fire of the enemy, who made use of the natural advantages of the terrain to take a dreadful toll. This battle decided that the ultimate victory would go to the North.

The British Expeditionary Force in France in August 1914 contained the finest infantry shots ever to go into action. This was the result of the intensive drill and rapid fire practice evolved by Lieutenant-Colonel Mac-Mahon of the Royal Fusiliers who was Chief Instructor at the School of Infantry at Hythe before the war. Denied the machine guns that common sense decreed, by the short-sighted conservatism of the War Office, he concentrated on building up the fire power and accuracy of the infantry. During the retreat the German troops were subjected to such well aimed and such rapid fire that they thought they were opposed by massed machine guns. The Regular Army virtually ceased to exist during the first months of the war but it gained a respite for Kitchener's volunteer battalions to be recruited, trained and to take their place in the line of battle.

Although the Mexican Mondragon self-loading rifle had been manufactured in Switzerland by SIG Ltd, prior to World War I, most nations entered World War II with bolt action rifles. The American Army had the Garand which was a gas-operated 8-shot SL rifle and this led the way. The Russians had the Simonov and Tokarev SL rifles. The Tokarev was made in quantity but was not very successful. The Germans developed a semi-automatic rifle in 1941 and later in the war produced the revolutionary concept of the Assault Rifle with the MP43 and MP44 but most of the German armies were equipped with the Mauser bolt action rifle developed in 1898.

The story of the British effort to introduce a lower powered intermediate cartridge to replace the ultra powerful .30-06 is dealt with in the discussion of British rifles, later in this section, and of the EM 2 rifle in particular. This was rejected largely because the USA insisted on the adoption of the T65 case and the 7.62 bullet and although this produced a standard cartridge it was never very popular. The Russians went to the intermediate cartridge immediately after the Second World War and their rifles, the AK-47 and the AKM, have been the most successful of any introduced in this period.

The Vietnam War involved the US Army and the terrain and the short ranges involved for the rifleman led to the adoption in that theatre of the M16A1 rifle in 5.56mm calibre. Shortly afterwards the American Army announced its intention of adopting the 5.56mm cartridge on a world-wide basis. Thus the pendulum swung fully and the Americans emerged as the champions of the small calibre.

This decision has cut straight across the Stanag on rifle ammunition and set in train a series of developments in several countries aimed at establishing a new NATO standard for the 1980s. Some of the results of these developments are described later in this section.

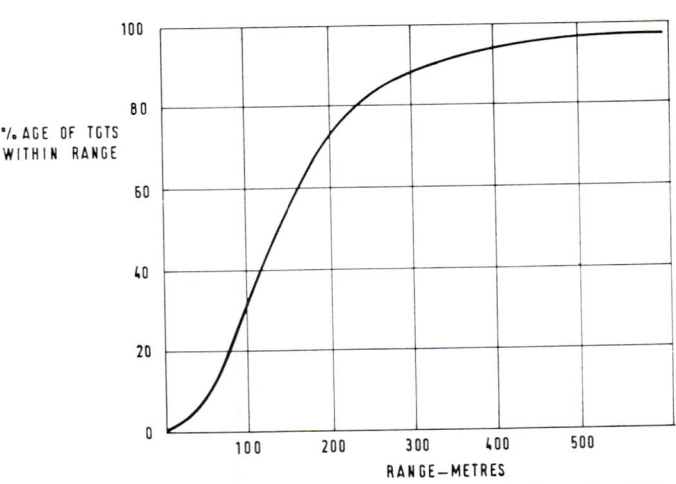

A cumulative frequency diagram (or ogive) showing the expected range for rifle fire engagements

It seems likely – indeed, having regard to the magnitude of American influence in NATO affairs, it is almost certain – that the new NATO standard will specify a light bullet of smaller calibre than 7.62mm. It is also likely that several non-NATO countries will see the commercial wisdom of following the NATO lead. The technical justification for this change rests on two contentions: first, that an infantryman seldom needs to engage a target at a range of more than 400 metres; and, secondly, that a reduction in the recoil energy that has to be absorbed by the firer will substantially increase his chances of hitting his target. There is also the operational justification of a reduction in the infantryman's equipment load; but sceptics suggest that any such reduction is more likely than not to be treated as a reason for requiring the soldier to carry an equivalent load of other paraphernalia.

Statistics of infantry engagements produced by US authorities are demonstrated in the accompanying graph which shows that some 30 per cent of all target engagements occur at ranges of 100 metres or less, about 72 per cent at 200 metres or less, about 88 per cent at 300 metres or less and about 88 per cent at 400 metres or less. If these figures are accepted as valid for all likely infantry engagements, therefore, there is clearly little point in burdening the infantryman with a weapon and ammunition capable of killing a man at 2000 metres when they will only rarely be used to engage targets at ranges in excess of 400 metres. In fact, the figures are not universally recognised as having the required validity: nevertheless, in the absence of a convincing refutation, they are extremely persuasive.

The argument in favour of reducing the recoil energy of the infantryman's principal weapon is, if anything, rather stronger. It is widely agreed that the problem of training a soldier to shoot with a rifle becomes increasingly difficult as the energy level goes up. High speed cine films have shown that even with soldiers of some experience there is a pronounced tendency with some to flinch, and even to close both eyes, whilst waiting for the squeezing of the trigger to release the round.

It has been demonstrated that a satisfactory reduction in recoil energy, coupled with adequate lethality at ranges of 400 metres or so, can be achieved by using a bullet of 5.56mm calibre or possibly less. The suggestion that the performance of the basic infantry weapons should be thus reduced – even if the underlying argument is accepted without reservation – has, however, raised doubts. The infantry section, or squad, traditionally has riflemen and a light machine gun. These are complementary and in the field the riflemen support the gunners with fire as they advance or retire and then the LMG provides supporting fire when the riflemen move. If the LMG is to carry out its normal tasks it undoubtedly needs a greater effective range than 400 metres. The accompanying figure shows machine gun ranges against a number of engagements and is read in the same way as the preceding figure. From this it is seen that the average range i.e. that

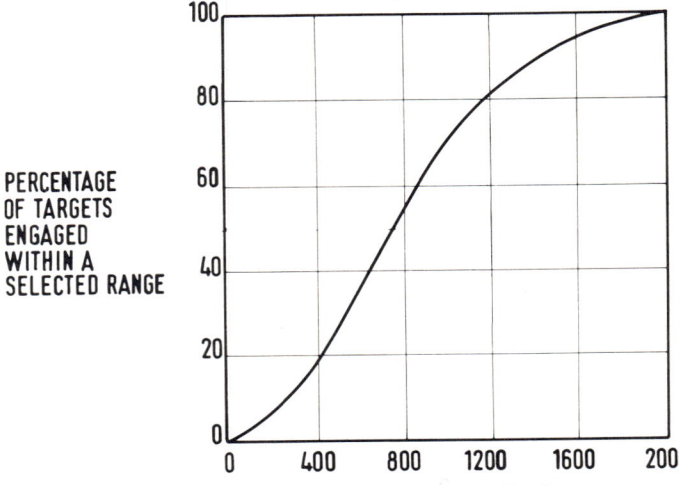

PERCENTAGE OF TARGETS ENGAGED WITHIN A SELECTED RANGE

Expected range for machine gun engagements

range which is exceeded on 50 per cent of the occasions when the gun is used, is about 750 metres and clearly the machine gun cannot use the same ammunition as the rifle.

This use of two natures of ammunition at the lowest level in the infantry battalion is difficult to justify. It causes difficulties in action when the rifleman cannot supply the machine gunner and it causes logistic difficulties in supply.

Two possible approaches to this problem are currently being considered. One, a compromise solution, is to accept a somewhat larger rifle bullet than the ideal, and to use this in the LMG. The other is to adopt 5.56mm or less as the standard calibre both for the infantryman's personal weapon and for a relatively short-range section automatic weapon (probably eliminating the SMG at the same time); and to retain a larger calibre, which might conveniently be 7.62mm, for use in the longer-range roles of the present GPMG, probably reducing the scale of issue of the heavier weapon.

It is too early to forecast the outcome of the discussions and trials that are currently in progress and which will continue long after these words appear in print. Two things can, however, be said with some confidence: first, that it is unlikely that the final decision will be taken solely on military grounds: politics are almost certain to intrude. Secondly, whatever NATO may decide to do, the world at large will continue to use most of the weapons and ammunition described in this book for many years to come.

ARGENTINA

7.62mm FN-PATTERN RIFLES

Formerly equipped with Mauser-type 7.65mm rifles, the Argentinian Army has for some time now used the FN FAL Nato-pattern rifle and the FN heavy-barrelled rifle which are made under FN licence at the ordnance factory at Rosario.

It is understood that three versions of the FN FAL are made at Rosario – the FN 50-00 standard pattern with fixed stock and the FN 50-61 (standard 533mm barrel) and FN 50-63 (short 436mm barrel) both of which have folding stocks. Details of these weapons and of the heavy-barrelled weapon will be found in the entries for the corresponding Belgian weapons.

Manufacturer: Fabrica Militar de Armas Portatiles 'Domingo Matheu', Rosario, Sante Fe.

Status: In production and in service in Argentina.

AUSTRALIA

7.62mm RIFLES L1A1 and LIAI-FI

The Australian Army obtained its rifles from the UK before World War I. In 1912 the Australian Government set up a factory for making rifles at Lithgow, New South Wales, and manufactured the No 1 Mk III* rifle. After World War I the UK authorities introduced the No 4 rifle but manufacture continued in Australia of the No 1 rifle.

A lightened version called the No 6 rifle (Australian) was produced in limited numbers during the war. The production of the No 1 rifle ceased in 1955 with a total of 640,000 manufactured at Lithgow and two subsidiary plants at Orange and Bathurst.

The standard Australian rifle is the LIAI manufactured at Lithgow and conforming in most respects to the British 7.62mm rifle. This is still current in spite of the use of the USA M141A1 5.56mm which was employed by Australian troops in Vietnam only as a replacement for the F1 SMG.

LIAI-FI

An interesting variant of the LIAI rifle was manufactured at the request of the Papua and New Guinea Forces for the use of their troops. This was a shortened and lightened version of the LIAI rifle. A new combined flash eliminator/muzzle brake was designed and this, with a short butt, has reduced the weapon length by some 70mm and the recoil energy by about 20 per cent. As explained below the energy reduction has resulted in an improved grouping capacity, but the primary reason for introducing the modification was to make the weapon more suitable for use in close environments and by troops of relatively small stature.

The redesigned flash eliminator reduces the length by 63.5mm and provides:
(i)   Flash elimination (approximately 95 per cent efficient);
(ii) Muzzle brake (20 per cent reduction in recoil energy);
(iii) A standard fitting for all muzzle attachments; blank firing attachment, grenade launcher, bayonet etc.

A short butt 6.35mm shorter than the LIAI butt completes the length reduction. The modified flash eliminator/muzzle brake is as effective as the standard eliminator, producing no more flash than the gas port, and combines the reduction in recoil with minimum concussive effect to the firer. At 45 and 90 degrees to the rifle the pressure/noise level is less than with the standard LIAI rifle.

The reduction in total length of the barrel assembly has reduced the 'jump' of the rifle barrel, producing a smaller angle of deviation between the layed axis of the bore and the actual line of departure of the bullet and thus improving grouping capacity at shorter ranges.

'Jump' can only be identified scientifically by analysing the differences obtained between the line of departure of the bullet and the static axis of the bore in relation to the velocity of each specific shot, fired from a fixed rest. It should not be confused with the angular displacement of the muzzle, caused by the reaction of the rifle on firing about the point of contact of the butt with the firer's shoulder. This latter displacement, which can be detected by the firer, affects the time taken to relay the rifle on the same aiming point during rapid fire and is sometimes referred to incorrectly as 'jump'.

In the modified rifle, the vertical displacement of the muzzle for a single shot has been reduced because the flash eliminator/muzzle brake is also an effective muzzle compensator. This is achieved because the bottom slot is omitted, as standard practice, to avoid signature effects from sand and dust, and the slots of the muzzle brake are designed to force the barrel down as well as forward.

Compensation, which results from the effect of barrel jump on the line of departure of the bullet for different velocities, is present when the barrel vibrations have a positive phase at bullet ejection in which case the lower the velocity, the higher the muzzle of the barrel will point. This compensates for the lower velocity as compared with the higher velocity bullet, which will be ejected when the barrel is in a lower part of its positive phase of displacement. The magnitude of the 'jump' in the standard LIAI rifle is large and the range at which it is said to compensate is 600 metres. This is the range at which the high and low velocity rounds are closest together, and form the tightest group. In the modified rifle, because the magnitude of the jump is reduced, and is closer to the normal lie of the barrel, the compensating range is shorter, and hence the grouping capacity is better at shorter ranges.

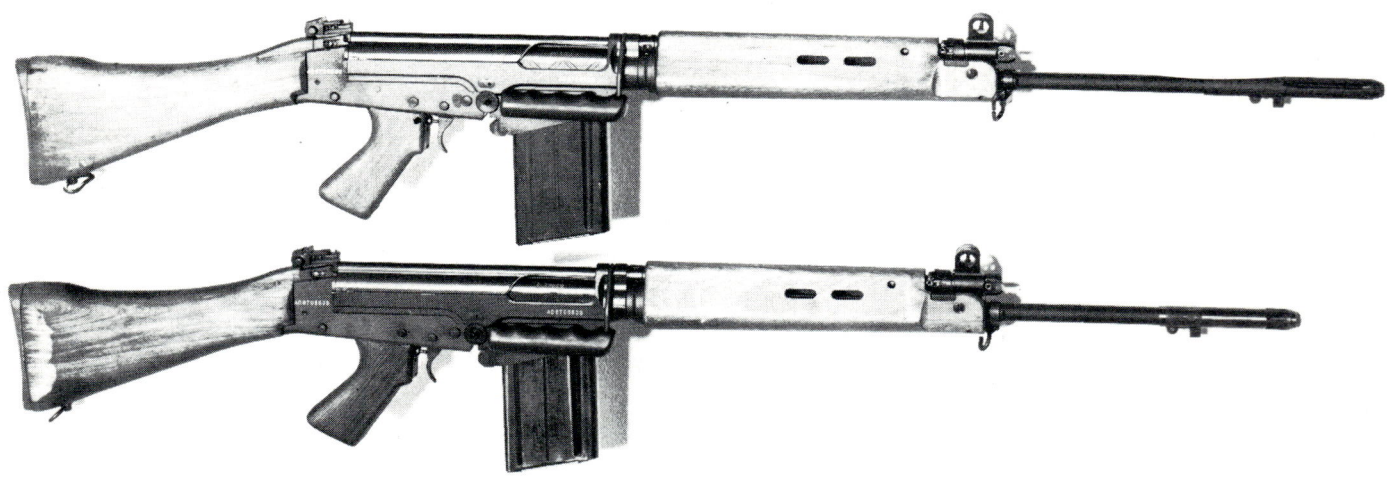

LIAI (top) and LIAI-FI shortened version (Australian Army photograph)

DATA
(LIAI)
Cartridge: 7.62mm × 51
Method of operation: Gas
Method of locking: Tilting block
Method of feed: 20-round box magazine
Method of fire: Single shots
Weight: 4.97kg
Length: 1143mm
Barrel: 533mm
   Rifling: 6 grooves RH
Sights: Foresight: Blade
   Rearsight: Aperture. 200-600 metres
Muzzle velocity: 838 metres/sec
Muzzle energy: 334mkp
Recoil energy: 1.45mkp
Rate of fire: SS: 40 rounds/min
Range, maximum effective: 600 metres
Manufacturer: Small Arms Factory, Lithgow, New South Wales
Status: Still manufactured. In service

SHORT RIFLE (LIAI-FI)
As LIAI except:
Weight: 4.91kg
Length: 1,073mm
Recoil energy: 1.17mkp

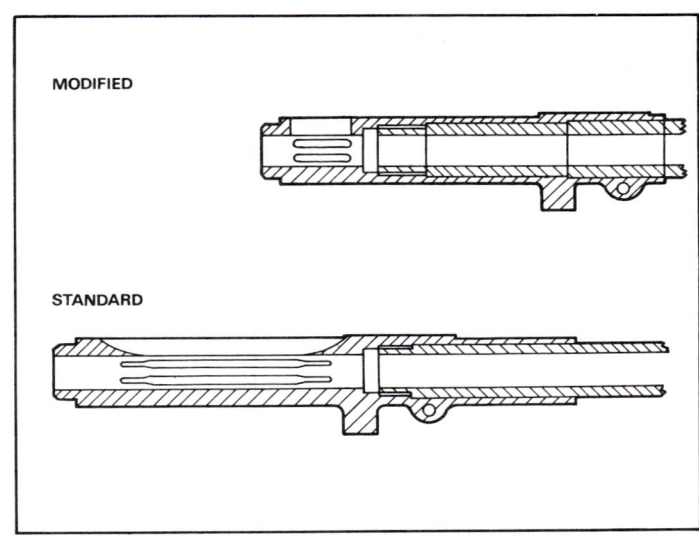

MODIFIED

STANDARD

The standard and modified flash eliminator

7.62mm RIFLE L2AI

This is a heavy-barrelled version of the LIAI rifle used to give some measure of supporting fire to units other than infantry.

Infantry are equipped with the 7.62mm L4A4 Bren LMG.

This rifle is very similar to the standard FN HB rifle and the Canadian C1 HB rifle.

DATA
Cartridge: 7.62mm × 51
Method of operation: Gas
Method of feed: 30-round detachable box magazine
Method of fire: Selective
Weight: 6.9kg
Length: 1,137mm

Barrel: 533mm
   Rifling: 6 grooves RH
Sights: Foresight: Blade
   Rearsight: Aperture
Muzzle velocity: 838 metres/sec
Muzzle energy: 334mkp
Recoil energy: 1mkp
Rate of fire: Cyclic: 675-750 rounds/min
   Bursts: c75 rounds/min
   SS: 40 rounds/min
Range, maximum effective: 800 metres
Manufacturer: Ordnance Factory, Lithgow, New South Wales
Status: No longer manufactured. In service

L2A1 Heavy Barrelled Rifle (Australian Army photograph)

MAGAZINE FILLER FIAI

To enable soldiers to load the magazines used with the LIAI and L2AI rifles more quickly and with less effort, the Australian Army Design Establishment at Maribyrnong, Victoria, has developed a magazine filler which will accept either loose rounds or 5-round chargers. By using this device, it is said, the time to load a 20-round magazine is reduced from a minimum of 30 seconds to 10 seconds and the soldier has full control of the rounds during the loading process.

As is clearly indicated by the accompanying illustration the filler is fitted over the magazine and charged either with loose rounds – up to four at a time – or a 5-round clip: the rounds are then pressed out of the filler and into the magazine. Smooth operation is obtained by coating the filler with Nylon II.

The filler weighs 57 grams and measures 79 × 69 × 25mm and has been adopted by the Australian Army.

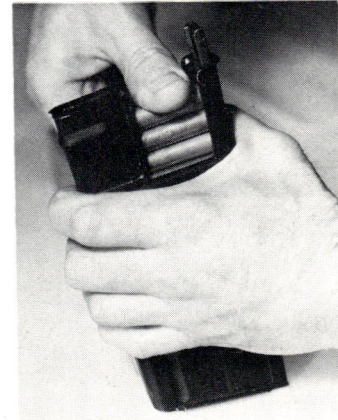

The magazine filler can be charged either with loose rounds or with clips as shown here

Using the magazine filler

7.62mm SNIPING RIFLE

The Australian Army uses the Spartco M44 Sniper Rifle made by the Omark firm in St Mary's, South Australia. This firm make the Omark Target rifle and the Spartco 44 is an improved version of this rifle with a conventional turn bolt action. It has forward locking with three massive lugs. There is no provision for magazine loading and each round is placed in the chamber individually.

The rifle is shown with the standard telescope.

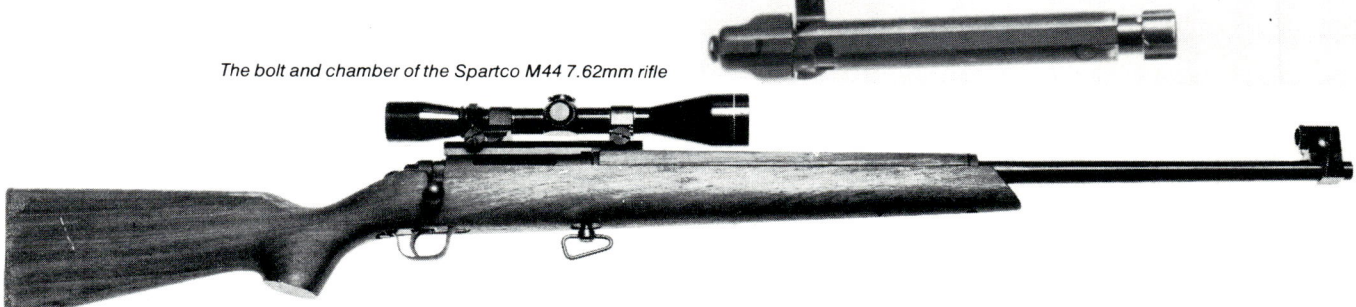

The bolt and chamber of the Spartco M44 7.62mm rifle

Spartco M44 sniper rifle

AUSTRIA

7.62mm (AUSTRIAN) FAL RIFLE

From 1885 until after the First World War the Austrian Army was equipped with Mannlicher rifles of various calibres and patterns.

After the Second World War there was an interim period during which the Austrian Army had a motley collection of weapons from the UK, USA and USSR which have now been replaced by the Belgian FN FAL. Originally this rifle was supplied by Fabrique Nationale but it is now manufactured by Steyr-Daimler-Puch.

Manufacturer: Steyr-Daimler-Puch AG Arms Division, PO Box 4, A-4400, Steyr

Status: In production and in service

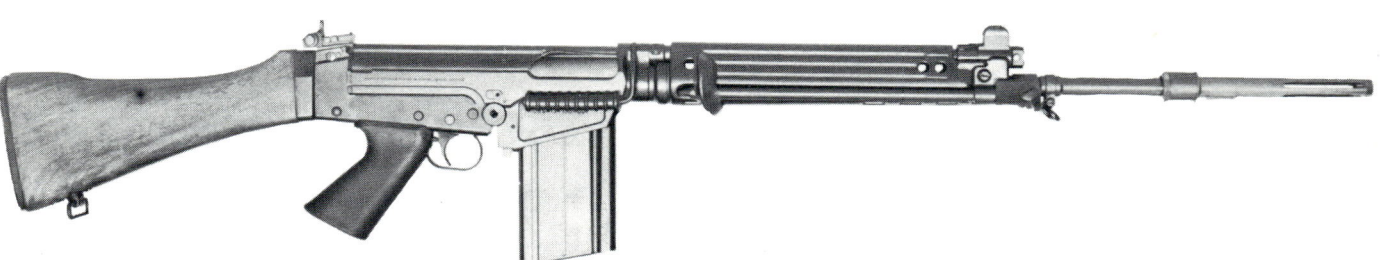

The FN FAL supplied to Austria in 1958

7.62mm SSG 69 RIFLE

This is now the standard sniping rifle for the Austrian Army. It is called the Steyr-Mannlicher-Scharfschützen-Gewehr and is manufactured by Steyr-Daimler-Puch AG at their factory at Steyr. The Austrian Army calls it the Scharfschützengewehr 69 (SSG 69).

It has some features of interest. The barrel is made by the cold forging process – or hammering – in which the billet is placed on a mandrel with the rifling raised in relief. A series of hammers forces the rifling onto the tube and form the external contour simultaneously. This process, originally developed by Steyr and now used by many barrel makers, results in work hardening both the bore and the outside surface of the barrel. It also allows, as in the case of the SSG 69, a slightly tapered bore.

The bolt is manually operated and moves through 60 degrees. It has six rotating locking lugs, symmetrically arranged in pairs, set at the rear. Rear locking, although it allows a shorter bolt movement than the Mauser front locking system, has always been considered to be somewhat less desirable since the whole body of the bolt is placed in compression rather than the bolt head. Also the body of the weapon is weakened by the cut-out on the right hand side of the body in front of the locking shoulders. This in the SSG 69 has been offset to some extent by strengthening the receiver and also by lengthening the receiver to give the barrel seating a length of 5cm which places the chamber within the receiver and so makes the barrel-receiver group very rigid.

The trigger mechanism gives a double pull. The length and weight of the pull are both adjustable externally. The safety catch on the top right of the rear of the receiver is of the sliding type. It locks the bolt and the firing pin.

The standard magazine, holding five rounds, is of the rotating spool type which has been used on Mannlicher sporting and military rifles for many years. The rifle can, however, be used with a 10-round box magazine.

The stock on the sniping rifle is made of a synthetic material. It can be adjusted for length by the addition or removal of the butt pad giving a long, medium or short butt.

The receiver has a longitudinal rib machined on the top to take the Kahles Helia 6S2 telescope of six magnifications. It is graduated up to 800 metres and internally adjusted. The sight is attached by lever clamped rings onto the rib. There are also iron sights brazed onto the barrel for emergency use

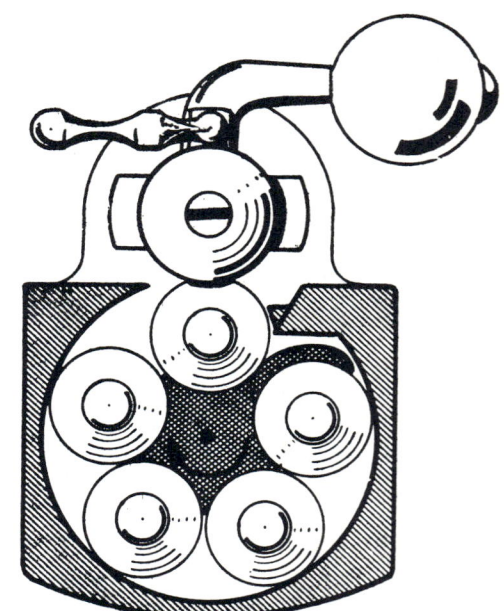

A representative Mannlicher-Schönauer magazine (The Austrian SSG69 rifle holds 5 rounds.)

only. An infra-red night sighting system may also be fitted, or an image intensifier sight.

The same rifle with a heavier barrel and a differently shaped butt-stock is available for competition shooting. The stock may be obtained either in the same material as the SSG 69 or in walnut. This rifle has match sights – Walther tunnel front and rear Walther micrometer.

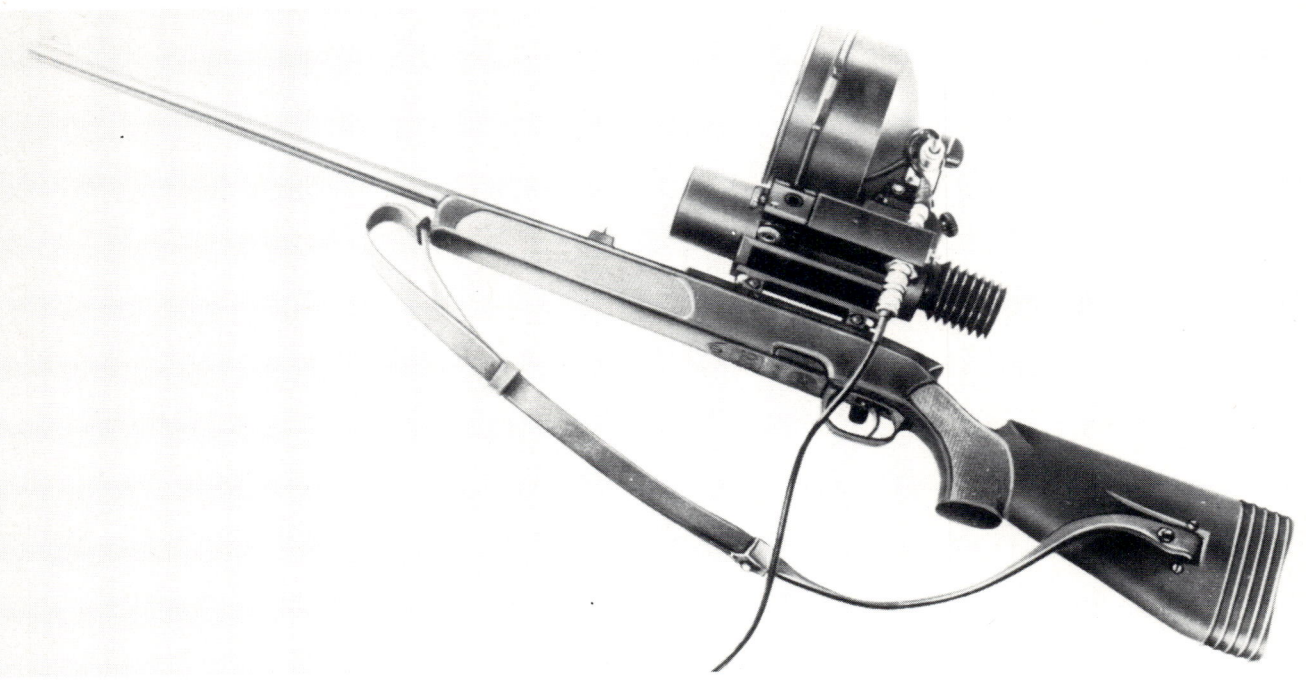

SSG fitted with infra-red sight

Using RWS match rounds the manufacturer claims the following grouping figures:

5 shots at 100 metres 15mm
10 shots at 300 metres 90mm
10 shots at 400 metres 130mm
10 shots at 600 metres 200mm
10 shots at 800 metres 400mm

DATA
Cartridge: 7.62mm × 51
Method of operation: Manual
Method of locking: Rotating bolt
Method of feed: 5-round rotary magazine (or 10-round box)
Method of fire: Single shots

WEIGHTS
Rifle with empty magazine: 3.9kg
Rifle with empty magazine and telescopic sights: 4.5kg
Magazine empty: 0.065kg
Magazine loaded: 0.19kg

LENGTHS
Rifle: 1,130mm
Barrel: 650mm
Sights: Telescopic: 4 ×, internally adjusted to 800 metres
    Reticule: Inverted pointer and broken cross wires
    Iron sights: V backsight. Blade foresight (Emergency use only)

The trigger mechanism

FIRING CHARACTERISTICS
Muzzle velocity: 860 metres/sec
Muzzle energy: 362mkp
Recoil energy: 1.66mkp
Chamber pressure: 3,460kg/cm²
Range, maximum effective: 800 metres
Manufacturer: Steyr-Daimler-Puch AG, Steyr
Status: In production. In service with the Austrian Army

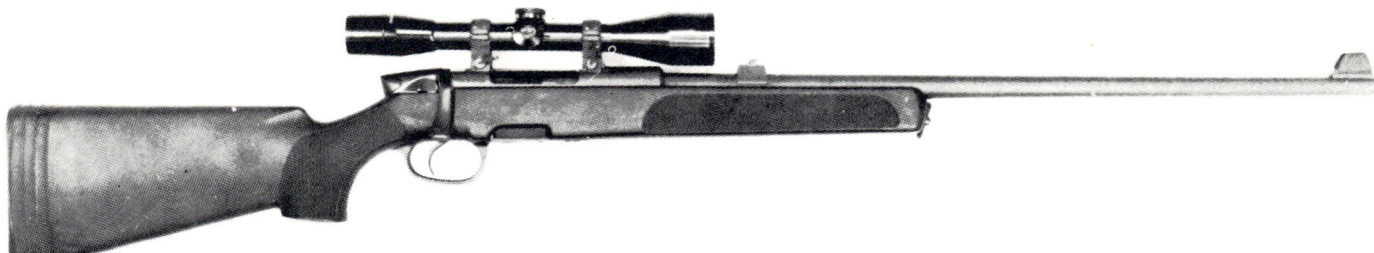

The SSG69 sniping rifle

The Steyr sniping rifle (model SSG) cal. 7.62 × 51 (308) fitted with Smith & Wesson Star-Tron image intensifier

STEYR 5.56mm UNIVERSAL WEAPON

This rifle, of very recent origin, was tested in late 1972. It was produced by Steyr-Daimler-Puch and, as its name indicates, the basic mechanism supports more than one class of weapon. As originally designed, a carbine, an assault rifle and a light machine gun comprise the group of weapons using the basic body group and firing mechanism.

The basic concept is that of a 'Bull Pup' weapon, the barrel and breech projecting well to the rear and being superimposed above the butt. The magazine is situated to the rear of the pistol grip and trigger assembly, in a manner generally reminiscent of the British .280in calibre EM2 rifle.

The weapon system is chambered for the 5.56mm × .45 cartridge, and the magazine is made of transparent synthetic material, holding basically 30 rounds, although consideration has been given to the development of similar magazines of 40- or 50-round capacity.

Much use has been made in the body of aluminium, in an attempt to reduce weight to the absolute minimum, and to this end the stock is manufactured in synthetic material.

DATA

	Machine carbine	Assault rifle	Light machine gun
Calibre:	5.56mm	5.56mm	5.56mm
Method of operation:	Gas	Gas	Gas
Method of feed:	Magazine	Magazine	Magazine
Weight (without magazine):	3.13kg	3.36kg	3.43kg
Length of barrel (without flash hider):	407mm	508mm	610mm
Weapon length:	680mm	790mm	880mm
Rifling:	6 grooves RH	6 grooves RH	6 grooves RH
Rate of fire:	Approx 650rpm	Approx 650rpm	Approx 650rpm
Manufacturer: Steyr-Daimler-Puch AG, Steyr			

BELGIUM

.30in FN RIFLE MODEL 1924/30

Mauser bolt-action rifles were adopted by Belgian armed forces in 1889 and were manufactured by Fabrique d'Armes de l'Etat and Fabrique Nationale d'Armes de Guerre (now known simply as Fabrique Nationale, or FN). The first such rifle was the 7.65mm M1889 which was an improved version of the Mauser Reich-Commission rifle of 1888 and remained in Belgian service until 1935.

Next came the 7.65mm M1935 which was substantially the same as the German Kar 98K service rifle described later in this section. This in turn was

followed by the 7.65mm M1936, a conversion of the M1889 using a wooden hand-guard and having a sleeve for the bolt head similar to that of the Kar 98K. Finally there was the .30 FN Model 1924/30 which was a copy of the M98 Mauser which was used in limited numbers by the Belgian Army in the years immediately after World War II.

None of these weapons is currently in service in Belgium, but it is probable that many still exist.

.30in AUTOMATIC RIFLE M1930

FN manufactured the Browning automatic rifle for export to Chile, China, Poland and Sweden. The Belgian gun differs from the US 1918 A1 BAR in having a finned barrel and a much more convenient gas regulator. A few guns were made with a quick-change barrel.

Manufacturer: FN, Herstal
Status: No longer in production or in Belgian Army service. BARs made in Belgium have been seen, together with the corresponding American weapons, in South-East Asia and might be encountered elsewhere.

.30in AUTOMATIC RIFLE TYPE D

The FN developed Type D was introduced after the Second World War. It is an improvement over the US M1918 A2 automatic rifle, has a good quick change barrel and can be stripped rapidly. The stock is hinged and after removing the trigger assembly, the piston slide and bolt assembly can be removed. The quick stripping facility was the result of design changes by FN, taking the return spring from the pistol slide assembly and placing it in the butt. There are alternative rates of automatic fire using an escapement mechanism with a powerful clock spring – not the buffer system of the M1918 A2. There are dust covers for the ejection and magazine ports. Fitted with a bipod, the weapon can be used with a butt monopod.

The Model D was used in Belgium in .30-06 calibre and was purchased by Egypt in 7.92mm calibre in 1949. It remained in Egyptian service until displaced in first line service by Russian weapons.
DATA
Cartridge: US .30-06 or 7.92mm Mauser
Method of operation: Gas

Method of locking: Rising link
Method of feed: 20-round detachable box magazine
Method of fire: Automatic (2 rates)
Weight: 9.2kg
Length: 1,143mm
Barrel: 500mm
Rifling: 4 grooves RH
Sights: Foresight: Post
Rearsight: Tangent
Muzzle velocity: (.30-06) 854 metres/sec
Muzzle energy: 361mkp
Rate of fire: 700 and 400 rounds/min
Range, maximum effective: 800 metres
Manufacturer: Fabrique Nationale, Herstal
Status: No longer manufactured. No longer in service in Belgium though probably still held in reserve stocks. Still in second-line service in Egypt.

FN production of the Browning automatic rifle Type D (RMCS)

7.92mm SAFN M49 RIFLE

Before the Second World War, FN was working on a self-loading rifle. The designer was D. J. Saive, and when the Germans invaded Belgium in 1940 he and several of his colleagues went to England to work in the Design Department of the Royal Small Arms Factory at Enfield. After the war the rifle was produced as the ABL (Arme Belgique Légère) and as the SAFN (Saive Automatique FN) in 7.92mm, 7.65mm, .30-06in and 7mm calibres and was sold to several countries in some of which it is still in service.

A gas-operated weapon with a semi-automatic action, the M49 uses a tilting-block locking system of the Tokarev type. The mechanism is piston-operated and there is gas regulator which is adjusted by a sleeve to which access is obtained by removing the front hand-guard. The rifle is fired from the closed-breech position and the hammer spring guide, projecting from the trigger guard, acts as a cocking indicator. A 10-round magazine is used and this is loaded with either 5-round charges or loose rounds. The action is held to the rear when the magazine is empty: there is also a manual

ABL (Arme Belgique Légère) 7.92mm. The first post-war commercial gun

hold-open device to enable the rifle to be loaded with single rounds.

The standard design had a tangent aperture rear sight adjustable for elevation and windage but there was also a sniper version with a telescopic sight. A bayonet lug was a standard fitting and some models had a muzzle brake.

DATA

Calibre: 7.92mm, 7.65mm, .30-06 or 7mm
Operation: Gas
Locking: Tilting Block
Feed: 10-round charger-loaded magazine
Fire: Semi-automatic

Weight: 4.5kg
Length: 1201mm
Barrel: 589mm
Sights: Foresight: Shielded post
        Rearsight: Tangent aperture
Muzzle velocity: 730m/sec
Effective range: 700m
Manufacturer: FN, Herstal
Status: No longer in production. Supplied to Argentina, Brazil, Colombia, Egypt, Indonesia, Luxembourg, Turkey, Venezuela and Zaire and still in service in some of these countries.

7.62mm FN FAL RIFLE

As a successor to the ABL/SAFN development a more modern type of rifle, incorporating the Saive breech mechanism, was developed by FN. The initial model used the German 7.92mm Kurz cartridge and was demonstrated in February 1948: subsequent weapons were chambered for the British .280 (7mm) cartridge. It is of interest to note that originally the rifle was developed in two forms – a conventional rifle with a fixed wooden butt and a 'Bull Pup' design in which there was no butt. In this latter weapon the butt plate was attached directly to the rear end of the receiver and the recoil went directly into the firer's shoulder. The magazine was placed as far back as possible – leaving only sufficient space for the length of the bolt and a small sear over-run behind it. The trigger had to be the conventional distance forward of the butt plate and so came in front of the magazine. The straight-through design necessitated raised sights. This 'Bull Pup' design was abandoned in Belgium, and design effort was concentrated on the conventional weapon. Eventually the British .280, or 7mm, cartridge was

rejected and Saive, assisted by Ernest Vervier, re-designed the rifle for the American 7.62mm cartridge which became the NATO standard. This rifle was called the FAL – Fusil Automatique Légère – and became a great success. It was adopted by over 70 countries including the Netherlands, West Germany, Luxembourg, New Zealand, Chile, Venezuela, Peru, Ecuador, Ireland and Cuba. It was produced in Belgium, United Kingdom, Canada, Australia, India, Israel, Austria and Argentina. These various countries introduced many modifications to suit their own needs. A consignment was sent to the USA for troop trials but the rifle – known as the T48 – was not adopted.

The basic design of the FAL incorporates gas operation, a 20-round magazine, selective fire, and a rigid butt stock. Variations include a shorter barrel and a folding stock and a version with a bipod and a heavy barrel which in some countries is used tactically as a squad automatic or light machine gun.

The .280 rifle fired in the USA trials

Prototype .280 long model (1949)

Prototype FAL cal. .280 short model (1949)

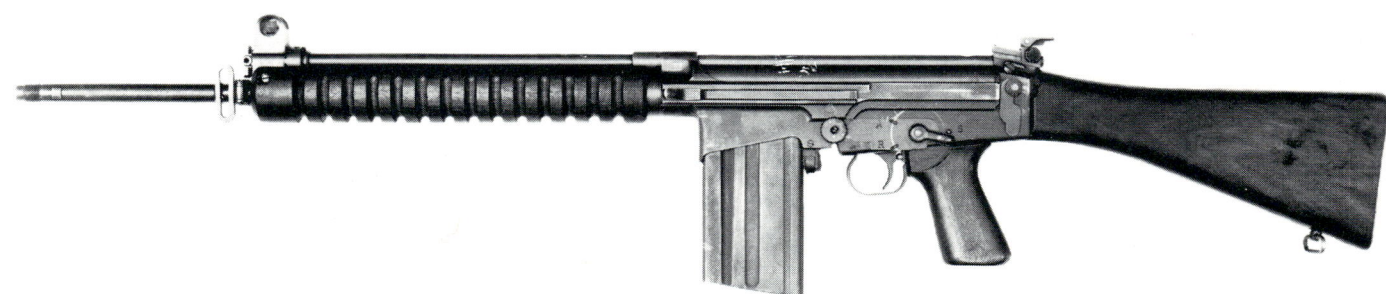

Prototype Cal 280 (1951)

FAL – prototype cal. .280 long model with carrying handle (1951)

FN 7.62mm FAL

The T48 rifle using the .30 T65 cartridge (1953)

LAR with folding butt (1955)

LAR (FALO) heavy barrel (1973)

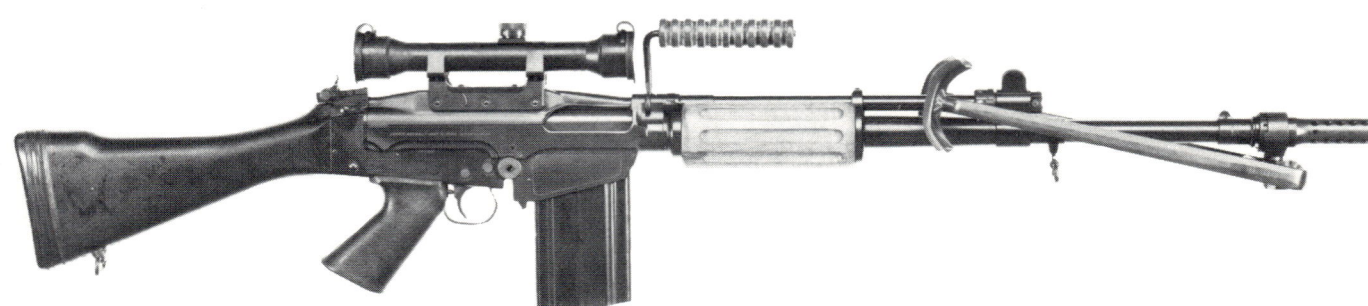

LAR (FALO) heavy barrel (1973). The carrying position

OPERATION

To load the FAL, the magazine catch, located behind the magazine and under the receiver, is operated to remove the magazine. The loading process requires no filler and the firer places a round on the magazine platform and forces it down until it is displaced sideways under one of the feed lips. This process is repeated until 20 rounds are inserted. The front end of the magazine is placed in the housing and the rear end rotated back and up until the magazine catch clicks in to lock it in position.

The selector lever is located above the pistol grip on the left hand of the receiver and is operated by the thumb of the right hand. The 'safe' position is at the top, 'repetition' lies below it and 'automatic' is further forward. (In the British, Canadian, Indian and Netherlands, versions, there is no automatic fire.) The cocking handle is on the left side of the receiver. In some models it folds flat and must be pulled back to extend it at a right angle before it can be used. When the cocking handle is retracted fully and then released, the bolt picks up the top round from the magazine and chambers it. The weapon always fires from the closed breech position. The type of sight used varies somewhat from country to country. The usual backsight is an aperture. It is adjusted for any range by pressing in the lock and sliding it along its base until the required range, shown in hundreds of metres, is reached. The UK rifle used the 'Hythe' night sight which is described in the sub-section on British rifles.

When the trigger is pulled the hammer contacts the firing pin and this, in turn, hits the cap to ignite the propellant charge. When the bullet passes the gas port in the top of the barrel, some of the propellant gas is diverted into the gas cylinder where it expands and drives back a light, spring-loaded piston. This piston strikes the top of the front face of the bolt carrier, transfers its energy, and after a short travel is returned by its spring to its forward position. The carrier is driven rearwards and has about six millimetres of free travel during which the chamber pressure is dropping to an acceptably low level. After this idle motion – known as 'mechanical safety after firing' – the unlocking cam of the carrier moves under the bolt lug and lifts the rear end of the bolt out of the locking recess in the floor of the receiver. The bolt and carrier travel back together, compressing the return spring. The extractor withdraws the empty case from the chamber and holds it on the face of the bolt until it strikes the fixed ejector and is thrown out of the rifle to the right, through the ejection port.

The return spring drives the carrier and bolt forward; the feed rib on the bolt pushes the top cartridge out of the magazine and over the bullet guide into the chamber. The extractor snaps into the extraction cannelure of the cartridge case and the bolt can travel forward no further. The carrier continues on and the locking cam rides over the bolt, forcing the rear of the bolt down into a recess in the receiver floor and holding it there. The final forward movement of the carrier trips the automatic sear. If the trigger is pressed, the hammer will drive the firing pin into the cartridge cap.

TRIGGER AND FIRING MECHANISM

The trigger and firing mechanism of the FN FAL is ingenious, fool-proof and copied, in principle, by many other manufacturers. It consists of a sear mounted on a fixed pin which passes through an elongated slot. The sear is spring-loaded and moves forward – when it can – along its elongated slot. The trigger is pivoted at the top of the same fixed pin. When the trigger is

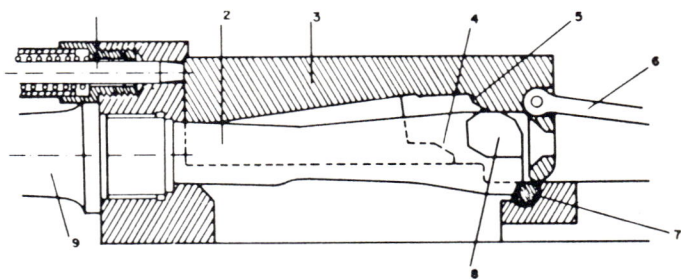

FAL bolt functioning: (1) Piston; (2) Bolt; (3) Bolt carrier; (4) Unlocking cam; (5) Locking cam; (6) Driving spring rod; (7) Locking seat; (8) Lugs; (9) Barrel

pulled a shoulder rotates up and forces the rear end – the tail – of the sear up. The front end is depressed and moves out of the hammer notch. The hammer rotates slightly but is held by the automatic – or 'safety' – sear until the bolt carrier is fully home and bolt locking is completed. When the automatic sear is depressed by the carrier the hammer is free to rotate and drive the firing pin into the cartridge cap. If the selector is set to 'auto' the trigger shoulder can rise sufficiently to hold the nose of the sear down clear of the hammer so that the hammer is controlled only by the automatic sear. If the selector is set to 'repetition' the trigger shoulder can rise only a short distance. The sear nose is depressed out of the notch and the hammer swings forward as before. The sear spring forces the sear forward along its elongated slot, the nose presses on the underside of the hammer, and the tail slips forward off the shoulder of the trigger. When the hammer is rotated back by the recoiling bolt carrier the nose of the sear is pressed into the hammer notch. The full force of the hammer spring overcomes the weaker sear spring and forces the tail of the sear back against the side of the shoulder and so another round cannot be fired. When the trigger is released the shoulder moves down and the hammer spring forces the sear further across and the tail moves onto the top of the shoulder of the trigger. Pulling

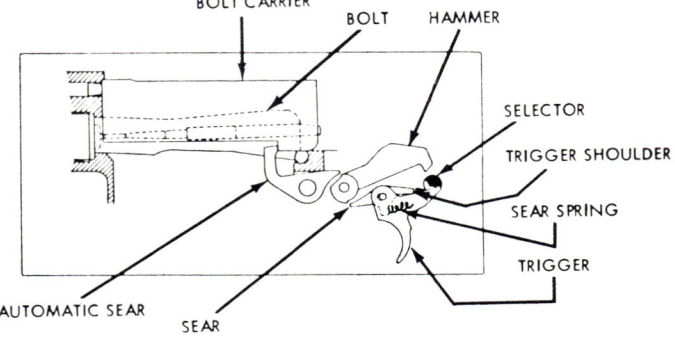

FAL firing mechanism

the trigger lifts the trigger shoulder which in turn lifts the tail of the sear and the nose moves down out of engagement with the hammer notch. The hammer will be held up by the automatic sear if the bolt carrier is not fully forward.

When the selector is placed at 'safe' the trigger shoulder is prevented from rising sufficiently to lift the tail of the sear.

When the ammunition is expended the bolt stop comes into action. The bolt stop is normally held down by a spring. When the last round is fired a rib on the magazine platform lifts the bolt stop into the path of the bolt. On the UK version the last 6mm of the bolt stop is ground off and thus the bolt is in the forward position when the ammunition is expended. By pushing up the bolt stop by hand when the bolt is to the rear, the bolt can be held open whenever required.

GAS REGULATION

The FN FAL has a gas regulator. It works on the 'exhaust to atmosphere' principle. When the gun is clean and firing under ideal conditions, a large proportion of the gas is passed through the regulator and out into the atmosphere. When the need comes to increase the gas pressure on the piston head, the regulator is screwed up and the gas diverted into the cylinder. There are two ways of setting the regulator according to the type fitted to the rifle. The older type has a square forward face and should be opened until the oval gas escape port behind the front sight is exposed. Starting from this point, the regulator should be screwed up 20 clicks. When this has been done a magazine with a single round should be inserted and the round fired. The bolt should be held to the rear after firing and if it does not come back far enough, the regulator should be closed five clicks and another single round fired from the magazine. This process should go on until the bolt is held to the rear. When this happens, five single rounds should be fired to check this setting. The regulator is then closed three clicks and tested with a full magazine. If reloading does not take place at semi-auto fire, then a further closing of the regulator by two clicks is required. The more modern regulator is much simpler to adjust and may be identified by an angled cut on its front face. The regulator is opened until the gas port is exposed and then a magazine with one round is emplaced. This is fired and if the bolt is not held to the rear, the regulator is closed by one click and the process repeated one click at a time until proper functioning is achieved. With the UK type weapon with no holding open device, the regulator is adjusted until the empty cartridge case is thrown out of the rifle to a distance of some three metres.

The gas plug must be rotated when firing grenades to ensure all the gas pressure goes to drive the grenade out and none goes on the piston. To do this the plunger is depressed and the plug rotated until the marking is on the bottom. After each grenade the bolt must be retracted by hand and a fresh cartridge loaded into the propelling chamber. Some FN FAL rifles have a combined flash eliminator – grenade launcher which is a cylindrical fitting on the muzzle. Others have a prong-type flash eliminator and with these a spigot launcher must be placed over the muzzle. Some of these have a sight but more modern grenades have the sight mounted integrally.

Zeroing the sights is achieved by screwing the front sight up or down to adjust for elevation and the back sight aperture can be moved across by loosening the screw underneath on the side to which movement is required and tightening the screw on the other side.

STRIPPING

To strip the rifle, the magazine is first removed. The bolt is then pulled back and the chamber and feedway checked to ensure no cartridge is in the weapon. The bolt is then allowed forward under control, the hammer remaining cocked. The take-down lever is located on the left side of the receiver at the rear. The lever may be of the old pattern which is vertical or the new pattern which is horizontal. In either case the lever is rotated anti-clockwise and the butt stock swung down to open the rifle. The bolt cover is then pulled to the rear off the receiver. The bolt assembly can then be withdrawn by pulling on the return spring rod, and the bolt removed from the carrier.

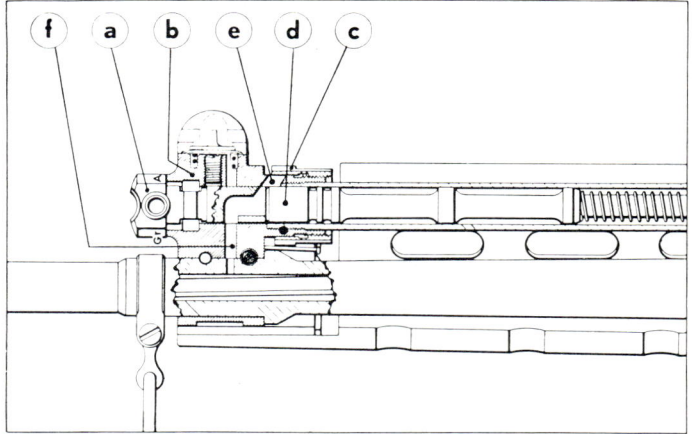

Gas regulation: **(a)** Plug; **(b)** Gas block; **(c)** Gas regulator; **(d)** Piston head; **(e)** Gas outlet; **(f)** Gas port

DATA

General characteristics and special characteristics of four versions of the weapon are given below. The four versions, with their FN reference numbers are:

FN 50-00: Standard model with fixed buttstock and standard barrel
FN 50-61: Model with side-folding buttstock and standard barrel
FN 50-63: Model with side-folding buttstock and short barrel
FN 50-41: Model with fired buttstock, bipod and heavy barrel

GENERAL CHARACTERISTICS

Cartridge: 7.62mm × 51
Operation: Gas
Locking: Tilting block
Feed: 20-round steel or light alloy box magazine
Weight: 0.25 or 0.12kg empty; 0.73 or 0.60kg loaded
Fire: Selective in standard model but several countries make or use it only as a self-loading weapon and FN offer this as a standard alternative
Barrel: Regulator: Exhaust to atmosphere system
    Rifling: 4 grooves RH. 1 turn in 305mm
    Cooling: Air
Sights: Foresight: Cylindrical post
    Rearsight: Aperture, sliding on bed, adjustable 200-600m × 100m; or flip aperture 150/250m; or fixed battlesight 300m (see table)
    Zeroing: Elevation: foresight screws up and down (click gives 1cm at 100m). Rearsight in dovetail
Rate of fire: SS: 60 rounds/min
    Automatic: 120 rounds/min
    Cyclic: 650-700 rounds/min
Effective range: 650m
Trigger pull: 3.6-4.1kp
Bayonet: Length: 290mm
    Weight: 221g
Scabbard: 132g steel. 56g plastic

SPECIAL CHARACTERISTICS

Type	50-00	50-61	50-63	50-41
Length (without bayonet)	1090mm	—	—	1050mm
(with bayonet)	1260mm	—	—	—
(without bayonet and stock extended)	—	1095mm	998mm	—
(without bayonet and stock folded)	—	845mm	748mm	—

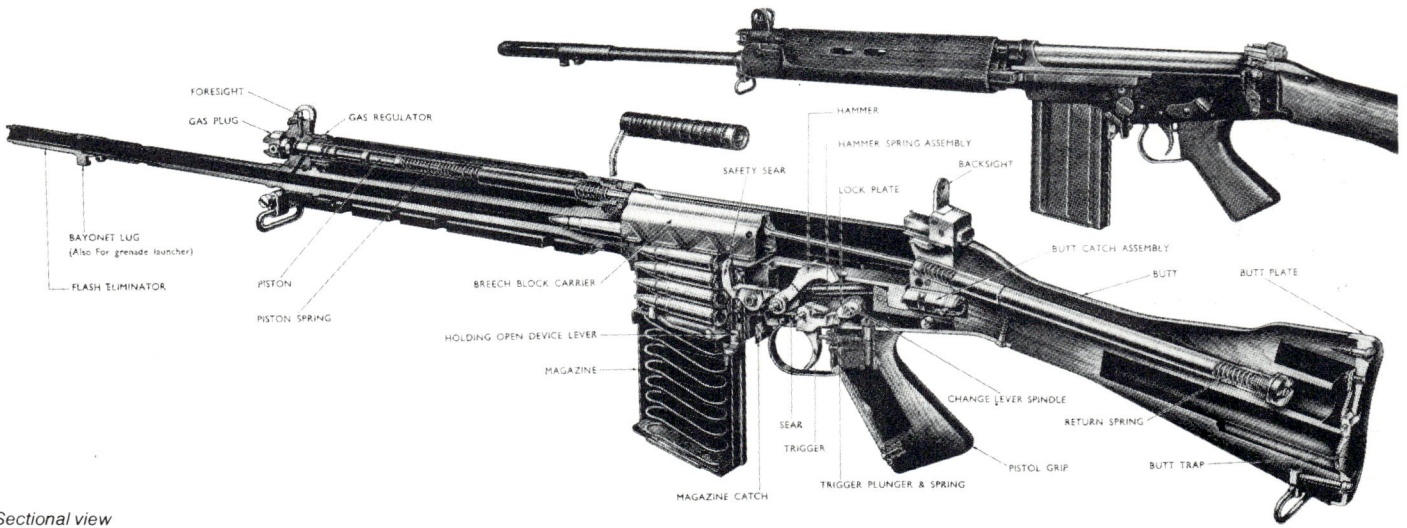

Sectional view

(with bayonet and stock extended)	—	1265mm	1168mm	—
Weight (without bayonet or magazine)	4.25kg	3.9kg	3.75kg	6.00kg
Barrel length	533mm	533mm	436mm	533mm
Rearsight type	Sliding	Flip	Fixed	Sliding
Sight radius	553mm	549mm	549mm	553mm
Muzzle velocity	840m/s	840m/s	810m/s	840m/s
Muzzle energy	335mkp	335mkp	310mkp	335mkp

Manufacturer: Fabrique Nationale, Herstal, Nr Liège, Belgium
Status: The FAL has been or is still in production not only in Belgium but also in a number of other countries such as Argentina, Australia, Austria, Canada, India, South Africa, Norway and the UK. Included in the countries using the FN FAL are: Argentine, Australia, Austria, Belgium, Brazil, Burundi, Chile, Cuba, Dominica, Ecuador, India, Indonesia, Ireland, Israel, Kuwait, Liberia, Libya, Luxembourg, Morocco, Mozambique, New Zealand, Paraguay, Peru, Portugal, South Africa, Singapore, and the UK

7.62mm FN SNIPING RIFLE

Designed primarily for internal security use, this rifle is a recent addition to the FN range of weapons. It is based on the standard Mauser bolt action, and incorporates a special heavy barrel. The butt length is variable, and may be changed, to suit individual firers, at will.
DATA
Cartridge: 7.62mm × 51
Method of operation: Manual bolt
Method of locking: Rotating bolt

Method of feed: 4-round box magazine
Method of fire: Single shots
Weight, without sight: 4.9kg
Length of barrel: 610mm
Muzzle velocity: 850 metres/sec
Sights: Telescopic. No iron sights fitted
Manufacturer: FN, Herstal
Status: In production

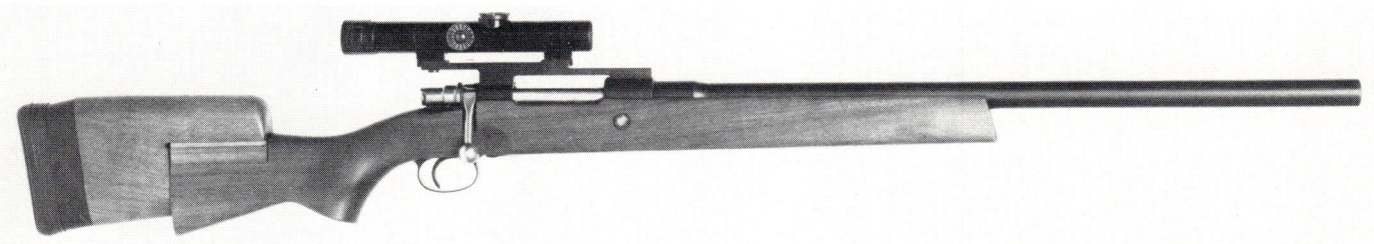

7.62mm FN Sniping Rifle

5.56mm CAL RIFLE

In 1966 FN produced a .223 rifle. It was one of the first European small calibre rifles and it was considered at this time that the .223 cartridge would be adopted by most European countries. This may still be so but the transition period has already dragged on for nearly a decade and in that period various other rounds have made their appearance.

The FN CAL was designed by Ernest Vervier and represents one of the neatest and most effective of the 5.56mm rifles.

DESCRIPTION

The CAL is a gas-operated rifle using the familiar FN gas regulator system in which the exhaust to atmosphere principle is employed. It is a locked breech weapon using not a multi-lug system but a double interrupted thread on the bolt head which is engaged behind a similar thread in the barrel extension and secured in place when the bolt is rotated. The return spring is wrapped round the short stroke piston to enable any type of butt configuration to be used.

The trigger mechanism is similar to that used in the US M1 Garand. The change lever gives safe, single shot, and full automatic and also has as standard a three-round burst control. This provides the firer with an enhanced chance of a first round hit. The duration of the burst is only 0.211 seconds and in this short period of time the muzzle does not rise excessively. The use of full automatic fire with a high impulse cartridge and a lightweight rifle must cause the muzzle to accelerate upwards and the FN burst fire control is designed specifically to cope with this problem by restricting the number of rounds fired to the controllable optimum which in this case, at a cyclic rate of 850 rounds/min, is three. This also allows time to re-align the barrel after each burst.

The trigger guard can be folded back against the pistol grip to allow the use of arctic mittens.

The rifle is equipped with a holding-open device which retains the bolt carrier to the rear when the magazine is empty. When a loaded magazine is inserted, the carrier is released by pressing in the release catch situated above the rear edge of the magazine on the left side of the receiver.

The front sight is a cylindrical post and the rear sight is a two position flip aperture giving ranges of 0 to 250 metres, and 250 to 400 metres.

The flash hider does not take the usual pattern of the prong type almost universally used today but is a plane cylinder with three holes bored on each side at the front. These deflect some gas backwards and so produce a muzzle brake effect. Rifle grenades can be placed over the flash hider and located on the raised rings on the barrel.

The CAL bayonet

Flash hider, grenade launcher and blank firing device

The receiver and fore-end, and trigger and magazine holder, are made of steel pressings. The bolt, carrier and piston are machined from forgings. The breeching-up of the barrel is unusual. The barrel extension – containing the locking threads – is of greater diameter than the barrel and is coned at its forward end. The barrel is pushed through the front of the receiver from the rear and the cone of the barrel extension fits into a similar cone in the reinforced front face of the receiver. The barrel is screw threaded. When it is pushed fully forward a nut is dropped down from the muzzle and tightened into the cone seating on the front of the receiver. This holds the barrel rigidly in the receiver. Rotation is prevented by a key in the bottom of

CAL with folding buttstock

the receiver engaging in a keyway on the underside of the barrel extension. This system of course allows no simple adjustment of the cartridge head space but in current rifles the CHS is very rarely adjustable because experience has shown that with modern steels there is virtually no wear of the locking system.

In the CAL the bolt head locks directly into the barrel extension and so the stress path is very short and is limited to the barrel extension and bolt head. The remainder of the bolt, bolt carrier and receiver are virtually unstressed. The buttstock and pistol grip are made of nylon. If required a folding buttstock can be fitted.

OPERATION

The magazine catch lies on the left of the magazine holder. The magazine takes 20 rounds and is loaded with individual cartridges pressed straight through the magazine lips. The magazine is pressed straight up into the well until the catch is heard to click into position.

The cocking handle is located on the right of the receiver. The bolt carrier is withdrawn, compressing the return spring, and when released it flies forward. The lug on the underside of the breech face forces the top round out of the magazine, over the chambered bullet guide in the bottom of the barrel extension and into the chamber. The bolt head enters the barrel extension and comes to rest. The bolt carrier continues forward and a cam groove causes a cam pin on the bolt to rotate the bolt about its longitudinal axis. The interrupted buttress threads on the bolt head are rotated in front of the corresponding threads in the barrel extension and the bolt is pulled slightly forward and locked. The final forward motion of the bolt carrier exposes the firing pin, which is slightly proud of the rear of the bolt, and also trips the safety sear.

When the trigger is operated, with the selector lever set to any of the three fire positions, the sear is rotated off the hammer bent and the hammer rotates forward and strikes the firing pin which is driven forward onto the primer cap. When the bullet moves past the gas vent bored in the top of the barrel, 17cm from the muzzle, some of the gas passes through the vent and into the regulator. The regulator is of the same pattern as the FAL. Normally most of the gas is exhausted to atmosphere but closing the regulator escape holes, by screwing up the sleeve, allows a larger proportion to impinge on the piston head. The piston is driven back and contacts a lug above the front face of the bolt carrier. The carrier moves back. There is a free movement of about five millimetres whilst the cam slot moves across the stationary cam pin. This provides the mechanical safety after firing and allows the chamber pressure to drop to a safe level. The cam slot then engages the pin and this rotates the stationary bolt. The lead on the locking threads retracts the bolt slightly as it rotates and this provides primary extraction to unseat the cartridge case in the chamber. When the cam pin reaches the top of the cam slot the bolt is fully unlocked and is pulled back with the carrier. The case is fully extracted and ejected to the right. The return spring is fully compressed and the bolt carrier is forced forward. Provided ammunition remains in the magazine and the selector is set to 'auto' or 'burst fire' the cycle will repeat. If the selector is set to 'single shot' or the last round of a three-shot burst has been fired, the hammer will be caught and held back by the sear.

TRIGGER MECHANISM

The trigger extension carries two spring-loaded sears. The back sear is the secondary sear, the front one is the primary sear. When the gun is cocked manually the hammer is held on the forward sear. When the bolt carrier is fully forward it operates a safety sear which holds the hammer back at all times when locking is not completed.

SINGLE SHOT FIRE

With the bolt carrier fully forward the hammer is held on the front sear. When the trigger is pulled the trigger housing rotates forward and the front sear frees the hammer which goes forward to fire the round. When the hammer is rocked back by the recoiling carrier, the trigger is still pressed and the hammer is caught by the rear sear. To fire another round the hammer must be released. The housing moves back, the sears move with it, and the hammer is caught by the front sear. When the trigger is pulled the sear goes forward and another round is fired. This process is repeated shot by shot.

AUTOMATIC FIRE

When the change lever is set to 'automatic' the shaft locks the rear sear which then plays no part in the action at all. The hammer is rotated back and held by the safety sear. As soon as the bolt carrier goes fully home the safety sear releases the hammer and the gun fires. When the trigger is

CAL showing selector lever and telescopic sight

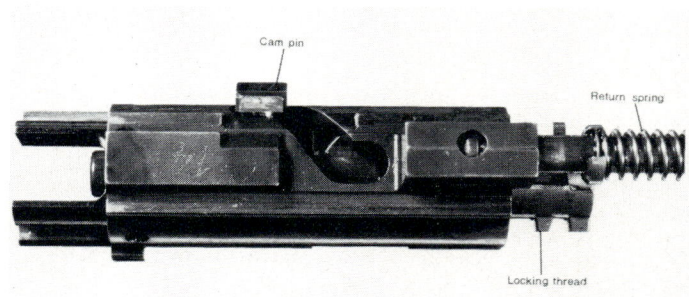

Bolt and carrier of the FN CAL (RMCS)

released the hammer is caught by the safety sear and as soon as the bolt carrier is fully forward the safety sear is operated and the hammer moves into the front sear where it remains until the trigger is pulled again to fire rounds at automatic fire.

THREE-SHOT BURST FIRE

The 3-shot burst fire mechanism is a removable device fitted inside the receiver. It has a U cut out at the front to fit round the hammer spindle and the change lever spindle passes through it and locates it at the rear end. The mechanism has an arm with a three-tooth ratchet at one end which contacts a spring-loaded pawl on the hammer axis. At the other end is a similar ratchet. When the change lever is set to '3' the rear sear is freed but is held back by the rear of the ratchet device. As each round is fired the ratchet is rotated and after the third the rear end slips off the catch on the rear sear which moves forward and holds the hammer back. When the trigger is released – at any time during the operation – the hammer slips to

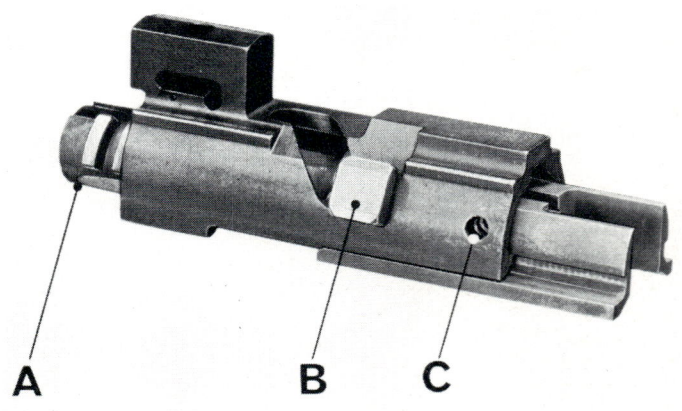

A   B   C

Bolt and bolt carrier: (a) Locking thread; (b) Cam pin; (c) Pin retaining firing pin

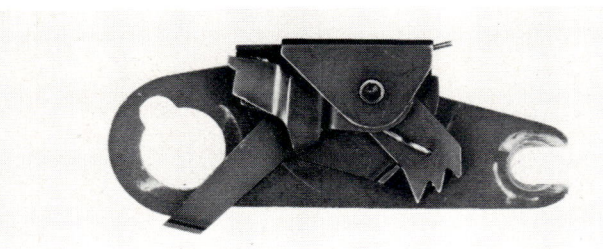

FN burst fire control

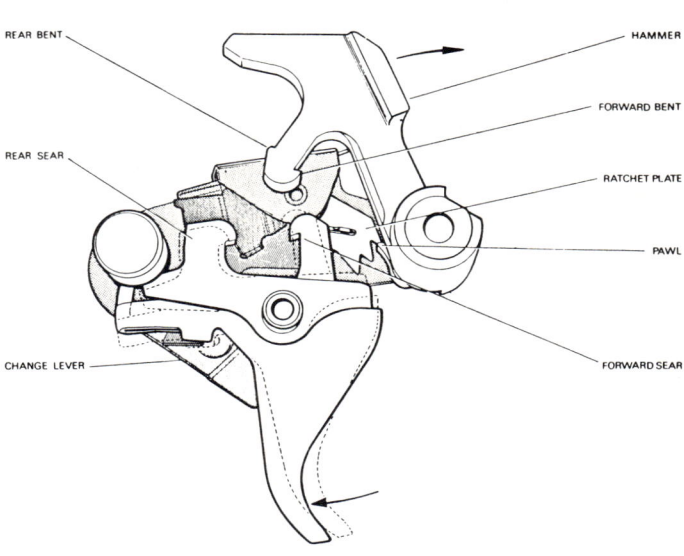

FN burst fire controller shown with hammer (RMCS)

the forward sear as the housing is rotated and the gun is ready to fire another burst.

GRENADE LAUNCHING

There are two separate and distinct ways in which grenades can be fired. Firstly the conventional, muzzle-launched grenade can be employed. This has a 22mm internal diameter boom which fits over the flash hider and barrel. To project this grenade a propelling cartridge is employed and the gas valve on the front of the gas regulator is rotated so that all the gas pressure is used on the grenade and the piston receives no gas.

Secondly FN make a grenade launcher of the underslung type which can be used as a separate launcher of the USA M79 type or attached under the front of the fore-end. It has its own sight and firing mechanism. Until the sight is erected the firing pin is locked. This launcher fires the USA 40mm M406 grenade. This launcher is no longer being produced.

STRIPPING

The magazine is removed and the cocking handle retracted to allow the chamber to be checked. This also cocks the hammer which makes it easier to remove the bolt carrier later.

The take-down pin is located just behind the selector lever. When it is pushed through the action can be opened up like a shot gun.

The bolt carrier and bolt are removed to the rear using the cocking handle.

DATA
Cartridge: 5.56mm × 45
Method of operation: Gas
Method of locking: Rotating bolt
Method of feed: 20-round box magazine
Method of fire: Selective and 3-round burst

WEIGHTS
Gun, without magazine or sling: 3kg
Empty magazine (steel): 155g
Empty magazine (alloy): 85g
Filled magazine (steel): 390g
Filled magazine (alloy): 320g
Gun with full magazine (steel) and sling: 3.5kg
Bipod: 175g
Trigger pull: 4.3kp

LENGTHS
Gun, overall: 980mm
Barrel (without flash hider): 467mm

CAL stripped (RMCS)

MECHANICAL FEATURES
Barrel: Rifling: 6 grooves RH. 1 turn in 305mm
     Cooling: Air
Sights: Foresight: Cylindrical post
     Rearsight: Flip aperture. 0.250 metres. 250-400 metres. Windage Nil
     Zeroing: Front sight
     Sight radius: 460mm

FIRING CHARACTERISTICS
Muzzle velocity: 970 metres/sec
Muzzle energy: 170mkp
Muzzle momentum: 0.351kps
Rate of fire: 650-700 rounds/min cyclic
Recoil energy: 0.76mkp
Accessories: Bayonet – tubular handle; Bipod; Blank firing attachment; Infra-red sight
Manufacturer: Fabrique Nationale, Herstal, Nr Liège
Status: Not being manufactured. Not in service. Available if ordered

CANADA

7.62mm C1 RIFLE
From the middle of the First World War, after the withdrawal of the Ross rifle, to the end of the Second World War the Canadian forces were equipped with Lee Enfield rifles, initially from UK sources but latterly from Long Branch Arsenal where some 962,000 rifles – mainly the Lee Enfield No 4 – were manufactured during the Second World War.

After the war the Canadian authorities tried a number of variants on the FN FAL before settling on the C1 in June 1955. The FN rifles known as the X8E1 and X8E2, were tested in Canada as well as in UK.

Canadian C1 rifle. Note charger guides and disc rearsight (RSAF)

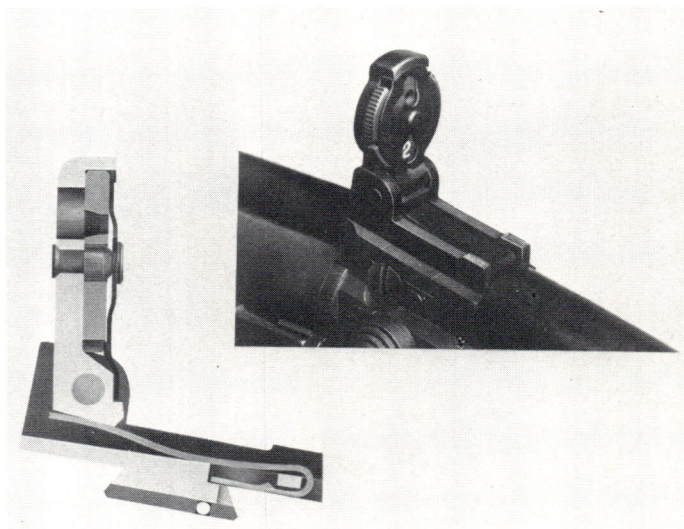

The Canadian disc rear sight

The Canadian C1 differs from the L1A1 in having an opening in the feed cover through which the magazine can be re-charged using chargers and guides. It also has a rearsight which is a disc offering five different ranges, from 200 to 600 metres, by 100-metre intervals, by rotating the outside of the disc. The range appears in an aperture at the bottom of the front face of the disc.

CIAI MODIFICATION

In 1960 the British L1A1 was found to be firing rounds before the breech was closed. This was found to be due to the long firing pin bending on firing and failing to withdraw into the breech-block. When the next round was chambered the projecting firing pin could fire the cap. The long firing pin was replaced by a two-part firing pin. In Canada this modification produced the CIAI rifle which also had a plastic carrying handle.

DATA
Cartridge: 7.62mm × 51
Method of operation: Gas
Method of locking: Tilting block
Method of feed: 20-round box magazine
Method of fire: Semi-automatic
Weight: 4.25kg
Length: 1,136mm
Barrel: 533mm
Sights: Foresight: Post
          Rearsight: Aperture, disc
Muzzle velocity: 840 m/sec
Muzzle energy: 335mkp
Rate of fire: SS: 35 rounds/min
Range, maximum effective: 400 metres
Manufacturer: Long Branch Arsenal, Ontario
Status: No longer in production. In service with Canadian Forces

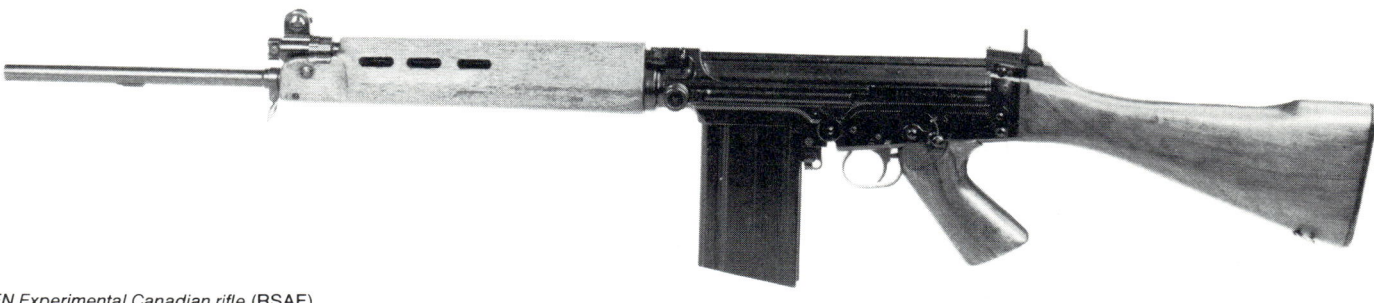

FN Experimental Canadian rifle (RSAF)

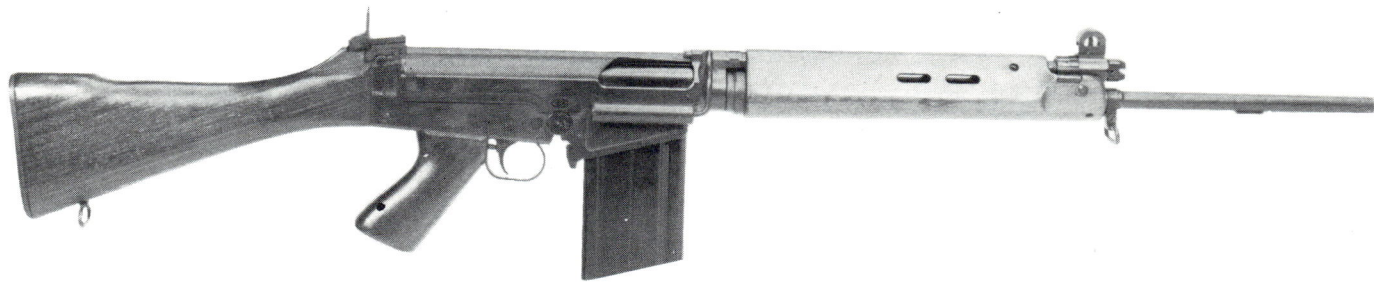

The Canadian C1 prototype

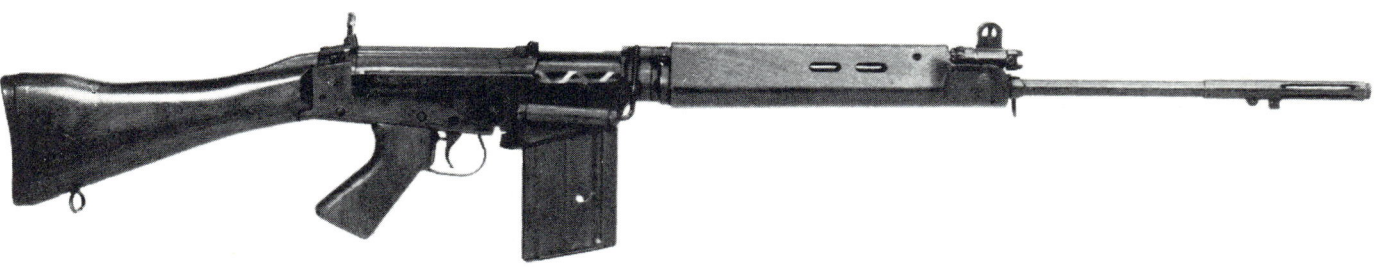

The Canadian C1

7.62mm AUTOMATIC C2 and C2A1 RIFLES

The heavy-barrelled FN rifle was taken by the Canadian Army as their Squad Light Automatic. It has selective fire allowing either single shots or full automatic. There are box magazines holding 20 and 30 rounds. The rearsight is a conventional tangent aperture.

The C2 rifle may readily be recognised by the uncovered gas cylinder over the forward grip. The gas regulator takes a light bipod.

The C2 rifle was modified by the substitution of a two-part firing pin and a plastic carrying handle, and known as the C2A1.

Canadian C2 heavy Barrelled Rifle (RMCS)

DATA
Cartridge: 7.62mm × 51
Method of operation: Gas
Method of locking: Tilting block
Method of feed: 30-round box magazine
Method of fire: Selective
Weight: 6.93kg
Length: 1,136mm
Barrel: 533mm
Sights: Foresight: Post
     Rearsight: Tangent, aperture 200-1,000yds

Muzzle velocity: 854 metres/sec
Muzzle energy: 346mkp
Rate of fire: Cyclic: 710 rounds/min
         Auto: 60 rounds/min
          SS: 35 rounds/min
Range, maximum effective: 600 metres
Manufacturer: Long Branch Arsenal, Ontario
Status: No longer in production. In service with Canadian Forces

7.62mm C3 SNIPING RIFLE

Canada has recently introduced into a service a new sniper rifle. This is the Parker Hale Model 1200Tx modified slightly to meet Canadian requirements. The stock is fitted with four ½in spacers to permit length adjustment. The rifle has two male dove-tail blocks on the receiver, to accept either the Parker Hale 5E vernier rearsight, or the Austrian Kahles six-power telescope. All exposed metal parts of the rifle are non-reflective.

The Canadian designation for this rifle is 'Rifle 7.62mm C3'

DATA
Cartridge: 7.62mm × 51
Manufacturer: Parker Hale
Status: In service

CHILE

LOCAL MANUFACTURE

Changes in Chile's international political alignment have introduced an element of confusion into the pattern of the country's military equipment, largely because of the attempt made during the Allende regime to replace what were predominantly NATO-pattern weapons by Russian weapons. At one time it was decided that the FN FAL and the heavy barrelled version would be the standard rifle and LMG and that the weapons would be made in Chile to replace existing US M1 rifles in first-line service at least. Subsequently, however, some SIG rifles and Rheinmetall LMG were purchased and subsequently again some Russian AK-47 Kalashnikov rifles were acquired.

CHINA (PEOPLE'S REPUBLIC)

7.62mm TYPE 53 CARBINE

The Chinese authorities use type numbers corresponding to the Western calendar and so this copy of the Russian Model 1944 Carbine was produced in 1953. The Russian weapon is derived from the Mosin-Nagant rifle Model 1891-30 – and may readily be identified by its tapered magazine, short straight bolt handle and the large flanged cocking piece. It has a long, tapering cruciform folding bayonet. The Chinese version differs only in the Chinese characters stamped into the receiver. The Type 53 fires the large Russian 7.62mm × 54R cartridge. Full details of the weapon are given in the pages on Russian weapons and the Chinese version is the same.

DATA
Cartridge: 7.62mm × 54R
Method of operation: Manual – bolt

Method of locking: Rotating bolt
Method of feed: 5-round internal magazine
Method of fire: Semi-automatic
Weight: 3.92kg
Length (bayonet folded): 1,029mm
Length (bayonet extended): 1,327mm
Barrel: 520mm
     Rifling: 4 grooves RH
Sights: Foresight: Post
     Rearsight: Tangent. Notch
Muzzle velocity: 766 metres/sec
Muzzle energy: 287mkp
Rate of fire: 10-15 rounds/min
Range, maximum effective: 400 metres
Manufacturer: State factories
Status: No longer produced. In service with Chinese Militia Units and may well be found elsewhere in Chinese client countries

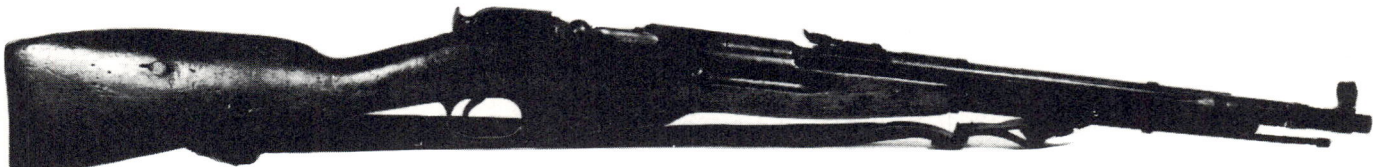

The PRC Type 53 carbine is a copy of the Russian 1944 carbine

7.62mm TYPE 56 CARBINE

This is a Chinese copy of the Soviet Simonov SKS SL carbine. The rifle may be identified by the symbol 五六式 (Type 56) located on the left front of the receiver. The weapon is fashioned and functions in exactly the same way as the SKS Russian carbine which is described in the section on Russian weapons. Later versions of the Type 56 have a spike bayonet replacing the folding blade of conventional shape used on all other SKS variants.

Chinese Type 56 (SKS) markings

Chinese militia receiving instruction on the T56 carbine

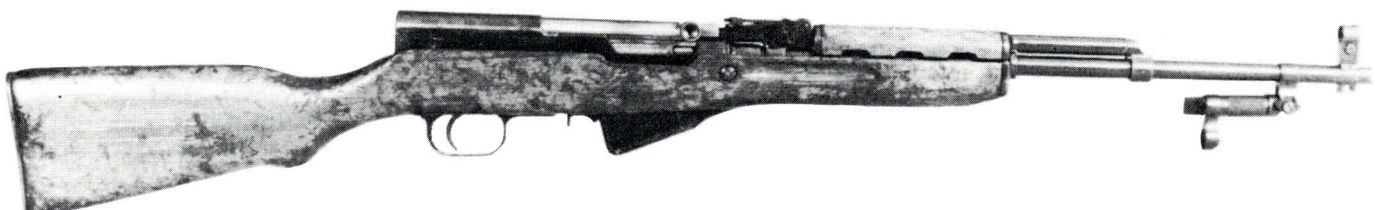

Chinese SKS Type 56 with knife bayonet (RSAF)

DATA
Cartridge: 7.62mm × 39
Method of operation: Gas
Method of locking: Tilting block
Method of feed: 10-round internal magazine
Method of fire: Semi-automatic
Weight unloaded: 3.86kg
Length (bayonet folded): 1,021mm
Barrel: 521mm
       Rifling: 4 grooves RH
Sights: Foresight: Cylindrical post
       Rearsight: Tangent. Notch
Muzzle velocity: 735 metres/sec
Muzzle energy: 215mkp
Rate of fire: c. 20 rounds/min
Range, maximum effective: 400 metres
Manufacturer: State factories

The T56 carbine seen here has the spike bayonet

Status: No longer in production. In service with Chinese Militia and may well be found elsewhere in Chinese client countries

7.62mm TYPES 56 AND 56-I ASSAULT RIFLES

The Type 56 Assault Rifle is a copy of the later model of the Soviet AK-47 in which the rear end of the top surface of the receiver is straight. (Earlier models had a down slope on the top rear surface of the receiver.) This model is identified by the Chinese characters on the right hand side of the receiver showing the positions of the selector lever. The upper position (full auto) of early production models shows 冲 The lower position (single shot) shows 单. Later production models show 'L' for the full auto marking and 'D' for single shot.

There is also a Type 56-1 Assault Rifle which has a folding metal stock. This may be distinguished from the Russian AK-47 not only by the Chinese markings or 'L' and 'D' for auto and single shot respectively, but also by the prominent rivets in the arms of the buttstock, which are not present in the Russian version.

Some of these models carry a permanently attached spike bayonet folding back under the muzzle.

DATA
Cartridge: 7.62mm x 39
Method of operation: Gas
Method of locking: Rotating bolt
Method of feed: 30-round detachable box magazine
Method of fire: Selective
Weight: 4.3kg
Length: 869mm

Chinese Type 56 (RSAF)

Chinese Type 56

Barrel: 414mm
     Rifling: 4 grooves RH
Sights: Foresight: Cylindrical post
     Rearsight: Tangent. Notch
Muzzle velocity: 710 metres/sec
Muzzle energy: 203mkp
Rate of fire: Cyclic: 600 rounds/min
     Auto: 100 rounds/min
     SS: 40 rounds/min
Range, maximum effective: 300 metres
Manufacture: State factories
Status: In production. In service with Chinese troops. Supplied to some
S.E. Asian countries, Pakistan and Ethiopia

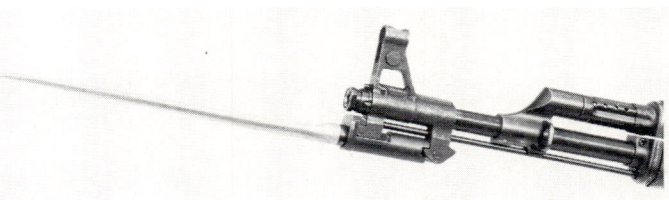

Chinese Type 56 with bayonet in place

Chinese Type 56-1. Note rivets in arms of buttstock (RSAF)

7.62mm TYPE 68 RIFLE

This is a native-designed rifle that has recently come into service with the Army of the People's Republic of China. In general appearance it resembles the Type 56 (SKS) but the barrel is longer, the bolt action is based on that of the AK-47 and the rifle provides selective fire. It has a two-position gas regulator. It normally uses a 15-round box magazine but if the bolt stop is removed, or ground down, the 30-round magazines of the AK-47 and AKM can be used.

There are two versions of the Type 68. The earlier version has a receiver machined out of the solid whereas the later version has a pressed steel receiver. It can be recognised by the large rivets in the side of the receiver.

OPERATION

The Type 68 can be loaded in one of four ways. First, using an empty 15-round magazine, cocking the action holds the bolt to the rear; a ten-round SKS type stripper clip can then be put into the feed guides and the rounds forced down. Five further rounds can then be pressed in from the next clip. Secondly, if stripper clips are not available, 15 rounds can be forced down, one after the other, into the magazine. Thirdly, the 15-round magazine can be pre-loaded off the gun and placed in position when the need arises. Lastly if the bolt stop has been removed or ground down the bigger magazines can be used but they must be pre-filled off the gun as the bolt will automatically close on the empty chamber and close off the top feed opening.

When the bolt is retracted over the loaded magazine and released, the top round is fed into the chamber as the bolt flies forward.

The selector lever is located directly in front of the trigger on the right. When the selector is pulled to the rear – reading 'O' – the trigger is locked. The bolt however can be pulled back if required. The middle position, marked '1', with the lever vertical, provides semi-automatic fire and when the lever is fully forward, the gun will fire at full automatic. This position is marked '2'.

The sights are adjusted by pressing in on the side locks and moving the sight bar along the leaf to the required range. The position marked III is a battle sight position for all ranges up to 300 metres.

Normally the gas regulator will be set with the smaller of the two holes nearer the barrel. If it is necessary to use the large hole to increase the gas flow when the gun is slowed down by the entry of dirt, or fouling, the procedure is quite simple. The gas regulator retainer is pressed in towards the cylinder. When it disengages from the hand-guard, the retainer is pulled out of the gas cylinder and then the regulator is rotated to select the other hole. The retainer is replaced and rotated and the gun should then be ready to fire.

The bayonet is like that of the SKS. The handle is forced back against the spring and the bayonet then rotated forward and locked at the muzzle.

To fire the weapon, the selector lever is placed on 1 or 2. If full auto (2) is selected, the burst should be restricted to three to five rounds in length. When the trigger is pulled the hammer reaches the firing pin and the cap is crushed. Some of the propellant gas passes through the vent and into the gas cylinder above the barrel. The piston is forced back, and the bolt carrier starts to move to the rear and rotate the hammer back. The action is similar to that of the Russian AK-47. After a period of free travel of about 6mm, the cam cut in the bolt carrier reaches the operating lug of the bolt. The bolt is rotated – providing initial extraction – and the bolt is withdrawn. The fired case is held to the bolt face by the extractor until the ejector pivots it out to the right of the gun. The return spring is compressed. The bolt carrier hits

the rear wall of the receiver and rebounds. As it goes forward the next round is fed and chambered. The extractor clips over the cartridge rim and the bolt comes to rest. The carrier continues on and the cam forces the operating lug across and rotates the bolt into the locked position. The carrier, in its final forward motion, after the bolt is fully locked, releases the safety – or automatic – sear and then stops as it reaches the front of the receiver.

THE TRIGGER AND FIRING MECHANISM

The automatic (or safety) sear is located forward of the hammer and the latter is held back until the bolt is fully home and locked.

The trigger sear is to the right behind the hammer and moves with the trigger. The semi-automatic sear is on the left and functions only when the selector is set to '1'. The gun can never fire – regardless of the selected mode – until locking is completed. The safety (automatic) sear is then contacted by the carrier and driven off the hammer. When the trigger is pulled the trigger sear releases the hammer. The round is fired and the recoiling carrier forces the hammer back. As soon as the carrier starts to move back the spring-loaded automatic sear holds the hammer up. At single shot the semi-automatic sear is engaged and holds the hammer back. Since the trigger is held back after the round has been fired it must be released before another shot. When this happens the semi-automatic sear moves off the hammer. The hammer starts to move forward but is caught by the trigger sear. This is another variation on the Garand M1 trigger mechanism. When the trigger is pulled the hammer is released and if the bolt is locked the hammer will hit the firing pin. If the bolt is not locked the hammer is held back by the auto sear.

When the selector lever is set for automatic fire, the semi-auto sear is held clear of the hammer and plays no part. The trigger sear moves off the hammer and the round is fired. When the hammer comes back it is held by the automatic sear and only when the bolt is fully closed does the gun fire. When the trigger is released the trigger sear catches the hammer and holds it back.

When the selector is in the safe position – 'O' – the selector shaft blocks movement of the trigger sear and so the hammer is held.

STRIPPING

Remove the magazine, retract the bolt, inspect the chamber. Press in the catch on the left rear of the receiver cover and pull the cover back off the receiver.

If the gun is an early model, the return spring guide rod can be lifted out of the machined receiver. If the gun has the stamped receiver of the later model, the driving spring rod must first be eased forward before lifting out. Pull back the cocking handle. As the carrier reaches the rear end of the receiver press down on the cocking handle and it will disengage from the receiver. The carrier can then be lifted out. The bolt can be rotated and removed from the carrier.

The piston comes out of the gas cylinder when the gas regulator retainer is removed. The hand-guard and heat shield are free to come off.

Rotate the catch at the rear of the trigger guard and lift the trigger group out.

DATA

Cartridge: 7.62mm × 39
Method of operation: Gas
Method of locking: Rotating bolt

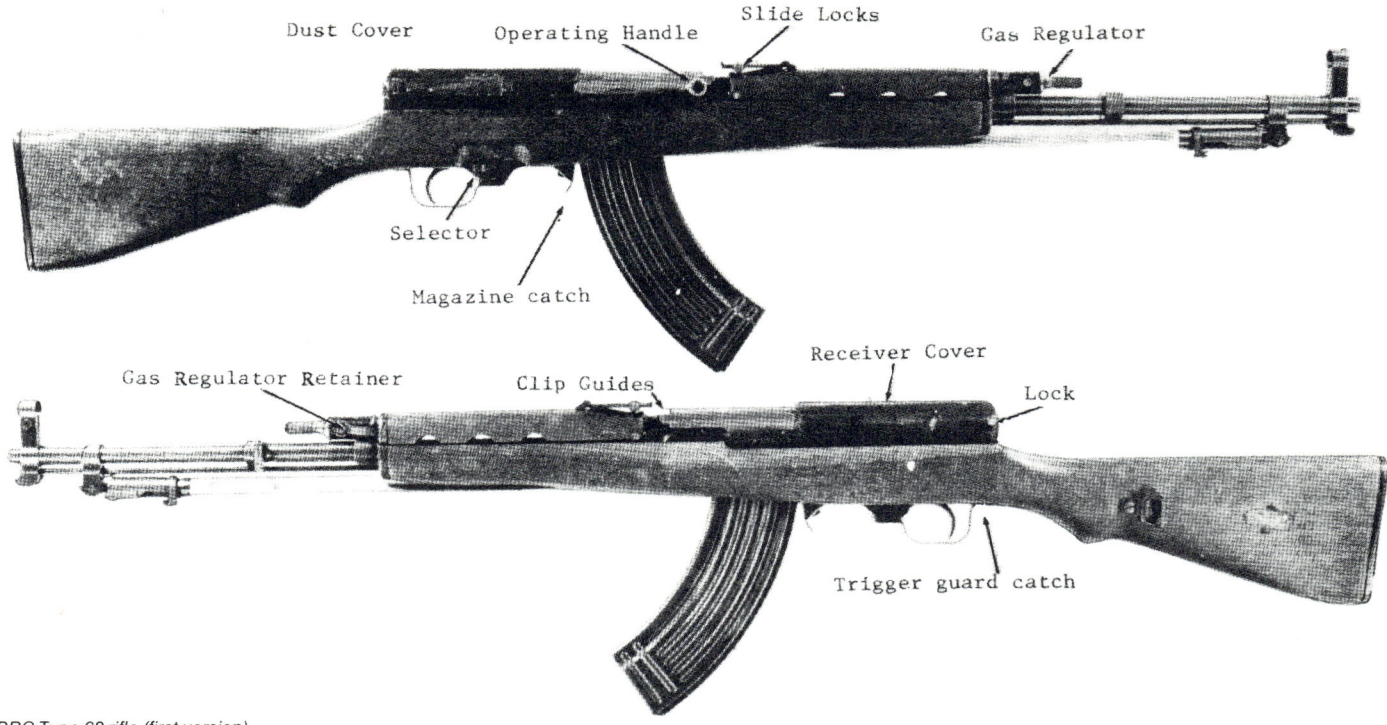

PRC Type 68 rifle (first version)

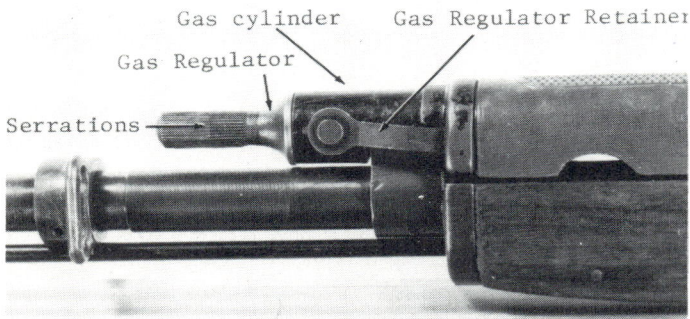

The gas regulator of the PRC Type 68

Method of feed: 15-round detachable box magazine (30-round box magazine from the AK-47, AKM can be used only if the holding open stop is removed)
Method of fire: Selective
Weight: 3.49kg
Length: 1,029mm
Barrel: 521mm
        Rifling: 4 grooves RH
Sights: Foresight: Cylindrical pillar
        Rearsight: Tangent notch
Muzzle velocity: 730 metres/sec
Muzzle energy: 215mkp
Rate of fire: Cyclic: 750rpm
        Auto: 85rpm
        SS: 40rpm
Range, maximum effective: SS 400 metres; Auto 200 metres
Manufacturer: State factories
Status: In production. In service with Chinese troops at least

CHINA (TAIWAN)

LOCAL MANUFACTURE

The Nationalist forces brought a mixture of weapons and calibres with them to Taiwan. These included Japanese rifles originally in 7.7mm and later bored out to 7.92mm; there were also Belgian FN 1924 and M1930 rifles in 7.92mm and 7.92 Czech and German Mauser rifles.

During World War II the Americans supplied M1903 rifles and M1 Garands in .30-06 calibre. Numbers of M1 carbines were also supplied.

The collection of weaponry naturally led to logistic problems and it is reported that the Nationalists are now producing the M14 rifle in quantity.

5,000 M16 rifles were obtained from the USA and these equip the Taiwan Special Forces.

CZECHOSLOVAKIA

7.62mm Vz52 and 52/57 SL RIFLES

The Czech Vz 52 was designed and production planned in that short period that elapsed after World War II before Czechoslovakia came under Russian domination. It was designed to use the native 7.62mm intermediate cartridge known as the M52. This round differed from the M43 in many respects and was in no sense interchangeable with it. The Czech cartridge is somewhat longer than the Russian and has both a higher bullet weight and charge weight. This produced a higher muzzle velocity and a greater effective range. All the same the Russians forced the Czechs to abandon this round and later versions of the rifle are chambered for the Russian M43 cartridge and are known as the Vz 52/57. The change has not improved the accuracy, consistency or range of the rifle although of course it has furthered the cause of standardisation.

The following lists the salient characteristics of the two rounds M52 Czech and M43 Russian respectively:

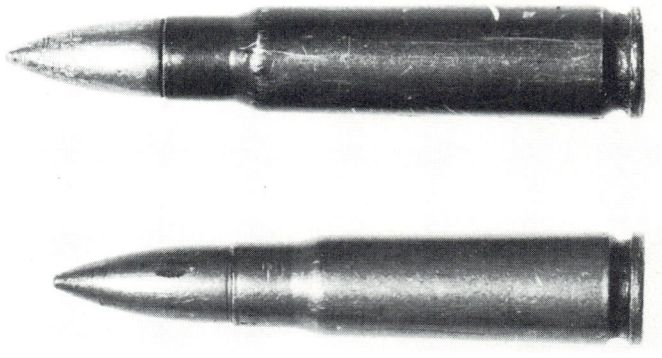

Top. Czech M52 7.62mm × 45. Bottom. Russian 7.62mm × 39

	M52	**M43**
Weights:		
Complete round:	19g	16.4g
Bullet:	8.6g	7.9g
Charge:	1.75g	1.62g
Lengths:		
Round:	59.7mm	51.3mm
Case:	45mm	39mm
Diameters:		
Bullet:	7.9mm	7.92mm
Case (base):	11.2mm	11.25mm
Muzzle velocity:	744m/sec	710m/sec

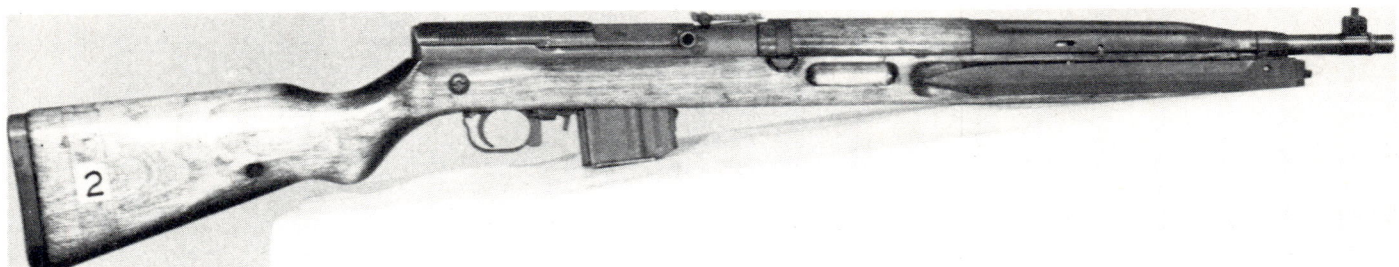

Vz 52

METHOD OF OPERATION

The rifle is gas operated. There is a gas vent located 23cm from the breech face and after the bullet has passed this point a small proportion of the gas is diverted through this hole into the gas cylinder. Unlike the great majority of gas operated weapons there is no circular section cylinder containing a piston but a sleeve surrounds the barrel and this carries out the functions of the conventional piston. Gas enters the space between a gas stop and the gas sleeve, expands and drives the sleeve to the rear. There is a short metal semi-cylinder connecting the gas sleeve to an actuator and this transmits the sleeve movement backwards. The actuator receives this impulse and passes it via a pair of springloaded horns directly to the breech block carrier.

If it is required to vary the gas force to allow for adverse operating conditions, the gas stop is screwed in towards the sleeve which has the effect of reducing the expansion chamber volume and so increasing the working pressure. Similarly the violence of the action can be diminished by screwing the gas stop out and increasing the volume available for expansion of the gases. The gas stop is held in position by a lock nut which is shown in the photograph.

FIRING CYCLE

A forward locking downward tilting breech block is employed. This too is a feature rarely encountered. The forward locking gives a short stress path in the block and the receiver and is conducive to accuracy. However in this type of design the maximum vertical movement of the block occurs at the front end when locking or unlocking takes place and this makes the positioning and securing of the cartridge in the extractor difficult. To cope with this problem the extractor is made stirrup shaped and a locking bar is cammed down to grip the case from above, as locking is completed.

After a round is fired there is a short delay whilst the bullet travels up to the gas port and then, as already described, the actuator horns are driven back by a sharp impulsive blow against the front face of the bolt carrier. There is a small initial idle movement of the carrier which is part of the mechanical safety after firing, and then a cam path on the inside surface of the hollow carrier engages with lugs formed on the outer surface of the breech block. The front end of the breech block is then lifted out of engagement with its recess in the floor of the body. The carrier and block then move to the rear as one unit as soon as the unlocking is completed. The small spiral spring forces the actuator, connector and the sleeve back into position whilst the block is still moving backwards. It is thus a short stroke piston action.

The bar above the extractor stirrup is cammed down when locking occurs and the case is gripped very firmly. During initial extraction, which occurs when the front face of the breech block is lifted from its recess, the bar is held down but as soon as relative motion occurs between the carrier and the body, it is released. The ejector is a pushrod which is stopped abruptly when its rear end strikes a projection in the floor of the body. The continued rearward movement of the bolt causes the ejector to project from the breech face and the cartridge case is rotated around the bar and thrown upwards. The cover over the carrier and bolt deflects the case and it flies

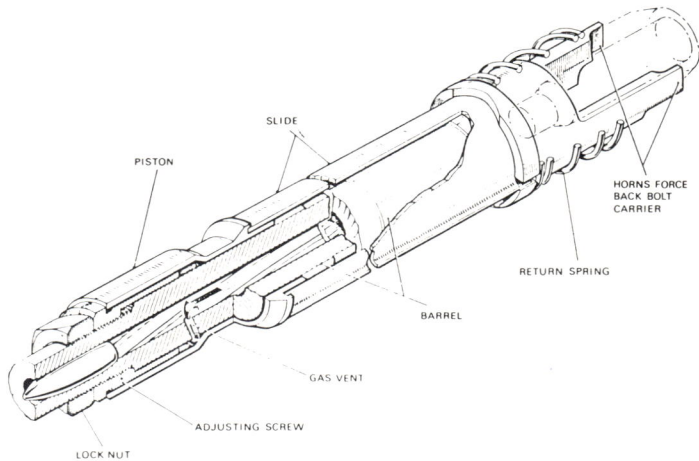

Wrap-around piston system – Czech SL rifle, 7.62mm Vz 52

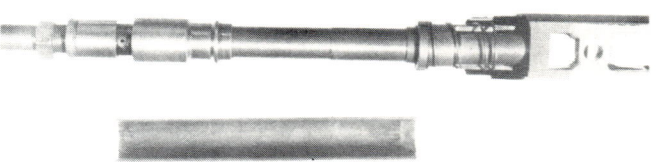

Elements of the gas system

over the firer's left shoulder.

The hammer is rotated by the recoiling bolt and held down by the sear. The return spring stores energy which is utilised before the bolt carrier reaches the rear of the body, to drive the working parts forward again. On this forward stroke a round is picked up from the magazine, fed into the chamber, and the front of the bolt is then forced down by the carrier to lock into the body. After the bolt is locked the carrier still has a small forward motion which provides the mechanical safety before firing by preventing trigger action until it is completed.

TRIGGER AND FIRING MECHANISM

The trigger and firing mechanism is obviously based on that employed in the American M1 Garand. It incorporates a hammer with two bents and a main and auxiliary sear. The disconnector action used to provide single shot fire holds the hammer on an auxiliary sear when it is rotated by the recoiling bolt. To fire another round it is necessary to release the trigger and in so doing the bent slips off the auxiliary sear and is retained by the primary sear ready for the next round to be fired.

When the ammunition in the magazine is expended the action is held to the rear by a holding open device operated by the rising magazine platform.

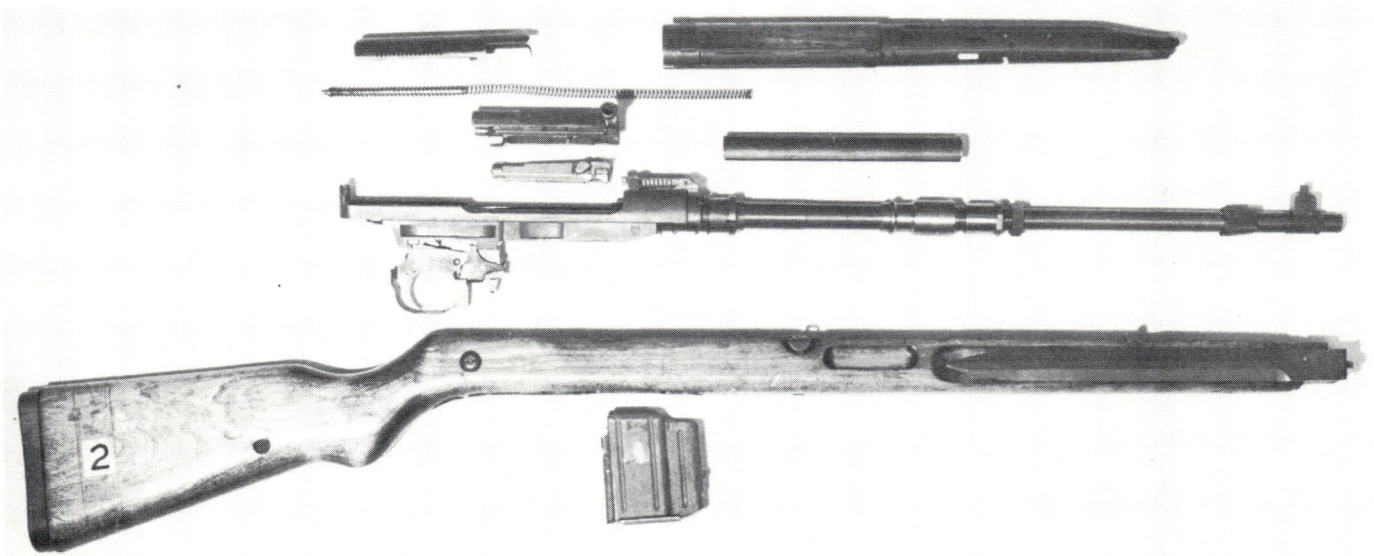

The Vz 52 field stripped

STRIPPING

First the weapon must be made safe and this is done by removing the magazine, cocking the action and inspecting the chamber. The process of disassembly is as follows:

(1) Remove the top cover. This is accomplished by forcing it forward, pressing in the plunger projecting from the rear of the cover, and then lifting the cover straight up out of the body grooves. The plunger and return spring can now be eased to the rear.

(2) Pulling back on the cocking handle brings the carrier and bolt to the rear and pressure to the right causes the carrier to move over into a cut away section from which it can be removed from the body of the gun.

(3) Remove the bolt from its carrier by pushing it to the rear, pulling down on the front end and then pulling it out of the carrier.

(4) Remove the hand guard by pressing in the metal clips in front of the rearsight and lifting the guard off.

(5) Remove the trigger group. This action is achieved by pulling the rear of the trigger guard back and when it is unlocked it can be swung forward and slid into the magazine opening and removed.

(6) To remove the stock use the point of a bullet to press in the plunger under the hole in the bayonet and slide the barrel band forward. The stock can now be detached.

(7) The gas assembly can now be broken down. The connector can be forced back against the actuator and then lifted off.

To reassemble, the process follows logically from that used to strip.

HANDLING AND FIRING

The weapon is heavy and bulky for the round it fires. This results in a low level of recoil and it is very comfortable to fire. It can be carried comfortably using the sling but is not well enough balanced to be easily secured at the point of balance.

If it becomes necessary to adjust the gas system during firing, this is a somewhat tedious process because the foregrip has to be removed, the gas stop moved to a new position and the locking nut replaced. Since there is no way of knowing how much effect is being achieved by any given change of cylinder volume, it may be necessary to make several alterations before the required effect is achieved.

There are, basically, three ways of loading the rifle. These are:

(a) Using a five-round charger to load the magazine from the top; charger guides are machined into the front face of the bolt carrier.

(b) Replenishing the magazine by feeding in individual rounds from the top.

(c) Replacing the magazine as required with one pre-filled. The magazine is filled by stripping rounds from the charger and then feeding them individually into the ten-round box.

CONCLUSIONS

The claims made for the Vz52 rest mainly on two technical features of design. These are:

(a) The wrap-around piston.

(b) The forward locking tilting block.

The wrap-around piston was used by the Germans in World War II. The idea was first used in the Gew 41(W) which was a Walther design with an annular piston at the muzzle, and subsequently in the MKb 42(W) which was an early version of the MP43. The idea had the attraction of distributing the mass of the gas cylinder and piston all round the thrust line of the barrel and so eliminating the turning moment caused by the movement of offset masses. In practice the complication and expense of manufacture nullified such advantages as were there.

The forward locking block again has advantages which are more theoretical than practical and here again the extraction and feed problem present difficulties.

Generally, the bulk, weight and complexity of the weapon detracted from such advantages as were given by a very good cartridge and it cannot really be claimed to have been a great success.

DATA

Cartridge: 7.62mm × 45 (Czech M52)
Method of operation: Gas
Method of locking: Tilting block
Method of feed: 10-round box magazine
Method of fire: Self-loading

WEIGHTS

Rifle, no magazine: 4.1kg
Empty magazine: 181g
Loaded magazine: 363g
Rifle with full magazine: 4.5kg
Trigger pulls: 1st 2.5kp 2nd 3.4kp

LENGTHS

Rifle, bayonet folded: 1,003mm
Rifle, bayonet extended: 1,204mm
Barrel: 523mm

MECHANICAL FEATURES

Barrel: Rifling: 4 grooves RH. 1 turn in 305mm
   Regulator: Annular sleeve under fore-end
   Cooling: Air
Sights: Foresight: Blade
   Rearsight: Leaf Tangent U
   Graduation: 1-9 by 50-metre increments
   Zeroing: Line. Foresight on dovetail Elevation. Change foresight blade
   Sight radius: 488mm

FIRING CHARACTERISTICS

Muzzle velocity: 744 metres/sec
Muzzle energy: 241mkp
Recoil energy: 0.76mkp
Rate of fire: 30 rounds/min
Range, maximum effective: 400 metres
Manufacturer: Ceskoslovenska Zbrojovka, Strakonice
Status: No longer manufactured. No longer in Czech Army service and virtually obsolete

---

7.62mm Vz58 ASSAULT RIFLE

Most countries of the Warsaw Pact make weapons based on Russian designs and the armies of most of them are equipped with locally-made versions of the AK-47 or AKM rifles. Not so the Czechoslovakian Army, the soldiers of which are equipped with the Vz58 which is an indigenous product of original Czech design. The earliest known versions had wooden butts, pistol grips and fore-ends, but the current issue weapons use a wood fibre filled plastic for those parts. There are two standard versions – the Vz58P with a solid butt and the Vz58V which has a butt which is a rod folding flat alongside the right-hand side of the gun.

The Vz58 bears a superficial resemblance to the Soviet AK-47 but a close look immediately reveals considerable differences.

SYSTEM OF OPERATION

The arm is gas-operated with a vent, located 215mm from the breech face, opening into a cylinder located above the barrel. The cylinder is 25mm long. There is no gas regulator and the full gas force is exerted on the 13mm diameter piston head. The entire piston is chromium-plated and so remains free of fouling. The gas pressure can only drive the piston back 19mm and

Czech Vz58P solid butt version

The V258V

the shoulder on the shank then butts up against the seating and no further movement is possible. There is a light return spring held between the piston shoulder and the seating which returns the piston to its forward position. The cylinder is vented on the underside and the gas pressure gives the piston an impulsive blow before exhausting to atmosphere after the piston has gone back 16mm. There is a protective metal heat shield over the piston which has a covering of the wood-filled plastic which is used throughout for the furniture. This in shape is exactly the same as that in the AK-47 and it is removed by the withdrawal of a pin passing through the rearsight block in which the piston sits.

The short tappet-like stroke of the piston impinges on the breech-block carrier and drives it rearwards. After 22mm of free travel during which the chamber pressure falls to a very low level, an inclined plane on the carrier moves under the locking piece and lifts it out of engagement with the locking shoulders in the steel body of the gun. The locking piece swings and this movement around the periphery of a circle provides the slow powerful leverage required for primary extraction. The breech-block is then carried rearwards extracting the empty case from the chamber. A fixed ejector in the receiver passes through a groove cut in the underside of the bolt and the case is rotated around the extractor and flung upwards clear of the gun. The continued rearward movement of the carrier and the bolt compresses two double coiled helical springs. The larger of these fits into the top hole of three drilled in the carrier and the smaller rests in the hollow steel tube which acts as a hammer. The carrier is driven forward and the feed horns on the underside of the bolt face, force a round out of the magazine and into the chamber. When the round is fully chambered with the extractor sprung over the cannelure, the carrier still has 16mm of travel and as it advances, a transverse cam face forces the locking piece down and the two lugs enter the locking shoulders in the body. There is a strong similarity in this locking system to that used in the Walther P.38 SL pistol. It should be noted that the arm can be assembled and fired without the locking piece and this could lead to a grave accident.

TRIGGER AND FIRING MECHANISM

Unlike the very great majority of self-loading and automatic rifles the Vz58 does not have a rotating hammer which strikes a firing pin: the hammer is a steel bar hollowed from one end almost throughout its full length to take the hammer spring. At the open end is welded a bent and there is a groove cut in each side of this to slide on the receiver guideways. The hammer enters the hollow bolt and drives forward a fully floating firing pin.

The trigger mechanism consists of two sears located side by side with the left sear slightly in front. The right-hand sear is connected to a forward sear trip operated by the carrier. Unless the bolt carrier is fully forward – i.e. locking is completed – the trip holds up the right-hand sear and the hammer is held back. The left-hand sear works with a disconnector to provide single shot fire.

The selector is located on the right-hand side of the receiver and like most modern Czech weapons single shot is indicated by '1' and full auto by '30'. When the selector is rotated forward to full auto the disconnector is lowered and is disengaged from the semi-automatic sear. When the carrier is fully forward the right-hand sear is depressed and the hammer is held on the semi-auto sear only. As soon as the trigger is operated the trigger bar is moved forward and the left-hand sear is depressed to release the hammer. So long as the trigger is pressed and there is ammunition in the supply the firing of the gun is controlled by the bolt closure. Each time the bolt recoils the automatic sear rises and holds up the hammer and as soon as the locking is completed the right-hand sear drops and the gun fires.

When the selector is rotated to the rear to the semi-auto position the trigger bar is lowered and forced clear of the semi-automatic sear but the disconnector is allowed to rise to engage the semi-automatic sear.

Trigger operation fires one round. The carrier then recoils and the automatic sear rises. The carrier strikes the disconnector and lifts the semi-automatic sear. The hammer is held by the automatic sear which is released when the bolt carrier goes fully forward, and since the auto sear is 1.5mm behind the semi-auto sear, the bolt then goes forward and is held up by the semi-auto sear.

To fire another round it is necessary to release the trigger to allow the disconnector to move back and up to engage under the semi-automatic sear. The trigger can now be pressed and the hammer will go forward off

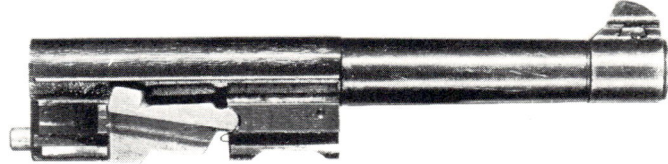

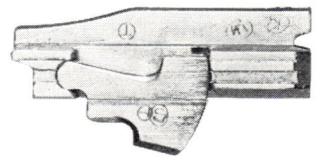

A comparison of the locking systems of the V358 and the German P38 pistol (RMCS)

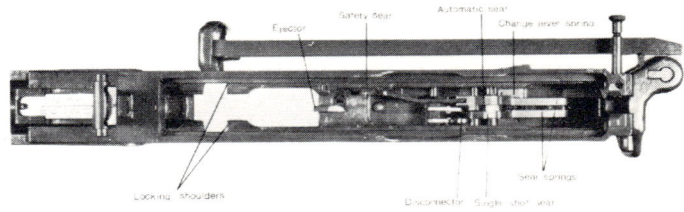

V358 trigger mechanism (RCMS)

the semi-auto sear.

At the 'safe' position with the selector pointing vertically downwards, the trigger bar and the disconnector are lowered and so there is no connection between the trigger and the semi-automatic sear which holds the hammer.

To see how safe this was, a loaded gun was dropped 20 times from six feet on to a concrete slab to see if the semi-auto sear could be jarred off the bent. There was no release of the hammer.

One feature of the trigger mechanism worthy of note is that no coil springs are employed. Both sears are held up by flat leaf springs.

STRIPPING

Make sure the weapon is safe. This is done by removing the magazine, operating the bolt and checking the chamber.

The magazine is removed by rotating the release catch forward. This is located immediately in front of the trigger guard and can be recognised by the shaped portion of the guard intended for the insertion of the left thumb. The buttstock must next be swung out to the braced position.

The receiver cover is pinned to the receiver and is released by moving the locking pin, at the top rear, fully to the right. The cover is pressed forward and when the rear end is lifted it can be slid back and removed with the hammer spring and return spring.

Withdraw the cocking handle and at the end of the carrier travel rotate the cocking handle upwards. As the front of the carrier lifts, place the middle finger under the bolt and lock to prevent them falling out, and remove the assembly. The hammer can be taken out by pulling it fully to the rear and then moving it forward about ¼in until it will rotate anti-clockwise. It can then be withdrawn.

The handguard over the gas piston can be released as soon as the pin under the back sight is forced across to the right. The piston head can be lifted when the piston is fully retracted and when tilted the piston and spring can be taken out.

Re-assembly is based on reverse order to stripping and presents no problems. Note that the hammer spring attached to the receiver cover goes into the hollow hammer and the return – or driving – spring goes into the top hole of the three drilled in the carrier.

ACCESSORIES

The usual accessories are available consisting of a sling, bayonet, cleaning rod, oil bottle, and zeroing tool.

V358 with buttstock folded and field stripped (RMCS)

In addition to these however are the unusual adjuncts of a flash hider and a bipod. Either or both can be fitted. The muzzle nut is removed by depressing its retaining plunger and screwing off and the cone shaped flash hider screwed on. The bipod slides over the bayonet mount under the foresight and when in position is held by a locking plunger engaging in a hole in the base. When the bipod legs are folded forward the bipod can be removed. When the legs are folded back they can be stowed for carriage.

A blank firing attachment can be placed over the muzzle. This replaces the muzzle nut and has a small orifice which passes a limited amount of gas and allows the build-up of enough pressure to operate the gas system.

METHOD OF MANUFACTURE

Rather surprisingly, the receiver is machined from the solid. The exterior finish is good but grooves in which the bolt carrier slides carry very pronounced milling cuts and are not as well finished as one would expect. The bolt carrier again is machined from the solid and the interior tool marks are very noticeable. The cutter marks are very much in evidence on the bolt but the lock is very cleanly finished and chromium plated. The receiver cover is a light gauge pressing carrying a single coil return spring and a double coil hammer spring. The double column magazine is pressed out, bent over and spot welded. The holding open device is operated by an attachment to the follower and this has led to a rather unusual shaped magazine which although it takes the Russian rounds cannot be interchanged with the AK-47 magazine.

The buttstock is an I-section casting, welded to the shoulder plate and when extended it is very rigid.

The use of light material and wood filled plastic has kept the weight down and the overall impression is of a well made gun with no effort spent on an unnecessary degree of finish.

The Vz 58V is a well conceived, well constructed arm of modern design. It is robust, accurate, and safe when used by trained firers. The performance is comparable with the latest American designs and with the butt folded it is easier to carry.

It has been produced to be sold abroad and appeared in Vietnam. No doubt it will soon be seen in a number of the emergent states where its very competitive price will be attractive.

DATA
Cartridge: 7.62mm × 39
Method of operation: Gas

Method of locking: Pivoting locking piece
Method of feed: 30-round box magazine
Method of fire: Selective

WEIGHTS
Rifle, empty: 3.14kg
Magazine, empty: 185g
Magazine, full: 681g
Rifle, loaded: 3.82kg
Trigger pull: 3.2-3.5kg

LENGTHS
Rifle, stock extended: 820mm
Rifle, stock folded: 635mm
Barrel: 401mm

MECHANICAL FEATURES
Barrel: Regulator: Nil
    Rifling: 4 grooves RH. 1 turn in 240mm
    Cooling: Air
Sights: Foresight: Cylindrical post
    Rearsight: Tangent leaf V sight. Battle sight position denoted by 'U'. Windage – Nil
    Graduation: 100 to 800 metres by 100 metre increments
    Zeroing: Elevation. Front sight screws up and down Line. Front sight on eccentric
    Sight radius: 356mm

FIRING CHARACTERISTICS
Muzzle velocity: 710 metres/sec
Muzzle energy: 203mkp
Recoil energy: 1.17mkp
Rate of fire: Cyclic: 800 rounds/min
      Auto: .90 rounds/min
      SS: .40 rounds/min
Range, maximum effective: 400 metres
Manufacturer: Ceskoslovenska Zbrojovka, Strakonice
Status: Currently manufactured. In service with the Czechoslovakian Army. Commercially available. Has been used by Palestine Liberation Army and the Black September Group

7.62mm URZ SYSTEM

The Czechoslovakian URZ system was produced in 1970. The abbreviation stand for 'Universal Small Arms' and it could well be that the basic idea came from a study of the Stoner 63 system (qv). The system comprises:
An automatic rifle (AP)
A light machine gun (LK)
A medium machine gun (TK)
A tank machine gun (T)
These weapons have a common design, the fundamentals of which appear to be based on the Czech Vz59 GPMG. Although the system has

been discussed in Czech magazines, not a great deal is known about it. The photographs shown reveal, when examined and scaled, that the weapons are almost certainly chambered for the NATO 7.62mm × 51 cartridge. This would be in line with Czechoslovakian policy with the other weapons such as the Skorpion in .32 calibre and the Vz 59 offered in 7.62mm × 51. The purpose of this is claimed to be an effort to obtain Western currency. However if the system is adopted – which does not seem likely – it could well (in addition to the NATO cartridge) use two natures of ammunition – the 7.62mm × 39 and the 7.62mm × 54R. The automatic rifle and the light machine gun would be firing the 7.62mm × 39 M43 cartridge and the medium machine gun and the tank gun would be chambered for the big Russian 7.62mm × 54R.

Automatic Rifle (AP)

This rifle is intended to replace the existing Vz 61 SMG (the Skorpion) and the current assault rifle the Vz 58. It is quite heavily constructed and when unloaded weighs 3.9kg which is heavier than the Vz 58. This weight seems excessive for a rifle chambered for the 7.62mm × 39 cartridge and leads to the assumption that at least some of these rifles use the larger round or, as in the Stoner 63 rifle, the excess weight comes from using components which have to be heavy to carry out a more exacting role in the other weapons.

The barrel is comparatively light – considerably lighter than those of the other weapons – and is not chromium plated. The bayonet is of the knife type and, like that of the AKM utilises the scabbard to incorporate a wire cutter. The rifle has a separate magazine to take ballistite cartridges for grenade projective and the selector on the left hand side of the body, gives safe, semi-automatic which argues that a separate control is used for grenade firing.

Light Machine Gun (LK)

The LMG is basically similar to the rifle in its magazine feed. The barrel is heavier, has a quick change facility and a chrome lining. There is a carrying handle and a folding bipod. The LK weighs 5.2kg unloaded. This weight seems to indicate that the 7.62mm × 39 is used and it would appear that the weapon would have a performance similar to that of the RPK but with a greater capacity for sustained fire.

Medium Machine Gun (TK)

The TK is a tripod-mounted version of the LK, with an optical sight, using the Czech 250-round open pocket continuous link belt. The tripod is lightweight and can be quickly converted into an anti-aircraft mount. The gun and its tripod together weigh only 11kg.

Tank Machine Gun (T)

This is a vehicle-mounted co-axial machine gun. It is solenoid-controlled and belt fed. It weighs 5.7kg and is fitted with the heavy barrel necessary for the large volume of fire required from an AFV gun.

COMMON CHARACTERISTICS

The AP, LK and TK have some features which are common to all of them.

SIGHTS

They have adjustable foresights and leaf backsights with 9 range settings. The optical sight of the TK MMG can be fitted to the rifle and light machine gun. It is a metascope and not only gives indication of infra-red surveillance but is sufficiently accurate in its location of an active IR source to allow fire to be directed at it.

FEED

All three weapons have a 50-round light alloy drum magazine and are fed from vertically below the receiver. In addition the TK MMG is normally belt fed without removing the magazine. There is some evidence that belt feed can also be used, similarly, in the other two guns.

The URZ system

GRENADE LAUNCHING

All three weapons carry a grenade sight permanently fitted to the foresight block. They have a small box magazine for the ballistite cartridges and all have rubber pads fitted to the buttstock to reduce the recoil force from grenade firing.

DATA	AP	LK	TK	T
Cartridge:	7.62mm × 39	7.62mm × 39	7.62mm × 54R	7.62mm × 54R
Method of operation:	Gas	Gas	Gas	Gas
Method of feed:	50-round drum	50-round drum	250-round belt	Belt
Weight (less magazine):	3.9kg	5.2kg	11kg (with tripod)	5.7kg
Length (less bayonet):	995mm	995mm	1,200mm	877mm
Muzzle velocity:	717 metres/sec	717 metres/sec	800 metres/sec	800 metres/sec
Muzzle energy:	204mkp	204mkp	300mkp	300mkp
Rate of fire: Cyclic:	800rpm	800rpm	800rpm	1,100rpm
Auto:	150rpm	120rpm	200rpm	200rpm
SS:	35rpm	—	—	—
Manufacturer: Ceskoslovenska Zbrojovka, Strakonice				
Status: Probably experimental				

DOMINICAN REPUBLIC

.30 LIGHT RIFLE CHRISTOBAL MODELS 2 and 62

The Dominican Army was equipped with the M1908 7mm Mauser rifle. These have now been sold and the Dominican Republic Arsenal has produced a weapon for its forces. The Hungarian designer Pal Kiraly who was responsible for the 39M and 43M Hungarian SMGs went to South America after the Russians occupied his country. In 1948 he came to an agreement with the Government of Dominica and he started up a factory at San Christobal to manufacture arms. The plant was established with extensive help from the Italian firm of Pietro Beretta and the Beretta SMG was at first produced. Kiraly then designed the Christobal Carbine Model 2, using the .30 cartridge of the US M1 carbine and this was produced. Kiraly died in the early 60's.

This is a delayed blowback rifle using the system familiar from the Hungarian 39M SMG. It fires from an open breech. A light weight bolt head carries a lever, one end of which is engaged in the floor of the receiver and the other end bears against the heavy bolt body. The bolt head is restrained by the lever when the pressure is high and the heavy bolt body is acceler-

ated backwards. When the lever is rotated out of the receiver the entire bolt is blown back. On the feed stroke the two parts of the body must come together and rotate the lever into the receiver before the bolt body can drive the firing pin, in the bolt head, into the cap of the cartridge.

Model 62

Subsequently a Model 62 was made which was a gas operated assault rifle firing the 7.62mm × 51 cartridge. It was not manufactured in quantity.

DATA (Model 2)
Cartridge: .30 M1 Carbine
Method of operation: Delayed blowback
Method of delay: Lever and two part bolt
Method of feed: 25- or 30-round detachable box magazine
Method of fire: Selective

The Christobal selective fire carbine Model 2

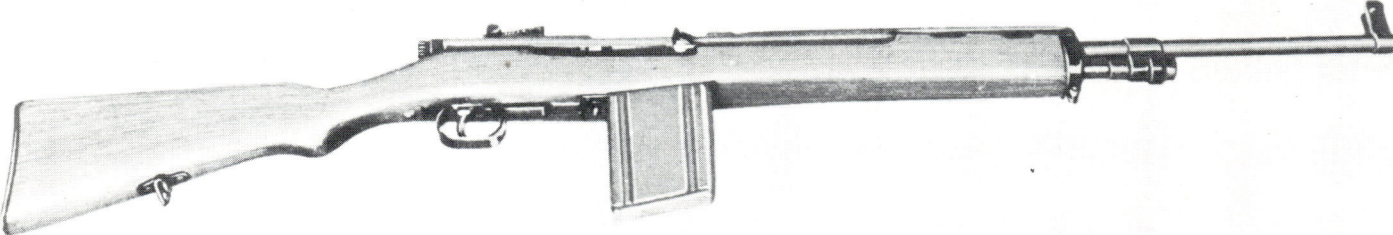

The Dominican M62

Weight: 3.52kg
Length: 945mm
Barrel: 409mm
    Rifling: NK
Sights: Foresight: Blade
    Rearsight: Notch
Muzzle velocity: 572 metres/sec
Muzzle energy: 118mkp

Rate of fire: Cyclic: 580 rounds/min
    Automatic: 120 rounds/min
    SS: 40 rounds/min
Range, maximum effective: 300 metres
Manufacturer: San Christobal Arsenal
Status: No longer manufactured. In service with Dominican troops. In limited service in Cuba

FINLAND

7.62mm M60 and M62 ASSAULT RIFLES

The Finnish Assault Rifle is essentially a Russian AK 47 manufactured at Valmet. The Finns adapted the design in the late 1950s and the first small pilot batch required for troop trials bore the designation M60. After some minor changes the Finnish Defence Forces adopted the weapon under the designation M62.

The M60 differs from the AK 47 in several respects. There is no wood on the M60. The metal fore-end and the pistol grip are both plastic covered. The buttstock is a cylindrical tube with a cross bar riveted on for the shoulder piece. The cleaning rod and brush are carried in the tube of the stock. The forearm of the Model 60 has 10 large holes and 10 small holes to allow dissipation of heat. The receiver is made from stampings riveted and welded. The barrel has a three prong flash eliminator. The foresight is a

Finnish 7.62mm assault rifle M62

Finnish M60 assault rifle

hooded post located over the front end of the gas cylinder. The rearsight is a tangent aperture protected by two wings. Since, unlike the USSR practice, an aperture rearsight is used, it is located at the back of the receiver cover. There is no trigger guard, but a protective bar is dropped down in front of the trigger to prevent accidental release of the magazine. The safety catch and selector lever on the right of the receiver is exactly the same as that of the AK 47. The semi automatic marking is a one dot, and next comes full auto with three dots.

The 1962 modifications were not of great significance. The fore end is now made of plastic, ribbed, with 24 large cooling holes. A trigger guard is fitted. The pistol grip is ribbed plastic and now sweeps back further at the rear upper end. The fitting of the shoulder piece to the tubular stock has been amended somewhat.

The M62, selective-fire, weapon is stricfly a military rifle. For commercial sale, however, the manufacturers make a semi-automatic version, the M62/S, which is available with either a metal buttstock, like the M62, or a wooden stock.

DATA (M62)
Cartridge: 7.62mm × 39
Method of operation: Gas
Method of locking: Rotating bolt
Method of feed: 30-round detachable box magazine
Method of fire: Selective
Weight, empty: 3.5kg
Weight, loaded: 4.7kg
Length: 914mm
Barrel: 420mm
   Rifling: 4 grooves RH
Sights: Foresight: Hooded blade
   Rearsight: Tangent aperture
Muzzle velocity: 719 metres/sec
Muzzle energy: 208mkp
Rate of fire: Cyclic: 650 rounds/min
   Auto: 120 rounds/min
   SS: 40 rounds/min
Range, maximum effective: 350-400 metres
Manufacturer: Valmet Oy, Punanotkonkatu, Helsinki
Status: In production. In service with Finnish Forces

5.56mm M71/S RIFLE

This is essentially a cost-reduced but very well made version of the earlier Valmet M62/S rifle but in 5.56mm × 45 calibre. Its appearance is not thought to presage a change in standard calibre for the Finnish forces: it appears to have been designed primarily to supplement the range of weapons available for export.

In addition to the change of calibre several improvements on the M60/M62 design have been incorporated and cost has been held down by the extensive use of castings and sheet-metal work in the construction, keeping machining operations to a minimum. Stripping has been simplified by dispensing with the carbon scraper behind the gas piston so that the piston and bolt-carrier assembly can be withdrawn without removing the gas cylinder. The sights have been moved forwards relative to those of the M62, the tangent rear sight (100-500m × 100m) being mounted on the receiver ring and the foresight at the muzzle. Both sights incorporate tritium light sources for use in poor light.   The M71/S is a semi-automatic weapon – as the S suffix indicates – and is sold with a fixed plastic stock. No doubt the manufacturers are in a position to make a selective-fire version for military sales if required; at present, however, it appears that the weapon is being made to order for commercial sales through Interarms.

M71/S rifle

Operation: Gas
Locking: Rotating bolt
Feed: 30-round detachable box magazine
Fire: Semi-automatic
Sights: Foresight: Hooded blade
   Rearsight: Tangent aperture 100-500m × 100m
Manufacturer: Valmet Oy, Punanotkonkatu 2, Helsinki
Status: Production. See text.

DATA
Cartridge: 5.56mm × 45

FRANCE

8mm M1916 RIFLE and CARBINE

Long obsolete in Europe, this rifle and carbine still exist as operational weapons in some former French territories – notably in Asia. Several variants may be found but the following data are typical.

DATA
Cartridge: 8mm French M1886 rimmed
Operation: Manual, bolt action

Feed: 3- or 5-round magazine
Weight: 3-4kg
Length: 945mm
Sights: Foresight Blade
   Rearsight: Adjustable leaf
Rate of fire: 8-10 round/min
Status: No longer made but still encountered

7.5mm MAS 36 RIFLE

Introduced in 1936, this manual bolt-action rifle still survives in a training role in France and as an operational weapon in many former French

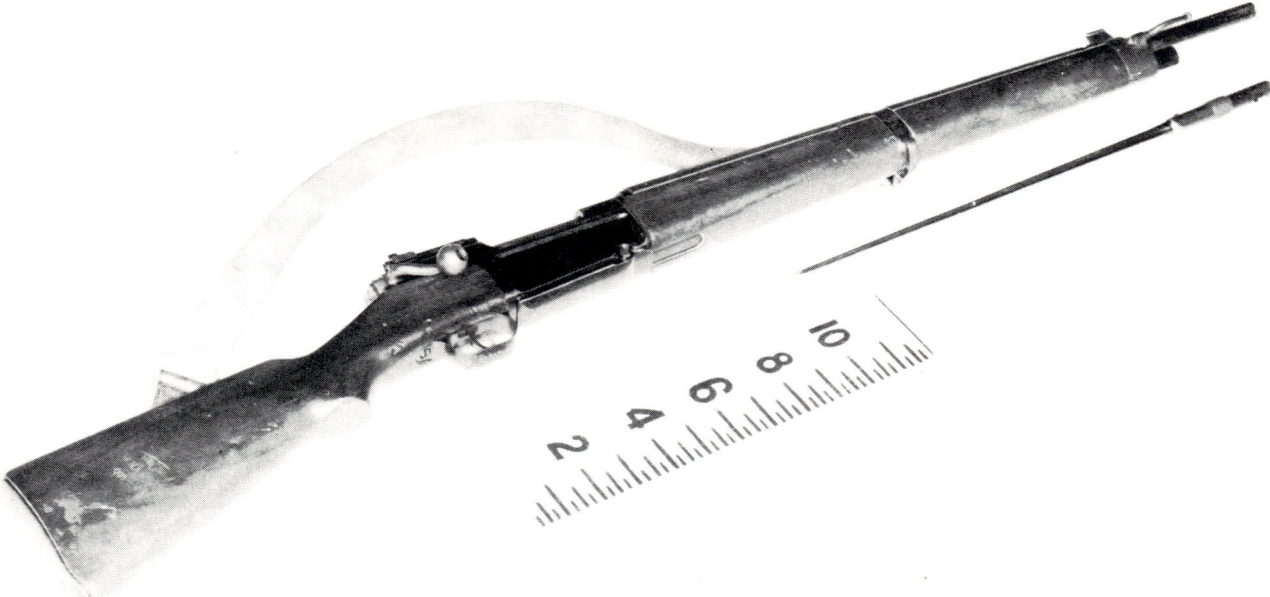

The MAS 1936 carbine

territories. Its bolt action is similar to that of the Mauser but has its locking lugs at the trigger end, to give a short bolt stroke, instead of in the stronger breech position. The 5-round magazine is loaded using a charger or individual rounds. A bayonet can be fitted or stowed.

Two variants of the basic design were a parachute version (M36CR39) with a folding stock and shorter barrel and a post-war version (M36M51) with a built-in grenade launcher. The rifle also formed the basis of the FR-F1 sniper's rifle.

DATA (M36 unless otherwise specified)
Cartridge: 7.5mm M29

Operation: Manual bolt-action
Feed: 5-round integral magazine
Weight: 3.8kg (CR39, 3.6kg)
Length: 1018mm (CR39, 886mm or 617mm)
Barrel: 574mm (CR39, 450mm)
Sights: Foresight: Hooded barleycorn
         Rearsight: Aperture and ramp
Muzzle velocity: About 800m/sec
Effective range: 500m (CR39, 450m)
Status: No longer made. Used for training and in service in some former French territories

7.5mm MAS 49 RIFLE

The MAS 49 is a self-loading rifle using gas operation but dispensing with the gas piston and cylinder which are normally employed. The gas is diverted back, over the barrel, and impinges on the bolt carrier to drive it to the rear. The carrier moves back freely for about ¼in and then lifts the back of the breech block out of its locking recess in the receiver and carries it to the rear. This system reduces the overall weight of the weapon but is generally regarded as producing a lot of fouling. However it seems to be effective with the MAS 49.

The weapon is typical of its period using wooden furniture, a limited capacity magazine and a ball round ranging out well beyond the soldier's capacity to make use of it. There is a grenade sight mounted on the left side just behind the muzzle. A graduated spigot can be moved in and out, and thus by variation of the length of shot travel, the range can be varied.

DATA
Cartridge: 7.5mm Model 1929
Method of operation: Gas – direct action
Method of locking: Tilting block
Method of feed: 10-round detachable box magazine
Method of fire: Semi-automatic
Weight: 4.7kg
Length: 1,100mm
Barrel: 580mm
         Rifling: 4 groove LH
Muzzle velocity: 823 m/sec
Muzzle energy: 311mkp
Rate of fire: SA 30 rounds/min
Range, maximum effective: 600 metres
Status: No longer manufactured. In service in some of the former French Colonies

7.5mm MODEL 49/56 RIFLE

This rifle is a modified version of the MAS 49 which was adopted by the French Army after World War II to re-equip their infantry units which had a miscellany of obsolescent French rifles and wartime Allied weapons. The Model 49/56 differs from the 49 in the following ways:
(a) The wooden fore-end is shortened.
(b) The integral grenade launcher has been replaced by a new combined muzzle brake/grenade launcher.

OPERATION

The MAS 49/56 is a self-loading gas-operated rifle with a ten-round box magazine. Part of the propellant gas is deflected into a gas tube which lies along the top of the barrel, below the wooden furniture, and emerges over the breech. The gas passes along the tube and is delivered into the bolt carrier. The gas expands inside the carrier and forces the carrier back. The carrier moves back ⅜in and then cam grooves at the back of the carrier contact lugs on the side of the bolt and the tilting block is lifted out of engagement with the locking recess in the receiver and this rocking motion provides primary extraction of the case. The carrier collects the bolt and the

assembly moves rearwards as an entity. The return spring is compressed, the empty case is withdrawn from the chamber and the hammer is rotated back against its spring. The fired case, held by the extractor, strikes the ejector and is expelled to the right of the rifle. The back end of the bolt carrier reaches the end of the receiver and stops. The compressed return spring then drives the carrier forward, loading a round and locking behind it.

TRIGGER AND FIRING MECHANISM

The trigger/firing mechanism is in principle the same as that employed in the USA Garand M1 and later in the M14 rifle, using a hammer with two bents and a primary and secondary, spring loaded, sear mounted on the trigger extension. When the weapon is ready for firing the hammer bent is held by the primary sear. Pulling the trigger moves the primary sear out of the main notch – or bent – of the hammer and the hammer spring rotates the hammer forward. When the hammer is brought back by the recoiling bolt carrier its rear hook is caught by the spring-loaded secondary sear and held. It is not possible to fire another round as the trigger is still held back.

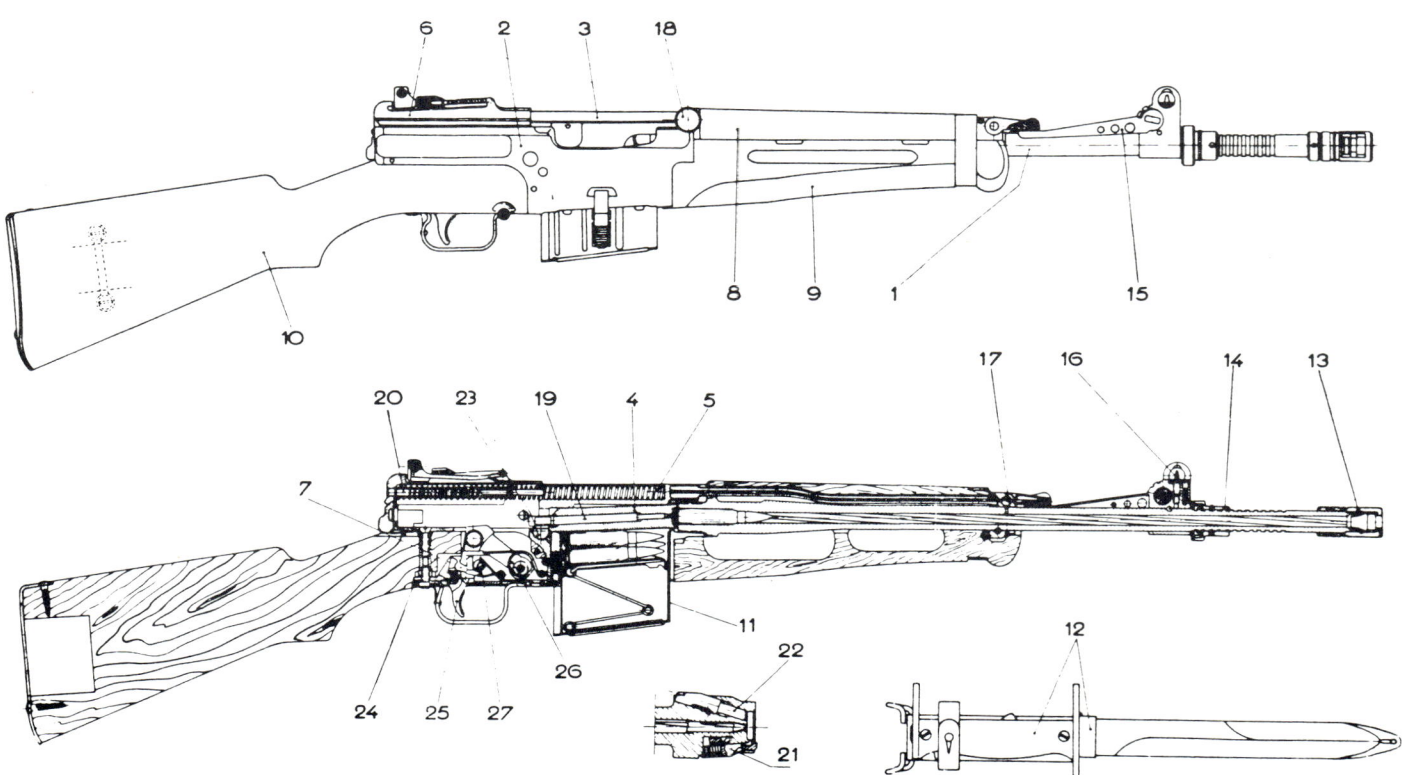

Section through the 7.5 MAS 49/56 rifle. Key: (1) Barrel; (2) Receiver; (3) Breech cover; (4) Bolt; (5) Return spring; (6) Breech cover; (7) Trigger mechanism; (8) Hand guard; (9) Lower hand guard; (10) Butt; (11) Magazine; (12) Bayonet; (13) Flash hider; (14) Grenade fitting; (15) Grenade sight; (16) Sight; (17) Gas passage; (18) Cocking handle; (19) Firing pin; (20) Spring guide rod; (21) Extractor; (22) Ejector; (23); (24); (25) Trigger; (26); (27) Safety

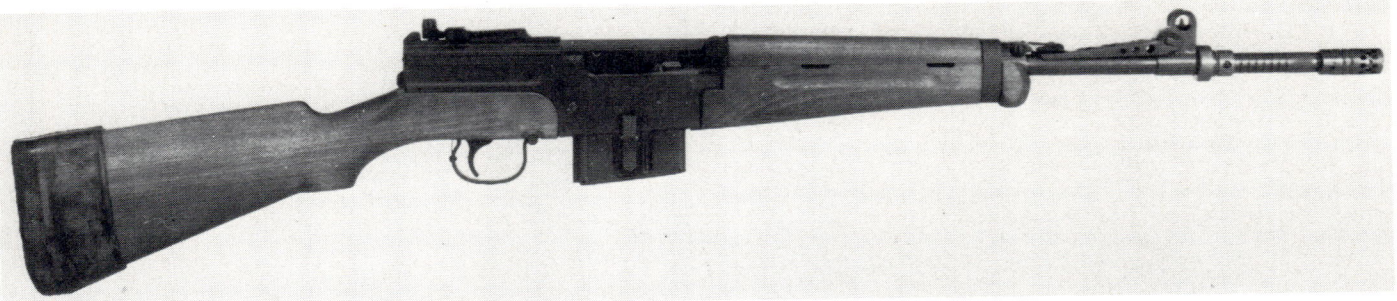

The MAS 49/56 rifle

When the firer releases the trigger the upper end of the trigger revolves back and the spring loaded secondary sear releases the hammer but before it can clear the trigger mechanism the primary bent is caught by the primary sear and the hammer is held. Pulling the trigger releases the hammer and the cycle starts again.

After the ammunition in the ten-round magazine is expended, the carrier will be held to the rear by the holding device operated by the magazine platform. The magazine catch on the right side of the magazine can be depressed, the magazine removed and replaced with a full one or alternatively two five round clips can be loaded via charger guides at the front of the bolt cover. The bolt can then be pulled back and when released will fly forward to chamber the top round.

GRENADES
To discharge a grenade, the rifleman must first remove the magazine and ensure the chamber is clear. A ballistite grenade cartridge is manually loaded, the bolt closed and the safety applied. The grenade is slid over the muzzle, which is also the launcher, as far as it will go.

To lift the main grenade sight to the vertical postion it is first necessary to move the small covering leaf. The gas used to operate the automatic mechanism of the rifle has to pass through a hole drilled in the spindle to which this leaf is attached; when the leaf is raised, rotation of the spindle blocks the gas path to the breech block carrier and allows all of it to be used in driving the grenade. The safety catch is moved up and the firer can then take aim. The grenade sight is aimed by aligning the appropriate range arc with the greatest body diameter of the grenade and placing the arc on the target. After firing, the sight is folded back, the leaf rotated to clear the gas track and after inspection of the chamber, the magazine can be re-inserted in readiness to fire ball ammunition. It is important to ensure that a ball cartridge is not fired with a grenade in place on the launcher.

STRIPPING
Stripping the M1949/56 rifle is straightforward. After the magazine has been removed and the chamber checked, the cover catch at the rear of the receiver is pressed and the receiver cover pushed forward until the rear end can be lifted out of the receiver. If it is then withdrawn the cover can be removed. The return spring is then exposed and can be lifted out. If the cocking handle is pulled back the bolt carrier assembly can be lifted out. The bolt can then be removed from its carrier.

Accessories include a telescopic sight and a night sight. The telescopic sight is the M53 bis. It fits onto the sight base on the left of the receiver, sliding on from rear to front, and is locked by swinging the adaptor lever forward. Further details of this sight are given in the FR-F1 Sniping Rifle entry below. The night sight is put on over the flash suppressor and

foresight and the clamping wing nut is tightened.

The M49/56 rifle takes the French 7.5mm × 54 cartridge and both ball and tracer rounds can be used. Armour piercing ammunition is available but produces considerable barrel wear. A few rifles were manufactured to fire the NATO 7.62mm x 51 cartridge.

DATA
Cartridge: 7.5mm × 54
Method of operation: Gas (direct action)
Method of locking: Tilting block
Method of feed: 10-round box magazine
Method of fire: Self-loading

WEIGHTS
Rifle, without magazine: 3.9kg
Magazine, empty: 200g
Magazine, full: 432g
Rifle, loaded: 4.34kg
Bayonet: 500g

LENGTHS
Rifle: 1,010mm
Barrel: 521mm

MECHANICAL FEATURES
Barrel: Rifling: 4 grooves RH. 1 turn in 12in. (305mm)
     Regulator: Nil
     Cooling: Air
Sights: Foresight: Blade
     Rearsight: Leaf tangent. Aperture
     Graduation: 2-12 by 100 metre increments
     Zeroing: Line. Back sight screws across block
     Elevation: Back sight screws up and down
     Sight radius: 569mm

FIRING CHARACTERISTICS
Muzzle velocity: 817 metres/sec
Muzzle energy: 306mkp
Recoil energy: 1.52mkp
Rate of fire: SS: 30 rounds/min
Range, maximum effective: 600 metres
Status: No longer manufactured. No longer in service with the French Army. Used in countries which were at one time French Dependencies: Cameroun, Chad, Dahomey, Ivory Coast, Malagasy Republic, Rwanda

---

FR-F1 SNIPER'S RIFLE
The French sniping rifle, the Fusil à Répétition Modele F1, is a ten shot, manually-operated bolt-action rifle based on the action of the now obsolete 7.5mm Model 1936. It has a detachable 10-round box magazine. A few parts of the old rifle – firing pin and spring, bolt plug, extractor, sear and spring, and bolt stop – are still used.

The rifle was specifically designed for sniping but two other versions are in existence. The three models are known as:
(a) Tireur d'Elite – the sniping rifle
(b) Tir Sportif – the target rifle with target sights and a 3.3 to 4.2 pound

trigger pull
(c) Grande Chasse – which is described as being designed for big game hunting: it has an APX model 804 telescopic sight and a 2-2.5kg trigger pull

OPERATION
The bolt is manually operated with a turn down knob on the right hand side. No left handed version is made. The locking lugs are rear mounted. Assuming the rifle to have been fired, lifting the bolt handle cams back the

The French sniping rifle, Model F1

firing pin and compresses the spring. Initial extraction is produced by the rotation of the bolt; as the bolt handle comes up, a cam at its root bears against a cam surface located at the rear of the receiver and a slow powerful leverage is exerted to loosen the fired case in the chamber. Continued rotation takes the locking lugs of the bolt out of engagement with the recesses in the receiver. Withdrawal of the bolt allows the extractor to pull the case out of the chamber and it is held against the bolt face until it strikes a fixed ejector located on the left of the receiver. The case is then ejected clear of the rifle to the right. The bolt is prevented from rotating during its reciprocating movement by the spring loaded stop riding against the bottom of the bolt. Backward motion is terminated when a shoulder on the bottom of the bolt face reaches the bolt stop. As the bolt is forced forward it feeds the top round into the chamber and as it is closed the extractor grips the rim of the cartridge. At the same time the sear holds up the firing pin lug to retain the firing pin in the cocked position.

When the trigger is operated it rotates back around the trigger pin joining the trigger and sear until the trigger stud reaches the bottom of the receiver. Continued pressure pivots the sear and compresses its spring. When the top of the trigger adjusting screw reaches the receiver the first pressure is felt. When the second pressure is taken the sear releases the lug of the firing pin which goes forward under its own spring to hit the cap. The lock time is very short. It should be noted that if the trigger is held back and the bolt operated, the bolt stop which pivots on the trigger pin, is depressed against its spring and the bolt comes freely out of the receiver.

Telescope Modele 53 bis

THE TELESCOPIC SIGHT

The FR-FI sniping rifle uses the Modele 53 bis telescopic sight which is carried, with its adjusting tool, in a transit case. On the right of the mount are 2 lugs which fit into dovetails on top of the receiver. A lug on the left of the mount is for a groove between the dovetails. The mount is located with the locking lever to the rear and when in place it is secured by rotating the lever forward. To zero the telescope the screws at the bottom of the mount ring are loosened, the elevation knob set to 2 and the rifle is bore-sighted on a distant object. The plastic rings between the telescope and the mount rings are rotated until the telescope reticle is on the aiming mark with zero windage set. When the bore and reticle are aligned on the same aiming mark the screws on the mount rings are tightened. A 3-round check firing at 200 metres should then be carried out to ensure that the reticle is on the mean point of impact. If not, the adjusting tool is used to loosen the elevation knob locking screws. Rotate the elevation zero ring and windage knob until the reticle is on the point of impact. The elevation zero ring is gripped, the elevation knob put to 2, and the three screws tightened. The windage knob screws are loosened and the knob rotated until the red line is on the index. The screws are then tightened. A further check group should be fired. Once the sight is correctly zeroed it may be dismounted, cased, and re-mounted without change of zero.

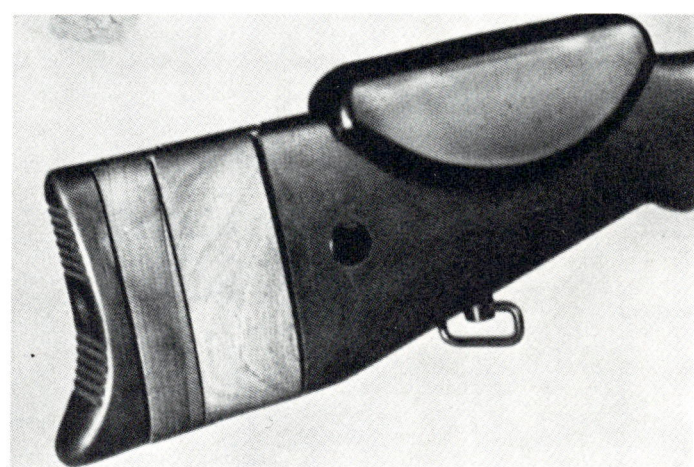
The butt of the French sniping rifle

PREPARATION FOR FIRING

The rifle is issued to one man in the sniping section and he fits the weapon to suit his own physical characteristics. The length of the buttstock can be increased by fitting one or both of the wooden spacers provided. The smaller is 20mm and the other 40mm thick. The butt plate screw is removed and the spacer fitted to mate the contour of the buttstock. The butt plate is then screwed on again. Next the cheek pad is fitted. There are two heights, 8 or 17mm. The cheek pad has pins on the underside which mate into holes on the comb of the stock. A hide mallet or other soft hammer may be needed to fit the cheek pad flush to the stock. It should be noted that it is essential not to damage the pins on the cheek pad because this fitting has to be removed from the rifle before the bolt can be withdrawn.

Lastly the armourer should adjust the weight and length of the trigger pull to suit the firer. The adjusting screws are on the trigger extension and make contact with the top of the receiver when the trigger is operated, thus fixing the length of pull and first pressure. Second pressure is automatically determined by the contact area between the sear and cocking lug of the firing pin and can only be adjusted by honing the mating faces to change the manufacturer's angles.

The magazine catch on the right of the receiver is pressed to release the magazine. The magazine holds ten rounds. If it is to be replaced in the rifle the rubber cap is left on the bottom but if the magazine is being carried as a loaded replacement the rubber cap is placed over the top to keep out dust and put back on the bottom – if time permits – when the magazine is placed in the rifle. It is possible to load single rounds through the bolt way to replenish a partially expended magazine but this procedure is not recommended in action.

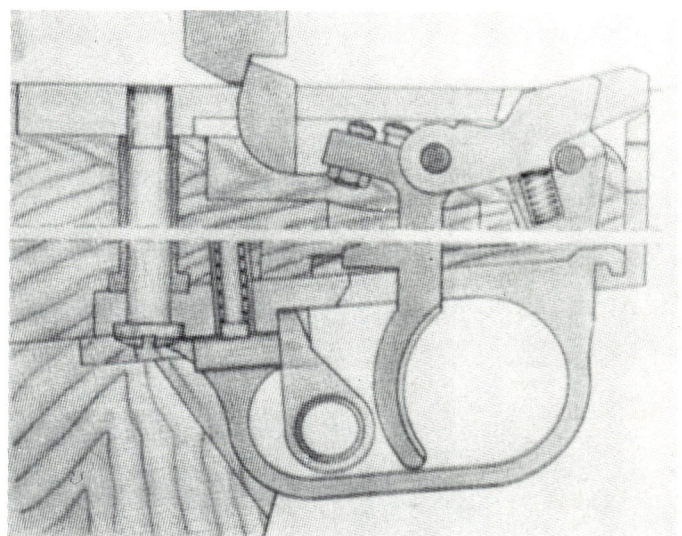
The trigger arrangement of the French sniping rifle

If the flash eliminator has been removed it is necessary to fire a check series to ensure maximum accuracy when it is replaced. This is done by loosening the locking collar when the eliminator has been replaced on the rifle, and using a soft copper bar or a wooden rod through the prongs of the eliminator, to screw the eliminator fully home. Tighten the collar by finger pressure only and fire a five shot group. Loosen the collar, unscrew the eliminator two turns and again hand tighten the collar.

Fire another group. Loosen the collar, tighten the eliminator by one turn, tighten the collar by hand and fire again. Using the setting for the smallest group of the three firings, adjust by half turns until the minimum group size is established. Then lock the collar using a strap. It is found that the setting of the flash eliminator is very critical.

The bipod is permanently fixed at the rear of the fore-end and the rifle is carried with the bipod legs swung forward and fitting into recesses on each side of the forearm. The bipod is always used unless firing over cover such as a low wall. The bipod legs can be lengthened by twisting the knurled

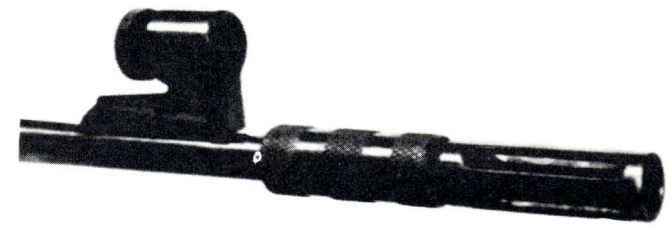
The flash eliminator

collar above the spade and rotating it back when the spring loaded lower leg has extended sufficiently. The legs should be fully retracted for stowing the bipod along the forearm.

There may be occasions when the telescope cannot be used. The front and rear sights are normally laid flat and must be raised. The rear sight is a square shouldered notch. The foresight is a flat topped pyramid. The shoulders of the rearsight and the centre of the foresight have luminous green dots and at night the three dots are evenly spaced in a horizontal line and placed on the target. To use the iron sights the telescope must first be dismounted.

The FR-FI uses match quality 7.5 × 54mm ball ammunition and the use of tracer or armour piercing ammunition, which will damage the bore, is prohibited. The FR-FI is also manufactured in 7.62 × 51mm NATO and the marking 7.5mm or 7.62mm is inscribed on the left hand side of the receiver.

DATA

Cartridge: 7.5mm × 54 or 7.6mm × 51

Method of operation: Manual
Method of locking: Rotating bolt
Method of feed: 10-round box magazine
Method of fire: Single shots

WEIGHTS
Rifle, empty: 5.2kg
Magazine, empty: 220g
Trigger pull: 2.05-2.5kp

LENGTH
Overall, without spacers: 1.138mm
Barrel: 552mm

MECHANICAL FEATURES
Barrel: Rifling: 4 grooves RH. 1 turn in 305mm
Sights: Optical: × 4
    Iron Foresight: Flat topped pyramid. With luminous spot.
    Rearsight: Square shouldered notch with luminous spots.
    Zeroing: Elevation. Change foresight Line. Foresight on dovetail.

FIRING CHARACTERISTICS
Muzzle velocity: 852 metres/sec
Muzzle energy: 333mkp
Recoil energy: 1.38mkp
Rate of fire: 10-15 rounds/min
Range, maximum effective: 800 metres
Manufacturer: Groupement Industriel des Armements Terrestres, 10 Place Georges Clémenceau, 92211 Saint-Cloud, France
Status: No longer being manufactured. In service with French Army

---

5.56mm FA MAS

The FA MAS 5.56 rifle is intended as the soldier's personal weapon. It can produce semi-automatic, automatic and burst firing using any of the 5.56 cartridges meeting the requirements of the NATO specification and can also project anti-tank and anti-personnel grenades with an inside boom diameter of 22mm, using a special ballistite cartridge.

The bull pup design of the British EM2 appears again but unlike the British design the MAS weapon can be fired from either shoulder without the difficulties produced in the EM2 of ejection of the spent case.

The bolt face has two extractor positions. The rifle is issued with the extractor on the right and the spring loaded ejector rod mounted centrally inside the bolt face, then rotates the empty case around the extractor on the other side of the bolt face and move the dummy extractor across to replace it. The ejector will now pivot the case out to the left. The cheek rest can be removed and positioned on the other side of the buttstock where it closes off the ejection slot provided for operation on the other side. The ability to fire the weapon off either shoulder is an advantage that removes one of the major objections to the bull pup design.

The cocking handle is placed centrally above the receiver to permit operation by either hand (in a manner similar to that used on the Armalite AR-10 rifle) and the centrally mounted sights can be used regardless of the shoulder the soldier uses.

ACCURACY

The maker claims that at 200 metres the horizontal spread plus vertical spread of 10 rounds, does not exceed 400mm .

DESCRIPTION

The weapon is made up of the following component groups.

The barrel assembly with the receiver, cocking mechanism and return spring.

The working parts consisting of the breech-block, carrier, and delay lever.

The trigger assembly
The buttstock and cheek rest
The carrying handle
Bipod, bayonet and sling

BARREL

The barrel is of plain steel, with no evidence of chrome plating. It has a fluted chamber. The forward end carries a series of rings which seat the grenade and with an adjustable collar control the position of the grenade and so vary the muzzle velocity. A flash hider is fitted to the muzzle.

The receiver is of light alloy and the other assemblies are pinned to it.

WORKING PARTS

The breech-block fits into the carrier. It is drilled to take the firing pin and the ejector rod and spring, and has a detachable front section carrying the extractor and a dummy extractor plug. This front section is easily removed by levering out a securing pin on top of the breech-block with the aid of a cartridge case.

The carrier has grooves at the bottom of the rear end which enable it to slide in the receiver. It carries the breech-block. It is drilled at the top of the front face to take the cylinder containing the return spring. This is secured by a transverse pin which can be pushed out using the nose of a round.

The delay lever has two parallel, angled, arms joined by a cross piece. The arms connect the breech-block to the carrier and the cross piece controls the position of the firing pin. The lower ends of the arms bear against a hardened steel pin across the receiver and the upper ends rest against the back face of the breech-block carrier. It is the means of holding up the breech-face, whilst the chamber pressure is high, and transferring energy to the carrier. It also controls the trigger mechanism by operating the safety sear.

THE TRIGGER ASSEMBLY

The mechanism is self contained in a plastic box which is pinned to the receiver. It provides single shots, automatic fire and three-round bursts but the selector process is somewhat different to that used in the CAL and the AR-15. There are two selector controls – the usual 'safe', 'semi' and 'auto' control which is located near the trigger and the burst fire controller located under the trigger mechanism. This arrangement is said by the manufacturer to be used because the burst fire escapement is kept completely separate from the basic mechanism and if the burst fire device cannot operate due to the entry of mud etc, it in no way affects the primary means of fire.

There are three types of fire available:
Semi-automatic: Fire selector on '1'; Burst selector on '0'
Automatic fire: Fire selector on 'R'; Burst selector on '0'
Three round bursts: Fire selector on 'R'; Burst selector on '3'

The weapon is 'safe' when the selector lever is on 'S', and parallel to the barrel axis.

The trigger guard can be pulled down from the pistol grip and rotated through 180 degrees to allow the use of arctic mittens.

THE SIGHTS

The foresight is mounted on a column pinned to the barrel. It is raised to allow for the straight through contour of the buttstock. The foresight blade is mounted on a leaf spring and can be moved across the pillar, by using a

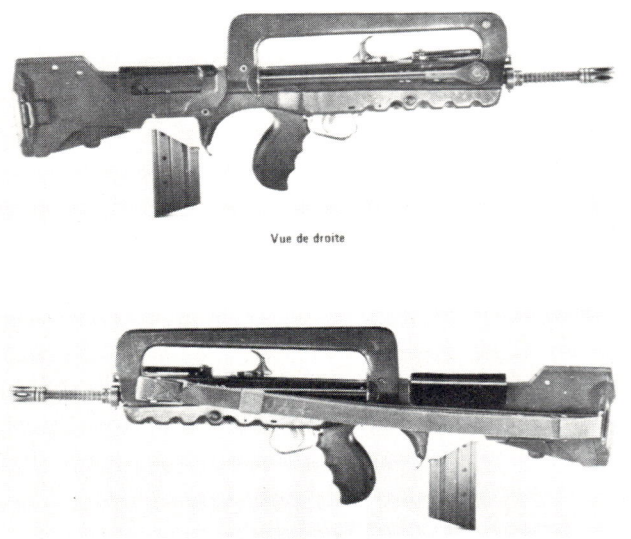

The MAS 5.56mm rifle

Vue de droite

Vue de gauche

Bolt, bolt carrier and delay lever of the MAS rifle

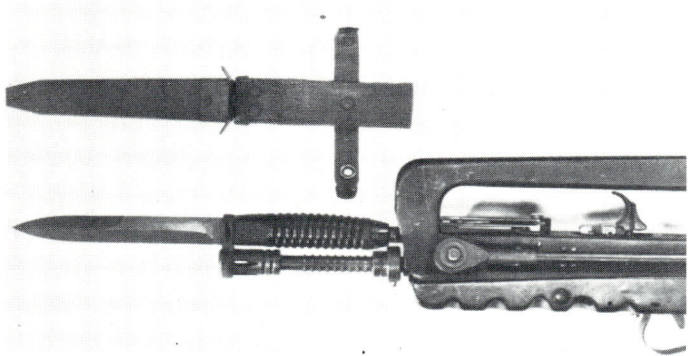

The bayonet of the MAS 5.56mm rifle

notched screw to compress the spring into the pillar, moving the foresight to the right and releasing the screw to allow the spring to carry the foresight to the left. Each notch on the screw head moves the mpi 4cm at 200 metres (0.2 mils).

There is a foresight cover with a luminous bead for night firing and a detachable open sight for direct laying of anti-tank and anti-personnel grenades.

The rear sight is also on a column, above the return spring cylinder. It is an aperture with the choice of two diameters selected by the use of two hinged plates, one on the front of the sight column and one on the rear. For conditions of good light both plates are up and the eye selects the small aperture on the front plate. When the light is poor the front plate is hinged down and the large aperture of the rear plate is used. At night both shutters are lowered and the top of the pillar makes a large aperture which is used in conjunction with the luminous bead on the foresight support.

The backsight is adjustable for elevation. There is a milled screw which compresses a spring to raise and lower the sight cradle. One turn of the screw moves the mpi 7cm at 200 metres (0.35 mils).

THE FURNITURE

The plastic buttstock carries a spring buffer in the top half. This cushions the blow of the working parts as they recoil and is compressed by about 25mm. There is a rubber shoulder pad to reduce the impact on the firer's shoulder. The cheek pad is held in place, on the selected side of the buttstock, when the buttstock is pinned to the receiver in front of the magazine housing. The empty case is ejected sideways through a slot in the buttstock.

The carrying handle is of plastic. It provides:
(a) Protection for the sights against accidental damage.
(b) Protection for the return spring cylinder.
(c) Protection against barrel heat.

It carries the sight for the indirect fire of grenades at 45 degrees or 75 degrees, the detachable sight for direct grenade fire, and the bipod legs.

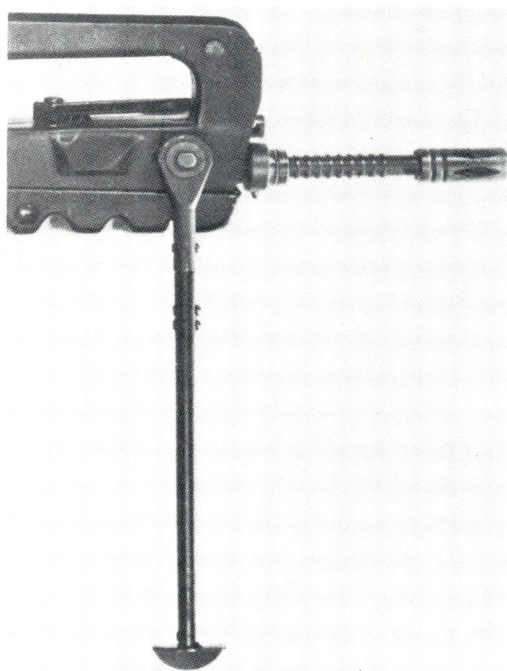

The bipod of the MAS rifle

OPERATION

The magazine holds 25 rounds, which may be loaded individually or by using a modified USA loader, and when loaded it is placed in the weapon by locating the front end in the well and rotating it rearwards to engage the magazine catch. The magazine has holes drilled in the sides to indicate that it contains (from top to bottom) 5, 10, 15, 20 or 25 rounds.

If the weapon is not to be fired immediately, the safety catch should be set to 'S'. The cocking handle is gripped with one or two fingers and pulled to

The foresight of the MAS 5.56mm rifle

the rear as far as possible and then released. The first movement releases the bolt lever and thus neutralises the anti-set back arrangement. The cylinder is sealed and lubricated for life. The piston is connected by a removable pin to the bolt carrier and the bolt carrier, as it is retracted, withdraws the bolt. When the cocking handle is released it flies forward under the pull of the compressed return spring and the feed lug under the front face of the bolt pushes the top round into the chamber. As the bolt comes to rest the extractor slips over the rim of the cartridge and the bolt carrier bears against the top of the arms of the delay lever, causing it to

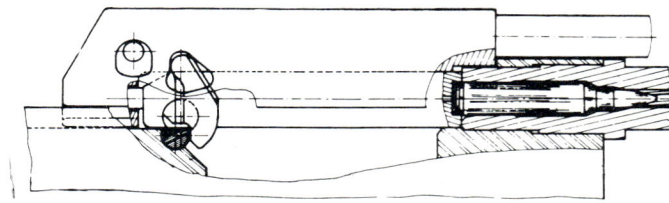

The action of the delay lever

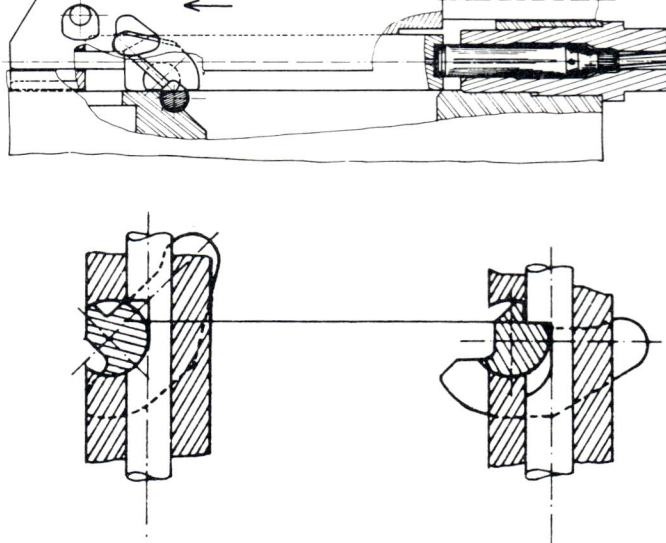

Firing pin retraction

rotate forward, with the pin in the body acting as a fulcrum, until it assumes a vertical position. When it does this the bottom end of the left arm of the lever presses down on a spring loaded rod which releases the safety sear and at the same time the centre cross bar, connecting the two arms, rotates out of a notch in the firing pin, which is then free and can be driven forward when struck by the hammer. When the trigger is operated (with the selector set to a fire position) the hammer flies forward and hits the firing pin which goes forward between the top arms of the delay lever and crushes the cap of the cartridge.

The pressure developed by the expanding gases forces the cartridge case back against the breech face and the bolt starts to move back. The lower arms of the delay lever lie below the bearing pin in the receiver and the force exerted by the breech-block causes the delay lever to rotate backwards. The top ends of the arms bear against the inside of the bolt carrier and since the top lever arms are longer than the bottom arms, a velocity ratio exists and the carrier is accelerated back relative to the bolt which moves only a very short distance. During the first 45 degrees of backward rotation of the delay lever, the following occur:

(a) The bolt carrier is accelerated backwards.
(b) The cross bar of the delay lever engages in the notch in the firing pin and withdraws it into the bolt
(c) The bottom of the left arm of the delay lever moves off the rod leading to the safety sear which is then released so that the hammer is held back regardless of the position of the trigger or the firing sear.
(d) The movement of the breech-block is retarded and this ensures that the cartridge case does not emerge, unsupported, from the chamber whilst the gas pressure is high.

When the delay lever has rotated some 45 degrees, it clears the pin in the receiver and the residual pressure in the chamber forces the cartridge case and bolt rapidly back. The bolt and its carrier then travel back together with the piston compressing the return spring in the cylinder. The empty case is rotated around the extractor, by the centrally mounted ejector as soon as it is clear of the chamber. It then flies out of the ejection port on the side opposite to the cheek rest, clear of the gun.

The back of the bolt carrier hits the buffer and compresses it by some 25mm and the bolt carrier and bolt are then reversed in direction and, impelled by the return spring, go forward to repeat the cycle.

THE TRIGGER AND FIRING MECHANISM

Due to the bull pup design the trigger is well forward of the hammer and is connected by a long rod. When the trigger is pulled the connecting rod moves forward. When the selector is set to 'single shot' (1) the forward movement of the connecting rod is limited. The rod carries a sleeve which rotates the manual sear off the hammer. If the delay lever is vertical it presses down the spring loaded rod bearing on the safety sear and the safety sear is lifted off the hammer. The hammer flies forward and the round is fired. The recoiling bolt carrier goes back and rotates the hammer over. It is held by a third sear which is rotated into engagement by the spring. When the trigger is released the sleeve on the connecting rod moves back. Since the trigger spring is powerful the spring of the third sear is overcome and the hammer is then held by the manual sear. When the trigger is pulled another round is fired.

When the selector is set to automatic, the connector rod is able to move further forward. The manual sear is moved off the hammer and the increased travel of the sleeve holds the third sear back and the hammer is held by the safety sear. When the delay lever reaches the upright position it releases the safety sear and another round is fired. Thus at automatic the fire is controlled by the safety sear only.

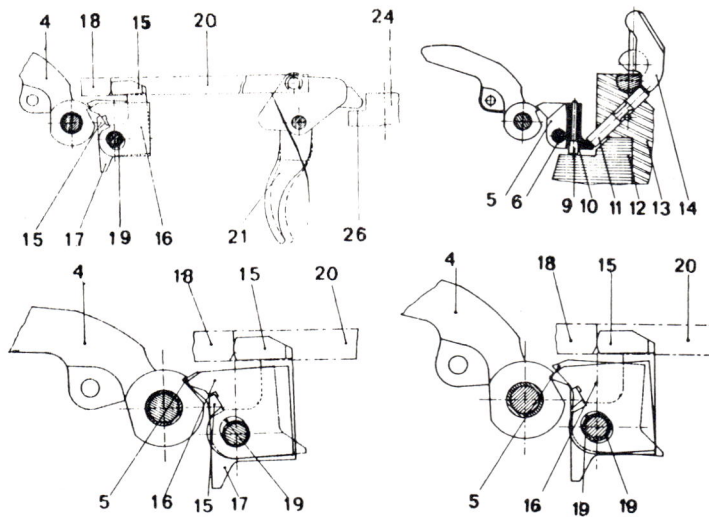

The trigger mechanism

ACTION OF THE BURST FIRE CONTROLLER

Attached to the hammer is a rod which for lack of a better name is translated literally as the 'percussion' rod. Each time the hammer goes back the percussion rod bears on an operating rod which causes a ratchet wheel to rotate.

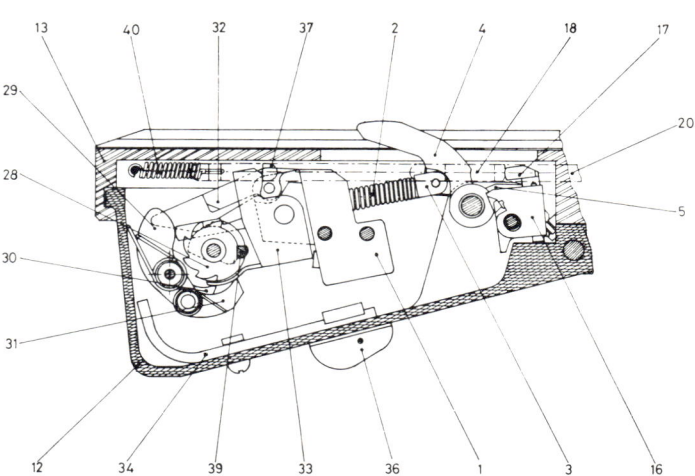

The F.A. MAS 5.56: **(1)** *Hammer stop;* **(2)** *Percussion spring;* **(3)** *Percussion rod;* **(4)** *Hammer;* **(5)** *Automatic sear;* **(6)** *Shaft for 3 sears;* **(9)** *Sear pusher;* **(10)** *Sear springs;* **(11)** *Automatic sear drive;* **(12)** *Trigger-guard casing;* **(13)** *Receiver;* **(14)** *Amplifying lever;* **(15)** *Driven sear notch;* **(16)** *Cam;* **(17)** *Driven sear;* **(18)** *Driven sear drive;* **(19)** *Cam slot;* **(20)** *Connecting rod;* **(21)** *Trigger;* **(24)** *Selector;* **(26)** *C/C face;* **(28)** *Ratchet wheel;* **(29)** *Limiter operating piece;* **(30)** *Hold down pawl;* **(31)** *Driving pawl;* **(32)** *Stop pawl;* **(33)** *Ratchet release;* **(34)** *Bolt;* **(35); (36)** *Operating knob;* **(37)** *Ratchet release pusher;* **(38)** *Ratchet release spring casing;* **(39)** *Ratchet wheel stop;* **(40)** *Rod return spring;* **(41)** *Stop pawl spring*

A pawl limits the movement to one tooth and a further pawl prevents counter rotation. When the percussion rod has completed its backward stroke it releases the operating rod which re-positions itself, bearing on the ratchet. After the third shot the percussion rod does not release the operating rod and firing ceases. When the trigger is released the wound up ratchet goes back to the starting position and the hammer is held on the manual sear.

SAFETY

The mechanical safety of the weapon is dependent on the delay lever which exercises control as follows:

(a) The firing pin cannot go forward until the delay lever is vertical. If through some mechanical failure the hammer is able to fall, the blow is taken by the firing pin which pushes the lever into the vertical position but at the same time loses so much energy that a misfire is inevitable.
(b) After the round is fired, the delay lever rotates and withdraws the firing pin. The firing pin is held back until the delay lever re-assumes the vertical position.
(c) Until the delay lever is vertical the safety sear holds up the hammer.
(d) If the delay lever is left out when the rifle is assembled the safety sear will remain in contact with the hammer and hold it up.

FIRING GRENADES

The ballistite cartridge is packed with each grenade. The procedure for preparing the rifle is taught as a drill. The soldier:

(a) Makes safe.
(b) Selects his aiming system – which can be either:
(1) Direct fire, in which case he puts the detachable sight on the rifle.
(2) Indirect fire, in which case he swings out the grenade sight, attached to the top of the receiver behind the forward post of the carrying handle, to the desired angle of 45 degrees or 75 degrees.
(c) Sets the grenade projector ring, around the barrel, as far back as possible for direct fire and forward at the required setting for indirect fire.
(d) Removes the grenade safety pin.
(e) Pushes the grenade fully home up to the grenade projector ring.
(f) Loads the ballistite cartridge.
(g) Cocks the rifle.
(h) Sets the change lever to 1 and the burst fire control to 'O'

At direct fire the recoil taken by the soldier is considerable and is absorbed by placing the buttstock under the arm where it can move back without obstruction and by using the sling across the chest and over the left elbow. The right thumb does not go round the pistol grip but lies on top of the forefinger along the side of the pistol grip; alternatively the grip may be supported. Similarly the left hand is placed on top of the carrying handle, forward of the cocking handle.

At indirect fire the weapon is turned sideways and the butt must be placed against a firm object or dug into the ground.

STRIPPING

(1) Remove the magazine and check that the chamber is empty. The only tool required is a cartridge.
(2) Remove the butt by pushing out the pin located in front of the magazine well and pulling the butt back. To remove the cheek rest, push it straight back.
(3) Remove the handguard by pushing out the pin which enters the back sight column. The handguard is then rotated forward and lifted off.
(4) Remove the trigger mechanism by pushing out the pin located behind the magazine well.

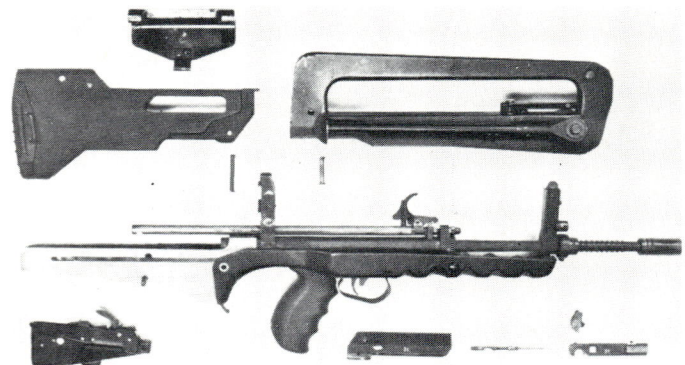

F.A. MAS 5.56 stripped

(5) Remove the working parts by pulling back the cocking handle and hold it whilst the pin securing the piston to the bolt carrier is pushed out. The cocking handle goes forward under control and the bolt carrier assembly is drawn off to the rear.

(6) Separate the working parts by moving the block in the carrier until the delay lever is vertical and the bolt will separate from the carrier. Remove the locking lever by rotating it until the upper arms are lined up with the centre line of the bolt. The firing pin comes out to the rear.

STRIPPING THE BOLT
To remove the detachable bolt head – to change the extractor from one side to the other – prise out the pin on top of the breech-block.

DATA
Cartridge: 5.56mm x 45
Method of operation: Delayed blowback
Method of delay: Vertical delay lever
Method of feed: 25-round box magazine
Method of fire: Selective and three round bursts

WEIGHTS
Rifle without magazine, sling or bipod: 3.38kg

Empty magazine: 0.15kg
Loaded magazine (25 rounds): 0.425kg
Bayonet and scabbard: 0.43kg
Sling: 0.140kg
Bipod: 0.170kg

LENGTHS
Rifle without bayonet: 757mm
Barrel: 488mm

MECHANICAL FEATURES
Barrel: Regulator: Nil
        Rifling: 6 grooves RH. 1 turn in 305mm
        Cooling: Air
Sights: Foresight: Blade
        Rearsight: Aperture 0-300 metres
        Zeroing: Line. Foresight. Elevation. Rearsight
        Sight radius: 330mm

FIRING CHARACTERISTICS
Muzzle velocity: 960 metres/sec
Muzzle energy: 167mkp
Recoil energy: 0.760mkp
Chamber pressure: 3,622kg/cm²
Rate of fire: Cyclic: 900-1,000 rounds/min
        Auto: 125 rounds/min
        SS: 50 rounds/min
Range, maximum effective: 300 metres
Spread: At 200 metres H + L (10 round group) 400mm

GRENADE FIRING
A/Tk grenades: Normal operating range: 80 metres
A/Personnel: Direct fire; Normal operating range: 120 metres
        Indirect fire 45 degrees: Minimum 140 metres; Maximum 360 metres
        Indirect fire 75 degrees: Minimum 70 metres; Maximum 180 metres
Muzzle velocity: 960m/sec
Grenade weight: 500g
Manufacturer: Manufacture d'Armes de St. Etienne, St. Etienne
Status: Not yet in production in quantity

GERMANY (FEDERAL REPUBLIC)

MAUSER RIFLE MODEL 98

This rifle was produced for the German forces as the Gewehr 98; it was made under licence, in Belgium, China, Czechoslovakia, Poland, Spain, and Yugoslavia; and it was used as the design basis of the US M1903 and M1917 rifles and the British Pattern 14 rifle (No 3 Mk 1). The last production model was the Yugoslav M1948 rifle. The ammunition has varied with the individual countries concerned but the majority have used the 7.92mm × 57. The United States M1906 cartridge (the .30-06) has also been used in large numbers.

In 1935 the Model 98K carbine – the Kar 98K – was adopted. The 'K' stands for Kurz and the new rifle which was to serve the German forces throughout the 1939-45 War, the Kar 98K, was reduced to an overall length of 43.6in from the full length of 49.2in in the 98 rifle.

The Mauser is a bolt-operated rifle with a forward locking lug arrangement. The internal magazine holds five rounds. When the bolt is fitted a cam forces the firing pin nut and the firing pin to the rear and compresses the firing spring, i.e. cocking occurs on the rearward movement of the bolt. The initial extraction, to unseat the cartridge case in the chamber, is provided by the base of the bolt handle acting on the receiver. When the bolt is withdrawn the empty case is extracted and comes up against the fixed ejector in the left of the receiver which rotates the case around the extractor and throws it out of the rifle to the right.

The forward movement of the bolt pushes a round forward into the chamber. The bolt head is enclosed in a shroud as it reaches the end of forward travel and the rotation of the bolt handle forces the two lugs on the bolt head behind abutments in the receiver.

The manual safety forces back the firing pin nut and withdraws the firing pin from the sear, and at the same time, rotating the safety catch, locks the bolt in the closed position.

In addition the firing pin cannot go forward unless the bolt is fully closed. If the bolt is not closed the energy of the firing pin spring is used to close it when the firing pin nut engages a cam in the bolt.

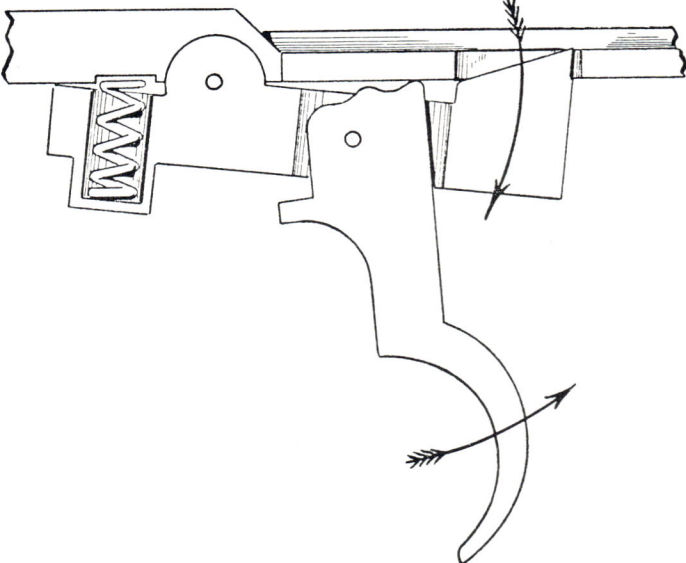

Trigger mechanism of the Mauser 98. Note the two humps on the trigger extension giving two pulls

The trigger produces two pulls. This is done by having two humps on the trigger which bear on the bottom of the receiver. When the trigger is pressed the first hump produces a light trigger pull as the sear moves down the bent face. When the second hump comes in contact with the receiver

Mauser Kar 98K

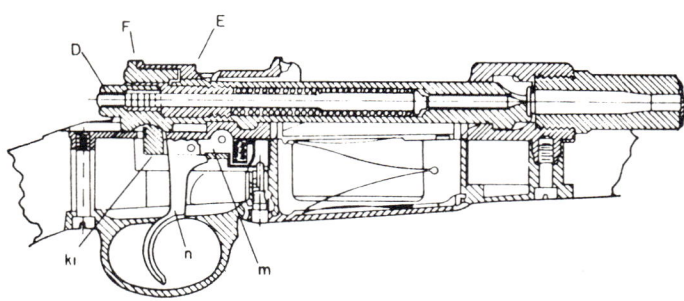

Sectional view of the Kar 98U

DATA
Cartridge: 7.92mm x 57
Method of operation: Manual – bolt
Method of locking: Rotating bolt
Method of feed: 5-round internal box
Method of fire: Single shots
Weight: 3.89kg
Length: 404mm
Barrel: 597mm
    Rifling: 4 groove RH
Sights: Foresight: Blade
    Rearsight: Tangent Notch
Muzzle velocity: 754 metres/sec
Muzzle energy: 372mkp
Rate of fire: 10 to 15 rounds/min
Range, maximum effective: 600 metres
Manufacturer: Mauser-Werke A.G. and many others
Status: No longer in production. Still in service in Turkey, Indonesia and some African and South American countries and still held in reserve stocks elsewhere.

the mechanical advantage is reduced and the pull becomes heavier resulting in an increased trigger pull as the sear disengages from the bent.

7.92mm SL RIFLE 41 (W)

The two big German firms Mauser and Walther each produced trial batches of self loading rifles in 1941. The Gew 41 (M) was not accepted and the Walther model was developed into the Model 43 rifle which was mass produced.

The Gew 41 (W) had an expansion chamber at the muzzle with a hole at the front which was sealed as the bullet passed through. The build up of pressure drove back an annular piston wrapped round the barrel and this in turn pushed a piston back which imparted energy to the breech block carrier.

The bolt of the rifle was locked into the receiver by two hinged flaps which were pushed out by the firing pin and pulled in as the carrier moved back.

The fixed magazine held ten rounds loaded in five round chargers.

The weapon was expensive to produce, was muzzle heavy and the differential expansion between the barrel and the annular piston led to stoppages. It was never made in large quantities and production ceased when the Gew 43 was available.

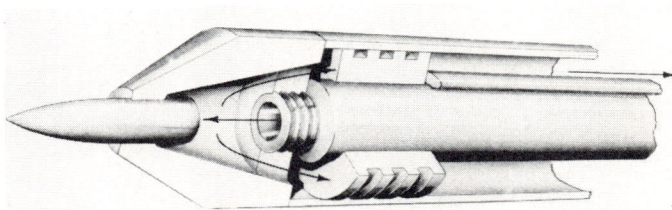

Gas system of the Gew 41 (W) (RMCS)

DATA
Cartridge: 7.92mm × 57
Method of operation: Gas
Method of locking: Projecting lugs
Method of feed: 10-round integral box magazine
Method of fire: Self-loading
Weight: 5kg
Length: 1,124mm

Barrel: 546mm
    Rifling: 4 grooves RH
Sights: Foresight: Barleycorn
    Rearsight: Tangent leaf. Notch
Muzzle velocity: 777 metres/sec
Muzzle energy: 395mkp
Rate of fire: Semi-auto: 40 rounds/min
Range, maximum effective: 600 metres
Manufacturer: Carl Walther Waffenfabrik A.G. Zella-Mehlis
Status: No longer manufactured. Only briefly in service

Gew 41 (M) (RMCS)

Gew 41 (W) (RMCS)

7.92mm SL RIFLE MODEL 43

A derivative of the Walther Gew 41(W) this rifle used the same bolt but had a totally different gas operation system. A Tokarev system with a short stroke piston was placed over the barrel and when the bullet passed under the gas vent, some 32cm from the muzzle, the piston drove the operating rod back and this in turn imparted energy to the bolt carrier. A spring around the operating rod returned it to the forward position.

The carrier moved back, carrying the firing pin housing with it, and after a short period of free travel the firing pin housing withdrew the locking lugs and the bolt was carried back.

The standard of finish of the G43 deteriorated as the war progressed. The steel castings of the receiver and bolt carrier progressively received less finishing. The woodwork became poorer in quality and eventually was replaced by plastic.

Gas system of the Gew 43 (RMCS)

There was a telescope mounting on top of the receiver to take the × 1½ ZF41 telescope and the rifle was used on the Russian Front as a sniper's weapon.

After the war it was used by the Czech army, as a sniper's rifle, for several years.

DATA
Cartridge: 7.92mm x 57
Method of operation: Gas
Method of locking: Projecting lugs
Method of feed: 10-round detachable box magazine
Method of fire: Self-loading
Weight: 4.34kg
Length: 1,118mm
Barrel: 549mm
     Rifling: 4 grooves RH

Sights: Foresight: Barleycorn
     Rearsight: Tangent leaf. Notch
Muzzle velocity: 777 metres/sec
Muzzle energy: 395mkp
Rate of fire: Semi-auto: 40 rounds/min
Range, maximum effective: 800 metres
Manufacturer: Carl Walther Waffenfabrik A.G. Zella-Mehlis Gustloff-Werke, Weimar
Status: No longer produced. Virtually obsolete but a few may still be in service outside Germany.

7.92mm Gew model 43 (RMCS)

7.92mm MP43 and MP44 ASSAULT RIFLES

In 1934 the requirement for a cartridge less powerful than the 7.92mm × 57, led to a development contract being placed with Polte Werke of Magdeburg who, in 1941 produced the 7.92mm Infanterie Kurz Patrone. This had a 7.92 case cut down from 57mm to 33mm, a powder charge reduced from *c.* 47 grains to 24.6 grains and a 7.92mm bullet reduced in weight from 198 grains to 123 grains.

In 1938 the C.G. Haenal factory at Suhl was given a contract to develop 50 prototypes of a light automatic rifle to fire this cartridge. Hugo Schmeisser was in charge of the project.

In January 1941 the firm of Carl Walther at Zella-Mehlis was given a contract to produce, by August 1942, 200 prototypes of their own weapon for the cartridge. The project engineer was Brauning.

The Haenal weapon was called the MKb42(H) and the Walther gun was known as the MKb42(W). 10,000 Haenal guns were made and some 8,000 of the Walther model.

The Walther weapon was gas-operated with an annular piston wrapped round the barrel. There was a forward-locking, tilting block, design for the breech and prominent high set sights necessitated by the straight-through action. The gun can readily be identified by the cylindrical, metal, ventilated fore-end.

It was tried on the Russian front and the annular piston design was not considered satisfactory.

The MKb42(H) was tried on the Russian front, modified somewhat and large-scale production was started with the weapon known as the MP43. In 1944 the name was changed to MP44 and later to Sturmgewehr 44 (assault rifle 44).

The Haenal weapon designed by Hugo Schmeisser was a gas-operated weapon with the cylinder over the barrel. The breech-block achieved positive locking by tilting down at the rear end and engaging in front of an abutment in the floor of the receiver. The top rear end of the bolt was shaped into a hook facing forward. Under the rear of the piston was another hook, facing back. When the gas pressure drove the piston back, the two hooks engaged and the rear of the bolt was first lifted and then the bolt was carried back. There was no regulator but cleaning was simple and the whole design was robust.

The differences between the MKb42(H) and the MP43 were as follows:
(1) The MKb42(H) had a longer piston. It was mounted in a separate tube over the barrel with a clear air space between the two. In the MP43 the fore-end stamping included the gas cylinder.
(2) The MP43 did not have a cut-out on the receiver for the bolt handle. It did not have a bayonet lug.

The designation 'MP' – Machine Pistol – is said to have been used in the early stages of the design project to deceive Hitler and his entourage about the nature of the weapon as it was known he would oppose a light bulleted rifle.

The MP44 remained in service after the 1939-1945 War with the East German Border Guards. It has now been replaced by the German AK47.

German 7.92mm Kurz and standard 7.92 × 57 rifle cartridge (RMCS)

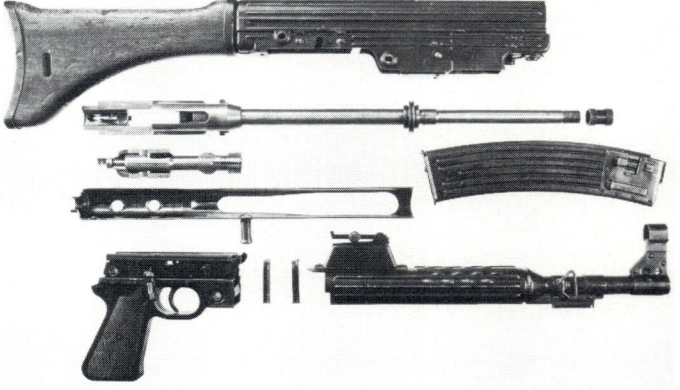

MKb42(W) field stripped

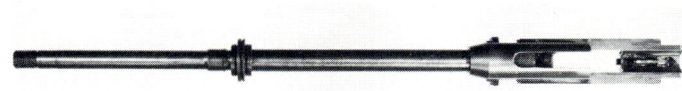

The piston wrapped round the barrel of the MKb42(W)

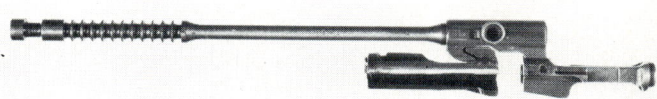

The Haenal locking system

DATA	MKb42(W)	MKb42(H)	MP43, MP44, StG44
Cartridge:	7.92mm × 32	7.92mm × 33	7.92mm × 32
Method of operation:	Gas – annular piston	Gas – conventional piston	Gas – conventional piston
Method of locking:	Tilting block	Tilting block	Tilting block
Method of feed:	30-round detachable box magazine	30-round detachable box magazine	30-round detachable box magazine
Method of fire:	Selective	Selective	Selective
Weight:	4.43kg	5kg	5.22kg
Length:	933mm	940mm	940mm
Barrel:	409mm	365mm	419mm
Rifling:	4 grooves RH	4 grooves RH	4 grooves RH
Sights: Foresight:	Hooded Barleycorn	Hooded Barleycorn	Hooded Barleycorn
Rearsight:	Tangent. Notch	Tangent. Notch	Tangent. Notch
Muzzle velocity:	650 metres/sec	640 metres/sec	650 metres/sec
Muzzle energy:	170mkp	166mkp	170mkp
Rate of fire: Cyclic:	600 rounds/min	500 rounds/min	500 rounds/min
Automatic:	120 rounds/min	120 rounds/min	120 rounds/min
SS:	40 rounds/min	40 rounds/min	40 rounds/min
Range, maximum effective:	500 metres	500 metres	500 metres
Manufacturer:	Carl Walther Wf	C.G. Haenal AG	C.G. Haenal AG Mauser-Werke and others

Status: No longer produced. The StG44 has been in service since 1965 with factory militia in East Germany and might be encountered elswhere.

The Haenal MP43

MKb42(W) (RMCS)

The MP43 'mit Krummlauf' A curved barrel, with sights to shoot round corners (RMCS)

MP43 field stripped

7.62mm G3 RIFLE

After the Second World War certain German designers went to the Centro de Estudios Tecnicos de Materiales Especiales, Madrid, (CETME) and participated in the design of a delayed blowback operated rifle known as the CETME. Subsequently development of this rifle continued in Spain using an unusually long bullet in 7.92mm calibre. The firm of NWM at s'Hertgenbosch were interested in developing the rifle and obtained rights to do so but the German Army considered the design had potential and the development of the weapon was transferred to Heckler and Koch at Oberndorf/Neckar near Stuttgart. Work was continued there and in 1959 the FN FAL rifle used by the Bundeswehr was replaced by the Heckler and Koch G3 rifle.

DESCRIPTION

The receiver is a steel pressing, grooved on each side to guide the bolt and seat the back plate. The receiver carries the barrel which lies below the tubular extension, spot-welded on to the receiver, holding the cocking lever and the forward extension of the bolt. The cocking lever runs in a slot cut in the left side of this tubular housing and can be held in the cocked position by a transverse recess. The barrel is screw-threaded at the muzzle with a serrated collar to engage the retaining spring of the flash eliminator or blank firing attachment. The rifling is orthodox and the chamber carries twelve longitudinal flutes extending back from the lead to 6mm from the chamber face.

The bolt is ⌐ shaped. The long forward extension is hollow and takes the return spring. It extends into the tube above the barrel. The bolt head carrier and bolt head are located on the barrel axis. The bolt head carrier has long bearing surfaces on each side which slide into the grooves in the sides of the receiver. The bolt head carries two rollers which project on each side and are forced out by the inclined front faces of what the manufacturer calls the 'locking piece'. (This term will be used but as will be seen it is really a misnomer since the breech is never truly locked.) When out, the rollers engage in recesses in the barrel extension. The bolt head and locking piece seat in the bolt head carrier and are held by the bolt head locking lever to prevent bounce on chambering the cartridge. The trigger mechanism fits into a separate assembly secured to the receiver by a locking pin.

OPERATION

The weapon is carried ready for action with the cartridge in the chamber, the bolt head supporting the base of the round, and the rollers held out in the recesses in the barrel extension by the front face of the locking piece. The hammer is cocked and held by the trigger sear.

When the trigger is squeezed the sear is lowered out of the hammer notch and the hammer flies forward and drives the firing pin through the hollow locking piece to fire the cap. The pressure generated in the chamber forces the cartridge case rearwards and exerts a force on the breech face which tends to drive the bolt head back. Before the bolt head can go back,

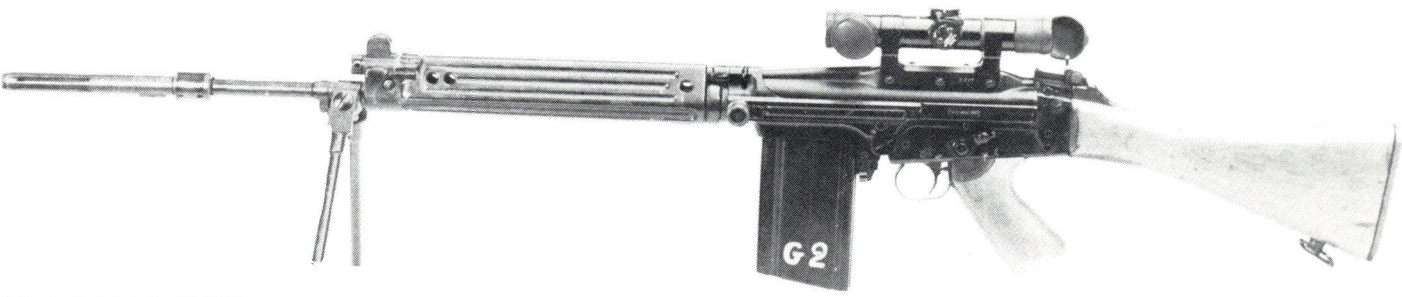

FN FAL German rifle (RSAF)

G3 A3

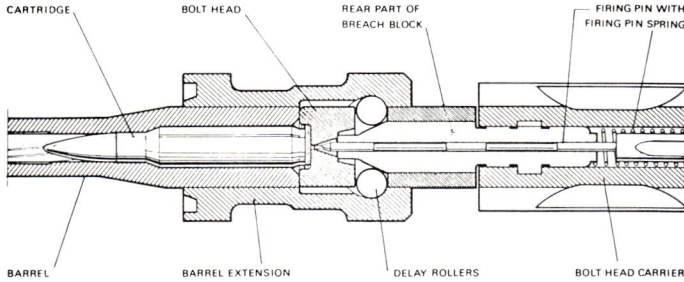

Rifle loaded, ready to fire

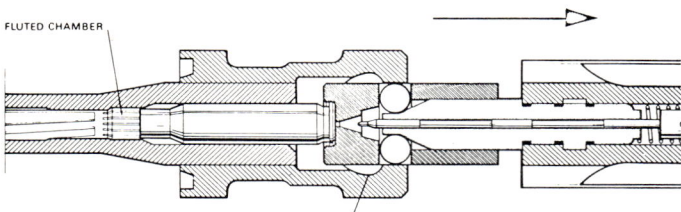

The G3 rifle. Method of operation

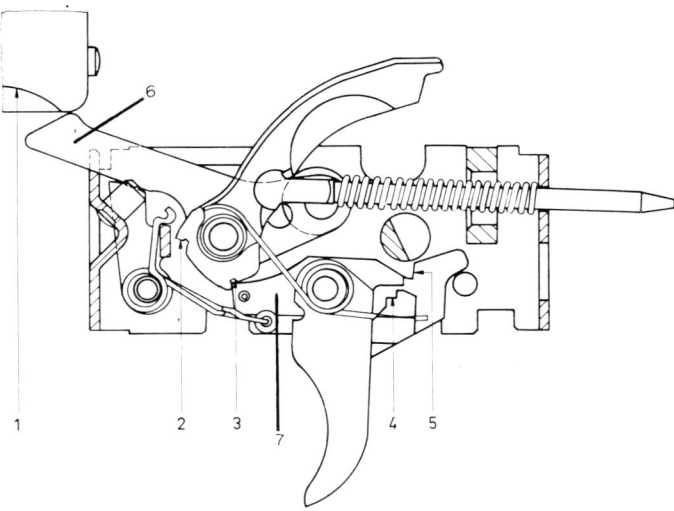

The selective fire lever set at "E" single fire. The safety pin permits a limited trigger pull. Key: (1) Cam surface; (2) Notch for burst; (3) Notch for single fire; (4) Notch for the sear; (5) Recess for single fire; (6) Safety sear; (7) Sear

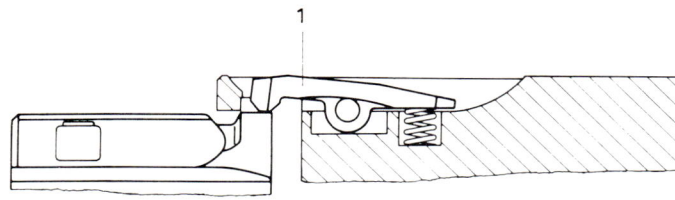

Disengagement of the bolt-head locking lever: As the bolt head carrier travels backward, the bolt-head locking lever (1) is simultaneously pressed over the bolt-head shoulder against the pressure of its spring. After the round has been chambered, the bolt-head stops at the mouth of the barrel. The bolt-head carrier continues forward until the locking piece presses the locking rollers into engagement in the barrel extension. The bolt-head locking lever now engages the bolt-head shoulder thus preventing it from rebounding

the rollers must be driven inwards. The rollers, which are carried in the bolt head, are pushed back and the angle of the recesses in the barrel extension is such that the rollers are forced inwards against the inclined planes on the front of the locking piece. In turn this inward force drives the locking piece back and with it the bolt head carrier. The angle of the locking piece face is such that the velocity ratio between bolt head carrier and bolt head is 4:1. Thus while the rollers are moving backwards and inwards the bolt head carrier is travelling back four times as far as the breech face. As the carrier moves back the bolt head locking lever is disengaged. After the bolt face has moved back a little over a millimetre the rollers are clear of the recesses in the barrel extension, the entire bolt is blown back by the residual pressure with the bolt head and bolt carrier maintaining their relative displacement of about 5mm. The bolt head carrier cocks the hammer and compresses the return spring. The cartridge case, held by the extractor, hits the ejector arm and is thrown out to the right. The rear end of the carrier hits the buffer. The buffer action, assisted by the return spring, drives the bolt carrier forward. The front face of the bolt head strips a cartridge from the magazine and chambers it. The extractor springs over the extraction groove of the cartridge and the bolt head comes to rest. The locking piece and bolt carrier then close up the gap of 5mm and the rollers are pushed out into the recesses of the barrel extension. The bolt head locking lever engages the bolt head shoulder thus preventing bounce. The weapon is then ready to be fired again.

TRIGGER AND FIRING MECHANISM

The trigger mechanism is in principle the same as that employed in the Belgian FAL 7.62mm rifle.

A spring-loaded sear has an elongated slot in which the trigger pin fits. The spring tries to drive the sear forward over the trigger. At the same time another spring holds up the nose of the sear. The rifle can never be fired unless the bolt carrier is fully forward. Completion of the forward movement moves a safety sear off the hammer bent.

In single shot firing the bolt is closed and the trigger sear holds up the hammer. When the trigger is operated the sear is rotated down at the front and out of the hammer notch. When the hammer rotates to fire the round, the spring-loaded sear slips forward and its tail drops down off a fixed step called the pull-off surface; but the firer is still holding the trigger back. The hammer is rotated back by the bolt and catches the nose of the sear. The hammer spring overcomes the sear spring and pushes the sear back against the side of the pull-off surface. The hammer is held by the auto sear until the bolt closes and releases it. The hammer is held by the sear but the trigger is already pulled and another shot cannot be fired. When the trigger is released the rear end – or tail – of the sear is allowed to rise and the spring forces it back and the elongated hole allows it to move onto the pull-off surface. When the trigger is pulled another round is fired.

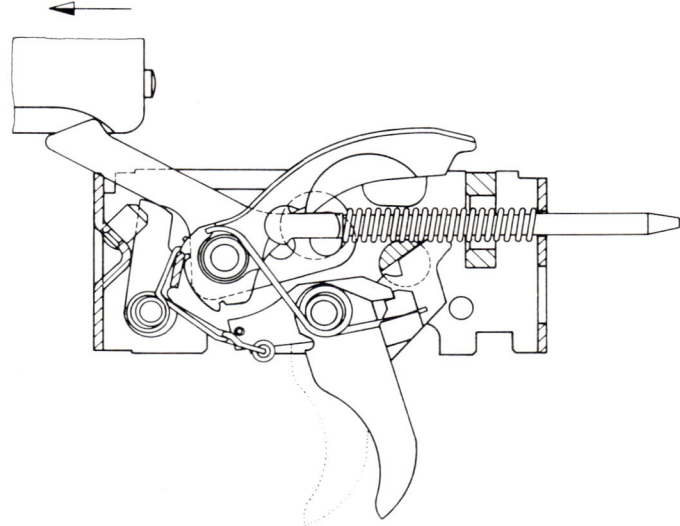

Burst function: Setting the selective fire lever at "F" = automatic results in a longer trigger travel, which is required only for automatic fire. When the trigger is pulled, the first shot is fired in the same manner as if the selective fire lever were at "E" = single fire. However, the longer trigger travel swivels the sear so far downward that it can no longer catch the hammer. The hammer is now held only by the catch. As the bolt snaps forward, it pushes the safety sear downward, disengages the catch and releases the hammer. As this function repeats, it results in automatic fire. When the trigger is released, the front of the sear swivels upward again and engages the "single fire" notch in the hammer

When the change lever is put to auto, the rotation of the change lever spindle allows the sear tail to rise so high that the nose of the sear does not engage the notch on the hammer at all and the hammer is held by the auto sear only. As soon as the bolt carrier travels fully forward the auto sear is released and the hammer is freed. When the change lever is set to 'safe' the spindle prevents any upward movement of the sear and so the nose cannot drop out of engagement with the hammer notch.

ACCESSORIES

The G3 rifle has a number of accessories and training aids. First there is a telescopic sight with a mount which clips over the receiver on prepared surfaces. The sight is basically for sniping out to 600 metres, or surveillance, or observation of fire at longer ranges.

There is also an infra-red sight. This is an active sight with an infra-red illuminator and a power source. The IR sight is attached to the telescopic sight mount by two screws and the entire assembly can be quickly clipped on or removed. The infra-red device comes from Eltro and the Rank Cintel Image Intensifier can also be fitted. A blank firing attachment may be screwed on the muzzle instead of the flash eliminator. It has a retaining circlip which grips the serrations on the muzzle and prevents the attachment working loose. The attachment consists of an open-ended cylinder with a cross bolt which closes the opening entirely. A groove is cut across the bolt so that by rotating the bolt the amount of gas escaping can be regulated to produce correct functioning of the rifle. This device has a dull chromium plated finish to prevent confusion with the flash hider.

A special bolt marked 'PT' replaces the normal bolt and is used for firing plastic training ammunition. This works on pure blowback and has no delay rollers. It is not suitable for use with service ammunition. The normal magazine is used for plastic ammunition.

G3 A3 ZF

To conserve ammunition and allow troops to train in confined and built-up areas, a sub-calibre training device is available. It consists of a sub-calibre tube with a special bolt and magazine. The ammunition used is 5.6mm × 16 (.22LR). The sub-calibre tube is inserted from the breech and locked with a spring ring. In addition the tube is secured by a bolt on the magazine engaging in the end of the chamber face of the tube. The extractor enters a groove in the chamber face. The bolt assembly carries out the normal functions of chambering, supporting, firing, extracting and cocking the hammer. The magazine for 20 5.56 × 16 cartridges fits into the normal G3 magazine. The G3 rifle can be used to project rifle grenades of the Mecar or Hispano-Suiza type. To use the grenade, the magazine is removed and the ballistite cartridge placed in the open chamber. The bolt is closed and the grenade placed over the flash hider until it reaches the front sight holder.

The standard grenade is of German manufacture and comes complete with folding sight with ranges of 50, 75 and 100 metres and so no separate sight on the rifle is required. All NATO grenades with the standard tail boom

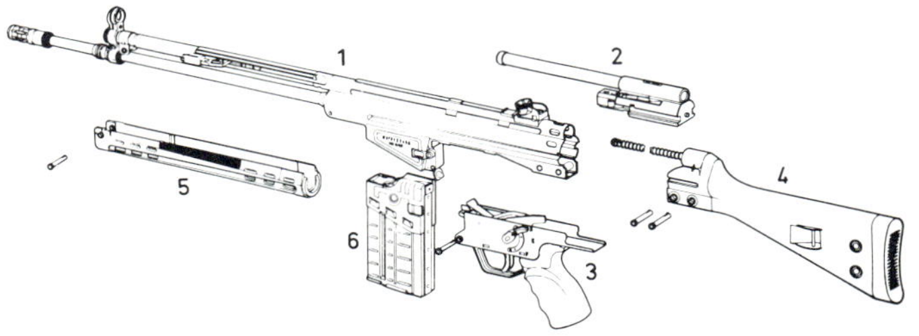

Assembly groups. Key: **(1)** *Barrel with receiver;* **(2)** *Bolt;* **(3)** *Grip assembly with trigger and safety mechanisms;* **(4)** *Back plate with buttstock;* **(5)** *Handguard;* **(6)** Magazine*

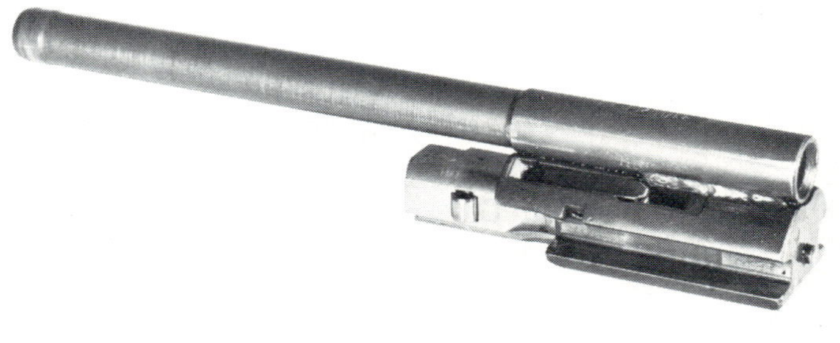

The breech block of the G3 rifle

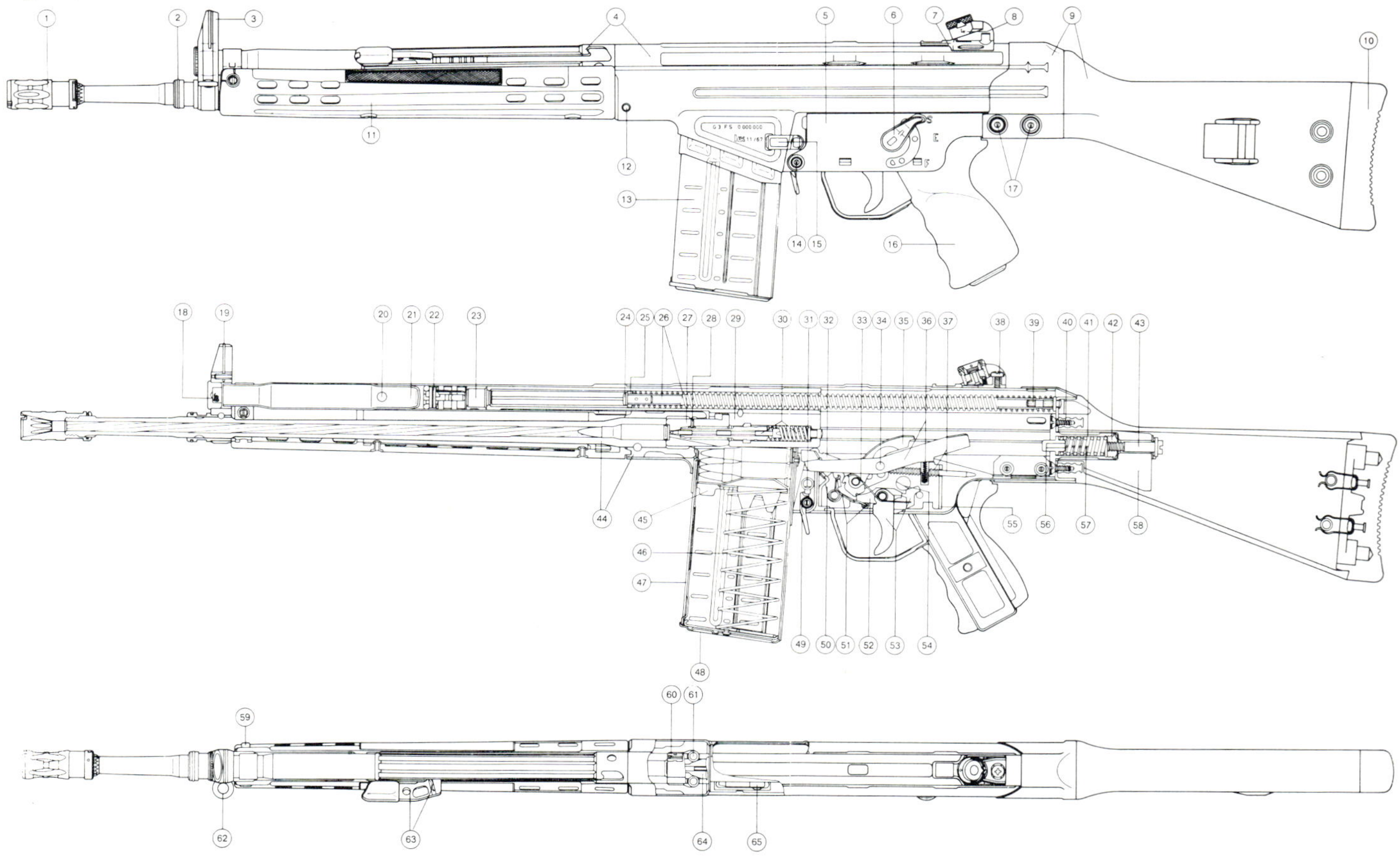

The G3 automatic rifle, calibre 7.62mm (NATO). Key: **(1)** *Flash suppressor (grenade launcher) with retaining spring for flash suppressor;* **(2)** *Snap ring to mount grenade;* **(3)** *Front sight holder;* **(4)** *Receiver and operating housing;* **(5)** *Grip assembly;* **(6)** *Safety;* **(7)** *Sight base;* **(8)** *Rotary rear sight;* **(9)** *Back plate with buttstock;* **(10)** *Butt plate;* **(11)** *Handguard;* **(12)** *Cylindrical pin;* **(13)** *Magazine;* **(14)** *Grip assembly locking pin;* **(15)** *Magazine catch;* **(16)** *Grip;* **(17)** *Buttstock locking pins;* **(18)** *Cap;* **(19)** *Front sight;* **(20)** *Stop pin;* **(21)** *Stop abutment;* **(22)** *Operating handle spindle;* **(23)** *Operating handle support;* **(24)** *Stop pin for recoil spring;* **(25)** *Recoil spring guide ring;* **(26)** *Recoil spring tube with recoil spring;* **(27)** *Bolt head;* **(28)** *Clamping sleeve and holder for locking roller;* **(29)** *Bolt body with recoil spring tube;* **(30)** *Firing pin with firing pin spring;* **(31)** *Contact piece;* **(32)** *Release lever;* **(33)** *Elbow spring for trigger;* **(34)** *Ejector spindle;* **(35)** *Hammer;* **(36)** *Ejector with ejector pressure spring;* **(37)** *Pressure shank and pressure spring;* **(38)** *Fixing screw;* **(39)** *Stop pin for spring guide;* **(40)** *Countersunk screw;* **(41)** *Buffer housing;* **(42)** *Buffer closure;* **(43)** *Screw for buffer;* **(44)** *Barrel with barrel extension;* **(45)** *Follower;* **(46)** *Follower spring;* **(47)** *Magazine tube;* **(48)** *Magazine floor plate;* **(49)** *Magazine release lever;* **(50)** *Catch;* **(51)** *Elbow spring with roller;* **(52)** *Sear;* **(53)** *Trigger;* **(54)** *Safety pin;* **(55)** *Trigger assembly;* **(56)** *Buffer pin;* **(57)** *Buffer spring;* **(58)** *Support for buffer housing;* **(59)** *Handguard locking pin;* **(60)** *Extractor with extractor spring;* **(61)** *Locking roller;* **(62)** *Eyebolt;* **(63)** *Operating handle with elbow spring;* **(64)** *Locking piece;* **(65)** *Bolt head locking lever*

internal diameter of 22mm can be used including the bullet trap type. Heckler and Koch have developed their own 'slip in' bullet trap so that any grenade can be discharged using ball ammunition.

STRIPPING

Stripping the G3 rifle is very simple. After removing the magazine and checking that the chamber is clear, press out the two locking pins holding on the back plate and remove the buttstock and its back plate. The trigger grip assembly can be dropped down and removed by pushing out the single holding pin. Retracting the cocking handle allows withdrawal of the bolt assembly. The flash hider and handguard can be removed at will. The bolt head can be rotated from the carrier by holding the carrier and rotating the head. When the locking piece is rotated within the bolt head, the firing pin and spring can be taken out of the locking piece.

VARIANTS ON THE G3 RIFLE

The standard rifle is known as the G3A3 and has a plastic buttstock and plastic handguard.

When a telescopic sight is fitted to this rifle it is called the G3A3ZF.

When the plastic buttstock is replaced by a retractable butt it is called the G3A4.

DATA
Cartridge: 7.62mm × 51
Method of operation: Delayed blowback
Method of delay: Rollers
Method of feed: 20-round box magazine
Method of fire: Selective

WEIGHTS
Rifle, fixed butt, without magazine: 4.25kg
Rifle, retractable butt, without magazine: 4.50kg
Aluminium magazine, full: 625kg
Steel magazine, full: 753g
Trigger pull: 3.6-4.1kp

LENGTHS
Rifle with fixed butt: 1,020mm
Rifle with retractable butt: 800mm
Barrel: 450mm

MECHANICAL FEATURES
Barrel: Regulator: Nil
Rifling: 4 grooves RH. 1 turn in 305mm
Chamber: 12 flutes
Cooling: Air

Sights: Foresight: Post
Rearsight: U battle sight at 100 metres. Apertures for 200, 300 and 400 metres.
Zeroing: Elevation. Adjust range drum with tool. Line. Backsight moves laterally.
Sight radius: 572mm

FIRING CHARACTERISTICS
Muzzle velocity: 780-800 metres/sec
Muzzle energy: 290-300mkp
Recoil energy: 1.52mkp
Rate of fire: Cyclic: 500-600 rounds/min
Automatic: 100 rounds/min
SS: 40 rounds/min
Range, maximum effective: 400 metres
Manufacturer: Heckler and Koch GmbH, Oberndorf/Neckar
Status: In production. In service with the German Army. The armed forces and/or police forces of the following countries have adopted HK rifles and are completely or partially equipped with them:

EUROPE	AFRICA	CENTRAL AND SOUTH AMERICA
Denmark	Chad	Bolivia
France*	Ghana	Brazil*
Germany	Ivory Coast	Chile
Italy	Kenya	Colombia
Netherlands	Malawi	Dominican Republic
Norway*	Morocco	El Salvador
Portugal*	Niger	Guyana
Sweden*	Nigeria	Haiti
Switzerland	Senegal	Peru
Turkey*	Sudan	
	Tanzania	
	Togo	
	Uganda	
	Upper Volta	
	Zambia	

NEAR AND MIDDLE EAST	FAR EAST
Abu Dhabi	Brunei
Bangladesh	Burma
Dubai	Indonesia
Iran*	Maylasia
Jordan	Thailand*
Pakistan*	
Qatar	
Saudi Arabia*	
Sharja	

*Countries marked with an asterisk are producing Heckler and Koch rifles under licence. The rifles are also produced by the Royal Small Arms Factory, Enfield, England although they are not in UK service.

G3 A4

G3 SG/1 SNIPING RIFLE

The G3SG/1 Sniping rifle is used by the German police. It is basically the G3A3 but has some differences. During proof and testing of the standard rifles, those that demonstrate their ability to place the mean point of impact correctly and produce minimum groups are set aside for modification to

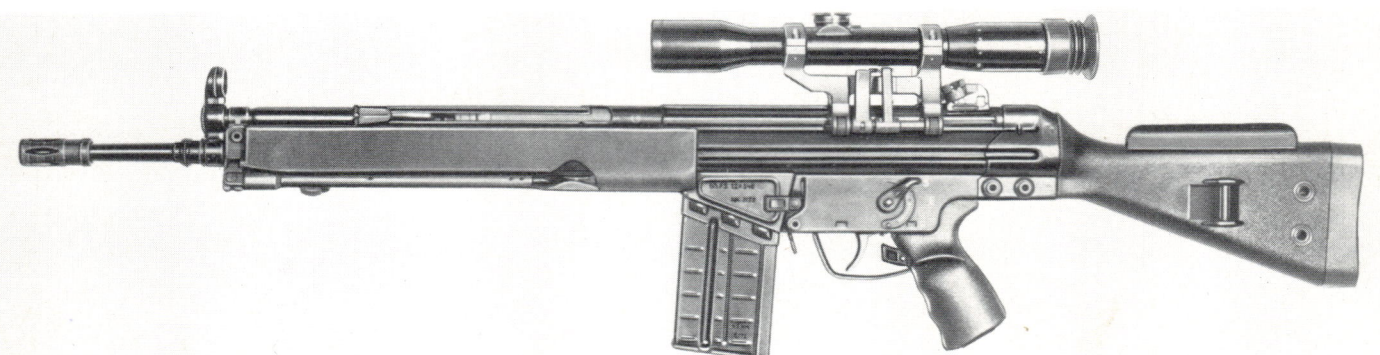

G3 SG/1 sniping rifle

sniper rifles. The sniper rifle is fitted with a special trigger unit. This incorporates a set trigger which has a pull-off which can be varied between 0.5 and 1.5kp. Setting the trigger can only be done when the selector lever is set to E. After firing one round the trigger can be re-set or the rifle can be fired again using the ordinary trigger setting which has been reduced to 2.6kp. If the trigger has been set, it is automatically released as soon as the selector lever is changed from 'single shot' to 'safe' or 'auto'.

The sight is not that normally used by the G3 but is a special Zeiss with variable power from $1.5\times$ to $6\times$, with windage and range adjustment 100-600 metres. The standard mount is employed which fits over the receiver and allows use of the iron sights without dismounting the telescope. The reticle pattern is based on the use of the mil i.e. the angle subtended by one unit of length at a distance of 1,000 units. e.g. one metre at 1,000 metres subtends one mil. This system enables the firer to set the correct range provided he can align the telescope on an object of known size. For example a car of approximately 5 metres length subtends 25 mils on the telescope. The range therefore is $^5/_{25}\times 1,000 - 200$ metres.

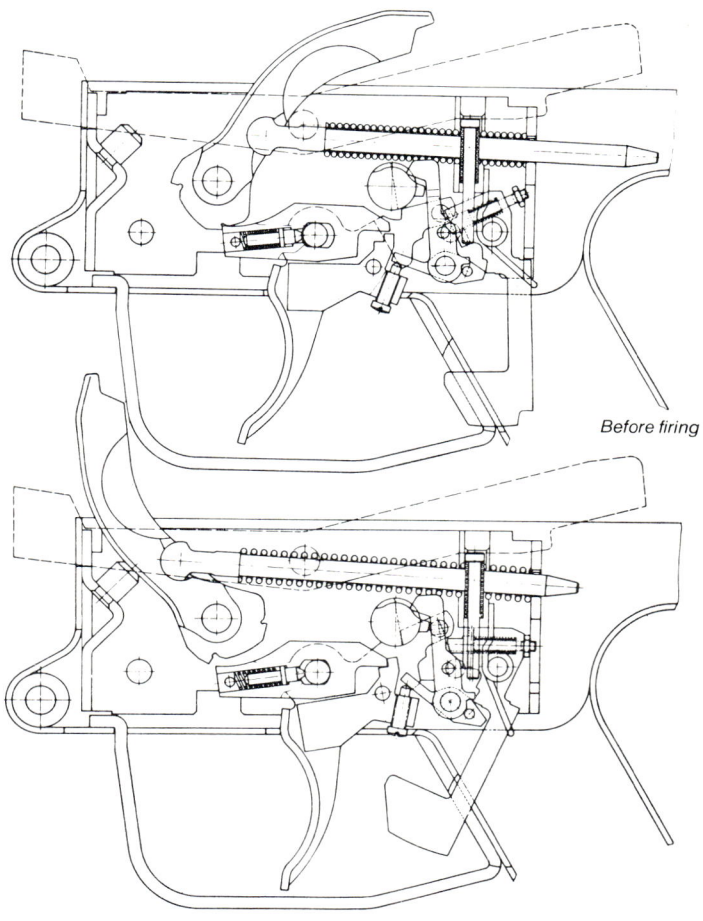

Before firing

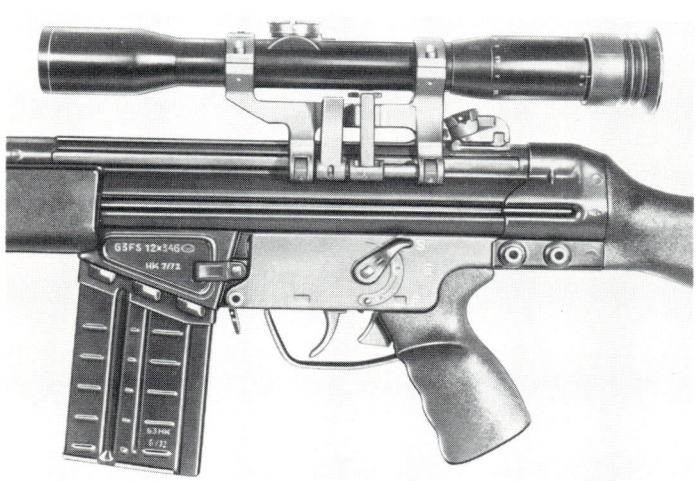

The sights and trigger of the G3 sniping rifle

After firing

7.62mm × 39 HECKLER AND KOCH HK32 RIFLE

The Group III weapons in the Heckler and Koch listing fire the Russian 7.62mm M43 cartridge which has a case length of 39mm. These weapons have been produced in experimental and prototype forms to test the system but they have not been manufactured in quantity. A substantial order would present no problems to the firm but the cost of tooling up for manufacturing the weapon and the continuous metal belt for the machine guns, make a small order uneconomic. The weapons in this group are the HK32A2 automatic rifle, the HK32A3 retracting butt version and the short automatic HK32KA1.

The functioning and characteristics of the HK32 rifles are similar to those of the G3 rifle.

DATA
Cartridge: 7.62mm × 39
Method of operation: Delayed blowback
Method of delay: Rollers
Method of feed: 20-, 30- or 40-round box magazine
Method of fire: Selective

WEIGHTS	A2	A3	KA1
Rifle, no magazine:	3.55kg	3.88kg	3.88kg
20-round magazine, empty:	140g	140g	140g
30-round magazine, empty:	150g	150g	150g
40-round magazine, empty:	160g	160g	160g
Rifle, with loaded 30-round magazine:	3.99kg	4.34kg	4.29kg
Cartridge:	247 grains (16g)		

LENGTHS	A2	A3	KA1
Rifle:	920mm	940mm	864mm
Butt retracted:	NA	729mm	670mm
Barrel:	390mm	390mm	322mm

MECHANICAL FEATURES
Barrel: Regulator: Nil
Sights: Foresight: Post
          Rearsight: 100-metre 'V' battlesight. Apertures for 200, 300 and 400 metres. Adjustable for windage

The HK32KA1 automatic rifle

Zeroing: Elevation. Adjust range drum with tool
Line. Backsight moves across
Sight radius: 400mm

FIRING CHARACTERISTICS

	A2	A3	KA1
Muzzle velocity:	730 metres/sec	730 metres/sec	690 metres/sec
Muzzle energy:	215mkp	215mkp	192mkp

Recoil energy: 1.1kp   1.1kp   1.1kp
Rate of fire: Cyclic: 750 rounds/min
 Automatic: 100 rounds/min
 SS: 40 rounds/min
Manufacturer: Heckler and Koch GmbH, Oberndorf/Neckar
Status: Design proved and demonstration models made. Available if ordered

5.56mm HECKLER AND KOCH HK33 RIFLE

Heckler and Koch manufacture a series of rifles using the 5.56mm × 45 cartridge. These are the HK33A2, HK33A3 and HK33KA1 and they form part of a weapon family all firing this cartridge and made up of rifles, a sub-machine gun and machine guns. This group of weapons is designated by the manufacturer as 'Group II'. 'Group I' comprises the 7.62mm × 51 group of weapons and 'Group III' is that collection of weapons intended to fire the Russian 7.62mm × 39 cartridge.

OPERATION

The basic operating principle of the HK33 rifle is that of delayed blow-back, firing from a closed breech, using the Heckler and Koch system which employs a two-part bolt. The bolt head contains two rollers which are forced outwards into recesses in the barrel extension by angled faces on the more massive bolt body. When the round is fired, the gas pressure exerts a force on the bolt face which tends to drive it back but the two rollers must move inwards before the bolt head can move. The shape of the recesses is such that the slight backward movement permitted to the rollers drives them inwards but this movement is resisted by the mass of the bolt body, and the force of the return spring, transmitted to the rollers by way of the angled faces lying between them. The angled faces are driven rearwards and the bolt body moves back four times as far as the bolt face whilst the rollers are moving in. As soon as the rollers clear the recesses in the barrel extension, the residual pressure in the chamber forces the two parts of the block back together, the two parts still displaced relatively by the rollers. The cartridge case is held to the bolt face and is thrown to the right of the gun when it strikes the ejector.

The HK33 is a scaled-down version of the 7.62mm G3 rifle and uses exactly the same trigger and firing mechanism as the larger rifle. This is described in some detail in the previous account of the G3 rifle. The mechanism provides automatic fire, single shot fire and a 'safe' position.

The sights fitted to the .223 (5.56mm) rifle give a V backsight for battle setting and apertures for 200, 300 and 400 metres. Adjustment is available for windage. Zeroing for elevation and line is carried out on the rearsight. Optical sights can be fitted in a standard mount producing a four-power magnification with adjustment by hundreds of metres from 100 to 600. Infra-red and other special sights can also be accepted by the same mount.

The HK33A2 has a rigid plastic butt, the HK33A3 has a double strut telescoping butt, the telescopic sight version is known as the HK33ZF; the HK33KA1 is a shortened version. All have the same basic operating system and all strip in the same way as the G3. The basic data relating to these weapons is shown below.

DATA

Cartridge: 5.56mm × 45
Method of operation: Delayed blowback
Method of delay: Rollers
Method of feed: 20- or 40-round box magazine
Method of fire: Selective

WEIGHTS

HK33A2, no magazine: 3.65kg
HK33A3, no magazine: 3.98kg
HK33KA1, no magazine: 3.98kg

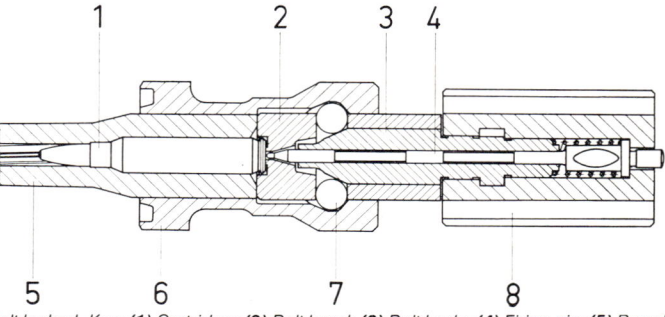

Bolt locked. Key: *(1)* Cartridge; *(2)* Bolt head; *(3)* Bolt body; *(4)* Firing pin; *(5)* Barrel; *(6)* Barrel extension; *(7)* Delay roller; *(8)* Bolt head carrier.

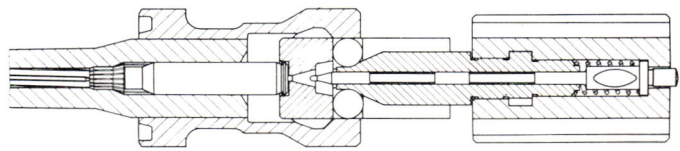

Bolt unlocked

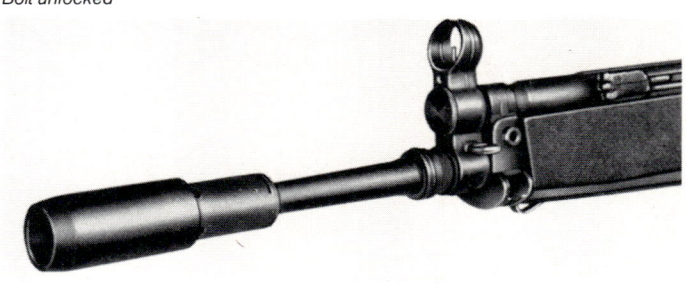

The HK33 with blank attachment with bullet trap

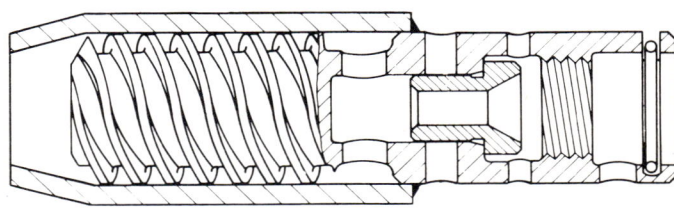

A cross-section of the blank attachment with bullet trap

Aluminium magazine 20 rounds empty: 113g
Aluminium magazine 40 rounds empty: 159g
Cartridge: 11g

HK33A2

LENGTHS
HK33A2: 920mm
HK33A3 Butt stock retracted: 735mm
HK33A3 Butt stock extended: 940mm
HK33KA1 Butt stock retracted: 680mm
HK33KA1 Butt stock extended: 863mm

MECHANICAL FEATURES
Barrel: Regulator: Nil
      Rifling: 6 grooves RH. 1 turn in 350mm
      Chamber: 16 flutes
      Cooling: Air
Sights: Foresight: Post
      Rearsight: V battlesight 100 metres. Apertures 200, 300 and 400 metres
      Zeroing: Line. Backsight moves across on screw thread Elevation. Adjust range drum with tool
      Optical: 4 × Telescope. 6 range increments from 100-600 metres. Adjustable for windage
      Sight radius: 480mm

FIRING CHARACTERISTICS (HK33A2 HK33A3)
Muzzle velocity: 920 metres/sec

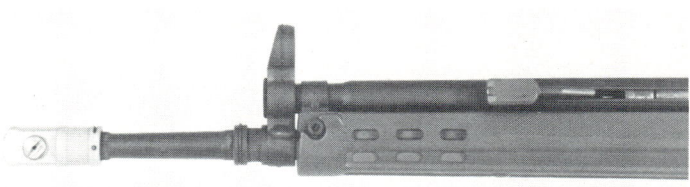

Standard blank attachment for G3, HK33 and other rifles, here shown fitted to a G3 rifle

Muzzle energy: 150mkp
Recoil energy: 0.76mkp
Rate of fire: Cyclic: 750 rounds/min
      Automatic: 100 rounds/min
      SS: 40 rounds/min
Range, maximum effective: 400 metres
Manufacturer: Heckler and Koch GmbH, Oberndorf/Neckar
Status: In production in Germany. In production in Thailand. Adopted by Thailand, Malaysia and by Brazilian Air Force. Also sold in varying quantities elsewhere

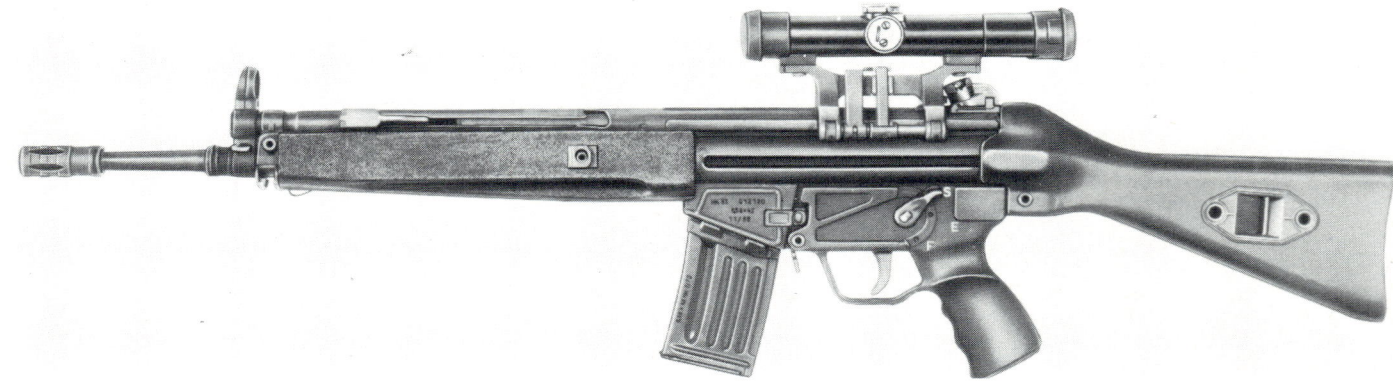

HK33ZF

HK33KA1

HK33A3

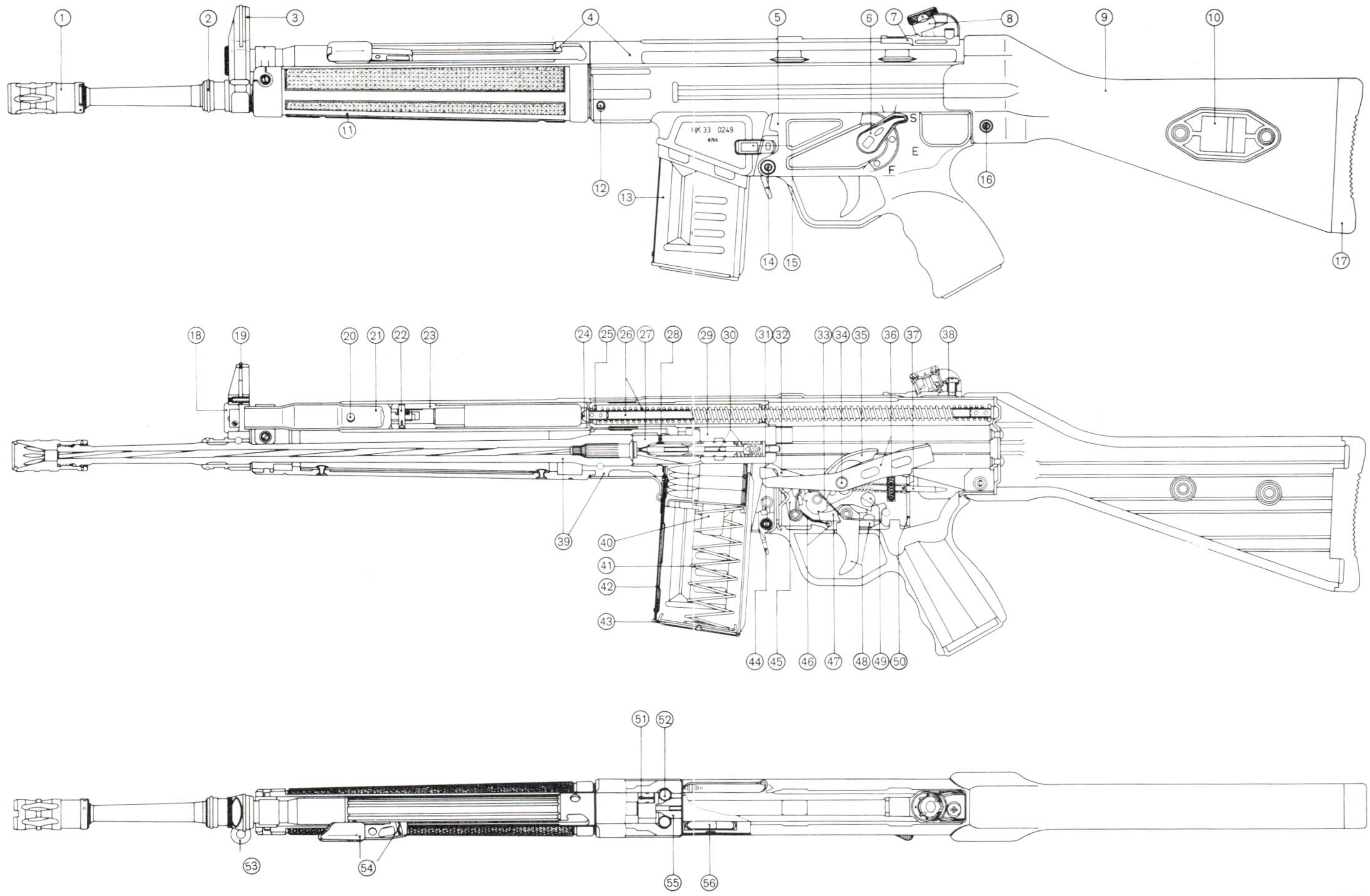

(1) Flash-hider; (2) Spring ring to mount the rifle grenade; (3) Front sight holder; (4) Receiver with cocking lever housing; (5) Grip assembly; (6) Selector; (7) Rotary rear sight; (8) Sight support; (9) Butt stock; (10) Support for sling; (11) Locking pin for handguard; (12) Handguard; (13) Spring hook; (14) Magazine; (15) Locking pin for grip; (16) Magazine catch; (17) Locking pin for butt stock; (18) Cap; (19) Front sight; (20) Stop pin; (21) Stop abutment; (22) Axle for cocking lever; (23) Support for cocking lever; (24) Stop pin for recoil spring; (25) Recoil spring guide ring; (26) Recoil spring guide rod; (27) Recoil spring; (28) Bolt head; (29) Clamping sleeve and holder for locking rollers; (30) Bolt head carrier with recoil spring tube; (31) Firing pin;

(32) Firing pin spring; (33) Contact piece for magazine catch; (34) Release lever; (35) Trigger spring; (36) Axle for ejector; (37) Hammer; (38) Ejector with compression spring; (39) Binding screw; (40) Back stop; (41) Barrel with barrel extension; (42) Follower; (43) Follower spring; (44) Magazine housing; (45) Spring floor plate; (46) Magazine floor plate; (47) Magazine release lever; (48) Catch; (49) Elbow spring with roller; (50) Sear; (51) Trigger; (52) Safety axle; (53) Pressure shank with pressure spring; (54) Trigger housing; (55) Extractor with extractor spring; (56) Locking roller; (57) Eyebolt; (58) Cocking lever with elbow spring; (59) Locking piece; (60) Bolt head cocking lever

4.6mm HECKLER AND KOCH HK36 ASSAULT RIFLE

The HK36 represents an approach to the next generation of rifle to succeed the current weapons based on the 5.56mm × 45 cartridge. The design, produced by a team led by Herr Moeller, was based on the requirements set out below.

(1) A reduced-impulse cartridge providing a small muzzle momentum. A straight-through action which with the low impulse would produce a negligible turning moment tending to raise the muzzle. This would allow the soldier to control the weapon at automatic fire.

(2) A reduced combat weight to eliminate fatigue due to carrying the weapon and at the same time provide the soldier with a realistic quantity of ammunition for a combat situation that might prevent immediate re-supply. The reduction in weight would be associated with the maintenance of mechanical strength by the use of the high strength plastics and alloys.

(3) An effective range of 300 metres. This of course would permit a substantial reduction in the mass of the bullet and so contribute to the reduced muzzle impulse.

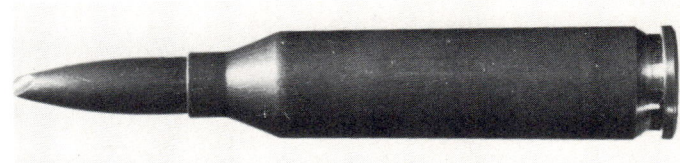

HK 4.6mm cartridge (RMCS)

(4) A flat trajectory which would reduce the height of the mid-range ordinate and allow a single sight setting. This in turn would eliminate range finding errors.

(5) A high chance of a hit due to the combination of the reduced recoil energy provided by the low muzzle impulse, the flat trajectory, and a burst fire control producing three rounds for a single trigger operation. These three rounds would be fired at a high cyclic rate calculated to

HK36 assault rifle Cal. 4.6 × 36

produce the minimum angular deviation at the muzzle.

(6) The target effectiveness would be optimised by producing one bullet with a high chance of incapacitating the lightly protected soldier and another bullet with an ability to penetrate cover and armoured targets. The anti-personnel bullet would achieve its end by utilising a new design of nose calculated to produce maximum tumbling within the human target whilst maintaining complete stability in flight due to a high sectional density and an adequate rotational velocity.

The anti-hard target bullet would achieve success by using a high density tungsten carbide core.

DESCRIPTION

The HK36 is a rifle of distinctive appearance. The receiver, pistol grip and buttstock are plastic covered and the carrying handle incorporates the sight unit. The buttstock is of the telescopic retracting type and the barrel is unencased and has a flash suppressor. The magazine is of original design. It consists of a metal box mounted permanently attached below the receiver. The ammunition is supplied in a wrap-around box with neither top nor bottom and is kept in this container by a tape. The magazine – which it is repeated is integral with the gun – is charged as follows. At the bottom, on each side, is a milled button attached to a spring-loaded chain carried inside the magazine. When the buttons are pulled down the chain is extended and held out. This pulls down the magazine platform and compresses the magazine spring. The rear of the magazine is open and the 30-round box is placed in, on top of the follower. A further pull on the chain releases the holding catch. The magazine platform rises under the cartridges and passes inside the containing box. The chain is taken up into the magazine.

The first round is now positioned for loading and when the bolt comes forward the top cartridge is fed into the chamber. The magazine is sealed against the entry of dirt, snow etc. As subsequent rounds are fired the magazine spring drives the follower further up inside the ammunition box until when the last round is fired the bolt is held open. When the chain is pulled down, the empty box is ejected, the magazine spring is fully compressed and the platform is pulled down to allow room for the next ammunition pack to be inserted.

This system is claimed to reduce weight and cost. The ammunition is factory packed in plastic boxes which are expendable in time of war. No dirt can reach the ammunition before loading.

The weapon is fitted with a reflex sight for daylight use and a beta light is used for conditions of poor visibility at dusk and dawn.

The HK36 uses the roller system of delayed blowback utilised in all Heckler and Koch rifles and machine guns and described in the entry for the G3 rifle above.

STRIPPING

To strip the rifle, the ammunition box is removed, the bolt is retracted, using the cocking handle on the left at the top of the receiver wall, and the chamber is inspected.

The collapsible butt is then removed, the take-down pin on the left rear of the receiver is pressed through and the receiver and stop removed. The return spring comes out with it and the bolt can be withdrawn by retracting the cocking handle.

DATA
Method of operation: Delayed blowback using rollers
Ammunition supply: Box feed from below
Modes of fire: Single shot. Automatic fire. Controlled burst (Can be 2, 3, 4 or 5 rounds)
Rate of fire: Cyclic: 1,100-1,200 rounds/min
Case ejection: Right and forward
Sights: Reflex sight with daylight screen and Beta light for poor light conditions
Sighting: 300 metres – fixed sight setting

WEIGHTS
Rifle with feed unit: 2.85kg
Ammunition box for 30 rounds: 51g
Ammunition box with 30 rounds: 282g
Rifle with 30 rounds: 3.14kg
Rifle with 90 rounds: 3.68kg

DIMENSIONS
Length of rifle, butt stock extended: 890mm
Length of rifle, butt stock retracted: 796.6mm
Height, including feed unit: 195.5mm
Width: 40.8mm
Length of barrel: 398.8mm
Length of barrel, without flash suppressor: 381mm
Length of rifling: 345.4mm
Twist of rifling: 1 turn in 160mm (1 turn in 35 calibre)
Direction of twist: RH
Angle of twist: 5° 7'
Bore diameter across grooves: 4.7mm
Bore diameter across lands: 4.57mm
No. of grooves: 6
External diameter of barrel: Breech: 16.0mm
                                              Centre: 14.0mm
                                              Muzzle: 12.9mm
Diameter of flash suppressor: 16mm
Length of ammunition box: 139.8mm
Height of ammunition box: 55.8mm
Width of ammunition box: 20.3mm

MISCELLANEOUS
Bolt position on firing: Closed
Bolt position – ammunition expended: Open
Distance of bolt recoil to buffer: 84.0mm
Distance of bolt recoil to rear of cartridge: 73.6mm
Sear over-run: 5.1mm
Recoil energy: 0.32mkp
Recoil momentum: 0.4kg/sec
Trigger pull: 3.5kp

4.3mm SALVO WEAPON

Among new weapons and ammunition being offered as possible NATO standards is a German project embodying several of the newer ideas in small-arms design.

First, it uses caseless ammunition, the bullet being set in a block which comprises the propellant charge and its primer and which is completely consumed (in theory at least) when the round is fired. Because no spent cases have to be ejected the weapon, once loaded, can be sealed against dirt everywhere except at the muzzle. Secondly, the effective range of the weapon is limited to about 300-400 metres, because of the belief that this is the practical maximum requirement for most infantry engagements today: this permits the use of a light bullet and small propellant charge. Thirdly, the weapon uses the salvo techniques of using a single charge to fire several (in this instance three) bullets in tandem so as to increase the hit probability. By using a small bullet the resultant recoil forces can be contained within the compass of a small weapon mechanism.

Some special problems arise from the use of caseless ammunition apart from the obvious danger of incomplete combustion leading to excessive fouling. One is the difficulty of obtaining adequate obturation of the breech; another is the climatic protection of the ammunition; and a third is the danger of cook-off resulting from the enclosure of the system and the low thermal conductivity of the propellant block compared with that of a metal cartridge case. This last difficulty can be somewhat reduced by using a propellant with a high ignition temperature.

Other details from the limited range of available information regarding the new weapon are that the ammunition is loaded in 10-round packs into a fixed internal magazine holding 50 rounds; that the individual bullet weight

4.3mm Salvo Weapon (bottom) and G3 Rifle

is 2 grammes and the muzzle velocity imparted to it some 1100m/sec; that the standard daylight sight is a 1:1 reflex optical device with a crosswire which can be illuminated; and that the weapon is some 77cm long.
Status: Trials

GERMANY (DEMOCRATIC REPUBLIC)

7.62mm KARABINER — S

This is a copy of the Russian Simonov Semi Automatic Carbine (SKS). It differs from the Soviet original only in having a hole through the stock to attach the lower end of the sling. In all other respects it is the same and the details will be found in the entry covering Soviet equipment.

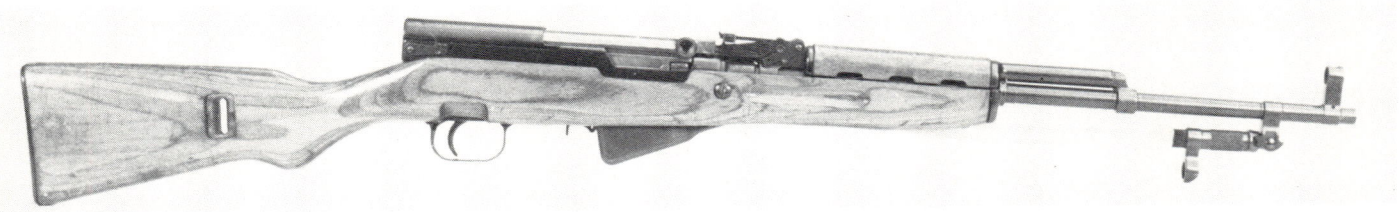

The 7.62mm East German Karabiner S. Note slot in butt for sling (RSAF)

7.62mm MPiK ASSAULT RIFLE

This is the East German version of the Russian 7.62mm AK assault rifle; it has a fixed wooden stock and may be distinguished from the Russian or any of the satellite weapons by the distinctive fire selector markings. The upper (full auto) position is marked 'D' and the lower position which indicates single shot is marked 'E'. The East German MPiK is the only AK copy which does not have a built-in recess in the butt for cleaning kit, and neither does it have a cleaning rod under the barrel. The piston and bolt are finished to a very high standard and are chromium plated. Details of weight and performance are the same as the Russian AK and will be found in the Russian section.

MPiK

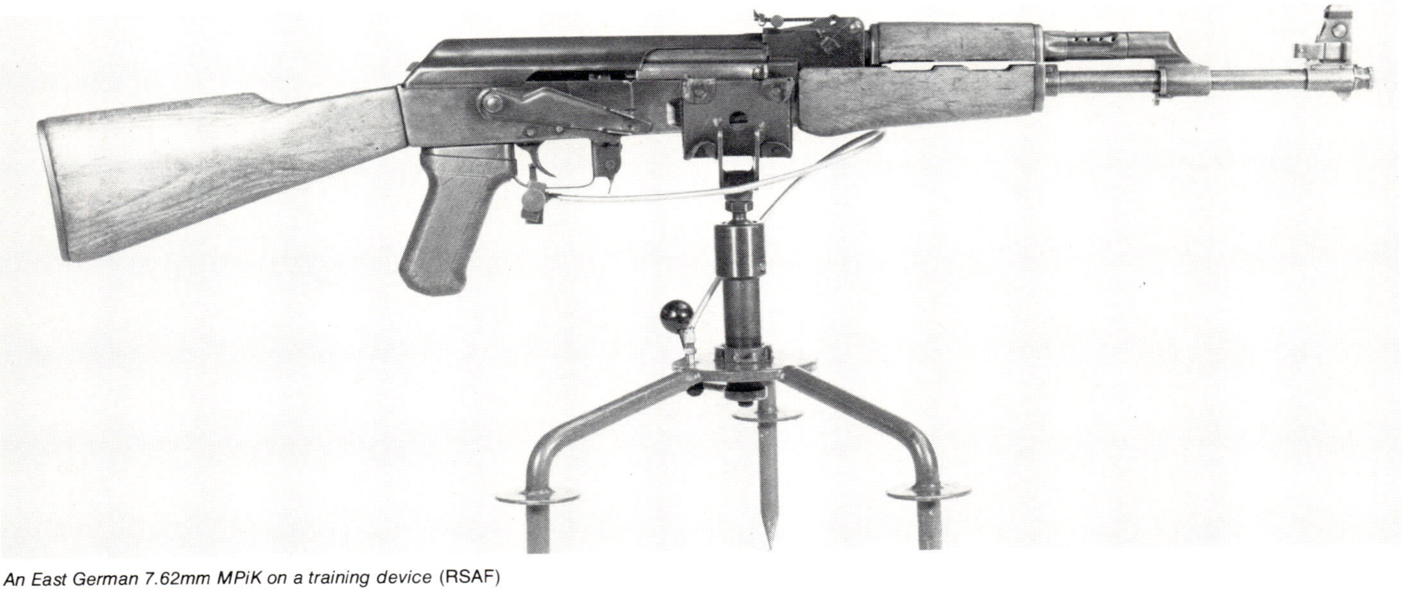

An East German 7.62mm MPiK on a training device (RSAF)

The East German MPiKS (RSAF)

7.62mm MPiKS

This is the German copy of the AK with the folding stock. Again it has the individualistic markings and the chromium-plated piston and breech block. Like the MPiK it has neither cleaning rod nor provision for cleaning kit.

7.62mm MPiKM

This is the East German copy of the Russian AKM assault rifle, the modernised AK. It exists in two forms. The earlier has a wooden, fixed, stock and a solid wooden non laminated lower handgrip to the fore arm. The rear pistol grip is plastic and the top half of the forearm is made of the same material.

The later version has a plastic stock, pistol grip and handguard with the grip and the stock having prominent studs. It does not have the Russian compensator. The other details will be found in the section on Russian rifles.

The East German MPiKM with plastic furniture (RSAF)

7.62mm MPiKMS

The MPiKMS is the folding stock version of the Russian AKM. It has no differences, except the fire selector markings, from the Russian gun. It does not have the Russian compensator.

KKMPi69

This is an East German training rifle. It is chambered for the .22RF cartridge (5.6mm x 16). It would appear to be used for all forms of field exercise and is carried by troops on assault courses, route marches, and all preliminary training on weapon handling and familiarisation is done on this rifle.

Note that the selector lever, sights, magazine and pistol grip are made as far as possible, to resemble those of the full bore rifle.

The 5.6mm KKMPi 69

HUNGARY

HUNGARIAN RIFLES

The Hungarian Army is equipped with the standard Warsaw Pact rifles. The AK-47 is now largely relegated to reservists and the AKM is in service.

The Hungarian AKM has design differences from the standard Russian and other Communist countries'. There are two pistol grips and these together with the buttstock are made of pale blue nylon. The forearm, extending forward under the barrel for some four inches from the forward pistol grip, is made of perforated metal sheet. There is no handguard around the gas cylinder which is noticeably grooved and extends back to

Hungarian AK-47. The selector markings are '1' and '∞' (RSAF)

Hungarian troops training with the AMD

join the receiver below the rearsight block.

The Hungarians also produce the short barrelled AMD rifle which with its large and prominent muzzle brake and single strut folding stock is easily recognised. Since there is, as mentioned above, a long barrel AKM in the Hungarian forces, the AMD is employed – tactically – as a sub-machine gun and a full description of it will be found in the section on Hungarian SMGs.

Hungarian AKM assault rifle

Hungarian AKM

INDONESIA

INDONESIAN RIFLES

The Dutch used the 6.5mm Mannlicher rifle in the East Indian colonies and many of these were left behind when Indonesia became independent.

The Japanese 7.7 rimmed cartridge and the .303in rimmed cartridge were sufficiently available in Indonesia to make it worth their while to convert the 6.5mm rifles to take these cartridges.

The US M1 rifle was obtained in some quantity both from Beretta and directly from the US. Beretta also manufactured their BM 59 in Indonesia.

The Russian AK-47 and the SKS were obtained and later the Indonesians were one of the first Asian countries to obtain a large number of the US AR-15 rifle which they used in their confrontation with the British over Borneo in 1963.

Indonesia is also one of the many countries now using the G3 rifle designed by Heckler and Koch in West Germany.

ISRAEL

5.56mm GALIL ASSAULT RIFLE

The Israeli army has been largely equipped with 7.62mm FN FAL rifles and also used the Heavy Barrelled rifle as the squad LMG. After the Six Day War of 1967 it was decided to adopt a rifle using the 5.56mm x 45 cartridge. A series of tests was carried out to determine the best rifle. The weapons considered were:

The M16A1 – USA
The Stoner rifle – NWM, Holland
The Heckler and Koch – HK 33 – Germany
The AK-47 – USSR
The rifle designed by Lt Col Uziel Gal – tc7 'New UZI'
The Galil Rifle – developed jointly by Yaacov Lior and Israel Galili.

Other rifles were tried at various stages but the above were the most serious contenders. Most of the firing was conducted in desert terrain, and great emphasis was laid on reliability and functioning under adverse conditions. The Galil most nearly met the stringent requirements, and the rifle won the Annual Israeli Defence Award. In 1972 a decision was taken to adopt the Galil and the weapon is now in service, but by no means on a universal basis, in the Israeli Defence Forces. Other countries have also shown interest in buying the Galil.

DESCRIPTION

The Galil ARM was designed to fill the roles of the sub-machine gun, assault rifle and light machine gun. It can also be used to project anti-tank and anti-personnel grenades from the shoulder and illuminating and signal grenades, with the butt on the ground. The buttstock may be fixed and

made of either wood or plastic: there is alternatively a folding tubular stock which lies along the right side of the weapon.

In addition to the ARM there is a short barrelled sub-machine gun, with a folding stock, known as the SAR – Short Assault Rifle.

There are three magazine capacities – 12, 35 and 50 rounds. The 12-round magazine is used with the ballistite cartridges required for grenade launching, and the 35-round magazine is generally employed in the rifle role. When the weapon is employed as a light machine gun the 50-round magazine is used. The bipod is carried lying under the barrel and fitting into a groove under the foregrip. The powerful leverage that can be obtained when the bipod legs are swung down to the vertical position, is used to provide a wire cutter. Any barbed wire placed under the hook at the bipod fulcrum can be sheared – usually in one movement of the bipod legs.

The sights enable the weapon to produce aimed fire out to 500 metres. The foresight is a cylindrical post which can be screwed up or down for zeroing and the rear sight is a flip aperture with the choice of 0-300 metres and 3-500 metres. There are also night sights set for use at 100 metres and these are normally folded, but when lifted produce a pattern of three luminous spots. The centre spot is that of the foresight, and three luminous aiming marks are lined up horizontally and placed on the target.

There is little doubt that the Galil in many respects is modelled on the AK-47 series and most nearly approximates to the Finnish M62 assault rifle. It is a gas-operated rifle with no regulator. The gas block is pinned to the barrel and the gas track is drilled back at 30 deg. into the gas cylinder. The piston head and shank are chrome-plated. The bolt carrier is an

The fixed stock of the Galil can be wood or plastic

The Galil rifle with folding stock

extension of the piston end and is hollowed out over the bolt to take the return spring. The bolt has a cam pin operating in a slot in the carrier and has two locking lugs which are rotated in locking recesses to support the cartridge before firing. The cocking handle is attached to the bolt carrier to give positive bolt closure. It emerges from the right side of the receiver and is bent upwards to allow cocking with either hand. The change lever on the right of the receiver, like that of the AK-47, is a long pressing which when placed on 'safe' both closes up the cocking way against the entry of dirt and restricts the carrier movement. It is possible to retract the bolt sufficiently to inspect the chamber but not enough to feed a round.

Firing a grenade from the shoulder

OPERATION

The Galil fires from a closed bolt position. The magazine, fitting under the gun, is placed in position and held by the magazine catch located in front of the trigger guard. The change lever is taken off 'safe' and the cocking handle pulled to the rear. When it is released the carrier is driven forward and the top round pushed out of the magazine into the chamber. The bolt comes to a halt and the further forward travel of the carrier causes the cam pin – engaged in a cam slot in the carrier – to rotate the bolt. The bolt forces the cartridge forward, the extractor slips over the rim and the gun is ready for firing.

When the trigger is pulled, the hammer drives the firing pin forward and the cap is crushed. Some of the propellant gas escapes through the gas vent into the cylinder and drives the piston rearwards. There is a brief period of free travel, whilst the gas pressure drops, as the width of the cam slot passes the cam pin. The slot then engages the pin which is rotated as the carrier proceeds back. The rotation of the bolt provides primary extraction and then the case is withdrawn as the bolt retracts. The return spring is compressed, the empty case is ejected and then the return spring energy drives the carrier forward and the cycle starts again.

TRIGGER AND FIRING MECHANISM

The system used is that employed in the MI Garand rifle, the AK series and many others, in which the hammer has two bents and the trigger extension carries two sears. The hammer is initially held by the main sear and when the trigger is pulled the trigger extension rotates forward and down and the hammer is freed. Provided that the carrier is fully forward the hammer can continue on to strike the firing pin. At semi-auto the hammer is re-cocked by the recoiling carrier and is caught by the spring loaded auxiliary sear. The bolt goes forward but since the trigger is already pulled nothing further happens. When the firer releases the trigger, the trigger extension moves back and up as it rotates and the hammer slips out of the auxiliary sear and is caught by the main sear. When the trigger is pulled another round is fired.

At full automatic the rear, spring-loaded, auxiliary sear is held back. The first round of the burst is fired off the front sear and the carrier comes back and rocks the hammer over. Until the carrier is fully forward the safety sear holds the hammer back. As soon as the carrier travels fully forward the safety sear is knocked off and the hammer rotates to fire a further round. So after the first round the trigger sear plays no part. When the trigger is released the hammer is caught by the main sear and held back.

If the safety catch is applied the trigger extension is locked and neither sear can be depressed.

The bipod of the Galil ARM weighs 250gm, and is constructed to serve as a wire cutter

STRIPPING

The Galil breaks down into six parts for field stripping. The procedure follows that of the AK series. First the magazine is removed and the chamber checked; then the guide rod of the return spring is pushed forward and the receiver cover lifted off.

The return spring and road are removed. The cocking handle is withdrawn and the carrier and bolt lifted up out of the receiver. The bolt is then rotated out of the carrier.

DATA (ARM or SAR)
Cartridge: 5.56mm x 45
Method of operation: Gas
Method of locking: Rotating bolt
Method of feed: 33- and 50-round box magazine
Method of fire: Selective

SAR with pistol grip

The short-barrelled Galil SAR

WEIGHTS
Gun, empty: 3.9kg or 3.5kg
Gun with bipod and carrying handle: 4.3kg
35-round magazine, empty: 390g
35-round magazine, loaded: 710g
50-round magazine, empty: 440g
50-round magazine, loaded: 1kg

LENGTHS
Stock extended: 970mm or 820mm
Stock folded: 740mm or 600mm
Barrel: 460mm or 330mm

MECHANICAL FEATURES
Barrel: Rifling: 6 grooves RH 1 turn in 305mm
　　　　Regulator: Nil
　　　　Cooling: Air
　　　　Change: Nil
Sights: Foresight: Cylindrical post
　　　　Rearsight: Flip aperture 0-300m 300-500m
　　　　Graduation: Nil
　　　　Sight radius: 475mm
　　　　Night sights: Folding, luminous, set for 100m

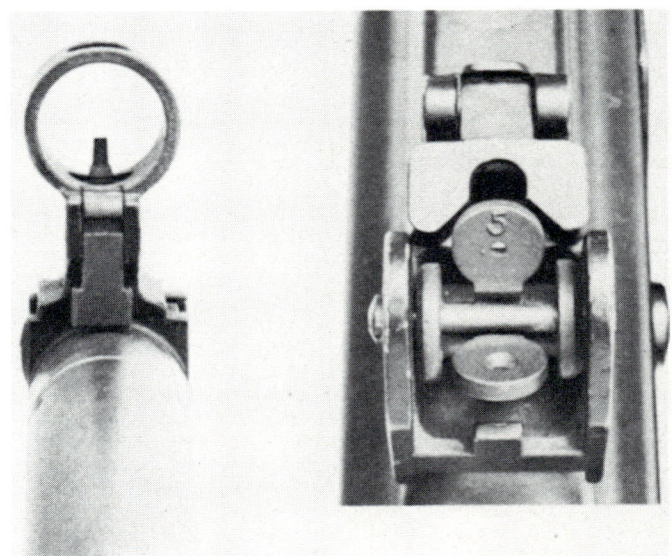

The sights of the Galil rifle consist of a post-type foresight and aperture "L" flip-type rearsight, set for 300m and 500m. Night sights are standard on all Galil models. The sights are provided with luminous spots, set for 100m

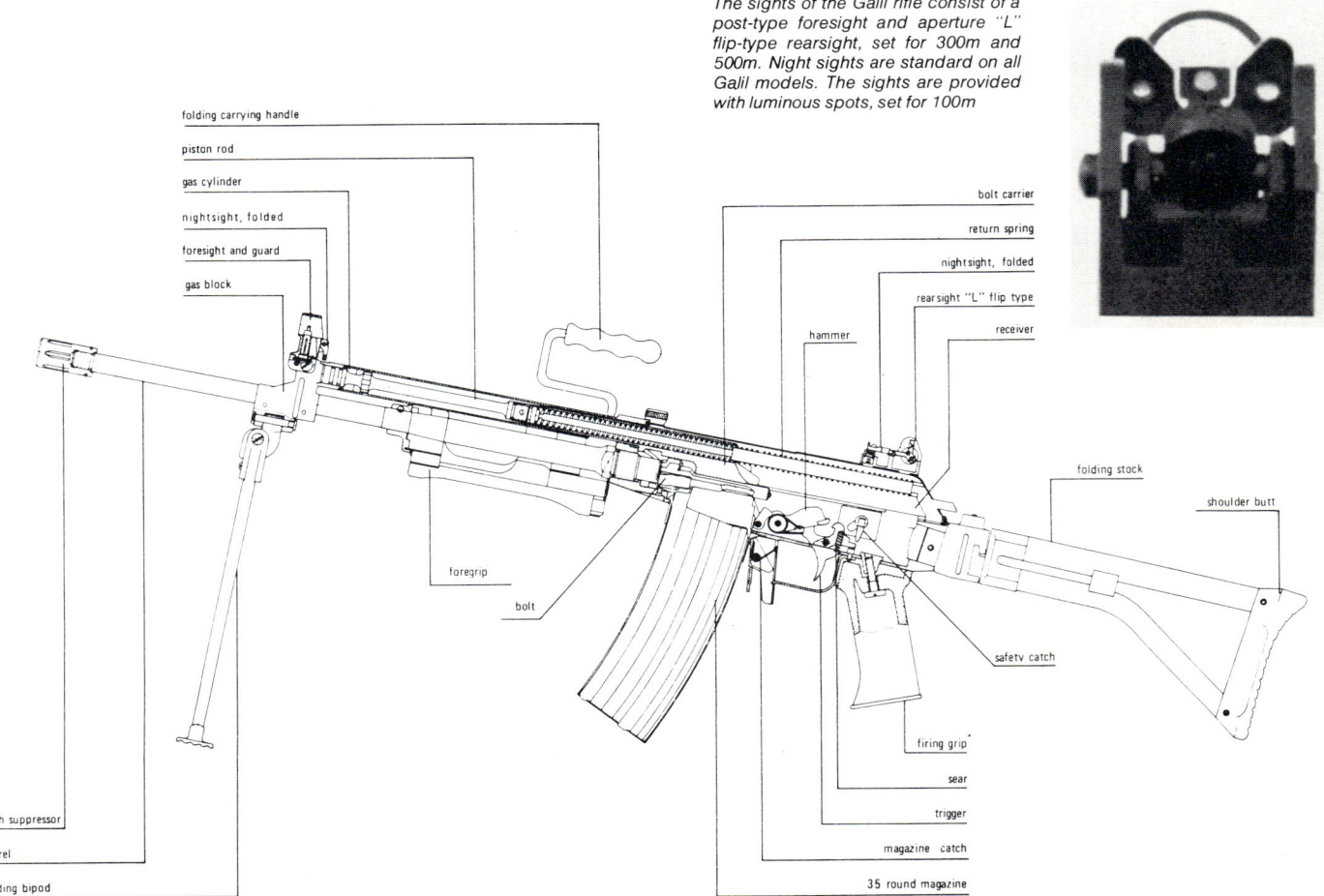

folding carrying handle
piston rod
gas cylinder
nightsight, folded
foresight and guard
gas block

bolt carrier
return spring
nightsight, folded
rearsight "L" flip type
receiver
hammer

folding stock
shoulder butt

foregrip
bolt

safety catch

firing grip
sear
trigger
magazine catch
35 round magazine

flash suppressor
barrel
folding bipod

The Galil rifle

FIRING CHARACTERISTICS
Muzzle velocity: 920 metres/sec or 980 metres/sec
Muzzle energy: 154mkp or 176mkp
Chamber pressure: 3,622kg/cm²
Rate of fire: Cyclic: 650 rounds/min
          Automatic: 105 rounds/min
          SS: 40 rounds/min

Range, maximum effective: 600 metres or 400 metres
Manufacturer: Israel Military Industries, Tel Aviv
Status: In production and in service with Israeli forces. Tested by other armies.

The Galil stripped

ITALY

7.62mm BM 59 RIFLE

At the end of World War II the firm of Pietro Beretta at Gardone-val-Trompia, began to construct the US M1 .30 Rifle – the Garand – for the Italian Army. These rifles were later supplied to Indonesia and Denmark. Some 100,000 rifles were produced by 1961.

The need to compete with weapons of more modern design (the M1 rifle came into USA service in 1936) led to the production of a modified M1 rifle firing the NATO 7.62mm x 51 cartridge. Studies to convert the Garand into a modern selective fire weapon were commenced in 1959 under the direction of Domenico Salza and completed by Vittorio Valle.

The earliest versions were given letter suffixes. The first BM 59 was a Garand, lightened and shortened, modified to take a twenty-round detachable box magazine.

Next came the BM 59 R which had a device to slow down the rate of fire. This was followed by the BM 59 D with a pistol grip and bipod and the BM 59 GL with a grenade launcher. The BM 60 CB had a three-round burst fire controller.

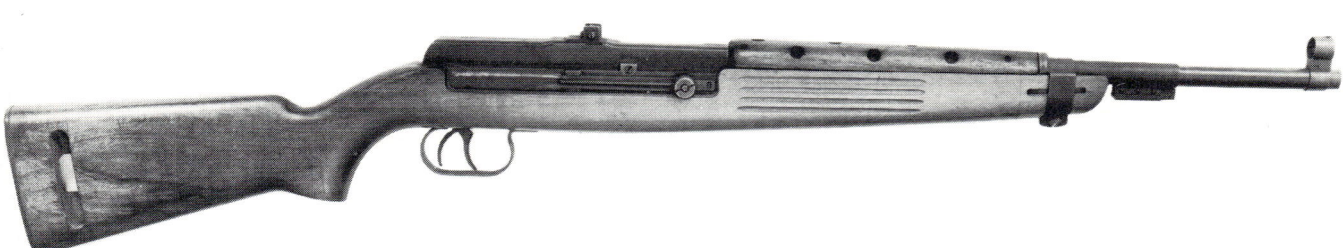

A .30 carbine made for Morocco. Although this looks like the USA M1 carbine it has a tilting block

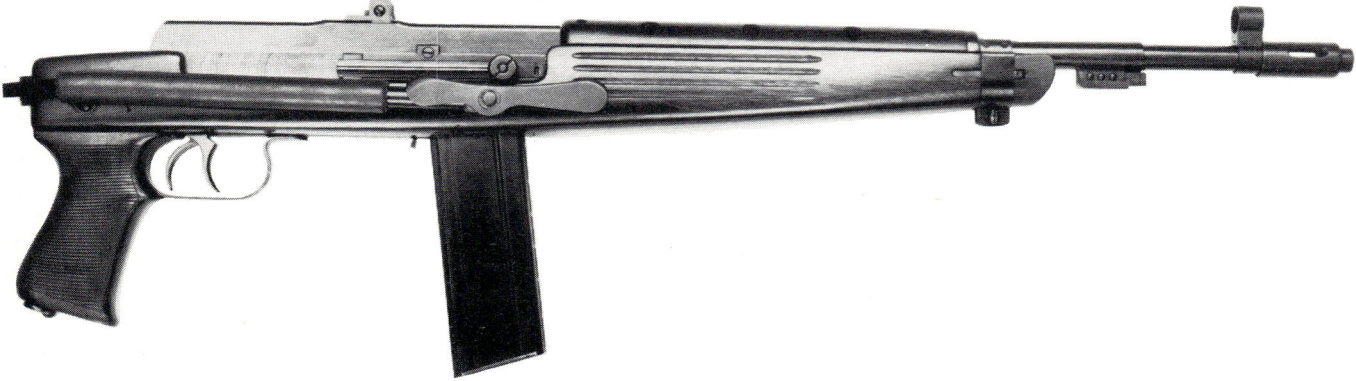

The folding butt version of the .30 carbine

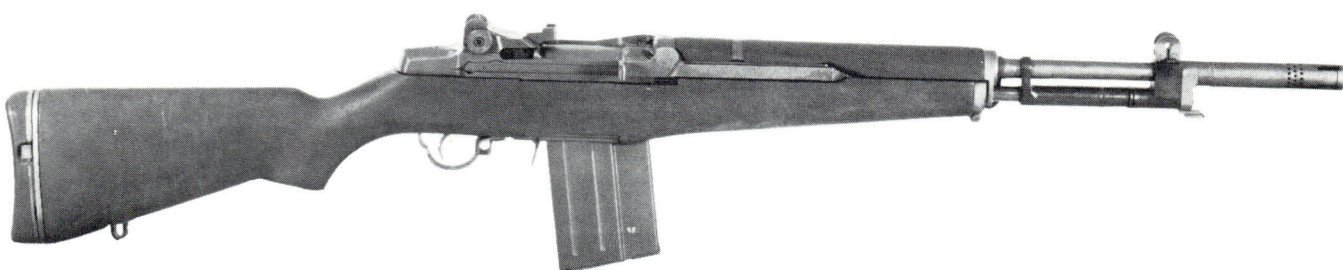

The BM 59 Mark I

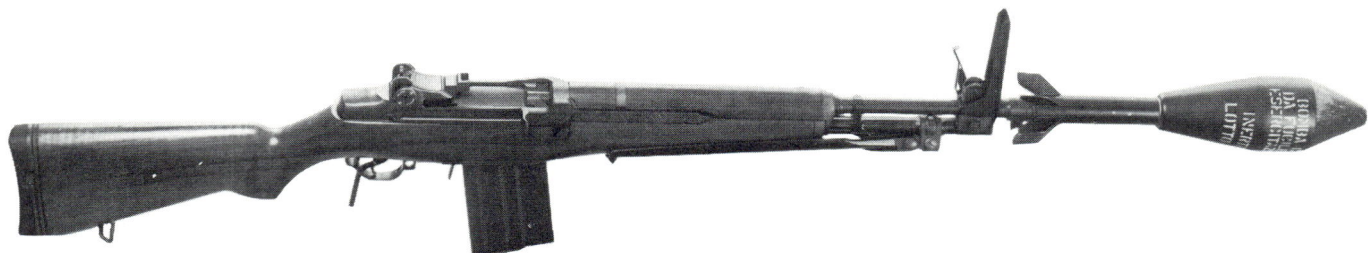

BM 59 GL with permanently attached grenade launcher and sights. Note the winter trigger

BM 59 Mark Ital.

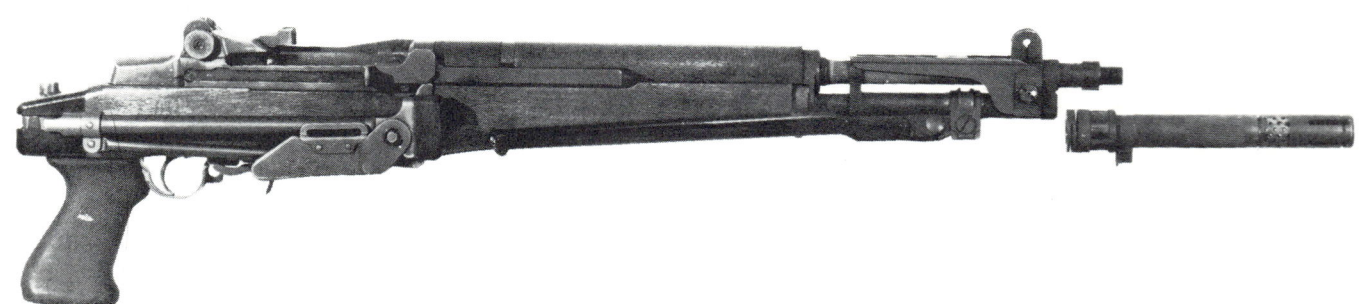

BM 59 Mark Ital. Para – the Parachutists' rifle

Of the BM 59 series the Mark E was the cheapest since it used the Garand barrel and gas cylinder. In all the others the barrel and gas cylinder was a Beretta design. The current series is as follows:

The BM 59 Mark I is a fixed wooden-stocked rifle with the gas cylinder under the barrel. There is a 20-round detachable box magazine which can be loaded and replenished using chargers and guides built into the receiver. The corresponding Italian Army version is known as the BM 59 Mark Ital and has a light bipod fitted to the gas cylinder. The BM 59 Mark II is like the Mk I but has a pistol grip, a winter trigger and a bipod.

The BM 59 Mark III has a folding metal stock and two pistol grips.

The Italian Army BM 59 Mark Ital TA and the BM 59 Mark Ital Para were derived from the Mark III. The Mark Ital TA is for Alpine troops and the Mark Ital Para is for airborne use.

The BM 59 Mark IV is a heavy-barrelled version intended for the squad light automatic role. It has a plastic buttstock and a hinged buttplate and a pistol grip. There is no forward pistol grip.

The BM 59 will fire any anti-personnel or anti-tank grenade with a boom with an inside diameter of 22mm. Where the grenade launcher is fitted it is not intended that it should be removed, except for the Mark Ital TP – the Parachutists' rifle. The erecting of the grenade sight automatically cuts off the gas supply to the gas piston. A ballistite cartridge is used for the grenade and it is particularly dangerous with this rifle to fire a ball round into a grenade.

DATA (BM 59 Mark Ital)
Cartridge: 7.62mm x 51
Method of operation: Gas
Method of locking: Rotating bolt
Method of feed: 20-round detachable box magazine
Method of fire: Selective
Weight: 4.6kg
Length: 1,095mm
Barrel: 4 groove RH
　　Rifling: 490mm
Sights: Foresight: Blade
　　Rearsight: Aperture. Adjustable for range and windage

Muzzle velocity: 823 metres/sec
Muzzle energy: 322mkp
Rate of fire: Cyclic: 750 rounds/min
　　Auto: 120 rounds/min
　　SS: 40 rounds/min
Range, maximum effective: 600 metres
Manufacturer: Pietro Beretta SpA, Gardone-val-Trompia
Status: No longer in production. In service with Italian Army. Manufactured under licence in Indonesia and Morocco. The Nigerian Government had a licence to manufacture but this was not taken up when the Biafran civil war started

BM 59 Mark Ital. TA for Alpini

5.56mm BERETTA 70/223 RIFLE

In early 1968 Pietro Beretta at Brescia started an initial survey for a new assault rifle. The design team was headed by Mr Vittorio Valle, head of the Beretta R & D Department, under the direct supervision of Mr P.C. Beretta, the General Manager. Work included a detailed evaluation of existing 5.56mm systems, including the AR 15 and the Stoner.

Eventually a gas-operated system was adopted. It was decided to have a conventional piston and cylinder system with the gas port as far forward as possible. The length of the piston could lead to excess weight or lack of strength and the designers decided to attach the piston to the bolt carrier and to wrap the return spring around the piston so that it would be compressed between the piston head and the forward end of the receiver. With the magazine under the gun the piston rod, spring and cylinder must be above the barrel and this has the advantageous effect of raising the centre of gravity of the weapon towards the barrel where it is ideally located. No gas regulator is incorporated which detracts from the value of a gas-operated system. The designers next looked at the type of bolt they were going to use. They wanted symmetrical support so the tilting block of the FN FAL was not considered. With the rejection of roller locking systems along with blowback operation, a rotating bolt solution became inevitable. The multi-lug system used by the M16, Stoner and FN CAL rifle was not adopted because it was considered that it was difficult to ensure that all the lugs were engaging in their recesses and taking their fair share of the stress and so the forward locking, two-lug system of the Garand, .30 calibre Carbine, and the Russian Kalashnikov AK-47, was adopted. One of the advantages of forward locking, in a modern design, is that the bolt can lock directly into the barrel extension. Thus only the barrel and bolt head are stressed and must be of high tensile material but the rest of the bolt and the receiver need

not be produced from such expensive steel. However Beretta have chosen to weld a sleeve into the receiver and the bolt lugs close into recesses cut in this. This system is used in the Russian AKM with a similar bolt lock and results inevitably in a heavier weapon.

Fairly early on in the design stage it was decided that the cartridge – the M193 – could be used for a Squad Automatic using the same heavy gauge steel pressings but with a heavier barrel capable of dealing with the heat transfer problem associated with the higher rates of fire demanded from a light machine gun. At the other end of the scale a folding butt carbine was also impossible. These three weapons are all available but interest seems to be centred largely on the AR70.

OPERATION

The operating system of the AR70 is quite simple. On firing, the gas pressure drives the bullet forward up the bore and the entire rifle recoils back into the firer's shoulder. After a bullet travel of approximately 33cm the gas passes through the vent into the cylinder and drives the piston rearward. There is a free travel of the piston for about 9mm before the carrier starts to rotate the bolt and produce unlocking. This delay – mechanical safety – allows the pressure to drop. The bolt is cammed through 30 degrees and is fully unlocked; it travels back with the carrier, extracts the spent case, compresses the operating spring around the piston and as the latter re-asserts itself the working parts go forward, feeding a new round into the chamber. When chambering is complete the bolt comes to a stop but the carrier continues forward and the cam rotates the bolt into the locked position. The trigger and firing mechanism are orthodox in their action. Single shot is obtained using a disconnector between the trigger

The Beretta 70/223 rifle

The Beretta 70/223 rifle

The Beretta 70/223 with grenade and bayonet

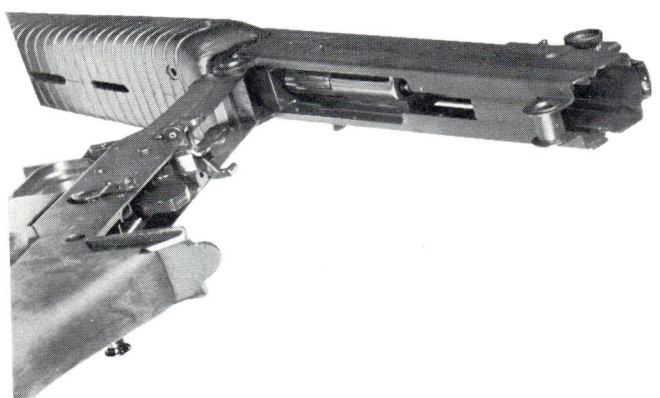

First stage of stripping

The telescopic sight attachment

and the sear; the latter operates in a bent near the hammer axis. When firing at full auto the hammer is controlled by a safety sear which is operated by the bolt carrier in its last forward motion. This ensures locking is completed before the hammer is released and it operates also in single shot, i.e. if the bolt is not locked the hammer cannot move.

In the design of the weapon as an assault rifle it was considered – wisely – that all openings should be sealed to prevent the ingress of dirt when the rifle was ready to fire. A cover was provided over the slot in the receiver in which the cocking handle comes back (*not* the ejection opening) and this flies up as the firer initially cocks the weapon. This cocking handle is the only connection between the bolt carrier and the piston; if it is lost during stripping, the rifle becomes useless.

STRIPPING

The rifle strips easily. A take-down pin is located on the left of the receiver above the rear surface of the pistol grip and is pushed through with the nose of a round. The butt group drops down and the cocking handle catch is released and the cocking handle pulled out. The bolt and carrier come out to the rear. The fore-end is spring-retained. The flash eliminator can be removed and then the gas cylinder, piston and spring. The only snag in re-assembling the gun is ensuring that the slot in the piston, to connect it with the bolt carrier, is properly lined up.

It should be noted that the rear aperture sight and the foresight are both on the same side of the separating surfaces as the weapon breaks. Thus wear in the take-down pin or in the mating surfaces does not – unlike some current rifles – produce sloppiness in the sight. A telescopic sight can be fitted if required.

The rigid stock of the AR70 can easily be detached and replaced with the folding butt of the SC model.

The rifle fires the MECAR 40mm grenade. To assemble the grenade over the flash eliminator a lever lying horizontally over the muzzle, must be raised. This closes a valve, ensuring all the gas from the ballistite cartridge is used to drive the grenade, and the normal gas system is non-operative.

DATA
Cartridge: 5.56mm × 45
Method of operation: Gas
Method of locking: Rotating bolt
Method of feed: 30-round box magazine
Method of fire: Selective

WEIGHTS (AR Assault Rifle)
Rifle, alone: 3.41kg
Magazine, empty: 255g
Magazine, loaded: 0.586kg
Rifle, loaded: 3.99kg
Bayonet: 284g
Trigger pull: 2.04kg

LENGTHS (AR Assault Rifle)
Rifle without bayonet: 940mm
Rifle with bayonet: 1,077mm
Rifle, butt folded, no bayonet: 858mm
Barrel: 450mm
Bayonet: 292mm

MECHANICAL FEATURES
Barrel: Regulator: Nil
　　　　Rifling: 4 grooves RH. 1 turn in 305mm
　　　　Cooling: Air

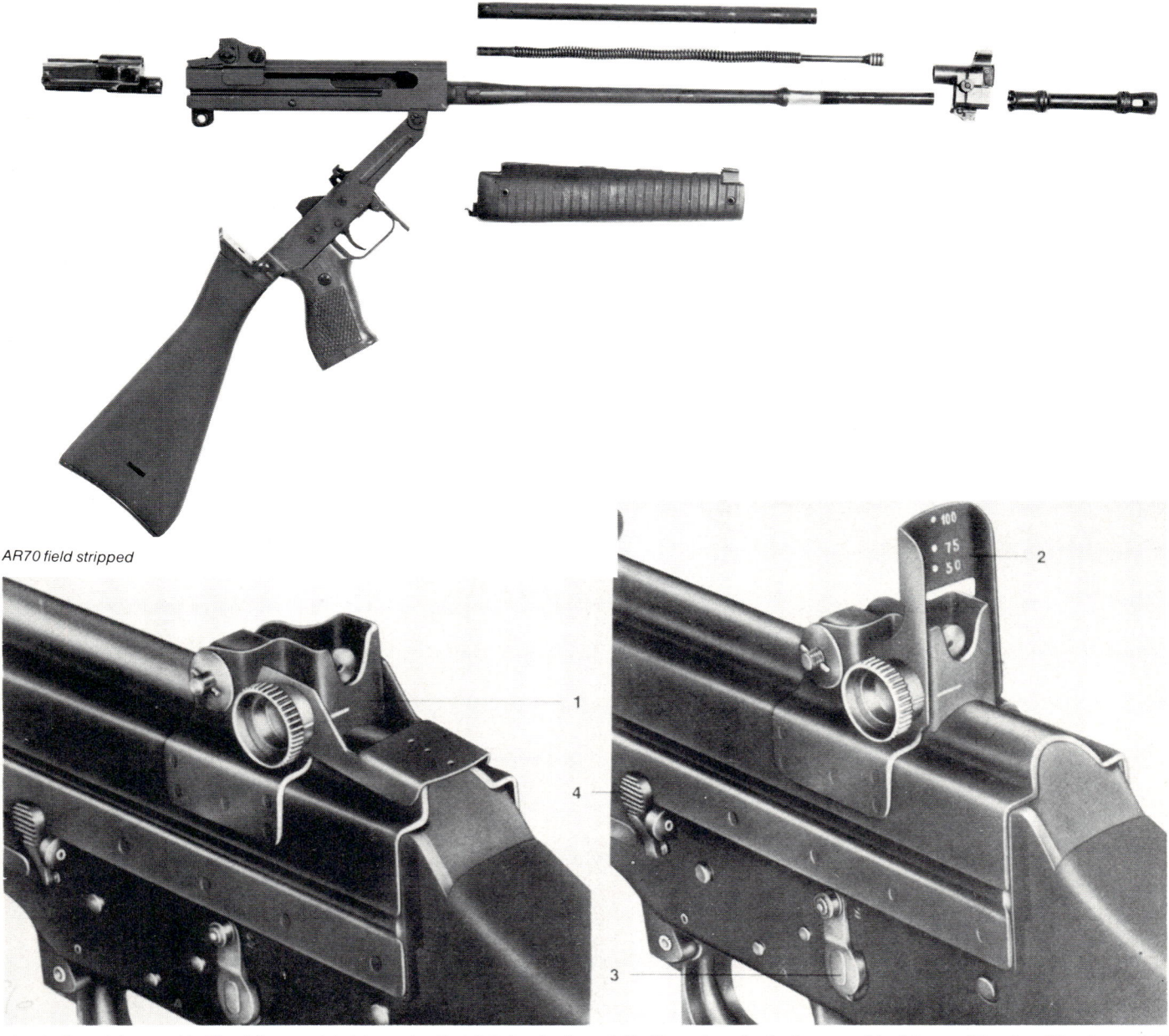

AR70 field stripped

Key: **(1)** Rear sight assembly. The pinion rear sight is located on the left; its function is to adjust the elevation of the aperture. The rear sight is adjustable for windage by use of the front screw; **(2)** Grenade launcher sight. To launch the grenade the special sight with apertures for the three possible distances (50 metres, 75 metres and 100 metres) is raised; **(3)** Selector. S safety, I single fire, A automatic fire; **(4)** Bolt latch

Sights: Foresight: Cylindrical post
   Rearsight: Aperture flip. 0-150 metres; 150-300 metres
   Grenade sight: 50-70-100 metres
   Graduation: Nil
   Zeroing: Elevation. Front sight screws up and down
      Line. Back sight on bolt
   Sight radius: 527mm

FIRING CHARACTERISTICS (AR Assault Rifle)
Muzzle velocity: 970 metres/sec
Muzzle energy: 171mkp
Recoil energy: 0.760mkp
Chamber pressure: 3,622kg/cm²
Rate of fire: Cyclic: 630 rounds/min
   Automatic: 100 rounds/min
   SS: 40 rounds/min

Range, maximum effective: 400 metres
Manufacturer: Pietro Beretta SpA, Gardone-val-Trompia, Brescia
Status: Production

DATA (SC Special Carbine)
As AR except:
Weight, carbine alone: 3.52kg
Length, without bayonet: 935mm
Length, without bayonet and with butt folded: 734mm
Recoil energy: 0.663mkp

DATA (LM Light Machine Gun)
As AR except:
Weight, LMG alone: 4.06kg
Recoil energy: 0.732mkp
Status: Not yet in production

5.56mm BERETTA 70/223 SHORT RIFLE

This is similar to the standard rifle but has a shorter barrel. The gas port has been moved black slightly and the length of the operating rod has been shortened. This of course results in a lack of interchangeability of parts between the two models. The short rifle is very compact and is claimed to have the advantages of an SMG whilst retaining the virtues of a rifle.

The weapon was designed to be used inside an armoured vehicle or anywhere where space is restricted.

The changes which have been made with respect to the standard rifle are:

	Standard Rifle	Short Rifle
Total length, butt open:	940mm	820mm
Total length, butt folded:	734mm	598mm
Length of barrel:	450mm	320mm
Weight:	3.65kg	3.45kg

734 m/m

598 m/m

Beretta 70/223 standard and short rifles compared

JAPAN

6.5mm TYPE 38 RIFLE

This was one of the standard Japanese infantry rifles during the Second World War and was very widely distributed throughout Asia where it may still be found. Carbine and short rifle derivatives probably also still exist.

DATA
Cartridge: 6.5 Type 38 (Some rifles modified to take the 7.92mm Mauser round)
Operation: Manual, bolt action

Feed: 5-round integral magazine
Weight, loaded: 4.2kg
Length: 1275mm
Sights Foresight: Blade
　　　　　Rearsight: Tangent V-notch leaf
Rate of fire: 10-15 rounds/min
Effective range: 400m
Status: No longer made but still likely to be encountered in Asian countries.

7.7mm TYPE 99 RIFLE

This rifle was introduced as an improved successor to the 6.5mm Type 38 which it resembles in many respects. Many of the rifles have been converted to use 7.92mm Mauser ammunition (in China) or .30-06 ammunition. The principal recognition features are the large circular safety knob at the rear of the bolt and the egg-shaped bolt handle.

DATA
Cartridge: 7.7mm (Japanese). See text
Operation: Manual, bolt action

Feed: 5-round integral magazine
Weight: 4kg
Length: 1143mm
Sights Foresight: Blade
　　　　　Rearsight: Adjustable aperture leaf
Rate of fire: 8-10 rounds/min
Effective range: 500m
Status: No longer made. In service, modified or unmodified, in various parts of Asia

7.62mm TYPE 64 RIFLE

The formation of the Japanese Self Defence Force led to the requirement for a new series of weapons and the Howa Machinery Company of Nagoya received a contract to develop a rifle. The project Leader and Designer was General K. Iwashita. Several designs and modifications to those designs were produced until eventually the Type 64 emerged. This was the weapon accepted for the Japanese Self Defence Force.

Considering that the NATO 7.62mm cartridge is probably not the best round for any Asiatic nation, the Type 64 rifle finds an ingenious answer to many of the problems. The cartridge used is a reduced load 7.62mm x 51. The propellant charge has been reduced to 90 per cent and the bullet has a purple tip. The reduction in the powder charge leads to a reduced muzzle impulse and as no effort has been made to reduce the weight significantly, the recoil energy that the soldier has to absorb is itself less than that experienced by troops using the conventional 7.62mm cartridge. If it should be necessary to employ the full charge NATO round then the gas regulator must be set to reduce the amount and pressure of the gases reaching the piston head. The rifle has been designed to launch rifle grenades and the gas regulator includes a facility to cut off the gas supply to the piston

entirely, so that the available energy goes to the grenade and also to ensure that the excessive gas produced by the ballistite cartridge does not damage the piston and bolt.

The rifle is orthodox in appearance and action. The gas cylinder and piston are located above the barrel. The locking system incorporates a tilting block, lifted into engagement and subsequently lowered and carried back by the bolt carrier.

The butt is a straight through action and this, with the bipod under the front of the fore end, and the muzzle brake, produces extremely accurate single shot fire. The gun fires at 500 rounds a minute at full automatic and this relatively slow rate assists in maintaining the burst on the target. There is no regulator on the gun and the rate of fire cannot be adjusted.

The very short length of the rifle of only 99cm makes it distinctive and easily recognised. This small overall dimension (13cm less than the USA M14) and the reduced velocity and recoil force make the Type 64 a very good weapon for the initiation of recruits and their subsequent advanced musketry training.

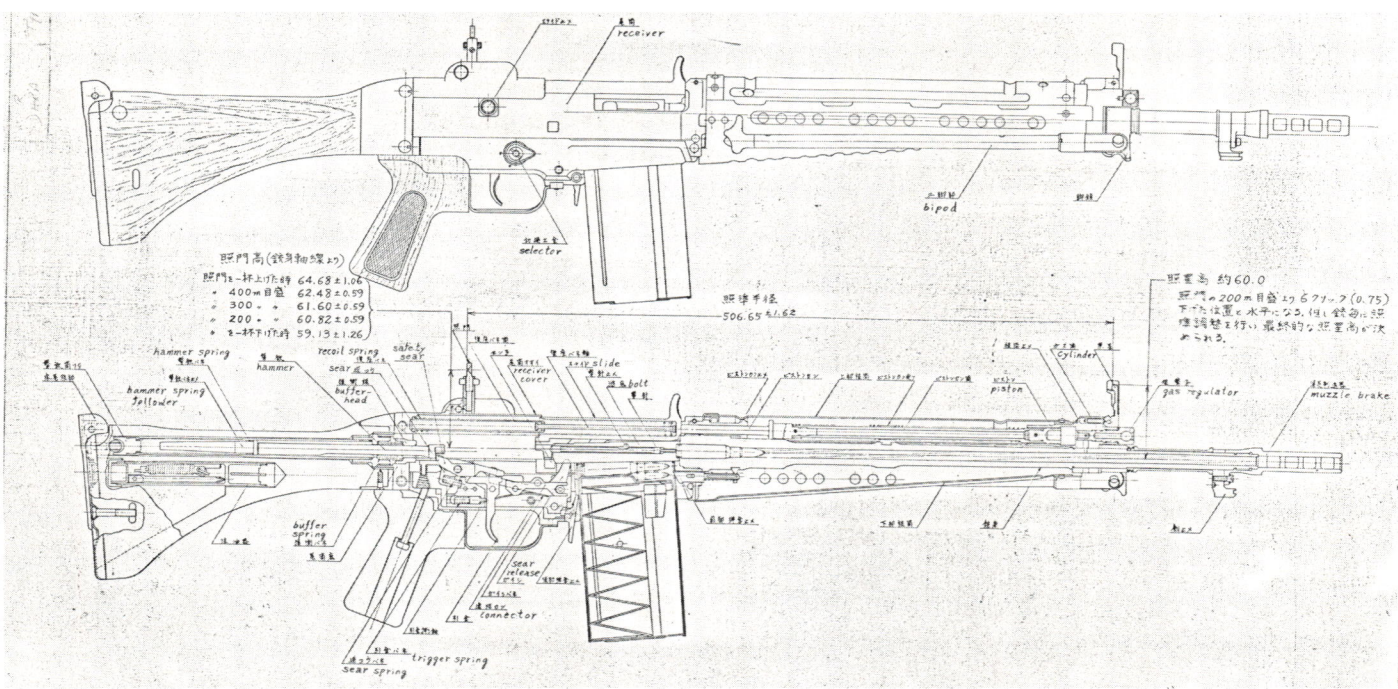

Composition of the Type 64 rifle

Japanese Type 64 rifle

DATA
Cartridge: 7.62mm x 51 (Reduced load)
Method of operation: Gas
Method of locking: Tilting block
Method of feed: 20-round detachable box magazine
Method of fire: Selective

WEIGHTS
Gun only, with bipod: 4.4kg
Magazine, empty: 0.24kg
Magazine, full: 0.72kg

LENGTHS
Rifle: 990mm
Barrel: 450mm

MECHANICAL FEATURES
Barrel: Regulator: Nil

Rifling: 4 grooves RH
Cooling: Air
Sights: **Foresight:** Blade
Rearsight: Aperture
Graduation: 200, 300 and 400 metres. Windage scale
Zeroing: Backsight

FIRING CHARACTERISTICS
Muzzle velocity: Reduced charge 700 metres/sec
Full charge 800 metres/sec
Muzzle energy: Reduced charge 243mkp
Full charge 317mkp
Rate of fire: Cyclic: 500 rounds/min
Emergency 100 rounds/min (limited to one minute)
Sustained rate 20 rounds/min
Range, maximum effective: 400 metres
Manufacturer: Howa Machinery Ltd, Shinkawacho, near Nagoya, Japan
Status: In production. In service with the Japanese Self Defence Force

KOREA (NORTH)

7.62mm TYPE 68 ASSAULT RIFLE

The regular army of North Korea is largely equipped with the Type 68 Assault Rifle. This is based on the Russian AKM but has distinct differences. Internally it does not have a rate of fire reducer but, like the AK-47, has no restraint on the hammer. Externally the forestock is not shaped with the two recesses – one on either side – for the fingers, that are a feature of all other AKM derivatives. However the greatest source of difference is the folding stock which consists of two perforated rails joined at the shoulder piece. This makes the North Korean Type 68 the lightest of the AKM rifles.

The North Korean copy of the Soviet AK-47 is still retained for use with militia units and support troops.

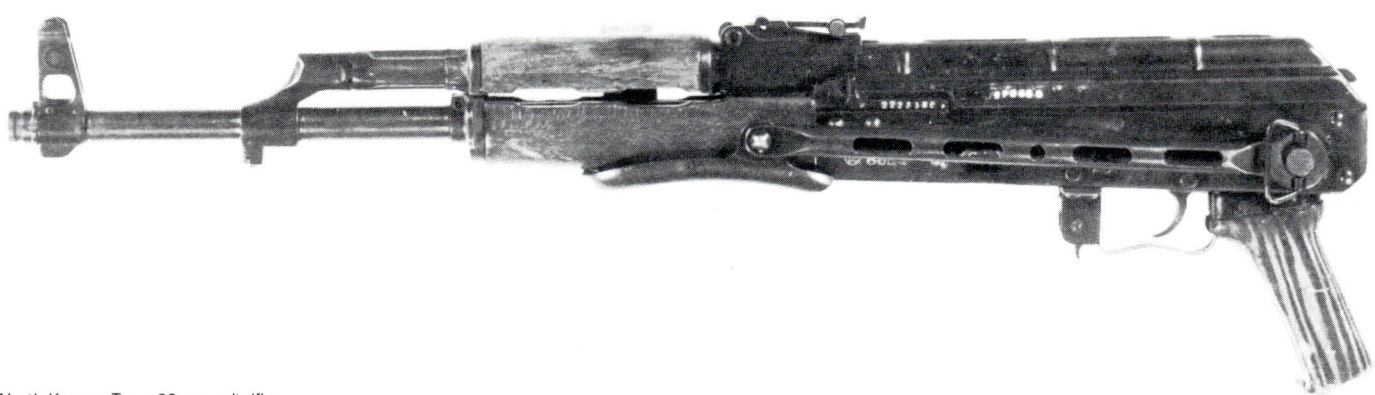

North Korean Type 68 assault rifle

PERFORATIONS

NO RAILS

North Korean Type 68 assault rifle. Note the perforated buttstock

North Korean AK-47 (RSAF)

NORWAY

NORWEGIAN RIFLES

The Norwegian Army was equipped with the Krag-Jorgensen rifle from Denmark, used with the 6.5mm rimless Mauser cartridge, made by Kongsberg. These were largely lost during the German Occupation in 1940.

After the war the Norwegian Army decided to adopt the German G3 rifle to replace the American, British and Mauser rifles that they had. The G3 is produced at Kongsberg. It differs from the standard Heckler and Koch in that to allow silent cocking, when required, the bolt is allowed forward under control and then finally closed by finger pressure on the grooves cut in the side of the bolt.

The Norwegian sniping rifle is also the Heckler and Koch.

Manufacturer: A/S Kongsberg Våpenfabrikk, N-3600 Kongsberg.

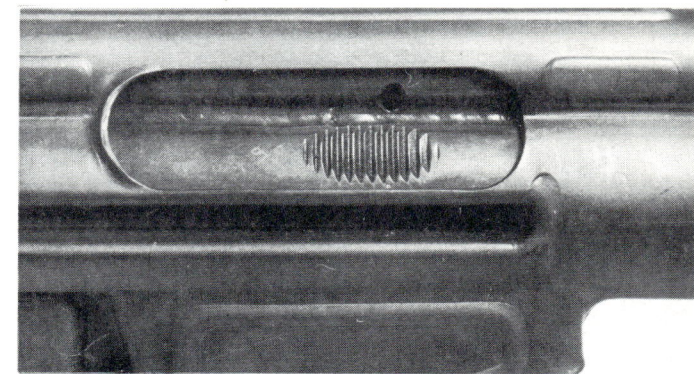

Norwegian G3 bolt closure

The G3 sniping rifle

POLAND

7.62mm PMK ASSAULT RIFLE

The bolt-operated rifles used by Poland between the two World Wars were basically Mauser, and similar to the German 98 pattern weapons.

After the Second World War the Polish Forces were equipped with the Mosin-Nagant Rifles but these were displaced by the Kalashnikov assault rifles as soon as these appeared.

The Polish-built copy of the Russian AK-47, known as the PMK, does not differ significantly from the Russian original. The variant described as the DGN-60 is described below.

The Polish AK-47 (RSAF)

7.62mm PMK-DGN-60 ASSAULT RIFLE

This is the PMK modified for grenade launching. The muzzle has been made cone shaped and threaded to take the LON-1 grenade launcher which is externally of 20mm diameter.

The gas cylinder has been modified to take a gas cut-off valve which prevents gas from the grenade cartridge reaching the operating piston. A special grenade-launching sight is attached to the standard rearsight. A 10-round magazine, which will hold only grenade cartridges, is used for

grenade launching. To absorb the considerable recoil the butt has been modified in shape and a boot fitted which goes into the firer's shoulder. The only mechanical change is the fitting to the rear of the breech cover of a securing catch to the return spring rod. This must be released before the rod can be pushed in to allow removal of the breech cover.

The Polish-made F1/N60 anti-personnel and the PGN-60 anti-tank grenades are used with the Polish PMK-DGN-60 rifle. It should be noted

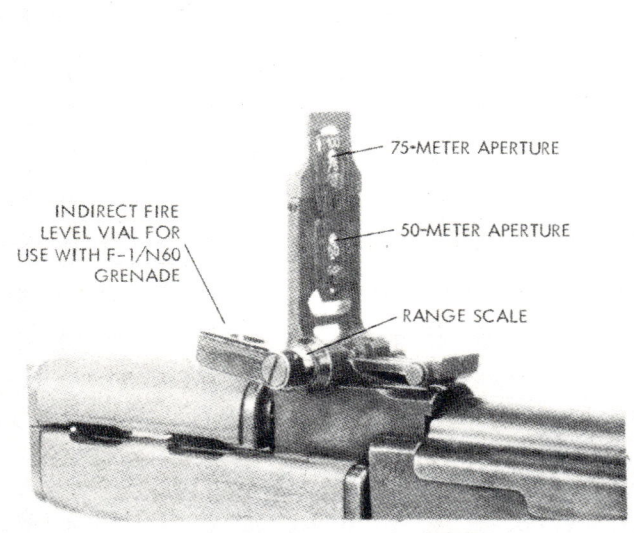

INDIRECT FIRE LEVEL VIAL FOR USE WITH F-1/N60 GRENADE

75-METER APERTURE

50-METER APERTURE

RANGE SCALE

(a) FOR 50- AND 75-METER FIRING (LEAF DOWN)

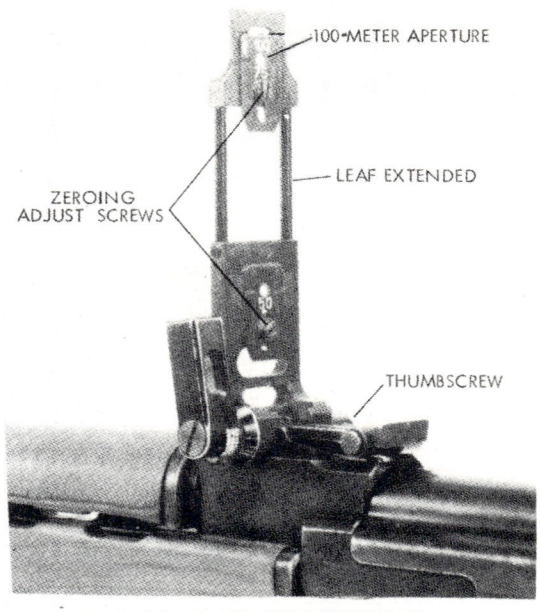

100-METER APERTURE

LEAF EXTENDED

ZEROING ADJUST SCREWS

THUMBSCREW

(b) FOR 50- AND 100-METER FIRING (LEAF UP)

Grenade launching sights (T. Smith)

that these grenades have 20mm internal diameters and will fit no other launcher. Similarly the conventional grenade with an internal diameter of 22mm should never be used from the Polish rifle.

The head of the grenade screws on to the tail boom. The F1/N60 anti-personnel grenades have no fins on this boom but the PGN-60 does.

The grenade cartridge is white tipped and crimped. Under no circumstances should any other cartridge be used.

Polish PMK-DGM-60 with LON-1 grenade launcher (RSAF)

7.62mm PMKM ASSAULT RIFLE

This is the Polish copy of the Soviet AKM. Like the latest Russian models it is fitted with a compensator at the muzzle. It cannot launch grenades and the muzzle is not coned.

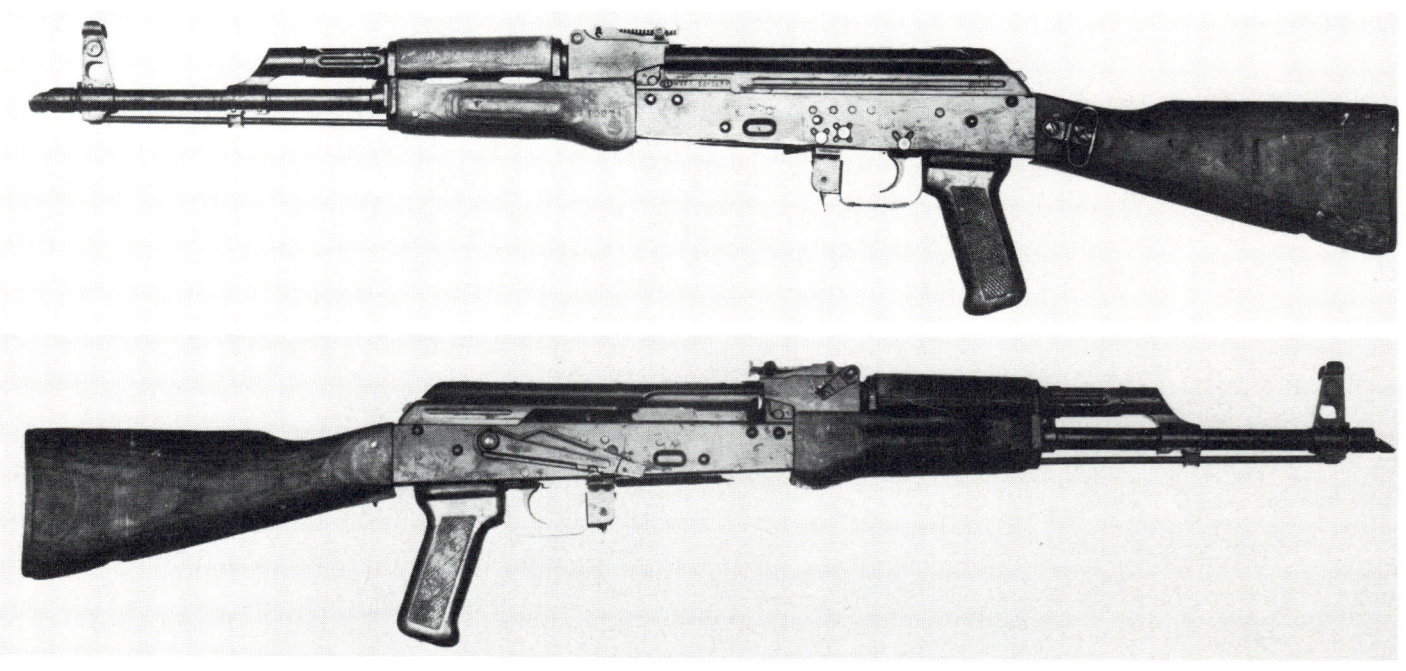

The Polish 7.62mm × 39mm PMKM is a copy of Soviet AKM. Note compensator

POLISH AK-47-BULGARIA

The Polish arsenals produced a number of copies of the Russian AK-47 which were manufactured for the Bulgarian Army. It is not known why this was done. It may have been a purely commercial transaction or there may have been some political significance.

The Bulgarian AK-47 produced in Poland

ROMANIA

ROMANIAN RIFLES

The Romanian Army has been equipped with the locally produced AK-47 copy, but this has now been relegated to Militia and reserve use.

The current assault rifle is the copy of the Soviet AKM. This may be readily recognised because it has a wooden forward pistol grip made from laminated material. In addition the usual Romanian markings appear on the selector – 'FA' for full auto and 'FF' on the lower position for single shot.

Romanian soldier with Romanian-built AKM

Romanian AKM

SPAIN

7.92mm CETME RIFLE

In 1944 and 1945 work was done in Germany to produce a cheap simple rifle. The StG 45(M) was developed by Mauser at Oberndorf am Neckar. The weapon was also known as the Gerat 06H or the MP 45(M)

The gun was of a delayed blowback type using a two-part bolt and a roller delay device. (The detail of how this works will be found in the section on the German G3 rifle.) After the war the French investigated this system at their development centre at Mulhouse and took the Mauser engineer Ludwig Vorgrimler to work on the project. He produced two breech mechanisms using the American .30 carbine cartridge.

After some years in France, Vorgrimler went to Spain and worked at the Centro de Estudios Tecnicos de Materiales(CETME) at Madrid. The development, started in 1950, was aimed at an operational requirement calling for an effective range of about 1,000m, an all-up weight of about 4kg and a recoil force for automatic fire, of about 0.75kg.

The last requirement ruled out the 7.92mm Mauser round which was the standard for rifles and LMGs in the Spanish forces. Instead, the round chosen, though still of 7.92mm calibre, used a very long, light, pointed bullet. This cartridge proved to be successful and the Dutch firm of Nederlandsche Wapen En Munitiefabrick of s'Hertenbosch took out an exploitation licence for the system. (This permitted them to demonstrate the rifle and supply it either by manufacture or through CETME.)

The development programme was set up to produce two assault rifles, the Model 1 with positive locking and a gas-operated mechanism and the Model 2 which used a delayed blowback system derived as indicated above, and described in more detail below. After a series of trials it was decided to adopt the Model 2 system.

The method of operation of this delayed blowback rifle is, briefly, as follows. The bolt consists of a light head and a more massive body. The head carries two rollers and the front of the bolt body is wedge-shaped. This forces the rollers out into the recess in the barrel extension. The rear part moves forward between the rollers bringing the firing pin to a position where it can reach the cap of the cartridge when it is struck by the hammer.

The gas pressure drives the cartridge case back in the fluted chamber

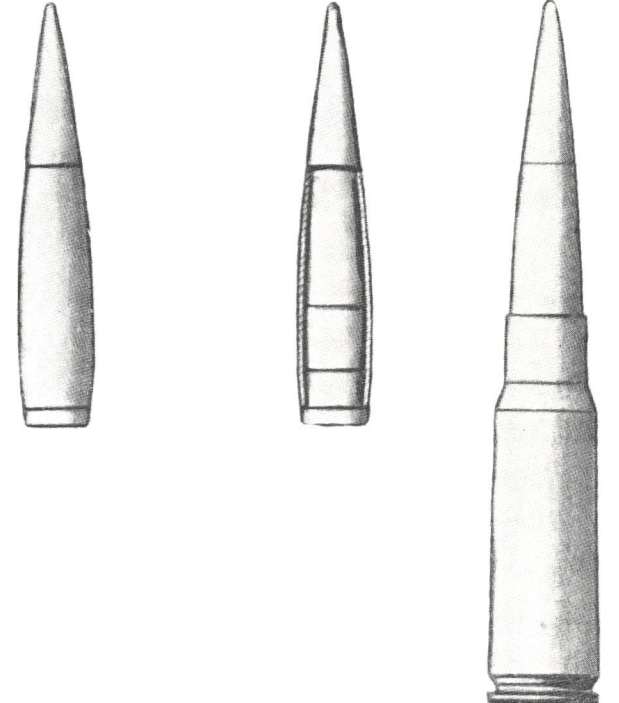

The CETME 7.92mm cartridge

CETME Assault Rifle Model 1 (gas operated)

CETME Assault Rifle Model 2. This was the delayed blowback weapon which was adopted as the basis for further development

and the base presses against the breech face. The rollers prevent movement of the bolt head but the recesses are so shaped that the rollers are forced in and press on the inclined planes of the bolt body and drive the bolt body back. When the rollers are fully in, the breech head and body are both driven back with a gap between them. The empty case is ejected and the return spring drives the bolt forward. The top round is fed into the chamber and the bolt face comes to rest. The wedge of the heavy bolt body drives the rollers out into their recesses and the gun is ready to fire again.

Model 2 was developed to operational standard and an experimental quantity was made having the following general characteristics.

Length: 970mm
Barrel: 435mm
Weight: 4.25kg without magazine
Magazine: 20-round or 30-round detachable box
Weight of empty magazine: 0.38 or 0.48kg
Rate of fire: 550 rounds/min cyclic. Selective fire mechanism
General: Minimal use of mechanical parts. Folding bipod usable as a handguard when folded

This was the first roller delay device rifle (RSAF)

7.62mm CETME ASSAULT RIFLES
MODELS A, B, 58, C and E

When the NATO countries decided to standardize the 7.62mm × 51 cartridge for small arms, the Spanish authorities decided that it would be advisable to use the same calibre for Spanish military weapons. It was considered, however, that the standard NATO round was unnecessarily powerful: accordingly, a new cartridge was developed having the same external dimensions as the NATO round but having a lighter bullet, a smaller charge and thus a lower muzzle velocity and energy than the NATO round. The characteristics of this round are compared with those of the standard NATO round, the short Mauser round and the CETME round developed for their 7.92mm rifle are compared in the following table. It should be noted, however, that the external dimensions of the two 7.62mm cartridges were made the same despite the other differences.

	Light CETME	Short Mauser	CETME/ NATO	NATO
Calibre:	7.92mm	7.92mm	7.62mm	7.62mm
Bullet weight:	6.8g	12.8g	7.3g	9.4g
length:	46mm	35mm	31mm	32.5mm
Charge weight:	1.8g	2.9g	1.8g	2.8g
Cartridge weight:	18g	27.4g	19g	24.5g
Muzzle velocity:	800m/s	750m/s	760m/s	780m/s
Muzzle energy:	222mkp	367mkp	215mkp	292mkp
Recoil impulse:	0.74kgs	1.26kgs	0.74kgs	1.04kgs

MODELS A & B

CETME developed a series of rifles in 7.62mm calibre. The first of these, the Model A, entered production in 1956 and was identical in most respects with the 7.92mm Model 2 described in the previous entry. It was followed, in 1958, by the Model B, also known as the Model 58, which incorporated several improvements including a grenade-launching fitment; the elimination of the hold-open feature whereby the gun was fired from the open-breech position (the objection to which was its mechanical complexity and the disturbance to the firer's-aim as the action went forward); and the compensating additions of a metal jacket to assist cooling and serve as a foregrip in place of the folded bipod. Model B was taken into service with all Spanish armed forces in 1958, and in the same year the licence previously held by NWM in the Netherlands was transferred to Germany and the development of what became the G.3 rifle was put in hand there.

In 1964 it was decided that the Spanish forces should adopt the standard NATO 7.62mm × 51 cartridge in place of the CETME/NATO round. Before this more powerful round could be used, however, certain modifications to the Model B/Model 58 rifle were necessary; and the result of this was the Model C, which is the current production and service version.

MODEL C

This is a selective-fire weapon using a 20-round detachable box

CETME Rifle Model A

magazine (5-round boxes are available for training) and, using the roller-locked delayed blowback system developed for the earlier weapons. The rifle is fitted with a combined flash eliminator/grenade launcher attachment, may be fitted with a bayonet, a telescopic sight or an infra-red sight, and has a case for cleaning tools in the cocking handle guide tube.

Two versions of the Model C are made: the standard version has a wooden handgrip and no bipod and the alternative version has a bipod and a metal handgrip. Accessories for either version include a magazine filler and a blank firing attachment which replaces the flash eliminator.

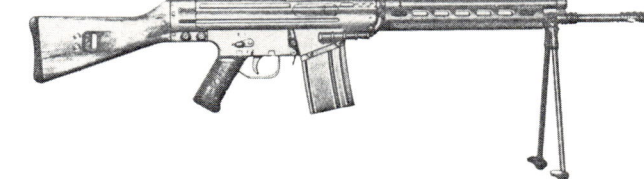

CETME Model B (Model 58)

OPERATION

The weapon is loaded by inserting the leading edge of a loaded

7.12in CETME Model C

magazine into the front of the magazine well and rotating it rearwards until the magazine catch engages (to remove the magazine the catch must be released either by pushing the magazine catch lever forward or by pressing the pushbutton located behind the magazine well.) With the magazine in position set the selector lever to either T (semi-automatic) or R (automatic) and pull the cocking handle (on the left of the rifle) fully to the rear and release it. When it is released, the bolt moves forward, strips a round from the magazine, chambers it and cocks the action, and the weapon is ready to fire. To render the weapon safe move the selector lever to S. When the weapon is thus cocked the cocking lever may be folded down.

If required the weapon may also be set in a safe condition with the bolt to the rear. To achieve this the first part of the cocking process is performed as before; but then, instead of the cocking lever being released it may be turned upwards into a recess at the rear of the guide tube, whereafter the action may be locked as before by setting the selector lever to S.

The arrangement of the roller locking device is shown (in the locked position) in the accompanying drawing. When the round is fired, the pressure on the bolt head is transmitted to the bolt carrier through the rollers. Until these rollers are clear of the recesses in the barrel extension the locking piece and bolt carrier are caused to move backwards faster than the bolt head, thus giving a substantial mechanical advantage to the return spring (not shown) and introducing the required initial delay. When the rollers are clear of the recesses the bolt head, locking piece and carrier move rearwards together, extracting the spent case, ejecting it and then returning to chamber a fresh round.

STRIPPING
(a) Remove the magazine.
(b) Draw the cocking handle to the rear, ensure that no round remains in the chamber and release the cocking handle.
(c) Remove the two attaching pins from the buttstock and store them in the hole drilled in the buttstock for the purpose.
(d) Withdraw the buttstock and return spring.
(e) Tilt the handgrip forwards, draw the bolt to the rear by means of the cocking handle and withdraw the bolt through the rear of the receiver.
(f) To strip the bolt, press the bolt head back until it is stopped by the carrier, then rotate it 180° anti-clockwise and remove it.
(g) Rotate and remove the locking piece.
(h) Extract the firing pin and spring.

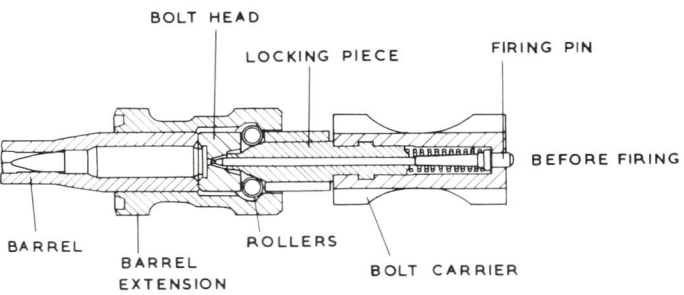

The CETME delay action and locking piece

No further field stripping should be attempted. Assembly is in the reverse order. After re-assembly the action should be checked by cocking and firing on an empty chamber before inserting a magazine.

DATA (Model C)
Cartridge: 7.62mm × 51 NATO
Operation: Delayed blowback using rollers
Feed: 20-round box magazine
Fire: Selective
Weight: 4.2kg with wooden handguard. 4.5kg with bipod and metal hand-guard
Weight of empty magazine: 0.275kg
Length: 1015mm
Barrel: 450mm
    Rifling: 4 groves RH. Twist 305mm
Sights: Foresight Protected blade
    Rearsight Turning leaf with V notch for 100m and aperture leaves for 200, 300, and 400m
    Sight radius 580mm
Muzzle velocity: 780m/sec
Muzzle energy: 23mkp
Rate of fire: 550-650 rounds/min cyclic
Effective range: 600m

CETME Model E

MODEL D

The designation Model D was applied to an intermediate development stage between Models C and E and was used only within the CETME organisation.

MODEL E

This is the latest in the CETME 7.62mm series and embodies several improvements over the Model C. These include improved extraction, improved sights, the introduction of a plastic handgrip and the provision of a hold-open device when the magazine is empty. An experimental quantity has been made but the weapon is not in production.

Manufacturer (all models): Centro de Estudios Tecnicos de Materiales Especiales – INI (CETME), Padilla, 46-Madrid.

Status:

Models A & B. No longer made and obsolete
Model C. In production and in service in Spain
Model D. Never in production
Model E. Experimental only at present
General. CETME rifles have been supplied at various times to Denmark, Norway, Pakistan, Portugal and Sweden.

5.56mm CETME ASSAULT RIFLE MODEL L

This selective-fire weapon in 5.56mm (.223) calibre embodies CETME's extensive experience in developing their range of similar weapons in 7.92mm and 7.62mm calibre. A special feature is the introduction of a controlled burst facility in addition to the usual semi-automatic and automatic functions.

Two versions of the weapon have been designed – a standard model with a fixed buttstock and a short-barrelled version with a telescopic stock. Standard magazine capacity is 20 rounds but 10-round and 30-round magazines can be supplied. Standard sights are calibrated for 100, 200, 300 and 400m but a variety of more elaborate telescopic or night sights may be fitted.

OPERATION

Operation of the automatic mechanism is by a delayed blowback system substantially the same as that used on earlier CETME weapons, delay being achieved by the use of rollers as before. An important departure from the earlier systems, however, is the incorporation of an additional spring-loaded locking lever in the bolt support assembly to provide additional initial resistance to the blowback pressure. When the breech is locked a projection on the forward end of this lever, which is spring-loaded at its rear end and pivoted on the bolt support assembly, is interposed between a rearward-inclined upward projection at the rear of the bolt head and a downward projection from the upper part of the bolt support. When, after firing, the roller action produces the normal differential rearward motion of the bolt head and the firing-pin holder, the bolt support moves with the firing-pin holder and then applies pressure to the forward face of the locking lever to close the gap between the bolt support and bolt head projections. This pressure causes the forward projection on the locking lever to ride up the inclined face of the bolt head projection and thus rotates the lever about its pivot against the pressure of its spring. In so doing it adds to the resistance to the initial rearward motion of the bolt mechanism: after the lever projection has reached the top of the bolt head projection, however, it slides back to the top of this projection, thus permitting the gap between the bolt head and bolt carrier projections to be closed and offering no further resistance to the recoil action. When the bolt comes forward again at the end of the automatic cycle the locking lever projection is re-inserted into its gap by the pressure of its spring.

TRIGGER MECHANISM

In general principle, the operation of the trigger mechanism for single shots (T) or normal automatic fire (R) is similar to that of the German G3 rifle: similarly the safety setting (S) of the selector lever provides a conventional impediment to the operation of the trigger. The short burst (r) mechanism employs a ratcheted sear mechanism (which is disengaged for the other three settings of the selector) but is unusual in that it is operated by the tail of the spring-loaded ejector.

STRIPPING

To strip the Model L first remove the magazine and check that there is no round in the breech, then proceed as follows.

(a) Remove the two buttstock attachment pins and store them in the spare holes in the buttstock.
(b) Holding the forepart of the weapon with one hand, pull the buttstock to the rear to release it and the recoil damper assembly.

5.56mm CETME Model L Assault Rifle

Short version of the Model L with stock retracted

(c) Pull the cocking handle backwards and withdraw the complete bolt assembly from the rear of the receiver.
(d) Remove the handgrip pin and pull the handgrip back about 1.5mm along the axis of the weapon until it comes to its stop. Remove the safety pin and withdraw the firing mechanism by pulling the handgrip at right-angles to the barrel.
(e) Remove the handguard pin and pull the handguard towards the muzzle to separate the handguard and main body assemblies.
(f) To disassemble the bolt assembly, first hold the bolt support firmly in the left hand and press the bolt head with the left hand until the rollers emerge, then rotate the bolt head 180° anticlockwise and pull to separate it from the support.
(g) Turn the firing pin carrier 90° clockwise whereupon the tail end of the carrier will be driven out into the bolt support trough by the firing pin spring. The pin and spring can then be easily withdrawn.
(h) No further stripping is recommended for normal field operation. Assembly is in the reverse order.

DATA

(Characteristics peculiar to the short versions shown in parenthesis)
Cartridge: 5.56mm
Operation: Delayed blowback
Delay: Rollers and locking lever
Feed: 20-round detachable box magazine as standard. 10-round and 30-round versions available.
Fire: 3-selective – semi-automatic, controlled burst and automatic
Weight (unloaded): 3.4kg
Weight of empty 20-round magazine: 0.2kg
Length: 925mm (665mm or 860mm)
Barrel: 400mm (320mm)
   Rifling: 6 grooves RH. Pitch 305mm

CETME Model L with bipod and telescopic sight

Sights: Foresight Protected conical post
       Rearsight Rotating disc with open notch for 100m and apertures
       for 200, 300 and 400m
       Zeroing Elevation: adjust foresight. Line: rearsight has adjustable
       spindle
       Sight Radius 440mm
Muzzle velocity: 920m/sec (850m/sec)
Rate of fire: 700-800 rounds/min cyclic
Manufacture: Centro de Estudios Tecnicas de Materiales Especiales-INI
(CETME), Padilla, 46-Madrid.

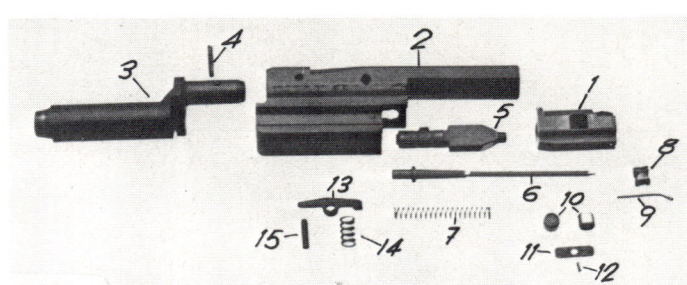

Components of the bolt sub-assembly **(1)** *Bolt head;* **(2)** *Bolt support;* **(3)** *Bridge;* **(4)** *Pin;* **(5)** *Firing pin holder;* **(6)** *Firing pin;* **(7)** *Firing pin spring;* **(8)** *Extractor;* **(9)** *Extractor spring;* **(10)** *Rollers;* **(11)** *Rollers' support;* **(12)** *Elastic pin;* **(13)** *Locking lever;* **(14)** *Locking lever spring;* **(15)** *Locking lever pivot pin*

SWEDEN

6.5mm AG42 (LJUNGMAN) RIFLE

The AG42 was in service in 1942 and was the first rifle to use the principle of direct gas action. No piston was employed but the gas travelled back along a tube and impinged on the bolt carrier which was driven to the rear. After a short free travel the carrier picked up the bolt and lifted the rear end out of engagement with the locking surface in the bottom of the receiver. The carrier then moved the bolt to the rear. The empty case was extracted and ejected; the return spring drove the bolt forward to chamber the next round and the bolt dropped to lock into the receiver.

From this design came a number of weapons using the same principle – the French MAS 49 and 49/56 and, more recently, the Armalite AR-10 and AR-15.

The AG42 was found to need modifications to the trigger and it was then re-named the AG 42B. The Ljungman rifle was taken into service in Denmark as the Madsen-Ljungman rifle. This differed in having the gas tube wrapped around the barrel. It was also manufactured in Egypt as the Hakim using the 7.92mm cartridge.

DATA
Cartridge: 6.5mm × 55

Method of operation: Gas-direct action
Method of locking: Tilting block
Method of feed: 10-round non detachable box magazine
Method of fire: Self-loading
Weight: 4.71kg
Length: 214mm
Barrel: 622mm
       Rifling: 6 grooves RH
Sights: Foresight: Barleycorn
       Rearsight: Leaf. Aperture
Muzzle velocity: 750 metres/sec
Muzzle energy: 258mkp
Rate of fire: SS: 40 rounds/min
Range, maximum effective: 600 metres
Manufacturer: Carl Gustafs, Gevrärsfactori, Eskilstuna
Status: No longer manufactured. Being replaced by the Swedish-manufactured G3. See text.

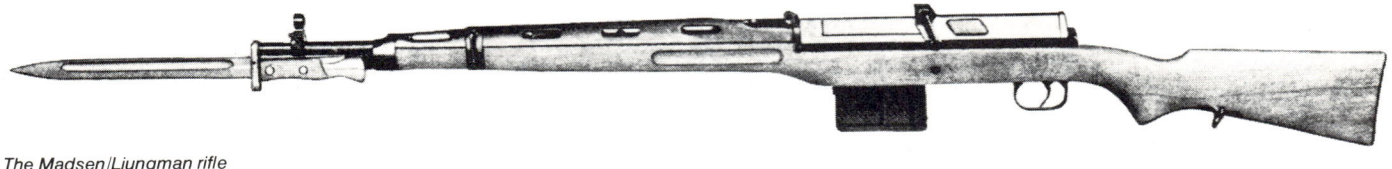

The Madsen/Ljungman rifle

7.62mm G3 RIFLE

The German G3 rifle is made in Sweden by FFV – Forenade Fabriksverken, Huvudkontoret at Eskilstuna. In all essentials it is the standard weapon.

5.56mm MKS ASSAULT RIFLE

One of several recently-introduced weapons exhibiting radical departures from conventional rifle design concepts, the Swedish MKS assault rifle has been developed with the dual objectives of providing a handy and effective weapon for use in modern combat conditions and of being suitable for manufacture in the less technologically advanced countries of the world – the latter objective being, of course, related to the Swedish restrictions on arms exports.

A light, compact, gas-operated, selective-fire weapon, the MKS features a combined pistol grip and magazine holder, a folding butt – which, in the folded position provides the firer with a forward handgrip for use when firing from the hip – and a choice of rifle or carbine band lengths. The weapon fires from a closed breech in the positive forward locking by a six-lug rotary bolt; the gas system is piston-operated and the gas flow can be regulated: the cocking lever is on the top of the receiver and is thus equally convenient for right-handed or left-handed firers.

Because the receiver is not subjected to high firing stresses it is made of light-gauge metal but the general construction of the weapon is robust: weight reduction has been achieved by compact design, not by the use of light alloys or insufficiently strong components. An important feature is the compact design of the receiver and firing mechanism, the latter being positioned below the breech instead of in the customary rear position.

DATA
(Characteristics of the carbine, where they differ from those of the rifle are shown in parenthesis).
Cartridge: 5.56mm × 45
Operation: Gas, piston-operated with regulator
Locking: Rotating lugs
Feed: 30-round detachable box magazine in pistol grip

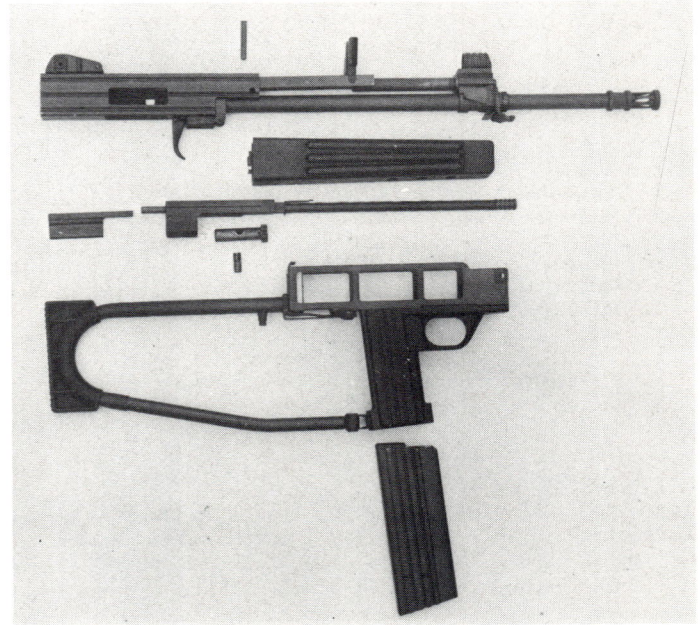

MKS stripped

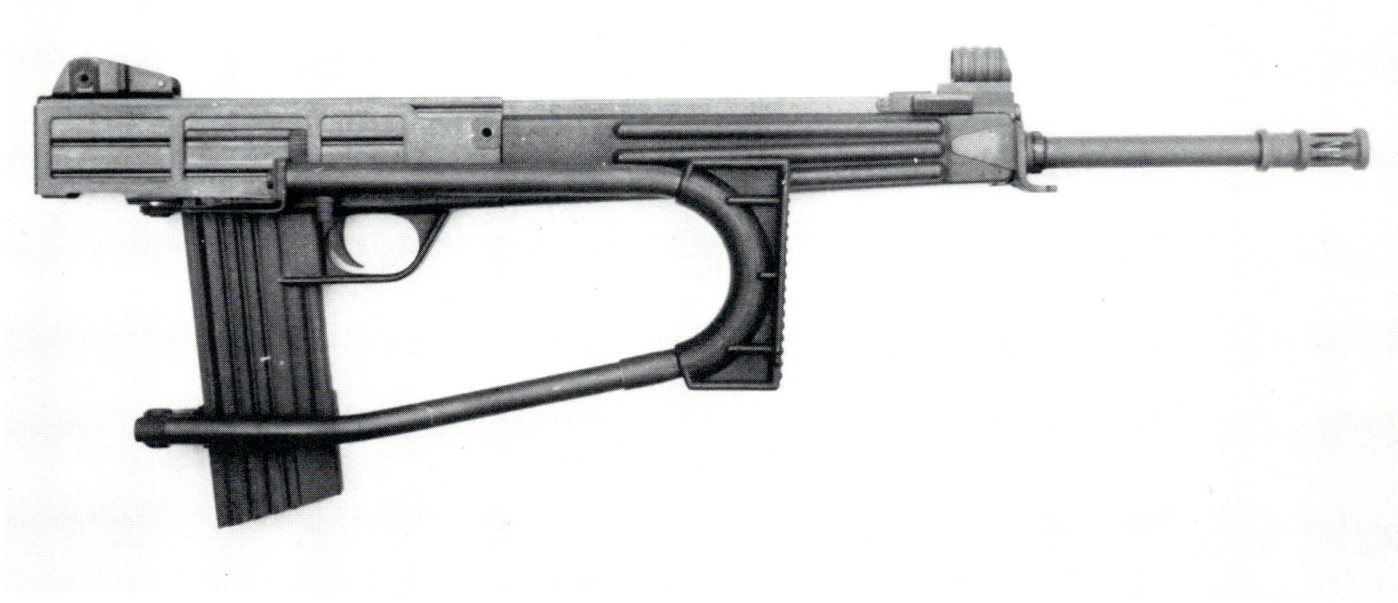

MKS Assault Rifle with stock folded to give forward grip

MKS Carbine with stock extended

Fire: Selective
Weight, empty: 2.75kg (2.36kg)
      loaded and with sling: 3.36kg (2.97kg)
Length: 868mm (751mm) with stock open: 634mm (517mm) with stock folded
Barrel: 467mm (350mm)
Sights: Foresight: Blade
      Rearsight: Aperture 250 or 400m
      Sight radius: 435mm

Muzzle velocity: 975m/sec (925m/sec)
Rate of fire: 700-1100 rounds/min, cyclic
Manufacturer: Interdynamic AB, Stockholm
Status: Not known

SWITZERLAND

7.62mm SG510-4 RIFLE

The SIG Swiss Industrial Company of Neuhausen Rhinefalls started manufacturing infantry weapons in 1860. It made the Swiss National rifle, the Vetterelli, designed by the Director of the SIG small arms factory, in 1869.

When the Swiss Army adopted the Schmidt-Rubin straight pull rifle in 1889 SIG made some of the parts. In 1906 SIG entered into consultations with General Mondragon of Mexico and in 1911 they produced the Mondragon SL rifle for the Mexican Army. They can probably claim that they were the first firm to mass produce a self-loading rifle.

After this SIG developed a number of rifles and sub-machine guns and the names of famous designers such as Kiraly, Endel and Gaetzi became associated with their weapons.

In the early 1950s their director Rudolf Amsler, produced the AM55 which was a blowback-operated rifle using a roller-action delay and was based to some extent on the German Sturmgewehr 45 assault rifle. This rifle was adopted by the Swiss Army as the Stgw 57 and replaced the Schmidt Rubin bolt-operated rifle.

The SG 510 series was developed from the AM55 and consisted of:

The SG 510-1 firing the 7.62 × 51 NATO cartridge.

The SG 510-2 firing the same cartridge but lighter in construction with a correspondingly high recoil.

The SG 510-3 firing the Soviet 7.62 × 39 cartridge and

The SG 510-4 using the 7.62 × 51 NATO round.

The SG 510-3 and 510-4 differ only in the cartridge they use and the resulting dimensions and weights.

DESCRIPTION

The SG 510-4 is a delayed blowback-operated rifle utilising a two-part block and delay rollers to hold up the breech face.

The body of the gun is made from pressings wrapped round and hard-soldered. The rear end of the receiver has been strengthened to take the butt, with the return spring, and the front end has a strengthened section to house the breech and the roller seatings. The roller seatings may be taken out and replaced when worn or when the feeler gauge, inserted between the two parts of the breech block when closed, shows excessive play.

The barrel is made by the cold swaging or 'hammering' process. In this the conventional process of deep drilling the forging and then rifling the interior of the barrel by drawing a cutter through the bore, is not followed. Instead the forging is made about half the length of the finished barrel and considerably thicker. It is drilled and a mandrel inserted. This has the rifling grooves raised on its surface. When the mandrel is in place a series of hammers strikes the outside of the barrel. The barrel is gradually elongated as the mandrel passes up until it is full length. The 'clapping' process impresses the rifling into the barrel and at the same time not only is a very good surface imparted but both the bore and the outside surface are work hardened. The grain flow is also improved.

The barrel has integral gas rings for grenade launching off the muzzle, and a muzzle brake to reduce recoil velocity is incorporated in the barrel. This also acts as a flash suppressor. The rear part of the barrel is surrounded by a perforated casing. A bipod is suspended behind the foresight and can be stowed, if so required, by folding the legs and rotating the bipod until the legs lie along the top of the barrel.

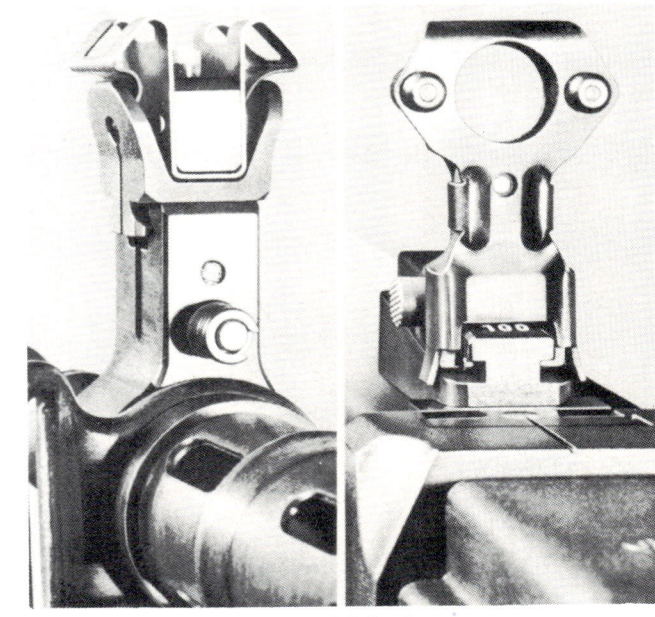

*Night front sight **(left)** and night rear sight fitted*

The foresight is a pillar and the rearsight an aperture. The rearsight has press locks which allow the frame to be moved up or down the sight bed to the selected range. The front sight mount can be moved across in a dovetail for lateral zeroing. For elevation zeroing the Allen key provided is used to screw the pillar in or out.

Night sights can be fitted. The front sight fits into the protectors and is held by springs. The aiming point is a luminous spot. The rearsight fits over the sight frame and has a large aperture. The sights together with the tools, gauge, sight spanner and cleaning kit, go into the pistol grip for stowage.

The telescopic sight is carried on a mount which clamps on to the top of

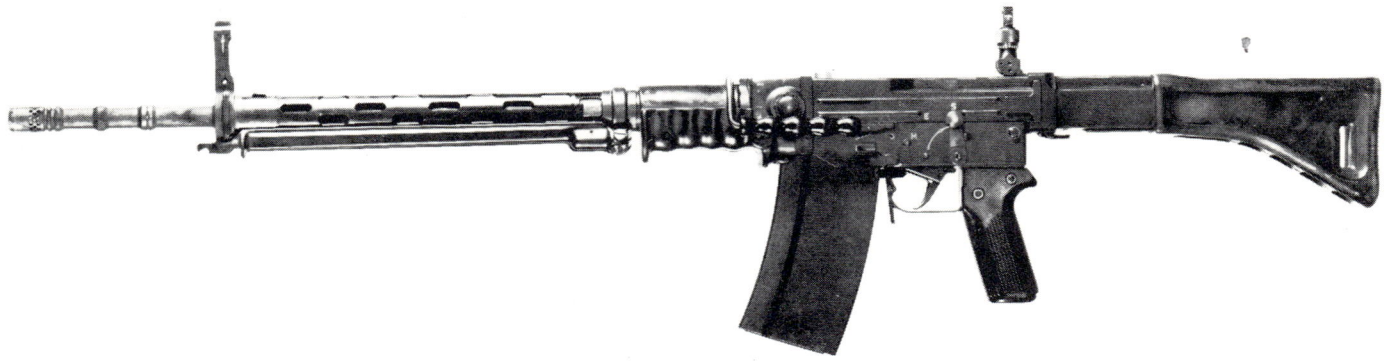

The Swiss service rifle. The 7.5mm StGW 57

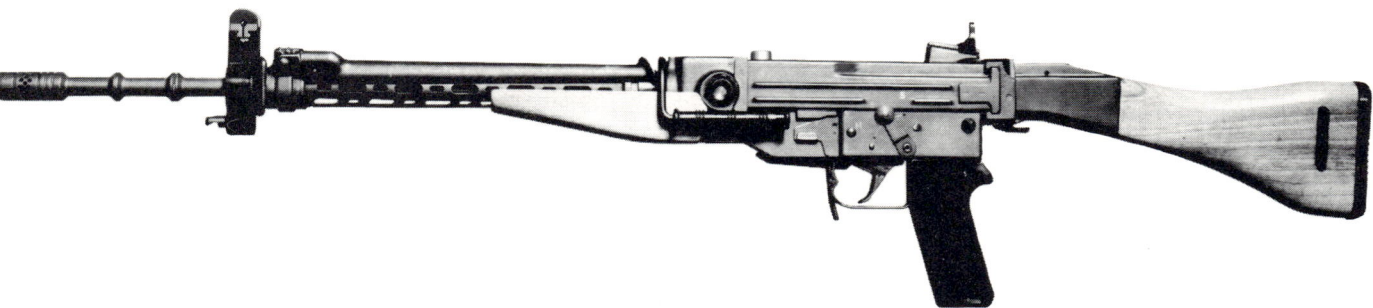

The SIG 510-4 7.62mm rifle

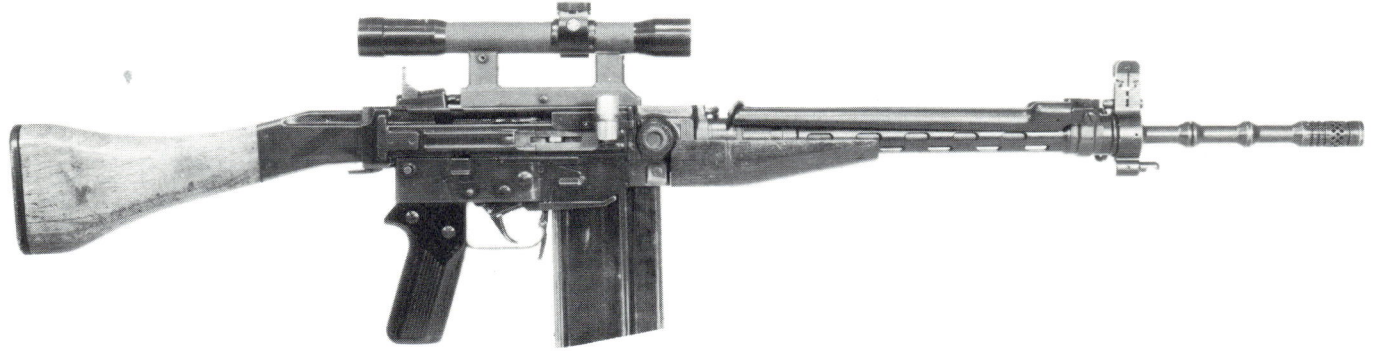

SIG 510-4 with infra-red sight

Sniping version

the receiver. It has a 4× magnification. An infra-red sight or an image intensifier sight can also be fitted.

A long arctic trigger is permanently fitted. It is also used for grenade firing. When not in use it hinges up flat under the receiver. When pushed down it has a short projecting arm which operates the normal trigger.

A blank firing device can be fitted over the muzzle for training. A bayonet can be fitted to the lug under the collar below the foresight. A ring fits over the muzzle brake.

The rifle will fire Energa type grenades using a ballistite cartridge. These are usually contained in a special magazine which takes the place of the normal one. This helps to ensure a ball round is not fired into the grenade.

The SG510-4 has been exported extensively to South America. It is the standard weapon for the Military Forces of Chile and the Bolivian Army.

OPERATION

The magazine is withdrawn from the rifle by pressing the release catch situated in front of the trigger guard. The magazine holds 20 rounds and is loaded normally by pressing the cartridges in, one at a time, from the top. There is a magazine filler issued with the rifle which allows filling from chargers. The loaded magazine is placed in the magazine well and pushed home until the catch clicks. The gun is loaded by pulling back and then releasing the T-shaped cocking handle; the bolt comes back, the hammer is cocked and held by the sear. On its forward travel the bolt chambers the cartridge, the extractor grips the cannelure and the gun is ready for action. The bolt is a two-part type with a light bolt and a heavier body. The bolt head

carries two light rollers. These are of unusual shape since they are not simply cylindrical in section but have small pivoting pieces. These are engaged in the bolt head. When the round is chambered the bolt head movement ceases and the bolt body forcing forward is able to pass between the rollers. The front face of the bolt body is wedge-shaped and the rollers are rotated out into recesses in the receiver. The gun fires from a closed breech and so the cartridge remains in the chamber, held by the bolt face, until the trigger is operated.

When the gas pressure is developed the bullet is forced up the bore and the cartridge case is driven back. The chamber is fluted and the case floats on a film of gas. This cuts down the friction between case and wall and prevents the elongation of the case caused when the neck expands and grips the wall and the gas pressure forces the cartridge head back. This can well produce separated cases.

The gas pressure on the breech face forces the rollers to the rear face of their recesses and the angle of the recesses forces the rollers inwards against the inclined faces of the bolt body. Due to the selected angle of the wedge, the bolt body is accelerated back and the two parts of the bolt are separated. When the rollers are clear of the recesses the entire bolt is drawn back by the residual impulse with a displacement between the two parts. The empty case is held to the breech face by the extractor. The ejector is of an unusual type. It is a rocking system attached to the top of the bolt head and as the bolt recoils the ejector contacts a ramp on the left wall of the receiver and the case is pushed through the ejection slot on the right of the receiver. This method is less violent than the usual fixed ejector system. The return spring is compressed.

The bolt comes up against the rear plate and the compressed return spring forces it forward. The bolt picks up the next round and chambers it.

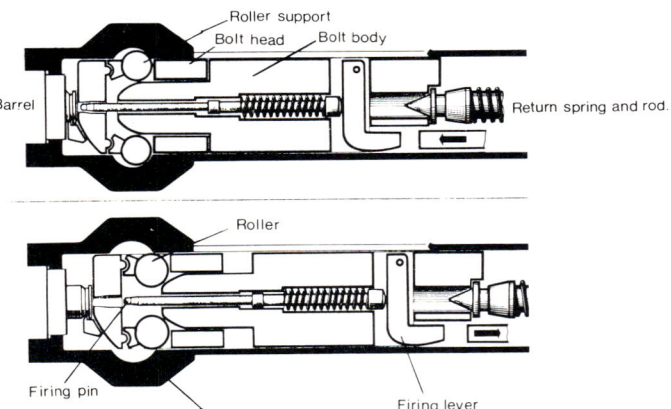

Before and after firing

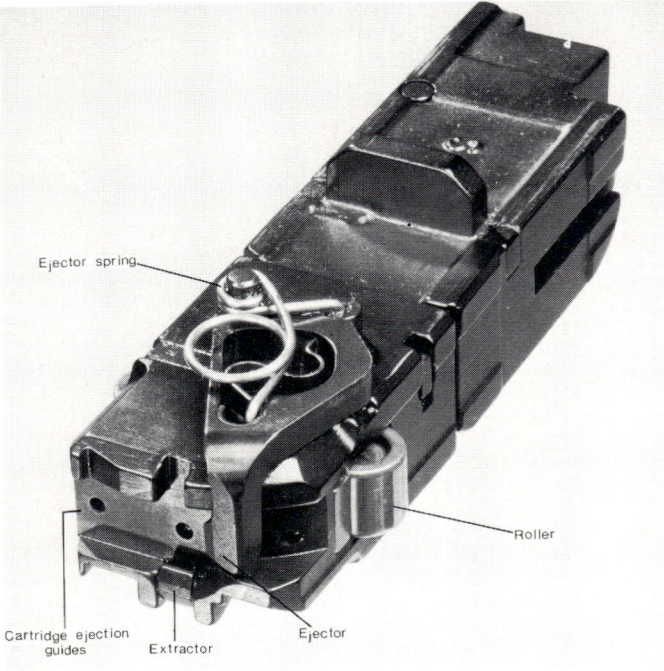

The bolt of the SIG SG510-4

THE TRIGGER AND FIRING MECHANISM

The rifle produces selctive fire, i.e. it can be fired at either single shot or full auto. The trigger mechanism is of simple design and unlike most modern rifles does not owe its origin to Garand's design for the M1 .30-06 rifle. It is based on the provision of a sear with an elongated slot through which passes an axis pin. A spring tends at all times to force the sear forward. The trigger is a pressing with a step at the rear. When the trigger is rotated the step lifts the rear end of the sear and the nose moves down out of the notch in the hammer and the hammer rotates forward to fire a round.

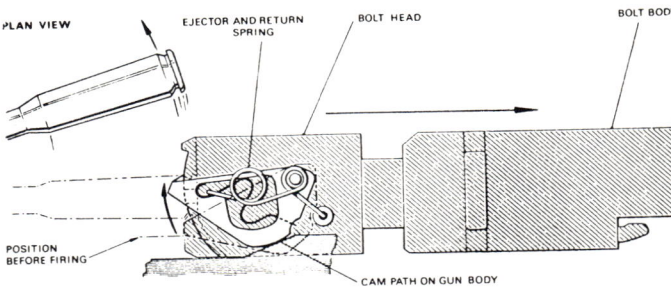

The ejector of the SG510-4

SINGLE SHOT FIRE

As soon as the hammer has gone forward the sear is pushed forward by its spring and it moves off the step of the trigger and lies on the flat portion in front of it. When the hammer is rotated back it is caught by the sear engaging in the notch. The powerful hammer spring pushes the sear back against the front face of the step. Another round cannot be fired until the trigger is released. As soon as the trigger step drops, the sear is able to move back over the top of it. Pulling the trigger lifts the tail of the sear, depresses the nose, and another round is fired – provided the bolt is fully home and the rear part has closed fully up to the front part.

AUTOMATIC FIRE

When the change lever is rotated to 'auto', the step at the rear of the trigger is able to rise considerably higher and this depresses the nose of the sear much further when it moves out of the hammer notch. As a result, when the hammer comes back it has no contact at all with the sear. It is caught by a quite separate safety sear and held back until the rear part of the two-part block comes forward to push the rollers out into their recesses. This final forward movement depresses the safety sear and releases the hammer. Thus the firing is controlled by the bolt closing position which satisfies the requirement for mechanical safety before firing. As soon as the trigger is released the sear moves up and catches the hammer on its next rearward rotation, and holds it back.

When the selector lever is rotated to 'safe', the shaft rotates over the rear of the trigger and prevents it from rising.

The massive hammer is mounted on the left of the receiver very close to the wall. It is therefore not operating down the centre line of the bore and it cannot reach the firing pin. Instead it hits the short end of an L-shaped bar which reaches right across the breech block and is pivoted on the far side from the hammer. The centre of the transverse bar hits the firing pin and this in turn hits the cap of the case.

STRIPPING

(1) The magazine is removed by pressing in the catch behind the magazine. The cocking handle is withdrawn and the chamber and feedway inspected.
(2) The catch under the receiver, behind the pistol grip, is lifted. The butt can then be rotated anti-clockwise through 45 degrees and pulled off to the rear.
(3) The cocking handle can be retracted and the bolt withdrawn.
(4) The trigger group and pistol grip come off after sliding the releasing pin to the right.
(5) Separate the two parts of the bolt.

The Stgw 57 stripped

DATA (SG 510-4)
Cartridge: 7.62mm × 51
Method of operation: Delayed blowback
Method of delay: Rollers
Method of feed: Magazine (20-round)
Method of fire: Selective

WEIGHTS
Gun only: 4.25kg
Sling: 114g
Magazine empty (20-round): 300g
Bayonet and scabbard: 300g
Telescopic sight and mount: 840g
Gun with bipod: 4.45kg

LENGTHS
Gun overall: 1,016mm
Barrel: 505mm
Rifling: 305mm

MECHANICAL FEATURES
Barrel: Rifling: No regulator. 4 grooves RH. 1 turn in 305mm
Sights: Foresight: Cylindrical post
Rearsight: Aperture
Graduation: 100-600 metres with 100-metre increments
Zeroing: Foresight
Sight radius: 593mm

DATA (SG 510-3)
As SG 510-4 except
Cartridge: 7.62mm × 39
Method of feed: Magazine (30-round)

WEIGHTS
Gun only: 3.75kg

Magazine empty (20-round): 343g
Telescopic sight and mount: 797g
Gun with bipod: 4.0kg

LENGTHS
Gun overall: 887mm
Barrel: 420mm
Rifling: 240mm

MECHANICAL FEATURES
Sights: Graduation: 100-500 metres with 100-metre increments
Sight radius: 508mm

FIRING CHARACTERISTICS
Muzzle velocity:	SG510-4,	790 metres/sec
	SG510-3,	700 metres/sec
Muzzle energy:	SG510-4,	305mkp
	SG510-3,	200mkp
Recoil energy:	SG510-4,	1mkp
	SG510-3,	0.7mkp
Chamber pressure:	SG510-4,	465kg/cm²
	SG510-3,	3,465kg/cm²
Rate of fire: Cyclic:	SG510-4,	600 rounds/min
	SG510-3,	525 rounds/min
Auto:	SG510-4,	80 rounds/min
	SG510-3,	90 rounds/min
SS:	SG510-4,	40 rounds/min
	SG510-3,	40 rounds/min
Range, maximum effective:	SG510-4,	600 metres
	SG510-3,	400 metres

Accessories: Telescopic sight. Blank firing attachment. Cleaning Kit. Night sights. ATk grenade sight
Manufacturer: SIG Swiss Industrial Co., Neuhausen Rhinefalls
Status: No longer in production. Order for Swiss Army completed. In service (Stgw 57) with Swiss Army. In service in Chile. In service in Bolivia

5.56mm SG530-1 RIFLE

When the .223 (5.56mm) cartridge was adopted by the US Army, various European countries manufactured rifles in this calibre in the hope – and in some cases expectation – that this cartridge would be adopted for NATO.

Amongst the firms producing a .223 rifle was SIG. At the time (1963) they were collaborating with Beretta who were producing parts for the SG510-4 and a joint study was set up between the two firms. It was soon found that agreement could not be reached on such technical essentials as the method of operation and type of locking. With their experience of the SG510-4 SIG favoured blowback operation using a roller delay whilst Beretta considered a gas-operated weapon would prove to be best. Eventually the two firms parted company and SIG produced the SG530-1 and Beretta the AR 70/.223. Externally there is some similarity between these weapons so early studies may at least have been partially fruitful.

SIG found their blowback design was very prone to 'cook off' and also that even with the fluted chamber there were extraction problems. Eventually they retained the rollers but converted them to locking rollers (no longer delay rollers) and introduced gas operation.

The weapon was eventually produced in very limited numbers but no substantial sales have been made. This is in part due to the high cost but also because very few countries are making a move to change from the 7.62mm × 51 NATO cartridge to any other until such time as NATO produces a firm STANAG on small arms ammunition for a future system.

OPERATION
The 30-round magazine is removed by pushing forward the catch in front of the trigger guard. The cartridges are pressed straight in and the magazine replaced by putting the front end into the magazine well and rotating the magazine until the catch engages.

The cocking handle is located well forward on the top left of the barrel housing. When it is retracted the bolt travels back over the rounds in the magazine and when it is released the bolt is driven forward and chambers the cartridge. The extractor grips the rim of the case. The rifle fires from the closed breech position and when the round is chambered it remains in the breech until the trigger is operated. The firing pin strikes the cap and some of the resultant propellant gas is diverted into the cylinder above the barrel and drives back the piston. There is a short delay whilst the gas pressure is falling and then the piston pulls back a locking bar which holds the rollers out into recesses in the receiver. As soon as the locking bar has moved back and is no longer holding the roller the residual pressure on the breech face forces the block back and the rollers are driven in. The piston, with the assistance of the blowback force, carries the breech block to the rear. The empty case remains on the bolt face until the fixed ejector throws it out to the right of the gun. The return spring lies inside the piston and has a long guide with a back plate which is attached to the rear of the receiver casing. This allows any selected butt to be fitted. As the piston moves rearward the return spring is compressed and drives the piston and bolt forward at the end of the recoil stroke. The bolt picks up a round and after chambering it comes to rest. The piston continues on and the locking bar pushes the rollers out and then continues forward to lock them in position.

The rifle can be loaded with a ballistite cartridge to launch the Strim grenade. The grenade – anti-personnel or anti-tank – slips straight over the flash eliminator and no spigot is required.

STRIPPING
The magazine is removed, the weapon is cocked and the chamber checked.

The take-down pin is located at the rear of the receiver. It is pushed right through and the butt stock forced down. The return spring can be withdrawn and cocking the weapon withdraws the piston and bolt.

Re-assembly is in reverse order.

The first SG530-1 had a short barrel and plastic furniture. Note the shape of the magazine

The short-barrelled rifle field stripped

DATA
Cartridge: 5.56mm × 45
Method of operation: Gas
Method of locking: Rollers
Method of feed: Magazine
Method of fire: Selective

WEIGHTS
Gun only: 3.27kg
Magazine empty: 0.66kg
Gun loaded 30-round magazine: 3.86kg
Trigger pull: 3.18kg

LENGTHS
Overall length, fixed butt: 953mm
Barrel: 391mm

MECHANICAL FEATURES
Barrel: Regulator: Nil

Rifling: 4 grooves RH. 1 turn in 305mm
Sights: Foresight: Cylindrical post
Rearsight: Aperture. Flip
Graduation: 100 and 300 metres
Sight radius: 470mm

FIRING CHARACTERISTICS
Muzzle velocity: 877 metres/sec
Muzzle energy: 155mkp
Recoil energy: 0.7mkp
Chamber pressure: 3,620kg/cm²
Rate of fire: Cyclic: 600 rounds/min
Auto: 90 rounds/min
SS: 30 rounds/min
Range, maximum effective: 400 metres
maximum, approx: 2,500 metres
Manufacturer: SIG Swiss Industrial Co, Neuhausen Rhinefalls
Status: Not in production. Not in service. Trial quantities only manufactured

The short-barrelled version was also made with wooden furniture

Long barrel, solid stock plastic furniture. Note shape of cocking handle

SG530-1 long barrel, folding stock. Note grenade positioning device

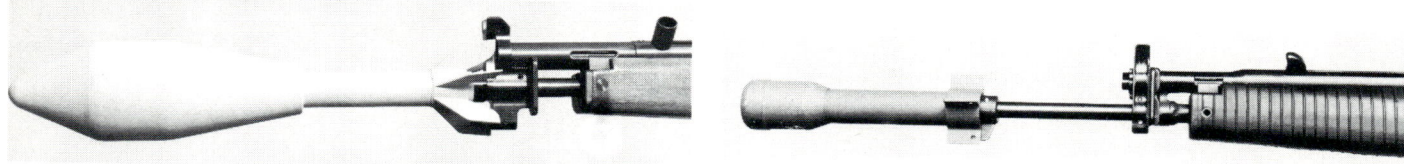

Short-barrelled rifle. Note the extent of the grenade

Long-barrelled rifle. Note position of grenade

SG-540 SERIES ASSAULT RIFLES

The latest rifles produced by SIG are the SG540, 542 and 543. The SG540 and 543 are chambered for the 5.56mm × 45 cartridge and the SG542 for the 7.62mm × 51 NATO round; but all three are made to the same basic design.

The rifles are gas-operated with a rotating bolt. The cocking handle reciprocates with the bolt and provides a means of closing the bolt if for some reason the return spring is unable to force it fully home. The gas regulator is mounted at the front of the cylinder and has a milled cap which can be rotated to one of the positions marked respectively 0, 1 and 2. At '0' the valve is fully closed, no gas passes to the cylinder, and the entire gas force is used to project a grenade from the muzzle. The normal firing position is with the regulator set to '1', and '2' is an oversized port reserved for those occasions when the weapon is lacking in energy due to fouling or the entry of sand or snow etc.

The weapon can be fired at single shot, full auto or with a three-round burst controller which provides for the release of three rounds at a high cyclic rate of 725 rounds a minute from a single trigger operation. When firing at single shot, accuracy is improved by the provision of a double pull trigger.

When the weapon is used in extremely cold conditions demanding the use of Arctic mittens, the trigger guard can be rotated so that the hand has direct access to the trigger. The trigger guard is similarly rotated when grenades are fired.

When the ammunition is expended the magazine platform operates a holding-open device. When a new, loaded, magazine is inserted the action can be released by a slight backward movement of the cocking handle and when this is released the bolt will chamber the next round. Alternatively the device may be released by pressing in a catch located on the left of the receiver above and behind the magazine.

The foresight is a pillar which may be rotated up or down to allow for elevation zeroing. The rearsight is an aperture in a tilted drum which may be rotated to give ranges of 100 to 500 metres for the .223 rifle and 100 to 600 metres on the SG542. Each rifle has range alteration in increments of 100 metres.

A bipod is mounted under the front of the barrel casing. This is normally stowed under the barrel and is pulled down when needed.

The flash suppressor is the closed prong type and when grenades are used these are slid straight down onto the barrel. The spike bayonet has a tubular handle which fits over the flash suppressor.

A telescopic sight, an infra-red sight or an image intensifier can be fitted.

The use of plastics for the butt, trigger guard, pistol grip and fore-end has reduced the weight and cost of the weapon without detracting from its efficiency in any way.

A conventional butt or a tubular one folding flat alongside the right hand side of the receiver, can be fitted.

STRIPPING

The magazine is removed by pressing on the catch in front of the trigger guard and the bolt retracted by pulling on the fixed cocking handle on the right. The chamber and feedway can then be inspected.

There is a takedown pin located above the pistol grip just behind the change lever and when this is pressed through the butt can be forced down with the lower receiver and the trigger group. The cocking handle is pulled back to bring the bolt to the rear. The handle is then withdrawn sideways from its slot and the bolt withdrawn.

SG540 with fixed butt and 30-round magazine

DATA
Cartridge: SG540 and 543, 5.56mm x 45
SG542 7.62mm x 51
Method of operation: Gas
Method of locking: Rotating bolt
Feed: Magazine
Method of fire: Selective

WEIGHTS
Rifle with fixed butt: SG540, 3.26kg
SG542, 3.55kg
SG543, 2.96kg
Rifle with folding butt: SG540, 3.31kg
SG542, 3.55kg
SG543, 2.96kg

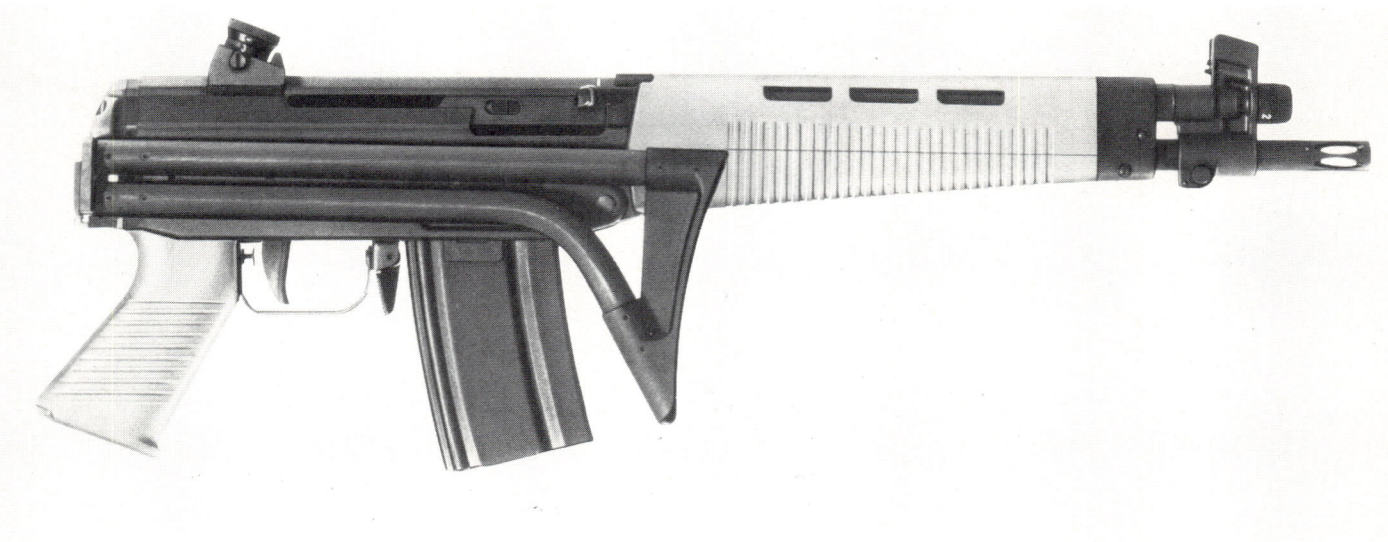

SG543 with folding butt and 20-round magazine

Additional for bipod: SG540/542, 0.28kg
Empty magazine: 20 rounds: SG540/543, 0.20kg
    SG542, 0.24kg
    30 rounds: SG540/543, 0.24kg
Full magazine: 20 rounds: SG540/543, 0.43kg
    SG542, 0.73kg
    30 rounds: SG540/543, 0.585kg
Muzzle energy: SG540, 175mkp
    SG542, 325mkp
    SG543, 140mkp
Rate of fire: 650/800 rounds/min
Effective range: 400m

LENGTHS
Overall with fixed butt: SG540, 950mm
    SG542, 1,002mm
    SG543, 805mm
Overall with folding butt: SG540, 720mm
    SG542, 754mm
    SG543, 569mm

Barrel length (without suppressor): SG540, 460mm
    SG542, 465mm
    SG543, 300mm

MECHANICAL FEATURES
Barrel: Rifling: 4 grooves RH. 1 twist in 305mm. 2-position regulator
Sights: Foresight: Cylindrical post
    Rearsight: Aperture
    Graduation: 100m increments to 500m (SG542, 600m)
    Zeroing: By foresight
    Sight radius: SG540/543, 495mm
    SG542, 528mm

FIRING CHARACTERISTICS
Muzzle velocity: SG540, 980m/s
    SG542, 820m/s
    SG543, 875m/s
Manufacturer: SIG Swiss Industrial Co, Neuhausen, Rhinefalls
Status: All the models are available from the manufacturers and production has commenced in France

SG542 with fixed butt and 20-round magazine

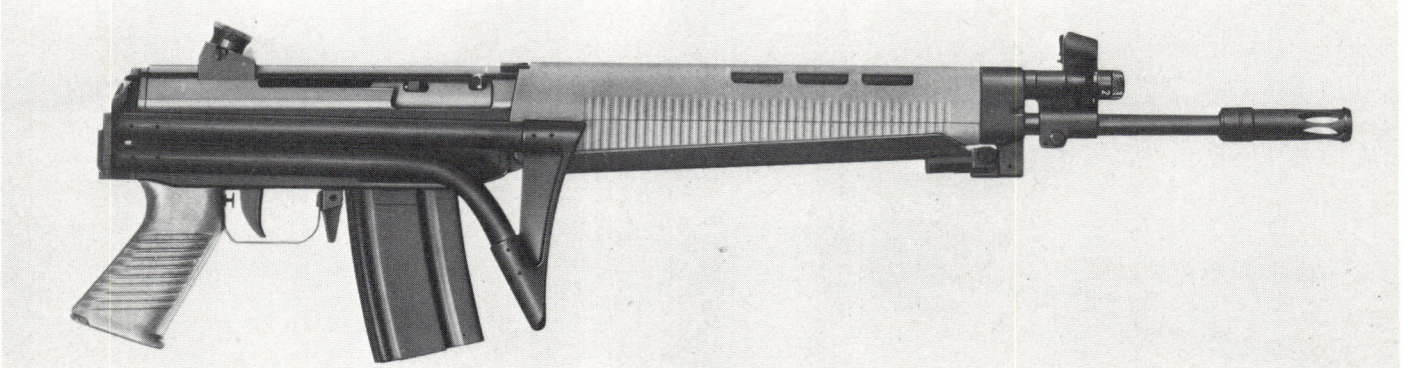

The 5.56mm SG540, with folding stock

SG540 sniping rifle

UNION OF SOVIET SOCIALIST REPUBLICS

7.62mm MOSIN-NAGANT RIFLE

This rifle was designed by the Belgian Nagant brothers, Emile and Leon, and Colonel Sergei Mosin of the Russian artillery. The two Nagants and Colonel Mosin had both designed rifles of their own and the final Russian rifle of 1891 appears to be the action of Mosin and the magazine system of the Nagant brothers. The weapon was made to fire the Russian 3-line cartridge, line being a Russian measurement of length equal to 2.54mm.

The rifle was stocked almost to the muzzle and took a socket bayonet – probably the last European rifle to be so equipped. The rifle was originally sighted for the round nosed 7.62mm cartridge and when the spitzer type light bullet (L) was introduced in 1908, the sight was changed.

The bolt of the Mosin is of original and unique design. The removable bolt head rotates with the bolt body and locking is achieved by two lugs on the bolt head moving into recesses in the receiver. When the bolt is locked the two locking lugs are horizontal.

The cocking occurs as the cocking piece is held back by the sear as the bolt goes forward. Safety is achieved by pulling back on the cocking piece and rotating it anti-clockwise. This moves a lug into a recess in the bolt and also withdraws the striker point through a cylinder in the bolt head; the striker point has two flats and so when turned it cannot pass between the flats in the inside of the cylinder to move towards the cartridge cap.

The magazine is very unusual in that when the top round has been chambered, the second round is held down and prevented from rising under the bolt until the final rotation of locking removes the feed interruptor and the cartridge is pressed up under the bolt.

There were a number of models following the original model of 1891, at least some of which may still be encountered – particularly in S.E. Asia.

DATA
Cartridge: 7.62mm × 54R
Method of operation: Manual – bolt
Method of locking: Rotating bolt
Method of feed: 5-round integral box
Method of fire: Single shots

	Rifle M1891/30	Sniper Rifle M1891/30	Carbine M1938	Carbine M1944
Weight:	3.95kg	5.05kg	3.47kg	4.03kg
Length:	1,232mm	1,232mm	1,016mm	1,016mm
Barrel:	729mm	729mm	508mm	518mm
Sights: Foresight:	Post. Tangent	Post. Tangent	Post. Tangent	Post. Tangent
Rearsight:	Notch	Notch	Notch	Notch
Muzzle velocity:	811 metres/sec	811 metres/sec	766 metres/sec	766 metres/sec
Muzzle energy:	321mkp	321mkp	287mkp	287mkp

Rate of fire: 9-10 rounds/min
Range, maximum effective: 800 metres
Manufacturer: Various State Arsenals, including Sestorets and Tula.
Status: Not in service in Europe but still found in various models elsewhere

7.62mm M1891/30

The sights of this rifle were calibrated in metres rather than the arshins of the earlier weapons. (One arshin equalled 0.71 metres). The M1891/30 was made from 1930 to 1944 and was issued to the Soviet infantry in the

Second World War. It was simply a model of the 1891 type modified for easier production by having a cylindrical receiver.

Mosin-Nagant 7.62mm M1891/30 rifle.

7.62mm M1891/30 Sniping Rifle

This was a M1891/30 rifle specially selected for accuracy. The bolt handle was lengthened and turned down

Until the advent of the Dragunov sniping rifle in the Soviet Army in the late 60s, this rifle, fitted with a PU telescope, was the standard sniping rifle. The

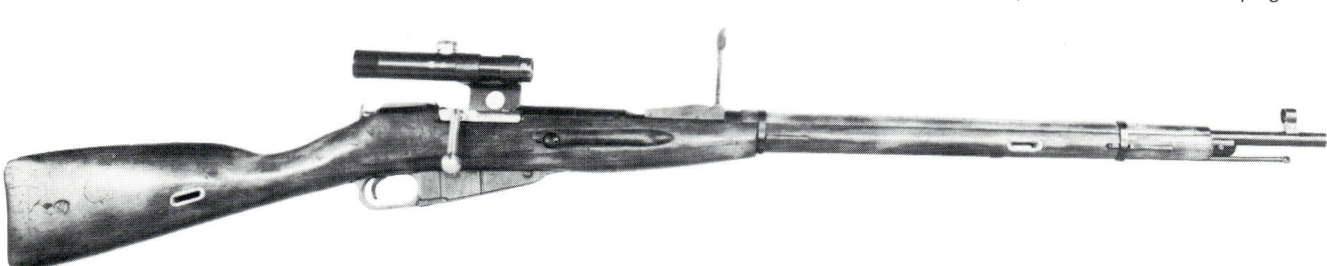

Mosin-Nagant 7.62mm M1891/30 sniping rifle (RMCS)

3.5 power telescope was supported at its forward end by a sight mount dovetailed into the left of the receiver. It was not a popular military sight – although used subsequently with success as a sporting telescope on the Russian 'Bear' rifle which is a 9mm copy of the Dragunov sniping rifle – and was replaced by the 4 power PE which has conventional ring mounts.

A copy of the rifle, the Vx 54 was made in Czechoslovakia. It can be recognised by the sporting type stock and the exposed barrel.

A Soviet soldier sniping with the 7.62mm M1891/30 rifle in 1943 (Novosti)

7.62mm M1938 Carbine

This replaced the M1910. It had the cylindrical receiver and tangent rearsight of the M1891/30. It did not have a bayonet.

7.62mm M1944 Carbine

In 1944 a folding cruciform shaped bayonet was added to the M1938 carbine. The barrel was increased in length by half an inch but apart from these there were no changes. This carbine is still in use with some Asian Communist countries. It has also been produced by the People's Republic of China as the Type 53 carbine.

Mosin-Nagant carbine M1938 (Novosti)

7.62mm SIMONOV SL RIFLE (SKS)

Sergei Gavrilovich Simonov was one of the last old guard Russian designers. He was born in 1894 and started work at the Tula Arsenal whn he was 30. In 1926 he was an inspector of quality control at the Arsenal and in 1927 he worked in the Design and Development Department under Federov. He designed a rifle which was accepted as the AVS but was not made in quantity. He designed an anti-tank rifle, the PTRS, of 14.5mm calibre in World War II and after the war he produced a scaled-down version of this which was a light self-loading short rifle – or carbine – and was the first weapon to fire the new 7.62mm × 39 M43 cartridge.

It is a gas-operated rifle of very conventional design with a charger loaded 10-round box magazine enclosed inside the receiver. There is a catch below the receiver, behind the magazine, which when pressed releases the bottom plate of the magazine to allow quick emptying. It has a permanently attached, folding blade bayonet.

It is now obsolescent in the Soviet Army, but has been manufactured by several Communist countries and is still in use with several of these. In East Germany the rifle is known as the Karabiner-S. It can be identified by the year of manufacture and the serial number on the left front of the receiver and the fact that there is a hole through the butt for the sling. It does not carry the cleaning rod. In Yugoslovia it is called the M59/66 and is recognised by the permanently attached grenade launcher at the muzzle and the folding grenade sight behind the launcher. The Chinese PLA call it the Type 56 SA carbine and the later version has a triangular section bayonet in place of the flat blade. The symbol is carried on the left front of the receiver. The North Korean forces use the name 'Type 63' carbine and the receiver cover has '63' stamped into it.

OPERATION

To load the rifle the cocking handle on the right of the bolt is retracted. This is permanently attached to the bolt. If the magazine is empty the bolt will be held to the rear. The ammunition comes in 10-round chargers and is placed in the charger guides in the front of the bolt carrier and pressed fully down. When the 10 rounds are in the magazine the charger is removed; the bolt is pulled slightly back and released; and goes forward to chamber the top round. The magazine can, if necessary, be loaded or topped up as required, by using individual rounds.

Soviet soldiers using the SKS for ceremonial purposes in the Red Square, Moscow, during the parade to commemorate the 55th anniversary of the October Revolution on 7 November 1972. The nearer man's rifle has the magazine open (Novosti)

The safety catch is located along the rear of the trigger guard and is pushed forward and up for 'safe' where it indicates its presence by obstructing the trigger finger as well as blocking the trigger.

Pulling the trigger releases the hammer which drives the firing pin into the cartridge cap. Some of the gases following the bullet up the bore are diverted through the gas port and impinge on the head of the piston. The piston is forced rearwards and the tappet strikes the bolt carrier. It is a short stroke action and the spring returns the tappet and piston to their forward position. The carrier is driven back and after about 8mm of free travel, during which the gas pressure drops, it lifts up the rear end of the bolt out of engagement with the floor of the receiver. The bolt assembly then moves rearward as an entity. The hammer is rocked back to its cocked position and the return spring progressively compressed. The extractor holds the empty case to the bolt face until it contacts the ejector and is expelled through the port on the right of the receiver.

The return spring drives the bolt assembly forward; the bolt picks up the top round in the magazine and chambers it. The extractor enters the cannelure of the cartridge case and bolt motion ceases. The carrier continues forward for about 8mm and forces the rear of the bolt down into its recess in the receiver.

TRIGGER AND FIRING MECHANISM

When the trigger is squeezed the trigger bar pushes the spring-loaded sear block forward and clear of the hammer. Provided the bolt carrier is fully forward, and the bolt is locked, the hammer rotates and hits the firing pin. The round is fired. The bolt moves rearward and rotates the hammer back.

Bolt closed

Hammer released

Bolt recoiled

Trigger and firing mechanism of the SKS (RMCS)

The underside of the hammer forces down the disconnector which in turn pushes down the trigger bar to a level below the sear. The sear spring forces it back under the hammer and over the trigger bar. The hammer is held and cannot move. To fire another round the trigger must be released. The trigger bar is forced to the rear and the hammer/trigger spring forces it up so that it lies against the rear surface of the sear. When the trigger is pulled the trigger moves forward and pushes the sear forward against its spring, the hammer rotates and the cycle is repeated. Unless the bolt carrier is fully forward the safety sear holds up the hammer but the final closure of the carrier depresses the safety sear which is then moved clear of the hammer.

The rifle continues to fire single shots until the ammunition is expended. The magazine platform then rises and a small stud pushes up a bolt retaining catch which holds the bolt to the rear. When the magazine platform is depressed by the insertion of ammunition, the catch continues to hold the bolt to the rear until the bolt is pulled slightly back – when the catch drops – and is released to feed the top round.

SIGHTS

The rearsight is a U notch. The range is set by depressing the slide catch and moving the sight along the leaf until the leading edge is lined up with the line below the desired range figure. There is a battle sight setting on the leaf which covers all ranges up to 300 metres.

The foresight can be adjusted for zeroing and to do this the combination tool, issued with the rifle, is required. The spanner fits over the foresight which is screwed up to lower the point of impact and vice versa.

STRIPPING

The magazine catch is pulled back to swing the magazine open and so remove the cartridges. The bolt is retracted and the chamber checked.

The receiver cover pin on the right rear of the receiver is rotated to the vertical position and pulled as far as possible out of the rifle. The receiver cover can now be brought back and the return spring removed. The bolt carrier and bolt come back when the cocking handle is pulled rearwards and can be lifted out of the receiver and separated.

The gas cylinder tube retaining pin can be rotated upwards and the rear of the upper handguard lifted. The gas cylinder tube and piston can then be removed. The piston will drop out of the tube.

DATA

Cartridge: 7.62mm × 39
Method of operation: Gas
Method of locking: Tilting block
Method of fire: Self-loading
Method of feed: 10-round internal box magazine
Weight, empty: 3.85kg
Length: 1,021mm
Barrel: Rifling: 4 grooves RH
Sights: Foresight: Post
Rearsight: Tangent notch
Muzzle velocity: 735 metres/sec
Rate of fire: 20 rounds/min
Range, maximum effective: 400 metres
Manufacturer: State factories
Status: No longer manufactured. No longer used in the USSR except for ceremonial purposes. Still used in some Asian countries

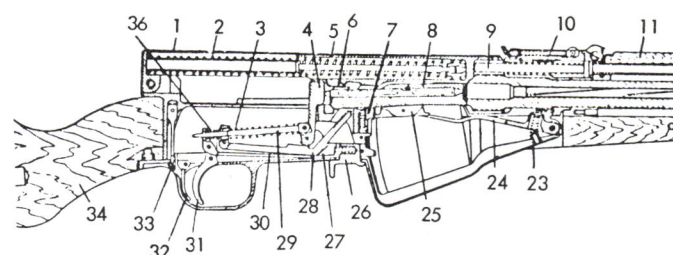

Sectional view of the SKS: (1) Bolt cover; (2) Driving spring; (3) Hammer spring; (4) Hammer; (5) Bolt carrier; (6) Locking cam; (7) Last-round stop; (8) Bolt; (9) Tappet; (10) Tappet return spring; (11) Handguard; (23) Follower spring; (24) Follower arm; (25) Follower; (26) Magazine catch; (27) Sear; (28) Disconnector; (29) Hammer spring plunger; (30) Trigger bar; (31) Trigger; (32) Safety; (33) Latch; (34) Stock; (36) Disconnector spring

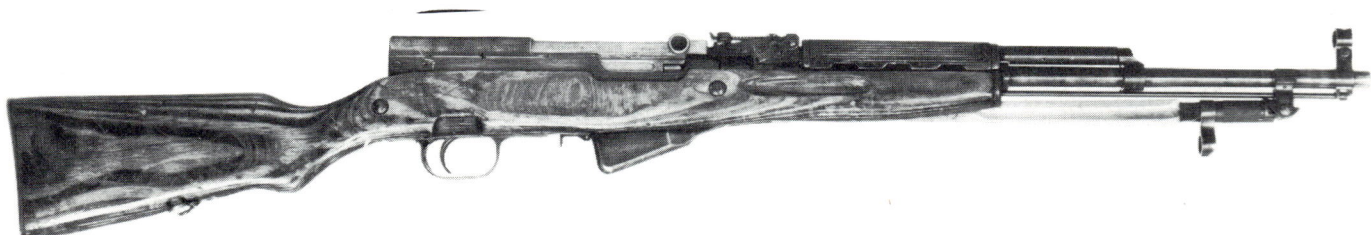

The SKS (RMCS)

7.62mm AK-47 ASSAULT RIFLE

The AK-47 has been the most outstandingly successful rifle in service since World War II. The designer was Mikhail Kalashnikov, who took up weapon design after being badly wounded, in 1941, as a tank commander in the battle for Byransk. During his convalescence he designed a sub-machine gun which was not taken into service and then a carbine which again was not accepted.

He continued designing and his model of 1947, the AK-47 came into service in 1951. In 1959 he improved the methods of production and his new automatic rifle was called the AKM. The basic principles of the AK-47 rifle have been applied to a family of light machine guns (RPK), general purpose machine guns (PK), medium machine guns (PKS) and the tank machine gun called the PKT.

Kalashnikov has been awarded the title of Hero of Socialist Labour as an appreciation of his inventions.

GENERAL

The AK-47 Assault Rifle is a gas-operated rifle which could well be taken

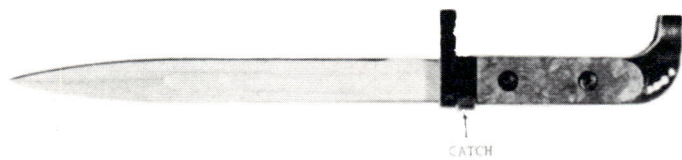

AK-47 bayonet

The Russian short 7.62mm × 39 M43 assault rifle cartridge compared with the long 7.62mm × 54R rifle and machine gun cartridge (RMCS)

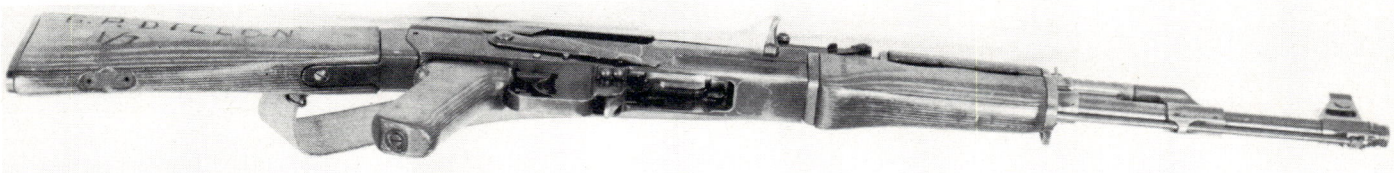

Romanian AK-47 showing laminated woodwork (RSAF)

AK-47 with folding double strut stock. The example shown here is East German (RMCS)

SELECTOR MARKINGS FOR AK47 ASSAULT RIFLES

Upper or Full Auto Symbol	Lower or Semi Auto Symbol	Producer	Native Name, etc.
AB	0 ⌐	Soviet	AK-47, AKM and AKMS
AB	E ⌐	Bulgaria	AK-47 and AKM
C	P	Poland	PMK, PMK-DGN, KbK AK
D	E	E. Germany	MPK, MPiKmS – Rifles do not have cleaning rods. MPiKM and MPiKMS have cleaning rods
FA	FF	Romania	Has "S" at top for safe postion
禾	荓	China (P.R.)	Early Production
L	D	China (P.R.)	Type 56 and 56-1 Assault Rifle (Late Production)
∞	1	Hungary	
· · ·		Finland	RYNNAKOKIVAARI – applies to M60 and M62
ㄹL	ㄷL	North Korea	Types 58 and 68 Assault Rifle
R	J	Yugoslavia	M64 series – has U at top for safe position
30	1	Czechoslovakia	M58 Assault Rifle

to exemplify the type. It is a compact weapon, capable of selective fire, robust, reliable and producing a remarkably consistent grouping and accuracy for such a short-barrelled weapon.

The Warsaw Pact countries have now largely replaced it with the AKM – a modernised and improved version – but it is still held for mobilisation in European Communist countries. It has been issued in immense numbers to the Middle East countries and the Egyptian, Syrian, Iraqi and Tunisian Armies – among many others – have it as standard equipment. It has been used extensively in most of the world's trouble spots including the Congo, Nigeria, Vietnam (by both sides) and in the Egyptian-Israeli war.

The AK-47 has been manufactured not only in the USSR but also in Bulgaria, Communist China, East Germany, Hungary, North Korea, Poland, Romania and Yugoslavia. The Finnish M60 and M62 rifles are variants of the AK-47. The easiest way to determine the country of origin is to examine the selector markings for 'single shot' and 'full auto' on the receiver.

The AK-47 is supplied in two configurations, one with a rigid butt and one with a double strut folding metal buttstock controlled by a simple press button release above the pistol grip.

There are also early and late production models. The early model has a built-up receiver which has an angular shape to the rear end, sloping noticeably down to the butt.

Early and late versions of the AK-47. The differences are arrowed on the respective receivers (US Army)

Hungarian AK-47 with wooden stock and hand grips (RSAF)

Chinese Type 56 rifle with attached bayonet

Chinese Type 56 with folding butt and no bayonet. Note rivets in stock arms (RSAF)

The later type has a straight receiver.

The various countries in the Warsaw Pact have produced a whole variety of materials for buttstocks and forearms ranging from laminated sheets of plywood to various types of plastic and all-metal construction. On the whole the standard of material employed for furniture is not up to that of the American or West European weapons.

The USSR AK-47 has a separate bayonet which slips over the muzzle and moves down until the catch locks onto the muzzle nut.

The Chinese AK-47 is known as the Type 56 rifle. Early models had wooden butts and were almost identical with the late – straight receiver – USSR weapons, but later Type 56 rifles have a permanently attached folding cruciform bayonet.

The Chinese folding stock model, known as the Type 56-1 assault rifle, has no bayonet and is generally similar to the Russian rifle but can be distinguished at a glance by having extra rivets through the metal struts, one about 4cm from the butt catch and one about 5cm from the folding shoulder piece.

The Poles produce two versions of the AK-47. One is similar to the Russian gun and is known as the PMK. The other is the PMK-DGN which takes the LON-1 grenade launcher and can be distinguished by a gas cut-off valve located at the gas tap-off into the cylinder.

Unlike the Russian AK-47 the East German MPK does not carry a cleaning rod under the muzzle extending into the fore-end. Nor does it have a recess in the butt to carry cleaning tools.

The Finnish M60 and M62 rifles have combined flash suppressor – bayonet mountings, foresights moved back to the gas cylinder and an aperture rearsight fixed to the back of the receiver cover.

OPERATION

The magazine is loaded by placing the cartridge between the feed lips and pressing it down. The magazine is located in the rifle by placing the front end into the magazine well until the lug engages and then rotating the rear end back and up until the magazine catch can be heard to grip it. The cocking handle is permanently fixed to the right of the bolt carrier and reciprocates with it. This allows manual bolt closure if for some reason the bolt carrier does not go fully forward. If the cocking handle is retracted and released, the top round is fed into the chamber. When the trigger is operated the hammer hits the floating firing pin and drives it into the cap of the cartridge. Some of the propellant gases are diverted into the gas cylinder on top of the barrel. There is no gas regulator. The piston is driven back and the bolt carrier, built into the piston extension, has about 8.5mm of free play whilst the gas pressure drops to a safe level. A cam slot in the bolt carrier engages the cam stud on the bolt and the bolt is rotated through 35 degrees to unlock it from the receiver. There is no primary extraction, during bolt rotation, to unseat the case and so a large extractor claw is fitted which grips the empty case and holds it to the bolt face until it contacts the fixed ejector formed in the guide rail and is thrown out of the right-hand side of the gun. As the bolt travels back it rocks the hammer over and also compresses the return spring. The bolt is brought to a halt by hitting the solid rear end of the receiver. The helical return spring drives the bolt forward, another round is chambered, the extractor claw grips in the cannelure at the back of the case and the bolt comes to rest. The carrier continues on for about 5.5mm after locking is completed. This is sufficient to prevent carrier bounce unlocking the bolt when the carrier hits the receiver

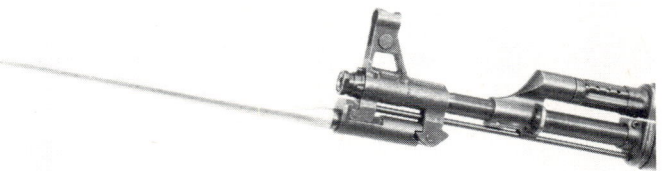

Chinese Type 56 Bayonet

Polish AK-47 with grenade launcher LON-1. This model is called the PMK-DGN
(RSAF)

stop. During this last forward movement of the carrier the safety sear is released and control of the hammer is returned to the trigger sear.

TRIGGER AND FIRING MECHANISM

The trigger and firing mechanism is based on that of the USA M1 Garand rifle. The hammer has two working surfaces on the bent and there are two sears which are hook shaped. When the hammer is cocked and the weapon is ready to fire, the main bent, which is the forward one, is held by the trigger sear which is part of the trigger lever. When the trigger is pulled the trigger lever rotates forward and the sear is disengaged from the hammer which is free to rotate, under the influence of its spring, into the firing pin.

When a single shot is set on the change lever, the hammer, when it is rocked back by the recoiling bolt carrier, is caught by the spring-loaded auxiliary sear. Since the trigger is already back another round cannot be fired. When the trigger is released the trigger lever carrying the main sear moves back and catches the hammer as it is released when the auxiliary is rotated clear of the secondary bent. Thus control of the hammer is restored

to the main sear and provided the bolt carrier is fully forward, pulling the trigger will release the hammer to fire another round.

To provide mechanical safety, which implies that the bolt must be fully locked before the cartridge can be fired, a safety sear is fitted. Until this is disconnected by the carrier, in its final forward movement after locking is completed, it engages the hammer and holds it up.

When the change lever is set to automatic fire, a boss on the shaft presses against the spring-loaded auxiliary sear and it is forced back so far that it plays no part in controlling the hammer.

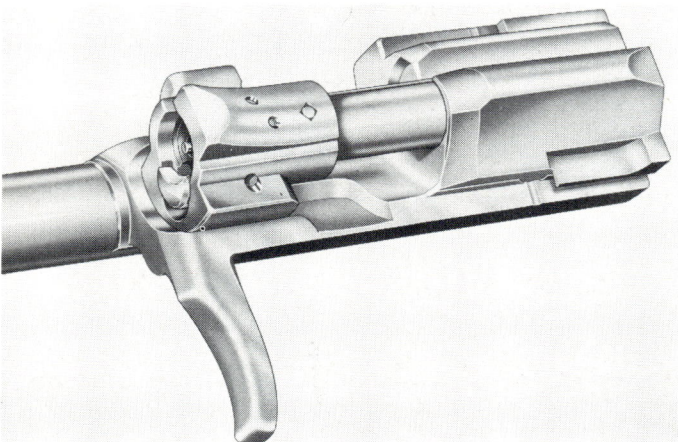

The bolt of the AK-47 (RMCS)

Polish PMK (RSAF)

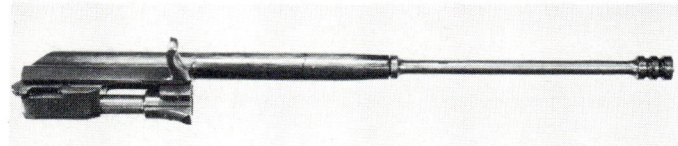

The piston mounted over the bolt (RMCS)

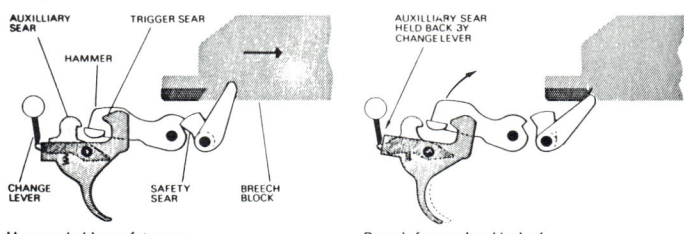

Hammer held on safety sear
Change lever set for automatic fire

Breech forward and locked
Trigger pressed, gun fires

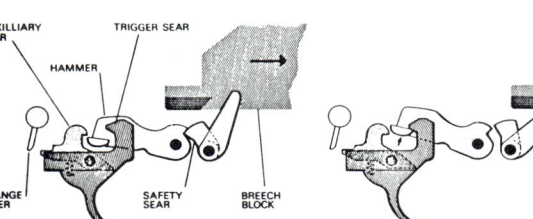

1 Hammer held on safety sear
(Breech unlocked)

2 Hammer held on trigger sear
(Breech locked)

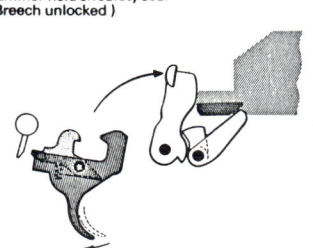

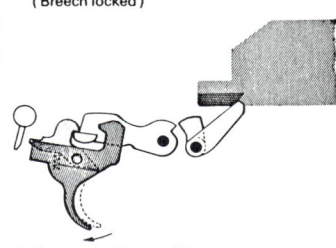

3 Trigger pressed; hammer released;

4 Hammer held on auxilliary sear

Trigger and firing mechanism of the AK-47

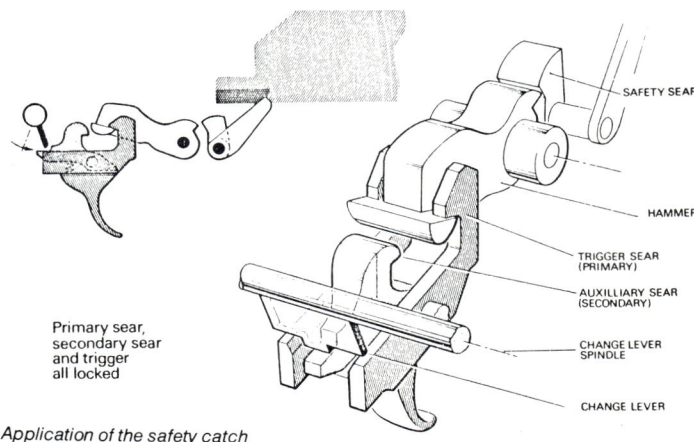

Primary sear,
secondary sear
and trigger
all locked

Application of the safety catch

When the trigger is pressed, the hammer is released from the trigger sear and goes forward to fire the first round. The recoiling carrier rotates the hammer back and it is held by the safety sear. As soon as the carrier is fully forward the safety sear is disengaged, the hammer is freed, and another round is fired. So long as the trigger is pressed, ammunition is available in the magazine, and the bolt carrier goes fully forward, the gun will continue to fire at its cyclic rate.

The change lever is mounted on the right-hand side of the receiver and is unique in its design. It is a long pressed-out bar pivoted at the rear and applied by the firer's thumb. The top position is 'safe'. Here it locks the trigger and physically prevents the bolt from coming back sufficiently to pass beyond the rear of a cartridge in the magazine, but does allow sufficient movement for the soldier – or his NCO – to check that the chamber is clear.

The lever produces automatic fire at the centre position and single shots when fully depressed. It is invariably stiff to operate, noisy in functioning and extremely difficult to manipulate when wearing Arctic mittens.

SIGHTS

The foresight is a cylinder, screw-threaded for adjustment when zeroing. The spanner in the combination tool kit is used for this. Lateral adjustment for zeroing is achieved by moving the foresight block in a dovetail.

The rearsight is an open U-shaped notch which will allow ranges up to 800 metres by means of a slide and ramp. There is a battle sight setting for all ranges up to 200 metres.

For night work, wire clips, each containing a luminous dot, are fixed over the foresight and below the backsight. These are lined up and superimposed one on the other and on the target. They may readily be removed when not required.

MANUFACTURE AND MATERIALS

The AK-47 is manufactured by conventional machine tools and the only notable metal pressings are the receiver cover, magazine and safety catch. Nearly everything else is machined from the solid and is demanding both on machines and labour.

The steels used are of good quality and in many cases where stressed parts are involved, alloy steels have been employed adding considerably to the cost of the weapon. Chromium plating is employed extensively and all parts in contact with the gases are so treated.

STRIPPING

Remove the magazine, check that the chamber and feedway are clear.

Press the end of the return spring guide into the rear end of the receiver cover and lift the receiver cover off the receiver. (The Polish PMK-DGN has a lock on the return spring guide which must first be depressed.)

Push the return spring guide forward to clear its rear housing and remove from the gun.

Pull the cocking handle to the rear and remove the bolt carrier and bolt. Remove the bolt from the carrier.

Rotate the gas cylinder lock, mounted on the right of the rearsight block, and free the gas cylinder and upper handguard.

FIRING

The AK-47 has a short sight base and a short barrel. In spite of these disadvantages it will produce single round groups at ranges out to 400 metres when fired by the 'average' shot which are not noticeably inferior to those produced by the same soldiers firing British or American rifles. In the hands of an expert the deficiencies of the AK-47 become more apparent.

When fired at automatic, again by 'average' shots, in short bursts, it produces smaller groups than weapons using the NATO 7.62mm × 51 rifle cartridge but it is inferior to the USA AR-15 (M16).

The steel core of the bullet can give extremely good penetration.

When considering these figures the remarkable thing is that the AK-47, designed in 1947 and in service in 1951, is still able to compete on more or less equal terms with the American M16 rifle designed in 1957 and brought into quantity service in the middle 60s.

DATA
Cartridge: 7.62mm x 39
Method of operation: Gas
Method of locking: Rotating bolt
Method of feed: 30-round detachable box magazine
Method of fire: Selective

WEIGHTS
Rifle only: 4.3kg
Magazine empty: 322g
Magazine loaded: 827g
Trigger pull: 2.72kp

LENGTHS
Gun, butt extended: 869mm
Gun, butt folded: 699mm
Barrel: 414mm

MECHANICAL FEATURES
Barrel: Regulator: Nil
       Rifling: 4 groove RH. 1 turn in 235mm

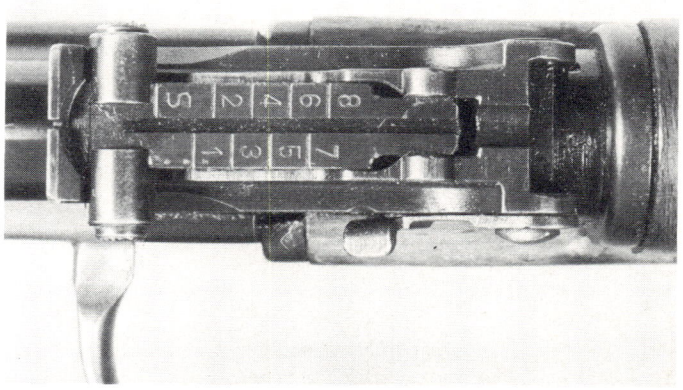

The Polish AK-47 showing battle sight marked S. This is a setting for up to 200 metres (RSAF)

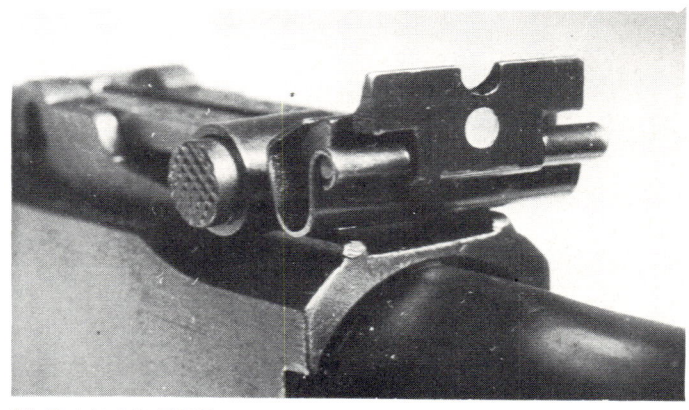

AK-47 night sight (RSAF)

AK-47 night sight (RSAF)

Sights: Foresight: Pillar
    Cooling: Air
    Graduation: 100-800 metres; Battlesight up to 200 metres
    Zeroing: Elevation. Rotate foresight. Line. Foresight on eccentric
    Sight radius: 376mm

FIRING CHARACTERISTICS
Muzzle velocity: 710 metres/sec
Muzzle energy: 202mkp
Recoil energy: 0.64mkp

Chamber pressure: 2,850kg/cm^2
Rate of fire: Cyclic: 600 rounds/min
    Automatic: 100 rounds/min
    SS: 40 rounds/min
Range, maximum effective: 300 metres
Manufacturer: State factories
Status: No longer produced in USSR. Widely used in Asian countries and in Egypt and Syria. Still used in reserve units in Warsaw Pact countries. First line weapon in Yugoslavia.

AK-47 field stripped (RMCS)

7.62mm AKM ASSAULT RIFLE

The AKM is a modernised version of the AK-47, produced in 1959. The forged and machined receiver of the AK-47 has been replaced with a body of pressed steel construction with riveting employed extensively to join the 1mm thick U section to the inserts which house the locking recess, the barrel bearing, and the backsight block at the front and the butt at the back. It should be noted that the bolt now locks into a sleeve and not directly into the receiver as in the AK-47. The slides on which the breech-block reciprocates are pressed out and spot welded inside the receiver walls. The results of these changes are reduced manufacturing costs and reduction in weight from 4.3kg to 3.13kg.

The AKM is produced with a wooden stock. It is also made with a folding butt stock and is then known as the AKM-S.

The AKM incorporates a rate of fire reducer which lies adjacent to the trigger and replaces one of the double hooks which are a feature of the AK-47. The rate reducer holds the hammer back after the carrier has

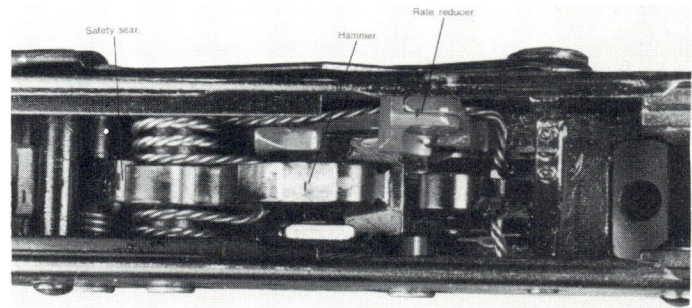

The AKM rate reducer (RMCS)

Identification of the AKM (RMCS)

depressed the safety sear and relies for its effect on the inertia of the system. In practice it seems of dubious value particularly since it consists of some five components – one of them of quite intricate shape – and the reduction in the cyclic rate is not significant.

There are several features which distinguish the AKM from the AK-47 and allow visual recognition. These are:

A There is a small recess in each side of the receiver centrally over the magazine. This is a magazine guide.
B The lower handguard has a groove for the firer's fingers.
C The receiver cover has transverse ribs.
D The bayonet lug under the gas tap-off point.
E The four gas escape holes on each side of the gas cylinder have been omitted.
F The sight is graduated to 1,000 metres instead of 800 – except in the case of the Hungarian short assault rifle.
G A small compensator is fitted to the muzzle as a recent modification.

Versions of the weapon are made in several Warsaw Pact countries. They differ in furniture details but in all essentials they are the same.

The East German AKM is in two versions. The earlier has a plastic grip and upper handguard. The later version has a plastic stock as well and the grip and stock have noticeably protruding studs.

The Romanian AKM has a laminated wooden foregrip which forms part of the fore-end and is shaped like a pistol grip.

The Hungarian AKM has a perforated sheet metal forearm with a nylon foregrip and no upper hand guard. The butt stock and pistol grip are of pale blue plastic. There is also a short assault rifle version – it could even be called a sub-machine gun – with a pronounced muzzle brake and no bayonet lug. The single strut folds sideways and the rear sight is graduated

only to 800 metres. The plastic stock and grip are brown in colour.

OPERATION

There is no essential difference between the functioning of the AKM and that of the AK-47. The rate reducer is the only different mechanical feature.

ACCESSORIES

The AKM and AK-47 carry the same accessories which are:
(a) bayonet
(b) blank firing device
(c) combination tool kit
(d) magazine carrier
(e) night firing sight
(f) oil bottle and cleaning fluid
(g) sling

The bayonet of the AKM is quite different in shape from that of the AK-47. Whereas the AK-47 bayonet has an even taper to the point on each side, that of the AKM has an undercut reverse edge. The AKM bayonet has a slot in the blade into which a lug on the scabbard fits. The scabbard is electrically insulated and has a shearing edge so that, with the bayonet, an effective wire cutter is made. The blank firing device goes onto the muzzle

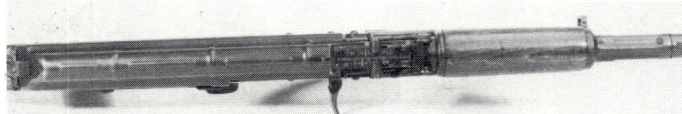

The Russian AKM sights (RMCS)

The Romanian AKM (RSAF)

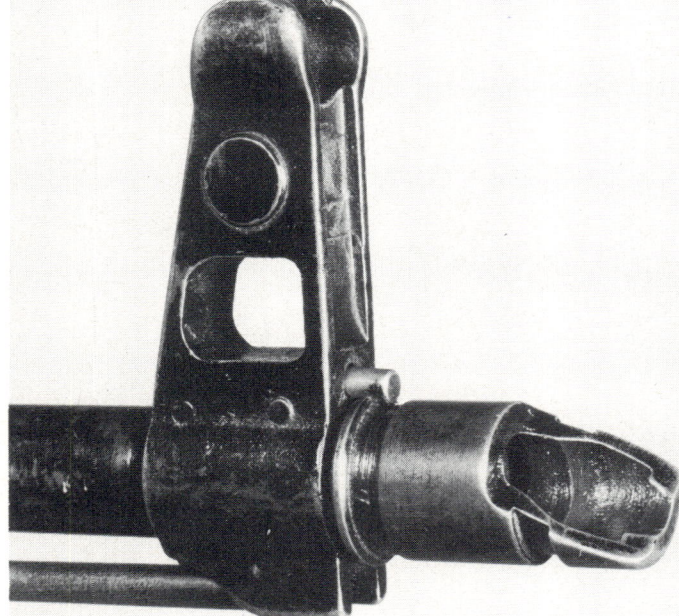

The compensator. Note it not only keeps the muzzle down but prevents any rightish tendencies (RMCS)

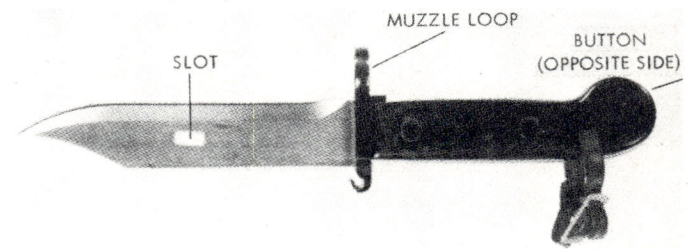

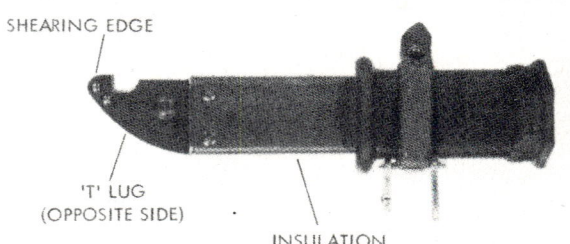

AKM bayonet

Russian AKM (RMCS)

Soviet 7.62 x 39mm assault rifles AKM and AKMS

The East German MPi KM showing plastic furniture (RSAF)

Hungarian short rifle (RSAF)

thread which lies under the muzzle nut. It produces sufficient pressure in the bore to operate the piston.

The combination tool kit fits under the butt plate. It is contained in a case which also acts as a handle for the cleaning rod. The combined drift, screwdriver and spanner is used, amongst other things, to adjust the front sight.

There are several magazine carriers. Some hold three and others four magazines.

The night sights are the same as those on the AK-47.

The Russian soldier carries a double oil container. One part carries lubricating oil, the other has bore-cleaning solvent. The kit is held not on the rifle but in a small pouch.

GRENADE LAUNCHING

The only AK-47 or AKM that launches a grenade is the Polish AK-47 known as the PMK-DGN 60. Details of this are given in the section on Polish Rifles.

STRIPPING

The AKM strips in exactly the same way as the AK-47.

DATA

Cartridge: 7.62mm × 39
Method of operation: Gas
Method of locking: Rotating bolt
Method of feed: 30-round detachable box magazine
Method of fire: Selective
Weight: 3.15kg
Length: 876mm
Barrel: Rifling: 4 groove RH. 414mm
Sights: Foresight: Pillar
     Rearsight: U Notch
     Graduation: 200-1,000 metres
Muzzle velocity: 715 metres/sec
Muzzle energy: 205mkp
Rate of fire: Cyclic: 600 rounds/min
     Automatic: 100 rounds/min
     SS: 40 rounds/min
Range, maximum effective: 300 metres
Manufacturer: State factories
Status: In production. In service with Soviet Forces and all satellites. Supplied to Egypt and Syria

The AKM stripped (RMCS)

7.62mm DRAGUNOV SNIPING RIFLE (SVD)

The Russian Army used the Mosin-Nagant M1891 as the standard infantry and sniping rifle in World War I and in the Second World War they employed an improved version, the M1891/30. The round for this rifle was first introduced in 1908 and is generally referred to as the 7.62mm x 54R, which indicates a calibre of 7.62mm, a case length of 54mm and a rimmed head. It is a good round and will produce very accurate shooting in skilled hands up to 1,000m.

After the war the rifle remained in service until the introduction of the Dragunov in about 1967.

DESCRIPTION

The rifle is a single shot – or semi-automatic – arm with a 10-round magazine. It is gas-operated with a cylinder located above the barrel. There is a two-position gas regulator which may be adjusted using the rim of a cartridge case as a tool. The first position is employed in the usual operation of the rifle and the second is for extended use at a rapid rate or when conditions are adverse.

The bolt system is, in principle, exactly the same as that used in the AK-47, AKM and RPK, but the Dragunov bolt cannot be interchanged with that of the other weapons which fire the M43 7.62mm x 39 intermediate round. However the assault rifle and LMG are operated on a long stroke piston principle which is somewhat heavy for a rifle since the movement of

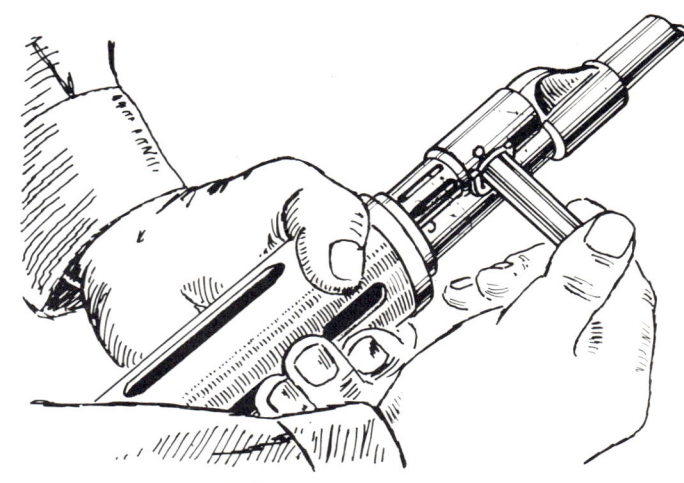

Adjusting the gas regulator

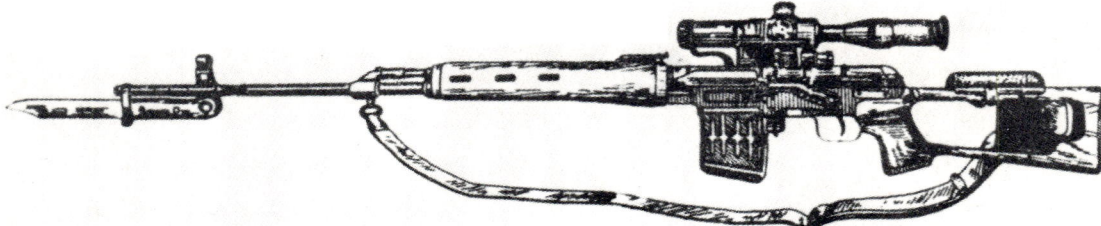

The 7.62mm sniper rifle, Dragunov (SVD)

the fairly heavy mass with the attendant change in the centre of gravity militates against extreme accuracy. Therefore in the Dragunov the designer has gone to a short stroke piston system. The piston, of light weight, is driven back by the impulsive blow delivered by the gas force and transfers energy to the bolt carrier which moves back and a lug on the bolt, running in a cam path on the carrier, rotates the bolt to unlock it. The carrier and the bolt go back together; the return spring is compressed and the carrier comes forward and locks the bolt before firing can take place. Mechanical safety is produced by the continued movement of the carrier after bolting is completed. When the carrier is fully home a safety sear is released and this frees the hammer which, when the trigger is operated, can come forward to drive the firing pin into the cap.

Since the trigger mechanism has to provide only for single shot fire, it is a simple design utilising the hammer, the safety sear controlled by the carrier, and a disconnector. The disconnector ensures that the trigger must be released after each shot to re-connect the trigger bar with the sear.

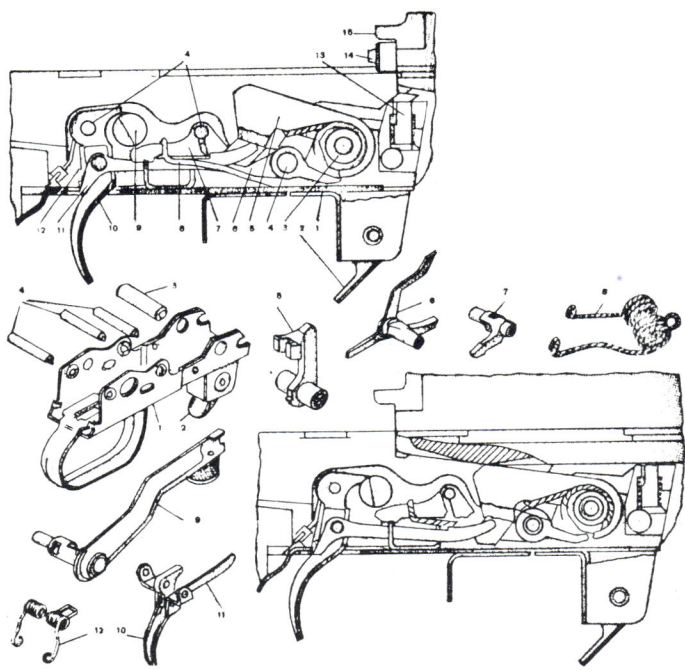

SVD. Parts of the trigger mechanism: (1) trigger housing; (2) magazine catch; (3) hammer pin; (4) mechanism pins; (5) hammer; (6) safety sear; (7) sear; (8) hammer spring (9) safety (10) trigger; (11) trigger bar; (12) trigger spring; (13) bolt stop; (14) firing pin; (15) bolt safety lug

SIGHTS

The Russian sniper uses the PSO-1 sight. This is a telescopic sight of four magnification with power for reticle illumination supplied by a small battery. It is rather longer than most modern telescopic sights at 375mm but a rubber eyepiece is included in this length. The firer's eye is in contact with this rubber which automatically gives the correct eye relief of 68mm. The field of view – true – is 6 degrees which is comparable with that obtained in most military telescopes of modern design. The optics of this sight are good. The blooming used on the lenses to reduce light loss on the interchange surfaces is extremely effective and the depth and uniformity of the deposit compares favourably with any other similar sight in service.

The sight incorporates a metascope – i.e. it is capable of detecting an infra-red source. There is some doubt whether this is sufficiently developed to be used as a passive infra-red sight but reports have appeared in the German technical press that not only can it be used passively but it can be employed in conjunction with an infra-red light source for target illumination.

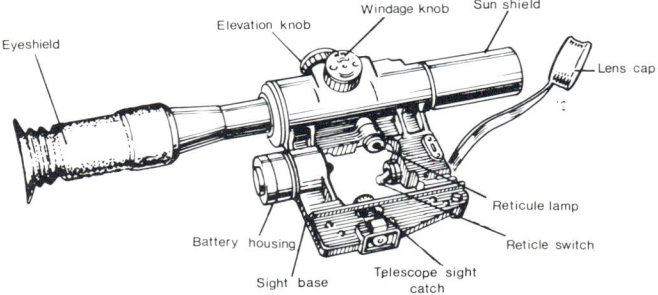

PSO-1 telescopic sight

WEAPON CONFIGURATION

The shape of the butt with a cut-out section provides a ready means of identification when the weapon is slung over the shoulder of the marching soldier. The cheek rest is readily detachable and some pictures have appeared with this missing. The pistol grip is incorporated in the shoulder stock frame in a manner which is unique to this weapon. The trigger guard is

of sufficient size to allow the use of Arctic mittens.

The flash eliminator on the muzzle has five prongs arranged with three apertures at the top so that some measure of compensation is achieved to force the muzzle down by the emergent gas force at the top exceeding that from the two apertures at the bottom. The forward end of the flash eliminator prongs is so shaped that the run out on the taper produces an inclined plane which deflects some portion of the gases to reduce the recoil. Rather surprisingly all the Russian photographs show the arm with a bayonet attached. Possibly the additional weight at the muzzle tends to hold it down but one would have thought that a bayonet, as such, would be the last piece of equipment demanded by a sniper!

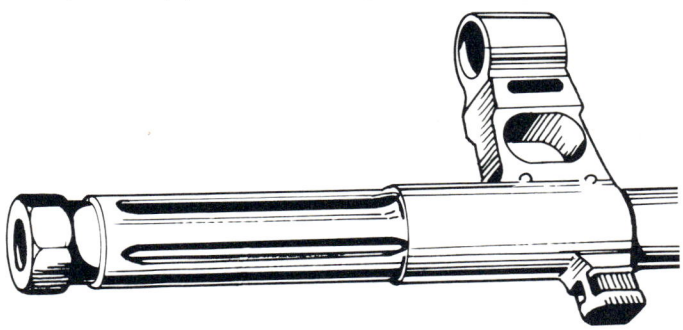

Flash eliminator

Polish soldiers with Dragunov sniping rifles

DATA
Cartridge: 7.62mm × 54R
Method of operation: Gas. Short stroke piston
Method of locking: Rotating bolt
Method of feed: Magazine
Method of fire: Self-loading

WEIGHTS
Rifle with telescope: 4.3kg
Magazine (10-round): 0.085kg
Bayonet: 0.57kg

LENGTHS
Rifle without bayonet: 1,225mm
Rifle with bayonet: 1,370mm
Barrel: 547mm

MECHANICAL FEATURES
Barrel: No regulator
　　　　Rifling: 4 grooves RH 1 turn in 254mm
Sights: Telescopic-type PSO-1 Metascope
Length including eyepiece: 375mm
Height: 132mm

Width: 70mm
Exit pupil diameter: 6mm
Entrance pupil diameter: 24mm
Magnification: 4x
Eye relief: 68mm
Field of view (true): 6°
Field of view (apparent): 24°

Reticle – pointer and cross wire – battery illuminated
FIRING CHARACTERISTICS
Muzzle velocity: 830metres/sec
Muzzle energy: 337mkp
Recoil energy: 1.84mkp
Rate of fire SS: 20 rounds/min
Range, maximum effective: 1,300metres

UNITED ARAB REPUBLIC

7.92mm HAKIM RIFLE

The Egyptian Army has historically used the same rifle as the British. In 1949 the Egyptians became independent and purchased a number of Saive-designed FN self-loading rifles.

The 7.92mm Hakim rifle was manufactured in Egypt. It was essentially a copy of the 6.5mm AG42 Ljungman rifle, made by Carl Gustaf in Sweden, but adapted to take a 7.92mm round. In 1954, Egypt started to obtain substantial assistance from the USSR and amongst the weapons so obtained were the Czech Vx 52 SL rifle (qv) and the Russian SKS SL carbine. These apparently appealed to the Egyptians who manufactured a self-loading carbine with an attached folding bayonet, using the Russian 7.62mm x 39 cartridge, which they called the Raschid rifle. This was based on the Hakim rifle using the modified Ljungman system of direct gas action. Few were made and the weapon, if still in service, is not used by first-line troops. Some of the 7.92mm Hakim rifles were also modified to take the 7.62mm round; but these too are at best obsolescent weapons.

The weapons most widely used by the Egyptian Army today are the Russian AK-47 and AKM rifles.

The sights and gas tube of the Egyptian Hakim rifle (RMCS)

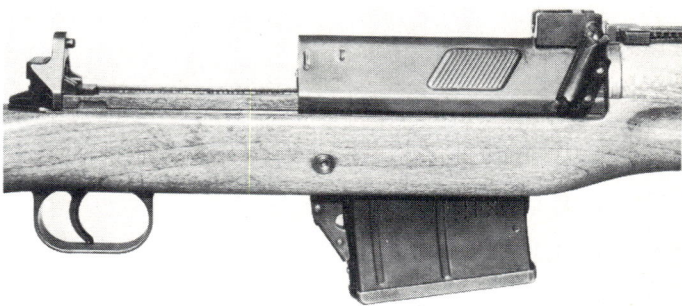

Cocking the Hakim Raschid

Hakim 7.92mm rifle

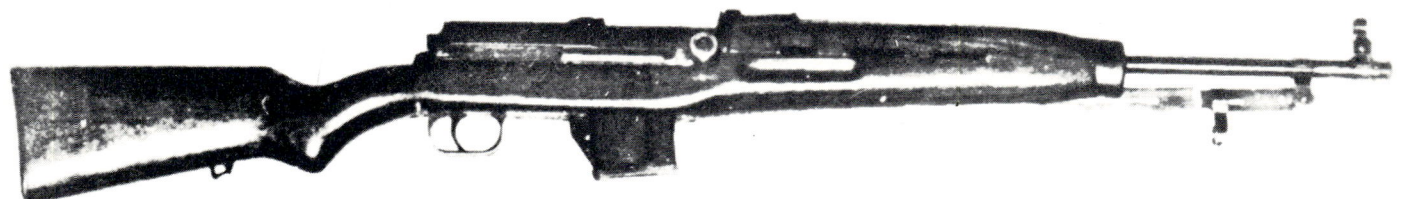

The Raschid rifle

UNITED KINGDOM

.303in LEE-ENFIELD RIFLES

The short magazine, Lee-Enfield rifle was approved for service on 23 December 1902 to take the place of the magazine Lee-Metford and the magazine Lee-Enfield – generally referred to as the 'Long' Lee-Enfield. The Lee-Metford had been recommended for adoption in January 1888. It had a muzzle velocity of 564m/sec with a bullet of 14g. When cordite became available in 1892 the velocity was raised to 610m/sec. The Lee-Metford Mk I held eight cartridges in Lee's magazine and the Mk II held ten. The fine, very shallow grooves of the Metford rifling were readily eroded by cordite

propellant and in 1896 the earlier pattern of shallow grooves with square edges was re-adopted. It had previously accumulated fouling with black powder charges but when used again, with bands of equal width to the grooves and the rifling depth increased to 0.165mm, it was successful. The rifle was known as the Lee-Enfield Mk I.

During the South African War there was a demand for a shortened rifle and a committee recommended the adoption of the SMLE Mk I which was 5 inches shorter than the Lee-Enfield Mk I and had a charger guide on the bolt

Rifle-303 No 1. Mk III 1907 (RMCS)

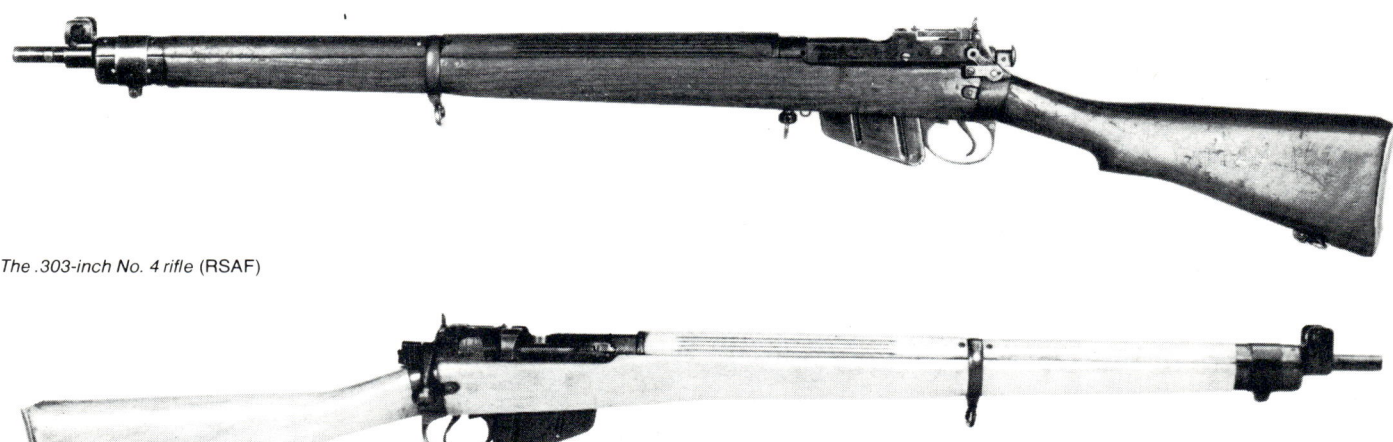

The .303-inch No. 4 rifle (RSAF)

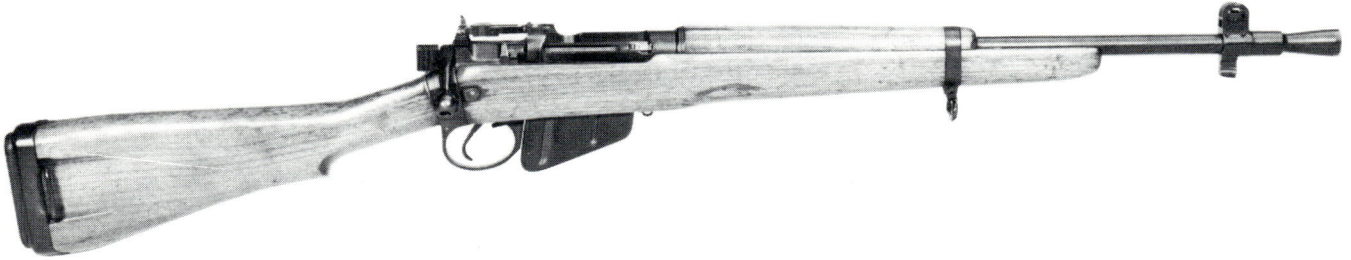

The .303 No. 4 Mk 2 rifle (RSAF)

head. The SMLE Mk II was a rifle made by conversion from the Lee-Metford Mk II* and the Lee-Enfield rifle. The Mk III rifle in January 1907 embodied charger guides on a bridge spanning the body.

From 1910-1913 work was carried out on a new Mauser-type rifle with a calibre of .276in (7mm), known as the Pattern 13 rifle. The cartridge was semi-rimless and bottle necked and gave a muzzle velocity of 711m/sec. The P13 had a thicker stronger barrel than the SMLE and the stocking did not extend to the nose cap. When war broke out in 1914 the .276 cartridge was abandoned and the rifle was produced in America for the British Army and was called the 1914 Pattern rifle. When America came into the war in 1917, this rifle was made for the US forces, with the .30-06 cartridge, and was known as the US Rifle Cal .30 Model of 1917. It was generally referred to as the 'Enfield'. In 1918 the magazine cut-off and the long range sight were abolished and the resulting weapon was called the Mk III.

After World War I the British Army continued with the SMLE. Old models were converted to produce the Mk IV – similar to the Mk III.

The Mk V was provisionally accepted in 1922. It was an improved Mk IV with an aperture rearsight but was never produced in quantity. The Mk VI SMLE was an improvement on the Mk V and came into service as the No 4 rifle.

The No 4 rifle was used throughout World War II and saw service in every theatre in which British or Colonial troops were engaged. It differed from the No 1 rifle in having an exposed length of barrel at the muzzle. It was an accurate weapon and consistently placed a 5-round diagram in a circle of 4 inch (102mm) diameter at 200yds (183m).

The No. 5 Jungle Carbine was developed for use in the Far East.

DATA (No. 4 Rifle)
Cartridge: .303 Mk VII ball (11.3g) or equivalent
Operation: Manual, bolt action
Feed: 10-round detachable box magazine
Weight: 4.1kg loaded
Length: 1130mm
Sights: Foresight: Protected blade
           Rearsight: Adjustable aperture
Muzzle velocity: 751m/sec
Rate of fire: Up to 20 rounds/min
Effective range: 500m
Manufacturer: Royal Small Arms Factory, Enfield
Status: No longer in production (but see entry for L39A1 rifle). No longer in service with UK forces but stocks still held. In service with some former British territories and may be encountered elsewhere.

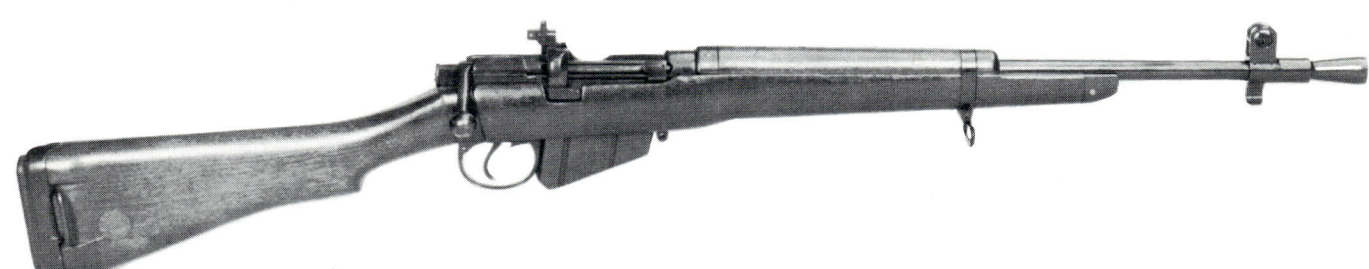

The .303 No. 5 Mk 1 rifle (RMCS)

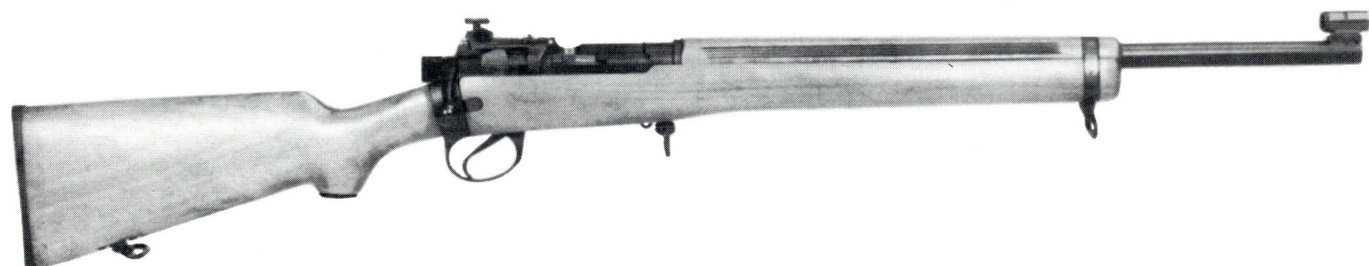

The .303 No. 5 Mk II rifle (RMCS)

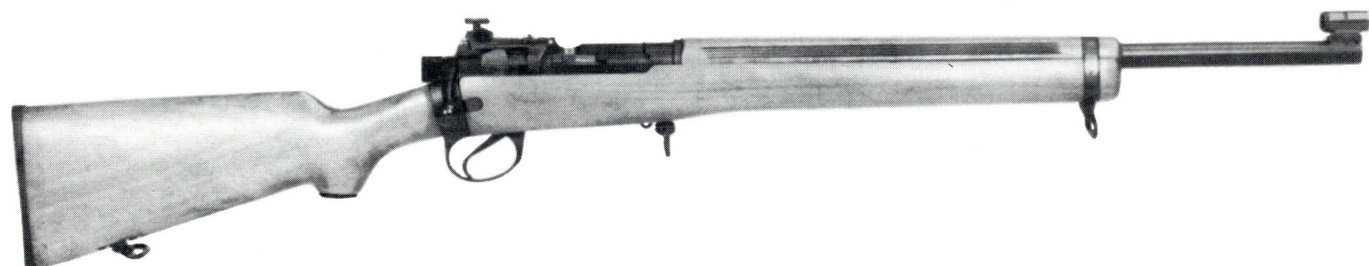

The .22 No. 8 rifle. Still in service (RSAF)

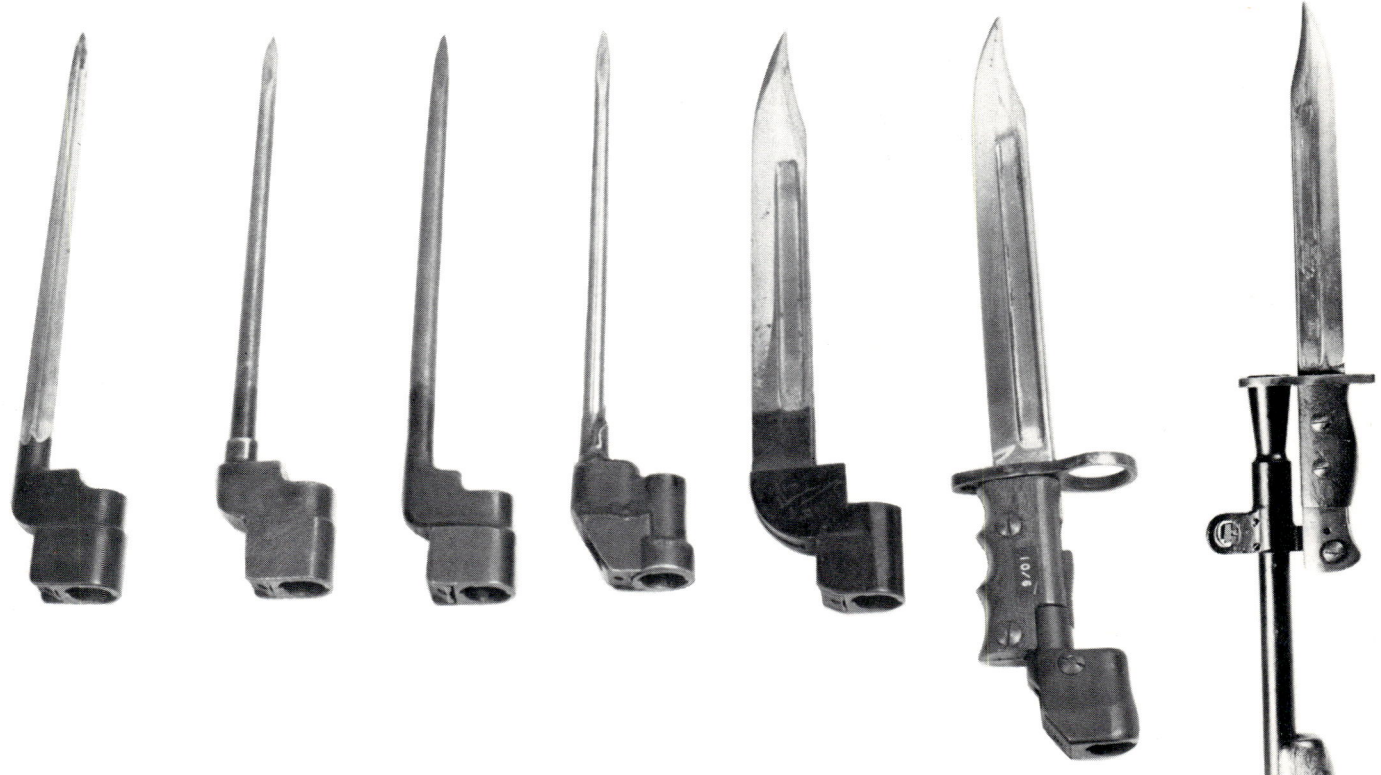

L. to R. Bayonets No. 4 Mk I, No. 4 Mk II, No. 4 Mk II, No. 4 Mk III, No. 7 and No. 9 (RSAF)

Rifle No. 5 with bayonet No. 5 (RSAF)

7mm ENFIELD EM RIFLES

In 1945 it was decided that a self-loading rifle was required by the British Army. The US Army had been issued with the M1 Garand (qv) in 1936 and by the end of the war most major powers were using self-loading rifles. The Germans had the Gw41 and 43 in 7.92mm and the MP44 in 7.92mm Kurz. The Russians had the Tokarev and Simonov rifles in the 7.62mm × 54R cartridge and produced a short 7.62mm × 39 cartridge in 1943 and the Simonov carbine in the 1944.

The calibre of the new British rifle was established at .276 inches (7mm) by the "Ideal Calibre Committee". This was the same calibre as that selected for the British 1913 rifle and for the American rifle trials in the early 1930s when the Pedersen .276 cartridge with a bullet weight of 8.1g and a muzzle velocity of 762m/sec was generally expected to become the standard round.

British effort was devoted initally to two rounds – one of .270 (6.85mm) calibre, a bullet weight of 6.5g and a muzzle velocity of 838m/sec and the other of .276 calibre with a bullet weight of 8.4g and a muzzle velocity of 731m/sec. Both cartridges had rimless cases. The .270 was found to lack energy and was too much affected by cross winds and was abandoned. All subsequent effort was applied to the .276 round. The bullet finally reached 731m/sec with a 9.1g bullet. Eventually this round became known as the 7mm Mk I Z at a velocity of 771m/sec. This round is generally referred to as the .280 – although .276 is the true diameter – and is known in Belgium as the British Intermediate Cartridge. FN were concerned in the development of this round which was used initially in the two FN rifles – the FN Light Rifle short model (the Bullpup) and the long model (the FAL). (See entry on Belgian rifle.)

British design was centred on the Royal Small Arms Factory and the Project Leader was Mr Noel Kent-Lemon. He had four independent design teams each working on a somewhat different concept of the Infantry Personal Weapon which was intended to replace the pistol, SMG and rifle and, with a heavier barrel, the LMG. This approach necessitated a short weapon but one with a capacity for accurate fire – i.e. a long barrel. To get these two parameters the 'Bullpup' approach was used in which the wooden stock was eliminated and a shoulder rest placed at the end of the receiver. Thus the recoiling parts came back to the firer's shoulder, his face was directly against the chamber and the direction of ejection made it impossible to fire the weapon from the left shoulder.

The first design – the Enfield Model 1 (EM1) – was the responsibility of Mr Stanley Thorpe who had many years of experience behind him and was later to become Manager of the Design and Development Establishment at Enfield. His weapon was gas-operated and positively locked using the German system of roller locking employed in the Sturmgewehr 45 assault rifle. The rifle employed pressings and production from steel sheet and was designed to cut down costs and time.

The EM1 was never fully developed and the difficulties experienced in getting subcontractors to produce pressings in time for trials, led to the abandonment of the project. The mechanism of the rifle was complicated and the field stripping procedure was complex. A collection of data on the EM1 is included for interest.

DATA (EM1 rifle)
Cartridge: 7mm Mk IZ
Method of operation: Gas
Method of locking: Rollers
Method of fire: Selective
Method of feed: 20-round box magazine

WEIGHTS
EM1 rifle with magazine empty: 4.66kg
Barrel and gas cylinder: 1.59kg
Trigger pull: 1st pressure 1.82kp 2nd pressure 5.22kp

LENGTH
Rifle: 914mm
Barrel: 622mm

MECHANICAL FEATURES
Barrel: Rifling: 5 grooves RH. 1 turn in 305mm
Sights: Optical: Unit magnification. 100-900yds (91-823m)
   Iron: (Emergency only)
      Foresight: Post
      Rearsight: Aperture
   Sight radius: 295mm

FIRING CHARACTERISTICS
Muzzle velocity: 771metres/sec
Muzzle energy: 275mkp
Recoil energy: 1.03mkp
Chamber pressure: 3,385kg/cm^2
Rate of fire: Cyclic: 600 rounds/min
      Automatic: 120 rounds/min
      SS: 40 rounds/min
Range, maximum effective: 825 metres
      maximum practical: 1,850metres
Accuracy: 8in (20cm) group at 200yds (183m)
Penetration: Steel helmet at 700yds (640m)

AMMUNITION
Calibre: 7mm
Type: Ball (AP. Tracer. APT and observation rounds were also developed)
Bullet weight: 9.09g
Charge weight: 1.91g NRN
Case weight: 10.48g
Round weight: 20.4g

In charge of the second Enfield Design Team was Stefan Kenneth Janson who came from Poland, and had worked at Radom and Stalowa Wola.

The Enfield Model 2 (EM2) turned out to be mechanically extremely

The EM1 .280 rifle (RSAF)

successful and politically extremely controversial.

It was another Bullpup design, gas-operated, with a locking system of some complexity in the field, in which the firing pin sleeve forced out two locking lugs into recesses in the receiver wall. Since the trigger was forward of the magazine, the trigger linkage was long and somewhat complicated – although perfectly effective.

The EM2 originally fired a 8.42g bullet at 732m/sec and was ready for full scale trials at the end of 1948. It was then tested throughout 1949 in the UK. In March 1950 it was taken to the USA and given engineering trials from March to May at Aberdeen Proving Ground. From May to November it underwent troop trials at Fort Benning against the FN .280 rifle and the American T25, with the M1 Garand as control. The EM2 rifle fired 56,800 rounds, 37,000 at full automatic, and stoppages averaged 4.54 per 1,000 rounds fired overall, and 3.4 per 1,000 rounds fired a semi-automatic. This was better than the M1 Garand which, firing single shot only, averaged 3.84 stoppages per 1,000 rounds fired, from a total of only 16,700. The EM2 was also the most accurate of the rifles fired.

The US Ordnance authorities made it clear that they considered the .276 cartridge to be lacking in power and its low muzzle velocity productive of too high a vertex height. In spite of increasing the bullet weight to 9.079g and the muzzle velocity up to 771m/sec the cartridge was not accepted.

In April 1951 Emanuel Shinwell, Minister of Defence, announced the intention of adopting the EM2 rifle in the British Army as the No 9 rifle. The Canadian Defence Minister Brooke Claxton managed to convene a meeting of the Defence Ministers of USA, UK, Canada and France which was held in the Pentagon on 2 August 1951. The net result was an agreement to preserve the status quo and that standard weapons and ammunition should continue in production but a new round would be adopted for NATO standardisation as soon as possible.

It was clear that the .280 round would never be accepted and Winston Churchill – who was then Prime Minister – announced suspension of the decision to adopt the EM2 rifle for British service.

The 7.62mm × 51 NATO cartridge was adopted on 1 May 1957 and this was the end of the EM2 rifle. Janson left England and went to work in the USA and eventually became Director of Weapon Research and Development with Winchester. Kent-Lemon died and the Design Team eventually disintegrated.

DATA (EM2 rifle)
Cartridge: 7mm Mk IZ
Method of operation: Gas
Method of locking: Projecting lugs
Method of fire: Selective
Method of feed: 20-round box magazine

WEIGHTS
EM2 rifle without magazine or sling: 3.55kg
Sling: 113g
Empty magazine: 223g
Loaded magazine: 653g

The EM1-280 rifle (RSAF)

EM2 rifle with full magazine and sling: 4.31kg
Barrel: 865g
Trigger pull: 1st pressure 2.95kp 2nd pressure 4.78kp

LENGTHS
Rifle: 889mm
Barrel: 622mm
EM2 rifle and No 7 bayonet: 1,092mm

MECHANICAL FEATURES
Barrel: Rifling: 5 grooves. LH. 1 turn in 254mm
Sights: Optical: Unit magnification 100-900yds. External zeroing on sight
Iron: (Emergency only)
Foresight: Post
Rearsight: Aperture. Set for 200 yds (184m)

Sight radius: 292mm
FIRING CHARACTERISTICS
Muzzle velocity: 771metres/sec
Muzzle energy: 275mkp
Recoil energy: 1.03mkp
Chamber pressure: 3,385kg/cm²
Rate of fire: Cyclic: 600-650 rounds/min
Automatic: 120 rounds/min
SS: 60 rounds/min
Sustained rate: 40 rounds/min
Range, maximum effective: 823 metres
Range, maximum practical: 1,892 metres
Accuracy: Standard rifle: 6 in group at 200yds (152.4mm at 183 metres)
Sniping rifle: 3in group at 200yds (76.2mm at 183 metres)
Penetration: Steel helmet at 700yds (640 metres)

The EM2 .280 rifle (RMCS)

The EM2 field stripped (RMCS)

7.62mm L1A1 RIFLE

When the 7.62mm cartridge was adopted as a NATO standard it was decided that the British Army should adopt the FN FAL rifle (qv). This had been developed initially to fire the 7.92mm Mauser cartridge and was well capable of using the less powerful 7.62mm × 51 NATO round.

The initial weapon from FN had been taken on troop trials in 1955 and there were two types of rifle known initially as types 'A' and 'B' and later as the X8E1, and X8E2. The type 'B' rifle had the unit magnification optical sight of the EM1 and EM2. This had an inverted pointer to be used for ranges up to 200yds and two range lines for 400 and 600yds, etched on the lens inside the sight. The type B rifle could be loaded only by inserting a loaded magazine: the magazine could not be topped up on the gun. The type 'A' had a breech charger guide and an opening in the breech cover to permit topping up or loading without removing the magazine from the gun. The cartridges were held in a horseshoe-type clip. The type 'A' rifle had a leaf aperture back sight. Both of the rifles fired the standard NATO 7.62mm cartridge at either automatic or single shot and both had the flash eliminator integral with the bayonet. A holding open device was incorporated. The rear projection on the magazine platform engaged a stud and forced up a pillar to arrest the bolt.

The X8E5 was also subject to troop trials. It differed from the E1 and E2 in having a modified firing pin.

The X8 rifles were used against the Mau-Mau in Kenya and, as a result of after-action reports and troop trials, the weapons were modified for eventual acceptance as the L1A1 rifle. The action is generally similar to that of the FN FAL rifle.

DATA (X8 Rifle)
Cartridge: 7.62mm × 51
Method of operation: Gas
Method of locking: Tilting Block
Method of fire: Selective
Method of feed: Type A. Clip loading into the 20-round box magazine.
Type B. Magazine loading

WEIGHTS
Rifle type 'A' no magazine: 4.05kg
Rifle type 'B' no magazine: 4.14kg
Magazine empty: 234g
Magazine loaded: 718g
Rifle type 'A' with full magazine: 4.76kg
Rifle type 'B' with full magazine: 4.86kg

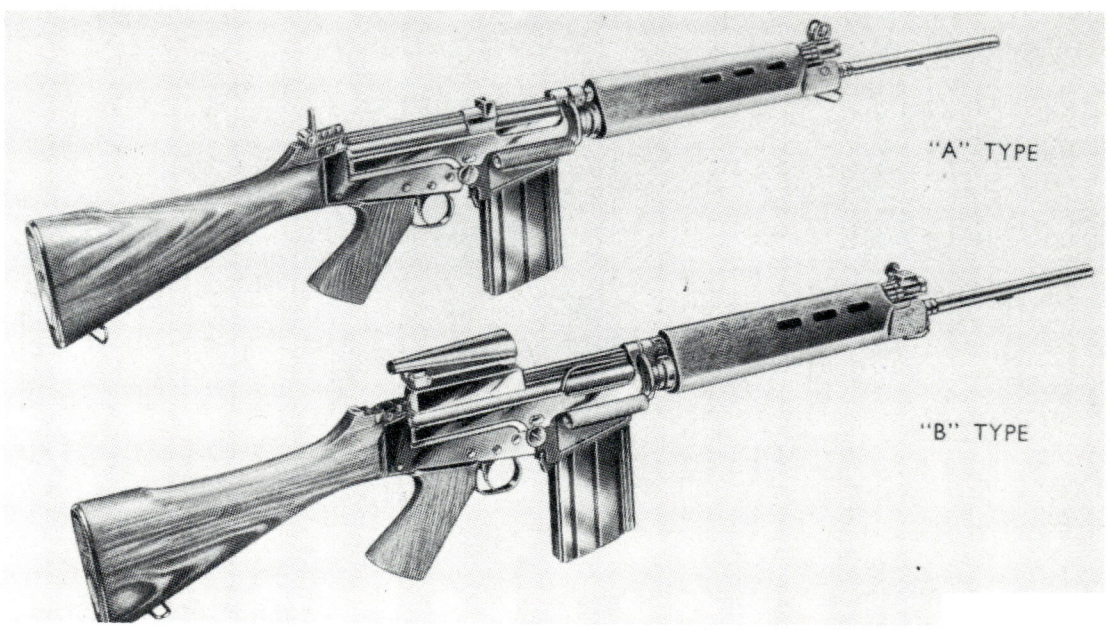

Experimental FN rifles used in troop trials in the British Army

LENGTH
Rifle: 1,054mm
Barrel: 533mm

MECHANICAL FEATURES
Barrel: Rifling: 4 grooves. RH. 1 turn in 220mm
Sights: Unit magnification: (Type B)
    Graduations: 200, 400, 600yds (184, 369, 554 metres)
    Zeroing: External controls
    Iron: Type A
    Foresight: Cylindrical post
    Rearsight: Aperture
    Zeroing: Elevation. Foresight. 1 click=.4in at 100yds (101mm at 90 metres)
        Line. Rearsight moves in dovetail

FIRING CHARACTERISTICS
Muzzle velocity: 853 metres/sec
Muzzle energy: 346mkp
Recoil energy: 1.66mkp
Chamber pressure: 3,465kg/cm²
Rate of fire: Cyclic: 650-700 rounds/min
    Automatic: 80 rounds/min
    SS: 40 rounds/min
Range, maximum effective: 800 metres

DATA (L1A1 rifle)
Cartridge: 7.62mm × 51
Method of operation: Gas
Method of locking: Tilting block
Method of fire: Single shots
Method of feed: 20-round box magazine

WEIGHTS
Weight, rifle only: 4.3kg
Weight, rifle and full magazine: 5kg
Magazine, empty: 255g
Magazine,full: 738g

LENGTHS
Rifle alone: 1,143mm
Barrel: 554mm

MECHANICAL FEATURES
Barrel: Regulator: Exhaust to atmosphere type
    Rifling: 6 grooves RH 1 turn in 305mm
    Cooling: Air
Sights: Foresight: Trilux
    Rearsight: Apertures
    Graduation: 200 to 600 yards (183-549m)
    Zeroing
    Sight radius: 554mm

Sight Unit Infantry Trilux (SUIT) may be fitted

FIRING CHARACTERISTICS
Muzzle velocity: 838metres/sec
Muzzle energy: 325mkp
Recoil energy: 1.65mkp
Chamber pressure: 3,465kg/cm²
Rate of fire: Semi-automatic: 40 rounds/min
Range, maximum effective: 600m with SUIT
Manufacturer: Royal Ordnance Factory, Fazackerley. Royal Small Arms Factory, Enfield Lock, Middlesex
Status: No longer manufactured. In service with British forces

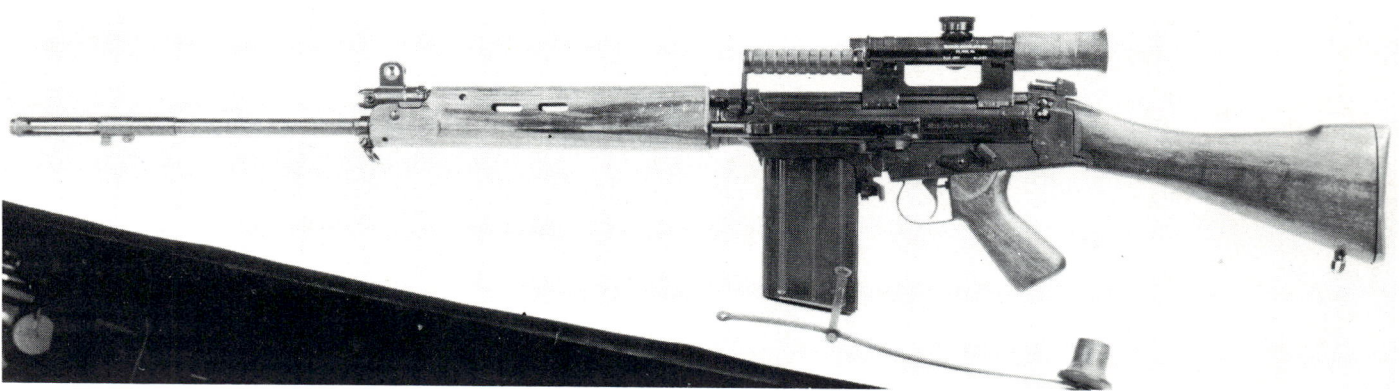

L1A1 with No 74 telescope (RSAF)

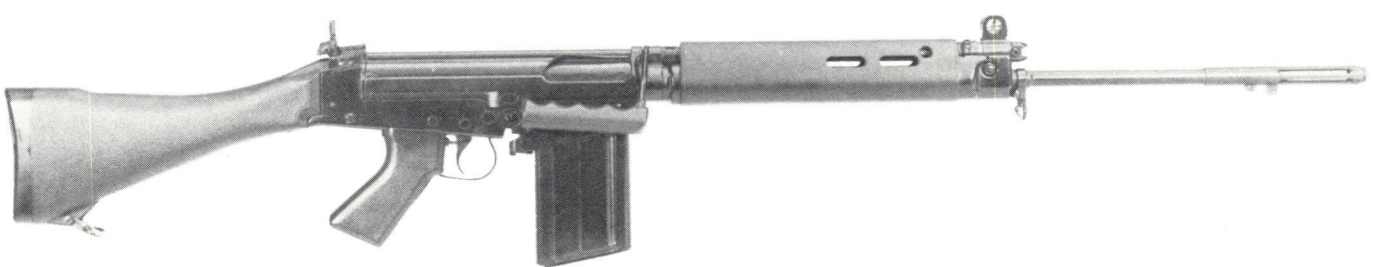

The L1A1 rifle with nylon furniture. This is the current design (RSAF)

7.62mm RIFLE L39A1

DESCRIPTION

The L39A1 rifle was introduced to provide a satisfactory target rifle for competitive shooting for units of the British Forces who normally would be equipped with the 7.62mm L1A1 rifle. The L1A1 rifle is unsuitable for serious target shooting and the decision was made to produce target rifles from the .303 No 4 Rifles held in Ordnance Depots. The No 4 rifles chosen for the conversion were the Marks 1/2 and 2. The choice of these marks of the No 4 rifles was made because the trigger is mounted on the receiver and not on the trigger guard as on some earlier marks. With changes in the woodwork due to temperature variation and moisture content, a trigger attached to the trigger guard does not give a consistent pull off.

The L39A1 is a manually-operated bolt action single shot rifle with a heavy 7.62mm barrel, manufactured at the Royal Small Arms Factory at Enfield, and the necessary modifications carried out on the extractor and receiver to permit the use of 7.62mm ammunition.

The barrel is produced using the Steyr cold forging process with the mandrel, carrying the rifling in relief, inserted in the drilled forging. The outside of the barrel is hammered and as a result is elongated and the grooves impressed on the inner surface. Both inner and outer skins are work-hardened and the pattern of the hammering is clearly visible on the external surface of the barrel. A foresight block is soldered to the barrel but no foresight is fitted. Commercial target sights are fitted by the using unit.

The barrel projects from the wooden fore-end for 15in (381mm). The fore-end comes from the No 4 .303 rifle, cut down to half an inch of the lower band. The butt is unchanged from the No 4 rifle except that a recess has been machined under the knuckle to take a container holding spare foresight blades. The handguard comes from the .22 No 8 rifle, suitably modified.

The rifle is proofed for 7.62mm ammunition which produces a higher chamber pressure than the .303 Mk VII, and in addition to the usual military proof marks of crown, ER and crossed flags with the letter P, the receiver, bolt and bolt head are stamped 19T. There are four sizes of bolt head available, marked 0, 1, 2 and 3 in ascending size, for ensuring correct cartridge head space.

The prime purpose of the weapon is competition shooting, and since rounds are usually hand-fed into the chamber the only service required from the magazine is the provision of a platform to support the round while this is done. For this purpose the original .303 magazines are retained. There is no positive ejector when this magazine is used. A groove in the left of the receiver shallows towards the rear and the friction between the side of the case and the groove tips the mouth of the case to the right and the extractor loses its grip. As an alternative a 7.62mm magazine holding ten rounds can be provided. It has an ejector plate spot welded to the lip at the left rear.

OPERATION

The round is placed on the platform and when the bolt is pushed forward the cartridge is fed into the chamber. The extractor snaps over the rim of the case into the cannelure. As the bolt goes forward the front bent of the cocking piece is in contact with the long arm of the sear and the cocking piece and striker are held to the rear. The main spring in the bolt is compressed between the collar of the striker and the rear inner surface of the bolt.

When the bolt is fully forward, the firer rotates the bolt lever down. The resistance lug on the bolt working in the cam groove and the resistance column in the bolt working on the resistance shoulder, force the bolt forward, seat the cartridge in the chamber, and then lock the bolt. The long cam groove in the rear of the bolt is lined up with the stud on the cocking

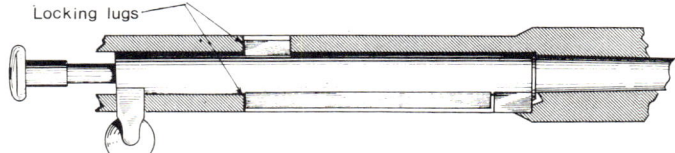

The Lee rear locking bolt

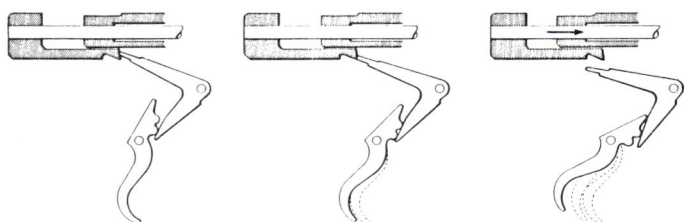

The double pull of the No. 4 rifle

piece and the action is fully cocked and ready for firing.

The trigger carries two ribs and when the trigger is squeezed the bottom rib pressing on the short arm of the sear rotates the sear about its axis and the nose of the sear moves down the face of the cocking piece. This first pull takes up the overlap which ensures that the sear cannot be accidentally jarred off the face of the bent. The top rib of the trigger then meets the short arm of the sear. This results in a reduced lever effort and the increased force needed to move the sear further, is the second pull. The second pull disengages the long arm of the sear cleanly from the bent with no drag.

The compressed main spring drives the cocking piece and striker forward until the striker point projects through the bolt head and strikes the cap to fire the round. The collar of the striker reaches the tenon of the bolt head which limits the striker travel.

After firing, the bolt lever is raised to unlock the bolt. The bolt head cannot rotate as it is engaged in the guide rib on the right of the body and the cocking piece is restrained by its groove in the body and cannot rotate. The bolt rotation withdraws the cocking piece, as its stud moves from the long to the short cam groove in the bolt, and the striker point is withdrawn from the cap of the fired case. The resistance lug on the underside of the bolt, working in the cammed groove in the body, produces the slow strong leverage which withdraws the bolt and bolt head and provides the force to loosen the cartridge case in the chamber, i.e. primary extraction.

When the bolt is fully rotated the resistance column is lined up with the slot in the body and the bolt can be pulled back. The empty case is withdrawn and ejected to the right.

As the cocking piece clears the long arm of the sear, the latter rises ready to hold the cocking piece when the bolt is pushed forward. The rearward motion of the bolt is stopped when the bolt head meets the resistance shoulder in the body.

MECHANICAL SAFETY

The mechanical safety before firing comes from the provision of two cam grooves in the rear of the bolt with a stud between them, and a stud on the cocking piece.

If the bolt lever is not fully closed when the stud on the cocking piece goes forward, it hits the right side of the stud on the bolt and closes the bolt.

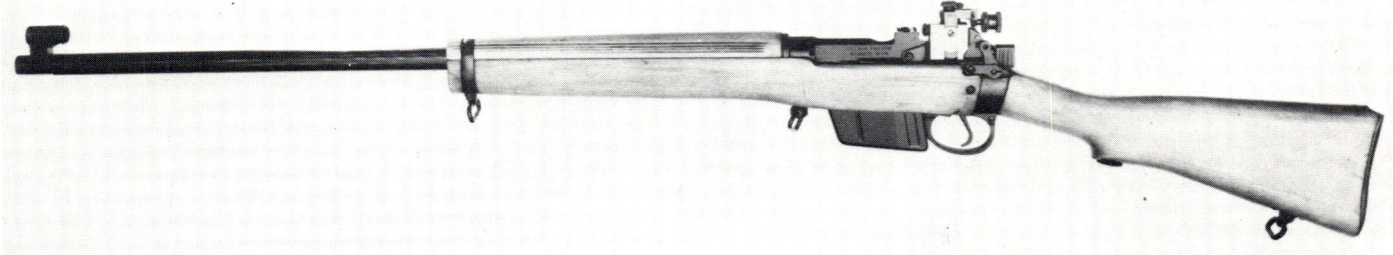

The 7.62mm L39A1 rifle (RSAF)

Possibly a misfire may occur if the cocking piece dissipates excessive energy in closing the bolt.

If the bolt is half closed the two studs are lined up and the striker cannot move forward. The sear has been released from the cocking piece and lies beneath it. When the firer closes the bolt the striker can move forward and the sear engages the half bent of the cocking piece and the two studs lie side by side. The bolt cannot be opened and as the sear is in the half bent of the cocking piece, the trigger cannot be pressed. The cocking piece must be manually withdrawn to allow the sear to engage the full bent.

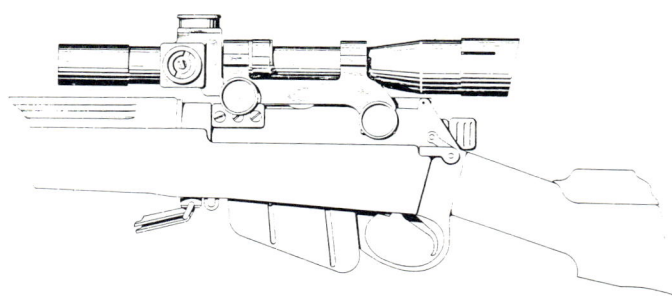

The telescope No. 32 Mk 3 on the No 4 rifle

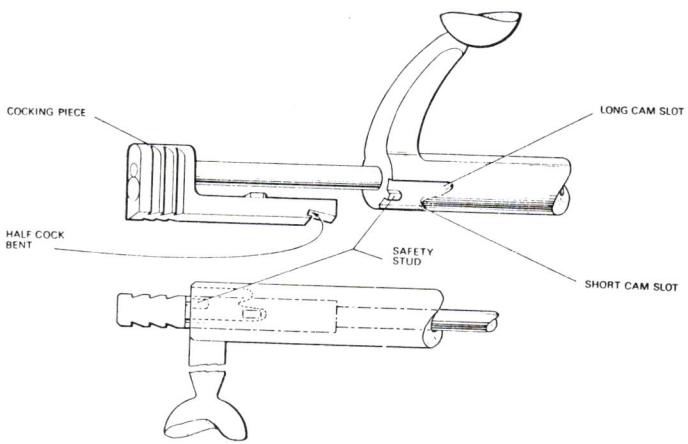

Mechanical Safety

APPLIED SAFETY

The safety is at the left rear of the body. It can be applied with the action cocked or fired. Applying the safety with the action cocked pulls the cocking piece back from the sear and locks it to the rear. With the action in the fired position, the cocking piece is withdrawn and locked so that it cannot be pulled back to the cocked position.

DATA

Cartridge: 7.62mm × 51
Method of operation: Manual

Method of locking: Rotating bolt
Method of feed: Either single round or 10-round box magazine
Method of fire: Single shots

WEIGHTS
Rifle: 4.42kg
Trigger pull: First pull 1.13-1.59kp
Second pull 1.81-2.04kp

LENGTHS
Rifle: 1,180mm
Barrel: 700mm

MECHANICAL FEATURES
Barrel: Rifling: 4 grooves RH 1 turn in 305mm
Sights: Competition sights attached as required by user

FIRING CHARACTERISTICS
Muzzle velocity: 841 metres/sec
Muzzle energy: 332mkp
Recoil energy: 1.67mkp
Chamber pressure: 3,465kg/cm²
Manufacturer: Royal Small Arms Factory, Enfield Lock, Middlesex
Status: Manufactured as required. In service with British Troops

7.62mm ENVOY TARGET RIFLE

Designed primarily as a target rifle which meets the specification of the British National Rifle Association, the Envoy rifle is based on the No 4 rifle but incorporates a number of special target shooting features.

The barrel is free floating and is manufactured from high-grade alloy by precision swaging, giving a non-reflecting, hammered external finish and an accurate rifling profile; and the chamber is made to close tolerance and tight so as to permit minimum case expansion. The receiver and bolt are of No 4 rifle pattern and the body and barrel are carefully stocked for high firing accuracy. A 10-round magazine is fitted as standard. Other features include a centre swivel for a target shooter's sling, a built-in container for the front sight insert and a butt plate made of shock-proof vulcanised chloroprene rubber.

DATA

Cartridge: 7.62mm × 51

Operation: Manual bolt action
Feed: 10-round magazine or hand loading
Weight: 4.75kg (barrel 1.7kg)
Trigger pull: 1.8-2.05kg
Length: 1186mm (barel 699mm)
Rifling: 4 grooves RH. Pitch 305mm. Depth 0.110mm. Width 4.3mm
Sights: Foresight: Tunnel with replaceable elements
Rearsight: Aperture micrometer with optional ¼ or ½ minute clicks for elevation and windage
Sight Radius: 830mm
Height of Sight Line above Bore Centre Line: 27.5mm
Manufacturer: Royal Small Arms Factory, Enfield, Middlesex
Status: Available to order

RSAF Envoy Rifle

7.62mm RIFLE L42A1

The L42A1 rifle came into service to meet the need for a sniper's rifle.

It is a conversion from the .303 No 4 rifle using Rifle No 4 Mk I(T) or Mk I*(T). These No 4 rifles were equipped originally with the Telescope Sighting No 32 Mk 3, and were used for sniping.

The conversion in all major aspects is similar to that used for the L39A1 rifle. However the trigger is pinned to the trigger guard – not mounted on the receiver. There is an additional swivel, secured by the front trigger guard screw.

The magazine on the L42A1 takes ten 7.62mm × 51 cartridges and has an ejector plate, spot welded to the left rear lip.

There are differences between weapons converted from the No 4 Mk I

and the No 4 Mk I*. The bolt head has a catch on the Mk I which must be depressed to permit the bolt head to engage or disengage with the guide rib. The Mk I* has a break in the guide rib but no catch.

Telescope brackets are fitted to the left side of the body to take the Telescope, Straight, Sighting, L1A1 which is modified from the Telescope Sighting No 32 Mk III of the No 4 (T) rifle. Those brackets also allow use of the image intensifier sight.

The open sights of the No 4 Rifle have been retained and the Mk I backsight is used. To allow for the different ammunition the datum line has been lowered by 0.070in and the modified slide marked 'm' on the right side.

The foresight is a spit block sweated to the barrel and it has an adjusting screw allowing the foresight to be clamped to the block. There are eight sizes of foresight from – 0.03in to 0.075in by increments of 0.015in (0.76-2-1.905mm×0.381mm) for zeroing.

ACTION
The action of the L42A1 is exactly the same as that of the L39A1 except for the ejector function.

DATA
Cartridge: 7.62mm × 51
Method of operation: Manual
Method of locking: Rotating bolt
Method of feed: Either single round or 10-round box magazine
Method of fire: Single shots

WEIGHTS
Rifle: 4.43kg
Trigger pull: First pull 1.36-1.81kp
Second pull 2.27-2.95kp

LENGTHS
Rifle: 1,181mm
Barrel: 699mm

MECHANICAL FEATURES
Barrel: Rifling: 4 grooves RH 1 turn in 305mm

Straight sighting telescope L1A1 mounted on the 7.62mm L42A1 rifle

Sights: Nil. Telescope L1A1 attached

FIRING CHARACTERISTICS
Muzzle velocity: 838metres/sec
Muzzle energy: 332mkp
Recoil energy: 1.67mkp
Chamber pressure: 3,465kg/cm²
Manufacturer: Royal Small Arms Factory, Enfield Lock, Middlesex
Status: In production. In service with British forces

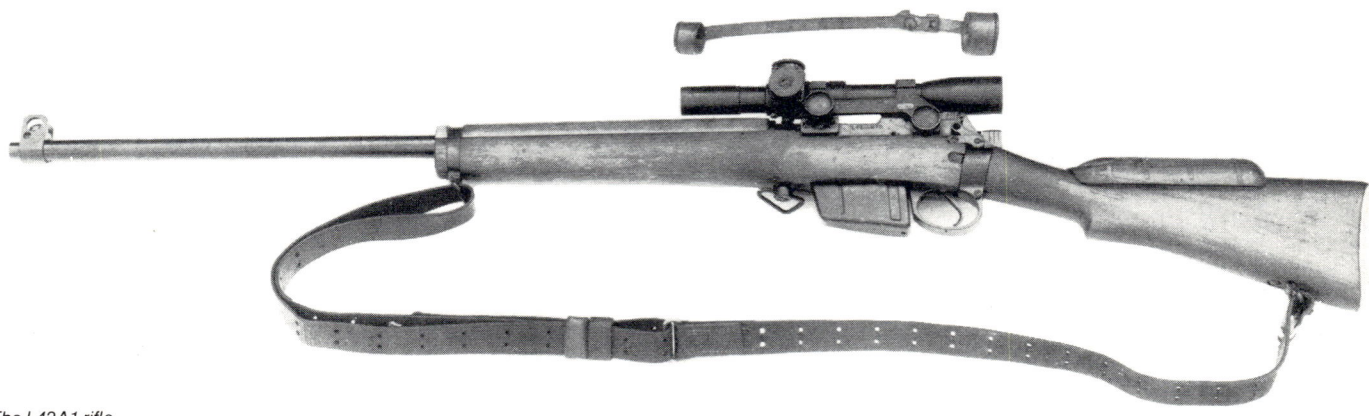

The L42A1 rifle

5.56mm STERLING LIGHT AUTOMATIC RIFLE

The Light Automatic Rifle was designed by Mr Frank Waters who is Sterling's Chief Designer.

It is gas-operated using a piston operating onto a bolt carrier in which is held a rotating bolt. Rotation is achieved with a cam path in the bolt carrier in which is engaged a cam pin projecting from the bolt. As the carrier is projected forward to feed a round from the magazine into the chamber, the bolt is prevented from rotating but when feed is completed and the bolt can go no further forward, the continued movement of the carrier rotates the seven lugs on the bolt head in front of abutments in the barrel extension and the bolt is locked to the barrel. The hammer is controlled by a safety sear which ensures that until the bolt is fully closed and locked, the hammer is held back. In the unlikely event of mechanical failure allowing the hammer to go forward before the bolt is fully closed, it strikes the rear end of the carrier, which masks the firing pin until the carrier has completed its forward movement, and dissipates its energy in pushing the carrier forward. After firing, the carrier is forced back by the piston, which lies above the barrel and after a short period of delay whilst the gas pressure falls, the cam slot engages the bolt cam pin and rotates the bolt. This rotation provides primary extraction and loosens the case in the chamber. The unlocked bolt is carried back, the case is extracted and ejected to the right of the gun, and the return spring is compressed. The bolt carrier runs out, the next round is fed and, if the trigger is still depressed, fired. If the ammunition supply is exhausted the bolt carrier is held to the rear by the magazine operated holding open device.

There is a simple 3-position gas regulator at the front of the cylinder and the muzzle carries a flash hider which also serves to centre a grenade over the barrel.

The sights of the rifle consist of a post at the front which has lateral adjustment for zeroing and a rearsight with apertures for 200 metres and 400 metres and a vertical adjustment for zeroing. There is a mount for a telescopic sight or an image intensifier.

Fire is selective and there is a three-round burst facility.

DATA
Cartridge: 5.56× 45
Method of operation: Gas
Method of locking: Rotating bolt
Method of feed: 20-round box magazine
Method of fire: Selective

WEIGHTS
Rifle: 3.4kg
Magazine empty: 85g
Magazine loaded: 285g
Rifle loaded: 3.685kg

LENGTHS
Rifle, fixed butt stock: 970mm
Rifle, butt extended: 970mm
Rifle, butt folded: 755mm

MECHANICAL FEATURES
Barrel: Regulator: 3 gas tracks and cut off position for grenade launching

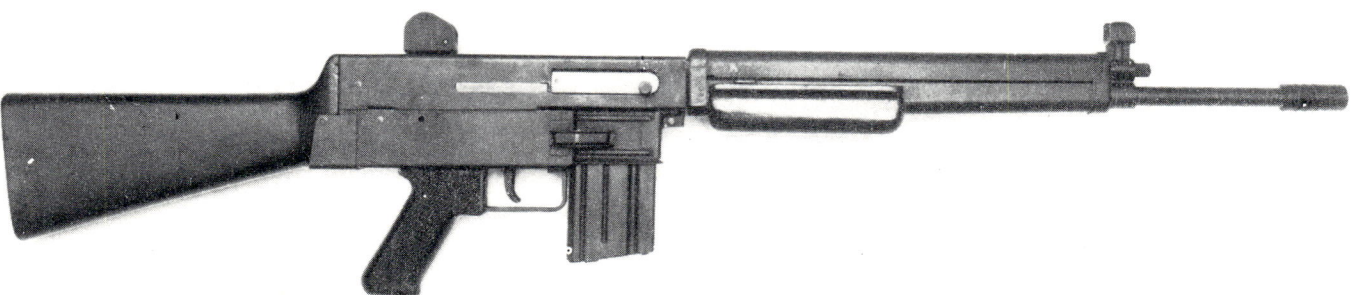

The Sterling light rifle

Rifling: 6 grooves. RH 1 turn in 305mm
Cooling: Air
Sights: Foresight: Post
Rearsight: Apertures for 200 and 400 metres
Zeroing: Line. Foresight on dovetail; Elevation. Rearsight
Sight radius: 520mm

FIRING CHARACTERISTICS
Muzzle velocity: 990 metres/sec
Muzzle energy: 178mkp
Recoil energy: 0.7mkp

Chamber pressure: 3,622kg/cm^2
Rate of fire: Cyclic: 650 rounds/min
Automatic: 100 rounds/min
SS: 40 rounds/min
Range, maximum effective: 400metres
Accessories: 30-round magazine. Bayonet. Bipod. Sling
Manufacturer: Sterling Armament Co, Dagenham
Status: Following the negotiation of the agreement with Armalite it now seems unlikely that Sterling will proceed with this weapon. The experience gained with it will doubtless be of value, however, in their further development of the Armalite series.

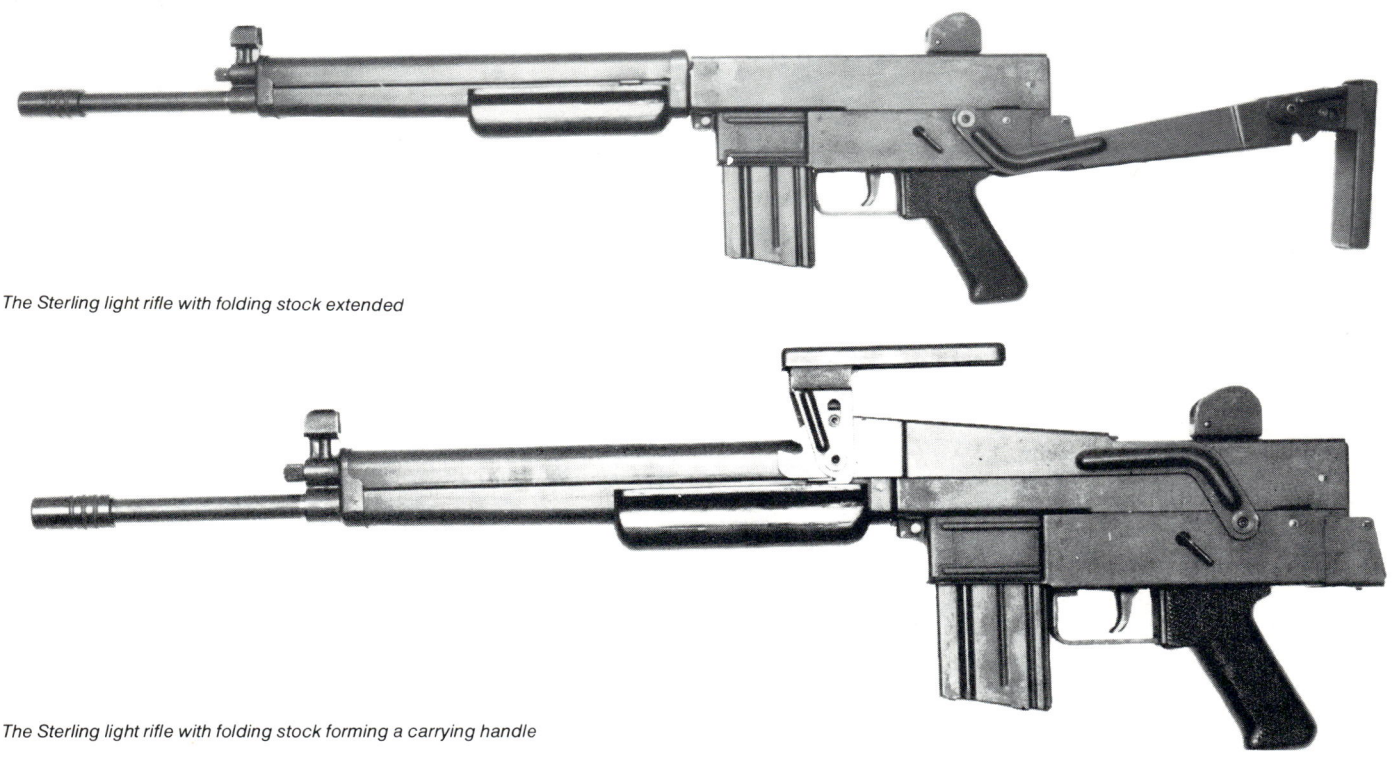

The Sterling light rifle with folding stock extended

The Sterling light rifle with folding stock forming a carrying handle

4.85mm INDIVIDUAL WEAPON

In June, 1976, two new weapons were demonstrated by the British Army at the School of Infantry, Warminster. Designated, at present, simply the Individual Weapon (IW) and the Light Support Weapon (LSW), both are in 4.85mm calibre and have been developed as possible replacements for most of the existing range of British infantry small arms and as the British entries for the 1977-78 series of NATO finals which is aimed at establishing new standard weapons and ammunition for the 1980s.

Both weapons were developed at the Royal Small Arms Factory at Enfield: the Project Manager was Colonel John S. Weeks and the RSAF team leader Mr. E. I. Kirkpatrick. Some 80% of the components of the weapons are common to both; but as the intended role of the LSW is as a replacement for the current 7.62mm Bren LMG and for the 7.62mm GPMG in its light support role it is described in a separate entry in the Machine Gun section of this book. It should be noted here, however, that, although the standard magazine for the IW holds 20 rounds and that for the LSW 30 rounds, the two magazines are interchangeable, also that the LSW is light enough to be fired from the shoulder without bipod support.

AMMUNITION

A new 4.85mm round has been developed for use with both weapons. It

has a brass case, weighs 11.6g and produces a muzzle velocity of 900m/sec (IW) 930m/sec (LSW). Ball, tracer and blank rounds had been developed up to the time of the demonstration; and armour-piercing, grenade-launching, drill, inspection and proof rounds were under development. During trials a 4.85mm round penetrated a 3.4mm NATO mild steel plate at 500m whereas a standard 5.56mm round fired under the same conditions did not.

CONSTRUCTION

Apart from the forestock, the IW is made entirely of steel but with a minimum of mechanical parts. The forestock is made of nylon and is in two parts which are held together with a quick-release clip. The weapon is gas-operated and locked by a rotating bolt engaging in lugs immediately behind the breech. The cocking handle is on the right and the magazine is located behind the pistol grip. The barrel is provided with a flash eliminator.

A ×4 SUSAT optical sight is fitted as standard and there is an open battle sight on top of the optical sight. No range performance data have so far been released but the weapon probably has an effective range around 500m. Mecar-type grenades can be fired directly from the muzzle. A bayonet is under development.

Firing the 4.85mm Individual Weapon (UK MoD)

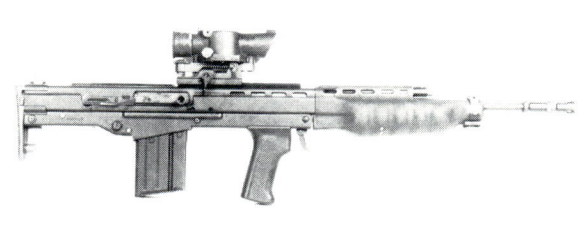

4.85mm Individual Weapon (British Army official)

This new rifle is light and handy and has the advantage of looking more like a soldier's weapon than some recently proposed devices. Considered as a replacement for the present 9mm SMG and the 7.62mm SLR used by British forces, it can provide a much bigger punch than the former and is much better suited to the combat situations in which British troops have recently been engaged than the latter.

COMPARATIVE DATA (IW and SLR)

	Individual Weapon	Self Loading Rifle			
Ammunition:					
Calibre:	4.85mm	7.62mm	**Loaded Magazine (20 rounds):**	.398kg	.755kg
Types:	Ball	Ball	**Weapon (complete with**		
	Tracer	Tracer	**loaded magazine):**	4.12kg	5.65kg
	Blank	Blank	**Length:**		
		Ballistite	**Barrel (including**		
Round Weight:	11.6 grams	24.6 grams	**flash hider):**	51.85cm	62.2cm
Method of Operation:	Gas	Gas	**Weapon:**	77cm	114cm
Type of Locking:	Rotary Bolt	Falling	**Mechanical Features:**		
	Forward	Breech Block	**Rifling: Grooves:**	4	4 or 6
	Locking	Rear Locking	**Turns:**	1/125mm	1/305mm
Method of Feed:	Magazine	Magazine	**Trigger Pull:**	3.12-4.5kg	3.12-4.5kg
Method of Fire:	Selective	Semi Automatic	**Firing Characteristics:**		
Weight:			**Muzzle Velocity:**	900m/s	835m/s
Weapon (less Magazine			**Recoil Energy:**	3.7J	16.58J
and Optical Sight):	3.12kg	4.29kg	**Rate of Fire (Cyclic):**	700-850r/m	Single Shot
Optical Sight:	.6kg	.6kg	**Manufacturer:**	RSAF	RSAF
Empty Magazine:	.174kg	.263kg	**Status:**	Trials	Service

5.56mm STERLING AR-18 BP COMBAT RIFLE

Since acquiring manufacturing and commercial exploitation rights for the Armalite AR-18 rifle and AR-18S machine carbine, Sterling have put in hand the development of two new versions of these weapons, the AR-18 BP Combat Rifle and the AR-18 LMG. The former is a 'bull pup' version of the AR-18 having a very short buttstock, the trigger group and pistol grip well forward and the magazine well located between the butt and the pistol grip.

Manufacturer: Sterling Armament Co, Dagenham, Essex
Status: Development

UNITED STATES OF AMERICA

.30in M1903 (SPRINGFIELD) RIFLE

One of the most famous of American rifles, this weapon is still to be found in several countries. Based on the Mauser rifle, of whose virtues the US forces had become aware in the Spanish-American war, it was first used with the .30 M1903 ball cartridge, but later the M1906 (.30-06) cartridge was adopted and earlier weapons re-chambered for it. There were several versions of the rifle but the following data are typical.

DATA
Cartridge: .30-06, .30 M1, .30 M2
Operation: Manual, bolt operated
Locking: Rotating bolt, forward lugs
Feed: 5-round internal box magazine

Weight: 4.0kg
Length: 1100mm
Barrel: 610mm
    Rifling: 4 grooves LH. Pitch 254mm
Sights: Foresight: Blade
    Rearsight: Leaf or ramp aperture or telescopic
Muzzle velocity: 700-850m/sec according to type and ammunition
Muzzle energy: 330-360mkp
Rate of fire: 10 rounds/min
Effective range: 800m
Manufacturer: Springfield Armoury and others in the USA
Status: No longer made but still in use outside Europe and North America

.30in M1903 rifle

.30in M1917 (ENFIELD) RIFLE

Known as the 'Enfield' because of its British (RSAF) origin, this rifle is almost identical to the British P14 which was produced in the USA in .303in calibre in plant commissioned by the British Government early in the First World War. When the USA entered the war in 1917 the rifle was produced (in much larger numbers) in .30-06 calibre for the US forces.

The P14 weapons were used for training and for British Home Guard

M17 rifle with telescopic sight

units during the Second World War and were popular with marksmen. Most of the surviving weapons, however, are almost certainly the US version and are believed to be widely distributed.

DATA
Cartridge: .30 M1906
Operation: Manual, bolt-operated
Locking: Rotating bolt, forward locking
Feed: 5-round internal box magazine
Weight: 4.17kg
Length: 1082mm
Barrel: 660mm
    Rifling: 5 groove LH. Pitch 254m
Sights: Foresight: Blade
    Rearsight: Leaf aperture
Muzzle velocity: 862m/sec
Muzzle energy: 368mkp
Manufacturers: Winchester Repeating Arms Co. and others
Status: No longer made but still exists in large numbers

.30 Cal RIFLE M1

John C. Garand began his design career during World War 1. He started with a light machine gun actuated by the set back of the primer in its pocket in the head of the cartridge case. The primer pushed the firing pin and this unlocked the bolt.

The war ended and in 1919 Garand started work at Springfield Armoury on a new, primer-actuated rifle. The introduction of the new progressive burning powder, known as Improved Military Rifle, which has a slower pressure rise, produced insurmountable problems for the primer actuation system which Garand had then to abandon. Instead, he designed a gas-operated rotating-bolt rifle which was tested at Springfield Armoury in 1926-29. He died at Springfield, Massachusetts on 16th February 1974 aged 86, after a long, successful and distinguished career in small arms design.

In 1929 a comparative test was held at Aberdeen Proving Ground between the Garand, the Pedersen delayed blowback rifle, the Thompson, also a delayed blowback weapon, a Colt-manufactured short recoil Browning rifle, the Belgian Browning, the Czechoslovakian Zb 29 designed by Vaclav Holek, and a gas-operated toggle joint lock rifle produced by the German designer Heinemann. The Garand in .276 (7mm) calibre was considered the best and 20 rifles were made for detailed testing. This was concluded in 1932 and the Garand was recommended for adoption in .276 calibre. General MacArthur vetoed the adoption of the .276 cartridge, however, and the weapon was standardised, after further tests, on 9 January 1936, as the US Rifle calibre .30 M1.

Production got under way in August 1937 and by August 1939 some 50,000 had been made. The early models had a muzzle cap screwed on and this was drilled to allow the passage of gas back to the piston. So in effect the bullet had left the muzzle before any gas was diverted. The standard production models had a conventional gas tapping near the muzzle.

A number of modifications were made to the M1 rifle in various versions. Those denoted with a letter suffix were adopted.

M1E1 Had a more gradual cam angle in the operating rod handle.
M1E2 This was an experimental sniping rifle with a telescopic sight.
M1E3 The bolt cam lug had a roller lug attached and the cam angle of the operating rod was altered. This idea, although not accepted in the **M1**, was adopted in the later M14 rifle.
M1E4 The gas system was changed to the self-regulating gas cut off expansion system.
M1E5 Short barrelled, 18 inch (457mm) version with a pantograph type stock. There was excessive muzzle blast and flash although accuracy out to 300yds (274m) was acceptable.
M1E6 This had an offset telescopic sight.
M1E7 This had a M73 (Lyman Alaskan) or M73B1 (Weaver 330) telescope on a Griffin and Howe mount. This was standardised as the **M1C.**
M1E8 (MID) Another telescope mounted sniping rifle.
M1E9 This was the same as the M1E4 except that the piston was separate from the actuating rod and drove it back. This system was retained in the M14 rifle.

The early version of the Garand (RSAF)

Standard M1 .30 Rifle

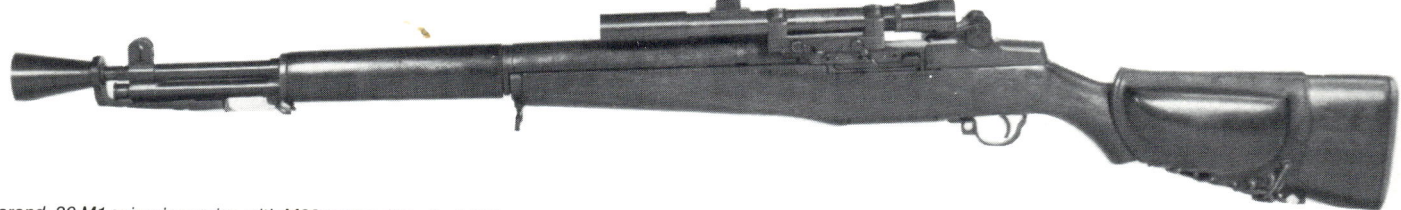

Garand .30 M1 sniper's version with M82 scope. Note flash hider

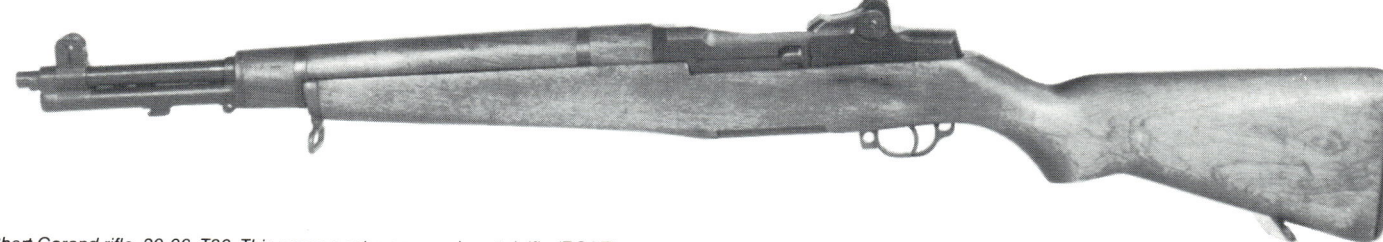

Short Garand rifle, 30-06, T26. This was a post-war experimental rifle (RSAF)

OPERATION

The cartridge clip takes eight .30 calibre cartridges. These are loaded into the clip so that the base of each round rests on the back wall of the clip and the extractor groove of each cartridge engages the inner rib of the clip. If the nose of any round is allowed to protrude, loading becomes difficult.

The operating rod handle is retracted and the rod held to the rear by the catch. The clip is placed on the follower and pushed in with the thumb until it engages the clip latch. When this occurs the follower arm rotates the accelerator which in so doing forces down the front end of the operating rod catch. The operating rod is released and is driven forward. The front end of the bolt engages the top cartridge and pushes it forward into the chamber. The extractor engages the groove in the base of the cartridge. The bolt is rotated clockwise by the camming recess in the operating rod and the two lugs on the bolt engage in locking recesses in the receiver. The ejector spring is compressed.

When the trigger is operated the hammer strikes the firing pin and this hits the cap of the cartridge. Some of the propellant gases are diverted through the gas port into the cylinder. The piston and operating rod are driven to the rear, compressing the return spring under the barrel. There is an initial free movement of 5/16 inch (8mm), allowing the gas pressure in the chamber to drop, until the camming surface of the recess in the operating rod contacts the bolt lug and lifts it up, rotating the bolt to the left and unlocking the lugs from their recesses in the receiver. The rotation and slight withdrawal of the bolt face loosens the case in the chamber, cams the hammer away from the firing pin and withdraws the firing pin from the cap into the bolt.

The bolt is carried back by the operating rod, the empty case is pulled out of the chamber by the extractor and when the mouth of the case emerges from the chamber, the compressed ejector spring can expand and the ejector emerges from the bolt face to throw the case out of the rifle to the right front.

The hammer is cocked, the return spring fully compressed and the bolt passes over the rim of the top round in the magazine. The return spring exerts pressure on the follower arm which lifts the follower and forces the cartridges upwards in the clip. The end of the operating rod strikes the front face of the receiver, goes forward and the bolt chambers the next round.

When the last round in the clip is fired the operating rod comes back and is caught by the operating rod catch and held to the rear. The clip is ejected by the clip ejector, emitting a low 'ping' in the process.

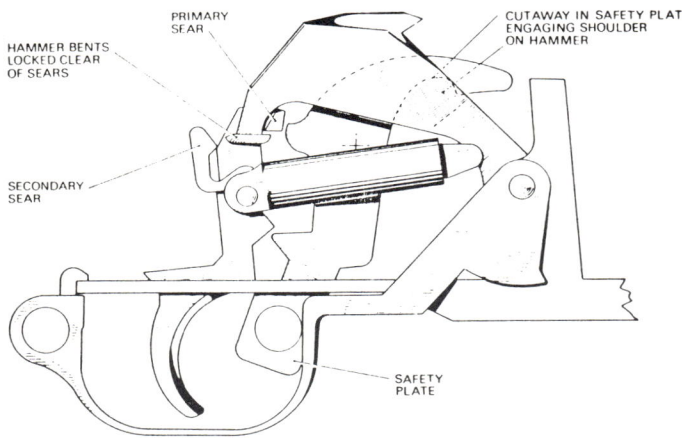

The action of the applied safety mechanism (RMCS)

TRIGGER AND FIRING MECHANISM

The Garand trigger and firing mechanism has been very widely copied and is now found in various forms in many other American and some Soviet weapons.

The trigger has an extension, the primary sear, which is shaped like a hook and moves backward and forward as the trigger is operated. Mounted on this extension and behind it is a spring loaded secondary sear.

The hammer carries two bars – or bents – and when it is rotated fully back, these lie horizontally, one reaching forward, the other back. The forward one is the primary bent, the rearward one the secondary bent.

When the hammer is cocked the primary sear engages the primary bent. When the trigger is rotated the primary sear goes forward and releases the hammer and the round is fired. The hammer is rocked back by the bolt and since the trigger is still pulled, the primary bent passes behind the primary sear but the secondary bent is caught by the spring loaded secondary sear and is held to the rear. To fire another round the trigger must be released. The backward movement frees the secondary sear and the hammer starts to rotate but is immediately caught by the primary sear as it moves back.

When the trigger is operated again the primary sear moves forward, the hammer is free and rotates onto the firing pin.

However if the bolt is not fully rotated and locked, the tang of the firing pin is blocked by the receiver bridge. When locking is completed the tang is aligned with a slot in the bridge and can move forward. Also unless the bolt is fully locked the hammer cannot reach the firing pin but will drive the bolt forward and close it, and when it does reach the pin it will have insufficient energy to fire the cap and a misfire will result.

The safety catch is located in front of the trigger guard. When it is pulled back to the 'safe' position a cutaway engages a shoulder in the hammer to lock it. The hammer is also forced back and disconnected from the sear. The safety plate, when it is fully back, also prevents any movements of the trigger.

STRIPPING

(1) Remove the loaded clip from the receiver by pulling back the operating rod handle. Place the fingers of the left hand over the receiver, press in the clip latch with the left thumb and the clip will be ejected into the left hand.

(2) Check no round remains in the chamber and then allow the operating rod to go forward under control.

(3) Turn the rifle over, grasp the rear end of the trigger guard and pull backwards and upwards on the guard. Take care not to rotate more than 90 degrees and then withdraw the trigger group by pulling directly upwards.

(4) Lift the stock group from the receiver by pulling upwards on the butt end of the stock. This breaks the weapon into barrel and receiver group, the trigger housing group and stock group. These can be further disassembled if required.

DATA

Cartridge: .30 M2
Method of operation: Gas
Method of locking: Rotating bolt
Method of feed: 8-round clip
Method of fire: Self-loading

WEIGHTS
Rifle, empty: 4.3kg
Rifle with bayonet M1905: 4.8kg
Trigger pull: 2.5-3.41kp

LENGTH
Rifle, overall: 1106mm
Barrel: 610mm
Rifling: 587mm

MECHANICAL FEATURES
Barrel: No regulator
    Rifling: 4 grooves RH. 1 turn in 254mm
    Cooling: Air
Sights: Foresight: Blade
    Rearsight: Aperture. Windage scale
    Graduation: 200-1,200yds (183-1097m)
    Zeroing: Line. Move foresight block on dovetail. Elevation. Rearsight drum
    Sight radius: 27.9in at 100yd setting (710mm)

FIRING CHARACTERISTICS
Muzzle velocity: 865metres/sec
Muzzle energy: 367mkp

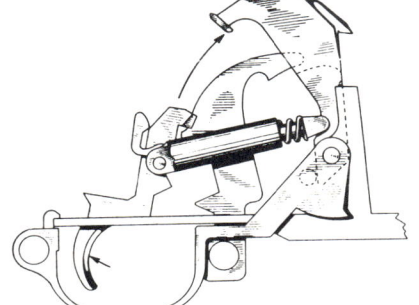
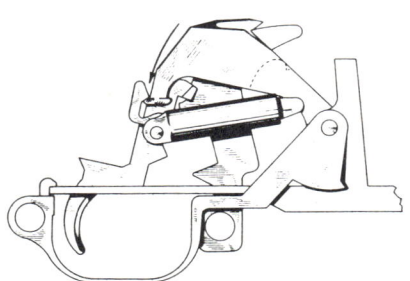
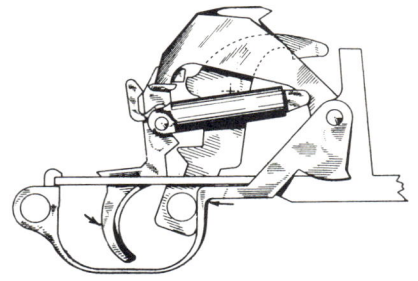

The trigger and firing mechanism: (1) The trigger is pulled, the trigger extension goes forward and the hammer is released; (2) The hammer is rotated by the recoiling bolt. The rear bar catches in the spring loaded sear; (3) When the trigger is released the hammer is transferred to the main sear (RMCS)

Recoil energy: 1.66mkp
Chamber pressure: 3523kg/cm²
Rate of fire: 30 rounds/min
Range, maximum effective: 600metres
Maximum (approx): 3,200m
Accessories: Bayonet, M1905. Bayonet scabbard M3. Bayonet scabbard

M1910, Sling
Manufacturer: Springfield Armoury, Springfield, Mass. Harrington & Richardson Arms Co. Worcester, Mass. International Harvester
Status: No longer manufactured in USA. In service in USA with National Guard Battalions. In service (modified to 7.62mm) in Italy

.30 M1 CARBINE

On 1 October 1940 the US Ordnance Department issued a specification for a light rifle – weight not to exceed 5½lbs (2.5kg) and capable of either self-loading or automatic action. This weapon was required to replace the pistol and sub-machine gun in arms other than infantry.

The cartridge for this weapon was developed by Winchester Repeating Arms Co from their .32 self-loading rifle cartridge of 1905 from which it deviated only very slightly in external measurements. It was known as Calibre .30 SR M1 where SR stood for 'Short Rifle'.

The contenders for this design were Springfield Armoury, Reising, Winchester, Auto-Ordnance Co, Woodhull, Turner, Hyde, Savage Arms Co and Harrington and Richardson.

After preliminary firing in May 1941 the requirement for selective fire was abandoned.

The Winchester design was based on their experimental model rifle produced for test in 1940. This weighed 4.2kg and incorporated a new form of gas operation, developed by David M. Williams, and now universally referred to as "short stroke piston operation". Winchester it is reported, produced their carbine in an extraordinarily short period of time and it was submitted for test on 15 September 1941 and proved the best of the contenders.

It was accepted in October 1941 as the US Carbine Caliber .30 M1 and eventually more of these carbines were produced than any other single US model. Published production quantities for Carbines M1, 2 and 3 are:

Winchester	828,059
Inland Manufacturing Division of General Motors	42,097
Underwood-Elliot-Fisher	545,616
National Postal Meter	413,017
Rock-ola Manufacturing Corporation	228,500
Quality Hardware and Machine Co	359,666
Standard Products Co	247,160
Saginaw Steering Gear Division of General Motors	517,212
IBM	346,500

Total   3,527,827

These weapons were issued to all theatres of operations in which US troops were employed.

The M1 Carbine was a self-loading carbine.

The M1A1 Carbine, standardised in May 1942, had a side folding stock.

The M1A2 Carbine, standardised in 1942, had a modified receiver to accommodate a ramp back sight in place of a flip over type. It was never produced.

The M1A3 Carbine, standardised but not produced, had a pantograph type stock.

The M2 Carbine was standardised in November 1944 as a selective fire carbine.

The M3 was a M2 with no sights and a flash hider. It was intended specifically to carry the Infra-red "Sniperscope".

A lot of experimental models were made but were not adopted. The M8 grenade launcher was standardised for use with all the carbine models in November 1943.

Various forms of the carbine have been produced in Italy by Beretta as the Model 1957, in Dominica as the Cristobal carbine M2 and in Morocco, a home-produced version of the Beretta model 1957.

OPERATION

The magazine is loaded with 15 rounds and pushed up into the magazine well. The cocking handle is on the right and retraction and subsequent release chambers the top round in the magazine.

When the trigger is squeezed the hammer is released and the firing pin is driven into the cap of the cartridge. The gas pressure forces the bullet up the bore and some of the gas following it is diverted through a gas vent about 114mm from the chamber. The pressure is high and it impinges on a very small piston which is driven back only 3.6mm before its movement is stopped. It contacts the operating slide which acquires the momentum of the piston and moves back. There is a delay to allow the chamber pressure

US Army .30 cal. carbine M2

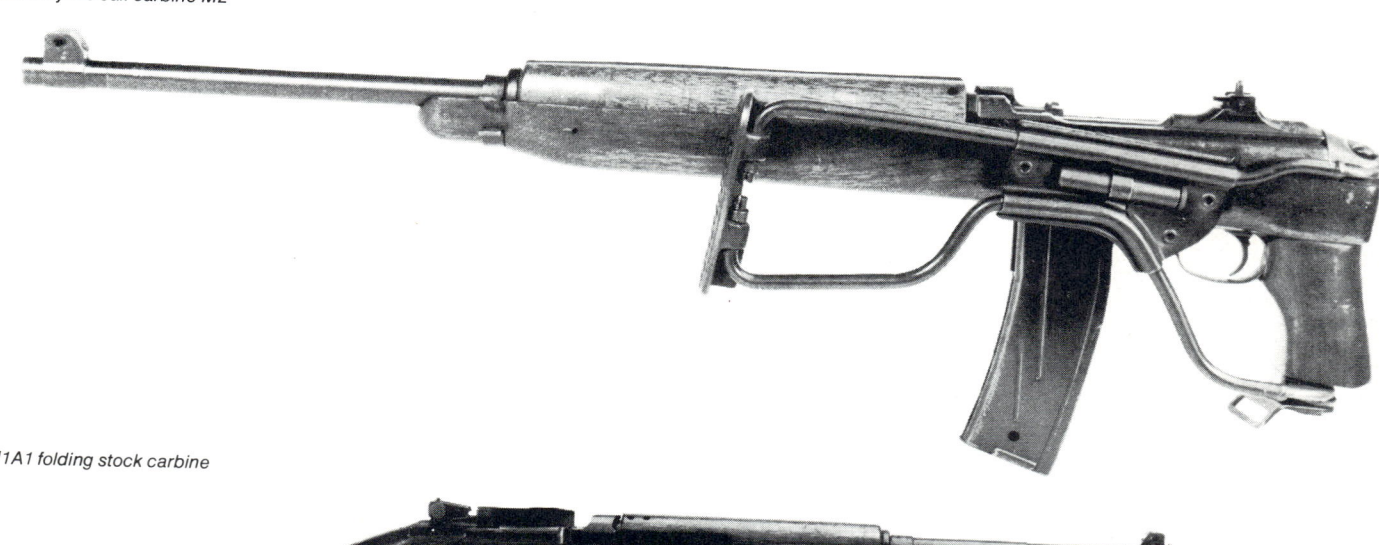

M1A1 folding stock carbine

M2 carbine modified to take a cartridge deflector

to fall whilst the slide travels back a little over 7.6mm and then a cam recess engages the operating lug on the bolt. The bolt is rotated – providing primary extraction of the near parallel sided case – and then unlocked. This rotation starts the cocking action on the hammer and also retracts the firing pin. The empty case is pulled out by the extractor and then the spring loaded ejector in the bolt throws it forward to the right of the carbine. The hammer is now cocked and the return spring is compressed to drive the bolt forward.

The bolt chambers the round and rotates to the locked position, the operating slide pushes the piston forward inside its cylinder and the weapon is ready to fire again. Should the self-loading action fail, the cocking handle can be used to operate the cycle by hand.

TRIGGER AND FIRING MECHANISM (M1 CARBINE)

The trigger is pivoted about the trigger pin located at its top front corner so when it is pulled the shoulder at the rear end rises. The tail of the sear rests on top of the shoulder and when it is lifted the nose is depressed out of the hammer notch. The sear pivots on the trigger pin and has an elongated notch which provides sufficient clearance for the sear to move forward and disengage itself from the trigger shoulder. When the hammer is cocked, the rearward pressure exerted by the hammer, and resulting from the forward pressure of the hammer spring acting above the hammer pivot, overcomes the presence of a small spring acting on the sear and maintains the sear in contact with the trigger shoulder: when the trigger is operated and the sear is disengaged from the hammer, however, the sear spring drives it forward and the tail of the sear slips off the shoulder of the trigger. When the bolt recoils it rotates the hammer, and the notch on the underside is held by the sear. To fire another round the firer must release the trigger. The shoulder drops and the hammer spring overcomes the sear spring and forces the tail of the sear back over the top of the trigger shoulder and when the trigger is pulled, another round can be fired.

When the firing pin goes forward a tang must enter a cut out portion in the bridge of the receiver and this can only occur when the bolt is fully rotated and locked. If the hammer goes forward when the bolt is not fully closed, the hammer energy is absorbed in rotating the bolt into the locked position and there may not be enough energy to fire the cap – resulting in a misfire.

The safety is a push through type located just forward of the trigger guard. When it is pushed to the left a slot in the plunger allows the forward end of the trigger to be depressed thus allowing the rear shoulder to rise. When it is pushed to the right the solid diameter of the plunger moves under the forward end of the trigger and prevents it from moving down.

The M2 version of the carbine has selective fire. A lever, operated by the slide as it reaches the forward limit of its travel, lifts the sear out of engagement with the hammer bent at automatic fire.

STRIPPING

(1) Remove the magazine, cock the action and inspect the chamber.
(2) Push back the sling swivel against the fore end. Loosen the front band screw – using a screwdriver or the rim of a cartridge case. Press the front end of the locking spring rearwards and pull the front band forward over the spring. Slide the upper fore end forward and lift it clear of the barrel.
(3) Lift the muzzle and pull the barrel receiver and trigger group forward and out of the stock.
(4) Push out the pin located at the front of the trigger guard. Pull back the operating slide spring guide free of the operating slide. Pull it forward and to the right and the spring and guide are free.

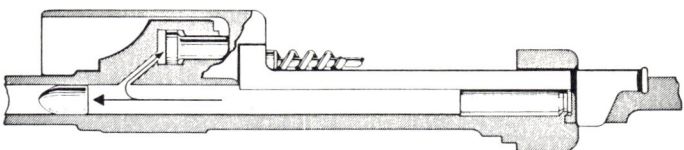

The action of the short stroke piston (RMCS)

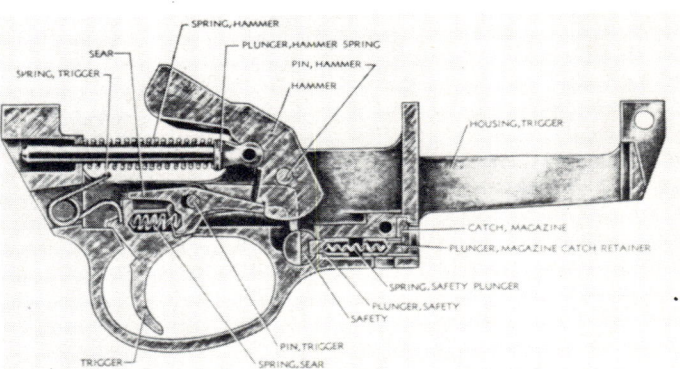

Sectional view of M1 and M1A1 trigger group seen from the right. The hammer is cocked and the sear in its rearward position with its tail on the trigger shoulder

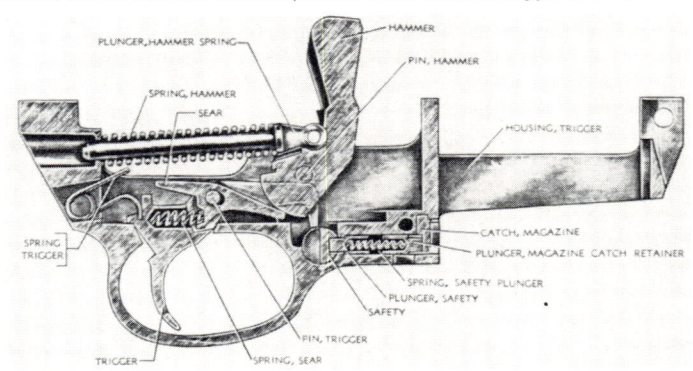

In this picture the hammer is shown forward and the sear disengaged from the hammer and in its forward position clear of the trigger shoulder

(5) Remove bolt by rotating it anti-clockwise, lift it at the front, rotate and remove.
(6) Pull the housing forward to clear the grooves in the receiver and lift it out. Remove slide from barrel.
(7) Re-assemble in reverse order.

DATA
Cartridge: Carbine Cal .30 M1
Method of operation: Gas
Method of locking: Rotating bolt
Method of feed: Magazine
Method of fire: M1 – self-loading, M2 and M3 selective

M3 with Sniperscope and flash hider (RSAF)

M2 carbine modified to take a grenade launcher sight mounted on left side

WEIGHTS
M1 Carbine with unloaded magazine: 2.36kg
M1 Carbine with loaded magazine and sling: 2.63kg
M1A1 Carbine with unloaded magazine: 2.53kg
M1A1 Carbine with loaded magazine and sling: 2.77kg
M2 Carbine with unloaded magazine: 2.36kg
M2 Carbine with loaded magazine and sling: 2.63kg
Magazine empty: 0.074kg
Magazine loaded (15 rounds): 1.25kg
100 cartridges: 2.68kg
Trigger pull: 1.82-73kp

LENGTHS
M1 Carbine: 904mm
M1A1 Carbine, stock extended: 905mm
M1A1 Carbine, stock folded: 648mm
Barrel: 458mm

MECHANICAL FEATURES
Barrel: No regulator
   Rifling: 4 grooves RH 1 turn in 508mm
   Cooling: Air
Sights: Foresight: Blade
   Rearsight: Flip aperture 0-150, 150-300. Leaf slide on M2 models
   Zeroing: Backsight slides in dovetail for line adjustment
   Sight radius: 546mm

FIRING CHARACTERISTICS
Muzzle velocity: 607metres/sec
Muzzle energy: 95mkp
Recoil energy: 0.56mkp
Chamber pressure: 2,280kg/cm²
Rate of fire: Cyclic: (M2 and M3 only) 750 rounds/min
   Auto: (M2 and M3 only) 75 rounds/min
   SS: 40 rounds/min
Range, maximum effective: 300 metres
   Maximum: 2,000 metres

.30 CALIBRE BROWNING AUTOMATIC RIFLE

John M. Browning was probably the most successful gun designer in history. He was born in Ogden, Utah in 1855. His father was a gunsmith and John Browning and his brother Matthew were brought up with the background to become weapon designers. John Browning's first rifle was a dropping block design, 600 of which he produced before selling the guns and the manufacturing rights to the Winchester Arms Co. The Browning brothers set up a sporting goods store in Ogden, Utah with a workshop on the floor above. In 1884 he designed a lever action, tube magazine rifle in .45 calibre. This was marketed by Winchester as the Model 1886 and led to an association between Browning and Winchester that lasted until they had a disagreement over a self-loading shotgun. Browning went to Europe and produced a series of weapons for FN, including pistols, that were produced in USA by Colt.

In 1890 Browning offered a gas-operated machine gun to Colt. This was tested by the US Navy and adopted by them in 6mm calibre (the cartridge for the Lee rifle). This gun is generally referred to as the 'Potato Digger' since the operating lever below the barrel swept out an arc below the gun – making it difficult to use in the prone position. The Army was still content to use the Gatling gun.

Browning returned to the USA and in 1917 gave a demonstration of two new weapons – the Browning water-cooled machine gun and his Automatic Rifle. The tests at Congress Heights of the BAR on 27 February 1917 were very impressive. The rifle was fired at semi-automatic, automatic and whilst carried by a walking soldier. In addition it was completely stripped down to its basic 70 components and rapidly re-assembled.

Colt's held the rights to Browning's design and they provided the draw-

ings and gauges to enable other companies to manufacture the Browning Automatic Rifle (BAR). Browning returned to Winchester's plant and there the working drawings were produced. Production started in February 1918 and in November of that year when the war ended, Winchester were producing 300 guns a day. Other guns were made by Marlin-Rockwell who were turning out 200 a day when the war ended. Colt made a total of 9,000 to bring the overall figure up to 52,000 guns. The weapon first saw action on 13 September 1918.

The BAR model remained the same until 1937 when the Model 1918A1 was introduced. (In 1922 a few guns were modified for cavalry use but this Machine Rifle Model 1922 was never very successful in this role and was made obsolete in 1940.) The Model 1918A2 was introduced in 1941 and remained in service after World War II. It was used in Korea and finally went out of US Army service when the M60 GPMG was introduced in 1957. These models all have basically the same mechanism and are distinguished as follows.

Model 1918. This has a smooth barrel, slightly tapered, with no bipod. It produces selective fire.

Model 1918A1. This has a bipod attached to the gas cylinder just forward of the forearm. An outer butt plate is hinged to swing over the top of the firer's shoulder. The rearsight is adjustable for elevation only.

Model 1918A2. The flash hider is changed and incorporates a bearing for the bipod. The rearsight has both elevation and windage adjustment controlled by large knobs with a click mechanism. There is a stock rest under the buttstock. There is a cyclic rate mechanism to reduce the rate of fire from 500 to 300 rounds a minute. Two rates of automatic fire can be

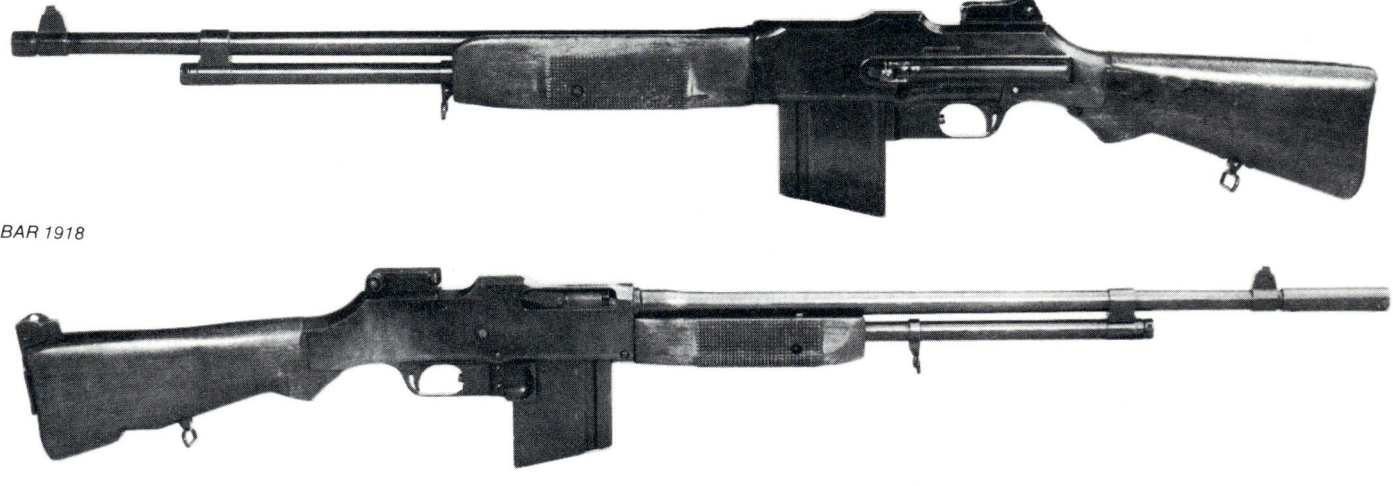

BAR 1918

BAR, long barrel – 1918, modified

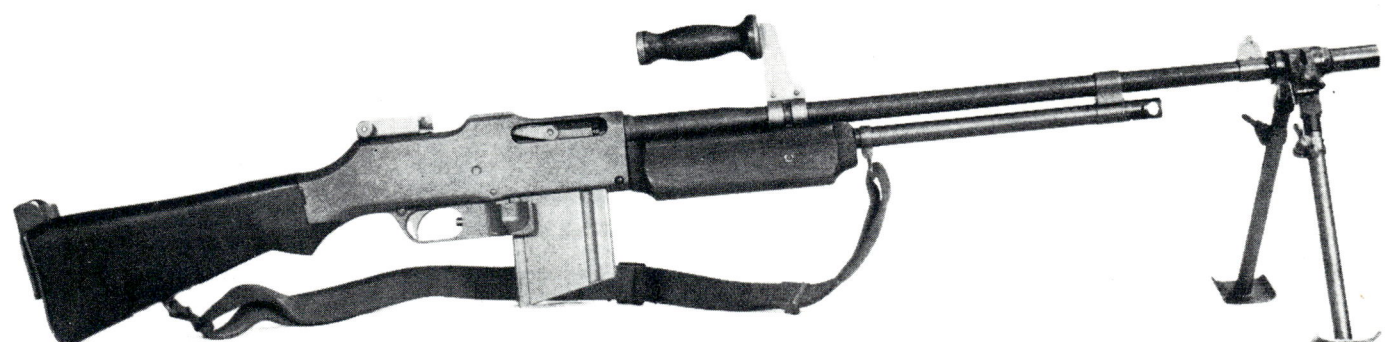

BAR .30 M1918M2

obtained but there is no semi-automatic ability. There is a metal heat shield in the forearm to protect the return spring.

Machine Rifle Model 1922. This had a heavy, finned barrel. The stock rest clamped round a groove in the butt.

T34 Automatic Rifle. This was a conversion to the NATO 7.62mm × 51 cartridge carried out in 1949. It was never in service.

Colt produced a commercial model of the M1918A2 called the R75 which had selective fire. It had a bipod fitted to the gas cylinder. It weighed 20¼lb. They later marketed the 'Monitor' which was an improved version of the R75. It had an 18inch barrel and a compensator but no bipod. It weighed 16.25lb and was used by some US Police Departments. The BAR was also produced by FN before World War II as the Model 30 and the Model D came out after the Second World War. This has a quick-change barrel and the return spring is housed in the butt. It was also manufactured in Sweden and Poland.

The last production of the BAR in USA occurred during the Korean War when the Royal McBee Typewriter Co produced 61,000 M1918A2 rifles.

OPERATION

The BAR is a gas-operated weapon with a locking piece which enters a recess in the roof of the receiver.

The 20-round box magazine is removed by pressing forward the release catch located inside the front edge of the trigger guard. The magazine is loaded by placing the filler over the magazine with the grooves over the magazine catch rib. The clip is placed over the filler and the round pressed straight down with the thumb. If no filler is available individual cartridges are loaded one by one until the magazine is full. The magazine is replaced in the receiver in front of the trigger guard and pressed up until the catch locks it in position.

The rifle is cocked by pulling back the cocking handle on the left of the receiver. The cocking handle is then returned to the forward position leaving the working parts to the rear.

The change lever is marked 'S' for safe. On the Models 1918 and 1918A1, 'F' gives semi-automatic fire and on the Model 1918A2 – which has no semi-automatic fire – it will produce the slow rate of automatic fire (350 rounds per minute). When set to 'A' all models give automatic fire – the Model 1918A2 giving the higher rate of fire of 500-650 rounds/minute.

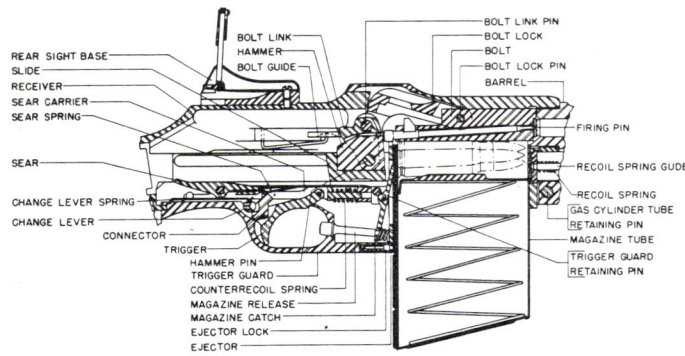

A section through the receiver of the BAR

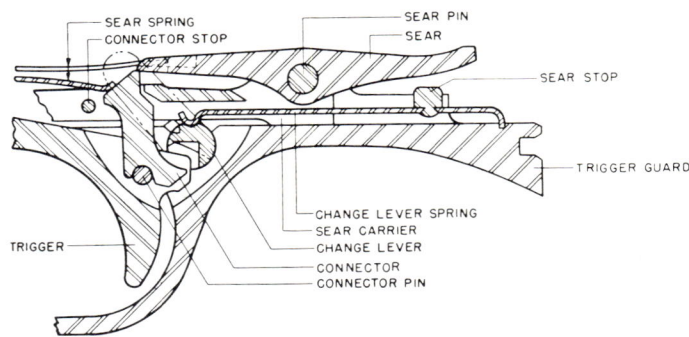

The change lever set to semi-auto

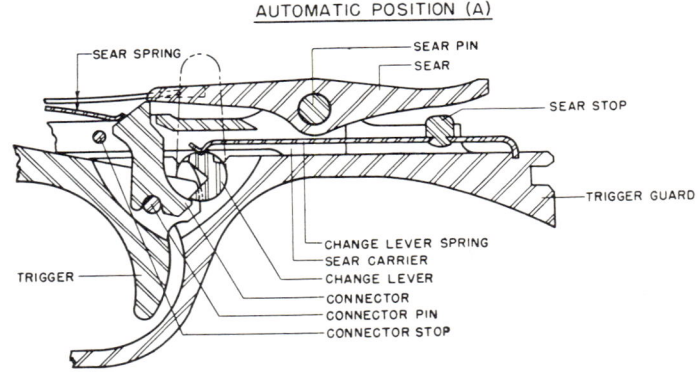

The change lever at "automatic"

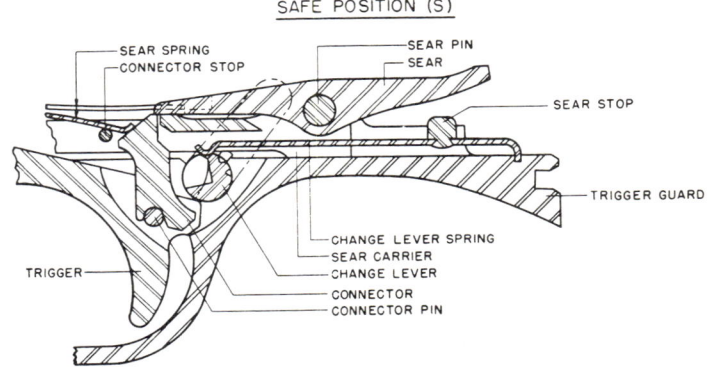

The change lever at "safe"

With the change lever moved from 'safe', when the trigger is operated the sear is depressed from its notch in the slide which goes forward, pulled by the compressed return spring. The rear end of the slide contains the hammer which is connected to the bolt by a link. The feed rib under the bolt engages the base of the top cartridge in the magazine and pushes it forward against the bullet guide and up into the chamber. As it emerges from the magazine lips the base of the cartridge slides across the bolt face and into the extractor.

When the slide is about 5cm from its forward position the bolt lock begins to ride over the rear shoulders of the bolt supports which are riveted into the sides of the receiver. These cam up the rear end of the bolt lock. The bolt link pin passes over dead centre with respect to the bolt lock pin and the bolt lock is forced up by the link, attached to the hammer pin, into the locking recess in the top of the receiver and thus levers the bolt home. The hammer pin passes dead centre under the bolt link pin. At this point the firing pin is released from its slot in the under side of the bolt lock and is positioned to be struck by the hammer. The hammer, attached to the slide, moves forward a further 2.5mm and drives the firing pin ahead of it whilst it makes its last 1.5mm forward travel. The firing pin hits the cap and some of the propellant gas passes through the gas port drilled down through the barrel 15cm from the muzzle, through the gas cylinder tube bracket and into the gas cylinder. The cylinder has three gas ports which are rotated into position, when the gas pressure on the piston head needs to be changed, using the combination tool. Usually the smallest port is employed but if the gun is carboned up or very dirty the second or third port is used. The gas cylinder body, at the front of the gas cylinder tube, is screwed right in and then rotated back so that the symbol – a large, medium or small circle – is towards the barrel.

The gas pressure drives the piston back. The piston is attached to the slide which carries the hammer and bolt. At the moment of firing the hammer pin is 5mm in advance of the link pin, and the hammer is slightly behind the head of the firing pin. When the slide moves back the hammer is carried back 5mm until the hammer pin is under the link pin. This is the mechanical safety after firing which allows the gas pressure in the chamber

to drop to a safe level. The link is then revolved forward around the hammer pin and draws the bolt lock down out of the locking recess in the receiver. By the time the slide has travelled back 3cm the bolt lock is completely clear of the locking recess. As the bolt lock revolves down from its locked position it cams the firing pin back from the face of the bolt. The movement of the circular cam surface on the lower part of the bolt lock passing over the bolt supports in the receiver, produces primary extraction which loosens the cartridge in the chamber. The bolt moves back and the extractor on the right of the bolt face holds the empty case on the breech face until it strikes the ejector on the trigger group. The cam is rotated about the extractor and through the ejection port on the right. It strikes the receiver about an inch behind the ejection port and is deflected to the right front of the rifle.

The end of the slide hits the buffer and rebounds about 2.5mm before engaging the sear. If the change lever is at 'A' the cycle is repeated.

TRIGGER AND FIRING MECHANISM (M1918 and M1918A1)

The trigger carries a connector which rises into contact with the sear. When the change lever is set in the forward position to 'F' and the trigger is operated the connector raises the front end of the sear thus depressing the rear end and releasing the slide. As the trigger is further retracted into a cutaway on the change lever, the connector is cammed from under the sear by a cam on the sear carrier and the end of the sear drops resulting in the nose rising and arresting the slide in the rear position. The trigger must be released to allow the connector to be pushed back by the sear spring under the tail of the sear.

When the change lever is set to 'A', vertically, and the trigger is operated, the connector rises and pushes up the tail of the sear. The connector comes into contact with a solid segment of the change lever and so does not come into contact with the cam on the sear carrier. The nose of the sear is depressed and the slide moves forward. It continues to reciprocate until the trigger is released or the ammunition is exhausted.

When the change lever is positioned at 'safe' the trigger cannot rotate back at all, but is locked.

BAR 1918A2

M1918A2

The M1918A2 differs in that the trigger mechanism will produce two rates of fully automatic fire but there is no provision for single shots.

STRIPPING

Remove magazine and cock weapon. Ensure chamber is empty.

Rotate the gas cylinder retaining pin, at left front of receiver, and withdraw it from its socket.

Pull forearm and gas cylinder tube forward and remove.

Return working parts forward.

Rotate retaining pin at front of trigger guard and withdraw it.

Withdraw trigger mechanism.

Remove return spring guide by pressing right index finger on checkered surface of its head and turning it until the ends are clear of retaining shoulders. Remove return spring.

Line up hammer pin holes on receiver and operating handle by inserting point of dummy round in hole in operating handle with right hand, pressing on hammer pin, and pushing operating handle back with left hand. Push hammer pin through. Pull operating handle to rear and remove.

Push slide to rear and push hammer forward out of its sear on the slide. Lift hammer out of receiver.

Push slide forward, with bolt link down, out of the receiver, taking care to avoid striking gas piston or rings against gas cylinder tube bracket.

Force bolt guide out with left thumb. Lift out bolt, bolt lock and bolt link by pulling them slowly to rear end of the receiver and up, with right thumb and forefinger. Pull out firing pin from its way in bolt. Push out bolt link pin and remove bolt link.

Remove extractor by pressing point of dummy round against the claw and exerting pressure upward and to the front. Remove extractor spring.

Re-assembly is in reverse order.

DATA

Cartridge: .30 Cal M1 or M2
Method of operation: Gas
Method of locking: Projecting lug
Method of feed: 20-round box magazine
Method of fire: M1918, M1918A1 – selective
M1918A2 Two rates of automatic fire.

WEIGHTS
Gun only M1918: 7.26kg

M1918A1: 8.41kg
M1918A2: 8.82kg
M1922: 8.74kg

LENGTHS
Gun overall M1918: 1,194mm
M1918A1: 1,194mm
M1918A2: 1,215mm
M1922: 1,040mm
Barrel: 610mm except M1922 – 457mm

MECHANICAL FEATURES
Barrel: Regulator: 3 positions
Rifling: 4 grooves RH
Cooling: Air. No quick change barrel in US models
Sights: Foresight: Blade
Rearsight: Tangent leaf with aperture backsight
Windage: M1918A2 and M1922
Graduation: 1-16 by 100yd (91.4m) increments
Zeroing: Elevation: Change foresight. Line: Foresight moves in dovetail
Sight radius: 782mm

FIRING CHARACTERISTICS
Muzzle velocity: 860 metres/sec
Muzzle energy: 366mkp
Recoil energy: 1.1mkp
Chamber pressure: 3,460kg/cm²
Rate of fire: Cyclic: 550 rounds/min
Slow auto (M1918A2 only): 350 rounds/min
Single shot (except M1918A2): 350 rounds/min
Single shot (except M1918A2): 40 rounds/min
Range, maximum effective: 600 metres

Manufacturer: Colt Patent Firearms, Hartford, Connecticut. Winchester Repeating Arms Co., New Haven, Connecticut. Marlin-Rockwell Corporation, New Haven, Connecticut. IBM, Poughkeepsie, New York. New England Small Arms Corp. Royal McBee Typewriter Corp.
Status: No longer manufactured. Still in service with Greek Army

---

7.62mm M14 SL RIFLE

The US .30 calibre rifle M1 (Garand) was introduced into the US Army on 9 January 1936. It served the US forces well in World War II but was considered to be somewhat heavy and its 8-round clip was inadequate. An improved gun was designed in 1944, known as the T20. This was an M1 rifle with a 20-round box magazine, a selective fire capacity and a compensator. It was not adopted. American research was devoted to a new SL rifle, produced at Springfield Armoury, called the T25 which had a tilting block design locking in the top of the receiver. The T25 had a 20-round magazine and a muzzle brake-compensator. It had an upswept buttstock. It fired a new cartridge using a case known as the T65, which was simply a shortened .30-06 case. Various projectiles were available. In 1950 it was decided to purchase 5,000 T25 rifles for troop trials but the order was cancelled and the Belgian FN rifle and the British EM2 rifle were tested against the T25. The T25 was not a success and the T47 was introduced to

replace it; the British .280 cartridge used in the EM2 and the FN rifle was considered lacking in power. Springfield Armoury then produced the T44 which was a modernised M1 Garand rifle with the gas port moved nearer the breech. It fired a 7.62mm ball and used the T65 cartridge case using a 20-round box magazine. The T47 was abandoned in 1952 and the T44 developed further. The Belgian FN rifle was produced using the 7.62mm ball and T65 cartridge case and this did well in tests in America. It was given the name T48 and 3,000 were purchased from FN for troop trials together with 200 heavy-barrelled guns to be tested as squad automatics. At the same time tests were made on the large scale production of both the T44 and T48. 500 T48s were made by Harrington and Richardson, at Worcester, Mass and 500 T44s were produced by Springfield Armoury. During the winter firing programme of 1953-4 the T48 developed troubles in extremely cold conditions. These were corrected before the follow-up winter trials of

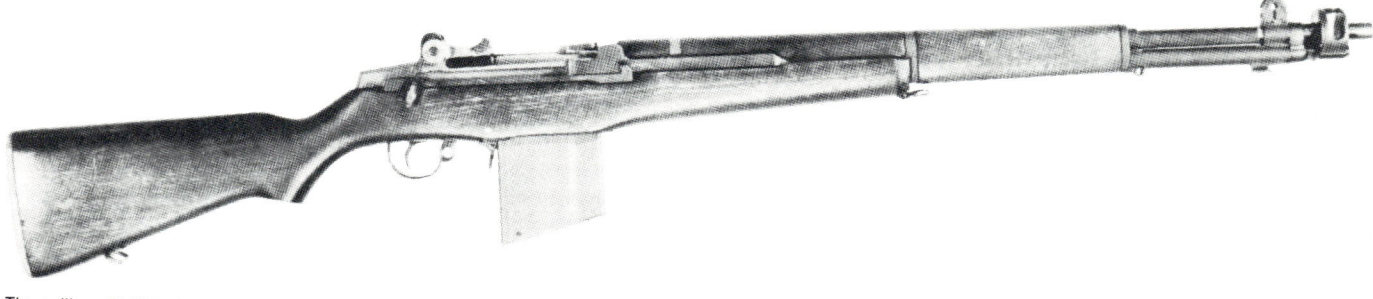

The calibre .30 T20 rifle (T. Smith)

1954-5 but in so doing, further faults showed themselves during temperate climate endurance tests. The British, Australian, Canadian and Belgian Armies had all adopted the FN FAL rifle (qv) and so were concerned at these failings. Eventually in April 1956 the T44 and T48 were both considered ready for production but the home product, the T44, was considered to be lighter, easier to produce, and using a system, developed from the M1 rifle, that was known to suit American needs.

On 1 May 1957 the US Secretary of the Army announced the adoption of the T44 rifle in two versions, ie the Rifle Calibre 7.62mm M14 and the Rifle Calibre 7.62mm M15. The M14 would be a light-barrelled semi-automatic rifle and the M15 would be a heavy-barrelled selective fire rifle.

In December 1959 the M15 project was abandoned and it was decided that a selector would be produced and fitted to a proportion of M14 rifles. These would have a bipod and be capable of selective fire.

Later the M14E1 and M14E2 rifles were developed. The M14E1 was simply a M14 with a folding stock and only a few were made for trial.

The M14E2 went into service and in March 1968 was re-designated "Rifle 7.62mm M14A1". This rifle is capable of selective fire but is designed primarily for automatic fire. It differs outwardly from the M14 rifle in that it has a straight line stock with a rear pistol grip and a folding front handgrip which lies flat along the underside of the stock. The front handgrip has five positions with one inch spacings to accommodate firers of all sizes.

There is also a rubber recoil pad and a hinged shoulder rest which can be swung out to lie on the shoulder to control the butt of the rifle: and at the muzzle there is a stabiliser assembly consisting of a perforated steel sleeve which slides over the flash suppressor and is fastened to the muzzle over the bayonet lug by a screw and lock nut. This stabiliser – together with the weight of the M2 bipod – keeps the muzzle down at automatic fire.

Production of the M14 rifle ceased in 1964. Deliveries were as follows:

Springfield Armoury, Springfield, Mass	167,100
Harrington and Richardson, Worcester, Mass	537,582
Thompson-Ramo-Wooldridge, Cleveland, Ohio	319,163
Winchester-Western, New Haven, Connecticut	356,501

OPERATION

To load the rifle one of four procedures can be followed:

(1) Loading the magazine out of the rifle.

To remove the magazine place the right thumb on the magazine catch, located behind the magazine, press in and rotate the base of the magazine forward with the right hand, out of the magazine well.

(a) Each round is placed on the magazine platform and pressed down into the magazine against the spring force, until the magazine contains the full quota of 20 rounds.

(b) To use the 5-round charger, a magazine filler is required. The filler slides over the top rear portion of the magazine and a 5-round charger is inserted. The rounds can be pushed in by using the thumb or the open end of the combination tool. When the first five rounds are in the magazine the charger can be removed and the process repeated until 20 rounds have been inserted. The filler is then removed.

(2) Loading the magazine in the rifle.

To retract the bolt, grasp the cocking handle with the right hand and pull it fully to the rear. Press in the bolt lock located on the left side of the receiver to hold the bolt to the rear.

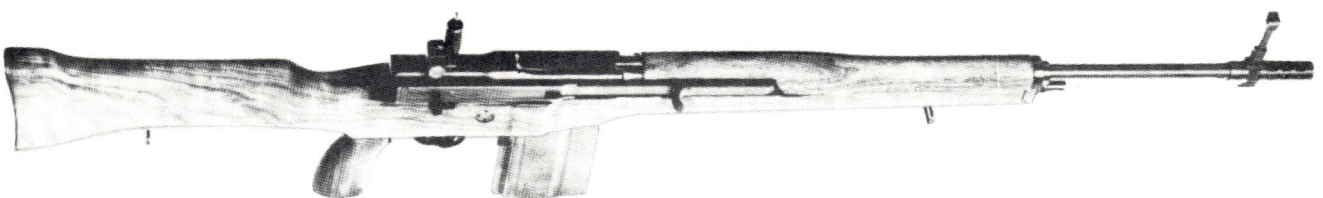

The .30 T25 rifle

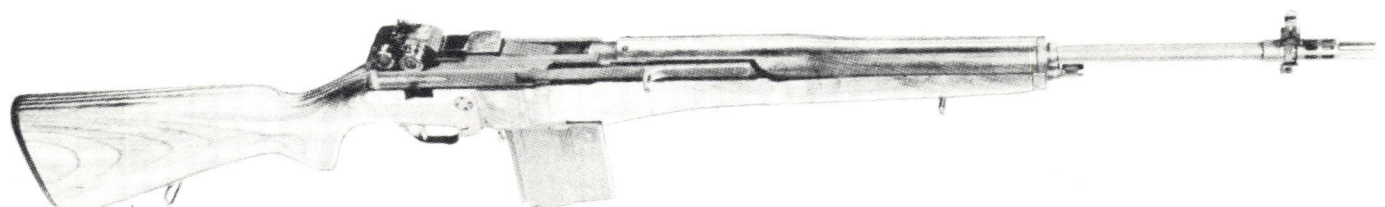

Cal .30 T47 rifle (T. Smith)

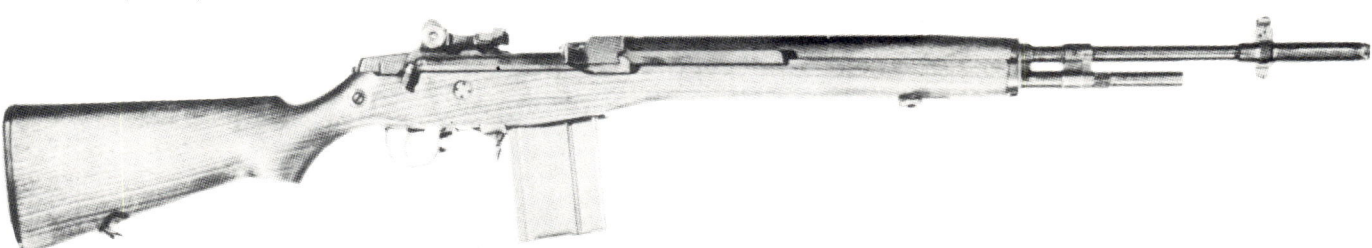

The .30 Cal T44 rifle (T. Smith)

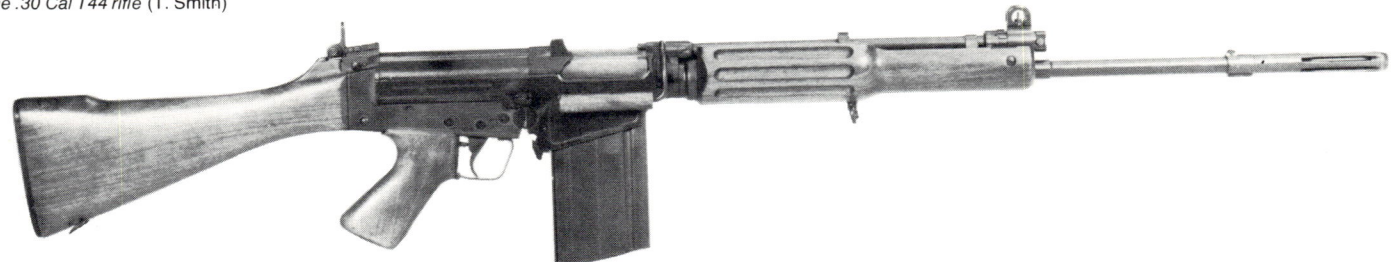

The 7.62mm T48 rifle (RMCS)

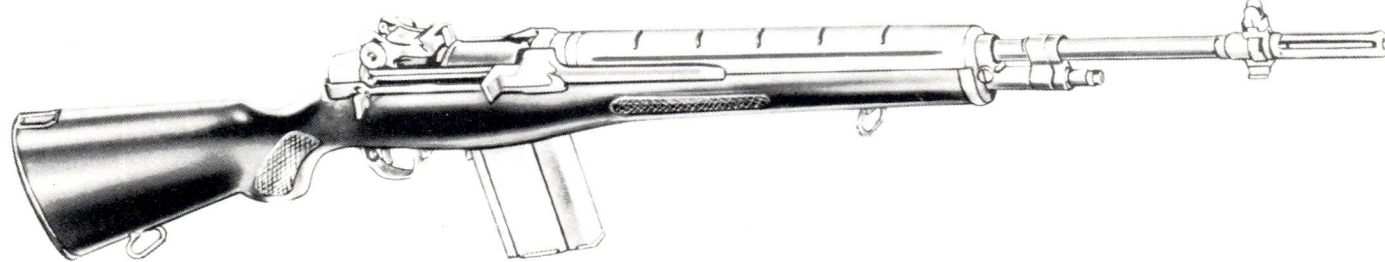

The 7.62mm M14 rifle

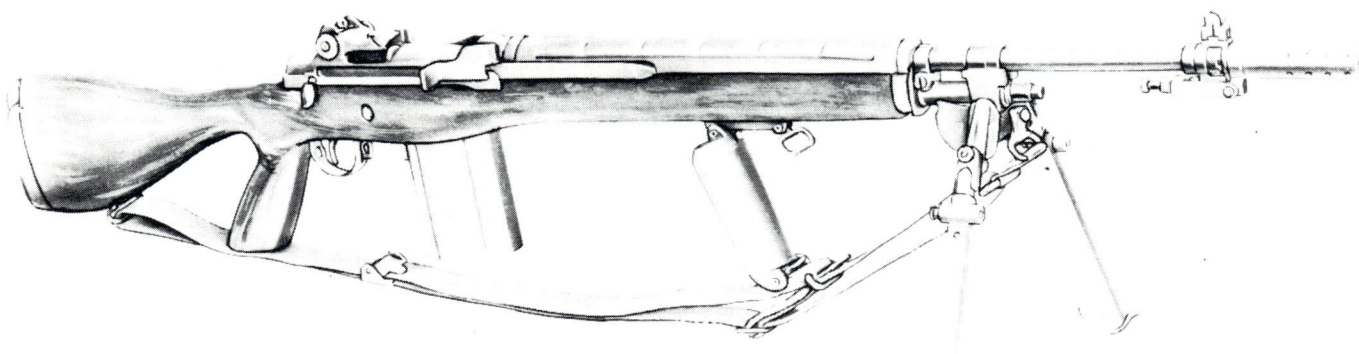

The 7.62mm M14A1 rifle (formerly M14E2) (US Army photograph)

(a) The magazine can be loaded through the top of the receiver with a 5-round charger. The charger is placed in the charger guide and the 5 rounds forced down into the magazine. This procedure is repeated four times.

(b) Single rounds can be placed in the magazine through the top of the receiver. Each round is pressed down and fully seated until the full capacity of 20 rounds is achieved.

The magazine is placed in the rifle by inserting the front end first and then rotating the rear until the magazine catch snaps into engagement with an audible click.

If the cocking handle is pulled back and released, the bolt will pick up the top round and chamber it. The safety catch is located in the front of the trigger guard and is pulled back for 'safe'.

The sights consist of a blade foresight and an aperture rearsight graduated from 200 metres to 1,100 metres. The elevation control is on the left of the backsight and is rotated clockwise to elevate. The windage control is on the right of the rearsight. The foresight can be moved across on its block in a dovetail for lateral zeroing. The range scale can be adjusted for elevation zero.

The normal M14 will fire at semi-automatic only. If a selector is fitted it must be rotated according to the type of fire required. When it is positioned with the face marked 'A' to the rear (rear type projection up) the rifle is set for automatic fire.

When the safety is pushed forward and the trigger squeezed, the hammer is able to rotate forward and drive the firing pin into the cap. The bullet

passes up the bore and some of the gas passes through a port drilled in the bottom of the barrel. It passes through the spindle valve which is designed to cut off the gas when firing grenades – and through the side walls of the piston. The hollow interior of the piston head is filled with gas and the piston is forced rearwards, driving the operating rod and bolt with it, as soon as sufficient pressure has been developed to overcome the friction forces and the return spring tension. After the piston has travelled back slightly less than 4mm, the gas ports are no longer aligned and no further gas can enter. This system – attributed to the White SL rifle of 1929 – requires no gas regulator, as by design the pressure available to move the actuating rod back will automatically increase until it is sufficient to overcome the resistance to motion. The piston moves back 38mm and the exhaust port in the bottom of the gas cylinder is then exposed to allow the expanded gases to escape to atmosphere.

The operating rod has a free travel of about 9.5mm to allow the chamber pressure to fall and then the camming surface inside the hump forces the bolt roller upward disengaging the locking lugs on the front of the bolt from the locking recesses in the receiver. This rotation of the bolt provides the primary extraction to loosen and unseat the case in the chamber. The bolt is pushed back, the empty case is extracted and held to the bolt face. As the bolt continues back the mouth of the case emerges from the chamber. As soon as this occurs the compressed spring of the ejector is able to thrust the ejector – contained within the bolt body – forward and the case is revolved around the extractor and thrown out of the gun to the right. The empty case on its way out is struck by the forward face of the hump of the operating rod

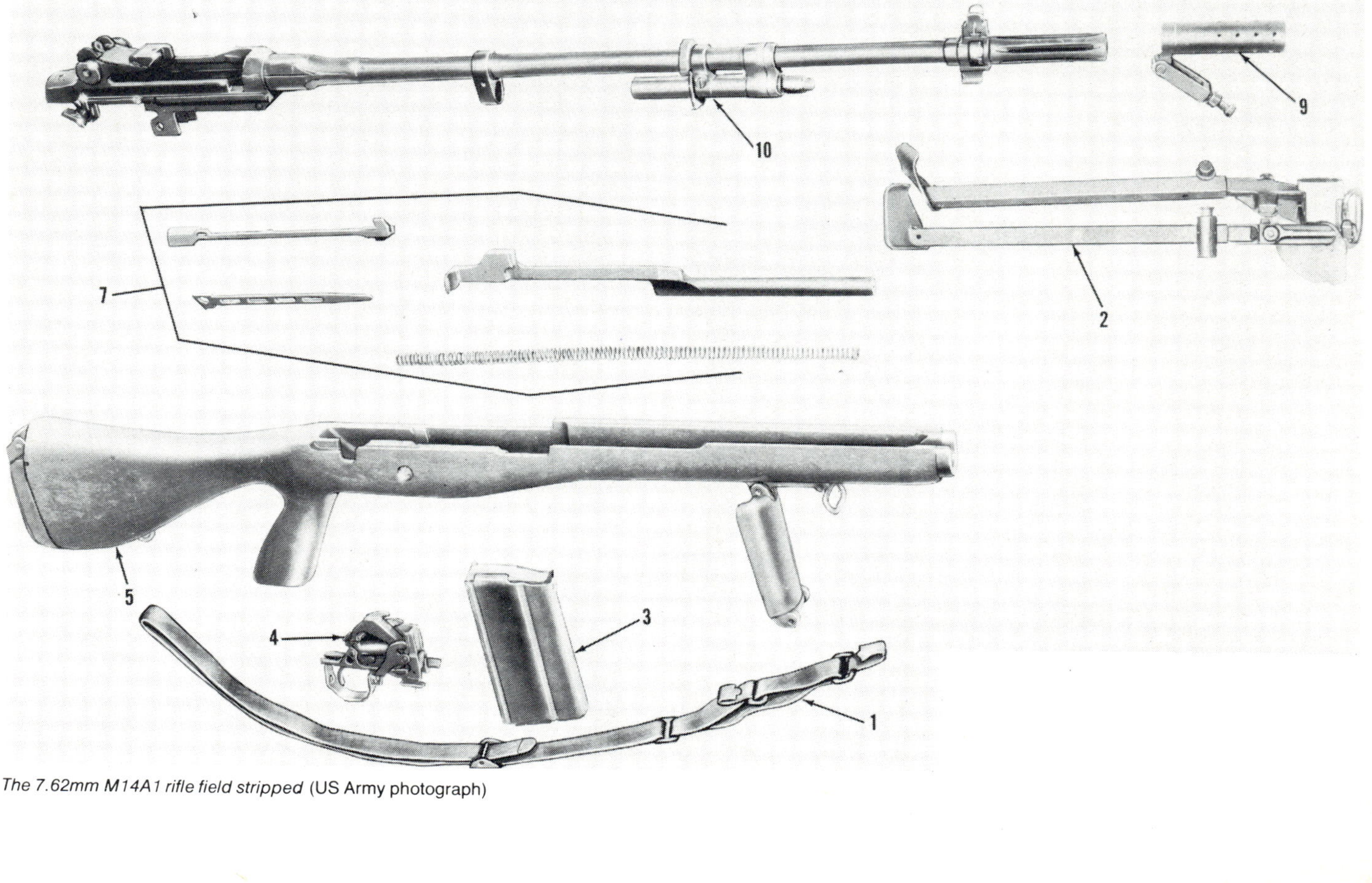

The 7.62mm M14A1 rifle field stripped (US Army photograph)

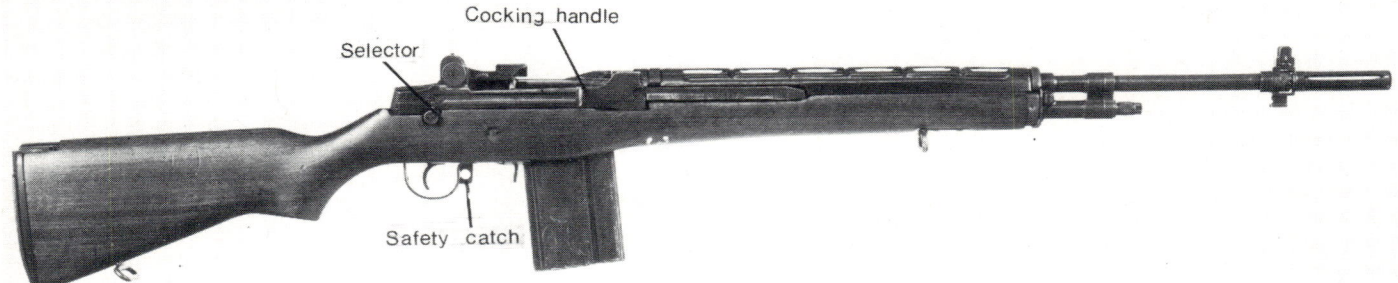

The 7.62mm M14 rifle

which helps in speedy ejection. The compressed return spring forces the operating rod forward and the bolt chambers another round and is rotated into the locked position.

When the ammunition is expended the magazine follower operates the bolt lock and the bolt is held to the rear ready for a fresh magazine to be inserted.

TRIGGER AND FIRING MECHANISM

This mechanism came to the M14 straight from the M1 Garand. It consists of a hammer with two bents on it (hooks, in US nomenclature), a trigger with a trigger extension which is the main sear, and a spring loaded auxiliary sear mounted behind it. When the gun is ready to fire, the main sear holds the bent of the hammer. When the trigger is pulled, the trigger extension which is the main sear moves forward off the hammer bent and the hammer spring drives it forward. When the round is fired the bolt rides over the hammer and rotates it back. The main sear is still forward and cannot catch the hammer bent which is caught by the auxilliary spring-loaded sear.

At semi-auto, another round cannot be fired until the trigger is released. When this happens the auxiliary sear moves back and the hammer slips off and starts forward but is caught by the main sear and held ready for the next round to be fired. At full auto the hammer is held on the spring-loaded auxiliary sear – as before – and the hammer is released by the final closure of the bolt. This is achieved by having the shoulder on the operating rod engaging the hook of the connector assembly and forcing it forwards. This rotates the sear release on the selector shaft causing the flange on the sear release to push the auxiliary sear to the rear and release the hammer. Thus the rifle fires a round every time the bolt closes – provided the trigger remains pressed.

STRIPPING

(1) Remove magazine, cock action, check chamber and feedway clear.
(2) Allow action forward under control.
(3) To remove the trigger mechanism grasp the rear of the trigger guard with thumb and forefinger of the right hand and pull down and out, making certain that the trigger guard is not rotated more than 90 deg. Lift out the firing mechanism.
(4) To separate the barrel and receiver from the stock, grasp the receiver in the left hand, sights upwards, and with the right hand strike sharply down on the buttstock, separating the barrel and receiver from the stock. This separates the rifle into the three main groups, firing mechanism, barrel and receiver, and the stock.

Re-assembly follows in the natural reverse order.

ACCESSORIES

Blank Firing Attachment: This consists of the M12 muzzle attachment and the M3 breech shield. The tubular portion of the attachment is inserted into the muzzle opening of the flash suppressor and is secured by the bayonet lug and a spring clip. The shield is secured to the cartridge guide by a lug with a spring plunger.

The Winter Trigger Kit M5 consists of an arctic trigger and an arctic safety installed to the pistol grip with screws. The winter trigger is a flexible grip lying under the small of the butt and attached to the trigger. Grasping the small of the butt with the right hand enables the fire to reach the flexible link and squeezing it up to the buttstock fires the rifle.

The Winter Safety is an extension piece reaching forward 38mm outside the trigger guard and long enough to be used with arctic mittens.

The M2 Bipod is a light folding mount which slips onto the gas cylinder and gas cylinder lock and is secured using the combination tool to tighten the self-locking bolt.

The M6 Bayonet Knife and M8A1 Bayonet Knife Scabbard. The groove of the bayonet handle slips over the bayonet lug on the flash suppressor and the ring goes over the flash suppressor. The bayonet is pushed back until the lugs of the latching lever snap over the bayonet lug.

The M76 Grenade Launcher is secured by sliding the launcher over the flash suppressor and pushing the clip latch rearward to secure it to the bayonet lug. The launcher has nine annular grooves numbered 6-1, 2A, 3A and 4A. These allow different ranges by placing the grenade at different positions on the launcher where it is retained by a spring clip prior to launching. The spindle valve must be rotated to the horizontal position to cut off gas to the piston before a grenade is fired.

The M15 Grenade Launcher Sight can be used for both low angle and high angle firing. The mounting plate for this sight is installed by workshops on the left hand side of the receiver over the magazine. The plate has

notches into which the spring tips of the sight fit. The sight is turned clockwise until the index line of the sight is aligned with the 0 deg. index on the mounting plate and the levelling bubble should then be central. The sight is then turned to the required elevation, and to level the bubble the muzzle must be elevated.

DATA

Cartridge: 7.62mm × 51
Method of operation: Gas
Method of locking: Rotating bolt
Method of feed: Magazine
Method of fire: M14 self-loading – some selective. M14A1 – selective

WEIGHTS

M14 rifle with full magazine and cleaning kit: 5.1kg
M14 rifle with full magazine, selector, bipod and cleaning kit: 5.9kg
M14A1 rifle with full magazine: 6.6kg
Empty magazine: 0.226kg
Full magazine: 0.68kg
Cleaning equipment: 0.3kg
M2 bipod: 0.79kg
Grenade launcher M76: 0.2kg
Grenade launcher sight: 0.136kg
Bayonet knife M6: 0.34kg
Scabbard for bayonet M8A1: 0.11kg
Blank firing attachment M12 with breech shield M3 (M14 only): 0.11kg
Kit winter trigger with winter safety: 0.11kg
Trigger pull: 2.5-3.4kp

LENGTHS

M14 overall with flash suppressor: 1,120mm
M14A1 overall with stabliser: 1,120mm
Barrel: 559mm

MECHANICAL FEATURES

Barrel: Regulator: None
      Rifling: 4 grooves RH 1 turn in 305mm
      Cooling: Air
Sights: Foresight: Fixed post
      Rearsight: Tangent aperture
      Graduation: 2-11 by increments of 200 metres (One click of elevation or windage moves the bullet 0.7cm at 25 metres)
      Zeroing: Rearsight for elevation. Line. Foresight
      Sight radius: (100yd setting) 678mm

FIRING CHARACTERISTICS

Muzzle velocity: 853metres/sec
Muzzle energy: 364mkp
Recoil energy: M14 1.7mkp M14A1 1.5mkp
Chamber pressure: 3,465kg/cm²
Rate of fire: Cyclic: 700-750 rounds/min
Standard rates of fire: Semi-automatic: 1 minute – 40 rounds/min
      3 minutes – 30 rounds/min
      10 minutes – 20 rounds/min
      30 minutes or more – 15 rounds/min

Automatic: 1 minute – 60 rounds/min
      5 minutes – 40 rounds/min
      10 minutes – 30 rounds/min
      30 minutes or more – 20 rounds/min

Ranges:
Maximum effective semi-auto without bipod: 460 metres
Maximum effective semi-auto with bipod: 700 metres
Maximum effective automatic with bipod: 460 metres
Maximum range: 3,725 metres
Manufacturer: Harrington and Richardson Arms Co, Worcester, Massachusetts. Thompson-Ramo-Wooldridge, Port Clinton, Ohio. Winchester – Western Arms Division of Olin Mathieson Corp., New Haven, Connecticut. Springfield Armoury, Springfield, Massachusetts.
Status: No longer manufactured. Issued to selected CONUS and overseas US Army units. Standard weapon for most US Army Reserve, Army National Guard and ROTC units.

US RIFLE 7.62mm M21

This is the current sniping rifle in the US Army. It was called, until recently, the US Rifle 7.62mm M14 National Match (Accurised).

The differences between this rifle and the M14 are:

(1) Barrels are gauged and selected to ensure correct specification tolerances. Barrels are not chromium plated.

(2) The stock is of walnut and is impregnated with an epoxy resin.

(3) The receiver is individually fitted to the stock using a fibre glass compound.

(4) The firing mechanism is hand fitted and polished to provide a crisp hammer release. Trigger pull is between 2 and 2.15kg.

(5) The suppressor is fitted, and reamed to improve accuracy and to eliminate misalignment.

(6) The gas cylinder and piston are hand fitted and polished to improve operation and reduce carbon build up.

(7) The gas cylinder and lower band are permanently attached to each other.

(8) The rifle must group consistently with an average extreme spread for a ten-round group, not exceeding 6 inches (15cm) at 300 metres.

(9) A suppressor is fitted at the muzzle. This does not affect the bullet velocity but reduces the velocity of the emerging gases to below that of sound. This makes location of the firer very difficult.

THE SNIPER'S TELESCOPE

The telescope uses a principle first employed by Lt Leatherwood. On the telescope are two stadia on the horizontal reticle (graticule) which subtend 60 inches (1.5m) at 300 metres when viewed with the telescope variable magnification ring set to 3 power. On the vertical reticle are two stadia which subtend 30 inches (76cm) at 300 metres when the telescope is set to 3 power. As an illustration of this, the distance from the soldier's waist belt to the top of his helmet can be taken to be 30 inches (76cm). At 300 metres' range the two stadia on the vertical reticle will, with a 3X setting, rest on the waist belt and top of the steel helmet. If the range is greater than 300 metres the power ring is used to increase the size of the picture until once again the two stadia lines rest on the waist belt and steel helmet. Clearly the range is proportional to the power used, for example since the 3X magnification just places the stadia on belt and helmet at 300 metres then the 9X magnification will put the stadia on belt and helmet at 900 metres.

This can be used to give the sniper a range read-out which he can use in reporting enemy locations etc. However, in the Leatherwood system, the use of this principle is carried one stage further and a ballistic cam is attached to the telescope power ring. This cam is cut for the cartridge in use and so the act of placing the stadia in the correct position not only records the range but displaces the telescope axis and so automatically applies the

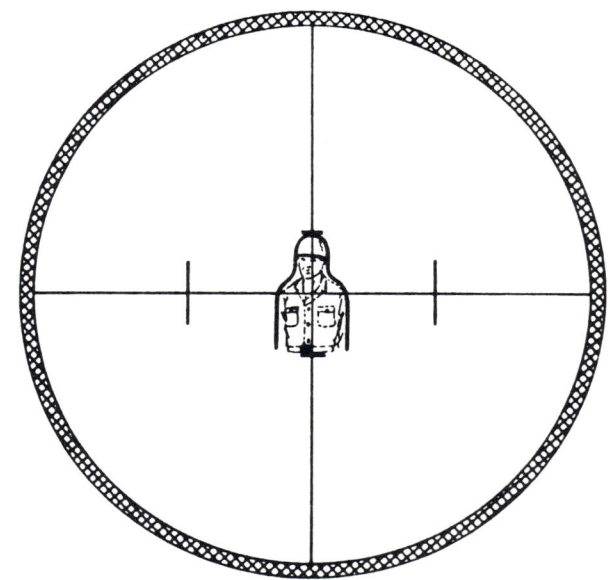

The sniper's sight picture-stadia correctly adjusted

correct tangent elevation to the rifle.

This is done by locating the ballistic cam – normally cut for the M118 match ammunition – on the cam base of the telescope mount and holding it in place by a spring located in the mount. Thus any alteration of the power ring – and the ballistic cam attached – automatically applies the correct range provided the object lying between the stadia lines is 30 inches (76cm) high.

Clearly with experience, the sniper can use an object 15 inches (38cm) high and fit it between the horizontal reticle and one stadia, or an object 20 inches (51cm) high and filling two-thirds of the space between stadia. If more appropriate he can use the stadia on the horizontal reticle with an object 60 inches (152cm) long.

TELESCOPE DATA
Weight (with cam): 455g

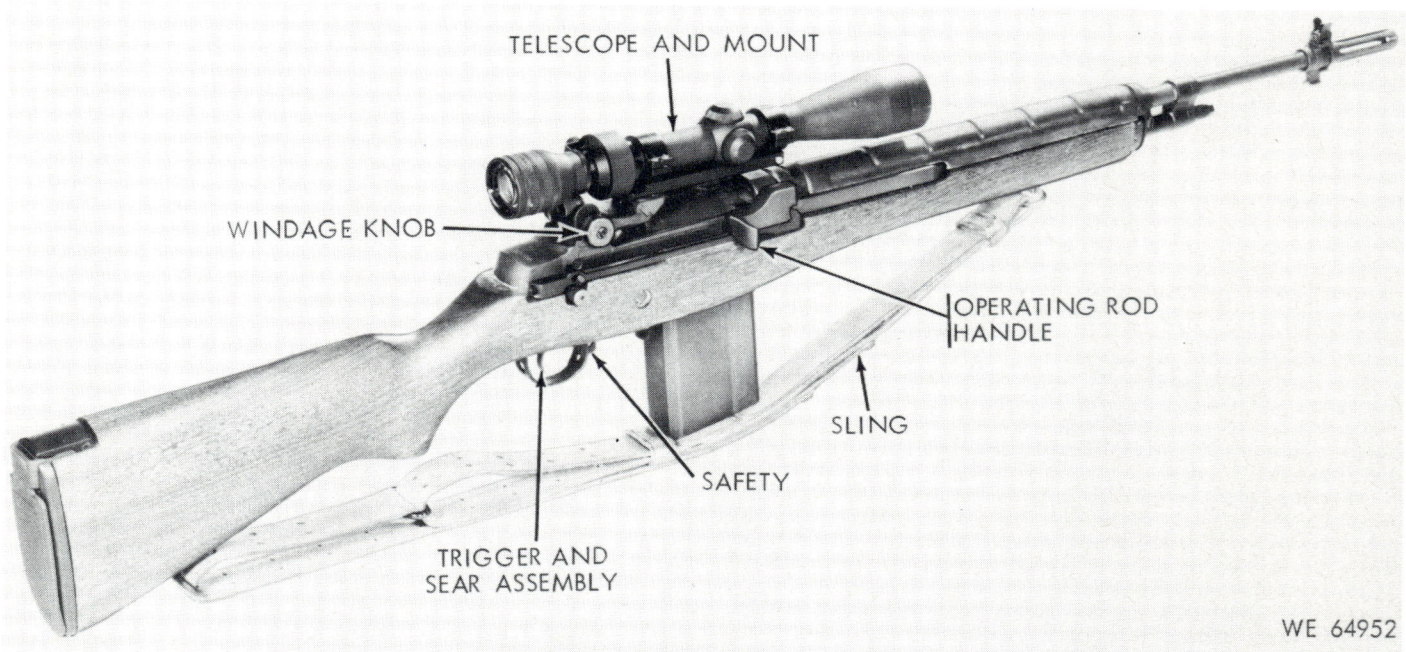

The 7.62mm M21 rifle (US Army photograph)

The suppressor on the M21 rifle (US Army photograph)

Length: 324mm
Magnification: Variable 3X to 9X
Eye reliefs: 76.2mm-95.3mm
Adjustments: Internal. ½ minute graduations for elevation and windage
Reticle (Graticule): Crosshairs with stadia marks
Ballistic cam: For M118 match ammunition
Objective lens diameter: 46mm
Eyepiece diameter: 34mm
Finish: Black matt anodised
Mount: Weight: 170g
　　　　Material: Aluminium
　　　　Operation: Hand fixed, spring loaded base
　　　　Finish: Black matt anodised
Manufacturer: Redfield, Denver, Colorado. (A Division of Outdoor Sports Industries)

The Redfield range-finding telescope (the rifle is NOT an M21)

THE NIGHT VISION SIGHT, INDIVIDUAL SERVED WEAPON, AN/PNS-2

This sight is a portable, battery powered, electro-optical instrument that can be hand held for surveillance purposes or mounted on the rifle for aimed fire at night.

It is completely passive and cannot be detected by the enemy. It functions by magnifying electronically the background light which is present as moonlight, starlight or skyglow and allows the user an image – varying in detail with the ambient light – sufficiently clear on all but the most overcast night to enable him to observe, identify and engage a target.

The sight can be zeroed by day or night. It cannot easily be zeroed at dusk. This is because in daylight the lens cap cover is left on. At night the lens cap cover is removed. At dusk the light level can still be high enough to operate the automatic cut-off which protects both the operator's eye and the image intensifier tube.

THE NIGHT VISION SIGHT AN/PVS-3 and AN/PVS-3A

This sight is a miniaturised and improved version of the AN/PNS-2. It is a portable, battery powered, electro-optical instrument which consists of the night sight, a carrying case, and a battery tray. When used at night, the night sight amplifies reflected ambient light: it does not project a visible or infra-red light and, therefore, cannot be detected by the enemy. The sight consists of a main body assembly which includes the objective lens assembly, eyepiece assembly, image intensifier tube, and power supply. An eyeshield is attached to the eyepiece assembly, and an attenuator lens cap fits on the objective lens assembly.

The attenuator lens cap reduces the amount of light entering the image intensifier tube during daylight operation. The eyeshield aids in security by preventing light leaks on the operator's face caused by visible glow from the eyepiece assembly. Rubber flaps in the eyeshield close completely to prevent light leakage when the operator removes the eyeshield from his eye.

TECHNICAL CHARACTERISTICS
Type: Portable, hand-held viewing device
Power source: Battery tray (two cells)
Operating conditions: Temperature range of −65 deg F (−55 deg C) to +115 deg F (+46 deg C). Humidity range of 0 to 100 per cent
Focusing range: From 4 metres to infinity
Field of view: 10 deg
Weight: 1.36kg (with battery tray installed)
Length: 343mm
Battery type: Mallory RM-930 (two)
Voltage: 2.8 volts dc
Shelf life: 9 months

7.62mm AR-10 ASSAULT RIFLE

In 1952 George Sullivan – an attorney – and Charles Dorchester started a firm to develop high quality sporting guns. They obtained the interest of Richard Boutelle, President of Fairchild Engine and Airplane Corp and on 1 October 1954 the Armalite Division of Fairchild was set up and Charles Dorchester was made Manager.

Eugene Stoner was taken on as Chief Engineer and the company, located at Costa Mesa in California, set out to produce sporting weapons. A development programme was started and a number of prototypes produced. Then the US Air Force asked the firm to produce a survival rifle. This was to have a light weight, a simple mechanism and enough power to enable an airman, who had parachuted into a hostile environment, to obtain food and, if necessary, defend himself. The cartridge chosen was the Hornet .22 which was a high velocity round well suited for the task. The rifle was designed so that the bolt action receiver and barrel could be separated from each other and lodged in the hollow glass fibre buttstock together with the magazine. With the rubber shoulder pad keeping out dirt, snow etc, the rifle made a neat and handy package. The entire weapon floated and was easily attached to a waist belt leaving the hands free.

The AR-5 was tested by the US Air Force at Stead Air Force base in Nevada. After incorporating a few suggested minor modifications the rifle was accepted by the USAF as the MA-1 Survival Rifle. Large orders did not materialise for this rifle and a civilian version, the AR-7, was made in 1958 and is still selling. It was made for the .22LR cartridge, used a blowback action, and like the AR-5 was stowed in the buttstock. It weighs only 1.25kg and makes a good adventure training rifle. It is called the Explorer.

A number of other weapons were developed in prototype form. They were:

AR-1. A Mauser bolt action rifle firing the 7.62mm × 51 cartridge; it was intended for sporting use or military sniping. Prototype only.

AR-3. An SL 7.62mm rifle, it had an aluminium receiver and a fibre glass stock. It introduced a multi-lug rotating bolt head which was the only part of the rifle to be developed intensively.

AR-5. Survival rifle.

AR-7. Explorer.

AR-9. A 12 bore shotgun with an aluminium barrel and receiver. Prototype only.

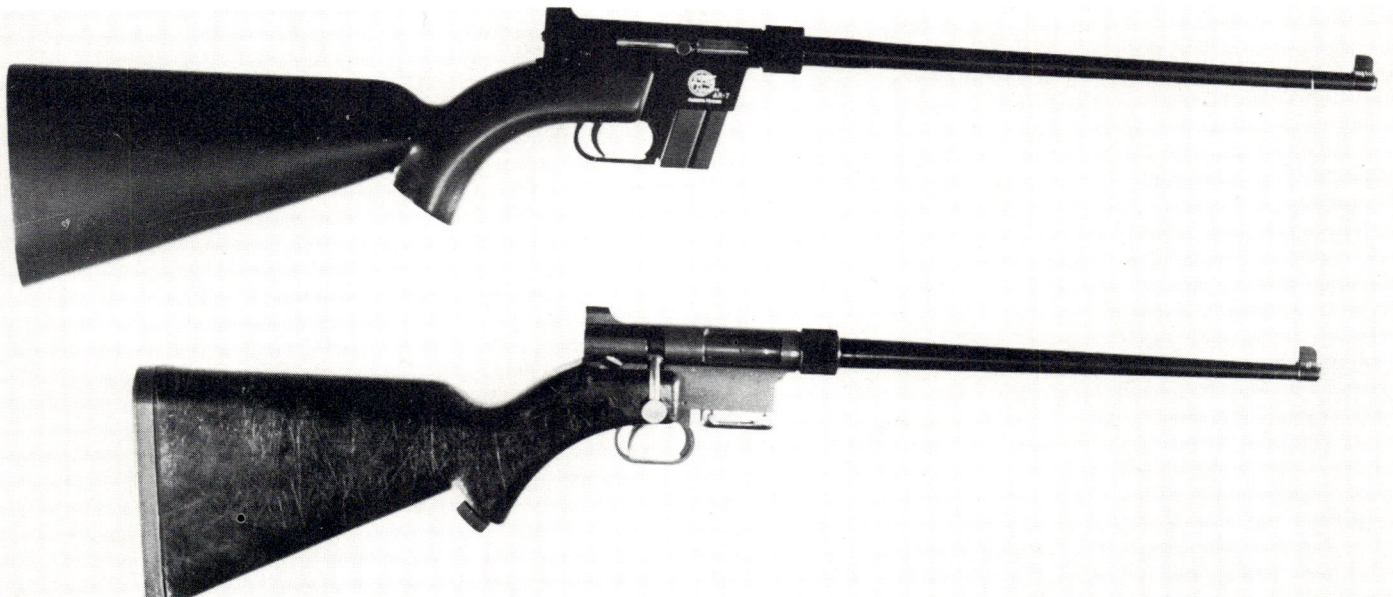

Top: *The AR-7 "Explorer".* **Bottom:** *The AR-5A Survival rifle*

AR-10 Development

The AR-10 was designed from the outset as an assault rifle. It was a project started before Stoner joined Armalite, and was originally based on the .30-06 cartridge but in 1955 it was decided to change to the 7.62mm × 51 cartridge. A number of prototypes were made, all of them incorporating straight line actions and high sight lines. Most of them had alloy magazines recognised by the square patterns made by the fullering of the pressing. (The term "waffle" type is used in the USA to describe this configuration.) A ribbed fore-end was used also.

A third version used a titanium liner inside an aluminium sleeve. This was not a success and the designer reverted to a plain steel barrel.

In 1957 Artillerie-Inrichtingen (now Eurometaal), the Netherlands Arsenal at Hembrug agreed to produce the AR-10 rifle. The necessary changes to the drawings to convert to metric measurements were made and Stoner simplified the design in some respects.

Unfortunately tooling up did not proceed very rapidly – mainly because the Dutch Army were not sufficiently impressed by the rifle and did not adopt it. The funds for setting up the production line were slow in materialising. In the meantime Fairchild started an advertising campaign and set up a complex sales organisation involving three arms companies – Cooper-MacDonald of Baltimore, Interarmco of Alexandria, Virginia, and Sidem International centred on Bonn in Germany. Due to the delay the countries who were interested chose rifles more readily available. A few AR-10s were sold to Nicaragua; the Sudan, and Burma. About 1,200 guns were sold to Portugal in 1959. It appears that at this time – 1959 – there was some disagreement between Fairchild and Artillerie-Inrichtingen and their agreement was not renewed.

The prototype of a modified rifle called the AR-10A was made in 1958-9 with a larger diameter bolt and a cocking handle moved to the rear of the receiver. This was never developed.

In 1959 a production contract was signed with Colt's Patent Firearms Corp to make the AR-10A and also the AR-15. Colt's began to assemble a production line for the AR-10A but sales demonstrations in the Far East showed the AR-15 to be better received and Colt did not proceed with production of the AR-10A.

DESCRIPTION

The AR-10 is a gas-operated rifle. The feature of greatest interest in the weapon is the gas system selected which differs considerably from the conventional system. Instead of the gas, directed from the barrel through a gas vent, impinging on the face of a piston, it travels back along a tube and enters the interior of the bolt carrier. This system, however, is not new. It was used in the Swedish Ljungman rifle and its derivatives and the French incorporated it in the MAS 49.

The AR-10 pioneered many features which subsequently appeared in the AR-15 which as the M16 and M16A1 rifle is described thereunder. However a brief description of the action of the AR-10 follows.

OPERATION

To load the rifle the magazine is removed by pressing the magazine release catch on the right of the receiver. It is filled with twenty 7.62mm × 51 cartridges and replaced in the magazine well. The cocking handle stands above the receiver and is enclosed by the carrying handle. Pulling back on the vertical, trigger-like cocking handle rotates the hammer back, and compresses the return spring. When the cocking handle is released the bolt

The AR-10 carrying handle, rearsight and locking handle

goes forward, feeding a round into the chamber.

When the trigger is operated the hammer strikes the cap, the propellant burns and the resulting pressure drives the bullet up the bore. The gas follows the projectile and enters a stainless steel tube above the barrel, leading back into the space in the cylindrical shell of the bolt carrier. Here it forces the carrier back. After about 3mm of free travel to allow the chamber pressure to fall, a cam path cut in the carrier causes a pin on the bolt to revolve about the longitudinal axis of the bolt and thus rotate the bolt locking lugs out of engagement with the barrel extension. The carrier then pulls the bolt bodily to the rear to start the operating cycle. There is no primary extraction and the empty case is pulled sharply out of the chamber and ejected from the gun. The bolt carrier stores energy in the return spring and comes forward again to chamber a round from the 20-round box magazine. When the cartridge is fully chambered the seven locking lugs on the bolt head are rotated through 22½ degrees and lock behind abutments in the barrel extension. The weapon will fire at either single shot or full automatic with a selector lever on the left of the body. The aperture back sight is in the rear pillar of the carrying handle and is raised or lowered by a horizontal drum graduated from 200 to 700 metres by 100 metre divisions. Stripping the AR-10 is a simple matter. After the gun is made safe a pin located at the rear of the body is pulled out. The upper receiver then pivots up and the bolt and carrier assembly can be withdrawn and separated.

The AR-10 features the use of alloy forgings in the two parts of the receiver, fibreglass pistol grip and a plastic butt. The magazine is of light alloy. These materials allow an unloaded weight of 4.1kg.

Some variations on the AR-10 have been made. The principal variations are, short barrelled carbine, magazine fed LMG, and a belt fed LMG. None of these is in production.

DATA
Cartridge: 7.62mm × 51

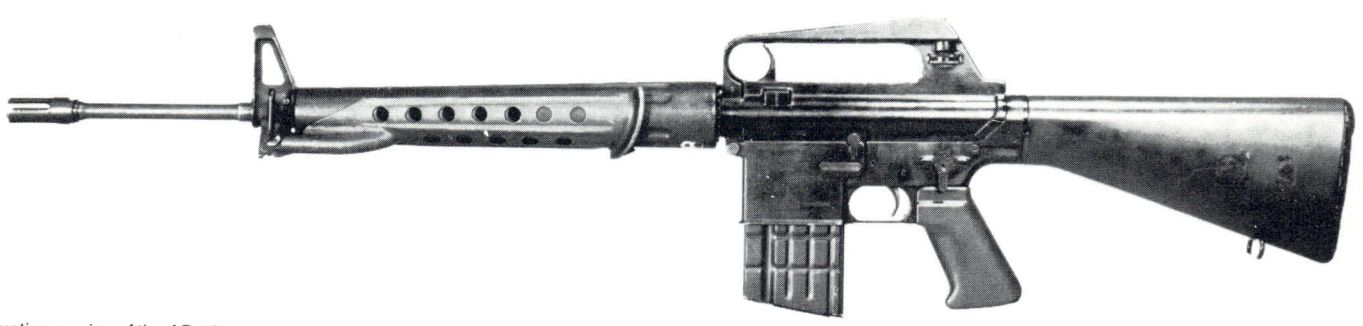

Production version of the AR-10

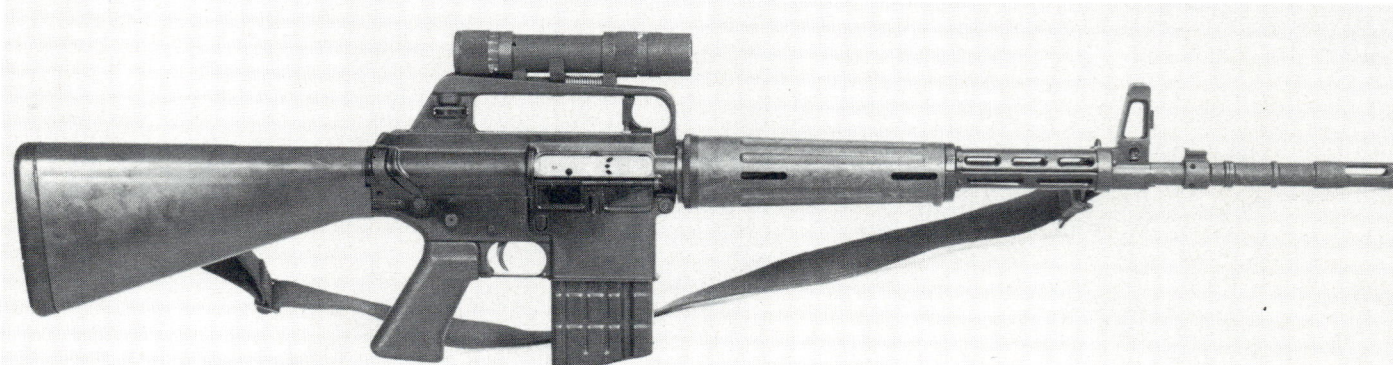

AR-10 with sniper's scope and grenade launcher – no bipod

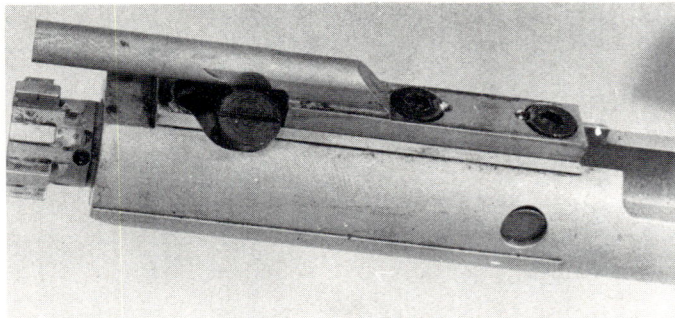

The AR-10 bolt head, gas tube and actuating cam pin

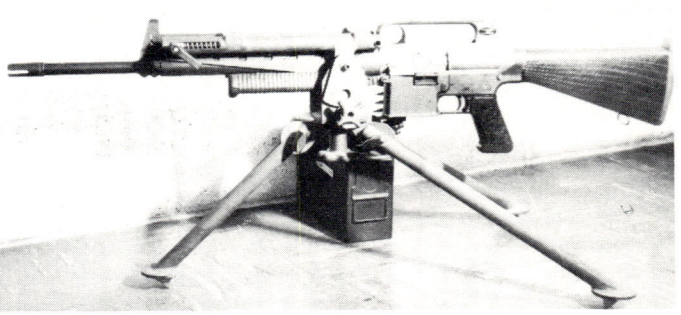

The AR-10 belt-fed LMG

WEIGHTS
AR-10 only: 4.1kg
Sling: 0.18kg
Magazine empty: 0.14kg
AR-10 with 20 round magazine: 4.82kg
Trigger pull: 3.4kg

LENGTH
AR-10: 1,029mm
Barrel length: 508mm
AR-10 with bayonet: 1,169mm

MECHANICAL FEATURES
Barrel: Gas regulator: Nil
       Rifling: 4 grooves. RH 1 turn in 254mm
Sights: Foresight: Fixed blade
       Rearsight: Aperture
       Graduations: 200-700 metres
       Windage: Nil
       Zeroing: Rearsight
       Sight radius: 527mm

FIRING CHARACTERISTICS
Muzzle velocity: 845 metres/sec
Muzzle energy: 324mkp
Recoil energy: 1.34mkp
Chamber pressure: 3,465kg/cm²
Rate of fire: Cyclic: 700 rounds/min
       Automatic: 80 rounds/min
       SS: 40 rounds/min
Manufacturer: Armalite Division of Fairchild Engine & Airplane Co., Costa Mesa, California. Artillerie Inrichtingen, Hembrug, Zaandam, Holland. Colt's Patent Firearms Manufacturing Co Inc, Hartford, Connecticut
Status: No longer produced. Small quantities sold to Nicaragua, Sudan, Burma and Portugal

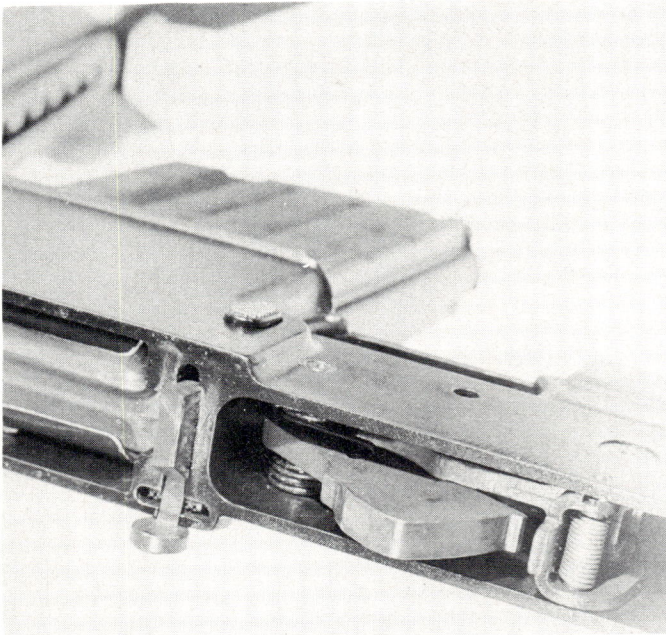

The AR-10 hammer, hammer sear, bolt release and magazine catch

Method of operation: Gas
Method of locking: Rotating bolt
Method of feed: Magazine
Method of fire: Selective

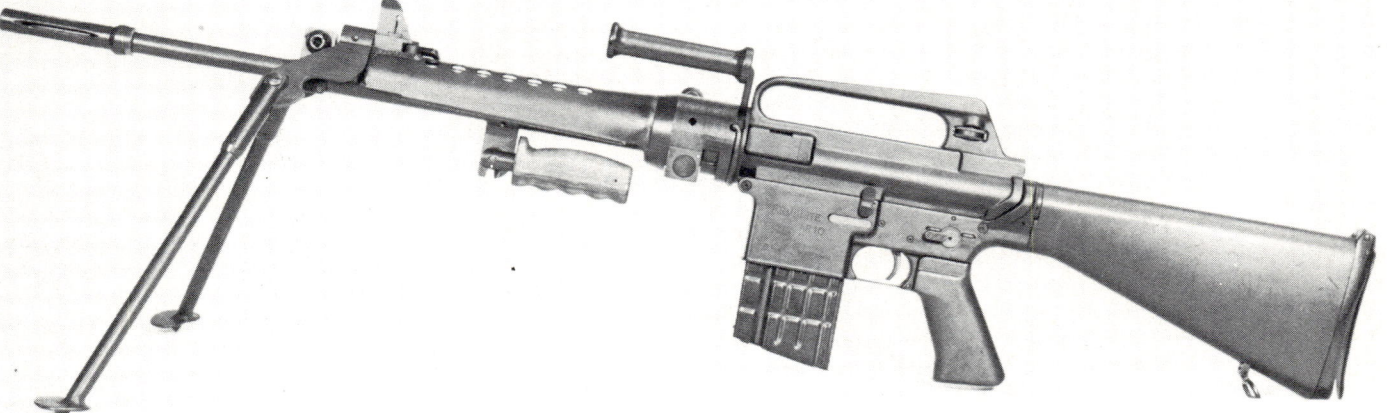

AR-10 LMG. Note underhand barrel change lever

AR-10 LMG. Note barrel lowered for changing

5.56mm AR-15 (M16) RIFLE

The .223 (5.56mm) AR-15 was designed by Eugene Stoner, then an employee of Armalite Inc. It uses the same method of gas operation as the AR-10 and, broadly, is derived from that gun. To understand the reason for the adoption of this gun it is necessary to be aware of the user's needs. The Infantry Board, Fort Bennings, laid down the following as its requirements:

(1) Loaded weight not to exceed 6lb. (2.7kg)
(2) Accuracy and maximum height of trajectory to be at least equal to that of the M1 rifle at ranges up to 500 yards (457m).
(3) Selective fire capability.
(4) Penetration of body armour, steel helmet or 10-gauge steel plate at 500 yards.
(5) Lethality not less than the M1 carbine at 500 yards.

These led to the design of a lightweight, low impulse rifle firing a lightweight bullet at high velocity. No round of a suitable type existed so Armalite had to start by obtaining a cartridge. Whether the calibre and weight – .223in (5.56m) and 55 grains (3.56g) – selected were the best possible, is open to debate. In retrospect a calibre of .26in (6.6mm) and perhaps 80 grains (5.18g) would have produced a round which could have the range and lethality required for a light machine gun. As a result of the requirements and the acquisition of a cartridge the AR-10 was scaled down for testing. The earliest prototypes even had the cocking handle on top of the body. Ten AR-15 rifles were delivered to the Infantry Board on 31 March 1958. They were tested at Aberdeen Proving Ground with satisfying results and the Board recommended that the AR-15 be considered as a replacement for the M147 .62mm rifle. After Arctic tests at Fort Greely modifications were made including strengthening the barrel to allow for firing with water in the bore; the trigger guard was modified to allow firing in Arctic mittens and the cocking handle was removed from inside the carrying handle and located behind it.

Various other tests followed and a procurement programme started. The US Air Force was very interested and Lt Col Burton T. Miller, then serving, tested the AR-15. The Air Force took 8,500 in 1961, the Army took 85,000 in the same year followed by 85,000 in 1963, 35,000 in 1964, 100,000 in 1965 and a further 100,000 in 1966. The Vietnam struggle undoubtedly increased the demand. Colt's Patent Firearms Company had been licensed to produce the gun in January 1959 and they manufactured the quantities mentioned. On 30 June 1967 the US Government and Colt made a contract whereby the Government agreed to pay $4,500,000 for a licence to use technical data and all patents relating to the M16 rifle. This enabled them to set up additional production from other firms and both General Motors and Harrington and Richardson have each manufactured the AR-15. Only Colt are currently producing the M16 rifle.

The original AR-15 was designated the M16. The Air Force version still has this nomenclature but the Army rifle was modified in 1966 to become the M16E1 and in 1967 this became the M16A1. The differences are chiefly that the M16A1 has a bolt with serrations on the right hand side and a plunger which protrudes from the body and can be used to force the bolt home if the return spring for some reason is unable to do so. This device, the forward assist assembly, allows the firer to close his bolt when a dirty cartridge produces a high friction force and thus saves fitting a reciprocating cocking handle such as that used on the Russian AKM. Whether such a

device is correct in principle is doubtful, because eventually forcing rounds into the chamber ignores the reason for the difficult chambering, and may result in scoring the chamber, feeding a malformed cartridge or otherwise damaging the mechanism.

The original AR-15 had a twist of rifling of one turn in 14 inches (356mm). An unclassified US report produced by the Ballistics Laboratory entitled *Exterior Ballistics of the AR-15 Rifle* showed that although the bullet was marginally stable in air at 60 deg F, it was totally unstable when fired in Arctic conditions. This led to the production of a twist of one turn in 12 inches (305mm) and with this increased rotation of the bullet it is now just stable at below-zero air temperatures. This has resulted in some loss of lethality but not to a significant degree.

When the M16 was initally issued to troops in Vietnam – and particularly to the US Marines – they were told that the gun was self-cleaning. A spate of complaints about the case failing to eject led to a Congressional Enquiry. The causes were found to be associated with an unannounced change from tubular IMR propellant to ball propellant, and lack of cleaning. There is no doubt that the effects of ball powder differ from those of IMR in several respects. Chiefly, these are an increased rate of fire and depositions of fouling in the cavity between the bolt carrier and the bolt head. This carbon when hot is soft but cools after a short while and hardens to produce a bond strong enough to prevent the bolt unlocking; nor can the rifle be hand-operated. As a result the weapon becomes inoperative.

Following this enquiry several changes were made. The soldier was issued with a cleaning kit, the buffer was modified to reduce the rate of fire and the chamber was chromium plated. The net result of these innovations was to produce a rifle which now is at least as reliable as any other in service.

OPERATION

The rifle operates as follows: the cocking handle, located behind the carrying handle, is withdrawn to cock the hammer. If the magazine is empty the magazine follower will rise under the force of the magazine spring and hold the bolt carrier to the rear. When a loaded magazine is in place the carrier will be driven forward by the return spring and the lugs on the bolt will pick up a round from the magazine and feed it into the chamber. As the bolt locking lugs enter the barrel extension the ejector is compressed against the left side of the cartridge head and the extractor rides over the extractor groove and engages on the right side of the cartridge.

As the bolt motion stops when the cartridge is fully chambered, the carrier continues forward to contact the rear face of the barrel extension and the cam slot cut in the carrier rotates the cam pin of the bolt. This causes the bolt to rotate anti-clockwise (viewed from the rear) and the eight locking lugs move behind abutments in the barrel extension. The rifle is now ready and if the fire control selection on the left side of the receiver is set either to 'auto' or 'semi', operation of the trigger will fire the round. When the trigger is pulled, the sear, extending forward of the trigger, is rotated down and moves out of the hammer notch – or bent – under the hammer close to the hammer pivot; the hammer is then rotated forward by its spring and hits the firing pin which in turn strikes the cartridge cap and so fires the round. As the bullet passes the gas port some of the gas passes back along a stainless

The AR-15 .223 rifle

AR-15 carbine version

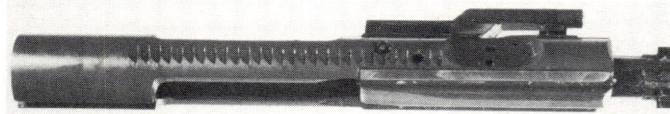

Bolt serrations for closure device

The bolt closure device (RMCS)

steel tube and through the bolt carrier key into the hollow interior of the carrier. The expanding gas forces the carrier back and the movement of the cam slot moves the cam pin, and the bolt is made to rotate about its longitudinal axis and so unlock as the lugs move out from behind the abutments in the barrel extension. The momentum acquired by the carrier enables it to carry the bolt to the rear at a slightly reduced velocity. There is no primary extraction and the extractor withdraws the cartridge from the chamber; the spring-loaded ejector rod emerges from the left of the bolt face and rotates the case around the extractor as soon as the case clears the chamber, and the case passes through the ejection port on the right side of the receiver and so out of the rifle. The carrier continues rearward compressing the return spring and cocking the hammer. The action of the buffer and the assistance of the return spring, force the carrier forward and the cycle starts again.

TRIGGER AND FIRING MECHANISM

The trigger mechanism of the M16 is based on that of the M1 Garand. The hammer has a bent near its axis of rotation in which the trigger sear engages and a further bent on the underside which enables the hammer to be held by the spring-loaded disconnector sear, at semi-auto fire. With the selector set to 'semi' the carrier rotates the hammer back. The trigger is still held to the rear and the disconnector is therefore rotated forward by its spring, and its hook-shaped sear holds the upper inside bent of the hammer. To fire another round the firer must first release the trigger and the trigger sear moves back into its notch on the hammer. The release of the trigger moves the disconnector sear clear of the hammer which then is held only by the trigger sear. This process is repeated for each shot fired at 'semi'.

When 'auto' is engaged and the trigger is operated, the hammer is released as before but the disconnector is prevented from moving forward to catch the hammer by a cam on the fire selector lever and so plays no part in the control of the hammer.

To ensure that the hammer will not contact the firing pin until the bolt is fully locked, an auto sear holds it up until released by the bolt carrier in its final forward movement. Should the trigger be released during firing, the hammer is released from the auto sear but caught by the trigger sear so terminating firing.

STRIPPING

The M16 is field stripped as follows: Remove the magazine, cock the action and check that the chamber is empty. The takedown pin on the left rear of the receiver is pushed through and the butt and lower receiver dropped down. The bolt carrier assembly and cocking handle can then be

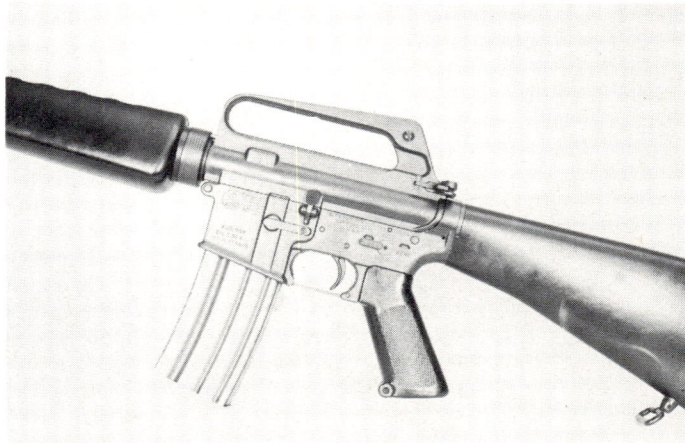

AR-15 with burst fire control

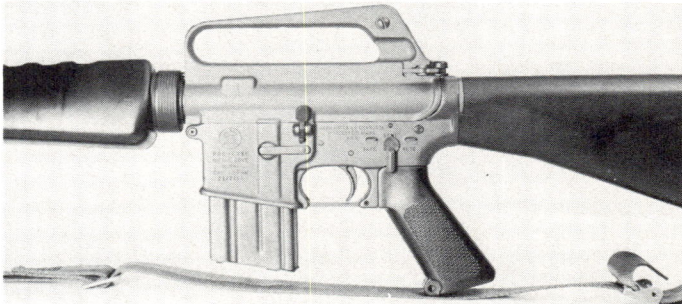

The M16A1, made by Harrington & Richardson

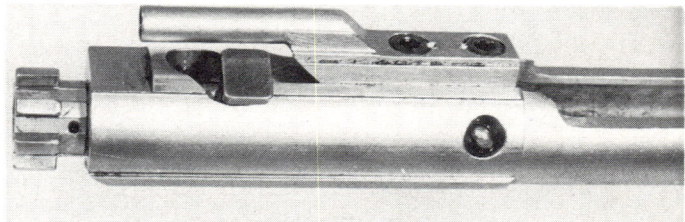

The locking lugs of the bolt head, bolt carrier and bolt cam pin (RMCS)

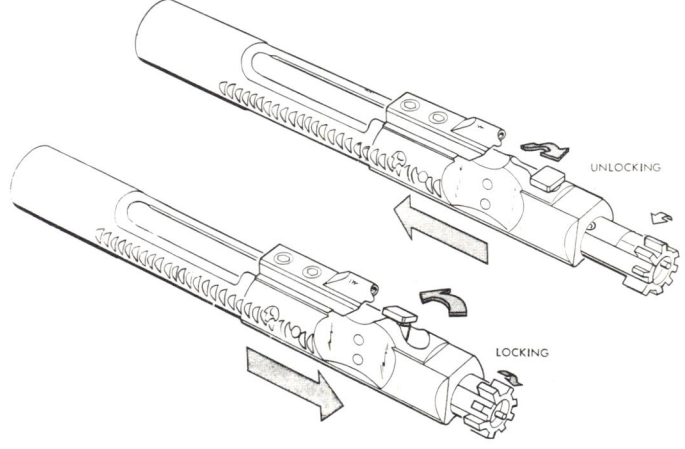

Locking and unlocking the M16 rifle (US Army photograph)

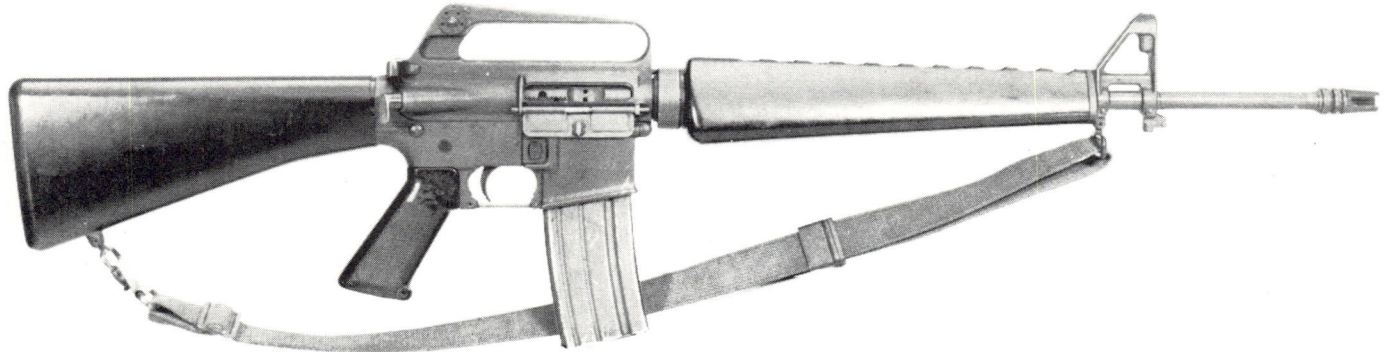

The M16A1 rifle (RMCS)

slid onto the rear and the bolt separated from the carrier. The handguard is removed next, followed by the buffer and return spring.

Re-assembly is in reverse order.

DATA
Cartridge: 5.56mm × 45 M193 ball M196 tracer M199 dummy M100 blank
Method of operation: Gas-direct action
Method of locking: Rotating bolt
Method of feed: 20- and 30-round box magazine
Method of fire: Selective

WEIGHTS
Model M16 Rifle without sling or cleaning equipment: 3.1kg
Model M16A1 Rifle: 3.18kg
Empty 20-round magazine: 91g
Empty 30-round magazine: 117g
Loaded 20-round magazine: 318g
Loaded 30-round magazine: 455g
Sling: 182g
Model M16 rifle with sling and loaded 20-round magazine: 3.6kg
Model M16 rifle with sling and loaded 30-round magazine: 3.73kg
Model M16A1 rifle with sling and loaded 20-round magazine: 3.68kg
Model M16A1 rifle with sling and loaded 30-round magazine: 3.82kg
Trigger pull: 2.3kp-3.8kp

LENGTHS
Rifle with flash suppressor: 990mm
Rifle with bayonet knife M7: 1,120mm
Barrel: 508mm
Barrel with flash suppressor: 533mm

MECHANICAL FEATURES
Barrel: Rifling: 6 grooves RH 1 turn in 305mm
  Regulator: None
  Cooling: Air
Sights: Foresight: Cylinder on threaded base
  Rearsight: Flip aperture
  Graduation: 0-300 :300-500
  Zeroing: Elevation. Depress detent and rotate post. Line. Rotate drum on right side of backsight.
Sight radius: 501mm

FIRING CHARACTERISTICS
Muzzle velocity: 1,000 metres/sec
Muzzle energy: 176mkp
Recoil energy: 0.75mkp
Chamber pressure (max): 3,660kg/cm²
Rate of fire: Cyclic: 700-950 rounds/min
  Automatic: 150-200 rounds/min
  Semi-auto: 45-65 rounds/min
  Sustained: 12-15 rounds/min
Range, maximum effective: 400 metres
  maximum: 2,650 metres

ACCESSORIES
Bayonet knife M7
Projector grenade M203
Rifle grenades

AMMUNITION
Calibre: 5.56mm (Cal .223)
Type: Ball, blank, dummy and tracer

The following grenades are authorised for use with the M16A1 rifle with the use of additional accessories:
(a) Rifle grenades
  (1) M19A1 WP
  (2) M22A2 Smoke series
  (3) M23 Smoke streamer series
(b) Hand grenades with M2A1 grenade projection adaptor, M7A3CS

Manufacturer: Military Firearms Division of Colt's Industries, Hartford, Connecticut
Status: In service with US Forces. Supplied to many US Allies, including Taiwan, UK and the Philippines. A quantity was also supplied for use by Australian troops in Vietnam. Manufactured under licence in Philippines and Singapore

M16A1 rifle stripped

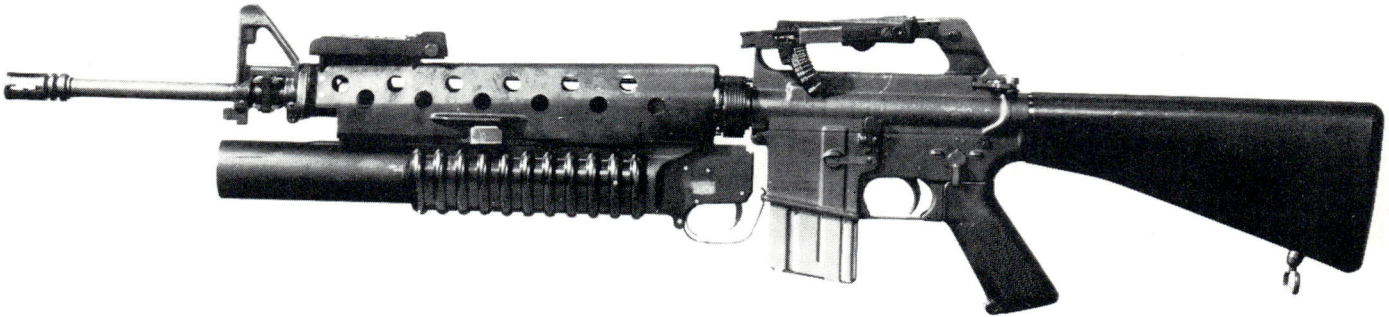

M16A1 rifle with M203 grenade launcher (RMCS)

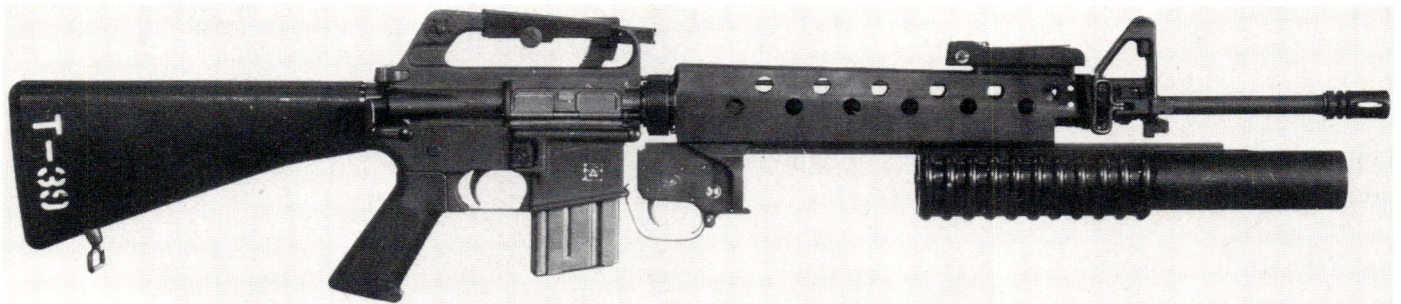

M16A1 rifle with M203 grenade launcher shown in loading position RHS

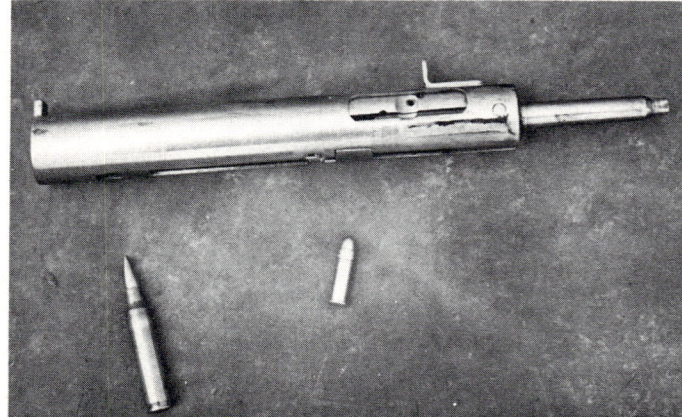

The Atchisson/MAC replacement bolt, enabling .22 LR cartridges to be used for training purposes. The barrel has the same external contour as the 5.56mm cartridge (RMCS)

Replacement magazine allowing the use of .22LR cartridges (RMCS)

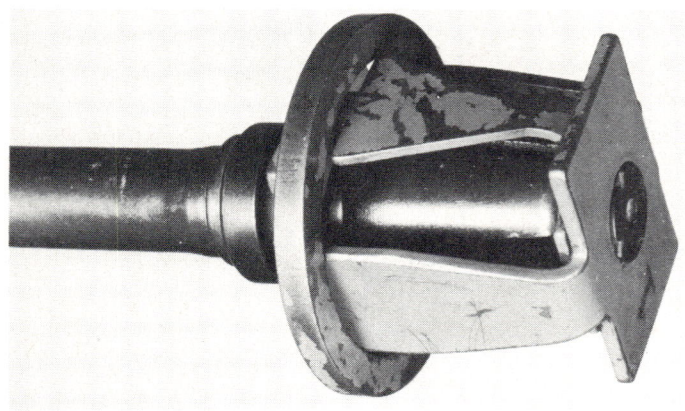

Blank firing attachment. This restricts the gas flow sufficiently to build up enough pressure to operate the bolt (RMCS)

5.56mm AR-18 RIFLE

The firm of Armalite Inc was established by Charles Dorchester, the present Chairman of the Armalite Board, and George Sullivan, an attorney. These two individuals established the firm's connection with the Fairchild Engine and Airplane Corporation on 1 October 1954. Later Eugene Stoner was hired as Chief Engineer for Armalite and produced a series of weapons of which the AR-15 (qv) was the most successful. As the M16A1 it is the current US Army rifle.

In 1961, at the time Armalite left the Fairchild Corporation, Eugene Stoner left Armalite to act as a consultant with Colt and to pursue various other enterprises such as the Thompson-Ramo-Wooldridge 25mm gun.

The new Chief Engineer was Arthur Miller. He came in at a time when the Army was buying the AR-15 in large numbers and it became the objective of Armalite Inc to produce a strong reliable rifle which would utilise the latest and most advanced manufacturing techniques to keep production costs to a minimum. It was considered at this time that a cheap, simple and reliable rifle would be ideal for issue to the many countries – particularly in SE Asia – that needed military aid.

The patents for the rifle designed by Arthur Miller were ascribed to Messrs Dorchester, Sullivan and Miller.

Armalite arranged for the AR-18 to be tested by the well known HP White Laboratory at Belair, Maryland to provide a disinterested verdict on its performance. The US Army conducted tests of ten prototype models at Aberdeen Proving Ground and at Fort Benning in 1964. In 1965 a further twenty-nine were manufactured in some haste and tested by the US Army. In 1967 the US Air Force tested some 75 rifles. It seems from these tests that although the AR-18 offers some advantage over the AR-15 the numbers of AR-15 rifles already manufactured and the cost of purchasing production rights from Colt make it unlikely that the United States Army will make any considerable purchase of the AR-18.

In 1967 Howa Machinery Co of Nagoya, Japan started production of the AR-18 rifle. Japanese law requires that their rifles be sold only to non-combatant nations, and Japan would not countenance export to the USA during the Vietnam war.

The AR-18 has been produced at Costa Mesa, California, since 1968. Three distinct weapons are made. These are the AR-18, the AR-18S which is the short barrelled sub-machine gun version, and the AR-180 which was specifically designed to be capable of firing full automatic except by major reconstruction of the trigger group.

In the latter part of 1974 an agreement was concluded between Armalite Inc and the Sterling Armament Co Ltd of Dagenham, England under which the AR-18, AR-18S and AR-180 would be produced in Dagenham.

IRA terrorists in Northern Ireland include in their armoury a number of AR-180 rifles, of Japanese origin, which have been acquired indirectly. A very limited number of US manufactured AR-180 rifles have also been used by the IRA, and these also were illicitly acquired.

SYSTEM OF OPERATION

The weapon is gas-operated with a vent located 32.5cm from the breech face and 13.5cm from the muzzle. The cylinder is of stainless steel mounted above the barrel with 5mm clearance. It is 41mm long. The cylinder takes the form of a hollow spigot over which fits a female piston 48mm long. The stationary spigot has 3 gas rings around the end. When the piston has moved back 13mm, 4 vents pass over the gas rings and the gas is evacuated to the air. The actuating rod is in two parts: a short head 25mm long, which fits into the main rod 25cm in length. This rod has a collar 88mm from the end which forms the forward housing of the actuating rod return spring. This short-stroke piston action is similar in design principle to that of the German wartime Gewehr 43. There is no gas regulator.

The rod is in contact with the top of the front face of the bolt carrier and in its half-inch movement imparts enough energy for the completion of the entire cycle of operations.

The Armalite AR-18 .223 rifle (RMCS)

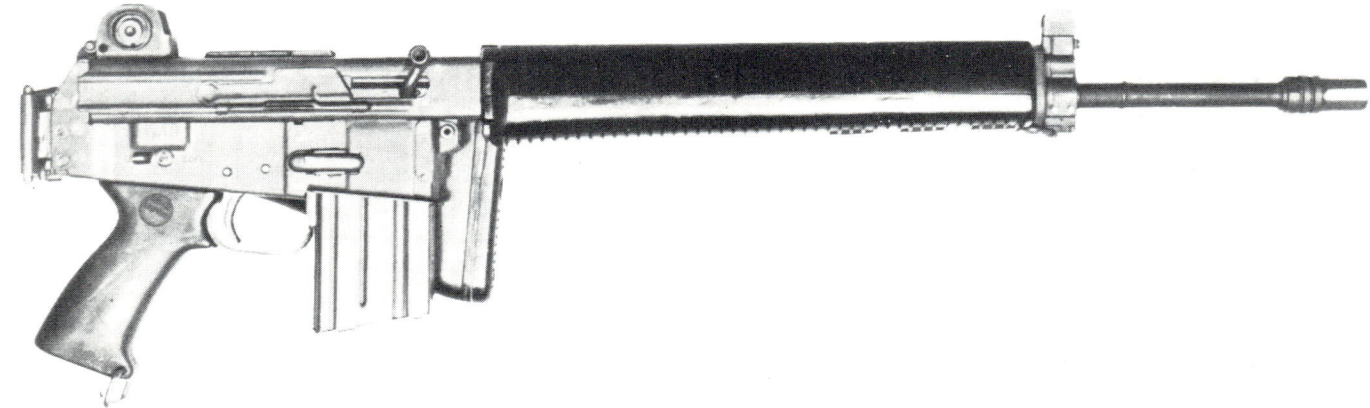

AR-18 with butt folded

AR-18 locking lugs of bolt, cam pin of bolt carrier. (RMCS)

The bolt head carries seven locking lugs which are rotated for locking through 22½ degrees to engage in front of corresponding locking shoulders in the barrel extension. On the shaft of the bolt is a pin which projects to enter a cam way on the carrier. When the carrier moves back impelled by the piston thrust, the pin first moves across the width of the camway – a distance of 3mm – to provide mechanical safety, and is then forced down to rotate and unlock the bolt head. The pin rides in a spot welded guideway which prevents any movement. The continued rearward movement of the carrier pulls the bolt with it to the rear. The extractor is mounted at 3 o'clock on the bolt face and withdraws the empty case which is ejected through an opening on the right of the receiver by the action of a spring-loaded plunger set in the bolt face at 9 o'clock which acts as soon as the case is free of the barrel extension. The bolt moves back along the guide rods which pass through it, compressing the two return springs mounted around the rods.

On the forward movement of the carrier the lowest of the bolt locking lugs pushes the top round of the 20 in the magazine forward and it is guided up into the chamber. The bolt reaches the limit of its forward travel and is then rotated to lock by the action of the camway on the pin. After locking is completed the carrier travels forward a further 3mm to provide mechanical safety before firing. Until this last 3mm is completed the firing pin mounted in the carrier cannot reach the cap. The firing pin is strongly spring retracted and so 'g' forces cannot produce an unintentional firing – as was the case in the early AR-15 which had a heavy free floating pin.

TRIGGER AND FIRING MECHANISM

The weapon will fire at either single shot or full automatic.

Full Auto

Lying along the bottom of the receiver is a spring-loaded rod which at its front end carries a vertical hook which is driven forward by the bolt carrier as locking is completed. This forward movement rotates the automatic sear backwards and releases the hammer. Thus the weapon can only fire when locking is completed. Pulling the trigger lowers the trigger extension which is engaged on a bent on an extension of the hammer below its axis pin. This fires the first shot. Thereafter firing is controlled, whilst the trigger remains pressed, by the spring-loaded rod which activates the automatic or 'safety' sear.

Single Shot

The trigger extension releases the hammer and the round is fired. The hammer comes back and through a hole in it passes a secondary sear which is spring-loaded and grips the front edge of the aperture in the hammer. The trigger must be released to free this sear and the hammer is then gripped by the trigger extension. This in principle is an adaptation of the double bent system used on the Garand and M14 rifles. Putting the change lever to "semi" rotates the spindle which holds the safety sear out of operation. In theory this means that the trigger can be operated with the bolt only partially forward; and that the hammer energy is then used to close the bolt, resulting in a misfire. In practice, however, the problem is of little consequence since the firer cannot operate the trigger fast enough to produce the effect described.

SAFETY

The hammer must be cocked before the safety can be applied. The change lever spindle forces the secondary sear down and locks it. At the same time it rotates over a backward extension of the trigger and locks that. One small feature is noteworthy. If the gun is fired at semi-auto, putting the change lever to 'safe' with the trigger depressed, depresses the secondary sear and the gun fires.

STRIPPING

Ensure the weapon is safe by:
(a) Removing the magazine.
(b) Cocking the action and inspecting the chamber.

Replace working parts in the forward position, leaving the hammer cocked. Behind the back sight bracket is a 'T' piece with a spring-loaded plunger on the end of the right arm of the 'T'. Depress this plunger and press the entire 'T' forward between the backsight protectors. Lower the butt away from the receiver keeping the thumb firmly on the 'T' piece to prevent the return springs under control and take out the springs and their guide

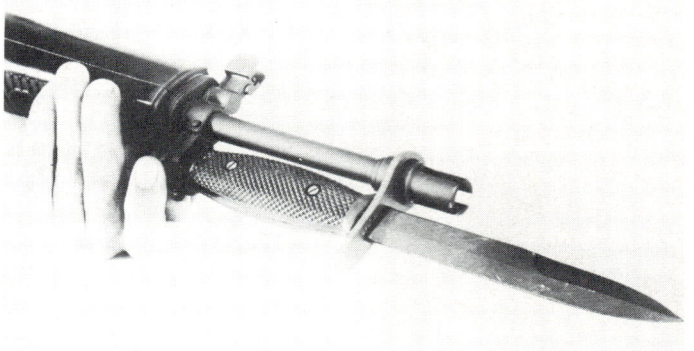

Knife bayonet

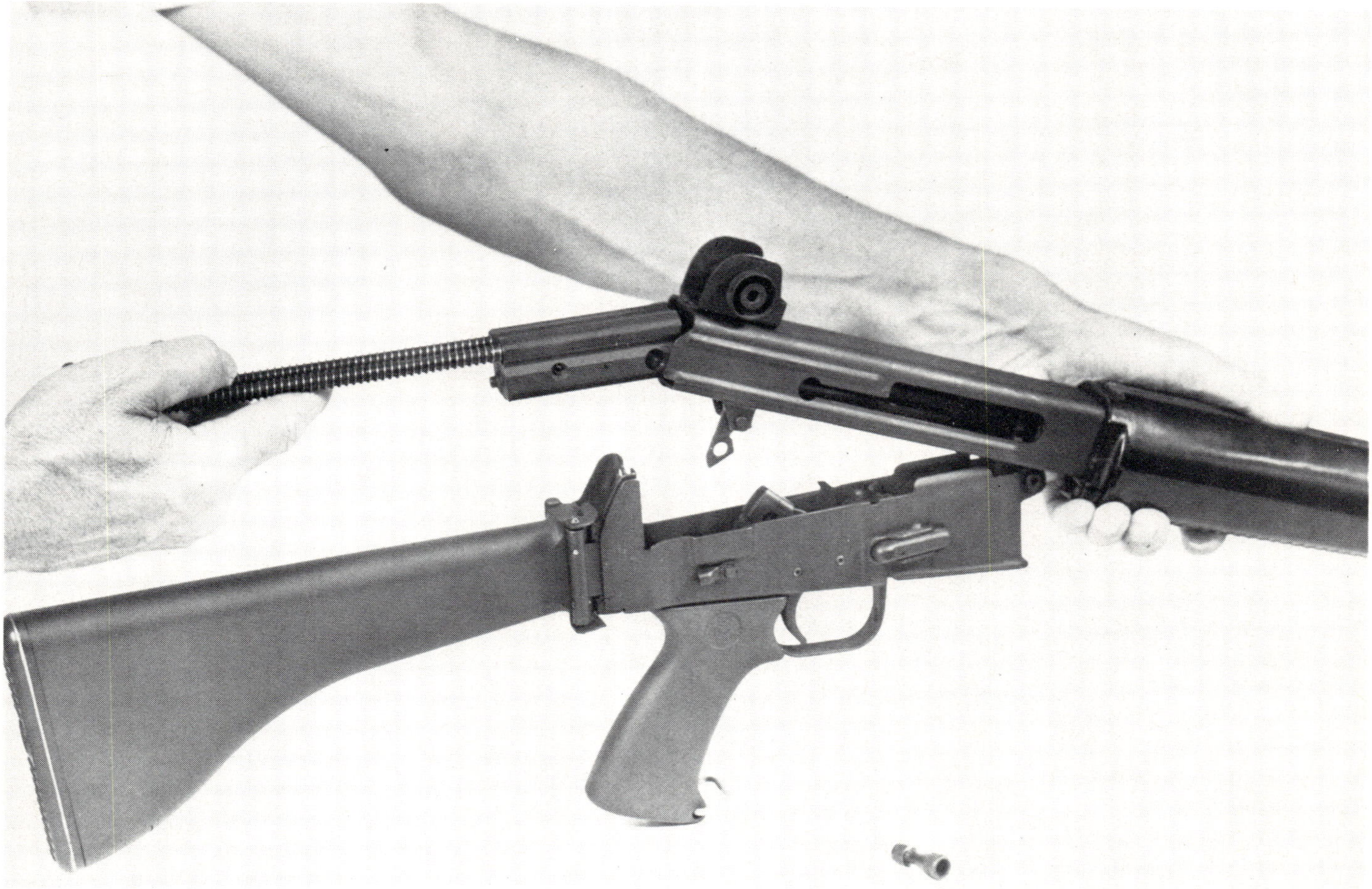

Stripping the AR-18

rods with the 'T' piece. Withdraw the cocking handle to enlarged hole in the receiver and withdraw the handle. The bolt can then be removed.

Push out the pin connecting the butt group to the receiver. The top foregrip will lift off. The bottom half of the foregrip cannot be field stripped.

The actuating rod can be pushed in against the spring and the piston, connecting piece and rod lifted out forward.

The bolt is stripped by pushing out the single transverse pin from right to left. The striker and spring then come out, the pin producing bolt rotation lifts out and finally the bolt head.

This is the limit of normal stripping.

Re-assembling is in the logical reverse order, but a few points need attention. Make certain the upper half of the foregrip is properly positioned before inserting the return spring guides which hold it in place. Be sure the holding open catch is in place before closing the butt group to the receiver, as it can rotate backwards and jam on the closure. Make certain the bolthead is fully forward or else the pin will not enter its guideways. Lastly ensure the hammer is cocked before closing up the mechanism.

CONSTRUCTION

The system of manufacture of the AR-18 is very different from that of the AR-15. Steel stampings are used instead of alloy forgings to simplify manufacture and reduce costs.

The body of the gun is made from one sheet of metal, stamped out, wrapped and welded on the underside. The guide ribs for the bolt rotating pin are spot welded along the left-hand side. The foregrip is made in top and bottom halves both of fibreglass. Underneath each half is a metal heat shield with a generous clearance around the barrel and with holes for heat to escape. The butt and pistol grip are of glass-impregnated nylon, virtually unbreakable, and the magazines are of a very light gauge alloy. A telescopic sight mount is spot-welded on top of the receiver.

The trigger mechanism is made of very light metal, the sear and bent being case-hardened.

Many of the parts can be made on automatic screw machines and ease and cheapness of production by factories not necessarily specialising in armament production was a major factor in the design.

DATA
Cartridge: 5.56mm × 45
Method of operation: Gas
Method of locking: Rotating bolt
Method of feed: Magazine
Method of fire: Selective

WEIGHTS
Gun empty: 3.17kg

Discharging an anti-tank grenade from the AR-18

Empty 20-round magazine: 0.027kg
Loaded 20-round magazine: 0.312kg
Gun with loaded 20-round magazine: 3.58kg
Gun, loaded with telescopic sight: 4.0kg

LENGTHS
Gun, stock extended: 940mm
Gun, stock folded: 736mm
Barrel: 464mm

MECHANICAL FEATURES
Barrel: Regulator: Nil
　　　　Rifling: 6 grooves RH 1 turn in 12in (305mm)

Cooling: Air
Sights: Foresight: Cylindrical post
Rearsight: Aperture flip
Graduation: 200 and 400 metres
Windage: Milled knob produces clicks
Zeroing: Elevation on foresight Line on windage scale
Sight radius: 496 and 508mm

FIRING CHARACTERISTICS
Muzzle velocity: 1,000 metres/sec

Muzzle energy: 179mkp
Recoil energy: 0.58mkp
Chamber pressure: 3,560kg/cm²
Rate of fire: Cyclic: 800 rounds/min
Auto (bursts): 80 rounds/min
SS: 40 rounds/min
Range, maximum effective: 460 metres
Manufacturer: Armalite Corporation, Costa Mesa, California, USA. Sterling Armament Co. Ltd., Dagenham, England
Status: Production

5.56mm M16A1 AUTOMATIC RIFLE, SQUAD AUTOMATIC WEAPON

This is a modified M16A2 weapon offered for sale by WAK Inc., Dayton, Ohio. The modifications were carried out by Maxwell Atchisson.

The principal differences between the Defence Systems weapon and the standard M16A1 are as follows:

The modified M16A1 fires from the open bolt position which ensures that in a gap between rounds or bursts the chamber is empty and there is no risk of cookoff.

The strength of the buffer has been increased. The return spring is more powerful and the muzzle attachment reduces the recoil.

The weapon is also offered with a heavy barrel, making it a passable LMG, or with a standard M16 barrel.

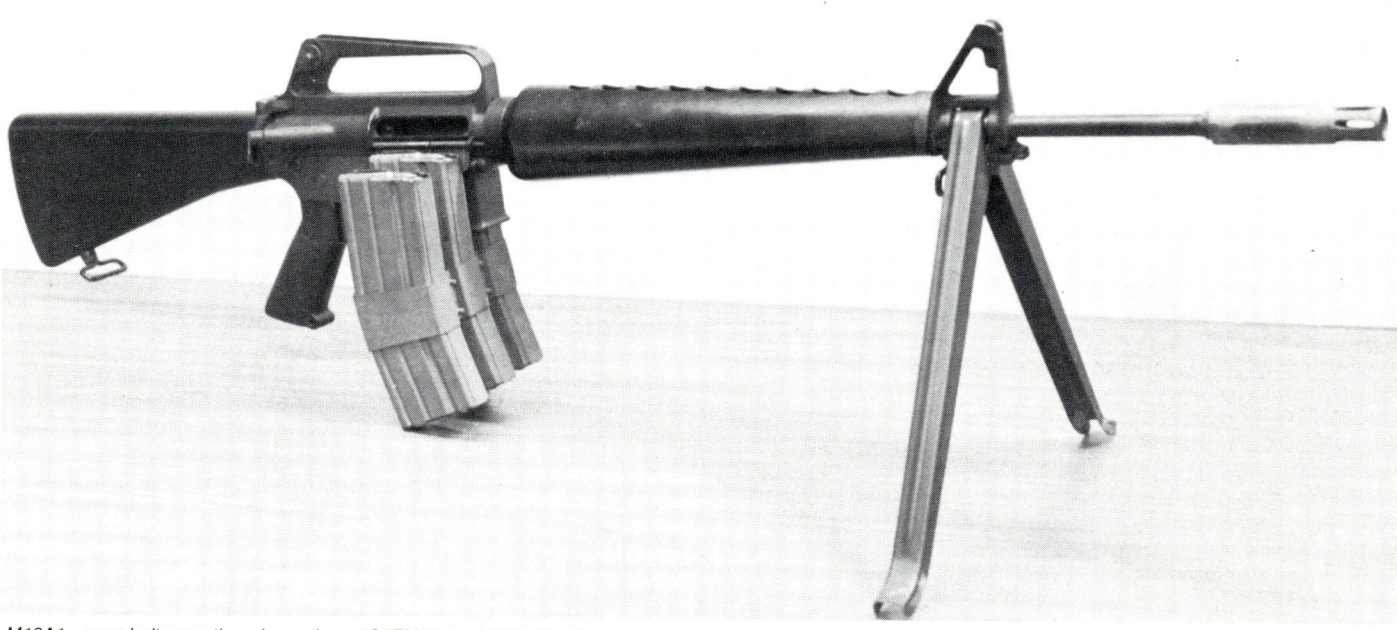

M16A1 – open bolt operation – heavy barrel CETME bipod (B.B. Bintliff)

Open bolt M16, automatic bolt catch release and assault Tri-Mag with auxiliary magazine catch (B.B. Bintliff)

The Atchisson M16 night sight (B.B. Bintliff)

To increase the fire power the German MP 40 idea of two magazines on a gun has been taken a step further and a 3-tier magazine has been made. When the first magazine has been emptied, the next can be moved straight across followed by the third in due course. When the magazine is inserted, the automatic bolt release allows the bolt to move forward onto the sear. With the heavy barrel and a 90-round capacity, the inventor claims it is a very practical light machine gun.

A practical luminous night sight consisting of a rear aperture and a front spot can be fitted into the top channel of the carrying handle.

DATA		
(Maker's figures)	**M16A1**	**Open bolt M16A1**
Weight empty:	3kg	2.4kg
		(or 3.8kg with
		heavy barrel)
Overall length:	991mm	1041mm
Cyclic rate of fire:	700-800 rpm	600-700 rpm
Automatic rate:	150-200rpm	250-300rpm
Maximum rate with		
"Tri-magazine":	—	310-360rpm
Magazine empty:	—	0.45kg
Magazine loaded:	—	1.47kg
Manufacturer: WAK Inc., 4326 Webster St. Dayton, Ohio		
Status: Available		

5.56mm WAK M16 FIRING-PORT WEAPON

Against a US Army requirement for a firing-port rifle primarily for use in mechanical infantry combat vehicles (MICV), but also suitable for use outside the vehicle in an emergency, WAK have produced a modified 5.56mm M16 rifle.

This weapon achieves a lower rate of fire (620rounds/min) than the standard M16 and incorporates a number of non-standard components including the bolt carrier and receiver extension. It is shown in the accompanying illustration with a detachable shoulder stock for use outside the vehicle.

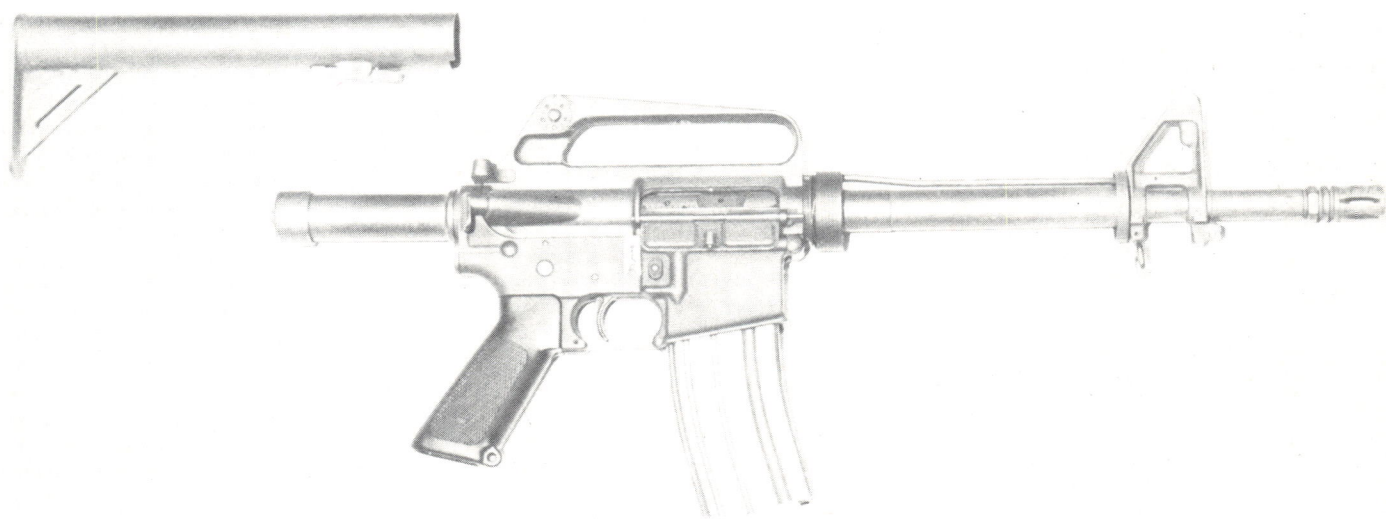

M16 Firing-port Weapon and detachable shoulder stock

12 GAUGE ATCHISSON ASSAULT RIFLE

This is a selective-fire shotgun firing any of the many available loadings of shotgun cartridge from the rifled slug to a conventional game size.

It has been designed by Maxwell Atchisson who is convinced that experience has shown that in situations such as those which were common in Vietnam, the leading man in an infantry patrol needs more fire power at short range than can be supplied by a conventional rifle.

The Assault shotgun has a 20-round magazine and as can be seen from the accompanying photograph the weapon has a straight through butt and the action of the bolt and return spring accords with normal military practice. The gun is operated by blowback, using the advanced primer system of ignition. The magazine is spring operated and may be either a drum shape or a 5-round single column box.

DATA
Method of operation: Blowback
Method of locking: Nil
Method of feed: 20-round drum magazine or 5-column single column box magazine
Method of fire: Selective
Weight empty: 5.2kg
Weight with 20-round magazine: 7kg
Overall length: 990mm
Barrel length: 475mm
Rate of fire: Cyclic: 360 rounds/min
Manufacturer: WAK Inc., 3426 Webster St, Dayton, Ohio
Status: Available

Atchisson 12 Gauge assault shotgun with 20-round drum magazine (T. Swearingen)

5.56mm FOOTE ASSAULT RIFLE

J.P. Foote is one of the younger USA gun designers. He has been associated with Ingram and Atchisson and connected with the Military Armament Corporation at Marietta, Georgia. He has designed the FAC-70 (Foote Automatic Carbine 1970) in 5.56mm calibre. The rifle has been tested in England by Sterling Arms Co at Dagenham but it appears to be unlikely that they will manufacture the gun. The FAC-70 follows the R-68 Assault Rifle which was similar in many respects

The FAC-70 is a selective-fire gas-operated rifle, using a rotating-bolt multi-lug system. The magazine comes from the AR-180 self-loading rifle. The forestock is of wood but could be produced in plastic for large scale manufacture. The cocking handle is over the gas cylinder to allow cocking with either hand and the safety is unusual in being placed in the bottom of the trigger guard.

DATA
Cartridge: 5.56mm × 45
Method of operation: Gas
Method of locking: Rotating bolt
Method of feed: 30-round box magazine

WEIGHT
Gun unloaded: 3.73kg

LENGTH
Rifle without stock: 718mm
Rifle with stock: 960mm
Barrel: 457mm

FIRING CHARACTERISTICS
Muzzle velocity: 976metres/sec
Muzzle energy: 173mkp
Rate of fire: Cyclic: 600 rounds/min
      Auto: 120 rounds/min
      SS: 40 rounds/min
Range, maximum effective: 350metres

*From **left** to **right**, John Foote with his FAC-70 assault rifle, Cal. .223, Gordon Ingram with his silenced Ingram Model 10 sub-machine gun and Maxwell Atchisson, designer of the Atchisson Model 57 sub-machine gun and the modified M16 system*

SPECIAL PURPOSE INDIVIDUAL WEAPON (SPIW)

This US concept originated in the late 1950s and was the subject of intensive research and development effort. There were a number of government agencies and a small number of manufacturing firms directly concerned in the SPIW programme.

The US Ordnance Weapons Command was initially responsible for the work carried out by the Research and Development Division and various Arsenals, Frankford, Springfield, Picatinny and the Ballistics Research Laboratories. The civilian firms concerned were Aircraft Armament Industry (AAI), Remington, Whirlpool Corporation, Harrington and Richardson, Technik Inc, Winchester and Olin Mathieson.

The basic concept was generated as a result of Exercise Salvo and, stripped of all non-essentials, amounted to one of projecting a light fin-stabilised projectile at a very high muzzle velocity. The muzzle impulse would be very low due to the low mass of the projectile and this would result in a weapon capable of producing controlled bursts of fire with a very high chance of a hit.

Subsequently the lightness of the weapon and its ammunition led to the idea of placing an area weapon under the barrel to allow the soldier to deal with targets not in the direct line of sight.

A significant part of the development work in the SPIW programme was concerned with the ammunition. A discussion of the development of the flechette round which is central to the SPIW development will be found in the section of this book which deals with ammunition; all that need be said here is that the requirement of producing the light fin-stabilised projectile is met by using a cartridge of conventional shape but containing a finned dart or flechette which is saboted at the end remote from the cartridge base. The

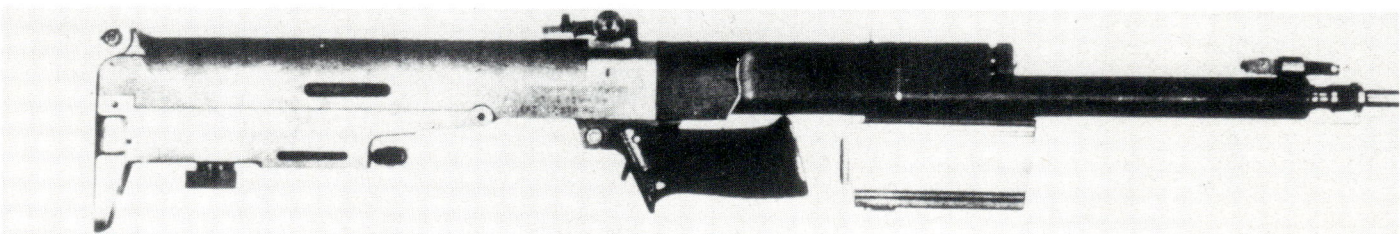

Experimental 5.6mm Springfield Arsenal Special Purpose Individual Weapon of 1962

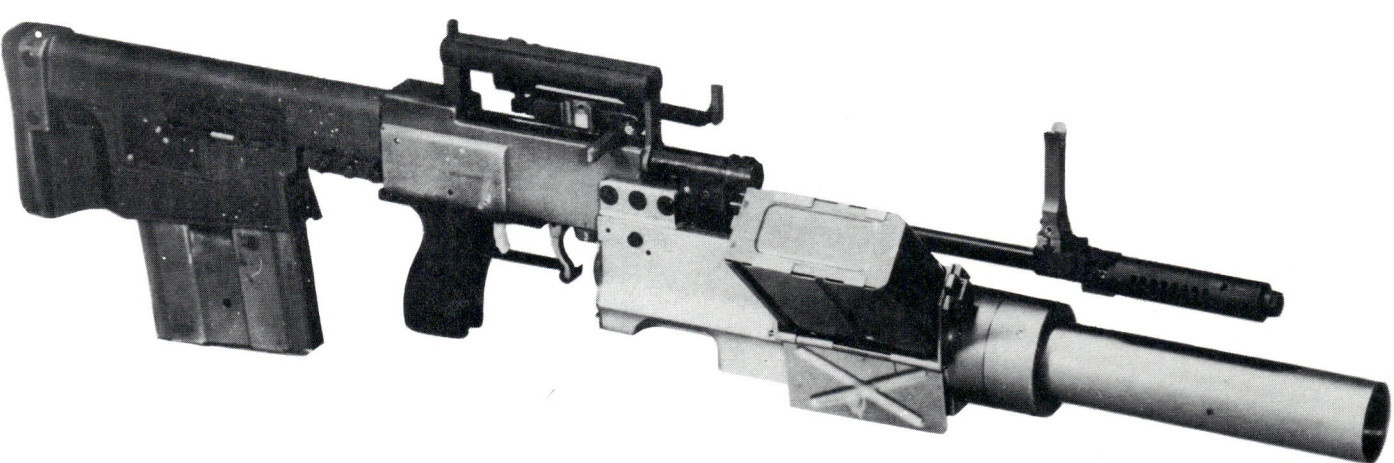

The first Springfield Armoury SPIW (1964) (Courtesy Dr. E. Ezzell)

The first AAI Corporation SPIW (1964) (D. E. Ezzell)

sabot provides an adequate cross-section for the propellant gases to act upon while the saboted projectile is in the bore and is cut away as the projectile emerges from the barrel.

During 1962 it was established that a 10-grain (650mg) flechette propelled in this way possed the ability to incapacitate a human target and also to defeat all known types of body armour. It was considered nearly equal to the NATO 7.62mm 150-grain (5.7g) bullet out to ranges in excess of 500 metres and it was believed possible to extend its effectiveness to 1,000yds.

To increase the chances of a hit, it was also shown that the best results came from firing three rounds each trigger pull, delivered at a very high cyclic rate.

This produced an extreme spread of about four mils. If dispersion increased, the kill probability decreased until at about 20 mils extreme spread the current level of the M14 was reached.

At this time there were two cartridge contenders and several rifles. The cartridges were the XM110 and the XM144. The difference between them lay principally in the primer used. The XM110 cartridge used a standard light pistol primer in a pistol primer layout to provide initial energy to drive back the firing pin although research and development studies by AA1 showed that a one-piece blowback primer was also possible. The XM144 needed a conventional primer but one of smaller size than any developed at that time.

It is also worthy of note that at this time the flechette cost $0.33 and sabots cost $0.76. The introduction of moulding for sabot production and centreless grinding for both components was expected to reduce the cost to $0.03 for projectiles and $0.05 for sabots.

Also in 1962, while trials of the various contending weapons were under consideration for the SPIW role, the Armalite AR-15 emerged as a serious challenger. The objection to it, from the viewpoint of those concerned with the SPIW project, was that it had less long-term development potential; but in the short-term it offered a greater probability of incapacitating a soldier with a random hit as the following figures show.

Weapon	Probability of Inflicting Incapacitating Wound
M14:	0.4
AR-15:	0.26
Flechettes:	
10.2gr (661mg) (MV 1432m/s):	0.14
12.6gr (816mg) (MV 1432m/s):	0.16
18.5gr (1199mg) (MV 1158m/s):	0.10

AREA WEAPONS

The area weapon was also being developed as a detachable launcher to be connected to the barrel of the point fire weapon. The cartridges for their programme were also being developed. The M406 was in service with troops and was fired from the M79 grenade launcher to a range of 375 metres. This used fuze PDM551 with an arming distance of 45ft. The cartridge M407E3 was a practice round for the M79.

The cartridge XM434 with fuze PIBD XM550 was also being developed. This was a shaped charge round designed to penetrate two inches of steel, four inches of aluminium armour and seven inches of reinforced bunker concrete.

Cartridge XM398, with fuze XM536, was a ground impact/airburst round which had a 120 millisecond delay. When set as an airburst it detonated five feet above the target. There was a proposed 30mm cartridge designed to have the same lethality as the 40mm cartridge. This would have much the same weight and filling as the 40mm and would therefore be longer.

When weapon tests started in 1964 there were five contenders. The first was designed and manufactured by Springfield Armoury. It was a 'bullpup' design with no buttstock and the trigger in front of the magazine. An advantage claimed for this layout was that it was possible to produce a very long barrel within an overall length of 40in. With the grenade launcher in position the centre of gravity lay between the firer's hands. Without the launcher the centre of gravity was at the pistol grip as in a well-designed sub-machine gun. This design carried a bayonet knife.

The second design, also by Springfield, was conventional. It had a bipod and carried a knife bayonet.

The third contender was designed by AAI. It had a slightly dropped buttstock and a vertical drum magazine carrying 50 rounds which were fired in three-round bursts. The barrel casing was perforated and a launcher was slung under the muzzle.

The fourth contender was produced by Olin-Winchester. It was of orthodox appearance.

Lastly there was the Harrington and Richardson weapon; but this was withdrawn from the competition because the high chamber pressure required to obtain the 4700ft/sec MV was considered unsafe.

From March-May 1964 the comparative evaluation of four models took place. The control weapons were the M14, the AR-15, and an M16 modified to take a two-shot burst control and a muzzle brake-cum-compensator. The M79 was control for the launcher firings using cartridges M407E2 and M407E3 – both practice rounds.

The trials revealed the basic unreliability of all contenders.

The Springfield bullpup design had a stoppage rate of 1 failure per 21.3 rounds fired. The AAI contender's rate was 1/23.5 and the Olin Winchester was 1/10.8.

Various aspects were criticised on all models. The weight distribution, bulk, sights and methods of loading all had unfavourable mention.

The three shot launchers also had a high stoppage rate. The Springfield was 1 in 12.9, the Olin-Winchester was 1 in 2.1 and the AAI was 1 in 4.66. The only satisfactory solution was advanced by Springfield Armoury and this was a single-shot launcher which had no stoppages.

Further testing was carried out and improved reliability was demonstrated. The XM10 cartridge was shown to operate the mechanism of the rifle correctly only when it was lubricated and this was considered unac-

The Olin-Winchester SPIW (1964)

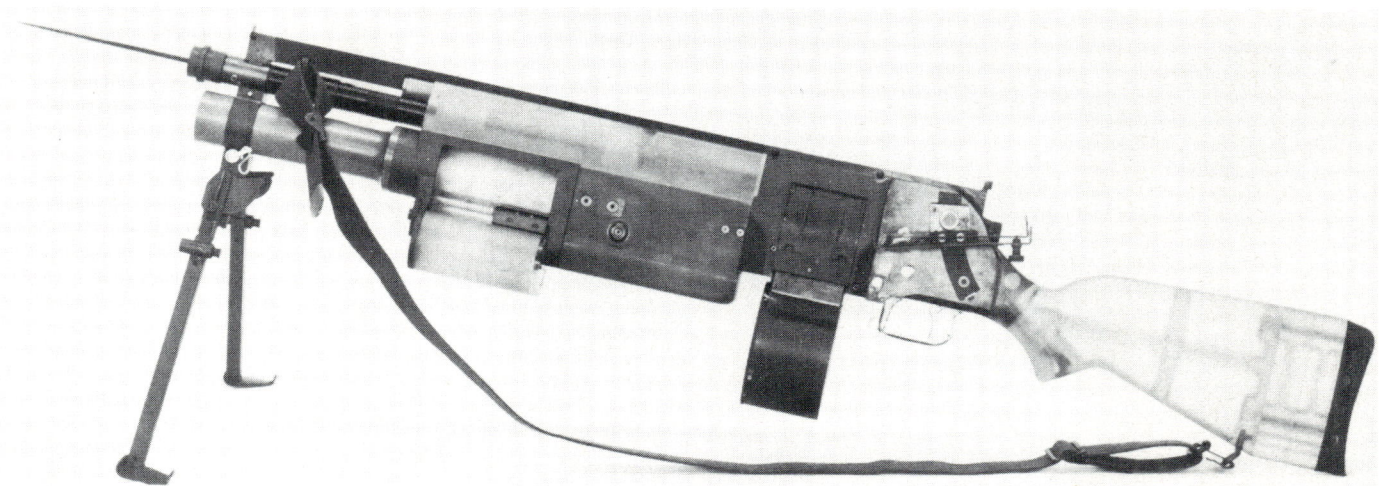

Harrington and Richardson SPIW (1964) (Dr. E. Ezzell)

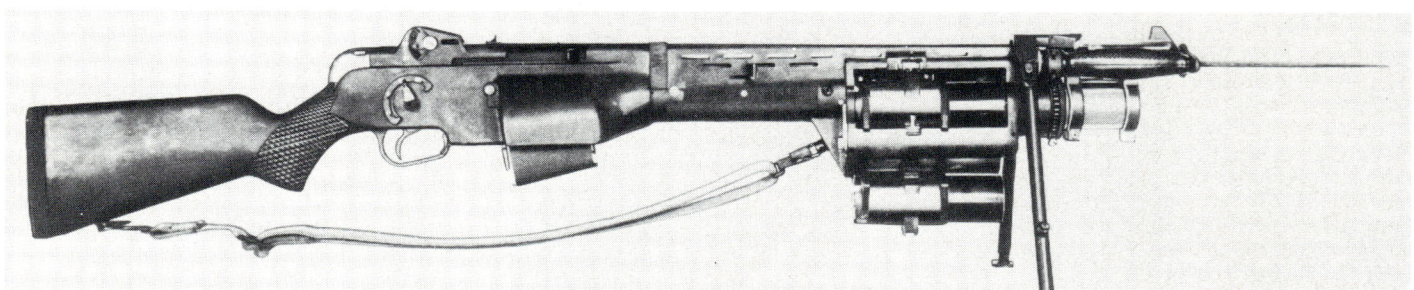

The second AAI Corporation SPIW (Dr. E. Ezzell)

The second Springfield Armoury SPIW (1966) (Dr. E. Ezzell)

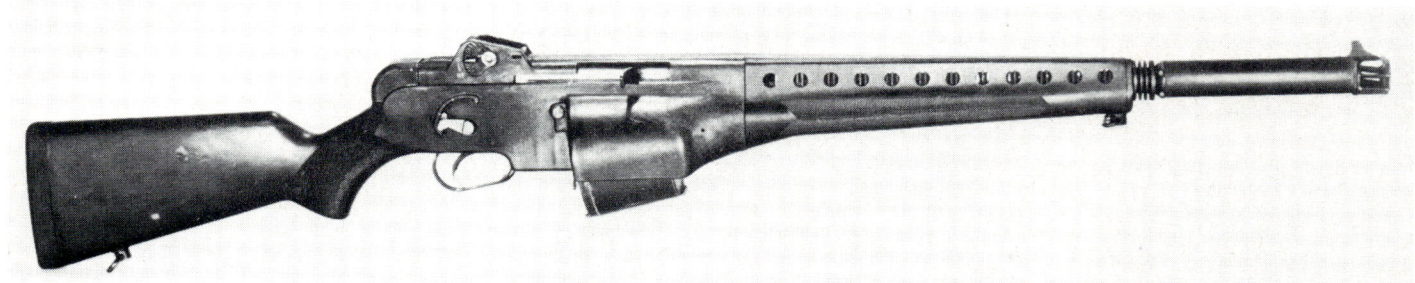

The AAI SPIW rifle

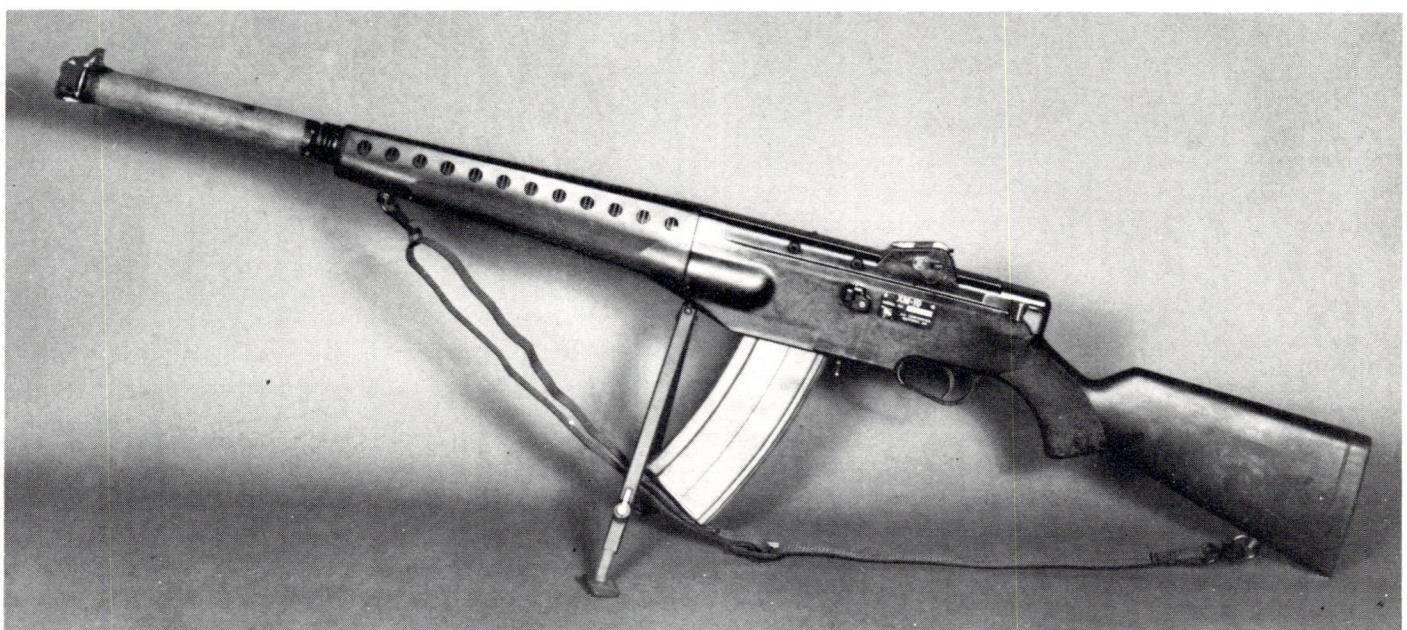

The XM 19 5.6mm Serial Flechette rifle (US Army photograph)

ceptable. The XM144 performed well.

The Engineering Design Model tests concluded that all the models had some good points but the AAI version was considered the most promising. The US Army Infantry Board said that the AAI version was considered the most promising but that features from other weapons should be incorporated.

HQ US Army Materiel Command did not accept these views and instead decided to appoint a project manager for all "New Rifle Systems" with a brief to cover conventional bullet firing weapons as well as SPIW. A vigorous development and testing programme was laid down and the basic requirements were re-evaluated by Combat Development Command. Engineering and service tests and field trials were to be carried out on 5.56 cartridge weapons – including the AR-15, AR-18, Stoner 63, and SPIW. Springfield Armoury and AAI were asked to design improved weapons and meet a new timetable, leading to the choice of one of their submissions and the manufacture of 100 of the chosen weapon by December, 1966.

It was considered that the AAI weapon did not require a great amount of modification but that Springfield had to put in more design effort and would find it hard to meet the dates.

The grenade launcher programme was revised and AAI were asked to provide a three-shot pump action launcher, and Springfield a semi-automatic action.

AAI were now using an improved ball cartridge, the FA T 209, and the FA T 197 was their new tracer round.

The Springfield, conventional primer, ball cartridge was now the XM 216 (FA T 187) and the tracer was the FA T 201. A great deal of work had been done on the grenade cartridge and the existing types were:

In production:
M406: Anti-personnel
M407: Practice
In development:
XM463: Anti-personnel
Similar to M406 but with an expanding metal diaphragm to contain smoke and flash.
XM434: Anti-personnel
A shaped charge round. About 75% as effective as the M406 against personnel.
Under study:
XM534: Anti-personnel
Rocket-assisted round to 800m XM434 war head

Multiple anti-personnel shotgun-type cartridge

A further development was the Disposable Barrel Cartridge Area Type

Ammunition (DBCATA), using a disposable metal or plastic barrel. The range was still 400 metres but it was less accurate than the conventional system.

Further tests and comparative evaluation of the SPIW contenders led to the elimination of all except the AAI SPIW rifle. From this was developed the XM 19 Rifle which externally differs little from the previous model.

The XM 19 was tested and in 1973 it was announced that it would not meet the requirement. This was largely due to the problems always associated with the earlier SPIW contenders of clean severance of the sabot. With the XM 19 this was largely overcome but in so doing a further hazard was introduced. This was the risk that the firer might ingest the dust which resulted from the detaching of the plastic sabot from the steel flechette.

The next AAI project is the XM-70 Serial Flechette Rifle. This is a lightweight, low-impulse weapon which will fire from the open bolt position and operate in two modes of fire: semi-automatic and three-round controlled burst. Other features of the XM70 Rifle are the use of a reflex collimator sight and a muzzle attachment to suppress noise and flash, provide compensation and reduce impulse. The compensation and lower impulse characteristics are instrumental factors in controlling the dispersion of the three-round burst. The system employs an aluminium, box-type magazine with a capacity of 50 XM645 cartridges.

One of the unique features of the XM 70 weapon – XM 645 ammunition systems is the manner in which gun cycling is accomplished. Instead of the conventional gas-operated system, a piston primer housed in the cartridge case imparts the energy necessary to function the mechanism. Under the pressure developed in the chamber, the piston is forced rearward through a fixed stroke within the cartridge case. The firing pin continues aft extracting and ejecting the spent case and feeding the next round on its return to battery. Some of the salient characteristics of the weapon are listed below.

Weight of rifle: 3.36kg
Weight of magazine: 0.5kg
Total weight: 3.86kg
Mode of operation – Semi-Automatic: 3-rounds controlled burst
Overall length: 1,076mm
Muzzle velocity: 1,418metres/sec
Impulse (compensated): 4lb/sec

Currently, interest in flechette, both in the USA and elsewhere, is at a low level of intensity. The possibility of using both flechette ammunition and standard ammunition in the same weapon, (as may be possible in weapons such as the XM 70 having rifled portions to the barrel) continues to be of interest, but in the main, the solution to the "ideal rifle" problem is being sought elsewhere.

FUTURE RIFLE SYSTEM (FRS)

This is the name of the United States Army programme to provide a basic infantry weapon system (both point and area fire) for the 1980-85 time frame. The requirement has been laid down in great detail but a few of the required characteristics are listed below.

PERFORMANCE CHARACTERISTICS
1. Extend capabilities of the M16A1 rifle and the M203 Grenade Launcher.
    (a) Better reliability and maintainability.
    (b) Point and area fire of equal importance.
2. Must be capable of functioning reliably whilst delivering the following fire

– repeated each 6 hour period in a 24 hour combat day.
    (a) Point fire ammunition.
(1) 540 rounds point ammo at the sustained fire rate with cooling between missions.
    (a) 180 rounds automatic.
    (b) 135 rounds burst fire (if applicable).
    (c) 45 rounds semi-automatic.
    (d) 180 rounds automatic.
(2) At least 10 per cent tracer.
(3) Target ranges.

(a) 50 m to maximum effective range.
(b) 50 per cent in 200-300 metres range.
(c) 30 per cent in 50-300 metre range – moving targets.
(d) Area ammunition – 15 rounds.
3. Point Fire Effectiveness.
(a) Probability of incapacitating at least 25 per cent better than the M16A1 rifle.
(b) Probability of a hit =0.3-0.5 per trigger pull with a target size 34.5 × 19.5in (876×496mm) (kneeling man), range 300-500 metres, aiming error 1 mil linear standard deviation.
(c) Lowest recoil, smoke, flash and blast, commensurate with required performance.
(d) Tracer as good as M196 cartridge (current 5.56mm tracer) at ranges 300-500 m.
(e) Accept bayonet for emergency situation.
4. Area Fire Effectiveness
(a) Deliver fragments or projectiles in optimum pattern at ranges of 400m.
(b) Smaller calibre than current 40mm cartridge.
(c) Neutralise point target at 35-200m.
(d) Engage area targets with indirect fire at 150-400m.
(e) Lethality not less than 40mm M406 grenade.
(f) Probability of a hit = 0.5 for 1m square vertical target 100-150 metres.
(g) Probable range error at 200-300m not to exceed 9 metres.

PHYSICAL CHARACTERISTICS
1. Simple design and construction.
2. Point fire system usable when separated from area fire system.
3. Loaded weights (point and area fire components) not to exceed 9-11lbs.
4. Sights.
(a) Simple, durable, minimum motion by firer for day or night use.
(b) Superior to M16A1 rifle and M203 grenade launcher.
(c) Improved chance of a hit at ranges up to 500 metres.
(d) Operable in winter clothing or protective clothing.

RELIABILITY
1. Mean rounds between stoppage:
(a) Point fire – 1,000 minimum for first 10,000 rounds.
(b) Area fire – 500 minimum for first 5,000 rounds.
(c) Parts replacement.
    (1) Point fire maximum 0.1 average parts per 1,000 rounds in first 10,000 rounds.
    (2) Area fire – on average, no parts in first 1,000 rounds.
2. Resist fungus, sand, salt water, rust, corrosion in use. Non-fouling and non-corrosive ammunition.
3. Standard interchangeable parts.
4. Field stripping without tools.
5. Barrel life, point fire, 20,000 rounds.

A number of possible alternative approaches to these requirements have been formulated. Amongst them the following have been publicly mentioned.

SFR – Serial Flechette Rifle
This is a weapon firing three flechettes (see previous entry on SPIW for definitions) in a controlled burst. It is also capable of semi-automatic and automatic fire. The XM19/70 is the current example of this kind of rifle. (It is illustrated in the preceding entry on SPIW). Current released data for the XM19 is as follows:
Velocity: 1,478 metres/sec
Cyclic rates
Burst fire: 1,800 rounds/min
Full automatic: 600 rounds/min
Weapon weight: 3.18kg with 60 rounds
Cartridge weight (brass case): 115 grains (7.45g)
Flechette weight: 10.2 grains (0.66g)
Recoil momentum – per round: .03kgm/sec
Mid range ordinate to 500 metres: 254mm
Dispersion (Linear Standard Deviation): 1.0mils
Three round burst (Extreme Spread): 7.0mils
Maximum range to penetrate steel helmet: 800 metres

The current problems with the SFR are mainly:
Ammunition cost and difficulties in production.
Waterproofing primer piston assemblies.
Round to round dispersion.
Personnel hazards from sabot separation and fragments.
Personnel hazards from eye and lung irritation produced by fine particles of sabot.
Sabot design to eliminate need for a stripper.
Tracer reliability.
Heat dissipation.
Extraction at high rates of fire.

SBR – Serial Bullet Rifle
This is a rifle firing a controlled burst of three bullets of calibre 4.32mm. There are two types of rifle in use for experimental work. One is a modified version of the XM19 and the other is a modified M16A1.
The SBR will fire a burst of three 27-grain (1.75g) conventional bullets of

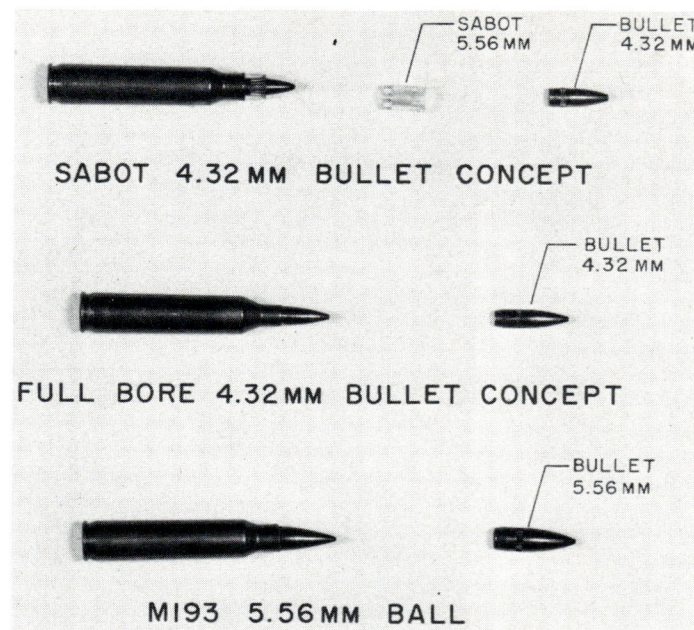

The ammunition for the Serial Bullet Rifle (US Army photograph)

4.32mm at 1,190m/sec. It will also fire at single shot or full auto. The lightweight bullet produces a low muzzle impulse and the high cyclic rate of fire of 1,800-2,000 rounds a minute with a muzzle compensator-brake, produces minimum dispersion. A rate reducer is used on full automatic fire. With 60 rounds it should weigh about 3.18kg. The cartridge weight is 120 grains (7.7g).
An alternative version fires the 4.32mm saboted ammunition from a standard 5.56mm barrel. The sabot is stripped aerodynamically at the muzzle. This produces few problems since the round is spun and the centrifugal force is available for separation. The small size of the bullet leads to the same problem as that experienced with the flechette where the size of the tracer element is so small that tracer burn-out occurs at unacceptably short ranges.

DCR – Dual Cycle Rifle
In 1971 the United States Army Small Arms Systems Agency (USASASA) under the direction of Col R. S. Isenson, the Commander, and Technical Director I. R. Ambrosini produced the concept of the Dual Cycle Rifle (DCR). In brief this is a rifle in which the burst is fired at a very high cyclic rate but the functions of feed and extraction are carried out at a fraction of that speed. The idea was presented to American Industry and fifteen companies produced proposals. Eventually after analysis of the designs, the field was reduced to two contenders. Both use a single barrel. Multiple barrels were rejected due to unfavourable strength to weight figures. Conventional ammunition is used and fired in three round bursts at a rate of about 4,500 rounds/minute. Both divide the cycle of operations into 'fire' and 'clear' sequences.
Both designs work on the principle that although the cyclic rate of fire is high the translational velocities of the reciprocating parts must be kept low, with maximum velocity not exceeding 9m/sec (peak velocities in a weapon like the XM19 are of the order of 18m/sec).
Both designs use rotating cylinders and both use box-type magazines with the ammunition stacked in three vertical columns so that three rounds can be loaded into the chambers at one time. The following description of the operation of the two Dual Cycle Rifles is based on an account "Dual Cycle Rifle" by Lester W. Roane, Chief of the Industrial and quality Assurance Division, USASASA, Aberdeen Proving Ground, which appeared in the *Army Research and Development News Magazine* of May-June 1973.

DESIGN A
A three-chambered asymmetrical rotating cylinder is used. The magazine is located below the receiver.
The system functions with the firing of round one using stored spring energy.
The operating rod is driven to the rear by gas energy. Round two is indexed into the firing position and the striker cocked by the recoiling operating rod. Round two is fired and the operating rod given further energy which is used to index and cock the striker. When round three is fired the chambers are opened for extraction. The energy of the operating rod is used to extract the cases. The operating rod picks up additional moving parts and rebounds from the buffer, three rounds are stripped from the magazine, the three empty cases are ejected forward and the chambers are charged. Round one is indexed for firing and the action is completed until the trigger is operated again.

DESIGN B
The operating rod shuttles back and forth over a short distance during the fire function and over a much linger distance for the clear/reload functions. A nine-chamber symmetrical rotating cylinder is used. There are three extract/eject stations, none of which is coaxial with the barrel. At least five of

the chambers are empty at all times. The magazine is on the left side. Starting from a freshly loaded and cocked condition (i.e. three chambers loaded with live rounds; chamber number one in the firing position; chambers four-nine empty) a simplified firing sequence is as follows:

Fire round one (using stored spring energy).

Launch operating rod to the rear (using propellant gas energy).

Partially index round two and fix the firing pin to the operating rod. The hammer is not used to fire rounds two and three.

Return operating rod to the forward position and complete indexing of round two (using stored spring energy and residual momentum from the chamber drum).

Fire round two and launch operating rod to the rear.

Index round three and return operating rod. Fire round three and launch operating rod to the rear for its "long" stroke cycle.

Extract/eject empty cartridges from chambers one and two. Compress drive spring. Stop operating rod on buffer. Launch operating rod forward.

Feed rounds four, five and six, index round four into firing position, and rest for next trigger pull

Repeat the above cycle with only one change. Indexing of round four puts the empty round three case into an extractor position. Then when the next clear/reload cycle is initiated, three empty cases (three, four and five) will be extracted and ejected.

The four flechettes are launched at about 1370/sec and versions have been tested with both puller and pusher sabots. The bore of the weapon is smooth and the sabots are stripped aerodynamically. This system provides four rounds per trigger pull and so there is no need for a burst fire capability.

LRAR – Low Risk Alternative Rifle

This rifle is of conventional design and represents a fall back solution (i.e. there is no risk of failure) if none of the foregoing alternatives is found to be acceptable. Amongst the possibilities being considered is the open bolt rifle of which the Low Maintenance Rifle (LMR) (qv) is an example.

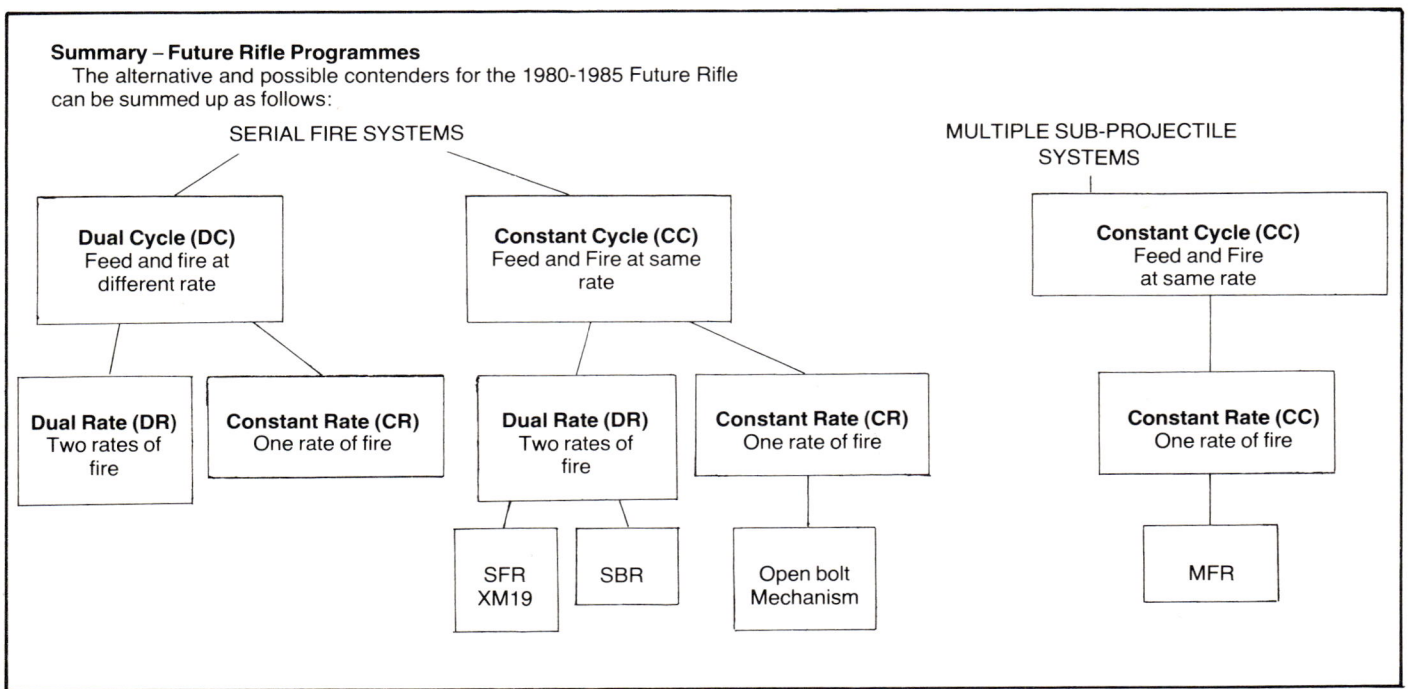

Summary – Future Rifle Programmes

The alternative and possible contenders for the 1980-1985 Future Rifle can be summed up as follows:

SERIAL FIRE SYSTEMS — MULTIPLE SUB-PROJECTILE SYSTEMS

Dual Cycle (DC) Feed and fire at different rate

Constant Cycle (CC) Feed and Fire at same rate

Constant Cycle (CC) Feed and Fire at same rate

Dual Rate (DR) Two rates of fire

Constant Rate (CR) One rate of fire

Dual Rate (DR) Two rates of fire

Constant Rate (CR) One rate of fire

Constant Rate (CC) One rate of fire

SFR XM19

SBR

Open bolt Mechanism

MFR

5.56mm TRW LOW MAINTENANCE RIFLE

The Small Arm Weapon Systems programme in the USA has led to the development of several new Infantry arms and amongst these the Low Maintenance Rifle (LMR) has some very interesting concepts.

The originating company was the systems group of Thompson, Ramo, Wooldridge Inc at Redondo Beach, California (TRW) and the project was completed in March 1973.

The principal designer of the LMR was Donald Stoehr who was also the project manager. The arm has some features which are extremely unusual in a rifle and well worthy of comment. These are listed, without being in any particular order as:

Open bolt firing.

Full automatic fire only.

Control of dispersion of fire by low cyclic rate, straight through stock and compensator.

Semi-permanent dry film lubrication.

Extensive use of corrosion resistant materials and finishes.

OPEN BOLT FIRING

It has always been considered an essential feature of rifle design to keep the lock time to a minimum, that is to say that the interval between trigger operation and cap initiation should be minimal. This has been justified as the only way of ensuring accuracy. The argument, in brief, is that the firer can rarely maintain a steady aim in action for long so that response, after squeezing the trigger, must be as nearly immediate as possible. After trigger operation there should be minimum movement of parts and these should be of the smallest possible weight to keep down any changes in the centre of mass of the weapon and to prevent the setting up of vibrations in the barrel which could cause variation in the natural amplitude and frequency of the tube movement. These considerations point to an arrangement in which the breech bolt or block is fully forward and locked prior to trigger action which itself led to the movement only of a firing pin and sometimes a hammer. Thus – and only in this manner – could accuracy and consistency be maintained. A series of single shots obtained under identical conditions led to the optimum chance of a hit.

The LMR has a different approach. Reliance is placed on increasing the chance of a hit by firing several rounds which are sufficiently well spaced out in time to allow correction between shots. The first shot fired from the open breech position is likely to be less accurate than that from a closed

breech but the difference in lock time is not more than some 20 milliseconds and the bolt – as will be seen – is designed to produce minimum disturbance on locking while in its action, unlike that of most contemporary rifles, produces no torque. Lastly the open breech system is a complete answer to any possibility of cook-off.

FULL AUTOMATIC FIRE

There are three basic approaches to the question of increasing the chance of a hit from a rifle. The first and most orthodox has the experience of the ages behind it and is to fire a series of aimed single shots. The second idea is to release a group of 3-5 rounds at a high cyclic rate with one operation of the trigger. The justification for this is simply that the interval between shots does not permit any appreciable target movement and the low impulse associated with the modern small calibre cartridge does not lead to significant barrel lift in this short period of time. The third – and least frequently met – is to fire a series of rounds at full automatic at a slow cyclic rate. This view is justified by its advocates who point out that the interval of time between successive shots is ample to correct the aim after each round and to counter the lift of the barrel. This view was advanced some years ago at the Design and Development Department of the Royal Small Arms Factory at Enfield, England.

CONTROL OF DISPERSION

Apart from the question of rate of fire, two other considerations loom large when considering dispersion. These are the effect of the position of the centre of gravity of the weapon relative to the line of the barrel and the position of the support in the shoulder, again relative to the thrust line of the barrel. The LMR – it will be noticed a little later – has the gas cylinder and piston alongside the barrel and the magazine functioning horizontally on the opposite side. The centre of gravity of the weapon is therefore in the same horizontal plane as the barrel. The butt is a direct continuation of the line of the barrel. These factors almost entirely offset the lift of the muzzle produced by the low impulse of the 5.56mm cartridge but to ensure there is no appreciable upward acceleration a compensator is fitted with the flash eliminator.

DRY FILM LUBRICATION

The ability to dispense with fluid lubrication leads to advantages in desert

The Low Maintenace Rifle. Note magazine and piston on side of weapon to keep centre of mass on bore (D. Stoehr)

terrain, where sand and oil make an effective grinding paste, in Arctic climates where oil readily freezes and in situations where maintenance support is lacking. The dry film lubricant can readily be sprayed on periodically from aerosol type containers to maintain the skin and there is no need for daily oiling as with conventional lubricating methods.

CORROSION RESISTANT MATERIALS AND FINISHES

The use of these materials and finishes leads to the requirement for only minimal maintenance to ensure reliable and continuous functioning under adverse conditions. The fact that components are either corrosion-resistant or have protective finishes is of particular value when fighting in hot damp tropical climates. The barrel, bore and chamber are hard chrome plated which minimises not only corrosion but also erosion from automatic fire and the build-up of carbon from the products of combustion of the propellant. As a general result of these measures, cleaning of moving parts is minimised and, in general, powder fouling, brass dust from cases, dirt and dust do not adhere to these prepared surfaces and can be removed with no more assistance than that of a damp rag.

DESCRIPTION

The LMR is a gas-operated rifle, firing at full automatic only at a cyclic rate of 450 rounds per minute and functioning from the open bolt position. The ammunition supply is from 20- and 30-round magazines of the M16 rifle.

CYCLE OF OPERATION

The cycle starts with the bolt head held to the rear in the open position, held by the sear against the bolt face. When the trigger is squeezed the sear is lowered and the return spring, wrapped round the operating rod, drives the operating slide and the bolt forward. A cartridge is stripped from the magazine, which extends horizontally from the left side of the body, and is fed into the chamber. As the cartridge ceases its forward motion the extractor claw moves over the rim of the case and springs into the cannelure.

The movement of the operating slide is conveyed to the bolt by a stud, which passes through an elongated slot in the side of the bolt; this stud enters a wedge shaped firing pin inside the bolt. The wedge bears against two rollers in the bolt – one at the top and one at the bottom – but since the rollers have nowhere into which they can move outwards, the wedge cannot move past them and merely pushes the whole bolt forward. When the bolt is fully forward there are recesses in the top and bottom of the body

into which the rollers can move. The wedge drives the rollers outwards to lock the bolt to the body and further forward movement of the operating slide moves the stud along the elongated slot in the side of the bolt, carrying the wedge shaped firing pin forward to project through the bolt face to contact and fire the cap of the cartridge. The gas pressure drives the bullet up the bore. As the bullet passes the gas vent on the right side of the barrel near the muzzle, some of the gas enters a cylinder lying parallel to the barrel on the right of the gun, and drives back the piston attached to the operating slide. The first 6mm of rearward free travel of the operating slide provides mechanical safety. The stud on the slide then starts to withdraw the locking wedge, which maintains the rollers in a locked position for a further 8mm. The pressure is very nearly down to ambient level when, after 9mm of slide travel, the stud reaches the end of the elongated slot and pulls the bolt to the rear. The unsupported rollers are forced into the body of the bolt, the empty case is extracted, and after 8cm of bolt travel a fixed ejector contacts the base of the case, and throws it through a port in the operating slide and out of the gun. The slide and bolt continue rearwards and pick up the ejection port cover which is pulled back to close the port. If the sear is held down the cycle is repeated. If the sear is up it holds the bolt and the ejection port is covered, and no dirt or mud can enter the action.

STRIPPING

The magazine is removed and the gun checked for safety. The pin holding the buttstock to the receiver lies on the top surface in front of the shoulder piece and can be removed after depressing the centre lock pin. The buttstock will then slide to the rear.

There is a latch on the rear of the gas cylinder. This, when pushed forward and rotated a quarter turn clockwise, releases the slide assembly, bolt and locking wedge. The bolt can then be removed from the stud and the firing pin-locking wedge withdrawn. If it is necessary to remove the trigger group, the retainer spring on the right is removed, the pin holding the group to the receiver is then withdrawn and the group is free.

The gas cylinder plug comes out using the ⅝in (16mm) open ended spanner provided, and this completes field stripping.

TESTING

The LMR was tested against the M16A1 and an M16A1 modified by fitting a straight stock, a muzzle brake and reducing the rate of fire. The test programme produced some very interesting results.

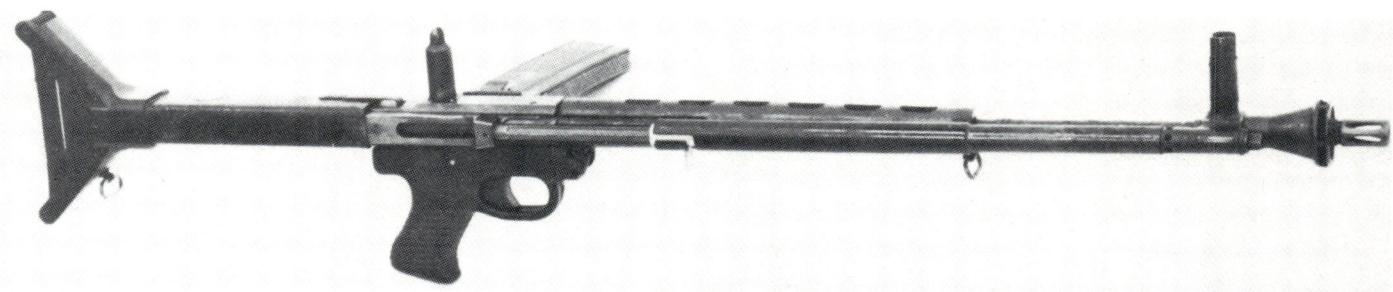

LMR with different muzzle attachment (D. Stoehr)

RELATIVE DISPERSION OF THE RIFLES IN SINGLE SHOT MODE

Rifle	Sample size	Standard Deviation 5 Mils		
		H	V	$\sqrt{V^2+H^2}$
LMR	10	.45	.58	.73
M16	10	.25	.31	.40

The firing was deliberate single shot from the prone position with a forearm rest. The difference between the weapons here is attributed to the effects on the LMR of firing from an open breech.

THREE-ROUND BURST DISPERSION DATA

Rifle	Position	Shooter	Average Extreme Spread Mils Five 3-round Bursts		
			V	H	$\sqrt{V^2+H^2}$
M16	Prone	Mean of	24	11	26
	Standing	4 Shooters	29	23	37
Modified M16	Standing	Mean of 3 Shooters	8.2	9.0	12
LMR	Standing	A	13.0	8.4	15
		B	9.2	5.5	11
	Prone	A	11.0	5.2	12
		B	5.8	7.5	9.5

The LMR, firing 3-round bursts, produces an extreme spread equal to that of the modified M16 and an average less than half that of the standard M16.

FULL AUTOMATIC FIRE RESULTS

Rifle	Position of Firer	Burst Length	Standard Deviation (mils)		
			H	V	$\sqrt{H^2+V^2}$
LMR	Standing	30	5.2	6.2	8.1
	Prone	30	4.5	5.4	7.0
M16	Standing	20	9.5	10.5	14.2
M16 Modified	Standing	20	6.3	6.3	8.9

It can be seen – comparing the results from the standing position – that the LMR was appreciably more effective in the automatic mode than the M16 and its modified counterpart.

The LMR was found to be markedly superior in terms of reliability and far less maintenance was required. This was to be expected since the entire design was centred on this aspect.

DATA
Cartridge: 5.56mm × 45
Method of operation: Gas
Method of locking: Projecting lugs
Method of feed: 30-round box magazine
Method of fire: Automatic

WEIGHTS
Rifle without magazine: 3.3kg
Empty magazine (30 rounds): 0.11kg
Full magazine (30 rounds): 0.34kg
Rifle, loaded: 3.64kg
Bayonet M6: 0.27kg
Scabbard M8A1: 0.14kg

LENGTHS
Rifle with flash suppressor: 871mm
Rifle and bayonet M6: 1,016mm
Barrel, without flash suppressor: 493mm

MECHANICAL FEATURES
Barrel: Regulator: Nil
     Rifling: 4 grooves RH 1 turn in 305mm
     Cooling: Air
Sights: Foresight: Post
     Rearsight: Apertures. 0-300 metres. 300-500 metres
     Zeroing: Line. Front sight; Elevation. Front sight.
     Sight radius: 533mm

FIRING CHARACTERISTICS
Muzzle velocity: 990m/sec
Muzzle energy: 178mkp
Chamber pressure: 3,655kg/cm^2
Rate of fire: Cyclic: 450 rounds/min
         Automatic: 120 rounds/min
         Sustained: 30 rounds/min
Range, maximum effective: 460 metres
Maximum: 2,425m
Manufacturer: Thompson, Ramo, Wooldridge, Redondo Beach, California
Status: Evaluation

LMR field stripped

5.56mm RUGER MINI-14 RIFLE

The firm of Sturm, Ruger and Co introduced in 1973 a new 5.56mm carbine known as the Mini-14. When first produced it was a self-loading rifle only but in the very near future a weapon fitted with a selector switch to allow full auto fire and controlled three-round bursts, will be available. This is in its final stages of testing and should enhance the military value of the rifle considerably.

The Ruger 5.56mm Carbine is clearly based on the design principles established by John C. Garand when the Cal 30 M1 rifle was standardised on 9 January 1936. The M14 using the 7.62mm × 51 cartridge used the same breech but a different gas system.

The rotating bolt design is extremely strong but at the same time it can be made quite short and compact. It is easily manufactured and because of the limited number of components it is not expensive to produce. The total number of Garands made by Winchester and Springfield Armoury during World War II was 4,028,395. The number of failures of the components of the breech mechanism was extremely small and the system was shown to be both reliable and durable.

The major drawback from the viewpoint of the United States Infantry was that both the .30-06 and the 7.62mm × 51 cartridges had a high level of impulse which made it almost impossible to control either the Garand M1 or the M14 at full automatic fire.

The 5.56mm × 45 cartridge has a much lower muzzle impulse and therefore, provided the weapon is made at the correct weight, it can readily be fired at full automatic with a worthwhile chance of hitting.

It should not be assumed that the Ruger Mini-14 is only a scaled-down version of the M1-M14 system. The chamber pressure of the 5.56mm cartridge at approx 3,620kg/cm² is higher than that of the 7.62mm × 51, which is 3,515kg/cm², and so the forces imposed – whilst reduced by the smaller areas involved – are still high and direct scaling is not possible. The reductions found possible and savings made by more modern high tensile alloy steels have resulted in a light handy rifle with all the advantages conferred by the flat trajectory of the 5.56mm cartridge.

OPERATION

The magazine containing five or twenty rounds is detached from the rifle by pressing forward the magazine catch located immediately behind the magazine. It is filled by pressing the cartridges in individually until the staggered double column box is full. The magazine is pressed up into the well until the magazine catch clicks home to hold it.

The cocking handle is on the right of the gun, attached to the slide and reciprocating with it. To load the first round the cocking handle is pulled right back and released. The compressed return spring drives it forward and the

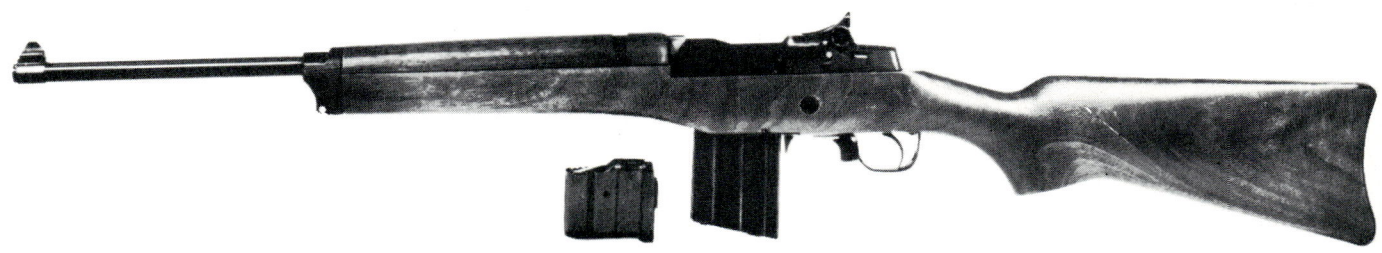

Ruger Mini-14, Calibre 223. 20-Shot magazine shown in rifle. 5-shot magazine shown also.

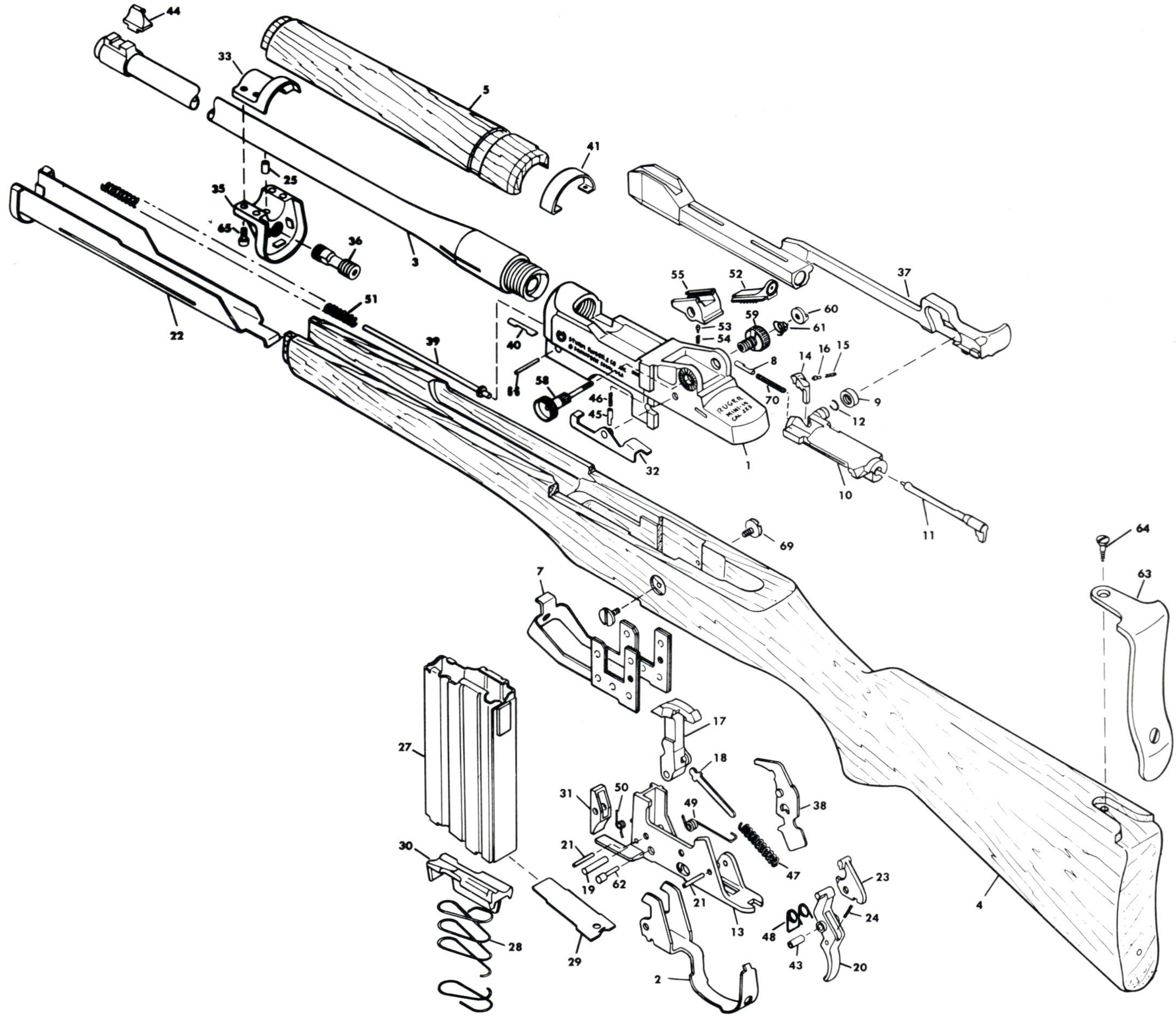

An exploded view of the Ruger 5.56 carbine (Mini-14)

bottom face of the bolt picks up the top cartridge in the magazine and pushes it forward into the chamber. The extractor springs into the cannelure of the cartridge case and the ejector is forced back into the bolt face, compressing its spring. The slide carries a cam path in which the bolt roller engages. When the round is chambered the bolt comes to rest but the slide continues on and the bolt is rotated clockwise so that the two bolt locking lugs move in front of abutments in the receiver. The slide continues on for approximately 6mm over the bolt roller and when the end of the cam path contacts the roller all forward movement ceases and the gun is ready to fire.

When the trigger is pulled the hammer drives the firing pin against the cap and the round is fired. The gas pressure forces the bullet up the bore and the gas follows it up towards the muzzle. Some of the gas passes down through a vent drilled radially through the barrel wall and through a stationary piston to impinge on the hollow interior face of the slide. The slide is driven back and the straight action of the cam path moves over the bolt roller. This free travel of approximately ¼ in allows the chamber pressure to drop to atmospheric before the roller is lifted by the cam path and the bolt is rotated. The firing pin is cammed back. The rotation of the bolt dislodges the cartridge case in the chamber and provides the slow powerful leverage required for primary extraction. The bolt is then carried to the rear and the case is held to the bolt face by the extractor. As soon as the case is clear of the chamber the compressed ejector spring is able to push the ejector out, rotating the case about the extractor and throwing it out of the gun to the right and forward. The bolt continues back over the rounds in the magazine and the return spring is fully compressed. The spring reasserts itself and drives the slide forward to repeat the cycle.

If the ammunition is expended the magazine follower operates the bolt holding open device. This can be released either by operating the bolt release on the left of the receiver, or by withdrawing the magazine, replacing with a full magazine and pulling back slightly on the cocking handle. When it is released the bolt will go forward and chamber the top cartridge.

TRIGGER AND FIRING MECHANISM

The trigger has a forward extension which is shaped to be the hook-like main sear. When the trigger is pulled this sear rotates forward. Mounted on the trigger bushing is a secondary sear which is spring-loaded forward.

The hammer carries two bents which themselves are hook-like projections. When the hammer is rotated back by the underside of the recoiling bolt, the main sear catches the main hammer bent and holds the hammer back. When the trigger is pulled the main sear is rotated forward and the hammer is free to go forward to fire the round. When the hammer is pressed back, as the bolt moves rearward, the secondary bent is caught by the spring-loaded secondary sear. However since the trigger remains pressed from firing the previous round it must be released. This action moves the secondary sear back and it releases the hammer which starts to rotate forward. However it is then caught by the main sear in readiness for the firing of another round.

Should the hammer be released before the bolt is fully closed, a tang on the rear end of the firing pin will not go forward but will come into contact with the back of the bolt and dissipate the hammer energy by pushing the bolt forward into the locked position. Only when the bolt is fully rotated to the locked position can the firing pin reach the cap.

The applied safety lies in the front of the trigger guard and can be operated by the movement of the forefinger of the trigger hand. It is pushed forward to 'fire' and pulled back to 'safe'. When at 'safe' it blocks the hammer and pushes it down off the sear which is thus disconnected. When the weapon is set to 'safe' the slide can be retracted and the weapon loaded.

DATA

Cartridge: 5.56mm × 45 M193 or any commercial counterpart
Method of operation: Gas
Method of locking: Rotating bolt
Method of feed: 5- or 20-round box magazine
Method of fire: Self-loading

WEIGHTS
Gun empty: 2.9kg
Gun loaded (20 rounds): 3.1kg
Trigger pull: 2kp

LENGTHS
Gun: 946mm
Barrel: 470mm

MECHANICAL FEATURES
Barrel: **Regulator:** Nil
    Rifling: 6 grooves RH 1 turn in 305mm
    Cooling: Air
    Change: Nil
Sights: **Foresight:** Bead on post
    Rearsight: Aperture. Adjustable for elevation and windage. Clicks of 1 min of angle (1 min is approx 3cm at 100m)
    Zeroing: Elevation. Rearsight; Line. Rearsight
    Sight radius: 561mm

FIRING CHARACTERISTICS
Muzzle velocity: 1,005 metres/sec
Muzzle energy: 184mkp
Recoil energy: 0.76mkp
Chamber pressure: 3,650kg/cm²
Rate of fire: SS: 40 rounds/min
Range, maximum effective: 300 metres
Maximum: 2,750 metres
Manufacturer: Sturm, Ruger and Co Inc., Southport, Connecticut
Status: In production

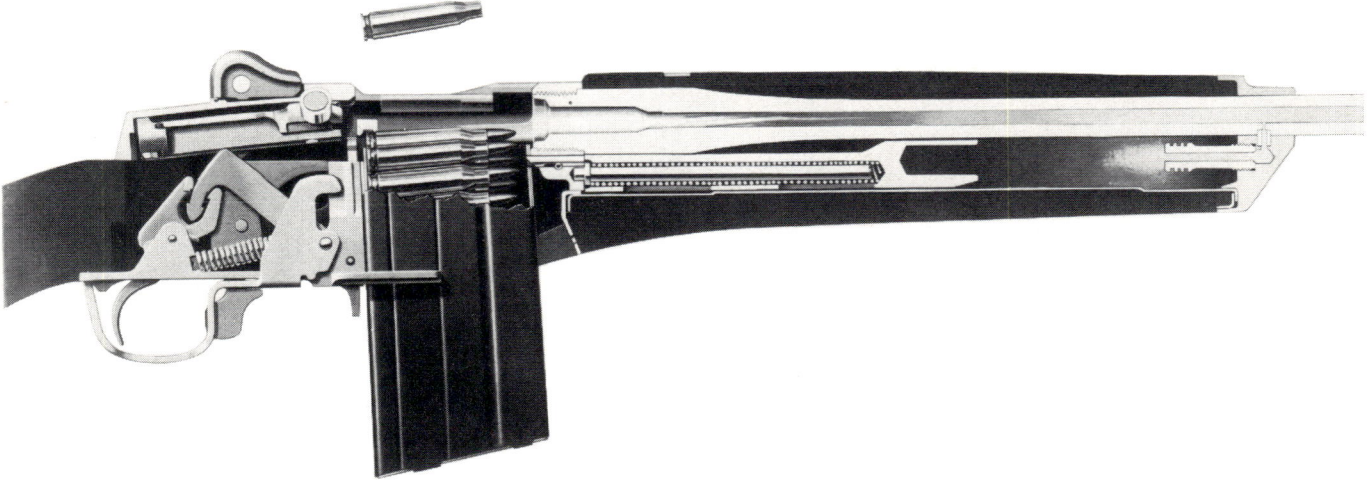

Ruger Mini-14, Cal. .223 – cutaway view. Mechanism shown in full recoil. Bolt will be driven forward under pressure of the main spring to chamber next cartridge. Note that gas pressure drops to zero before bolt is unlocked.

5.56mm STONER 63 and 63A RIFLES

When Eugene Stoner left Armalite Inc he produced a family of weapons known as the Stoner 63 System. These weapons are described in the section on Machine Guns but in brief the 63 System consisted of some basic parts to which could be added, as required, a barrel, feed system, butt and trigger mechanism to enable the construction of a series of weapons. This system was later improved but there were few offers for it either in America or in Europe where it was marketed by NWM at s'Hertgenbosch in Holland.

Eventually the rifle was offered as a separate unit and was widely tested and tried by a number of countries. During the long and involved series of evaluation trials in Israel, the Stoner rifle performed particularly well.

As might be expected the bolt and locking system are closely related to those of the AR 15 (M16). There are seven lugs on the bolt head which move in front of abutments on the barrel extension and are turned to lock by the action of a cam pin on the bolt turning in a cam path cut in the bolt carrier.

The gas vent leads gas through into a cylinder on top of the barrel to drive back a piston. The piston is latched on to the bolt carrier and so the action is that of a long stroke piston. The rearward motion of the bolt carrier carries the cam path to the rear. There is a short period of free travel while the width of the slot passes over the cam pin and then the pin is rotated and the bolt is unlocked. There is no primary extraction and a large extractor is fitted to ensure the case comes out cleanly. The empty case is ejected to the right of the gun, the return spring is compressed and the bolt carrier is driven forward to chamber another round and lock the bolt.

The weapon has the same bolt as that used in the machine gun version and as a result is slightly heavier than most of the 5.56mm rifles in service. It has been shown to be very reliable and has rather less recoil than its counterparts, due to its slightly greater weight, which make it a very comfortable rifle to fire. It carries a 30-round steel magazine with an aluminium alternative. The standard 22mm grenade can be fitted and it is necessary to cut off the gas supply to the piston.

As a result of trials various improvements were made and the rifle was then known as the 63A. The barrel is now gas nitrided to improve its durability, a cover has been placed over the ejection port and a very practical rifle has resulted.

DATA
Cartridge: 5.56mm
Method of operation: Gas
Method of locking: Rotating bolt
Method of feed: 30-round box magazine

Method of fire: Selective
Weight, empty: 3.7kg
Weight, loaded with sling: 4.4kg
Length: 1,022mm
Barrel length: 508mm
Rifling: 4 grooves RH 1 turn in 305mm
Sights: Foresight: Post
      Rearsight: Flip 0-300 and 300-500yds
Muzzle velocity: 990 metres/sec
Muzzle energy: 178mkp
Rate of fire: Cyclic: 750 rounds/min
      Automatic: 90 rounds/min
      SS: 40 rounds/min
Range, maximum effective: 400 metres
Manufacturer: Cadillac Gage Company, PO Box 1027, Warren, Michigan 48090, USA; NWM, s'Hertgenbosch, Netherlands
Status: Has not been produced since 1971. Not in service

The Stoner 63A rifle

5.56mm LOCKLESS RIFLE/MACHINE GUN

An interesting recent development in the field of small-calibre weapons in the LRMG – Lockless Rifle/Machine Gun – developed by Hughes Helicopters.

Available information on this project will be found in a corresponding entry in the machine gun section of this book. The accompanying illustra-

tion, however, shows the appearance of the weapon.
Manufacturer: Hughes Helicopters Division of Summa Corporation, Culver City, California 90230
Status: Development

Hughes 5.56mm Lockless Rifle

YUGOSLAVIA

EARLY WEAPONS

The Czech 7.92mm Model 24 rifle – which was the same as the Mauser 98 in most respects – was widely used in Yugoslavia before World War II. It was manufactured at Kragujevac to supplement purchases from Brno.

After the 1939-45 war, the Yugoslavs had German Mauser 98s, and weapons obtained from the Italians. The USSR supplied some old Mosin-Nagant 1891/30 rifles and Model 1944 carbines.

7.62mm M59/66 RIFLE

The Yugoslav M59/66 rifle is their copy of the Russian SKS Carbine (qv). It has a spigot type grenade launcher attached permanently to the muzzle and a folding grenade launching sight which is normally folded flat behind the front sight. To launch grenades it is necessary firstly to be sure that they are of the correct type with a boom of internal diameter of 22mm. The gas supply must be cut off from the gas piston by pressing in the catch and rotating it to the top of the gas cylinder. The grenade sight is then erected. The grenade cartridge is lodged in the tail boom of the Yugoslav grenade and is loaded individually into the chamber.

The sighting process is standard for this type of grenade, using the appropriate range arc aligned with the largest diameter of the grenade and placed on the target.

It is imperative that only the ballistite cartridge is used for grenade launching. If a ball round is used there is a very considerable chance that it will cause the grenade to explode on the launcher.

The M59/66 followed the M59 which was a straight copy of the SKS.

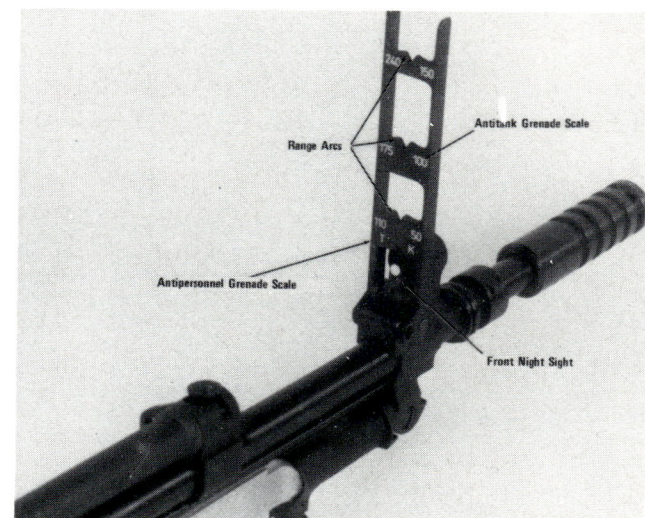

Yugoslav M59/66 with grenade sight erected

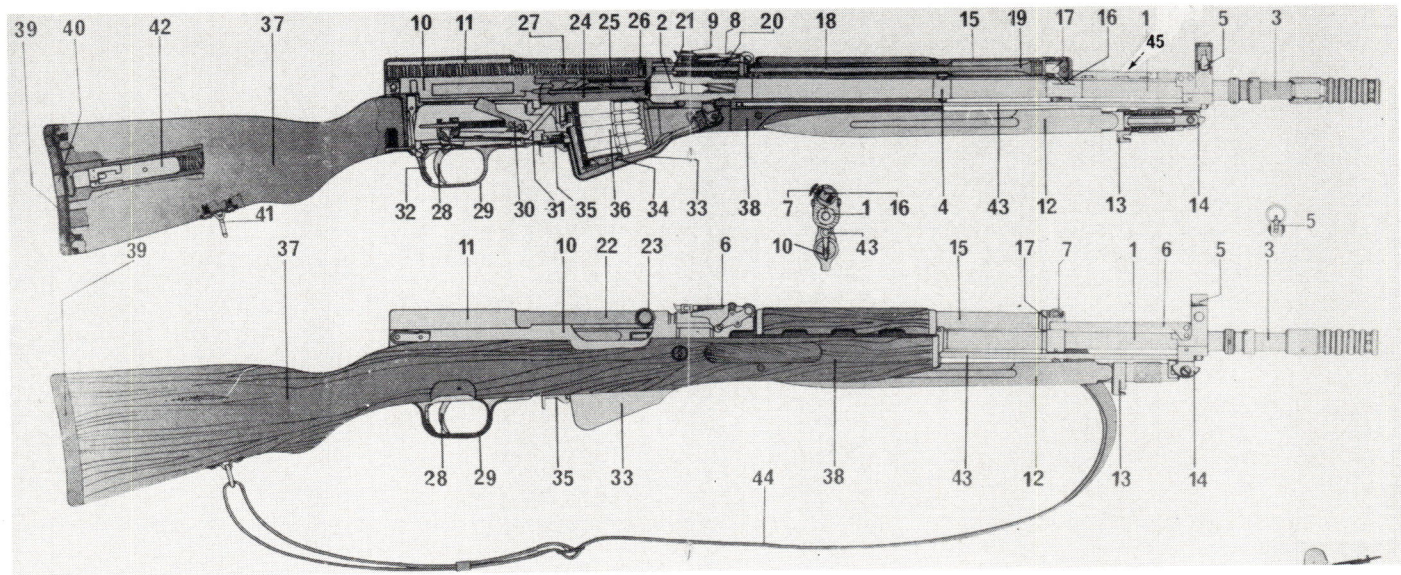

Yugoslav M59/66 rifle. The points of interest are: **3** – Grenade launcher; **45** – Grenade sight; **16** – Gas cut-off valve. There are also night sights – not shown – after the Russian pattern

Yugoslav troops demonstrating an improvised river crossing. The rifle is the 7.62mm M59/66

7.62mm M64 ASSAULT RIFLE (Model 70)

This is the Yugoslav version of the AK-47 assault rifle. There are three versions. The M64 has a 508mm barrel and a fixed wooden stock. The M64A has a 414mm barrel and fixed wooden stock. The M64B has a 414mm barrel and a folding metal stock.

All these Yugoslav M64 rifles have a folding grenade sight on the gas cylinder which, when moved to the vertical position, cuts off the gas supply to the piston. There is a built in grenade launcher.

The M64 is unique in the AK series in that it has a holding-open device.

The Yugoslav M64B is now called the model 70A. Note the grenade launching sight and the compensator. The compensator is screwed off for the grenade launcher to be used (J. Smith)

This means that the standard magazine, used by Warsaw Pact countries, cannot be used and a 20-round magazine is employed instead of the usual 30-round type.

The Yugoslav export agency, Jugo Import, describes these weapons as being part of the "Faz" family which also includes the 65A and 65B Light Machine Guns.

The Model 64A is now called the Model 70. It has the wooden stock and characteristics of the AK 47.

The Model 64B is now called the Model 70A and differs from the Model 70 in having a folding metal stock. The Model 70 weapons can have the grenade launcher with an external diameter suitable for the 22mm grenade. They have also been seen with a compensator which is unscrewed and replaced with the grenade launcher.

MACHINE GUNS

INTRODUCTION

The need to increase firepower has been recognised from earliest times and when gunpowder became known to the warring nations of Europe, it was not long before efforts were devoted to the problem of increasing the number of projectiles that could be delivered in a given period of time.

The practice of putting a number of muskets together on a frame or, later, on a cart and firing them in succession, was frequently adopted; but the difficulty of reloading in the face of an active enemy and the physical effort involved in moving the assembly encouraged the search for a more practical arrangement. Several weapons resulted from this search, all of dubious value and all accorded an undue amount of publicity. The most famous was undoubtedly Puckle's Gun which was, essentially, a large flint-lock revolver on a very modern-looking tripod. The cylinder was rotated by hand and lined up with the barrel; and a half turn of the handle behind it screwed the whole cylinder forward and the tapered end of the chamber entered the barrel and made a gas-tight fit. It was in fact extraordinarily modern in its conception. It was reported in the London Journal of 31 March 1722, that the machine was discharged in the Artillery Fields 63 times in seven minutes. This was accomplished by a single man during a rain storm. The inventor declared his intention of firing round bullets against Christians and square ones against Turks. The plan came to nothing but the weapon is still in the Tower of London as a memorial to a remarkable idea for its time.

The next development was the battery gun evolved during the American Civil War. This differed little from the earlier organ gun in principle and consisted of a series of barrels lying flat on a carriage. The most successful was the Billinghurst Requa Battery Gun which had 25 barrels of .58in calibre. An open powder train connected the breeches of all 25 barrels and a single percussion cap provided the ignition impulse to fire them in one volley. The barrels could be adjusted for height and spread and the three-man crew was said to be able to fire off seven volleys in a minute. The gun weighed 1,300lb. This type of gun was designed to assist in the defence of bridges which were frequently covered and ideal for the employment of such a weapon.

Another Civil War invention was the Gatling Gun. Whilst the war was in progress Doctor Gatling received no encouragement but when the fighting stopped, interest started to appear and eventually the weapon was widely adopted throughout the civilised world and lasted well into the 20th century. It had a number of barrels, initially six, which were arranged on a central axis around which they revolved. The barrels were rotated by hand cranking and the ammunition dropped into place from a hopper. In recent years the Gatling principle has returned to favour in the design of aircraft and anti-aircraft weapons, such as the US Vulcan gun, which use a rotating multi-barrel assembly to give a very high rate of fire. The essential difference between such weapons – often described as Gatling-type guns – and the original, however, is that the mechanical functions in the modern weapon are performed automatically.

Several other hand-operated guns, such as the American Gardner and the Nordenfelt (invented by Heldge Palmcranz) were also widely adopted; but all such weapons became obsolete when Hiram S. Maxim invented the Maxim Gun. This gun differed from all its predecessors in one simple respect. It derived its energy to carry out the cycle of operations, not from the muscular efforts of its operator, but from the propellant itself. This revolutionised the weapons industry and started a train of events that in their consequences have had as much effect on the history of Europe and America as any other single event, including the invention of the atomic weapon.

The machine gun in the 1914-1918 War denied to both infantry and cavalry the ability to move above ground during the daytime. The machine gun caused such casualties in that war that it is almost impossible for us, two generations later, to comprehend the magnitude of the disaster it brought. As a single example, and by no means unique, on the first day of July 1916 the British Army started its Somme offensive. At the end of that day its casualties, mainly due to the German Maxim guns, were 57,000.

The Maxim gun was what would now be called a medium, or sustained fire machine gun. The First World War saw the development of the light machine gun, carried by one man and served by one other. It also saw the heavy machine gun, of first .5in and then 20mm, develop into a reliable and practical weapon for use in tanks or on aeroplanes and eventually in anti-tank and anti-aircraft roles.

The principles employed in the design of automatic weapons were established before the end of the 19th century. Maxim covered nearly all the possible approaches in a series of patent applications, many of which have been taken into use. Some of them still remain to be exploited but almost all the big discoveries were made early on, and since then the improvements have largely been due to the improved knowledge of metallurgy and the use of improved and lightened materials. It is still the deficiencies in materials used that prevent improvements in weapon design that are long overdue. For example the most pressing problem has always been that of heat dissipation from the machine gun barrel. The effect of undue heat accumulation is to degrade the barrel steel and to reduce its physical strength until erosion of the softened material has enlarged the bore to the extent that accuracy is no longer obtainable and eventually, safety is impaired.

Maxim solved the heat problem for the first generation of machine guns by using water cooling and surrounding the barrel with a jacket. This was effective but it made the gun heavy, water was sometimes difficult to obtain and the system produced a revealing plume of steam when used for sustained fire. Modern guns, using cartridges of the same calibre, have the same basic heat problem; but the desire for light and highly mobile equipment has led to the adoption of air cooling in place of water cooling. This change, however, has resulted in a considerable loss of firepower; whereas the Browning, Maxim and Vickers guns of the First World War were all capable of about 10,000 rounds an hour for extended periods of time – depending in fact almost entirely on the back-up they received in ammunition and barrels – the modern machine gun can barely provide one-third of this volume of fire at greatly reduced range. The reason is simply that the machine gun is no longer as uniquely important as it was. The mortar, the light support gun, the tank and the aircraft have effects which are not confined to rear areas; they can also be used in the immediate battle and as a result the role of the machine gun has been significantly reduced in importance.

However the quest for lightness and portability can be carried too far and there are signs that this has been realised in the United States. In the Soviet Union there has never been quite the same problem because the Russian medium machine gun fires the 7.62mm x 54R cartridge which has a very good long range performance; and their light machine guns have used the 7.62mm x 39 intermediate round which has a performance superior to that of the current USA 5.56mm cartridge at the longer ranges.

Thus the current USA Squad Automatic Weapons programme is based on a slightly larger cartridge of 6.0mm which should give a better performance at ranges between 600 and 1,200 metres where the current rifle cartridge in 5.56mm is noticeably lacking in energy and incapacitating power.

Clearly the machine gun is very unlikely ever to return to its former dominant position; but there seems to be some hope that the potentiality of the weapon can be used to better effect in Western armies than it would be if the clamour for lightweight weapons were continued too long. So far as NATO countries and their close associates are concerned, however, much depends on the outcome of the small arms trials which are designed to establish a NATO calibre for the 1980s. Undoubtedly there will be strong pressure, on grounds of costs and logistics, to minimise the number of different types of small-arms ammunition required by infantry formations; and it is to be hoped that the need for adequate firepower will be equally strongly pressed.

AUSTRALIA

7.62mm M60 GPMG

Currently in service in Australian infantry formations the 7.62mm M60 GPMG is purchased from the USA. The weapon itself is fully described in the appropriate US entry later in this section; but two Australian developments, designed to provide more satisfactory methods of handling ammunition in what are considered to be the most likely combat conditions, are briefly described here.

MAGAZINE BELT BOX

This is a metal box which holds 40 rounds of 7.63mm ammunition in standard belt form. It is so designed that it can be permanently attached to the gun without impeding the use of continuous belt ammunition, and so that the feed can be changed from external belt feed to boxed belt feed without opening the gun feed top cover.

The 40 rounds held by the magazine include those on the clipping platform of the magazine lid (see photographs); and the lid performs the additional function of a belt stop pawl – so that the belt can be loaded into the magazine and retain these exposed rounds in position in one operation without having to thread the belt through a gate.

To load the magazine the box portion is simply pressed downwards to open the spring-loaded lid and a suitable length of belt is lowered into it. Holes in the rear side of the box enable the gunner to see roughly how many rounds there are in the box. To bring the magazine ammunition into operation, if the gun is empty, the magazine belt is simply drawn out of the box by the top clipping round and loaded in the normal way. If the gun has been firing rounds from an external belt, however, the top round on the clipping platform is clipped to the end of the belt protruding from the gun, any surplus length of the other belt having first been unclipped.

OPERATIONAL USE

Two important uses are envisaged. First, the firer can keep the belt box loaded with ready ammunition. If he then needs to move without his No. 2, either he or the No. 2 can break the external belt at a suitable length and clip it to the magazine belt. Alternatively, if the belt box is empty, the external belt can be broken at a suitable length and the loose end dropped into the box without either removing the belt from the gun or having to thread it through a gate.

The box is made of aluminium and is nylon coated to reduce noise, avoid corrosion and provide a dry lubricant. It weighs 343g.

BANDOLIER

To provide a convenient method of carrying GPMG belt ammunition with adequate camouflaged protection for the belt a special 50-round bandolier has been developed. Made of PVC-coated nylon it provides waterproof protection for the ammunition, is sufficiently durable to be re-used and cheap enough to be treated as expendable in appropriate circumstances. Three bandoliers will fit into an M19A1 ammunition box.

Alternative fastenings are provided which enable the effective length of the bandolier to be varied or two or more bandoliers to be joined together so that it or they can be worn in any convenient way.

To load the gun from the bandolier it is necessary to withdraw only a few rounds from its mouth (which can be identified by touch at night) thus leaving the bulk of the rounds in protective covering. There are then two ways of removing the remainder of the rounds for firing: either the bandolier cover can be pulled off like a sock – in which case it remains in a re-usable condition but the rounds are unprotected – or a gutting strip can be used to lay the whole belt open quickly, the opened cover remaining under the rounds to protect them from picking dirt up from the ground.

Manufacturer: Commonwealth of Australia Department of Manufacturing Industry, Canberra, ACT 2600
Status: In service with Australian forces

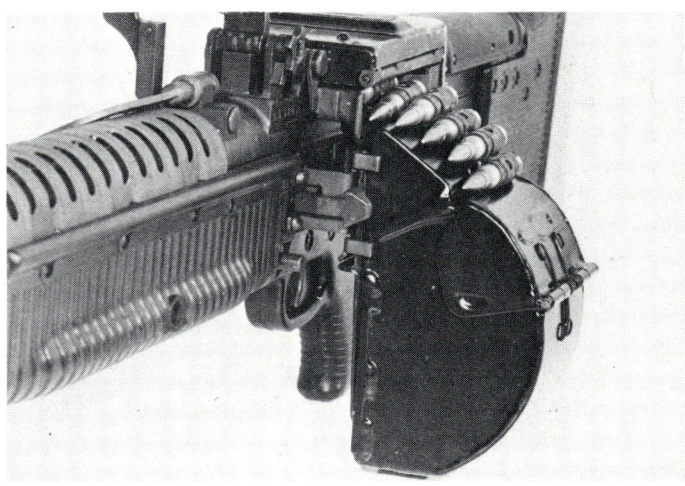

The 40-round box is shown here mounted on the GPMG with its belt coupled to the belt in the gun

The 40-round box loaded and ready to attach to the GPMG. Note the three rounds on the clipping platform and the internal rounds visible through the holes in the side of the box

AUSTRIA

SCHWARZLOSE 8mm MO7/12 MACHINE GUN

This machine gun was invented by Andreas Schwarzlose in 1902 and manufactured by Steyr in 1905. The weapon was water-cooled, belt fed, and delayed blowback operated. From the designer's point of view it is one of the more interesting of the early machine guns because the relationship between barrel length, muzzle velocity and the proportions of the lever members of the delay device is so critical. The delay is provided by two lever arms; one is attached to the breech-block and the other to a fixed pivot in the receiver. When the breech is closed, both extend forward and their junction forms a swinging pivot. Thus the gas pressure on the breech face starts to move the block back; but for the block to go back the swinging pivot must rotate, which requires a force at right angles to the arms. In the initial bolt movement when the two arms are nearly coincident and almost parallel to the barrel, this rotating force is very small and so the swinging pivot rotates slowly. As the breech opens the force increases and the pivot swings faster. Thus initially the high breech pressure is resisted strongly, but when it drops the resistance also falls and the block can more easily be forced back.

This system works very well for a selected cartridge and a given barrel

Yugoslavian troops using the Schwarzlose 07 on manoeuvres

Schwarzlose 8mm M07/12 MMG

length, but if the barrel is shortened slightly the pressure drops too soon and there is insufficient energy to carry the bolt fully to the rear. If the barrel is lengthened to increase the muzzle velocity then the breech opening is harsh. A similar effect is obtained by varying the powder charge. It can readily be seen that once the cartridge and barrel length were decided it was impossible to change either without redesigning the delay device. The powerful return spring played a greater part than is usual in delayed blowback designs.

The feed sprocket arrangement provided a very precise method of positioning the cartridge.

The Schwarzlose was probably the only delayed blowback gun to function during World War I with any measure of success. It was used in World War II in Austria and Italy and more recently, probably in very limited numbers, by Frelimo in their revolt against the Portuguese.

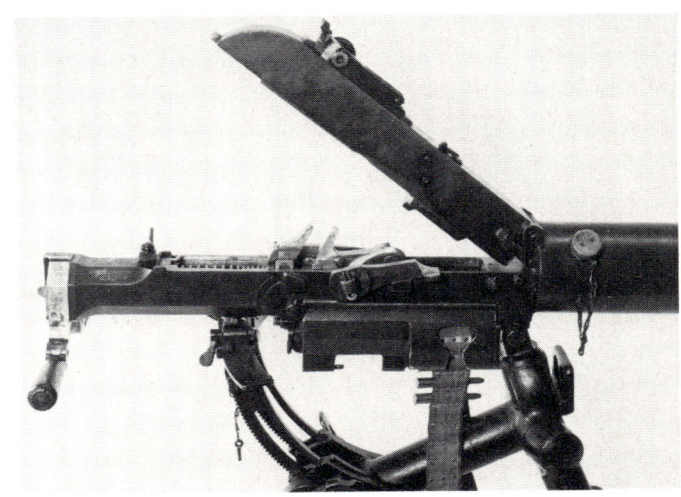

Delay system of the Schwarzlose 8mm MG

DATA

Cartridge: 8mm x 50R
Method of operation: Delayed blowback
Method of delay: Toggle joint
Method of feed: 250-round fabric belt
Method of fire: Automatic
Weight: 20kg
Tripod: 20kg
Length: 1,067mm
Barrel: 527mm
    Rifling: 4 grooves RH.
    Cooling: Water
Sights: Foresight: Barleycorn
    Rearsight: Tangent. Notch.
Muzzle velocity: 610 metres/sec
Muzzle energy: 300mkp

Rate of fire: Cyclic: 400 rounds/min
    Automatic: 200 rounds/min
Range, maximum effective: 2,000 metres
Manufacturer: Waffenfabrik, Steyr
Status: No longer manufactured. Not known to be in service with any regular formation but some have been in use by irregular forces in recent years (see text)

BELGIUM

7.62mm FN MAG

The first machine gun of significance produced in Belgium was the Lewis. Colonel Isaac Newton Lewis brought five demonstration guns to Europe and the first manufacture was at "Armes Automatiques Lewis" in Liège. With German occupation in 1914 the production was removed to England where BSA manufactured the weapon.

The range of Browning machine guns from the Browning Automatic Rifle through the .30 calibre air and water cooled guns to the Heavy barrelled .50 calibre guns, have all been made by FN at Herstal and sold very widely. Amongst the buyers have been Argentina, Belgium, China, Greece, Israel, Thailand, Sweden and the UK.

FN designed the Mitrailleuse à Gaz (MAG) in the early 1950s and in the middle of that decade it became recognised as one of the best general purpose machine guns available. It was designed by M. Ernest Vervier who retired from FN in 1973, with this gun as his crowning achievement. The FN MAG is gas-operated and belt-fed and has a quick-change barrel. It is light enough to be carried by the infantrymen in the section and is capable of producing sustained fire over considerable periods when mounted on a tripod.

It is a sturdy reliable gun with a regulator which will allow the weapon to function well and overcome adverse operating conditions. It fires the standard NATO 7.62mm cartridge from a disintegrating link belt of the US M13 type; alternatively the 50-round continuous articulated belt can be used but the two types of belt are not interchangeable. It has been made in other calibres – notably for Sweden in a calibre of 6.5mm for the M58 GPMG.

RECEIVER

The receiver is made of sturdy pressings riveted together to make a rectangular section of considerable strength. It is reinforced at the front to take the barrel nut and gas cylinder and at the rear end for the butt and buffer.

Along the inside of the receiver are ribs which support and guide the breech block and piston extension in their reciprocating movement. The breech block guides are shaped to force down the locking lever when the breech block is fully forward, and in the floor of the receiver is a substantial locking shoulder against which the locking lever rests when locking is completed.

There is a cut out section on the right of the receiver in which the cocking slide operates and the bottom of the receiver has a slot for the ejection of the empty case.

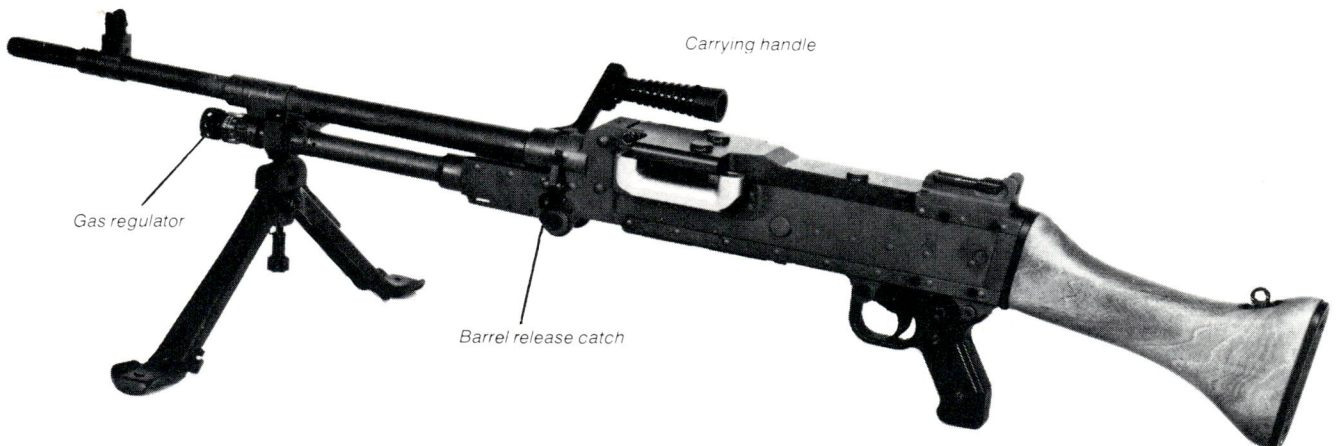

The 7.62mm FN MAG

BARREL

The barrel is threaded externally at the rear end to fit into the barrel locking nut. This has an external interrupted buttress thread to engage into the receiver and is prevented from rotating by the barrel locking catch attached to the left side of the receiver. The carrying handle sleeve is engaged on flanges in the barrel locking nut and rotating the carrying handle locks the nut into the receiver. Pushing the carrying handle forward disengages the barrel locking spindle from the barrel locking nut and allows the carrying handle to be swung sideways out of the line of sight.

A gas vent is drilled through the barrel leading down into the regulator. The gas comes into the regulator which has a surrounding sleeve inside which is a gas plug with three gas escape holes. When the gun is clean and cold most of the gas passes out through these three holes and only the minimum required to operate the gun passes back to the piston head. As the need arises to increase the gas pressure to overcome the frictional resistance caused by the expansion of heated components, gas fouling or the ingress of sand etc., the gas regulator knob is rotated, the gas regulator sleeve slides along the gas block and the three holes are progressively closed until eventually all the gas is diverted to the piston head. This same arrangement can be used to vary the rate of fire within the limits of 600 to 1,000 rounds a minute.

At the muzzle is the foresight block and the screw threaded flash eliminator of the closed prong type. The bore is chromium plated.

BARREL CHANGE

The gun stops firing in the breech open position when the trigger is released whilst ammunition remains in the belt. The breech is closed on an empty chamber when the last round is fired.

The safety catch is pressed through to the right to the 'safe' position and to do this the breech block must be to the rear; so if the gun is empty the action must be cocked.

The top cover plate is lifted if a loaded belt remains in the gun and the belt is removed. The actuating catch of the handle is engaged in the recess of the barrel locking nut, the head of the barrel locking catch – on the left of the receiver – is pressed in, the carrying handle is rotated to the vertical position and pushed forward. The barrel is then moved forward and lifted off.

To replace the barrel the carrying handle is held vertically up, the barrel is rested on the V formed by the forepart of the gas cylinder and, with the barrel locking catch pressed in, the barrel is slid back. The gas regulator goes into the gas cylinder and the interrupted thread of the barrel enters the barrel nut.

The carrying handle is rotated to the right to engage the threads of barrel and nut. The body locking catch is released and the barrel is secure.

THE PISTON AND BREECH-BLOCK

The piston is attached to the piston extension which has a cut out section at the front to allow passage of the ejecting case from above. At the rear is a massive piston post attached to which is the locking lever link which in turn is connected to the locking lever. Finally the locking lever is pinned half way along the breech block. When the block is travelling forward the locking lever lies in recesses in both sides of the block. The block is hollowed to take the firing pin which is mounted in the piston post. On the front face is the extractor. The return spring fits into the hollow interior of the piston extension.

THE TRIGGER MECHANISM

The trigger is centrally pivoted at its top edge so when it is pulled the rear end rises. Resting on the rear end of the trigger is a long, centrally pivoted sear. When the trigger is pulled the front end of the sear – the tail – is forced up and the rear end – the nose – drops down out of engagement with a bent on the bottom of the piston extension. Also on the front top edge of the trigger is a pivoting tripping lever which projects up into the piston way. This tripping lever has a spring which pivots it forward. On its front face is a step.

When the trigger is pulled the central pivot causes the front, carrying the tripper, to go down and the back to rise, lifting the tail of the sear. As the tail of the sear rises, the spring loaded tripping lever moves forward underneath it and holds it up.

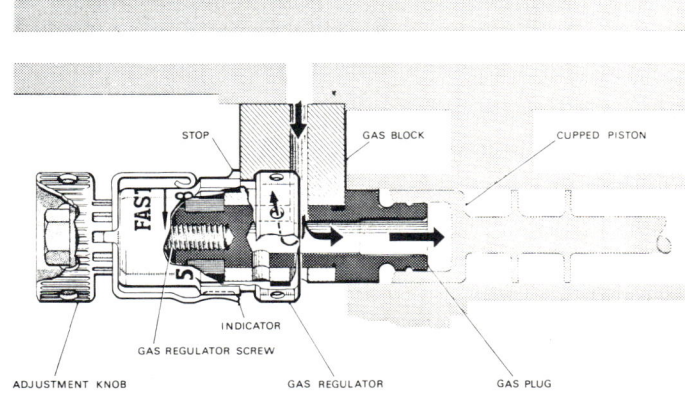

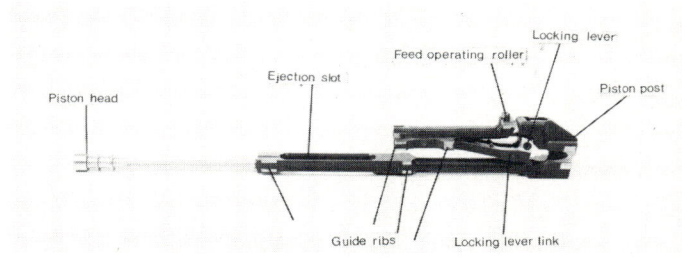

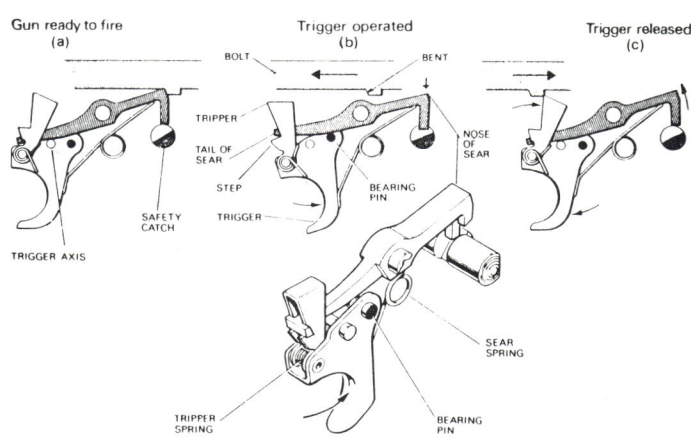

When the trigger is released the tripping lever rises with it and holds up the tail of the sear so the nose cannot rise to engage the piston and hold it back. The tripping lever, as it rises, re-enters the bolt way. As the piston comes back it hits the top of the tripping lever and rotates it back against the spring. The tail of the sear flies down and its nose rises. The piston going back passes over the sear but when it comes forward again it is caught by the full force of the sear and the area of contact is large enough to prevent any chipping or bending.

The safety catch is a push-through plunger. When at 'safe' it rests under the sear nose and prevents it falling. At 'fire' a cut out section allows full sear movement.

THE FEED MECHANISM

This is a two-stage system with the belt moving half way across on the forward motion of the bolt and moving the other half pitch during bolt recoil. The top of the breech block carries a spring-loaded roller which engages in a curved feed channel in the feed cover over the receiver. This channel is pivoted near its rear end and at its front end is attached to the end of a short feed link. This link swings about its centre so that as one end goes in towards the centre line of the gun the other end moves out. It carries an inner feed pawl at one end and two outer feed pawls at the other. Thus as the breech block travels forward the roller will first travel down a straight section of the feed channel, whilst the cartridge is forced out of the stationary belt, and then enter the curved portion. This forces the feed channel to the right. This swings the feed link to the left and rotates it about its centre so that the inner feed pawl moves out over the waiting cartridge and the outer pawls force it in half the distance to the gun centre line.

As the breech block moves back, the roller swings the front of the channel to the left. The feed link swings to the right so that the inner pawl comes in, bringing the belt across half a pitch, and the first round comes up against the cartridge stop and is positioned for chambering.

The outer pawls move out over the next cartridge. Thus each set of pawls acts alternately as feed and stop pawls and the cartridge moves half way across for each forward and backward movement of the breech block.

THE BUFFER

The buffer assembly consists of a bush which receives the impact of the piston extension and moves back into a cone which it expands outwards. This grips the walls of the buffer cylinder and also moves back slightly. In moving back it flattens a series of eleven Belleville washers. These saucer shaped washers store the kinetic energy of the piston as strain energy and in returning to shape they drive the cone and bush forward and force the piston forward again. This makes for a hard buffer with a high coefficient of restitution.

THE SIGHTS

The foresight is a blade mounted on a screw-threaded base which fits into a block mounted on a transverse dovetail.

The backsight is a leaf which can be used folded down for ranges marked from 200 to 800 metres by 100 metre increments. A slide with two spring catches allows the aperture backsight to be set to the correct range.

When the leaf is raised ranges are marked from 800 to 1,800 metres at intervals of 100 metres. There is a V backsight on the slider.

Elevation zeroing is carried out on the foresight by lifting the securing stirrup, rotating the blade through multiples of 180 degrees movement and then replacing the stirrup. A tool is needed.

Lateral zeroing is achieved by moving the foresight bodily in the dovetail. The securing screw is loosened on one side and tightened on the other.

OPERATION

Disintegrating belts come factory-packed and are not intended to be re-filled in the field. The continuous 50-round link belt can be re-filled by placing cartridges in the open pocket of the belt with the nib pressing into the extraction groove. Lengths of belt – of either type – can be joined to increase the ammunition available without stopping firing to change belts. With the continuous belt the loop in the leading link is placed in the slot of the last link of the previous belt and a cartridge is inserted to hold the two belts together. With the M13 type links, the single loop of the last round is placed between the two loops of the link of the leading round and a round is pushed in to hold the two belts together. The belts may be held in a 50-round belt box attached to the left of the gun or kept in a 250-round box placed beside the gun on the left.

The gun is cocked by pulling the cocking handle fully to the rear and then replacing it in the forward position. When the gun is cocked – and only then – the safety catch can be set to 'safe' by pushing it from left to right through the gun body. The letter 'S' can then be read on the right side of the plunger, facing the firer.

The top cover is opened by squeezing in the two catches at the back and rotating the cover forward to the vertical position. The loaded belt is then inserted – open side down – across the feed tray so that the leading cartridge rests against the cartridge stop on the right. The top cover is then lowered. (In practice it helps to tilt the gun clockwise on the bipod so the rounds tend to fall into rather than out of the gun whilst the cover is being closed.)

The safety catch is pushed through from right to left. The letter 'F' then shows, facing the firer, on the part of the catch projecting from the left side of the gun. When the trigger is pressed the nose of the sear drops and the piston extension is forced forwards by the compressed return spring, carrying the bolt with it. The feed horn on the top edge of the breech block pushes the first round in the belt straight through the belt link and the bullet is directed down into the chamber by the bullet guide. The top surfaces of the locking lever are forced down when they hit the underside of the top breech block guide. The cartridge is fully chambered, the extractor slips into the groove and the base of the cartridge seats into the recessed face of the breech block. The ejector is forced back and the ejection spring is compressed. The breech block stops.

The piston extension continues forward. The locking lever continues to

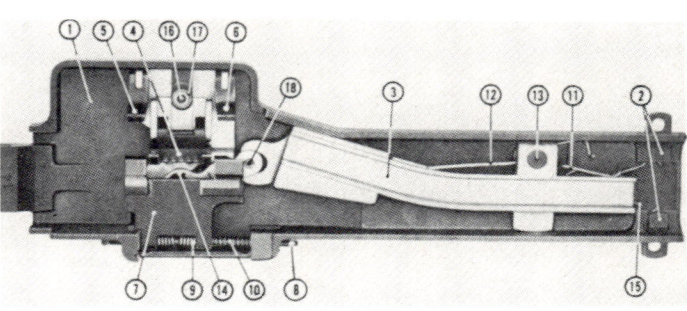

The inside of the feed cover: **(1)** *Cover;* **(2)** *Cover securing catches;* **(3)** *Feed arm;* **(4)** *Inner feed pawl;* **(5)** *Outer feed pawl (front);* **(6)** *Outer feed pawl (rear);* **(7)** *Cartridge guide pawl;* **(8)** *Pin securing cartridge guide pawl;* **(9)** *Spring, cartridge guide pawl;* **(10)** *Control spring, cartridge guide pawl;* **(11)** *Feed arm control spring;* **(12)** *Feed arm retaining spring;* **(13)** *Pivot, feed arm;* **(14)** *Spring, circlip, feed pawl assembly;* **(15)** *Catch spring;* **(16)** *Pivot, feed actuating rollers;* **(17)** *Rollers;* **(18)** *Bush, feed pawl assembly*

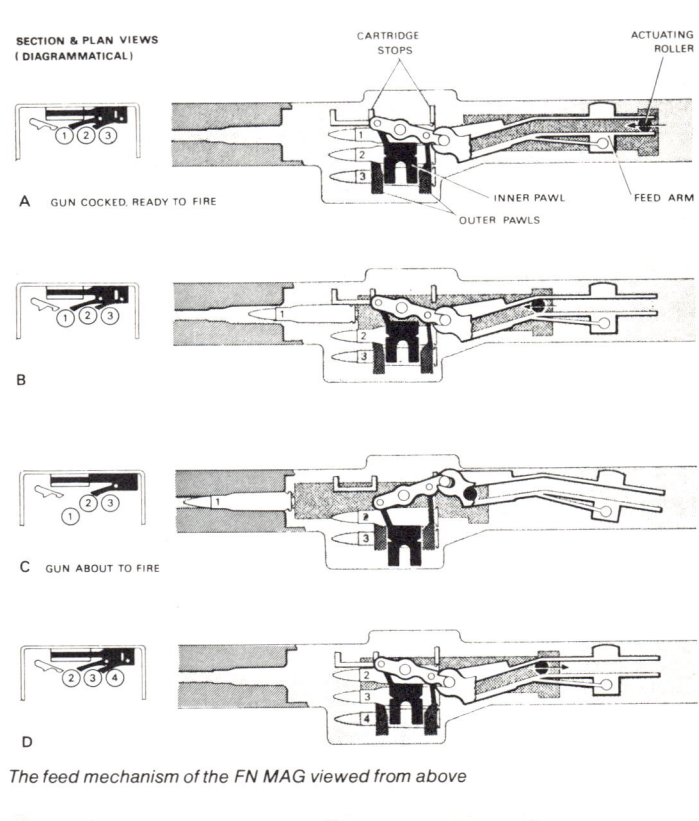

The feed mechanism of the FN MAG viewed from above

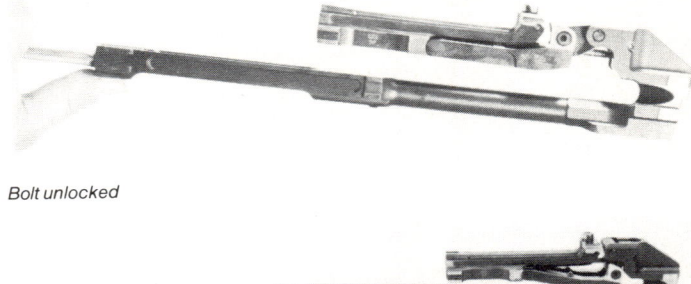

Bolt unlocked

Bolt locked. The locking lever is down and supported by the locking face

move down and drops in front of the locking shoulder in the bottom of the receiver. Further forward movement of the piston extension causes the locking lever link to rotate forward past the vertical position. The final forward movement of the piston post pushes the long firing pin through the front face of the breech block and the cartridge cap is crushed and the propellant ignited. The forward motion of the piston extension ends when its shoulder hits the stop face of the gas cylinder. The gas pressure forces the bullet up the bore and on past the gas vent and some of the gas flows through the vent into the gas regulator and then to the piston head which is driven back.

The piston post withdraws the firing pin into the breech block. The locking lever link is rotated back to the vertical position. The bullet is now well clear of the muzzle and the chamber pressure has dropped to a safe low level. The continued movement of the piston post rotates the link further and this lifts the locking lever out of contact with the locking shoulder. The locking lever then pulls the breech block rearward, the empty case is loosened in the chamber and withdrawn and as soon as it is clear of the chamber the compressed ejection spring pushes forward the ejector which hits the top of the cartridge base and rotates the case down, around the extractor, through the slot in the piston extension and out through the bottom of the gun. The rearward motion of the piston extension compresses the return spring. The piston extension hits the buffer and is thrown forward. If the trigger is still pressed the cycle starts again.

THE MOUNTS

The bipod is mounted on the forward end of the gas cylinder and can rotate from side to side to allow firing across a slope – i.e. one leg higher than the other with the sights vertical. The legs are not adjustable for height.

The bipod can be folded back for carrying. A hook on each leg engages in a slot in the side of the receiver and is held securely in place by a sliding retainer catch.

The tripod mount is a spring buffered assembly to which the gun is attached by two gudgeon pins fitting into the rings on the underside of the receiver, and a push-through pin which enters a hole above the trigger guard.

The tripod has a coarse traverse and a locking handle and a fine traverse control which has a clicker giving 1 mil for each click. The fine traverse gives a 30 mil control. The gun is put on line using the coarse control which is then locked and fine adjustment made with the fine control which can also be locked. There is a scale of 0-600 mils on either side of zero. There are traverse stops. Both locks can be released for traversing fire.

Elevation is obtained by means of an elevating arc which is controlled by a handwheel. This also can be locked. The arc gives 30 degrees of elevation (530 mils).

The gun can also be used with the Danish DISA series of tripods.

STRIPPING

(1) Lift the top cover plate and remove the belt.
(2) Cock the gun and check the chamber is clear. Return the working parts under control.
(3) Remove the butt by depressing the butt catch and lifting the butt upwards.
(4) Remove the return spring by pushing the rear end of the return spring rod forward and then lifting it. It is then pulled out of the rear end of the receiver.
(5) Remove the piston, piston extension and breech block by retracting the cocking handle and withdrawing these parts.
(6) Remove the barrel.
    Re-assemble in reverse order.

DATA
Cartridge: 7.62mm x 51
Method of operation: Gas
Method of locking: Dropping locking lever
Method of feed: Belt
Method of fire: Automatic

WEIGHTS
Gun without butt or bipod: 10.1kg
Gun with butt and bipod: 10.85kg
Barrel with flash suppressor and carrying handle: 2.75kg
Belt – 50 rounds: 1.47kg
Trigger pull: 3.6-6.3kg

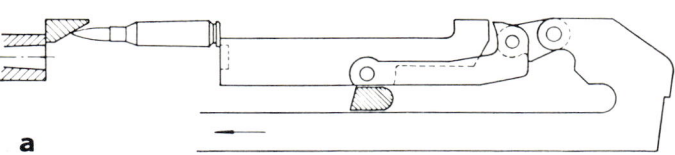

a
Beginning of feed.

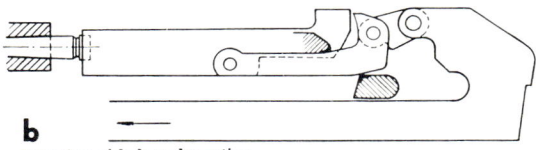

b
Lowering of bolt under action of front breech-block guides.

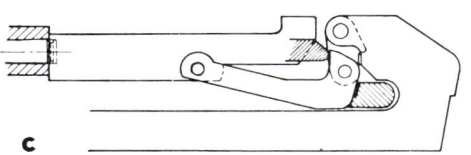

c
Locking and firing.

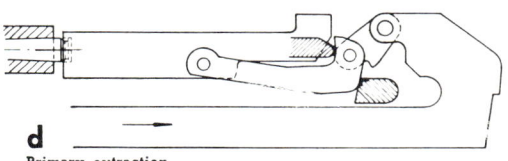

d
Primary extraction.

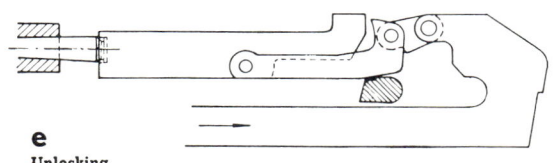

e
Unlocking.

The operating cycle

LENGTHS
Gun with flash suppressor: 1,255mm
Barrel: 545mm

MECHANICAL FEATURES
Barrel: Regulator: 4 positions
         Rifling: 4 grooves RH. 1 turn in 305mm
         Cooling: Air. Quick change barrel
Sights: Foresight: Blade

The MAG on its spring tripod

The FN MAG mounted on the Mark ⁵204 DISA tripod

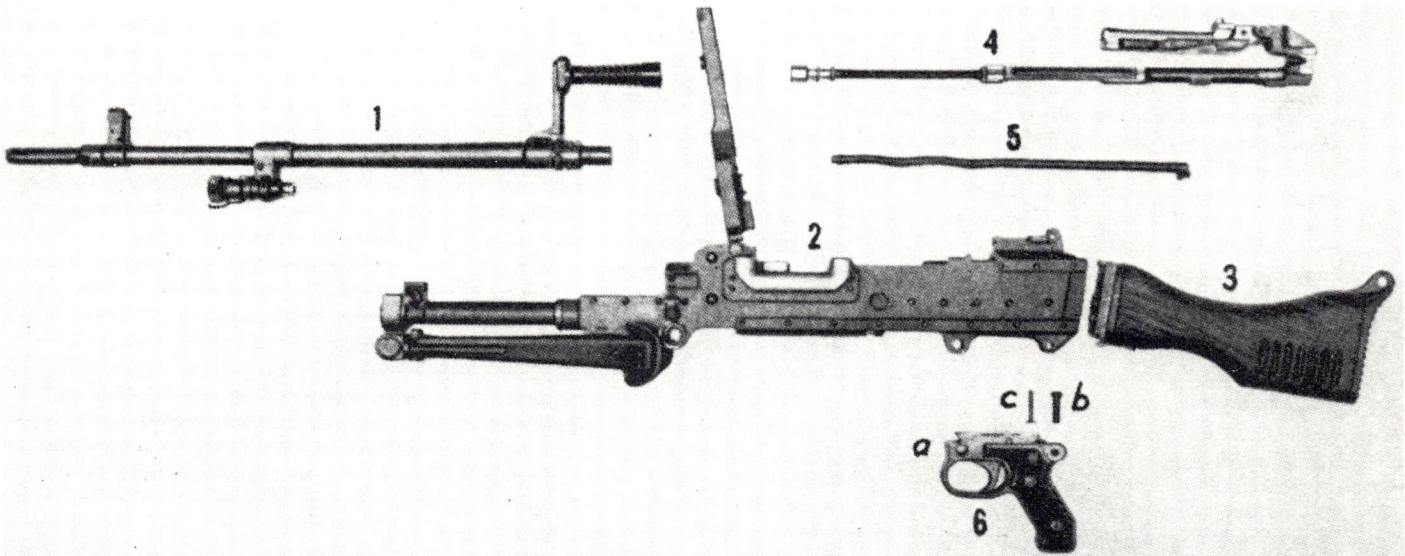

The machine gun split into its principal assemblies: (1) Barrel assembly, with gas regulator and carrying handle; (2) Body with bipod and cover; (3) Butt; (4) Breech block mechanism and piston; (5) Return spring assembly; (6) Trigger assembly: (a) Trigger frame (b) Joint pin, trigger grip (c) Retaining pin, joint pin

Rearsight: Aperture when leaf is lowered; U notch when leaf is raised
Graduation: 200-800 metres by 100 metre increments when leaf is flat; 800-1,800 metres by 100 metre movements when leaf is raised
Zeroing: Line. Foresight. Block moves on dovetail. Elevation. Foresight screws up and down
Sight radius: Sight folded down 848mm; Sight raised 785mm
Traverse (bipod): 50° (880mils)

FIRING CHARACTERISTICS
Muzzle velocity: 840 metres/sec
Muzzle energy: 345mkp
Chamber pressure: 3,465kg/cm²
Rate of fire: Cyclic: 600-1,000 rounds/min
          Auto: 250 rounds/min
Range, maximum effective: 1,200 metres

TRIPOD DATA
Weight: 10.5kg
Maximum height of barrel axis: 720mm
Minimum height of barrel axis: 254mm
Total traverse: 67° (1,200mils)
Total elevation: 30° (530m ls)

ACCESSORIES
Combination tool; Extractor remover; Sight key; Bore cleaning brush; Chamber cleaning brush; Gas regulator tool; Set of drifts

Manufacturer: Fabrique Nationale, Herstal, Liège, Belgium

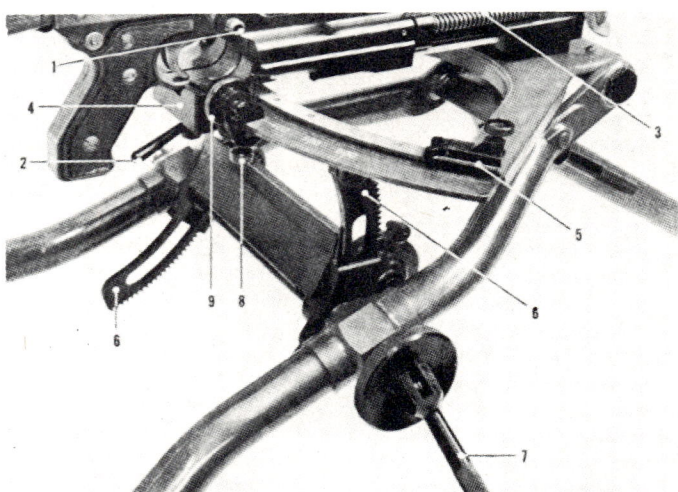

The tripod controls: (1) mounting pin; (2) traverse locking lever; (3) recoil spring; (4) traversing slide; (5) traversing stop; (6) elevation rack; (7) elevation lock; (8) fine control lock; (9) fine control handwheel (bearing)

Status: In production. In service with forces of Argentina, Belgium, Cuba, Ecuador, India, Israel, Kuwait, Libya, Netherlands, New Zealand, Peru, Qatar, Rhodesia, Sierra Leone, South Africa, Sweden, Tanganyika, Uganda, UK, Venezuela and elsewhere

5.56mm MINIMI LIGHT MACHINE GUN

As part of a logical step on the part of Fabrique Nationale to introduce a 5.56mm LMG to match their CAL rifle in the same calibre, the Minimi has recently been developed, and was unveiled late in 1974. This development has taken place against a background of uncertainty as to the future small arms calibre likely to be adopted by NATO. While it is far from certain that the 5.56mm × 45 cartridge will become a NATO standardised round, FN are taking comparatively little risk in producing this new weapon in this particular calibre, since there are reasonable prospects of the manufacturers' being able to substitute any new NATO cartridge for the 5.56mm should the choice of cartridge for standardisation ultimately go against 5.56mm. In particular, FN have produced a round (S101) with a 4g bullet of great penetrating power in place of the standard 3.5g bullet and this round can be fired from the Minimi.

The Minimi, whatever its family characteristics may be externally, is claimed as a new weapon, incorporating features not found in previous FN designs.

The gun is gas-operated, utilising gas tapped from the forward part of the barrel in conventional fashion. The rotary gas regulator is of a new simple design, based on the earlier MAG type, and having three basic settings (normal, emergency and grenade firing). Adjustment is by hand, even with a hot barrel.

The breech locking mechanism is of a new FN design, where the bolt is locked into the barrel extension by a rotational action. This action is initiated by a cam in the bolt carrier.

Normal gas operation, in which the gas piston is forced to the rear, moves the bolt carrier back, leaving the bolt still locked to the barrel extension. The residual chamber pressure has become virtually zero by the time the cam action referred to earlier unlocks the bolt. Primary extraction of the spent case begins only when the bolt has unlocked.

The ammunition feed system on the Minimi incorporates new FN designs, and here the disintegrating link belt is held in a box magazine of transparent material, which, apart from acting as an ammunition carrier when not on the gun, locks firmly to the gun and becomes virtually integral with it when in action. Two types of magazine exist, one of 100 rounds and the other of 200 rounds.

The gun is normally bipod mounted but can, if required, be mounted on a tripod. It can also be used with either a fixed or a folding stock. In addition, for use as a port-fire weapon in the MICV (Mechanised Infantry Combat Vehicle) the Minimi can be used without any stock. The weapon can be used either on full automatic or, if required, using a burst control device giving bursts of three-six rounds.

DATA
Cartridge: 5.56mm × 45 or S101 (see text)
Method of operation: Gas
Method of locking: Rotating bolt head
Method of feed: 100- or 200-round belts, in box magazine
Method of fire: Full automatic or controlled bursts

WEIGHTS
Weight with bipod: 6.5kg
Weight with 200 rounds: 8.8kg
Weight of spare barrel: 2.1kg

LENGTHS
Length of weapon: 1000mm with fixed stock; 815mm with metal folding stock, 650mm without stock
Length of barrel: 468mm
Rate of fire: 750-1250 rounds/min
Barrel twist: 1 in 9
Muzzle velocity: 895m/sec (S101 ball) or 780m/sec (L-102 tracer)
Manufacturer: Fabrique Nationale Herstal SA
Status: Production

FN Minimi 5.56 LMG

CHINA (PEOPLE'S REPUBLIC)

CHINESE MACHINE GUNS

The Armed Forces of the Chinese People's Republic have very largely been equipped with copies of weapons produced originally elsewhere. The weapons they hold are described individually in the sections devoted to the country of origin. These are:

Chinese Name	Origin
Type 24	German 7.92mm Maxim M08 MMG
Type 26	Czechoslovakian 7.92mm Zb26 LMG
Type 53	Russian 7.62mm DPM LMG
Type 54	Russian 12.7mm Model 38/46 HMG
Type 56	Russian 7.62mm RPD LMG
Type 57	Russian 7.62mm SG-43 MMG
Type 58	Russian 7.62mm RP-46 Coy MG
Type 63	Russian 7.62mm SGM MMG

Status: Types 53, 54, 56 and 58, at least, are believed to be manufactured in China. Types 24 and 26 were certainly manufactured there at one time and may still be. All appear to remain in service although some are probably used only by reserve units or the People's Militia.

Training with the Chinese Type 56 LMG (Russian 7.62mm RPD)

TYPE 67. 7.62mm LIGHT MACHINE GUN

The Type 67 appears to be a weapon produced in China and used in that country to replace the Type 53 LMG and the Type 58 Coy Machine Gun. It has also been issued to the North Vietnamese and was used against American and South Vietnamese troops.

The gun is gas-operated and belt fed and may be used with either a bipod or a tripod. Its design is a mixture of features from the other guns in the above list and the part each has played in its design is as follows:

Type 24	(Maxim)	Feed mechanism
Type 26	(Zb26)	Bolt and piston
Type 53	(DPM)	Trigger mechanism
Type 56	(RPD)	Gas regulator
Type 57	(SGM)	Barrel change system

The Type 67 uses the 7.62mm × 54R cartridge, and has an open pocket metal belt with the pockets joined by spring metal coils. Each pocket carries a nib, extending to the rear, with a bent over tab. The round is pressed into the link with the tab against the rear face of the cartridge. This type of belt allows the bolt to push the round out of the link and straight into the chamber.

OPERATION

The belt is loaded. The feed cover catch at the rear of the receiver is pressed and the feed cover lifted about its front hinge. The cocking handle on the right of the receiver is normally folded vertically downwards and must be lifted up through 45 degrees before it can be pulled back to cock the action. (Before cocking it is essential to check the safety catch is back to 'fire'. If forward to 'safe' the sear will jam on the underside of the piston.) It is then replaced in the forward position and rotated down. The belt is placed in the feedway with the open side of the link facing down. (If the belt is inverted an immediate stoppage results.) The first round is in the feedway slot. The cover is closed.

The safety catch is located on the right of the receiver immediately above the trigger and functions in the usual Degtyarev fashion with 'safe' in the forward position and the catch rotated to the rear for 'fire'.

The rearsight – of similar shape to that of the Czech Vz59 – has an elevation knob on the left and a windage knob on the right. There is a clicker system with each click on the elevation knob corresponding to 25 metres up to 1,000 metres range and 20 metres thereafter. The windage knob produces one click for each minute of angle i.e. one inch at 100 yds.

The gun will fire always from the open bolt position and when the ammunition is expended the bolt closes on an empty chamber.

When the bolt goes forward the cartridge is pushed into the chamber. The bolt movement ceases. The piston continues forward and the rear of the bolt is lifted up to lock into the ceiling of the receiver. The piston continues forward after locking is completed and the flat face of the piston post drives the firing pin into the cartridge cap.

After firing, the bullet travels up the bore and some of the gas following it is diverted into the gas cylinder, below the barrel, where it drives the piston rearward. There is a period of free travel allowing the gas pressure to drop, before the ramp on the rear face of the piston post pulls the rear end of the bolt down out of its recess in the top of the receiver. The piston then carries the bolt to the rear; the empty case is extracted and then ejected downwards out of the gun. The return spring is compressed along its guide rod. When the piston comes to rest the return spring drives it forward and the cycle is repeated.

The belt is fed into the gun from the right and the feed mechanism is operated by having a cam track on the top side of the piston extension at the front – in a manner reminiscent of the Czech Vz52. This forces a roller on the bottom of the lower feed arm to move out and the rotation of the lower feed arm is transmitted by a vertical shaft to the upper feed arm. As the upper feed arm moves, a slot in it engages a roller on the feed slide and the feed slide moves outward to engage a round in the belt. The similarity between this system and that used in the Vickers gun is readily apparent.

As the piston extension moves forward it carries the bolt which forces a cartridge forward through the belt and into the chamber. As the piston extension continues forward the lower feed arm is moved back to its original position and this in turn pulls the upper feed arm and the next cartridge is pulled across from right to left by the feed slide and moved into the slot in the feed tray where it is pressed down by a pair of cartridge guides in the cover. A spring loaded stop pawl on the feed tray prevents the belt from slipping out as the feed slide oscillates.

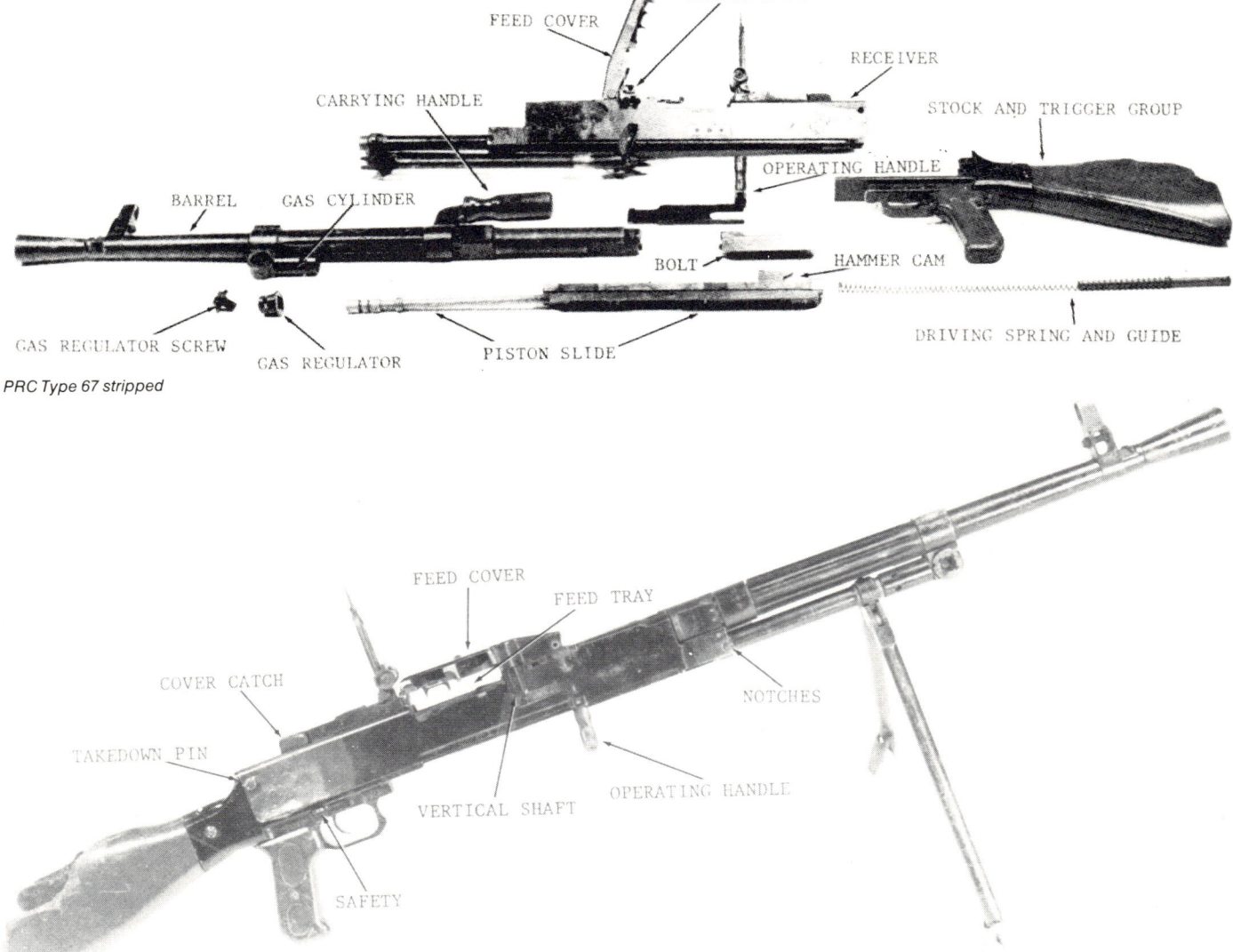

PRC Type 67 stripped

PRC Type 67 LMG

The barrel will normally be changed after two minutes firing at the rapid rate (which takes three 100-round belts). The procedure is to lift the top cover plate, remove the belt if any cartridges remain in it, and then press the barrel retaining catch to the left – as in the Russian SGM. Grasp the carrying handle and push the barrel forward off the gun. Place the new barrel in position, with the gas cylinder in the gas cylinder tube, and pull the barrel back. Push the retaining catch across to the right. Put in a new belt. Close the top cover plate and resume firing.

The same micrometer adjustment for cartridge head space is used in this gun as in the SGM.

The gas regulator works in the same way as that in the RPD. The nut on the left side of the regulator is loosened and then the regulator is pushed through to the right. This disengages it from the index pin and the regulator can then be rotated to the selected position. There are three settings – 1, 2 and 3 – of which the first is that usually employed. The regulator is then pushed back and the nut tightened.

STRIPPING

Lift the top cover plate, remove the belt, check that the chamber and feedway are clear. Remove the barrel.

Press the takedown pin, at the rear of the receiver, to the right. Pull the butt to the rear. Remove the return spring and guide.

Pull the cocking handle back and remove the piston and bolt.

Re-assembly is in reverse order. It will be noted that the above procedure is exactly the same as that used in the Bren, derived from the Czech Zb26.

ANTI-AIRCRAFT MOUNTING

The anti-aircraft sights consist of a pillar permanently attached to the top of the stirrup-like rearsight and a speed ring foresight, which fits into dovetails in the top of the receiver and is held by a spring catch. The tripod is up-ended and the gun attached by fitting the notches on the underside of the front of the receiver on to the pins in the mount and rotating the gun down until the catch locks on the front of the trigger guard.

DATA
Cartridge: 7.62mm × 54R
Method of operation: Gas
Method of locking: Tilting block
Method of feed: 100-round continuous open pocket metal belt
Method of fire: Automatic
Weight: 9.9kg
Length: 1,143mm
Barrel: 597mm
          Cooling: Air. Quick change barrel
Sights: Foresight: Pillar
          Rearsight: Leaf Notch. Adjustment for windage
Muzzle velocity: 835 metres/sec
Muzzle energy: 341mkp
Rate of fire: Cyclic: 650 rounds/min
          Automatic: 150 rounds/min
Range, maximum effective: 800 metres
Manufacturer: State factories
Status: In production. In service in China at least

CHINA (TAIWAN)

MACHINE GUNS IN TAIWAN

The Chinese Nationalists carried to Taiwan a collection of machine guns, all of foreign origin. They included:

Type 24   — German 08 Maxim made in China
Type 26   — Czech Zb 26 made in China
Type 30   — Czech Zb 30 made in China
Madsen 7.92mm   — Danish Madsen
Bren guns 7.92mm   — Canadian manufacture

Browning .30 M1919A4 — USA manufacture

Subsequently further supplies of Browning .30 M1919A4 machine guns were provided.

The USA supplied to the Taiwan Government the necessary machinery to manufacture the M60 machine gun and this is now being produced.
Status: The M60 is in production and in service. None of the others are known to be made in Taiwan but some are probably still in service there.

CZECHOSLOVAKIA

7.92mm MODELS 26, 27 & 30 LMG

The Czechoslovakian armament firm of Ceskoslovenska Zbrojovka, Brno, has an extremely high reputation. It produced a series of excellent light machine guns which were manufactured in large numbers and very widely exported. They were also produced under licence by a number of different countries.

The designer Vaclav Holek designed a machine gun known as the Praga Model 24. This was modified and eventually became the Model 26. The Models 26, 27 and Model 30 were virtually the same weapon in principle but had detail changes which prevented the interchanging of parts.

The guns carry the markings 'Lehky Kulomet ZB VZ 26 (27 or 30)' on the right side of the receiver and 'BRNO' on the left.

The Model 26 is a gas-operated LMG with a 20-round box magazine mounted over the receiver. The gas cylinder carrying the bipod reaches right out to the muzzle of the finned barrel. There is no regulator. The barrel may be changed rapidly, by rotating the barrel locking lever and using the carrying handle to push the barrel forward.

The gun has the bolt mounted on the piston extension. The piston extension carries a piston post which is seated in the hollow interior of the bolt and controls its position as the piston reciprocates. The bolt is raised at its rear end at the conclusion of the feed stroke, to lock into a recess in the ceiling of the receiver. When the chamber pressure is reduced sufficiently, the ramp on the rear of the piston post lowers the bolt and carries it to the rear. The gun fires from the open breech position.

The gun will fire at single shot as well as automatic. The trigger mechanism is illustrated and explained in some detail in the description of the Bren gun (qv).

The Models 26, 27 and 30 machine guns made extensive use of machined parts and were expensive to produce.

The weapons were made in China, Iran and Romania as well as in Czechoslovakia; and a variation on the Model 30, which had a knurled section at the rear of the barrel, was manufactured in Yugoslavia as the Model 30J. Altogether some 24 countries used the Model 26-30. When the Germans occupied Czechoslovakia in 1939 they continued production of the Models 26 and 30 and these guns were used in the German Army usually with reserve formations – as the MG 26 (t) and MG 30 (t).

The British Bren was a derivation of the Czech series and the relationship is described in the relevant UK entry.

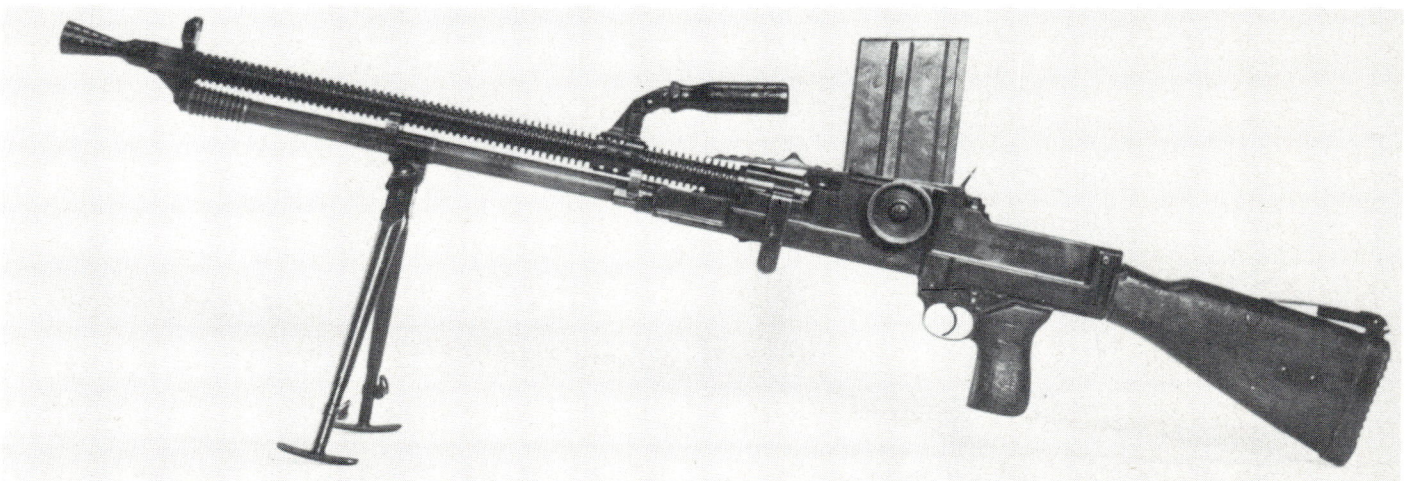

VZ 26 7.92mm (RSAF)

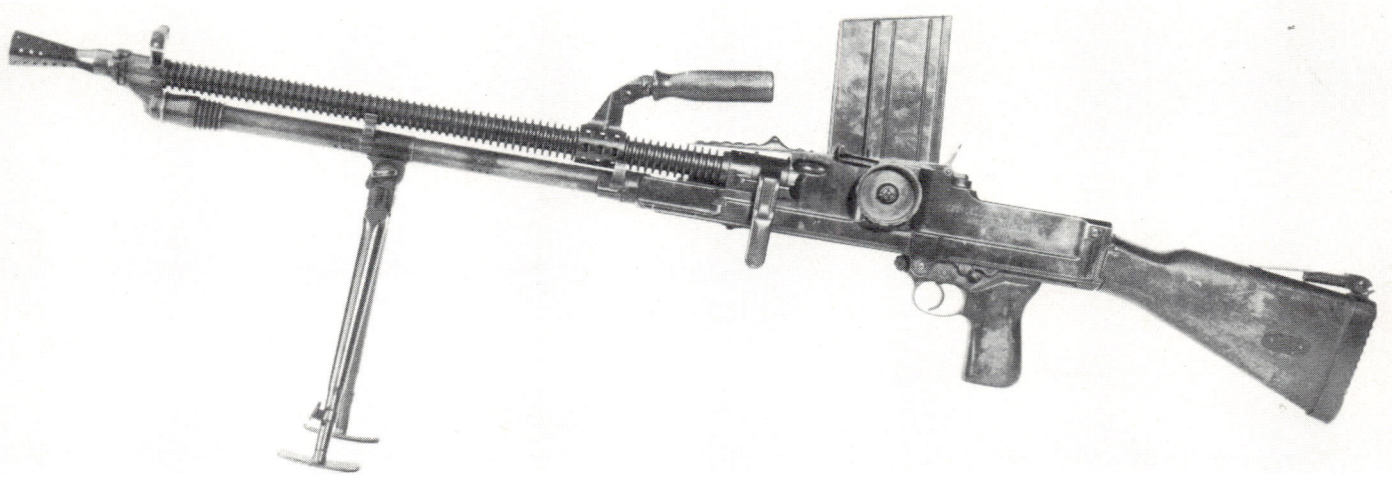

VZ 27. 7.92mm LMG

DATA
Cartridge: 7.92mm × 57
Method of operation: Gas
Method of locking: Tilting block
Method of feed: 20-round detachable box magazine
Method of fire: Selective
Weight unloaded: 9.69kg
Length: 1,163mm
Barrel: 602mm
    Rifling: 4 grooves RH.
    Cooling: Air. Quick change barrel

Sights: Foresight: Blade
        Rearsight: Tangent aperture
Muzzle velocity: 762 metres/sec
Muzzle energy: 380mkp
Rate of fire: Cyclic: 500 rounds/min
        Automatic: 120 rounds/min
        SS: 50 rounds/min
Range, maximum effective: 700 metres
Manufacturer: Ceskoslovenska Zbrojovka, Brno
Status: No longer manufactured. No longer in first-line regular service but in world-wide service with reserve and irregular forces

VZ 30

7.92mm MODEL 37 MMG

This gun was manufactured in 1937 and its nomenclature in the Czech army was the Model 37. It was sold commercially as the VZ 53.

It was an air-cooled, belt fed gun, gas-operated and very sturdy. The action was much the same as the Model 26 but the bolt locked to the barrel extension and not into the receiver. The barrel and block could recoil together within the receiver before unlocking occurred. This in no way affected the method of operation of the gun nor the cycle of operations. It was intended to reduce the trunnion pull by dissipating energy before the whole gun recoiled and so reduce the load on the tripod or vehicle mount.

The Model 37 fed from the right and could use either a metal or a fabric-cum-metal continuous open pocket belt. It introduced the cocking system which later was used on Models 52 and 59, in which the trigger mechanism is pushed forward and the sear used to pull the piston and breech block to the rear. This system was used on the British wartime BESA Tank MG and has recently been employed in the Colt CMG-2 LMG.

The Model 37 could be employed on its tripod as a medium machine gun or as an anti-aircraft gun. The British version, manufactured by BSA, was a tank MG. The German Army used it both as a tripod-mounted MMG and in their tanks as the MG 37(t). It had two rates of fire, a buffer device, sometimes misleadingly called the 'accelerator' being interposed to shorten the recoil distance and to return the bolt forward at high speed. Without the device the rate of fire was about 450 rounds/min and with it the firing rate

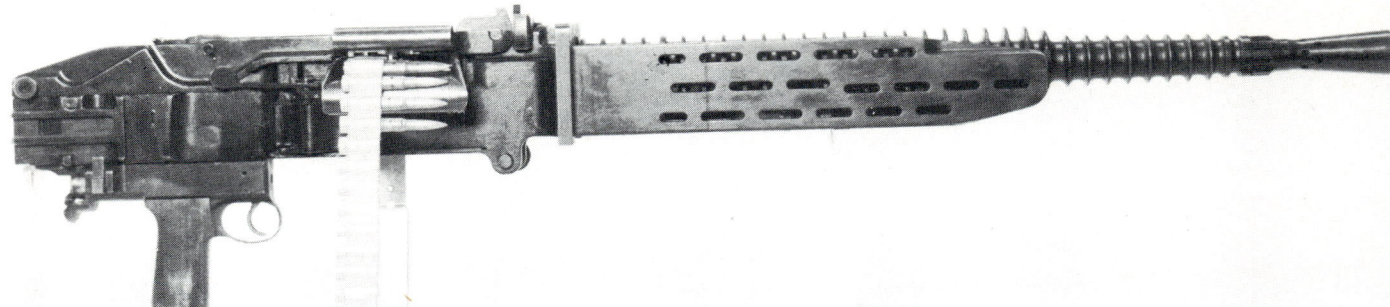

The Czech VZ 37 MMG

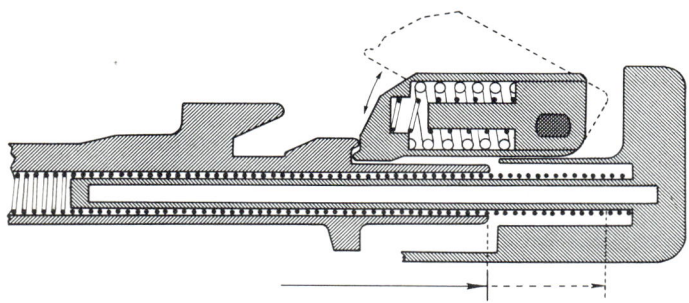

The 'accelerator'

The rate-of-fire controller of the 7.92mm is seen here, above and to the rear of the pistol grip, in the 'high' position

went up to about 700 rounds/min. In many ways this was an ideal arrangement for a tank gun. In British manufacture the idea was dropped at an early stage to simplify production.

The Czech gun can be distinguished from all but the very earliest British BESA guns by the perforated side plates of the receiver. The British guns had plain slab sides.

DATA
Cartridge: 7.92mm × 57
Method of operation: Gas
Method of locking: Tilting block
Method of fire: Selective
Weight: 18.82kg
Length: 1,105mm
Barrel: Rifling: 678mm
     Rifling: 4 groove RH.
     Cooling: Air. Quick-change barrel
Sights: Foresight: Blade
     Rearsight: Leaf Graduated from 300 to 2,000 metres; Battlesight at 200 metres
Muzzle velocity: 793 metres/sec
Muzzle energy: 410mkp
Rate of fire: Cyclic: 450 or 700 rounds/min
     Automatic: 200 rounds/min

Biafran troops with the Czech VZ37 MMG in the Civil War in Nigeria in 1968 (UPI)

SS: 50 rounds/min
Range, maximum effective: 1,000 metres
Manufacturer: Ceskoslovenska Zbrojovka, Brno
Status: No longer produced. In use in Nigeria at least

7.62mm MODEL 52 LMG

Last of a line of Czechoslovakian machine guns which were adopted or copied by many of the major powers, Model 52 is a development of the traditional Czech light machine gun and is only now being totally superseded by the Model 59 which is a GPMG.

Model 52 was originally chambered for the Czech 7.62 7.62mm short round but was subsequently modified to take the Russian 7.62mm M43 round and in this version it is known as Model 52/57.

The gun itself is small, neat and compact. The design is extremely sophisticated and manufacture is complex. The tolerances on the body fabrication are very tight indeed and keeping to them has produced a lot of difficulty.

OPERATING SYSTEM

The gun is gas-operated. Some of the propellant gas enters a very short vented cylinder about 18cm from the chamber and drives back a light piston on which is carried the bolt. The bolt itself has been greatly reduced in size compared with that of the Bren gun and so the moving mass has very little inertia. This leads to very rapid acceleration and an extremely high rate of fire. The gun uses either a magazine feed or a belt and the rates of fire obtained are 900 rounds per minute with magazine and 1,200 rounds per minute with belt feed. The difference is accounted for by the frictional resistance encountered when forcing rounds out of a spring-loaded box magazine which is greater than that presented by a round in a belt. This is somewhat surprising because it is generally accepted that the effort of lifting the belt is greater than that required to feed from a magazine.

There is a gas regulator of conventional multi-track design containing four passages within a rotating block. The gun is normally fired on the smallest diameter passage and the larger sizes are used when the weapon is either dirty or has become carbon fouled after prolonged firing. In practice, however, there seems to be little sign of fouling after two 100-round belts and the regulator would appear to be of use only when the gun is employed in adverse conditions.

The return spring is a single coil twelve inches long, which is housed in a tube inside the wooden butt. There is a buffered back plate to return the recoiling parts and unlike the Bren the butt is not buffered.

The locking system differs from that of the Bren and is nearer to that used in the BESA. The ramp at the rear of the piston has a vertical step cut in the front face and the locking surfaces of the wedge shaped block are in contact with this step as the piston drives the block forward. This means that there is no tendency – as there is on the Bren – for the block to be lifted during the forward stroke of the piston. This reduces friction and helps in the production of the high rate of fire. The locking surfaces of the bolt project outwards from the bolt body and when the bolt is almost fully forward they ride up inclined slots cut in the side of the receiver. The rear of the bolt is thus raised into the locked position and the rear faces of these bolt projections form the locking surface. The centre and top of the bolt – unlike the Bren and BESA – are not used to lock in to the body. This reduction of the bearing surface is possible because of the reduced power of the Czech short 7.62mm round compared to the .303 and 7.62mm NATO round.

FIRING SYSTEM

The gun fires from an open breech. The firing pin is contained within the body of the bolt and is strongly spring retracted. The bolt is carried forward by the piston and feeds a round from the magazine or belt and chambers it, after which the rear end of the bolt is lifted and locked into the body. The piston post has a further 6 millimetres of free travel before it strikes the firing pin and drives it into the cap. The method is precisely that used in the Bren and is simple, safe and reliable.

MAGAZINE FEED

This is a conventional arrangement. The magazine of 25 rounds capacity is slightly curved and fits on top of the weapon. The magazine opening has a spring-loaded cover which is operated by pushing forward the magazine catch. This cover when down is very close fitting and will keep dust out of the mechanism. The cover is attached to the barrel nut and when raised can be rotated clockwise to disengage the interrupted thread of the nut from that of the barrel and so permit a quick barrel change.

BELT FEED

The belt is of the German continuous link pattern and carries 100 rounds. It is placed in position by lifting the feed cover and the belt ejection cover, laying the belt in place over the pawls and then closing the magazine cover. The belt can be locked by depressing the feed cover lever and this effectively closes off the feed opening against dirt and dust. The arrangement for feeding the belt across from right to left as the bolt reciprocates is extremely neat, simple and effective. On the right hand side of the piston the two guides running in the body of the gun are machined with a double taper. The bottom guide is thinned off at the rear and undercut. A roller mounted on the simple bell crank feed lever is pushed out as the piston comes back and a feed pawl mounted on the top of the bell crank is moved inwards to force the belt across the gun from right to left. The upper guide has a bevelled edge on which a flat projection from the bell crank rests. As the piston goes forward this projection is lifted by the bevelled surface and the top end with its spring-loaded pawl is forced outwards under the belt. This system ensures that the feed lever is always positively located relative to the position of the piston. There are two double sets of spring loaded stop pawls to prevent the belt from falling out of the gun as the piston goes forward. This system is extremely efficient; there is a minimum of friction and the very high rate of fire is evidence of how successful it is. The inventor of this feed system was Heinrich Von Wimmersperg who took out a series of European patents before World War II.

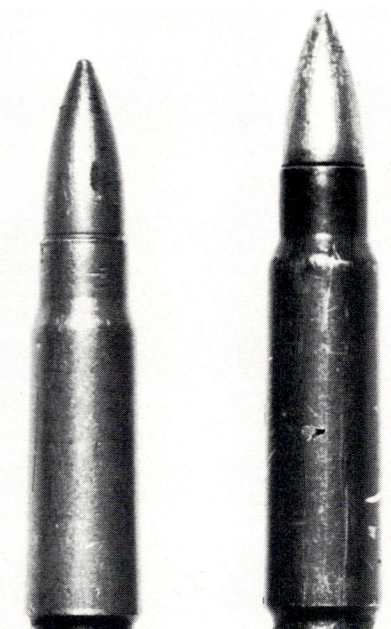

Right: *The Czechoslovakian M52 cartridge.*
Left: *The Soviet M43 cartridge*

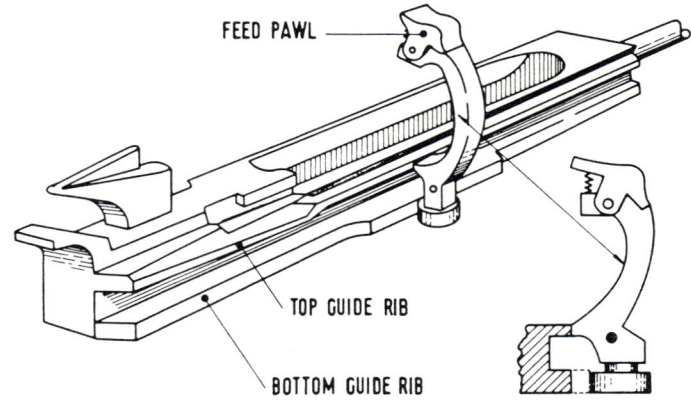

Feed arrangements

COCKING THE GUN

There is no cocking handle attached to the piston, the system being similar to that of the BESA. A thumb catch on the left of the gun and above the pistol grip is depressed to unlock the trigger group from the underside of the receiver. The pistol grip is pushed forward until the sear rides under the bent on the underside of the piston. The piston grip is pulled rearwards and the interlock of sear and bent retracts the piston and with it the bolt, to the cocked postion. The trigger group locks back into the body and the gun is ready to fire. It is noteworthy as evidence of the lengths gone to keep out dirt that when the butt is pushed forward it pulls a cover out with it to seal off the ejection opening on the underside of the body.

Czech 7.62mm VZ 52 LMG, magazine fed (RMCS)

The Czech 7.62mm VZ 52 LMG – belt fed (RMCS)

SAFETY CATCH

The safety catch is located on the left of the gun behind the cocking catch. It can be operated when the pistol grip is fully forward and when it is fully back. In the forward position the act of pushing up the safety lever forces a small projection on the lever itself into a recess in the underside of the body thus locking the grip forward together with the piston and bolt. The underside of the weapon is now completely sealed off and this would appear to be the normal way of carrying the gun when immediate action is not required.

With the pistol grip to the rear, when the safety catch is lifted to the 'safe' position two things happen. A lug attached to the lever is rotated directly under the sear and prevents it from moving down and also the same lug rests on the trigger housing to prevent any movement of the cocking catch. Thus the trigger group as a whole is locked in postion and the sear also is locked.

This safety catch is of a very satisfactory design and in addition to being foolproof can easily be operated from the firing position by the right thumb only, leaving the hand to control the alignment of the weapon.

TRIGGER AND FIRING MECHANISM

There is a facility for either single shot or continuous fire controlled respectively by the top half and bottom half of a single trigger. This system is extremely neat and works well. Like all these Czech mechanisms it is very simple and beautifully designed.

To set continuous fire the lower half of the trigger is pulled and in so doing two forces are applied simultaneously. The trigger bar is moved back, and through the simple linkage arrangement the sear is rotated to release the bent on the piston. At the same time the extension on the trigger bar presses against the tripper extension and rotates it anti-clockwise. This causes the tripper head to move down out of the path of the piston. The sear is held clear and fire continues as long as the trigger is pressed. When it is released the spring under the sear forces it up and it catches the bent on the next forward movement of the piston.

Single shot operation is obtained when the top half of the trigger is pulled. The upper half of the trigger rotates the trigger bar as before and the sear is rotated out of engagement with the bent. But the tripper extension is NOT now rotated and remains up. The piston bent hits it and drives it down. As it goes down it is forced to rotate anti-clockwise. This allows the sear to rise but as it does so a step comes up under the sear and holds it. Thus no further rounds can be fired. To fire again the trigger is released and the springy linkage forces the step out from under the sear and the mechanism is prepared for further firing when the trigger is pressed.

BARREL CHANGING

The barrel of the VZ52 is very substantial and this together with the belt feed leads to the supposition that it is intended to produce a considerable rate of sustained fire. This necessitates a quick barrel change. The method adopted is the one used in the Bren with a nut, containing an interrupted thread, in the body of the gun. The magazine opening cover acts as a barrel change lever and is connected directly to the nut. The nut is rotated clockwise and the barrel is withdrawn straight forward as soon as the nut has been rotated.

The arrangement for mating the gas regulator spigot and the gas cylinder are the same as those for the Bren.

SIGHTS

The sight line is offset 35mm to the left because the top-mounted magazine prevents a clear view over the barrel.

The foresight is a blade mounted on a dovetail for lateral movement. Some models have a circular removable hood to protect the foresight blade, others have the blade alone.

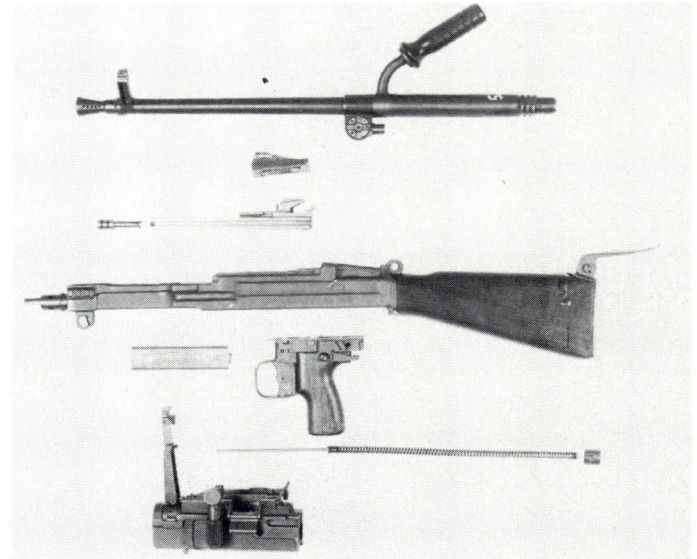

VZ52 stripped

The backsight consists of a tangent sight incorporating a U cut in a plate mounted at a slant on top of a pillar graduated from 200 to 1,200 metres by hundreds. There is a visual marker for the range and also a clicker. The number of clicks between successive 100 metre graduations is not constant but increases with range. This prevents sight setting by ear at night since each click represents a fixed increase in quadrant elevation.

The backsight has a lateral adjustment for windage.

Zeroing is carried out by sliding the foresight in its dovetail and the armourer's scribing mark can be seen when the sight is examined. Zeroing for elevation is achieved by change of foresight blade.

STRIPPING

This is not an easy weapon to strip. The design is very unusual in that the receiver, which is stamped from medium gauge sheet steel, holds a machined body containing the barrel nut and feed mechanism. There is no cocking handle and, unlike most LMGs, the butt is permanently secured to the receiver and can be detached only in a workshop.

The procedure to strip is best carried out as follows. Ensure the working parts are forward. Lift up the butt strap, rotate the return spring securing cap in the butt plate and remove the spring and guide rod. Lift the magazine opening cover to the vertical position and rotate it to the right. The barrel can then be withdrawn forward. Using the thumb catch pull back until the piston head is just clear of the gas cylinder. Put one finger inside the barrel nut and the whole body with the piston and block can be rotated up and out to reach the position shown. The trigger group can be slid forward bringing with it the bottom opening cover. The sub-assemblies can now be further stripped at leisure.

When this procedure is followed the most noticeable feature is the extremely tight press fit between the machined body and the pressed steel receiver. It is remarkably close and examination shows that it has been obtained by making the interior diameter of the receiver slightly low and surface grinding to get a slight interference fit.

When re-assembling, the procedure is reversed but assembly is made easier because there is a small catch built into the body which drops when the gun is inverted and holds the piston in the correct place to enable the machined body to be inserted under the rear of the pressed receiver and rotated down to fit in.

In general the very close tolerances and the high standard of machining produce a weapon outstandingly well made. Final fitting of receiver and body is probably by selective assembly to obtain such tight machining. Stripping in the field – particularly at night – would not be at all easy.

FIELD HANDLING

The gun weighs 8kg. The carrying handle is rigidly attached to the barrel. This ensures that the full weight of the gun is not held by a single tooth. It does not rotate to the side and it does not collapse flat. The angle of the handle to the barrel makes it reasonably comfortable to carry in its pronounced butt-heavy position. With a full box magazine or a 100-round belt this butt heaviness is accentuated. Rather surprisingly there is no arrangement by which a container can be secured on the right hand side of the gun to hold a single belt whilst firing on the move and the length is left dangling when firing like this. In very close country the belt could easily get caught up.

The bipod is very similar to that of the Bren, but is bent backwards. The sleeve fits over the cylinder vent holes and from time to time it must be swivelled round to cut the carbon which collects outside the vents.

The gun has a forward tripod mounting carrying a horizontal pin directly below the gas cylinder, with the block welded on to the underside of the receiver. The mounting drops into a recess in the tripod and the pin is then rotated through 90 degrees to secure it. The rear mounting is on top of the butt end of the receiver and takes a pin to connect gun and tripod. There is also a rear sling swivel attached to the butt strap but no sign of a forward sling swivel. The sling however can conveniently be looped round the carrying handle.

The flash hider is a perforated cone with the holes drilled radially. This imparts a small backward velocity to the emergent gases which tends to reduce the recoil of the weapon but at the expense of also producing a pronounced circle of flash around the muzzle when firing at night. It is rather surprising that a flash eliminator has not been fitted; but the mouth of the cone has been built up leaving only a bore-sized aperture so that, when the bullet is passing through, the gases are forced out of the side perforations. The system would seem to meet the requirements of the Czech ammunition which incorporates a considerable amount of potassium chlorate to suppress flash.

RELIABILITY

As already noted the gun is manufactured to very close tolerances. When it is used in dirty conditions great care must be taken when stripping to ensure that no mud or dust gets into the receiver. In particular, dust in the boltway slows the gun down very quickly.

The working parts are light and rely on the kinetic energy acquired during a very short cyclic period to push dust, etc. out of the way. They can be stopped in conditions in which a Bren would continue to function perfectly well.

Under active service conditions where the gunner cannot always choose the precise ground on which to use his weapon it would produce a large number of stoppages. It should however be pointed out that the Model 52 is no worse in this respect than any other LMG firing the Czech or Russian short rounds.

DATA

System of operation: Gas
Barrel: Long stroke piston, 4-track regulator
     Bore diameter: 7.62mm
     Overall length: 581mm
     Weight: 2.33kg
     Rifling: 4 grooves RH
     Depth of groove: 0.1524mm
     Width of groove: 4.45mm
     Pitch: 254mm
Gun: **Weight:** 8kg
     Overall length: 1,041mm
Sights: Foresight: Blade (Bren type)
     Rearsight: Tangent rearsight with U
     Sight radius: 551mm
     Graduation of rearsight: 200-1,200 by 100 metres
Rate of fire: Cyclic: Belt fed 1,200 rounds/min; magazine fed 900 rounds/min
Muzzle velocity: 755 metres/sec
Muzzle energy: 250mkp (M52 cartridge)
Recoil energy: 0.248mkp
Ammunition: Czech 7.62mm M52 Cartridge. (Model 52) or Russian 7.62mm M43 cartridge. (Model 52/57)
Manufacturer: Ceskoslovenska Zbrojovka, Brno
Status: In service in Czechoslovakia but being superseded by the Model 59 GPMG

7.62mm MODEL 59 GPMG

This Czechoslovakian machine gun followed the Model 52 and uses the same general approach but is somewhat simplified in operation and considerably less complicated to produce.

It is a true general purpose machine gun and can fulfil a variety of roles. It fires the Russian 7.62mm × 54R cartridge.

As a squad automatic weapon with a light barrel and bipod it is known as the VZ59L. As a light machine gun with a heavy barrel and bipod it is still known as the VZ59L.

As a medium machine gun with a heavy barrel and a light tripod it is called the VZ59. This tripod also enables the gun to produce anti-aircraft fire.

As a tank coaxial machine gun, fitted with a solenoid, it is referred to as the VZ59T.

The gun is also manufactured to use the NATO 7.62mm × 51 cartridge and is then designated the VZ59N. The different cartridge contour leads to a different chamber and bolt face.

The gun fires only from the open pocket metal non-disintegrating Czech belt. The open pocket allows the Russian rimmed cartridge to be pushed straight through the belt and the advantages obtained by having a push-through feed are clearly demonstrated when comparing this system with the complex arrangements for the Russian PK GPMG.

The continuous metal belt can be re-loaded as required, and a belt filler which can be clamped on an ammunition box is available.

In the LMG role a 50-round metal box can be hung from the right hand side of the gun. This is used for firing on the move during the assault. In the MMG role a box holding 250 rounds in 5 belts is available.

To join two belts together remove the loop used for pulling the belt through, from the leading link of one belt. Take the last link of the other belt which is 'T' shaped in this leading link and use a cartridge to join the two belt lengths together. The belts should be placed in the container with the link openings down and the loop at the top of the box.

The rearsight for the early model LMG is a horse-shoe shaped bar with odd ranges on the left hand arm and even ranges on the right. The V notch is adjusted up and down by means of knobs on each side. The sight reads from 1 to 20 in hundreds of metres. Later models, and particularly the VZ59N, have a light folding frame backsight of conventional design with spring thumb catches for setting the range.

The foresight is a cylinder mounted eccentrically on a screw threaded base and has a hooded protector. All zeroing is carried out on the foresight.

The bipod clamps into its seating below the foresight. It will pivot back along the barrel by closing the legs when they are hanging vertically below the gun and laying them under the barrel. The lower part of each leg telescopes into the upper part to allow adjustment for height and to permit firing across a slope when one leg must be longer than the other. A catch allows movement of the legs. When released it holds the leg in position.

The VZ59 tripod in the AA role (G. Brown)

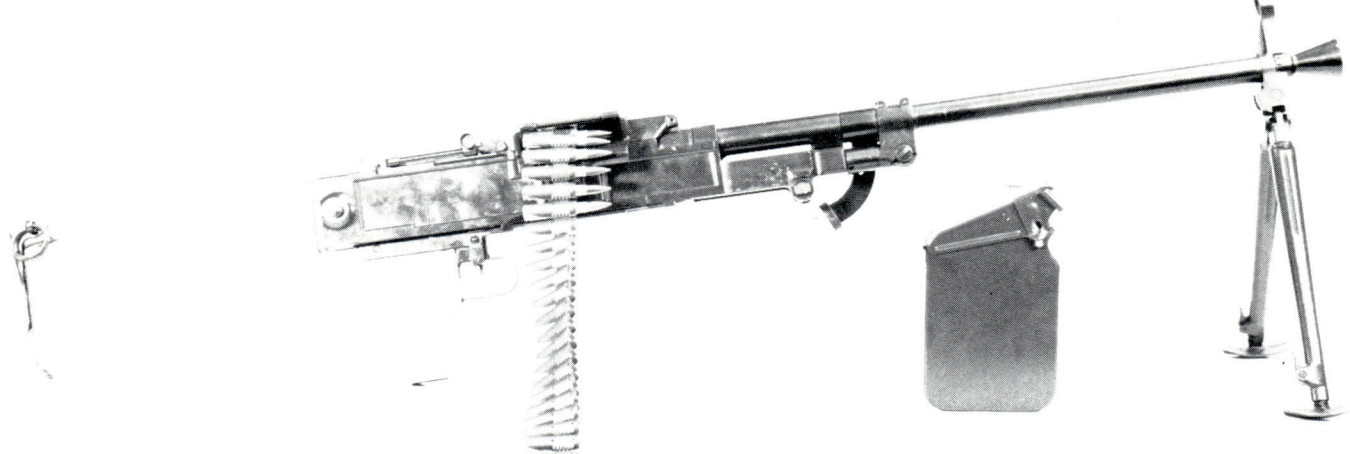

VZ59N (RSAF)

OPERATION

The belt is loaded by pressing the cartridges into the open tray links. Each link has a tab at its rear which fits up against the base of the cartridge – not into the cannelure if rimless NATO ammunition is being used.

The 50-round box has two grooves into which fit two lugs at the end of the feed tray on the right of the gun. When the box is fitted into place the cover will spring open. Pull out the loop fitted at the leading end of the belt. Press the cover catch, on top of the cover, forward and lift the cover. Press the belt exit cover back and it will fly open. Place the belt in position with the open side of the link downwards. It will be retained in the gun by the stop pawl when the cover is closed.

To cock the gun pull down the trigger group latch which is the cone shaped projection mounted on the left side of the receiver above the pistol grip. This releases the trigger grip from the receiver. When the trigger is pressed the sear goes down and the pistol grip can be pushed fully forward. The trigger is then released and the sear rises. It engages in the bent under the piston and when the pistol grip is withdrawn again, the sear acts as a catch and pulls the piston and bolt rearwards compressing the return spring. The trigger group is reconnected to the receiver and the weapon is cocked.

The safety catch also lies on the left of the receiver behind the trigger group latch. When pressed up it locks the sear. When the safety catch is moved down and the trigger is pressed the sear is depressed and the piston goes forward carrying the breech block. The feed ribs on top of the block force a cartridge through its link and into the chamber. The extractor snaps over the rim of the cartridge and the rim of the round hits the breech face and the breech block can advance no further. The piston continues on and the two ramps force the locking piece to rotate upwards and into two recesses in the receiver side walls. They ride under the locking piece and hold the lock in position. When locking is complete there is a short delay providing mechanical safety before firing and then the piston post hits the rear of the breech block, driving the firing pin into the cap. (The similarity with the locking system of the VZ58 rifle is clear.)

The gun fires and some of the propellant gases are diverted into the gas port. The piston is driven to the rear. The piston post moves away from the breech block and the spring-loaded firing pin is retracted. The central unlocking cam has an inclined plane which pulls the lock down out of its recesses in the receiver and the piston carries the bolt back with it. The empty case is held to the bolt face and ejected downwards through the cut-away section in the piston. The return spring is compressed by the piston and rearward motion ceases when the back of the bolt hits the rather soft buffer.

If the trigger remains pressed the cycle will be repeated.

FEED SYSTEM

The feed system owes its design to the Model 52 and is copied in the Russian PK GPMG. In this system, originated by Von Wimmersperg prior to World War II, the flat sides of the piston are raised to form cam paths on which runs a roller attached to a feed arm. The cam forces the roller outwards. The roller in turn pushes out the bottom end of a feed arm, mounted vertically on the receiver, which is pivoted at its centre point. As the bottom goes out, the top of the lever must go in and the feed pawl attached to it forces the belt in towards the feeding position on the centre line of the gun, until the leading cartridge comes up against the cartridge stop of the feed tray.

When the piston goes forward another cam path controls the feed lever and it is positively actuated and the top is pivoted out. The feed pawl, which is spring-loaded, slips over the next round in the belt. The belt cannot slip back because it is held up to the gun by a stop pawl on each side of the feed pawl. There is also another pair of stop pawls on the feed tray.

TRIGGER MECHANISM

The trigger mechanism, like that of most guns firing only at automatic, is simple. The trigger is ⌐ shaped and when it is pressed the top arm rises

The heavy-barrelled version on its tripod with the 250-round container (G. Brown)

VZ59N (RSAF)

and lifts the front of the sear. The sear is centrally pivoted and the rear end falls, allowing the piston to go forward.

Incorporated in the trigger mechanism is a controlled sear device to ensure that the sear rises to present a full mating surface with the bent of the piston. It consists of a sear catch powered by the trigger spring. The catch lies beneath the top arm of the trigger and passes through it. It presses up on the front end of the sear and so keeps the nose down. When the trigger is pressed the spring pressure on the catch is increased. When the trigger is released the trigger arm rises but the sear catch holds the sear tail up (and the nose down) until the spring pressure is sufficiently reduced and the trigger levers the sear catch clear of the sear. The sear rises rapidly and there can be no question of a slow return even if the firer releases the trigger extremely slowly. In this way the chipping of the sear face resulting from partial engagement, is reduced.

The safety catch, on the left of the receiver, is pushed up to engage and in pivoting it blocks the sear which cannot fall; at the same time a flange at its upper edge slides in a slot in the receiver and locks the trigger group. This prevents the gun from being cocked.

GAS REGULATION

The gas regulator in all the VZ59 guns except that chambered for NATO ammunition has two positions. The normal position is marked '1' and this is changed to '2' using the combination tool.

The NATO guns have a four-position regulator. This is of unusual design in that movement is controlled by the carrying handle. To unlock the regulator press the carrying handle lock (which lies parallel to the barrel at the foot of the handle) and twist the carrying handle and then rotate it until the pointed lug at the front of the handle can be lined up with the notch at the top rear of the gas cylinder. Position 1 is used when the gun is functioning normally. The pointer on the right of the regulator is rotated to '1' and the regulator pressed fully in to the left. To get to position '2' the regulator is pressed to the right and rotated until the pointer is aligned with '2'. To get to '3' the regulator is rotated backwards still being held to the right, and the pointer is at '3'. The position '4' is reached by pressing the regulator to the left and rotating it forward. To lock the regulator in the selected position, press the carrying handle lock, then twist and rotate the carrying handle. It should be noted that position '4' produces a very high rate of fire and was intended for anti-aircraft use.

BARREL CHANGING

To change the barrel the procedure is the same as that followed with the Model 52. Press the cover catch forward, pivot the cover up about its front hinge and then push the cover sideways so that it rotates to the right. The cover is attached to the barrel nut and this is rotated out of engagement with the interrupted threads on the barrel.

Grasp the carrying handle and push the barrel forward out of the receiver. Remove the bipod by squeezing the legs together and swinging them forward until the legs are at right angles to the barrel. Put the bipod on a cool barrel and insert it into the gun.

STRIPPING

(1) Set the safety catch up to 'safe', press the cover catch forward, lift the cover and remove the belt. Check no cartridge remains in the chamber or feedway.

(2) Set the safety to 'fire'. Depress the trigger group latch and control the forward movement of piston breech block and trigger group.

(3) Push the takedown pin at the rear of the receiver, fully to the left and remove the buttstock to the rear.

(4) Pull the trigger group back and the group will come out of the gun together with the piston and breech block.

TELESCOPE

A telescopic sight is available and can be used with the gun, mounted either on its bipod or a tripod. The telescope is attached to the receiver by means of a clamp. The sight can be adjusted for windage and elevation. The reticle can be illuminated at night and the telescope has a dovetail to accept the lamp housing. An active infra-red source and receiver can also be used with the gun.

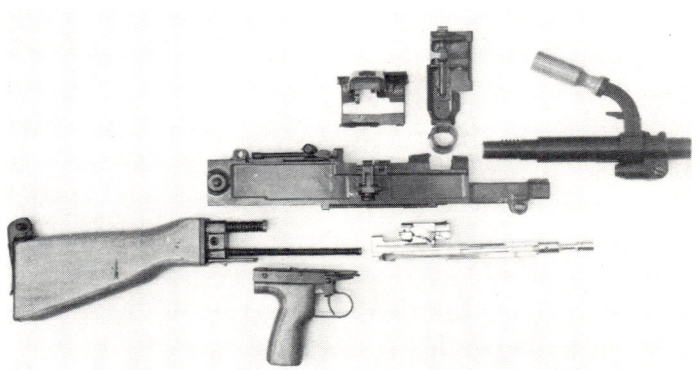

VZ59 stripped

MOUNTS

The bipod is standard with the light guns. To mount the gun on the tripod, the rear sight is lifted and the gun passed under the traversing arc and the mounting lugs on top of the rear of the receiver are then pinned to corresponding lugs under the main frame of the mounting. There is provision for free traverse and traversing stops are also provided. The tripod height can be adjusted.

If required the tripod can be used for anti-aircraft firing by using extension pieces.

DATA
Cartridge: 7.62mm × 54R or 7.62mm × 51
Method of operation: Gas
Method of locking: Swinging lock

LENGTHS
Gun with heavy barrel: 1,215mm
Gun with light barrel: 1,116mm
Heavy barrel with flash hider: 693mm
Light barrel with flash hider: 593mm
Sight base (heavy barrel): 744mm
Height of weapon: 225mm

WEIGHTS
Weapon with bipod, empty: 8.67kg
Weapon with tripod: 19.24kg
Heavy barrel: 3.79kg
Tripod: 9.93kg
Loaded 50-round belt: 1.38kg
50-round belt container: 0.60kg
250-round container: 2.22kg
Container with 5 × 50-round belts: 6.90kg

MECHANICAL FEATURES
Sights: Foresight: Pillar. Adjustable for zeroing both line and elevation
      Rearsight: V notch. Adjustable from 100 metres to 2,000 metres by 100-metre increments.
Rifling: 4 grooves RH. 1 turn in 240mm

FIRING CHARACTERISTICS
Muzzle velocity (light bullet):
      Heavy barrel: 830 metres/sec
      Light barrel: 810 metres/sec
Muzzle velocity (heavy bullet):
      Heavy barrel: 790 metres/sec
      Light barrel: 760 metres/sec
Rate of fire: Cyclic (ground targets): 700-800 rounds/min
      (Anti-aircraft): 1,000+ rounds/min

Rate of fire practical
Heavy barrel: 350 rounds/min
Light barrel: 150 rounds/min
No of rounds before barrel change
Heavy barrel: 500 rounds
Light barrel: 350 rounds
Maximum range (practical)
Tripod: 1,500 metres
Bipod: 1,000 metres
Maximum range: 4,800 metres
TRIPOD
Minimum barrel height: 300mm
Maximum barrel height: 500mm

Height of gun in AA role: 1,440mm
Maximum elevation: 21° 36′
Maximum traverse between stops: 43° 12′
TELESCOPE
Magnification: ×4
Field of view: 8°
Length of telescope: 200mm
Length of telescope with eyepiece, lens hood: 280mm
Eye relief: 61mm
Weight of telescope: 0.38kg
Manufacturer: Ceskoslovenska Zbrojovka, Strakonice
Status: In production. In service with the Czechoslovakian Armed Forces. Available for sale in 7.62mm × 54R or 7.62mm × 51.

DENMARK

7.92mm MADSEN LMG

The famous firm of Dansk Industri Syndikat started manufacturing machine guns in the very early years of the 20th century. They continued until they went out of the weapon business in 1970. The great majority of their guns were based on a single system – the automatic version of the Martin-Henry (Peabody in the USA) rifle. This was a single-shot, hinged-block system still used for competition purposes in .22LR. Since there was no reciprocating block it became necessary to fit a separate rammer. The magazine was above the receiver.

The Madsen action is unique and in spite of its complexity it worked well with rimless ammunition but not so well with rimmed cartridges.

The barrel recoils and the block has a stud which is forced back and after ½in of free travel it moves up on a non-recoiling switch plate. The combined extractor-ejector then levers the empty case out of the chamber and down the underside of the breech block and out of the gun. The stud continues along the top of the plate and the block cocks the hammer and stores

energy in a spring operating a recoil arm. When the stud reaches the end of the top surface of the switch plate, the block is forced down by the powerful cover spring. A pivoted feed arm rotates forward and forces the first round in the inverted magazine forward and into the chamber. The breech block is then forced forward and follows the track in the switch plate. It rises and is guided into a horizontal path which locks the breech block. The hammer drives the firing pin forward and the cap is fired.

This action does not really follow the usual pattern of automatic operation. It is neither a long recoil operation, since the barrel does not recoil a distance exceeding that of an unfired cartridge, nor a short recoil operation. It is a system of its own and the surprising thing is not that it works so well but that it works at all.

The Madsen was used in many countries and during World War II was even converted by the Germans into a belt-fed gun.

Apart from this conversion several models of the Madsen were made,

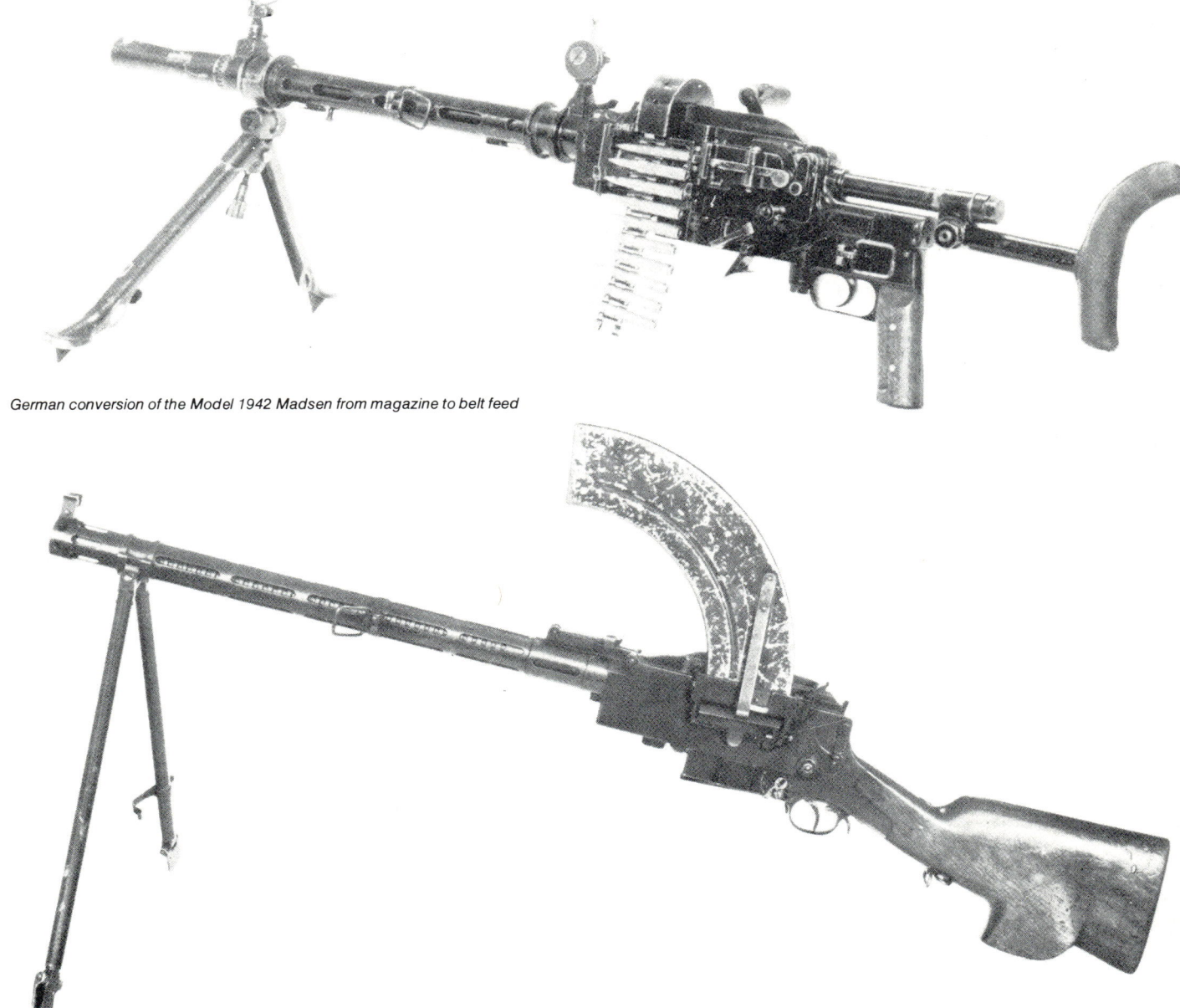

German conversion of the Model 1942 Madsen from magazine to belt feed

Model 1950 Madsen LMG (RMCS)

including one in 6.5mm which was used by the former Dutch East Indies Army. The following brief data are typical of the 7.92mm models.

DATA
Cartridge: 7.92mm Mauser
Method of operation: Recoil (see text)
Method of feed: 30-round detachable box magazine (or belt – see text)
Method of fire: Selective
Weight: About 11.8kg

Length: About 1 metre
Sights: Blade foresight and adjustable V-notch rearsight
Rate of fire: 125 rounds/min
Effective range: 800m
Manufacturer: Dansk Industri, Syndikat AS-(DISA)- 22, Mileparken, DK-Skovlunde, Denmark
Status: No longer in production or in European service. Versions of the Madsen LMG have been widely distributed, however, and still exist in many countries. In South-East Asia, in particular, Danish-made weapons in 7.92mm and possibly in 6.5mm may be encountered.

7.62mm MADSEN-SAETTER GPMG

This GPMG was the last of the Madsen series of machine-guns and was introduced in the 1950s. Since then the makers of the series, Dansk Industri Syndikat AS, have ceased making weapons, although they still make machine-gun mountings.   The gun is gas-operated with a simple locking system involving a lug on each side being forced out of the bolt and into recesses in the receiver. It is, unfortunately, possible to assemble and fire the gun with the lugs missing.

The manufacturing techniques employed the use of pressings, the barrel was chromium plated, and the weapon was well made. It was a contender in the British GPMG trials in 1958 but did not there prove itself to be reliable. It came into the field rather too late and the cream of the market was taken by FN. It was made in limited numbers at the Bandung arsenal in Indonesia.

It is no longer in production. A prototype .5 version was produced but this was never put on the market.

DATA
Cartridge: 7.62mm × 51
Method of operation: Gas
Method of locking: Projecting lugs

Method of feed: Belt. Usually 50 rounds. Continuous links but can be modified for disintegrating links
Method of fire: Automatic
Weight: 10.1kg
Length: 970mm
Barrel: 564mm
 Rifling: 4 grooves RH
 Cooling: Air. Quick-change barrel
Sights: Foresight: Blade
 Rearsight: Tangent notch
Muzzle velocity: 838 metres/sec
Muzzle energy: 334mkp
Rate of fire: Cyclic: 750 rounds/min
 Automatic: 200 rounds/min
Range, maximum effective: 800 metres
Manufacturer: Dansk Industri Syndikat AS-(DISA)- 22, Mileparken, DK-Skorlunde, Denmark. (Also made in Indonesia)
Status: No longer manufactured. No longer in European service. Locally manufactured weapons in service in Indonesia.

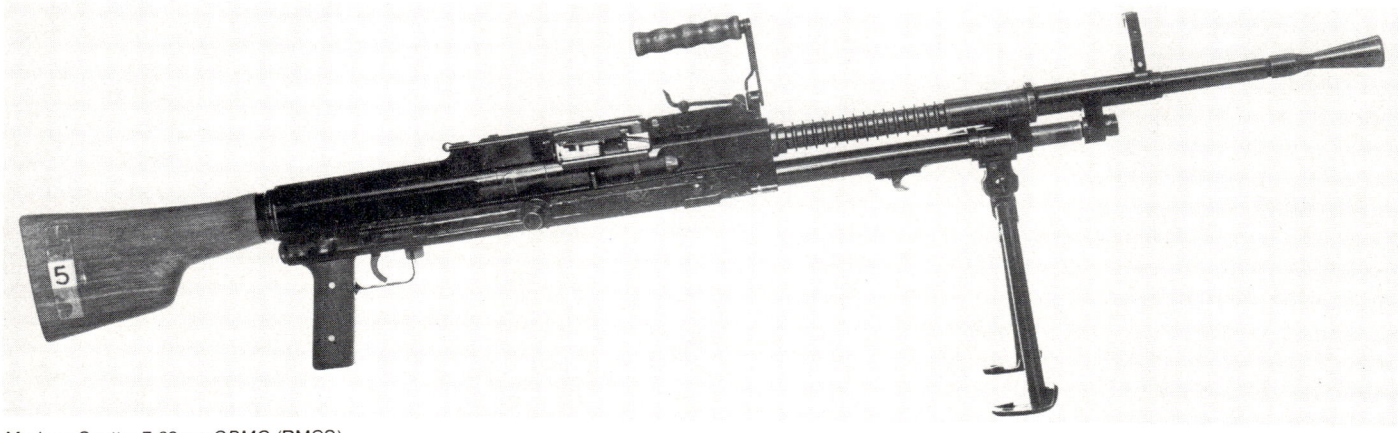

Madsen-Saetter 7.62mm GPMG (RMCS)

FINLAND

7.62mm LMG KK 62

This is a gas-operated light machine gun which, although it bears little superficial resemblance to it, is based on the Czech Zb 26 series and has a tilting block which locks into the roof of the receiver of the gun. It was started as a project in 1957 and the prototype was started in 1960. Trials were completed in 1962 and the LMG came into service with the Finnish Forces in 1966. The gun is manufactured by Valmet Oy and is used only in Finland. It is belt-fed and uses the Russian 7.62mm M43 cartridge with a 39mm case length. It fires only at fully automatic at a high rate of fire, and is unusual in modern machine guns in feeding from the right. Its weight of 8.3kg empty suggests that, with the cartridge it uses and a quick change barrel, it should be capable of a large volume of fire.

DATA
Cartridge: 7.62mm × 39
Method of operation: Gas
Method of locking: Tilting block
Method of feed: 100-round continuous link belt
Method of fire: Automatic
Weight, empty: 8.3kg
Weight with full belt: 10.6kg
Length: 1,085mm
Barrel: 470mm
 Rifling: 4 grooves RH.

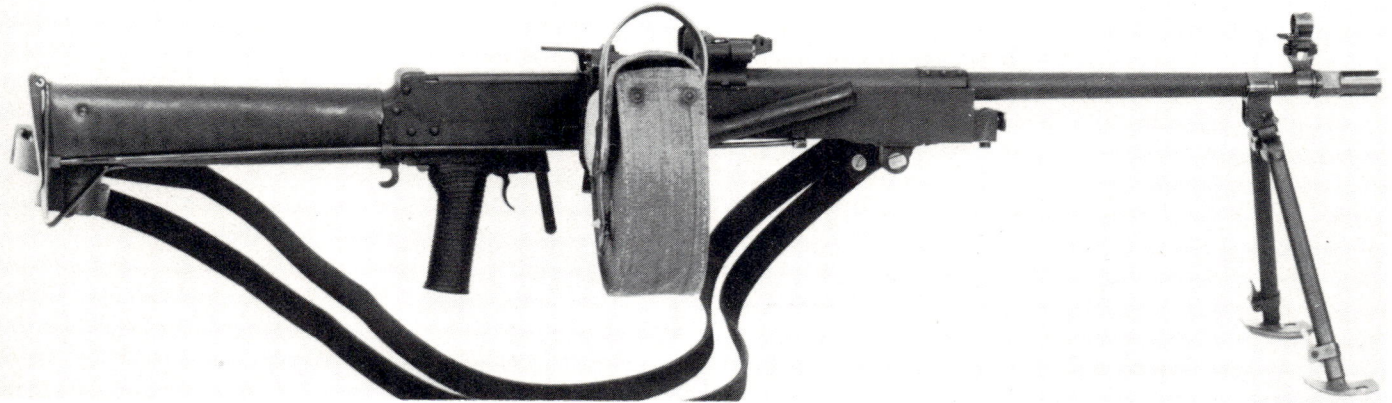

The 7.62mm KK 62 LMG

Sights: Foresight: Pillar
          Rearsight: Aperture
Range setting: 100 metres – 600 metres by 100 metre steps
Muzzle velocity: 730 metres/sec
Muzzle energy: 220mkp

Rate of fire: Cyclic: 1,000-1,100 rounds/min
                 Practical: 300 rounds/min (maker's figures)
Range, maximum effective: 350-450 metres
Manufacturer: Valmet Oy, Paakonttori, Punanotkonkatu 2, Helsinki
Status: Production complete. In service with Finnish Forces

7.62mm MACHINE GUN M/32-33 MAXIM

One of the two machine guns currently in service with the Finnish Army, the M/32-33 Maxim is a typical example of the old water-cooled medium machine gun which was used so effectively in the 1914-1918 war. The accompanying illustration shows a Finnish Army weapon but, since the Maxim originated in the UK, the detailed description of the weapon will be found among the UK entries below.

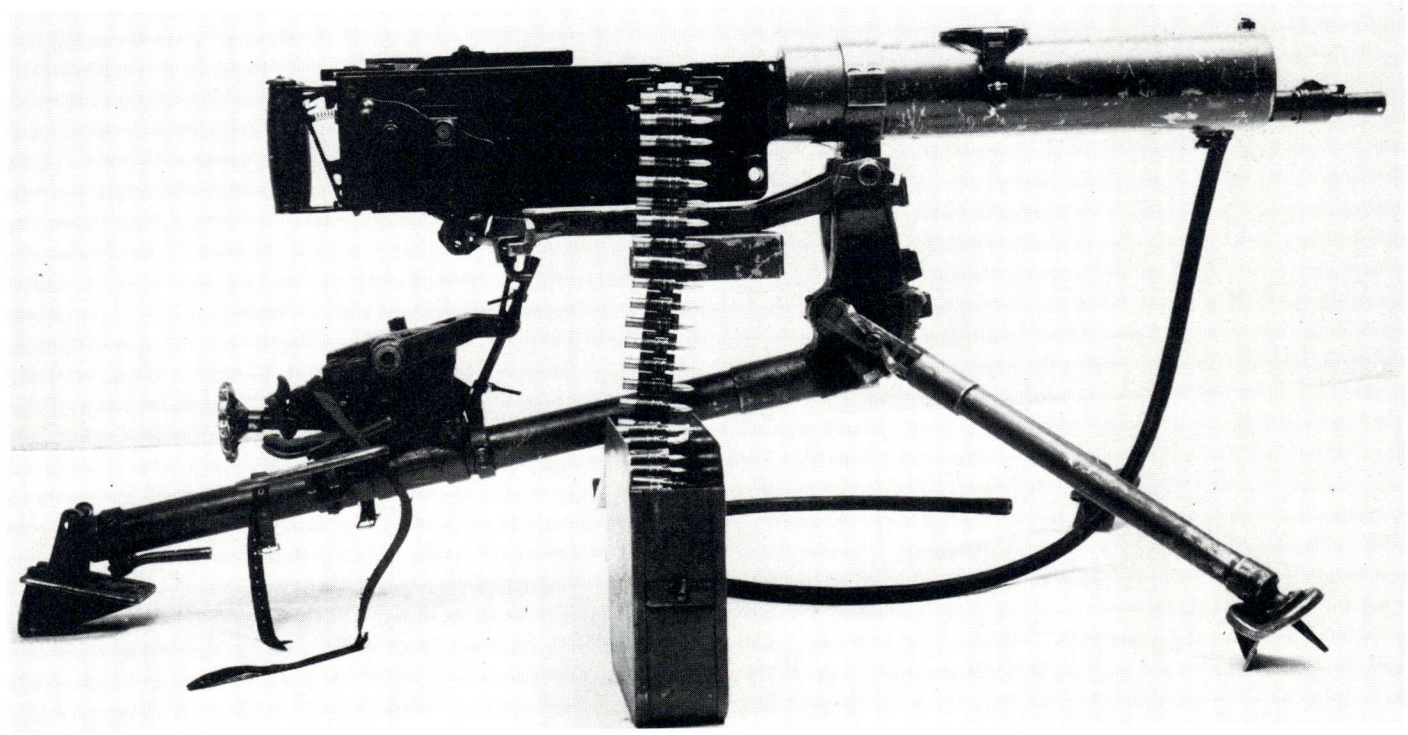

Finnish Maxim MMG

FRANCE

7.5mm MODEL 24/29 LMG

The Chatellerault was the standard French machine gun at the beginning of World War II and after that war it was put back into production to supply the French Army in Indo-China. It is no longer used by the French but was employed extensively by the Viet Cong in the Vietnamese war.

The gun is gas-operated with a top-mounted magazine holding 26 7.5mm × 54 cartridges. The action is sturdy and reliable. The barrel cannot be removed without the use of a spanner to rotate the barrel out of the receiver. The locking action is that of the tilting bolt. Two triggers are employed. Semi-automatic fire comes from the front trigger and full automatic from that of the rear.

A monopod can be fitted into the underside of the butt to make an improvised tripod.

American sources speak highly of the effectiveness of the weapon in Vietnam.

DATA
Cartridge: 7.5mm × 54
Method of of operation: Gas
Method of locking: Tilting block
Method of feed: 26-round top-mounted detachable box magazine
Method fire: Selective
Weight: 9.2kg
Length: 1082mm
Barrel: 500mm
          Rifling: 4 grooves LH
Muzzle velocity: 850 metres/sec
Muzzle energy: 330mkp

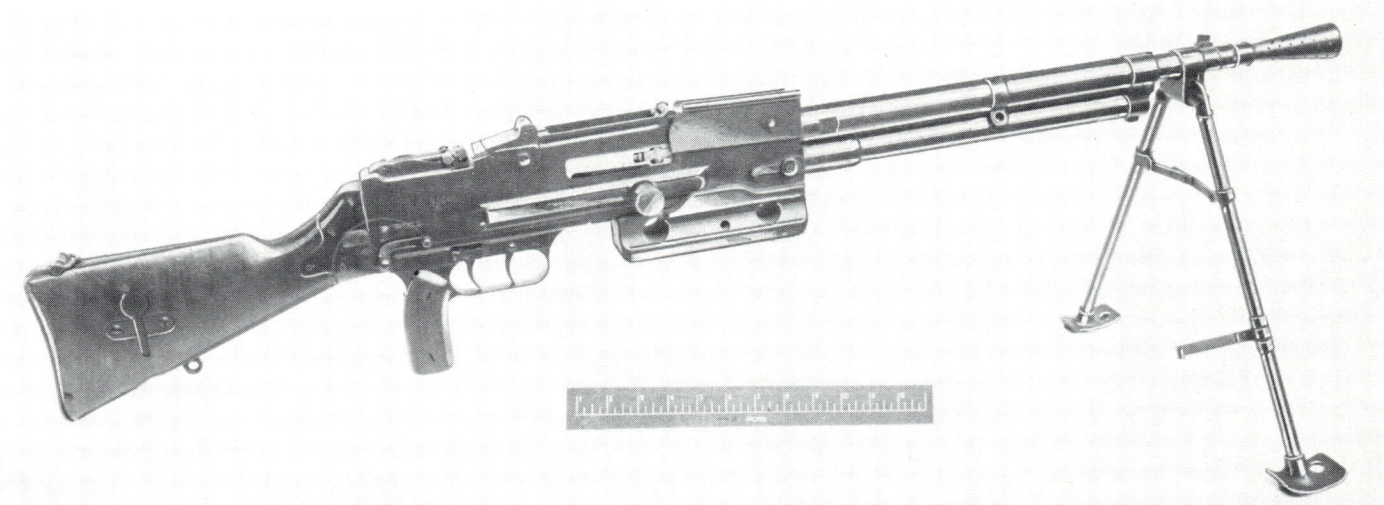

The French Chatellerault 7.5mm LMG M 1924/29

Rate of fire: Cyclic: 500 rounds/min
           Automatic: 125 rounds/min
           SS: 52 rounds/min
Range, maximum effective: 800 metres
Status: No longer manufactured. No longer in European service but is probably still to be found in South-East Asia and possibly on former French

Territories elsewhere. A development of the M24/29 – the M1931A – may also be found, usually on a French M1945 or US M2 tripod: it has a heavier barrel, a drum or side-mounted box magazine and a prominent ejector housing on top of the receiver and is capable of automatic fire only using a single trigger.

7.5mm AA 52 AND AA 7.62 NF-1 GPMG

After World War II the French Army had no modern weapons of native design but was equipped with a variety of British, American and German guns. This diversity of weapons and the difficulty of supplying spare parts contributed to their disaster in Indo-China.

The Arme Automatique Transformable Model 52 – GPMG model 1952 – was designed for ease of production, using stampings wherever possible. The receiver of the gun is made of fabricated semi-cylindrical shells welded together. It fires the French 7.5mm × 54 cartridge of 1929. A version firing the 7.62mm × 51 cartridge is also made and known as AA 7.62 NF-1. For both versions there is a choice of light and heavy barrels.

OPERATION

The French 7.5mm cartridge develops about 3.500kg/cm². This pressure forces the case outwards against the chamber walls and drives the base backwards. If the brass case expands beyond its elastic limits it will not return to its original dimensions and when the steel chamber contracts it will grip the case very tightly. If this happens the base will be driven back by the internal pressure and the case will separate at its weakest section. To prevent this and to allow the case to move back, intact, inside the chamber, there are a number of longitudinal grooves in the neck of the chamber running out halfway towards the mouth. Gas enters these grooves and the case 'floats' with equal pressure on each side of the brass wall and can move comparatively freely.

To prevent premature movement whilst pressure is still high a two-part block is employed. The front part carries a lever. The short end of the lever rests in a recess in the side of the receiver and the long arm of the lever bears against the massive rear part of the block. Gas pressure exerts a force on the bolt face and the lever is forced to rotate thus accelerating the rear part of the block but restraining the front part until the lever is clear of the recess. The entire bolt is then blown back by the residual pressure. The empty cartridge case is held by the extractor to the bolt face until it strikes the double ejectors on the bottom rear of the feed tray and is deflected down through the bottom of the gun.

It is found that the cartridge head space is critical and when wear occurs the bearing surface in the receiver can be quickly replaced. In spite of this

The bulge produced in the cartridge case. Note fluting grooves in neck (RMCS)

the ejected cases are deformed where they expand into the bullet guide. Any relaxation of the tolerances in case manufacture and increase in head space will result in a blow out.

In Europe, blowback-operated guns are popular because they are cheaper to produce than gas-operated guns, but it should be noted that there is no reserve of power to deal with the friction caused by the ingress of sand or dirt nor with the build up of carbon in the bolt way to which all blowback actions are subject.

The AA 52 fires from an open breech. The firing pin floats freely in the front part of the block and is forced forward only when the rear part of the block closes up to the front part. This can only occur when the lever – which holds the two parts separated – can rotate into the recess in the receiver at the end of forward travel. Thus the round cannot be fired until the delay device is properly positioned to hold up the front face of the block.

FEED

The 7.5mm AA52 gun uses a French disintegrating link belt based on the US M13 pattern but somewhat more flexible and having a smaller extension for a given load. The AA 7.62 NF-1 can use either this type of belt or the M13-NATO belt. Unlike the system used in most current GPMGs where the rounds are moved over one half pitch for each stroke of the reciprocating bolt, the French gun uses a pawl to collect the next round on the forward stroke of the bolt and positions it for firing as the bolt goes back. The AA 52 cannot use the usual system of a roller in a feedway to operate the feed pawl since the two parts of the bolt separate after firing and remain with a gap between them until immediately before firing the next round. A cam groove on top of the bolt accommodates a lever which is swung from side to side to operate the feed pawl. Unlike the FN MAG or the British L7A2 GPMG the AA 52 must be carried with the gun cocked when a loaded belt is in place.

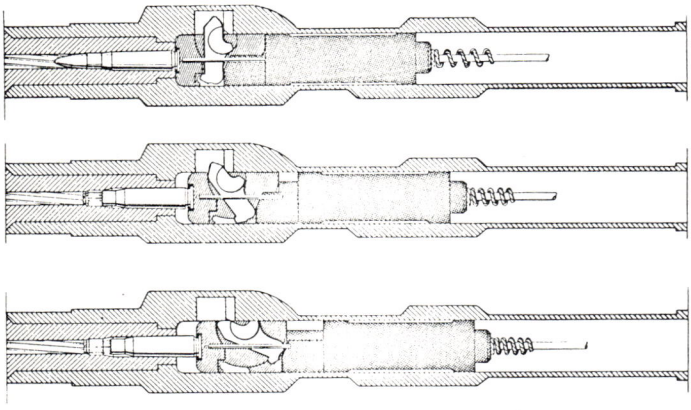

AA52 two-part bolt action
Top: *Gun fires – Lever engaged in receiver.* **Middle:** *Bolt body moving back.*
Bottom: *Lever rotated clear of receiver (RMCS)*

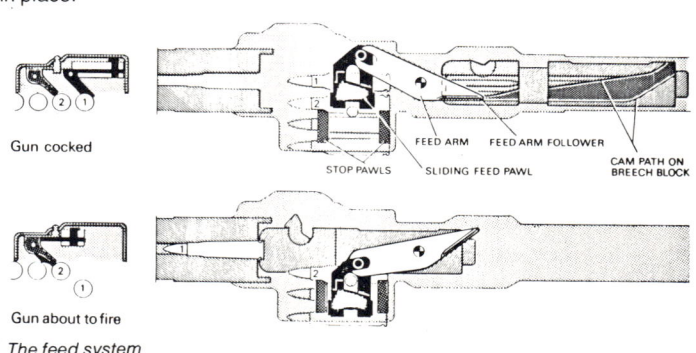

Gun cocked

FEED ARM   FEED ARM FOLLOWER

STOP PAWLS   SLIDING FEED PAWL   CAM PATH ON BREECH BLOCK

Gun about to fire

The feed system

AA52 (RMCS)

AA52 on the US M2 tripod for sustained fire (RSAF)

TRIGGER AND FIRING MECHANISM

The gun is designed to fire at 900 rounds a minute at full automatic only, when clean. A soft buffer in the rear end of the bolt keeps the forward acceleration of the bolt down. To ensure that the sear and bent mate on full engaging surfaces when the trigger is released, a "controlled sear" is used which incorporates a tripper to release the sear at a pre-determined position whilst the bolt is moving forward. This works as follows. The sear is an arm pivoted at its mid point. The rear end engages the bolt and this is known as the nose of the sear. The front end (tail) is over the trigger. When the trigger is pulled the tail of the sear is pushed up and the nose falls. The bolt is freed and starts to reciprocate. Attached to the trigger is a sear catch – or tripper – which moves down when the trigger is pulled and has its own spring which rotates it under the tail of the sear. When the trigger is released the tripper goes up but it prevents the tail of the sear from falling. When the bolt next comes back it hits the tripper, revolves it back against its spring, and frees the tail of the sear to fall. The nose of the sear rises, the bolt going back rides over it, and the full face of the sear is presented to the bent of the bolt as it comes forward. This prevents chipping of the sear due to contact of reduced mating areas.

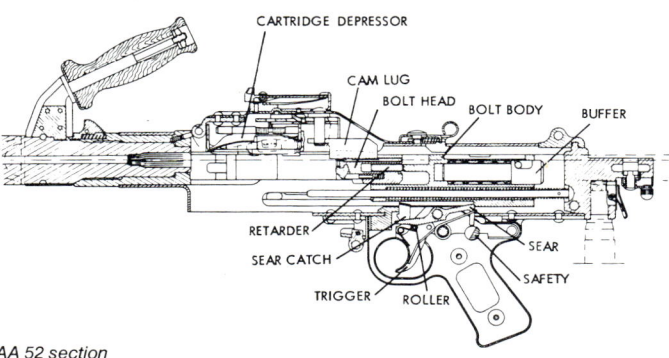

AA 52 section

BARREL CHANGE

In a modern machine gun using a charge with a calorific value of about 1,000 calories per gram, a barrel equilibrium temperature of about 600°C will be reached after 600-800 rounds have been fired at 200 rounds/min. Therefore the barrel must be changed at intervals of not more than four minutes, otherwise the barrel steel will be degraded, leading to loss of velocity, inaccuracy, a considerable drop in the trajectory and permanent barrel damage. The barrel change arrangements of the AA52 are awkward if the gun is being fired off its bipod. A barrel release catch must be pressed in (in earlier guns, pulled back), and then the wooden barrel-carrying handle rotated clockwise and pushed forward. Since the bipod is permanently attached to the barrel, once the barrel is drawn off there is no forward support for the gun and the gunner is left holding a very hot gun.

SIGHTS

The foresight is a hinged block with a slot in the top. For firing by day the slot is used and at night the entire foresight block is fitted into the notch of the rearsight, the sights being luminescent.

The rearsight is graduated from 200 to 1,400 metres by 50-metre divisions and 1,500 to 2,000 metres by 100-metre divisions. It can be offset for wind, drift or allowance for a moving target. Zeroing is carried out on the foresight. The dovetail is moved across for lateral adjustments and the block is changed for vertical adjustment. Having all the zeroing on the foresight allows the barrels to be zeroed before going into action.

STRIPPING

The gun was designed for parachute use with a butt which telescopes into the body but a heavy blow may jam the butt forward and the gun cannot then be cocked or stripped. The butt must be pulled back into the extended position by putting a sling loop around a groove in front of the shoulder piece and pulling back.

To strip, the gun is made safe and then the butt is removed by rotating a catch underneath. The monopod has a catch at the back. The rear plate of the receiver, and the spring rod, spring and bolt can be withdrawn by six revolutions of the actuating handle.

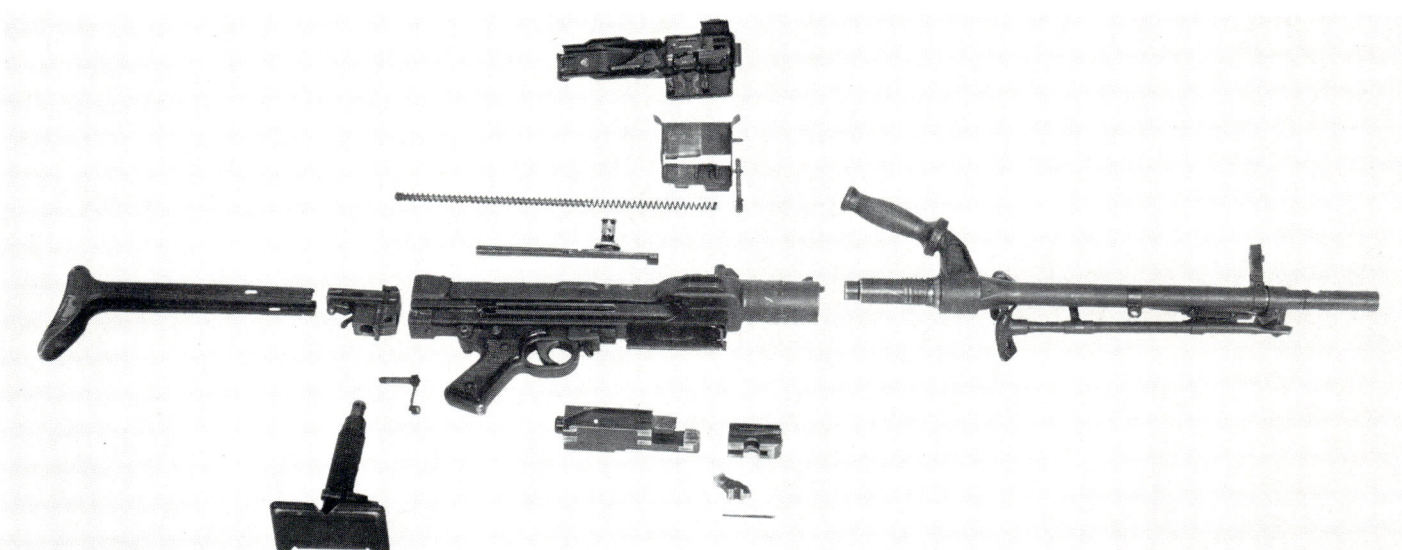

AA52 field stripped (RMCS)

HANDLING

The gun is butt-heavy when carried by the wooden carrying handle. The greater the ammunition load the more the centre of gravity moves back. When used as a squad automatic, a box holding 50 rounds is hung on the hook on the left of the cartridge guide and this makes movement through undergrowth easier. The bipod, of the 'music stand' type is permanently attached to the fore-end of the barrel and not only hinders barrel changing but reduces the arc of fire. There is a monopod at the rear of the gun which can be pinned to the ground and the gun can be raised or lowered using a milled handgrip.

One target can be recorded for night firing, using the micrometer type setting on the rear monopod. When the gun is used for sustained fire it is mounted on a tripod – usually the US M2 tripod with an adapter.

Both the heavy barrel for sustained fire and the light barrel for squad use are plain steel using neither stellite liners nor chrome plating – presumably for cheapness.

DATA (Common to both versions unless otherwise indicated)
Cartridge: 7.5mm M/29 or 7.62mm NATO
Method of operation: Delayed blowback
Method of feed: Disintegrating link belt (see text)
Sights: Foresight: Slit blade
Rearsight: Leaf graduated 200-2,000 metres
Sight radius: 19in (483mm)
BARREL
Bore diameter: 7.5mm or 7.62mm
Overall length without flash hider
  Light barrel: 500mm
  Heavy barrel: 600mm
Rifling: 4 grooves RH. 1 turn in 297mm
Width of grooves: 4.34mm

Depth of grooves: 0.89mm
GUN
Weight (light barrel, no bipod): 9.15kg
  (light barrel, bipod and flash hider): 9.7kg
  (heavy barrel, bipod and flash hider): 11.15kg
Length (light barrel, butt extended): 1145mm
  (light barrel, butt retracted): 980mm
  (heavy barrel, butt extended): 1245mm

BALLISTICS
Rate of fire: Cyclic: 900 rounds/min
  Practical (heavy barrel): 250-700 rounds/min
  (light barrel): 150 rounds/min
Muzzle velocity: 800 metres/sec
Muzzle energy: 350mkp
Practical range (heavy barrel): 1200m
  (light barrel): 800m
Maximum effective range: 3000m

Ammunition	7.5mm M/29	7.62mm NATO
Complete round weight:	363g	375g
Bullet weight:	139g	144g
Charge weight:	44g	44g
Round length:	76mm	71.2mm
Case length:	54mm	51mm
Bullet diameter:	7.5mm	7.62mm
Case diameter:	12.2mm	11.8mm

Manufacturer: Originally developed and produced by Manufacture Nationale d'Armes de Chatellerault (MAC). Production subsequently transferred to Manufacture Nationale d'Armes de Tulle. Enquiries to GIAT 10, Place Georges Clémenceau-92211 Saint-Cloud, France.
Status: Production complete. In service with the French Armed Forces

---

GERMANY (FEDERAL REPUBLIC)

7.92mm MG34

The MG34 was designed by Mauser-Werke at Oberndorf and was intended as a dual purpose ground and anti-aircraft machine gun. Later it was employed with even greater flexibility and was used as a light machine gun with a bipod and as a sustained-fire machine gun using a sturdy buffered tripod and a dial sight.

The gun was a short recoil design using a rotating bolt head with an interrupted buttress thread at the front. The rear end of the barrel carried two cams which accelerated the bolt rearwards after it was unlocked from the barrel.

The trigger of the standard version produced full automatic fire from the bottom half and single shots from the upper surface. Some, however, were made with a single trigger action producing automatic fire only (see below).

The belt was pulled through the gun by a feed pawl operated by a curved belt feed lever which fitted under the top cover plate, resting between two studs on the upper surface of the bolt. As the bolt reciprocated the curved lever oscillated across the gun and, through an intermediate feed lever,

moved the feed slide out for a pawl to collect a round, and then moved it in again to bring that round up to the cartridge stop and position it for the bolt to ram it out of the belt and into the chamber.

The MG34 was modified in 1941 in an effort to increase production rates. The modifications involved non-standard parts which could not be interchanged, and were not carried out on a large scale. They included:

MG 34S. A shorter barrel version with a simplified bolt using lugs to lock. The arrangement for control of the firing pin was simplified. The gun fired only at full automatic and could use only the belt feed.

MG 34/41. This carried the simplification process further and lightened the bolt to produce a higher rate of fire.

The MG 34 remained in service throughout the 1939-45 war and was then taken into service by a number of countries such as Czechoslovakia, France, Israel and, for a time, the East German militia. It has been used by the Viet Cong and North Vietnamese militia, mainly in an anti-aircraft role, and was said to be in use with second-line Portuguese units in Angola.

MG34 on a buffered tripod with automatic traversing and searching device

DATA
Cartridge: 7.92mm × 57
Method of operation: Short recoil
Method of locking: Rotating bolt
Method of fire: Selective
Method of feed: 50-round continuous link belt or 75-round saddle magazine
Weight: 12kg
Length: 1,224mm
Barrel: 629mm
      Rifling: 4 grooves RH
Sights: Foresight: Blade
      Rearsight: Leaf notch
Muzzle velocity: 755 metres/sec
Muzzle energy: 372mkp
Rate of fire: Cyclic: 900 rounds/min
      Auto: 200 rounds/min
      SS: 60 rounds/min
Range, maximum effective: Bipod 550 metres; Tripod 1,800 metres
Manufacturer: Mauser-Werke AG Oberndorf; Steyr-Daimler-Puch, Steyr
Status: No longer in production. No longer in regular European service but has been seen in use in Vietnam and Angola and might be found in other parts of Africa or Asia.

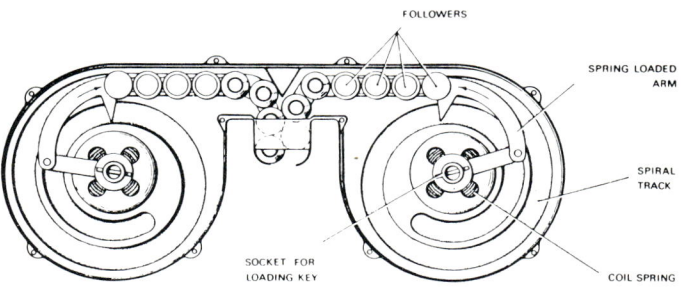

The 75-round saddle drum magazine (RMCS)

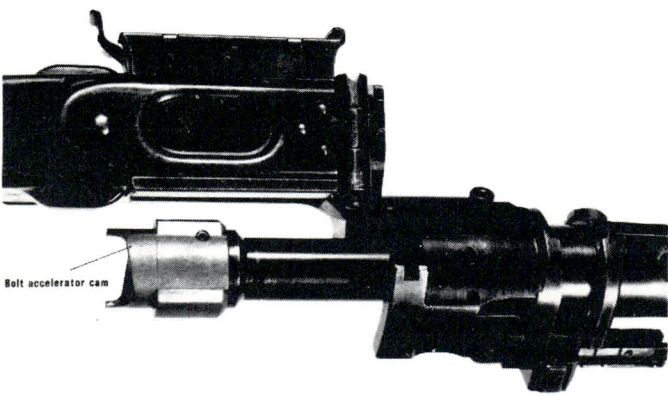

MG34 barrel change

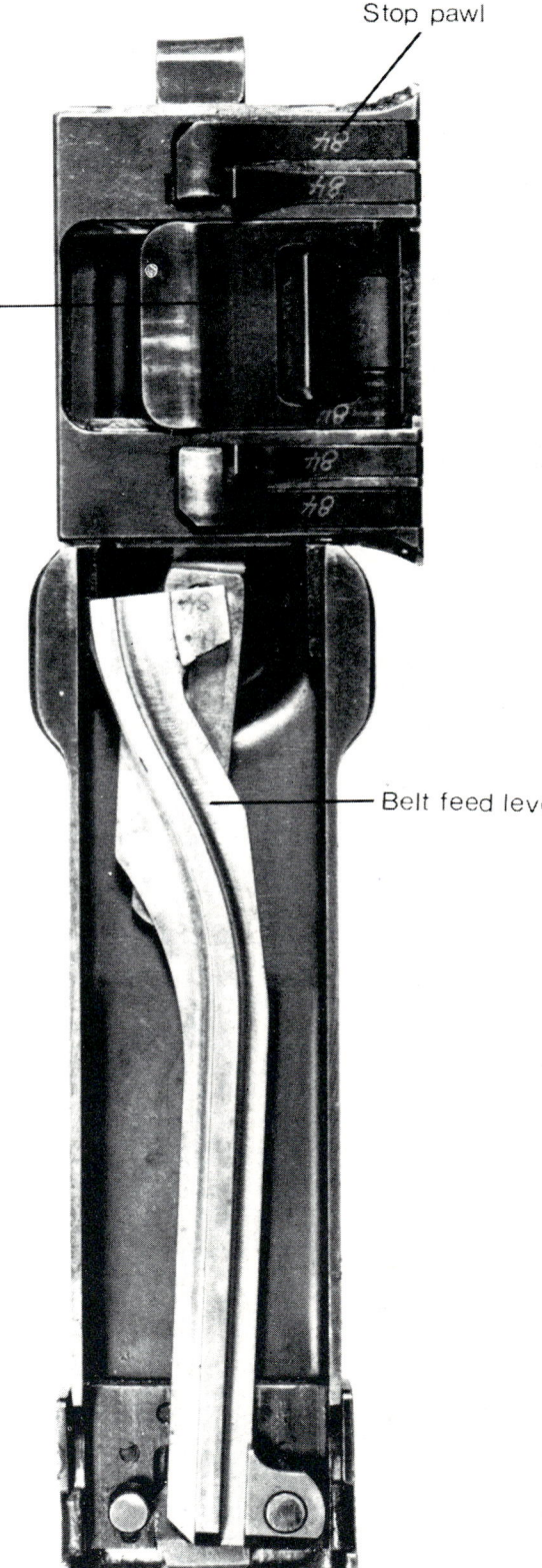

Stop pawl

Feed pawl

Belt feed lever

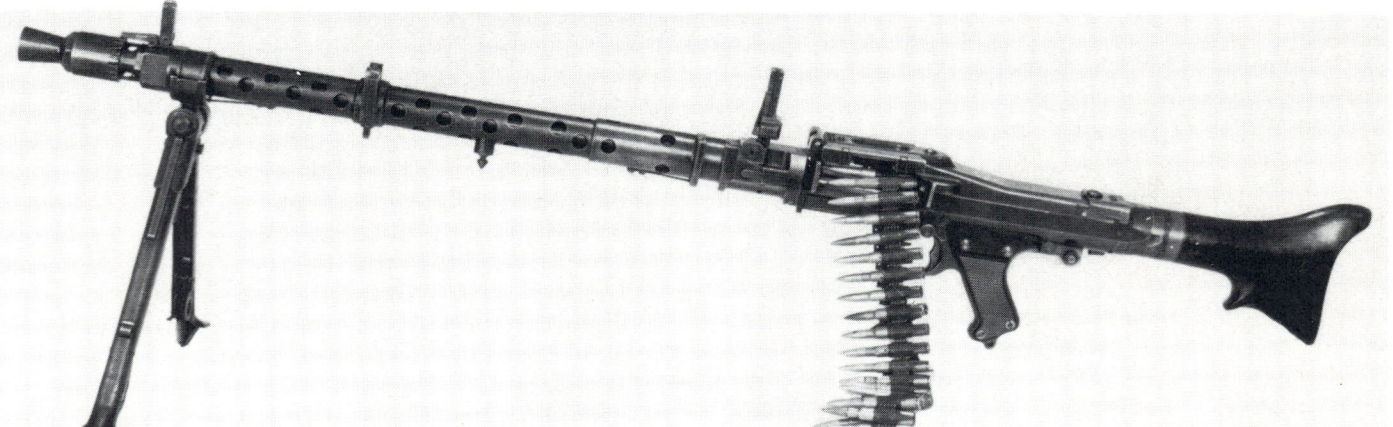

The feed arrangements of MG34

The 7.92mm MG34 – bipod controlled (RMCS)

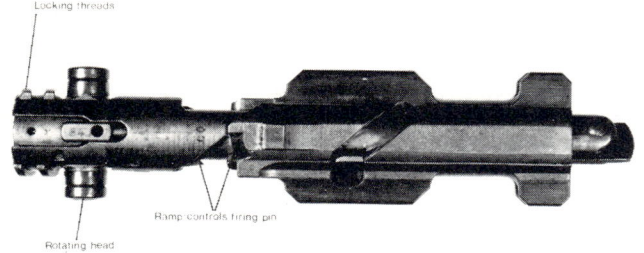

MG34 – bolt unlocked (RMCS)

The simplified bolt on MG34/41 (RMCS)

7.92mm MG42 LIGHT MACHINE GUN

One of the best-known automatic weapons of the Second World War, the MG42 was introduced to meet a German Army requirement for an inexpensive and reliable weapon to replace the MG34. How successful a replacement it was may be judged from the fact that nearly a million had been made by the end of the war.

Brief data are given below and the weapon is illustrated here but a more detailed discussion will be found in the entry for the 7.62mm MG1, 2 and 3 machine guns later in this section.

DATA
Cartridge: 7.92mm × 57
Method of operation: Gas-assisted recoil
Method of Feed: 50-round continuous link belt
Method of fire: Automatic

Weight: 11.6kg
Length: 1,230mm
Band: 566mm
Sights: Foresight: Folding blade
       Rearsight: Tangent with V-notch
Rate of fire: Cyclic, 1,100-1,200 rounds/min
Effective range: 800m from bipod
Manufacturer: Mauser-Werke AG, Oberndorf-Neckar and others
Status: No longer made in Germany. Some were converted to 7.62mm calibre as the MG-2; some others were taken into service by the French Army. The latter were replaced by the AA 52 weapon but some may still survive outside France. The Yugoslav Army uses a version of the gun called the SARAC M1953 which fires the 7.92mm × 57 cartridge and is believed still to be in production

MG42 (RMCS)

7.92mm and 7.62mm MG81

During the Second World War Mauser-Werke at Oberndorf produced the MG81 in 7.92mm. It was designed initially for aircraft use and to increase its fire power, the weapon was built as a twin-barrelled machine gun (MG 81Z) with one common receiver and trigger. This twin-barrelled gun produced 1,700 to 1,800 rounds/min/barrel. Three such twin-barrelled guns were used in an additional pod attached to a Ju 88 or Do 217. In some cases as many as 6 pods were attached to a Ju 88 giving a fire power of 60,000

rounds/min.

The lack of penetration of the 7.92mm bullet led to the development of larger calibre machine guns and the MG81 was used for airfield defence and installed on S-boats for AA protection. About 200,000 MG81s were made. Many were equipped with a shoulder stock and sights and used as ground machine guns.

After Germany came into NATO Mauser resurrected the MG81 rebuilt to

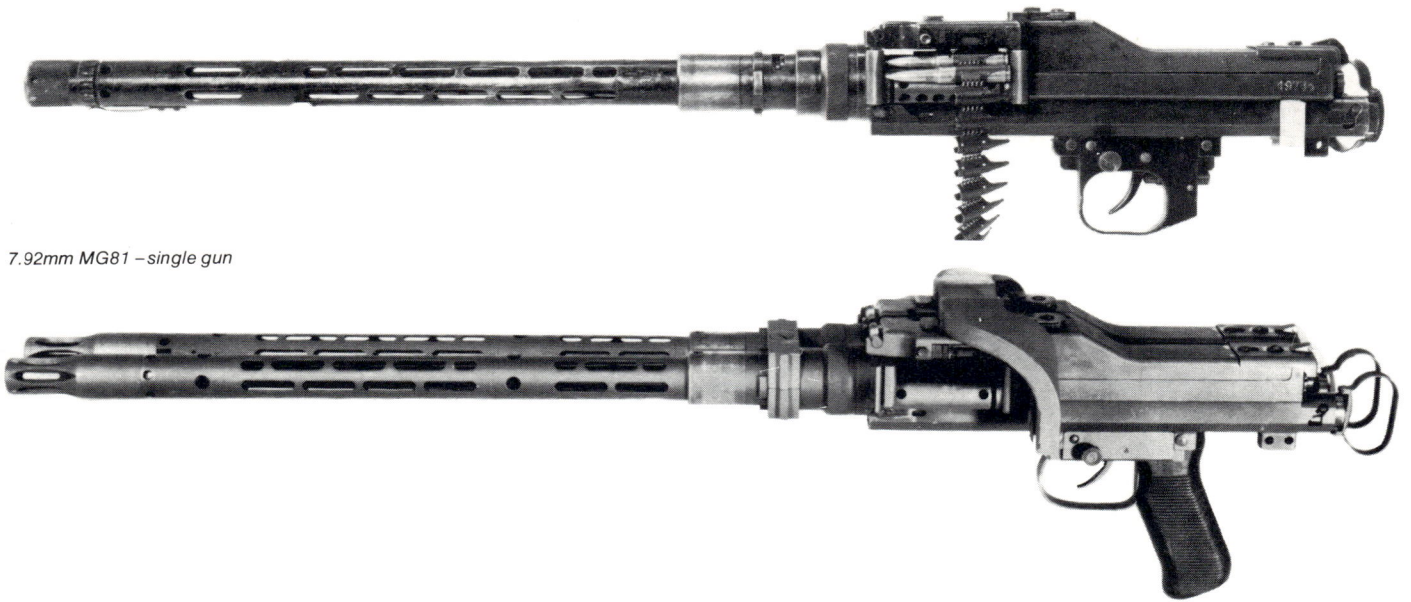

7.92mm MG81 – single gun

MG81Z – twin gun

7.62mm × 51 NATO. The gun was aimed first at the helicopter market where the value of a fast-firing light machine gun would be appreciated. With a twin-barrelled MG81Z on each side of the helicopter the pilot would have a fire power of 6,800-7,000 rounds/min.

The second possibility was to use the gun in the ground role with a reduced rate of fire of 1,200 rounds/min. The gun – as shown here – is very light and occupies little space.

The MG81 operates, in principle, in the same way as the MG34 with a rotating bolt head. The recoil action is the same but rather a lot of gas assistance is used at the muzzle.

DATA

Cartridge: 7.62mm × 51
Method of operation: Short recoil with gas assistance
Method of locking: Rotating bolt head
Method of feed: Either disintegrating link belt or 100-round continuous belt.
Method of fire: Automatic

	MG81	MG81Z
Weight (helicopter version):	6.5kg	12.9kg
Weight (ground role)	8.5kg	—
Trigger pull:	5.0kg	7.5kg
Length (inc. flash hider)	940mm	940mm
Barrel:	475mm	475mm
Distance between bores:	—	56mm
Sights: Foresight:	Pillar	Pillar
Rearsight:	Notch	Notch
Muzzle velocity:	838 metres/sec	838 metres/sec
Muzzle energy:	348mkp	348mkp
Rate of fire:		
(helicopter version)	1,700 rounds/min	3,400 rounds/min
(ground version)	1,200 rounds min	
Range, maximum effective:	800 metres	
Manufacturer: Mauser-Werke, Oberndorf, Neckar		
Status: Available for production		

7.92mm MG81 adapted for general use

7.62mm MG81

7.62mm HECKLER AND KOCH HK21 GENERAL PURPOSE MACHINE GUN

Heckler and Koch produce a series of weapons which they divide into groups according to calibre. Group I consists of a 9mm SMG and rifles and machine guns in 7.62mm × 51 NATO calibre. Group II uses the USA 5.56mm × 45 cartridge and Group III the Russian 7.62mm × 39 cartridge.

The HK21 is a belt-fed GPMG using the 7.62mm × 51 NATO cartridge. This will normally be carried in the disintegrating link belt and the gun will function using either the German DM6 belt, the USA M13 belt or the French belt. However, the continuous link belt – DM1 – can also be used if required. Furthermore by changing the barrel, the belt feed plate and the bolt, the gun can be converted to firing the 5.56mm × 45 or the 7.62mm × 39 cartridge i.e. from Group I to Group II or Group III. The utility of the weapon is further increased by the ability of the user to insert a magazine adapter in place of the feed mechanism, to take any of the Heckler and Koch 7.62mm magazines intended for the G3 rifle or the HK11 LMG.

The gun has a practical and effective quick-change barrel that enables it to produce sustained fire when required. The weapon can be employed as:
(a) Belt-fed light machine gun, bipod-mounted.
(b) Magazine-fed light machine gun, bipod-mounted.
(c) Belt-fed sustained-fire machine gun, tripod mounted.
(d) Belt-fed sustained-fire machine gun for vehicle installation.

The light bipod can be fitted directly in front of the feed system, which increases the amount of traverse available but tends to reduce the accuracy: alternatively it can be mounted at the front of the body which increases the accuracy but reduces the amount of traverse available.

HK21 with belt feed system

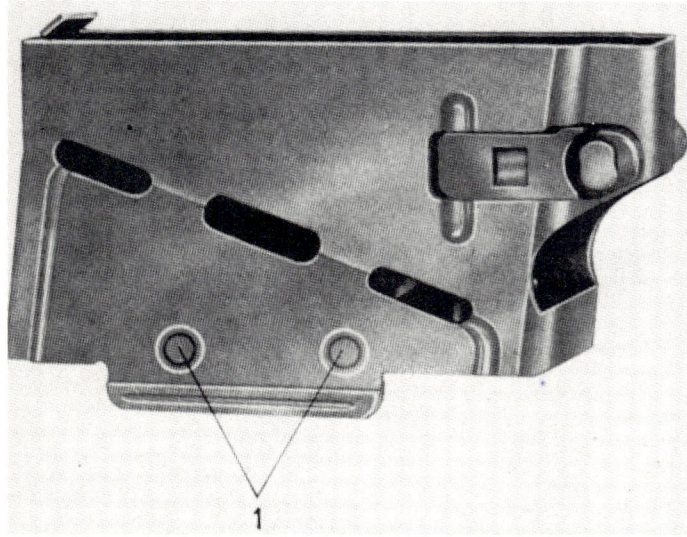

The magazine attachment unit makes the use of the G3 rifle magazine possible. It is installed in the receiver in lieu of the belt feed insertion unit and is held by the locking pins (1)

OPERATION

The method of operation of the HK21 is the same as that used in the G3 rifle (qv) employing the two-part breech block and the delay rollers. The delayed blowback system, with a fluted chamber for easy cartridge movement, operates from the closed breech position with a round in the chamber when the gun is ready to fire. The feed system of the belt-fed gun functions as follows:

If the disintegrating belt has a feed tag this is pushed through the feed tray from left to right and pulled until the first round reaches the cartridge stop. Since the bolt will pass over the belt the open side of the belt links must be placed uppermost before the tag is inserted. This point is worthy of note since most operators who are accustomed to the German MG3 or the British L7A2 (where the bolt passes under the belt) will have acquired the habit of positioning the belt with the open side downwards. The cocking handle is then pulled fully back and released – the cartridge is then driven into the chamber.

Where the belt has no tag the procedure is somewhat different. The gun is first cocked and the cocking handle held to the rear in the recess of the cocking slideway. The feed mechanism catch is depressed and the mechanism moved over to the left. The first round is placed in the feed sprocket and this is rotated to the right until it locks. The first cartridge is now in place and the feed unit can be pushed in. Releasing the cocking handle will feed the first round from the belt into the chamber.

There is a curved cam path in the underside of the bolt body which engages an actuating stud in the feed mechanism. As the bolt moves back after firing, the twin sprockets are rotated and a round positioned in the boltway. The loose link from the previous round is pushed out of the gun. As the bolt comes forward it re-positions the actuating stud on the left. The sprockets can revolve only to the right unless released by the hand-operated catch already mentioned.

If required the belt feed unit can be withdrawn completely and replaced with a magazine unit. This fits up into the receiver and is held by two locking pins. The unit allows the use of the 20-round magazine or the 80-round double drum plastic magazine.

The gun may be fired at single shot or full automatic. The selector lever is located above the pistol grip and the trigger mechanism, disconnector and automatic sear are the same as those used in the G3 rifle.

STRIPPING
(1) Remove belt or magazine.
(2) Check chamber is empty.
(3) Push out butt retaining pins. Remove butt stock and return spring by pulling butt to the rear.
(4) Withdraw cocking handle to rear. Remove bolt.
(5) To remove the feed block press down the rear end of the locking plate on the right of the mechanism and simultaneously push catch at front left bottom. Feed mechanism can then be slid out to the left.
(6) To remove the barrel pull the barrel catch back, rotate barrel anti-clockwise and push forward. Once the barrel is clear it is withdrawn to the rear.

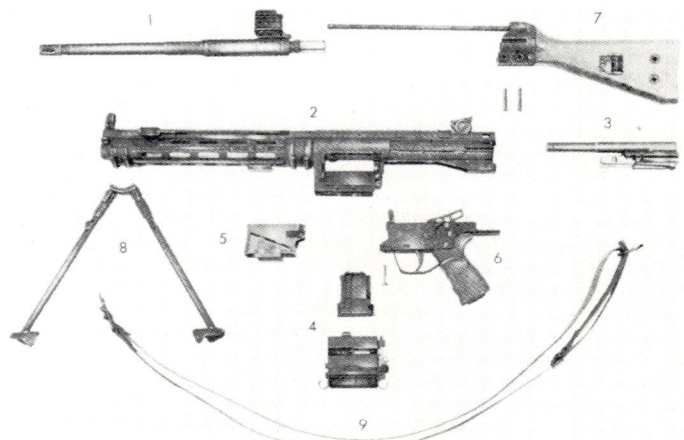

HK21 field stripped. Major assembly units: (1) Barrel; (2) Receiver, operating mechanism and sights; (3) Bolt; (4) Belt feed insertion unit; (5) Magazine attachment unit; (6) Grip assembly unit; (7) Back plate with buttstock; (8) Bipod; (9) Combat carrying sling

RE-ASSEMBLY

In general this follows the reverse order to stripping but the following points must be observed.
(1) When inserting the feed mechanism of the HK21 only that catch on the front left bottom corner must be depressed.
(2) Bolt head must be pushed forward from bolt body before inserting into body.

The HK21 can be stripped in 1 minute and re-assembled in 1½minutes.

DATA
Cartridge: 7.62 × 51mm or 5.56mm × 45 or 7.62mm × 39
Method of operation: Delayed blowback
Method of delay: Rollers
Method of feed: Belt
Method of fire: Automatic

WEIGHTS
Gun without bipod: 7.32kg
Gun for vehicle use: 7.11kg
Barrel: 1.70kg
Bipod: 0.6kg

LENGTHS
Gun with butt: 1,021mm
Gun without butt (for vehicle use): 820mm
Barrel: 450mm

MECHANICAL FEATURES
Barrel: Regulator: Nil
Rifling: 4 grooves RH. 1 turn in 305mm
Cooling: Air. Quick-change barrel
Sights: Foresight: Blade
Rearsight: Aperture drum. Clicks every 100 metres. Adjustable
for windage
Graduation: 200-1,200 metres by 100-metre increments
Zeroing: Line. Backsight moves across on screw.
Elevation. Adjust range drum with tool
Sight radius: 589mm

FIRING CHARACTERISTICS

	7.62mm × 51	5.56mm × 45	7.62mm × 39
Muzzle velocity:	800 metres/sec	973 metres/sec	750 metres/sec
Muzzle energy:	304mkp	171mkp	226mkp
Range, maximum			
effective:	1,200 metres	600 metres	800 metres
Rate of fire: Cyclic: 900 rounds/min			
Automatic: 200 rounds/min (2 barrels)			

Manufacturer: Heckler and Koch GmbH, Oberndorf, Neckar
Status: In production. In service with Portuguese Army

HK21 with magazine feed adaptor

7.62mm HECKLER AND KOCH HK 21A1 GPMG

This is the latest development in the HK21 series. The gun is shown
below and incorporates a fold-down feed mechanism which is shown in the
accompanying photograph in its lowered position. Also shown here is a
drawing and functional description of the Hinged Belt Feed Insertion Unit
(HBFIU) in its .223 version.

This new feed facility makes the task of loading the gun easier, makes it
simpler to remove a belt when required and, if a stoppage should occur,
makes rectification a lot quicker.

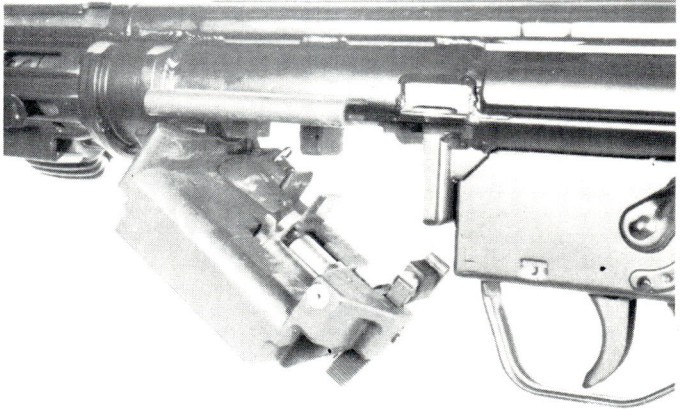

A close-up view of the HK21A1 fold-down feed mechanism

7.62mm HK21 A1

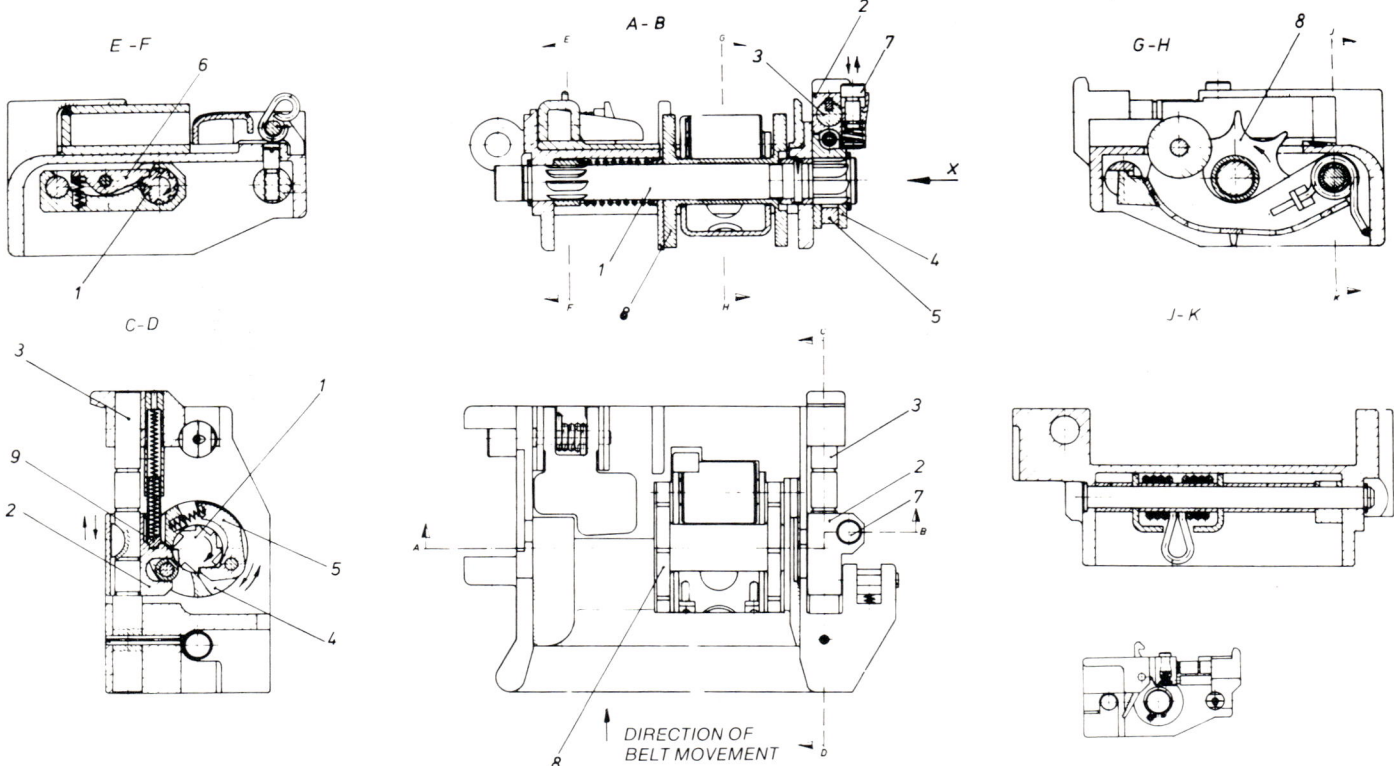

Hinged Belt Feed Insertion Unit (HBFIU)
(1) Control spindle; (2) Control slide; (3) Control slide spindle; (4) Control ring; (5) Ratchet; (6) Catch; (7) Control wheel; (8) Sprocket wheel; (9) Compression bolt.
Summary of the functioning sequence during firing:
1 The bolt head, in forward travel moves the control slide (2) and control wheel (7) to the right. This occurs as the control wheel follows the guideway in the bolt head carrier.
2 The control slide (2) turns the control ring (4) which rotates the control spindle and sprocket wheel in a clockwise direction.

3 Before the end of the belt movement, the catch (6) engages in the control spindle and prevents counter clockwise movement of both the control spindle and belt.
4 In rearward travel, the bolt, through the action of the guideway in the bolt head carrier, moves the control slide (2) left, and guides it by means of the compression bolt and spring (9) into its starting position. At the same time the control slide (2) of the control ring (4) moves without resistance the ratchet (5), one notch of the control spindle, which it engages just before the end of control slide travel.
5 The control slide (2) is now in position to perform the next loading sequence.

MOUNTINGS FOR THE HK 21 GPMG

In the light role the bipod can be mounted directly in front of the feed system or at the front of the barrel casing.

TRIPOD MOUNT 1100

For the sustained fire ground role the tripod mount 1100 is used. This is a spring buffered tripod which can be folded and carried into action on the shoulders of one man. When set up its height (measured as bore centre line above ground) can be adjusted between 750mm and 350mm. This allows fire over low cover and where no cover is available the gun is sufficiently low to present a small target and also prevent any overturning moment. The rear legs of the tripod can be folded to allow use in a small weapon pit.

There is a traversing arc between the two rear legs which allows an arc of

43 degrees. The rear attachment of the gun to the arc is by the elevating column which permits an elevation of 14 degrees. If required the elevating column can rapidly be disconnected to allow a 360 degrees traverse of the gun.

Attached to the elevating column housing is a dial sight with a periscopic optical viewing eye piece allowing the gunner to operate the weapon without unduly exposing himself. The sight can be levelled by spirit level and, by reference to an aiming mark, it can be used to engage targets, the

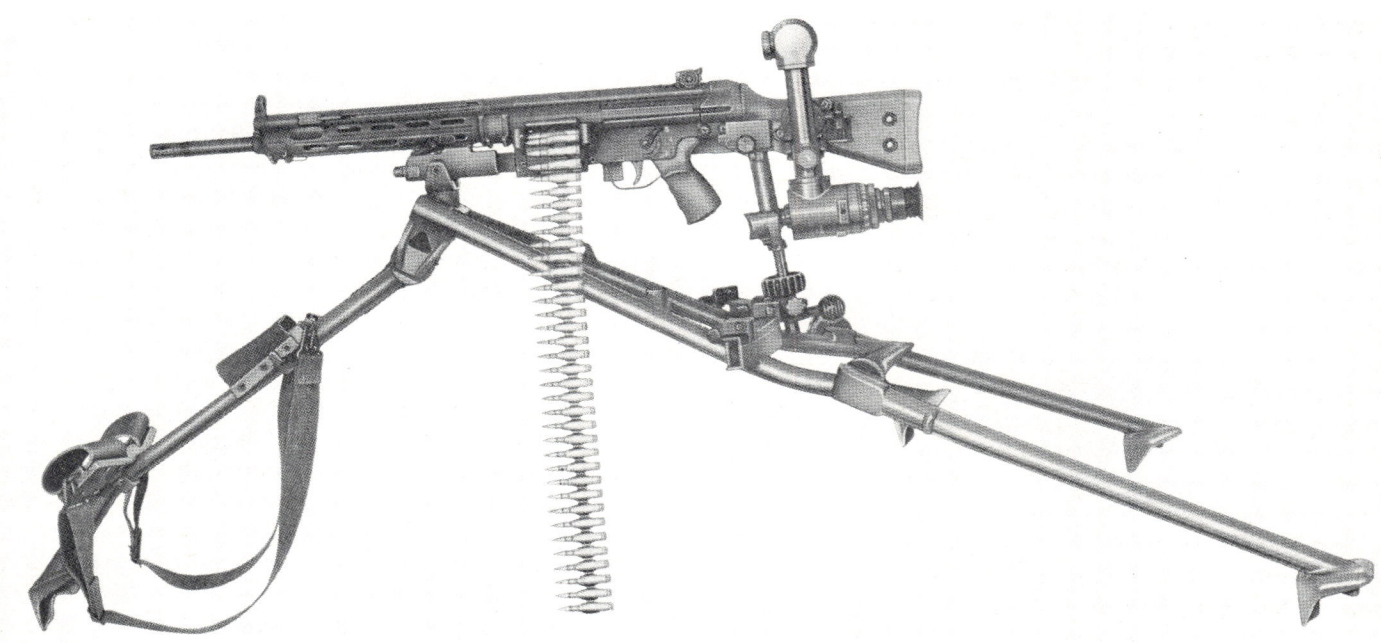

Tripod mount

bearing and elevation of which have been previously recorded after ranging.

The sight also allows the gunner to produce traversing fire between set stops on the traversing arc, and searching fire.

DATA
Dimensions, folded:

Length: 770mm
Width: 570mm
Height: 230mm
Weight: 9.2kg
Max traverse: 43°
Max elevation: 14°

COLUMN MOUNT 2400

This mount is basically intended for use on a light vehicle. It is a spring balanced system and with the butt of the weapon replaced by a receiver end cap, the weapon can be traversed rapidly and elevated up to 75 degrees or depressed to –15 degrees. The amount of traverse varies with the type of vehicle and the restrictions imposed by vehicle design, but with an open vehicle such as the jeep or Land Rover, the gun can get 90 degrees of fire on either side whilst the vehicle is moving. If the vehicle is stationary and the firer can leave his seat, the mount allows complete 360 degree traverse.

The same mounting can be used for a static anti-aircraft defence system.

Ground target fire with the column mount

AA fire with the column mount

ANTI-AIRCRAFT/GROUND MOUNT 2700

This system is designed for use with armoured vehicles providing a top hatch. The weapon can be rotated rapidly through 360 degrees and from –10 degrees up to 75 degrees. At any point it can be locked in position for the engagement of ground targets.

The gun is used without the buttstock and is so mounted that no turning moments are produced when firing.

The anti-aircraft/ground mount 2,700

CIRCULAR TRACK MOUNT

This mount is designed to go onto unarmoured vehicles of load carrying types. It can be fitted above the passenger seat in the cab of a lorry and allows the gun to deal with either ground or aerial targets.

The circular track rotates throughout 360 degrees and allows rapid traverse. When it is locked in position the gun has a traverse of some 180 degrees and can be elevated from –15 degrees to +75 degrees. The buttstock is removed and the rear of the gun is supported in prolongation of the barrel axis. Thus there is no turning moment when the gun is firing. The 100-round belt is located in a box below the gun. To use the HK21 in a dismounted role, the gun can be disengaged from the mounting, the buttstock fitted and the bipod positioned, in a very short while.

The circular track mount. Ground target fire

DATA
Weight of the circular track mount: 33.5kg
Outside diameter: 762mm
Inside diameter: 647mm
Diameter of hole: 725mm
Height of mount above roof: 310mm
Height with gun fitted: 325mm

These mounts are also available with cradles for other MGs.

AA fire

7.62mm HECKLER AND KOCH HK11 LIGHT MACHINE GUN

The HK11 is a light machine gun using the 7.62mm × 51 NATO cartridge.

It operates on the delayed blowback system using the roller delay system common to many of the Heckler and Koch weapons. It is in many respects similar to the G3 Rifle and a number of the parts are interchangeable. The barrel can readily be changed and this adds considerably to the ability to produce sustained fire.

The HK11 can be fed from an 80-round double drum magazine or from a 20-round magazine of conventional form. The bipod can be located at the front of the receiver casing or directly in front of the magazine.

DATA
Cartridge: 7.62mm × 51
Method of operation: Delayed blowback
Method of feed: Magazine – 80-round dual drum or 20-round box
Method of fire: Selective

Weight without bipod: 6.2kg
Barrel: 1.7kg
Bipod weight: 600g
Length: 1,020mm
Barrel length: 450mm
Sights: Foresight: Blade
       Rearsight: Aperture
       Setting: 200-1,200 metres. Click adjustment per 100 metres
Muzzle velocity: 800 metres/sec
Muzzle energy: 300mkp
Rate of fire: 850 rounds/min
Range, maximum effective: 800 metres

Manufacturer: Heckler and Koch, Oberndorf, Neckar
Status: In production and in service in Africa and South America

The 7.62mm × 51 HK11

5.56mm HECKLER AND KOCH HK13 LIGHT MACHINE GUN

The HK13 is a light machine gun using the 5.56mm × 45 cartridge and therefore falls into the Heckler and Koch Group II list of weapons.

It is largely the same as the G3 rifle (qv) and operates in exactly the same way. Its physical dimensions are very much the same but it has the heavier quick-change barrel necessary for its light machine gun role.

The HK13 will take the 20-, 30- and 40-round magazines used in the HK33 rifle and will also take the plastic double drum magazine holding 100 rounds.

A bipod may be fitted either at the front of the barrel casing or at a centre point just in front of the magazine.

The LMG will produce selective fire. The change lever is located above the pistol grip on the left of the receiver. The trigger and firing mechanism functions in the same way as that of the G3 rifle.

The HK13 strips in the same manner as the G3.

DATA
Cartridge: 5.56mm × 45
Method of operation: Delayed blowback
Method of delay: Rollers
Method of feed: 20-, 30- and 40-round box magazines; 100-round double drum magazine
Method of fire: Selective

HK13 field stripped

5.56mm HK13 LMG with a double drum magazine. The bipod is mounted forward

WEIGHTS
Gun, without bipod or magazine: 5.4kg
Bipod: 0.6kg
Barrel: 1.7kg
20-round box magazine, empty: 110g
30-round box magazine, empty: 140g
40-round box magazine, empty: 160g
100-round double drum, empty: 1.35kg
Cartridge: 11g

LENGTHS
Weapon: 980mm
Barrel: 450mm

MECHANICAL FEATURES
Barrel: Regulator: Nil
    Rifling: 4 grooves RH. 1 turn in 305mm
    Cooling: Air. Quick change barrel
Sights: Foresight: Blade

Rearsight: 100 metre V backsight. Apertures for 200, 300 or 400 metres. Adjustable for windage
Zeroing: Elevation. Adjust sight drum
Line. Back sight moves across
Sight radius: 541mm

Note: A telescopic sight can be fitted.

FIRING CHARACTERISTICS
Muzzle velocity: 950 metres/sec
Muzzle energy: 162mkp
Chamber pressure: 3,620kg/cm²
Rate of fire: Cyclic: 750 rounds/min
      Automatic: 100 rounds/min
      SS: 60 rounds/min
Range, maximum effective: 400 metres

Manufacturer: Heckler and Koch, Oberndorf, Neckar
Status: In production and in service in South-East Asia

HK13 with box magazine and telescopic sight

7.62mm MG1, 2 & 3 MACHINE GUNS

The German Army went into World War II in 1939 with the MG34 as its principal ground machine gun both in the infantry squad and in armoured vehicles. It was a slow and expensive gun to produce with forgings machined to close tolerances, and it had long been evident that a successor would be needed. Prototypes of a new gun – which subsequently became the highly successful MG42 – were made in 1938 with the maximum use of stampings and the very minimum of forgings. Efforts were made to reduce the use of alloy steels as much as possible. The only component using nickel or chrome alloy steel was the extractor. It is said that Dr Peter, who was in charge of the project, interested Dr Gruner, of the Johannes Grossfuss firm, in the possibilities of stamping a machine gun body. Dr Gruner who knew a lot about stamping and deep drawing steel containers but rather less about machine guns, spent three weeks with the Army studying the MG34 and other weapons and then returned to his firm at Dobeln in Saxony. He came to Berlin quite soon with a roughed out pressing, and this led to a programme of development culminating in a fully pressed receiver.

The method chosen to lock the bolt head to the barrel was unique. The idea of using line contact for force transmission had been discussed before but no practical experience was available. The details of who actually designed the locking system are a matter for debate. It is believed that Louis Stange of Rheinmetall-Borsig – designer of the MG34 – was responsible for the MG42 locking system; although Lt Col G.M. Chinn in 'The Machine Gun' has ascribed it to Edward Stecke of Warsaw whose patent was registered in the USA in 1937. This patent, however, covered a lever-operated delayed-blowback system whereas in the MG42 the initial recoil motion occurs with the breech locked. The characteristic sound of the MG42 – like tearing linen – was first heard in action in May-June 1942 when Rommel's Panzer Grenadiers engaged the British 8th Army positions at Gazala in the Western Desert. From then until the end of the War it was met on every battle front where the German Army was in action. It achieved a great reputation – so much so that an American copy, the .30 T24, was made by the Saginaw Steering Gear Division of General Motors from captured models and tested in October 1943-February 1944. This was not a successful venture due to incorrect dimensioning.

When the German forces came into NATO they decided to modify the MG42 design from 7.92mm calibre to 7.62mm × 51 and adopt it as their standard General Purpose Machine Gun. It was manufactured by Rheinmetall in 1959 and called by them the MG42/59. The Bundeswehr called it the MG1. The earliest MG1 fired the 7.92mm × 57: the MG1A1 was

MG42 on its tripod. This tripod can be made to search automatically, operated by the recoil of the gun

chambered for the 7.62mm × 51 contained in a continuous belt and the barrel was chrome plated. The MG1A2 could be fed from the German 50 round continuous belt known as the DM1 or the US M13 disintegrating link belt: the MG1A3 had some small changes intended to speed production including the rounded muzzle booster and will only fire the continuous belt.

In parallel with this development process, some of the original MG42 weapons were converted from 7.92 to 7.62 calibre and were redesignated MG2. The current weapon, however, is a further development known as the MG3 which came into service in 1968; it has the external shape of the MG1A3 and can be fed from the German DM1 continuous belt or either the German DM6 or the US disintegrating link belts. It has an AA sight and a belt retaining pawl to hold the belt up to the gun when the top cover plate is lifted.

The original MG42 was used by the French Army for several years until the AA52 came into service. The Yugoslav Army uses a gun called the SARAC M1953, which fires the German 7.92mm × 57 wartime cartridge, and is still manufactured in Yugoslavia. The MG42/59 is used by Austria, Denmark, Spain (where it is made under licence at Oviedo), Chile, Turkey, Iran and Pakistan (where it is manufactured as the MG1A3). It is manufactured in Germany for the Bundeswehr. In Italy it is manufactured by a consortium of Beretta, Luigi Franchi, and Whitehead Moto Fides. Beretta makes the bolts, Franchi the barrels and Whitehead the trigger mechanisms. The guns are assembled at Beretta in Rome and at Whitehead's.

FUNCTIONING OF THE MG3

The disintegrating link belt of the US M13 or the German DM6 type can be used in the MG1A2 or the MG3. It is factory filled and is not intended to be refilled after use. The continuous belts of the German DM1 type which are the only type used in the SARAC M53, the MG42, MG1 and MG1A3, and can also be used in the MG1A2 and MG3, can be refilled after use. To load these belts, cartridges are placed in each semi-circular link with the nib on the belt fitting into the extraction groove of the cartridge. The belts can be joined by using the last cartridge in one belt as a hinge pin to join the last link of that belt to the first link of the next belt.

The earliest MG42s had a straight cocking handle. The great majority of MG42s and all subsequent guns have a T-shaped cocking handle. The cross bar of this T is grasped and rotated back. The shaft is used as a lever to unlock the bolt from the barrel. The cocking handle is then pulled straight back and the bolt cocked. When the bolt is to the rear – and only then – the safety catch above the pistol grip can be pushed through to the left to lock the sear.

The ammunition must be placed in the gun with the open side of the links downward so that the belt is above the cartridges. If it is put in with the link down, an immediate stoppage will result. If a feed tab is fitted this can be pushed straight through the gun. If not, the top cover plate must be lifted and the belt laid across the feed tray, cartridges downwards. When the rear of the cover plate is pressed down, the gun is ready for action. Pushing the safety catch from left to right with the side of the right thumb puts the gun in the 'ready to fire' position. The driving spring is compressed. The ammunition is held in the belt passing through the gun from left to right. When the trigger is pressed, the sear, which engages the bent of the bolt, is lowered and the bolt goes forward, forcing a round out of the belt into the chamber.

The locking system of the gun is its most interesting and original feature. The bolt head has an undercut slot on each side extending forward and inwards. In each of the undercuts rests a locking roller. The rollers are shaped like the wheel on a wheel barrow, i.e, a shaft and roller in one piece. As the bolt goes forward, the striker sleeve, impelled by the return spring,

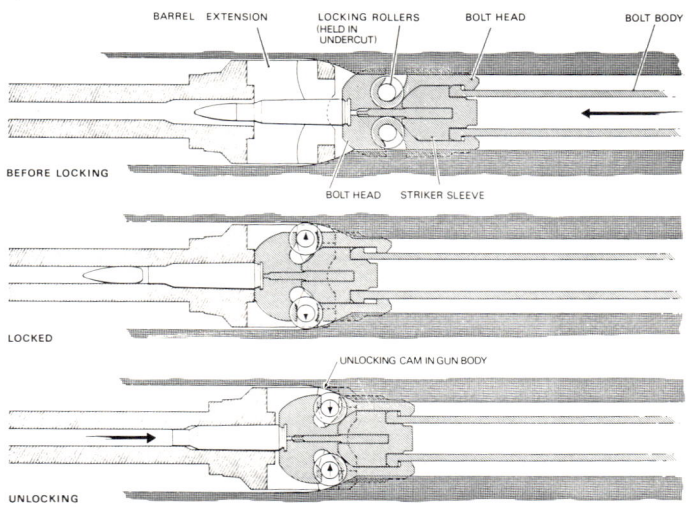

BARREL EXTENSION   LOCKING ROLLERS (HELD IN UNDERCUT)   BOLT HEAD   BOLT BODY

BEFORE LOCKING

BOLT HEAD   STRIKER SLEEVE

LOCKED

UNLOCKING CAM IN GUN BODY

UNLOCKING

The locking and unlocking process (RMCS)

The MG42 lock in the locked position

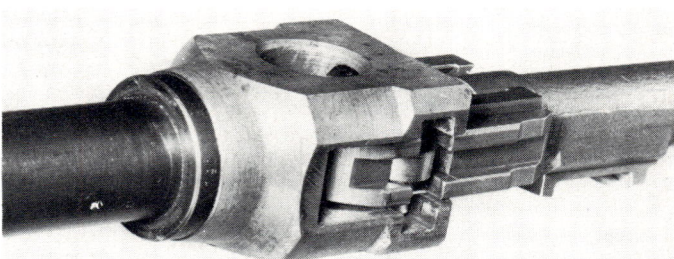

The MG42 lock at the moment of unlocking

forces the rollers forward into the undercut in the slots and completely clear of the receiver. There is therefore no contact between the rollers and the receiver, and no friction. The bolt head enters the barrel extension and the rollers enter cammed slots which drive them back out of the undercut and

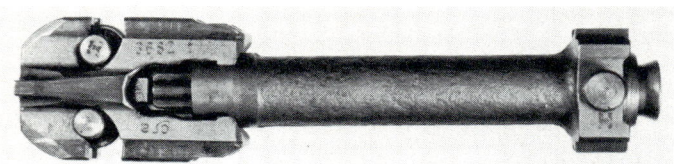

MG42 bolt (RMCS)

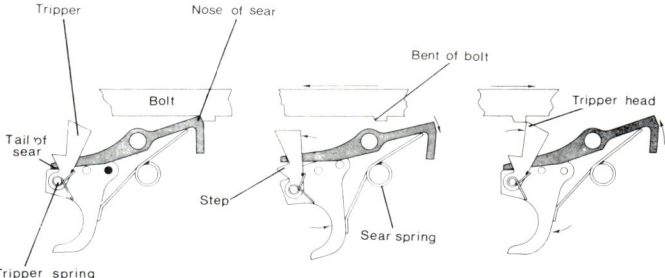

Trigger mechanism

then outwards. The outward motion is accelerated by the angled face of the striker sleeve which is driven forward by the full force of the return spring. The rollers move out not only along the cam grooves in the barrel extension but also along their grooves in the bolt head and so the barrel extension and bolt head are firmly locked together. As soon as the rollers are fully out the striker sleeve, carrying the striker, drives forward between them and the cap is struck.

The gas pressure developed in the chamber forces the breech face back but as the bolt head is locked to the barrel, which is free to move, the barrel is pulled back with it. Gas pressure produced in a muzzle booster, or recoil intensifier, gives further energy to the barrel.

The muzzle booster is a device first used on the British Vickers Gun in 1911. An expansion chamber is formed beyond the muzzle and this is momentarily made a closed vessel as the bullet seals off the exit. The gas pressure rises rapidly to about 620kg/cm² and the pressure is applied to the barrel face. The barrel is accelerated rearwards and since the barrel is locked to the bolt, the bolt velocity is also increased.

The shafts of the rollers hold the bolt head to the barrel extension during firing and during the subsequent 8mm of free recoil. The rollers then contact cam paths in the non recoiling receiver and the rollers are forced inwards along the cam paths in the barrel extension and the bolt head; the striker sleeve is forced back and the bolt is accelerated away from the barrel.

This acceleration of the bolt is an essential feature of all short recoil operated machine guns of rifle calibre to impart sufficient energy to the bolt to carry out the cycle of operations. In the MG3 it is accomplished during the process of unlocking the bolt from the barrel. The roller shafts travel in both the barrel extension and the bolt head and complete their travel in both components in the same time. However the length of their two paths is not the same and since the distance along the path in the barrel extension is greater than that in the bolt head, the bolt head must travel faster than the barrel and so is accelerated relative to it.

As the bolt is freed from the barrel extension, after a total travel of 21mm, the barrel return spring drives the barrel forward to its run out position and the empty case in the chamber is held by the extractor on the bolt face as the bolt continues rearwards. The ejector is a two piece rod. The rear portion strikes the buffer spring and the front portion is forced out of the top of the breech face to pivot the case about the extractor and out of the bottom of the gun. The buffer spring is very powerful and having a coefficient of restitution of nearly unity returns the bolt to the forward position at a high velocity.

The belt movement is produced by a stud on top of the bolt riding in a curved feed channel in a feed arm. This feed arm rests under the top cover plate and is pivoted at its rear end. As the bolt reciprocates, the front of the feed arm moves across the receiver and operates a lever attached to the belt feed slide. This slide has two sets of spring loaded pawls mounted one on each side of the centrally postioned slide pivot. Thus when one set of pawls is moving out and springing over the rounds in the belt, the other set is pulling the belt in. Each set of pawls in turn moves the belt across one half pitch. This sharing of the load reduces the forces on the belt and the feed mechanism. It produces a smooth belt flow rather than a series of jerky belt movements.

TRIGGER AND FIRING MECHANISM

Due to the high rate of fire the bolt velocity is very considerable and the connection of the trigger sear and bent of the bolt must take place with a full face engagement. If the sear is only partly up when the bent hits it, there will be chipping of the mating surfaces. To prevent this the mechanism incorporates a controlled sear which rises at a predetermined point relative to the position of the bolt to ensure full area contact of the two parts.

The arrangement of the sear is shown in the diagram. The trigger carries a light, pressed-steel tripper which has its own spring forcing it forward. The tail of the sear passes through the tripper and a T-bar on its end limits the forward rotation of the tripper. The front face of the tripper has a step projecting forward. When the firer pulls the trigger, the trigger rotates and the tail of the sear is pushed up and the other end of the sear – the nose – pivots down and disengages from the bent of the bolt. The bolt is driven forward by the double wound return spring. The spring of the tripper rotates it forward and the step rides under the T-bar of the raised tail of the sear. When the firer releases the trigger the tail of the sear can only fall as far as the step on the tripper and it comes to rest on the step. The nose of the sear therefore cannot rise to intercept the bolt. The rotation of the trigger pushes the tripper – which is attached to it – up into the path of the bolt which rides over it on the forward stroke and fires another round. On the recoil stroke the bolt hits the tripper head and rotates it back. This moves the step from

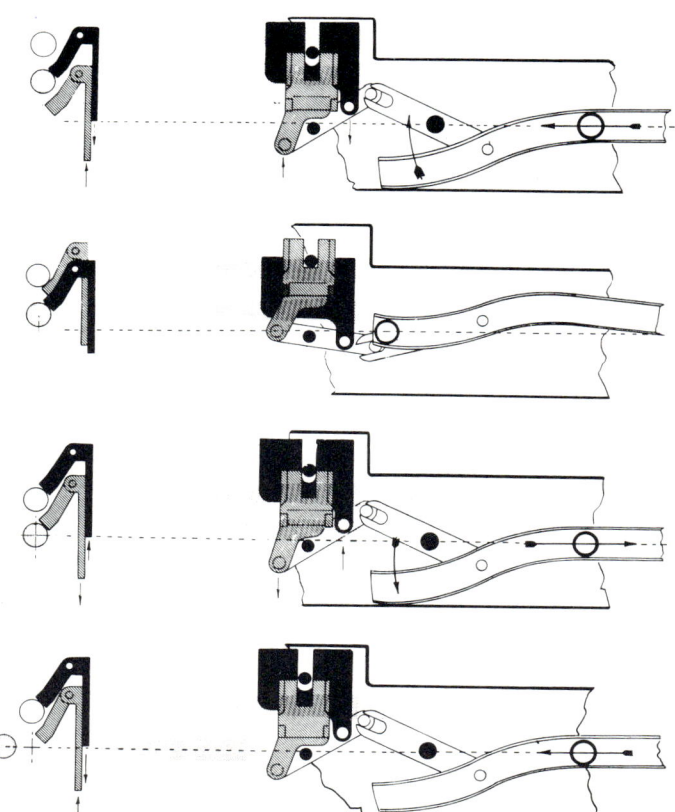

The reciprocating motion of the bolt pulls the belt across the gun (RMCS)

under the tail of the sear which then falls and the nose of the sear rides up into the path of the bolt. The bolt rides over it as it moves back and continues back on its over-run. By the time the bolt comes forward again the nose of the sear has risen fully and presents its full frontal area to the bent. By this means the damage caused by high velocity contact and inadequate surface areas, is avoided.

RATE OF FIRE

The gun in its original form as the MG42 fired at about 1,200 rounds a minute.

The standard bolt used in the MG1A1, MG1A3 and the MG3 weighs 550g and produces this rate of fire. The MG1A2 uses a heavy bolt weighing 950g and this produces rates of fire of about 900 rounds a minute. The German Army uses the lighter bolt but the Italian MG42/59 uses the heavier bolt. If another rate of fire were required this could be obtained by changing the bolt, buffer spring or muzzle booster appropriately.

SIGHTS

The foresight is mounted on the front end of the barrel casing and hinges flat. The rearsight is a U notch that is mounted on a slide moving on a ramp. Graduation is from 200 to 1,200m on the MG3. (The MG-42 was from 200 to 2,000m.) Since the foresight is not on the barrel zeroing must be carried out on the rearsight.

BARREL CHANGE

The barrel must be changed at frequent intervals. Firing in short bursts at a rate of about 200-250 rounds a minute, the barrel should be changed after

MG42/59 (RMCS)

150 rounds, ie three 50-round lengths. The barrel change is very quick and simple. The gun is cocked, and the barrel catch on the right of the barrel casing is swung forward. The breech end of the hot barrel swings out and can be removed by elevating the gun. A cool barrel is pushed through the barrel catch and the muzzle bearing. When the catch is rotated back the barrel is locked.

STRIPPING

The process of stripping is uncomplicated. The bolt is retracted, the chamber checked and the bolt returned to the forward position. A catch below the receiver allows a 90 degrees rotation of the butt and buffer spring out of the receiver. The large T-shaped cocking handle on the right of the receiver will withdraw the bolt and the return spring. The barrel catch moves outwards on the right of the breech to permit withdrawal of the barrel. The bolt can be further broken down by holding the bolt head stationary with the rollers fully out and then rotating the bolt body through 90 degrees. The bolt body and head can be separated and the ejector and spring loaded insert removed.

The rearsight of the MG3. Note the bold figures and compare with the US M60 GPMG (RMCS)

ACCESSORIES

A buffered tripod to allow sustained fire is available. A dial sight allowing engagement of unseen targets and recording of previously registered targets can be fitted to the tripod. A blank firing attachment can be fitted in lieu of the normal recoil booster at the muzzle.

DATA
Cartridge: 7.62mm × 51
Method of operation: Short recoil
Method of locking: Roller locking
Method of feed: Belt
Method of fire: Automatic

WEIGHTS
MG3 without bipod: 10.5kg
Bipod: 550g
Barrel: 1.8kg

LENGTHS
MG3 overall without butt: 1,097mm
MG3 overall with butt: 1,225mm
Barrel with extension: 565mm
Barrel without extension: 531mm
Length of shot travel: 475mm

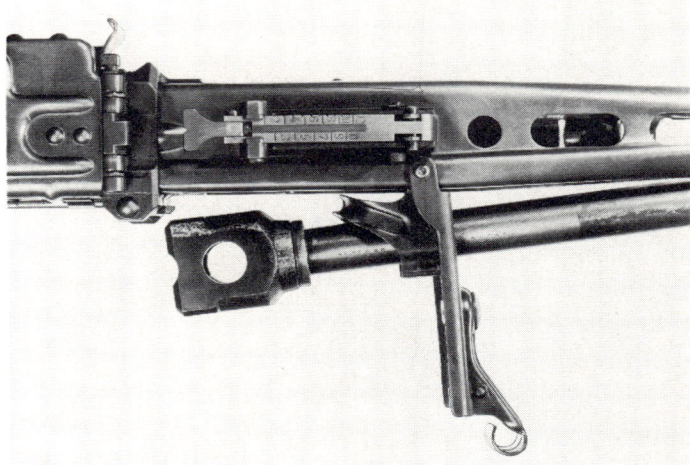

Barrel change (RMCS)

MG3. Note shape of muzzle booster

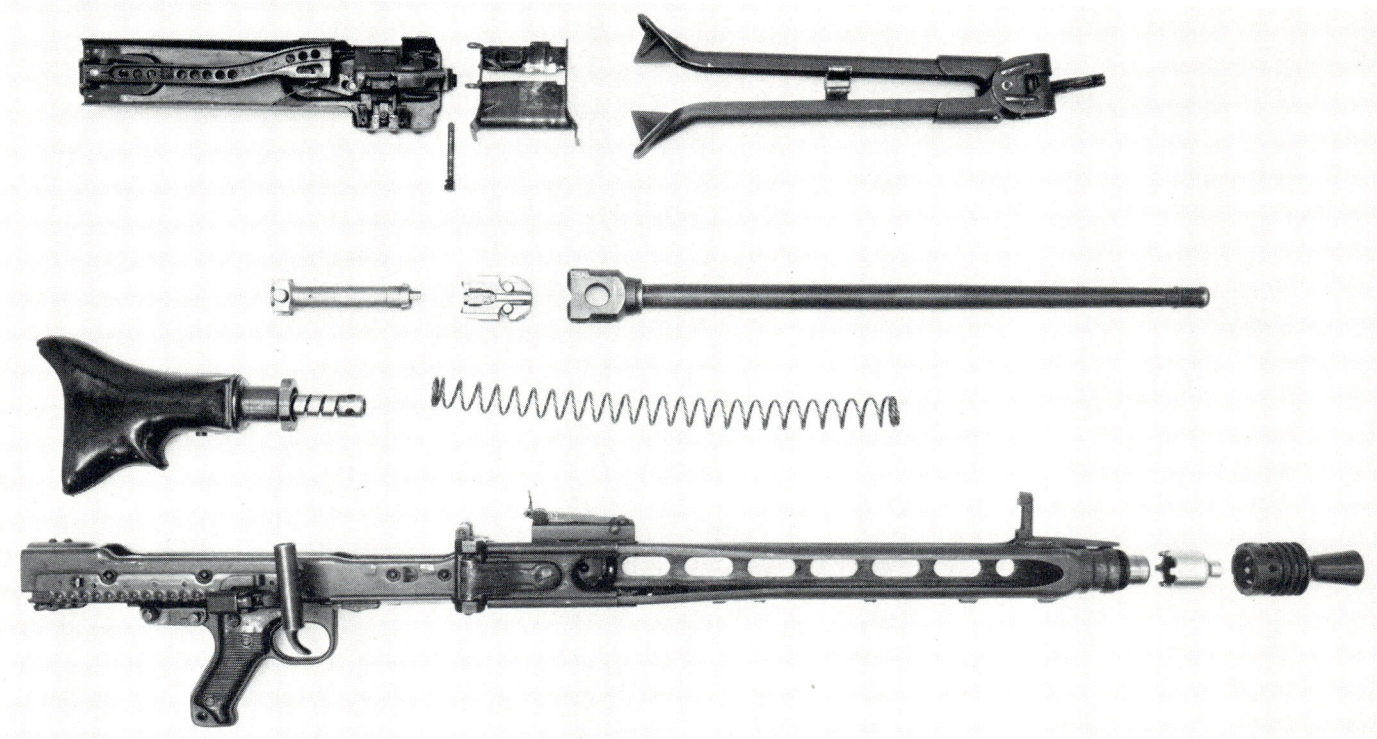

MG42/59 stripped (RMCS)

MECHANICAL FEATURES
Barrel: Regulator: Nil
            Rifling: Polygonal rifling (Barrels by Heckler and Koch, GMBH)
            Cooling: Air. Quick change barrel
Sights: Foresight: Barleycorn
            Rearsight: Notch
            Zeroing: Elevation. Change foresight
            Line: Foresight on dovetail
            AA sight: Folds flat when not in use
            Sight radius: 430mm

FIRING CHARACTERISTICS
Muzzle velocity: 820 metres/sec

Muzzle energy: 300mkp
Chamber pressure: 3,300kg/cm^2
Rate of fire: Cyclic: 700-1,300 rounds/min
            Automatic: 250 rounds/min
Range, maximum effective: Bipod 800 metres, Tripod 220 metres

Manufacturer: Rheinmetall, Dusseldorf
Status: In production in Germany. Also produced in Italy by Beretta, Luigi Franchi and Whitehead Moto-Fides, and in Spain, Portugal and Pakistan. Also in service with the forces of Austria, Denmark, Chile, Turkey, Iran, Norway and the Sudan. MG42 produced in Yugoslavia as SARAC M1953 M1963

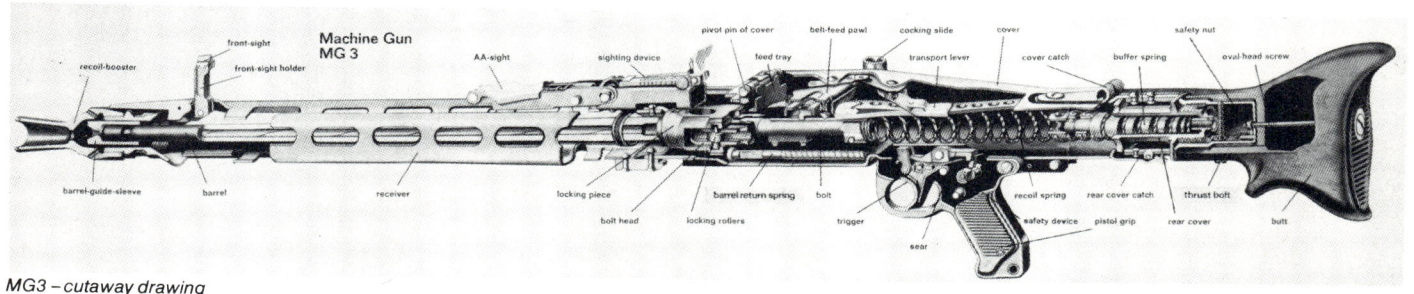

MG3 – cutaway drawing

GERMANY (DEMOCRATIC REPUBLIC)

7.62mm LMG K

This is the East German version of the Russian RPK LMG. It is identical to the Russian gun and all details will be found in the entry on Soviet weapons.

Similarly, the East Germans use the PK as their General Purpose Machine Gun and tank gun, and details will be found in the section on Soviet arms.

ITALY

7.62mm 42/59 MG

This is the standard Italian General Purpose machine gun and is manufactured under license from Rheinmetall.

Data are given in the section on German weapons.

Manufacturers: Pietro Beretta SpA, Brescia, Luigi Franchi SpA, Brescia, Whitehead Moto-Fides, SpA, Livorno
Status: In production and in service

5.56mm BERETTA AR70 LMG

This is the LMG version of the AR70 Rifle. In method of operation it is identical to the rifle and details of the weight etc., are given in the section on Italian rifles.

Manufacturer: Pietro Beretta, SpA, Gardone-val-Trompia, Brescia

AR70 LMG with bipod, carrying handle, heavier barrel and rigid stock Weight 8lb 15oz

JAPAN

6.5mm TYPE 96 LMG

In 1936 Nambu introduced the Type 96 LMG to replace the Taisho 11. The hopper was replaced by a 30-round box magazine, the gun had a quick change barrel and the 6.5mm cartridge was oiled not, as before, on the gun but by an oiler built into the magazine loader. The gun was frequently fitted with a 2½ × telescope mounted on the top left side of the receiver and had a bayonet as an accessory. The Type 96 never replaced the Taisho 11 but the two LMGs were both used.

DATA
Cartridge: 6.5mm Arisaka rifle (Type 38)
Method of operation: Gas
Method of locking: Rising block
Method of feed: 30-round box magazine
Method of fire: Automatic
Weight: 9.1kg

Length: 1,054mm
Barrel: 551mm
    Rifling: 4 grooves RH
    Cooling: Air. Quick change barrel
Sights: Foresight: Barleycorn
    Rearsight: Tangent. Aperture
    Telescopic: 2.5X
Muzzle velocity: 732 metres/sec
Muzzle energy: 353mkp
Rate of fire: Cyclic: 550 rounds/min
        Automatic: 120 rounds/min
Range, maximum effective: 500 metres
Manufacturer: Shin Chuo Kogyo Co. Ltd., 4-18-18 Omori-nishi, Ohta-ku, Tokyo 143
Status: No longer manufactured. Still in use with North Korean militia

The Japanese Model 96 6.5mm (RMCS)

7.7mm TYPE 99 LMG

The introduction of the 7.7mm rimless round precipitated a hasty search for a LMG to fire it. A number of current weapons were modified and lightened and eventually it was decided to modify the Type 96. The Type 99 had a flash hider, a rear monopod support adjustable for elevation (both of which features distinguish it from the Type 96) and, most important of all, the quick-change barrel had a genuine headspace adjuster which, with an adequate primary extraction, allowed the use of unlubricated ammunition for the first time. There was also a long bayonet fitted to the front of the gas cylinder.

The resulting gun was much nearer to the European and American concept of a LMG and had it been developed earlier than 1942 it would have been very effective.

An easily disassembled version was made by Nagoya Arsenal for parachutists. It broke into its component groups and could be put together with great speed.

Many of these weapons were left in the countries which the Japanese had occupied during the war. Some were subsequently converted to 7.9mm calibre by the Chinese.

DATA
Cartridge: 7.7 rimless Type 99 or 7.92mm (see text)

Method of operation: Gas
Method of locking: Rising lock
Method of feed: 30-round detachable box magazine
Method of fire: Automatic
Weight: 10.5kg
Length: 1,187mm
Barrel: 546mm
    Rifling: 4 grooves RH
Sights: Foresight: Barleycorn
    Rearsight: Tangent. Aperture
Muzzle velocity: 731 metres/sec
Muzzle energy: 246mkp
Rate of fire: Cyclic: 850 rounds/min
Range, maximum effective: 600 metres

Manufacturer: Shin Chuo Kogyo Co. Ltd., 4-18-18 Omori-nishi, Ohta-ku, Tokyo 143

Status: No longer manufactured. Still used by North Korean militia and may be encountered in any country occupied by the Japanese during the Second World War

The Type 99 7.7mm LMG (RSAF)

7.62mm MACHINE GUN MODEL 62

This gun started as the model 9M and was accepted into service with the Japanese Self-Defence Force in 1962.

The gas cylinder and piston are below the barrel. The locking system is very unusual in that it is a tilting block with the front of the bolt forced up by cams on the piston extension (slide) to lock. Two wings level with the centre line move into recesses in the receiver and the bolt is held in position by the piston extension under it. The final movement of the piston, after locking is completed, carries the firing pin, fixed to the piston post, through the block, into the cartridge cap. Until the front of the block has risen there is no hole for the firing pin.

After the round has fired, some of the propellant gas passes through the gas port and drives the piston to the rear. The firing pin is withdrawn and the front of the bolt is first cammed down and then pulled back.

The extraction is unusual. There is no spring-loaded extractor hook but whilst the round is in the chamber, before firing, there is a spring-loaded plunger forced up into the cannelure from below. When the front end of the

bolt is carried down, a fixed hook on the bolt face above the firing pin hole, drops down and grips the cannelure of the cartridge head. When the bolt starts back the case is withdrawn. There appears to be no primary extraction.

The feed system uses a bolt-operated feed arm which oscillates as the bolt reciprocates and the belt is drawn across in two stages corresponding to the extraction and feed strokes.

The barrel retaining catch is depressed by lifting the top cover plate. The carrying handle is rotated and then the barrel can be pushed forward. Whilst the top cover plate is lifted it prevents the front of the bolt from rising into the locked position and so the firing pin hole is blocked. This prevents the feed and firing of a round when this is unlocked or there is no barrel in position.

The Model 62 is a somewhat complex gun but has a reputation for reliability and accuracy.

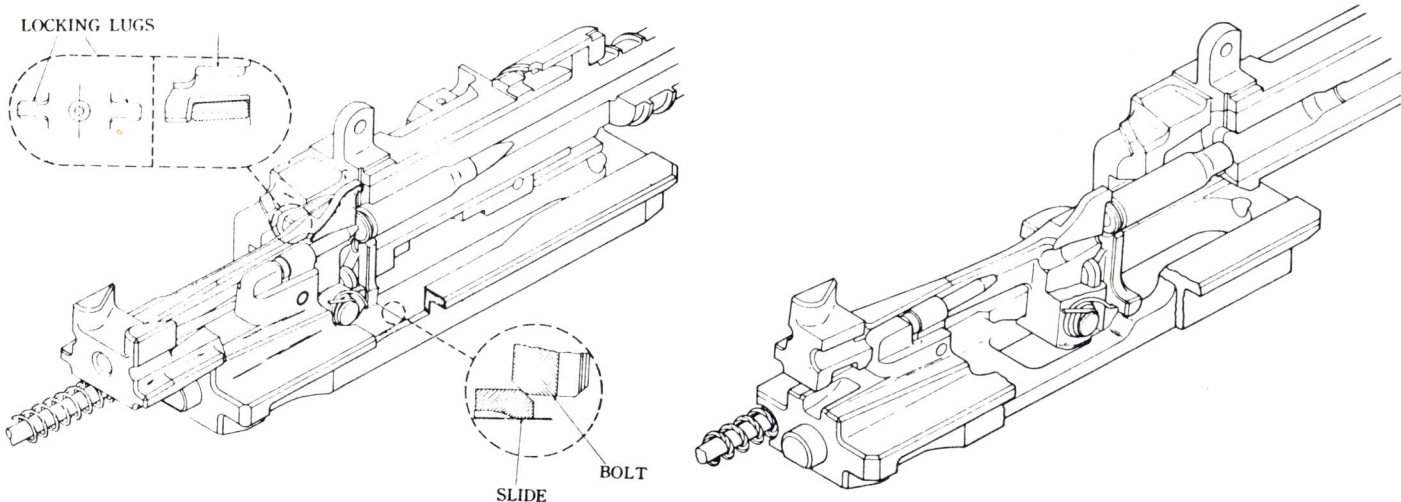

Locking mechanism

Assured extracting

DATA
Cartridge: 7.62mm × 51
Method of operation: Gas
Method of locking: Front tilting block
Method of feed: Disintegrating link belt
Method of fire: Automatic
Weight: 10.7kg
Barrel weight: 2.0kg
Length: 1,200mm
Barrel: 635mm
     Rifling: 4 grooves RH. 1 turn in 254mm

Cooling: Air. Quick change barrel
Sights: Foresight: Blade
     Rearsight: Leaf Aperture
     Sight radius: 590mm
     Telescopic sight: Cranked
Muzzle velocity: 855 metres/sec
Muzzle energy: 346mkp
Rate of fire: Cyclic: 550 rounds/min
Range, maximum effective: Bipod 600 metres; Tripod 1,100 metres
Manufacturer: Nittoku Metal Industry Co Ltd.
Status: In production. In service

The 7.62mm M62 GPMG

MEXICO

.30in RM2 LIGHT MACHINE GUN

This is a very light LMG, designed and built in Mexico by Productos Mendoza, and is an improved version of an earlier weapon known as the Model 45. The RM2 is currently in service with Mexican forces.

A simple gas-operated weapon, the RM2 has a top-mounted detachable box magazine, a permanently-attached bipod and a muzzle brake. The action provides a selective fire option; but it should be noted that the barrel cannot be changed so that the weapon's capacity for sustained automatic fire is limited. The firing pin can be reversed in case of breakage; and access to the working parts, for this or any other reason, is obtained by hingeing the butt and trigger mechanism down: all the working parts may then be drawn to the rear in much the same way as they can on the Type D BAR. The action is locked by a turning bolt.

DATA
Cartridge: .30-06in

Method of operation: Gas
Method of locking: Rotating bolt
Method of feed: 20-round detachable box magazine
Method of fire: Selective
Weight: 6.4kg
Length: 1100mm
Barrel: 610mm. No barrel change
Sights: Foresight: Hooded barleycorn
     Rearsight: Aperture
Rate of fire: 600 rounds/min cyclic (see text)
Effective range: 800m

Manufacturer: Productos Mendoza SA. Bartolache 14, Mexico City
Status: In service with Mexican forces

SWITZERLAND

7.5mm M25 LIGHT MACHINE GUN

This is an elderly recoil-operated weapon which is still in limited service in the Swiss Army. Compared with the post-war MG42-derived M51 weapon described below it has a very slow rate of fire, but it has the merit of being somewhat lighter and thus better-suited to the needs of the foot-soldier.

DATA
Cartridge: 7.5mm M11
Method of operation: Recoil

Method of feed: 30-round detachable box magazine
Weight: 10.8kg with bipod
Length: 1160mm
Sights: Foresight: Blade
     Rearsight: Tangent 100-2000m
Rate of fire: Cyclic 450 rounds/min
Effective range: 800m from bipod
Status: No longer made. In limited Swiss Army service and obsolescent

7.5mm M51 LIGHT MACHINE GUN

Currently a standard LMG of the Swiss Army, this weapon was designed by the government establishment at Berne. The design is largely based on the German MG42 of Second World War fame; but, largely because the design calls for machined parts in many places where the MG42 uses stampings, it is better made but it is also more expensive and more than 4kg

heavier.

Features of the design include a quick-change barrel arrangement and a belt feed system, both of which are similar to those of the MG42. The locking system is also based on that of the German weapon but the Swiss design uses flaps instead of the rollers used on the MG42. Accessories include a tripod mount which can be fitted with an optical sight and a drum attachment which enables a 50-round belt to be carried conveniently.

DATA
Cartridge: 7.5mm M11
Method of operation: Gas-assisted recoil
Method of locking: Flaps
Method of feed: 50 or 250-round link belt
Method of fire: Automatic

Weight: 16kg with bipod
Length: 1,270mm
Barrel length: 560mm
Sights: Foresight: Folding blade
        Rearsight: Tangent
Rate of fire: 1000 rounds/min cyclic
Effective range: 800m from bipod
Manufacturer: SIG-Swiss Industrial Company – Neuhausen Rheinfalls
Status: In Swiss Army service, chiefly in motorised units

7.62mm SIG 710-3 GPMG

In 1945 Allied Intelligence Officers questioning German employees in Small Arms Factories interrogated Dr Niemann, chief of research at Mause Werke. He gave some information of a new German machine gun called the MG45 which worked on the delayed blowback principle. His description of the gun was interesting because it tied up with details supplied by Dr Grunow of the Grosfoss plant at Dobeln in Saxony. Unfortunately no gun was found for examination. Nothing more was heard of this weapon but in 1961 the Swiss Industrial Company at Neuhausen produced their delayed blowback machine gun, the SIG 710-3, which tallies in nearly all respects with the known details of the MG45.

The SIG 710-3 is a General Purpose Machine Gun designed to fire the NATO 7.62mm round. It makes use of modern manufacturing techniques, employing pressings wherever possible and it is probably one of the most advanced GPMGs today.

OPERATION

When the gun is fired the high pressure developed in the cartridge drives the case back hard against the bolt face. This same pressure also forces the case out against the chamber walls. There is a hardness gradient along the brass cartridge varying from 100 D.P.N. at the neck to 175 D.P.N. near the cannelure. The wall thickness also increases from front to rear. The soft neck of the case expands beyond the elastic limit and suffers permanent deformation but the rest of the case returns to its original dimensions and is therefore free in the chamber when the pressure drops. This however is not good enough in a blowback operated gun where the case must move back when the pressure is still fairly high, to operate the system. The large amount of friction between case and chamber wall will prevent case movement and if there is excessive cartridge head space, bulging of the rear of the case or a case separated near the small cone will result. To reduce this friction and also to provide extra force to drive the bolt back, the chamber is fluted. Gas escapes from the mouth of the case when the bullet begins to move and this gas runs into the grooves, thus partially neutralising the internal pressure and floating the case in a film of gas. This reduces the area of metal-to-metal contact. The fluting runs out just beyond the small cone so obturation is still obtained.

The net effect is to allow the case to move back and maintain a force against the breech block. This is the source of energy to carry out the cycle of operation.

The method of operation of the breech is very interesting. The basic principle of any delayed blowback system is to maintain the support of the base of the cartridge case and prevent excessive backward movement of the case whilst the pressure is high. This usually entails, in addition to the breech system, a fairly short barrel to allow a rapid pressure drop, which itself produces lower ballistics than could otherwise be obtained.

The NATO 7.62mm cartridge chamber pressure is 3510kg/em² and over the full shot travel to the muzzle the mean effective pressure is near enough to 1,575kg/cm². This pressure exerted over the bore area of 0.48cm² produces a backward force of 762kg. The breech block of the 710 weighs 0.8kg and so the velocity produced with an unlocked breech would not be less than 14m/sec. This velocity would be excessive and damage to the weapon would result and the emerging high pressure gas could injure the firer.

The breech block has three major parts: (1) the forward part which

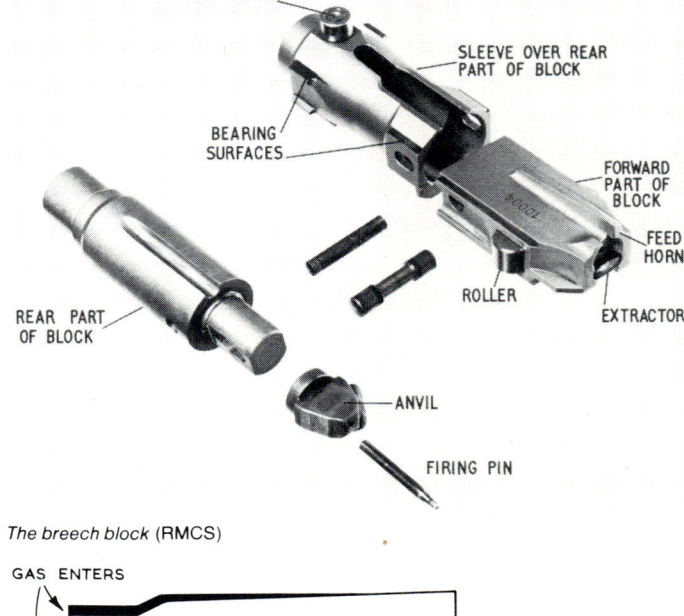

The breech block (RMCS)

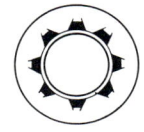

SIDE ELEVATION OF THE CHAMBER

END ELEVATION
The fluted chamber (RMCS)

contains the rollers, (2) the rear part which supports the anvil on which the rollers bear and (3) a sleeve which surrounds the rear part.

At the moment of firing the rollers in the forward part of the bolt are forced outwards into the recesses in the body of the gun by the anvil which itself is held forward by the rear part of the bolt.

The backward force exerted by the gas drives the cartridge rearwards and the front part of the bolt starts to move. This movement is transmitted to

An early version of the SIG710-3 with a wooden butt (RMCS)

the body of the gun through the rollers. The reaction of the body to this applied force has a component which drives the rollers inwards. When they start to move in, they force the inclined plane of the anvil shoulders back and the rear part of the block is driven back. This movement is resisted by the inertia of the rear part of the block, including its sleeve, and the force exerted by the return spring. The rear part of the block moves back a greater distance than the front due to the angles of the anvil shoulder and is therefore accelerated with respect to the front part. When the rollers have moved in and are clear of the body the whole block moves back under the force exerted on the cartridge case by the residual pressure of the gases.

Using the system the mean velocity of the breech block is reduced to a little over 3m/sec, and the dangers of hasty breech opening are averted.

When the return spring is fully compressed the bolt hits the buffer. The bolt then travels forward with the two parts still separated because the rollers are held in by the body guide ribs. When the round is fully chambered the rollers come opposite the recesses cut into the body. The rear part of the bolt has its own momentum and is also being impelled by the return spring. The anvil is driven forward between the rollers which are forced out into the body. When they are fully out (and not until then) the anvil can go far enough forward to strike the free floating firing pin which then gives the cap an impulsive blow.

The part played by the sleeve around the rear part of the bolt is unique in this type of mechanism. When the cap is struck the rear part of the block has reached the limit of its forward travel but the sleeve has a further 5mm of forward movement. The kinetic energy it contains is used for two purposes. First it prevents any bounce of the bolt which may occur if there is a slight hang-fire in the ignition of the propellant and secondly it is still moving forwards when the backward thrust is developing in the chamber so that its forward momentum must be destroyed before there can be movement of the front part of the bolt. This provides another – although small – check to bolt movement when the pressure is high.

TRIGGER AND FIRING MECHANISM

The trigger mechanism is developed directly from that used in the MG42. The moment at which the sear rises when firing is discontinued is carefully controlled to ensure that the bent of the bolt, which is moving quite fast, encounters the full face area of the sear. This prevents chipping and general wear of the bent and sear which is quite common on guns where the sear can rise into the bolt path at any moment.

The arrangement of the sear is shown. The trigger carries a tripper which is forced forward by its own spring. When the trigger is rotated the tail of the sear goes up and the nose of the sear disengages from the bent of the bolt. The spring of the tripper drives it forward and a step rides under the tail of the sear. When the trigger is released the tail can fall only a little way because it is held up by the step on the tripper, and the nose of the sear cannot rise. The rotation of the trigger pushes the tripper up into the path of the bolt which rides over it on the forward stroke but on the rearward stroke (having fired another round) drives the tripper backwards. This moves the step from under the tail of the sear which then is free to fall and the nose of the sear rises into the bolt path. The bolt rides over the sear on its way back but the sear rises to present its full face to the bent on the next forward stroke. This mechanism is very successful in saving the bent and sear from damage but if the tripper is released it can produce a hazard to safety when the safety catch is set to 'safe' with the bolt forward.

The applied safety consists of a bolt pushed across the body of the gun to prevent the nose of the sear from being depressed. Since the nose of the sear is held down until the tripper is pushed back, it follows that the gun must be cocked before the safety can be applied.

FEED SYSTEM

The feed system is the same in all essential details as that developed for the MG42. A roller is mounted on top of the sleeve over the rear of the bolt to engage in a rear pivoted track, or feed way, carried under the top of the feed cover. As the belt reciprocates the feedway swings about its pivot and moves from side to side across the gun.

Attached to the forward end of the feedway is a short lever pivoted near its centre point, about which it oscillates as the feedway moves back and forth across the gun. The lever carries the inner and outer feed pawls both of which are spring-loaded. They are attached to opposite sides of the centre pivot so that they are always moving in opposite directions, i.e. the inner pawls move in when the outer pawls move out and vice versa.

When the gun is cocked and ready to fire the next round is held up to the cartridge stop by the inner feed pawl. The bolt goes forward and the roller moves down the feedway. It moves at first down the straight section whilst the bolt is driving the round out of the belt, and the feed pawls are stationary. When the round is clear of the belt the roller enters the curved position of the feedway and the feedway is forced across to the right. This pivots the attached lever and the inner feed pawl is moved out. The outer pawl moves in, pulling the belt up, and bringing the nearest round towards the weapon. The gun fires and at this moment the next round is held by both the inner and outer feed pawls. When the bolt moves back the roller is still in the curved portion of the feedway but now forces the feedway in the opposite direction to that in which it moved before firing. Then the inner feed pawl is moved in to bring the round up to the cartridge stop whilst the outer pawl is forced over the next round in the bolt.

The most noteworthy feature of this system is its simplicity and the fact that the feed is carried out in two half stages as the bolt goes forward and back, with the round moved one half pitch each phase. This produces a smoother continuous feed motion with a considerable reduction in the

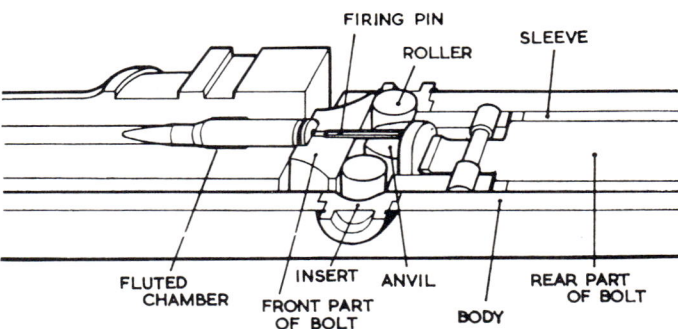

The breech in firing position

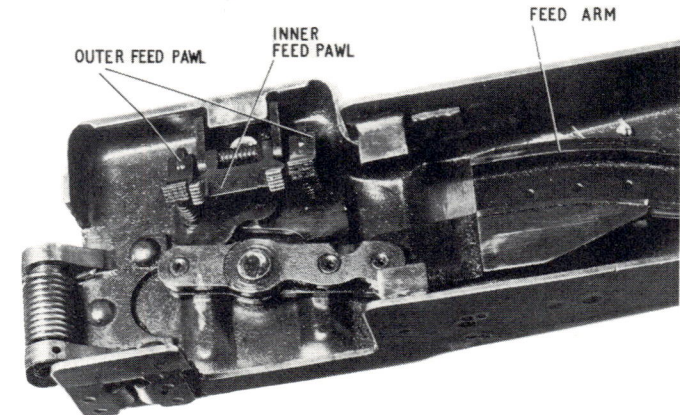

The feed system (RMCS)

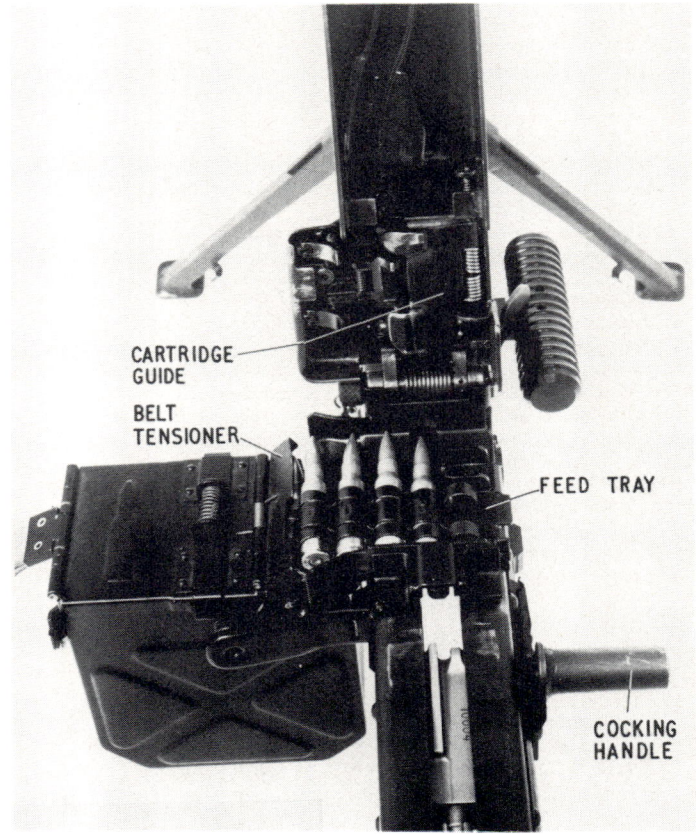

Loading the SIG710-3 (RMCS)

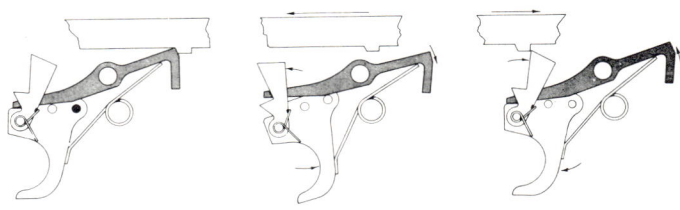

The trigger and sear (RMCS)

accelerations and decelerations of the bolt and the forces imposed on both feed pawls and links. The roller on the bolt is not spring-loaded and so the gun must be cocked, to line up the feedway and the roller, before the top cover plate is closed down. This means that the gun can never be carried with the bolt forward and a belt in position. Any attempt to do so will damage the feed mechanism when the gun is cocked.

The gun has a considerable reserve of energy for feeding and under good conditions will lift a belt length of 1.2 metres.

One very useful feature is the gun's ability to cater for rounds held either in NATO disintegrating links of the USA M13 pattern or in the German type continuous metal belt.

To change from one type of belt to the other requires a change of the feed tray and the cartridge guide. The whole operation takes less than 60 seconds.

BARREL AND SIGHTS

The barrel change arrangement is very good. The barrel release catch on the right of the barrel casing is pushed and the barrel pulled out and back. It can be done with one hand and the change is definitely faster than that of the German MG3. This is probably the fastest change yet produced. The barrel handle is a good heat insulator and even when the barrel is cherry red the change is neat and simple.

The foresight is a blade fixed between protectors and the whole slides in a dovetail on the barrel casing. The rearsight is a leaf working on a ramp. It is graduated from 100 to 1,200 metres by hundreds and has good bold figures.

Zeroing presents a difficult problem in that the foresight is attached to the body casing and zeroing for elevation means a change of foresight. This means of course a different zero for every barrel and a different foresight. A foresight on the barrel is obviously a better arrangement because then all barrels can be zeroed on the foresight before going into action. This however could produce difficulties in the barrel change system.

STRIPPING

Stripping is a simple process. With the bolt forward and the top cover plate lifted, the forward of the two catches below the neck of the butt is pressed and the butt rotated. The butt, buffer, and return spring, rod and casing are withdrawn. A sharp jerk on the cocking handle throws out the bolt. The trigger group requires the extraction of one pin. The barrel catch releases the barrel and the weapon is then field stripped.

When the two pins in the bolt are pressed out the bolt is fully stripped. The rollers are held in by a low strength wire spring and can be released with the fingers. The top cover plate is held to the body by a pin incorporating a flat. When the punch marks on pin and top cover plate are lined up, the pin can be withdrawn.

The feed mechanism can be stripped by:
(1) Removing cartridge guide. Push forward, rotate and remove hinge pin.
(2) Remove feedway by compressing spring plate at the pivot end.
(3) Remove feed pawls.

The trigger mechanism is easily stripped and assembled and the procedure is straightforward when the gun is seen.

HANDLING

The weapon weighs 9.25kg. The barrel handle on the side cannot be used for carrying and so the weapon must be carried either using the sling around the firer's neck or at the high port position. The weapon is well adapted to firing from the hip, holding the bipod legs with the left hand.

When used as a section LMG the 100 round belt carrier is extremely useful. It protects the ammunition from mud and sand, it prevents undergrowth from catching the belt, it simplifies firing on the move and it is easy to detach and refill. The lid acts as a tensioner on the belt.

The bipod legs cannot be adjusted.

When used as a sustained fire weapon there are several changes to be made. The main ones are: Replace light barrels and use heavy barrels. Remove belt carrier.

TRIPOD

The tripod carries a dial sight weighing 2.5kg incorporating a telescope of

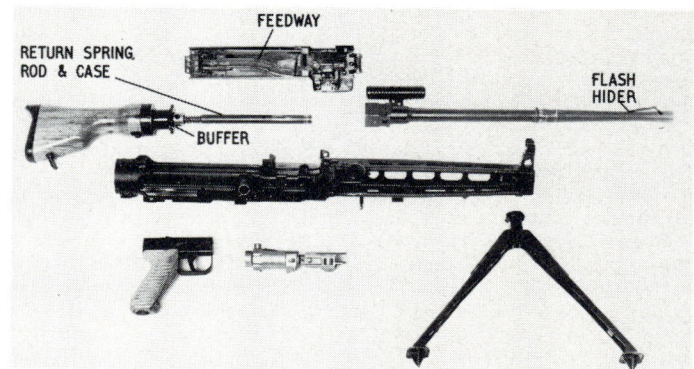

The SIG710-3 field stripped (RMCS)

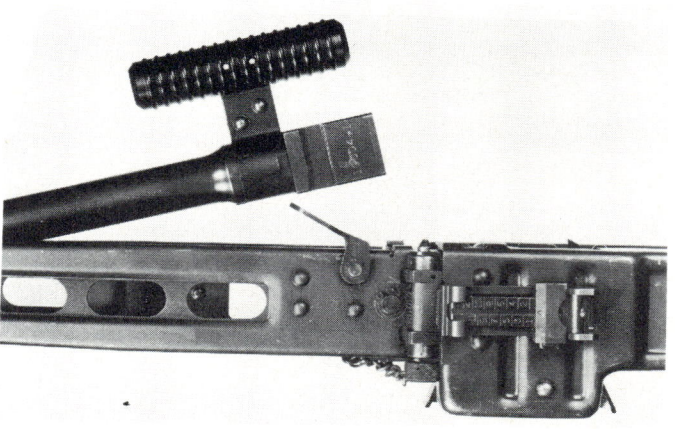

Changing the barrel (RMCS)

2½ magnification. There is also an infra-red night sight. The tripod is SIG L810. It is a sprung tripod. The gun recoils when the first round is fired and the springs are compressed. Before the gun is fully forward again the next round is fired and thereafter the gun quivers in a state of near equilibrium.

There is an automatic device for dispersing fire in either elevation, line or both. This in principle shows a distinct similarity to that used on the MG42 during World War II.

The tripod can be mounted at any height between 30.5 and 70cm and it weighs 10.3kg. It folds up and can be carried by one man on his back.

The weapon has of course, the usual cleaning kit but there are also one or two very useful ancillaries. There is a blank firing barrel which operates the gun very well using standard 7.62mm NATO blank of the British pattern. This is carried in a metal case. There is also an extremely good belt filler for the German type belt.

DATA

Cartridge: 7.62mm × 51
Method of operation: Delayed blowback
Method of delay: Rollers
Method of feed: Belt. Disintegrating link type or continuous link belt
Method of fire: Automatic

WEIGHT

Gun: 9.25kg
Heavy barrel: 2.5kg
Standard barrel: 2.04kg

SIG710-3 with belt carrier and current butt

Blank firing barrel: 1.89kg
Belt carrier: 0.8kg

LENGTH
Gun overall: 1,143mm
Barrel: 559mm

MECHANICAL FEATURES
Barrel: Regulator: Nil
      Rifling: 4 grooves RH. 1 turn in 305mm
      Cooling: Air. Quick change barrel
Sights: Foresight: Blade
      Rearsight: Leaf notch.
      Graduation: 100-1,200 metres, in 100 metre steps
      Zeroing: Elevation. Rear sight. Line. Foresight on dovetail
      Sightbase: 412mm
      Telescopic sight: ×2.5

FIRING CHARACTERISTICS
Muzzle velocity: 790 metres/sec

Muzzle energy: 300mkp
Recoil energy: 0.4mkp
Rate of fire: Cyclic: 600 rounds/min
      Automatic: 200 rounds/min
Range, maximum effective: Bipod 800 metres; Tripod 2,200 metres

TRIPOD CHARACTERISTICS
Designation: Tripod Mount L810
Minimum firing height: 305mm
Maximum firing height: 700mm
Weight: 10.3kg
Maximum elevation: 500mils
Maximum traverse: 800mils
Dimensions folded: 82 × 46 × 27cm
Weight of telescope: 1.45kg
Weight of telescope mount: 400g
Accessories: Blank firing barrel, belt carrier, ammunition box, sling, cleaning kit, belt filler
Manufacturer: Swiss Industrial Co., Neuhausen Rhine Falls, Switzerland
Status: Available

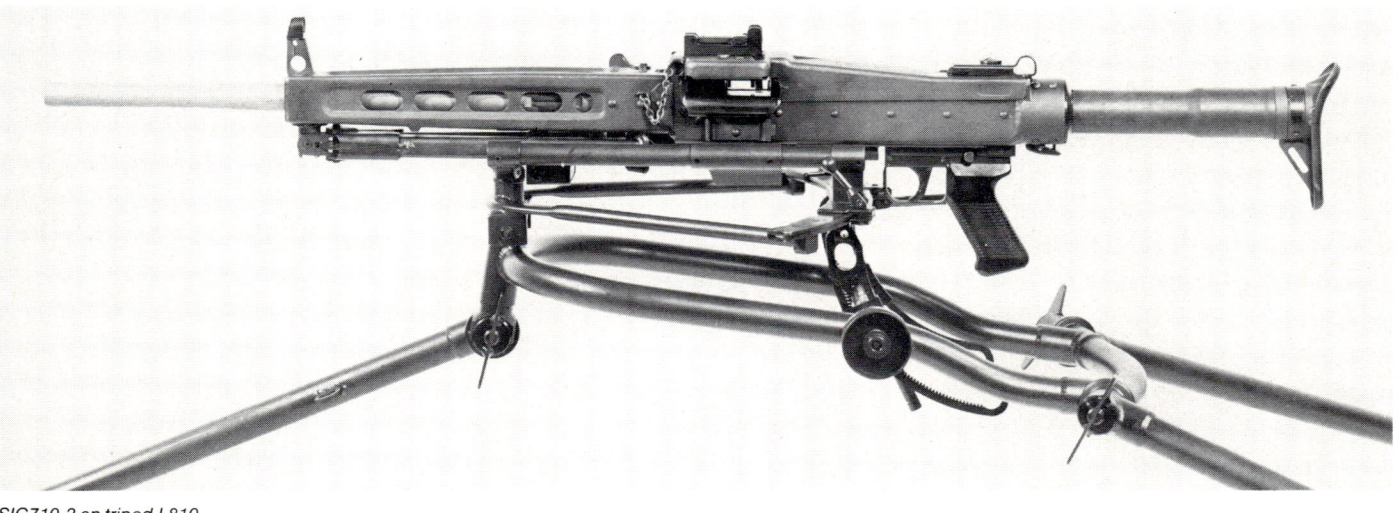

SIG710-3 on tripod L810

UNION OF SOVIET SOCIALIST REPUBLICS

7.62mm MAXIM MMG

The earliest models of the Maxim Medium Machine Gun purchased by Imperial Russia were made in England, and it was not until 1905 that manufacture commenced at the Tula Arsenal. The first guns had a bronze jacket and were excessively heavy. In 1910 production started of the steel jacketed model which remained in service until the end of the Second World War and was used in Korea by the Chinese and in Vietnam by the Viet Cong.

The Maxim gun used by the Russians differs from the British and German guns in non-essential details but the Russians did have a mount that was unique. This was known as the Sokolov and remained in service until the gun itself was obsolete. Vast numbers of the Maxim were made and even as late as 1944 270,000 were produced.

Details of the operation of the Maxim gun are given under British Machine Guns.

Status: No longer in service in Warsaw Pact countries, but still to be found in Asian countries at least.

The Maxim Model 1910 on the Sokolov mount (RMCS)

Russian Maxim machine-gun carts in the anniversary parade on November 7th 1931 (Novosti)

7.62mm DEGTYAREV DP AND DPM LMG

The Degtyarev Pekhotnyy was designed by Vasily Alexeyevitch Degtyarev in the early 1920s and was completed in 1926. Production began in 1933 at Tula Arsenal. The weapon was used extensively in the Spanish Civil War where it was found that the basic design was sound. The return spring housed under the barrel became excessively hot but this was cured by perforating the barrel casing. The 49-round flat horizontally-mounted drum gave trouble. The magazine was subsequently loaded with 47 rounds and functioned satisfactorily. The capacity of the drum is marked on the top surface. It was used throughout World War II and similar models were used in aircraft – DA and DA-2 (which was a twin-barrelled version) – and in tanks where it was known as the DT. This had a heavier barrel, a 60-round drum, a telescoping shoulder stock and a pistol grip. The grip safety of the DP was replaced by a safety lever. It had a bipod and a detachable front sight to allow it to be used in the ground role.

In 1944 the DP was modified by H. Shilin and known as the DPM – DP modernised. The return spring was taken from under the barrel and placed in a cylindrical housing behind the receiver, projecting back over the small of the butt. A pistol grip was added. The grip safety was replaced by a safety lever mounted on the right of the receiver just above the trigger.

The two weapons differ only in these details and will be treated as one. The DPM has been manufactured in China as the Type 53 Light Machine Gun.

DESCRIPTION

The DP has 65 parts, is of very simple construction and was intended for manufacture by unskilled labour. The design has many large flat bearing surfaces which mate during operation and the friction caused by the introduction of dirt causes stoppages in action. The barrel in the earliest versions had annular cooling fins but these were omitted during the war to speed production. The barrel of the earliest DP was fixed and so overheated readily. To get the barrel out required the unscrewing of the flash hider and gas cylinder nut. The cylinder was then slipped back and two pins holding the barrel in place knocked out with a drift. The barrel could then be rotated, using a tool on the flats at the muzzle, and pulled out.

In 1940 a replaceable barrel of more modern design was fitted. When the gun is cocked the barrel lock – located on the left side of the receiver – is pressed in and an open-jawed spanner placed over the flats near the muzzle. The barrel is rotated through 60 degrees and then pulled forward out of the barrel jacket.

The barrel casing is made of two tubes welded together. The top tube takes the barrel and the bottom one contains the gas piston and the return spring in the DP. The gas regulator is of the variable gas track type and has

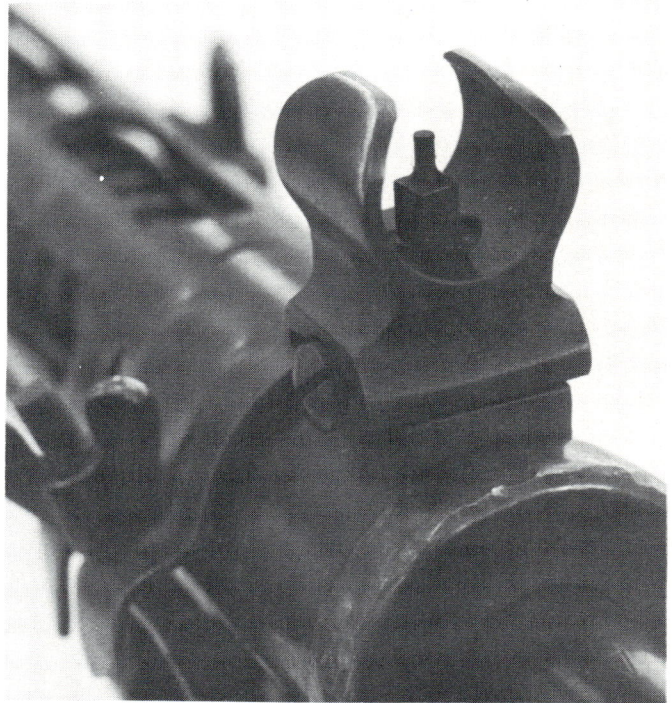

DP foresight (RMCS)

three passages of 2.7mm, 3.3mm and 4.0mm. To change the setting remove the cotter pin, unscrew the nut, move the regulator out and re-set. Replace the regulator, tighten the nut and replace the cotter pin. The piston is a rod attached to the slide which carries the breech block. The slide has a slot to allow passage of the extracted cartridge and is machined at the rear end to provide cams to force the locking lugs in to unlock the bolt. The cocking handle projects from the right side of the slide and reciprocates with it. The breech block is rectangular in shape. Along each side is a locking lug. In the centre is the firing pin which is attached to the slide. Camming

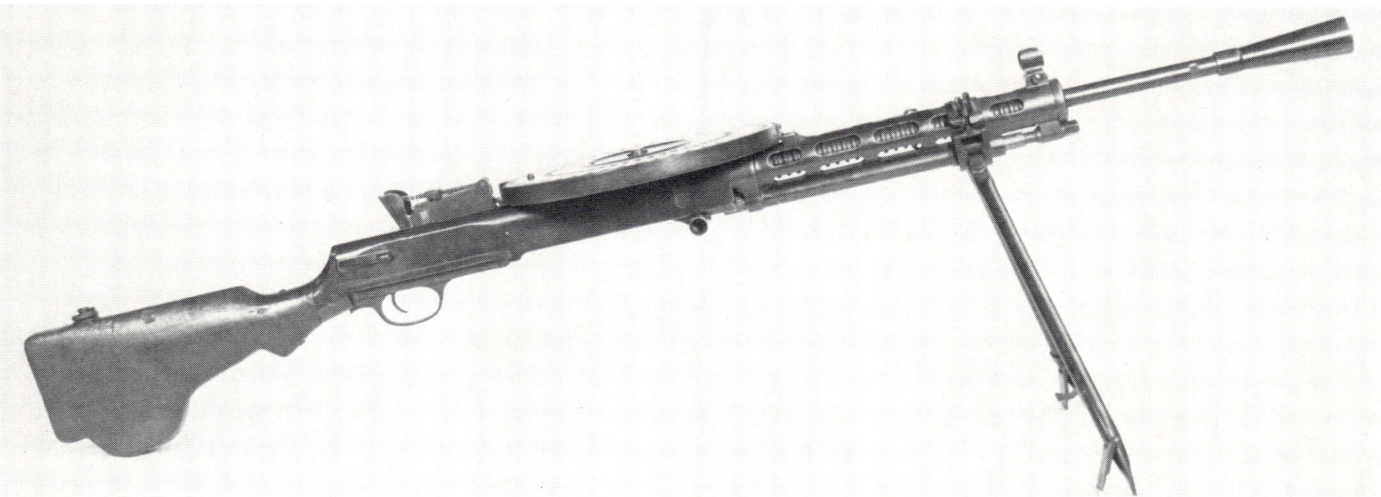

DP 7.62mm Degtyarev (RMCS)

shoulders on the firing pin force the two locking lugs outward into recesses in the sides of the receiver as the slide continues forward after the breech block has chambered the round and come to rest.

The foresight is a post with two foresight protectors. The rearsight is a leaf tangent V. It is adjusted by pressing in the side catches and moved along the bar to the appropriate range. The magazine catch is located at the back of the rearsight block.

OPERATION

The drum magazine is loaded by inserting cartridges, nose towards the centre, into the feed mouthpiece, on top of the empty case which is used as a follower. The magazine is rotated by pulling round the leather tag. This will often have been torn off and rotation must be accomplished by pressure on the small stud that holds the leather tag. Separate positions are provided for each cartridge.

Slide forward the dust cover and place the fork, at the front of the magazine, into the T slot on top of the barrel jacket. The rear of the magazine is then dropped down in front of the rearsight block. Check that the catch is holding the magazine. Pull the cocking handle to the rear. The magazine spring will place a round in the magazine lips.

The DP has a grip safety. The DPM has a rotating lever above the trigger on the right side of the gun and this is rotated to the rear for 'fire'.

When the trigger is pulled the return spring forces the slide forward carrying the breech block. The feed piece of the breech block drives a cartridge from the drum into the chamber. The cartridge is rimmed and comes to rest against the barrel face and the extractor on the bolt face snaps over the rim as the bolt motion ceases. The slide continues on and the firing pin moves on with it and cams out the locking lugs on the sides of the bolt into recesses in the receiver sidewalls. The firing pin continues on and strikes the cap of the cartridge. It is prevented from emerging too far and piercing the cap when its shoulders strike the interior of the bolt.

The bullet passes up the bore and some of the gases following it pass through the gas port and impinge on the front face of the piston. The piston moves back and the slide which is attached to it carries the firing pin back. The slide has cams machined in its top surface and after a period of free travel whilst the gas pressure drops, these force the locking lugs out of the recesses in the receiver and into the sides of the bolt. The slide then carries the whole bolt rearwards compressing the return spring. The extractor holds the empty case to the breech face until the ejector revolves it down through the aperture in the slide and out of the bottom of the gun. The rear of the slide hits the rear wall of the trigger housing, stops and is driven forward again by the compressed return spring.

The bolt picks up another round and the cycle is repeated as long as the trigger is pressed and the drum contains ammunition.

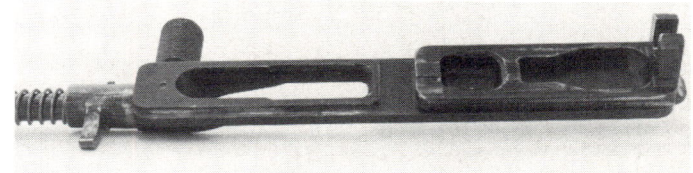

DP piston and slide

DP rearsight (RMCS)

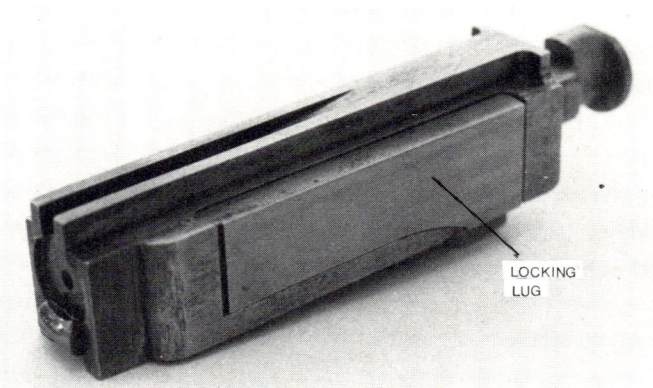

LOCKING LUG

DP bolt (RMCS)

The Chinese Type 53 DPM (RMCS)

TRIGGER AND FIRING MECHANISM

Since the gun fires only at full automatic the trigger system is rudimentary. The trigger has a hook at its upper end, extending forwards over the sear. When the trigger is pulled the hook depresses the sear which drops out of engagement with a bent in the underside of the slide.

The grip safety of the DP is located immediately behind the trigger and blocks its rotation until it is lifted by the firer's grip and frees the trigger.

STRIPPING

Remove the magazine by depressing the catch behind the rear sight block and lifting the rear end.

Check the chamber is clear.

Next the return spring must be disconnected or removed.

The DP has the return spring under the barrel and this must be unlocked by pressing the handle on the left front of the receiver forward and then down.

On the DPM the spring is housed in a tube behind the receiver. Pull back the detent on the tube, rotate the tube, remove it and withdraw the spring. Unscrew and remove the body locking pin at the right rear side of the receiver. Force down the butt.

Pull the cocking handle to the rear and withdraw the slide, bolt and firing pin. Lift the bolt up off the slide.

The grip safety and trigger of the DP

DATA

Cartridge: 7.62mm × 54R
Method of operation: Gas
Method of locking: Projecting lug
Method of feed: Drum
Method of fire: Automatic

WEIGHTS

Gun empty: 9.1kg
Bipod: 0.7kg
Flash hider: 0.2kg
Barrel: 2.0kg
Empty magazine: 1.6kg
Loaded magazine: 2.8kg

LENGTHS

Gun overall: 1,270mm
Flash hider: 127mm
Barrel: 605mm
Rifled length: 532mm

MECHANICAL FEATURES

Barrel: 3 position regulator
    Rifling: 4 grooves RH. 1 turn in 254mm
    Cooling: Air. Quick change barrel
Sights: Foresight: Cylindrical post
    Rearsight: Leaf tangent with a V backsight
    Graduation: 1,100-1,500 metres by 100 metre increments
    Zeroing: Front sight
    Sight radius: 616mm

FIRING CHARACTERISTICS

Muzzle velocity: 840 metres/sec
Muzzle energy: 337 mkp
Chamber pressure: 3,100 kg/cm²
Rate of fire: Cyclic: 600 rounds/min
        Auto: 80-90 rounds/min
Range, maximum effective: 800 metres
Manufacturer: State Arsenals
Status: No longer manufactured. No longer in service in Warsaw Pact countries. Copied by the Chinese as Type 53 (see text) and weapons from either source may be found in parts of Asia. Widely used in Africa.

7.62mm RP-46 COMPANY MACHINE GUN

During World War II the Russians felt the need for a machine gun held at company level to produce a greater volume of fire than that supplied by the DPM, and yet light enough to be carried forward in the assault. During 1944 the Soviet designers W. Shilin, P. Poliakov and A. Dibinin worked on the DPM and eventually produced a version which could be belt fed for sustained fire and by changing the top cover could make use of the flatdrum of the DPM during the assault. Although the design was finalised during the war it did not come into service until 1946 and the gun was known as the RP-46.

The RP-46 was officially adopted by the Russian Army but it has been very little in evidence. The Chinese Communists manufactured the gun and called it the Type 58. The North Korean version is known as the Type 64. Apart from the markings the guns are the same.

In order to convert the DPM for belt feed the magazine has been removed and a feeder located over the receiver by utilising the magazine lug at the front and the magazine catch at the rear. The belt feeder is operated by a somewhat crude use of the cocking handle which, as in the DP, is fixed to the right hand side of the slide and reciprocates with it. The handle fits into the claw like feed operating slide and causes the feed slide to move backwards and forwards. The internal diameter of the claw is three times that of the cocking handle and so the slide is able to accelerate to its full velocity in either direction before the feed slide is operated. This enables

the full power of the gun to be utilised for unlocking the gun and accelerating the bolt back in one direction and similarly the full power is available to accelerate the bolt and push a round into the chamber.

The feed slide moves back, and a diagonal feed groove cut in the top surface moves the belt feed pawl inward, and the first round in the belt is moved up to the cartridge stop. The round is held by a retaining pawl in the top feed cover when the feed slide moving forward forces the feed pawl out to the right to slip over the next round to be fed.

The feed slide carries a pair of jaws which grip the rim of the case and extract it from the belt as the feed slide travels back. The cartridge is pulled back under a spring loaded depressor arm mounted under the top feed cover plate and this arm pushes the cartridge down into the feedway where the bolt feed piece can drive it forward into the chamber.

This process of loading the belt into the gun at one level, withdrawing the cartridge backwards and then lowering it to another plane where it is lined up with the chamber and subsequently fed, is a relic of the early days of Maxim and Browning where the closed belt system made this procedure inevitable.

The RP-46 takes a 250-round continuous closed pocket metallic belt. The cartridge is simply placed in the conical pocket as far as it will go. The belt is usually carried in a metal box.

The dust cover over the feedway on the gun is lowered. The belt is loaded

RP46 Company MG (RMCS)

into the gun by inserting the feed tab into the feedway on the right of the gun and pulling the tab through until the first round reaches the stops. To load the gun the cocking handle must be pulled twice. The first time the bolt is retracted the jaws cannot grip the cartridge rim. The second time the leading round is pulled back and forced down into the feedway. The gun is then cocked and ready to fire.

If for any reason the belt feed device is not required it can readily be removed from on top of the receiver by pressing the magazine catch behind the rearsight block. The cocking handle must be pulled back until it lies in the centre of the claw. Tilting the feeder forward frees it from the cocking handle. The front end is held by the T lug and can be moved back to free the feeder completely from the gun. If required a DP or DPM 47 round drum magazine can then be used on the gun.

The RP-46 differs from the DPM in some other minor details. There is a barrel release lever on the left of the receiver to depress the barrel lock. The gas regulator has a catch that engages one of the three grooves in the bottom of the gas block and can be moved from position 1 to 2 and then 3 as required.

The Chinese Type 58 originally had this type of regulator but it was later changed to a rotary type similar to that used in the RPD LMG. (qv).

DATA
Cartridge: 7.62mm × 54R
Method of operation: Gas
Method of locking: Projecting lugs
Method of feed: Magazine then belt
Method of fire: Automatic

WEIGHTS
Gun, empty: 13kg
Barrel: 3.2kg

LENGTHS
Gun: 1,283mm
Barrel: 607mm

MECHANICAL FEATURES
Barrel: 3 position regulator
    Rifling: 4 grooves RH. 1 turn in 254mm
    Cooling: Air. Quick barrel change
Sights: Foresight: Cylindrical post
    Rearsight: Leaf tangent with a V backsight
    Graduation: 1-15 by increments of 100 metres
    Zeroing: Foresight
    Sight radius: 635mm

FIRING CHARACTERISTICS
Muzzle velocity: 840 metres/sec
Muzzle energy: 337mkp
Chamber pressure: 3,100kg/cm²
Rate of fire: Cyclic: 600 rounds/min
        Auto: 200 rounds/min
Range, maximum effective: 800 metres
Manufacturer: State arsenals
Status: No longer in production. No longer in service in Warsaw Pact countries. Copied by the Chinese as Type 58 and made in North Korea as Type 64. Still in service in parts of Asia and Africa.

The Chinese Type 58 (RMCS)

7.62mm RPD LMG

Design work was started on the RPD by Degtyarev in 1943 to make use of the newly developed 7.62mm × 39mm cartridge. The urgent needs of the armed services – all of whom used Degtyarev machine guns firing the 7.62mm × 54R cartridge – caused slow progress to be made but, shortly after the war ended, production of the new short cartridge was accelerated and the RPD was the first machine gun to use this cartridge.

The RPD was manufactured in large numbers and it formed the standard squad automatic for the Russian Army and also its satellites. It was manufactured by Communist China as the Type 56 and Type 56-1 and by North Korea as the Type 62 light machine gun.

It is now obsolescent in the Warsaw Pact countries but is still used by the Communist countries in South East Asia and by partisan forces in Africa.

DESCRIPTION

The RPD is a belt-fed automatic weapon. It is gas-operated and has a locking system which, in priciple, is like that of the DP; it uses locking lugs of the same sort but they are pushed out to lock, not by the firing pin but by a wedge on top of the slide. The belt is a continuous, metal, open pocket design. The links are connected by a short metal spiral spring link. The cartridge goes into the pocket and the nib at the rear of the belt fits into the extraction groove at the rear of the case. Some belts have no nib but a right angled projection fits against the base of the cartridge. The 50-round belt can be joined to another by putting the end link of one belt against the joining link of the other. A cartridge is used to keep the two belts together. The cover on the belt carrier is opened and the belt placed in, from the left, with the loading tab outside. The belt carrier is slid onto the mounting bracket under the gun, from the rear. The mounting bracket lock is swung down to secure the belt carrier in place. On the Chinese Type 56-1 the dust cover over the feedway must be swung down and locked into place to act as a belt carrier bracket.

The gun is fed by a feed arm oscillated across the receiver by a roller carried on the slide.

There is a regulator mounted in a block under the gas vent. It is adjusted by loosening the nut on the left side of the regulator and pressing it to the right. The regulator has three settings marked 1, 2 and 3 and is rotated to align the required number with the index pin. The regulator is then pushed

back to the left and the nut tightened.

The barrel is fixed and cannot be changed.

The foresight is a post. The rearsight is a tangent U. The rearsight leaf registers from 100 to 900 metres by 100 metres steps.

For zeroing, the front sight is screwed in or out for elevation adjustment. For line, the locknut must be loosened and the slide moved across its dovetail. The rearsight has a separate windage knob.

VARIANTS

During its service life several small variations were made to the RPD and as a result there are five recognised versions of the gun. These are:
First version: Female gas piston fitting over male gas spigot. No dust cover. Rigid, reciprocating cocking handle. Windage knob on right of rearsight.
Second version: Male gas piston fitting into female cylinder. No dust cover. Rigid, reciprocating cocking handle. Windage knob on left of rearsight.
Third version: Male gas piston, female cylinder. Dust cover on feed mechanism. Folding non-reciprocating cocking handle. This is the version copied by the Chinese as their Type 56.
Fourth version: Male gas piston, female cylinder. Longer gas cylinder. Extra friction roller on piston slide. Dust cover on feed mechanism. Buffer in butt. (Sometimes called RPDM)
Fifth version. As fourth version but with folding feed cover belt carrier. Multi-piece cleaning rod carried in butt trap. (Also Chinese Type 56-1.)

OPERATION

After loading the belts and placing one, or two joined together, in the belt carrier, locate the belt carrier under the gun. Push the loading tab through the feedway from left to right and pull through to seat the first cartridge under the retaining pawl. If no loading tab is fitted the feed cover must be lifted and the belt put – open side down – on the feedway. The belt has a nib – already mentioned – fitting into the extraction cannelure, and there is also another nib at the front end level with the shoulder of the case. This nib must fit over a guide which pushes the nose of the bullet down for locating, ready for feeding. If the belt is not so located a stoppage is inevitable.

When the belt is in place and the top cover replaced, the cocking handle

Russian Marines using the RPD. Note the grip used by the soldier (Novosti)

Russian RPD Model 1 with a female piston (RMCS)

Russian RPD Model 2 with male piston (RMCS)

RPD Model 3, Chinese Type 56 – with folding cocking handle and folding cover over exit (RMCS)

can be retracted; the cocking handle stays to the rear on the first two versions of the gun but is pushed forward and folded upward on the later models. The gun is then ready to fire. When the trigger is pulled the slide is driven forward carrying the bolt which pushes the first round out of the belt and into the chamber. The extractor slips into the extraction groove and the bolt comes to rest. The slide goes on and the solid wedge at the rear drives beween the locking lugs and forces them out into the locking recesses in the receiver walls. The bolt is now firmly secured to the receiver. The slide goes on and the wedge hits the rear of the light firing pin in the bolt. The cap is struck, the propellant ignited and the bullet driven up the bore. A proportion of the gas passes through the gas port, and after giving the piston head a sharp blow, disperses to atmosphere from the open cylinder. The slide is attached to the piston and when it goes back there is a period of idle movement in which the breech block remains firmly locked whilst the chamber pressure drops to a safe level. Then the locking lugs, which rest in cam slots cut in the top face of the slide are forced inwards against the sides of the bolt and unlocking is completed. The slide carries the breech block back. The empty case is held to the breech face and ejected downwards out of the gun when the ejector strikes the top of the base of the case and revolves it round the extractor. The return spring is fully compressed and the slide is driven forward again.

FEED MECHANISM

The slide carries a feed roller which, mounted on the left hand side, fits into the feed arm under the top cover plate.

Pivoted at the centre of the feed arm is a feed slide which carries a spring loaded feed pawl. When the feed arm is moved to the right, the feed pawl is moved to the left.

Starting with the gun cocked and ready for action, the cartridge is positioned by the feed pawl against the cartridge guide. It is lined up with the bullet guide and is ready for chambering.

When the trigger is pulled the bolt goes forward and pushes the round out of the belt into the chamber. During this action the cartridge belt must be stationary so the roller runs down a straight portion of the feed arm. As soon as the cartridge is clear of the belt, the roller pushes the feed arm to the right

and the feed slide moves out of the gun to the left. The stop pawl on the feed tray prevents the belt being pushed to the left out of the gun as the spring loaded feed pawl rides over the round in the belt. At the end of the forward stroke of the bolt the round is fully chambered and the feed pawl is gripping the next round in the belt.

The round is fired. The piston is driven to the rear. The roller moves back and there is an initial free travel before it bears on the feed arm. The feed arm is then pulled to the left, the feed slide is pivoted to the right. The feed pawl pulls the round it is gripping to the centre line of the gun where it is held by the cartridge guide and the feed pawl.

In brief the gun brings the belt across during the recoil stroke and positions the feed pawl over the next round, ready for feeding, during the firing stroke.

TRIGGER AND FIRING MECHANISM

Since the gun fires only at full auto the trigger mechanism is not complex. The trigger has a hook at the front end which enters a window in the sear. When the trigger is pulled the hook pulls the sear down. The safety catch is on the right of the receiver, directly above the trigger. When it is applied, i.e. put forward, it locks the sear in the up position. If an attempt is made to cock the gun with the safety forward (at safe) the underside of the slide will jam on the immovable sear and remain locked. The gun will then be useless until the slide can be driven forward again. This presents no problem with the early version guns with fixed cocking handles but is not easy with non reciprocating cocking handles.

STRIPPING

(1) Lift the top cover plate by pushing forward on the catch at the rear end and then rotating the cover forward and up. (It will only elevate about 45 degrees.)
(2) Remove belt. Check chamber is clear. Return bolt to forward position.
(3) Press out the locking pin at the rear of the receiver. Slide butt and trigger group rearwards.
(4) Pull cocking handle rearwards and take slide and bolt out. Lift bolt off slide.

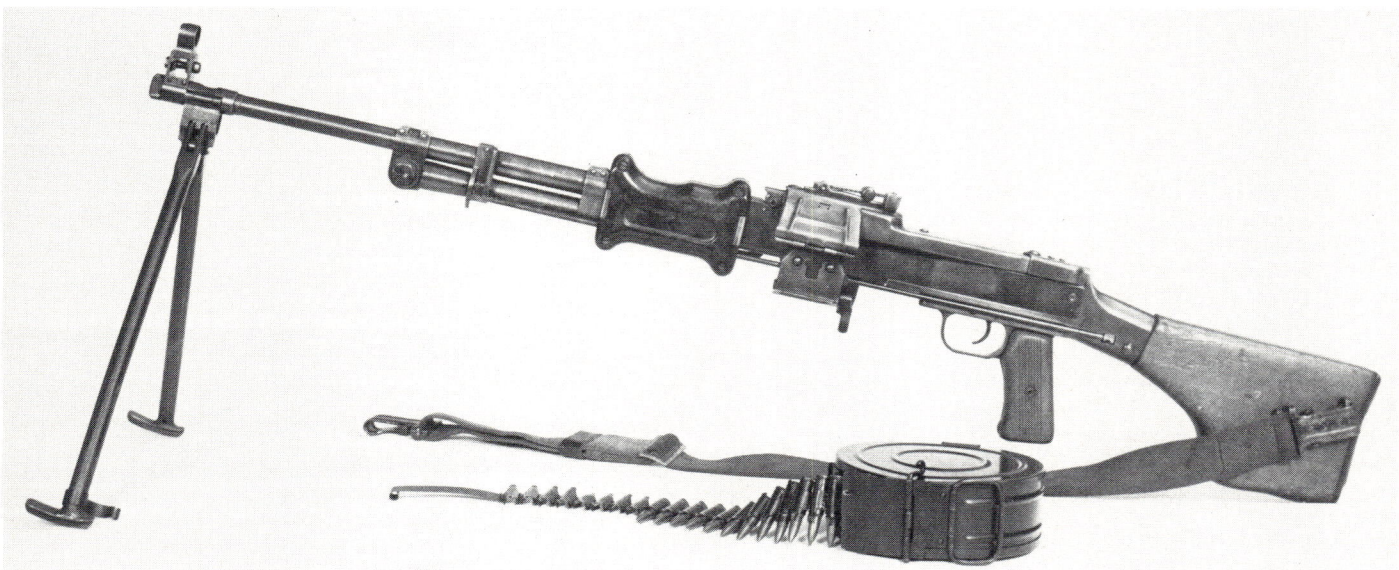

RPD Model 4 (Hungarian) with anti-friction roller on the back of the bolt and enclosing gas cylinder (RSAF)

RPD Model 5 without cleaning rod. The deflector and drum bracket become the cover (RSAF)

REASSEMBLY
(1) Put locking lugs in bolt; place bolt on slide with feet of locking lugs in cam slots.
(2) Push forward on slide; insert slide rails in grooves in receiver walls and push forward.
(3) Slide butt and trigger group into the receiver. Replace locking pin.

DATA
Cartridge: 7.62mm × 39
Method of operation: Gas
Method of locking: Projecting lugs
Method of feed: Belt
Method of fire: Automatic

WEIGHT
Gun only: 7.1kg

LENGTHS
Gun: 1,036mm
Barrel: 521mm

MECHANICAL FEATURES
Barrel: 3 position regulator
        Rifling: 4 grooves RH. 1 turn in 254mm
        Cooling: Air. Fixed barrel
Sights: Foresight: Cylindrical post
        Rearsight: Leaf tangent with V backsight
        Windage Graduation: 1-9 by increments of 100 metres
        Zeroing: Foresight
        Sight radius: 600mm

FIRING CHARACTERISTICS
Muzzle velocity: 700 metres/sec
Muzzle energy: 200mkp
Recoil energy: 0.55mkp
Rate of fire: Cyclic: 700 rounds/min

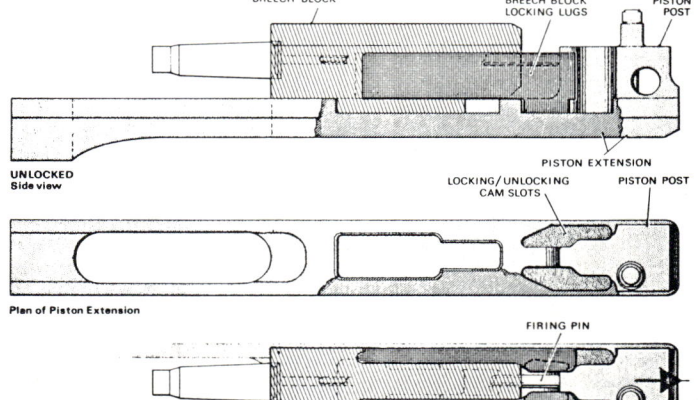

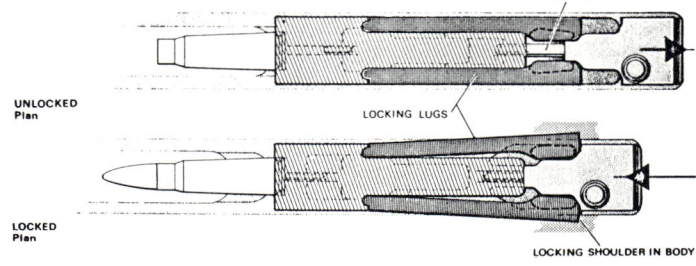

RPD locking system (RMCS)

Automatic: 150 rounds/min
Range, maximum effective: 800 metres
Manufacturer: State Factories of the Soviet Union and all European Satellites. Made in China and North Korea
Status: No longer in production. No longer used by European Communist Armies. Still in use in Pakistan, Egypt, China, North Korea and Vietnam and in parts of Africa

---

7.62mm SG43 AND SGM (GORYUNOV) MMG

The Russian designer Peter Maximovitch Goryunov produced his SG43 to supplement the fire of the DP and DPM. The gun was modified and improved until there were eventually six versions of the gun with comparatively minor differences. These guns are:
SG43. This has a smooth barrel with no fins at all. It has the cocking handle lying horizontally between the two vertical spade grips of the firing gear.

The sear is attached to the return spring guide. The barrel lock is a simple wedge which comes out to the side. There are no dust covers over the feed and ejection openings.
SG43B. This has a micrometer barrel lock and dust covers over feed and ejection openings.
SGM. This has longitudinal fins and a separate sear housing. Dust covers are on late production models. The cocking handle is on the right hand side of receiver.
SGMT. This is the tank version of SGM with a solenoid on the back plate of the receiver.
SGMB. Similar to SGM but has dust covers over the feed and ejection ports.
Hungarian SG GPMG. This gun has a RPD buttstock with a pistol grip. It has an external resemblance to the PK GPMG but there is no hole in the buttstock and the ejection slot is lozenge shaped rather than rectangular.

The Goryunov guns have been used by Communist countries in Europe and Asia and have been issued to Arab countries in the Middle East.

The Communist Chinese version of the SG43 is known as the Type 53 and the SGMB is called the Type 57 heavy machine gun. The Czech version has the marking Vz43 and the Polish gun is stamped Wz43.

DESCRIPTION
The Goryunov is a sturdy, simple and reliable gun. It is gas operated, belt fed and fires from a wheeled tripod which can be man handled or pulled by a draught animal or vehicle. It has a variable track gas regulator.

The barrel is changed readily. The SG43 has a simple wedge which drives into a dovetail slot on top of the barrel. All other Goryunov MGs have a milled catch on the barrel lock which must be depressed before the lock can be withdrawn. The headspace of all these weapons except the SG43 is adjusted by the micrometer barrel lock. The tool provided in the tool kit for this purpose is used to rotate the square socket screw. The gun is adjusted only at base workshops. The barrel is pulled back until the breech block will just lock into its locking recess on the right side of the receiver wall.

The belt is the standard Russian, closed pocket type, used in the RP46, holding 250 7.62mm × 54R cartridges. It is loaded by forcing the rounds into the metal pockets as far as they will go.

The gun fires from the open breech position and since it has the closed pocket belt, the cartridge is withdrawn from the belt, lowered to the level of

SG43. Note the smooth barrel and cocking handle between the spade grips (RMCS)

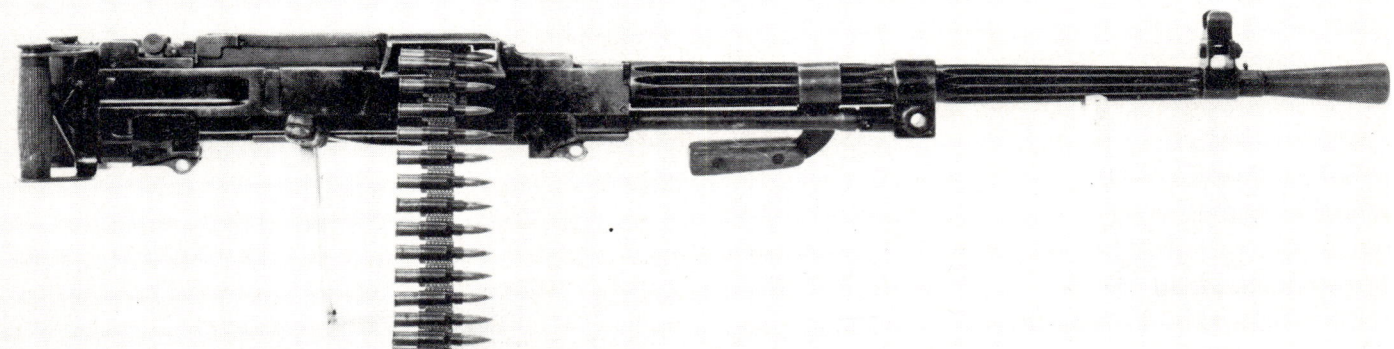

SGM. Note the cocking handle on the right-hand side on the fluted barrel (RMCS)

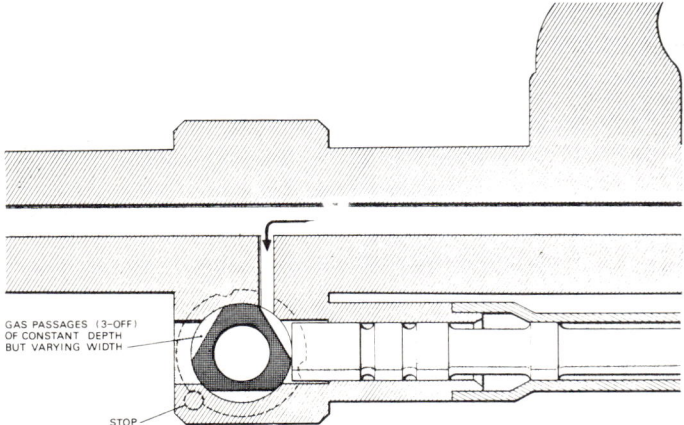

GAS PASSAGES (3-OFF) OF CONSTANT DEPTH BUT VARYING WIDTH

STOP

Gas regulator of the Goryunov M43 (RMCS)

the barrel and then rammed by the bolt.

It fires at automatic only and the massive barrel and the easy change make it possible to sustain a good rate of fire. There is no dial sight as used in the German or British MMGs of the period. The wheeled mounts incorporate coarse traverse and elevating gears and a fine elevating knob. The mounts have separate lock levers for elevation and traverse which are normally secured before firing but the traverse lock lever can be released so that free traverse through 360 degrees is possible.

The sights are simple and easily adjusted. The foresight is a cylinder mounted between two protectors. It is zeroed for elevation by screwing in and out, and for line by undoing the nut at the base and pushing the foresight on its dovetail into the required position. The rear sight is a U notch mounted on a tangent leaf. The leaf is placed upright before firing. It is graduated from 2-23 on the left and 2-20 on the right by 100s and adjustment is made by using the elevating knob at the top of the scale. There are figures on both sides of the frame. Those on the right are for use with light bullets Type L or LPS weighing 148 grains (9.6g). Those on the left are for heavy bullets, yellow-tipped, weighing 182gr (11.8g). There is a windage scale on the rearsight.

OPERATION

The feed cover is lifted to the vertical position and the belt is placed in the feedway from right to left with the first round located so that its rim lies inside the claws of the cartridge gripper. The cover is lowered and the gun cocked. The cocking handle on the SG43 and SG43M lies horizontally between the

The late Major F.W.A. Hobart (Editor of the first edition of this book) beside the SGMB with tripod in AA position (RSAF)

grips and on the others projects from the right of the receiver.

To fire the gun the trigger locking lever must first be raised with the left thumb and then the trigger can be operated with the right thumb.

The return spring drives the slide forward carrying the bolt. The bolt picks up the cartridge which is lying above the feedway, with the nose slightly down, and pushes it into the chamber. As it enters the chamber the extractor on the boltface grips the rim. The bolt comes to rest but the slide continues on. The raised piston post moves up the hollow interior of the bolt and forces the rear end out into a locking recess in the right hand wall of the receiver. The piston post then continues on and strikes the firing pin which is driven into the cap of the cartridge.

As the slide travels forward the diagonal grooves cut in its top surface engage ribs in the feed slide which is pushed out to the right and the feed pawl slips over the next cartridge in the belt.

Lying under the feed cover is the lower feed cover. Resting on top of this lower feed cover, with a lug which reaches down to the bolt, is the cartridge gripper. The lug engages in the bolt so the cartridge gripper reciprocates above it. The cartridge gripper has a pair of spring loaded claws which grip over the rim of the cartridge in the belt when the bolt goes fully forward.

The gases push the bullet up the bore and some are diverted into the gas cylinder and force the piston and slide rearwards. The piston post on the slide moves back along the hollow interior of the bolt. There is a period of free travel whilst the chamber pressure drops to a safe level and then the piston post forces the rear end of the bolt out of the locking recess and carries it back. The empty case is held to the breech face and is ejected through the lozenge shaped port on the left of the gun.

As the bolt goes back the cartridge grippers pull the round out of the belt and withdraw it. The spring loaded depressor arm projecting down from the underside of the feed cover forces the round down into the lower feed cover where it rests, nose slightly down, in the feedway where it can be fed by the next forward movement of the bolt.

As the slider goes back the grooves on the top surface pull the feed pawl inwards and the next round is moved over into position for the cartridge grippers to seize it at the end of the next feed stroke.

SG43 barrel lock (RMCS)

SGM backsight (RMCS)

SGM Micrometer CHS adjuster and lock (RMCS)

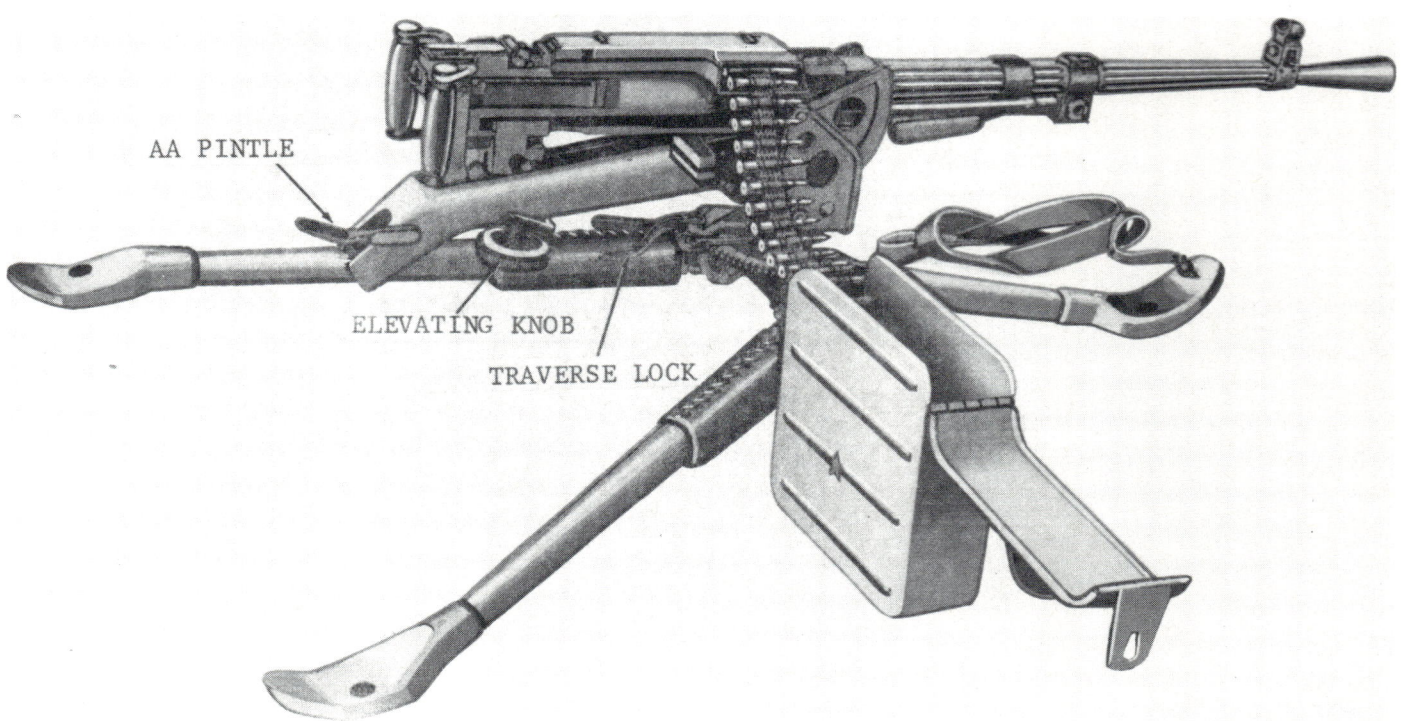

AA PINTLE

ELEVATING KNOB

TRAVERSE LOCK

SGM on the Sidorenko-Malinovski tripod

STRIPPING
(1) Lift the feed cover. Remove the belt. Ensure the chamber is clear.
(2) With the SG43 or SG43M pull the takedown pin on the lower right rear of the receiver to the right and remove the backplate.
With the SGM, SGMB or SGMT depress the detent in the latch at the top of the backplate. Slide the latch back. Rotate the backplate clockwise and remove it.
Withdraw the return spring.
(3) With the SGM, SGMB and SGMT remove the sear housing out of the back of the receiver.
(4) Grip the cocking handle and pull it rearwards. Remove the bolt and slide. The bolt can be lifted off the slide. The belt feed slide comes out of the receiver to the right. The cartridge gripper can be slid along the lower feed cover until it reaches the cutaway section and can then be removed.
To reassemble the gun the procedure is as follows:
(1) Put the cartridge gripper back in the lower feed cover with the lug at the back projecting down.
(2) Put the belt feed slide in the receiver. Push the ejector forward in the bolt.
(3) Put the bolt as far forward as possible over the piston post on the slide.
Put the cocking handle forward and place piston and bolt in the receiver.
(4) Slip the sear housing of the SGM, SGMB and SGMT – sear forward – into the sear.
(5) Put the return spring into the slide. Put the guide in the spring. Close up the backplate.
(6) Close the lower feed cover and adjust the lug of the cartridge gripper in the bolt. Close the feed cover.
(7) Pull the cocking handle and ensure everything works!

ACCESSORIES
There are several accessories issued with the guns. The chief ones are Cleaning rod. Chamber clearing brush. Two compartment oil and solvent container. Combination tool. Punch. Separated case remover. Barrel lock micrometer adjuster. Wooden mallet.

DATA
Cartridge: 7.62mm × 54R
Method of operation: Gas
Method of locking: Tilting block
Method of feed: Belt

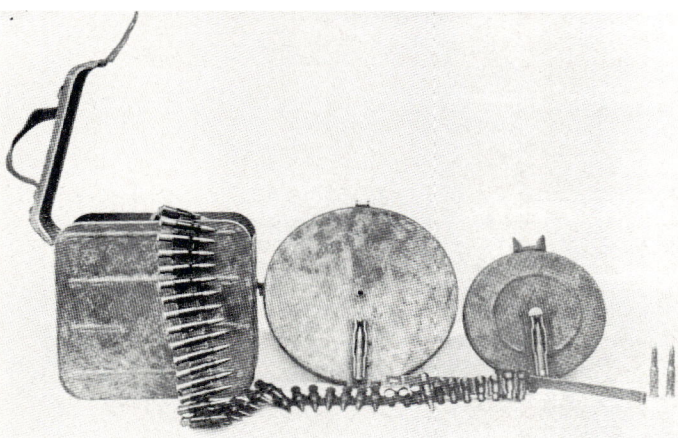

Left: The box and belt for the SG43. **Centre:** The drum for DP. **Right:** The drum for DT and the DA

SG43 foresight

SG43. The spade grips and the cocking handle located below and between them. The trigger locking lever and trigger are shown (RMCS)

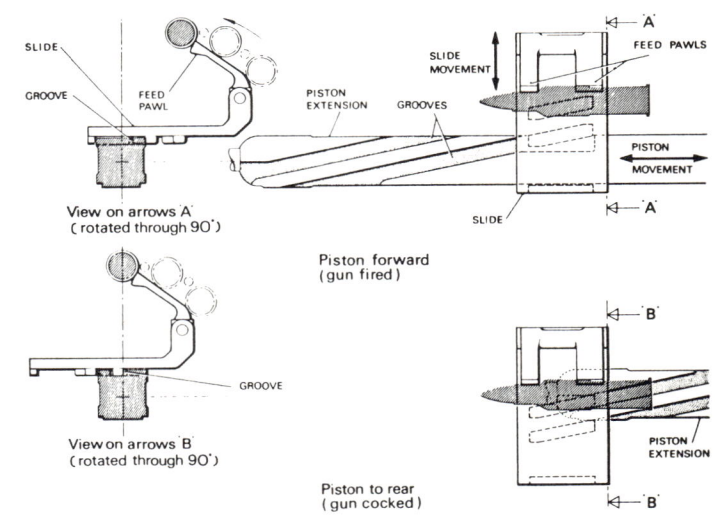

The feed system of the Goryunov MMGs (RMCS)

WEIGHTS
Gun empty: 13.6kg
Barrel: 4.8kg
Trigger pull: 4.6kp

LENGTHS
Gun: 1,120mm
Barrel: 719mm

MECHANICAL FEATURES
Barrel: 3 position regulator
    Rifling: 4 grooves RH. 1 turn in 228mm
    Cooling: Air. Quick change
Sights: Foresight: Cylinder on dovetail
    Rearsight: Tangent leaf with U backsight
    Graduation: 2-23 on left of sight frame by increments of 100
        metres
        2-30 on right of sight frame by increments of 100
        metres
    Zeroing: On foresight
    Windage: On rearsight
    Sight radius: 850mm

FIRING CHARACTERISTICS
Muzzle velocity: 800 metres/sec
Muzzle energy: 388mkp
Chamber pressure: 3,081kg/cm²
Rate of fire: Cyclic: 650 rounds/min
        Practical: 250 rounds/min
Range, maximum effective: 1,000 metres
Manufacturer: State Factories in Russia, Czechoslovakia and Poland
Status: No longer in production. No longer in service with Warsaw Pact forces. Used in considerable numbers by Egyptian and Palestinian and

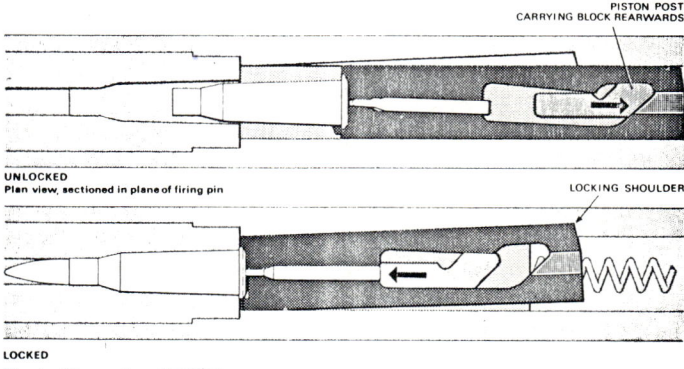

The locking action (RMCS)

other Middle Eastern forces and in Vietnam. Copied by the Chinese as Type 53 and 57 and may be encountered anywhere in the Far East. Widely used in Africa

7.62mm RPK LMG

Since the AK47 Assault Rifle was introduced, Russian policy has been to replace the older weapons with modern counterparts designed by Kalashnikov. The light machine gun in the Soviet infantry section has been, for several years, the RPD – a Degtyarev design. This has now been replaced by the RPK – the Ruchnoi Pulemet Kalashnikov. It was first seen in large numbers carried in the May Day Parade in the Red Square in Moscow in 1966 although its existence was known before this. The picture here shows a model stamped 1964 and there are no indications that it is other than a standard gun. The RPKS differs from the RPK in having a folding butt.

The RPK – like its predecessor the RPD – has no barrel change and therefore its capacity to produce sustained fire – even using a comparatively low heat input cartridge – must be limited to about 80 rounds a minute. Its low weight of 5kg and its magazine feed would indicate that it is intended more as a heavy barrelled rifle than as a light machine gun. However it replaces a belt-fed LMG, also without a barrel change, and with a capacity of 75 rounds in its drum magazine it is almost certainly employed as a light machine gun.

The RPK is basically an AKM with a longer and sturdier barrel. The bolt from the AKM can be placed in the RPK and will function perfectly satisfactorily in some 80 per cent of cases. The deciding factor is the question of the cartridge head space and experiments have shown that in 5 cases out of 6 a bolt from the rifle will have a satisfactory cartridge head space when inserted in the RPK. This gives great tactical advantages and means that the RPK gunner can call for a replacement bolt from the rifle section. Similarly the RPK will take the magazines from the AK47 or the AKM. It also has a 40-round box magazine of its own and a 75-round drum magazine. The 75-round drum magazine takes some while to fill and it appears that it would be used initially in action but thereafter replaced, during the assault or the early stages of defence, by the 40-round magazine. The box

The 75-round drum magazine of the RPK

magazines are loaded by placing a cartridge between the feed lips and pressing down. The drum magazine has a loading lever on the front which is used to compress the magazine spring before each round is inserted into

The RPK LMG with 40-round box magazine (RMCS)

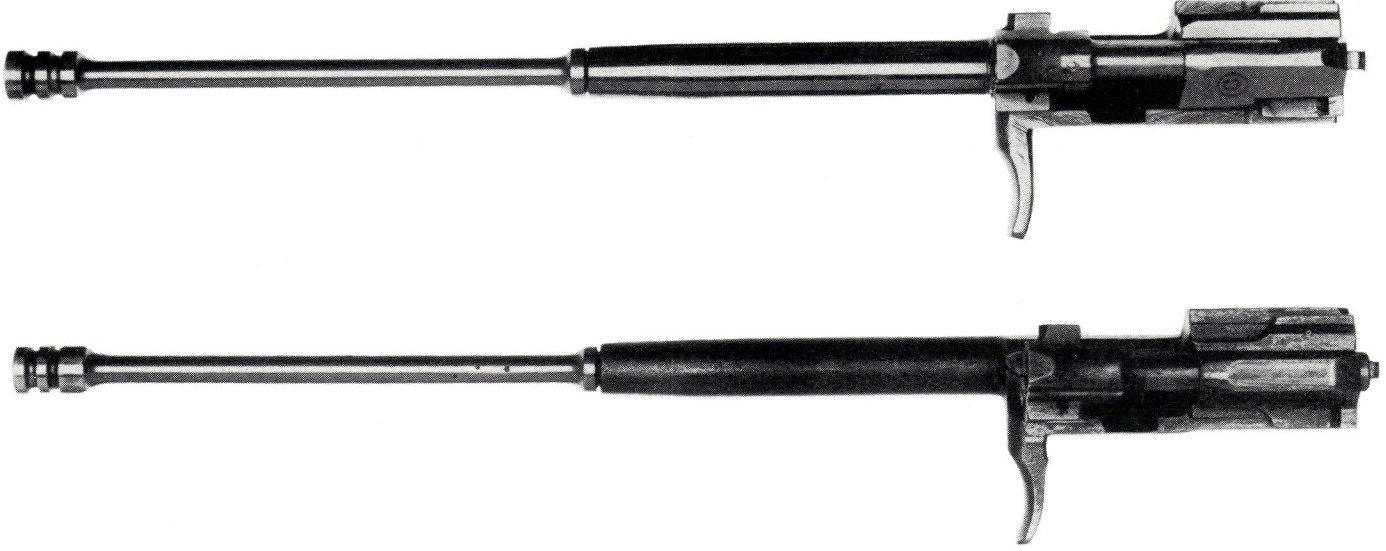

RPK and AKM bolts. **Top:** *Bolt and piston from the AK-47.* **Bottom:** *Bolt and piston from the RPK (RMCS)*

the feed lips. It is released after each round is loaded. The drum has an extension piece which is inserted in the magazine-well under the gun, in the same way as a box magazine. The magazine rests across the gun, sloping forward at about 45 degrees.

ACTION

The RPK is gas-operated with a vent located 21.5cm from the commencement of rifling and 28cm from the muzzle, opening into a cylinder located above the barrel. There is no gas regulator – which results in a slightly harsh action and a vigorous ejection to the right rear when the gun is clean, and a gradual slowing down of the rate of fire and force of ejection as firing progresses and fouling accumulates. The piston is forced back by gas pressure in the cylinder and there is a short period of free travel whilst the width of the cam slot cut in the piston extension travels across the unlocking lug of the bolt head and then the two locking lugs are caused to rotate anti-clockwise out of engagement with the locking shoulders. After unlocking is completed the piston carries the bolt to the rear.

The loading stroke of the bolt chambers the round; the bolt movement then ceases and further forward movement of the piston rotates the bolt to enable the locking lugs to engage in front of the locking shoulders.

The firing pin floats freely in the bolt. It cannot be reached by the hammer which comes up against a stop until such time as locking is completed. If the hammer is released early the bolt is forcibly closed and the reduced blow on the firing pin produces a misfire. The control of the hammer will be mentioned when discussing the trigger mechanism.

The cocking handle is integral with the bolt carrier and reciprocates as the gun fires. This gives a positive closure if adverse conditions of sand or mud prevent completion of locking. Whether this feature is entirely desirable is a matter of opinion. It can be maintained that brute force will close the bolt but it does not necessarily remove the cause of the stoppage and may well produce worse trouble by damaging the round which it is desired to force into the chamber.

There is a single extractor which is located on the right hand side of the bolt face which itself is recessed so that the base of the round is always fully supported in the chamber. A fixed ejector in the body runs along a groove in the bolt producing a strong ejection to the right rear of the gun. The barrel and chamber are both chromium plated.

There is no holding open device so the mechanism always stops in the forward position.

FIRE SELECTION

The selector is on the right hand side of the machined receiver and is a long lever of similar shape to that in the rifle. There are three positions: fully automatic at the middle position of travel, single shot at the bottom and safe at the top.

The selector arm in the 'safe' position carries out two functions. Its spindle carries an arm which when rotated to 'safe' covers the trigger extension and prevents trigger movement. The selector itself comes up to block the cocking lever and thus prevents the weapon being cocked whilst set at 'safe'. The limited bolt movement does not pass over the base of the round in the magazine but is sufficient for the firer to check that his chamber is empty either by visual inspection by day or by feeling at night.

THE TRIGGER MECHANISM

The weapon employs a system embodying a hammer with a cross bar at the top which forms two bents – one on the left arm and one in the centre. The function of the right extension on the cross bar will be dealt with later.

The nose of the trigger carries a single hook sear which engages in front of the left arm of the hammer bar, and a secondary spring loaded sear is rotated with the trigger.

The mechanism, in principle, is the same as that employed in the US M1 Garand and the M14. It is derived from that used in the Russian AK.47 but is

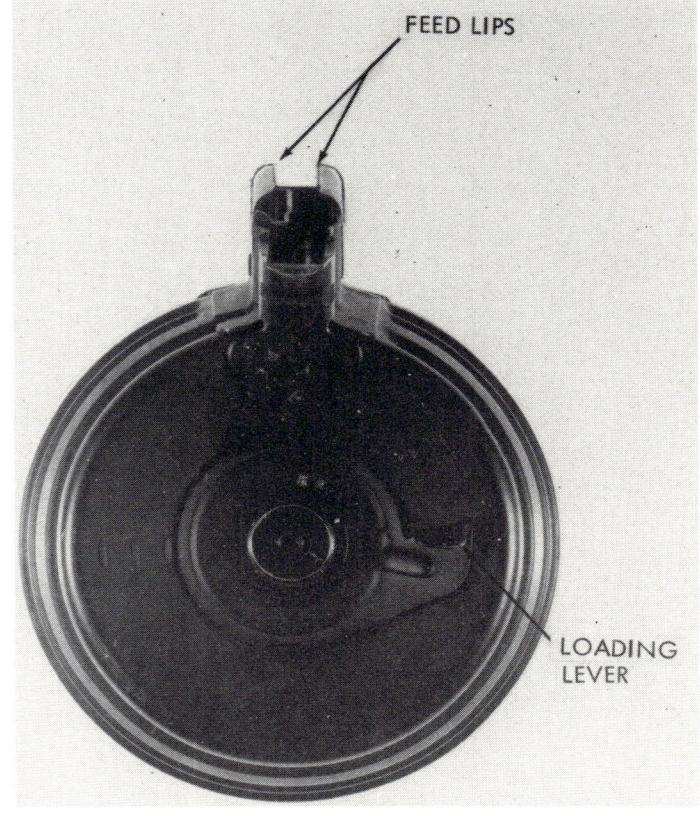

75-round drum of the RPK showing the loading lever which must be depressed for each round loaded

considerably modified. There is a safety sear which always holds back the hammer until the bolt carrier is fully forward when this rotates the safety sear clear of the hammer notch near the hammer axis.

When "single shot" is selected i.e. the bottom position of the selector lever, and the weapon is loaded and locking is completed, the hammer is held back only by the nose of the trigger. Rotation of the trigger moves the nose forward, the hammer bent is disengaged and one round is fired. The hammer is rotated back by the rearward movement of the bolt and the T bar at the top of the hammer is held back by the spring loaded secondary sear engaging the centre of the cross bar of the T. Since the trigger is still held back by the firer another shot cannot be fired until the trigger is released. The nose of the trigger moves up and holds the left hand arm of the hammer head and at the same time releasing the trigger moves the secondary sear clear, leaving the firer free to rotate the trigger which will, if locking is complete, allow the hammer to go forward under the influence of the two-strand multiple wire spring. This disconnector action occurs with every round fired.

When "auto" is selected the spindle on the selector lever is rotated. This carries an attachment which forces the secondary sear back and it is no longer contacted by the hammer in its rearward rotation. The fire is controlled entirely by the safety sear. When the bolt carrier is fully forward it rotates the safety sear extension which releases the hammer to fire another round. The process continues until the ammunition is expended (in which case the hammer remains forward) or the trigger is released and the hammer is held

RPK field stripped (RMCS)

back by the nose of the trigger and the safety sear.

The trigger-firing mechanism is obviously based on the Kalashnikov AK-47 but the following changes taken from the AKM have been incorporated. Instead of a double-hook – as on the AK-47 – the nose of the trigger has only the one which is on the left hand side. Mounted on the trigger axis and lying on the right side of the receiver is a spring loaded pawl which is struck by the right arm of the T of the hammer cross bar every time the hammer rises. The pawl is linked to another hook which moves over the hammer when the pawl is struck and holds the hammer down. The long curved face of the pawl results in the hook holding the hammer for an appreciable time. When the spring snaps the pawl back and releases the hook, the hammer rises but the delay reduces the cyclic rate.

SIGHTS

The rearsight is a leaf sliding on a ramp. It has, like all Soviet hand held weapons, a U backsight. There is also a night sight with an enlarged U with a fluorescent white spot. The backsight is graduated in hundreds of metres from 1 to 10. There is a windage scale.

The foresight is a cylindrical post which can be screwed up or down for elevation adjustment, when zeroing.

There is a battle sight which is a coarse U covering 100-300 metres.

STRIPPING

The RPK strips in exactly the same way as the AK-47 and AKM.

ACCESSORIES

The same accessories are carried as the AK-47 and AKM but there is no bayonet. A bipod is mounted well forward which can be folded under the barrel and clipped in place.

Some RPKs mount an infra-red night sight.

DATA

Cartridge: 7.62mm × 39
Method of operation: Gas
Method of locking: Rotating bolt
Method of feed: 40-round box magazine or 75-round drum. Can also use 30-round rifle magazine
Method of fire: Selective

WEIGHTS

Weapon: 5kg
30-round magazine, empty: 340g
30-round magazine loaded: 850g
40-round magazine empty: 368g
40-round magazine loaded: 1.13kg
75-round drum empty: 0.9kg
75-round drum loaded: 2.1kg

LENGTH

Weapon: 1,035mm
Barrel length: 591mm

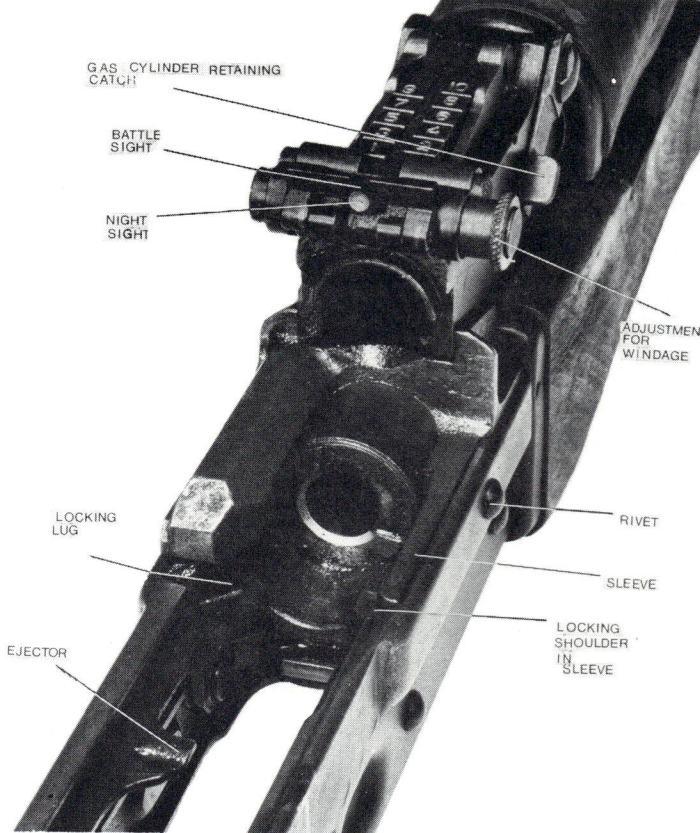

The rear sights and breech of the RPK (RMCS)

MECHANICAL FEATURES

Barrel: Regulator: Nil
    Rifling: 4 grooves RH. 1 turn in 241mm
        Diameter across lands 7.65mm
        Depth of grooves 0.1524mm
        Width of grooves 4.06mm
    Cooling: Air. No barrel change
Sights: Foresight: Cylindrical post
    Rearsight: Leaf notch
    Graduation: 1 to 10 by 100 metre steps
    Zeroing: Elevation and Line. Foresight screws up or down
    Sight radius: 570mm

FIRING CHARACTERISTICS
Muzzle velocity: 732 metres/sec
Muzzle energy: 216mkp
Recoil energy: 0.83mkp
Rate of fire: Cyclic: 660 rounds/min

Automatic: 80 rounds/min
S.S.: 40 rounds/min
Range, maximum effective: 800 metres
Manufacturer: State factories
Status: In production. In service in the USSR and East Germany at least

7.62mm PK MACHINE GUN FAMILY

As the family of Kalashnikov weapons replaced those of Degtyarev the time came for the replacement of the RP46 and the SGM series by a Kalashnikov design. The weapon selected for this task was the PK. It is a mixture of components and ideas from other weapons. The rotating bolt comes from the other Kalashnikov weapons, the AK47 and RPK, the cartridge gripper comes from the Goryunov SGM and so does the barrel change. The system of feed operation using the piston to drive the feed pawls comes from the Czech VZ52 LMG. The trigger comes from the Degtyarev RPD. The gun is obviously something of a mixture. Probably had Kalashnikov been allowed a rimless cartridge and an open pocket belt, a gun rather like a bigger RPK would have been produced which – with a good barrel change – would have been simple and easy for troops to understand.

DESCRIPTION

The Soviet 7.62mm PK machine gun first came to the notice of the United States intelligence in mid-1964 and, at that time, was believed to be the replacement for the even-then obsolescent RP46 Company Model machine gun. Since that time, however, the Russians have modified and improved the basic PK machine gun so that it now has supplanted not only the RP46, but also the SGM heavy machine gun. The following versions of the PK machine gun exist:

PK: the basic gun with a heavy fluted barrel, feed cover constructed from both machined and stamped components and a plain butt plate. The PK weighs about 9kg pounds.

PKS: the basic gun mounted on a tripod. The lightweight tripod (4.75kg) not only provides a stable mount for long range ground fire, it also can be quickly opened up to elevate the gun for anti-aircraft fire.

PKT: the PK as altered for coaxial installation in an armoured vehicle. The sights, stock, tripod, and trigger mechanism have been removed, a longer heavy barrel is installed, and a solenoid is fitted to the receiver back plate for remote triggering. An emergency manual trigger and safety is fitted.

PKM: a product improved PK, with a lighter weight, unfluted barrel, the feed cover constructed wholly from stampings, with a hinged butt rest fitted to the butt plate. Excess metal has been machined away wherever possible to reduce the weight down to about 8.4kg.

PKMS: PKM mounted on a tripod (similar to the PK).

PKB: The PKM with the tripod, buttstock, and trigger mechanism removed and replaced by twin spade grips and a butterfly trigger similar to those on the SGMB. This gun may possibly be known as the PKMB.

The PK and PKM machine guns are infantry support guns normally fired from their bipod mounts; however both versions can be installed in the front firing ports of the Soviet BMP infantry combat vehicle. The PKS also is an infantry gun and is used in the classic role of a heavy machine gun to provide long range area fire, cover final protective lines, and, in addition, provide anti-aircraft fire. The PKT is used in coaxial installations on most modern Soviet tanks and armoured personnel carriers. The PKM, although about one pound lighter than the PK, is used in the same role as the PK. The PKB (PKMB) is probably used as a pintle mounted gun on older SPCs such

PKS (US Army photograph)

as the BRDM, BTR50, and BTR60 similar to the manner in which the old SGMB was utilised.

The PK family of machine guns are gas-operated, rotary bolt locked, (Kalashnikov system), open-bolt fired, fully automatic, belt fed machine guns. The 7.62 × 54mm rimmed cartridge is fired and this is available in plain ball, steel-cored ball, armour piercing, armour piercing-incendiary and incendiary-ranging types. The steel-cored ball cartridge bullet weighs 147gr (9.5g) and has a muzzle velocity of 825 metres per second. The ammunition is fed by non-disintegrating metallic belts: current belts are composed of joined 25-round sections but earlier feed belts were made of one 250-round length. The belts are held either in 250-round ammunition boxes, in special large capacity boxes on tanks (for the PKT) or in a 50-round assault magazine attached to the bottom of the gun's receiver. The PK, PKM, and PKB guns are effective against area targets at ranges to 1000 metres. They have a cyclic rate of 650 shots per mintue. When set up on tripods for anti-aircraft fire and tracer control is used, these guns have an effective range of about 600 metres against army type aircraft. Limited US firing tests indicate that the PK has a very mild recoil effect and practically no muzzle climb which makes the weapons easily controllable by the gunner. The component parts of the PK are individually simple.

The receiver is constructed of stampings riveted up. It carries the very simple, auto-only, trigger mechanism and the belt feed mechanism.

The barrel is chrome plated and has a change system which is not as quick as that employed in most modern guns. To operate it, the gun must be unloaded; the feed cover comes up when the return spring guide is pressed and the feedway pivots up on the same pin. The barrel lock comes out to the side in the same way as the SGM and the barrel can be pulled forward out of the receiver – presumably with an asbestos glove. The new barrel goes in,

PK GPMG (US Army photograph)

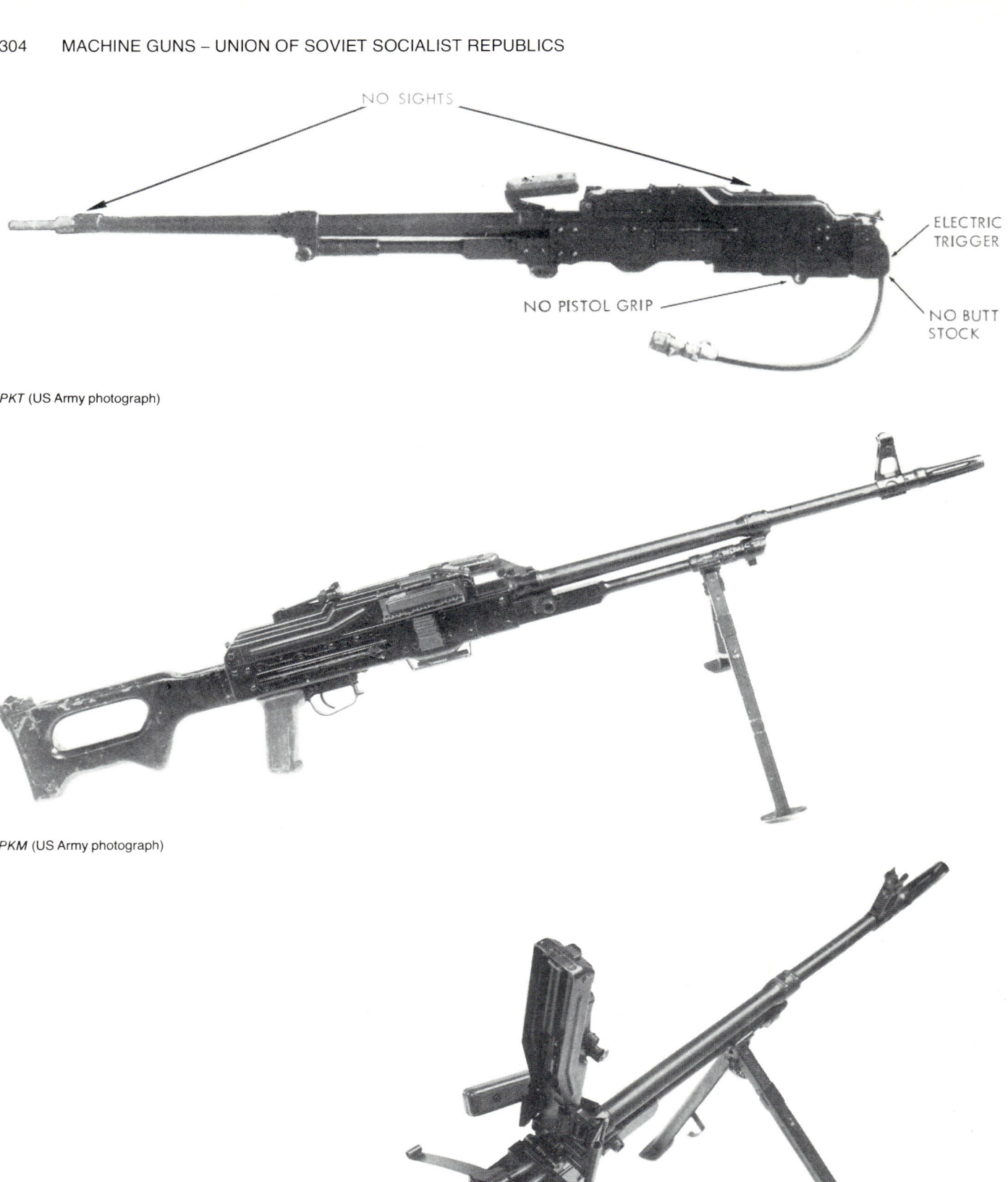

NO SIGHTS

ELECTRIC TRIGGER

NO PISTOL GRIP

NO BUTT STOCK

PKT (US Army photograph)

PKM (US Army photograph)

Loading the PKM. Note that the gun feeds from the right (US Army photograph)

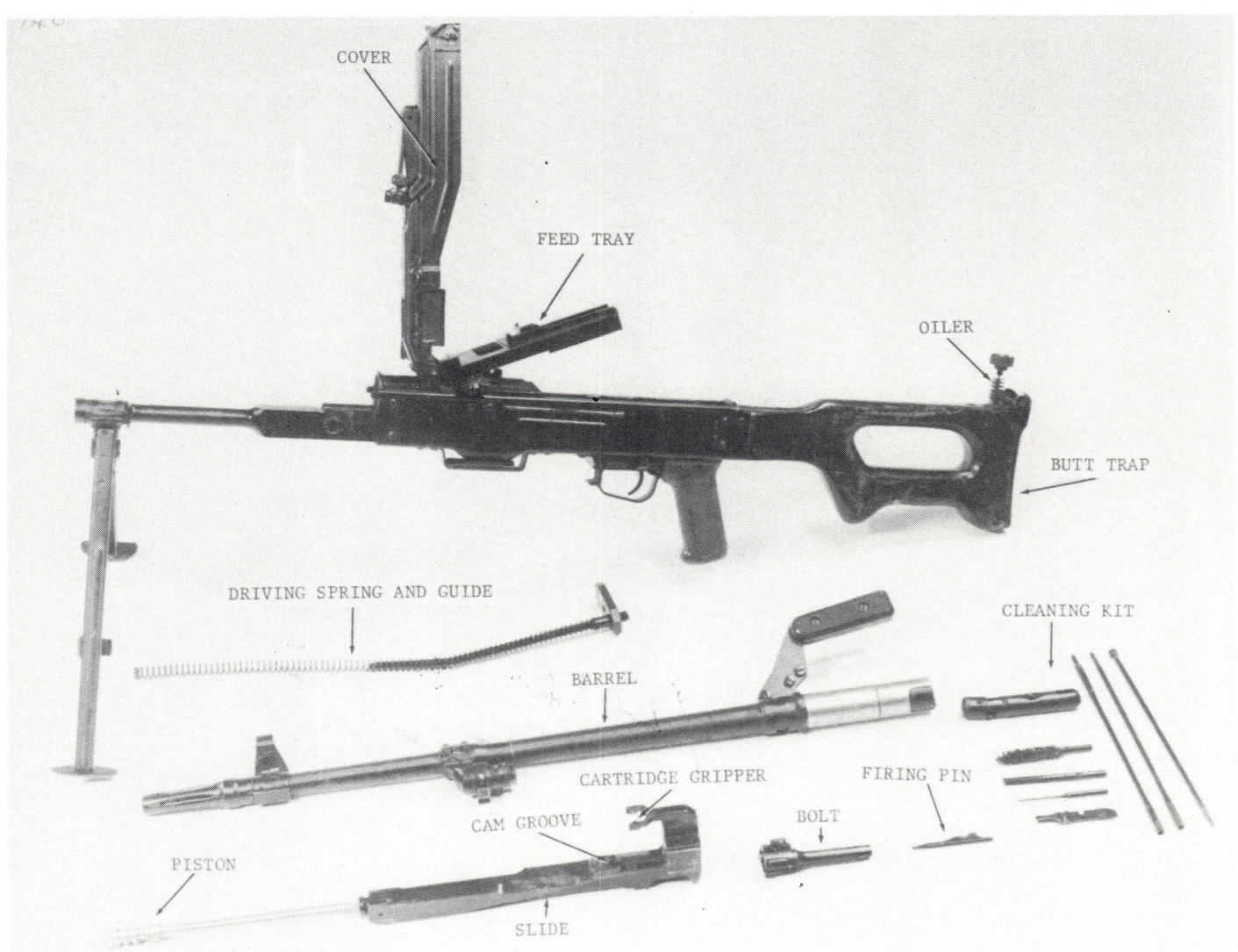

PKM field stripped (US Army photograph)

the lock is replaced, the feedway is lowered, belt replaced and feed cover lowered and the gun is ready to fire. A gas regulator is fitted. It is a variable track type with three numbered positions, similar to that in the Goryunov, and the head of the regulator is disengaged from its detent and moved to the selected number.

The gas piston is attached to the slide. Running along the length of the slide is a cam path on which bears the roller of the belt feed lever. The roller follows the cam as the slide goes back and the feed lever pivots outward causing the feed pawl attached to it to move in with the next cartridge in the belt. This is placed in position ready for the cartridge gripper. As the bolt goes forward a second cam path forces the feed lever in at the bottom, out at the top and the spring loaded feed pawl moves out over the next cartridge.

On the top of the slide is the bolt carrier. The relationship between this carrier and the bolt is exactly the same as that in the AK47. As soon as the bolt stops moving forward – having chambered the round – the cam path on the carrier engages the cam pin on the bolt and rotates it to lock into recesses.

At the rear of the slide, projecting forward over the bolt, is the cartridge gripper. When the bolt is fully forward the two spring-loaded claws of the gripper slip over the rim of the cartridge in the belt. When the bolt recoils the cartridge is pulled out of the belt and back. The spring-loaded cartridge depressor arm pushes the cartridge down out of the claws and it is held in the feed lips waiting for the bolt to drive it forward into the chamber.

OPERATION

The 250-round belt is loaded in the same way as the RP46 or the Goryunov. The feed cover of the gun can be lifted when the return spring guide is pressed. The belt is placed in the feedway – coming in from the right – with the first round gripped in the claws of the cartridge gripper. The feed cover is closed, the safety catch set to 'fire', and the cocking handle on the right of the receiver is retracted and returned to the forward position. If the safety catch is left in the rear position at 'safe' the gun cannot be cocked.

With the safety at 'fire', pulling the trigger releases the sear and the compressed return spring drives the slide forward. The bolt picks up the round in the feed lips and chambers it. The extractor grips the rim and bolt movement ceases. As the slide goes forward the cam path along the side forces the feed pawl outwards over the next cartridge in the belt. The bolt carrier moves forward with the slide after the round is chambered and the bolt is rotated 30 degrees to the locked position. The firing pin is carried on the bolt carrier and it comes through the bolt to fire the cap.

The gases force the bullet up the bore. Some of them pass through the gas vent and drive the piston and slide back. The bolt carrier moves back and the firing pin is retracted. There is a period of free travel whilst the pressure drops and then the cam slot on the bolt carrier engages the cam pin on the bolt and the bolt rotates to become unlocked. The bolt recoils. The empty case is held on the bolt face and the slide compresses the return spring. The cartridge gripper pulls the cartridge out of the belt and carries it back. The cam path on the side of the bolt carrier forces the feed roller outwards and the upper end of the pivoted feed arm moves inwards so the feed pawl pushes the belt into the gun and the next round reaches the cartridge stop where it remains for the gripper to come forward again.

The empty case is ejected by the fixed ejector. The depressor arm forces the live round down into the feed lips, waiting for the bolt to go forward again. The cycle is repeated as long as the trigger is pulled and ammunition remains in the gun.

STRIPPING

(1) Press forward the return spring guide and lift the feed cover. Remove the belt and check the chamber. Remove the barrel by slipping the lock out and pulling the barrel forward.
(2) Press in the return spring guide and ease the return spring with its guide upwards, out of the gun. Hold the cartridge grippers and pull the bolt carrier, bolt slide and piston out of the gun.
(3) Pull the bolt forward and rotate it free of the carrier. Lift the firing pin out of its recess in the carrier.

RE-ASSEMBLY

(1) Put the firing pin in its recess in the bolt carrier. Put the bolt back over the firing pin on to the bolt carrier.
(2) Pull the bolt forward on the slide, place the piston in the gas cylinder. Pull the trigger and push the bolt carrier home. Put the return spring into its seating in the slide and press the guide forward until it seats against the rear wall of the receiver. Replace the barrel and lock it. Close the feed cover.

ACCESSORIES

The largest accessory is the tripod which although primarily designed for general use, can be quickly adapted for anti-aircraft fire.

Belt boxes for 50-, 200- and 250-round belts are issued. The 50-round box can be attached to the underside of the PK for the assault role.

Spare parts and the usual combination tool and the oil-solvent container are carried.

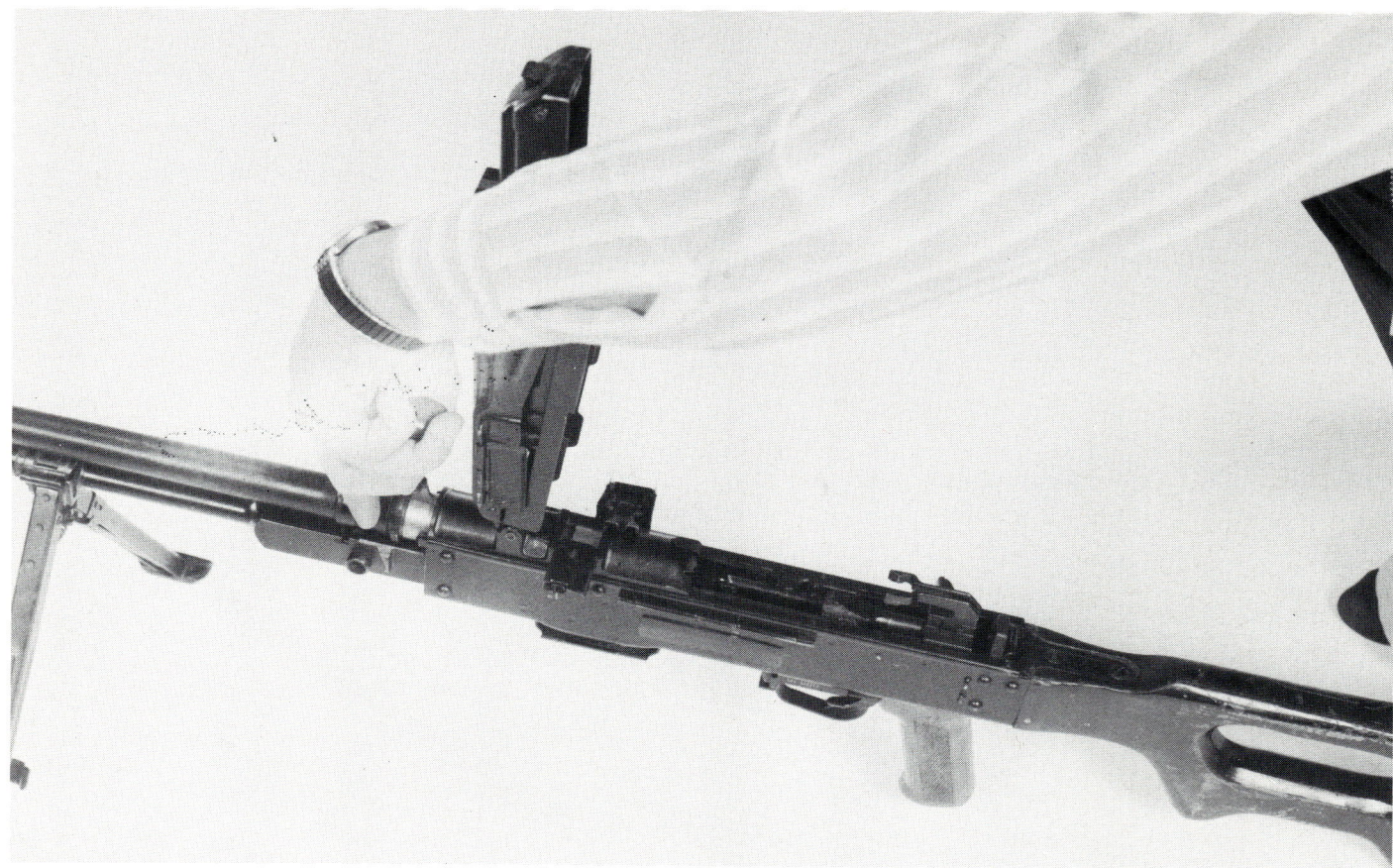

Changing the barrel of the PKM (US Army photograph)

DATA (PKS)
Cartridge: 7.62mm × 54R
Method of operation: Gas
Method of locking: Rotating bolt
Method of feed: Belt. 50, 100, 200 and 250 rounds
Method of fire: Automatic

WEIGHTS
Gun, empty: 9kg
Tripod: 7.5kg
Belt of 50 rounds: 1.22kg

LENGTHS
Gun: 1,160mm
Gun on tripod: 1,267mm
Barrel: 658mm

MECHANICAL FEATURES
Barrel: Bore: Chromium plated
Regulator: 3 position
Rifling: 4 grooves RH
Cooling: Air. Quick change
Sights: Foresight: Cylindrical post
Rearsight: Vertical leaf. Windage scale
Zeroing: Vertical: foresight. Lateral: foresight on dovetail

FIRING CHARACTERISTICS
Muzzle velocity: 825 metres/sec

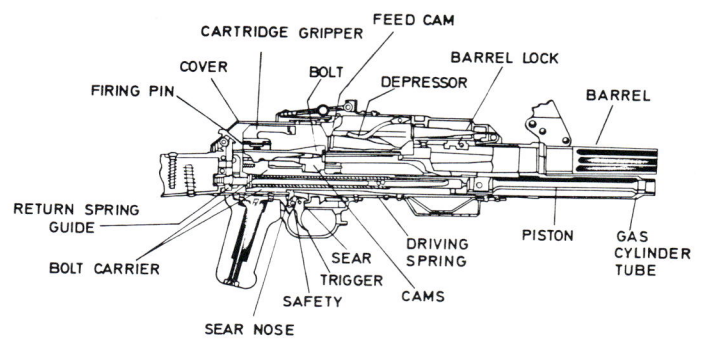

PK section

Muzzle energy: 395mkp
Chamber pressure: 3,081kg/cm²
Rate of fire: Cyclic: 650 rounds/min
Automatic: 250 rounds/min
Range, maximum effective: 1,000 metres
Manufacturer: State factories
Status: Current manufacture. In service with Russian and allied armies

12.7mm DEGTYAREV HMG
(DSh K-38 and Model 38/46)

The DSh K-38 was designed by Degtyarev and was based on an earlier model of his, the DK, which was produced in very limted numbers in 1934. Although the main design was that of Degtyarev, the feed was designed by G. S. Shpagin who achieved a considerable reputation and became a Lieutenant-General in the Red Army. Shpagin's feed system was a rotary type in which the rounds in the belt were successively removed from the links and then fed through a feed plate and collected by the bolt in its forward travel. This was a complicated process and required skill and training if stoppages were to be avoided.

In 1946 the rotary feed was replaced by the conventional shuttle type feed used on the Degtyarev model RP46. This difference produces a ready recognition feature as the DSh K-38 has the large circular drum like feed mechanism and the Degtyarev Model 38/46 has a flat rectangular feed cover. There is no interchangeability between the parts of the two guns.

The 12.7mm (0.5in) guns have been used extensively by European and Asian Communist countries. The European countries who originally used

the gun on a tripod now fit it into a number of vehicles for anti-aircraft and anti-soft skin vehicle duties. It is still used on the ground mount by the Asian Communist countries. The Chinese Communist version is a copy of the Model 38/46 known as the Type 54 HMG and can be identified by the Chinese characters on the receiver behind the feeder. The Czechs make a towed four-gun anti-aircraft assembly.

The DSh K-38 feeds from the left and has a fixed barrel. The Model 38/46 can readily be adapted for feed from either side, by changing some parts in the feed mechanism, and it has a quick change barrel.

OPERATION

The belt is a continuous metallic link type holding 50 rounds. Each link takes a cartridge which is located by the nib on the belt entering the groove of the cartridge. Moving the ammunition is facilitated if it is placed in a box.

The cover latch of the DSh K-38 is located at the rear of the cover and it permits the cover to be rotated about the hinge at the front.

The Russian 12.7mm DSh K on a Sokolov mount (RSAF)

The belt is placed in the gun from the left with the first link under the link stripper and the first cartridge in the top compartment of the rotating feed drum. The weight of the ammunition is taken off the feed drum and the ammunition and drum pushed round through some 120 degrees. When the drum will rotate no further the feed cover is closed. The cocking handle between the spade grips is retracted and the slide held to the rear on the sear. The compartments of the rotating feed drum are now full and the first round is pressed through the feed plate into the path of the bolt.

The Model 38/46 should be regarded as a large version of the RP46. The belt tab is inserted into the feed guide and pulled through until the first round passes over the stop pawl which will prevent it from falling out. When the cocking handle is fully retracted the gun is ready to fire.

When the trigger is pressed it raises the rear end of the sear release lever which pivots and forces down the sear out of engagement with the slide. The compressed return spring drives the slide and bolt forward. The feed rib on the bolt passes under the feed drum of the DSh K-38 and picks up the round which is projecting through the feed plate. In the Model 38/46 the round is held up to the catch stop. The round is pushed forward and into the chamber. The extractor grips into the cannelure at the base of the cartridge and the bolt comes to rest. On each side of the bolt is a long locking lug which is pivoted at the front end into a recess in the side of the bolt and opens out from the bolt at the rear end – like a flap – as the firing pin, which is attached to the slide, drives forward. The projecting lugs are cammed out by shoulders on the firing pin and engage in recesses in the side walls of the receiver. The firing pin goes in a further 16mm after locking is completed and the cap is fired.

The bullet passes up the bore and the gases following it enter the cylinder and drive the piston back. The slide carrying the firing pin is retracted and there is about 16mm of free play whilst the chamber pressure drops. The recesses cut into the top surface of the slide, bolt and firing pin go back as one unit. The empty case comes out on the bolt face and is ejected through the bottom of the receiver. The return spring is compressed to provide

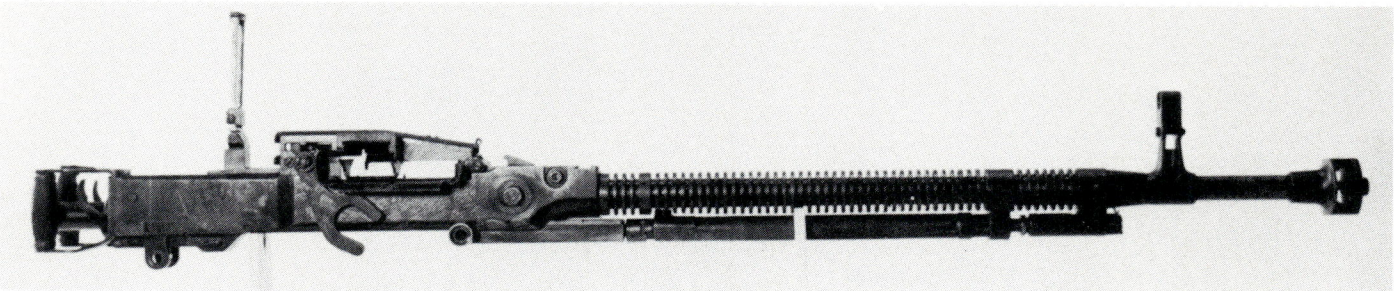

12.7mm Degtyarev 38-46 HMG (RMCS)

energy for the next forward stroke.

As the operating stud on the slide comes back it enters the open stirrup of the feed lever and rotates it back. On the Model 38/46 this operates the feed slide as in the RP46. A cam path moves the belt feed slide inward and the feed pawl brings the next round up to the cartridge guide and over the stop pawl. As the feed slide goes forward with the operating stud, the feed pawl is moved out to engage the next round in the belt.

On the DSh K-38 the backward movement of the operating stud rotates the feed lever and a pawl bears on a ratchet in the feed drum causing it to rotate. (In a manner not unlike the revolving chamber of a pistol revolver). At the same time another pawl prevents counter rotation. The rotation of the drum draws the belt into the gun. The first cartridge is pressed along the lips in the feed plate and is subsequently forced forward on the next feed stroke of the bolt.

STRIPPING

(1) Lift the feed cover and remove the belt.
(2) Check the feed drum of the DSh K-38 is empty.
(3) Check the chamber is clear.
(4) Push out the locking pin at the rear of the receiver and detach the back plate from the receiver.
(5) Remove the sear through the back of the receiver.
(6) Force the gas cylinder forward and rotate it clockwise to free it from the barrel.
(7) Retract the cocking handle. Remove gas piston and slide with bolt and firing pin. Remove gas cylinder.
(8) On the Model 38/46 unscrew the barrel lock securing nut. Remove barrel lock to the side. Pull barrel forward out of the receiver.

RE-ASSEMBLY

(1) Assemble the firing pin in the bolt and place locking lugs on the sides. Place bolt on slide and push into receiver.
(2) Pull gas cylinder forward and rotate anti-clockwise to re-connect it with the barrel.
(3) Slide sear mechanisms into receiver. Drop back plate. Replace locking pin.
(4) On Model 38/46 replace barrel, barrel lock and searing nut.

ACCESSORIES

The following are issued with the 12.7mm HMG's.

(1) Cleaning rod.
(2) Chamber cleaning brush.
(3) Oil and solvent container.
(4) Combination tool.
(5) Punch.
(6) Separated case extractor.

SIGHTS

The ground sights are of orthodox configuration. The front sight is a pillar which screws up and down for zeroing. The bolt through the base of the front sight can be loosened and the sight moved totally for zeroing.

The rearsight has vertical twin pillars with a U backsight between them. When the sight is upright the elevating screw is at the top. Rough setting of the sight is achieved by pressing the slide catch and moving the slide connecting the pillars, up or down until the upper edge is aligned with the required range reading which is shown in hundreds of metres. The elevating screw gives fine adjustment. There is a windage knob at the base of the

After the Six Day War (UPI)

sight.

The anti-aircraft sight Model 1943 requires the concerted action of two men. The No 2 rotates his sight and lines it up along the fuselage of the target and so indicates the approach angle. He does this by rotating the target course hand crank. The drive shaft also rotates the No 1's sight. The No 1 lines up the rear, peep sight with an aim off lead determined by his estimate of the target speed.

MOUNTINGS

The basic mount for both the D.Sh. K38 and the Model 38/46 is the model 1938. This is a two wheeled mount that can be moved by man, mule or motor. A shield is sometimes provided for ground use. The traverse and elevation are coarse with a fine elevation adjustment. The gun is locked in position before firing.

The mount can be converted for AA use by removing the gun and shield and then taking off the wheels and axle. The three legs are spread, the gun mounted above them on the saddle and the sight inserted in the dovetail on the left side of the receiver.

DATA
Cartridge: 12.7mm × 108
Method of operation: Gas
Method of locking: Projecting lugs
Method of feed: Bolt
Method of fire: Automatic

WEIGHTS
Gun: 35.7kg
Barrel: 12.7kg

LENGTHS
Gun: 1,588mm
Barrel: 1,070mm

MECHANICAL FEATURES
Barrel: Regulator: 3 position
　　　Rifling: 8 groove RH. 1 turn in 394mm
　　　Cooling: Air. M38-46 has changeable barrel
Sights: Foresight: Cylindrical post
　　　Rearsight: Vertical leaf with U backsight
　　　Graduation: 0-33 by 100 metres increments
　　　Zeroing: On foresight
　　　Sight radius: 1,111mm

FIRING CHARACTERISTICS
Muzzle velocity: 860 metres/sec
Rate of fire: Cyclic: 575 rounds/min
　　　　　Practical: 80 rounds/min
Range, maximum effective: 2,000 metres

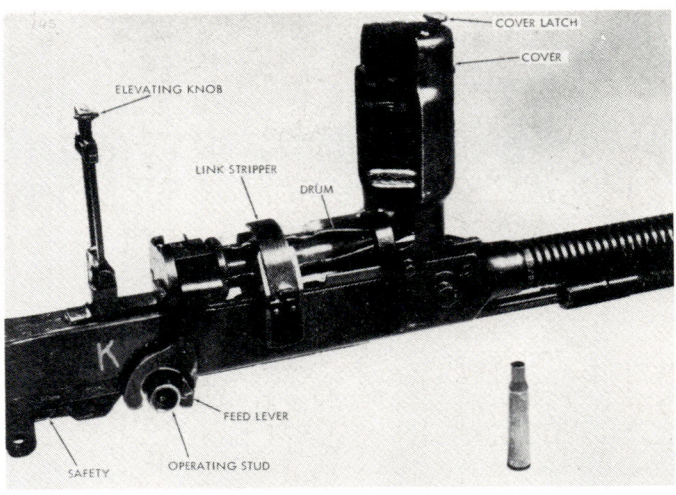

DSh K 12.7mm HMG drum feed arrangements (RSAF)

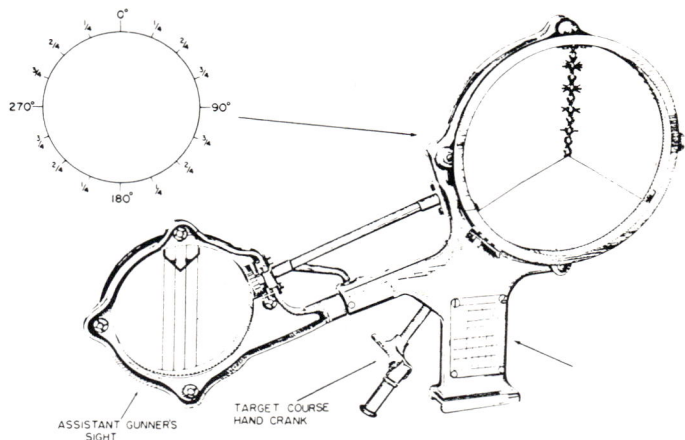

M 1943 AA sight

Manufacturer: Soviet State Factories
Status: No longer manufactured. Still in service in Russian and allied armies. Used by Chinese (as Type 54), Arab and Vietnamese forces and has been seen with Zimbabwean guerrillas

---

14.5mm KPV HEAVY MACHINE GUN

This gun was designed immediately after World War II by Vladimirov expressly to fire the high velocity round produced for the PTRD-41, Degtyarev, anti-tank rifle. It is a very well made, solid weapon with some characteristics and ideas new to Soviet weaponry.

METHOD OF OPERATION

The gun is short recoil operated with gas assistance supplied by a muzzle booster. Before firing the bolt assembly is securely locked to the barrel. The locking lugs consist of 8 rows of castellated form each 1.65mm deep which are rotated to lock into corresponding recesses on the barrel extension. The pressure build up forces the breech block rearwards and this in turn draws the barrel back with it against the resistance offered by the inertia of the assembly and the force of the return spring. Since the barrel has its own run out spring this also opposes the rearward movement. When the projectile reaches the hole in the muzzle cap the gases are briefly sealed and the resulting pressure build up inside the booster drives the barrel backwards to give increased momentum to the recoiling parts. The breech block and barrel have a free recoil of slightly less than 5mm which provides the mechanical safety after firing and allows the bore pressure to fall to a safe level. The bolt head carries a roller on each side running in a curved cam path in the bolt body and these rollers come up against curved cam paths in the body of the gun. The rotation imposed on the bolt head unlocks it from the barrel. There is a 6mm pitch on the locking lugs and whilst the bolt head is being rotated it is drawn back this distance which provides the slow powerful leverage required for the initial extraction of the cartridge case. At the same time the firing pin is withdrawn. The unlocking is completed when the barrel and bolt have recoiled together for 18mm. As the rollers are rotated by the cams in the body they are running in the slots in the bolt body and thus accelerate the bolt body to the rear. The relative displacement between the bolt head and bolt body is slightly less than 18mm.

The fired case is held in a T slot in the bolt head which grips the rim and extractor groove, and the rearward movement of the unlocked bolt withdraws the expended case from the chamber.

The next round to be fed is held by two claws which move back with the bolt and extract this round from the closed pocket metal belt. When the bolt head is rotated to unlock, the T slot is then lined up to receive the next round

which is forced down by a cam operated arm and displaces the case of the previous fired round which falls out of the bottom of the gun. However this system cannot operated when the gun fires single shot or the last round of the belt is fired. To cater for these circumstances a spring loaded arm is fitted behind the cam which depresses the cartridge feed arm down far

The belt is pulled through by the pawl on the tray, moved over by the action of the reciprocating gas piston

The bolt of the KPV. The rotation of the roller in the cam slot rotates the bolt head which locks into the interrupted threads in the barrel

KPV 14.5mm Heavy machine gun

enough to eject the empty case.

During bolt recoil the belt is fed across and a live round positioned ready to be gripped by the claws above the bolt, as the latter comes forward.

When the bolt has reached its rearmost position energy is stored in the return spring and the buffer. This carries the bolt forward, driving a round into the chamber and slipping the feed claws over the waiting round in the belt. The bolt head – as with all rotating bolt recoil operated machine guns – must be correctly positioned to allow the locking lugs to enter the recesses in the barrel extension. This is accomplished in the KPV by locking the bolt head and releasing it to be free for rotation when the locking latch hits a cam in the body. The two bolt head rollers run on to locking cams in the side walls of the body and are rotated to lock the bolt head to the barrel. The bolt body then closes up to the bolt head and the firing pin is driven through into the cap and the round is fired. As the bolt goes forward the feed pawl is moved outwards to slip over the next round in the belt ready to draw it towards the barrel on recoil.

The system is not as complex as it may sound and the weapon is obviously designed for ease of manufacture.

LOADING

To load the gun it is necessary to allow the claws that withdraw the round from the belt to grip the rim. Since the claws are mounted 51mm behind the bolt face and the round is held in the belt at the shoulder it is necessary to withdraw the bolt about 63mm before inserting the belt and pulling it fully through . The bolt is then released and the return spring will force it forward and allow the extractor claws to ride over the rim of the positioned round.

The bolt is then withdrawn fully to the rear until held by the sear. This cocking movement must be continuous. If the bolt is checked half way back the live round will fall off the T slot and out of the gun.

TO UNLOAD

Cock the gun.

Lift the feed tray.

Pull back the round which is in line with the bolt, release the belt stop pawls and withdraw the belt.

Allow the bolt forward under control until the round on the bolt face reaches the extraction position where it will fall out of the T slot. In a hot dirty gun it will probably need to be pushed down and out of the gun. Continue to control the bolt until it is fully forward.

TO REMOVE THE BARREL

Unload.

Cock the gun.

Rotate the triangular barrel catch 45 degrees clockwise. This rotates the locking sleeve and the barrel is then taken out forward using the handle provided.

STRIPPING

The gun is designed to be field stripped without the use of any special tools. The procedure is simple.
(1) Raise the top cover.
(2) Cock the gun.
(3) Remove the barrel.
(4) Rotate the cover through 60 degrees and lift the front end up.
(5) Lift the feed tray out of the body.
(6) Control the bolt until it is fully forward to release the compressed return spring.
(7) Release the catch and rotate the body end plate controlling it against the return spring which will then come out.
(8) Depress the sear and withdraw the bolt. The bolt head can then be removed from the body.

GENERAL IMPRESSIONS

The gun was designed for simplicity of manufacture. The body is a simple metal cylinder to which the various attachments are rivetted. There is some welding. There is considerable use of stampings e.g. the feed tray.

There is no lack of strength and all the components are both robust and well finished. Apart from the ejection opening it is well sealed against

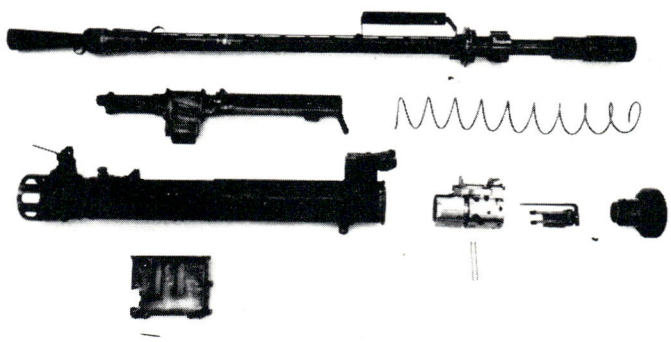

The KPV stripped

ingress of dirt and dust.

Whilst the gun was designed initially as an anti-aircraft gun it is extremely suitable as an armoured fighting vehicle gun. It has a very short inboard length (60cm) which is less than the .5 Browning, the belt feed system which allows breakdown in 10 round lengths is very suitable for vehicle use and so is the alternative left or right hand feed but the forward barrel change is not an advantage in this role although it is difficult with a 135cm barrel to devise any suitable alternative.

MOUNTING

Towed carriage mountings exist for one, two or four guns: they are known as ZPU-1, ZPU-2 and ZPU-4 respectively; There is also a self-propelled four-gun mounting. These have all been very successful and the twin-towed and four-gun towed assemblies were used extensively in North Vietnam.

DATA

Length of gun: 2,006mm
Weight of gun: 49.1kg
Length of barrel: 1,346mm
Weight of barrel with jacket: 19.5kg
Inboard length: 597mm

SIGHTS

Front: Cylindrical post
Rear: Tangent leaf U.200-2,000metres by 100 metre intervals
Zeroing
Elevation: Front cylindrical post screws up or down
Line: Moveable dovetail base to front sight
Radius: 736mm

BARREL

Chromium plated – no sign of liners. Fitted muzzle booster and flash hider.
Air cooled, quick change
Rifling: RH one turn in: 406mm
Bore diameter: 14.55mm
Groove diameter: 14.93mm
Groove width: 4mm
Land width: 1.83mm

FEED

Left or right hand
Ammunition: AP1 or HEIT
Belt: Continuous metallic closed pocket. Breaks down into groups of 10 rounds. Can be fed either way up
Bullet weight: 923 grains (60 grams)
MV: 1,000metres/sec
Cyclic rate of fire: 600rpm
Cartridge Head Space: Non adjustable
Manufacturer: State factories
Status: In widespread service and client countries

UNITED KINGDOM

.303in MAXIM MACHINE GUN

Hiram C. Maxim was an American who came to England in 1881 and set himself up at 57D Hatton Garden and, with some American machine tools, not only invented but also manufactured the first true machine gun. In 1884 he demonstrated his first model which was a large, heavy, and clumsy piece of equipment some 1.45mm long and 1.07mm high on its tripod; but the model, although of great technical interest, was never produced. Instead Maxim simplified it, greatly modified the action, lightened it and improved the feed. The production model was ready for demonstration in 1884; and in the same year Maxim approached Vickers, the armament and ship building firm, and the Maxim Company was formed with Albert Vickers as Chairman. The manufacturing works were at Crayford in Kent.

The gun was demonstrated extensively in 1887 and 1888 to the United Kingdom, Austria, Hungary, Germany, Italy, Russia, Switzerland and the USA. The trials were successful – in spite of many difficulties put in Maxim's way – but orders were slow. The British Government for example purchased three guns and it was not until 1891 that a scale of two guns per battalion was authorised for the regular army.

The Germans and Russians set up manufacturing plants of their own.

The Maxim gun was first used in action in the Matabele War of 1893. They were very successful in the Sudan campaign and were employed extensively by both sides in the Boer War. The Russo-Japanese war of 1904 showed the potentialities of the gun but it was in the first World War that the Maxim used by the German Army, and the British Maxim and Vickers – a derivative of the Maxim – were so terribly effective.

In the First World War the Maxim gun was manufactured at the Royal Small Arms Factory at Enfield Lock until 1917.

DATA
Note: The following data relate to the British-made Maxim but they are generally representative of all manufacturers.
Cartridge: .303 Mk VII
Method of operation: Short recoil
Method of locking: Toggle joint
Method of feed: 250 round fabric belt
Method of fire: Automatic
Weight: 18.2kg
Length: 1,181mm
Barrel: 718mm
        Rifling: 4 grooves RH
        Cooling: Water
Sights: Foresight: Blade
        Rearsight: Leaf notch
Muzzle velocity: 744 metres/sec
Muzzle energy: 318mkp
Rate of fire: Cyclic: 600 rounds/min
        Automatic: 200 rounds/min
Range, maximum effective: 2,770 metres
Status: No longer manufactured. Not in regular military use. In service with Chinese militia (Type 24), and in Vietnam

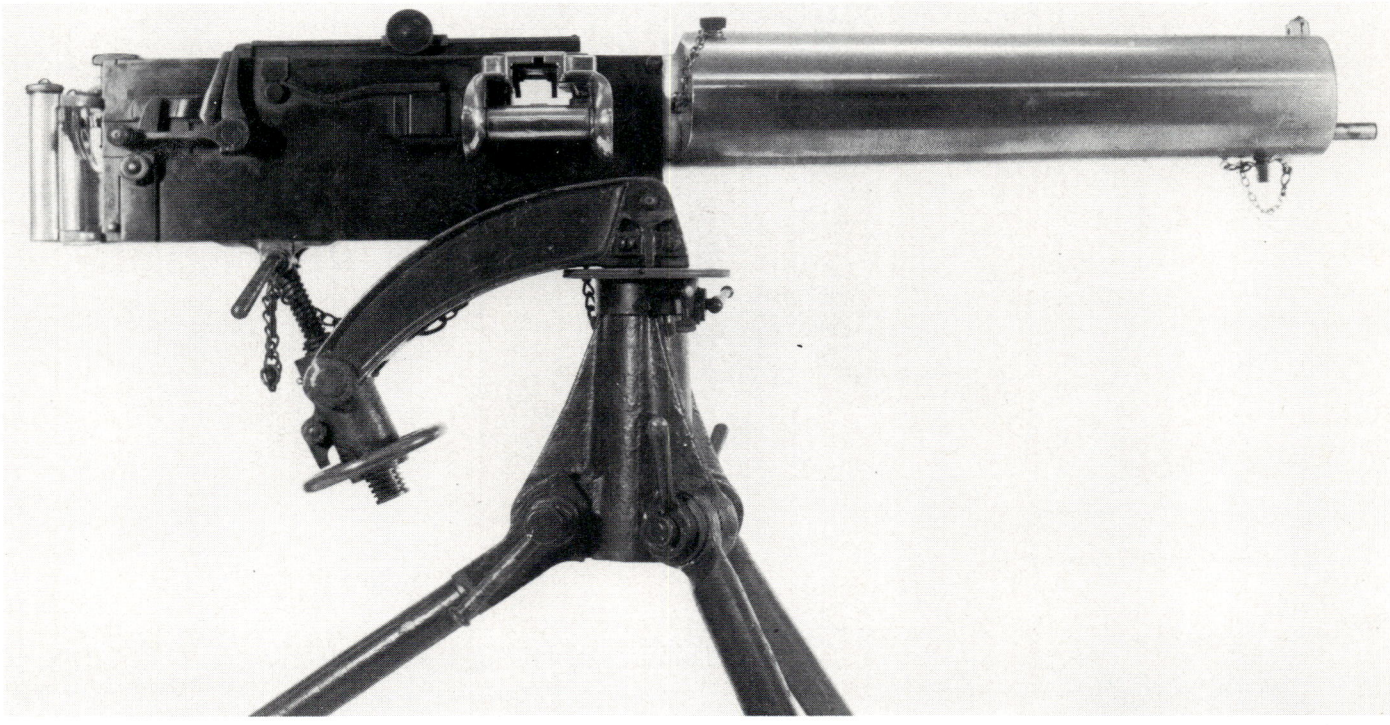

This brass-jacketed Maxim was manufactured at the Royal Small Arms Factory at Enfield. Production of this model continued until 1917

.303in VICKERS MK 1 MACHINE GUN

'The Vickers Machine Gun was a modification to the Maxim carried out by Vickers at Erith. It was an improvement on the original design being both more efficient and lighter. It was adopted by the British Army in November 1912.

The Vickers gun operated on the short recoil principle. The locking device was a toggle joint. The front arm was attached to the breech block – or 'lock' as it was called – and the rear arm was secured to a rearward extension of the barrel. Each of these arms could pivot at the joint and also at their point of junction. When the gun was ready for firing the junction of the two arms lay on the floor of the receiver and below the other two pivots. Thus to break the toggle joint an upward force was required at the central pivot.

When the gun fired, the gas pressure forced the lock back. The two toggle arms were pushed back and the barrel extension was driven rearwards.

When the bullet left the muzzle it very temporarily sealed off an expansion chamber fixed to the non recoiling barrel casing. The muzzle pressure of about 630kg/cm² was exerted on the enlarged face of the barrel and thrust the barrel back. This increased the energy available to the bolt and barrel to enable the bolt to carry out the cycle of operations. The lock and the barrel moved back together, securely attached, for a distance just over 6mm whilst the pressure in the chamber fell to a safe level. A tail on the rear toggle arm to rotate thus lifting the centre pivot and breaking the joint.

As the lock came back it withdrew the empty case from the chamber and

a live round from the belt. The recoiling side plate rotated a bell crank which moved the feed slide out to the right for the feed pawl to pass over the next round in the belt. The shape of the cam path on the tail of the rear toggle arm then forced the barrel forward and the feed slide brought the belt across as the barrel went forward. Thus the entire process of collecting and positioning the round was achieved whilst the breech block was moving back. The fusee spring, by then fully extended, returned the lock to the forward position.

The extractor, on the lock face, was forced down by ramps on the top cover plate and the live round it carried was lined up with the chamber and forced in as the lock moved forward.

When the toggle joint dropped to the locked position the extractor on the lock face was levered up, uncovering the firing pin hole, and the T slot on the extractor face passed round the rim of the round in the belt.

If the trigger was pressed, the final movement of the toggle joint below the horizontal fired the gun.

The water jacket held 4.1 litres. After three minutes firing at the rapid rate of 200 rounds a minute the water boiled. This so called nucleate boiling assisted the heat transfer from the barrel to the water by providing bubbles which increased convection cooling. The water then evaporated at the rate of 0.9 litre/1,000 rounds fired.

There was a steam tube with an outlet to a flexible pipe which led off to a can where the steam was condensed and collected. At a suitable gap in the firing programme it was replaced in the jacket.

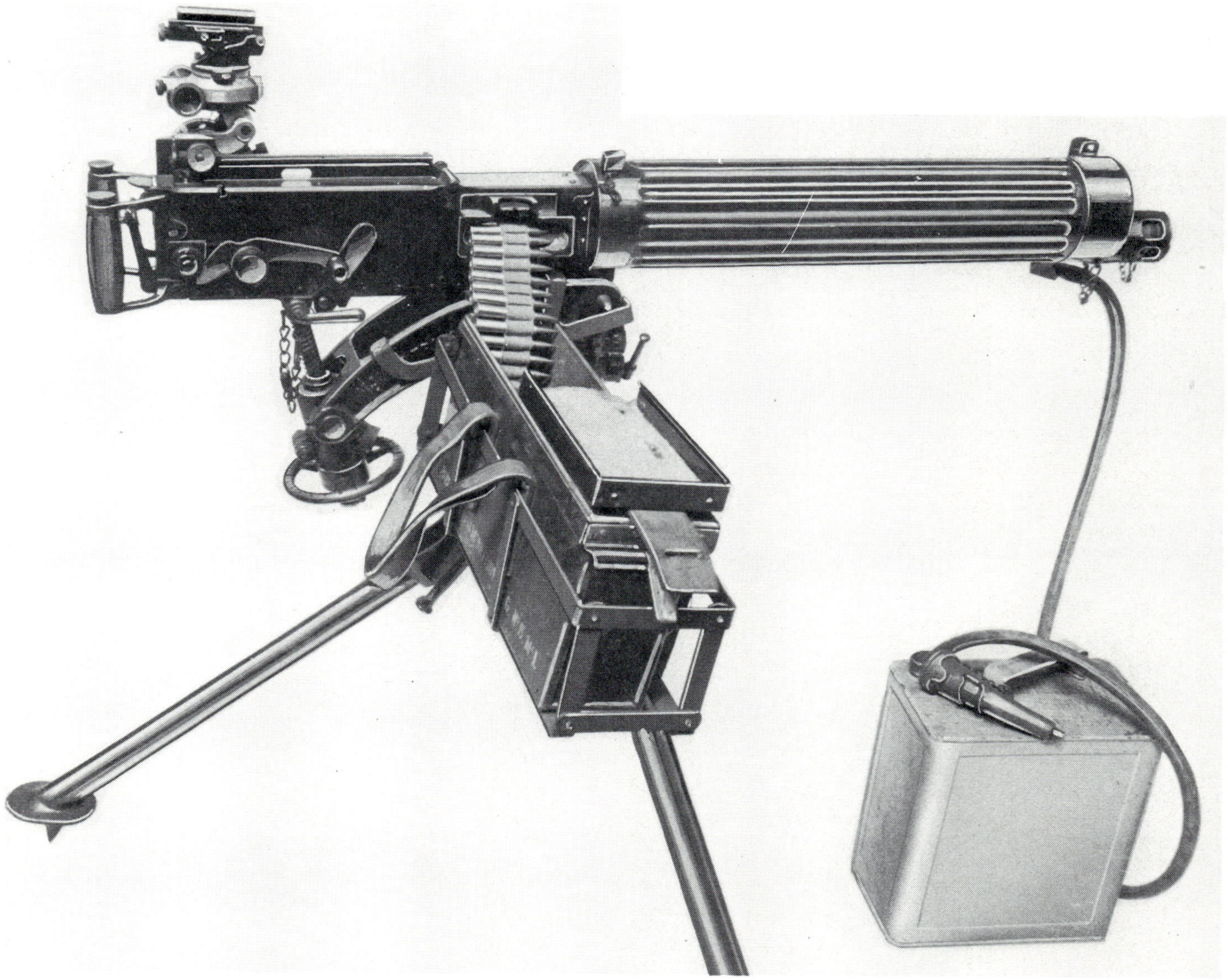

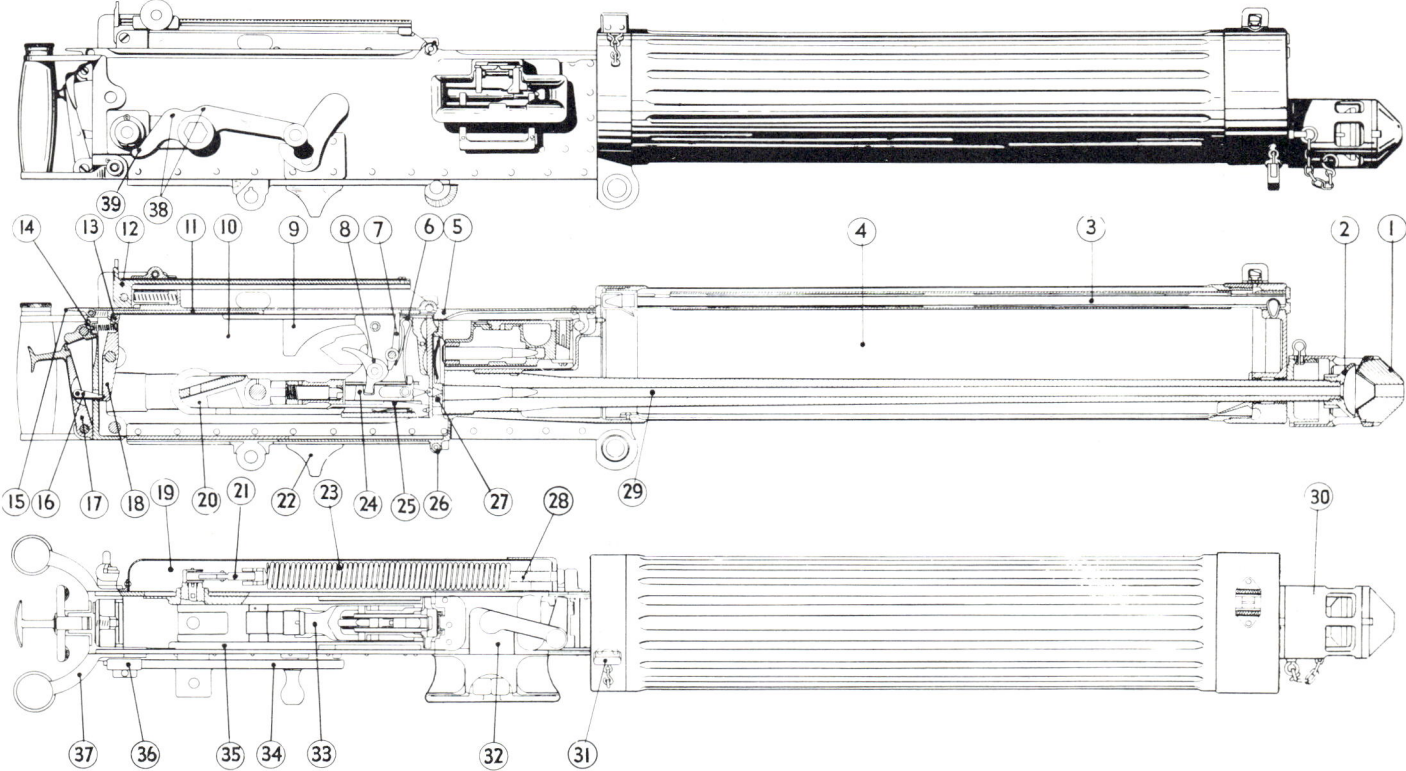

Vickers .303 in Mk 1 with Dial Sight

The Vickers gun: **(1)** front cone; **(2)** muzzle cup; **(3)** steam tube; **(4)** barrel casing; **(5)** front cover; **(6)** lock spring; **(7)** trigger; **(8)** tumbler; **(9)** ramps; **(10)** breech casing; **(11)** rear cover; **(12)** tangent sight; **(13)** trigger bar; **(14)** safety catch; **(15)** gun cover; **(16)** firing lever pawl; **(17)** firing lever; **(18)** trigger bar lever; **(19)** fusee spring box; **(20)** crank; **(21)** fusee; **(22)** elevation stop; **(23)** fusee spring; **(24)** firing pin; **(25)** sear; **(26)** sliding shutter; **(27)** extractor; **(28)** fusee spring adjusting screw; **(29)** barrel; **(30)** muzzle attachment; **(31)** filler plug; **(32)** feed block; **(33)** lock; **(34)** crank; **(35)** RS side plate; **(36)** roller; **(37)** rear cross piece; **(38)** First and second hump; **(39)** tail of crank handle

The gun was heavy, subject to ammunition stoppages, and when hot emitted a plume of steam which revealed its position. However in spite of these shortcomings the machine gunners swore by it and indeed, mounted on the Mk IV tripod, it was capable of feats of endurance that almost matched those of the men that fired it.

It could fire at 10,000 rounds an hour for as long as it could be supplied with water, ammunition and replacement barrels. The barrel was changed every 10,000 rounds – i.e. every hour and a good detachment rarely took much over two minutes for this task and lost only the water that entered the new barrel as it was pushed in from the rear. Using the Mk 8Z streamlined bullet it could provide deadly, indirect fire on to reverse slopes and enemy forming up places as much as 4,500yds (4.1km) away – a feat no NATO machine gun of 7.62mm calibre can accomplish today, 60 years later.

The Vickers remained in British service until declared obsolete in 1968. The last recorded instance of its use in British service was by the 3rd Battalion The Parachute Regiment during the operations in the Radfan.

The ammunition for this gun was reported as still being made in Czechoslovakia for export to Pakistan where the gun was used in the war with India in 1972.

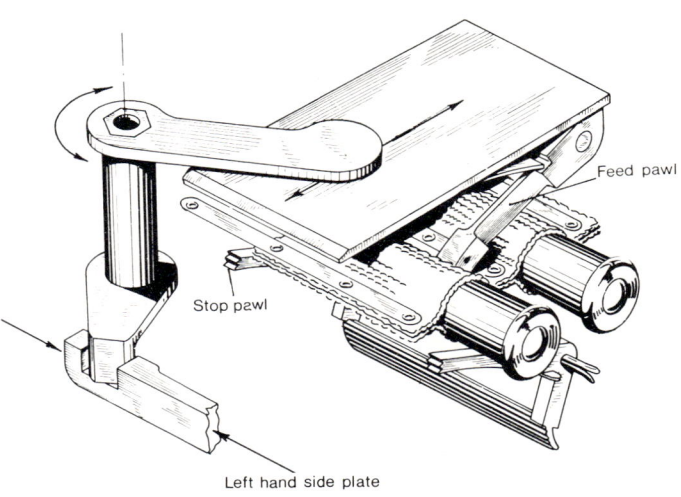

The Vickers' feed. The feed pawls pull the belt across and the stop pawls prevent it from falling back

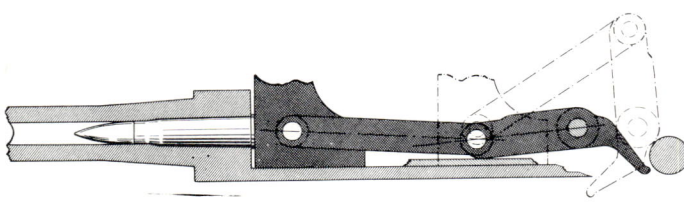

The principle of the toggle lock

DATA

Cartridge: .303 Ball Mk 8Z
Method of operation: Short recoil
Method of locking: Toggle joint
Method of feed: 250 round fabric belt. (Earlier belts had metal spacers)
Method of fire: Automatic
Weight without water: 15kg
Weight with water: 18.2kg
Weight of tripod: 22.7kg
Length: 1,156mm
Barrel: 724mm
      Rifling: 4 grooves RH.
Sights: Foresight: Blade
      Rearsight: Leaf aperture
Muzzle velocity: 744 metres/sec
Muzzle energy: 318mkp
Rate of fire: 450-500 rounds/min
Range, maximum effective: 4.1km with Mk 8Z ammunition
Manufacturer: Vickers Sons and Maxim, Erith; Vickers-Armstrong Ltd. Crayford; Ordnance Factories

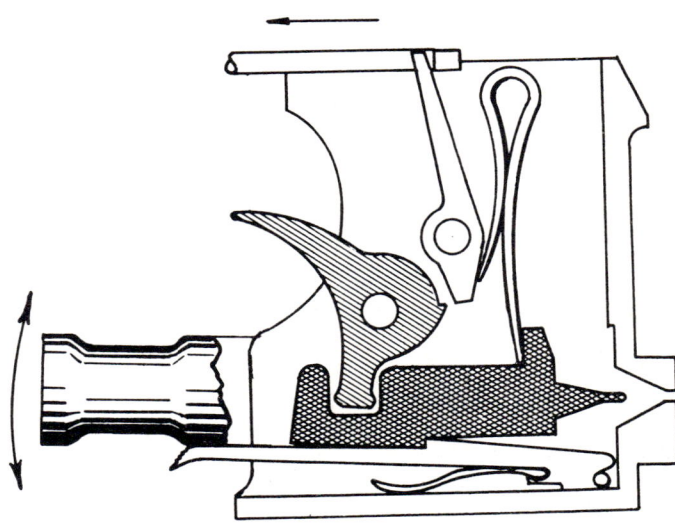

The lock

Status: No longer manufactured. No longer in British service. In use with Arab Emirates and Tonga. Used in Pakistan as recently as 1972

.303in VICKERS BERTHIER LMG

In 1925 Vickers acquired manufacturing rights for the machine gun originally invented by General Berthier and tested, but not accepted, by the US authorities in 1917. The resultant series of guns, known as the Vickers-Berthier, was made both in the UK and in India and some were still in service in India as recently as 1972.

The gun was gas-operated, with the piston under the barrel, and had a tilting block locking system. Manufacture started at the Crayford plant of Vickers in 1928 (Mk 1) and a Mk 2 was introduced in 1930. This was a strong contender in the trials for the replacement of the Lewis Gun in the British Army and was in the final short list – but of course the Bren was the winner.

A lightened version of the Mk 2 was produced for the Indian Government

Vickers-Berthier Mk 3 LMG on the Vickers tripod

but was not adopted. Shortly afterwards, however, a version known as the Mk 3 went into production at the Ishapore Rifle Factory and remained in production until the end of the Second World War. During this process a Mk 3B was introduced as a local modification, the change involving the gas regulator of the original design by an exhaust-to-atmosphere system with a screw-up regulafor.

DATA
Cartridge: .303 Mk 7
Method of operation: Gas
Method of locking: Tilting block
Method of feed: 30-round detachable box magazine
Method of fire: Selective
Weight: 10kg

Barrel: Quick-change, air-cooled, 597mm
Sights: Foresight: Blade
Rearsight: Aperture leaf
Muzzle velocity: 744m/sec
Muzzle energy: 318mkp
Rate of fire: Cyclic: 600 rounds/min
Automatic 120 rounds/min
SS 60 rounds/min
Effective range: 600m
Manufacturer: Vickers Armstrong Ltd Crayford. Ishapore Rifle Factory, India
Status: No longer made. Probably still a reserve weapon in India and possibly to be encountered elsewhere in Asia

---

.303in BREN GUNS

When the 1914-1918 war ended the British Army possessed large quantities of the Vickers MMG Mk 1 and the Lewis gun. The Vickers gun was generally recognised as being the best gun of its kind in the world but the Lewis gun had several drawbacks. Its weight, its bulk, the nature of its feed system and its proneness to feed stoppages all made it unsatisfactory as the infantry section LMG and it was agreed that a replacement was required. It was decided in 1922 that the Browning Automatic Rifle – somewhat modified – should be accepted into service as the Browning Light Machine Gun. This decision was never implemented in full and various sporadic trials of other LMGs were carried out in a rather desultory way for some years. In December 1922 the Small Arms Committee arranged comparative trials of the Browning, Madsen, Beardmore-Farquhar, Hotchkiss and the Type 'D' Lewis Gun. The trials of the Hotchkiss and Madsen, which were considered cavalry LMGs, were carried out by the 13th Hussars, the remainder by 1st Bn Dorset Regt. The Browning was considered to be the most suitable gun.

In 1924 the Beardmore-Farquhar Mk II LMG was tried and rejected, and in 1925 the French Chatellerault 7.5mm LMG was examined and in 1926 a Swiss Furrer LMG was purchased, tried, and "no further trials recommended". In 1927 the McCrudden LMG and Erikson LMG were examined and in 1928 the new Madsen was tried. The McCrudden gun was resubmitted in 1929 but was not acceptable.

On 29 October 1930 comparative trials were arranged for the Browning .303 LMG, Darne .303 LMG, Vickers-Berthier LMG, Kiraly-Ende 7 LMG, the Madsen .303 LMG and the Zb 26 LMG of 7.92mm calibre. Of these the Browning came from USA, Darne from France, Madsen from Denmark, the

In April 1931 the Zb 27 was ordered in .303in calibre. The conversion was carried out on a Zb 30 and incorporated several small improvements over the Zb 27.

In June 1931 a programme of trials for the ZGB30, (as it was called) Vickers-Berthier and Darne was recommended. These consisted of:
(a) Long range accuracy trials at Hythe consisting of 3 series of shoots at 500, 1,000, 1,500, 2,000 to 2,500yds.
(b) Endurance trial at Enfield of 30,000 rounds.
(c) A special trial of a new heavy barrel for the Vickers-Berthier.

The trial report (SAC Minute 1188) runs to 88 foolscap pages. It is one of the most interesting and comprehensive reports that one can imagine. The final conclusion on the Zb 30 was:

"That the Zb gun . . . is of such outstanding design, workmanship and material as to warrant further serious consideration.

Its performance during the trials has been remarkable having in view the fact that it was designed primarily for a rimless cartridge and a nitro-cellulose charge. The present defects of the weapon are:
(a) Excessive fouling due to the present position of the gas port which is not suitable for a cordite charge.
(b) Ejection is faulty due to the gun having been converted at short notice to fire the rimmed Mk VII .303 cartridge."

In May 1932 Mr Staller of the Zb company took the gun back to Brno and it was modified by moving the gas block towards the chamber, fitting a new gas block, cylinder and front half of the piston. The gun was brought to England by its designer Vaclav Holek. It was tested and 18,936 rounds were fired; it functioned perfectly. During the 15,000 round endurance trial

.303 ZGB 30 (RSAF)

V-B was British made, the Kiraly was made by SIG of Switzerland and the Zb came from Czechoslovakia. The Zb 26 came to the notice of the Small Arms Committee via a report from the Military Attaché at Prague. The cost of one Zb 26 for trial was £75.25p and 10,000 rounds of 7.62mm ammunition cost £52.34p. With a packing and delivery charge of £7.52p the cost of equipment for the trial – which turned out to be of great importance – was £135.10p. The MA at Prague also reported on the Kosar recoil reducer and stabiliser and a tripod fitted with this gear was ordered at a cost of £74. In 1930 the decision was made to replace both the Vickers MMG Mk 1 and the Lewis Gun with one weapon capable of carrying out both roles. In view of this, the date of the trials of the LMGs was brought forward and the weapons were fired as they became available. The Darne arrived too late for inclusion. The Czech firm of Ceskoslovenska Zbrojovka Akciova Spolecnost of Brno did NOT supply a Zb 26 as ordered but sent instead the Zb 27 which was an improved version. So the Zb 26 was never officially tried in this country. The trials were exhaustive and long drawn out.

In a detailed summary of the mechanical features of the Zb 27 after firing 10,986 rounds, the wear was described as "negligible" and the barrel diameter had increased by 0.005in (0.13mm).

The V-B report was not so good but concluded "These and other minor points are all remedial and, properly developed, it should be the equal of the Zb gun". Further trials were recommended.

ZGB 30 fitted with gas regulator and flat gas deflector plate (RSAF)

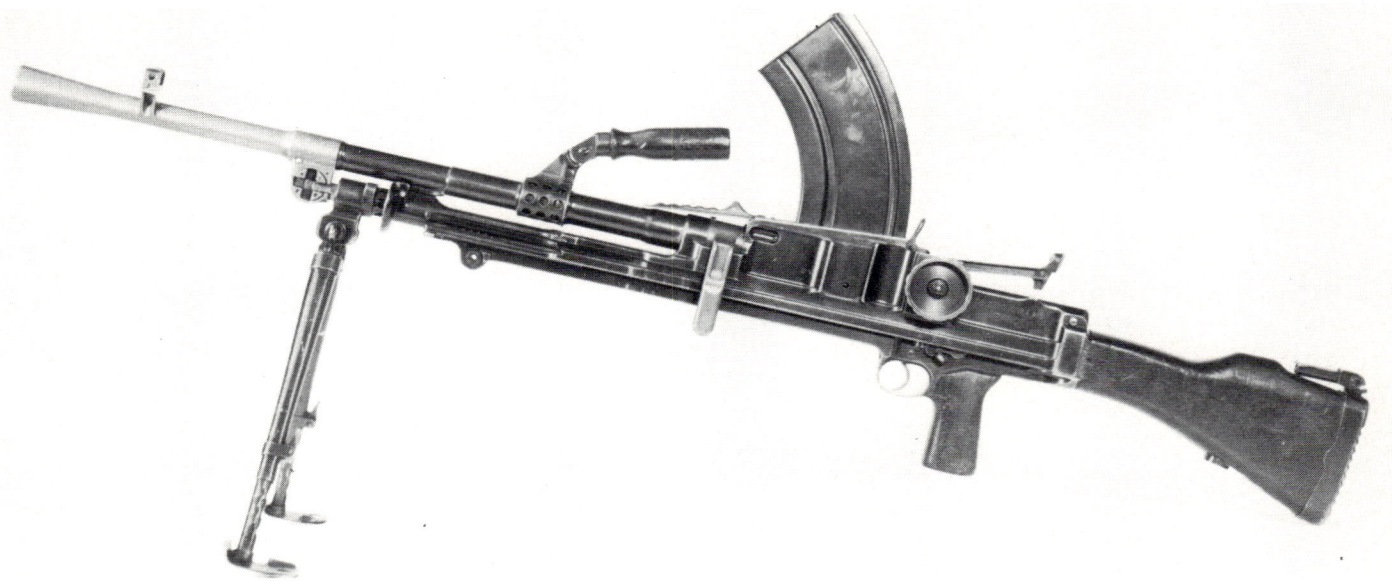

ZGB 33 (RSAF)

there were 90 stoppages; 61 were caused by loose caps in the ammuntion. The Committee asked for a 30-round magazine instead of the 20 fitted and ordered 10 guns incorporating the improvements – and known as the ZGB – which with spare barrels, spare parts and accessories were to cost £175 per set. Whilst the ZGB guns were being made the Director of Munitions visited Brno between 14 January 1933 and 22 January 1933, and as a result of discussion with Mr Holek the designer and the Superintendent of the Royal Small Arms Factory, a Czech design change was incorporated to allow the piston buffer to take the recoil not only of the piston but of the barrel and body. This movement of about 2mm reduced the recoil felt by the firer.

The ZGB so modified was called the ZGB 32 and was given preliminary testing at Enfield by firing some 500 rounds and was then sent to Hythe for a 4,000-round endurance test, and finally fired a further 25,000 rounds at Enfield for functioning and wear. Whilst at Enfield a modified ejector designed as a chisel to burr brass over the cap and prevent 'caps out' was tried with complete success. The ZGB 32 was satisfactory but the committee decided further improvements were possible and should be incorporated in a modified version to be known as the ZGB 33. There were 25 modifications of which the most important were:

Speed of gun to be reduced from 600 rounds a minute to 480 rounds a minute.

Sights to read to 2,000yds by 50s. No fins on barrel. Length of barrel to be reduced by 48mm. Gas exhaust shield to be cupped. Modified cocking handle. Modified butt slide catch. Modified comb to butt. Lengthen idle movement of piston to delay breech opening. New ejector.

Two of the ZGB 33s were ordered and an extra 6 spare barrels were also asked for so that the weapons could undergo the following tests:

Acceptance tests 1,000 rounds.

Endurance of mechanism 150,000 rounds.

Accuracy and other tests 50,000 rounds.

The trials were fired on 29 January 1934 with success. The speed of the gun was reduced, the locked period of the breech was increased, accuracy was improved and over 140,000 rounds were fired before any part failed.

Two models of the ZGB 33, known as the ZGB 34, were purchased on 14 April 1934. A 50,000 round endurance test was then fired in August 1934 to compare the ZGB 34 with the latest heavy barrelled Vickers-Berthier. This proved finally and conclusively that the Czech Zb was the better gun. This trial was reported at great length in SAC minute 1545. From the description it is clear that the Zb gun was extremely thoroughly tested and hundreds of thousands of rounds were fired before it was adopted.

The decision to use this gun to replace both the Vickers gun and the Lewis gun was rescinded in 1937 when it was expected that the Zb 53 air cooled gun (later known as the BESA) of 7.92mm calibre would replace the Vickers and the ZGB take over the light role.

BREN .303 SERIES

When the acceptance committee expressed themselves as fully satisfied, arrangements were made for the production of the gun at the Royal Small Arms Factory at Enfield. The gun was named the BREN from BRno and ENfield. The drawings had to be converted from metric measure to inches and this was completed in January 1935. During 1934 Mr Robinson the Factory Superintendent planned the production line, installed machine tools and the tool room started on the gauges. Some idea of the immensity of the task can be gained from the fact that there were 270 operations on the body alone and for this ‘550 gauges were required each made to an accuracy of 0.0125mm. The gun was made by conventional machining from the solid and the first gun was finished in September 1937. This was a very creditable performance indeed. By December 1937 42 guns were completed and by July 1938 production was 300 a week – rising to 400 a week in September 1939.

By June 1940 more than 30,000 guns had been produced and issued.

The gun was manufactured only at Enfield and one air raid would have been absolutely catastrophic in its effect. Magazines were manufactured by BSA and the Austin Motor Works. These gave trouble because they would only function with 29 rounds instead of 30. This was found to be a drawing error in the conversion from the rimless 7.92mm cartridge design.

After Dunkirk only about 2,300 Bren guns remained in England, and Enfield worked flat out to produce more. By 1943 production at Enfield had reached 1,000 guns a week. Production was started in 1940 by John Inglis in Canada and by the Lithgow Small Arms Factory in Australia which produced 150 guns a week by 1942. Inglis also manufactured the gun in

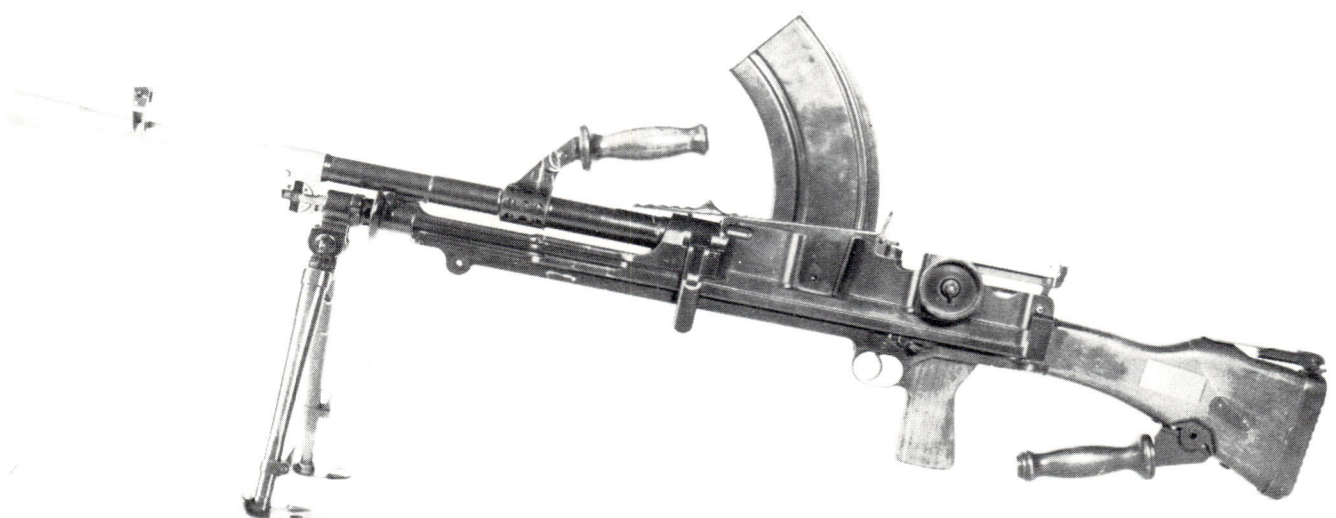

The first Bren Mk 1 (RSAF)

7.92mm by Inglis, for China (RSAF)

7.92mm for China. In 1952 the Inglis version of the Mk II Bren was manufactured in Taiwan as the M41 in .30-06.

The original gun was designated the Mk I. The Mk II gun had the same length barrel, a simplified rear sight, and the flash hider/gas regulator/front sight which was originally a single stainless steel fabrication was produced as three separate units with only the regulator in stainless steel. The bipod was made with non-telescoping legs and the handle below the butt was omitted. These changes to assist production increased the weight from 10.04kg to 10.52kg. The Mk III simplified production, reduced barrel length, and also the gun weight was reduced to 8.76kg. The Mk IV had the shorter barrel and weight was reduced to the minimum compatible with the stresses imposed by the .303 Mk VII cartridge.

The differences can be summarised as:

	Barrel length	Overall Length	Weight
Mk I	635mm	1,156mm	10.04kg
Mk II	635mm	1,156mm	10.52kg
Mk III	565mm	1,090mm	8.76kg
Mk IV	565mm	1,090mm	8.68kg

Further data on these weapons and a description of the Bren mechanisms will be found in the entry for the 7.62mm L4 series below.

7.62mm L4 BREN SERIES

When the decision was made to adopt the 7.62mm NATO round various conversions of the .303 Bren gun were made to adapt it for 7.62mm. These generally employed the breech block made for the Canadian 7.92mm guns, with new barrels.

A brief summary of the L4 series follows:

L4A1: Converted Mk III .303 Bren. First known as the X10E1. Two steel barrels Bipod Mk 1. Now obsolescent.

L4A2: Converted Mk III .303 Bren. First known as the X10E2. Two steel barrels. Light bipod. Land and Naval use. Now obsolescent.

L4A3: Converted Mk II .303 Bren. One chromium plated barrel. Now obsolescent for land service.

L4A4: Converted Mk III .303 Bren. One chromium-plated barrel. Current weapon all services.

L4A5: Converted Mk II .303 Bren. Two steel barrels. Obsolescent for land and air service. Still in Naval service.

L4A6: Converted L4A1. One chrome-plated barrel. Introduced only for land service. Now obsolescent.

L4A7: Conversion of Mk I .303 Bren. None made but drawings prepared for the Indian Army. One chrome-plated barrel.

OPERATION

The Bren Light Machine Gun is a magazine fed, gas operated gun using a tilting block locking system lifting the rear end of the breech block into a locking recess in the top of the body.

During the period of initial pressure build up, the body, barrel, breech block, gas cylinder and bipod recoil on the butt slide approximately 6mm. The movement is buffered by the piston buffer and spring. When this energy has been absorbed the piston buffer spring reasserts itself and returns the body, barrel, cylinder and bipod to their normal positions on the butt slide. This recoil and run out of these assemblies reduces the shock experienced by the firer and makes for less breakages in the affected components.

When the gun is fired the gases force the bullet up the bore and a small proportion of them is diverted through a tapping in the barrel, passes through the regulator and impinges on the piston head. The piston is driven back.

Attached to the piston by a flexible joint is the piston extension on which is supported the breech block.

A piston post on the extension fits into the hollow interior of the breech block and 2 ramps hold the rear of the block up into the locked position engaged in the locking recess at the top of the body.

When the piston extension moves back there is a movement of about 32mm during which the bolt remains fully locked. Further movement removes the ramp support under the block and then an inclined surface on the rear of the piston post forces the back end of the bolt down and unlocking is completed.

The tilting motion of the breech block provides primary extraction and the cartridge case is first unseated in the chamber and then withdrawn by the extractor claw as the breech block moves back. A fully fixed ejector rides in a groove on top of the block and it is chisel shaped so that as it strikes the brass of the cartridge case above the primer cap, brass is burred over the cap to prevent the latter falling out and causing a stoppage. The empty case is pushed through a cut-away section in the piston extension and thrown

Bren Mk II (RSAF)

Bren Mk III (RSAF)

The 7.62mm Bren L4A1 was originally called the X10E1 (RSAF)

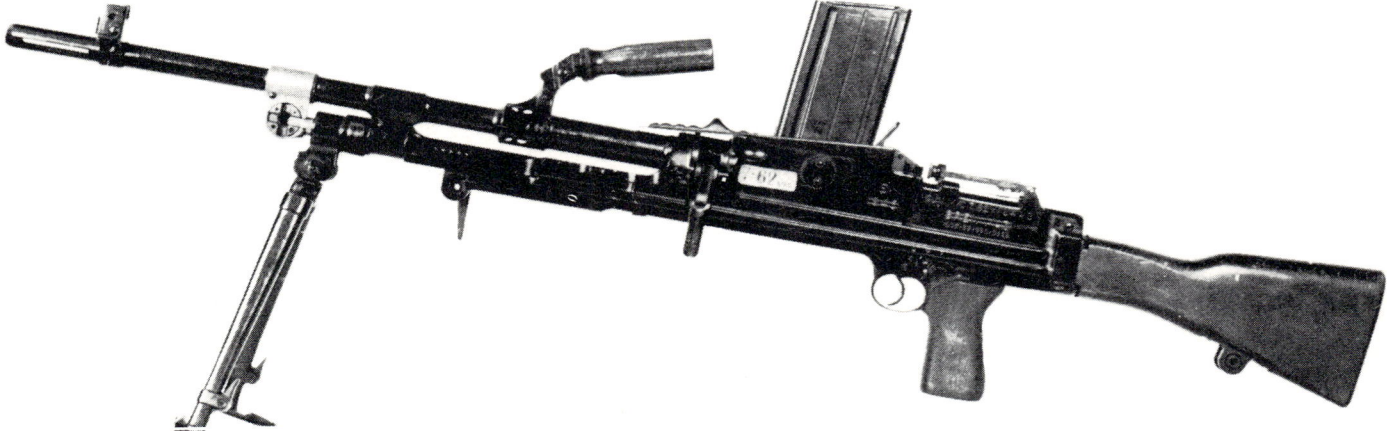

The 7.62mm Bren L4A2, converted from the Mk III .303 Bren and originally called the X10E2 (RSAF)

downwards out of the gun: As the piston goes back the return spring is compressed, storing energy, and this plus the action of the soft buffer throws the piston forward again. The soft buffer has a low coefficient of restitution and so the piston speed forward is not excessive and this keeps the cyclic rate to about 500 rounds a minute. The feed horns on top of the front of the block push a round out of the 30-round box magazine mounted vertically above the gun and the bullet is guided downwards into the chamber. As the cartridge goes forward the extractor claw clips over the rim of the round. When the round is fully chambered bolt movement ceases. The piston continues forward under its own momentum, and the remaining force in the return spring, and the two ramps at the rear end lift the rear of the breech block so that the locking surface on top of the rear of the block rises into the locking recess in the body. The ramps remain under the block and hold it locked. The forward movement of the piston continues for another 32mm and the front face of the piston post acts as a hammer to drive the spring retracted firing pin into the cap at the base of the cartridge. It can be seen from the accompanying diagram that the system is extremely simple. It has one mechanical imperfection in that the locking ramps at the rear of the piston extension are attempting to lift the rear of the breech block against the top of the gun body throughout the forward stroke. This increases the friction force and it is noteworthy that in later guns of Czech manufacture such as the Zb 53 – BESA – and Vz 52 these ramps have been made with a vertical leading edge and the initial bolt raising is produced by cams in the sides of the hollow block. Mechanical safety on the gun is provided before firing by the initial non-alignment of the cartridge and the firing pin in the bolt and subsequently by the free movement of the piston post of 32mm after locking is completed before it contacts the firing pin. Mechanical safety after firing comes from:

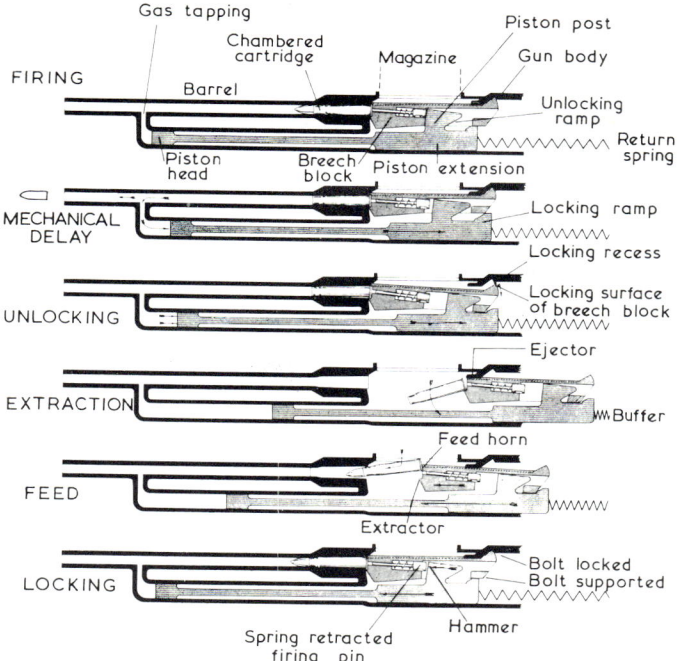

The action of the Bren gun (RSAF)

(a)   The location of the gas vent which is 15in from the breech face.

(b)   The free travel of 32mm of the piston post before the inclined ramp starts to pull the block down out of the locked position.

It is interesting to note that in 1933 when "caps out" was first observed in the ZGB 32 it was considered to be due to excess residual pressure caused by unduly early unlocking. A series of electrical contacts was set up in the gun and it was found that the bullet was 67cm from the muzzle when unlocking began and 4.02m from the muzzle when unlocking was complete. Nevertheless the free travel of the piston was increased in the ZGB 33.

The applied safety disconnects the trigger from the sear by holding the trigger lever in the middle of the sear window.

In theory this is not a satisfactory arrangement as a heavy jar caused by dropping the gun could dislodge the sear from the piston bent. In practice

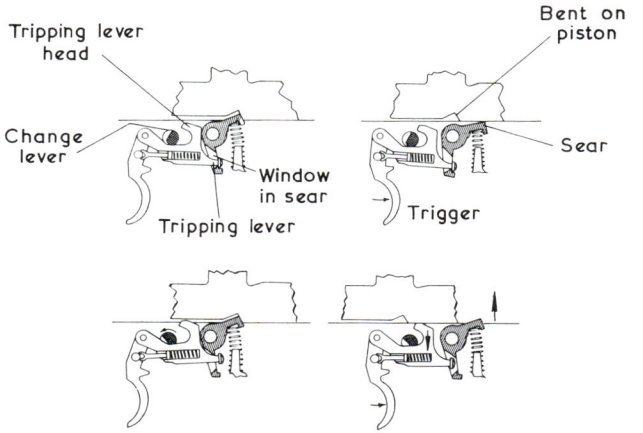

The fire selector of the Bren gun (RMCS)

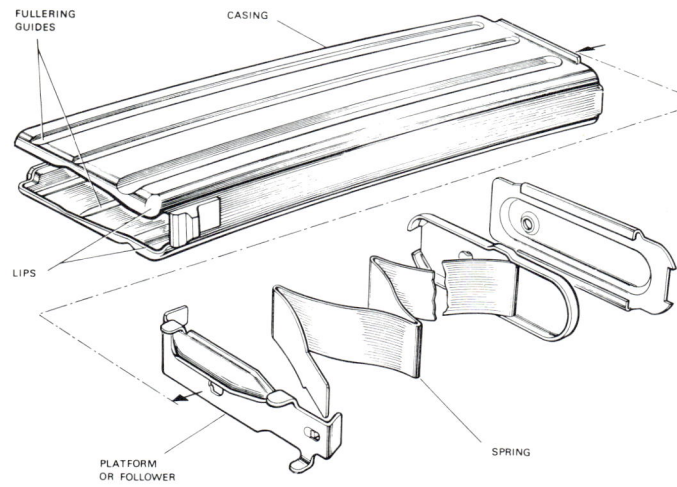

The 7.62mm Bren gun magazine (RMCS)

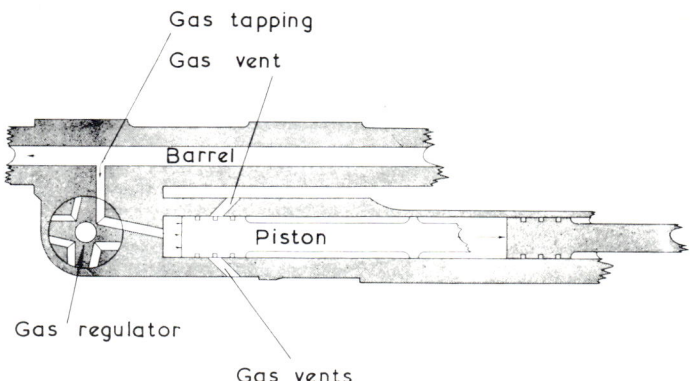

The gas system of the Bren gun (RSAF)

there is no record that this has ever happened.

The gas regulator was installed in the Bren gun – it was not in the early Zb series – to give greater flexibility when the gun is firing under adverse conditions produced by sandy terrain, mud, firing at elevation or depression. The regulator has 4 tracks and a larger diameter gas track can be rotated into position as required. It should be noted that the gas impulse is only applied for a very short distance and then the gas escapes to atmosphere through vents bored in the cylinder walls. If excessive fouling occurs the bipod can be twisted and this cuts away any build up of carbon which is then dispersed by the next blast of gas. This feature produces an extremely reliable gun even after prolonged firing.

The barrel can be changed in a matter of seconds by raising the barrel latch and pulling the barrel forward using the carrying handle. With the gun fired at 120 rounds – 4 magazines – a minute, the barrel requires changing every 2½min. The hot barrel can be cooled by air after removal from the gun or as often happened in action by laying it in wet grass or even in a stream.

TRIGGER MECHANISM

The weapon can be fired either at full automatic or at single shot. The latter facility is employed to conserve ammunition, prolong barrel life and for tactical deception. The selector mechanism is illustrated. The sear has a window through which projects the tripping lever. When the change lever is rotated to 'single shot' the tripping lever bears against the upper surface of the window in the sear and its tripping head is raised into the path of the gas piston which depresses the tripping head as it comes forward. This forces the tripping lever down away from the sear window and the sear is released to rise and hold the piston to the rear. Releasing the trigger re-positions the tripping lever against the top surface of the sear window and operating the trigger fires one more shot. When the change lever is set to 'auto' the tripping lever is forced down to bear on the bottom side of the sear window and the tripping lever head is pulled down clear of the piston. The gun continues firing as long as ammunition remains in the magazine and the trigger is depressed.

MOUNTING

The gun is usually employed as a light machine gun using a bipod but during the war a tripod was available. This enabled the gun to fire on fixed lines and could also be adapted readily for anti-aircraft use. The Mk 2 and Mk 2/1 tripods were of Czech design. The 30-round box magazine was universal but had to be loaded with the care as overlapping rims could cause stoppage. A 100-round high speed drum magazine was produced for anti-aircraft fire early in World War II but was not widely used because it was heavy, difficult to load quickly and also awkward to carry.

The Mark I gun had a tangent drum backsight but to simplify production a vertical leaf backsight was installed on subsequent marks.

The Mk I gun also had a handle under the butt for a left hand grip and a strap on the butt plate to rest over the shoulder. Both these features were abandoned for later marks.

STRIPPING

(1)   Remove the magazine. Cock the action. Check chamber and feedway clear.

(2)   Push body locking pin, at rear of body from left to right.

(3)   Pull back the butt and trigger group.

(4)   Pull back the cocking handle and remove the piston and breech block. Re-assemble in reverse order.

Mk I
Cartridge: .303 Mk 7
Method of operation: Gas
Method of locking: Tilting block
Method of feed: 30-round box magazine
Method of fire: Selective

WEIGHTS
Gun: 10.04kg
Magazine, empty: 0.48kg
Magazine, full (30rds): 1.25kg
Magazine, drum (100rds) empty: 2.92kg
Magazine, drum (100rds) full: 5.41kg
Barrel, assembled: 2.85kg
Trigger pull: 2.72kp

LENGTHS
Gun: 1,156mm
Barrel (Mk I): 635mm

MECHANICAL FEATURES
Barrel: Regulator: 4 position
Rifling: 6 grooves. RH. 1 turn in 254mm
Width of grooves: 2.23mm
Depth of grooves: 0.1,447mm
Cooling: Air. Quick change
Sights: Foresight: Blade
Rearsight aperture, drum operated arm: Aperture, tangent leaf
Graduation: 200-2,000yd (1829m) by 50yd increments
Zeroing: Elevation. Change foresight blade. Line: Foresight on dovetail.
Sight radius: 788mm

FIRING CHARACTERISTICS
Muzzle velocity: 744m/sec
Muzzle energy: 318mkp
Recoil energy: 0.55mkp
Chamber pressure: 2,900kg/cm²
Rate of fire: Cyclic: 500 rounds/min
Auto: 120 rounds/min
S.S.: 40 rounds/min
Range, maximum effective: 600m
Maximum: 3,000m

Mk II
As Mk I except
Gun: 10.52kg
Barrel: 2.93kg
Trigger pull: 3.18kp
Rearsight: Tangent leaf, 200-1800yds (1,646m) × 50yds
Sight radius: 782mm
Cyclic rate: 540 rounds/min

Mk III
As Mk I except
Gun: 8.76kg

Barrel: 2.31kg
Trigger pull: 2.72kp
Gun: 1,090mm
Barrel: (Mk 4) 565mm
Rearsight: As Mk II
Sight radius: 694mm
Cyclic rate: 480 rounds/min

Mk IV
As Mk III except
Gun: 8.68kg
Barrel: (Mk 5) 2.27kg
Trigger pull: 3.18kp
Cyclic rate: 520 rounds/min

L4A4
As Mk I except
Cartridge: 7.62mm × 51
Gun: 9.53kg
Magazine, empty: 0.45kg
Magazine with 30 rounds: 1.18kg
No drum magazine:
Barrel: 2.72kg
Trigger pull: 1.8-3.6kp
Gun: 1,133mm
Barrel: 536mm
Rearsight: As Mk III
Sight radius: 743mm
Muzzle velocity: 823m/sec
Muzzle energy: 332mkp
Chamber pressure: 3,465kg/cm²
Cyclic rate: 500 rounds/min

Manufacturer: Royal Small Arms Factory, Enfield; John Inglis Ltd., Toronto, Canada; Small Arms Factory, Lithgow, New South Wales, Australia
Status: No longer manufactured. In service (L4A4) in UK for non-tooth arms. Still widely used in British Commonwealth and other countries in .303 (users include Pakistan and the Lebanon) 7.62mm (users include Australia and India) and 7.92mm (probably only in China).

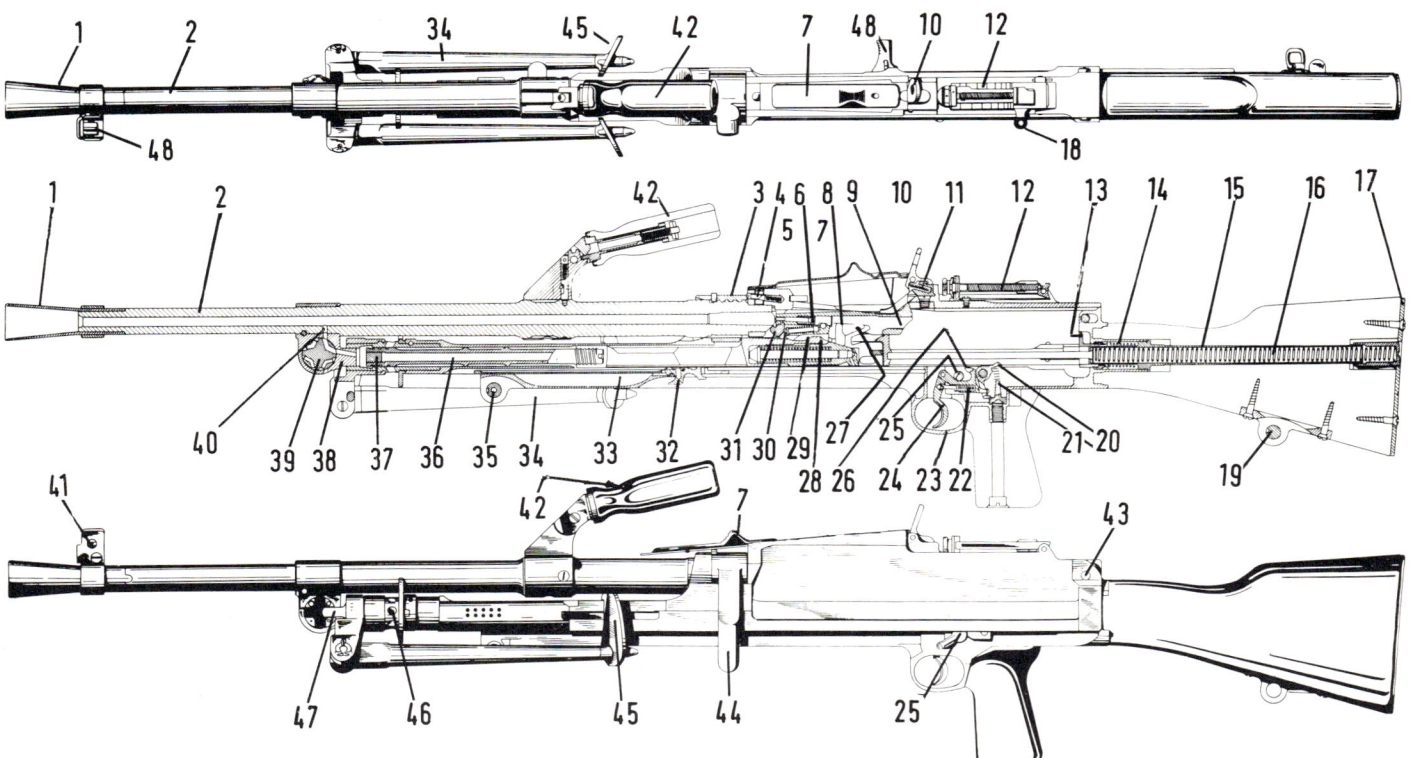

Sectioned view of the Bren gun: (1) Flash hider; (2) Barrel; (3) Barrel nut; (4) Barrel nut retainer; (5) Firing pin; (6) Firing pin spring; (7) Magazine opening cover; (8) Breech block; (9) Ejector; (10) Magazine catch; (11) Magazine catch spring; (12) Backsight leaf; (13) Piston, Buffer; (14) Spring, Buffer; (15) Return spring tube; (16) Return spring; (17) Butt plate; (18) Backsight; (19) Rear mouning pin; (20) Sear; (21) Sear spring; (22) Trigger spring; (23) Trigger guard; (24) Trigger; (25) Change lever; (26) Tripping lever; (27) Piston post; (28) Piston post bufferspring; (29) Extractor stay spring; (30) Extractor stay; (31) Extractor; (32) Ejection opening cover catch; (33) Ejection opening cover; (34) Bipod leg; (35) Front mounting pin; (36) Piston; (37) Piston head; (38) Gas regulator block; (39) Gas regulator; (40) Gas vent; (41) Foresight assembly; (42) Carrying handle; (43) Body locking pin; (44) Barrel nut; (45) Bipod foot; (46) Gas vents; (47) Gas cylinder locking bar; (48) Foresight blade

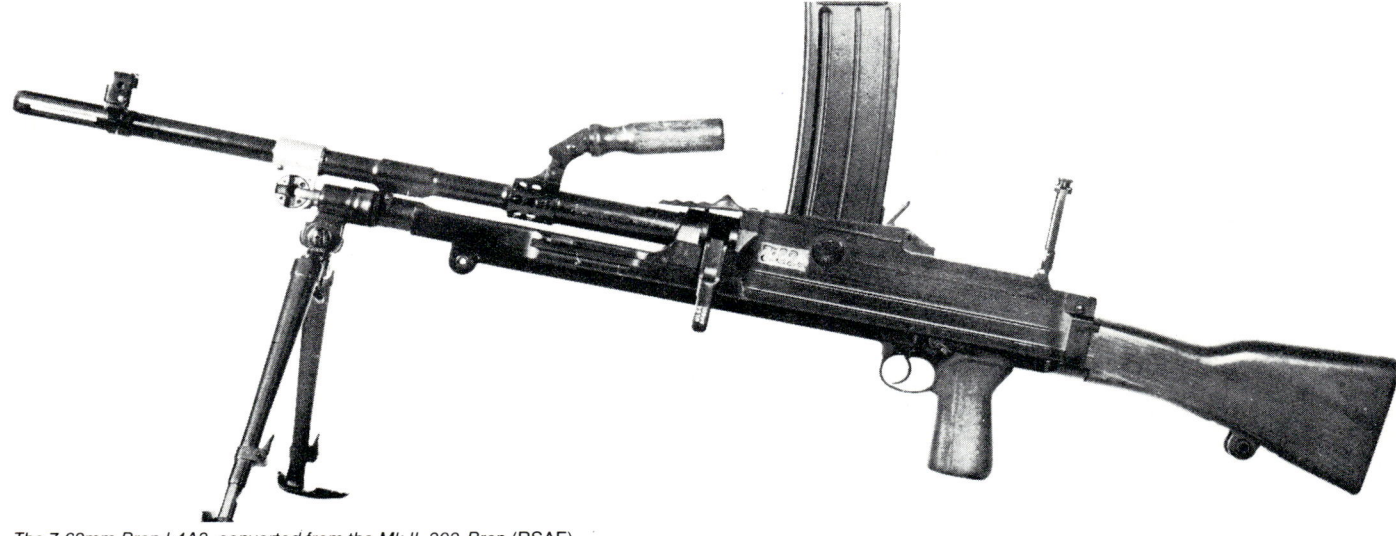

The 7.62mm Bren L4A3, converted from the Mk II .303 Bren (RSAF)

7.62mm Bren L4A4 converted Mk III .303 Bren. Known originally as the X10E6 (RSAF)

7.62mm L7A1 AND L7A2 GPMGs

The British Army ended the Second World War in 1945 with the Vickers MG Mk 1 as its sustained fire weapon and the Bren gun as the section LMG. Both guns used the .303 in cartridge – the Vickers employing the Mk 8Z and the Bren the Mk 7.

For several years there was a concentration of effort on the .280 cartridge – or 7mm Mk 1Z as it was eventually called – as a universal round for the Infantry. It was intended to use this cartridge in the single weapon to replace the pistol, SMG, rifle and LMG and to feed the new sustained fire machine gun known as the Taden, designed by Turpin at Enfield.

With the demise of the .280 project in 1952 and the subsequent NATO standardisation on the 7.62mm round, the Taden was scrapped and a series of sustained fire machine guns was developed using the NATO cartridge. The final design was the X11E2. This was basically a Bren gun converted to belt feed with the piston operating the feed mechanism. The weapon had a quick change barrel and was produced by the Design and Development Department of the Royal Small Arms Factory at Enfield. There was a good degree of co-operation between Enfield and the School of Infantry and the weapon went some way to meeting the users' requirement. The long barrel and the accompanying long sight radius produced accurate fire but – as was subsequently revealed – the feed system which

involved the rotation of the vertical feed shaft, by the piston, into the feed slide – produced a lot of friction and under adverse conditions, or firing in elevation, the gun would not lift the belt through any significant height.

A preliminary trial to determine the future GPMG of the British Army was held at Enfield between 24 April and 30 May 1957. The contenders were:

7.62mm SFMG X11E2 UK.
7.62mm MAG made by FN in Belgium.
.30 M60, USA.
7.62mm Madsen-Saetter, Denmark.
7.62mm AA 52, France.
7.62mm SIG MG 55-2, Switzerland.
7.62mm SIG MG 55-3, Switzerland.
7.62mm Bren Control, UK.

Each gun was provided with a tripod and a bipod and two spare barrels. The FN MAG also had a heavy barrel.

The trial consisted of examination, functioning at single shots (where applicable) and full auto, accuracy, mud test and sand test. Representatives from each of the countries or firms concerned were allowed to prepare and maintain their weapons. None of the weapons behaved badly. The FN was considered best and the X11E2 next. In July further preliminary test

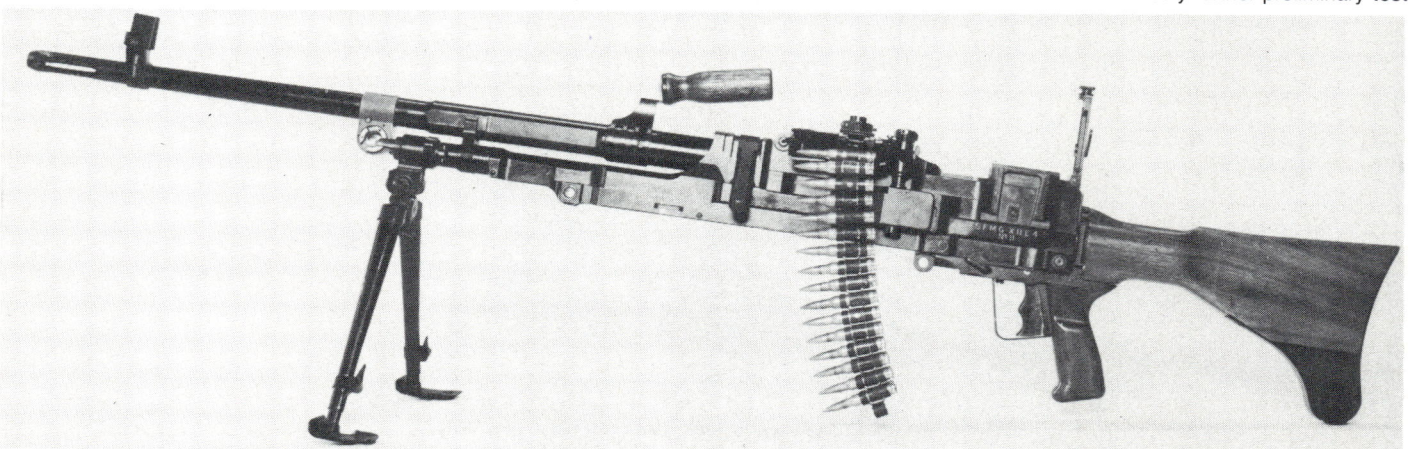

The X11E4 SF MG – this was almost identical to the gun tested (RMCS)

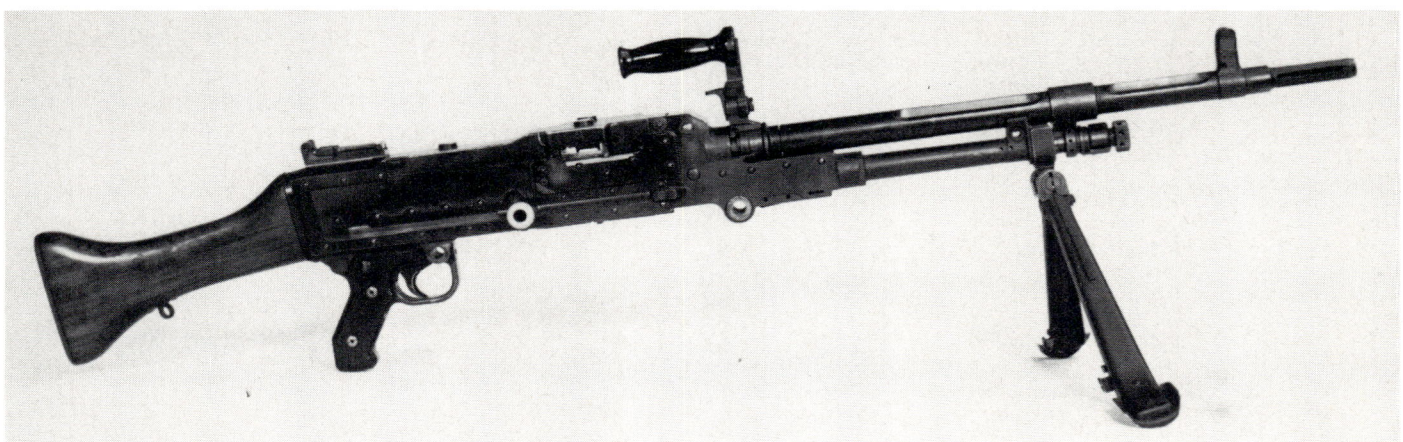

L7A1 – heavy barrel. This can be identified by the flutes on the upper surface of the barrel (RMCS)

firings were carried out by the School of Infantry at Netheravon. The trial was designed to test (a) reliability of functioning and (b) accuracy in both MMG and LMG roles.

The X11E2 was considered the best gun on this occasion followed by the FN MAG. In October 1957 FN supplied a weapon for further tests at Enfield and in January 1958 further trials were conducted of the British gun. In June 1958 the War Office decided to abandon the Enfield design and concentrate on the FN model.

Almost immediately the FN barrel showed it was inadequate for sustained fire and in December 1958 FN were asked to develop a heavy barrel with a stellite liner. Whilst this was being done further tests showed piston bounce and the possibility of firing with an unlocked breech so in July 1959 the piston and locking lever design was modified. This led initially to a high rate of piston failure and further re-design was carried out which led to successful trials in October 1960. At the same time the heavy barrel was accepted and a succession of Troop Trials were carried out in the UK, Middle East and Far East. It is perhaps significant that there was a preference expressed in the Far East for the lighter, magazine-fed Bren rather than the heavy belt fed GPMG. The Final Acceptance of the gun took place at a meeting held in Northumberland House on 11 July 1961. An order for 1,500 guns was placed with FN on 1 November 1961 and the last of these was delivered in February 1962. Towards the end of 1963 RSAF Enfield started production.

It was intended that the gun, fitted with a light barrel and fired off its tripod, should be able to give accurate and effective fire at 730m. When fitted with the stellite-lined heavy barrel and fired from a tripod it was required to give sustained effective fire up to 1,830m and harassing fire out to 2,740m. Unfortunately the production stellite lined barrel was shown to fail after prolonged firing. This was found to be due to the manufacturer's inability to maintain the very close tolerances required. The liner was an interference fit and after a while gas from the end of the liner found its way back between the liner and the steel barrel and eventually eroded the barrel steel at the stress raising angle at the the thin section in front of the chamber. The stellite liner was abandoned when success was in sight and it was decided to chrome plate all barrels. For the sustained fire role a conversion kit would be kept at Company HQ enabling any selected gun to produce sustained fire. The conversion kit consists of:

Mounting Tripod 7.62mm MG L4A1. Sight unit C2 and accessories. Buffer recoil 7.62mm MG Mk 1. Barrels – 2. Aiming post, lamp and accessories. Spare return spring. Holdalls.

This enables the gun to register and record engaged targets which can then subsequently be re-engaged without further ranging under conditions of darkness, smoke or fog.

The gun was accepted in 1961 as the GPMG 7.62mm X15E2 on tripod X2E2. In service it was known initially as the L7A1 and after certain

changes were found to be necessary, these were incorporated and the designation changed to L7A2. The major changes were:
(1) Fitting two bents on the sear. This was found necessary to ensure that when the bolt was brought back sufficiently far to feed a round, it would be caught and held if by accident it should slip from the firer's hand.
(2) Fitting two part cartridge pawls to give a better alignment with the cartridge and a better control of the rounds in the belt.
(3) Fitting a 50-round cartridge box on the left of the gun for use in the close quarter battle.

There were several minor changes amounting to twelve in all and dealing with a variety of small points such as changing the carrying handle, strengthening the bipod legs, changing the inner feed pawl for the M13/2 link.

The functioning of the L7A2 is indistinguishable from that of the FN MAG (qv).

DATA (L7A2)
Cartridge: 7.62mm × 51
Method of operation: Gas
Method of locking: Dropping locking lever
Method of feed: Belt
Method of fire: Automatic

WEIGHTS
Gun in LMG role: 10.9kg
Barrel: 2.73kg
Ammunition (100 rounds linked): 2.95kg
Wallet, spare parts and tools: 1.02kg
Trigger pull: 3.6 to 6.3kg

LENGTHS
LMG: 1,232mm
SFMG: 1,048mm
Barrel: (includes 5cm overhang of carrying handle)
    With flash hider: 679mm
    Without flash hider: 597mm

MECHANICAL FEATURES
Barrel: Regulator: Escape to atmosphere type. 10 positions.
    Rifling: 4 grooves RH. 1 turn in 305mm
    Cooling: Air. Quick change
Sights: Foresight: Blade
    Rearsight: Aperture
    Graduation: 200-800 metres by 100-metre increments; 800-1,800 metres by 50 metre increments

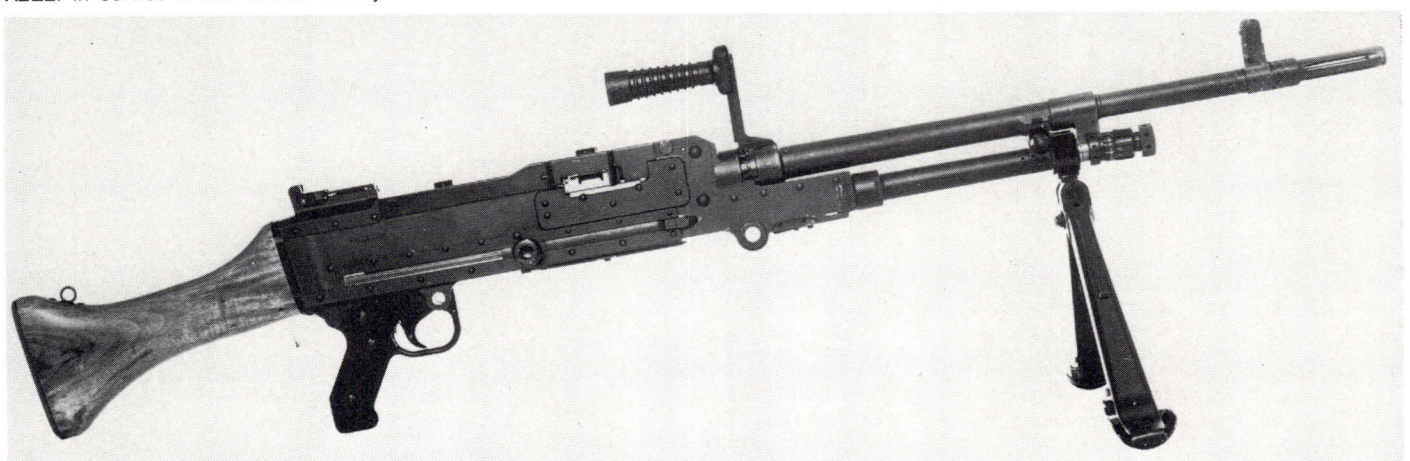

The L7A2 GPMG in the light role (RMCS)

Zeroing: Elevation. Screw foresight up or down through 180deg ·
steps. Line. Move foresight housing in dovetail
Sight radius: LMG role (sight down) 851mm; SFMG role (sight
up) 787mm

FIRING CHARACTERISTICS
Muzzle velocity: 838m/sec
Muzzle energy: 334mkp
Chamber pressure: 3,465kg/cm²
Rate of fire: Cyclic: 750-1,000 rounds/min
Operational normal: LMG role 25 rounds/min; SFMG role

100 rounds/min
Operational rapid: LMG role 100 rounds/min; SFMG role 200
rounds/min

ACCESSORIES
50-round, belt feed box. Blank firing attachment L3A1 with blank ammunition guide plate. Cover muzzle 7.62mm MG L1A2. Wallet, spare parts,
filled. Chest, carrying, 7.62mm Mk 1.

Manufacturer: Royal Small Arms Factory, Enfield, Middlesex
Status: Production schedule complete. In service with British forces

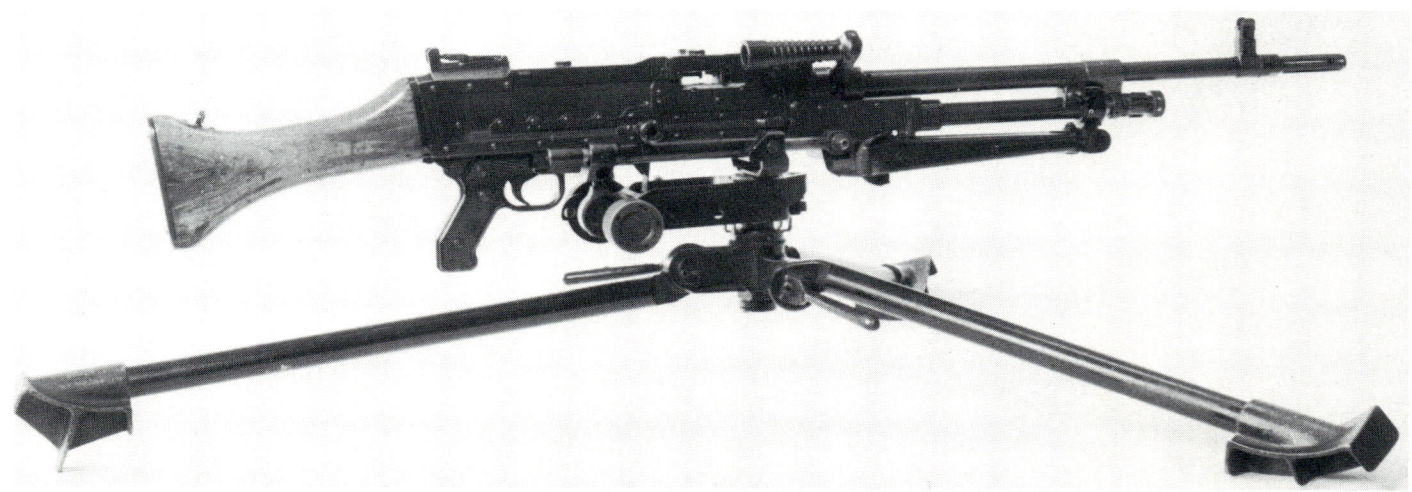

L7A2 GPMG in the sustained fire role on tripod mounting 7.62mm MG L3A1 (RMCS)

GPMG BUFFERED TRIPOD MOUNTING

To provide a strong and stable yet small and light mounting for the L7
GPMG the Tripod Mounting, 7.62mm MG, L4A1 was developed at the
Royal Small Arms Factory at Enfield. Details of this mounting are given
below; but it should be noted that the RSAF have now produced basically
similar mountings adapted for use with a wide variety of other machine
guns.

The mounting incorporates its own recoil buffer unit, permitting all round
traverse and has a quick release mechanism allowing free traverse,
elevation and depression.

(a) Three legs – two short, one long
(b) Tripod head
(c) Cradle and recoil unit
(d) Elevating mechanism
(e) Traversing mechanism.

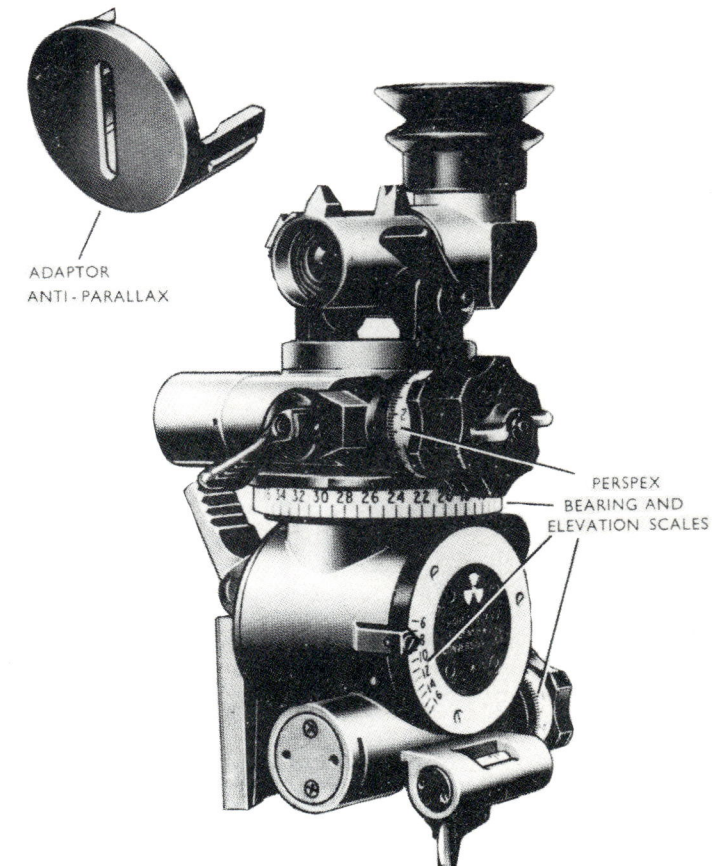

Sight unit, C2, Trilux and adaptor, anti-parallax

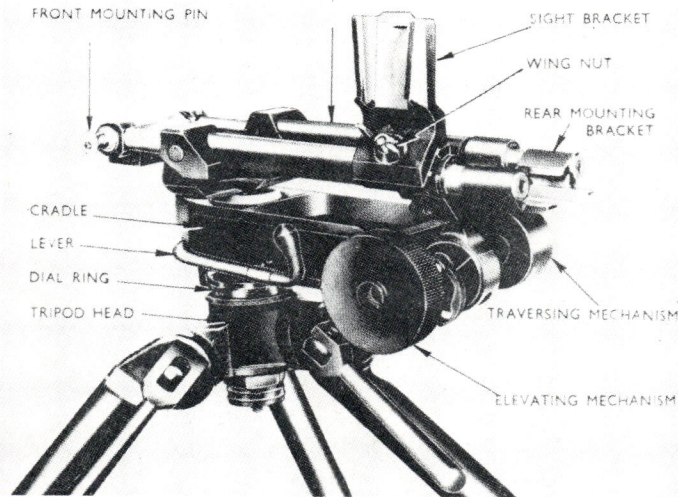

The cradle and recoil unit (RSAF)

The three tubular legs support the tripod head. At the foot each leg has a
shoe to give an improved ground grip. Each leg is locked by a cam lever
which when pushed inwards secures the leg in any desired position. When
the locking levers are pulled outwards the clutch faces are forced out by coil
springs and the leg is free. The tripod can be set to 'high' or 'low' and these
settings are notched on the legs and on the tripod head at the junction of the
clutches. There are three lugs on the tripod head to take legs. The dial ring
is held in position by friction and can be rotated by hand. It has a traverse
scale of 0-3,200 mils in each direction with graduations every 250 mils,
numbered every 1,000 mils. The indicator moves with the head and a line
on it indicates the traverse on the scale. The cradle and recoil unit is

*This illustration shows the contour of the tripod feet, which ensures maximum
anchorage on all types of ground from all tripod heights (RSAF)*

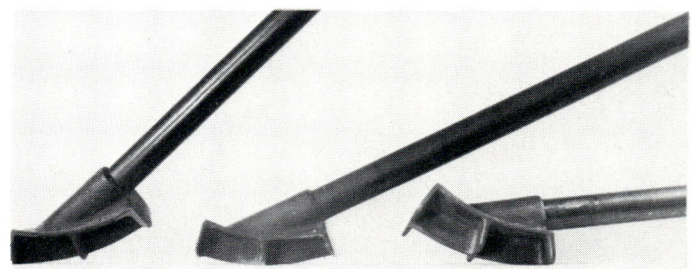

mounted on the tripod head. The cradle is attached to the tripod head by a ball joint which can be locked; when free it allows 600 mils elevation and all round traverse. The gun is secured to the recoil unit by front and rear mounting pins. The cradle has an enclosed buffer system of tubes, buffers and springs. When the first round is fired, the whole gun recoils and then the buffer returns it to battery. Before run out is completed the next round is fired and thereafter the gun movement is extremely small as it rests in equilibrium imposed between the recoil force and the buffer unit.

The elevation mechanism provides a fine adjustment using the handwheel on the left. It is controlled and locked by an eccentric cam tightened by a thumb lever. The fine traversing mechanism is controlled by the handwheel on the right. The range of controlled traverse is 200 mils and one turn of the handwheel traverses the gun through 6.6 mils. A clicker control operated by a sliding sleeve gives 2.2 mils to each click i.e. three clicks per turn. If desired the sleeve may be pushed in to give a smooth, silent control.

The dial sight is the 'Sight unit C2, Trilux' which is also used with the 81mm mortar. It has a right angled telescope with a magnification of 1.7X and a field of view of 180 mils. The eyepiece may be rotated 1,600 mils (90deg) right or left from the vertical. The bearing assembly comprises the coarse and fine bearing scale rings and a worm gear. The coarse bearing ring has a scale reading from 0 to 6,400 mils (0-360deg) and is numbered every 200 mils in a clockwise direction. The fine bearing scale ring is assembled on the worm spindle and has a slipping scale graduated in single mils from 0-100 and numbered every 10 mils. The two bearing scales allow the gun to be laid onto a selected zero line and then bearings read off to the nearest mil from that zero line. The sight can then be locked if so required.

The elevation assembly has a coarse scale plate and a fine scale ring. A worm gear allows the completed sight unit to be rotated up or down and the angle of elevation can be read to the nearest mil. The worm gear can be locked in a similar way to that for bearing.

The elevation and cross levelling bubbles are mounted below their corresponding coarse scales.

The sight unit is fitted with perspex bearing and elevation scales which, with the telescope graticule and the levelling bubbles, are Trilux illuminated by sealed in beta sources, using Tritium gas, which lose half their brightness in 10 years.

When the L7 machine gun is used on the tripod the butt is removed and the recoil buffer is employed in its place. This carries out the same function as the buffer assembly and carries the same braking cone and ring together with the Belleville compression washers as those on the buffer assembly of the gun in the LMG role.

DATA
Mounting: Tripod L4A1

WEIGHTS
Tripod: 13.61kg
Sight unit, cased: 2.58kg
Conversion kit, complete: 32.66kg

LENGTHS
Legs spread:
Distance across short legs: 1,118mm
Distance front to rear: 1,118mm

Height of sight line above ground: 330 to 635mm
Folded dimensions: 813 × 191 × 191mm

MECHANICAL FEATURES
Free traverse: 360 degrees (6,400mils)
Mechanical traverse (max): 11 degrees (200mils)
Clicker control (angle/click): 7mins (2.2mils)
Elevation (max): 22 degrees (400mils)
Mechanical elevation (max): 2 degrees 48min (50mils)
Depression (max): 11 degrees (200mils)
Mechanical depression (max): 2 degrees 48 min (50mils)

Manufacturer: Royal Small Arms Factory, Enfield
Status: Production. In service with British Armed Forces

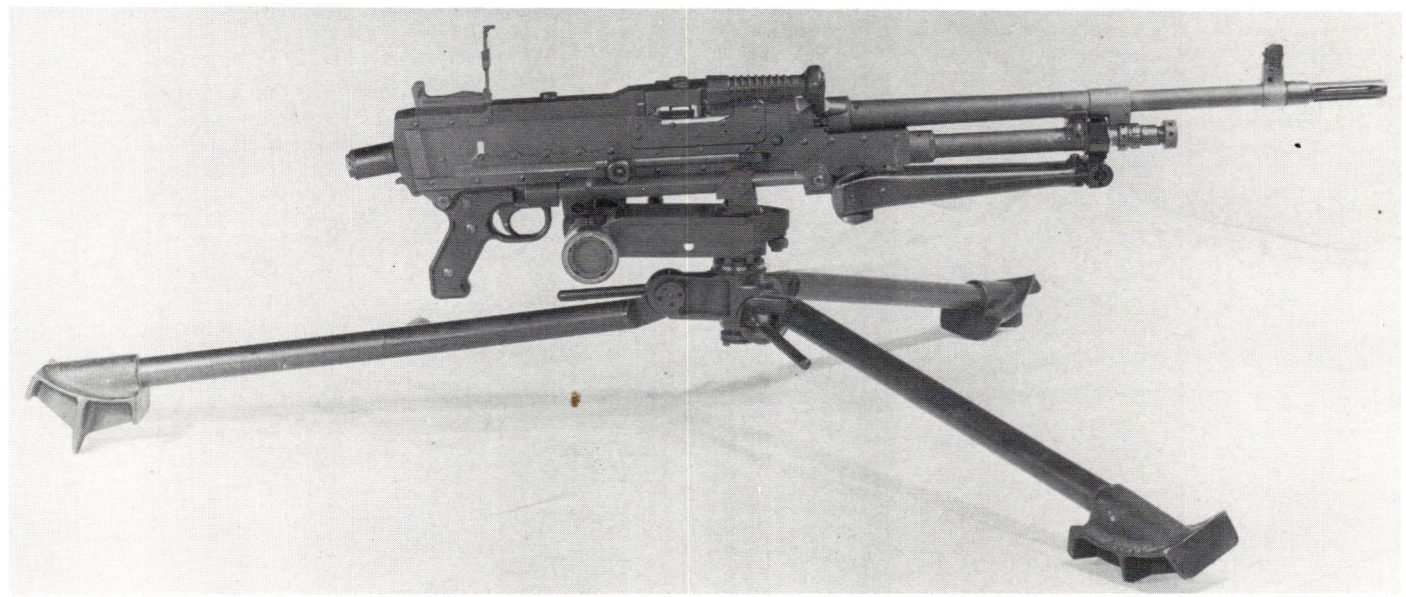

The 7.62mm L7A2 MG mounted on the Mounting Tripod 7.62mm MG L4A1. Note the butt has been removed and the buffer, recoil, inserted (Courtesy RSAF)

7.62mm L8A1 TANK MG.

During World War II the standard British tank gun was the 7.92mm BESA which was developed from the Czech Model 37(Zb53). After the war it was decided to abandon the 7.92mm cartridge and British Armoured Fighting Vehicles were largely equipped with the cal .30 Browning M1919A4 tank machine gun. Prior to the introduction of the Chieftain tank it was decided to adopt a machine gun using the 7.62mm × 51 NATO cartridge and the USA M73 machine gun was evaluated. It was not considered to be a satisfactory gun for British service and the decision was made to adapt the L7 machine gun for tank use.

The L7 GPMG can be fed only from the left; its gas system is of the 'exhaust to atmosphere' type, and to remove the belt from the gun it is necessary to lift the top cover plate, housing the feed mechanism.

All of these factors make it unsuitable for tank use. The necessity to feed from the left dictates the position of a coaxial machine gun relative to the main armament and this is not always the position the designer or the user would prefer.

Any gas-operated gun releases fumes to the immediate surrounding area through gas vents and the 'exhaust to atmosphere' system is particularly bad because when the gun is operating under the most favourable conditions the amount of gas escaping through the regulator is at its greatest. For this reason it is frequently not possible to use blank cartridges in a tank machine gun.

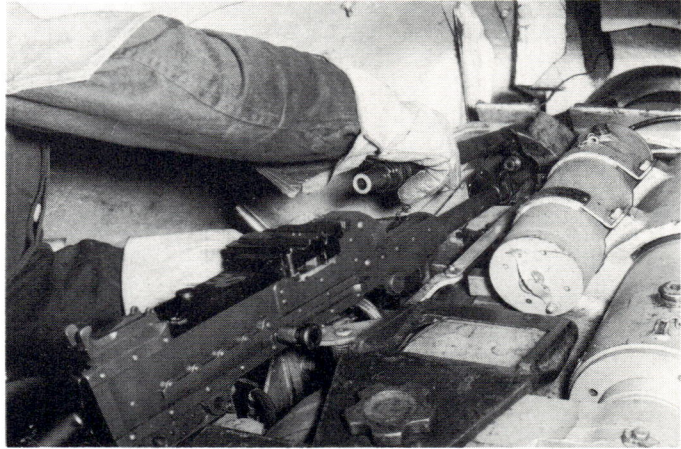

Changing the barrel of the L8A1 Tk MG in a Chieftain tank. The whole gun must be withdrawn into the tank to allow the barrel to go forward (RMCS)

The interior of a tank turret can be very cramped and the machine gun may have to be mounted with insuffficient clearance to allow the top cover plate to be lifted sufficiently to allow the belt to be removed. The ideal gun, has its hinges along both sides of the upper surface of the receiver so that the cover requires the miniumum overhead clearance and can be opened to either side.

The L8 machine gun embodies the necessary changes to improve the L7 for tank use but embodies the same basic design features.

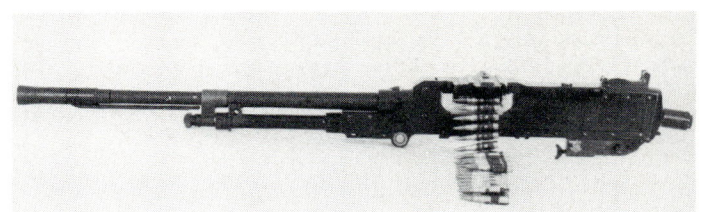

L8A1 tank MG (RMCS)

GAS SYSTEM

The gas regulator plug has three radial gas ports, 1, 2 and 3 of increasing diameter and fits into a conical seating to eliminate any gas leakage. Also to exclude gas from the interior of the AFV, the usual gas escape holes are omitted from the gas cylinder. Since a feature of this weapon is the exchangeable barrel requirement, the inevitable small escape of gas via the close clearance fit of the gas plug in the front end of the gas cylinder is dealt with by a fume extractor tube fitted into the conical flash suppressor and led back to the regulator spindle nut. The gases emerging from the muzzle pass the forward end of the excess gas tube and create an area of low pressure, thus sucking out any gas in the tube originating in the gas plug.

When it is desired to change the gas setting, the gun is cocked, the regulator spindle nut turned back and regulator plug turned to align the required gas port with the barrel vent in the gas block. When the regulator spindle nut is tightened, the flat on the regulator plug prevents the plug rotating. The spindle is serrated to engage the spring of the spindle to prevent rotation of the nut.

THE FEED PAWL DEPRESSOR

This is a sheet metal plate which is fitted over the feed pawls. When the depressor is moved to the left, the spring loaded feed pawls are free to work in the normal manner and the belt cannot move to the left. When the depressor is moved to the right the feed pawls are pushed up against their springs and the belt can be pulled to the left out of the gun.

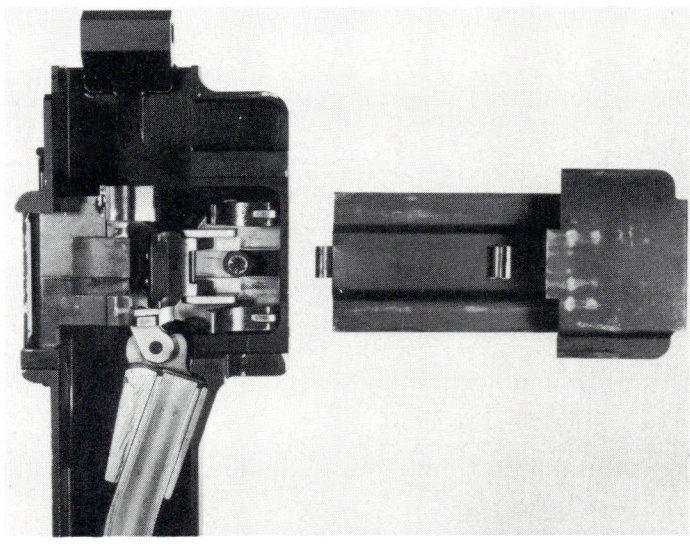

The pawl depressor taken off the gun to show the components (RMCS)

L8A1 IN THE GROUND ROLE

Dismounting of the L8A1 for use in the ground role is not contemplated except in extreme emergency. The gun when used in the co-axial role needs neither sights, nor bipod, nor butt. When the gun is removed from the tank and employed for ground use the bipod is attached to the front of the gas cylinder. The barrel is removed, the bipod sleeve goes over the front of the gas cylinder with the legs out horizontally and when the legs are rotated down the lugs of the gas cylinder engage in the recesses of the bipod adaptor. The recoil buffer is removed and the wooden butt slipped into the grooves at the rear of the receiver. As no foresight is fitted proper sighting is impossible.

In all other respcts the L8A1 is similar to the L7A2 and operates in the same way as the FN MAG (qv).

The pawl depressor moved to the right and pawls depressed so the belt can be removed without lifting the feed cover (RMCS)

DATA
Cartridge: 7.62mm × 51
Method of operation: Gas
Method of locking: Dropping locking lever
Method of feed: Belt
Method of fire: Automatic

WEIGHTS
Gun, complete: 10.43kg
Barrel: 3.06kg
Trigger pull: 8.16kg

LENGTHS
Gun: 1,099mm
Barrel (including flash suppressor and 5cm overhang of carrying handle): 737mm

MECHANICAL FEATURES
Barrel: Regulator: 3 position
Rifling: 4 grooves. RH. 1 turn in 305mm
Cooling: Air. Quick change
Sights: Foresight: Post mounted in flash suppressor
Rearsight: Aperture
Graduation: 200-800 metres by 100 metre increments; 800-1,800 metres by 50 metre increments
Zeroing: Nil
Sight radius: Sight down 851mm Sight up 787mm

FIRING CHARACTERISTICS
Muzzle velocity: 838m/sec
Muzzle energy: 334mkp
Chamber pressure: 3,465kg/cm²
Rate of fire: Cyclic: 650-1,000 rounds/min
Accessories: Wallet S.A. spare parts and tools No. 2 Mk 1 – filled; Spare parts box containing: Spare barrel, bipod, butt, breech block and piston assembly, return spring assembly
Manufacturer: Royal Small Arms Factory, Enfield
Status: In production. In service

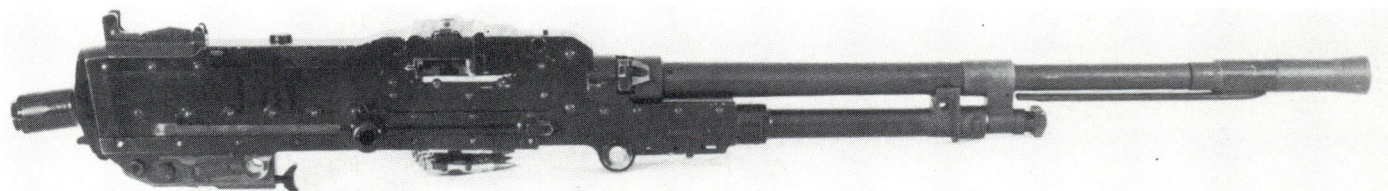

L8A1 TK MG. Note the vestigial barrel handle which makes the use of an asbestos glove essential (RMCS)

7.62mm L37A1 TANK MG

This is a machine gun based on the L8. It is intended that the gun will be used in Armoured Fighting Vehicles, Scout Cars and APCs and also have a capability for use in a dismounted, ground role.

The gun is basically the L8 Machine Gun and to enable it to carry out its ground role it carries L7 MG sub assemblies. The gun is made up of the following items:

L8 Machine Gun Body assembly. This normally has an electrically controlled solenoid trigger.

L8 Machine Gun Barrel assembly. This barrel, the L3A2, does not have a foresight, or an insulated barrel carrying handle.

L7 Machine Gun Trigger mechanism. This replaces the normal L8 trigger.

L7/L8 Machine Gun Buffer, recoil assembly Mk I.

The accompanying illustration shows the gun as it would be in the tank. There is a back sight fitted on the tank gun body.

To convert the gun to its ground role, parts of the gun equipment needed are: L7 Machine Gun Barrel assembly. This barrel, the L1A2, has a foresight and a carrying handle.

L7 Bipod assembly.
L7 Butt assembly.

DATA (Where differing from the L8 Machine Gun)
Gun:
Weight: 9.53kg
Length: 1,075mm

Barrel L3A2 (AFV Role):
Weight: 2.7kg
Length: 663mm

Barrel L1A2 (Ground Role):
Weight: 2.7kg
Length: 711mm

Sights (Ground Role):
Rear: Aperture
Front: Adjustable blade

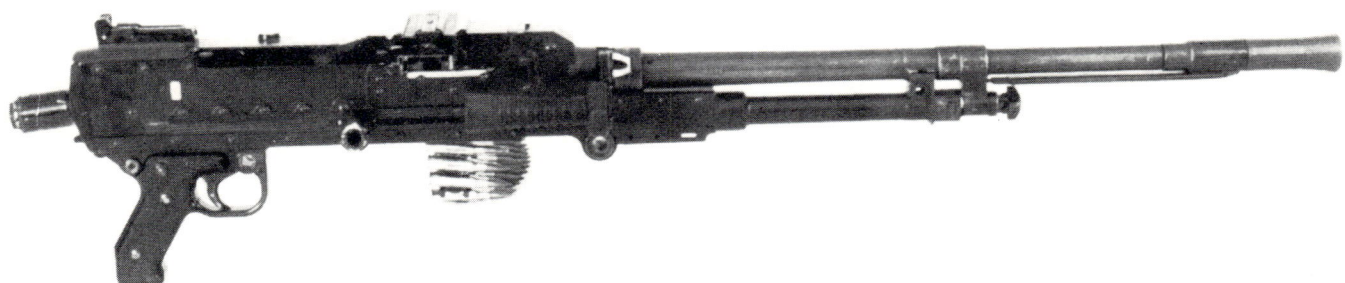

L37A1 in its tank configuration (RMCS)

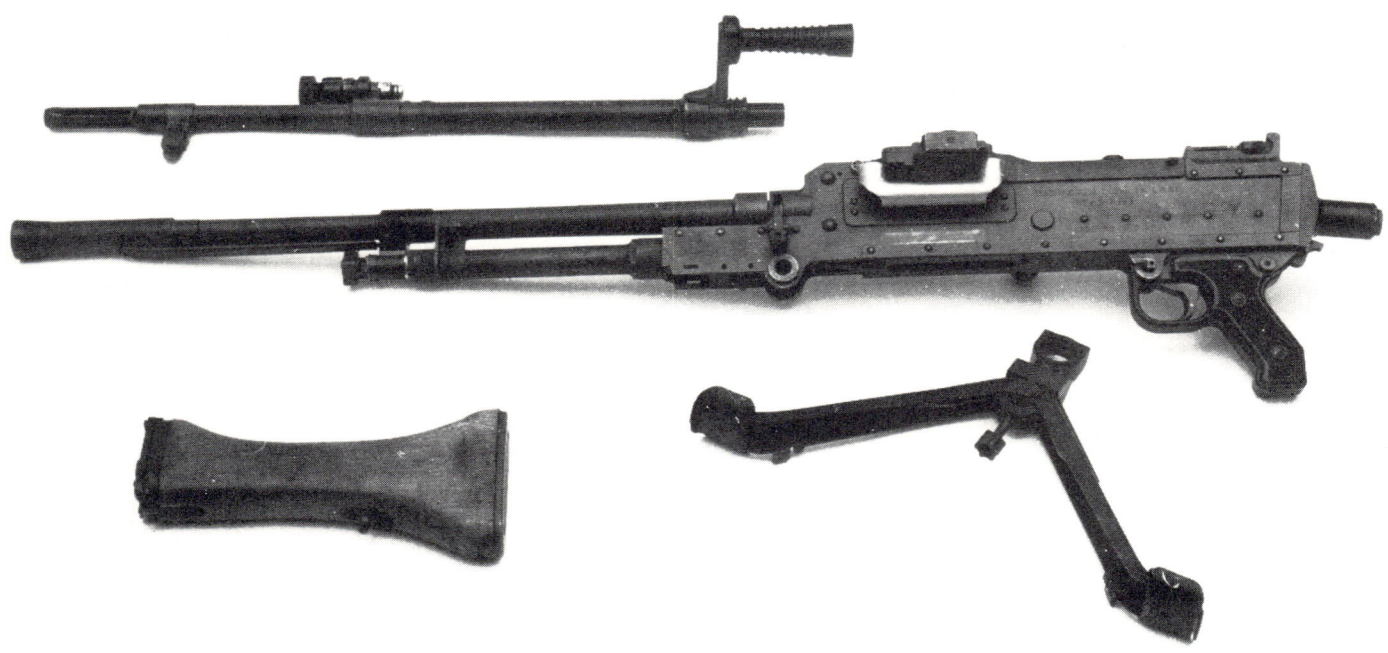

L8 with the attachments for converting it to the L37, including an L1A2 barrel (RMCS)

7.62mm L20A1 MG

This gun is a modification of the L8 Tank Machine Gun to enable it to be used in a helicopter. The trigger is electrically controlled, there is no sighting system and the barrel does not have the flash hider and gas tubes of the L3A2 barrel. It has the gas system of that barrel but uses a prong type flash eliminator. The gun can be fed from either side by changing the feed cover with the feed pawls and feed arm and the feed plate.

A duct is installed to convey the expended links into a bag.

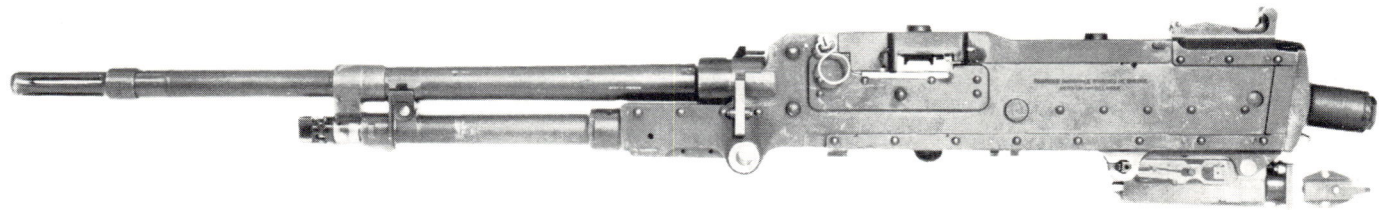

The 7.62mm L20A1 MG with right-hand feed (RMCS)

7.62mm L41A1 DPMG

This is the Drill Purpose gun made up from the L8 Tank Machine Gun. From the right hand side little can be seen to indicate that the gun is to be used, as its name implies, for drill purposes only, but from the left hand side it can be seen that the barrel is no longer of much use. In addition the firing pin has been shortened and no longer protrudes, and the firing hole bush has been plugged.

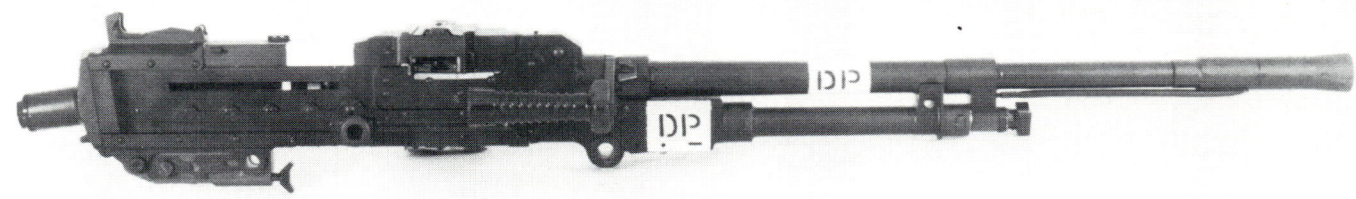

The L41A1 DP gun viewed from the right (RMCS)

7.62mm L43A1 RANGING MACHINE GUN

Until very recently it had not been possible to combine the role of the ranging tank machine gun with that of the co-axial machine gun. To some extent barrel wear suffered by the co-axial MG resulted in loss of consistency, essential to a ranging gun, but in addition a problem existed with the movement of the MPI (mean point of impact) of a group of shots from a cold to a hot gun. This was critical since effective ranging is essential with the gun either cold or hot. The L43A1, with its barrel bearing, was specially developed to reduce this MPI shift to an acceptable level. This bearing is located between the gas block and the muzzle, and supports the barrel at the forward end. The L43A1 doe not have the flash hider and gas tube of the L3A2 barrel.

The L43A1 is used in Scorpion to range the 76mm gun.

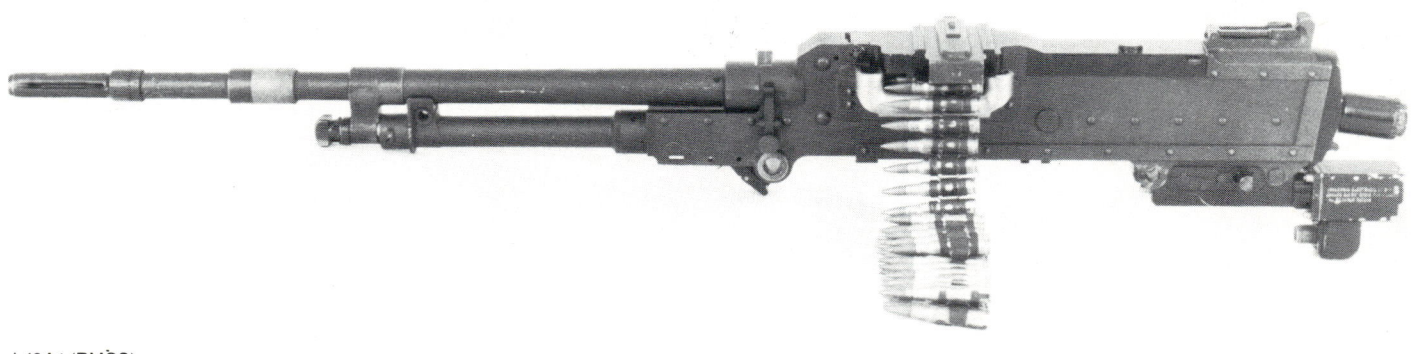

L43A1 (RMCS)

7.62mm L46A1 DPMG

This is a conversion of the 7.62mm L7A1 and L7A2 for drill purposes. The firing hole bush has been plugged. The firing pin has been shortened. The barrel has been plugged and welded and material has been taken from the locking shoulders of the bolt to ensure that it will not fit into any other gun.

4.85mm LIGHT SUPPORT WEAPON

Two new weapons in 4.85mm calibre were publicly demonstrated by the British Army in June, 1976. Constituting the British entry for the 1977-79 NATO trials, the weapons are intended to perform the functions which are at present performed by the SMG, SL rifle and the GPMG in its LMG role.

Known at present as the Individual Weapon (IW) and the Light Support Weapon (LSW), the two weapons share the same basic design and some 80% of their components are interchangeable. The LSW is the larger of the two: it weighs just over a kilogram more than the IW and differs from it

Firing the Light Support Weapon (bipod folded) (UK MoD)

mainly in having a larger barrel and consequently a higher muzzle velocity and longer effective range. It is expected normally to be used with a 30-round magazine but this is interchangeable with the 20-round magazine of the IW.

Tabulated below are comparative data for the LSW and for the GPMG which the LSW is intended to replace in its LMG role. Some further information on the two weapons will be found in the entry for the IW in the section dealing with rifles.

DATA

AMMUNITION	LSW	GPMG
Calibre:	4.85mm	7.62mm
Types:	Ball	Ball
	Tracer	Tracer
	Blank	Blank
Round weight:	11.6 grams	24.6 grams

WEIGHT		
Weapon (less Magazine and Optical sight):	4.08kg	10.9kg
Optical sight:	.6kg	.62kg
Empty magazine:	.242kg	N/A
Loaded Magazine:	.584kg	.870kg
(filled with)	(30 rds)	(30 rd Belt)

Weapon (complete with loaded magazine):	5.26kg	12.39kg

LENGTH		
Barrel (including flash hider):	64.6cm	62.9cm
Weapon:	90cm	123cm

MECHANICAL FEATURES		
Rifling: Grooves	4	4
Turns	1/125m	1/305m
Trigger Pull:	3.12-5kg	3.6-6.3kg
Method of operation:	Gas	Gas
Type of Locking:	Rotary Bolt	Dropping Link
	Forward Locking	Rear Locking
Method of Feed:	Magazine	Belt

FIRING CHARACTERISTICS		
Muzzle Velocity:	930m/s	843m/s
Recoil Energy:	3.78J	8.65J
Rate of Fire (Cyclic):	700-850r/m	650-900r/m

Manufacturer: Royal Small Arms Factory, Enfield, Middlesex
Status: Trials

UNITED STATES OF AMERICA

.30 CALIBRE BROWNING MODEL 1917

In 1900 Browning obtained a patent for a short recoil-operated machine gun. The US Army Board evinced little interest and Browning turned to continued work on commercial weapons for Fabrique Nationale d'Armes de Guerre in Belgium. In 1910 Browning returned to his machine gun and produced a prototype at Ogden, Utah, which differed from the 1901 patent in having bottom ejection, a buffer, and a revised trigger mechanism.

It was only in 1917 that the US Army awoke to the realisation that it was ill prepared for war and that its machine guns were inadequate both technically and numerically. It had 282 Maxim guns of the 1904 pattern, 158 Colt Model '95 (Potato Diggers) and 670 Benet-Mercier gas operated LMGs. (These were a French, Hotchkiss pattern). This total of 1,100 obsolete machine guns was not of much use for the clearly impending clonflict.

Browning demonstrated his water cooled machine gun to a gathering of press, politicians, and allied attaches, on 27 February 1917 at Congress Heights, Washington DC. It was a great success and a further demonstration in May was even more convincing. First it fired 20,000 rounds at 600 rounds a minute without stoppage and, to convince the doubters, repeated the performance with a further 20,000. To show this was not due to any special preparation of the gun, another weapon was brought up and fired for 48 min 12 sec at 600 rounds a minute – a total of 28,920 rounds were fired before all the available ammunition was expended. Browning then stripped and re-assembled a gun whilst blindfolded.

Contracts for manufacturing the gun were placed very promptly. Colt's produced the drawings and gauges very rapidly for all the contractors. Westinghouse produced 30,150 and by Armistice Day, November 11 1918, had a production rate of 500 guns a day. Remington Arms Co. made 12,000 and with the Colt contribution, a total of 56,608 was produced – a truly remarkable figure but one that made little difference to the progress of the war since the first 12 Divisions of the US Army sent to France were equipped with machine guns purchased from France. The next 11 had .30 calibre Vickers guns made by Colts and the last 12 had Browning .30 Model 1917 machine guns. The Browning saw little service but was used by a unit of the 79th Division in September 1918.

It was discovered that the bottom plate of the receiver was not strong enough and a strengthening stirrup was fitted to modify some 25,000 guns in 1920-1921.

In 1936 the Model 1917 was modified to the 1917A1. The changes included:
(a) A new bottom plate
(b) A new cover latch assembly which remained open
(c) A new belt feed lever
(d) A new backsight for the .30-06 and M1 ammunition
(e) A modified tripod known as the M1917A1 tripod

During World War II further modifications were added to improve durability and allow use of the calibre .30 M2 ball cartridge. These included the flash hider M8 and a detachable carrying handle.

The M1917A1 was used throughout World War II. It was an excellent weapon. After the war experimental models were made using the T65 cartridge in both .30 calibre and 7.62mm. These guns operated successfully as the T214 series but work terminated in 1956 when it became clear that the T161E3 prototype of the M60 would be adopted.

DESCRIPTION

The receiver consists of pressings, riveted together. At the bottom is the breech lock cam which pushes the breech block up to the locked position and holds it there. At the forward end is the barrel which can be screwed in and out of the barrel extension to adjust the cartridge head space. The barrel extension continues to the rear for several inches. The breech lock is mounted in a vertical slot in the rear of the barrel extension.

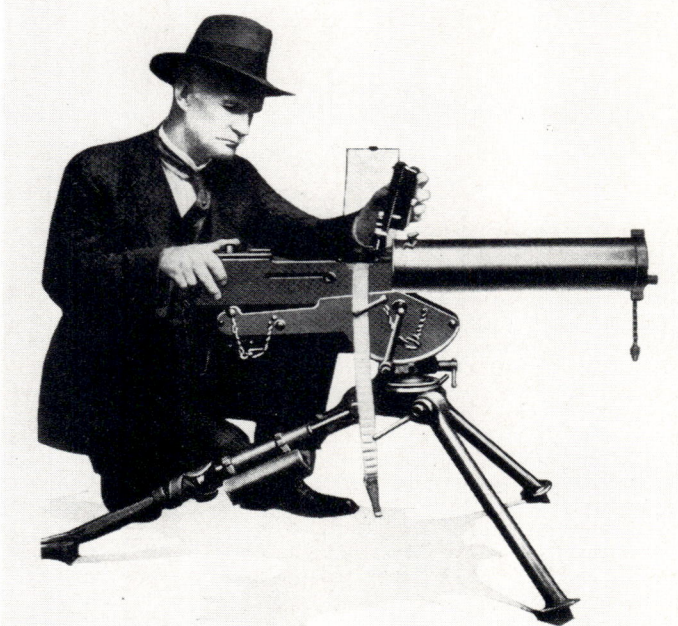

Browning and his Model 1917 machine gun

Attached inside the rear part of the receiver is the lock frame which carries the accelerator and two unlocking ramps.

The bolt contains the firing mechanism, the extractor for removing the cartridge from the belt, and along the top is a cam groove which causes the bolt feed lever to swing across the gun as the bolt reciprocates. The return spring and its guide rod are contained in the bolt. A T slot is cut in the front face of the bolt to hold the live round before firing and the empty case after firing.

The barrel is surrounded by a water jacket containing 7 pints of water. There is a steam escape tube, connecting piping and a condenser can.

The foresight is a blade dovetailed into the base to allow lateral movement for zeroing.

The rearsight is a vertical leaf aperture, offset to allow for drift, graduated from 100 to 3400 yds by 50 yd increments.

A windage scale is provided which rotates the centre sight base. Zeroing for elevation is accomplished by moving an adjusting plate.

OPERATION

Before loading the M1917A1 machine gun, the weapon should be quickly examined to ensure that all is in order. The water jacket and condenser can should be full with no leaks from the muzzle gland or rear barrel packing. The cartridge head space should be checked since the gun will not fire if it is too small and bulged or split cases will result from excessive space. Ammunition belts should be inspected before loading. The tripod should be checked for stability and security and care taken that the vertical and horizontal locking levers are secure.

The ammunition box is placed on the left of the gun and the tag of the belt pushed through the feedway from left to right and pulled to the right until the

US Cal. 30 MG, Model 1917A1 (RMCS)

first round is positioned on the right of the belt holding pawl. The cocking handle is fully retracted and released, twice. A cartridge is then in the chamber and the gun is ready to fire.

When the trigger is pulled the front end of the trigger bar goes down and forces the sear down against the sear spring until the shoulder of the firing pin is released by the sear notch. The firing pin spring then forces the firing pin forward to strike the primer.

The gas pressure pushes the bolt back. The bolt is locked to the barrel extension and both barrel and bolt recoil together for 8mm. The breech lock holding the barrel extension to the bolt then moves off the breech lock cam in the floor of the receiver. The inclined planes of the front projections of the lock frame drive down the breech lock by contact with the breech block pin which stands out on each side of the lock. When the breech lock drops, the bolt is freed from the barrel extension.

As the barrel extension moves back, the barrel plunger spring is compressed and the rear of the barrel extension strikes the accelerator and rotates it backwards. The tips of the accelerator strike projections on the bottom of the bolt. The energy of the barrel and barrel extension is transferred to the bolt which is accelerated backwards. The accelerator, at the end of its travel, locks the barrel extension to the lock frame and so the barrel remains in its recoiled position with the barrel plunger spring compressed.

The bolt continues rearward, compressing the return spring, bringing with it a live round from the belt, held in the extractor, and an empty case held in the T slot on the bolt face. The extractor is forced down as the bolt recoils. The stud on the pivoted belt feed lever moves to the right in the cam groove on top of the bolt and the belt feed slide is forced to the left. The belt pawl engages on the left of the first cartridge which is positioned by the bent holding pawl.

The cocking lever is fastened by a transverse pin inside the bolt and its top, protruding through the top of the bolt, is rotated forward by the top cover of the receiver. The rear end of the cocking lever moves back carrying the firing pin to the rear and compressing the firing pin spring. The firing pin engages a notch in the sear which has been forced up by the sear spring.

When the rear of the bolt strikes the buffer plate its remaining energy is absorbed in the fibre discs and expended as heat as the brass buffer ring is forced over the buffer plug and expanded against the inner wall of the grip. The return spring then forces the bolt forward.

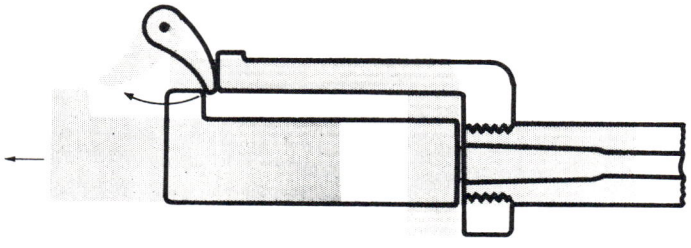

The action of the accelerator (RMCS)

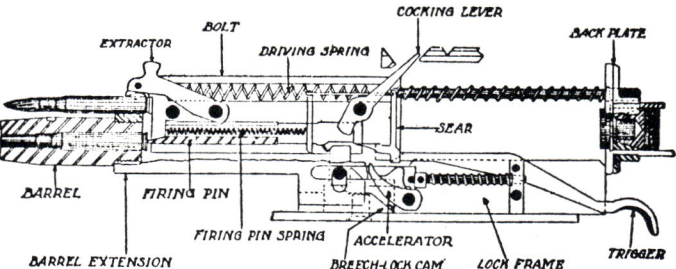

The relation of the parts in the forward position

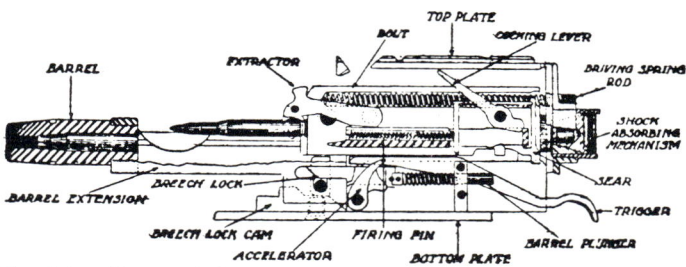

The relation of the parts in the rearward position

As the bolt moves forward the extractor, holding the live round, is guided down, the empty case is knocked from the T slot out through the bottom of the gun and the live cartridge is forced into the T slot on the bolt face and lined up with the chamber.

The upper end of the cocking lever, protruding from the top of the bolt, is forced back by the receiver, causing the lower end to move forward away from the rear of the firing pin. If the firing pin should be prematurely released, it is re-engaged by the cocking lever and eased forward so that the firing pin cannot contact the primer until the breech is locked.

As the bolt goes forward the projections on the under side strike the accelerator and revolve it forward. This unlocks the barrel from the lock frame and the combined force of the bolt impact on the accelerator and the compressed plunger spring, drive the barrel and barrel extension fully forward.

The stud on the pivoted belt feed lever moves to the left in the cam groove on top of the bolt forcing the feed slide to the right. The belt feed pawl carries the first cartridge to the right against the cartridge stops, ready to be gripped by the extractor. The next cartridge is carried over the belt holding pawl which rises behind it and holds it in position to be engaged by the feed pawl on its next movement to the left.

The extractor rises as the bolt concludes its forward movement, leaving the live round in the chamber, still gripped by the T slot. The extractor grips the first round in the belt and is held down firmly by the extractor spring in

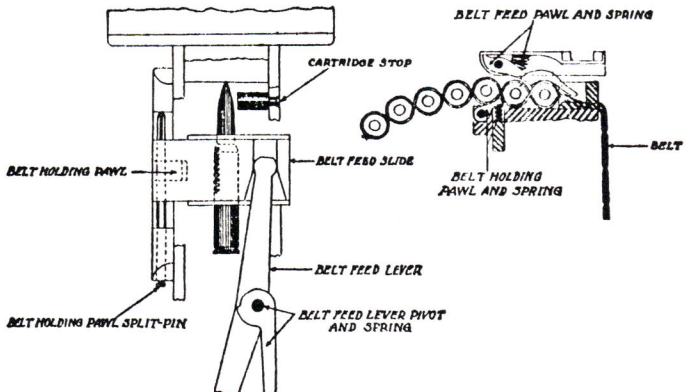

The belt-feed mechanism

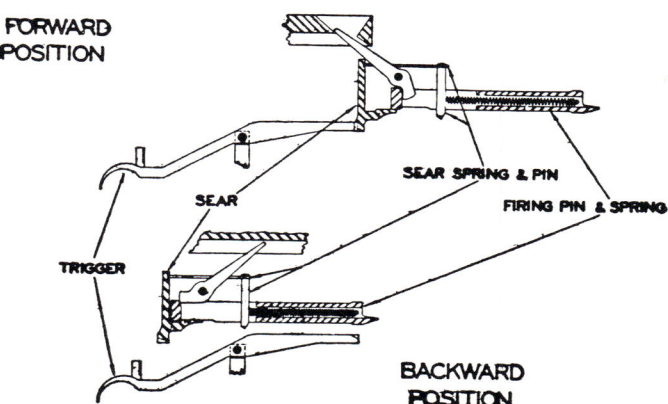

The trigger mechanism

US 3rd Army troops at Coblenz, 17 March 1945 (Imperial War Museum)

the cover. The breech lock is forced upwards into a recess in the bottom of the bolt by the cam in the bottom of the receiver, and locks the barrel extension to the bolt just before the recoiling parts reach the firing position.

The sear cam meets the trigger cam and the sear is pulled down, releasing the firing pin and the round is fired.

THE TRIGGER AND FIRING MECHANISM

The trigger is a long bar, pivoted in the lock frame, with a curved portion for the firer's finger at the rear end. This is lifted to fire the gun. At the fore end is an inclined plane cut into the width of the bar and called the trigger cam. The firing pin is a long cylinder with the firing pin spring inside. When the firing pin is cocked the rear end of the compressed spring rests against the sear pin. Extending back from the top of the sear pin is a flat sear spring which engages in a notch in the top of the front of the vertical arm of the sear and tends to lift it. The forward extension of the sear lies under the firing pin and has a step which engages in a notch in the firing pin and holds it in the cocked position. The bottom of the vertical arm of the sear carries an inclined plane – the sear cam.

The cocking lever is a pivoted arm in the bolt. The bottom end enters a slot in the firing pin and can thus bear on the pin to withdraw it to the cocked position. The top end projects through a hole in the top of the receiver so that it is pushed backwards and forwards as the bolt reciprocates.

As the bolt goes back after firing, the cocking lever is pushed forward and holds the firing pin back in the cocked position.

When the trigger is lifted the front end drops. When the bolt reaches the firing position – and not until then – the trigger cam mates with the sear cam and the forward movement of the bolt causes the two inclined planes to move over each other and the sear is pulled down. The forward extension of the sear releases the firing pin which goes forward and hits the cap whilst the bolt is still moving forward and has about 1.5mm to travel.

One feature of the trigger-sear design is that they can only meet when the bolt is in the correct position and if by chance the sear is jammed down and releases the firing pin, the cocking lever controls the rate at which the pin goes forward and the gun will not fire.

STRIPPING

Remove the belt, retract the bolt and withdraw the round in the chamber.
(1) Remove the back plate. Pull the latch and raise the cover. Pull back the cocking handle and bolt to the rear. Insert the rim of a cartridge case (or a screwdriver if available) in the slot at the end of the return spring rod. With the slot horizontal push the rod in as far as it will go and turn the rod clockwise through 90 degrees – i.e. the slot is vertical. This engages lugs on the rod in recesses in the bolt and locks the spring in compression. Push the cocking handle forward about an inch to free the end of the spring rod from the back plate. Push the latch forward and lift the back plate out.
(2) Remove the cocking handle. Pull the cocking handle fully back and remove it from the bolt.
(3) Remove the lock frame. Push in on the trigger pin, through the hole on the right of the receiver, with the nose of a round. Grasp the trigger and pull the lock frame, bolt, barrel extension and barrel rearwards. Remove the bolt. Hold the lock frame firmly and press forward on the accelerator to separate the lock frame and barrel extension.
(4) Strip the bolt. With the base of the cartridge push in the head of the driving spring rod and turn it 90 degrees to the left. The return spring is compressed and must be released with care. Push out the cocking lever. Turn the bolt over, push up the sear with the bullet to release the firing pin spring. Push it over to the left, lever the spring into the locking recess and the sear will drop out. Push the sear spring back again and the pin and spring may be pushed out. The firing pin and its spring can be dropped out of the back of the bolt. The extractor should be turned and pulled out to the left.

Re-assembly follows the reverse pattern. Re-assemble the bolt and insert and lock return spring with its rod. Attach the lock frame to the barrel extension by rotating the accelerator and compressing the barrel plunger spring. Push the assembly into the receiver until the trigger pin comes against the side of the receiver. Push in the trigger pin and slide the whole assembly forward until the trigger pin springs into its hole in the receiver. Slide the bolt in with the cocking lever forward. Insert the cocking handle and slide it forward sufficiently to allow the back plate to be inserted. Pull

right back on the cocking handle and hold it hard back whilst the return spring rod is rotated 90 degrees anti-clockwise to release the spring. Allow the bolt forward under control.

DATA
Cartridge: .30 M1 or M2
Method of operation: Short recoil
Method of locking: Projecting lug
Method of feed: 250 round belt
Method of fire: Automatic

WEIGHTS
Gun: 18.6kg
Gun, no water: 14.8kg
Barrel: 1.36kg
Trigger pull: 3.18-5.45kp

LENGTH
Gun: 981mm
Barrel: 607mm
Rifling: 543mm

MECHANICAL FEATURES
Barrel: Rifling: 4 grooves RH. 1 turn in 254mm Depth of grooves 0.1016mm Cross-sectional of area of bore 47.74mm²
Cooling: Water 3.3 litres
Sights: Foresight: Blade
Rearsight: Leaf aperture. Windage scale
Graduation: 100-3,400 by 50yds increments (91-3,109m × 46m)
Zeroing: Line. Foresight Elevation. Rearsight
Sight radius: 668mm

FIRING CHARACTERISTICS
Muzzle velocity: 854metres/sec
Muzzle energy: 361mkp
Chamber pressure: 3,465kg/cm²
Rate of fire: Cyclic: 450-600 rounds/min
                    Automatic: 250 rounds/min
Range, maximum:
   Cartridge ball .30 M2: 3,450yds (3,154 metres)
   Cartridge ball .30 M1: 5,500yds (5,029 metres)
   Cartridge ball .30 1906: 3,450yds (3,184 metres)
   Cartridge tracer .30 M1: 3,450yds (3,155 metres)
   Cartridge armour piercing .30 M2: 4,500yds (4,115 metres)
   Cartridge armour piercing .30 M1: 4,000yds (3,691 metres)

ACCESSORIES
Tripod M1917A1
Belt loading machine
Clinometer M1917
Aiming circle M1916
Aiming circle tripod, type G
Range finder 80cm base, M1914 or
Range finder 80cm base, M1917

Manufacturer: Colt's Patent Firearms Manufacturing Company, Hartford, Connecticut. Remington Arms – Union Metallic Cartridge Co, New England
Status: No longer manufactured. No longer in service with the army of any major power but a few survive elsewhere – notably in South America.

.30 CALIBRE BROWNING MODEL 1919A6

The M1919A6 is a belt fed, air-cooled, recoil operated machine gun. It can have a muzzle mounted bipod or be mounted on the M2 tripod. It is similar to the model M1919A4 except for the following modifications:
(1) A removable metal shoulder stock has been added.
(2) The cover latch has been modified to provide for easier opening.
(3) The return spring has been lightened to make bolt retraction easier.
(4) A removable handle has been added to enable easier carrying of a hot gun.
(5) The barrel jacket has been modified to mount a front barrel bearing, a removable bipod assembly and a lock ring.
(6) The bolt latch has been removed.
(7) The M7 flash-hider has been incorporated.

The M1919A6 has a barrel which can be changed when hot by. grasping the muzzle and (preferably with asbestos mittens) unscrewing the barrel and sliding it forward out of the jacket. The new barrel is slid into the jacket and screwed into the barrel extension. The cartridge head space is adjusted by screwing the barrel in until the bolt will just close and then backing off two clicks on the ratchet. The following data is that where the M1919A6 differs from the M1919A4.

Weight with metal stock and bipod: 14.74kg
Weight of metal stock: 0.79kg
Weight of barrel: 2.11kg
Trigger pull: 3.86kg
Length overall: 826mm
Status: No longer manufactured. No longer in US service though probably held in reserve. Still in widespread use and likely to be encountered in any country that has benefited directly or indirectly from US military aid programmes.

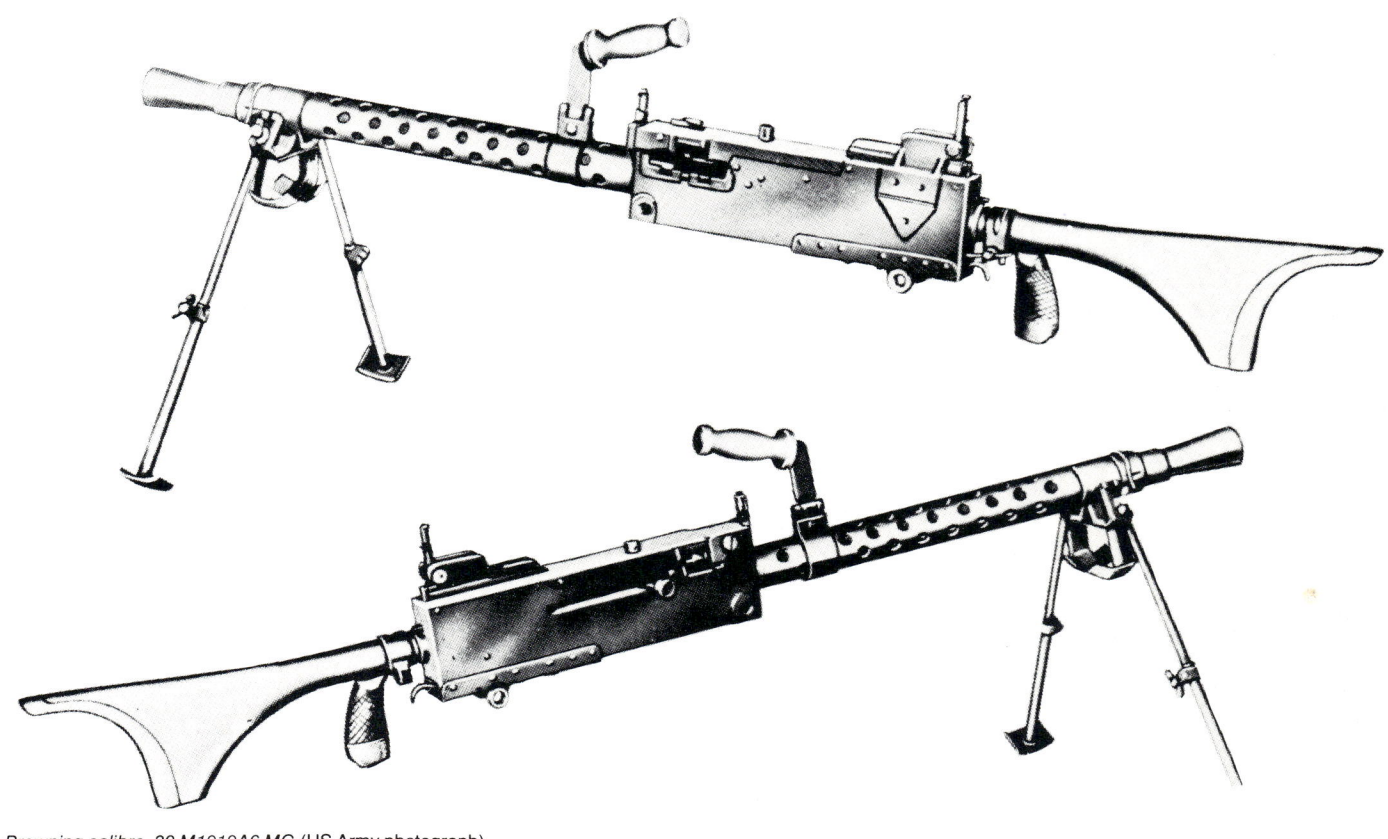

Browning calibre .30 M1919A6 MG (US Army photograph)

.30 CALIBRE BROWNING MODEL 1919A4

The Model 1919A4 was used as a fixed gun in tanks in World War II and on many post-war AFV's. The flexible gun was used by infantry as a company level weapon, mounted on the M2 tripod, with the flash hider M6 and a detachable carrying handle. The evolution of the M1919A4 can be traced back to the .30 calibre Browning tank machine gun which itself was derived from Browning's air-cooled aircraft machine gun designated the M1918.

The mechanism of the Model 1919A4 is identical with that of the M1917 already described.

The differences between the M1919A4 and the M1917 and M1917A1 are that it is air cooled, has a perforated steel barrel casing and no water jacket. The M1919A4 has a heavier barrel but has a lower capacity for sustained fire. The sights of the two weapons are different.

DATA
Cartridge: .30 M1 or M2
Method of operation: Short recoil
Method of locking: Projecting lug
Method of feed: 250 round belt
Method of fire: Automatic

WEIGHTS
Gun: 14.06kg
Barrel: 3.33kg
Trigger pull: 3.18-5.45kg
M2 tripod: 6.35kg

LENGTH
Gun: 1,044mm
Barrel: 610mm
Rifling: 543mm

FIRING CHARACTERISTICS
Muzzle velocity: 860 metres/sec
Muzzle energy: 367mkp
Chamber pressure: 3,465kg/cm²
Rate of fire: Cyclic: 400-500 rounds/min
            Automatic: 120 rounds/min
Range, maximum effective: 1,000 metres

MECHANICAL FEATURES
Barrel: Rifling: 4 grooves RH. 1 turn in 254mm Depth of grooves 0.1016mm Cross sectional area of bore 47.74mm^2
Cooling: Air

Sights: Foresight: Blade
Rearsight: Leaf aperture. Windage scale
Zeroing: Line foresight. Elevation rearsight
Sight radius: 354mm

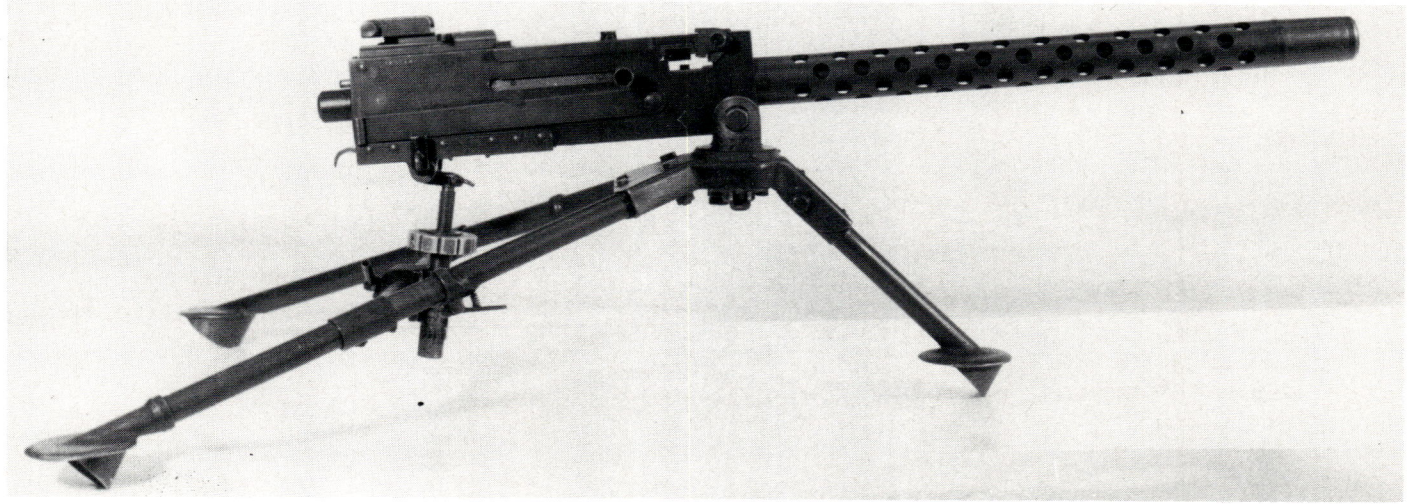

Browning calibre .30 Model 1919A4 on tripod M2 (RMCS)

.5in CALIBRE BROWNING MACHINE GUNS

Towards the end of 1917 it became apparent that the .30 calibre machine gun could not be expected to penetrate the improved protection that was being used in France on vehicles, gun shields and even on soldiers, and General Pershing initiated a requirement for a larger calibre, more powerful machine gun. The officer in charge of the American Machine Gun School in France, obtained samples of the French Hotchkiss 11mm HMG and its ammunition and these were sent to America for evaluation. Browning worked with the Winchester Repeating Arms Co to develop a new cartridge at New Haven. The earliest rounds had a trimmed case but this solution was not accepted by General Pershing and on 15 October 1918 the Browning .5 Machine Gun was fired for the first time, using a bullet of 707 grains (45.8g) with a muzzle velocity of 2,200ft/sec (670m/sec). This low velocity was ascribed to the short barrel of only 775mm, which was the longest that Winchester could rifle. When an order was placed for guns with a longer barrel the result was disappointing. The gun, although it weighed 72.6kg on its tripod, was difficult to control and had a poor penetration.

The German Mauser 13mm anti tank rifle ammunition, which had a good armour penetration, was examined and Winchester made use of the ideas found there to improve their cartridge. Eventually the Browning .5 Machine Gun and its improved cartridge were accepted into service. The gun was known as the US Machine Gun Calibre .50 M1921. It was similar in nearly all respects to the .30 M1917; but because of the large recoil energy of the breech block it was found necessary to install an oil buffer. This was based on artillery practice and the piston was driven to the rear against the resistance of the oil which passed through notches cut in the periphery of the piston head, to return to the other side of the piston. There was an adjustable valve to control oil flow and so vary the rate of fire.

In 1930 the capacity of the water jacket was increased and the gun was designated the M1921A1. Three years later the M2 gun was introduced. This had an improved performance with a 1143mm barrel and better water circulation. This gun was in service throughout the Second World War in the anti-aircraft role.

The air-cooled .5 Browning was first fired on 12 November 1918. It was developed for aircraft use and was adopted in 1923 as the Model 1921. In 1933 it was re-named the M2 and subsequently it was found necessary to increase the mass of the barrel. The .50 HB M2 has been used extensively and is still in service. It has been employed in fixed, flexible and anti-aircraft roles and has been one of the most successful guns of all time. It has a tripod mount for one ground role weighing in all some 44.5lbs.

DATA
(M2AA except where otherwise stated)
Cartridge: .5 M2 Ball
Method of operation: Short recoil

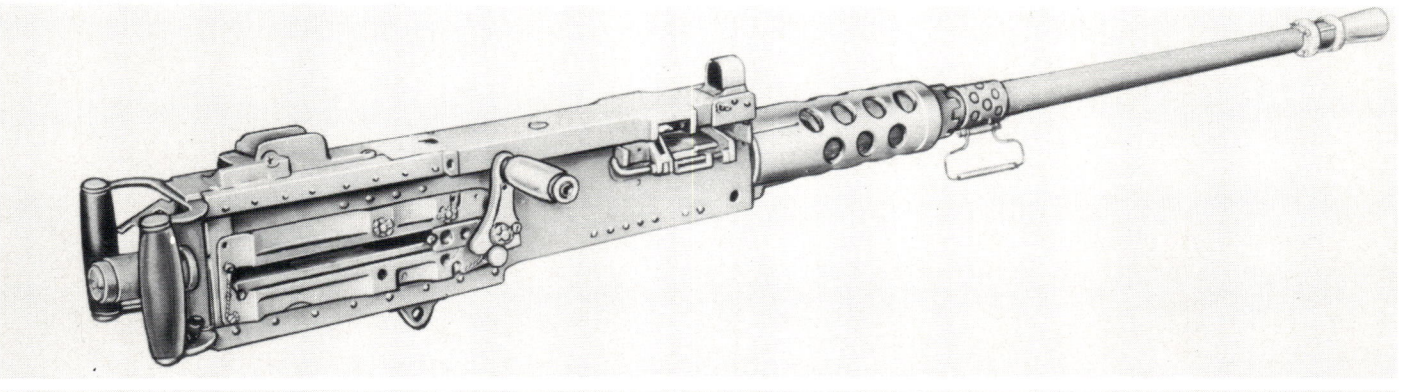

A - RIGHT REAR VIEW.

B - LEFT FRONT VIEW.

M2 cal .50 Browning, flexible (US Army photograph)

M2 cal .50 ground mount, M3 tripod (US Army photograph)

Method of locking: Projecting lug
Method of feed: Disintegrating link belt
Method of fire: Automatic. **M2HB:** Selective
Weight: 54.9kg (including water) **M2HB:** 38.1kg
Length of gun: 1.676mm **M2HB:** 1,653mm
Length of barrel: 1,143mm
Rifling: 8 grooves RH: Pitch 381mm
Sights: Foresight: Blade
   Rearsight: Leaf aperture

Rate of fire: Cyclic: 500-650 rounds/min **M2HB:** 450-550 rounds/min
Muzzle velocity: 893 metres/sec
Muzzle energy: 1,867mkp
Manufacturer: Frigidaire, AC Spark Plug, Saginaw Steering Gear, Brown-Lipe-Chapman, Savage Arms Company and the Buffalo Arms Company have all produced the M2 as well as Colt's Patent Firearms Manufacturing Company, Hartford, Connecticut
Status: Still in use by US forces and by those of a good many other countries.

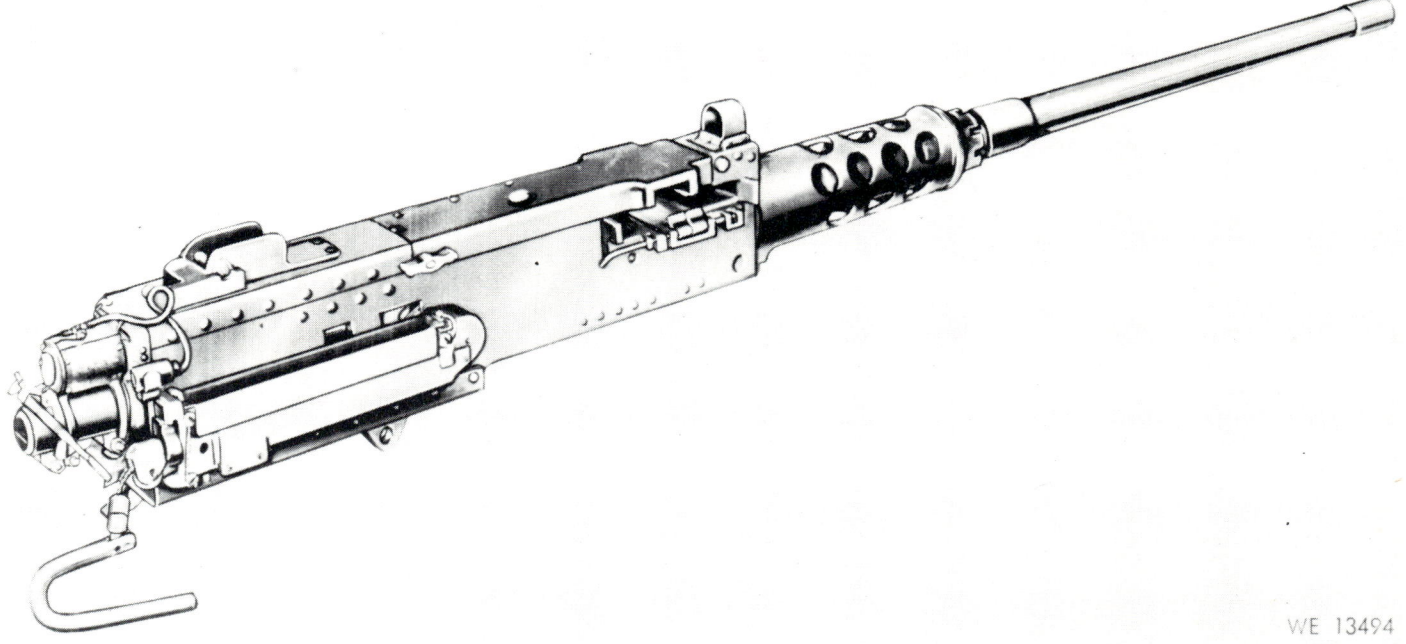

WE 13494

M2 cal .50 HB turret type (commander's cupola) (US Army photograph)

7.62mm M60 GPMG

The American army ended the 1939-45 war still using weapons which owed their origin to the genius of John M. Browning. The infantry squad weapon was the Browning .30 Automatic Rifle M1918A2 (the BAR) and sustained fire came from the Browning Cal .30 M1917A1 machine gun. The Browning Calibre .30 M1919A4 was widely used in its flexible form. All of these weapons gave wonderful service in their day but the need to reduce the number of infantry weapons and to produce lighter substitutes led to the decision to replace all of these weapons by one General Purpose Machine Gun. When the war in Korea came, the new GPMG was still on the drawing board but the design was hastened along and most of the development work was done by the Bridge Tool and Die Manufacturing Co, of Philadelphia together with the Inland Manufactuirng Division of General Motors.

The basic design was originated in the closing stages of World War II and the first working model was the T44. This gun was based almost entirely on the German models and combined the belt fed mechanism of the MG42 with the complete piston and bolt assembly of the FG42. The weapon was not satisfactory and the piston arrangements were changed. The modified gun was called the T52. The T52 itself hung about for some while and further modifications were done to the feed. It was eventually re-designated

the T161. Finally the design was considered to be satisfactory and was sealed as the M60. The prime producer has been the Maremont Manufacturing Co of Saco in Maine.

It will be seen that stampings and fabrications are used extensively and that rubber and plastics are often employed in place of wood and steel.

OPERATION

The M60 is a gas-operated weapon. The barrel is drilled radially downwards at 8in from the muzzle and after the bullet has passed this point a small proportion of the propellant gas passes through the vent.

The gas enters the gas cylinder, passes through a drilling in the side wall of the piston and expands to fill the interior of the piston and the forward section of the gas cylinder. When sufficient pressure has built up the piston is forced rearwards. As soon as it moves the radial drillings through the piston are moved out of alignment with the gas vent and no further gas enters the cylinder. This is shown diagramatically below.

The piston moves back and drives the operating rod, which carries the bolt rearwards. The action is that of a short stroke piston since the piston travel is limited to 60mm, and a sharp impulsive blow is given to the

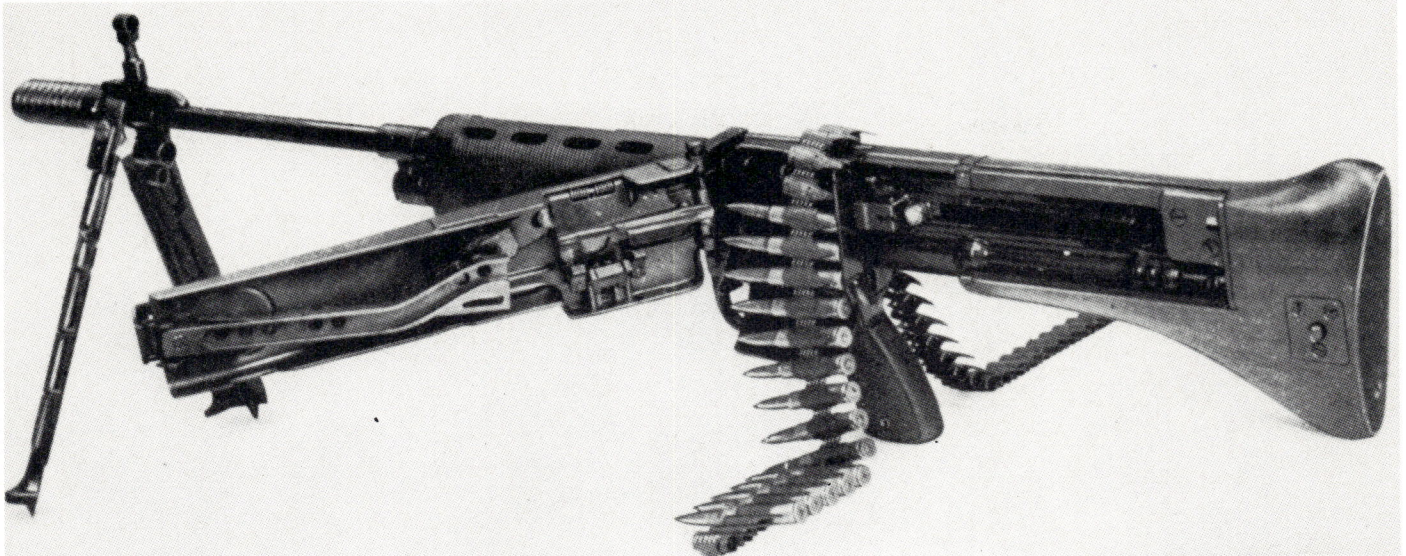

The 7.92mm calibre T44 LMG

operating rod which imparts enough energy to carry out the complete cycle of operations.

There are some aspects of this system worthy of comment. The generally accepted view is that the greatest single advantage of gas operation is its flexibility and by that is meant the ability to overcome adverse conditions of operation ie mud, sand and fouling, by increasing the volume of gas directed against the piston head and so increasing the operating force. In order to do this, gas-operated weapons use a gas regulator of one sort or another to enable the firer to produce this extra operating force as and when required.

There are many types of regulators and the most common are (1) the multi-track type – such as that used in the Bren gun – where the gas can be directed through vents of different size and so vary the volume available in a given time, or (2) the expansion to atmosphere type where a quantity of gas is tapped off and a rotating valve is used to allow a regulated quantity to escape to atmosphere whilst the remainder does useful work on the piston head. This system is used in the FN MAG.

The M60 has no method of gas adjustment. There is no regulator of any sort adjustable by the firer. The general theory of operation is that the piston will move back when enough energy has been supplied to overcome fouling and external friction. When the piston moves, it automatically cuts off its own gas supply and can be said to be self regulating. It is often referred to as a constant volume system. It must be emphasised however that the piston can be driven back slowly without acquiring enough energy to function under the most adverse conditions that can be encountered and by the very nature of the system there is no way of increasing the energy level. There is much to be said in favour of allowing adjustment to remain in the hands of the firer. Since there is no adjustment available for the gas force it follows that there is no way of bringing the rate of fire up if it starts to drop due to increased friction forces caused by dirt, sand, etc.

After the gas cylinder has been stripped for cleaning the piston can be inserted on reassembly into the cylinder, the wrong end first. If this happens the holes in the piston do not line up with the gas port and the weapon fires one round after which it stops with the working parts forward. This provides an interesting test of the No 1's knowledge of his weapon because this is not listed in "Trouble Shooting" in the US Technical Manual and after re-cocking by hand the fault occurs again. It is obviously a bad design

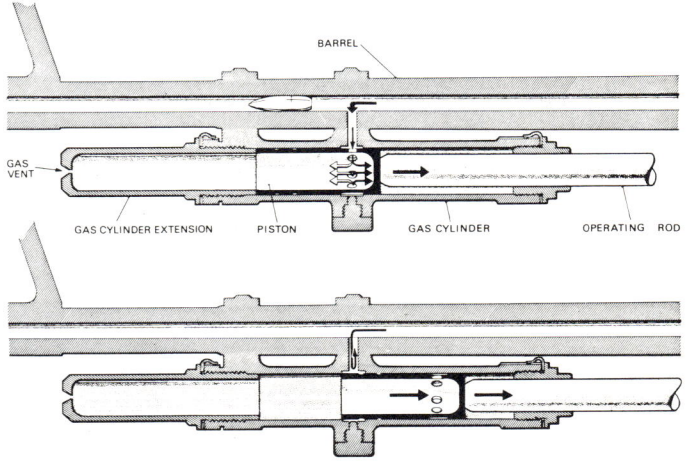

The constant energy gas regulator (RMCS)

feature that the piston can be incorrectly assembled in the cylinder.

It will be noted that the gas cylinder is permanently attached to the barrel. This is done because there is a requirement for an easy change barrel. Mating a gas cylinder and barrel whilst using this design of constant volume gas regulation would be exceedingly difficult. It is also true that changing the barrel provides a clean gas cylinder. Every spare barrel carries a gas cylinder which adds to the weight of the spare barrel and also adds to the overall cost of gun and spares. From the same figure it will be seen that every barrel also carries a bipod permanently attached and this also adds both weight and cost.

Reverting to the sequence of operations, as already noted the piston gives a sharp impulsive blow to the operating rod. The operating rod assembly has a post which rides in the hollow interior of the bolt and it is noteworthy that this post carries an anti-friction roller which is the bearing surface against the camway cut in the bolt. The bolt, in principle, is exactly

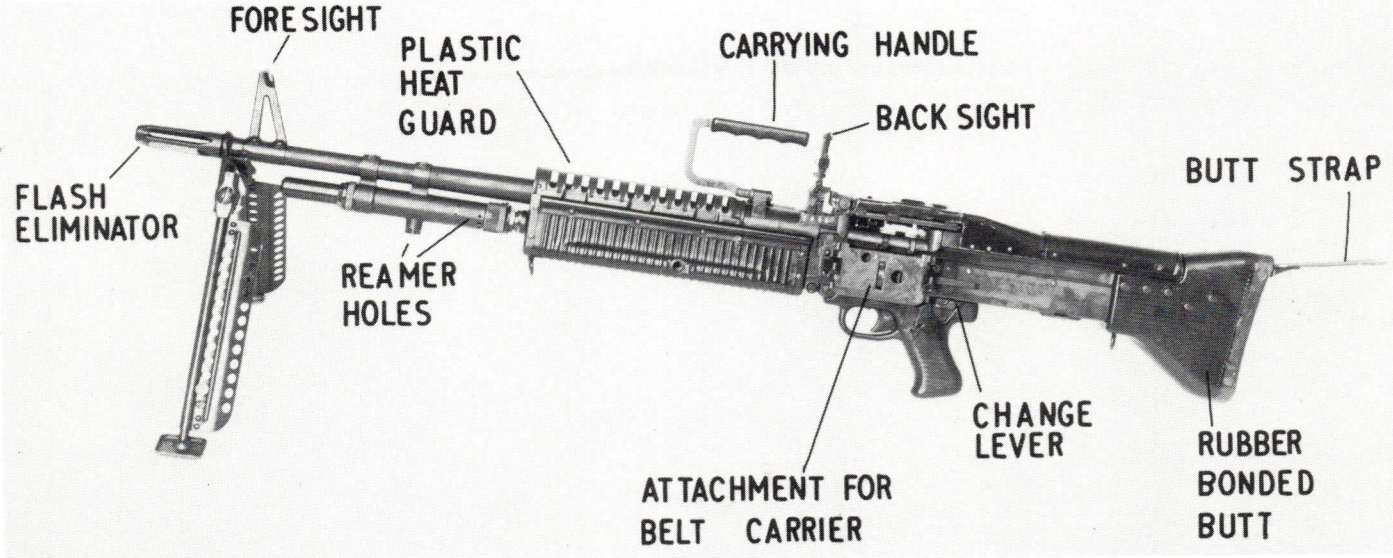

The cal 7.62mm M60 GPMG (RMCS)

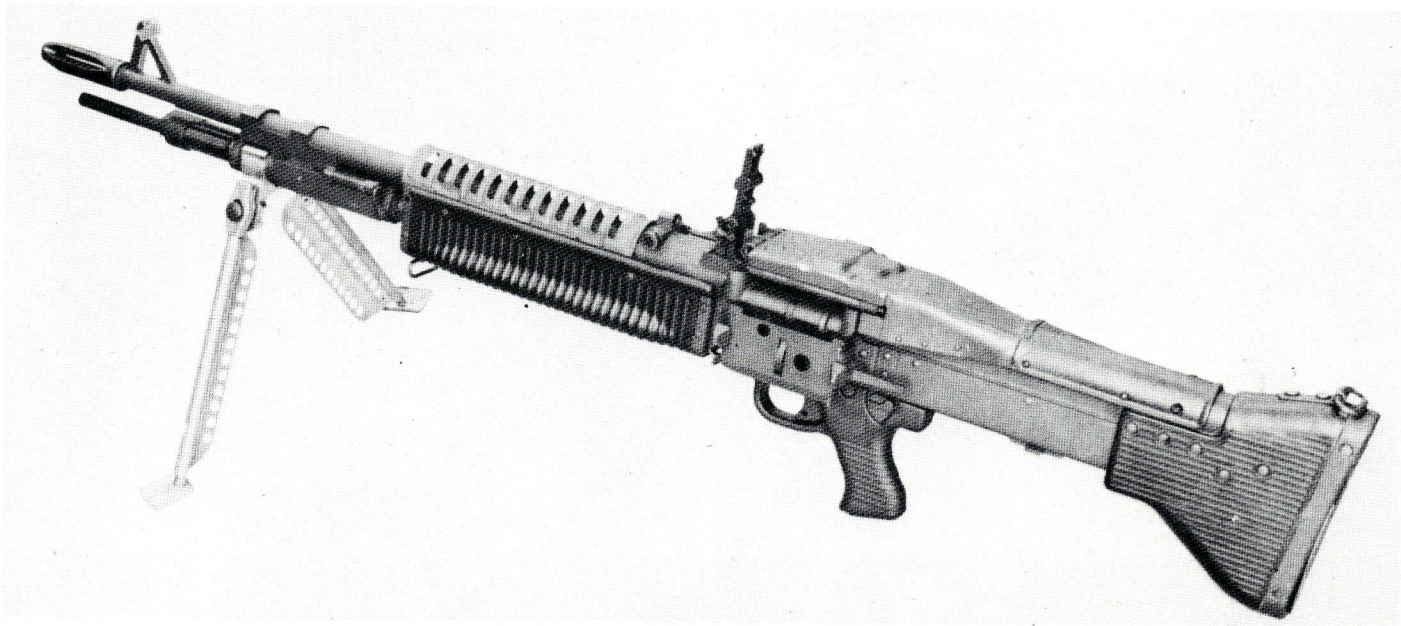

M60 fitted with gas evacuator tube for use in AFVs

the same as that of the American Lewis gun. The post rides initially in the curved portion of the cam slot and tries to rotate the bolt which is restrained by the forward locking lugs riding in longitudinal grooves in the gun body. When the bolt is fully forward it can rotate clockwise and lock in the curved cam patch cut in the barrel extension. When the rotation is completed the post is able to enter the last inch of the cam slot, which is parallel to the longitudinal axis, and travel straight forward. The firing pin, which is carried on the post, then strikes the cap.

The requirements for mechanical safety before firing are very adequately met by the system. The round is fully chambered and the base is supported by the locked breech before the firing pin enters the last, straight section of the cam path. There is no foreseeable way in which the cap can be struck prematurely.

After firing, mechanical safety demands that the support of the chambered case should be maintained whilst the pressure is high and that this support cannot be removed until the pressure has dropped to a safe low level. In the M60 this is achieved in the following fashion. The projectile reaches the gas port which is only 203mm from the muzzle and until this point is reached there is no tendency for the bolt to be rotated. The gas pressure forces the bolt back but the two lugs on the bolt are held firmly in the cam slot in the barrel extension and there is no component of force to produce rotation. After the bullet has passed the gas port the pressure starts to build up in constant volume cylinder. Before there is sufficient pressure to move the piston the bullet has left the muzzle. The gas impinges on the operating rod and this moves back 21mm before unlocking commences. The general effect is to produce complete mechanical safety and in fact the delay after firing before the bolt opens is largely the cause of the rather slow rate of fire compared to most modern GPMGs, eg the British L7A2 fires at 750-1,000 and the German G3 fires at 1,200 rounds/min on the higher rate.

A further contributing factor to the slow rate of fire is the design of the buffer. There are, in general, two basic kinds of buffer. One is designed to absorb energy and reduce the recoil force transmitted to the firer's shoulder whilst the other type is designed to absorb no energy but to fling the working parts forward with the maximum possible velocity. This produces a high rate of fire and also plenty of energy to clear dirt out of the boltway. The American buffer falls into the first category. It absorbs energy. The operating rod contacts the buffer plunger which transfers the energy to a series of rubber pads. The pads are squeezed out and force friction surfaces against the walls of the buffer tube. The buffer springs are compressed and the

friction of the pads on the tube wall dissipates energy as heat. From this it is evident that the coefficient of restitution is low and the forward velocity of the operating rod and bolt is less than its contact velocity with the buffer. The USA technical manual places great stress on the necessity to keep the buffer free of all solvents or cleaning fluids, which might be expected to attack the rubber pads.

The M60 is designed to fire full auto only, at a cyclic rate of 550 rounds/min. This is a slow enough rate for an accomplished firer to get off a single round. The tactical rate 'rapid' is 200 rounds/min. The propellant has a high calorific value (71.5 cals/grain-1103 cal/g) and after one minute's firing at the rapid rate the barrel gets so hot that a round will "cook-off" in the chamber in under ten seconds. Thus the weapon must fire from an open breech system.

FEED SYSTEM

The M60 started out with the German MG42 feed system. The MG42 was the first gun to come into large scale use employing a system of inner and outer feed pawls driven by a bolt operated feed lever, which were arranged to move in opposite directions and move the belt in two stages as the bolt moved back and forward again. The advantage of the German system is that the belt can be moved when the energy level available is at its greatest. Just after the round has been fired the bolt has available plenty of energy as it begins its rearward stroke and when the bolt has reached the last inch and a half of its forward travel its velocity is high and the kinetic energy it possesses is absorbed in part by doing work on the belt and moving it across, rather than being absorbed by crushing up the case.

If the belt is being moves as the bolt goes both back and forward, it must obviously move only half a pitch each time and this in itself means a reduction in the acceleration of the belt and therefore the forces required to move the belt and also the forces produced in the belt, are kept low.

As the M60 was progressively developed the feed system was changed. The friction roller at the back of the bolt was retained and also the feed arm located in the top of the feed cover in which it operated. The best feature – the inner and outer pawl system – was abandoned and a single pawl system substituted. In this the roller carried by the bolt moving forward swings the feed arm to the right. The feed arm is pivoted so the front end carrying the feed pawl slips to the left over the next round to be fed. As the bolt goes back the pawl moves to the right and lifts the entire weight of the belt through one complete pitch. Naturally this increases the load on the gun and although the Americans claim the gun can lift 100 rounds vertically,

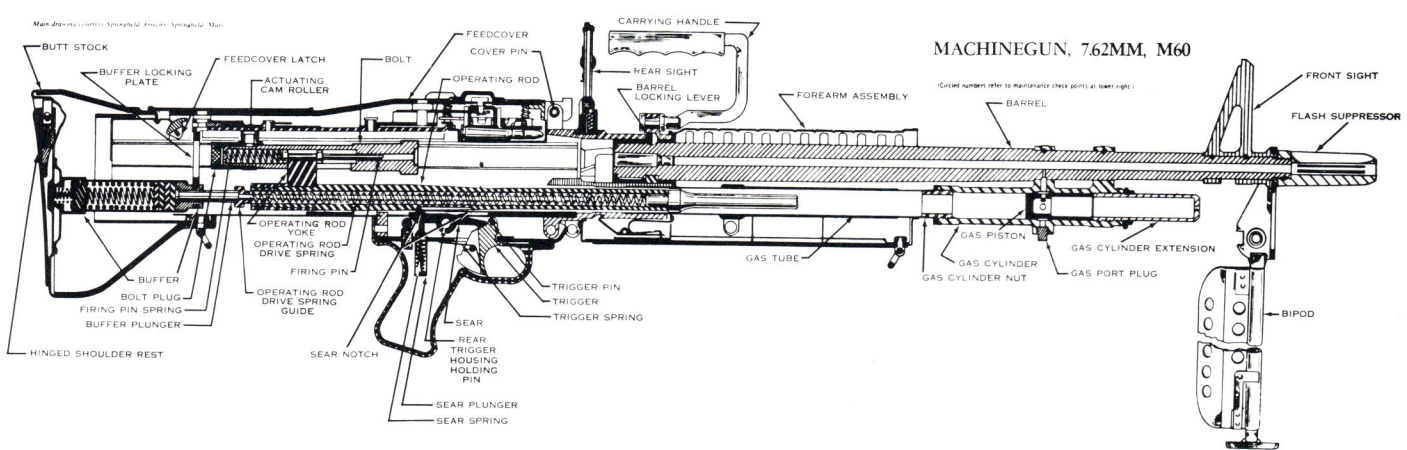

Sectional view of the M60 GPMG

this becomes difficult when the gun is dirty.

TRIGGER AND FIRING MECHANISM

The main problem in designing the trigger and firing mechanism of a modern GPMG which invariably fires from an open breech, is to ensure that the bent and sear do not meet with such force distributed over a small contact area that chipping occurs. There are two ways in which this can be avoided:

(a) The use of a controlled sear. This is the system used on the German G3, the Swiss SIG-710, the British L7A2 and in fact most modern GPMGs.

(b) The buffer sear. In this system the sear is spring buffered so that the energy possessed by the moving part is transferred to the body of the gun via the sear over a period of controlled travel. This system is used in heavy machine guns such as the Hispano Suiza 20mm.

The M60 uses no such device to control bent and sear engagement. The firer can release the sear at any moment and it will rise into the path of the bent. The sear, as a result, can wear quite quickly. The photograph above illustrates this.

The applied safety catch is a simple arrangement by which a cross pin is rotated. A cutaway section comes under the sear extension at "fire" and the body of the pin locks the sear at "safe". It is reliable and robust. The safety catch – like the trigger – cannot easily be operated in the far north if the firer is wearing an arctic mitten.

BARREL ASSEMBLY

The gas cylinder and the bipod are both permanently attached to the barrel. Thus the member of the gun crew who carries the spare barrel has to cope with a kilogram or so of weight which could be on the body of the gun.

The barrel is chromium plated and also has a stellite liner in the six inches of barrel forward of the chamber. The practice of depositing chromium plating in the barrel has been universal since the last war as a means of prolonging barrel life by reducing both gas erosion and mechanical wear but the M60 is the first gun to make successful use of a stellite liner. Stellite is a proprietary alloy which possesses the extremely useful virtue of retaining its mechanical strength at high temperatures. It is made of cobalt, chromium, tungsten and molybdenum with traces of iron. The approximate percentages are:

Cobalt – 60%
Chromium – 25%
Molybdenum – 5%
Tungsten – 10%

The liner is produced by the investment casting process and the maximum length that can be produced is about 15cm. No heat treatment is required after manufacture but it is absolutely essential that the correct amount of interference fit is maintained between the liner and the barrel.

The alternate heating and cooling of the barrel and liner can allow gas to penetrate between the liner and barrel interfaces if the machining is not carried out to precise tolerances. If this happens the barrel steel is gradually eroded until eventually the barrel fails.

BARREL CHANGING

This feature is not good. The belt must be removed, the gun cocked and the barrel catch lifted before the barrel can be pulled forward out of the body. It must be remembered that in a GPMG producing sustained fire the exterior barrel temperature could be as high as 500 degrees – i.e. just glowing in the dusk. There is a carrying handle on the body by which the gun itself can be held off the ground but the barrel has no means by which it can be pulled out other than the bipod legs. If these are used two men are required for the change. The official method is shown in the accompanying photograph. The No 2 of the gun is issued with "Mitten Asbestos M1942 – quantity one", and he pulls the barrel out whilst the No 1 presses down on the stock with his right hand lifts the fore-end with his left hand.

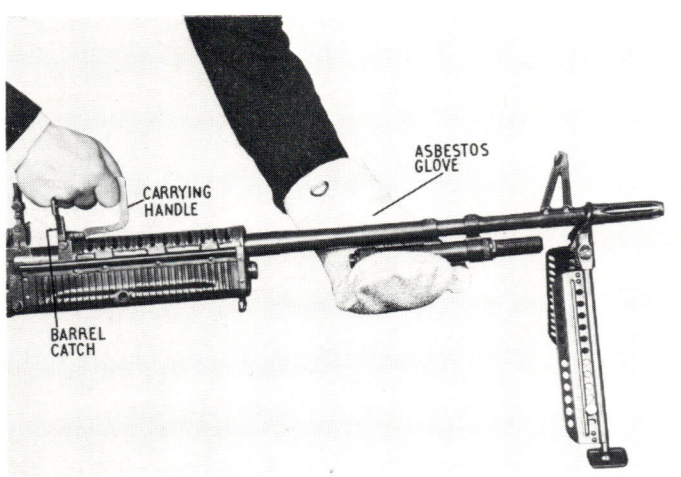

Changing the barrel (RMCS)

SIGHTS

The sights on this gun are not good. The figures on the backsight are so small that even in the bright light of day they are almost indistinguishable. The backsight of the M69 is graduated from 200yds to 1,200yds (1,097m) by 100yd steps. There is a windage scale. The foresight is raised up on a

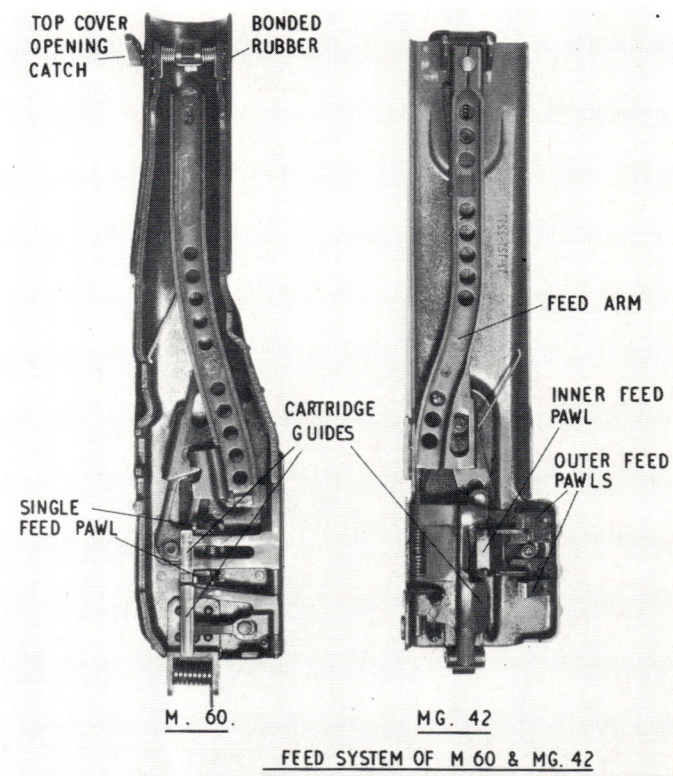

The feed system of M60 and MG 42 (RMCS)

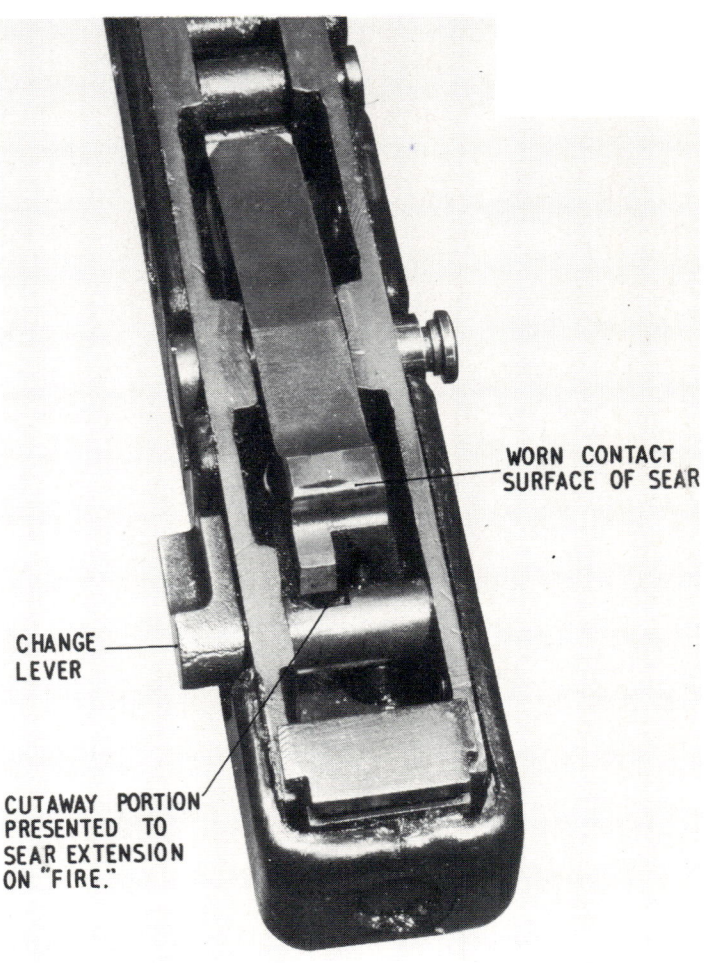

Trigger mechanism (RMCS)

pillar and is non-adjustable.

The sleeve that holds the foresight is also the bipod stop. As the bipod is rotated around the barrel it comes up against the stop and eventually the securing pins on the sleeve weaken. The foresight then has 10 degrees of play on either side of the vertical. This is not conducive to accuracy.

When a machine gun is supplied with several barrels some arrangement should be made for zeroing so that whichever barrel is placed on the gun the zeroing for that barrel is achieved without adjustment. This logically implies that all zeroing should be done on the foresight so that all the barrels can be zeroed prior to going into action and the change of a barrel as and when required, needs no further adjustment to the weapon to produce accurate fire.

The M60, having a fixed foresight, makes adjustment for zeroing on the backsight. This means that the No 1 on the gun must first recognise which barrel is in the gun and secondly know the correct zero setting for both elevation and line for that barrel. Thirdly, he must produce a screwdriver and change the zeroing scale. In practice this inevitably means all barrels are fired from a common zero and the consequent loss of accuracy is accepted.

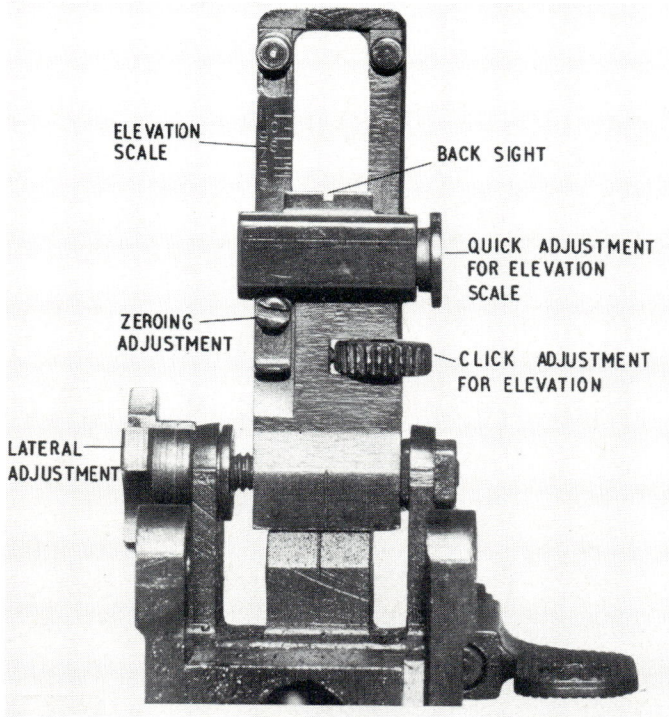

The backsight of the M60. The figures on the scale are very small (RMCS)

STRIPPING

The Technical Manual lists 20 stages in stripping the weapon and re-assembling it. In practice it is a fairly straightforward procedure although care must be taken in removing the bolt operating rod assembly as the captive spring bearing on the piston post will cause the operating rod to come out and twist when the bolt is halfway out. This can be painful if the fingers are caught.

The general procedure for stripping is as follows: Check the gun is safe and the bolt forward. Lift the shoulder strap, depress and rotate the bolt driving spring clutch to remove the spring. Rotate the latch lever assembly to lift the top cover plate. Remove the buffer yoke, remove the butt. Slide the bolt and operating rod out sufficiently far to insert the yoke into the bolt. This holds the bolt spring in place. Remove the bolt and operating rod.

Rotate the barrel catch and remove the barrel.

The trigger group can be removed by displacing the leaf spring and pushing the retaining pin through the body.

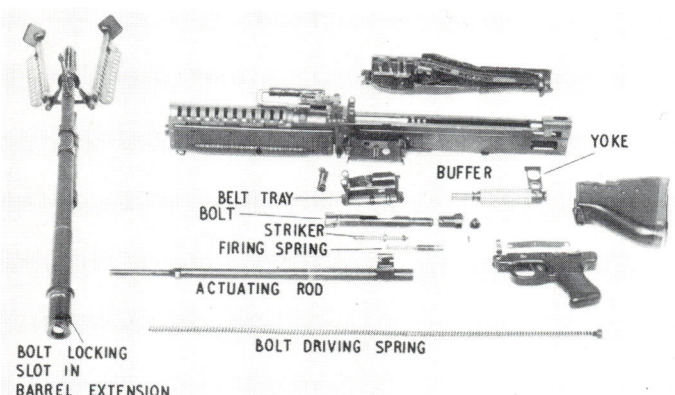

The M60 stripped (RMCS)

The above order of events is not that taught officially but it does have the advantage that taking the barrel off at the end allows the bipod to support the front end of the weapon whilst the bolt etc is being removed.

Re-assembly is straightforward. The bolt driving spring is a long sloppy single wound spring which tends to belly and must be controlled whilst being inserted.

HANDLING IN THE FIELD

The gun weighs nearly 10.5kg and is carried by a handle mounted on the

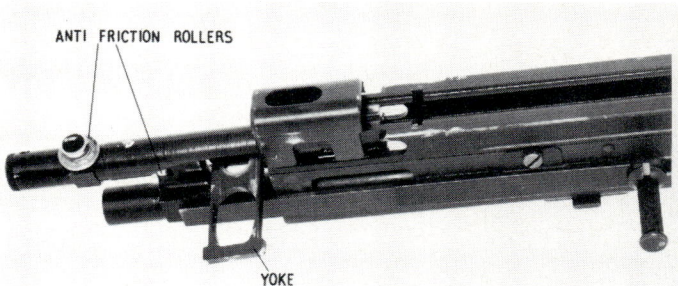

Removing the bolt (RMCS)

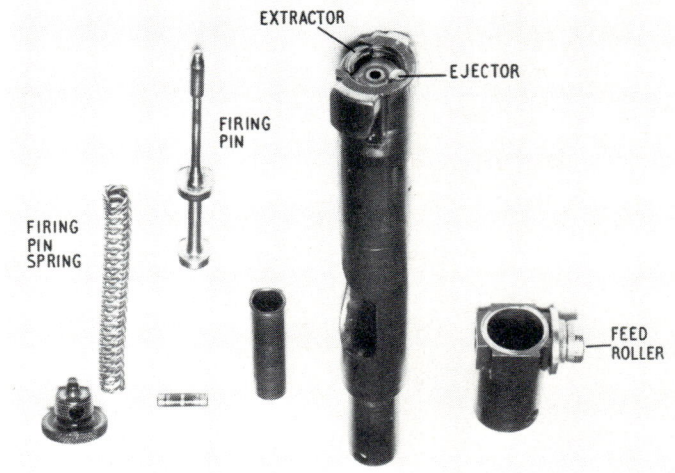

The bolt

body. This handle is flimsy and barely adequate to the task required of it. When the gun is empty the carrying handle is at the centre of gravity. The addition of belted ammunition brings the centre of gravity back and the muzzle rises. When the gun is used in the squad LMG role a canvas belt carrier is fixed on the left hand side of the gun to take a 100 round belt. This is of considerable assistance in jungle terrain as it prevents the loose end of the belt from catching in undergrowth, branches and other obstructions. There is a sling for a long carry which is generally used when moving forward, and a canvas carrying case for transport.

The bipod mount of pressed steel is an integral part of the barrel group and is not removed at unit level. The bipod yoke fits around the barrel and is held in position by the flash suppressor. The bipod legs are normally laid along the barrel when the gun is carried. The legs are lowered by pulling each in turn to the rear – compressing the lock spring – and pushed down. The length of the leg is increased by pulling down on the foot. The leg plunger engages a notch in the bipod leg extension and holds it in place. The length of the bipod leg is shortened by depressing the bipod leg plunger and pushing up on the bipod foot. The bipod is positioned in the up position by pulling down on the bipod leg to compress the lock spring and raising it until it locks into position alongside the barrel.

When the M60 is used in the sustained fire role the M122 tripod is employed. This is made up of the tripod assembly, the traversing and elevating gear and the pintle and platform group.

The tripod assembly consists of the tripod head and pintle bush and lock, one front leg and two rear legs. The traversing bar connects the two rear legs and supports the elevating and traversing mechanisms. Engraved on the bar is a scale divided into 100 mil major divisions and 5 mil subdivisions giving 450 mils to the left and 425-430 mils to the right of the centre. The traversing handwheel has a one mil click device built in. On the traversing handwheel is engraved a scale which covers 25 mils in 1 mil increments and the gun can be traversed 50 right and left of centre on the handwheel. The elevating handwheel has a one mil click device built in. Engraved on the handwheel is a scale of 5 mil and 1 mil divisions. Using the upper elevation screw allows a total of 400 mils of elevation.

The M60 uses the M4 pedestal mount for the M151 quarter-ton truck

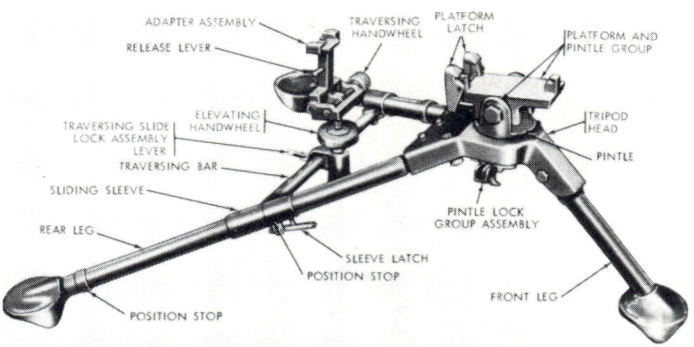

M122 tripod (US Army photograph)

(Jeep). The M142 gun mount (part of the M4 mount) which serves as a cradle for the gun can be used in other vehicles. It has a platform identical to that in the M122 tripod mount.

For training purposes there is a blank firing attachment (M13). This screws on to the muzzle and is secured to the foresight by a wing nut. It restricts gas flow from the muzzle and allows pressure to build up to operate the gas action. It is inadvisable to fire the gun with the attachment in place.

If the barrel is changed every 500 rounds the gun will produce 60 minutes firing at 125rpm from two barrels.

The barrel does not dissipate heat rapidly and the chamber gets hot enough to allow a cook-off in 10 seconds after two minutes firing at 125 rounds/minute.

DATA
Cartridge: 7.62mm × 51
Method of operation: Gas
Method of locking: Rotating bolt
Method of feed: Disintegrating link belt
Method of fire: Automatic

WEIGHTS
Gun: 10.48kg
Barrel (incl bipod and gas cylinder): 3.74kg

LENGTH
Gun, overall: 1,100mm
Barrel (excluding flash hider): 560mm

MECHANICAL FEATURES
Barrel: Regulator: Self regulating
    Rifling: 4 grooves RH. 1 turn in 292mm
    Cooling: Air. Quick change barrel
Sights: Foresight: Fixed blade
    Rearsight: U notch
    Graduation: 200-1,200 metres by 100 metre steps
    Zeroing: Backsight
    Sight radius: 540mm

FIRING CHARACTERISTICS
Muzzle velocity: 860metres/sec
Remaining velocity at 500 metres: 492metres/sec
           3,700 metres: 108metres/sec
Muzzle energy: 366mkp
Remaining energy at 500 metres: 141mkp
           3,700 metres: 5mkp
Rate of fire: Cyclic: 550 rounds/min
    Automatic: 200 rounds/min
Range, maximum effective: Bipod: 800 metres **Tripod:** 1,800 metres
Maximum: 3,700 metres

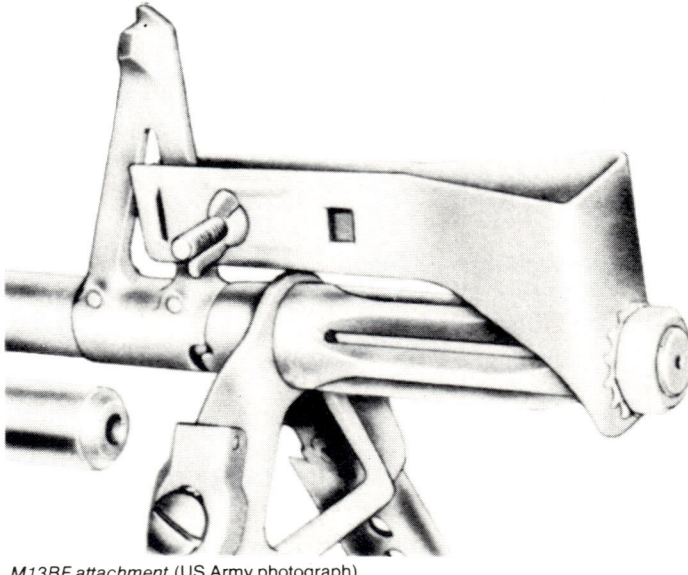

M13BF attachment (US Army photograph)

MOUNT
Weight: 6.8kg
Length: Extended: 825mm
Folded for transportation: 685mm
Spread of rear legs: 762mm
Height: 358mm
Traversing range using traversing bar: 50 deg
Free: 360 deg (6400mils)
Traversing bar, graduated: (875mils)
Elevating range free: +28 deg 30′ +28 deg 45′
Locked: +14 deg −12 deg 35′
Least increment: 1mil
Elevating handwheel, graduated: 1mil

Manufacturer: Bridge Tool & Die Manufacturing Company, Philadelphia. Inland Manufacturing Division, General Motors, Dayton, Ohio. Maremont Corporation, Saco, Maine
Status: Manufacture completed. In service with US forces and in Australia, Taiwan and Vietnam

7.62mm M73 TANK MACHINE GUN

This was a purpose-built tank machine gun. It was designed by R. Colby and I. Lockhead, and manufactured by the General Electric Co of New York.

The designers set out to provide a number of the desired characteristics of the coaxial machine gun. These were:
  a. Short inboard length
  b. Feed from either side
  c. Barrel change inside the vehicle with no displacement of the gun
  d. All adjustments to be carried out without displacing the gun
  e. Top cover hinged on either side
  f. No fumes
  g. Dismountable for ground use

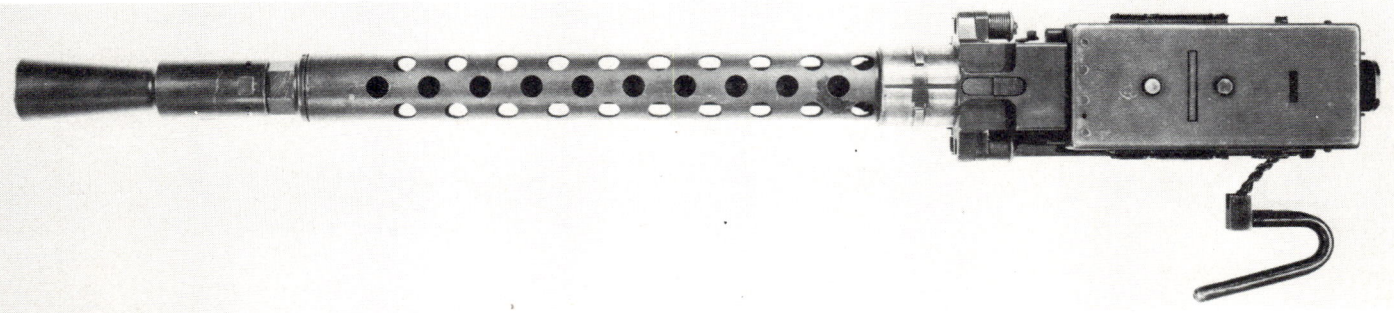

M73 from above (RMCS)

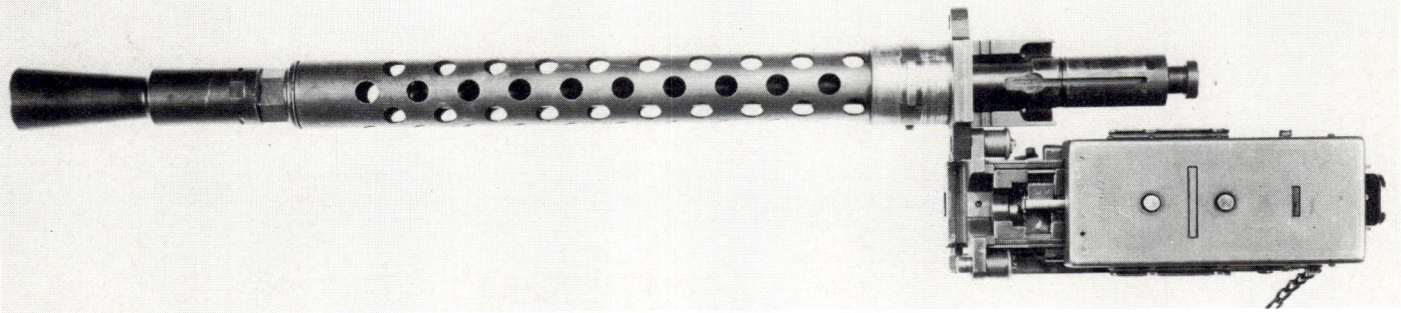

M73. The casing remains stationary and the receiver is rotated. The barrel is shown partly withdrawn. The receiver hinges on either side (RMCS)

The M73 had a small sliding breech block and a separate rammer. The barrel recoiled and a lug under the block ran in a cam path in the receiver and the breech block moved over to the right. Thus a short inboard length was obtained. However, with no reciprocating bolt, extraction was complicated and the case was withdrawn by an extractor which transferred it to a carrier which moved back and then rotated down so that the case lay nose forwards under the breech block. When the rammer drove the next round into the chamber it forced the case off the carrier and into a bag.

The kinematic path of the empty case was viewed with suspicion when the gun was initially produced, and the gun was first modified as the M73A1 and then replaced with the M219.

The receiver of the gun could be rotated to the left or right with the barrel casing locked into the mantlet and so the barrel could be withdrawn straight to the rear. This feature was borrowed from the German MG34 tank machine gun.

The top cover was hinged on either side. This reduced the space required overhead to a minimum and allowed all adjustments to be carried out inside the turret.

The rate of fire was kept down to 500-600 rounds a minute. This slow rate meant that the breech block was slow in opening and so the amount of fumes brought into the crew compartment was minimal.

The gun normally fired from the left but an 8 step process allowed conversion to right hand feed.

The gun could be used as a coaxial gun, in the Commander's cupola or with a bipod, and a pistol grip and trigger linkage as a ground gun.

DATA
Cartridge: 7.62mm × 51
Method of operation: Short recoil with gas assistance
Method of locking: Sliding breech block
Method of feed: Disintegrating link belt
Method of fire: Automatic
Weight: 14kg
Weight of barrel: 2.4kg

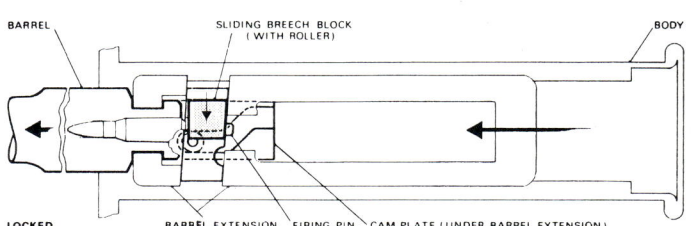
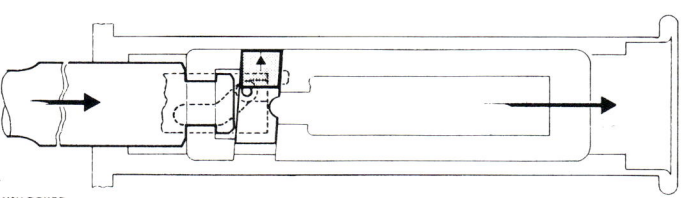

The action of the M73 and M219 Tk machine guns (RMCS)

Length: 889mm
Barrel: 559mm
Rifling: 4 grooves. 1 turn in 305mm
Sights: None
Muzzle velocity: 854 metres/sec
Muzzle energy: 361mkp
Rate of fire: Cyclic 500-625 rounds/min
Range, maximum effective: 900 metres
Manufacturer: General Electric Co of New York, Burlington, Vermont. Rock Island Arsenal, Rock Island, Illinois
Status: No longer in production. Still in service

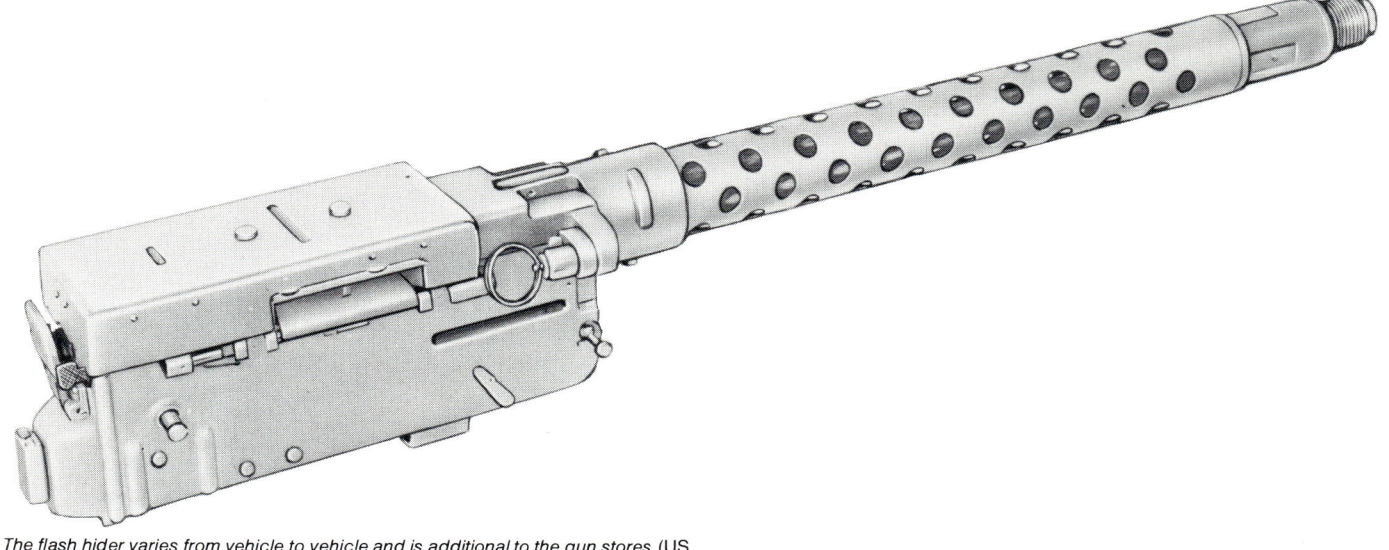

The flash hider varies from vehicle to vehicle and is additional to the gun stores (US Army photograph)

7.62mm M219 TANK MACHINE GUN

The M73 machine gun experienced considerable stoppages and was modified to correct these. The modified gun was initially called the M73E1 and subsequently the M73A1. The degree of modification required was such that the final version of the gun was given the nomenclature M219. The new gun is very similar in appearance to the M73 but any attempt to interchange assemblies must be approached with some care. The barrel extension assembly of the M73 is not interchangeable with that of the M73A1/M219 and any attempt to carry out such interchange will result in malfunction.

There are several variations between the two guns due to the redesign of the extractor, rammer and rammer assembly, the feed tray assembly and the addition of new cams to the M219 receiver which alter the timing of extraction, ejection and ramming and are intended to reduce the stoppage rate.

The M219 is normally issued as a left hand feed gun. However in some vehicles the gun must have a right hand feed and there is a conversion involving 11 stages which allows the change. Similarly, regardless of the direction of feed, the charging assembly, which is a handle and chain, is normally on the left of the receiver but can be changed over to the right. The tactical role of the M219 is the same as that of the M73 and both are fixed guns in coaxial positions in main battle tanks or flexible guns in lighter vehicles.

The M219 is slightly lighter than the M73 but otherwise there is no difference in their respective data.
Status: Currently in service with the United States Army

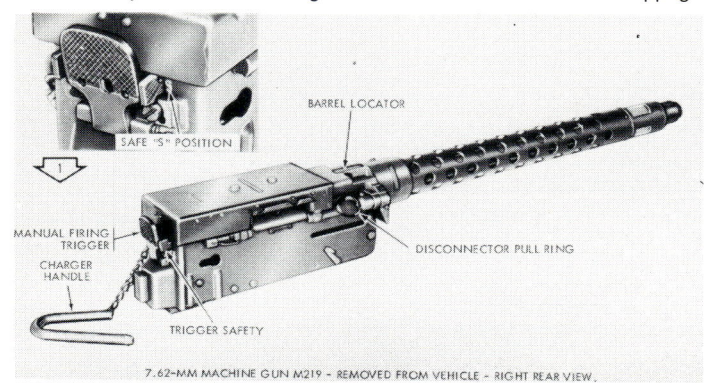

M219 7.62mm Tk MG (US Army photograph)

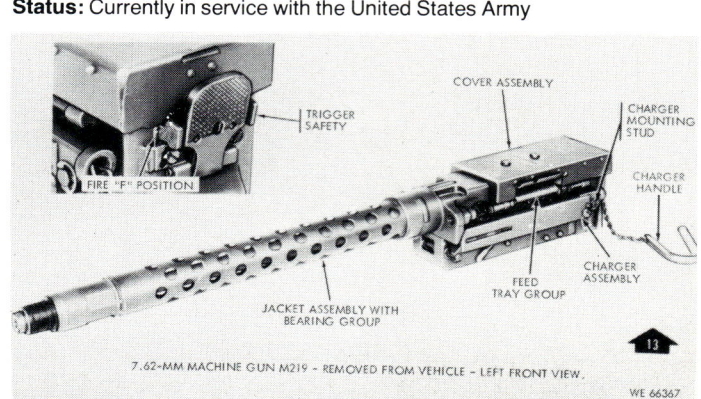

7.62mm MINIGUN M134

The General Electric Co of Burlington, Vermont, came into the machine gun field with the production of the Minigun which was specifically planned for use in the aircraft and helicopter in the Vietnam conflict. It was based on the 20mm Vulcan gun which armed many types of American aircraft.

This weapon is based on the Gatling gun principle in which a high rate of fire was achieved by having a number of rotating barrels which fired in turn when the 12 o'clock position was reached. The loading, firing and extractor sequences of the Gatling are shown.

The first Gatling was made in 1862 so possibly the progress made in the last 100 years is not as great as some would believe. The original Gatling gun was hand cranked and could produce a cyclic rate of 1,000 rounds a minute for a very brief period. The delays in loading etc. normally meant about 250 rounds/min was the optimum.

The minigun is driven by a 28 volt electric motor and produces a steady rate of fire which varies according to the type from between 4,000 and 6,000 rounds per minute as a top rate, down to 300 rounds/min as the slowest rate of fire. At a steady 6,000 rounds/min the drive motor draws 130 amperes.

The gun itself consists of 4 groups:

a. the barrel group
b. the gun housing
c. the rotor assembly
d. the bolt assembly

BARREL GROUP

The six 7.62mm barrels fit into the rotor assembly and each is locked by a 180 degree turn. They pass through the barrel clamp which grips the barrel using a special tool to secure the bolt. The barrels are normally parallel but

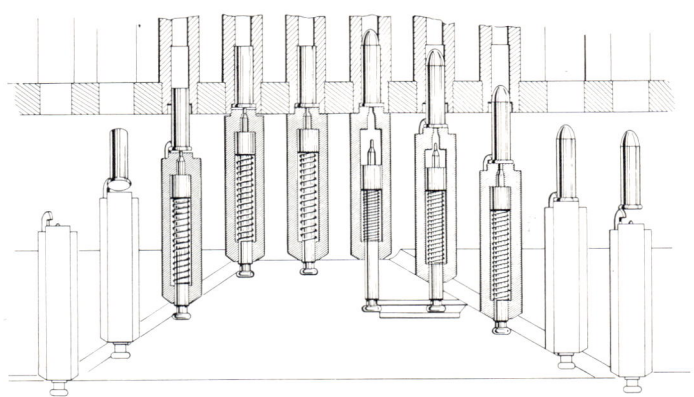
The loading, firing and extraction sequence of the Gatling gun (RMCS)

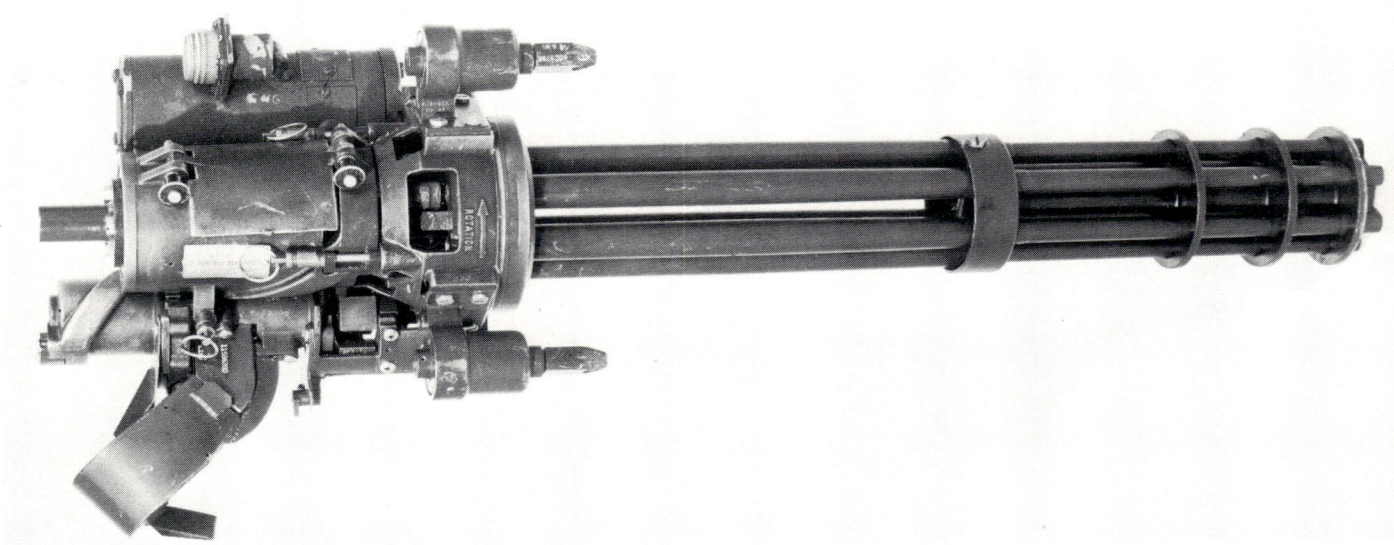
The GE 7.62mm Minigun (RMCS)

there are other clamps available which are designed to produce varying dispersion patterns by ensuring that the barrels converge at some selected range.

GUN HOUSING

This is a one piece casting which holds the rotor assembly and provides a mounting for the "safety sector" and the guide bar. The function of these two components will be mentioned later. There is an elliptical cam path on the inner surface in which the bolt bearing roller runs.

ROTOR ASSEMBLY

This is the main structural component of the gun and is supported in the gun housing by ball bearings. The front part of the rotor assembly holds the six barrels. Six bolt tracks are cut into the rotor and six removable tracks are bolted on to the ribs on the rotor. Each bolt track carries an S shaped triggering cam which cocks and fires the firing pin of one bolt.

BOLT ASSEMBLY

There are six bolts each of which is mated to a barrel and locks into the barrel by means of a rotating head: when each is unlocked and withdrawn from the barrel the empty case is pulled out by a fixed single extractor. The firing pin is spring operated and carries a projection or 'tang' at the rear end. This tang engages the S shaped triggering cam on the rotor. The side slots on the bolt engage in the bolt tracks of the rotor and this causes the bolt to move round with the rotor.

GUN OPERATION

The red master switch cover must be elevated to expose the switch which controls all the electrics. The firing button on the left hand trigger grip

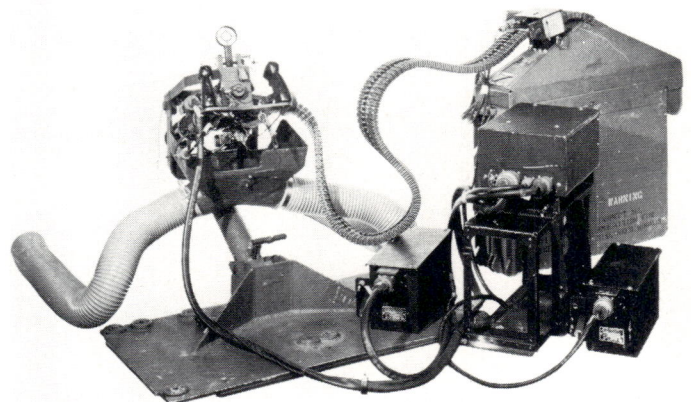
The ammunition and power supply for the Minigun. Note the elephant trunks to convey the empty cases clear (RMCS)

starts the rotor assembly and barrel assembly rotating in an anti-clockwise direction viewed from the rear. As the rotor assembly turns, the roller on each bolt follows the elliptical cam path on the inner surface of the gun housing. Each bolt in turn picks up a live round from the guide fingers of the guide bar.

As the bolt is carried round, the roller, working in the groove, moves the

The GE 7.62mm Minigun on a pedestal mount developed for aircraft use (RMCS)

bolt forward to chamber the round. The bolt head is now rotated by the cam path in the bolt body and locks into the barrel. The firing pin has been cocked by the tang action in the triggering cam in the rotor and at the top position of the bolt the S shaped groove releases the firing pin and the round is fired.

The elliptical cam path in the gun housing has a flat profile – or dwell profile – which holds the bolt locked until the bullet has gone and the pressure has dropped to a safe level. The bolt assembly roller enters the reverse segment of the path and the bolt head is unlocked. The cam path carries the bolt to the rear, extracting the empty case which is pushed away by the guide bar and ejected. The bolt has now completed a 360 degree cycle and is ready to pick up another live round. All six bolts repeat the same procedure in sequence.

Ammunition boxes carry a normal load of 4,000 linked rounds. This is pulled up a plastic chute to the gun. If the length of this chuting exceeds five feet or the radius of the curve is small it is advisable to have another motor on the top of the ammo boxes driving a sprocket which helps by pushing the belted ammunition up to the gun.

It will be noted that since the entire gun is driven by an external source, a misfired round is simply ejected and thrown down the large section hose with the empties either into a box or more usually out over the side.

It is equally possible to use unlinked ammunition and feed it up from the boxes.

When the gun ceases firing the bolts cease to pick up ammunition from the guide bar and the bolts close on an empty chamber. Thus there is no danger of a cook-off during the second it takes the barrels to come to rest.

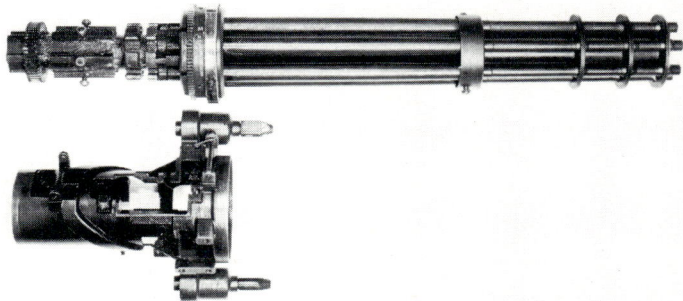

The barrel group disconnected from the rotor assembly (RMCS)

DATA
Cartridge: 7.62mm × 51
Method of operation: External power
Method of locking: Rotating bolt
Method of feed: Linked belt or linkless
Method of fire: Automatic

WEIGHTS
Basic gun: 15.9kg
Drive motor: 3.4kg
Recoil adapters (2): 1.36kg
Barrel (6): 1.09kg each
Feeder: 4.8kg

LENGTHS
Gun, overall: 800mm
Barrel: 559mm

MECHANICAL FEATURES
Barrel: Regulator: Nil
  Rifling: 4 groove RH. 1 twist in 254mm
  Cooling: Air
Sights: Vary with employment
Recoil force: Average at 6,000 rounds/min 136kp
Peak at 6,000 rounds/min 163kp
Recoil: At 6,000 rounds/min 4.1mm
Runout: At 6,000 rounds/min 1.6mm
Power required: At 6,000 rounds/min (steady rate) 130 amp
Starting load: 260 amp for 100 m sec

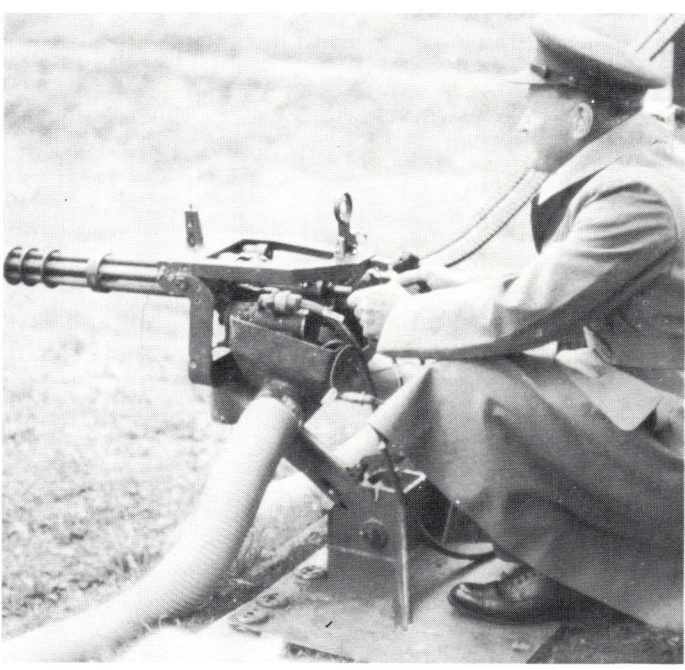

The Minigun firing on the range using an improvised mounting (RMCS)

Reliability (gun only): Not less than 200,000 rounds/stoppage
Gun life: 1,500,000 rounds minimum

FIRING CHARACTERISTICS
Muzzle velocity: 869 metres/sec
Muzzle energy: 373mkp
Rate of fire: Up to 6,000 rounds/min
Manufacturer: General Electric Co., Burlington, Vermont
Status: In production. In service

5.56mm XM-214 GUN AND SIX-PAK

The success of the M134 has led GE to produce a lightweight version in 5.56mm intended for use in vehicles, small boats, or emplaced on the ground. It is similar in general arrangement to the M134 but several design innovations have been made. These are:
(1) An access cover lever/safing lever that allows the gun to be made incapable of firing when the lever is in the "safe" position.
(2) Bolts that are removable from the gun without tools.
(3) A clutch mechanism that stops the feeder drive gear upon trigger release.
(4) A case ejection sprocket.

SIX-PAK

The XM214 has been produced in a complete lightweight system intended for use on the M122 tripod or from a vehicle. The system with 1,000 rounds of ammunition weighs 85lbs and can be quickly broken down into two equal loads for carrying. Called by GE, the Six Pak, it consists of three major components, the XM214 gun, the ammunition package, and the power module.

AMMUNITION PACKAGE

Linked ammunition is stored in 500-round cassettes and two cassettes are held in the ready for use position on the ammunition rack. When the gun is firing the feeder pulls ammunition to the gun from the front cassette through a length of flexible chuting. When the first cassette is emptied, ammunition is supplied from the second cassette and this trips a visual warning system, indicating to the gunner the need to add another cassette.

The ammunition package is removed from the system by using snap off connectors. The chute is removed from the gun feeder by using a quick disconnecting lever. When the ammunition is placed on the gun, this lever locks the first round to the adaptor in a position where it will be picked up by the gun feeder. As the chute is snapped on to the feeder, the lever is automatically disengaged and the first round is positioned in the feeder sprocket.

POWER MODULE

This contains the 24V dc plug-in battery and an 0.8 HP motor together with the solid-state electronic controls. The battery is nickel-cadmium and is rechargeable in 15 minutes. If the gun is operating on a vehicle the battery can be plugged in and the charge maintained. The battery will fire 3,000 rounds from one charge. It contains a "no-spill' electrolyte paste and has a life of over 1,000 recharges.

The solid sate printed circuit panel in the power module controls the burst-limit, firing rate and the automatic clearing of the gun.

DATA

Cartridge: 5.56mm × 45
Method of operation: Battery power
Method of feed: Linked belt
Method of fire: Automatic. One of two selected rates between 400 and 4,000 rounds/min

WEIGHTS
Complete system (including 1,000 rounds): 38.6kg
Gun: 12.25kg

LENGTHS
Overall: 1,041mm
Gun: 686mm
Width (incl. ammunition case): 444mm

MECHANICAL FEATURES
Barrel: Regulator: Nil
       Rifling: 4 groove RH 1 turn in 305mm
       Cooling: Air
Sights: Telescopic
Recoil force: At 4,000 rounds/min 45.4kp
Power required: At 4,000 rounds/min 60 amp
Reliability: 25,000 rounds/stoppage
Barrel life: 100,000 rounds

FIRING CHARACTERISITCS
Muzzle velocity: 991 metres/sec
Muzzle energy: 178mkp
Rate of fire: 400-4,000 rounds/min

Manufacturer: General Electric Co, Burlington, Vermont
Status: Evaluation

The XM-214 with its ammunition pack

0.5in M85 MACHINE GUN

This is a recoil operated .5 calibre machine gun designed for use in an AFV either coaxially mounted or located in a cupola. It may be dismounted and fired from the tripod. The gun has a dual rate of fire from ground and anti-aircraft use. It was designed by the Aircraft Armament Corporation of Cockeysville and is manufactured by the General Electric Co of New York.

The M85 takes the disintegrating link belt which must be placed in the gun open side downwards. It is cocked by pulling back the cocking handle and when at the rear the bolt is held by the sear in the open position.

The gun is fired by using the firing switch or the hand trigger but in either case the solenoid plunger rotates the sear out of engagement with the bent of the bolt carrier. The bolt as it goes forward strips the first round out of the belt and pushes it up against the bullet guide where it is deflected down into the chamber. When the round is fully chambered the bolt comes to rest as the extractor grips over the cannelure in the bottom of the cartridge.

The bolt carrier comes forward and forces the locking lugs out into their recesses in the receiver. The firing pin mounted on the bolt carrier can then project through the bolt and fire the round.

The gas pressure, exerted through the base of the cartridge case, drives the bolt rearwards. The bolt is locked to the barrel extension and the barrel also recoils. As the barrel recoils it strikes the accelerator and the accelerator lever bears on the bolt carrier, projecting it rearwards. The carrier moves away from the bolt and cams in the locking lugs. The bolt is then free of the barrel and is lifted back by the bolt carrier, pulling the empty case out of the chamber. The barrel and the accelerator are returned to the forward position by their own springs. At the end of the recoil stroke the bottom extractor is forced off the extraction groove of the cartridge and the bolt rotates the ejection lever which rotates, Lewis gun fashion, to push the empty case around the side extractor and out of the gun on the left.

The bolt carrier is then driven forward off the buffer and the cycle is repeated. The gun firing thus at the high rate, fires some 1,050 rounds/min.

When the low rate of fire is required the rate selector lever is turned to the right and the delay lever is struck by the bolt. This starts the time delay drum revolving. The rotation of the drum retracts the solenoid plunger and the sear holds up the bolt and carrier to the rear. The drum continues to rotate and winds up a torsion spring.

The energy of the rotating drum is taken up by the torsion spring. When the drum strikes the stop the spring acts on it to reverse its rotation. The drum strikes the delay lever and re-positions it for the next stroke and then releases the solenoid plunger. The bolt carrier goes forward and the next round is fed forward. The slow rate produces about 400 rounds/min.

The delay is produced by the drum as described but since the bolt carrier and bolt are fired off the sear and are being projected by the return spring only with no buffer assistance, the time for forward travel is also increased.

DATA
Cartridge: .50 M2 Ball
Method of operation: Short recoil
Method of locking: Projecting lugs
Method of feed: Disintegrating link belt
Method of fire: Automatic. Two rates of fire
Weight: 27.9kg
Length: 1,384mm
Barrel: 914mm
Sights: None (coaxial with main armament)
Muzzle velocity: 866 metres/sec
Muzzle energy: 1,754mkp

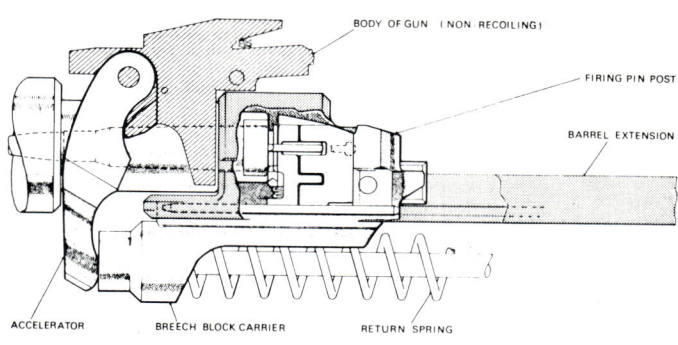

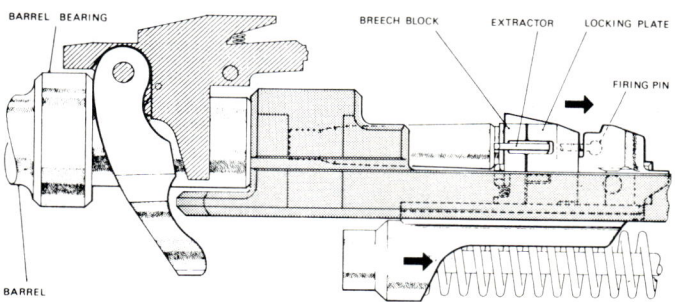

The short recoil action and accelerator of the M85 HMG (RMCS)

Rate of fire: Cyclic: High rate: 1,050 rounds/min
Low rate: 400 rounds/min
Range, maximum effective: 1,000 metres
Manufacturer: General Electric Co of New York, Burlington, Vermont
Status: In service with United States forces

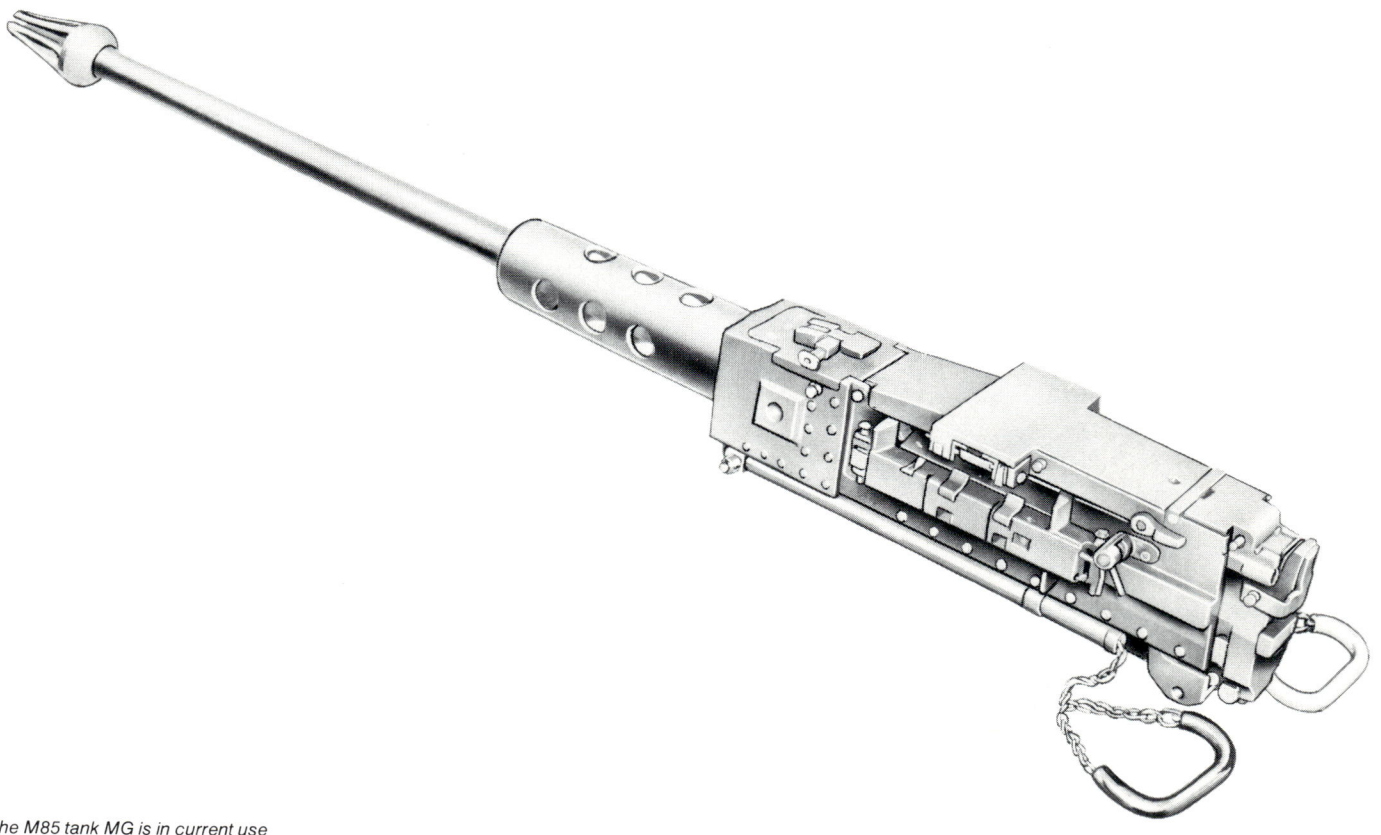

The M85 tank MG is in current use

5.56mm COLT CMG-2 LIGHT MACHINE GUN

The Colt Machine Gun-2 is designed as a belt-fed LMG with a number of features carefully selected from other machine guns. The cocking arrangements are taken from the system used in a whole series of Czechoslovakian guns – starting with the Zb50 and culminating in the Vz52 and 59 – in which the pistol grip is slid forward and when the catch is released the sear rises to engage the bent on the bolt carrier: withdrawing the pistol grip cocks the action. The gas system is the same as the M60 in that gas is taken into the piston head through a port on the top. When the piston moves back the gas is automatically cut off and that operating on the piston head leaves the cylinder through vents.

This system eliminates any form of manual gas regulator controllable by the firer. The gas port, expansion chamber, exhaust port, and forward barrel support are all integral with the fixed foresight which is permanently secured to the barrel. It is questionable whether a fixed foresight is suitable for a light machine gun with interchangeable barrels. Zeroing must be carried out on the back sight and a change of zero – which is frequently required when barrels in different states of wear are used – means a delay in production of accurate fire. An adjustable foresight which can be zeroed is generally regarded as preferable for a machine gun – certainly for a light machine gun.

The feed mechanism is based on the Czech Vz52. Cam paths are machined into the left side of the bolt carrier and as the carrier moves back a roller on the feed accuator follows the lower cam path to move the feed pawl in and a lug above the roller follows the upper cam path to force the feed pawl out during the return stroke. Thus as the carrier moves back the belt is drawn into the gun and held there and as the carrier goes forward the spring loaded feed pawl moves out under the belt to grip the next round ready for feeding.

There are however features of the gun which are unusual and interesting. There are two bolt carrier driving springs each wrapped around the guide rod, mounted on each side of the receiver, which support and guide the rear of the bolt carrier. The front of the bolt carrier is supported by the piston. There is no spring loaded extractor but a slot is machined into the front face of the bolt, forming a recess into which the cartridge slides, on feeding, with a retaining lip. A spring loaded plunger is depressed as the cartridge slides down and resets itself to project over the base of the round to prevent it moving up again.

The ejector is based on the Lewis principle. It is a spring loaded arm positioned above the round. When the carrier moves back after firing, a lug depresses the arm which forces the case down, off the bolt face, and out through a cutaway in the piston and a hole in the bottom of the receiver. The operation cycle, in brief, is as follows, The belt, held in a 150 round drum, is positioned in the feed tray and the pistol grip pushed forward. After the latch is released the grip is pulled back to cock the gun. The safety catch is a push through cross bolt, which, when pushed from right to left, locks the sear and prevents disengagement from the bent in the bolt carrier. To fire the gun the safety is moved to the right and the trigger pulled. The action is fully automatic and there is no provision for single shots. The two driving springs force the carrier forward with the bolt held to it by a sturdy connecting pin. The bolt feeds a round from the M13 type disintegrating link belt and this cartridge slides down the bolt face and is held there by the retaining lip and the spring loaded plunger as it is chambered. The connecting pin holding the bolt to the carrier is depressed by a cam path and the bolt is rotated by the same pin acting on a helical groove in the bolt. The bolt rotates through

The Colt CMG-2 5.56mm LMG

CMG-2 showing feed drum

CMG-2 field stripped

22½ degrees and the 8 locking lugs move behind locking recesses in the barrel extension. The firing pin, fixed to the bolt carrier, continues forward to fire the cap. This firing pin is pointed at both ends and so can be inserted either way. This simplifies changing the pin particularly in action at night.

After the bullet passes the gas port – integral with the foresight – gas enters the piston head through a hole in the top and expands to drive the piston rearwards thus cutting off the gas supply. After the piston has gone back 15mm the gas is evacuated at pressure to scavenge the expansion chamber and remove carbon fouling. The carrier attached to the piston, has 9.5mm of free travel to give mechanical safety after firing, and the bolt is then rotated and withdrawn. The connecting pin, in the carrier moves up, locking the bolt to the carrier. The spring loaded ejector arm is forced down when a lug on the side of the carrier contacts it and the case is pushed downwards through the piston and bottom of the receiver. The ejector returns to its normal position under the action of its torsion spring.

As the carrier goes back the feed actuator moves in through 30 degrees as the roller moves over the cam path and the next round is positioned ready for feeding. The backward movement of the bolt carrier is cushioned by a soft hydraulic buffer which absorbs the energy of the recoiling parts as its piston deflects through a 19mm travel.

The carrier moves forward under the influence of the return (driving) springs, the feed pawl moves out to position itself under the next round and the cycle continues.

Pre-production models of the CMG-2 have been tested and evaluated. The gun has been demonstrated extensively. It utilises proved ideas largely introduced in earlier weapons and with its quick change barrel system it should be a successful gun.

Perhaps the most significant factor of all is the choice of bullet. Colts intend this gun to fire a 68 grain (4.41g) projectile. This lies between the 55 grains (3.56g) of the standard M193 5.56mm ball and the 77 grain (5.0g) Mauser-IWK. To produce stability in this bullet the barrel has a twist of 1 turn in 225mm. (The standard 55 grain bullet is effectively stabilised over short ranges by 1 turn in 305mm. The longer-range Mauser-IWK bullet requires 1 turn in 203mm). This means that the M193 ball will be over spun and must lose some lethality if fired through the CMG-2 barrel at short ranges. Thus two natures of 5.56mm ammunition will be current in the Infantry sub-unit which is one of the features which it is most desirable to eliminate.

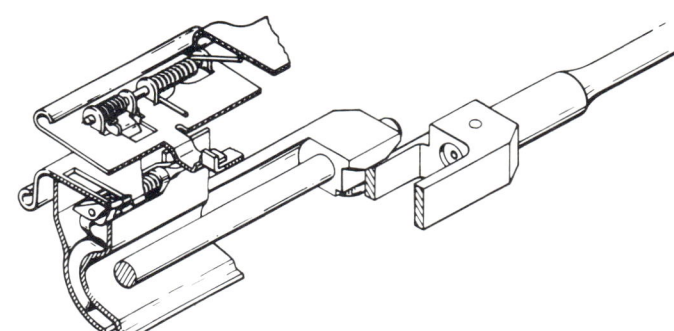

The feed mechanism

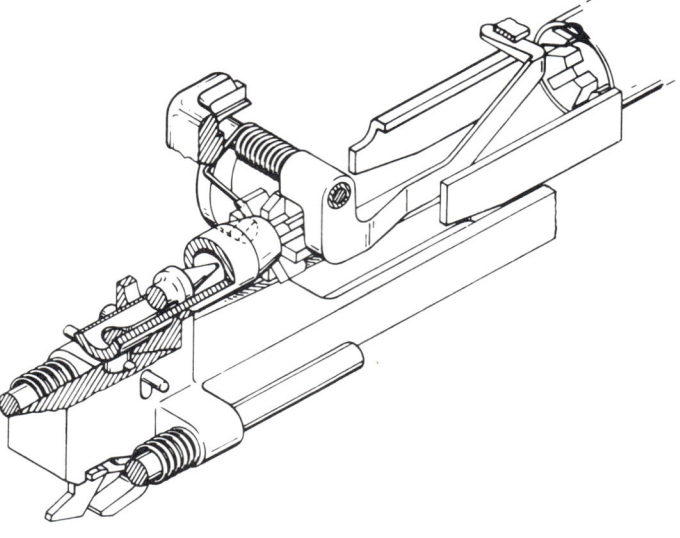

Firing pin, bolt and ejector

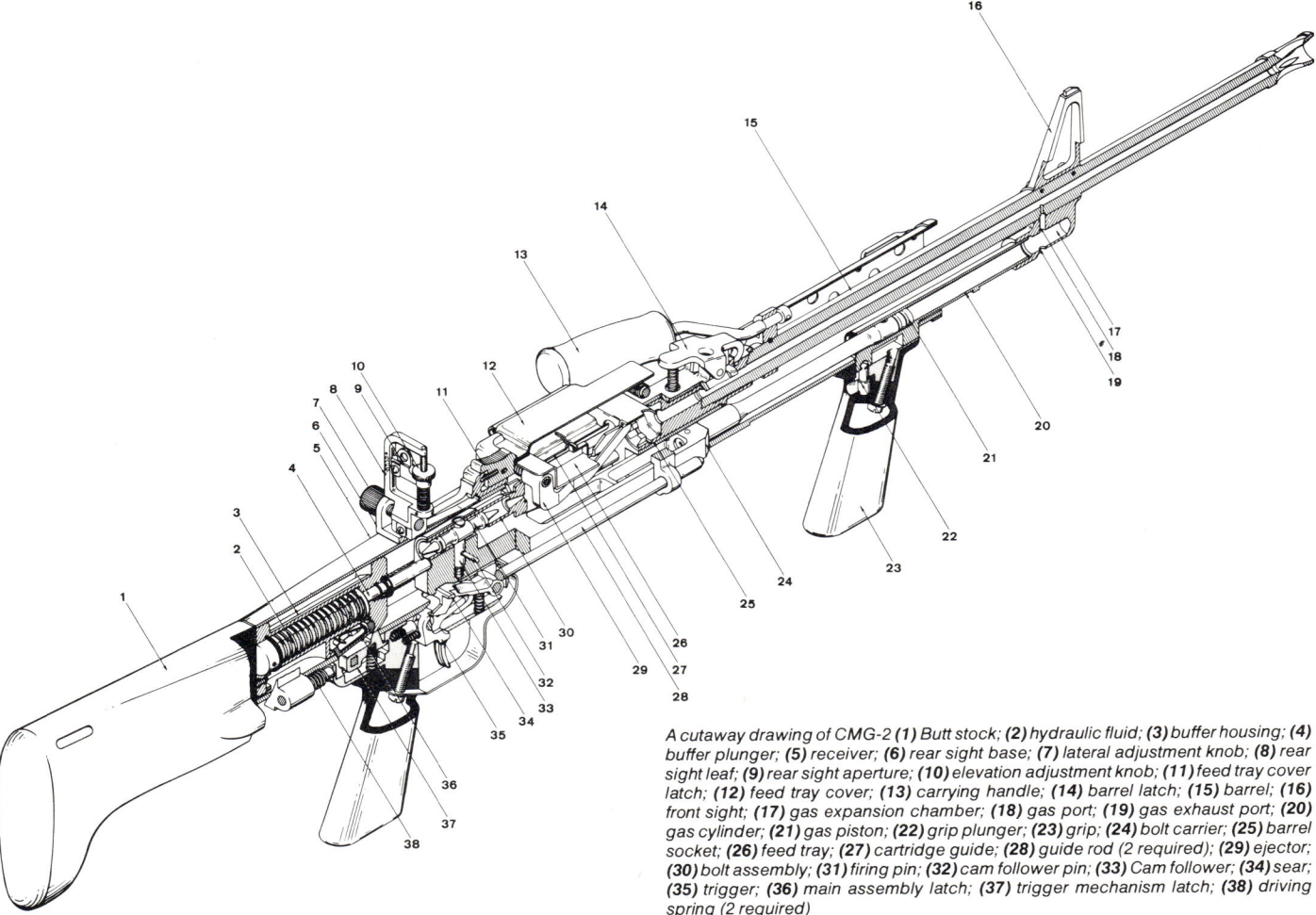

A cutaway drawing of CMG-2 **(1)** Butt stock; **(2)** hydraulic fluid; **(3)** buffer housing; **(4)** buffer plunger; **(5)** receiver; **(6)** rear sight base; **(7)** lateral adjustment knob; **(8)** rear sight leaf; **(9)** rear sight aperture; **(10)** elevation adjustment knob; **(11)** feed tray cover latch; **(12)** feed tray cover; **(13)** carrying handle; **(14)** barrel latch; **(15)** barrel; **(16)** front sight; **(17)** gas expansion chamber; **(18)** gas port; **(19)** gas exhaust port; **(20)** gas cylinder; **(21)** gas piston; **(22)** grip plunger; **(23)** grip; **(24)** bolt carrier; **(25)** barrel socket; **(26)** feed tray; **(27)** cartridge guide; **(28)** guide rod (2 required); **(29)** ejector; **(30)** bolt assembly; **(31)** firing pin; **(32)** cam follower pin; **(33)** Cam follower; **(34)** sear; **(35)** trigger; **(36)** main assembly latch; **(37)** trigger mechanism latch; **(38)** driving spring (2 required)

DATA
Cartridge: 5.56mm × 45. Ball MG (68 grains) Ball M193 (55 grains) Tracer M196
Method of operation: Gas
Method of locking: Rotating bolt
Method of feed: Belt
Method of fire: Automatic

WEIGHTS
Gun without bipod: 5.9kg
Bipod: 709g
Barrel: 1.871kg
Belt drum: 709g

LENGTH
Gun: 1,065mm

MECHANICAL FEATURES
Barrel: Regulator: Nil
    Rifling: 6 grooves RH. 1 turn in 225mm
    Cooling: Air. Quick change barrel
Sights: Foresight: Fixed post
    Rearsight: Aperture
    Zeroing: Rearsight

FIRING CHARACTERISTICS
Muzzle velocity: 991m/sec (M193 ball)
    884m/sec (68 grain ball)
Muzzle energy: 55 grain ball 177mkp
    68 grain ball 176mkp
Rate of fire: Cyclic: 650 rounds/min

Feed and ejection

Sustained: 120 rounds/min
Range, maximum effective: (68 grain ball) 800 metres
    (55 grain ball) 600 metres
Manufacturer: Military Arms Division. Colt Industries, Hartford, Connecticut
Status: The CMG-2 was one of the weapons considered in the Squad Automatic Weapon System (SAWS) programme (qv) but was eliminated.

5.56mm FOOTE MG-69

This General Purpose Machine Gun was produced in prototype in 1969 by J.P. Foote. The weapon has been offered to a number of American firms but no production has resulted.

The weapon is strongly reminiscent in appearance of SIG design but the method of operation is gas – rather than blowback. The cocking handle is on the right and there is a push through safety. The gas regulator is at the front of the cylinder.

DATA
Cartridge: 5.56mm × 45mm
Method of operation: Gas

Method of feed: Belt

WEIGHT
Gun: 6.6kg
Barrel: 1.7kg

LENGTH
Gun without stock: 876mm
Gun with stock: 1,060mm
Barrel: 508mm
Barrel with extension and flash hider: 554mm

FIRING CHARACTERISTICS
Muzzle velocity: 1,018 metres/sec
Muzzle energy: 180mkp

Rate of fire: Cyclic: 700 rounds/min
Automatic: 250 rounds/min
Status: Prototype

MG-69, 5.56mm (J.P. Foote)

DUAL FEED ARMOUR MACHINE GUN

This tank machine gun was designed by Maremont and developed by them under contract awarded by the US Weapons Command. The weapon was intended to be a replacement for the M73, M73A1 and the M219 and to be employed in the coaxial role as well as being cupola mounted. If required it can be dismounted and fitted with a shoulder stock and bipod or a tripod.

The gun is short- recoil operated, has a quick-change barrel, and has a dual ammunition feed. This has obvious uses in the armoured battle but it is of interest to note that the manufacturer describes the dual capacity facility by saying "Chambered for the 7.62mm calibre, it can fire either NATO ammunition or armour piercing flechettes as selected by the user". Each of the two belt fed modules can be supplied from either left or right side, utilising common components.

Since the gun may well fire ammunition of differing muzzle impulse, an impulse control device is fitted to the gun which can effectively cope with mounts having spring rates which vary widely in value.

DATA
Cartridge: 7.62mm NATO of any type (Ball AP etc) or armour piercing flechette
Method of operation: Short recoil
Method of locking: Rotating bolt
Method of feed: Dual disintegrating link belt
Method of fire: Automatic
Length: 874mm
Muzzle velocity: 845 metres/sec
Muzzle energy (7.62mm): 361mkp
Rate of fire: Cyclic: 500-650 rounds/min
Rapid: 200 rounds/min
Sustained: 100 rounds/min
Range, maximum effective: 1,000 metres
Manufacturer: Maremont Corporation, Saco, Maine, USA
Status: Evaluation

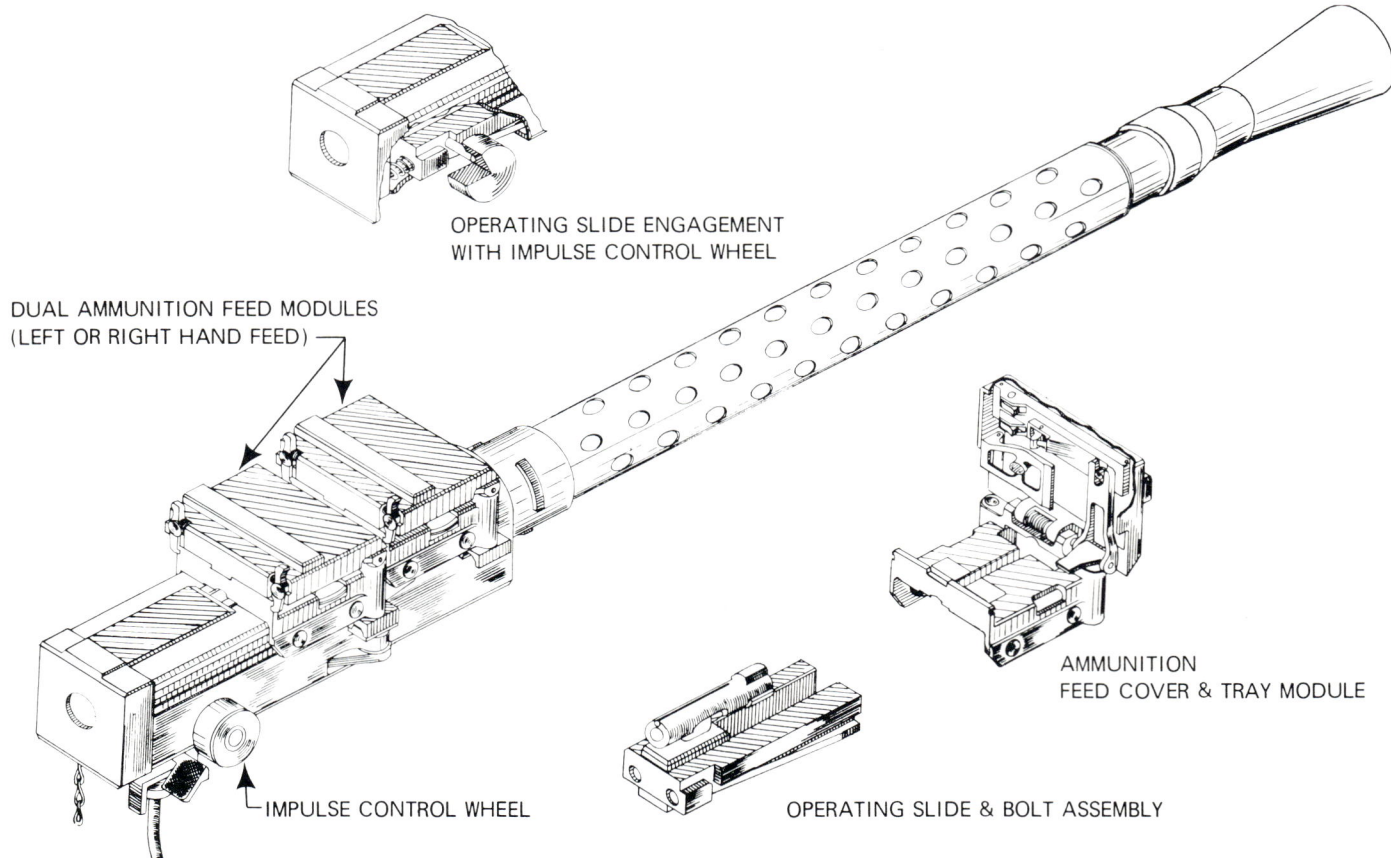

OPERATING SLIDE ENGAGEMENT
WITH IMPULSE CONTROL WHEEL

DUAL AMMUNITION FEED MODULES
(LEFT OR RIGHT HAND FEED)

AMMUNITION
FEED COVER & TRAY MODULE

IMPULSE CONTROL WHEEL

OPERATING SLIDE & BOLT ASSEMBLY

7.62mm Armour Machine Gun components

7.62mm dual ammunition feed Armour Machine Gun

7.62mm MAREMONT UNIVERSAL MACHINE GUN

The Maremont Universal Machine Gun is intended as a lightweight weapon to be used against personnel, either as an infantry LMG replacing the M60 or as an armour machine gun replacing the M73, M73A1 and the M219. In both the infantry and armour roles it offers significant gains in terms of reduced weight and bulk and greater simplicity.

The gun can be either recoil operated or gas operated by changing the minimum number of parts. Some 85% of the parts are basic to either type weapon. It could also be built if the need arose with the ability to switch from one type of operation to another as and if required.

The gun fires from an open bolt which rotates to lock and has three forward locking lugs. The belt feed mechanism can be altered to feed from the other side with little difficulty. The barrel is a quick change design, air-cooled.

DATA
Cartridge: 7.62mm × 51 NATO

Method of operation: Gas and short recoil – changeable at will
Method of locking: Rotating bolt
Method of feed: Disintegrating belt – fed from either side
Method of fire: Automatic
Weight without bipod: 6.8kg
Length with stock and flash suppressor: 940mm
Length as fixed MG in tank: 879mm
Inboard length (front of feed to rear of receiver): 203mm
Maximum width and height less sights, carrying handle bipod and pistol grip: 95mm
Muzzle velocity: 854 metres/sec
Muzzle energy: 361mkp
Rate of fire: Cyclic: 500-650 rounds/min

Manufacturer: Maremont Corporation, Saco, Maine
Status: Evaluation

Universal Machine Gun

6mm US ARMY SQUAD AUTOMATIC WEAPONS SYSTEM (SAWS)

The US Army Weapons Command held a competition, which ended in 1974, to gain information which was intended to lead to the next Squad Automatic Weapons System (SAWS). A number of weapons were entered, some originating in the USA and some from FN in Belgium and Heckler and Koch in West Germany.

The US weapons entered fired one of the 6mm cartridges developed by Frankford Arsenal, details of which are given in the Ammunition section. The cartridge chosen was the XM 732 (the tracer equivalent of which was the XM 734). The XM 732 was designed to give a longer range capability

than the 5.56mm M193 cartridge, and a lethality equal to the 5.56mm. The cartridge was to be suitable ultimately for use in a rifle. An outline of the shape of the 6mm XM 732, and a comparison with the 5.56mm and 7.62mm ball cartridges is given below.

Three US entries took part in the trials, which were completed successfully in 1974. They were the Maremont XM233, the Philco-Ford XM234 and an entry from Rodman Laboratory, Rock Arsenal. The 5.56mm Colt CMG-2 and Stoner weapons were also considered.

Maremont's entry was based on their Universal Machine Gun design in its gas-operated mode. The weapon is illustrated here and a few performance data are given below. Similar information is given for the Philco-Ford entry and there is little that can usefully be added to what is apparent there.

The Rodman Laboratory weapon is a bullpup design with a very pronounced straight-through action. It is gas operated with the gas cylinder above the barrel, and the cocking handle located on the gas piston on the right of the gun. The return spring is wrapped around the gas piston, and the right hand side of the casing around the barrel has a long, piano-type hinge allowing the casing to be dropped for access. The ammunition belt is contained in a drum on the left side of the gun and bent around the weapon. The safety catch is to the right of the pistol grip, above the trigger. It is pushed up to "F" for firing and down to "S" for safe. A selector switch located above the safety allows for single shots or full automatic fire. Dust covers are fitted over the ejection slot and the belt entry port.

DATA
6mm Maremont LMG XM 233
Cartridge: 6mm
Method of operation: Gas
Fires from open bolt

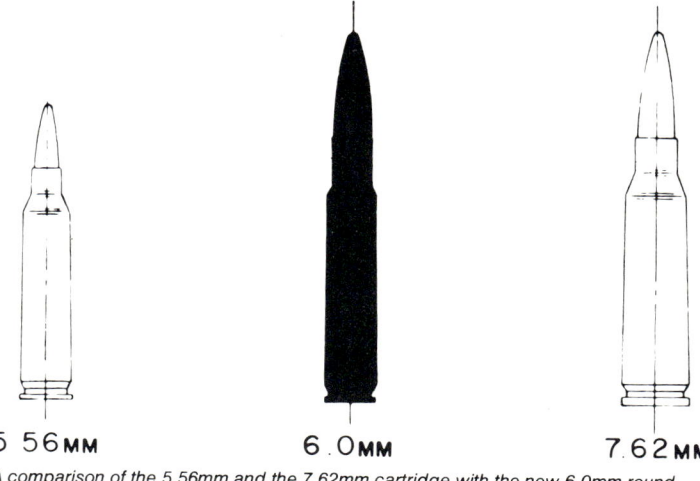

5 56MM   6.0MM   7.62MM

A comparison of the 5.56mm and the 7.62mm cartridge with the new 6.0mm round XM 732

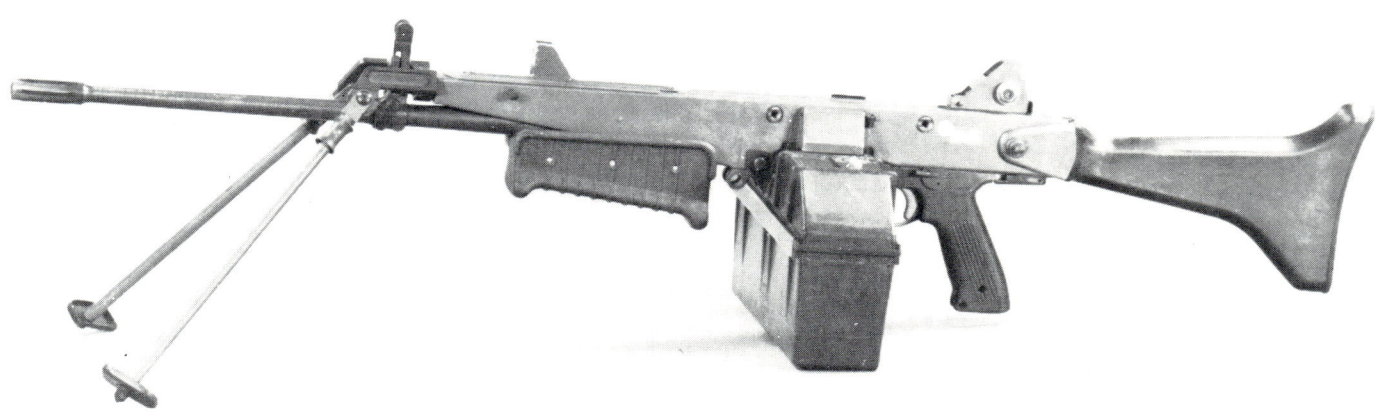

The 6mm Maremont LMG. XM 233 (US Army photograph)

The Philco-Ford 6.0mm LMG XM 234 (US Army photograph)

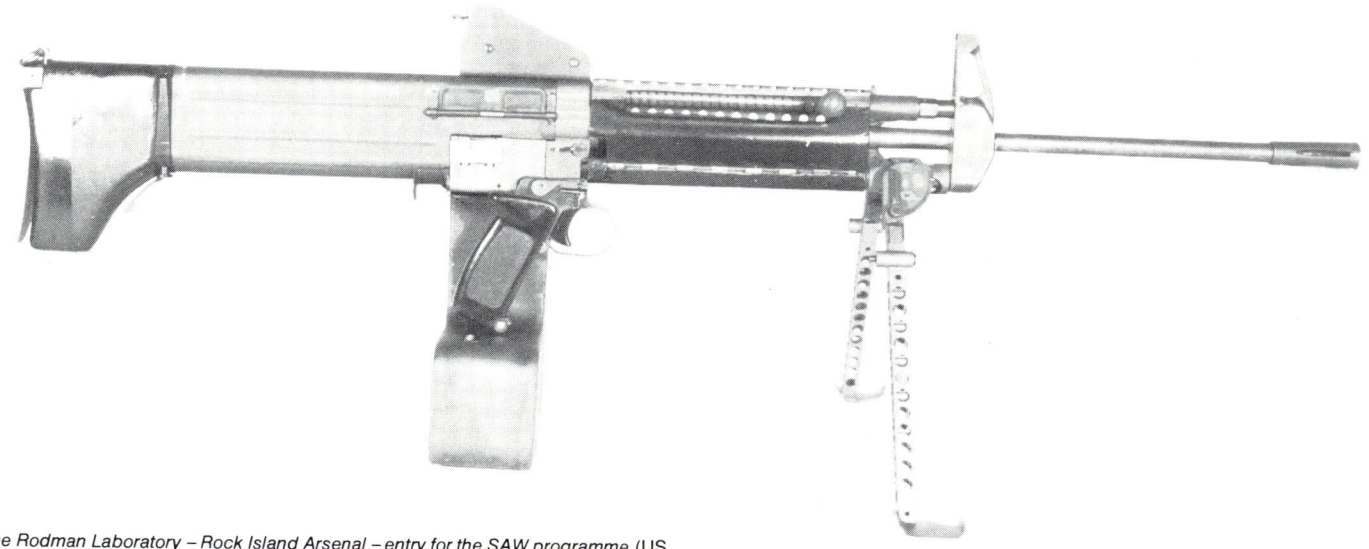

The Rodman Laboratory – Rock Island Arsenal – entry for the SAW programme (US Army photograph)

Method of feed: Disintegrating belt
Muzzle velocity: Approx 762 metres/sec
Rate of fire: 450 rounds/min
Number of manufactured parts: 150
Length: 1,067mm
Weight, with 200 rounds: 11.45kg
6mm Philco-Ford LMG XM 234
Cartridge: 6mm
Method of operation: Gas
Fires from open bolt
Method of feed: Disintegrating belt

Muzzle velocity: Approx 762 metres/sec
Method of fire: Full automatic only
Rate of fire: 500 rounds per minute
Number of manufactured parts: 125
Length: 1,067mm
Weight with 200 rounds: 10.2kg
Status: Following the successful completion of the SAWS trials in 1974, when the contestants were reduced – or so it seems – to the Rodman US entry and the FN Minimi, the project was shelved by the US authorities. Presumably it may be revived when the probable outcome of the NATO small-arms trials (in 1977-78) is clearer.

5.56mm STONER 63 SYSTEM

When Eugene Stoner left Armalite Inc to become a consultant with Colt's Patent Firearms Corp he took with him his two principal design aides, Robert Fremont and James L. Sullivan. (This Sullivan was not the attorney George Sullivan who, with Charles H. Dorchester, founded Armalite Inc.) Stoner is a man of wide and vivid imagination and having been in the US Marines he also had a firm grasp of the tactical requirements of infantry. Stoner's concept was to build a weapon system which could be easily modified as occasion demanded. Starting with certain basic parts these could be fitted with different barrels, feed systems and trigger mechanisms to permit the construction in the field of a number of different weapons to meet varying tactical demands. Starting with a receiver, a bolt and piston, and a return spring, together with a trigger and firing mechanism, a short barrel, folding butt and box magazine could be added to make a sub-machine gun. This could be transformed into a rifle by the addition of a longer barrel, and a fixed butt. Similarly the rifle could be transformed to a light machine gun with suitable changes of barrel, firing mechanism, and where required, feed mechanism. The medium machine gun could be developed from this.

Whilst working for Armalite he had become acquainted with Howard Carson who was a Vice-President of Cadillac Gage and in charge of their West Coast plant, in Costa Mesa, making pneumatic and hydraulic machinery. Stoner explained his ideas to Carson and later to Russel Bauer, President of Cadillac Gage. Bauer considered the scheme worthwhile and a small arms development centre was established near the Costa Mesa plant. Here Stoner, Sullivan and Fremont worked. The first practical weapon was produced in 1962 and called the Stoner 62. It was manufactured to fire the 7.62mm × 51 cartridge and proved mechanically sound. However it became clear that there was a distinct likelihood that the 5.56mm × 45 cartridge was going to replace the larger cartridge and all subsequent work was carried out with that round.

The system was eventually known as the Stoner 63 system.

DESCRIPTION

The system as originally proposed comprised six weapons. These were the Assault Rifle, the Sub-Machine Gun, the Medium Machine Gun, the fixed (tank) Machine Gun and two Light Machine Guns (magazine-fed and belt-fed).

The gas system used for the AR 10 and AR 15 was not used. Instead a conventional piston utilising a long stroke was employed. The advantage of this system applies mainly to the machine guns – which make up two-thirds of the system. The need to use the movement of the bolt to provide the energy to lift and feed belt loaded ammunition makes a sustained pressure on the piston preferable to a sharp impulsive blow and the increased mass – and consequently the momentum – of the moving parts, helps to maintain a steady belt feed.

The rifle and the SMG are both hammer fired from a closed bolt position and have selective fire. The magazines are below the receiver. They have holding open devices. The machine guns fire from the open bolt position

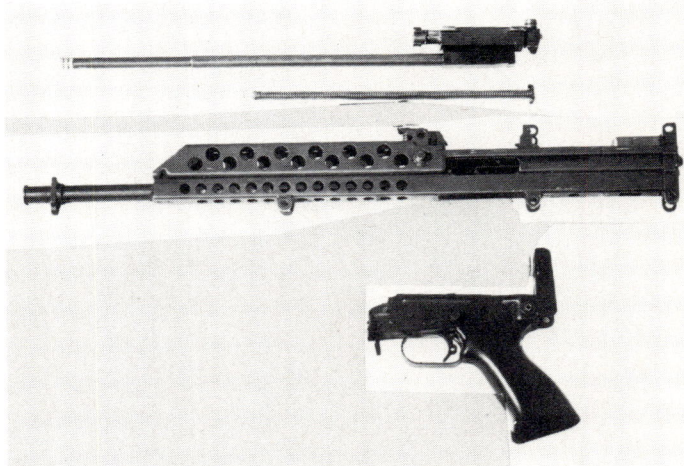

The basic components of the Stoner system

and have fixed firing pins controlled by the piston extension. The magazine feed gun has its magazine on top which necessitates the piston being below the bolt. In all the machine guns the receiver is inverted.

STONER 63A AND 63A1

The Stoner 63 system was manufactured by Cadillac Gage who granted a licence to Mauser-IWK. This was later transferred to NWM Kruitoorn at s'Hertgenbosch in Holland. The Dutch firm did a great deal of work in Europe publicising the system and produced some very interesting and far sighted pamphlets on the "Soldier of the 70s". In spite of these efforts the system was not widely adopted. The US marines tested the weapons and some improvements were effected. These took the form of:

a. Larger gas port opening.
b. Chromium plated chamber.
c. Stronger and better fitting dust covers.
d. A relieved breech block cam pin.
e. A gas nitrided bore.

The modified guns were known as the Stoner 63A weapons.

In spite of these improvements the guns were not sold in large numbers and it was decided to concentrate on the rifle and the light machine guns as separate weapons in their own right, and to abandon production of the Stoner System.

The rifle has been tested as the XM22. Some details of it will be found in the section dealing with rifles.

The LMG was re-designed. The direction of feed was changed from left

ASSAULT RIFLE XM22 5.56MM

BUTTSTOCK FOLDED

The Stoner 63 5.56, Assault Rifle XM22 with buttstock folded

ASSAULT RIFLE XM 22 5.56MM

BUTTSTOCK AND BIPOD EXTENDED

Stoner 62 Assault Rifle XM22 5.56mm with buttstock and bipod extended

to right. The reason for this was that with the attached ammunition box on the left, the soldier frequently banged his knee on it. A new box is more centrally mounted. The 63A1 has been extensively tested as the XM207 LMG by the US Marines and adopted as the Mk 23 (Commando MG) for their SEAL teams.

This SEAL team version was used in Vietnam. The gun with 800 rounds of belted ammunition weighed only 35lb (16kg) and was very popular for patrols.

THE LIGHT MACHINE GUNS

As already noted, the LMGs can be either magazine or belt fed. The magazine fed gun has offset sights to allow vision past the magazine. The belt fed gun requires the addition of the belt feed group.

In changing from the closed breech firing of the rifle and SMG to the open bolt position of the LMG the following is involved.

180 degrees rotation of the receiver and working parts. Removal of three parts from the trigger and firing mechanism, and replacement by dust excluder. Rotation of feed roller lug to the top. Positioning of firing pin to make it fixed relative to the bolt carrier instead of floating with spring retraction for hammer operation as in rifle and SMG role.

OPERATION

The Stoner LMGs are gas operated using a conventional piston system located in a stainless steel cylinder. On firing, the gas following the bullet up the bore is tapped off through a vent in the barrel wall and enters the gas cylinder. The sharp impulsive blow delivered to the piston drives it rearward and the piston movement is communicated to the bolt carrier. The bolt head has to be rotated to unlock it after firing and this is done by having a cam pin

projecting from the bolt head and entering a curved path in the carrier. To ensure mechanical safety after firing, the cam path has an initially straight action. When the bolt moves back it takes the carrier with it and the straight portion of the slot moves over the cam pin and so there is no rotation of the bolt. This extends for about 5mm and allows the gas pressure to drop off. The curved portion of the cam slot then engages the cam pin and causes bolt rotation. The bolt is completely unlocked after some 6mm of carrier travel.

Unlike most multi locking-lug rotating bolt heads, there is no pitch on the locking lugs and so no primary extraction occurs during unlocking. This leads to a rather violent extraction of case and considerable stressing of the extractor.

The extractor does not rotate about a pivot pin but has a fulcrum at its rear end. A deep seating is provided which permits the use of a longer spring which being located in line with the bolt axis provides an efficient leverage.

The ejector is located in the body and being springloaded is held out into the bolt way. The bolt passes over it and the empty case is ejected to the left and deflected downwards by a plate to ensure that the empty case does not come into contact with the belt feed.

The rearward motion of the carrier compresses the return spring on its rod. The design of the basic Stoner system – which requires the butt to be changed for the different roles – located the return spring not, as is usual, in the butt but in the body.

To maintain a reasonable rate of fire and to give sufficient energy to the bolt carrier and piston to overcome frictional resistance, a buffer is used. This consists of a number of Belleville washers which are deformed by the piston energy and which on returning to their original shape release strain energy which helps to accelerate the piston and carrier assembly forward.

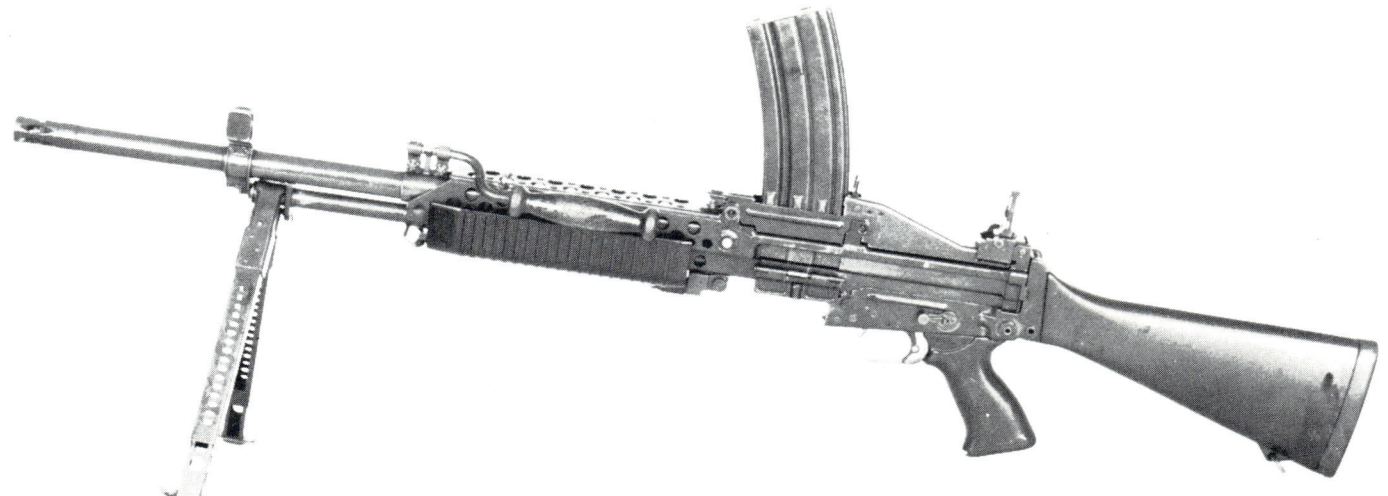

The Stoner 63A LMG with magazine feed (RMCS)

LMG (MAG FED)
BUTT
HANDGUARD
BODY COVER (WITH BACKSIGHT
AND MAG CATCH)
BARREL (WITH OFFSET SIGHTS
AND CARRYING HANDLE)
MAGAZINE
BIPOD
MAGAZINE ADAPTOR

Major components of the Stoner 63A

Stoner 63 LMG belt-fed (RMCS)

LMG (MAG FED) → LMG (BELT FED)
CHANGE OF BARREL
MAGAZINE ADAPTOR AND BODY COVER
REPLACED BY
BELT FEED COVER (WITH BACKSIGHT)

*The change from magazine feed to belt feed for the Stoner 63. **Picture shows:** Change barrel; Magazine adaptor and body cover replaced by belt feed cover (with backsight) (RMCS)*

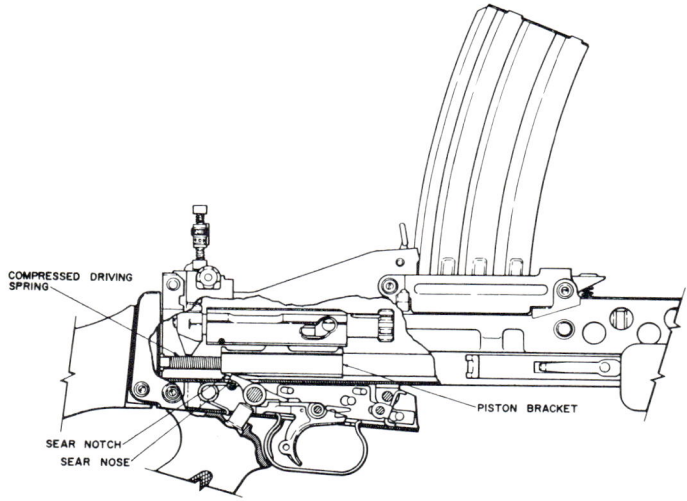

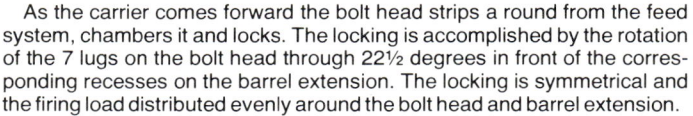

Sear nose engaged in the sear notch of the piston bracket

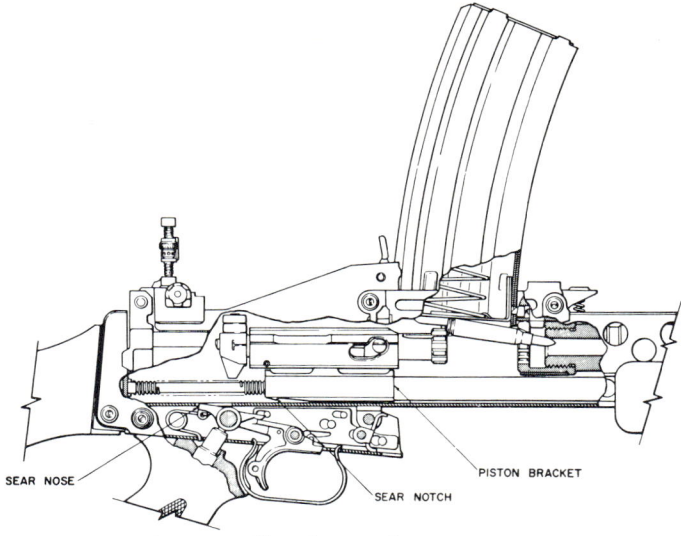

The bolt picking up the top round from the magazine

As the carrier comes forward the bolt head strips a round from the feed system, chambers it and locks. The locking is accomplished by the rotation of the 7 lugs on the bolt head through 22½ degrees in front of the corresponding recesses on the barrel extension. The locking is symmetrical and the firing load distributed evenly around the bolt head and barrel extension.

TRIGGER AND FIRING MECHANISM

In both the magazine and the belt fed versions the gun operates from an open breech. This enables the barrel and chamber to cool between bursts and keeps the ammunition in the supply system – i.e. the magazine or belt – and out of the hot chamber until the bolt in its forward movement strips the round out, feeds it into the chamber and after locking, fires it.

SIGHTS

The front sight is a pillar which can be rotated to raise or lower the sight for zeroing adjustment for elevation. On the magazine-fed gun the sight is offset to the left since the magazine is set vertically above the gun body on the centre line.

The rearsight is a folding leaf tangent slight with, once again, the magazine-fed gun having the rearsight aperture offset to the left.

Graduation of the rearsight is from 200 to 1,000 metres by 100m increments with an audible clicking system to give a positive indication of setting. There is a windage adjustment on the rearsight which is of the micrometer type. This is used for zeroing for line and has a centre mark and clicker operation.

The rearsight apertures are:

Magazine-fed gun	2.28mm
Belt-fed gun	1.52mm
Belt-fed gun – battle sight	2.28mm

FEED

The magazine feed is placed above the gun. The standard magazine contains 30 rounds and is made up by welding two pressings. This mounting position, although producing a fairly high silhouette, does allow the adoption if required of a larger capacity magazine without the disadvantage experienced with under-mounted magazines of coming into contact with the ground.

The belt fed version takes a disintegrating spring steel link belt, fed from the left. The method of moving the belt across is taken from the German MG42.

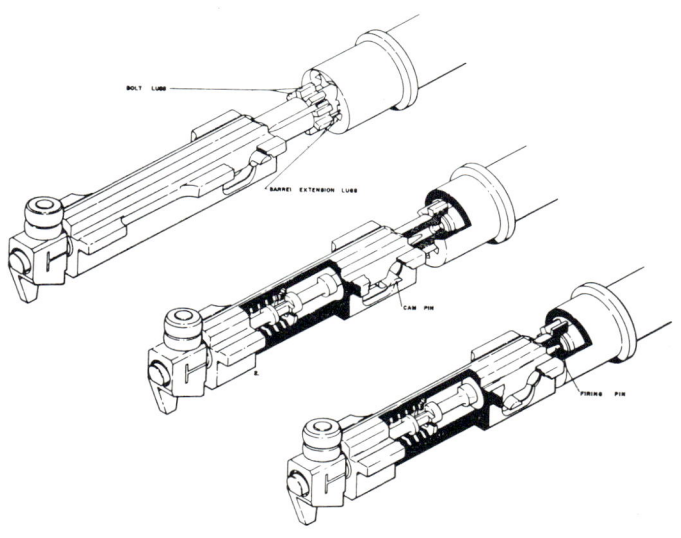

The three positions of the bolt locking: (1) bolt entering barrel extension; (2) bolt rotated half way; (3) bolt locked

STRIPPING

The weapons are designed to strip easily with the use of no tools other than the nose of a standard 5.56mm round. The procedure is:

(1) Ensure the arm is safe by removing the ammunition supply, cocking the action and checking that the chamber is clear. Let the working parts go forward under control.
(2) Push the take down pin through the body from left to right as far as it will go.
(3) Pivot down the trigger housing and butt and withdraw the return spring.
(4) Raise the muzzle and allow the bolt carrier assembly complete to slide out of the body.
(5) Remove the barrel.

XM207 5.56mm MG

Re-assembly is carried out in the reverse order. There are two points to observe:
(1) The bolt cam pin must be correcly located in its recess before the working parts can be inserted.
(2) The barrel must never be replaced with the working parts forward.

DATA
Cartridge: 5.56mm × 45
Method of operation: Gas
Method of locking: Rotating bolt
Method of feed: Magazine or belt
Method of fire: Automatic

WEIGHTS
LMG – magazine fed: 5kg
LMG – belt fed: 5.4kg
Barrel: 1.81kg
Sling: 0.17kg
Magazine – empty: 0.2kg
Magazine – with 30 rounds: 0.54kg
50 rounds disintegrating belt: 0.68kg
100 round belt box – empty: 0.14kg
100 round belt box – loaded: 1.5kg
150 round belt box – loaded: 1.95kg
LMG with full magazine and sling: 5.7kg
LMG with 150 round belt in box and sling: 7.03kg
Trigger pull: 3.97kg

LENGTH
LMG: 1,022mm
Barrel: 508mm

MECHANICAL FEATURES
Barrel: 3 port regulator (belt fed only)
　　　　Rifling: 6 grooves RH. 1 turn in 305mm
　　　　Cooling: Air – quick change
Sights: Foresight: Cylindrical post
　　　　Rearsight: Tangent leaf. Folding
　　　　Graduation: 200-1000 metres by 100 metre increments
　　　　Zeroing: Elevation. Frontsight. Line. Rearsight on wedge
　　　　Sight radius: 565mm

FIRING CHARACTERISTICS
Muzzle velocity: 1,000 metres/sec
Muzzle energy: 186mkp
Recoil energy: Magazine feed: 0.386mkp
　　　　　　　Belt feed: 0.346mkp
Chamber pressure: 3,650kg/cm²
Rate of fire: Cyclic: 750 rounds/min
　　　　　Automatic: 60 rounds/min
Range, maximum effective: 800 metres
Maximum: 2,650metres
Manufacturer: Cadillac Gage Company, PO Box 1027, Warren, Michigan 48090.
Status: Not made since 1971. In service (modified) with US marines.

5.56mm Mk 23 COMMANDO MG

As noted in the discussion of the Stoner 63 system, a somewhat modified version of the bolt-fed Stoner LMG was adopted by the USMC for use by their SEAL teams in Vietnam. This version of the weapon is illustrated here: general information on its design will be found in the preceding entry.

Manufacturer: Cadillac Gage Company, PO Box 1027, Warren, Michigan, 48090
Status: In service

The US Navy's Mk 23 5.56mm machine gun (Commando MG)

5.56mm HUGHES LOCKLESS LMG

Sponsored initially by the Advanced Research Projects Agency, and now the subject of a contract with the U.S. Army Command, this Hughes-developed weapon utilises a lockless action incorporating a sliding sleeve and a special plastic cased, fully telescoped cartridge also of Hughes design. This type of weapon removes the need for the conventional sealing function provided by the usual metallic cartridge case, and significant savings in cartridge weight also accrue.

DATA
Cartridge: Special 5.56mm plastic cased cartridge
Method of operation: Gas
Action: Lockless, with sliding sleeve
Method of feed: 200-round magazine
Weight with 200 rounds: 8.2kg
Length: 1,091mm
Muzzle velocity: 915 metres/sec

Hughes 5.56mm Lockless LMG prototype

Rate of fire: 420 shots per minute
Manufacturer: Hughes Helicopters, Division of Summa Corporation, Culver City, California, USA
Status: Prototype

7.62mm CHAIN GUN

Hughes Helicopters and Ordnance Systems have developed a 7.62mm version of their well-known 30mm Chain Gun. The latter weapon is discussed at some length in the sub-section dealing with cannon and the following notes deal only with the state of progress of the 7.62mm weapon at mid-1976.

At that time some 100,000 rounds had been fired by two prototype weapons, the first firing having taken place in May 1975. These firings

included turret firings (5000 rounds), firing under field conditions (20,000 rounds) a 2000-round burst with a water-jacketed barrel, 10,000 rounds of 'foreign' ammunition fired without stoppage or malfunction and over 75,000 rounds fired from the first prototype with only one broken part.

The gun is physically interchangeable with the coaxial weapon used in M-48 and M-60 tanks and is envisaged by the manufacturers as appropriate to future US armoured vehicles from APC's to main battle tanks.

Manufacturers: Hughes Helicopters and Ordnance Systems, Culver City, California
Status: Advanced development as a private venture. A programme to make further prototypes for user evaluation had been approved by mid-1976 and customer support was being sought.

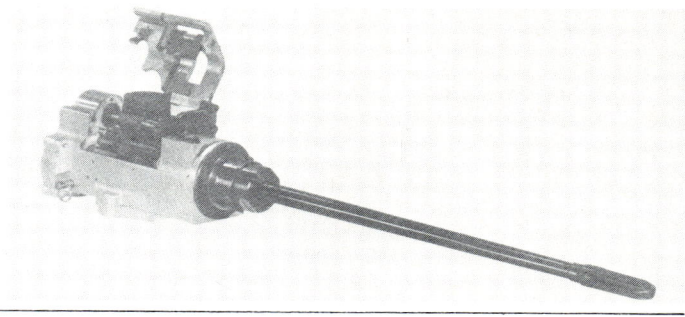

Hughes 7.62mm Chain Gun

VIETNAM

7.62mm TUL-1 LMG

This light machine gun looks very much like the Russian RPK and carries a 75 round drum magazine below the receiver in the same way as the RPK. It is in fact a weapon produced within the country and is based on the Chinese PRC Type 56 Assault Rifle which itself is built with the characteris- tics of the Russian AK-47. So, the TUL-1 has the receiver of the AK-47 and also has the same trigger mechanism without the rate controller which is a feature of the AKM and RPK designs.

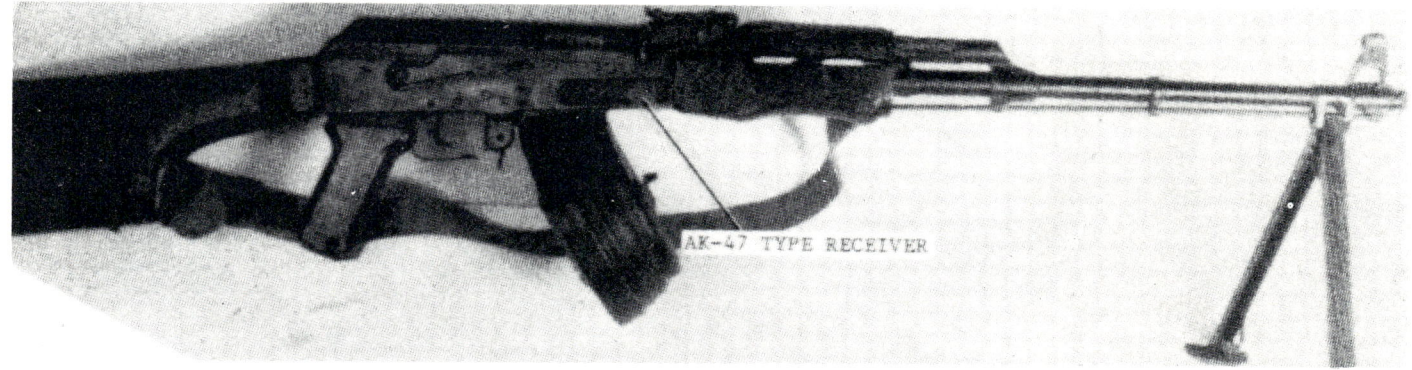

The Vietnamese 7.62mm TUL-1 LMG

YUGOSLAVIA

7.62mm M65A AND M76B LMGs

These two LMGs are both heavy barrelled versions of the Yugoslav Assault Rifle, the M64 which itself is the Yugoslav version of the Soviet AK-47.

The difference between the two weapons is that the M65A has a fixed barrel and the M65B has a quick change barrel. The barrel of the M65B has a series of annular fins extending back from the gas tap off point. The barrels of both guns have cone shaped flash hiders and carry a light bipod.

The two LMGs function in the same manner as the AK-47 (qv). They differ in the same fashion but have a small retainer securing the return spring, which is located at the left rear of the receiver. This must be depressed before the return spring guide rod can be removed.

The barrel change of the M65B is accomplished by pressing in the barrel retaining catch located on the lower end of the barrel nut handle and then lifting the handle up to the limit of its travel. The barrel can then be pushed forward and removed. After inserting the new barrel, it is locked by turning the barrel nut handle down and making certain that the retaining catch has locked.

Both guns use 30-round magazines. The equipment issued with the guns is limited to a leather sling, an oil container and a Soviet AK-47 type combination tool. The M65B has one spare barrel.

DATA
Cartridge: 7.62mm × 39

Method of operation: Gas
Method of locking: Rotating bolt
Method of feed: 30-round detachable box magazine
Method of fire: Selective
Weight: 5.45kg
Length: 1,095mm
Barrel: 470mm
Rifling: 4 grooves RH
Cooling: Air. M65B has quick change barrel.
Sights: Foresight: Cylindrical post
         Rearsight: Leaf, Notch
Muzzle velocity: 732 metres/sec
Muzzle energy: 215mkp
Rate of fire: Cyclic: 600 rounds/min
         Automatic: 120 rounds/min (M65B)
         Automatic: 80 rounds/min (M65A)
         SS: 40 rounds/min
Range, maximum effective: 600 metres

Manufacturer: Crvena Zastava, Kragujevac
Status: In production. In service

7.92mm M53 GPMG

The current Yugoslav General Purpose Machine Gun is the SARAC which is the German MG42. The weapon has not been changed from the gun used by the German Army in World War II. Details will be found in the section on German weapons.

DATA
Cartridge: 7.92mm × 57
Method of operation: Short recoil. Gas assisted
Method of locking: Projecting lugs
Method of feed: 50-round continuous metal link belt
Method of fire: Automatic
Weight: (with bipod) 11.6kg
Tripod: 19.2kg
Length: 1,219mm
Barrel: 533mm
         Cooling: Air. Quick change barrel
Sights: Foresight: Barleycorn
         Rearsight: Tangent. Notch
Muzzle velocity: 756 metres/sec
Muzzle energy: 374mkp
Rate of fire: 1,200 rounds/min
Range, maximum effective: Direct fire 800 metres. Indirect fire 3000 metres

Yugoslavian troops on manoeuvres

Manufacturer: Crvena Zastava, Kragujevac
Status: No longer manufactured. In serivce

CANNON

INTRODUCTION

Although nomenclature is by no means universally consistent, it is fairly common practice to refer to the group of automatic weapons having calibres in the region of 20-30mm as 'cannon'. There is some operational validity in making a distinction between such weapons and machine guns of about 15mm calibre downwards, on the one hand, and quick-firing guns of about 35mm calibre upwards on the other hand, the former group being fairly generally associated with infantry operations and the latter with those of the artillery; but there are many exceptions to this rough and ready classification. Marines, paratroops and such special formations as the RAF Regiment which in many respects resemble infantry formations may well be called upon to operate weapons – light howitzers or 40mm AA guns, for example – which are not customarily thought of as infantry weapons; and

machine guns and cannon are extensively used as secondary armament or on special vehicles of armoured formations. The extent to which cannon are used – often but not necessarily on infantry armoured vehicles – by the infantry nowadays certainly justifies their inclusion in this book, however; and the differences between these weapons and those classified as machine guns are thought to justify their treatment as members of a separate weapon category.

Many of these weapons are used operationally in elaborate mountings – notably those designed for anti-aircraft operations. The entries which follow, however, are primarily concerned with the basic weapon: information on special mountings will be found in the section dealing with anti-aircraft and anti-tank weapons.

FRANCE

20mm GUN M621

This is an electrically powered cannon of light weight and low recoil designed for use on a small ground vehicle or a cargo carrier. It also has applications in any field where its two major characteristics of light weight and low recoil are at a premium. It is therefore found in helicopters and rivercraft.

The locking system of the gun makes use of two swinging locking pieces, one in each side of the bolt, projecting outwards into the boltway and engaging in recesses in the body. After the round is fired these locking pieces are retracted by gas action. There is a gas vent on each side of the barrel located some 650mm from the breech face: gas from these drives back two pistons which force back the supports that secure the locking pieces: these are then driven inwards and the residual gas pressure enables the bolt to move back. When the locks are fully in, the block is blown to the rear.

The gun can fire at single shot from a closed breech or at 300 rounds/minute or 700 rounds/minute. These rates of fire are controlled electrically. In the event of a misfire there is an automatic re-cocking system which uses a blank firing cartridge to provide the necessary power after a delay of 0.3 seconds to allow for a hangfire. It is also possible to re-cock the gun by hand using a wire cable provided with a T handle.

The gun uses mainly the USA 20mm M56 cartridge (or the M55 or M53), all of which are electrically fired and allow ready variation of the rate of fire and also permit both open and closed breech firing. These rounds are used in the USA M39 20mm Gun and in the Vulcan M61 20mm Gun. The USA M12 link is employed.

The feed systems of the gun provide its chief technical interest. The first of the different modes is the usual flat feed with the belt coming in from one side and the empty links ejected on the opposite side. The direction of feed can be reversed by the reversal of the sprocket feed and by changing several parts. The second method is referred to as the "enveloping feed mechanism". It uses the same arrangements except that the axis of the sprocket drive has been raised so that the rounds enter the gun from a slightly elevated position and the links are ejected on the same side as the feed and are flung out under the incoming belt. The third system is a flat feed system but a generator is built into the gun and no external power is required. Lastly, there is a double feed with two belts, one on each side. The gunner is able to select which of the two belts he requires and so can change from HE to AP at will. With all four methods of feed, the electrical control box enables the firer to select single shot fire with a closed breech operation, or automatic fire from an open breech. At automatic the length of the burst can be fixed and a record maintained of the rounds fired.

20mm Gun M621

Twin belt feed arrangement of the M621

DATA
Calibre: 20mm
Weight of weapon: 45.5kg
Weight of cradle: 12.5kg
Length of gun: 2,207mm
Width of gun cradle: 202mm
Height of gun in cradle: 245mm
Height of gun with selective feed mechanism: 425mm
Rate of fire: 730 or 300 rounds/minute
Voltages:
Capping: 250volt
Re-cocking: 24volt
Feed: 24volt
Ammunition: AP, HE, tracer, HE

The light infantry mount which can be towed behind a jeep or moved by helicopter

Manufacturer: Designed by AME (Atelier de Fabrications de Mulhouse), developed by EFAB (Etablissement d'Etudes et de Fabrications de Bourges) and produced by MAT (Manufacture Nationale d'Armes de Tulle). Enquiries to GIAT, 10 Place Georges-Clémenceau, 92211 Saint-Cloud
Status: In production and in service

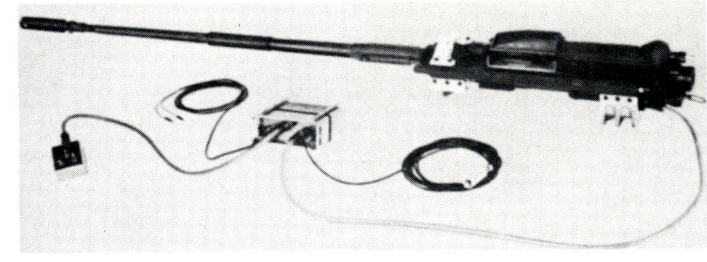

Flat feed mechanism on the left

20mm GUN MODEL F2 (M693)

The F2 is a gas operated cannon with two gas vents, one on each side of the barrel, and a short gas piston in each of the cylinders which is driven back as the gas passes through the vents. The gun is locked by two swinging locking pieces which are used in the locked position as struts between the block and the body of the gun. The gas pressure, after firing, drives back the two pistons and they in turn move back the supports which hold the locking pieces in place, and the residual gas pressure forces the breech block rearwards.

The gun fires cartridges with the mechanical primer of the Hispano Suiza HS820 family – as opposed to the M621 which uses the electrically primed USA M56 cartridge. The feed system allows the choice of two types of ammunition. These are held in belts fed in from each side and rapid change from one to the other is possible using a manually operated switch. The feed on each side is known to the manufacturer as "enveloping" and this entails the ejection of the links from the same side as the belt feed. The feed mechanism is driven mechanically by the recoiling movement of the breech block slides, through a ratchet and pawl assembly. The weapon when used with a power source can provide remote control. The control box allows the selection of single shot, automatic fire or a limited burst.

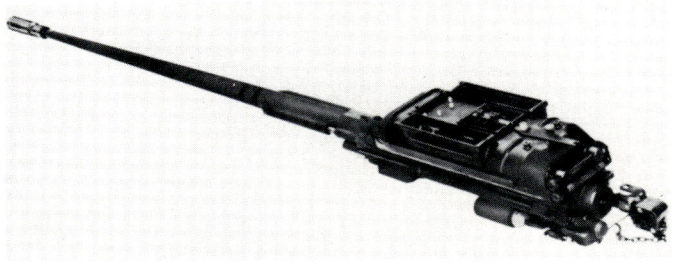

Model F2 20mm gun

DATA
Calibre: 20mm
Length: 2,695mm
Width: 205mm
Height: 236mm
Weight: 70.5kg
Weight of barrel with muzzle brake: 25kg
Length of barrel with muzzle brake: 2,065mm
Weight of cradle: 10.5kg
Weight of control box: 1.25kg
Muzzle velocity of HS820 HE,
Incendiary and practice ammunition: 1,050metres/sec
Muzzle velocity of 693 APDS: 1,300metres/sec

AMMUNITION
The gun will fire all types of ammunition of the HS820 family
Manufacturer: GIAT, 10 Place Georges-Clémenceau, 92211 Saint-Cloud
Status: In service as the Model F2

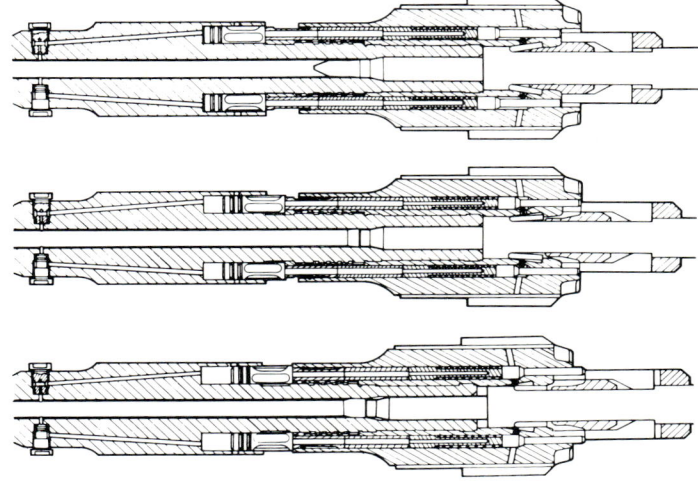

The locking arrangements of the F2

Top: Gun ready to fire. Breech locked. **Middle:** Gun Fired. Gas moving pistons back. **Bottom:** Breech unlocked

20mm GUN MODEL F1

Designed by the Etablissement d'Etudes et de Fabrications de Bourges (EFAB) and made by the Manufacture Nationale d'Armes de Tulle, (MAT) this 20mm cannon fires the HS 820 range of ammunition, and equivalent ammunition of French manufacture, which is mechanically fired.

Similar in many respects to the M621 and F2 weapons the F1 features a central box giving a choice of single shot, limited burst or full automatic operation, a double feed mechanism which ejects from the same side as the belt enters and thus gives a choice of two types of ready ammunition, and an optional electric recocking device.

DATA
Calibre: 20mm
Length: 2,600mm
Width: 204mm
Height: 260mm without feed guides; 228mm without cradle
Weight: (with cradle and feed guides): 80kg
Rate of fire: 700-750 rounds/min cyclic
Manufacturer: See text. Enquiries to GIAT, 10 Place Georges-Clémenceau, 92211 Saint-Cloud
Status: In production and in service

GERMANY (FEDERAL REPUBLIC)

MK20 RH202 20mm GUN

This gun is designed to be used either as an anti-aircraft weapon or against ground targets. In the former role it relies on its very rapid traverse and elevation and high rate of fire to deal with those targets that ground-air missiles find so elusive.

The gun is gas operated and uses a system of breech locking in which two locking levers, or flaps, project outwards into the body of the gun. This symmetrical locking system has much to commend as pressure and this function is independent of bolt travel or barrel recoil. The gun will fire either single shots or automatic and when set to "safe" the bolt is locked and the sear is secured to prevent accidental discharge.

The gun fires whilst the working parts are still moving forward and a large part of the recoil energy is taken to arrest and then reverse this motion. This "floating" firing and the use of a muzzle brake keep the recoil force down to 550–700kg.

The low recoil force and the use of gas pressure instead of recoil to operate the feed lead to a low trunnion pull, so that the gun can be installed in a very light mounting on a vehicle which normally would be overstressed with a 20mm gun of conventional recoil force. The gun has two different belt feed systems. Each is mounted on a hinged frame which is separate from the gun and absorbs the forces involved in the passage of the ammunition. The Type 2 belt feed mechanism allows two belts to be fed in together, side

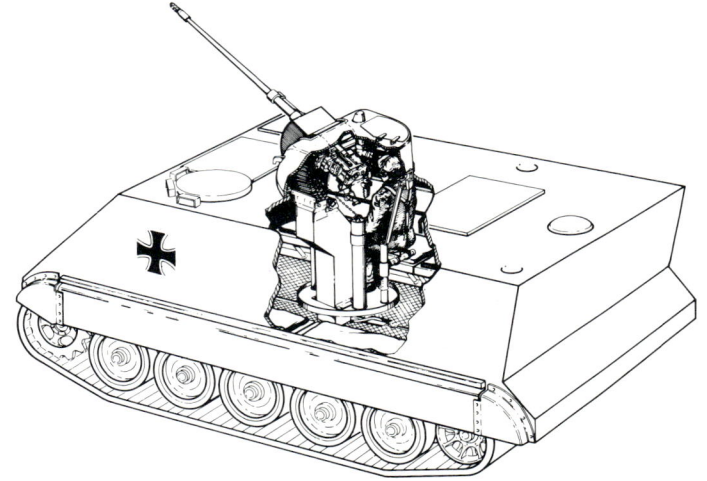

Layout of the MK 20 Rh 202 in the M113

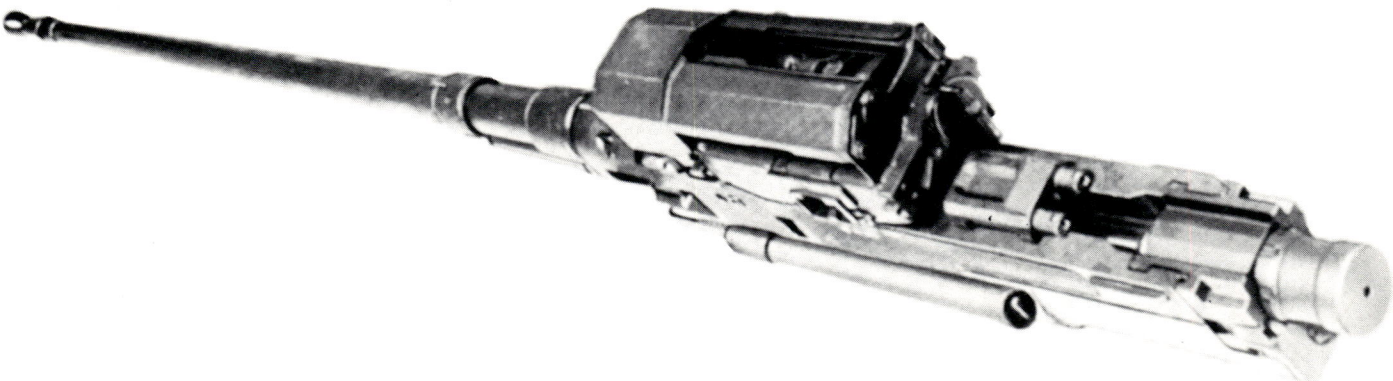

The belt feed mechanisms Type 2 and Type 3

by side, into the top of the gun. These belt feeds originate one on each side of the weapon and allow a very rapid change from one nature of ammunition to the other, merely by throwing over a switch on the feed mechanism.

The Type 3 belt feed mechanism allows the feed of two belts one from each side and at the same time a magazine can be inserted from the top. This normally takes only 6–10 rounds but there appears no reason why more should not be fed in this way. It is possible with the Type 3 feed to fire alternate rounds from two belts in turn. This can be done manually or an external source of electric or hydraulic power can be used. The barrel life of the gun is estimated to be about 8,000 rounds, and a special barrel is available for firing plastic blank ammunition. This has a reduced area muzzle opening to allow the build up of gas pressure to enable the gas system to operate the mechanism.

APC MOUNTING
Rheinmetall has developed a one man armoured turret for the M113 APC. This is called the TS Rh10. The weapon compartment in the turret with belt chute and ammunition box is separated from the gunner by a bulkhead to prevent the ingress of carbon monoxide. The turret can be entered from the crew compartment and also has a hatch on top. The gun has an electronically controlled device providing a series of single shots at a rate controllable within 60 to 360 rounds/minute and with a device to limit the number of rounds to any number selected, between 1 and 99 rounds. The turret holds 200 rounds of ammunition – 150 in one belt and 50 in the other using the Type 2 feed.

DATA (GUN)
Cartridge: 20mm × 139
Method of operation: Gas
Method of locking: Protecting lugs
Method of feed: Alternative of 2 belts (Type 2) or 2 belts and magazine (Type 3)
Method of fire: Selective. Single shot or automatic

WEIGHTS
Gun complete: 81.5kg
Recoiling parts (weapon housing complete and barrel): 61kg
Belt feed mechanism Type 2: 17.5kg
Belt feed mechanism Type 3: 11kg
Barrel: 28kg
Muzzle brake: 4kg
Ejector assembly: 0.7kg

DIMENSIONS
Overall length of gun including muzzle brake: 2,610mm
Height of gun with Type 2 feed: 261mm
Height of gun with Type 3 feed: 259mm
Width of gun: 110mm
Overall width with Type 2 feed: 241mm

FIRING CHARACTERISTICS
Muzzle velocity
  High Explosive Incendiary (HEI): 1,050metres/sec
  Armour piercing: 1,100 metres/sec
Rate of fire: 800-1,000 rounds/minute
Muzzle energy: 5,600-7,000mkp
Effective Range: Up to 2,000metres
Maximum range: 7,000metres
Penetration-AP-1,000metres
  Normal impact (Angle of obliquity 0°): 32mm
  Angle of obliquity 30°: 24mm
  Angle of obliquity 60°: 8mm
Manufacturer: Rheinmetall GmbH, 4 Dusseldorf 1
Status: In production. In service with German Forces. Also in use with Norwegian Forces

---

SWITZERLAND

OERLIKON AND HISPANO-SUIZA
For many years two Swiss arms firms of Hispano-Suiza of Geneva and Oerlikon of Zurich dominated the world markets in fast firing 20 and 30mm guns used for anti-aircraft fire and mounted on armoured fighting vehicles for the attack of lightly protected targets. In 1971 Oerlikon obtained a controlling interest in Hispano-Suiza and the products of the two firms have since been controlled from Zurich. As a result of this takeover, the guns of Hispano origin now being produced by Oerlikon have been redesignated.

20mm BELT FED CANNON KAA— (FORMER DESIGNATION OERLIKON TYPE 204 GK)
This is a blowback operated gun which has a locked breech. This type of arrangement is rarely met outside 20mm guns (although the Breda 6mm Model 30 and the Johnson Light Machine gun are examples of this method in smaller guns). Whilst the breech is locked the receiver recoils within the cradle.

OPERATION
The gun fires from the open breech position and when the trigger is pressed the sear which holds up the bolt is rotated out of engagement and the return springs drive the bolt forward. The bolt forces a round through the link of the belt and into the chamber, and comes to rest when the front face encounters the bolt stop which is a replaceable insert. The rear part of the bolt – called by the manufacturer the "tail" – continues forward under its own inertia and forces out two pivoting locking pieces which engage in recesses in the replaceable locking shoulders in the body. The tail of the bolt is held in place by a spring loaded detent to prevent it from bouncing and it holds the locking pieces out into engagement. The firing pin attached to the tail, hits the cap and the round is fired. This occurs when the receiver is still moving forward in the cradle, giving floating firing. The gas pressure forces the shell up the bore and as it passes the gas port which is located close to the breech face, the gas pressure forces back a piston which in turn drives the return spring housing back. This has a lug which engages the bolt tail and this is withdrawn. This withdraws the firing pin and the support for the locking pieces. The bolt is then blown back by the residual pressure in

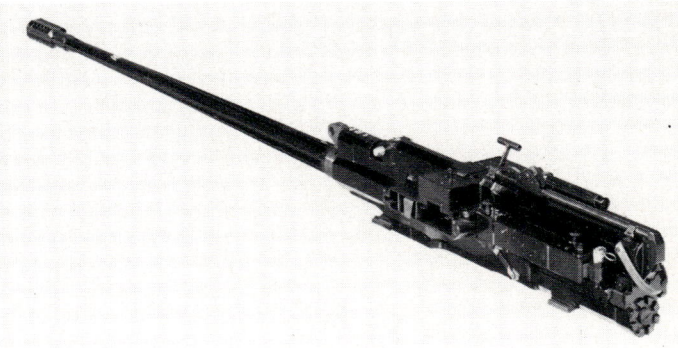

The Oerlikon 20mm belt fed cannon KAA. This was formerly designated 204 GK

the bore. The chamber is fluted to reduce extraction friction. The empty case is held by the extractor on the bolt face and driven down out of the gun as the bolt passes under the fixed ejector. The bolt moves back onto the spring buffer. If the change lever is at "single shot" the sear holds up the bolt to the rear. The sear is spring loaded to cushion the shock of arresting the bolt. If the change lever is at automatic, the bolt goes forward to fire again.

The feed mechanism is operated by the return spring housing. A lug on the housing engages in a spiral slot in the feed cylinder and the cylinder rotates first in one direction and then in the other. At the front end of the cylinder, teeth are cut which engage in the feed slide and move it across the gun and back. As it moves in, the feed pawls attached to it bring the next round in front of the bolt. The belt is prevented from slipping back by the stop pawl as the feed slide moves out to collect the next round.

DATA
Cartridge: 20mm (Types listed separately)
Method of operation: Blowback with a locked breech
Method of locking: Pivoting locks
Method of feed: Belt – disintegrating link type
Method of fire: Selective

Weights
Barrel with muzzle brake: 26.6kg (Heavy barrel is 5.67kg heavier)
Receiver: 26.4kg
Bolt: 4.1kg
Bolt feed plate: 4.5kg
Cover group: 20kg
Trigger mechanism: 5.4kg
Complete gun: 87kg
Length of barrel: 85 calibres (170mm)
Rifling: 12 grooves. Increasing twist 0° to 6° 30'
Force required to cock gun: 7-10kg
Trunnion pull: 2,400kg
Muzzle velocity: 1,050metres/sec
Rate of fire, cyclic: 1,000 rounds/min
Manufacturer: Machine Tool Works Oerlikon Bührle Ltd., Zurich
Status: In production and in service

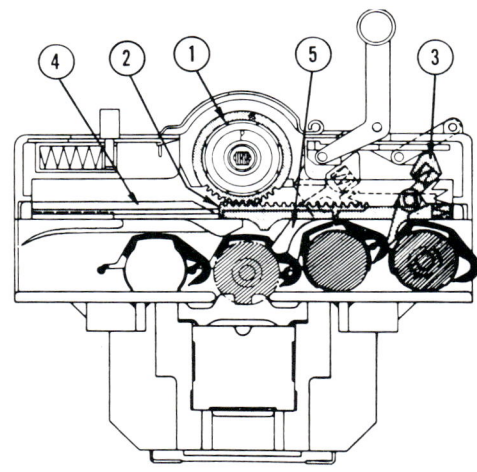

Sectioned view showing ammunition feed: (1) Feed roller; (2) Belt feed slide; (3) Feed pawls; (4) Stop; (5) Holding pawls

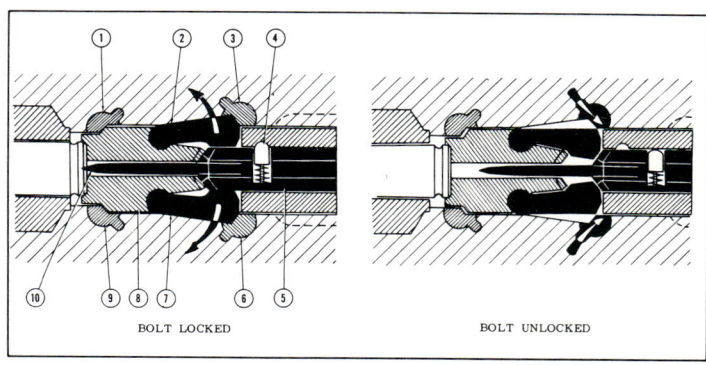

BOLT LOCKED   BOLT UNLOCKED

Sectioned view showing the bolt action of the KAA 20mm cannon: (1) Stop insert; (2) Pivoting lock; (3) Lock insert; (4) Detent; (5) Bolt tail; (6) Lock insert; (7) Pivoting lock; (8) Bolt head; (9) Stop insert; (10) Firing pin

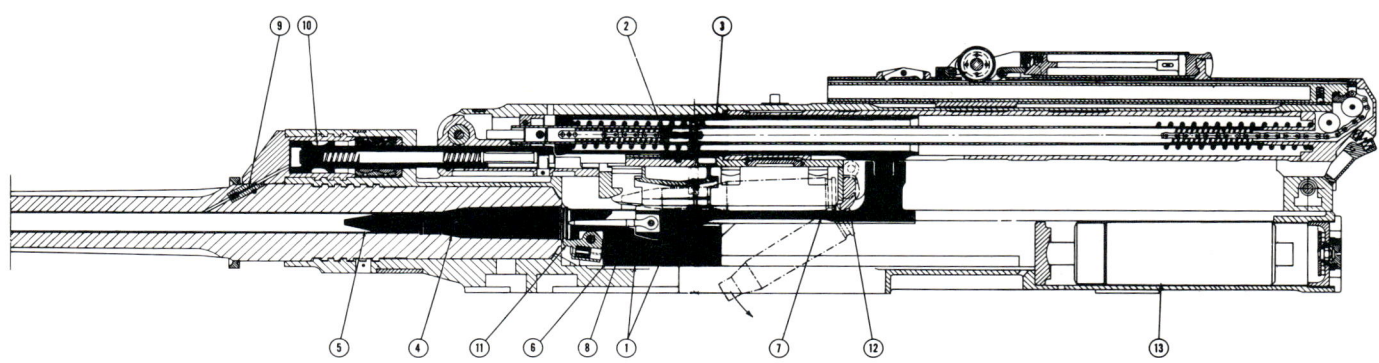

Sectioned view of the KAA 20mm cannon: (1) Bolt; (2) Charging spring; (3) Spring housing; (4) Cartridge; (5) Chamber; (6) Bolt head; (7) Bolt tail; (8) Firing pin; (9) Gas port; (10) Gas piston; (11) Extractor; (12) Ejector; (13) Bolt buffer

20mm AUTOMATIC CANNON KAB-001 (FORMER DESIGNATION 5TG)

This is a positively-locked gas-operated gun suitable for AA or ground target applications. It is mechanically fired and uses a mechanical trigger, for either single-shot or automatic operation, with a trigger locking device which prevents the bolt from moving forward without feeding a round into the chamber. Ammunition feed is by either drum or box magazine. The barrel has Oerlikon progressive rifling and is fitted with a 4-stage muzzle brake. The gun may be field-stripped without tools.

DATA
Calibre: 20mm

Barrel length: 2400mm
Weights:
Cannon: 109kg (including barrel)
Barrel: 51.6kg
20 round drum magazine, empty: 17.0kg
50 round drum magazine, empty: 24.5kg
8-round box magazine, empty: 4.5kg
Single round: 320-340g according to type
Rifling: 12 grooves RH. progressive 0° to 6°
Mean recoil force: 800kp

The Oerlikon 20mm cannon type KAB. This was formerly the 5TG. Note the box magazine

The Oerlikon 20mm canon type KAB with drum magazine

Recoil travel: 10mm
Muzzle velocity: 1100-1200m/sec
Rate of fire: approx. 1000 rounds/min

Manufacturer: Machine Tool Works Oerlikon Bührle, Zurich
Status: In production and in service

20mm CANNON KAD— (FORMER DESIGNATION HS 820)

The Hispano-Suiza designed HS 820 has been one of the most successful 20mm guns ever produced. It has been used in a number of mounts for a variety of tasks by a variety of nations including USA and Germany, and the same mechanism has been adopted for a 30mm gun, the HS 831. The current Oerlikon equivalents are the KAD-AO1, which can have either drum or box magazine feed, and KAD-B which is the general designation of a family of belt-fed weapons. Of this family the KAD-B13-3 and KAD-B17 have right-hand feed and the KAD-B16 left-hand feed; and the B13-3 has an axially-mounted recoil buffer whereas the other two have offset buffers.

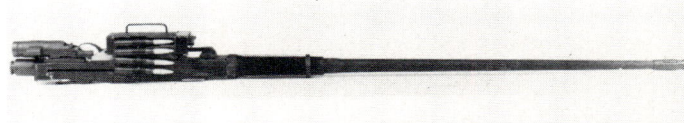

The original Hispano-Suiza HS 820

OPERATION

The gun fires from the open breech position. When the weapon is cocked and ready to fire, the breech block is held to the rear by the sear engaging in the locking piece. When the trigger is operated the bolt is driven onward by the compressed return spring and the feed horn on top of the front face forces the first round out of the magazine and it is guided into the chamber. As the block reaches the end of its travel, the locking piece is forced down by guides on the inside of the receiver and the locking piece drops in front of a locking shoulder in the bottom of the gun. As soon as the locking piece moves down it frees two locking plates which are driven forward by their springs to ride over the locking piece and ensure it cannot rise. The bolt is halted. The locking piece acts as a strut and holds the breech block firmly in place. The firing pin goes forward and the round is fired.

The whole gun recoils as the projectile goes up the bore. After a short travel the shell passes under a gas vent and the gas pressure is used to force back a tappet which pushes the locking plates back off the top of the locking piece. The angles between the locking piece and the locking shoulder are such that once this has happened the locking piece is lifted and the bolt is freed from the receiver. The residual pressure drives back the bolt and the empty case is held to the breech face until it hits the spring loaded ejector and is thrown down out of the gun. The rear end of the breech block strikes the buffer and is thrown forward. If the trigger is still depressed, the cycle is repeated. Release of the trigger allows the buffered sear to rise and hold the bolt to the rear.

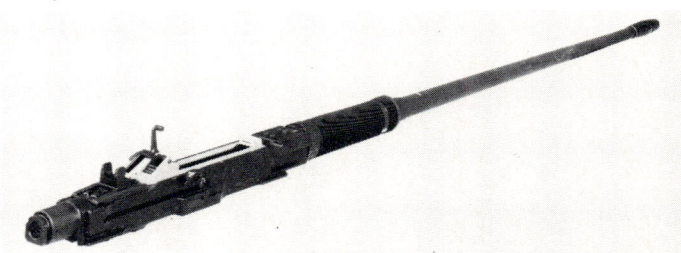

The Oerlikon 20mm cannon type KAD-B13-3. This was formerly designated the HS 820

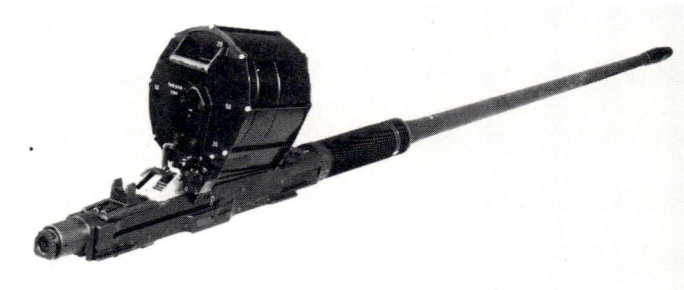

The Oerlikon 20mm cannon type KAD-AO1 with drum magazine

DATA

Cartridge: 20mm
Method of operation: Blowback with a locked breech
Method of locking: Locking piece drops into locking shoulder
Method of feed: 10-round box or 50-round drum (KAD-AO1) or belt (KAD-B)
Method of fire: Selective
Weights:
Gun without magazine or feed mechanism: 61kg (AO1) 57kg (B)
Empty drum/box magazines: 20kg/4.8kg (AO1)
Feed mechanism: 8.5kg(B)
Barrel: 35kg (AO1) 31kg (B)

Lengths:
Total: 2,975mm (AO1) 2,565mm (B)
Barrel: 2,316mm (AO1) 1,906mm (B)
Rifling: 15 grooves RH. 5° (AO1) 7° (B)
Recoil distance: 22mm
Recoil force: 830kp
Muzzle velocity: 1,040-1,050m/sec
Rate of fire: 1,000 rounds/min maximum
Manufacturer: Machine Tool Works Oerlikon Bührle, Zurich
Status: KAD models in production and service. HS820 no longer made but still used

25mm AUTOMATIC CANNON TYPE KBA-B

This gun was based on the 25mm cannon produced by the American firm of Thompson, Ramo, Wooldridge (TRW). The original concept was designed by Eugene Stoner and incorporated the rotating bolt lock which is a feature of his smaller calibre M16 Rifle. The USA weapon was originated in 1964 for the USA Bushmaster trials but was also tested extensively throughout Europe. It was known as the TRW 6425. It was the first gun to incorporate a dual feed system. When the Bushmaster programme was postponed during the Vietnam War the European patent rights were taken up by Oerlikon. Further development work was carried out and the gun was modified from a recoil operated weapon and converted to a gas operated gun.

In the USA the TRW 6425 is being developed by Philco Ford.

OPERATION

The gun fires from the open breech position. The bolt and the bolt carrier are held to the rear in the waiting position and the ammunition is held up to the gun. When the trigger is operated the carrier is driven forward by the compressed return springs. The bolt is mounted in the top of the carrier and pushes the first round out of the belt and into the chamber. When the round is fully home the seven locking lugs on the bolt head have moved forward and lie in front of the locking shoulders in the rear of the barrel extension. A pin on the side of the bolt projects through a cam slot in the bolt carrier and as the carrier continues forward the cam slot forces the pin round and the bolt is rotated around its longitudinal axis and the lugs move in front of the locking shoulders and the breech is secured. The final forward movement of the bolt carrier moves the firing pin against the base of the round and the gun fires. The firing pin cannot reach the cap until locking is completed and so provides mechanical safety before firing.

The gas pressure drives the shell up the bore and also forces back the breech block which pulls the barrel with it for a distance of 25-30mm. The projectile passes the gas port on the underside of the barrel and the short stroke piston is driven back against the front face of the bolt carrier. The bolt

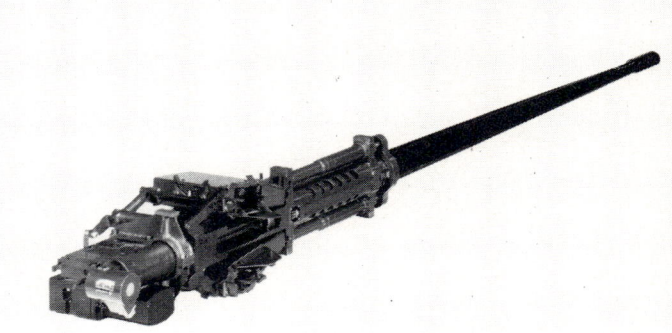

Oerlikon 25mm gun type KBA-CO1

carrier is accelerated away from the recoiling barrel and the cam slot rotates the bolt out of engagement with the barrel extension and carries it to the rear. The residual gas pressure pushes the case out of the chamber and it is held by the extractor until the rear end of the bolt reaches the buffer and the ejector rod is forced forward to rotate the empty case round the extractor and out of the top of the gun. The barrel is returned to the battery position by two buffers, one on each side, made up of belleville washers which store strain energy. The belt feed arrangements are simple and very effective. The two belts are fed up on each side of the receiver and are linked so that when one side is feeding, the other is free. The bolt carrier has a guideway on each side sloping down from front to rear and this causes the feed pawl to move up and down and on the upward stroke the belt is lifted and on the downward movement – as the carrier goes forward – the spring loaded pawl moves down over the next round and positions itself to move the round up on the next recoil stroke. This dual feed system permits a switch from one nature of ammunition to another without having rounds in the feedway which must be fired off first.

DATA
Cartridge:
25mm HEI; HEI-T; SAPHEI; SAPHEI-T; TP; TP-T; APDS-T; APP-T
Method of operation: Gas
Method of locking: Rotating bolt
Method of feed: Dual selective belt
Method of fire: Selective

WEIGHTS
Complete gun: 108kg
Barrel: 37kg

LENGTHS
Gun, overall: 2,806mm
Barrel: 2,173mm
Rifling: 80 calibres (2,000mm)

MECHANICAL FEATURES
Barrel
Regulator: Nil
Rifling: 18 grooves RH. 0° – 7° 30'
Cooling: Air, Quick change

FIRING CHARACTERISTICS
Muzzle velocity: 1,100metres/sec SAPHEI-T; SAPHEI; HEI-T; HEI; TP-T; TP
1,325metres/sec APDS-T; APP-T

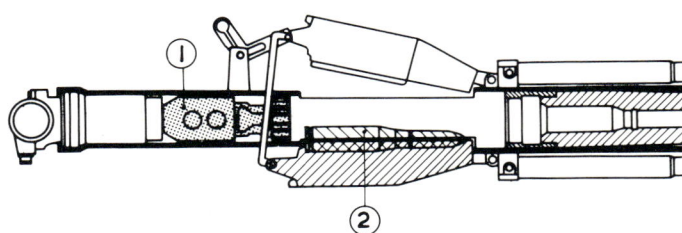

The KBA-B 25mm cannon showing how the feed is switched from one belt to that on the other side: *(1)* Bolt; *(2)* Round in belt

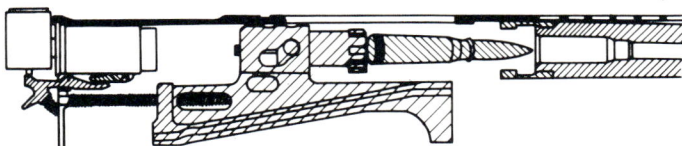

The KBA-B 25mm cannon showing the sloping ramp which controls the belt movement

Muzzle energy: 11,544mkp SAPHEI-T; SAPHEI; HEI-T; HEI; TP-T; TP
Recoil force: 2,500kp
Rate of fire: 570 rounds/min
Manufacturer: Machine Tool Works Oerlikon, Bührle, Zurich
Status: In production and in service

25mm AUTOMATIC CANNON TYPE KBA-CO1

This gun operates in the same way as the KBA-B. It is a gas operated gun with a recoiling barrel to reduce the trunnion pull. It differs from the KBA-B in that it is intended to be used with a ground mount and with such a mount the dual feed takes the ammunition in from the top. A feature of the gun is the greatly reduced recoil forces which are of course essential for a ground mount.

DATA
Cartridge: 25mm HEI; HEI-T; SAPHEI; SAPHEI-T; TP; TP-T; APDS-T; APP-T
Method of operation: Gas
Method of locking: Rotating bolt
Method of feed: Dual selective belt. Feed from above
Method of fire: Selective
Weight: 38kg

LENGTHS
Gun overall: 2,916mm
Barrel: 2,182mm
Width of gun: 272mm
Height of gun: 355mm

MECHANICAL FEATURES
Barrel
Regulator: Nil
Rifling: 18 grooves RH. 7° constant pitch
Cooling: Air. Quick change

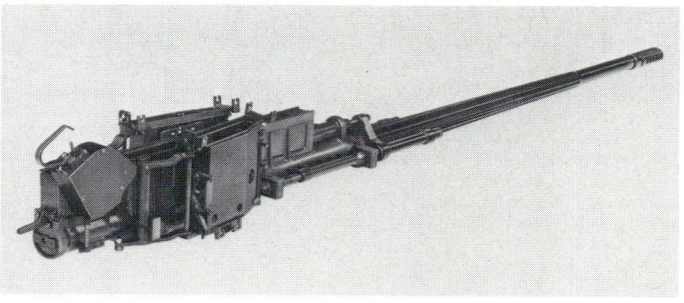

Oerlikon 25mm gun. Type KBA-CO1

FIRING CHARACTERISTICS
Muzzle velocity: 1,100 metres/sec SAPHEI-T; SAPHEI; HEI-T; HEI; TP-T; TP
1,325 metres/sec APDS-T; APP-T
Muzzle energy: 11,544mkp SAPHEI; SAPHEI-T; HEI-T; HEI; TP-T; TP
Recoil force
Maximum rearward: 820kg
Maximum forward: Nil
Rate of fire: 600 rounds/min
Manufacturer: Machine Tool Works Oerlikon Bührle Ltd., CH-8050 Zurich
Status: In production and service

30mm CANNON KCB

The 30mm KCB functions in exactly the same way as the HS 820 20mm gun. It feeds either from a clip feed mechanism containing 8 clips of 5 rounds each or a left-hand or right-hand belt feed mechanism, and fires at 600-650 rds/min.

DATA
Calibre: 30mm
Muzzle velocity of projectile: 1,080m/sec
Rate of fire: 650 rounds/min

Length of bore: 75 calibres
Overall length of weapon: 3,570mm
Length of gun barrel: 2,600mm
Weight of weapon: 136kg
Weight of gun barrel: 61kg
Recoil of weapon: 45mm
Manufacturer: Machine Tool Works Oerlikon Bührle Ltd., CH-8050, Zurich
Status: In production and in service

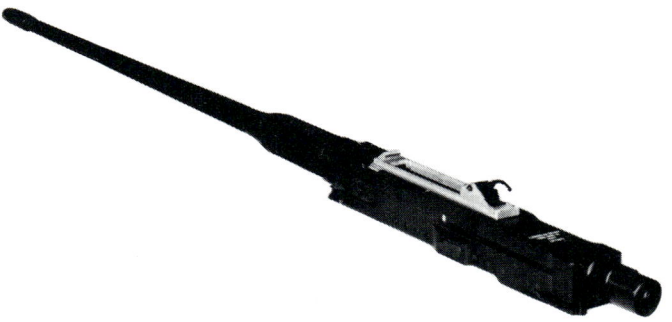

The Oerlikon 30mm cannon type KCB. The former designation was the HS 831

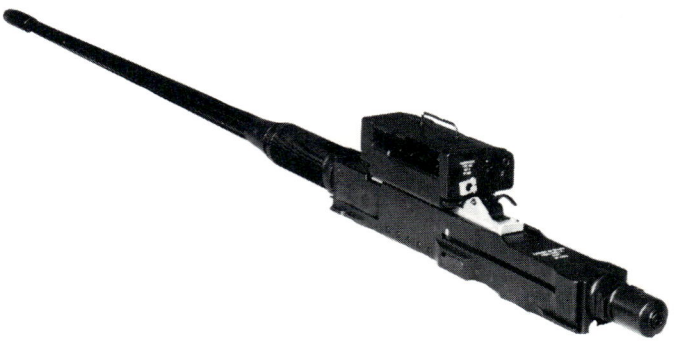

The Oerlikon 30mm cannon type KCB with feeder

UNION OF SOVIET SOCIALIST REPUBLICS

23mm ZU-23 CANNON

The Russian 23mm ZU-23 is a gas operated gun with a vertically moving breech block-locking system which drops to unlock. The breech block is raised and lowered in guideways in the body of the gun and its position is controlled by cams on the piston extension.

OPERATION

The gun stops firing with the working parts held to the rear on the sear. When the trigger is operated and the sear is lowered, the return spring drives the working parts forward. A round is rammed by the separate rammer and extractor through the link and into the chamber. As the piston extension moves forward three diagonal grooves cut across the top surface move a cross feed slide outwards and the feed pawls are retracted. The extractor on the rammer engages the rim of the round in the chamber and the breech block is raised up and pushed slightly forward by the cams on the piston extension raising it in the inclined guideways in the gun body. The firing pin is released during the last 20mm of breech block movement. The piston extension holds the block in position and is prevented from bouncing. The gun fires and some of the propellant gases are diverted through the gas regulator at a point 368mm from the commencement of rifling. The regulator is chromium-plated and has two ports of 3.2mm and 3.4mm diameter. The gases enter the gas cylinder which is also chrome plated. The gas piston (chrome plated) is driven back, and after 10mm of free piston movement the breech block is lowered by cams on the piston extension. The block moves back as it goes down and moves the extractor back to provide primary extraction. As the piston continues back, the extractor withdraws the empty case which is forced down through guides and out of the bottom of the gun. The further movement of the piston draws the feed slide across and the one-piece spring-loaded feed pawl pulls the belt across. The piston extension is checked by the buffer and thrown forward. If the ammunition is depleted a last round lever, operated by the linked round, and connected to the firing mechanism ensures that the last round is left on the feed tray ready for ramming; so that the mechanism need not be re-cocked before a new belt is placed in the feed tray.

The gun can be fed from either side and, to effect the change, only the feed pawl, the 3-tracked cam plate on the piston extension and the retaining pawls have to be changed.

The receiver and feed of the ZU-23 cannon

The ZU-23 twin AA gun

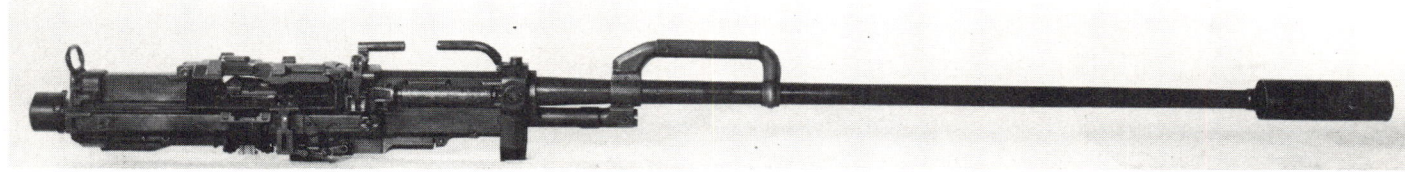

The Zu 23mm cannon

EMPLOYMENT

The ZU-23 is frequently employed in a twin gun system mounted on a light towed carriage.

The towing vehicle is the Russian jeep which provides a good cross country performance. The ZU-23 in the twin gun version is air transportable and air droppable. It is held by one Battery of the AA Battalion in the Motor Rifle Regiment.

DATA

Cartridge: 23mm HEI-T and API-T
Method of operation: Gas
Method of locking: Vertically rising block
Method of feed: Disintegrating link belt
Method of fire: Automatic

WEIGHTS

Gun: 75kg
Barrel with muzzle attachment: 27.2kg
Recoiling parts: 6.14kg

LENGTHS

Gun overall: 2,555mm
Barrel and muzzle attachment: 2,010mm
Barrel: 1,880mm
Receiver: 953mm
Inboard length (front face of feed opening to rear of weapon): 565mm

MECHANICAL FEATURES

Barrel
Regulator: 2 position
Rifling: RH. 10 Grooves increasing over 920mm from 1 turn in 1,150mm to 1 turn in 575mm. Then constant to muzzle
Chamber: Chromium plated. 12 flutes
Cooling: Air. Quick change

FIRING CHARACTERISTICS

Muzzle velocity: 970 metres/sec
Muzzle energy: 9,145mkp
Chamber pressure: 3,100kg/cm²
Rate fof fire: 800-1,000 rounds/min
Maximum range: 2,200 metres

AMMUNITION

Length of round: 236mm
Length of case: 152mm
Nature of case: Steel
Maximum diameter of case (across belt): 34.5mm
Weight of complete round: 6,944 grains (450g)
Weight of propellant: 1,177 grains (76.5g)
Weight of projectile
  HEI-T: 2,908 grains (188.5g)
  API-T: 2,932 grains (190g)
Weight of 50 rounds in belt: 25.5kg
Fuze for HEI-T: Spin actuated. Self destruction after approx. 5sec
Manufacturer: State factories
Status: Widely used in various mountings by Russian, allied and client forces

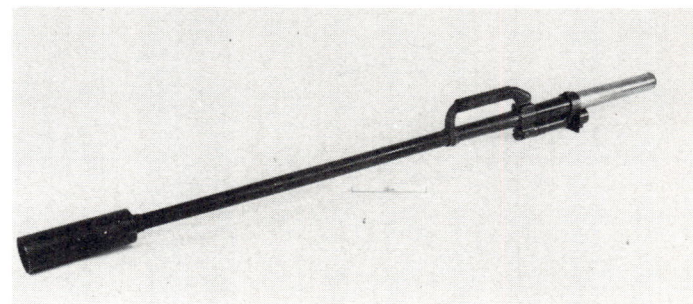

The barrel of the ZU-23

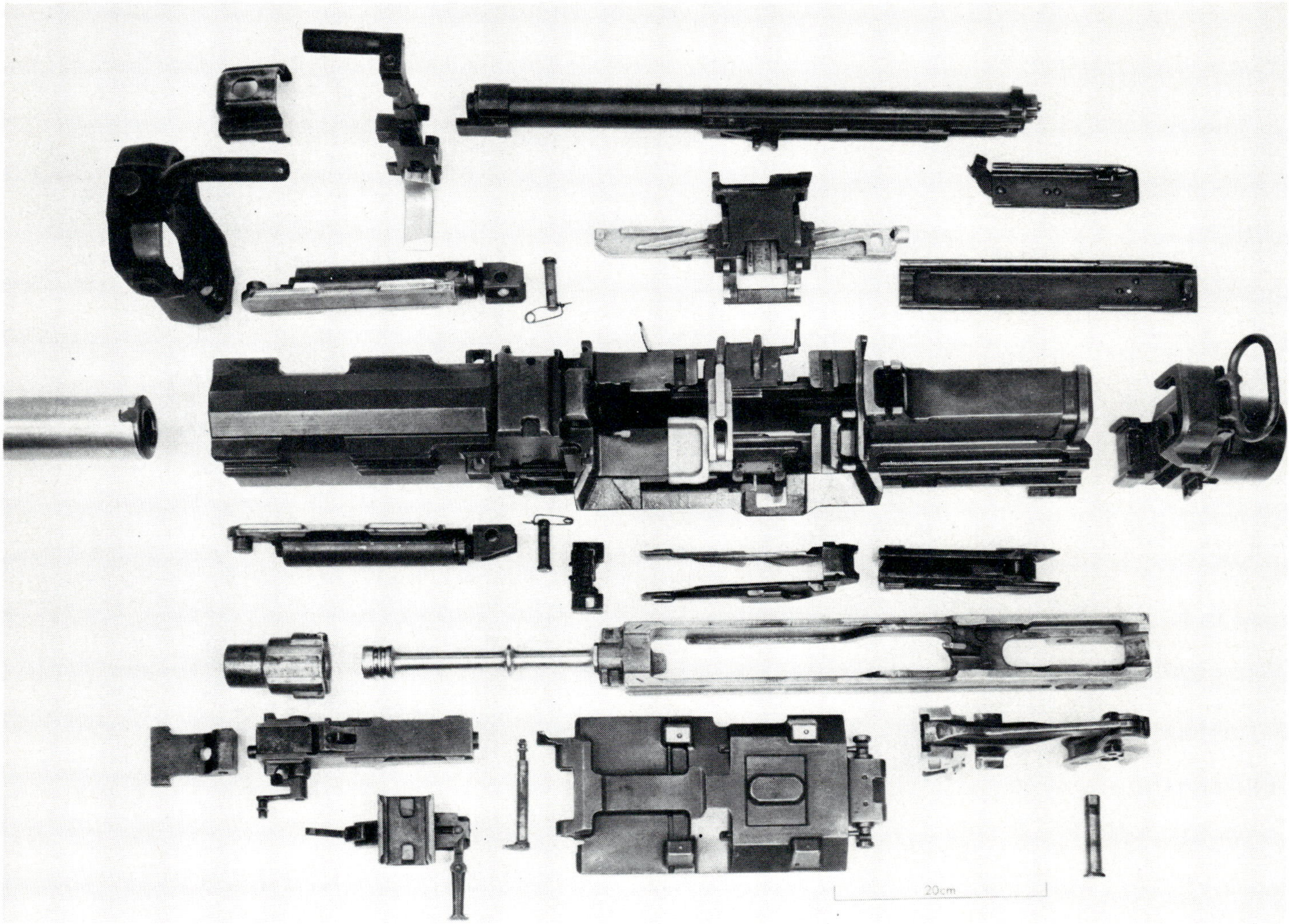

The ZU-23 cannon stripped

UNITED KINGDOM

RARDEN 30mm CANNON (L21A1)

The concept of the Rarden cannon dates from the early 1960s. The initial study concentrated on the defeat of APC's at a range of 1,000 metres and a deterrent effect against low flying and slow flying aircraft. The then current Soviet APC, the BTR-50P, had armour plate 14mm thick sloping back at 45 degrees from the vertical. It was considered that by the time the project came to fruition, the armour plate of comparable vehicles could have been increased to 40mm and it was on this basis that the Rarden calibre was decided. Examination of current weapons and their penetration led to the view that 30mm was the minimum acceptable calibre. The principal requirements influencing the design of the weapon were: (i) accuracy, (ii) low trunnion pull, (iii) short inboard length, (iv) low weight, and (v) low toxicity. The decision was made to design a completely new 30mm gun to meet these requirements with the design work done at the Royal Small Arms Factory at Enfield. The designer was Mr Norman Brint. The name RARDEN derives from the initials of the Royal Armament Research and Development Establishment and Enfield.

The role of the gun was defined, in order of priority, as:

(a) Attack of Armour. This includes destruction of APC's from any angle at 1,000 metres range and penetration of the side armour of the main battle tank.

(b) Attack of soft targets including B vehicles and troops in the open or behind light cover.

(c) Deterrence of low, slow-flying aircraft, including helicopters.

It was decided that a new APDS round would be required for the primary role of the weapon and that this would be designed by RARDE. For the remaining roles it was decided to use the Hispano-Suiza 831L ammunition and the chamber design was based on this round.

The greatest obstacle to the required low trunnion pull and short inboard length was a high rate of fire. A high rate of fire demands that the recoiling parts be rapidly arrested and returned to the run out position as quickly as possible. To do this requires a high trunnion pull and this needs a very heavy mounting. Also a high rate of fire means that the barrel is still vibrating after the previous round and consistency cannot be obtained. The high rate of fire requires a large ammunition supply and this is not possible in a vehicle where space is very limited.

Since the primary requirement was accuracy, however, the weapon was

The 30mm Rarden gun. The handle at the rear cocks the action, the clips are inserted from the back and the empty cases are ejected from the chute on the left. The casing of the gun is sealed and no fumes come into the crew compartment

designed as an automatic, aimed, single-shot weapon which had a resulting automaticity of some 90 rounds/min and a correspondingly low trunnion pull. No attempt was made to degrade the accuracy to achieve a higher rate of fire. To cut down the inboard length it was decided to load from the rear. The requirement for low toxicity was met by arranging for forward external ejection of the empty case and by enclosing the entire gun mechanism.

The final design was a gun operated on a long recoil system with a sliding block to reduce the length behind the breech and clip fed, rear loaded ammunition.

GUN MECHANISM

The gun operates on the long recoil system. When the gun fires, the breech block, breech ring, rammer, barrel, buffer cylinder and recuperator cylinder all move back some 33cm inside the non-recoiling casing, against the buffer, compressing the air in the recuperator.

The breech block remains locked for the first nine inches of recoil and is then opened by a cam attached to the block rolling round a radial wall of twice its own diameter, in the breech ring. This produces a movement of the breech block at right angles to the barrel axis, and at the same time the rammer is drawn down to grip the empty case.

When the recuperator drives the barrel and ring forward, the empty case is left on the rammer at the rear. The breech block is held open. After eight inches of run out, the rammer is rotated to line up with the feed slide which then moves across from right to left pushing the empty case into the ejector way, and moving a live round into the rammer claw.

The final forward movement of the breech ring ejects the empty case from the previous round forward out of the chute, out of the gun. The rammer is rotated to carry the live round down into line with the bore and then forward to feed the round into the chamber. The rammer releases the sliding block which pushes it into a recess in the breech ring. The gun is now ready to fire and the firing hammer is released from the sear by the gunner operating either the firing button or a solenoid.

Mechanical safety before firing is controlled by the breech block which pushes out a safety plunger when it is fully home. This releases the safety sear and leaves the hammer held by the sear. After firing, the free recoil of 23cm ensures that the pressure is down at atmospheric before the breech opens.

The feed mechanism is designed to take two three-round clips. The clip releases the rounds as soon as they are pushed in from the rear. For lightness the gun body is made of cast aluminium alloy in two sections. The bottom casing contains the recoiling masses and the top case houses the feed, firing and cocking mechanisms.

The barrel is of monobloc construction and it is made of high-yield steel,

Rarden mounted on Scimitar Tracked Reconnaissance Vehicle

threaded at the breech end for attachment to the breech ring and at the muzzle for a flash suppressor. A barrel catch engages serrations at the breech end to prevent barrel rotation. The use of high quality steel has produced a very light barrel of only 24.5kg with a length of 244cm. As with all light, long barrels, the paramount problem in obtaining accuracy and consistency is to control the vibration pattern on loading and firing. This is done in the Rarden with a front bearing situated about one quarter of the barrel length from the breech. This slides in the barrel sleeve. The vibrations are damped by four damping pads at the end of the barrel sleeve. Clearance between pads and the barrel is 0.076mm.

Changing the barrel is a simple operation. The flash suppressor is screwed off, the barrel catch is lifted and the barrel screwed out. The breech end is then pushed forward, lifted and then pulled back. The barrel will normally be removed during long, non-operational moves and stowed on the hull of the vehicle.

Application of the gun in British Army service include the Fox armoured car, the Scimitar combat reconnaissance vehicle and some of the AFV 432 APCs. The gun can also be mounted in a two man turret in the US M 113A1. In all these vehicles the gun is compatible with day and night sighting systems including image intensifiers and infra red sights.

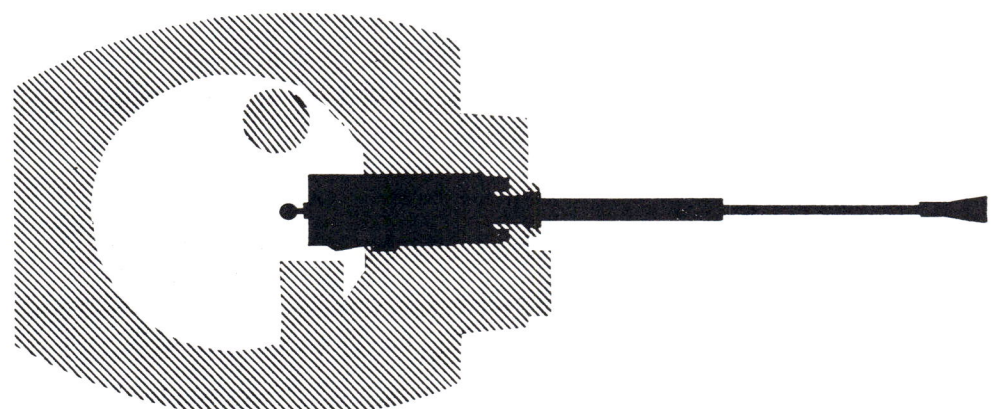

There is a very short inboard length of the gun inside the Fox turret

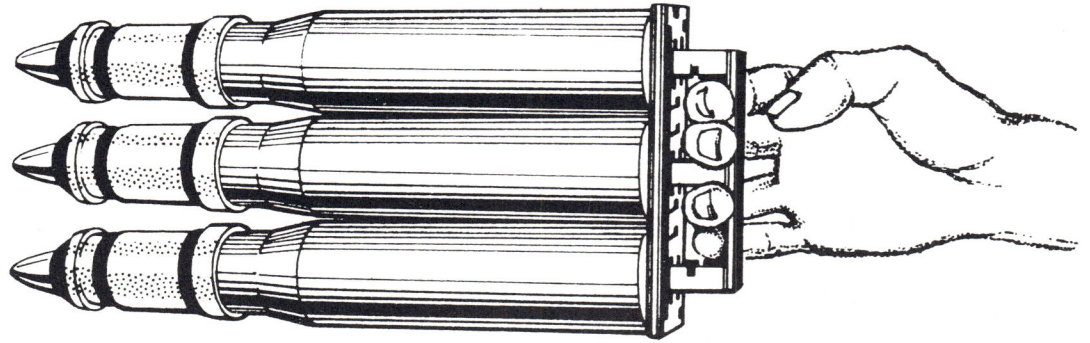

The ammunition is held in clips of three. When the rounds are pushed in, the clip becomes detached

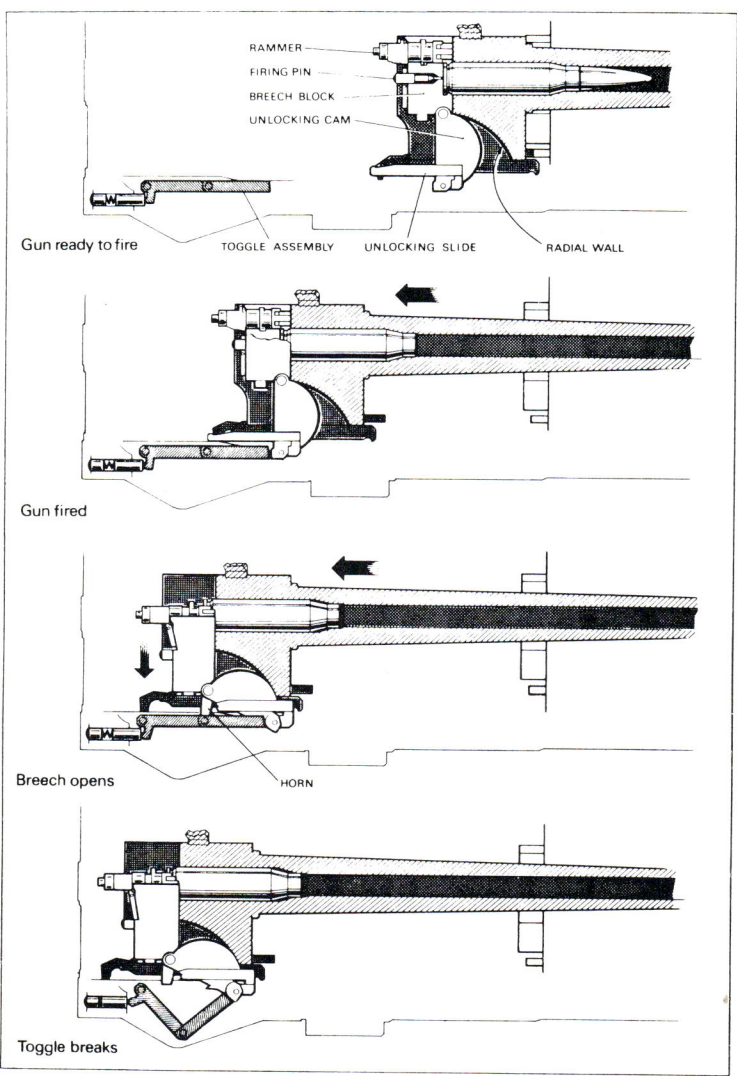

The sequence of events to completion of recoil is shown. Note that when the toggle assembly makes contact with the unlocking slide, the unlocking cam is rotated around the radial wall which moves the block across at right angles to the barrel axis

DATA
(APDS ammunition)
Weight: 95.25kg (approx)
Length: 2.959 metres
Calibre: 30mm
Weight of barrel: 24.5kg
Weight of barrel with flash hider: 26.8kg (approx)
Length of barrel: 2.44 metres

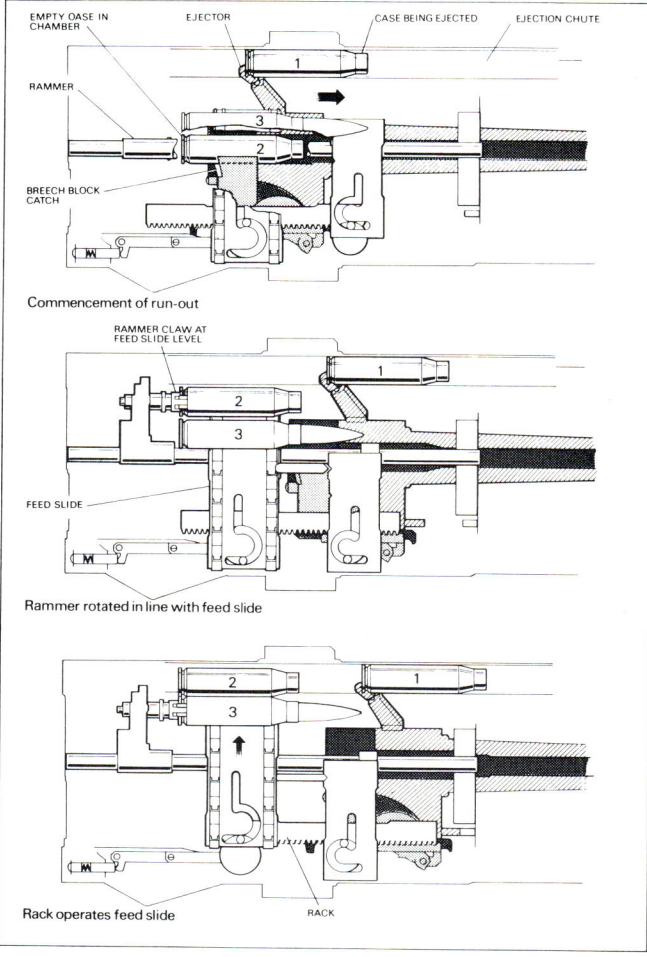

The runout sequence and positioning of the next round for firing

Trunnion pull: 1,360kp
Rifling:
    Number of grooves: 18
    Twist of grooves: 6° RH constant pitch
    Depth of grooves: 0.6mm
    Width of lands: 3.0mm
Weight of complete round: 780g
Weight of projectile: 290g
Weight of three rounds in clip: 2.72kg
Length of complete round: 285.7mm
Weight of projectile: 360g
Manufacturer: Gun. Royal Small Arms Factory, Enfield Lock, Middlesex; Ammunition. British Manufacturing and Research Co., Grantham, Lincs.
Status: In production and in service with the British, Belgian and Nigerian armies

UNITED STATES OF AMERICA

30mm (and 25mm) HUGHES CHAIN GUNS

Developed by Hughes Helicopters and Ordnance Systems, the 30mm XM230 Chain Gun is a single barrel externally powered weapon which incorporates a rotating bolt mechanism driven by a simple chain drive. The gun fires from an open breech and has a variable rate of fire up to 800 rounds a minute.

It was originally intended for the US Army Advanced Attack Helicopter and is now considered to be suitable for use on US Army ground vehicles. The weapon was started as a private venture in January 1973. It was first fired in April 1973 and burst fired in May of that year. A 2,500 round feasibility trial sponsored by the US Army was successfully completed in September 1973 and by December 1973 4,000 rounds had been fired.

Firing trials have since continued through four generations of development models, and by mid-1976 the total had reached 250,000 rounds. Illustrated here are the third ('C') and fourth ('D') development models: the C model is designed for use with linkless ammunition and is the version intended for use with the Advanced Attack Helicopter: the D model is that currently intended as the basis of armoured vehicle applications.

In a chain gun system, since all moving parts are strictly mechanically related, all mechanical operation are closely timed and controlled. It is thus possible to use a single operational cycle without sacrifice of safety and with considerable savings in manufacturing cost. Furthermore, the gun function is independent of ammunition ballistics: this means not only that the rate of fire can be varied at will within wide limits but also that the number of highly stressed components is small: the receiver function is limited to ammunition handling and the receiver itself experiences no loads resulting

from chamber pressure or buffer impacts. This feature also contributes to cost reduction: it also means that the amount of redesign involved in producing a weapon that will fire a more powerful round is quite small.

The basic mechanism provides for either forward or side ejection and is readily modified to incorporate a dual feeder. The bolt lock time is relatively long (up to 20 milliseconds) and this means that gas efflux from the breech is negligible and the risk of a hangfire accident virtually eliminated.

Firing to date has been with XM639 ammunition, one of the WECOM 30 family. Because the US Army is considering a change to the XM788/789 family which will be interoperable with the European 30mm ADEN/DEFA ammunition, Hughes are modifying their design accordingly: this involves a small increase in weapon size over the figures given below for the current ammunition.

Hughes are also currently under contract to develop a 25mm weapon, designated XM242, and 15 prototypes are to be delivered to the US Army by February 1978. At mid-1976 firing was being carried out on a test fixture and the first gun firing was scheduled for late 1976.

DATA (30mm C Model)
Cartridge XM-552/639: 30mm Dual Purpose: Brass, steel and aluminium cases
Method of operation: Externally powered
Method of locking: Rotating bolt
Method of feed: Disintegrating link belt
Method of fire: Fully automatic – variable rate

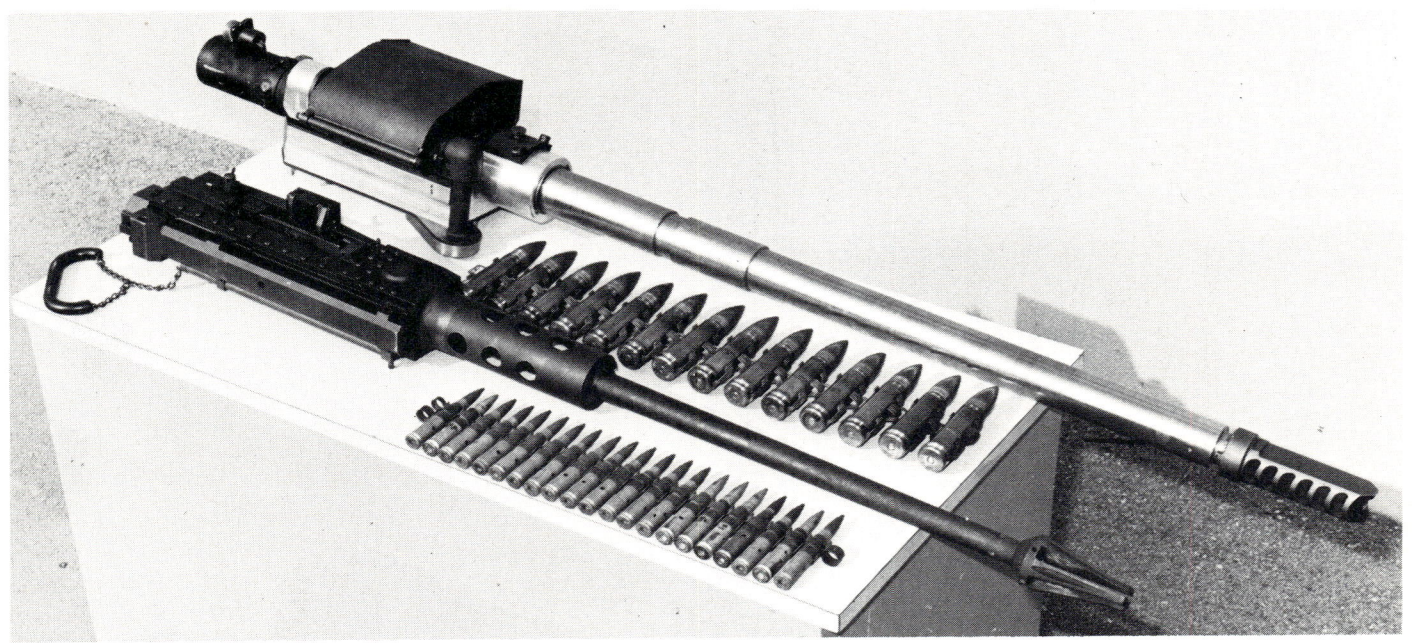

The Hughes Chain gun displayed beside the M85.5in Machine Gun. For a 30mm gun it is remarkably compact

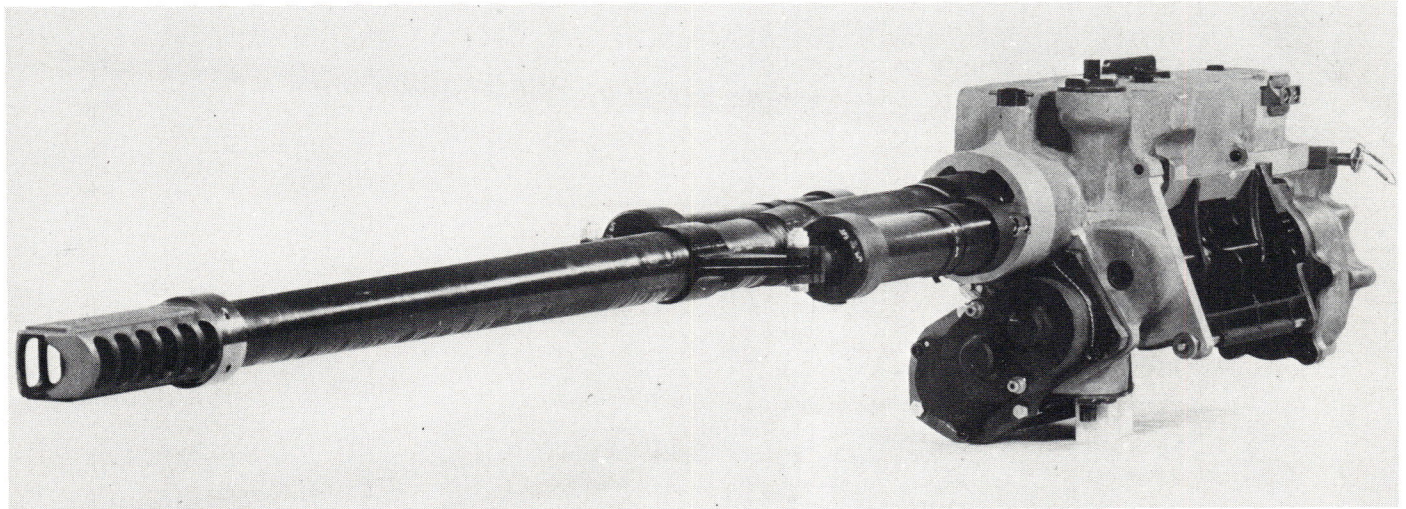

XM230C Chain Gun for linkless ammunition

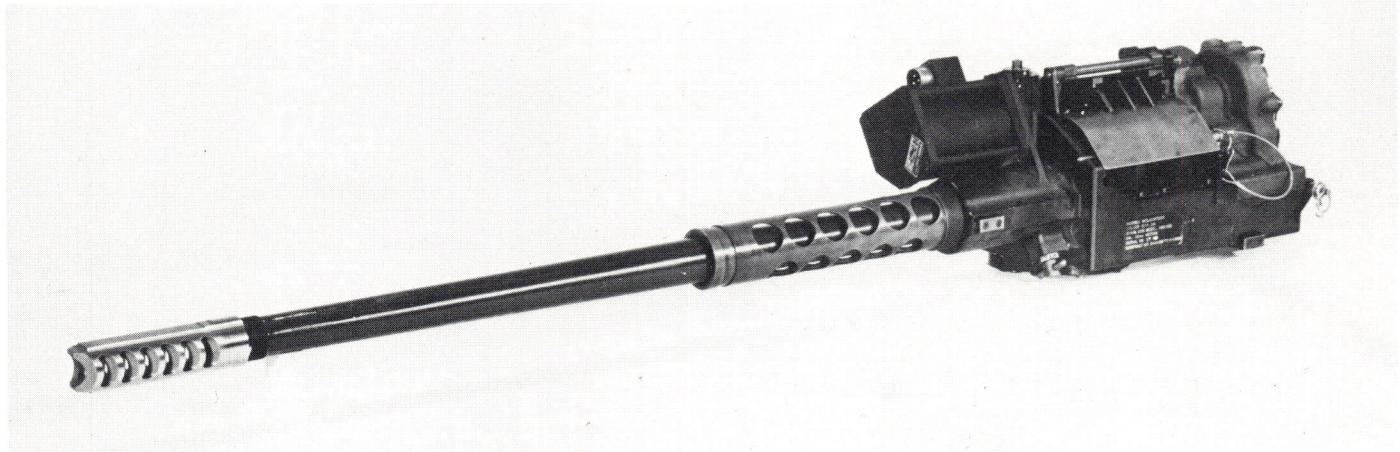

XM230D Chain Gun

WEIGHTS
Barrel: 13.6kg
Gun: 27.2kg

LENGTHS
Barrel: 1,067mm
Gun: 1,600mm
Length behind feed: 136mm
Width: 254mm
Height: 279mm

FIRING CHARACTERISTICS
Muzzle velocity: 671 metres/sec
Rate of fire: 1 – 1-800 rounds/min. Normal rate 620 rounds/min
Maximum effective range: 3,000 metres

MOTOR
Power provided: 5HP
Time to full power: 0.1sec
Manufacturer: Hughes Helicopters and Ordnance Systems, Culver City, California 90230
Status: 30mm at advanced stage of development. See text for details of 25mm weapon programme

20mm (SIX-BARRELLED) M168 GUN

This is a modified form of the M61A1 airborne weapon. Like the M61A1 it is externally powered with a cluster of six barrels. The rate of fire has been modified from 6,000 rounds/minute in the M61A1 and the M168 is capable of firing at 1,000 or 3,000 rounds/minute. The gun is basically a Gatling type mechanism in which each of the six barrels fires only once during each revolution of the barrel cluster. Barrels are attached to the gun rotor by interrupted threads and no headspace adjustment is required. The muzzles are held in a muzzle clamp which allows the dispersion of shot to be spread into a flattened ellipse. The gun rotor rests on bearings inside the stationary outer housing and contains the six gun bolts. As the bolts rotate around the rotor, a cam follower on each bolt follows a stationary cam path fixed to the housing and this causes the bolt to reciprocate and carry out the functions of feeding, chambering, locking, firing, unlocking, and extraction. Since each barrel only fires once for each revolution i.e. 500 rounds/minute/barrel, there is no chance of cook off. Any misfires are thrown out of the gun – and so are hangfires! When the gun stops firing, the bolts are held back and so the chambers are left empty. Alternatively a declutching feeder can be used which permits firing of all ammunition actually in the gun. The gun weights 136kg and the weight of mounting, ammunition etc. varies with the carriage.

Manufacturer: Aircraft Equipment Division, General Electric Co, Burlington, Vermont

Status: In production and in service

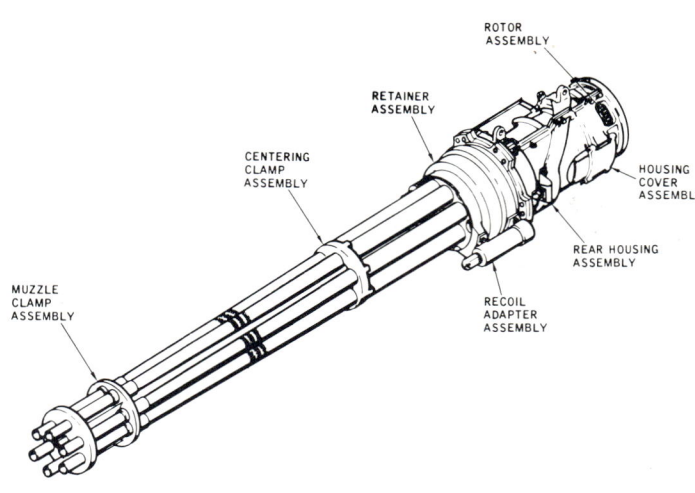

M168 20mm cannon

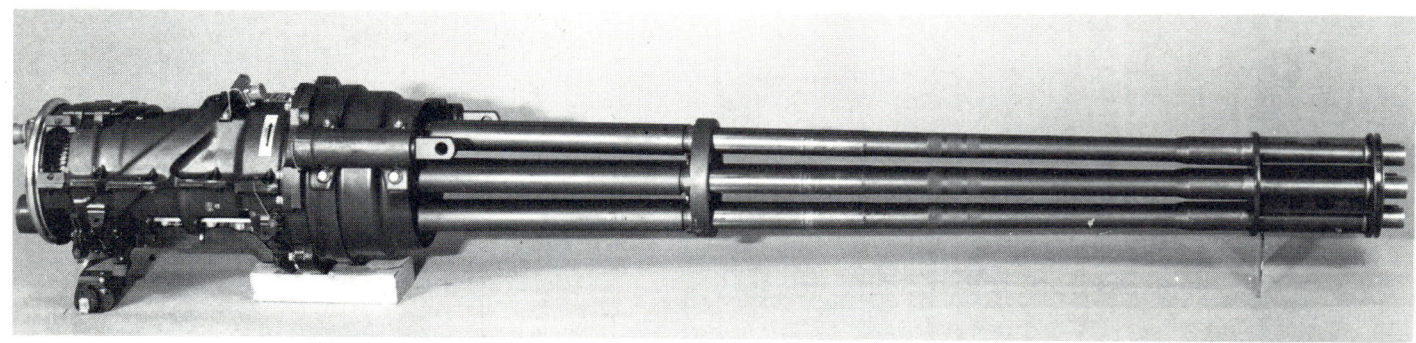

M168 20mm 6 barrelled canon is a modified M61A1 Vulcan gun

20mm GE120 GUN

This is a private venture 20mm gun which is expressly produced to allow use of a variety of types of ammunition and also to employ a dual feed permitting choice of two natures without reloading. To achieve the use of different natures, the barrel must be changed and minor modifications to the feed system are needed. Feed can be from either side. The gun is recoil operated.

DATA	Types of Ammunition		
	HS-820	**Mk100**	**M50**
Length:	2273mm	2108mm	2007mm
Barrel length:	1788mm	1626mm	1524mm
Length from front of feed to rear of gun:	394mm	373mm	368mm
Weight:	49kg	44.5kg	43.5kg
Barrel Weight:	18.1kg	13.6kg	12.7kg

Note: Flash suppressor adds 1.1kg and 152mm

Recoil travel (Receiver): None
Recoil travel (Barrel): 51mm
Overall height: Dual Feed 188mm; Single Feed 160mm
Overall width: Dual Feed 198mm; Single Feed 168mm
Firing rate: 400-700 shots per minute. Selectable firing rates available – using pulse solenoid. Semi-automatic or automatic fire at gunner's option
Ignition: Electric or Percussion
Gun life (excluding barrels): 50,000 rounds (minimum)
Parts replacement: 5,000 rounds (minimum)
Feed system: Link belt feed, dual or single sprocket feed, reversible right or left side
Manufacturer: General Electric Co, Lakeside Avenue, Burlington, Vermont
Status: Prototypes only

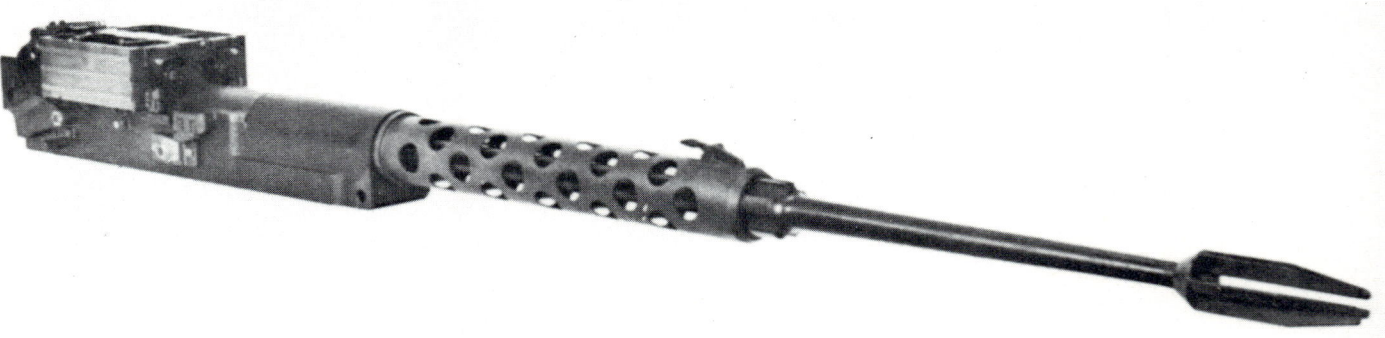

The GE-120 20mm automatic gun

20mm EX-29 GUN

Ex-29 20mm gun. This is the single feed version which can have the belt feeding from either side

The EX-29 is a single-barrelled recoil-operated gun which can fire at a rate of either 250 or 550 rounds/minute with a mechanical rate reducer; alternatively, with a pulsed solenoid, any rate up to 550 rounds/minute can be selected.

The gun is produced with either single or dual feed systems. Using a single feed system the feed can be from either left or right hand. The dual feed is intended to allow rapid and easy change from API to HEI ammunition. The ammunition can be either percussion or electrically fired and it is possible to change from one type to the other in the field.

The gun has been selected by the US Marine Corps as the primary armament on the LVTP-7 amphibious vehicle.

DATA

Gun	Single feeder	Dual feeder
Length	1,930mm	1,892mm
Width	165.1mm	235mm
Height	218mm	218mm
Weight	57.3kg	59.1kg

Gun life: 50,000 rounds
Bore: 20mm
Barrel:
   Length: 1,219mm
   Weight: 13.6kg
Ammunition: M50 series and the MK147; EX-157 – 163 (percussion primed)
Method of operation: Short recoil, modified Browning cycle
Feeder: Sprocket type, uses M14 link
Rate of fire
   Electrically pulsed: Variable to 550 rounds/min
   Mechanical rate reducer: 250 or 550 rounds/min
Muzzle velocity: 1,006ft/sec
Recoil force (on rigid stand): Peak 3,273kp; rms 1,727kp
Power required
Firing Solenoid: 28Vdc – 20amps
Electric Primed Ammunition: 300Vdc – 0.5amps
Manufacturer: General Electric Co, Lakeside Avenue, Burlington, Vermont
Status: Production linked to progress of LVTP-7 programme

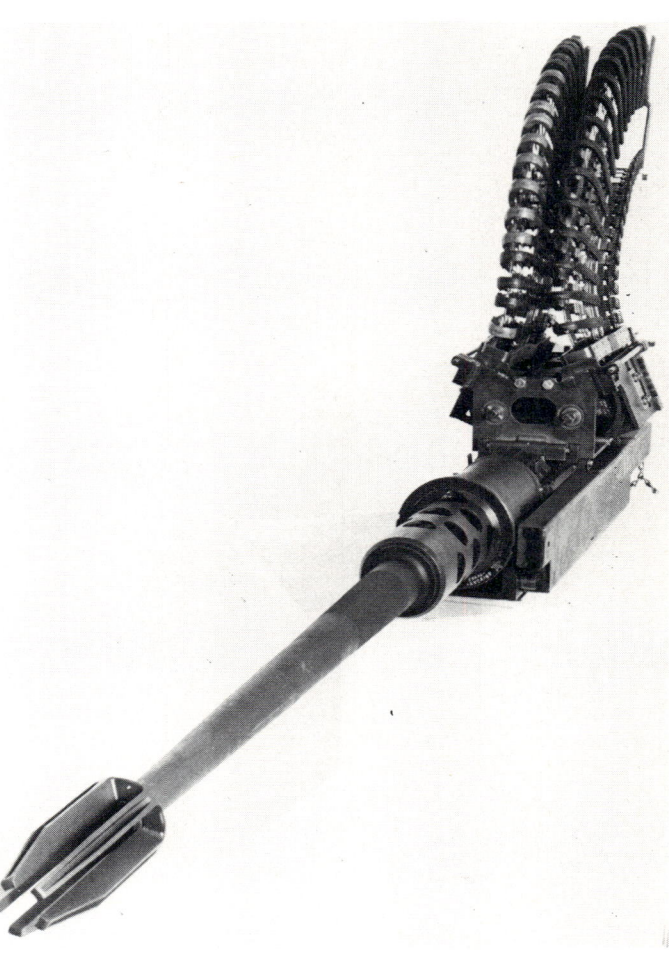

Dual feed EX-29. The gun can be switched quickly from one type of ammunition to another as the tactical situation demands

M197 20mm GUN

The M197, 20mm gun is a three barrel, externally powered, lightweight version of the M61A1 Vulcan gun. It is currently in the US military inventory for use in applications requiring a lightweight, highly reliable gun capable of firing at rates of up to 1,500 shots-per-minute.

The gun operation is based on an externally powered, rotating cluster of barrels. Each barrel has its own bolt which sequentially rams, locks, fires, unlocks, and extracts rounds during one revolution of the barrel cluster. The barrels are installed in the gun rotor with a ⅓ twist; no head space adjustment is necessary. The gun rotor rotates within a stationary gun housing which contains the main cam. The bolts, which slide within tracks on the gun rotor, are driven fore and aft by the controlling action of the main cam. Each barrel fires only once during each revolution of the gun rotor. This reduced rate for each barrel contributes to a long weapon life and high reliability.

A total peak recoil load of less than 2,600 pounds allows the weapon to be mounted in many configurations including turret, pod and pintle.

The gun fires standard M50 series ammunition. It is at present used only in the air application but can form the basis of a lightweight infantry anti-aircraft system.

The M197 20mm gun is a three barrelled version of the M61A1 Vulcan. It is light and reliable

DATA
Gun (Including Delinking Feeder)
   Length: 1,829mm
   Width: 405mm
   Height: 342mm
   Weight: 66.5kg
Number of barrels: 3
Gun Life: 75,000rds
Calibre: 20mm
Barrel
   Length: 1,524mm
   Weight: 8.18kg
Barrel Life (per set of 3): 15,000rds

Ammunition: 20mm M50 series
Method of operation: Externally powered; Gatling type
Feed system: Linked or linkless
Rate of fire: 400-1,500 rounds/min
Muzzle velocity: 1,030 metres/sec
Average recoil force: 681.8kp at 1,500 rounds/min
Power required: 3hp at 1,500 rounds/min
Reliability: 30,000 minimum rounds before failure
Manufacturer: General Electric Co, Lakeside Avenue, Burlington, Vermont
Status: In production for the USMC and for Iranian and Korean forces in airborne applications

30mm XM-188 GUN

This 30mm, three-barrel gun is a Gatling-type weapon much like the 6-barrel, 20mm Vulcan Gun currently in production. A cluster of three barrels rotates on bearings within a fixed housing. The barrels are retained in a rotor assembly which carries a bolt for each barrel. Interaction of bolt guide rollers with an internal cam in the housing provides the reciprocating action to ram and extract the cartridges. A rotary cam on the rotor cocks the firing pin spring and fires the rounds. A drop lock secures the bolts for firing.

The gun fires the XM552 HEDP round and is designed to fire at a nominal firing rate of 2,000 shots per minute, but is capable of rates as low as 400 shots per minute.

The gun feeder, which mounts on the housing, strips the links from the ammunition belt and feeds rounds into position on the rotor. The feeder incorporates a de-clutching feature which assures a cleared gun at the end of each burst. A linkless feeder is also available.

A single firing-pin spring, mounted on the housing cover, supplies the energy for firing the percussion primers. A manually-operated safety lever provides a positive safety feature by unloading the firing pin spring.

Power for the gun, supplied from external sources, is either hydraulic or electric (ac or dc). The drivers are interchangeable on the basic gun without modification. The gun can be completely disassembled for field maintenance without the use of special tools.

DATA
Number of barrels: 3
Barrel length: 1,067 or 1,372mm (Gain Twist Rifling)
Firing rate: Variable up to 2,000/min
Weight: 42.9kg (with 1,067mm barrels, less drive and feeder)
       44.7kg (with 1,372mm barrels, less drive and feeder)
Length: 1,473mm (with 1,067mm barrels)
Width: 473mm
Height: 305mm with electric drive
Drives: Electric (AC or DC), or Hydraulic; Mutually interchangeable on basic gun
Average recoil force: 636kp at 2,000 rounds/min
Peak recoil force: 1,182kp at 2,000 rounds/min
Feeder: Side stripping or linkless, declutch clearing
Accuracy: 80% circle 8 mils
Round: XM-552, 30mm HEDP Round
Muzzle velocity: 671 metres/sec
Firing impulse: 19kg sec/round
Chamber Pressure: 2,103kg/cm² approx
Manufacturer: General Electric Co, Lakeside Avenue, Burlington, Vermont
Status: Selected by Bell Helicopter for their YAH-63 AAH helicopter. The gun is in advanced development

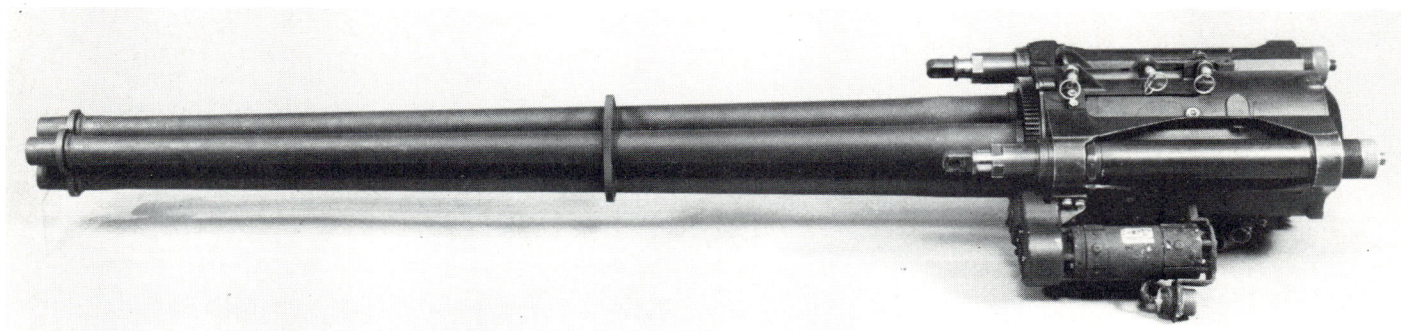

The XM188 30mm cannon is designed to fire up to 2,000 rounds a minute.

GUN, AUTOMATIC, 20mm M139

This is the US copy of what was formerly known as the Hispano Suiza HS820. Details of the gun are given in the section on Swiss guns.

DATA
Calibre: 20mm
Muzzle velocity: 1,050 metres/sec
Rate of fire: 960 rounds/min
Weight without feeder: 57kg
Maximum rearward force: 830kp
Maximum forward force: 800kp

Recoil distance: 16-22mm
Barrel
No of grooves: 15
Direction of rifling: RH
Twist: 5° constant
Weight: 32kg
Life: 10,000 rounds
Manufactuer: US Arsenals
Status: In service

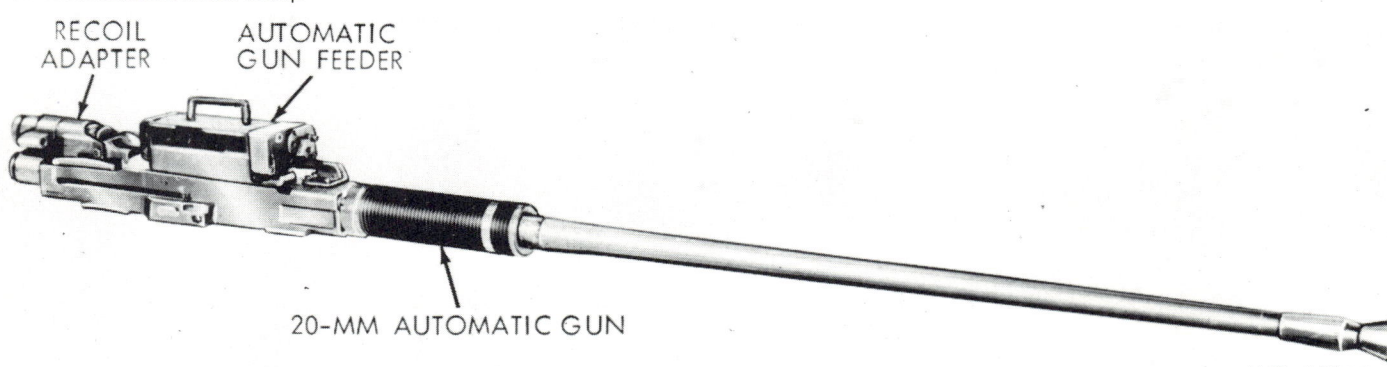

M139 20mm automatic gun

AMMUNITION

FOR SMALL ARMS AND OTHER WEAPONS
UP TO 35 MILLIMETRE CALIBRE

SMALL-ARMS AMMUNITION

Metallic centre-fire military ammunition dates, in general, from the 1860-1870 period, by the end of which decade most armies had adopted, even if only on a limited scale, breech-loading infantry arms. Initially, for these breech-loading arms, black powder propellant and lead projectiles were universal, with calibres generally around 11mm to 12mm following the pattern established by the muzzle loading rifles which preceded these breech-loaders. The ballistics of all these rifles followed a well established pattern, the requirement being for the fairly heavy lead bullet having good ranging properties to be propelled long distances. Since fighting ranges for infantry at this time were well in excess of 1,000 metres, and since the black powder propellant imposed a low muzzle velocity, the bullets described a high trajectory. Correct weapon sighting was of paramount importance and volley firing was widely accepted as a means of achieving satisfactory target effect.

With the introduction of smokeless powder in the mid-1880s, there was a move, originating largely in France and Switzerland, towards jacketed projectiles of reduced calibre. These reduced-calibre bullets, then often called "composite" bullets, were mostly between 7mm and 8mm calibre, and their adoption was completed, in most parts of the world, by about 1900. By that time most of the major powers had selected the basic rifle calibres that were to remain standard, for the countries concerned, for the next 40 years or so.

The reduction in calibre was accompanied, largely through the medium of the new smokeless propellants, by significant increases in velocity, from a norm of about 380 metres per second for 11mm black powder cartridges, to about 760 to 850 metres per second with the 7mm to 8mm range of cartridges. This increase in velocities resulted in flatter trajectories and a corresponding effectiveness in terms of the "dangerous space", within which an unprotected man was vulnerable to fire. Sighting errors, because of the low trajectory, became far less important. The smokeless propellant played a further part in changing infantry tactics by eliminating the masses of tell-tale smoke which hitherto had indicated the firers' position, and which, in addition, had sometimes obscured vision and rendered fire control difficult. All this, together with the advent of the rifle-calibre machine gun, changed the nature of infantry warfare, a fact not fully comprehended until 1914.

The Inter-War Years

Small arms ammunition development between 1918 and 1939 did little to alter the basic design of the rifle cartridges of the major powers, most of whom entered the 1939-1945 war with the same rifle cartridges as they had been equipped with in 1900. Of the major powers, Russia, France and the United Kingdom tended to use the rimmed cartridge case, which was far from ideal for feeding in automatic weapons, while Germany, Italy, Japan and the United States favoured rimless cartridges for most of their infantry rifle calibre weapons.

In three other areas, however, the inter-war years did result in changes of calibre and tactics. These areas were heavy machine guns; anti-tank rifles; and sub-machine guns.

Large calibre machine guns were adopted by most major powers between the wars. Such weapons were often first specified for aircraft or tank use; but their potential as anti-aircraft or anti-armour weapons was soon appreciated by infantry. Large calibre machine guns tended to be of calibre 0.5in (12.7mm) or close thereto.

Anti-tank rifles were developed in parallel with these large calibre machine guns, but whereas the machine guns were used by specialised units or sub units, the anti-tank rifles were usually intended for use with normal infantry rifle platoons or equivalent sub units. These anti-tank rifles were usually of calibre 12.7mm to 14.5mm calibre, and trace their lineage back to the 13mm anti-tank rifle developed and used by Germany late in the 1914-1918 war. During and just prior to the 1939-1945 war, various countries experimented with large capacity anti-tank rifle cases, necked to take the standard rifle calibre bullet, believing that ultra-high velocity was the key to armour penetration.

Sub-machine guns were first adopted for infantry by Germany late in the 1914-1918 war, when the 9mm Bergmann was taken into service. Germany, Russia, and later the United States became the chief proponents of such weapons, which later spread into universal service. With few exceptions, these weapons were chambered for the 7.62mm Tokarev cartridge, the 9mm Parabellum cartridge or the 0.45in A.C.P. cartridge.

The 1939-1945 war saw changes in infantry tactics, including a reduction in fighting ranges, widely accepted by the war's end as being about 400 metres maximum (the range at which a rifleman could see, identify and hit his opponent). Coupled with this was the widespread desire to see infantrymen armed with automatic or semi-automatic rifles. Prior to the war, only the USA had adopted such a rifle as standard, although the USSR equipped certain units and individuals with equivalent rifles during the war, and Germany, later in the war, adopted the new 7.92mm Sturmgewehr (MP 44). This weapon greatly influenced post-war cartridge development, since it fired a new, short case 7.92mm cartridge of intermediate power.

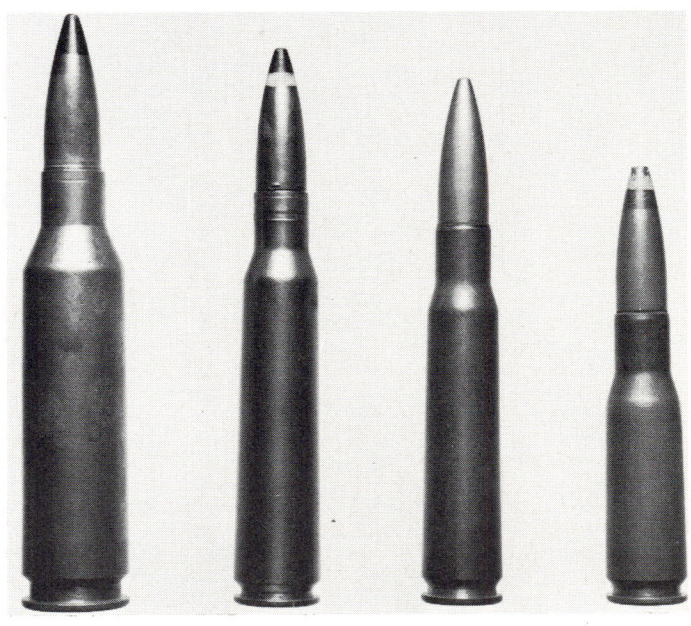

Some larger types of small-arms ammunition. **Left to right:** *14.5mm, USSR; 12.7mm, USSR; 12.7mm (.50in) Browning, USA; .50in Spotter, T48A1, USA*

Apart from the obvious saving of raw material and reduction in the soldier's burden, this cartridge had the advantage of enabling the rifle to be fired at full automatic, effectively, out to full fighting ranges, something impossible either with rifles firing normal full power rifle cartridges or with sub-machine guns. Weapon designers saw, in intermediate power, short cased cartridges, the means to develop whole new families of infantry weapons, and most post 1945 cartridge development reflected this German design. It would however be wrong to credit the Germans with having been the only nation to tread this path during the war, since the USSR also developed a new intermediate power cartridge in 1943. The difference perhaps was that Germany used the 7.92mm "Kurz" cartridge extensively during the last two years of the war, whereas the Russians hardly used their Model 1943, 7.62mm, cartridge during the war at all, largely because the new weapons designed to fire the cartridge were insufficiently developed at the time.

In the five years following the 1939-1945 war, Switzerland, France, Spain, Czechoslovakia, the United States and the United Kingdom all developed new, intermediate-powered short cartridges, for use in new self-loading rifles, and light machine guns. Most armies wished to reduce the number of cartridge types in use within the infantry battalion and, in some instances at least, it was the intention that the new cartridge be used in the rifle, light machine gun and sub-machine gun role and, if possible, in the medium machine gun role also. Nowhere has this ideal been achieved in practice: the nearest approach has been made by the armies of the Warsaw Pact.

Post 1945 Assault Rifle cartridges, main developments. **Left to right:** *7.92mm MP 43, German; .280in (7mm), UK; 7mm High Velocity, UK; 7.65mm, French; 7.5mm, Czech Model 1950; 7.5mm, Swiss; 7.92mm CETME, Spain*

The post-1945 developments referred to led to the adoption, by the Western-oriented political/military treaty organisations (NATO, CENTO, and SEATO) of a new rifle calibre cartridge, in 7.62mm calibre, for use in rifles and machine guns (light and medium). This cartridge is generally referred to as the "7.62mm NATO" or "7.62mm × 51mm" cartridge, and has also been adopted by a large number of countries elsewhere. The decision to adopt this cartridge as the NATO standard was and remains controversial. So far as can be determined, the balance of expert opinion was heavily in favour of a less powerful cartridge and a smaller calibre; and it seems that it was mainly high-level pressure in the USA that secured the adoption of the 7.62mm round.

The Warsaw Pact Armies, together with the armies of the People's Republic of China and its satellites, have all adopted, as standard, the Russian model 1943 cartridge in 7.62mm calibre, also known generally as the "7.62mm × 39mm" cartridge. This cartridge has also been adopted by several other countries.

After 1945, and before the adoption on a wide scale of the two 7.62mm cartridges just discussed, many of the armies of the world were re-equipped with the existing arms and ammunition of the USSR the USA and the UK. For this reason the old basic rifle and pistol cartridges of these powers, the 7.62mm × 54 (USSR) 7.62mm Tokarev (USSR), .30in-06 (USA) .30in. Carbine (USA) .45in. ACP (USA) .303in. (UK) and .380in (UK), are found in all corners of the globe, often locally manufactured, but also imported from either the original country of origin, or from one of the major ammunition producing countries.

The adoption by much of the world of one of the three basic case types (the third being the 5.56mm × 45, covered in detail later) by no means represents the end of current cartridge development. Increasing efforts have been made, particularly in the United States, to increase hit probability and wound effect. This originally led to the development programmes of "Salvo", "Flechette", and "Salvo Squeezebore" and indirectly to the 5.56mm Armalite development, and more recently into research on "micro-calibres" – small calibres down to about 3mm, with cases of size and capacity less than those of the 5.56mm Armalite case. These recent developments have been carried out not only in the United States, but also in most West European countries.

Project Salvo

This US project originated in 1952, and is an important factor in the appreciation of the then current US search for a more effective rifle cartridge. From Salvo sprang the later 5.56mm M.16 rifle programme.

Approaching the basic problem of how, when, where and why infantry suffered casualties, the US made an exhaustive analysis of a large number of their own casualty reports. This study influenced thought both on weapon and ammunition design and on infantry tactics. The random nature of hits on human targets that was shown by the US analysis, led to the conclusion that hits were as often as not the result of unaimed fire. It was also widely accepted that, for each bullet hitting a target, considerable expenditure of ammunition had taken place. All this cast doubts upon the traditional belief in the need for a high precision rifle, since the precision inherent in most military rifles, was, apparently, rarely used effectively, and certainly not beyond a hundred metres range or so. The US investigation concluded that an infantry weapon capable of dispersing its shots would neutralise human error, and significantly increase the hit ratio out to normal maximum infantry fighting ranges of 300 to 400 metres. This concept was contrary to the then current US ordnance programme for a high velocity, long range, selective fire self-loading rifle, using a full power large calibre conventional cartridge. Nevertheless the Salvo project went ahead, the project specification requiring that –

(1) for each trigger pull a salvo of small, high velocity, projectiles be fired;
(2) the projectiles describe a circular pattern on the target;
(3) all the projectiles be lethal at 400 metres; and
(4) the salvo have enough projectiles to secure one hit, at least, on a man sized target at ranges up to 400 metres.

The Salvo programme covered cartridges up to .30in calibre, fired from weapons designed to give dispersed shots, fired in rapid succession or simultaneously. Dispersion was achieved in a variety of ways, by multi-barrelled weapons, by single barrelled weapons with muzzle adaptors, and by cartridges firing more than one projectile.

Salvo was carried out over a period of several years, and many of the weapons involved were chambered for high velocity .22in cartridges. It was the high effectiveness of this type of cartridge that led to further US interest in this calibre, and this interest culminated in the .223in (5.56mm) series of weapons and cartridges. Apart from high velocity .22in ammunition, the Salvo trials included duplex and triplex ammunition in .30in or 7.62mm calibre. As the name suggests, duplex cartridges contained two bullets in tandem, and triplex thee bullets in tandem. There was nothing new in this idea, duplex cartridges in .303in calibre having been tested in the UK and USA in the early 1900s while Greener triplex .303in ammunition was tested in the UK in 1918.

To begin with, .30in (.30in-06) cases with elongated necks, giving a case length of 74mm, were used for both duplex and triplex loadings, the necks being considered necessary to hold the lower bullets, but the later T.107 duplex round successfully utilised the standard .30in-06 case, which was also subsequently used for triplex. The bullets for the .30in duplex and triplex were of short, conical shape, the bullets touching, head to tail. The long necked .30in case was also necked down to .22in calibre, and triplex loaded.

7.62mm NATO cases were also used in these Salvo experiments, duplex loadings both with conical bullets and with bullets of conventional contour being produced. The best known of these, the T.314E3 duplex, was later standardised in the US Army, as the M.198. This cartridge, with a standard 7.62mm × 51mm case, was loaded with two 80-grain (5.2g) bullets of conventional ogive, both flat based, but with the rear bullet's base being canted at an angle of 9 degrees. The velocity of the leading bullet at 25 metres was 850 metres per second and that of the second bullet 790 metres per second. The canting of the second bullet's base gave controlled dispersion. The canted base of the rear bullet was a feature common to most of the duplex loadings in the Salvo project.

Later in the Salvo programme, special 6.35mm single ball and duplex ammunition was manufactured by Frankford Arsenal (FA-T 124 and FA-T 127). Made in 1959, the rimless cases were 52.6mm long, and the bullets of both types weighed 70 grains (4.5g) each. In the same year, Winchester also provided .25in or 6.35mm ammunition for the Salvo project. The Winchester ammunition employed rimless cases 47.6mm long, and the bullets for both the single ball and duplex versions weighed 68 grains (4.4g). The simplex version was designated the FA-T 115 and the duplex was FA-T 116. The duplex version, like the previously mentioned FA-T 127 and the 7.62mm M.198 duplex were identified by green bullet tips.

Included in the Salvo project were single flechette and multi-flechette cartridges as well as flechette "shot" cartridges. These flechettes, discussed in detail later, were felt to show much promise and be worthy of extra development.

Salvo Squeezebore (SSB)

In 1962, the Salvo project was halted and in the same year Salvo Squeezebore (SSB) came into the picture. Because of the priority then being given to flechettes, however, SSB tended to be overlooked.

Salvo Squeezebore, although that was not his name for it, had in fact been invented, in 1948, by Russell S. Robinson, a New Zealander, who was at that time working as a consultant to the UK Ministry of Supply at Fort Halstead. His original work was done on a larger calibre – 20mm squeezed to 0.5in – and lack of obvious application caused him to shelve the idea although he had found it to work reliably. It was only when, in 1961, while working with the USAF, he heard of the US Army's Salvo project that he applied his original idea to small-arms calibres and found that it worked well.

SSB bullets were cone shaped, hollow projectiles, in tandem, head-to-tail, enclosed usually in plastic, and held in the case neck. These cartridges were fired through taper barrels, the tapering being achieved in different ways. The barrel could be of normal type with the front portion merging into a smooth bored tapered section. A refinement on this was to have a further cylindrical rifled portion forward of the tapered portion. The third method, and the one bestowing most flexibility on the rifle, was that in which the tapered portion was a removable extension that could be screwed onto any weapon, thereby giving SSB capability to that weapon.

The reducing calibre, or tapered barrel, causes the cone shaped, hollow metal bullets to be swaged into a longer form, in the reduced calibre, the cross-sectional area of the bullet being reduced to about one quarter of its original value in the process. It was found that only a little of the velocity of the bullets was lost in the swaging process, but it was found that the front bullets travelled faster than those following, a fact that could be compensated for by increasing the weight of the front bullet.

Between two and eight bullets per cartridge were successfully fired under trial conditions, in the United States, although in fully developed ammunition the number usually ranged between three and five. Depending on the requirement, the SSB ammunition offered a fair amount of choice. A greater number of bullets of light weight gave a shorter lethal range but a greater hit probability. Fewer but heavier bullets gave increased range, while for very long range a single squeezebore bullet could be used. This last arrangement, however, ceased to be a salvo system and was essentially similar to many single-projectile squeezebore arrangements reaching back to the work done on tapered barrel systems by Janacek, Gerlich and others which had formed the basis of many studies and trials in Britain, France, Germany, the United States and other countries before and during the 1939-45 war.

Initial faults to do with excessive bullet dispersion and the fragility of the forward bullet in automatic feeding weapons were overcome by 1965, as was the problem of excess wear to the tapered portion of the barrel.

Salvo Squeezebore was publicly tested first in 1962, when .50 to .30in (.50in, bullets swaged in firing down to .30in calibre) and .30 to .15in cartridges were successfully fired. Over the next five years a number of other SSB cartridges were developed, but funds were not made available for the programme to be fully pressed home. Nonetheless, in 1967 the United States Navy, who were responsible for riverine operations in support of the Army in Vietnam, invested in .50 to .30in and used SSB machine guns in such operations. As was pointed out at the time, SSB gave .50in calibre machine guns, with a normal rate of fire of 600 rounds/min, a capability of 3,000 shots/min.

Representative SSB cartridges had the following make up:
(1) .50 to .30in cartridge, with five projectiles each weighing 140 grains (9g). Velocity of front bullet 930 metres/second;
(2) .30 to 15in cartridge (7.62mm × 51 case) with three bullets each weighing 20 grains (1.3g). Velocity of front bullet 1,220 metres/second;
(3) .45 to .38in pistol (Colt) with three bullets each weighing 80 grains (5.2g).

Salvo Squeezebore arrived on the scene at an unfortunate time, was overshadowed by Flechette, and finally died as an infantry project. It is, however, currently being considered for use in the 0.5in secondary armament of AFV – the idea being to offer the gunner a choice of salvo squeezebore or single squeezebore projectiles.

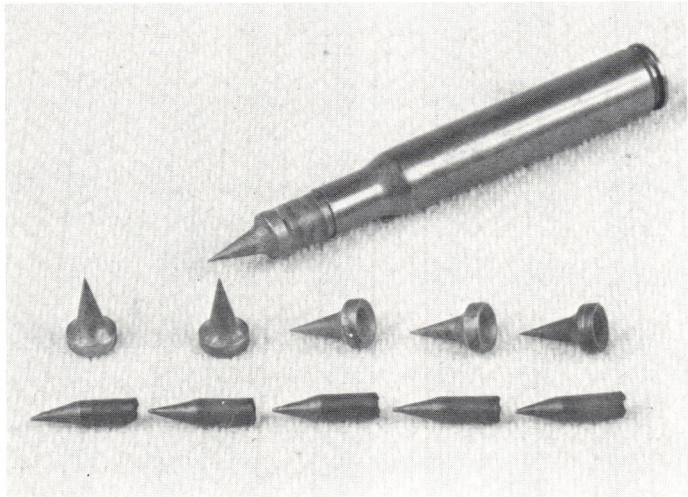

Salvo Squeezebore cartridge shown with bullets before and after firing (Russell S. Robinson)

SPIW Flechette

Deriving from the Salvo project, the SPIW (Special Purpose Individual Weapon) project was launched late in 1962. SPIW, like Salvo, was a United States concept and was based on the replacement of the conventional projectile by one embodying a 'flechette'. Although the project itself dates from 1962, Aircraft Armaments Inc. (AAI) had tried an experimental single flechette as early as 1959. This had been fired in a modified Model 70 Winchester rifle, having a smooth-bore barrel and muzzle stripper. Prior to this, in 1957, AAI had produced "shotshell" multiple flechettes based on 12 gauge shotgun cartridges.

Flechette ammunition, as the name implies, was ammunition in which a dart or arrow took the place of the conventional bullet. The flechette was of small diameter and weight, and was designed to be fired at very high velocity. At shortish ranges the combination of projectile length and weight and high velocity, gave the flechette a wound effect of a very high order, the flechette being unstable and tumbling upon impact. The flechette was intended, as far as the single flechette cartridge was concerned, to be fired at high rates of fire, controlled as to length of burst by an automatic setting on the weapon. The flechette therefore satisfied one of the original Salvo requirements by giving projectile dispersion at the target. It was appreciated, however, that flechette cartridges were not "maids-of-all-work" and that conventional ammunition would be required to meet some infantry needs.

In fact, and in spite of its early promise, the Flechette programme has run into trouble, both on grounds of cost, and on technical grounds including accuracy. Flechette ammunition has not come into general service anywhere, although the US Army made use of certain types of flechette ammunition in Vietnam, primarily by the "Point man" of an infantry section operating in jungle country, the flechettes here being usually fired from a shot gun type weapon.

Single flechette ammunition, on which most research effort has been spent, consists of a small metal cartridge case, commonly of nominal 5.6mm calibre, into the neck of which is placed the flechette itself, with the narrow body of the arrow secured at the point by a sabot, filling the gap between the case neck and the flechette. The full length of the flechette is contained within the cartridge case, the fins being positioned almost on the inner base of the case. When fired the sabot is discarded at the muzzle by means of a stripper, integral with the muzzle, allowing the flechette to continue on its fin-stabilised flight.

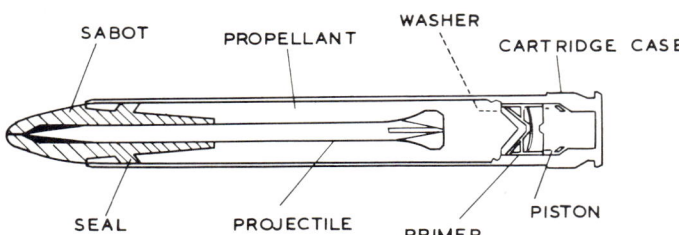

Typical Piston Primed Single Flechette Cartridge

To reduce weapon weight and achieve simplicity in what are weapons with exceptionally high cyclic rates of fire, some flechette cartridges are piston primed. In such cartridges the primer is fired by a small piston actually contained in the base of each cartridge case. After firing the piston is forced back by gas pressure, and in turn forces back the firing pin on the rifle. This unlocks the breech block, and residual gas pressure drives the cartridge case back and gives sufficient energy to the breech block to carry out the cycle of operations. This system obviates the necessity for a

conventional gas system in the weapon, but piston-primed ammunition is difficult and costly to make.

Various flechette cartridges to fit the Salvo and SPIW projects have been made in the United States. Apart from single flechette types with metal cases, a number of different multi-flechette cartridges, usually based on commercial shotgun cartridges, have been made, usually with cases of plastic material. Apart from normal flechette, proof, tracer and dummy cartridges have been produced in a variety of case types. Sabots have generally been made of nylon or fibreglass, and have caused much trouble because fine particles may blow back into the firer's eyes when the discarded sabot disintegrates at the muzzle.

The flechettes themselves are usually made of steel, but other materials have also been used. A particular aim has been to use a metal with as high a density as possible, and bi-metal flechettes have also been used, where the front portion has been of the heavier metal, leaving the tail light, and the centre of gravity far forward.

A characteristic of single flechette ammunition, apart from the high velocity given to the dart, is the low weight of the dart and of the complete cartridge. A typical 5.6mm flechette cartridge (the XM.144) weighs 93 grains (6g) in all, with the flechette itself weighing between 8 and 10 grains (0.5-0.65g) plus about 7 grains (0.45g) for the sabot. Even the longer XM.110, with its piston primer, has a total cartridge weight of only 98 grains (6.35g). Muzzle velocities of single flechette cartridges with darts weighing 8 to 10 grains range between 1,370 and 1,430 metres per second and, surprisingly, these light projectiles have a good armour piercing performance. Fired against 6.3mm and 3.15mm hard steel plate, as well as aluminium plate, at 130 metres range, at angles of attack of 90 degrees and 60 degrees, the 10 grain flechette achieved penetration and compared very favourably with 5.56mm M.193 ball and M.80 7.62mm ball. Flechettes were found to retain striking effect out to 500 metres but were inaccurate – a fault which continued to dog the entire flechette programme.

When the flechette emerges at the muzzle, the fragments of the sabot, having a poor ballistic shape and little mass, soon fall to the ground. The flechette itself, with a launch velocity of 1,430 metres per second, loses velocity rapidly as it proceeds down range, due to its light weight. It would arrive at a target 400 metres distant with a residual velocity of about 1,030 metres per second. At this point the flechette's remaining energy is about 25 kilogrammetres. The wounding efficiency of the flechette is of a high order in that, due to its shape and the fact that this shape degrades immediately upon impact with flesh, this remaining energy is quickly given up to the target. (Flechettes tend to buckle into a hook upon impact with flesh, and since this is a very poor ballistic shape, and since flesh is about 800 times denser than air, the buckled flechette gyrates and gives up its energy very rapidly, thus earning high marks as an effective projectile).

In the search for the optimum weight flechette in rifle calibre, darts weighing 18.5 grains (1.2g) were produced, giving muzzle velocities of around 1,160 metres per second.

A requirement existed for tracer flechette, with ignition at 25 metres from the muzzle, and good day and night trace to 500 metres. Despite a number of different approaches to this, the requirement was found impossible to meet. The small cross section of the flechette made the conventional trace chamber ineffectual. Apart from trying the conventional chamber, other solutions included coating the entire rear of the dart with trace composition, and also making the rear of the dart entirely of magnesium.

A wide variety of US flechette cartridges were made, the most frequently encountered being the following:

XM.110. 5.6mm single flechette. Belted, rimless, bottlenecked case with piston primer. Case length 52.8mm. Overall length 58.8mm

XM.144. 5.6mm single flechette. Rimless bottlenecked case. Conventional primer. Case length 43.9mm. Overall length 49.6mm. Head diameter 8.1mm

XM.215. 5.6mm single flechette. Rimless bottlenecked case. Conventional primer. Case length 43.9mm. Overall length 49.3mm. Head diameter 8.5mm. The XM.215 was a wide-case variant of the XM.144

XM.645. 5.6mm single flechette. Belted, rimless, bottlenecked case with piston primer. Case length 57mm. Overall length 62.5mm. This cartridge will be found with Canadian arsenal headstamps.

Each of the above was manufactured in variant forms. These variants incorporate a number of changes from the basic, including case taper differences, size of primer, wall thickness, type of flechette and tracer. In addition the basic forms (and probably some of the variants too) were produced in proof and dummy loadings.

The potential of multi-flechette loadings was realised early on, and AAI tried, in 1957, a multi-flechette cartridge based on a 12 gauge shotgun case. In flechette form: these cartridges were often referred to as being of 18.5mm calibre. The 1957 AAI cartridge, known as type "A-LI" had 32 flechettes, each of 13 grains (0.84g) weight. Muzzle velocity was 426 metres per second.

At least two other types of 18.5mm shot-shell flechettes existed, in the following forms:

(1) 26 flechettes, of normal finned type. with total weight of 240 grains (15.55g). Muzzle velocity 548 metres per second.

(2) 18 flechettes of "mass stabilised" type, having a thicker form than normal, the pointed front end having heavier metal than the rear. The rear had no fins. Total weight of flechettes 390 grains (25.27g). Muzzle velocity 518 metres per second.

Flechette cartridges in 10.4mm, 7.62mm NATO and .45in ACP have also been manufactured in the United States. Apart from the cartridges listed above, which were strictly military in origin, Amron Corporation in the

United States, with interests in the armaments area, produced a number of flechette types. Of particular interest was their 8.35mm multi-flechette. This utilised a large capacity, conventional type case with normal primer. The bottlenecked rimless case measured 68.7mm in length, overall length being 79.2mm. A cluster of four flechettes was positioned in the neck of the case by a single sabot. This cartridge was manufactured with brass and aluminium cases.

Development of SPIW/Flechette was carried out in the United States by AAI, Winchester Western, Harrington and Richardson and Springfield Armoury. This field of four was narrowed down to AAI and Springfield Armoury, a number of different weapon designs, many of unconventional appearance, being produced. By 1970 the programme had been further narrowed down to one weapon considered suitable for limited field tests, namely the XM.19 rifle, developed by AAI, although two further weapon designs were still then under development. The XM.19 was, like many of the other weapons produced for flechette, smooth-bored, and fired the XM.645 single flechette cartridge, the weapon being recoil-operated. It was intended that this weapon fire three-round controlled bursts, but sustained bursts of automatic fire were also possible. Total weight for rifle and 200 rounds of ammunition was intended to be within the set limit of 12lb (5.44kg). The XM.19 achieved grenade launching capability by means of a detachable launcher.

Flechettes have been used for a variety of larger weapons also, including heavy machine guns, 20mm cannon, and light artillery, flechette in the latter weapon being close to the original concept of "grapeshot". Flechette in rifle calibre has also been the subject of trials elsewhere in the West. Basically however, in the rifle role, it has not fulfilled yet the hopes originally placed in it.

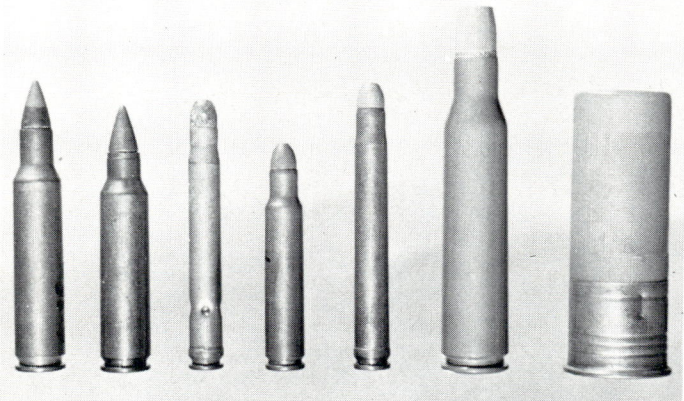

SPIW/Flechette ammunition. **Left to right:** *6.35mm FA-T 124 (52.6mm case); 6.35mm Winchester (47.6mm case); XM110 flechette (USA); XM645 flechette (USA; 8.35mm Amron multi-flechette (USA); Multi-flechette (USA)*

Micro-Calibre Ammunition

The 5.56mm x 45mm Armalite cartridge, described separately later, has attracted great interest and – partly, no doubt, because of the unilaterial decision, taken by the US authorities in 1960, to adopt it for first-line infantry use in place of the 7.62mm NATO round – it has been taken into service and seriously considered by many countries. Despite this trend, however, several countries, including the United States, have been, and still are, involved in experimental programmes with even smaller calibres. Such work commenced, in the United States, as part of the earlier projects already mentioned, in the early 1960s, but the bulk of the experimental work, both in the USA and elsewhere, has taken place since about 1968.

Most interest has been concentrated on calibres between 3mm and 5mm, some of the ammunition being based upon necked down 5.56mm Armalite cases, but others being based upon smaller shorter cases. Much of the work had been concentrated in Germany and the United States, but most other leading Western countries are involved also, Belgium for example producing 3.5mm ammunition (for high-speed revolver-type automatic weapons) and 4.8mm ammunition, and Spain producing various 4mm designs.

The arguments which currently surround the adoption of micro-calibre ammunition are similar in principle to those which surrounded the original 5.56mm cartridge. The advantages of light cartridge weight and light weapons, with low recoil and ease of control, are considerable. The high rates of fire, possibly automatically controlled, can give Salvo effect if required. Against this, short effective range, and vulnerability to wind may make at least some micro-calibre ammunition less suitable for general infantry purposes than the 5.56mm and larger calibres. Nevertheless, the entries for the 1977-79 NATO trials include 4.85mm weapons and ammunition from the UK and a 4.3mm weapon firing caseless ammunition from Germany.

As an indication of the typical characteristics of ammunition made in these smaller calibres, the following details of 4.6mm Heckler and Koch experimental ammunition may be helpful. The case length is 35.6mm.

(a) with 54 grain (3.5g), tungsten carbide core bullet, muzzle velocity of 780 metres/sec;

(b) with 42 grain (2.7g), lead core bullet, muzzle velocity of 840 metres/sec.

With increases in case length and capacity, and/or significant further reductions in calibre, no doubt the above velocities can be greatly exceeded, and the resultant long, thin bullet would have good short range wound effect. Much of the recent micro-calibre experimental work however has not been concerned with the extreme cartridge possiblities, and the above German cartridges seem to represent the median.

Micro-calibre ammunition. **Left to right:** *Rem UMC .13in USA; .17in FA-T 216 USA; 4mm Germany; 4.6mm Germany/Spain; 4.9mm Germany*

Squad Automatic Weapon Project (SAW)

An interesting indication of the existence of conflicting currents of thought regarding the best way of arming the infantryman is provided by the US Squad Automatic Weapon (SAW) project which ran from 1972 to 1975. It involved the development of weapons and ammunition of notional 6.15mm calibre with a view to providing a light automatic weapon capable of engaging targets out to 1,000 metres or so but not capable of performing the MMG function of providing sustained fire at significantly greater ranges.

To those who believe firmly that any engagement of an enemy at a range of more than 400 metres is a job for either an MMG or a mortar, the SAW programme appeared as a retrograde movement. It is fairly widely agreed that the abolition of the need for more than one type of ammunition to be issued to the smallest fighting units is desirable; and the obvious way to achieve this end is to make the soldier's individual weapon handy enough to perform the functions of both rifle and SMG. The relatively powerful 6.15mm cartridge would not lend itself readily to such an amalgamation and would, so the argument runs, put an unnecessary burden on the soldier.

On the other hand, there are many who think that the trend in recent years has been in the direction of too great a reduction of fire-power in the infantry section or squad and that the scale of issue and tactical availability of MMG, mortars and other longer-range weapons is and always will be too low to enable troops to exploit opportunities of engaging an enemy at ranges beyond 400 metres when they arise. No doubt those who hold such views include the spiritual successors of those who imposed the 7.62mm standard on a reluctant NATO alliance; but it is not necessary to leap from a 400 metre maximum to 2,000 metres or more; and there are many who would like to see a compromise which might well be in the region of 1,000 metres.

Moreover, although the SAW project was explicitly aimed at the development of a weapon in the LMG category, there is also a respectable case to be stated for considering a calibre of around 6mm for a GPMG or light MMG role while retaining the principle of equipping the infantry generally with a smaller-calibre weapon.

Be all that as it may, the SAW project is currently shelved and is likely to remain on the shelf at least until the conclusion of the 1977-79 NATO trials: it has indeed been suggested that one reason for shelving it was that to have continued with it would have implied a criticism, from within, of the US decision to abandon the NATO standard and adopt 5.56mm as the calibre for individual infantry weapons.

Although the SAW project was strictly American, it is worth noting here that the parallel British development of individual and light support weapons with the new 4.85mm round is intended to cover all infantry section weapon functions from SMG to LMG. Full performance data have not been released, but it has been released that the new round is capable of perforating a 3.4mm NATO mild steel plate at a range of at least 500 metres.

In the United States, more than one basic 6mm case design was developed in the SAW trials. Case materials used were brass, aluminium and steel, and the best known cartridge to emerge was the XM 732. This design had a 45mm case length, with larger case diameter and capacity than the 5.56mm × 45mm cartridge, and a long, high sectional density bullet weighing 106 grains (6.87g) and having a muzzle velocity of 762 m/s.

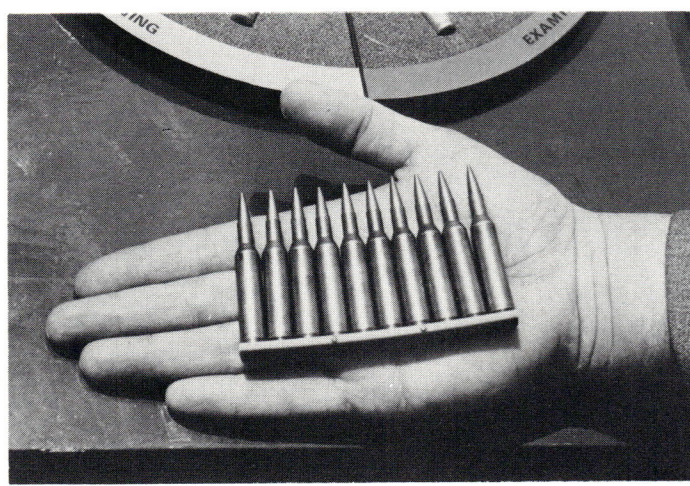

The British 4.85mm ammunition introduced with the Individual Weapon and Light Support Weapon in 1976. The round weighs 179 grains (11.6g) and produces a muzzle velocity of 900-930 metres/second according to the weapon used (C.F. Foss)

Left to right: *7.62mm × 51 with depleted uranium core; 6mm SAW with aluminium case (USA); 6mm SAW XM 732 with steel case (USA); 5.56mm caseless (USA); 9mm caseless (USA)*

Future Trends in Small Arms Ammunition

Since the introduction of metallic cased military ammunition over a hundred years ago, the individual components, while changing their shape, weight and composition, have remained essentially the same, and the same in number. The four components are case, cap (with composition), propellant and projectile. Attempts have been made, for a number of years, and in a number of countries, to reduce the number of components. Mainly this was to achieve savings of cartridge weight, to save strategic raw material (such as brass) and to allow changes in weapon design. The last factor has, perhaps, predominated, and a cartridge that, by its design, allows a simplified form of feed and extraction in automatic weapons has been the ideal.

A modified case design, of plastic, with conventional primer, where the case is triangular in form has been tried, essentially in automatic weapons of the revolver feed type, in the United States, the cartridges usually being referred to as "trounds". This cartridge offered savings in weight, and lent itself to modified forms of feed. Apart from ball loadings, trounds were produced in flechette form.

Caseless ammunition of the rocket variety has been experimented with for a number of years, in Germany, the UK and the US. The most recent manufacture in this area was "Gyrojet" (manufactured in the United States, and France) where the projectiles carry solid rocket propellant in the projectile itself, acting through nozzles in the base of the projectile. This system, while allowing a completely new feed system to be applied to the weapons (pistols basically) and while eliminating some of the components found in conventional ammunition, has not been found satisfactory on grounds of cost, low velocity, range and effect.

The area in which a significant breakthrough is currently being sought is in caseless ammunition. This is not a new concept, and even in the small arms and aircraft cannon area has been the subject of considerable work, in years past, in Japan, Germany, Spain, the UK and the USA, and no doubt elsewhere also.

Current interest in caseless ammunition is at a high level, particularly in

the United States and Germany, both for small arms and for aircraft cannon. Caseless ammunition offers savings in cartridge brass, and therefore in weight, and offers the chance of being able to dispense with the extraction process in the weapon itself. Caseless ammunition, at least so far as current developments in ammunition for small arms are concerned, consists of a projectile or group of projectiles, the rear of which or the whole of which is embedded in solid propellant, which in turn is shaped in cartridge case form, and which embodies a priming composition inset into the base. The exterior of the solid charge is treated to give anti-damp and flame retardant characteristics, and to give sufficient strength and hardness to withstand the forces and friction encountered in handling, loading and feeding. Upon being fired, the case and priming composition are completely consumed, the bullet being propelled up the barrel in the normal way.

The major problems associated with caseless ammunition are, and have always been (a) achieving complete case combustion; and (b) achieving good breech obturation. The latter problem is the greater, and various chamber systems have been developed to cope with this. An additional problem, that of the vulnerability of loose cartridges carried in the soldier's pouch to accidental ignition, caused by the impact of an enemy bullet or otherwise, has recently come very much to the fore.

5.56mm fully-telescoped cartridge developed for the Hughes Lockless rifle/LMG. The 68 grain (4.4g) round is surrounded by the propellant and the whole is encased in plastic material.

Recent examples of new types of small-arms ammunition are the caseless round developed for the German 4.3mm Salvo Weapon and the fully-telescoped round developed in the USA for the Hughes 5.56mm Lockless Rifle/LMG.

Although there is a considerable body of opinion which regards the introduction of careless ammunition as the next logical step in small-arms development, there are many who disagree with this view.

They point out that shortage of case material is hardly likely to become a compelling reason to force a switch to caseless ammunition, and existing brass or steel cases will continue to offer the most robust and reliable system in weapons that, by virtue of the conventional cartridge, are simple in design and manufacture, and simple to maintain under average field conditions. The weight saving factor claimed by the caseless school may be a delusion, in that the long suffering infantryman will, if necessary, and without being consulted, be required to carry whatever weight of ammunition results from the number of rounds that the current doctrine obliges him to fire.

Musketry Improvements

Bound up with the questions relating to improvements in ammunition and weapons design are other questions relating to the proficiency and fire discipline of the individual soldier and the fire unit. It is generally accepted that musketry standards in most major armies have declined considerably since the early years of this century: it is also probably true to say that the widespread adoption of automatic individual weapons has led to a prodigious waste of ammunition in unaimed (and often undisciplined) fire. It is at least arguable, therefore, that both the weight and the cost of soldier-carried ammunition could be reduced more effectively by improving the way in which weapons and ammunition are used than by the relentless pursuit of technological innovation. In this context it is worth noting that the British Army, at least, have recently instituted a programme designed to raise musketry standards from what experience in Northern Ireland indicated was a deplorably low level.

NATO Trials

Several references have already been made to the NATO small arms trials which are to take place in 1977-79 and are intended to establish new NATO standards for the 1980s. Full details of these trials are not available at the time of writing, but the following summary covers what is currently known or surmised concerning them.

First, it appears that, despite the reservations which many people have concerning a limitation of 400 metres (or possibly, according to some schools of thought, 600 metres) on the required effective range of all weapons up to and including the LMG, some such limitation will be the basis of the trial programme. Rather surprisingly, in view of the current popularity of the concept of NATO standardisation, however, it also appears that there is to be no prior commitment by the participants – or by non-participating NATO countries – to acceptance of the results of the trials as the basis of future national standards.

Secondly, it appears that no new weapon is to be entered by the USA. The control weapon for the trials will be the US M16 rifle firing the 5.56mm M193 ball and M196 tracer ammunition. It is believed, however, that the US authorities are very interested in the 5.56mm S101 round developed by FN in Belgium for the Minimi LMG. This round has a ball projectile weight of 4g (62 grains) instead of the 3.5g (55 grain) bullet used with the M16. With a faster rifling twist of one turn in 9in (229mm) instead of 12in (305mm) this bullet has good stability and penetrating power out to about 900 metres. Heavy bullets designed for barrels with 1 in 8in (203mm) twist have also been developed in the USA (see the general entry on 5.56mm ammunition). The French FA MAS uses the standard 5.56mm round.

Apart from 5.56mm, the calibres to be considered seem likely to be the German 4.3mm caseless round as used in their Salvo Weapon, the German 4.6mm conventional round with the HK 36 Assault Rifle and the British 4.85mm round with the Individual and Light Support Weapons. Having regard to the extensive investment in 5.56mm weapons in Belgium, Germany and the USA and the less extensive but still significant investment in Italy and the UK, however, it seems that a very good case will have to be made out for the adoption of one of the smaller calibres if the 5.56mm position is to be undermined.

LARGER CALIBRES

Developments in ammunition for heavy machine guns and cannon in recent years have been much more orderly and subject to fewer policy fluctuations than those outlined above in the discussion of small-arms ammunition. No doubt there are many reasons for this; but perhaps one of the most important is that the relatively small (though still substantial) size of the market for these heavier weapons has encouraged the concentration of development work in fewer localities with consequent reduction in temptation to indulge in competitive innovation.

Again, the tactical circumstances in which the weapons are likely to be used are less vigorously disputed than are those which may be relevant in the discussion of smaller weapons. Standard targets are troops at long range, aircraft and vehicles and the weapons are commonly mounted on prime movers or substantial trailers and often fitted with elaborate sighting devices; so that accuracy, range, effectiveness and volume of fire are more important than extreme portability of either the weapon or its ammunition.

Finally, and especially at the upper end of the calibre range, there is scope for quite substantial alterations in ammunition characteristics by modifying the construction of the projectile without altering the mechanism of the weapon. The .05in (12.7mm) armour-piercing cartridge developed by Eurometaal in the Netherlands, for example, can be used in conjunction with the types of ammuniton of the same calibre in the same weapon even though its effect on the target is quite different: indeed a common feature of some modern weapons is their ability to accept multiple feeds of separately belted ammunition so as to give the gunner the opportunity of switching from one type of ammunition to another without delay.

To a far greater extent than small arms, the heavier weapons have applications in ships and aircraft in addition to their land force roles: indeed many of the cannon now used by land forces were originally developed for use in aircraft or are derivatives of airborne weapons. The US General Electric multi-barrel Vulcan gun, for example, began as an aircraft weapon, came down to earth as part of a land-mobile anti-aircraft system and has since gone to sea as a component of a 'last-ditch' close-in weapon system (CIWS) for anti-aircraft and anti-missile defence. For this third application the idea of using bullets with depleted uranium cores was put forward to increase the effectiveness of the anti-missile defence; and since it was found that such ammunition produced a significant 'burn-through' effect when it struck armour at high velocity the possibility of using such bullets, in various calibres down to 7.62mm, in the land role was considered. For various reasons, including cost and emotional objections to the use of even depleted uranium on the battlefield, nothing may come of this project; but it provides a useful example of the kind of inter-service cross-fertilisation that can occur in this area of weapon development.

Liquid Propellants

A potentially important development, at least for vehicle-mounted weapons, is foreshadowed by the work that is being done on liquid propellants. The use of such propellants for artillery weapons has been the subject of experimental work for several years; but the recent work on 25mm weapons carried out by Grumman Aerospace for the US Navy brings the technique within the orbit at least of motorised infantry.

The weapon under study is a four-barrel inverse-Gatling device in which the barrels, with their propellant injection apparatus, remain stationary relative to the gun cradle and there is a rotating bolt assembly which loads the projectiles into each barrel in turn and closes the breech while the propellant is injected and consumed. With such a system a firing rate of 4,000 rounds/min can be achieved using a lighter structure than is required for a more conventional weapon. Many problems remain to be solved before the gun could become a practical infantry weapon, but its potential is interesting.

WOUND BALLISTICS*

No introductory survey of small-arms ammunition development would be complete without some reference to that aspect of ammunition design which is concerned with the effect of the bullet on the human target. The scientific study of such effects, wound ballistics, is of comparatively recent

*This section of this introduction is a modified and shortened version of the article contributed by Major P. Labbett to the 1976 edition.

development as an organised discipline but has made considerable progress, since the Second World War, in replacing guesswork and false assumptions by some hard facts.

Ballistic Shape

For small arms ammunition, three general bullet shapes apply. Bullets with round noses (which, except for pistol or sub-machine gun ammunition, are virtually obsolete), bullets with pointed noses and flat bases, and bullets with pointed noses and streamlined or boat-tailed bases. The two classes of pointed bullet represent the norm of conventional rifle calibres. Apart from these three general bullet shapes, new developments in ammunition have led to bullets with asymmetrical ogives, and to flechettes or similar projectiles.

Spin

The bullet spin is induced by the rifling of the weapon, and is the rotation of the bullet about its axis. At the commencement of flight, the rate of spin is very great – around 200,000 revolutions per minute for a 7.62mm NATO rifle bullet. This spin will prevent a conventional bullet (but not a sphere) from tumbling along the line of flight. It also tends to maintain the axis of the bullet during flight parallel to the axis of the bore of the weapon firing it, and not parallel to the ground.

Yaw

Yaw is the deviation of the longitudinal axis of the bullet from the line of flight. It will vary significantly in degree at various points along the trajectory, and will continue, still in varying degree, when the bullet enters the denser medium represented by the tissue of a body. Yaw commences soon after the bullet leaves the barrel since, passing through the barrel, the centre of gravity of the bullet is forced to travel in a circle and is not on the axis of the bore, whereas, upon leaving the bore, the rotation centres on the centre of gravity. Inherent or induced asymmetry in a bullet is an important factor in the production of yaw, and this in turn materially affects the wounding characteristics of the bullet.

Centre of Gravity

In a conventionally shaped bullet, this tends to be towards the rear. Since under normal conditions of mass production total accuracy is impossible, the centre of gravity is usually not on the axis of symmetry of the bullet.

Centre of Pressure

In a conventionally-shaped bullet forces tending to retard the bullet in flight are focussed on a point along the axis of the bullet towards the nose. This point is the centre of pressure.

Overturn Couple, or Lever Arm

The distance between the centre of gravity and the centre of pressure is known as the overturning couple or the lever arm, and through this the stabilising forces deriving from spin operate. Since neither of these two centres lies exactly on the axis (due to normal manufacturing errors) the result is yaw. The greater the distance between the two centres, the more stable the bullet tends to be, and therefore a longer bullet tends to be more stable than a short one.

The Bullet in Flight

Upon leaving the muzzle, spin imparted by the barrel rifling prevents the bullet tumbling base over tip, and it also preserves the bullet's axis parallel to the line of the bore. Yaw at the muzzle, in a properly made bullet, will only be a maximum of two or three degrees, and may be as little as a few minutes of angle. Yaw however does not remain a constant figure during flight, and will increase, typically reaching its maximum at about fifteen feet (about 5 metres) from the muzzle, at which point spin reasserts itself, and yaw diminishes. Thereafter there is a cycle of increasing and diminishing yaw throughout the range of engagement, and at longer ranges this becomes more potent as the effect of spin diminishes. At long ranges, as yaw becomes more potent, and as the spin has kept the axis of the bullet in line with the line of the bore, the bullet tends to approach the target, assuming the target to be in the vertical plane, otherwise than at right angles. This in itself influences the effectiveness of the bullet, but the resultant asymmetry of the atmospheric retardation also has the effect of further increasing the degree of yaw.

Impact With The Human Target

The bullet entering tissue produces a permanent track or tunnel, the missile leaving cut and torn tissue in its wake.

While cutting through the tissue, the bullet also imparts shock waves and radial velocity to these tissues, which absorb energy given up by the bullet. The pressure developed with these shock waves can be of the order of one thousand pounds per square inch (approx: 70 kilogrammes per square centimetre). In absorbing this energy some tissues, more elastic than others, react so that they move outwards and create a large temporary cavity. This cavity, in the space of a few milliseconds, goes through several pulsations, expanding and retracting, before reverting to a semi-permanent shape. All this takes place before the victim, if he still lives, can comprehend the detail of what is occurring.

The shape of the permanent path may not always be obvious from the mere examination of the entry and exit holes of the bullet. Depending upon the part of the body struck, and the proximity of more solid obstacles such as bone, and the degree of yaw, etc., the bullet may or may not create a simple "tunnel" wound, of permanent diameter only slightly less than that of the bullet itself. Quite possibly however the bullet, after entry, may cause a large permanent cavity within the limb or body, and this in turn may be accompanied by a large exit hole (if the bullet exits at all) or by a deceptively small exit hole. The existence of large permanent cavities, accompanied by gaping exit (or entry) holes has often, in the past, led to accusations, entirely false in fact and based upon faulty ballistic knowledge, that the enemy at the time was using explosive or expanding bullets.

As has been stated, a bullet develops yaw along its path through the air, this yaw reappearing at intervals along the trajectory. The bullet will continue to yaw, if it is yawing already, when it hits the target. Alternatively it can commence its cyclic yaw after entry. The effect of the denser medium of the human tissue will accentuate the angle of the yaw, and trials have shown that a bullet having very slight yaw at impact may develop yaw within the target of anything up to fifty or even one hundred degrees. This therefore plays a large part in creating a permanent cavity of far greater size than the diameter of a simple tunnel wound, with dire consequence to the victim. It is often the case that spin reasserts itself when the bullet is still within the body, reducing yaw, so that the bullet makes a small clean exit hole. Often the reverse is true. Yaw will further change as obstructions of varying density are met, such as bone. Since yaw effect is greater in tissue or bone than in air, yaw augments retardation of the missile, and therefore helps the kinetic energy to be given up in the wound, all of which increases wound efficiency.

Apart from the permanent cavity, (which, in spite of its name, and assuming the victim lives and is medically tended, will largely heal up) mention has been made of the temporary cavity. The shape of this temporary cavity is, except where yaw has taken effect, in the form of an ellipse. Its volume may be as much as twenty-six times the volume of the permanent cavity at its widest point. Surrounding the temporary cavity is an area in which the tissue is to a greater or lesser extent damaged. This tissue will, if kept clean, tend to revitalise itself. If not kept clean, and under battlefield conditions cleanliness may be difficult or impossible, the damaged tissue becomes a breeding ground for bacteria, and this in turn is responsible for such things as gas gangrene, and relatively simple casualties may then become more seriously stricken, or die. The temporary cavity vanishes quickly (in milliseconds), leaving only an area of damaged tissue surrounding the permanent track.

Apart from causing the cavities referred to, high-velocity bullets with the shock waves which accompany them, can cause secondary damage to bones, etc., not directly in the path of the bullet. Simple fractures therefore may be caused to bones without direct impact having taken place, and the same can happen to blood vessels not directly struck. In the main however, it has been noted that blood vessels tend to survive, even when close to the cavity.

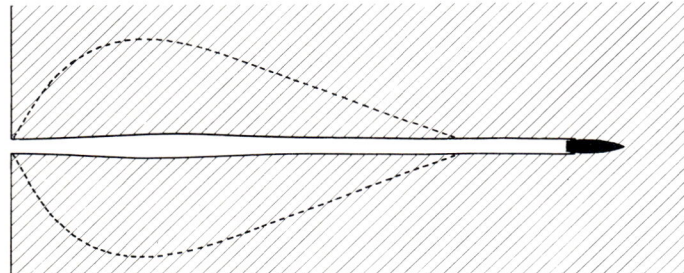

Diagram of a wound track (no yaw on the bullet). The permanent cavity and track is shown by the continuous line, and the temporary cavity is shown by the broken line.

Shock waves, in tissue, arise at the point of impact. In tissue the velocity of these shock waves is about 4,800 feet per second (1,462 metres per second). Shock can incapacitate and, in extreme cases, can kill.

The slowing down or retardation of a bullet as it traverses tissue is an important factor in determining how that missile delivers up its energy to the tissue, and how effective therefore it is as a wounding and shocking force. A missile of large presentation area and small mass gives up its energy rapidly, and will produce a wide but short temporary cavity. This is a factor in the wound efficiency of the flechette type of projectile.

Obviously, a projectile loses energy to the atmosphere during flight and it is its residual energy on impact with the target that is important.

The Human Target

A man, standing erect, has a total target area which may be calculated in different ways, but an area of approximately 0.42 square metre is generally accepted. In general the rear of a man offers better "in-built" protection to the vital organs, by means of tissue, bones and so on, the front being more vulnerable. Of the total area, the vulnerable portion has been calculated as 40 per cent, the vulnerable areas being organs, canals, nerve centres, and major blood vessels, etc. The probability that a bullet will pierce through to the vulnerable area increases with the bullet's energy and velocity.

Target analyses in the Second World War and Korea, supported by US experience in Vietnam, shows that the three sub-divisions of the vulnerable area (head, chest and abdomen) account for 40 per cent of hits, and the extremities (legs, arms, hands, feet, etc.) account for the balance. The victims in this analysis were unprotected by body armour, the advent of which has radically changed the pattern, since casualties now incurred show a preponderance of head and possibly lower abdomen wounds (depending upon the type of armour) and extremities, since hits on chest and upper abdomen, while still occurring, are largely ineffective. In any case, it must be stated that the above figures represent an analysis of hits inflicted by all weapons and not just small arms, and except in certain types of campaign, or in certain types of engagement, gunshot wounds account for, at best, under 30 per cent of the total hits, and in some areas have been as little as 10 per cent. However, much of the survey work was upon

casualties suffered by "friendly" troops, and here, particularly in Korea and Vietnam, these forces had a superfluity of supporting arms and weapons, ranging from direct air support, including napalm, to heavy artillery, while the enemy had not, and a corresponding analysis of enemy casualties in those conflicts may have shown an even smaller percentage of wounds inflicted by small arms. As against that however, underdeveloped countries in the future will, if they are engaged in hostilities, probably not equip their infantry with body armour, and, since such countries may often be rich only in manpower, "human wave" attacks, such as sometimes occurred in Korea, could present a situation where the volume of wounds caused by defending small arms rose to high levels.

From the point of view of the defensive battle, the object of small arms fire is currently often expressed in terms of incapacitation, such that the enemy soldier will receive a wound that renders him incapable, within 30 seconds, of continuing the assault. The "30-second assault" can, of course, be readily translated into tactical situations other than one in which the target is carrying out the assault.

The range at which the human target is engaged depends upon the tactical situation. On the one hand, enemy infantry forced to dismount from their APC at extreme range, perhaps 1,000 metres, present a target totally different from that presented by either the urban guerrilla or an enemy soldier who falls into an ambush on a jungle trail at a range of 30 metres. Effective maximum infantry ranges of about 300 metres are now generally accepted as the standard, both to identify the enemy as hostile (it may be obvious anyway) and to engage him with effective fire from platoon weapons. The enemy may be, but probably is not, currently wearing body armour, but in all probability he is festooned with the various items of equipment and personal kit that infantry everywhere are encumbered with and which also offer some protection. A moving infantryman, at 300 metres and partially protected in this way, may not easily be effectively hit by the average rifleman, and even if he is, 60 per cent of the hits are likely to be extremity hits only, and may not stop the assault. Current weapon and ammunition development is intended to improve this effective hit ratio.

Ammunition Design and Wound Effectiveness

The Hague Convention of 1899 ruled illegal bullets which have jackets with slits or an opening at the point which would permit the jacket to strip upon impact with the target, allowing the lead core to mushroom, causing very serious entrance wounds. The intention of the Convention was clear, and the elimination of "dum-dum" type wounds was an admirable idea, except that the fundamental ballistic thinking behind the remedy put forward by the Convention lacked a full appreciation of all the factors involved, and was based more on supposition and random observation than upon scientific study. This is hardly surprising since wound ballistics as a science had not begun to develop. It was not then appreciated that yaw played the part it did in causing cavity wounds, neither was it realised that "conventional" looking small arms bullets, having full metal jackets, could, by their internal structure, cause large complicated wounds similar to those caused by open-nosed bullets. Even less probably did the convention recognise the importance of velocity in the wound effect equation.

Two bullets may be cited as possessing, under certain circumstances, peculiar wounding characteristics. The first, and unintentionally severe, bullet was the British .303in Ball Mark 7. In this design, in order to place the centre of gravity as far to the rear as possible, the nose filling consisted of a small aluminium plug. This plug, under wartime conditions in 1914-18 when aluminium needed to be conserved, was replaced by wood, china, wire, etc., the basic lead/antimony core being unchanged. The nose of the Mark 7, irrespective of the type of nose filling chosen, tended to break off and could cause, in a wound, break up of the bullet with consequent serious wounding effect. The intention behind this design however had been no more than to improve the external ballistics of the bullet, by placing the centre of gravity far back.

The second example was the 6.5mm Japanese rifle round, where, probably intentionally from the wounding point of view, the lead core was thickened considerably at the base compared to the upper portion. This bullet, in spite of its small calibre and lowish velocity, tumbled badly upon hitting tissue, and caused serious wounds.

In recent years, bullet design has been concerned not only with exterior ballistics and accuracy, but wound effect. Designers, for the first time, have had at their disposal the benefit of specific research into wound ballistics. Some of the solutions offered are shown below, often in conjunction with the weapon solutions already referred to.

HIGH VELOCITY, SMALL CALIBRE BULLETS

Here the solution, embodied in such cartridges as the US M 193 cartridge in 5.56mm x 45 calibre, centres upon high velocity, and high residual kinetic energy. The small 55 grain (3.5g) bullet is conventional in shape, lead-cored, and with pointed nose and boat-tailed rear. Initial velocity is 1,005 metres/second and muzzle energy 184mkp. At 400 metres range, velocity has fallen to about 518 metres/second and striking energy is down to about 55mkp. It is an accepted "wound ballistic yardstick" that, to cause a casualty, a bullet needs to deliver up to the target, at the moment of impact, about 8mkp of energy. The 5.56mm bullet, at this range, is thus an effective solution. (It is less acceptable against other criteria not connected with wound ballistics.) Experience in the past few years has shown that the M.193 bullet, at high impact velocities (i.e., at short range) can break up in the wound and, apart from any other results, causes a very large wound.

HIGH VELOCITY HIGH SECTIONAL DENSITY BULLETS

These bullets, usually of calibre smaller than 5.56mm, are being developed currently in a number of Western countries. Ballistics at the muzzle for this class tend to follow fairly closely those of the 5.56mm, but the bullets have a greater length in relation to their diameter, (i.e. they are long and thin). These projectiles should be stable in flight, because of the length of the "overturning couple" but are intended, upon impact, to tumble quickly and give up their energy. The advantage in this class of bullet, compared to the M.193, is likely to be in the exterior ballistics area.

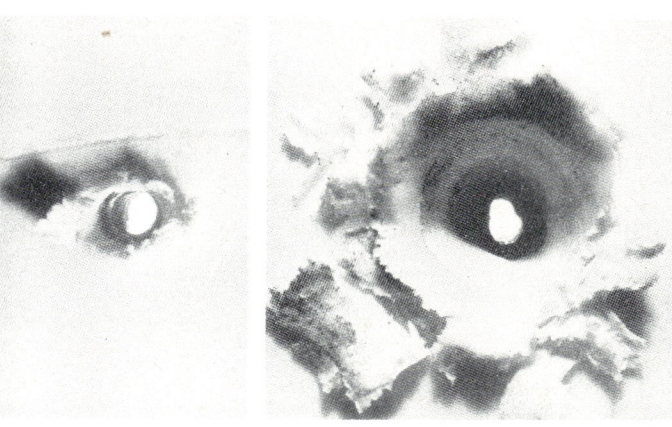

FLECHETTE

Flechettes are in fact an extension of the high sectional density theory, coupled with fins for stability in flight (most flechette weapons are smooth-bore) and a non-composite body construction (at least for the most part, although some composite body flechette rounds have been produced). The short range, ultra-high velocity flechette (velocity around 1,372 metres/second) performs well as a wounding agent at short range. The long dart, not unlike a simple nail in construction, deforms easily and quickly upon impact, and gives up its residual energy in a very satisfactory manner. At 400 metres a typical single flechette will have a residual velocity of about 1,036 metres/second and striking energy of about 26mkp, well above the "norm" of 8mkp.

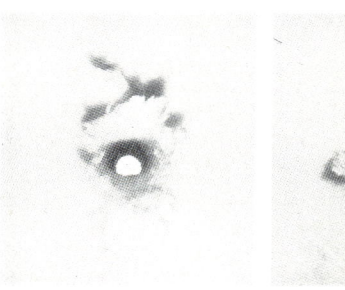
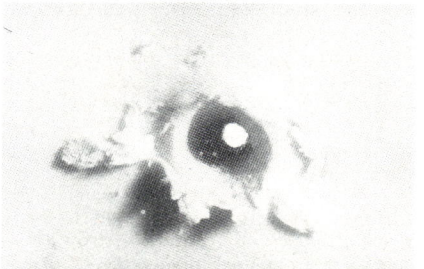

HECKLER AND KOCH SPOON-POINT

In West Germany, Heckler and Koch have recently developed a new small calibre bullet with a *Löffelspitz* (spoon-point). Here the ogive of the bullet is assymetrical, and into one side is scooped out a depression, similar to the imprint left by the base of a spoon. This design is intended to cause the bullet to incline as soon after impact as possible, and so give up its energy as efficiently as possible. Heckler and Koch claim that the spoon point does not cause the bullet to tumble, but merely accentuates the tumble and causes it to occur as close to, or on, the surface as possible. This design is specifically to increase the incapacitating effect of wounds caused in legs and arms, where otherwise the bullet may have made its exit without yawing. These bullets are made with both lead and tungsten cores, and do not lose accuracy because of the ogive, or at least do not lose it to any significant degree.

Conclusion

Short of actual war, the theory of wound ballistic development is often difficult to prove completely, since only in war can the full effect of new designs be seen on the casualties caused. Most of the proof of designs so far considered (with the exception of the 5.56mm M 193) has been carried out with artificial media, or sometimes with dead or drugged animals. Neither artificial media, nor animals can completely reproduce the effect upon human targets. Human targets in any case vary in size, weight and durability, and it is doubtful if completely typical conditions can ever be determined. Bullet design will continue to improve, in terms of lethality, but there must be serious doubts that total hit ratios will or can significantly improve, or that the hit efficiency ratio will also change greatly, especially if body armour becomes accepted on a world-wide basis.

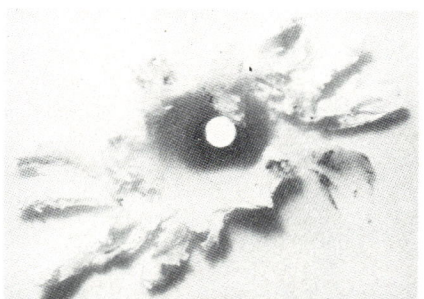

The above illustration depicts the effect on a soap cake target (thickness 4.7in) of various types of ammunition, at a range of 30m. Entrance hole on the left and the exit hole on the right. **Top:** *4.6mm × 36, Heckler and Koch Löffelspitz ammunition, displaced volume 0.002³ in.* **Middle:** *5.56mm × 45 ammunition, displaced volume 0.001³ in.* **Bottom:** *7.62mm × 51 ammunition, displaced volume 0.0013³ in*

INTERNATIONAL STANDARD SMALL-ARMS AMMUNITION

7.62mm × 39mm CARTRIDGE (M.1943)

The 7.62mm × 39mm cartridge was developed during the 1939-45 war, by the USSR and, from the date of its emergence, was designated as the Model 1943 cartridge. It was used, according to Russian sources, on a very minor scale, in the closing stages of the war, but does not seem to have been issued in quantity until the early 1950s; probably because the new family of Russian small arms designed to fire the new round were themselves not fully developed until the early 1950s.

The M.1943 cartridge is now the standard small arms cartridge of the Warsaw Pact countries, of Communist China and its satellites, and of a number of other states, not necessarily politically aligned with Moscow or Peking. This medium-powered cartridge is used in a variety of self-loading rifles and light machine guns, and comes close to providing the answer in the search for the universal infantry cartridge. It is still in the MMG role that the USSR and other Eastern Bloc countries use the old 7.62mm × 54mm cartridge.

Most, but not all, Communist made 7.62mm × 39mm ammunition is steel cased (either lacquered or copper washed), with comparatively few brass case producers. Plastic cased blank and short-range practice ammunition has also been produced in this calibre in Finland and Norway.

The 7.62mm × 39mm cartridge has a rimless, bottlenecked case 39mm long. The rim diameter is 11.2mm.

The standard Russian ball-bullet, Type PS, weighs 123 grains (8g), and in steel-cored (M.S.) and boat-tailed. Propelled with a charge of 25 grains (1.6g) nitrocellulose type powder, the muzzle velocity is 10 metres/second. Muzzle energy is 205mkp. There also exists a Finnish 123 grain flat based lead cored ball-bullet, presumably of similar ballistics.

7.62mm × 39mm M.1943 ammunition. **Left to right:** *Ball (Type PS); API (Type BZ); In: ranging (Type ZP); Tracer (Type T.45); Blank; Blank, plastic; Blank, wood bullet*

7.62mm × 39mm ammunition produced in Warsaw Pact countries will normally be found with standard USSR colour codes. Communist China originally used this code also, in its entirety, but in recent years has commenced in some instances to vary the Russian code. Finland uses its own code.

Known producers of the 7.62mm × 39mm cartridge include:

Belgium	Germany	Indonesia	Norway (Plastic)	Romania	USSR
Bulgaria	Egypt	Iraq	Korea (North)	Sudan	Yugoslavia
China	Finland	Israel	Pakistan	Syria	
Czechoslovakia	Hungary	Netherlands	Poland	United States	

7.62mm × 51mm AMMUNITION (NATO)

This cartridge is a direct descendant of the United States T.65 .30in. Light Rifle cartridge, which, in its standardised form, was adopted by the North Atlantic Treaty Organisation in 1953.

The US T.65 cartridge was not, as were the German 7.92mm Kurz, the Russian 7.62mm × 39mm or the British .280in, an intermediate power cartridge. The T.65 was, in effect, a cartridge having the ballistic characteristics of the old .30in. M.2 cartridge, but with a shorter case. The United States therefore, in its desire to stick with the desirable characteristics, i.e. effective range, muzzle velocity, bullet weight, penetration, etc., accepted the remaining, but far less desirable characteristic of the M.2, – its heavy recoil in a light weight rifle. In accepting the latter they were forced to accept a heavier rifle than desirable, and, worse still, in the interests of NATO unity, the other NATO powers accepted the same liability.

The T.65 series of .30in. cartridges came originally in three case lengths, 47mm, 49mm and finally 51mm, and it was the last of these that became the case of the new 7.62mm NATO standard cartridge in 1953.

In much the same way as the 7.62mm × 39mm cartridge has been adopted by countries outside the main communist blocs, so the 7.62mm × 51mm cartridge has been adopted or manufactured not only by NATO, CENTO and SEATO but also by a large number of countries belonging to none of these three treaty organisations, many of whom are not even politically sympathetic to those organisations.

Most 7.62mm × 51mm ammunition, irrespective of source, is brass cased, although Belgium, France, and the United States also produce some steel cased ammunition, with the United States also producing limited quantities with light alloy cases, Germany, France, Norway, Austria and Australia also produce plastic cased blank, grenade or short range practice ammunition.

The 7.62mm × 51mm cartridge has a bottlenecked rimless case, 51mm long, with a 11.9mm diameter rim. With a standard 44 grain (2.8g) nitrocellulose charge, the 144 grain (9.3g) boat-tailed ball-bullet gives a muzzle velocity of 838 metres/second with muzzle energy of 332mkp. This high powered cartridge, used in rifle, light machine gun and medium machine gun, is not, in a hand held rifle of reasonable weight, without bipod, suitable for full automatic fire.

Apart from standard 144 grain ball with lead core, mild steel core ball and other ball varieties have been produced in different countries. Spain, for example, has produced special light ball ammunition for use in CETME self-loading rifles, having a bullet weight of 94 grains (6.1g). The United States has produced special heavy ball for match use, with bullet weights of 175 grains (11.3g) and 200 grains (13g), and Japan has produced special low recoil ball ammunition. In short, a very wide assortment of ammunition has been produced, based on the NATO case, which is non-standard, and which conforms to no NATO specification.

NATO colour codes will be found on most 7.62mm × 51mm ammunition, but these codes are not universally used in all parts of the world, and certain non treaty countries still use their own individual codes.

Countries producing 7.62mm × 51mm ammunition include:

Argentina	Iran	Sudan
Austria	Israel	Sweden
Australia	Italy	Taiwan
Belgium	Japan	Turkey
Brazil	Malaysia	United Kingdom
Bulgaria	Morocco	USA
Canada	Nepal	W. Germany
Chile	New Zealand	*Potential producer in near future*
Czechoslovakia	Norway	Abu Dhabi
Denmark	Pakistan	Philippines
France	Peru	South Korea
Greece	Portugal	
Holland	South Africa	
India	Spain	

*7.62mm × 51, NATO ammunition. **Left to right:** US T.65. 45mm case; US T.65. 47mm case; US T.65. 51mm case; Spanish, CETME bullet; Short range practice, German; Short range practice (plastic), German; Blank, Blank; plastic*

5.56mm × 45mm AMMUNITION

The Salvo project already referred to had one very important result. It led to growing interest in the US Army and Air Force in .22in calibre weapons. Included in the Salvo programme were weapons chambered for the .222in Remington cartridge, and the US Military, or at least influential parts of it, concluded that much of the original advantage that would have come from Salvo would still be achievable if a .22in calibre self-loading rifle were to be adopted. Such a weapon and ammunition offered low weight, high velocity, low trajectory, low recoil and therefore good control when fired full auto, and effective killing power at fighting ranges.

Winchester, and the Armalite Division of the Fairchild Corporation were both asked to develop a high velocity .22in weapon. The Armalite weapon was preferred and led to the AR 15 rifle in .223in calibre, which in turn became the M.16 rifle firing the M.193 ball cartridge in 5.56mm calibre.

The original .222in Remington cartridge was slightly modified, and used as the basis of the new cartridge. The case capacity was enlarged, and with a 55 grain (3.5g) bullet gave a muzzle velocity of 1,005 metres per second. It was this cartridge, then known as the .223in, that finally became the M.193.

Although the 5.56mm cartridge has not been adopted as a standard round by any of the Western treaty organisations, this cartridge has been adopted, with a variety of light weapons, on an individual basis, by countries all over the world, outside the communist blocs. It ranks therefore alongside the 7.62mm × 39mm and the 7.62mm × 51mm cartridges as a cartridge in semi-universal use. In addition, it has been the departure point for a series of experimental "Micro-calibre" cartridges in various parts of the Western world.

Most 5.56mm × 45mm ammunition is brass cased, but steel cases have been produced by Belgium, France and the United States, the United States also producing limited quantities with light alloy cases. In addition a range of blanks and short range practice rounds with plastic cases have been produced, notably by Germany. 5.56mm caseless ammunition has also been produced experimentally in the United States.

*5.56mm × 45 ammunition. **Left to right:** Remington Magnum; .224in E.2; 5.56mm ball, M.193; 5.56mm ball, heavy spire bullet; 5.56mm short range practice; 5.56mm granade blank; 5.56mm blank, plastic*

The original ball bullet weight, for the M.193 cartridge, was 55 grains, the bullet having a normal ogive and being designed for barrels having a 1 in 12 twist. Produced later (mainly by IWK and NWM and in the United States) was a spire-pointed heavy bullet (weight between 68 and 77 grains or 4.4 and 5g) designed for 1 in 8in (203mm) twist barrels, giving better long range accuracy.

In the past year or so, Fabrique Nationale have produced a heavier 5.56mm bullet with standard ogive, weighing 62 grains (4g), designed for better all range performance, and intended for 1 in 9in (229mm) twist barrels.

The 5.56mm case is bottlenecked and rimless, 44.6mm in length, with a 9.5mm rim diameter. With a standard charge of 25 grains (1.6g) of ball powder, the 55 grain boat-tailed M.193 ball bullet develops a muzzle velocity of 1,005 metres/second with a muzzle energy of 184mkp. The standard US propellant is ball powder, although the US and other countries have used other N.C. powders.

5.56mm ammunition produced in the US and in Western Europe usually has the NATO system of colour codes, but it does not follow that 5.56mm ammunition produced elsewhere is similarly marked.

Known producers of the 5.56mm × 45mm cartridge include:

Australia (limited)	Netherlands
Austria	Norway
Belgium	Singapore
Brazil	Spain
Canada	Sweden
Finland	Thailand
France	UK (limited)
Israel	USA
Italy	West Germany

SERVICE AMMUNITION – CALIBRES BELOW 20mm

Shown here are the main details of service ammunition in use throughout the world since 1945. These details should, where applicable, be read in conjunction with the references to identification codes, and the history of the main "Pact" or "Treaty" cartridges now in service in many parts of the world. The following text does not cover the many types of training ammunition which may be found in all calibres including blanks, drill or dummy, and short range practice cartridges. In the tabulations that follow, muzzle velocities are given in both imperial and metric measures but weights are expressed only in grains. One grain is approximately 0.065 gramme; and the accompanying simplified conversion table will help to make conversions.

More than 50 countries are known to manufacturer military ammunition for their own purposes and many of them export ammunition to other countries. Information available regarding these activities varies considerably from country to country and the following listings should not be regarded as exhaustive.

Grains	Grammes	Grains	Grammes	Grains	Grammes
1	0.06	10	0.65	100	6.48
2	0.13	20	1.30	200	12.96
3	0.19	30	1.94	300	19.44
4	0.26	40	2.59	400	25.92
5	0.32	50	3.24	500	32.40
6	0.39	60	3.89	600	38.88
7	0.45	70	4.54	700	45.36
8	0.52	80	5.18	800	51.84
9	0.58	90	5.83	900	58.32

ARAB MILITARY INDUSTRIES ORGANISATION

This organisation was set up on 29th April 1975, with an initial funding of one billion dollars, to create a central arms manufacturing organisation for the Arab countries. Signatories of the agreement were Egypt, Qatar, Saudi Arabia and the United Arab Emirates. The agreement was preceded by a series of discussions, initiated by a resolution of the Arab Industrial Development Centre, passed in mid-1971 to establish an Inter-Arab Military Industries Authority, between the Arab Chiefs of Staff in 1974; and it was followed by further discussions, including some with French and British manufacturers, during which the programme of activities was developed and modified.

Although it is quite conceivable that the programmes will be modified again, the most recent agreement known is that reached early in 19? when the Presidents of France and Egypt met in Cairo on 15th Januar 1976. The programme then set out envisaged the establishment of manufacturing organisation with headquarters in Cairo, financed by t four participants enumerated above (but with most of the money comi from Saudi Arabia) all having the benefit of French technological a business participation. This company could initially concentrate on aircr manufacturing activities, ammunition production and the manufacture spare parts. So far as ammunition production is concerned the new orga sation starts with the benefit of Egyptian experience and facilities – discu sed in the United Arab Republic entry below.

ARGENTINA

Argentina now makes and uses 7.62mm × 51mm ammunition, but for a considerable period of time her basic rifle calibre has been the 7.65mm Mauser. The 7.65mm cartridge was produced in a number of bullet variations, as shown below.

7.65mm CALIBRE

Argentinian cases were of brass, with Berdan type primers. Cases we rimless, bottlenecked, and 54mm long. The ball bullet of 154 gains wei gave a muzzle velocity of 2,750f/s. The following 7.65mm bullet types w in Argentine service.

Type	Designation
APT	Type LP (Luminosa Perforante)
Spotter	Type R (Reglase)
AP	Type P (Perforante)
Smoke Tracer	Type TH (Trazante Humosa)
Light Tracer	Type TL (Trazante Luminosa)
Incendiary	Type QI (Quimica Incendiaria)

AUSTRALIA

7.62mm × 51 ammunition for the rifles and machine guns in service in the Australian Army is made in Australia. While the 5.56mm M16 rifle was being us Australian troops in Vietnam there was also a limited production of ammunition for it but this has probably now ceased.

AUSTRIA

Austrian munitions manufacture is known to include 7.62mm × 51 and 5.56mm × 45 rifle ammunition and the 9mm Parabellum. Ammunition in other ca is probably made also.

BELGIUM

At the close of the 1939-1945 war, Belgium discarded her pre-war basic rifle calibre cartridge, the 7.65mm Mauser, and remained armed with weapons and ammunition acquired from her allies. During the immediate post-1945 period therefore Belgian ammunition fell into five categories, all of which were manufactured in Belgium by Fabrique Nationale. These categories were, .303in (British), .30in-06 and .30in Carbine (USA) for rifles and machine guns, with .50in (12.7mm) ammunition for heavy machine guns. For pistol and sub-machine gun use, the 9mm Parabellum cartridge, which had been manufactured pre-1939, was retained.

From 1954 Belgium, although heavily engaged on the British .28 project, and involved also with the 7mm intermediate cartridges, adop the 7.62mm NATO cartridge which then replaced the earlier British and designs in Belgian service. Belgium also produces large quantities 5.56mm × 45 ammunition.

Although neither Britain nor Belgium adopted any of the 7mm in mediate cartridges which appeared around 1952, Belgium did succee selling SL rifles, chambered for one of these 7mm cartridges, to Venezu

Since then this 7mm cartridge has been made and sold commercially, and is described below. Other Belgian ammunition is not covered in detail here, since it conforms to NATO, British or US standard ammunition already described.

7.62mm CALIBRE (7.62mm NATO)

Belgian ammunition in this calibre will be encountered with standard NATO type cases, made in brass and steel. Primers are of Berdan type. Belgian 7.62mm cartridge nomenclature relates to the bullet fitted to the NATO case, and the following types are in service:

Type	Designation
Ball	SS.77
Tracer	L.78
AP	P.80
API	PI.86

.50in BROWNING (12.7mm CALIBRE)

Belgian .50in ammunition corresponds to US specifications, and Belgium currently produces counterparts of the following US cartridges: Ball M2 and M33; Tracer M17, AP M2, API M8, and API/T M20.

7mm INTERMEDIATE CALIBRE (7mm MEDIUM)

This cartridge is basically the British 7mm second optimum cartridge, which appeared on an experimental basis in 1952. It failed to win approval as the cartridge for adoption by NATO, for which purpose it was manufactured by both Britain and Belgium. Subsequently however Belgium made and sold this cartridge to Venezuela. Cases are of brass, rimless and bottlenecked. 49mm long. Primers are of the Berdan type. Details of the ball cartridge, sold to Venezuela as the "bala para fusil automatico" are:

Type	Designation	Charge	Bullet description and weight	Muzzle velocity
Ball	S12	39 grains	Flat-based, pointed, lead core. 140 grains	2,750f/s (840 metres/sec)

5.56mm × 45 CALIBRE

Originally Belgium produced 5.56mm which conformed with the corresponding United States designs. This ammunition was brass-cased with Berdan primers, and carried the following Belgian designations:
Ball: SS92; Tracer: L95; AP: P96
In addition a special Gendarmerie ball bullet was designated the RN100.
Within the last two years new bullet designs have been produced by FN with heavier bullets than the original 5.56mm designs, but using the same cartridge case. The heavier bullets, fired from 1 in 9 twist barrels give good long range accuracy. The two new cartridges are:

Type	Designation	Charge	Bullet description and weight	Muzzle velocity
Ball	SS101	24.7 grains (1.6 grammes)	61.7 grains (4 grammes)	2,932f/s (895 metre/sec)
Tracer	L102	22.2 grains (1.44 grammes)	63.9 grains (4.14 grammes)	2,559f/s (780 metres/sec)

OTHER CALIBRES

Apart from the cartridges mentioned above, Belgium, as one of the major ammunition exporters of the world, makes and exports a number of other calibres, which will usually bear the same head-stamp marks as ammunition for domestic use. Included in this category are 7.5mm French Model 1929C ammunition (made with Syrian head-stamps), 7.65mm Mauser, 7.92mm × 57mm Mauser, 6.5mm Mannlicher and a number of different pistol calibres.

BRAZIL

Ammunition currently produced in Brazil is known to include 7.62mm × 51 and 5.56mm × 45 rifle ammunition and various types of pistol ammunition. A programme to establish and produce standard small arms and ammunition for all military services was initiated in 1974 and may well be nearing fruition.

BULGARIA

In common with most other Warsaw Pact countries, Bulgaria produces at least the 7.62mm × 39 and LMG ammunition used by its own armed forces and probably other types as well. Among the latter is believed to be the 7.62mm × 51 round.

CANADA

Canadian Arsenals make a wide range of small arms including 5.56mm and 7.62mm rifles, 7.92mm (Bren) LMG .50 Browning MG and 9mm Browning pistols. Ammunition for most if not all of these weapons is also made and recent developments have included work on new .50 ammunition.

CHILE

Little is known about Chilean ammunition production. The 7.62mm × 51 round is certainly made there; but the mix of weapons in service in Chile is such that it is likely that other types are made also.

CHINA (PEOPLE'S REPUBLIC)

Communist China manufactures many of the main cartridge types described under USSR and in general appears to make such ammunition against Russian specifications. Chinese nomenclature however is different, and takes the form of a type number for each calibre, relating to the year in which the cartridge was adopted. The following nomenclature applies:
7.62mm × 39mm, Type 56; 7.62mm × 54mm, Type 53; 7.62mm Tokarev, Type 50; 12.7mm HMG, Type 54; 14.5mm HMG, Type 56.
Communist China took over from the Nationalists large quantities of 7.92mm weapons chambered for the 7.92mm × 57mm cartridges. These cartridges were manufactured in China with both pointed and round-nosed bullets, the cases being of brass. A description of typical 7.92mm ammunition is contained elsewhere in this chapter, and further description of the Chinese made ammunition is unnecessary.

CHINA (TAIWAN)

Following the admission of the People's Republic of China to the UN and Taiwan's consequent departure, a series of small-arms projects was put in hand in 1972 to compensate for the loss of arms supplies from the USA. It is known that the 7.62mm × 51 round is currently made on the island but it is probable that the range of local manufacture extends beyond this by now.

COLOMBIA

Details of current Colombian ammunition manufacture are not known; but it is believed that the 7.62mm × 51 round is made there and possibly also the .30-06.

CZECHOSLOVAKIA

Prior to the 1939-1945 war, the standard Czechoslovakian rifle cartridge was the 7.92mm × 57mm Mauser, and she continued to make this calibre after the war, and after her adoption of the Russian 7.62mm M1943 cartridge. As an arms exporting country of note, Czechoslovakia makes a considerable variety of ammunition, and apart from exporting 7.92mm ammunition, makes and exports 7.62mm × 54mm Russian, .303in British and 7.62mm × 51mm (NATO) ammunition. These various calibres are covered in detail elsewhere, and further description here is therefore unnecessary.

Czechoslovakia today is armed with weapons chambered for the cartridges described in detail under "USSR" (with the possible exception of some weapons chambered for 9mm Parabellum and 7.65mm S.L. pistol cartridges). However, in the early 1950s the Czechs developed their own 7.62mm medium power assault rifle cartridge, which was exported to certain countries aligned to the Communist Bloc. This Czech 7.62mm cartridge was not interchangeable with the Russian M43 cartridge, and as a member of the Warsaw Pact, and in the interests of standardisation, the Czechs did not retain their own cartridge in service.

7.62mm MODEL 1952 CARTRIDGE (also known as the 7.62mm × 45mm cartridge)
This cartridge has been made with both steel and brass cases. Steel cases, lacquered, predominate. The case is rimless and bottlenecked, and 44.7mm long. Primers are of the Berdan type. Although other loadings may have existed, ball and tracer seem to be the two types actually in service.

Type	Designation	Charge	Bullet description and weight	Muzzle velocity
Ball	M52	27 grains	Boat-tailed, pointed, steel core. 130 grains	2,440f/s (744 metres/sec)
Tracer	M52	27 grains	Flat-based, pointed. 130 grains	2,440f/s (744 metres/sec)

7.65mm BROWNING CARTRIDGE
This SL Pistol cartridge was in service in Czechoslovakia prior to the 1939-1945 war. In recent years it has made a reappearance in Czechoslovakia for use in machine pistols or sub-machine guns. The 7.65mm case is straight sided with a semi-rimless base, 17mm long.

Type	Designation	Charge	Bullet description and weight	Muzzle velocity
Ball	M1927 (original Czech designation, probably now changed)		Flat-based, round-nosed, lead core. Weight varies according to mfg. 55 to 75 grains	990f/s (302 metres/sec)

DENMARK

Ammunition for at least some of the weapons used by Danish forces is made in Denmark. Rounds made include the 7.62mm × 51 NATO and 9mm Parabellum.

DOMINICAN REPUBLIC

Little information is available on Dominican ammunition manufacture, but it is believed that .30 M1 Carbine ammunition is made for the Cristobal M2 weapon used by the army.

FINLAND

Finland, while not a member of the Warsaw Pact, has for a considerable period of time used ammunition whose design originated basically in the USSR. Since 1945 two basic rifle calibre cartridges have been in service, the Russian 7.62mm × 54mm and the Russian 7.62mm × 39mm, both manufactured in Finland.

Finnish ammunition in these calibres is interchangeable with that made in the USSR, but bullet designs vary. Finnish cases are usually of brass, and Berdan primers are generally used, although Boxer ignition has appeared in some Finnish productions.

The standard Finnish S.L. pistol or sub-machine gun round is the 9mm Parabellum.

Finnish 7.62mm × 54mm ammunition conforms to the following designations:

Ball: Type D166 (having a 200 grain boat-tailed bullet, with velocity of 2,300f/s (701 metres/sec))
Tracer: Type D278
AP: Type D277
Incend: Type S276

Finnish 7.62mm × 39mm ammunition conforms to the following designations:
Ball: Type S309. Differs from USSR type, and has a flat-based lead cored bullet which weighs 124 grains
Tracer: Type VJ313. Different ogive to USSR type. Flat-based bullet weighing 124 grains.

FRANCE

Since 1945 the small arms ammunition picture in France has been a confused one. In all, thirteen different categories of ammunition have been in use, and for ease of reference these may be split into three classes. Firstly there are pre-1939 designs, which comprise the 8mm and the 7.5mm rifle calibres, and the 7.65mm Pistol calibre.

Secondly there are the calibres which, during and just after the war France pressed into service, to augment her own designs. Most of this second category were made in France in post-war years, and the second class includes US .30in Carbine ammunition, .30in and .50in. Browning ammunition and .45in ACP ammunition, British .303in calibre ammunition and .380in revolver ammunition, and finally German 7.92mm × 57mm ammunition (for MG use) and 7.92mm Kurz ammunition. The third class covers post-war adoptions, which comprise the 7.62mm NATO cartridge and the 9mm Parabellum cartridge.

Many of the above types have completely vanished from French service today, while others have been relegated to reserve. France retains in first line service the 7.5mm and the 7.62mm NATO cartridges for rifles and machine guns, the 9mm Parabellum cartridge, and the .50in (12.7mm) Browning heavy machine-gun cartridge. Apart from the thirteen categories mentioned, France has, within the last two years, adopted the 5.56mm × 45 cartridge. This is now manufactured in France.

Covered below in detail are those calibres in use since 1945 which are not already covered in in other parts of this section.

7.5mm CALIBRE (known also as the 7.5mm MAS or 7.5mm Model 1929.C)
This cartridge, which was being progressively introduced at the outbreak of the 1939-1945 war, is still the basic French rifle and machine gun cartridge. It is in service in Metropolitan France and elsewhere with the exception of Germany, where the French Army uses the 7.62mm NATO cartridge. The 7.5mm cartridge will be found with both lacquered steel and with brass cases, the cases being bottlenecked and rimless, and 53.5mm long. Primers are of the Berdan type. Principal loadings in current service include:

Type	Designation	Charge	Bullet description and weight	Muzzle velocity
Ball	Mle 1929 "O"	44.8 grains	Flat-based, pointed, lead core. 140 grains	2,600f/s (793 metres/sec)
Tracer	Mle 1949 "TO"	—	Steel core, lead sleeve (red bullet tip). 145 grains	—
Tracer	Mle 1949A "TO"	—	Steel core, lead sleeve (red bullet tip). 145 grains	—
Tracer	Mle 1950 "TO"	—	Lead core, (green bullet tip). 140 grains	—
Tracer	Mle 1950A "TO"	—	Lead core, (green bullet tip). 140 grains	—
Tracer	Mle 1958A "TO"	48.8 grains	Lead core, plastic tracer cover, (violet bullet tip). 140 grains	—
Tracer	Mle G.59 "TO"	—	Lead core. Has longer trace than Mle 58. (Red tip). 140 grains	—
AP	Mle 1949 "P"	—	Hardened steel core. 145 grains	—
AP	Mle 1949A "P"	—	Hardened steel core. 145 grains	—
APT	Mle 1949 "TP"	—	Originally white band, black tip.	—
APT	Mle 1949A "TP"	—	Now red band, black tip	

NOTE: A short range 7.5mm Observation cartridge also exists, for use with the 75mm recoilless gun. The 7.5mm round, without a tracer component has a yellow bullet tip and if fitted with a tracer component, has a red band with a yellow tip. This cartridge is the "Cartouche de tir reduit Mle 1954".

8mm CALIBRE (also known as the 8mm Lebel cartridge)

Although no longer in service in France, this cartridge may appear in other parts of the world, especially those in which France has, or has had, a military presence. The 8mm cartridge, except for small batches of German controlled production during the 1939-1945 war, has always been brass cased. The cases are rimmed, bottlenecked, and 51mm long. Primers are of Berdan type. Principal recent loadings include:

Type	Designation	Charge	Bullet description and weight	Muzzle velocity
Ball	Balle D	47 grains	Boat-tailed, pointed, solid bronze. 198 grains	2,400f/s (732 metres/sec)
Ball	Balle N	47 grains	Boat-tailed, pointed, lead core. 199 grains	
AP	Balle P	49 grains	Flat-based, pointed, steel core. Blackened envelope	
Tracer	Balle T	46 grains	Boat-tailed, pointed, tin washed envelope. 174 grains	

(Note: A further tracer design in 8mm calibre existed, the T Mle 51.)

7.62mm NATO CALIBRE

Although not now a member of NATO, France developed her own series of cartridges in 7.62mm NATO calibre, at an early date, and her forces currently stationed in Germany carry weapons chambered for this cartridge. Basically the French 7.62mm ammunition conforms to NATO ballistics, and French ammunition is proved in NATO test centres together with that of NATO members.

French 7.62mm ammunition is found with lacquered steel and with brass cases, the steel predominating. The bottlenecked rimless 51mm case is standard, and fitted with Berdan type primers. The following French 7.62mm NATO cartridges are, or have been, in service:

Ball Designated	Balle O. Mle 1951
Ball Designated	Balle O. Mle 1954
Ball Designated	Balle O. Mle 1960
Ball Designated	Balle O. Mle 1961
AP Designated	Balle P. Mle 1960
API Designated	Balle Pl. Mle 1960
Incendiary Designated	Balle I. Mle 1960
Tracer Designated	Balle T. Mle 1951
Tracer Designated	Balle T. Mle 1954
Tracer Designated	Balle T. Mle 1960 Observation

12.7mm MODEL 1947 (.50in BROWNING)

Apart from US ammunition taken into French service, France has produced its own design of 12.7mm cartridge, whose bullets vary from the US designs. The French cartridge cases, made in brass and steel, conform to the external measurements of the US case. Principal French loadings are:

Type	Designation	Charge	Bullet description and weight	Muzzle velocity
Ball	"O" Mle 47	231 grains	Mild steel core. 687 grains	2,867f/s (875 metres/sec)
AP	"P" Mle 47	231 grains	Hard steel core. 687 grains	2,867f/s (875 metres/sec)
APT	"PT" Mle 47	231 grains	Hard steel core. 700 grains	2,818f/s (860 metres/sec)
Tracer	"T" Mle 47	231 grains	Mild steel core. 700 grains	2,818f/s (860 metres/sec)
Incend	"I" Mle 47	231 grains	Mild steel sleeve, filled with composition. Base pad of lead. 633 grains	2,998f/s (915 metres/sec)

5.56mm CALIBRE

For the past few years France has produced development quantities of 5.56mm × 45 ammunition, together with a new rifle chambered for this round. In 1973 the Le Mans arsenal produced the first batches of production ammunition. Two loadings have been produced, the Balle "O" (Normal ball) and Balle "T" (Tracer). As far as is known, the projectiles and ballistics for both are standard for this class of ammunition. French 5.56mm ammunition is produced with both lacquered steel and brass cases.

7.65mm CALIBRE (7.65mm MAS or 7.65 M.1925)

This French designed round was for use in SL pistols and sub-machine guns. It was made with both brass and steel cases, the cases being straight sided and rimless. 19.5mm long. Primers were of the Berdan type.

Type	Designation	Charge	Bullet description and weight	Muzzle velocity
Ball		Balle L	Round-nosed, flat-based, lead core. 85 grains	1,200f/s (366 metres/sec)

9mm PARABELLUM

French 9mm ammunition for S.L. pistols and sub-machine guns uses standard 9mm Parabellum cases, which were made both in brass and steel. Cases are straight sided and rimless, 19mm long. Primers are of the Berdan type. Two service 9mm cartridges have been in service, as under:

Type	Designation	Charge	Bullet description and weight	Muzzle velocity
Ball	Balle O	6 grains	Flat-based, round-nose, lead core. 124 grains	1,300f/s (396 metres/sec)
Tracer	Balle T	6 grains	Flat-base, round-nose, originally had white bullet tip, later changed to red. 124 grains	1,300f/s (396 metres/sec)

GERMANY (FEDERAL REPUBLIC)

West German small arms ammunition since 1945 has been standardised on NATO or US cartridges. Currently in use is 9mm Parabellum ammunition for S.L. pistols and sub-machine guns, 7.62mm NATO ammunition for rifles and machine guns and 50in (12.7mm) Browning ammunition for heavy machine guns. In addition Germany has produced a number of different 5.56mm × 45mm cartridges, although the weapons chambered for this round have not been adopted by the Bundeswehr. Much of West Germany's early ammunition requirements was originally met by contract supply from Portugal, Spain, and Belgium, particularly in 7.62mm calibre.

Since German small arms ammunition is standard, it is not covered in separate detail here. German 9mm Parabellum ammunition is brass cased and with 124 grain bullets, with standard ballistics. German 7.62mm ammunition is also brass cased, with standard NATO ballistics, the individual cartridge types being identified by the following nomenclature: Ball, mild steel core: DM.1; Ball, lead core: DM.41; Tracer: DM.21; Short range, plastic: DM.18; Blank, plastic: DM.28.

See also the note on German and Japanese World War II ammunition at the end of this section.

GREECE

Greek requirements for small arms ammunition are largely met by manufacture within the country. It is known that the 7.62mm × 51 and 9mm Parabellum rounds are made there, but the range may be wider than this.

HUNGARY

In common with most other Warsaw Pact countries, Hungary has its own munitions plant which produces at least some of the small-arms ammunition used by Hungarian forces. This certainly includes the 7.62mm × 39 M1943 round.

INDIA

Indian manufacture of small arms has a long history; but, in the past fifteen years or so, manufacturing capacity has been increased to near the point of self-sufficiency. Standard Indian military weapons fire the 7.62mm × 51, .303in and 9mm Parabellum rounds, all of which are made in India.

INDONESIA

Indonesian forces are equipped with a wide variety of small arms for which several different types of ammunition are required. Some of this, and certainly the 7.62mm × 39 and 9mm Parabellum rounds, is made in Indonesia as also are some of the weapons.

IRAN

Although the most spectacular aspect of Iranian defence operations in recent years has been the gigantic programme of weapon and equipment purchases from the USA and Europe, there has been a persistent move towards the establishment of an indigenous armament industry. The manufacture of small arms ammunition has formed part of this operation and at least 7.62mm × 51 and 9mm Parabellum rounds are made in Iran.

IRAQ

Little is known about small arms ammunition manufacture in Iraq. It is believed, however, that 7.62 M1943 rounds are made there for the Russian weapons with which the Iraqi forces are mainly equipped and that some .303in rounds are made for weapons originally supplied by the UK.

ISRAEL

Israel has a substantial munitions industry which makes ammunition for home consumption and for export in the main NATO, Warsaw Pact and former British calibres. Rounds known to be made are 5.56mm × 45, 7.62mm × 39 M1943, 7.62mm × 51 NATO, .303in British, 7.92mm Mauser and 9mm Parabellum, but there are probably others.

ITALY

Italy had a very large assortment of rifle or machine gun calibres in service during the 1939-1945 war, involving eight different case designs. After 1945 Italy retained in service three of these designs, the 6.5mm calibre, 7.7mm (.303in) calibre, and the 8mm machine gun calibre. Taken into service also were the .30in Carbine and .30in-06 cartridges, for the US weapons supplied to Italy. Subsequently Italy took into service the 7.62mm NATO cartridge, which, together with the 9mm Parabellum cartridge and the .50in (12.7mm) Browning cartridge now comprise Italy's main categories of ammunition. Covered below in detail are those cartridges which are peculiar to Italy.

6.5mm CALIBRE (6.5mm M91)

This was originally the standard Italian rifle calibre cartridge, and was still manufactured in Italy in the mid-1950s. The case was usually of brass but post-war manufacture utilised steel cases. The case was rimless and bottlenecked, and 52.5mm long. Primers were of the Berdan type.

Type	Designation	Charge	Bullet description and weight	Muzzle velocity
Ball	M91	34 grains	Round-nosed, flat-based, lead core. 162 grains	2,300f/s (701 metres/sec)

7.7mm CALIBRE (.303in)

This cartridge was originally in service, before and during the 1939-1945 war, with the Italian Air Force. The case is identical with the British .303in cartridge, and British ammunition chambered in Italian weapons. After the war Italy did not retain this calibre in her Air Force, but since the Italian Army were supplied with British No 4 rifles and Bren LMG in .303in calibre, Italy retained this calibre and continued to manufacture it. Post-1945 7.7mm ammunition was brass cased, the cartridge being rimmed and bottlenecked, with a case length of 56.2mm. Ball and tracer were the two standard loadings produced, the ammunition corresponding basically with that of British make.

*Miscellaneous service ammunition. **Left to right:** (1) 7.92mm × 57mm Mauser, ball; (2) 7.92mm × 33 MP43 ball, Germany; (3) 8mm Breda, Italy; (4) 6.5mm Mannlicher Carcano, Italy; (5) 7.65mm × 54mm Mauser, Argentina; (6) 9mm Largo, Spain*

8mm CALIBRE (8mm MODEL 35 or 8mm BREDA)

This cartridge, of Italian design, was the standard medium machine gun cartridge during the 1939-1945 war, and retained in service by Italy after the war. Originally steel and brass cases were produced, but brass predominated. The case was rimless and bottlenecked, 59mm long. Primers were of the Berdan type. Post-war loadings of this cartridge were as follows:

Type	Designation	Charge	Bullet description and weight	Muzzle velocity
Ball	M35	49 grains	Flat-based, pointed. 208 grains	2,600f/s (793 metres/sec)
Tracer	M56	49 grains	Flat-based, pointed red bullet tip	

9mm PARABELLUM (9mm M38)

Italy has long been the user of 9mm Parabellum ammunition, of which two distinct loadings exist in Italy. The basic current cartridge is the Model 1938 which is used for sub-machine guns and which produces pressure of about 16 tons per square inch. The M38 cartridge is unsafe to fire in the old Glisenti S.L. pistol with which the Italian Army was once equipped, and a lower powered 9mm cartridge, using the same case was used in this pistol. Italian M38 ammunition is normally brass cased, although steel cases have also been used. Details of the two classes of Italian ammunition are:

Type	Designation	Charge	Bullet description and weight	Muzzle velocity
Ball	M1910	5 grains	Flat-based, truncated flat-nose. 124 grains	1,000f/s (305 metres/sec)
Ball	M1938	7 grains	Flat-based, round-nosed. 115 grains	1,450f/s (462 metres/sec)

JAPAN

A note on German and Japanese ammunition of the Second World War appears at the end of this list. Current production of ammunition is known to include the 7.62mm × 51 cartridge with reduced charge, for use in the Type 64 rifle, and probably covers other types.

KOREA (NORTH)

It is probable that the North Koreans now make most of their own small-arms ammunition. They certainly make the 7.62mm × 39 round and probably the 7.62mm × 54R also.

KOREA (SOUTH)

South Korean forces are equipped entirely with small arms of US design and have recently set up a plant in Pusan to make the 5.56mm M16A1 rifle. It is probable that they are or will shortly be making ammunition for this and probably the 7.62mm × 51 round also. It is known that the country intends to be self-sufficient in small arms manufacture at least by 1981.

MALAYSIA

Since 1972 Sharikat Explosives have been making small arms and ammunition and it is believed that ammunition production is in the order of 20 million rounds per annum. The company is jointly owned by the Malaysian Government, Oerlikon of Switzerland, Dynamit Nobel of West Germany and three Malaysian companies. Products certainly include the 7.62mm × 51 round and probably the 5.56mm × 45 and 9mm Parabellum rounds.

MOROCCO

It is known that the 7.62mm × 51 round is made in Morocco but no details or other information are available.

NEPAL

A munitions plant was established in Nepal in 1975 and is known to be producing the 7.62mm × 51 round.

THE NETHERLANDS

The Netherlands has a substantial munitions industry which supplies the requirements of the country's armed forces – at least so far as small arms are concerned – and exports some types of ammunition. Types produced are 5.56mm × 45, 7.62mm × 51 NATO (ball, tracer and AP including belted rounds for the FN MAG), .30-06, .303in, 9mm Parabellum and .50 Browning plus a .50 hard-core round (.50 AP-HC armour-piercing and .50 AP-HC1 armour-piercing incendiary) which was introduced by Eurometaal of Zaandam (then known as Artillerie-Inrichtingen) in 1971. This round can be fired from all weapons suitable for the .50 M2 ball ammunition and has an armour-piercing penetration of at least 10mm at 800 metres and 45° incidence. It has a bullet weight of 679 grains (44g) and a muzzle velocity, with a 45in (1,143mm) barrel of 920m/sec (3,018ft/sec). The round can be mixed with other types of .50 Browning ammunition.

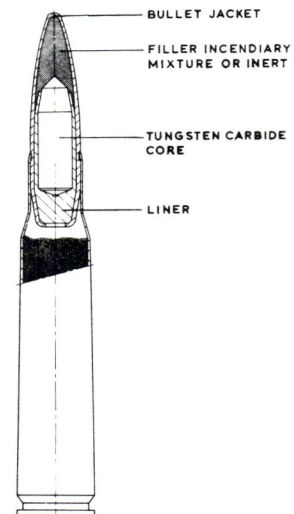

BULLET JACKET

FILLER INCENDIARY MIXTURE OR INERT

TUNGSTEN CARBIDE CORE

LINER

Sectional view of Eurometaal .50 AP-HC round

NEW ZEALAND

Most of the small arms used by New Zealand forces use the 7.62mm × 51 NATO round and this is manufactured locally. It is not known that any other ammunition is made.

NORWAY

NATO 7.62mm × 51 ammunition is extensively used by the Norwegian armed forces and is manufactured in the country. 5.56mm × 45 and 9mm Parabellum rounds are also made.

PAKISTAN

Nine factories are now producing small arms and ammunition in Pakistan, the first having been built with Chinese help in 1970, and the country achieved self-sufficiency in this respect in 1975. Ammunition produced includes 7.62mm × 51 NATO, 7.62mm × 39 M1943 Russian pattern and .303in British pattern.

PERU

In common with most other South American states, Peru is building up a defence industry which includes munitions manufacture. Ammunition known to be produced at present is the 7.62mm × 51 NATO round but there may be others.

PHILIPPINES

At least three-quarters and possibly as much as nine-tenths of the small arms and ammunition used by the armed forces of the Philippines are now made in the country. The main thrust towards self-sufficiency dating from as recently as 1975. No details are available, but it is probable that the 7.62mm × 51 round is in production and possible that the 5.56mm × 45 round is also.

POLAND

Polish ammunition production is known to include the 7.62mm × 39 M1943 and the 9mm × 18 pistol round. These two rounds cover all Polish requirements other than that for the 12.7mm HMG. It is not known that the latter round is made in Poland.

PORTUGAL

Portugal maintains a thriving small arms ammunition industry, and has become one of the major exporters of ammunition in a variety of calibres. Capacity exists in Portugal to supply ammunition of obsolescent design, which can, upon request, be marked on the head with whatever stamp the ultimate user requires, which can mean that the country of origin remains undetected. This practice also extends to ammunition of modern design.

Such ammunition as is ordered from Portugal is loaded to give whatever ballistics the buyer wishes, which means in practice that Portugese ammunition is loaded to the standard ballistics normally found with the calibre in question.

Apart from a wide variety of pistol calibre ammunition, Portugal has produced large quantities of 7.62mm × 51mm NATO ammunition, and .303in ammunition.

ROMANIA

Apart from the fact that the 7.62mm ×39 M1943 round is made there, no   details of Romanian ammunition production are known.

SINGAPORE

5.56mm × 45 ammunition for the M16 rifles made in Singapore is also   made there. It is not known that other types are made but they may well be.

SOUTH AFRICA

Manufacture of small arms and ammunition in South Africa has been on an increasing scale for the past fifteen years or more and almost all the country's requirements in these respects are now met by home manufacture.

SPAIN

Since 1945 Spain has used two basic rifle calibre cartridges, the 7.92mm × 57 mm Mauser cartridge, and the 7.62mm × 51mm cartridge. For pistol and sub-machine gun use Spain employs the 9mm Largo cartridge.

Spanish 7.92mm Mauser ammunition is conventional in type and is not covered here.

7.62mm × 51mm CALIBRE (NATO CASE)

Spain makes two basic 7.62mm cartridges, both utilising the standard NATO 51mm case. One of these is the cartridge loaded with standard weight projectiles and loaded to NATO specifications. The second category was designed specially loaded to give ballistics suitable for the Spanish CETME Model 1958 rifle, which is a delayed blowback design. Spanish 7.62mm NATO cased ammunition is brass cased, with Berdan type primer.

Type	Designation	Charge	Bullet description and weight	Muzzle velocity
Ball	CH.001	30 grains	Boat-tailed, spire point. 95 grains	2,500f/s (762 metres/sec)

9mm LARGO CALIBRE (also known as 9mm BERGMANN – BAYARD)

This powerful cartridge is the basic Spanish pistol and SMG cartridge. It has a rimless case with straight sides, 23mm long. Cases are of brass, with Berdan primers. Details are as follows:

Type	Charge	Bullet description and weight	Muzzle velocity
Ball	6 grains	Flat-based, round-nosed, lead core. 130 grains	1,150f/s (350 metres/sec)

SUDAN

Little is known about Sudanese ammunition manufacture but it appears   that both NATO and Russian pattern 7.62mm rounds are made.

SWEDEN

Swedish small arms ammunition from 1945 covers the following categories: 9mm Parabellum, for S.L. pistols and sub-machine guns; 6.5mm ammunition for rifles and machine guns; 8mm ammunition for medium machine gun use, and 12.7mm (.50in) Browning Model 1945 ammunition; and in addition Sweden, although not a member of NATO, has produced 7.62mm × 51mm ammunition.

6.5mm CALIBRE (also known as 6.5mm Mauser, or 6.5mm M94)

Most 6.5mm Swedish ammunition has been produced with brass cases, the cases being rimless, bottlenecked, 55mm long. It has been produced over a long period of time, and in a variety of loadings, the current loadings being:

Type	Designation	Charge	Bullet description and weight	Muzzle velocity
Ball	PRJ. M.41	41 grains	Boat-tailed, pointed, lead core. 140 grains	2,600f/s (793 metres/sec)
AP	PPRJ. M.41	41 grains	—	
Tracer	SLPRJ. M.41.B	41 grains	Flat-based, pointed. 120 grains	

8mm CALIBRE (8mm Model 1932, also known as 8mm Bofors)

This powerful 8mm cartridge is peculiar to Sweden. The case, of brass, is rimless and bottlenecked, 62.7mm long. Primers are of Berdan type. Loadings include:

Type	Designation	Charge	Bullet description and weight	Muzzle velocity
Ball	PRJ. M.32	55 grains	Boat-tailed, pointed. 218 grains	2,500f/s (762 metres/sec)
Tracer	PPRJ. M.39	55 grains	Boat-tailed, pointed, steel core. 182 grains	2,700f/s (824 metres/sec)
AP	SLPRJ. M.39	55 grains	Pointed. 170 grains	2,560f/s (780 metres/sec)
Incend	Brand. PRJ. M.41	55 grains	Boat-tailed, pointed	

9mm PARABELLUM

The Swedish 9mm cartridge is designated the M39 cartridge, and has a 115 grain bullet. Most cases are of brass, with some steel cases, brass washed, also employed. Ballistics for Swedish 9mm ammunition are standard for the calibre.

SWITZERLAND

Switzerland is armed with the same basic infantry cartridges that were in service during the period of the 1939-1945 war. The basic pistol and sub-machine gun cartridge is the 9mm Parabellum cartridge (replacing the earlier 7.65mm Parabellum). The rifle and machine gun cartridge is the 7.5mm round, the larger calibres being the .50in (12.7mm) Browning cartridge and the .50in Spotting rifle cartridge (based on the US M48.A.I).

7.5mm CALIBRE

This cartridge, similar to, but preceding the French 7.5mm cartridge, is designated the Model 1911, and may be encountered with brass, steel or alloy cases. The case is rimless and bottlenecked, 55.4mm long. Primers are Berdan type. The principal loadings are:

Type	Designation	Charge	Bullet description and weight	Muzzle velocity
Ball	G.P. II	50 grains	Boat-tailed, pointed, lead core. 175 grains	2,600f/s (793 metres/sec)
AP	St: Kern II	49 grains	Boat-tailed, pointed, steel core. 175 grains	
Tracer (AA)	FLAB. L'spur II	46 grains	Boat-tailed, pointed. 148 grains	
Tracer	L'spur 11	51 grains	Flat-based, pointed. 156 grains	

A further 7.5mm Swiss cartridge may be encountered which resembles a normal rifle cartridge. It is the cartridge for the sub calibre spotting tube used on 90mm anti-tank weapons. The case is rimmed and bottlenecked, and the bullet fired is a tracer bullet. The case length of this particular cartridge is 55.4mm, and it bears a close resemblance to the 7.5mm Model 1911 case. Two variants exist, as follows:

Type	Designation	
Tracer	L'spur 50	vary with regard to velocity
Tracer	L'spur 57	

9mm PARABELLUM

Swiss made 9mm Parabellum ammunition is standard with regard to ballistics compared to ammunition of similar type made elsewhere. The Swiss cartridge is designated "Pistolen Patrone 41", and is readily identified by the bullet contour which is more rounded and "heel shaped" than other makes. The bullet weight is 124 grains, and cases are normally brass, although some aluminium cased ammunition was also issued at one time.

SYRIA

It is known that at least some of the ammunition for the 7.62mm Russian rifles used by Syrian forces is made in Syria as also ammunition for their 9mm SMG. 12.7mm ammunition may also be made there.

THAILAND

Thailand uses a variety of US cartridges, at the present time, of standard type. In addition however, Thailand has had in service for a long time, a rifle cartridge of local design, which was manufactured as recently as the late 1950s. This 8mm cartridge has a case superficially similar to the pre-war 8mm Austrian Mannlicher cartridge, but not interchangeable with it. The Thai 8mm cartridge has a rimmed, bottlenecked case, 51.5mm long. Primers are of the Berdan type.

Type	Designation	Charge	Bullet description and weight	Muzzle velocity
Ball	Type 66	49 grains	Flat-based, pointed, lead core. 180 grains	—

TURKEY

Turkey has been making small-arms ammunition for many years, and recent events – notably the embargo on US military supplies following the invasion of Cyprus – have probably encouraged measures to ensure self-sufficiency. Ammunition types known to have been made are 7.63mm × 51 and 7.92mm × 54.

USSR

Since 1945, seven different categories of small arms ammunition have been in service with the USSR. In the main, other Communist States, including China, have used the same categories, although many such States also used other categories, notably 7.92mm × 57mm ammunition, in the years immediately succeeding the 1939-1945 war.

Two basic rifle calibre cartridges have been in USSR service – the 7.62mm × 54mm cartridge, and the 7.62mm × 39mm cartridge. For S.L. pistol and sub-machine gun the 7.62mm Tokarev cartridge was used. Two further pistol cartridges have been used, the 7.62mm Nagant revolver cartridge, and the more recent 9mm Makarov S.L. pistol cartridge. In the heavy machine gun role, two cartridges have been used: the 12.7mm and the 14.5mm cartridges.

Evidence exists to show that, at least on a development basis, the USSR has produced 5.6mm ammunition in recent years. The standard M.43 cartridge has been necked down to 5.6mm calibre, the resultant combination is fairly well known as a match or competition cartridge. Reports of this same basic cartridge with special loadings such as tracer indicate that the 5.6mm × 39 cartridge has formed part of a military programme.

7.62mm × 54mm CALIBRE (also known as the 7.62mm Moisin Nagant)

Ammunition in this calibre made in the USSR will be encountered with both brass and copper washed steel cases, steel cases predominating in recent years. Cases are rimmed, bottlenecked, with a length of 54mm. Primers are Berdan type. Principal loadings are:

Type	Designation	Charge	Bullet description and weight	Muzzle velocity
Ball	M1930 Type D	47 grains	Boat-tailed, pointed, lead core. 182 grains	2,680f/s (818 metres/sec)
Ball	Type LPS	48 grains	Boat-tailed, pointed, steel core. 149 grains	2,850f/s (870 metres/sec)
AP	M1930 Type B30	48 grains	Boat-tailed, pointed, steel core. 170 grains	2,790f/s (851 metres/sec)
API	M1940 Type BS40	48 grains	Flat-based, pointed, tungsten core. 187 grains	2,575f/s (785 metres/sec)
API	M1932 Type B32	50 grains	Boat-tailed, pointed, steel core, flat based. 154 grains	2,850f/s (870 metres/sec)
APT	Type BT	49 grains	Pointed. 157 grains	2,800f/s (855 metres/sec)

Incend/Ranging	Type ZP	47 grains	Boat-tailed, pointed. 160 grains. Internal striker mechanism	2,710f/s (827 metres/sec)
AP/I/T	Type BZT	48 grains	Flat-based, pointed. 142 grains	2,850f/s (870 metres/sec)
Tracer	M1930 Type T	45 grains	Flat-based, pointed. 148 grains	2,740f/s (837 metres/sec)
Grenade		24 grains		

(Note: A later type of tracer in 7.62mm × 54mm exists, the Type T46)

7.62mm × 39mm CALIBRE (M1943 Cartridge)

Ammunition in this calibre made in the USSR is made entirely with steel cases, copper or brass washed. Cases are rimless and bottlenecked, and 39mm long, with Berdan type primers. Principal loadings are:

Type	Designation	Charge	Bullet description and weight	Muzzle velocity
Ball	Type PS	25 grains	Boat-tailed, pointed, steel core. 123 grains	2,330f/s (710 metres/sec)
Tracer	Type T45	25 grains	Flat-based, pointed. 115 grains	
API	Type BZ	25 grains	Boat-tailed, pointed. 120 grains	
Incend/Ranging	Type ZP	25 grains	Flat-based, pointed with tracer. 102 grains	

7.62mm TOKAREV (also known as the 7.62mm × 25mm cartridge)

Most USSR made ammunition in this calibre is brass cased, the case being rimless and bottlenecked, 24.5mm long. Primers are of the Berdan type. Three service loadings exist:

Type	Designation	Charge	Bullet description and weight	Muzzle velocity
Ball	Type P	9 grains	Flat-based, round-nosed, lead core. 85 grains	1,500f/s (457 metres/sec)
API	Type P41	9 grains	Flat-based, round-nosed, steel core. 74 grains	
Tracer	Type PT	9 grains	Flat-based, round-nosed. 85 grains	

7.62mm NAGANT REVOLVER

All ammunition in this calibre is brass cased, the case being rimmed, and bottlenecked, 38.7mm in length. Primers are of the Berdan type. This cartridge is unusual in that the bullet is entirely contained within the case. The necking may be either a true bottleneck, or a very sharp neck taper. The bullet, upon being fired, forces out the neck. This cartridge is still in use as a revolver match cartridge.

Type	Designation	Charge	Bullet description and weight	Muzzle velocity
Ball	Type R	6 grains	Flat-based, rounded contoured nose with flattened tip. 106 grains	950f/s (290 metres/sec)

9mm MAKAROV

This post-1945 cartridge for use in Makarov and Stechkin SL pistols may be found with lacquered steel, copper washed steel or brass cases. The case is rimless, with straight sides, and 17.8mm long. Berdan type primer.

Type	Designation	Charge	Bullet description and weight	Muzzle velocity
Ball	—	4 grains	Flat-based, round-nosed. 93 grains	1,100f/s (335 metres/sec)

12.7mm CALIBRE

This heavy machine gun cartridge has been the standard HMG round for a long period of time. USSR production is brass cased, the case being rimless and bottlenecked. Case length is 107mm. Primers are of the Berdan type. Principal loadings are:

Type	Designation	Charge	Bullet description and weight	Muzzle velocity
Exp/Incend	Type ZP	255 grains	Brass fused projectile. 685 grains	
AP	Type B30	270 grains	Boat-tailed, pointed, steel core. 810 grains	Velocity of AP and API
API	Type B32	250 grains	Boat-tailed, pointed, steel core. 710 grains	is approx. 2,750f/s
API	Type BZ	235 grains	Boat-tailed, pointed, steel core. 740 grains	(840 metres/sec)
APIT	Type BZT	265 grains	Flat-based, pointed, steel core. 680 grains	

(Note: a further API cartridge exists in 12.7mm calibre, the Type BS41)

USSR and Czech service ammunition. **Left to right:** 7.62mm × 54mm, USSR; 7.62mm × 45mm Model 1952, Czech; 7.62mm × 39mm Model 1943, USSR; 7.62mm Tokarev; 7.62mm Nagant revolver; 9mm Makarov

14.5mm CALIBRE
This heavy machine gun cartridge has a rimless bottlenecked case 114mm long.

Type	Designation	Charge	Bullet description and weight	Muzzle velocity
API	Type B32	470 grains	Boat-tailed, pointed, steel core. 980 grains	
API	Type BS41	485 grains	Pointed, tungsten carbide core. 980 grains	
APIT	Type BZT	485 grains	Pointed, steel core. 919 grains	Approximately
APIT	Type BST	470 grains	Pointed, tungsten carbide core. 1,065 grains	3,200f/s (976 metres/sec)
IT	Type ZP	478 grains	Pointed, steel core. 921 grains	
HEI	Type MDZ	467 grains	Gilding metal clad steel envelope, lead liner. 903 grains	

UNITED ARAB REPUBLIC (EGYPT)

As noted in the entry for the Arab Military Industries Organisation, the production of ammunition in and for Egypt may be expected, in future if not already, to be co-ordinated with activities in and for the other three participating countries. Meanwhile it is to be assumed that production is continuing under Egyptian auspices.

Egyptian attempts to achieve self-sufficiency in ammunition production cover a period of some 25 years and, barring the heavy demands made during the Arab-Israeli wars, they have probably attained this objective in at least some calibres: certainly they have been making enough of some types to export them to other Arab states and to other African countries. Calibres known to have been produced are 7.62mm × 39, .303in, 7.92mm × 57 and 9mm Parabellum.

UNITED KINGDOM

Since 1945, ten basic categories of small arms ammunition have been used by the United Kingdom. Of these the .303in cartridge and the 7.62mm (NATO) cartridge have been in universal service at different times, in rifles and machine guns. The 7.92mm BESA cartridge and the .30in Browning cartridge have both been in general service for armoured vehicle machine guns only, the 7.92mm BESA being in fact obsolescent by 1945. Two further rifle calibre cartridges have been used on a "special-to-theatre" basis; the .30in Carbine cartridge and the 5.56mm Armlite cartridge being both used in very specialised areas only, mainly in the Far East.

Of the remaining four basic types, two relate to use in pistols or sub-machine guns, the 9mm Parabellum cartridge being used in both roles, and the .380in cartridge being used only in revolvers. In the heavy machine gun role, the .50in Browning cartridge has been in general service by the UK since the 1939-1945 war. In more recent years the .50in Spotting Rifle cartridge has also been adopted by the UK.

The 7.92mm BESA cartridge is not covered in detail here, since it has long since passed out of service, and in basic design is similar to 7.92mm × 57mm Mauser ammunition described elsewhere. The .30in Carbine ammunition and the 5.56mm ammunition used on the "special-to-theatre" basis are either of US manufacture or produced against US specifications, and are already covered in the US ammunition section. This also applies to British .50in Spotting Rifle ammunition, which, to date, has been of US standard production.

Summarised below are details of the nomenclature and the characteristics of the remaining six categories of UK ammunition.

British and French service ammunition. **Left to right:** .303in ball, Mark 7, UK; .303in G Mark 8 tracer, UK; .303in H Mark 1 grenade cartridge, UK; .380in ball mark 2, revolver, UK; 8mm Ball, France; 7.5mm Ball, France; 7.65mm pistol/SMG, France; 9mm tracer, France

.303in CALIBRE (also known as the 7.7mm × 56mm)
All British and Commonwealth service .303in ammunition has been made with brass cases only. The case is rimmed and bottlenecked, with a length of 56.2mm. Primers of all British and Commonwealth .303in ammunition are, with the exception of some Canadian manufacture, of the Berdan type. Principal loadings are:

Type	Designation	Charge	Bullet description and weight	Muzzle velocity
Ball	Mark 7	37 gr. Cordite	Flat-based, pointed, aluminium tip filler, lead core. 174 grains	2,440f/s (744 metres/sec)
Ball	Mark 8.z	40 gr. NC	Boat-tailed, pointed, lead core. 175 grains	2,550f/s (777 metres/sec)
A.P.	W Mark I	37 gr. Cordite	Flat-based, pointed, steel core. 175 grains	2,500f/s (762 metres/sec)
Incend	B Mark 7	36 gr. Cordite	Flat-based, pointed, steel sleeve. 177 grains	2,370f/s (722 metres/sec)
Tracer	G Mark 2	35 gr. Cordite	Flat-based, pointed, lead tip filler, flame tracer. 154 grains	2,300f/s (701 metres/sec)
Tracer	G Mark 8	36 gr. Cordite	Flat-based, blunt pointed ogive, dark ignition tracer. 169 grains	2,370f/s (722 metres/sec)
Grenade	H Mark I.z	30 gr. Ballestite		
Grenade	H Mark 2	43 gr. Cordite		
Grenade	H Mark 7.z	35 gr. Bofors Powder		

7.62mm CALIBRE (also known as 7.62mm NATO and 7.62mm × 51mm)
British and Commonwealth 7.62mm service ammunition has been issued only with brass cases. Cases are rimless and bottlenecked and 51mm long. British and Commonwealth cases, except for Canada, are Berdan primed. The nomenclature below covers UK production only, and corresponding Commonwealth ammunition may bear different nomenclature.

Type	Designation	Charge	Bullet description and weight	Muzzle velocity
Ball	L.2.A.2	44 grains	Boat-tailed, pointed, lead core. 144 grains	2,700f/s (823 metres/sec)
Tracer	L.5.A.3	41 grains	Flat-based, pointed, lead tip filler. 135 grains	2,620f/s (799 metres/sec)
Grenade	L.I.A.2	39 grains		

In addition, two further 7.62mm Ball rounds may be encountered. Ball L.2.A.4. corresponds with L.2.A.2 except that the propellant is ball powder. Ball L.II.A.I corresponds also with L.2.A.2 but was made under contract by Raufoss Arsenal, Norway.

.30in BROWNING

For use in AFV machine guns only, this category of ammunition was originally supplied to Britain by the USA. Since 1945 however British manufactured ammunition has entirely replaced that from the US, although the characteristics remain largely unaltered. British .30in ammunition is all-brass cased, the case being rimless and bottlenecked, 63mm long. British cases are Berdan primed. Principal loadings are:

Type	Designation	Charge	Bullet description and weight	Muzzle velocity
Ball	Mark 4.z	52 grains	Flat-based, pointed, lead core. 150 grains	2,800f/s (855 metres/sec)
Tracer	G Mark 1.z	50 grains	Flat-based, pointed, lead tip filler. Unlike US production, trace composition is held in metal canister. 150 grains (dim ignition tracer)	
Incendiary	B Mark 2.z	50 grains	Flat-based, pointed, steel sleeve. 7 grains composition. 154 grains	2,850f/s (870 metres/sec)

.50in BROWNING

For use in AA machine guns, and in AFV's, this category of ammunition was originally supplied in Britain by the USA. Since 1945 however British manufactured ammunition has entirely replaced that from the USA. British .50in Browning ammunition is all brass cased, the cases being rimless and bottlenecked, 99mm long. British cases are Berdan primed. Principal loadings are:

Type	Designation	Charge	Bullet description and weight	Muzzle velocity
Ball	Mark 3.z	235 grains	Boat-tail, pointed, steel core. 710 grains	2,700f/s (823 metres/sec)
Tracer	G Mark 6.z	240 grains	Flat base, pointed, lead tip filler, dark ignition tracer. 685 grains	2,700f/s (823 metres/sec)
Incendiary	B Mark 2.z	245 grains	Flat-base, pointed, steel sleeve. 710 grains	2,600f/s (793 metres/sec)
API	Mark 1.z	240 grains	Boat-tailed, pointed, steel core. 660 grains	2,850f/s (870 metres/sec)
MG Observing	L.II.A.1	240 grains	Boat-tailed, pointed, steel core. 626 grains	3,000f/s (914 metres/sec)
MG Observing	L.II.A.2	240 grains	Boat-tailed, pointed, steel core. 626 grains	2,965f/s (903 metres/sec)
MG Observing	L.13.A.1	240 grains	Boat-tailed, pointed, steel core. 965 grains	

.380in CALIBRE

This cartridge, for the Enfield revolver and other revolvers subsequently adopted for service, has been made in Britain and most parts of the Commonwealth. Only brass cases have been used, these being rimmed with straight sides, 19.3mm long. Except for Canadian made ammunition, all .380in ammunition is Berdan primed. Only one service loading has been in use since 1945.

Type	Designation	Charge	Bullet description and weight	Muzzle velocity
Ball	Mark 2	4 gr. Cordite	Flat-based, round-nosed, lead core. 197 grains	600f/s (183 metres/sec)

9mm CALIBRE (also known as 9mm Parabellum or 9mm × 19mm)

For use in the Browning S.L. pistol and in sub-machine guns, this cartridge has been made in Britain and most parts of the Commonwealth. Only brass cases have been used, these being rimless, with straight sides, 19mm long. Except for Canadian ammunition, all 9mm ammunition is Berdan primed. Only one service loading has been in use since 1945.

Type	Designation	Charge	Bullet description and weight	Muzzle velocity
Ball	Mark 2.z	6 grains	Flat-based, round-nose, lead core. 115 grains	1,300f/s (396 metres/sec)

UNITED STATES OF AMERICA

Since 1945, seven basic categories of small arms ammunition have been used by the United States. These are the .30" (.30-06), 7.62mm (NATO) and 5.56mm cartridges for rifles and machine guns, the .30in. Carbine cartridge, the .45in. ACP cartridge for use in pistols and sub-machine guns, the .50in. Browning Heavy machine gun cartridge, and the .50in Spotting Rifle cartridge. Summarised below are details of the nomenclature and the characteristics of these cartridges.

CALIBRE .30 (known commonly as the .30in-06 or the 7.62mm × 63mm cartridge).

US ammunition in this calibre will be encountered with both brass and steel cases. Primers are of the Boxer type. The .30in case is rimless and bottlenecked, with a length of 63mm. Principal loadings in recent years are:

Type	Designation	Charge	Bullet description and weight	Muzzle velocity
Ball	M2	50 grains	Flat-based, pointed, lead core. 152 grains	2,740f/s (837 metres/sec)
AP	M2	53 grains	Flat base, pointed, steel core. 165 grains	2,715f/s (829 metres/sec)
API	M14	50 grains	Flat base, pointed, steel core. 150 grains	2,780f/s (849 metres/sec)
Incendiary	M1	54 grains	Flat-based, pointed, steel sleeve. 140 grains	2,950f/s (901 metres/sec)
Tracer	M1	50 grains	Flat-based, pointed, lead point filler, bright ignition. 152 grains	2,700f/s (824 metres/sec)
Tracer	M25	42 grains	Flat base, pointed, lead point filler, dim ignition. 146 grains	2,665f/s (814 metres/sec)
Frangible	M22	43 grains	Flat-based, solid construction of powdered lead and bakelite. 108 grains	1,300f/s (396 metres/sec)
Grenade	M3	43 grains		

(Note: All US service .30in ammunition matched their ballistics at 600 metres)

CALIBRE 7.62mm (known commonly as the 7.62mm NATO or the 7.62mm × 51mm cartridge)

US ammunition in this calibre will be encountered with both brass and steel cases. Primers are of the Boxer type. The 7.62mm case is rimless and bottlenecked, with a length of 51mm. Principal loadings are:

Type	Designation	Charge	Bullet description and weight	Muzzle velocity
Ball	M59	47 grains	Boat-tailed, pointed, steel core. 150 grains	2,750f/s (840 metres/sec)
Ball	M80	47 grains	Boat-tailed, pointed, lead core. 149 grains	2,750f/s (840 metres/sec)
AP	M61	47 grains	Boat-tailed, pointed, steel core. 150 grains	2,750f/s (840 metres/sec)
Tracer	M62	47 grains	Chamfered bullet, pointed, lead tip filler. 141 grains	2,750f/s (840 metres/sec)
Grenade	M64	41 grains		

CALIBRE .30 CARBINE (also known as the 7.62mm × 33mm cartridge)
US ammunition in this calibre will be encountered with both brass and steel cases. Primers are of the boxer type. The .30in carbine case is rimless and has slightly tapered straight sides. The case length is 32.6mm. Principal loadings are:

Type	Designation	Charge	Bullet description and weight	Muzzle velocity
Ball	M1	13 grains	Flat-based, round nosed, lead core. 108 grains	1,900f/s (579 metres/sec)
Tracer	M16	13 grains	Chamfered base. Round-nosed, lead tip filler. 107 grains	1,850f/s (564 metres/sec)
Tracer	M27	13 grains	Chamfered base, round-nosed, lead tip filler, dim ignition. 101 grains	1,800f/s (549 metres/sec)
Grenade	M6	20 grains		

CALIBRE 5.56mm (also known as .233in or 5.56mm × 45mm)
Most US 5.56mm ammunition is brass cased, although some steel cased ammunition has been manufactured. Primers are of the Boxer type. The 5.56mm case is rimless and bottlenecked, and 44.5mm long. Principal loadings are:

Type	Designation	Charge	Bullet description and weight	Muzzle velocity
Ball	M193	24 grains	Boat-tailed, pointed, lead core. 55 grains	3,300f/s (1,005 metres/sec)
Tracer	M196	24 grains	Chamfered bullet, lead tip filler. 53 grains	
Grenade	M195			

CALIBRE .45in (also known as .45in ACP)
US ammunition in this calibre will be encountered with brass and steel cases. The .45in case is rimless and straight sided, with a length of 22.7mm. Primers are of the Boxer type. Principal loadings are:

Type	Designation	Charge	Bullet description and weight	Muzzle velocity
Ball	M1911	5 grains	Flat-based, round-nosed, lead core. 234 grains	820f/s (250 metres/sec)
Tracer	M26	6 grains	Flat-based, round-nosed, lead core. 208 grains	850f/s (259 metres/sec)

CALIBRE .50in BROWNING
US ammunition in this calibre will be encountered with brass and steel cases. The .50in case is rimless and bottlenecked, with a length of 99mm. Primers are of the Boxer type. Principal current loadings are:

Type	Designation	Charge	Bullet description and weight	Muzzle velocity
Ball	M2	235 grains	Boat-tailed, pointed, steel core. 710/722 grains	2,810f/s (858 metres/sec)
Ball	M33	237 grains	Boat-tailed, pointed, steel core. 662 grains	2,910f/s (888 metres/sec)
AP	M2	235 grains	Boat-tailed, pointed, steel core. 708/718 grains	2,900f/s (885 metres/sec)
Tracer	M10	240 grains	Flat-based, pointed, lead tip filler. 643 grains	2,860f/s (873 metres/sec)
Tracer	M17	225 grains	Flat-based, pointed, lead tip filler. 643 grains	2,860f/s (873 metres/sec)
Tracer	M21	240 grains	Flat-based, pointed, lead tip filler. 699 grains	2,840f/s (867 metres/sec)
API	M8	233 grains	Boat-tailed, pointed, steel core. 649 grains	2,910f/s (888 metres/sec)
APIT	M20	230 grains	Boat-tailed, pointed, steel core. 612 grains	2,910f/s (888 metres/sec)
Incendiary	M1	240 grains	Boat-tailed, pointed, steel sleeve. 633 grains	2,950f/s (901 metres/sec)
Incendiary	M23	237 grains	Flat-based, pointed, steel incendiary container. 512 grains	3,400f/s (1,036 metres/sec)

(Note. Except for Incendiary M23, the ballistics of all .50in match at 600 metres)

US Service ammunition. **Left to right:** .30in M2 Ball; 7.62mm × 51mm, NATO; .30in carbine; 5.56mm × 45mm; .45in ACP

CALIBRE .50in SPOTTING RIFLE
This ammuntion is manufactured only with brass cases. The case is rimless and bottlenecked, and is 76mm long. Powder ignition is via a long flash tube extending up into the case from the primer vent. Only one service type has been issued in the United States.

Type	Designation	Charge	Bullet description and weight	Muzzle velocity
Spotter Tracer	M48AI	110 grains	Flat-based, pointed, with a trace chamber in the base. An incendiary charge of 32 grains is held in an aluminium container in the forward portion of the bullet	1,745f/s (532 metres/sec)

VIETNAM

Small arms and ammunition have been produced in Vietnam for a decade or more. No details are known, but it is reasonable to assume that standard Warsaw Pact calibres predominate.

YUGOSLAVIA

Yugoslavia is currently using standard Warsaw Pact ammunition, and in addition manufactures and exports ammunition in other military calibres. Prior to the adoption of the Russian 7.62mm × 39mm cartridge, Yugoslavia made and used 7.92mm × 57mm ammunition for the many German weapons that she retained in use after the war.

7.92mm × 57mm CALIBRE
Yugoslav ammunition in this calibre examined has been steel cased, and is generally believed to conform to the normal ballistics for this type of ammunition.

.303in CALIBRE
Yugoslavia manufactures and exports what appears to be standard .303in British ball ammunition, equivalent to Ball Mark 7 and Ball Mark 8.z.

7.62mm × 39mm CALIBRE
Yugoslavia is fairly unusual among communist countries in that at least some of her production in this calibre is brass cased, and employs a lead cored flat-based bullet in place of the usual USSR pattern.

Cases are head-stamped with the British mark number, and the cases are of brass.

9mm PARABELLUM
Yugoslavia has exported quite large quantities of this calibre, all brass cased and of conventional appearance. Some has been head-stamped in commercial fashion, but some has been head-stamped with East Bloc military factory codes.

GERMANY AND JAPAN 1939-1945

A very large quantity of German arms and ammunition dating from the 1939-1945 war has remained in service during the period covered by this review, and some has appeared, in the late 1960s, in Vietnam, coming probably by way of the USSR.
In the same way some Japanese arms and ammunition remained in use after the war ended, mainly in China, and, together possibly with old Nationalist Chinese 7.92mm weapons and ammunition could still be held in reserve. A brief summary therefore of the principal types of such ammunition is given below.

7.92mm × 57mm CALIBRE
German 7.92mm calibre ammunition was made with brass and steel cases, the latter being mainly lacquered, but also copper washed. The cases were rimless and bottlenecked, 57mm long, with Berdan type primers. A large variety of loadings were produced in Germany, some of the principal ones being as follows:

Type	Designation	Charge	Bullet description and weight	Muzzle velocity
Ball	s.S.	44 grains	Boat-tailed, pointed, lead core. 198 grains. (Identified by green primer annulus)	2,500f/s (762 metres/sec)
Ball	SmE	44 grains	Boat-tailed, pointed, iron core. 178 grains. (Blue primer annulus)	2,800f/s (855 metres/sec)
API	PmK	45 grains	Boat-tailed, pointed. 156 grains (red primer annulus, or red band on base. Later type had black annulus)	2,750f/s (840 metres/sec)
APT	Smk.L'spur	44 grains	Boat-tailed, pointed. 156 grains. Red primer annulus with black bullet tip	2,720f/s (830 metres/sec)

7.92mm KURZ (7.92mm Pist: Patr: 43, also referred to as the 7.92mm × 33mm cartridge)
This was the first assault rifle cartridge (i.e. a short cased intermediate power cartridge) to be used on a wide scale. It influenced post-war cartridge design in a positive way, and was used (and manufactured) after the war, in East Germany, by units of the Factory Militia. Although varieties other than ball were produced, only ball ammunition was widely issued. Cases were of lacquered steel, rimless and bottlenecked, 32.8mm long. Primers were of the Berdan type.

Type	Designation	Charge	Bullet description and weight	Muzzle velocity
Ball	Pist: Patr 43.m.E	24 grains	Boat-tailed, pointed, iron core. 124 grains	2,350f/s (716 metres/sec)

9mm PARABELLUM (Pist: Patr: 08)
German 9mm Parabellum ammunition, for SL pistols and SMG use was produced with brass and steel cases, the latter normally being lacquered, but sometimes copper washed. The rimless case, 19mm long, was standard for this class of cartridge, and was Berdan primed. Three basic ball variations were in service, as under:

Type	Designation	Charge	Bullet description and weight	Muzzle velocity
Ball	Pist: Patr: 08	6 grains	Flat-based, round-nosed, lead core. 124 grains	1,300f/s (395 metres/sec)
Ball	Pist: Patr: 08.m.E	5 grains	Flat-based, round-nosed, steel core, blackened envelope. 98 grains	1,475f/s (450 metres/sec)
Ball	Pist: Patr: 08.m.SE	5 grains	Flat-based, round-nosed, solid sintered iron bullet. 91 grains	1,500f/s (457 metres/sec)

6.5mm CALIBRE (Type 38 ammunition, also known as 6.5mm Arisaka)
This was the basic Japanese rifle calibre cartridge. Brass cased, the semi-rimmed bottlenecked design had a case length of 50.8mm. Berdan type primer.

Type	Designation	Charge	Bullet description and weight	Muzzle velocity
Ball	Type 38	34 grains	Flat-based, round-nosed, lead core. 138 grains	2,500f/s (762 metres/sec)

7.7mm CALIBRE
In all, Japan used three different types of 7.7mm ammunition. One was identical, with regard to case dimensions, to the British .303in, and need not be discussed further here. The other two types were the 7.7mm semi-rimmed, Type 92, and the 7.7mm rimless, Type 99. Steel and brass cases may be encountered, the cases in both designs being 57.7mm long and bottlenecked. Apart from the rim design, they are very similar. They differed however in bullet design, as shown below:

Type	Designation	Charge	Bullet description and weight	Muzzle velocity
Ball	Type 92	43 grains	Boat-tailed bullet, pointed. 203 grains. Pink band around case mouth	2,200f/s (671 metres/sec)
Ball	Type 99	43 grains	Flat-based bullet, pointed. 181 grains. Pink band around case mouth	2,300f/s (701 metres/sec)

The Type 92 was for use in machine guns only, while the Type 99 was used in rifles and machine guns.

Different identification codes were used by the Japanese Navy and Army. Japanese Naval small arms ammunition (7.7mm rimmed) had the following code:
Ball: Black primer annulus
AP: White primer annulus
Tracer: Red primer annulus
Incendiary: Green primer annulus
Explosive: Purple annulus
Japanese Army ammunition (7.7mm semi rim, 7.7mm rimless and 7.92mm × 57mm) had the following code:
Ball: Pink band around case mouth
Tracer: Green band around case mouth
AP: Black band around case mouth
Incendiary: Magenta band around case mouth
Explosive: Purple band around case mouth (on Type 92)
Explosive: White band around case mouth (on 7.92 x 57)

*Miscellaneous service ammunition: **Left to right:** 6.5mm Swedish Mauser; 8mm ball, Sweden; 7.5mm ball, Swiss; 6.5mm ball, Japan; 7.7mm semi rim, Japan; 7.7mm rimless, Japan*

SERVICE AMMUNITION – 20mm CALIBRE UPWARDS

20mm × 110 OERLIKON

This ammunition, and the anti-aircraft weapons for it, is generally regarded as obsolescent, although in some countries it is still in military and naval service. For the greater part, such weapons are likely to be found with ammunition of British or US manufacture, although Swiss or Italian ammunition may still exist. British ammunition in this calibre was originally introduced for naval and land service, whereas US ammunition was naval in origin.

The rebated rimless cartridge case dates back to pre-1939, and bears a strong resemblance to the original Becker. It is 110mm long and may be of brass or steel. The primer is percussion. Projectiles vary in weight, depending upon type, but average about 130 grammes.

US MANUFACTURE 20mm × 110
Ball: Unfuzed steel projectile, inert filled
AP: Unfuzed, solid shot
HE/I: Fuzed with Mark 26 DA fuze. Filled with either Tetryl or Pentolite
HE/T: Fuzed with Mark 26 DA fuze. Filled with Tetryl. Trace for 4 seconds
HE/I/T: Fuzed with Mark 26 DA fuze. Filled with Tetryl. Traces for 4 seconds

BRITISH MANUFACTURE 20mm × 110 (Land Service)
HE/I: Fuzed with No 258 Mk I DA fuze. Filled TNT and SR 379. Designed to self-destroy
HE/I/T: Fuzed with No 254 Mk 2 DA fuze. Filled TNT and SR 379. Not self-destroying
Semi-AP/HE/I: Steel nose piece. Filled TNT and SR 379 incendiary composition
Tracer: Unfuzed steel body, inert filled except for trace composition at rear
Practice: Unfuzed steel body
For colour coding, see general description of US and British codes.

Left to right: 20mm Oerlikon, British, 1939-1945; 23mm case for Zu 23 (USSR); 20mm Vulcan (USA)

20mm × 139 (M139 or HSS820A)

This post-war design is manufactured in Switzerland, West Germany and France, and represents the updating of the earlier 20mm × 110 Oerlikon. It is intended for anti-aircraft and ground use.

The cartridge case is usually of lacquered steel, and is rimless, bot-

tlenecked and 139mm in length. Overall cartridge length is 213mm. Projectile weights vary but, except for APDS, centre around 120 grammes. Primers are percussion. Muzzle velocity is around 3,445 feet per second (1,050 metres per second). Propellant weight is about 52 grammes.

GERMAN MANUFACTURE 20mm × 139
DM51AI; HE/I/T: Fitted SD fuze DM131AI. Filled Hexal 60/40
DM43; AP/I/T: Steel body enclosing AP core. Projectile fitted with ballistic cap
DM48; Practice: Steel body, inert filled tracer cavity. Dummy fuze and alloy filler
DM48AI; Practice tracer: As for practice, but base cavity filled with tracer
For colour coding, see general description of German codes.

SWISS MANUFACTURE 20mm × 139
UIA; HE/I: Fitted SD fuze. Filled 10 grammes Trinalite
UIAT; HE/I/T: Fitted SD fuze. Filled 8.5 grammes Trinalite. Trace to 2,000 metres
RIA; AP/HE/I: Fitted SD base fuze. Filled 4.5 grammes Trinalite
RINT; AP/I/C/T: Tungsten carbide core. 2.5 grammes Incendiary pellet. Trace to 900 metres
ET; Practice tracer: Steel body with inert plug filling. Trace to 2,000 metres
EP; Practice tracer: Steel body with inert plug filling
RT; AP/T: Have also been manufactured
RI; AP/I: Have also been manufactured
For colour coding, see general description of Swiss codes.

FRENCH MANUFACTURE 20mm × 139
OE; HE/I: Fitted SD fuze. Filled 16 grammes Hexal
OET; HE/I/T: Fitted SD fuze. Filled 6 grammes Hexal
OPTSOC; AP Discarding sabot: Total projectile weight 90 grammes
OXT; Practice tracer: Inert filled steel body
OX; Practice: Inert filled steel body

20mm × 128 OERLIKON

This Swiss design, produced in a wide variety of loadings, is intended for anti-aircraft and ground use.

The cartridge case of lacquered steel is rimless and bottlenecked, 128mm long. Overall cartridge length is 203mm. Projectile weights vary, but centre around 120 to 130 grammes. Primers are percussion. For 85-calibre barrels the muzzle velocity is 3,445 feet per second (1,050 metres per second) and for 120-calibre barrels is 3,609 feet per second (1,100 metres per second). The propellent charge is about 53 grammes.

SWISS MANUFACTURE 20mm × 128
SSB/K; HE/I: Fitted SD nose fuze, KZ 0152. Filled 12 grammes Hexal
SSBL/K; HE/I/T: Fitted SD nose fuze, KZ 0152. Filled 7.6 grammes Hexal. Traces for 2.5 seconds
MSB/K; HE/I (Mine): Fitted SD nose fuze, KZV 0199. Filled 18 grammes Hexal. Total projectile weight only 102 grammes
MSBL/K; HE/I/T (Mine): Fitted SD nose fuze, KZV 0199. Filled 12 grammes Hexal. Total projectile weight only 110 grammes. 2.5 second trace
BSBH/B; AP/HE/I: Fitted SD base fuze, BZ 0144. Heat treated steel body, with ballistic cap. Filled 5.4 grammes Hexal
PKLH; AP/Hard Core/T: Tungsten carbide core, with ballistic cap 1.7 second trace
SU; Practice: Iron body
SUL; Practice tracer: Iron body with tracer sleeve
For colour coding see general description of Swiss codes.

The term "Mine" (Minengeschoss) with the HE/I and HE/I/T types above refers to a class of projectile originally developed in Germany during the second world war. In this type, which requires a high standard of projectile design, high quality metal and manufacturing techniques, and rigorous inspection, the projectile walls are thinner than with standard HE/I or HE thus giving lighter projectile weight and greater space for a larger HE or HE/I filling, which in turn increases terminal effect.

20mm × 102 (US M56)

This cartridge, of US design, is used both in ground roles, such as with the French 20mm gun M621, and in aircraft. The ammunition is manufactured in the United States, in France and in Belgium.

The cartridge case is of brass or steel, and is rimless and bottlenecked, 102mm long. Overall length is 167mm. The primer is electric. Projectile weights are 100 grammes, and muzzle velocity approx. 3,280 feet per second (1,000 metres per second). The charge weight is approximately 40 grammes.

US MANUFACTURE 20mm × 102
M55A1; Practice ball: Steel body fitted with dummy fuze
M56A3; HE/I: Fitted with fuze PD.M505. Filled RDX pellet with incendiary composition
M53; AP/I: Steel body, with alloy nose. Filled 5.5 grammes incendiary composition
For colour coding, see general description of US codes.

FRENCH MANUFACTURE 20mm × 102
AP/T: Traces to 1,200 metres
HE/T: Fitted SD fuze. Filled 6.5 grammes explosive. Traces to 1,500 metres
HE: Fitted SD fuze. Filled 7.8 grammes explosive

23mm × 153 (USSR)

This cartridge is used, by various WTO countries and others receiving Soviet military aid, in Zu 23 and ZSu 23-4 anti-aircraft equipments.

The cartridge case may be brass or steel and is belted, rimless and bottlenecked. The case is 153mm long, and the overall length is 235mm. Primers are percussion. Projectile weights are approximately 190 grammes. Charge weights are about 77 grammes. Muzzle velocity is approximately 3,180 feet per second (970 metres per second).

USSR MANUFACTURE 23mm × 153
BZT; AP/I/T: Steel body, filled 4.6 grammes incendiary composition
MG25; HE/I/T: Steel body, filled 20.1 grammes HE/I composition
For colour coding, see general description of USSR codes.

25mm × 137 OERLIKON

Of Swiss design, this calibre represents what is now often thought to be the optimum calibre in the 20mm to 35mm bracket. It is intended for anti-aircraft and ground use.

The cartridge case is of lacquered steel, rimless and bottlenecked and

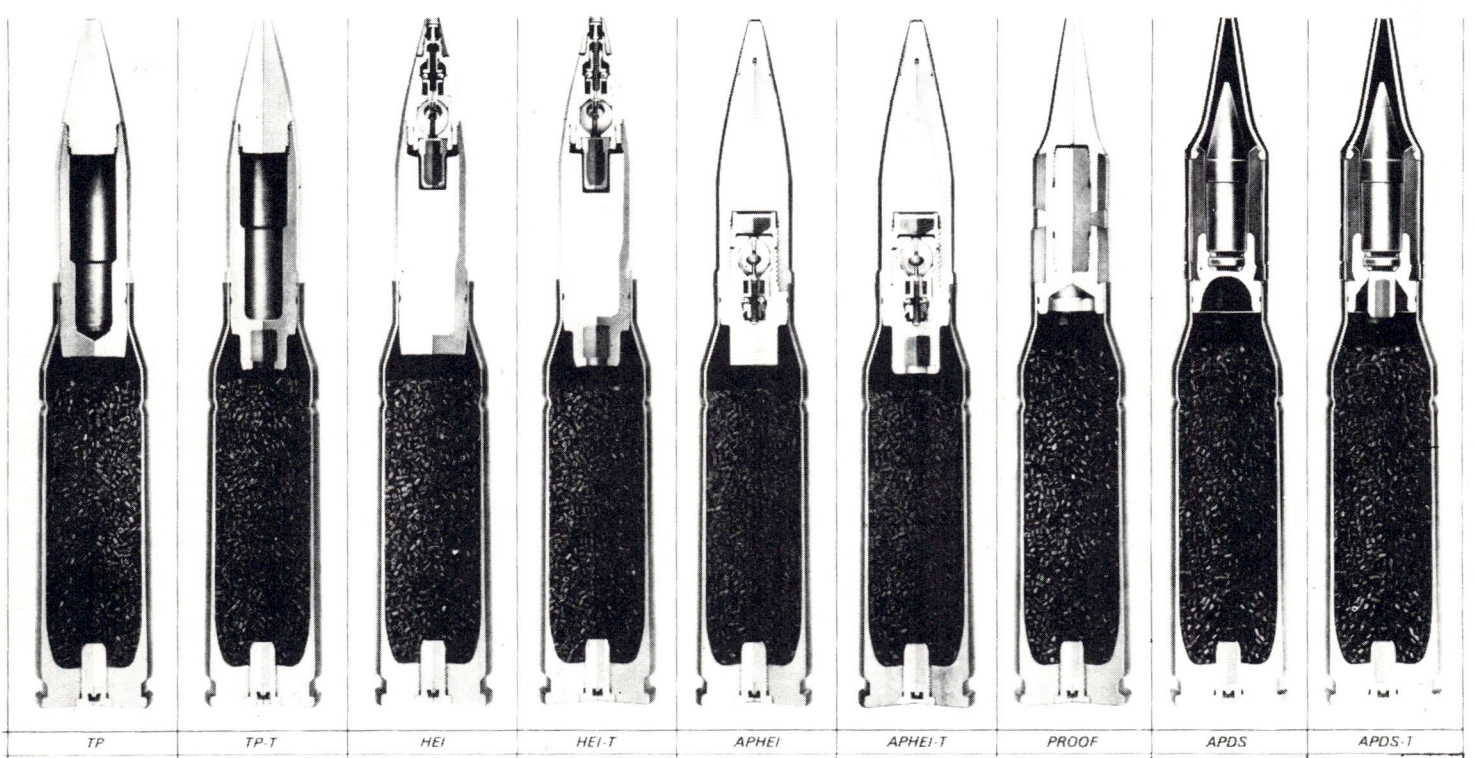

| TP | TP-T | HEI | HEI-T | APHEI | APHEI-T | PROOF | APDS | APDS-T |

Swiss ammunition for the 25mm gun (25mm × 137)

137mm long. Overall cartridge length is 224mm. Projectile weights vary, but centre around 180 grammes. Primers are percussion. The charge weight is about 90 grammes except for APDS where it is 98 grammes. Muzzle velocity is approximately 3,600 feet per second (1,100 metres per second) for 180 gramme projectiles, but the lighter APDS has a velocity of 4,800 feet per second (1,463 metres per second).

*Swiss ammunition. **Left to right:** 25mm × 137 KBA; 20mm × 128 KAA – KAB; 20mm × 139 KAD (820)*

SWISS MANUFACTURE 25mm × 137

SU; Practice tracer: Steel body with dummy fuze. Trace to 1,300 metres
SUL; Practice: Steel body with dummy fuze
SSB/K; HE/I: Fitted SD fuze KZB 311. Filled 27 grammes Hexal
SSBL/K; HE/I/T: Fitted SD fuze KZB 311. Filled 26 grammes Hexal. Trace to 1,300 metres
PSBH/B; AP/HE: Fitted SD base fuze 317 or 318. Ballistic cap. Filled 11 grammes Hexal
PSBLH/B; AP/HE/T: Fitted SD base fuze 317 or 318. Ballistic cap. Filled 11 grammes Hexal. Trace to 1,300 metres
PKHT; AP Discarding sabot: Sintered tungsten carbide core. Plastic sabot
PKLHT; APDS/T: Sintered tungsten carbide core. Plastic sabot. Trace to 1,000 metres
For colour coding, see general description of Swiss codes.

30mm × 170 (HSS 831L or RARDEN)

This Hispano-Suiza (now merged with Oerlikon) design of ammunition for anti-aircraft and ground use is manufactured in France, Switzerland and Britain.

The cartridge case is usually of lacquered steel, but is also made in brass, and is rimless and bottlenecked, 170mm long. Overall cartridge length is 285mm. Projectile weights vary, but except for APDS tend to centre around 360 grammes. Primers are percussion. Charge weight is approximately 160 grammes, and muzzle velocity, except for APDS in a 75 calibre barrel about 3,540 feet per second (1,080 metres per second). Practical range is approximately 3,000 metres.

SWISS MANUFACTURE 30mm × 170 (HSS 831L)

EP; Practice: Inert filled steel body
ET; Practice tracer: Inert filled steel body. Trace to 3,100 metres
UIA; HE/I: Fitted SD nose fuze. Filled 42 grammes Trinalite
UIAT; HE/I/T: Fitted SD nose fuze. Filled 28 grammes Trinalite. Trace to 3,100 metres
RIA; AP/HE/I: Fitted SD base fuze. Filled 28 grammes Trinalite
RID; AP/I: Filled 38 grammes Incendiary composition
RINT; AP/I/C/T: Filled 13 grammes Incendiary composition. Trace to 1,700 metres
For colour coding, see general description of Swiss codes.

BRITISH MANUFACTURE 30mm × 170 (RARDEN)

L5AI; AP/SE/T: Specially hardened steel body. Alloy ballistic cap. The special explosive (SE) produces a smoke effect. Trace to 1,500 metres
L6AI; AP/HC/T: AP shot with hard core (HC) of tungsten carbide. 10.5 grammes Incendiary composition for spotting effect. Trace to 1,500 metres
L7AI; Practice tracer: Steel body with dummy fuze and inert filling. Trace to 2,000 metres
L8AI; HE/T: Fitted SD percussion fuze L86A2. Steel body. Filled 25.6 grammes of Torpex 2. Trace to 2,000 metres
(not allocated); APDS: Projectile weight is only 290 grammes. Velocity 3,940 feet per second (1,200 metres/second)
For colour coding, see general description of British codes.

FRENCH MANUFACTURE 30mm × 170

OE; HE/I: Fitted SD fuze, PAD 57. Filled 45 grammes Hexal
OET; HE/I/T: Fitted SD fuze, PAD 57. Filled 28 grammes Hexal
OX; Practice: Steel body
OXT; Practice tracer: Steel body, with trace cavity

35mm × 228 OERLIKON

This is the largest of the current calibres for land service covered, and is of Swiss design.

The cartridge case is rimless, bottlenecked, and of lacquered steel. Case length is approximately 230mm and overall length is 387mm. Projectiles weigh 550 grammes, with muzzle velocity of approximately 3,852 feet per second (1,175 metres per second). Practical range is 4,000 metres.

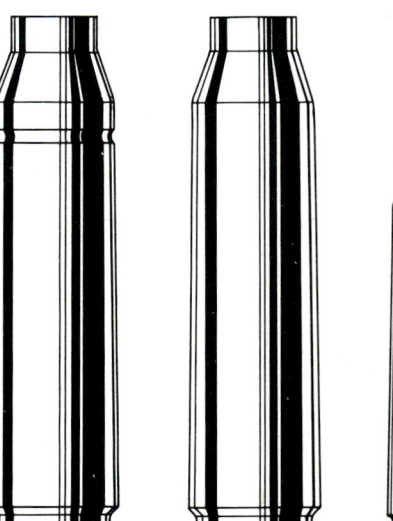 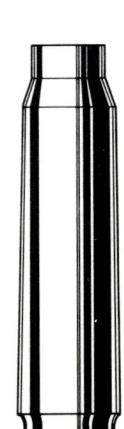 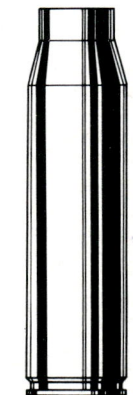

*Swiss ammunition. **Left to right:** 35mm × 228 KDA; 35mm × 228 KDM – KDC; 30mm × 173 KCA (aircraft ammunition for comparison only); 30mm × 170 KCB (831)*

SWISS MANUFACTURE 35mm × 228

MSBL/K; HE/I/T: Fitted SD fuze, KZVD 0242. Filled 98 grammes composition. Trace for 4.5 seconds
MSBK; HE/I: Fitted SD fuze, KZVD 0242. Filled 120 grammes composition
PKLH; AP/HC/T: Fitted with special hard core. Trace for 2 seconds
PSBH/B; AP/HE/I: Fitted base fuze, BZD 0266. Filled 22 grammes composition
SUL; Practice tracer: Inert filled steel body. Trace to 4,400 metres
For colour codes, see general description of Swiss codes.

IDENTIFICATION CODES

Specialised forms of small arms ammunition (armour piercing, tracer, etc) are usually identified by colour codes, the colour generally being applied to the bullet tip. In addition, certain countries, principally the UK and Commonwealth, used coloured primer annulus codes, which were originally in lieu of, and additional to, bullet tip colours. The UK and Commonwealth are largely alone in also using headstamp codes to identify different cartridge types.

NATO COLOUR CODES

The NATO colour code is based very largely on the old US Army code, and is as follows:
Red tip: Tracer bullet
Black tip: Armour piercing bullet
Silver tip: Armour piercing incendiary bullet
Blue tip: Incendiary bullet
Yellow tip: Observation bullet
Yellow tip, red band: Observing/tracer bullet

In most instances the coloured primer annulus found on NATO ammunition has no special coding significance, an exception to this being British ammunition in NATO calibres, where the old British annulus code has been

retained by the UK in addition to the tip colours shown above (except that .30in Browning and some .50in Browning have no annulus code).

Ammunition accepted as standard against a NATO specification bears in the head-stamp the NATO mark of a cross within a circle. This mark is used wrongly on some non-standard ammunition within NATO and also on some ammunition made and used outside NATO.

ARGENTINE COLOUR CODE

Argentina uses its own system of coloured bullet tips, for ammunition of under 20mm calibre, as follows:
Blue tip: Light tracer bullet
Yellow tip: Smoke tracer bullet
Green tip: Armour piercing tracer bullet
Red tip: Armour-piercing bullet
Black tip: Spotter bullet
White tip: Incendiary bullet

CHINESE (PEOPLE'S REPUBLIC) COLOUR CODES

Prior to about 1967 the Chinese used the USSR system of colour codes. From about 1967 Chinese ammunition began, with certain types, to be marked with a simplified and modified Russian code. This modification stemmed apparently from the realisation that small arms armour-piercing ammunition was unlikely to be required in future, and therefore the original black tip used to denote AP was available for use. It is now used to indicate armour-piercing incendiary ammunition instead, and the old API code of black over red tip has lapsed. Other tip colours in China appear to be unaltered from the USSR code.

Chinese small arms ammunition is often to be found with pink primer annuli and with pink case neck seals.

FINNISH COLOUR CODE

Although the basic infantry cartridge in Finland is the Russian 7.62mm × 39mm, Finland has not adopted the Soviet colour code system. The basic Finnish code is:
White tip: Tracer bullet
Blue tip: Armour piercing bullet
Black/red tip: Armour piercing incendiary bullet
Red tip: Observation bullet

FRENCH COLOUR CODE

Prior to the introduction of the 7.5mm rifle and machine-gun cartridge before the 1939-45 war, France relied little on head-stamp codes or bullet tip colours to identify special bullet types. Since the adoption of the 7.5mm cartridge, colour tip codes have been introduced, and these were consolidated after the 1939-45 war into the following code. Apart from this colour code, French ammunition is fairly informative with its head-stamps, which often show calibre, date, place of manufacture of the cartridge, and the origin of the case material.
Violet tip: Tracer bullet
Red tip: Tracer bullet
White tip: Tracer bullet (certain types only, largely superseded)
Grey tip: Ball (12.7mm)
Black tip: Armour-piercing bullet
Blue tip: Incendiary bullet
Yellow tip: Observation bullet
Silver tip: Armour-piercing incendiary bullet
Silver/red tip: Armour-piercing incendiary tracer bullet
Yellow/red tip: Observation/tracer bullet
Black/red tip: Armour piercing tracer bullet
Black/white tip: Armour piercing tracer bullet
Green tip: Tracer bullet.

The above codes apply to French domestic ammunition, and offer a variety far wider than applies in NATO. Although not now a member of NATO, France arms her troops stationed in Germany with weapons chambered for the 7.62mm NATO cartridge, and French made 7.62mm ammunition bears normal NATO codes, which in any case fall within the pattern shown above. French made 7.62mm NATO ammunition seems to have simpler head-stamp code than other calibres made in France, and shows only date, manufacturer and the NATO standard mark.

SWEDISH COLOUR CODES

The Swedish system of identification is basically by bullet tip colours, although use is made of colouring devices on the cartridge head itself. The basic Swedish code is:
Blue tip: Ball (match)
Red tip: Tracer bullet
Black tip: Armour piercing bullet
White tip: Tracer bullet
Orange tip: Armour piercing incendiary bullet

SWISS COLOUR CODE

Switzerland has been unusual in denoting the type of loading on rifle calibre cartridges mainly by lacquering the whole of the base of the round a distinctive colour, as follows:
Plain base: Ball
Purple base: Armour piercing bullet
Red base: Tracer bullet
Recently the above method was abandoned, and Swiss ammunition now uses coloured tips as identification, as under:
Red tip: Tracer bullet (7.5mm calibre)
Silver tip: API bullet (12.7mm Browning)
Red tip, silver band: APIT bullet (12.7mm Browning)
Plain tip, white band over red band: Spotter bullet (12.7mm Browning)
White tip, red band: Spotter bullet (12.7mm short case spotter)

UK COLOUR CODES AND HEAD-STAMP CODES

The original British system of colour and head-stamp codes applies on all small arms ammunition, except 7.62mm × 51mm (NATO), .30in. Browning and most of the .50in. Browning and .50in. Spotter series. The colour annulus code dates, in part, from the 1914-18 war, and the original bullet tip code from 1939-45. The original British head-stamp code dates, in part, from 1916.

The original British colour tip code, as under, was often omitted, and was subordinate to the annulus code which was rarely omitted.
Blue tip: Incendiary bullet
Black tip: Observation bullet
Green tip: Armour-piercing bullet
White tip: Tracer bullet, according to type

Grey tip: Tracer bullet, according to type
Red tip: Tracer bullet, according to type
The British primer annulus colour code was the major colour code, rarely omitted, except in the .30in. (Browning series) and still retained today, on the appropriate types of cartridge. The annulus code was:
Purple annulus: Ball or practice ball
Red annulus: Tracer bullet
Green annulus: Armour piercing bullet
Blue annulus: Incendiary bullet
Black annulus: Observation and explosive bullets
Yellow annulus: Proof, or ballistic standard cartridges
The British practice of stamping the heads of cartridge cases with code letters to indicate bullet type, propellant type, etc., commenced in a limited way in the last century, and evolved into a full code during and just after the 1914-1918 war. This code survives today on those cartridges whose design dates approximately from before the 1950s (except the .30in. Browning series). That part of the original head-stamp code that may be found on ammunition still in service is as follows:

Head-stamp letter "B": Incendiary bullet
Head-stamp letter "D": Drill cartridge
Head-stamp letter "G": Tracer bullet
Head-stamp letter "H": Grenade or line throwing cartridge
Head-stamp letter "L": Blank cartridge
Head-stamp letter "O": Observation bullet
Head-stamp letter "Q": Proof cartridge
Head-stamp letter "R": Explosive bullet
Head-stamp letter "U": Inspectors' dummy cartridge
Head-stamp letter "W": Armour-piercing bullet
Head-stamp letter "Z": Nitrocellulose propellant

The head-stamp letter code was used additionally to the coloured annulus code, and apart from use by Britain, was in use on Commonwealth small arms ammunition also.

The old British head-stamp letter code is gradually being replaced with new head-stamp codes, described below. British made 7.62mm NATO ammunition, .50in. Spotter ammunition, and parts of the .50in. Browning, .30in. Browning and 9mm Parabellum series bear the new head-stamp codes, these being additional to the NATO bullet tip colour code. (In addition British 7.62mm NATO ammunition carries, on the appropriate loadings, the British annulus colour code.) 7.62mm NATO ammunition and 9mm Parabellum ammunition also bear the NATO head-stamp mark (a cross within a circle).

The new British head-stamp code describes basic ammunition types under an "L" prefix and variations within that type under an "A" suffix. Confusion arises from the fact that the "L" number used in one calibre to denote a basic type need not be the same number used in another calibre to denote the same basic type. The existing "L" numbers currently used on the head-stamps of British ammunition of recent design are as follows:

	7.62mm NATO	9mm Para	.30in Browning	.50in Browning	.50in Spotter
L.1	Grenade and Drill	Inspection	—	Drill	—
L.2	Ball	—	—	—	—
L.3	Inspection	—	—	—	—
L.4	Proof	—	—	—	—
L.5	Tracer	—	—	—	—
L.10	Blank	—	Blank	—	Drill
L.11	Ball	—	—	M.G. Observing	—
L.12	—	—	—	Proof	—
L.13	Blank	—	—	M.G. Observing (Heavy)	—

The suffix letters and numbers after the "L" number denote different "marks" of that cartridge. Thus in 7.62mm calibre, the L.2.A.1 and the L.2.A.2 denote the first and second variation or "mark" of the basic L.2 ball cartridge.

Commonwealth produced ammunition, for the most part, does not follow too closely the new British head-stamp code. Canada has adopted simple US type head-stamps and relies on the bullet tip code for bullet identification. New Zealand and Australia began with the same code, on their 7.62mm ammunition, but Australia in particular now employs a significantly different variation on the same basic theme.

USSR COLOUR CODE

The USSR colour code is used within the Warsaw Pact Armies. It was also used, until about 1967, by Communist China, but since then the Chinese have modified and simplified the code somewhat. Some other countries, which have been supplied with Communist arms have also adopted the Russian code system.
Yellow tip: Heavy ball, Type "D" (7.62mm × 54mm ammunition)
Silver tip: Heavy ball, Type "LPS" (7.62mm × 54mm ammunition)
Black tip: Armour-piercing bullet
Green tip: Tracer bullet
Black tip on red bullet: Armour-piercing incendiary bullet (tungsten carbide core)
Black tip, red band: Armour-piercing incendiary bullet (steel core)
Black tip, yellow band: Armour-piercing incendiary bullet (Type BZ in 12.7mm calibre) .

Purple tip: Armour-piercing tracer bullet
Purple tip, red band: Armour-piercing incendiary tracer bullet
Red tip: Incendiary ranging bullet
Crimped blank, white tip: Grenade blank (7.62mm × 39mm) Polish, and possibly others

Normally, Communist small arms ammunition bears no special annulus code, but ammunition intended for tropical use may have red or pink annuli or case mouth-seals.

OLD US COLOUR CODE

For the greater part, US service ammunition has always used a simple head-stamp, denoting manufacturer and date of manufacture only. The colour primer annulus holds no special significance, and identification of bullet type has been through the medium of coloured bullet tips. The old US code parallels the newer NATO code (which the US has adopted) and was as follows:

Black tip: Armour-piercing bullet
Silver tip: Armour-piercing incendiary bullet
Blue tip: Incendiary bullet
Brown tip: Tracer bullet
Red tip: Tracer bullet
Orange tip: Tracer bullet
Green tip; white band: Frangible bullet
Green tip: Duplex bullet loading
Red tip, silver band: Armour-piercing incendiary tracer bullet

HEADSTAMP MANUFACTURERS CODES POST-1945

A	Altdorf, Switzerland
A.74	South Africa (74 probably refers to date)
AA	Ammunitionsarsenalet, Denmark
AC	San Cristobel, Dominican Republic
AD	Indonesia
AE	Israel (early)
AI	Artillerie Inrichtingen, Holland
AMA	Ammunitionsarsenalet, Denmark
AMF	Sweden
AOC	Italy (code for BPD)
ASC	Portugal
AYM	Czechoslovakia
AYR	Raufoss Arsenal, Norway
B. MARCO	British Manufacturing and Research Co, UK
BPD	Bombrini Parodi Delfino, Italy
BXN	Czechoslovakia
CAC	Colonial Ammunition Co, New Zealand
CBC	Brazil
CDM	Mexico
CIS	Chartered Industries, Singapore
CMC	Romania
DA	Dominion Arsenal, Canada
DAC	Dominion Arsenal, Canada
DAG	Dynamit AG, West Germany
DC	Dominion Cartridge Co, Canada
DI	Defence Industries, Canada
DWM	Deutsche Waffen und Munitionsfabrik, West Germany
E	Israel
EK	Greek Powder and Cartridge Co
EMK	Greek Powder and Cartridge Co
EMZ	Eurometaal, Zandam, Holland
FA	Frankford Arsenal, USA
FC	Federal Cartridge Co, USA
FAME	Peru
FAMAP	Argentina
FMC	Argentina
FMCSF	Argentina
FMMAP	Argentina
FMSF	Argentina
FMSL	Argentina
FAMAE	Chile
FME	Chile
FMEP	Chile
FMG	Chile
FN	Fabrique Nationale, Belgium
FNM	Fabrica Nacional de Municiones de Armas, Portugal
FNM	Fabrica Nacional de Municiones, Mexico
FNP	Palencia Arsenal, Spain
FNT	Toledo Arsenal, Spain
FNAM	Morocco
FNCM	Brazil
FR	Brazil
G	Genschow, West Germany
GB	Greenwood and Batley, UK
GB	Chartered Industries, Singapore
GECO	Genschow, West Germany
GFL	Fiocchi, Italy
H	Hirtenberger, Austria
HA	Haerens Ammunitionarsenalet, Denmark
HK	Heckler and Koch, West Germany (Custom made)
HXP	Greek Powder and Cartridge Co
ICI	Kynoch (Imperial Chemical Industries Ltd) UK
IMI	Israel
IMPA	Argentina
IM	Colombia
IK	Yugoslavia
IVI	Industrie Valcartier, Canada
IWK	Industrie Werke Karlsruhe, West Germany
JTE	Japan
JAO	Japan
K	Kynoch (Imperial Chemical Industries Ltd) UK
K	Karlsborg, Sweden

KA	Pusan, South Korea
KF	Kirkee, India
Lapua	Lapua, Finland
LBC	Leon Beaux, Italy
LC	Lake City Arsenal, USA
LM	Le Mans Arsenal, France
MAC	Military Armament Corp., USA (Custom made)
MAL	Malaysia
MEN	Maschinenfabrik Elisenhutte, Hessen, West Germany
MF	Footscray, Australia
MKE	Turkey
MMM	Spain
MNAM	Morocco
MR	Manhurin, France
MS	Manusear, Budingen, West Germany
NK	Yugoslavia
NNY	Yugoslavia
NP	Sweden
NR	Yugoslavia
NWM	Nederland Wapen & Munitiefabriek
OE	Oerlikon, Switzerland
OFN	Nigeria
OFV	India
OJP	Oesterreich Jagdpatronenfabrik, Austria
ORBEA	Cartucheria Orbea, Argentina
PMP	Pretoria Metal Pressings, South Africa
P	Palencia Arsenal, Spain
POF	Pakistan Ordnance Factory
PP	Yugoslavia
PPU	Yugoslavia
PPL	Yugoslavia
PPYU	Yugoslavia
PS	Seville Arsenal, Spain
PSM	Indonesia
QC	South Vietnam
R	Brazil
RA	Raufoss Arsenal, Norway
RA	Remington Arms, USA
RD	Dominican Republic
RG	Radway Green Royal Ordnance Factory, UK
RL	Royal Laboratory, Woolwich, UK
RPA	Philippines
RPR	Romania
RTA	Royal Thai Arsenal, Thailand
RY	Etablissement Rey a Nimes, France
Rem-UMC	Remington UMC, USA
RWS	RWS, Nürnberg, West Germany
S	Sako, Finland
S	Seville Arsenal, Spain
SAKO	Sako, Finland
SAM	South African Mint
SB	Sociedad Santa Barbara, Spain
SBLT	Spain
SF	Gevelot (Formerly SFM), France
SGA	Singapore Arsenal
SM	Sweden
SMI	Societa Metallurgiça Italiana
SO	Sako, Finland
SR	Spennymore Royal Ordnance Factory, UK
SYI	Societa Metallurgica Italiana
T	Toledo Arsenal, Spain
T	Thun Arsenal, Switzerland
TA	Israel
TE	Japan
TE	Toulouse Arsenal, France
TS	Atelier de Construction de Tarbes, France
TW	Twin Cities Ordnance Plant, USA
VE	Valence Arsenal, France
VPT	Lapua, Finland
WRA	Winchester Repeating Arms, USA
W-W	Winchester Western, USA
Z	Czechoslovakia
ZV	Czechoslovakia

It will be seen that few codes appear above for Warsaw Pact countries or for the People's Republic of China. In these countries a common system exists in which most ammunition factories are allotted code numbers. Most ammunition has the factory code number in the "12 o'clock" position. The following factory code numbers are known to apply to the countries shown:

0	Czechoslovakia
3	USSR
04	GDR
05	GDR
10	USSR and Bulgaria
11	China and Yugoslavia
12	Yugoslavia
14	Yugoslavia
17	USSR
21	Poland and Romania
22	GDR and Romania
23	Hungary and Romania
179	USSR
184	Believed USSR
188	USSR
270	USSR
304	USSR
321	China
343	Poland
451	China
513	USSR
529	USSR
539	USSR
540	USSR
30	USSR
31	China
38	USSR
41	China
46	USSR
50	USSR
58	USSR
60	USSR
61	China
71	China
81	China
93	North Korea
121	China
541	USSR
543	USSR
545	USSR
547	USSR
611	USSR
661	Believed China
671	China
710	USSR
711	USSR
791	China
21215	China

Other headstamps include devices other than letters and numbers. North Korean ammunition makes use of triangles and squares, and early Chinese marks (probably dating from Chinese Nationalist times) include swastikas and other symbols.

IDENTIFICATION-LARGER CALIBRES

Large calibre projectiles readily lend themselves, because of size and the consequent relative ease of manufacture, to complicated or compound fillings. These projectiles have relied on painting to protect the steel of the shell body from rust, and to afford the most convenient method of identification, by colour coding, of the type of shell or its filling. Apart from identifying the type of shell by the basic colour code, the shells are large enough to have stencilled, in addition to the basic code, supplementary information such as filling date, lot number and so on.

Apart from armour-piercing, and some categories of practice ammunition, most ammunition in the calibre band under discussion is fuzed. These are usually nose, but may be base fuzes, and therefore hidden from view in a complete round. Most modern ammunition of the fuzed variety has a self-destruct mechanism incorporated so that, after firing, if the target is not struck, the shell destroys itself before coming to earth. This self-destruct mechanism may be a feature of the fuze itself, or it may be activated by the burning through of the tracer compound in projectiles having trace capability.

ARGENTINA

Argentine codes, used on 20mm Oerlikon ammunition and valid for calibres up to 60mm are:

BASIC CODE
Armour-Piercing projectile: White
Practice projectile: Red
HE (fragmentation) projectile: Pale green
Incendiary projectile: Grey
AP/Incendiary projectile: White with grey tip

SUPPLEMENTARY CODE
Flame tracer: Blue
Smoke tracer: Yellow

These two colours appear on the tips of projectiles, in conjunction with the appropriate main code.

BELGIUM

All Belgian cannon ammunition, unless marked specially at the customer's request, bears the following codes, similar to those of other NATO members.
Practice: Light blue
AP/I or SAP/I: Black with red band
HE/I or HE/I/T: Yellow (may also have red band)

WEST GERMANY
Practice projectile: Blue
Armour-piercing projectile: Black
AP/HE projectile: Black, with yellow lettering
AP/I projectile: Black, with red lettering
Explosive (M) projectile: Yellow, with black lettering

SWITZERLAND

The Swiss coding system is in two parts. There is a basic colour code which appears not only on the cartridges themselves but also on box labels and packages generally. The second part is a supplementary code which appears on the cartridge only. The cartridge or projectile code therefore may consist of both elements of the system.

BASIC CODE (Packages and projectiles)
Training ammunition: Black
Pyrotechnic: Pale blue
Blank: Green
Drill: Light brown
War munitions: Grey

SECONDARY CODE (Projectiles only)
HE filling: Yellow
Incendiary filling: Pink
Tracer: Red
Smoke: White

The application of these two codes can be confusing. For example a grey projectile with a red band is a service (war) projectile with a tracer component. A projectile with a yellow nose and a pink body is an HE/I shell, but is presumably a war projectile also.

UK
Practice projectile: Blue
Armour-piercing projectile: Black. With red band if fitted with incendiary pellet. With pale green band if having smoke capacity
HE: Yellow
The above British codes are for current 30mm projectiles, and do not cover older 20mm Oerlikon ammunition which may still be encountered. For surviving marks of 20mm Oerlikon ammunition, the following codes apply:
HE/I (self destroying) projectile: Pale blue
HE/I/T projectile: Bright green
Semi AP/HE/I projectile: Red body with white nose-piece
Tracer projectile: Green
Practice ball: Olive drab

USA

For US 20mm Oerlikon the following old codes apply:
Ball: Black
AP: Black
HE/I: Red (filled tetryl) or pink (filled pentolite)
HE/T: Grey (filled tetryl) or blue (filled pentolite)
HE/I/T: Bright Green

For the more recent 20mm Vulcan ammunition the codes are:
Practice Ball: Blue with white markings
AP: Black with white markings
AP/I: Black with red band, white markings
HE/I: Yellow, with red band, black markings. However, early HE/I ammunition in this calibre was originally coded by having a red body with olive drab ogive.

USSR (Zu 23 only)

For 23mm ammunition used in Zu 23 equipment.
AP/I/T: Black body with yellow tip
HE/I/T: Black body with red tip

SECTION TWO

AREA WEAPONS

GRENADES
  Combat Grenades
  Grenade Launchers
  Riot Control Munitions
  Pyrotechnics
ANTI-PERSONNEL MINES
FLAMETHROWERS
MORTARS

GRENADES

HIGH EXPLOSIVE GRENADES

The hand grenade is known to have been used in the fifteenth century where its principal employment was in the defence of walled cities and fortresses. It was in those days a primitive piece of equipment with a burning fuze which frequently led either to a premature explosion – to the discomfort of the thrower – or burned for so long that an intrepid defender had time to pick it up and hurl it back. It became the practice in European Armies to have companies of selected troops who handled these grenades and from their task came the name "Grenadier." These troops became an elite force in their own armies, as for example the Grenadier Guards in the British Army. With the demise of siege warfare the grenade went out of fashion but in the Russo-Japanese War of 1904 the grenade was improvised and used by both sides. In the First World War there was a great revival of the use of the weapon and in the prolonged period of trench warfare both sides developed hand grenades. In many places the trenches were close enough to allow an interchange of grenades and where they were separated by greater distances, fighting patrols carried grenades across No Man's Land to shower them into the enemy's firebays. As defences deepened and dugouts became both more frequent and elaborate, the grenade was found to be the ideal means of dealing with an enemy inaccessible to bullet or bayonet.

Eventually two distinct types of grenade were developed, referred to as "offensive" and "defensive". The offensive grenade was designed to be used by an assaulting infantryman who could throw it and continue to move forward without fear of suffering from his own missile. This effect was achieved by having a grenade with a high-explosive content but very thin walls which did not have a sufficient volume of metal to produce heavy fragments with large kinetic energies. The grenade would produce a very considerable blast effect which would daze and demoralise the defender and before he could recover the attacker would follow up his temporary advantage and press home his assault.

The defensive hand grenade is designed to produce a large number of fragments which are effective at a considerable distance from the point of impact. This makes it imperative for the man who throws the grenade to remain under cover himself and for his companions to be equally careful.

In recent years the efficiency of the current grenade has been questioned. Many countries have carried out tests and attempted to analyse the practical value of the grenades they use. The Mills Grenade is probably the best known of all hand grenades and it has been used by many armies. Many more, including the USA and the USSR, have developed grenades of a similar type. This type of grenade has a large high explosive content and a relatively thick, cast-iron body the exterior surface of which is deeply notched to produce segments about one inch square, which were considered, during the First World War, to be the size required.

When the grenade filling was detonated under controlled conditions, it was found that the exterior notching had almost no effect on the ultimate fragment size. The size of the resulting splinters was determined by the ratio of the charge to the body mass, the material selected for the body and the metallurgical treatment of that material.

Careful examination of the fragments coming from the typical Mills type grenade revealed that the base plug and part of the fuze remained almost intact after the detonation of the filling and that these were able to travel out to some 200yds from the point of explosion and could inflict fatal wounds up to that range. On the other hand a large part of the body of the grenade was blown into dust which had almost no wounding effect. Thus the Mills type grenade was considered to be suitable for neither offensive nor defensive use.

A further difficulty became apparent during the analysis of the results. There was found to be very considerable difference in the wounding capability of the grenade according to the orientation of the major axis. If the grenade is detonated with the major axis vertical the fragments sweep out sideways to produce a considerable wounding effect at fairly close range. The base plug is driven into the ground and does no harm. Similarly the fuze element is blown up into the air and is unable to do much harm. (Clearly if the grenade has the base plug on top at the moment of detonation of the filling, it is the plug that goes up into the air and the fuze that enters the ground, but the effect is unchanged.) The diagram shows this effect.

If the grenade is rotated through 90 degrees so that the major axis becomes horizontal, the pattern changes. The effect achieved now depends upon whether the axis is aligned across the thrower's front or points directly away from him. In the first case the plug and fuze are projected to his right and left and the fragmentation pattern forms a cylinder with a short radius of effect. When the axis of the grenade is along the direction of projection then the major danger to the firer is the very real one presented by the base plug or the fuze. Thus, to make any judgement of grenade effectiveness it is imperative to define the position and orientation of the grenade at the moment of detonation.

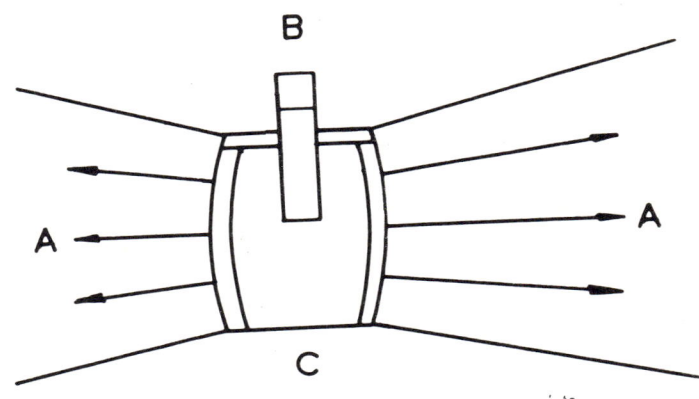

Fragment dispersion: A = radial fragment; B = fuze; C = base plate

Next comes the necessity to define clearly what the user wants the grenade to do. The criteria of effectiveness for a defensive grenade are obviously not the same as those for the offensive grenade. However it may be sufficient to define the requirement for the offensive grenade, and to relate the defensive grenade to that. For example, the user may say that his offensive grenade must guarantee incapacitation of an unprotected man at 10 metres from the point of burst but have no splinters with sufficient residual energy at 20 metres to penetrate the skin of a man. The defensive grenade criteria might perhaps be 20 metres and 40 metres. If this is an acceptable way of looking at the problem then the defensive grenade need be considered no further and attention can be focused on the offensive grenade in order to clarify the basic requirements.

Clearly there is a need to define what is required from the fragment to guarantee "incapacitation" and it is also necessary to define the chance of a hit. Lastly the statistical likelihood of getting both a hit and incapacitation must be examined. Traditionally the state of incapacitation is achieved when the target is unable to carry out his task. However it is not sufficient to say baldly that incapacitation is achieved unless the time which elapses between the wounding and the incapacitating is defined. Thus it is generally accepted that a reasonable time for the incapacitation of an assaulting infrantryman should be 30 seconds.

It is accepted that the minimum of energy that must be conveyed to the human target to produce incapacitation, is some 58ft/lb, or 8kgm, or 77 Joules according to the country concerned. This can be related to the penetration of some convenient material such as pinewood but it must be clearly understood that this system, widely used on the continent, is at best an approximation because the energy required to penetrate, say, one inch of pine depends on the size of the fragment. It is self evident that more energy is required in a large fragment of grenade to penetrate than is required in a small fragment. Thus to be truly indicative of the effect on the man, the fragment size should first be defined, and when that is done it is possible to quote a depth of penetration in a selected material, such as wood, that corresponds to incapacitation. This, however, is not done, so that many of the tests carried out by manufacturers are not in fact conveying a true picture, and the figure of penetration of one inch of pine can only be taken as a very rough approximation.

From the above – and ignoring the reservation on fragment size – it is possible to set up a simple test to give a reasonable estimate of the likelihood of getting an incapacitating wound. It is however much easier to test several different types of grenade made by different firms and make out some sort of order of merit, since the assumption can be made that those grenades producing large fragments with considerable lethality must produce less of them and so, in proportion, reduce the chance of a hit.

A typical test defines the position of the grenade as having its major axis vertical, the fuze uppermost, and the position of detonation 1 metre above the ground. This gives a very unrealistic picture because all the factors are in favour of the grenade. However it matters little if the object is to compare grenades, although in making an objective evaluation of any single grenade it gives an unrepresentative picture which flatters.

A series of wooden panels, usually one inch pine, are erected around the grenade at distances of 4, 6, 8, 10, 15 and 20 metres. Each panel is one metre wide and two metres high. After the grenade has been detonated statically, the perforations are counted and the number per square metre, for each range, are calculated. According to the design there should be a guaranteed incapacitation (one perforation in a square metre) at a certain range and no perforations at another range. (Note however that a lack of penetration does not indicate that the fragment is harmless at that range – only that it will not incapacitate.)

The following figure shows graphically the number of perforations per metre plotted against range. It will be seen that the figure of one perforation per metre was achieved at 9.5 metres and at 20 metres the chance of incapacitation was very slight indeed.

These figures were taken from a trial report* using the PRB 423 Grenade and the next illustration from the same source shows the layout of the panels.

The question of the fragment size is very important. The larger the fragment the further it will travel and the less the likelihood of achieving a nil incapacitation effect at a range as close as 20 metres. The ideal weight for the fragment is not universally agreed but few would argue with the figures 3-10 grains (0.2-0.65g). To achieve a consistency of fragment size within this range there are three methods available to the manufacturer. These are:

A pre-fragmented coil inside a very light casing;
A large number of steel balls held in a plastic liner inside a light casing;
A pre-notched interior to the metallic casing of the grenade.

All these methods are in current use in successful grenades today. All produce optimum fragment size but the random location of the grenade at the moment of detonation means that trials must rely on a fairly large sample before they become really meaningful.

The subject becomes somewhat more complicated if the grenades involved in testing are of difference in weights and shapes. The different weight affects the ability of the user to achieve range and accuracy and also affects the number of fragments. The shape affects the ability of the thrower to achieve range and also affects the distribution pattern of the fragments at the target.

The next figure shows the effect of weight and shape on range and is taken from the same source as the previous reference.

The effectiveness of the fragmenting grenade as a function of weight, is shown below.

This is a particularly interesting graph because the lighter grenade, shown as a dotted line (the NWM-40), weighed only one quarter as much as the heavier; but the result shows there is no directly proportional relationship between grenade weight and the chance of incapacitation. In fact it could be argued that the lighter grenades, of which more can be carried,

will, over several engagements, produce more casualties than the same weight of heavier grenades.

Lastly the question of fuzing should be considered. Ideally the fuze should function after a known period of time. There should also be the ability to have impact functioning after a given *distance* of travel (not time) and lastly there should be the means of selecting either time or impact. This latter is necessary because on occasion time is all important – i.e. rolling a grenade down into a dugout. On other occasions impact is the overriding requirement but some arrangement dependent on distance travelled is necessary to protect the man who drops the grenade at his own feet.

It would seem that the design and evaluation of the properties of the hand grenade have by no means reached perfection. Grenades are now safer and more reliable for the user and certainly more lethal than ever before but they are tending to become more expensive in attempting to achieve all that is required. The best grenade may now stand less chance of adoption simply because it is marginally more expensive than a less safe, slightly less lethal and somewhat less reliable grenade.

The introduction of the projected grenade of the M406 type has widened the possibilities and the next generation of projected grenades may well be smaller, cheaper and equally as effective as current hand grenades. It does seem, however, that in this field the adoption of the new ring aerofoil grenades may introduce an entirely new dimension into hand grenade design and the familiar shape of the hand grenade may disappear for ever.

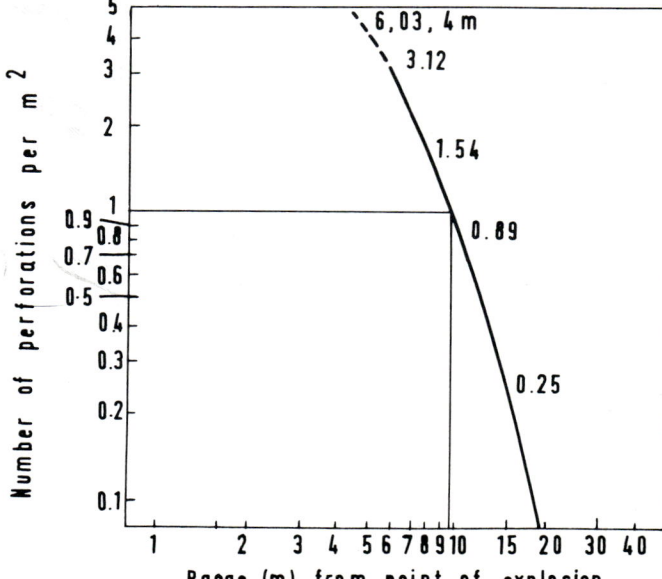

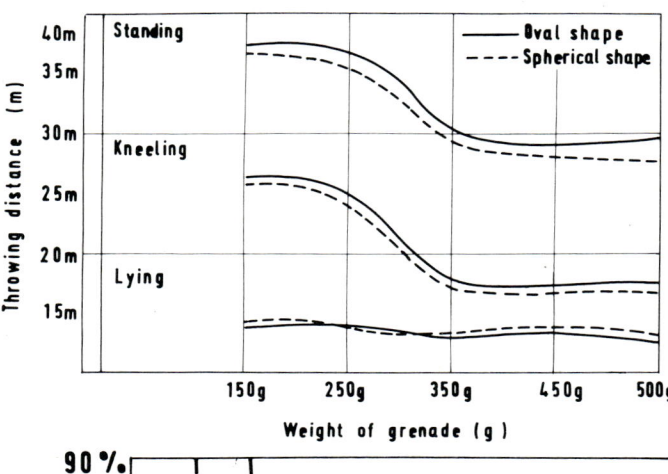

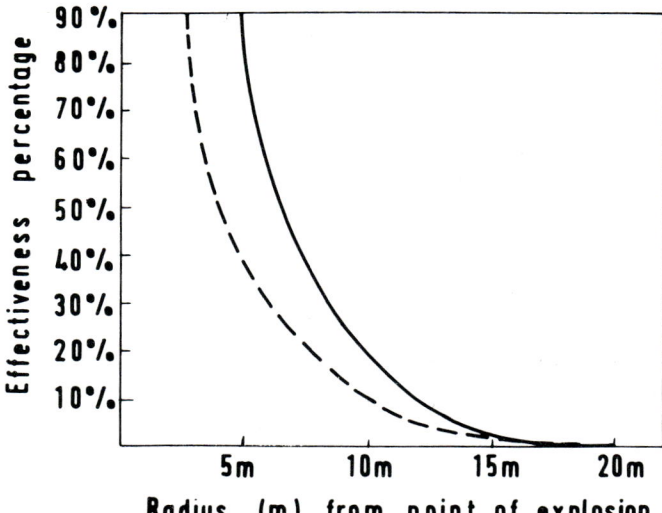

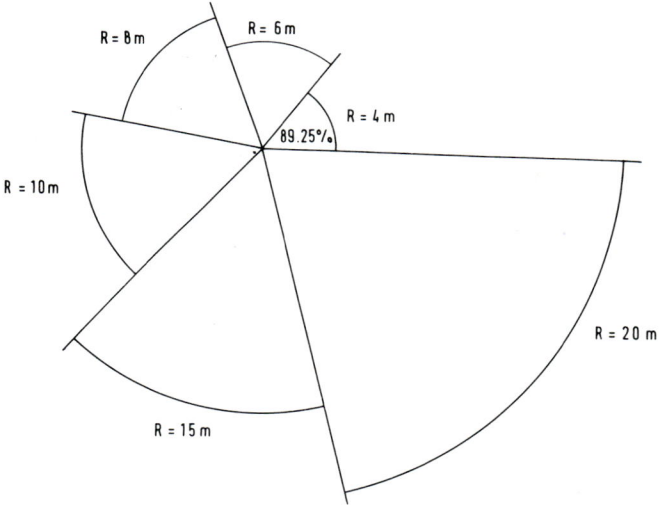

Grenade lethality. Position of grenade – point zero vertical 1m above the ground: fuze upwards

* "Anti-Personnel Hand Grenades" by Lt. Col. P. Crevecoeur. International Defence Review, June 1973.

SMOKE GRENADES

Although the term 'grenade' was long applied exclusively to an explosive device, the techniques applied both to the design of igniters and fuzes for such weapons and in the development of methods of projecting them in the direction of the enemy have been found equally useful in the development and use of many other combat devices, many of which are now loosely classed as grenades.

An important group of such devices are those that produce smoke of various kinds for concealment or signalling purposes. There is a wide variety of such smoke generators – so wide, indeed, that it is not easy to group them in a manner that is both convenient and informative. At one extreme there are those that contain white phosphorus and are designed to burst and scatter their contents in the target area: such devices not only produce smoke but also have significant incendiary effects and can incapacitate personnel nearby: at the other extreme there are substantially harmless containers of smoke-producing chemicals which are used almost exclusively for signalling. While it is evidently reasonable to classify these extreme examples as grenades on the one hand and pyrotechnics on the other, the satisfactory location of a dividing line in the range of intermediate devices is not easy.

In grouping the entries in this section an arbitrary division has been made between smoke grenades which are primarily intended to confuse or incapacitate the enemy and those that are primarily intended for signalling to friendly troops or co-operating aircraft. The former groups have been amalgamated with the entries for various types of HE grenade and the latter group has been incorporated with a sub-section on pyrotechnics. A third group closely associated with riot control operations is discussed further below.

ANTI-TANK GRENADES

A problem of a different kind arises in the classification of the now large number of explosive grenades designed to penetrate armour or fortifications. From one point of view it would be reasonable to group these with the special anti-tank weapons (rockets, missiles and so forth) described in a later section of the book: on the other hand, since many of these grenades are members of families of munitions that include anti-personnel or smoke grenades it has seemed more appropriate to keep the families together. Anti-tank grenades are therefore grouped with the HE grenades.

GAS GRENADES

Poison gas generators and dispensers producing lethal or incapacitating agents of kinds proscribed by the Geneva Convention are not described in this book. No doubt they exist: but so far as is known they are not a service issue in any regular armed force covered here. Generators and dispensers of lachrymatory gases used for riot control and similar purposes are discussed below.

GRENADE LAUNCHERS

Attachments to rifles to enable them to project grenades to distances beyond the limits of hand throwing have been in use for many years. More recently several special-purpose launchers have been designed for projecting various types of grenade. Some of these – such as those used with the US 40mm grenades – are primarily military combat weapons, although they may have other applications: others have been designed primarily for use by either soldiers or police for riot control.

Since there is some overlap of functions both types have been grouped together in a sub-section. It should be remembered, however, that these special launchers are not the only means whereby grenades may be projected (as distinct from thrown) towards an enemy: several types of grenade are now available for use with rifles incorporating simple standard launching fitments, and some of these types can be launched using standard ball ammunition in the rifle.

RIOT CONTROL

Reference has already been made to tear gas grenades and these are

A Fordson Pyrene Water Cannon in Northern Ireland

now available in great variety and are intended mainly for use in civil disturbances. Associated, on a 'family' basis, with some of these are some smoke generating devices and this association has been maintained by including both gas and smoke grenades in a sub-section dealing with riot control munitions, although this arrangement involves a slight inconsistency with the other grouping system for smoke grenades.

For what is hoped will be the convenience of the reader this riot control sub-section also includes the range of solid projectiles, loosely described as 'rubber bullets', which have been much used for riot control in recent years. These munitions cannot in any way be described as grenades but the launchers used to project them can also be used for launching grenades.

There are, of course, many other riot control weapons in police and security force inventories: they range from truncheons to aerosol sprays. For the most part, however, these weapons are not used by military forces and are not described here. One famous weapon, the water cannon, is however illustrated in this introductory section.

PYROTECHNICS

Signalling and illuminating devices are now available for battlefield and other military or para-military uses in great variety. A final sub-section of this section describes some of these aids, but it must be emphasised that this listing is intended to be indicative only.

MISCELLANEOUS DEVICES

Grenades and pyrotechnics lend themselves more readily than most military stores to ingenious improvisation and 'home-made' bombs and incendiary devices have been a feature of conflict from very early times. The weapons, munitions and aids described in the following pages, however, are such as are made in substantial quantities in an organised fashion: no attempt has been made to record the ingenuities of amateur or irregular grenadiers.

ARRANGEMENTS

The various subdivisions of this section described above have been arranged in the following sequence.
Combat Grenades – anti-personnel, anti-armour and 'combat' smoke.
Grenade Launchers – for combat and other grenades and riot control munitions
Riot Control Munitions – grenades and solid projectiles
Pyrotechnics – signalling and illuminating devices

COMBAT GRENADES

ARGENTINA

HAND GRENADE GME-FMK2-MO

The GME-FMK2-MO hand grenade was designed by Fabricaciones Militares. The body design is based on a nodular iron technique which is claimed by the company to be unique. Its final characteristics are the result of its metallic structure (Fe, C, Mg, Mn, etc.) and the post-casting heat treatment used.

The fuze body consists of one piece in aluminium which can be produced by drop forging or injection moulding. It incorporates the detonator and firing mechanism and can be removed from the grenade body as a single unit.

On explosion, the fuze body is reduced to fragments, in most cases of a weight of 3-5g. These will not endanger the thrower whose throw in the prone position is limited to about 10m, or 30m if kneeling.

Firing is initiated by percussion, and the powder train produces a delay of 3.6-4.5 seconds between the throwing of the grenade and the moment of explosion.

The bursting charge consists of a mixture of recrystallised hexogene and flaked TNT in proportions which can be varied to suit fragmentation requirements. The net weight of the charge varies between 75 and 79g.

The grenade GME-FMK2-MO

SAFETY DEVICES
The hand grenade has two safety devices. One is a specially shaped spring steel wire securing the grenade in transit, and the other consists of two split pins on the safety pin ring. The first can be removed at any time and the grenade can continue to be handled with perfect safety. It is released by firm thumb pressure and must always be removed before issuing the grenades.

The split pin is the last safety device on the grenade and once it is removed the grenade is ready for throwing. Should the safety lever come away on pulling out the pin, the grenade will explode.

RANGE
(a) The effect of the fragments can put out of action anyone within a range of 5m.
(b) The effect of the shock wave at a distance of 2-3m will be to produce at least violent concussion (assuming that the fragments have been absorbed by furniture etc).
(c) Fragment spread is effective up to 10m. with a density of distribution of 10-15 fragments per square metre and over the surface of a sphere.
(d) Fragments will perforate a steel helmet at a distance of 1m.
(e) A 4mm thick steel sheet is perforated at a range of 50-100cm from the point of explosion.

OPERATION
The delay period varies between 3.6-4.5 seconds, figures which have been arrived at after rigorous testing.

During this time lapse, the travel of a grenade thrown by an average man can vary between 30 and 50m and the delay period allows a safety distance between thrower and grenade of an average of 40m.

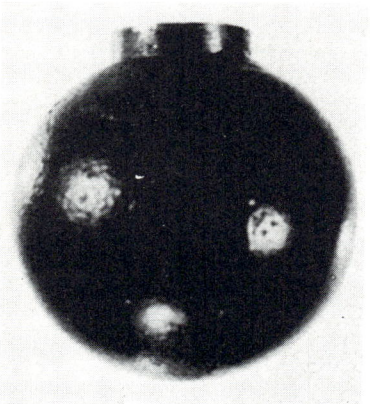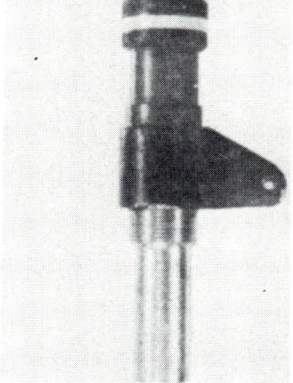

Grenade body and fuze

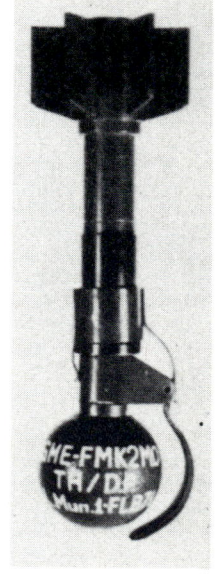

Grenade and launcher

PACKING AND TRANSPORT
The hand grenades are packed in wooden cases with grid support which secures each individual grenade by the body and the fuze cap.

Each box contains 25 grenades and is of a weight and size suitable for easy handling. Should it be likely that boxed grenades will be exposed for long periods in unfavourable weather conditions special packaging can be supplied with grenades wrapped individually in polythene.

GRENADE USED WITH RIFLE LAUNCHER
If a launching device is used with the grenade, it can be fired to a distance of 350-400m, to explode either at ground level or at varying heights, according to the degree of skill acquired by the soldier in practice.

The launcher is provided separately, complete with its propellant cartridge.

To fire:
(a) Make sure the grenade is firmly in its seating and that the safety lever is in place;
(b) Place grenade and launcher in the muzzle of the automatic light rifle (FAL). There is no need to use a muzzle adaptor;
(c) Rotate gas vent plug to close;
(d) Load rifle with the propellant cartridge provided with launcher;
(e) Remove safety split pin;
(f) Aim and fire.

PRACTICE AND DRILL GRENADES
Grenade and fuze bodies of FMK 2 are used, which has the following features:
(1) Inert detonator and weighted body;
(2) Supplied with 5 spare safety levers, creep springs and safety pins in case of loss or damage to those fitted;
(3) Painted in white;
(4) Markings as on original with addition of the letters EJ after letters GM;
(5) Fitted with safety wire for transport.

DATA
Weight: Grenade body: 165g
      Fuze body: 40.8g
      Charge: 75.79g
Length overall: approx 120mm
Body diameter: approx 55mm
Delay: 3.6-4.5sec
Manufacturer: Fabrica Militar de Armas Portatiles 'Domingo Matheu' Cabildo 65, Buenos Aires
Status: In production and service

INSTRUCTIONAL HAND GRENADE GMINS-FMK4-MO
This is similar to the operational FMK2 grenade but has the following special characteristics:
(a) Smoke emitting powder train which, on ignition (3.6-4.5 seconds) indicates the moment of explosion of the grenade.
(b) Grenade body perforated to allow smoke emission.
(c) A set of interchangeable smoke emitting powder trains in quantities established by the instruction programme requirements.
(d) A spare fuze body.

The fundamental feature of this grenade is that, though the powder train must be changed each time, the grenade body can be used indefinitely whilst in good condition, giving it unlimited life.

Manufacturer: Fabrica Militar (see above)
Status: In service

AUSTRIA

DEFENSIVE AND OFFENSIVE HAND GRENADES TYPE 69
Two hand grenades are produced in Austria. These are the HdGr 69 and the HdGrO 69. Both are egg shaped and both have plastic bodies. The difference between them lies in their different tactical roles and the differ-ences incorporated to cater for these. The HdGr 69 is a defensive hand grenade and the HdGrO 69 is an offensive hand grenade. In both cases the outside body is made of a rigid plastic which is claimed to withstand the

forces generated by impact with hard surfaces, such as roadways or tree trunks.

The fuze has a plastic body into which is screwed the tube, with the delay compound pressed in, and at the end of the tube the detonator is crimped. The functioning of the grenade is not very different from many others. The safety pin is withdrawn, with the safety lever held firmly against the grenade body, and the striker rotates under the influence of the compressed striker spring. The action of the striker forces the lever off the grenade and the striker moves on to the detonator cap. The design allows the lever to rotate through 45 degrees before it is cleared from the plastic housing and until this rotation has taken place the grenade remains completely safe. It is possible, should the need arise, to replace the pin and the grenade can be replaced in the soldier's carrying pouch with complete safety. After the striker hits the cap an ignition train is started which burns for 4.0 + 1.0 − 0.5secs. This sets off the detonator which in turn initiates the main filling. In the case of the HdGrO 69 the fact that the fuze housing and the body walls are made of plastic ensures that there are no fragments and the full effect of the grenade comes from the blast effect. This grenade can also be used for training and simulating the burst of artillery or mortar fire.

The fragmentation grenade has 3,500 steel balls contained in a plastic matrix surrounding the high explosive filling. These are driven out at about 6,000ft/sec. Virtually the entire chemical energy of the HE filling is used to impart kinetic energy to the balls and almost none is wasted in breaking up the plastic casing of the grenade. Due to their shape the balls lose velocity quickly. In the immediate vicinity of the point of burst, the balls will penetrate a steel plate 12mm thick. At 5 metres from the grenade there is near 100 per cent chance of lethality. At 20 metres the chance of being hit by a ball with sufficient residual energy to produce incapacitation is virtually nil.

DATA
Fragmentation Type:
Length: 115 ± 2mm
Diameter: 60 ± 1mm
Weight: 485g ± 30g

The HdGr 69 fragmentation grenade   The HdGrO 69 offensive hand grenade

Weight of filling: 65g ± 5g
Delay time: 4 ± 0.5 sec
Length of the detonator assembly: 70.5mm
Offensive Type:
As Fragmentation Type except;
Weight: 220g ± 30g
Weight of filling: 40g ± 5g

Manufacturer: Arges Accessories Co Ltd., A-4690 Schwanenstadt/Rustorf, Austria
Status: In service with the Austrian Armed Forces

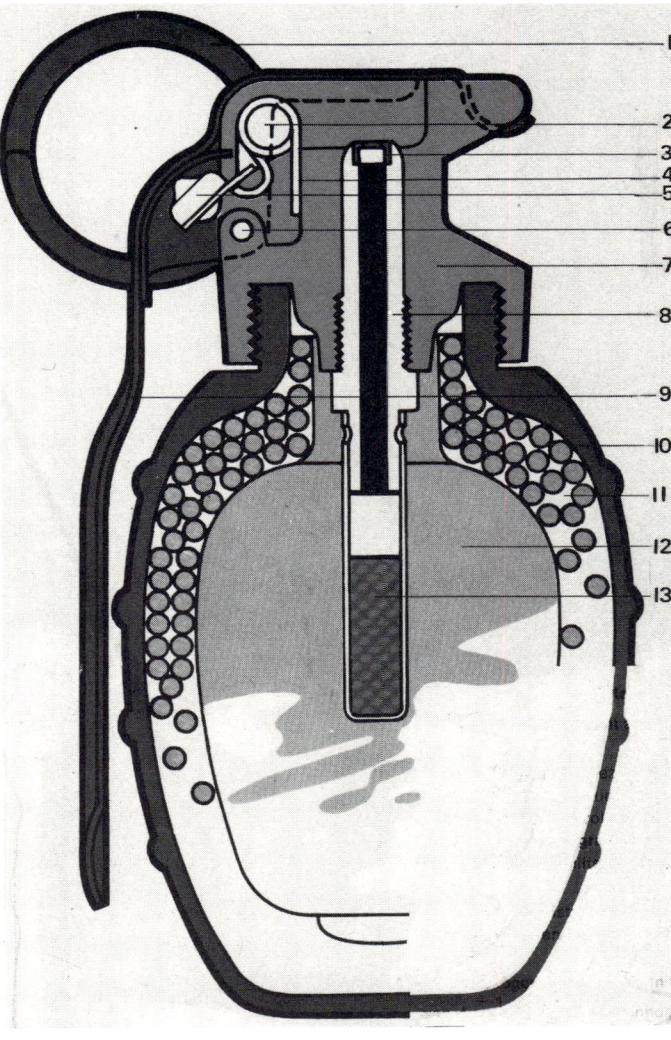

A section through the HdGr 69 fragmentation grenade, showing detonator assembly: (1) Ring of the safety pin; (2) Striker axis pin; (3) Igniter cap; (4) Striker spring; (5) Striker head; (6) Safety pin; (7) Detonator holder; (8) Delay composition; (9) Safety lever; (10) Plastic body of the grenade; (11) Balls packed in plastic; (12) High explosive filling; (13) Detonator

BELGIUM

MANUFACTURERS

Grenades are made in Belgium by three companies whose products are listed below. To avoid tedious repetition, their full names and addresses are given here only and their products are identified by incorporating 'FN', 'MECAR', or 'PRB' in the title of each entry. The three companies are:

Fabrique Nationale Herstal SA B.4400, Herstal
Mecar SA 6522-Petit-Roeulx-lez-Nivelles
Société anonyme PRB Département Défense, Avenue de Tervueren 168, Bte 7, 1150 Bruxelles.

FN-STRIM RIFLE GRENADES

Fabrique Nationale manufactures two types of rifle grenades, with explosive charge, under STRIM licence: anti-personnel grenade calibre 40mm types, AP 32Z, AP 32 ZA and AP 23 ZB, and anti-tank grenade calibre 65mm, type 65 AC 28 R2.

These are designed for launching by means of a special grenade cartridge, fired from an infantry rifle. If the latter has a grenade launcher as a permanent fixture, it can be used immediately, otherwise all that is required is the correct removable type of launcher fitted to the muzzle.

Every type of live grenade has its corresponding inert practice grenade for training purposes.

These practice grenades have the same outward form and practically the same ballistic characteristics and require the same launching technique as the live grenades.

PROPULSIVE CARTRIDGES

The various types of grenade are launched by means of cartridges, each consisting of a capped case, the mouth of which is sealed by star crimping with wax or by a plug sealed with varnish. Every grenade is supplied with its special cartridge which is retained in a rubber plug in the tail of the grenade.

Type 32ZA is supplied with both long and short range grenade cartridges. The latter is marked with a circular groove midway and can thus be recognised even in the dark.

Grenades 65 AC 28 R2, AP 32 ZA and AP 32 ZB are supplied with an auxiliary charge contained in a small case of combustible material housed in the bottom of the tail of the grenade.

The table below gives an indication of the propulsive powder charges for each grenade cartridge and its auxiliary.

Type of grenade	Propulsive charge in grams	
	Cartridge	Auxiliary
65 AC 28 R2	2.30	0.30
AP 32 Z	2.30	—
AP 32 ZA Direct fire short range cartridge	1.70	0.70
AP 32 ZA Curved fire long range cartridge	3.30	0.70
AP 32 ZB	3.30	0.70

DISCHARGING THE RIFLE GRENADES

The FN rifle grenades can be fired by any rifle which has either a built in launcher or has one fitted to the muzzle. The internal diameter of the grenade boom is 22mm.

As a typical example, the FN FAL rifle fitted with either a fixed or removable grenade launcher, projects the four types of grenade accurately in direct fire. Sighting is by means of a special grid as described below.

For curved fire, projected at an angle of 40deg, the anti-personnel grenade AP 32 Z has a range of more than 380m. For grenades 32 ZA and 32 ZB, the maximum range is 600m.

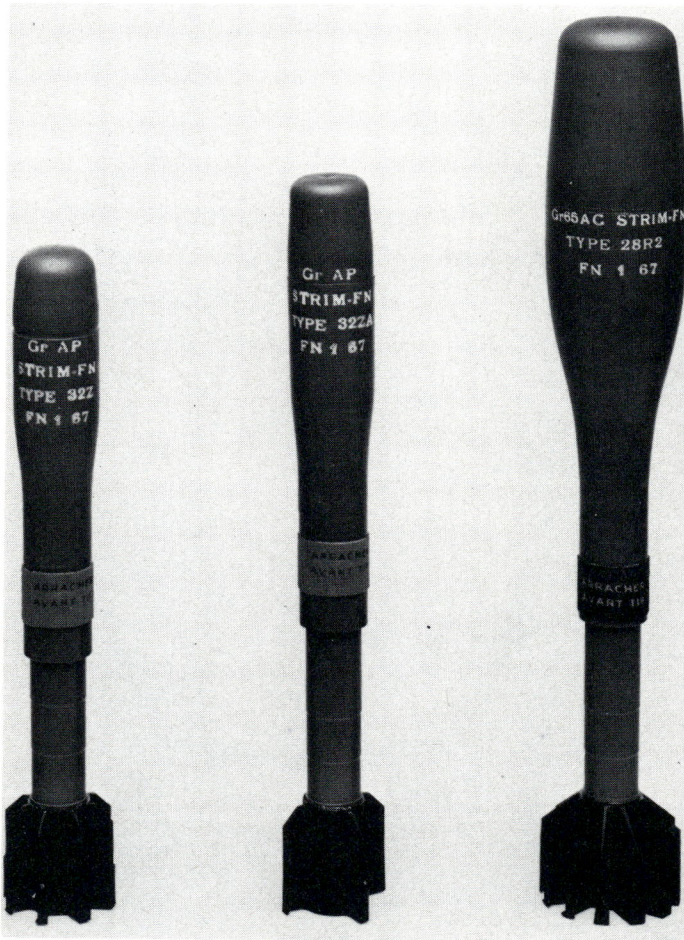

Left to right: Grenade AP 32 Z; Grenade AP 32 ZA or ZB; Grenade 65 AC 28 R2

Left to right: Cartridge, long range, for grenades AP 32 ZA and AP 32 ZB; Cartridge for grenades 68 AC 28 R2 and AP 32 Z; Cartridge, short range, for grenade AP 32 ZA

SIGHTING

Sighting for direct fire is by alignment of the objective, the visible tip of the grenade (or centre point of the grenade) and the correct graduation on the sighting scale.

The graduations marked on the right side of the grid are for the 65 AC 28 R2 grenade.

Those on the left side of the grid refer to the 32 Z and 32 ZA grenades.

For sustained fire, the same technique as for mortar firing is used. The firer holds the weapon, feeds the grenade cartridges and pulls the trigger.

The loader positions the grenade on the launcher, takes observations and makes the necessary corrections.

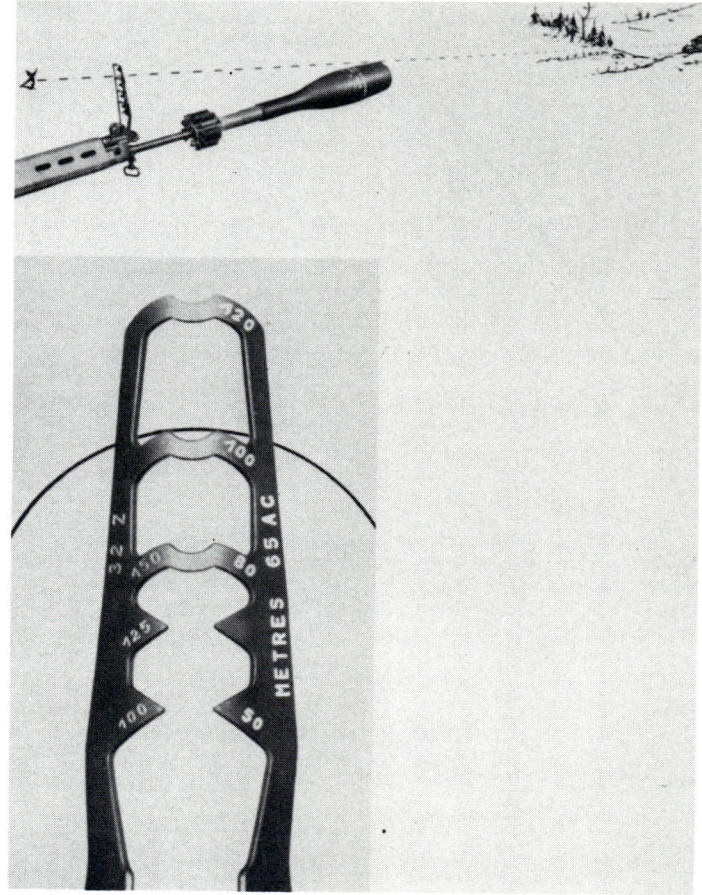

The Sights

FN 40mm ANTI-PERSONNEL RIFLE GRENADE
AP 32 Z

This grenade has a steel body which, under the explosive effect, breaks up into a considerable number of fragments of varying dimensions. Based on the shaped-charge principle, this grenade also has the power to penetrate a minimum of 100mm of armour plate.

DATA
Diameter of body of grenade: 40mm

Length: 315mm
Average weight: 515g
Initial velocity (with the FAL): 69m/sec
Effective range, direct fire: 150m
Range (angle of fire=40deg): More than 380m
Status: In production. In service

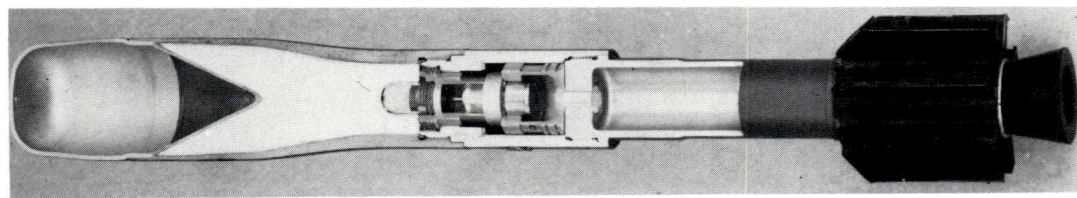

Grenade AP 32 Z

FN 40mm ANTI-PERSONNEL RIFLE GRENADE
AP 32 ZA

The anti-personnel explosive grenade AP 32 ZA is characterised by an increased anti-personnel effect due to a controlled fragmentation of the body; on explosion, more than a thousand spherical projectiles of equal size are dispersed in all directions at supersonic speed. The average diameter of these treated steel projectiles is approx. 3.2mm. They retain high efficiency within a wide radius around the point of impact and a good power of perforation, sufficient to penetrate 80mm of armour plating.

This grenade can be launched with either of the two following propulsive cartridges.

Short range grenade cartridge used for direct fire up to 150m with the standard sight for the 32 Z.

Long range grenade cartridge used for curved fire up to the maximum range.

Characteristics for both A and B grenades are given in the following entry.

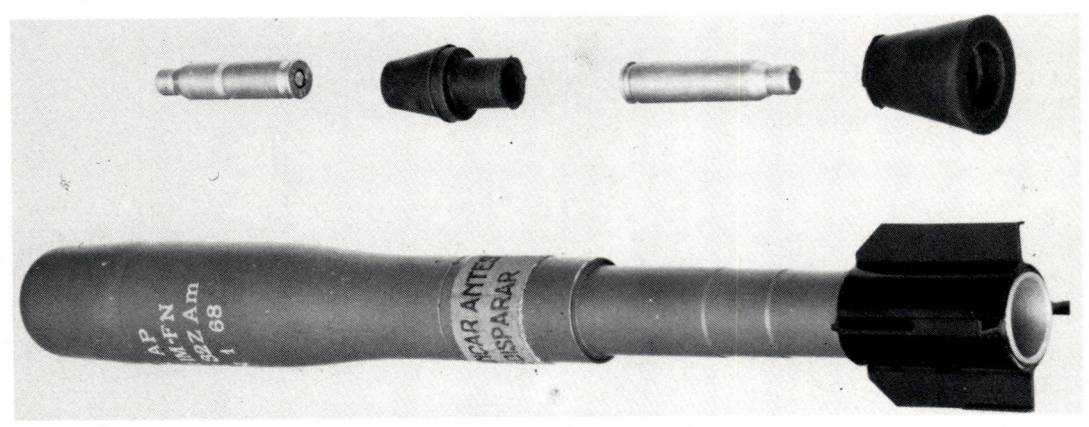

Grenade AP 32 ZA with short range and long range cartridge, and rubber plugs to locate detonator

FN 40mm ANTI-PERSONNEL RIFLE GRENADE
AP 32 ZB

The anti-personnel explosive grenade AP 32 ZB is not armour-piercing but the anti-personnel effect is greater than that of the AP 32 ZA, due to the increased number of projectiles contained in the controlled fragmentation body.

This is launched only with the long range grenade cartridge which is used for both direct and curved fire.

DATA
Diameter of body of grenade: 40mm

Diameter of tail unit with 4 vanes: 53.5mm
Overall length: 350mm
Average weight: 495kg
Perforation: 80mm
Minimum quantity of anti-personnel projectiles: 1,250 (1,050 for AP 32 ZA)
Range:
Direct fire: 150m
Curved fire (firing angle=40deg): 600m
Status: In production. In service

FN 65mm ANTI-TANK RIFLE GRENADE 65 AC 28 R2

The anti-tank grenade 65 AC 28 R2 is remarkable for its exceptional perforating power in relation to its weight and diameter.

At the normal angle of incidence, against armour plating the penetration power averages 300mm.

Its extreme sensitivity and the instantaneous action of its fuze enable this grenade to function at high angles of incidence against armour plate surfaces: at an angle of 60deg it is still effective and the limit is only reached at an angle of 70deg. Its high power of penetration against armour is matched by its efficacy against concrete; thus it can be used successfully against shelters, blockhouses, light fortifications etc.

DATA
Diameter of body of grenade: 65mm
Length: 420mm
Average weight: 735g
Initial velocity (with the FAL): 59m/sec
Effective range, flat trajectory: 120m
Status: In production. In service

FN-LUCHAIRE-STRIM LIGHT RIFLE GRENADES

FN have developed a new family of rifle grenades, suitable for launching from 7.62mm rifles using special grenade cartridges, but primarily intended for use with 5.56mm rifle firing ball ammunition, the grenades being fitted with FN bullet traps.

Part of this development work has been carried out in conjunction with Luchaire-STRIM in France and embraces the STRIM series of light grenades which are described in the appropriate French entry. Another part of the development has concerned the AP 1640 grenades which are described below.

FN AP 1640 GRENADES

Apart from the FN-Luchaire-Strim family, a further class of rifle grenade for 5.56mm calibre weapons has been developed and produced by FN. These are the AP 1640 grenades of which two types exist. Arming is initiated by the propulsion force (modified by the bullet trap where appropriate) and delayed by an escapement mechanism.

Rifle Grenade AP 1640.S

This grenade is launched from the rifle by means of a special grenade cartridge, normally housed, in transit, in the tail of the grenade. The grenade may also be fired from 7.62mm rifles.

DATA
Range: (with 5.56mm rifle): 400 metres
Certain arming distance: 15 metres
Muzzle velocity: 74 metres/second
Weight of grenade: 345g

Rifle Grenade AP 1640.N

This grenade may be launched either with a special grenade cartridge or, if the grenade is fitted with a bullet trap, by a normal 5.56mm ball cartridge. It is not intended for use with 7.62mm ball cartridges.

DATA
Range: 375 metres
Certain arming distance: 15 metres
Muzzle velocity: 67 metres/second
Weight of grenade: 385g

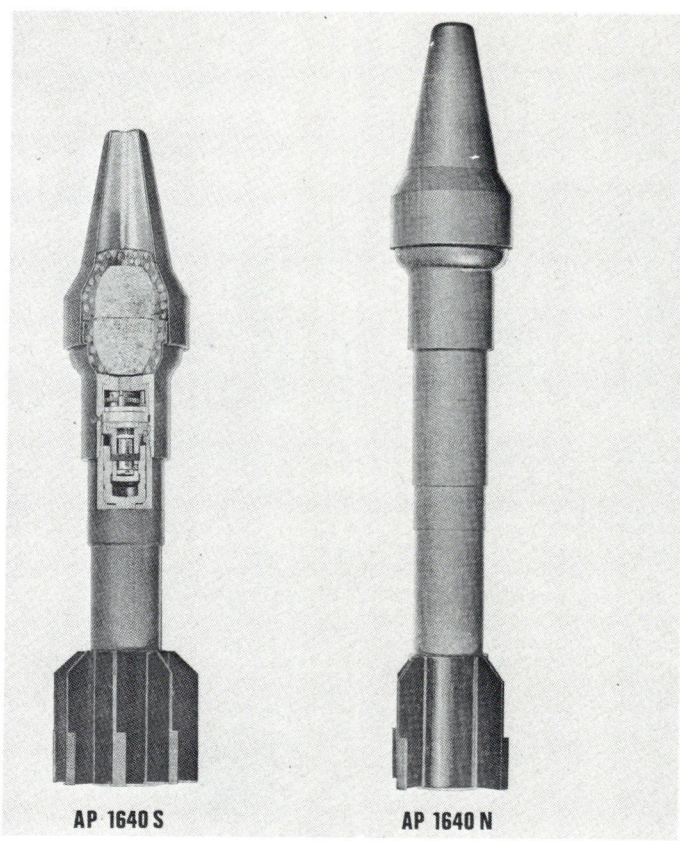

AP 1640 S   **AP 1640 N**

AP 1640 rifle grenades. The S grenade has been sectioned to show the arming mechanism and warhead arrangement

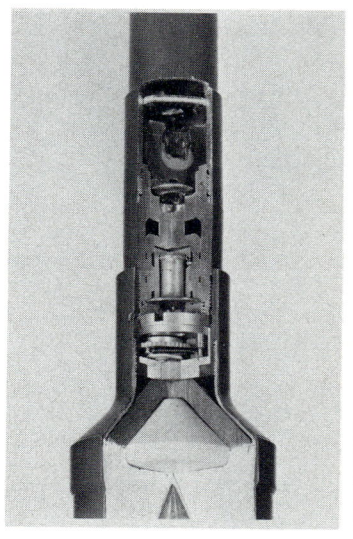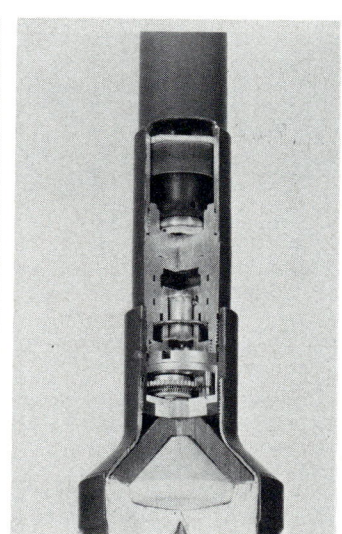

Sectioned view of the grenade bullet trap before and after firing a 5.56mm ball bullet into it

MECAR RIFLE GRENADE DESIGNATIONS

Mecar grenade designations for their older rifle grenade designs have functional codes. These have the following meanings:
ARP – armour piercing
BT – fitted with a bullet trap
FRG – fragmentation
N – cartridge propelled
PFL – parachute flare

RFL – rifle-launched
SIG – signalling
SMK – smoke
5.56 – for use with 5.56mm rifle
7.62 – for use with 7.62mm rifle
40 – 40mm calibre grenade

MECAR 40mm ANTI-TANK RIFLE GRENADE ARP-RFL-40 N

The ARP-RFL-40 N armour-piercing rifle grenade is designed to defeat armour and armoured personnel carriers. The Mecar rifle grenades eliminate the need for separate grenade launchers and offer each rifleman a simple, rapid and uniform means of handling a variety of combat situations. The ARP-RFL-40 N weighs only 226 grams (7.9oz). It can be fired accurately at distances of 200 metres and it will pierce armour of up to 125mm thickness. In its standard configuration it is provided with a super quick, point detonating fuze which operates at angles of incidence as steep as 70 degrees from the normal. This fuze arms after sixteen metres of grenade travel, and actions at impact on a moderately firm surface. For special applications, the ARP-RFL-40 N can be furnished with Mecar's super sensitive fuze which will detonate even when striking soft targets such as water, mud or sand. This super sensitive fuze can be further supplied in a triple safe configuration including an external shield which, when in place

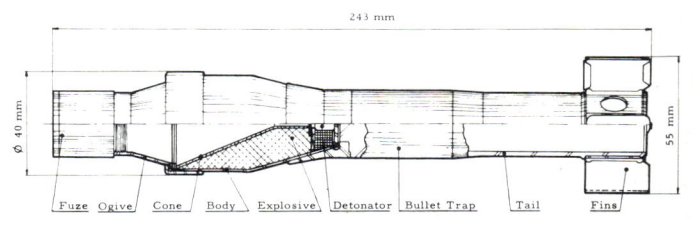

ARP-RFL-40 N

provides a positive, visible safety indication that the strike is out of line with the detonator.

The low recoil of the ARP-RFL-40 N permits firing from the shoulder or from any other conventional rifle position.

The ARP-RFL-40 N fits directly on any combat rifle of the proper calibre provided with a 22mm muzzle diameter. For other rifles, Mecar offers suitable adapters. Each grenade is furnished with one special cartridge and one direct fire aiming grid for the rifle in use.

DATA
Calibre: 40mm
Length: 243mm
Weight: 226gm
Fuze: Super quick, point detonating
Rifle: Any
Aiming grid: Provided with grenade
Special cartridge: Provided with grenade
Operational range:
  Moving targets: 150 metres
  Fixed targets: 200 metres
  Maximum range (at 45°): 500 metres
Target penetration:
  Armoured steel: 125mm
  Concrete: 400mm
  Maximum angle of impact (from normal): 70°
Accuracy at 150m (height + width): 1.5 + 1.5 metres
Launch velocity (nominal): 100m/sec
Arming distance: 16 metres
Recoil energy (nominal): 7kpm
Operating temperature range: −32°C to + 52°C
Status: In production. In service

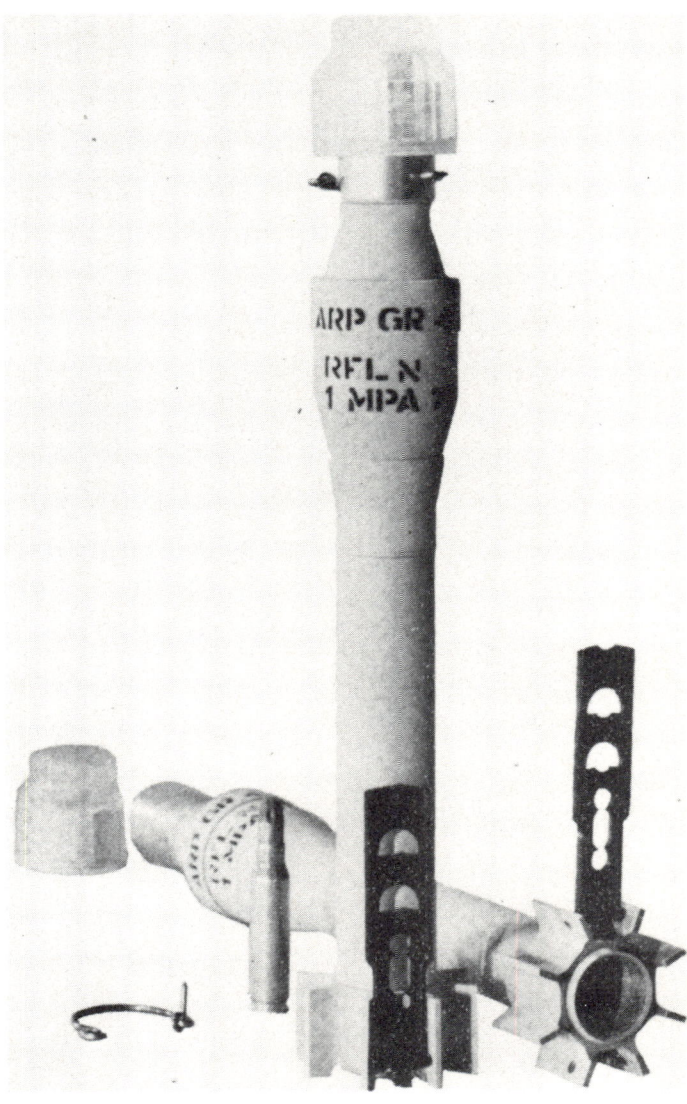

The 40mm armour-piercing rifle grenade. Normal

MECAR 40m ANTI-TANK RIFLE GRENADE ARP-RFL-40 BT 5.56 (and 7.62)

The ARP-RFL-40 BT 5.56 armour piercing rifle grenade with bullet trap will defeat armour and armoured personnel carriers. The bullet trap enables the rifleman to fire the 40mm rifle grenades in direct sequence with live ammunition and by eliminating the need for separate grenade launchers, offers a simple, rapid and uniform means of handling a variety of combat situations. The ARP-RFL-40 BT 7.62mm rifle grenade is also available.

The ARP-RFL-40 BT 5.56 weighs only 264 grams. It can be fired accurately at distances of 100 metres and it will pierce armour of up to 125mm thickness. In its standard configuration it is provided with a super quick, point detonating fuze which operates at angles of incidence as steep as 70 degrees from the normal. This fuze arms after eight metres of grenade travel and actions at impact on a moderately firm surface. For special applications, it can be furnished with Mecar's super sensitive fuze. The low recoil permits it to be fired from the shoulder or from any other conventional rifle position.

DATA
Calibre: 40mm
Length: 243mm
Weight: 264gm
Fuze: Super quick, point detonating
Rifle calibre: 5.56mm
Aiming grid: Provided with grenade
Cartridge: Regular ball ammunition
Operational range: 100 metres
Maximum range (at 45°): 275 metres
Target penetration:
  Armoured steel: 125mm
  Concrete: 400mm
  Maximum angle of impact (from normal): 70°
Accuracy at 100m (height + width): 1.5 + 1.5 metres
Launch velocity (nominal): 60m/sec
Arming distance: 8 metres
Recoil energy: 4.33kpm
Operating temperature range: −32°C to +52°C
Status: In production. In service

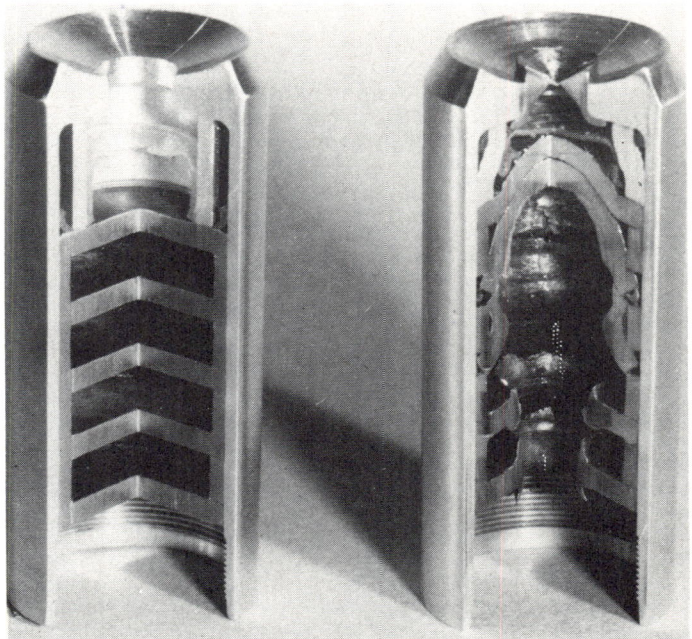

The bullet trap before and after firing

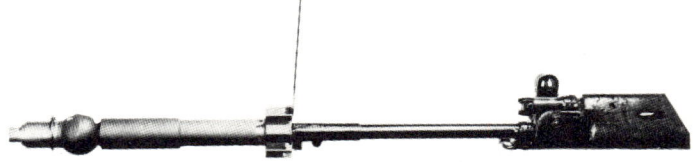

The Mecar 40mm Bullet Trap Grenade

MECAR 40mm FRAGMENTATION RIFLE GRENADE FRG-RFL-40 N

The FRG-RFL-40 N fragmentation rifle grenade is intended for accurate direct fire against enemy concentrations and for indirect fire against concealed positions. It weighs only 200 grams and can be fired out to ranges of 500 metres. At impact, its serrated spherical war head of soft steel will break into more than 300 fragments travelling at 1,200 metres per second. The lethal radius extends to five metres and fragments can remain effective out to 30 metres. In its standard configuration the FRG-RFL-40 N is equipped with a super sensitive fuze which operates on hard targets as well as on soft targets such as water, mud or sand, even when striking at grazing angles. This super sensitive fuze which arms after nine metres of grenade travel can be further supplied in a triple safe configuration including an external shield which, when in place, offers a positive, visible safety indication that the striker is out of line with the detonator.

The FRG-RFL-40 N fits directly on to any combat rifle of the proper calibre provided with a 22mm muzzle diameter. For other rifles, Mecar offers suitable adapters. Each grenade is furnished with one special cartridge and one direct fire aiming grid for the rifle in use. Indirect fire sights or special sights can be supplied.

DATA
Calibre: 40mm
Length: 195mm
Weight: 200gm
Fuze: Super sensitive
Rifle: Any
Aiming grid: Provided with grenade
Special cartridge: Provided with grenade
Maximum range (45° launch angle): 500 metres
Number of fragments: >300
Average fragment size: 0.14m
Lethal radius: 5 metres
Maximum effective radius: 30 metres
Launch velocity (nominal): 100m/sec

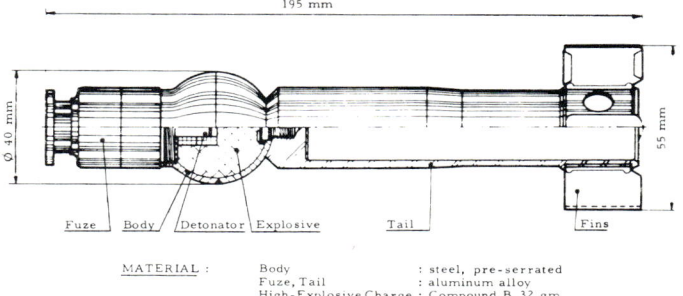

FRG-RFL-40 N

Arming distance: 9 metres
Recoil energy (nominal): 6.4kpm
Operating temperature range: −32°C to +52°C
Status: In production. In service

Rifle grenade, 40mm, fragmentation. Normal

MECAR 40mm FRAGMENTATION RIFLE GRENADE FRG-RFL-40 BT 5.56 and 7.62

The FRG-RFL-40 BT 5.56 fragmentation rifle grenade with bullet trap is intended for accurate direct fire against enemy concentrations and for indirect fire against concealed positions. The Mecar bullet trap enables the rifleman to fire the 40mm rifle grenades in direct sequence with live ammunition. There is a similar grenade, for use with 7.62mm rifles, designated the FRG-RFL-40 BT.7.62mm.

The FRG-RFL-40 BT 5.56 weighs only 240 grams and can be fired out to ranges of 300 metres. At impact, its serrated spherical war head of soft steel will break into more than 300 fragments travelling at 1,200 metres per second. The lethal radius extends to five metres and fragments can remain effective out to 30 metres. In its standard configuration it is equipped with a super sensitive fuze which operates on hard targets as well as on soft targets such as water, mud or sand, even when striking at grazing angles. This fuze, which arms after eight metres of grenade travel, can be further supplied in a triple safe configuration including an external shield which, when in place, offers a positive, visible safety indication that the striker is out of line with a detonator.

The FRG-RFL-40 BT 5.56 fits directly on to any combat rifle of the proper calibre with a 22mm muzzle diameter. For other rifles, Mecar offers suitable adapters. With each grenade is supplied one direct fire aiming grid matched to the rifle in use. Indirect fire sights or special sights can also be supplied.

For training an inert fragmentation grenade simulating the live grenade in all aspects the shape, weight, balance and trajectory.

DATA
Calibre: 40mm
Length: 195mm
Weight: 240gm
Fuze: Super sensitive

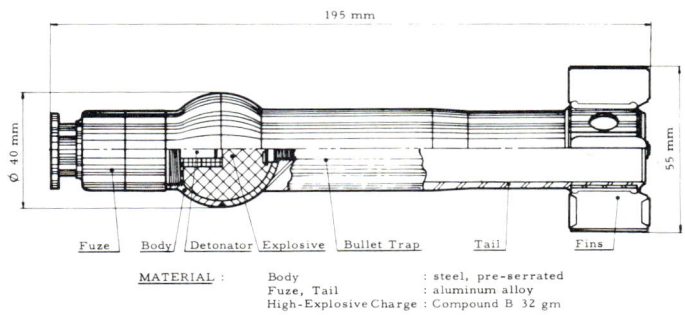

RFG-RFL-40 BT 5.56

Rifle Calibre: 5.56mm
Aiming grid: Provided with grenade
Cartridge: Regular ball ammunition
Maximum range (at 45°): 310 metres
Number of fragments: >300
Average fragment size: 0.14gm
Lethal radius: 5 metres
Maximum effective radius: 30 metres
Launch velocity (nominal): 64m/sec
Arming distance: 8 metres
Recoil energy (nominal): 4.2kpm
Operating temperature range: −32°C to +52°C
Status: In production. In service

Rifle grenade, 40mm fragmentation, with bullet trap

MECAR 40mm SMOKE GENERATING RIFLE GRENADE SMK-RFL-40 N

The SMK-RFL-40 N smoke producing rifle grenade is intended to create a persistent, opaque smoke screen. It weighs only 350 grams and can be fired out to ranges of more than 300 metres. The grenade contains a short delay which is started at the instant of grenade launch. During its operation SMK-RFL-40 N slowly releases over a period of 150 seconds a thick, white, opaque smoke. For combination smoke-screening/signalling Mecar also offers SMK-RFL-40 type of orange coloured smoke.

DATA
Calibre: 40mm
Length: 225mm
Weight: 350gm
Rifle: Any
Special cartridge: Provided with grenade
Maximum range (at 45°): 315 metres
Ignition delay: 5sec
Duration of smoke screen: 150sec
Smoke colours available: Orange, White
Operating temperature range: −32°C to +52°C
Status: In production. In service

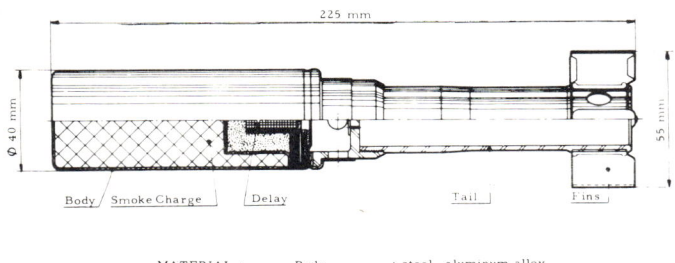

SMK-RFL-40 N

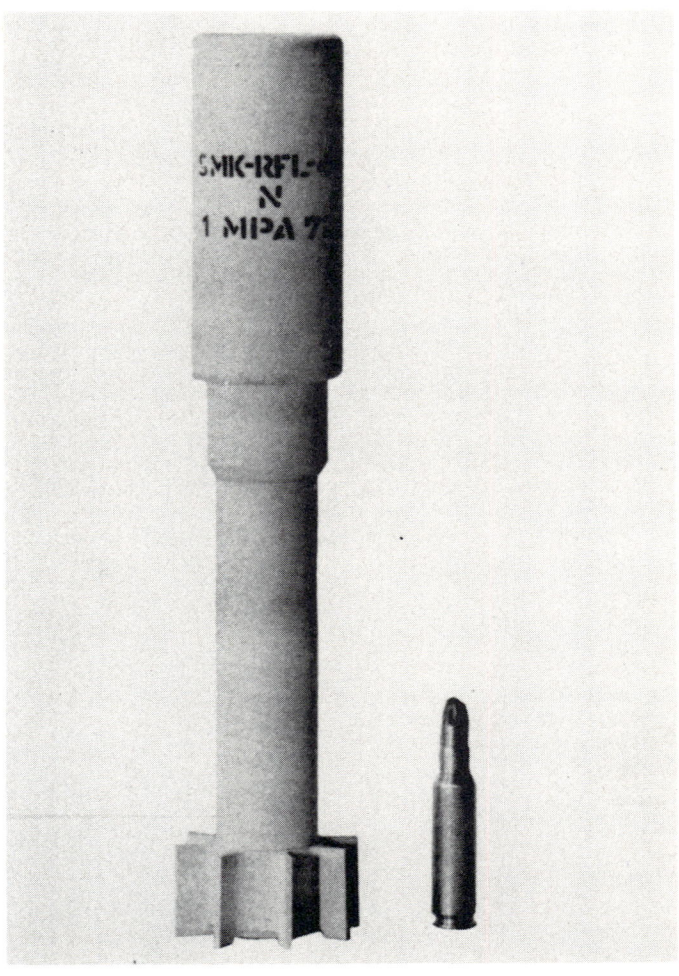

Rifle grenade, 40mm, smoke generating. Normal

MECAR 40mm SMOKE GENERATING RIFLE GRENADE SMK-RFL-40 BT 5.56 (and 7.62)

The SMK-RFL-40 BT 5.56 smoke producing rifle grenade with bullet trap is provided to create a persistent, opaque smoke screen. There is a similar 7.62mm model called the SMK-RFL-40 BT 7.62mm. The bullet trap eliminates the need for separate grenade launchers.

The grenade weighs only 390 grams and can be fired out to ranges of 150 metres. It contains a short time delay which is started at the instant of grenade launch. During its operation the SMK-RFL-40 slowly releases a thick, white, opaque smoke over a period of 150 seconds. For combination smoke-screening/signalling, Mecar also offers an SMK-RFL-40 type of orange coloured smoke. The grenade fits directly any combat rifle of the proper calibre with a 22mm muzzle diameter. For other rifles, Mecar offers suitable adapters.

DATA
Calibre: 40mm
Length: 225mm
Weight: 390gm
Rifle calibre: 5.56mm
Cartridge: Regular ball ammunition
Range, maximum effective (at 45°): 150 metres

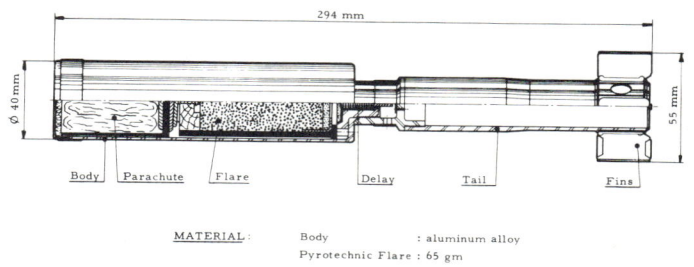

SMK-RFL-40BT 5.56

Ignition: 5sec
Duration of smoke screen: 150sec
Smoke colours available: Orange; White
Operating temperature range: −32°C to + 52°C
Status: In production. In service

MECAR 40mm ILLUMINATING PARACHUTE RIFLE GRENADE PFL-RFL-40 N

The PFL-RFL-40 N rifle grenade is a classic paraflare which provides an average of 30 seconds of high intensity illumination. It weighs 290 grams and its flare will burn for 30 seconds with an intensity as high as 60,000 candles. Flare colours of yellow, red and green are available which permit the PFL-RFL-40 to be used both for illumination and for signalling. The grenade is supplied in two versions, one with an ignition delay of 5 seconds for high angle launch and the other with a 2 seconds delay for flat trajectories. When launched at 45 degrees to illuminate wide areas, flare ignition will occur at an altitude of 120 metres and the parachute will carry the flare aloft throughout the entire burning time. The PFL-RFL-40 N with 2 seconds delay is used to illuminate ground targets at close range. The flare burns after either settling on the ground or being suspended in brushwood by its parachute lines.

The PFL-RFL-40 N fits directly on any combat rifle of the proper calibre with a 22mm muzzle diameter. For other rifles, Mecar offers suitable adapters. Each grenade is furnished with one special cartridge for the rifle in use.

DATA
Calibre: 40mm
Length: 294mm
Weight: 290gm
Rifle: Any
Special cartridge: Provided with grenade
Maximum range: 250 metres

PFL-RFL-40 N

Flare colours available: Yellow, red, green
Illuminating intensity: Yellow 60,000 and 25,000 candles; Red 25,000 candles; Green 25,000 candles
Duration of flare: 30sec
Ignition delay: 2 and 5sec
Height of flare release (at 45°): Approx 120 metres
Height of end signal: Approx 50 metres
Operating temperature range: −32°C to +52°C
Status: In production. In service

MECAR 40mm ILLUMINATING PARACHUTE RIFLE GRENADE PFL-RFL-40 BT 5.56 (or 7.62)

The PFL-RFL-40 BT 5.56 rifle grenade with bullet trap is a standard paraflare which provides an average of 30 seconds of high intensity illumination. There is also a similar grenade for use with 7.62mm rifles. The Mecar bullet trap enables the rifleman to fire either grenade with appropriate ball ammunition. The PFL-RFL-40 BT 5.56 weighs 330 grams. Its flare will burn for 30 seconds with an intensity as high as 60,000 candles. Flare colours of yellow, red and green are available which permit to be used for both illumination and signalling. The grenade is supplied in two versions, one with an ignition delay of 3 seconds for high angle launch, and the other with a 2 seconds delay for flat trajectories. When launched at 45 degrees to illuminate wide areas, flare ignition will occur at an altitude of 65 metres and the parachute will carry the flare aloft throughout the entire burning time. The grenade with 2 seconds delay is used to illuminate ground targets at close range. The flare burns either after having settled on the ground or when remaining suspended in the undergrowth by its parachute lines.

DATA
Calibre: 40mm
Length: 294mm
Weight: 330gm
Rifle calibre: 5.56mm
Cartridge: Regular ball ammunition
Maximum range: 110 metres

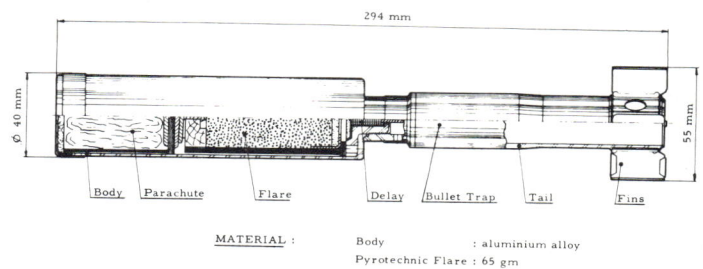

PFL-RFL-40 BT 5.56

Flare colours available: Yellow, red, green
Illumination intensity: Yellow 60,000 and 25,000 candles; Red 25,000 candles; Green 25,000 candles
Duration of flare: 30sec
Ignition delay: 2 and 3sec
Height of flare release (at 45°): Approx 65 metres
Operating temperature range: −32°C to +52°C
Status: In production. In service

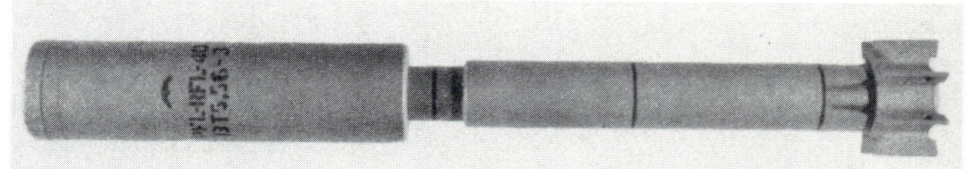

Rifle grenade, 40mm, illuminating, parachute, with bullet trap

MECAR 60mm DUAL PURPOSE ANTI-PERSONNEL GRENADE

This grenade has been designed in such a way that it can be either thrown by hand or launched from a rifle using a regular ball round. For the latter purpose the tail is fitted with the Mecar bullet trap. The grenade is time-fused so that air bursts are possible.

DATA
Hand grenade
Diameter: 60mm
Height: 85mm
Weight: 422g
Explosive weight: 132g
Delay: 4sec
Number of fragments: 500
Lethal radius: 8 metres

Tail
Weight: 195g
Interior diameter: 22mm
Length: 215mm

Rifle Grenade (Hand grenade + Tail)
Total weight: 617g
Muzzle velocity: 58m/sec
Recoil energy: <15kgm
Maximum range: corresponding to 4sec flight duration (up to 225 metres)
Operating temperature range: −32°C to +52°C

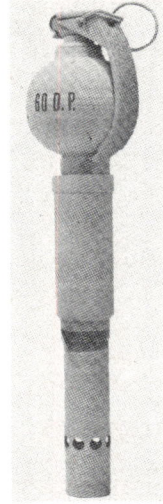

Hand and rifle launched version of the 60mm dual purpose grenade

MECAR 60mm LONG RANGE ANTI-PERSONNEL GRENADE

This long-range (up to 700 metres) weapon in intended to perform many of the functions currently performed by the smaller mortars. The warhead is designed to give a highly effective fragmentation pattern.

DATA
Calibre: 60mm
Length: 320mm
Weight: Total: 636g
       Warhead: 336g
Launch velocity: 47-55m/sec
Operational range: 700m
Number of fragments: >500

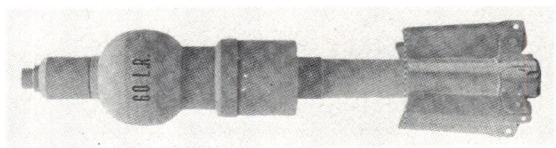

60mm long-range anti-personnel grenade

Lethal radius: 8 metres
Maximum effective radius: 30 metres

MECAR 60mm REBOUNDING ANTI-PERSONNEL GRENADE

This grenade is designed to give an enhanced anti-personnel effect by rebounding from its first impact and bursting while in the air after the rebound. For the purpose the warhead nose has a spring-loaded plunger which provides the rebound and which initiates the explosion of the grenade so that it bursts about one metre from the ground.

In other respects the grenade is similar in design to other members of this new Mecar series. In the form detailed and illustrated here the grenade has an operational range of some 260 metres. A long range version is also available, however: this has a range of some 600 metres and retains the rebounding feature.

DATA
Calibre: 60mm
Length: 290mm
Weight: Total: 560g
       Warhead: 336g
Launch velocity: 53m/sec

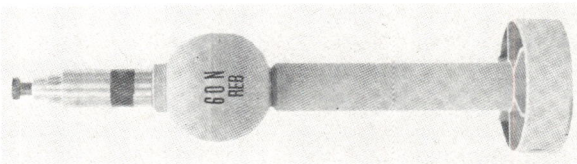

Standard version of the 60mm rebounding anti-personnel grenade

Height of bursting: about 1 metre
Operational range: 260m
Number of fragments: >500
Lethal radius: 8 metres
Maximum effective radius: 30 metres
Recoil energy: 9kgm

MECAR 75mm LONG-RANGE ANTI-PERSONNEL RIFLE GRENADE

Similar in general design to other members of the new Mecar grenade family, this long-range device carries a more powerful warhead producing more fragments with a greater lethal range. This combined with the substantial range of some 500 metres makes the weapon suitable for many of the roles otherwise performed by a light mortar.

DATA
Calibre: 75mm
Length: 330mm
Weight: Total: 935g
       Warhead: 638g
Launch velocity: 40m/sec
Operational range: 500m
Number of fragments: >700

75mm long-range grenade

Lethal radius: 10m
Maximum effective radius: 35 metres

PRB 406 ILLUMINATING RIFLE GRENADE

The grenade consists of a light alloy body closed by a plastic ballistic cap, or ogive, and a stabilising boom with fins. The body holds an igniter set off by the propellant gases, a delay element, an expelling charge for the parachute and the illuminating charge. The tail boom enables the grenade to be used with any rifle with a launcher, or flash eliminator, of 22mm external diameter.

4.5 seconds after firing the grenade, the delay device ignites the expelling charge which expels the illuminating charge and the parachute. The parachute deploys and descends at a maximum rate of 2 metres/second.

Fired at 45 degrees the grenade illuminates a circle of 260 metres radius, centre located 300 metres from the firer the expelling height being 100 metres. The illuminating area is thus 212,372 square metres and the illuminated area extends from 40 metres in front of the firer to a distance of 560 metres.

DATA
Weight: 375g

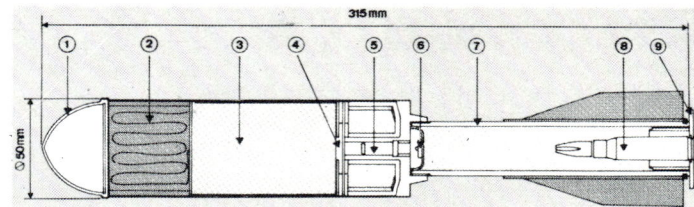

The PRB 406 illuminating rifle grenade: **(1)** *Ogive;* **(2)** *Parachute;* **(3)** *Illuminating charge;* **(4)** *Expelling charge;* **(5)** *Delay element;* **(6)** *Igniter;* **(7)** *Tail boom;* **(8)** *Ballistite cartridge;* **(9)** *Cartridge holder*

Candle power: 150,000 candelas
Burning time: 30 seconds (minimum)
Ejection delay: 4.5 seconds
Rate of descent: 2 metres/second maximum

PRB 412 SMOKE RIFLE GRENADE

This grenade has a steel body with a rear closing plug. This plug is drilled to form smoke channels and it also carries the tail boom with the stabilising fins. The tail boom allows the grenade to be used with any rifle with a 22mm external diameter launcher or flash suppressor.

The boom carries the ballistite cartridge which sets off the igniter which, in turn, ignites the delay element. This burns for about 3 seconds and then ignites the ignition booster. This is in contact with the main charge which ignites the smoke filling of hexachlorethane. This comes out through the channels in the base plug and forms a thick cloud of white smoke which provides a screen. The emission time is not less than 30 seconds. The duration of the screen depends on the weather conditions, temperature, wind etc.

DATA
Weight: 720g
Maximum range: 300 metres

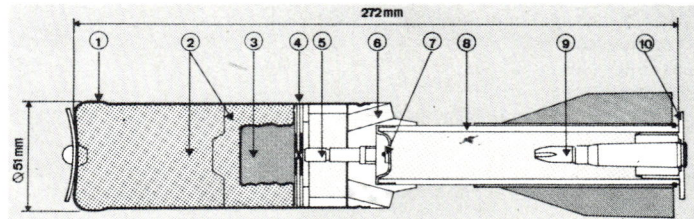

The PRB 412 smoke rifle grenade: **(1)** *Steel body;* **(2)** *Smoke charge;* **(3)** *Ignition charge;* **(4)** *Ignition booster;* **(5)** *Delay element;* **(6)** *Smoke hole;* **(7)** *Igniter;* **(8)** *Tail boom;* **(9)** *Ballistite cartridge;* **(10)** *Cartridge holder*

Ignition delay: 3 seconds
Time of emission: 30 seconds minimum

PRB 434 ANTI-PERSONNEL RIFLE GRENADE

The PRB 434 can be fired from standard NATO rifles fitted with a removable grenade launcher or a flash supressor of 22mm standard external diameter. There are two launching cartridges. Maximum range is achieved with the rifle butt on the ground, and using the long range cartridge this gives a range of 400m. With the rifle being used in the 'sling around the arm' position, the short range cartridge is used; this gives a maximum range of 150m.

PRB 434 consists of three components, a thermoplastic body loaded with 100g of compound B, a fragmentation sleeve surrounding the body and a fin stabiliser containing the fuze. The launching tube is fitted with fins to stabilise the trajectory; this results in increased range and an impact angle greater than 70°.

The grenade is provided with a "super-quick" impact fuze. Its arming delay provides a muzzle safety of ±30m. The fuze acts as a connecting piece between the launching tube and the warhead. On firing, the fuze body absorbs the set-back of the fragmentation sleeve. A safety pin, which must be withdrawn before firing, prevents any accidental arming of the fuze during handling and transportation.

DATA
Weight of grenade: 555g
Weight of fragmentation sleeve: 300g
Weight of explosive charge: 100g
Length of grenade: 278mm
Maximum range – long range cartridge: 400m
Maximum range – short range cartridge: 150m
Safety distance: 30m
Unit pack: Two grenades per fibre container and sixteen containers per case

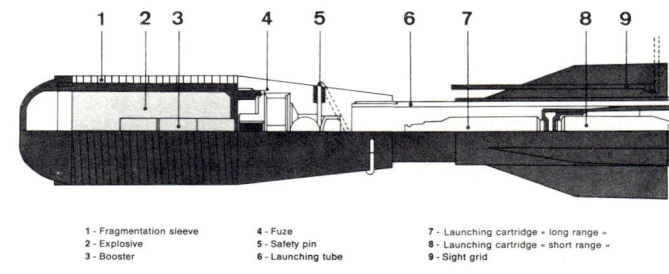

1 - Fragmentation sleeve
2 - Explosive
3 - Booster
4 - Fuze
5 - Safety pin
6 - Launching tube
7 - Launching cartridge « long range »
8 - Launching cartridge « short range »
9 - Sight grid

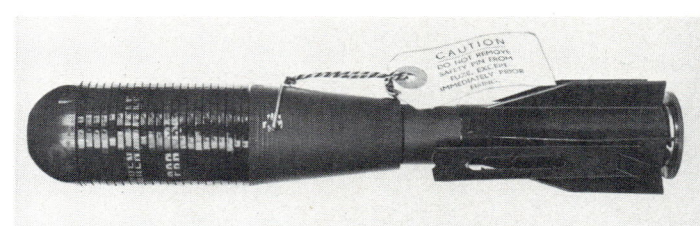

PRB 434 Anti-Personnel rifle grenade

PRB 404 ANTI-PERSONNEL FRAGMENTATION GRENADE

This grenade consists of a thermoplastic body loaded with 100g of Compound B manufactured by PRB; a notched coil fragmentation sleeve placed around the body; a fin stabilising tube containing the Jet Shot and the fuze. The fuze for the PRB 404 grenade is a super quick impact type functioning at all impact angles. The arming delay provides a muzzle safety of 10 to 45 metres depending on the time of delay which can vary from 0.3 to 1 second. The fuze acts as a connecting piece between the tube carrying the fins and the warhead. The fuze body absorbs the set back of the fragmentation sleeve and transmits the impulse of the Jet Shot to the warhead.

The components of the PRB 404 grenade can be used to make up either a conventional offensive or defensive hand grenade. The defensive hand grenade consists of the thermoplastic body and the notched coil fragmenting sleeve which is held on to the body by a ring screwed on to the lower part of the case. The offensive hand grenade is made up of the thermoplastic

body only, which with its 100g filling produces a very considerable blast effect.

DATA
Length: 250mm
Weight: 520g
Weight of jet shot: 200g
Total weight: 720g
Weight at beginning of flight: 560g
Fragmenting sleeve weight: 300g
Explosive charge weight: 100g
Average range at 45°: More than 400 metres
Muzzle velocity: 70 metres/sec
Muzzle safety:
0.3 second delay: 10 metres

1 second delay: 45 metres
Safety distance: 30 metres
Launchers: Disposable mortar PRB 424; Single hand launcher; Multi spigot PRB 426; Rifle (not yet developed)
Ignition: Electrical or percussion
Packing: 24 grenades with Jet Shot in one wooden case
Net weight: 16.5kg
Gross weight: 24kg
Volume: 0.08 metres^3

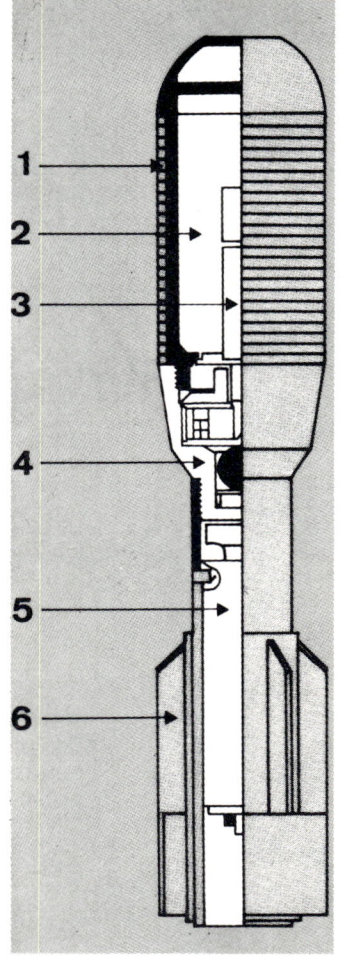

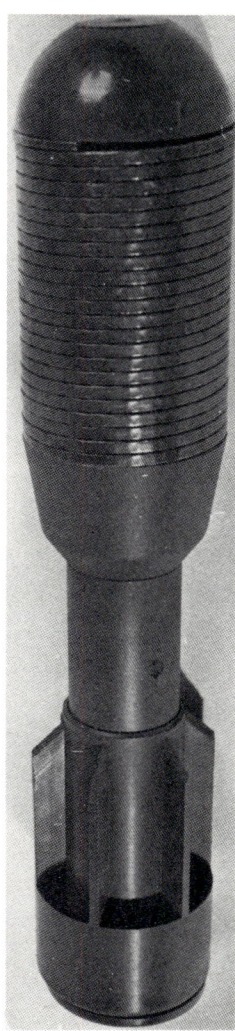

The PRB 404 grenade (1) fragmentation sleeve; (2) explosive; (3) booster; (4) fuze; (5) Jet Shot cartridge; (6) fin assembly

The PRB 404 grenade

PRB 422 HI-BLAST GRENADE

The grenade PRB 422 is designed to produce an extremely high blast effect. The shape of the warhead and the explosive employed (trialene) give a maximum shockwave effect. The makers envisage this grenade being used to attack bunkers, underground shelters, covered trenches and light structures.

DATA
Grenade:
Length: 265mm
Weight: 630g
Weight of Jet Shot: 200g
Total weight: 830g
Weight at beginning of flight: 670g
Explosive charge weight: 350g
Average range at 45°: 300 metres
Muzzle velocity: 60 metres/sec
Muzzle safety (1 second delay): 45 metres
Launchers: Disposable mortar PRB 425; Single hand launcher
Ignition: Electric or percussion

The Hi-Blast grenade PRB 422

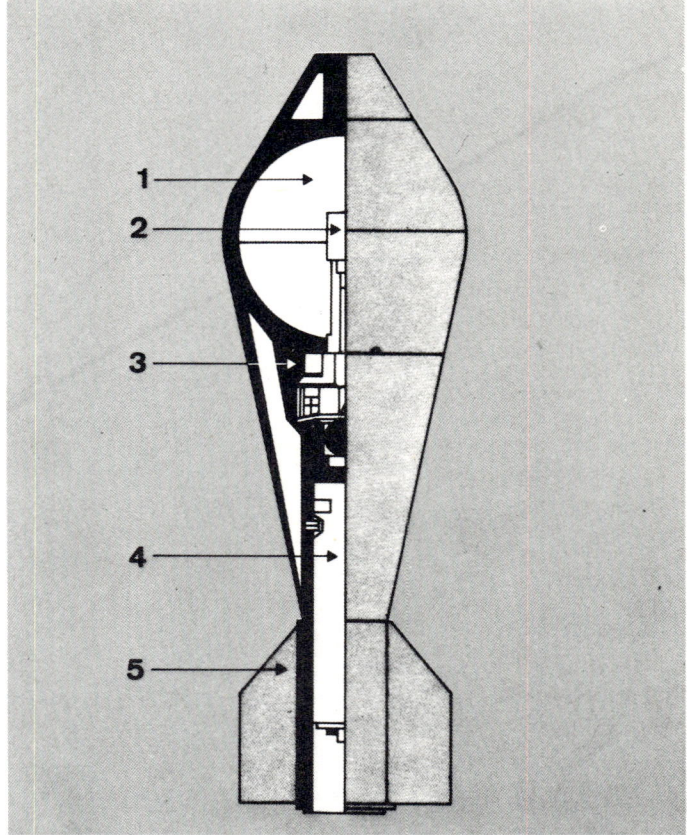

PRB 422: (1) explosive; (2) booster; (3) fuze; (4) Jet Shot Cartridge; (5) fin assembly

PRB 423 HAND GRENADE

GENERAL DESCRIPTION

The hand grenade PRB 423 produces a controlled fragmentation due to the number and shape of the splinters and to the weight and type of the explosive used.

The very high efficiency at close range and the very short safety radius are the two main characteristics of the PRB 423 grenade.

The dispersion of the effective splinters is obtained in a homogeneous manner and is uniform in the space around the point of impact whatever the position of the grenade may be at the moment of explosion.

The safety radius allows the soldier to remain unsheltered when he launches the grenade at 20 metres minimum.

This results in an important logistic advantage as the same grenade can be used as an offensive and as a defensive one.

GRENADE BODY

The egg-shaped grenade is composed of five elements:
(a) an outer plastic case of olive green colour with transversal and longitudinal ribs ensuring a good grip;
(b) a fragmentation sleeve lining the inside of the case; this sleeve is made of a spirally wound steel wire of rectangular section. This wire is prenotched (according to a PRB patent) at regular intervals, inside the coil formed, so as to fragment into about 900 splinters during the explosion;
(c) 22 steel balls placed in the bottom closing plug and 30 in the upper part of the case to reduce the dead angles when the grenade explodes in horizontal position;
(d) a very powerful explosive filler;
(e) a plastic closing plug of olive green colour.

THE FUZE

The PRB 432 time fuze has a 4sec gasless delay. This delay is sufficient to allow the soldier to throw the grenade without danger, but is too short for an enemy to throw it back.

DATA

Weight of the grenade body: 180g
Weight of the time fuze: 50g
Weight of the complete grenade: 230g
Explosive filler weight (Comp B): 60g
Fragmentation sleeve weight: 65g
Number of fragments, average weight of one splinter: 0.105g

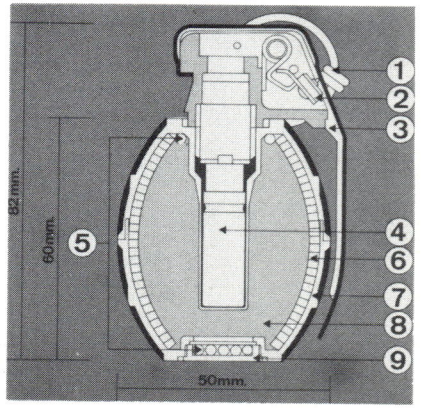

The PRB 423 grenade: **(1)** safety clip; **(2)** striker; **(3)** lever; **(4)** detonator; **(5)** balls; **(6)** fragmentation sleeve; **(7)** plastic shell; **(8)** explosive; **(9)** plug

Number of steel balls: 52
Average weight of each steel ball: 0.1g
Lethal radius: 9m
Safety radius: 20m

PRB 423 PRACTICE HAND GRENADE

The practice hand grenade is intended for training soldiers in the use of the live controlled-fragmentation hand grenade PRB 423.

It has the same weight (230grs) and shape and the same outside aspect. However it looks different from the live grenades due to its colour, marking, materials and elements used.

The effect produced is noise, simulating an explosion, and a small quantity of smoke.

The functioning does not produce any projection of metallic elements, consequently its use does not require any special safety provisions.

This grenade has two separate components:

GRENADE BODY

The body is of aluminium alloy. This part has a through channel in which is screwed the fuze with its deflagrator and which permits the evacuation of the gases produced when functioning.

This body can be re-used (minimum 100 times) without other maintenance than simple cleaning with a rag.

TIME FUZE

The practice time fuze is identical in all respects to the PRB 432 (4sec) gasless delay time fuze used with the PRB 423 live grenade; its use and functioning are the same. The only difference is that the detonator has been replaced by a deflagrator which produces noise and smoke. No dangerous projections are produced by its functioning. Like the PRB 432 time fuze, the practice time fuze cannot be re-used as it is destroyed upon functioning.

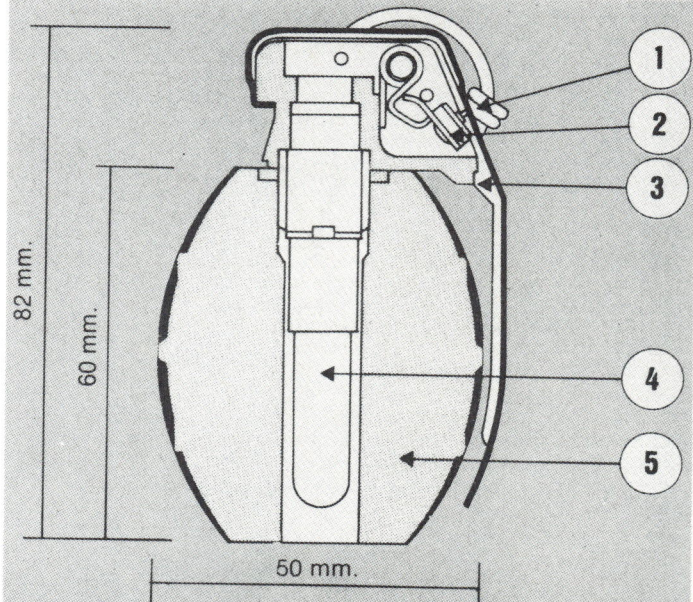

The practice hand grenade PRB 423: **(1)** safety clip; **(2)** striker; **(3)** lever; **(4)** deflagrator; **(5)** grenade body

PRB 446 OFFENSIVE HAND GRENADE

The purpose of the offensive hand grenade PRB 446 is to produce a powerful blast effect without fragments.

It has been developed with elements of the controlled fragmentation hand grenade PRB 423. Its outside shape is identical, the only difference being the colour and marking as well as a lighter weight: 165grs instead of 230grs.

All the components that can produce dangerous fragments, particularly the fragmentation sleeve and the balls, have been removed.

The same explosive is used, compound B, but in larger quantity, 85grs instead of 60grs, in order to increase the power of the shock wave (same

power as that of 110grs of cast TNT). This grenade uses the PRB 432 time fuze of 4sec gasless delay which is also used with the PRB 423 controlled fragmentation hand grenade.

DATA

Weight of the grenade body: 115g
Weight of explosive (comp B): 85g
Weight of time fuze: 50g
Total weight of the grenade: 165g

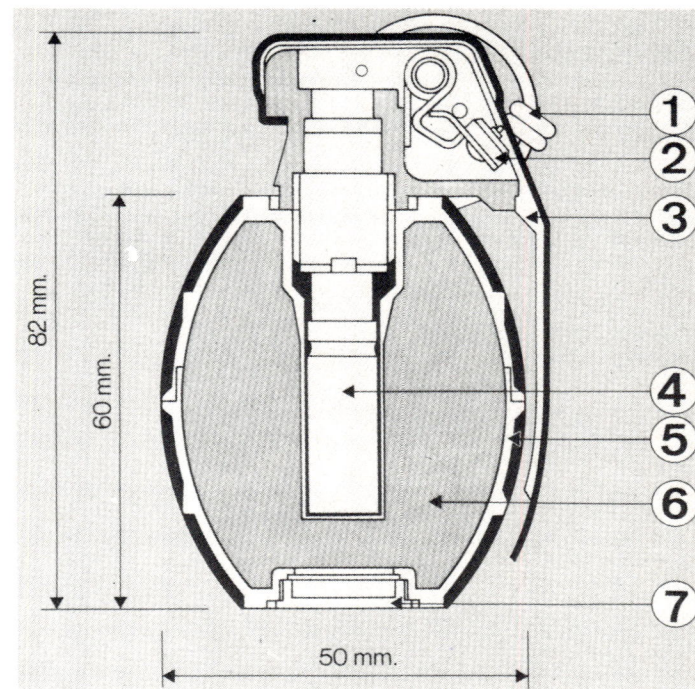

Offensive hand grenade PRB 446: (1) safety clip; (2) striker; (3) lever; (4) detonator; (5) plastic shell; (6) explosive; (7) plug

PRB 8 (or 7) BIVALENT HAND GRENADE

The PRB 8 grenade is composed of thermoplastic case containing the explosive and of a fragmentation sleeve. This fragmentation sleeve is a steel wire of square section, which is pre-notched and spirally wound. It can be withdrawn to change the PRB 8 defensive grenade into the PRB 7 offensive grenade.

Use of this fragmentation sleeve makes the anti-personnel efficiency of the PRB 8 grenade very high.

The grenade uses the PRB 433 time fuze with 4.5 sec gasless delay.

DATA
Diameter: 50mm
Height: 112mm
Weight:
  Grenade body PRB 7: 116g
  Explosive (TNT): 80g
  Fragmentation sleeve: 300g
  PRB 433 time fuze: 43g
  Total weight of the grenade PRB 8 with its time fuze: 485g
Lethal radius: 12m
Safety radius: 40m

PRB 8 and PRB 7 grenades and components

PACKING
48 grenades PRB 8 and 48 time fuzes PRB 433 separately per no nail wooden case.
Gross weight of one case: 28kg
Volume of one case: .055m³

PRB SMOKE GRENADES

Two smoke grenades are currently made by PRB. One, type PRB 405, is a 'bursting' type of white phosphorus grenade creating a dense cloud of white smoke and having an associated incendiary effect and an anti-personnel effect within a 15 metre radius of the explosives.

The charge is contained in a waterproof can and is detonated by a 4.5 second time fuze intiated by a conventional spring-loaded plunger secured by a lever and split pin with pulling ring.

Type HC is a hexachlorethane grenade containing some 200g of composition and emitting a cloud of dense, white, clinging smoke. Non-explosive, it can be fitted either with a ring and plunger mechanism with a 4.5 second delay to ignition or with a friction igniter with a 4 second delay.

DATA	PRB 405	HC
Diameter:	50mm	63mm
Height:	103mm	125mm
Weight: Complete:	330g	320g
Time fuze assembly:	50g	50g
Smoke emission:	c. 45sec	c. 90sec
Danger zone:	15m radius	—
Packing: Grenades:	54/case	50/case
Fuzes:	108/case	—
Average packed weight:	500g	520g

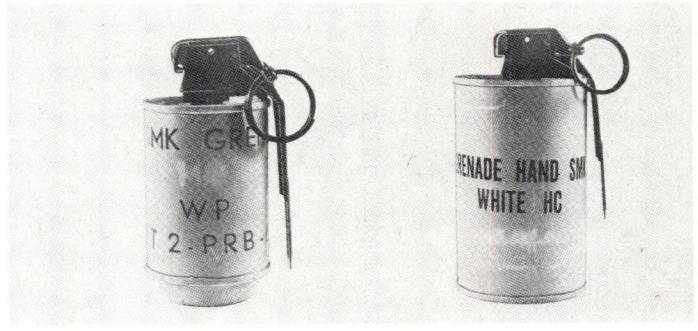

Smoke grenades PRB 405 (left) and HC

CHINA (PEOPLE'S REPUBLIC)

CHINESE GRENADES

The armed forces of the People's Republic of China use a variety of grenades of both Chinese and Russian manufacture. The Chinese grenades are similar in design to the Russian models, except that in most cases they have different dimensions; and as the same design is often made by a number of factories there are minor differences between copies of the same type of grenade.

TYPE 42 (OFFENSIVE/DEFENSIVE) HAND GRENADE

This is a direct copy of the Russian RG-42 grenade and its method of operation is identical.

DATA
Weight: 385g
Length: 127mm
Diameter: 58mm
Weight of filling: 110g
Type of filling: Pressed TNT
Fuze delay: 3-4sec
Effective fragmentation radius: 15m
Unit pack: 20 grenades and 20 fuzes
Weight of pack: 14.97kg

TYPE 1 (DEFENSIVE) HAND GRENADE

This is a copy of the Russian F1 grenade

DATA
Weight: 581g
Length: 125mm
Diameter: 57mm
Weight of filling: 55g
Type of filling: Cast TNT
Fuze delay: 3-4sec
Effective fragmentation radius: 15m
Unit pack: 20 grenades and 20 fuzes
Weight of pack: 19.5kg

TYPE 59 (DEFENSIVE) HAND GRENADE

This is similar in design to the Russian RGD-5 grenade and operates in the same manner.

DATA
Weight: 308g
Length: 115mm
Diameter: 54mm
Weight of filling: 110g
Type of filling: TNT
Fuze delay: 3-4sec
Effective fragmentation radius: 20m
Unit pack: 20 grenades and 20 fuzes
Weight of pack: 19.5kg

STICK GRENADES

The Chinese have manufactured a wide variety of stick grenades for defensive operations. Scored, serrated and plain types have been encountered. Their contents have included picric acid, mixtures of TNT or nitroglycerin with potassium nitrate or sawdust, and schneiderite. Method of operation is that the cord of the pull-friction fuze, which is located underneath the cap at the end of the throwing handle, is pulled. This ignites the delay element which lasts between 2.5 and 6 seconds, after which the detonator explodes the main charge. These grenades are generally packed in boxes of twenty already fuzed.

A typical example of a defensive stick grenade is illustrated here and is known to be still in use. It is a fragmenting type with a serrated head made of grey cast iron. This produces a small number of large fragments and a very large number of fragments so small that they could well be described as "dust". The filling is picric acid which was discarded as an explosive filling in the West many years ago, principally because it forms dangerous and unstable compounds. (In the UK this was the HE Lyddite which was used in World War I). It is essential that the inside of the container is varnished.

DATA
Weight: 500g
Length: 228mm
Diameter: 50mm
Weight of filling: 99g
Type of filling: Picric Acid
Fuze delay: 2.5-5sec
Effective fragmentation radius: 10 metres

A Chinese, serrated, fragmenting, defensive stick grenade

CZECHOSLOVAKIA

RG 34 and RG4 ANTI-PERSONNEL HAND GRENADES

The Russian hand grenades in current service are also used in Czechoslovakia. In addition two native grenades have been produced. These are both impact anti-personnel grenades. They are described as offensive hand grenades but the sheet metal bodies also produce some fragmentation. If required, each of these grenades can be fitted with a fragmentation sleeve.

RG 34

The RG34 is a steel bodied cylindrical grenade, distinguished by the serrations around the mid section.

DATA

Type: Blast
Weight (without fragmentation sleeve): 340g
Length: 76mm
Maximum diameter: 64mm
Body material: Steel
Filler weight: 100g
Filler material: TNT
Fuze type: Impact. All ways.
Range thrown: 35 metres
Effective fragment radius: 13 metres
Effective fragment radius with fragmentation sleeve: 25 metres

RG 4

The RG4 has replaced the RG34 in the Czechoslovakian Army. It has a cylindrical steel body which is completely smooth. It can be converted to a defensive grenade by adding a fragmentation jacket. This grenade is unusual in containing an upper and lower bursting charge.

DATA

Type: Blast
Weight (without fragmentation sleeve): 320g
Length: 84mm
Maximum diameter: 53mm
Body material: Steel
Filler weight: 105g
Filler material: TNT
Fuze type: Impact
Fragmentation radius: 13 metres
Fragmentation radius with fragmentation sleeve: 25 metres

The Czechoslovakian Model RG34 hand grenade

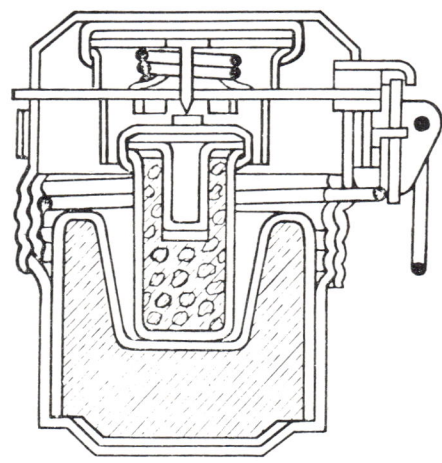

The Czechoslovakian Model 34, defensive hand grenade

The Czechoslovakian RG4, defensive hand grenade

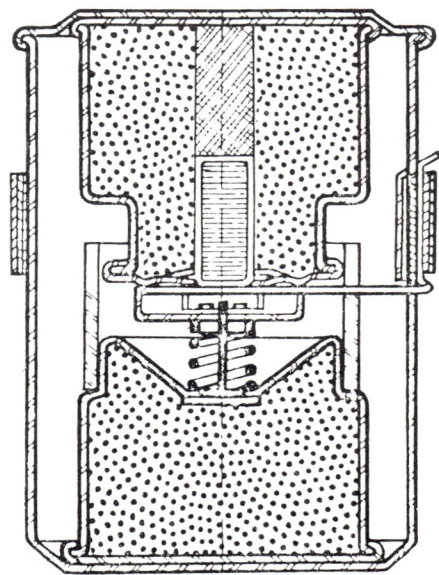

The Czechoslovakian RG-4 hand grenade

FRANCE

STRIM 5.56 LIGHT RIFLE GRENADES

These grenades were developed to meet a growing need for grenades suitable for launching from 5.56mm light automatic rifles. For such rifles, fitted with a standard 22mm holder, the grenades can be launched using normal ball amunition. They can also be launched from 7.5mm or 7.62mm rifles fitted with 22mm holder; but for such weapons a grenade-launching cartridge must be used. Four types of operational grenade and a practice grenade have been developed.

Light Anti-tank Grenade – has a combat range of 80-100 metres and an accuracy (5 grenades at combat range) of 100 cm (H+L). Penetration is 350mm steel armour; NATO single target, heavy tank, at 65°; NATO double target – medium tank – at 60°; concrete 100-120cm.

Light Anti-personnel Grenade – suitable for flat or curved fire, it has a combat range at 45° up to 300 metres and provides uniform scattering and wound effects up to 15 metres from point of burst.

Light Smoke Grenade – uses TICL 4 composition with an emission time of 30 seconds. Suitable for flat or curved fire it has a combat range at 45° up to 300 metres.

Light Illuminating Grenade – a parachute illuminator providing illumination greater than 0.75 lux on the perimeter of an area 240 metres in diameter. Flight delay to operation in 3.5 seconds and the illuminating time is 20 seconds. Lighting density is 150,000 candles.

Practice Grenades – for training.

DATA (common to all grenades)
Calibre: 58mm
Length: 380mm
Weight: 500g
Muzzle velocity: 65m/s
Manufacturer: Luchaire S.A., Division Armement, Département Materiels STRIM, 180, boulevard Haussmann, 75382 Paris CEDEX 08
Present status: Pre-production. French Army evaluation imminent late 1976

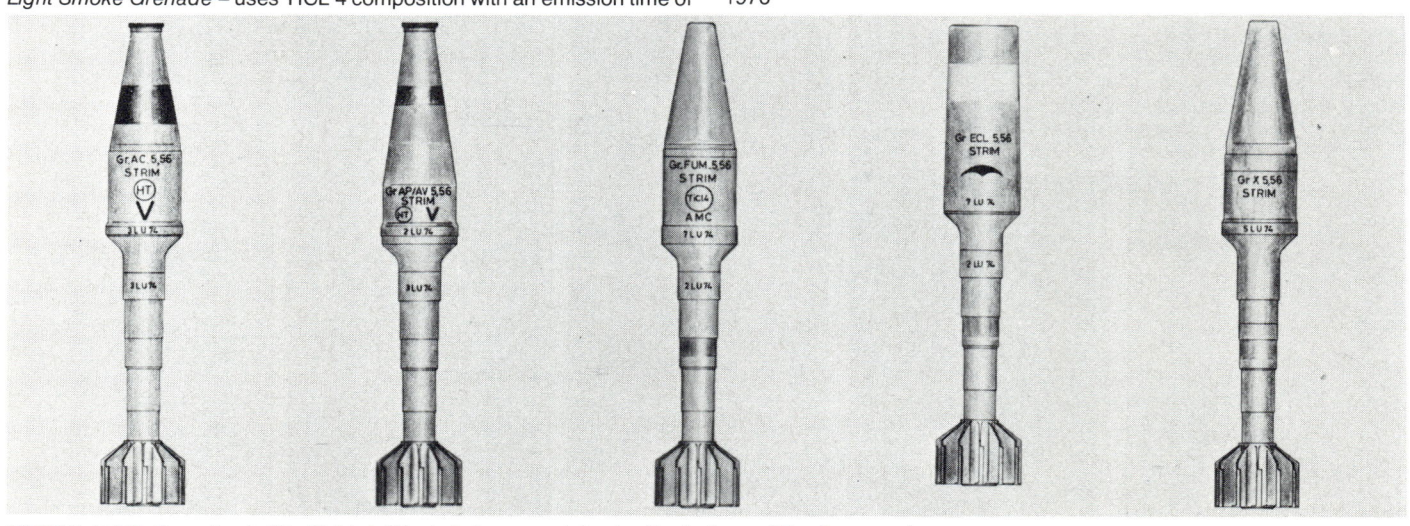

STRIM Light Rifle Grenades. **Left to Right:** *Anti-tank, Anti-personnel, Smoke, Illuminating and Practice grenades*

SERAT 63mm A.C. RIFLE GRENADE TYPE GRAFAC

This anti-tank hollow charge rifle grenade is designed for close-combat against armoured vehicles.

Very light, it has been specially designed to be launched from the 5.56mm MAS rifles that are to be allotted to the French Armed Forces in the very near future. However, it can also be launched from the 7.5mm rifles now in service.

In both cases, the rifles will be provided with the standard 22mm launching sleeve. Special launching cartridges, without bullet, are made for each type of rifle. The penetration is the same as that of the most recent grenades in service with the French Armed Forces and with the Armed Forces of many foreign countries.

CHARACTERISTICS

The effective range, for a 2.50m vertex height, i.e. the tank height, is equal to approximately 100 metres.

The fuze includes an electromagnetic generator and the muzzle safety exceeds 6m. It complies with the transport and handling safety requirements of the NATO specifications (safety device in case of accidental fall or cocking, igniter train cut-out device, etc). The grenade can fall from 5m high, without any risk of burst. It is hermetically sealed. Properly packed, it can be parachuted.

The grenade is supplied with a ballistite cartridge without bullet, corresponding to the calibre of the rifle for which it is provided.

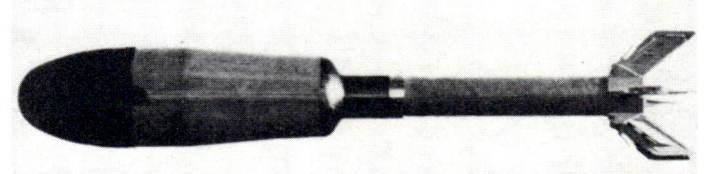

SERAT 63mm A.C. rifle grenade, type Grafac

DATA
Max. diameter of body: 63mm
Total length, when stored: 365mm
Weight of grenade: 515g approx.
Muzzle velocity: 65m/s approx.
Effective range with a flat-trajectory fire: 100m approx.
Max range with a 45° angle: 350m approx
Penetrating power with a zero angle of incidence: 300mm
Manufacturer: Société d'Etudes, de Réalisations et d'Applications Techniques, 134 boulevard Haussmann - 75008 Paris, France
Status: Under development

40mm PRACTICE RIFLE GRENADE

This is designed to train men in the use of rifle grenades. It consists of a body, fin assembly, dummy safety pin and detonating charge. To operate it, place the grenade on the rifle, load the rifle with a blank cartridge and then remove the safety pin. The rifle is then fired. The gases released by the cartridge eject the grenade from the rifle to a range of 5-15 metres depending on the angle selected, and simultaneously fire the explosive charge simulating ejection of a grenade. The grenade is re-usable after insertion of a fresh explosive charge.

DATA
Body diameter: 40mm
Fin diameter: 53mm
Length: 292mm
Weight: 515g
Manufacturer: Societe E. Lacroix, 31 Murret, Route de Toulouse, or Direction Commerciale, 75 Paris IV, 18 Rue Malher

65mm TRAINING RIFLE GRENADE MODEL F1

The 65mm Training Rifle Grenade Model F1 (also known as the Model 61), is used to train troops in the use of rifle grenades. It can be used with any 7.5mm or 7.62mm rifle having the 22mm attachment and firing blank ammunition. It is composed of an oval body made of plastic, tube of light alloy, tail stabiliser consisting of 12 plastic fins and a dummy firing pin.

DATA
Calibre: 65mm
Length: 420mm
Weight: 775g
Manufacturer: Groupement Industriel des Armements Terrestres, 10, place Georges Clémenceau, 92211 Saint Cloud.
Status: In service with the French Army

POLYVALENT RIFLE AND HAND GRENADE MDF

The Losfeld-Industries polyvalent grenade can be used in any one of the three following forms:

Anti-personnel rifle grenade, MDF;
Defensive hand grenade, MD;
Offensive hand grenade, M.

The transformation is immediate, the grenade MDF being a combination of three entirely detachable elements: the explosive body M, the pre-fragmented metallic sleeve D and the finned tail-assembly F.

The PFA 5 fuze permits manual pre-selection of any of the three modes of functioning: on impact, on delay (4 seconds after projection) or on impact/delay (the delay system serving principally to ensure the self-destruction of the hand grenade).

With the selector set on "impact" the functioning is instantaneous for launching by hand or by rifle. It should be noted that with the selector set on delay or impact/delay, the MDF grenade can be launched by rifle so as to explode above the enemy.

Transportation safety is by interruption of the fire channel.

Handling safety is by the presence of the fuze-cover, of the safety tape and of the tape-tightener.

Launching or dropping safety is by unrolling of the tape.

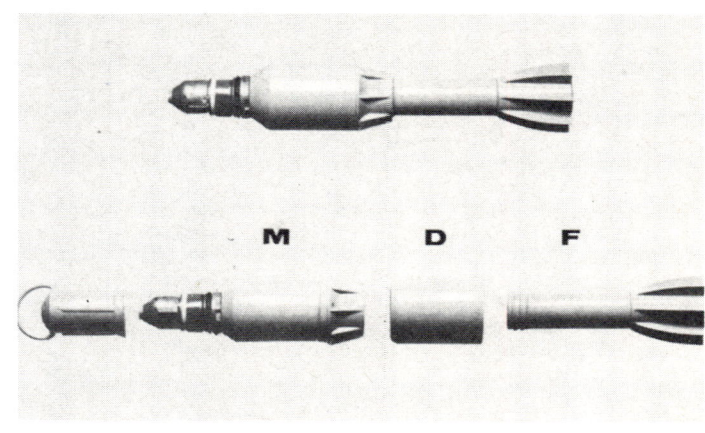

Polyvalent rifle and hand grenade MDF

DATA
Maximum range of the grenade MDF: 400m, with a dispersion of less than 4m in direction
Characteristics, with PFA-5 fuze (without waterproof cover):
Grenade MDF weight: 490g
Length: 270mm
Grenade MD weight: 414g
Length: 150mm

Grenade M weight: 262g
Length: 150mm
The efficiency of each of the three forms is claimed to be equivalent to that of the best grenades.
Manufacturer: Losfeld-Industries 13-15, rue Thiebault, 94220 Charenton (France)
Status: In production
French Army designation: GR.POL.EXPL.F1

MODEL F4 50mm SMOKE RIFLE GRENADE

The Model F4 50mm Smoke Rifle Grenade comprises a fore-body of cylindrical ogival shape ending with a nose piece, the rear of which consists of a plug provided with an empenned tube cartridge case. Before the grenade is fired the safety pin must be pulled out of the nose.

The Mk F4 is fired from the French 7.5mm 49-56 rifle by means of a ball-less 7.5mm cartridge. It can however also be launched from 7.62mm weapons by means of a 22mm sleeve and a ball-less 7.62mm cartridge.

Fired at an angle of 74 degrees it has a range of 80m, whilst fired at an angle of 45 degrees it has a range of 400m. It will lay a smoke screen 4 or 5 metres high for a minimum period of 45 seconds, depending on the wind speed.

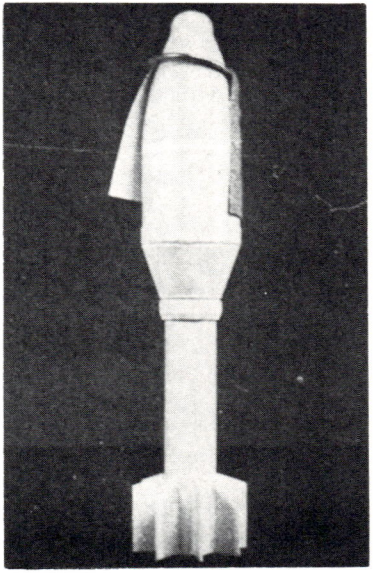

Model F4 50mm smoke rifle grenade

DATA
Total length: 290mm
Maximum diameter of body: 51mm
Average weight: Approx 470g
Packaging: Individual containers grouped in quantities of 4 in partitioned layout of 6 partitions in wooden cases of 24 grenades (weight: approx. 44kg)
Minimum range: Approx. 80 metres
Maximum range: Approx. 400 metres
Time of smoke discharge: 45 seconds
Manufacturer: Etablissements Ruggieri, Direction Commerciale Armement 122 rue La Boetie, 75008 Paris (France).
Status: Mass production. Equipment in service in the French Army

DEFENSIVE AND OFFENSIVE GRENADES WITH METALLIC OR PLASTIC IGNITERS

There are two basically different types of these grenades:
(a) Thin metal wrapping (offensive grenade – photo No. 1) or thick metal wrapping (defensive grenade – photo No. 2), loaded with tolite and used with Mk 35 lead igniter.
(b) Plastic wrapping, small and large models (photos No. 3 and 4) loaded with compressed tolite and to be used with plastic igniter with ejectable lever ALSETEX Mk 67.

Grenade:	No. 1	No. 2	No. 3	No. 4
Diameter:	60mm	55mm	50mm	55mm
Total height with igniter:	95mm	100mm	100mm	120mm
Total weight with igniter:	140g	540g	220g	310g
Weight of the tolite:	90g	56g	150g	225g

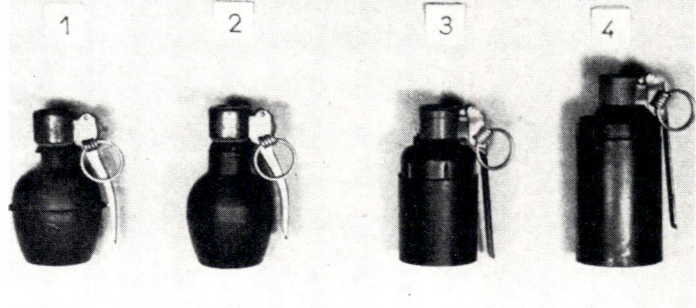

Defensive and offensive grenades with metallic or plastic liners

PERFORMANCE
These grenades explode with a delay of about 5 seconds after being thrown. The grenade marked '2' is a fragmentation grenade.

Those marked 1, 3 and 4 alternative cause a blast effect the importance of which depends on the charge. That marked '4', particularly, with its heavy charge can lead to relatively heavy damage.

The adoption of the very light ALSETEX plastic igniter with ejectable lever, combined with a wrapping almost entirely of plastic material, allows a large charge weight.

Note: There are practice grenades.
Manufacturer: Société Alsacienne d'Etudes et d'Exploitation (ALSETEX) 4, rue de Castellane – 75008 Paris (France)
Status: Mass production. The metal grenades are used in the French Army. Plastic grenades are used in some other countries.

OF 37 HAND GRENADES

These standard French grenades are made in three types: offensive, defensive and practice and training.

The OF M 1937 offensive grenade is made of aluminium with a two-part body, and contains 90 grams of TNT. The M 1935 fuze for this grenade is packed separately.

The DM 46 defensive grenade has a cast-iron body. The loading is similar to the one of the offensive. The fuze is identical, packed the same way.

The training and practice grenade has the same aluminium made body as the above mentioned OF M 2937 grenade. Loaded with plaster, the grenade contains an ignition device of black powder. This permits the grenades to open upon bursting. The fuze is packed as above.

Manufacturer: Luchaire S.A., 180, boulevard Haussmann – 75382 Paris Cedex 08 (France).
Status: Standard production made to order.

OF 37 hand grenades

OFFENSIVE M OR DEFENSIVE MD HAND GRENADE

The offensive form of this Losfeld-Industries grenade is known as type M and the defensive type is MD. The pre-fragmented metallic sleeve, D, placed on the attack grenade M transforms the latter into the defensive grenade.

The grenades are equipped either with the igniter model 1935 or with the impact and/or delay fuze PFA 5.

The grenade M is composed of a body in plastic charged with 87 grams of explosive. Its weight is 129 grams and its maximum diameter is 48mm.

The sleeve D, which weighs 152 grams can be fitted in place or removed without the need to detach the fuze PFA 5 or its waterproof cover.

The exercise attack grenade Mx consists of the same body as the grenade M, and can therefore use the sleeve D, the igniter model 1935 or the fuze PFA 5.

The grenades M, Mx and MD can always be fitted with the finned tail-assembly F for rifle launching (as with the Polyvalent Grenade MDF).

The fuze PFA 5 (see Polyvalent Grenade MDF) functioning on impact and/or delay by selection possesses an allways impact system.

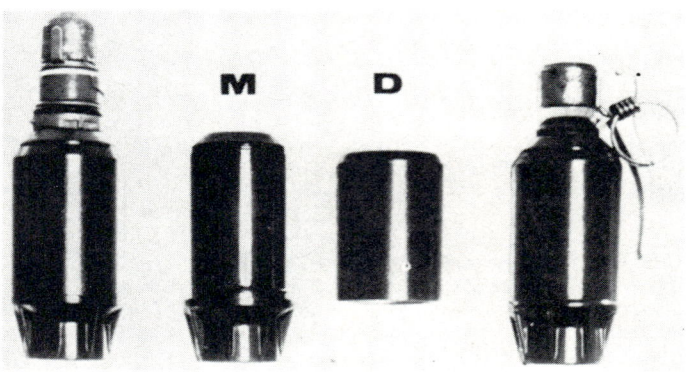

Offensive M or defensive MD grenade

DATA

Grenades	Attack form M Weight	Defensive form MD Weight	Attack form M and defensive MD Length
With igniter Model 1935:	266g	418g	128mm

With fuze PFA 5 (without cover): 262g   414g   150mm
Manufacturer: Losfeld-Industries, 13-15 rue Thiebault, 94220 Charenton (France)
Status: Mass production. It is called the GR.MA.EXPL.F1 by the French Army

COLOURED SMOKE GRENADE TYPE LXT 290

The LXT 290 is designed for target designation purposes. It can be dropped from an aircraft or helicopter or used on the ground. It consists of four main components – cylindrical body, stabilising cover, smoke producing composition and the delay igniter component.

DATA
Diameter: 51mm
Overall height: 260mm
Weight: 500g
Delay of composition igniter: 4 seconds
Duration of smoke emission: 135 seconds
Colour of smoke: Red, green, yellow, white, orange, blue, purple, black
Manufacturer: Ste. E. Lacroix, Route de Toulouse – 31600 Muret (France) 18 rue Malher – 75004 Paris (France)
Design stage: Completed

Coloured smoke grenade type LXT 290

SMOKE GRENADE MODEL 56 AND 1 Kg SMOKE POT F1

Each of these smoke generators is equipped with a spoon firing plug and a 2.5 second delay (no detonator) with intensifier. The Model 56 grenade has a threaded extension piece which enables several grenades to be screwed together to extend the emission time. The F1 smoke pot can be supplied with an electric ignition plug.

Manufacturer: Société Nationale des Poudres et Explosifs, 12 quai Henri IV, 75181 Paris 04
Status: In production and service with the French Armed Forces
DATA

	Smoke grenade	Smoke pot
Diameter:	60mm	100mm
Height:	190mm	130mm
Total weight:	400g	1.35kg
Maximum duration of smoke:	2min 30sec	2min 50sec
Minimum duration of smoke:	1min 40sec	2min 10sec

SNPE Model 56 smoke grenade (left) and smoke pot type F1

PLASTIC PRACTICE GRENADE MODEL F1

The Plastic Hand Grenade F1 consists of three components – a plastic body filled with chalk or talc, the plastic sheath containing the explosive charge and an igniter set. It operates as follows: the safety pin is pulled out and the operating lever is held against the body of the grenade. The grenade is then thrown and 5 seconds later the composition explodes causing the grenade to burst and scatter the contents.

DATA
Diameter: 56mm
Length: 73mm
Weight: 240g
Delay: 5 seconds
Manufacturer: Ste E Lacroix, Route de Toulouse – 31600 Muret (France), 18, Rue Malher – 75004 Paris (France)
Status: Mass production. Operational in the French Army

Plastic practice grenade, model F1

RTE GRENADE FUZE TYPE 960

This fuze is designed for grenades, in particular for lachrymatory grenades, to be thrown by hand or fired from a rifle (with an adapter).

PERFORMANCE

The fuze is pressure operated when thrown by hand, or pressure set back operated when fired from a rifle, depending on the arrangement of the grenade in the adapter.

CHARACTERISTICS
Overall length: 68mm
External length (protruding from the grenade): 38mm
Overall diameter: 24mm
Weight: about 20g
Delay: 3 or 4 seconds
Manufacturer: Etablissements Ruggieri, Department Armement, 122 Rue la Boetie 75008 Paris (France)
Status: Now being developed

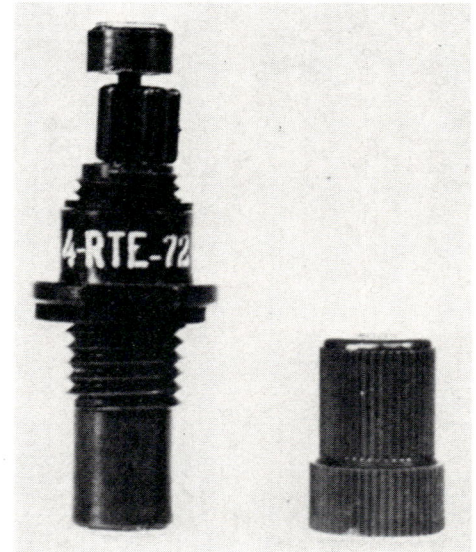

RTE grenade fuze, type 960

SUNDRY IGNITERS AND DELAYS

ALSETEX make a wide variety of igniters, delays and similar devices for military and para-military use. Nine of them are illustrated here and the descriptions that follow relate to the numbered items in the illustrations.
1. 2.5 second delay with black powder reinforcer for use with rifle-launched powder tear-gas grenades. Made of plastic.
2. 6 second delay with detonator for use with rifle-launched liquid tear gas grenades. Made of plastic.
3. Igniter plug and release lever with black powder reinforcer for Criquet-type powder tear-gas hand grenades. Made of plastic.
4. Igniter plug and release lever with detonator for liquid tear-gas hand grenades. Made of plastic.

5. Transmission relay with black powder reinforcer for connecting smoke pots together. Made of plastic.
6. Traction igniter plug for use with heat pots for spiking guns. Made of lead.
7. Igniter plug with horizontal lever and black powder reinforcer for use with large static smoke pots. Made of lead.
8. Igniter plug with lever for AEI dredger with 5 second delay detonator. Made of lead.
9. Electric igniter plug with black powder reinforcer
Manufacturer: ALSETEX SA, 4 rue de Castellane 75008, Paris
Status: Generally in production and service

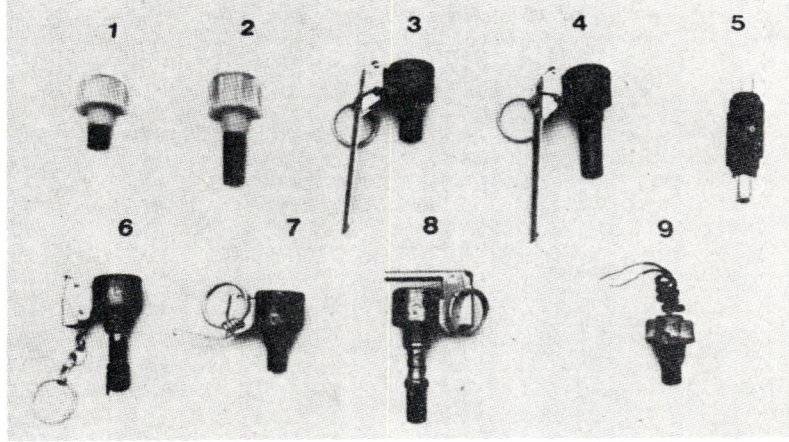

OLDER GRENADES

ANTI-PERSONNEL RIFLE GRENADE, M1948
DATA
Rifle: 7.5mm Mle 1936 G and LG48
Weight: 485g
Length: 20cm
Exterior diameter: 5cm
Practical range: 80 – 260m
Lethal area: 10m (fragment range 25m)

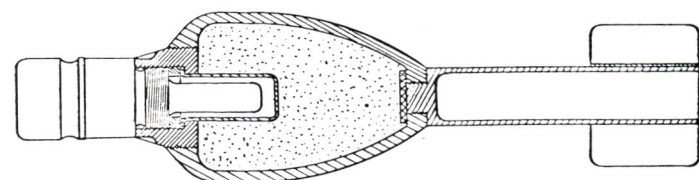

The model 1948 anti-personnel rifle grenade

ANTI-TANK RIFLE GRENADE, 73mm, M1950
DATA
Weight: 800g
Length: 40.5cm
Exterior diameter: 73mm
Launch speed: 50m/sec
Practical range: 75m (240m maximum)
Penetration: 30cm of steel – 90cm of concrete
Max angle of incidence: 70°

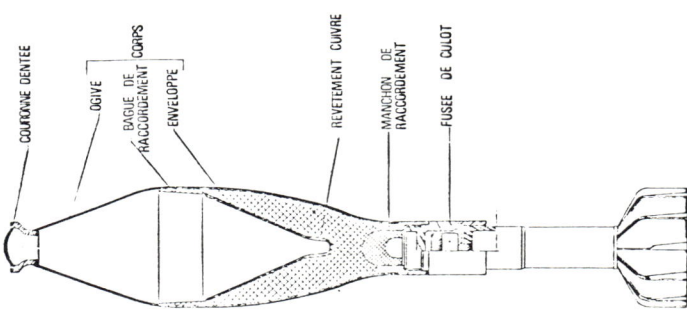

The 73mm, model 1950, anti-tank rifle grenade

ANTI-PERSONNEL RIFLE GRENADE, 34mm, M1952, MODIFIED 1960
DATA
Weight: 500g
Length: 27cm
Exterior diameter: 34mm
Launch speed: 70m/sec
Range: 100 – 400m
Lethal area: 10m (fragment range 30m)

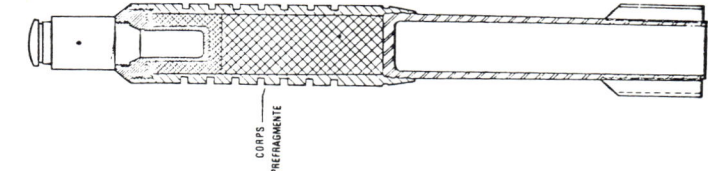

MULTI-PURPOSE RIFLE GRENADE, 40mm, M1956
DATA
Weight: 510g
Length: 30.5cm
Launch speed: 70m/sec
Practical range: 100m anti-tank; 100 – 400m anti-personnel
Lethal area: 10m (fragment range 30m)
Penetration: 12cm of steel – 36cm of concrete
Max angle of incidence: 60°

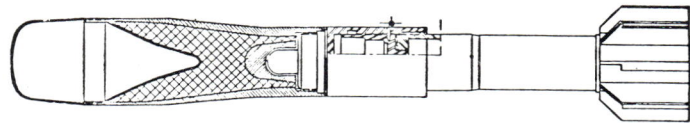

Manufacturer: Luchaire SA, Département STRIM, 175 boulevard Hauss-mann, 75008 – Paris

GERMANY (FEDERAL REPUBLIC)

M-DN 11 GRENADE

One of three defensive hand grenades made by Diehl (the others are the M-DN 21 and 31) the M-DN 11 grenade is barrel shaped and made of plastic. The thick wall contains 3,800 steel balls which are embedded in the plastic. The outside of the grenade body has longitudinal and transverse ribs which are raised from the surface to improve the user's grip and generally to improve handling under adverse conditions such as sub-zero temperatures or in mud. The interior is filled with plasticised nitropenta.

At the top a fuze thread is cut into the plastic material, and in this the grenade takes the DM 82 fuze. This has the same external appearance as previous fuzes made by Diehl and consists of a spring actuated hammer, held back by a long safety lever from hitting the primer cap, and a delay pellet above a detonator and a booster located in the bursting charge.

When the safety pin is withdrawn the torsion spring (item **2** in the accompanying drawing) forces the hammer **(3)** round and it hits the DM 1024 primer cap **(4).** The spring force throws off the protective cap and the safety lever. The flash of the percussion primer ignites the delay pellet **(7)** in its delay tube **(8).** After about 2.5 seconds burning time the heat melts a solder ring **(9)** and so disconnects the delay tube **(8)** from the detonator holder **(10).** The pressure spring **(11)** then forces the detonator holder and

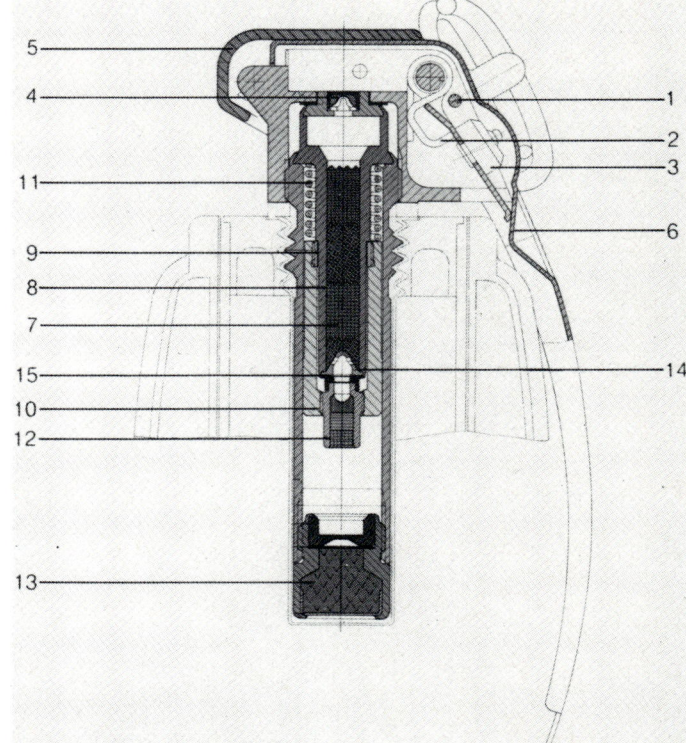

A sectioned view of the DM 82 fuze assembly

DM 1066 detonator **(12)** down on to the DM 1034 booster **(13).** After 4 seconds burning time the flash from the delay pellet passes through two holes in the cup over the detonator and reaches the detonator. The detonator sets off the booster which in turn ignites the main charge.

The M-DN 11 hand grenade

DATA
M-DN 11 hand grenade: 470g
DM 82 fuze: 63.5g
Grenade body, empty: 364g
HE filling: 42.5g

Ball diameter: 2.5-3mm
Number of balls: 3,800
Manufacturer: Diehl Wehrtechnik, 8505 Rothenbach, Fischbachstrasse 20, W. Germany

M-DN 21 GRENADE

This is a smaller edition of the M-DN 11. It functions in exactly the same way but uses the M-DN 22 fuze.

DATA
M-DN 21 hand grenade: 225g
M-DN 22 fuze: 62g
Grenade body, empty: 118g
HE filling: 45g
Ball diameter: 2-2.3mm
Number of balls: 2,200
Manufacturer: Diehl Wehrtechnik, 8505 Rothenbach, Fischbachstrasse 20, West Germany

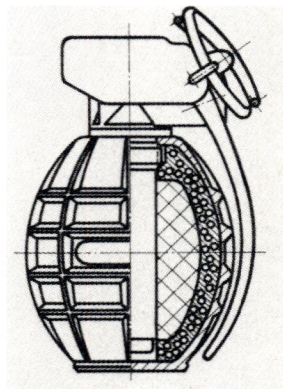

M-DN 21 grenade

M-DN 31 GRENADE

This grenade fits between the two others in size and functions in a manner similar to that of the M-DN 21 grenade.

DATA
M-DN 31 hand grenade: 248g
M-DN 22 fuze: 62g
Grenade body, empty: 151g
HE filling: 35g
Ball diameter: 2-2.3mm
Number of balls: 3,000
Manufacturer: Diehl Wehrtechnik, 8505 Rothenbach, Fischbachstrasse 20, West Germany

M-DN 31 grenade

OFFENSIVE-DEFENSIVE HAND GRENADE DM 51

This dual purpose grenade consists of two major elements: a high explosive hand grenade body and a fragmentation surround. The body can be used separately as an offensive grenade, and when the jacket is placed around it the two parts together make up a defensive grenade. The parts are connected and held by a bayonet fixing in which the outer jacket is turned through 90 degrees and the base portion of the jacket locks on to the central body. The HE grenade body has the shape of a hexagonal prism. It consists of a water tight plastic container filled with compressed nitropenta. The top end of the container is screw threaded to take a detonator. The fragmentation surround is cylindrical and is made of plastic, with fragmentation inserts, in the same way as the defensive grenades described above. The two major parts – HE centre and surround – can be joined and separated as often as required. Several grenade bodies can be jointed to make up a cluster charge or connected end to end to make up a Bangalore torpedo for assault engineer applications.

The offensive-defensive DM 51 hand grenade has been adopted by the West German Army under the nomenclature "Handgranate Spreng/Splitter DM 51 mit Handgranaten-Zünder DM 82".

DM 51 hand grenade

DATA
DM 51 hand grenade: 435g
DM 82 fuze: 64g
Fragmenting jacket: 290g
HE hand grenade (without fuze): 81g

Manufacturer: Diehl Wehrtechnik, 8505 Rothenbach, Fischbachstrasse 20, West Germany
Status: In production

PRACTICE HAND GRENADE

A practice hand grenade has been developed for the DM-51 offensive-defensive grenade. It is of the same construction as the DM 51 and the two parts can be used separately or together, as with the DM 51, and have the same weights. The central body contains a practice fuze and a practice HE filling. These can be used up to 50 times either with or without the fragmentation jacket.

The practice charge can easily be replaced by screwing out the practice fuze and the fuze can be prepared by cocking the striker, mounting the safety lever and disarming by the safety pin.
Packaging: The M-DN 11 and DN 31 are carried by the soldier on a belt with four individual containers with a polyurethane cover. The DM 300 boxes take 10 DM 51 hand grenades. The box is made of plastic.
Manufacturer: Diehl Wehrtechnik, 8505 Rothenbach, Fischbachstrasse 20, West Germany

The practice hand grenade for the DM 51

DM 19 INCENDIARY HAND GRENADE (IHG)

One of several smoke and incendiary grenades made by Buck KG, this is designed to produce a cloud of dense smoke and at the same time to ignite the incendiary charge contained within its plastic case. It is described as a 'Blend-Brand-Hand grenade' which means a burning smoke ('Blinding and Burning') hand grenade. It is packed inside a cylindrical cardboard casing for travelling. The grenade is plastic bodied and is armed by unscrewing the plastic cap and pulling out the safety wire. It is then thrown and the plastic body breaks up on contact. The fuze DM82 provides instantaneous combustion of the phosphorus filling. This produces a very vivid flash and a dense cloud of smoke. The temperature of the grenade is said to be 1,200 degrees C and the smoke lasts for several minutes.

The practice version of the DM 19 is called the DM 38 A1 and has a fuze that does not contain a primer and delay unit as the live grenade does. Instead of the incendiary charge the grenade contains an inert lime dust compound which simulates an effect on the target.

DATA
Weight: 320g
Length: 135mm
Diameter: 67mm
Weight of incendiary charge: 260g
Manufacturer: Buck KG, 7844 Neuenberg/Baden, W. Germany
Status: In production and in service

The DM 19 incendiary hand grenade (IHG)

HC SMOKE GRENADE

This is designed to be discharged from the smoke projectors of an armoured vehicle or thrown by hand after pulling away the "tear off fuze". It produces a dense smoke cloud all round a vehicle and makes possible a tactical withdrawal under its cover. If the grenade is projected its range is from 40-70 metres and if hand thrown it is about 30 metres. The projected grenade starts to emit smoke after 2½ seconds of flight. The hand-thrown grenade starts producing smoke in 2½ seconds after the fuze is torn off. The smoke emission in each case lasts for 2½ minutes.

The grenade has a metal body, a smoke compound filling and an electric ignition system and propellant charge. The weight of the grenade is 1,200g and the weight of smoke filling is 900g.

HC smoke grenade

PRACTICE SMOKE GRENADE SG-ACC

This is used for training purposes. It gives off less smoke than the SG-HC but burns without any flame and so can be used on heathland without risk of fire. It weighs the same as the HC Smoke Grenade and has the same dimensions.

Manufacturer: Buck KG, 7844 Neuenburg-Baden

HAND GRENADES DT 11B1

This is a high explosive offensive grenade relying on blast effect. It uses the detonator set DT 12A1B1 and consists of a cylindrical cardboard body containing 200 grams of TNT. The total weight of the grenade is 330 grams. It can be thrown about 30 metres.
Manufacturer: Believed to be identical in all material respects with the No 14 grenade made by Israel Military Industries, Tel Aviv, Israel
Status: In service with West German forces

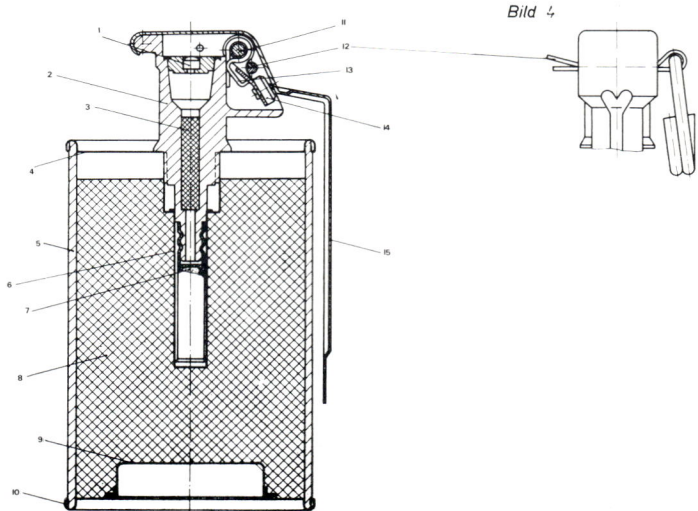

Bild 4

Sectioned view of the DT 11B offensive hand grenade (blast grenade): (1) Primer cap DM 1024; (2) Fuze head; (3) Delay column; (4) Sheet metal cover with thread for fuze; (5) Enclosure of pasteboard; (6) Case; (7) Detonator; (8) Explosive composition (TNT flakes); (9) Base plug; (10) Sheet metal base; (11) Spring bolt; (12) Safety split pin with ring; (13) Striker spring; (14) Striker; (15) Lever

Hand grenade DT 11 B1

HAND GRENADES DM 21 and DM 41

DM 21 is a high explosive blast grenade used in the offensive role. It has a cement impregnated fibre body, cylindrical in shape, containing 200 grams of TNT. It uses the DM 42 detonator set and weighs 355 grams.

DM 41 is a fragmentation grenade employed as a defensive weapon. It uses the DM 72 fuze. It has a light steel body with a spiral notched coil lining It has 150 grams of Composition B. The total weight is 450 grams. Both grenades have been declared obsolete.

HAND GRENADE DM 48

This is intended to be used in training the soldier to throw hand grenades. It has a hollow, cast iron body. When the DM 62 detonator functions it produces only a puff. It can be re-primed for repetitive use. It weighs 425 grams.

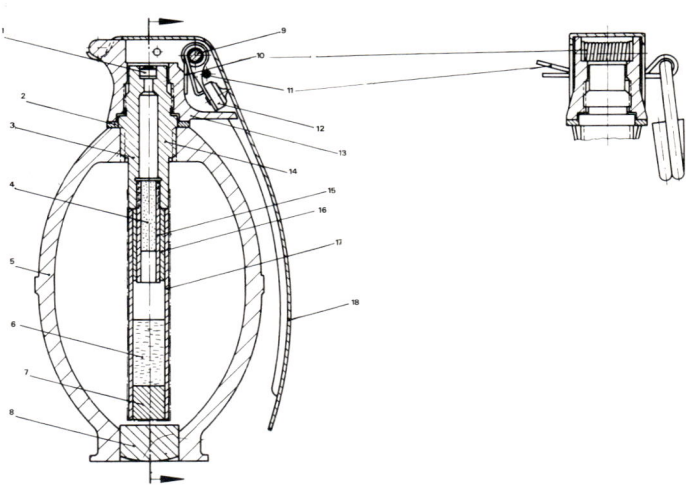

Training grenade DM 48: (1) Primer cap DM 1023; (2) Sealing; (3) Fuze body with training charge (training charge with fuze bottom part); (4) Delay column; (5) Grenade body; (6) Explosive set; (7) Closing plug; (8) Closing plug; (9) Spring bolt; (10) Striker spring; (13) Fuze head (fuse top part); (14) Fuze body; (15) Brass case; (16) Divider case; (17) Explosive set case; (18) Safety lever

GERMANY (DEMOCRATIC REPUBLIC)

GRENADES IN EAST GERMAN FORCES

East German troops are equipped almost entirely with grenades of Russian design but two smoke grenades of East German design and manufacture, described below, are still in use.

ES-32 SMOKE HAND GRENADE

This is a cardboard cylinder. It is ignited by the user rubbing the ignition pellet with a friction cap which activates the 7 second delay fuze. The grenade continues to emit black smoke for 1.5-2 minutes. The grenade weighs 250g.

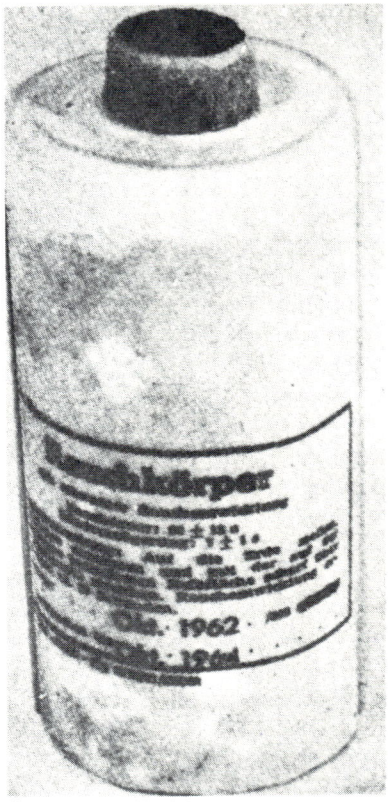

East German S-32, smoke, hand grenade

S-53 SMOKE HAND GRENADE

The S-53 smoke grenade is of similar construction to the S-32 but differs in having a handle like a conventional stick grenade. The grenade weighs about 300g and burns for 30 seconds producing a white smoke cloud. It will continue to burn even if submerged in water.

East German S-53, smoke, hand grenade

HUNGARY

M42 GRENADE

The only grenade of Hungarian design in current service is the M42. This is an offensive stick-type hand grenade. It employs a delay fuze. One unusual feature of M42 is the provision of a male thread at the top of the grenade and a female thread at the bottom which permits the junction of several grenades to provide a small demolition charge. There are three half inch wide red bands around the body.

DATA
Type: Blast:
Weight: 310g
Length: Head: 2.98in (76mm)
     Stick: 4.64in (118mm)
     Total: 7.62in (194mm)
Maximum diameter: 48mm
Body material: Steel
Filler weight: 134g
Filler material: TNT
Fuze type: Delay
Fuze delay: 3.5-4.5 seconds
Range, thrown: 30 metres

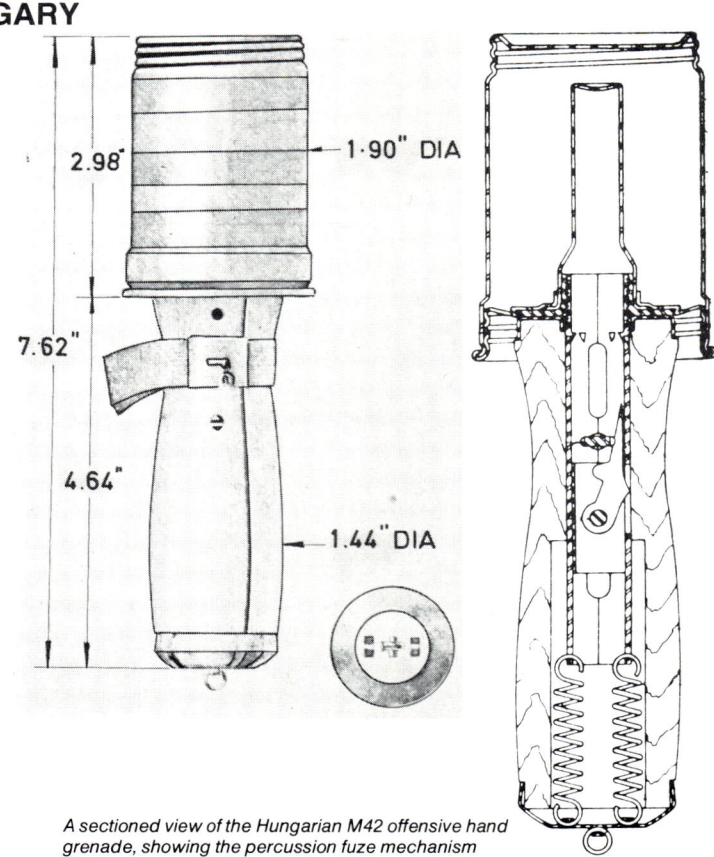

Hungarian M42 offensive hand grenade

(Dimensions in inches. See text for metric equivalents)

A sectioned view of the Hungarian M42 offensive hand grenade, showing the percussion fuze mechanism

ISRAEL

NO. 5 HAND GRENADE - SMOKE

This grenade is used for signalling and also to produce a local smoke screen. The grey smoke is emitted for slightly less than 2 minutes and, being of hexachlorethane, has less tendency to pillar than some of the phosphorus smokes. The grenade consists of a tin plated cylinder and is operated in the conventional fashion with a fly off lever restrained by a safety pin.

DATA
Smoke colour: Grey
Smoke mixture: Hexachlorethane 46% + ZnO 46% + A18%
Mixture weight: 600g
Body material: Steel sheet
Functioning: Delay fuze 2sec ± 1sec
Height: 150mm
Diameter: 62mm
Weight: 800g
Actuation: On removal of safety pin
Application: Local smoke screen and signalling
Smoke emission: 110-120sec
Packing: 24 grenades, each in a hermetically sealed can, in a wooden box
Manufacturer: Israel Military Industries, Tel Aviv

No. 5 hand grenade – smoke

NO. 14 HAND GRENADE - OFFENSIVE

This grenade is used by assaulting infantry who need to close with the enemy immediately after the blast and so require the radius of effect of the grenade to be comparatively small without the production of splinters. The grenade operates in the usual way with a fly off lever and safety pin.

DATA
High explosive filling: TNT flakes
Weight of HE filling: 200g
Body material: Laminated paper with sheet metal ends
Functioning: Delay fuze 4.5 ±0.5sec
Height: 95mm without fuze; 115mm with fuze
Diameter: 64mm
Weight: 325g
Actuation: By removal of safety pin
Application: Offensive hand grenade
Packing: 50 grenades, each in a sealed plastic bag, in a wooden box. 8 cartons of fuzes, 25 in each, in a wooden box
Manufacturer: Israel Military Industries, Tel Aviv

No. 14 hand grenade – offensive

M 26 HAND GRENADE - FRAGMENTATION

This is a copy of the United States grenade, made under licence. It is a fragmentation grenade with a notched coil inside the tin plate cover.

DATA
High explosive filling: Composition B. Cast
Weight of HE filling: 150g
Body material: Sheet steel
Fragmenting material: Spirally wound steel coil, pre-notched
Number of fragments: 1,000
Functioning: Delay fuze 4.3 ±0.5sec
Height: 107mm
Diameter: 62mm
Weight: 425g
Actuation: Removal of the safety pin
Application: Thrown by hand
Lethality: 50% chance of a hit – lying man – at 10 metres
Packing: 8 cartons of five grenades, each in a fibre container, in a wooden box
Manufacturer: Israel Military Industries, Tel Aviv

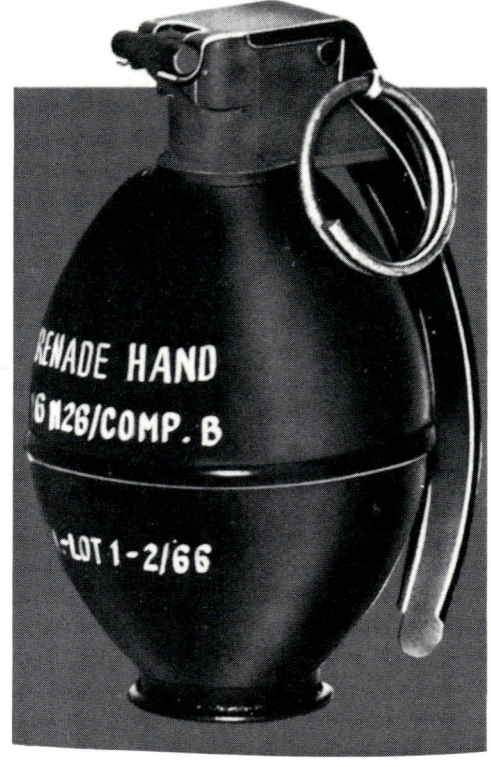

M 26 hand grenade – fragmentation

NO. 5 HAND GRENADE - COLOURED SMOKE

This grenade is employed for ground position indication or ground to air indication. It is also used for the production of local smoke screens.

DATA
Smoke colours: Red, yellow, green and blue
Body material: Sheet metal
Height: 150mm
Diameter: 62mm
Weight: 450g
Smoke charge: 300g
Type of fuze: Delayed ignition
Delay time: 1 to 3 seconds
Smoke emission: 45-85 seconds
Application: Position marking and local smoke screen
Functioning: When the safety pin is withdrawn, the fly off lever is discarded and the firing pin is driven against the percussion primer to ignite the delay element of the fuze
Packing: 16 grenades, each individually sealed in a metal cannister, in a wooden case
Manufacturer: Israel Military Industries, Tel Aviv

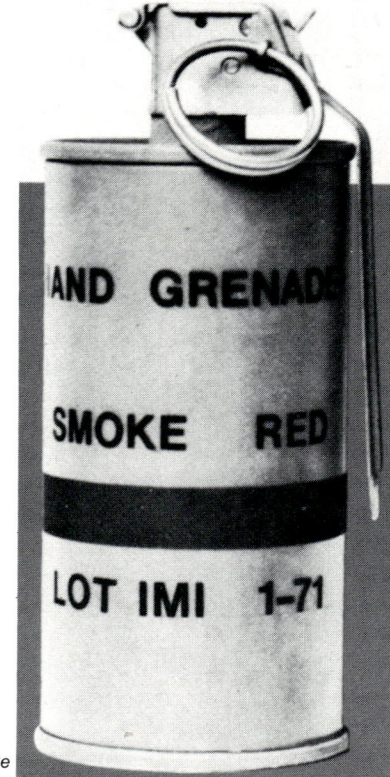

No. 5 hand grenade – coloured smoke

ITALY

ENERGA-TYPE TRAINING GRENADE

Although the Energa grenade is no longer made by Mecar in Belgium, it and similar anti-tank rifle grenades are still in service in many armies including the Italian Army.

Tirrena SpA make a training grenade which resembles the Energa in all operational respects except that it does not have a high-explosive warhead. Instead it has a head made of shock-resistant plastic with a coloured filling; and this can be used, with 7.62mm rifles for grenade firing practice in two ways. Because the missile is stoutly constructed, it will not break on impact with soft surfaces, so that when fired over ground that is free from rock or other hard obstructions the grenade can be collected and used again. On striking an object that is sufficiently hard to rupture the grenade head, however, a coloured cloud indicates the point of impact.

The grenade can thus be used economically for giving soldiers practice in the process of firing the grenade without, in most instances, destroying it: alternatively it can be used for practice in firing grenades against moving manned tanks.

DATA
Weight of grenade: 640g
Length: 357mm
Calibre: 65mm
Range: Using a (Garand) M1 rifle with an Energa type barrel and a US rifle cartridge, maximum horizontal range is 240-250 metres (45° elevation)
Manufacturer: Tirrena SpA, Via del Quirinale, 22 00187 Roma
Status: In Italian Army service since 1958

NETHERLANDS

NETHERLANDS GRENADES

At the conclusion of World War II and with the formation of NATO it was decided that all Netherlands ammunition packages and individual munitions should be marked in Dutch and in English. That is why many of the grenades shown have their titles printed in English and is not, as is sometimes claimed, that the grenades were made in the UK for use in the Netherlands.

Between 1955 and 1958 a French hand grenade was used. Until 1960 some British and some American grenades were used.

Since then the bodies of Dutch grenades have been made in the country. There are two major manufacturing plants, Eurometaal (formerly known as Artillerie Inrichtigen) and NWM (Nederlandse Wapen en Munitie Fabrickes). Both of these plants had extensive filling facilities but the filling of munitions, including grenades, is now forbidden by Dutch law and only powder is made. All HE filling is now carried out in Germany or Belgium. Fuzes are filled in Switzerland and larger types of ammunition are filled in France.

FRAGMENTATION HAND GRENADE NO. 1

This grenade is egg-shaped with a smooth exterior surface and no serrations or indentation. It is painted olive green and has yellow markings.

For bulk transit the grenades are packed in green-painted wooden boxes, stencilled "40 HGR No. 1" in yellow letters. Each box also contains an airtight green tin with 40 fuzes. During transit the grenade is sealed with a bakelite plug which is removed, for the insertion of the fuze, immediately before use. The firer checks the detonator and fuze before screwing the assembly, as a whole, into the hand grenade. The cast iron body has a plug at the top and inside this is screwed a bakelite tube to take the No. 12 Fuze assembly.

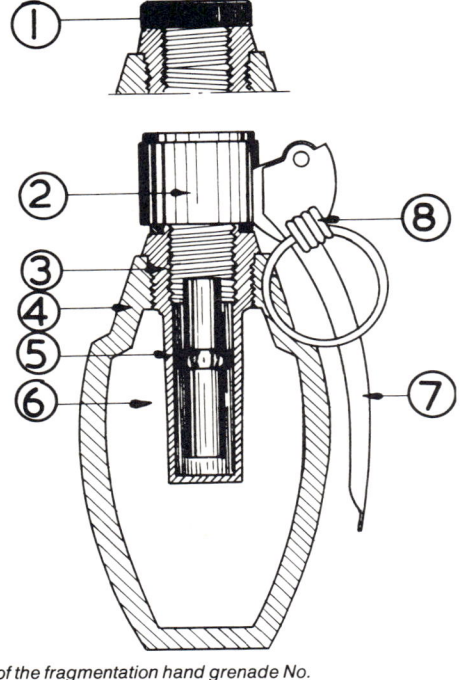

Sectioned view of the fragmentation hand grenade No. 1: (1) Fuze holder sealed during transit; (2) Fuze No. 12; (3) Bakelite insert; (4) Body of the grenade; (5) Shank of the bakelite tube; (6) High explosive filling; (7) Safety lever; (8) Safety pin and ring

Fragmentation hand grenade No. 1

FRAGMENTATION HAND GRENADE NO. 1C1

This is extremely similar to the No 1 grenade. Internally it differs in having the fuze assembly 19C1 or 19C2.

Fragmentation hand grenade No. 1C1 with fuze assembly No. 19C2/20

GRENADES

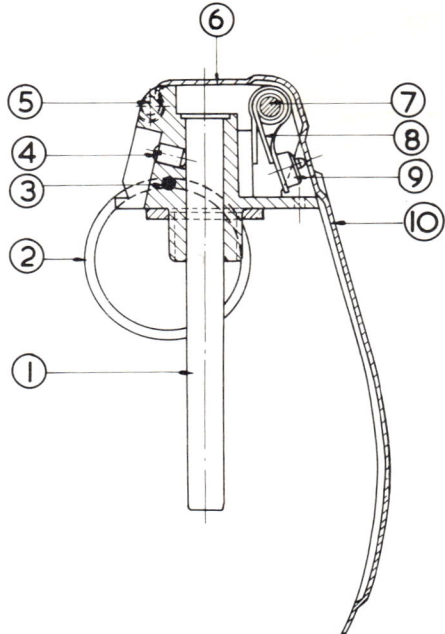

Fuze No. 19: (1) Delay train; (2) Safety pin with ring; (3) Safety pin; (4) Retaining screw; (5) Safety lever axis; (6) Fuze No. 191C; (7) Firing pin axis; (8) Firing pin spring; (9) Firing pin; (10) Safety lever

The No 19 fuze mechanism is intended to be the standard Dutch fuze for all future grenades adopted by the Armed Forces. The original fuze is the No 19. The first modification was numbered 19C1 and the second 19C2. A typical designation for a fuze assembly – ie fuze plus detonator – is 19C1/ 20. This indicates that the Fuze No 19 including the 1st modification is being used with detonator No 20. The fuze/detonator combinations are used as follows:

19C1/20 for offensive, defensive and explosive smoke grenades.
19C2/17 for smoke, incendiary and tear gas grenades.
19/9 for practice fragmentation grenades.

The No 19 fuze is very orthodox in its functioning. When the safety pin is withdrawn the striker rotates and the lever is forced off the grenade body.

The striker ignites the detonator cap which in turn ignites a length of slow match which takes about three seconds before the main filling is detonated.

There is no indication that the No 19 Fuze has been initiated and neither smoke, flame or sound are apparent.

DATA
Body: Cast iron
Filling: 55gm TNT powdered
Diameter: 56mm
Height: 122mm
Weight: 670g

FRAGMENTATION HAND GRENADE MK 2

This is a copy of the USA Mk 2 grenade which although obsolescent in US land service is still used in the US Navy.

This grenade like the British 36M and the Soviet F1 is heavily notched on the outside of the cast iron body with the idea of producing fragments about one inch square and of the thickness of the grenade body. In spite of this the high explosive filling detonates to produce a lot of dust and a few excessively large pieces of casing. The fuze and the filler plug can be lethal at ranges up to 200 metres. The fuze assembly is the No 19C2/20.

DATA
Body: Cast iron
Filling: 55g TNT powdered
Diameter: 57mm
Height: 114mm
Weight: 630g

Fragmentation hand grenade Mk 2 with fuze assembly No. 19C2/20

OFFENSIVE HAND GRENADES NO.s 13 & 17

Hand grenade No 13 is a cylindrical steel-bodied grenade, made of rolled tinplate. It contains an HE filling which produces a considerable blast effect. There is virtually no fragmentation effect. Fuze assembly No 23 is used.

The No 13 Grenade has now been declared obsolescent and production has ceased. It is being replaced by the No 13 C1 which is superficially similar. This uses the No 19C2/20 fuze assembly. It can be thrown about 30 metres and has a five second delay after fuze initiation.

DATA
Body: Cardboard with tinned bottom
Filling: 225g
Diameter: 54mm
Height: 143m
Weight: 475g

Offensive hand grenade No. 13

Offensive hand grenade No. 17 with fuze assembly No. 19C2/20

Offensive hand grenade No 17 is a conventional cylindrical hand grenade. It uses fuze assembly No 19C2/20. It can be thrown about 30-40 metres and produces a considerable blast effect with an effective radius of 5 metres.

DATA
Body: Plastic
Filling: 205g
Diameter: 56mm
Height: 125mm
Weight: 475g

INERT HAND GRENADES

Three types of inert hand grenade are produced. The first is a copy of the No 1 fragmentation grenade. The body is of cast iron and is painted white. There is neither charge nor fuze but a safety pin is fitted. It is used for throwing practice only.

The second grenade is an instructional hand grenade. Externally it is similar to the current fragmentation grenade – No 1C1. It carries the number but has no charge and the fuze is rendered harmless. The grenade body and the fuze are recognised by a red letter "O" painted on each of them.

The Practice Fragmentation Grenade No 6C1 has an egg shaped body made of cast iron and painted blue. The grenade has a fuze mechanism which blows out a cork at the bottom of the body to make a report. The fuze functions as the standard No 19.

SMOKE HAND GRENADES

Several smoke hand grenades of broadly similar characteristics are in service. No 7 is typical of the range, it is lighter than the fragmentation grenades and can be thrown further. It is provided with a fuze assembly No 25. Smoke production commences 2-3 seconds after the grenade is thrown. The smoke is dark grey and lasts for 1-2 minutes.

The body of the grenade is grey with a yellow band, letters and figures.

DATA
Body: Tinned steel
Filling: 405g
Diameter: 63mm
Height: 151mm
Weight: 660g
Smoke: Grey, 1-2 mins

M8 is similar to the Smoke Hand Grenade No 7 in shape, size and functioning but uses the Fuze No E7R6 which differs from the No 25. It emits a light coloured grey smoke. The grenade body is painted grey with yellow markings.

No 9 is also similar to the Smoke Hand Grande No 7 but has a 200g filling and weighs 440g. It uses the fuze No 25 and gives off yellow smoke for 50-80 seconds. It is painted yellow.

No 10 Smoke Hand Grenade produces green smoke for 50-80 seconds. It has the same physical dimensions and method of operating as the No 7 and the No 9 grenades and the same filling and weight as No 9. It is painted green.

No. 11 grenade emits red smoke for 50-80 seconds. It has the same external appearance as Nos. 7, 9 and 10 but is painted red. It weighs only 360g and has a 145g filling.

Smoke Hand Grenade is also still in use and is produced in yellow, green or violet. The colour of the smoke is marked on the body of the grenade. Smoke starts 2-3 seconds after throwing and lasts for 1-2 minutes. Like the M8 Smoke Hand Grenade it uses the E7R6 fuze.

Smoke grenade No. 10 with fuze assembly No. 25

INCENDIARY HAND GRENADE NO. 12

This can be thrown about 40 metres. It functions in the same way as the smoke hand grenades but some 2 seconds after the grenade is activated, burning phosphorus produces the incendiary effect which is sustained for about one minute.

DATA
Body: Tinned Steel
Filling: 380g
Diameter: 63mm
Height: 153mm
Weight: 735g
Duration: 40-80sec

Incendiary grenade No. 12 with fuze assembly No. 25

PHOSPHORUS SMOKE GRENADES NO. 16 & NO. 80 MK 1

Phosphorus Smoke Grenade No. 16 has fuze assembly No. 27. The cylindrical steel case contains phosphorus pellets. After the grenade is thrown there is a delay of about 4 seconds and then the detonator sets off a small bursting charge which opens the body and ejects the phosphorus. When it comes into contact with the air, the phosphorus produces a dense white cloud.

The grenade is thrown about 40 yards and, depending on wind strength, a screen for local protection can be formed from 2-3 grenades. The body of the grenade is painted grey with a yellow band, letters and figures.

Phosphorus smoke grenade No. 80 Mk 1 with fuze mechanism No. 2 Mk 1/1 and delay detonator No. 75 Mk 2

DATA
Body: Tinned Steel
Filling: 180g white phosphorus
Diameter: 50mm
Height: 101mm
Weight: 284g

Phosphorus Hand Smoke Grenade No 80 Mk 1 is the UK smoke grenade. It produces white smoke when the case bursts and the phosphorus is ejected into the air. Fuze mechanism No 2 Mk 1/1 and delay detonator No 75 Mk 2 are used.

Phosphorus smoke grenade No. 16 with fuze assembly No. 27

RIFLE GRENADES

The Dutch Army uses the Rifle Grenade HEAT No. 4. This is based on the Belgian Mecar Energa Hand Grenade.

PRACTICE GRENADES

There are two practice rifle grenades. These are the Practice Rifle Grenade No. 5 and the No. 18. The latter has a white powder marker head.

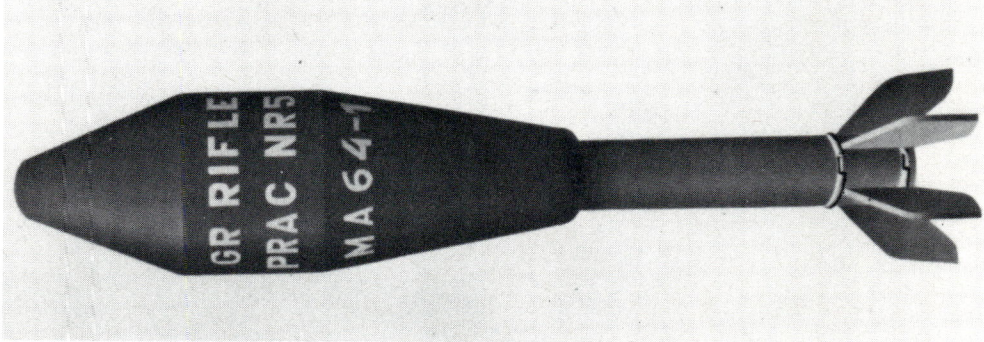

Practice rifle grenade No. 5

EUROMETAAL EMZ HAND GRENADE

The Eurometaal EMZ hand grenade, developed for the Royal Netherlands Army, consists of a plastic body with an inner lining of steel balls and an HE charge. It is fitted with the standard 19C3 mechanical fuze with pyrotechnical delay, which is a member of what has been the standard range of fuzes of the Netherlands Army for some years. The safety-pin blocks the lever. This lever in turn blocks the firing pin, which, when released, ignites the percussion primer. The primer then ignites the rest of the explosive train.

During trials it was found that the grenade exploded into about 2,100 fragments at an initial velocity of 1,600 metres per second and that it had a lethal area of approx 14m².

DATA
Length: 103mm
Diameter: 60mm
Weight of hand grenade with filling: 330g
Weight of fragmentation body: 120g
Weight of filling: 120g (Composition B)
Fuze: 19C3
Delay: 3.5sec ± 0.5sec
Packing: 18 grenades per box
Weight of box: approx 9.5kg
Volume of box: approx 0.023m³
Manufacturer: Eurometaal NV, Postbus 419, Zaandam, Holland

Eurometaal EMZ grenade (full size)

V40 MINI-GRENADE

NWM de Kruithoorn NV have produced what is probably the smallest hand grenade currently manufactured. It is officially named the V40 Grenade but is generally referred to as the "Mini" grenade. It is spherical with a diameter of 37mm. The body is made of steel and pre-notched on the inside. This ensures that the fragments obtained when the filling charge detonates are all of optimum size and there are no large pieces which travel a long way and constitute an unwanted hazard. Equally there is no production of fragments so small that they constitute dust and have no lethal effect at all. An analysis of the grenade fragments shows that the 78 gram body breaks up into splinters with the following distribution of mass.

Mass	No.	% Mass
0.3 gram	10	4.4
0.2 gram	112	33.0
0.15 gram	198	43.7
0.10 gram	60	8.8
0.05 gram	138	10.1
	518	100.0

It is probable that the smallest fragments of 0.05 gram lose their velocity rather too quickly to make a significant contribution to the lethality of the grenade and anyone near enough to be hit by them would receive a more crippling wound from a larger fragment. This leaves a total of 380 incapacitating pieces which are impelled radially outwards at a velocity of 1800m/sec. Due to their limited mass they lose a significant proportion of their velocity by the time they have travelled 5 metres and at 25 metres the likelihood of danger is too small to be significant.

The makers set themselves a rigorous criterion in demanding an average of 2.5 penetrations per metre as their measure of incapacitation. Their tests have been conducted using 5 ply laminated wood panels set up 3, 4 and 5 metres from the grenade and from these it has been demonstrated that 100 per cent casualties are assured at 3 metres from the point of burst.

The grenade weighs only 120 grams. This is about 2/5 of the weight of a conventional grenade and so on a weight basis of comparison the V40 emerges very favourably. The functioning of the grenade is straightforward. The safety pin is unusual in that in addition to passing through to hold the lever against the spring, it has a 'U' shaped addition which fits over the lever and prevents accidental withdrawal. To use the grenade, the pin is rotated to free the safety arm mentioned above and illustrated, and with the lever held firmly against the grenade body, the pin is withdrawn. The grenade remains safe so long as the lever is not released and if the immediate tactical situation changes, the pin can readily be replaced. When the grenade, pin withdrawn, is thrown, the spring forces the striker round in an arc, the lever is forced clear, and the striker goes on to crush the cap of the detonator. There is then a four second delay before the booster sets off the main charge.

The grenades are packed in bandoliers each holding five, and the bandoliers are packed in the standard US box M548. The bandolier weighs 650 grams and the box of thirty-two bandoliers (160 grenades) weighs 32kg.

A tail boom can be attached to the mini-grenade and it can then be

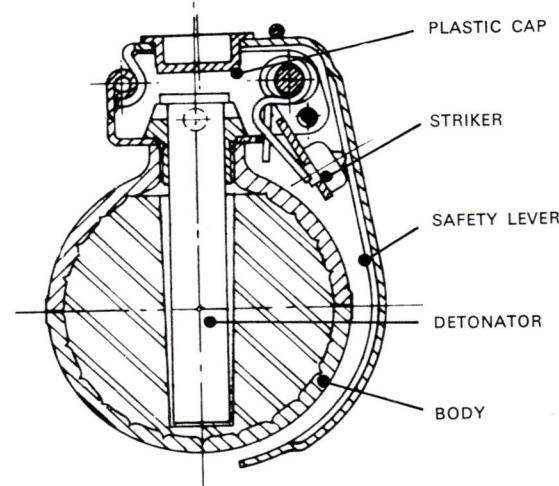

PLASTIC CAP

STRIKER

SAFETY LEVER

DETONATOR

BODY

Cut-away view of the NWM V40 mini-grenade

The V40 mini-grenade. This is the practice version

projected as a rifle grenade to 225 metres with an initial velocity of 90 metres/sec using a 7.62mm grenade launching cartridge or at 75 metres/sec using a 5.56mm grenade launching cartridge.

Manufacturer: NWM de Kruithoorn NV, PO Box 1050, 's-Hertogenbosch

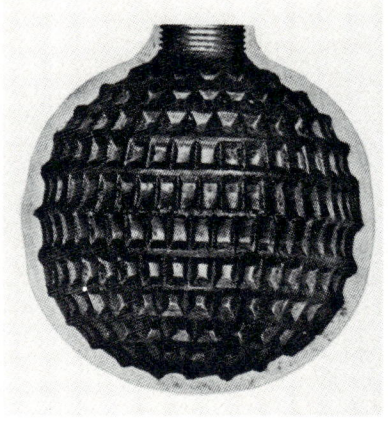

Section through the V40 mini-grenade showing the pre-notched form of the interior

POLAND

POLISH GRENADES

The Polish Army still uses the Model 31 hand grenade. This is a fragmentation grenade of similar appearance and function to the Soviet F1 hand grenade. The latter is used by the Polish Army, too, as also is the Soviet RC-42 anti-personnel hand grenade.

Poland is the only Warsaw Pact country to equip its forces with rifle grenades. These are launched from the Polish model of the Russian AK47 assault rifle, the PMK-DGN/60. The muzzle of the rifle is coned to take the Polish LON-1 grenade launcher and the rifle has a gas cut off to ensure that the gas energy is devoted to grenade launching and at the same time the piston is not subjected to excessive pressure from the grenade launching cartridge. The LON-1 has an external diameter of 20mm and therefore should not be used with the more normal 22m grenades usually projected from rifles. The two grenades, the F1/N60 anti-personnel grenade and the PGN-60 anti-tank grenade, with their internal diameter tubes of 20mm cannot be launched from any Western rifle – all of which have 22mm launchers.

The F1/N60 rifle grenade is a Polish adaptation of the Soviet F1 fragmentation grenade. The delay fuze has been replaced with an impact fuze and an unfinned stabilising boom has been added. The sights of the PMK-DGN/60 rifle show ranges of 100-240 metres.

The PGN 60 HEAT anti-tank rifle grenade is of Polish design and the shaped charge warhead has a finned stabilising boom, and is employed out to ranges of 100 metres.

DATA

	F-1/N60	PGN 60
Weight, fuzed:	632g	580g
Length:	270mm	405mm
Diameter:	55mm	67.5mm
Weight of HE filler:	45g	218g
Fuze type:	Impact	Impact
Maximum range:	240 metres	100 metres
Effective range:		50 metres
Fragment radius:	15-20 metres	100mm

Polish Model 31, defensive, fragmenting, hand grenade

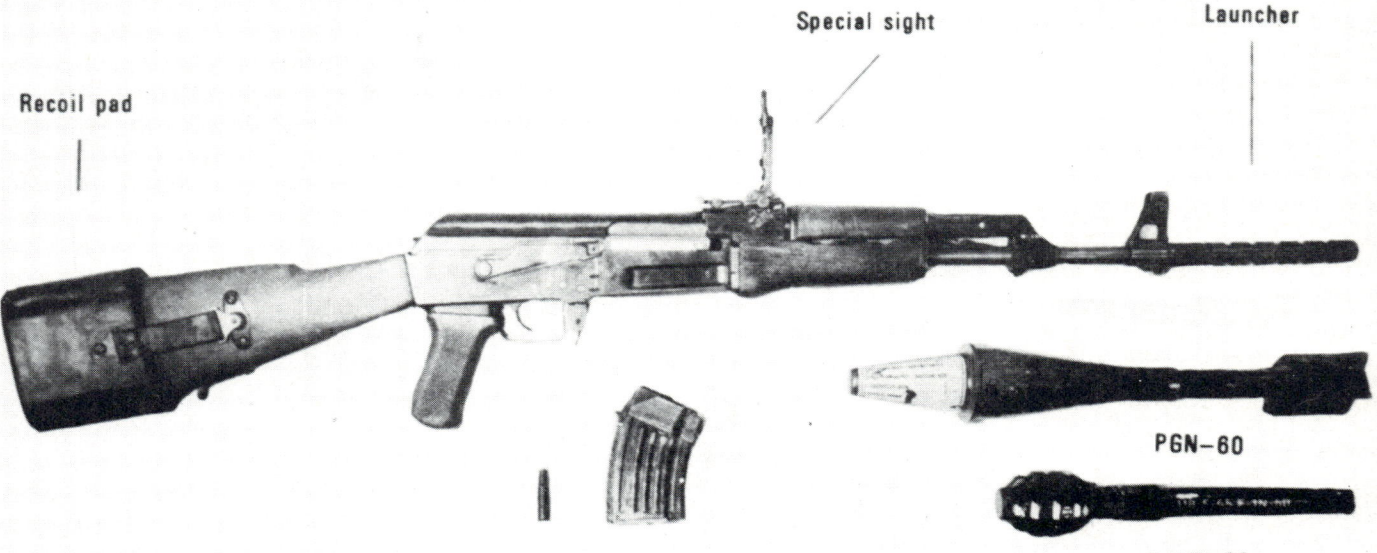

Polish PMK-DGN/60 rifle with the associated grenades, PGN-60 (top) and F1/N60

SPAIN

HAND GRENADES MODELS PO 1, 11 AND 111

These grenades are manufactured by Plasticas Oramile of San Sebastian, Spain. They are generally produced as high explosive grenades but, on order, smoke and incendiary fillings can be produced. All of them are thrown by hand.

Model PO 1 has a black bakelite casing. It is an offensive grenade and acts very largely by blast effect. Maximum effect is obtained at 2 metres and it is said to be effective at 3.5 metres with a deterrent effect at 10 metres radius.

Model PO 11 has a grey metal body and is regarded as a dual purpose weapon capable of either defensive or offensive application.

Model PO 111 is the Model 1 with an 18mm metal coil. Its normal application is in the offensive role but it can be transformed into a defensive grenade by the addition of an external metal coil. As an offensive weapon the shock wave is said to be effective at 3.9 metres. As a defensive grenade it produces a fragmentation effect out to 8 metres.

DATA
Explosive charge: Compressed trilite
Booster: Tetralite
Firing arrangement: Tape, striker and spring, inertia ball and detonating cap
Fuze: Mechanical impact type
Safety: **(a)** Tape must be fully unwound; **(b)** Inertia ball prevents fuze functioning at ranges less than 7 metres from the user; **(c)** If the grenade is armed by the tape unwinding and it fails to explode, the fuze is left in a safe condition and the grenade can be lifted

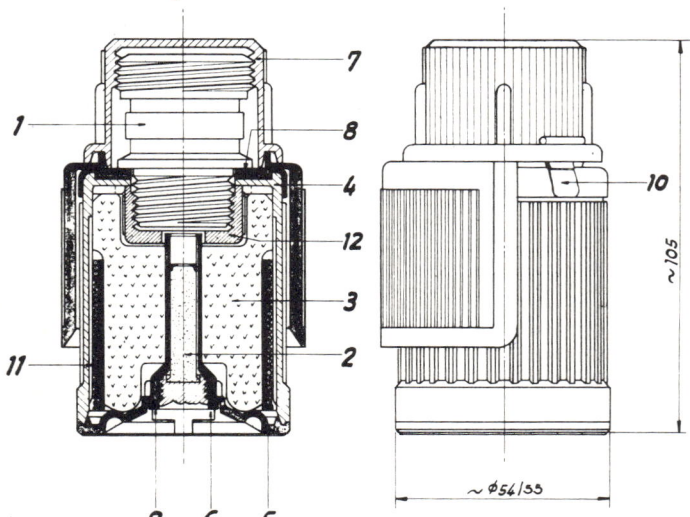

Dimensions:	PO 1	PO 11	PO 111
Length:	105mm	105mm	105mm
Diameter:	54mm	52mm	54mm
Weight:	285g	255g	325g
High explosive:	114g	114g	88g

Manufacturer: Plasticas Oramile, San Sebastian

PO 111 hand grenade

A sectioned view of the PO 111 hand grenade: **(1)** Percussion fuze; **(2)** Detonator; **(3)** Explosive charge; **(4)** Body; **(5)** Base of the grenade; **(6)** Detonator plug; **(7)** Safety cap; **(8)** Joint of the fuze; **(9)** Joint of the detonator; **(10)** Seal (welded to the joint); **(11)** Metal coil; **(12)** Nut of the fuze

POSARE VI AND VII GRENADES

These are offensive grenades but the POSARE VII may be converted to a defensive grenade by the addition of a metal coil around the body and a conical cap around the top of the grenade. The POSARE VI is a "mini" grenade and the POSARE VII is of conventional size.

Both grenades work in the same way. In the accompanying sectioned drawing the grenade is shown as it would be issued to troops. The safety pin **(1)** is through the lever **(3)** and the ring on the safety pin is strapped to the body of the grenade **(2)**. The detonator assembly consisting of the pyrotechnic delay **(5)** and the gaine **(7)** is forced down by its spring **(8)** against the shutter **(9)**.

When the safety pin is withdrawn the shutter spring rotates the lever free of the body and the shutter is ejected. (Until this happens an accidental initiation will be kept from the main filling by the shutter). The detonator assembly is driven down by its spring and the fixed pin initiates the thermal delay **(5)**. The spring **(4)** around the firing pin then reasserts itself, after having been compressed by the descending detonator assembly, and forces the detonator assembly clear of the firing pin. The main filling is initiated and the grenade functions. If it fails to function, it can be lifted since the detonator assembly is held clear of the firing pin.

The Posare VI differs from the Posare VII in that it contains metal fragments (6) in the space which is left empty in the latter.

DATA	Posare V1	Posare V11
Outside diameter:	60mm	60mm
Height:	80mm	100mm
Weight:	170g	210g
Weight of TNT filling:	60g	125g

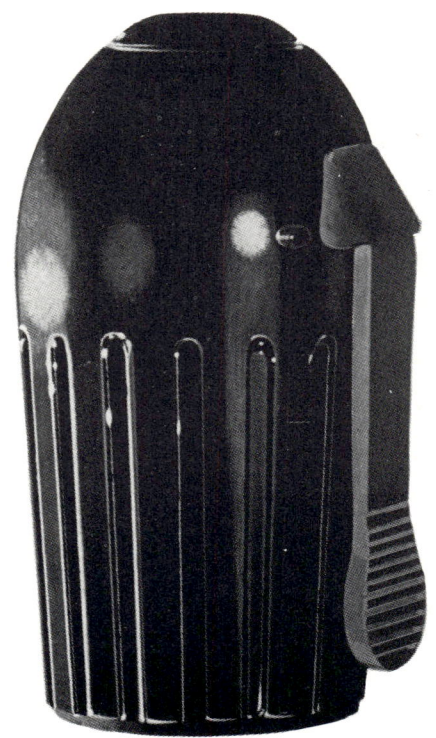

Posare VII

Posare VI

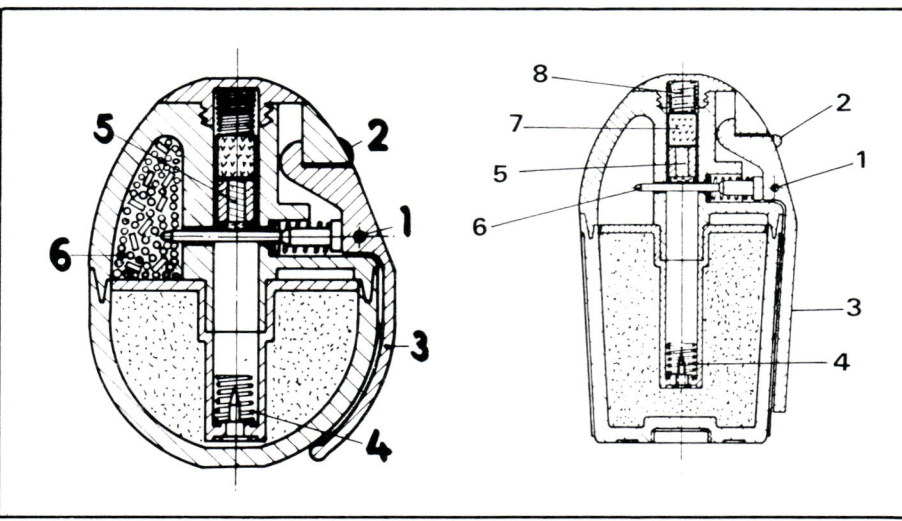

Sectioned views of Posare VI and VII

POM SERIES GRENADES

Derivatives of the PO series described above, the POM series of grenades is also manufactured by Plasticas Oramile. The POM-I is a development of the PO 111 and incorporates both a percussion and a delayed action fuze. It weighs 326g.

The POM-II-R is the latest hand grenade in the series and is a modified version of an earlier POM-II. It consists of a cylindrical body filled with explosive, this being closed by a cap containing the fuze. It is operated in a manner similar to that of other grenades in the series, in that a tape must be unwound before the safety pin can be removed, and it has an allways percussion fuze. The POM-II-R can also be fired from a sub-machine gun with the aid of a special attachment.

It can be converted into a defensive hand grenade by fitting a steel splinter collar around the body of the grenade, this gives it an effective radius of 50m. The design of the POM-II-R is such that it can also be adapted for use as a trip grenade.

Manufacturer: Plasticas Oramile, San Sebastian

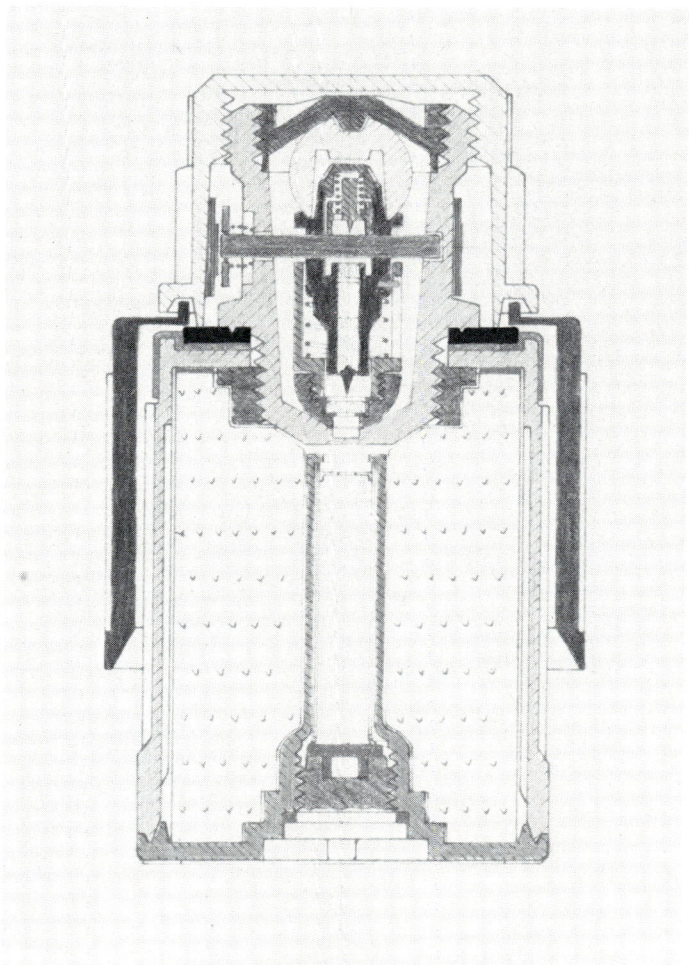

Sectioned view of the POM 11-R Grenade

POM1 grenade (Courtesy J. Allen)

HAND GRENADE E.A. M5

Manufactured by Explosives Alaveses SA "Expal" Vitoria, Spain, this is an offensive grenade which can be converted to a defensive type by the addition of a metal sleeve. It can be thrown by hand or launched from a rifle with the standard 22mm launcher.

The fuze can be set to either of two positions. These produce (a) Delayed action only and (b) Percussion and delayed operation. This latter arrangement is intended to produce a self destruction aspect.

It cannot function at a distance of less than 6 metres and if projected no further than this, it will become inert after 1.5 seconds. The makers claim that it is completely waterproof and will function on impact on any surface at any angle of incidence.

DATA
Length: 100mm
Diameter: 50mm
Weights:
Offensive grenade: 290g
Defensive grenade: 500g
High explosive filling: 135g
Maximum range (rifle projected): 260 metres
Radius of effect: 5 metres

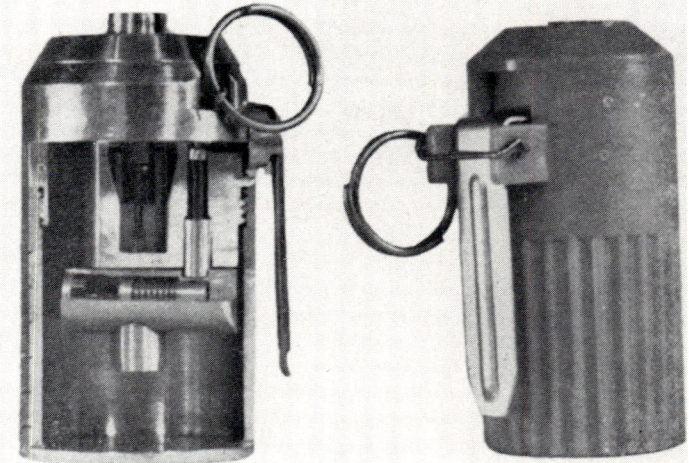
Hand grenade E.A.M5

Three training models of the grenade are produced. These are:
(a) Inert instructional grenade. This is yellow with a distinctively embossed surface which can be distinguished from the HE grenade both by touch and sight. It can be fully dismantled for instructional purposes;
(b) Inert launching practice grenade. This is grey and made to be launched and recovered. After replacing the spring of the firing lever it can be used again. Its weight and range are the same as the combat grenade;
(c) Blank grenade. This functions on impact producing a small report and giving off smoke which can be seen by both the firer and an observer.
Manufacturer: Explosives Alvases SA, Vitoria

RIFLE GRENADE G.L. TYPE 1. MODEL 61

This grenade, manufactured by Instalaza, is an anti-tank grenade with a shaped charge warhead. It can penetrate up to 250mm of armour plate and 650mm of concrete. It was intended to be used with the CETME Models B and C rifles but can be employed with any rifle with a launcher or flash eliminator of 22mm.

DATA
Diameter: 64mm
Length: 395mm
Internal diameter of fin assembly: 22m
Weight ready for firing: 650g
Weight in carrying case: 820g
Weight of projecting charge: 1.9g
Maximum range: 54 metres/sec
Muzzle velocity: 300 metres
Effective range: 100 metres
Fuze: Time and percussion
Projecting cartridge: 7.62mm contour with 5 pointed, crimped, ends
Minimum range: 10 metres
Time of flight: 50 metres (0.9sec); 75 metres (1.41sec); 100 metres (1.94sec)
Manufacturer: Instalaza SA, Zaragoza

A practice grenade is produced for training purposes. The body is made of bitumenised, rolled paper. The fin assembly is made of high strength alloy steel and allows the practice grenade to be used on many occasions. The grenade is painted black.

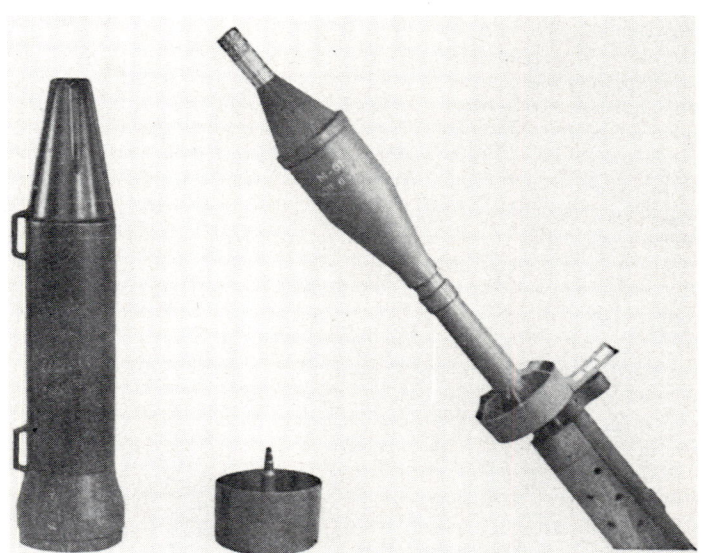
Rifle grenade G.L. type I, model 61

RIFLE GRENADE G.L. TYPE II MODEL 63 B

This grenade is manufactured by Instalaza.

It is a shaped charge, fragmentation grenade for use against tanks and personnel which will produce penetration of armour plate of up to 150mm and up to 400mm in concrete. It was intended for use with the CETME Models B and C but may be used with any rifle with a 22mm flash eliminator, or launcher of that dimension.

The sights are graduated from 75 to 200 metres for direct fire and, with indirect fire, read 150, 200, 250, 300, 350, 400 and 425 metres.

DATA
Calibre: 40mm
Overall length: 333mm
Internal diameter of fin assembly: 22mm
Weight of grenade: 510g
Weight of grenade in case: 600g
Weight of projection charge: 1.9g
Weight of HE filling: 88g
Maximum range: 425 metres
Muzzle velocity: 70 metres/sec
Effective radius against personnel: 6 metres
Manufacturer: Instalaza SA, Zaragoza

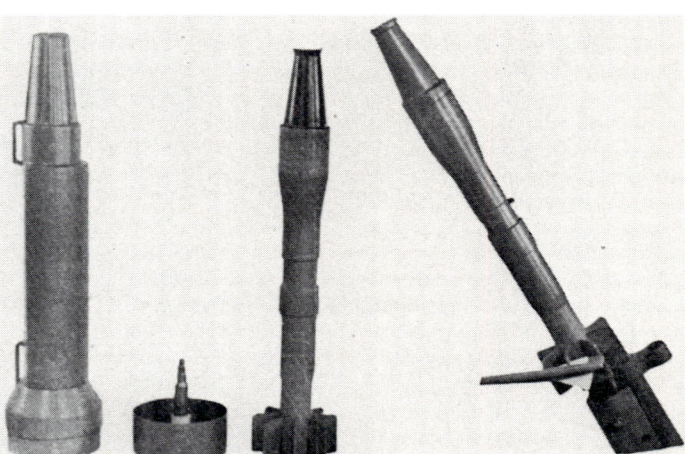
Rifle grenade G.L. type II, model 63B

SWEDEN

FFV 915 SMOKE RIFLE GRENADE

The FFV Smoke Rifle Grenade is fired from a standard 7.62mm automatic rifle by a special cartridge of the rosette crimped type loaded in a magazine holding 20 cartridges.

It is normally projected in a low angle fire to its intended impact point, and the smoke grenade will start emitting smoke before it hits the ground if the range is above 250 metres. The smoke screen produced by the grenade under normal weather conditions will extend 20m wide and 4m high within 10 seconds.

The smoke composition of titanium dioxide and hexa-chloroethane is ignited by means of black powder discs. Effective smoke is produced immediately. Because the smoke is emitted through an outlet channel adjacent to the fins at the rear of the grenade, emission is assured even in soft ground and snow.

FFV 915 Smoke Rifle Grenade

DATA
Weight: 570 grams
Length: 272mm
Smoke emission duration: 50sec (approx)

Weight of smoke composition: 320 grams
Range: 300m
Operational temperature range: −40°C to +60°C
Manufacturer: Forenade Fabriksverken, Eskilstuna, Sweden

UNION OF SOVIET SOCIALIST REPUBLICS

ANTI-PERSONNEL HAND GRENADES

The Soviet Union has a number of anti-personnel hand grenades. Those produced prior to the Second World War are all officially obsolete but some of them have found their way to the Far Eastern area and have been used in Vietnam. Amongst these very early grenades are the RDG-33 and RPG-40.

RDG-33

This is a hand grenade with a delay detonator, functioning in both offensive and defensive roles. In the offensive mode it is a seamed tin plate cylindrical grenade with a screw thread to allow the attachment of a metal throwing handle. As an offensive grenade it has a lethal radius of 5 metres. When converted to the defensive role a metal sleeve is placed over the cylindrical body holding the 85g TNT filling and a stud on the metal cylinder engages in a recess in the sleeve to retain it in position. The sleeve is pre-notched in a diamond pattern. It then has a lethality radius of 25 metres. Without the jacket it weighs 508 grams and with the jacket 722 grams. The delay time is 3.2-3.8 seconds. Blinds are very dangerous with this grenade and should be destroyed in situ. The grenade is obsolete in USSR but was used in Vietnam.

RPG-40 hand grenade

RGD-33 hand grenade

RPG-40

This is an anti-tank hand grenade, using an HE filling to produce a blast effect. It has a separate primer detonator fitted into a recess in the head of the grenade. It is stabilised in flight by a ribbon which streams behind it. It is effective against soft skinned and load carrying vehicles but has little chance of success with armoured vehicles of modern construction. It weighs 1,105g and has an instantaneous allways fuze. The 794g of TNT gives an effective fragmentation radius of 20m. The Soviet wartime grenade are still encountered with militia units of the Warsaw Pact countries.

RG-42 ANTI-PERSONNEL HAND GRENADE

This is a fragmentation concussion hand grenade which was used in the Second World War and was retained for some years in the Soviet Army. It was adopted by the Chinese Army as the Hand Grenade Type 42. Since then it has been taken by all the Satellite countries and used by them for several years. It has now been relegated to the various militia bodies of these countries.

The grenade body is a plain steel, light gauge, cylinder with no serrations. It encloses a separate fragmentation sheet that is formed into a pre-grooved diamond shaped pattern. The grenade is employed in much the same way as any other delay fuzed type and should be thrown from behind cover. The UZRG fuze gives a delay of 3-4 seconds and the pressed TNT filling drives the fragments out to an effective radius of 25 metres.

The grenades are packed, unfuzed, 20 to a wooden box, with the fuzes packed in a separate container in the same box. The packed box weighs 16kg.

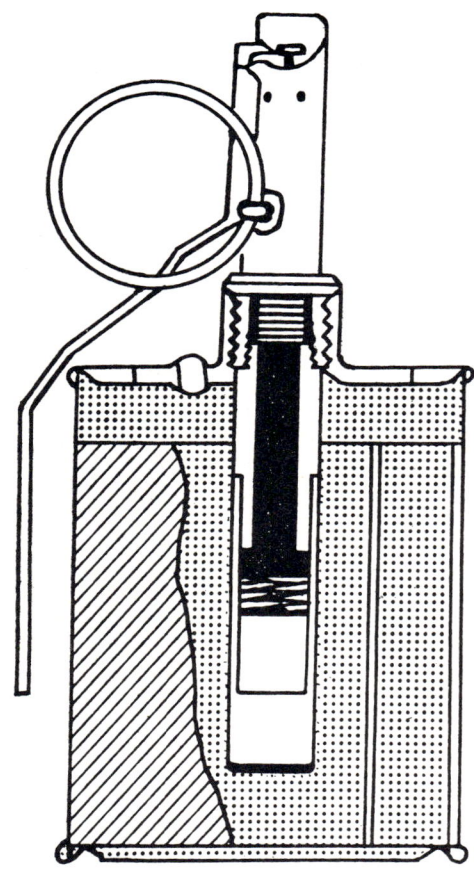

A sectioned view of the Soviet RG-42 grenade

DATA
Type: Fragmentation
Weight: 436g
Length: 121mm
Maximum diameter: 54mm
Body material: Steel
Filler weight: 118g
Filler material: Pressed TNT
Fuze type: Delay

RG-42 anti-personnel hand grenade

Fuze delay: 3 to 4 seconds
Identifying markings: P-42
Range thrown: 35 metres
Effective fragment radius: 25 metres

F1 ANTI-PERSONNEL HAND GRENADE

This grenade was introduced during the Second World War. It is a fragmentation grenade with a cast iron body notched into cubes on the outside surface in a manner reminiscent of the United States Mark II Grenade or the British Mills 36 Grenade. It suffers from the same defects as the latter and produces a number of fragments from the base plug and filler which can be lethal out to 200 metres and so the thrower would be well advised to throw the grenade from under cover.

The Polish Army has also introduced this grenade in a modified form with an impact fuze as the F-1/N 60 rifle grenade.

DATA
Type: Fragmentation
Weight: 600g
Length: 124mm
Maximum diameter: 55mm
Body material: Cast iron
Filler weight: 60g
Filler material: TNT
Fuze type: Delay
Fuze delay: 3.2-4.2 seconds
Range thrown: 30 metres
Effective fragment radius: 15-20 metres

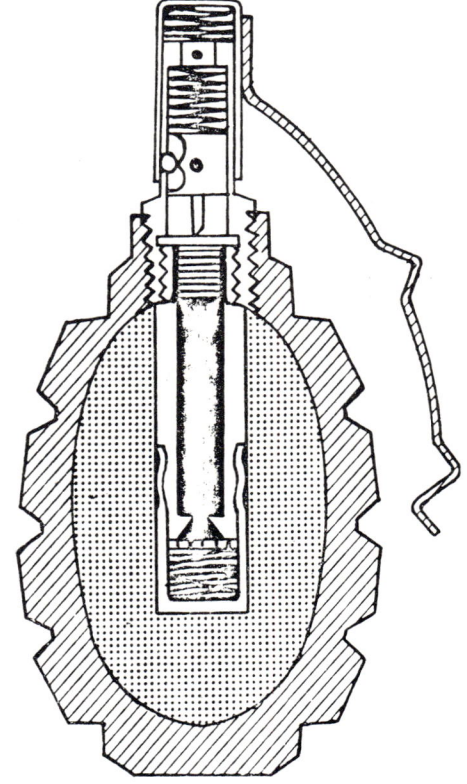

A sectioned view of the Soviet F1 defensive hand grenade

F1 fragmentation grenade. This grenade is usually painted olive green

RGD-5 ANTI-PERSONNEL HAND GRENADE

This is an egg shaped anti-personnel fragmentation grenade with a smooth exterior surface to the two piece steel body and with a serrated fragmentation liner. It is a compact, easily handled grenade which can be thrown slightly further than the earlier Russian defensive hand grenades. It uses the fuze UZRG. The detonator assembly protrudes.

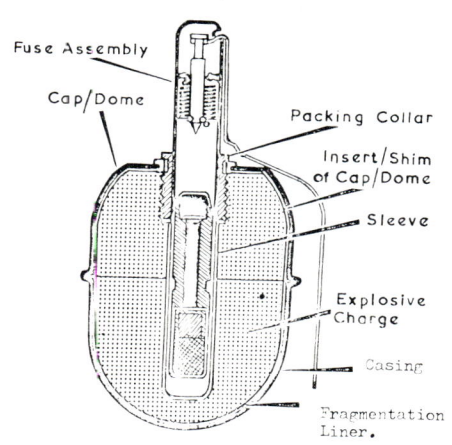

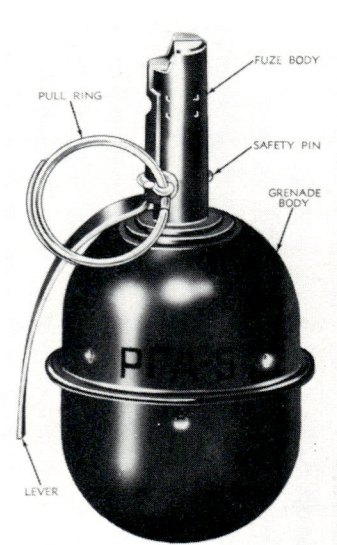

A sectioned view of the Soviet RGD-5 hand grenade

RGD-5 anti-personnel hand grenade

DATA
Type: Fragmentation
Weight: 310g
Length: 114mm
Diameter: 57mm

Weight of filling: 110g
Type of filling: TNT
Fuze: 3.2-4.2 second delay UZRG
Range thrown: 30 metres
Effective fragment radius: 15-20 metres

RPG-6 ANTI-TANK HAND GRENADE

This anti-tank grenade was used in the Second World War by the Russian Infantry and was subsequently adopted by most of the Eastern Bloc including the People's Republic of China.

It has several features in common with the RPG-43. It has four trailing cloth strips to stabilise it in flight. These are dragged out by the safety lever from the throwing handle, when the grenade is thrown. The RPG-6 can be distinguished by its hemispherical head on the cone shaped casing over the shaped charge. It is a more efficient anti-armour grenade than its predecessor, and because of its pronounced fragmentation effect it can be used as an anti-personnel grenade.

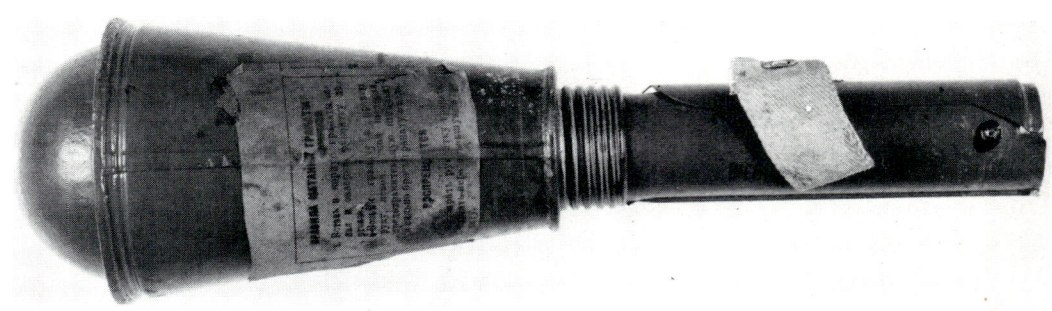

HEAT hand grenade, RPG-6

DATA
Type: Anti-tank
Weight of grenade with fuze: 1,100g
Weight of HE filling: 562g
Type of HE filling: TNT
Penetration: 100mm

Type of fuze: Instantaneous. Impact
Effective fragment radius: 20m
Throwing distance: 15-20m
Length: 343mm
Diameter: 102mm

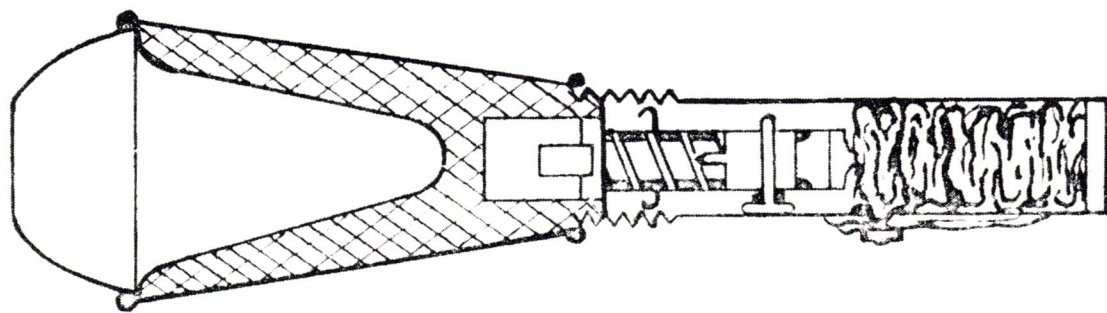

A sectioned view of the Soviet RPG-6 anti-tank grenade

RPG-43 ANTI-TANK HAND GRENADE

This is the earliest of the Soviet Anti-Tank Hand Grenades. It was intended for employment at very close ranges, against armoured vehicles and defensive, protected positions. To ensure that the head of the grenade strikes the target there is a stabiliser consisting of two fabric strips which pull a conical metal sleeve, open at both ends, which trails behind the grenade during its flight through the air.

The fuze is instantaneous impact type. The grenade was used by the Egyptian troops in the October War of 1973 with the Israelis.

DATA
Type: Anti-tank
Weight of grenade with fuze: 1,200g
Weight of HE filling: 612g
Type of HE filling: TNT
Penetration: 75mm
Type of fuze: Instantaneous impact
Effective fragment radius: 20 metres
Length: 279mm
Diameter: 102mm

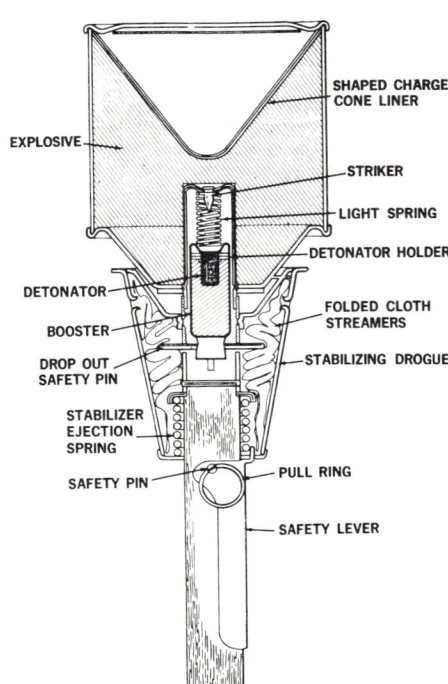

SHAPED CHARGE
CONE LINER

EXPLOSIVE

STRIKER

LIGHT SPRING

DETONATOR HOLDER

DETONATOR

FOLDED CLOTH
STREAMERS

BOOSTER

DROP OUT
SAFETY PIN

STABILIZING DROGUE

STABILIZER
EJECTION
SPRING

SAFETY PIN

PULL RING

SAFETY LEVER

A sectioned view of the RPG-6 anti-tank grenade

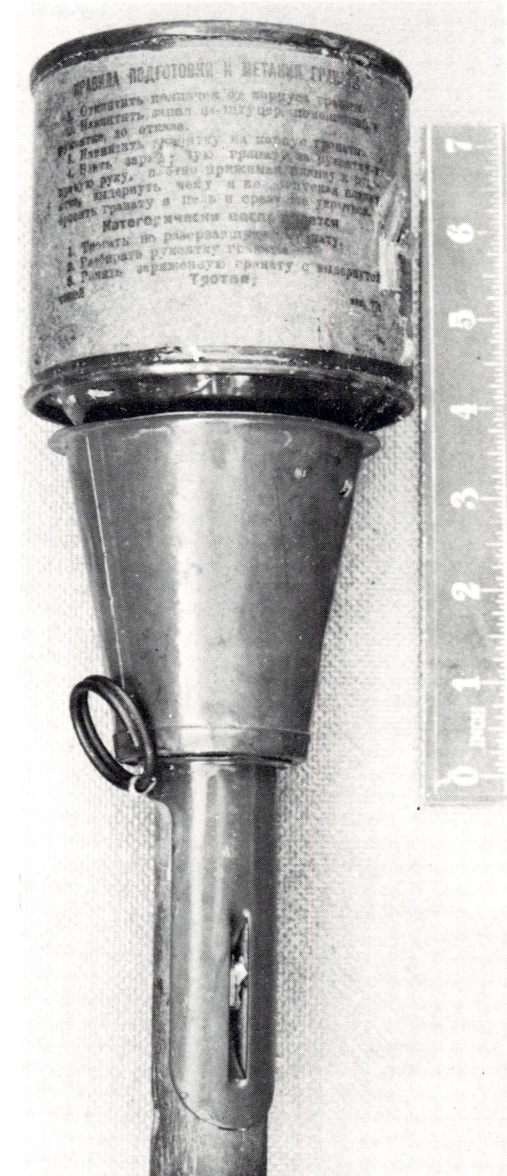

The Soviet RPG-43 anti-tank hand grenade

RKG-3 ANTI-TANK GRENADES

The family of RKG-3 grenades has now replaced the RPG-40, RPG-43 and RPG-6 anti-tank grenades in the Eastern Bloc and in the People's Republic of China.

The RKG-3 is a more modern type of grenade and is more efficient than those grenades it replaces. It is stabilised in flight by a four panelled fabric drogue which is pulled out from the handle when the grenade is thrown. The drogue development completes the arming of the grenade. The drogue also ensures that it is possible to drop the grenade on the top of an armoured vehicle.

The earliest member of the family was the RKG-3 and this was capable of penetrating just under 5in. Two further versions – the 3M and the 3T – have been produced. The RKG-3M has a copper cone instead of the steel liner of the first version and the 3T also has a different cone liner. The RKG-3M was used extensively in the 1973 October war and was shown to penetrate 165mm of armour.

DATA
Type: Anti-tank
Weight of grenade with fuze: 1.07kg
Weight of HE filling: 567g
Type of HE filling: TNT/RDX
Penetration:
RKG-3: 125mm
RKG-3M: 165mm
Type of fuze: Instantaneous impact
Effective fragment radius: 20 metres
Length: 362mm
Maximum diameter: 55.6mm

UPG-8 PRACTICE GRENADE
This is a practice anti-tank grenade used in training in place of the RKG-3 series of anti-tank grenades.

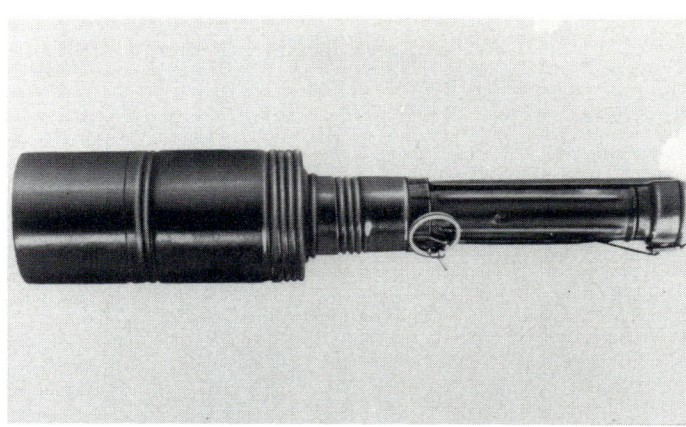

RKG-3 anti-tank grenade

Russian troops training with the anti-tank grenade (Novosti)

SMOKE HAND GRENADE RDG-1

This is a stick type grenade. The earliest version adopted about 1948, was made of grey moulded cardboard. Later versions are said to have a wooden handle. There is an inner cardboard tube with an igniter at each end and in the middle. The friction igniter is rubbed on the match head fuze at the wide end of the grenade to ignite the filling which can be either a white or a black smoke mixture. The grenade will float and can be used to produce screening smoke during the progress of a water crossing operation.

DATA
Weight: 500 grams
Length: 222mm
Throwing distance: 35 metres
Average smoke area: 460 sq. metres
Burning time: 1-1½ minutes

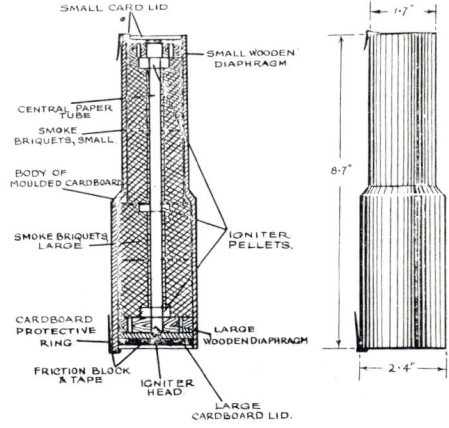

RDG-1 smoke hand grenade

SMOKE HAND GRENADE RDG-2

This grenade has been in service since the early 1950s and has been adopted by all the Soviet Bloc countries. It is a tactical grenade and is used to conceal the movements of small bodies of Infantry or Engineers. It is made of cardboard with a cardboard tube down the centre. It is filled with a burning type filler and a friction fuze. It is waxed and is damp proof but it cannot be used to produce smoke over water. It produces a dense white smoke approximately 20 metres long and 8 metres wide.

DATA
Length: 240mm
Diameter: 46mm
Weight: 500g
Throwing range: 35 metres
Smoke area: 160 sq. metres
Duration of smoke: 1½mins.

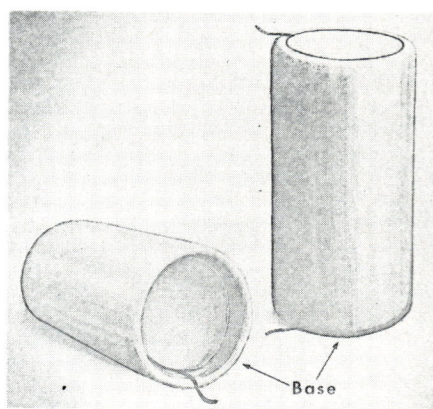

RDG-2 smoke hand grenade

UNITED KINGDOM

UK GRENADE NOMENCLATURE

Readers are warned that the alphanumeric references used in the titles of many modern British weapons are unique only within the range of variants of one type of weapon; the same alphanumeric reference can be applied to two different types of weapon. If the two types are very different no problem arises; but in this section it is important to realise that, for example, the Grenade, Hand, CS Anti-Riot Irritant L2A1 is entirely different from the Grenade, Hand-Rifle, Anti-Personnel L2A1, and that a reference out of context to the "L2" or "L2A1" Grenade can be misleading.

HAND GRENADE NO. 36M

The Grenade, Hand, No. 36M is an improved form of the Grenade, Hand, No. 36, modified for service in Mesopotamia and especially sealed against moisture. It is an anti-personnel grenade which is projected by hand. It has a thick, cast iron, body which is notched on the outside. The original idea was that the body would break up into pieces corresponding to the notched segments but it was found that the fragment size is in no way related to the notches and in fact the grenade produces a relatively limited number of very large fragments and also a lot of cast iron dust. The large fragments and the base plug give rise to a danger area which extends about 275 metres from the point of burst and the thrower must be under cover. Weight of the filled grenade is 774g.

The grenade was also used as a rifle grenade and in this role was fitted with a gas check plate of steel. A cup launcher was used on the rifle. In this role the grenade had a range of about 180 metres and was fitted with a seven second delay fuze. The components used in the rifle projected version have now been declared obsolete.

The Grenade, Hand, No. 36M is now being replaced by the Grenade, Hand/Rifle, Anti-Personnel, L2A1.

DRILL GRENADE NO.36 M Mk 4

This drill grenade consists of the empty components of the service grenade. It is painted white and holes are drilled through the body. There are two holes in the bracket above the retaining pin and a wire is strung between them to retain the striker lever when the grenade is thrown.
Manufacturer: Royal Ordnance Factories
Status: Obsolescent but still in widespread service

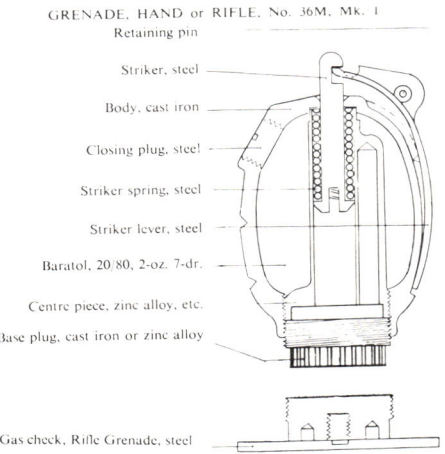

GRENADE, HAND or RIFLE, No. 36M, Mk. I

Retaining pin
Striker, steel
Body, cast iron
Closing plug, steel
Striker spring, steel
Striker lever, steel
Baratol, 20/80, 2-oz. 7-dr.
Centre piece, zinc alloy, etc.
Base plug, cast iron or zinc alloy
Gas check, Rifle Grenade, steel

Grenade, hand or rifle, No 36M, Mk 1

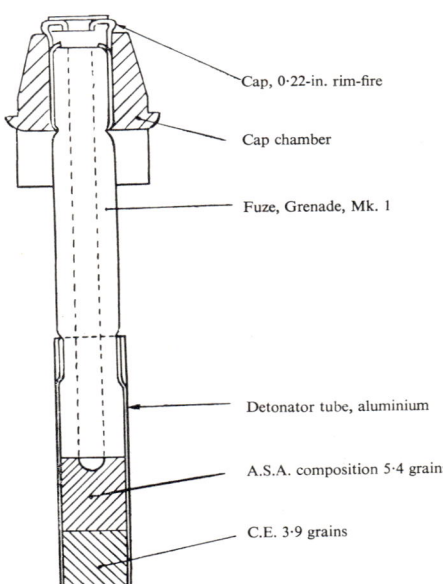

Grenade, hand, 36M

GRENADE NO. 80 WP Mk 1
AND Mk 1/1

The Grenade Hand/Discharger No. 80 WP is intended to produce screening smoke and may be either thrown or projected from a multi barrel discharger on an AFV, using a Fuze, electric, No F103. It has a tinplate body filled with white phosphorus, Detonator No. 75 and Striker Mechanism Grenade No. 2. It is being replaced by the Grenade XL21E1 (qv).

STRIKER MECHANISM GRENADE NO. 2

This consists of an adapter with a screwed in housing for a spring operated striker which is retained in the cocked position by a fly off lever and safety pin.

DETONATOR NO. 75

The Detonator No. 75 consists of a .22in rimfire cap attached to a 1.5in (38mm) length of Fuze Grenade No. 1 and a cap chamber. The fuze gives a delay of 2.5 to 4 seconds and then initiates a Detonator No. 63 Mk 2 or No. 78 Mk 1.

FUZE ELECTRIC NO. F 103

This has a brass gunpowder magazine, containing Gunpowder G 20, closed by a brass cover into which is set a Fuze Electric No. 53 Mk 2.

DRILL GRENADE HAND/DISCHARGER NO. 80 Mk 1

This is the body of a service grenade with an inert filling.

DRILL DETONATOR NO. 75 Mk 1

This is an empty .22 rimfire cap in a cap chamber and connected to a dummy fuze and an empty detonator tube. It is painted white with a hole through the tube of the detonator.

Manufacturer: Royal Ordnance Factories

Cap, 0·22-in. rim-fire
Cap chamber
Fuze, Grenade, Mk. 1
Detonator tube, aluminium
A.S.A. composition 5·4 grains
C.E. 3·9 grains

Detonator, No. 75 Mk 2

Status: Obsolescent

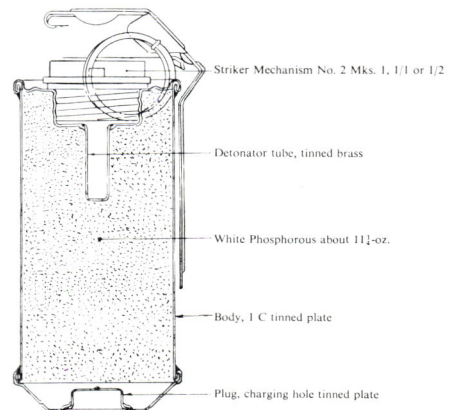

Striker Mechanism No. 2 Mks. 1, 1/1 or 1/2

Detonator tube, tinned brass

White Phosphorous about 11¼-oz.

Body, 1 C tinned plate

Plug, charging hole tinned plate

Grenade, No. 80 WP Mk 1

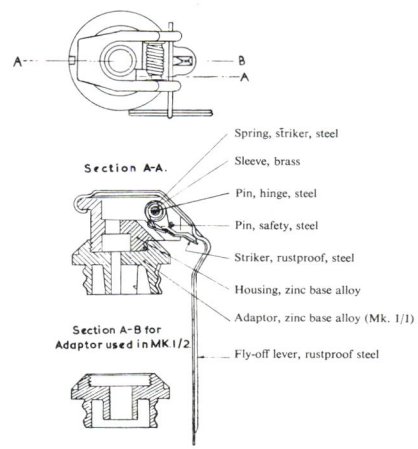

A—   B
—A

Section A-A.

Spring, striker, steel

Sleeve, brass

Pin, hinge, steel

Pin, safety, steel

Striker, rustproof, steel

Housing, zinc base alloy

Adaptor, zinc base alloy (Mk. 1/1)

Section A-B for
Adaptor used in MK 1/2

Fly-off lever, rustproof steel

Striker mechanism, No. 2, Mks 1/1 and 1/2 (plan with fly-off lever removed)

Grenade, hand/discharger No. 80 W.WP Mk 1

DRILL GRENADE (DISCHARGER) SMOKE L1

This grenade is inert and will be used for practising all of the grenades in the series used with dischargers. It uses empty components and is painted Oxford blue.

The body of the L1A1 version of this grenade is similar to that of the L5 grenade and is filled with cement to a weight of 425-485 grams.

The L1A2 version differs from the L1A1 in the method of body construction and has an increased weight of filling (880-890g).

GRENADE, HAND-RIFLE, ANTI-PERSONNEL, L2

The Grenade L2 is a high explosive anti-personnel grenade based on the US M26 Grenade and closely resembling it in appearance and performance. It differs in having a separate fuze assembly. It was designed to be thrown by hand or projected from a rifle but due to various difficulties it is no longer intended that rifle projection should be used.

The L2 Grenade has superseded the Grenade 36M. It exists in two variants, L2A1 and L2A2, but the only significant difference between the two is in the design of the fuze holder which was modified to assist production.

The grenade consists of a two part, tinned plate outer casing, a coil of notched wire, a fuze (L25), holder, cap and HE filling.

The body assembly (upper and lower) holds the fuze holder in the upper part and the two parts are 1.6in (upper) and 1.45in (lower) in length and circular in section. The coil is made from steel wire 0.094in in section and notched at intervals of 0.125in. The HE filling consists of 6oz of RDX/TNT.

There are a number of models of the L25 fuze. Currently issued are the L25A3 and L25A4. The fuze consists of a striker assembly and an adapter assembly with detonator, delay pellet and cap housing.

Grenade, hand or rifle, anti-personnel, L2A1

PRACTICE AND DRILL GRENADES

Practice grenades L3A1, 2 and 3 and drill grenades L4A1 and 2 are similar in construction and appearance to the operational grenades. Practice grenades are inert and are painted light blue. Drill grenades are fitted with Drill Fuze, Grenade, Percussion L30 and are painted dark blue.

Full titles are Grenade, Hand-Rifle, Practice, Inert L3A1 etc. and Drill Grenade, Hand-Rifle, L4A1 etc.

Manufacturer: Royal Ordnance Factories
Status: In service

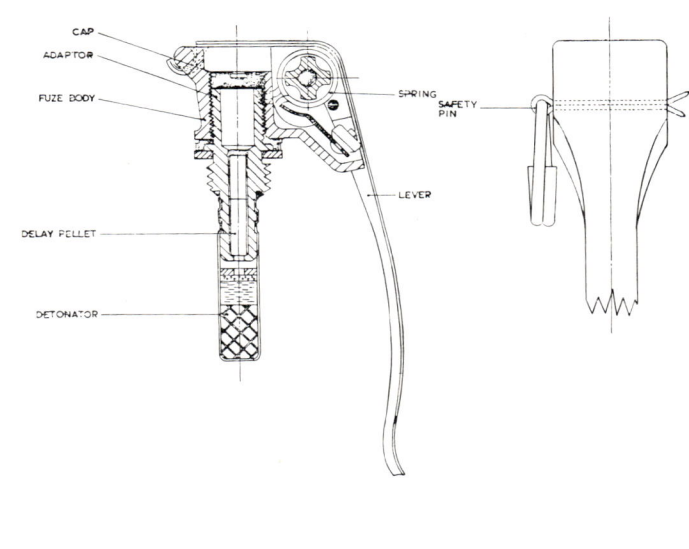

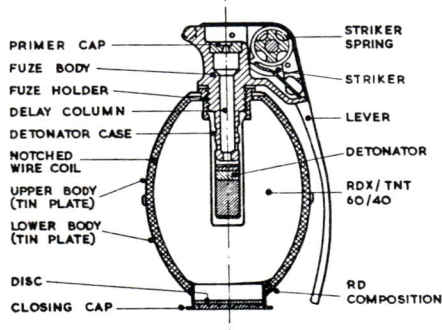

Fuze, grenade, percussion, L25A3

SMOKE GRENADES XL21E1 (XL5E1) AND XL6E1

Grenade, Hand, Screening Smoke, XL21E1 is the replacement for the No. 80 WP grenade. It is a rubber bodied, red phosphorus-filled, smoke grenade weighing about 450kg. It was originally called the Grenade Hand XL5E1.

UNITED STATES OF AMERICA

GRENADES, HAND: FRAGMENTATION, DELAY, M67 and M33

Hand Grenade M67 is Hand Grenade M33 with a safety clip. Each grenade is assembled with a fuze that initiates the explosive charge. These grenades detonate at the expiration of 4 to 5 seconds after release of the safety lever.

Grenade body: Bodies of the M67 and M33 are identical. The shape is essentially spherical. The body measures 63.5mm in diameter. Bodies contain a high-explosive filler.

Fuze, hand grenade M213: Hand Grenade Fuze M213 is a pyrotechnic delay-detonating fuze. The body contains a primer and pyrotechnic delay column. Assembled to the body are a striker, striker spring, safety lever, safety pin and pull ring, safety clip, and a detonator assembly. (Older models do not have the safety clip.)

Safety clip: The hand grenade safety clip is designed to keep the safety lever in place, should the safety pin be unintentionally removed from the grenade. It is an additional safety device used in conjunction with the safety pin.

The hand grenade safety clip, of spring-steel wire, is shaped in a special configuration for installation on the grenade. It consists of a clamp, which fits around an extension of the fuze body and the safety lever, holding the safety lever snugly against the fuze body.

Clips of older design consist of a loop, which fits around the neck of the grenade, and a clamp which fits over the safety lever.

The training model of the M67 is designated Grenade, Hand, Practice, Delay, M69. This consists of the grenade body, fuze, hand, grenade, practice, M228 and primer M42 (as used in the M67). The body itself is empty. The M69 has identical physical characteristics to the M67 but is painted blue with a brown band. They are packed 50 per carton, one carton per carrier bag and one carrier bag per wooden box.

Its functioning is identical to the M69 except that it emits a loud report, similar to that of a firecracker, and this is followed by a puff of white smoke.

FUNCTIONING

Hand grenade M67. Release of the safety clip, and removal of the safety pin permit release of the safety lever. When the safety lever is released, it is forced away from the grenade body by a striker acting under the force of a striker spring. The striker rotates on its axis and strikes the percussion primer. The primer emits a small, intense spit of flame, igniting the delay element. The delay element burns for 4 to 5 seconds, then sets off the detonator. The detonator explodes, thus initiating the explosive charge. The explosive charge explodes, rupturing the body and projecting fragments.

Hand grenade M33. Except for release of the safety clip, functioning is the same as that for the M67.

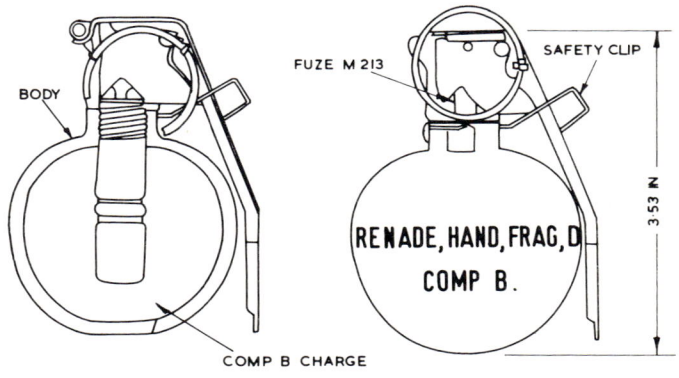

Fragmentation hand grenade M67

DATA
Grenade (with fuze):
Models: M67, M33
Body: Steel
Weight: 398g
Length (max): 89.7mm
Diameter: 63.5mm
Colour: Olive drab w/yellow markings
Packing: 1 per fibre container; 30 per packing box
Filler:
Type: Comp B
Weight: 185g
Fuze:
Model: M213
Type: Pyrotechnic delay-detonating
Primer (percussion): M42
Detonator: Lead azide, lead styphnate, and RDX
Delay time: 4,5sec
Weight: 71g
Length: 85mm
Colour, safety lever: Olive drab w/black markings
Safety devices:
Pull ring and safety pin: Grenade M33
Pull ring and safety pin, and safety clip: Grenade M67

GRENADE, HAND, FRAGMENTATION, DELAY, M61, M26A1 and M26 and M62 (and M30 PRACTICE)

Hand Grenade M61 is Hand Grenade M26A1 with a safety clip. The M26A1 is the M26 with preformed tetryl pellets around the fuze well liner. Each grenade is assembled with a fuze that initiates the explosive charge. These grenades detonate a nominal 4 to 5 seconds after release of the safety lever although it has been reported that the delay is commonly nearly twice as long as this. The Grenade, Hand, Practice, Delay, M62 and Grenade, Hand, Practice, M30 are the training models of the grenades M61/M26/M26A1. The grenade body is identical to that of the M61/M26/M26A1, and is fitted with either the M205A1 or M205A2 pyrotechnic igniting fuze. The functioning of the grenade is similar to the M61/M26/M26A1 except that the igniter initiates the black powder charge (when installed). The stopper (when installed) is forced from the base of the body. A loud report, like that of a firecracker, and a puff of white smoke follows. The grenade is painted blue with a brown band and white markings, or no markings at all. It is packed one per container, 30 per packing box. Igniters are packed in boxes of 360.

Grenade body: Bodies of the M61, M26A1 and M26 are identical. The body constructed of two pieces of thinwall sheet steel, has a notched fragmentation coil liner.

Fuzes, hand grenade, M204A1 and M204A2: Fuze M204A1 and Fuze M204A2 are pyrotechnic delay-detonating fuzes. They differ only in body construction. The body contains a primer and a pyrotechnic delay column. Assembled to the body are a striker, striker spring, safety lever, safety pin with pull ring, and a detonator assembly. The split end of the safety pin has an angular spread or diamond crimp.

Safety clip: The hand grenade safety clip is designed to keep the safety lever in place should the safety pin be unintentionally removed from the grenade. It is an additional safety device used in conjunction with the safety pin.

The safety clip, of spring steel wire, consists of a loop which fits around the fuze body and a clamp which fits over the safety lever.

Safety clips on Hand Grenades M61 and M67 are not interchangeable.

DATA (combat grenades)
Grenade (with fuze):
Models: M61, M26A1, M26
Body: Thin-wall sheet steel w/inner fragmentation coil
Weight: 454g
Length (max): 99mm

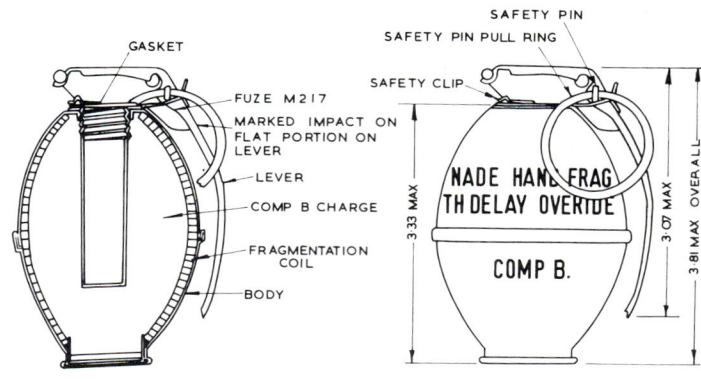

Fragmentation hand grenade M61

Diameter: 57mm
Colour: Olive drab w/yellow markings
Packing: 1 per fibre container; 30 per packing box
Filler:
Type: Comp B w/tetryl
Pellets: M61, M26A1
Comp B: M26
Weight:
M61, M26A1 Comp B: 156g
Tetryl pellets: 8g
M26 Comp B: 165g
Fuze:
Models: M204A1, M204A2
Type: Pyrotechnic delay-detonating
Primer (percussion): M42
Detonator: Lead azide, lead styphnate, and RDX
Delay time: 4 to 5sec (see text)
Weight: 73g
Length: 102mm
Colour, safety lever: Olive drab w/black markings

GRENADE HAND: FRAGMENTATION, Mk2

Hand Grenade, Mk2 is now authorised for U.S. Navy use only.

Because of its shape and the deep serrations of its body, Hand Grenade Mk2 was dubbed "pineapple". These serrations were intended to delineate fragmentation of the body when the grenade exploded; but the intention was no better realised with this than with the British 36 or F1.

Grenade body: The body is of cast iron. It contains a high-explosive filler.

Fuzes, hand grenade, M204A1 and M204A2: See description in the entry for the M61 grenade above.

Safety clip: Safety clips are not used with Hand Grenade Mk2.

The training model of the Grenade Hand: Fragmentation Mk2 is designated Grenade, Hand: Training, Mk1A1. It has identical physical characteristics to the Mk2 except that it has no filler or fuze. Unlike other training grenades the Mk1A1 does not emit smoke or noise and is non-functioning. The M1A1 is painted black and is packed in boxes of 24 grenades.

DATA
Grenade (with fuze):
Model: Mk2
Body: Cast iron
Weight: 596g
Length (maximum): 114mm
Diameter: 57mm
Colour: Olive drab, or olive drab w/yellow band around top of fuze well
Packing: 1 per fibre container; 30 per packing box
Filler:
Type: TNT (flaked or granular)
Weight: 56g

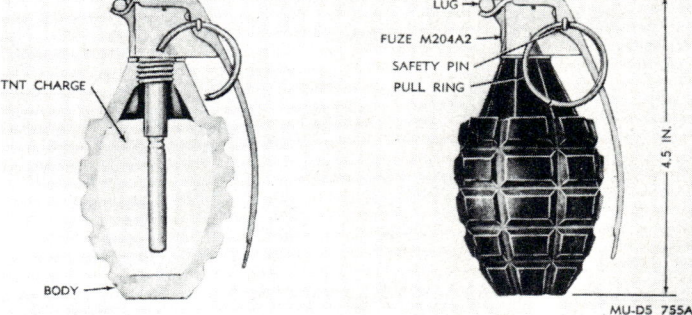

Fragmentation hand grenade Mk 2

Fuze:
Model(s): M204A1, M204A2
Type: Pyrotechnic delay-detonating
Primer: M42
Detonator: Lead azide, lead styphnate, and RDX
Delay time: 4-5 seconds (see note on M61 etc grenades)
Weight: 3g
Length: 101mm
Colour, safety lever: Olive drab w/black markings
Safety device:
Pull ring and safety pin: Grenade Mk2

GRENADE, HAND: FRAGMENTATION, IMPACT M68 and M59

Hand Grenade M68 is Hand Grenade M59 with a safety clip. Each grenade is assembled with an electrical impact fuze.

Grenade body: Bodies of the M68 and M59 are identical and are the same as those of Hand Grenades, Fragmentation, Delay, M67 and M33. The shape is essentially spherical. The body measures 2.5 inches (57mm) in diameter and contains high explosive filler.

Fuze, hand grenade, M217: Fuze M217 is equipped with a safety pin, the split end of which is either spread or has a diamond crimp, and a pull ring. **Impact** is embossed on the safety lever. (Older models had red safety levers with or without **Impact** painted thereon in black.) The major components are as follows: a bouchon assembly, a fuze body assembly (which contains a thermal power supply, an arming delay thermal switch, a delay-

detonation thermal switch assembly, an impact switch assembly and an electric detonator), and a booster pellet. The bouchon assembly consists of a striker, striker spring, striker hinge/pin, safety lever and safety pin with pull ring. The fuze body is hermetically sealed.

Safety clip: The hand grenade safety clip is designed to keep the safety lever in place, should the safety pin be unintentionally removed from the grenade. It is an additional safety device used in conjunction with the safety pin.

Clips, of spring steel wire, consist of a loop, which fits around the neck of the grenade, and a clamp, which fits over the safety lever.

The safety clips on Hand Grenades M68, M61, M67 and M57 are not interchangeable.

DATA
Grenade (with fuze):
Models: M68, M59 (M33 w/fuze M217) (M33A1)
Body: Steel
Weight: 398g
Length (maximum): 126mm
Diameter: 64mm
Colour: Olive drab w/yellow markings
Packing: 1 per fibre container; 30 per packing box
Filler:
Type: Comp B
Weight: 184g
Fuze:
Model: M217
Type: Electrical impact w/overriding delay function feature
Primer: M42
Detonator: Lead azide, lead styphnate, PETN
Delay time: 3 to 7 seconds
Weight: 169g
Length: 76.2mm
Colour, safety lever: Olive drab hand w/**Impact** embossed on lever, red lever w/ or w/o **Impact** stencilled in black on lever
Safety devices:
Pull ring and safety pin: Grenade, M59 (M33 w/Fuze M217)
Pull ring and safety pin, and safety clip: Grenade, M68
At high temperature (+125°F), arming time may be as short as 1 second;

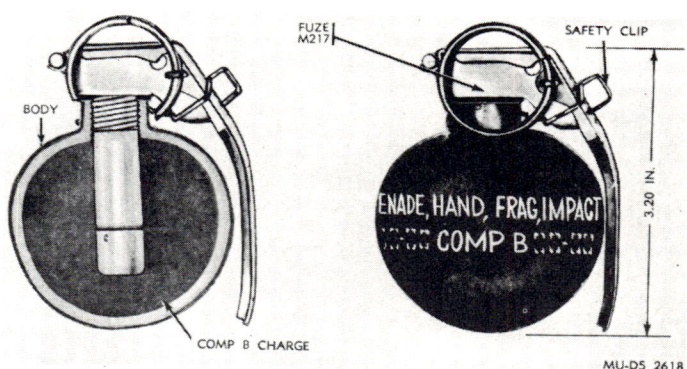

Fragmentation hand grenade M68

at low temperature (−40°F), as long as 2 seconds. The secondary pyrotechnic delay feature functions within 3 to 7 seconds throughout the temperature range of −40°F to −125°F.

If the grenade does not detonate on impact (after proper arming time), the grenade will be detonated by the secondary pyrotechnic delay feature. If the fuze fails to function after release of the safety lever, the fuze power supply will become inactive within 30 seconds.

GRENADE, HAND: FRAGMENTATION, IMPACT M57 AND M26A2

Hand Grenade M57 is Hand Grenade M26A2 with a safety clip. Each grenade is assembled with an electrical impact fuze.

Grenade body: Bodies of the M61, M26-A1 and M26 are identical to the M26A2 except the fuze threads are different. The body, constructed of two pieces of thinwall sheet steel, has a notched fragmentation coil liner. Bodies contain a high explosive filler. Bodies of the M61, M26A1 and M26 contain booster pellets and are longer and narrower than those of the M26A2 and M57. Bodies of M26A2 and M57 do not contain booster pellets.

Fuze, hand grenade, M217: See description in the entry for the M68 grenade above.

Safety clip: The hand grenade safety clip is designed to keep the safety lever in place, should the safety pin be unintentionally removed from the grenade. It is an additional safety device used in conjunction with the safety pin.

Clips, of spring steel wire, consist of a loop, which fits around the neck of the grenade, and a clamp, which fits over the safety lever.

The safety clips on Hand Grenades M68, M61, M67 and M57 are not interchangeable.

DATA
Grenade (with fuze):
Models: M57, M26A2
Body: Thin-wall sheet steel w/notched fragmentation coil
Weight: 454g
Length (maximum): 99mm
Diameter: 57mm
Colour: Olive drab w/yellow markings
Packing: 1 per fibre container; 30 per packing box
Filler type: Comp B w/tetryl pellets
Comp B weight: 156g
Tetryl pellets weight: 8g

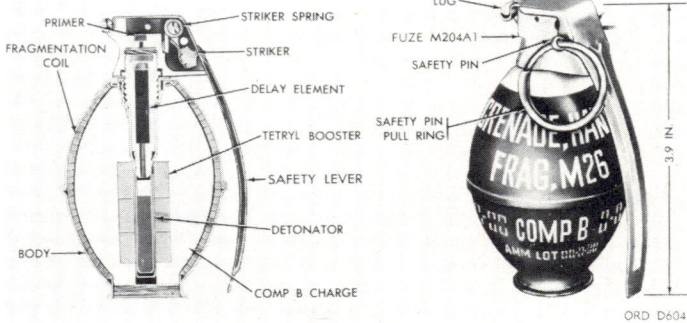

Hand grenade M26 (US Army Photograph)

Fuze:
Model: M217
Type: Electrical impact w/overriding delay function feature
Primer: M42
Detonator: Lead azide, lead styphnate PETN
Delay time: 3 to 7 seconds
Weight: 76g
Length: 76.2mm
Colour, safety lever: Red hand w/**Impact** embossed, in lever; red lever w/ or w/o **Impact** stencilled in black on lever
Safety devices:
Pull ring and safety pin: Grenade, M26A2
Pull ring and safety pin and safety clip: Grenade, M57
Arming: The note in the description of the M59 and M68 grenades applies

GRENADE, HAND: OFFENSIVE, Mk3A2

Hand Grenade Mk3A2 is the only offensive hand grenade authorised by the US Army for issue and use. It is about the same size as the fragmentation hand grenade, but has a cylindrical body made of pressed fibre. The shape of the fuze safety lever is slightly different from that of a fragmentation grenade and conforms to the shape of the body of the grenade. The Mk3A2 may be issued fuzed with or without safety clips, or unfuzed.

Grenade body: The grenade body is a cylinder made of pressed fibre and contains high explosive TNT.

Fuzes, hand grenade, M206A1 or M206A2: Fuze M206A1 and Fuze M206A2 are pyrotechnic delay-detonating fuzes. They differ only in body construction. The body contains a primer and a pyrotechnic delay column. Assembled to the body are a striker, striker spring, safety lever, safety pin and pull ring, and a detonator assembly. The split end of the safety pin has an angular spread or diamond crimp.

DATA
Grenade (with fuze):
Model: Mk3A2
Body: Asphalt-impregnated fibre
Weight: 443g
Length (maximum): 134mm
Diameter: 54mm
Colour: Black w/yellow markings
Packing: 1 per carton; 20 cartons per wooden box
Filler:
Type: TNT (flaked)

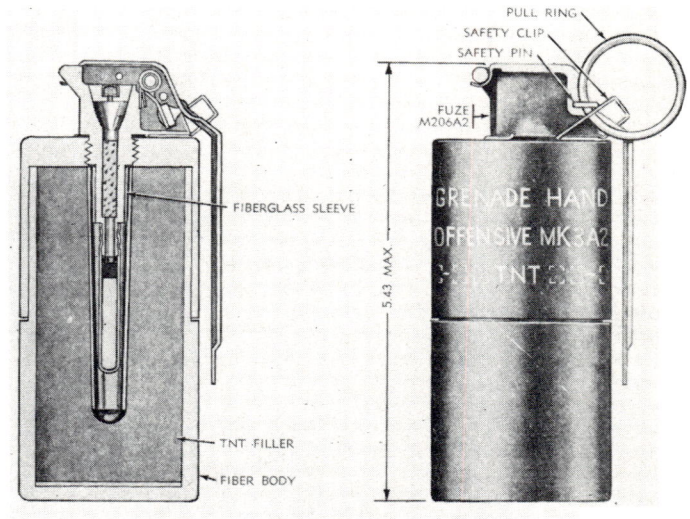

Offensive hand grenade Mk 3A2

Weight: 227g
Fuze:
Model: M206A2
Type: Pyrotechnic delay-detonating
Primer: M42
Detonator: Lead azide, lead styphnate, and RDX
Delay time: 4-5 seconds

Weight: 73g
Length: 109mm
Colour: Olive drab w/black markings
Packing: 25 per carton; 8 cartons per wooden box
Safety devices*: Pull ring and safety pin: Fuzed grenades
Pull ring and safety pin, and safety clip: Fuzed grenades
*Unfuzed grenades have no safety devices

GRENADE, HAND: ILLUMINATING, Mk1

Hand Grenade Mk1, is the only illuminating hand grenade authorised by the US Army for issue and use. In outward appearance, the Mk1 resembles fragmentation hand grenades of the M26 series.

Grenade body: The body is made in two pieces. The illuminating charge is pressed into the lower half of the body and covered with a layer of first-fire composition. This, in turn, is covered with an igniter charge.

Fuze: The fuze is an integral part of the grenade. The body contains a primer and quickmatch bushing. Assembled to the body of the fuze are a striker, striker spring, safety lever, and safety pin with pull ring. The split end of the safety pin has an angular spread

Safety clips: Safety clips are not required with illuminating hand grenades.

DATA
Grenade (with fuze):
Model: M7, M7A1
Body: Sheet metal
Weight: (M7) 482g; (M7A1) 525g
Length: 145mm
Diameter: 63.5mm
Colour: Grey w/1 red band and red markings
Packing: 1 per container; 16 per packing box
Filler:
Type: CN–Pyrotechnic composition
Weight: (M7) 291g (M7A1) 355g
Fuze:

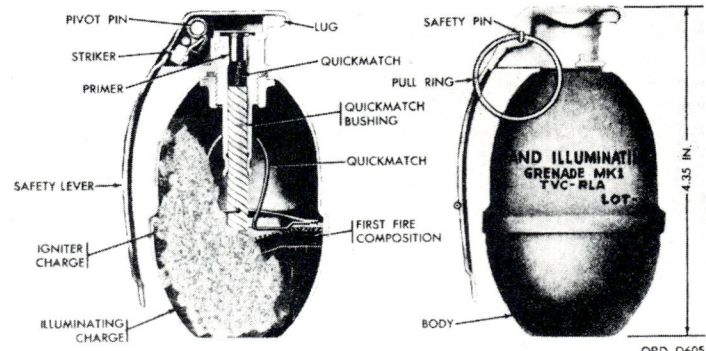

Illuminating hand grenade Mk1

Model: M201A1
Type: Pyrotechnic delay-igniting
Primer: M39A1
Ignition mixture: Iron oxide, titanium, zirconium
Delay time: 0.7–2sec
Weight: 42g
Length: 99mm
Colour: Grey or olive drab w/black markings
Safety device: Pull ring and safety pin

GRENADE, HAND: SMOKE, HC, AN-M8

HC Smoke Hand Grenade AN-M8 is a burning type grenade used to generate white smoke for screening activities of small units. It is also used for ground-to-air signalling. The duration of smoke screen or signal is 105 to 150 seconds.

Grenade body: The grenade body is a cylinder of thin sheet metal. It is filled with HC smoke mixture topped with a starter mixture directly under the fuse opening.

Fuze hand grenade, M201A1: Fuze M201A1 is a pyrotechnic delay-igniting fuze. The body contains a primer, first-fire mixture, pyrotechnic delay column, and ignition mixture. Assembled to the body are a striker, striker spring, safety lever and safety pin with pull ring. The split end of the safety pin has an angular spread.

Safety clips: Safety clips are not required with these grenades.

DATA
Grenade (with fuze):
Model: AN-M8
Body: Sheet metal
Weight: 681g
Length: 145mm
Diameter: 63.5mm
Colour: Light green w/black markings
Packing: 1 per container; 16 per packing box
Filler:
Type: HC (type C)
Weight: 539g
Fuze:
Model: M201A1
Type: Pyrotechnic delay-igniting
Primer: M39A1

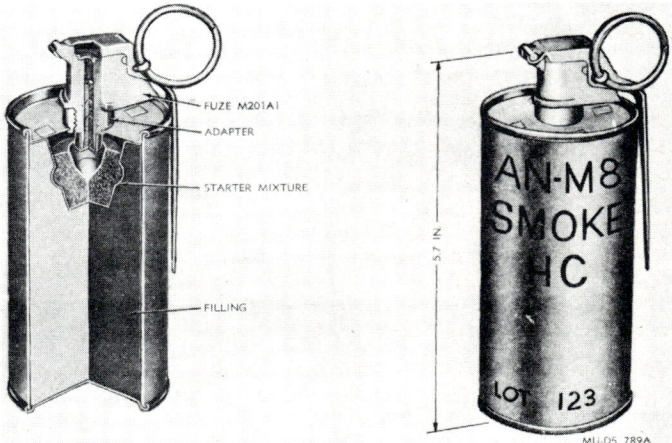

HC smoke hand grenade AN-M8

Ignition mixture: Iron oxide, titanium, zirconium
Delay time: 0.7 – 2 sec
Weight: 43g
Length: 99mm
Colour (safety lever): Grey or olive drab w/black markings
Safety device: Pull ring and safety pin
Function: Similar to M7A1

GRENADE, HAND: INCENDIARY, TH3, AN-M14

TH3 Incendiary Hand Grenade AN-M14 is used primarily to provide a source for intense heat to destroy equipment. It generates heat to 2,200 deg C. The grenade filler will burn from 30 to 45 seconds. This was developed by the Chemical Warfare Service in response to a military requirement for a hand held incendiary device that would allow the individual soldier to destroy equipment. Over 800,000 M14's were built, with final deliveries by Ordnance Products Incorporated in 1970. The grenade is normally hand thrown, although it may be rifle launched by using a special M2 series projection adapter.

Grenade body: The grenade body, of thin sheet metal, is cylindrical in shape. It is filled with an incendiary mixture, Thermite TH3 and First Fire Mixture VII.

Fuze, hand grenade, M201A1: See description in the entry for the AN-M8 grenade above.

Safety clips: Safety clips are not required with these grenades.

DATA
Grenade (with fuze):
Model: AN-M14
Body: Sheet metal
Weight: 909g
Length: 145mm
Diameter: 63.5mm
Colour: Light red w/black markings
Packing: 1 per container; 16 per packing box
Filler:
Type: Igniter mixture III, delay mixture V, FF mixture VII, incendiary mixture, Thermite, TH3, and Thermite, plain
Weight: 752g
Fuze:
Model: M201A1

Type: Pyrotechnic delay-igniting
Primer: M39A1
Ignition mixture: Iron oxide, titanium, zirconium
Delay time: 0.7-2 seconds
Weight: 42g
Length: 99mm
Colour: Grey or olive drab w/black markings
Safety device: Pull ring and safety pin

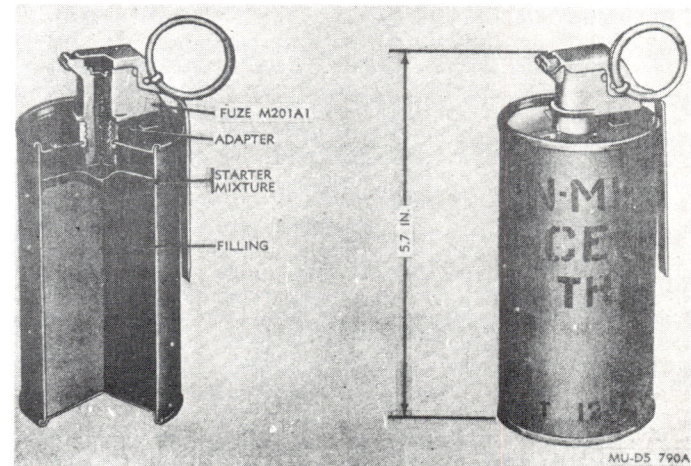

TH3 incendiary hand grenade AN-M14

GRENADE, HAND: SMOKE, WP, M15

WP Smoke Grenade M15 is a bursting type grenade used for signalling, screening and incendiary purposes. The screening effect of the smoke is limited because WP (White Phosphorus) burns with such intense heat that the smoke tends to rise rapidly. Pieces of WP will burn for about 60 seconds, igniting any flammable substance contacted. Since WP burns the flesh, it is effective against personnel. The effective casualty radius is 15 metres (49.2 feet).

Grenade body: The grenade body, of sheet steel, is cylindrical in shape. The body has a fuze liner and is filled with WP.

Fuze, hand grenade, M206A1 and M206A2: See description in entry for Mk 3A2 offensive grenade above.

Safety clips: Safety clips are not required with these grenades.

DATA
Grenade (with fuze):
Model: M15
Body: Sheet metal
Weight: 880g
Length (maximum): 114mm
Diameter: 60mm
Colour: Grey w/1 yellow band and yellow markings
Packing: 1 per container; 16 per packing box
Filler: WP 425g
Fuze:
Models: M206A1, M206A2
Type: Pyrotechnic delay-detonating
Primer: M42

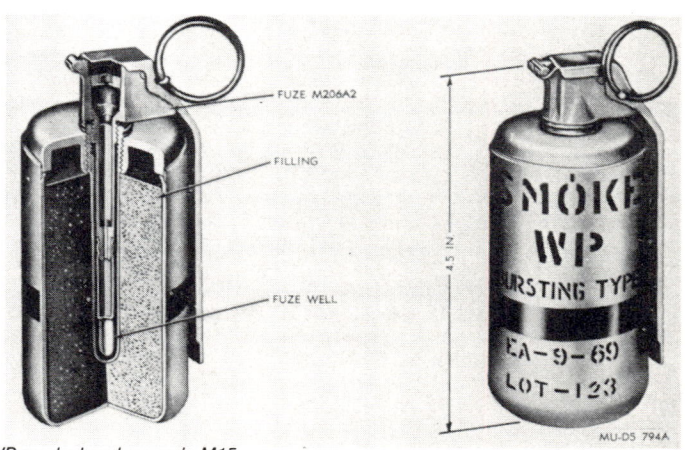

WP smoke hand grenade M15

Detonator: Lead azide, Lead styphnate, RDX
Delay time: 4-5 seconds
Weight: 73g
Length: 109mm
Colour: Olive drab w/black markings
Safety device: Pull ring and safety pin

GRENADE, HAND-RIFLE, SMOKE, WP, M34

Hand-Rifle Grenade M34 is used for signalling, screening and incendiary purposes. The screening effect of the smoke is limited because WP (White Phosphorus) burns with such intense heat that the smoke tends to rise rapidly. Pieces of WP will burn for about 60 seconds, igniting any flammable substance contacted. Since WP burns the flesh, it is effective against personnel. The effective casualty radius is 25 metres (82ft). It is normally thrown but can also be used as a rifle grenade with the M1A2 adapter.

Grenade body: The grenade body, of serrated steel, is cylindrical in shape. The serrations assure body breakup. The body has a fuze well liner and is filled with WP.

Fuze, hand grenade, M206A2: Fuze M206A2 is a pyrotechnic delay-detonating fuze. The body contains a primer and a pyrotechnic delay column. Assembled to the body are a striker, striker spring, safety lever, safety pin with pulling ring, safety clip and a detonator. (Older models do not have the safety clip). The split end of the safety pin has an angular spread or a diamond crimp.

DATA
Grenade (with fuze):
Model: M34
Body: Steel
Weight: 681g
Length: 132mm
Diameter: 60mm
Colour: Light green w/1 yellow band; light red markings
Packing: 1 per can; 16 cans per packing box
Filler: WP 426g
Fuze:
Model: M206A2
Type: Pyrotechnic delay detonating
Primer: M42
Detonator mixture: Lead azide, Lead styphnate and RDX
Delay time: 4 to 5 seconds

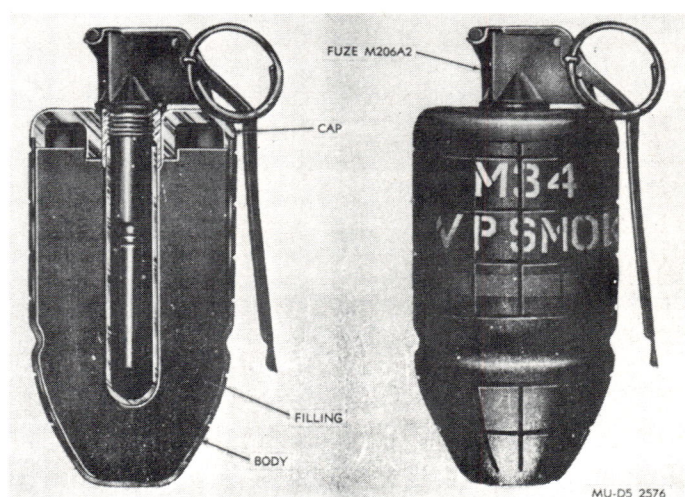

WP smoke hand-rifle grenade M34

Weight: 74g
Length: 109mm
Colour: Olive drab w/black markings
Safety device: Pull ring and safety pin (older models). Pull ring, safety pin, safety clip (newer models)

GRENADE, RIFLE: HEAT, M31

This rifle grenade is a point-initiated, base-detonated (PIBD), high-explosive, anti-tank (HEAT) grenade. It employs a shaped charge to defeat armour plate or concrete, and will function against targets at all angles of obliquity up to 65 degrees. The grenade uses a piezoelectric assembly which generates an electric current when crushed on impact with the target. This action initiates the explosive train. Only Rifle Grenades M31, which are assembled with modified nose assembly have a positive ground between the piezoelectric crystal and the metal nose protector cap.

General: Rifle Grenade M31 consist of three basic parts; the cylindrical body with conical ogive and conical rear section; the fuze; and the stabiliser. The ogive contains a piezoelectric assembly in the nose. A lead wire (in conduit) connects this assembly to the fuze, in the base of the body. The body contains Comp B moulded against a copper shaped charge liner. A booster is contained in the fuze at the base of the body. Fuze M211 consists of a base, spring-driven detonator rotor and a cover. The detonator rotor contains an electric detonator. The base contains a setback leaf assembly. The cover contains a booster pellet. The aluminium stabiliser consists of a stabiliser tube, with an adapter at its forward end (for connection to the body), and a fin assembly at the other end. When assembled, the fuze is held within the adapter.

OPERATION

An inertia-actuated setback leaf assembly prevents alignment of the detonator with the booster in the fuze until the rifle grenade is launched. Prior to arming, the detonating circuit within the fuze is grounded. Thus, current cannot pass through the detonating circuit, and current from an accidentally crushed or stressed crystal is short circuited to the body of the grenade. The detonating switch is contained within a small rotor which is locked into the short-circuit position by a setback leaf assembly. When the grenade is launched, the setback leaf assembly releases the rotor. The rotor turns 90 degrees, opening the shorting switch and closing the firing switch. Upon launching, the grenade functions as follows:

(1) Inertia setback causes the first of the three setback leaves in the setback leaf assembly to overcome the tension of its spring. This releases the second leaf.

(2) The second leaf rotates, releasing the third leaf.

(3) The third leaf rotates, releasing a rotor assembly containing the firing circuit.

(4) The rotor assembly turns 90 degrees to close the firing circuit, thus arming the grenade.

(5) Upon impact with the target the crystal is crushed and generates an electrical impulse.

(6) The electrical impulse is conducted through a lead wire in the conduit to the electric fuze.

(7) The electrical impulse passes through a resistance wire in the detonator, initiating the explosive train.

(8) The detonator detonates the booster and, in turn, the shaped charge.

(9) The principal explosive force of the shaped charge is directed forward to penetrate the target.

DATA
Model: M31
Type: HEAT

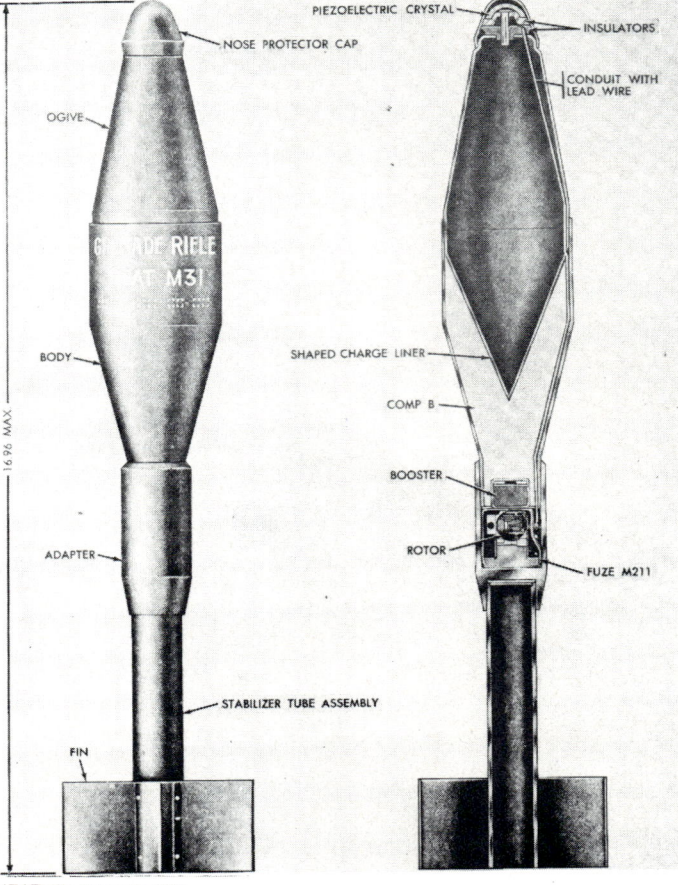

HEAT rifle grenade M31

Weight (as issued): 709g
Explosive charge: (COMP B) 254g
Diameter: 56mm
Height: 430mm
Body: Steel
Fuze: M211
Type: PIBD
Colour: Olive drab w/yellow marking
Packing: 1 per container; 10 containers per packing box with 20 grenade cartridges M3

GRENADE, RIFLE: SMOKE, WP, M19A1

WP Smoke Rifle Grenade M19A1 is filled with WP (White Phosphorus). This chemical agent ignites spontaneously when exposed to air, producing a yellow-white flame and giving off a dense cloud of white smoke. When used as an antipersonnel weapon, Grenade M19A1 has an effective casualty radius of 10 metres. Grenade M19A1 has a maximum range of approximately 195 metres.

WP Smoke Rifle Grenade M19A1 consists of three basic parts: a steel stabilizer tube assembly, an integral fuze and a body. After the grenade is launched, the fuze functions on impact. It bursts the body and scatters particles of burning WP over a large area.

Grenade and fuze function as follows:
(1) The grenade ogive strikes the ground or other resistant object.
(2) Inertia of the firing pin overcomes spring tension and the firing pin strikes the primer.
(3) The primer emits a small, intense spit of flame.
(4) Flame from the primer explodes the detonator.
(5) Explosion of the detonator ruptures the body. Fragments of the body and particles of WP scatter over an area with a radius of approximately 10 metres.

(6) Particles of WP ignite upon coming into contact with air and produce a dense cloud of white smoke.

DATA
Model: M19A1
Type: Smoke (WP)
Weight: 681g
Diameter: 51mm
Height: 287mm
Charge (WP): 241g
Body: Sheet steel
Fuze: Integral
Type: Mechanical impact detonating
Colour: Light green w/yellow band; red marking
Packing: 1 per container; 10 containers per packing box

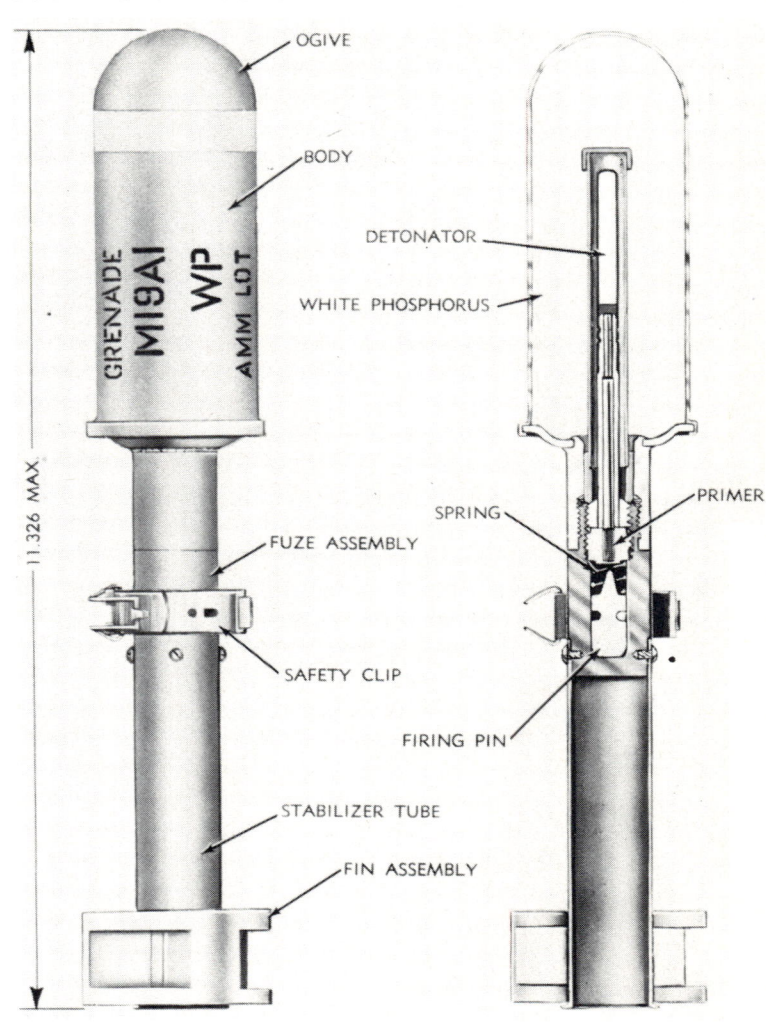

OGIVE

BODY

DETONATOR

WHITE PHOSPHORUS

GRENADE M19AI WP AMM LOT

11.326 MAX

SPRING

PRIMER

FUZE ASSEMBLY

FIRING PIN

SAFETY CLIP

STABILIZER TUBE

FIN ASSEMBLY

WP smoke rifle grenade M19A1 (US Army Photograph)

GRENADES, RIFLE: SMOKE, GREEN, RED, VIOLET OR YELLOW, M22 and M22A2

Coloured Smoke Rifle Grenades M22 and M22A2 are launched from a rifle. These grenades, used only for signalling and for laying smoke screens, produce green, red, violet or yellow smoke. The M22 and the M22A2 differ only in minor features. Both have a range of over 200 metres.

The two grenades resemble WP Smoke Rifle Grenade M19A1 but are somewhat smaller. The M22 and M22A2 consist of three basic parts: a steel stabiliser assembly, an integral fuze and a body. The fuze is a mechanical impact-igniting type. The body is filled with a burning-type smoke charge which contains a dye to colour the smoke. The surfaces of the smoke charge within the body are coated with a starter mixture charge to facilitate ignition. A small opening or air hole in the nose of the ogive is covered by a nose closing plug.

OPERATION

Coloured Smoke Rifle Grenades M22 and M22A2 function on impact, emitting a cloud of coloured smoke for approximately one minute.

DATA

Models: M22 or M22A2
Type: Smoke (coloured)
Weight: 572g
Diameter: 45mm
Height: 272mm
Charge: A mixture of baking soda, potassium perchlorate, sugar and a dye to colour the smoke
Weight of charge: 336g
Body: Sheet steel
Fuze: Integral
Type: Mechanical impact igniting
Colour: Light green w/colour of smoke produced painted on body union; black marking
Packing: 1 per container; 10 containers per packing box
Function: Similar to M19A1 but primer ignites starter mixture charge and case is not ruptured. Smoke is emitted through holes in the base.

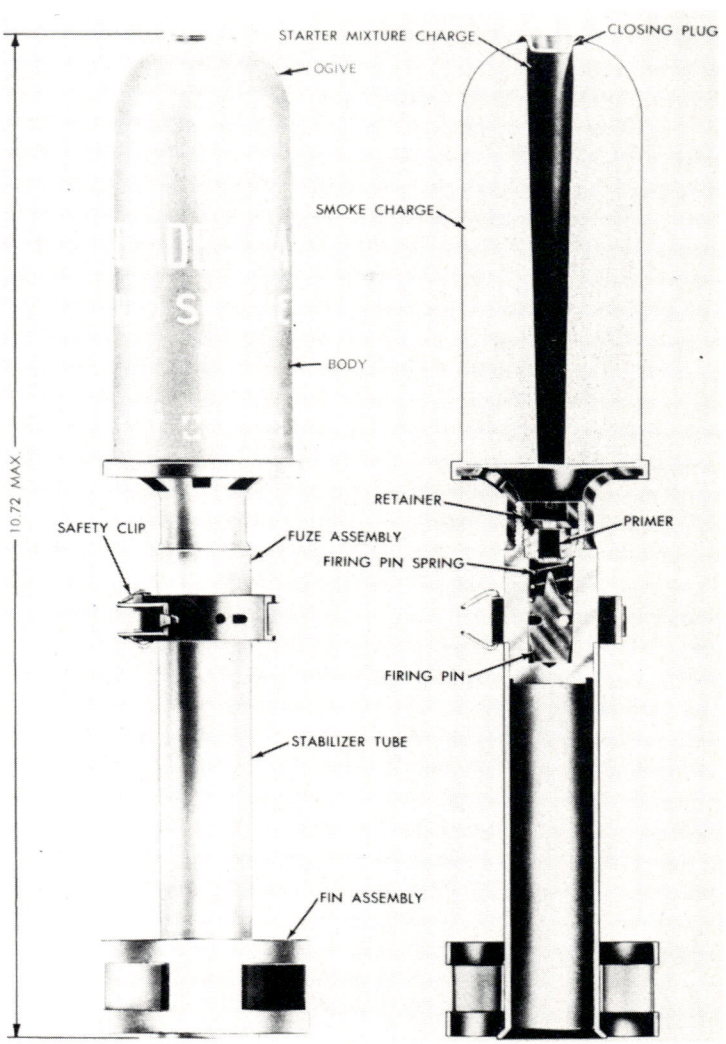

STARTER MIXTURE CHARGE

CLOSING PLUG

OGIVE

SMOKE CHARGE

U S

BODY

10.72 MAX

RETAINER

PRIMER

SAFETY CLIP

FUZE ASSEMBLY

FIRING PIN SPRING

FIRING PIN

STABILIZER TUBE

FIN ASSEMBLY

Coloured smoke rifle grenade M22A2 (US Army Photograph)

GRENADES, RIFLE: SMOKE, GREEN, RED, VIOLET OR YELLOW, STREAMER, M23 AND M23A1

Coloured Smoke Streamer Rifle Grenades M23 and M23A1 are projected from a rifle assembled with a grenade launcher, using a grenade cartridge. These grenades, used only for signalling purposes, produce green, red, violet or yellow smoke streamers. The M23 and M23A1 differ only in minor features and both have a range of over 200 metres.

The grenades are fabricated from the same metal parts (except for the fuze) as Coloured Smoke Rifle Grenades M22 and M22A2. The M23 and M23A1 consist of three basic parts: a steel stabiliser tube assembly, a fuze and a body. The body is filled with a burning-type smoke charge which contains a dye to colour the smoke. The surfaces of the smoke charge within the body are coated with a starter mixture charge (to facilitate ignition). A small air hole opening in the nose of the ogive is covered by a piece of tape (to protect the filler against moisture). The tape must be removed prior to firing.

OPERATION

Coloured Smoke Streamer Rifle Grenades M23 and M23A1 function on firing, emitting a steam of coloured smoke over the entire trajectory. Upon firing the grenade cartridge in the rifle, these grenades are launched and function as follows:

(1) Flash from the grenade cartridge passes from the rifle through orifices launched in the fuze to ignite the igniting charge in the fuze.
(2) The igniting charge ignites the starter mixture charge.
(3) The starter mixture charge ignites the smoke charge.
(4) The smoke charge begins to burn, generating coloured smoke.
(5) Air entering the air hole in the nose of the grenade forces smoke out of holes in the base of the body, producing streamers of coloured smoke.
(6) The smoke charge continues to burn, producing smoke over the entire trajectory of the grenade, and for a few seconds after striking the ground. (Total burning time approximately 12 seconds).

DATA

Models: M23, M23A1
Type: Coloured smoke streamer
Weight: 527g
Diameter: 45mm
Height: 251mm
Charge: A mixture of baking soda, potassium perchlorate, sugar and a dye to colour the smoke 182g
Body: Sheet steel
Fuze: Integral
Type: Igniting
Colour: Light green w/colour of smoke produced painted on body union; black marking
Packing: 1 per container; 10 containers per packing box

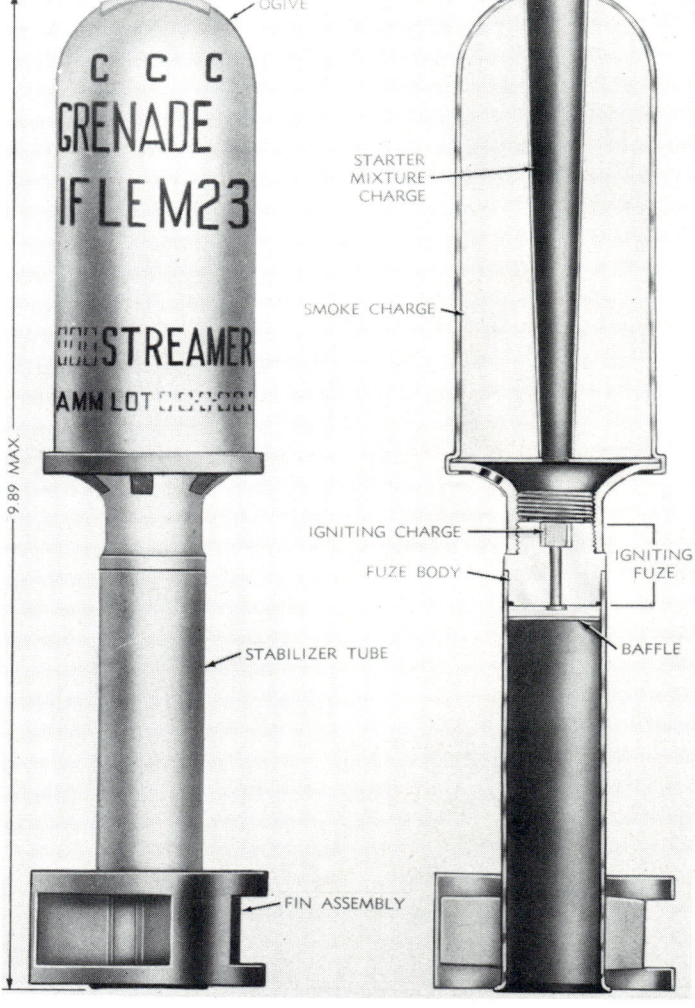

Coloured smoke rifle grenade M22A2 (US Army Photograph)

GRENADE, RIFLE: AT, PRACTICE, M29

Practice AT Rifle Grenade M29 has no filler or fuze. It may be fired at a target without danger to the target other than from impact and may be used repeatedly if the stabiliser tube fin assembly is replaced when it becomes damaged. It has a maximum range of approximately 150 metres.

The grenade consists of two parts: a body and a stabiliser tube-fin assembly of steel. A separately issued stabiliser tube-fin assembly is available for replacement purposes.

DATA

Model: M29
Type: Practice AT
Weight: 681g
Diameter: 76mm
Height: 368mm
Charge: None
Body: Cast iron
Fuze: None
Colour: Black w/white markings or blue w/white markings

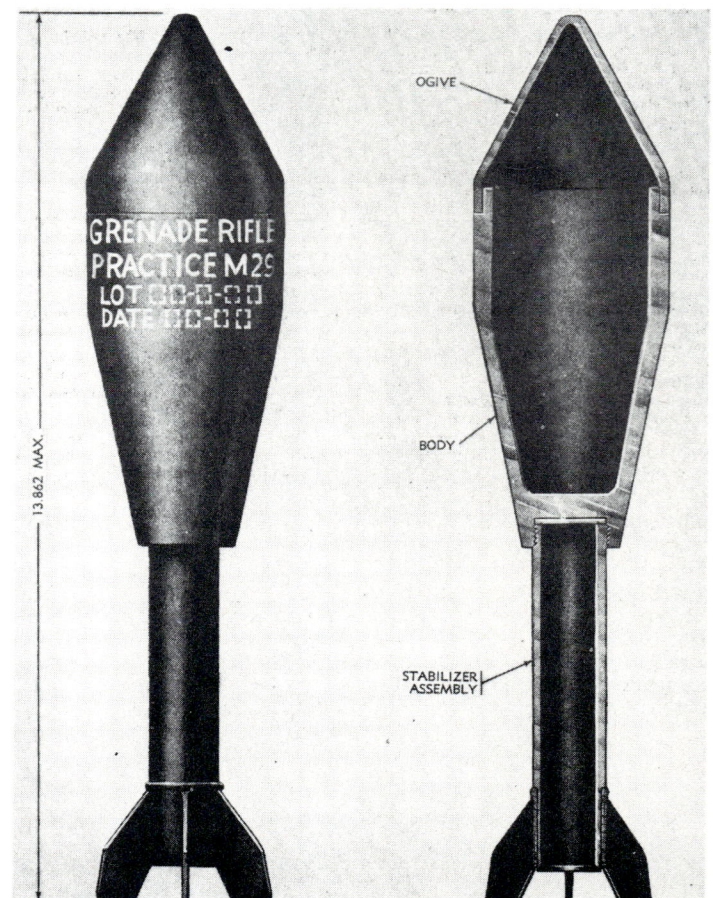

Practice AT rifle grenade M29

40mm GRENADE CARTRIDGES

There is a wide range of 40mm grenade cartridges suitable for use with M79, M203 and XM174 grenade launchers. The 40mm cartridge is a fixed munition consisting of a cartridge case and a projectile.

The cartridge case is made of aluminium and has an integral propellant retainer into which is inserted a thin-walled brass cup, containing the propellant, followed by an aluminium base plug which seals the base of the cartridge case. This arrangement is the basis of the high-low propulsion system required to propel a 40mm projectile from a shoulder-fired weapon. When the firing pin strikes the cartridge primer the propellant in the brass powder cup is ignited and generates a pressure in the region of

2,500kg/cm². This causes the brass case to rupture at a ring of vent holes in the propellant retainer, allowing gas to flow into the remainder of the cartridge case which thus forms a low pressure chamber (around 200kg/cm²). This pressure is adequate to propel the projectile and does not produce excessive recoil. The grenade leaves the launcher with a muzzle velocity of 76 metres/second and is spin stabilised by the launcher rifling. The spin also provides the rotational force necessary to arm the fuze.

Grenades known to be in the series are listed below and it will be seen that they include high-explosive, riot control, practice and a variety of smoke, signalling and illuminating types.

40mm Cartridges   Colour Identification

Cartridge	Body	Ogive*	Lettering
40mm, HE M381 and M406	Green	Gold	Yellow
40mm, HE M386 and M441	Green	Gold	Yellow
40mm, HE M463 (smokeless, flashless)	Green	Black	Yellow
40mm, HE M397 (airburst)**	Green	Gold	Yellow
40mm, HE M433 (dual purpose)**	Green	Gold	Yellow
40mm, practice, M382 and M407A1	Green	Silver	Yellow
40mm, multiple projectile, M576E1	Green	Black (SABOT)	White
40mm, multiple projectile, M576E2	Green	None	White
40mm, green smoke parachute, XM658	Green	Green	Black
40mm, white star parachute, M583	White	White	Black
40mm, red smoke parachute, XM659	Green	Red	Black
40mm, white star cluster, M585	White	White	Black
40mm, yellow smoke parachute, XM660	Green	Yellow	Black
40mm, violet smoke parachute, XM669	Green	Violet	Black
40mm, tactical CS, XM651E1	Green	Grey	Black
40mm, yellow smoke streamer, XM696	Green	Yellow	Black
40mm, green star parachute, XM661	White	Green	Black
40mm, green smoke streamer, XM697	Green	Green	Black
40mm, red star parachute, XM662	White	Red	Black
40mm, orange smoke streamer, XM698	Green	Orange	Black
40mm, green star cluster, XM663	White	Green	Black
40mm, red smoke streamer, XM699	Green	Red	Black
40mm, red star cluster, XM664	White	Red	Black
40mm, brown smoke streamer, XM700	Green	Brown	Black
40mm, yellow smoke canopy, XM676	Green	Yellow	Black
40mm, violet smoke streamer, XM701	Green	Violet	Black
40mm, green smoke canopy, XM679	Green	Green	Black
40mm, white smoke canopy, XM680	Green	White	Black
40mm, violet smoke canopy, XM681	Green	Violet	Black
40mm, red smoke canopy, XM682	Green	Red	Black
40mm, riot control CS, XM674 (E24)***	Grey	N/A	Black
40mm, riot control CS, XM675 (E25 RS)***	Light Green	N/A	Black
40mm, orange star parachute, XM695	White	Orange	Black

*The ogive is the nose end of the cartridge.
**The M397 (airburst) and M433 HE DP cartridges are ⁵⁄₃₂in longer than the standard cartridges.
***Not authorised for use with M203 grenade launcher.

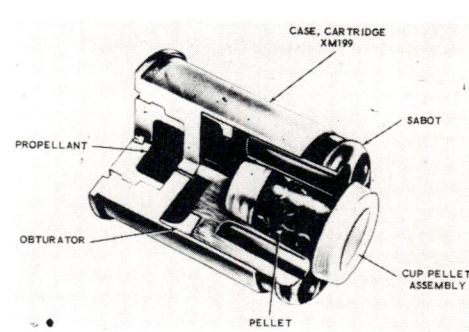

40mm, multiple projectile, XM576E1 cartridge (US Army Photograph)

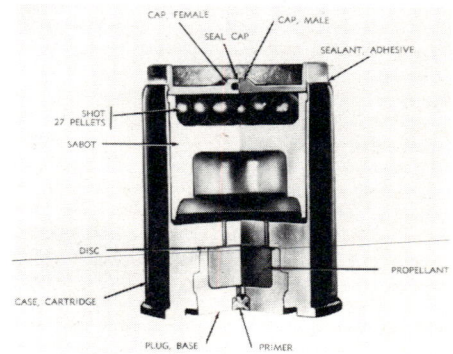

40mm, multiple projectile, XM576E2 cartridge (US Army Photograph)

IDENTIFICATION

The HE (M406), HE (M463) and TP (M407A1) are identical in size and shape. However, the weight of the M463 is slightly greater than the M406 or the M407A1. There are two notches on the rim of the M463 to identify it during the hours of limited visiblity. The appearance of the HE airburst round differs from the M406, M463 and M407A1, in that the skirt is longer and the ogive is smaller. However, the size and weight of the HE airburst and the HE (M433) dual purpose round are almost identical. The M406, M433 and M397 have gold coloured ogives, while the M407A1 has a silver coloured ogive and the M463 has a black coloured ogive.

FUZES

The M552 and M551 impact detonating fuzes are used with the HE and the TP rounds. The M552 fuze arms by a spin action and is armed about 3 metres from the muzzle. The M551 fuze arms by a spin and setback action and must travel between 14 and 28 metres before being armed. The HE airburst round is equipped with the M536 fuze that incorporates the same spin and setback action as well as the same arming distance as the M551

fuze. Upon impact the fuze ignites a separation charge assembly which ejects a grenade into the air. At a height of about 5 feet the grenade explodes into fragments.

EFFECTIVE CASUALTY RADIUS

The high explosive grenade has an effective casualty radius of 5 metres. The effective casualty radius is defined as the radius of a circle about the point of detonation in which it may be expected that 50 per cent of exposed troops will become casualties.

COMBAT LOAD

The recommended minimum combat load is 36 rounds of HE 40mm ammuntiion.

PACKING

All HE and TP ammunition is packed in wooden boxes containing 12 bandoliers of 6 rounds each for a total of 72 rounds.

A 40mm cartridge case and projectile

40mm HE M381 or HE M406 cartridge, and the 40mm, practice, M382 or, practice, M407A1 cartridge (US Army Photograph)

RING AEROFOIL GRENADE (RAG)

The experience of the Vietnam campaign showed that there was a need for a shoulder fired grenade that would have a relatively flat trajectory, thus reducing foliage interference when firing at extended ranges under the dense overhead canopy of trees encountered in many South East Asian countries. It was not possible to increase the muzzle velocity of the grenade launcher and still retain a shoulder fired weapon due to the greatly increased recoil forces produced on the firer's shoulder. It appeared therefore that some aerodynamic means was required to offset the gravity drop and obtain a flatter trajectory without any appreciable increase in launch velocity. This required introducing a lift force to overcome gravity drop.

The characteristics of the ring aerofoil have been studied by aeronautical engineers in the past and it was known that ring aerofoil shapes of a high aspect ratio had good lift to drag charactertistics and a series of such aerofoil rings was produced and tested. These tests were sufficiently favourable to lead on to the design of warheads. The basic concept was an outside pre-fragmented surface a of a heavily cambered aerofoil section and an inner surface with the high explosive sandwiched between. This allowed a good charge to mass ratio.

The first practical tests of the RAG were designed to test the lethality and fragment pattern of the grenade and to compare them with those of the 40mm M406 Grenade, which was at that time the only store with which comparison could be made.

Three sizes of RAG were fabricated and tested. These had outside diameters of 2, 2.5 and 2.75 inches (51, 63.5 and 70mm)and each had the outer wall based on the pre-fragmented wire size of the M406 grenade. It was discovered that the 2.5 inch RAG with an aerofoil thickness of 0.4 inch (10mm), although it gave a reduced charge to mass ratio when compared to the M406 grenade, gave an equal number of fragments in the target area and these had an initial launch velocity equal to those of the M406 ie about 790m/sec. To obtain the required flight characteristics the RAG had to be spun and tests showed that it could be sabot launched at the required spin rate and velocity with a charge weight no different to that of the M406 Grenade.

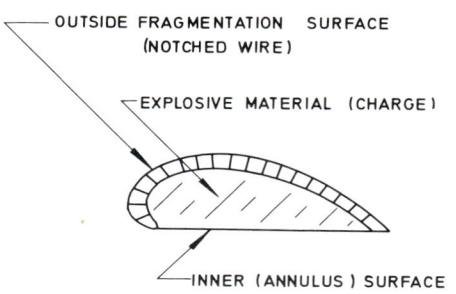

OUTSIDE FRAGMENTATION SURFACE (NOTCHED WIRE)

EXPLOSIVE MATERIAL (CHARGE)

INNER (ANNULUS) SURFACE

Basic warhead design

The RAG described above was known by its inventor, Mr Flatau, as RAG(B) and the following table lists its trajectory characteristics.

DATA
Projectile weight: 91g
Launch velocity: 137m/sec

Range (Metres)	Launch angle (Degrees)	Time of Flight (Sec)	Lateral Deflection (Metres)
100	.0	0.7	.0
200	0.6	1.5	0.4
300	0.9	2.4	1.1
400	1.2	3.2	2.5
600	1.5	5.0	6.7
800	1.8	7.0	13.4
1000	2.0	9.2	23.0

An illustration of the arrangement of the RAG and a comparison of its size with that of th M406 grenade is shown.

Further work on the RAG has led to the production of other fragmenting types and also designs for riot control.

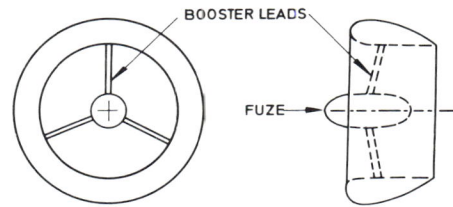

BOOSTER LEADS

FUZE

Intial fuze concept

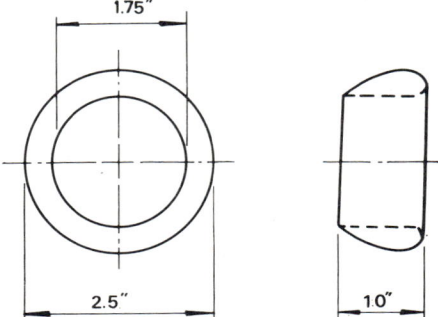

1.75″

2.5″

1.0″

RAG initial arena test series

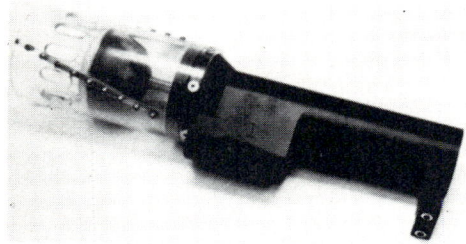

RAG grenade in launcher. This is the anti-riot weapon

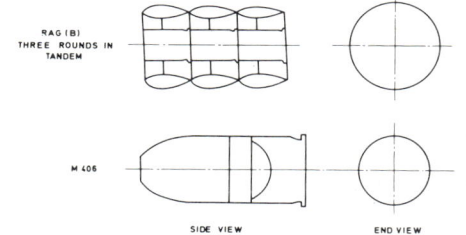

RAG (B) THREE ROUNDS IN TANDEM

M 406

SIDE VIEW   END VIEW

Size comparison of RAG (B) and M406

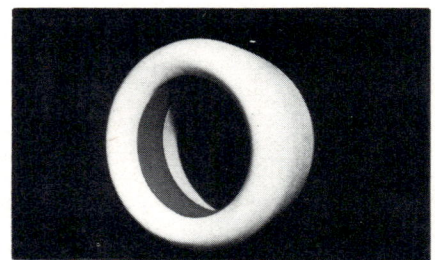

Soft RAG anti-riot grenade

VIETNAM

VIETNAMESE GRENADES

The North Vietnamese Army used a large variety of Chinese and Soviet hand grenades. Among the latter were the RPG-43, RPG-6, RG-42, F1, RPG-40 and the RDG-33. In addition many types of grenade of local design and manufacture were encountered in South Vietnam. Now that the conflict is over there will no doubt be some standardisation on Soviet and Chinese hand grenades, and local manufacture will be phased out. In addition the Vietnamese now hold large stocks of current American hand grenades as well as large quantities of the M79 Grenade Launcher.

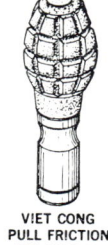

VIET CONG PULL FRICTION DELAY FUZE

U.S. MK2 STRIKER RELEASE DELAY FUZE

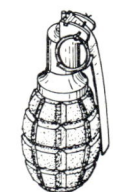

VIET CONG STRIKER RELEASE DELAY FUZE

BRITISH MILLS BOMB NO. 36M STRIKER RELEASE DELAY FUZE

VIET CONG PULL FRICTION DELAY DELAY FUZE

VIET CONG STRIKER RELEASE DELAY FUZE

VIET CONG STRIKER RELEASE DELAY FUZE

VIET CONG STRIKER RELEASE DELAY FUZE

VIET CONG STRIKER RELEASE DELAY FUZE

Some types of grenade used by Viet Cong forces

YUGOSLAVIA

YUGOSLAVIAN GRENADES

Yugoslavia uses both hand and rifle grenades. The hand grenades are egg shaped and they are basically of the same design. The earliest ones had an impact fuze but the later ones are all fitted with delay fuzes. Typical of the series is the M69 which weighs 600g and has a 4.5 second delay fuze.

The older M52R grenade is also still in service. There is also a stick smoke grenade which weighs 600g and emits smoke for up to two minutes.

The Mecar Energa rifle grenade was used in Yugoslavia for several years and was launched from a spigot attached to the muzzle of the M48 Rifle, which was bolt operated.

The M59/66 semi automatic rifle is now used to project the new grenades which were developed in the country. The Yugoslav M64 assault rifle, which is equipped with a grenade sight, takes a grenade launcher when the compensator is removed. Erecting the grenade sight automatically cuts off the gas supply to the piston. There are four Yugoslav rifle grenades, all of which are characterised by their rather small diameters. In addition to the anti-tank and anti-personnel grenades, there is an illuminating and a smoke grenade. The smoke grenade is 330.5mm in length and 40mm in diameter. It generates smoke for 90 seconds.

DATA

	A-Tk	A-Pers
Weight, fuzed:	0.602kg	0.52kg
Length:	390mm	307mm
Diameter:	60mm	30mm
Weight of HE:	235g	67g
Fuze type:	Impact	Impact
Max. range:	150metres	400metres
Effect range:		20-50metres
Penetration:	200mm	—

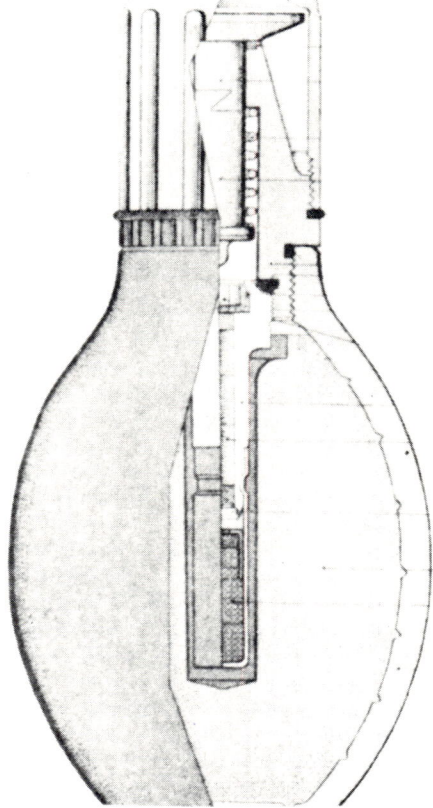

The Yugoslavian M69 anti-personnel hand grenade

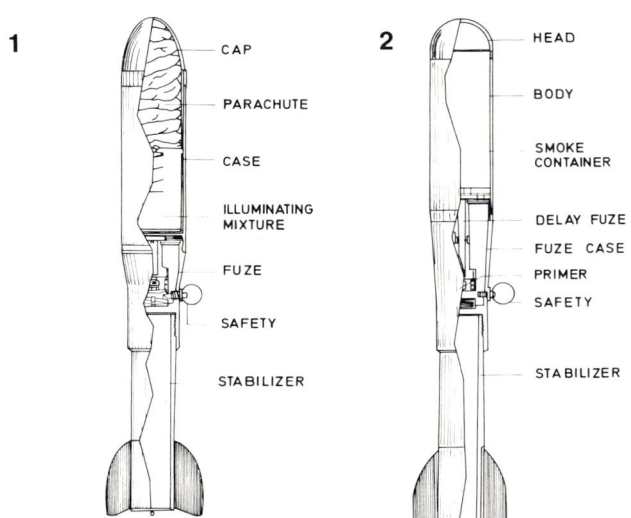
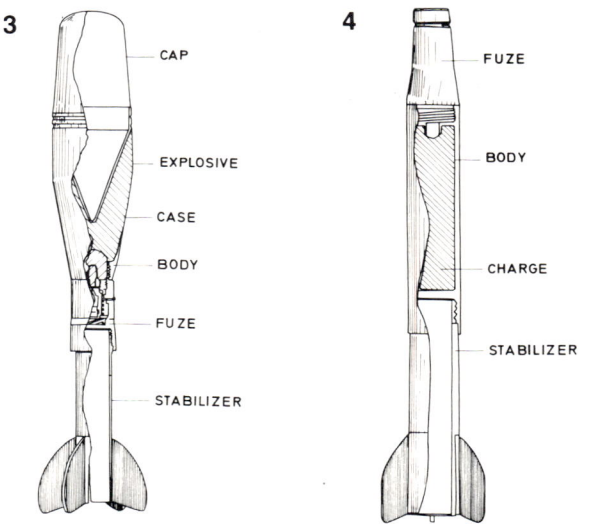

(1) Illuminating rifle grenade M62 (2) Smoke rifle grenade M62 (3) Anti-tank rifle grenade M60 (4) Anti-personnel rifle grenade M60

GRENADE LAUNCHERS

ARGENTINA

38.1mm FM GAS GUN

Designed to fire tear gas cartridges and similar munitions, this weapon consists of two sections, a barrel and breech section and a butt and firing mechanism, connected by a pivot and secured by a simple lever catch which also functions as a safety.

To load the weapon the top catch is released and the gun 'broken' to give access to the breech. A cartridge is then inserted and the gun closed. Until the lever catch is secured, however, the gun cannot be fired because there is a spring-loaded catch in the top of the trigger assembly which prevents trigger operation. This safety catch has a limb which projects through the top of the trigger assembly case; and only when this projection is forced down by the barrel locking catch does the safety catch pivot out of engagement with the trigger and permit the weapon to be fired. The barrel locking catch is spring-loaded.

A single pull on the trigger cocks and releases the firing mechanism. After firing, the gun is broken again and the act of so doing slides the extractor to

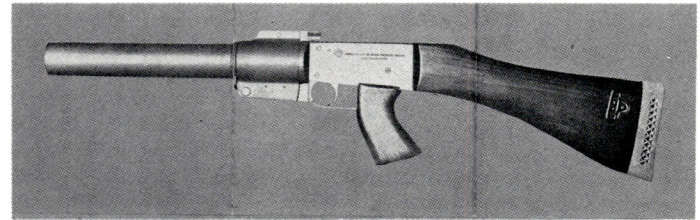

38.1mm FM Gas Gun

the rear for a short distance sufficient to permit removal of the cartridge by hand.

The gun is robustly constructed and all metal surfaces are treated for resistance to corrosion. Little maintenance is required other than routine cleaning and oiling.

Optional fittings are a sling swivel and a carrying handle.

DATA
Calibre: 38.1mm
Length: 743mm

Maximum height: without carrying handle: 185mm
with carrying handle: 230mm
Weight: without carrying handle: 3.35kg
with carrying handle: 3.45kg
Manufacturer: Fabrica Militar de Armas Portatiles 'Domingo Matheu' Cabildo 65, Buenos Aires

BELGIUM

MECAR MUROLA MULTI BARREL EXPENDABLE GRENADE LAUNCHER

This is a four-barrel portable grenade launcher firing 60mm grenades to a range of up to 400 metres and weighing less than 5kg. The expendable launcher alone weighs less than 2.5kg. An aiming grid is provided with each weapon.

DATA
Calibre (Projectile): 60mm
Length: Weapon: 530mm
Projectile: 250mm
Weight: Total: 4,700g
Projectile: 565g
Total volume: 160×215×530mm
Launch velocity: 75m/sec
Operational range: 400 metres

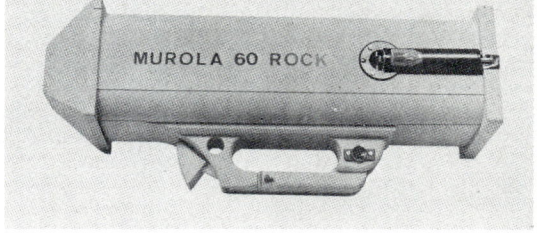
Mecar Murola expendable launcher

Lethal radius (1 round): 8 metres
Maximum effective radius: 30 metres

DISPOSABLE MORTARS PRB 424 and PRB 425

The idea of the disposable mortar has been considered on many occasions but the expense and the weight of the conventional mortar have always rendered the idea impractical. With the introduction of the Jet Shot the makers claim that a practical disposable mortar becomes possible.

The disposable Mortar PRB 424 fires the 404 grenade and the PRB 425 fires the 422 grenade. In both cases a pack consists of the disposable mortar and seven rounds. The PRB 404/424 set weighs 11.5kg and the PRB 422/425 set weighs 14kg. The disposable mortar with one grenade inside and three tubes each holding two grenades, is held between the base plate and a closing cover.

The pack is designed to be carried over the shoulder on the sling provided.

The disposable mortar is used as follows:

The cover is removed and the tubes taken out. The mortar is placed on its baseplate. The sling has the ranges marked on it. To get a required range the firer stretches the sling which is connected to the baseplate and the mortar tube. He then places his foot on the required range mark on the sling and the sling then makes a triangle – mortar-foot-base plate. The muzzle is raised until the sling is tight and the right angle of elevation is set. When the range and the line to the target are determined, a grenade is dropped down

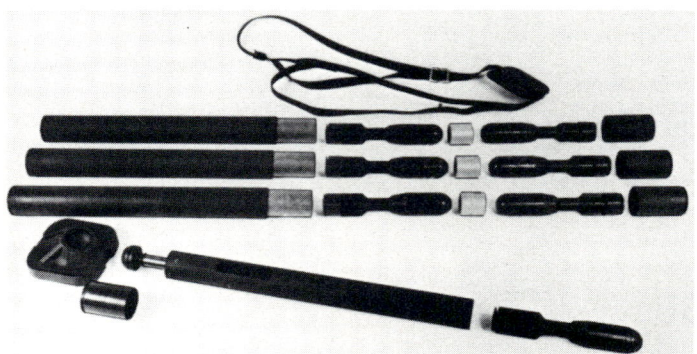
Disposable mortar PRB 424 with the 404 grenade. The mortar and seven grenades make up one pack

the muzzle. A trained mortar man can fire seven bombs before the first hits the ground.

PRB SINGLE HAND LAUNCHER

The single hand launcher is designed to fire the Jet Shot grenade, either electrically or by percussion.

The launcher is made from a cylindrical tube with a spigot on the front end over which the grenade is located. At the lower end of the tube is a base plate with a spike for use on hard ground. Between the spigot and the base plate is a carrying sling of fixed length which has an index mark. This mark is placed on the ground and held there by the firer's foot. This ensures that the tube is elevated to 45 degrees.

When electrical ignition is employed, a connection box is held on the sling. This has the firing switch and also contains a 1.5 volt alkaline dry battery for ignition. When percussion firing is used, a sleeve around the cylinder is forced down. This engages a hammer and carries it down to the bottom of the tube and at the same time extends a spring inside the tube. When the sleeve reaches the bottom of the tube the hammer and spring slip off and the hammer is carried up to strike the cap of the Jet Shot grenade. When the next grenade is placed on the tube the sleeve is moved up to engage the hammer and then forced down as before.

The single-handed launcher

PRB 426 MULTI-SPIGOT LAUNCHER

This is a device to allow the firing of 12 Jet Shot grenades, in pairs, on pre-determined bearings and elevations.

The spigots are on a plate which can be adjusted for elevation and bearing. The spigots are adjusted to control the spread of the grenades and at the setting giving a 50% chance of lethality – i.e. one fragment per metre² with sufficient remaining energy to penetrate 25mm of pinewood – the 12 grenades cover an area of 100 metres × 50 metres which is a half hectare.

The electric control box has a sequential device allowing control of the rate of fire. It is possible to fire the grenades at such a rate that all 12 are in the air together to obtain the maximum surprise.

The device can be attached to any vehicle or used on the ground with a separation between the launcher and the firer.

The multi-spigot launcher, loaded and ready to fire

PRB "JET SHOT" SILENT WEAPON SYSTEM

The Jet Shot cartridge consists of a thin wall tube made of a high tensile steel. At the rear end, the tube is sealed by the ignition device which may be either percussion or electric. Above the propellant charge is the piston which is driven up the tube when the powder is ignited. The piston reaches the end of the cylinder and is abruptly checked and brought to rest when it reaches a threaded ring screwed into the end of the tube. The cylinder is fully sealed and as no gas escapes there is neither noise nor flash.

The manufacturer explains the practical success of the device by stating that the dynamic pressure developed during the burning of the propellant builds up so rapidly that the material of the tube does not have time to expand sufficiently to produce failure. The piston moves up the cylinder at an extremely rapid rate and so the pressure drops again very quickly in the tube, and the grenade projected off the end of the piston carries on along its trajectory. The cartridge is left full of gas which slowly seeps out past the piston, over a period of time. The combustion efficiency with such rapid burning is claimed to be higher than that achieved in normal gun practice and as a result a comparatively small propellant charge produces a high velocity. The use of the dynamic pressure enables a lightweight tube to be used, so overall the system is light and convenient to handle. Finally the lack of gas expanding behind the projectile adds to the accuracy of the system.

This cartridge is claimed by PRB to have potential development promise in fields other than purely military and could be used for many purposes where silence, speed and light weight are required. Possible uses include:
(a) Projecting a line for any one of a countless number of uses. Examples include rescue from the sea, scaling a cliff or crossing an obstacle.
(b) Laying telephone lines over obstacles.
(c) Erecting high tension cables.

The Jet Shot cartridge has been tried with bigger loads and at longer ranges and one version has achieved a range of 1,200 metres with a projectile weighing 1.7kg.

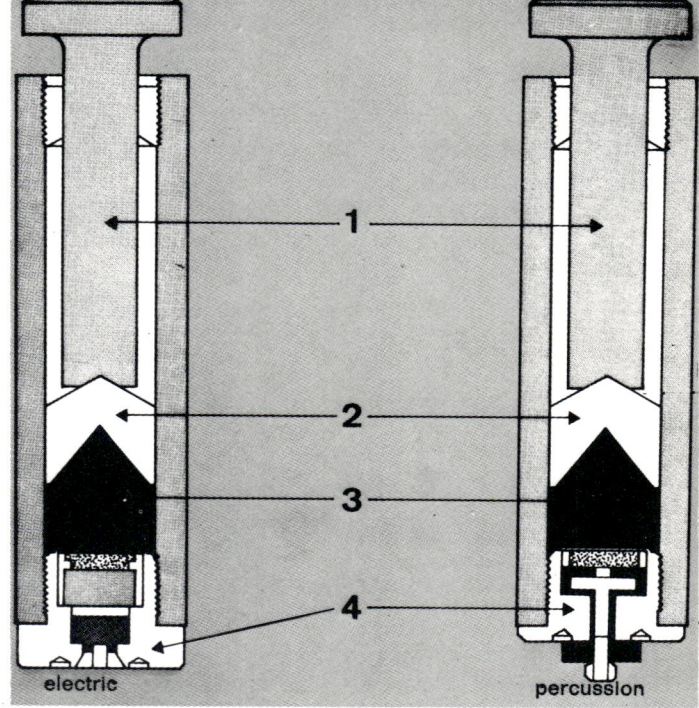

The Jet Shot System: (1) driving rod; (2) piston; (3) powder; (4) ignition device

GERMANY (FEDERAL REPUBLIC)

HAND FLAME CARTRIDGE LAUNCHER MODEL HAFLA-35L

This is manufactured by Buck KG and is in service with the German Army under the designation Flammpatrone, Hand, DM 34. It is a single shot, one man operated, throw away weapon designed to impel an incendiary smoke charge to a range of 70-80 metres.

The weapon comprises an aluminium launch tube and three compressed sections of incendiary smoke composition contained in a projectile. A pivotal handgrip fuze and firing assembly is fitted at one end of the tube and a plastic cover at the other end. The launcher is watertight. Three units are individually packed and moisture sealed in a plastic carrying case.

OPERATION
The HAFLA-35L is delivered with the handgrip in the safe position. By depressing the safety button (1), the grip (2) can be moved outwards exposing the trigger (3). The trigger cannot be activated until the grip is moved completely to the rear and is locked in position. The weapon is then ready to fire.

The trigger is depressed and the firing pin (4) strikes the primer which ignites the first propellant (5). Simultaneously the projectile is set in motion and the second propellant (6) is ignited and the aluminium capsule (7) is blown out of the tube.

As the second propellant burns, the delay fuze (8) begins to smoulder. This action concurrently activates the incendiary smoke payload (9). After some two seconds, the burning mixture in the delay fuze reaches the dispersion charge (10). An immediate burst then demolishes the projectile spreading burning fragments of incendiary smoke composition.

The projectile bursts after travelling 70 to 80 metres and burning particles will be spread over an area 10m in width and 15m in length. If however the projectile strikes a hard surface within a range of 8-70m, the incendiary smoke charge immediately scatters upon impact in a brilliant flash of blinding smoke and fire covering an area of 5-8m. In either case the combustion of hot (1,300°C) fragments continues for at least 2 minutes.

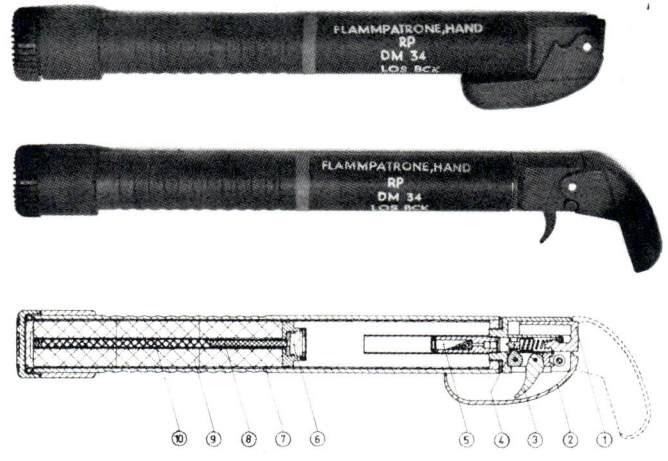

DATA
Weight: 625g
Weight of composition: 240g
Overall length: 445mm
Calibre: 35mm
Incendiary composition: Red phosphorus
Packing: 3 HAFLAs per pouch; 51 HAFLAs per crate

PRACTICE GRENADE
This has the same dimensions and weight as the HAFLA but has an inert filling of lime and a smoke marker to indicate the point of impact.

Manufacturer: Buck KG, 7844 Neuenberg-Baden

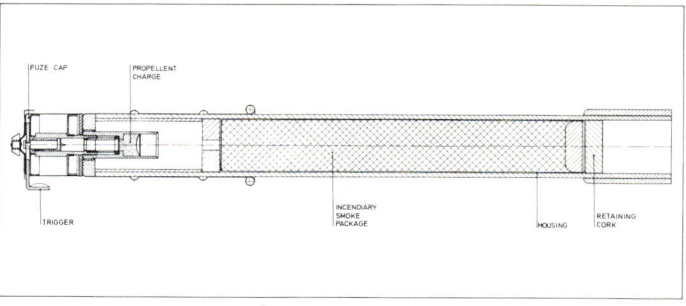

HAFLA-35L Cartridge launcher

HAND FLAME GRENADE LAUNCHER (HAFLA)
CALIBRE 30mm

The HAFLA (30mm) is manufactured by Buck KG. It consists of a hollow, pasteboard tube into which a combustible composition has been packed and sealed. The forward end of the tube is open and is reinforced by a circular pasteboard band. The rear of the tube is covered with a rigid, metal sleeve which contains a threaded aperture into which the fuze and firing unit is secured.

The weapon has a range of at least 30m and with an elevation of 30° a range of 60m can be reached. HAFLAs are packed in a sealed unit which contains five sealed plastic bags, each of which contains one launching tube and one fuze.

The German Army designation of the 30mm HAFLA is DM 24, and operational weapons are painted green. There is also a practice model which is painted blue and designated DM 28. This is identical in size, shape and fuzing to the live HAFLA but instead of an incendiary smoke charge it contains approximately 200 grams (7.1oz) of calcium carbonate, which clearly marks the point of impact.

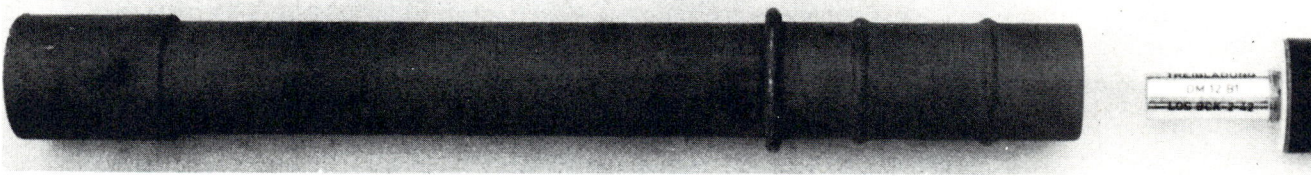

HAFLA 30mm Grenade launcher

DM 24 hand-held flame discharger (German Army Photograph)

OPERATION
There are two settings on the fuze cap, "S" for safety and "F" for fire. As the fuze cap is turned counter-clockwise to the "F" notch, the trigger is freed. When the trigger is depressed, the firing pin in the fuze unit strikes a primer which ignites the propellant charge. This in turn sets fire to the combustible mixture package as it is ejected from the launching tube along with the retaining cork. As the projectile hits a hard or firm surface it shatters, and the combustible mixture spreads and explodes.

DATA
Weight: 500g
Weight of composition: 200g
Overall length: 370mm
Calibre (inside diameter): 30mm
Incendiary composition: Red phosphorus
Manufacturer: Buck KG, 7844 Neuenberg-Baden
Status: In production and in service

INCENDIARY SMOKE LAUNCHER

This 182mm nebelwerfer is used to produce a mass of flame and smoke to blind and confuse the enemy. The angle of elevation can be adjusted to produce a maximum range of 220 metres. The incendiary smoke charge ignites in the air or on the ground and bursts after a time of flight of 5.5 to 6 seconds.

The smoke and flame covers an area of 30-50 sq metres in diameter and the temperature rises to 1,100-1,200 degrees C. The duration of the effect is about 3 minutes and although the smoke is not poisonous it causes a severe irritant coughing and causes all in the target area to wear a respirator.

The equipment consists of:
Launching tube and frame;
Projectile with incendiary smoke charge and propellant charge;
Electric fuse, power source and cable;
Total weight 10.5kg; Weight of incendiary smoke charge 5.6kg.
Manufacturer: Buck KG, 7844 Neuenburg-Baden

Incendiary smoke launcher

40mm GRENADE LAUNCHER TYPE HK 69AI

This is a light and handy weapon designed to fire grenades at either low or high angle and can project a 40mm grenade up to a range of 350 metres. It thus fills the gap between maximum hand throwing and minimum mortar range.

The grenade launcher is a single-shot, break-action weapon with a retractable butt stock, a fixed foresight and a folding ladder-pattern rearsight. The barrel is rifled.

To load the weapon, the cocking handle (on top of the receiver) is pulled back as far as it will go, thus cocking the action and breaking the barrel to the front. If there is a spent round in the breech it may be extracted manually, a recess cut in each side of the breech end of the barrel enabling the firer to grip and withdraw the spent case. When a new round is inserted, an indicator pin which extends into the chamber is pressed out and shows a red ring projecting from the rearsight support.

When the barrel is pivoted back into the receiver it is secured by locking bolts which engage a catch in the barrel. The action remains cocked and may be secured by applying a safety located on either side of the pistol grip.

Grenades may be launched with the butt stock either extended or retracted. To extend it, it is necessary only to pull it to the rear; to retract it a latch at the rear of the receiver must be pressed sideways. The ladder rearsight is raised for aiming if the range exceeds 100 metres.

HK 69AI Grenade launcher and round

DATA
Calibre: 40mm
Mode of fire: Single-shot manually loaded
Length: 430mm (stock retracted) or 610mm
Barrel: 320mm
    Rifling: 6 grooves
Weight: 1.8kg
Sights: Foresight: Fixed barleycorn
    Rearsight: Fixed rearsight for up to 100 metres. Folding ladder for 150-300 metres × 50 metres
    Sight radius: 275mm
Muzzle velocity: Approx. 75m/sec
Manufacturer: Heckler & Koch GmbH, 7238 Oberndorf-Neckar

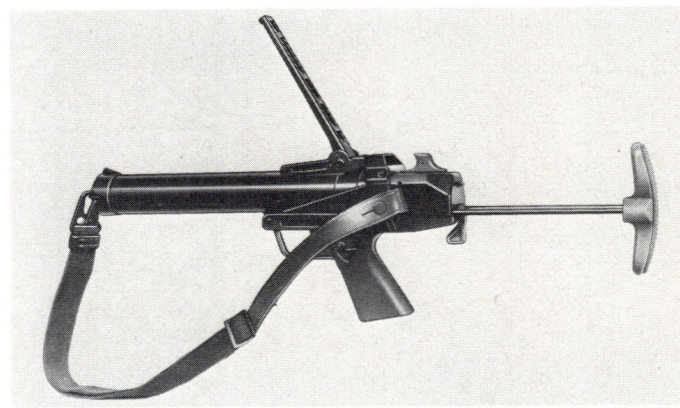

Grenade launcher with butt stock extended and ladder rearsight raised for aiming

---

26.5mm SIGNAL PISTOL TYPE P2AI

This is a single-shot break-action signalling pistol which can be simply adapted to fire tear gas grenades.

In its basic form the pistol comprises a seamless drawn steel barrel which is pivoted on a receiver and grip assembly. A locking stud at the rear of the barrel engages with a breech catch on the receiver to lock the barrel in position; to break the weapon for loading or unloading the breech catch at the top of the grip must be depressed. The action of opening the breech automatically partially ejects an empty case by means of the ejector at the bottom of the barrel.

After loading a cartridge in the chamber the barrel is snapped shut and the weapon is loaded and safe. To fire it the hammer must be thumb-cocked. There is no applied safety but the hammer may be lowered under control.

To convert the pistol to a grenade launcher two additional parts are required – a grenade launching cap and an insertion tube. The latter is threaded at the forward end and has an ejector at the rear end which mates with the ejector in the pistol barrel. To fit it, the pistol is first broken, then the tube is inserted from the breech end, ensuring that the two ejectors make contact. When the tube is fully inserted the launcher cap is secured on its forward end and the conversion is complete.

As a grenade launcher the weapon is loaded in the same way as is the pistol except that it is a propellant charge only and not a complete round that is inserted in the breech. The grenade canister is placed in the launcher cup.

The weapon is easily maintained but both barrel and insertion tube must be cleaned after firing. For protection in store any common gun oil may be used.

DATA
Pistol:
Calibre: 26.5mm
Weight: 0.52kg
Length: 200mm
Barrel: 155mm

Grenade launcher
Calibre of propellant charge (black powder): 7.62mm × 51
Weight of insertion tube: 0.35kg
Weight of grenade cup: 0.86kg
Total weight assembled: 1.73kg
Length overall: 380mm
Manufacturer: Heckler & Koch GmbH, 7238 Oberndorf-Neckar

P2AI signal pistol

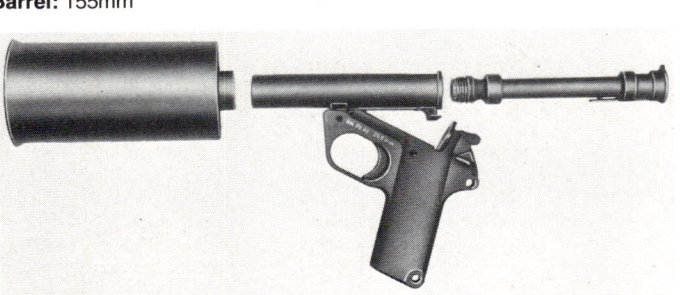

Illustrating the assembly of the grenade launcher to the pistol

The grenade launcher complete

SWITZERLAND

FALCONET

This is a prototype weapon being developed by Sarmac S.A. The designer is Francois Brandt, son of Edgar Brandt of mortar fame. It consists of a personal weapon of unusual design intended for employment in the infantry section. It has a maximum range of 600-700 metres. The first photograph shows the weapon in its normal configuration. The straight-through action chosen to eliminate the turning moment about the shoulder, is a noticeable feature. When the weapon is being carried, the barrel can be slid backwards so that the muzzle brake comes down to the hydraulico-pneumatic recoil absorber. The recoil mechanism is housed in a cylinder which can be seen above the barrel. This is shown on the other photograph. The bipod is folded under the fore-end. Two types of ammunition are available. The offensive grenade is a blast-effect projectile and the defensive grenade contains 12 small anti-personnel darts.

DATA
Calibre: 24mm
Method of operation: Mechanical, semi-automatic
Method of feed: 5-round box magazine
Method of fire: Single shots
Weight: 6kg
Weight of loaded magazine: 600g
Length: Ready fire position 1,100mm
　　　　　Barrel retracted 900mm
Sights: Iron sights – optical optional
Rate of fire: 1 round/sec maximum
Muzzle velocity: (offensive grenade) 400 metres/sec
　　　　　　　　　(defensive grenade) 600 metres/sec

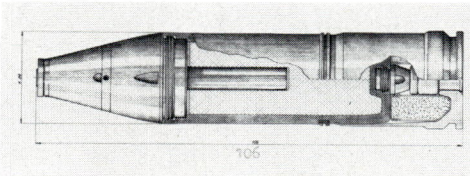

The offensive grenade

AMMUNITION
Offensive grenade
Weight: 115 gram
Bursting charge: 24 gram
Range: 600 metres
Fuze arming distance: 3 metres
Defensive grenade
Weight: 70 gram
Range: 150 metres
Sub-projectiles: 12 darts
Manufacturer: Sarmac SA., 54 bis route des Acacias, 1227 Carouge-Genève
Status: Development of prototypes in progress

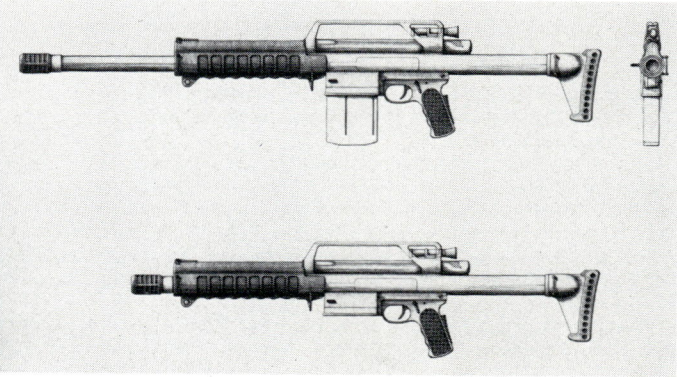

Falconet ready to fire (top), and folded for carriage (bottom)

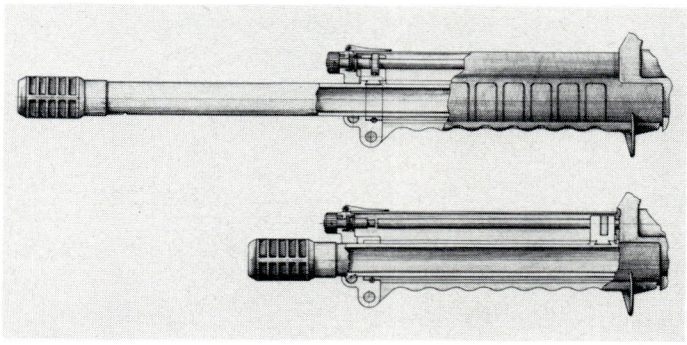

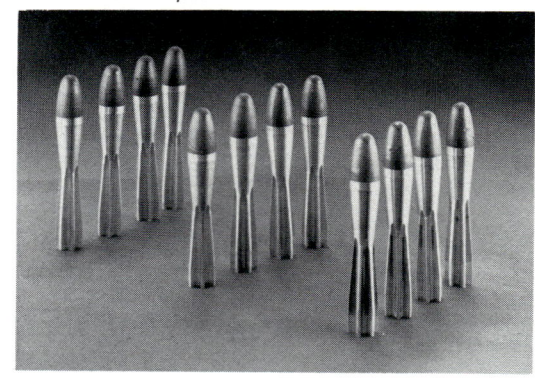

Detail of retracted barrel and folded bipod

The 12 darts for the defensive grenade

UNITED KINGDOM

GRENADE DISCHARGER L1A1

The Discharger Grenade L1A1, is a light single-shot muzzle loading, shoulder fired discharger, electrically operated, with a range of about 100 metres. A new range of grenades has been produced for use with this discharger. The new ammunition was introduced partly to remove the use of white phosphorus from service, and to replace the No. 80 grenade with its separately stored detonator, fuze and cover, by a single unit; but partly also to provide a better means of projecting CS gas into a riotous assembly from a distance beyond the range of hand-thrown retaliatory missiles and in a way that prevented the gas source from being smothered or thrown back.

The grenades already introduced are:
Smoke Screening, L5
Anti-Riot Irritant, L6
Smoke Screening, L7, Green
Anti-Riot Irritant, L9
Anti-Riot Irritant (Long Range), L11
Anti-Riot Irritant (Medium Range), L12
Practice Anti-Riot (Long Range), L14
Practice Anti-Riot (Medium Range), L15

The weapon is powered by two standard U2 dry cells and a large number of grenades can be fired before these need to be replaced. The power is used to ignite the propellant charge in the base of the grenade, whereby the grenade is projected from the the launching cup; and safe handling of the weapon is ensured by requiring that three actions must be performed, two of them simultaneously, to launch a grenade.

Discharger, grenade L1A1

First, the weapon must be cocked by pushing the cocking plunger, located at the fore end of the pistol grip and trigger assembly, to the rear. No contact is made when this is done; but when the trigger is pulled, and provided the safety button has been and remains pressed, a current pulse of approximately 10 milliseconds in duration is fed to the contact jack which mates with the base of the grenade. When the trigger is pulled the cocking plunger is released and returns to its uncocked position: no further current can therefore be transmitted to the contact jack until it has been re-cocked; so that in the event of a misfire a live grenade can be removed with safety.

The safety button is located immediately to the rear of the grenade cup and projects downwards; it thus cannot be operated, together with trigger, with one hand. This means that two hands are required to complete the firing circuit and the weapon cannot be fired accidentally while being loaded.

The grenade cup or barrel is removed by pressing a spring plunger near its base and on the left-hand side of the weapon and twisting it off. This enables both it and the contact jack to be cleaned easily in the field. A plunger at the rear underside of the stock enables the butt plate to be removed for battery replacement. The butt plate is fitted with a shock absorbent pad.

DATA

Grenade diameter: 66mm

Length of launcher: 695mm
Weight of launcher: 2.7kg
Operating voltage: 3V
Power source: 2 × U2 cells
Standard weight of grenade: 550g
Maximum range: 100m
Manufacturer: Royal Small Arms Factory, Enfield
Status: In production and service

ANTI-RIOT PROJECTORS

The intensive and prolonged use of troops in aid of the Civil Power in Northern Ireland has led to the deployment of anti-riot ammunition and projectors.

The British Army is equipped with various projectors.

The Pistol, Pyrotechnic, 1½in, No. 4, Mk 1/1 weighs 1.276kg, has a barrel length of 105mm and fires 1½in (38mm) gas cartridges and similar ammunition.

The Riot Gun, 1½in, XL 48E1 is expected to take over the role of projecting anti-riot baton rounds.

The USA 1½in Federal Riot Gun exists in several models of which the Model 201Z is the most commonly encountered.

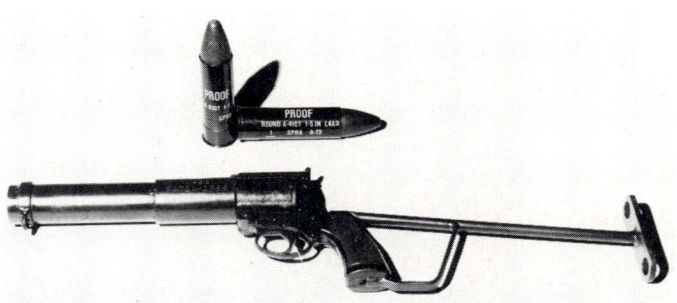

Riot gun XL 48E1

Pistol, pyrotechnic, 1.5in, No. 4, Mk 1/1

Federal riot gun, 1.5in, model 201Z

ANTI-RIOT GUN AND SIGNAL PISTOL

This Webley Schermuly lightweight smooth bore weapon is designed to give optimum performance with the variety of 1.5in (38mm) anti-riot cartridges and rounds now in service with, or under development for the British Army. It is a highly developed conventional, single-shot, break-open weapon with a double action firing mechanism.

As riot guns are primarily fired from the shoulder from a standing position the balance and handling characteristics of this weapon are intentionally similar to those of a high quality shot gun.

In addition, provision has been made to mount the gun in the turret of the Ferret, Saracen, and Shorland armoured vehicles in place of the Browning machine gun normally fitted.

CONSTRUCTION

The riot gun consists of four major components which are mainly of light alloy.

(1) *The basic assembly* is a light alloy casting housing the double action firing mechanism, barrel catch and pistol grip. When fitted with suitable barrels of 1in (25mm) or 1.5in (38mm) calibre the whole becomes a signal pistol.

(2) *The barrel* is also of light alloy and the present model is chambered for the standard U.K. alloy case anti-riot ammunition. The provision and fitting of alternative barrels of different lengths, calibres and chamber configurations is simple.

(3) *The foregrip* is a standard component in the riot gun configuration. In addition to protecting the firer's hand from any barrel heating it makes an important contribution to the handling and accuracy of the weapon. The foregrip is adjustable to cater for the firer's arm length and firing technique.

(4) *The butt assembly* consists of a selected hardwood butt strongly attached to the pistol assembly, and also mounts the back sight.

DATA
Anti-Riot Gun
Weight: 3.18kg

The Webley-Schermuly anti-riot gun

Length: 828mm
Height: 178mm
Width: 51mm
Effective ranges: Cartridge 1.5in Anti-Riot Irritant L3A2 up to 120 metres

Signal Pistol
Weight: 1.13kg
Length: 254mm
Height: 140mm
Width: 48mm
Effective ranges: Cartridge 1.5in signal-over 75 metres altitude
Manufacturer: Schermuly Ltd, High Post, Salisbury, Wiltshire

1.5in SIGNAL PISTOL

The Webley Schermuly 1.5 inch (38mm) pistol is chambered to fire all paper cased and alloy cased 1.5 inch signal and anti-riot cartridges. Of modern design it requires minimal maintenance and is simple and safe in use.

The weapon is constructed principally of high tensile aluminium alloy of rugged construction giving light weight and durability. The mechanism is of the double action type requiring a firm long trigger pull, the striker having automatic rebound to avoid accidental discharge when closing. The design also incorporates a safety interlock to ensure that the muzzle catch is fully engaged before the weapon can be fired.

To load the weapon it is necessary only to press down the serrated part of the barrel catch and allow the barrel to swing open through 90°; enter the round as far as the extractor will permit; and close the gun until the barrel catch fully engages.

DATA
Calibre: 1.5in (38mm)
Length: 254mm
Weight: 1.14kg
Manufacturer: Schermuly Ltd, High Post, Salisbury, Wiltshire

Loading and firing the signal pistol

UNITED STATES OF AMERICA

XM174 SERIES OF 40mm AUTOMATIC GRENADE LAUNCHERS

The XM174 Series was developed by the Aerojet Ordnance and Manufacturing Company of Downey, California under US government contract. It is a compact, direct blowback action, self-powered, magazine-fed weapon designed to fire standard US Army 40mm low-velocity grenade cartridges. Ammunition is fed into the launcher from a 12-round, spring operated magazine designed for quick installation and removal. Ammunition is fed into the launcher from the left and empty cases are ejected through a port on the right.

Firing is from a closed bolt position. The charging handle is located on the right of the launcher and the firing selector push-button is located in the pistol grip to permit selection of semi-automatic (single-shot) or full automatic fire.

The launcher delivers accurate fire to a range of 400m with standard ammunition; or up to 1000m with rocket-assist ammunition under development. It has a wide variety of applications, many of which have already been tested in combat. Bipod, tripod and pintle mountings are possible and installations have been made on helicopters, armoured vehicles and river patrol boats. It also can be fired from the hip (see picture). Recoil in this position is less than that of the M79 Launcher.

Standard 40mm ammunition includes the M43 HEDP, M406 HE, M397 HE Airburst, M407 practice, illuminating and signal cartridges. A full list of these cartridges will be found under the entry for the 40mm Grenade Launcher M79. In addition there have been under development the XM651E3 CS cartridge and an extended-range HEDP RAP cartridge.

The first model developed was the XM174 which was successfully used in combat in Vietnam. This was followed by the XM174E1 which incorporated modifications to prevent misassembly and to improve function.

The XM174E2 accepts the new M433 HEDP and M397 HE Airburst cartridges which are longer than the earlier cartridges. In addition, the bolt sear mechanism was redesigned, wear-resistant inserts were fitted to the receiver and an auxiliary extractor was added to the bolt.

The current model is the XM174E3 which has the additional capability of being able to fire rocket-assist ammunition. It has a stronger pistol grip and buffer necessary to accept the higher recoiling bolt velocities encountered with the RAP (Rocket Assisted Projectile) round.

DATA
Length overall: 712mm
Width without magazine: 219mm
Width with magazine: 387mm
Height without magazine: 158mm
Height with magazine: 216mm
Weight of launcher (without pintle adapter): 7.25kg

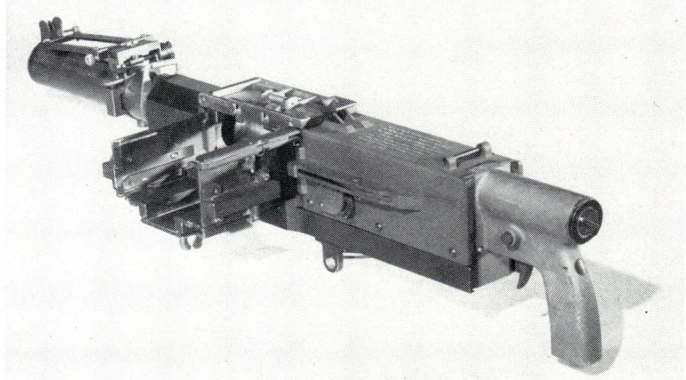

XM174 launcher without magazine or tripod

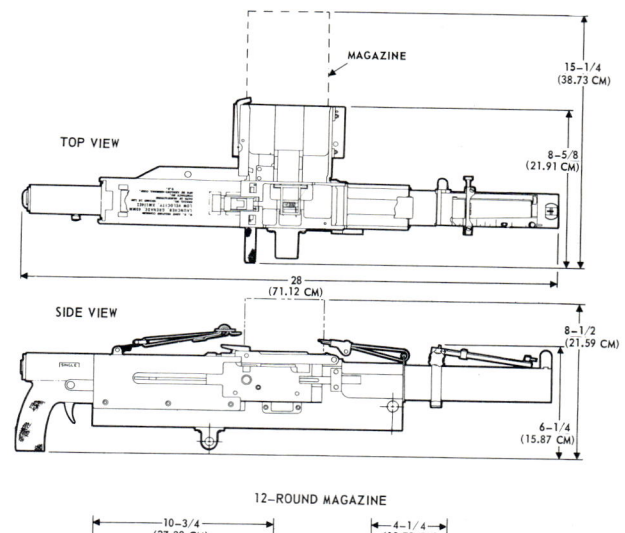

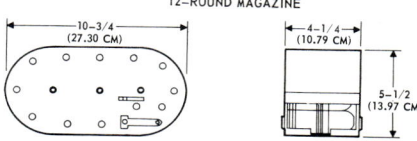

XM174E3 Automatic Grenade Launcher

Weight of launcher (with pintle adapter): 7.7kg
Weight of loaded magazine: 4.5kg
Capacity of magazine: 12 rounds
Cyclic rate of fire: 300 rounds per minute
Sustained rate of fire: 90/100 rounds per minute
Operation: Direct blowback
Function: Automatic or semi-automatic
Manufacturer: Aerojet Ordnance and Manufacturing Company, 9236 East Hall Road, Downey, California, 90241, USA
Status: The following quantities of XM174s have so far been delivered:

	XM174/XM174E1	XM174E2	XM174E3
US Army	21	0	0
USAF	160	1	0
USMC	43	7	1
AOMC	0	0	1
Total	224	8	2

Although the usefulness and general desirability of the XM174 series is not seriously in doubt no decision for large-scale procurement has been taken. Meanwhile the weapon is being studied by the West German authorities.

Position for firing the XM174 from the hip

Tripod-mounted XM174

40mm GRENADE LAUNCHER M203

The M203 Grenade Launcher was developed by the AAI Corporation of Cockeysville, Maryland under the direction of the United States Army Weapons Command. Development started in May, 1967 and it was type classified Standard "A" in August, 1969. The M203 is the successor to the M79 Grenade Launcher and is replacing this on a one for one basis. It fulfils the US Army requirement for a rifle/grenade launcher package, whereas the earlier M79 was only a grenade launcher.

The 40mm grenade launcher, M203 is a lightweight, single-shot, breech-loaded, pump-action (sliding barrel), shoulder-fired weapon attached to the M16/M16A rifle. It consists of a handguard and sight assembly group, receiver assembly, quadrant sight assembly, and barrel assembly.

The grenade launcher uses fixed ammunition. There are varieties of high explosive, training, multiple projectile (buck shot), illuminating, and signalling rounds (both standard and developmental types) available for use in the M203.

MECHANICAL DETAILS

The safety is just forward of the trigger, inside the trigger guard. To fire the launcher, the safety must be in the forward position.

Depressing the rear portion of the trigger guard allows the trigger guard to rotate down and away from the magazine well of the rifle thus allowing the grenadier to fire the weapon wearing gloves or mittens.

The barrel latch is on the left side fo the barrel. This latch locks the barrel and receiver together. To open the barrel, depress the barrel latch and slide the barrel forward.

QUADRANT SIGHT

The quadrant sight assembly mounts on the left side of the carrying handle of the M16/M16A1 rifle. It consists of a mounting screw, quadrant sight assembly clamp sight bracket assembly, sight latch, rear sight aperture, sight aperture arm, front sight post, and sight post arm.

The clamp and sight bracket hold the sight assembly to the carrying handle of the rifle and are secured by the mounting screw.

The quadrant sight arm mounts the sight aperture arm and the sight post arm. This permits the sight to pivot on the range quadrant to the desired range setting. The range quadrant is graduated in 25-metres increments from 40 to 400 metres. Rearward pressure on the sight latch unlocks the quadrant sight arm allowing it to move along the range quadrant so that the desired range number can be centred in the window of the quadrant sight arm.

The front sight post mounts on the quadrant sight arm by means of a pivot bracket that can be opened when the sights are in use or closed when not in use, to prevent damage to the sights. For elevation adjustments, turn the elevation adjustment screw on the sight post to the right to decrease elevation and to the left to increase elevation. One full turn will move the impact of the projectile 5 metres at a range of 200 metres.

The rear sight aperture connects to the sight aperture arm, which is attached to the rear portion of the quadrant sight arm. The rear sight aperture arm serves the same purpose as the sight post arm. The rear sight aperture can be adjusted for minor changes in deflection when zeroing the launcher. For windage adjustment, press the rear sight retainer and move the aperture away from the barrel to move impact to the left. One notch on the rear sight aperture will move the impact of the projectile 1½ metres at a range of 200 metres.

SIGHT LEAF ASSEMBLY

The sight leaf is a folding, adjustable open ladder design that permits rapid firing without sight manipulation and uses the front sight post of the M16/M16A1 rifle as the front aiming post.

The sight leaf base is permanently attached to the rifle hand guard by two mounting screws. It serves to protect the sight leaf from damage when the leaf is not being used and in the *down* position.

The mount is attached to the sight base and is used to raise or lower the sight leaf blade. The sight leaf is graduated in 50 metre increments from 50 to 250 metres and numbered at 100 and 200 metres.

The screw attaches the sight leaf to the sight mount. To make minor adjustments in elevation when zeroing the launcher, the sight leaf can be moved up or down by loosening the elevation adjustment screw. The rim of a 40-mm cartridge case may be used for this purpose. Raising the sight leaf increases the range and lowering it decreases the range. The elevation scale consists of five lines spaced equally apart on the sight leaf. The index line is on the left of the sight leaf. One increment will move the impact of the projectile 10 metres in elevation at a range of 200 metres.

A knob at its left end is used to turn the sight windage screw to adjust for deflection. The windage scale consists of a zero line in the centre of the scale and two lines spaced equally on each side of the zero line. When making minor adjustments in deflection while zeroing the launcher, one increment on the windage scale will move the impact of the projectile 1½ metres at a range of 200 metres.

AMMUNITION

40-mm ammunition for use with the launcher includes high explosive (HE), high explosive air-burst (HE air-burst), high explosive smokeless and flashless, high explosive dual purpose (HEDP), and training practice (TP), M576 multiple projectile, M583 white-star parachute and M585 white-star cluster.

The high explosive rounds contain a grenade 38mm in diameter with about 35g of explosive. The grenade is formed of rectangular-wrapped steel wire. The wire is notched at intervals to allow for fragmentation upon detonation of the grenade.

The practice round is ballistically matched to the high explosive (HE) round and is filled with a yellow dye powder. Upon impact, the fuze booster breaks open the grenade and disperses the powder as a puff of yellow smoke which is visible out to the maximum range of the launcher.

Both standard and developmental ammunition designed for the 40mm grenade launcher, M79, is normally adaptable to the M203 grenade launcher.

No attempt should be made under any conditions to fire 40mm high velocity ammunition in the M203 grenade launcher.

DATA

Weapon:
Length of launcher: 389mm
Length of barrel: 305mm
Weight (unloaded): approx 1.36kg
Weight (loaded): approx 1.56kg
Weight (loaded) (M16A1 and M203): approx 5kg
Trigger pull: 2.2kg
Ammunition:
Calibre: 40mm
Weight: approx 277g
Operational characteristics:
Action: Pump
Maximum range: 400 metres (approx)
Maximum effective range (area targets): 350 metres
Maximum effective range (point target): 150 metres
Minimum safe firing ranges (HE and TP):
Training: 80m
Combat: 31m
Manufacturer: Colt Industries, Hartford, Connecticut
Status: In production and in service

Typical 40mm grenades

M203 40mm grenade launcher on the M16A1 rifle (US Army photograph)

WE 69655

40mm GRENADE LAUNCHER M79

The 40mm grenade launcher, M79, is a single shot, breakopen, breech-loading, shoulder-fired weapon. It consists of a receiver group fore-end assembly, barrel group, sight assembly, and stock assembly. A rubber recoil pad is attached to the butt of the stock to absorb part of the recoil. A sling is provided to carry the weapon.

Standard and development ammunition designed for use with the 40mm grenade launcher M203 is also used with the M79. The grenadier carries part of his ammunition in two universal ammunition pouches, each of which can hold three rounds. Ammunition is also carried in the two-pocket bandolier in which the ammunition is packed. Each pocket contains a plastic support which holds three rounds.

SAFETY

To fire the launcher the safety must be in the forward position. In this position the letter F is visible near the rear end of the safety. When the letter S is visible just forward of the safety, the launcher will not fire. The safety is automatically engaged when the barrel locking latch is operated to open the breech.

REAR SIGHT ASSEMBLY

The adjustable rear sight assembly consists of a rear sight lock, a windage screw and windage scale, an elevation scale and lock screw, a sight carrier and retainer locknut, and elevating screw wheel and elevating screw, and a rear sight frame and fixed sight.

The rear sight lock is spring loaded and permits the rear sight frame assembly to be locked in either the *up* or *down* position. To unlock the sight frame push down on the flat surface of the rear sight lock. By releasing the pressure the frame is locked in the desired position.

A knob at its right end turns the windage screw to adjust the rear sight for deflection. One click of the screw will move the impact of the grenade about 28 centimetres at a range of 200 metres. For right windage turn the screw clockwise: for left windage turn it counterclockwise. The windage scale consists of a zero line in the centre of the scale and 10 lines spaced equally on each side of the zero line. The rear sight assembly can be moved 42 clicks right or left of centre.

The elevation scale is graduated from 75 to 375 metres in 25-metre increments and numbered at 100, 200, 300 and 375 metres. As the rear sight carrier is moved up the scale, the rear sight is cammed to the left compensating for the normal right-hand drift of the projectile. The lock screw holds the elevation scale in position.

A retainer locknut permits the sight carrier to be moved along the eleva-

tion scale and clamps it to the sight frame in the desired position. To move the sight carrier along the elevation scale turn the retainer locknut counter-clockwise until it can be pushed inward. This inward pressure unlocks the sight carrier allowing it to be moved along the elevation scale. To lock the sight carrier in position, release the pressure on the retainer locknut and turn the nut clockwise until it stops.

The elevating screw and wheel are used to make fine adjustments in elevation. Turning the wheel clockwise increases the elevation setting; turning the wheel counterclockwise decreases it. When the screw is turned it moves the sight carrier along the elevation scale. One complete turn (one click) will move the impact of the round about 2½ metres at a range of 200 metres.

When the rear sight frame is in the down position, the fixed sight may be used to engage targets, at ranges up to 100 metres.

FRONT SIGHT

The front sight consists of a tapered front sight blade and two front sight blade guards.

DATA

Weapon:
Length of launcher (overall): 737mm
Length of barrel: 356mm
Weight of launcher loaded: 2.95kg
Weight of launcher unloaded: 2.72kg
Ammunition:
Calibre: 40mm
Weight: 227g
Operational Characteristics:
Action: Breakopen, single shot
Sights: Front: Blade
　　　　　　Rear: Folding leaf, adjustable
Chamber pressure: 210kg/cm²
Muzzle velocity: 76 metres per sec
Maximum range: 400m (approx)
Maximum effective range (area targets): 350m
Maximum effective range (point targets): 150m
Minimum safe firing range:
Training: 80m
Combat: 31m

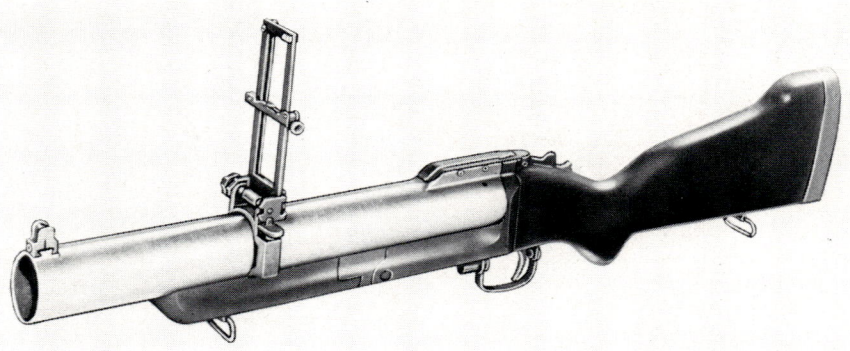

A 40mm cartridge case and projectile

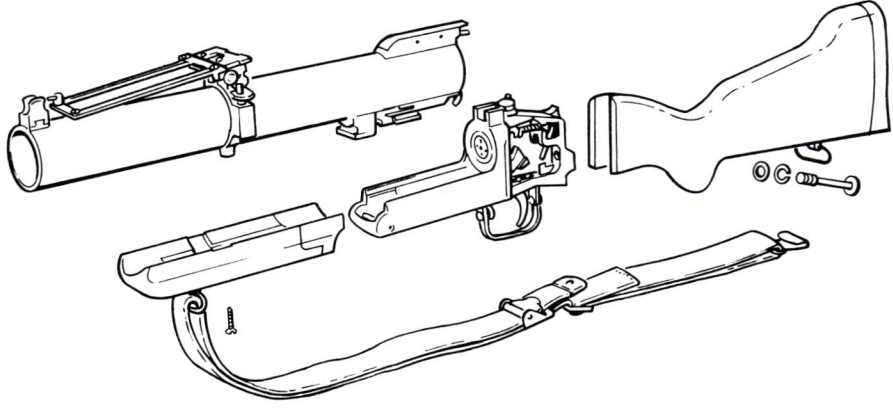

The major components of the M79 grenade launcher (US Army Photograph)

ADAPTERS, GRENADE PROJECTION, M1-SERIES

Grenade Projection Adapters M1-Series adapt fragmentation, practice, illuminating and WP smoke hand grenades for launching from a rifle. Three different models are available: the M1, the M1A1 and the M1A2. Adapter M1 can be used with Fragmentation Hand Grenade Mk2 only. Fragmentation hand grenades can be projected a maximum of 160 metres when launched from rifles using Grenade Projection Adapters M1-Series.

Adapter M1 is similar to the M1A1, except that it has four claws instead of three and does not have a cup at the base of the claws. The M1A1 and the M1A2 differ only in construction of the fin assembly. Adapters M1A1 and M1A2 consist of four parts: a fin assembly, a stabiliser tube, a cup and three claws. The adapter is fabricated from sheet steel with three spring-steel claws. These grip and hold the grenade in the adapter. The fin assembly is attached to one end of the stabiliser tube. The cup and claws are attached to the other end of the stabiliser tube. An arming clip is attached to the longest of the three claws.

OPERATION

After placing the grenade in the adapter and releasing the safety clip and removing the safety pin, the hand grenade with adapter is placed on the grenade launcher and is fired. It functions as follows:
(1) The arming clip moves rearward, striking a small extension of the arming clip retainer.
(2) Force of the arming clip's striking the small extension (made of brittle metal) breaks it, allowing the arming clip to fall free, thus releasing the safety lever.
(3) The fuze begins to function (see paragraph describing particular hand grenade for information on subsequent functioning).

DATA
Models: M1, M1A1, M1A2
Weight: 170g
Height: 178mm
Colour: Olive drab w/black markings
Packing: 24 per carton; 2 cartons (48 units) in packing box
Loaded packing box:
Weight: 22.2kg
Dimensions: 781 × 349 × 305mm
Volume: 0.083m³

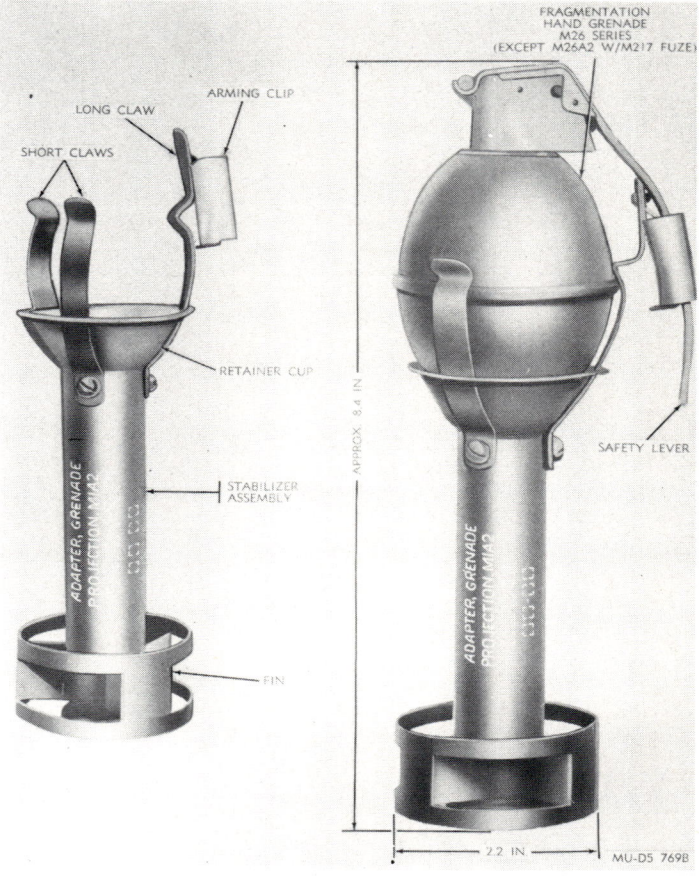

Fragmentation hand grenade, M26 series (US Army Photograph)

ADAPTER, GRENADE PROJECTION, M2-SERIES

Grenade Projection Adapters M2-Series adapt cylindrical hand grenades for launching from rifles. Two different models are available: the M2 and the M2A1.

Adapters M2 and M2A1 differ only in the method of attaching the claws and claw base plate to the stabiliser tube. Grenade Protection Adapters M2-series consist of five parts: a fin assembly, a stabiliser tube, a claw base plate, three claws, and a setback band. The adapter is fabricated from sheet steel. The three spring steel claws grip the lip of the base of the grenade body and hold the grenade in the adapter. The fin assembly is attached to one end of the stabiliser tube. The claw base plate and claws are attached to the other end of the stabiliser. The setback band is placed around the body of the grenade over the safety lever.

OPERATION

When the hand grenade with adapter placed on the grenade launcher is fired, it functions as follows:

(1) Set back force moves the setback band to the rear, releasing the safety lever.

(2) Fuze begins to function (see paragraph describing particular hand grenade for information on subsequent functioning).

DATA

Models: M2, M2A1
Height: 127mm
Colour: Grey with black marking
Packing: 50 per packing box

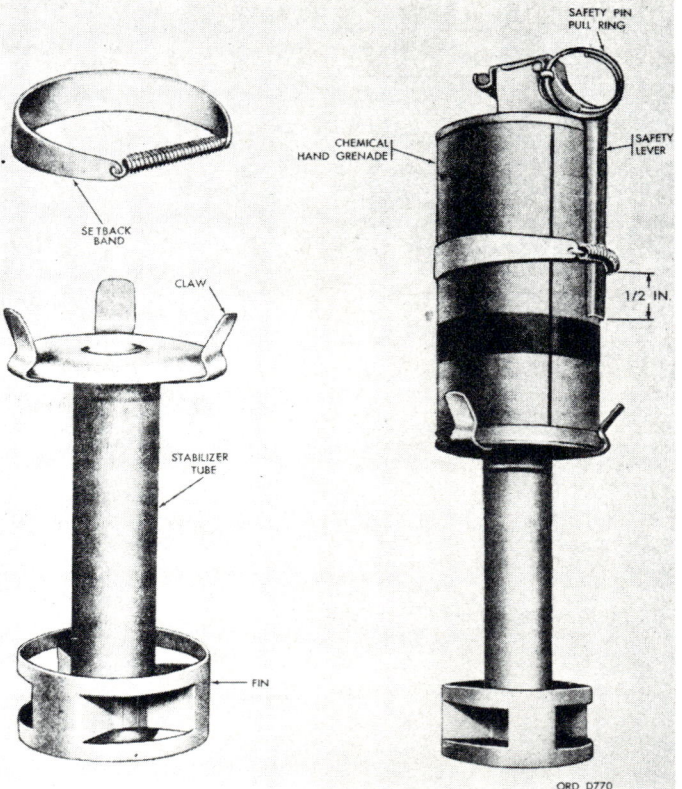

Grenade projection adapter M2A1 w/chemical hand grenade

SMITH & WESSON 37mm (1.5in) SHOULDER GAS GUN

This is a rugged weapon built on an all-steel N frame. It has a hardwood stock and a rubber recoil pad. It will fire with either single or double action and may be used to launch all S&W and other 37mm (1.5in) projectiles. The barrel is detachable for packing. The gun weighs about 2.7kg and is 74cm long.

Manufacturer: Smith & Wesson, 2100 Roosevelt Avenue, Springfield, Massachusetts 01101

SMITH & WESSON 37mm (1.5in) GAS AND FLARE PISTOL

Built on a heavy-duty S&W pistol frame this weapon is designed to fire all S&W 37mm (1.5in) projectiles and aerial flares except the No 12 fin-stabilized 'Tru-Flite' penetrating projectile which can be fired only from shoulder gas guns. The pistol will fire with either single or double action and is made of steel with a wooden grip.

Manufacturer: Smith & Wesson, 2100 Roosevelt Avenue, Springfield, Massachusetts 01101

SMITH & WESSON 12-GAUGE LAUNCHER No 33

This launcher is designed for use with 12-gauge police shotguns to launch S&W continuous discharge CN, CS or smoke grenades (No 2, calibre 67mm). It is made of steel and has a wing-nut clamp fitting. S&W 12-gauge No 35 launching cartridge must be used with this launcher.

Manufacturer: Smith & Wesson, 2100 Roosevelt Avenue, Springfield Massachusetts 01101

SMITH & WESSON 12-GAUGE LAUNCHER No 36

This launcher is designed for use with 12-gauge police shotguns to launch the S&W Rubber Ball (CN, CS or smoke) grenades (No 15, calibre 79mm). Apart from its larger diameter it is similar to the No 33 launcher and must also be used with the No 35 launching cartridge.

Manufacturer: Smith & Wesson, 2100 Roosevelt Avenue, Springfield, Massachusetts 01101

SMITH & WESSON .38 SPECIAL MIGHTY MIDGET GRENADE LAUNCHER

This launcher (No 99) is designed for use with .38 Special or .357 Magnum revolvers to fire S&W Mighty Midget CN and CS grenades (No 98, calibre 35mm). A knurled nut fastening clamps it to the barrel of the revolver and the grenade is fired using S&W .38 special launching cartridges.

Manufacturer: Smith & Wesson, 2100 Roosevelt Avenue, Springfield Massachusetts 01101

LIMITED LETHALITY WEAPON

The Limited Lethality Weapon has been designed by Mr. W. R. Blake of the Tulsa Ordnance Company. The weapon has been designed to deliver a painful to incapacitating impact without cutting the victim's arteries or penetrating the skin.

In appearance the weapon resembles a shot gun and is shoulder fired.

The weapon fires a standard golf ball which is propelled from the barrel by a standard .410 blank shot-gun cartridge. The magazine, which is under the barrel holds a total of six golf balls. The cartridges are loaded in a conventional bolt action fashion.

The manufacturers propose three different muzzle velocities using three differently colour-coded cartridges. Much higher muzzle velocities could be developed, but for riot duty the object is to deter or incapacitate temporarily and not to maim.

The Limited Lethality Weapon complete with six golf balls and six cartridges

By late 1975 the prototype had been completed and successfully completed its trials. Detailed engineering drawings have also been completed as have the engineering specifications.

DATA
Calibre: 43mm
Method of feed: 6 shot magazine
Weight empty: 2.949kg
Weight with full magazine: 3.288kg
Length: 1,016mm
Barrel length: 469mm
Barrel type: Smooth bore
Sight front: Blade

Sight rear: Open "V"
Muzzle velocity: 50m/s; 67m/s; 94m/s
Rate of fire: 1 shot in 2 seconds
Range maximum: 275 metres
Range effective: 70 metres
Manufacturer: Tulsa Ordnance Company, Box 52202, Tulsa, Oklahoma, USA, 74152
Status: Not yet in production or service

RIOT CONTROL MUNITIONS
BELGIUM

FN R40 RIOT CONTROL AMMUNITION

The projection system of the FN R40 ammunition allows various 40mm calibre projectiles to be fired from a rifle or sub-machine gun using a special cartridge. The device makes it possible to fire, at a high rate and with a conventional gun, types of projectile that are otherwise commonly fired from special guns.

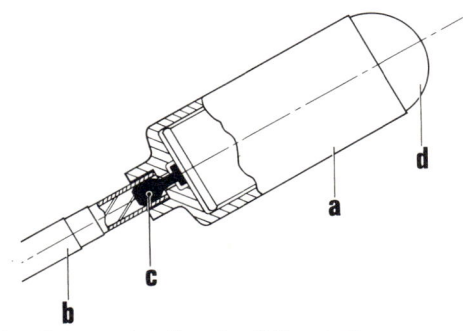

The R40 grenade (a) launcher; (b) barrel of the weapon; (c) fixture plug; (d) projectile

R40 ammunition

To date the R40 ammunition has been adapted to the following weapons:
Carbine .30 M1
Browning automatic rifle (BAR) Police model;
Weapon with grenade launcher: in calibre 7.62mm (FN FAL); in calibre 5.56mm (FN CAL):
Weapons with flash-hider; in cal 7.62mm (FN FAL);
UZI sub-machine gun, cal 9mm Parabellum;
Mauser rifle, cal 7mm.
Extension of this range is possible.

OPERATION
The R40 ammunition consists of a launcher fitted with one of the types of projectiles described below. The complete round is fitted on the muzzle of a rifle and is held in place by the elastic fixing plug which enters the bore. Both projectile and fixture plug are ejected by means of the gas in the propulsive cartridge. During this phase the launcher is subjected to recoil which effectively holds it in position in the barrel. When the projectile has left the launcher, the latter is blown off the barrel by residual pressure.

It is always possible to re-use the launchers and certain of the projectiles. As the propulsive cartridge is separate from the launching device, reloading does not require specialist aid and can be carried out at the firing point.

R40/01 – RUBBER BATON
DATA
Semi-hard rubber projectile
Weight: 150g
Diameter: 40mm
Range at 40°: 125 metres

USE
Owing to the projectile's high muzzle velocity, direct fire at short range is not recommended if one wants to avoid causing injuries.
Crowd dispersal will be more effective by ricochet fire at ranges below 30 metres and by direct fire beyond that distance.

R40/02 – RUBBER DISCS
DATA
Semi-hard rubber discs

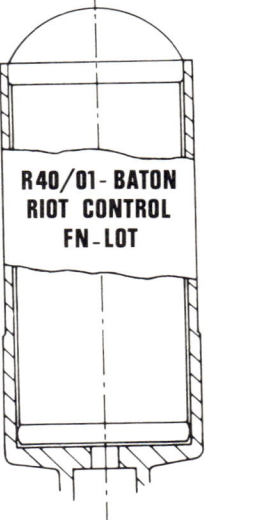

Shape and contents of R40 ammunition

Weight per disc: 29g
Number of discs: 5
Initial velocity: 60 to 70m/s (according to gun used)
Effective range: 40 metres

USE
This ammunition can be used for very short range direct fire without causing injuries. Owing to the quick dispersion of the discs into space, a wide zone is covered even at short range.

R40/03 – RUBBER BALLS
DATA
Semi-hard rubber balls
Weight per ball: 2.8g
Number of balls: 20
Effective range: 50 metres

USE
This ammunition can be fired at short range without causing injuries. Owing to their form, the balls maintain their velocity better than the discs of ammunition R40/02. The pattern is narrower.

Manufacturer: FN. Herstal, Liège

FN TEAR GAS GRENADE LAC M1 (M2 and M3)

These three grenades are similar in function but differ in size and in that two of them can be rifle-launched whereas the third can be thrown only by hand.

LAC M1

This grenade weighs about 230 grams. Gas emission lasts for approximately 15 to 30 seconds. It can either be thrown by hand, fired from a rifle, or even from certain sub-machine guns, without using a grenade launcher. It is believed to be the only type of grenade which can be launched by rifle, or from a riot shotgun, without any extra equipment.

Weapon	Calibre	Maximum range m
Rifles	7mm-7.62mm	100
	7.65mm-7.92mm	100
	.30-.303	100
	5.56mm	75
Riot gun, shortgun with		
50 cm barrel	12 gauge	100
US carbine	.30	50
Sub-machine gun UZI	9mm Parabellum	50

Type and calibre of the weapon must be specified when ordering, as the dimensions of the firing pin must be adapted accordingly, and the type of propulsive cartridge appropriately chosen.

The pin can also be supplied suitably adapted for use with a rifle which has a grenade launcher fixed to the muzzle of the barrel, although, in this instance, it is better to use the grenade LAC M2, specially designed for a weapon which has this fitment.

LAC M2

This grenade weighs about 475 grams and gas emission also lasts for approx 15 to 30 seconds. Its discharge is appreciably more than that of the LAC M1.

It is designed for firing from a rifle or sub-machine gun fitted with a launcher. Its maximum range is 160 metres. It can however be adapted for throwing by hand.

The M2 does not have a boom fitting over the muzzle but the muzzle is inserted into a hole in the body. This arrangement has been adopted to prevent a fired grenade being picked up easily by the tail and thrown further away. In this way the size of the grenade is considerably reduced and risk of injury on impact is minimised.

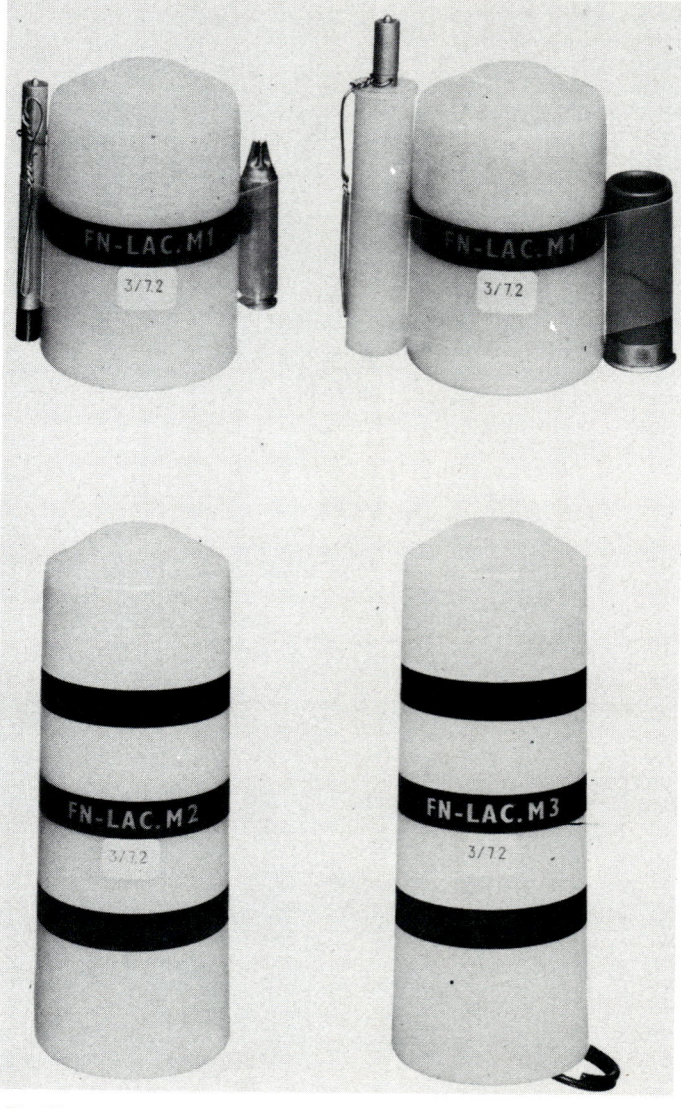

The FN tear gas grenades

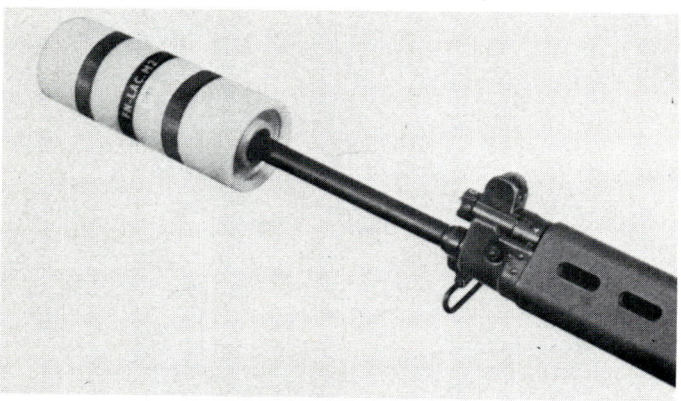

M2 Grenade on rifle barrel

The propulsive cartridge must, of course, be appropriate to the weapon used to launch the grenade, and the type of equipment must thus be specified when ordering.

LAC M3

This grenade weighs about 450 grams; its high output of tear gas is emitted in approximately 15 to 30 seconds.

It is designed for hand throwing only.

FN SMOKE GRENADES
FN-FUM.M1, FUM.M2, FUM.M3

Smoke and signal grenades marked FN-FUM.M1, FN-FUM.M2 and FN-FUM.M3 are the M1, M2 and M3 grenades with the tear gas compound replaced by a smoke forming compound.

The emission of gas, lasting approximately 20 to 30 seconds, produces an opaque cloud, tinted with red, blue, green or orange as required.

These grenades can be used to provide a light protective screen, or for signalling purposes.

Their other characteristics and methods of operation are identical to those of the FN – LAC grenades.

FRANCE

ALSETEX SMOKE AND LACHRYMATORY GRENADES

These grenades can be either rifle launched, using a blank cartridge, or thrown by hand. For rifle launching the operating delay is 6 seconds, for throwing it is 2.5 seconds. The primary purpose of both grenades is for riot control.

(A) Explosive, splinterless, lachrymatory grenade. Device made of 2 parts fitted one into the other. The ogive separates from the base on trajectory. Only expanded plastic ogive explodes, without creating dangerous splinters. (B) Tear-gas grenade with persistent effect. Consists of a perfectly tight casing containing a bulb of lachrymatory persistent liquid. The version on the left has a 6-second delay for rifle launching; the other has a lever igniter with a 2.5 second delay

DATA

	A	B
Diameter:	56mm	56mm
Length with delay element:	135mm	200mm
Total weight:	175g approx	250g approx
Weight of filling:	40g approx (explosive + lachrymatory)	140g approx
Range when fired from a rifle:	100m	100m

(A) Explosive splinterless lachrymatory grenade. The explosion of this grenade is very efficient from the psychological point of view and is accomplished by neither dangerous splinters nor effects. It causes a very efficient instantaneous lachrymatory emission.

(B) Tear-gas grenade with persistent effect. The liquid released during the functioning creates a persistent, effective, invisible lachrymatory cloud.

Manufacturer: Société Alsaciennce d'Etudes et d'Exploitation (ALSETEX), 4, rue de Castellane Foy – 75008 Paris (France)

Status: Mass production

TEAR GAS GRENADE "CRIQUET" MODEL F2

This grenade emits an orthochlorobenzalmalononitrile lachrymatory cloud. The active elements are contained in a composite case of cardboard and metal.

The grenade can be thrown either by hand by fitting with a spoon firing plug with a 2.5 second delay, no detonator, and with intensifier, or by rifle using a grenade sleeve adapted to the rifle. In this case it is fitted with an ignition transmission relay, with a delay of 2.5 seconds, and is propelled by a blank cartridge. The tear gas is discharged segmentally from three sections. This enhances the effectiveness of the grenade while rendering it harmless.

DATA

Length (without relay or firing plug): 155mm
Diameter: 55mm
Total weight: 345g
Weight of active mass: 150g
Duration of the operation: 50 to 60 seconds
Range when thrown by hand: 40m
Range by rifle projection: 80 to 100m
Packaging: Supplied in individual waterproof packing, in wooden cases of 32 units

Criquet' Model F2 tear gas grenade

Manufacturer: Société Nationale des Poudres et Explosifs, 12, Quai Henri-IV – 75181 Paris Cedex 04 (France)

Status: Mass production for the French Army

PLASTIC ANTI-RIOT GRENADE TYPE M.O. (RIFLE LAUNCHED)

This has been developed for the use of riot police. It consists of a plastic body filled with explosive, a sheath, igniter set and a stabiliser, and it is splinter proof. The grenade is fired by a rifle fitted with a discharger and a blank cartridge is used to fire the grenade.

DATA

Diameter: 57mm
Length: 113mm
Weight (with igniter set): 140g
Delay train time lag: 5 seconds
Range: 80-120m
Manufacturer: Societe E. Lacroix, 31 Muret, Route de Toulouse, or Direction Commercial, 75 Paris IV, 18 Rue Malher

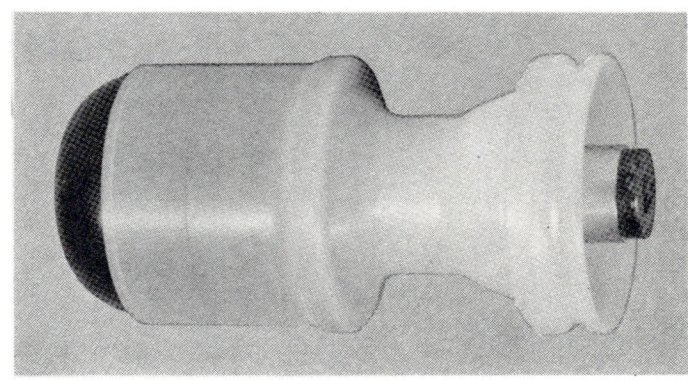

M.O. Rifle-launched grenade

PLASTIC ANTI-RIOT GRENADE M.O.

This splinter-proof grenade has been developed for the use of riot police. It consists of a plastic body filled with explosive or detonating composition, a plastic sheath and a hand operated igniter set. As combustion of the delay train ends, the igniter breaks away from the grenade whereupon the latter bursts, without splintering, 0.8 seconds later.

DATA

Diameter: 58mm
Length: 100mm
Weight (with igniter set): 250g
Time delay: 5 seconds
Manufacturer: Societe E. Lacroix, 31 Muret, Route de Toulouse, or Direction Commercial, 75 Paris IV, 18 Rue Malher

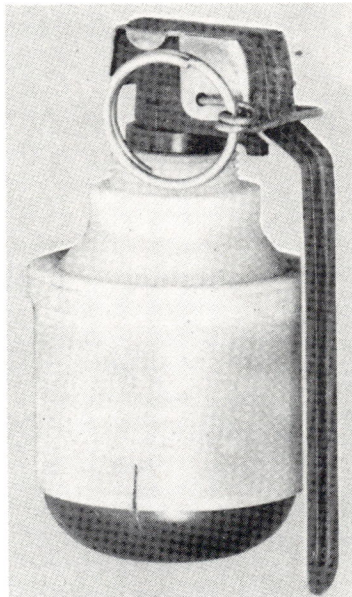

M.O. Hand grenade

CS AEROSOL CONTAINERS TYPES 39, 63 and 220

These three containers can be used either as hand-held aerosols or as hand grenades. In the former application the CS gas in the container is released by pressing a conventional aerosol button: for the latter application the valve is fixed open by percussion and the thrown canister will emit the full contents.

There are two versions of the Type 63, illustrated here. The emission time of the FDM version is 5 seconds longer than that of the CPM.

Manufacturer: Société Nationale des Poudres et Explosifs, 12, Quai Henri IV – 75181 Paris Cedex 04.
Status: In production for the French Army

DATA	Type 220	Type 63	Type 39
Diameter (mm):	50	35	27
Length (mm):	150	98	130
Capacity (cm³):	220	63	39
Total weight (g):	210	60	49
Action weight (g):	3	0.5	0.5
Operating time (sec):			
(approximate):	240	30(FDM) or 25 (CPM)	20

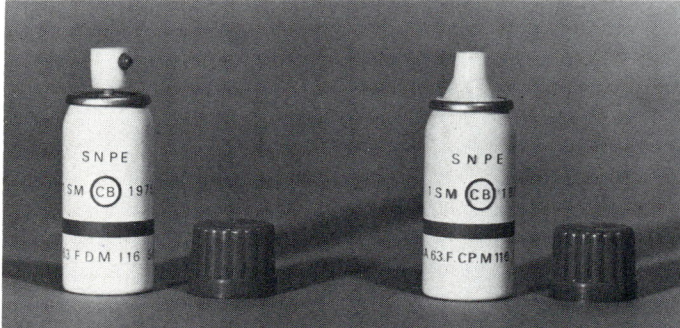

Type 63 containers FDM (left) ad CPM

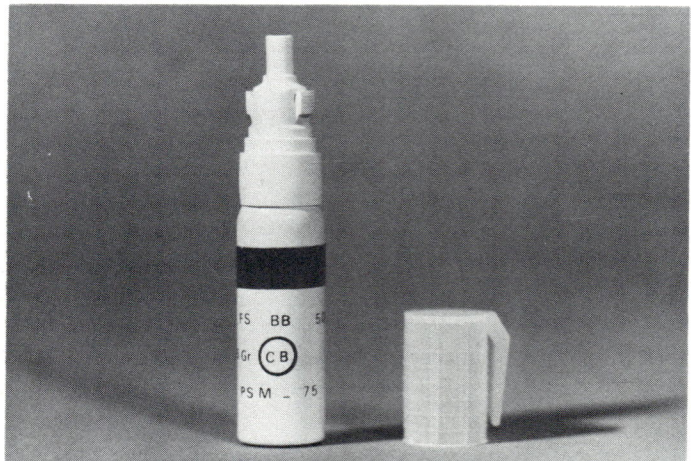

Type 220 container

NETHERLANDS

TEAR GAS HAND GRENADE NO. 14

This is a cylindrical grenade with a body of tinned rolled plate. It is painted grey with a red band, figures and lettering. It can be thrown about 40 metres and the fuze is initiated to puncture a gas cartridge which produces a stream of tear gas for about one minute.

It can be fitted with fuze assembly No. 25 or, in later production, with fuze assembly No. 19C2/17.

DATA
Body: Tinned Steel
Filling: 240g
Diameter: 73mm
Height: 158mm
Weight: 610g
Duration: 50-90sec

Tear gas grenade No. 14 and fuze assembly No. 25 or fuze assembly No. 19C2/17

UNITED KINGDOM

HAND GRENADE, NO. 91 (LACHRYMATORY)

The No. 91 Grenade is thrown by hand. It is initiated by the igniter, Grenade No. 1, Mk 1, operated by Striker Mechanism No. 3, Mk 1/3. The Mk 1 Grenade produced smoke so slowly that it could be thrown back by the recipient. The Mk 2 Grenade which is currently used produces a cloud of smoke lasting for about 25 seconds.

The body of the Mk 2 grenade is a cylinder of tinned plate about 114mm long and 57mm in diameter. The top is slightly dished and has a central recess about 25mm in diameter and 13mm in depth with a rolled thread to take the striker mechanism. There are four smoke emission holes, tape covered, around the top. An inner canister about 100mm by 50mm is perforated with 4mm holes, covered with paper, and there is a recess in the top corresponding to that in the top of the body. It has a filling of 185 grams of lachrymatory composition pressed in, in four pellets, with an igniting composition on top.

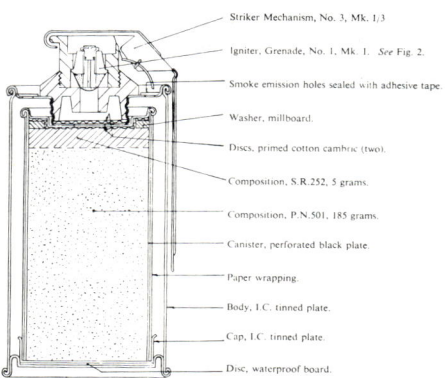

Grenade, hand, No. 91, Mk 2

Manufacturer: Royal Ordnance Factories
Status: In service

Grenade, hand, No. 91, lachrymatory

CS. ANTI-RIOT IRRITANT HAND GRENADES, L1A2 AND L2A1

The L1 grenade is hand thrown, or dispensed from light aircraft. It is initiated by an igniter operated by a striker mechanism.

The empty grenade consists of a tinplate cylinder with top and bottom closing plates, a perforated steel inner canister and a tin plate cap. The body is 114mm long and 57mm in diameter. The inner canister is 100mm long and 50mm in diameter. It is perforated all over with 4mm holes. The filling is a pressed composition pellet. The smoke lasts for 10-40 seconds.

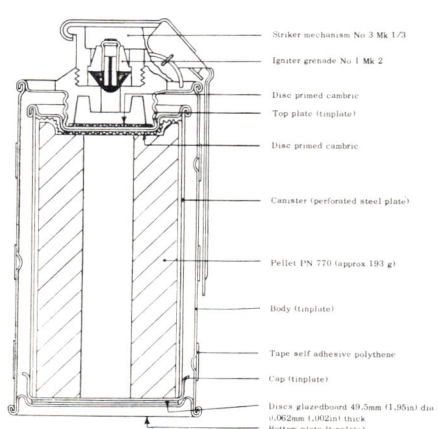

Striker mechanism No 3 Mk 1/3
Igniter grenade No 1 Mk 2
Disc primed cambric
Top plate (tinplate)
Disc primed cambric

Canister (perforated steel plate)

Pellet PN 770 (approx 193 g)

Body (tinplate)

Tape self adhesive polythene
Cap (tinplate)
Discs glazedboard 49.5mm (1.95in) dia
0.062mm (.002in) thick
Bottom plate (tinplate)

Grenade, hand, CS anti-riot irritant, L1A2

The L2 grenade is hand thrown and produces an explosion and a cloud of irritant smoke from the scattering of the irritant pellets that make up the main filling. This prevents the grenade being thrown back.

The body of the grenade is a hollow rubber cylinder with a centrally perforated tinplate lid which holds the striker mechanism. The interior of the body holds 400 pellets of a composition which burns to produce the irritant gas.

Manufacturer: Royal Ordnance Factories
Status: In service. The L2 grenade will be replaced by the more modern L13

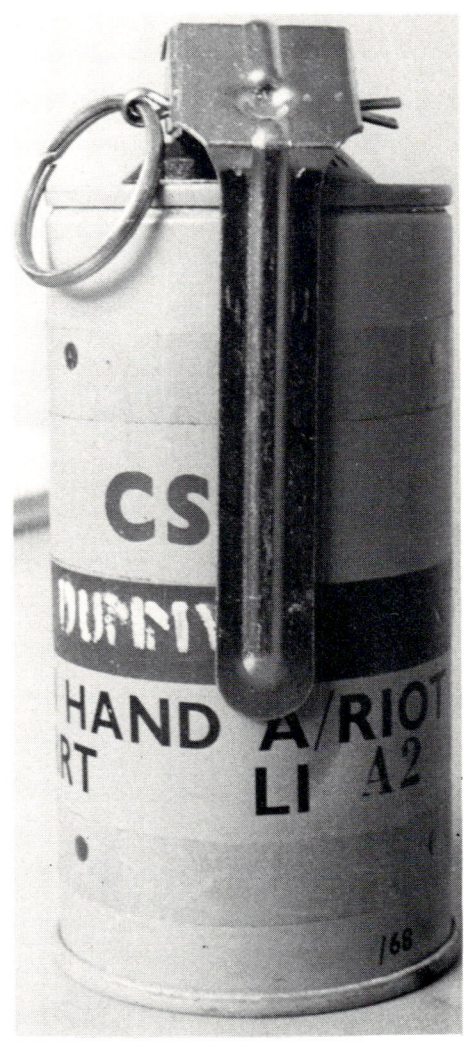

Grenade, hand, CS anti-riot irritant, L1A2

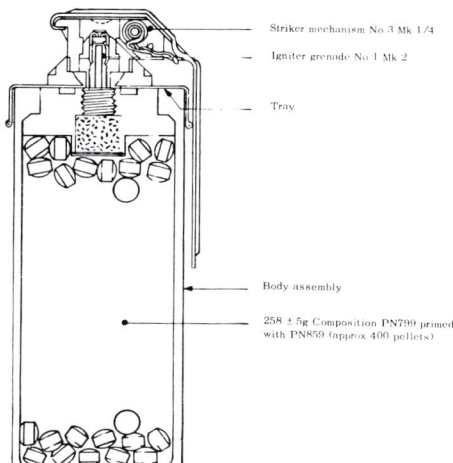

Striker mechanism No 3 Mk 1/4

Igniter grenade No 1 Mk 2

Tray

Body assembly

258 ± 5g Composition PN799 primed with PN859 (approx 400 pellets)

Grenade, hand, CS anti-riot irritant, L2A1

Discharger, grenade L1A1

SMOKE SCREENING GRENADE L5

There are two versions of this grenade, L5A1 and L5A2. The body is common to both and is a cold drawn seamless steel tube, open ended with a circular tin plate base. It is 178mm long and 63.5mm in diameter. The filling consists of three pre-pressed pellets of smoke composition.

The Fuze Electric 3 in F 52 Mk 1 is used with 2.6g of gunpowder (for the L5 A1) which gives a range of 50-60 metres. White smoke is emitted and lasts for 30-50 seconds. The L5A2 differs from the L5A1 in the construction of the filling and the gunpowder charge has been increased to 2.9g.

Manufacturer: Royal Ordnance Factories
Status: In service

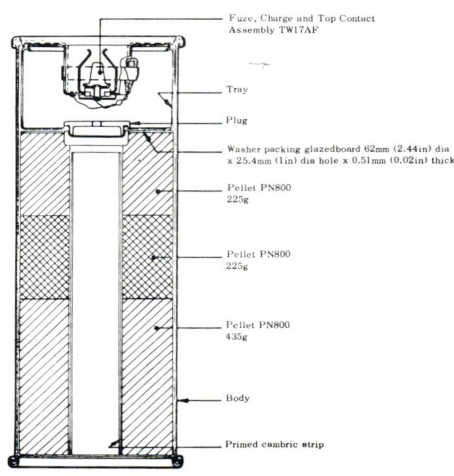

Fuze, Charge and Top Contact Assembly TW17AF

Tray

Plug

Washer packing glazedboard 62mm (2.44in) dia x 25.4mm (1in) dia hole x 0.51mm (0.02in) thick

Pellet PN800 225g

Pellet PN800 225g

Pellet PN800 435g

Body

Primed cambric strip

Grenade, discharger, smoke screening, L5A2

GRENADE L6A1, ANTI-RIOT IRRITANT

This is similar to the Smoke Screening Grenade L5 in construction. It has a filling of two pre-pressed pellets. It is used in the same way as the L5 with the F52 Mk 1 electric fuze and 2.6g of gunpowder giving it a range with the L1A1 discharge of some 50-60 metres.
Manufacturer: Royal Ordnance Factories
Status: In service

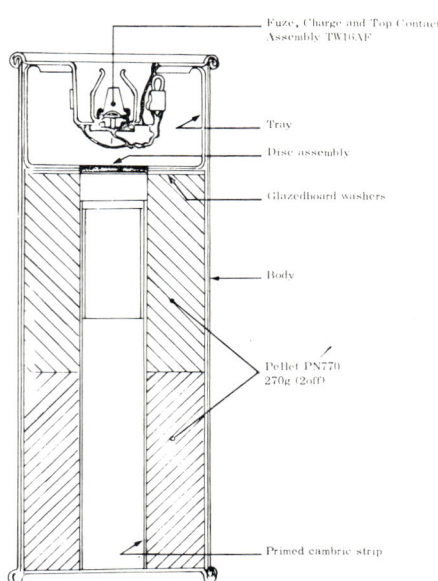

Fuze, Charge and Top Contact Assembly TW16AF

Tray

Disc assembly

Glazedboard washers

Body

Pellet PN770 270g (2off)

Primed cambric strip

Grenade, discharger, anti-riot irritant, L6A1

SMOKE SCREENING GREEN GRENADE L7A1

This is generally similar to the Grenade L5. It has a filling of two pre-pressed pellets and the gunpowder charge has been reduced to 2.25g.

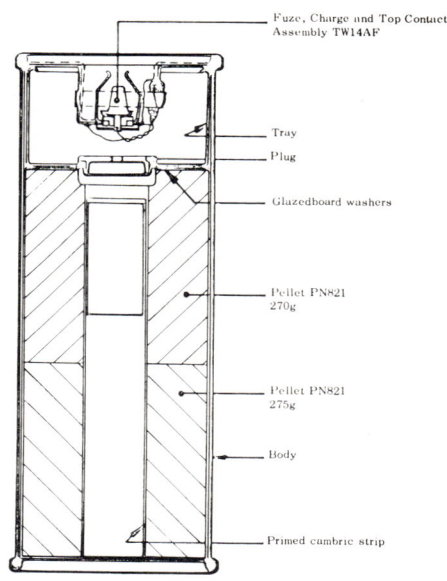

Grenade, discharger, smoke screening, L7A1, green

ANTI-RIOT IRRITANT GRENADES L9, L11 (LONG RANGE) AND L14

Each of these grenades comprises a rubber cylinder 66mm in diameter and 147mm long with a gunpowder propellant charge in the base which is ignited by Fuze, Electric, No. F92, Mk 2, Type C. The L9A1 grenade body contains 400 specially primed pellets of instant gas generating compound which weigh 18.5g and are ignited by the gunpowder charge. (4.5g). The charge propels the grenade from the L1A1 launcher to a range of 50-80 metres.

The L11 long range grenade has been designed to replace the L9. It is basically the same as the earlier grenade but has 23 aluminium-cased CS pellets of the type used in the L13 grenade. The grenade is projected to a distance of 50-80 metres.

The L14A1 is a practice version of the L11 Grenade and has a different filling which produces white smoke without any irritant effect.
Manufacturer: Royal Ordnance Factories
Status: In service. L9 obsolescent

Left to right: *anti-riot grenades L11 (medium range), L12 (long range) and L13 (hand) which serves a similar purpose but is not designed for use with the L1A1 launcher*

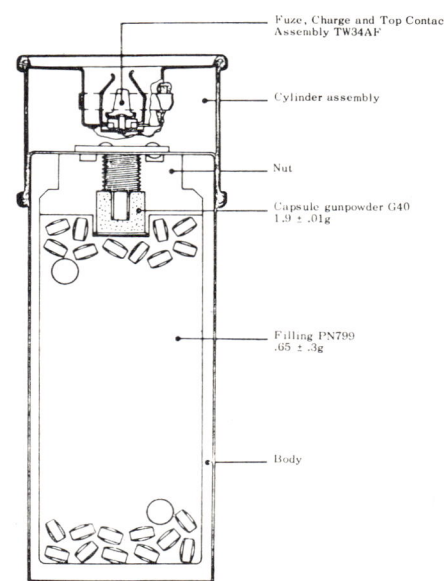

Grenade, discharger, anti-riot irritant, L9A1

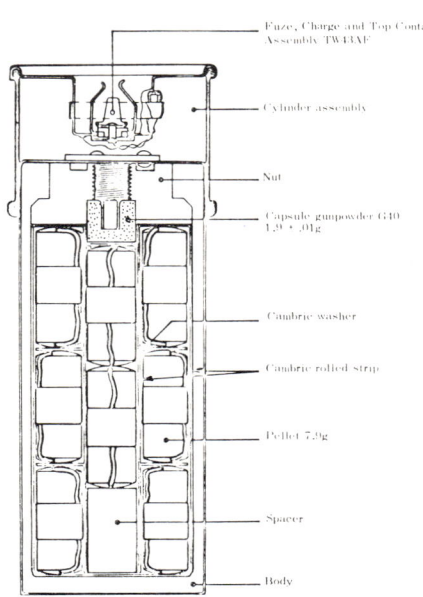

Grenade, discharger, anti-riot irritant, (long range) L11

Grenade, discharger, anti-riot irritant, (long range) L11A1

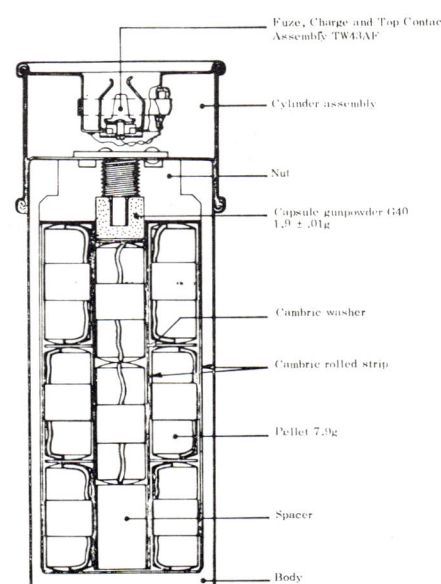

Grenade, discharger, practice, anti-riot, (long range) L14A1)

ANTI-RIOT IRRITANT GRENADES L12A1 (MEDIUM RANGE) AND L15A1

The L12A1 grenade has been introduced to cover the ground which lies between the maximum range of the hand thrown grenade (25 metres) and the minimum range of the L11 Grenade (50 metres).

It is similar to the L11 grenade differing only in the length of the delay increment and a reduction in the gunpowder propelling charge.

The L15A1 grenade is similar in design and action to the L14 (practice) grenade but has the same delay and propelling charge as the L12 grenade.

Manufacturer: Royal Ordnance Factories
Status: In service

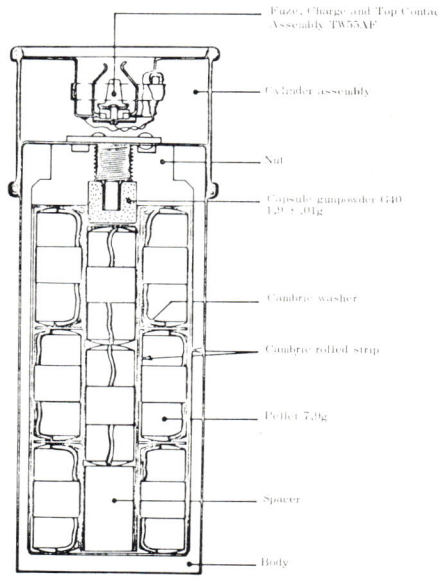

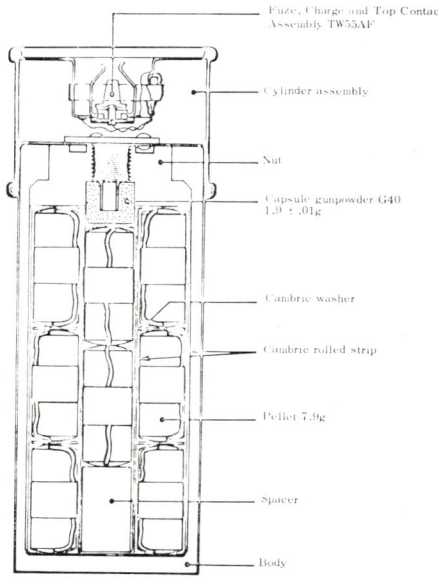

Grenade, discharger, anti-riot irritant, (medium range) L12A1

Grenade, discharger, anti-riot irritant, (medium range) L12A1

Grenade, discharger, practice, anti-riot, (medium range) L15A1

GRENADE, HAND, ANTI-RIOT IRRITANT, L13

The L13 anti-riot grenade has been designed to replace the L2 anti-riot irritant grenade (not to be confused with the L2 anti-personnel grenade). It differs in the nature of the filling. The rubber body and closing device are similar to those of the L2 grenade, but the filling consists of 23 aluminium cased CS pellets.

Manufacturer: Royal Ordnance Factories
Status: In production and in service

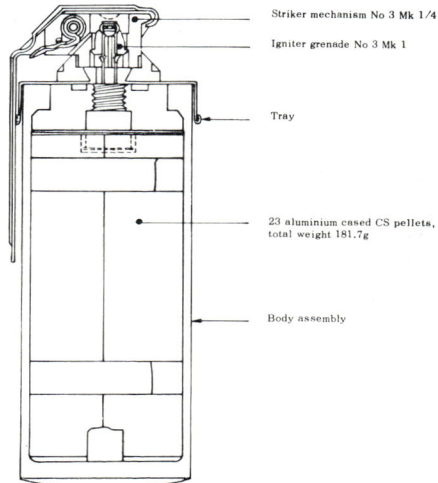

Grenade, hand, anti-riot irritant, L13A1

1.5in ANTI-RIOT BATON ROUNDS

These were designed to be fired from the existing Federal Riot Guns and Signal Pistols of 1.5in (38mm) and were intended to be used to break up riotous assemblies. The first rounds tried were made of wood and were based on the American design. They were replaced with rubber rounds intended to be fired directly into the target at ranges preferably not less than 25 metres. Between mid-1970 and mid-1972 studies carried out on some 33,000 rounds fired revealed a mortality rate of 1:16,000 which in Northern Ireland at the time was statistically less likely to produce deaths than the normal environmental hazards produced by traffic, falling chimney pots or runaway horses. A disability rate of 1:1,900 and a serious injury rate of 1:800, however, were not considered acceptable and a replacement grenade made in PVC was produced in 1972. This was lighter than the rubber round and somewhat more resilient but its major improvement was in its accuracy which enabled the projectile to be fired with a considerably greater chance of hitting a selected individual between ranges of 25 and 50 metres.

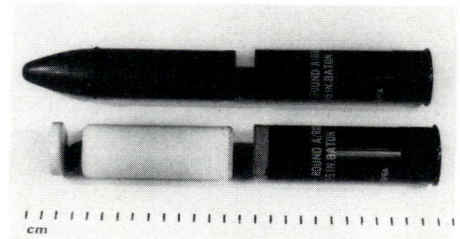

The rubber baton round and the PVC baton round

DATA

Material	Rubber	PVC
Weight:	150g	135g
Diameter:	38mm	38mm
Length of baton:	116mm	107mm
Weight of complete round:	212g	199g

The L5A1 PVC, 1.5in, anti-riot round

ANTI-RIOT, IRRITANT, HAND, GRENADE L1A3

This grenade generates a large, dense cloud of CS Smoke. Delay in ignition ensures that the thrower will not be affected by the emission; and the rate of emission is such that there is not enough time for the grenade to be retrieved and thrown back without considerable hazard.

A version with a reinforced base plate is available for use with rifle and vehicle-borne discharges and a red-smoke version is available for practice.

A cylindrical body of tin plate contains a solid block of CS-producing composition. The standard striker mechanism No. 3, Mk 1/3 is of the 'fly-off' lever type and is secured by a safety pin with pull ring.

DATA
Range: Up to 32 metres
Delay time: 1-5 seconds
Burning time: 8-40 seconds
Length: 140mm
Diameter: 64mm
Weight: 454g
CS composition content: 210g approximately
Packaging: Each grenade is sealed in an airtight tin which is opened by a turn key. 10 grenades, together with keys, are packed in a steel box.
Manufacturer: Schermuly Ltd, High Post, Salisbury, Wiltshire

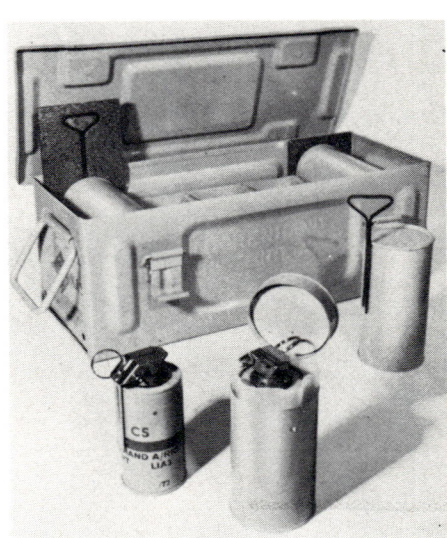

Grenade, hand, anti-riot irritant, L1A3

CARTRIDGE 1.5in ANTI-RIOT IRRITANT L3A1

These cartridges have been designed for the UK Government to replace the paper-cased L2A2 cartridge. The L3A1 carries a payload of CS smoke-producing composition and can be fired from standard 1.5in (38mm) pistols and riot guns. Two types are available: L3A1 for long-range firing; and for shorter ranges a similar cartridge with a reduced propellant charge.

There is also a practice version, pink-smoke-filled (L4A1).

When fired a delay composition is ignited by the propellant and emission of CS smoke beings a few seconds after firing.

An aluminium canister projectile holds the CS smoke-producing compositon and delay unit. This canister is contained within an aluminium cartridge case which incorporates the percussion cap in the base and a propellant charge.

DATA
(L3A1 and L4A1)
Range (nominal): 100mm
Delay time: 1-5 seconds
Burning time: 10-25 seconds
Length: 120mm
Diameter: 38.7mm stepped to 39.6mm
Weight: 200g
CS composition content: 93g
Muzzle velocity: Over 100 metres per second
Packaging: Rounds are packed 25 to a box with batches of 5 rounds secured by linked plastic grips.
Manufacturer: Schermuly Ltd, High Post, Salisbury, Wiltshire

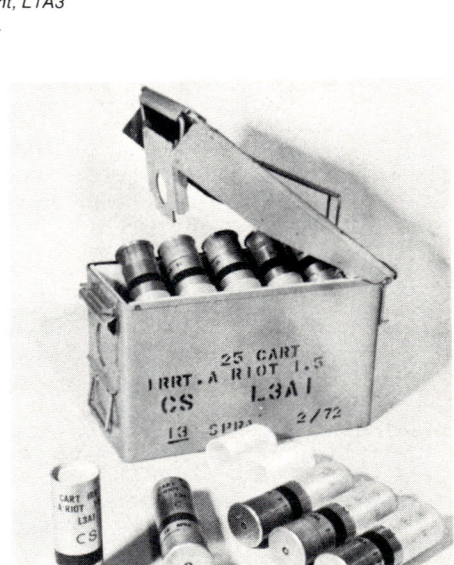

Cartridge, 1.5in, anti-riot irritant, L3A1

1.5in ANTI-RIOT BATON (RUBBER) L2A2

This riot control device consists of a rubber projectile capable of being fired from any 38mm (1.5in) calibre riot gun or pistol. Its main use is to break up riot crowds, severe bruising and shock being the maximum injury likely to be sustained by persons struck by this projectile when used at recommended ranges.

The complete round consists of an extended aluminium alloy cartridge case with a centre fire percussion cap, plastic charge capsule and a greased medium hard rubber projectile.

DATA
Range: Minimum 6 metres; Maximum 25 metres plus
Length (baton): 146mm
Length (complete): 165mm
Diameter: 38mm
Weight (baton): 149g
Weight (complete): 212g
Packaging: Rounds are packed 18 to a box in individual spacer tubes
Manufacturer: Schermuly Ltd, High Post, Salisbury, Wiltshire

Cartridge, 1.5in, anti-riot baton, L2A2

1.5in ANTI-RIOT BATONS (PLASTIC) L3A1 & L5A2

Each of these riot control munitions, successors to the anti-riot baton (rubber), consists of a plastic projectile capable of being fired from any 38mm (1.5in) calibre riot gun or pistol. Its main use is to break up riot crowds, severe bruising and shock being the maximum injury likely to be sustained by persons struck by this projectile when used at recommended ranges. The L3A1 is recommended for the larger ranges.

From the Webley Schermuly long-barrel riot gun, the plastic round can be effectively fired at ranges of 30m to 60m enabling law enforcement officers to direct fire at mob ringleaders. The long range cartridge is intended to out-range stone throwing rioters.

The complete round consists of an extruded aluminium alloy cartridge case with a centre fire percussion cap, plastic charge capsule and a polyvinylchloride (PVC) projectile. Minor differences of cartridge closure and propellant charge distinguish variations of the basic design produced to meet users' performance requirements.

DATA
Baton: Weight: 107g
   Length: 99mm
Round: Weight: 170g
   Length: 120mm
Diameter: 38mm
Packing: 25 rounds in steel H83 box. Weight 9kg approx.
Manufacturer: Schermuly Ltd, High Post, Salisbury, Wiltshire
Status: In production and service

UNITED STATES OF AMERICA

GRENADES, HAND: RIOT, CN, M7 and M7A1

Grenade M7 and Grenade M7A1 are burning type riot control agent grenades and may be used to simulate casualty agents during training. CN has a powerful lachrimal effect and is irritating to the upper respiratory passages. In high concentrations it is irritating to the skin, causing a burning and itching sensation. The onset of incapacitation is 15 to 30 seconds and duration from 5 to 20 minutes depending upon dosage concentration.

Grenade body: The grenade bodies of these grenades are of thin sheet metal and are cylindrical in shape. The filling is compressed into the grenade body, a tapered hole being formed through the body of the filling. The top surface of the filling and the tapered walls of the hole are coated with starter mixture (to aid ignition of the fuel by the fuze).

Fuze, hand grenade M201A1: Fuze M201A1 is a pyrotechnic delay-igniting fuze. The body contains a primer, first-fire mixture, pyrotechnic delay column and igniter mixture. Assembled to the body are a striker, striker spring, safety lever and safety pin with pull ring. The split end of the safety pin has an angular spread.

Safety clips: Safety clips are not required with these grenades.

OPERATION
Removal of the safety pin permits release of the safety lever. When the safety lever is released, it is forced away from the grenade body by a striker acting under the force of a striker spring. The striker rotates on its own axis and strikes the percussion primer. The primer initiates the first-fire mixture. The fuze delay element, igniting mixture, and grenade starter mixture and filler are initiated in turn by the preceding component. The pressure sensitive tape is blown off the emission holes and the CN agent is emitted for 15 or 30 seconds.

DATA
Grenade (with fuze):
Model: M7, M7A1
Body: Sheet metal
Weight: (M7) 17oz (482g); (M7A1) 18½oz (525g)
Length: 145mm
Diameter: 63.5mm
Colour: Grey w/l red band and red markings
Packing: 1 per container; 16 per packing box

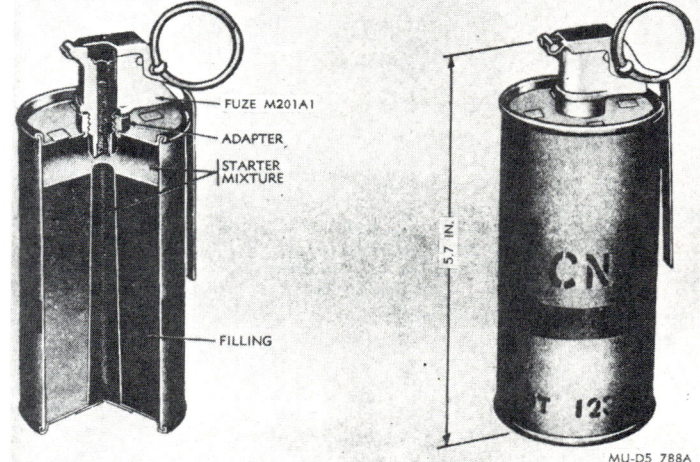

CN riot hand grenade M7A1

Filler:
Type: CN Pyrotechnic composition
Weight: (M7) 291g (M7A1) 355g
Fuze:
Model: M201A1
Type: Pyrotechnic delay-igniting
Primer: M39A1
Ignition mixture: Iron oxide, titanium, zirconium
Delay time: 0.7 – 2 sec
Weight: 42g
Length: 99mm
Colour: Grey or olive drab w/black markings
Safety device: Pull ring and safety pin

GRENADES, HAND: RIOT, CS, M7A2 and M7A3

Grenades M7A2 and M7A3 are similar in appearance to the M7A1. They are burning type riot control agent grenades and may be used to simulate casualty agents during training. CS has a powerful lachrimal effect and is irritating to the upper respiratory passages causing coughing, difficulty in breathing and chest tightness. Heavy concentrations will cause nausea and vomiting as well. The onset of incapacitation is 15 to 30 seconds and duration is less then 10 minutes after personnel are removed to fresh air. CS is more persistent and has a more severe reaction than CN.

Grenade body: The body is a cylinder of thin sheet metal. The filler is compressed into the grenade body with a starter mix.

Fuze, hand grenade, M201A1: See description in the entry for the M7 grenade above.

Safety clips: Safety clips are not required with these grenades.

DATA
Grenade (with fuze):
Models: M7A2, M7A3
Body: Sheet metal
Weight: 440g

Length (max): 45mm
Diameter: 63.5mm
Colour: Grey w/l red band; red markings
Packing: 1 per container; 16 per packing box
Filler:
Type: CS (156g)
Weight: (M7A2) 156g burning mixture and 99g powdered CS in gelatine capsules; (M7A3) 208g burning mixture and 127g pelletized CS agent
Fuze:
Model: M201A1
Type: Pyrotechnic delay-igniting
Primer: M39A1
Ignition mixture: Iron oxide, titanium, zirconium
Delay time: 0.7–2sec
Weight: 42g
Length: 99mm
Colour: Grey or olive drab, w/black markings
Safety device: Pull ring and safety pin
Function: Similar to M7A1

GRENADES, HAND: CN1, ABC-M25A1 AND ABC-M25A2

CN1 Hand Grenades ABC-M25A1 and ABC-M25A2 are bursting type grenades used for riot control and to simulate casualty agents during training. CN1 has a powerful lachrimal effect and is irritating to the upper respiratory passages. In higher concentrations, it is irritating to the skin, causing a burning itching sensation. The onset of incapacitation is from 15 to 30 seconds and the duration from 5 to 20 minutes depending upon dosage concentration.

Grenade body: The grenade body is spherical. It is made of two plastic hemispheres cemented together. The two pieces together form a burster well and slider housing.

Fuze: The fuze is a pyrotechnic delay-detonating type integral with the grenade body. The fuzing components consist of an arming sleeve, arming pin, firing spring, slider assembly and firing pin. The slider assembly contains a primer, pyrotechnic delay column and a detonator. The grenade is assembled with a safety pin and pull ring.

Safety clips: Safety clips are not required with these grenades.

DATA
Grenade (with fuze):
Models: ABC-M25A1, ABC-M25A2
Body: Plastic hemispheres (2)
Weight: 213g
Length (maximum): 86mm
Diameter: 74mm
Colour: Grey w/red band and red markings
Packing: 1 per can; 50 per packing box
Filler:

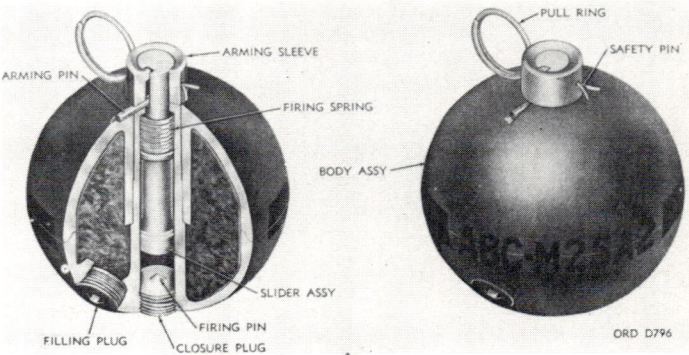

CN1 hand grenade ABC-M25A2

Type: CN1
Weight: 90g
Fuze:
Model: Integral
Type: Pyrotechnic delay-detonating
Primer: 2926a (Olin)
Detonator: Lead azide, Lead styphnate and tetryl
Delay time: 1.4-3 seconds
Safety device: Pull ring and safety pin

GRENADE, HAND: RIOT, CS1, ABC-M25A2

Grenade CS1, ABC-M25A2 is similar to Grenade, CN1 ABC-M25A2. It is a bursting-type riot control agent grenade and may be used to simulate casualty agents during training. CS has a powerful lachrymal effect and is irritating to the upper respiratory passages, causing coughing, difficulty in breathing and chest tightness. Heavy concentrations will cause nausea and vomiting as well. The onset of incapacitation is 15 to 30 seconds and duration from 30 minutes to several hours depending upon the dosage concentration. CS is more persistent and has a more severe reaction than CN.

Construction and fuzing are the same as for the CN grenades.

DATA
Grenade (with fuze):
Model: ABC-M25A2

Body: Plastic hemispheres (2)
Weight: 227g
Length: 86mm
Diameter: 75mm
Colour: Grey w/red band and red markings
Packing: 1 per can; 50 per packing box
Filler: CS1 57g (approx.)
Fuze:
Model: Integral
Type: Pyrotechnic delay-detonating
Primer: 2926a (Olin)
Detonator: Lead azide, Lead styphnate and tetryl
Delay time: 1.4-3 seconds
Safety device: Pull ring and safety pin

GRENADE, HAND: 8 TO 12 SECOND DELAY, CS, M54

Grenade, M54 is a burning-type riot control agent grenade and may be used to simulate casualty agents during training. CS has a powerful lachrimal effect and is irritating to the upper respiratory passages, causing coughing, difficulty in breathing and chest tightness. Heavy concentrations will cause nausea and vomiting as well. The onset of incapacitation is 15 to 30 seconds and duration is from 30 minutes to several hours, depending upon dosage concentration. CS is more persistent and has a more severe reaction than CN.

Grenade body: The grenade body is thin sheet steel, cylindrical in shape. The grenade is filled with a mix of CS pellets and fuel mixture. The filler is loaded through a flash hole in the centre. The sides of the flash hole and top of the sear are coated with a starter mixture.

Fuze, hand grenade M226: Fuze, M226 is a pyrotechnic delay-igniting fuze. The body contains a primer, first-fire mixture, delay column, and ignition mixture. Assembled to the body are a striker, striker spring, safety

CS 8 to 12 second delay hand grenade M54

lever and safety pin with a pull ring. The split end of the safety pin has an angular spread.

Safety clips: Safety clips are not required with these grenades.

DATA
Grenade (with fuze):
Model: M54
Body: Thin sheet steel
Weight: 454g
Length: 146mm
Diameter: 64mm
Colour: Grey w/red band, red markings
Packing: 1 per container, 16 containers per packing box

Filler:
Type: CS
Weight: 119g

Fuze:
Model: M226
Type: Pyrotechnic delay igniting
Primer: Percussion w/no designation
Igniter mixture: Iron oxide, titanium and zirconium
Delay time: 8 to 12 seconds
Colour: Olive drab w/black markings
Safety device: Pull ring and safety pin
Function: As M7A1

GRENADE, HAND: RIOT, POCKET, CS, XM58

CS Pocket Riot Hand Grenade XM58 is a burning-type riot control agent grenade and may be used to simulate casualty agents during training. CS has a powerful lachrimal effect and is irritating to the upper respiratory passages, causing coughing, difficulty in breathing and chest tightness. Heavy concentrations will cause nausea and vomiting as well. The onset of incapacitation is 15 to 30 seconds and duration is less than 10 minutes after personnel are removed to fresh air. CS is more persistent and has a more severe reaction than CN.

Grenade body: The body is a thin-walled, two-piece aluminium cylinder. It contains a CS-pyrotechnic composition. There is a hole in the base of the body which is used for agent emission after functioning.

Fuze, hand grenade M201A1E1: This fuze is similar to the fuze, M201A1. The body contains a primer, fire mixture, pyrotechnic delay column and ignition mixture. Assembled to the body are a striker, striker spring, safety lever and safety pin with pull ring. The split end of the safety pin has an angular spread.

Safety clips: Safety clips are not required with these grenades.

DATA
Grenade (with fuze):
Model: XM58
Body: Aluminium
Weight (approx): 114g
Length (max): 83mm
Diameter: 33mm
Colour: Grey w/red band and red markings
Packing: 10 per fibreboard box; 10 per packing box
Filler:
Type: CS-pyrotechnic composition
Weight: 39g
Fuze:
Model: M201A1E1

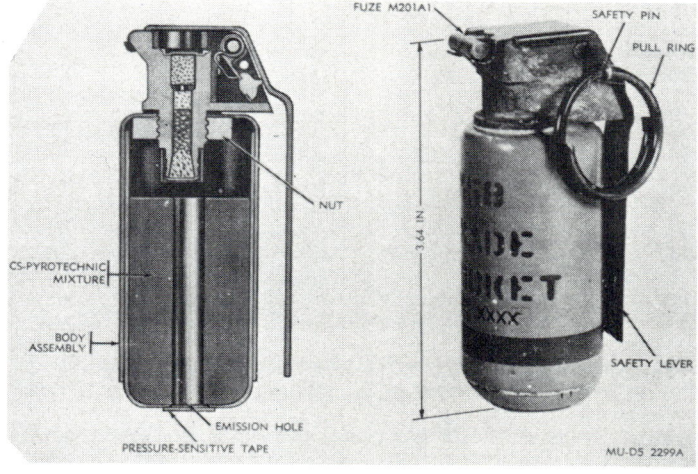

CS pocket riot hand grenade XM58

Type: Pyrotechnic delay-igniting
Primer: M39A1
Igniter mixture: Iron oxide, titanium, zirconium
Delay time: 0.7-2sec
Weight: 42g
Length: 76mm
Colour: Olive drab w/black markings
Safety device: Pull ring and safety pin
Function: As M7A1

S&W CONTINUOUS DISCHARGE GRENADES No 2

Designed to be either hand-thrown or launched from a shotgun launcher, these grenades are available with CN, CS or white smoke fillings and use military pattern fuzes.
DATA
Diameter: 67mm
Length: 152mm
Container: Aluminium

Fuze: M201A1
Delay: 1-2sec
Discharge time: 40-50sec
Discharge method: Burning
Manufacturer: Smith & Wesson, 2100 Roosevelt Avenue, Springfield, Massachusetts 01101

S&W MILITARY PATTERN CONTINUOUS DISCHARGE GRENADES No 3

Similar to the No 2 grenade but slightly smaller, fitted with a military-pattern pin safety and designed for hand-throwing only these grenades are available with CN, CS or white smoke fittings

DATA
Diameter: 63.5mm
Length: 140mm

Container: Tin Plate
Fuze: M201A1
Delay: 1-2sec
Discharge time: 35-45sec
Discharge method: Burning
Manufacturer: Smith & Wesson, 2100 Roosevelt Avenue, Springfield, Massachusetts 01101

S&W BLAST DISPERSION GRENADE No 5

Designed for hand-throwing only, this grenade is intended for use where an immediate and non-flammable discharge of CN or CS powder is required. It has the same dimensions as the No 2 continuous discharge grenade but has an integral fuse with a 3-second delay. The case is made of non-fragmenting aluminium so that the blast effect is devoted entirely to

scattering the CN or CS powder.

Manufacturer: Smith & Wesson, 2100 Roosevelt Avenue, Springfield, Massachusetts 01101

S&W RUBBER BALL GRENADE No 15

This grenade is designed for hand-throwing or launching from a shotgun launcher. It burns very rapidly, thus offering little opportunity for a rioter to pick it up and throw it back, and its rubber case minimises the chance of serious injury. It is available with CN, CS or smoke filling.

DATA
Diameter: 79mm
Height: 121mm

Container: Rubber
Fuze: M201A1
Delay: 1-2sec
Discharge time: 15-20sec
Discharge method: Burning
Manufacturer: Smith & Wesson, 2100 Roosevelt Avenue, Springfield, Massachusetts 01101.

S&W 'MIGHTY MIDGET' GRENADE No 98

These small grenades are designed for hand throwing or for launching from shotgun or revolver launchers. Available with either CN or CS fillings they have striker ignition fuzes.

DATA
Diameter: 35mm
Length: 127mm

Container: Aluminium
Fuze: Striker ignition
Delay: 3sec
Discharge time: 20-25secs
Discharge method: Burning
Manufacturer: Smith & Wesson, 2100 Roosevelt Avenue, Springfield, Massachusetts 01101

S&W 37mm RIOT CONTROL PROJECTILES

Smith & Wesson make a range of 37mm CN, CN and smoke generating projectiles and instantaneous gas discharge shells. With the exception of the 'Tru-Flite' penetrating projectile (which must be used with a shoulder-fired weapon) these rounds can all be used with 37mm (1.5in) S&W and most other gas guns and pistols. The main types are listed below and all are available with CN, CS or smoke fillings except No 21 which, for obvious reasons, is available only with CN or CS.

No 12 'Tru-Flite' Penetrating Projectile A fin-stabilized hand rubber projectile for accurate shooting will penetrate ⅝in (16mm) plywood at 100

yards (91.4m).
No 17 Long Range Projectile A low-recoil projectile available in 75 and 150 yard (68.5 and 137m) models
No 18 Long Range Rubber Projectile Similar to No 17 but having no external metal on the projectile
No 21 Short-Range Shell This pojects a dense cloud of CN or CS gas and smoke to a distance of 35 feet (about 11 metres) from the muzzle of the gas gun or pistol.
Manufacturer: Smith & Wesson, 2100 Roosevelt Avenue, Springfield, Massachusetts 01101.

12-GAUGE BARRICADE PIERCING PROJECTILE

Designed to be fired from 12-gauge cylinder bore police shotguns with 2¾ or 3in (70.1 or 76.2mm) chambers this 'Tru-Flite' projectile will penetrate ¾inch (19mm) plywood at 50 feet (15.25m) or window glass at up to 80 yards (73 metres) and disperse the CN or CS vapour behind the obstruction. The projectile contains a red dye marker to help to indicate hits; and an average shot can put a second round in a circle of diameter 2 feet

(61cm) at 80 yards (73m). Recoil is very low. The projectile contains no explosive or pyrotechnic and contamination risk is low. A protective cap, colour-coded for identification, is fitted to each round.
Manufacturer: Smith & Wesson, 2100 Roosevelt Avenue, Springfield, Massachusetts 01101

PYROTECHNICS
FRANCE

COLOURED SMOKE HAND GRENADES, RUGGIERI MODEL F1 AND MODEL F2

The coloured smoke hand grenades Models F1 and F2 are used for signalling during the hours of daylight. The Model F1 is suited for regrouping parachutists when they have landed whilst the Model F2 is used for marking dropping zones or determining the strength and direction of wind on the ground. The model F2 is sometimes dropped by aircraft or helicopter.Both types have the same type of cylindrical body of light alloy construction containing the smoke composition. The Model F1 is provided with a pressure igniter set protected in storage by a screwed cap, a safety valve line gland prevents untimely functioning.
The Model F2 is fitted with an automatic igniter set Model 35.

DATA

	Model F1	Model F2
Height of grenade body:	150mm	150mm
Total height with fuse:	pressure type, 175mm	spoon type, 175mm
Overall diameter with fuze lever:	55mm	63mm
Average weight:	0.450kg	0.530kg
Ignition delay:	about 2 seconds	about 2 seconds
Packaging:	wood containers of 40 grenades (weight of about 30kg)	metal boxes of 5 grenades and wood containers of 40 grenades (weight of about 35kg)
Time of smoke discharge:	a minimum of 2 minutes	a minimum of 2 minutes
Smoke colours:	red, orange, yellow, green, violet, blue, white	red, yellow, green

Coloured smoke hand grenades, models F1 (right) and F2

Manufacturer: Etablissements Ruggieri – Direction Commerciale Armement, 122 rue la Boetie – 75008 Paris (France)
Status: In production. Adopted by the French Army

COLOURED SMOKE HAND GRENADE MODEL F3

Similar in purpose to the F1 grenade the Ruggieri Model F3 is larger and has a longer emission time. Unlike the F1, however, it is fitted with an automatic igniter set, Model 35, as used on the Model F2.

DATA
Height: Total: 258mm
        Grenade body: 236mm
Diameter: Including igniter: 66mm max
        Grenade body: 58mm
Average weight: 0.7kg
Ignition delay: 2sec
Emission time: 2½ minutes
Colours available: red, green, orange, yellow, violet, blue or white
Packing: 5 grenades in sealed metal carrier
        8 carriers in wooden case
        Average weight (40 grenades) 42kg
Manufacturer: Etablissements Ruggieri – Direction Commerciale Armement, 122 rue la Boetie – 75008 Paris
Status: In production. Adopted by the French Army

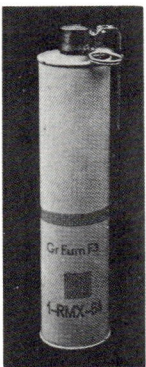

Model F3 smoke grenade

COLOURED SMOKE GRENADE TYPE 60

The Type 60 smoke grenade can be used for signalling, target designation or as a smoke grenade. It comprises the following components – cylindrical metal body, vented cover, the smoke producing mixture and a lever type delayed igniter set.

DATA
Diameter: 55mm
Overall height: 140mm
Weight: 700g
Delay of composition igniter: 4 seconds
Duration of smoke emission: 50 seconds
Colour of smoke: Red, green, yellow and white
Manufacturer: Societe E. Lacroix, Route de Toulouse, 31 Muret, or Direction Commerciale, 18 Rue Malher, 75 Paris IV

Type 60 smoke grenade

40mm HAND-DISCHARGED ILLUMINATOR RTE TYPE 709

This is a rocket propelled parachute flare which can be launched from its transport packing tube when this is either held in the hand or propped on a simple stand.

The rocket has a light alloy body with stabilising apertures at the rear and containing a propellant charge and the paraflare with its ejector. The rocket propellant initiates the paraflare ejection and ignites the illuminant.

The container has a cap at each end which is taped in position. The lower cap covers a percussion priming device controlled by an arming and fusing lever. Operation of this lever with both caps removed fires the rocket.

If fired at 45° the rocket will eject the parachute at a height of about 120 metres and a ground range of some 400 metres. The parachute and flare will then descend at about 5 metres/second.

DATA
Case length: 314mm
Rocket length: 270mm
Case diameter: 46mm
Rocket diameter: 40mm
Total weight: 500g
Rocket weight: 345g
Illumination: 80,000 candlas approx.
Duration: 18 seconds approx.

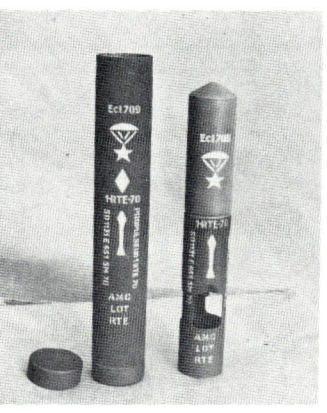 

The hand launcher and rocket and (right) a suggested launching arrangement

Manufacturer: Etablissements Ruggieri, Direction Commerciale Armement, 122 rue la Boetie – 75008 Paris

27mm HAND SIGNALLING DEVICES MODEL 1958

A range of 27mm disposable hand signalling devices is made by Ets Ruggieri. Each consists of a light alloy tube (length dependent upon signal type) containing the signal assembly, an ejector and the firing system. In each case the firing system comprises a traction igniter and delay and is operated by a pull-cord. The ignition system is protected by a plastic cap which carries symbols in relief on its outer surface so that the signal can be identified by night.

To fire the signal the launch tube is grasped by one hand with the protective cap towards the firer. This cap is then removed, using the other hand, and the ignition cord extracted from its housing. The firer should then kneel on one knee and, holding the device at arm's length and with the igniter side towards the ground and the tube inclined away from him, pull the ignition cord briskly. He should then immediately press the base of the tube firmly on the ground and hold it vertical as far away from himself as possible until it has fired. The delay from ignition to firing is approximately three seconds.

All the signals are enclosed in launch tubes of the same diameter but the tube length varies with the contents as shown below.

Signal	Length	Weight
Single light (white or green)	146mm	85g
Single light (red magnesium)	178mm	110g
Three lights (white, green or red)	193mm	120g
Six lights (white green or red)	273mm	160g
Parachute star (white, green or red)	273mm	160g
Parachute smoke (yellow, green red, orange or violet)	273mm	160g
Parachute caterpiller (white, green or red)	273mm	155g

Packing: Signals are packed in lots of 10 in sealed metal containers and the containers are packed in boxes of 100 signals (weight 23-27kg according to signal) except for the single white or green lights which are in boxes of 200 (weight 32kg).
Manufacturer: Etablissements Ruggieri, Direction Commerciale Armement, 122 rue la Boetie – 75008 Paris
Status: Production

UNION OF SOVIET SOCIALIST REPUBLICS

26.5mm SIGNAL PISTOL

This single-shot smooth bore weapon exists in several versions among the Warsaw Pact and client countries. Used for launching various types of signal or illumination flare they are now probably obsolescent in Eastern Europe, where modern hand-launched flare signals are now in service, but will certainly be encountered elsewhere.

DATA
Calibre: 26.5mm
Length: Typically 220mm
Weight: Typically 0.8kg
Status: Obsolescent

30mm & 40mm HAND FLARE SIGNALS

Hand flare signals and similar pyrotechnic devices are now in service in the Warsaw Pact armies. Consisting of hand-held disposable launchers containing propellant charges and stars or parachute flares they are not significantly different from many devices in service or available in other countries. It is believed that they are replacing signal pistols in most applications.

UNITED KINGDOM

HAND GRENADE, NO. 83 SMOKE

The Grenade, Hand, No. 83, is designed to be thrown by hand. It can also be thrown out of a light aircraft. It is used for signalling and produces a cloud of coloured smoke which may be blue, green, red or yellow. It is initiated by a striker setting off an igniter. The description below relates to Mk 2/1 and is followed by some details of the Mk 3 grenades.

The container is a tinplate cylinder with top and bottom closing plates and a smoke canister.

The body is 114mm long and 63.5mm in diameter. It is produced with flush seams and the top closing plate has a central recess 25.4mm in diameter and 12.7mm deep with a rolled thread for the striker mechanism. The base of the recess has a flash hole and four 6.3mm holes, covered with tape, are spaced around the top plate. These are smoke emission holes.

The smoke canister is a sheet steel cylinder 102mm long by 51mm diameter. It is perforated all over and covered with paper which has been shellac varnished. It has a tin plate top recessed to fit over the recess in the top closing plate of the body and has a flash hole to match that in the top of

the body. A tin plate cap closes the bottom of the canister after it has been filled.

The filling consists of three solid pellets each pressed in. The filled grenade is fitted with the striker mechanism and igniter.
GRENADE, HAND, NO. 83 Mk 3/1

The body is cylindrical with top and bottom closing plates, diaphragm, base and ignition tube. It is of tinplate similar to that of the Mk 2/1. The top closing plate is perforated at the centre and a zinc adapter for the striker mechanism, is fitted. The bottom of the body is closed by a tin plate base, copper diaphragm and then a tin plate closure disc. An ignition tube, 102mm long, is perforated along its length and the end fits over the projection on the base. The cloud of smoke lasts for about 25 seconds.

The filling is a perforated pellet pressed in.
Manufacturer: Royal Ordnance Factories
Status: In service

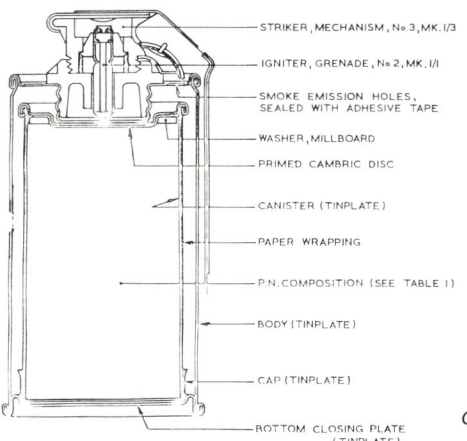

Grenade, hand, No. 83, smoke, Mk 3/1

Grenade, hand, No. 83, smoke, Mk 2/1

Grenade, hand, No. 83, smoke

Grenade, Hand, Coloured Smoke Marking XL6E1 is intended as the replacement for the No. 83 Grenade. It will weigh about 225g and be available with red, orange, or green smoke.
Manufacturer: Royal Ordnance Factories

SIGNAL, SMOKE, HAND THROWN

This smoke signal is designed for ground-air signalling, and for ground recognition marking. When actuated, a dense cloud of coloured smoke is emitted from the grenade for 10 to 20 seconds according to colour. An uncocked firing mechanism is incorporated ensuring maximum safety in handling and storage.

The body is a seamed metal canister, containing a solid block of smoke-producing composition. At the base of the canister is a rupture disc which is blown out to allow smoke emission.
DATA
Colours: Red, green, blue, yellow
Delay: 2-3 seconds
Burning: 10-20 seconds (colours vary)
Length: 92mm
Diameter: 54mm
Weight: 185g

Packaging: 180 units per case
Manufacturer: Schermuly Ltd., High Post, Salisbury, Wiltshire

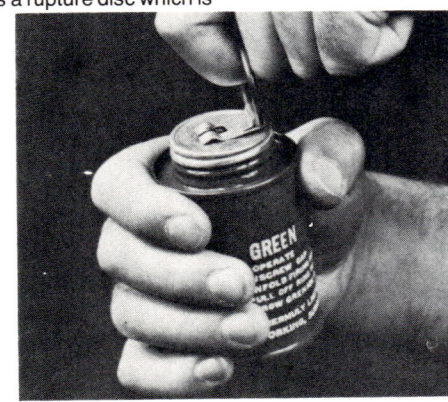

The Schermuly, hand-thrown, smoke, signal grenade

ROCKET 1.5in, HAND-FIRED PARACHUTE ILLUMINATING L3A2

Based on the well proved Schermuly 'Icarus' rocket, this hand-fired percussion ignition illuminator is able to define targets down to man-size at ranges between 100 and 300m. A high intensity flare suspended from a parasheet makes accurate small arms fire possible for the duration of the flare.

To use the rocket the adhesive tape securing the metal top cap is removed, leaving the cap itself in position. A similar cap at the base is removed and the firing lever is disclosed. Tape holding this ring lever is peeled away and the lever pulled out and held at the side of the rocket. Pressure on the lever activates the striker mechanism and the rocket is fired instantaneously. Maximum altitude is gained in about 5 seconds and the payload ejected. Variations in firing elevation are practicable, ranging from vertical ejection at 400m altitude to 30 degrees giving a ground range of over 300m.

The discharger is a resin-bonded weatherproof cylinder, with the lever operated percussion ignition system fitted in the base. Operating diagrams and instructions are printed on the discharger. The rocket is of light aluminium, housing the solid propellant and payload. The drum tail and slow spin imparted by the motor design ensure maximum accuracy and consistency in flight path.

DATA
Height (approx): 400 metres
Ground range: 320-412 metres
Illumination: 80,000cd
Length (complete): 266mm
Diameter (complete): 46mm
Total weight: 354g
Burning time (minimum): 25 seconds
Packaging: 100 rockets packed in wood Trade Pack
    12 rockets packed in waterproof polythene bottle service pack. 4 bottles per case (total 48 rockets).
Manufacturer: Schermuly Ltd, High Post, Salisbury, Wiltshire

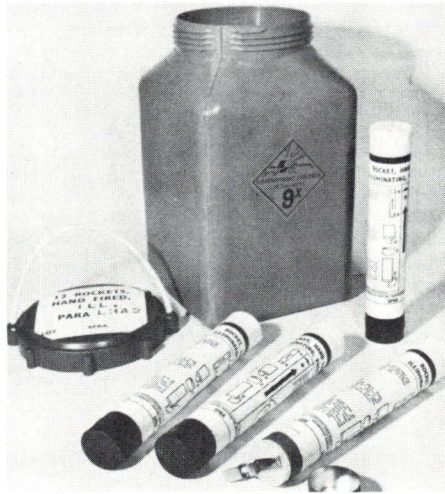
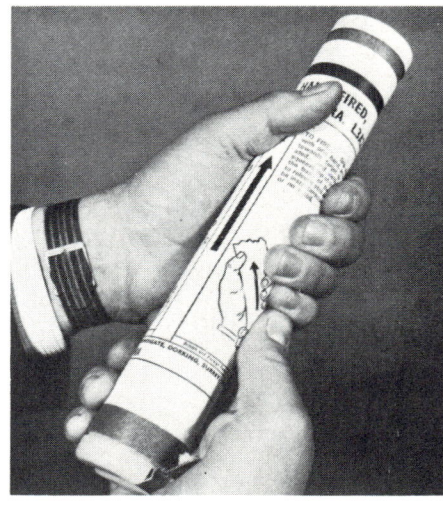

The Schermuly 1.5in, hand-fired, parachute, illuminating rocket, L3A2

HAND-FIRED, SIGNALLING AND ILLUMINATING ROCKETS

The basic unit of all Schermuly hand-fired rocket signalling and illuminating equipment is the 'Icarus' hand-fired rocket. It is drum-tail stabilised of light aluminium construction housing, centrally, the solid propellant motor and carrying the payload in the nose section.

The rocket is housed in a resin bonded weather-proof cylinder, which constitutes the igniter and dispensible discharger. It is fitted with a lever-operated percussion ignition device.

Variations of firing elevation to suit the terrain are practicable, ranging from a vertical ejection of approximately 412m to a 'gun' range of 320-412m.

DATA
Length of discharger: 266mm
Diameter of discharger: 46mm
Length of rocket: 266mm
Diameter of rocket: 38mm
Weight (total): 354g
Height of ejection: 412 metres approx.
Time of flight (power): 5 seconds approx.

Weight of payload: 141g maximum
Maximum ground range: 320-412 metres
Packaging: 100 rockets packed in wood Trade Pack weight 39kg.
    12 rockets packed in waterproof polythene bottle service pack. 4 bottles per case (total 48 rockets) weight 38kg.

Rockets available:
Single star – Red (Distress) L1A1
         – Green L2A1
         – Orange L4A1
Multi-star signals
Parachute illuminating L3A2 (qv)
Radar reflecting, distress (Radaflare)
Smoke streamer (orange, ascending or descending)
Maroon signal
Parachute target
Smoke puff, brown
Manufacturer: Schermuly Ltd, High Post, Salisbury, Wiltshire
Status: In production and service

SIGNAL CARTRIDGE, 26.5mm (1in)

This cartridge has been developed to meet the need for a cost effective signal and illuminating cartridge. Aluminium-cased, it will fit the standard one inch Verey pistol, as well as the 26.5mm pistol. It is available with red, green and illuminating stars.

The rim of the aluminium case is knurled where necessary for night colour identification. An aluminium cap is used to form a waterproof closure. Daytime identification is by means of a coloured star printed on the side of the casing.

DATA
Height: 76 metres
Burning time: 5-6 seconds
Calibre (nominal): 26.5mm
Length: 56mm
Colours and approximate intensity: Illuminating – 35,000 candles; Red – 23,000 candles; Green – 20,000 candles
Packaging: 50 boxes are packed in a wooden case, Trade Pack. Quantity per pack: 500. 10 cartridges are packed in a polystyrene box (Unit of order)
Dimensions of package: 580 × 330 × 300mm
Gross weight: 32kg
Manufacturer: Schermuly Ltd, High Post, Salisbury, Wiltshire

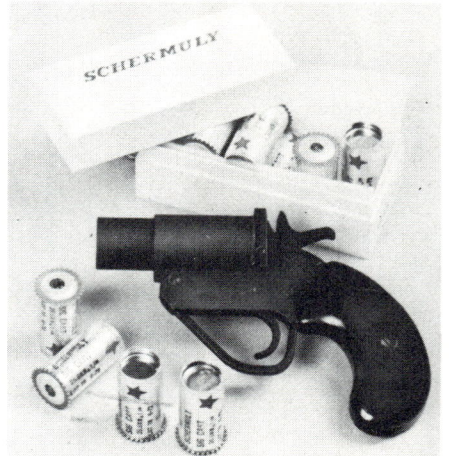

Cartridge, signal, 26.5mm (1in)

1.5in SIGNAL CARTRIDGE

This cartridge is larger in both dimensions than the 26.5mm/1in cartridge used with the standard Verey pistol and has corresponding improved performance. The cartridge consists of a rimmed aluminium casing into which the propellent charge and signalling or illuminating star are inserted and sealed with a weather-proof closing disc. The colour of the star is indicated on the side of the case and on a paper disc inserted into the mouth of the closing cup. Colours available are red, green and white (illuminating). The cartridges are intended for use with the Schermuly 1.5in (38mm) Signal Pistol and other launchers of the same calibre.

DATA
Calibre: 38mm
Length: 70mm
Trajectory height: 191 metres with signal pistol
Burning time: 7 sec minimum
Intensity of illumination: White – 80,000 CP
Red – 40,000 CP
Green – 25,000 CP
Packing: 12 cartridges in tinplate cylinder (12.7cm dia. × 23.5cm) with tape closure
Manufacturer: Schermuly Ltd., High Post, Salisbury, Wiltshire

---

DISTRESS SIGNAL (2 STAR RED) Mk 4

This signal is a compact item of equipment designed for carrying on the person. It ejects two red stars, at intervals, to signal distress.

The signal consists of a seamless aluminium cylinder, closed off at the top end with a screw cap. There is a PVC tape over the joint between the cap and the body. Beneath the cap is the 'D' ring percussion igniter mechanism.

The cylinder houses a mild steel tube, surrounded by a board insulator. Within this tube are the delay, the flash-through compositions and the two red stars.

OPERATION:
Remove the sealing tape. Remove screw cap. Holding the signal as high as possible, unfold and then twist the 'D' firing ring to release the striker. After releasing the striker, hold the signal firmly and vertically at the full upward extent of the arm until the two stars have been ejected.

DATA
Length: 127mm
Diameter: 33mm
Weight: 137g
Ejection height: 30m (approx.)
Burning time: 6-8 seconds
Intensity: 7,000 CP
Delay: 1-4 sec before firing: 5-7 secs between stars
Manufacturer: Schermuly Ltd, High Post, Salisbury, Wiltshire

SIGNAL KIT 16mm (MINIFLARE)

This kit comprises a pen-sized projector and eight screw-on cartridges in a weatherproof plastic pack. Each cartridge, a self-contained waterproof unit, has a propellant and a star emitting an intense light. For signalling use, Red, Green and White colour-coded cartridges are available. An important feature of the 'Miniflare' is that when fired vertically as a distress signal, the star burns out well above ground or sea level. With an effective range of 50 to 100m this system is an ideal illuminator for small patrol and ambush operations.

The cartridge consists of an aluminium case containing the propellant and star, the case also acting as a projection cup. A waterproofing disc seals the top of the cartridge and the threaded projection at the base contains the percussion cap.

The projector is anodised light alloy with a female thread at the top to take the male threaded cartridge. A trigger is attached directly to the spring-loaded striker.

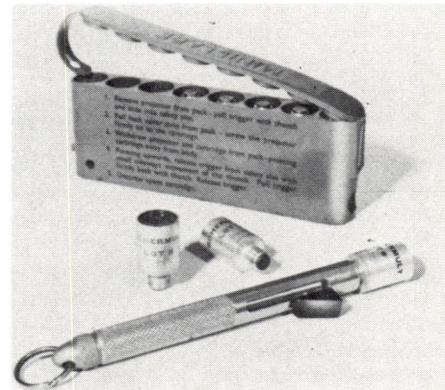

DATA
Height (approx): 65m
Burning time: 6-7 seconds
Projector: 120 × 13mm
Dimensions: Cartridge: 32 × 16mm
Pack: 152 × 63 × 19mm
Weight (complete): 255g
Colours and approx. intensity: Red – 4,800 candles; Green – 2,400 candles; White – 5,000 candles
Manufacturer: Schermuly Ltd, High Post, Salisbury, Wiltshire

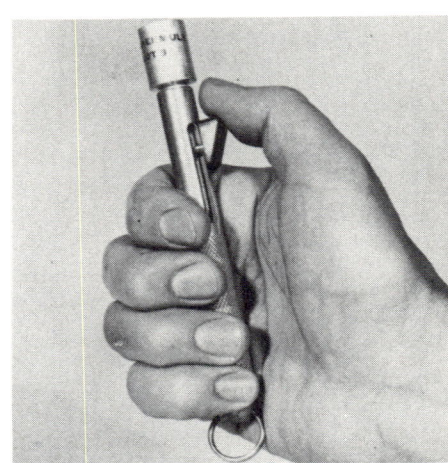

Miniflare 16mm signal kit

PAINS-WESSEX SMOKE GRENADE

The signal, smoke, 45 second, has been developed by Pains-Wessex as an alternative to the British Army No 83 Smoke Grenade. It has been designed for use under all climatic conditions.

The top cap has been designed so that it can be easily unscrewed when wearing Arctic clothing.

The signal is supplied to NATO colour coding. The colour of the cap indicates the colour of the smoke.

CONSTRUCTION
The signal consists of a tin plate metal body (1) containing the smoke composition pellet (2) and an integral, uncocked firing mechanism (3). Smoke emission is through vents (4) in the top of the signal. These vents being sealed in storage by the top cap (5).

METHOD OF USE
Unscrew the coloured top cap to which is attached the firing lanyard (6). Pull the cap sharply away from the signal until the lanyard is released from the signal. This action both energises and releases the striker and initiates the 3 second delay (7). Throw the signal at once.

DATA
Total weight: 245g
Weight of smoke composition: 142g
Burning time: 25sec, 45 sec or 75sec depending on requirements
Length: 105mm
Diameter: 55mm

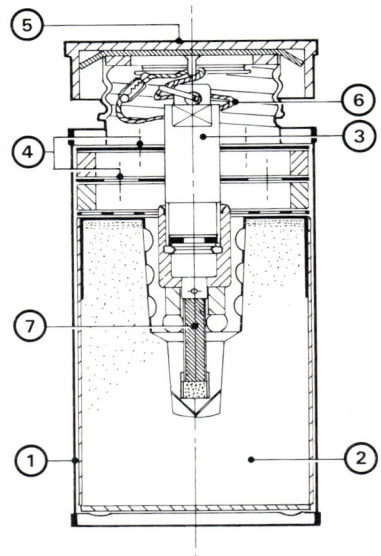

Pains-Wessex smoke grenade

UNITED STATES OF AMERICA

GRENADE, HAND: COLOURED SMOKE (RED, GREEN YELLOW OR VIOLET) M18

Coloured Smoke Hand Grenade M18 is used for ground-to-air or ground-to-ground signalling. Grenades may be filled with any one of four smoke colours: red, green, yellow or violet. Each grenade will emit smoke for 50 to 90 seconds.

Grenade body: The body, of thin sheet metal, is filled with red, green yellow or violet smoke composition. The filler is topped with a starter mixture.

Fuze, hand grenade, M201A1: Fuze M201A1 is a pyrotechnic delay-igniting fuze. The body contains a primer, first-fire mixture, pyrotechnic delay column, and ignition mixture. Assembled to the body are a striker, striker spring, safety lever, and safety pin with pull ring. The split end of the safety pin has an angular spread.

Safety clips: Safety clips are not required with these grenades.

DATA
Grenade (with fuze):
Model: M18
Body: Sheet metal
Weight: 539g
Length: 146mm
Diameter: 64mm
Colour: Light green w/black markings
Packing: 1 per container; 16 per packing box
Filler:
Type: Smoke composition
Weight: 326g
Fuze:
Model: M201A1
Type: Pyrotechnic delay-igniting
Primer: M39A1
Ignition mixture: Iron oxide, titanium, zirconium

Coloured smoke hand grenade M18

Delay time: 0.7-2 seconds
Weight: 42g
Length: 99mm
Colour: Grey or olive drab w/black markings
Safety: Pull ring and safety pin
Function: Similar M7A1

ANTI-PERSONNEL MINES

Anti-personnel mines are in a weapon category rather different from that of most weapons described in this book. Although they are frequently laid by infantry and all too frequently encountered by them, the laying process – at least so far as the larger devices are concerned – is commonly carried out with engineer support and advice: futhermore, although there are many standard types of mine in army inventories, the scope for elegant variation and ingenious improvisation in constructing obstacles that may range from a single booby-trap to an elaborate minefield is such that no comprehensive catalogue of the possibilities can be compiled.

There are, however, some general principles of construction and use that are applicable to a wide variety of such weapons; and by describing these principles it is at least possible to give some indication of the state of this branch of military technology.

Purpose

Anti-personnel (AP) mines are defensive weapons whose main functions are to slow down an enemy advance and reduce the possibility of a successful surprise attack. If unsupported by other weapons any array of mines can ultimately be cleared by the enemy by one means or another; but a well-sited, well-laid and energetically defended minefield can deny a piece of territory to any enemy for a time that may be of great tactical significance. It has to be recognised, however, that a minefield is a two-way obstacle and that in certain circumstances it may be preferable to use non-lethal devices (described below) in parts of it.

An important function that can be performed by the AP mine in addition to that of holding up infantry or soft-skinned vehicles is that of delaying the clearance of anti-tank minefields. Anti-tank (AT) mines are commonly adjusted to respond only to the presence of heavy vehicles – it being generally uneconomical and possibly tactically undesirable for them to respond to the pressure of a soldier's foot – and the process of hand clearance of a detected minefield can be delayed by sowing AP mines among the AT mines or using them as anti-lifting devices.

Blast Mines

There are two fundamentally different types of AP mine one of which depends for its effect solely on explosive blast while the other, fragmentation, type has effects similar to those of the various types of defensive grenade described in the preceding section.

AP blast mines are most commonly either buried or laid flat on the ground and are usually fitted with pressure-operated initiation mechanisms. Unless the mine is very large, therefore, its lethal or incapacitating effect is likely to be confined to the soldier who treads on it. This disadvantage, however, must be balanced against the advantages that the mines are easy to lay, difficult or impossible to see and, because their non-explosive components can be made almost entirely of wood or plastic material (or even cardboard for some small mines), difficult to detect by electromagnetic mine-detection methods.

Many mines of this type have adjustable pressure mechanisms and can thus be set to respond to vehicle pressure rather than to the pressure of the soldier's foot: it is also possible in many instances to replace the pressure mechanism by one that can be detonated with a tripwire or other form of initiation system.

Because of their localised effect, blast AP mines must be sown thickly if they are to constitute a major obstacle to the enemy. The possibility of sympathetic detonation thus becomes a problem and the explosives used in modern blast AP mines are specially chosen to guard against this hazard.

Blast mines are made in a wide range of sizes with explosive contents of from about 10g to 0.5kg or more. Some of the smaller ones are suitable for random scattering by hand or for dispersing from some mechanical contrivance. Worth noting in this context is the possibility of dispensing such mines from aircraft. The development in recent years of cluster bomb devices which are dropped as a single unit from an aircraft and scatter their bomblet payload over a wide area offers opportunities of overcoming some of the difficulties of satisfactory distribution; and while most cluster bombs carry percussion bomblets it is believed that the US Gator bomb is suitable for use with AP mines.

An important recent development is the British Ranger system whereby a large number of small non-lethal mines can be scattered in predetermined patterns by a multi-barrel projector.

Fragmentation Mines

There are two important subdivisions of the group of fragmentation AP mines. One sub-group comprises devices which are essentially tethered fragmentation grenades, picketed into the ground, mounted on a stake or free-standing: the other sub-group comprises devices resembling small mortars which, when triggered, propel a fragmenting weapon to a height of a metre or two so as to give it a wide radius of lethal or incapacitating action. Weapons in the first sub-group are commonly referred to as fragmentation mines without qualification: the others are generally known as bounding mines.

Because these weapons are effective over a wider area than blast mines they are commonly fitted with initiating mechanisms suitable for use with tripwires: some bounding mines, however, are buried and fitted with pressure initiators and fuze delays so that the mine bounds after the soldier has passed – unless, as is not unknown, he has the self-sacrificing courage to keep his foot on it.

Almost all fragmentation mines contain substantial quantities of metal and are therefore easy to detect electromagnetically. They can, however, be laid and wired with such ingenuity that their detectability offers little comfort to the man with the mine detector.

Special mention should be made of the directional type of fixed fragmentation mine exemplified by the Picatinny Arsenal Claymore (M18A1) mine used by US, German, Israeli, UK and now Vietnamese forces and the ALSETEX Mk F1 used by the French Army. Each is a free-standing remotely-actuated weapon loaded on one side with an array of steel balls – 700 for the Claymore and 500 for the F1 – which are projected in a fan of about 60° in the pointing direction. The Claymore is the larger of the two: it weighs about 1.6kg and contains 680g of C-4 explosive composition and is highly effective up to about 50 metres and dangerous to 250 metres: the French mine weighs only 1kg and is highly effective to some 35 metres. Both mines can be fired electrically: the Claymore will also operate with a tripwire. The Swedish (Bofors) AP12 is a device of size and performance similar to that of the Claymore.

Initiation

Within a minefield, the commonest methods of initiation are by pressure sensitive mechanisms or traction mechanisms associated with trip-wires; and, as already noted, some mines can be modified from one form of initiation to another and there are some mechanisms which respond both to traction and to pressure – the Israeli (IMI) No 12 mine and the Netherlands (Eurometaal) AP23 mine have initiation mechanisms of this type. Some mines, too, are designed so that they respond to pressure but use traction initiation: the Russian PMD-6 and 7 series works in this way, pressure on the hinged wooden lid causing the edge of the lid to apply traction to the striker-retaining fin of the mechanism, and the arrangement lends itself readily to booby-trapping.

Other types of initiation include electrical systems which may be either intruder-operated or controlled remotely by own troops and vibration sensitive devices. The latter are particularly troublesome because they cannot safely be lifted or neutralised and must be destroyed in place from a safe distance.

Pyrotechnic Mines

Available nowdays are several types of mine which respond to initiation (generally by tripwire) with illumination instead of explosions and thus expose the intruders to fire from supporting weapons. The advantage of using this type of device either to create a complete minefield adjacent to a defended area or to provide a non-lethal channel through a minefield is that it does little to help the enemy and may valuably reduce the impediment to a break-out or counter-attack.

Mines in Service

Tabulated below are some brief data on some mines that are believed to be currently in service. The list is intended only to be indicative, however: it does not purport to be exhaustive.

Country of Origin and Manufacturer	Designation	Functional Type	Common Method of Laying	Construction	Normal Initiation	Total Weight	Explosive Weight
Belgium/PRB	M35	Blast	Buried	Plastic	Pressure	158kg	100g
	M409	Blast	Ground	Plastic	Pressure	183g	80g
	M413	Fragmentation	Picket	Plastic/Steel	Traction	640g	90g
Canada/Canadian Arsenals	C3A1	Blast	Buried	Plastic	Pressure	86g	9.5g
	M25	Blast	Buried	Plastic	Pressure	86g	9.5g
Czechslovakia/—	NA-Mi-Ba	Blast	Various	Plastic	Pressure or Traction	2.4kg	—
	PP-Mi-Sb	Fragmentation	Stake	Steel/ Concrete	Traction	2.1kg	75g
	PP-Mi-Sr	Bounding	Buried	Steel	Pressure or Traction	3.2kg	325g
France/ALSETEX	Mk 59	Blast	Buried	Plastic	Pressure	130g	70g
	Mk 61	Blast	Buried	Plastic	Pressure and anti-lifting traction	125g	57g
	Mk 63	Blast	Buried	Plastic	Pressure	100g	30g
	Model 55	Bounding	Buried	Metal	Traction or Electrical	4kg	400g
	F1	Directional	Free-standing	Plastic/ Steel Balls	Electrical	1kg	—
France/Lacroix	F1A	Illuminating	Various	Plastic	Traction or Electrical	2.4kg	(6min illumination–1 hectare)
France/Ruggieri	Model 1950	Illuminating	Buried	Plastic	Traction	465g	(45sec illumination–3 hectares)
	Type 424	Warning and Illuminating	Various	Plastic	Traction	1.7kg	(3min illumination–3 hectares)
Germany (E)/—	K-2	Bounding	Ground	Plastic/ Steel Balls	Traction	5kg	—
Hungary/—	M49	Blast	Ground	Wood or Plastic	Traction	300g	75g
	—	Bounding	Stake	Steel/ Steel Balls	Traction	3.6kg	800g
Israel/IMI	No 10	Blast	Ground or Buried	Plastic	Pressure	120g	50g
	No 12	Bounding	Picket	Metal/Balls	Traction	3.5kg	250g
Netherlands/Eurometaal	AP23	Bounding	Picket or Buried	Steel	Pressure and Traction	4.5kg	500g
Sweden/Bofors	AP12	Directional	Free-standing	Plastic/ Steel Balls	Traction or Electrical	1.4kg	—
UK/EMI	Ranger	Blast (non-lethal)	Scattered	Plastic	Pressure	—	10g
USSR/—	AKS	Blast	Ground or Buried	Steel	Traction by tilt-rod	9kg	6.8kg
	DM	Blast	Buried	Wood	Vibration	1.8kg	1.2kg
	MZD	Blast	Buried	Wood	Various including Vibration	Various	Up to 10kg
	OZM	Bounding	Buried	Metal	Various	18.6-45.4kg	1.8-6.3kg
	PMK-40	Blast	Scattered	Cardboard	Pressure	90g	50g
	PMN	Blast	Scattered	Plastic	Pressure	600g	240g
	PMD-6	Blast	Ground	Wood	Pressure/ Traction	400g	200g
	PMD-7	Blast	Ground	Wood	Pressure/ Traction	300g	75g
	POM-7	Fragmentation	Stake	Cast Iron	Traction	1.7kg	75g
USA/—	M7A2	Blast	Buried	Metal	Pressure plus anti-lifting Traction	2.2kg	1.6kg
	M16A1	Bounding	Buried	Cast Iron/ Steel	Traction	3.6kg	500g
	M18A1 (Claymore)	Directional	Free-standing	Plastic/ Steel Balls	Traction or Electrical	1.6kg	700kg

Manufacturers: Manufacturers noted in the tabulation are:
  PRB SA, Avenue de Tervueren 168, B-1150 Brussels, Belgium
  Canadian Arsenals Ltd, PO Box 717, Postal Station B, Ottawa, Canada
  ALSETEX, 4 rue de Castellane, 75008 Paris, France
  Société E. Lacroix, Route de Toulouse – 31600 Muret, France
  Ets Ruggieri, Direction Commerciale Armement, 122 rue la Boétie –
  75008 Paris, France
  Israel Military Industries, Tel Aviv, Israel
  Eurometaal NV, PO Box 419, Zaandam, Netherlands
  EMI Electronics Ltd, 135 Blyth Road, Hayes, Middlesex, England
  AB Bofors, S-690 20 Bofors, Sweden

FLAMETHROWERS

Although flamethrowers, in forms recognisably related to current types have been available for use by foot soldiers since the early years of this century, and have been used in both world wars and some others, development of such weapons has received comparatively little attention. Nor for that matter, has the development of larger vehicle-mounted weapons been very energetically pursued, apart from a flurry of activity, during the Second World War, leading to the production of such weapons as the British tank-mounted Crocodile.

It may reasonably be assumed that the relatively low priority accorded to such developments is a reflection of the limited range of combat situations in which the portable flamethrower, at least, can be used to better effect than other weapons; and it is evident that the preoccupation of many military planners with preparation for high-speed warfare in open country will have generated little enthusiasm for a weapon that is virtually useless in such circumstances. If, as it reasonably might, it should be decided that extensive operations in urban areas are a probable feature of future warfare, however, it is possible that some attention will be paid to the flamethrower.

A few flamethrowers are described below. Most of these are man-portable devices but one larger (Russian) manhandled weapon has been included. Mention may also be made of the US M132 flamethrower which is mounted on an APC and which might be used as a supporting weapon with armoured infantry vehicle formations.

M132 self-propelled flamethrower

FRANCE

MODEL 1954/57 PORTABLE FLAMETHROWER

The Model 1954/57 is the standard flamethrower of the French Army and has been designed and manufactured by the French GIAT/DTAT. It consists of an air bottle, two fuel bottles, hose and flame gun. The two fuel bottles hold 10 litres of fuel which is sufficient for one continuous burst of 5-6 seconds or six one-second bursts. Eight igniters are provided. Basically the high pressure bottle sends a 120 bar compressed air stream to a reducing valve, from which gas at the lower pressure of 18-22 bars forces the fuel from the tanks through the hose to the flame gun itself. The following fuels can be used:
Gellified petrol

Oilgel (gellified oil and petrol)
Liquid Fuel (petrol and smoke oil)

DATA
Weight, loaded: 20.3kg
Weight, empty: 12.9kg
Maximum range (with gellified fuel): 60 metres
Effective range (with gellified fuel): 40 metres
Manufacturer: GIAT, 10 place Georges Clémenceau, 92211 Saint Cloud
Status: In service with the French Army

MODEL 1958 FLAMETHROWER

This weapon was developed some years ago for the French Army and was last shown at the 1971 Satory Exhibition. It is believed, however, that it has not been placed in production.

Two versions of the Model 1958 were developed, one with a steel tank and the other with a light alloy tank. Each consists of a single tank with the flamegun mounted directly on it, instead of being connected through a hose. The tank itself has two compartments, one being spherical and containing air (at 30 bars pressure) and being connected with the other compartment, which contains the fuel, by way of a valve. When the operator presses the valve trigger fuel starts to flow and the igniter operates. The tank holds 3 litres of fuel which is sufficient for about six seconds of continuous use: it can also be fired in bursts. The fuel used is either liquid or gellified petrol.

DATA
Weight empty (steel construction): 5.1kg
Weight empty (alloy construction): 3.7kg
Weight loaded (steel construction): 7.3kg
Weight loaded (alloy construction): 5.9kg
Tank height: 49cms
Tank diameter: 14cms
Length of flamegun: 24cms
Maximum range with gellified fuel: 45 metres
Effective range with gellified fuel: 30 metres
Manufacturer: GIAT, 10 place Georges Clémenceau, 92211 Saint-Cloud
Status: Believed development only

GERMANY (DEMOCRATIC REPUBLIC)

MODEL 41 FLAMETHROWER

The Model 41 flamethrower is carried on the infantryman's back and consists of two cylindrical tanks, one containing the fuel and the other being the pressure tank. The flamegun is connected to the tank by a hose and consists of a long cylinder with a smaller cylinder on the side. No details of the performance of the Model 41 have become available but its maximum range is probably about 20 metres. It is unusual in that its tanks are carried horizontally.
Status: In service

HUNGARY

MODEL M-51 FLAMETHROWER

This consists of two vertical tanks carried on the man's back and connected to the flamegun by a hose. It is believed that the weapon is operated by first pressing the fuel lever towards the rear of the flamegun and then pressing a second lever to ignite the fuel. No details of the range of the Model M-51 have become available but its maximum range is probably about 20 metres.

Status: In service

ITALY

PORTABLE FLAMETHROWER MODEL T-148

The Tirrena T-148 flamethrower is a portable equipment comprising a shoulder-borne assembly (the tank) with three cylindrical containers, an electronically-ignited flame gun and a flexible hose which couples the other two assemblies. The all-up weight of the loaded weapon is 29kg.

TANK

The shoulder-borne tank consists of three cylindrical sheet steel containers, galvanized inside and outside. The central one contains nitrogen compressed at 28 atmospheres, while the other two contain a gel mixture prepared from petrol and napalm. Each container has a screw plug on top. The plug of the central container serves as a union for coupling the nitrogen charging tube through a pressure reducing valve calibrated at 28 atmospheres; and there is a check valve inside the plug to avoid partial emptying of the container when the flexible tube is removed.

The first of the gel containers, the one in direct communication with the central container, has a plug with a safety valve calibrated at 34 atmospheres $\pm 10\%$. This container has an elbow on the bottom with a rotary union for attaching the flexible tube which connects it to the flamethrower and is closed with a simple screw plug. In the upper part of the shoulder-borne tank there is a small tap on the metal pipeline connecting the nitrogen container with the first gel container for the release of pressure if necessary. The rotary union and the one on the back of the flamethrower are mounted on steel ball bearings so that even when the pressure inside the weapon is high it is possible to rotate the flexible tube easily at both ends, to facilitate aiming.

FLAMETHROWER

The weapon consists of two superimposed tubes. The lower one has a larger diameter and contains the obturator, while the upper one houses the set of batteries which supply power for the electronic ignition of the jet: the set consists of eight intense-discharge flash-type batteries cased in stainless sheet-steel. The batteries must be inserted in the upper tube with their positive poles pointing towards the front.

The obturator, which opens and closes the jet, has a fixed valve and a mobile tubular seat: it is controlled by the rear handgrip, which opens the obturator when drawn back.

The tendency of the pressure to operate the valve is almost totally compensated, so as to require a controlled opening force and a reliable automatic return of the handgrip when the jet is being closed.

The front handgrip of the flamethrower is fixed and has a push-button which operates the electronic igniter. This is housed in the special shock-resistant case fixed to the front part of the flamethrower: its electronic components are completely incorporated in a plasticized insulating mass, so that the igniter will continue to function even if the weapon has been immersed in water.

This igniter has an incendiary power much superior to that of the cartridges used on many other types of flamethrower and has an electric arc which lasts for several minutes instead of a few seconds. Moreover, incendiary cartridges have to be ignited a few seconds before flamethrowing can begin, consequently revealing the operator's presence to the enemy, whereas electronic ignition is silent and practically invisible.

LOADING

The flamethrower is loaded in three stages:

(a) Put eight batteries into the upper tube of the weapon and check the efficiency of the scintillator.

(b) Put the inflammable gel into the two side containers of the shoulder-borne tank.

(c) Charge the central container with compressed nitrogen, using the special flexible tube with its pressure reducer calibrated at 28 atmospheres.

These operations are carried out as follows:

(1) The eight batteries must be inserted into the upper tube of the weapon with the positive pole pointing forwards after unscrewing the rear plug of the tube.

The efficiency of the scintillator is then checked by pressing the push button on the front handgrip: an arc of blue-violet-reddish sparks should form on one of the two pairs of scintillator points. A weak light blue spark means that the batteries are low and should be replaced.

(2) The gel is transferred into the two cylinders of the shoulder-borne tank by means of the hand-pump on the lid of the gel container. The pressure of the hand-pump can transfer the gel easily along the transparent flexible tube into the shoulder-borne tank; and the tank should be filled to a level about 6 or 7cm below the mouth of each container. Care must be taken to tighten the two screw plugs (by hand), because once the compressed gas has been inserted it is impossible to tighten them.

(3) The central container is charged with compressed nitrogen by means of the special flexible tube with its threaded unions, the nitrogen being obtained from an ordinary high-pressure gas cylinder, with the pressure reducer calibrated at 28 atmospheres.

As the nitrogen is inserted, the pressure inside the flamethrower rises, and the gauge stick in the centre of the safety valve in the plug of the first container in the shoulder-borne tank comes up. When the pressure has reached 28 atmospheres the gauge stick will be level with the top of the plug.

OPERATION

The following operations are to be carried out:

(1) Throwing must be carried out with the left foot in front and the right foot behind and the body leaning slightly in the direction of the jet: otherwise the operator will not sustain the recoil of the weapon when it is throwing.

(2) Press the trigger controlling the sparks in the special hole in the side of the nosepiece.

(3) Operate the rear handgrip for single throwing or for several consecutive throwings, keep the front trigger pressed and direct the throwing towards the objective.

(4) When the gelatine throwing is finished it is advisable, both to clean the weapon and to extinguish residual flames in the nozzle, to release the remaining nitrogen gas through the nozzle, without pressing the trigger.

After firing the inside of the flamethrower should be cleaned by washing with petrol or diesel, but care should be taken to remove the batteries first, to avoid danger of fire.

DATA
Weight of empty tank and hose: 13.6kg
Weight of flamegun: 3.65kg
Total unloaded weight: 17.25kg
Weight of napalm charge: 11.25kg
Weight of batteries: 0.5kg
Total loaded weight: 29kg
Manufacturer: Tirrena SpA, Via del Quirinale, 22 00187 Roma

UNION OF SOVIET SOCIALIST REPUBLICS

ROKS-2 FLAMETHROWER

Very few of these remain in service as they have been replaced by the ROKS-3 or the more recent LPO-50 flamethrowers. The ROKS-2 consists of a rectangular fuel container, with a smaller compressed air bottle attached to it, a hose and a flamegun which has the appearance of a rifle. Like the ROKS-3, the ignition cartridges are carried in a cylinder mounted on the muzzle of the flamegun and are activated by pressing the trigger. The fuel tank holds 10 litres of fuel, which is sufficient to give a maximum of 7-8 one second bursts and a maximum range of some 35 metres can be achieved in favourable conditions.

Status: Obsolescent but still in service with some Warsaw Pact armies

ROKS-3 FLAMETHROWER

The ROKS-3 flamethrower has been replaced in almost all of the Warsaw Pact countries by the more recent LPO-50 flamethrower. It consists of a cylindrical fuel tank which holds 8 litres and has a filling aperture on top with the hose outlet at the base. The cylindrical compressed air tank is attached to the side of the fuel tank. The hose is connected to the gun which resembles a rifle in appearance. Mounted at the muzzle of the flamegun is the ignition cylinder containing ten 7.62mm ignition cartridges: as the weapon is fired the cylinder advances automatically and brings a new cartridge into position. When the operator pulls the trigger a spring-loaded shut off valve opens and allows the fuel to be ejected, a further pull releases the firing pin which ignites the ignition cartridge. When the trigger pressure is released the flamegun stops. There is sufficient fuel for ten 5-second bursts.

DATA
Weight filled: 23.5kg
Maximum range with thickened fuel: 35 metres
Maximum range with unthickened fuel: 15 metres
Status: Obsolescent but still in service in some Warsaw Pact armies.

LPO-50 FLAMETHROWER

The LPO-50 is currently the standard flamethrower in Warsaw Pact armies having largely replaced the earlier ROKS-2 and ROKS-3 flamethrowers. It consists of a tank group, hose and gun group. There are three tanks, on the top of each of which are an excess pressure relief valve and a cap for the filling aperture which also contains the chamber for the pressurising cartridge.

Wires from the three containers are combined in a harness which is fastened to the hose and attached to the gun group. Outputs from the three tanks are connected to a manifold, through one-way valves which prevent fuel flowing from one tank into another, and this manifold is connected to the hose.

Ignition is by means of a slow-burning pyrotechnic cartridge, three of which are grouped below the muzzle of the flamegun. A selector lever is mounted forward of the trigger guard on the gun and, when the trigger is pressed, energy is supplied from a power pack of four 1.5V cells to one of the ignition cartridges and simultaneously to one of the tank pressurising cartridges. Pressure from the latter drives fuel from the tank through the appropriate non-return valve into the manifold and thence by way of the hose to the flamegun where it is ignited by the pyrotechnic cartridge. The firer can thus fire three shots, changing the selector lever position between shots. The tank capacity in 3.3 litres which is sufficient for a flame burst of 2-3 seconds. A trigger safety is fitted.

DATA
Fuel capacity: 3 × 3.3 litres
Weight, empty: 15kg
Weight, loaded: 23kg
Maximum range with liquid fuel: 20 metres
Maximum range with thickened fuel: 70 metres
Status: In service with Warsaw Pact forces

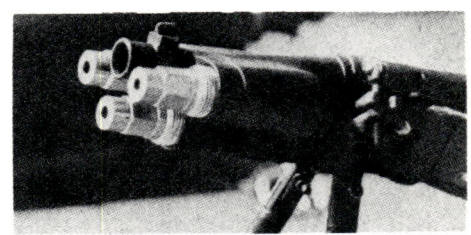

Firing the LPO-50 flamethrower

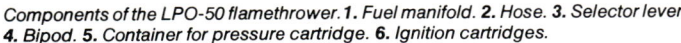

Components of the LPO-50 flamethrower. 1. Fuel manifold. 2. Hose. 3. Selector lever.
4. Bipod. 5. Container for pressure cartridge. 6. Ignition cartridges.

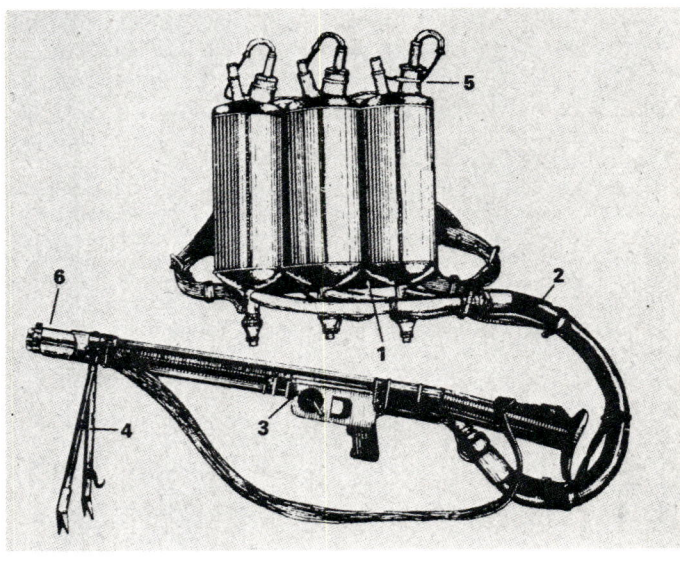

TPO-50 CART-MOUNTED FLAMETHROWER

The TPO-50 cart consists of a two-wheeled handcart with three identical flamethrowers mounted horizontally on top, a recoil spade is provided at the rear of the cart. Each flamethrower holds 21 litres of fuel and they can be fired together or individually. If required the cylinders can be dismounted for ground use. Folding front and rear sights are provided on each cylinder and the cylinders can be elevated from +2° to +50°, traverse being carried out by moving the cart.

Each of the cylinders has a screw-on head and mounted on this is the discharge nozzle, cartridge holder and a relief valve. The fuel is forced out of the cylinder by gas pressure which is produced by an electrically ignited cartridge.

The ignition cartridge is the same as that used with the PLO-50 infantry flamethrower and ignites the fuel as it leaves the nozzle. Both the igniter and pressure cartridges are simultaneously ignited electrically from a 6V (4 × 1.5V) power pack which can be located remotely to enable the TPO-50 to be fired from behind cover if required.

DATA
Crew: 2
Weight loaded: 170kg
Weight empty: 130kg
Maximum range with thickened fuel: 180 metres
Maximum range with unthickened fuel: 65 metres
Status: In service

UNITED STATES OF AMERICA

ABC-M9-7 PORTABLE FLAMETHROWER

The ABC-M9-7 flamethrower consists of the M9 fuel and pressure unit, M7 flamethrower gun and the M8 fuel hose which connects the other two units.

The fuel and pressure unit consists of two connected aluminium fuel tanks, a spherical steel pressure tank and valves, and a pressure regulator. Compressed air enters the tops of the fuel tanks and forces thickened fuel through the hose to the gun under 25kg/cm² pressure. Four US gallons (15.14 litres) of fuel is ejected 40 to 55 metres in 8 seconds in a continuous stream or in a maximum of five bursts. The fuel is ignited by an incendiary charge from an ignition cylinder as it leaves the nozzle of the gun barrel, five incendiary charges being contained in an ignition cylinder which fits over the forepart of the barrel.

DATA
Weight, empty: 11.8kg
Weight, full: 22.7kg
Fuel capacity: 15.14 litres
Range: 40-55 metres
Status: Obsolescent

M2A1-7 PORTABLE FLAMETHROWER

The M2A1-7 portable flamethrower is carried on the soldier's back and consists of the M2A1 tank group, M7 flamethrower gun and M8 hose group. The latter connects the tank group to the gun.

The tank group consists of a pressure tank and two fuel tanks. Compressed air enters the tops of the fuel tanks and forces thickened fuel through the hose to the gun. Under pressure approximately 15 litres of fuel is ejected to a distance of between 40 and 55 metres. The flame lasts for ten seconds if fired in a continuous stream or can be delivered in five two-second bursts. The fuel is ignited by an incendiary cylinder as it passes from the nozzle of the gun barrel, there being five incendiary charges in the ignition cylinder which fits over the forepart of the barrel. To fire the gun a lever on the rear grip must be pressed as well as the forward trigger.

DATA
Fuel capacity: 15 litres
Range: 40-55 metres
Status: Obsolescent

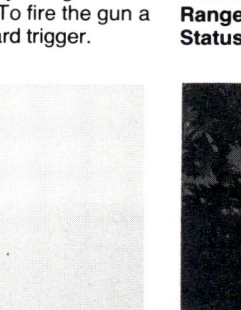

Firing position for the M2A1-7 (USMC)

The M2A1-7 portable flamethrower

M9A1-7 PORTABLE FLAMETHROWER

This is the replacement for both the M2A1-7 and the M9-7 flamethrowers. It consists of a tank group, a hose group, a gun group and a separate carrier group. The tank group comprises a tubular frame with two interconnected fuel tanks, a protective cover, a flame gun holster and carrying straps. A high-pressure sphere is mounted beneath the smaller of the two fuel tanks. Air pressure from this sphere is distributed to the fuel tanks through a pressure regulator mounted between the tanks. The hose group supplies fuel from the tanks to the gun group. The fuel is then ignited by a replaceable ignition cylinder in the nozzle end of the gun group. Each cylinder contains five incendiary charges.

The carrier group consists of a frame, protective cover and carrying straps. Four spare high pressure spheres and two ignition cylinders are stowed in the carrier group, each of these cans contains two ignition cylinders.

The principle of operation is the same as for the M2A1-7 and M9-7 flamethrowers.

DATA
Weight of complete portable flamethrower: empty: 11.3kg
loaded: 22.7kg
Weight of carrier group: empty: 13.6kg
loaded: 17.2kg
Fuel capacity of flamethrower: approx 15 litres
Range: about 50 metres
Status: In service

US Marine wearing ABC protection clothing and carrying the M9A1-7 portable flamethrower (USMC)

MORTARS

INTRODUCTION

The mortar was one of the early forms of artillery and is known to have been used by Mohammed II at the time of the siege of Constantinople in 1451. It was known in Europe as the bombard and consisted of a metal pot secured to a timber base. It was used for the reduction of fortresses and cities under siege and also for action against ships close in to shore. The weapon was not popular and, by bursting on discharge, it may well have killed more friends than foes. As artillery developed the bombard fell out of favour and disappeared from service. During the Russo-Japanese War of 1904/1905, devices were used to project improvised grenades to distances greater than those to which they could be thrown by hand, but little real advance was made until the advent of trench warfare made some sort of mortar imperative.

In 1908 the German Army had a mortar which consisted of a smoothbore steel tube on a wooden base. The weapon is said by some experts not to have been a mortar at all since it fired only at low angles, less than 45 degrees. In 1912 the firm of Krupp developed a trench howitzer which had a large, circular, explosive head, mounted on a rod. It was known inevitably to the troops as a "Toffee Apple Mortar".

The greatest name in mortar design is undoubtedly that of Mr Wilfred Stokes who was managing director of a firm of agricultural engineers named Ransomes and Rapier. His mortar contained all the elements of all subsequent weapons of this type. The barrel was a steel tube with an internal diameter of three inches (76mm); it rested on a steel baseplate and there was a bipod with elevating and traversing gears. His bomb was a cylinder, with no tail fins, and at the back end there was a 12 bore shot gun cartridge filled with Ballistite. The fusing arrangements were based on those of the 36 grenade – the Mills bomb. The fly-off lever was held by a safety pin and a spring loaded plunger. Before the bomb was dropped down the barrel of the mortar, the safety pin was removed. The set-back on firing caused the removal of the support afforded by the spring loaded plunger and the fly-off lever was held only by the interior of the barrel. When the bomb emerged, the lever flew off and the safety fuse was ignited. This meant a constant time interval between firing and bomb burst. This was not practical and it was quickly superseded by an "all ways" fuze which detonated the main charge on impact. The 3-inch mortar was followed by the 4-inch (102mm) which was adopted by the American Army on its entry into the War in 1917. The 4-inch mortar was used for the projection of gas bombs as well as HE.

Mortars increased in size until both British and French armies were using 9.45-inch or 240mm weapons.

During the 1930's the Brandt and the Stokes Mortars were the principal contenders and the USA adopted the Brandt mortars in 60 and 81mm

The German 8cm M42 Granatwerfer 42. This is about the smallest size to which a medium mortar can be reduced, firing a standard bomb. This mortar had about half the range, 1,200yds (1,100 metres) of the standard German 8cm Gr. W34

calibre. The German mortar, the 8cm Granatwerfer 34, was basically of the same design as the Stokes and Brandt. The mortars used by the belligerents in World War II were basically of the same pattern, varying only in calibre and detailed design.

DEFINITIONS

By definition a mortar is a high trajectory fire weapon in which the recoil force is passed directly to the ground through a baseplate. There have been some heavy mortars using a recoil system but this in no way invalidates the basic definition.

The "conventional" mortar which is found in most in-service weapons, is muzzle loading, smooth bore, firing a fin stabilised, subsonic bomb, and establishing zones of fire by variation of charge weight. Range is adjusted by alteration to the tangent elevation.

Mortars are usually divided into three classes – light, medium and heavy – with the following general characteristics. (This includes only conventional mortars. The use, for example, of rocket assisted bombs, can increase the maximum range considerably.)

Light Mortars: Calibre up to 60mm (2.36in). Total weight up to about 40lb (18.2kg). Bomb weight 1 to 3lb (0.454 – 1.36kg). Maximum range 500-

A typical Stokes-Brandt mortar. The UK 3in mortar

The German 50mm Model 36. (5cm Gr. W36) shows how complicated a light mortar can be. This mortar has cross levelling gear, elevating gear, traversing gear and levelling bubbles for the sight

On the other hand the mortar can be very simple indeed – a tube, in fact, with no other appurtenances except a miniscule base plate

2,000yds (461-1,845m).

Medium Mortars: Calibre 60mm-100mm (2.36in-4in). Total weight 75lb – 150lb (34 – 68kg). Bomb weight 7lb – 15lb (3.2 – 6.8kg). Maximum range 2,000yds – 6,000yds (1,846 – 5538 metres).

Heavy Mortars: Calibre in excess of 100mm (3.94in). Total weight in excess of 200lb (91kg). Bomb weight above 15lb (6.8kg). Maximum range up to 9km (9,750yds).

CONSTRUCTION

The very great majority of mortars have only four main parts. These are: the barrel, the baseplate, the mounting, and the sight.

The barrel is a steel tube with one end closed by the breech-piece. This is screwed on or into the barrel. To prevent the escape of gases a copper washer is inserted as an obturating ring to produce a seal.

With very few exceptions, the interior of the bore is smooth. The exterior surface is also generally left plain although a few mortars incorporate radial finning to assist cooling. The firing mechanism is in the breech-piece. It may take the form of a fixed semi-spherical stud on which the bomb is dropped by gravity or in some cases it may be spring operated. In many mortars the applied safety allows the retraction of the firing pin. This is a highly desirable feature. In most mortars of medium size the misfire drill necessitates lifting the base end of the barrel to let the bomb drop out of the muzzle into the hands of a waiting member of the detachment. If by mischance the bomb should be allowed to drop back onto the projecting firing pin during this procedure and it fires on the second impact, the effect could be disastrous. In heavier mortars a tool is lowered to grip the bomb by the fuze, to withdraw it, and here too it is not a good thing to have the bomb dropping back onto the proud pin.

The baseplate is necessary to take the downward force of the explosion and to distribute it over as large a flotation area as is considered practical. This reduces the ground pressure and the tendency of the plate to sink. In wet or soft soil it is not unknown for a medium mortar baseplate to sink four feet into the ground. This not only prevents the use of the mortar but it also makes it a long laborious task to get the baseplate out. Since the mortar is often deployed in areas inaccessible to vehicles, this means physically digging it out. To prevent this happening, it may be necessary to place timber, turf, or stones under the baseplate, or to increase its effective area by the use of an auxiliary plate which fits round the normal one.

The baseplate can also slip sideways when the mortar is deployed on the slope of a hill and the use of a bedding-in round to make sure the plate is firmly in place is standard technique in most armies. Surprisingly in these days of mortar locating radar, there still appears to be no bedding-in round in service which disintegrates after it has applied the necessary impulse to the plate. There are square plates, rectangular plates and, most popular of all today, circular plates which, if properly bedded in, will allow 360 degree traverse. All base plates are ribbed to provide strength, prevent buckling and to ensure that the baseplate does not slip. Some sort of carrying handle is essential – particularly for winching out the plate when a hasty move becomes imperative.

The mounting will normally be a bipod, although a few tripods are in service. The mounting supports the barrel and carries the elevating and traversing gears. In many mortars a shock absorber is incorporated in the mounting. This will consist of one or two cylinders usually containing springs, although, in some heavier mortars an hydraulic system may be employed. These cylinders are interposed between the barrel collar and the bipod and after the barrel has recoiled and been pushed back by the reaction of the ground and plate, the springs ensure that the relative positions of barrel and bipod remain unchanged. The bipod contains the cross levelling gear. The object of this is to enable the sights to be placed upright regardless of the slope of the ground on which the mortar is emplaced.

The sights of a mortar have grown in complexity as the years have passed and particularly in the heavier calibres of mortar, where bombs are expensive and available in limited numbers, they approximate to the sights of an artillery piece in functioning. The target will very, very rarely be in view of the mortar position and, in fact, for the mortar detachment commander so to site his weapon that direct fire can be brought to bear on his detachment,

would show a lack of appreciation of the characteristics of the mortar as well as a lack of commonsense. The sight will, therefore, be laid on some selected aiming point which can be a prominent and easily recognised feature such as a church tower or it can be an aiming post put out for the purpose. With the correct angle between the line to the target and the line to the aiming post, set on the sight, the barrel of the mortar will be pointing at the target. This will enable fire to be brought down and corrections to the line can be made. However, it is a cumbersome way of adjusting fire and does not allow of ready recording of target data for subsequent engagement of the same target on call. A slipping scale is therefore introduced. This enables the sight to be laid on any selected aiming point with the correct angle to the centre of the azimuth arc on the main scale, and the slipping scale recording zero. Then all subsequent switches can be made with respect to the zero line. This enables all target data to be recorded with reference to the zero line even though the aiming point may have been changed or become obscured. (It should be noted however that since meteorological data are not available at the mortar position, true data can never be deduced and stored.) The actual sighting device that is aligned on the aiming post may be a collimator or it may be a telescope.

CHARACTERISTICS

Simplicity. The limited number of components and the unsophisticated fire control system make the mortar easy to handle and reduce the time taken to train detachments. They make for ease and speed of production and reduce unit costs.

High trajectory fire. This is probably the main characteristic of the mortar. It enables the weapon to be placed behind hills, in ravines or in small deep pits and to bring plunging fire to bear on similar enemy positions.

Mobility. The light weight and ease with which the mortar can be moved, allow rapid changes of position. With the development of mortar locating radar, this may be the only way of producing effective fire and avoiding concentrations of counter mortar fire.

Flexibility. The simple design of the mortar leads to the ability to make rapid switches of target virtually anywhere in the 360 degree arc. The mortar communication and control system in use with all major powers allows the rapid concentration of the fire of a number of units on a single target and their immediate dispersion either to a number of individual targets or to another concentration which may well be considerably removed both in direction and range. Their mobility adds to their flexibility by allowing the rapid concentration and subsequent dispersion of a number of fire units in any desired locality.

Fire Power. The simple design of the bomb and its ease of loading make possible the maintenance of a high rate of fire. The weight of bombs delivered in unit time can be very large. Due to the steep angle of descent of the bomb its lethal radius is more nearly circular than that of the shell where the flat angle of impact means that a high proportion of the fragments go into the ground and many are thrown high into the air, producing on the ground the typical "butterfly wing" pattern, with areas of immunity in front of and behind the point of burst. The use of the airburst VT fuze can increase the effectiveness of the mortar bomb, against troops dug in, by a factor of up to 100%.

COMPARISON WITH ARTILLERY WEAPONS

In comparison with land service artillery of similar calibre, the mortar has the following characteristics in its favour:
(a) simplicity and cheapness;
(b) high trajectory;
(c) high rate of fire;
(d) mobility – particularly in unfavourable terrain;
(e) low chamber pressure;
(f) negligible barrel wear;
(g) small dimensions – leading to ease of concealment;
(h) bomb with excellent anti-personnel characteristics;
(j) low equipment-bomb weight ratio.

There are however several areas in which the mortar does not compare favourably with artillery. These are:
(a) Accuracy;
(b) Consistency;
(c) Range;
(d) Ability to produce predicted fire;
(e) Versatility (Mortars, at present, are limited to operations against personnel in the open. They cannot attack tanks, troops under cover or highly mobile targets such as APC's.)

MORTAR DISPERSION OF FIRE

The mortar has a reputation for dispersing its fire over a wide area and although this is no longer anything like as true as it was, it still has sufficient validity to warrant the observation.

The conventional mortar is muzzle-loaded. There must be, therefore, a clearance between the bomb and the interior of the bore to allow the escape of air compressed as the bomb falls. This difference in diameter is known as "windage" and the relevant area difference is "windage area". The escape of gases past the bomb through the windage area, reduces the muzzle velocity, and due to the manufacturing tolerances on the guide band of the bomb, this effect on the velocity varies from bomb to bomb. This produces a dispersion on the ground. Due to the clearance between bomb and barrel, the bomb chatters its way up the barrel and this bouncing effect inevitably means that it emerges with a random yaw, and although its centre of mass

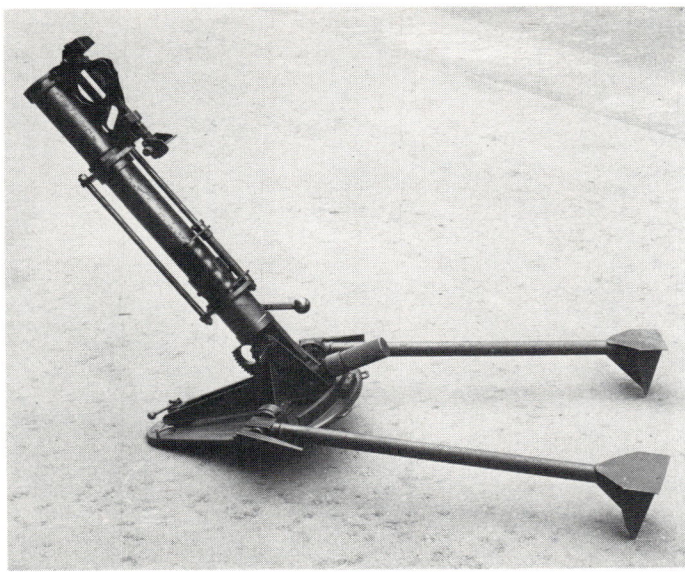

The Madsen 51mm light mortar

The Madsen mortar in its anti-tank role

is moving in prolongation of the barrel axis, the longitudinal axis of the bomb and that of the barrel are not aligned.

When the bomb leaves the barrel, the gases emerging from the muzzle flow over it from rear to front, and in this intermediate zone the fin stabilizing effect of the bomb increases the yaw because of the separation of the centres of mass and pressure relative to the direction of air flow. Since the initial yaw is a random effect, the dispersion on the ground is also random but in a barrel with considerable windage it can be a significant proportion of the range. (For example the British 3in mortar could produce a 50% zone on charge 2 at 45 degrees, of 4.38% of range). The differences in dimensions and weights from bomb to bomb due to manufacturing tolerances play an important part in causing dispersion by varying both velocity and yaw. During World War II and subsequently in equipment developed during that time, there was experienced a phenomenon known as the "sporadic short round" in which for no obvious reason a bomb would drop very short and inevitably land either on own troops or on the controlling OP. A great deal of effort was put into finding the cause of this effect and observers were put into balloons to watch the bomb sail past at the apex of its trajectory.

It was eventually found by RARDE – The Royal Armament Research and Design Establishment – to be due to spin yaw resonance. In this effect a rotation imparted to the bomb by a damaged fin coincided in frequency with the yaw oscillation and the build up of yaw due to the resonance so established, eventually increased the aerodynamic drag of the bomb to the extent of causing it to fall some 1,000yds (900m) short.

It can be seen from the above that the dispersion of the fire of the mortar is due to windage and to variations in bomb weight and size. In modern mortars both of these causes have been largely eliminated. Probably the best example of the way this has been done is the British 81mm mortar which will produce a 50% zone comparing favourably with many guns in service. In this equipment, the bomb has been given an expanding guide band which allows the escape of air during the bomb's fall and closes the windage gap when the mortar fires. The dimensions of the bomb have been very carefully controlled and this, although increasing cost, has contributed immensely to the accuracy and consistency of the weapon.

PREDICTED FIRE

The mortar cannot produce predicted fire. The reason for this is the lack of meteorological data at the time of initial engagement or preliminary ranging. The mortar bomb is fin stabilised which makes wind direction and velocity of more importance than is the case with the spin stabilized shell. The effect of wind is of particular importance when the mortar bomb has been fired at a high angle of elevation and has reached the apogee of its trajectory. Here it will have no vertical velocity and a low forward velocity so that the wind effect is extreme.

During the process of ranging, both line and angle of projection will be adjusted until the mean point of impact of the bombs is centred on the target, and the co-ordinates of the target can be produced from the bearing and range of the mortar. Unfortunately these co-ordinates cannot be corrected to take into account the effect that has been produced by wind speed and direction, air density etc. at the time of ranging and at a subsequent time when the wind has changed, the mean point of impact of the bombs will be shifted by a considerable amount. This may be sufficient not only to render the fire ineffective, it may also make it hazardous to own troops.

The answer to this is clearly the extension of meteorological data to mortar positions.

TARGET VERSATILITY

The conventional mortar cannot be used as an anti-tank weapon. It would add greatly to its value if it could. The simplest way of doing this is demonstrated in the accompanying photographs of the Madsen 51mm light mortar, but this direct fire engagement is not a practical proposition for a large mortar; neither is it cost-effective to leave mortars in position to be overrun by tanks and their accompanying infantry.

There are, however, two ways in which larger conventional mortars are likely to be used against tanks in future. One method involves the use of a conventionally-aimed mortar bomb which produces an anti-armour effect over a wide area; this is the basis of a Hotchkiss-Brandt development described in the French section below; the other is to provide the bomb with some form of terminal guidance – such as infra-red homing, a laser designator-seeker arrangement or a TV or imaging infra-red (IIR) system. Applications of these techniques to mortar bombs as well as to other missiles and projectiles are among the ideas being studied in an extensive series of programmes in the USA at least.

UNCONVENTIONAL MORTARS

The conventional mortar was said to be muzzle loading, smooth bore, firing a fin stabilized sub-sonic bomb and having charge zones. Range was said to be adjusted by altering the tangent elevation. Any mortar which departs from this definition is considered to be unconventional. The development of the highly successful Brandt and Tampella rocket assisted bombs may eventually lead to the acceptance of this method of increasing range – even though it reduces the lethality of the bomb by inserting the rocket motor into the volume of high explosive filling. The US 4.2in (107mm) mortar has used a rifled barrel and spin stabilization for many years. The Brandt 120mm rifled mortar has introduced the system into Europe and although the method used, of pre-engraved bands, is quite different, the end effect is much the same.

The large calibre mortars of 160mm and 240mm used by the USSR have barrels far too long to allow conventional muzzle loading and they are lowered for breech loading. All these unconventional designs have been produced to overcome the constraints imposed by the orthodox approach which cannot cope with the need for extremes of size, range or accuracy insisted upon by some countries. Only in the field of range adjustment is the conventional mortar still supreme.

There have been several attempts to vary range by controlling pressure. The Russians used this system in their 50mm pre-war light mortars and exactly the same system was used by the French in their 50mm "Lance Grenade". In both of these approaches gas was allowed to escape to give lower muzzle velocities and ranges, and as the range was extended the gas bleed was closed off. The elevation of the mortar remained unchanged throughout the range band. The French mortar is illustrated on the next page.

The French 50mm "Lance Grenade" mortar. This fired at a constant angle and regulated gas pressure by bleeding it off through vents under the range collar

FUTURE MORTARS

There may well be two types of mortar in use in the future. One could be an extension of the conventional mortar and would be deployed by the infantry in terrain inaccessible to vehicles. This sort of mortar would be used by mountain divisions, parachute troops and commandos. The second type of mortar would be linked to a vehicle and would not be dismountable. It would be fired at a fixed elevation and would make use of liquid propellant. This is thermodynamically more efficient than current solid propellants. The system would use a black box to evaluate the effects of meteorological data, barrel wear, barrel temperature, charge temperature and bomb weight and shape and the Detachment Commander would dial the required range. The "fire" button would inject the correct amount of fuel and ignite it immediately. Such a system would allow the use of a variety of projectiles and allow totally predicted fire with no ranging process. There would be a need for better target position data but this is already available from the laser range finder and the vehicle position indicator. It can be well argued that the adoption of such a mortar would remove the virtues of simplicity and cheapness and a liquid propelled gun would be both more effective and little more expensive but the cardinal value of the mortar, its ability to deliver fire over almost any kind of crest situated almost anywhere on the trajectory, will always make it an essential weapon for the infantry in conventional warfare.

The Japanese "89 Type" 50mm mortar. This had a rifled, tapered bore, with a rod on the inside, which moved forward as the range decreased and increased the chamber volume and decreased the shot travel. It was known as the 'Japanese Knee Mortar' and if fired off the leg would almost certainly guarantee a broken thigh – if nothing worse

The Italian Brixia 45mm mortar. This varied range by: (a) Varying angle of elevation; (b) Varying shot travel; (c) Varying chamber volume; (d) Bleeding gas off to atmosphere. It was a very complicated mortar which sent a very small bomb to a maximum range of 323yds

BELGIUM

PRB 431 60mm HIGH EXPLOSIVE MORTAR BOMB

PRB SA manufacture 60mm, 81mm and 4.2 inch (107mm) mortar bombs. These are exported all over the world.

The PRB 431 mortar bomb has a watertight thin metallic casing which contains a patented fragmentation sleeve and explosive charge. PRB claim that the 431 is twice as effective as the American M49A2 mortar bomb.

The fins, which are made of light alloy, hold a primary cartridge with an "improved" ignition cap. The supplementary charges are held by spring blades fixed on the fin tube and are shorter than the fin blades.

The PRB 431 can use all fuzes standardised on the American 1.5in (38mm) fuze well. It has been designed for firing from the American M19 mortar, although according to PRB, it can also be fired from breech-loaded mortars.

In addition, the loading of the mortar bomb can be modified so that the smoke produced by the explosion is red, yellow or green.

DATA

Total weight: 1.37kg
Weight of TNT explosive: .15kg
Length of bomb with US M52A2 fuze: 255mm
Length of bomb without fuze: 195mm
Lethal radius: 13.5m
Propelling charge: 4 increments (powder M8) and 1 primary cartridge
Maximum range (M19 mortar): 1,800m
Packing: 1 shell per fibre container, ten containers per wooden case
Manufacturer: PRB SA, Avenue de Tervueren 168, B-1150, Brussels

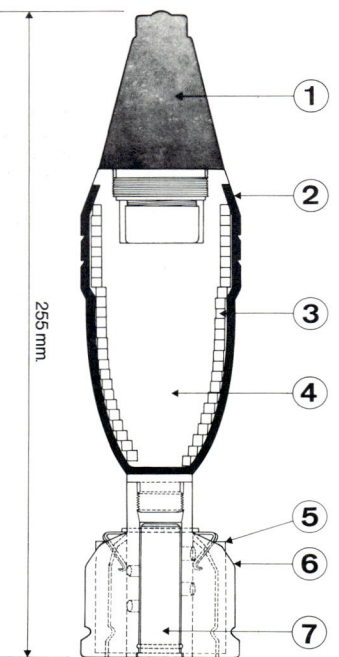

PRB 431 60mm Mortar Bomb: (1) Fuze (2) Sheath (3) Fragmentation body (4) Explosive (5) Increment charges (6) Fin assembly (7) Primary cartridge

PRB 414 81mm HIGH EXPLOSIVE MORTAR BOMB

The PRB 414 mortar bomb is made of a watertight, thin metallic sheath which contains a patented fragmentation sleeve and an explosive charge. The light alloy fins and the use of a hunting type primary cartridge have enabled the manufacturers to give the bomb maximum HE content.

The supplementary charges are held by spring blades staked on the fin tube and are shorter than the fin blades. The PRB 414 can use all standard American fuzes as it has a 1.5in fuze well. The loading of the mortar bomb can be modified so that the smoke produced by the explosion is red, green or yellow.

The mortar bomb has been designed to be fired from the American M1 or M29 mortar, as well as being a replacement for the American M43A1 bomb. PRB claim that their bomb is twice as effective as the American bomb.

DATA

Total weight: 3.25kg
Weight of TNT explosive: .50kg
Length of bomb with US M54A2 fuze: 338mm
Length of the bomb without fuze: 275mm
Lethal radius: 21m
Propelling charge: 6 increments (powder M8) and 1 primary cartridge
Maximum range (M1 mortar): 3,000m

The ranges of the PRB 414 shell, when used with the American mortars M1 and M29 or any foreign mortars of the same geometrical characteristics (105cm, low pressure-600 bars), are given by the American firing table for the M43A1 shell with the fuze M52A2. PRB can also supply super charges

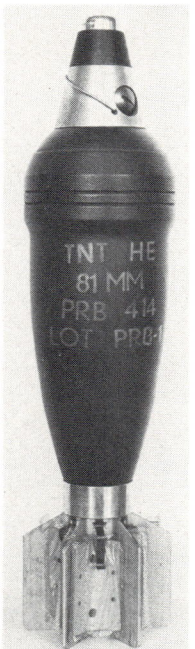

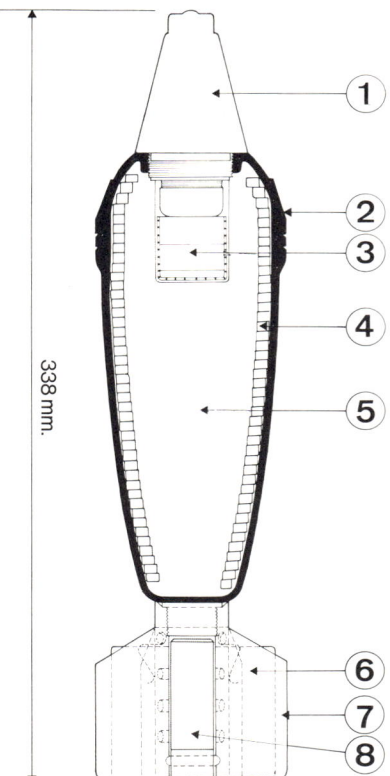

for use in medium pressure (800 bars) and high pressure (1,000 bars) mortars.
Packing: 1 shell per fibre container, ten containers per wooden case
Manufacturer: PRB SA (see above)

PRB 414 81mm Mortar Bomb: (1) Fuze (2) Sheath (3) Booster (4) Fragmentation body (5) Explosive (6) Increment charges (7) Fin assembly (8) Primary cartridge

CHINA (PEOPLE'S REPUBLIC)

60mm TYPE 31 AND VARIANTS

This was originally a Chinese Nationalist weapon and is a copy of the United States Mortar M2. Both the M2 and the Type 31 weapons resemble the pre-war French Stokes-Brandt M1935 mortar. All three have a square baseplate, a handcrank on the end of the elevating screw housing and a cross-levelling mechanism of two-piece construction. Recognition features are brass feet on the Chinese Nationalist weapon and a folding handcrank on the traversing knob of the French and US versions which can be distinguished from each other by the markings.

DATA	Type 31	M2	M1935
Calibre	60mm	60mm	60mm
Barrel length	675mm	726mm	700mm
Firing weight	20.2kg	19.0kg	17.6kg
Max.range	1530m	1820m	1760m
Rate of fire	20-30 rounds/min		
Status	All three weapons are strictly obsolete but all may still be encountered in service in parts of Asia		

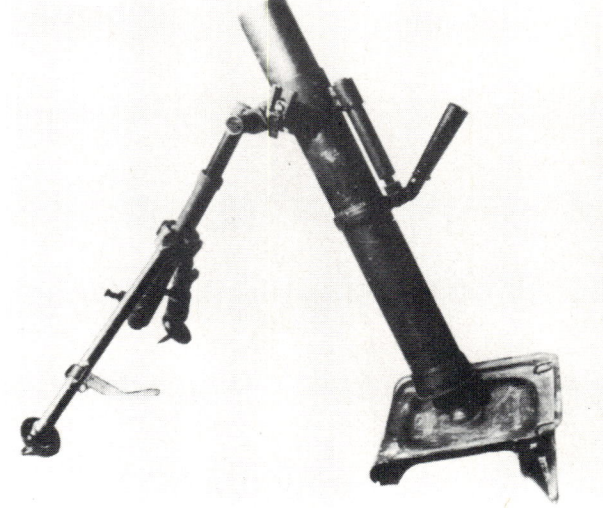

The Chinese 60mm mortar, Type 31

60mm MORTAR TYPE 63

The Type 63 light mortar is essentially an updated model of the earlier Type 31 mortar. It is lighter and has only one recoil cylinder, its baseplate is smaller and rectangular in shape (on the Type 31 the baseplate is square), the bipod and mortar barrel are shorter and a carrying handle is provided on the barrel, just below the recoil system. It has the same operational range as the Type 31.
DATA
Calibre: 60mm

Weight in firing position: 12.39kg
Length of barrel: 610mm
Rate of fire: 15-20 rounds per minute
Range: 1,530m
Ammunition: HE
Muzzle velocity: 158m/s
Status: In service with Chinese forces and in Albania, Vietnam and some African Liberation Armies

82mm TYPE 53

This is a copy of the Russian M1937 which is still the current mortar of this calibre in the USSR. China has exported this to Cambodia, Pakistan, Tanzania, Uganda, Vietnam.
Status: In service

120mm TYPE 53

This is a copy of the Russian M1943, and is also used by Pakistan, Tanzania and Vietnam.
Status: In service

160mm MORTAR

This is a copy of the Russian M1943.
Status: In service

81mm FRAGMENTATION PROJECTILES

There are two 81mm bombs in service. Both are based on the US M43A1 projectile, one being a direct copy and the other a variant. The direct copy has the characteristics given below.

DATA
Calibre: 81mm
Type: Fragmentation
Weight (fuzed): 3.22kg
Bursting charge: 0.56kg TNT
Fuze: (?) point detonating
Known using weapons: Mortars, Models 20 and 53

The variant version has the following characteristics.

DATA
Calibre: 81mm
Type: Fragmentation
Weight (fuzed): 3.20kg
Bursting charge: 0.35kg TNT
Fuze: (?) point detonating
Known using weapons: Mortars, Models 20 and 53

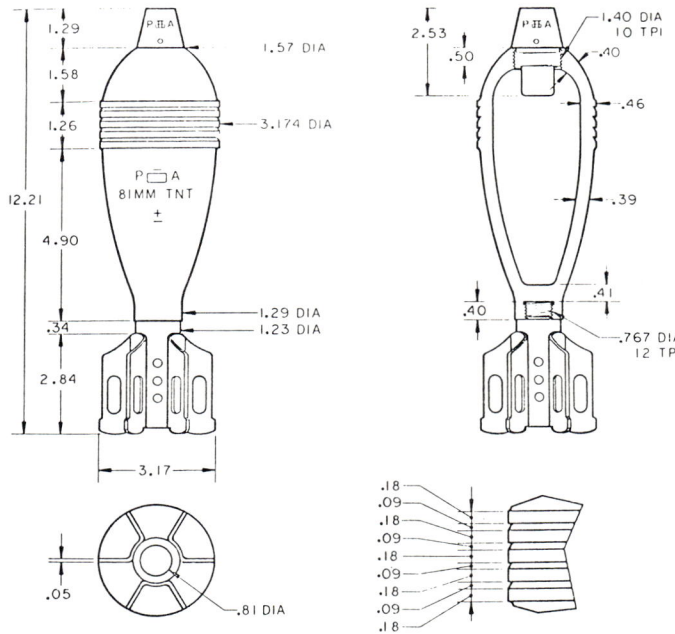

Chinese 81mm fragmentation projectile, a copy of the US M43A1 (all dimensions in inches)

Chinese 81mm fragmentation projectile and the US M43A1 (variant) copy (all dimensions in inches)

82mm HE PROJECTILE

DATA
Calibre: 82mm
Type: HE
Weight (fuzed): 3.86kg
Bursting charge: 0.38kg TNT
Fuze: (?) point detonating
Known using weapons: Mortars, Models 20 and 53

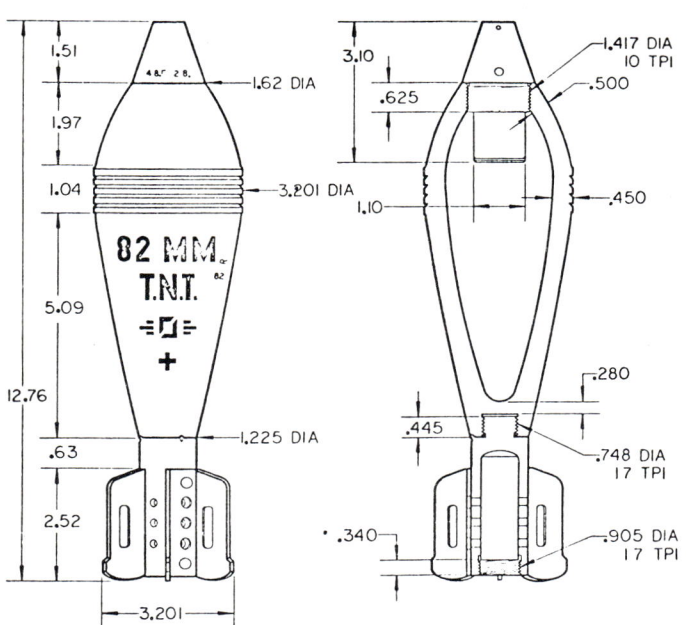

Chinese 82mm HE projectile (all dimensions in inches)

82mm FRAGMENTATION PROJECTILE, MODEL M30

DATA
Calibre: 82mm
Identification: M30
Type: Fragmentation
Weight (fuzed): 3.14kg
Bursting charge: 0.42kg TNT/dinitronapthalene
Fuze: Model 6 point detonating
Known using weapons: Mortars, Models 20 and 53
Remarks: Fuze is a copy of the Soviet Model M-6

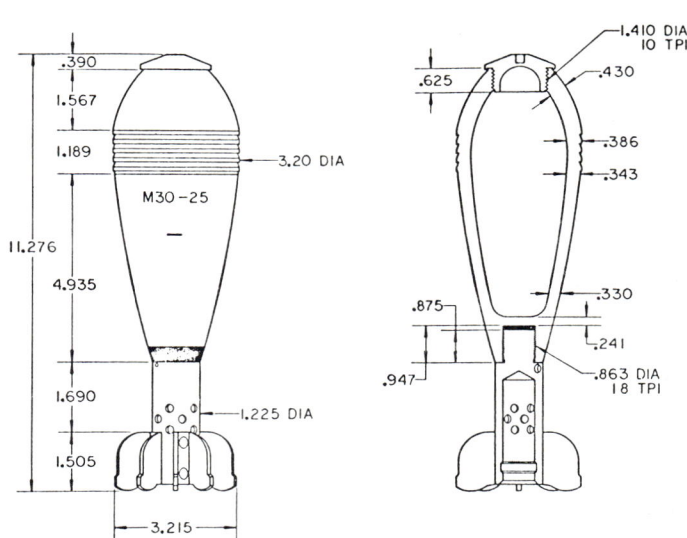

Chinese 82mm fragmentation projectile, Model M30 (all dimensions in inches)

82mm FRAGMENTATION PROJECTILE

DATA
Calibre: 82mm
Type: Fragmentation
Weight (fuzed): 3.82kg
Bursting charge: 0.14kg commercial dynamite
Fuze: Model 9 point detonating
Known using weapons: Mortars, Models 20 and 53

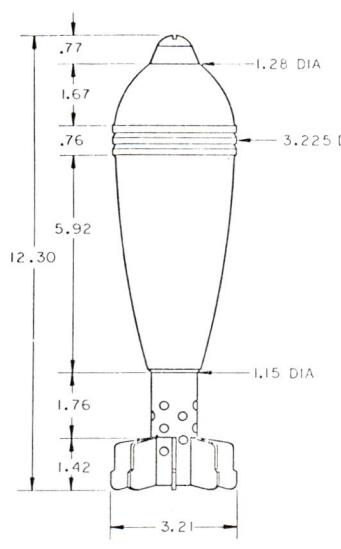
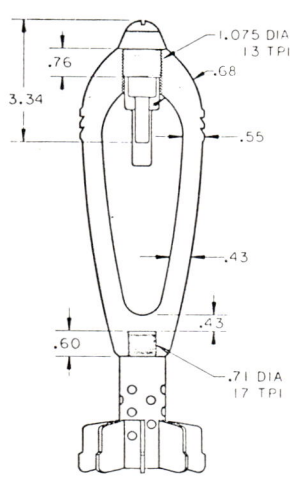

Chinese 82mm fragmentation projectile (all dimensions in inches)

82mm FRAGMENTATION PROJECTILE

DATA
Calibre: 82mm
Type: Fragmentation
Weight (fuzed): 3.72kg
Bursting charge: 0.25kg TNT
Fuze: Model 8 point detonating
Known using weapon: Mortar, Model 20

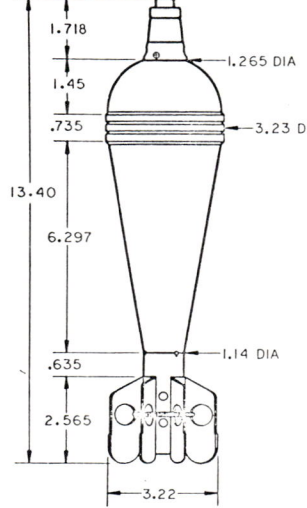
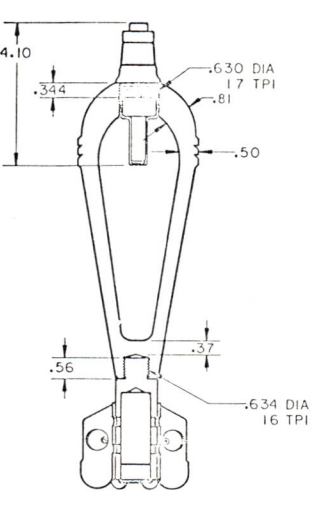

Chinese 82mm HE projectile (all dimensions in inches)

82mm HE PROJECTILE

DATA
Calibre: 82mm
Type: HE
Weight (fuzed): 3.88kg
Bursting charge: 0.31kg TNT and potassium nitrate
Fuze: Models 8 and 9 point detonating
Known using weapon: Mortar, Model 20
Remarks: The projectile is illustrated without fuze

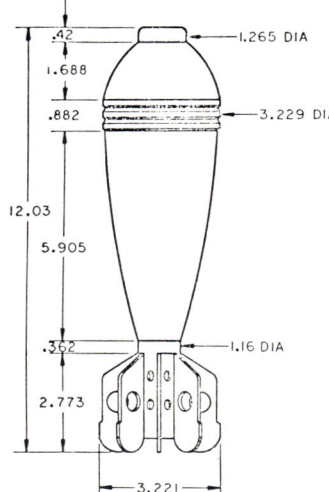
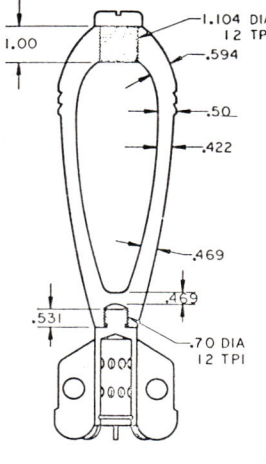

Chinese 82mm fragmentation projectile (all dimensions in inches)

CZECHOSLOVAKIA

CZECHOSLOVAKIAN MORTARS

During and shortly after World War II the Skoda Works produced a series of interesting and unusual mortars including some of very considerable size. A 305mm mortar with breech loading obturation was tried but work ceased at the end of the war. The last unorthodox mortar was the B19 which was a breech loading mortar with a large double cylinder recoil and recuperator system. It was a 21cm mortar but not unduly heavy for such a bore. It was not easily or rapidly switched from target to target. The B24 was

a 120mm mortar which until recently at any rate was still in use with some territorial formations. It appears to be similar to the Brandt mortar and was towed into action on a very light carriage. It fired a 13kg bomb out to some 7km, and in the firing position weighed approximately 250kg.

In 1948 a short 120mm mortar was produced. This was intended for airborne use and to equip troops engaged in fighting in the mountains or over other terrain where weight assumed major importance. The bipod is of

The B19 21cm heavy mortar. Note the recoil cylinders and the long recoil of the barrel

The current 81mm mortar, the M1948

The B24 mortar on its travelling carriage. This 120mm mortar is not in service with first line troops

the same shape as the B24 with the curved members joining at the back of the elevation gear case and pinched in together at their junction.

The 120mm M1948 mortar is no longer in front line service, although quantities are probably held in reserve. It fires an HE bomb weighing 16.3kg to a maximum range of 5,900m. Ammunition is the same as that used for the 120mm B24 mortar. Total weight of the M1948 is 317.5kg and maximum rate of fire is stated as 6 rounds/min.

Only two Czech mortars are in current service with first line troops and both of these are 81mm calibre. Both are said to have performances much the same as the Russian M37 and they use the same ammunition. These two mortars are the M1948 and the M1952.

The mortar breaks down into three man pack loads for easy transportation, ie barrel, baseplate and bipod. The M1948 fires a 3.63kg HE bomb to a maximum range of 3,700m. Total weight of the mortar is 63.5kg and maximum rate of fire is 10-12 rounds/min. No data on the M1952 mortar is available at the present time.

The short 120mm mortar, M1948

FINLAND

FINNISH ARMY MORTARS

Mortars produced to designs by Oy Tampella AB in Finland are among the most widely-used of such weapons. Because of political difficulties in the way of direct arms trading, however, the exploitation of their designs is now mainly by licence to manufacturers in other countries. The most extensively used of such licences is that to Soltam Ltd. in Israel, a company which was founded in 1950 and is largely concerned with mortar manufacture and sale. At least one other licence is known to have been issued: this was to Sweden for the manufacture of the 120mm M-40 mortar.

Tampella have been making mortars for the Finnish Army since the 1930s. Their designs have been found to be reliable; and the earlier weapons at least have been adopted, with or without modification, by several countries. It is known that Tampella designed a new range of weapons in the 1960s and early 1970s, but no data have been made available: meanwhile the mortars currently used by Finnish forces appear to be the earlier M-38 and M-56 81mm, the M-40 120mm and M-58 160mm mortars, designed and built by Tampella, the Russian-designed M-38 120mm weapon built under licence by Tampella and, possibly, the Russian M-37 82mm mortar obtained from the Soviet Union.

Manufacturer: Oy Tampella AB, Pääkonttori, Lapintie 1, SF-33100 Tampere 10, Finland. Details of the licence-built Soltam weapons are included in the Israeli entries.

81mm M-38 AND M-56 MORTARS

These two mortars are believed to be currently operational with Finnish forces. From the limited data available it is not possible to say what, if any, external differences there are between the two weapons and their superficial appearance is very much like that of the short 81mm mortar of the current Tampella/Soltam series. The reported characteristics of the older weapons are, however, significantly different from the 81mm Tampella/Soltam mortars: they are reported to be substantially heavier and to have less range. The brief details set out below appear to be common to the M-38 and M-56 weapons.

DATA
Calibre: 81mm
Weight in firing position: 60kg
Range: 3000m
Rate of fire: 20 rounds/min
Weight of bomb: 3.5kg
Crew: 3-4
Manufacturer: Tampella
Status: Believed to be in service only in Finland

120mm M-40 MORTAR

This is an early Tampella-designed mortar which is also produced under licence in Sweden. In the Swedish version the stand was changed in 1956 from the original Tampella design to a Hotchkiss-Brandt design (also made in Sweden) and in 1972 the Swedish mortars were fitted with new sights. It is improbable that either of these modifications was carried back to the Finnish version.
DATA
Calibre: 120.25mm

Weight in firing position: About 285kg
Barrel length: 200cm
Elevation: 45-80°
Range: 6,400m maximum
Rate of fire: 12-15 rounds/min
Weight of bomb: 13.3kg
Manufacturer: Tampella (see above)
Status: In service in Finland and in modified form in Sweden

160mm HEAVY MORTAR M-58

This is the largest mortar currently in service in Finland. Designed by Tampella, it appears to be significantly lighter than the 160mm Soltam mortar which is based on a Tampella design but may well incorporate locally designed modifications.
DATA
Calibre: 160mm

Weight in firing position: 1,350kg
Weight of bomb: 40-45kg
Maximum range: 10,500 metres
Rate of fire: 10 rounds/min maximum: 4 rounds/min practical
Manufacturer: Tampella
Status: In service in Finland at least

FRANCE

60mm "COMMANDO" MORTAR

This is the lightest and most portable of the Hotchkiss-Brandt mortars. It is produced in two variants, type "V" and type "A". Both have small spades and do not use a mounting. They are controlled for both line and elevation directly by the firer.

The type "V" has a short barrel and a fixed firing pin. As soon as the muzzle loaded bomb reaches the firing pin it is automatically fired. A sighting unit is fitted and this is a simple clamp on type which has a bubble fitted on the right hand side. The firer sets the range on a drum and when the bubble is levelled the sight is elevated for the correct tangent elevation for the selected range. A white line is inscribed along the front of the barrel and the azimuth is applied by lining up this mark with the target. A broad webbing strap is located around the barrel to provide a grip for the firer's left hand which would otherwise find it difficult to control the hot barrel. A webbing sling is provided for carriage of the mortar and a muzzle cover is supplied to keep out the dirt, sand etc. which greatly increase barrel wear. The spade is small and button shaped.

The mortar will fire at a rate of 12 to 20 rounds a minute. There is a two charge system providing a maximum range of 1,050 metres and a minimum range of 100 metres. The overall length of the mortar is 680mm and the barrel itself is 650mm. The total weight is 7.7kg.

The type "A" is longer and a breech piece located below the barrel holds the firing mechanism and is connected to a small trough shaped spade. The mortar is controlled by a firing lever which has a trip-over action. The bomb is dropped in from the muzzle and rests on the firing pin. The user pulls back on the lanyard attached to the firing lever, the firing pin is retracted, the spring is compressed and then the pin trips over and is driven forward to fire the round. There is no sight fitted and the soldier lying behind the mortar lines up the barrel to control his fire for azimuth and estimates the correct

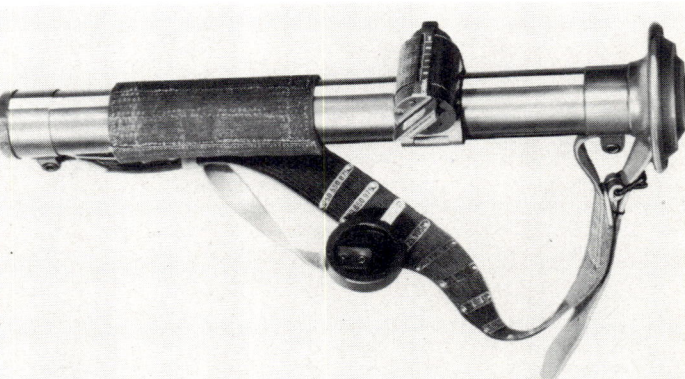

60mm Commando Type 'V'. This has a fixed firing pin and fires the bomb as soon as it drops. Note the button shaped spade

quadrant elevation for his first round. Subsequently fire is corrected by the observation of burst.

The type "A" mortar has an overall length of 861mm but the barrel length is the same as that of the type 'V' mortar. The weight is 10kg.

AMMUNITION
The Commando mortars have a range of 60mm ammunition.

HE BOMB Mk 61
The body of this mortar bomb is made of perlitic, malleable iron. It is filled with pressed TNT and is fitted with the V9 fuze. The total length of the bomb is 317mm, and it weighs 1.720kg. Using Charge II it is propelled to 1,050 metres.

HE BOMB Mk 72
This bomb is made of the same material. It is 321mm in length and has a total weight, with its TNT filling, of 1.730kg. It has the V9 fuze.

HE COLOUR MARKER BOMB Mk 61 AND Mk 72
These bombs are used for ranging and target indication and consist of the normal HE filling but mixed with it is colouring matter which may be green, yellow or red. The bombs have the same physical characteristics as the normal HE bombs.

SMOKE BOMB Mk 61 AND Mk 72
These bombs, filled with liquid titanium chloride, produce an effective smoke screen. The weight, length etc. of these bombs is the same as those of the HE bombs. The same fuze is used.

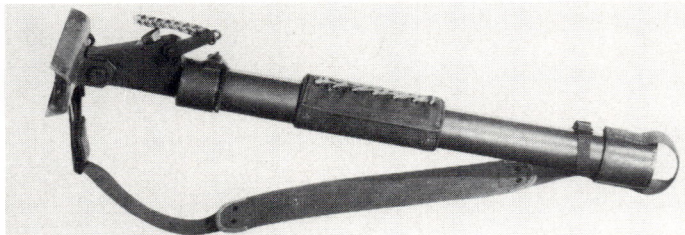

60mm Commando Type 'A'. Note the lanyard attached to the firing lever. Note the trough shaped spade

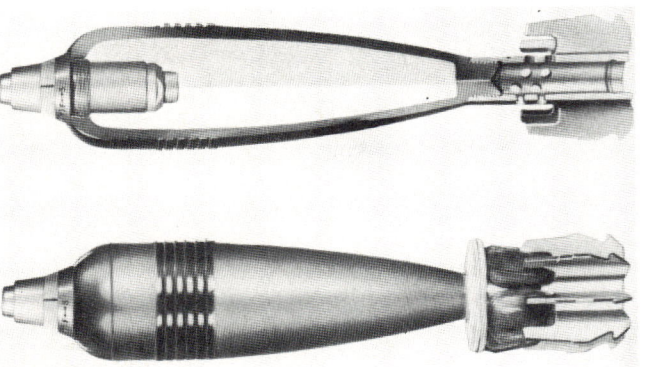

60mm HE bomb, Mk 61, fuzed V9

60mm HE bomb, Mk 72 with fuze V9

The 60mm parachute illuminating Bomb, Mk 63

PRACTICE BOMBS Mk 61 AND Mk 72

These bombs are partly filled with hexachlorethane and ballasted with a dummy head. Alternatively they may be filled completely with a mixture of sulphur/napthalene. Again they have the same ballistics as the HE bomb, and the V9 fuze.

ILLUMINATING BOMB Mk 63

This bomb has a magnesium based filling and is hung on a parachute. The light persists for a minimum of 30 seconds and produces 180,000 candelas. It provides illumination over an area with a radius of 150 metres. The round is 333mm long, weighs 1.550kg and has a clockwork fuze.

Manufacturer: Thomson-Brandt – Branche Hotchkiss-Brandt Armements, 52 Avenue des Champs-Elysées 75 008-Paris
Status: Production. The Commando mortar was developed in 1966 and has been adopted by the armed forces of some 20 major countries, the majority of whom use the Type A mortar

---

60mm LIGHT MORTAR

This mortar was produced as a private venture by Hotchkiss-Brandt who started work on it in 1963. It has proved to be a very successful light mortar and is still in production.

The weapon is of orthodox configuration with a baseplate, barrel and bipod mounting. The barrel is smooth bored, made of nickel chrome steel and can be supplied chromium plated if required. The base of the barrel is threaded to take the breech piece. The breech piece is made of steel and is screwed into the barrel. It is pinned in place and can be removed only by an armourer. The striker is dome headed and screws into the breechpiece from the rear. It protrudes into the base of the chamber and projects about 1.5mm. The bombs are dropped on the striker.

The baseplate is an equilateral triangle reinforced by three webs forming a star round the central cone. On the top surface there is a socket into which fits the breech piece.

The barrel is locked into position by rotating it in the socket. The baseplate allows all-round traverse and the webs give good stability in very wet soil. A lifting handle is fitted. The bipod supports the barrel. It has two legs made of aluminium alloy hinged to a cross piece at the top. The legs can be moved out or in and the width between the feet is controlled by an adjustable chain. Passing upwards from the centre of the crosspiece, in a tube connecting the two bipod legs, is the elevating screw. This is attached to the yoke.

The yoke carries the traversing gear and at the end of it is the traversing handle. On the top of the yoke is the cradle into which the barrel fits, and at the other end to the traversing handle is the sight bracket.

The sight in use on the 60mm Light Mortar is the F9. This has an elevating scale graduated from 40 to 60 degrees at 1 degree intervals. The deflection micrometer is divided into 300 mils in 5-mils graduations.

The mortar can be brought into action very quickly even on an unprepared platform. The baseplate should be level. If possible the first round should be fired at an angle greater than 60 degrees and serves to bed the plate in.

If the ground is soft the baseplate will sink in but using the barrel as a lever it can be withdrawn speedily. The detachment can move on foot carrying the mortar over considerable distances.

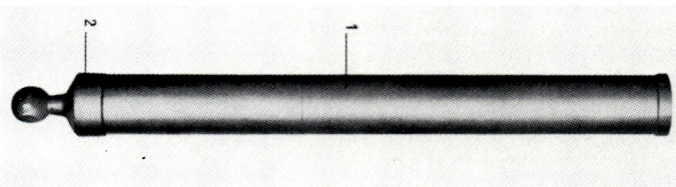

The barrel of the 60mm light mortar. The breech piece (2) is pinned in place and carries the striker

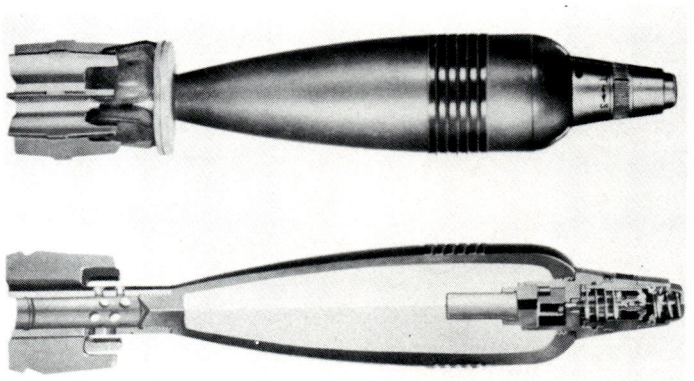

Mk 60/61 bomb with the V9 fuze

DATA
Weight: 14.8kg
Length of barrel with breech piece: 724mm
Weight of barrel: 3.8kg
Weight of baseplate: 6kg
Weight of bipod: 5kg

The 60mm light mortar, showing the maximum and minimum angle of depression

The mortar in position on rough ground

Mk 61 ammunition range. Note the shape and position of the secondary charges

Top traverse: 300 mils
Elevation: 40°-85°
Minimum range: 100 metres
Maximum range: 2,000 metres

AMMUNITION
The 60mm Light Mortar was designed for the Hotchkiss-Brandt Mk 60/61 bomb.

The details of the round are:
Body, forged steel. Length, 317.5mm. Filling, pressed TNT, (31g). Weight of complete round, 1.65kg.

The primary cartridge (LZ) is in a case of 24mm diameter and 65mm long. The charge is 4.2 grams made of two types of Ballistite.

The secondaries which lie between the eight fins of the tail unit, are made up of 3.5 grams of Ballistite.

The supercharge is horseshoe shaped and is made up of 5 grams of Ballistite. It lies around the primary cartridge housing beneath the secondaries.

The maker claims a very efficient fragment pattern for the 60mm bomb

The sight of the 60mm mortar: (1) Bearing scale; (2) Sighting tube; (3) Cross level bubble; (4) Sight catch; (5) Elevation scale; (6) Elevation fine scale; (7) Elevation bubble

with the largest mass of fragments weighing between 1 and 2 grams.

The mortar will also fire the US 60mm bomb (old type), the old Hotchkiss Mk 35/47, the Mk 61 coloured marker, smoke and practice bombs and the Mk 63 illuminating bomb described in the entry for the 60mm Commando mortar (above).

Manufacturer: Hotchkiss-Brandt Armement (see above)
Status: In production and in service with several armies

60mm LONG RANGE MORTAR

The Hotchkiss-Brandt Long Range Mortar has been developed to combine the flexibility of the 60mm Light Mortar and the firepower of the 81mm Mortar. For ease of transport it can be broken down into three components: barrel, baseplate and bipod.

It can fire the standard Brandt Mk 61 and Mk 72 ranges of HE, smoke, practice and illuminating bombs. In addition a new long range projectile called the LR has been developed for this mortar. The LR is of malleable perlitic cast iron, has unfolding fins and a fuze which detonates under any angle of impact, including grazing fire. The LR bomb weighs 2.2kg and has a total length with fins folded of 367mm. It has a tolite charge which gives the bomb comparable efficiency to the 81mm mortar bomb.

DATA
Calibre: 60mm
Total weight: 23kg
Length of barrel including breech: 1350mm
Weight of barrel: 8.4kg
Weight of baseplate: 8.8kg
Weight of bipod: 5.8kg
Traverse: 300 mils
Elevation: 40° to 85°
Maximum range: 5,000m
Manufacturer: Hotchkiss-Brandt Armement (see above)
Status: Pre-production

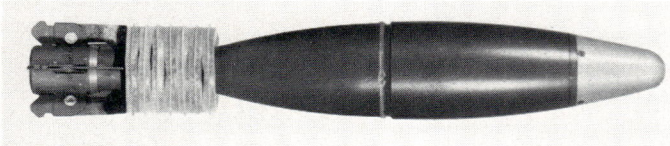

60mm long-range bomb Type LR

60mm Hotchkiss-Brandt Long-Range Light Mortar

60mm GUN-MORTAR

The 60 MC HB mortar has been developed for use in an armoured personnel carrier. It was started in 1970 and has now been fitted to a number of vehicles – such as the AML-Panhard – used by infantry.

The weapon can be muzzle loaded from outside the vehicle. The firer drops the bombs down the smooth bore tube.

When this procedure is followed the mortar can be regarded as conventional and the bomb drops onto a fixed firing pin. It then can be fired in the upper register (45 degrees-90 degrees) at a rate of 12 to 20 rounds a minute.

The mortar is equipped with a falling block breech mechanism. There are different ways of opening the breech to fit in with the available space in different vehicles. One is by using a lever breech mechanism, or alternatively a simple hand bar may be positioned across the rear of the block and then rotated back and down to operate the breech.

As soon as the breech block is unlocked the firing pin is withdrawn and will not emerge again until the block is locked. This ensures that the mortar cannot be loaded from the muzzle and fired whilst the breech block is unlocked.

When the firing is controlled from within the vehicle, either electrical or mechanical firing can be provided through a trigger lever.

Since the recoil force must be taken on the trunnions, a hydraulic buffer is provided. This allows a recoil of 135mm. The maximum recoil force is kept down to 1.7kg. The recoiling mass is 42kg and this of course makes a major contribution to keeping down the velocity of recoil.

AMMUNITION

The gun mortar will fire the old Mk 35/47 bomb, the standard Mk 61 bomb and the long range Mk 72 bomb.

The Mk 63 illuminating bomb is used for target illumination, and the Mk 61 smoke bomb for the provision of immediate cover.

The bombs used in this mortar have the V9 fuze (except the illuminating bomb which has a clockwork time fuze) which has a safe and fire setting. In addition a modified V9 fuze can be provided to give arming closer to the muzzle. This provides functioning at 20metres and will also give graze functioning for horizontal firing.

DATA
Length of weapon: 1,210mm
Bomb travel: 905mm
Elevation: −11° to +75°
Maximum range
Mk 72 bomb: 2,600metres

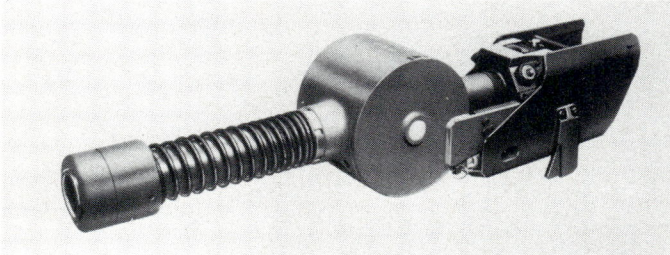

Hotchkiss-Brandt 60mm gun mortar

Muzzle loading from outside the vehicle

Mk 61 bomb: 2,050metres
Flat trajectory: 300metres
Manufacturer: Hotchkiss-Brandt Armement (see above)
Status: Mass production. Has been exported to at least one country

60mm MC 60 on Panhard M3 APC. The lever breech mechanism is on the left of the breech

60mm GUN MORTAR MODEL LR

This mortar can be turret mounted in a variety of vehicles such as the Panhard M3 armoured personnel carrier, in addition it can also be mounted in riverline or coastal patrol craft. It can be breech-loaded or muzzle-loaded. It has a lever breech mechanism with an automatic withdrawal of the firing pin during breech opening. It incorporates a safety mechanism which ensures that the firing pin is clear from the front face as long as the breech is not locked.

It can be fired either electrically or mechanically through a trigger mechanism or by gravity when muzzle loaded.

It can fire the LR long range standard Mk 61 and Mk 72 and Mk 35/47 bombs and the Mk 63 illuminating bomb.

DATA
Calibre: 60mm
Total length of barrel: 1,800mm
Total length of bomb travel: 1,500mm
Length of recoil: 170mm
Maximum recoil thrust: 2,800kg
Weight of recoiling mass: 75kg
Elevation: −11° to +75°
Maximum ranges as a mortar:
    LR Bomb: 4,000metres
    Mk 72 Bomb: 3,000metres
    Mk 61 Bomb: 2,300metres
Maximum ranges with flat trajectory:
    LR Bomb: 400metres
    Mk 72 Bomb: 300metres
Manufacturer: Hotchkiss-Brandt Armement (see above)
Status: Pre-production

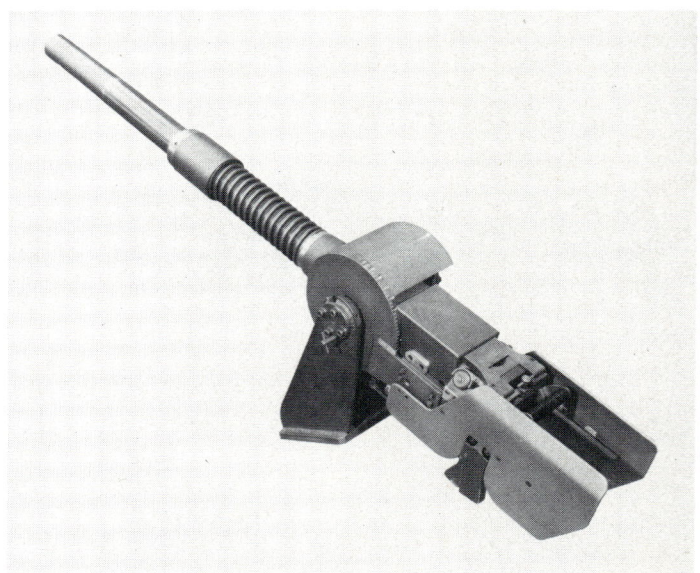

Hotchkiss-Brandt 60mm Gun Mortar Model LR

60mm ANTI-TANK MORTAR BOMB

This bomb has been developed by Hotchkiss-Brandt to be fired from the 60mm Gun Mortars, thus giving these weapons a full range of ammunition; i.e. HE, Illuminating, Smoke, Practice and Anti-tank. A similar 120mm mortar bomb has also been developed. The mortar bomb has a piezo-electric fuze which gives it a 10m muzzle safety, i.e. the bomb is not armed until it is 10m away from the weapon.

Although the hollow charge will penetrate almost 200mm of armour or concrete, it still has a good anti-personnel capability.

60mm anti-tank mortar bomb

DATA
Weight of complete round: 1.54kg
Total length: 343mm
Charge: Hexotolite
Muzzle velocity: 200m/s
Range, stationary target: 500metres

Range, moving target: 300metres
Manufacturer: Hotchkiss-Brandt Armement (see above)
Status: Pre-production

81mm LIGHT MORTAR

This mortar was designed in 1961 and has been in service for several years. It exists in two versions. These are known as MO 81-61 C and MO 81-61 L. The two versions have barrels of 1,150mm and 1,450mm respectively. The mortar is typical of its type and consists of barrel unit, mounting and baseplate. The barrel is made of steel, reinforced at the rear end and chrome plated internally. At the rear end is screwed on the breech piece which holds the firing gear. This allows the user to retract the firing pin when required in the safe position or allow it to protrude in the firing position. The end of the breech piece contains the ball which fits into the socket on the baseplate. It has two flats which allow for the insertion of the knob and subsequently its rotation.

The mounting consists of the bipod, elevating gear, traversing gear, cross levelling gear, and the barrel clamp. The bipod legs can be splayed at will and the distance between them is controlled by the chain connecting the feet. The elevating screw thread is enclosed in a tube. The tube is connected by a rod to the left bipod leg. By sliding the tube along the rod the elevating screw column is tilted and so the mortar is cross levelled. The traversing gear is enclosed in a tube. The traversing handle is at one end of the tube and the sight mounting is at the other.

The baseplate is made of chrome molybdenum steel. It has, on the top surface, a socket in which the knob of the breech piece fits. This socket is moveable to allow the equipment to rotate around the baseplate. The underside of the baseplate has three ribs which radiate outwards from under the socket and provide the strength to prevent the baseplate from buckling as the impulsive loading is applied.

The mortar may be carried in any suitable vehicle. It can also be broken down into mule loads or even carried by the detachment in framed ruck-sacks.

The sustained rate of fire for the mortar is 12-15 rounds/minute.

In addition to the standard HE bombs, M57D and Mk 61, the following variants are available in both series: *Coloured, HE, target marker bomb:*

The Hotchkiss-Brandt 81mm light mortar

(Green, yellow or red) filled TNT and colouring material. *Smoke bomb:* Filled liquid titanium tetrachloride. *Practice bomb:* Filled with sulphur/napthalene mixture and with dummy fuze.

THE VIG and V19 Pa FUZES
The V19 Fuze may be set for instantaneous action or to function with a delay. The mechanism is arranged so that there is complete safety in the bore. The fuze cannot detonate the main filling until 0.8sec after firing. This means that on Charge 0 the bomb will have travelled 55 metres and at charge 6 it will have travelled 200 metres before the main filling can be detonated. In the event of double loading the bombs have been proved safe.

V19 P fuze showing the arm and safe switch and the instantaneous/delay setting

DATA

	Short barrel	Long barrel
Total weight:	39.4kg	41.5kg
Length of barrel:	1.15 metre	1.45 metre
Weight of barrel:	12.4kg	14.5kg
Weight of base plate:	14.8kg	14.8kg
Weight of mount:	12.2kg	12.2kg

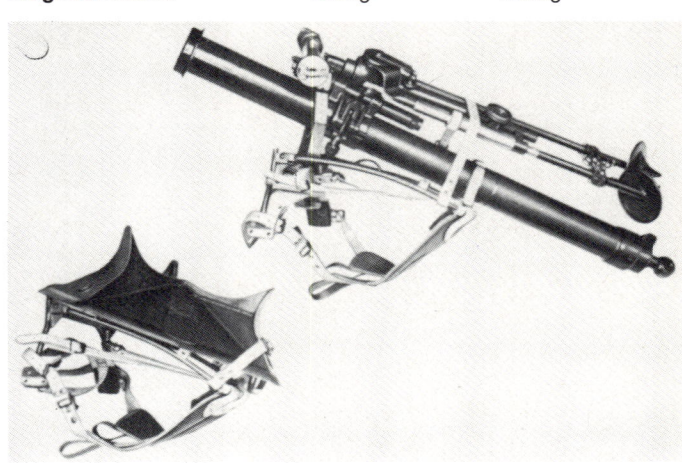

81mm mortar man pack

HE bombs, smoke and illuminating. Note the difference in size between the M57D and Mk 61 bombs

AMMUNITION

	Short barrel	Long barrel
HE bomb	M57D	Mk 61
Material:	Steel or malleable perlitic cast iron	
Fuze:	V19 Pa	V19 P
Length:	382mm	414mm
Total Weight:	3.3kg	4.325kg
Filling:	TNT	TNT
Minimum range:	120 metres	75 metres
Maximum range:	4,100 metres	5,000 metres
Illuminating bomb	Mk 62	Mk 68
Total length:	390mm	417mm
Weight of complete round:	3.15kg	3.5kg
Filling:	Magnesium based illuminating composition	
Illuminating power		
(candelas):	250,000	750,000
Minumum burning time:	35sec	30sec
Radius of illumination:	250 metres	250 metres
Range:	3,400 metres	4,200 metres
Fuze:	Clockwork time	

Manufacturer: Hotchkiss-Brandt Armement (see above)
Status: In production and in service with the French Army (short barrel) and several others

81mm mortar moved by mule

120mm LIGHT MORTAR (MO-120-60)

The 120mm Light Mortar is a simple mortar in which mobility and firepower have been allied. It fires a variety of ammunition and provides all-round fire from a minimum range of 600 metres out to 6,610 metres.

The mortar is made up of the barrel, mounting and baseplate.

The barrel is smooth bore and has a breech piece screwed over the end. The firing mechanism is enclosed in the breech piece and the firing pin can be set to protrude, thus firing a bomb dropped on it under gravity, or alternatively the pin can be retracted into a safe position. The bottom of the breech piece has a spherical ball, with two flats, which enables it to be secured in the baseplate. The mounting consists of the bipod legs, the elevating gear, the traversing gear, cross levelling gear and the barrel clamp, which contains a shock absorbing buffer. The bipod consists of two legs, each terminating in a shoe with a spike, and the spread of the legs is controlled by the length of an adjustable chain. The elevating gear in its tube is connected to the top of the bipod and reaches up to connect with the traversing gear. The traversing mechanism consists of a yoke which holds the traversing screw and also connects the elevating gear to the barrel clamp. On the right of the yoke is the traversing handwheel and on the left is the sight mounting.

To enable the sight to be upright at all times, there is a cross levelling mechanism made up of the rod connecting the elevating screw tube to the left bipod leg. This can be moved across by a control on the bipod leg and so the elevating screw column can be moved to the vertical position regardless of the slope of the ground on which the mortar is standing.

The baseplate is triangular in shape with a socket in the centre to take the breech piece ball and underneath are three ribs which provide the complete rigidity required and also prevent the baseplate slipping.

The mortar has been designed to be operated in the simplest way possible and can be brought into action and maintained with three men in the detachment. The baseplate must be dug in if it is not possible to fire the initial round at an angle of elevation greater than 60 degrees. If this can be done there is no need for a bedding in round but there will be a 5-8% reduction in range in this first round.

In the event of a misfire, the firing mechanism can be set to 'safe' which withdraws the firing pin and then the bomb extractor can be used to remove the bomb from the tube.

The 120mm Light Mortar can be moved by vehicle, mule, man pack or by air.

DATA
Total weight of equipment: 94kg
Weight of barrel: 34kg
Weight of bipod: 24kg

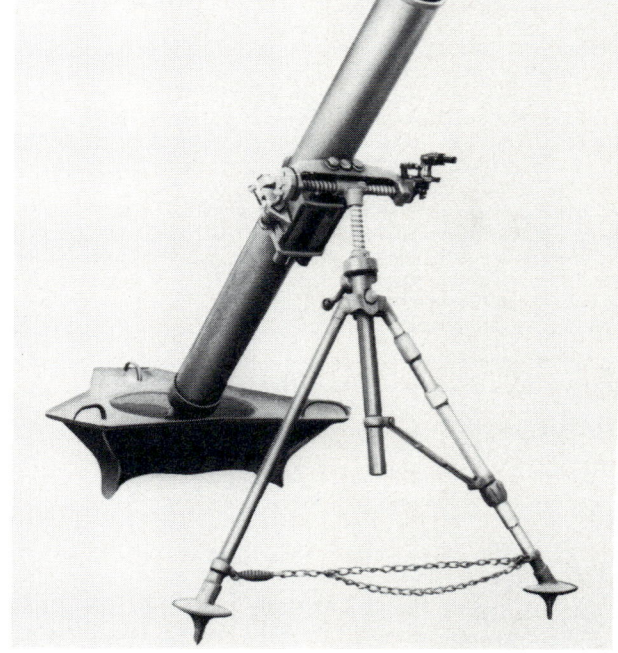

120mm light mortar

Weight of baseplate: 36kg
Length of barrel with breech piece: 1,632mm
Elevation: 40° –85° (711 – 1,511mils)
Traverse: 360° (6,400mils)
Range of fire: Normal 8 rounds/min for 3min; 15 rounds/min for 1min

M44 HE BOMB

This is a conventional high explosive bomb, fuzed V19 P, weighing 13kg and filled TNT. It is 679mm long, minimum range is 500 metres and the maximum is 6,650 metres. There is a practice bomb and a HE marker bomb with the same weight and performance as the M44 bomb.

Mk 62 SMOKE BOMB

This is a canister type smoke bomb with a time fuze, FH81, which is filled HCE. The range of this bomb is 500 to 6,650 metres. The minimum smoke time is 2 minutes.

The M44 bombs

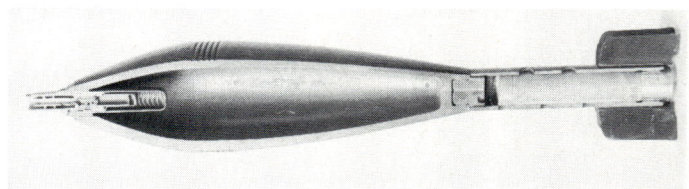

The M44 bomb sectioned

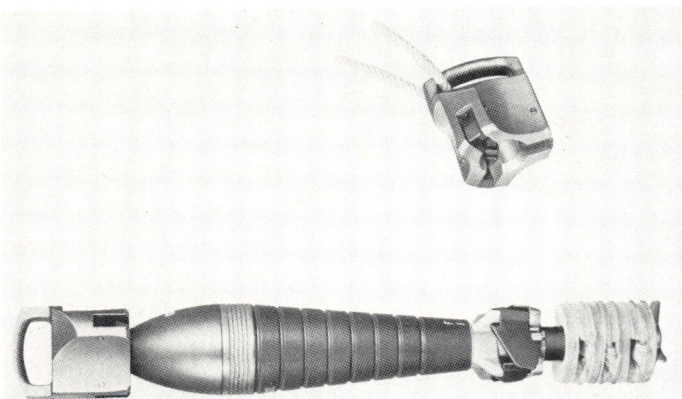

Mk 62-ED ILLUMINATING BOMB

This has a mechanical time fuze, type FH81-B

DATA
Total length: 800mm
Total weight of complete round: 13.65kg
Filling: Illuminating compound-magnesium based
Power: 700,000 candelas
Burning time: 1 minute
Radius of illumination: 300 metres
Manufacturer: Hotchkiss-Brandt Armement (see above)
Status: In production and in service in the French Army and several others

The bomb extractor which is used to remove the bomb from the barrel in the event of a misfire. It is lowered from the muzzle and grips over the fuze

PEPA BOMB

This bomb consists of a steel body, an HE filling, an internal solid fuel rocket motor and the V19 P fuze. The propelling charge made up of the primary and secondary charges is located at the rear. The body **(3)** is made in two parts, screwed together, with the tail assembly **(10)** screwed on to the rear part of the body.

The HE content **(2)** is 2kg of hexogenetolite cast inside the cavity and around the solid fuel motor. The solid fuel motor **(5)** of star shaped section, is housed in a tube **(4)**, externally inhibited, with a venturi at the end **(6)**. The venturi is secured at the tail end by an obturator containing an optional delay **(7)** and a selection lock **(8)** which allows the use of the solid fuel propulsion unit if required. A spring catch **(13)** holds the selection lock in the required position.

The propulsion charge consists of the primary cartridge **(11)** and up to 7 augmenting cartridges. The tube **(10)** holding the primary cartridge contains the flash holes communicating with the secondary charges. This tube is ejected after the bomb is fired.

In use the order of events is as follows. The bomb is removed from the container and the charge system adjusted by the removal of unrequired secondaries. If the rocket assistance is required the tube containing the primary cartridge is rotated clockwise. The fuze V19 P is then set for instantaneous action or delay.

The ranges obtainable with the PEPA are as follows. 'R' indicates rocket assistance.

Charge	Elevation Max°	Range metres min	Elevation Min°	Range metres max
1	74	600	45	1,350
2	72	1,000	45	1,900
3	69	1,700	45	2,560
4	67	2,200	45	3,175
5	70	2,500	45	3,560
6	69	2,800	45	4,250
3R	66	4,000	55	4,800
4R	66	4,600	55	5,500
5R	63	5,300	50	6,100
6R	62	5,700	45	6,550

From this table it can be seen that the maximum range without rocket assistance is 4,250 metres. The muzzle velocity is 240 metres/sec. The maximum range with rocket assistance is 6,550 metres. The muzzle velocity is increased by 110 metre/sec.

Manufacturer: Hotchkiss-Brandt Armement (see above)
Status: In production and in service

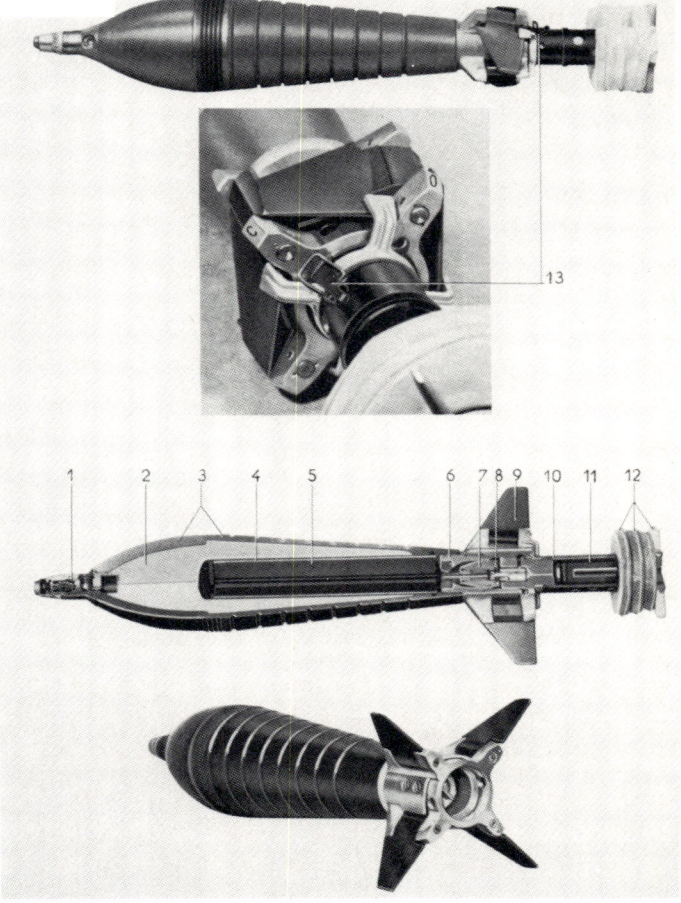

120mm PEPA bomb: (1) Fuze V 19 P; (2) HE filling; (3) Steel body; (4) Tube containing rocket assistance; (5) Rocket motor; (6) Venturi; (7) Optional delay; (8) Selection lock; (9) Spring opened tail fin; (10) Tail assembly; (11) Primary cartridge; (12) Secondary charges; (13) Spring catch holding the selection lock in place

120mm LIGHT, STRENGTHENED, MORTAR (MO-120-M65)

This 120mm mortar uses the baseplate and mount of the Light 120mm Mortar but the barrel is reinforced and weighs some 10 kilograms more than that of the light mortar. There is also a difference in the method of moving this mortar. A trolley with pneumatic tyres and elastic suspension is used on which the entire mortar rests. A muzzle cap with a towing eye is used to enable the mortar to be pulled by a light vehicle of the jeep type. Alternatively if the necessity arises, the mortar can be dragged along by the detachment, using the towing handle which is also part of the muzzle cap. When the mortar is brought into action, the baseplate is lowered on to the required position and the bipod is used to connect the barrel to the baseplate. The mortar is not fired from the wheels.

The mechanism of the mortar allows conventional gravity firing but there is a spring controlled firing pin which allows the bomb to be loaded into position and fired by means of a lanyard attached to the firing lever. The firing mechanism also allows the firing pin to be withdrawn as a safety measure. The mortar has an all round field of fire without need to move the baseplate and with the barrel clamp giving an angle of elevation of 60 degrees, there is a top traverse of 300 mils.

120mm strengthened light mortar (MO-120-M65)

PEPA/LP bomb

PEPA/LP sectioned

The mortar in motion

DATA
Total weight of equipment mounted on carriage: 144kg
Total weight in firing position: 104kg
Weight of barrel and breech piece: 44kg
Weight of mount: 24kg
Weight of baseplate: 36kg
Weight of trolley and muzzle cap: 40kg
Length of barrel and breech piece: 1,640mm
Rate of fire: 8 rounds/minute for 3 min; 12 rounds/min for 1 minute

AMMUNITION
The mortar can use the following bombs: HE bomb M 44/66; the illuminating bomb MK ED; the smoke, practice, and marker bombs corresponding to the M44; the PEPA bomb – described in the previous entry – and the PEPA/LP bomb. The PEPA/LP is of the same size as the PEPA and is also a rocket assisted bomb, somewhat lighter than the PEPA, but with a lower minimum range and a longer maximum range.

DATA
Total length with tail assembly: 758mm
Total weight of complete round: 13.42kg

Filling: RDX/TNT
Minimum range: 500 metres
Maximum range using rocket propulsion: 9,000 metres
Manufacturer: Hotchkiss-Brandt Armement (see above)
Status: Production

MO-120-AM 50 HEAVY MORTAR
This mortar is mounted on a heavy wheeled carriage and can be fired either on the wheels with the axle locked, or off the bipod. The very heavy barrel allows a rate of fire of 8 rounds/min for a prolonged period and 12 rounds a minute for a short time. This mortar is no longer in production and is being replaced by the MO-120-LT which was designed in 1970.

AMMUNITION
This mortar will fire the M44 HE bomb. The practice bomb, the HE marker (red, yellow or green), the smoke bomb (white phosphorus or titanium tetrachloride) and the Mk 62 smoke and illuminating bombs, can also be fired.

DATA
Total weight of equipment including the wheeled carriage: 402kg
Total weight of equipment without the wheeled carriage: 242kg
Weight of barrel (including the towing eye): 76kg
Weight of mount: 86kg
Weight of base plate: 80kg
Weight of wheeled carriage: 137kg
Length of barrel: 1.746 metres
Elevation: 45°-85°(800 mils-1,511 mils)
Top traverse (60° elevation): 17° (300 mils)

Mortar in action on its bipod

Mortar in action position on its wheels

120mm heavy mortar, MO-120-AM-50

Manufacturer: Hotchkiss-Brandt Armement (see above)
Status: No longer in production. In service in the French Army and several others but being replaced, in the French Army at least, by the MO-120-LT

120mm BRANDT MORTAR MO-120-LT
This mortar was introduced to replace the MO-120-AM 50. It has a massive baseplate and is transported on a wheeled carriage. The carriage is substantial, with pneumatic tyres and torsion bar suspension, but the mortar is fired off the bipod mount. It is claimed that the mortar on its carriage can be pulled by two men but this can only be over short distances on favourable terrain.

AMMUNITION
This mortar fires all the ammunition used by the AM-50:
PEPA/LP long range rocket assisted bomb
The HE bomb M44/66
The illuminating bomb Mk 62-ED
The smoke, practice and marker bombs corresponding to these.

The ammunition for the mortar

DATA
Total weight of equipment with the wheeled carriage: 203kg
Total weight in firing position: 170kg
Weight of barrel: 65kg
Weight of mount: 25kg
Weight of baseplate: 80kg
Weight of travelling carriage: 48kg
Weight of towing attachment (barrel cap and eye): 7kg
Length of barrel and breech piece: 1.700metres
Elevation: 45°-85° (711 mils-1,511 mils)

The 120mm Brandt mortar, MO-120-LT

Top traverse (60 elevation): 17° (300 mils)
Firing: Gravity or controlled firing. Pin can be withdrawn for safety
Rate of fire: Normal 8 rounds/min; Maximum 12 rounds/minute
Manufacturer: Hotchkiss-Brandt Armement (see above)
Status: Production

120mm RIFLED MORTAR MO-120-RT-61

The 120mm rifled mortar is probably the most complex of modern mortars and in some aspects approaches very closely to the gun. It can be fired only off its wheels and can be deployed only in areas to which the towing vehicle has access. It is a massive piece of equipment which fires a heavy bomb out to 13 kilometres. It has a rifled barrel and is muzzle loading. To cope with the windage problem it has a pre-engraved driving band.

Main components are the barrel, cradle and undercarriage, and the baseplate. The barrel is a substantial forging equipped at the muzzle to take the towing eye by which it is attached to the vehicle. The outside is radially finned to increase the surface area for heat dissipation. The interior is rifled and with the pre-engraved driving band imparts rotation to the shell to produce stability throughout the trajectory.

The cradle consists of a steel tube connecting the two wheels and carrying the torsion bar suspension. The traversing gears are totally enclosed to exclude foreign matter. The elevating handwheel rotates a worm which passes through a nut to pivot an arm attached via a collar to the barrel. The collar sliding along the barrel produces the necessary change of elevation. The sight unit is attached to the collar and is tilted by a cross levelling shaft.

The baseplate is very heavy with massive webs on the underside. After a prolonged period of firing the baseplate can be extricated by using the barrel as a lever and employing the towing vehicle to pull the baseplate up.

DATA
Total weight of the equipment: 582kg
Barrel:
Length of barrel: 2.080 metres
Weight of barrel: 114kg
Weight of towing eye: 17kg
Mount:
Weight of mount: 257kg
Elevation: 30°-85°
Top traverse at 60° elevation: 250 mils
Baseplate:
Weight of baseplate: 190kg
Clamping collar: 4kg
Dimensions of the equipment:
Wheel base: 1.734 metres
Overall width: 1.930 metres
Overall length: 3.015 metres
Height in running position: 1.335 metres
Ground clearance: 0.325 metres
Wheel diameter: 0.7 metres
Time into action: 1.5 minutes
Time out of action: 2 minutes
Normal rate of fire: 10/12 rounds/minute
Maximum rate of fire: 15-20 rounds/min – for a very limited period

AMMUNITION
Since this is a rifled mortar, none of the other 120mm bombs can be used in this weapon. A rocket assisted bomb is available. This has a tube carrying the secondary charges. An anti-tank bomb has also been developed and is described in the next entry.

DATA
PRPA Bomb (Projectile rayé à propulsion additionelle)
This has rocket assistance which comes into action after a delay of 10 seconds, and a pre-engraved driving band.
Length with tail tube: 918mm
Weight: 18.7kg
Filling: RDX/TNT

The rifled 120mm mortar, MO-120-RT-61

Maximum range with rocket assistance: 13,000 metres
Minimum range without rocket assistance: 1,100 metres
Fuze: PDM 557

PR-14 Bomb
No rocket assistance. Pre-engraved driving band.
Length including tail tube: 897mm
Weight of complete round: 18.7kg
Filling: RDX/TNT
Maximum range: 8,135 metres

The 120mm rifled mortar in action

The ammunition for the rifled mortar

Minimum range: 1,100 metres
Fuze: PDM 557

Illuminating bomb PRECLAIR
Overall length: 886.5mm
Total weight of complete round: 15.7kg
Filling: Magnesium based compound
Fuze: FR 55 A clockwork
Fuze setting: 2 to 55 seconds

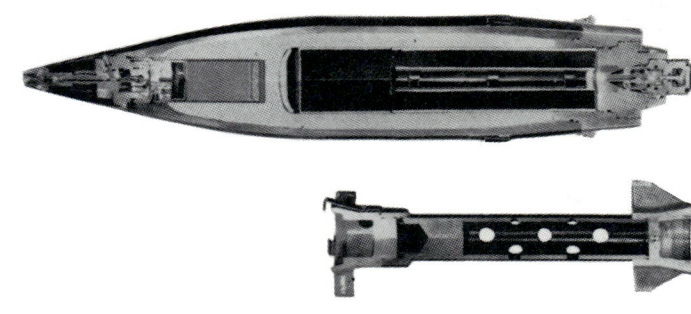

Sectioned PRPA Bomb

Optimum height of functioning: 300 metres
Rate of fall of illuminant: 5 metre/sec
Radius of illumination: 500 metres
Minimum burning time: 60 seconds producing 1,050,000 candelas; 40 seconds producing 1,600,000 candelas
Manufacturer: Hotchkiss-Brandt Armement (see above)
Status: The mortar is in production and in service with the French Army and several others. The three bombs are all in production: the PR-14 has been adopted by the French Army and it and the PRPA have been exported

120mm RIFLED ANTI-TANK BOMB

This has been developed by Hotchkiss-Brandt to extend the range of 120mm mortar ammunition. The basic idea is that the mortar bomb hits the ground almost vertically and sprays a large number of fragments out sideways. According to Hotchkiss-Brandt, if the new mortar bomb lands at an angle of 70° or more and 15 metres or less away from the target, the fragments will penetrate 12mm of armour to a height of approx 1.5m. Although this would fail to knock out a main battle tank it would obviously cause some damage, and it would cause considerable damage to armoured personnel carriers and armoured cars.

120mm anti-tank bomb

DATA
The following data have been released on this mortar bomb:
Weight of complete round: 18.7kg
Total length including tail: 897mm

Charge: Hexotolite
Maximum range: 13,000 metres with rocket assistance
Minimum range: 1,100 metres without rocket assistance
Status: Production

HOTCHKISS-BRANDT MORTARS – COMPARATIVE CHARACTERISTICS

The range of mortars extending from 60mm through 81mm to 120mm has been designed to give a range overlap as the calibre increases and units equipped with these mortars are able to produce effective fire from a minimum range of 100 metres out to 13,000 metres.

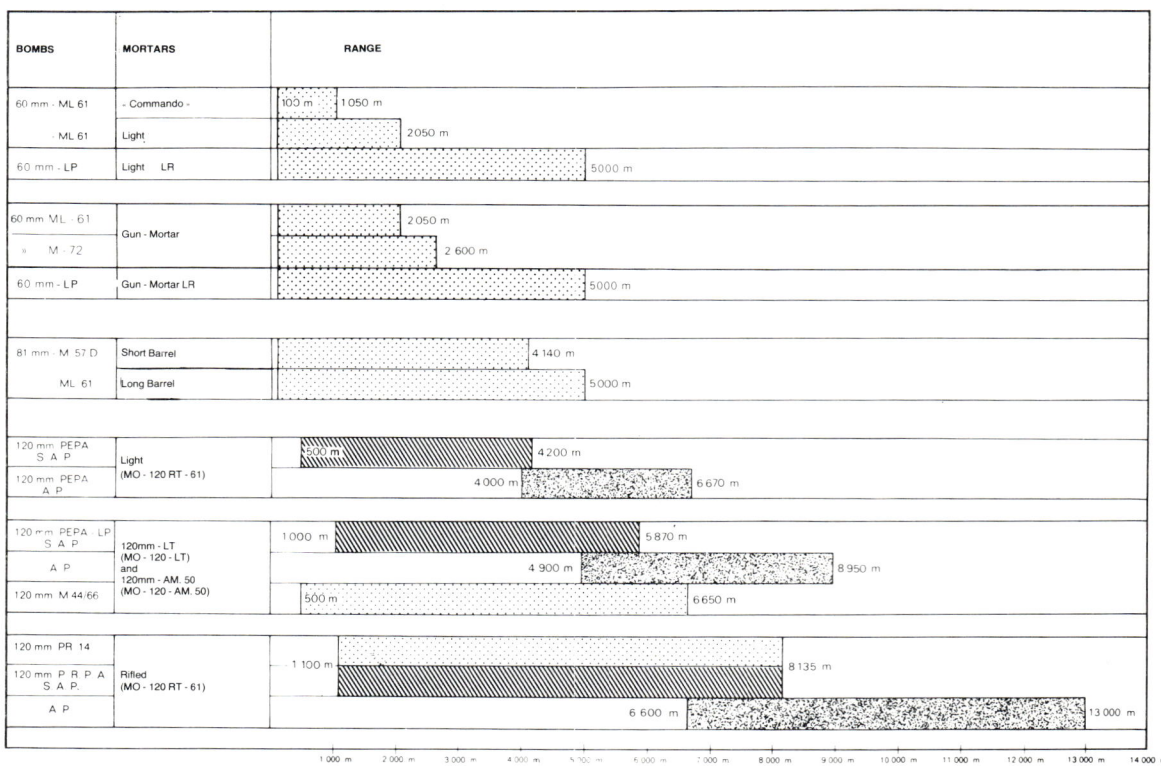

The range overlap on the Hotchkiss-Brandt mortars

GERMANY (FEDERAL REPUBLIC)

GERMAN ARMY MORTARS

The German Army used the mortar with considerable success during both world wars; and the British Army regarded the German mortars, and the way they were used, with great respect. Surprisingly, however, the Germans looked on the Russians as the masters in this field and they copied the Russian 120mm mortar and also shared the same design of 82mm mortar.

After the Germans came into NATO they again adopted the mortar. They did not accept any kind of light mortar (50-60mm) or a medium mortar (81mm) but purchased, from France and from Israel, 120mm mortars made, respectively, by Hotchkiss-Brandt and Soltam. The Israeli mortar is made to a design produced by the Finnish firm of Tampella (qv). The current mortars of the German Army are illustrated below. Complete details are given in the entries on the originating countries.

The Panzer Mörser M113. This US Armoured Personnel Carrier has been adapted by the Bundeswehr to carry the 120mm Tampella mortar. This mortar is intended to be used, as far as possible, directly from the vehicle. It can, if necessary, be deployed dismounted from the armoured carrier. It has a range when mounted in the vehicle of 450-6,350 metres.

It is used by Armoured Infantry, Mountain Infantry, Light Infantry, Armoured Reconnaissance units, and Tank Regiments.

The Tampella 120mm mortar can be broken down to mule loads for deployment in mountainous terrain. The barrel and bipod make up one mule load and the heavy baseplate together with the sight and two rounds make up another.

When the mortar is deployed in mountainous country a special baseplate is available for rocky surfaces. This makes, with the simple bipod, a very basic mortar.

The Panzer Mörser HS 30 has been modified from its primary role as an Armoured Personnel Carrier and is shown here with the 120mm Brandt Mortar. It has the ability to engage targets between 400 and 6,150 metres. The weapon as shown is used by Home Defence units of the Territorial Army.

The 120mm Tampella Light Mortar is used by the mortar detachments of the Airborne Infantry Regiment. Its range zone is 450-6,350 metres.

The 120mm AM50 Brandt Mortar is used by the Light Infantry units of the Territorial Army. It is carried on the mortar trailer which is towed by a 30cwt lorry. The mortar can engage targets between 425 and 6,150 metres.

The 120mm Tampella Mountain Mortar. Everything that can be lightened, has been. Note the special baseplate for rocky terrain

The sight, ammunition and the bipod of the Tampella mortar are in view. The barrel is on the other side

The 120mm Brandt in the HS30

120mm Brandt towed by a 30cwt lorry

M113 carrier with 120mm Tampella mortar

NICO-PYROTECHNIK MORTAR TRAINING SYSTEM

The Nico-Pyrotechnik Mortar Training System has been designed to provide the infantryman with realistic training without having recourse to isolated ranges. The system consists of a reusable sabot and sub-calibre ammunition calibrated to simulate the full size ammunition. Sub-calibre ammunition may be obtained as standard for the various zone charges and calibres. In general, the system is gauged for a 10 to 1 ratio for range and azimuth, for example a weapon sighted for a range of 2,000 metres would fire a sub-calibre round to a range of 200 metres. The various zone charges for the various calibres result in ranges from 70 metres to 500 metres.

Ammunition and sabots have been manufactured for the following calibres: 60mm, 81mm, 82mm, 120mm, 160mm and 4.2in.

The sabot is identical is size and shape to the standard mortar bomb. It also has a simulated fuze with a safety cotter pin and a screw for selecting N/D (no delay) and W/D (with delay). Adaptors simulating the propellant charges of the live round can also be attached. All operations performed in combat are carried out with the training round, including unloading a mortar bomb from the barrel.

A manoeuvre cartridge has also been recently developed. This, when fired, has a sound equal to that of a live round.

Status: The system was first adopted by the Federal Republic of Germany and subsequently the following countries have adopted the system: Belgium, Burundi, Ghana, Nigeria, Switzerland. Recently the United States conducted a competition for a sub-calibre training system and the NICO system was adopted by the United States Army.
Manufacturer: Nico-Pyrotechnik, Hanns-Jurgen Diederichs KG, 2077 Trittau, Bez Hamburg, Germany. The company also make sub-calibre training devices for anti-tank weapons including the M-72, Panzerfaust and the Bazooka.

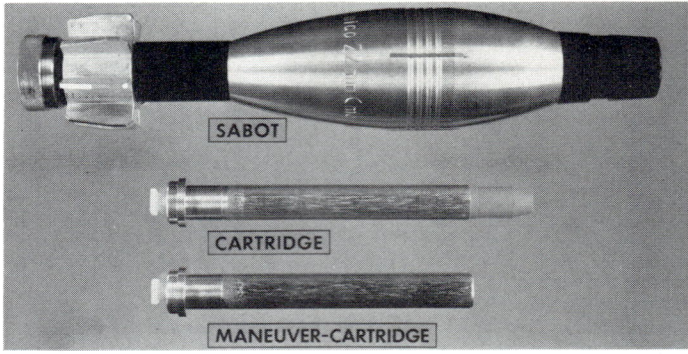

The 81mm mortar training system

ISRAEL

ISRAELI MORTARS AND AMMUNITION

The firm of Soltam Ltd. manufacture mortars made to the Finnish Tampella designs. These are sold to a very large number of countries. Soltam also manufacture ammunition for their mortars.

Israel Military Industries (IMI) was set up by the Israeli Government to manufacture those items of military equipment that the resources and skills of the country are able to provide. They produce the Galil rifle, hand grenades and a wide variety of munitions for the Artillery and Tank Corps.

However, unnecessary duplication of effort is avoided and agreements with Soltam and other manufacturing concerns have been made so that IMI produce stores which are not made elsewhere in the country. The entries that follow list the IMI products relevant to this section of the book.

Care should be taken, when using the abbreviation IMI, to avoid confusion with Imperial Metal Industries in the UK which is also known by that abbreviation.

52mm MORTAR

This is a conventional smooth-bore muzzle loaded mortar. It is of very simple design, consisting of a tube and a trough-like baseplate mounted across the base of the barrel. Connecting the barrel to the baseplate is the breech piece which contains the firing mechanism. The firer operates the firing mechanism by rotating the small wheel on the right of the barrel. There are no sights as such and aiming is carried out by using the white line on the barrel to align the bore. The mortar can be used for low angle or high angle fire, is easily managed by one man, and has a carrying handle and a muzzle cover. High explosive, illuminating and smoke bombs are all fired.

DATA
Overall length: 637mm
Barrel length: 490mm
Baseplate dimensions: 150mm × 85 × 35mm
Baseplate weight: 1.3kg
Overall weight: 7.9kg
Range, minimum: 130 metres
Range, maximum: 420 metres
Elevation: 20°-85° (178mils-755mils)
Rate of fire: 20-35 rounds/min

The 52mm mortar made by IMI
Manufacturer: Israel Military Industries, POB 7055, Tel Aviv, Israel
Status: In production. In service with Israeli forces

52mm IMI SMOKE BOMB

DATA
Length: 240mm
Weight: 920g
Charge weight: 400g
Filling material: Hexachlorethane, zinc oxide, and aluminium powder
Propelling charge: Primary cartridge with 4g Ballistite
Muzzle velocity: 78 metres/sec
Maximum range: 400 metres
Time delay: 7.5sec
Time of smoke generation: 100sec

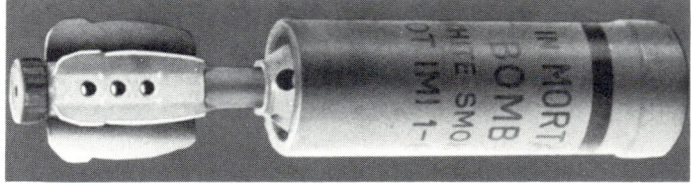

52mm smoke bomb
Manufacturer: IMI (see above)
Status: In production. In service

52mm IMI HE BOMB
DATA
Length: 250mm
Weight: 1.02kg
Charge weight (TNT): 150g
Propelling charge: Base ignition cartridge containing 3g of ballistic

powder
Fuze: No. 161
Muzzle velocity: 78m/s
Maximum range at 45° elevation: 460-480m
Manufacturer: IMI (see above)
Status: In production. In service

52mm IMI ILLUMINATING BOMB

DATA
Overall length: 260mm
Weight of complete round: 800g
Illuminant charge: 150g
Nature of illuminant charge: Pyrotechnic composition
Propelling charge: Primary cartridge with 4g Ballistite
Muzzle velocity: 78 metres/sec
Parachute opening: Range 350 metres; Height 100 metres; Time 8sec
Illuminating power: 100,000 candles
Minimum burning time: 30sec

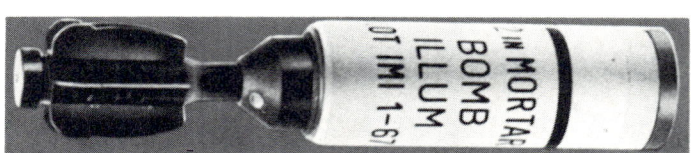

52mm illuminating bomb

Manufacturer: IMI (see above)
Status: In production. In service

60mm SOLTAM MORTAR

This mortar was designed to fulfil two roles. Equipped with a bipod it was intended to be used in the normal way as a company support weapon; alternatively, without the bipod, it could be used as a light mortar in the assault role.

In the standard role, the mortar consists of the three elements of barrel, bipod and baseplate. The barrel is made of alloy steel and the bore is given a particularly smooth finish. Screwed to the bottom of the mortar tube is the breech piece. This is rounded off at its lower end into a ball which fits into the socket of the baseplate. The striker pin is contained in the breechpiece. It is of the fixed, non-retractable type, and has no control mechanism. The impact of the bomb on the fixed striker is enough to set off the cap of the primary cartridge. A canvas sleeve is placed around the barrel to act as a heat shield and to allow the attachment of a carrying handle. Around the muzzle is a simple drum sight which is used only in the attack or "Commando" role.

The bipod is of conventional design with the spread of the legs limited by the construction of flanges in the plates where they are joined at the top of the legs. Passing up through the bipod is the elevating screw and the elevating column which is joined to the yoke. This carries the traversing screw. At the left end is the sight bracket, whilst the right hand end has the traversing handwheel. The cross levelling gear connects the left leg of the bipod to the bottom of the elevating gear. Thus when the mortar is brought into action on uneven ground, the elevating screw and column can be swung to allow the sight to be brought to the upright position. Two recoil cylinders are interposed between the barrel collar and the yoke. The sight has a clamp which will normally be placed around the tubular yoke but can also be placed around the barrel when so required. There is a bearing scale which runs from zero round to 6,400 mils. The target or aiming post is viewed over a collimator. The elevation scale is set out in five columns corresponding to the ranges achieved by the primer and the four charges and the range reader is scribed on a perspex plate attached to the body of the sight. When the range is applied, the body of the sight is thrown out of level and to centre the elevation bubble the barrel must be elevated or depressed.

The baseplate is of welded construction with a flat, dished top plate and three webbed ribs which enable the baseplate to take the recoil force without slipping. In the centre of the baseplate is a socket to take the ball at the bottom of the breech piece. The socket has a clamping ring with a securing screw that can be used to clamp the barrel rigidly to the baseplate. The construction of the baseplate is such that a 360 degree traverse can be obtained. The second way of using the mortar is in the assault role. Here the bipod is not used. The normal sight can be secured to the muzzle or a simple drum sight can be used. The barrel is controlled by hand until it is required to go to fire for effect, and then the clamp on the base plate is used to lock the barrel at the required elevation in the desired line.

AMMUNITION

The HE bomb is made from a steel forging, and machined to shape. The tail unit is made from an extruded aluminium tube. The secondaries are arranged around the tail boom above the fins and when the bomb is

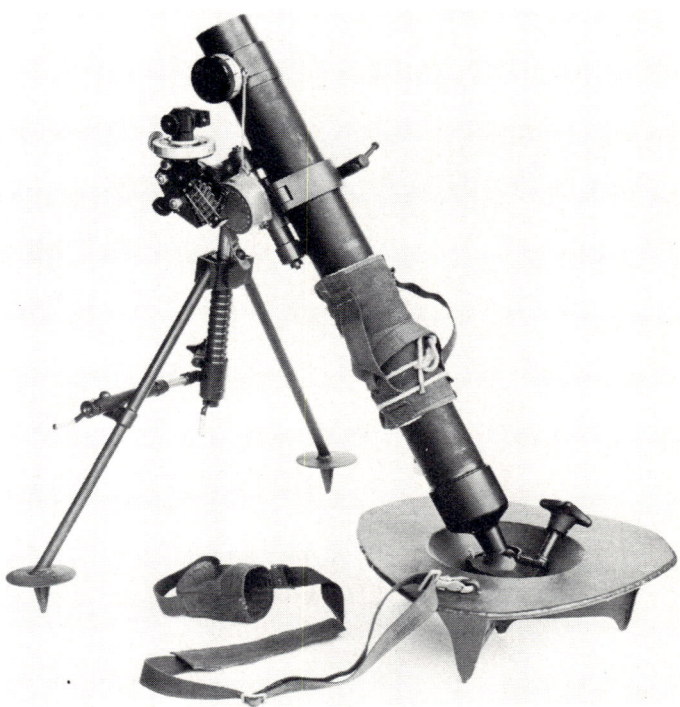

The 60mm Soltam mortar set up as a conventional company support weapon. Note the sight on the bipod and also the drum sight at the muzzle

60mm HE bomb

dropped into a hot barrel the secondaries do not contact the walls of the tube, and there is no danger of a cook off.

The ballistics of the smoke bomb are the same as the HE. There are two smoke fillings, white phosphorus and titanium tetrachloride. The white phosphorus is used also for ranging at night.

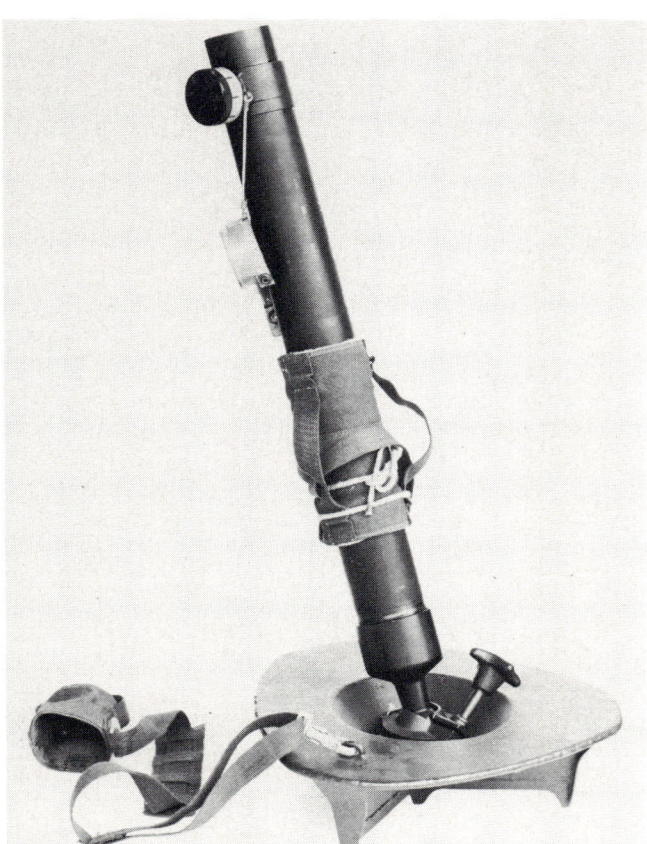

The 60mm Soltam mortar used without bipod in the assault role

The 60mm mortar packed up for carriage

DATA
Bore diameter: 60.75mm
Total weight of mortar, with bipod, in firing position: 14.5kg
Total weight of mortar (without bipod) in Commando role: 10kg
Weight of barrel with sight: 6.6kg
Weight of bipod: 4.5kg
Weight of baseplate: 3.4kg
Overall length of barrel from breech to muzzle: 740mm
Traverse, without moving baseplate: 360°
Top traverse without moving bipod: at 50° elevation 116mils; at 70° elevation 137mils
Elevation: 40° 79°
Ranges — Primary only: 140-400metres
    Charge 1: 350-1,080metres
    Charge 2: 550-1,600metres
    Charge 3: 1,000-2,085metres
    Charge 4: 1,500-2,555metres
Weight of bomb: 1.59kg
Maximum intial muzzle velocity: 220m/s
Minimum intial muzzle velocity: 63m/s
Manufacturer: Soltam Ltd.
Status: In service in Israel at least

The sight. This is normally attached to the yoke of the bipod but can be attached to the barrel

81mm M-64 MORTAR

This is a mortar of conventional design but incorporating some features providing a choice of parameters. The mortar is produced in three versions. These are:

(a) Mortar with short barrel;
(b) Mortar with long barrel;
(c) Mortar with a barrel that breaks into two sections.

The barrel is of alloy steel with a good interior finish. There is a breech piece at the bottom which fits into the socket of the baseplate. This breech piece carries a fixed firing pin. It is possible to have a controllable firing pin incorporated in the breech piece with a safety catch which retracts the firing pin, but this is an "optional extra". The three alternative barrels each have their own advantages and disadvantages. The short barrel is the lightest and easiest to move but does not achieve the range of the long barrel. The long barrel is heavier and less mobile but produces the longer range. The break down barrel is the most easily carried by the man on foot and takes up less length in a vehicle. It achieves the same range as the long barrel but is heavier. The choice of barrels is one that must be examined carefully by the user.

The bipod is of orthodox pattern but has some interesting features. The two legs of the bipod have spiked feet and the distance between them is controlled by an adjustable chain. The elevating column is attached to the yoke and has a cross levelling gear connecting it to the left tripod leg. The elevating screw thread is totally enclosed within the elevating tube and so is protected from the ingress of dirt, sand and snow. The yoke carries the traversing screw and protects it. The traversing handwheel is on the left and

81mm Soltam with long barrel

the sight mounting on the right. There is a shock absorbing unit consisting of two cylinders joining the yoke to the barrel clamp.

The baseplate is of circular shape with welded ribs on the underside. The socket takes the ball of the breech piece and allows a full 360 degree traverse without need to move the baseplate. A carrying handle is attached and is needed to get the baseplate out when coming out of action.

The sight is graduated in mils and covers the full 6400 traverse. There is also a slipping scale. This enables the sight to be used on an aiming post and the target recorded in terms of a bearing rather than a switch from the point of aim. This permits registration of the target and subsequent engagement of the target without further ranging. If meteorological information is available, then the target data can be corrected and stored in a true form. The elevation scale and the cross levelling are controlled by bubbles and a collimator is used for sighting. A quick release is available for the traversing scale.

The mortar fires an HE round, a smoke round with similar ballistics and a practice round. There is an illuminating, parachute, round.

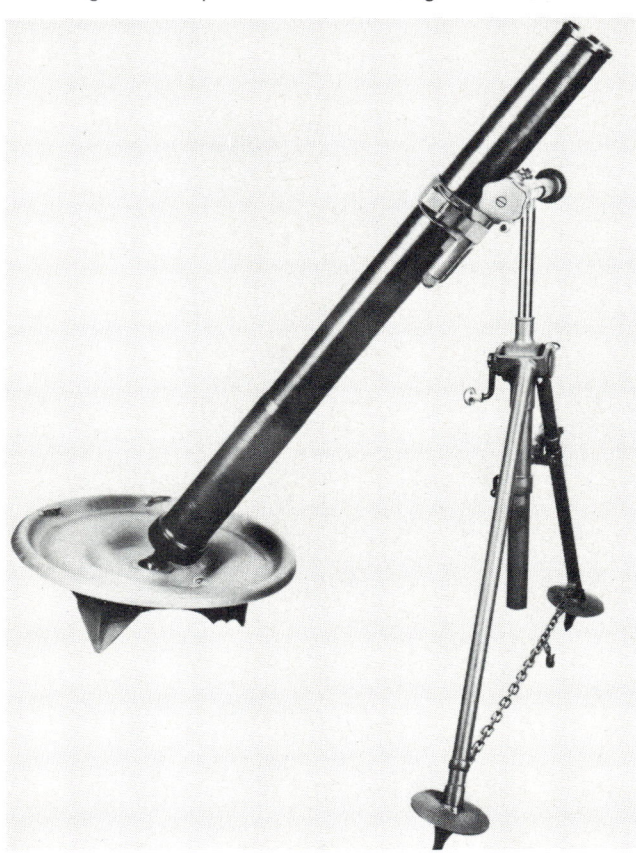

81mm Soltam with short barrel

DATA
MORTAR
Calibre: 81mm
Total weight of mortar with short barrel: 37kg
Total weight with long barrel: 40kg
Total weight with "break down" barrel: 43kg
Range with short barrel
    Minimum: 150metres
    Maximum: 4,000metres

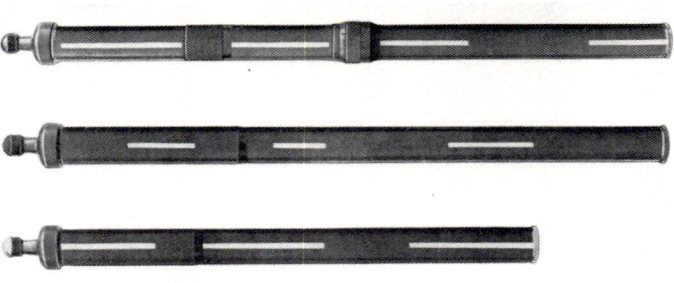

The three barrels of the 81mm mortar

81mm Soltam with the break down barrel

Range with long barrel
Minimum: 150metres
Maximum: 4,600metres
Range with break down barrel
Minimum: 150metres
Maximum: 4,600metres
Elevation: 43°-80°
Traverse: 360°
Top traverse at 45°: 100mils
Maximum rate of fire: 20 rounds/min (very limited duration)
Maximum working pressure: 827kp/cm²
Barrel:
Weight of short barrel: 11.5kg
Weight of long barrel: 14.5kg
Weight of break down barrel: 17.5kg
Overall length of short barrel: 1,155mm
Overall length of long barrel: 1,455mm
Overall length of break down barrel: 1,455mm
Bipod:
Weight complete: 12.3kg
Overall length: 960mm

Baseplate:
Weight complete: 13.2kg
Sight
Weight: 1.57kg
Graduation of traversing scale: 0-6,400mils
Graduation of elevating scale: 700-1,600mils (40°-90°)

AMMUNITION
HIGH EXPLOSIVE BOMB
Weight of complete round: 4kg
Body. Forged steel construction: 2.9kg
Tail unit: 200g
  Fuze: Point detonating. Super quick and delay: (Arming safety 0.8sec)
  Weight: 200g
  Firing. TNT: 540g
  Charge system: Primary and 6 secondary cartridges
Overall length of round: 370mm
Chamber pressure at maximum charge: 827kp/cm²
Range bracket
  Minimum: 150metres
  Maximum: 4,600metres
Muzzle velocity
  Minimum: 60metres/sec
  Maximum: 260metres/sec
  Consistency: 50% zone can be taken as 1% of range

SMOKE BOMB
  FM round. Filled Titanium Tetrachloride. Weight of filling 540g
  WP round. Filled White Phosphorus. Weight of filling 540g
  PWP round. Filled Plastic White Phosphorus. Weight of filling 540g
  All other data as the HE round.

PRACTICE BOMB
  Weight of smoke charge (to mark point of impact) 100g
  Weight of inert filling 440g

The sight

The 81mm mortar broken down to a three man load using the break down barrel

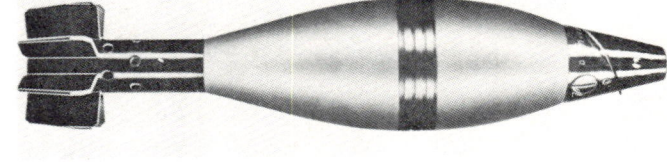

Ammunition for the 81mm Soltam mortar

All other data as the HE round.

Manufacturers: Soltam Ltd., Israel
Status: In service in Israel at least

81mm IMI ILLUMINATING BOMB Mk 1

DATA
Overall length: 570mm
Weight of complete round: 4.8kg
Weight of illuminant: 650g
Propelling charge: Primary cartridge and 4 increments
Muzzle velocity: 180 metres/sec
Minimum range: 400 metres
Maximum range: 1,800 metres
Illuminating power: 250,000 candlepower
Minimum burning time: 40sec
Rate of descent: Approx 6.8 metres/sec
Height of parachute opening: 650 metres

81mm illuminating bomb, Mk 1

Actuation: The bomb is designed to be used with a British type 3in Mortar or the Long Barrel Soltam. With the latter, the striking pin must be removed from the primary cartridge
Manufacturer: IMI
Status: In production. In service

81mm IMI ILLUMINATING BOMB Mk 2

This illuminating bomb is a great improvement on the Mk 1 bomb. It functions with a clockwork fuze which at a pre-determined point initiates a small propelling charge. The pressure developed by this charge shears the pins holding the two parts of the bomb body, ignites a small rocket motor and the pyrotechnic charge. The rocket motor drives the illuminant forward and this pulls the auxiliary parachute out of the rear section of the bomb. The main parachute is also pulled out but remains attached to the rear section of the bomb. The auxiliary parachute slows the illuminant assembly and the rear part of the bomb goes past and pulls the main parachute from its bag. The main parachute opens and the illuminant descends gently.

DATA
Overall length: 570mm
Weight of complete round: 4kg
Weight of illuminant: 800g
Muzzle velocity: 260 metres/sec
Maximum range: 4,000 metres
Rate of descent: 5 metres/sec
Illuminating power: 700,000 candlepower for 60 seconds; 1,000,000 candlepower for 40 seconds
Manufacturer: IMI (see above)
Status: In production. In use with Israeli forces. Tested by several European armies.

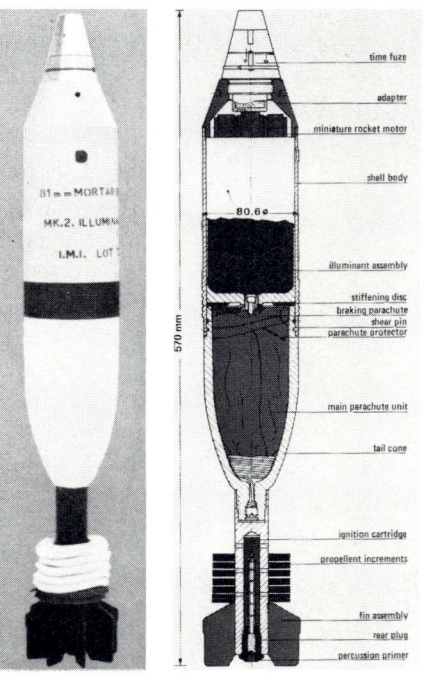

81mm illuminating bomb, Mk 2

120mm SOLTAM LIGHT MORTAR

This mortar was designed to provide infantry with a mortar capable of firing the very lethal 120mm ammunition but sufficiently light to enable it to be moved by a vehicle of the "jeep" type, transported by a mule, carried by a detachment of three soldiers, moved in a helicopter or dropped by parachute. The light mortar can fire all the 120mm bombs available including the rocket assisted bomb.

BARREL

The barrel is an alloy steel tube with a honed interior. The lower end is externally screw threaded to take the breech piece. The breech piece holds the striker. This is a fixed stud on which the bomb falls under gravity. However, to ensure safety whilst dealing with a misfire, there is a safety catch which, when rotated, draws the pin back into the interior of the breech piece. The lower end of the breech piece is shaped into a ball which enters a socket in the baseplate. The barrel can be carried by a single man. However, it weighs 43kg so it is not likely that he will want to carry it very far.

BIPOD

The two legs have spikes at the bottom and are joined at the elevation gear housing. The distance between the legs is controlled by an adjustable length chain. The lower end of the elevation column, which contains the elevation screw thread, is attached to the left leg of the bipod by a cylinder containing a screw thread. The rotation of the handle at the end of this thread moves the elevation column out of the vertical and so allows the mortar to be cross levelled to allow for irregularities in the ground. At the top end of the elevating column is the yoke which holds the sight at the left and the traversing handle at the right. The thread of the traversing gear is, like all the threads in this mortar, completely enclosed. The yoke is connected to the barrel clamp by a pair of shock absorbing units which ensure that the barrel-yoke position does not change as the barrel recoils and then returns to its original firing position.

BASEPLATE

The baseplate is a heavy, welded, steel dish which has a socket at the centre to take the breech piece. The mortar can traverse through 360 degrees without need to shift the baseplate. It is generally unnecessary to prepare the baseplate position extensively, but if the first rounds are being fired at a low angle of elevation the possibility of the baseplate tilting is removed if it can be dug in to ground level. The ribs welded on to the underside of the plate prevent the baseplate from slipping sideways.

120mm Soltam light mortar in firing position

SIGHT

This incorporates a 360 degree (6,400mils) traverse scale and a slipping scale. Thus when the zero line has been recorded the slipping scale can be adjusted to zero. The mortar can therefore engage targets, register at the conclusion of the action, and re-engage without recourse to further ranging. Large switches are made easier by the incorporation of a quick release lever which enables the sight head to be rotated rapidly onto a new bearing without laborious rotation of low geared hand wheels. Elevation and cross-level are controlled by bubbles and a collimator is used to lay on the aiming post.

TOOLS

The tools supplied include a tool which can be inserted from the muzzle to engage around the fuze of a bomb and is used to withdraw it in the event of a misfire.

CARRIAGE

This is a lightweight two-wheeled vehicle with a torsion bar suspension. It enables the mortar to be pulled by troops. It is parachutable and can be towed behind any vehicle with a towing hook of the right height and size. In some roles the carriage is not used and the mortar is brought into action without it. In addition to supporting the mortar, the carriage carries the spare parts and tools for the weapon and also has six metal containers set across the axle, allowing the carriage of that number of ready to use bombs.

AMMUNITION

The mortar takes the M58F and M58FF series of rounds. However, it can also use the new Super (ST) ammunition and the rocket assisted bomb.

DATA
MORTAR
Calibre: 120mm
Total weight of the mortar in the firing position: 108kg
Total weight of mortar in the travelling position: 218kg
Length in travelling position: 2.17metres
Width in travelling position: 1.5metres
Height in travelling position: 0.98metres
Range with conventional round M58F: 400-6,200metres
Range with conventional round M58FF: 400-7,000metres
Elevation: 45°-80° (800mils-1,422mils)
Traverse: 360° (6,400mils)
Top traverse at 45 degrees: 4.7° (83mils)
Top traverse at 75 degrees: 9.4° (166mils)
Chamber pressure, maximum: 950kp/cm^2
Maximum rate of fire: 10 rounds/min (for limited duration)
Normal rate of fire: 5 rounds/min
Barrel
Weight of barrel with breech piece: 43kg
Length of barrel with breech piece: 1.73metres
Bipod
Weight: 37kg
Overall length: 1,000mm
Baseplate
Weight: 38kg
Diameter: 740mm
Sight
Weight: 1.57kg
Graduation of bearing scale: 0-360 (0-6,400mils)
Graduation of elevating arc: 40-90 (700-1,600mils)
ROUND M58F-HE
Weight of round complete: 12.9kg
Body, Forged Steel: 9.3kg
Tail unit: Aluminium alloy 700g
Fuze: Super quick/delay. Arming safety 0.8sec; weight 200g
Filling: TNT 2.3kg
Charge system: Primary cartridge + additional charge + 8 secondary charges
Overall length of round: 580mm
Muzzle velocity
Minimum: 115metres/sec
Maximum: 310metres/sec
Maximum chamber pressure: 900kp/cm^2
Range
Minimum: 400metres
Maximum: 6,200metres
Consistency: 50 per cent zone can be taken as 1 per cent of range

ROUND M58F – SMOKE
FM round. Filling: Titanium Tetrachloride. Weight of filling 2.3kg
WP round. Filling: White Phosphorus. Weight of filling 2.3kg
PWP round. Filling: plastic White Phosphorus. Weight of filling 2.3kg
All other data are the same as for the M58F-HE round.

ROUND M58F – PRACTICE
Weight of smoke indicator charge: 200g
Weight of inert filling: 2.1kg
All other data are the same as for the M58F-HE round.

ROUND M58FF – HE
Weight of round complete: 13kg
Body. Forged steel: 9.3kg
Tail unit: Aluminium alloy 700g
Fuze: Super quick/delay. Arming safety 0.8sec 200g
Filling: TNT 2.3kg
Charge system: Primary cartridge + additional charge + 10 secondary charges

The travelling carriage of the 120mm Soltam light mortar. The containers on the axle tree carry six rounds ready for use

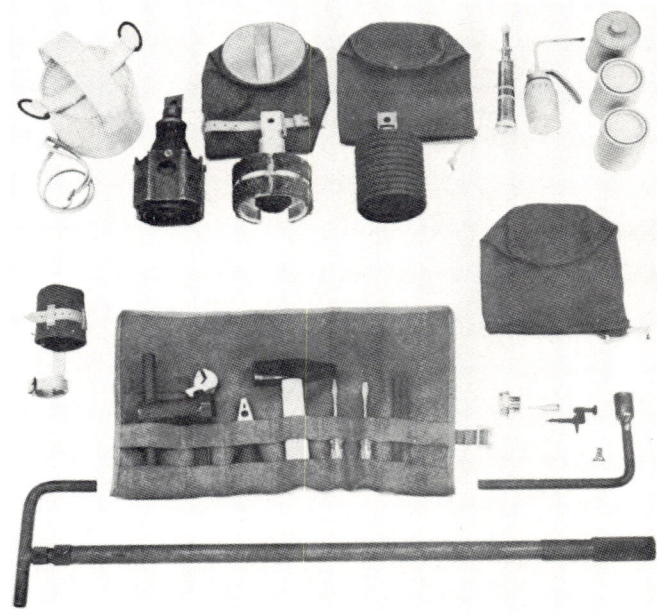

The tools issued with the mortar. Note the misfire tool, top left, and its rod, bottom

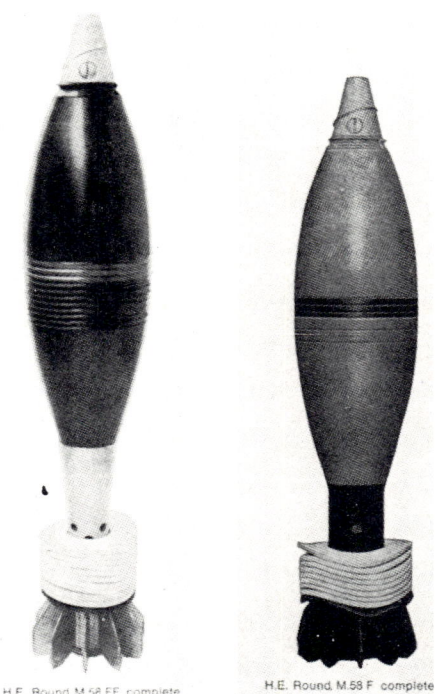

H.E. Round M58 FF complete   H.E. Round. M58 F complete

The M58F (right) and M58FF rounds

Overall length of round: 635mm
Muzzle velocity
    Minimum: 90metres/sec
    Maximum: 315metres/sec
Maximum chamber pressure: 850kp/cm^2
Range
    Minimum: 400metres
    Maximum: 7,000metres

ROUND M58FF – SMOKE

FM round. Filling: Titanium Tetrachloride. Weight of filling 2.3kg
WP round. Filling: White Phosphorus. Weight of filling 2.3kg
PWP round. Filling: Plastic White Phosphorus. Weight of filling 2.3kg
    All other data are the same as for the M58FF-HE round.

ROUND M58FF – PRACTICE

Weight of smoke indicator charge: 200g
Weight of inert filling: 2.1kg
    All other data are the same as for the M58FF-HE round.
Manufacturer: Soltam Ltd., Israel
Status: In service in Israel at least

120mm SOLTAM M-65 STANDARD MORTAR

The standard 120mm is a substantial mortar which can be used in the traditional way and can also be mounted in an APC or similar vehicle. Such a vehicle should be able to carry sufficient ammunition to make full use of the very considerable fire power of the weapon.

BARREL AND BREECH PIECE

The barrel is made of high tensile alloy steel and is given a very good internal finish. The breech piece screws into the bottom of the barrel and holds the firing mechanism. The spring loaded striker is fired by pulling a firing lever which cocks the spring before allowing it to trip over to fire the bomb. The firing pin can be retracted to a safe position and this is of particular value when clearing a misfire. The ball shaped end of the breech piece fits into the socket of the baseplate. At the front end of the barrel is a bayonet-type catch into which the towing eye is secured. This is sprung to reduce the shocks of travelling.

BIPOD

The bipod is, in principle, similar to that of the light 120mm mortar. All exposed and sliding components are either chromium plated or made of stainless steel to resist wear or corrosion and all the gears and screw threaded columns are totally enclosed.

BASEPLATE

This is a circular dish-shaped plate of steel with strengthening ribs welded on. There are also carrying handles and eyes for securing the baseplate to the carriage welded onto the upper side of the baseplate.

SIGHT

The sight employed on the standard mortar is the same as that used on the 120mm light mortar.

CARRIAGE

This is a more substantial carriage than that used with the light mortar. It is of box construction made up of welded steel sheet. The top portion carries the barrel clamping collar and baseplate clamping hooks. The wheels are of standard jeep size and type. Drag rings are mounted on the wheel hubs for man handling the mortar across country. The frame of the cross member is boxed in to take tools and has a lid. There are welded attachments to which can be secured the cleaning rods, carriage stay, and base plate levering rods, during transit.

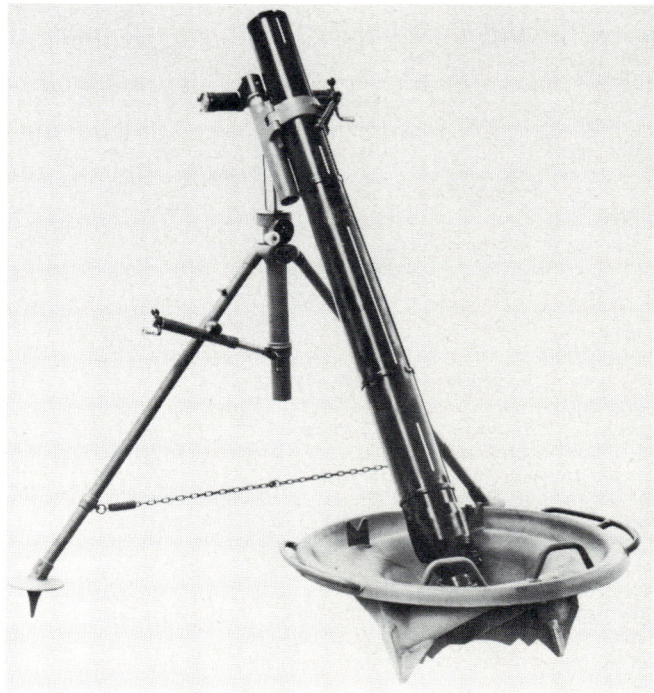

Soltam 120mm standard mortar in the firing position

120mm standard mortar mounted in an Israeli half-track

Removing a misfired bomb from the 120mm mortar

DATA
MORTAR
Calibre: 120mm
Total weight of mortar in travelling position (without any accessories): 365kg
Weight of mortar in firing position: 220kg
Length in travelling position: 2.65 metres
Width in travelling position: 1.53 metres
Height in travelling position: 1.05 metres
Range with standard round M58F: Minimum 400 metres; Maximum 6,200 metres
Range with new conventional round (ST) Maximum: 8,300 metres
Elevation: 45° 80° (800-1,422 mils)
Traverse: 360° (6,400 mils)
Top traverse: 13.5° (240 mils)
Maximum chamber pressure: 1,250kp/cm²
Maximum rate of fire: 10 rounds/min

Normal rate of fire: 5 rounds/min
Barrel with breech piece:
Weight: 82kg
Overall length: 1.94 metres
Bipod
Weight: 66kg
Length: 1.74 metres
Baseplate
Weight: 72kg
Diameter: 960mm
Sight
Weight: 1.57kg
Graduation of bearing scale: 0°-360° (0-6,400 mils)
Graduation of elevating arc: 40°-90° (700-1,600 mils)
Carriage
Weight: 129kg
Trail eye: 16kg
AMMUNITION
   Data for the M58 series of 120mm ammunition are given in the preceding entry (120mm Light Mortar).
Manufacturers: Soltam Ltd., Israel
Status: In service in Israel at least

The 120mm standard mortar in the travelling position

Standard 120mm bomb

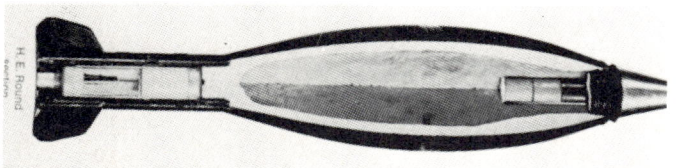

Sectioned view of the HE bomb

120mm IMI HE BOMB
   This is a rocket assisted bomb which will reach 9,800 metres. It can be fired from any current 120mm mortar.

DATA
Overall length: 744mm
Complete round weight: 16.7kg
Propelling charge: Primary and 8 increments
Rocket propellant: 1.15kg
High explosive filling: 2.45kg
Nature of filling: Compound B
Maximum range: 9,800 metres
Manufacturer: IMI (see above)

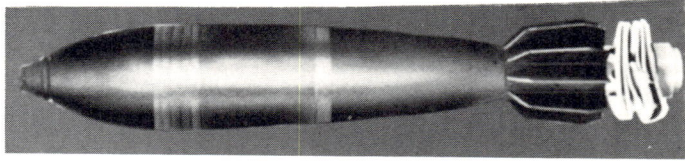

120mm high explosive bomb

Status: In production. In service with Israeli forces. Tested by some other armies

120mm IMI ILLUMINATING BOMB
   This operates in the same way as the 81mm Mk 1 illuminating bomb.

DATA
Overall length: 580mm
Weight of complete round: 12.6kg
Weight of illuminant: 1.1kg
Propelling charge: Primary and 8 increments
Muzzle velocity (max): 315 metres/sec
Minimum range: 1,200 metres
Maximum range: 5,700 metres
Illuminating power: 1,000,000 candlepower
Minimum burning time: 52sec
Rate of descent: 7.8 metres/sec

120mm illuminating bomb

Height of parachute opening: 600 metres
Manufacturer: IMI (see above)
Status: In production. In service with Israeli forces. Tested by some other armies

160mm SOLTAM M-66 MORTAR
   The 160mm mortar fires a 40kg bomb out to 9,300 metres. To do this requires a heavy weapon (1,700kg in the firing position) and one requiring a detachment of 6-8 men. It is a matter for the individual user-country to decide whether a mortar offers advantages over a gun when these factors and the order of accuracy of the mortar (50% zone of approximately 1% of the range) are considered.

BARREL
   This is a high tensile strength, alloy steel, tube. At the bottom end is the breech piece which contains the firing mechanism. This is operated by a firing lever which allows the spring loaded striker to trip off the sear and go forward to fire. The striker can be withdrawn to provide safety – particularly in the case of a misfire.

CARRIAGE
   There is no bipod mounting for this weapon and instead the barrel is elevated and depressed by a single column which is part of the carriage. The very heavy weight of the bomb makes conventional loading difficult and it is necessary to lower the barrel to a loading position. This is done by folding back the elevating strut from a hinge at its midpoint. There is a counterbalance mechanism which makes it easy to elevate the barrel each time it is loaded. This consists of steel cables attached to the barrel some two metres from the muzzle and led over sheaves into the lower pair of tubes that make up the chassis of the carriage.

The mortar in travelling position

   The axles allow the road wheels to be turned in and locked by a cam plate attached to the axle tube. The offside road wheel incorporates a clutch and handle to allow slow traverse. The carriage rolls on its wheels through a complete 360 degree circle without moving the baseplate.

BASEPLATE
   This is a heavy flat disc welded up with a number of webs to give stiffness and to prevent the tendency to slide sideways. Four handles are welded to the top plate to allow carrying the baseplate and they are used to get the

Soltam 160mm mortar in firing position

160mm mortar on modified Sherman chassis as used by Israeli Army

baseplate out of the ground. There is a central socket into which the tail of the breech piece fits. This allows a full 360 degree traverse without movement of the baseplate. There is a spring loaded locking arrangement to ensure that the breech piece cannot leave the baseplate.

SIGHT

Two types of sight are available. The "A" sight, is of simple design with a 360 degree scale, cross levelling bubble, elevation bubble and a lensatic sight. The type "B" sight has a slipping scale and so can be adjusted to permit direct bearing readings from any selected aiming point.

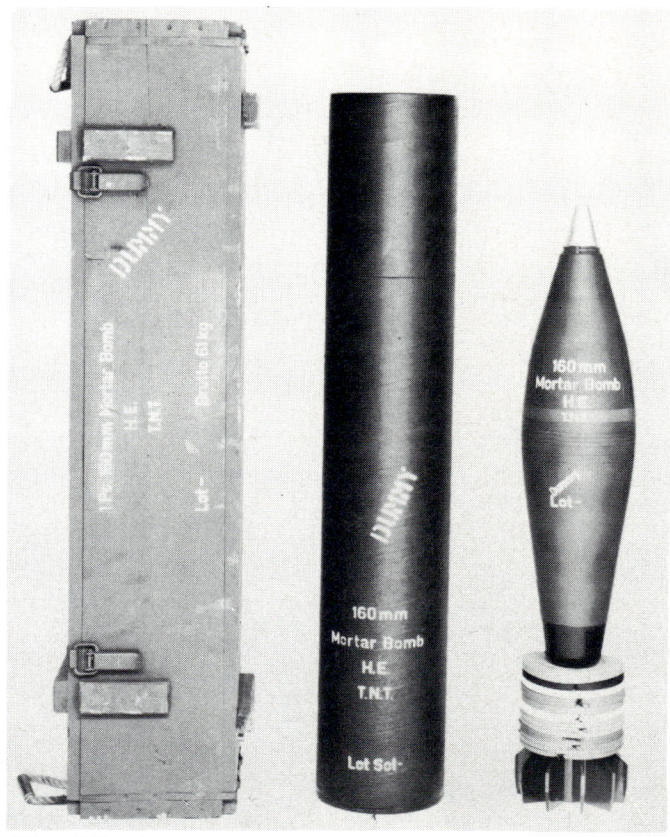

160mm HE bomb

AMMUNITION

The HE bomb is made from forged steel. The tail unit is made from extruded aluminium. The secondaries, which are flat discs, do not protrude beyond the diameter of the fins and so do not come into contact with the barrel wall. This reduces the chance of a cook-off, even with a barrel temperature as high as 1,200 degrees F. The high explosive filling is 5kg of TNT. The propellant system is made up of the primary cartridge and nine secondaries. The Diehl fuze gives a direct action or a slight delay.

There are two kinds of smoke bomb. One has a titanium tetrachloride filling and the other plastic white phosphorus. The WP bomb can be used also as a night ranging bomb.

DATA
Calibre: 160mm
Weight of mortar in travelling position (excluding baseplate): 1,450kg
Weight of baseplate: 250kg
Total weight of mortar in firing position: 1,700kg
Length of barrel: 2,850mm
Maximum range: 9,300 metres
Elevation: 43°-70° (764-1,244 mils)
Traverse: 360° (6,400mils)

Sight:
Weight type "A": 1.45kg
Weight type "B": 1.57kg
Traversing scale: 360° (6,400 mils)

Ammunition:
Weight of bomb complete: 40kg
Weight of HE filling: 5kg
Rate of fire: 5-8 rounds/min
50% zone: ¾-1¼% of range

Manufacturers: Tampella (see above). Soltam Ltd., Israel
Status: In service in Finland and Israel at least

SPAIN

60mm MORTAR, MODEL L

All the mortars used by the Spanish Army are manufactured by Esperanza y Cia., SA, under the general trade designation ECIA. Some of these mortars have also been sold to Portugal for use by Portuguese forces overseas; so it is likely that since the decolonisation process some of them have now come into the possession of the armed forces of former Portuguese territories such as Angola or Mozambique.

Model L is a Company mortar, easily carried by one soldier and capable of producing high explosive fire, smoke or illumination.

The barrel of the mortar is of steel with a thread turned on the outside of the lower end, over which the breech piece fits. The breech piece contains the tigger mechanism. This allows the firer the choice of gravity firing or trigger operation. There is a safety device which withdraws the pin when

required. At the bottom of the breech piece is a ball shaped extension which fits into the socket of the baseplate. The baseplate is circular. Webs are welded on to the bottom to stiffen the body and prevent any slipping when the mortar is fired at a low angle of elevation. In the centre is the socket which takes the ball of the breech piece. This socket can revolve and so the mortar has a complete 360 degree traverse.

The mount is unusual in so small a mortar in being a tripod. It is normally located with two legs to the rear and one forward. The three legs are pinned into a fabricated tripod head and can be closed together when the mortar is brought out of action. There is no cross levelling gear and the legs of the tripod cannot be varied in length. The tripod head contains the elevating handle which raises or lowers the elevating column which is fixed to the

60mm mortar in carrying position

The 60mm mortar, Model L, in the firing position

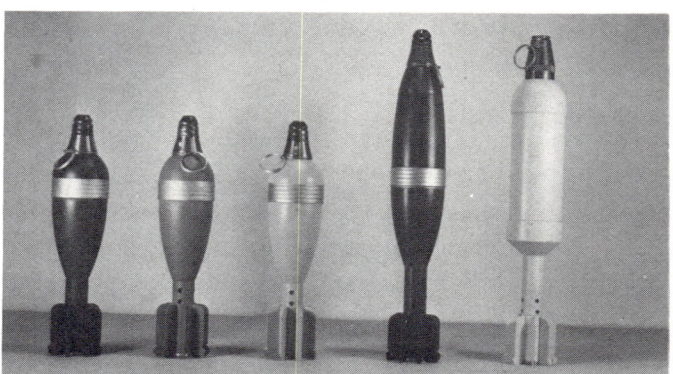

*Ammunition for the 60mm mortar. **(Left to right)** HE, exercise, smoke, high capacity and illuminating bombs*

yoke. The yoke carries the traversing screw which passes through a nut attached to the barrel. The traversing handle is on the left end of the traversing screw and when the handle is turned the thread is rotated, and the nut is pulled across, drawing the barrel with it. The sight is attached to the barrel collar. The sight has a telescope for viewing the aiming mark and elevating and traverse scales. There is no slipping scale.

DATA
Calibre: 60mm
Barrel length: 650mm
Weight of barrel and breech piece: 4.2kg
Weight of baseplate: 2.8kg
Weight of mount: 3.9kg
Weight of sight: 1.1kg
Maximum rate of fire: 30 rounds/min
Maximum range: 1,975 metres
Number of charges: 5

AMMUNITION
DATA
HE round:
Length: 263mm
Weight: 1.43kg
Filling: TNT 232g
Manufacturer: Esperanza y Cia., SA, Marquina (Vizcaya), Spain
Status: In production and in service

60mm COMMANDO MORTAR

This is a light section mortar operated and carried by one man. The barrel is a plain tube with a small circular button type baseplate at the bottom. There is no mount. The soldier supports the barrel with his left hand, grasping the canvas sleeve placed around it to protect his hand. A rudimentary sight is held on the right of the tube by a "hose clip" fastener.

Of all the light mortars in use today, this must be one of the simplest.

DATA
Calibre: 60mm
Barrel length: 650mm
Weight of barrel and breech: 3.1kg
Weight of baseplate: 2.8kg
Weight of sight: 520g
Maximum rate of fire: 30 rounds/min
Maximum range: 1,070 metres
Number of charges: 2
Ammunition: As 60mm Model "L"
Manufacturer: Esperanza y Cia., SA (see above)
Status: In production and in service with Spanish forces

60mm Commando mortar in action

60mm Commando mortar in carrying position

81mm MORTAR, MODELS L-N and L-L

The differences between these models are very slight and amount to the elevation and traversing screws being fully enclosed on the model L-L. The legs of the tripod are linked by chain.

The barrel is a steel tube, strengthened at the rear end, and screw threaded on the outside of the bottom to take the breech piece. This contains the firing mechanism and allows either gravity or controlled firing. The ball extension of the breech piece fits into the socket of the circular baseplate and is held by a spring latch. Two different barrel lengths are available.

The tripod follows the same pattern as the that of the 60mm mortar, with the three legs arranged one forward and two to the rear, fitting into the fabricated tripod head. The mortar is designed to be man portable in three loads.

DATA
Mortar:
Weights:
Barrel and breech piece: standard barrel: 17kg
                              long barrel: 19kg

Distribution of the 81mm mortar, broken down to man loads

81mm mortar Model L-N in firing position

81mm mortar Model L-L in firing position

Baseplate: 13.5kg
Mount: Model L-N: 10.5kg
      Model L-N: 11.5kg
Sight: 2kg
Length: Normal barrel: 1,150mm
      Long barrel: 1,450mm
Maximum rate of fire: 15 rounds/min
Maximum range: Normal barrel - NA bomb: 4,125 metres
      Long barrel - NA bomb: 4,600 metres
      Normal barrel - N bomb: 4,270 metres
      Long barrel - N bomb: 5,200 metres
Ammunition:
HE bomb Model NA:
      Length overall: 343mm
      Weight: 3.2kg
      TNT filling: 496g
HE bomb Model N:
      Length overall: 381mm
      Weight: 4.13kg
      TNT filling: 675g
Number of charges: 6
Manufacturer: Esperanza y Cia., SA (see above)
Status: In production and in service

*Model N series ammunition. **Left to right:** HE, exercise, smoke, high-capacity and illuminating rounds.*

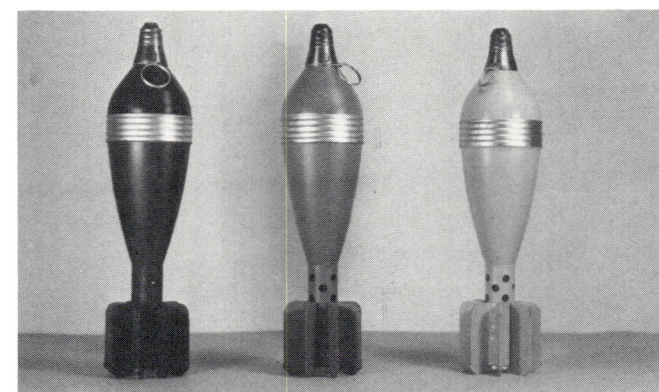

*Model NA series ammunition. **Left to right:** HE, exercise and smoke rounds*

105mm MORTAR, MODEL L

The 105mm Mortar is a scaled up version of the 81mm. It has a similar type of tripod adjusted in the same way and the same sighting unit. Firing is either by gravity or trigger. The main difference in the 105mm mortar is that it is carried on a small trolley or carriage which is normally towed behind a Land Rover. There are two varieties of carriage of which that most commonly seen carries the mortar, tripod and sight directly over the axle with the baseplate on a platform in line with the towing eye. No ammunition is normally carried on the mortar although in emergency some could obviously be carried in a box on the baseplate.

The second type of carriage has 12 rounds carried in cylinders, one round to a cylinder, located in lockers mounted inboard of the pneumatic tyred wheels. The baseplate rests on a shelf on the shelf on the centre of the axle with the barrel, tripod and sight above it.

DATA
Weights:
Barrel and breech piece: 35.7kg
Baseplate: 43kg
Mount: 24.25kg
Travelling carriage: 111kg
Length of barrel: 1.5 metres
Maximum rate of fire: 12 rounds/minute
Maximum range: 6,000 metres
Number of charges: 5
Ammunition:
Overall length: 546mm
Weight of HE bomb: 9.4kg
HE filling: TNT, 1.704kg
Manufacturer: Esperanza y Cia., SA (see above)
Status: In production and in service

105mm mortar, Model L, in the firing position

The light carriage for the 105mm mortar

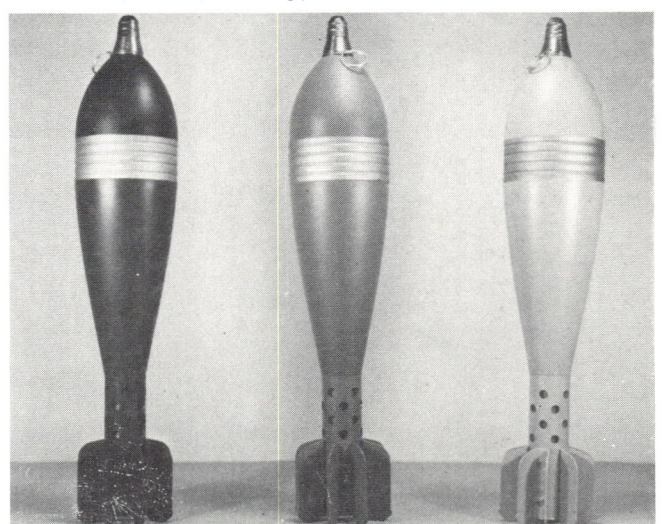

*105mm mortar ammunition. **Left to right:** HE, exercise and smoke*

120mm MORTAR, MODEL L

Model L is the standard 120mm mortar. It has all the characteristics of the other ECIA mortars with the tripod mount, simple barrel and circular baseplate. It can be fired either by gravity drop or by trigger control. The mortar is transported on a carriage towed by a Land Rover or M113 APC.

The baseplate lies over the axle and is held in position by a number of clips. The barrel and mount rest on a frame above the baseplate and are held in position by straps.

DATA
Mortar:
Weights:
Barrel and breech piece: 61kg
Baseplate: 100kg
Mount: 40kg
Sight: 2kg
Carriage: 125kg
Length of barrel: 1.6 metres
Maximum rate of fire: 12 rounds/min
Maximum range: Bomb N: 5,700 metres
            Bomb L: 5,940 metres
Number of charges: 5
Ammunition:
Bomb N: Length overall: 668mm
            Weight: 16.745kg
            Filling: TNT 3.175kg
Bomb L: Length overall: 604mm
            Weight: 13.195kg
            Filling: TNT 2.34kg
Manufacturer: Esperanza y Cia., SA (see above)
Status: In production and in service

120mm mortar, Model L, in the travelling position

*N series ammunition. **Left to right:** HE, exercise and smoke bombs*

120mm Model L in the firing position. Note the massive baseplate

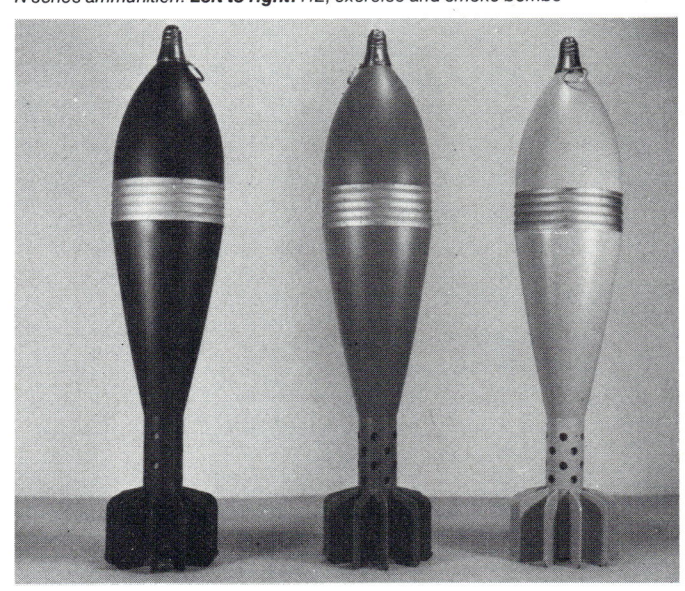

*L series ammunition. **Left to right:** HE, exercise and smoke bomb*

120mm MORTAR, MODEL SL

This is a light version of the 120mm Mortar Model L. Weight has been saved at the expense of range and rate of fire. The carriage used is the light model of the 105mm mortar.

DATA
Weights:
Barrel and breech piece: 47kg
Baseplate: 43kg
Mount: 26kg

The light carriage for the SL mortar. Note how weight has been saved compared with that for the Model L

Sight: 2kg
Carriage: 111kg
Length of barrel: 1.6 metres
Maximum rate of fire: 12 rounds/min
Maximum range: Bomb N: 5,000 metres (4 charges)
Bomb L: 5,940 metres (5 charges)
Ammunition: As for 120mm Mortar Model L
Manufacturer: Esperanza y Cia., SA (see above)
Status: In production and in service

The 120mm mortar, Model SL, in the firing position

SWEDEN

81mm MORTAR m/29(1929)

The 81mm mortar m/29(1929) is the standard light mortar of the Swedish Army and has been in service almost 50 years. It is basically the French 81mm Stokes/Brandt Model 1917 mortar produced under licence in Sweden. In 1934 the French sights were replaced by sights of Swedish design. In appearance the mortar is similar to most other mortars of that period – rectangular base with carrying handle, bipod with chains connecting the legs and an anti-cant device on the left leg.

DATA
Barrel calibre: 81.4mm

Weight in firing position: 60kg
Barrel length: 1,000mm
Elevation: +45° to +80°
Traverse: 90°
HE bomb weight: 3.5kg
Maximum m/v: 190m/s
Minimum m/v: 70m/s
Maximum range: 2,600 metres
Rate of fire: 15-18 rounds/minute
Status: In service with Swedish forces and in the Irish Republic

120mm MORTAR m/41C(1941)

The 120mm mortar m/41C(1941) is the standard heavy mortar of the Swedish Army. It is basically the Finnish Tampella Model 1940 120mm mortar built in Sweden. In 1956 Sweden built a number of Hotchkiss-Brandt M-56 baseplates under licence to replace the earlier Tampella baseplates. More recently the sights have been replaced. The mortar is issued on the scale 8 per mortar company of the infantry brigades and 6 per mortar company of the Norrlands brigades.

DATA
Barrel calibre: 120.25mm
Weight travelling: 600kg
Weight in firing position: 285kg
Barrel length: 2,000mm
Elevation: +45° to +80°
Traverse: 360°
HE bomb weight: 13.3kg
Maximum m/v: 317m/s
Minimum m/v: 125m/s
Maximum range: 6,400 metres
Rate of fire: 12-15 rounds/minute
Status: In service with Swedish forces and in the Republic of Ireland

120mm Mortar m/41C

FFV 266 120mm SMOKE BOMB

This mortar bomb is provided with a parachute which slows down the smoke container (the rear part of the shell body) so that it reaches the ground at low velocity, without risk of re-bound or shattering against hard ground, and with little risk of sinking into soft ground. The speed of descent is constant at all ranges, which means that the full smoke function is achieved over the whole firing range of the mortar. The FFV 266 is provided with a mechanical time fuze and its trajectory is almost identical to that of the corresponding HE mortar bomb so that no extra ranging shots are required for smoke mortar fire.

The smoke composition consists of hexachloroethane, zinc oxide and calcium silicide which rapidily produces a dense and persistent smoke screen. On open terrain, with a wind speed of 5m/s it has been proved that

the smoke covers an area 200m long and approx. 50m in width to a height of over 15m.

The full sequence of events of the bomb in its downward trajectory is as follows: (1) The fuze ignites a turning charge and the gas produced is forced out through two nozzles to turn the shell 15° to 30° from the tangent to the trajectory. (2) The front part of the bomb is shot away by a separation charge and, simultaneously, the parachute with its pilot chute and harness is withdrawn from the parachute canister. The smoke composition is ignited. (3) When the parachute with its harness has been extended by the pilot chute the latter is released by the breaking of the thread which holds the rigging lines of the parachute together, whereupon the parachute opens. (4) The rear part of the shell body falls tail forward towards the ground and is slowed down by the parachute. The smoke composition is burning. (5) Smoke is produced with full effect when the shell reaches the ground.

DATA
The 120mm FFV 266 is available in two versions depending on the configuration of the tail assembly. FFV 266-S has a steel tail assembly: FFV 266-T has an aluminium tail assembly of the Tampella type.

FFV 266-S
Weight of smoke mortar shell without increments: 13.3kg
Weight of smoke composition: 3kg
Weight of smoke mortar round in container: 15kg
Effective burning time: 5 minutes
Maximum firing range: 6,000 metres
Maximum remaining velocity on separation: 235m/s
Speed of descent: 30m/s
Operational temperature range: −40°C to +60°C
m/v charge 10(max.m/v): 317m/s
m/v charge 1: 124m/s
P max charge 10: 1,000 bars

FFV 266-T
Weight of smoke mortar shell without increments: 12.6kg
Weight of smoke composition: 3kg
Weight of smoke mortar round in container: 14.2kg
Effective burning time: 5 minutes
Maximum firing range: 6,000 metres
Maximum remaining velocity on separation: 230m/s
Speed of descent: 30m/s
m/v charge 8(max m/v): 301m/s
m/v charge 0: 111m/s
P max charge 8: 820 bars
Manufacturer: Forenade Fabriksverken, Eskilstuna, Sweden

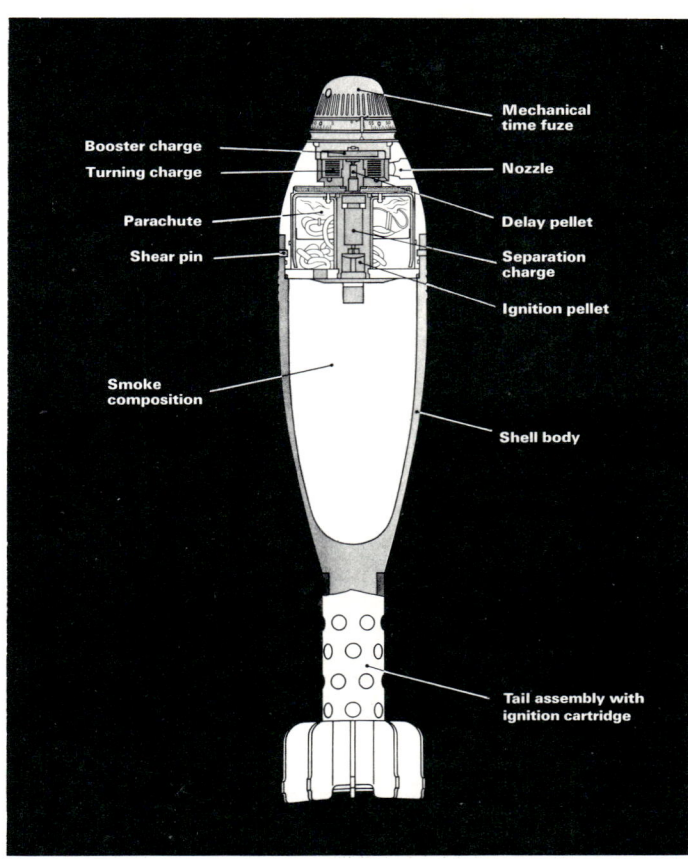

FFV 266 Smoke Bomb

LYRAN 71mm ILLUMINATING SYSTEM
This illuminating system has been developed in order to meet the primary requirements of small units for battlefield illumination. The objective has been, using only one type of ammunition, to design a simple, portable version, primarily intended for infantry use, and a version for use on various types of combat vehicles, an essential requirement then being that it should be possible to mount the system on existing types of combat vehicles, without any major vehicle modifications.

INFANTRY VERSION
The infantry version consists of two packs, comprising a launcher and six mortar flare shells.

Pack 1 consists of a plastic mounting containing the barrel and two mortar flare shells. Before firing, the barrel is erected on the mounting. The elevation of the barrel is set with the aid of a spirit level. When firing, the operator is seated on the mounting.

Operating the Lyran launcher

The two Lyran packs can be carried by one man

Combat vehicle installation of Lyran

Pack 2 consists of four mortar flare shells, individually packed in plastic tubes which can be connected together.

The mortar flare shell is provided with a pyrotechnical fuze which can be set for ranges of 400, 800 and 1,300 metres (refers to horizontal range to flare).

DATA
Total weight, pack 1: 9kg
Total weight, pack 2: 8kg
Ranges (elevation 47°): 400 and 800 metres
Mortar Flare shell:
Weight: 1.17kg
Length: 340mm
Muzzle velocity: 115m/sec
Luminous intensity (mean): 600,000 candelas
Descending speed (mean): 3m/sec
Burning time: 30sec
5-lux illumination (diam): 500 metres

COMBAT VEHICLE VERSION

The combat vehicle version consists of a launcher intended for permanent mounting, firing device and ammunition packs.

The launcher, which is fired from the crew compartment of the vehicle, is provided with an electromechanical firing device. The launcher is connected via the firing device to the electric system of the vehicle. It is fastened with four screws, either directly to the top of the vehicle, or on a special fastening device and it is so located that, during combat, it can be served by the crew without anyone having to leave the crew compartment.

Before combat operations commence, the launcher is loaded, the elevation (45°) is set, and the safety device on the launcher is released.

In the transport position the barrel is swung down to protect it from being damaged.

A control unit is used for firing the launcher from inside the vehicle. Its design depends on the number of launchers to be mounted on the vehicle: there is a firing button for each launcher. When the mechanical safety of a launcher has been released, firing can take place immediately: the firing buttons are provided with covers to prevent accidental firing.

The vehicle ammunition pack is the same as pack 2 for the infantry version except that the mortar flare shells are provided with extra propellant charges. These charges are used to obtain a range of 1,300 metres. The connection devices on the individual packing tubes can be utilised for attaching extra ammunition on or in the combat vehicle.

DATA
Weight of launcher: 17kg
Power requirements: 24V DC
Elevation settings: 5° steps
External dimensions of baseplate: 205 × 110mm
Total length: 885mm
Firing elevation: 45°
Mortar Flare Shell: as for infantry version
Muzzle velocity with extra propellant charge: 153m/sec
Manufacturer: AB Bofors, Ordnance Division, Box 500, S-690 20 Bofors, Sweden
Status: In production

SWITZERLAND

81mm MORTAR, MODEL 1933

This mortar is very similar to the German, US and Russian mortars produced in this calibre in the 1930s. In the shape of the baseplate, the rather complicated arrangements for the socket and the layout of the elevating and traversing screws, it has much in common with the US M1 mortar. The bipod legs, with their spiked feet, are positioned by the chain connecting them. The cross levelling gear is operated from the left leg of the bipod and the elevating gear tube is displaced as the connecting rod is moved across. The tube passes through the junction of the bipod legs and there is a gear case at the junction from which projects the elevating handle. The top of the elevating column is attached to the nut through which passes the traversing screw. The wheel on the right hand end of the traversing screw rotates the thread which moves the nut along and with it goes the barrel. The sight is connected to the left end of the yoke. There are two shock absorbers interposed between the barrel latch and the yoke and they ensure that the yoke is correctly positioned before a round is fired.

DATA
Weights:
All up: 62kg
Barrel: 21kg
Mounting: 18kg
Baseplate: 21kg
Sight mount and sight: 2kg
Lengths:
Barrel: 1,265mm
Shot travel: 1,155mm
Mount: 940mm
Baseplate: 680 × 410mm
Top traverse: 8°
Traverse, moving bipod: 45°-56°
Elevation: 45°-90°

81mm mortar, model 1933

Ammunition

Types:	HE	Smoke	High Capacity Fragmentation Bomb
Fuzing:	Point detonation or slight delay	Percussion	Point Detonation
Weight:	3.17kg	3.67kg	6.89kg
Filling:	Trotyl	Smoke composition	Trotyl
Charges:	0-6	0-6	1-4
Muzzle velocity:	70-260m/sec	70-260m/sec	64-110m/sec
Maximum range:	4,100 metres	3,000 metres	1,070 metres

Manufacturer: Waffenfabrik, Bern
Status: In Swiss Army service, designated 8.1cm Mw 33

81mm MORTAR, MODEL 1972

This is an improved mortar. The baseplate is a flat disc with webs welded on to the under side. The bipod has been cleaned up by having the screw threads fully enclosed and the cross levelling gear, although working in exactly the same way, is much easier to operate. A very considerable weight saving has been made. Like its predecessor, the mortar breaks down into three man portable loads.

DATA
Weights:
All up: 45.5kg
Barrel: 12kg
Mounting: 15kg
Baseplate: 16.5kg

Sight mounting and sight: 2kg
Lengths:
Barrel: 1,267mm
Shot travel: 1,154mm
Mount: 930mm
Baseplate diameter: 550mm
Top traverse: 10°
Traverse, moving bipod: 360°
Elevation: 45°-90°
Ammunition: As for Model 33
Manufacturer: Waffenfabrik, Bern
Status: In Swiss Army service, designated 8.1cm Mw 72

81mm mortar, Model 72

120mm MORTAR, MODEL 64 IN MORTAR CARRIER M106

This mortar is normally fired from inside the carrier using a special baseplate built into the structure of the vehicle. A conventional baseplate is carried externally on the side of the vehicle and if necessary the mortar may be dismounted and brought into action as a conventional infantry mortar.

An 81mm sub-calibre training device is used which consists of a tube inserted in the barrel and enables firings to be carried out on smaller ranges and at reduced cost.

The 120mm mortar is muzzle loaded and the firing mechanism is manually controlled using an external firing lever.

The 120mm mortar carrier, M106, with the mortar just visible

DATA
Weights:
Overall weight of the equipment: 239kg
Barrel weight: 87kg
Mounting: 51kg
Baseplate: 95kg
Sight mounting and sight: 3kg
Lengths:
Barrel length: 1,770mm
Shot travel: 1,524mm
Mount: 1,400mm
Baseplate: 950mm
Top traverse: 10°
Traverse, moving bipod: 60°
Elevation: 45°-85°
Ammunition:
Fuze: Point detonation and slight delay (HE); Point detonation (Incendiary/Smoke)

The interior of the carrier showing the 120mm mortar, M64, and its ammunition ready for use

Weight: 14.33kg
Filling: Trotyl (HE); White phosphorus (Incendiary/Smoke)
Charges: 1-8
Muzzle velocity: 128-420m/sec
Maximum range: 8,000 metres
Manufacturer: Waffenfabrik, Bern (mortar)
Status: In Swiss Army service, designated 12cm Mw Pz 64

120mm MORTAR, MODEL 74 ON 2 WHEEL CARRIAGE

This mortar in this form was produced in 1972. The mortar itself is the same as that used in the carrier – i.e. the Model 64. The equipment is designed to be towed by a light vehicle or carried as an underslung load on a helicopter. The carriage is of a simple design with a cross axle on which the weight of the mortar is taken. Alongside the mortar is an ammunition box allowing 12 ready for use rounds to be carried on the mounting.

The mortar itself is of orthodox construction and is a scaled-up version of the 81mm weapon.

DATA
Weights:
Carriage with mortar: 620kg
Carriage unloaded: 208kg
Drawbar weight: 15kg
Lengths:
Length with mortar on carriage: 2,350mm
Length unloaded: 1,140mm
Overall width: 1,510mm
Height loaded: 1,130mm
Height unloaded: 970mm
Wheel base: 1,285mm
Ground clearance: 240mm
Towing speeds, on roads up to: 80km/hr
Ammunition: As for Model 64
Manufacturer: Waffenfabrik, Bern
Status: In Swiss Army service

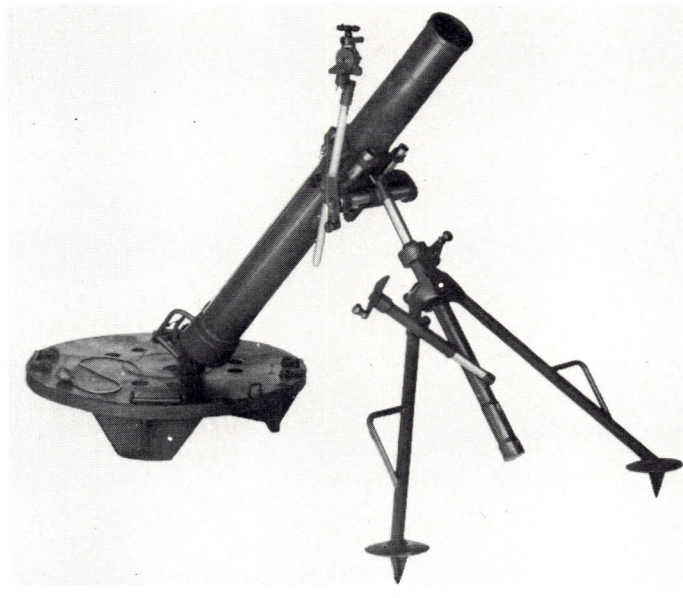

120mm mortar, Model 74, in action position

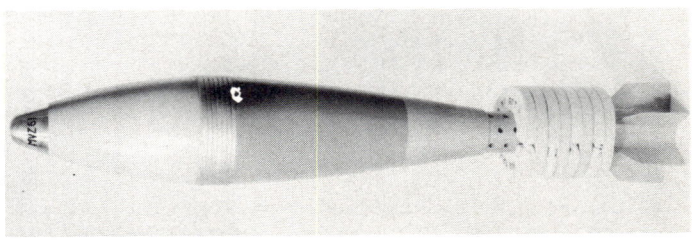

120mm mortar ammunition (HE)

The 120mm mortar, Model 74, on its 2-wheel carriage

RATTLEBOX

This is a lightweight rocket launcher intended in attack to support the infantry and in defence to break up the enemy attack. It can also be used to cover prepared obstacles with fire. It weighs only 7kg and the three rocket packs of four missiles each bring the weight to 30kg. It has a two-man crew and can be carried forward into position, using a small hand trolley. It can be set up very quickly and can be fired from an electrically operated control box.

The rockets are 50mm diameter and four of them are placed in a container which itself is the launcher. There are several different types of rocket, including anti-personnel, illuminating and smoke. An armour-piercing rocket is also available.

DATA
Weapon – less containers: 7kg
Weight with three container/launchers: 30kg
Height at maximum elevation: 900mm
Maximum elevation: 85°
Minimum elevation: 20°
Traverse: 360°
Laying: Manual
Time into action: 1 minute
Time to fire 12 rounds: 1 second
Ammunition:
Weight: 1.3kg
Weight of warhead: 260g
Length: 550mm
Diameter: 50mm
Propellant weight: 60g
Burning time: 0.01sec
Muzzle velocity: 100 metres/sec
Maximum range: 800 metres
Armour penetration: 250mm
Manufacturer: SARMAC S.A., 54 bis, route des Acacias, 1227 Carouge-Geneva

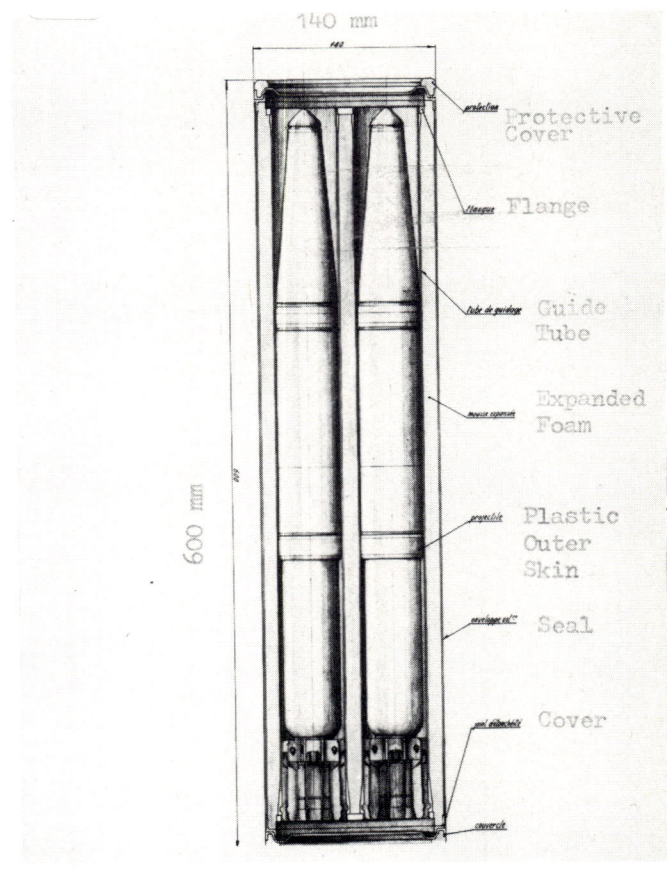

The rockets in their launcher boxes

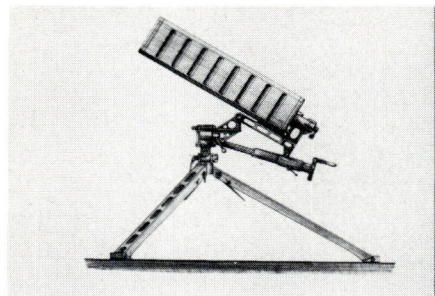

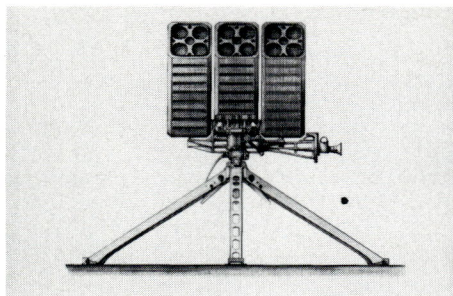

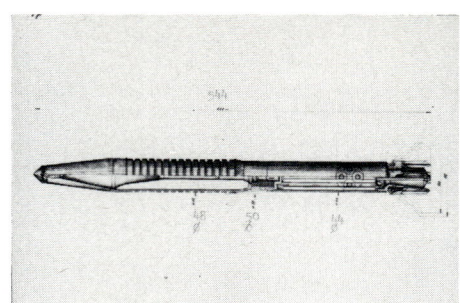

Side elevation of Rattlebox

Rattlebox, showing three launchers of four rockets each

The pre-formed anti-personnel rocket

UNION OF SOVIET SOCIALIST REPUBLICS

50mm MORTARS

In the late 1930s and early years of the following decade, the Russians developed the M38, M39, M40 and M41 mortars.

M38

This was a smooth bore, muzzle loaded mortar with a fixed firing pin. The range adjustment was carried out by rotating a sleeve around the base of the mortar and this opened or closed a series of gas ports allowing the gas pressure to be evacuated to atmosphere to obtain short ranges. The mortar fired only at 45 degrees and at 75 degrees. The sight was a simple aiming circle-clinometer. The usual baseplate was a small oval shaped plate which was replaced in mountain warfare by a rectangular one. The ammunition was of a conventional finned type but there was only the primary and no secondaries.

M39

This was an improved version of the M38 using a conventional system of range control in which the barrel was raised or lowered to achieve variation of the fall of shot. The same sight as that in the M38 was employed.

M40

The M40 retained the variable gas system to adjust the range and the accompanying fixed elevation. The bipod and the baseplate were made of simple sheet metal stampings. The bipod was unique in design with an unusual means of cross levelling in which the adjustable linkage varied the angle of the traversing gear axis relative to the elevating gear, by rotating the sleeve on the drop arm. The sight, like that of the M38, was a simple device with bubbles that levelled at 45 degrees and 75 degrees.

A three-barrel version was made but apparently only in limited numbers. In this the centre barrel had the usual spherical ball mounting fitting into the socket in the centre of the base plate and the other two were attached to it and linked in parallel. A lanyard-operated latch was situated over the muzzle and when it was pulled, all three bombs dropped together.

DATA **(M40)**
Calibre: 50mm
Total weight in firing position: 11.5kg
Total weight in travelling position: 12.25kg
Length of barrel incl. base cap: 788mm
Diameter of baseplate: 254mm
Maximum range at 45 degrees: 800 metres
Maximum range at 75 degrees: 130 metres
Total traverse: 5.5 degrees
Ammunition: HE

M41

This mortar dispensed with the usual bipod mount and shock absorber assembly and a supporting yoke, mounted on the baseplate, provided adjustment for elevation, traverse and cross level. Like the M38 and M40

Soviet 50mm mortar, model 1940

the mortar fired at 45 degrees or 75 degrees and had a gas pressure regulator. The gases resulting from the burning of the propellant were ducted away from the gas regulator through a pipe under the barrel. The sight was simplified.

DATA
Calibre: 50mm
Total weight firing: 10kg
Total weight travelling: 12kg
Length of bore: 564mm
Baseplate dimensions: 260 × 430mm
Maximum range: 800 metres
Total traverse: 12 degrees
Ammunition: HE
Manufacturer: State factories
Status: None of these mortars is now in service in Warsaw Pact countries. The M40, however, was used during the war in Vietnam and may possibly still be in service in that region

82mm M36 MORTAR

This was the first of the Soviet 82mm Mortars. It was very similar to the US 81mm Mortar M1 and the German 82mm was based on this design. The ammunition was conventional with a primary cartridge and six increments. Three different types of sight were used, the MP-1, the MP-82 optical sights and a sheet metal aiming circle clinometer.

DATA
Calibre: 82mm
Total firing weight: 57.3kg
Total length of barrel: 1288mm
Maximum range: 3,100 metres

Ammunition: HE and Smoke
Manufacturer: State factories
Status: Largely superseded by later models but probably still to be found outside Europe

The Soviet 82mm mortar, model 1936. This mortar is almost identical to the USA and German patterns.

82mm M37 MORTAR

This was a modification of the M36 having a circular baseplate. It may be distinguished by the cross levelling and connecting rod on the right leg rather than the left. However when using this as an identifying feature the position of the elevating handle should be noted. This should emerge from the gear case at the rear. If not the bipod gear will be on the left. The circular baseplate was a great success and although a rectangular plate has been used in the mountain divisions, it is rarely seen. The sight is the MPM 44.

DATA
Calibre: 82mm
Length of barrel: 1220mm
Weight: 56kg
Elevation – maximum: 85 degrees
           – minimum: 45 degrees
Top Traverse: 6 degrees
Rate of fire: 15-25 rounds/min
Bomb weight: 3.05kg
Muzzle velocity: 211 metres/sec
Maximum range: 3,000 metres
Minimum range: 100 metres
Detachment: 5
Manufacturer: State Factories
Status: Standard 82mm Mortar in the Warsaw Pact countries. Produced in Communist China as the Type 53

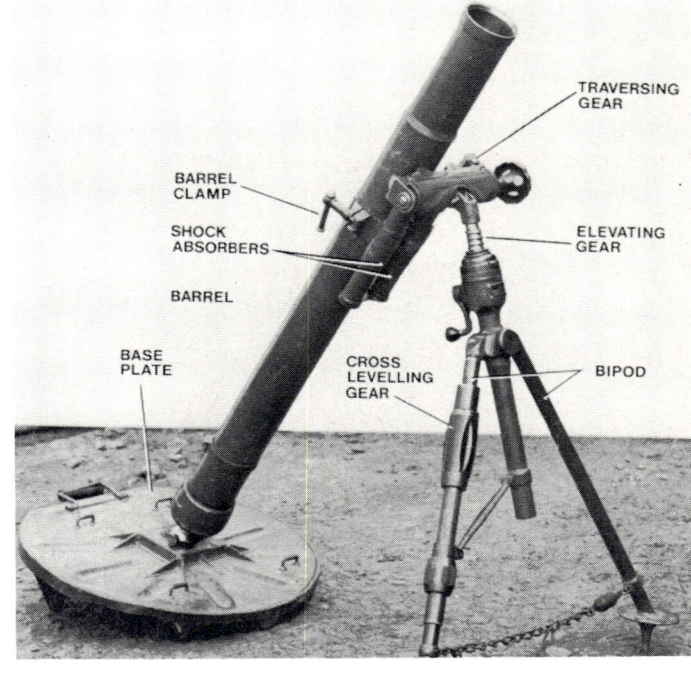

The M37 was restored to favour after the 1941-45 war. Apart from the muzzle safety device the 'new' M37 has the same general appearance

82mm M41 MORTAR

This was introduced to improve the performance and mobility of the M37 mortar. Instead of the conventional bipod and yoke, two short legs supported the long elevation column and the traversing gear. Cross levelling was accomplished in the same way as the M40 50mm mortar, with a linkage between the elevating shaft and the traversing screw. At the foot of each bipod leg was a stub axle to which a wheel could be fitted. When the mortar came out of action the bipod was folded back and clamped to the circular baseplate. The wheels were attached and the mortar was towed from the muzzle end by whatever type of transport was available – man, mule or motor.

DATA
Calibre: 82mm
Length of barrel: 1,220mm

Weight in firing position: 52kg
Weight in travelling position: 58kg
Elevation – maximum: 85 degrees
           – minimum: 45 degrees
Top traverse: 5 degrees
Rate of fire: 15-25 rounds/minute
Bomb weight: 3.05kg
Muzzle velocity: 211 metres/sec
Maximum range: 2,550 metres
Minimum range: 100 metres
Detachment: 5
Manufacturer: State Factories
Status: No longer in production. Still in service with some satellite countries and in North Korea. The M41 was discontinued largely because it was found to be less stable than the M37.

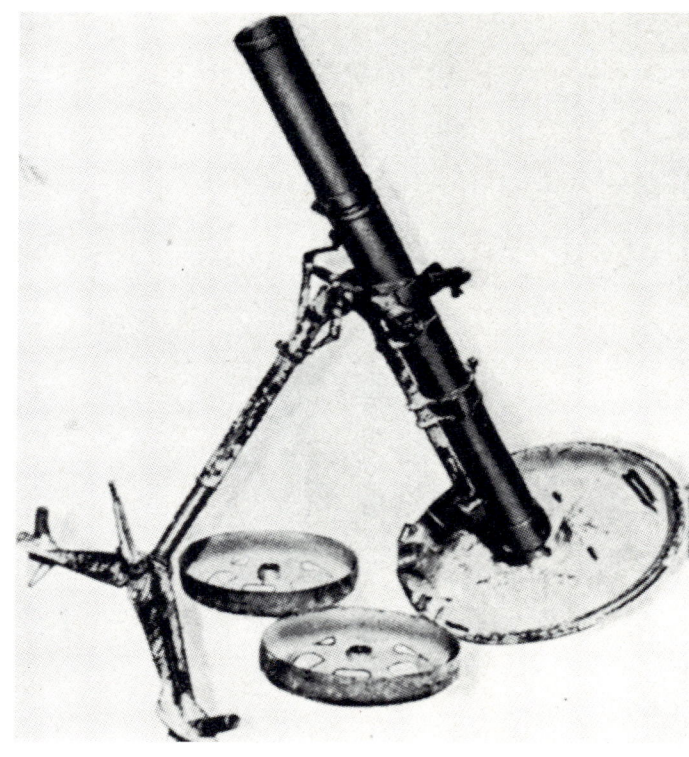

The M41, 82mm mortar, has an unconventional mount with short legs and a long elevation column. The wheels were removed before firing.

82mm M43 MORTAR

This mortar differed from the M41 in that the wheels remained attached to their stub axles and were not detachable before firing. The weight in the firing position was the same as that in the travel position and was 58kg. The M43 was also discontinued in favour of the M37.

The M43, 82mm mortar, retained its wheels in action

82mm 'NEW' M37 MORTAR

This is the current 82mm mortar. It is the same as the original M37 but has a lightened tripod and baseplate. The muzzle is fitted with a double loading stop which prevents the possibility of dropping a second bomb down before the first has cleared the muzzle.

The ammunition for the 82mm mortar has remained unchanged since its inception in 1936, however the Vietnamese used a bomb fitted with a chemical delay fuse. The firing pin was held back against the spring by a plastic arrestor. A corrosive solution attacked the plastic and when it was sufficiently weakened the firing pin drove forward into the cap and the filling was detonated. This was achieved by having the acid solution in a glass tube loaded into the detonator just before firing. When the detonator was tightened in its housing the glass tube was broken. The fuze was safe until impact.

Status: Soviet 82mm mortars of one type or another are used in Albania Bulgaria, China (produced in China as the Type 53), Cambodia, Congo, Cuba, Cyprus, Czechoslovakia, East Germany, Egypt, Ghana, Indonesia, Iraq, North Korea, Syria, Vietnam, Yugoslavia (it has also been made in Yugoslavia with a slightly different rectangular baseplate). The East Germans have developed a two wheeled carriage to carry the mortar and its ammunition.

A muzzle safety device is fitted to the "new" M37 to prevent double loading

107mm M38 MORTAR

This mortar was produced after the 120mm mortar and is a reduced size copy of that weapon designed for mountain use, and animal transport. The weapon is carried complete on a two wheeled trolley. It has now been replaced with the M-107 which is an improved version.

DATA
Calibre: 107mm
Length of barrel: 1,670mm
Weight in firing position: 170kg
Weight in travelling position: 340kg
Elevation Maximum: 80 degrees
Elevation Minimum: 45 degrees
Top traverse: 3 degrees
Rate of fire: 15 rounds/minute
Bomb weight:
HE Heavy: 9.0kg
HE Light: 7.9kg
Muzzle velocity:
HE Heavy: 302 metres/sec
HE Light: 263 metres/sec
Maximum range:
HE Heavy: 5,150 metres
HE Light: 6,300 metres
Minimum range:
HE Heavy: 800 metres
Detachment: 5
Manufacturer: State Factories
Status: No longer in production. Still in service with Mountain Divisions and in China, North Korea and Vietnam

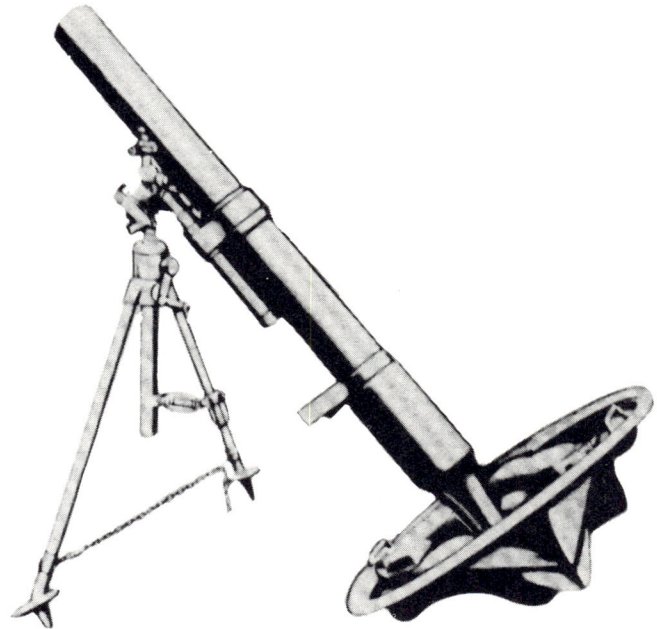

The 107mm mortar, M1938

120mm M38 MORTAR

The Russian 120mm Mortar occupied the same place in the Infantry Division as the 107mm in the Mountain Division. During World War II and afterwards the 120mm Mortar was found in the divisional artillery as well as in the separate non divisional artillery units. In recent years it has also found a place in the motorised rifle battalions of some divisions.

The M38 was a great deal more mobile than most mortars of that calibre. It was lifted bodily on a two wheeled transporter and towed behind any suitable vehicle. It can be broken down to three loads for animal pack transport. It can be fired directly by dropping the bomb down on a protruding firing pin, or alternatively, a trigger device can be employed.

The M38 is also fitted with the muzzle safety device

120mm mortar, M1938, in travelling order

120mm M43 MORTAR

Although the M38 was a very successful mortar and was copied by the German Army, it was modified into the M43. This differs in having longer shock absorber cylinders and retains both the very efficient base plate of stamped circular form and the two wheeled carriage. The M43 is produced in Communist China as the Type 55.

DATA
Calibre: 120mm
Length of barrel overall: 1,854mm
Weight in firing position: 274.8kg
Weight in travelling position: 500kg
Width in travelling position: 1,548mm
Height in travelling position: 1,206mm
Track: 1,210mm
Elevation: 80 degrees
Maximum/Minimum: 45 degrees
Top traverse: 8 degrees
Rate of fire: 12-15 rounds/min
Bomb weight: 15.4kg
Muzzle velocity: 272 metres/sec
Maximum range: 5,700 metres
Minimum range: 460 metres
Detachment: 6
Manufacturer: State Factories

120mm mortar, M1943

The M1943 in travelling order

Status: No longer in production. Soviet 120mm mortars are still used by the following countries:— Albania, China, Czechoslovakia, East Germany, Egypt, Iraq, North Korea, Romania, Soviet Union, Syria, Vietnam, Yemen and Yugoslavia. The Austrians have a mortar based on the M1943 called the 12cm Granatwerfer M-60

120mm mortar, M1943

160mm MORTARS

The Russian Army introduced the 160mm M1943 to provide the infantry divisions with a weapon producing a heavy weight of high explosive but not making undue demands on the hard pressed manufacturing resources. It was the heaviest mortar used by the Soviet Army during the Second World War. Because of the long barrel it had to be a breech loading weapon and the barrel pivoted for loading about trunnions located not far from the centre point. It was towed by the muzzle, using either an APC or a heavy lorry. After the war it was used by Poland, Romania and Bulgaria and deployed in troops of four mortars. It has now been replaced throughout the Warsaw Pact countries by the 160mm Mortar M-160. This is very similar in design and the method of breech loading has been preserved but it has a longer barrel and a greater range. It was originally used as a divisional mortar in all types of division but is now employed with the mountain divisions where its range, explosive shell capacity and high angle of fire are all very useful.

DATA	M43	M160
Calibre:	160mm	160mm
Length of barrel:	3030mm	4550mm
Weight in firing position:	1170kg	1300kg
Weight in travelling position:	1270kg	1470kg
Length in travelling position:	3985mm	4860mm
Width in travelling position:	1770mm	2030mm
Height in travelling position:	1414mm	1690mm
Track:	1750mm	1750mm
Elevation: Maximum:	80 degrees	80 degrees
** Minimum:**	45 degrees	50 degrees
Traverse:	25 degrees	24 degrees
Rate of fire:	3 rounds/min	2-3 rounds/min
Bomb weight:	40.8kg	41.5kg
Muzzle velocity:	245 metres/sec	343 metres/sec
Maximum range:	5150 metres	8040 metres
Minimum range:	630 metres	750 metres
Detachment:	7	7

The 160mm mortar, M1943

Detail of the trunnions about which the barrel is lowered for loading

The 160mm mortar, M160

Status: Neither model is now in production. The 160mm M43 is still used by Albania, China, Czechosovakia, East Germany, Egypt, North Korea, Syria and Vietnam. The 160mm M160 is still used by China, Egypt and Syria

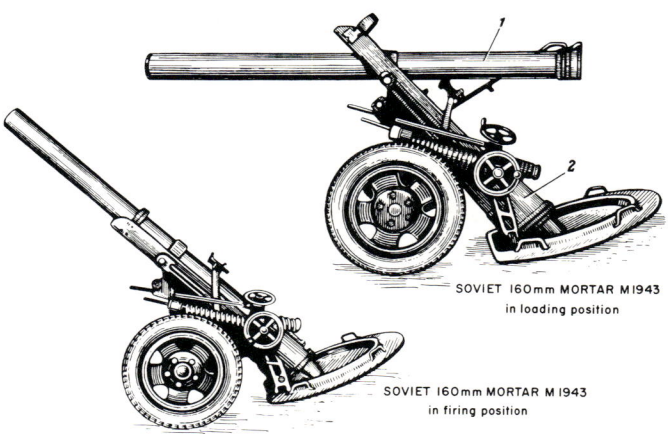

SOVIET 160mm MORTAR M1943
in loading position

SOVIET 160mm MORTAR M1943
in firing position

The 160mm mortar, M1943, in the loading and firing positions

240mm MORTAR M-240

This is the largest mortar employed in the Soviet Army. It was first seen when it appeared in the 7th November Parade, 1953, in Moscow together with the M160 Mortar. It functions in the same way as the 160mm mortar and is breech loaded in a similar fashion. It is towed by the muzzle but can be distinguished from the M160 by its much larger baseplate, the firing platform under the barrel, the vertical cylinders on either side of the barrel just above the axle, and the collar around the tube in which the trunnions are located.

DATA
Calibre: 240mm
Length of barrel: 5340mm
Weight in firing position: 3610kg
Length in travelling position: 6510mm
Width in travelling position: 2490mm
Height in travelling position: 2210mm
Elevation
Maximum: 65 degrees
Minimum: 45 degrees
Traverse: 18 degrees
Rate of fire: 1 round/minute

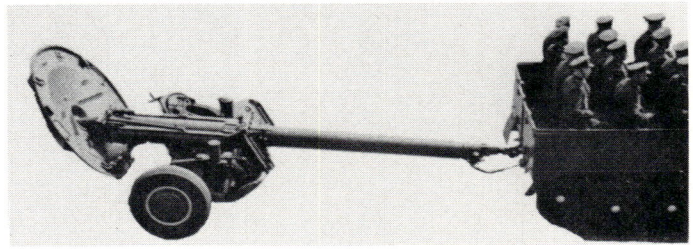

240mm mortar, M240

Bomb weight: 100kg
Muzzle velocity: 362 metres/sec
Maximum range: 9700 metres
Detachment: 9
Manufacturer: State Factories
Status: No longer produced. In service in Bulgaria, China, Romania and USSR

MORTAR AMMUNITION
82mm Fragmentation Projectile, Model 0-832

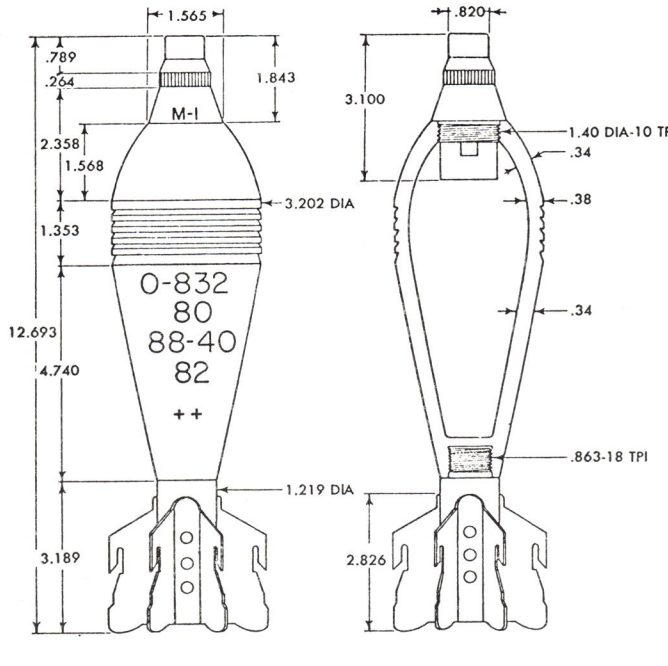

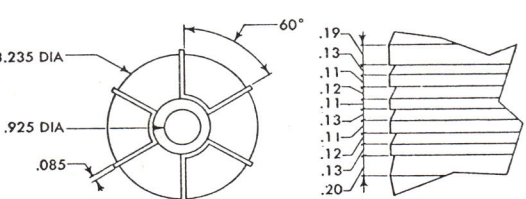

ALL DIMENSIONS IN INCHES

The Russian 82mm fragmentation projectile, Model 0-832

DATA
Calibre: 82mm
Identification: 0-832
Type: Fragmentation
Weight (fuzed): 3.4kg
Bursting charge: 0.4kg Schneiderite
Fuze: Model M1 point detonating
Known using weapon: Mortar M1937 (1942-1943 version)
Remarks: Also uses Models M-2, M-3, M-4, MP-82, and MP point detonating fuzes.

82mm Fragmentation Projectile Model 0-832D

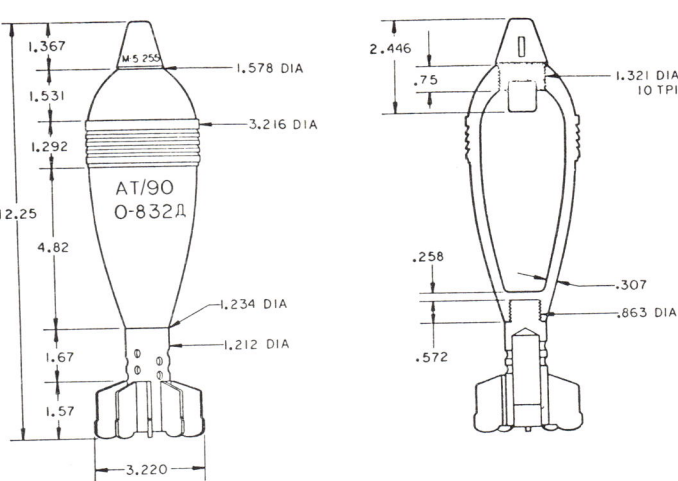

The Russian 82mm fragmentation projectile, Model 0-832D

DATA
Calibre: 82mm
Identification: 0-832D
Type: Fragmentation
Weight (fuzed): 3.1kg
Bursting charge: 0.41kg TNT/amatol
Fuze: Model M-5 point detonating
Known using weapon: Mortar M1937 (1942-1943 version)
Remarks: Also uses Models M-1, M-2, M-3, M-4, MP-82, and M-6 point detonating fuses.

82mm Fragmentation Projectile Model 0-832 DU

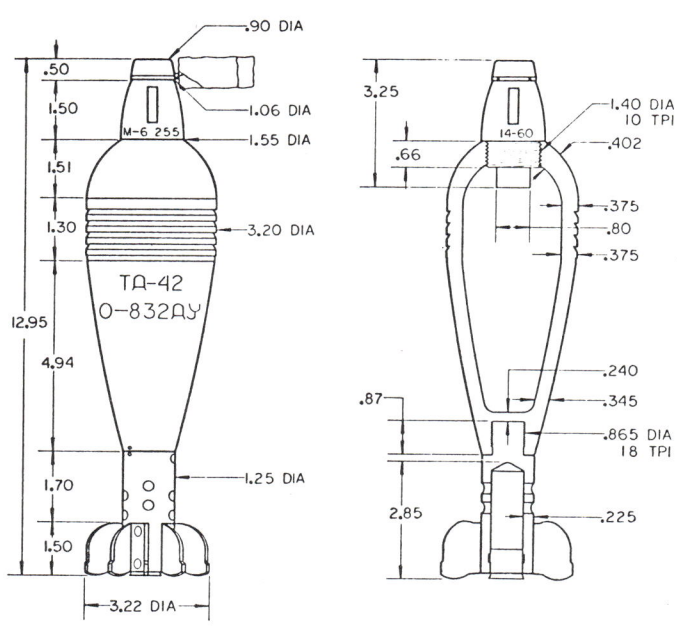

Russian 82mm fragmentation projectile, Model 0-832DU

DATA
Calibre: 82mm
Identification: 0-832 DU
Type: Fragmentation
Weight (fuzed): 3.2kg
Bursting charge: 0.435kg TNT/dinitronapthaline
Fuze: Model M-6 point detonating
Known using weapon: Mortar M1937 (1942-1943 version)
Remarks: Also uses Models M-1, M-2, M-3, M-4, M-5, and MP-82 fuzes

107mm Fragmentation – HE Projectile Model OF-841

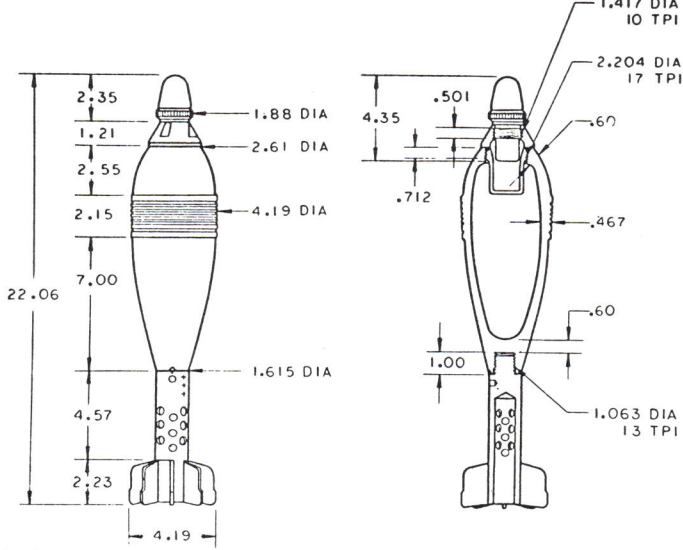

Russian 107mm fragmentation – HE projectile, Model OF-841A

DATA
Calibre: 107mm
Identification: OF-841
Type: Fragmenting – HE
Weight (fuzed): 7.9kg
Bursting charge: 2.1kg TNT/Schneiderite
Fuze: Model GVMZ point detonating
Known using weapon: Mountain-pack regimental mortar M1938
Remarks: Also uses Model GVMZ-1 point detonating fuze

107mm Fragmentation – HE Projectile, Model OF-841A
DATA
Calibre: 107mm
Identification: OF-841
Type: Fragmenting – HE
Weight (fuzed): 9.1kg
Bursting charge: 1.0kg TNT/amatol
Fuze: GVMZ-7 point detonating
Known using weapon: Mountain-pack regimental mortar M1938
Remarks: Also uses Models GVMZ and GVMZ-1 point detonating fuzes.
Fuze is shown with shipping cap installed

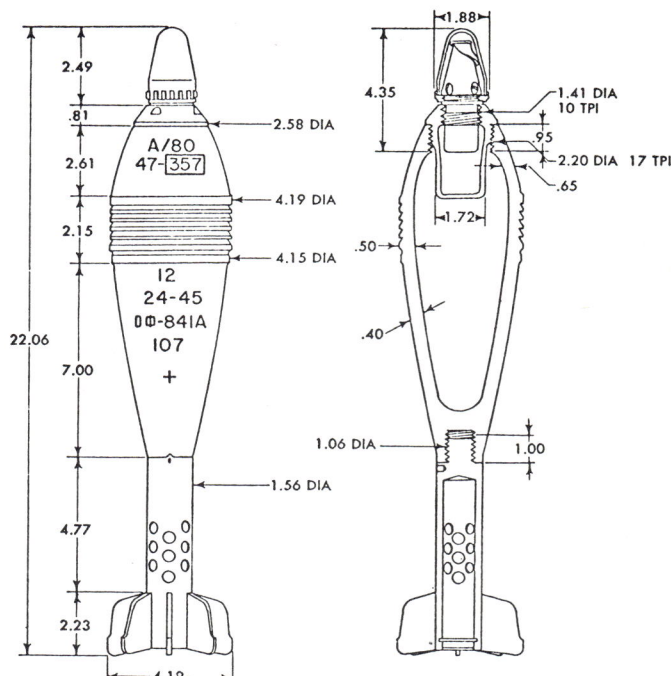

Russian 107mm fragmentation – HE projectile, Model OF-841

120mm HE Projectile, Model F-843

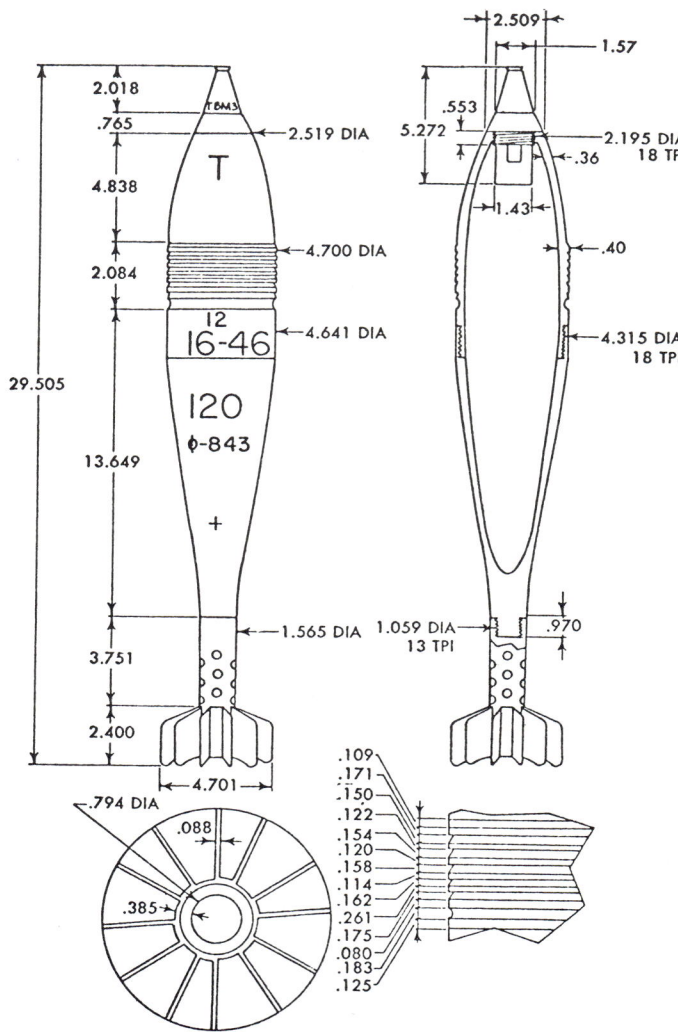

Russian 120mm fragmentation – HE projectile, Model OF-843

DATA
Calibre: 120mm
Identification: F-843
Type: HE
Weight (fuzed): 16.4kg
Bursting charge: 3.9kg TNT
Fuze: Model GVMZ point detonating
Known using weapons: Regimental mortars M1938 and M1943
Remarks: Also uses Model M-1 point detonating fuze

120mm Fragmentation – HE Projectile, Model OF-843

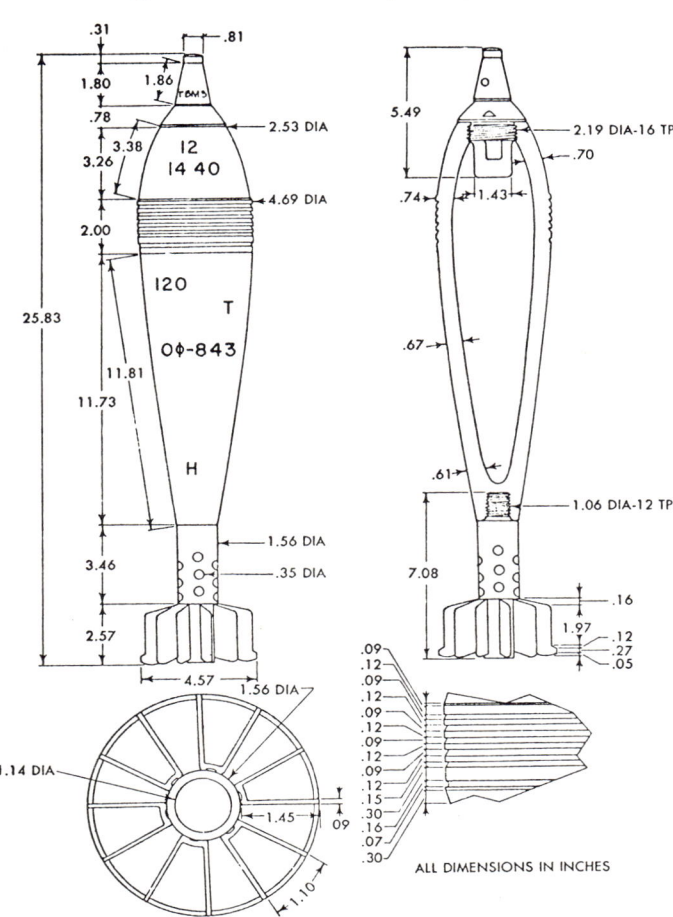

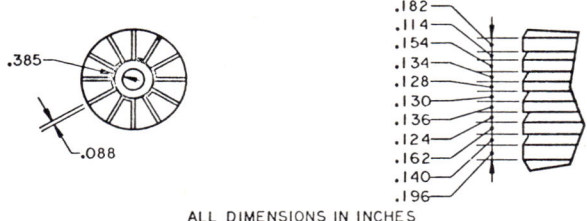

ALL DIMENSIONS IN INCHES

Russian 120mm fragmentation – HE projectile, Model OF-843A

DATA
Calibre: 120mm
Identification: OF-843A
Type: Fragmenting – HE
Weight (fuzed): 16kg
Bursting charge: 1.58kg amatol 80/20
Fuze: Model GVMZ-1 point detonating
Known using weapons: Regimental mortars M1938 and M1943
Remarks: Also uses Model M-4 point detonating fuze. Illustrated with nose plug instead of fuze.

160mm HE Projectile, Model F-852

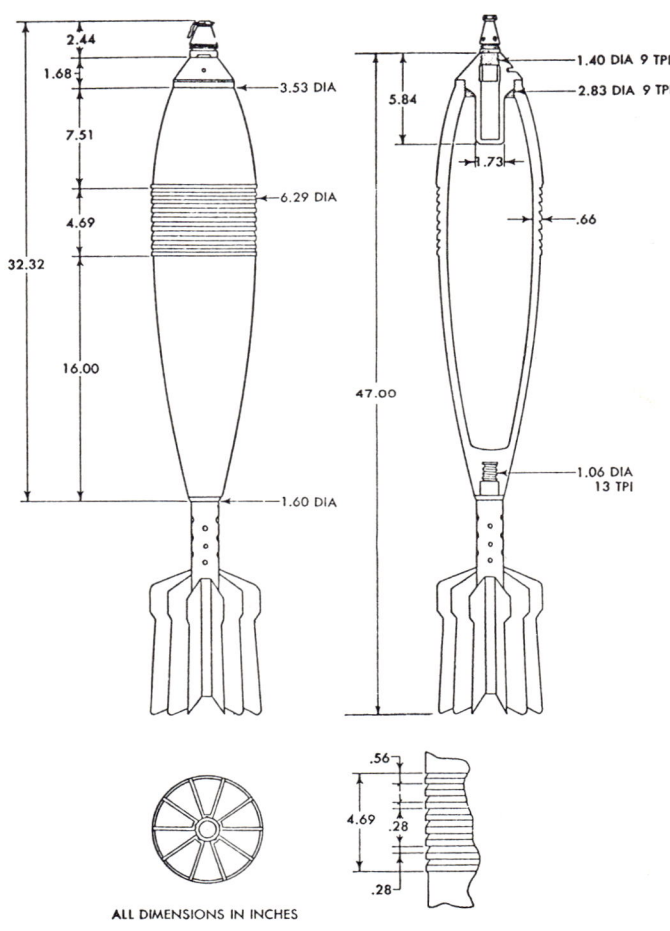

ALL DIMENSIONS IN INCHES

Russian 160mm HE projectile, Model F-852

DATA
Calibre: 160mm
Identification: F-852
Type: HE
Weight: 40kg
Bursting charge: 7.38kg TNT
Fuze: Model GVMZ-7 point detonating
Known using weapon: Mortar M1943

Soviet 120mm fragmentation – HE projectile, Model OF-843

DATA
Calibre: 120mm
Identification: OF-843
Type: Fragmenting – HE
Weight (fuzed): 16kg
Bursting charge: 2.675kg TNT
Fuze: Model GVMZ point detonating
Known using weapons: Regimental mortars M1938 and M1943
Remarks: Also uses Models M-1 and M-4 point detonating fuzes

120mm Fragmentation – HE Projectile, Model OF-843A

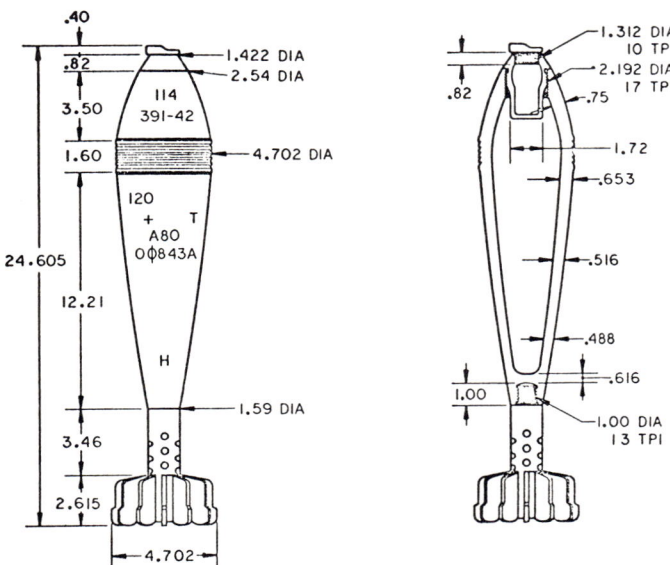

UNITED KINGDOM

ML 2 INCH MORTAR

The Muzzle Loading 2 Inch Mortar was introduced into the British Army before the Second World War and is still in service. It is hoped that it will be replaced by the new 51mm Mortar in the near future.

Several different models have been in service. The current model in the British Army is the Mark 8* which is used by infantry and consists of a barrel 543mm long, a breech piece and a spade. The earlier and now obsolete Mk 7* and 8 airborne models had a shorter barrel 356mm long and the earlier and also obsolete model intended for use with the Universal Carrier had a rectangular baseplate.

The barrel is a steel tube with a bore 51.2mm, in diameter. The breech piece closes the rear end and contains the firing mechanism which is operated by a firing lever. It is attached to the rear end of the barrel by screw threads and secured by a barrel catch. The spade has a bracket attached to the breech piece and the spade itself is shaped like an inverted trough and is at right angles to the breech piece.

The mortars used with the universal carrier had elevating and traversing clamps and used a sight (Sight No 4 Mark 1). This had a range scale graduated in the upper and lower registers from zero to 525 yards. The infantry and airborne mortars were attached directly to their base spades and had no sights. A white line was painted down the length of the barrel to allow it to be aligned on the target and adjustment of fire was carried out by observation of burst.

The ammunition for the mortar is filled with high explosive or produces smoke or illumination. The Mark 1 bomb was filled TNT or amatol 50/50. It

The 2 inch mortar Mk 7. This was used in the Universal Carrier

had a zinc alloy or steel tail. The Mark 2 bomb carried smoke compositon and had either a zinc alloy or steel tail. It had a 3.24g cartridge. If an aluminium alloy tail was fitted a 3.05g cartridge was used. The Mark 2 bomb had a variety of fillings apart from smoke. There were single stars, red or green and multi stars red, green or white. There was also an illuminating bomb fitted with a parachute.

The fuze used is the Fuze, Percussion Direct Action No 161 Mark 1. This fuze has a safety pin which must be withdrawn before firing. There is a spring loaded detent which prevents a ball from moving outwards. The ball fits into a groove in the striker and whilst it is in place the striker cannot move. On firing, the detent sets back and the ball is able to travel outwards and downwards. This allows the striker to move forward under its spring and it releases the shutter which is rotated by its own spring to bring the detonator immediately below the point of the striker. On impact the cap is crushed in and forces the striker point onto the detonator; the resulting detonating wave is amplified and sets off the main filling. The fuzes 151 and 151A used in the early life of the mortar had no safety pin, and became obsolescent.

The 2 inch mortar was used by the British Army and the troops of the Commonwealth throughout the Second World War. Its maximum range of 525 yards and the small capacity of the HE bomb led to the discontinuance of the HE round at the end of the war but the smoke and illuminating rounds were retained. The black-painted illuminating round was issued to illuminate ground and targets in front of the section position and particularly it was used to illuminate targets for the anti-tank weapon of the time – the PIAT. The bomb was extremely susceptible to wind effects and could well drift on its parachute to illuminate the user and leave the enemy hidden in the dark. The smoke bomb has a green body with a red ring round it. When it is fired, a delay pellet prevents smoke emission for about five seconds. The bomb produces smoke which will screen for about two minutes.

In the 1960s the HE bomb was re-introduced. The mortar and its ammunition have long been due for replacement.

2 inch mortar Mk 8. This is used by the infantry*

The 2 inch mortar Mk 8, in action

DATA (Mk 7** and 8*)
Barrel:
Dimensions:
Diameter of bore: 51.2mm
Length: Muzzle to front of firing-hole bush: 509mm
        With breech piece: 669mm
        Without breech piece: 543mm
Weight:
With breech piece: 4.14kg
Without breech piece: 2.3kg
Base Plate:
        Depth: 22mm
        Length: 165mm
        Width: 165mm
        Weight: 682g
Firing mechanism: Percussion
Ammunition:
Bombs, Mark 1:
Weight of HE bomb: with zinc alloy tail: 1,022g
            with steel tail: 994g
Filling: Amatol 50/50, TNT or baratol 20/80
Bombs, Mark 2:
Smoke: 909g
Illuminating with parachute: 965g
Signal multi-star (with cartridge)
Green, red, red and green: 511g
White: 909g
Signal single star (with cartridge):
Green: 539g
Red: 511g

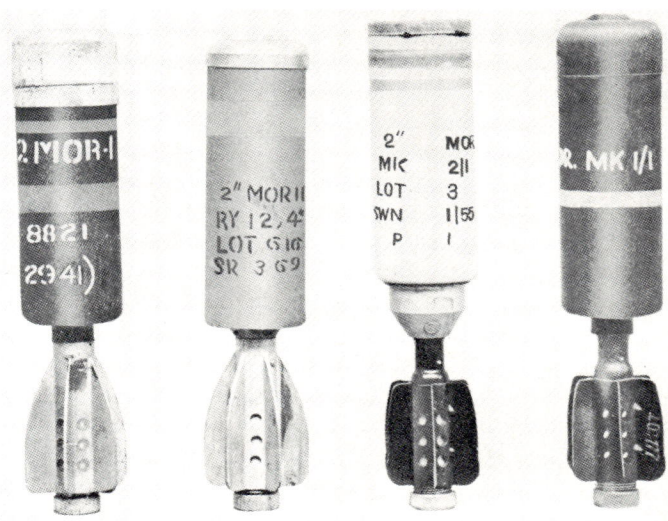

ML, 2 inch mortar bombs

Cartridge: Ballistite 3.05, 3.24 or, 3.56g (3.56g obsolescent)
Fuzes used (Percussion D.A.): Nos 161, 151A or 151 (Nos 151 and 151A obsolescent)
Manufacturer: Royal Ordnance Factories
Status: In service but obsolescent

51mm MORTAR

This mortar has been developed to replace the 2in Mortar which has rendered such sterling service over so many years. It is hoped that it may come into service soon. The mortar has been designed by the Royal Armament Research and Development Establishment (RARDE) at Fort Halstead.

The 51mm Mortar has been designed as a simple weapon which can be operated by one man. The barrel is a steel tube of orthodox design, bell mouthed to increase strength at the muzzle and to facilitate loading. At the lower end is the breech piece. This contains the firing mechanism which is, in principle, the same as the 2in mortar but differs considerably in detail. It is cocked by hand, the firing mechanism is totally water-proofed and the firing button on the top is enclosed in a rubber boot. The baseplate is of steel and is of unusual shape. This is apparently the result of trials carried out on a number of designs and materials. The shape of the road grader was also considered in these studies.

There is a monopod held under the barrel by a jubilee clip. This has a telescoping leg which can be rotated up into the main cylinder of the monopod to achieve the required length. If the mortar is to be used for low angle fire, the monopod can be folded up to lie along the underside of the barrel and employed as a hand grip by the firer.

The sight is held to the barrel by a hose clip in the same way as the bipod. It allows fire in both high angle or low angle and allows for windage. A simple bubble system is used in conjunction with direct reading scales. A tritium source is incorporated to allow the use of the sight by night as well as by day.

The most interesting part of the design is probably the means adopted to

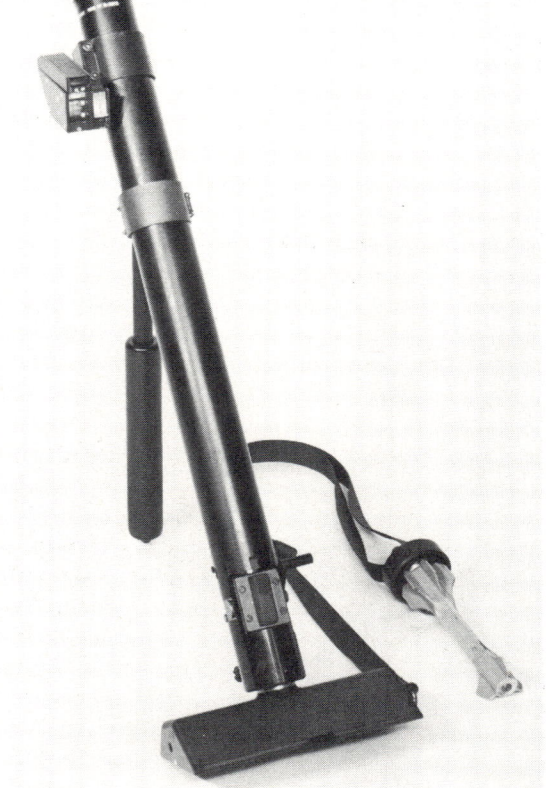

The RARDE designed 51mm mortar

Sight unit of the 51mm mortar

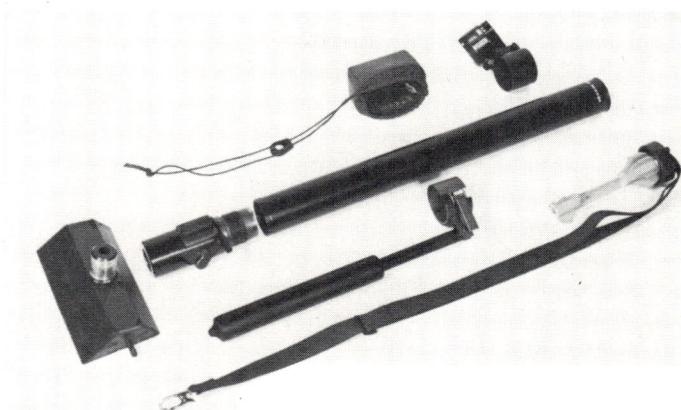

51mm mortar broken down into its major components

achieve the minimum range of 200 metres. This is a short range insert which is dropped into the barrel from the muzzle. It is a rod with a long firing pin along its longitudinal axis. The lower end of the firing pin rests on the firing pin in the breech piece and is driven forward when the mortar is fired. Thus the bomb does not reach the bottom of the tube and the short range is achieved by increasing the chamber volume and so reducing the working chamber pressure: at the same time there is a reduction in shot travel.

The bomb is of advanced design and the high explosive body is pre-notched to produce fragments of optimum size. The smoke and illuminating bombs have also been proved.

DATA
Barrel: calibre: 51.25mm
weight: 1.5kg
length overall: 700mm
outside diameter: 55mm
Breech piece assembly: weight: .99kg
length: 155mm
Sight unit weight: .36kg
Monopod support weight: .48kg
overall length folded: 207mm
extended: 420mm
Baseplate weight: .76kg
HE Bomb L1A1:
Weight: .79kg
Length: 272mm
Maximum muzzle velocity: 106m/s
Maximum range: 800m
Minimum range: 150m
50% zone for maximum range (approx): 25m
Filling: 60/40 RDX/TNT
Fuze: L98E2 point detonating, delayed arming fuze is said to be under development
Smoke Bomb L1A1: This has the same body as the HE round but without the fragmentation coil. Filling is Hexachlorethane and smoke duration is 120 seconds.
Illuminating L1A3: Same body as the smoke bomb. Burst height at 800m is 250m, rate of descent 5 metres per second. Duration of burning about 30 seconds. Output 25,000 candle power peaking to 40,000 for 12 seconds.
Practice Bomb: This can have either an inert filler or a small smoke charge with fixed time delay.
Manufacturer: Royal Ordnance Factories
Status: Expected to enter service in the near future

Sectioned view of the HE bomb

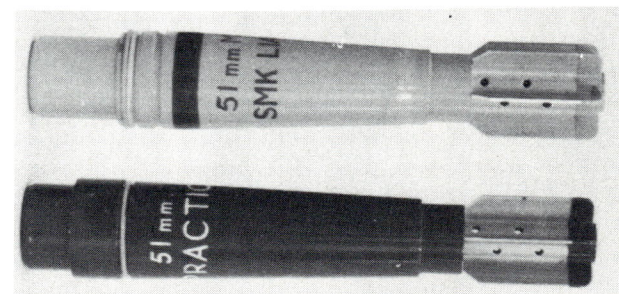
The practice bomb and the smoke L1A1 bomb

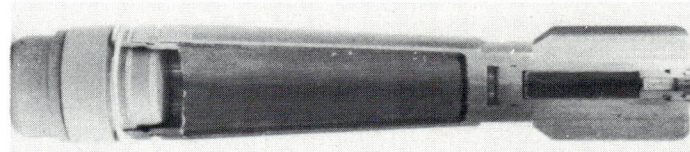
Sectioned view of the smoke bomb

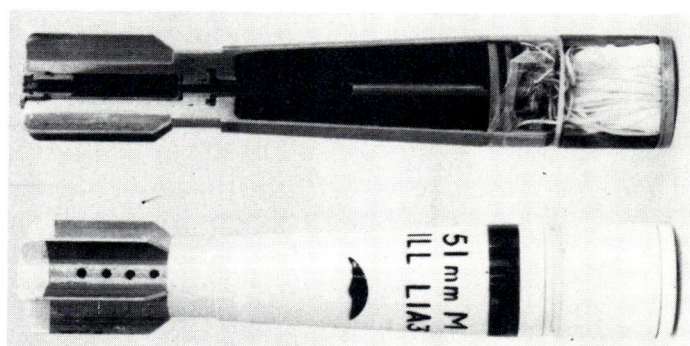
The illuminating bomb L1A3 and a sectioned view

HE L1A1 bomb

3in MORTAR

The Muzzle Loading 3 Inch mortar was introduced into British Service in 1936. It has now been replaced by the 81mm Mortar in the British Army but remains in service in many other countries.

The Mark 1 barrel, initially introduced with the equipment, was reduced in diameter at the breech end and screw threaded over the reduced diameter to take the breech piece and striker stud. The Mark 1A barrel and the Mark 2 barrel were modified in the form of the breech piece; this had two flats to facilitate assembly and stripping. The striker stud was long and rounded. The Mark 4 barrel was designed to take a heavier charge. It was marked with a 2 inch (51mm) black band with the figure 3 in red on the band, and it had a clinometer plane.

The Mark 5 barrel was lighter and stronger than its predecessors. The full diameter of the tube was screw threaded to take the breech piece. The striker stud was modified to allow the firing of German and Italian 81mm bombs during the war.

When first issued, the mortar had a maximum elevation of 80 degrees giving a range of 275 yards (250 metres) with the lowest charge. At 45 degrees it had a range of 1,600 yards (1,450 metres) with the top charge and 865 yards (800 metres) with the bottom charge. The baseplate progressed from the No 1 to the No 6 and became progressively lighter as the years passed. The first service mounting was the Mark 3. The last was the Mark 5.

The mortar was originally issued with the Mark 1 sight which was graduated from 0 to 180 degrees right and left in multiples of ten degrees. The Mark 2 sight had a range scale drum instead of the range scale strip, and the lensatic sight had a vertical slot in lieu of a triangular aperture.

PERFORMANCE
In its final form the weights of the equipment were: Mark 5 barrel 41lb (18.6kg), No. 6 base plate 36lb (16.3kg), Mark 5 bipod mounting 48lb (21.8kg). The ranges attainable were:
Charge I 500yds to 1,500yds (457-1,372 metres)
Charge II 950yds to 2,800yds (869-2,560 metres)

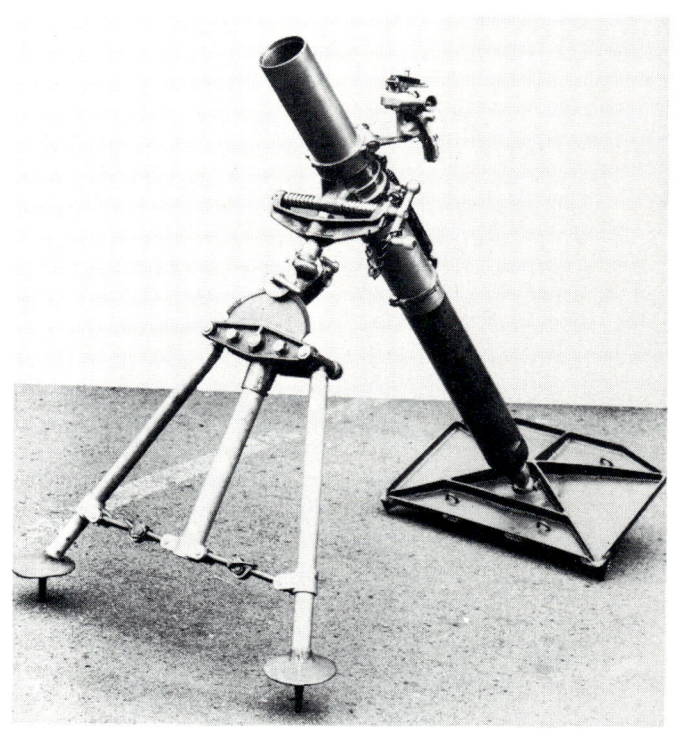
The early 3 inch muzzle loading mortar. This comprises: Ordnance, ML, 3 inch mortar, Mk 2; Mounting, 3 inch mortar, Mk 3; Plate, Base, 3 inch mortar, No. 1; Mk 1 sight

The beaten zones at the target were:
Charge I 300yds long by 60yds wide (274 × 55 metres)
Charge II 600yds long by 100yds wide (549 × 91 metres)
The accepted rates of fire were:
Rapid 12-15 rounds a minute
Normal ·7-10 rounds a minute
Slow 3-5 rounds a minute
Time of flight for charge I was about 20 seconds. For charge II it was 30 seconds.

The mortar fired high explosive and white phosphorus smoke bombs. In each case two charges were available. Charge I consisted of the primary cartridge and three secondaries and Charge II consisted of the primary cartridge and six secondaries. The final version of the HE Bomb was the Mark 6, and the last WP was the Mark 11.

Various other bombs were used with the 3 inch mortar during the 1939-45 war and shortly afterwards. These were:
Bomb ML Screening Smoke, Base Ejection, 3 inch Mortar, 10lb (4.535kg). This had the No 390 time fuze, which was common for all the Base Ejection bombs.
Bomb ML, Coloured Smoke, Base Ejection, 3 inch Mortar, 10lb.
Bomb ML, Flare, T.R. Base Ejection, 3 inch Mortar, 10lb.
Bomb ML, Star, 3 inch Mortar, 10lb with Parachute.
The use of white phosphorus filling enabled both the high explosive and the smoke bombs to use Fuze Direct Action No 162 Mark 1/1. This had considerable advantage over the previous practice of using the No 390 time fuze for base ejection smoke rounds.

DATA (Mark 5 except where specified)
MORTAR:
Barrel:
Calibre: 81.48mm
Length:
Muzzle to front of striker stud: 1,150mm
With breech piece: 1,266mm
Without breech piece: 1,162mm
Total weight: 20kg (Mk 4 22.2kg)
Mounting:
Depth over traversing gear: 206mm (Mk 4 165mm)
Length, with sight removed and cradle swung over: 914mm (Mk 4 978mm)
Weight including cradle: 20.5kg
Traverse, angle of left and right: 5.5 degrees
Means of firing: Striker stud
Base Plate: No. 5; (Mk 4 has No. 6)
Depth: 203mm
Length: 521mm
Width: 368mm
Weight: 19.5kg (Mk 4 15.54kg)
Range: 450-2,560 metres (see text for details)

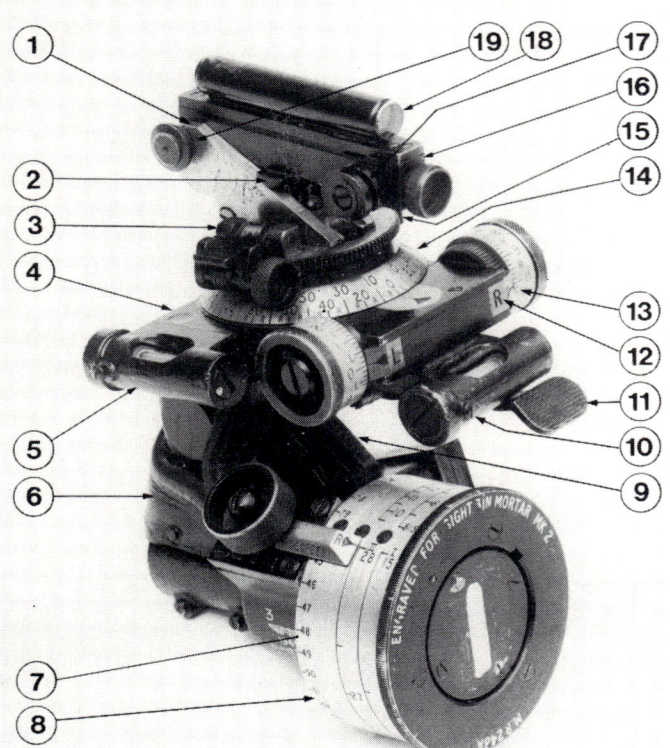

Mk 2 3in mortar sight. Note the range drum. The maximum range had reached 2,950 with the Mk 6 bomb. (1) Sight supporting bracket; (2) Sight carrier nut; (3) Latch; (4) Azimuth gear bracket; (5) Longitudinal bubble; (6) Azimuth gear elevating arm; (7) Range scale reader; (8) Range scale drum; (9) Tangent elevation gear bracket; (10) Cross level bubble; (11) Azimuth gear quick release latch; (12) Micrometer drum reader; (13) Micrometer drum; (14) Azimuth gear dial; (15) Worm wheel carrier; (16) Sight carrier; (17) Rear sight; (18) No. 2 Lensatic sight; (19) Foresight

The "Ordnance 3 in Mortar" with Mk 5 barrel, No. 6 baseplate and Mk 5 bipod

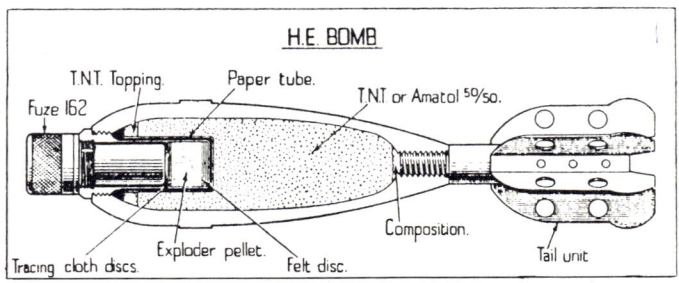

The Mk 4 bomb, HE. This contains either 270g or 80/20 Amatol or 540g of TNT, or Amatol 50/50

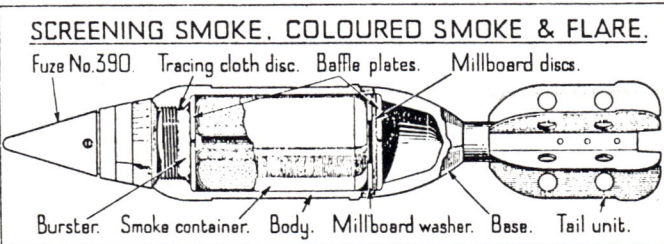

The Mk 1 bomb, screening, smoke

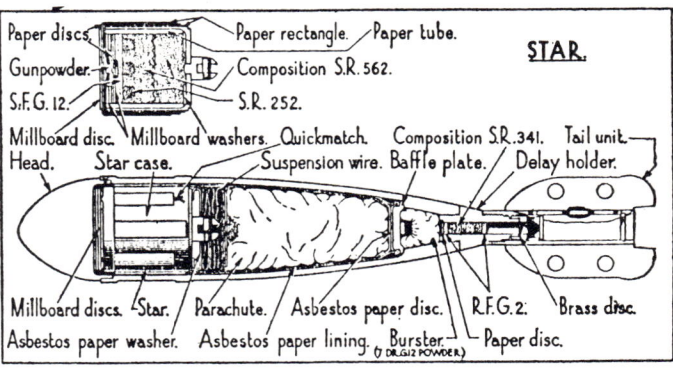

The star bomb

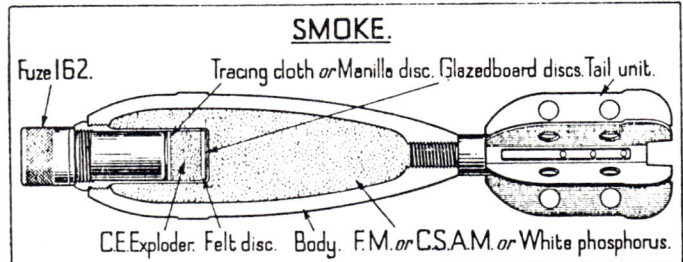

The Mk 1 bomb with parachute

3in mortar and detachment

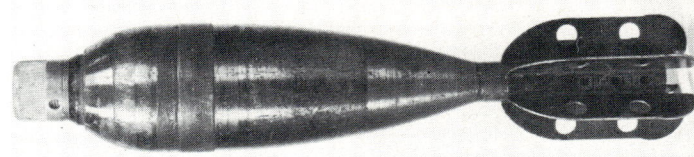

HE bomb

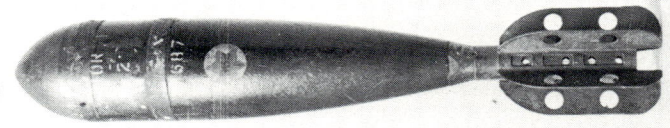

Bomb, ML, 3in mortar, star

Rate of fire: Up to 15 rounds/min (see text for details)
AMMUNITION:
High explosive Mk 4:
Filled 80/20 amatol (Type 42):
Maximum weight (complete, approx): 4.42kg No. 3 tail; 4.51kg No. 6 or No. 8 tail
Minimum weight (complete, approx): 4.31kg No. 3 tail; 4.37kg No. 6 or No. 8 tail
Filled 80/20 amatol (Type 43)
Maximum weight (complete, approx): 4.51kg No. 3 tail; 4.59kg No. 6 tail; 4.56kg No. 8 tail
Minimum weight (complete, approx): 4.39kg No. 3 tail; 4.48kg No. 6 tail; 4.45kg No. 8 tail
Filled TNT or 50/50 amatol

Maximum weight (complete, approx): 4.48kg No. 3 tail; 4.56kg No. 6 or No. 8 tail
Minimum weight (complete, approx): 4.37kg No. 3 tail; 4.45kg No. 6 tail; 4.42kg No. 8 tail

Other bombs:
In addition to the HE bombs there are smoke, screening smoke, coloured smoke, flare, star, practice, inert and drill bombs. Smoke bomb fillings are white phosphorus (various marks) titanium tetrachloride (FM) or chlorsulphonic acid/sulphur trioxide (CSAM)
Manufacturer: Royal Ordnance Factories
Status: No longer in production. In service in Bangladesh, Burma, Cameroon, Egypt, India, Indonesia, Malaysia, Nigeria, Oman, Pakistan, Saudi Arabia, Sri Lanka and Yemen.

MORTAR, ML 81mm L16

The 81mm Mortar has been a great success. It has greatly extended the infantry's ability to produce their own support by providing both an increased range over the 3in mortar and a bomb with an increased lethality. It has been shown to be both more accurate and more consistent than its predecessor with the added advantage to the user of being lighter and more easily handled.

The 81mm Mortar has been a great success. It has greatly extended the infantry ability to produce their own support by providing both an increased range over the 3in mortar and a bomb with an increased lethality. It has been shown to be both more accurate and more consistent than its predecessor with the added advantage to the user of being lighter and more easily handled.

It is normally deployed as part of a section used conventionally in a prepared position on the ground. It has also been developed to be fired from the FV 432 which greatly increases its immediate mobility and enables speedy movement to another site at the conclusion of an engagement. It can be carried in a Land Rover and when necessary it can be broken down into three loads of 25, 25, and 26lbs (11, 11 and 12kg approx.) which can be carried by the mortar section.

BARREL

To enable the mortar to fire bombs with the hot propellants used by some NATO countries, a barrel slightly heavier than that originally specified was adopted. Firing the British bomb, the mortar can fire 15 rounds a minute for 15 minutes, at the end of which the barrel temperature has reached an equilibrium value of 1,000°F. This is believed to be a considerably better performance than can be obtained from any other mortar of this calibre. It can be argued that this is a performance that will never be required under the conditions of mobile warfare envisaged in the future. But since the predictions of the experts have a disquieting habit of being wrong, it could be that in the future, as in the past, the ability of a mortar to produce a large volume of fire in a short space of time, will be of great importance.

The barrel is made up from a forged steel tube which has been reduced in diameter at the bottom and to save weight it has been screw threaded internally for the insertion of a breech plug. The lower half of the barrel has been finned to increase the surface area available for heat dissipation, and the top half of the barrel has been left plain. There is a collar at the mouth of the barrel to strengthen the section there and a small internal taper is provided to assist in loading the bomb.

BREECH PLUG

This fits into the barrel at one end and has a ball shape to fit into the socket of the baseplate. It carries a longitudinal hole screw threaded to take the firing pin.

MOUNTING

This is of unusual shape and has been referred to as a 'K' mount. The shape was adopted because with the elevating screw incorporated in one of the legs there is a significant weight saving and no loss of function. All the screw threads associated with elevation and traverse of the mortar have been enclosed and this reduces wear and increases life.

The 81mm mortar carried by its detachment

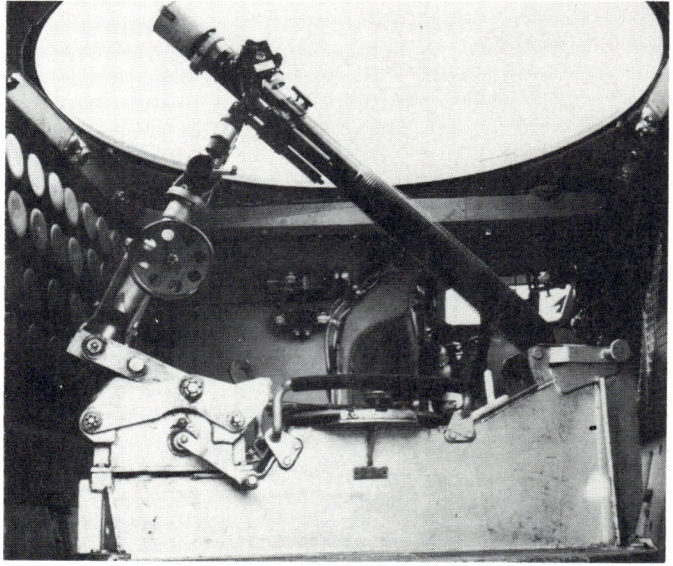

The 81mm mortar mounted in FV 432

ML 81mm mortar

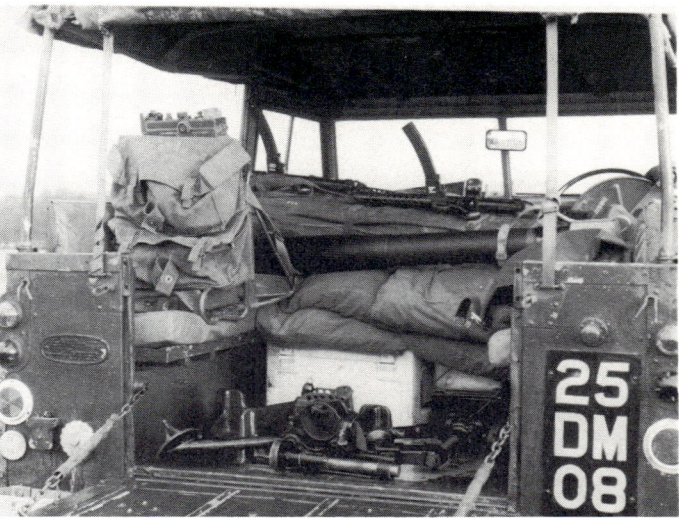

The 81mm mortar in the Land Rover

Soldiers of the 1st. Bn., the Royal Regiment of Wales, using the 81mm mortar

BASE PLATE

This is of Canadian design and is of forged aluminium. The design was produced by the Canadian Armament Research and Design Establishment. It is light and handles easily and is strong enough for the equipment. It produces an adequate flotation area and the design of the web prevents any tendency for the plate to slip sideways. The base plate was originally designed to have replaceable sockets – one to take the RARDE barrel and the other to take the US 81mm barrel. In both designs the circular base plate allowed all round traverse without need to disturb the plate.

SIGHT

This is the Canadian C2 sight. It fits not only the mortar but also the General Purpose Machine Gun for use in the sustained fire role. It allows either direct laying or indirect laying using a 45 degree angled telescope of some 1.7 magnification. In the near future the sight will be illuminated for night use with a tritium source providing a beta light.

AMMUNITION

The mortar has a high explosive round, the L15A3, fitted with Fuze No. 162. It was planned initially to develop a VT fuze but the various economy cuts that have been introduced since the mortar was first projected have eliminated these. The US and Norwegian Raufoss VT fuzes have been studied, and the virtues of such a fuze and the increased anti-personnel efficiency that they bring are well appreciated, but the cost is likely to prevent significant advance in the near future.

The standard HE bomb is of a highly streamlined shape and has been

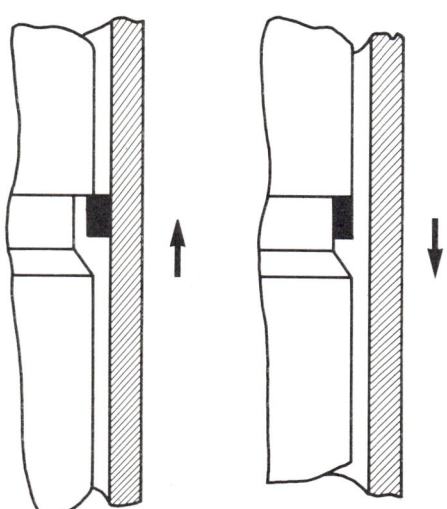

The sealing ring is driven out to close the windage gap when the pressure is developed

designed to produce the maximum number of fragments of the optimum size, which is considered to be 10-50 grains (0.6-3.2g). A study of cast iron, forged steel, and spheroidal graphite cast iron, showed the third to be the best material. The 81mm bomb has also gained in velocity and consistency from the incorporation of a sealing ring. This allows adequate windage as the bomb drops down the tube but the pressure produced by the burning propellant forces the macrolan ring outwards against the interior wall of the mortar tube and so prevents gas leakage. The ring also centres the bomb to prevent the yaw at the muzzle associated with conventional mortars and which leads to both inaccuracy and inconsistency. The ring also, by preventing the escape of hot gas past the bomb in the bore, reduces the barrel temperature and allows more bombs to be fired at the selected rate.

The white phosphorus smoke bomb has been highly successful. It has the same weight and shape as the HE bomb and so eliminates the need for false ranges to be set for smoke.

The illuminating bomb has become more important in recent years and provides the infantry with their best source of white light for the night engagement of enemy troops and armour. The Hotchkiss-Brandt 81mm Illuminating Bomb has been used but it is hoped that there will be a British illuminating bomb in service soon. The practice bomb is the L27A1. It has a maximum range of 80 metres when an obturating ring is fitted.

A special bomb is required for target marking, signalling, indicating etc in countries where tropical jungle prevents observation of the target area and a Sky Trail bomb which leaves an indicating path behind it, has been under development for some time; but with the British withdrawal from the Far East, the need is no longer so pressing.

DATA
Barrel: OML L 16
Weight: 11.88kg
Overall length: 1270mm
Outside diameter: (1) Muzzle: 86mm
                     (2) Breech: 94mm
Calibre: 81mm
Construction: Steel monobloc forging

Mounting, L5:
Weight: 11.36kg
Overall length (folded): 1143mm
Construction: Steel and light alloy

Traverse: 5° left and right of zero at 45° elevation (89 mils right and left at 800 mils elevation)
Elevation: Minimum 45° (800 mils)
Maximum 80° (1422 mils)

Performance: HE round

Baseplate Canadian Mk 1

Weight: 11.36kg
Diameter, overall: 559mm
Socket size: 50.8mm
Construction: Forged aluminium alloy

Ammunition: HE Bomb L15A3

Calibre: 81mm
Fuze: No 162
Length overall: 510mm
Weight complete: 4.26kg
Bomb body weight: 2.45kg
Tail weight: 0.27kg
Filling weight: 0.68kg
Filling: 60/40 RDX/TNT
Construction:
Body: Cast
Tail: Extruded light alloy
Propellant: NC porous discs in celluloid containers

Smoke Bomb L19A4

This has the same body and tail as the HE Bomb L15 and ranges are the same. Filling, White Phosphorus. Fuze 162 Weight complete 4.26kg.

Illuminating round.

Hotchkiss-Brandt Mk 68. Fuzed F.H. 81. Rounds are issued complete with Charge 5.

Bomb, smoke, L19

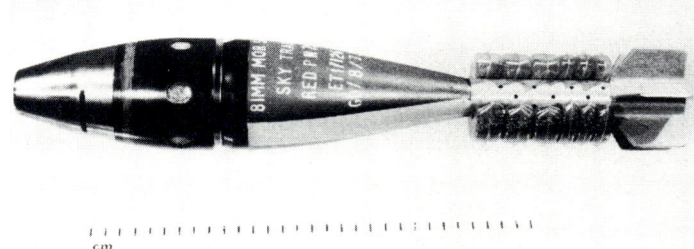

The "Red Sky Trail"

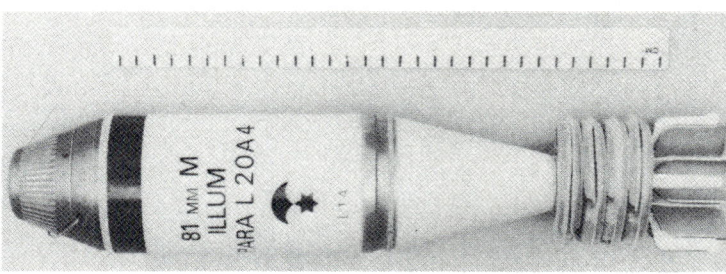

Illuminating bomb L204A1

Performance: HE round

	Augmenting Cartridges			Muzzle velocity (Metres/sec)		Range (Metres)		50%
	Small	Intermediate	Large	L5 Mounting	FV 432	Minimum	Maximum	Zone (metres)
Primary	0	0	0	73	73	180	520	15×2
Charge 1	1	0	0	110	110	390	1120	30×5
Charge 2	2	0	0	137	139	580	1710	30×5
Charge 3	3	0	0	162	163	780	2265	30×5
Charge 4	3	1	0	195	197	1070	3080	40×10
Charge 5	3	2	0	224	227	1340	3850	50×15
Charge 6	3	3	0	250	255	1700	4680	60×20
Charge 7	1	0	4			1900	5255	
Charge 8	1	0	4			2100	5660	

Performance – Illuminating round

Charge	Cartridges	MV m/sec	Range (m) Min	Range (m) Max	50% Zone (m) L	50% Zone (m) W	50% Zone (m) H
Charge 1	1	125	100	1000	35	20	30
Charge 2	2	158	700	1700	35	20	40
Charge 3	3	186	800	2200	35	20	45
Charge 4	4	212	1000	2700	40	25	55
Charge 5	5	236	1200	3200	55	30	60

Bomb, HE, L15A1

Manufacturer: Royal Ordnance Factories
Status: In service in Abu Dhabi, Austria (Austrian designation is 8cm Granatwerfer 70), Bahrain, Canada, Great Britain, Guyana, India, Kenya, Malaysia, Oman, New Zealand, Nigeria, Qatar, Ras Al Khaimah and Yemen.

4.2 INCH MORTAR

The Mark 2, S.B. 4.2 inch mortar was used in the Second World War by Artillery units of the Royal Artillery. Anti-tank regiments were equipped with the mortar as an alternative weapon.

The mortar consisted of barrel, mounting and a variety of baseplates.

The Mark 2 barrel was a steel tube with a bore of 4.2 inches (107mm) diameter and a length of 60 inches (1,524mm) without breech piece. The rear end was screw threaded to take a cap. The cap was screwed on to the barrel and reduced in diameter at the rear end and screw threaded to take the breech piece. The breech piece screwed on to the cap and the rear end was spherical to fit into the rebound socket of the standard baseplate, and into the socket of the mobile baseplate. There was a spring locking catch to ensure that the barrel did not leave the baseplate during firing. The striker stud was screwed into the breech piece.

The standard baseplate was 25 inches (635mm) wide, 22 inches long (559mm) and 11 inches deep (279mm). It weighed 117lbs (53.2kg) and in spite of these dimensions and weight it sank into soft ground very rapidly and an auxiliary baseplate, which fitted round it to increase the flotation area, was issued with it. This itself weighed 185lbs (84kg). There was a mobile baseplate with stub axles, pneumatic tyred wheels and a towing bar. This weighed 756lb (348kg). It was 51.5 inches long (1,308mm), 40 inches wide (1,016mm) and 26.5 inches deep (673mm).

The Mark 3 mounting was the last in service. This was a tripod mount with a cradle, elevating and traversing gears and a sight bracket.

The Mark 3 sight was graduated from zero to 180 degrees right and left. It had a range scale drum and could be used with an aiming post to produce predicated fire. It superseded the Mk 1 sight which was of the range scale strip variety.

An ammunition trailer accompanied the mortar.

There were two charges. Charge 1 comprised the primary cartridge and four secondaries. The top charge, Charge 2, comprised the primary cartridge and six secondaries. There were also cylindrical and streamline bombs. Charge 1 would give a range of 2,750yds (2,538 metres) with the streamline bomb and 2,250yds (2,075 metres) with the cylindrical bomb. Charge 2 produced 4,100yds (3,785 metres) with the streamline bomb and 3,250yds (3,000 metres) with the cylindrical. The beaten zone was 280yds (258 metres) by 140yds (129 metres) with Charge 2.

AMMUNITION

There were two marks of high explosive bomb. The Mark 2 bomb, which was the last in service, was a streamline bomb with the tail unit attached directly to the rear of the bomb body. It was filled with TNT or Amatol 150/50. The bomb was fuzed with the 162 fuze.

The 4.2in mortar was last used in Borneo when six mortars were rushed out. In general the mortar was phased out of service in the 1950s. It was large and heavy weapon very prone to drop its bomb about one thousand yards short. This was found – much later – to be caused by a phenomenon known as spin-yaw resonance (see introduction).

4.2in mortar in action. The lifting bars fitted into the stub axle brackets to raise or lower the platform

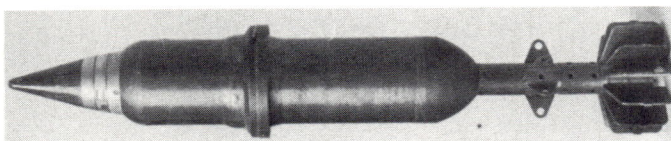

Bomb, Mk 1, ZSB, smoke, BE, DS, 4.2in mortar

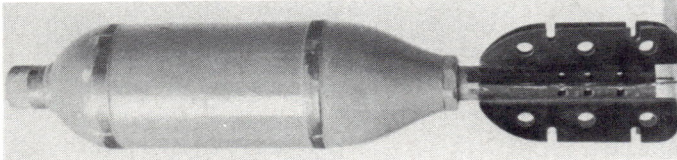

Bomb, Mk 2, SB, smoke, 4.2in mortar

Bomb, Mk 2, SB, smoke, 4.2in mortar, FM or CSAM

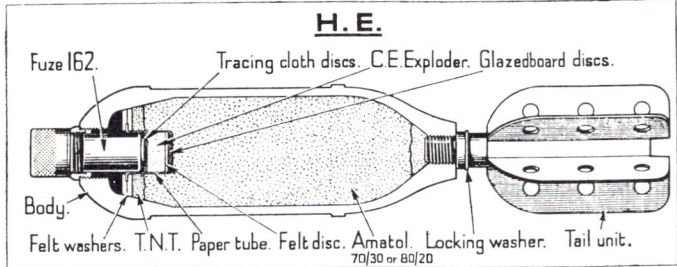

Bomb, Mk1, SB, HE, cylindrical, 4.2in mortar

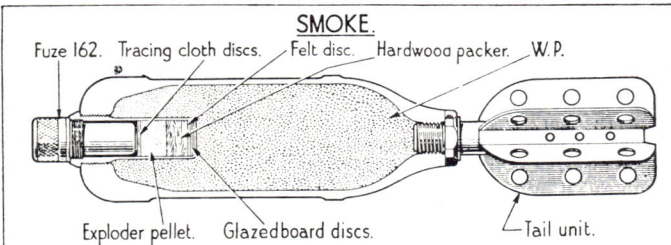

The Mark 2 bomb contains some 2.7kg of white phosphorus

The 4·2in mortar on the mobile baseplate

DATA

Equipment:
Barrel (Mark 2)
Diameter of bore: 4.2in (107mm)
Length:
Muzzle to front of striker: 1,537mm
Total with breech piece: 1,734mm
Total without breech piece: 1,613mm
Total weight: 41.5kg
Baseplate:
Standard Mark 3:
Depth: 298mm
Length: 559mm
Width: 644mm
Weight: 53kg
Auxiliary:
Depth: 229mm
Length: 940mm
Width: 711mm
Weight: 84kg
Mobile:
Depth: 673mm
Length: 1,308mm
Width: 1,016mm
Weight: 343kg
Weight of tripod: 36kg
Weight of lifting bars: 20kg
Mounting (Mark 3):
Depth over traversing gear: 152mm
Length with sight removed and cradle swung over: 1,511mm
Width legs folded: 254mm
Width legs splayed: 1,702mm
Width over traversing gear: 318mm
Weight including cradle: 27kg
Traverse, angle of, left and right:
Standard baseplate: 7° to 21°

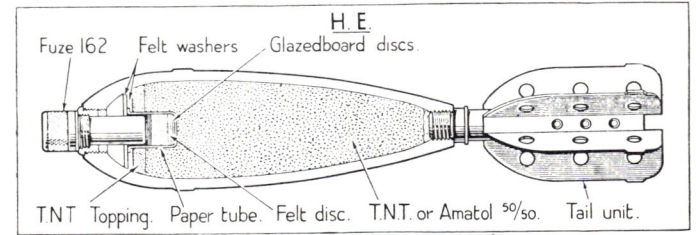

Bomb, Mk2, SB, HE, streamline, 4.2in mortar

Mobile baseplate: 7° to 21°
Elevation: 45° to 80° Q.E.
Means of firing: Striker stud
Shipping tonnage (mobile baseplate complete): 444kg
Maximum speed limit: 50km/h
Ammunition:
Weight of complete round:
High explosive:
Mark 2 (streamline): 9.1kg
Mark 1 (cylindrical): 9.3kg
Smoke:
Mark 2 (white phosphorus): 10.2kg
FM: 9.7kg
CSAM: 9.9kg
Smoke, BE, DS (screening): 8.9kg

Manufacturer: Royal Ordnance Factories
Status: No longer made. No longer in UK service but a few may still be encountered elsewhere

4.2in mortar on mobile baseplate in travelling position

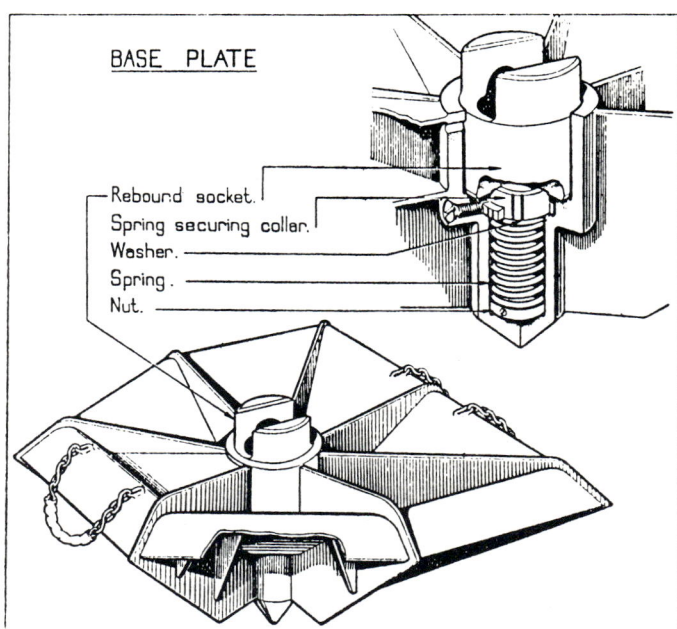

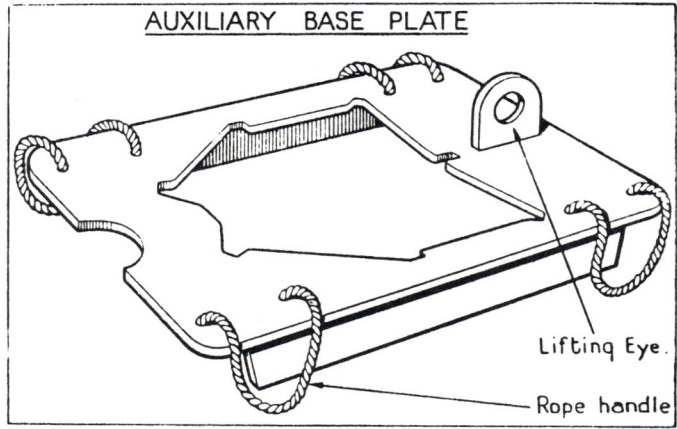

Baseplates, 4.2in mortar

UNITED STATES OF AMERICA

60mm M19 MORTAR

The M19 mortar is a conventional smoothbore, muzzle loading weapon designed to produce high angle fire. The equipment consists of the barrel M19, bipod M2, and baseplate. The bipod and baseplate together make up the M5 mount.

M19 BIPOD

The barrel is a steel tube with an external thread at the lower end to take the basecap. The firing mechanism is contained in a housing which is attached to the base cap by a threaded adaptor. The barrel is fitted to the baseplate by a spherical projection which fits into a socket and is locked in place. The firing mechanism consists of the firing pin, a spring, a trigger and pawl and a firing lever. A firing selector acts as a cam on the rear end of the firing pin and allows firing the mortar with or without the firing lever.

BIPOD

This consists of the two legs, the elevating mechanism assembly and the traversing gear. The bipod legs are connected by a clevis joint which limits the spread of the legs. The elevating screw tube passes through the junction of the legs and connects up with the yoke. The left leg of the bipod carries the sleeve of the cross levelling gear. When the sleeve is moved up or down the leg the connecting link which is attached to the elevating tube forces the elevating tube out of the vertical. This in turn moves the yoke out of the horizontal. Thus when the mortar comes into action on uneven ground and the two spiked feet on the bipod legs are on different levels, the cross levelling gear enables the yoke to be made level and the sight which is fitted into a dovetail slot in the yoke is upright.

The elevating gear consists of the screw thread in the tube with a handle at the bottom. This enables the yoke to be pushed up or down and the barrel clamp, mounted on the yoke, raises or lowers the muzzle of the barrel.

The traversing gear consists of a nut which is moved across inside a tube by the rotation of the traversing handwheel. This displaces the yoke to one side or the other. The lower half of the barrel clamp has two shock absorber cylinders which permit movement between the yoke and clamp assembly during firing.

BASEPLATE

This is a rectangular plate with ribs on the underside and a centrally mounted socket to take the spherical end piece of the barrel. The barrel is held in place by a locking lever.

Checking the lay before the HE bomb is dropped

The mortar is fired by dropping a bomb down from the muzzle. The setting of the selector lever determines the method by which the firing takes place. If the firing pin is locked out, the primer drops on it and the bomb is fired. If the firing pin is retracted, the firing lever must be pulled back to compress the firing spring so that when the firing pin trips off the lever, it is driven forward to fire the round. At high angles of elevation either method may be used. At low angles only lever fire will provide the necessary impulse to fire the cap.

There is a small M1 baseplate which may be attached to the barrel and the weapon can then be hand held and fired without the bipod.

The M4 sight has an elevating scale covering the arc from 40° to 90°, by 10° divisions. The micrometer scale is divided up into 40 divisions each one representing ¼°. The traversing scale has 60 graduations each of 5 mils. The graduations are numbered every 10 mils from 0 to 150 on each side of the zero position.

Ammunition

HE

The high explosive round is the M49A2. This has a steel body containing 154g of TNT. A fin assembly is screwed on the rear end of the body and a fuze is inserted in the nose. The fins envelop four secondary cartridges. The fuze is the M525 or 525A.

SMOKE

The M302 is used as a screening, signalling or incendiary round. It is filled with white phosphorus and has a burster charge. The fuze is the M82 which has a superquick action. The round is being replaced by the M302A1 with Fuse PD M527B1.

PRACTICE

The M50A2 is the practice round. It differs from the HE round in colour and filling. It has the same ballistic characteristics and has a small black powder charge to indicate the point of fall.

ILLUMINATION

Bombs M83A1, A2 and A3 are all in service. The illuminant assembly is expelled after 14.5secs flight and drifts down on its parachute to illuminate the ground below.

The illumination lasts for a minimum of 25 secs with a minimum of 330,000 candlepower.

TRAINING

The M69 training bomb has a solid cast iron body and the normal tin assembly. Only the primary cartridge is used and the maximum range is 225 metres.

DATA
Weights
Mortar complete: 20.5kg
Mortar with M1 baseplate: 9.3kg
Barrel: 7.26kg
Bipod: 7.44kg
Baseplate: 5.81kg
Baseplate M1: 2.04kg
Overall length: 819mm
Elevation
With M5 mount: 40° – 85° (710mils to 1,510 mils)
With M1 baseplate: 0° – 85° (0mils to 1,510mils)
Traverse right or left: 125mils
Rate of fire
Maximum rounds per minute: 30
Sustained rounds per minute: 18

M19 60mm mortar. This mortar was developed from the M2 in 1942. It is no longer in service in the USA but large numbers were used in Vietnam. It has been replaced in US Army service by the M29 81mm mortar

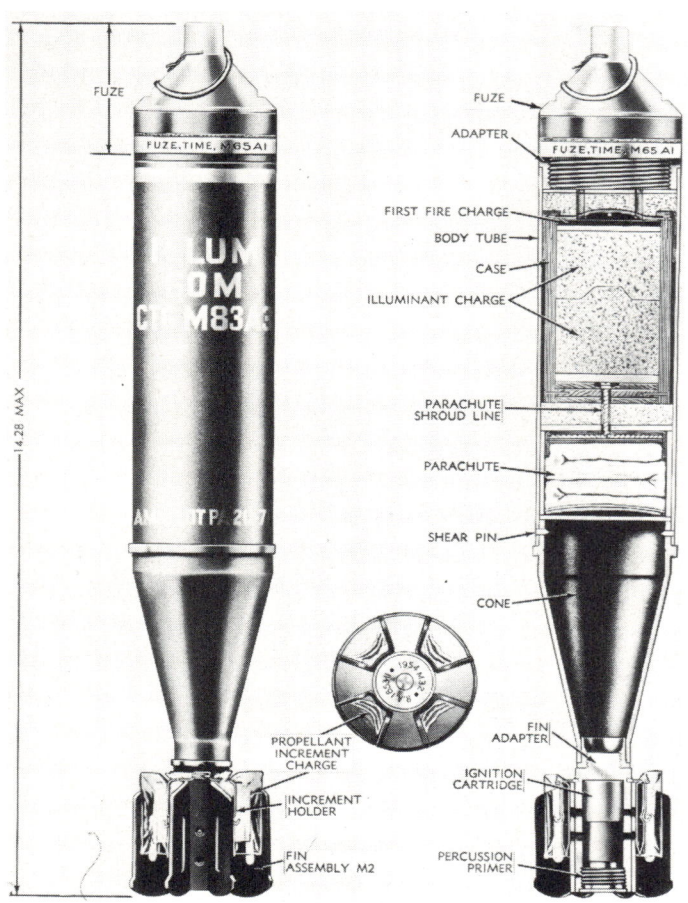

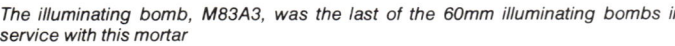

The illuminating bomb, M83A3, was the last of the 60mm illuminating bombs in service with this mortar

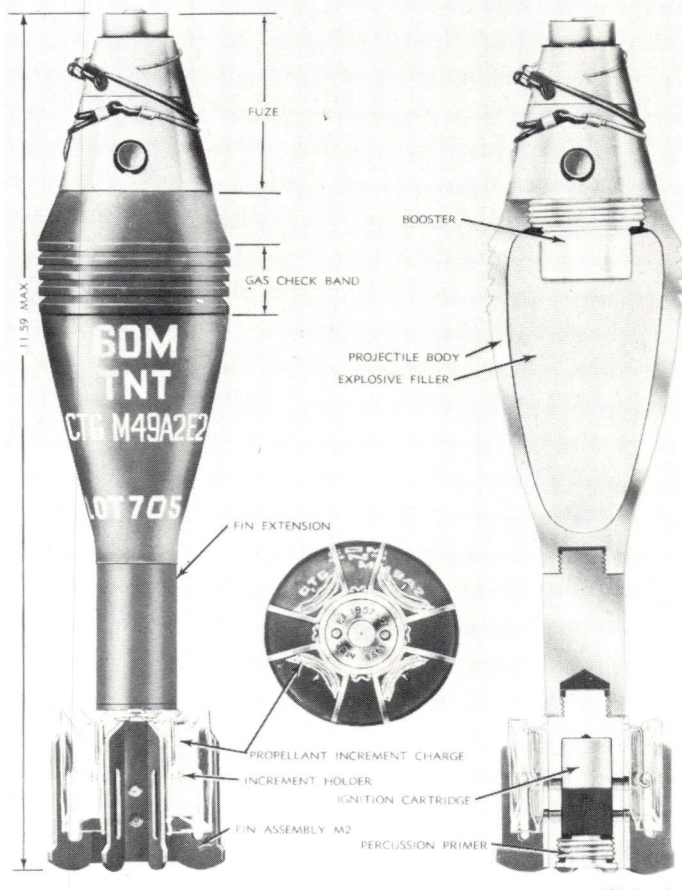

M49A2E2 high explosive bomb. The suffix E2 indicates that it is the second experimental development of the M49A2 bomb

Ammunition
M49A2 HE Bomb

Weight: 1.36kg
HE filling: TNT
Weight of HE filling: 154g
Propelling increments: 4
Maximum range: 1,790 metres

M302 WP Smoke Bomb

Maximum range: 1,450 metres

M50A2 Training Bomb

Maximum range: 1,790 metres

M69 Training Bomb

Maximum range: 255 metres

M83A1 Illuminating Bomb

Weight: 1.88kg
Maximum range: 1,000 metres

The M19 60mm Mortar is now obsolescent in the US Army and is no longer in issue. However large numbers were supplied to US allies in South East Asia and it is still a current weapon in South Korea and, presumably, in Vietnam.

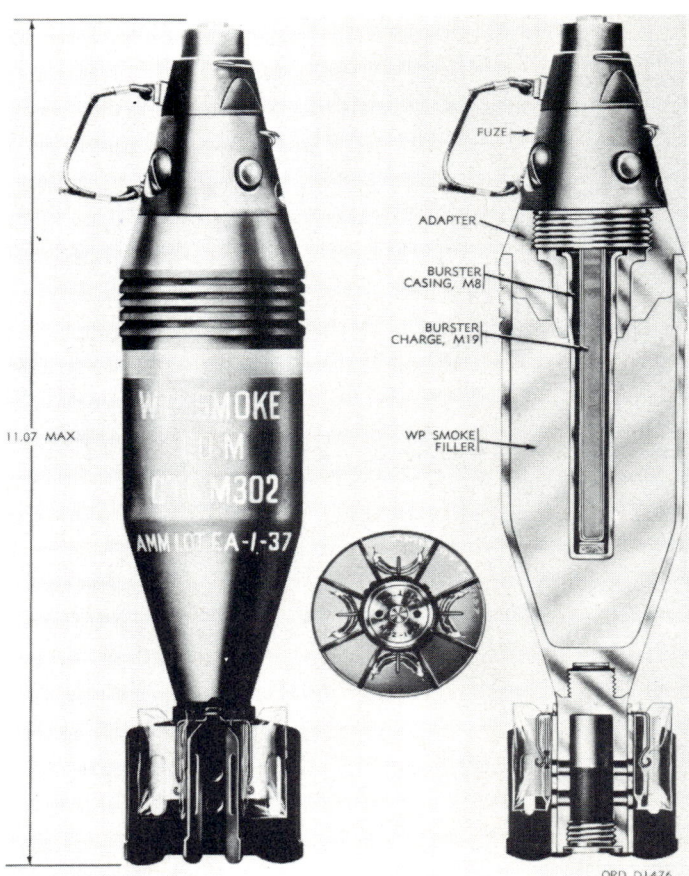

White phosphorus smoke bomb, M302

XM 224 60mm LIGHTWEIGHT COMPANY MORTAR

During the Vietnam campaign, the US Infantry found the 81mm Mortar to be excessively heavy and unwieldy for use outside the firebases. As a result patrols had to rely for their own support on the 60mm M19 mortar which was then obsolescent. In December 1970 the XM224 mortar was approved for development to succeed the 81mm Mortar in the Infantry, Airmobile Infantry and Airborne Infantry. It was intended to be a light portable weapon capable of providing the volume of fire required by the infantry and of operation at either high or low angle fire.

The mortar has been developed at Watervliet and Picatinny Arsenals: the advanced development objective was approved in 1971, engineering tests were completed at Aberdeen Proving Ground in 1972 and the engineering design was approved in 1973. The weapon was tested at Fort Benning and it was anticipated that it would be approved for service before the end of 1976. The FY1976 request was for further 3.6 million dollars for further development work and 2.9 million dollars were in the FY 1977 requests for the provision of 300 mortars. The AN/GVS 5 laser rangefinder has been placed in production for the United States Army and United States Marine Corps.

To achieve the range required an improved propellant has been adopted: this is hotter than that used in the M19 mortar and also develops a higher working pressure. The lower part of the tube has been radially finned to increase the surface for heat dissipation and the wall thickness has been kept to much the same value as that of its predecessor by the use of a higher tensile steel. The baseplate is circular in shape with a pronounced web on the underside, and is an aluminium forging. This provides strength, rigidity and light weight. There is also a light rectangular baseplate – the XM8 – which is used when the weapon is hand held to provide both high angle and direct fire. In this method of employment the weight of the mortar is only 7.8kg. The firer supports the barrel towards the muzzle by gripping a canvas sleeve and at the rear there is a handle which holds the trigger mechanism. The mortar can be fired by either gravity or a spring loaded firing pin controlled by a firing lever which cocks and fires the pin in one movement. In the conventional employment using a bipod the entire mortar weighs 20.4kg. The bipod has alloy legs and the elevating screw thread is contained in an alloy elevating tube. Attached to this tube is the connecting rod of the cross levelling gear which is moved across by a sleeve on the left leg of the bipod. The object of this gear is to get the sight upright when the mortar is brought into action on a slope or on irregular ground. The M53 sight used on the 81mm mortar weighs 2.8kg. The new XM64 sight developed for the XM224 mortar weighs only 1.1kg and is both simpler and lighter than that of the larger mortar. For easy transport the mortar breaks down into two man loads, the heavier being 11.8kg.

To reduce the number of different sorts of fuze required – running at 15 different types with the 81mm mortar – a multi-option fuze was developed. This allows the user to select airburst, near surface burst, direct action and delay. The fuze uses techniques developed in the design of micro-circuits for the 40mm high-velocity aircraft round. The arming process requires air pressure and set back. The ram effect operates the electronic circuits and

The 60mm company lightweight mortar. This is an early prototype

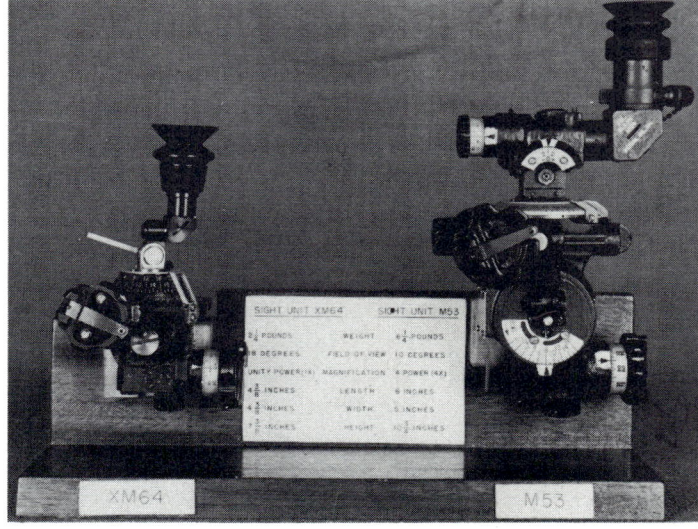

A comparison of the M53 sight used on the 81mm mortar with the XM64 used on the XM224 60mm mortar

the set back removes the safety locks that guarantee safety up to that point. The fuze has been so designed that if the airburst fails to function, the near surface burst operates. If the firer has selected the near surface burst and this fails to function, the point detonation action becomes operative. Lastly if direct action has been selected, delay is obtained if the required setting fails. A plastic cover over the fuze must be removed before the round is fired but if it is inadvertently left in place, air pressure tears it off. The nose ring of the fuze (see photograph) provides the method of selection. The value of a mortar lies largely in the element of surprise. A number of bombs dropping without warning onto a target produces more casualties and is said to have a greater morale effect than four times that number preceded by a slow ranging series. To try to obtain this surprise effect, a 2.3kg laser range finder, the AN/GVS 5, will be used. This enables a range to be read with an accuracy of 10 metres at any range up to 10,000 metres. So, knowing his own position and having a compass, the Mobile Fire Controller or Forward Observation Officer, can find the co-ordinates of the target position with sufficient accuracy to justify elimination of the ranging process.

Manufacturers: Apart from Watervliet and Picatinny Arsenals, contributors to the programme so far have been Frankford Arsenal, Aberdeen

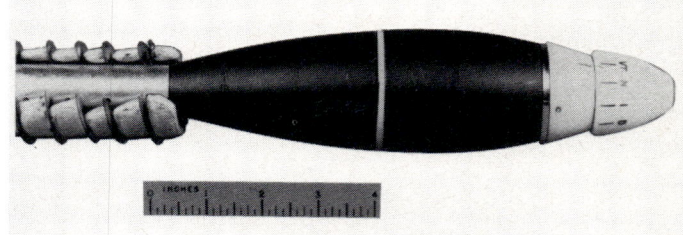

High explosive bomb XM720 fitted with the multi optional fuze

Proving Ground, Harry Diamond Laboratories (Washington D.C.), Eastman Kodak (Rochester N.Y.), Bergman Mfg. Co. (Garland, Tex), IITRI (Chicago, Ill.), Ruoff Inc. (Runnemede, N.J.), Norris Industries (Los Angeles, Calif.), and Notre Dame University.
Status: Pre-production. Initial Operational Capability scheduled for mid-1979

81mm MORTAR M1

The 81mm Mortar M1 consists of the Cannon (barrel) M1 and the Mount M1. The Cannon consists of a tube, base cap and a firing pin. The base cap is hollowed and threaded to screw on the barrel. It ends in a spherical projection flattened on two sides, which fits into and locks in the socket of the baseplate. The firing pin is screwed tightly into the base cap against a shoulder. The firing pin protrudes a little over a millimetre through the base cap into the barrel.

The Mount consists of a bipod and a baseplate. The bipod consists of the leg assembly, the elevating mechanism assembly and the travelling mechanism assembly. The baseplate is a rectangular pressed steel body to which are welded a series of ribs and braces, a front flange, three loops, a link, two handles and the socket. The sight fitted is the M34A2. The mortar is also mounted in a variety of vehicles including the M4 and M21 half-tracks.

DATA
Calibre: 81mm
Weight of barrel: 20.18kg
Weight of mount: 19.27kg
Weight of baseplate: 20.41kg
Total weight: 59.87kg
Barrel length overall: 1266mm
Length of barrel: 1155mm
Elevation: +40° to +85°
Traverse: 5° left and right

Type of firing mechanism: Fixed firing pin
Rate of fire normal: 18 rounds per minute
Rate of fire maximum: 30 rounds per minute
Ammunition types: HE, Illuminating, Smoke – FS, WP and TP
Range at 45° elevation:
HE (M43A1) and TP(M43A1): 3016 metres
HE (M56 and M56A1): 2317 metres
HE (M362 – 5 increment max): 2467 metres
Illuminating (M301A1, M301A2) (51¼°): 2102 metres
Smoke FS (M57 AND M57A1): 2216 metres
Smoke WPM (57 and M57A1): 2568 metres
M68 training, ignition charge only: 283 metres
Muzzle velocity at 45° elevation
HE (M43A1) and TP(M43A1): 211m/s
HE (M56 and M56A): 174m/s
HE (M362): 234m/s
Illuminating (M301A1/A2) (51¼°): 174m/s
Smoke FS (M57 and M57A1): 174m/s
Smoke WP (M57 and M57A1): 174m/s
M68 training ignition charge only: 53m/s
Status: No longer in production, still used by Austria, Belgium, Brazil, Cambodia, Cuba, Denmark, Greece, India, Italy, Indonesia, Japan, Liberia, Luxembourg, Netherlands, Norway, North Yemen, Pakistan, Philippines, South Korea, Spain, Taiwan, Thailand, Trinidad, Turkey, Vietnam and Yugoslavia

---

81mm MORTAR M29/M29A1

This 81mm Mortar is a smooth bore, muzzle-loaded, high-angle of fire weapon. It consists of the barrel, the mount and the baseplate. It may be used in the conventional way or mounted in the M125A1 carrier.

The barrel is made up of the tube, externally threaded at the rear to take a base plug which has a ball shaped projection on its lower end to fit into the socket of the baseplate. There are 2 white lines painted 432 and 533mm from the muzzle for the location of the mount attachment ring. The exterior of the barrel is radially finned to increase the cooling area. The mount is either the M23A1 or the M23A3 and comprises the bipod legs, elevating mechanism and the traversing mechanism. The bipod has two tubular steel legs hinged at the sides of the elevating mechanism: they have spiked feet and their spread is limited by an adjustable chain with a spring to relieve the shock on the legs during firing. The right leg has no moving parts but the left leg has the cross level mechanism on a sliding bracket mounted on the leg with a locking sleeve and an adjusting nut. The sliding bracket is connected to the elevating housing by a connecting rod. When the mount is located on uneven or sloping ground, the sliding bracket is moved across by rotation of the sleeve on the bipod leg and this in turn moves the elevating mechanism assembly across taking the barrel with it. This enables the sight, located at the left end of the yoke, to be moved into an upright position. The elevating mechanism assembly includes a vertical elevating screw moving inside the elevating housing assembly. There is a handle projecting back from the gear case located at the junction of the bipod legs, and rotation of this handle elevates or depresses the mortar barrel.

The traversing assembly consists of the yoke assembly, traversing mechanism, and shock absorber. The yoke body supports the upper end of the barrel when the mortar is assembled. The older models of the mortar had a yoke with a levelling bubble. The sight unit is mounted in the dovetail sight slot on the left side of the yoke. The traversing mechanism is an internal screw shaft operating within a nut and tube. The handwheel turns a screw which forces the nut to traverse the yoke and take the barrel with it. The tube over the nut is connected to the elevating shaft which protrudes from the gear case of the bipod. The shock absorber is a compression spring, mounted in the yoke. When the barrel is located to the yoke by the barrel clamp the shock absorber connects the barrel to the bipod.

The baseplate was the M3. This is a one-piece unit made of aluminium alloy. In the centre is the barrel socket which rotates through 360 deg. The current version is the M23A1 which is a 2-piece unit: when it is assembled for use the inner ring assembly and outer ring assembly are secured

The mortar, 81mm M29, ground mounted with the M53 sight

together by 3 latches. This baseplate is now in service with the latest (product-improved) version of the mortar which was redesignated M29A1 in 1970.

Sight units M53 or M34A2 are used with the mortar. The M53 is now the standard sight and has very largely replaced the M34A2. Each incorporates a telescope mount and an elbow telescope fastened together into one unit. Both have fixed and slipping scales.

The 81mm mortar with sight M53 and a boresight fitted

DATA
Calibre: 81mm
Weights:
Barrel: 12.7kg
Mount: 18.14kg
Baseplate M3: 11.34kg
Baseplate M23A1: 21.8kg
Sight unit M53: 2.4kg
Sight unit M43A2: 1.81kg
Elevation: 800 – 1500mils
Traverse. Right or left from centre: 95 mils
Traverse moving mount: 6400mils
Length: 1,295mm
Method of fire: Muzzle-loaded, drop-fired
Muzzle velocity: 268.3m/s
Max. range: 4,737 metres
Ammunition: HE, smoke and illuminating
Crew: 5

Rate of fire Bomb	Mortar	Maximum rounds/min	Sustained rate of fire
M362	M29	15 for 2 min	4
		27 for 1 min	
M362	M29A1	25 for 2 min	5
		30 for 1 min	
M374 and M375	M29	18 for 2 min	5
M374 and M375	M29A1	25 for 2 min	8
		30 for 1 min	

Manufacturer: Watervliet Arsenal, Watervliet, N.Y.
Status: In production since 1953 the M29 and M29A1 mortars have been and are used extensively by US forces and by many other countries including Australia, Austria, Italy and Vietnam

The 81mm mortar mounted in the M125 carrier

81mm MORTAR AMMUNITION
AUTHORIZED ROUNDS
(1) High Explosive, M43A1, M43A1B1, M362A1, M362, M374, M374A2
(2) White phosphorus, M57A1, M370, M375, M375A2
(3) Illuminating, M301A1, M301A2, M301A3
(4) Training Practice, M43A1, M68.

HE M374 and M374A2
The peralitic malleable iron projectile is loaded with approximately 0.95kg of Composition B. The rear of the bourrelet section of the projectile is fitted with an obturator ring with a circumferential groove. The aluminium fin assembly, M149, consists of an ignition cartridge housing and 6 extruding fins canted counterclockwise 5 deg. at the rear to stablize the round in flight.

HE M362
The steel forged projectile is loaded with approximately 0.95kg of Composition B. The aluminium fin assembly is the M141.

HE M43A1
The complete round consists of a relatively thin-walled shallow-cavity steel projectile containing a TNT bursting charge and PD fuze.

WP M375 & M375A2
The M375 WP round is ballistically identical to the M374 HE round and otherwise similar except that it is loaded with approximately 725g of white phosphorus, and contains a one-piece aluminium burster casing (M158) prefilled to the forward end of the body. The burster casing houses a central burster tube containing RDS.

WP M370
The M370 WP round is ballistically identical to the M362 HE round and

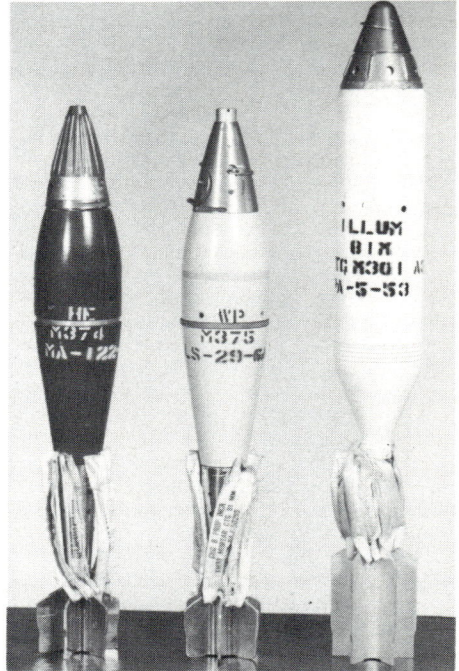

*81mm bombs. **Left.** HE bomb M374. **Centre.** White phosphorus smoke bomb M375. **Right.** Illuminating bomb, M301A3*

otherwise similar except for the white phosphorus filler.

Illuminating Ammunition
M301A3
The complete round consists of a time fuze, a thin-walled steel body-tube containing the parachute and illuminant assembly, and a steel tail cone and fin assembly.

This round is designed to be fired with a minimum of 2 propelling charge increments and not more than 8. It has a burst height of 600 metres and will illuminate a 1200 metre area for a minimum of 60 seconds.

M301A2
Illuminating cartridge M301A2 is similar to the M301A3 except that it has a tail fin that is 2.27in shorter than the M301A3. The round is designed to be fired with a minimum of 2 propelling charge increments and not more than 4 increments. The height of burst is 400 metres and it will illuminate an 1100 metre area for a minimum of 60 seconds.

M301A1
Illuminating cartridge M301A1 is similar to the M301A2 except that it has gas check bourrelet grooves and some minor dimensional differences in metal parts.

Target Practice Ammunition (TP)
M43A1
Target practice cartridge M43A1 is intended for use in training only and is similar to the M43A1 HE except for the projectile filler and its colour. The target practice projectile is loaded with an inert material (plaster-of-paris and stearic acid) and a 0.05 pound pack powder pellet. On impact, the black powder pellet and fuze booster charge provide a spotting charge for observation purposes. The projectile is loaded to simulate the weight of the high explosive projectile and has the same ballistic characteristics.

81mm HE bomb M43A1

Sectioned view of the M43A1 bomb

4.2in MORTAR M2A1
The 4.2in mortar M2A1 was designed and developed during the Second World War. It consists of the barrel and shock absorbing mechanism, baseplate with sliding handles on each side and a standard. The standard supports the mortar when the mortar is in the firing position and is connected to the baseplate by two connecting rods, one each side. The elevating wheel is on the standard as also is the very limited traversing mechanism. If required, the weapon can be broken down in three loads for easy transportation – barrel, baseplate and standard. During the war it was normally carried on a two-wheeled hand cart.

DATA
Calibre: 107mm
Weight of barrel: 47.6kg
Weight of baseplate: 77.1kg

4.2in MORTAR M30
The 4.2in mortar, M30, is a rifled, muzzle-loaded, drop-fired weapon which can be hand-carried for short distances when disassembled into five loads. The complete weapon comprises a barrel, a standard, a bridge assembly, a rotator assembly, a baseplate and a sight unit. The design is such that the recoil forces are absorbed by the main mechanical assemblies as a whole.

The barrel is a rifled tube 60in (152.4cm) long with an inside diameter of 106.7mm (4.2in) between lands. This rifling consists of 24 lands and 24 grooves of which the first 9in (22.86cm), as measured from the base inside the barrel, are straight. The twist increases to the right from zero at this point to one turn in 84in (213cm).

The standard assembly, consisting of the elevating, traversing and recoil mechanism, connects the barrel and the bridge assembly.

The elevating gear handle, located in front of the mortar at the top of the standard assembly is used to elevate or depress the mortar throughout either the low or high ranges of elevation.

Fuzes
Point Detonating Fuzes (PDF)
(1) M524 Series. Dual purpose fuze M524A5, superquick or 0.05 second delay, is used with M362 series HE cartridges and M374 or with WP cartridges M370 and M375.
(2) M525, M525A1. These fuzes are modifications of M52 series fuzes. The modification consists of the substitution of a head assembly containing a delayed arming device in addition to the firing pin mechanism. These fuzes are used for M43 HE and TP series ammunition.
(3) M526 series. These fuzes, which are replacing PF fuze M519, consist of the former M52 series fuzes modified, as in the M525 series, with an arming delay and, in addition, fitted with an adapter containing booster pellets to adapt to a newer design ammunition. This fuze may be used instead of PD fuze M524A1 in cartridges M362 and M374 HE and M370 and M375 WP.
(4) PD fuze M519, which is a combination of PD fuze M525A1 and a fuze adapter, is a single action type with a direct action firing device for use with cartridges M362 HE and M370 WP.

M532
The M532 is a radio-doppler fuze which is standard for the M374 HE round and may also be used on the M362 HE or the M375 WP round. It provides an airburst at or near a height for optimum effectiveness by employment of the radio doppler principle of target detection. A clock mechanism provides a nominal 9 seconds of safe air travel (610 to 2,340 metres travel along trajectory for charges 0 to 9, respectively). It can also be set superquick (point detonating) to eliminate the proximity function.

The proximity fuze can be converted to a point detonating fuze action by rotating the top of the fuze more than 120 deg. in either direction.

M517
This proximity fuze is provided for use with the M362 high-explosive round. It will not function in the M374 or M375 rounds because of the spin. The M517 fuze's operating principles are similar to the M532, differing primarily in the arming system. The minimum time (after firing) to arm for an impact function is in excess of 1.5 seconds. The minimum time (after firing) to arm for proximity function is 3.2 seconds. This fuze does not provide a PDSQ option.

Mechanical Time Fuze, M84
This fuze is a single-purpose, powder train, selective-time type used with the 81mm illuminating cartridges M301A1 and M301A2. It has a time setting of up to 25 seconds.

Mechanical Time Fuze M84A1
This fuze is a single-purpose, tungsten ring, selective time type used with the 81mm illumination cartridge M301A3. It has a time setting of up to 50 seconds.

Weight of standard: 24.9kg
Total weight: 149.7kg
Elevation: 80mils to 1080mils
Traverse: 300mils left and right
Rate of fire – normal: 5rpm
Rate of fire – maximum: 20rpm
Ammunition HE weight: 11.56kg
        Smoke: 14.5kg
Maximum range HE: 4022 metres
Maximum range smoke: 2926 metres
Minimum range: 546 metres
Status: No longer used by the United States Army. Still used in many parts of the world including Belgium, Ethiopia, India, Italy, Japan, Netherlands, Norway, Pakistan, Philippines, South Korea, Spain, Turkey and Vietnam

The elevating mechanism cam locks the elevating screw housing assembly in either its low or high range position. This assembly cannot be locked in any intermediate position.

The traversing mechanism consists of an enclosed screw and bearing located at the top of the standard assembly. It is operated by turning the traversing crank on the left side of the mechanism.

The recoil mechanism consists of a series of springs mounted in the lower section of the standard assembly. These are designed to ease the downward shock of firing and return the mechanism to its pre-firing position.

The bridge assembly consists of two pieces joined by a swivel joint. One end receives the cap at the base of the barrel: the other is fitted with a spade which facilitates the digging action of the bridge assembly during firing.

The rotator assembly is approximately 20in (50.8cm) in diameter. It carries the barrel end of the bridge piece on its upper side and pivots on the baseplate.

The baseplate assembly is approximately 38in (96.52cm) in diameter. A recess in the centre receives the bottom insert of the rotator assembly. The lower surface contains six ribs to increase the area in contact with the ground. Each rib has a depth of approximately 6½in (16.51cm). Two carrying handles are provided.

Sight Units, M53 and M34A2

The M53 sight unit is the standard sighting device. It replaced the M34A2. It consists of an M128 telescope mount and an M109 elbow telescope fastened together into one unit for operation.

The M109 telescope is a lightweight 4 power, fixed focus instrument, with a 10 deg. field of view that provides the optical line of sight for aiming the weapon for line and elevation. There is a coarse elevation scale on the left side of the sight body with 18 graduations, each of 100mils, numbered every 200mils. The elevating knob has an adjustable micrometer with 100 graduations each of 1 mil and numbered every 10 mils from 0 to 90. The deflection micrometer scale has 100 graduations numbered from 0 to 90. It is fastened to the deflection knob. There is a coarse deflection slip scale and an adjustable micrometer deflection slipping scale. There are two levelling bubbles located at 90 deg. to each other on the main sight housing.

Ammunition

Ammunition for the 4.2in mortar M30, is issued in the form of semifixed complete rounds. Semifixed ammunition is characterized by an accessible propelling charge which may be adjusted for firing. The propelling charge consists of an ignition cartridge and 41 propellant increments assembled in a bag and sheets. To adjust the charge, the individual increments are removed from the cartridge container or cartridge container extension.

The 4.2in mortar ammunition is stablized in flight by rotation rather than by fins as in the case of the 60mm and 81mm mortar ammunition.

The NATO colour code is used in accordance with NATO STANAG Number 2321.

The table below contains information on the standard rounds authorized for the 4.2in mortar, M30. Depending on the type of projectile filler, ammunition is classified as high explosive (HE), smoke (PWP or WP), gas (CG, CV, CNB, CNS, H, HD or HT) and illumination.

The mortar, 4.2 inch, M30: The gunner is checking the line with the boresight

Bomb Type	Range (m) Min	Max	Weight (kg)	Effective Area (m)	Burning Time (s)	Rate of Descent	Filler and Designation
HE M329A1:	920	5650	12.28	40×20	n/a	n/a	TNT
HE M329:	870	5420	12.28	40×20	n/a	n/a	TNT
HE M3A1:	870	4620	12.22	40×20	n/a	n/a	TNT
HE M3:	870	4620	12.22	40×20	n/a	n/a	TNT
Smoke Me28A1:	920	5650	13.00	n/a	n/a	n/a	WP
Smoke M328:	870	5420	13.00	n/a	n/a	n/a	WP
Smoke M2A1:	870	4620	11.30	n/a	n/a	n/a	WP
Smoke M2:	870	4620	11.30	n/a	n/a	n/a	WP
Illum M335A2:	400	5490	12.11	1500 dia	90	5 m/sec	—
Illum M335A1:	640	5290	12.11	800 dia	70	10 m/sec	—
Illum M335:	640	4800	12.11	800 dia	60	10 m/sec	—
Gas M2A1:	870	4540	11.19	n/a	n/a	n/a	HD
Gas M2:	870	4540	—	n/a	n/a	n/a	H,HD,HT
XM630 Tactical CS:	n/a	5650	—	n/a	60	n/a	CS

GENERAL DATA
Calibre: 4.2in (106.7mm)
Weights:
Barrel M30: 71.0kg
Bridge assembly: 76.7kg
Baseplate assembly: 87.5kg
Standard assembly: 27.0kg

Firing the 4.2 inch mortar from an M106A1 carrier (US Army)

The M30 mortar mounted in the M106 carrier

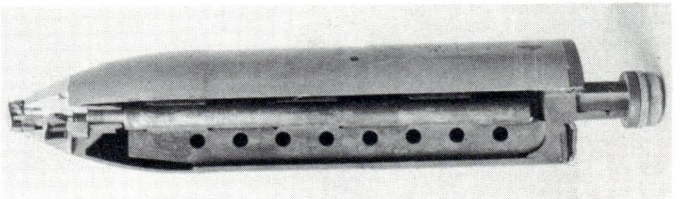

White phosphorus smoke bomb, M328A1

Rotator Assembly:
  Cast magnesium: 26.1kg
  Welded steel: 40.4kg
Sight equipment:
  M34A2: 1.8kg
  M53: 2.4kg
Mortar complete: 305.0kg with welded
steel (latest model) rotator and M53 sight.
Length of Barrel: 1524mm
Rifling: 24 grooves
Ammunition: See text and table above
Range:
Maximum: 5650 metres (M329A1 ammunition)
Minimum: 920 metres (M329A1 ammunition)
Elevation:

	Low range	High range
Maximum:	933mils	1156mils
Minimum:	706mils	919mils
Firing elevations:	800 or 900mils	1065mils
Per turn of elevating handle (approx):		13mils

Shifts:
Per turn of traversing crank (approx): 10mils
On traversing mechanism (right or left from centre): 125mils
  Rate of fire. The maximum rate of fire is 18 rounds per minute for the first minute and 9 rounds per minute for the next 5 minutes. This can be followed by a sustained rate of fire of three rounds per minute for prolonged periods.
Status: In service with US forces and in Austria, Canada and Zaire

The mortar, 4.2 inch, M30, ground mounted with the M53 sight

YUGOSLAVIA

50mm MORTAR M8

This is very similar to the British 2in mortar but differs in having a supporting and carrying handle at the point of balance. The barrel is a plain steel tube internally screwthreaded at the bottom to take the breechpiece which holds the trigger and firing mechanism. The weapon is fired by a lever on the right of the breech piece. The sight is a simple pointer with a bubble to indicate when it is horizontal and a range scale. The baseplate is trough shaped and lies across the barrel axis. The mortar M8 fires an HE bomb weighing about 1kg, a smoke bomb and an illuminating bomb.

DATA
Calibre: 50.0mm
Weight: 7.3kg
Maximum range: 480 metres
Minimum range: 135 metres
Rate of fire: 25-30rounds/min
Muzzle velocity: 80 metres/sec
Manufacturer: State Factories
Status: In service with Yugoslav forces

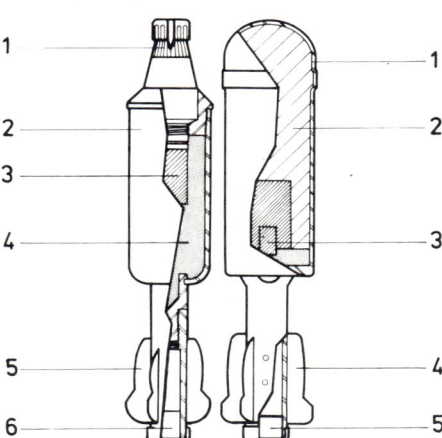

50mm ammunition. **Left.** *A high explosive bomb.* (1) *Fuze;* (2) *Steel body of the bomb;* (3) *Detonator;* (4) *High explosive filling;* (5) *Tail fin;* (6) *Primary cartridge.* **Right.** *An illuminating bomb.* (1) *Body casing;* (2) *Smoke composition;* (3) *Smoke igniter;* (4) *Tail fin;* (5) *Primary cartridge*

50mm, M8 mortar

60mm MORTAR M57

This was developed from the US M2 60mm mortar which is now obsolete. The breech piece is screw threaded to fit over the bottom of the barrel, and has a ball-shaped end to fit into the socket of the rectangular baseplate. The bipod has a cross levelling gear operated by a sleeve on the left leg and connected to a rod attached to the elevating gear. This is attached to the

yoke which carries the traversing screw and the shock absorbing spring cylinders. At the right hand end of the yoke is the traversing handwheel and on the left is the sight. This has no slipping scale but allows switches from a chosen aiming point.

The mortar fires HE, smoke and illuminating bombs.

DATA
Calibre: 60.75mm
Weight of barrel: 5.50kg
Weight of bipod: 4.50kg
Weight of baseplate: 8.85kg
Weight of sight: 1.00kg
Muzzle velocity: 159 metres/sec
Minimum range: 75 metres
Maximum range: 1700 metres/sec
Rate of fire: 25-30 rounds/min
Weight of bomb: 1.35kg
Manufacturer: State Factories
Status: In service

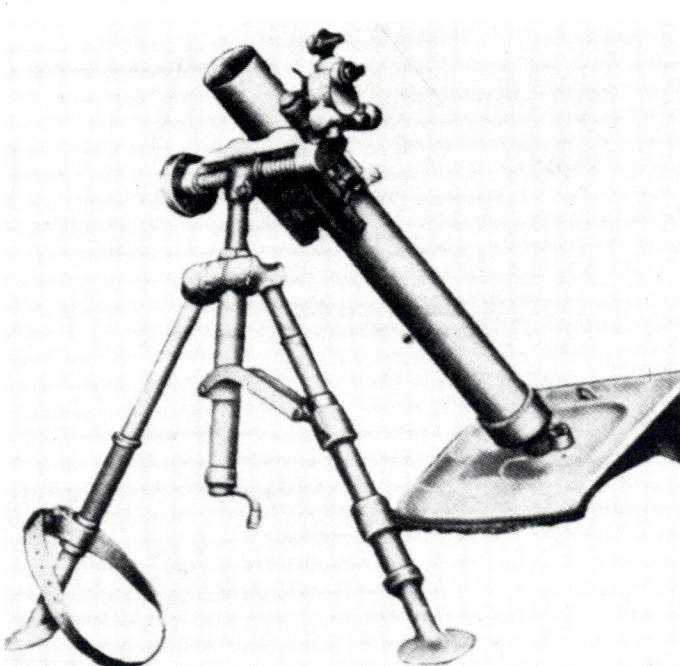

60mm, M57 mortar

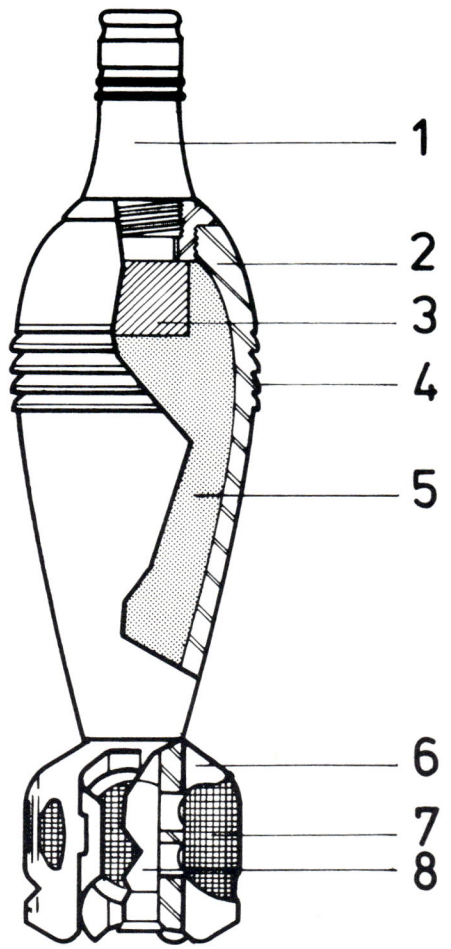

60mm HE bomb. (1) Fuze; (2) Steel body; (3) Detonator; (4) Guide rings; (5) High explosive filling

81mm MORTAR M31

This is a copy of the US M1 81mm mortar. It has a plain steel tube, a rectangular baseplate and a simple bipod with the spread of the legs controlled by a chain. The cross levelling gear is controlled from the right leg of the bipod.

DATA
Calibre: 81mm
Weight of barrel: 21kg
Length of barrel: 1,310mm
Weight of bipod: 19kg
Weight of baseplate: 20kg
Weight of sight: 1.5kg
Rate of fire: 20rounds/min
Maximum range: 4,100 metres
Minimum range: 85 metres
Muzzle velocity: 300 metres/sec
Ammunition:
Weight of light HE bomb: 3.2kg
Weight of TNT filling: 650g
Weight of heavy HE bomb: 4.2kg
Weight of TNT filling: 750g
Smoke bomb. As heavy HE bomb: Produces smoke for 2-4mins
Illuminating bomb. As heavy HE bomb: Produces 300,000 candlepower for 30 secs and illuminates a circle of diameter 250-300 metres
Manufacturer: State Factories
Status: In service

The 81mm mortar, M31

81mm MORTAR M68

Although similar in appearance to the French Hotchkiss-Brandt MO-81-61L mortar, the Yugoslav M68 is of Yugoslav design and construction.

DATA
Calibre: 81mm
Weight of barrel: 16kg
Length of barrel: 1,640mm
Weight of bipod: 13kg
Weight of baseplate: 11kg
Weight of sight: 1.5kg
Rate of fire: 20rounds/min
Maximum range: 5,000 metres
Minimum range: 90 metres
Muzzle velocity: 300 metres/sec

Ammunition:
HE bomb:
Weight (fuzed): 3.3kg
Bursting charge: 463g TNT
Fuze: Model UT M45P1 point detonating
Manufacturer: State factories
Status: In service

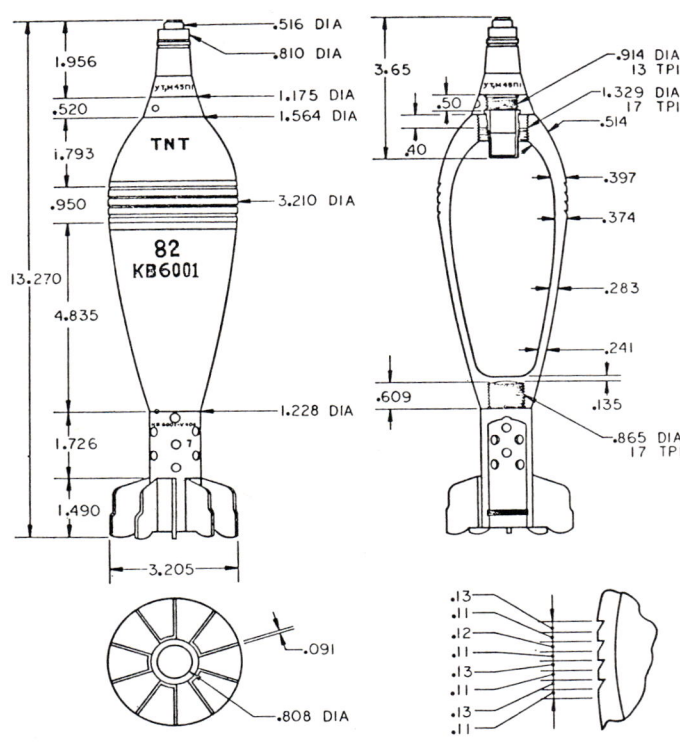

ALL DIMENSIONS IN INCHES

81mm HE bomb. (The Yugoslavian 82mm HE projectile, Model M31)

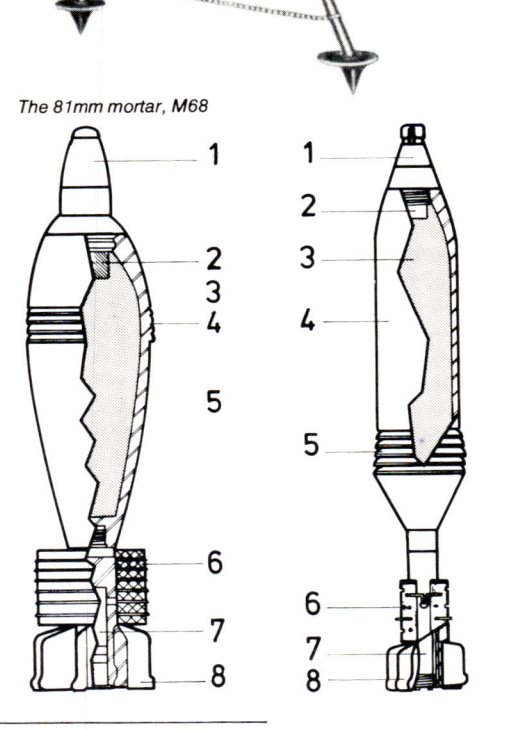

The 81mm mortar, M68

81mm mortar ammunition. **Left.** *The high explosive bomb.* **(1)** *Fuze;* **(2)** *Detonator;* **(3)** *Steel casing;* **(4)** *Guide rings;* **(5)** *High explosive filling;* **(6)** *Secondary charges;* **(7)** *Primary cartridge;* **(8)** *Tail fin.* **Right.** *The high capacity high explosive bomb.* **(1)** *Fuze;* **(2)** *Detonator;* **(3)** *High explosive filling;* **(4)** *Steel casing;* **(5)** *Guide rings;* **(6)** *Secondary charges;* **(7)** *Primary cartridge;* **(8)** *Tail fin*

120mm MORTAR UBM 52

The 120mm UBM 52 is of Yugoslav design and construction. Some reports have suggested that the mortar, is in fact, the French 120mm Hotchkiss-Brandt MO-120-AM50 built in Yugoslavia but both Hotchkiss-Brandt and the Yugoslav Ministry of Defence have informed **Jane's Infantry Weapons** that this is not the case. It is apparent from the photographs that there is little resemblance between the Yugoslav and French mortars.

The UBM 52 has been designed for both field and mountain deployment. For field use it is normally towed by its muzzle by a 4×4 truck, for example the Zastava AR-51. For transport in rough country it can be quickly broken down into five loads and carried by animals.

When in the firing position the wheels are retained and the hydro-elastic recoil system permits immediate commencement of fire once in position. The mortar, which is smooth bore, can also fire the Russian 120mm mortar round. It can be fired either by conventional drop firing or by a trigger. The mortar has a crew of five.

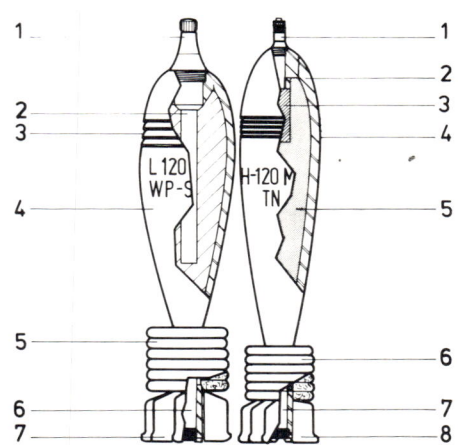

120mm mortar ammunition. **Left.** *The white phosphorous smoke bomb.* **(1)** *Fuze;* **(2)** *Smoke composition igniter;* **(3)** *Guide rings;* **(4)** *Bomb casing;* **(5)** *Secondary cartridges;* **(6)** *Primary cartridge;* **(7)** *Tail fin.* **Right.** *The light fragmentation bomb.* **(1)** *Fuze;* **(2)** *Bomb casing;* **(3)** *Detonator;* **(4)** *Guide rings;* **(5)** *The high explsoive filling;* **(6)** *Secondary cartridges;* **(7)** *Primary cartridge;* **(8)** *Tail fin*

DATA
Calibre: 120mm
Weight of complete equipment: 400kg
Maximum range (Heavy bomb): 4,760 metres
Minimum range (Heavy bomb): 195 metres
Maximum range (Light bomb): 6,010 metres
Minimum range (Light bomb): 225 metres
Ammunition:
Light bomb, HE Model 56:
Weight (fuzed): 12.2kg
Bursting charge: 2.5kg TNT
Fuze: Model 45UTU point detonating (a copy of the Brandt M1945 mortar fuze)
Heavy bomb, HE Model 49:
Weight (fuzed): 15.1kg
Bursting charge: 3.1kg

Fuze: Model 45TU point detonating (modified version of the Brandt M1945 mortar fuze)
Smoke bomb: Produces smoke for 2-4 minutes
Illuminating bomb: Burns for 30 secs and produces 1,100,000 candle power

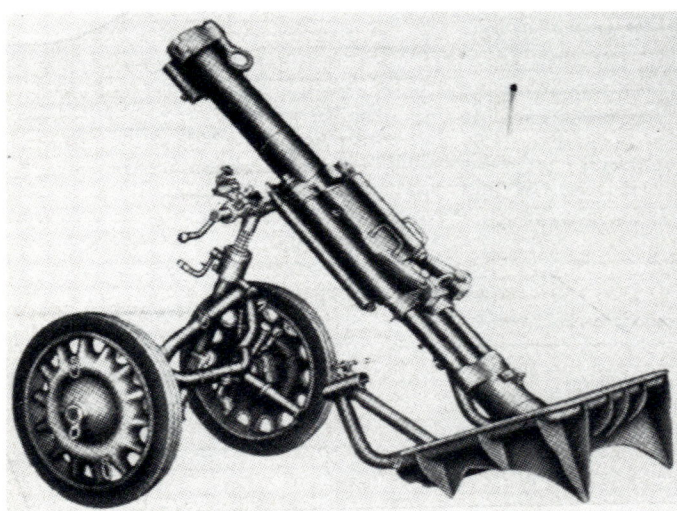

120mm mortar, UBM 52

Loading the 120mm UBM 52 mortar

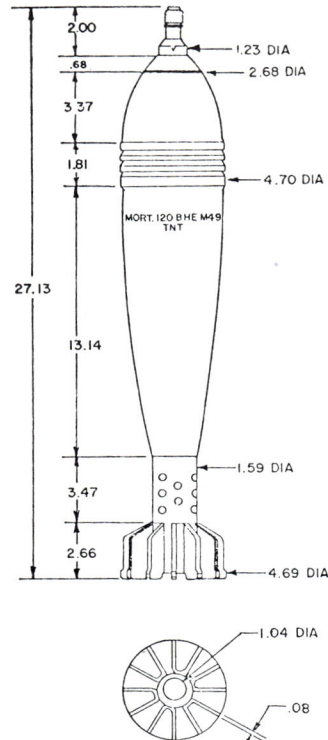

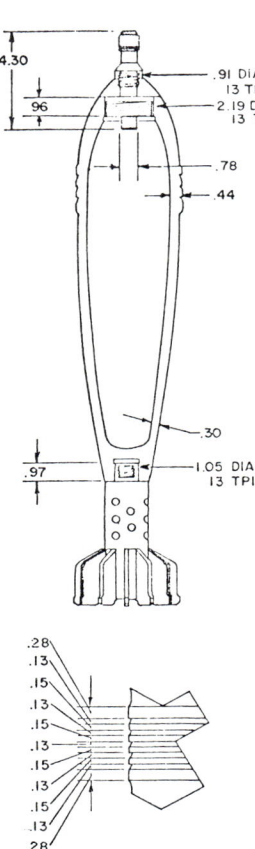

Yugoslavian 120mm HE projectile, Model 49

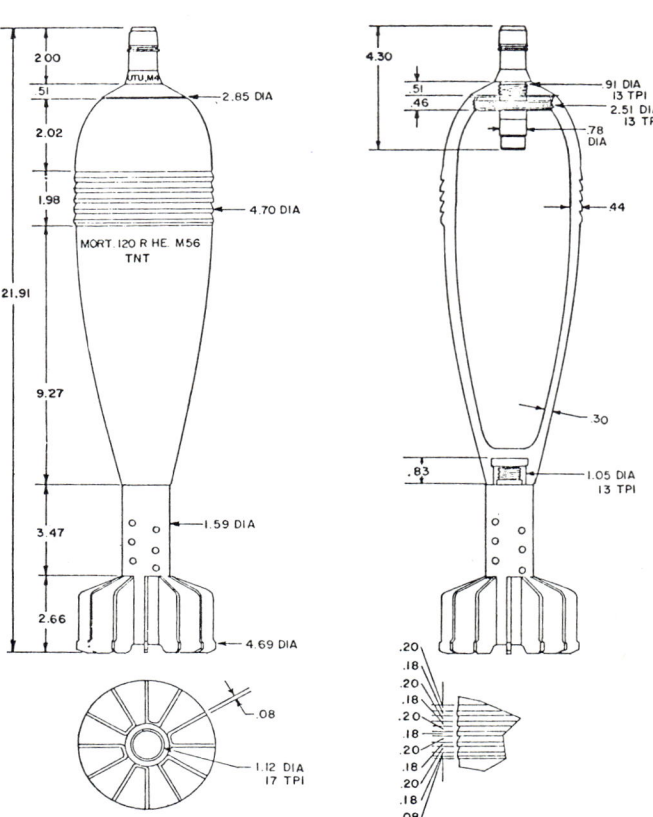

Yugoslavian 120mm HE projectile, Model 56

SECTION THREE

ANTI-AIRCRAFT AND ANTI-TANK WEAPONS

ANTI-AIRCRAFT AND ANTI-TANK WEAPONS

INTRODUCTION

This section deals with two groups of relatively specialised weapons which infantry units may be called upon to use against aircraft or armoured fighting vehicles. Selection of weapons for inclusion in the section presents a number of difficulties because the structures of different armies and the allocation of operational responsibilities within them varies so widely that there are no universally clear-cut distinctions between the functions of infantry (pedestrian or motorised) and those of artillery, engineer, and armoured units.

Arbitrarily, therefore, we have excluded from this section all anti-aircraft guns of 40mm or greater calibre (and a few others); all surface-to-air guided missiles other than those that are designed to be man-portable; and all anti-aircraft systems involving main battle tank chassis. We have also omitted anti-aircraft mountings for machine guns, of 7.62mm calibre or less, which have already been described earlier in the book.

On the other hand we have included anti-aircraft mountings for the heavy machine-guns and cannon described in previous sections. This is because such mountings often incorporate elaborate apparatus for aiming and controlling the weapon, the description of which is inappropriate to the entry describing the basic weapon – the more so since one basic weapon may be used in several different mountings of varying degrees of complexity.

From the range of possible entries in the anti-tank part of this section we have omitted detailed descriptions of all high-velocity anti-tank guns with a calibre of more than 90mm; tank-mounted weapons again; flamethrowers

and other fluid incendiary devices, hand grenades and their rifle-launched derivatives (all of which are described in earlier sections); and detailed descriptions of mines, demolitions and destructive obstacles. Mines, however, are dealt with in summary form.

Even with these arbitrary exclusions – or perhaps because of them – there are still some areas of uncertainty in the classification and we would welcome reader comments.

Very few of the weapons which have been designed primarily for use against armoured land vehicles can be employed in an anti-aircraft role with any hope of success: on the other hand many anti-aircraft weapons can be used effectively against light armoured ground targets and may occasionally disable a heavier vehicle. For this reason, the first sub-section of this section is devoted to anti-aircraft weapons and includes those that have a dual capability: whereas the second sub-section, on anti-tank weapons, contains descriptions of weapons which may be used effectively against tanks and fortifications but not against aircraft.

Apart from the foregoing all that need be said about this classification and arrangement of the anti-aircraft weapons is that, as in other sections of the book, they are arranged under their country headings in ascending order of calibre and with the cannon preceding the missiles. In the anti-tank sub-section, however, the reader's attention is drawn to the introductory note which contains some general observations of relevance to many of the entries that follow.

ANTI-AIRCRAFT WEAPONS

CHINA (PEOPLE'S REPUBLIC)

CHINESE LAA WEAPONS

Several light anti-aircraft weapons are in service with the PLA. Reference has already been made, in the section on machine guns, to the Type 54 HMG which is the Chinese version of the Russian DShK 38/46 weapon; and there are various AA guns of Russian design and calibres of 37mm upwards which lie outside the scope of this book.

Between these limits it is evident that the Chinese have in service 14.5mm weapons of Russian design and it is probable that at least some of these have been or are being manufactured in China. Machine guns of the KPV 14.5mm pattern have been seen in quadruple, twin and single mountings apparently identical with the Russian ZPU-4, ZPU-2 and ZPU-1 mountings respectively.

Descriptions will be found among the USSR entries later in this section.

A Chinese worker militia at Talien training on a quadruple 14.5mm AA mounting similar to the Russian ZPU-4

CZECHOSLOVAKIA

QUADRUPLE 12.7mm HEAVY MACHINE GUN MOUNTING M53

This is a mounting designed and built in Czechoslovakia to mount the Soviet DShK 38/46 HMG in a 2×2 arrangement similar to that used in the ZPU-4 14.5mm quadruple mounting. It is a two-wheeled mount with levelling jacks at the front and the rear and is recognisable by the four drum magazines used to feed the guns and the prominent muzzle brakes on the barrels. Further information on the basic gun will be found in the appropriate USSR entry.

DATA
Calibre: 12.7mm
Dimensions, travelling: 2.9m long × 1.6m wide × 1.78m high
Track: 1.5m
Weight, travelling: 640kg

Weight in combat order: 628kg
Elevation: −7° to +90°
Traverse: 360°
Maximum range
  Horizontal: 6,500metres
  Vertical: 5,500metres
Effective vertical range: 1,000metres
Cyclic rate of fire: 550-600 rounds/barrel/min
Practical rate of fire: 80 rounds/barrel/min
Feed: 50-round drum for each barrel
Status: No longer in service in Czechoslovakia. Believed to be in service in Cuba and Vietnam

KULOMET 15mm HEAVY MACHINE GUN ZB-60

This weapon is primarily intended for infantry fire support but has also a limited anti-aircraft use. It is a larger version of the well-known ZB Vz53 7.92mm weapon and has much the same appearance in outline. The earlier weapon was copied in the UK and extensively used in the Second World War and known as the BESA. The ZB-60 was also copied in the UK for use in armoured cars but only a small quantity was made.

DATA
Calibre: 15mm
Lengths
  Weapon: 205cm
  Barrel: 109cm

Weight: 159kg including tripod
Operation: Gas
Sights
  Front: Blade
  Rear: Aperture
Feed: belt, 40 rounds, metal links
Muzzle velocity: 905 metres/sec
Range: 2,400 metres
Rate of fire: 430 rounds/min cyclic
Manufacturer: Ceskoslovenska Zbrojovka
Status: No longer in service in Europe. Believed to be in service in the Middle East.

TWIN 30mm AA CANNON M-53/59

Two versions of this twin 30mm AA mounting are in service in Czechoslovakia. The M-53 is an open mounting on a light four-wheel trailer: the M-59 is a partially-enclosed mounting, which gives the gunner some protection, installed on an armoured version of the Praga 6×6 V3S truck.

DATA (M-53)
Calibre: 2 × 30mm
Barrel length: 2430mm
Elevation: −10° to +90°
Traverse: 360°

Firing Weight: 2,000kg
Ammunition: HE or API (Projectile 0.45kg. Complete round0.9kg)
Muzzle velocity: 1000m/sec
Rate of fire: Cyclic 450-500 rounds/min. Automatic 100 rounds/min
Range: 2,000m practical. Maximum about 10,000m
Armour penetration: (ground role) 60mm at 500m
Crew: 4
Status: In service in Czechoslovakia. Not normally used by infantry formations

DENMARK

DISA AA MOUNTINGS FOR LIGHT AUTOMATIC WEAPONS

DISA (Dansk Industri Syndikat A/S) make a range of special mountings to enable LMG or MMG to be used effectively against aircraft. Both field and vehicle mountings are included in the range, the design objective being the creation of a robust and extremely stable mount which yet permits the gunner, working single-handed, full freedom of weapon aiming. This requirement is met in the field mountings by a pivot mount on a tripod which, although light in weight, can be adjusted to suit any terrain and gunner's position while still remaining highly stable.

The vehicle mountings employ a patented lever arm system comprising two lever arms. One of these is a rigid horizontal bar vertically pivoted at one end on the mounting baseplate and joined by a vertical pivot at the other end to the second arm. The second (upper) arm is a spring-loaded vertical parallellogram which carries the gun on a combined horizontal and

vertical pivot at the end remote from the junction with the lower lever arm. The parallellogram can be locked, if required, at any of five different gun levels. This arrangemet gives a wide freedom of aiming movement to the gunner.

Vehicle mounts need not be specially adapted to vehicles except for the baseplate fixing. Differences in weight and dimensions of machine guns, however, make some modification of the basic design neccessary.

DATA (Typical)
Weight of field mounting: 10.15kg
Height to gun pivot: 1530mm maximum
Minimum muzzle height: 510mm
Weight of vehicle mounting: 15.85kg

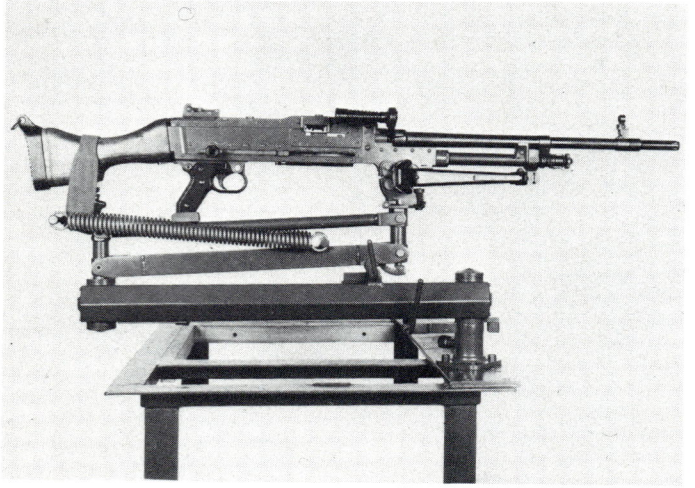

DISA vehicle mounting for FN MAG

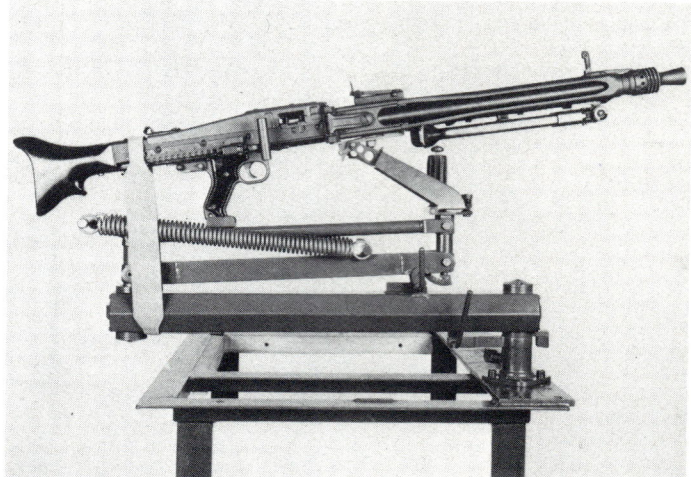

DISA vehicle mounting for German MG3

Height range of gun pivot: 514-985mm
Elevation limits: −10° to +90°
Manufacturer: Dansk Industri Syndikat A/S, 22 Mileparken, DK-2740 Skorlunde
Status: In service in several armies and undergoing trials in others

DISA mounting emplaced on an AFV

FRANCE

TOUCAN MOUNTING FOR 20mm M693 CANNON

Several mountings have been devised for the 20mm M693 weapon. An important one is the Toucan APC mounting in which the basic weapon can be associated with a 7.62mm NATO co-axial MG and various optional items such as smoke dischargers and a searchlight. Developed by GIAT for the French Government the Toucan mounting can also accommodate the M621 cannon, the Rheinmetall Rh202 or the Oerlikon 20mm cannon. It is in service with the M693 in the French Army.
Manufacturer: GIAT, 12, place Georges Clémenceau, 92211 Saint Cloud
Status: In service with the French Army

The gun in a Toucan mounting

20mm LIGHT TOWED AA MOUNTINGS TYPE 53

Two light towed AA mountings, 53T1 and 53T2, have been developed for the 20mm F1 cannon, the only significant difference between them being the ammunition supply arrangements. Each is a one-man-operated unit which, weighing only 650kg, can be towed by any vehicle. Significant features are optional manual or hydraulic laying and the possibility of incorporating a 'taboo' facility which establishes non-firing zones in elevation and azimuth.

DATA
Calibre: 20mm
Gun Data: See Cannon section
Crew: 1

Weight: 650kg
Azimuth limits: Unlimited
Elevation limits: −8° to +83°
Hydraulic laying rates: Zero to 80 deg/sec in azimuth and elevation
Sights: AA: Unit magnification
         Ground: ×5.2 telescope
Ammunition supply: 53T1: 130HE + 30AP
                53T2: 80HE with quick-change ammunition bin + 30AP
Manufacturer: GIAT, 10, place Georges-Clémenceau, 92211 Saint-Cloud
Status: Trials

20mm TWIN TURRET FOR M621 CANNON

The SAMM S.530-A turret is a light simple equipment intended to be fitted to any small AFV to provide an anti-aircraft gun mounting with secondary ground attack capability. It carries two 20mm M621 cannon (see Cannon section).

The turret and turret basket carry most of the mechanical electrical and hydraulic equipment for laying and firing the guns together with the main ammunition supply. Sighting is optical and comprises the AA sight (M411) which is carried in an armoured cupola on the turret roof and an APX episcope (L794B) for use when engaging ground targets. Four smoke pot launchers are fitted.

DATA
Weight in combat order: approx 1,700kg
Crew: 2
Armour: 7mm
Elevation limits: −10° to +70°
Elevation speed: 40 deg/sec
Traverse: 360°
Traverse speed: 80 deg/sec
Guns: 2 × M621 20mm cannon
Ammunition supply: 300 rounds/gun in turret basket
Manufacturer: Société d'Applications des Machines Motrices (SAMM) 224, quai Stalingrad – 92130 Issy-les-Moulineaux
Status: Production. In service with one army outside France

SAMM turret for the M621 cannon

20mm TWIN TURRET FOR F2 CANNON

The SAMM TG 522 is a twin-gun AA turret, with secondary ground attack capability, suitable for installation on light and medium armoured vehicles. It is of the rotating casemate type and is operated by two men. Its hydraulic 'speed' aiming control system, optical gunsights and ammunition feed system together permit smooth tracking and continuous engagement of moving targets. Provision is made for the installation of radio and any one of a variety of sights and fire control systems.

DATA
Weight, in combat order: 1800kg

Crew: 2
Elevation limits: $-8°$ to $+75°$
Traverse: 360°
Training speed: 0.8-80 deg/sec
Guns: $2 \times$ F2 20mm cannons
Ammunition supply: 240 rounds HE and optional 40 rounds AP per gun
Manufacturer: Société d'Applications des Machines Motrices (SAMM) 224, quai Stalingrad – 92130 Issy-les-Moulineaux
Status: Prototypes

20mm ANTI-AIRCRAFT TURRET MOUNTING TYPE TA20

The TA20 turret has been designed for installation on light armoured vehicles and comprises twin 20mm cannon and a 7.62mm machine gun with associated sighting and aiming equipment which can include a combined surveillance and acquisition radar. The cannon can be either the Oerlikon HSS 820 or the DTAT M621 or 693.

The turret is built by CNMP-Berthiez and features welded plastic shielding, stable positioning on a wide-diameter bearing support hub and hydraulic servo drives (by Officine Galileo) with emergency manual controls. Targets are acquired either by two target-designation optical sights which permanently view the whole horizon or by the EMD X-band pulse doppler radar. Targets are designated by either system to the gunner's optical sight; and by keeping this trained on the target the gunner causes the Galileo system computer to calculate lead angle and command the gun to the appropriate direction.

DATA
Turret weight with guns, radar and ammunition: 1900kg
Track diameter: 1,500mm
Armour plating: 8-10mm
Elevation limits: $-5°$ to $+85°$
Elevation speed: 80 deg/sec maximum. Acceleration 100 deg/sec² maximum
Traverse: 360°
Traverse speed: 90 deg/sec maximum. Acceleration 100 deg/sec² maximum
Sights: Galileo computer sight type P56T. $\times 5$ with 12° field
6 Episcopes L794B. Field 11° vertical by 32°
Ammunition supply: 300 rounds/gun in belts plus 100 rounds for the MG
Radar: X-band pulse doppler. Range in excess of 8km
Manufacturers: Turret: CNMP – Berthiez, 15, avenue d'Eylau – 75116 Paris, France
Guns: Machine Tool Works, Oerlikon Bührle Ltd, CH-8050 Zurich, PO Box

The TA20 AA turret installed on a Panhard M3 vehicle

888, Birchstrasse 155 Switzerland
or GIAT, 12, place Georges Clémenceau, 92211 Saint-Cloud, France
Computer Sight and Servo Drives: Officine Galileo, Divisione Sistemi, 50134 Firenze – Via C. Bini 44, Italy
Radar: Electronique Marcel Dassault (EMD), 55 quai Carnot, 92214 Saint-Cloud, France
Status: A prototype installed in a Panhard M3 vehicle was exhibited at the French Army exhibition at Satory in 1973 and again in 1975 at which time it was said that prototype tests had been completed

GERMANY (FEDERAL REPUBLIC)

20mm AA TWIN MOUNTING FOR Rh 202 GUN

Two anti-aircraft mountings for the Rheinmetall Rh202 20mm cannon have been developed. One of these, and the main subject of this entry, is the 20mm AA Twin Gun developed by Rheinmetall for the Federal German Department for Ordnance Technology and Procurement: the other is an AA field mounting developed co-operatively by Rheinmetall, Hispano-Suiza (now Oerlikon), Kern & Co. and Kongsberg Våpenfabrikk and described in a separate entry (see Norway).

AA TWIN MOUNTING

This is an Air Defence Gun producing accurate fire against low flying targets out to 2,000 metres. All round traverse is provided and elevation between 5 degrees and 83 degrees. Rate of traverse is 100 degrees/sec and elevation 55 degrees/sec. The power for operation is hydraulic but in the event of failure, control can still be maintained using manual operation. This mounting has a computer-aided sight which incorporates a 'taboo' facility which prevents the gun from being fired in prohibited directions – thus avoiding the commonly encountered danger of firing on friendly troops when operating any kind of aided laying system. The arrangement permits the specification of an elaborate series of prohibited azimuth and elevation combinations.

FIRE CONTROL SYSTEM

The fire control system is the well-known P56 computing sight and gun laying equipment made by Officine Galileo in Italy. It consists of the following main assemblies:
1. Monocular optical sight with swivelling objective prism for laying the gun against air and ground targets.
2. Electronic analogue computer for the calculation of kinematic lead values.
3. Joystick with two degrees of freedom for speed control of the line of sight.
4. Input panel for the target speed and crossing point distance of air targets or the target distance of ground targets.
5. Hydraulic servo drive for the gun traversing and elevating gears.
6. Manual traverse and elevation mechanism.
7. Mechanical auxiliary sight:
physically associated with which, but not part of the P56 system, is a

The AA twin mounting. The firing position

petrol-electric generator producing power for the complete gun system.

To engage an air target the gunner first sets estimated target speed and aiming point distance on the input panel then acquires the target in his open sight using the joystick to control the gun. He then changes over to the optical sight and used the joystick to bring the reticle into coincidence with the nose of the aircraft. Holding the sight in this relative position by means of the joystick he then presses the joystick down to put the guns under control of the computer. Thereafter he keeps the optical sight on the target and the computer points the guns with the degree of lead needed for successful firing. Firing will, however, be inhibited, when appropriate by the taboo programme.

When engaging ground targets it is necessary only to set the estimated range on the input panel and to bring the target into the reticle of the optical sight before firing.

DATA
Twin Gun System
Dimensions in travelling position
   Length: 5,035mm
   Width: 2,360mm
   Height: 2,075mm
Swing radius of guns at 0° elevation: 2,510mm
Muzzle height at 0° elevation: 735mm
Weights:
   In travelling position without ammunition: approx. 2,170kg
   In firing position, with 550 rounds of ammunition: approx. 1,640kg

Automatic cannon
Type: Mk 20 Rh 202
Calibre: 20mm
Rate of fire: 1,000 rounds/min
Muzzle velocity: 1,050-1,260m/sec
Recoil force: 550-700kg

Laying system
Laying range
   Traverse: unlimited
   Elevation: −7.5° to +85.5°
Laying speed
   Traverse: max. 80°/sec
   Elevation: max. 48°/sec
Acceleration
   Traverse: max. 120°/sec^2
   Elevation: max. 75°/sec^2
Optical system
   Magnification: × 5
   Field of view: 12°
Lead computer: Electronic analog system
Estimated data input
   Target speed (air targets): 60 to 350m/sec
   Crossing point distance (air targets): 100 to 600 metres
   Target distance (ground targets): 100 to 2,000 metres

The AA twin mounting coming into action

Power supply system
Drive engine: System NSU-Wankel, air cooled with centrifugal governor, manual starter
   Power: 6kW at 4,500rpm

Ammunition
Type: 20mm × 139
Ammunition boxes: 2 × 275 belted rounds
Belt frame: 2 × 10 belted rounds

Trailer
Number of wheels: 2
Electrical system: 24V or 12V
Towing-eye adjustable in height: ±200mm
Manufacturer: Rheinmetall GmbH, 4000 Düsseldorf 1, Ulmenstrasse 125
Status: In production and in service with the German Army and other NATO forces

NORWAY

AA FIELD MOUNT HS 669 N with 20mm Rh 202 GUN

The Anti-Aircraft Field Mount HS 669 N with Automatic Gun 20mm Rh 202 was developed co-operatively by Rheinmetall GmbH, Hispano-Suiza (Suisse) S.A. (now Oerlikon), Kern & Co AG and A/S Kongsberg Våpenfabrikk. It is a further development of the Hispano-Suiza mount HS 669, containing the A/S Kongsberg Våpenfabrikk designed cradle with ammunition cases and flexible belt feed channels, all adapted to the Automatic Gun 20mm Rh 202, developed by Rheinmetall. The optical sight was developed by Kern & Co AG. The project was closely supervised by technical representatives of Bundesamt für Wehrtechnik und Beschaffung, Federal Republic of Germany and of Hærens forsyningskommando, Norway.

The mount may be used against ground targets as well as air targets, is simple and easy to handle and operate, and may be brought into action quickly.

The mount is primarily designed for towing by truck, but may also be transported by helicopters or ordinary transport-planes. No special tools are required for dismantling it into suitable loads for man-pack transportation.

Rh 202 GUN

A full description of the Rh 202 gun will be found in the German entry in the section dealing with cannon.

CRADLE

The cradle, which carries the gun and guides the recoiling mass, is made of cast aluminium alloy and is bedded in the upper mounting. It contains the recoil brakes and components forming part of the fire selector and trigger mechanism.

The frame assembly contains the feeder mechanism and the belt guides. For the inspection of the gun, the frame assembly may be raised and is automatically locked in the gun inspection position. To dismount the feeder mechanism, the frame should be rotated to its forward position. The cocking crank is placed on top of the cradle. Both sides of the cradle are fitted with a clamping device for holding the ammunition cases and the flexible belt channels in position.

The spring loaded case covers are kept raised to ease the attachment of the ammunition cases to the cradle. The cases contain 75 rounds each and may be used on either side. The belts of ammunition are completely free and unguided in their cases, and are prevented from running back by a locking device in the feed mechanism.

Together with a 10 round magazine, which is inserted on top of the gun, the total in-mount ammunition amounts to 160 cartridges. Inserting ammunition belts or changing between left and right belt and magazine is done quickly.

HS 669 N mount with Rh 202 gun

UPPER MOUNTING WITH SEAT

The upper mounting holds the cradle and contains the parts of the elevating and traversing mechanism, partly consisting of adjustable twin gears to prevent play in the transmission. The upper mounting is quickly assembled to or disassembled from the lower mounting by a special locking device.

The optical sight is mounted on the upper mounting between the elevating and traversing handwheels.

The seat, which has been primarily designed for use of the gun against air targets, can also be folded to provide the gunner with a comfortable prone position support when using the gun against ground targets.

LOWER MOUNTING
The lower mounting includes the central base with the three trails, of which the two shorter side trails may be disconnected as required for transport or storage purpose. When towing the mount, the forward trail serves as the carriage drag link.

CARRIAGE
The carriage is a 2-wheel trailer. The towbar may be set in several positions to compensate for differences in towing hook height and thereby keeping the mount approximately in a horizontal position when being towed.

The wheels are mounted on pivots and are supported by springs with hydraulic dampers.

OPTICAL SIGHT
The FERO-Z13 sight is used for both air and ground targets. Lead angle curves are provided to assist with the engagement of air targets; for ground targets the sight is calibrated for ranges of 500, 1,000 and 1,500metres.

DATA
Calibre: 20mm
Rate of fire: 800-950 rounds per min
Maximum range: 7,000metres
Effective range: 500-2,500metres
Optical sight: 18kg
  Magnification, ground targets: 5x
  Magnification, air targets: 1,5x
  Visible field, ground targets: 200metres at 1,000metres
  Visible field, air targets: 700metres at 1,000metres
Weights
  Gun with feeder and recoil brakes: 72kg
  Cradle complete, without ammunition: 112kg
  Upper mounting: 100kg
  Shield: 33kg
  Lower mounting: 125kg
  Carriage: 160kg
  Optical sight: 18kg
  Total weight: 620kg
Manufacturer: (complete mount) A/S Kongsberg Våpenfabrikk N-3600 Kongsberg
Status: In service

SWEDEN

RBS 70 PORTABLE AA MISSILE SYSTEM

RBS 70 is a portable anti-aircraft missile system, intended for defence of mobile army units.

The system consists of three units – stand, sight and missile in container – and is separated into these three units for transport. As it is portable, RBS 70 can be deployed in such favourable places for anti-aircraft defence purposes as hilltops, roofs or towers and can be deployed and made ready for firing in less than 30 seconds. The actual engagement of targets is carried out by one man but to fire several missiles in rapid succession a loader is needed.

IFF equipment can be connected to the system and automatically blocks the sight if an attempt is made to engage a target which the IFF equipment has found to be friendly.

The system can be coupled to a search radar to receive accurate target indication information enabling the operator quickly to acquire the target in the sight telescope. This gives a shorter reaction time, and means that a greater number of targets can be engaged – and more efficiently – than if there is no search radar.

Missile guidance is based upon the optical beam rider principle. A laser beam, invisible to the eye, is generated in the sight unit and aimed by the operator at the target. The missile is fired into the guidance beam, which it thereafter follows automatically to the target. This principle involves a high degree of aiming accuracy, and good anti-jamming properties.

The stand carries the sight and the missile, and is provided with a seat for the operator. The sight generates the guidance beam, and is provided with a telescope, the line of sight of which coincides with the centre of the guidance beam. The line of sight and the guidance beam are aimed with the aid of a servo-controlled and gyro-stabilised mirror. This is controlled by a lever which the operator operates with his right thumb.

The missile is stored with folded control surfaces and fins in the container. It is fired from the container by a booster motor, which burns out in the container and is thereafter jettisoned. A few metres from the sight the sustainer motor is ignited, which accelerates the missile to supersonic speed. The sustainer motor has smokeless powder, and does not interfere with the guidance beam.

The missile contains electronics which detect deviations of the missile from the axis of the guidance beam, and generate signals to the control surfaces to keep the missile on the beam.

The warhead of the missile is prefragmented, and is initiated either by a direct-action fuze or by a jam-proof laser proximity fuze.

An important feature claimed for the system is its resistance to jamming. Optical beam riding in combination with advanced signal technology is said to make jamming practically impossible. Also claimed for it is a high kill probability resulting from a high degree of precision in the aiming system and the highly effective warhead.

Material for training in handling and firing of the system is also available. This includes a simulator with which the operator can be trained in all phases of the operation of the system, including target tracking.

RBS 70 system ready for action

DATA
Range: 5,000 metres
Altitude covered: 3,000 metres
Deployment time: 30sec

Reloading time: 10sec
Weight
  Stand: 22kg
  Sight: 35kg
  Missile in container: 23.5kg
Length of missile: 1,320mm
Diameter of missile: 106mm
Guidance: Optical beam rider
Proximity fuze: Laser type
Warhead: Prefragmented
IFF: Can be connected
Target indication: Can be received from search radar
Manufacturer: AB Bofors, Ordnance Division, Box 500, S-690 20 Bofors, Sweden
Status: Development is complete and production deliveries began in 1976

SWITZERLAND

20mm OERLIKON GUN TURRET TYPE GAD-AOA

This armoured, one-man, multi-purpose gun turret is equipped with a single Oerlikon 20mm cannon type KAA (former designation 204GK) details of which are given in the appropriate cannon entry. The turret is armour-plated to give protection against small-arms fire and is sealed against chemical and radioactive particle hazards. The cannon itself is mounted outside the turret thus permiting freedom of movement within and preventing the ingress of fumes. The height of the seat and platform can be adjusted to suit the gunner.

Ammunition is belt-fed from the right and the gun can be reloaded with the hatch closed and full armour protection, the last chance to reload with such protection being indicated by a warning lamp on the gunner's forehand support. A large ammunition capacity coupled with these reloading arrangements enable the turret to be kept ready for action over long periods. Gun laying is by handwheel.

The turret is suitable for installation in a variety of armoured vehicles. Known installations are the Mowag Piranha APC and Tornado MICV (both illustrated here) and the Austrian Saurer APC.

GAD-AOA turret on the Mowag Piranha APC

Firing the KAA cannon

GAD-AOA turret on the Mowag Tornado MICV

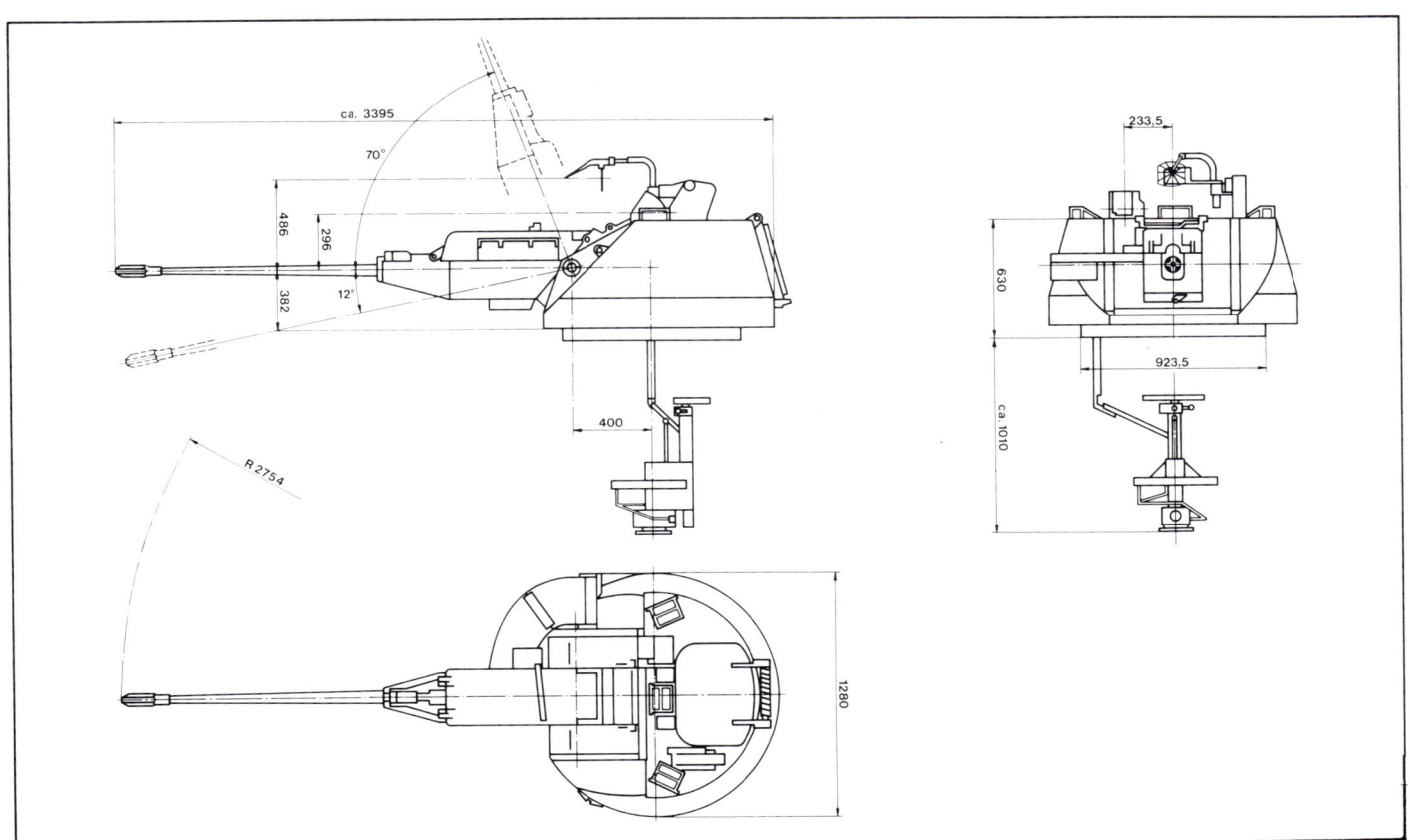

Layout and dimensions of the GAD-AOA turret

DATA
Weights:
Turret with rotating platform: 927kg
Cannon with barrel: 88kg
100 round belt: 40kg
Total weight (ready for action): 1,055kg

Aiming:
Traverse arc: unlimited
Elevation arc: −12° to +70°
Turning radius at 0° elevation: 2754mm

Armour:
Front against 90° impact: 20-35mm
Other surfaces: 8-20mm

Cannon:
Calibre: 20mm
Rate of fire: approx. 1,000 rounds/min
Barrel length: 1856mm
Muzzle velocity (according to type of ammunition): 1100-1200m/sec

Ammunition:
Types: SLA, SBA, MLA, MSA, HLA, PSA, ULA, UGA
Length of round: 203.5mm
Weight of round according to type: 320-340g
Weight of shell according to type: 102-128g
Manufacturer: Machine Tool Works, Oerlikon-Bührle Ltd, CH-8050 Zurich, PO Box 888, Birchstrasse 155
Status: In production and in service

20mm OERLIKON INFANTRY AND AA GUN TYPE GAI-BO1

The GAI-BO1 (formerly designated 101 La/57G) is a dual purpose gun designed to operate against ground and aircraft targets. It is towed behind any suitable vehicle and can be very rapidly brought into action in either of its two roles. Similarly, it can be changed from anti-aircraft fire to ground action or vice versa. In the ground role it can be fired off its wheels or dropped into action on its frame. It has a very good cross country performance and with its wide track, large tyres and a ground clearance that can be adjusted from 230mm to 370mm it can traverse most terrain.

DATA
Gun: Oerlikon Cannon KAB-001 (formerly known as the 5TG).
Muzzle velocity: 1,100-1,200metres/sec
Rate of fire (cyclic): 1,000 rounds/min
Weight without magazine: 103kg
Weight of filled drum magazine (50 rounds): 41.5kg
Weight of filled box magazine (8 rounds): 8kg
Weight of barrel: 51kg

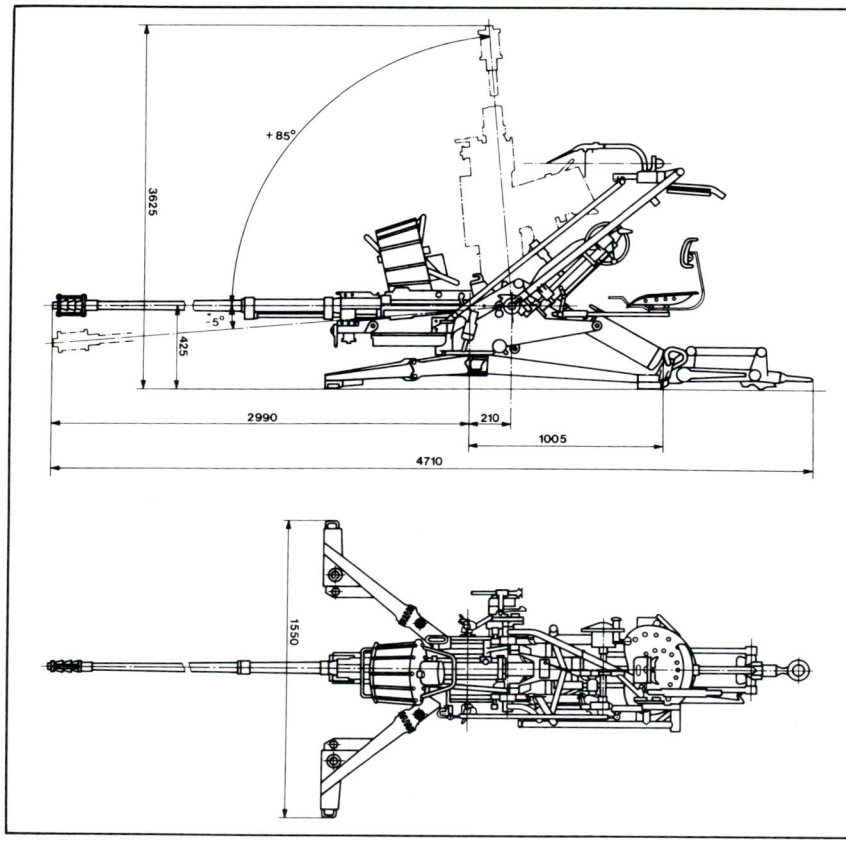
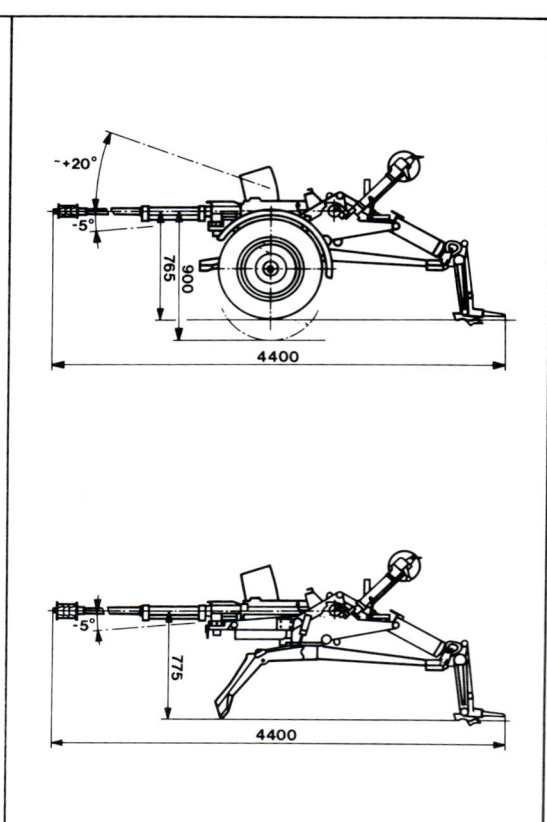

Layout and dimensions of the GAI-BO1

The Oerlikon 20mm Type GAI-BO1 in ground target configuration

The Oerlikon 20mm infantry and AA gun type GAI-BO1

OPERATIONAL TIMINGS
Travelling position to anti-aircraft position: 25sec
Travelling position to ground action: 20sec
Anti-aircraft position to ground position: 6sec
Changing drum magazines: 3sec

Elevation from −5° to 85°: 2sec
Traverse through 360°: 3sec
Manufacturer: Machine Tool Works Oerlikon-Bührle Ltd, CH-8050 Zurich,PO Box 888, Birchstrasse 155
Status: In production and in service

20mm OERLIKON KAD MOUNTINGS

The Oerlikon 20mm cannon KAD formerly known by its Hispano-Suiza designation, HS 820, has been used in many different mountings, some of which are described below.

Oerlikon GAI-C Single Mounting

Formerly designated HS 669A, this was a mobile single gun mounting from which three men could get the gun into action against aircraft in 20 seconds and get out again after action in a further 20 seconds. The weight of the complete equipment in the travelling position was 512kg and in the firing position 370kg. The dimensions were kept to a very reasonable size and amounted to a length in the travelling position of 4.04metres and when in the firing position the width was 1.70metres and the distance from the pivot to muzzle was 2.65metres. The mounting has since been superseded by the GAI-CO1 and GAI-CO3 single mountings.

HS 665 Triple Mounting

This was a mobile mounting with self-contained fire and power control equipment for three type HS 820 guns, enabling them to be used in the anti-aircraft and anti-armour roles as well as being able to engage soft targets. There is a two wheeled carriage which can easily be withdrawn when the equipment is brought into action by its detachment (including the driver) of four. Only a gunner and a loader are needed to maintain fire. On the ground the gun is supported on three spades to form a wide and rigid base. The gunner controls the fire from the back of the mounting and uses a joystick assembly. There are two prismatic sights fitted – one for anti-aircraft use and one for ground targets. Hydraulic power is used to elevate and rotate the gun. The system used was devised by Officine Galileo of Florence.

DATA
Triple 20mm Field Mounting Type 665

DIMENSIONS
Overall length of mounting in transport position: 4,590mm
Overall width of mounting in transport position: 1,860mm
Overall height of mounting in transport position: 2,340mm
Height above ground of ring in horizontal position: 880mm
Track: 1,580mm
Total length of mounting in horizontal firing position: 4,610mm
Total height of mounting in vertical firing position: 3,180mm
Height above ground of baseplate (transport position): 430mm
Firing height: 575mm
Maximum spread of spades
　Rear: 1,555mm
　Front: 1,130mm
　Radius from trainging axis to end of barrels: 3,055mm

WEIGHTS
Carriage: 150kg
Base with spades: 160kg
Rotating part with seat: 120kg
Control unit: 110kg
Cradle: 130kg
Armour: 35kg
3 guns type 820-L (57kg each): 171kg
3 magazines type 520-A, full (33kg each): 99kg
Total weight of mounting with guns and magazines
In transport position: 1,570kg
In firing position: 1,230kg

OPERATION
Maximum recoil of gun in cradle: (25mm)
Elevation limits
　Mechanical: −5° to +83°
　Hydraulic: −3° to +81°
Training limits: 360°
Maximum angular velocity in elevation: 60°/sec
Maximum angular velocity in training: 110°/sec
Maximum acceleration in elevation: 60°/sec²
Maximum acceleration in training: 120°/sec²
Time required to traverse 180°: 2.4sec
One turn of emergency handwheel
　Elevation: 4°
　Training: 9°

Oerlikon Single Mountings GAI-CO1 and GAI-CO3

Successors to the GAI-C (HS 639A) mounting mentioned above, these two light single mountings differ in only two significant respects: the GAI-CO1 is belt-fed and incorporates the KAD-B13-3 85 calibre cannon whereas the GAI-CO3 is drum-fed and has the longer-barrelled 105 calibre KAD-AO1 cannon.

The Oerlikon 20mm infantry and AA gun type GAI-CO1. The former designation HS-639-B 3.1

The Oerlikon 20mm triple barrel AA gun type 665

Oerlikon GAI-CO3 mounting. The former designation was HS639-B4.1

Both are one-man operated and tripod-mounted, with detachable two-wheeled travelling gear which has an adjustable towing eye. They have reflector sights for use against air and ground targets with a fixed arrangement of lead markers and lead curves which automatically follow the elevation movements of the gun.

DATA
(Common to both mountings unless otherwise indicated)
Gun: KAD-B13-3 (CO1) or KAD-AO1 (CO3)
Rate of fire: 1,050 rounds/min
Muzzle velocity: 1,050m/sec
Barrel length: 1,840mm (CO1) or 2,240mm (CO3)
Feed: 75-round belt (CO1) or 50-round drum (CO3)
Weights:
　Travelling without ammunition: 512kg (CO1) or 495kg (CO3)
　Firing position, loaded: 370kg (CO1) or 342kg (CO3)
　Ammunition and container/drum: 44kg (CO1) or 36kg (CO3)
Gun laying:
　Traverse: Unlimited (free movement or with foot pedal)
　Elevation: −7° to +83° (handwheel 8°/revolution)

Rotation radius at zero elevation: 2,650mm (CO1) or 3,060mm (CO3)
Sights: Delta IV reflector sight with telescopic sight for ground targets
Graticule illumination by daylight or electric battery
Graticules: High-speed targets to 900km/h and low speed to 200km/h

Field of vision: AA sight 1,060 mils: telescopic sight 300 mils
Magnification: AA sight × 1: telescopic sight × 2.5
Ammunition: Types MSA, MLA, PLA, HLA, UGA, ULA
Weight of round: 314g

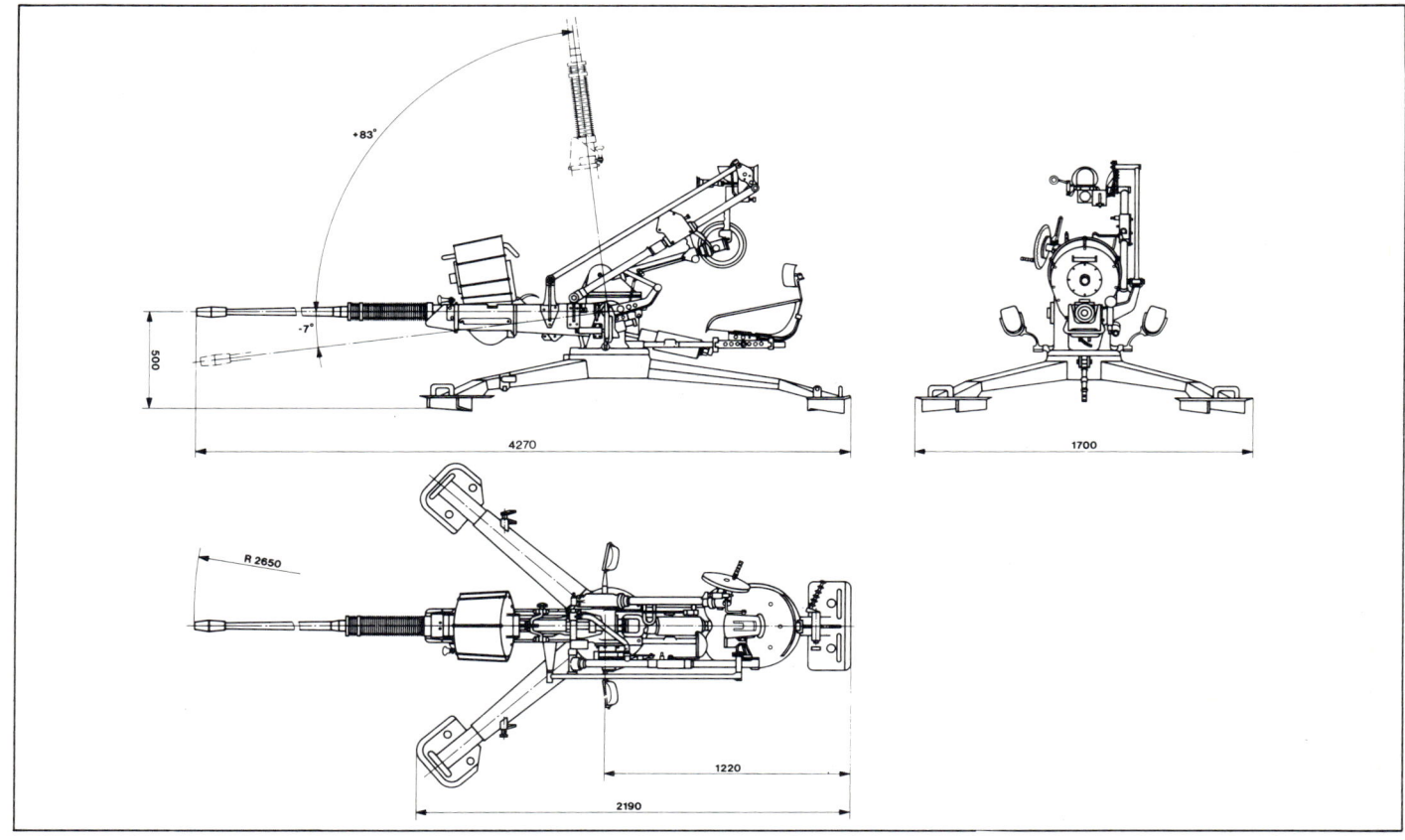

Layout and dimensions of the GAI-CO3 mounting. The GAI-CO1 mounting is similar but has an overall length of only 3,870mm, because the cannon barrel is 400mm shorter, and a boxed belt feed in place of the drum

Oerlikon GAI-DO1 Twin Mounting

This is a Hispano Oerlikon twin barrel mounting using the HS 820 (KAD) cannon for low level air defence. The gun mounting has hydraulic power control using the Galileo control unit P56 with a joystick for traverse and elevation. The ammunition is contained in boxes on the outside of each gun. The former designation was HS 666.

DATA
Gun: Twin HS 820-SL (KAD)
Calibre: 20mm
Rate of fire: 1,000 rounds/barrel/minute
Muzzle velocity: 1,050 metres/sec

EQUIPMENT
Weight in travelling position: 1,540kg
Weight in firing position, with ammo.: 1,200kg
Traverse: 360°
Rate of traverse: 80°/sec
Elevation: −3° to +81°
Rate of elevation: 48°/sec
Tactical range: Up to 2,000metres
Manufacturer: All the above mountings are or have been manufactured by

The Oerlikon 20mm twin barrel AA gun type GAI-DO1. (Former designation HS 666)

Machine Tool Works Oerlikon-Bührle Ltd, CH-8050 Zurich, PO Box 888, Birchstrasse 155

25mm OERLIKON TURRET TYPE GBD

This turret has been developed for use with the Oerlikon 25mm Automatic Cannon type KBA-B. It is an overhead mounting that can be installed in any type of armoured vehicle and enables the gun to be used in a ground or anti-aircraft role. Only one man is required to operate and fight the turret. Known installations are the GBD-AO5 for the M113 C&R vehicle and the GBD-B20 on the M113 APC version.

Oerlikon 25mm gun turret GBD-AO5 mounted on the M113 C&R vehicle

DATA
Weight of turret- without ammunition: 940kg
- with ammunition: 1,055kg
Traverse: 360° (6,400 mils)
Traverse velocity: Up to 70°/sec (1,244 mils/sec)
Elevation: −15° to +55° (−267 to 978 mils)
Sights- Day: Aiming periscope for ground and AA use:
×6 or ×2 magnification
- Night: Infra-red aiming periscope, ×4 magnification
Manufacturer: Machine Tool Works Oerlikon-Bührle Ltd, CH-8050 Zurich,
PO Box 888, Birchstrasse 155

Turret type GBD-B20 on M113 APC

25mm OERLIKON MOUNTING TYPE GBI

This infantry mounting incorporates the 25mm KBA-CO1 cannon, details
of which are set out in an entry in the cannon section of this book. The
mount is a tripod, giving all-round traverse and an elevation range from −10
to +70 degrees, which is mounted on a two-wheel trailer. The gun is
traversed by a handwheel, which can be declutched to give a free swing
when required, and elevated by a second handwheel. A box containing 40
rounds of belted ammunition is mounted on each side of the gun which is
fed from both sides. The gun is served by a three-man crew and can be fired
off its wheels in an emergency. The mount can be broken down into
convenient loads for transport over difficult terrain.

DATA
Cannon: 25mm Type KBA-CO1
Weight of complete mounting- travelling position: 550kg
- firing position: 410kg
Weight of trailer: 140kg
Manufacturer: Machine Tool Works Oerlikon Bührle, CH-8050 Zurich, PO
Box 888, Birchstrasse 155

Oerlikon 25mm infantry mounting type GBI

30mm OERLIKON MOUNTING TYPE GCI

This mounting was designed for use with the weapon formerly known as
the HS831 cannon and now bearing the Oerlikon designation KCB. Details
of the weapon will be found in the section of this book dealing with cannon:
details of the mounting (formerly known as the HS661) are given below.
Suitable for the engagement of both airborne and ground targets the
system is mobile on a two-wheel trailer and can be brought into action
rapidly.

DATA

DIMENSIONS
Overall length of mounting transport position: 5,400mm
Overall width of mounting in transport position: 1,860mm
Overall height of mounting in transport position: 2,400mm
Height above ground of ring in horizontal position: 560-880mm
Track: 1,340mm
Total length of mounting in horizontal firing position: 5,150mm
Total height of mounting in vertical firing position: 430mm
Firing height: 575mm
Maximum spread of spades
Rear: 1,555mm
Front: 1,130mm
Radius from training axis to end of barrels: 3,595mm

WEIGHTS
**Total weight of mounting with gun and feed mechanism in transport
position:** 1,540kg
In firing position: 1,150kg

OPERATION
Maximum recoil of gun in cradle: 60mm

The Oerlikon 30mm AA gun type GCI (Former designation HS 661)

Elevation limits
Mechanical: −5° to +83°
Hydraulic: −3° to +81°
Training limits: 360°
Maximum angular velocity in elevation: 60°/sec
Maximum angular velocity in training: 110°/sec
Time required to traverse 180°: 24sec
One turn of emergency handwheel
Elevation: 4°
Training: 9°
Manufacturer: Machine Tool Works Oerlikon-Bührle Ltd, CH-8050 Zurich,
PO Box 888, Birchstrasse 155

35mm AUTOMATIC CANNON KDC

This twin barrelled gun of advanced design was formerly known as the
Oerlikon MK and with the Contraves Super-Fledermaus fire control equipment was referred to as the Oerlikon-Contraves 35mm twin barrelled AA
gun system with the designation 2ZLA-353-MK. The equipment is now
known as the GDF-001. It is a fully automatic radar controlled anti-aircraft
gun.

The Oerlikon 35mm automatic gun is positively locked and gas operated.
Its rate of fire is 550 rounds/min and its muzzle velocity is 1,175metres/sec-
ond. The body of the gun, with the barrel, moves back on the cradle slides
during recoil. The gun cover which contains the feed mechanism is held by
the magazine and does not recoil. There is a muzzle brake and to this is
secured a muzzle velocity measuring device.

The guns fire during the counter recoil movement and so the action is that
of floating firing whereby the recoil force is reduced. The weapon can be
said to oscillate without abrupt changes of direction and therefore a reduction of accelerations, and their corresponding forces, is achieved.

With a twin barrelled gun with a high rate of fire and a heavy round,
ammunition supply is very difficult to maintain. On this gun 56 rounds are
held in the feed hopper for each barrel. There is a reloading hopper for each
barrel and during firing under automatic control the two members of the
detachment transfer ammunition from the reloading hoppers to the feed
hoppers on the gun. Reloading is simple and quick for an ammunition clip
with 7 rounds weighs about 11.5kg and can be moved into the feed hopper
whilst the gun is firing. Thus replenishment from outside the gun only

becomes essential when the complete supply of 238 rounds on the gun has been fired.

The gun is provided with automatic levelling for the platform by remote control. The three levelling spindles are actuated by oil pressure supplied by electrically driven oil pumps or, in the event of power failure, by hand. A pilot light indicates when the platform is level. Using power the gun can be brought into action with a three man detachment in 1.5 minutes or by one man on his own in 2.5 minutes. In emergency when there is no power it can be brought into action by hand. The time for this is not known.

During firing the muzzle velocity of the gun is measured by firing through a coil and measuring induction changes.

The Oerlikon twin 35mm AA gun type GDF-001. The former designation was 2ZLa/353 MK. This is the travelling position

DATA
Calibre: 35mm
Barrel length: 3,150mm (90 calibres)
Shell weight: 550g
Weight of bursting charge: 120g
Muzzle velocity: 1,175metres/sec
Rate of fire per barrel: 550rds/min
Rate of fire of twin gun: 1,100rds/min
Weight of shells fired per second: 10.1kg
Weight of explosive fired per second: 2.2kg
Time of flight for
2,000metres: 2.19sec
3,000metres: 3.78sec
4,000metres: 5.97sec
Elevation: −5° to +92°
Traverse: Unrestricted

	Min	Max
Rate of elevation:	0.05	60°/sec
Rate of traverse:	0.05	120°/sec
Elevation acceleration:		120°/sec²
Traverse acceleration:		180°/sec²

Traverse and elevation drive:
Electric, by remote control
Electric by gunlayer, by joystick, with auxiliary sight
Manual drive by gunlayer, with ground sight telescope

Ammunition supply (rounds):	**per barrel**	**per twin gun**
Ready in feed hoppers:	56	112
In reloading hoppers on gun:	63	126
	119	238

Reloading from reloading hoppers
(1 man per barrel) approx.: 150 rounds/min
Weight of 7-round ammuntion clip: 11.5kg
Weight of twin gun without ammunition: 6,000kg
Gun in firing position with 238 rounds
(Approx 390kg): 6,400kg
Height of gun axis in firing position, approx.: 1,280mm
Overall height in firing position, approx.: 1,720mm
Overall height in travelling position
with barrel locked at +15°, approx.: 2,600mm
Overall length, towing lug to muzzle: 7,870mm
Overall width in travelling position: 2,260mm

The Oerlikon twin 35mm AA gun GDF-001 in firing position. Note the velocity recording device on the muzzles

Track width: 1,900mm
Wheel base: 3,800mm
Ground clearance: 330mm
Automatic levelling range: 7°
Manufacturer: Machine Tool Works Oerlikon-Bührle Ltd, CH-8050 Zurich, PO Box 888, Birchstrasse 155
Status: In service

UNION OF SOVIET SOCIALIST REPUBLICS

14.5mm ZPU-1, ZPU-2 AND ZPU-4 MOUNTINGS

The Russian KPV 14.5mm heavy machine gun and the Chinese copy thereof have been extensively used in single, twin and quadruple towed and vehicle mountings for anti-aircraft purposes. Most commonly encountered is probably the ZPU-4 four-gun system which is certainly in service in Russia and probably in other allied and client countries of the USSR: it is

A Chinese ZPU-4-pattern mounting with a twin 37mm AA mounting behind it

also still in service in China (as either an imported or locally-made weapon) and both it and the twin-gun ZPU-2 were used extensively by North Vietnamese forces during the war in Vietnam. Details of the basic gun are given in an earlier section: the accompanying illustrations show some of its applications.

Twin 14.5mm AA mounting for the KPV on a Russian BTR-152V APC. (Novosti)

Close-up of a Russian ZPU-4 in firing position

23mm ZU-23 AND ZSU 23-4 MOUNTINGS

The Russian 23mm ZU-23 gun is used in two important mountings. One is the standard towed mount comprising two guns and associated feed system and laying gear all mounted on a two-wheel collapsible trailer: the other is the AFV-mounted radar-controlled quadruple gun system known as the ZSU 23-4 or Shilka.

ZU-23

Details of the basic gun are given in the cannon section earlier in the book and the standard twin mount is illustrated here. It may be used to engage either ground or air targets.

ZSU 23-4 in a Moscow parade with 57mm ZSU-57 SP guns following. The ZSU 23-4 is an early version: more recent models exhibit minor external differences in the hull and turret. (Tass)

ZU-23 twin mounting in action position

ZSU 23-4 vehicles in an Egyptian parade. These are of a modern pattern which is also in service in Russia (SIPA Press)

ZSU-23-4

This is the 4 gun version mounted on a modified PT/76 hull. It is used by one 4 gun Battery of the AA Battalion in the Motor Rifle Regiment.

In this version the guns are water cooled and the rate of fire remains at 900-1000 rounds per barrel giving some 4000 rounds/minute which is the greatest weight of fire produced by any light anti-aircraft gun in current service. The ammunition is limited to 500 rounds per gun but 3000 more are carried in the support vehicles.

The associated Gun Dish fire-control radar will pick up a low flying target at 5 miles range. The gun is at its best when dealing with a low level attack but having no IFF it is limited in its engagement of targets in conditions of poor visibility.

After the 1973 October War the Israeli low level aircraft losses were first attributed to the SA-7. Subsequent analysis shows that a high proportion of the Arab success should be credited to the ZSU 23-4 gun.

Manufacturer: State Factories

Status: In production. In service in the USSR, East Germany, Hungary, Poland, Egypt and Syria

SA-7 SURFACE-TO-AIR MISSILE

SA-7 is the US alphanumeric code for a man-portable shoulder launched anti-aircraft missile which is also known by the NATO code-name Grail. It was first seen in action in Egypt after the Six Day War but was not very effective. It was used in Vietnam with more success against the piston engined aircraft in use there. It was also employed against helicopters.

The missile is very similar to the American Redeye missile and although somewhat less sophisticated has a comparable performance. It consists of an infra-red seeker, a warhead, a control section, a propulsion unit and various electronics. The infra-red seeker is an uncooled lead sulphide type which needs a strong signal to function well and so tends to chase the exhaust pipe of a hot engine. In the 1973 October War in Israel, an Israeli military spokesman was quoted as saying that a lot of tail pipes were bent but little other damage was done.

There are four spring loaded tail fins which stabilise the missile in flight and two canard fins at the front control it.

The warhead is RDX/AP and there is a graze fuze as well as a direct action fuze but no proximity fuze or IFF is fitted.

The acquisition procedure is similar to that of Redeye. When the operator locates a target he removes the end cap of the launch tube and points it at the target. The trigger has two stages of operation. The first movement switches on the thermal battery; and when the missile is receiving an acceptable level of infra red, an audible warning is given and a light comes on. The trigger is pulled right back when the target is in range. The missile is ejected by a motor which burns out before the tail of the missile leaves the tube. The booster accelerates the missile and the sustainer then functions.

A Polish soldier firing the SA-7

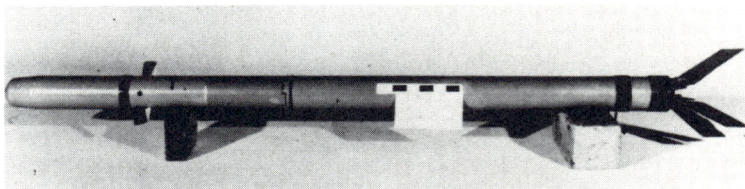

The Grail missile

DATA

Launcher length: 1,346mm
Launcher diameter: 100mm
Launcher weight: 10.6kg
Weight of missile: 9.2kg
Length: 1,300mm
Diameter: 70mm
Rocket motor: Solid. Three stage
Guidance system: Infra-red passive
Warhead: HE. DA/Graze fuze
Maximum range: 3.5km
Maximum height: 2.0km
Minimum height: 50metres
Manufacturer: USSR State factories

Status: In production. In service with the Warsaw Pact forces. Used in Vietnam and against Israel by Egyptian and Syrian Armies. Used by Warsaw Pact countries and several others.

UNITED KINGDOM

BLOWPIPE AA MISSILE

Blowpipe is an anti-aircraft missile made by Short Bros & Harland Ltd of Belfast. It was selected from three contenders to meet the General Staff Requirement for a lightweight hand held weapon capable of providing protection for all arms against low flying aircraft, and is very considerably more effective than the GPMG which is all the Infantry have at present.

The basic conception was that of an extremely light compact and portable equipment that could be carried by one man. It consists of the missile, contained within its launching canister, and the aiming unit. It is entirely self contained and requires no external power or assistance either to launch or control it. The canister is issued as a complete entity and the aiming unit contains all the required launching and guidance equipment. The canister is 1,400mm long and it weighs 14kg. The aiming unit is 280×229×102mm and weighs 7kg. Included in this weight is the optional IFF interrogator which enables the firer to determine whether or not an aircraft is hostile. The canister and the aiming unit are connected together, giving a complete system weight of 21kg.

To use the equipment, the operator places it on his shoulder with the left hand supporting the front of the canister and his right hand on the grip on the aiming unit. The hand grip has a firing trigger and the thumb operated missile controller. The target is viewed through the monocular sight and the operator pulls the trigger. This generates electrical impulses which energize the thermal batteries to provide power for the aiming unit and for the missile. The battery which powers the aiming unit is fitted in the canister. A sequence device in the aiming unit ensures that all systems are activated and it then fires the first stage motor in the missile. The missile is on its way one second after the trigger is pulled. The first stage motor burns only for sufficient time to get the missile under way and is burned out before the missile emerges. This is to protect the firer. The missile coasts to a safe

The missile coasting as it leaves the launcher tube

distance and then the main motor is ignited to accelerate the missile to supersonic velocity. The missile is fitted with flares which enable the firer to follow the missile by eye and also are detected by a sensor in the aiming unit. The error signals generated in the sensor are transmitted by a radio transmitter in the aiming unit and an aerial in the canister, to the missile. A receiving system in the missile transmits these signals to the control unit and the missile is automatically gathered into the centre of the field of view and onto the line of sight. This automatic guidance is of limited duration and is effected by the brightness of the flares and by their relative brightness against the background. Its value lies in its ability to gather the missile to allow engagement of targets at very close range. After initial gathering the missile is controlled by the firer who uses the thumb control to keep the missile on the line of sight to the target. Under some circumstances it may even be advisable to control the missile from launch entirely by hand and in that case the automatic control is switched off before firing.

The missile is controlled in flight by the nose mounted control surfaces. One pair produces roll and the other pair produces lateral movement. The process is described as "twist and steer".

The fuzing system of the missile is in the nose and the high explosive warhead is mounted in the centre section. The fuze will function on direct contact with a target and in addition there is a proximity fuze which will initiate the warhead if the missile passes within a certain distance of the target.

After engaging a target the operator separates the aiming unit from the empty canister. A new canister is clipped to the aiming unit and the missile system is ready for another engagement.

A trainer set, suitable for both initial and continuation training, is available. It simulates the full effect of a missile launch and provides aiming practice. For initial training it will of course be necessary for the soldier also to fire a practice missile.

DATA
Canister
Length: 1,400mm
Weight: 14kg
Aiming unit
Dimensions: 280 × 229 × 102mm
Weight: 7kg
Type: Man portable, shoulder controlled surface to air missile
Guidance principle: Radio command. Optical tracking
Guidance method: Twist and steer using nose mounted control surfaces
Propulsion: Two stage solid motor
Warhead: High explosive with direct action and proximity fuzing
Manufacturer: Short Bros and Harland Ltd., PO Box 241, Airport Road, Belfast
Status: In production. In service with the British Army and Canadian Armed Forces

Blowpipe man-portable anti-aircraft weapon   *Aiming the weapon*

UNITED STATES OF AMERICA

M163 20mm VULCAN AIR DEFENCE SYSTEM

The Vulcan Air Defence System is based on a modified form of the Vulcan M61A1 20mm aircraft gun. This gun is an externally powered version of the Gatling gun and in the aircraft version fires at rates of up to 6,000 rounds/minute. The gun is mounted on an electrically driven turret and fitted with a range only radar which feeds into a computing gun sight. The ground defence system was tested in 1964-65 and adopted with the Chaparral to form composite Air Defence Battalions. The self-propelled version is the M163, the towed version is the M167. Both towed and SP versions have been in production since 1967. The latest system, which can be either towed or vehicle mounted, is the Autotrack Vulcan Air Defence System (AVADS).

The APC system is mounted in a modified M113/M163. This vehicle is designated the M741. The major components of the system are the M168 20mm Vulcan gun, the linkless ammunition feed system, the M61 Gyro Lead Computing Sight, the VPS2 Range-only radar developed by Frankford Arsenal and made by Lockheed Electronics, and a one man controlled, electrically driven turret. Boresighted with the gun is the XM134 straight telescope for day time spotting and the AN/TVS2B image intensifier sight is provided for night vision. If the gun is firing at the higher rate of 3,000 rounds/minute, a burst limiting device controlled by the gunner can be set at 10, 30, 60 or 100 rounds. There is no burst limit at the lower rate. The linkless ammunition feed system stores 1,100 rounds in a ready to fire condition. (These may be the M246 air defence round or the M50 series round. For practice the M220 round is used.) The vehicle carries a reserve of 800 rounds. The linkless ammunition system provides control of the rounds and removes malfunctions caused by defective links and excessive belt pull. The system is loaded with linked ammunition and a loader mechanism delinks the rounds and guides them into the storage drums. The discarded links drop into an empty ammunition box. The fire control

The M163 Vulcan Air Defence System

consists of the gyro lead computing gunsight, a range radar and a sight current generator.

The gunner visually acquires and tracks the target with the gyro lead-computing gunsight. The antenna axis of the radar is slaved to the optical line-of-sight. The radar supplies target range and the range-rate data to the sight current generator. These inputs are then converted to the proper current for use in the sight.

With the range, range rate, and angular tracking of the optical line-of-sight (measured by a freely gimballed gyro), the sight automatically computes the future target position and adds the required superelevation to hit the target. The lead angle is equal to the angular rate of the target multiplied by the time of flight of the projectile to the future target position.

The turret fire control is a disturbed line-of-sight system. The sight case and gun bore are physically fixed in alignment. The sight reticle, which defines the optical line-of-sight, is positioned by the gyro and is displaced from the gun bore as the gunner tracks the target, thereby establishing the proper lead angle. The amount of optical line-of-sight displacement is dependent on the range and range rate inputs to the sight. The required tracking time to establish the lead angle is one time of flight of the projectile.

The range-only radar, is a coherent doppler, moving target indicator (MTI) radar. It will acquire and track in range, targets as far as 5,000 metres away. A green light appears in the sight optics signalling that the radar has acquired the target and that the target is within the effective range of the turret system. The gunner acquires the target in the sight reticle, tracks it, and fires after the green light appears.

The electric drive of the turret is controlled by three solid state servo-amplifiers. These servo-amplifiers and the d.c. motors they control are interchangeable and easily replaced.

Azimuth slew rate of the turret is 60 degrees/second, and the elevation slew rate is 45 degrees/second, with accelerations in excess of 160 degrees/second^2 in both drives. The tracking control enables the gunner to maintain steady, continuous motion of the turret during firing.

Power for the system is provided by three, 24-volt nickel-cadmium batteries; two drive the Vulcan gun and the third drives the turret. The batteries are charged either by the vehicle generator or a portable auxiliary unit.

DATA
Weapon Coverage
Azimuth: 360°
Elevation: +80° −5°
Total System Weight: 2,363kg
Recoil Force Average
  At 3,000spm: 818kp
  At 1,000spm: 172kp
Turret Slewing Rate
  Azimuth: 60°/sec
  Elevation: 45°/sec
Standby Power Requirement: 500 watts
Manufacturer: General Electric Company, Burlington, Vermont
Status: In production and service

M167 20mm VULCAN AIR DEFENCE SYSTEM

The towed version (M167) of the Vulcan Air Defence System is mounted on a gun carriage and is a lightweight version of the M163 self-propelled VADS. The towed VADS has the advantage of being helicopter transportable and can be used in those situations where use of a tracked vehicle would be impractical. This system has been in production since 1967.

The system is made up of the 20mm, M168 Vulcan Gun, a linked ammunition feed system and a fire control system, all mounted in an electrically-powered turret. The towed VADS contains its own batteries and is equipped with a petrol generator for recharging.

Firing rates for the Vulcan gun with the linked feed system are 3,000 and 1,000 shots per minute. The high firing rate provides effective defence against low-flying, subsonic aircraft. The lower firing rate provides effective fire against ground targets such as personnel, trucks, and lightly armoured vehicles.

Fire control consists of a gyro lead-computing gunsight, a range-only radar, and a sight current generator. The gunner visually acquires and tracks the target. The radar supplies range and range-rate data to the sight current generator. These inputs are converted to proper current for use in the sight. With the current the sight computes the correct gun lead angle and adds the required superelevation. The towed VADS system uses the M61 gyro lead-computing gun sight.

DATA
Weight (Loaded with 500 rds): 1,500kg
Height on wheels: 2,032mm
Height emplaced: 1,727mm
Wheel track: 1,765mm
Ammo box capacity: 300 rounds of 500 rounds
Firing rates
  High: 3,000spm
  Low: 1,000spm
Weapon Coverage

The M167 Vulcan Air Defence System is a towed equipment, but has all the essential elements of the self-propelled system

Azimuth: 360°
Elevation: +80° −5°
Recoil Force Average
  At 3,000spm: 718kp
  At 1,000spm: 239kp
Turret Slewing Rates
  Azimuth: 60°/sec
  Elevation: 45°/sec
Manufacturer: General Electric Company, Burlington, Vermont
Status: In production and service

AUTOTRACK VULCAN AIR DEFENCE SYSTEM (AVADS)

The Autotrack Vulcan Air Defence System (AVADS) was developed by General Electric as a private venture experimental programme and was then evaluated by the US Army with good results against airborne targets. The system is an independent, self-contained turret consisting of the gun, feed, drive, ammunition storage, power, and fire control subsystems. This turret retains many of the features of the proven VADS turret and is directly interchangeable with it. AVADS provides the additional features of:

(a) Automatic tracking
(b) Aided visual acquisition
(c) Higher performance turret servo drives
(d) New fire control computation

The system retains the VADS ability to provide effective fire against ground targets while affording an improved anti-aircraft effectiveness. The AVADS turret can deliver accurate firepower at rates of up to 3,000 shots-per-minute from armoured vehicles, towed gun carriages, and fixed ground mounts.

HELMET SIGHT

The helmet sight consists of a collimated reticle, a linkage magnetically coupled to the helmet and set of synchros. With this device, the gunner directs the electrical boresight of the radar to follow his line of sight. The radar antenna is slaved to the helmet sight line during acquisition.

RADAR

The standard VADS VPS-2 range-only radar has been modified to track in angle as well as range. It consists of a rear feeding, low sidelobe, polarised twist, cassegrain reflector enclosed in a fibreglass front plate; a gearless, gyro-stabilised electric drive; and signal processing and interface electronics, most of which have been proven in VPS-2 radar.

The Autotrack Vulcan Air Defence System with helmet sight

FIRE CONTROL COMPUTER

The new solid-state, analogue fire control computer performs two functions; it computes the proper lead angle and designates time to fire. The computer can process the ballistics of each of several different 20mm rounds through a simple switch setting. The computer automatically compensates the ballistics selected for air density changes. In any future major design revision it is planned to replace the analogue computer by a digital computer.

SELF-TEST UNIT

A self-test unit, mounted in the turret, monitors important system functions. Lights indicate any antenna servo motor overcurrent or overheating, erroneous angle track or range jamming or radar fade conditions.

SYSTEM OPERATION

Depending on the mission, component availability and gunner choice, the AVADS turret is capable of operating in five distinct modes:
(1) Helmet sight acquisition/automatic track.
(2) Ring sight acquisition/automatic track.
(3) Helmet sight track/range-only radar.
(4) Helmet sight track/estimated range and range rate.
(5) Ground mode.

As the gunner, aided by his helmet sight, searches for the target, the radar antenna (not radiating) and the turret (in low gain mode) follow his line of sight. The gunner acquires the target by placing the sight reticle on it. He then turns over control of the engagement to the system by actuating the trigger; at that time the radar will radiate. When the radar has locked on, control of the antenna is transferred from the helmet sight to the radar angle track circuitry. The fire control computer calculates the correct lead angle and directs the turret to a position required to hit the target. When the gun bore reaches the proper line and the target's future position is within gun range, logic circuits in the computer command the gun to fire a 2-second burst (approximately 100 rounds), pause, fire another burst, and so on until the gunner releases the trigger. Upon trigger release, system control returns to the helmet sight.

In each of the other four modes the amount of system automation is reduced in relation to that of the first mode.

DATA
Gun: M-168, 20mm Vulcan
Weight
 Feed system: 545kg
 Mount: 1,399kg
 Gun: 136kg
 Ammunition: 282kg
 Total: 2,363kg
Firing Rate: 1,000/3,000spm
Ammunition Capacity: 1,100rds
Feed System: Linkless, single-ended
Drive System: Electric
Power Requirements: On-station batteries require 500 watts standby
Ammunition: M50 series
Barrel Life (Per set): 20,000 rounds
Slewing Rates: Azimuth 80°/sec; Elevation 60°/sec
Train/Azimuth Limits: None, 360° continuous
Elevation Limits: +80°; −5°
Recoil Force (Average)
 At 3,000spm: 818kp
 At 1,000spm: 272kp
Fire Control
Radar: X Band, pulse doppler tracks in range and angle. 200-5,000 metre range
Computer: Linear straight line prediction, solid-state, provides ballistics for 5 different projectiles
Helmet sight: Electro-mechanical used for acquisition, allows gunner to perform 360° search
Manufacturer: General Electric Company, Burlington, Vermont

REDEYE ANTI-AIRCRAFT GUIDED MISSILE SYSTEM

Redeye is a man-portable, shoulder fired air defence guided missile system designed to provide combat units with the capacity to destroy low flying aircraft.

It resulted from a feasibility study carried out in 1958 and a development programme begun in 1959. A production contract was placed with the General Dynamics Corporation, Pomona Division, Pomona, California, in 1964 and the delivery schedule was completed in 1970.

The Redeye weapon consists of three major components – the launcher, the missile, and the launcher battery/coolant unit. The missile is sealed in the launcher and is not removed in the field before firing. The launcher houses the missile and provides the controls and power and coolant channels necessary for target acquisition and firing. The launcher battery/coolant unit is inserted immediately before firing. The Redeye launcher consists of the launch tube, open sight assembly and gripstock. It provides the means of transporting, aiming and firing the missile. The electrical connection between the launcher and the missile is made through the umbilical assembly. The launcher is discarded after the missile is fired.

The launch tube is a cylinder containing the missile, in a constant low humidity environment. The front end seal is transparent to infra red radiation to allow the missile to sense the target.

The open sight assembly allows the operator to aim the weapon, track the target, estimate range and apply tangent elevation (or "superelevation"). The sight carries an audible and vibratory indicator to show that the missile seeker has acquired the target.

The Redeye missile is supersonic, using passive infra red homing and proportional navigation guidance. It contains the seeker section with the IR detector which converts the target IR radiation into an electrical signal which locks the seeker on the target and generates guidance commands for the missile during flight. The seeker tracks the IR source after the gyro is uncaged.

It also houses the controls and the motor driven fins. One pair of fins is stationary during flight and the other is moved in response to the signals from the seeker section. The missile battery is inert at ambient temperatures. When the trigger is pressed an electric squib ignites a thermite charge which melts the electrolyte to develop a 40 volt output within 0.5sec. The fuze timer ignites the sustainer motor, arms the warhead and prepares it for detonation.

The warhead, when armed, can be detonated in one of three ways. (a) When it penetrates a metal object a firing pulse is generated, (b) When it decelerates on contact with a solid object, and (c) It destroys itself after 15 seconds flight. The rocket motor section consists of the ejector motor and sustainer motor.

OPERATION

No IFF (Identification-Friend or Foe) is fitted to Redeye and target identification is carried out solely by the firer.

The operator sees the target and if he decides to engage, the following sequence occurs and must be completed within 30 seconds. When the target is in range the safety and actuator device is operated. This activates the battery coolant unit and Freon gas flows to the seeker and expands to cool the infra red detector unit to 100°F which is its most efficient working temperature. The sight is place on the target and the IR radiation received is focused on the detector cell. When sufficient energy is received to enable the seeker to track, an audible tone is generated and the gyro which has spun up to speed, is uncaged as soon as the uncaging switch is held down. The ejector motor fires and the exhausting gas impinges on the tail fins –

Redeye in launching position

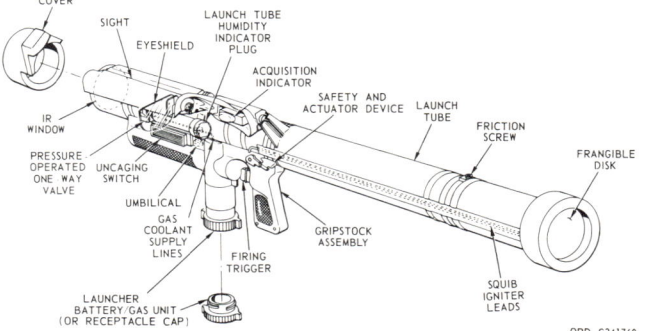

Redeye launcher

which are still folded – and the missile spins at full rate inside the launcher. When the ejector produces a missile acceleration of 28g an inertial switch in the fuze timer closes and the fuze timer starts. The missile emerges from the launcher under the force of the ejector motor and coasts for about 7 metres until the sustainer motor fires. (This is to protect the operator.) The fuze arms the warhead 1.6 seconds after the fuze timer starts and simultaneously the self destruction cycle is initiated.

The seeker section detects any difference between the gyro line of sight and the source of IR energy. The tracking error signal is then used in a tracking servo-loop to reposition the seeker so that it is aimed at the target. The fins are moved by the control section activated by the seeker signals.

When the target is struck the warhead is activated. If the target is missed the self destruction circuit functions.

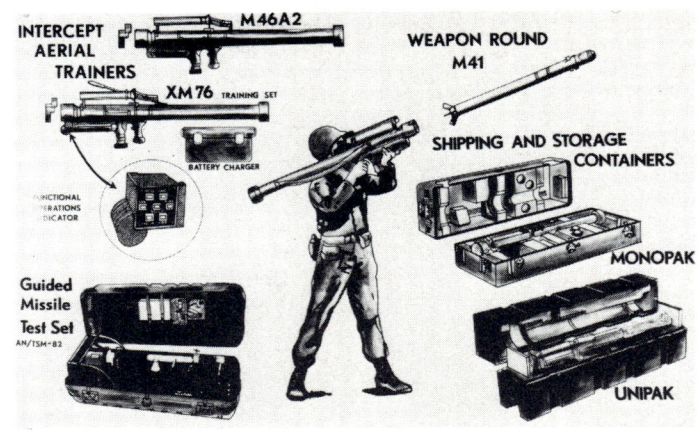

The Redeye weapon system

DATA
Redeye weapon (complete with cover and launcher battery/coolant unit M41)
   Length: 128.3mm
   Width: 119mm
   Height: 277mm
   Weight: 13.1kg
Missile
   Length: 1,206mm
   Diameter: 70mm
   Weight: 8.2kg
Launcher (without cover, sling or coolant unit)
   Length: 754mm
   Diameter: 92mm

   Weight: 3.9kg
M41 launcher battery coolant unit
   Length: 152mm
   Diameter: 47mm
   Weight: 0.5kg
Manufacturer: General Dynamics, Pomona Division, P.O. Box 2507, Pomona, California 91766
Status: In service with US forces and in Israel, Sweden and West Germany

STINGER ANTI-AIRCRAFT GUIDED MISSILE SYSTEM

Stinger is a man-portable, shoulder-fired guided missile system which enables the soldier effectively to engage low altitude jet, propeller driven and helicopter aircraft. Developed by the United States Army Missile Command in conjunction with General Dynamics Pomona Division, Stinger is the successor to the Redeye weapon system which has been operational in the US Army and US Marine Corps and elsewhere. Designed for the threat beyond the 1980's, Stinger has all-aspect engagement capability, an IFF system, improved range and manoeuvrability and significant countermeasures immunity. The system is a fire-and-forget weapon employing a passive infra-red seeker and a proportional navigation system. The missile contains a high explosive, hit-to-kill warhead, an electric control system and a dual-thrust rocket motor and employs a separable eject motor which launches the missile to a safe distance from the gunner prior to rocket motor ignition.

The missile, packaged within its disposable launch tube is delivered as a certified round, requiring no field testing or direct support maintenance. A separable, reusable gripstock is attached to the round prior to use. The gripstock contains the launch electronics and an IFF antenna and is used for multiple firings; the launch tube is discarded after each firing. The IFF interrogator is worn on the firer's belt.

The weapon can be carried and fired by one soldier. An aluminium weapon round container provides shipping and storage protection for a complete weapon (missile in launch tube, separable gripstock and battery coolant units) and can be integrated with a variety of military vehicles to enable rapid deployment by motorised troops. A wooden missile round container provides transport protection for missile rounds (missile in launch tubes and 3 battery coolant units) each round being enclosed in a protective bag.

Stinger engagement techniques are similar to those used for Redeye. Upon visually acquiring the target, the gunner finds it in the optical sight, initiates the missile functions, performs IFF interrogation, and launches the missile against aircraft identified as hostile. IFF interrogation can occur at any time during this sequence prior to launch. Upon launch, the missile guides itself automatically to the target.

TEST AND TRAINING EQUIPMENT
Since Stinger is delivered as a certified round, no test equipment is required at ammunition supply points or at field level.

Guided Missile Training Set XM134 (Tracking Head Trainer) simulates full launch procedures and allows an instructor to monitor a soldier's performance.

Field Handling Trainer XM60 is used for system handling deployment and sighting exercises.

A Moving Target Simulator M-87 (MTS) is used in conjunction with Guided Missile Training Set.

Stinger in launching position

DATA
Type: Man-portable, shoulder-fired surface-to-air guided missile
Guidance: Optical aiming – Infra-red homing
Propulsion: Solid Propellent Dual Thrust Rocket Motor with separable boost motor
Warhead: High explosive
Length: 1,524mm
Weight: 13.4kg
Diameter: 70mm

Speed: Supersonic
Range: Not disclosed
Crew: Normally a team of two, each being equipped to fire independently
Manufacturer: General Dynamics, Pomona Division, PO Box 2507, Pomona, California 917666
Status: Production go-ahead expected early in 1977

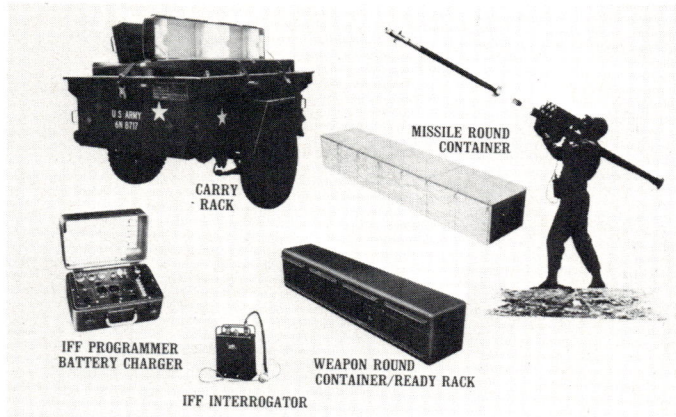

Stinger system components

Firing the Stinger missile

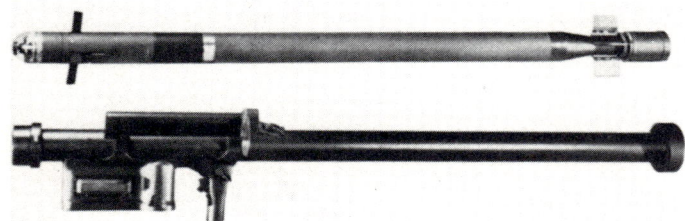

The Stinger launcher and missile

YUGOSLAVIA

20mm AA CANNON M1955

Based on the Hispano-Suiza (now Oerlikon) HSS 804 20mm cannon design this is a triple-barrelled weapon designed in Yugoslavia and manufactured there since 1955. It is extensively deployed in the Yugoslav Army and a version of it is used on many of the country's smaller naval vessels. The three barrels are fed by drum magazines and the weapon may be fired either on its two-wheel carriage or, with the wheels raised, from a tripod mount

DATA
Calibre: 3 × 20mm
Feed: 3 × 60-round drum magazines
Ammunition: HEI, HEI-T, API, API-T, AP, Practice
Rate of fire: 800 rounds/barrel/min cyclic
Range: AA: 1,200m
　　　　Ground: 2,000m
Penetration: (AP): 25mm at 1,000m
Status: In service and believed to be still in production

M1955 three-barrelled 20mm AA Cannon

ANTI-TANK WEAPONS

INTRODUCTION

As explained in the general introduction to this section, this anti-tank sub-section is devoted to weapons which have been designed primarily for use against armoured vehicles. Most of them can, of course, be used effectively against a variety of other land targets; and alternative warheads have been developed for some of them to extend their usefulness. Hardly any of them, however, can be used with any great hope of success against aircraft.

Early attempts to defeat the tank in battle involved the use of high-velocity rifles or guns and relied on the shape, hardness and kinetic energy of the projectile to pierce the tank armour. Projectiles designed for use with such weapons were, and still are called simply armour-piercing (AP) projectiles. Most large tanks still carry guns designed to fire high-energy projectiles and there are still many other high-velocity weapons in service in various parts of the world; but the range of types of munition suitable for use against tanks has been considerably extended in recent years and few weapons of calibre greater than 30mm and firing high-velocity rounds are nowadays handled by infantry. A few such weapons, however, are briefly noted in this section.

Modern Projectiles

An important version of the AP round is that known as APDS (armour-piercing discarding sabot). In this round the armour piercing element is a hard core of calibre significantly smaller than that of the complete projectile and shaped for maximum anti-armour effectiveness. This is surrounded by a much lighter casing, or sabot, which breaks up as the projectile leaves the gun barrel. The point of this arrangement is that the core can have a shape which differs considerably from that of the complete projectile and, not having been scored by the rifling in the barrel, is aerodynamically clean. Moreover, since it is very much heavier than the sabot, the core acquires most of the kinetic energy of the complete projectile; and indeed it acquires a greater energy than could be imparted to it if it were fired, without sabot, by a gun of appropriate calibre and the same chamber pressure as that of the larger gun.

A tank clad experimentally with 'Chobham' armour. British Chieftain tanks supplied to Iran will be the first operational AFV to be armoured in this way (UK MoD)

High explosive (HE) rounds with contact fuzes can also be used against tanks and may, if they are large enough, be effective against exposed portions of the tank mechanism (such as the tracks) but will not in general be effective against heavy armour. Two modern refinements of the HE round may be effectively used in some circumstances: they are the HEAP (high-explosive armour piercing) and HESH (high-explosive squash-head) rounds. The HEAP round has a projectile of relatively high velocity, a hardened case and a high-explosive charge which is contact fuzed with a very short delay. The effect of the arrangement is that the projectile either embeds itself in the armour or passes through it and then explodes with an effect which is more damaging than that of the simple HE round.

HESH rounds can be used with lower-velocity weapons, and are so designed that the nose of the shell crumples on impact to make a large contact area before the explosive is detonated. Such rounds will not in general pierce armour, but the explosion sets up shock waves in the armour which in themselves can incapacitate the crew and may also cause pieces of metal to break away from the surface remote from the explosion. Such

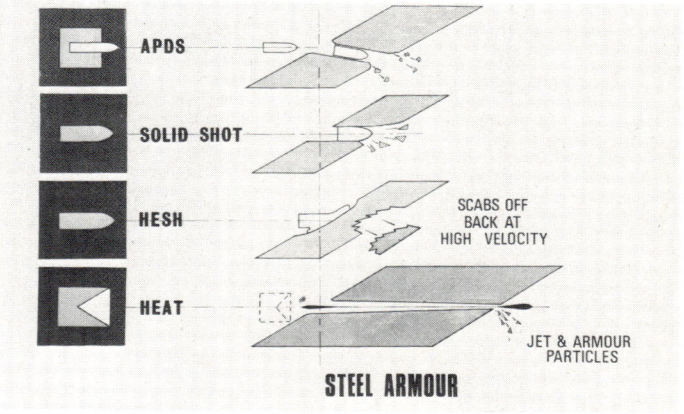

Diagram illustrating the effects of current anti-tank projectiles on conventional steel armour (MVEE)

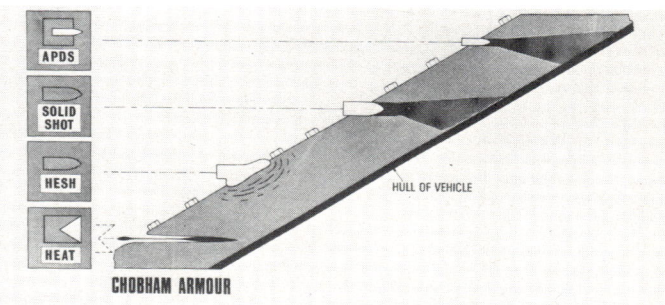

Diagram illustrating the effect of anti-tank projectiles on 'Chobham' armour (MVEE)

fragments fly off at high velocity and can do great damage inside a tank turret.

Most widely used in infantry weapons, however, is the projectile (which may be a shell, a rocket, a grenade or a guided missile) with a shaped-charge warhead frequently described as a HEAT (high energy anti-tank) round. This type of projectile is designed to be effective with only a moderate impact velocity and depends for its effect on the design of the warhead and fuze. The explosive charge occupies the rear portion of the warhead and is formed round a hollow cone with its apex to the rear. The base of the cone is of approximately the same diameter as the warhead at that point and in front of it is an air space enclosed by the rounded or pointed head of the projectile on which the fuze igniter is mounted. On impact this hollow portion crumples, bringing the base of the cone to the surface of the armour; at the same time the fuze ignites the charge at the rear and the conical shape of the front of the charge causes the explosion to be focussed into a high-velocity high-temperature gas jet. Such a jet will penetrate solid armour plate to a depth typically, for a large projectile, of 30cm or more; and if this amounts to perforation a jet of hot gas and molten metal is squirted into the interior of the tank.

Which of these various types of projectile will be most effective against armour depends on the design and thickness of the armour. Against solid armour the HEAT round is particularly effective; but in certain circumstances a sandwich construction is likely to be more vulnerable to an APDS round. There is therefore a good deal to be said for having a mix of projectiles available for satisfactory defence against tanks.

Before leaving this subject it is appropriate to mention a recent British armour development, the 'Chobham' armour (so called because it was developed at the Military Vehicles and Engineering Establishment at Chobham). This is claimed to offer greatly enhanced resistance to all forms of projectile as is indicated by the accompanying illustrations. Details of the construction of this armour have not been released, but it seems probable that it is a sandwich made up of two sheets of armour plate separated by a highly dispersive, possibly granular, filling.

Merits of Anti-Tank Weapons

For some years now there has been a continuous and often acrimonious debate both on the viability of the tank as a weapon system in a modern weapons environment and on the relative merits of different kinds of anti-tank weapon. In the first part of the argument, rivalry between the cavalry, infantry, and artillery arms has been obtrusive: in the second, the very large expenditure potentially involved in major anti-tank weapon procurements and the prestige attached thereto has exacerbated these rivalries and introduced commercial and national rivalry; it has also, since there is a school of thought that maintains that tanks are best destroyed from the air, stimulated inter-service rivalry; and the demands of other public services on national budgets have brought the debate into the political arena. In all these circumstances it is not surprising that objectivity should be in short supply.

What makes matters worse is that there is very little hard information on which to base a judgement. Anti-tank weapons of modern types have not been much used against modern tanks in actual combat. Guided missiles were used by the Israelis in 1956 and again, with rather poor results, in the war between India and Pakistan in 1971; they were used briefly but with some success in Vietnam and with moderate success in the 1973 Arab-Israeli war. Although first reports created a contrary impression, however, the majority of tank casuallties in the 1973 war were caused by the guns of other tanks.

It is no part of the function of this book to attempt to arbitrate in this controversy or to support any of the contending factions; and it is not suggested that the comment just made on the 1973 war tends either to prove or disprove any point in the argument: it is simply a matter of setting the record straight. The main body of this section is concerned with what are believed to be factual descriptions of the very large number of anti-tank weapons currently available: it is for others to decide which, if any, are appropriate to the particular requirements of particular armies. As with most other weapons, the skill and morale of the soldier in the tank or behind the anti-tank weapon are every bit as important as the merits of the weapons they employ.

ATGW Systems

Concerning the important group of guided anti-tank weapons (ATGW), however, some comment on system nomenclature is necessary. The practice of applying 'generation' labels to successive devices designed to meet a particular requirement is widespread among those who make, use or write about weapons. When used to denote a simple time sequence of devices there is no great harm in the practice; although the common assumption that a higher generation number denotes a superior article can lead to misunderstanding even when the sequence is very simple. When the label is used to distinguish between different sub-species instead of, or in addition to, denoting the sequence in time the results can be most misleading; and the use of 'generation' labels for anti-tank missiles has led not only to confusion but also to misunderstandings which may yet prove to have quite serious consequences.

What makes the confusion so bizarre is that it has arisen from the application of only the first two terms in the series. It is generally agreed that those relatively simple, early, and manually guided weapons, such as the British Vigilant, the French SS10 or the German Cobra, are devices of the first generation: they are also widely known as MCLOS (for manual command to line-of-sight) systems. The disagreement arises because some people describe a later and more sophisticated MCLOS system such as the British Swingfire as a second-generation weapon whereas others reserve the term for weapons incorporating a semi-automatic command-to-line-of-sight (SACLOS) guidance system – examples being the American TOW and the Franco-German Milan. Others again reserve the second-generation term for systems in which the missile is not wire-guided (as are all those mentioned above) but receives optical, or radio, commands – examples here being the Russian 'Swatter' MCLOS missile and the Italian SACLOS Sparviero development. At this stage, however, the idea of a third generation begins to emerge: some writers describe a SACLOS system without wire as a third-generation weapon: others reserve the term for a more extensively automated (ACLOS) system.

PREFERRED NOMENCLATURE

Because of this confusion it is evidently easier to refer to ATGW as MCLOS, SACLOS and ACLOS systems and the entries in this sub-section are labelled MCLOS or SACLOS; there are no infantry ACLOS weapons yet. It is also necessary, in our view at least, to dispel the widely held belief that SACLOS systems are intrinsically superior to MCLOS systems. This belief is, quite properly, encouraged by those who make SACLOS systems; and in the following discussion we do not seek to deny the positive claims that are made by the SACLOS advocates: our purpose is simply to demonstrate the existence of other arguments tending to an opposite conclusion.

GENERAL ATGW PRINCIPLES

In any ATGW system the guidance process necessarily comprises three elements:

(a) a method of determining the direction of the target from the missile control post;

(b) a method of assessing the nature and extent of the departure of the missile in flight from the path determined by (a); and

(c) a method of influencing the flight of the missile so as to eliminate any departure detected at (b).

In an MCLOS system (a) and (b) are provided by the operator who, with or without the aid of a telescope or binoculars, observes the target and the missile and the deviation of the latter from the sight line to the former. He also provides the calculating and initiating functions of (c); using a manual control lever or joystick, he makes what he thinks is an approximate correction and, having observed the result of that, makes further corrections as required until the missile is on course.

If the sight line is rotating (as it will be for all crossing targets and some others) the missile must, if it is commanded to the line of sight, fly a curved course: in such instances manual course correction will be required almost up to the time of impact. If the sight line is not rotating, however, no corrections will be required after the missile has been brought on course; and in some systems it is thereafter possible for the missile to be flown 'hands-off'.

It is important to notice that the only system element influencing the flight of the missile is the operator's manual controller and that the avoidance of sudden violent manoeuvres is dependent only on smooth operation of this control: there is no need for smooth optical tracking; and temporary loss of vision will of itself not influence the behaviour of the missile.

SEPARATION IN MCLOS SYSTEMS

In most MCLOS systems it is possible for the operator to be located some distance from the point from which the missile is launched; it is also often possible for a single operator, in these circumstances, to be in charge of several prepositioned missiles which he can launch and control sequentially without changing his own position. When a remotely located missile is launched, of course, it must initially be caused to execute quite vigorous manoeuvres, in order to 'gather' it into the operator's operational field of view: in most systems this is readily achieved by an initial large left or right command by the operator; but if the operator-missile displacement is such as to preclude such a simple manoeuvre (as is possible in the more sophisticated applications of the Swingfire system) an initial preprogrammed gathering operation can be built in to the system as an automatic function.

How important the separation facility can be in practice was demonstrated during the 1973 Arab-Israeli war. After they had recovered from their initial surprise at being opposed by ATGW (among other anti-tank weapons) the Israeli tank commanders rapidly developed the practice of getting off a quick round in the direction of any puff of dust or mark which might indicate the launching of an ATGW in their direction. Since the mean velocity of a shell from a tank gun over any practical ATGW range is far greater than that of any current guided anti-tank missile, a well-aimed shell would be likely to reach the missile launching area before the missile reached the tank; and if the operator were close to the launch point there would be a good chance of at least causing him to miss his target.

It should be noted that ATGW manufacturers are conscious of the need to reduce the 'signature' of a weapon so as to minimise the chances of a successful riposte by the tank commander: nevertheless, even if the missile itself emits little in the way of visible vapour it is impossible to ensure that the rocket efflux does not kick up dust (or snow or sand) when launched close to the ground.

SACLOS CHARACTERISTICS

In a SACLOS guidance system, element (a) of the basic triad is again provided by the operator; but, whereas the MCLOS operator merely informs his own brain of the direction of the target, the SACLOS operator designates it as precisely as he can to the remainder of the guidance system by aligning an optical sight on the target and maintaining that alignment throughout the engagement.

Elements (b) and (c) are provided automatically by apparatus located at the control site; and it is this automatic operation that distinguishes the SACLOS from the MCLOS system. It is possible to envisage a variety of ways in which the missile direction could be measured but all systems of which guidance details are known use infra-red tracking apparatus (the infra-red source being in the tail of the missile) to measure the deviation with respect to a reference direction. This reference direction is determined by and is ideally identical to the direction established by the operator's optical sight.

From these deviation measurements, apparatus at the control site generates information signals which are communicated to the missile and there acted upon in such a way as to eliminate the deviation of the missile from the reference direction.

SYSTEM CONSTRAINTS

Because the automatic operations of a SACLOS system are referenced to the effective infra-red (or equivalent) measurement axis, whereas the operator is associated exclusively with the optical aiming system, it follows that the axis of the latter must be closely aligned with the guidance reference axis if the target is to be successfully engaged. With a stationary target and the optical sight clamped on a central aim, a modern long-range SACLOS ATGW will not hit a target at maximum range unless its optical and reference axes are aligned to better than 0.5mil (about 1.7 minutes of arc). Because the combined sighting and tracking assembly necessarily comprises several mechanical piece-parts which are capable of relative movement under stress and because the direction of the reference axis is determined by both electrical and mechanical components, the alignment of the two axes cannot be regarded as fixed. It must be checked frequently.

It is not essential that the missile launcher of a SACLOS system should be co-located with the aiming and tracking assembly. It is essential however, that the missile should come swiftly into the effective field of view of the tracker. Because of the difficulty of arranging this without considerable additional equipment elaboration all current SACLOS systems, other than those that are installed in land vehicles or aircraft, use a combined launcher tracker and sighting unit. This eliminates the possibility of moving the operator to a safe distance from the launcher but it may have the compensation of enabling the weapon to be brought into action quickly. It also means, however, that the operator must reload before he can fire another missile.

SUMMARY

As pointed out earlier, the purpose of the foregoing discussion has not been to demonstrate the superiority of any particular type of ATGW guidance system. Both MCLOS and SACLOS systems have their advantages and their disadvantages, and the choice between them must to some extent depend on the nature of the requirement, the purchaser's facilities for training and maintenance, the type of terrain in which the missiles are most likely to be used and so forth. A brief summary of the main technical and operational considerations is given below.

TRAINING

SACLOS systems can be operated with less training than MCLOS systems. The skill required to operate an MCLOS system, however, is probably one that can be acquired by most people.

RELIABILITY

Less can go wrong in an MCLOS than in a SACLOS system having comparable facilities and there is no MCLOS requirement for axis alignment.

OPERATOR SECURITY

In certain circumstances the separation possibility available with an MCLOS system may give the operator more protection from enemy fire than is available to a SACLOS operator.

TIME INTO ACTION

Because MCLOS systems are generally designed to take advantage of the separation facility whereas SACLOS systems usually have integral arming and launching assemblies, SACLOS systems can probably be brought into action more quickly (other things being equal) than MCLOS systems.

SEQUENTIAL FIRING

Provided he has time to set out his missiles before he comes under fire, an MCLOS operator can fire several missiles (up to 18 in one instance) sequentially without any pause for reloading. Operators of currently available man-portable SACLOS weapons, on the other hand, must reload after each firing. Which is the more advantageous arrangement depends on the circumstances.

DISTRACTION

Provided he does not jerk his manual control, it does not matter if the MCLOS operator is momentarily distracted by enemy fire. If the SACLOS operator's concentration is broken, however, and his aim thereby deflected, the missile will be commanded automatically to a new direction. Whether or not it can be commanded back to the original course depends on the amount of flight time that remains. For similar reasons the SACLOS operator's tracking of a moving target must be smooth.

JAMMING

Both systems are equally vulnerable or invulnerable to jamming on the command link. Both systems can be deflected by a smoke screen or other visual obstacle (though greater sophistication, already available in other departments of weapon technology, may overcome this disadvantage). A flare fired by a threatened tank is unlikely to upset the aim of an MCLOS operator but might influence the automatic tracker of a SACLOS weapon. The more sophisticated types of SACLOS system, however, are designed to discriminate against such interference.

OPERATIONAL EXPERIENCE

ATGW have not so far been used much in combat. The most extensive use was possibly that against Israeli tanks in the 1973 war when Russian MCLOS weapons were used with moderate success by what appear to have been very thoroughly trained and regularly practised Egyptian troops. The SACLOS TOW system was used successfully in an air-ground role in Vietnam and the Israelis fielded some late in the 1973 war. Available data, however, are too meagre for a comparative evaluation to be made with any confidence.

STATUS

MCLOS systems are currently widely deployed in armed forces around the globe but SACLOS systems are gaining ground. Notable advances are the adoption of the TOW and Dragon SACLOS systems by the US forces, the adoption of TOW by many other countries and the decision of the British authorities to purchase the Franco-German SACLOS Milan: the latter decision means that Britain, France and Germany are likely to be very largely if not totally equipped with SACLOS infantry weapons before long ▸ and will presumably be joined in this respect by Italy when the Sparvien missile comes into production.

It is, however, likely that MCLOS infantry systems will persist in many areas – especially those using the smaller weapons like Bantam and Cobra/Mamba. There is so far no sign of any Russian intention to introduce a SACLOS system although their willingness to equip other countries with the currently-known systems may mean that they have something better available for their own troops.

Types of Infantry Anti-tank Weapon

The following main categories of weapon may be distinguished.

Grenades Most anti-tank grenades are nowadays launched using either a rifle or a special grenade launcher. The idea of applying the grenade to the tank by hand, however, has not been totally abandoned. Grenades and launchers are described in the Area Weapon section.
Rockets There are many man-portable rocket launchers in service throughout the world. Known current weapons are described in this section.
Recoilless Weapons Recoilless rifles and guns are widely used although some are in process of being replaced by ATGW. Descriptions of known current weapons are included in this section.
High-velocity Anti-tank Guns Very few major armies deploy such weapons in infantry formations nowadays but they still exist in substantial numbers. Details of some of the better-known weapons are included here but it is not claimed that the coverage is exhaustive.
ATGW Descriptions of current weapons are included among the entries in this section.
Anti-tank mines A few of the commoner types are listed in tabular form as an indication of the variety of available devices. Here again, however, the listings are certainly not exhaustive.

This picture of a US 106mm M40 recoilless rifle at the moment of firing illustrates clearly the relative magnitude of the forward and rearward blast effects of this type of weapon. The vehicle is the FMC XR311

ARGENTINA

105mm RECOILLESS GUN MODEL 1968

Work on recoilless weapons in Argentina dates back to the late 1940s or early 1950s, the first such weapon in Argentine service having been the 75mm recoilless gun which entered service in 1952. This Argentine Model 1972 was designed and developed under the direction of Engineer Alejandro Czekalski of the Research and Development Department of the Direccion General de Fabricaciones Militares (FM) of the Argentine Ministry of Defence.

Described here is the 105mm Recoilless Gun Model 1968 – F.M. Czekalski, which was developed in a similar way and built entirely by the Rio Tercero military factory of F.M.

The gun has a cylindrical perforated combustion chamber and a centrally hinged breech block. The back plate has a venturi mounted on it in such a way as to be easily replaced; and there are two spiral vanes in the body of the diffuser to compensate the terminal force resulting from the interaction of the barrel rifling and the shell. An additional peripheral chamber permits the use of a lower-density charge and gives optimum combustion of the powder and efficient use of the resultant gases. A mechanically-operated firing pin detonates the primer at the base of the shell and an ignition transmission line ignites the propelling charges. Either HE or hollow-charge (ECH) ammunition can be fired.

Several different firing positions are available to meet different operational requirements. When mounted on its towing carriage the gun can be fired with the axle high, half-lowered or low: while still on its wheels it can also be from its or standard Unimog 421 ½-ton carrying vehicle and with its muzzle forward: it can also be fired from a tripod. Minimum height to the centre of the barrel in the low-axle position is 62cm.

Aiming is by means of a telescope which is calibrated up to 1,800 metres and fitted with a stadiametric ladder anti-tank sight. An auxiliary spotting rifle (7.62mm FAP – heavy automatic rifle) is fitted.

The two-wheeled gun-carriage can be fitted with conventional or puncture-proof tyres. It has a torsion bar suspension.

DATA
Gun calibre: 105mm
Barrel length: 3.00m
Overall length: 4.02m
Height in road trim: 1.07m
Minimum height of barrel: 0.62m (low angle position)
Weight
Weapon with carriage and normal tyres: 397kg
Spotting rifle: 6.4kg
Additional for puncture-proof tyres: 56kg
Vertical field of fire: −7° to +40° 30′
Maximum range: 9,200m
Range of spotting rifle: 1,200m effective
Sight field of view: 12°
Magnification: 4×
Rear danger zone: 40m (90°)
Crew: 4
Rate of fire: 3-5 rounds/minute

Ammunition:	HE Shell	Hollow charge (ECH) Shell
Weight:	15.6kg	11.1kg
Muzzle velocity:	400metres/sec	400 metres/sec
Internal pressure at breech:	930kg/cm²	830kg/cm²
Penetration:	—	200mm

Manufacturer: Rio Tercero Military Factory, Direccion General de Fabricaciones Militares, Cabildo 65, Buenos Aires
Status: In service with Argentinian forces

AUSTRIA

106mm RECOILLESS RIFLE M40A1 (towed)

The US M40A1 recoilless rifle is in service with the Austrian Army in two forms. One of these is as a vehicle-mounted weapon – as it is in its US Army applications: the other is as a towed weapon on an Austrian-designed two-wheeled carriage. The carriage is notable for having two stable firing positions, the barrel being 26cm higher in one position than it is in the other.

DATA
Calibre: 106mm
Barrel length: 340cm
Elevation: −17° to +65°
Traverse: 360°
Weight of rifle in combat order: 113.9kg
Weight of shell: 7.71kg
Weight of carriage: 170kg
Muzzle velocity: 503 m/sec
Maximum range: 6,900 m
Rate of fire: 5 rounds/min
Status: In service with the Austrian Army

M40A1 on Austrian-designed carriage. This picture illustrates the bistable nature of the design

---

BELGIUM

RL-83 (BLINDICIDE) ROCKET LAUNCHER

This widely-used multi-purpose weapon has been in service for several years, and its simplicity and cheapness ensure that it will be many years yet before it becomes obsolete – the more so since the recent introduction of a new long-range anti-tank rocket for use with the weapon.

The weapon is a simple, mechanically-fired launcher capable of a wide range of 83mm ammunition. There are three sighting systems – an open sight or an optical sight with provision for angular correction, both up to 400m, and an auxiliary sight for ranges up to 900m. The launch tube folds to a little over half of its full length for ease of carriage.
DATA
Standard weapon:
Calibre: 83mm
Length of launcher: Open: 170cm
Folded: 62cm
Weight of launcher: 8.4kg complete with 900m sight
Firing mechanism: Mechanical

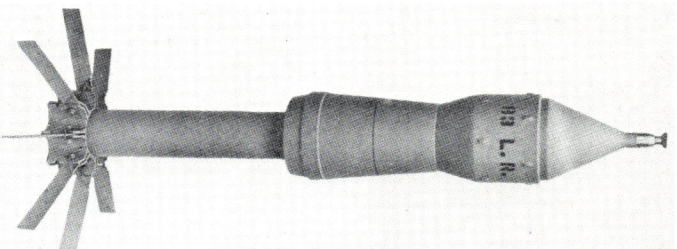

83mm long-range anti-tank rocket

Range: Up to 900m depending on type of ammunition
Muzzle velocity: 100metres/sec

Ammunition: Hollow charge anti-armour, HE anti-personnel combined HEAP/HEAT, illuminating, smoke and incendiary
Crew: 2
Long-range Anti-tank Rocket:
Length: 570mm
Weight: Total: 2.4kg
       In flight: 2.05kg

Launch velocity: 120m/sec
Maximum velocity: 300m/sec
Operational range: 500m with very flat trajectory
Penetration: Armour, 300mm; Concrete, 1m

Manufacturer: Mecar SA, 6522 Petit-Roeulx-lez-Nivelles
Status: The weapon is still in widespread service

MECAR BI-TUBE ROCKET LAUNCHER MPA 75

This is a highly-portable expendable infantry weapon for use against tanks, fortifications or troop concentrations. It comprises a twin-tube launcher with a single set of sights, an applied safety to enable the weapon to be carried safely between shots and a transportation safety which renders the weapon safe in its operational pack. The launcher is supplied in this pack with two anti-tank/anti-personnel rounds emplaced ready for use.

After removing the launcher from its pack all that is necessary to make it ready for firing is to cock it, which disengages the transportation safety, and erect the sights. The trigger is located in the upper central portion of the launcher, and when pressed it detonates the firing cap of a rocket and ignites its propellant charge. The propellant is entirely consumed while the rocket is in the launch tube so that there is no discharge of gas towards the firer when the rocket emerges. A second shot can be fired immediately after the first: alternatively the safety can be applied while the firer moves to another position. When both rockets have been fired the launcher is discarded.

DATA
Calibre: 75mm
Length of launcher: 510mm
Total weight with two rockets: 2.6kg
Weight of rocket: 950g
Initial velocity: 60m/sec

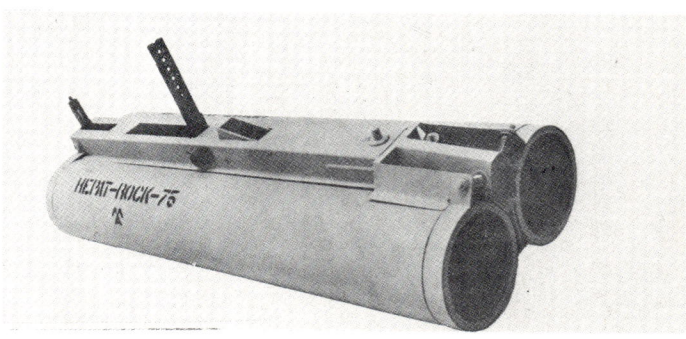

Mecar MPA 75 bi-tube launcher

Operational range: Anti-tank: 100m
           Anti-personnel: 300m
Penetration: Steel armour: 270mm
           Concrete: 600mm
Anti-personnel effect: 17 fragments/m² at 4m
Manufacturer: Mecar SA, 6522 Petit-Roeulx-lez-Nivelles

PRB 415 3.5in HE ANTI-TANK AND ANTI-PERSONNEL ROCKET

Among a wide range of military products (mostly rockets, ammunition and explosive devices) made by the PRB Group is a series of ground-launched rockets. In 60mm and 3.5in (94mm) calibres they make HEAT, smoke and incendiary rounds. They also make dummy, blank and sub-calibre practice rounds.

An interesting development in the 3.5in range is the dual-purpose PRB 415 replacement for the standard American M28A2 super-bazooka rocket. The novel feature of the Belgian round is that its warhead is designed to be effective in both anti-personnel and anti-tank roles. This has been achieved by slightly reducing the size of the normal hollow-charge arrangement and incorporating an anti-personnel fragmentation sleeve made of spirally-wound steel wire which has been prenotched by a patented process. At the same time the rocket propellant and igniter have been improved. The same modification has been developed for the 60mm rocket and could be easily adapted to other HEAT heads.

SUB-CALIBRE TRAINING DEVICE

PRB also make, and have widely exported, a training round which is externally identical in appearance to the 3.5in rocket but fires a 20mm projectile. It can be used with M20B1 or M20A1B1 launchers. The sub-calibre launch tube is rifled and the projectile is a tracer round having ballistics similar to those of the real rocket. Handling and firing procedures are the same as for the real rocket and the dummy rocket is ejected by recoil from the rear of the launcher.

DATA (Operational weapon)
Calibre: 89mm
Weight of rocket: 4kg
Weight of explosive charge: 0.6kg
Type of explosive charge: Composition B
Lethal radius (50%): 20m
Penetration: 200mm
Range at 45°: 735m
Muzzle velocity: 95m/sec
Fragmentation sleeve: 1,250 fragments
Manufacturer: PRB S.A., Avenue de Tervueren 168, B-1150 Brussels, Belgium
Status: Production. 3.5in RL are very widely deployed

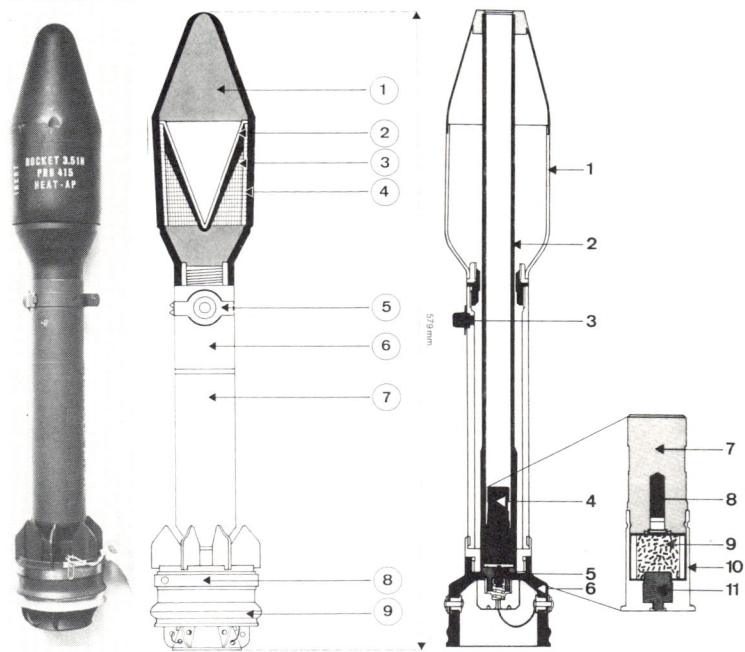

Left to right: PRB 415 3.5in dual-purpose rocket; drawing showing the construction of the PRB 415; drawings showing the construction and arrangement of the sub-calibre training rocket
Key to PRB 415 drawing: (1) Head; (2) Copper cone; (3) Explosive charge; (4) Fragmentation sleeve; (5) Safety band; (6) Base fuze M404A1; (7) Motor; (8) Contact ring; (9) Groove
Key to training rocket drawing: (1) Body; (2) 20mm barrel; (3) Dummy safety; (4) Cartridge; (5) Electrode; (6) Breech; (7) Bullet; (8) Tracer; (9) Powder; (10) Cartridge case; (11) Electric primer

90mm MECAR LIGHT GUN

This weapon is designed primarily for anti-tank defence but can fire various other types of ammunition as well as a HEAT round. Because of its low recoil force (about 2,000kg) and light construction, the gun is particularly suitable for light armoured vehicles, small gun-carriages and difficult access positions. If required a muzzle brake can be fitted. Two versions of the gun are available, one (CAN-90H) being somewhat heavier than the other and having a correspondingly lower recoil speed. The lighter weapon is the CAN-90L.

DATA
Gun without carriage:

Weight: 285kg (90L) 416kg (90H)
Calibre: 90mm
Height overall: 350mm (90L) 400mm (90H)
Width overall: 290mm (90L) 450mm (90H)
Barrel length: 2.9m
Length of chamber: 368mm
Chamber volume: 2,560ml
Maximum pressure: 1,200kg/cm²
Maximum recoil distance: 420mm
Maximum recoil velocity: 10.2m/sec (90L) 7.8m/sec (90H)
Barrel life: up to 10,000 rounds

Ammunition
HEAT round: **Weight:** 2.28kg (projectile) 3.54kg (round)
  Length: 635mm
  Muzzle velocity: 633m/sec
  Range: 3,500m maximum: 1,000m effective
  Arming distance: 16m
  Penetration: 350mm armour: 1200mm concrete
Fragmentation/tracer: **Weight:** 4.1kg (projectile): 5.21kg (round)
  Length: 520mm
  Muzzle velocity: 338m/sec
  Range: 4,200m maximum

  Arming distance: 40m
  Effective radius: 50m from impact
Smoke/tracer: As fragmentation round but payload produces smoke screen 40m wide
Canister round: **Weight:** 5.95kg (round)
  Length: 373mm
  Range: 300m operational
  Warhead: Canister containing 1,120 spheres weighing 3.6g each
Manufacturer: Mecar SA, 6522 Petit-Roeulx-lez-Nivelles

BRAZIL

ANTI-TANK MISSILES

For several years there were regular reports to the effect that an anti-tank guided weapon was being developed in Brazil as one of a range of rocket and missile projects controlled by the Comissao Central de Misseis (CCM). The project is believed to have started around 1967 and it has been reported that some prototypes had been completed by 1970.

No recent confirmation of the continued existence of this project has been received; nor has it been reported that any such project has been terminated. After so long a period it seems unlikely that there is now, if indeed there ever was, such a project in hand and the repeated references to it in standard reference annuals may be no more than a self-sustaining mutual copying process. On the other hand there is no doubt that the CCM have a continuing missile development programme; and there would appear to be no reason why they should not develop an anti-tank missile if they wished to do so.

It is known that MBB in Germany issued a production licence to Brazil for the manufacture of the Cobra wire-guided ATGW. It is just possible that this gave rise to the belief that there was a new missile in development; but the one statistic that accompanied the earlier reports gave the range of the new missile as 3km whereas Cobra's range is only about 2km. The Cobra licence was issued in 1973 – a date which is consistent with the abandonment of the indigenous project.

CHINA (PEOPLE'S REPUBLIC)

TYPE 56 40mm ANTI-TANK GRENADE LAUNCHER

This is a copy of the Soviet RPG-2 launcher and has the same weight and dimensions. It fires the Chinese Type 50 grenade which was designed and produced in that country. This is a better round as far as penetration is concerned than the Russian PG-2 HEAT but its superiority is apparent only at normal impact: at 45 degrees it may be less efficient.

DATA
Calibre of launcher: 40mm
Calibre of warhead: 80mm
Overall length of launcher: 1,194mm
Weight empty: 2.83kg
Maximum effective range: 150m
Type of ammunition: Type 50 HEAT
Projectile weight: 1.84kg
Rate of fire: 4-6rounds/min
Armour penetration: Type 50 HEAT 265mm at normal (0° obliquity)
(USSR PG-2 HEAT 150-175mm at normal)
Manufacturer: State factories
Status: Probably no longer manufactured. Supplied to North Vietnam

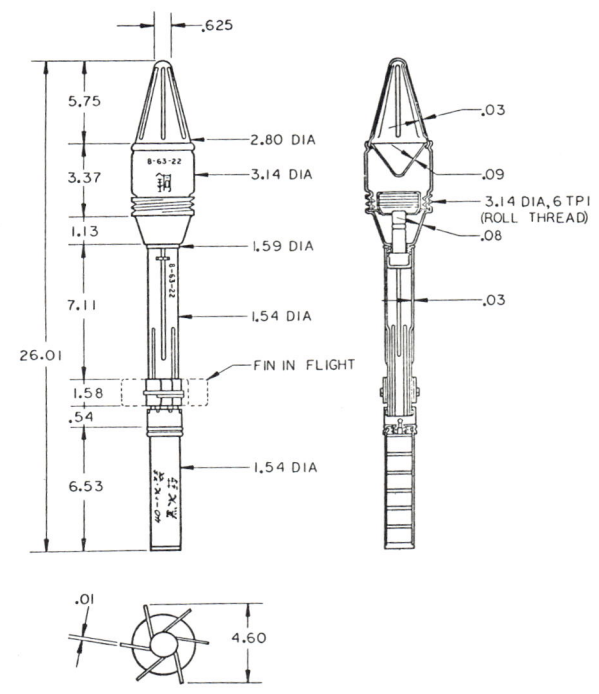

ALL DIMENSIONS IN INCHES

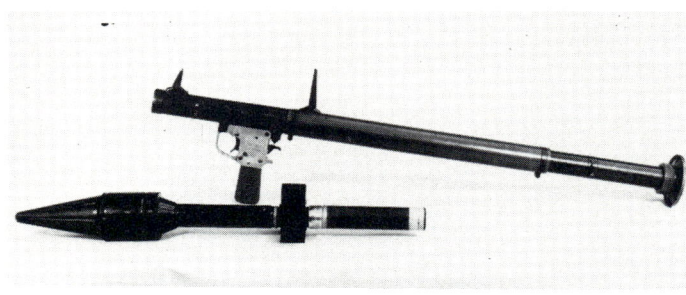

The RPG-2. This has been manufactured in China and is a copy of the Soviet weapon. It is shown with a practice grenade of Chinese origin

A sectioned drawing, showing the dimensions of the Chinese round

---

TYPE 69 40mm ANTI-TANK GRENADE LAUNCHER

This is a copy of the Soviet RPG-7 launcher and was not seen until 1972. It has the same performance as the Russian version.

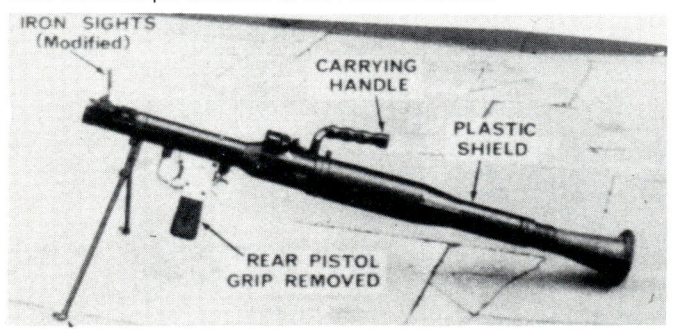

The Chinese Type 69 rocket launcher opposite has a carrying handle and no rear pistol grip. A small bipod is permanently attached. The RPG-7 shown above is of Bulgarian manufacture. It has the typical European layout including a wooden heat shield whereas the Chinese have used plastic

DATA
Calibre of launcher: 40mm
Calibre of projectile: 85mm
Length of launcher: 990mm
Weight of launcher: 7kg
Weight of grenade: 2.25kg
Muzzle velocity: 300 metres/sec
Range, static target: 500m
Range, moving target: 300m
Range, to self destruction: 920m
Penetration of armour at normal (0° obliquity): 320mm
Manufacturer: State factories
Status: In production and in service

Chinese Type 69 launcher

57mm ANTI-TANK GUN TYPE 55

This is a Chinese copy of the Russian M-43 gun. There are no known differences in construction and performance between the two weapons.

Available details will be found among the Russian entries.
Status: In service

57mm RECOILLESS RIFLE TYPE 36

This is a copy of the US M18A1. The United States sent the drawings to Nationalist China and gave technical assistance. When the Nationalists were forced off the mainland the Communists took over the factory and produced the Type 36 57mm RCL Rifle. This is a breech loading single shot weapon using a HEAT round against armour and an HE or canister round against personnel. The Chinese weapon will fire the American 57mm round but the converse is not true and the Chinese ammunition can be used by no-one else. The weapon can be fired from the shoulder but is usually fired from the rear bipod – front monopod system. It can also be mounted on a tripod – usually a Czech-pattern ZB26 or ZB30.

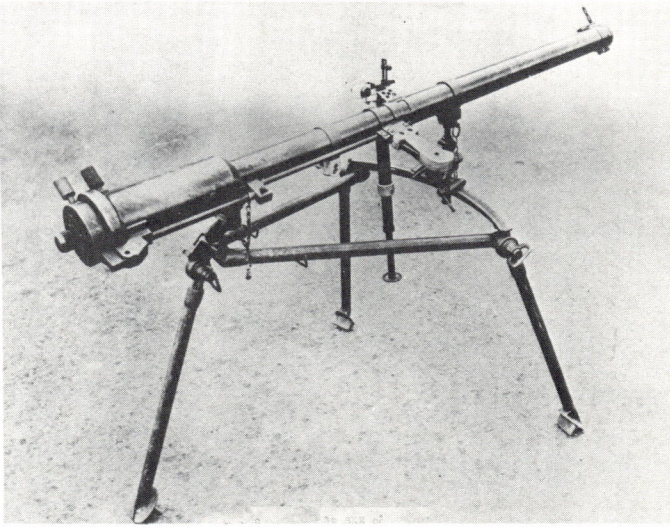

Tripod-mounted Type 36

DATA
Calibre: 57mm
Method of operation: Recoilless
Overall length in firing position: 1,549mm
Weight: 35.4kg
Maximum HE range: 450m
Ammunition: HE and HEAT
Armour penetration: 63.5mm
Manufacturer: State factories
Status: No longer in production. No longer used by front line troops

57mm recoilless rifle in action

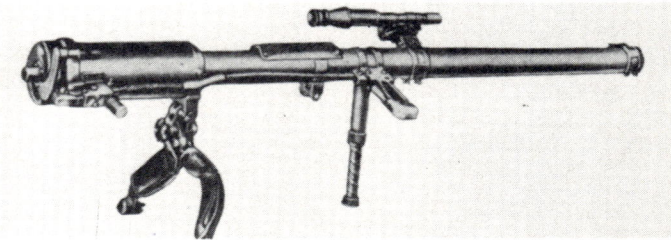

57mm recoilless rifle Type 36

75mm RECOILLESS RIFLE TYPE 52

This is a copy of the obsolete US M20 Recoilless Rifle and no improvement over the American weapon has been obtained. The gun can fire either Chinese or US ammunition.

The weapon is towed on a pair of solid wheels and a tripod with extendable legs is used for firing.

There is also a Type 56, which is a slightly improved version of the Type 52 and will fire only the Chinese ammunition.

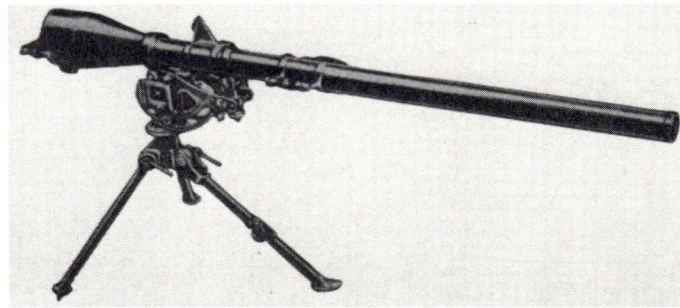

75mm recoilless rifle M20 (Type 52)

Chinese 75mm recoilless rifle Type 56

American troops using the M20

DATA
Calibre: 75mm
Method of operation: Recoilless
Overall length in the firing position: 2,132mm
Weight with US type mount: 85.1kg
Type of ammunition: HE or HEAT
Maximum range of HE shell: 6,675 metres
Maximum effective anti-tank range: 800 metres
Armour penetration: 228mm

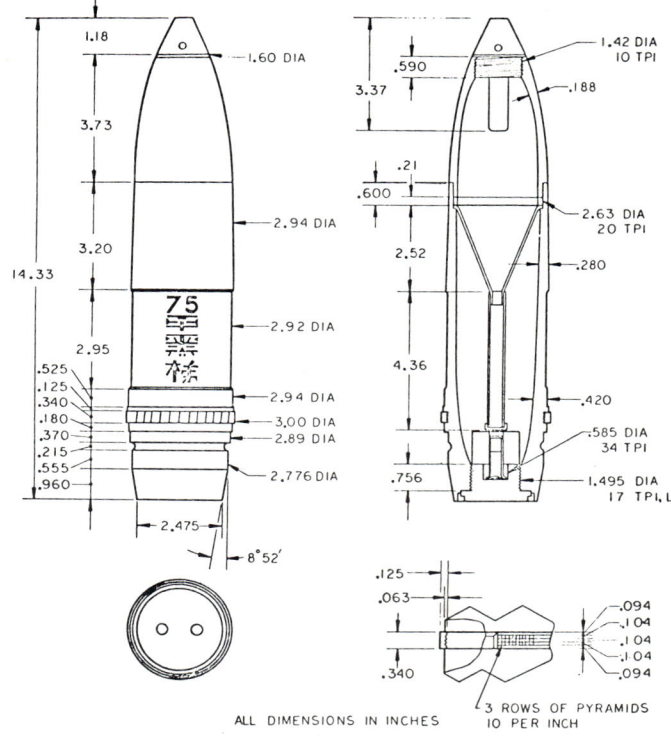

The HEAT shell for the RCL guns Types 52 and 56

ALL DIMENSIONS IN INCHES

90mm ANTI-TANK ROCKET LAUNCHER TYPE 51

This is a copy of the US 3.5in Rocket Launcher. It has the same performance and the same physical parameters. It breaks into two parts for carriage in the same way.

DATA
Length of launcher assembled for firing: 1,530mm
Length of launcher broken for carriage: 762mm
Weight of launcher: 5.45kg
Type of firing mechanism: Electrical
Range: 1,200m
Penetration: 267mm
Muzzle velocity: 98.6m/sec

Type 51 90mm anti-tank rocket launcher. This is a copy of the USA 3.5in RL (89mm M20)

82mm RECOILLESS GUN TYPE 65

This is a copy of the Russian B10 Recoilless Gun. The performance of the Chinese version is the same as that of the Russian weapon.

DATA
Cartridge: 82mm
Method of operation: Recoilless, with multi-vented breech block with enlarged chamber section
Length of barrel: 1,659mm
Overall length: 1,677mm
Weight in travelling position: 87.6kg
Weight of HE round: 4.5kg
Weight of HEAT round: 3.6kg
Muzzle velocity: 320m/sec
Maximum range HE round: 4,470m
Maximum effective anti-tank range: 390m
Armour penetration: 240mm
Rate of fire: 6-7 rounds/min

The Type 65 82mm RCL gun. This is a copy of the Soviet B10

CZECHOSLOVAKIA

45mm ANTI-TANK GRENADE LAUNCHER TYPE P-27 ("PANCEROVKA")

This is a Czech version of the Russian RPG-2 grenade launcher. The ammunition is not interchangeable with that of the Russian weapon and the launcher has a folding bipod under the muzzle. It is a more substantial and heavier weapon than the Russian. The propellant contains iron filings which increase the momentum of the gases leaving the rear end.

DATA
Calibre (Launcher): 45mm
Calibre (Projectile): 120mm
Method of operation: Rocket
Overall length of projector: 1,092mm

Type of ammunition: HEAT
Projectile weight: 3.3kg
Maximum effective range: 100metres
Armour penetration: 250mm
Rate of fire: 3-4 rounds/min
Manufacturer: Skoda
Status: No longer in Czech Army service. Replaced by the Russian RPG-7V. Still in service in Asia

P-27 45mm Anti-tank Grenade Launcher "Pancerovka"

82mm RECOILLESS GUN TYPE T-21 ("TARASNICE")

This is a smooth bore gun firing a fin stabilised projectile. The gun is mounted on two pressed steel wheels of very small diameter and can be fired either off the wheels or from the shoulder. It was also mounted on the Czech APC OT-62. It was exported in quantity to the Middle East and Vietnam but seems now to be obsolescent generally and probably obsolete so far as European forces are concerned.

DATA
Calibre: 82mm
Method of operation: Recoilless with a multi-vented breech block. No extractor
Overall length: 1,473mm
Barrel length: 1,204mm
Weight in travelling position: 20kg
Weight in firing position: 17.3kg
Projectile weight: 2.13kg
Muzzle velocity: 267m/sec
Maximum effective range: 457metres
Ammunition: HEAT
Armour penetration (at normal): 228mm
Manufacturer: Skoda
Status: No longer in production. No longer in service with Czech Army. Sold to Middle East armies but now almost entirely phased out. May still be in service in the Far East

T-21 82mm RCL Gun "Tarasnice"

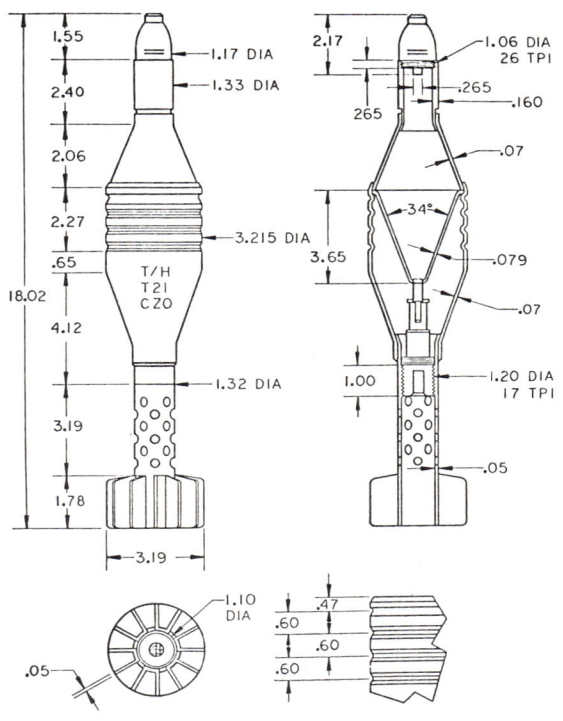

ALL DIMENSIONS IN INCHES

Tarasnice in action

Czechoslovakian 82mm HEAT round Model T-21

82mm RECOILLESS GUNS M59 and M59A

These are two versions of a recoilless gun, smooth bored, breech loaded, firing fin stabilised ammunition. The original M59 had a smooth exterior and the M59A differs only in having a radially finned section over the chamber to dissipate the heat. Each is capable of being towed behind an APC (usually OT-810) or any other suitable vehicle. It can be mounted on top of an OT-62 APC and has been seen inside. It can be manhandled over quite long distances with two men, with a towing harness, pulling on the bar across the muzzle. In addition to the HEAT anti-tank round it fires an HE shell in either direct or indirect roles. It is the only Warsaw Pact gun using the ranging rifle technique.

DATA
Calibre: 82mm
Method of operation: Recoilless
Overall length (firing position): 4,597mm
Weight: 385kg
Type of ammunition: HE and HEAT
Projectile weight: 6kg

The M59 A 82mm Recoilless Gun

Maximum effective anti-tank range: 1,200metres
Maximum HE range: 6,657metres
Armour penetration: 250mm
Manufacturer: State factories
Status: No longer in production. Still in service with units of the Czech Army

The M59 82mm Recoilless Gun

FINLAND

55mm RECOILLESS ANTI-TANK GRENADE LAUNCHER M-55

This weapon, which is the current light anti-tank weapon of the Finnish Army, is of rather more elaborate construction than many such man-portable recoilless launchers. The weapons are issued on a scale of six per company in the motorised battalions. The weapon was developed in Finland.

DATA
Calibre: 55mm
Launcher length: 94cm unloaded: 124cm with grenade in place
Weights
Weapon: 8.5kg
Grenade: 2.5kg
Effective anti-tank range: 200metres
Rate of fire: 3-5 rounds/min
Penetration: 200mm
Status: In service with the Finnish Army

Finnish 55mm light recoilless rifle

95mm RECOILLESS ANTI-TANK GUN M58

This is the only heavy recoilless weapon known to be in service with the Finnish Army. It is mounted on a two-wheel carriage for towing and the wheels remain in position for firing. Carrying handles are fitted on either side of the barrel close to the breech and the muzzle and stabilising legs are fitted front and rear.

The weapon was designed and built in Finland.

DATA
Calibre: 95mm

Barrel length: 3.2metres
Weight in combat order: 140kg
Muzzle velocity: 615metres/sec
Effective anti-tank range: 700-1,000metres
Armour penetration: 300mm
Crew: 3
Status: In service in heavy weapon companies of Finnish infantry battalions

FRANCE

68mm SARPAC ANTI-TANK ROCKET LAUNCHER

Primarily designed as an anti-tank weapon, the SARPAC portable rocket launcher may also be used successfully against fortifications. It can also be used to fire anti-personnel or illuminating rounds.

The launcher consists of a telescopic tube to which are attached a sight, a percussion firing mechanism and a shoulder butt. When the tube is retracted for carrying the firing mechanism is rendered inoperative and the weapon can be carried safely with a round in the tube. The sight is hinged with a parallelogram motion and lies flat against the tube in the carrying position. The folded weapon is carried by a sling harness.

Fin-stabilised ammunition is used, the eight fins of each type of round being folded when the rocket is in the tube and springing out after launch. The rocket is armed by gas pressure during launch but a delay element ensures that it is not fully armed until it is about 10 metres from the launcher.

SARPAC is designed for engagement of armoured targets, using a HEAT round, at ranges up to about 200 metres. With a HEAP or illuminating round, however, it can be used at ranges of 650-700 metres. With a loaded weight of 3-4kg according to ammunition type it can be fired comfortably

from the shoulder in standing, kneeling or lying positions.

Originally, SARPAC was envisaged as a disposable anti-tank weapon and the launcher was designed for extreme simplicity and cheapness. Since then an improved design, capable of being used for up to 20 rounds, has been produced. This type can also be fitted with a sight suitable for use with the HEAP and illuminating rockets up to the ranges mentioned above.

DATA (Improved Launcher)
Launcher
Calibre: 68mm
Length open: 997mm
Length closed: 734mm
Weight, empty with sling: 1.9kg
Ammunition
HEAT round (ROCHAR)
Weight: 1.09kg
Initial velocity: 150metres/sec

Effective range: 150-200metres
Armour penetration: 300mm at 0°
Maximum obliquity: 70°
HEAP round (ROCAP)
Weight: 1.8kg
Initial velocity: 92metres/sec
Effective range: 650metres
Illuminating round (ROCLAIR)
Weight: 1.3kg
Initial velocity: 138metres/sec
Effective range: 700metres
Burn time: more than 30 sec
Candle power: more than 180,000
Manufacturer: Thomson-Brandt, Branch Armement et Mécanique Général, 52 Avenue des Champs Elysees, 75008 – Paris
Status: In quantity production and in foreign service

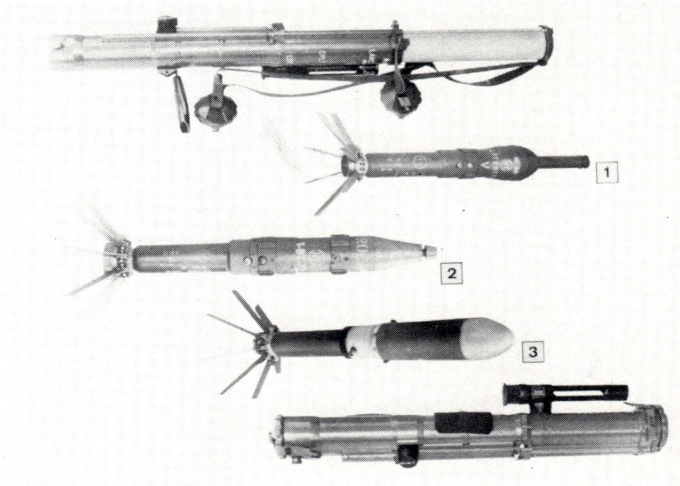

SARPAC and its ammunition. The launcher is shown in its open and closed positions and the three rockets are numbered (1) ROCHAR, (2) ROCAP, (3) ROCLAIR

ARPAC DISPOSABLE ANTI-TANK WEAPON

The "Arme Individuelle de Proximite Antichar" was developed for DTAT as a disposable individual close-in anti-tank weapon. It was intended to be issued in quantity to the infantry and on a lesser scale to supporting arms, for the engagement of tanks at ranges less than 100 metres, with 50 metres as the optimum range.

A full description of the weapon appeared in the 1976 edition of JANE'S INFANTRY WEAPONS. The weapon was last seen in public at the 1975 Satory exhibition but it was not adopted by the French Army and the project has now been discontinued.

80mm ACL-APX ANTI-TANK SYSTEM

The study of this concept began in 1964 when the Direction Techniques des Armaments Terresteres (DTAT) instructed Atelier de Construction de Puteaux (APX) to produce a feasibility study on a rocket assisted anti-tank weapon. This led to the Arme collective légère (ACL) and eventually the weapon itself, ACL-APX, was produced.

The weapon consists of a recoilless rifle which fires a fin stabilised projectile which is accelerated by rocket assistance and carries a shaped charge warhead. The weapon comprises a high tensile steel tube whose walls vary from 1 to 2mm in thickness. The tube is rifled and there is a chamber at the rear end which is enlarged to take a cartridge case which fits around the rear end of the rocket motor. The design allows rapid loading and locking of the breech and the extraction of the fired case when the breech is next opened.

The APX M326 optical sight has a field of view of 200 mils and a magnification of 3× and weighs 400 grams. It has range markings from 200 to 1600 metres. At the position corresponding to 580 metres two lines are drawn. One is for temperate climates (0-50 degrees C) and the lower is for cold climates of 0 to −30 degrees C. The top line will be the normal battle sightline. This is based on the fact that the rocket burns in all for 1.25 secs which corresponds to a distance of 580 metres, and the corresponding ordinate height is 1.8 metres which is less than the height of the target. At 580 metres range the rocket is still supersonic and although this represents the optimum range, it is possible to engage tanks out to 800 metres.

There is a forward handle under the barrel, a firing handle incorporated in a pistol grip and a shoulder support under the weapon which can be adjusted for comfort. The nozzle of the breech extends well back to ensure there is no danger to the firer.

AMMUNITION

The cartridge as supplied is a fixed round. The rear of the projectile is contained inside a cartridge case with a convergent-divergent nozzle at the rear end. The fins are folded inside the cartridge case, and are flung out into position by the initial centrifugal force generated by the rifling. They then lock into position and as they are offset they continue the rotation of the rocket at later stages of the trajectory. The missile is accelerated within the barrel by a charge consisting of several sticks of tubular propellant and emerges at a velocity of 400 metres/sec. Since the recoilless gun principle is used, it is not essential to have "all burnt" within the bore. When the projectile is clear of the muzzle a rocket motor is ignited and this increases the velocity to 545 metres/sec at 200 metres down range. This rocket assistance is, technically of great interest because it has been located inside the ballistic cap, which normally is empty, and does not reduce the amount of HE which is available for the shaped charge. It also helps stabilise the projectile in the early stage of flight by pushing the centre of mass forward and so increase the moment arm between the centre of mass and the centre of pressure. If the charge is detonated before the rocket motor is burned out, it is claimed that the effect is in no way degraded. The front of the ballistic cap carries a piezo-electric generator which produces a small voltage when the nose is crushed on impact, and this initiates the base detonator in the explosive filling of the shaped charge.

In addition to the anti-tank ammunition there are also anti-personnel rounds, illuminating and smoke rounds. None of these has the rocket assistance but uses the space to increase the useful load. There is a sub-calibre training device which is a dummy projectile placed in the launcher and allowing 7.5mm tracer to be used for 500 metres or a plastic bullet for firing on a 30 metre range.

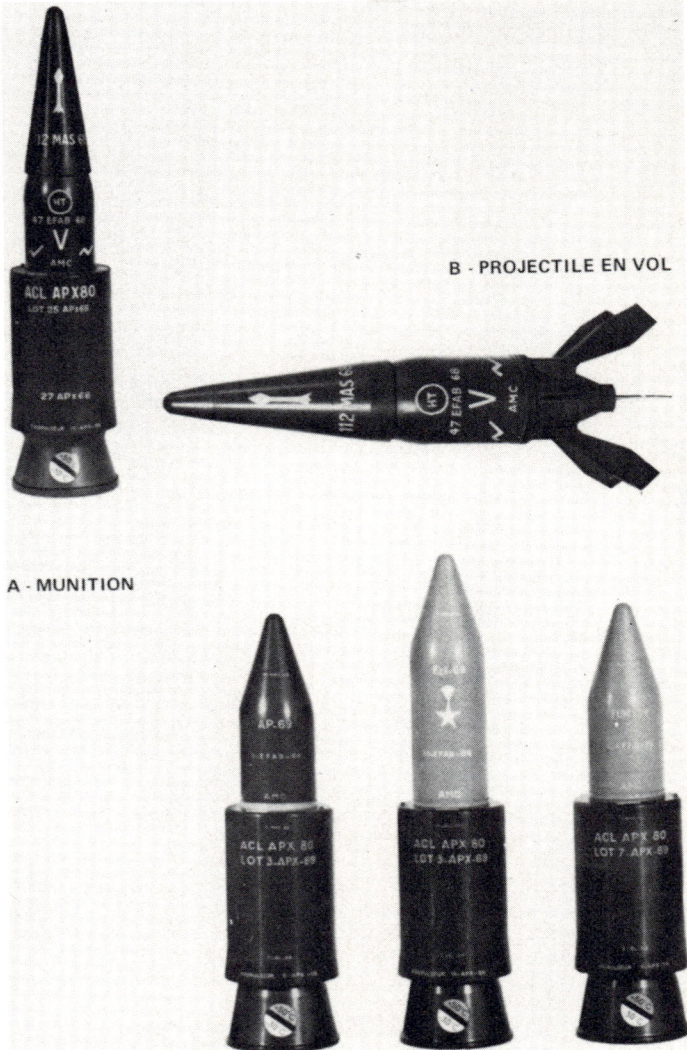

B - PROJECTILE EN VOL

A - MUNITION

*Top: The anti-tank round and the projectile in flight. **Bottom (left to right):** the HE round, the parachute illuminating round and the smoke round*

OPERATION

The soldier receives the missile in a plastic container holding two rounds. For bulk storage these containers are packed three in case. The soldier carries the weapon by the external handle when a short carry is involved. For a long patrol he uses the sling provided. Two men make up the crew. The missile is removed from the container by the loader and loaded into the breech. The locking system is a simple ring, rotated into position by a handle. The firer can adopt any convenient firing position but the kneeling position probably allows him more scope to acquire and track the moving target.

DATA
WEAPON
Overall length: 1,400mm
Weight including sight: 8.6kg
Overall weight of loaded weapon: 13kg

AMMUNTION (anti-tank)
Calibre: 80mm
Overall length: 530mm
Total weight: 3.6kg
Projectile weight: 1.85kg
Weight of hollow charge: 0.55kg
Cone diameter of hollow charge: 75mm

AMMUNITION (anti-personnel)
Total weight: 3.5kg
HE filling: 1.0kg
Muzzle velocity: 320metres/sec

FIRING CHARACTERISTICS
Muzzle velocity: 400metres/sec
Maximum velocity: 555metres/sec
Range to maximum velocity: 200metres
Effective battle range: 580metres
Time of flight to 580 metres: 1.25sec

Penetration: The warhead will penetrate the standard NATO heavy tank target which consists of:
(a) a single plate of 120mm at 65 degrees to the vertical and
(b) double plates of 40mm and 110mm at 65 degrees to the vertical
Manufacturer: Atelier de Construction de Puteaux (APX), Puteaux
Status: In production. In service with the French Army

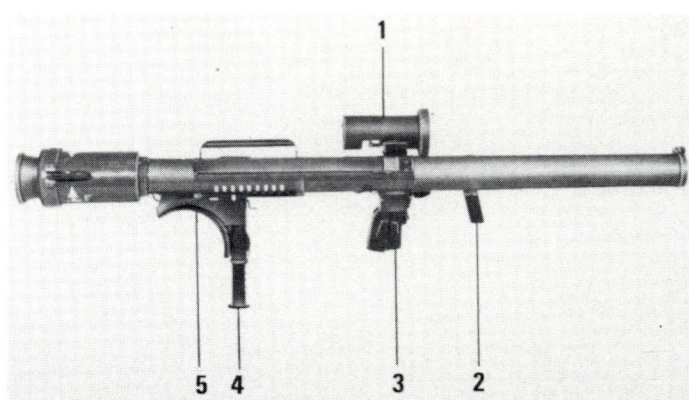

ACL-APX Launcher. (1) The APX M 326 sight; (2) Fore grip; (3) Firing handle; (4) Telescopic bipod; (5) Adjustable shoulder stock

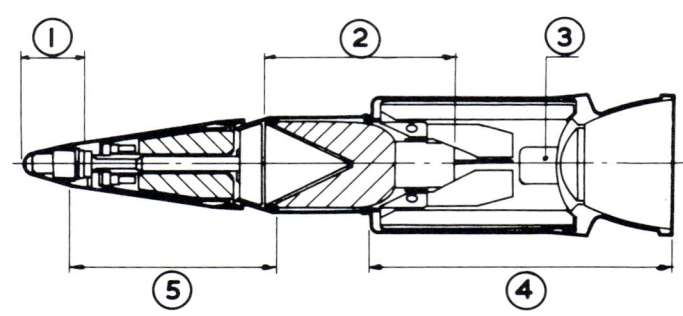

The ACL-APX anti-tank round. (1) The piezo-electric generator; (2) The warhead; (3) Igniter; (4) Rocket motor; (5) The rocket assistance

89mm STRIM ANTI-TANK ROCKET LAUNCHER

At the same time as APX was asked to investigate the possibility of an anti-tank system the Direction Technique des Armements asked a private firm, Societe Technique de Recherches Industrielles et Méchanique, (STRIM) to carry out a similar task. The solution produced by STRIM was for a rocket system, sub-sonic, lightweight and accurate out to 400 metres. It is called the "Lance-Roquette Anti-Char de 89mm".

The launching tube is made of glass fibre and plastic. It carries an adjustable shoulder piece which can be moved fore and aft to fit the firer and from the bottom of this comes a small bipod which may be pulled out and secured by a spring loaded catch. The fore hand grip may also be moved forward or back at will. The pistol grip contains the firing mechanism. This has a mechanical safety catch and when this is off, the action of pulling the trigger generates the current to launch the rocket. The telescopic sight is carried on the left side of the launcher. There are also iron sights and a carrying sling.

The APX M 290 sight is graduated in ranges of 100 metres to 1000 metres. The NATO requirement is for a maximum ordinate of 1.8 metres and a corresponding time of flight for this is 1.25 seconds and a range of 315 metres. The sight is arranged with the horizontal cross wire corresponding to this range and with two parallel lines engraved to give the combat elevation, i.e. 315 metres for temperatures of −10 degrees C (winter firing) and +30 degrees C for summer firing. The horizontal cross wire is marked 10, 20 and 30 on each side of the vertical centre line and these give the correct lead for a tank travelling at 10, 20 or 30 kilometers/hr, at the combat range (315m). Two stadia lines are provided to allow range assessment. This works on the subtension angle produced by a 6 metre tank. The two lines are set to straddle a crossing tank and this gives the range. In the head-on position width of the tank is taken to be 3 metres and so the tank is held between the centre line and the stadia.

THE ROCKET

The rocket is contained within a cylindrical carrying tube. The tube is made of glass fibre and laminated resin. It has end caps and three annular shock absorbers. The front cap is removed and the launcher tube is then attached to the rear end of the launcher with the rocket still inside, to complete the firing assembly. The rear plug is left in position to waterproof the rocket, until ready for use. Until it is removed the rocket cannot be fired but when it is taken off the firing circuit is completed.

The propulsion system uses a number of long sticks of tubular propellant and they give a constant pressure burning and therefore a constant acceleration of the missile. Burning is completed before the tail of the rocket leaves the tube and this ensures that no hot effluvia are thrown back into the firer's face. The rocket motor body and the nozzle are made of lightweight alloy. There are nine tail vanes folded forward along the body and these are forced out by centrifugal force and so emerge into the airstream as soon as the missile leaves the launcher.

The warhead contains a shaped charge with an aluminium cone. Forward of the charge is a ballistic cap and at the front of this is a piezo-electric generator which is connected through a transformer to the base fuze. The fuze cannot function until the rocket container is screwed

The 89mm STRIM anti-tank launcher and the round

into the launcher, and it is then armed by the propellant gas when the motor is fired. The system provides a good bore safety distance of some 10 metres.

The penetrative effect of the warhead enables it to meet the NATO heavy tank requirement of penetrating a single plate of 120mm set at 65 degrees and a double plate of 40mm followed by a 110mm plate, both set at 60 degrees, and 150mm apart. The head has been demonstrated penetrating 400mm of plate at normal (0 degrees obliquity).

TRAINING DEVICES

The training devices consist of:
(a) A dummy rocket.
(b) A practice rocket with an inert head and impact marker.
(c) A blank shot trainer.

The dummy rocket is intended to instruct soldiers in loading and unloading. The practice rocket is similar in all respects to the live round except that it is inert and marks the point of strike by the emission of talc. It can be fired against a tank without danger to the crew or damage to the vehicle.

The blank shot trainer consists of a dummy rocket fitted in a container identical with that of the anti-tank rocket. A cartridge is fitted into the electrical firing circuit and this produces the noise and smoke of discharge.

OPERATION

The weapon is normally served by a three man crew which consists of an

NCO, the firer and the loader, but it can be kept in action and fired by one man. The loading of the detachment is normally:

NCO: 2 rockets (held in one carrier)
Firer: 2 rockets and the launcher
Loader: 4 rockets

To bring the launcher into action the firer observes the following sequence.

First the weapon is taken out of its carrying case, and the muzzle cover taken off. The electrical system is then checked by pressing the trigger and the resulting flash in the rear end is seen through the telescope which is located, for travelling, in the rear of the tube. The telescope is twisted anti-clockwise and then withdrawn, and placed on the weapon. The fore grip and shoulder piece are adjusted as necessary, and the bipod in the shoulder piece is pulled out and locked. The weapon is then ready for loading.

A rocket container is taken out of its carrier and the adhesive tape at front and rear, removed. The front plug is removed and the container inserted. It has to be indexed and this is done by lining up two yellow arrows – one on the container and one on the launcher. The container is rotated clockwise through 60 degrees and this completes the electrical connections. As long as the rear plug is extracted, the weapon is ready for firing. If firing does not occur, the rear plug is replaced and then the container can be removed and returned to the storage condition.

MASCOT MOUNTING

The weapon can be incorporated in a vehicle-mounted cupola, known as Mascot, developed by GIAT. The cupola's primary application is with 7.62mm or 12.7mm MGs but the 89mm ACL can be fitted instead.

DATA
WEAPON
Calibre: 88.9mm
Length during transport: 1.168metres
Length in firing position: 1.600metres
Weight in transport condition: 4.5kg (incl. 0.5kg for telescope)
Weight loaded: 7.3kg

ROCKET
Calibre: 88.9mm
Length: 600mm
Length of container: 626mm
Weight without container: 2.2kg
Weight with container: 3.2kg
Weight of propellant: 300g
Diameter of shaped charge: 80mm
Weight of high explosive in warhead: 365g

FIRING CHARACTERISTICS
Muzzle velocity: 300metres/sec
Combat range for time of flight 1.25sec (maximum ordinate 1.9metres): 330metres
Combat range for time of flight 1.36sec (maximum ordinate 2.2metres): 360metres
Combat range for time of flight 1.55sec: 400metres
Maximum effective anti-tank range: 600metres
Maximum range at 45°: 2,300metres
Penetration:
Steel plate at normal (0 degrees obliquity): 400mm
Concrete: 1,300mm
Manufacturer: Manufacture Nationale-d'Armes de Saint Etienne, 3 Rue Javelin-Pagnon, (42) Saint Etienne. Sales handled by Hotchkiss-Brandt
Status: In production In service with the French Army as LRAC de 89mm Mle F1

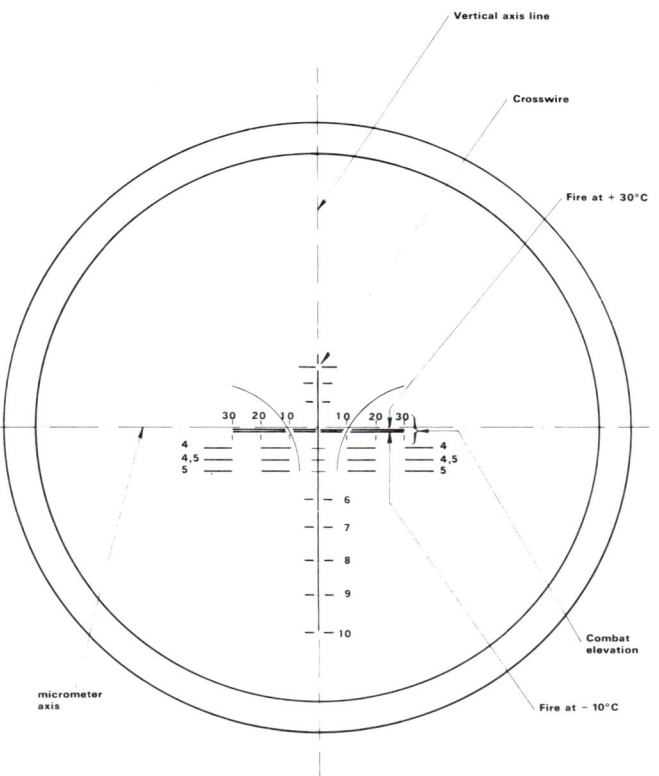

APX M 290 sight

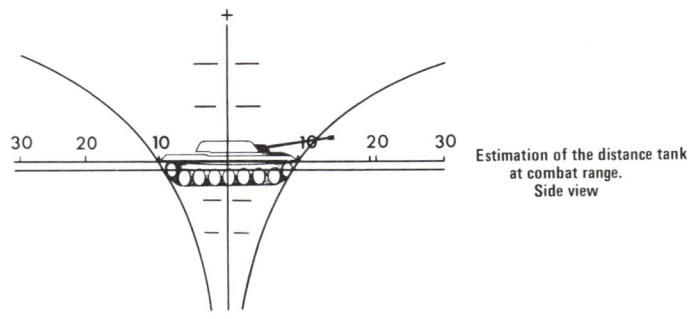

The sight picture with a tank at 315 metres which is the combat range

Estimation of the distance tank at combat range. Side view

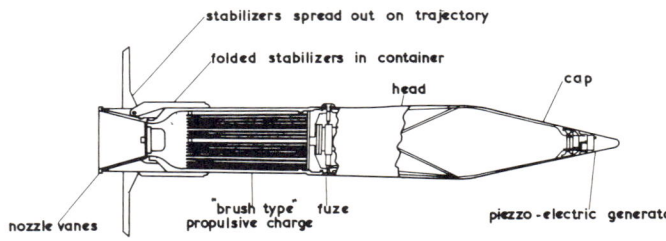

The missile for the STRIM anti-tank weapon

ACAR 100 and 200 ANTI-TANK REPEATERS

These two weapons were featured in the biennial exhibition of French Army equipment at Satory in 1975. They are unguided rocket-launching devices, differing from functionally similar weapons mainly in the possibility of firing two rounds in quick succession. Fired from the ACAR 100 the effective range of the two missiles is 100 metres; from the slightly larger ACAR 200 the range is 200 metres.

The missiles, with their hollow-charge warheads, are housed in transport tubes which act as launchers. Two such tubes are coupled together in an assembly which incorporates a single set of firing accessories (generator handle, aiming unit, shoulder strap, etc.) which is used to launch both missiles. For the more powerful ACAR 200 missile an extension tube is coupled to the launcher/transporter. The following data are all that have so far been made available.

DATA

	ACAR 100	ACAR 200
Calibre:	63mm	67mm
Velocity:	87m/s	177m/s
Effective range:	100m	200m
Time of flight:	1.2sec	1.2sec
Total weight:	2.5kg	3.5kg

Manufacturer: SERAT, Société d'Etudes et d'Applications Techniques, 134 Boulevard Haussmann – 75008 Paris
Status: Study project

ENTAC ANTI-TANK MISSILE

The Engin Teleguide Anti-Char was developed by the Direction Technique des Armements Terrestres and is produced by Aerospatiale. It was adopted by the French Army in 1957 and the Model 58 has been purchased by a number of armies.

This infantry anti-tank equipment consists of a four-missile launcher, a carrying vehicle such as a jeep (see, for example, the SAMO entry below), the necessary ancillary equipment for circuit testing and the missiles. The operator can be separated from the launching position by up to 110 metres

and he can control up to 10 missiles.

The missile is wire guided and the operator uses an optical sight into which he gathers the missile and controls it along the line of sight with a manual control (MCLOS system).

DATA
Missile length: 820mm
Missile diameter: 150mm

Launch weight: 12.2kg
Maximum speed: 84.7metres/sec
Range
    Minimum: 400metres
    Maximum: 2,000metres
Penetration: 650mm
Warhead: Shaped charge
Warhead weight: 4kg
Type: Wire guided Infantry anti-tank system
Guidance principle: Command to line of sight (MCLOS)
Guidance method: Optical sight, wire link control to spoilers on missile wings
Propulsion: Two-stage solid propellant motor
Manufacturer: Société Nationale Industrielle Aerospatiale, Division des Engins Tactiques, 2 a 18 rue Beranger, 92, Chatillon-sous-Bagneux
Status: In service with the armies of France, Australia, Belgium, Canada, Indonesia and USA; 140,000 missiles have been produced. Production has now ceased

ENTAC missile

SS10 ANTI-TANK WEAPON SYSTEM

SS10 is a wire controlled anti-tank missile. It was one of the first to go into service and was used successfully by the Israeli Army in action against the Egyptians in 1956. It has now largely been superseded by more modern weapons.

The missile is launched from a simple ramp launcher and is guided to its target by a manual control used in conjunction with a simple optical sight (MCLOS system).

DATA
Length: 851mm
Body diameter: 165mm
Wing span: 750mm
Launch weight: 14.8kg
Range
    Minimum: 900metres
    Maximum: 1,500metres
Maximum speed: 79metres/sec
Type of missile: Infantry anti-tank
Guidance principle: Command to line of sight (MCLOS)
Guidance Method: Optical tracking. Manual wire control to wing root spoilers

SS10 on its tubular launcher

Propulsion: Two stage solid propellant rocket motor
Warhead: High Explosive; 5.5kg filling
Manufacturer: Nord Aviation (now Aérospatiale)
Status: No longer in production. Largely replaced by more modern missiles

SS11 ANTI-TANK MISSILE

The SS11 is a line of sight wire-guided missile launched from either a vehicle or a ramp. The operator uses an optical sight and gathers the target to the line of sight. It is then kept there by means of a joystick control and the flares on the rear end of the missile help in this task.

In 1962 the SS11 B1 was introduced using transistorised firing equipment. This system provides a number of different warheads. There are anti-armour warheads (Type 140AC), anti-personnel (Type 140AP59), the Type 140APO2 which penetrates 10mm of plate at 3,000 metres and explodes 2 metres behind the plate, and an inert practice head.

The SS11 has been extensively installed as a helicopter-borne anti-tank weapon.

DATA
Missile length: 1,210mm
Missile diameter: 164mm
Wing span: 500mm
Launch weight: 29.9kg

Cruise speed: 100metres/sec
Range
    Minimum: 500metres
    Maximum: 3,000metres
Penetration
(Type 140AC): 600mm
Type: Wire guided Infantry anti-tank system
Guidance principle: Command to line of sight (MCLOS)
Guidance method: Optical sight, wire link control varying thrust of sustainer
Propulsion: Two stage solid propellant motor
Manufacturer: Société Nationale Industrielle Aérospatiale, Division des Engins Tactiques, 2 a 18 rue Beranger, 92 Chatillon-sous-Bagneux
Status: Still in production. Total production 166,000 at last available count. Used by Belgium, Canada, France, Germany, India, Iran, Israel, Italy, The Netherlands and the USA. Used also by 17 other countries. Manufactured under licence in India, West Germany and the USA.

SS11 missiles deployed in New Brunswick, Canada, ready for firing by the anti-tank troop of No. 42 Commando, Royal Marines, during exercise Grey Goose 75 (Royal Marine photo – May 1975)

HARPON ANTI-TANK SYSTEM

The Harpon vehicle-mounted ATGW was the first in the Aérospatiale series to be controlled by the infra-red TCA (SACLOS) system. A description of Harpon appeared in the 1976 edition of JANE'S INFANTRY WEAPONS but it is understood that the system has now been declared obsolete.

1160 SAMO WEAPON SYSTEM

The SAMO mount is intended to be used on the Land Rover type of vehicle. It can also be mounted on an armoured vehicle. The SAMO mount has two arms, each of which has four missiles. Normally the arms and the missiles they carry will be carried inside the hood of the vehicle but they take only four seconds to be extended using the power of a 24 volt battery.

The missiles carried can be Entac or SS11. Binoculars linked to the firing mount control the initial elevation of the missile. The vehicle is aligned so that it points either at the target or into the centre of an arc it is covering. It is not possible to fire the missile if the arms of the mount are not fully extended.

The missile when launched is wire controlled, according to its type, in the usual way.

Missiles can be launched and controlled if required, from a position some 20 to 100 metres away where the controller can, for example, see over a crest. The launcher complete with 4 launching ramps, weighs some 150kg.

The design was started by SAMO (Société d'Applications Mécaniques et d'Outillages) in 1964 as a private venture and the first prototype appeared in the following year. Trials were completed in 1967 and it came into service in 1969. It has since been adopted by several foreign armies.

Manufacturer: Société d'Application Mécaniques et d'Outillages, (SAMO) 150, Avenue de Verdun, 92130 Issy-les-Moulineaux.

A jeep equipped with 1160 SAMO firing mount and missiles. Left: Travelling position. Right: Firing position.

OFF-ROUTE ANTI-TANK MINE MODEL F1

Now in production for the French Army, this weapon is essentially an automatic remotely-operated missile launcher of advanced design. The basic idea is one that has been used, for example, in the US M-24 anti-tank mine, where a launcher located by the side of a road or other likely vehicle path is triggered by a passing vehicle: the special feature of the French device is the provision of an acoustic/infra-red influence fuze on the launcher in addition to the more conventional remote pressure switches. Since the launcher can be located as much as 80 metres from the expected position of the target, a concealed launcher using only the acoustic/infra-red detector would be difficult to find and clear.

The projectile is a hollow charge which is capable of perforating 70mm of armour plate at 80 metres with a 30 degree angle of incidence. The launcher is 265mm long, 190mm in diameter and weighs 10kg.

Manufacturer: GIAT, 10, place Georges Clémenceau, 92211 Saint-Cloud
Status: Production. Adopted by the French Army

VERTICÁLLY- AND HORIZONTALLY-ACTING ANTI-TANK WEAPON

This is a new type of anti-tank mine which is currently being studied for the French authorities by SERAT. It is intended for use in narrow defile.

The weapon is essentially a small but powerful gun firing a solid metal projectile at the AFV from short range. As its name implies, it can be set to fire either vertically (buried in the ground) or horizontally from the side of the defile and is triggered by a pressure igniter. It can also be fired by manual remote control and can be set to neutralise itself after a predetermined interval.

DATA
Length of launcher: 200mm
Weight of charge: 5kg
Width of defile effectively guarded: 10m
Manufacturer: SERAT, 134 boulevard Haussmann 75008 Paris
Status: Study project

GERMANY (FEDERAL REPUBLIC)

PZF 44 (LANZE) PORTABLE ANTI-TANK WEAPON

The PZF 44, also known as Lanze and often simply referred to as the Panzerfaust, is a recoilless, one man, weapon designed for close range anti-tank engagement.

The idea of such a weapon dates back to the closing stages of the last war and the PZF 44 has been in service since the early 1960's. Dynamit Nobel have recently produced a greatly improved ammunition which has extended the useful life of the Panzerfaust.

The weapon consists of a tube, open at both ends, with a pistol grip and firing mechanism underneath at the point of balance. At the front end is a forward pistol grip. The telescopic sight is mounted on the left side just forward of the rear pistol grip.

The ammunition is in two parts. It consists of the warhead and rocket motor, and the propelling charge and counterweight system contained in a tubular cartridge.

The propellant cartridge is inserted into the muzzle of the launcher and pushed down until only the top is projecting. The rear end of the rocket motor housing is then pushed down into a detent on the top of the propellant cylinder and the two are locked together. The rocket body is then pushed down until only the warhead is protruding. The precise position is determined by a stop under the warhead.

When the weapon is fired the propellant charge is ignited and a genuine

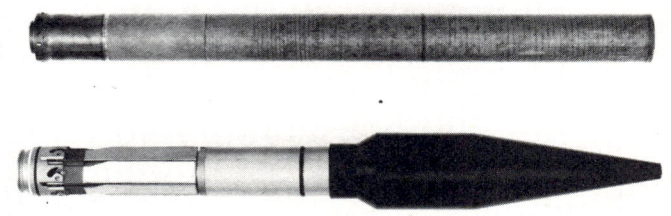

The warhead and propelling charge of the PZF 44

recoilless effect is obtained by the missile being discharged in one direction and a nearly equal mass of powdered iron being driven to the rear. This iron consists of a very large number of small particles with little mass and soon drops to the ground. As soon as the missile is free of the tube the six fins are extended, driven by a spring loaded sleeve. The propellant ignites the rocket motor which burns when it is clear of the firer and the rocket is accelerated as it moves towards the target. The acceleration forces arm the detonator which is fired by a piezo-electric voltage induced when the nose strikes the target.

DATA
Weapon:
Calibre: 44mm
Length in travelling position: 0.888 metres
Length in firing position: 1.162 metres
Weight of telescope: 0.75kg
Weight of weapon with telescope and carrying case: 7.8kg
Weight in firing position: 10.3kg
Grenade:
Diameter of warhead: 67mm
Length: 550mm
Weight: 1.5kg
Propellant charge:
Diameter: 44mm
Length: 538mm
Weight: 1kg
Firing characteristics:
Initial velocity: 168 metres/sec
Maximum velocity: 210 metres/sec
Penetration at normal (0° obliquity): 370mm
Combat range – stationary targets: 400 metres
Combat range – moving targets: 300 metres
Manufacturer: Dynamit Nobel, 5 Koln 80 Dellbruck. Diehl Wehrtechnik, 8500 Nurnberg 1
Status: In service with the Germany Army

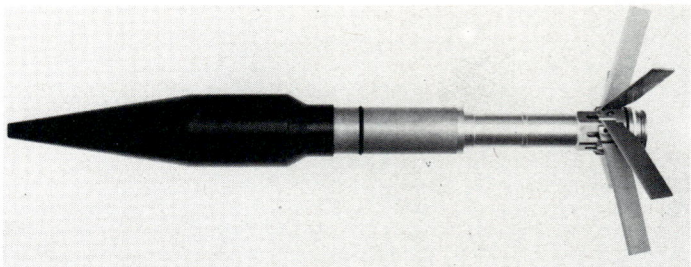

PZF 44

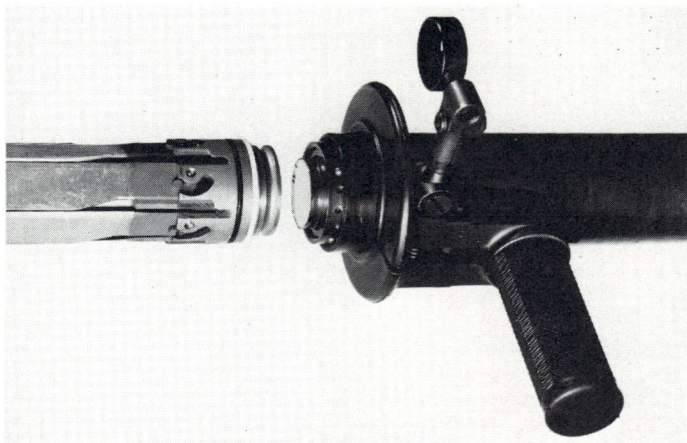

The propellant has been inserted in the launcher and the warhead is being attached

PZF44 can be conveniently fired from the shoulder

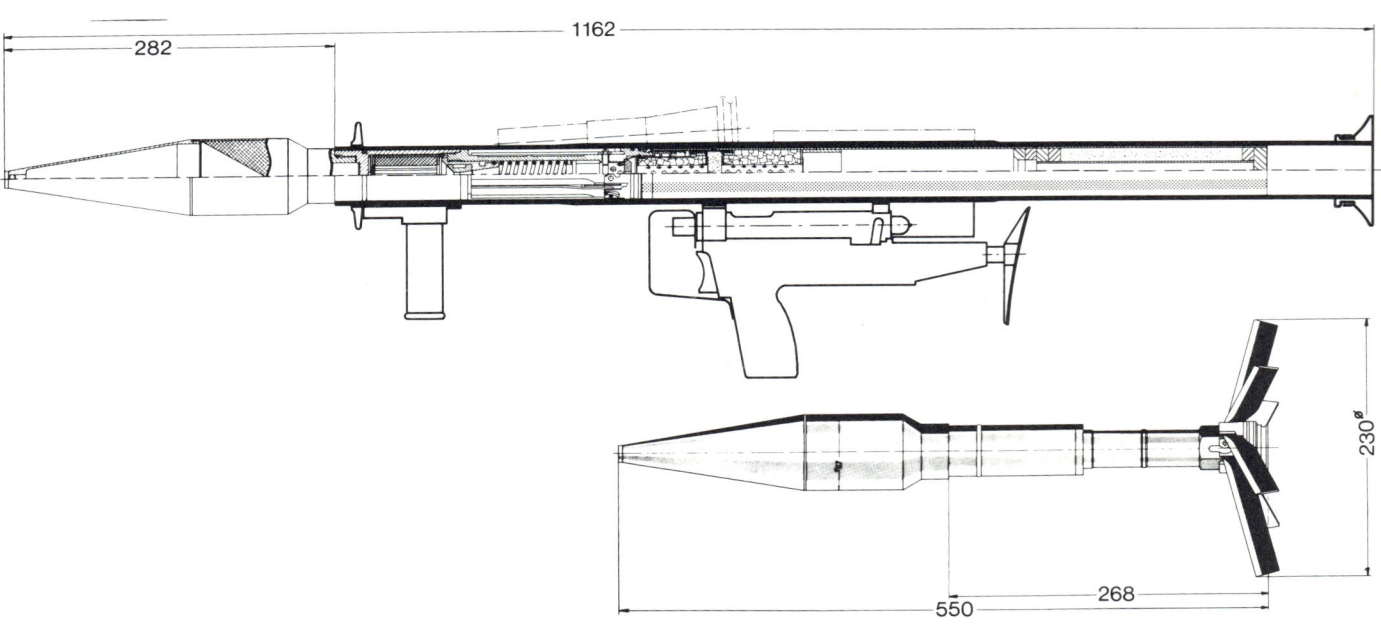

The launcher and projectile

ARMBRUST DISPOSABLE ANTI-TANK WEAPON

Armbrust (Crossbow) is a man-portable, shoulder-fired, recoilless expendable weapon with a maximum range of about 1,500 metres and an operational range against armoured vehicles of up to 300 metres using a HEAT round. An anti-personnel fragmentation round is also available.

Important characteristics of the weapon include the absence of flash, smoke and blast when fired and a firing noise similar in type and intensity to a pistol shot. It can be safely fired from a small enclosed space with a wall as close as 80 centimetres behind the firer. When fired from the prone position the firer presents no better target than does a rifleman.

Unlike many modern recoilless weapons, which rely for their recoilless action on the rearward expulsion of a large volume of high-velocity gas, Armbrust balances the forward momentum of the projectile by ejecting a counter-mass to the rear. This technique was in fact employed in the earliest recoilless weapons; but the particular ingenuity of the Armbrust system is that, whereas in the early weapons the two masses were expelled from an open tube by the propellant gases, the Armbrust projectile and counter-mass are propelled by pistons. These pistons are themselves driven by the propellant gases; but they are prevented from emerging from the tube by braking recesses at each end into which the piston cups expand and by which they are halted. As the projectile and counter-mass emerge from the tube, therefore, the pistons seal the ends of the tube, thus eliminating flash, smoke and blast and substantially reducing the firing noise relative to that of an equivalent open-ended weapon.

The counter-mass is made up of some 5,000 small plastic flakes which fan out as they leave the launch tube and fall harmlessly to the ground about 10 metres behind it. They will not rebound from the close wall mentioned above.

The Armbrust projectile has a reasonably flat trajectory, the apogee for 200 metres range being a little over one metre and that for 300 metres being about 3.5 metres. The sight reticle has three range lines – for 0-200m, 200-250m and 250-300m giving a maximum height error of only one metre within these brackets and thus giving the firer considerable latitude in his range estimation. The weapon is shoulder-fired, being held by the pistol grip and a handle behind it. Ignition is piezo-electric.

Armbrust is supplied to the firer as a sealed round and no maintenance or pre-firing drills are necessary. Two rounds can be clipped together and one man can comfortably carry four rounds. After firing the pressurised launch tube is discarded: it is hot, but not dangerously so, and the pressure does not constitute an explosion hazard.

DATA
Length of weapon: 850mm
Maximum tube diameter: 78mm
Warhead calibre: 67mm
Weight: weapon: 6.3kg
warhead: 0.99kg
Muzzle velocity: approx 220 m/sec
Flight time to 300m: approx 1.5sec
Armour penetration (HEAT round): more than 300mm
Maximum obliquity for detonation: 73°
Manufacturer: Messerschmitt-Bölkow-Blohm GmbH, Postfach 801149 AV 01, D-8000 München 80
Status: Not yet in service. Has undergone trials in West Germany and the USA at least

One possible Armbrust firing position

*Firing sequence for Armbrust from pre-ignition (**top**) to the expulsion of the missile and counter-mass with the pistons locked (**bottom**)*

75mm ANTI-TANK GUN M-40

This was a highly successful anti-tank gun used by the German Army in the Second World War. Long obsolete in its country of origin it is now believed to be in service only in Yugoslavia.

DATA
Calibre: 75mm

Weight in firing order: 1,500kg
Weight of shell: 5.7kg
Muzzle velocity: 550 m/sec
Maximum range: 7,700m
Manufacturer: Rheinmetall GmbH, 4 Düsseldorf 1
Status: In service in Yugoslavia

BO810 COBRA 2000 ANTI-TANK MISSILE

This missile was first started in 1957 by Bölkow GmbH and went into service three years later. The designation "2000" comes from the range. Although some 150,000 have gone into service in the last 14 years, it is now being replaced by Mamba and Milan.

Cobra is a one man, wire guided, anti-tank missile. It is set up by being placed on the ground in any convenient space, preferably pointing in the required direction. When it is launched, it is given a vertical boost that gets it into the air and then the sustainer takes over.

The operator can set up eight missiles and they are connected via a junction box to the control box which enables selection and launch of any particular missile. When the missile is launched the operator gathers it onto his line of sight and maintains it there by using a joy stick, the commands being transmitted to the missile through the cable which is dispersed from it.

The missile is shown in section with the description of the various parts, numbered with the key alongside. The warhead has a shaped charge with good penetrative ability. It is locked to the body of the missile by means of an adaptor ring. Behind the adaptor ring is the receiver gyro assembly which stabilises the missile in flight. The booster rocket, located between the lower wings, is used to launch the missile. A carrying handle located between the two upper wings is provided to enable one soldier to transport two rockets simultaneously. The battery lies behind the handle and it carries the guidance flares. The wire dispenser carries 2,000 metres of cable. There are two solid rocket motors and the nozzle of the booster is deflected downwards to give the missile its sudden jump at launch, and this enables it to be set up in almost any terrain.

DATA
Weight at launch: 10.3kg
Weight at burn out: 8.0kg
Length: 950mm
Wing span: 480mm
Body diameter: 100mm
Type of guidance: Command to line of sight (MCLOS)
Control: Spoilers in wings

Cobra deployed

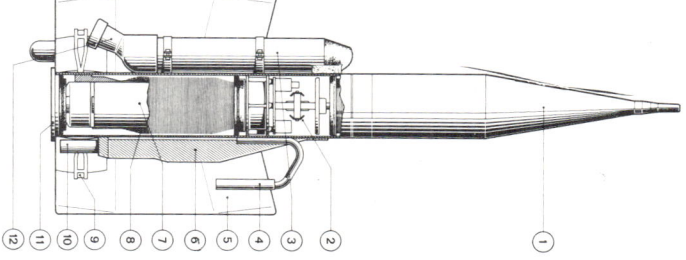
Cobra – sectioned view: (1) Warhead; (2) Receiver gyro assembly; (3) Booster rocket; (4) Carrying handle; (5) Wing; (6) Thermal battery; (7) Rocket sustainer motor; (8) Wire dispenser; (9) Spoiler; (10) Flare; (11) Sealing disc; (12) Booster motor duct

Propulsion: Solid booster; Solid sustainer
Warhead: Hollow charge
HE Content: 2.7kg
Penetration: 500mm
Manufacturer: Messerschmitt-Bölkow-Blohm GmbH, Ottobrun bei München
Status: No longer in production. Sold to 18 countries, including Denmark, Germany, Italy, Pakistan, and Turkey; manufactured under licence in Brazil, Pakistan and Turkey. Was used in combat during the war between India and Pakistan

Cobra – showing flares and wing root spoilers

MAMBA PORTABLE ANTI-TANK MISSILE

The Mamba is an improved successor to the Cobra 2000 missile. Of the same general type as the earlier weapon it differs from it in two major respects – the introduction of a new and improved controller and the use of a propulsion system which provides an element of jet lift throughout the flight. The weapon makes use of the warhead and is compatible with the control unit of the Cobra so that countries who have purchased the Cobra system can improve it by adding the new missile.

The launch system of the Cobra has been preserved and the jump start of the latter is still available. If required, a frame has been produced to enable Mamba to be launched directly from a vehicle. The new control unit is independent of battery and can handle 12 missiles; a selector switch enables choice of the required missile. The control unit incorporates a wide angle monocular telescope with an obliquely set eyepiece which facilitates the change from direct vision to telescopic without fear of losing the missile. Missiles connected to the control box can be tested by using a test key.

To fire a missile, a crank handle is rotated to store energy in a spring which actuates a generator to provide the launching current. The missile can be separated from the control box by up to 120 metres.

The Mamba missile can be operated against targets between 300 metres and 2,000 metres, and can be vectored through 45 degrees after launch.

Two types of warhead are available and either can be fitted, or an exchange made, in a short space of time. The first type is a conventional shaped charge for attacking armour and this will penetrate 475mm of plate. It is also claimed to be successful in penetrating spaced armour. The other type is the anti-tank shrapnel warhead. This has a shaped charge which will penetrate 350mm of armour and has a fragmentation effect in addition. It is therefore recommended for use against soft skinned vehicles and infantry.

There are several training devices for use with the Mamba system. First there is a dummy missile which is a replica of the Mamba without motor, electronics or warhead. It is used for training troops in tactical handling.

Mamba

Next comes the missile with a dummy head which is used to train controllers in the final stages of their course. Lastly there is a simulator which is used as a training aid. The 112/1-SU simulator is an indoor training device. There is an instructor's control unit, an adaptor cable for connecting the control unit to the simulator and a power line. The missile is represented by a blob on the screen of a CRO. The target is shown as a circle of light on the same screen and it is the trainee's task to direct his blob onto the circle and maintain it there.

1 Inter-changeable Warhead
2 Engine
3 Handle
4 Wing
5 Electronics and gyro
6 Guiding Wire
7 Flare
8 Spoiler with cover
9 Thermic battery
10 Cover with starting cable

Sectioned Mamba: (1) Inter-changeable Warhead; (2) Engine; (3) Handle; (4) Wing; (5) Electronics and gyro; (6) Guiding Wire; (7) Flare; (8) Spoiler with cover; (9) Thermic battery; (10) Cover with starting cable

DATA
Weights
Launching weight: 11.2kg
Warhead: 2.7kg

DIMENSIONS
Overall length: 955mm
Wing span: 400mm
Cross section with wings: 288mm × 288mm
Diameter of fuselage: 120mm
Diameter of warhead: 100mm

PERFORMANCE
Speed at end of launching phase: 55metres/sec
Speed at 2000 metres: 140metres/sec
Flight time to 500metres: 6sec
Flight time to 1,000metres: 10sec
Flight time to 2,000metres: 17.5sec
Range
Minimum: 300metres
Maximum: 2,000metres
Manufacturer: Messerschmitt-Bölkow-Blohm, Ottobrun near Munich, 8000 Munich 80, P.O. Box 801149
Status: In production

HUNGARY

PLATE CHARGE ANTI-TANK MINE

This is one of several remotely-operated projectile-launching anti-tank devices which have been introduced in recent years. Said to be capable of piercing 100mm of armour at a range of 20 metres, the projectile in this instance is a steel disc, 180mm in diameter, armed with a steel spike. It is projected, spike foremost, from a shallow aluminium bowl, three-quarters filled with explosive and propped on a framework so that the spike points in the likely operational direction. The bowl is 380mm in diameter, 80mm deep and the disc is secured to it by shear bolts. The mine is triggered by a remote pressure igniter as manual remote control.
Status: In service with Hungarian forces

INDIA

INDIAN ANTI-TANK MISSILES

So far as is known, the Indian authorities have not yet undertaken the design and development of any anti-tank missiles. The budgeted defence expenditure under the Five-Year Plan which started in April 1974, however, included a substantial sum for the provision of guided missiles, including anti-tank missiles.

In 1970/71 the firm of Bharat Dynamics Ltd was set up to undertake work on guided missiles for the Indian forces and specifically to implement a 1970 licence agreement with Aérospatiale, in France, and covering a programme aimed at Indian production of the SS-11 anti-tank missile.

Over a period from March 1971, to September 1973, the French manu-facturers supplied information, parts and engineering assistance; and the first batch of missiles made from sub-assemblies supplied by Aérospatiale was delivered from the Indian production line twelve months after the licence agreement was concluded. By the end of 1973 it was announced that the Indian company was in a position to make the complete missiles, without French assistance.

It is also understood that a licence was issued for the manufacture of Harpon, but no details are available and Harpon has now been declared obsolete in France.
Manufacturer: Bharat Dynamics Ltd, Hyderabad, India.

INTERNATIONAL

HOT VEHICLE-MOUNTED ANTI-TANK WEAPON SYSTEM

The High subsonic Optically tracked Tube launched weapon known as HOT is a heavy anti-tank missile developed jointly by Messerschmitt-Bölkow-Blohm and Aérospatiale. The name Euromissile is given to the organisation jointly formed by the French and German principals to market both HOT and other jointly-developed weapons including the Milan porta-ble anti-tank weapon described below.

HOT has been designed to be launched from a vehicle, a helicopter or an infantry position. The weapon system consists of:

a. The missile which is carried in, and fired from, a factory sealed tube. The round of ammunition consists of a fully assembled missile, factory loaded with its wings folded into a sealed tube which serves as storage container, transport container and launching tube.

b. The launching installation which is not standardised but may be on a vehicle, aircraft or ground position.

c. The control position where the optical/infra red sight, guidance command computer and electronic controls are located.

THE MISSILE
The missile comprises a warhead, containing a shaped charge and fuze, a motor section and a control and guidance section. The motor section contains a solid-propellent boost motor, which discharges through four boost nozzles at the rear of the missile, and a solid-propellent sustainer motor which discharges through a central tube passing through the boost motor compartment and terminating in a central sustainer nozzle. An external single jet deflector, controlled by the missile guidance equipment, controls the direction of thrust of the sustainer efflux; commands received through the guidance wires are decoded in the missile and referenced to a missile-borne gyro. In addition to the signal decoder unit and gyro the control and guidance section of the missile contains the wire dispenser bobbin and the internal power supply. The missile carries an infra red flare which is detected by the tracking system at the launcher.

When the boost motor is ignited the missile is launched from its tube, the folded fins emerge to stabilise it in flight and it attains a velocity of 280 metres/sec. The sustainer motor keeps it at this speed. The fins cause the missile to rotate in flight; and the signal decoder and gyro system interpret the guidance commands and synchronise their output with the missile rotation.

TRACKING AND GUIDANCE
In the launcher and control system there is a periscopic sight with a built in infra red detector. The axes of the optical and infra red elements must be aligned to within a few minutes of arc; and a test set is provided for checking this alignment at second echelon. The optical sight provides a magnifiied view, 4 x or 12 x, and cross hairs which the operator keeps aligned on the target, by manipulating a small joystick. A night sight with an image conver-

HOT Launching Gear 800 (Manual) mounted on a M113 APC. The aiming periscope can be seen between the two missile tubes

ter tube and a magnification of 6 x is available. The flare on the missile emits an infra red signal and the infra red detector measures the angular devia-tion of the missile from its reference direction and passes proportionate error signals to the guidance command computer. This, in turn, calculates and transmits the required guidance signals to the missile through the cables.

LAUNCHING ARRANGEMENTS
Installations vary considerably with the type of unit employing the missile and the type of transport, if any, available. The makers produce two types of launcher.

Launching Gear 800 (Manual). This is particularly suitable for light vehicles. The missile launching tube is manually locked to the ramp and the ramp is itself aligned in the required direction. When the missile is launched it is gathered by the controller into his field of view and directed at the target. The next container is placed in position by hand.

Launching Gear 800 (Hydraulic). The launch tube is locked hydrauli-cally and the ramp is elevated and rotated by hydraulic power whilst the target is tracked through the periscope.

For vehicle use the tubes are held in boxes on the exterior of the turret and the turret is turned to align the missile.

DATA

Guidance: Command to line of sight (SACLOS). Optical aiming with automatic infra red tracking
Method of guidance: Wire guidance control of jet spoiler
Propulsion: Solid booster motor and sustainer
Missile at launch
  Weight: 20kg
  Length: 1,275mm
  Diameter: 136mm
  Wing span (unfolded): 310mm
Container/Launcher Tube
  Weight (empty): 5kg

Weight (loaded): 25kg
Length: 1,300mm
Diameter: 175mm

OPERATIONAL PERFORMANCE
Sustained velocity: 260metres/sec
Time of flight to maximum range: 16secs
Effective range: 75metres to 4,000metres
Warhead: Shaped charge said to penetrate any known tank
Manufacturer: Messerschmitt-Bölkow GmbH, Ottobrunn bei München, Germany; Aérospatiale, 2 à 18, Rue Béranger Chatillon-sous-Bagneux, France
Status: In production. Not yet in service but adopted by French Army, by the German Army for limited AFV use and ordered by Kuwait and two other countries

MILAN PORTABLE ANTI-TANK WEAPON

The Missile d'Infanterie Léger Anti-char (Milan) is designed to be used by infantry from a defensive position and the emphasis is placed on this use rather than on vehicle mounting. Milan is a SACLOS wire-controlled missile and the task of the operator is to keep his cross hairs on the target. The flare on the missile emits an infra red signature which enables the computer to measure the error between its position and the line of sight. The velocity is twice that of most early portable missiles and allows the Milan missile to reach 1,500 metres in 10 seconds and 2 kilometres in 13 seconds.

The complete weapon system is made up of two units as follows:
(a) *A round of ammunition,* consisting of a missile, factory loaded into a sealed launcher/container tube.
(b) *A combined launching and guidance unit,* consisting of a launcher combined with a periscopic optical sight and an infra red tracking and guidance system, the whole being mounted on a tripod.

The round of ammunition comprises an assembled missile, factory loaded with wings folded into a sealed tube which serves the dual purpose of storage/transport container and launching tube.

The container/launcher tube is fitted with mechanical and electrical quick-connection fittings and a self-activating battery is mounted on the outside to provide electrical power for the firing installation.

THE MISSILE

The missile is an assembly of the following main components:
(a) an ogival head containing a shaped charge and fuze.
(b) a two-stage solid propellant motor discharging through an exhaust tube to a central nozzle located at the rear of the missile.
(c) a rear part containing the jet spoiler control system and guidance components. The guidance components include:
(1) a gas driven, turbine operated gyro
(2) an infra red flare
(3) a spool carrying the two guidance wires in one cable
(4) a decoder unit
(5) a self-activating battery for internal power supply

The missile is launched from its tube by a booster charge gas generator which is contained in the tube and burns for 45 milliseconds. Initial velocity is 75m/s.

The recoil effect is compensated but a part of it is used to eject the tube to the rear of the gunner to a distance of approximately 2 metres.

The two-stage propulsion motor burns for 13.0secs and increases the velocity of the missile, at first rapidly, then more slowly to 200m/s. The operator must keep his sight cross-hairs on the target throughout the engagement.

Guidance is achieved by means of a single jet spoiler operating in the sustainer motor exhaust jet. The jet spoiler operates on guidance command signals generated automatically by the launcher/sight unit (by measurement of the angular departure of the missile from the reference directions of the infra red tracker in the right unit) and transmitted to the missile via the guidance wires which unwind from the missile. In this respect Milan resembles HOT.

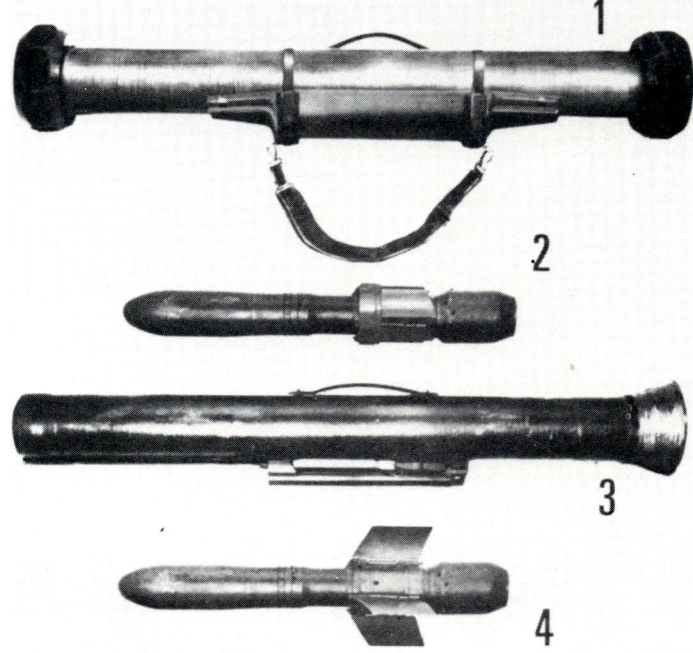

MILAN. *(1) "Packed" missile round; (2) Missile with wings folded; (3) Launcher-transport tube; (4) Missile in flight configuration*

The guidance commands are decoded by a transistorised decoder unit within the missile. The self-activating battery which provides internal power is designed for long-term storage and use in world-wide temperature conditions.

SAFETY ARRANGEMENTS

The missile is locked inside its tube and the solid propellant gas generator cannot be ignited until the missile is unlocked by the gunner.

The sustainer motor ignites when the missile is released from the tube and the wings have unfolded.

The fuze cannot arm until:
(a) the sustainer motor is ignited;
(b) an electrical safety device functions when the missile has flown approximately 20 metres

Note how the sight enables the operator to keep below the protection in front of the launcher

MILAN tactically sited

DATA
Missile
Weight (ready to fire): 6.65kg
Length: 769mm
Midbody diameter: 90mm
Warhead diameter: 103mm
Wingspan (wings unfolded): 265mm
Warhead, with fuze, weight: 2.98kg
Warhead filling: 1.45kg
Cone diameter: 103mm
Fuze: 0.3kg
Ammunition (Tactical package)
Weight in carrying condition: 11.8kg
Weight, ready to fire: 11.3kg
Length: 1,260mm
Body diameter: 133mm
Diameter at rear across flare cone: 182mm
Launching/Guidance Unit (folded)
Weight: 16.4kg
Length: 900mm
Height: 650mm
Width: 420mm
Traverse: 360°
Elevation: up to 20°

OPERATIONAL PERFORMANCE
Velocity
At launch: 75metres/sec
At 2km: 200metres/sec
Time of flight to maximum range: 13sec
Effective range: 25metres to 2,000metres
Chance of a hit 0-250metres: 75% (average)
250-2,000metres: Greater than 98% (Makers' figures)
Warhead: Shaped charge. Detonated by electrical connection produced by crush-up of ogive when missile hits. Minimum performance is the triple penetration of NATO heavy tank plate

Manufacturer: Aérospatiale, 2 a 18, rue Béranger, 92 Chatillon-sous-Bagneux, France; Messerschmitt-Bolkow Blohm 8012 Ottobrunn bei München, FRG; Marketed by Euromissile, 37 boulevard de Montmorency 75016-Paris

Status: In production. In service in France and Greece and ordered by seven other countries including Germany, South Africa (delivered 1974), Sweden (evaluation quantity) and the United Kingdom (including a production licence arrangement). The production rate initially planned had to be increased by 25% to cater for the demand. Some 22,000 missiles had been produced (at the Bourges plant of Aérospatiale) by the beginning of 1976

ITALY

MOSQUITO

Mosquito was produced by Contraves Italiana SpA as a one-man Infantry Anti Tank weapon. A relatively early MCLOS system it is optically-aimed, wire-guided and roll-stabilized.

It entered production in 1961 and was in service in the Italian Army for many years. Production ceased some years ago, however, and the missile must now be regarded as obsolete. A description appeared in the 1976 edition of JANE'S INFANTRY WEAPONS.

Mosquito man-portable anti-tank missile

FOLGORE ANTI-TANK WEAPON

This infantry section weapon is under development by Breda Meccanica Bresciana with the collaboration of Snia Viscosa. The projectile is fired from a light recoilless gun and after a short period of free flight, a rocket motor is ignited to give rocket assistance. The fin-stablised projectile has a hollow charge warhead.

Two men – aimer and loader – operate the weapons. An aiming device attached to the launcher enables the aimer to estimate target range and speed in a few seconds.

Folgore recoilless anti-tank weapon

DATA
Launcher
Length: 150cm
Weight: 10.8kg
Complete round
Length: 60cm
Weight: 4.2kg
Rocket
Calibre: 8cm
Weight: 2.8kg
Maximum velocity: 650metres/sec

Minimum range: 75metres
Maximum range: 1,000metres
Maximum trajectory height
At 500metres: 170cm
At 700metres: 210cm
Manufacturer: Breda Meccanica Bresciana, Via Lunga 2, Brescia, Italy
Status: Advanced development. Service entry planned for 1977

SPARVIERO

Sparviero (Hawk) is the name given to a long-range anti-tank weapon system, of advanced SACLOS type, conceived by Breda Meccanica Bresciana, with collaboration by Officine Meccaniche Galileo, and under development for the Italian Army. Service entry is planned for 1977.

An automatic infra red beam-riding guidance system will be employed, the guidance transmitter and optical sight forming part of a tripod-mounted launching assembly. The system will be crew-portable and operated by two men.

The missile container will also be the launching tube and the rocket will be propelled by three sequential solid-propellant motors – launcher, booster and sustainer. A hollow-charge warhead will be fitted.

Future developments envisaged include AFV, soft vehicle and helicopter mountings.

DATA
System weight with one missile: 69kg
Missile weight: 16.5kg
Length of the launcher/container: 140cm
Launcher/container calibre: 20.6cm
Missile length: 138cm
Body diameter: 13cm
Maximum range: More than 3,000metres
Minimum range: 75metres

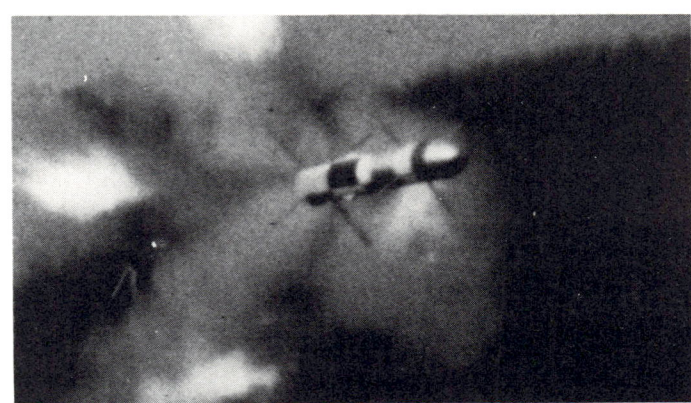

Sparviero missile in flight

Maximum speed: 290metres/sec
Manufacturer: Breda Meccanica Bresciana, Via Lunga 2, Brescia, (IR guidance by Officine Meccaniche Galileo SpA)
Status: Advanced development. Service entry planned for 1977

3.5in PRACTICE ANTI-TANK ROCKETS

Realistic training in the use of 3.5in (88mm) bazooka rocket launchers has been facilitated for many years by the use of the Tirrena practice rocket head. This head replaces the warhead of the combat round, being screwed on the propellant section of the round and glued in place.

When fired, the practice round thus constructed has the same trajectory and launching characteristics as the combat round and the weight is the same. It is handled and launched in exactly the same way as the combat round and may be fired directly at a tank without endangering the occupants. On impact the head disintegrates into harmless fragments but produces a readily-visible burst and makes a coloured mark on the target at the point of impact.

Although the practice head is made primarily for the 3.5in round, the same constructional technique can be used for rockets of other calibres.

DATA
Calibre: 3.5in (88mm)
Length: 598.1mm
Weight: rocket: 4kg
head and dummy fuze: 2.5kg
Initial velocity: 99m/sec
Combustion period: 0.03 sec
Maximum range: 750m
Practical range: 100-150m

Manufacturer: Tirrena SpA, via del Quirinale, 22-00187 Roma
Status: In widespread service

JAPAN

KAM-3D ANTI-TANK SYSTEM

Work started on this MCLOS anti-tank guided missile in 1957. The prime contractor was Kawasaki Heavy Industries, who were responsible to the Technical Research and Development Institute of the Japanese Defence Agency. The missile was finally called the Type 64 ATM and after prolonged trials it was adopted as standard equipment in the Japanese Ground Self Defence Forces. It now equips all thirteen of the JGSDF Divisions.

The missile has a cylindrical body with cruciform wings incorporating full width spoilers for control. It carries a flare which enables the operator to track it by day using an optical system using a thumb-button control box. By night the sustainer rocket exhaust provides the required illumination. The missile is placed on a metal frame launcher, which gives an angle of 15 degrees, by the two man crew. When launched, a booster motor accelerates the missile to cruising speed (85metres/sec) in 0.8sec, after which a sustainer motor maintains this speed.

Missiles can be fired singly or in multiple units by infantry or from jeeps or helicopters.

During trials it was found that three out of four unskilled operators were able to hit a target with their first round after completion of a two-week training course. Skilled operators could score 19 hits in 20 firings.

A field test set (KAM-3TE) and a simulator (KAM-3TP) are made by the main contractor.

DATA
Length: 1,015mm
Body diameter: 119mm
Wing span: 610mm
Launch weight: 15.7kg
Cruising speed: 85metres/sec
Range
Minimum: 350metres
Maximum: 1,800metres
Crew: 3
Manufacturers: Prime contractors, Kawasaki Heavy Industries Ltd, World Trade Centre Building, 4-1 Hamamatsu-cho, 2-Chome, Minato-ku, Tokyo Japan
Status: In production and in service with Japanese forces

KAM-3D missile on its launcher

Jeep mounting for KAM-3D missiles

KAM-9 (TAN-SSM) ANTI-TANK MISSILE SYSTEM

KAM-9 is an extended range SACLOS anti-tank weapon having a higher performance than the KAM-3D and suitable for use against armoured targets on both land and water.

The missile is launched from a tubular container which is used also for transport and storage. A solid-propellant launch motor ejects the missile from the container to a safe distance from the operator: the flight motor then ignites and accelerates the missile to its cruising speed in a few seconds.

Prior to launching the container is placed on the launching and tracking unit which comprises the firing mechanism the sight unit and the missile checkout device. The optical sighting device is designed to be operated by one man who, during the missile's flight, keeps his sight trained on the target. Sensors in the sight unit translate any course deviation by the missile into electrical signals which are fed into a computer; and this calculates and generates course correction signals which are communicated to the missile by way of the guidance cable.

The missile is currently under development for the Japan Ground Self-Defence Force and full operational details have not yet been released. It is believed, however, that the following data are substantially correct.

DATA
Missile
Length: 150cm
Diameter: 15cm
Span: 33cm
Container
Length: 170cm
Diameter: 20cm
Propulsion: Solid propellant booster and sustainer
Guidance: SACLOS. Optical sighting; Probably infra-red tracking; Wire command
Warhead: Hollow charge. Piezoelectric fuze or semi-armour piercing/HE with contact/electromagnetic fuze
Range: Not released. Presumably in the 3-4,000m region

Manufacturer: Kawasaki Heavy Industries Ltd. World Trade Center Building, 4-1 Hamamatsu-cho, 2-Chome, Minato-ku, Tokyo
Status: First design study 1964. Now at operational testing stage

SPAIN

88.9mm ANTI-TANK ROCKET LAUNCHER M-65

This is a Spanish-developed weapon of conventional design similar to that of the US M-20 bazooka and fired from the shoulder in the same way. It can use the American 3.5 inch ammunition.

DATA
Calibre: 88.9mm (3.5in)
Launcher length: 1,600mm in firing order: 830mm closed for carriage

Weight: weapon: 5.4kg
rocket: 2.0kg to 3.1kg according to type
Weight of 3-round carrier, empty: 1.5kg
Time into action: 15 seconds
Firing mechanism: Electrical by trigger-operated magneto
Ammunition: Anti-tank (CH M66), anti-personnel/anti-armour (MB 66) incendiary (FI M66), or practice (MI 66)

	CH M66	MB 66	FI M66
Rocket weight:	2.0kg	3.1kg	2.7kg
Initial velocity:	230m/sec	155m/sec	155m/sec
Maximum range:	2,500m	1,500m	1,500m
Effective anti-armour range:	450m	300m	—
Penetration: armour:	330mm	250mm	—
concrete:	800mm	700mm	—

Manufacturer: Instalza SA, Zaragoza
Status: In service in the Spanish Army

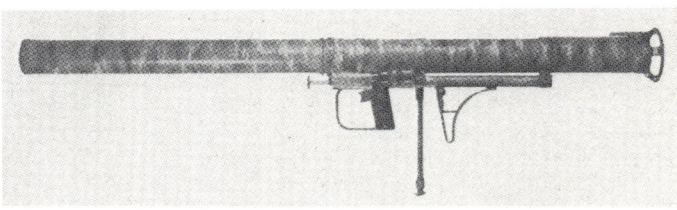

88.9mm Rocket Launcher M-65

SWEDEN

MINIMAN LIGHT ANTI-ARMOUR WEAPON

The Miniman is a one shot, throw-away, recoilless gun intended to be issued to infantry to enable them to have an effective defence against close in tanks. It arrives in the forward area with the projectile already in place and the soldier has simply to estimate range, and speed, cock his firing mechanism, lay on the target and fire.

The barrel is made of filament wound, glass reinforced plastic. Attached to the outside is a descriptive label giving simple illustrated instructions which make easy the process of applying the correct lead to a moving target and demand from the firer only that he judges the range, out to 150 metres, to the nearest 25 metres. The speed of the target is classified as very slow (6km/h), slow (20km/h) or fast which is 30km/h, and the firer is called upon to place his target in one of these categories, and that at a range not exceeding 150 metres is not excessively difficult.

The Miniman launching tube is of filament wound fibre and the projectile and charge are inside

The HEAT shell in the barrel is linked to the igniter by a breakable joint and the igniter is at the front of the combustion chamber which is made of high strength aluminium alloy and contains the igniting and propellant charges. The combustion chamber is cylindrical and perforated. Behind the combustion chamber the barrel is opened out to form a venturi. The firer cocks the weapon by moving the cocking lever over to the right. When he pushes the firing button forward the firing rod goes rearward and the pin ignites the primer. The flame travels down the ignition transmission line and reaches the igniting and propelling charges. The system works on the high-low pressure system. The pressure in the combustion chamber is at a high level and the gases escape through the holes into the barrel where the pressure is reduced. The pressure in the barrel breaks the joint between the combustion chamber and the shell and the shell moves forward whilst the gases emerge from the rear and the combustion chamber remains in the barrel. The momentum of the gases escaping through the venturi is equal to the momentum of the shell and gases going forward and so the gun remains stationary.

The HEAT shell consists of:

The distance tube at the front, made of alloy and responsible for establishing the stand off distance.

The shell body with copper liner and shaped charge of octol.

The stabilising tube of light alloy. In the rear of this tube are four H shaped slots and these form eight flaps which are forced out by gas pressure to form four fins to stabilize the shell.

When the shell strikes the target the body is compressed and the piezo crystal produces a voltage which initiates the electric detonator. The shaped charge is initiated from the rear and the resulting jet penetrates the armour plate.

There is also a sub-calibre device using a 9mm tracer round which is used for training or, with standard 9mm Parabellum, it can be used against miniature targets and for indoor firing against projected film targets.

DATA
Weight of weapon loaded: 2.9kg
HEAT shell, calibre: 74mm
　　　　　weight: 880g
　　　　　length: 325mm
　　　　　weight of explosive: 300g
Length of weapon: 900mm
Weight of package containing two weapons: 7.1kg

PERFORMANCE
Muzzle velocity: 160metres/sec
Armour penetration: 300mm

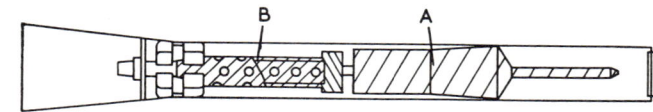

The projectile and propellant in the tube: (a) Projectile; (b) Propellant, contained in metal case. Note the breakable link between projectile and propellant case

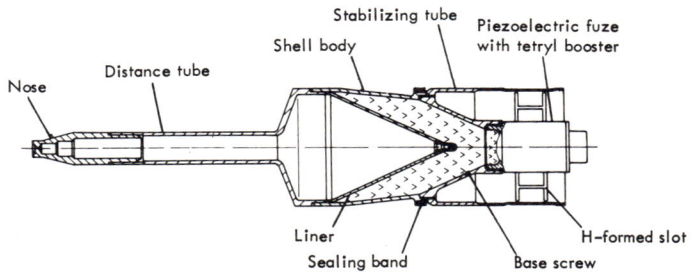

The projectile

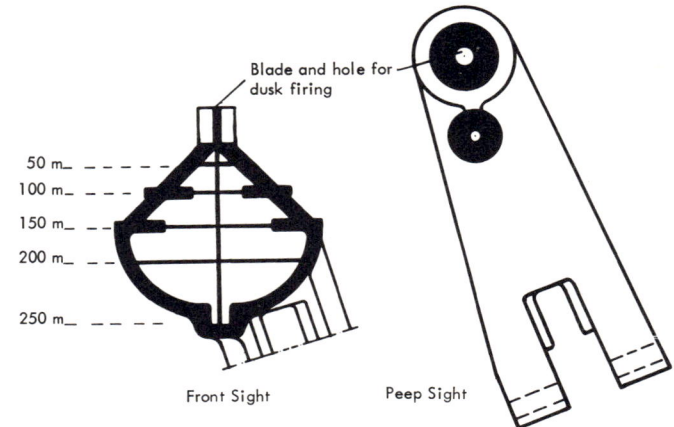

The sighting system

The development of the tail fins. The gas pressure forces them out into the air stream

Range, moving target: 150metres
　　　　stationary target: 250metres
Time of flight for 150metres: 1.2sec
Manufacturer: Forenade Fabriksverken (FFV), Eskilstuna
Status: In production. In service

84mm CARL GUSTAF M2 RCL GUN

This recoilless gun is intended to be used by Infantry as a Medium Anti-armour Weapon (MAW). It can also be employed to deliver HE, smoke or illuminating rounds which are particularly effective when used to illumi-nate armour targets at night. The range of the illuminating round is 2,300metres, that of the smoke is 1,300metres and the HE is effective out to 1,000metres. A stationary tank can be engaged with the HEAT round at

500metres and an armoured vehicle on the move at ranges up to 400metres. A practical rate of fire of up to 6 rounds/minute can be achieved.

The weapon is best served by a two man detachment. One fires the gun and the other carries ammunition and loads. The gun is breech loaded and is opened by releasing the venturi fastening strap and rotating the venturi sideways. The empty case is loosened in the chamber and the next round can be loaded straight in. Until the breech is rotated to the fully closed position the firing mechanism is inoperative. Since the round is percussion fired, it is necessary to index it into the chamber by a tongue and a notch.

The firing mechanism is contained in a tube on the right side of the barrel and is cocked when the cocking lever, behind the pistol grip, is pushed forward to compress the main spring. The safety catch is on the right side of the pistol grip. The RCL can be fired from the shoulder or from the prone position or it can be rested on the edge of a trench or fired from a mount on an APC. When fired off a flat surface the weapon is supported on a flexible bipod located immediately in front of the shoulder piece.

There is an open sight but the usual sighting system is a 2x telescope with a 17 degree field of view. This is fitted with a temperature correction device and luminous front and rear adaptors are available for night work.

The cartridge is of a light metal alloy. It contains a double-base propellant in strip form and a priming charge container. The rear closure of the case is a plastic disc which is blown out when the projectile starts to move down the bore. The HEAT shell carries a tracer compound and it is aerodynamically stabilised. There are no fins and the driving band is designed to rotate independently of the body and so ensures that the shell is not spun at a rate sufficiently high to degrade the HEAT effect. A piezo electric fuze is situated at the front of the tube which projects forward from the nose to obtain the correct stand-off distance, and this fires the hollow charge from the rear. The High Explosive shell has a time fuze and contains a large number of metal balls. Like the smoke and illuminating rounds, it is spin-stabilised. There is an inert filled target practice tracer projectile which matches the trajectory of the HEAT round.

For both range practice and field training the FFV219 9mm sub-calibre adaptor can be used. It has the same shape and dimensions as the HEAT round and can be used to fire either a 9mm tracer round which has the same trajectory as the HEAT round out to 400metres or a standard 9mm round for short range practice. The adaptor is reloaded outside the gun for each round.

DATA
Weapon
   Calibre: 84mm
   Length: 1,130mm
   Weight: 15kg
Telescope
   Weight: 1kg
   Magnification: 2x
   Field of view: 17°
HEAT Ammunition
   Weight of complete round: 2.6kg
   Weight of shell: 1.7kg
   Muzzle velocity: 310metres/sec
Ranges
   HEAT: 450metres
   HE: 1,000metres
   Smoke: 1,300metres
   Illuminating: 2,300metres
   Armour penetration: 400mm
Manufacturer: Forenade Fabriksverken, Eskilstuna, Sweden
Status: In service with Swedish forces and in Austria, Canada, Denmark, Dubai, Germany, Ghana, The Irish Republic, The Netherlands, Norway and the UK

84mm Carl Gustaf M2 RCL gun

The two-man crew can fire about 6 rounds a minute

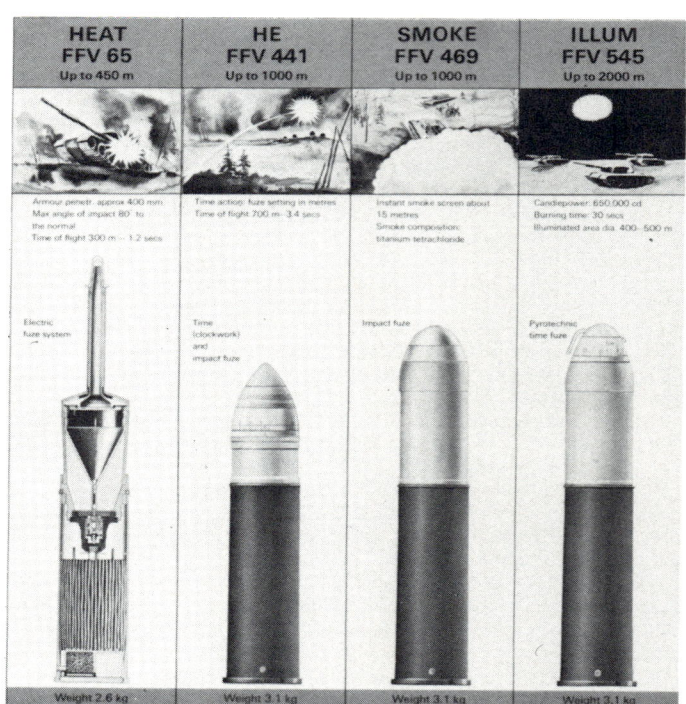

HEAT FFV 65 Up to 450 m	HE FFV 441 Up to 1000 m	SMOKE FFV 469 Up to 1000 m	ILLUM FFV 545 Up to 2000 m

The ammunition for the Carl Gustaf M2

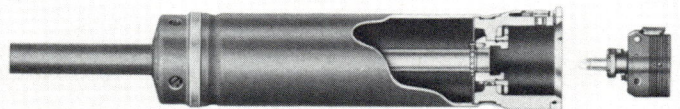

9mm sub-calibre practice device, with a 9mm round in position for loading

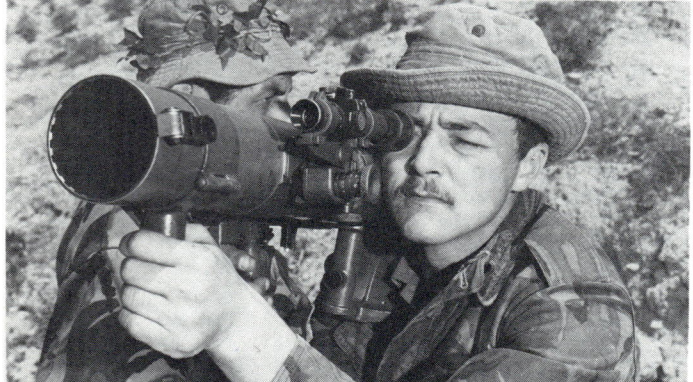

Soldiers of the Royal Anglian Regiment training with Carl Gustaf in Cyprus (UK MoD, 1973)

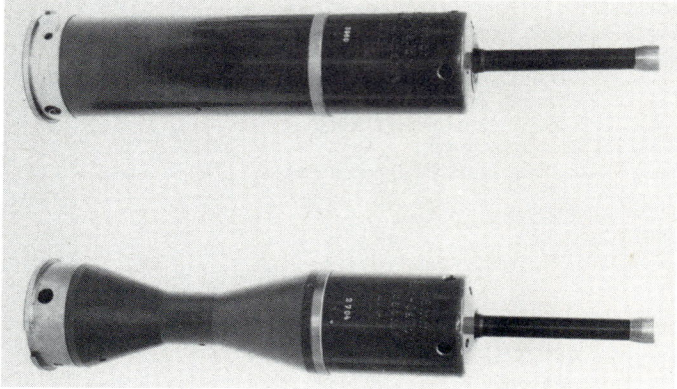

The earlier sub-calibre practice devices had a calibre of 6.5mm

84mm CARL GUSTAF M2-550 RCL GUN

The 84mm Carl Gustaf M2-550 is an improved version of the M2. The differences lie in the sighting system and the round fired in the anti-armour role. The modified weapon is also referred to as the Anti-Tank System FFV 550.

The FFV 555 range and lead finding sight replaces the telescope of the earlier model. The two main elements of this sight are the range finder and the lead finder.

The range finder is of the coincidence type with a horizontal dividing line which splits the image. The range finding handle is turned until a single image is produced. The range can then be read off if required. As the range handle is turned the line of sight of the telescope is moved to correspond to the elevation needed for the type of ammunition previously selected. Thus the graticule does not move in the telescope.

The lead finder is an electronic unit, battery powered, housed in the lower part of the telescopic sight. When the range has been found to the target for the selected shell, the electronic unit generates a series of light pulses separated in time by a period equivalent to the time of flight to the range of the selected shell (HEAT or HE). These are superimposed on the sight picture. The firer uses the trigger switch to start the pulses and also has a rheostat control to control the brightness. He lays on the centre of the target as the first light pulse occurs and he observes the position of the target when the next pulse occurs. This shows him, in terms of angular travel or lead, how far the target moves during the time of flight of the shell and so that amount is set on the lead sight as an aim off.

The lead finder functions between the ranges of 150 to 700metres with an accuracy giving a maximum deviation not exceeding 4% of the time of flight within the temperature range of −40 degrees to +60 degrees C. The battery is a re-chargeable sealed, nickel cadium cell usable down to −40 degrees C. At temperatures down to −20 a standard 1.5V dry battery may be used.

The 84mm FFV551 HEAT round is fin stabilized and rocket assisted. The fins are folded within the unfired round and emerge shortly after the round leaves the muzzle. After a travel of about 18metres, a rocket motor becomes operative and burns for 1.5sec. This increases the velocity from 290metres/sec at the muzzle to a maximum flight velocity of 380metres/sec. The FFV551 is not spin stabilized and has the same slipping driving band system as the earlier round. The ammunition employed with the M2 RCL can be fired with the M2-550 weapon.

A sub-calibre adaptor, FFV553, which has a calibre of 7.62mm fires tracer ammuntion with a trajectory similar to that of the HEAT 551 round and is externally similar to that round.

The 84mm Carl Gustaf M2-550 RCL gun (FFV 550)

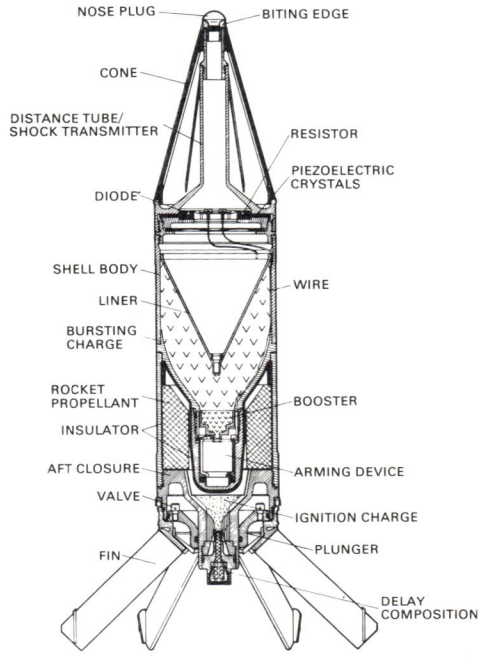

Sectioned view of the 84mm HEAT shell FFV 551

DATA
Weapon
Calibre: 84mm
Length: 1,130mm
Weight: 15kg

TELESCOPE
Length: 280mm
Width: 300mm
Height: 240mm
Weight (complete sight unit): 3.4kg
Magnification: 3x
Field of view: 12°

RANGE FINDER
Base: 250mm
Magnification: 4x
Range: 150-1,000metres
Accuracy: Standard deviation of 1m at 100metres; Standard deviation of 50metres at 1,000metres

AMMUNITION (HEAT)
Weight of complete round: 3.0kg
Weight of shell: 2.2kg
Muzzle velocity: 290metres/sec
Maximum velocity (see text): 380metres/sec
Maximum ordinate at 400metres: 1.8metres
Time of flight to 400metres: 1.2sec
Time of flight to 700metres: 2.1sec
Maximum effective range: 700metres
Armour penetration: 400mm
Manufacturer: Forenade Fabriksverken, Eskilstuna
Status: In production and in service with Swedish forces

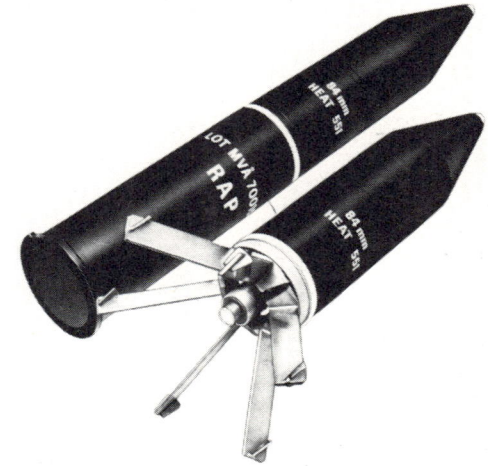

Left: The round as loaded. **Right:** The projectile after it has left the launcher and the fins have sprung out

---

90mm RECOILLESS RIFLE PV-1110

This weapon is employed either mounted on a light wheeled vehicle or on a two-wheel trailer. In the latter version the rifle is mounted on a turntable which forms part of the carriage and serves as an arm-rest for the gunner who fires from a kneeling position.

DATA
Calibre: 90mm
Barrel length: 3.7metres
Elevation: −10° to +15°

Traverse: 75°-115° according to elevation
Weight in combat order: 260kg as a trailer
Weight of shell: 3.1kg
Muzzle velocity: 715metres/sec
Effective range: 900metres
Penetration: 380mm armour at 90°
Rate of fire: 6 rounds/min
Crew: 3
Status: In service in Sweden and in the Irish Republic

Trailer-mounted version of the PV-1110 recoilless rifle

BANTAM PORTABLE ANTI-TANK MISSILE

This is a small, one man, wire guided, MCLOS anti-tank missile. The missile container holds the missile and a 20metre control cable. The missile is launched directly from the container and the cable connects the missile to the control unit. The control unit will take up to three missiles but it is also possible to connect a distribution box with outlets for 6 missiles to each of the control cables from the control unit which can thus be used to fire up to 18 missiles. The control unit consists of test facilities, a missile selector, safety and firing buttons, a monocular optical sight and a joystick to control the missile in flight.

The missile container has a carrying harness and is carried on the soldier's back. To bring it into action the container is placed on the ground and the control unit connected. If necessary extra cable can be used to displace the control unit by 120 metres from the missile. The operator carries out his tests of the battery and transmitter and then selects the missile. Each missile carries four guidance flares and according to the degree of visibility, the firer selects the required number of flares, one or all four. He then turns the safety to the off position and the transmitter starts operating. The firing button is pressed. The missile battery is made operative by the bursting of the electrolyte container. The gyro starts and the booster is ignited. After the gyro has run up to speed, it is uncaged after the missile has travelled about 30mm. The spools on the missile each contain 2,000metres of wire which is reeled out as the missile moves forward. A microswitch is mounted in each spool. One of the micro switches ignites the sustainer motor and the tracers after 40metres of wire has reeled out and the other arms the warhead fuze after 230metres.

When the missile leaves the container, the wings, which are folded in the launcher, open and the angled corners cause the missile to roll. The signals transmitted by the operator along the wires are communicated to the spoilers on each pair of wings. Since the missile is rolling, the spoilers on each pair of wings switch from transverse guidance to elevation guidance and vice versa at every ¼ revolution.

DATA
Type: Infantry, one man anti-tank missile
Type of guidance: Wire guidance (MCLOS)
Method of guidance: Manual commands transmitted to spoilers on wings

Bantam emerging from the launching/carrying box

Propulsion: Booster and sustainer solid motors
Warhead: Hollow charge; Capacitor-triggered exploding wire
Penetration: 500mm
Weights of system
  Container with missile: 11.5kg
  Container with missile: 20metre of cable and harness: 14kg
  Control unit with monocular sight: 5kg
  Reel with missile selector and 100metre cable: 10kg
Range: Less than 300metres to 2,000metres
Cruising speed: 85metres/sec
Manufacturer: Aktiebolaget Bofors, Bofors, Sweden
Status: In production. In service with Swedish and Swiss forces

SWITZERLAND

83mm ROCKET LAUNCHER M-58

Based on the Mecar (Belgium) Blindicide rocket launcher this weapon is a lightened version of an earlier (M-50) and generally similar device and is made at the state arsenal at Berne. Its principle of operation and the munitions fired are the same as those of the Mecar weapon.

DATA
Calibre: 83mm

Length: 1,300mm
Weight: weapons: 7.5kg
    round: 1.82kg
Initial velocity: 100metres/sec
Range: 200-300metres

83mm ROCKET LAUNCHER M-75

This is an improved version of the M-58 weapon and fires a projectile with flip-out stabilising fins to a range of 400-500 metres.

No other details were available in time for publication in this edition.

BB-65 ANTI-TANK MISSILE

This is the Swiss designation of the Swedish Bantam ATGW which is the only weapon of its kind currently in service with the Swiss Army. No indigenously-designed ATGW has been deployed in Switzerland but some of the early work on the Italian Mosquito missile was done by Contraves AG in Switzerland before the project was transferred to Contraves Italiana SpA.

90mm ANTI-TANK GUNS PAK 50 AND 57

These two light towed anti-tank guns are no longer in production but both are in service with infantry formations of the Swiss Army. The more recently developed of the two (Model 57) is heavier and has a somewhat higher performance; but the two are functionally similar and both fire a HEAT round. Comparative data are given below.

DATA	PAK 50	PAK 57
Calibre	90mm	90mm
Weight, complete with day and night sights	631kg	716kg
Weight of shell	1.95kg	2.7kg
Weight of propellant	250g	400g
Type of warhead	HEAT	HEAT
Minimum range (from cover)	20m	20m
Practical minimum range	200-300m	200-300m
Maximum range	600m	800m
Time of flight to maximum range	1.5 sec	1.5 sec
Maximum rate of fire	20 rounds/ min	20 rounds/ min

Crew   5-6 men   5-6 men
Sights (both models): Sighting telescope for daylight. Infra-red night sight
Manufacturer: Eidgenössische Konstruktionswerkstätte, CH 3602 Thun
Status: The PAK 50 entered service around 1953 and the PAK 57 around 1958. Both remain in service but production ceased in 1956 and 1959

PAK 57 gun in firing position

PAK 57 on tow

PAK 50 anti-tank gun in firing position

PAK 50 with trail folded for towing

UNION OF SOVIET SOCIALIST REPUBLICS

RPG-2 PORTABLE ROCKET LAUNCHER

The RPG-2 was developed from the German Panzerfaust of the Second World War. It fires a fin stabilised HEAT projectile which is loaded into the muzzle of the launcher. The fins are made of a stiff flexible sheet and they can be rolled around the cylindrical container of the motor and retained in place with a ring. As the fins are pushed down into the barrel the ring is slid off. The fins spring out and are held against the inside of the launcher. As soon as the missile leaves the muzzle the fins extend fully. The metal tube of the launcher has a wood-encased section in the middle to protect the firer against heat and also to make the weapon easier to hold when it is used in cold climates. The firing mechanism is a spring-loaded hammer and this means that the round has to be indexed into position to ensure that the hammer and the cap are in line. The diameter of the head of the rocket is twice that of the launcher tube.

The rear end of the tube is usually a plain cylinder but some have been seen with a flange-like blast deflector at the rear of the launcher.

The Chinese have manufactured the RPG-2 as the Anti-tank Grenade Launcher Type 56 and they have also a round of their own known as the Type 50. This round has an excellent performance when it hits at normal but at 45 degrees it is said to be less efficient than the USSR round.

DATA
Calibre of launcher: 40mm
Calibre of warhead: 82mm
Overall length of launcher: 1,494mm

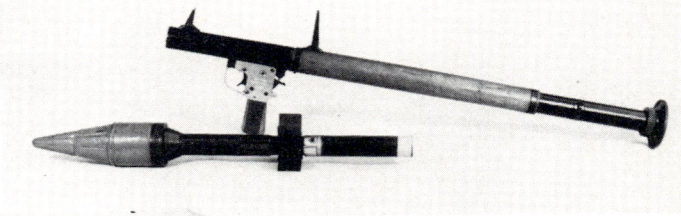

RPG-2 rocket launcher with grenade PG-2

Weight empty: 2.83kg
Maximum effective range: 150metres
Type of ammunition: Soviet PG-2 HEAT; PRC Type 50 HEAT
Projectile weight: 1.84kg
Rate of fire: 4-6 rounds/minute
Armour penetration: Russian round 150-180mm: Chinese round 265mm
Manufacturer: Soviet State Arsenals. PRC State Factories.
Status: No longer manufactured in USSR. Doubtful if still manufactured in China. In service with PRC Armies, North Korea, North Vietnam and the Arab armies.

RPG-7 PORTABLE ROCKET LAUNCHERS

Rocket launchers of the RPG-7 pattern were first seen in the Moscow Parade of 7 November 1962. The new weapon was at first thought to be an improved version of the RPG-2 and was called the M62; but it was subsequently realised that the general similarity in appearance concealed some important differences.

The RPG-7 is similar to the RPG-2 in having a tube of 40mm but the maximum diameter of the PG-7 grenade is 85mm at its widest. The RPG-7 has a stadia line, subtension type, range finding optical sight for day use and an image intensifier sight for night firing. It is percussion fired with a positively indexed round. The gases emerge from the convergent-divergent nozzle at high velocity and the weapon rests on the firer's shoulder. The original version of the weapon, referred to simply as RPG-7 was rather larger than the current model and fired a smaller projectile. The current model is known as the RPG-7V and has a variant (see below) called the RPG-7D.

The grenade has large knife-like fins which spring out when the projectile

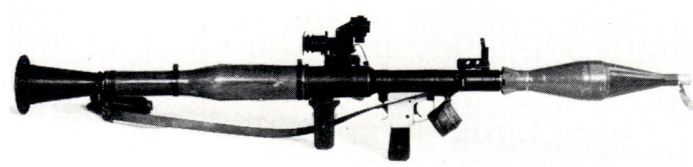

The RPG-7 loaded. The safety pin is still in place on the fuze

emerges from the tube. At the rear end of the missile are some small offset fins which give a slow rate of roll to improve stability. After a travel of 10 metres the rocket motor fires. This gives a small increase to the velocity then sustains it out to 500 metres. The point at which the rocket assistance comes in is very consistent and this regularity is a major factor in obtaining round-to-round matching of trajectory.

The penetration of the PG-7 grenade is very good. However the fuze is a piezo-electric type which produces a voltage when the nose of the round is crushed against an inner skin. This provides a means of rendering the missile inoperative by shorting out the fuze – for example, by placing wire in front of the target so that the nose cone, in touching two strands of the mesh, shorts out the fuze. The HEAT warhead of the missile will then not function. If it is fired into sandbags the self destruction element of the fuze will function but the main HEAT charge will by then have broken up and the target effect is virtually nil.

The procedure for firing is as follows. The user screws the cardboard cylinder containing the propellant to the missile. He then inserts the grenade into the muzzle of the launcher with the small projection mating with the notch in the muzzle to line up the cap with the percussion hammer. The nosecap is then removed and the safety pin extracted. The cocked hammer is released when the trigger is fired and the missile is launched.

The missile has reasonable accuracy if there is no cross wind but with a cross wind it is erratic. Whilst the rocket motor is burning and producing an up wind thrust greater than the down wind drag, the missile heads into wind and moves up wind. When the motor produces less up wind thrust than the down wind drag, or has burnt out, the rocket heads into wind, as would be expected with a fin stabilised projectile, but is blown bodily down wind. Another operational problem is that the weapon is very noisy.

In 1968 a folding version of the RPG-7V was seen. This was initially taken to be a new launcher and was tentatively named the RPG-8 but when it was realised it was a variant of RPG-7V, it was named the RPG-7D. It is employed by airborne troops and is carried through the parachute harness. The standard B41 projectile has been reported to have a fragmentation sleeve fitted for anti-personnel use.

The PGO-7 and PGO-7V optical sights are marked with ranges from 200 to 500 metres at intervals of 100 metres. They have a 13 degree field of view with a 2.5 magnification. They have, as already mentioned, a rangefinding stadia type sight. The NSP-2 infra red night sight can also be used.

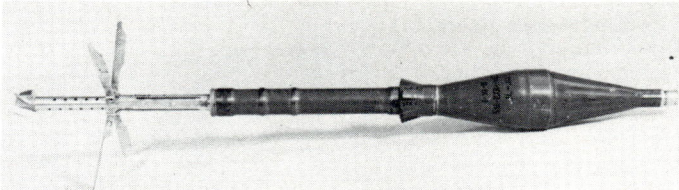

The PG-7 grenade. The knife like fins are folded flat until the rocket clears the muzzle. The gases from the rocket assistance are emitted from the ducts behind the warhead

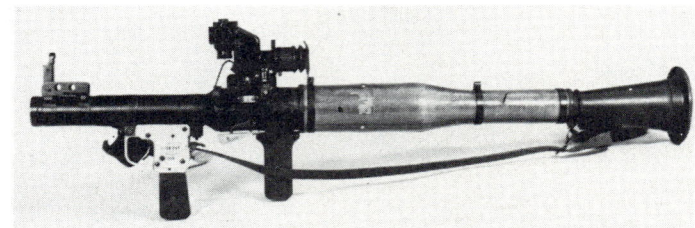

RPG-7V. This has a range finding optical sight

An RPG-7 made by El Fateh in Egypt

The markings on the El Fateh launcher

DATA
Calibre of launcher: 40mm
Calibre of projectile: 85mm
Length of launcher: 990mm
Weight of launcher: 7kg
Weight of grenade: 2.25kg
Muzzle velocity: 300metres/sec
Range, static target: 500metres
Range, moving target: 300metres
Range to self destruction: 920metres

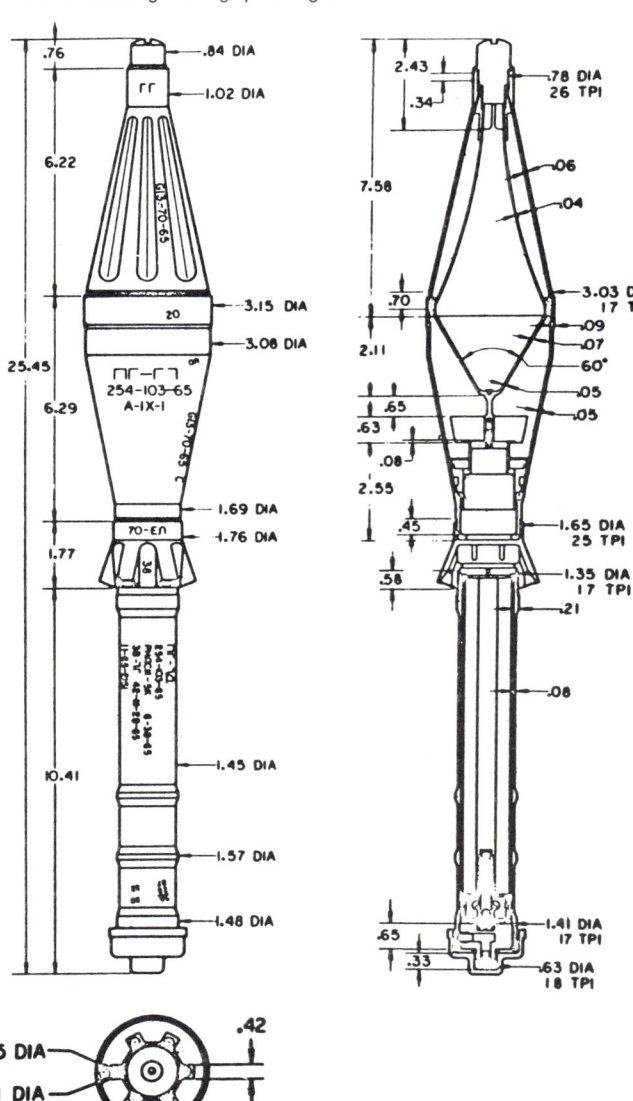

Dimensioned drawing of the PG-7 all dimensions in inches

Penetration of armour at normal: 320mm
Manufacturer: State Factories.
Status: In production. In service. Used by all Warsaw Pact forces and in widespread use in the Middle East, Africa and Vietnam. Also supplied to a variety of revolutionary organisations and 'freedom' fighters.

45mm ANTI-TANK GUN M-37

Believed now to be deployed only in Albania, this is a Second World War weapon of the Russian Army.

DATA
Calibre: 45mm
Barrel length: 46 calibres
Elevation: −8° to +25°

Traverse: 60°
Weight in firing order: 510kg
Shell weight: 1.43kg
Muzzle velocity: 760 metres/sec
Rate of fire: 30 rounds/min
Penetration: 60mm at 500metres and 90°
Status: In service only in Albania

57mm ANTI-TANK GUN M-43 (ZIS-2)

This is an elderly gun which is probably no longer used by first-line troops in Russia but continues in service in some other Warsaw Pact countries and has been copied in China as the Type 55. Its penetration capability is no longer sufficient for use against modern battle tanks, but light tanks and other armoured vehicles would be vulnerable to it. A version with an auxiliary power unit and known as the M-55 probably still exists.

DATA
Calibre: 57mm

Weight: 1,420kg (M-43) or 1,800kg with auxiliary motor (M-55)
Elevation: 5° to 25°
Traverse: 54°
Ammunition: HE, APHE, AP, HVAP with shell weights from 1.75kg to 3.74kg
Muzzle velocity: 700 metres/sec (HE) 1,270 metres/sec
Penetration: 100mm armour (HVAP)

Status: In service in Warsaw Pact countries and in China

85mm ANTI-TANK GUN M-1945 (D-44)

This gun was developed towards the end of the Second World War. Two models are in service, one being a towed weapon with split trails and the other a self-propelled version with a trail-mounted motor. Firing characteristics are the same for both weapons but the SD-44 self-propelled version weighs 525kg more than the D-44. The weapon is used in many countries and is standard equipment of Russian parachute regiments.

DATA
Calibre: 85mm
Weight: 1,725kg
Length: 1.78metres
Elevation: −7° to +35°
Traverse: 54°
Projectile weight: 9.5kg (HE): 9.3kg (APHE): 5kg (HVAP)
Muzzle velocity: 792 metres/sec (HE, APHE): 1,030 metres/sec (HVAP)
Range: 1600metres
Penetration: 102mm armour at 1,000metres (APHE) or 130mm (HVAP)
Status: In service in Russia and at least 20 other countries

Manhandling the 85mm D-44 gun (Tass)

73mm SPG-9 RECOILLESS GUN

The SPG-9 is a lightweight anti-tank gun, normally carried by two men and mounted on a tripod for firing. It can be towed using a small two wheel carriage. It is now used not only by the Motor Rifle Battalions of the Soviet Army but is also in service in Poland, Bulgaria, East Germany and Hungary.

It fires a fin stabilised round with a HEAT warhead. The propellant charge is carried in a case attached behind the fins and so it makes a very long round. However not only does this system produce a high muzzle velocity but the projectile is rocket assisted and the velocity is further increased.

The device mounted over the barrel, and resembling a spotting rifle, is in fact a sub-calibre training device.

DATA
Calibre: 73mm
Weight of launcher: 47.5kg
Weight of bipod: 12.0kg
Length of launcher: 2,110mm
Height of launcher: 800mm
Ammunition: HEAT, rocket assisted
Muzzle velocity: 435metres/sec
Velocity with rocket assistance: 700metres/sec
Maximum range: 1,300metres
Penetration: More than 390mm
Manufacturer: State Factories.
Status: In production. In service with Warsaw Pact countries.

SPG-9 with a sub-calibre training device. Note the length of the fixed round

The SPG-9 is the latest of the Russian RCL guns. It is 73mm calibre, rocket assisted and very efficient

---

82mm SPG-82 ROCKET LAUNCHER

This is a conventional rocket launcher of the type exemplified by the USA 3.5in RL, mounted on an axle with a pair of solid wheels and carrying a light shield. It is now obsolete so far as Warsaw Pact armies are concerned but was used in the Korean War, was seen in the early days of the war in Vietnam and may still be in service in Afghanistan and Syria.

DATA
Calibre: 82mm

Overall length: 2,150mm
Weight of weapon: 38kg
Weight of round: 5kg HEAT or HE
Maximum practical range: 275metres
Penetration: 230mm
Crew: 2

Status: See text

The 82mm SPG-82

B-10 82mm RECOILLESS GUN

This is a smoothbore recoilless gun. The projectile is fin stabilised and at first sight can easily be taken for a mortar bomb. It has a HEAT warhead. The weapon is towed on two wheels which are removed for firing, and the gun is fired off a tripod which is folded under the barrel in the travelling position and lowered when the gun is emplaced. If necessary the weapon can be fired from the wheels. A bar attached to the muzzle is used to enable the weapon to be dragged into position. The gun has an optical sight without range finding capability.

It was standard equipment in the Russian Army until the early 60's and then it was gradually phased out until now it is used only in the parachute battalions of the airborne divisions. It has been used for some years by the Egyptian and Syrian armies, it was copied by the Chinese as the Type 65 RCL Gun and is to be found in the armies of several Asian countries.

DATA
Cartridge: 82mm
Method of operation: Recoilless, with multi vented breech block with enlarged breech section
Length of barrel: 1,659mm
Overall length: 1,677mm
Weight in travelling postion: 87.6kg
Weight of HE round: 4.5kg
Weight of HEAT round: 3.6kg
Muzzle velocity of HE round: 320metres/sec
Armour penetration: 240mm
Maximum Range HE: 4,500metres
Maximum effective anti-tank range: 400metres
Rate of fire: 6-7 rounds/minute
Status: In limited European service but widely used in the Middle and Far East

The B10 on wheels. It is easily pulled for short distances by two men

The B10 82mm recoilless gun

B-11 107mm RECOILLESS GUN

Like the B-10 this is another smooth bore recoilless gun firing a fin stabilised mortar-like round. It is towed by the muzzle from a vehicle. The

The B11 107mm recoilless gun. This is a bigger piece of equipment than the B10 and is normally vehicle-towed from the muzzle. The larger wheels make a ready distinguishing feature

tripod legs are folded under the barrel in the travelling position and it is brought into action and fired normally off the tripod; but in an emergency it can be fired off the wheels with reduced accuracy. It can be employed as an anti-tank weapon but the sights also allow it to be used in the indirect fire role with an HE round. It is no longer in use with the Soviet army but is found in the armies of several countries including Bulgaria, East Germany and Egypt and several Far Eastern countries.

DATA
Cartridge: 107mm
Method of operation: Recoilless, with multi vent breech block and enlarged chamber section
Length of barrel: 2,718mm
Overall length: 3,314mm
Weight: 305kg
Weight of HE round: 13.6kg

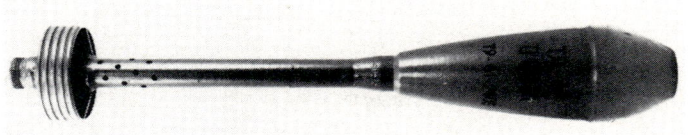

The fin stabilized bomb of the B11

Weight of HEAT round: 9kg
Maximum range HE: 6,650metres
Effective anti-tank range: 450metres
Armour penetration: 380mm
Rate of fire: 6 rounds/min

SNAPPER ANTI-TANK GUIDED MISSILE 3M6

Snapper is the NATO code-name given to the earliest of the Russian anti-tank guided missiles. It is also known by the US alphanumeric designation AT-1 and is believed to be designated 3M6 by the Soviet authorities.

Generally similar in function and layout to the French SS-10 missile it has, like its counterpart, been almost completely displaced by later weapons and is now unlikely to be encountered in Europe at least. One of the weapons supplied to the Arab armies in the early days of Russian involvement in the Arab-Israeli contest, it was employed during the Six-Day War.

Snapper is a MCLOS wire-guided missile and has always been seen mounted on a vehicle but can be controlled by an operator located in a remote position. Early mountings were on the GAZ-69 vehicle, but later the BRDM-2 was used.

DATA
Length: 1,130mm
Body diameter: 140mm
Wing span: 775mm
Launch weight: 22.25kg
Cruising speed: 53.6metres/sec
Range
Minimum: 370metres
Maximum: 2,700metres
Type: Infantry anti-tank system
Guidance principle: Command to line of sight. (MCLOS) Optical tracking of rear-mounted flares. Joystick control
Method of guidance: Wire control using spoilers in the trailing edge of the wings. Roll stabilized
Warhead: Hollow charge weighing 5.25kg. Direct action fuze
Penetration: 350mm
Manufacturer: State Factories
Status: No longer manufactured. No longer in service with Warsaw Pact forces

Loading Snapper on the BRDM-2

Snapper fired off GAZ-69

Snapper is now no longer used by Russian forces. The pointed nose and wide wing span make it easily recognised

SWATTER ANTI-TANK GUIDED MISSILE

Swatter is the NATO code-name for the Russian anti-tank missile which is also known by the US alphanumeric designation AT-2. It is an MCLOS vehicle-mounted system and is unusual in that radio command guidance is used, there being two radio frequencies on the command link as an ECCM measure.

The missile has two pairs of fins at the rear and two canard fins at the front. The canard fins are lined up with one pair of rear fins and these are parallel to the ground when the missile is in flight. The fins have controllable surfaces. Two flares are attached to one pair of fins. Propulsion is from a solid rocket motor which both boosts and sustains.

There have been two versions of the missile. The earlier version known as Swatter A had two sustainer nozzles, one on each side. The Swatter B missile does not have the sustainer nozzles and has larger flares – presumably indicating a longer time of flight.

BRDM INSTALLATION
The BRDM reconnaissance vehicle has been modified to take Swatter. The crew compartment has been widened and an optical sight has been installed. The missiles have been placed in the crew compartment which has three light covers over the top. There are four missiles with launchers in the missile compartment together with the erector gear. The missiles are on rails which can be elevated and depressed.

DATA
Weight at launch: 26.5kg
Length: 1,130mm
Diameter: 130mm
Rocket motor: Solid
Guidance: Manual Command. Radio Link

Control: Control surfaces on fins
Warhead: Heat. DA fuze
Range: 600-2,500metres
Penetration: 400mm +
Manufacturer: State Factories
Status: In service with USSR and Warsaw Pact Armies and in Yugoslavia

Swatter on BRDM in foreground.

SAGGER ANTI-TANK GUIDED MISSILE

Sagger is the NATO code-name for the Russian MCLOS anti-tank missile, also known by the US alphanumeric designation AT-3, which is now extensively deployed in Europe and elsewhere. Currently it is known to be used in at least three ways:
(1) As a man-portable missile
(2) Mounted on BRDM
(3) Mounted on BMP

MAN-PORTABLE SYSTEM

This is used in the motor rifle and airborne units. The detachment consists of an NCO and two men. The missile is carried into action in a fibreglass case in which the warhead is separated from the motor. The lid of the case forms a base for launching the missile which has a launch rail on the underside of the motor section. The two parts are taken out of the case and the front legs of the rail on the motor section are slotted in the lid so that there is a small angle of elevation. This is done to ensure that the missile enters the operator's field of view when launched. The warhead is then clipped to the body. The missile is aligned on the target or the centre of the primary arc, and the launcher is strapped to stakes driven into the ground. The leads from four missiles are taken to the control box and connected up. At the back of the control box are the batteries. The periscopic sight emerges from the centre and the control stick is in front of it.

The NCO is the operator. If the target is under 1,000 metres distant he does not use the sight but guides the missile to the target by eye. If the target is further away he gathers the missile to a line above the target and then controls it through the 10 magnification periscopic sight.

The method of guidance is line of sight command guidance and the corrections are transmitted through a multi core cable fed out from the missile. There is a flare between the two upper fins. The missile has two solid propellant motors. The front annular motor is a booster. The rear motor controls the missile through two jetavator nozzles at the rear which swivel according to the commands transmitted through the wire. The four plastic fins are folded when the missile is towed in the case. The warhead is a HEAT design.

BRDM MOUNTED SYSTEM

The BRDM reconnaissance vehicle is modified to take a rectangular hatch lifted by a centrally mounted hydraulically operated column. Six launch rails are attached to the underside of the hatch and missiles are clipped to these rails. Elevation, depression and swivelling are possible. The sight and control unit is located between the two forward hatches. Control of the missiles is carried out in the same way as with the man-portable system. Eight missiles are carried as a reserve in the vehicle.

BMP MOUNTED SYSTEM

In this single mounting guide rail of the missile is fitted into a bracket above the 73mm gun. The guide rail can be elevated and traversed at will. The missile is fired from inside the vehicle and controlled in the same way as the man-portable version.

Putting the warhead on the body

The final connection between missile and control box

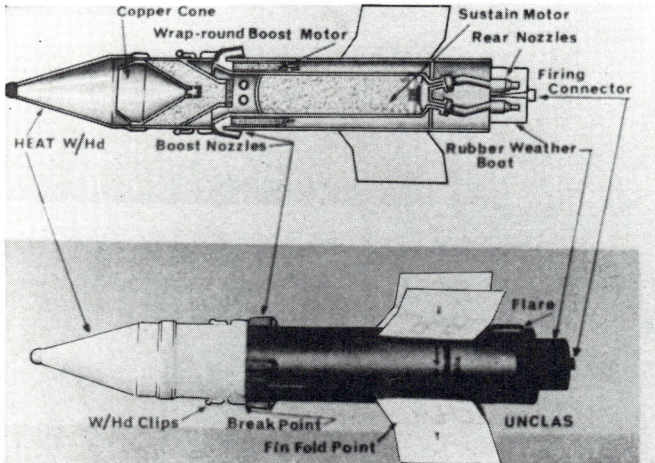

Sectioned view of the Sagger missile. Note the wrap round booster motor

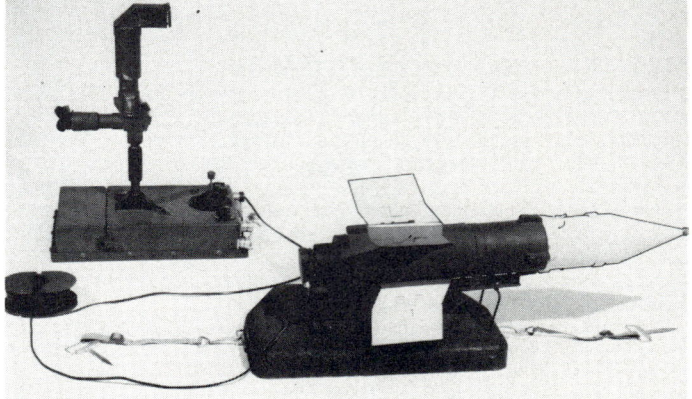

Sagger set up on its carrying case – launching ramp, connected to the control box. The control stick and periscopic sight are clearly seen

DATA
Weight at launch: 11.3kg
Length: 880mm
Diameter: 120mm
Rocket motor: Two, solid
Guidance system: Line of sight command (MCLOS) wire link
Control: Jetavator nozzles. Roll rate stabilised
Warhead: HEAT. Piezo-electric fuze
Range: 500-3,000metres
Pentration: 400mm +
Manufacturer: State Factories
Status: In production. In service with USSR units, Warsaw Pact countries, Egypt, Syria and Yugoslavia

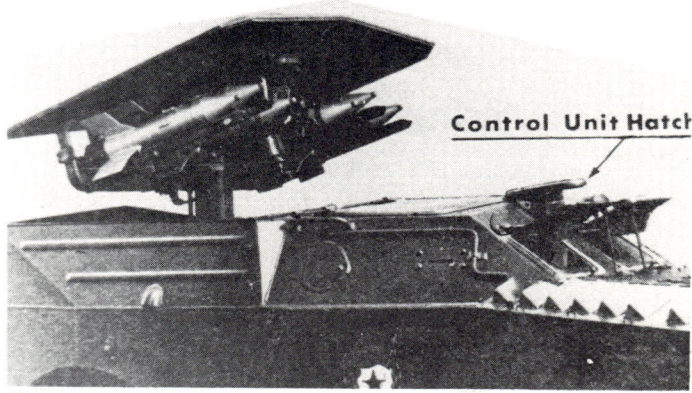
Sagger on BRDM

Sagger mounted over the 73mm smooth bore gun on BMP

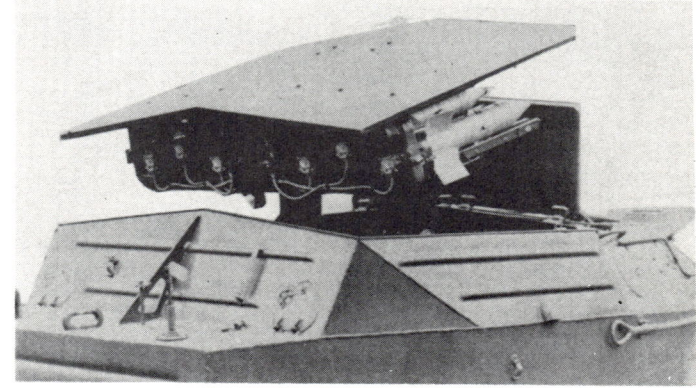
Sagger on BRDM

UNITED KINGDOM

6-POUNDER ANTI-TANK GUN

No longer in UK service, this weapon was developed around the outbreak of the Second World War as a replacement for the 2-pounder weapon then widely deployed. It was used both as a tank gun and, trailer-mounted, in the anti-tank role. It may still be encountered in various parts of the world. It was succeeded by the 17-pounder (76mm) weapon, details of which are given below for purposes of comparison. The US M-1 57mm gun was produced to the same design as the 6-pounder.

DATA	6-pounder	17-pounder
Calibre:	57mm	76.2mm
Weight:	1224kg	3040kg
Length:	4724mm	7540mm
Elevation:	−5° to +15°	−6° to +16.5°
Traverse:	90° total	60° total
Muzzle velocity:	900 m/sec (standard)	950 m/sec (standard)
Range:	9000m	10,500m
Rate of fire:	20 rounds/min	20 rounds/min
Penetration:	118mm at 475m	222mm (APDS) at 1000m

Status: The 6-pounder and its US equivalent are still in service in many countries. The 17-pounder is believed to be in service in Burma, Egypt, Israel, Pakistan and South Africa

WOMBAT 120mm BATTALION ANTI-TANK GUN

At the end of the Second World War, the standard anti-tank gun used by the British infantry battalion was the 17-pounder (76.2mm calibre). This had given good service and with its APDS (Armour Piercing Discarding Sabot) ammunition it had dominated the ground in front of British positions in 1943 but when the war ended it had to be replaced. It weighed three tons and it was a physical impossiblity for its detachment to manhandle it.

It was decided that the 32-pounder, weighing six tons and based on the 3.7in (94mm) AA gun, which had been designed to replace it, was out of the question and a recoilless gun was developed, called the Battalion Anti Tank Gun – the "BAT" (120mm BAT L1). This fired a 120mm Squash Head shell and the target effect was extremely good. The gun had an armoured shield and was designed with a large factor of safety on all its components and as a result it was excessively heavy. It weighed 1,000kg and once separated from its towing vehicle it was almost as immobile as the gun it was designed to replace. Although its weight was only one third of that of the 17-pounder it was decided that there was room for improvement and a later version was developed known as the 'Mobat' (Modified BAT) (120mm BAT L4).

The Mobat was much lighter, mainly because of the removal of the shield and the traversing gear, and used the spotting rifle technique for ascertaining the range. This extended the range at which a first round hit could be assured to 900yds (850metres). The all up weight of the Mobat was 764kg and this too was considered to be a lot too heavy. There was a requirement to portee the weapon on a long wheel base Land Rover and a further programme of lightening was undertaken. This resulted in the "Wombat" (120mm BAT L6).

The accompanying table shows the development of the Wombat from the BAT. The two earlier types had a vertically sliding block and this was replaced by a light, rotating ring lock on the Wombat. The use of a .5in spotting rifle pushed the range of engagement out to 1,200yds (1,100metres).

The overall weight of the Wombat is 295kg. The low weight has been achieved by making use of light alloys in the carriage and high grade steel in the barrel in order to reduce the barrel wall thickness. A new, lighter breech was designed and the greatest possible simplification made in the general

The Wombat is carried in the Land Rover and can be fired from it

design. An improved sub-calibre ranging device has been added.

The gun has a monobloc barrel, at the muzzle end of which there are manhandling bars which fold back when the gun is in action. The simple screw breech has a long venturi which is designed to carry away the back blast from the gun when it is fired from a pit.

The cradle is a sleeve, shrunk on the barrel and is not removable. It provides mounting surfaces for the trunnions, the rear mounting of the spotting rifle, and the sighting telescope. The forward mounting of the spotting rifle and the lugs on the underside of the barrel are all attached to the barrel by dovetail joints.

The barrel, cradle and spotting rifle assembly can be removed from the

The 120mm Wombat and its round. In this early picture the weapon is fitted with a .303in Bren instead of the standard .5in spotting rifle

cradle for air dropping purposes. This assembly weighs 200kg.

The carriage is made from light alloy castings and weighs 90kg. It is provided with 50.8cm diameter pneumatic tyred wheels. Two struts with adjustable pads give the carriage a four point suspension when the gun is in action. In the travelling position the struts fold upwards out of the way.

The gun has a free all-round traverse and is provided with a clamp so that it may be laid in any desired direction. It has an elevating gear which is disconnected for travelling.

The 120mm round has an electrical ignition system. The gun is fired by a circuit energised by small batteries enclosed in the firing arm. The spotting rifle is fired mechanically by a cable in a flexible conduit.

The gun is laid with an optical sight which has an adjustable graticule for range and line correction settings. Provision is also made for fitting an open sight use in emergency, an infra red sight and a dial sight for indirect fire.

The spotting rifle ranging device provided with the gun is the United States M8 5in (12.7mm) spotting rifle. It is gas operated and has a ten round magazine. It fires a bullet which has both a trace and an explosive head which marks the strike of the bullet with a white puff.

The trajectories of the 120mm shell and the .5in spotting rifle are matched so that they run within 63.5cm of each other over the range of the weapon. The layer adjusts his fire from observations of the trace of succes-

sive rifle shots until he achieves a hit on the target. He can then fire the main armament with a good chance of a first round hit. This permits a fighting range of 1,000 metres. Extension of this range may be achieved by the use of an improved ranging device.

The low weight of the equipment enables it to be handled, moved and fired by a detachment of two men. It is laid and controlled in action by one man, the second acting as loader. The pneumatic wheels give it good stability on rough ground and allow it to be handled comfortably by the detachment.

The gun with six rounds of ammunition can be transported in a long wheel base Land Rover, together with the detachment of two men, the driver, the men's kit and gun stores. The Fighting Vehicles Research and Development Establishment, Ministry of Supply, has designed a winch, loading ramp and ammunition racks for fitting in a standard vehicle. The gun can be fired from the vehicle if required.

The Wombat like all recoilless guns has a pronounced back blast and a typical signature on the ground. It is doubtful if it could be fought effectively in Northwest Europe where its position would be revealed as soon as it fired and and it would be engaged by tanks with a much longer effective range. It is being replaced in UK service by Swingfire.

COMPARATIVE DATA	BAT 120mm BAT L1	MOBAT 120mm BAT L4	WOMBAT 120mm BAT L6
Overall Weight	1,000kg	764kg	295kg
Length	402cm	404cm	386cm
Height	119cm	117cm	109cm
Width	157cm	153cm	86cm
Height of axis of bore	94cm	94cm	86cm
Wheel track	122cm	122cm	86cm
Wheel diameter	74cm	74cm	57cm
Ground clearance	28cm	24-25cm	18cm
Barrel weight	315kg (338 with towing eye)	199kg (338 with towing eye)	186kg
Elevating mass detachable from mounting	Not detachable	Not detachable	201kg
Ranging device and mounting weight	Not applicable	8.3kg	15.2kg
Carriage weight	660kg	425kg	91kg
Elevation limits	24°E, −6°D	30° 35'E −6° 40'D	17°E −8°D
Traverse limits	40°	360° (free)	360° (free)
Ranging			
Device	Not applicable	Bren	M8 US Spotting Rifle
Calibre	Not applicable	.303in	.5in
Weight	Not applicable	8.3kg	11.3kg
Maximum Range for first round hit	About 450metres	825metres	1,000metres

Length of bore: 234cm
Design pressure: 1,181kg/cm²
Muzzle velocity: 462m/sec
Projectile weight: 12.8kg
Propellant weight: 4.5kg
Complete round: 27.2kg
Calibre: 120mm
Manufacturer: Royal Ordnance Factory
Status: Wombat is the standard BAT in UK service and is also used in Australia. Mobat is still in limited UK service and has been supplied to Jordan, Kenya, Malaysia and New Zealand

Wombat on exercises

SWINGFIRE ANTI-TANK GUIDED MISSILE

Swingfire is a long range command controlled (MCLOS) wire-guided, anti-tank weapon system. It was specifically designed for use by armoured formations and was intended to be mounted on a vehicle. It is capable of destroying the armour on any known tank. It is, however, also suitable for infantry use.

The missile carrying vehicle can be placed in direct view of the target or it may be placed behind a crest in such a way that only the periscopic sight projects. The operator may also place his vehicle in a totally concealed position and place himself in a suitable position, not further than 100 metres away, and not more than 10 degrees above the vehicle where he can see the target. Alternatively the controller can be 23 metres above the vehicle launch. The target can be up to 45 degrees on either side of the launch bearing and up to 20 degrees above or below the horizontal axis of the vehicle. For use by armoured regiments and mechanised infantry the system is installed in FV 438, where there is the advantage that the missiles can be reloaded from inside the vehicle. This means that the crew are largely protected from small arms fire and, since the vehicle has its own air filter system, they also have NBC protection. The Swingfire system is adaptable to almost any vehicle and can readily be installed in a removable crew-portable arrangement for infantry use or on a helicopter. Another established installation is on the Combat Reconnaissance Vehicle "Striker". This combination is extremely effective and is the version ordered by the Belgian Government. Finally, the manufacturers have developed a one-missile trolley launcher ('Golfswing') which can be towed by the soldier and which has the sight unit strapped to it.

Swingfire is fired from its launching box which forms a primary package for the missile and hermetically seals it up to the moment of launch. In the FV 438 the launcher boxes are housed in armoured bins for protection against shell splinters and small arms fire and are lowered into the vehicle for reloading and elevated to the fire position. The launch box weight is 25lbs. No traversing or elevating gears are required and the launching bins are attached at the correct launching angle. If the vehicle is tilted, this is compensated for by a special vehicle tilt compensating unit.

The Swingfire missile is gathered, after launch, in the operator's field of view, close to the line of sight to the target, by an automatic programme generator built into the ground equipment. The data which is fed into the

Infantry version of Swingfire. The system is crew portable and can easily be removed from the vehicle and fired from the ground. The arc of fire, mounted or dismounted, is 90°

programme generator depends on the relative positions of the launch vehicle, operator and target. When firing takes place directly from the launch vehicle, the operator turns the vehicle sight on the target and the required angles of elevation and azimuth are then automatically fed into the

Swingfire separation and concealment. The AFV 438 is positioned near the right hand end of the clump of trees. The controller is camouflaged in position in the foreground

programme generator. When the controller is taking up a position separated from his vehicle, he pays out the separation cable and sets up the sight with its reference mark parallel to the line of launch. At the vehicle additional data is passed to the programme generator:

(a) Vehicle tilt angle (automatic compensation)
(b) The angle of elevation to the point of the crest over which the missile will pass to the target.
(c) Azimuth angle between the line of the launcher box and the separation sight.
(d) Separation distance from launcher to sight.

The angle of elevation and azimuth to the target are read off from the separation sight and passed to the programmer as before.

When the selector switch is set to "Direct Fire" or "Separate Fire" the automatic programmer brings the missile towards the line of sight to the target and into the operator's field of view; and thereafter the operator controls the missile manually.

The Swingfire missile command system is one of velocity control. In the missile autopilot there are two gyros, one for pitch and one for yaw. In the absence of commands from the controller the autopilot maintains the missile on a constant course. When the joystick is moved from the central position, the missile alters course and continues to do so until the stick is centralised. It then maintains its current heading. So the operator moves the joystick until he sees the missile framed in the target and moving towards it. He then centres the stick and the missile continues on its course to the target.

The controller's demands, communicated by the trailing wire link, are interpreted in the missile by altering the direction of thrust of the main motor.

DATA
Length overall: 1,060mm
Maximum body diameter: 170mm
Span with wings open: 373mm
Range
Minimum: (dependent on separation and launch azimuth angle); Less than 150metres at direct fire; Less than 300metres with 50metres separation
Maximum: 4,000metres
Guidance principle: Optical sighting. Programmed gathering to line of sight. Wire guidance (MCLOS)
Guidance method: Thrust deflection of main motor
Propulsion: Solid rocket motor giving low initial acceleration during gathering phase
Warhead: Shaped charge
Manufacturer: British Aircraft Corporation, Guided Weapons Division, Stevenage
Status: In production. In service with British and Belgian Armies. Ordered by Egypt.

Swingfire just after launch from the FV 438

Swingfire launched from the CVR(T) vehicle 'Striker'. The combat reconnaissance vehicle and the missile have also been ordered for the Belgian Army

An Infantry Swingfire quadruple launcher is shown here in the Argocat 8-wheel helicopter-transportable vehicle. The complete system including the lightweight periscope sight and launch controller is light enough to be carried slung beneath a Lynx helicopter or delivered by parachute on a suitable pallet

Infantry Transportable Swingfire. One of these trolleys can be moved by a single soldier even over rough terrain. The controller and sight is strapped to the missile container for transport.

VIGILANT ANTI-TANK GUIDED MISSILE

Vigilant (Visually Guided Infantry Light Anti-Tank missile) was developed by Vickers-Armstrong (Aircraft) Ltd in 1956 as a private venture. Prototypes were constructed in 1957 and trials completed in 1960. In 1963 it came into service with the British Army.

Vigilant is a light wire guided (MCLOS) anti-tank missile. It was designed for use by infantry and is fully man-portable. It consists of the missile, its launcher box, the selector box, the sight controller and a connecting cable. The launcher box is set down, pointing in the general direction of the expected enemy approach, and the firer can be up to 63 metres away with the sight controller. The missile can engage targets 35 degrees either side of the launch line. Also available is a traversable launcher which works with a modified selector unit and allows remote slewing of the launcher box (340 degrees in 8 seconds), which greatly reduces the minimum range of the missile. Control of the missile is by velocity control, using a thumb cup. After the firer launches the missile he controls it along the line of sight to the target. Displacement of the thumb cap in any direction causes the missile to move, relative to the line of sight, in the direction of displacement and with a rapidity determined by the amount of the displacement; when the cup is returned to the central position the missile is flying on its original bearing but has been displaced laterally. The controller therefore moves the missile until it is framed in the target and then centralises the control. If the direction

The fire control sight and the thumb control can be seen

of flight is not parallel to the sight line (either because of initial displacement or because the target is moving) the missile will tend to move out of frame; but this tendency can be corrected by further adjustment of the thumb cup.

Tracking is assisted by the flare that is located at the rear of the missile.

The signals transmitted from the thumb cup are transmitted through the guidance wires to the missile where they are combined with signals generated by the missile-borne autopilot. The resulting signals go to a roll-resolving commutator which ensures that whatever the roll attitude of the missile, the correct pair of control surfaces is actuated so that the missile movement is in the same direction as the thumb movement. As the missile changes direction the gyros in the autopilot measure the change in direction and reduce the control surface positioning signals as the missile approaches the direction required by the firer.

DATA
Weight of missile: 14.76kg
Weight of launcher: 6.71kg
Minimum range: 200metres
Maximum range: 1,375metres
Time of flight to maximum range: 12.5sec
Operator separation: 63metres
Guidance principle: Wire guided (MCLOS)
Guidance method: Serov controlled surfaces to pairs of fins
Propulsion: Two stage solid motor
Warhead: Hollow charge
Weight of warhead and fuze: 5.22kg
Manufacturer: British Aircraft Corporation, Guided Weapons Division, Stevenage
Status: Production ceased in 1974. In service with the British Army and in Abu Dhabi (1971); Finland (1963); Kuwait (1963); Libya (1968) and Saudi Arabia (1964)

Vigilant twin traversable launcher. Note the selector unit by the firer's left hand. (UK COI photo, 1973)

Vigilant and the operator in position

Possible vehicle mountings include one on the Short Bros and Harland 'Shorland' armoured car

UNITED STATES OF AMERICA

57mm M18A1 RECOILLESS ANTI-TANK MISSILE LAUNCHER

No longer in service with US forces but still to be found in several other armies, the M18A1 rocket launcher is by today's standards a relatively cumbersome and ineffective weapon. In its day, however, it was a valuable anti-armour weapon.

DATA
Calibre: 57mm
Length: 157cm
Weight: 20.2kg
Sight: Optical

Muzzle velocity: 360metres/sec
Range: 450metres effective
Ammunition: HEAT or HE
Crew: Two

Status: Obsolescent, but still in service outside USA. Countries known to have used the weapon and many of whom still have it in service are Austria, Brazil, China, Cuba, Cyprus, France, Greece, Honduras, India, Italy, Japan, Korea, Laos, Netherlands, Norway, Taiwan, Thailand, Turkey, Vietnam, Yugoslavia and Zaire.

57mm ANTI-TANK GUN M-1

This was a copy of the UK 6-pounder high-velocity anti-tank gun and was produced in the USA both as a towed weapon and, in smaller quantities, in various vehicle mountings.

The weapon and its UK equivalent are no longer in service with either American or British forces, but both versions were supplied to many countries and some are fairly certainly still in service.

66mm HEAT ROCKET LAUNCHERS, M72, M72A1, M72A2

The 3.5 Rocket Launcher was a cumbersome piece of equipment with limited range, accuracy or effectiveness. To give the soldier a modern, lightweight anti-tank weapon the M72 rocket launcher was developed. The M72 is now obsolescent and has been replaced by the M72A1 and M72A2.

The M72 series are one man, throw away type rocket launchers. Each consists of two concentric tubes. The outer tube carries the trigger housing assembly on the top, the trigger assembly, trigger safety handle, rearsight and foresight assemblies and the rear cover. The inner tube of aluminium will extend telescopically along a channel assembly which rides in an alignment slot in the trigger housing assembly. The channel assembly houses the firing pin rod assembly and locks the launcher in the extended position. The firing pin rod assembly locks under the trigger assembly and cocks the weapon when the inner tube is extended.

FIRING MECHANISM

The trigger, on the top rear of the outer tube, is a bar which must be depressed to release the tension on the firing pin rod assembly which then strikes the centre of the primer.

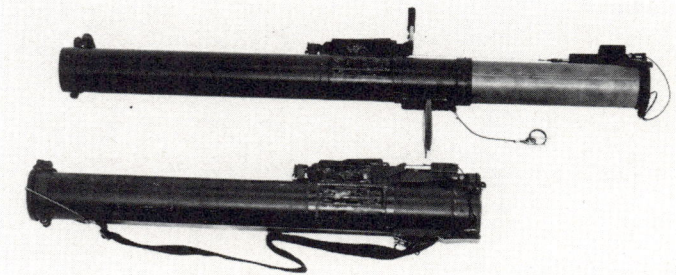

The launcher in its extended and retracted positions

The firing pin housing is fixed to the top rearmost portion of the inner tube. Closely associated with the housing is the firing pin rod assembly, firing pin rod spring, primer block and primer. The primer is in line with the firing pin.

The trigger safety handle must be pushed forward to the release or "arm" position before the trigger bar can be depressed. When the safety is at "safe" the firing pin rod assembly cannot move to the rear to strike the primer. Cocking is accomplished only in the last inch of travel of the inner tube as it is extended and so the inner tube must be pushed in at least one inch and pulled out again if re-cocking is necessary – for example after a misfire.

SIGHTS

The front sight of the M72A1 and M72A2 consists of a central vertical range line with ranges from 50 metres to 350 metres by 25 metre increments. There is a rangefinding device consisting of two stadia lines which subtend the length of a 20ft tank at that range. The tank is assumed to be twice as long as it is wide.

On either side of the central range line is a series of crosses which give the correct aim-off, or lead, for a 15 miles per hour (24km/h) directly crossing target. The rearsight of the M72A1 and M72A2 launchers, consists of the bracket, a plastic rearsight and a rubber rearsight cover. Inside the plastic rearsight is an aperture plate which is attached to a spring that automatically compensates for a temperature change.

ROCKET

The rocket is made up of the 66mm HEAT warhead M18, the point-initiating-base detonating fuze M412 and the rocket motor M54. Attached to the nozzle of the rocket motor are six spring loaded fins which are folded forward along the motor when the rocket is in the launcher. When the rocket emerges these fins spring out to stabilise the rocket in flight. The rocket motor is designed to ensure all the propellant is fully burnt before the rocket leaves the launcher, even under Arctic conditions where the propellant burns more slowly. The difference between the M72A1 and M72A2 rockets lies only in the improved armour penetrating capability of the latter.

The HEAT rocket warhead M18 consists of a tapered lightweight steel body, cylindrically shaped, containing ¾lb of octol. The cone is of copper. The nose cap contains a piezo-electric crystal which is crushed on impact and generates a small electric charge which is led to the detonator of the base fuze.

The rocket and launcher are identified by colour markings. The HEAT rocket is black with yellow stencilling.

Five rocket launchers, complete, are packed in a fibre board inner package and three such packs are contained in a wirebound wooden box. The inner pack weighs 12.5kg and the outer pack containing 15 launchers weighs 54.4kg.

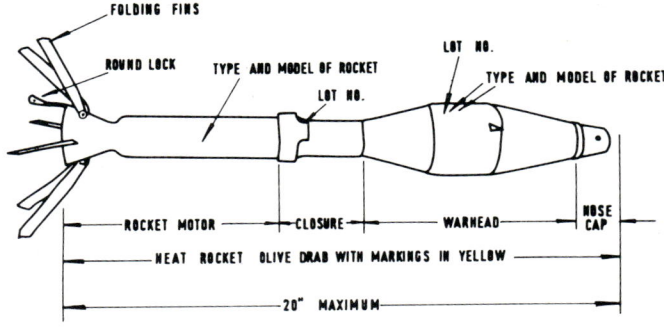

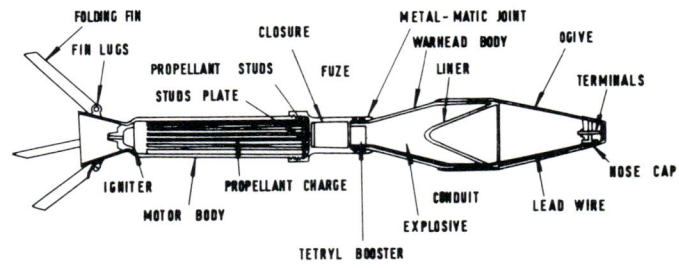

The 66mm High Explosive anti-tank rocket

Sectioned view of the 66mm HEAT rocket

The firing position with fingers on the trigger

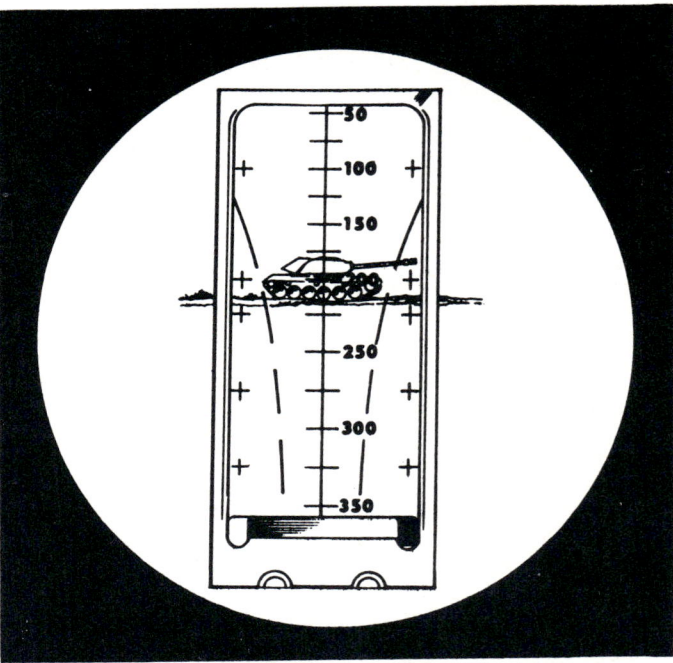

The front sight using the stadia lines for range estimation. When the tank is straddled by the stadia lines, the range is marked. Here the tank is at 200 metres

DATA
Rocket: M72A1, M72A2 with 66mm Heat warhead M18 PIBD Fuze M412; Motor M54
Launcher: M72A1, M72A2
Method of operation: Rocket
Method of feed: Single shot and discard
Method of fire: Percussion

WEIGHTS
Launcher only: 1.36kg
Rocket: 1kg
Complete assembly: 2.36kg

LENGTHS
Launcher closed: 655mm
Launcher extended: 893mm
Rocket: 508mm

MECHANICAL FEATURES
Launcher: Smooth bore
Sights: Front: Reticle, Graduated
    Rearsight: Peepsight. Adjusts automatically to temperature change
    Graduations of front sight: 50-350 metres by 25 metres increments
    Zeroing: Nil; Lead; 15mph (24km/h) marking
    Sight radius: 490mm

FIRING CHARACTERISTICS
Muzzle velocity: 145metres/sec at 24°C
Recoil energy: Nil
Range, maximum effective: Stationary targets 300metres; Moving targets 150metres
Maximum: 1,000metres approx
Penetration: Approx 305mm of steel plate
Manufacturer: Developed by the Hesse Eastern Company, Brockton Mass. Prime contractor, US Army Munitions Command
Status: In service

M71A1, M71A2 TRAINING DEVICE

This device was introduced for instructional purposes. It consists of the M190 sub-calibre launcher and the M73 sub-calibre rocket. It is a light-weight shoulder fired rocket launcher used to simulate the M73A1, M73A2 series weapons. Although much smaller in calibre, length, and weight than the M73A1, A2 it simulates the noise, smoke, blast and flight trajectory of the tactical rocket.

DESCRIPTION
The M190 sub-calibre launcher is a tubular, telescoping, smooth bore, open breech weapon. Its external appearance resembles the M72A1, M72A2 launcher. It has a re-usable sub-calibre inner tube for launching the M73 sub-calibre rocket. The sub-calibre inner tube is re-usable.

The M73 sub-calibre rocket is 35mm calibre and consists of a detonating head, a motor closure, a rocket motor and an igniter assembly. The detonating head, made of rigid plastic, contains 1.5 grams of M80 composition mix. The forward end of the motor closure contains a base detonating fuze and an M26 stab primer. The steel motor casing contains three tubular grains of M7 propellant. The rocket is stabilised by six moulded plastic fins.

The M73 sub-calibre rocket is launched in exactly the same way as the 66mm rocket. When the head strikes a target an inertia driven firing pin sets off the M26 stab primer which sets off the spotting head, producing noise, flash and white smoke.

The launcher controls, sights, and operation are the same as for the M73A1, M73A2 system.

The training device can be used against stationary or moving targets. It penetrates 3mm of steel plate or 20mm of soft wood.

DATA
Rocket: M73 sub calibre 35mm with base detonating fuse, rocket motor and detonating head
Launcher: M190 sub calibre
Method of operation: Rocket
Method of feed: Single shot. Reloaded by hand
Method of fire: Percussion

WEIGHTS
Launcher only: 2.28kg
Rocket: 0.17kg
Complete system: 2.46kg

LENGTHS
Launcher closed: 643mm
Launcher extended: 899mm
Rocket: 225mm

MECHANICAL FEATURES
Launcher: Smooth bore
Sights: As M72A1, M72A2

FIRING CHARACTERISTICS
Muzzle velocity: 153metres/sec at 21°C
Recoil energy: Nil
Range, maximum effective: 325metres
Penetration: 3.17mm steel plate

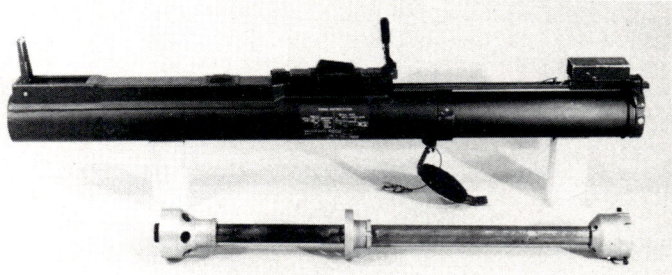
The sub-calibre training device

The M72 is not now in production. It differs from the M72A1, M72A2 in several respects.

THE SIGHTS
The rear sight is of two piece construction. The fixed portion is marked COLD and NORM and has two apertures. The moving slide is moved according to the temperature and thus a window is lined up with one of the rearsight apertures. "Norm" is above 0°C and "Cold" is below.

The foresight is graduated from 100 metres to 300 metres. It has lead marks but no range-finding stadia.

THE FIRING MECHANISM
There is a firing pin cable and firing pin on the M72 which carry out the functions of the firing pin rod assembly of the M72A1,A2. There is a re-cocking latch used to cock the launcher before extending it and to re-cock when the launcher has failed to fire. After a misfire the trigger is pressed again, and after a 10 second delay the trigger safety is re-set and the safety pin is inserted in front of the primer block. Note that if the safety pin hole for the rear safety pin is obstructed by the firing pin NO attempt should be made to replace the pin or collapse the launcher. It must be discarded at once. If the M72 is prepared for firing but has not been fired it can be restored to the carrying position. Re-set the safety and replace the rear safety pin. Depress the barrel detent and partially collapse the launcher – ensuring that the heel of the right hand is against the rear safety pin. Fold down the rearsight and foresight and replace the front cover and sling assembly.

It is essential that the rear safety pin be retained in place until the launcher is fully extended and that it is replaced before the barrel detent is pressed when re-assembling. If the safety pin is not replaced before the launcher is collapsed the firing pin may strike the primer with sufficient energy to fire the rocket.
Status: The M72 is obsolescent. The M72A1 and M72A2 are used by Canada, Australia, Norway, UK, Holland as well as United States troops. It has been used in Vietnam and by Israeli troops. It is manufactured by Raufoss in Norway.

75mm RECOILLESS RIFLE M-20
No longer in US Army service but still in use all over the world and much copied this is a breech-loading portable RR designed to be fired from an MG tripod mount. Design started in March 1944 and the weapon was first produced in 1945.

DATA
Calibre: 75mm
Weight: 52kg excluding mount: 67kg on the US M-74 mount
Length: 2,083mm

Ammuntion: HE, HEAT, HEP, WP
Muzzle velocity: 305 m/s (HEAT) to 427m/s (HEP)
Range, maximum: 3,200m (HEAT) to 6,560m (HEP)
Crew: 2-3

Status: No longer in US service. Believed to be in service in Argentina, Austria, Bangladesh, Brazil, France, Greece, Italy, Japan, Korea, Netherlands, Norway, Pakistan, Philippines, Saudi Arabia, Taiwan, Thailand, Turkey, Vietnam, Yemen, Yugoslavia and Zaire. Built in China as Type 52

ROCKET LAUNCHER, 3.5in M20
The Rocket Launcher M20 (sometimes called the Super Bazooka) followed the 2.36in (60mm) M9A1 Rocket Launcher. The 3.5in (89mm) calibre launcher is a two-piece tube, open at both ends, and with a smooth bore. Its function is to ignite the rocket which it launches and to give initial direction to its flight. Ignition is electrical.

To reduce the weight, the tube is made of aluminium and breaks into two sections for ease of carrying. The barrels of the M20 and M20A1 models are made from aluminium tube and the component parts are fastened by means of screws. The barrels of the M20A1B1 and M20B1 are aluminium castings and many component parts are cast integrally with the barrel. The sight is attached to the left side of the rear tube. It consists of a single lens and a graticule fitted into a housing. The graticule consists of a single broken vertical line, up the centre of the lens, and five broken horizontal lines. Each section of the vertical line and each space between sections represents 50 yards (45.7m). The horizontal lines are marked in hundreds of yards and the appropriate range is laid on the target. Each section of the horizontal line and each space between the sections, represents 5 miles/hr. The appropriate aim off is applied when firing at a moving target.

The current to fire the rocket is provided by a magneto: the movement of the armature being produced when the trigger is pulled and also when it is released. Thus a firing impulse is produced for both movements of the trigger and a rocket that fails to fire when the trigger is pulled, may fire when the trigger is released.

The rocket HEAT 3.5in is issued assembled and is loaded into the launcher as a unit. It consists of a rocket head, a fuze and a motor to which

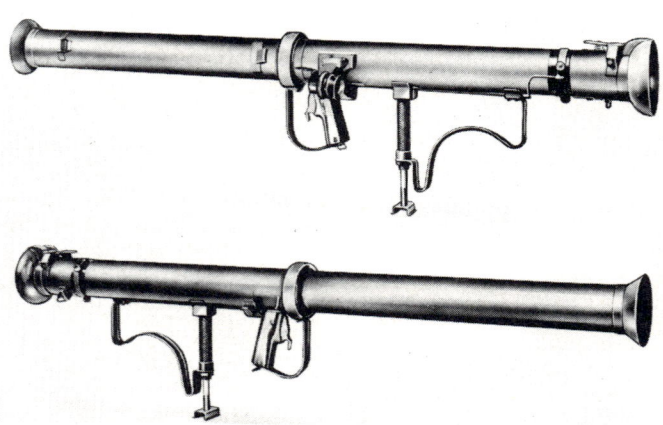
The rocket launcher M20. This 3.5in rocket launcher was used during the Korean War

is attached a tail assembly. The head is cylindrical with a ballistic head made of steel. The fuze is a base percussion type. The motor is a steel tube with propellant held in spacer tubes. The tail assembly is attached to the rear.

The igniter is at the front of the propellant with two leads passing out through the nozzle at the rear. These convey the firing current from the magneto-trigger when connected up. When the rocket is fired, there is a flow of high velocity high temperature gas from the venturi at the rear and there is a triangular danger area with a base and height of 25 yards (23m). The firer should wear a face mask to protect his eyes from particles of unburnt propellant.

DATA
Calibre: 89mm
Length of launcher assembled: 1,549mm
Length of front tube: 768mm
Length of rear tube: 803mm
Weight of launcher: 5.5kg
Weight of front tube: 1.6kg
Weight of rear tube: 3.9kg
Maximum range against armour: 110metres
Maximum range: 1,200metres
Rocket HEAT 3.5in M28, 28A1, 28A2
Length: 10.7mm
Weight: 4.04kg
Rocket Warhead
Filling: Composition B
Weight of bursting charge: 0.87kg
Rocket Motor Propellant: M7
Weight of propellant: 163g
Fuze: Fuze Rocket BD M404, Percussion, Non-delay
Status: No longer manufactured but still in use in many countries. Copied by People's Republic of China as Type 51.

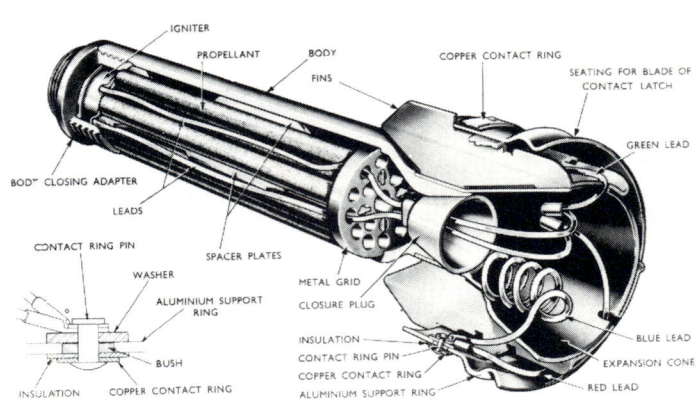
The motor and tail assembly

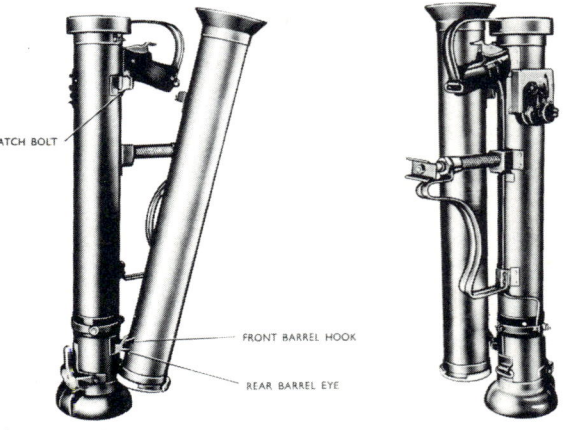
The launcher folds for ease of carriage

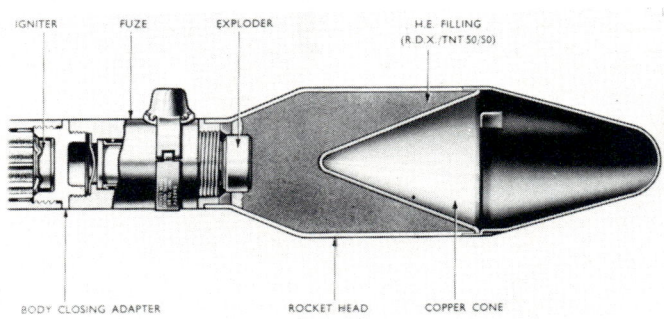
The warhead, filling and igniter

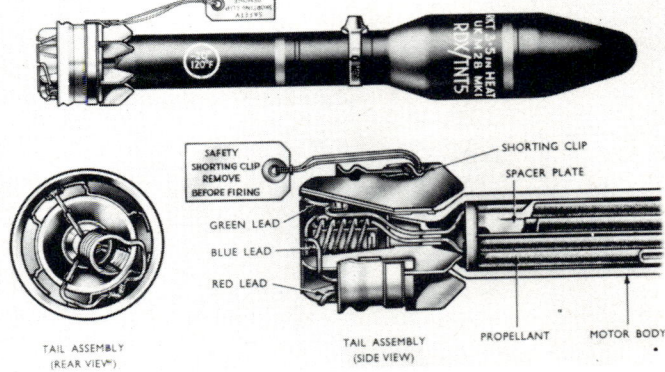

The 2.36in M9A1 rocket launcher. This was used in the North African Campaign by United States troops in 1943. It came out of service with the development of the 3.5in rocket launcher

The rocket and ignition system

90mm RECOILLESS RIFLE, M67

The 90mm recoilless rifle, M67, is a lightweight, portable, crewserved weapon intended primarily as an anti-tank weapon although it can also be employed against pill boxes or sandbag emplacement. It is designed to be fire from the ground off its bipod and monopod but may be fired from the shoulder. It is an air-cooled, breech loaded single shot weapon firing the high explosive anti-tank round M371E1. The rifle is equipped with a manually operated breech mechanism and a centrally located percussion type firing mechanism. It is designed for direct fire only. The M103 sight has a fixed focus, 3 power telescope with a field of view of 10 degrees. Its lead lines and stadia lines are provided for ranging on targets having a 10ft (3.05m) width and a 20ft (6.1m) length.

Some rifles used still in the Persian Gulf have the M103A1 sight. This is a sight modified for the experimental XM591 round which was only issued on a limited scale for a short while. The ranges on the left hand side of the sight remain unchanged but those on the right have been modified.

OPERATION
The breech block is hinged open to load the round but before this can be done the lock ring must be rotated clockwise. This withdraws the sear and forces the firing pin rearwards. The breech block can then be unlocked and swung clear of the breech opening. The firing pin and spring are housed in a bar crossing the hollow body of the breechblock. The round is placed in the breech and the block closed behind it. When the firing mechanism is operated the sear is withdrawn by a cable and the firing pin goes forward under the influence of the spring, and this strikes the cap and fires the round. The rear end of the cartridge case is made of frangible material and is blown out when the round fires. The gases pass out to the rear and flow over the firing pin housing, through the breech block.

The 90mm recoilless rifle. This has now been replaced in US service by Dragon

The shell is effective out to 400 metres. There is a 7.62mm sub-calibre training device which utilises a case blow-out arrangement with six equally spaced holes in the chamber shoulder to keep the pressure down and allow the trajectory to approximate to that of the 90mm round.

AMMUNITION
The ammunition of the M67 is a fixed round. The HEAT round M371E1 is a fin stabilized projectile with a shaped charge head. It has fuze PIBD M530. This is a point initiating, base detonating fuze with an inertially operated graze system. There is also a practice round with a small charge called TP M371.

DATA
Weight of complete system (unloaded): 16kg
Overall length: 1,321mm
Height, ground mounted: 432mm
Maximum range (approx): 2,100metres
Maximum sighted range: 800metres
Maximum effective range: 400metres

Rates of fire: Rapid: 10 round/min (max of 5 rounds); Sustained: 1 round/ min. When firing at the rapid rate, a 15 minute cooling period must be observed after every 5 rounds.

Status: Was in US and W. German service and is certainly still in service with US reserve formations. Replaced by Dragon in operational US formations.

105mm RECOILLESS RIFLES M-27, M-27A1

These are towed or vehicle-mounted recoilless weapon designed primarily for anti-tank operations. Originally developed for US Army use they are no longer in production or service in the USA but survive elsewhere.

DATA
Calibre: 105mm
Weight: 165kg excluding mount
Length: 341cm total; barrel 272cm

Ammunition: HE, WP, HEAT, HEP, HEP-T
Muzzle velocity: HE and WP 341 m/s; HEAT (M-324) 381 m/s; HEP 385 m/s; HEAT (M-341) 503 m/s; HEP-T 515 m/s
Range, maximum: 8,450m (HE). Effective anti-tank range 1,000m
Crew: 5, including two ammunition numbers

Status: Obsolescent and no longer in production. Believed to be in service in France, Israel, Japan, Morocco and Yugoslavia

106mm RECOILLESS RIFLE, M40

The 106mm Recoilless Rifle, M40 is a lightweight, recoilless weapon designed for both anti-tank and anti-personnel roles. It is air cooled, breech loaded, and fires fixed ammunition. The standard mount for the rifle is the M79 which serves also to attach the rifle to a carrier and to support the rifle when it is employed in its ground mounted role. A spotting rifle is used for ranging. The version most recently in service was the M40A2.

The barrel assembly consists of the tube, an enlarged reaction chamber and a mounting bracket. The tube is made of alloy steel, screw threaded at the back to take the reaction chamber. The breech block is a short cylinder with an interrupted screw thread to mate with the segmental thread in the interior of the recoil chamber. The breech block is hinged on the left side of the breech and is drilled to take the percussion firing mechanism. The mount M79 is basically a tripod. The two rear legs have carrying handles and clamps and the front wheel has a hard rubber tyre. The mount has the traversing and elevating gear and part of the firing mechanism. The two rear legs of the mount are adjustable for lateral expansion. The mount can be lifted at the rear by two men and pushed forward on the single wheel, like a wheelbarrow. The mount can also be clamped in position on a vehicle. The traversing mechanism allows 360 degrees of controlled or free traverse using the traverse knob. The elevating mechanism on the left of the mount provides slow or rapid rates of elevation. The handwheel gives rapid elevation (16mils/turn) whilst the firing knob gives slow elevation (3.8mils/turn). With the breech between the legs the gun can be elevated to +65 degrees and depressed to −17 degrees but over the legs the maximum elevation is 27 degrees. The .5 Spotting Rifle is a gas operated, magazine fed, self loading rifle, firing a bullet whose trajectory matches that of the recoilless rifle. The 106mm rifle is equipped with the M92D sight which is used for direct fire up to a maximum range of 2,200 yards (2,012m). The sight has a fixed focus, 3 power magnification and a field of view of 12 degrees 12'. The sight allows engagement up to 2,200 yards and has stadia lines based on a target of length 20 feet (6.1m) and width 10 feet.

OPERATION

The breech block is opened by depressing and rotating the breech operating lever and the round can then be loaded. When the breech operating lever is rotated back the breech block is locked. This connects the firing mechanism to the trigger. The .5 spotting rifle is used to determine range. The firer estimates range using, normally, the stadia lines and then when the target is thus considered to be in range the spotting rifle is fired. When a hit is obtained, the main armament is fired. Provided the same point of aim is used, the trajectory of the HEAT round will be the same as that of

M40 rifle, complete with spotting rifle, mounted on a M274 Mechanical Mule

the spotting rifle and a hit will ensue. (Note that the correct lead to allow for the target speed must be applied to the spotting rifle before a hit can be obtained.)

The sub-calibre device for training personnel on the 106mm RCL rifle consists of a case fitting into the chamber, carrying a .30 calibre barrel. This barrel has 24 holes drilled in it to reduce the velocity of the sub-calibre round, and, at the same time this creates a back blast which simulates that of normal discharge. The sub-calibre device is held in place by the breech block and fired by the gun firing pin. The cartridge case is extracted manually.

AMMUNITION

Ammunition for the 106mm rifle is issued in complete, fixed cartridges. Propellant is contained in a plastic bag within the cartridge case. The cartridge case is perforated to permit expanding propellant gases to escape into the enlarged reaction chamber. The cartridge case has a well around the primer to permit the breech to be closed. Proper headspace is

106mm recoilless gun M40

automatically provided for by the seating of the flange of the cartridge case againt the vent bushing.

Depending on the type of projectile, ammunition for the 106mm rifle is classified as high explosive anti-tank (HEAT), or high explosive plastic with tracer (HEP-T). Both projectiles are painted olive drab with yellow markings. These identifying colours are repeated on the sealing tape around the fibreboard container. Both rounds have a maximum range of 7,700 metres.

The spotting gun employs a spotter-tracer cartridge. The projectile contains a tracer element and an incendiary filler. On impact, the incendiary filler produces a puff of white smoke which aids in adjusting fire. The tracer burnout point is between 1,500 and 1,600 metres. The cartridge can be identified by the red and yellow marking on the nose of the projectile.

DATA
Calibre: 106mm
Weight: empty: 219.5kg
          loaded: 236kg
Overall length: 3,404mm
Height on M79 mount: 1,118mm
Width of M79 mount (legs spread): 1,524mm
    (Legs closed): 800mm
Length of bore: 2,730mm
Rifling: 36 grooves RH. Pitch 2,118mm
Type of breechblock: interrupted thread
Maximum range: 7,700metres
Maximum effective range: 1,097metres
Weight of HEAT round: 16.3kg
        HEAT projectile: 7.7kg
        HEP-T round: 17.2kg
        HEP-T projectile: 7.7kg

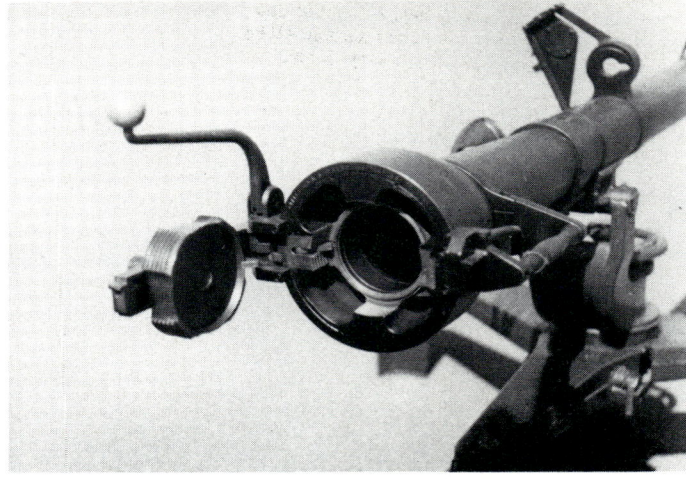

The breech arrangement of the M40

Manufacturer: Watervliet Arsenal, Watervliet, New York
Status: No longer in service with US forces. Has been used by the armed forces of at least 32 countries and is still in service in many of them. Has been built in Brazil, Israel, Japan and Spain as well as in the USA.

M47 DRAGON MEDIUM ANTI-TANK/ASSAULT WEAPON

The first mention of DRAGON (or MAW-Medium Anti-Tank/Assault Weapon) was in September 1966 when a full scale Engineering Development contract for $35 million was awarded to the McDonnell Aircraft Corporation (later to become the McDonnell Douglas Corporation). Contractor development continued until mid-1971 at which time the US Army took over the testing with a comprehensive series of Engineering Tests, Expanded Service Tests, and Operational Tests. More than 600 rounds were fired with a high success rate. In March 1972 the go-ahead was given to McDonnell Douglas for the first part of a multi-year procurement programme which has now reached the stage of competition with second source suppliers. Prior to 1975 production deliveries went to establish the training base in the USA. In February, 1975, Dragon became operational with the US Army in Europe.

The M47 Dragon is a tube-launched, optically-tracked wire-guided system operated by one man. It consists of the launching tube, the missile and the tracker. The front end of the smooth bore, fibreglass launching tube is supported on a stand and the firer normally sits with his legs extended forward, and the launcher resting on his shoulder. The missile is contained within the launcher and only the end of the warhead can be seen. The forward end contains the shaped-charge warhead and the fuze. The middle portion has 60 side-thrust rocket motors which operate in pairs. The rear section has the wire dispenser, the electronics, the battery, the flare assembly and the three folding fins which rotate outwards when the missile

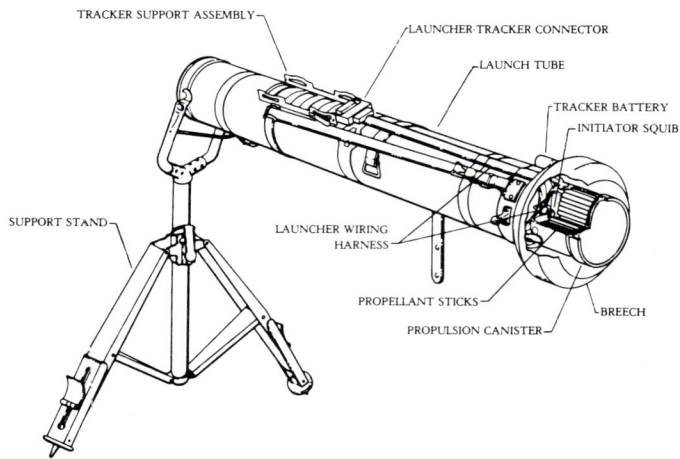

The launcher

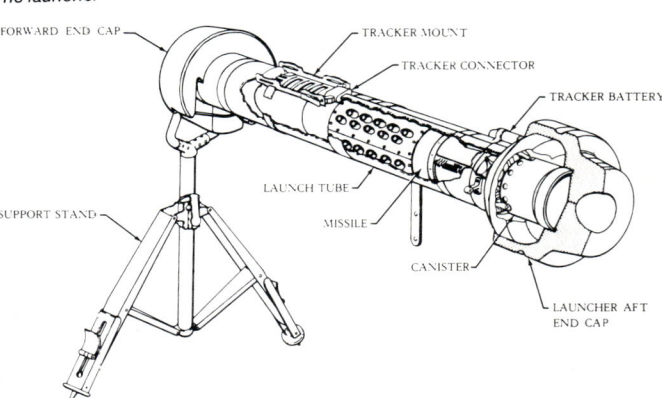

The round

leaves the launcher. The fins produce a slow roll which helps to stabilise the missile. The tracker has a 6X telescope and electronics to measure the displacement between the missile and the line of sight to the target, and to generate guidance commands which are passed along three wires to the missile. Kollsman Instrument Company is a second source for the tracker. The firer observes the target through the optical sight which has stadia lines which cover a 6 metre target at 1,000 metres. When the target is seen to be in range, the firer depresses a thumb switch safety and squeezes the trigger grip. The missile gyro is spun up to operating speed and then uncaged. A gas generator in the breech then launches the missile.

The operator has no task other than to keep his cross wires on the target. An infra red detector in the tracker picks up the signal from the flare in the missile tail and the displacement of this from the line of sight is measured. The corrective commands sent along the wires fire the side thrusting rockets which move the missile in the correct direction to bring it back to the

Dragon one-man anti-tank weapon

line of sight. If the missile strikes the target the chance of a kill is high. The manufacturer has demonstrated the ability to defeat the NATO medium and types I and III heavy tank targets.

At the conclusion of the engagement the operator removes the tracker unit from the empty launcher and places it on the next missile. The remainder of the round is discarded.

MAINTENANCE

The Dragon missile requires little field maintenance: visual inspection for damage and checking a humidity indicator at the front of the missile is about all that is necessary. The tracker assembly, however is a complex electromechanical, electronic and optical system and needs scheduled maintenance including, as with all SACLOS systems an axis alignment check. A field test set is available.

NIGHT SIGHT

A thermal imaging night sight has been developed for Dragon and is in production although quantities are as yet small relative to the missile

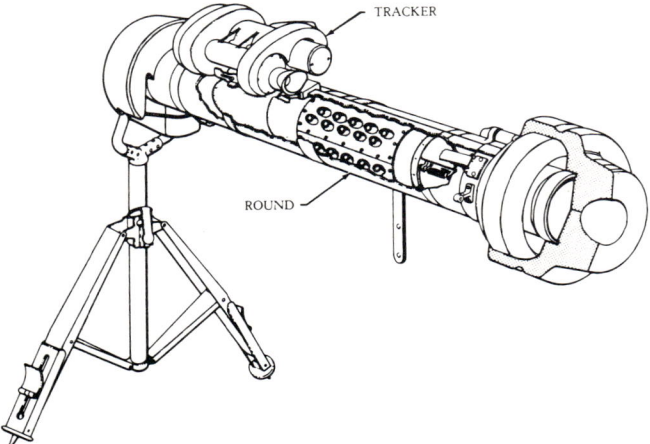

Dragon weapon system

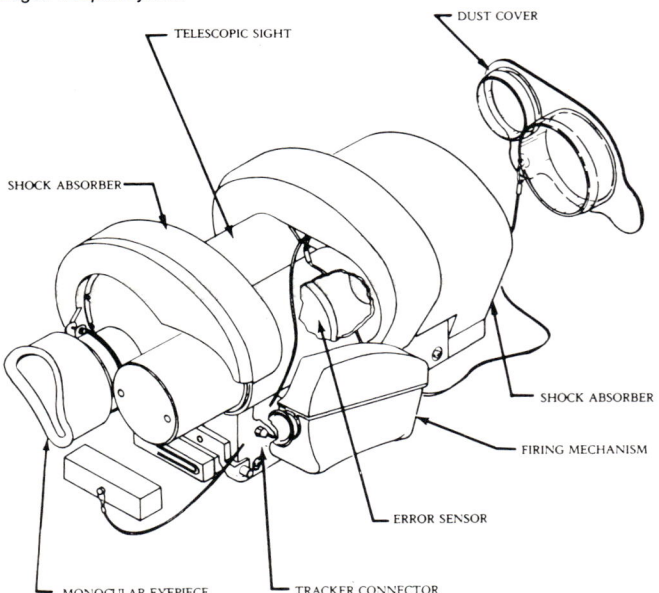

The tracker

Dragon operating position

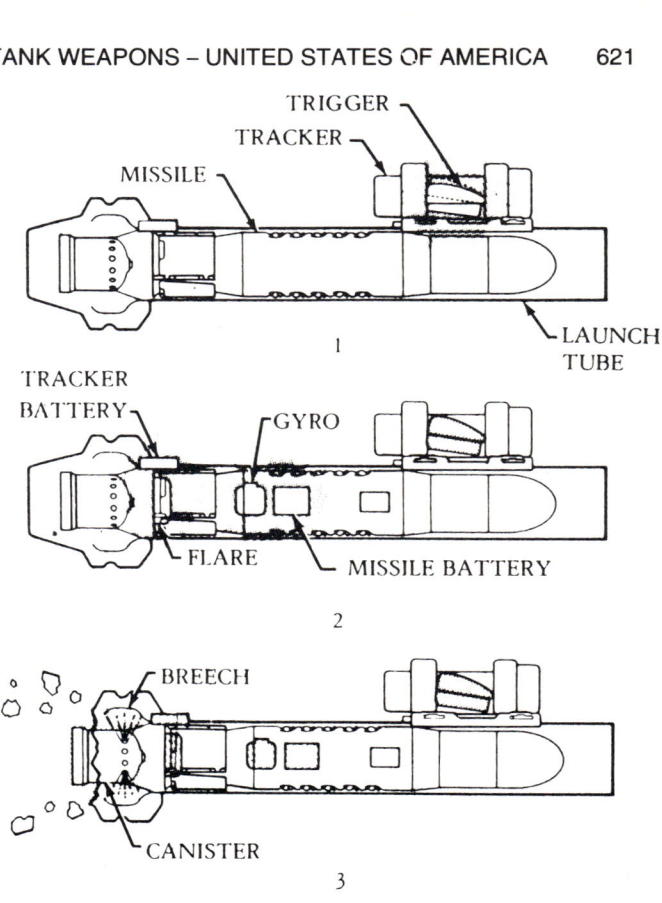

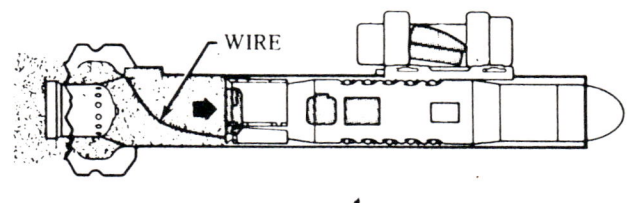

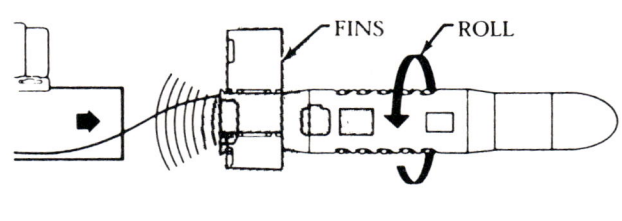

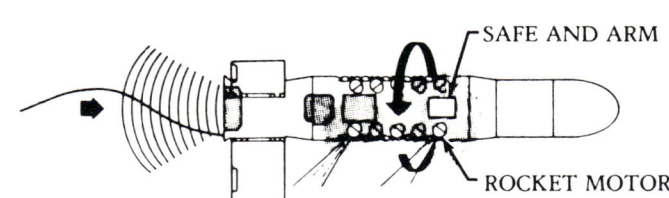

Launching the missile

procurement figure. Thermal imaging was decided upon after a competitive trial against a laser-illuminated gated system. The night sight weighs 4.5kg and is made by the Philips Broadcast Equipment Company.

FURTHER DEVELOPMENT

Another development envisaged is the replacement of the wire guidance system by a laser beam-riding system. This has been studied by the US Army's advanced research projects agency (ARPA) with associated development work by McDonnell Douglas.

DATA
Weapon
Guidance: SACLOS with infra-red tracking and wire guidance
Length: 1,230mm
Total weight (carry): 14.6kg
Launcher
Length: 1,154mm
Missile
Length: 744mm

Weight: 6.2kg
Propulsion: Gas launched, by 60 side-thruster solid-propellant motors in 30 pairs
Electronics: Solid state
Battery: Thermal 390 watts
Flare: Tungsten lamps
Gyro: Roll reference
Wire: 3 wire cable
Range: 1,000 metres
Lethality: Penetrates 3ft of reinforced concrete
Manufacturer: McDonnell Douglas Corporation, St Louis, Missouri. Second source for tracker for US Army and USMC is Kollsman Instrument Company, 575 Underhill Boulevard, Syosset, New York 11791.
Status: In service with the US Army

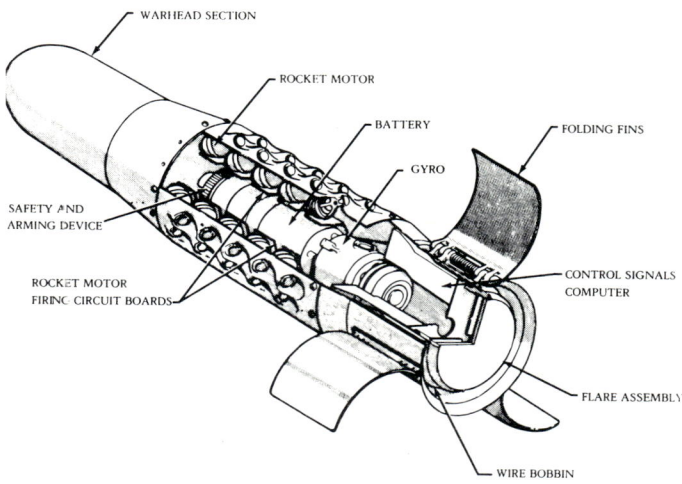

The missile

TOW HEAVY ANTI-TANK WEAPON SYSTEM

The TOW weapon system is a crew portable or vehicle mounted, heavy anti-tank weapon (HAW). The name is derived from its description as a Tube launched Optically tracked, Wire command link guided missile. Design work started in 1962, the first firings were carried out in 1968 and the weapon entered service in 1972.

The TOW weapon system, M 151E2, consists of six major units. These are: tripod, traversing unit, launch tube, optical sight, missile guidance set and battery assembly, housed in the missile guidance set.

The tripod provides a level and rigid mounting base for the traversing unit and allows levelling on ground sloping up to 30 degrees. The traversing unit is an electro-mechanical assembly attached to the tripod and is the mounting base for the optical sight and the launch tube. The launch tube is constructed of a lightweight honeycomb material, covered with laminated fibre glass. It provides initial guidance and stability to the missile and protects the gun crew from the missile launch blast on firing. The optical sight is used to track the target, and to detect the infra red signal from the missile in flight. The sight contains a 13 power telescope, boresighted to an infra red tracker, with a field of view of 5.5 degrees. The cross hairs in the eyepiece may be illuminated and the task of the gunner is to keep these cross hairs on the target. The missile guidance set consists of two rechargeable 50 volt batteries and one rechargeable 24 volt battery. These are nickel cadmium using potassium hydroxide electrolyte.

The missile is the BGM 71A. It consists of the launch motor, the flight motor, four control surfaces, the IR source, two wire dispensers, three batteries, a gyro, safety and arming devices, and the shaped charge warhead. The launch motor is at the rear of the missile and consists of 1.2lb of M7 double based propellant which is completely expended before the missile leaves the tube. The flight motor uses a solid propellant and is located near the centre of gravity of the missile. The burning gases emerge from a pair of nozzles at 30 degrees to the horizontal axis of the missile. This configuration eliminates interference with the wire link and minimises changes in the centre of gravity of the missile as the motor burns. The flight motor ignites about 12 metres in front of the launch tube to protect the gunner. The wire command link is a two wire system dispensed from two spools located at the back of the missile. These wires carry steering commands from the launcher to the missile, and they are applied, together with signals from the gyro, to the four control surfaces. The IR source provides a beacon which is detected by the IR tracker in the optical sight to determine the missile's position. The IR lamp current is modulated to allow discrimination against a background of other strong IR emitters such as the sun.

OPERATION

When the missile is installed in the launcher, the gunner uses the self test facility. This is a switch with seven positions and is used to check the circuitry associated with weapon functioning. When this is completed the

The component parts of the TOW launcher

operator connects the weapon system to the encased missile by raising the arming lever. When a target appears the gunner moves the sight to place the cross hairs on the target. When the target is in range the trigger is pressed. This activates the missile batteries and gas is released to spin the gyro up to speed. About 1.5 seconds later the launch motor is fired. This burns out completely within the tube but the missile acquires sufficient momentum to coast for about 12 metres. The missile wings and control surfaces are extended from the missile body. The IR source on the missile starts to operate and the two command-link wires are dispensed from the

The TOW missile

TOW tactically sited

internal spools. The first stage of arming the warhead occurs. The flight motor is activated at the end of the 12 metre coasting period and the war head is fully armed. The missile has then travelled about 60 metres.

GUIDANCE
The gunner operates the traversing unit and keeps the cross hairs of the optical sight on the target. The infra red sensor tracks the signal from the modulated lamp in the missile and detects any deviations from the line of sight path to the target. It provides continuous information over the wire link to the missile guidance set which produces signals which are delivered,

with those from the gyro, to the control surfaces to correct the flight path and bring the missile back to the line of sight.

TRAINING
The XM 70 training set utilises the TOW equipment. It consists of the instructor's console, a missile simulation round and a target set. An IR source is mounted on the training set vehicle to provide a reference for the target line of sight. The launcher/target line of sight error is detected and graded in the instructor's console from launch to simulated impact and the instructor is then able to correct, criticise or grade the gunner.

DATA

Designation:	BGM 71A
Type:	Heavy anti Armour Weapon (HAW)
Guidance Principle:	Automatic missile tracking and command to line of sight guidance from optical target tracker (SACLOS)
Guidance Method:	Wire command link controlling aerodynamic surfaces
Propulsion:	Two stage, solid propellant motor
Warhead:	HEAT

Item	Length	Width	Height	Weight
Launcher, tubular, guided missile, M 151E2:	2,210mm	1,143mm	1,118mm	78.5kg
Tripod (retracted):	1,064mm	645mm	569mm	9.5kg
Traversing unit:	297mm	518mm	511mm	24.5kg
Optical sight:	544mm	295mm	315mm	14.5kg
Launch tube:	1,675mm	191mm	191mm	5.9kg
Missile guidance set (with battery):	406mm	406mm	254mm	24kg
Battery Assembly:	394mm	117mm	178mm	10.9kg
Guided missile, surface attack BGM 71A:	1,285mm	221mm	221mm	24.5kg
Guided missile practice (inert warhead, live motor) XBTM 71A:	1,285mm	221mm	221mm	24.5kg
Missile velocity:	200 metres/sec			
Minimum range:	65 metres			
Maximum range:	3,750 metres			
Crew:	4			
Manufacturer:	Hughes Aircraft Co, Culver City, California.			
Status:	In production. In service with US Army. Purchased by Belgium, Canada, Denmark, West Germany, Greece, Iran, Italy, Jordan, Lebanon, Luxembourg, Morocco, Netherlands, Norway, Oman, Sweden (evaluation quantity), Turkey and the United Arab Emirates. Some were supplied to Israel during the 1973 war and others were supplied to South Vietnam.			

ANTI-TANK MINE M24
Although officially described as an anti-tank mine this weapon is in fact an automatically launched anti-tank missile. The system comprises a pressure-actuated switch which is placed, like a conventional anti-tank mine, in an appropriate position in the ground, a battery-operated (M-61) firing device and a plastic launch tube containing an M28 HEAT rocket. The launcher is aimed on a fixed line in the direction of the pressure switch; so that when the switch is actuated by a heavy vehicle the missile is launched towards the vehicle. Studies indicate that the hit probability verges on certainty for a vehicle travelling at between 8 and 56km/h at a range of 30 metres.

DATA
Switch: M2 Anti-tank mine discriminator
Firing device: M61 demolition firing device
Launcher: M143
Missile: M28A2 3.5in (89mm) HEAT rocket
Manufacturer: Picatinny Arsenal, Dover, N.J.
Status: In service. 50,000 were delivered to the US Army in 1968

YUGOSLAVIA

M 60 RIFLE GRENADE
Yugoslavia and Poland are the only two countries in the Eastern zone that use anti-tank rifle grenades and these are covered in detail in the sections on the grenades of those countries. The charactertistics of the Yugoslav M60 rifle anti-tank grenade are summarised below:

DATA
Calibre: 60mm

Overall length: 390mm
Weight: 602g
Range: 150 metres
Muzzle velocity: 60 metres/sec
Penetration: 200mm

M57 44mm ANTI TANK LAUNCHER (RB 57)
This is basically derived from the German Panzerfaust and is generally similar to the Czech P-27. The M 57 also has a permanently attached bipod and is served by a two man crew. The firer lies behind the weapon and the loader lies to his right.

Loading the RB-57

DATA
Calibre (Launcher): 44mm
Calibre (Projectile): 90mm
Length of launcher: 960mm
Weight of launcher: 8.2kg
Weight of projectile: 2.4kg
Type of projectile: HEAT
Maximum effective range: 200 metres
Penetration: 300mm

Yugoslavian troops with the M 57 44mm anti-tank rocket launcher RB-57

M 60 82mm RECOILLESS GUN

This gun was designed and developed in Yugoslavia. It is a light weight anti tank gun, firing a fin stablised round of native design. It can be towed behind a jeep-like vehicle or dragged into position by hand.

DATA
Calibre: 82mm
Length of weapon: 2,200mm
Overall weight: 122kg
Traverse: 360°
Elevation: −20° to +35°

Weight of projectile: 4.3kg
Muzzle velocity: 380 metres/sec
Maximum effective range (HEAT): 1,000 metres against moving targets: 1,500 metres against stationary targets
Armour penetration: 220mm
Crew: 5 men
Status: In service

The M-60 towed by the AR-51 jeep

The 82mm RCL gun M-60

M65 105mm RECOILLESS GUN

This is the Yugoslav produced replacement for the USA 105mm M 65. It is a rifled gun which can be towed or mounted on a vehicle. It uses a UB 12.7mm ranging machine gun. This uses a 20 round belt and can be fired single shot or full automatic at ranges between 100 and 600 metres. It has a muzzle velocity of 500 metres/sec. The direct fire optical sight graduated to 1,500 metres, is used for anti-tank firing and there is provision for indirect fire.

DATA
Calibre: 105mm
Method of operation: Recoilless:
Length of barrel: 4,155mm
Length of gun overall: 4,550mm
Width of travel position: 1,430mm
Height in travel position: 1,140mm
Weight in firing position: 280kg
Maximum range (HE): 6,000 metres
Maximum effective range anti tank (HEAT): 600 metres

The M-65 105mm recoilless gun

Armour penetration: 330mm
Rate of fire: 6 rounds/min
Manufacturer: State Factories
Status: Probably no longer in production. Still in service

ANTI-TANK MINES

Anti-tank mines are important items in the defensive armouries of most modern armies. Their function is not so much to inflict casualties on an enemy, although they may do so to a limited extent, as to slow his advance by causing him either to change direction to avoid a minefield or to bring forward suitable personnel or equipment to clear a path through the minefield – an operation which may take a considerable time, especially if those engaged in it are subjected to harassing fire by the defenders.

Most anti-tank mines consist of a large explosive charge which is detonated by a fuze mechanism which responds only to pressures of the order of magnitude associated with a tank or other heavy vehicle. In general, therefore, they will not respond to the pressure of a soldier's foot. In some circumstances the defenders may find it advantageous to lay a minefield in such a way as not to impede the progress of infantry or even light vehicles: if such impediment is required, however, it is usually provided by laying anti-personnel mines in the same minefield: reducing the operating pressure of the anti-tank mines, though possible in some instances, will in general be an uneconomical use of high explosive.

Instead of relying on the blast effect of a large explosive charge, several modern mines make use of the armour penetration possibilities of shaped charges either detonated in the ground or brought mechanically or explosively into contact with the target vehicle. The Hungarian shaped-charge mine is generally deployed in such a way as to be brought into contact with the armour by various improvised mechanical means: the American M-21 mine propels a saucer-shaped charge vertically against the underside of a passing tank.

For the best results, a shaped-charge mine should operate when the main body of the target is passing over it. One approach to meeting this requirement is exemplified by the French (STRIM) Model 1954 mine which has a trip-rod actuator and a 0.5 second delay; and an alternative arrangement (Model 1953) from the same source employs two similar mines laid to form the base of a triangle at the apex of which, in the direction of travel, is located a pressure-sensitive actuator which detonates both mines.

Early anti-tank mines were mostly metal-cased and it was to combat these that the electromagnetic mine detector was developed. To make such detection more difficult, many modern mines are either enclosed in plastic or other non-magnetic cases or made in caseless form by hardening and reinforcing the outer surface of the explosive charge: the only metal in such devices will thus be that which is essential to the functioning of the detonation mechanism and can be reduced to an amount that is difficult to detect. Even if the mine can be readily detected, however, its removal can be hindered by the use of anti-lifting explosive devices or other booby-trap arrangements. Provision is made in some mine designs for the incorporation of such mechanisms within the mine casing – which has the advantage of speeding the process of laying – but such provision is not essential to the booby-trapping process.

Clearance

Various techniques for the rapid clearance of minefields were developed during the Second World War, probably the most varied collection being that tried and operated by the British 79th Armoured Division under Major-General Sir Percy Hobart. Less successful devices in this collection were tank-propelled heavy rollers (which had also been tried with little success in the First World War) and various forms of plough: successful methods involved the use of flail tanks of various types and a device known as the Conger. The latter consisted of a rocket-drawn hose which was fired over the minefield, pumped full of explosive and detonated to clear a channel: there is a rather similar device in British Army service today known as the Giant Viper.

Another modern approach to minefield clearance is the use of Fuel-Air Explosive (FAE) munitions. The technique has other applications in addition to that of minefield clearance and numerous FAE projects are in hand or have been concluded in the USA at least. The technique involves the creation of an aerosol cloud of fuel-air mixture over the target area and detonating it to produce an explosion over a relatively wide area. The explosion can produce overpressures at ground level of 200kg/cm² or more; and it has been shown that the blast and heat thus generated will not only detonate conventional pressure-fuzed mines but also either detonate or neutralise mines whose fuzes are actuated by tripwires or by seismic, infra-red or electronic or magnetic influence devices. Many of the operational methods tested involve dropping the aerosol canisters from aircraft or helicopters; but at least two land systems have been tested, in one of which the aerosol cloud is drifted from the edge of the minefield and then exploded by remote control, which in the other (SLUFAE – Surface-Launched Unit FAE) the aerosol canisters are ripple-fired from a 30-tube multiple rocket launcher. The SLUFAE system has the advantages of clearing a longer path in one operation and being operable from a 600 metre stand-off position.

An extensive series of tests of FAE warheads against a variety of mines produced results showing total success up to a radius of 29 feet (8.8 metres) from point of impact for pressure-fuzed mines and 85 feet (25.9 metres) for pull-fuzed trip wire mines.

Special Mines

As indicated above, several different kinds of fuze have been developed to supplement or replace pressure fuzes in special circumstances, mainly for the purpose of making it more difficult for an enemy to make a path through a minefield without bringing up such special equipment as the Giant Viper or the SHUFAE rocket launcher. So far as the infantryman is concerned, however, the approach to clearance mainly involves the use of electromagnetic mine detectors (which are briefly discussed in the next

British Giant Viper rocket-propelled mine clearance system towed by a Combat Engineer Tractor (UK MoD)

Mine clearance by Fuel-Air Explosive charges. These three pictures show the aerosol canisters dropped from a helicopter, multiple mine detonation by the FAE explosion and the cleared minefield (US Army)

section) or probes.

Another departure from the familiar type of pressure-detonated buried charge is illustrated by a group of anti-tank weapons some of which are described in the main body of this section because, although commonly classified as anti-tank mines, they all operate as remotely fired missiles. The French (GIAT) Model F1, the Russian LMG grenade mine and the US M24 are clearly in this category, the Russian weapon dating from the Second World War and the other two being of more modern design. The French (SERAT) Vertically- and Horizontally-Acting Anti-tank Weapon project is conceptually similar to the other three but it and the Hungarian plate-charge mine differ in that their projectiles are solid.

Laying an anti-tank minefield by conventional means takes time which the defenders may ill be able to afford, especially during a withdrawal. Two methods of overcoming this difficulty may be mentioned here, although neither is very likely to be an infantry responsibility. One is the British Bar-Mine development: the other is the Astrolite liquid mine made by the Explosives Corporation of America. The Astrolite explosive is a liquid which is either poured or sprayed on the ground, is absorbed by the topsoil and can be detonated conventionally either locally, using a pressure sensitive device, or remotely. Apart from the ease and speed with which a minefield can thus be created the technique has the advantages that the explosive is extremely difficult, if not impossible, to detect and that it becomes inoperative – and thus presents no hazard to counter-attack operations – after about four days in the ground.

As its name implies the Bar-Mine (illustrated here) is an explosive device which is long in relation to its other dimensions and thus lends itself readily to the construction of gapless anti-tank defences. The mines are ploughed into the ground using a special towed trenching and covering dispenser which enables mines to be laid at a rate of 600-700 per hour using a single towing vehicle (typically an APC) and a crew of three men. A similar ploughing technique is being developed by GIAT in France for the HPD mine. The mine has been specially developed for this method of laying but is more nearly conventional in shape than the British mine. Because the Bar-Mine has a small cross-section, the trench required for buried mines can be produced with relatively low tractive effort: the shape is also convenient for stacking and results in a very economical use of explosive in relation to the extent of the obstacle created. The mine has a strong plastic case and contains very little metal and will break any tank track.

Finally, some mention should be made of the Russian Dog Mine, an idea borrowed from the German and Japanese armies in the Second World War and still operational. It involves using dogs which have been trained to run under the belly of an advancing tank and which, operationally, are caused to carry explosive charges which are detonated when a trip-lever catches on the tank.

Summary

The following table lists a range of mines and similar devices which are currently operational, available or under development in many countries. Here, as elsewhere, however, it should be stressed that the list is not exhaustive.

The British pressure operated Bar Mine (UK MoD)

Ploughing in a row of Bar Mines

Country/ Manufacturer	Designation	Type	Method of Initiation	Method of Laying	Case Material	Weight of Mine	Charge	Status
Czechoslovakia/-	PT-Mi-Ba	Blast	Pressure	Hand-buried	Plastic	7.6kg	–	In service
Czechoslovakia/-	PT-Mi-D	Blast	Pressure	Hand-buried	Wood	9kg	6.2kg	In service
Czechoslovakia/-	PT-Mi-K	Blat	Pressure	Hand-buried	Steel	7.2kg	5kg	In service
France/GIAT	F1	Missile-launching	Pressure or remote	Launcher above ground	Steel	10kg	6.5kg shaped	In service
France/STRIM	Model 1953	Twin fixed shaped charges	Pressure	Hand-buried	Metal alloy	1.9kg (pair)	0.6kg shaped	In service
France/STRIM	Model 1954	Single fixed shaped charge	Trip	Hand-buried	Metal alloy	0.9kg	0.3kg shaped	In service
France/TRT	HPD	Blast	Pressure, Timed self-arming and neutralising	Hand-buried or ploughed in	Plastic	6kg	–	In service
France/ALSETEX	MACI 51	Blast	Pressure	Hand-buried	Glass fibre-reinforced explosive	7kg	7kg	In service
France/ALSETEX	MACI 52	Blast (ventral)	Trip	Hand-buried	Glass fibre-reinforced explosive	9kg	9kg	In service
France/SERAT	–	Projectile-launching	Pressure	Launcher above or inserted in ground	Metal	–	5kg (propellant)	Project
Germany DDR/-	K-1/K-2	Blast	Pressure	Hand-buried	Plastic	11kg	7.5kg	In service
Hungary/-	Plate charge mine	Projectile-launching	Remote	Launcher above ground	Aluminium	–	–	In service
Hungary/-	Shaped-charge mine	Contact shaped charge	Mechanised trip or pressure	Mine above ground	Wood cardboard and canvas	5.7kg	about 5kg	In service
Sweden/Bofors	M101	Blast	Pressure	Hand-buried	Glass fibre-reinforced explosive	12.5kg	12.5kg	In service
Sweden/Bofors	M102	Blast	Pressure	Hand-buried	Glass fibre-reinforced explosive	8kg	8kg	In service
Sweden/Bofors	M103	Blast	Pressure	Hand-buried	Glass fibre-reinforced explosive	10kg	10kg	In service
USSR/-	LMG	Grenade-launching	Tripwire	Launcher above ground	Steel	9.5kg	0.187kg shaped	Obsolescent
USSR/-	TMB-2	Blast	Pressure	Hand-buried	Cardboard	7kg	6kg	In service, Obsolescent
USSR/-	TMSB	Blast	Pressure	Hand-buried	Cardboard	8kg	5.9kg	In service Obsolescent
USSR/-	TMD-B	Blast	Pressure	Hand-buried	Wood	7.7kg	5.7kg	In service, Obsolescent
USSR/-	TM46/TMN 46	Blast	Pressure	Hand-buried	Steel	8.7kg	5.5kg	In service
USSR/-	YaM-5	Blast	Pressure	Hand-buried	Wood	about 7kg	3.5-5kg	In service
USSR/-	YaM-10	Blast	Pressure	Hand-buried	Wood	11.8kg	10kg	In service
USSR/-	Dog Mine	Blast	Trip	Trained dog	Canvas	6.5kg	6kg	In service
UK/ROF	Bar-Mie	Blast	Pressure	Ploughed in	Plastic	–	–	In service
USA/-	M6A2	Blast	Pressure	Hand-buried	Metal	9.2kg	5.5kg	In service
USA/-	M15	Blast	Pressure	Hand-buried	Steel	13.6kg	9.9kg	In service
USA/-	M19	Blast	Pressure	Hand-buried	Plastic	12.7kg	9.5kg	In service
USA/-	M21	Shaped charge launching	Pressure	Hand-buried	Metal	7.7kg	4.9kg shaped projected charge	In service
USA/Picatinny	M24	Rocket launching	Pressure or remote	Launcher above ground	Metal	8.6kg	0.86kg warhead	In service
USA/Explosives Corp.	Astrolite	Blast	Pressure or remote, Self-neutralising	Poured or sprayed	None	Unlimited	Unlimited	Development

Manufacturers:
GIAT, 10 place Georges-Clémenceau-92211 Saint-Cloud, France
Luchaire SA, Département Materiels STRIM, 180 boulevard Haussmann 75832 Paris CEDEX 08, France
Société d'Armement et d'Etudes ALSETEX, 4 rue de Castellane-75008 Paris, France

SERAT, 134 boulevard Haussmann-75008 Paris, France
TRT, 88 rue Brillat-Savarin 75640 Paris CEDEX 13, France
AB Bofors, S-690 20 Bofors, Sweden
Picatinny Arsenal, Dover, New Jersey, USA
Explosives Corporation of America

SECTION FOUR

ARMOURED INFANTRY VEHICLES

ARMOURED INFANTRY VEHICLES

AUSTRIA

SAURER ARMOURED PERSONNEL CARRIERS

Development of the Saurer started in 1956 and after various prototypes had been built and tested the first production vehicle was completed in 1961, this being designated the 4K4F. Since then the 4K3KA and 4K4FA have also been built in quantity. Total production has amounted to some 450 vehicles of all types. A tank destroyer has also been developed which uses many Saurer APC components: this is called the Panzerjäger K.

The hull of the vehicle is of all-welded steel construction. The driver is seated at the front on the left side with the engine to his right, whilst the commander/gunner is seated behind the driver. The personnel compartment is at the rear of the hull and is provided with a bench seat down each side of the hull: there are two roof hatches and the infantry enter and leave the vehicle via the twin doors in the hull rear. The Saurer APC does not have a NBC system and is not amphibious.

The basic model is armed with a .50(12.7mm) Browning machine gun which is normally provided with a shield, or a turret-mounted 20mm Oerlikon Type 204 GK cannon. The latter model is known as the Saurer 4K4FA-G.

VARIANTS
4K 4FA-San: This is the ambulance model and has a crew of two and can carry four sitting patients and two stretcher patients
4K 3FA-FU: This is a command vehicle
4K 3FA-FU/A: An artillery command vehicle
4K 3FA-FU/FIA: This is an anti-aircraft command vehicle
4K 3FA-F2S: A radio vehicle
GrW1: This is an 81mm mortar carrier, the 120mm model was not adopted

DATA
Crew: 2 + 8
Weight loaded: 15,000kg (with 20mm turret)
12,500kg (with .50 machine gun)
Weight empty: 11,100kg
Length: 5.4 metres
Width: 2.5 metres
Height: 2.1 metres (with machine gun)
1.65 metres (hull top)
Ground clearance: 0.42 metres

Saurer Armoured Personnel Carrier
Track: 2.12 metres
Track width: 375mm
Length of track on ground: 2.9 metres
Ground pressure: 0.52kg/cm²
Maximum road speed: 61km/hr
Range: 370km
Fuel capacity: 184 litres
Fording: 1 metre
Gradient: 75%
Side slope: 50%
Vertical obstacle: 0.8 metre
Trench: 2.2 metres
Engine: Saurer 6FA, 6-cylinder diesel developing 250 HP at 2400 rpm
Armament: 1 × .50 (12.7mm) Machine Gun *or* 1 × 20mm Oerlikon 204 GK cannon
Armour: 8mm-20mm
Manufacturer: Steyr-Daimler-Puch AG, Vienna, Austria, (who took over Saurer-Werke in 1970)
Status: Production complete. In service only with the Austrian Army.

BRAZIL

URUTU EE-11 ARMOURED PERSONNEL CARRIER

The Urutu EE-11 has been designed for the Brazilian Army by the Engesa Company of Sao Paulo. The first prototype was completed in July, 1970 with the first production contract being awarded in 1972. The vehicle uses a number of components of the EE-9 Cascavel 6×6 armoured car which has also been developed by Engesa.

The hull is of all-welded construction. The driver is seated at the front of the hull on the left with the engine to his right. The commander's cupola/armament station is to the rear of the engine and driver's position. The personnel compartment is at the rear of the hull: this is provided with a total of six roof hatches, three each side, and normal exit is via the two side doors, one each side, or through the single door in the rear of the hull. Firing ports are provided in the sides and rear of the hull. The basic model is fully amphibious and is propelled in the water by its wheels. A special model has, however, been developed for the Brazilian Marines and has two propellers at the rear of the hull and various other modifications including bilge pumps and four schnorkel type tubes.

VARIANTS
No variants have been announced although obviously the vehicle is suitable for a wide variety of roles including armoured personnel carrier, load carrier, internal security vehicle and anti-tank missile vehicle. Vehicles have so far been armed with a .50(12.7mm) Browning machine gun on a open ring mount, an American Cadillac Gage turret with various combinations of weapons, including 7.62mm, and 12.7mm machine guns, and a 20mm cannon, or a Swedish Hägglunds turret with a 20mm cannon.

DATA
Crew: 2 + 13
Weight loaded: 11,800kg
Weight empty: 10,550kg
Length: 6 metres
Width: 2.59 metres
Height: 2.45 metres (with Commando type turret)
2.225 metres (top of hull)
Ground clearance: 0.5 metre
Track: 2.1 metres

Urutu EE-11 Armoured Personnel Carrier
Wheelbase: 2.093 metres + 1.415 metres
Tyres: 11.00 × 20 (bullet proof)
Turning radius: 7.7 metres
Maximum road speed: 95km/hr
Maximum water speed: 10km/hr
Range road: 600/700km
Range water: 60km
Fuel capacity: 250 litres
Fording: Amphibious
Gradient: 75%
Side slope: 30%
Vertical obstacle: 0.6 metre
Trench: 1.5 metre
Engine: Mercedes-Benz (Brazil) Model OM-352-A, four cycle, turbocharged six-cylinder diesel developing 165 HP at 2800 rpm.
Armament: See text
Armour: 6mm-12mm (estimate)
Manufacturer: Engenheiros Especializados SA, Sao Paulo, Brazil
Status: In production. In service with the Brazilian Army and Brazilian Marines

CHINA (PEOPLE'S REPUBLIC)

TYPE 55 ARMOURED PERSONNEL CARRIER

The Type 55 Armoured Personnel Carrier is the Chinese-built version of the Russian BTR-40 4×4 APC. It has similar characteristics but uses Chinese automotive components.

Manufacturer: Chinese State factories.
Status: Production complete. In service with Chinese Army and countries that have received Chinese aid

TYPE 56 ARMOURED PERSONNEL CARRIER

The Type 56 Armoured Personnel Carrier is the Chinese-built version of the Russian BTR-152 6×6 APC. It has similar characteristics but uses Chinese automotive components. As with the BTR-152, the Chinese have probably built anti-aircraft and command vehicles using the same basic

model.
Manufacturer: Chinese State factories
Status: Production complete. In service with the Chinese Army and countries that have received Chinese aid

TYPE K-63 ARMOURED PERSONNEL CARRIER

The K-63 was previously known as the M-1967 or M-1970 Armoured Personnel Carrier and has been in service for ten years. In appearance it is very similar to the American M114 Command and Reconnaissance Vehicle. The hull is of all-welded construction. The driver sits at the front on the left and the commander to the right of the driver. The engine is between the commander's and driver's positions. The personnel compartment is at the

rear of the hull and hatches are provided in the roof. Armament consists of a single 12.7mm Type 54 Heavy Machine Gun. The K-63 is fully amphibious, being propelled in the water by its tracks, and was used in combat in Vietnam. No accurate data are available at the present time.
Manufacturer: Chinese State factories
Status: Probably in production. In service in Albania, China, and Vietnam

CZECHOSLOVAKIA

OT-810 ARMOURED PERSONNEL CARRIER

During the Second World War the Germans set up a production line in Czechoslovakia to build their Kfz.251 half-track. When the war finished the Czechoslovakians took over this line and continued production for some years: in addition they rebuilt many vehicles that the Germans left behind. The Czech modifications included the installation of a more powerful engine, firing ports were provided for the rear troop compartment and the roof over this compartment was armoured.

VARIANTS

Anti-Tank: This has an 82mm M59A recoilless rifle mounted over the rear troop compartment, which can be fired from the vehicle or away from the vehicle as ramps are provided so that it can be quickly dismounted

DATA
Crew: 2 + 10
Weight loaded: 8500kg
Length: 5.8 metres

Width: 2.1 metres
Height: 1.75 metres (without armament)
Ground clearance: 0.3 metre
Ground pressure: 0.84kg/cm²
Maximum road speed: 52km/hr
Range: 320km
Fuel capacity: 160 litres
Fording: 0.5 metre
Gradient: 24°
Vertical obstacle: 0.255 metre
Trench: 1.98 metres
Engine: Tatra 6-cylinder diesel developing 120 HP
Armament: 1 × 7.62mm M59 machine gun
Armour: 7mm-12mm
Manufacturers: Various German and Czechoslovakian companies
Status: Production complete. In service with the Czechoslovakian and Romanian Armies

OT-62 ARMOURED PERSONNEL CARRIER

The Czechoslovakian OT-62 APC is basically the Russian BTR-50PK APC built in Czechoslovakia with a number of modifications, the most significant being the supercharged diesel engine and a complete NBC system. The hull is of all-welded steel construction. The commander is seated at the front of the hull on the left side with the driver to his right in the centre of the hull. The OT-62 has two projecting bays at the front of the hull, these being similar to the Russian BTR-50PU Model 2 Command vehicle. The troop compartment, which is to the rear of the commander and driver, is provided with roof hatches and most models have a door in each side of the hull. The OT-62 is fully amphibious being propelled in the water by two water-jets. Infra-red lights are standard equipment.

VARIANTS
OT-62A (or Model 1): This model is unarmed.
OT-62B (or Model 2): This has a small turret on the right bay, which is fitted with a 7.62mm M59T machine gun. The gun has an elevation of +20° and a depression of −10°; traverse is a full 360°. Mounted externally on the right side of the turret is a 82mm T-21 recoilless rifle. Total ammunition supply consists of 1250 rounds of machine gun ammunition and 12 rounds for the recoilless rifle.
OT-62C (or Model 3): This has been developed in Poland where it is called the TOPAZ 2AP. It has the same turret as is fitted to the OT-64C(2). This turret has a 14.5mm KPVT and a 7.62mm PKT machine gun with an elevation of +78° and a depression of −5°, traverse being 360°. Total ammunition carried is 500 rounds of 14.5mm and 2000 rounds of 7.62mm.
Command and Ambulance Models: These are known to exist.
WPT-TOPAZ: This is a special recovery vehicle developed in Poland. It is

provided with a winch and crane.

DATA (OT-62C)
Crew: 3 + 12
Weight loaded: 16,390kg
Length: 7 metres
Width: 3.225 metres
Height: 2.725 metres (turret)
Ground clearance: 0.425 metre
Track: 2.74 metres
Track width: 360mm
Maximum road speed: 60km/hr
Maximum water speed: 10.8km/hr
Range: 550km
Fuel capacity: 520 litres
Fording: Amphibious
Gradient: 70%
Vertical obstacle: 1.1 metres
Trench: 2.8 metres
Engine: PV-6, 6-cylinder supercharged diesel developing 300 HP at 1200 rpm
Armament: 1 × 14.5mm and 1 × 7.62mm machine gun
Armour: 14mm maximum
Manufacturer: Czechoslovakian State factories
Status: Probably in production. In service in Bulgaria, Czechoslavakia, Egypt, Hungary, India, Israel, Libya, Poland, and Romania

OT-64 SERIES ARMOURED PERSONNEL CARRIER

The OT-64 was designed from 1959 by both Czechoslovakia and Poland and uses many components of the Tatra 813 truck. It entered service in 1963/64 and is used by many countries in place of the similar Russian 6×6 BTR-60 series APC. The hull is of all-welded construction. The driver is seated at the front on the left side with the commander to his right. Doors are fitted in the sides and rear of the hull and roof hatches are also provided. There are different hatch arrangements according to when the vehicle was built and what armament is installed. The personnel are seated in the rear of the vehicle on seats which can be folded up so that the vehicle can be easily adapted to carry cargo. The OT-64 is fully amphibious being propelled in the water by two propellers at the rear of the hull. Other equipment includes a central tyre pressure regulation system, an NBC system and a full range of night driving and night fighting aids. A winch is mounted internally at the front of the hull.

OT64B (SKOT 2) with 12.7mm MG in turret

VARIANTS

OT-64A (or SKOT): The first model to enter service, some being armed with a 7.62mm machine gun on a pedestal mount.

OT-64B (or SKOT 2): Used only by the Polish Army. Armed with a 7.62 or 12.7mm machine gun on a pedestal mount with a curved shield.

OT-64C (or SKOT 2AP or Model 3): This has a more powerful engine and a fully enclosed turret which is the same as that fitted to the Soviet BTR-60PB and BRDM-2 vehicles. It is armed with a 14.5mm KPVT machine gun and a 7.62mm PKT machine gun: elevation limits are from −4° to +29°. Total ammunition carried is 500 rounds of 14.5mm and 2000 rounds of 7.62mm.

OT-64C(2) (or SKOT 2AP or Model 4): This has the same turret as is fitted to the OT-62C APC and has the same armament as the Model 3 but the machine guns can be elevated from −4° to +89½°, which enables them to be used in the anti-aircraft role.

OT-64 Anti-Tank Vehicle with Sagger ATGW: Two models have been seen so far. The first is the OT-64A with two Sagger ATGW mounted over the rear of the troop compartment whilst the second is the OT-64C with a Sagger mounted on either side of the turret, each being protected by a small vertical armoured plate.

OT-64 Command Vehicles: There are at least two models – the R2 and the R3.

DATA (OT-64A)
Crew: 2 + 18
Weight loaded: 14,300kg
Length: 7.44 metres
Width: 2.5 metres
Height: 2.03 metres (without armament)
Ground clearance: 0.46 metre
Track: 1.86 metres

OT64C (SKOT 2A) APC

Wheelbase: 1.3 metres + 2.15 metres + 1.3 metres
Tyres: 13.00 × 18
Maximum road speed: 94.4km/hr
Water speed: 9km/hr
Range: 710km (road)
Fuel capacity: 320 litres
Gradient: 60%
Vertical obstacle: 0.5 metre
Side slope: 2 metres
Engine: Tatra T 918-14, 8-cylinder diesel developing 180 HP at 2000 rpm
Armament: 1 × 7.62mm SGMB or M59 machine gun with 1250 rounds of ammunition
Armour: 10mm maximum
Manufacturer: Czechoslovakian State factories
Status: Probably in production. In service in Czechoslovakia, Egypt, Hungary, India, Libya, Morocco, Poland, Sudan, Syria, and Uganda

EIRE (IRISH REPUBLIC)

TIMONEY ARMOURED PERSONNEL CARRIER

The first prototype of the Timoney APC was completed in 1973 with a further two prototypes being completed in 1975. The vehicle has been designed to meet an Irish Army requirement for a vehicle capable of world-wide deployment as part of United Nations Forces. Other vehicles under development using many of the components of the APC include a 6×6 APC, a 4×4 reconnaissance vehicle and an amphibious load carrier.

The hull is of all-welded construction. Doors are provided in the sides and rear of the hull as are firing ports which enable the crew to fire their weapons from within the vehicle. Various armament installations are available. The Timoney APC is fully amphibious, being propelled in the water by its wheels: a propeller kit is being developed. Optional equipment includes a full air-conditioning system.

VARIANTS

The basic vehicle can be used as a cargo carrier, ambulance and radio/command vehicle.

DATA (Mk 3 APC)
Crew: 2 + 10
Weight loaded: 8164kg
Weight empty: 6350kg
Length: 4.95 metres
Width: 2.406 metres
Height with turret: 2.475 metres
Height to top of hull: 2.032 metres
Ground clearance: 0.381 metre
Track: 1.93 metres
Wheelbase: 2.867 metres
Tyres: 11.00 × 20 × or 12.00 × 20
Turning radius: 6.1 metres
Maximum road speed: 98km/hr
Maximum water speed: 4.8km/hr
Range: 483km

Timoney Mk 3 APC

Fuel capacity: 273 litres
Fording: Amphibious
Gradient: 60%
Side slope: 30%
Angle of approach: 35°
Angle of departure: 45°
Verticle obstacle: 0.762 metre
Engine: Chrysler 360, 8-cylinder water-cooled petrol engine developing 200 HP at 4000 rpm (as used in the M113 APC).
Armament: See text
Manufacturer: Technology Investments Limited, Gibbstown, Navan, Co Meath
Status: Prototypes built and tested. Ready for production

FRANCE

AMX VCI MECHANISED INFANTRY COMBAT VEHICLE

The AMX VCI (Véhicule de Combat d'Infanterie) was developed in the early 1950's and is based on the chassis of the AMX-13 light tank. The first prototype was completed in 1955 and the first production model in 1956. It is still in service with the French Army although it is slowly being replaced by the more recent AMX-10P MICV. It is still a useful vehicle and was really the forerunner of all modern MICV's.

The hull is of all-welded construction. The driver sits at the front of the vehicle on the left with the engine to his right. The commander's and gunner's positions are to the rear of the driver. The personnel compartment is at the rear of the hull and this is provided with twin doors in the rear. The infantry are seated facing outwards and there are two sets of hatches on each side. Each hatch is in two parts; the lower part has observation/firing ports and folds downwards whilst the upper part folds back on the roof of the vehicle.

Early models did not have an NBC system but most models in service have now been fitted with this. Night vision equipment is also provided but the AMX VCI does not have any amphibious capability. The basic vehicle is

normally armed with a 7.5mm or 7.62mm machine gun on a pintle mount, or a turret mounted 7.5mm or 7.62 machine gun, or a .50 (12.7mm) Browning machine gun on a ring mount which can be aimed and fired from within the vehicle. A recent model has been armed with the same turret as is used in the AMX10P.

VARIANTS

Listed below are the variants of the basic APC that are in service, this list does not include trials variants or other members of the AMX family such as the self-propelled guns.

81mm mortar carrier: This has an 81mm mortar, with a traverse of 40°, for which a total of 128 mortar bombs are carried. This model has a crew of six.

120mm mortar carrier: This has a 120mm mortar, with a traverse of 46°, for which a total of 60 mortar bombs are carried. It has a crew of five.

Battery Command Post: This is used to support self-propelled guns and can also tow an ammunition trailer.

Command Vehicle: This variant has additional radios.

Ambulance: This can carry four sitting and three stretcher patients plus a crew of four.

AMX VCA: This is used to support the 155mm SPG and carries the ammunition and the gun crew (ie driver and seven crew).

Anti-Tank Vehicle: The Netherlands Army have a number of AMX VCI fitted with the TOW missile installation.

ENTAC Anti-Tank Vehicle: This has two launchers for the ENTAC wire guided anti-tank missiles and a total of 26 missiles are carried.

Cargo Vehicle: The AMX VCI can be quickly adapted to carry cargo.

Combat Engineer Vehicle: This is known as the VCG and is provided with a dozer blade, winch, A frame and spades at the hull rear.

DATA
Crew: 1 + 12
Weight loaded: 14,000kg
Weight empty: 11,700kg
Length: 5.544 metres
Width: 2.51 metres
Height with turret: 2.32 metres
Ground clearance: 0.48 metre
Track: 2.159 metres
Track width: 250mm
Ground pressure: 0.7kg/cm²
Maximum road speed: 65km/hr
Range: 350/400km
Fuel capacity: 410 litres
Fording: 0.6 metre
Gradient: 60%
Vertical obstacle: 0.65 metre
Trench: 1.6 metres
Engine: SOFAM Model 8 GXb 8-cylinder petrol engine developing 250 HP at 3200 rpm
Armament: See text
Armour: 10mm-30mm
Manufacturer: Creusot-Loire at Chalon sur Saone. Enquiries to

Two views of the AMX VC1

Creusot-Loire, 15 Rue Pasquier, 75383 Paris, Cedex 08, France
Status: Manufactured as required. In service in Abu Dhabi, Argentina, Belgium, Ecuador, France, Indonesia, Italy, Netherlands, Venezuela

AMX-10P MECHANISED INFANTRY COMBAT VEHICLE

The requirement for a new vehicle to replace the earlier AMX VCI was drawn up in the early 1960s and the first prototype of the AMX-10P was completed in 1968. It entered production in 1972/73 and it has now started to replace the earlier vehicle.

The hull is of all-welded construction. The driver sits at the front on the left with the engine on his right. The commander and gunner are seated in the turret in the centre of the vehicle. The troop compartment is at the rear of the hull and the infantry are provided with individual seats which can be folded up so that stores can be carried. There are two roof hatches over the troop compartment and there is a large ramp in the rear of this compartment which is provided with two doors, each of which has a simple firing port. Periscopes are provided for the troop compartment. The AMX10P is fully amphibious and is propelled in the water by two water-jets. An NBC system is fitted as also is a full range of night fighting and driving equipment.

VARIANTS
AMX-10P with RATAC (Fire Control Radar for Field Artillery): In service with the French Army.

AMX-10P with HOT missile system: This is not yet in production and consists of a basic AMX-10P with a new turret mounting four HOT (two each side) anti-tank missiles in the ready-to-launch position with a further 15 to 20 missiles being carried in reserve.

AMX-10 TM: This model tows the 120mm Brandt mortar, a total of 60 mortar bombs being carried inside of the hull.

AMX-10PC (Command): This is a command model and has a total crew of six. It has additional radios and a generator.

AMX-10P (Training): This has no turret and is used for driver training.

AMX-10ECH (Repair): This is a light repair vehicle: it does not have a winch for recovery operations.

AMX-10P Ambulance: This is unarmed and can carry between four and nine casualties, either on stretchers or as sitting patients.

AMX-10 Wheeled vehicles: A 6×6 series of wheeled vehicles has also been developed using AMX-10P components: the first model to enter production will be the AMX-10RC reconnaissance vehicle. An APC designated the AMX-10RP was built as a prototype only in 1971.

AMX 10P on the move (ECP Armées)

AMX-10C Reconnaissance Vehicle: This is armed with a turret mounted 105mm gun.

DATA
Crew: 2 + 9
Weight loaded: 13,800kg
Weight empty: 11,300kg
Length: 5.778 metres
Width: 2.78 metres
Height overall: 2.54 metres

The troops and stores that can be carried by the AMX 10P

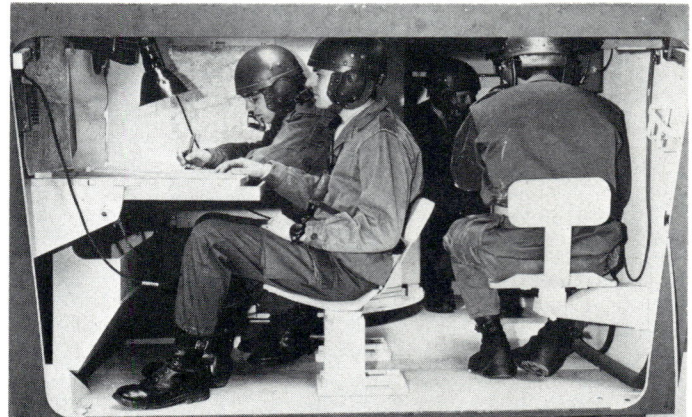

Internal layout of the AMX-10PC command post

Height top of hull: 1.87 metres
Ground clearance: 0.45 metre
Ground pressure: 0.53kg/cm²
Power to weight ratio: 20 HP/T
Maximum road speed: 65km/hr
Maximum water speed: 7.92km/hr
Range road: 600km
Fording: Amphibious
Gradient: 60%
Side slope: 30%

Vertical obstacle: 0.7 metre
Trench: 1.6 metres
Engine: Hispano-Suiza HS 115-2 8-cylinder diesel developing 276 HP at 3000 rpm
Armament: 1 × 20mm cannon with a co-axial 7.62mm machine gun
2 × 2 smoke dischargers
Manufacturer: Atelier de Construction Roanne. Sales handled by Groupement Industriel des Armements Terrestres, 10 Place Georges Clémenceau, 92211 Saint-Cloud, France
Status: In production. In service in France, Greece, and Saudi-Arabia

BERLIET VXB-170 ARMOURED PERSONNEL CARRIER

In 1968, Berliet Trucks built, as a private venture, a 4×4 wheeled armoured personnel carrier known as the BL-12. The French Army purchased one for trials but no production order was placed. Five modified vehicles were built for the French Gendarmerie in 1971 and these were known as VXB's. After trials the Gendarmerie ordered 50 vehicles and the first production order was completed in 1973/74. The Gendarmerie has a total requirement for about 400 VXB's.

The hull of the VXB is of all-welded construction. The driver sits at the front and the engine is at the rear of the hull on the left side. Doors are provided in the sides and rear, as also are firing ports. There are a total of four roof hatches, one of these being used for the armament installation. The VXB is fully amphibious and is propelled in the water by its wheels. The basic vehicle can have a number of optional extras including a winch with a capacity of 3500/4500kg, night vision equipment, NBC system, obstacle clearing blade, public address system and so on. Apart from the VXB there are three other basic versions – the VLC Light Combat Vehicle, the VRL Light Reconnaissance Vehicle and the Maintien de l'Ordre (Internal Security Vehicle.)

Berliet VXB

VARIANTS

The vehicle can be used as an APC, command vehicle, radio vehicle, ambulance and load carrier and the following armament installations are being offered:
Mortar vehicle with an 81mm mortar.
Turret-mounted 20mm cannon and co-axial 7.62mm machine gun.
Turret mounted twin 7.62mm machine guns.
Various 20mm, 12.7mm and 7.62mm weapons in open mounts.
Turret with 90mm gun as used in the AML armoured car.
Anti-Tank missile vehicle with HOT or Milan missiles.
Anti-aircraft gun vehicle with twin 20mm cannon.
Twin 80mm Oerlikon rocket launchers.
Turret mounted 60mm mortar and twin 7.62mm machine guns as used on AML.
Turret mounted 20mm cannon and 60mm mortar as used on AML.

VXB Swimming

DATA

Crew: 1 + 11
Weight loaded: 12,700kg
Weight empty: 9,800kg
Length: 5.99 metres
Width: 2.5 metres
Height without armament: 2.05 metres
Ground clearance: 0.45 metre
Wheelbase: 3 metres
Angle of approach: 45°
Angle of departure: 45°
Maximum road speed: 85km/hr
Maximum water speed: 4km/hr
Range: 750km
Fuel capacity: 220 litres
Fording: Amphibious
Gradient: 60%
Side slope: 30%
Engine: Berliet 8-cylinder diesel developing 170 HP at 3000 rpm
Armour: 7mm

The troops and stores that can be carried by the VXB

Manufacturer: Automobiles M Berliet at Bourg. Enquiries Automobiles M Berliet, 160, boulevard de Verdun, 92402 Courbevoie, France
Status: In production. In service in France and Senegal

PANHARD M3 ARMOURED PERSONNEL CARRIER

The M3 was designed by Panhard in 1968/69 to meet a requirement for an inexpensive armoured personnel carrier to undertake a range of roles including use as a command vehicle, APC, load carrier and ambulance. The first production M3 was completed in 1971 and large numbers have been built by Panhard, most of which have been for export. The M3 has about 95 per cent of its mechanical components identical to the Panhard AML series of armoured cars.

The hull of the M3 is of all-welded steel construction. The driver sits at the front of the hull and the engine is behind him. The personnel are seated along each side of the hull and at the rear. Doors are provided in the sides and rear of the hull. The basic model is fully amphibious, being propelled in the water by its wheels. The M3 does not have an NBC system but optional extras include night driving equipment and an air-conditioning system.

VARIANTS

The M3 can be used for the following roles and be fitted with the following armament installations:
Turret with twin 7.62mm machine guns.

The capacity of the M3 is evident from this picture

Turret with a single 7.62mm machine gun and 3 STRIM rocket launchers.
Turret with a single 7.62mm machine gun and 1 STRIM rocket launcher.
Ring mount with a 12.7mm machine gun.
Ring mount with a 7.62mm machine gun.
Turret mounted 20mm cannon.
Various machine guns can be mounted on the rear hatch including a 7.62mm weapon.
Mortar vehicle with an 81mm breech loaded mortar.
Repair vehicle called the VAT.
Ambulance called the VTS.
Command/radio vehicle called the VPC.
Cargo carrier.
Mortar vehicle with a 60mm turret-mounted mortar.
HOT anti-tank vehicle armed with four ready-to-launch HOT missiles with a further 10 missiles inside the hull.
M3 VDA anti-aircraft vehicle with turret mounted twin 20mm cannon.

DATA
Crew: 2 + 10
Weight loaded: 6100kg
Weight empty: 5300kg
Length: 4.45 metres
Width: 2.4 metres
Height: 2.48 metres (with turret)
        2 metres (without armament installed)
Ground clearance: 0.35 metre
Track: 2.05 metres
Wheelbase: 2.7 metres
Maximum road speed: 100km/hr
Maximum water speed: 4km/hr
Range: 600km
Fuel capacity: 165 litres
Fording: Amphibious
Gradient: 60%
Side slope: 30%
Vertical obstacle: 0.3 metre
Trench: 0.8 metre (with one channel)
        3.1 metres (with 5 channels)
Engine: Panhard 4 HD, 4-cylinder petrol engine developing 90 HP at 4700 rpm
Armament: See text
Armour: 8mm-12mm
Manufacturer: Société Constructions Mécaniques Panhard and Levassor, 18 Avenue d'Ivry, 75013, Paris, France
Status: In production. In service in Abu-Dhabi, Angola, Congo, France, Iraq, Ireland, Kenya, Lebanon, Malaysia, Portugal, Saudi-Arabia, Spain

M3 Armoured Personnel Carrier

M3 Mortar Vehicle

SAVIEM/CREUSOT-LOIRE VAB ARMOURED PERSONNEL CARRIER

In 1969, the French Army issued a requirement for a vehicle called the Véhicule de l'Avant Blindé (VAB). This was required to supplement the AMX-10P MICV in the battlefield area and would be used to carry troops and supplies: it would also be used for other roles such as command, ambulance, anti-tank and so on. Both Panhard and Saviem/Creusot-Loire built a number of prototypes in both 4×4 and 6×6 configurations. After trials the production order was awarded to Saviem/Creusot-Loire in 1975. First production vehicles will be delivered from 1977 and will be the 4×4 model: the 6×6 model will be placed in production later.

The hull of the VAB is of all-welded steel construction with the commander and driver at the front, engine in the centre and the personnel compartment at the rear. The personnel compartment is provided with seats which can be folded up so that supplies can be quickly loaded. Doors are provided in the hull sides and rear as are observation hatches. Hatches are provided over the commander's and driver's positions and over the troop compartment.

The VAB is fully amphibious, being propelled in the water by two water-jets. An NBC system is fitted as standard equipment. Optional equipment includes night vision equipment, air-conditioning system and a winch with 60 metres of cable.

Prototypes were armed with a .50 (12.7mm) Browning machine gun on a ring mount but it is expected that production vehicles will be armed with a 20mm turret mounted cannon. Saviem/Creusot-Loire have suggested that the VAB will be used for a variety of roles: 90mm turret as fitted to the AML, turret with twin 7.62mm machine guns, turret with a 20mm cannon and a 7.62mm machine gun, anti-aircraft gun or missile carrier, mortar vehicle with 81mm or 120mm mortar, recovery vehicle, command vehicle, ambulance, internal security vehicle and many other armament installations.

4 × 4 and 6 × 6 versions of the VAB

DATA (production vehicles may differ)

	4 × 4	6 × 6
Crew:	2 + 10	2 + 10
Weight loaded:	13,000kg	14,000kg
Weight empty:	11,000kg	12,000kg
Length:	5.98 metres	5.98 metres
Width:	2.49 metres	2.49 metres
Height without armament:	2.06 metres	2.06 metres
Ground clearance:	0.4 metre	0.4 metre
Track:	2.035 metres	2.035 metres
Wheelbase:	3 metres	1.5 metres + 1.5 metres
Tyres:	14.00 × 20	14.00 × 20
Maximum road speed:	100km/hr	100km/hr
Maximum water speed:	7km/hr	7km/hr
Range road:	1300km	1100km
Fuel capacity:	300 litres	300 litres

Fording:	Amphibious	Amphibious
Gradient:	60%	60%
Side slope:	30%	30%
Vertical obstacle:	0.6 metre	0.6 metre
Angle of approach:	45°	45°
Angle of departure:	45°	45°

Engine: Saviem Hm-71 2356 6-cylinder water cooled diesel developing 230HP at 2200rpm
Armament (prototypes): 1 × .50 (12.7mm) machine gun on ring mount
Manufacturer: Société Saviem/Creusot-Loire, 15 rue Pasuier, 75008, Paris, France
Status: In production for the French Army

GERMANY (FEDERAL REPUBLIC)

SCHUTZENPANZER SPZ 12-3 ARMOURED PERSONNEL CARRIER

In the 1950s the Swiss company of Hispano-Suiza built a self-propelled anti-aircraft gun. They then redesigned the chassis to meet a Germany Army requirement for an armoured personnel carrier. The first prototype was completed in 1957. The Swiss company could not, however, undertake large scale production so the production contracts were placed in Germany and Britain. The first production vehicles were completed in 1958 with final deliveries taking place in 1962. After the initial faults had been overcome the SPZ 12-3 (or HS 30 as it is also known) proved a useful vehicle, but it has been replaced in many units by the Marder MICV. The hull of the SPZ 12-3 is of all-welded steel construction. The driver is seated at the front of the vehicle on the left with the turret on his right. The turret-mounted 20mm cannon has an elevation of +75° and a depression of −10°, traverse being a full 360°. A 7.62mm MG 3 machine gun is normally pintle mounted and 8 dischargers are fitted. Total ammunition supply is 2000 rounds of 20mm and 3000 rounds of 7.62mm. The personnel compartment is in the centre of the hull and the infantry leave by jumping over the sides of the vehicle: there is a small two-piece door in the rear of the hull on the left side. The engine is at the rear on the right side.

The SPZ 12-3 is not amphibious. It is provided with an NBC system and most models have infra-red driving lights.

VARIANTS
Panzermörser SPZ 52-3: This is armed with a 120mm mortar in the troop compartment. A 81mm mortar carrier was built but not adopted for service.
Jagdpanzer Rakete JPZ 3-3: This has no turret and is armed with two launchers for the SS-11 ATGW.
SPZ 21-3: A command and radio vehicle.
SPZ 81-3 Feuerleitpanzer: This is an artillery fire control and command model.
Anti-tank Vehicle: This is armed with an American 106mm M40A1 recoilless rifle. For trials purposes an SPZ 12-3 has been fitted with the Milan ATGW system. There are also some vehicles in service with various radars.

DATA
Crew: 2 + 6
Weight loaded: 14,600kg
Weight empty: 11,700kg
Length: 6.31 metres (with armament)
5.56 metres (hull)
Width: 2.54 metres
Height: 1.85 metres with turret
1.63 metres without turret
Ground clearance: 0.4 metre
Track: 1.92 metres
Track width: 305mm
Ground pressure: 0.75kg/cm²
Maximum road speed: 58km/hr
Range road: 270km
Fuel capacity: 340 litres
Fording: 0.7 metre
Gradient: 60%
Vertical obstacle: 0.6 metre
Trench: 1.6 metres
Engine: Rolls Royce B81 Mk 80F 8-cylinder petrol engine developing 235 HP at 3800 rpm
Armament: 1 × 20mm cannon and 1 × 7.62mm machine gun, 8 smoke dischargers
Armour: 8mm-30mm
Manufacturers: Henschel and Hanomag in Germany and Leyland in Great Britain
Status: Production completed. In service only with the German Army

HWK 11 ARMOURED PERSONNEL CARRIER

The HWK series of vehicles was developed by Henschel-Werke of Kassel in the 1950s with the first prototypes being completed in 1963. The only model to enter production was the HKW 11 APC, and 40 of these were built for the Mexican Army.

The hull is of all-welded steel construction. The driver is seated at the front of the vehicle on the left, with the engine to his right. The commander is seated behind the driver. The personnel compartment is at the rear of the hull and the infantry are seated on benches five down each side of the hull. The personnel compartment is provided with two roof hatches and two rear doors. There is no provision for the crew to fight from within the vehicle apart from using the roof hatches.

The HWK-11 has no amphibious capacity and is not normally provided with either an NBC system or night vision equipment.

VARIANTS
HWK 10: Anti-tank missile launcher, not in service, armed with HOT or TOW missiles.
HWK 12: Anti-tank vehicle with turret-mounted 90mm gun, not in service.
HWK 13: Reconnaissance vehicle with turret-mounted 20mm cannon and 7.62mm mg, prototypes built but not in service.
HWK 14: Armed with a 81mm or 120mm mortar, not in service.
HWK 15: Command, radio or fire control vehicle, not in service.
HWK 16: Ambulance vehicle, not in service.

DATA
Crew: 2 + 10
Weight loaded: 11,000kg
Weight empty: 9,000kg
Length: 5.05 metres
Width: 2.53 metres
Height: 1.585 metres (without armament)
Ground clearance: 0.435 metre
Track: 2.2 metres
Track width: 330mm
Ground pressure: 0.55kg/cm²
Maximum road speed: 65km/hr
Range: 320km
Fuel capacity: 300 litres
Fording: 1.2 metres
Gradient: 60%
Vertical obstacle: 0.68 metre
Side slope: 30%
Trench: 2 metres
Engine: Chrysler 361 B 75M, 8-cylinder petrol developing 211 HP at 4000rpm
Armament: 1 × 7.62mm or 12.7mm machine gun
Armour: 8mm-14.5mm
Manufacturer: Rheinstahl Transporttechnik AG, Kassel 2, Germany
Status: Production complete. In service only with the Mexican Army

MARDER MECHANISED INFANTRY COMBAT VEHICLE

Without doubt the Marder is the most advanced vehicle of its type in production in the West. Its development can be traced back to 1959 when the German Army drew up its requirements for a new type of vehicle which would not only transport infantry about the battlefield but would also enable the infantry to fight from within the vehicle if required. Prototypes were built in the early 1960s by a number of Swiss and German companies. The first production order was placed in 1969 and the first Marder was completed in 1971. Since then well over 2000 have been built. The hull is of all-welded steel armour. The driver sits at the front on the left with the engine to his right and there is a further crew position to his rear. The commander and gunner are seated in the turret, which is armed with a 20mm cannon and a co-axial 7.62mm machine gun: traverse is 360° and elevation between −17° to +65°. The personnel compartment is at the rear and is provided with four roof hatches and four ball mounts in the side of the hull (two each side), which allow the infantry to fire their weapons from within the hull. Normal means of entry and exit for the infantry is via a ramp in the hull rear. There is also a remotely controlled 7.62mm machine gun over the rear troop

Marder MICV

compartment. Total ammunition carried is 1250 rounds of 20mm and 5000 rounds of 7.62mm. The Marder is provided with an NBC system and a complete range of night vision equipment. A schnorkel can be fitted for deep fording and an amphibious kit is being developed.

VARIANTS
Roland Anti-Aircraft Vehicle: This is now entering production and is armed with two launchers for the Roland SAM with a further 8 missiles inside the hull.
Marder with 120 mortar: Development only, no production.
Artillery Fire Control Vehicle: Development only, no production.
Marder with 105mm gun: Under development as a tank destroyer.
Marder radar vehicle: Not placed in production.
Marder with LWT-3 turret: This has a fully stabilised turret and is still under development.
    Other models developed to prototype stage included an ambulance, rocket launcher, reconnaissance tank and anti-aircraft gun vehicle.

DATA
Crew: 10 (commander, driver, 2 gunners and 6 infantry)
Weight loaded: 28,200kg
Length: 6.79 metres
Width: 3.24 metres
Height: 2.95 metres (including searchlight)
Ground clearance: 0.45 metre
Track: 2.62 metres
Track width: 450mm
Ground pressure: 0.8kg/cm²
Maximum road speed: 75km/hr

Marder carrying troops
Range (road): 520km
Fuel capacity: 652 litres
Fording: 1.5 metres
                2.5 metres with schnorkel
Gradient: 60%
Vertical obstacle: 1 metre
Trench: 2.5 metres
Engine: MTU MB 833 Ea-500 6-cylinder diesel developing 600 HP at 2200 rpm
Armament: 1 × 20mm cannon with a co-axial 7.62mm machine gun. 1 × 7.62mm machine gun at rear. 6 smoke dischargers on the turret
Manufacturers: Rheinstahl Transporttechnik AG, 35 Kassel 2, Germany, and Atlas MaK of Kiel
Status: In production. In service with the German Army

UR-416 ARMOURED PERSONNEL CARRIER

The UR-416 4×4 armoured personnel carrier has been designed by Rheinstahl to fulfil the need for a low-cost, easy-to-maintain vehicle suitable for use in a variety of roles. It consists of a standard Mercedes-Benz Unimog truck chassis with an armoured body. The driver is seated at the front on the left with the vehicle commander to his right. The eight infantry are seated in the rear of the vehicle, three each side facing outwards and two at the rear facing the rear. Doors are provided in each side of the hull and the rear. There are a total of ten firing ports in the hull. There are two hatches in the roof with the front hatch normally being used to mount the armament.

The UR-416 is used mainly in the internal security role and over 500 have so far been built, the first being completed in 1969. The vehicle is not amphibious and does not have an NBC system. Optional equipment includes run-flat tyres, a machine gun on the rear hatch, a winch, a heater and a fire extinguishing system and special MOWAG-type ball mounts enabling the crew to fire their weapons from within the vehicle with complete safety.

The vehicle is normally armed with a 7.62mm machine gun. This is provided with a small shield and is mounted on a ring mount enabling it to be traversed through 360°. Four smoke dischargers can be mounted if required.

VARIANTS
Ambulance: This can carry eight sitting or four sitting and two lying patients plus crew.
Command Vehicle: The vehicle can be used in both the command and fire control roles.
Reconnaissance: This is armed with a turret-mounted 7.62mm machine gun or 20mm cannon.
Anti-Tank: The models proposed include one with a Swedish 90mm recoilless rifle, another with Cobra ATGWs and finally one with the American TOW missile installation.
Repair Vehicle: This is provided with tools, welding equipment and so on.
Police Vehicle: Special models have been developed for the use of the police, and have obstacle clearing blades and special cupolas.

DATA
Crew: 2 + 8
Weight loaded: 6300kg
Weight empty: 4800kg
Length: 4.99 metres

Rheinstahl UR416 without armament
Width: 2.26 metres
Height: 2.24 metres (top of turret ring)
            2.52 metres (turret)
Ground clearance: 0.44 metre
Track: 1.616 metres
Wheelbase: 2.9 metres
Angle of approach: 47°
Angle of departure: 51°
Maximum road speed: 80km/hr
Range: 700km
Fuel capacity: 150 litres
Fording: 1 metre
Gradient: 70%
Vertical obstacle: 0.55 metre
Engine: Daimler-Benz Model OM 352 6-cylinder diesel developing 110 HP at 2800 rpm
Armament: 1 × 7.62mm machine gun
Armour: 9mm
Manufacturer: Rheinstahl Transporttechnik AG, 35 Kassel 2, Germany
Status: In production. In service with many countries including The Netherlands and Peru

ITALY

FIAT 6614 CM ARMOURED PERSONNEL CARRIER

The Fiat 6614 CM is a development of the earlier Fiat 6614 BM armoured personnel carrier. The hull of the 6614 CM is of all-welded steel construction. The driver is seated at the front of the vehicle on the left side with the engine to his right. Doors are provided in each side of the hull and there is a large power-operated ramp at the rear of the hull. A total of ten firing ports and vision blocks are provided for the personnel, one in each door, two in the ramp and three down each side of the hull. There are two hatches in the roof; the forward one normally mounts the main armament whilst the one at the rear can have a 7.62mm machine gun on a pintle mount. The first vehicles were armed with a standard Browning 0.50 machine gun but other armament installations are possible.

The Fiat 6614 CM is fully amphibious being propelled in the water by its wheels. Optional equipment includes infra-red night vision equipment and an NBC system.

VARIANTS
The Fiat 6614 CM can be used for a variety of roles including use as an ambulance, command vehicle and cargo carrier. A more recent model is the Fiat 6614M which is slightly larger and has a more powerful engine which develops 147 HP at 320rpm.

DATA
Crew: 2 + 8
Weight loaded: 7000kg
Weight empty: 5850kg
Length: 5.56 metres
Width: 2.37 metres
Height without armament: 1.68 metres
Ground clearance: 350mm

Track: 1.92 metres
Wheelbase: 2.8 metres
Tyres: 10.00 × 20
Turning radius: 6.8 metres
Angle of approach: 45°
Angle of departure: 45°
Maximum road speed: 96km/hr
Maximum water speed: 4.5km/hr
Range: 700km
Fuel capacity: 120 litres

Fording: Amphibious
Gradient: 60%
Side slope: 30%
Vertical obstacle: 0.45 metre
Engine: Fiat Model 8062 6-cylinder diesel developing 128 HP at 3200 rpm
Armament: 1 × .50 Browning machine gun (see text)
Armour: 6mm-8mm
Manufacturer: Fiat Company, Turin, Italy
Status: Available for production

JAPAN

TYPE SU 60 ARMOURED PERSONNEL CARRIER

Prototypes of the first post-war Japanese armoured personnel carrier were completed in 1957 by both Mitsubishi Heavy Industries and the Komatsu Manufacturing Company. The Mitsubishi vehicle was found to be the better of the two and this was placed in production as the Type SU 60 APC in 1960. Production continued until 1970 and the vehicle is now being replaced by the Type 73 MICV.

The hull is of all-welded steel construction. The driver is seated at the front of the hull on the right side with the bow machine gunner on the left. The commander is seated to the rear of the bow gunner's position, The .50 machine gun is mounted on the right side of the roof, to the rear of the driver, and is provided with a simple shield. The troop compartment is at the rear of the hull and this is provided with a three part roof hatch and twin doors in the rear of the hull. No provision is made for the infantry to use their weapons from within the vehicle. The Type SU 60 is not amphibious, nor does it have any night vision equipment or NBC system.

VARIANTS
Type SV 60: This has an 81mm mortar in the rear troop compartment and retains its bow and .50 machine guns.
Type SX 60: This has a 4.2 inch mortar mounted in the rear of the hull, it retains its .50 machine gun but the .30 bow machine gun is not fitted.

DATA
Crew: 2 + 8
Weight loaded: 11,800kg
Weight empty: 10,600kg
Length: 4.85 metres
Width: 2.4 metres
Height including machine gun: 2.31 metres
Height hull top: 1.71 metres
Ground clearance: 0.4 metre
Ground pressure: 0.57kg/cm²

Type SU-60 APC

Maximum road speed: 45km/hr
Range: 230km
Fording: 0.76 metre
Gradient: 60%
Vertical obstacle: 0.6 metre
Trench: 1.82 metres
Engine: Mitsubishi Model HA-21 WT 8-cylinder turbo-charged diesel developing 220 HP at 2400 rpm
Armament: 1 × .50 M2 machine gun on roof
      .30 machine gun in bow
Manufacturer: Mitsubishi Heavy Industries, Maruko, Tokyo, Japan
Status: No longer in production. In service only with the Japanese Army

TYPE 73 MECHANISED INFANTRY COMBAT VEHICLE

The Type 73 MICV is the replacement for the older Type SU 60 APC. The first prototype was completed in 1970 and the vehicle is now in service with the Japanese Army. The hull is of all-welded aluminium construction. The driver is seated at the front on the right side and the bow machine gunner is seated to his left. The commander is seated to the rear of the gunner's and driver's positions. The engine is on the left side of the hull with the main armament installation on the right. Hatches are provided in the roof and the infantry enter and leave the vehicle via the large ramp in the hull rear. Simple 'T' type firing ports are provided in the hull sides and rear. The armament consists of a .50 machine gun which can be aimed and fired from within the vehicle, and a .30 machine gun mounted in the bow. Smoke dischargers are mounted on each side of the hull roof at the rear. The Type 73 is fully amphibious being propelled in the water by its tracks. It is also provided with an NBC system and night vision equipment.

VARIANTS
No variants have been announced although variants are no doubt under development, including mortar carriers.

DATA (provisional)
Crew: 2 + 10
Weight loaded: 14,000kg
Length: 5.6 metres
Width: 2.8 metres
Height: 1.7 metres
Ground clearance: 0.4 metre
Maximum road speed: 60km/hr
Fording: Amphibious
Gradient: 60%
Vertical obstacle: 0.65 metre
Trench: 1.6 metres

Type 73 MICV

Engine: Mitsubishi V4 supercharged diesel developing 300 HP at 2200 rpm
Armament: 1 × .50 machine gun
      1 × .30 machine gun (bow)
      2 × 3 smoke dischargers
Manufacturer: Mitsubishi Heavy Industries Limited, Sagamihara, near Tokyo, Japan
Status: In production. In service only with the Japanese Army

NETHERLANDS

DAF YP-408 ARMOURED PERSONNEL CARRIER (8×4)

The prototype of the DAF YP-408 APC was completed in 1958 and the vehicle was in production from 1964 to 1968, about 750 being built. The hull of the YP-408 is of all-welded steel construction with the engine at the front. The driver is seated on the left and the commander/machine gunner on the right: both are provided with hatch covers. The ten infantry are seated in the rear of the vehicle, five down each side facing inwards. There are a total of six roof hatches and normal means of entry and exit is via twin doors in the

rear of the hull, each of these being provided with a firing port. The YP-408 is not amphibious and does not have an NBC system. Infra-red driving lights can be fitted as also can an infra-red searchlight to the machine gun. The .50 M2 machine gun can be fired from within the vehicle and can be traversed through a full 360°: elevation limits are +70° and −8°. Three smoke dischargers are mounted each side of the engine.

DAF YP-408 Armoured Personnel Carrier

VARIANTS

PWI-S (GR): This is the designation of the basic armoured personnel carrier.

PWI-S (PC) Platoon Commanders Vehicle: This is the basic APC with additional radios, and crew of nine.

PWCO (Company or Battalion Commander's Vehicle): This has additional radios and a folding table and a tent can be erected at the rear if required. The crew of six comprises driver, gunner and four staff members.

PW-GWT (Ambulance): This is unarmed and has a crew of three. It can carry two stretcher and four sitting patients.

PW-V (Freight): This has a crew of two and carries 1500kg of cargo.

PW-MT (Mortar Tractor): This tows the French 120mm Brandt mortar and carries 50 rounds of mortar ammunition. It has a crew of seven.

DATA

Crew: 2 + 10
Weight loaded: 12,000kg
Weight empty: 9,500kg
Length: 6.23 metres
Width: 2.4 metres
Height: 2.37 metres (with machine gun)
1.8 metres (top of hull)
Ground clearance: 0.518 metre
Track: 2.054 metres (front)
2.08 metres (rear)
Tyres: 11.00 × 20
Turning radius: 9 metres
Angle of approach: 42°
Angle of departure: 70°
Maximum road speed: 80km/hr
Range: 500km (road)
Fuel capacity: 200 litres
Fording: 1.2 metres
Gradient: 60%
Vertical obstacle: 0.7 metre

Soldiers deploying from the YP-408

Trench: 1.2 metres
Engine: DAF Model DS 575 6-cylinder diesel developing 165 BHP at 2400 rpm
Armament: 1 × .50 machine gun
2 × 3 smoke dischargers
Armour: 8mm-15mm
Manufacturer: DAF Company, Eindhoven, The Netherlands
Status: Production complete. In service only with the Netherlands Army

---

ROMANIA

TAB-70 ARMOURED PERSONNEL CARRIER

This is believed to be a Romanian version of the Russian BTR-60 6×6 armoured personnel carrier. Few other details are available.

Manufacturer: Romanian State factories
Status: In production and in service

SPAIN

PEGASO ARMOURED PERSONNEL CARRIERS

According to reports from Spain, the Pegaso Company of Madrid has built prototypes of 4×4 and 6×6 armoured personnel carriers, both of which are said to be amphibious and to use British aluminium armour.

Manufacturer: Pegaso S.A., Madrid Spain
Status: Trials

SWEDEN

PANSARBANDVAGN 302 ARMOURED PERSONNEL CARRIER

The first prototype of the Pbv.302 was completed in 1961 and the vehicle was in production for the Swedish Army from 1966 to 1971. It replaced the older Pbv.301 armoured personnel carrier. Hägglunds have developed a number of other vehicles using components of the Pbv.302 including an

ARV, Bridgelayer and the Ikv 91 tank destroyer.

The hull of the Pbv.302 is of all-welded steel construction and it is unusual in that the sides are double skinned. The commander is seated at the front of the vehicle on the right, the driver in the centre and the gunner on the left. The personnel compartment is at the rear of the hull and the normal means of entry and exit are the twin doors in the rear of the hull. There are two sets of hatch covers over the troop compartment and these are hydraulically operated. The Pbv.302 is armed with a turret-mounted 20mm cannon with an elevation of $+50°$ and a depression of $-10°$: traverse is a full 360°. A total of 505 rounds of 20mm ammunition are carried. 2×5 smoke dischargers are normally fitted.

The vehicle is fully amphibious, being propelled in the water by its tracks. Infra-red night driving lights are standard but the Pbv.302 does not have an NBC system.

VARIANTS

The basic vehicle can be quickly adapted for use as an ambulance, load carrier or recovery vehicle.

Stripv 3021 Armoured Command Vehicle: This is a command vehicle and has a total crew of seven, it is provided with additional radios and tables.

Epbv 3022 Armoured Observation Post Vehicle: This is a special vehicle and has an additional cupola with an optical rangefinder: it is also provided with a navigation system.

Bplpbv 3023 Armoured Fire Direction Post Vehicle: This has a crew of seven and has four radios and a fire direction computer.

Product Improved Pbv.302: Hägglunds have suggested that the following improvements could be made to the Pbv.302: a revised rear hull with firing ports and vision blocks; a more powerful Volvo THD 100C engine; an Allison automatic gearbox in place of the manual gearbox; a new steering system, and replacement of the 20mm gun by a 25mm gun with power traverse and full stabilisation.

DATA
Crew: 2 + 10
Weight loaded: 13,500kg
Length: 5.35 metres
Width: 2.86 metres
Height with turret: 2.5 metres
Ground clearance: 0.4 metre
Track: 2.42 metres
Track width: 380mm
Ground pressure: $0.6kg/cm^2$
Maximum road speed: 66km/hr

Pbv 302 APC

Maximum water speed: 8km/hr
Range: 300km
Fuel capacity: 385 litres
Fording: Amphibious
Gradient: 60%
Vertical obstacle: 0.61 metre
Trench: 1.8 metres
Engine: Volvo-Penta Model THD 100B 6-cylinder diesel developing 280 HP at 2200 rpm
Armament: $1 \times 20mm$ cannon and 2×5 smoke dischargers
Manufacturer: AB Hägglunds and Soner, Örnsköldsvik, Sweden
Status: Production complete. In service only with the Swedish Army

SWITZERLAND

MOWAG MR 8-01 SERIES ARMOURED PERSONNEL CARRIER

The MOWAG MR 8-01 series were designed in Switzerland in the 1950s and a small quantity was purchased by Germany for the use of the Border police. Subsequently about 350 were built in Germany and some have been transferred to the German Police. The hull is of all-welded steel construction. The driver is seated at the front of the vehicle on the left side. Entry doors are provided in the sides and rear of the hull. The vehicle is not amphibious and does not have any night vision equipment fitted.

VARIANTS

The vehicle is in service with the German Border Police in two models. The SW1(Kfz 91) is unarmed and is used as an armoured personnel carrier and carries seven men. The vehicles used by the German Police have slight modifications and some have an obstacle clearing blade mounted at the front. The SW2(Kfz 91) is armed with a turret mounted 20mm cannon and four smoke dischargers are mounted each side of the turret. This normally has a crew of four. MOWAG variants included anti-tank, rocket-launcher and mortar vehicles none of these however reached the production stage.

DATA
Crew: 3-5
Weight: 8200kg
Length: 5.31 metres
Width: 2.2 metres
Height with turret: 2.2 metres
Ground clearance (hull): 0.5 metre
Track: 1.95 metres
Wheelbase: 2.6 metres
Tyres: 10.00×20
Angle of approach: 45°
Angle of departure: 44°
Maximum road speed: 80km/hr
Gradient: 60%
Engine: Chrysler R361 6-cylinder petrol developing 161 HP
Armament (when fitted): $1 \times 20mm$ cannon
2×4 smoke dischargers
Manufacturers: MOWAG AG, Kreuzlingen, Switzerland. Henschel and Bussing in Germany
Status: Production complete. In service only with the German Border Police and German Police

MOWAG ROLAND ARMOURED PERSONNEL CARRIER

The Roland has been designed for use as an armoured personnel carrier, reconnaissance vehicle or internal security vehicle. Its hull is of all-welded construction. The driver is seated at the front. Entry doors are provided in each side of the hull and there is also a door in the rear on the right side. The engine is at the rear of the hull on the left. The turret is in the centre of the roof and there is a small hatch in the roof towards the rear on the right side.

The Roland is normally armed with a 7.62mm machine gun, although other armament installations are possible.

The vehicle is not amphibious and is not provided with an NBC system. Optional equipment includes a front mounted obstacle clearing blade, MOWAG type firing ports, bullet-proof tyres, infra-red driving equipment, searchlights and an air conditioning system.

VARIANTS

There are no special variants of the Roland although the vehicle can be used as a load carrier, ambulance or command vehicle.

DATA
Crew: 3 + 4
Weight loaded: 4700kg

Mowag Roland IS Vehicle with obstacle cleaning blade

Weight empty: 3900kg
Length: 4.44 metres
Width: 2.01 metres
Height with turret: 2.03 metres
Ground clearance: 0.4 metre
Track: 1.71 metres (front) 1.655 metres (rear)
Wheelbase: 2.5 metres
Tyres: 9.00 × 16
Angle of approach: 40°
Angle of departure: 36°

Maximum road speed: 110km/hr
Range: 550km
Fording: 1 metre
Gradient: 60%
Vertical obstacle: 0.4 metre
Engine: Chrysler 8-cylinder petrol developing 202 HP at 3900 rpm
Armament: 1 × 7.62mm machine gun
Manufacturer: MOWAG Motorwagenfabrik, Kreuzlingen, Switzerland
Status: In production. In service with many countries including Greece and Peru

MOWAG TORNADO (TAIFUN) MECHANISED INFANTRY COMBAT VEHICLE

The MOWAG Company have been designing tracked APCs and MICVs for over twenty years but so far none has entered procuction. The Tornado is also being marketed by Oto-Melara under the name of Taifun. The hull is of all-welded steel construction. The driver is seated at the front of the vehicle on the left side with the engine to his right. The vehicle commander is seated to the rear of the driver and the armament installation is in the centre of the vehicle. The main armament consists of a 25mm Oerlikon gun with an elevation of +60° and a depression of −12°: traverse is 360°. The personnel compartment is at the rear of the hull and the crew enter and leave this via a power operated ramp in the hull rear. There are two MOWAG-type ball mounts in each side of the hull which allow the crew to fire their weapons from within the vehicle. Secondary armament consists of two single 7.62mm machine guns on the top of the hull, at the rear, which can be laid and fired from within the personnel compartment.

The Tornado is not amphibious although a kit has been developed which enables it to ford to a depth of 1.8 metres. An NBC system is fitted.

VARIANTS
MOWAG have suggested that variants of the basic MICV could include an ARV, ambulance, command vehicle, anti-tank missile vehicle, 120mm mortar carrier, load carrier and ammunition vehicle.

Oto-Melara have proposed the following models for the Taifun:
Mk.1 would have a Scorpion turret with a 76mm gun.
Mk. 2 would have a turret armed with a 20mm cannon and a co-axial 7.62 mm machine gun. A 40mm grenade launcher would be mounted on the roof.
Mk. 3 would be armed with twin 20mm cannon in a turret with a traverse of 360°.

DATA
Crew: 10
Weight loaded: 20,500kg
Weight empty: 17,200kg

Mowag Tornado MICV

Length: 6.05 metres
Width: 3.15 metres
Height overall: 2.94 metres
Ground clearance: 0.45 metres
Track width: 450mm
Ground pressure: 0.6kg/cm²
Maximum road speed: 70km/hr
Range: 600km
Fuel capacity: 550 litres
Fording without preparation: 1.3 metres
Gradient: 60%
Vertical obstacle: 0.85 metre
Trench: 2.2 metres
Engine: MOWAG M 8DV-TLK 8-cylinder multi-fuel developing 430 HP at 2100 rpm
Armament: 1 × 25mm cannon
              2 × 7.62mm machine guns
Manufacturer: MOWAG Motorwagenfabrik AG, Kreuzlingen, Switzerland
Status: Manufacturers trials completed. Ready for production

MOWAG PIRANHA ARMOURED PERSONNEL CARRIER

The Piranha range of wheeled armoured vehicles has been developed by MOWAG to undertake a wide variety of roles including use as armoured personnel carriers, internal security vehicles, reconnaissance vehicles, command vehicles and load carriers. The range covers 4×4, 6×6 and 8×8 vehicles and all use many interchangeable components. Prototypes of all models have been built and tested and all are ready for production.

The hulls of these models are of all-welded steel construction. The driver is seated at the front of the hull on the left side with the engine to his right. The armament is installed in the roof of the vehicle and the roof is provided with hatches. Normal entry and exit is via the twin doors in the rear of the hull. A total of 6 MOWAG-type firing ports are provided, two in each side of the hull and one in each of the rear doors. All vehicles in the series are fully amphibious being propelled in the water by two propellers. Infra-red night vision equipment can be fitted and an NBC system is provided.

VARIANTS
4 × 4: Powered by a 190 HP petrol engine, this can be armed with various weapons up to a 20mm cannon.
6 × 6: Powered by a 300 HP diesel this can be armed with a variety of weapons including a 12.7mm machine gun, 20mm, 25mm and 30mm turret mounted cannon, a 90mm gun or an 81mm or 120mm mortar.
8 × 8: Powered by a 350 HP turbo-charged diesel, this can be fitted with a variety of armament installations. 20mm or 30mm cannon, twin 30mm anti-aircraft guns, twin 80mm rocket launchers or an 81mm or 120mm mortar can be mounted in the hull. A 7.62mm machine gun is also mounted on the roof towards the rear and this can be laid and fired from within the vehicle.

DATA

	4 × 4	6 × 6	8 × 8
Total crew:	9	12	14
Weight loaded:	7,000kg	9,600kg	12,500kg
Weight empty:	5,830kg	7,100kg	8,500kg
Length:	5.26 metres	5.84 metres	6.235 metres
Width:	2.5 metres	2.5 metres	2.5 metres
Height w/o armament:	1.85 metres	1.85 metres	1.85 metres

Mowag Piranha – 6 × 6 version

Ground clearance:	0.5 metre	0.5 metre	0.5 metre
Track:	2.18 metres	2.18 metres	2.18 metres
Wheelbase:	2.5 metres	2.04 metres + 1.04 metres	1.1 metres + 1.335 metres + 1.04 metres
Tyres:	11.00 × 16	11.00 × 16	11.00 × 16
Turning radius:	5.6 metres	5.65 metres	6.2 metres
Maximum road speed:	100km/hr	100km/hr	100km/hr
Maximum water speed:	9.5km/hr	10km/hr	10km/hr
Range roads:	750km	1000km	800km
Fuel capacity:	275 litres	300 litres	300 litres
Fording:	Amphibious	Amphibious	Amphibious
Gradient:	70%	70%	70%
Angle of approach:	45°	45°	45°
Angle of departure:	45°	45°	45°
Engine type:	Petrol	Diesel	Diesel
HP/RPM:	190/4000	300/2800	325/2800

Manufacturer: MOWAG Motorwagenfabrik AG, Kreuzlingen, Switzerland
Status: Manufacturer's trials completed. Ready for production.

MOWAG GRENADIER ARMOURED PERSONNEL CARRIER

This is another MOWAG vehicle which can be used for a wide variety of roles including armoured personnel carrier and armoured car. The hull is of all-welded steel construction. The driver is seated at the front on the left with the engine to his right. The personnel compartment is to the rear and normal means of entry and exit is via the twin doors in the hull rear. MOWAG-type firing ports can be installed if required. The armament is mounted in the roof of the vehicle and there is a small hatch in the roof towards the rear.

The Grenadier is fully amphibious being propelled in the water by a propeller at the rear of the hull. Optional equipment includes an air conditioning system, infra-red driving lights, electric ventilator and bullet-proof tyres.

VARIANTS

The vehicle can be armed with a variety of weapons including a 7.62mm machine gun, a 20mm cannon, an 8cm multiple rocket launcher and various anti-tank weapons.

DATA
Crew: 1 + 8
Weight loaded: 6100kg
Weight empty: 4400kg
Length: 4.84 metres
Width: 2.3 metres
Height with turret: 2.12 metres
Ground clearance hull: 0.4 metre
Track: 1.99 metres (front) 2 metres (rear)
Wheelbase: 2.5 metres
Maximum road speed: 100km/hr
Maximum water speed: 9km/hr
Range: 550km
Fuel capacity: 180 litres
Fording: Amphibious
Gradient: 60%
Angle of approach: 41°
Angle of departure: 36°
Engine: 8-cylinder petrol developing 202 HP at 3900 rpm
Manufacturer: MOWAG Motorwagenfabrik AK, Kreuzlingen, Switzerland
Status: Ready for production

UNION OF SOVIET SOCIALIST REPUBLICS

AT-P ARMOURED TRACKED ARTILLERY TRACTOR

The AT-P is used for a variety of roles including artillery towing vehicle, command vehicle, cargo carrier and (to a limited extent) as an armoured personnel carrier. The driver is seated at the front of the vehicle on the left side with the machine gunner's position to his right. The commander is seated behind the driver with the engine to his right. The personnel compartment is at the rear and is not normally provided with overhead armour protection. The AT-P is not amphibious; some models are provided with infra-red night driving equipment.

VARIANTS

AT-P (Command): This is provided with overhead armour protection for the personnel compartment at the rear and normal means of entry and exit is via two doors in the hull rear. The commander has a fully rotating cupola in place of the simple hatch cover of the basic AT-P.
AT-P (Fire Control): This is similar in appearance to the AT-P (Command).

DATA
Crew: 3 + 6

Weight loaded: 6300kg
Length: 4.45 metres
Width: 2.5 metres
Height: 1.83 metres
Ground clearance: 0.33 metre
Track: 2 metres
Track width: 300mm
Ground pressure: 0.4kg/cm²
Maximum road speed: 50km/hr
Range: 500km
Fording: 0.7 metre
Gradient: 60%
Vertical obstacle: 0.7 metre
Trench: 1.22 metres
Engine: ZIL-123R 6-cylinder petrol developing 110 HP at 2900 rpm
Armament: 1 × 7.62mm SGMT machine gun in bow
Armour: 12mm
Manufacturer: Russian State factories
Status: Production complete. In service only with the Russian Army

AT-P Tractors towing Sandal missiles

BTR-152 ARMOURED PERSONNEL CARRIER

The BTR-152 was the first Soviet post-war APC and entered production in 1950. It basically consists of a ZIL-151 6×6 truck chassis with an armoured body: later production models (from the BTR-152V) use the later ZIL-157 6×6 truck chassis. The BTR-152 is still used by most countries of the Warsaw Pact although it has been replaced in front line units by the BTR-60. The hull is of all-welded steel construction with the engine at the front, driver and commander behind the engine and the personnel compartment at the rear. Doors are provided for the commander and driver, and normal means of entry and exit for the crew is via a door in the hull rear. There are three firing ports in each side of the hull. The BTR-152 is not

amphibious and does not have an NBC system. Some have night vision equipment fitted. The vehicle is normally armed with a 7.62mm SGMB machine gun on a pedestal mount and a total of 1250 rounds of ammunition are carried.

VARIANTS

BTR-152: The first model to enter service. It has no winch and no central tyre pressure regulation system.
BTR-152V1: This has a winch mounted at the front and a tyre pressure regulation system with external air lines.

BTR-152V2: This is a modified BTR-152 with a tyre pressure regulation system with internal air lines.

BTR-152V3: This has a front mounted winch and a tyre pressure regulation system with internal air lines. Some have infra-red driving lights.

BTR-152K: This is a BTR-152V3 with overhead armour protection.

BTR-152 A/A: This is a BTR-152 chassis with twin 14.5mm KPV machine guns mounted in the rear. These have a traverse of 360°, elevation being from +80° to −5°. The Egyptians have some A/A BTR-152's armed with four 12.7mm MG53 machine guns.

BTR-152 ATGW: Some BTR-152s are reported to have Sagger ATGW mounted over the rear troop compartment.

BTR-152U: This is a command model with overhead armour and a roof much higher than that of the 152K.

DATA (BTR-152V1)
Crew: 2 + 17
Weight loaded: 8950kg
Length: 6.83 metres
Width: 2.32 metres
Height: 2.05 metres (without armament)
Ground clearance: 0.295 metre
Track: 1.742 metres (front) 1.72 metres (rear)
Wheelbase: 3.3 metres + 1.13 metres
Tyres: 12.00 × 18
Maximum road speed: 75km/hr
Range: 650km
Fuel capacity: 300 litres
Fording: 0.8 metre
Gradient: 30°
Vertical obstacle: 0.6 metre
Trench: 0.69 metre
Engine: ZIL-123 6-cylinder petrol developing 110 HP at 2900 rpm
Armament: 1 × 7.62 SGMB machine gun
Armour: 6mm-13.5mm
Manufacturer: Russian State factories

Soldiers deploying from a BTR-152 APC (Novosti)

Status: Production complete. In service in Afghanistan, Albania, Algeria, Bulgaria, Cambodia, Ceylon, China (built in China as the Type 56 APC), Congo, Cuba, Cyprus, East Germany, Egypt, Guinea, Hungary, India, Indonesia, Iran, Iraq, Israel, Mongolia, North Korea, North Yemen, PLA, Poland, Romania, Somalia, Soviet Union, Sudan, Syria, Tanzania, Uganda, and Yugoslavia

Russian motorised infantry and BTR-152 APCs on Exercise Yug in June 1971 (Novosti)

BTR-40 ARMOURED PERSONNEL CARRIER

The BTR-40 (4×4) APC entered service in 1951 and consists of a standard GAZ-63 truck chassis with an armoured body. As an APC it could carry eight infantry but it was normally used as a reconnaissance vehicle pending the introduction of the BRDM-1 vehicle. The engine is at the front of the hull, commander and driver are behind the engine and the personnel compartment is at the rear of the hull. Both the commander and driver are provided with doors and there are twin doors at the rear of the hull. Firing ports are provided in the hull sides and rear. A winch is mounted at the front of the hull. The 7.62mm machine gun has an elevation of +23½° and a depression of −6°, total traverse being 90°. The BTR-40 is not amphibious and does not have an NBC system or infra-red driving equipment.

VARIANTS
BTR-40K: This is a BTR-40 with overhead armour protection including four roof hatches each of which has a firing port.

BTR-40 A/A: This is a basic BTR-40 with twin 14.5mm KPV machine guns mounted in the rear. This mount is identical to that fitted in the BTR-152 AA. The guns have an elevation of +80° and a depression of −5°: traverse is a full 360°.

BTR-40kh: This is a BTR-40 with special equipment at the rear which enables it to dispense marking flags on the ground thus marking a passage for following vehicles through chemically contaminated ground.

DATA
Crew: 2 + 8
Weight: 5300kg
Length: 5 metres
Width: 1.9 metres
Height without armament: 1.75 metres
Ground clearance: 0.275 metre
Track: 1.588 metres (front) 1.6 metres (rear)
Wheelbase: 2.7 metres
Tyres: 9.75 × 18
Maximum speed: 80km/hr
Range: 285km
Fuel capacity: 120 litres

Fording: 0.9 metre
Gradient: 30°
Vertical obstacle: 0.47 metre
Trench: 0.7 metre with channels
Engine: GAZ-40 6-cylinder petrol developing 80HP at 3400 rpm
Armour: 8mm
Manufacturer: Russian State factories
Status: Production complete. In service in Afghanistan, Albania, Algeria, Bulgaria, China (built in China as the Type 55 APC), Cuba, Czechoslovakia, East Germany, Egypt, Guinea, Hungary, Indonesia, Iran, Iraq, Laos, Libya, Mali, North Korea, North Yemen, Poland, Somalia, Soviet Union, Sudan, Syria, Tanzania, Uganda, Vietnam, Yemen, Yugoslavia

BTR-50 ARMOURED PERSONNEL CARRIER

The BTR-50 basically consists of the PT-76 Light Tank chassis with a personnel compartment mounted on the forward part of the hull. It was first seen in 1957 and since then various models have been developed. The BTR-50 has also been built in Czechoslovakia in a modified form and known as the OT-62 (there is a separate entry for this model).

The hull is of all-welded steel construction with the personnel compartment at the front and the engine at the rear of the hull. The vehicle is fully amphibious and is propelled in the water by two water-jets at the rear of the hull. Most models have infra-red night vision equipment.

VARIANTS
BTR-50P: This was the first model to enter service. The troop compartment has an open roof. Some models are armed with a 7.62mm machine gun on a pintle mount. Most models of the BTR-50 can carry an anti-tank gun on the rear decking: this can be fired from the vehicle if required and ramps are provided so that the weapon can be quickly removed.
BTR-50A: This is similar to the BTR-50P but has a 14.5mm machine gun on a ring mount.
BTR-50PK: This model has full overhead armour protection and is normally unarmed. Some models have side doors and firing ports, the crew otherwise leave the vehicle via the roof hatches.
BTR-50PU Command Vehicle: There are two models, the Model 1 and the Model 2. Both have overhead armour protection and are provided with radios, map tables and a navigation system.

DATA (BTR-50PK)
Crew: 2 + 20
Weight loaded: 14,200kg
Length: 7.08 metres
Width: 3.14 metres
Height: 1.97 metres
Ground clearance: 0.37 metre
Track: 2.74 metres
Track width: 360mm
Ground pressure: 0.51kg/cm²
Maximum road speed: 44km/hr
Water speed: 11km/hr
Range: 260km
Fuel capacity: 250 litres
Fording: Amphibious
Gradient: 70%
Vertical obstacle: 1.1 metres
Trench: 2.8 metres
Engine: Model V-6 6-cylinder diesel developing 240 HP at 1800 rpm
Armament (if mounted): 1 × 7.62mm SGMB MG with 1250 rounds of ammunition
Armour: 10mm-14mm
Manufacturer: Russian State factories
Status: Production complete. In service in Afghanistan, Albania, Algeria, Communist China, Czechoslovakia (OT-62), East Germany, Egypt, Finland, Hungary, India, Iran, Israel, Libya, Poland, Romania, Somalia, Soviet Union, Sudan, Syria, Vietnam, and Yugoslavia

BTR-60 ARMOURED PERSONNEL CARRIER

The BTR-60 entered production in 1960 and was first seen the following year. It is normally employed by Motorised Rifle Divisions whilst Tank Divisions have the tracked BMP-1 or BTR-50.

The hull of the BTR-60 is of all-welded steel construction. The driver and commander are seated at the front and the personnel compartment is to their rear. The engines are at the very rear of the hull and are identical to those fitted to the BRDM-1 4×4 reconnaissance vehicle. All eight wheels of the BTR-60 are powered and the front four are used for steering. The vehicle is fully amphibious, being propelled in the water by a single water-jet at the rear of the hull. Infra-red night vision equipment has now been fitted to most BTR-60s and those with overhead armour are provided with an NBC system.

VARIANTS
BTR-60P: This was the first model to enter service and has an open top. It is normally armed with up to four machine guns, one 12.7mm and three 7.62mm weapons.
BTR-60PK: This has its troop compartment protected by an armoured roof and firing ports are provided in the sides of the hull. It is normally armed with a single 12.7mm or 7.62mm machine gun mounted on a pintle mount on the forward part of the roof. Only means of entry and exit are via the roof hatches.
BTR-60PB (also known as the BTR-60PKB): This is similar to the BTR-60PK except that it has a turret armed with 14.5mm and 7.62mm machine guns. This turret has full traverse through 360°, elevation being +30° and depression −5°. Total ammunition carried consists of 500 rounds of 14.5mm and 2000 rounds of 7.62mm. In addition this model has a side door in each side of the hull.
BTR-60PU Command Vehicle: This is the basic BTR-60P used for the command role and has additional radios and map boards.
BTR-60PB Forward Air Control Vehicle: This is a BTR-60PB which retains its turret (less armament) and is used in the FAC role.

BTR-60P (open top) APC on exercise (Novosti)

BTR-60 PK (hard top) in the foreground: BTR-60P behind (Novosti)

DATA

	BTR-60PK	BTR-60PB
Crew:	2+16	2+14
Weight loaded:	9980kg	10,300kg
Length overall:	7.56 metres	7.56 metres
Width:	2.825 metres	2.825 metres
Height:	2.055 metres	2.31 metres (with turret)
Ground clearance:	0.475 metres	0.475 metres
Track:	2.37 metres	2.37 metres
Wheelbase:	1.35m + 1.525 metres + 1.35 metres	

BTR-60 PB (turret model) in 1973 (Tass)

Tyre size:	13.00×18	13.00×18
Maximum road speed:	80km/hr	80km/hr
Water speed:	10km/hr	10km/hr
Range:	500km	500km
Fuel capacity:	290 litres	290 litres
Fuel consumption:	58 litres/100km	58 litres/100km
Gradient:	30°	30°
Vertical obstacle:	0.4 metres	0.4 metres
Trench:	2 metres	2 metres
Engines:	Both are powered by two GAZ-49B 6-cylinder petrol engines developing 90 HP (each) at 3400rpm	

BTR-60 PU Command Vehicle with a FROG missile section (Novosti)

Armament:	1×7.62mm MG	1×14.5mm & 1×7.62mm MG
Armour:	10mm	10mm (hull), 14mm (turret)

Manufacturer: Russian State factories
Status: Production complete. In service in Afghanistan, Algeria, Angola, Bulgaria, Cuba, East Germany, Egypt, Hungary, Iran, Israel, Libya, Mongolia, North Korea, Poland, Romania, Soviet Union, Syria, Vietnam, Yugoslavia

BMP-1 MECHANISED INFANTRY COMBAT VEHICLE

The BMP-1 was first seen in public in November 1967 and at that time was called the M-1967 and later the BMP-76PB. Its correct designation is now known to be the BMP-1. The BMP-1 was the first MICV to enter service with any Army and even today is the most well armed MICV in the world.

The hull is of welded magnesium construction. The driver is seated at the front of the hull on the left side with the engine to his right. The commander is seated behind the driver. The turret is in the centre of the vehicle with the personnel compartment at the rear. The latter is provided with four roof hatches and the infantry normally enter and leave the vehicle via twin doors in the rear of the hull. There are a total of ten firing ports and vision blocks, four in each side of the hull and one in each of the rear doors.

The turret is armed with a 73mm smooth bore gun, fed from an automatic loader, and a 7.62mm machine gun is mounted co-axially with the main armament. Over the 73mm gun barrel is a launcher rail for the Sagger ATGW. The gun has an elevation of +20° and a depression of −5°; traverse is a full 360°. Total ammunition carried is 30 rounds of 73mm, 1000 rounds of 7.62mm ammunition and five Sagger missiles. An SA-7 SAM is also normally carried inside the hull.

The BMP-1 is fully amphibious, being propelled in the water by its tracks. An NBC system is provided as also is a full range of night vision equipment.

VARIANTS
BMP-2: This is the latest production model. It has a lengthened bow and the deflector shroud at the rear has been extended, both modifications being made to improve its amphibious characteristics.
Polish BMP-1: Some of these are believed to be armed with a smaller gun.

BMP-1 APCs on parade in 1967 (Tass)

Fire Control Vehicle: This has a redesigned turret with a radar scanner at the rear.

Another view of the BMP-1 showing the Sagger missiles mounted above the 73mm gun (Novosti)

DATA
Crew: 3+8
Weight loaded: 12,500kg
Length: 6.75 metres
Width: 3 metres
Height: 2 metres
Ground clearance: 0.4 metres
Track width: 300mm
Ground pressure: 0.57kg/cm²
Maximum road speed: 55km/hr
Maximum water speed: 8km/hr
Range: 300km
Fuel capacity: 300 litres

Fording: Amphibious
Gradient: 60%
Vertical obstacle: 0.9 metres
Trench: 2.7 metres
Engine: Model V6 6-cylinder diesel developing 280 HP at 2000 rpm
Armament: 1×73mm gun
　　　　　1×7.62mm PKT machine gun co-axial with above
　　　　　1 Sagger ATGW launcher
Armour: 14mm maximum
Manufacturer: Russian State factories
Status: In production. In service in Czechoslovakia, East Germany, Egypt, Iraq, Libya, Poland, Soviet Union, Syria

GT-T/M-1970 ARMOURED PERSONNEL CARRIER

The GT-T was first seen in 1970 and at that time was given the provisional designation of M-1970. It is believed that the GT-T is the replacement for the older AT-P tracked vehicle. So far, the GT-T has been used as an armoured personnel carrier, prime mover for artillery, cargo vehicle, radio vehicle, fire control vehicle and command vehicle. The data given below are provisional.

The hull is of all-welded construction. The driver is seated at the front on the left side with the machine gun turret to the right. The personnel compartment is at the rear of the hull and this is provided with twin doors in the hull rear and roof hatches. Firing ports are provided in the hull sides and the rear doors.

The GT-T is fully amphibious and is propelled in the water by its tracks. A full range of infra-red night vision is provided as also is an NBC system.

VARIANTS
The only variant observed so far is one with the Pork Trough fire control radar system.

DATA
Crew: 3 + 10
Weight loaded: 10,000kg
Length: 6.35 metres
Width: 2.8 metres
Height: 2.25 metres
Ground clearance: 0.35 metre
Track width: 360mm

GT-T carriers on a winter exercise

Maximum road speed: 55km/hr
Maximum water speed: 5km/hr
Range: 400km
Fording: Amphibious
Gradient: 60%
Vertical obstacle: 1.1 metres
Trench: 1 metre
Engine: Model IZ-6 6-cylinder diesel developing 200 HP at 1800 rpm.
Armament: 1 × 7.62mm PKT machine gun
Manufacturer: Russian State factories
Status: In production. In service with the Russian Army

UNITED ARAB REPUBLIC (EGYPT)

WALID ARMOURED PERSONNEL CARRIER

The Walid APC was developed by Egypt in the early 1960s and is based on a standard civilian 4×4 truck chassis powered by a German Deutz air-cooled diesel engine. No accurate data are available on the Walid even though the Israelis have captured many and use them for internal security purposes. The hull is of all-welded steel construction with the engine at the front, the commander and driver sit behind the engine, and the personnel compartment is at the rear. The latter is not provided with overhead armour

protection. Firing ports are provided in the sides and rear of the hull. The Walid is normally armed with a 7.62mm or a 12.7mm machine gun on a pintle mount. It is not amphibious and has no NBC system.
Manufacturer: Egyptian Government factories
Status: Production of the Walid is now probably complete. It is in service with Algeria, Egypt, Israel, PLO, and Yemen

UNITED KINGDOM

HUMBER 1-TON TRUCK (PIG) ARMOURED PERSONNEL CARRIER

The Humber 1-ton truck basically consists of a Humber 4×4 chassis with an armoured body. These vehicles were built in the 1950s and were used by most arms of the British Army pending introduction of the Saracen APC. Today they are used only by the British Army for internal security duties in Northern Ireland. In 1972 it was found that the IRA were using AP rounds which would penetrate the armour of the vehicle. All the vehicles in Northern Ireland were brought back to England in batches where the armour protection was upgraded, at the same time a number of other modifications were carried out on the vehicle. The Humber truck is commonly known as the PIG.

The engine is at the front of the vehicle with the commander and driver being seated behind it: each is provided with a side door. The personnel compartment is at the rear of the hull and normal means of entry and exit are via twin doors in the rear of the hull. There are a total of six firing ports, two in each side of the hull and one in each of the rear doors.

VARIANTS
FV1611: This is the most common APC model.
FV1612: A radio model of which few remain in service.
FV1613: This is an ambulance of which few remain in service.

DATA
Crew: 2 + 6-8
Weight loaded: 5790kg
Weight empty: 4770kg
Length: 4.926 metres
Width: 2.044 metres
Height: 2.12 metres
Track: 1.713 metres

The Humber Pig APC in its original form

Wheelbase: 2.743 metres
Tyres: 11.00 × 20

Maximum road speed: 64km/hr
Range: 402km
Fuel capacity: 145 litres
Engine: Rolls Royce B60 Mk. 5A 6-cylinder petrol engine developing 120 HP at 3750 rpm
Armament: some have smoke or tear gas dischargers fitted
Manufacturer: Chassis by Humber and bodies by ROF's and GKN Sankey
Status: Production complete. In service in Britain and Portugal

The Pig with additional armour

ALVIS SARACEN ARMOURED PERSONNEL CARRIER (FV603)

The Alvis Saracen 6×6 armoured personnel carrier was developed shortly after the end of the Second World War and entered service with the British Army in 1953. Other members of the family include the Saladin Armoured Car, Stalwart load carrier and Salamander airfield crash tender. The Saracen is still used by the British Army, especially in Northern Ireland.

The hull is of all-welded armour construction with the engine at the front and the personnel compartment at the rear. The driver is seated behind the engine, and the commander in the turret: there is also a seat to the rear of and either side of the driver and four seats down each side of the hull. The crew enter and leave the vehicle via the twin doors in the rear of the hull. There are a total of eight firing ports, three in each side of the hull and one in each side of the rear doors. The Saracen is armed with a .30 machine gun in a turret with a traverse of 360°; the weapon has an elevation of +45° and a depression of −15°. A Bren LMG is mounted on a pintle mount to the rear of the turret. A three-barrelled smoke discharger is mounted on each side of the hull at the front. The Saracen does not have an NBC system, has no night driving equipment and is not amphibious.

Saracen 6 × 6 APC

VARIANTS
FV603 with reverse flow cooling: Designed for operations in hot climates and is recognisable by the cowl and the raised engine covers.
FV603 with open roof: These were built for Kuwait.
FV604 Command Vehicle: Used for the command role and most models have had their turrets removed. Map boards are provided inside, and a tent can be erected at the rear if required.
FV610 Command Vehicle: This has a higher roof than the FV604 and is provided with an auxiliary charging plant and extra batteries. A tent can be erected at the rear.

DATA
Crew: 2+10
Weight loaded: 10,170kg
Weight empty: 8,040kg
Length: 5.233 metres
Width: 2.539 metres
Height with turret: 2.463 metres
Height top of hull: 2 metres
Ground clearance: 0.432 metre
Track: 2.083 metres
Wheelbase: 1.524 metres + 1.524 metres
Tyres: 12.00 × 20
Ground pressure: 0.98 kg/cm²
Turning radius: 7 metres
Maximum road speed: 72km/hr
Range: 400km
Fuel capacity: 200 litres
Fording: 1.07 metres
Gradient: 42%
Vertical obstacle: 0.46 metre
Trench: 1.52 metres
Angle of approach: 53°
Angle of departure: 53°

Assault troop deploying from a Saracen. In the background, a Saladin armoured car (Central Office of Information)

Engine: Rolls-Royce B80 Mk 6A 8-cylinder petrol engine developing 160 HP at 3750 rpm
Armament: 1 × .30 Browing machine gun
          1 × 7.622mm Bren LMG
          2 × 3 smoke dischargers
Armour: 8mm-16mm
Manufacturer: Alvis Limited (now part of British Leyland), Coventry, England
Status: No longer in production. In service in Abu Dhabi, Brunei, Great Britain, Hong Kong, Indonesia, Jordan, Kuwait, Libya, Nigeria, Qatar, South Africa, Sudan, Thailand and Uganda

FV 432 ARMOURED PERSONNEL CARRIER

The FV 432 was developed from the FV420 series in the late 1950s and was in production from 1963 to 1971. It has a hull of all-welded steel construction. The driver is seated at the front of the hull on the left side with the engine to his right. The commander is seated behind the driver. The ten infantrymen are seated to the rear of the vehicle, five down each side of the hull. The personnel compartment is provided with a large door in the hull rear and a circular four-part hatch in the roof. The FV432 is provided with an NBC system and a full range of night vision equipment. A flotation screen is carried around the top of the hull and can be erected in five to ten minutes and the vehicle is then propelled in the water by its tracks. The FV 432 has proved itself to be a reliable vehicle in service and has been adapted for a wide variety of roles. The same basic chassis is used for the FV 433 Abbot SPG. The British have a MICV under development but this will not enter service until the 1980s.

VARIANTS
Ambulance: Designed to carry four stretcher patients or two stretcher patients and five sitting patients. It has a crew of two.
Cargo: The FV 432 can carry 3670kg of cargo.
Carl Gustav: A Swedish Carl Gustav anti-tank weapon can be mounted on a bar across the rear hatch.
Command: This has additional radios, and map boards and a penthouse can be erected at the rear of the vehicle.
Cymbeline: This is a FV432 with the EMI Cymbeline mortar locating radar system mounted on the roof of the vehicle with the operators controls inside the rear compartment.
FACE (Field Artillery Computer Equipment): Used by the Royal Artillery on the scale of one per self-propelled artillery battery.
Giant Viper: This is used by the Royal Engineers to tow the Giant Viper

FV 432 APC (Major R. P. Smith, RRW)

mine clearance system.

Minelayer: The vehicle can tow the Bar Minelaying System and the Ranger anti-personnel system can be mounted on the roof of the vehicle.

Mortar: This has an 81mm mortar mounted on a baseplate with a traverse of 360°: a bipod and baseplate are also carried enabling it to be used away from the vehicle.

Radar: The ZB 298 surveillance radar is often mounted on the roof of the FV432.

Rarden: A number of FV432s are being fitted with a Fox armoured car turret complete with the Rarden 30mm cannon.

Recovery: This has a winch with a maximum capacity of 16,270kg. An earth anchor is also provided.

Sonic Detection: Used by the Royal Artillery.

Wombat: This is armed with a 120mm Wombat recoilless rifle, which can be fired from the vehicle or away from the vehicle. It has a crew of four and carries 14 rounds of HESH ammunition.

7.62mm turret: Some FV432s are being fitted with a fully enclosed 7.62mm machine gun turret: in addition some are being fitted with twin 7.62mm GPMGs on the commander's position for use in the anti-aircraft role.

FV 434: A maintenance carrier used by the Royal Electrical and Mechanical Engineers.

FV436: This has the older Green Archer mortar locating radar system mounted at the rear of the hull and is being replaced by the Cymbeline radar.

FV 438 Swingfire ATGW Vehicle: This has two launcher boxes for the BAC Swingfire ATGW mounted on the roof of the hull and carries a total of 14 missiles. The commander is provided with a 7.62 machine gun.

FV 439 Signals: A specialised signals vehicle used by the Royal Corps of Signals.

DATA
Crew: 2 + 10

FV 432 with Wombat recoilless anti-tank gun

Weight loaded: 15,280kg
Weight empty: 13,740kg
Length: 5.251 metres
Width overall: 2.8 metres
Width over tracks: 2.527 metres
Height with machine gun: 2.286 metres
Height to roof: 1.879 metres
Ground clearance: 0.406 metre
Track: 2.184 metres
Track width: 343mm
Length of track on ground: 2.819 metres
Ground pressure: 0.78kg/cm²
Maximum road speed: 52km/hr
Maximum water speed: 6.6km/hr
Range road: 580km
Fuel capacity: 454 litres
Fording: 1.066 metres
Gradient: 60%
Vertical obstacle: 0.609 metre
Trench: 2.05 metres
Engine: Rolls Royce K60 No. 4 Mk. 4F, 6-cylinder multi-fuel engine developing 240 BHP at 2750 rpm
Armament: 1 × 7.62mm machine gun (see text)
Manufacturer: GKN Sankey Limited, Wellington, Shropshire, England
Status: Production complete. In service only with the British Army

SHORT SB.301 ARMOURED PERSONNEL CARRIER

The SB.301 has been designed as a companion vehicle to the Shorland armoured patrol car. The prototype of the SB.301 was completed in 1973 with the first production vehicle being completed the following year.

The basis of the SB.301 is a standard long wheel base Land Rover chassis fitted with a welded steel armour hull which provides the crew with protection from small arms fire. The driver and commander are seated at the front of the vehicle behind the engine and each is provided with a side door. The personnel compartment is at the rear of the hull and three men are seated down each side of the hull. Normal means of entry and exit for the passengers is via the twin doors in the rear of the hull. There are two firing ports in each side of the hull and one in each of the rear doors. The basic vehicle is unarmed although smoke dischargers can be provided if required. Optional equipment includes run-flat tyres and a ventilation system.

VARIANTS
The basic vehicle has been designed for internal security operations although it could also be adopted for other roles.

DATA
Crew: 2+6
Weight loaded: 3543kg
Length: 4.292 metres
Width: 1.764 metres
Height: 2.159 metres
Ground clearance: 0.21 metre
Track: 1.358 metres
Wheelbase: 2.768 metres
Tyres: 9.00×16
Turning radius: 8.87 metres

Short SB.301 APC

Maximum road speed: 96km/hr
Range: 368km
Fuel capacity: 100 litres
Engine: Rover 6-cylinder petrol developing 91 BHP at 4500 rpm
Armour: 8.25 metres
Manufacturer: Short Brothers and Harland Limited, Belfast, Northern Ireland
Status: In service in six countries. In production

SPARTAN ARMOURED PERSONNEL CARRIER

The Spartan (FV103) is based on the Scorpion chassis and entered service with the British Army in 1976; it is also in service with the Belgian Army. It is not the replacement for the FV432 but will be used by the Royal Artillery to carry Blowpipe anti-aircraft crews, as a missile re-supply vehicle to support the FV102 Striker and by other arms such as the Royal Engineers and Royal Armoured Corps.

Spartan APC (UK MoD)

Unloading a Spartan

It has a hull of all-welded aluminium construction. The driver is seated at the front of the hull on the left side with the engine to his right. The gunner is to the rear of the driver with the commander to his right. The gunner's cupola is provided with a 7.62mm machine gun which can be aimed and fired from within. The four infantrymen are seated in the personnel compartment at the rear of the hull and normal means of entry and exit is via the single door in the hull rear. In addition there is a two-piece roof hatch over the personnel compartment. No provision is made for the crew to fight from within the vehicle although the infantry are provided with viewing periscopes.

The Spartan is fully amphibious, being propelled in the water by its tracks. Before entering the water a flotation screen is erected, this being carried around the top of the hull. A full range of night vision equipment is fitted as also is an NBC system.

VARIANTS
The Spartan can be fitted with the ZB298 Ground Surveillance Radar and Alvis have suggested that the vehicle could be fitted with the TOW missile system.

DATA
Crew: 3+4
Weight loaded: 8172kg
Length: 4.839 metres
Width: 2.184 metres
Height: 2.25 metres
Ground clearance: 0.356 metre
Track: 1.7 metres
Track width: 432mm
Ground pressure: 0.345kg/cm²
Maximum road speed: 87km/hr
Maximum water speed: 6.4km/hr
Range: 644km
Fuel capacity: 364 litres
Fording: 1.067 metres (amphibious with screen)
Gradient: 70%
Vertical obstacle: 0.508m
Trench: 2.057 metres
Engine: Jaguar 6-cylinder petrol engine developing 195 BHP at 4750 rpm
Armament: 1×7.62mm machine gun with 2000 rounds of ammunition
Manufacturer: Alvis-British Leyland (UK) Limited, Coventry, England. Also built in Belgium at Malines
Status: In production. In service with the British and Belgian Armies

---

AT104 and AT105 INTERNAL SECURITY VEHICLES

In 1971 GKN Sankey built a 4×2 Internal Security vehicle called the AT100, but this was not placed in production and was followed by the AT104 in 1972. This was produced in quantity for the Dutch police and the Royal Brunei Malaya regiment. A further development has been the AT105, the first production model of this being completed in 1976.

AT104: AT104/AT105 are the best-protected of all of the Internal Security vehicles on the market at the present time. The AT104 vehicle has a hull of all-welded construction with the engine at the front. There are twin doors at the hull rear and a single door in each side, one of these being for the use of the driver. The commander's cupola is provided with a single-piece hatch and there are seven firing ports. The automotive components of the AT104/AT105 are standard Bedford commercial components.

AT105: This has a re-designed hull with the engine within the armour envelope. There are twin doors at the rear of the hull and a single door in each side, both of which can be used by the passengers. The commander's cupola has a single-piece hatch cover and is designed so that it can be removed as a complete unit to enable different armament installations to be fitted according to mission requirements.

VARIANTS
The AT104/AT105 can be fitted with a variety of armament installations including .30 and 7.62mm machine guns. Other optional equipment includes run-flat tyres, air conditioning, searchlights, winch, obstacle clearing blade, grenade dischargers and various radio installations.

DATA

	AT104	AT105
Crew:	2 + 9	2 + 8
Weight loaded:	8900kg	9144kg
Weight empty:	8000kg	8230kg
Length:	5.486 metres	5.17 metres

The original GKN Sankey AT 100 design

The AT 104 equipped for obstacle clearance

Width:	2.438 metres	2.489 metres
Height cupola:	2.489 metres	2.59 metres
Ground clearance:	0.457 metre (hull)	0.36 metre (hull)
Track:	2.076 metres (front)	2.06 metres (front
	2.057 metres (rear)	2.302 metres (rear)
Wheelbase:	3.302 metres	3.07 metres
Tyres:	12.00 × 20	12.00 × 20
Turning radius:	7.62 metres	7.15 metres
Maximum road speed:	80km/hr	88.5km/hr
Range:	640km	643km
Fuel capacity:	160 litres	160 litres
Fording:	0.7 metre	1.12 metres
Engine:	6-cylinder petrol	6-cylinder diesel
	developing 134 BHP	developing 146 BHP
	or	or
	6-cylinder diesel	8-cylinder petrol
	developing 98 HP	developing 164 BHP
Armament:	See text	See text
Armour:	6mm-12.5mm	6mm-12.5mm

Manufacturer: GKN Sankey Limited, Wellington, Shropshire, England
Status: AT104 in production and in service with Dutch Police and Royal Brunei Malaya Regiment. AT105 in production and service

The AT 105

UNITED STATES OF AMERICA

HALF-TRACK ARMOURED PERSONNEL CARRIERS

The Americans developed a whole range of half-track armoured personnel carriers before the Second World War and the first of these were in production by the time the USA entered the war. They were built by many companies and there are many variations on the basic vehicle. They have long been phased out of service with the American Army although they are still used by many armies even though the last vehicle was completed in 1945.

The hull is of all-steel construction with the engine at the front, commander and driver in the centre and the personnel compartment at the rear. All models have a door in the side for the commander and driver and most have a single door at the rear of the hull for the infantry. Some have a winch mounted on the front of the hull whilst others have a roller to assist the vehicle in overcoming obstacles. The troop compartment does not have any overhead armour protection. The armament is normally mounted around the sides of the troop compartment. The half-track is not amphibious and does not have an NBC system.

VARIANTS

There are many variants of the half-track including the M14, M16 and M17 with four 0.50 Browning anti-aircraft machine guns, the M13 with twin 0.50 machine guns, the M15 with two 0.50 and one 37mm gun, the M4 and M21 81mm mortar carriers and many local modifications. Israel has an anti-aircraft half-track with twin 20mm cannon, anti-tank vehicles with missiles, recoilless rifle or 90mm Mecar gun, command vehicles, special armoured ambulances and both 81mm and 120mm mortar carriers.

DATA (this relates to the M2A1)
Crew: 10
Weight loaded: 8890kg
Weight empty: 6940kg
Length: 6.137 metres
Width: 2.221 metres
Height: 2.692 metres
Ground clearance: 0.223 metre
Track: 1.637 metres (front) 1.722 metres (rear)
Track width: 305mm
Tyres: 8.25 × 20
Maximum road speed: 64km/hr
Range: 280km
Fuel capacity: 227 litres
Fording: 0.812 metre
Gradient: 60%
Vertical obstacle: 0.304 metre
Engine: White 160 AX 6-cylinder petrol developing 128 HP at 2800 rpm
Armament: 1×0.50 (12.7mm) maching gun in rear
              1×0.30 (7.62mm) machine gun in rear
Armour: 7mm-13mm
Manufacturers (all vehicles): Autocar Company, White Motor Company, Diamond T Motor Company, International Harvester Company
Status: Production complete. In service in Argentina, Belgium, Brazil, Colombia, Cuba, Dominican Republic, Greece, Guatemala, Israel, Italy, Japan, Mexico, Morocco, Portugal, Philippines, Spain, Taiwan, Thailand, Turkey, Uruguay, Venezuela and Yugoslavia

M75 ARMOURED PERSONNEL CARRIER

The M75 was developed shortly after the end of the Second World War and entered production in March, 1952, the final one being completed in February, 1954. It was replaced in the American Army by the M59 APC. The hull of the M75 is of all-welded steel construction. The driver is seated at the front of the hull on the left side with the engine on his right. The commander's/gunner's cupola is in the centre of the roof. The personnel compartment is at the rear and this is provided with two roof hatches, normal entry is via two doors in the hull rear. The 0.50 machine gun is on a pintle mount and has an elevation of +45° and a depression of −25°; 1800 rounds of 0.50 ammunition are carried. The M75 is not amphibious and does not have an NBC system; infra-red driving lights are provided. There is no provision for the crew to fight from within the vehicle.

VARIANTS

There are no variants of the M75 in service.

DATA
Crew: 2+10
Weight loaded: 18,828kg
Weight empty: 16,632kg

Length: 5.193 metres
Width: 2.844 metres
Height with machine gun: 3.041 metres
Ground clearance: 0.457 metre
Track width: 533mm
Ground pressure: 0.57kg/cm²
Maximum road speed: 71km/hr
Range: 185km
Fuel capacity: 568 litres
Fording without kit: 1.219 metres
Fording with kit: 2.032 metres
Gradient: 60%
Vertical obstacle: 0.457 metre
Trench: 1.676 metres
Engine: Continental AO-895-4 6-cylinder petrol developing 295 BHP at 2660 rpm
Armament: 1×0.50 (12.7mm) machine gun
Armour: 9.5mm-25.5mm
Manufacturers: FMC Corporation and International Harvester Company
Status: Production complete. In service only with the Belgian Army

M59 ARMOURED PERSONNEL CARRIER

The M59 was developed as a replacement for the earlier M75 APC and was in production from 1954 to 1959. It is no longer in service with the United States Army having been replaced by the M113 APC. The hull of the M59 is of all-welded steel construction. The driver is seated at the front on the left side and the commander on the right side. The personnel compartment is at the rear of the hull and this is provided with two roof hatches, normal entry and exit is via the hydraulically operated ramp in the rear of the hull. The vehicle has two engines, one being mounted in each side of the hull. The M59 is armed with a single 0.50 (12.7mm) Browning machine gun which is mounted on a pintle mount or in a cupola. The latter has a traverse of 360° and the machine gun can be elevated from −11° to +57°. 2000 rounds of machine gun ammunition are carried.

The M59 is fully amphibious, being propelled in the water by its tracks; infra-red night vision equipment is provided but there is no NBC system.

VARIANTS

The basic vehicle can be adapted for use as a load carrier, ambulance or command vehicle. The only other variant in service is the M84 mortar carrier. This is armed with a 4.2 inch (107mm) mortar and carries 88 mortar bombs.

DATA
Crew: 2+10
Weight loaded: 19,323kg

Weight empty: 17,916kg
Length: 5.163 metres
Width: 3.263 metres
Height cupola: 2.387 metres
Ground clearance: 0.457 metre
Track width: 533mm
Ground pressure: 0.51kg/cm²
Maximum road speed: 51.5km/hr
Maximum water speed: 6.9km/hr
Range: 164km
Fuel capacity: 518 litres

Fording: Amphibious
Gradient: 60%
Vertical obstacle: 0.46 metre
Trench: 1.676 metres
Engines: 2×GMC Model 302 6-cylinder petrol developing 127 HP at 3350 rpm each
Armament: 1×0.50 (12.7mm) M2 Machine Gun
Armour: 10mm-16mm
Manufacturer: FMC Corporation, San Jose, California
Status: Production complete. In service in Brazil, Ethiopia, Greece, Lebanon, Turkey and Vietnam

M113 SERIES ARMOURED PERSONNEL CARRIER

The M113 was designed by FMC as a replacement for the earlier M59 and M75 APCs. The first prototypes were completed in 1958 with the first production vehicles following in 1960. The first model was the M113 which was powered by a petrol engine: it was followed in 1963 by the first production M113A1 which is the current production model and is powered by a diesel engine. To date over 65,000 M113s have been built by FMC and the vehicle is also built in Italy by Oto Melara. Further development of the vehicle has resulted in the AIFV for which there is a separate entry. The M113 will be supplemented in the United States Army by the XM723 MICV which is still being developed by FMC, and should enter service in 1978.

The hull of the M113 is of all-welded aluminium construction. The driver is seated at the front of the hull on the left side with the engine to his right. The commander's cupola is in the centre of the roof and a .50 (12.7mm) Browning machine gun, is mounted on a pintle mount, has an elevation of +53° and a depression of −21°. 2000 rounds of .50 ammunition are carried. The personnel compartment is at the rear of the vehicle and normal entry and exit is via the hydraulically operated ramp in the hull rear: there is also a single hatch over the troop compartment. There is no provision for the crew to fight from within the vehicle.

The M113 is fully amphibious and is propelled in the water by its tracks: infra-red driving lights are provided: there is no NBC system in the basic vehicle.

VARIANTS

The basic vehicle can be adapted for use as a load carrier or an ambulance and there are a number of add-on kits such as NBC kit, heater kit, and gun shield kits. The following variants are in service but there are many local modifications also.

Bridgelayer: This has a scissors type bridge which unfolds over the front.
Australia: Has a number of modified M113s including M113 with Saladin turret, M113 with Scorpion turret, M113 with Commando armoured car turret.
Radar M113: The M113 has been adapted by various countries to mount different radar installations such as the British Green Archer.
M113 TOW: Many countries have fitted the M113 with the American TOW missile.
Swiss M113s: Some have the Hägglunds 20mm turret and Switzerland has her own mortar carriers (see Swiss mortar section for details).
M113 Fitters' Vehicle: This has a modified roof and is provided with a hydraulic crane.
M806A1 Recovery: This is a M113A1 with a winch mounted in the hull rear and it is also provided with spades.
M113 Bulldozer: This is a basic vehicle with a dozer blade mounted at the front of the hull.
Italian M113s: Oto Melara also offer various armament installations for the M113 and have developed a similar vehicle to the AIFV.
German M113s: The German Army has many modified M113s including over 500 with 120mm mortars in the rear and many special fire control vehicles.
M106/M106A1 Mortar Carrier: This is armed with a 107mm (4.2inch) mortar and carries a total of 88 mortar bombs.
M125A1 Mortar Carrier: This is armed with an 81mm mortar on a baseplate with a traverse of 360°. For full details of the M106 and M125 mortar vehicles refer to the mortar section.
M132A1 Flamethrower: This has the commander's cupola replaced with a flamethrower with a traverse of 360°. A 7.62mm machine gun is mounted co-axially with the flamethrower.
M577A1 Command Post: This has a much higher roof than the basic M113 and has additional radios and other equipment. A tent can be erected at the rear if required.
M163 Vulcan Air Defence System: This is armed with a turret mounted six-barrelled Vulcan anti-aircraft gun with a traverse of 360°, elevation is from −5° to +80°.
M548 Tracked Cargo Carrier: The basic M548 is used to carry cargo but there are many local modifications of this and the British Aircraft Corporation has developed a tracked Rapier A/A missile system on the M548. The M548 chassis is also used for the Lance SSM system, the Hawk Missile System and the Chaparral Missile System.

DATA (M113A1)
Crew: 2 + 11
Weight loaded: 11,156kg
Weight empty: 9,702kg
Length: 4.863 metres
Width: 2.686 metres
Height overall: 2.5 metres

M113 APC with M577A1 Command Post Vehicle behind (US Army)

M113 on a river crossing in Vietnam (US Army)

M113 made in Italy by Oto Melara

Ground clearance: 0.406 metre
Track: 2.159 metres
Track width: 381mm
Ground pressure: 0.55kg/cm²
Maximum road speed: 5.8km/hr
Range: 483km
Fuel capacity: 360 litres
Fording: Amphibious
Gradient: 60%
Vertical obstacle: 0.61 metre

Trench: 1.68 metres
Engine: GMC Model 6V53 6-cylinder diesel developing 215 BHP at 4000 rpm
Armament: 1 × .50 (12.7mm) Machine Gun
Armour: 12mm-38mm
Manufacturers: FMC Corporation, San Jose, California, USA. Oto Melara, Le Spezia, Italy

Status: In production. In service in Argentina, Australia, Bolivia, Brazil, Cambodia, Canada, Chile, Denmark, Ecuador, Ethiopia, West Germany, Guatemala, Greece, Haiti, Iran, Israel, Italy, Laos, Lebanon, Libya, Netherlands, New Zealand, Norway, Pakistan, Peru, Philippines, Somalia, South Korea, Spain, Switzerland, Taiwan, Turkey, United States, Uruguay, and Vietnam

XM723 MECHANISED INFANTRY COMBAT VEHICLE

In the late 1950s and early 1960s, a number of prototypes of a MICV were built in the United States but none were placed in production. Late in 1972, the FMC Corporation, who build the M113 series of APCs, were awarded a contract to design a MICV for the United States Army. The prototypes are now being tested and the XM723 should enter production in 1978. The XM723 will replace some but not all M113s; only a percentage of them will be replaced in what the American Army calls a high/low threat mix.

The hull is of all-welded aluminium construction with the front, vertical sides and hull rear having a sheet of steel armour added a short distance from the aluminium armour. This provides added protection against anti-tank weapons.

The driver is seated at the front of the vehicle on the left side with the engine on his right. The commander is seated behind the driver. The turret is in the centre of the vehicle with the troop compartment at the rear. Normal entry and exit is via a ramp at the hull rear and there is also a hatch over the compartment. There are six firing ports, two in each side of the hull and two in the ramp.

The armament on the prototypes consists of a 20mm M139 cannon with a co-axial 7.62mm machine gun. The guns have an elevation of +60° and a depression of −9°, total traverse being 360°. 600 rounds of 20mm and 3400 rounds of 7.62mm ammunition are carried. Production vehicles will be armed with a 25mm Bushmaster cannon although early production vehicles will have the 20mm weapon.

The XM723 is fully amphibious being propelled in the water by its tracks. An NBC system is provided and a full range of night vision equipment is fitted.

VARIANTS

The basic vehicle will be able to be used as a load carrier, ambulance or command vehicle. Other variants envisaged include an TOW-equipped anti-tank vehicle, a reconnaissance vehicle to replace the M114 and an anti-aircraft vehicle with Roland missiles, although there is now some doubt about this.

DATA

Crew: 11-12
Weight loaded: 19,500kg
Weight empty: 17,690kg
Length: 6.35 metres
Width: 3.2 metres
Height overall: 2.768 metres
Ground clearance: 0.482 metre
Track width: 533mm
Ground pressure: 0.49kg/cm²
Maximum road speed: 72km/hr
Maximum water speed: 6km/hr
Range: 483km
Fuel capacity: 746 litres
Fording: Amphibious
Gradient: 60%
Vertical obstacle: 0.914 metre
Trench: 2.54 metres

XM723 MICV prototype by FMC

An earlier prototype MICV built by Pacific Car and Foundry Co. (US Army)

Engine: Cummins VTA-903 diesel developing 450 HP at 2600 rpm
Armament: 1×20mm cannon
　　　　　　1×7.62mm co-axial machine gun
Manufacturer: FMC Corporation, San Jose, California, USA
Status: Trials. Not yet in production

ARMOURED INFANTRY FIGHTING VEHICLE (AIFV)

In the 1960s FMC built prototypes of a vehicle called the XM765. These were basically standard M113s adapted to undertake a MICV role. As a private venture FMC further developed this into a vehicle known as the Armoured Infantry Fighting Vehicle, or AIFV. This was demonstrated in Europe in 1973 and the vehicle is now in production for the Royal Netherlands Army; deliveries should start early in 1977 and run through to 1978. The AIFV uses many components of the standard M113A1 APC.

The hull of the AIFV is of all-welded aluminium construction with an additional layer of steel armour bolted to the sides of the hull. The space between the aluminium and steel has been filled with foam to give increased buoyancy.

The driver is seated at the front of the vehicle on the left side with the engine on his right. The commander is seated behind the driver with the personnel compartment at the rear. Normal entry and exit is via the hydraulically-operated ramp in the rear of the hull: there is also a hatch over the personnel compartment. There are five firing ports, two in each side of the hull and one in the ramp. Various armament installations are available: those being delivered to The Netherlands will be armed with a 25mm cannon and a co-axial 7.62mm machine gun which are mounted in a turret with an elevation of +55° and a depression of −10°: traverse is a full 360°. Total ammunition capacity consists of 315 rounds of 25mm and 1840 rounds of 7.62mm ammunition.

The AIFV is fully amphibious being propelled in the water by its tracks. A full range of night vision equipment is available. It is not fitted with an NBC system although a ventilation system is provided.

VARIANTS

Other armament installations are available including a low-profile installation of a 20mm cannon or a .50 machine gun. FMC have suggested that the vehicle can be used as a command post, TOW anti-tank vehicle, mortar vehicle towing a 120mm mortar, ambulance, cargo vehicle or recovery vehicle with a winch.

DATA

Crew: 10
Weight loaded: 13,470kg
Weight empty: 11,292kg
Length: 5.258 metres
Width: 2.819 metres
Height: 2.784 metres overall
Ground clearance: 0.432 metre
Track: 2.159 metres
Track width: 381mm
Ground pressure: 0.66kg/cm²
Maximum road speed: 61.2km/hr
Maximum water speed: 6.3km/hr
Range road: 490km
Fuel capacity: 416 litres
Fording: Amphibious
Gradient: 60%
Vertical obstacle: 0.635 metre

Trench: 1.676 metre
Engine: Detroit Diesel Model 6V53T diesel developing 264 BHP at 2800 rpm

Armament: 1×25mm cannon
        1×7.62mm machine gun co-axial with above
Manufacturer: FMC Corporation, San Jose, California, USA
Status: In production. On order for the Royal Netherlands Army

COMMANDO SERIES OF ARMOURED PERSONNEL CARRIER

The Commando series of 4×4 armoured vehicles were developed in the early 1960s by the Cadillac Gage Company. The first model was the V-100 which entered production in 1964. It was followed by the much bigger V-200, and this in turn has been followed by the V-150 which is essentially a modified V-100. Well over 2000 Commandos of all types have been built. They can be adapted for a wide variety of roles including use as an armoured personnel carrier, command/radio vehicle, internal security vehicle, anti-tank vehicle, mortar carrier and reconnaissance vehicle. The hull of the Commando is of all-welded construction. The driver is seated at the front of the vehicle on the left side. Doors are provided in each side of the hull and at the rear on the right side of the hull. The armament installation is in the centre of the roof and there are hatches in the roof to the front and to the rear of the turret. The engine is at the rear of the vehicle on the left side. There are nine firing ports arranged around the hull. The Commando is fully amphibious, being propelled in the water by its wheels. Infra-red driving lights are provided as also is a winch in the front of the hull. There is no NBC system.

Commando V-100 with twin MG turret

VARIANTS
V-100: (1) Fitted with a turret mounting twin .30 machine guns or a single .30 and a .50 machine gun; **(2)** Fitted with a pod and used in the command role; **(3)** Open top fitted with single 7.62mm or .30 machine gun; **(4)** Mortar carrier with 81mm mortar; **(6)** Anti-tank vehicle with TOW or Dragon missiles; **(7)** 7.62mm General Electric machine gun in a turret; **(8)** Recovery vehicle with A frame.
V-150: (1) APC; **(2)** Mortar carrier with 81mm mortar; **(3)** Reconnaissance vehicle with turret mounted 20mm cannon with a co-axial 7.62mm machine gun. A further 7.62mm machine gun is mounted on the roof for anti-aircraft defence; **(4)** Similar turret as before but with a 90mm Mecar gun; **(5)** Recovery vehicle; **(6)** Anti-tank vehicle with TOW or Dragon missiles; **(7)** Riot control vehicle; **(8)** IS vehicle.
V-200: Similar models to the above but there is also a 120mm mortar carrier.

Commando V-150 with 20mm cannon

DATA

	V-100	V-150	V-200
Crew:	12	12	12
Weight loaded:	7370kg	9550kg	12,730kg
Weight empty:	5910kg	6820kg	9298kg
Length:	5.689 metres	5.689 metres	6.121 metres
Width:	2.26 metres	2.26 metres	2.438 metres
Height turret top:	2.438 metres	2.54 metres	2.489 metres
Ground clearance:	0.406 metre	0.381 metre	0.431 metre
Track:	1.866 metres	1.942 metres	2.038 metres (front) 2.076 metres (rear)
Wheelbase:	2.667 metres	2.667 metres	3.263 metres
Tyres:	14.00 × 20	14.00 × 20	16.00 × 20
Maximum road speed:	100km/hr	88km/hr	96km/hr
Water speed:	4.8km/hr	4.8km/hr	4.8km/hr
Range road:	500/965km	500/965km	600km
Fuel capacity:	303 litres	303 litres	379 litres
Fording:	Amphibious	Amphibious	Amphibious
Gradient:	50%	60%	60%
Vertical obstacle:	0.609 metre	0.609 metre	0.609 metre
Angle of approach:	55°	55°	50°
Angle of departure:	53°	53°	50°
Engine:	Chrysler 361 petrol 200 HP	Chrysler 361 petrol 200 HP or Cummins diesel 155 HP	Chrysler 440 CID 275 HP

Commando V-200 with 90mm Mecar gun

Manufacturer: Cadillac Gage Company, Warren, Michigan, USA
Status: In production. In service in Bolivia, Ethiopia, Laos, Lebanon, Malaysia, Oman, Peru, Portugal, Saudi Arabia, Singapore, Somalia, Sudan, Turkey, United States, and Vietnam

LVTP-7 AMPHIBIOUS ASSAULT VEHICLE

In 1966 the FMC Corporation started to develop a vehicle to replace the LVTP-5 Amphibious Assault Vehicle then in use by the United States Marine Corps. The first prototype was completed in 1967 with the first production vehicles being completed in 1971 and final deliveries made in 1974. The hull of the LVTP-7 is of all-welded aluminum armour construction. The driver is seated at the front of the vehicle on the left side with the engine on his right. The commander is seated behind the driver and the gunner is on the right side of the hull. The personnel compartment is at the rear of the hull and entry to this is via a hydraulically operated ramp in the rear of the hull: in addition there are roof hatches. The LVTP-7 is fully amphibious and is propelled in the water by two water-jets. Infra-red night vision equipment is fitted but it is not provided with an NBC system. The armament consists of a .50 (12.7mm) machine gun in a turret with a traverse of 360°: elevation limits are from −15° to +60°: 1000 rounds of ammunition are carried.

LVTP-7 Amphibious Assault Vehicle

VARIANTS

The basic vehicle is used to transport Marines from ships offshore to the beach area and if required to inland areas. It can be quickly adapted for the cargo role or ambulance role. The other variants are listed below.

LVTR-7 (Landing Vehicle Tracked, Recovery Model 7): This is provided with a full range of repair equipment and a hydraulic crane with a maximum capacity of 4309kg. Crew of 5.

LVTC-7 (Landing Vehicle Tracked, Command, Model 7): This has a crew of 13 and is provided with additional radios, a generator and an air filtration system.

LVTE-7: This was an engineer model and has not been placed in production. There was also to have been a howitzer-armed model of the LVTP but this was not built.

DATA

Crew: 3+25
Weight loaded: 23,655kg
Weight empty: 18,257kg
Length: 7.943 metres
Width: 3.27 metres
Height overall: 3.263 metres
Ground clearance: 0.406 metre
Track: 2.609 metres
Track width: 533mm
Ground pressure: 0.57kg/cm²
Maximum road speed: 64km/hr
Maximum water speed: 13.5km/hr
Range land: 482km
Fuel capacity: 681 litres
Fording: Amphibious
Gradient: 70%
Vertical obstacle: 0.914 metre
Trench: 438 metres
Engine: Detroit Diesel Model 8V53T 8-cylinder diesel developing 400 HP at 2800 rpm
Armament: 1×M85 0.50 (12.7mm) machine gun
Armour: 6mm-35mm
Manufacturer: FMC Corporation, San Jose, California, USA
Status: Production complete. In service in Argentina, Italy, Spain, Thailand, and the United States

LVTP-7 on the beach

The vehicle's swimming prowess is evident

YUGOSLAVIA

M60 ARMOURED PERSONNEL CARRIER

The M60 APC has been in service with the Yugoslav Army since 1965. The hull is of all-welded steel construction with the suspension and track being based on the Soviet SU-76 SPG. The driver is seated at the front of the hull on the left side with the assistant driver on his right. The commander is behind the driver and the gunner is on the commander's right. The personnel compartment is at the rear of the hull and the normal entry to this is via twin doors in the rear: hatches are provided in the roof of the compartment. Firing ports are provided in the sides of the hull and there is also a single firing port in each of the rear doors. The top armament consists of a .50 M2 machine gun and there is also a 7.9mm M53 machine gun in the glacis plate firing forwards. The M60 is fully amphibious being propelled in the water by its tracks: it is not fitted with NBC or night vision equipment.

VARIANTS

There are no known variants of the M60 APC although it is probably used as an ambulance, cargo or command vehicle.

DATA

Crew: 3+10
Weight loaded: 9500kg
Length overall: 5.05 metres
Width: 2.75 metres
Height excluding machine gun: 1.8 metres
Ground clearance: 0.35 metre
Track: 2.37 metres

M90 APC on parade

Track width: 300mm
Maximum road speed: 45km/hr
Water speed: 6km/hr
Range: 400km
Fuel capacity: 130 litres
Gradient: 60%
Vertical obstacle: 0.6 metre

Trench: 2 metres
Engine: FAMOS 6-cylinder diesel developing 140 HP
Armament: 1×.50 machine gun on roof
          1×7.9mm machine gun in glacis plate
Armour: 10mm-25mm
Manufacturer: Yugoslav State factories
Status: Production complete. In service in Cyprus and Yugoslavia

M-980 MECHANISED INFANTRY COMBAT VEHICLE

The M-980 was first seen in Yugoslavia in 1975 and is now in service with the Yugoslav Army as the replacement for the older M-60 APC. In appearance it is similar to the Soviet BMP-1 MICV but in fact it uses some components of the new French MICV, the AMX-10P.

The hull is of all-welded steel construction although there is a possibility that some aluminium armour has also been used. The driver is seated at the front of the hull on the left side with the engine on his right. The commander is seated behind the driver and the turret is in the centre of the hull. The latter is armed with a 20mm cannon and a co-axial 7.92mm machine gun having a maximum elevation of 50° and a depression of −7°: mounted on the turret rear are two launcher rails for the Sagger ATGW. The troop compartment is at the rear and normal entry and exit is via the twin doors in the hull rear: there are also two roof hatches. The personnel compartment is provided with firing ports in the sides and rear. The M-980 is fully amphibious and is propelled in the water by its tracks. A full range of night vision equipment is provided, as is also an NBC system.

VARIANTS

There are no variants of the M-980 MICV.

DATA (Provisional)
Crew: 3+7
Weight loaded: 12,000kg
Weight empty: 11,000kg
Length: 6.25 metres
Width: 2.85 metres
Height: 2.16 metres
Track width: 300mm
Maximum road speed: 70km/hr
Maximum water speed: 8km/hr
Range: 500km
Engine: HS 115-2 8-cylinder diesel developing 276 HP at 3000 rpm
Armament: 1×20mm cannon
          1×7.92mm machine gun co-axial with main armament
          2 Sagger launchers
Manufacturer: Yugoslav State factories
Status: In service with the Yugoslav Army

SECTION FIVE

SIGHTING AND SURVEILLANCE SYSTEMS

SIGHTING AND SURVEILLANCE EQUIPMENT
BATTLEFIELD SURVEILLANCE RADARS AND INTRUDER ALARMS
REMOTE HANDLING EQUIPMENT
MINE DETECTORS

SIGHTING AND SURVEILLANCE EQUIPMENT

INTRODUCTION

In the first two sub-sections of this section are described several of the devices which have been developed in recent years to make it possible for the soldier to operate more effectively in difficult terrain or bad light. Some of these devices effect only a marginal improvement: some, for example, make it easier to aim a rifle accurately in conditions of visibility in which the target can be seen with tolerable ease. At the other extreme however, there are types of equipment now in or approaching service use which will often enable the soldier to determine with remarkable clarity what is happening even in pitch darkness or in thick vegetation.

The variety of instruments and equipments which could be said to contribute to the operation of surveillance or weapon sighting is very extensive; and in order to limit this section to a manageable size we have not attempted an exhaustive treatment of normal daytime optical devices (such as binoculars, telescopes or telescopic sights) and certain specialised devices which, although they may upon occasion (or even often) be used by infantry, are strictly appropriate to other specialist military operations. Three broad categories of these specialised equipments are briefly described below.

First there are numerous devices associated with the general problem of detecting, locating and removing or destroying explosive devices such as mines, booby-traps and other explosive apparatus. Specialised disposal techniques lie outside the range of normal infantry operations, but mine detecting and searching for bombs and booby-traps are tasks which may, (and recently frequently have) come the way of any soldier. In addition to the familiar mine detector recent developments have included explosive detection devices and the Wheelbarrow remotely-controlled viewing and handling machine which has achieved fame duri. g operations in Northern Ireland.

Secondly the many advances in the application of laser technology to the solution of military problems have included the introduction of several techniques whereby co-operating aircraft, 'smart' bombs, laser-guided shells and other munitions can be directed to a target by a man on the ground (or elsewhere) operating a laser designator – a gun-like device which projects a laser beam to the target which is reflected and detected by an airborne or projectile-borne homing system. A few representative entries in both these categories are included in the section.

Finally, there has been talk for many years of applying secondary radar techniques to the problem of locating and controlling men on the move. Not very much has so far been done, although the idea has been current for twenty years or more, but two small steps forward may be briefly mentioned: one proposal involves the carriage, by one member of a patrol, of a transponder which could be interrogated from time to time to locate the

Shown here is the patrol equipment of the PLRS – Position Locating and Reporting System developed for the USMC by Hughes Aircraft Company's ground systems group. Signals radiated by the manpack equipment are used by the master station to locate the patrol; and this information can be relayed to the patrol on request if it gets lost.

patrol and perhaps learn something of its activities with only a momentary breach of radio silence. Another and more recent suggestion involves almost exactly the reverse procedure to enable the patrol to locate itself when in blind country.

The bulk of the entries that follow are divided into two groups. In the first will be found descriptions of a variety of night sights, night viewing instruments and other optical devices (including a few laser equipments) arranged by country; in the second, and preceded by another brief introductory note, are descriptions of battlefield radars and some other surveillance systems. The section is completed by some short notes on remote viewing and handling devices and mine detectors.

FRANCE

NI-PE-38 INFRA-RED FIELD GLASSES MK 4

These field glasses are worn attached to the helmet, so as to leave the hand free, and consist of two separately attached identical optical and image conversion assemblies which can be spaced for maximum comfort.

The glasses must be used in conjunction with an infra-red searchlight or similar device. They may be used for any kind of infra-red viewing but are primarily intended for use by drivers.

DATA
Magnification: Unity
Field: 30°
Total weight: 1kg
Power supply: 1.5V battery
Practical range of vision: 50 metres
Manufacturer: Télécommunications Radioélectriques et Téléphoniques (TRT), 88 rue Brillat-Savarin, 75640 Paris Cedex 13
Status: In production and in French Army service

OB-24-A INFRA-RED BINOCULARS

These hand-held waterproof binoculars are designed primarily for use with an infra-red searchlight or similar source; but they can also be used in a passive role to detect infra-red sources up to a wavelength of 1.2 microns.

The binoculars comprise two parallel optical systems, with interpupillary distance adjustment, viewing a single image converter tube powered by a built in battery and power pack.

DATA
Magnification: ×4

Field: 15°
Recording power: Better than 1 mil at the centre of the field
Focussing: Centred on 500 metres, with sharp image from 300 to 1,000 metres
Interpupillary adjustment: 55-72mm
Weight: 2.5kg complete
Power source: 1.3V battery giving 40 hours operational life
Manufacturer: SOPELEM, 102 rue Chaptal, 92306 Levallois-Perret
Status: In production and in service with the French and several other forces

PORTABLE NIGHT OBSERVATION TELESCOPE

This is a small self-contained, hand-held, active infra-red viewing device designed for night observation to a distance of about 100 metres. It has been derived from the NI-PE-38 unit used in the driving binoculars of that reference. A single image converter is viewed through a single eyepiece, the whole being mounted above a housing which contains the built-in searchlight. The telescope is powered by a single small battery, the searchlight is also battery powered but by five cells.

DATA
Magnification: 1.1

Field of view: 28°
Searchlight field: 3° or 6° according to type of lamp
Objective focus: Fixed 1.5 metres or 20 metres
Range: 70-120 metres according to type of lamp
Power supply:Telescope: 1.5V cell giving 40 hours operational life
        Searchlight: 5 NiCd cells giving 1-1½ hour life with 6W lamp
Weight: About 1.6kg
Manufacturer: Télécommunications Radioélectriques et Téléphoniques (TRT), 88, rue Brillat-Savarin, 75640 Paris Cedex 13
Status: Production

DI-PT-7A INFRA-RED EQUIPMENT MK 2

This active infra-red equipment is designed to enable the Mk 49-56 7.5mm semi-automatic rifle to be fired in darkness and can easily be attached to such other rifles as the FN/FAL or M14. It comprises an infra-red searchlight mounted on a sighting telescope and image converter and a separate battery container. This combination of searchlight and sight make it possible to engage targets at ranges up to 200 or 250 metres according to atmospheric conditions.

DATA
Magnification: ×2.4

Field of sight: Approx. 12°
Sight dimensions: 290mm × 55mm
Projector dimensions: Length 110mm, diameter 170mm
Weight: Equipment mounted on weapon approx. 2kg; Battery and bag approx. 5kg
Manufacturer: Télécommunications Radioélectriques et Téléphoniques, 88, rue Brillat-Savarin, 75640 Paris Cedex 13
Status: Production and French Army service

PASSIVE MICROCHANNEL BINOCULARS

TRT have developed two types of passive night viewing binoculars using microchannel light intensifier tubes. One type has unit magnification and is light enough to be worn on the head while driving: the more recent type has ×4 magnification and can be either hand-held or tripod-mounted for longer-range viewing. A tank can be recognised at 500 metres with a luminosity of 1 millilux.

DATA

	Driving Glasses	Viewer
Magnification:	×1	×4
Field:	33°	8°
Focus:	Fixed	20m to infinity
Weight:	0.9kg	1.85kg

Power supply: Mallory 2.7V battery
Manufacturer: Télécommunications Radioélectriques et Téléphoniques (TRT) 88, rue Brillat-Savarin, 75640 Paris Cedex 13
Status: The driving glasses, designated OB-41-A. are in production and in French Army service. The viewer is in series production

TRT microchannel night driving glasses

PASSIVE NIGHT-VISION WEAPON SIGHT

This sight is designed for use with most of the larger infantry weapons, in starlight or moonlight, and is compatible with all such weapons that comply with NATO standards. Basically a straight-through image intensifier system it has an eyepiece that can be swivelled to suit special weapon requirements. A neutral filter enables the sight to be aligned, and the support adjusted, by daylight.

DATA
Magnification: ×4

Field: 10°
Graticule: Adjustable to ±5 mil in elevation and line
Focus: Adjustable from 10 metres to infinity
Typical range: 300 metres
Accessories: Light shield and lens diaphragm
Weight: 2.7kg
Manufacturer: SOPELEM, 102, rue Chaptal 92306, Levallois-Perret
Status: Production and service with French forces.

NIGHT DRIVERSCOPE

SOPELEM manufactures a range of night-driving episcopes for use on tanks, armoured cars and armoured personnel carriers such as the Panhard AML. They are rugged, watertight equipment capable of operating satisfactorily over a wide range of temperatures. The binocular unit is mounted above the driver's position and is coupled directly to the external objective lens system. A manual shutter control adjusts the brightness on the image intensifier photocathodes.

DATA
Field of view: 50°
Magnification: ×0.9

Resolving power: 1.5 mils
Interpupillary distance: 65mm (fixed)
Objective: f1.1
Focus: 30 metres (fixed)
Tube: Thomson-CSF THX458
Power input: 1.5V cell or 6V battery or vehicle power supply
Operating temperature: −40°C to +55°C
Weight: 3.7kg
Manufacturer: SOFELEM, 102, rue Chaptal, 92306 Levallois-Perret
Status: Quantity production

PASSIVE NIGHT OBSERVATION SIGHT VN6

Designed for long-range night observation, this passive sight has a wide-aperture catadioptric lens fully corrected for a spectral range of from 0.4 to 1.0 micron. It will provide observation under optimum conditions for any luminosity level over 10^{-5} lux. With a luminosity of only 10^{-3} lux a man can be seen at 700 metres and a tank at 1,300 metres.

DATA
Magnification: ×6

Field: 7°
Resolution: 0.2 mil at 10^{-2} lux
Operating temperature: −40°C to +55°C
Weight: 12kg
Manufacturer: SOPELEM, 102, rue Chaptal-92306 Levallois-Perret

PORTABLE LASER ILLUMINATOR IPY 43 AND RECEIVER RPL44

Developed under a French Government (DTAT) contract the IPY 43 is a portable illuminator for the designation of ground targets for destruction by laser-marked target-seeking weapons or by any other means which can utilise the laser marking. The equipment comprises an optical sighting telescope mounted on a laser transmitter, the operation of the latter being controlled by a trigger. The laser radiation is pulse modulated and the equipment is battery-operated.

RECEIVER

Although an obvious use of the illuminator is to designate targets for co-operating aircraft, it may be desirable for ground troops to locate the marked target and for this purpose the RPL 44 receiver has been developed. It is a small optical detector which gives the operator a clear visual indication when the marked target is in view. An aiming sight then enables him to locate it visually.

DATA

Illuminator IPY 43:
Wavelength: 1.06 micron
Pulse duration: 20 nanosec
Energy: 60 mJ
Peak power: 3.5MW
Divergence: 0.3 mrad
Repetition rate: 1-10 pulses/sec adjustable
Power supply: 24V battery
Weight: 10kg
Receiver RPL 44:
Range: 3km for a maximum distance of 3km between the illuminator and the target
Locating accuracy: better than 2 mrad
Receiver field of view: elevation: 30°
                      azimuth: 10°
Aiming sight: field of view: 5°
           magnification: ×8
           eyepiece diameter: 25mm
           diopter setting: −2 to +5

Power supply: battery
Weight: 2kg
Manufacturer: Compagnie Industrielle des Lasers, Route de Nozay, 91-Marcoussis

The RPL 44 marked target receiver

French IPY43 Portable Laser Illuminator. It is made by the Compagnie Industrielle des Lasers

GERMANY (FEDERAL REPUBLIC)

INFRA-RED NIGHT SIGHT TYPE B8-V

This is a conventional active infra-red equipment combining an infra-red illuminator and an image convertor sight with a separate power supply and suitable for installation on any conventional rifle or LMG. The sight has an illuminated graticule.

DATA

Sight magnification: ×4
Field of view: more than 7°
IR lamp: 35W
Operational range: more than 300 metres
Length: approx 320mm
Breadth: approx 175mm maximum
Height: approx 255mm maximum
Weight: about 2.6kg
Manufacturer: Eltro GmbH, Gesellschaft für Strahlungstechnik, Kurpfalzring 106, 6900 Heidelberg 1, Kurpfalzring Postfach 520
Status: In production and in service

Eltro B8-V active night sight

ORION 80 PASSIVE NIGHT SIGHT

This is a small-arm night sight using a three-stage image intensifier system. An adjustable reticle is projected into the image plane and its brightness can be increased or diminished to suit the target image.

DATA
Magnification: ×4
Field of view: 8°
Focus range: 20 metres to infinity
Reticle adjustment: ±5 mils in 0.5 mil steps
Eyepiece adjustment: ±5 diopters
Maximum diameter: 95mm approx
Length: 290mm approx
Weight: 1.8kg approx
Power source: 2.5V NiCd rechargeable battery giving 25 hours operation between charges
Manufacturer: Eltro GmbH, Gesellschaft für Strahlungstechnik, Kurpfalzring 106, 6900 Heidelberg 1, Kurpfalzring Postfach 520
Status: In service with West German forces

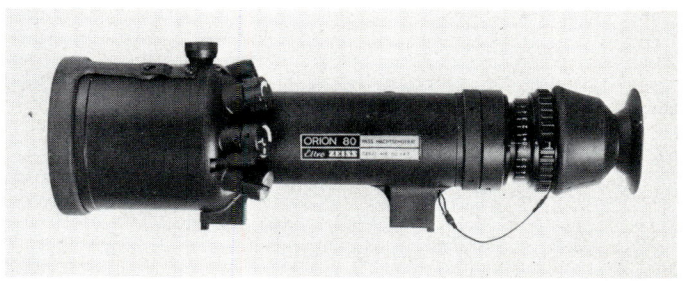

Orion 80 night sight

ORION 110 PASSIVE NIGHT SIGHT

This weapon sight is similar in operation to the Orion 80 sight but larger and having a performance appropriate to larger weapons. Some of the basic electro-optical components, however, are common to both sights.

DATA
Magnification: ×6
Field of view: 6°
Focus range: 40 metres to infinity
Reticle adjustment: ±5 mils in 0.5 mil steps
Eyepiece adjustment: ±5 diopters
Maximum diameter: 120mm approx
Length: 320mm approx
Weight: 2.4kg approx
Power source: 2.5V NiCd rechargeable battery giving 25 hours operation between charges
Manufacturer: Eltro GmbH, Gesellschaft für Strahlungstechnik, Kurpfalzring 106, 6900 Heidelberg 1, Kurpfalzring Postfach 520
Status: In service with West German forces

Orion 110 night sight

PASSIVE INFRA-RED TELESCOPE TYPE BN 21

This is a bi-ocular passive infra-red viewing device which is light enough to be hand held. It is battery-operated and uses a two-stage image intensifier tube.

DATA
Magnification: ×4.5
Field of view: 11°
Length: approx 340mm
Breadth: approx 150mm maximum
Height: approx 95mm maximum
Weight: approx 2.2kg
Manufacturer: Eltro GmbH, Gesellschaft für Strahlungstechnik, Kurpfalzring 106, 6900 Heidelberg 1, Kurpfalzring Postfach 520
Status: In production and service

Eltro passive IR telescope type BN-21

THERMAL DETECTION EQUIPMENT TYPE WZ1

This Eltro device comprises an objective lens and a battery-operated pyro-electric heat detector and is intended for use in conjunction with a night viewing device such as the BN 21 described in the previous entry.

DATA
Length: approx 165mm
Maximum diameter: 80mm
Weight: approx 0.55kg
Manufacturer: Eltro GmbH, Gesellschaft für Strahlungstechnik, Kurpfalzring 106, 6900 Heidelberg 1, Kurpfalzring Postfach 520
Status: In production and service

Eltro thermal detector type WZ1 mounted on a image intensifier telescope type BN 21S

LUNA-TRON NIGHT VISION EQUIPMENT

An extensive range of night sights, night viewing devices and night photography apparatus is made by Infrarot-Technik K. Eiselt of Stuttgart. It is believed that the firm caters largely for the civil sporting, security and police markets; but some of their products are suitable for use in conjunction with military weapons. As an example, the rifle night sight Type 303-Z is available with mounts for both sporting and military rifles and is of rugged construction. For this sight a choice of catadioptric objectives of 135mm f/1.6 or 128mm f/1.5 is available. These lenses are of especially high performance and are supplied in fully waterproof and shock-resistant

configurations appropriate to military use. With a 25mm eyepiece and the 135mm objective the Type 303-Z has a system magnification of ×5.4 and a field of view of nearly 8° and with it a man can be seen by moonlight at about 700 metres (30% target contrast) and by starlight at more than 500 metres.

Manufacturer: Infrarot-Technik K. Eiselt (IRT), 7000 Stuttgart-50 Waiblinger Strasse 5
Status: In production and available

NETHERLANDS

NIGHT VISION GOGGLES TYPE PG 1 MS

These goggles are primarily intended for use by drivers of armoured and soft-skin vehicles.

In a hatch-down position the AFV driver looks out through the central daylight prism. Its hands-free operation also provides paratroops, commandos, recce patrols, sentries and security forces with a useful aid at night.

A snap-on IR light source gives additional illumination for map reading and other short range tasks. If required FP (flash proof) tubes can be incorporated.

DATA
Weight: 900 grams
Magnification: Unity
Field of view: 47°
Focus range: adjustable from 25cms to infinity
Range: Typical up to 150 metres
Manufacturer: NV Optische Industrie "De Oude Delft" Delft, Holland
Status: In quantity production for NATO and other forces

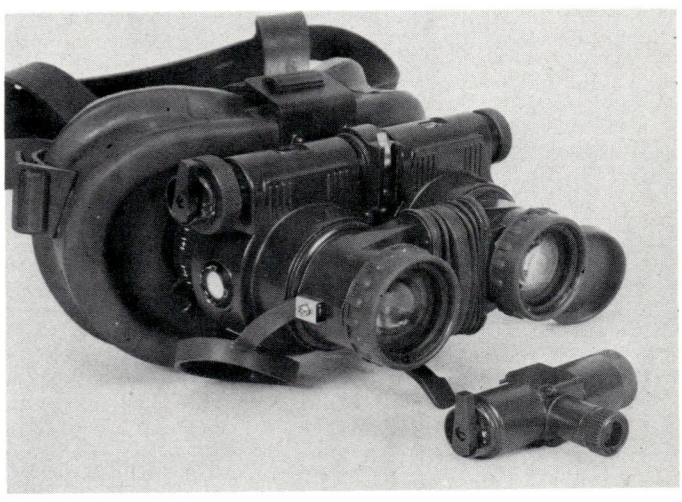

Night vision goggles type PG 1 MS

MINI WEAPON SIGHT TYPE RS 4 TS

This is a small, lightweight image intensifier system for observation and direct firing with weapons at night. Suitable for mounting on most basic infantry weapons, the sight can also be used as a hand-held viewer.

In its modular concept the sight teams up with the crew-served weapon sight having the central housing, incorporating tube and controls, in common.

Design features include automatic brightness control, an adjustable skylight diaphragm to suppress the disturbing effects of night sky illumination, a reticle with adjustable illumination and a manual gain control for operation at dusk and dawn.

For use as a night sight on personal anti-tank weapons the sight is provided with a flashproof (FP) image intensifier tube, preventing flash-burns on the phosphor screen.

DATA
Length: 360mm
Width: 135mm
Weight: 2.1kg
Magnification: ×4
Field of view: 10°
Focus Range: from 30 metres to infinity
Detection range: typically 500 metres on infantry and 1,500 metres on tanks
Manufacturer: NV Optische Industrie "De Oude Delft" Delft, Holland

Weapon sight type RS 4 TS

Status: In quantity production; deliveries to various military and paramilitary forces will start in 1977

PASSIVE BINOCULARS TYPE PB 4 DS

These binoculars are designed for general-purpose night surveillance by AFV commanders, outposts, recce-patrols, border guards, security and police forces. A single two-stage fibre-coupled image intensifier is used to produce a single image which is viewed through a bi-ocular eyepiece.

Included is a FP (flashproof) image intensifier with protection against tube damage resulting from an exposure to high intensity light sources.

DATA
Weight: 2.2kg
Magnification: ×4
Field of view: 10°
Focus range: adjustable from 4 metres to infinity
Detection range: typically 400 metres on infantry and 1,500 metres on tanks
Manufacturer: NV Optische Industrie "De Oude Delft" Delft, Holland
Status: In service with several armed forces and police; continued quantity production

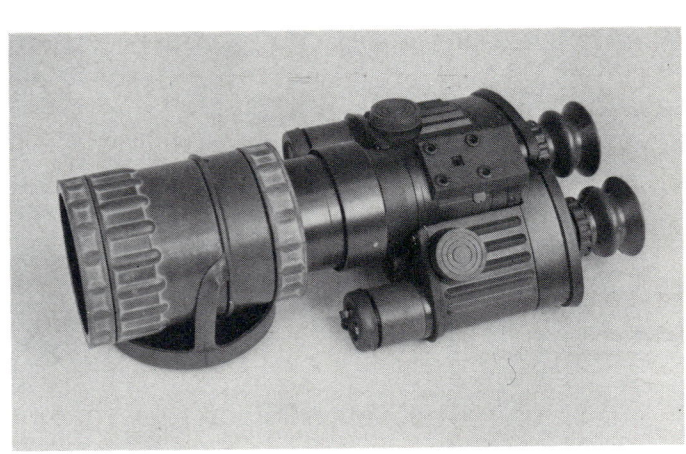

Passive Binoculars type PB 4 DS

CREW SERVED WEAPON SIGHT TYPE GS 6 TS

This night vision sight can be attached to all types of crew served weapons such as heavy machine guns, recoilless rifles and anti-tank guns. The modular design permits the use of either a straight or rectangular-eye piece. Reticles can be fitted matching the ballistics of the weapon concerned. The reticle illumination is adjustable. A sky-light diaphragm and an image brightness control switch have been incorporated for an optimal adaptation to the varying light conditions from dusk till dawn. To prevent tube damage when observing hits on armour special flash-proof tubes (FP) are fitted.

DATA
Length: 430mm
Diameter: 150mm
Weight: 3.2kg
Magnification: ×6
Field of view: 7°
Focus range: adjustable from 50 metres to infinity
Detection range: typically up to 800 metres on infantry and 2,500 metres on tanks
Manufacturer: NV Optische Industrie "De Oude Delft" Delft, Holland
Status: In quantity production for various armies

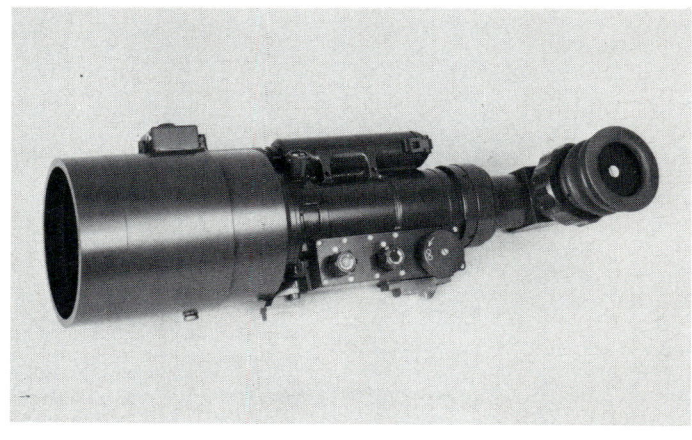

GS 6 TS crew-served weapon sight

NIGHT OBSERVATION AND AIMING DEVICE TYPE 7x200 AT

This is an image intensifier system designed for medium-range surveillance or for use with crew-served weapons. For surveillance the standard monocular eyepiece can be exchanged for a bi-ocular system. A rectangular monocular eyepiece is available to fit the device in a co-axial position on recoilless weapons

Design features include automatic brightness control, a manual gain control, a reticle projector with adjustable illumination, and an adjustable top and bottom field diaphragm to eliminate the disturbing effects of night sky illumination and a highly reflecting foreground.

The image intensifier tube is FP (flash-proof), a feature which prevents damage to the tube due to the observation of excessive light resulting from eg. the impact of APDS on hard targets.

DATA
Length: 550mm
Diameter: 252mm
Weight: 12.8kg
Magnification: ×7
Field of view: 7°
Focus range: adjustable from 50 metres to infinity
Detection range: up to 1,000 metres on infantry and 3,000 metres on tanks

Type 7x200 AT night observation and aiming device

Manufacturer: NV Optische Industrie "De Oude Delft", Delft, Holland
Status: In use with and in quantity production for various armies

NORWAY

SIMRAD HAND-HELD LASER RANGEFINDER LP7

This bi-ocular hand-held laser rangefinder, currently being developed by Simrad is one of several devices that have been produced recently by the manufacturers of laser-based equipment. Weighing only 1.6kg, the LP7 is the same size as a standard 7x50 binocular and as handy in use.

Manufacturer: Simrad as, PO Box 6114, Etterstad, Oslo 6
Status: Development

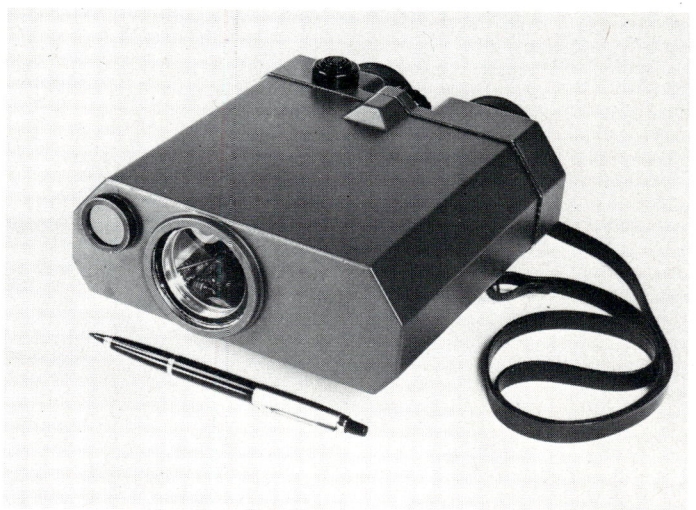

LP7 hand-held laser rangefinder

SIMRAD LASER RANGEFINDER TYPE LP8

The Simrad LP8 Laser Rangefinder is an extremely small, compact and light unit primarily intended for mounting on weapons or night observation devices. It contains all the electronic and optical units required to enable the operator to lay the instrument on a target, make a measurement and read the range to the target presented by the digital display on top of the instrument.

The transmitter is a miniaturized Q-switched Nd:YAG laser. The receiver uses a silicon PIN photodiode giving an operational range to typical military targets of approximately 3-4km when optical visibility is 10km. Unwanted nearby echoes may be gated out from the display by a minimum range control located on the operator's side of the instrument.

The range display is located on top of the instrument and shows the range of one target at a time to the nearest 5 metres. In addition there are two indicators to warn the operator either that more than one target has been detected or that one or more targets have been gated out by the minimum range control.

The display lights up when a range has been measured and switches off after 5 seconds. The rangefinder has been designed on modular principles to simplify repair and maintenance and is contained in a sturdy waterproof housing. Mechanical interfaces suitable for weapons, theodolites and night observation devices are available.

DATA
Dimensions: 78×85×200mm
Weight, excluding battery: 1.2kg
Operating temperature range: −30°C to +55°C
Transmitter:
Laser: Nd: YAG
Wavelength: 1.064 micron
Output energy: 5mJ nominal
Pulse width: 10 nsecs nominal
Pulses per minute: 12 (30 intermittent)
Beam width (90% energy): 1.5 mrad
Q-switch: Saturable dye
Receiver:
Field of view: 1.3 mrad
Type of detector: PIN photodiode optimized for 1.06 um. Optional: Avalanche photodiode
Aperture: 40mm
Clock frequency: 29.97 MHz
Range accuracy: ±5m. Optional: ±2m
Type of display: 7-segment LED
Minimum range setting: 200 metres to 3,000 metres continuous
Telescope:
Magnification: ×7
Field of view: Approximately 100 mils
Aperture: 40mm
Eye protection: Dichroic beamsplitter and absorption glass in eyepiece
Power Supply:
Recommended battery: NiCd-battery 12 volts/0.22 Ah rechargeable
Number of shots per battery before recharging: Approximately 300 at +25°C
Manufacturer: Simrad as, PO Box 6114, Etterstad, Oslo 6
Status: Trials

SWEDEN

AIMPOINT ELECTRONIC SIGHT

This electronic sight has been introduced by Aimpoint AB in Sweden and is claimed to enable the firer to aim more quickly and more accurately than he can with a conventional iron sight.

In the Aimpoint device the iron sights are replaced by a single battery-powered optical and electronic unit; and the eyepiece of this unit is designed to be viewed by one eye while the other eye remains open; the firer's field of view thus embraces more than can be seen through a telescope eyepiece; and the sight cover is less obtrusive than it is if only one eye is used. The electronics of the system cause a small bright red dot to appear in the field of view coincident with the point of aim of the weapon and the other eye associates this dot with a point in the field of view: in order to aim correctly, therefore, the firer has to bring this dot into coincidence with the desired target.

The position of the dot depends on the pointing direction of the weapon and is not altered by movement of the firer's head: when it is in coincidence with the target, therefore, the system is parallax-free.

Further development of the sight to introduce brightness control, improved battery life and provision for aiming off for movement is envisaged. In the meantime some encouraging trials have been conducted. During a test at FN in Belgium in which FN rifles fitted with Aimpoint Electronic sights were checked in late twilight against similar rifles with conventional iron sights, the inventor of the sight (Mr A. Ekstrand) and three professional marksmen each fired ten rounds in half a minute. With iron sights they scored 4 hits between them and with the new sight they scored 36.
Manufacturer: Aimpoint AB, Borrgatan 31, 211 24 Malmö.
Status: Production and commercial sales now in hand

PERISCOPIC RANGEFINDER TYPE A40P

This is a rugged but precisely made optical coincidence rangefinder which is light and handy enough to be carried and used conveniently by a foot soldier but which is capable of range measurement accuracy of 0.5 per cent at 400 metres or 2.3 per cent at 1,500 metres. Good results have been obtained in its large-scale use by the Swedish Army.

The rangefinder can be used either vertically or horizontally and is also a useful observation periscope. For rangefinding the projection beyond cover need be no more than 45cm. Ranges up to 1,500 metres are read directly from a scale close to the field of view in the eyepiece. Adjustment is by means of a conical roller which enables coarse and fine movements to be made with a single knob.

DATA
Measuring base: 40cm
Measuring range: 100-1,500 metres
Magnification: ×8
Field of view: 70×75 milliradians

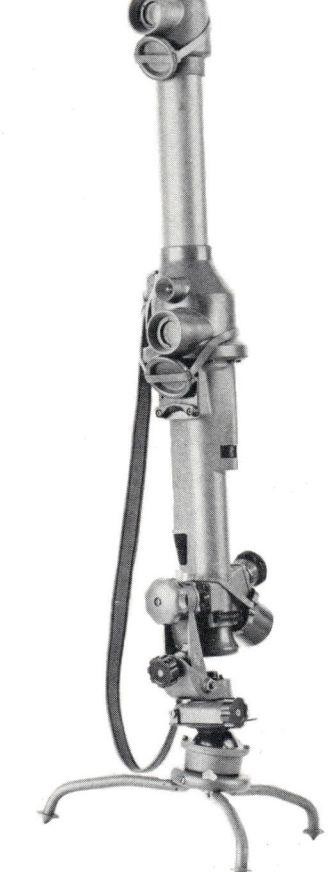

The A40P periscopic rangefinder with optional tripod

Measurement can be made vertically or horizontally

Exit pupil: Corresponds to a circle of 2.5mm diameter
Eye clearance: 20mm from outer lens surface
Periscopic height: 28 and 68cm
Eyepiece angle: +20° from horizontal plane
Best practical measuring accuracy: 400 metres range: 2 metres or 0.5%; 1,000 metres range: 16 metres or 1.6%; 1,500 metres range: 35 metres or 2.3%
Total length of instrument: 840mm
Total height in vertical position
　with simple support: 1,035mm

　with tripod: 1,095mm
Total height in horizontal position
　with simple support: 340mm
　with tripod: 405mm
Weight: 4.5kg
Outer dimensions of transport case: 940 × 265 × 210mm
Manufacturer: Jungner Instrument AB, Optical Division, Fack, S-171 20, SOLNA 1, Stockholm
Status: Production (5,000) complete. In service since 1965 in the Swedish Army

RS-322 TELESCOPIC SIGHT

This sight is intended primarily for use on such weapons as the Carl Gustaf M2 anti-tank rifle. It is of rugged construction, has a one-piece housing and exterior lenses made of hard crown glass.

The reticle of the RS-322 is provided with built-in betalight night illumination system which affords exceptionally high luminous efficiency. A special version of the sight can also be supplied with a bulb fitting for battery-operated illumination of the reticle. In this version the reticle is illuminated in such a manner that it will also stand out in daylight and against a light background.

The lateral and vertical boresighting adjustment of the reticle is made with the aid of two graduated knobs, which can be locked in position. In order to attain a high degree of mechanical strength and reliability in the boresighting mechanism, the reticle is mounted in a flexible tube instead of being suspended on riveted or screwed-down springs.

RS-322 Telescopic Sight

DATA
Length: 236mm
Diameter: 31-35mm including projections
Magnification: ×3
Field of view: 12°
Objective diameter: 22mm
Exit pupil: 7mm
Eye relief: 38mm
Eyepiece focus, fixed: −0.75 diopter
Manufacturer: Jungner Instrument AB, Optical Division Fack, S-171 20 SOLNA 1, Stockholm
Status: Production ceased recently but may be restarted. Sight is in Swedish Army service

ANTI-AIRCRAFT SIGHT TYPE KS-2

This is a small anti-aircraft sight for use with light automatic weapons and features a new type of optical presentation of lead angle.

The sight consists of a combination prism and a slightly reducing telescopic system. The image from the telescopic system is combined with the directly observed target in the combination prism so that the eye sees two images of the target one of which is larger than the other. When the sight is aimed at a fixed target the images should coincide and form one image only. When the sight is aimed at a moving target the larger image should chase the small image with a certain multiple of target lengths between them. This multiple is easy to learn and is taken from a precalculated table for each type of weapon.

The angle between the two images is a fictitious lead angle and forms only one-fifth of the real lead angle. One attractive feature of the sight is therefore that the eye needs to receive information from only a small part of the field of view.

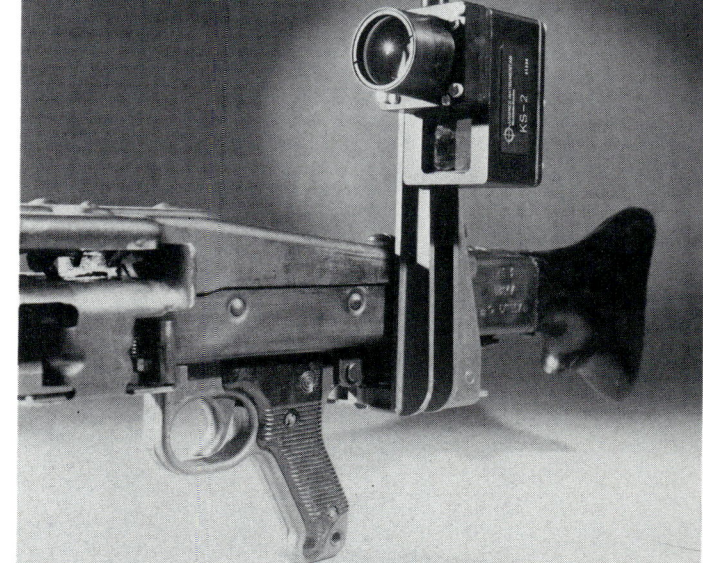

KS2 Sight on a German MG3

DATA
Free eye movement: approx 32 × 32mm
Field of view for 50mm eye-to-sight separation
　direct: 480 mils
　through telescope: 350 mils
Engagement range: 100-1,500 metres depending on visibility
Weight: 1kg including sight holder
Operating temperature: −40°C to +40°C
Manufacturer: Jungner Instrument AB, Optical Division, Fack, S-171 20 SOLNA 1, Stockholm
Status: Development since 1974

AS-1 RANGE AND LEAD-FINDING SIGHT

This advanced optical-electronic sighting system is the standard fitment on the FFV 550 84mm anti-tank weapon but could also be used with other weapons with suitable modifications.

Rangefinding, lead finding and aiming involve three distinct sequential operations. When the target is viewed through the eyepiece the images from the two objectives (see photograph) are displayed as a composite of which the upper section comes from one objective and the lower section from the other. By rotating the range drum of the sight any lateral displacement between the two parts of the target image can be corrected; this process in fact measures the range to the target but need not be read.

The sight trigger switch is then pressed and this causes light pulses (twinkles) to appear in the field of view. The spacing of these twinkles corresponds to the time of flight of the FFV 550 HEAT round to the range determined in the first operation. Any crossing motion of the target can be measured in terms of this time of flight, therefore, using a horizontal scale on the sight graticule.

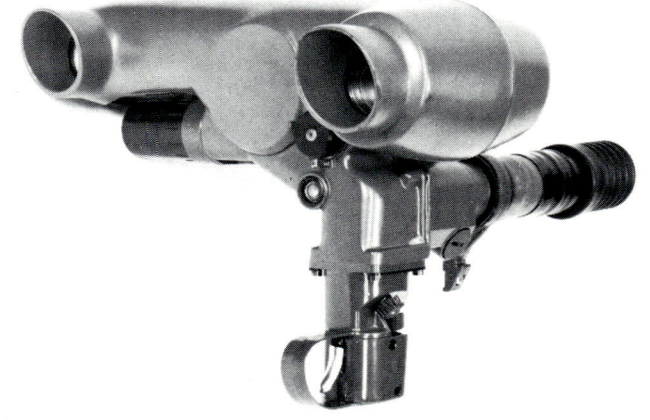

AS-1 Sight

Having made this measurement the gunner can then aim off by the required amount to secure a hit.

If the range to the target is known by other means the range drum can be preset to the appropriate range and the first measurement omitted. Conversely, it is also possible, of course, to use the rangefinder independently for purposes other than firing the FFV 550.

The sight incorporates an ammunition lever which selects the appropriate parameters, including sight elevation, for the FFV 551 HEAT shell, the FFV 441 HE shell and the FFV 569 Smoke shell.

AS-2 RANGE AND LEAD-FINDING SIGHT TYPE

Under development for use with the FFV 500 anti-tank weapon system, the AS-2 is an electrooptical sighting system by means of which range and lead can be determined and correct elevation automatically set. It consists of telescope, rangefinder, lead finder and computer integrated in one unit.

Distance measurements are made with the help of two bright horizontal lines, which are adjusted on top of and below the target. The expected target height is fed into the instrument before the engagement to give the correct distance between two horizontal lines in the field of view. With a zoom in the line projector the horizontal lines can be optically moved in range and when the target fills up the space between the projected lines the zoom setting gives the distance to the target. At the same time an aiming mark has moved downwards. The layer puts the aiming mark back on the target and thereby gets the correct elevation. The zoom does not change the appearance of the direct picture.

The lead is given by adjusting the speed of a line of moving bright spots to the target speed. This moves the aiming mark to the right lead angle.

DATA
Measuring range: 200-800 metres
Target base (vertical): 1-3 metres
Target speed: 0-45km/hour
Magnification: ×4
Field of view: 12°
Weight: 4.2kg
Dimensions: 355 × 260 × 113mm

RS-420 TELESCOPE GUNSIGHT

In service in the Swedish Army and used with the Bofors 90mm anti-tank RCL, the RS-420 is a collimator sight with a built-in elevation device.

For setting superelevation the objective is vertically adjustable by means of an elevation screw located at the bottom. It is provided with a circular scale graduated in distance. Calibration, if necessary, is carried out by adjusting the scale, which is locked in position by means of a locking-screw. In addition the scale can be changed to adapt the sight to different kinds of ammunition. The reticle is laterally adjustable by means of a knob. Turning the knob one dial unit moves the reticle one milliradian laterally. Beneath the lateral adjustment screw is a dovetail fitting for attaching the illuminating device, supplied with the sight, which comprises a housing with an incandescent lamp, a diaphragm to adjust the illumination intensity and a built-in battery. The lamp illuminates both the reticle and the elevation scale. The eyepiece is provided with a removable, bellows-type rubber eye-shield.

DATA
Magnifying power: ×4
Objective diameter: 20mm
Field angle: 10°
Exit pupil: 5mm
Distance between rearmost lens surface and exit pupil: 60 ±5mm
Resolving power: better than 15sec within a central field with a radius of 1.5°
Parallax with lateral adjustment set at centre: max ±0.5 milliradians
Diopter rating: −0.25 to 0.5 diopters
Manufacturer: Jungner Instrument AB, Optical Division, Fack, S-171 20 SOLNA 1, Stockholm

DATA
Weight: 3.4kg
Magnification: ×3
Field of view: 12°
Sight base: 250mm
Range measurement: 175-1,000 metres
Manufacturer: Jungner Instrument AB, Optical Division, Fack, S-171 20 SOLNA 1 Stockholm
Status: Production ceased recently but may be restarted. The sight is in service with Swedish and other forces.

AS-2 Range and lead-finding sight

Manufacturer: Jungner Instrument AB, Optical Division, Fack, S-171 20 SOLNA 1, Stockholm
Status: Development. Prototype completed in 1975

RS-420 Sight on a Bofors 90mm RCL

Status: Production (2,000) complete. In service in the Swedish Army since 1964

SWITZERLAND

AN/PVS-2 SYSTEM 75

Derived from the AN/PVS-2 Starlight Scope, System 75 is a family of night vision devices which exploits some of the important advances made in night vision technology since the original Starlight Scope was designed.

The basic instrument utilises a 18mm first generation three stage image tube intensifier with an integral automatic brightness control (ABC) circuit, a 95mm, catadioptric objective with high efficiency anti-reflection (HEA) coatings, an integral variable illuminated projected reticle, a highly accurate azimuth and elevation boresight adjustment mechanism, and a standard AN/PVS-2 25mm EFL, monocular eyepiece. Inherent in the design of the unit however, is the ability to use an 18mm first-generation, an 18mm second-generation, or a 25mm second-generation image intensifier tube.

In the following table are given data on the following members of the family:-

(1) 18mm first-generation sight (95mm objective)
(2) 18mm second-generation sight (95mm objective)
(3) 18mm first-generation crew-served sight (158mm objective)
(4) 18mm second-generation crew-served sight (158mm objective)

DATA

	1	2	3	4
Length (mm):	370	250	410	330
Diameter (mm):	86	86	150	150
Weight (kg):	1.9	1.36	4.0	2.7
Magnification (×):	3.8	3.8	6.32	6.32
Field of view (deg):	10	10	6.7	6.7
Focus range minimum (m):	4	4	10	10

The image tubes used are an 18mm 3-stage cascade type with ABC (**1** and **3**) and an 18mm MCP inverter type (**2** and **4**). The instruments are powered by Mallory 2.76V TR 132 cells with a normal operating life of 24 hours.
Manufacturer: ICW Systems, Gellerstrasse 163, CH-4052 Basel

MINI-NIGHTVIEWERS TYPES 4001 & 4002

These two instruments are light, portable, battery-operated passive night viewers. Type 4001 has a 75mm objective in a waterproof focussing mounting: Type 4002 is designed to enable the operator to use any standard C mount lens and is therefore not waterproof.

DATA
Length: 228mm
Width: 68mm
Diameter: 55mm
Mounting: Tripod or Pistol Grip

Weight: 1.2kg
Magnification (system): With 75mm f/1.4 lens ×3.5
Field of view: 13.7°
Monocular eyepiece: 10×
Image tube: 18mm cascade with ABC
Light gain: 35,000min, 60,000 typical
Power source: 2.76V Mallory TR132 or Mallory 3175 15-2 below 0°C
Operating time: 25 hours
Manufacturer: ICW Systems, Gellerstrasse 163, CH-4052 Basel

MIDI-NIGHTVIEWER TYPE 106

The Midi-Nightviewer is a passive image intensifier night vision system based on a 25mm electronic image intensification tube and a configuration suitable for both observation and sighting.

There are two versions (Types 105 and 106) which in essence perform the same function: however, the 106 is specially designed to meet the more rugged and exacting specifications of a military device.

The 105 can only accept commercial lenses, but the 106 can accept military lenses and therefore can be used as a fully operational military unit with special military lenses. The 106 can also be used as a high grade commercial unit with commercial lenses, but the action of fitting a commercial lens destroys part of the environmental engineering against water and humidity.

The Midi-Nightviewer may be hand-held, overhead slung, tripod mounted, rail mounted or carriage mounted, and used with military eyepiece, binocular "large screen" viewer or with any commercial reflex still or motion picture camera.

DATA
For standard instrument with 85mm f/1.7 objective
Magnification (system): ×3.5
Field of view: 28.5°
Monocular eyepiece magnification: ×12
Lens mount: Standard T
Image amplification: 35,000 minimum, 65,000 typical
Automatic brightness control: 400ft lamberts
Power source: 6.75V
Batteries: Mallory TR 235R
Operation duration (2 cells): 100 hours at 72°F (22°C)
Manufacturer: ICW Systems, Gellerstrasse 163, CH-4052 Basel

UNION OF SOVIET SOCIALIST REPUBLICS

NSP 2 AND PPN 2 INFRA-RED NIGHT SIGHTS

NSP 2 is a conventional active infra-red weapon sight comprising a small searchlight and an image converter viewed through an eyepiece. It is widely used in Warsaw Pact countries with such weapons as the AK-47 and AKM rifles and a LMG. It is also sometimes used with the RPG 2 and RPG 7 anti-tank rocket launches.

PPN 2 is similar in general design to the NSP 2 but is a larger and more powerful device used with longer-range weapons such as MMG and HMG.

Both sights are clumsy in appearance and bulky to hand, even the smaller NSP 2 extends nearly more than 20cm above the breech cover of the rifle.
Status: In service with Warsaw Pact forces.

UNITED KINGDOM

TRILUX NIGHT SIGHTS

Trilux night sights are simple modifications of rifle and machine gun iron sights and are designed to enable troops to fire accurately at dimly-distinguishable targets up to the maximum range of visibility. The principle involved is that of artificially enhancing the visibility of the foresight and enlarging the aperture of the backsight to allow for the expansion of the eye pupil in darkness.

The way in which the sighting principle is applied to a specific weapon depends on the design of the weapon's iron sights; and an indication of some of the different techniques is given by the accompanying illustrations. In all cases, however, the enhancement of the visibility of the foresight is achieved by incorporating a Betalight self-powered light source in the night foresight. This source, which is visible only to the firer, shows him the position of his foresight and enables him to align it with a shadowy target. The light source has a maintenance-free useful life of some 10-20 years.
Manufacturer: Saunders Roe Developments Ltd, Hayes, Middlesex
Status: Weapons for which sights are available include the FN FAL, the FN SLR L1A1, the G3 and the M16 rifles and the GPMG. The sights are currently in service with UK and many other forces

Appearance of the Betalight foresight by night and by day

Night sights for 7.62mm FN FAL rifle

Night sights for 5.56mm AR15 rifle

Night sights for 7.62mm L1A1 rifle

SINGLEPOINT DAY/NIGHT COMBAT GUNSIGHTS

Singlepoint sights embody the Singlepoint rapid-aiming principle in a highly-developed form.

The well-proven SP221 model for rifles and SMG is now being replaced by the new SP231 model which incorporates some minor modifications and has improved dusk/dark capabilities.

The sight is mounted in the rear sight position on a rifle or SMG and consists of a well-protected and nitrogen-filled collimator tube having a self-powered long-life light source at one end and a lens system at the other. The lenses have an external anti-reflective coating and an internal anti-condensation coating and are the optical elements of the sight eyepiece. The sight is adjusted so that the collimator tube is parallel to the weapon's line of fire.

Assuming that the weapon is fired right-handed, the firer positions his head with the right eye behind the sight and keeps both eyes open, so that he has an unobstructed view from his left eye and can see the same view with his right eye except where it is masked by the sight. From the sight emerges a narrow beam of light, originating in the light source and parallel to the weapon's pointing direction, and this beam of light is projected back into the right eye. The left eye, which has a clear view of the target, will now see the aiming light point projected out into the target area. To the firer it appears as though he is looking through the sight, whereas, in fact, the target and light point are superimposed in the brain by the natural process of binocular vision. The firer should relax and focus his eyes naturally on the target. The eye behind the lens becomes a gathering source, and the other eye sees the aiming point projected on the target.

The correct functioning of the sight does not depend on the eyesight of the firer: it is only necessary that he should be able to see the target with both eyes.

The sight housing incorporates horizontal and vertical adjustments so that the sight can be zeroed. The vertical adjuster incorporates a click mechanism.

The SP231 is available with standard mounting systems for the following weapons but can be made to fit most rifles or SMG's.

SP231/SLR	(SLR) L1A1 Rifle
SP231/FAL	FN FAL Rifle
SP231/M16	M16A1 Rifle
SP231/M14	M14 Rifle/Ruger Mini M14 Rifle
SP231/M1	.30 M1 Carbine
SP231/AR18	AR18 Rifle
SP231/G3	H & K Weapon Systems Group I, II and III
SP231/AKM	AKM Assault Rifle
SP231/ST4	9mm Sterling Mk 4 SMG
SP231/UZI	9mm UZI SMG
SP231/SDP	9mm S.D.P. M.Pi 69 SMC

DATA (Basic sight)
Length: 169.5mm
Diameter: Minimum 25.4mm, maximum 35mm
Weight: 271g
Optics: Glass AR-coated, dry nitrogen filled and sealed system
Standard operating range: Up to 300 metres

Singlepoint SP231/FAL

SP231/G3

Night light source: Approx. 10 year life
Manufacturers: Singlepoint Avionics Ltd, Kiln Acre, Wickham Road, Fareham, Hants. PO16 7HZ
Status: In production since mid-1960s and in widespread service. (SP221 and its predecessor)

RING SIGHT SYSTEM RC-7 (AND RC-25)

Following several years of investigation into small arms sighting problems, Ring Sights Ltd have developed a combined day and night collimated sight, for rifles and light automatic weapons, which is simple and robust and weighs very little.

The principle of operation is similar to that of some other collimated sights but the Ring Sight system differs from some in that the 'aiming' eye can see the target directly as well as the aiming mark which is projected at infinity into the field of view. For daylight firing the aiming mark is a circle which is generated, optically, using light reflected from the direction of the target and so adjusted that it always appears brighter than the target background. This ring marker is supplemented by a dot marker, in the centre of the ring, which is generated by an internal (Betalight) source. In full daylight conditions the intensity of illumination of the dot marker is too low for it to be perceived; but as the external light fades so its relative prominence increases until it becomes the dominant marker.

The fact that the firer, who can use one eye or both when aiming, can see the target as well as the marker with his aiming eye is claimed by the makers to have the advantages, over other types of collimating sight, of avoiding the problems of eye wander and retinal rivalry.

One of the accompanying illustrations shows the basic unit of the RC-7 rifle sight and a mount – for an FN rifle – complete with elevation and windage adjustments. The other illustration shows the graticule of a derived sight, the RC-25, which has been developed for anti-aircraft use.

Manufacturer: Ring Sights Limited, Woodyers, Wonersh, Guildford GU5 0PB
Status: Available to military or commercial order. The RC-7 sight is currently being used at the British Army Personnel Research Establishment as the unit power sight in a study of hand-held weapon sighting

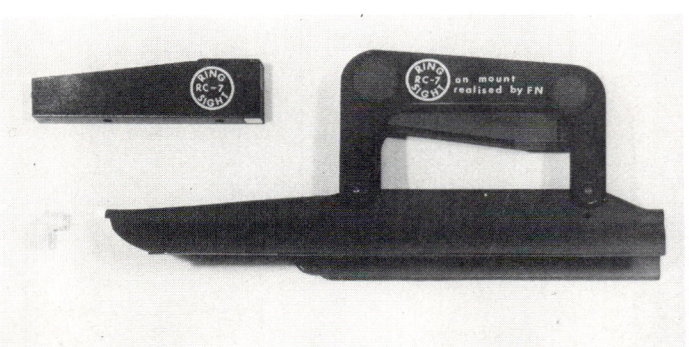

Left *The RC-7 sight unit.* **Right** *The sight unit incorporated in a mount for an FN rifle*

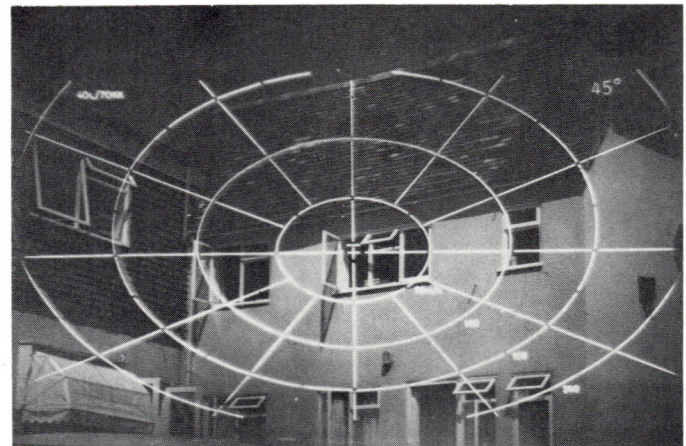

Graticule of the RC-15 sight as seen through the sight

TRILUX INFANTRY SIGHT UNIT (SUIT) L2A2

Designed and developed by the Royal Armament Research and Development Establishment (RARDE) in the UK this sight is now in production (Avimo Ltd) and in UK service. Its purpose was both to improve the effectiveness of infantry weapons in night fighting and to enable the user to identify and engage ill-defined targets in daytime at greater ranges than is practicable with open or simple telescopic sights.

The Trilux unit can be mounted on any of a wide variety of weapons and can be removed and replaced ready for firing without readjustment. The user views the target through a rubber eyepiece which excludes external light; and in his field of view instead of a conventional cross-wire graticule he sees an aiming pointer which is large enough to be unmistakable but not so large as seriously to obscure the target. This pointer is illuminated with red light from a trithium (Trilux) source which requires no external power supply: the intensity of the illumination can be varied from zero to maximum brightness by an external control on the sight body.

To zero the sight there are two adjusting screws (lateral and vertical) marked with 1 mil graduations. The adjustment requires a screwdriver or small coin. Range adjustment is provided by a two-position lever giving a choice of 0-400 metres and 400-600 metres.

DATA
Length: 188mm
Width: 76mm
Height: 69mm
Weight: 340g
Magnification: ×4
Objective aperture: 140 mils (8°)
Light transmission: More than 80%
Exit pupil: 6.6mm
Eye relief: 35mm
Environmental: −75° to +90°C
Manufacturer: Avimo Ltd, Optical Division, 140 Tottenham Court Road, London W1P 0JD

SUIT in use on a British SL rifle

Status: Development started in 1969 on a UK Government contract and the sight entered service use with the British Army in March 1974. Its service designation is Sight Unit, Infantry, Trilux (SUIT). Mountings have been produced for the 7.62mm FN Rifle and GPMG, the 5.56mm M16 Rifle, the 7.62mm G3 Rifle and the 84mm (Carl Gustav) Infantry Anti-Tank Gun. No details of sales or prospects outside the UK have been released.

DRY ZEROING DEVICE ZD3

The Avimo Dry Zeroing Device is a simple piece of apparatus which is gaining acceptance as a convenient method of rapidly zeroing individual infantry weapons. The device comprises an optical unit and a locating spud and incorporates an aiming mark which is optically projected to infinity. Zeroing is carried out by aiming through the weapon sights (which may be iron sights or, for example, a SUIT unit) for compatibility with this aiming mark. The sights are then adjusted by the armourer for elevation and deflection, until the weapon is 'sighted in' as required.

The instrument is vertically mounted on the weapon by simply inserting its spud into the muzzle. Separate interchangeable spuds are supplied for different weapon calibres. A socket spanner is provided with the instrument for quick change of the spuds.

Before use, the device must be calibrated against a master rifle previously zeroed on the range by a qualified marksman. Calibration is carried out by adjusting the aiming mark with the two recessed screws located under the front cap. Once calibrated, the device is ready for use – without the need for further adjustments – on weapons of the same calibre and type.

The device is supplied in a carrying case containing up to three spuds for

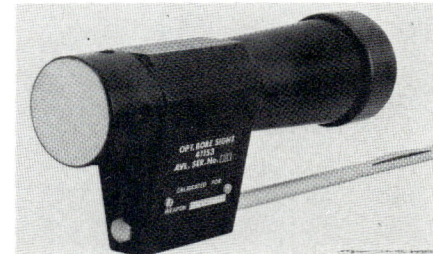

ZD3 Dry Zeroing Device

calibres as ordered by the customer, and an instruction sheet. Both the ZD3 and its case are made to meet applicable military specifications and environmental requirements.
Manufacturer: Avimo Ltd, 140 Tottenham Court Road, London W1P 0JD
Status: Private venture development, started in 1974. The equipment is in production but no sales details are known

MINI NIGHT VIEWER TYPE SS9076 MK 2

This is an extremely light hand-held device for passive night vision. Weighing only about 450 grammes it can be slung round the user's neck or carried in a pocket.

Most recent, as well as the smallest, in the range of Rank-Pullin night vision devices, it has been developed as a private venture starting in 1974.
Manufacturer: Rank Pullin Controls, Langston Road, Debden, Loughton, Essex

SS9076 Mini Viewer

LOW-LEVEL AIR DEFENCE SIGHTS NOs 78 & 81

LLAD Sight No 78 was developed by the Helio Mirror Company on a UK Government contract starting in 1974 and the sight was accepted for service use in June 1976. The No 78 sight is an operational device: sight No 81 is a version for training use only.

The sight fits firmly into the Individual Weapon Sight bracket on the General Purpose Machine Gun and the Light Machine Gun, ensuring simple and positive attachment to the weapon. Removal and fitting does not affect adjustment.

The incorporation of crossed polaroid filters is a major design feature. By rotating the eyepiece, field of view illumination can be reduced to almost zero, thus increasing contrast between reticle and target – an important consideration when engaging airborne targets against a bright background.

The reticle, which is optically injected into the field of view, provides for a wide range of target speeds and approach angles. The reticle fitted to the No 81 sight is designed for use with radio controlled, miniature aircraft targets.

Zeroing of the sight is accomplished by two adjusting dials, graduated in 2 mil divisions.
DATA
Overall length: 15cm

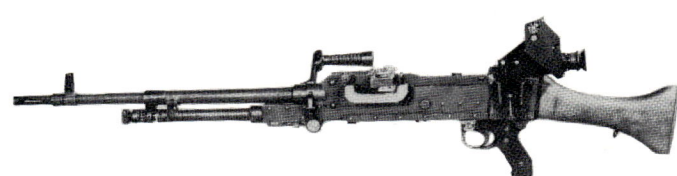

No 78 sight on British GPMG

Overall height: 16.5cm
Overall width: 6.2cm
Environmental: completely sealed: operation and storage between −40°C and +70°C
Weight: 624 gram
Magnification: ×1
Graticule illumination: ambient light
Manufacturer: Helio Mirror Company Ltd, 140 Tottenham Court Road, London W1P 0JD
Status: Developed in conjunction with MVEE and now accepted for British Army service

POCKETSCOPE PASSIVE NIGHT SIGHT

Designed particularly for small-scale military, para-military and security operations the PPE Pocketscope is a light hand-held passive night sight which can detect a man standing in clear starlight at a distance of 200 metres.

Weighing only 800 grammes the device is easily portable and achieves its performance in this small compass by using a micro channel plate image intensifier in conjunction with a catadioptric lens system.

DATA
Dimensions: 85mm × 67mm diameter
Weight: 0.8kg
Magnification: ×2.2
Field of view: 15°
Recognition range: 200 metres for a standing man under clear starlight
Manufacturer: Pilkington P.E. Ltd, Optical Division, Glascoed Road, St Asaph, Clwyd LL17 0LL
Status: Development started as a private venture in 1974 and the equipment went into production in 1975. It is now in service with some European military forces.

Pocketscope and case

NIGHT VIEWING GOGGLES TYPE SS70

These goggles are designed to enable the wearer to focus on a target in conditions of extremely low ambient lighting and to permit free use of his hands while he continues to observe the target.

The goggles weigh 1.13kg and can be focussed from 250mm (10in) to infinity. They are powered by a single 4.5V mercury battery with a working life of approximately 16 hours.

Development started on a UK government contract in 1971.
Manufacturer: Rank Pullin Controls, Langston Road, Debden, Loughton, Essex

SS70 goggles

PASSIVE INFANTRY WEAPON SIGHT UA 1116/00

This is a light passive sight for rifles, LMG and other light weapons which is capable of operating satisfactorily at illumination levels as low as one millilux (starlight). It is based on a ×1.5 magnifying multichannel tube which has been optimised for this kind of application. A rugged sealed unit it can be fitted with a variety of reticles to suit different weapons; its optical system incorporates automatic brightness control and protection against overload by bright sources.

DATA
Magnification: ×4
Field of view: 9°
Resolution (30% contrast) starlight: 1 mil (at 1 millilux)

moonlight: 0.5 mil (at 100 millilux)
Focus range: 25 metres to infinity
Eyepiece adjustment: −5 to +5 diopters
Reticle adjustment: 50 mils in elevation or azimuth in steps of 0.25 mil
Input voltage: 2.2-3.4V d.c. (dry cells)
Battery life: Approximately 35 hr in average use
Length: 312mm
Maximum diameter: 90mm
Weight: Less than 1.6kg
Manufacturer: The MEL Equipment Company Ltd, Defence and Avionic Systems Division, Manor Royal, Crawley, Sussex

PASSIVE NIGHT OBSERVATION SIGHT UA 1242/00

This is a light hand-held passive observation device based on the same ×1.5 magnifying multichannel image intensifier as is used in the same manufacturer's UA 1116/00 weapon sight and comprising also a high-speed catadioptric objective and a binocular eyepiece system. Its small weight makes it easy to use as a hand-held viewer but it can also be mounted on a tripod if required.

DATA
Magnification: ×4
Field of view: 7.5°
Resolution: starlight: 1 mil (at 1 millilux)
          moonlight: 0.5 mil (at 100 millilux)
Focus range: 25 metres to infinity
Eyepiece adjustment: −5 to +3 diopters: interpupillary distance 58-75mm
Input voltage: 2.3-3.4V d.c. (dry cells)
Battery life: Approximately 40 hr at 25°C
Weight, complete: 1.9kg
Length: 356mm
Manufacturer: The MEL Equipment Company Ltd, Defence and Avionic Systems Division, Manor Royal, Crawley, Sussex

MEL passive night observation sight

INDIVIDUAL WEAPON SIGHT TYPE SS20 MK 2

This infra-red night sight has been in service since 1970 and was one of the first in the Rank Pullin series of sight viewing devices. It was developed on a UK government contract starting in 1968.

The sight can be used for weapon aiming with any of a variety of individual weapons from rifles to rocket launchers and may also be used for surveillance. In its normal issue form it is contained in a light transit case complete with a universal adapter, carrying bag, batteries, cleaning equipment and operating instructions.

DATA
Dimensions: 477.5mm long × 110mm wide × 185mm high
Weight: 2.78kg including battery
Magnification: ×3.75
Field of view: 180 mils
Graticule pattern: Produced to suit weapon
Graticule adjustment: ±24 mils in both elevation and azimuth in half-mil steps
Operating range: Up to 700 metres in starlight for weapon aiming. 8-10km for surveillance depending on light level and terrain
Power supply: 6.75V mercury or rechargeable nickel-cadmium battery
Manufacturer: Rank Pullin Controls, Langston Road, Debden, Loughton, Essex
Status: In service in the British Army

SS20 weapon sight in use

TRILITE SMALL WEAPON NIGHT SIGHT

This sight is designed to meet the requirement for a weapon-fitting sight with a useful field of view and a recognition range of 400 metres for a starlit main battle tank, within the practical limits for man portability. The sight can be fitted to a variety of rifles, light, medium and general machine guns, small anti-tank guns etc., by the use of intermediate brackets. An adjustable graticule is fitted which has aiming points for specified ranges and leads for vehicle movement. A shutter eyeguard provides security during operation. The design is rugged and of modular construction to ease maintenance. Controls are the electrical switch and focus ring. Brightness control is automatic and a filter is provided for day training and zeroing.

DATA
Dimensions: 450mm × 100mm diameter
Weight: 3kg
Magnification: ×2.5
Resolution: 1.0 mRad at 10^{-8}ft Lambert
Field of view: 13°
Recognition range: Starlight 400 metres for main battle tank; Moonlight more than 1,000 metres for main battle tank
Power supply: 6.75V mercury battery with average 100 hour operating life
Manufacturer: Pilkington P.E. Ltd. Optical Division Glascoed Road, St Asaph, Clwyd LL17 0LL
Status: The project was part of a private venture programme started in 1970 and the sight has been sold to European, Middle Eastern and Far Eastern forces. A second-generation device using a channel plate intensifier is being developed

Trilite night sight on LMG

LOLITE SMALL SURVEILLANCE NIGHT SIGHT

This sight is designed to combine a useful surveillance range with a wide angle of view in a hand-held system. The Lolite gives recognition of a main battle tank at 600 metres in starlight and allows engagement with machine guns etc., at this range. Engagement at longer range is possible if lighting or camouflage is more favourable.

Aiming graticules can be fitted on the tube and various eyepieces for monocular, periscopic or biocular viewing are available.

Roles include infantry surveillance, SPC sighting, mortar shot fall observation and machine gun and rifle aiming.

Maintenance is minimised by the use of reliable components and modular construction.

DATA
Dimensions: 420mm × 100mm diameter
Weight: 3.4kg
Magnification: ×1.4
Resolution: 0.7 mRad at 10^{-8}ft Lambert
Field of view: 22°
Recognition range: Starlight 600 metres on main battle tank; Moonlight more than 1,500 metres for main battle tank
Power supply: 6.75V mercury battery with average 100 hour operating life
Manufacturer: Pilkington P.E. Ltd, Optical Division, Glascoed Road, St Asaph, Clwyd LL17 0LL
Status: The project was part of a private venture programme started in 1970 and the sight has been sold to European, Middle Eastern and Far

Lolite Night Sight

Eastern forces. Development of a second-generation device using a channel plate intensifier is planned

HAWKLITE MK III INFANTRY NIGHT SIGHT

The Hawklite Mk III sight was designed primarily to meet the requirement for a lightweight infantry night observation device. Weighing just 7.3 kilograms the device is capable of speedily acquiring targets at medium to long range. The 10° field of view and ×5 overall magnification enables a main battle tank to be recognised at around 1,200 metres under clear starlight conditions. Operational roles include heavy machine gun and anti-tank recoilless rifle applications. Bright or obscuration graticules can be fitted. Image brightness control is automatic.

DATA
Dimensions: 530mm × 168mm maximum diameter
Weight: 7.3kg
Magnification: ×5 (monocular). Biocular eyepiece available
Field of view: 10°
Recognition range: Starlight 1,200 metres for main battle tank; Moonlight more than 2,000 metres for main battle tank
Power supply: 6.75V mercury battery with average 100 hour operating life
Manufacturer: Pilkington P.E. Ltd. Optical Division, Glascoed Road, St Asaph, Clwyd LL17 0LL
Status: Development started as a private venture in 1971 and a prototype was completed in 1972. The sight is now in production and has been supplied to European and Middle East forces

Hawklite Mk III

CREW-SERVED WEAPON SIGHT TYPE SS30

This heavy weapon passive night sight was developed on a UK government contract placed in 1970 and is now in service with the British Army where is is known as the L3A1. It is designed for use with battalion anti-tank weapons but is also used in general surveillance applications.

A large diameter catadioptric objective system produces a high-definition image and an image of a variable-brilliance illuminated graticule is projected through the objective on the image plane. An automatic brightness control compensates for variations in ambient lighting but can be overridden by a manual control in some applications.

DATA
Dimensions: 635mm × 190mm diameter
Weight: 8.3kg
Magnification: ×5.7
Field of view: 108 mils (6°)
Objective focus: 50 metres to infinity
Power supply: 6.75V mercury or rechargeable nickel-cadmium cell
Manufacturer: Rank Pullin Controls, Langston Road, Debden, Loughton, Essex
Status: In service with UK forces

SS30 sight on anti-tank RR

NIGHT VIEWING DEVICE TYPE SS32 (TWIGGY)

Developed on a UK government contract placed in 1969 the 'Twiggy' passive night observation device is in service with UK forces in both surveillance and fire control (artillery and mortar) roles. It has a sophisticated lens system and a three-stage image intensifier powered by a battery. Operational life is at least 2,000 hours.

DATA
Dimensions: 610mm × 230mm maximum diameter
Weight: 10kg
Magnification: ×5
Field of view: 129 mils (7.5°)
Objective field: 20 metres to infinity
Power supply: 6.75 mercury cell (100 hour) or rechargeable nickel-cadmium cell
Manufacturer: Rank Pullin Controls, Langston Road, Debden, Loughton, Essex
Status: In service with UK forces where it is known as Telescope, Straight, Image Intensified L1A1. The name 'Twiggy' is unofficial.

SS32 night viewing device

STEADYSCOPE HAND-HELD VIEWER

The steadyscope is a hand-held gyro-stabilised sight designed to be used in place of conventional binoculars and to give the user a steady picture unaffected by hand tremor or vehicle vibration or other movement. It is a monocular instrument, of shape and size similar to that of standard binoculars, having two eyepieces one of which is blanked off. A flexible eyeshield can be reversed to enable the user to operate the instrument with either eye.

Stabilisation is accomplished by a gimbal-mounted mirror controlled by a gyroscope driven by a battery. In use the instrument may be held in any attitude and the user does not require any steadying support. An internal steering device provides effective tracking. The stabilisation is switched in by a push button: there is also an on-off push button switch, a focus ring and an eyepiece adjustment ring.

DATA
Magnification: ×7
Exit pupil diameter: 7.1mm
Eye relief: 22mm
Field of view: 7.4°
Eyepiece focus adjustment: −5 to +5 diopters
Eyepiece separation: 55mm adjustable to observers with 60-72mm eye separation
Maximum stabilised steering rate: 6°/sec
Weight: 2.0kg including battery
Length: 230mm
Width: 225mm
Height: 85mm
Power supply: 1.5V manganese alkaline cell with approximately 10 hours running time
Manufacturer: Precision Products Group, British Aircraft Corporation Limited, Electronic and Space Systems, Post Box 181, Stevenage, Hertfordshire SG1 2DA

THERMAL IMAGER

This is a portable infra-red day and night observation device which has been developed to a demonstration stage by Hawker Siddeley Dynamics and is currently proposed for a variety of military and security applications including use by infantry.

The Thermal Imager detects passive infra-red radiation from the scene and displays a real-time picture of eyepiece or larger size. The imager can detect objects invisible to the eye. It is superior to other observation devices when viewing personnel, vehicles or equipment under camouflage, or obscured by smoke, or against a complex background. The system may be used in total darkness with no artificial illumination.

When the equipment is mounted in a vehicle, independent monitors can be incorporated as an alternative or supplementary to the standard viewing system.

The field of view is scanned at 25 frames per second, giving a continuously updated picture. The system has no lag to degrade imagery when panning or due to motion and good resolution is obtained over a field of view at 15 deg azimuth and 6 deg elevation in the prototype. Other fields of view are possible.

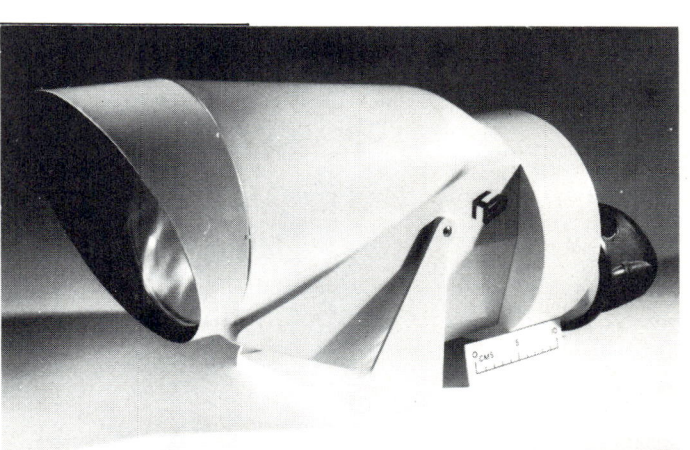

Model of projected production infantry version of the thermal imager

In operation, infra-red radiation from the scene is collected by an objective lens. After reflection the radiation passes through static transfer optics on to a cadmium mercury telluride detector. The detector scans lines in azimuth. There are several detector elements, enabling a number of lines to be scanned simultaneously. The scanning system is novel and produces a high resolution picture. The detector signals feed a set of light emitting diodes which are viewed via the display optics.

DATA (Provisional)
Size: 380mm × 180mm × 200mm
Weight: 12kg (excluding cooling pack and battery)
Power consumption: 15W at 6 V DC
Optics: Refracting system diameter 150mm. f/1.3 flocal length 200mm
Field of view: 15° azimuth, 6° elevation
Resolution: 0.15 milliradian over the whole field of view
Detector: Cadmium mercury telluride at 77K (50 elements)
Spectral band: 8-12 microns
Noise equivalent temperature: 0.2°C at 15°C
Display: 550 lines per frame; System magnification ×5; 25 frames per second; Gallium Phospide Diode Array; Processed to eliminate usual degradation of resolution by the TV raster; A cooling pack weighing 3 kilograms and containing high pressure air will last for 8 hours. A cooling pack containing a ½ litre of liquid nitrogen will give a mission duration of 3 days with 24 hours equipment operating time
Manufacturer: Hawker Siddeley Dynamics Ltd, Manor Road, Hatfield, Hertfordshire, AL10 9LL
Status: Development. The equipment has been demonstrated extensively under field conditions

Mid-range image obtained by the demonstration prototype

LASER TARGET MARKER AND RANGER

This equipment (LTMR) is designed for use either as the ground element of an air co-operation system for attacking ground targets or as the target designator for an attack employing ground-based artillery or other weapons. The equipment generates a pulsed laser beam of very low divergence which can be pointed at a target with a considerable precision. Energy reflected from the target can be detected by suitably equipped strike aircraft or by cannon-launched guided projectiles (CLGP) fired by artillery: it is also detected by the LTMR and used to determine the range of the target.

Development of the LTMR started in 1970 on a UK government contract and the first prototype was completed in 1972. Since then it has been the subject of extensive technical and operational trials and has now been adopted by the British Army, primarily for use by Forward Air Controllers but with a secondary ranging role for other forms of attack. In its primary role the FAC, having aimed the ranger accurately at the target, switches on the laser as the co-operating aircraft approaches. This enables the pilot of the aircraft to locate and identify the target accurately.

The equipment can conveniently be associated with night sights and similar devices and can be treated as either a man-portable or a vehicle-mounted device.

DATA
Marker/Ranger Unit:
Weight – including cables: 9.5kg
Maximum length: 224mm
Maximum width: 305mm
Maximum height: 142mm
Repetition rate: 10 or 20 pulses/sec
Ranging: ±5 metre accuracy to 10km (display limitation)
Endurance: Target marking for at least 20 minutes before recharge
Battery Unit:
Weight: 3.4kg
Dimensions: 183 × 125 × 68.5mm
Capacity: 24V 3.3 amp. hr
Manufacturer: Ferranti Ltd, Electronic Systems Department, Ferry Road, Edinburgh EH5 2XS
Status: Due in British Army service in 1978

Ferranti Laser Target Marker and Ranger

BETALIGHT ILLUMINATED DEFILE MARKER

Originally developed for use on the Medium Girder Bridge (MGB – made by Fairey) this self luminous marker is also suitable for minefield marking and similar purposes. It is a robust soldier-proof device which will retain its luminous properties for some 15-20 years. The plate carrying the luminous arrow is so mounted on the body of the device that it can be indexed to any of eight positions at 45 degree intervals. The arrow is clearly visible by day and by night.

The body is designed to be clipped on British Military Police mounting poles or other narrow supports, attached by screw to wood or threaded metal or suspended by its loop from any convenient projection. 12 markers can be carried in a standard 7.62mm ammunition box.

Manufacturer: Saunders-Roe Developments Ltd, Millington Road, Hayes, Middlesex UB3 4NB
Status: In production and in service in the UK and elsewhere

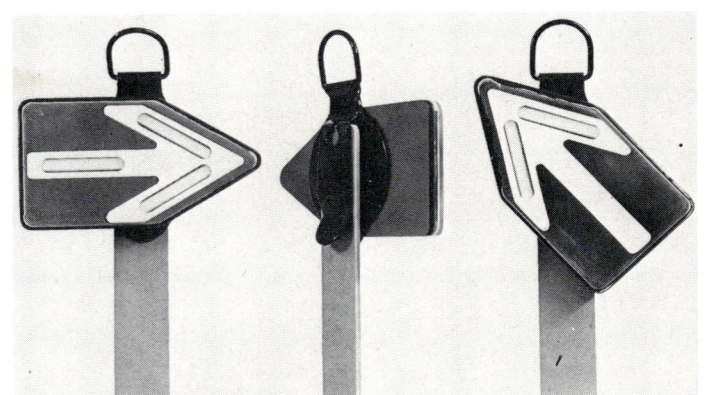
SRDL Betalight defile markers

SRDL AIMING POST LAMP

These aiming post lamps, which are in widespread service, are designed to be used to align mortars or artillery weapons during night firing. Their advantage over earlier types of aiming post lamp is that the Betalight source used is self-powered and reliable and weighs very little.

The lamps are supplied with either green or orange illumination and standard displays include a cross, a bar and an arrow. The lamps, which are small and light enough to be carried in the pocket, are designed to clamp on either square or round posts.

Using a combination of green and orange lamps it is possible to set up a series of mortars by planting a lamp to the front and rear of each. By using a C2 or similar sight each mortar can then be accurately aligned. By alternating orange and green lamps in both front and rear rows confusion between own and adjoining mortar lamps can be avoided.

Although designed primarily for weapon aiming, the lamp can be used for many other purposes either as a routine or in an emergency. Possible applications include route marking, map reading and minefield marking and the lamp can be used as a torch for close work or as a convoy tailboard lamp.

DATA
Length: 72mm or 75mm including mask
Width: 70mm including clamp
Diameter: 45mm
Clamping range: Round or square section posts from 13mm f38mm diameter
Weight: 230g complete
Normal working range: Up to 200 metres
Angle of view: 7.5° standard, 45° version available
Operating temperature: −60°C to +70°C
Manufacturer: Saunders-Roe Developments Ltd, Hayes, Middlesex, UB3 4NB
Status: In service with the British Army and many other armies

This illustration shows a range of military Betalight devices made by Saunders-Roe Developments and now in widespread use. The aiming post lamp and the defile marker (separately described) are seen: so is the necklight – a shielded continuously-operating torch which gives ample light for map-reading or for the adjustment of apparatus. The various devices are listed below and can be identified on the accompanying key.

1. Defile marker.
2. Aiming post lamp.
3. Betalight illuminated route marker.
4. SRDL Necklight self-powered torch.
5. Mortar sight illuminated by Betalights.
6. Illuminated peg light.
7. Map reader illuminated by Betalights.
8. SRDL Necklight.

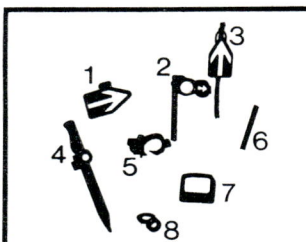

UNITED STATES OF AMERICA

AN/PVS-2 STARLIGHT SCOPE

Also known as STANO (Surveillance, Target Acquisition and Night Observation) No. 1, this is an image intensification device of conventional design which can be used as a hand-held visual observation instrument or as a night sight. In the latter role it can be fitted to most current infantry weapons. It was designed fairly early in the history of such devices, however, and although it remains in service as a reliable and adequate device it is out-performed by more recently-developed instruments.

DATA
Length: 440mm
Weight: 2.7kg
Magnification: ×4
Range: Starlight 300 metres; Moonlight 400 metres
Power supply: 6.75V disposable battery giving 72 hours continuous or 100 hour intermittent operational life
Status: In service with US forces since 1965, the AN/PVS-2 was developed by the US Army Electronics Command with the Wollensack Company as prime contractor.

AN/PVS-4 SECOND-GENERATION STARLIGHT SCOPE

Performing the same range of functions as the AN/PVS-2 Starlight Scope but with superior characteristics, the AN/PVS-4 is a light, passive night vision sight using a 25mm micro-channel plate inverter intensifier tube. The sight is easily attached to a number of different weapons or may be hand held for night reconnaissance.

An adjustable internally projected reticle and interchangeable reticle pattern allows the sight to be bore-sighted to the various weapons without having to move the sight.

Image tube gain and reticle brightness are manually adjustable to compensate for different levels of ambient lighting.

Automatic Gain Control circuitry is employed to maintain the viewed scene illumination constant during periods of changing light level conditions, such as the period from sunset to full darkness. This allows the operator of the sight to use the sight without having to readjust the tube gain control every few minutes during this period.

The tube features muzzle-flash protection which prevents the tube from being damaged by high intensity short duration flashes of light. The flash protection circuit is designed to recover in time for the observer to see the round hit the target.

DATA
Length: 24cm
Width: 12cm
Height: 12cm
Weight: 1.5kg
Mounting: Vee-block bracket
Magnification: ×3.7
Field of view: 14° 30′
Focus range: 25 metres to infinity
Objective focal length: 95mm
Eyepiece focal length: 25mm
Eye relief: 34mm
Diopter range: ±4
Power: 25ma at 2.65V
Battery life: 12 hours
Environment: −55°C to +45°C (operating): 98% RH 3,000 metres altitude
Manufacturer: Varo, Inc. Texas Division, 2201 W. Walnut St. PO Box 828 Garland, Texas 75040

NVS-700 SMALL STARLIGHT SCOPE

This second-generation individual weapon sight is now extensively used by military and police authorities in many countries. Both it and the NVS-800 Crew-served Weapon Sight (qv) use the same 25mm microchannel plate image intensifier tube and have almost all parts in common except the objective lens and associated fittings. The smaller NVS-700 is suitable for mounting on the 5.56mm M-16 rifle and similar weapons.

DATA
Magnification: ×3.5 (nominal)
Field of view: 253 mils
Viewing range
  moonlight: 25 metres to 600 metres
  starlight: 25 metres to 400 metres
Objective lens
  focal length: 95mm

focus adjustment: 25 metres to infinity
Reticle projector: illuminated
Reticle adjustment: 0.25 mil accuracy
Eyepiece
  focal length: 26.5mm
  focus adjustment: −6 to +4 diopters
Length: 292mm nominal
Diameter: 101.6mm nominal
Weight: 1.814kg
Operating temperature: −53°C to +49°C (with arctic kit)
Power supply: Mercury battery giving 12 hours operation at 20°C
Manufacturer: Ni-Tec Inc, 7426 Linder Avenue, Skokie, Illinois 60076
Status: In production and service

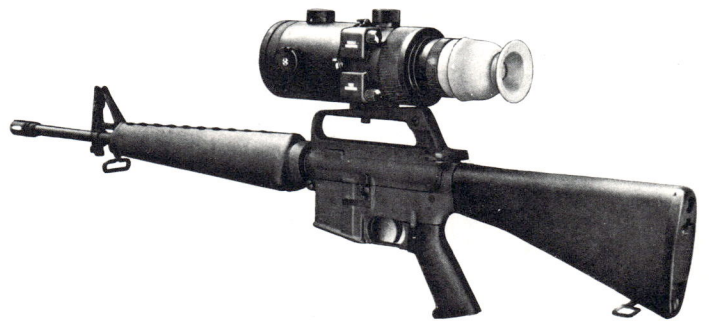

NVS-700 sight on M16 rifle

SCOTOS-I-RS INFANTRY WEAPON SIGHT

This light weapon sight has been designed for use with NATO individual infantry weapons and is also suitable for use with many others. The sight uses a relatively low magnification to compensate for tunnel effect and its image intensifier has automatic brightness control: it is thus simple to use.

Mounts are currently available for a variety of weapons and each is arranged so that all necessary zeroing adjustments are incorporated in the mount and none in the sight itself: a single sight (the expensive part) can thus be transferred from one weapon to another and, if the zeroing adjustments have been made previously, be immediately ready for use.

DATA
Dimensions: 380mm × 62.5mm diameter
Weight: 1.65kg
Magnification: ×1.4
Aperture: f/1.4
Field of view: 240 mils
Power supply: 2 × 2.8V mercury cells with average 200 hour intermittent operational use
Manufacturer: Aspheronics Inc. F., Fort Evans Road, PO Drawer 1134 Leesburg, Va 22075
Status: Developed as a private venture around 1970-71 and in production since January 1973. Supplied to Chile, Iran, Korea, Lebanon, Nepal, UK and USA

SCOTOS-I-RS sight on a Sterling L34A1 SMG on trial at Fareham, Hampshire, England

STAR-TRON NIGHT VISION SIGHTS

A range of night sights bearing the generic name Star-Tron has been produced by Smith & Wesson. This entry briefly describes the earlier devices in the range: another entry gives more detailed information on more recently developed sights.

Star-Tron passive sights have been widely used by police authorities in the USA; but they also have obvious military applications and the Mk 303A series also meets military weatherproofing requirements. Prior to the introduction of these sights the manufacturers marketed two ranges of weapon sight known as Mk 101 and Mk 202.

Sights in both early series employed first-generation image intensification systems comprising three image intensifier tubes in cascade (to give the necessary amplification) and connected by fibre-optic face plates. The Mk 101 with a 75mm f1.4 objective is 300mm in length, the Mk 202A with an 85mm f1.8 objective is a little shorter and both are longer than the Mk 323 second-generation device with a 170mm f1.4 objective.

Of these three series of first-generation sights the most highly developed is the Mk 303. Data for this sight with 135mm and 170mm objectives are given below; but it should be noted that other objective focal lengths from 75mm to 800mm are available.

DATA

	Mk 303A/135mm	Mk 303A/170mm
Objective focal lengths:	135mm	170mm
Aperture:	f1.6	f1.5
Magnification (standard):	×4.2	×5.3
Focus range:	8 metres to infinity	8 metres to infinity
Length:	283mm	332mm

Star-Tron Mk 303A sight

Weight, complete:	1.8kg	2.3kg

Battery: 2.6V mercury battery with operating life in excess of 50 hours
Manufacturer: Smith & Wesson, Springfield, Massachusetts 01101
Status: Production and police service at least

STAR-TRON MK 323 SIGHTS

This series of Smith & Wesson sights employs second-generation (microchannel plate amplifier) single-stage image intensifiers. The sights are thus significantly smaller than the sights with the triple cascaded image intensifiers in the Mk 101, 202 and 303 series. Data for sights with 135mm and 170mm objectives are set out below but it should be noted that other objectives from 75mm to 800mm are available.

	Mk 323/135mm	Mk 323/170mm
Objective focal length:	135mm	170mm
Aperture:	f1.6	f1.5
Magnification (standard):	×4.2	×4.3
Focus range:	8 metres to infinity	8 metres to infinity
Length:	187mm	236mm
Weight complete:	1.3kg	1.8kg

Battery: 2.6V mercury battery with operating life in excess of 50 hours
Manufacturer: Smith & Wesson, Springfield, Massachusetts 01101
Status: Production and police service at least

Star-Tron Mk 323 sight

STAR-TRON Mk-700 SERIES 1 PASSIVE NIGHT VISION RIFLESCOPE

Suitable for mounting on most modern military rifles, this small rifle sight incorporates an aiming reticle which can be seen equally well by day and by night. An integral daylight filter lens cap, used for daylight firing, protects the lens and helps to keep the night sight objective clean: for night firing this cap is flipped up.

Fitted as standard is a 100mm f/1.4 catadioptric objective which is spectrally corrected for night vision; but both larger and smaller objectives can be fitted if desired.

DATA
Objective
   standard: 100mm f/1.4 (T2) catadioptric
   optional: 95mm f/1.3 (T1.6), 130mm f/1 (T1.2) 135mm f/1.6 (T2.4), 170mm f/1.5 (T2)
Eyepiece: 27mm monocular
System magnification: ×3.7 standard
Intensifier: 19mm with minimum gain of 60,000
Sight adjustment: 0.25 mil per click: 18 clicks per revolution
Length
   without eyeguard: 263.5mm
   with eyeguard: 317.5mm
Weight: approx 1.6kg
Power Supply: 50-hour battery
Manufacturer: Smith & Wesson, 2100 Roosevelt Avenue, Springfield, Massachusetts 01101

SCOTOS-I-HH NIGHT VIEWING INSTRUMENT

This is a hand-held night viewing device which in its standard form has only a small magnification to compensate for tunnel effect but which will accept additional lenses if a magnified image is required.

A pistol-grip handle incorporates the batteries and a trigger on-off switch. The maximum objective aperture is f/1.3 and the minimum f/.22 and there is a focussing ring calibrated from 8 feet to infinity. The eyepiece is arranged to eliminate apparent image movement when the head is moved.

DATA
Dimensions: Tube 380mm × 60mm diameter (standard) grip 54 × 98 × 24mm
Weight: 1.7kg excluding carrying case (standard)

Objectives:	Standard	Alternatives	
Magnification:	1.23	2.27	0.82
Field of view:	240 mils	130 mils	360 mils
Diameter:	75mm	135mm	55mm
Aperture:	f/1.3	f/1.5	f/0.95

Minimum light: 5.0×10^{-5} ft candle (cloudy and moonless)
Resolution: 36 line pairs/mm
Eyepiece: Aspheric 50mm
Power supply: 2 × 2.8V mercury cells with average 200 hour intermittent operational life
Manufacturer: Aspheronics Inc. Fort Evans Road, PO Drawer 1134 Leesburg, Va 22075
Status: Developed as a private venture in 1970-71. In production since February 1972. Supplied to Chile, Iran, Oman, South Africa, UK and USA

SCOTOS II DIRECT IMAGING SPECTROSCOPES

Little information has so far been made available concerning these viewing devices which have been developed by Aspheronics to complement their range of SCOTOS night sights and night viewing devices.

Instruments in the SCOTOS-II range will be narrow-band imaging spectroscopes responding to selected frequency bands in the near-UV, visible and near-IR regions. Their purpose is to enhance selected target or terrain features by selecting the radiation band which contains the strongest emissions from such features and thus emphasising them in contrast with the remainder of the scene.

Manufacturer: Aspheronics Inc., Fort Evans Road, PO Drawer 1134, Leesburg, Va 22075
Status: Developed as a private venture. Scheduled for production in 1976

METASCOPE

This is a small monocular night vision device which can be used either in a passive role for infra-red viewing or, with a small IR source attached, for covert map-reading or similar purposes. In its passive role, its low magnification makes it more suitable for detecting the existence of IR sources than for examining them in detail. As an indication of its detection capability it is said that, when used in conjunction with a 1kW Xenon IR searchlight, it can detect a man at a distance of 350 metres.

DATA
Length: 152mm

Width: 108mm
Height: 114mm
Weight: 1.25kg including attached light source
Magnification: ×1.1
Field of view: 30°
Resolution: 3.75ft
Focus: Fixed, 30cm to infinity
Power supply: Mercury batteries with 24 hour duration (viewer) and 6 hour duration (light source)
Manufacturer: Varo Inc., Texas Division, PO Box 828, 2201 W Walnut St. Garland, Texas 75040

NOCTRON IV NIGHT VISION EQUIPMENT

Noctron IV is the name given to a range of night vision equipment developed by Varo Inc. for civil and military use. The basis of the system is a small hand-held night viewer to which can be added photographic equipment and other additional equipment as required. Most of the supplementary devices relate to functions remote from normal infantry use and data on only the basic instrument are set out here.

DATA
Length: 325mm

Width: 70mm
Height: 83mm
Weight: 1.3kg
Magnification: ×3.75
Field of view: 13.5°
Power supply: 2.65V mercury battery. Operating duration for two cells 100 hour at 22°C
Mounting: Pistol grip, tripod or camera
Manufacturer: Varo Inc., Texas Division, PO Box 828, 2201 W Walnut St, Garland, Texas 75040
Status: Production

SCOTOS-I-DS NIGHT DRIVING SIGHT

This is a new item in the SCOTOS range of night vision equipment developed by Aspheronics. It was developed as a private venture in 1975-76 and production is imminent at the time of writing.

Suitable as a night driving aid for all kinds of military vehicles the SCOTOS-I-DS features a wide-angle lens and a biocular stand-off eyepiece display.

Manufacturer: Aspheronics Inc, PO Drawer 1334, Leesburg, Virginia 22075
Status: Production scheduled for late 1976. No sales data yet available

HYPER-MINISCOPES MODELS 9821, 9823 AND 9823E

These night vision sights combine sophisticated optics with high resolution 18mm intensifiers. Model 9823 is intended primarily for use with individual weapons while Model 9823E is more suitable for crew-served weapons. The older Model 9821 is in US Army service as an individual weapon sight and is not greatly different from the 9823.

An important design feature common to both devices is the internal reticle projector. The projected reticle is fully adjustable to compensate for scene brightness and target contrast and it is especially effective under very dark conditions when a fixed blackline reticle would disappear. This reticle system is claimed to be more accurate than adjustable mounts.

Model 9823 can be attached directly to the M16 rifle and used with the other weapons listed below with the aid of simple adaptors. Model 9823E is similarly attached to crew-served weapons.

Interchangeable ballistic reticles and adaptors are available for the following weapons.

Model 9823	Model 9823E
FN Rifle	M2 0.50 MG
G3 Rifle	M85 0.50 MG
M14 Rifle	M139 20mm Gun
M16 Rifle	M40 106mm RR
Remington Model 700 Rifle	
Winchester Model 70 Rifle	
M60 MG	
M67 RR	
M79 Grenade Launcher	

DATA

	M9823	M9823E
Length (mm):	370	460
Diameter (mm):	86.5	150
Weight (kg):	1.75	3.95
Magnification (×):	3.5	5.7
Field of view (deg):	10.8	6.5
Objective focal length (mm):	98	155
Focus range, from (m):	10	25

COMMON DATA
Eyepiece focal length: 25mm
Diopter adjustment: −4 to +2
Image format: 18mm
Reticle accuracy: ¼ mil
Reticle adjustment: ¼ mil increments
Power source: 4x Mallory RM401
Operating life (20°C): 48 hours
Instrument operating temperature: −54° to +52°C
Manufacturer: Varo Inc., Texas Division, Box 828 2201, W Walnut St, Garland, Texas 75040
Status: Model 9821 in service. Models 9823 and 9823E in quantity production

Hyper-Miniscope Model 9823

NVS-800 CREW-SERVED WEAPON SIGHT

Designed for use on heavy automatic weapons, RCL guns and other armament of similar size, the NVS-800 sight closely resembles the NVS-700 (Small Starlight Scope) individual weapon sight (qv) but has a greater range capability resulting from the use of a larger objective lens. The eyepiece, 25mm second-generation image intensifier and associated components are common to both sights and the data given below relate only to the differences between the two.

DATA
Magnification: ×6 (nominal)

Field of view: 156 mils
Viewing range:
  moonlight: 25 metres to 1,200 metres
  starlight: 25 metres to 1,000 metres
Objective focal length: 155mm
Length: 355.6mm nominal
Diameter: 165mm nominal
Weight: 3.856kg
Manufacturer: Ni-Tec Inc, 7426 Linden Avenue, Skokie, Illinois 60076
Status: In production and service

CREW-SERVED WEAPONSIGHT

This is a versatile night vision sight for use with all types of crew-served weapons including the M2 MG and the 106mm RR. The sight mounts directly on the weapon and can be fitted with either straight-through or right-angle eyepieces – the latter being appropriate to such weapons as recoilless rifles.

The sight can also be mounted on a tripod and used for surveillance. With a light level as low as .0001 fc a tank can be detected at 1,000 metres and a man at 600 metres.

DATA
Length: 556mm

Width: 165mm
Height: 203mm
Weight: 8.25kg
Magnification: ×6.5
Field of view: 6°
Focus: Variable 50 metres to infinity
Diopter range: ±4
Power supply: 6.75V mercury battery with 72 hour life
Operating temperature: −54° to +46°C
Manufacturer: Varo Inc., Texas Division, PO Box 828 2201, W Walnut St, Garland, Texas 75040
Status: In service

AN/TVS-4 TRIPOD-MOUNTED NIGHT VISION SIGHT

Also known as STANO (Surveillance, Target Acquisition and Night Observation) No. 2, the AN/TVS-4 Tripod Mounted Night Vision Sight is designed to perform under conditions of darkness, utilising starlight and moonlight on observation and detection missions. It enables the individual soldier on outposts, listening posts, forward observation posts and patrols to detect, identify and observe friendly or enemy elements. It is also designed for use by artillery forward observers in adjusting indirect fire. It is portable and powered by a disposable battery.

DATA
Length: 838mm
Weight: 15.4kg (viewer only)
Magnification: ×7.5
Range: Starlight 1,000 metres; Moonlight 1,200 metres
Power supply: 6.75V battery with 72 hours continuous or 100 hours intermittent operational life
Manufacturer: Developed by US Army Electronics Command and produced by the Davidson Company
Status: Development started in 1961 and service entry with the US Army in 1965 as a replacement for the Infra-red Weapon Sight

AN/TVS-5 SECOND-GENERATION CREW-SERVED WEAPONSIGHT

This is a light passive night vision sight which uses 25mm micro-channel plate inverter intensifier tube. It can be used with a range of different crew-served weapons and can also be tripod-mounted for night reconnaissance.

An adjustable internally projected reticle and interchangeable reticle patterns allow the sight to be bore-sighted to the various weapons without having to move the sight.

Image tube gain and reticle brightness are manually adjustable to compensate for different levels of ambient lighting.

Automatic gain control circuitry is employed to maintain the viewed scene illumination constant during periods of changing light level conditions, such as the period from sunset to full darkness. This allows the operator of the sight to use the sight without having to readjust the tube gain control every few minutes during this period.

The tube features muzzle-flash protection which prevents the tube from

being damaged by high intensity short duration flashes of light. The flash protection circuit is designed to recover in time for the observer to see the round hit the target.

DATA
Length: 310mm
Width: 160mm
Height: 170mm
Weight: 3kg
Magnification: ×6.2
Field of view: 9°
Focus range: 25 metres to infinity
Diopter range: ±4
Power supply: 25 mA at 2.65V DC. Battery life 12 hour
Operating temperature: −54° to +46°C
Manufacturer: Varo Inc., Texas Division, PO Box 828, 2201 W Walnut St, Garland, Texas 75040

STAR-TRON Mk-606A SERIES 4 PASSIVE NIGHT VISION SYSTEM

This is a modern high-performance viewer for battlefield or frontier surveillance. For mobile operations its weight (around 30kg) is such that it can most conveniently be moved by vehicle; but it can be off-loaded and

man-handled over short distances for tripod-mounted surveillance. It is equipped with a yoke and trunnion mounting system which makes it possible to rotate the viewer vertically about its horizontal axis without moving its centre of gravity.

Features of the optical system include a 410mm f/1.5 catadioptric objective lens (which is available in both standard and specially lightened versions) an image intensifier with a minimum gain of 60,000, a choice of ×4 biocular or ×6.7 monocular viewers, automatic brightness control and broad-range gain control. A low military-type tripod is available.

DATA
Objective: 410mm f/1.5 (T2) catadioptric
Eyepiece: ×4 biocular or ×6.7 monocular
Systems magnification: ×7.07 or ×11
Field of view: 5.3°
Image intensifier: 40mm: minimum gain 60,000: maximum distortion (at 50% field) 10%
Length (withouth anti-backlight hood): 722.3mm
Maximum diameter: 287.3mm
Width (including yoke): 393.7mm
Height (with yoke but without tripod): 388mm
Height mounted on tripod: 516mm
Weight with standard objective: 28.83kg
Weight with lightweight objective: 24.90kg
Additional weight for tripod: 2.30kg
Power Supply: 6.75V mercury all with 50 hour life
Manufacturer: Smith & Wesson, 2100 Roosevelt Avenue, Springfield, Massachusetts 01101

Star-Tron Mk 606A Series 4 night viewer

NIGHT OBSERVATION DEVICE MODEL 229

This is a rugged, waterproof night-viewing equipment made to US military standards by Javelin Electronics on which information was released in 1975 although it appears that it was in military service before that.

Model 229 uses a second-generation image intensification system with an amplification factor of 100,000 and a performance superior to earlier devices made for the same purpose by the same manufacturer. It is

powered by an internal battery, has a built-in tripod which raises it some 30cm from the ground and is carried in a case which also meets military specification. The only performance information currently available is that it can precisely locate targets at ranges in excess of 1,000 metres.
Manufacturer: Apollo Lasers, Inc. Javelin Electronics Division, 6357, Arizona Circle, Los Angeles, California 90045
Status: In service with US and other armed forces

JAVELIN MODEL 223 NIGHT VIEWER

This is a heavy-duty second-generation night-viewing device recently introduced by Javelin Electronics and suitable for rough use either as a hand-held viewer or as a rifle-mounted sight. It meets US military specifications for such equipment.

There is a choice between 135mm or 170mm f1.6 catadioptric objective

lenses and the device features automatic brightness control, a secure eyeguard from which no light can be reflected on the operator, an automatic battery test indicator and an optional focal-plane iris.
Manufacturer: Apollo Lasers Inc., Javelin Electronics Division, 6357 Arizona Circle, Los Angeles, California 90045
Status: Production.

GROUND LASER LOCATOR DESIGNATOR

Hughes Aircraft Company is developing the Ground Laser Locator Designator (GLLD) for the US Army Missile Command. It is intended for use by ground troops to enable them to direct laser-guided munitions to targets designated by ground forces.

Two versions have been developed: the first is a tripod-mounted equipment containing a laser, a rangefinder, a telescopic sight and a tracking unit and is man-portable by a crew of two of whom only one is needed to operate the equipment: the later development is of a hand-held designator with fewer facilities. Provision is made for coding the marking laser energy in wavelength and pulse repetition frequency to permit weapons to discriminate between GLLDs. The use of the designators with co-operating aircraft is also being studied.

Manufacturer: Hughes Aircraft Company, California, USA
Status: 12 development units of the lightweight designator were delivered to the US Army Electronics Command in 1975 Field trials began in March 1976

Hughes Ground Laser Locator Designator currently under devlopment for the US Army

Hughes hand-held Ground Laser Locator Designator

AN/GVS-5 HAND-HELD LASER RANGEFINDER

Initially developed by the US Army Electronics Command and now the subject of a full development contract placed by the Army with RCA, the AN/GVS-5 is a hand-held laser system that enables the user to determine the range of a selected target in the space of about one second.

To operate the device the user first looks at the target through a monocular eyepiece and centres it in the telescope graticule: he then presses a "Fire" button and waits for the target range to appear on a light-emitting diode numerical display at the foot of his circular field of view. On either side of the display are warning indicators which are illuminated when the battery is low (left-hand indicator) or when the pressure of multiple targets is preventing the accurate measurement of range. The range measurement is made by measuring the round-trip time of a pulsed laser emission to the target and back; and if more than one target lies within the very narrow transmitted laser beam the right-hand warning indicator will light. To overcome this difficulty the equipment is fitted with an adjustable range gate which can be used to black out targets up to a range of 5km. As well as being adjustable this gate can be switched in and out at a predetermined setting.

The performance of the rangefinder is classified but the foregoing indicates that ranges in excess of 5km can be measured. Available physical data are summarised below and it should be added that the instrument's primary tactical rangefinding role can be supplemented by the provision of a tripod and az-el head to convert it to a surveying role.

Construction is modular, the design permits use in both low and high temperatures and the controls can be operated without removing arctic or other gloves. Normally powered by an internal battery, the instrument can also be powered from an external source.

AN/GVS-5 hand-held rangefinder

DATA
Weight: 5lb (2.27kg)
Emission wavelength: 1.06 microns
Beam divergence: 1.0 m rad
Range measurement limits: 20 metres to 9,990 metres
Range error: ±10 metres
Time to range: 1 second
Operating temperature: −46°C to +71°C including the effect of solar radiation

Power supply: Rechargeable nickel-cadmium battery or external power source
Range measurements per battery charge: More than 700 at 24°C; more than 350 at 71°C; more than 200 at −32°C
Manufacturer: RCA Automated Systems Division, Burlington, Massachusetts 01803
Status: Development. Award of a $1.5 million US Army contract covering the development and supply of twenty prototypes was announced in April, 1975.

BATTLEFIELD SURVEILLANCE RADARS AND INTRUDER ALARMS

INTRODUCTION

Over the past two decades or so, the advantages of equipping troops with some form of small radar to detect the presence of enemy troops or vehicles have been increasingly apparent to military authorities in many countries. Over the same period the willingness of these authorities to avail themselves of these advantages has been considerably stimulated by the great advances made in the development of miniaturised electronic equipment and the consequent possibility of producing radars small enough to be man-portable while offering facilities of real operational value.

A powerful stimulus to the development of such radars was the war in Vietnam in which American troops became acutely aware of the need for devices which would enable them to detect enemy movements in circumstances in which all kinds of optical observation were impossible. It is probable that the problem of detecting a creeping enemy in thick vegetation has not yet been finally solved: the combination of seismic sensors with the RCA Electromagnetic Motion Detector is a promising approach to a solution, however, and work on more elaborate multiple sensor systems is in hand in the USA. For detecting movement in less impenetrable environments, however, battlefield radars of many kinds have been and are being developed in the USA and parallel developments on a much more modest scale have occured in Europe.

As the entries in this section indicate, the currently and imminently available equipments range in size from devices small enough to mount on an individual weapon and having a detection range of a few hundred metres to crew-transported or vehicle-borne equipments capable of detecting men or vehicles at a distance of several kilometres. Although these devices differ widely in detail, however, there are a few basic principles of operation which may usefully be summarised here.

All these radars depend on the reflection by the target of electromagnetic radiation from the radar transmitter and principally on the Doppler effect whereby the reflected radiation from a radially moving target differs measurably in frequency from the incident radiation by an amount that depends on the relative radial velocity. By comparing transmitted and received frequencies, therefore, it is possible both to detect the presence of something moving and to make some assessment of the nature of the motion. The process is capable of very sensitive refinement and, when it is remembered that the component parts of a moving human body or vehicle are moving relatively one to another as well as being involved in a net translational motion, it can be seen that different types of target engaging in different types of motion will produce different patterns of frequency differences between the transmitted and received signals. In practice it is found that these patterns are recognisable in certain circumstances – even to the extent that under favourable conditions it is possible to detect a (radar) difference between men and women.

By itself this process detects only the presence and possibly the nature of a target. By making the transmitter radiation highly directional it is possible to determine the direction of a target; but of course this means that to survey an area of any significance the radiated beam must be swept regularly over the area of interest and most modern radars other than the smallest have some provision for systematic sector scanning. The final major refinement is to make provision for the measurement of range by impressing some form of modulation (pulse or frequency) on the transmitted radiation whereby the round-trip time to and from the target can be measured by standard radar techniques – which can incidentally also be used to detect stationary as well as moving targets if required.

In the simpler equipments the results of these processes are presented to the operator in the form of audible headphone signals. A common practice is for him to hear all the received moving-target signals while the radar is scanning the area as a general surveillance operation; then, when he hears an interesting signal, to take action to locate the target by restricting the scanning motion and by operating a range gate control which admits only signals from targets within prescribed distance limits, to measure the range. Various refinements of this basic procedure are made possible by additional circuits and devices, ranging from a simple visual indicator to simplify the determination of the bearing and range giving the maximum signal, to means of reading range or bearing or both from visual indicators while the radar continues to scan.

INTRUDER ALARMS

Included in this sub-section are descriptions of seismic and infra-red intruder alarms and the electromagnetic motion detector referred to earlier. Although these devices differ substantially from the battlefield radars their functions are similar and sometimes complementary to those of the radars when used (albeit temporarily) for static surveillance.

FRANCE

OLIFANT II PATROL RADAR

Olifant II is a Ku-band coherent pulse-doppler patrol radar designed to detect, locate and identify moving targets at short range. It is light enough to be carried and operated by one man and, if worn on the chest, can be used immediately after the operator stops moving. When on patrol, therefore, all that is required is for the operator to halt facing in the direction of interest and switch on the radar: and if there is a moving target within range in that direction he will hear an identifiable signal in his headphones. The radar can also be tripod mounted for more accurate measurements in a temporarily static role or for monitoring a road or other approach route.

DATA
Operating frequency: Ku-band
Detection ranges: Man crawling 400 metres; Man walking 1,800 metres; Moving vehicle 2,400 metres
Range accuracy: ±50 metres at 1,000 metres
Azimuth accuracy: ±10 mils
Weight: 9kg
Power supply: 12V rechargeable NiCd battery with 12 hour operating life between charges
Manufacturer: Thomson-CSF, Division Equipments, Avioniques et Spatiaux, 178 boulevard Gabriel-Péri, 92240-Malakoff
Status: Series production. An earlier patrol radar, called simply Olifant, was made by EMD

Olifant II in use on its tripod

RASIT BATTLEFIELD SURVEILLANCE RADARS

Three battlefield surveillance radars, all made by LCT, go under the name of Rasit. All are substantial devices, even the smallest of which has a range of 10 kilometres, and although all can be divided into man-packs for transport they are scarcely portable equipments in the ordinary source of the term. For vehicle mounting, however, or for relatively long-term installation in a defensive position they have evident advantages.

The three devices, in descending order of size are Rasit 72A (also known as Rapière), Rasit 72B and Rasit 72C. The first and last are similar in general configuration but differ in performance and facilities: Rasit 72B has the radar head mounted on the operating unit.

RASIT 72A/RAPIERE

Rasit 72A/Rapière is a long-range (20km) X-band coherent pulse doppler equipment using multiple range gates and filters for signal analysis. The antenna is remotely controlled and can be set to scan any sector or stopped and manually controlled. Targets are displayed on a B-scope and audibly in the operator's headphones and the operator can choose between scanning the full 20km range of the surveyed zone or any 2.5km range within the zone. The antenna is adjustable: elevation and fitted with a polarizer to give a choice of linear or circular polarizer. It is claimed that the equipment has very effective ECCM capabilities including a tunable transmitter. The radar head can be mounted on a tripod or vehicle and the control unit can be up to 50 metres away. Optional facilities include a remote TV slave monitor, automatic range tracking, remote control of antenna elevation and automatic surveillance over 360°.

Rasit 72/A

DATA
Operating frequency: Tunable over 200MHz in X-band
Peak power: 3kW
Detection ranges: Man walking 14,000 metres; Moving vehicle more than 20,000 metres
Accuracy: ±10 metres and ±8 mils
Display: B-scope daylight CRT showing polar UTM coordinates, plus numerical coordinate display, headphones and automatic acoustic alarm
Weight: 70kg total divisible into 4 loads of which the heaviest is 25kg
Power drain: 150W at 28V
Operating temperature: −40°C to +55°C

RASIT 72/B

Rasit 72/B weighs less than the 72/A and, as already noted, has its radar head mounted on top of the control unit, the antenna orientation being controlled by hand. It is particularly suitable for monitoring on a fixed axis.

DATA
Similar to Rasit 72A/Rapière except
Accuracy: ±20m and ±10 mils
Display: Linear solid state display, using light emitting diodes, of target range plus headphones
Weight: 50kg
Power drain: 100W

RASIT 72/C

Rasit 72/C is a shorter-range (10km) derivative of the 72/A with somewhat reduced facilities. The computer for polar/UTM coordinate conversion is offered only as an option and the power chain does not exceed 120W at 28V.

Manufacturer: Rasit 72 is made by Laboratoire Central de Télécommunications, (LCT), 18-20 rue Grange-Dame-Rose. 78140-Vélizy-Villacoublay and L.M.T. – Le Matériel Téléphonique, 46, Quai Alphonse Le Gallo 92103 Boulogne-Billancourt

Status: Two versions of Rasit 72A have been defined, Rasit 72A1 being an infantry-portable equipment (to which the title Rapière now appears to be confined) and Rasit 72A2 a vehicle-mounted system. There are, however, no known performance differences between the two. Prototypes of both

Rasit 72/B

versions have been tested by French and other armed forces and both were at the pre-production stage in mid-1975. Nothing has been heard recently of Rasit 72B or 72C

RASURA BATTLEFIELD SURVEILLANCE RADAR

Rasura, which is available in either portable (tripod-mounted) or vehicle-mounted versions, is an X-band autocoherent pulse-doppler radar providing both aural and visual indication of targets up to 2km (men) or up to 5km (vehicles) from the transmitter.

Detected targets are indicated to the operator by an aural signal and distance and bearing are displayed directly on the equipment indicator. Azimuth scanning is either manual or automatic in 4-degree steps. Range scanning may also be manual or automatic, there being a choice of three range sectors for automatic scanning.

DATA
Operating frequency: X-band
Peak power: 2-3kW
Antenna beamwidth: Azimuth 4°; Elevation 8°
Detection ranges: Men crawling 2,000 metres; Men walking 5,000-7,000 metres; Vehicles 7,000-10,000 metres
Accuracy: ±25 metres and better than ±17 mils
Range sectors: 0-2,000 metres, 1,500-3,000 metres and 3,000-5,000 metres
Weight: 3 × 20kg packs for the portable version
Power supply: NiCd battery or vehicle supply
Power drain: 60W
Operating temperature: −25°C to +50°C

Rasura battlefield radar

Manufacturer: Electronique Marcel Dassault, 55 Quai Carnot, 9221-4-Saint-Cloud
Status: In service with French, West German, Netherlands and Spanish forces

ITALY

SENTINEL RQT-9X PORTABLE INFANTRY RADAR

This is a light man-portable X-band frequency and phase-modulated CW doppler radar which will detect moving targets up to a range of about 4km. It is normally mounted on a tripod.

The equipment is operated in either a surveillance mode, with frequency modulation only for better clutter rejection, or a ranging mode with phase modulation added. In the former mode all targets within range and within the antenna beam are detected; in the ranging mode the operator can hear only targets lying within a manually variable range gate. The pseudo-random phase modulation code used ensures that the signal peaks sharply as the range gate control is operated, thus enabling range measurement to be made to a high degree of accuracy. The antenna is manually pointed and the signals are presented only in audible form.

DATA

Operating frequency: X-band
Power output: 40mW
Antenna beamwidth: Azimuth 4°; Elevation 12°
Detection range: Men 400metres; Vehicles 3,800metres
Weight: Approx. 5kg
Power supply: Battery
Manufacturer: Selenia-Industrie Elettroniche Associate SpA, Via Tiburtina, Km 12,400 Rome.
Status: In service with Italian and other forces.

Sentinel RQT-9X infantry radar

SENTINEL RQT-10X PORTABLE INFANTRY RADAR

This is a short-range patrol radar designed to detect moving targets up to a distance of about 5km. It comprises a combined transceiver and antenna unit and a small control unit which can be either mounted on the larger unit or operated up to 30m away from it. The equipment can be either carried on patrol or tripod mounted; in the latter instance it is possible to control the azimuth of the antenna remotely and for the antenna to execute a sector scan.

Solid-state circuitry is used throughout and operational features are said to include good ECCM performance, pseudo-random code modulation, a coherent receiver with code compression and audio frequency translation and simple target identification. Operating modes can be chosen from Search, Range-gated and Mixed and there is an optional optical alarm in addition to the normal audio tone signal output.

The operating frequency has not been disclosed. The transceiver and control unit together weigh 6.5kg and the tripod complete with scanning motor 2kg.

Manufacturer: Selenia Industrie Elettroniche Associate SpA, Via Tiburtina, Km 12,400 Rome.
Status: Production.

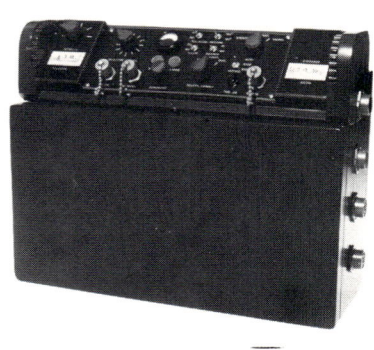

Sentinel RQT-10X patrol radar

SWEDEN

ISIDOR (UAP 40301) PORTABLE BATTLEFIELD RADAR

Isidor is a small portable CW radar which gives a visible and audible indication of moving targets up to at least 300m and possibly as much as 2km from the transmitter. The radar is normally tripod-mounted and the antenna manually steered, the radar being primarily intended for long-term monitoring of a particular point or line.

Operating headphones can be plugged into the radar head for direct monitoring; but a remote unit is also available which will accept output from up to four radar heads and indicate which, if any, is in contact with a target. When such an indication is given (by an indicator light) the operator can switch his headphones to listen to the output of the selected radar.

DATA

Operating frequency: 10.5GHz
Transmitter power: 10mW
Antenna beamwidth: 11°
Detection ranges: Men walking 300 metres; Moving vehicle 1,000-2,000 metres
Size: Main unit 10 × 20cm
Weight: 2.5kg excluding battery
Power consumption: 0.2A at 12V
Manufacturer: Telefonaktiebolaget L.M. Ericsson, M1 Division, S-431 20 Mölndal.

UNITED KINGDOM

PROWLER INFANTRY COMPANY RADAR

Prowler is a small self-contained patrol radar which can be carried by one man and may be tripod-mounted, chest-mounted or hand-held. Designed to a British Army specification it is suitable for use by infantry under battlefield conditions.

Electronically, Prowler is unusual in that in its two alternative operating modes, Search and Range, significantly different types of transmission are used. In the Search mode, in which the azimuths of all targets within range are sought, the radar uses a frequency-modulated CW doppler system: in the Range mode, in which target ranges are determined by an adjustable range gate, a pulse doppler system is used.

Only four controls are provided – an on/off switch, the Search/Range mode switch, the range gate control and a confidence switch to enable the operator to satisfy himself that the equipment is working correctly. This last switch also enables him to carry out a survey of his search area to detect any blind spots caused by ground screening.

DATA
TRANSMITTER AND ANTENNA SYSTEM
Operating frequency: Lower J-band
Polarisation: Horizontal

Antenna Beamwidth: 100 mils azimuth and elevation
Peak power (Pulse): 250mW
Mean power (FMCW): 25mW minimum

PRESENTATION
Audio system (Search and Range): Headset signals: operating audio response 40Hz to 1.7kHz. Audio gate position ganged to range gate in the range mode
Range: Direct reading scale calibrated from 75 to 3,000 metres in 25-metre steps. LED illumination

POWER SUPPLY SOURCE
Battery type: Secondary alkaline 24V 3.3amp/hour or 1amp/hour
Power consumption: Search 3W approx; Range 4W approx
Duration: 3.3amp/hour battery 33 hours;1amp/hour battery 12 hours

PERFORMANCE
Maximum range: Vehicle targets 3,000 metres; Men, good conditions 1,500 metres; Men, poor conditions 900 metres
Minimum range (Range mode only): 75 metres

Resolution: 100 metres
Target speed: Minimum 1.6km/hour; Maximum 64km/hour
Temperature range: Operating −32°C to +50°C; Survival −34°C to +70°C

PHYSICAL DIMENSIONS
Radar head: Height 280mm, Width 300mm, Depth 95mm
Tripod (collapsed): Length 600mm, maximum diameter 150mm
3.3amp/hour battery: Length 184mm, Width 127mm, Depth 73mm
1 amp/hour battery: Length 184mm, Width 52mm, Depth 73mm

WEIGHTS
Radar head: 3.5kg
Tripod: 3.5kg
Battery: 3.3amp/hour 3.5kg; 1amp/hour 1.1kg
Manufacturer: Marconi Radar Systems Ltd, Writtle Road, Chelmsford, CM1 3BN

Prowler Infantry Company Radar

ZB 298 BATTLEFIELD SURVEILLANCE RADAR

The ZB 298 Battlefield Surveillance Radar has been developed and manufactured by Marconi-Elliott Avionic Systems to meet a UK Ministry of Defence requirement for a portable battlefield radar, and has since been supplied to overseas customers. The radar can be transported by two soldiers and operated by one man to give an all weather, day and night facility to detect any significant movement on the battlefield. This includes the location and recognition of men singly or in groups, single or multiple vehicles and low flying helicopters. ZB 298 can also be used in a counter-insurgency role in keeping watch on sensitive areas such as an airfield.

The radar can be used in international border protection, particularly where the most vulnerable parts are only accessible on foot, by siting the radar near the border. Similarly, in its peace-keeping role, warnings of possible troop redeployment can be used to avert the danger of further conflict.

ZB 298 comprises a portable radar head, tripod, operator's display unit, power supplies, headset and cables with a system weight of 79lbs (35.8 kilograms). The system operates in the X-band with a peak transmitted power of 2kW and uses a flat antenna built as an integral part of the radar head.

The equipment takes only 2½ minutes to set up and be fully operational. It is extremely simple to operate from the display unit which can be situated up to 65ft (20m) away from the radar head. Alternatively, ZB 298 can be mounted on a soft-skinned or armoured vehicle.

To find and indentify a target the operator searches in range and bearing until the display shows the characteristic evidence of target presence. By moving the range markers over the target the range can be read off the numeric counters, and similarly, the bearing can be found from the reading on the bearing control. With little training, the operator can distinguish the nature of the moving target from its distinctive Doppler signature.

Supporting equipment for ZB 298 includes a training simulator to give realistic training on the classroom.

ZB298 in its infantry role

DATA
Range, maximum: 10,000 metres
       minimum: 50 metres
Azimuth coverage: 6,400 mils
Elevation coverage: ±355 mils
Range resolution: 35 metres
Azimuth resolution: 100 miles
Range accuracy: 25 metres
Azimuth accuracy: 15mils

Horizontal beamwidth: 90mils
Vertical beamwidth: 90mils
Manufacturer: Mobile Radar Division, Marconi-Elliott Avionic Systems Ltd., Elstree Way, Borehamwood, Hertfordshire, WD6 1RX.
Status: In service with UK and other forces.

BATTLEFIELD INTRUDER ALARM SYSTEM – IRIS

Marconi-Elliott Avionic Systems have designed the IRIS infra-red intruder alarm system for use out of doors in the protection of buildings and site perimeters. It is a lightweight, rugged, high reliability system requiring the minimum of technical skill to set up, making it particularly suitable for battlefield applications.

The basis of the system is an infra-red beam projected between a transmitter and a sensor. Interruption of the beam causes an alarm to be triggered at a remote monitoring unit. The beam is a narrow cylindrical pipe about 40mm (1½in) in diameter which is virtually impossible to detect without interrupting reception by the sensor. As the beam must be com-

pletely obscured to give an alarm, the transmitter and sensor can be hidden in light foliage, amongst small twigs and branches.

IRIS can be used both during the day and at night over ranges of 200 metres in average conditions. Even in fog, snow or tropical rain, a range of 50 metres may be obtained. The monitor unit is provided for control of up to four links with a counting facility to record the number of times that the beam is interrupted.

The system is designed to be 'fail safe' in that damage or destruction of the transmitter or sensor, disconnection of the battery, or the cutting of the signal cables leading to the monitor will automatically indicate an alarm condition.

Delay circuitry has been built in to overcome false alarms caused by such things as birds flying through the beam, which would reduce confidence in the equipment.

Power can be provided from any convenient 12 volt d.c. source.

Manufacturer: Mobile Radar Division, Marconi-Elliott Avionic Systems Limited, Elstree Way, Borehamwood, Hertfordshire, WD6, IRX.

Status: In service with UK forces.

IRIS Monitor Unit

BATTLEFIELD INTRUDER ALARM SYSTEM – TOBIAS

TOBIAS (Terrestrial Oscillation Battlefield Intruder Alarm System) has been designed by Marconi-Elliott Avionic Systems to provide a small, easily portable, all-weather day or night surveillance system which does not require line-of-sight conditions.

The system makes use of small, rugged, low-cost passive seismic sensors (geophones) which, because they are buried below ground level are virtually undetectable. The sensors are deployed near likely intruder approach routes or round a perimeter, if necessary, many miles from the display unit.

TOBIAS has four independent channels to each of which may be connected up to 20 geophones. Maximum detection distance of a man walking is seldom less than a circle of radius 50 metres round a single sensor. This will depend largely on the nature of the ground and the amount of natural and man-made seismic activity in the area, but distances in excess of 50 metres up to a radius of 300 metres are not uncommon. Therefore a considerable frontage can be protected by a single TOBIAS system.

To reduce the risk of false alarms with their resulting loss of confidence in the equipment, the display unit is equipped with adjustable sensitivity controls. These allow the operator to eliminate the background noise to permit maximum sensitivity on each channel, and if necessary will enable him to count the number of men or vehicles passing the sensor. Earphones are also provided in addition to the visual indication giving the operator the ability to listen to all four channels if he wants to and to recognise the nature of the movement near each sensor.

Power supplies are contained in the display unit giving a minimum of 72 hours continuous operation.

Manufacturer: Mobile Radar Division, Marconi-Elliott Avionic Systems Limited, Elstree Way, Borehamwood, Hertfordshire, WD6, IRX.

Status: In service with UK and other forces.

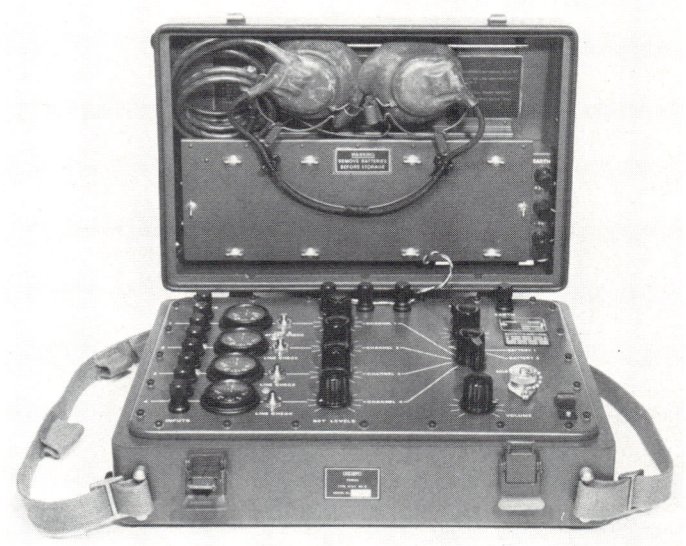

Control Unit for TOBIAS Military Intruder Alarm System

AIDA INTRUDER ALARM SYSTEM

AIDA – Automatic Intruder Detector Alarm – is an extension of and development from the Marconi-Elliott TOBIAS system described above. Like TOBIAS it uses passive seismic sensors which can be either buried in the ground or mounted on a fence to detect the vibrations caused by an intruder while discriminating against interference from such sources as machinery, traffic, trains or small animals. When a correct intruder vibration pattern is identified an alarm is automatically given at the central control point. The alarm can be in any convenient visible or audible form and can be remoted over considerable distances. Connections between the sensors and the control centre are made by buried cables; and any interference with them will also trigger the alarm circuits.

AIDA is primarily designed for the protection of permanent or semi-permanent installations, vehicle parks, compounds and similar potential targets for intruders where the area to be guarded is large. TOBIAS is more appropriate to small areas and temporary arrangements.

Manufacturer: Mobile Radar Division, Marconi-Elliott Avionic Systems Ltd, Elstree Way, Borehamwood, Hertfordshire, WD6 1RX

Status: Production

A central control panel for an AIDA installation

SHORROCK MICROWAVE FENCE

Shorrock Security Systems make a range of microwave intruder alarm systems generically described as microwave fences. Both static and mobile systems are available; and that which is most probably appropriate for military purposes is the Model 330, which is made in portable kit form, although the static systems may find applications in permanent or semi-permanent military installations – hutted camps and so forth.

A single kit of the Model 330 can protect an area of some 4,500 square metres and is so designed that it can easily be installed and tested by non-technical personnel in approximately 30 minutes.

On site the Microwave Fence units can be set up in the required pattern and are connected to a control unit. The range between transmitter and receiver is up to 80 metres and the invisible fence is typically 1.8-2.5 metres high and up to 2.5 metres thick in the centre. Once an intruder breaches the curtain of energy a discrete signal is initiated at the control unit.

Included in the system is a remote alarm unit which can be connected to the control and gives a warning signal audible up to 900 metres. Additional facilities are incorporated in the control unit which may be used to trigger external devices such as lights or radio links.

The microwave fences will operate satisfactorily in rain, fog, or snow, and have a high resistance to activation by birds, small animals and wind-blown debris.

COMPOSITION

Each kit comprises eight carrying cases, four microwave fence units complete with tripods, one control unit with visual and audible annunciators, four power units, nine cable reels, one remote alarm, one headset for use in certain military conditions, and one battery charging unit.

Each of the eight carrying cases is of sturdy metal construction, furnished with carrying handles and painted in olive drab.

Size:–   Length 1,200mm. Width 500mm
Depth 300mm. Weight (Empty) 26kg

The contents of each of the carrying cases are as follows:–

Case 1 Headquarters Case – 1 off.
1 Microwave Fence Receiver and Tripod.
1 Control Unit.
1 Battery Charging Unit.
1 Remote Alarm.
1 Headset.
1 Cable Reel.

Weight Gross: 61kg

Case 2 Receiver Case – 3 off, each containing:
1 Microwave Fence Receiver and Tripod.
1 Cable Reel.

Weight Gross: 51kg

Case 3 Transmitter Case – 4 off, each containing:
1 Microwave Fence Transmitter and Tripod.
1 Cable Reel.
1 Power Unit.

Weight Gross: 63kg

For transportation the eight carrying cases can be accommodated in a space of 1 metre × 1.2 metres × 1.2 metres.

Total Gross Weight: 465kg

Manufacturer: Shorrock Security Systems Ltd, Shadsworth Road, Blackburn BB1 2PR

UNITED STATES OF AMERICA

AN/PPS-5A BATTLEFIELD SURVEILLANCE RADAR

AN/PPS-5A is a versatile battlefield radar capable of detecting either moving targets only or both fixed and moving targets and featuring automatic sector scanning for long period surveillance. Physically portable in three manpacks from which the radar can be assembled in under 10 minutes, the system comprises a Ku-band non-coherent pulse doppler radar transmitter-receiver mounted with a parabolic antenna on a tripod and a remote display and control unit which can be located up to 6 metres from the radar.

The remote unit incorporates both A-scope and B-scope displays on which either moving targets or fixed and moving targets can be displayed. The MTI system used permits a high degree of discrimination against fixed targets while permitting the detection of moving targets down to about 1.6km/h radial velocity. Headphones can also be used either at the transmitter or at the remote unit to detect the characteristic tones of different kinds of moving targets.

A choice of sector scanning modes is available for surveillance; and targets thus detected can be located in range and bearing by stopping the scan, traversing the antenna to obtain maximum signal in azimuth and operating an adjustable range gate to obtain maximum signal in range.

DATA
Operating frequency: 16.0-16.5 GHz tunable
Range: Men 5km; Vehicles 10km
Accuracy: Azimuth ±10mils; Range ±20metres
Sector scans: 531, 1,062 or 1947mils
Weight: Radar 25.4kg; Remote unit 16kg
Power supply: 6V battery or 24VDC generator plus converter
Manufacturer: AIL Division of Cutler Hammer Inc., Deer Park, Long Island, New York 11729
Status: Originally entered US service as AN/PPS-5 in 1967 as a transistorised replacement for the AN/PPS-4 Silent Sentry made by Sperry. Production of the 5A improved MTI version was intiated by the US Army Electronics Command in 1974.

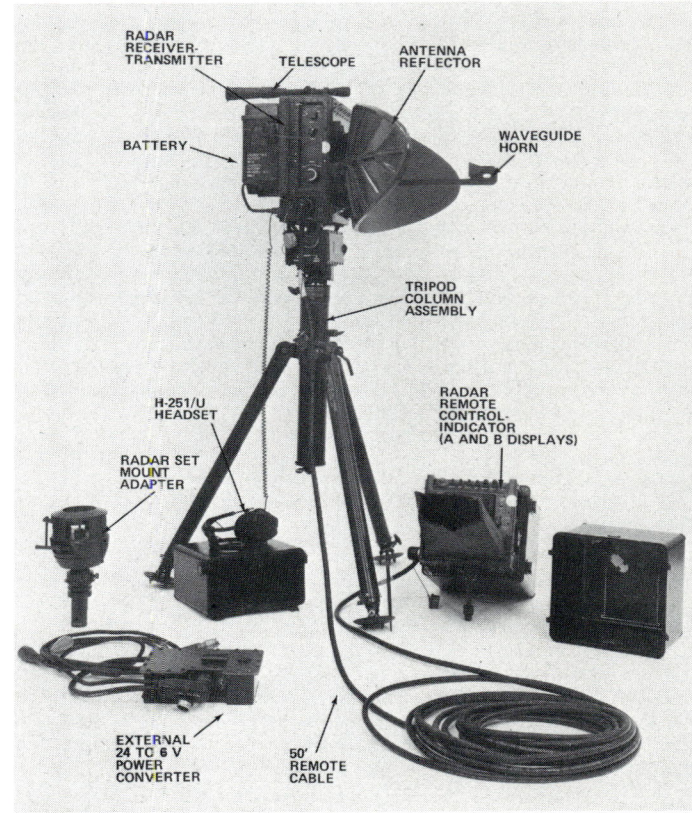

AN/PPS-5A

AN/PPS-5B BATTLEFIELD SURVEILLANCE RADAR

The AN/PPS-5, originally designed in the 1960-1963 period as a man-packed battlefield surveillance radar, is still doing world-wide duty in that capacity, having seen initial and extensive service from 1967 onwards in Southeast Asia. Between 1966-1971 AIL delivered a substantial quantity of AN/PPS-5's to the US Army and a modest quantity to international customers.

In Southeast Asia the AN/PPS-5 was put to many uses. Its first deployment was along the DMZ where it was used for general surveillance functions. At artillery bases it was used for perimeter defence and for providing target coordinates to the field artillery battery for direction of fire against approaching enemy patrols. It was also man-packed by foot patrols to forward areas for the acquisition of data on enemy troop movements.

During this same period, AIL made experimental models in a jeep-mounted configuration and in a 360° scan configuration, both of which were field-tested in Southeast Asia. The interest in the vehicle-mounted configuration continued, and the US Army developed a Pintle Mount Adapter to permit mounting the AN/PPS-5 on any military vehicle equipped with a 50-calibre machine gun mount. AIL's present contract with the US Army provides for the inclusion of this adapter with each AN/PPS-5B System.

The manufacturer reports that interest in greater mobility and transportability for the AN/PPS-5 has been steadily increasing, the argument being that by rapidly transporting the radar performance capability from one location to another, and requiring only a two- or three-man team, it can perform functions that could otherwise require a string of fixed installations, each with its own crew. This concept is particularly applicable along remote international border areas; and since most remote areas are not very accessible to large vehicles, the jeep appears to be the optimum vehicle.

Manufacturer: AIL Division of Cutler Hammer Inc., Deer Park, Long Island, New York 11729

Status: A small quantity is being produced for an oversea customer

AN/PPS-5B installed on an M-4 MG mounting in a jeep. To avoid unnecessary stress on the gearing the transmitter-receiver assembly is removed from the mounting while the vehicle is in motion

AN/PPS-6 BATTLEFIELD SURVEILLANCE RADAR

AN/PPS-6 is a man-portable tripod-mounted X-band non-coherent pulse doppler radar capable of automatic scanning and giving an audible indication of the presence of moving targets. The transmitter-receiver and small parabolic antenna form a single unit which, with the angular control assembly is mounted on a folding tripod and the user has the option of manual control of the pointing direction or any of three azimuth sector scans.

There is also a choice of range sectors. A range gate enables the user to search an area of 45 metres depth in range beyond a chosen range: in the automatic modes the equipment will either scan continuously an area extending in range for 315 metres beyond a chosen range or search, in alternate sweeps, this area and a further area extending from the 315 metre range to 630 metres beyond the chosen range. When a target is located its

coordinates can be determined by manually adjusting the antenna and range control for maximum signal and reading off the required angle and range.

DATA

Operating frequency: 9.0-9.5GHz

Range: Men 1,500 metres; Vehicles 3,000 metres

Accuracy: Azimuth ±18 mils; Range ±25 metres

Sector scans: 600, 900 or 1,200 mils

Weight: 20kg

Power supply: Battery

Manufacturer: General Instrument Corporation, 600 West John St, Hicksville, New York, N.Y. 11802

Status: In service with US forces

AN/PPS-9 HAND-HELD TACTICAL RADAR

AN/PPS-9 is a man-portable X-band coherent modulated CW doppler correlation radar designed for the US Army for combat surveillance and target acquisition. It provides a wide range of operational facilities within a very small compass. Weighing only 13lb (5.9kg), including the optional remote control unit and internal batteries to give 12 hours continuous operation, it may be hand-held or mounted on a tripod or vehicle pintle mount. Range performances of 1,500 metres on men and 3,000 metres on vehicles have been quoted.

Among the advantages claimed for the radar is a choice of all-range, fine-range, coarse-range and acquisition modes of operation; the coarse-range and all-range resolution being used for the surveillance of groups and large areas or fast-moving targets while fine-range resolution is

used for the separation of multiple targets and for high clutter rejection and detection through foliage. In the target acquisition mode targets can be observed simultaneously in all-range and discrete range channels.

Another important feature is the low background noise. Not only does this reduce operator fatigue but it also results in a low false-alarm rate when the radar is used to provide automatic target indication. A detailed description of the equipment principle of operation will be found in the AN/PPS-11 entry below. The equipment has been extensively tested and is approved for service. An MTBF of 3,000 hours is claimed.

Manufacturer: RCA, Missile and Surface Radar Division, Moorestown, N.J.

Status: In production for US forces

AN/PPS-10 PORTABLE BATTLEFIELD SURVEILLANCE RADAR

This is a very light (4.5kg) X-band coherent CW doppler radar designed to give an aural indication of targets in range. A choice of manual or automatic sector scan is available and the operator may choose between all-range surveillance and discrete range indication for target acquisition.

DATA

Operating frequency: X-band

Range: Men 1,500 metres; Vehicles 3,000 metres

Power supply: Disposable battery

Manufacturer: General Dynamics, Electronics Division PO Box 81127, San Diego, California 92138

AN/PPS-11 HAND-HELD TACTICAL RADAR

Formerly known as the Model 2019 M2 this battlefield radar uses an X-band modulated CW doppler correlation system and is the lightest of the RCA range of hand-held radars. The basic operating principle of these radars is described below and is common to the AN/PPS-9 and the AN/PPS-12 (Model 4019 M2).

The radar uses correlation of a phase-shifted pseudo-random code to determine range and to provide range resolution. A random code is generated in the code generator, a shift register with a feed-back loop. The code is then applied to a driver where an STC signal is introduced. The product of the two signals is then applied to the phase modulator section of the transmitter where the phase of the carrier is changed 180°.

The transmitter signal is applied to the circulator which permits simultaneous reception and transmission through the antenna. The reflected signal passes through the antenna and circulator and is superimposed on the transmitter signal attenuated through the reverse coupling of the circulator.

The two signals are detected in the mixer. Only the low-frequency signals are amplified in the video amplifier that follows. The product of the STC modulated code and its delayed replica with doppler modulation is introduced to the decoder. This signal and the product of the undelayed STC modulated code and the code delayed in a discrete time interval from the code generator are correlated in the decoder, leaving only a doppler-modulated STC signal at the amplifier.

The STC signal is next applied to the phase detector where correlation with a quadrature STC signal from the master oscillator provides weighting of amplitude, monotonically increasing with range. This provides low gain for close-in targets and high gain for long-range targets.

The signal containing only the modulation of the target is amplified by the audio amplifier and thresholded by a detector-gate combination for passing large signals to the sensor station. In the search mode, the clock rate is

used to generate the code. This provides a wide open range resolution of 1,000 metres. The range switch is placed in the first position, so that correlation occurs in the first range bin. The code provides a linear auto-correlation going to unity at 1,000 metres, voltage gain is hence linear with range. Since the STC action is also essentially linear with range, the system provides a fourth power range correction for constant power return from targets at any range.

The range selector switch may be placed on a specific range bin and the range resolution reduced to 25 metres by increasing the clock rate. This provides a 25-metre band of coverage at the range selected. An audio output of the doppler character of the target is provided to the radar operator.

Three controls only are required to operate the radar. One combines the on/off function with selection of the all-range (acquisition) or ranging (location) modes; a second selects the range segment for ranging and the third controls the signal volume in the headset. A manual battery check indicator is also provided.

DATA

Operating frequency: X-band 8.75GHz

Detection range: Men 500 metres; Vehicles 1,000 metres

Location range: 0-500 metres

Range resolution: 25 metres

Range accuracy: 8 metres

Weight: 4.5kg total

Power supply: 12V rechargeable NiCd battery

Manufacturer: RCA, Missile and Surface Radar Division, Moorestown N.J.

Status: In service with US forces

AN/PPS-12 HAND-HELD TACTICAL RADAR (TYPE 4019 M2)

Generally similar to the AN/PPS-11 radar, in the same equipment series, but larger and with added facilities, the RCA Type 4019 M2 is an X-band coherent modulated CW doppler correlation radar.

For the addition of about 2.6kg in total weight the user obtains an increase in maximum detection range from 1,000 metres to 3,000 metres, automatic scanning, automatic target warning and the facility for simultaneous surveillances and ranging. Apart from this the equipment function is the same as that described for the AN/PPS-11.

DATA
Operating frequency: X-band 8.75GHz
Detection range: Men 1,500 metres; Vehicles 3,000 metres

Range resolution: 25 metres
Ranging accuracy: ±8 metres
Sector scan: Selectable up to 270° 80 mil/sec
Look-listen facility: Indicator light and threshold meter provide visual indication of a detected target and relative measure of target signal strength corresponding to headphone aural signal. Combination of aural and visual indication provides continuous aural target monitoring while using visual signal to give target range.
Weight: 6.35kg total
Power supply: 12V internal NiCd battery
Manufacturer: RCA, Missile and Surface Radar Division, Moorestown N.J.

AN/PPS-15 PORTABLE BATTLEFIELD RADAR

This is an X-band coherent modulated CW doppler infantry radar which has been developed as a follow-on to the AN/PPS-10. Like the latter, it offers a choice of manual or selectable automatic sector scan and provides an aural indication of a target when searching which can be supplemented by a light indication when the range is measured by the manually-operated range gate. The radar also features a remote operation arrangement and a visual and aural alarm.

DATA
Operating frex-band
Detection ranges: 3,000 metres
Remoting: To 9 metres
Weight: 7.3kg
Power source: Internal disposable battery with 12 hour continuous operation capacity or external 24VDC
Manufacturer: General Dynamics Corporation, Electronics Division, PO Box 81127, San Diego, California 92138
Status: In service in the USA, Canada and Norway

AN/PPS-17 BATTLEFIELD SURVEILLANCE RADAR

This X-band non-coherent pulse doppler radar has been developed to meet a USMC requirement. It is in many respects similar to the AN/PPS-6 battlefield radar but differs from it primarily in its lower weight and in the addition of an IFF (Identification, Friend or Foe) facility.

DATA
Operating frequency: 9.0-9.5GHz

Detection range: Men 1,500 metres; Vehicles 3,000 metres
Range accuracy: ±25 metres
Azimuth accuracy: ±18 mils
Weight: Significantly less than 20kg
Manufacturer: General Instrument Corporation, 600 W John St, Hicksville, New York, N.Y. 11802
Status: Field trials

AN/PPS-18 BATTLEFIELD SURVEILLANCE RADAR

This pulse-doppler radar has been developed to meet the same USMC specification as has the AN/PPS-17 described above and is also similar to but lighter than the AN/PPS-6.

DATA
Operating frequency: 8.75GHz

Detection range: Men 1,500metres; Vehicles 3,000metres
Range accuracy: ±25metres
Azimuth accuracy: ±18mils
Weight: 15.8kg
Power supply: Battery
Manufacturer: RCA, Missile and Surface Radar Division, Moorestown NJ.

AN/TPS-21 and AN/TPS-33 PORTABLE BATTLEFIELD SURVEILLANCE RADARS

These two radars are X-band portable manpack pulse-doppler equipments used to detect troops and ground vehicles in motion. Scanning is either manual or automatic with choice of scanning sector. For the TPS-21 target detection is only by audible tone in the operator's headphones; in the TPS-33 there is also an A-scope display.

DATA
Operating frequency: X-band
Detection range: Men 10,000metres; Vehicles 18,000metres
Range accuracy: ±23metres or ±1% of range whichever is the greater
Manufacturer: Admiral Corporation, 3800 W. Cortland St., Chicago, Ill. 60647
Status: Both radars are in service with US forces. TPS-33 is also in service with the Bundeswehr.

ELECTROMAGNETIC MOTION DETECTOR

This solid state device is designed to detect moving targets in foliage and can operate either independently or in conjunction with a seismic system. Operated alone, the EMD is designed to indicate, within a radius of some 45metres, targets with radial velocities of from 30 to 240cm/sec in reasonably heavy foliage. On detecting a persistent target within the range of radial velocities the EMD generates a signal which is normally conveyed to a remote alarm indicator from which point the EMD is also normally switched on and off.

When used with a seismic network the EMD is so arranged that it is switched on when the network detects a seismic signal and it then searches for confirmation of the seismic signal. If a target showing net radial motion is detected an alarm signal is generated as usual and the EMD then switches itself off. If no target can be confirmed the EMD searches for a predetermined period and then switches itself off without transmitting an alarm signal.

An omnidirectional radiator is used in conjunction with a pulsed-band transmitter-receiver and doppler sense detector. Signal remoting can be by land line or radio link.

DATA
Operating frequency: 1,250MHz
Modulation: Pulse
Operating range: 3-46metres
Target velocity range: 30-240cm/sec
Size of unit: Approx. 20 × 20 × 15cm
Weight: Approx 2.75kg
Power supply: Mercury batteries giving nominal 30hr continuous operation
Manufacturer: RCA, Missiles and Surface Radar Division, Moorestown N.J.

R2000 PORTABLE BATTLEFIELD RADAR

This is a non-coherent pulse-doppler radar operating in the same frequency band as the AN/PPS-17 and similar to it in basic function. It differs from it, however, in being completely automatic in operation and remotely operable up to 30 metres by a control unit which can also be mounted on top of or behind the transmitter-receiver for hand-held or tripod-mounted operation respectively. A choice of automatic sector scans is available and there is a variable gate for range measurement. Target indication is aural supplemented by a visual light indication for coordinate measurement.

DATA
Operating frequency: 9.0-9.5GHz
Detection range: Men 1,500 metres; Vehicles 3,000 metres
Range accuracy: ±25 metres
Weight: 9.5kg
Power supply: Battery
Manufacturer: General Instrument Corporation, 600 W John St, Hicksville New York N.Y. 11802
Status: In service

R2010 BATTLEFIELD SURVEILLANCE RADAR

Similar to the R2000 radar but more powerful, the R2010 is an X-band non-coherent pulse-doppler equipment which, with its greater weight and substantially enhanced range performance is probably better suited to perimeter defence applications than to field operation. Like the R2000, it can be remotely operated up to 30m but there is also provision for a B-scope display in addition to the headphones at the remote unit.

DATA
Operating frequency: 9.0-9.5GHz
Detection range: Men 5,000metres; Vehicles 10,000metres
Range accuracy: ±25metres
Weight: 13.3kg
Power supply: Battery
Manufacturer: General Instrument Corporation, 600 W John St, Hicksville, New York N.Y. 11802
Status: Evaluation

PERSID-4A INTRUDER ALARM

PERSID-4A (Personnel Seismic Intruder Detector) is a 4-channel battery operated audio visual alarm system using passive geophone seismic sensors buried in the ground near likely intruder approach routes. The sensors are linked by wire to a control unit which can be located at a considerable distance from the sensors. Each sensor detects sub-audible ground vibrations made by men or vehicles and the resulting signals are amplified and processed at the control unit. The processed signals are reproduced in the operator's headphones and it is possible to interpret these signals by identifying particular signatures characteristic of men or types of vehicle.

Surveillance covering can be expanded by connecting up to six geophones to each of the four input channels; and the use of external selector switches on the input channels permits even greater expansion; it is also possible to arrange geophones in arrays which will have directivity if this should be of interest.

Geophones are robust and durable provided they are not exposed to acoustic overload such as could be caused by a nearby explosion.
Manufacturer: Defense Electronics Division of DEI Industries, Rockville, Maryland 20854
Status: In service with US forces

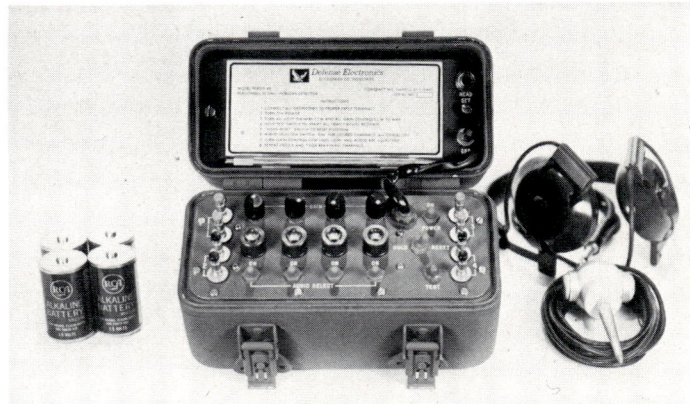

Persid system components

REMBASS BATTLEFIELD SENSOR SYSTEM

Currently the subject of a design study by RCA for the US Army Electronics Command, REMBASS – Remotely Monitored Battlefield Sensor System – has been conceived as a multi-faceted surveillance system for detecting the movements of wheeled and tracked vehicles and personnel over a wide area.

No detailed information on the project has so far been revealed; but it is understood that the intention is to use a variety of sensing devices – acoustic, seismic, magnetic, infra-red and probably others – so constructed that they can be deployed by hand, from the air, or by artillery projectiles or rockets. After deployment the sensors will report their findings to a central command post where the information will be processed and appropriate action initiated.
Manufacturer: RCA Government Systems Division, Moorestown N.J. 08057
Status: Study project for US Army Electronics Command, Fort Monmouth N.J. Although the award of the study contract was announced only in November, 1976, it is believed that other studies directed towards the same end preceded it.

REMOTE HANDLING EQUIPMENT

INTRODUCTION

In recent years considerable interest has been generated – largely as a result of operations in Northern Ireland – in the application of remotely controlled equipment to the solution of bomb disposal and related military and internal security problems. Two related categories of functions may be defined as Explosives Ordnance Reconnaissance (EOR) and Explosives Ordnance Disposal (EOD); the object of EOR being to use a robot vehicle to seek and examine suspected bombs or other hazards without risking the lives of the controlling personnel; and the object of EOD is to use the robot to lay demolition charges or otherwise dispose of the hazard with similar avoidance of risk.

It will be apparent that a similar basic vehicle can be used for both functions; but that for EOR the robot must be equipped with remote viewing apparatus (CCTV) while the EOD robot needs to have some remotely controllable mechanical handling capability.

Robot devices for these purposes first entered service with the British Army in Northern Ireland in 1971 and have been progressively developed since then. The first robot was named Wheelbarrow Mk 1 (so called because it was a three-wheeled vehicle): described below are the recent Mk 6 and Mk 7 developments in this progression, together with a conceptually related, but mechanically different, robot known as the Hunter.

WHEELBARROW Mk 6

Main items of this robot are the Trolley, Control Box, Monitor Unit, Control Drum and Accessory Assembly. The trolley is a tracked chassis containing the basic equipment – batteries, relays, electric motors, terminal board, spotlight and cover plate and attachment points for the mast, actuators and other ancillary equipment. The control box has controls for manoeuvring the vehicle and operating its various attachments: the monitor unit enables the operator to observe the scene viewed by the CCTV camera mounted on the boom of the vehicle. Accessories include straight and cranked boom extensions, a mast extension and an adaptor for a car hook and scissor attachment. Operational possibilities may be inferred from the description of the Mk 7 robot which follows

DATA
Length: 1,200mm
Width: 600mm
Height: approx 600mm minimum to 1,500mm
Weight: 180kg
Manufacturer: Morfax Ltd, Willow Lane, Mitcham, Surrey CR4 4TD, England
Status: In service

WHEELBARROW Mk 7

This is a developed version of Wheelbarrow Mk 6, the principal difference being an extension of the range and capabilities of its accessories. The equipment consists of a tracked vehicle which is powered by two lead-acid batteries carried on board. The motive power to the tracks is provided by two electric motors driven by an infinitely variable electronic speed control and the mechanical drive is transmitted by two worm drive gearboxes directly to the rear wheel axle. Also carried on board the main chassis are the electrical controls for the tractive and manipulating operations and an inverter to supply power to the television camera that is fitted on the manipulating mast. The vehicle is directed by a hand held control box, using positive switches which allow precise control of the vehicle and the boom with its attachments. Commands are transmitted to the vehicle by means of a fully protected trailing 18 way cable.

When an incident is reported, say a suspect parked car, Wheelbarrow can be taken speedily to the scene in a long wheelbase Land Rover or similar vehicle. It can then be driven off under its own power and the operator and ancillary equipment, including a CCTV monitor, deployed in a convenient defensive position. Using the control box the operator can manoeuvre the vehicle towards the car, using the TV system or by direct sight. On close approach the camera can be panned to facilitate a detailed inspection of the interior of the car. It may be necessary at this stage to break the car windows and this can be achieved by either a window breaking attachment or firing an automatic shotgun which are both fitted to the main boom assembly.

If it is decided to lay an explosive charge, this can be attached to the vehicle boom and placed in position, using the control box to operate an electro-mechanical release. Wheelbarrow will then withdraw trailing a firing cable. The charge can then be detonated using an independent plunger or by means of a special button on the control box which is protected by a cover to eliminate accidental operation. It may be more prudent to tow the car away before placing a charge or carry out further investigations. In this case a towing hook is attached to the boom and this is manipulated into position under the car. The hook is then released from the boom and Wheelbarrow withdraws trailing a tow rope in a similar manner to the firing cable. The car can then be towed, or dragged, away to a convenient position for further action.

Wheelbarrow's capability is not, of course, confined to the investigation of suspect cars. It can be equipped with various mechanical grabs for handling objects such as oil drums, milk churns etc. containing lethal devices. The vehicle's ability to climb stairs and negotiate rough ground has proved to be invaluable, particularly when it is called on to operate inside buildings. In this mode it is able to comply with one of the most elementary rules of strategy – always keep a path open for a tactical withdrawal.

This is achieved by nail guns on each side of the chassis which can be fired into the floor as the vehicle passes through doorways, preventing them from closing and obstructing its retreat.

DATA
Length: 1,220mm
Width: 690mm
Height: 820mm minimum (boom folded)
Weight: 195kg in operational configuration
Speed range: 0-33.5 metres/minute
Range: 100 metres with standard cable and drum
Power supply: 2×12V50A. HR lead/acid batteries
Endurance: 2hrs mean

Wheelbarrow Mk 7 with basic accessories

Wheelbarrow Mk 7 in action with a dustbin

CCTV Camera: Single lens. Power supplied by an inverter
Monitor: 9 inch (229mm)

Manufacturer: Morfax Ltd, Willow Lane, Mitcham, Surrey CR4 4TD, England
Status: In service. Details of sales are not available but since there was a potential sale of some 30 equipments to eight countries outside the UK as long ago as mid-1975 with at least five other countries then interested it may be assumed that there has been some movement since.

HUNTER REMOTELY CONTROLLED ROBOT VEHICLE

The Hunter is a self-powered, tracked, remotely-controlled vehicle developed for EOR and EOD operations. It consists of a battery-powered tracked chassis carrying a boom assembly to which can be fitted a wide variety of attachments. These include:

CCTV Camera reporting to a remote monitor
Car Hook with rope. The Hunter places the hook for remote towing
Scissors Grip. Long tongs for remote handling
Grapnel. For clearing loose obstructions or opening suspect packages
Scoop. For lifting and carrying suspect objects
Nail Gun. For securing doors
Tilting Arm. Remotely adjustable, this can be used to aim and operate a special shotgun for smashing windows or locks; to operate a window breaker; to place an incendiary or explosive charge; or to carry and pan the camera in EOR operations.

DATA
Length: 1,200mm
Width: 630mm
Height – without boom structure: 350mm
         – with boom lowered: 480mm
         – with boom raised: 1,300mm
Weight (chassis and boom): 115kg
Power Supply: 2 × 12V lead/acid batteries
Manufacturer: SAS R & D Services Ltd, Victoria House, Vernon Place, London WC1B 4DR, England

MINE DETECTORS

As noted earlier in this section, mine detection and clearance is a task which commonly has to be performed by infantry. When anti-tank and anti-personnel mines were first used the only practical method of hand clearance (and early attempts at mechanical clearance were so unsatisfactory in the their results that hand-clearance was virtually the only possibility) involved the use of simple probes with which the soldier prodded the earth and hoped to detect the mine without detonating it.

Came the electromagnetic mine detector; and for a brief period while many mines were made with metal cases the task of locating, if not lifting, them became much simpler. The extensive use of wooden cases, and more recently and increasingly plastic or fibre cases, however, restored the status quo so far as many blast mines were concerned; although fragmentation mines, provided the soldier can avoid the tripwires and other hazards, may be detected fairly readily. A possible modern counter to the plastic or wooden mine is the magnetic anomaly detector: used with care, such a device is likely to be able to detect a buried mine but is also likely to detect a lot of other buried objects and thus slow the clearance process. Moreover, there are now available in convenient form a variety of special mine initiation devices – such as those that are triggered by small vibrations – which can make any kind of hand-clearance operation extremely hazardous. Otherwise than in an emergency, therefore, such clearance techniques as the use of flail tanks, devices like the British Giant Viper or fuel-air explosions are likely to continue to be the most satisfactory ways of dealing with the perennially troublesome mine.

Early electromagnetic mine detectors, introduced before the invention of solid-state electronic circuitry, were fairly cumbersome devices: nowadays typical weights of portable detectors range from about 4kg to about 10kg depending on the performance required and the length of handle that is considered convenient. Some characteristics of modern detectors are compared below: 'range' in this context is the practical distance from the detection head at which a buried mine can be detected; and 'length' is the length of the handle on which the detector head is mounted.

Equipment	Range	Length	Weight
East German MSG 64	18cm	240cm	4.4kg
Russian IMP	100cm	200cm	9.7kg
British No 4C	51cm	128cm	5.0kg

Most electromagnetic mine detectors in service are one-man devices of types similar to those listed above. The Russians, however, have a vehicle-mounted arrangement (the DIM) which is intended for the rapid clearance of mines from roads. The detector head in this case is long and tubular and is propelled in front of a vehicle: when a buried metal object in the path of the vehicle is detected the brakes are automatically applied and a separate search process must be conducted to locate where, along the length of the detector head, the hazard is buried. The double search

The Plessey P6/2 is a pulsed induction metal detector which has been approved for British Army use. Interchangeable probes are available for a wide range of search applications

process is obviously time consuming to an unacceptable degree in a thickly sown minefield; but the system has some merit for checking a road where few, if any, mines are laid.

SECTION SIX

WEAPONS IN SERVICE

Country/Category	Type	Source etc
Mortar	82mm M37	
Anti-armour weapons	ZIS-3 ATk gun	
	82mm RCL B-10	
	40mm RPG-7	
	Sagger ATGW	
Anti-aircraft weapon	ZSU-23-4 Shilka	
Armoured vehicles	BTR-40, 50	

ARGENTINA

Pistol	Pistola Browning – HP 35 9mm NATO	The 9mm Browning FN. Made by Fabrica Militar de Armas Portatiles "Domingo Matheu"
	Pistola Ametralladora PA 0200/4 9mm NATO	Fabrica Militar
Sub-machine gun	PA-3-DM 9mm	Fabrica Militar
Rifles	Fusil Automatico Liviano F.A.L. 7.62mm NATO	Fabrica Militar
	Fusil Automatico Pesada F.A.P. 7.62mm NATO	Fabrica Militar. Heavy barrelled FN Rifle
General purpose machine gun	M.A.G. FN	Initially purchased from FN. Later manufactured by Fabrica Militar
Heavy machine gun	Browning 0.5in Heavy Barrelled. M2	USA
Grenade, anti-personnel	GME-FMK2-MO	Fabrica Militar
Grenades, anti-tank	PAF 62	Fabrica Militar
	PPP 26	Fabrica Militar
	PPF 26	Fabrica Militar
Grenades, tear gas	GLP-M1	Fabrica Militar
	GLP-M2	Fabrica Militar
	GCM-M1	
Mortars	Mortero Brandt calibre 81mm	Hotchkiss-Brandt, originally. Now manufactured by Fabrica Militar
	Mortero Brandt calibre 120mm	Now manufactured by Fabrica Militar
Anti-armour weapons	Canon sin Retroceso calibre 75mm DGFM	Copy of USA Recoilless Rifle 75mm, M20
	Canon sin Retroceso calibre 90mm DGFM	Copy of USA Recoilless Rifle 90mm, M67
	Canon sin Retroceso calibre 105mm DGFM	Designed and built in Argentina
	Cobra 2000 ATGW	Messerschmitt-Bolkow-Blohm, Germany
	SS-11 ATGW	Aerospatiale
	Hispano-Suiza 30mm HS 831 (towed)	Oerlikon-Bührle, Switzerland
Anti-aircraft weapon	AMX VCI MICV	Creusot-Loire, France
Armoured vehicles	M-113 APC	FMC, USA
	LVTP-7 AAV	FMC, USA
	Half-tracks	USA

AUSTRALIA

Pistol	9mm Pistol Browning L9A1	Stocks consist of pistols made by John Inglis, Canada. Replacements from FN Herstal, Liège
Sub-machine gun	9mm SMG F1	Commonwealth Small Arms Factory
Rifle	7.62mm L1A1	Commonwealth Small Arms Factory
	5.56mm M16	Military Division, Colts Industries
	7.62mm Omark M44	Sniping rifle. Made by Omark, Australia Ltd.
Light machine guns	7.62mm Heavy Barrelled FN Rifle L2A1	Commonwealth S.A. Factory: Not now used by Infantry
	7.62mm L4A4	Used in the Infantry Section. Manufactured at RSAF, Enfield
Sustained fire machine gun	7.62mm M60	USA
Heavy machine gun	.5in Browning Heavy Barrel M2	USA
Grenade, hand	M 26A2	Manufactured in Australia
Grenade, projected	40mm M406 using Grenade launcher M79 and M203 on M16 rifle	USA
Grenade, rifle	M26A2 with Adaptor Grenade Projection M1A2	Manufactured in Australia
Mortars	81mm Mortar F1	Consists of barrel and baseplate of USA 81mm mortar and mount of UK 3in mortar
	81mm Mortar F2	This is the UK L16A1 81mm mortar
Anti-armour weapons	66mm Light Anti-tank Weapon M72	Manufactured in Australia
	84mm Medium Anti-armour weapon L14A1	FFV, Sweden
	106mm M-40 RCL	USA
	120mm Wombat RCL	UK
Anti-aircraft missile	Redeye	General Dynamics, USA
Armoured vehicle	M-113	FMC, USA

AUSTRIA

Pistol	9mm Pistole 38	Steyr-Daimler-Puch
	0.45in M1911A1	Obtained from USA
Sub-machine gun	9mm MPi69	Steyr-Daimler-Puch
	9mm MP40	German origin
	7.62mm PPS-41	USSR
Rifles	7.62mm FN FAL	Steyr-Daimler-Puch
	7.62mm M1 Rifle	USA
	7.62mm M1 Carbine	USA
	7.62mm SSG69	Steyr-Daimler-Puch
General purpose machine gun	7.62mm M42/59	Rheinmetall, Germany

INTRODUCTION

In this section, weapons of various kinds and armoured vehicles all of which are believed to be currently in service with the armies, police and like forces of some one hundred and forty countries are listed, under country headings, together with such information regarding sources of supply as is available to us.

Generally, the weapons are such as are likely to be found in infantry formations, but some of the larger mortars and recoilless weapons and some of the anti-aircraft weapons may well be found more frequently elsewhere. In general we have tended to include too much rather than too little, both in this respect and in dealing with obsolescent weapons.

This survey in no way purports to be exhaustive: indeed the entries for some countries are vestigial. Had we restricted ourselves to countries of whose weapon inventories we were absolutely confident, however, the list would have been so short as to be of no practical value. We have therefore not hesitated to include a country even if our knowledge of its infantry equipment is limited to a single item.

It should be noted that the 'source' information given does not necessarily (and frequently does not) indicate the immediate source from which the present owner obtained the equipment concerned. There is a very substantial international market in military equipment through which articles may change hands several times before reaching the final customer; and this process is complicated by the substantial transfers of ownership by conquest that have occurred in recent years in the Middle East and South East Asia. Similarly, the mention of a manufacturer's name in the 'source' column does not necessarily mean that the manufacturer concerned was involved in the sale of the equipment to its present owner.

Country/Category	Type	Source etc
ABU DHABI		
Rifle	7.62mm G3	Heckler & Koch design
Mortar	81mm UK	UK
Anti-armour weapons	Vigilant ATGW	BAC, UK
	SS 11 ATGW	Aerospatiale, France
	Harpon ATGW	Aerospatiale, France
Armoured vehicles	AMX-VCI MICV	Creusot-Loire
	M3 APC	Panhard, France
	Saracen FV603 APC	Alvis/Leyland, UK

AFGHANISTAN

All current equipment is supplied by USSR. The initial supply started in 1956 and has continued since.

Pistol	7.62mm Tokarev Pistol (TT-33)	
Rifles	7.62mm Simonov SL Carbine (SKS)	
	7.62mm Kalashnikov Assault Rifle (AK 47)	
Light machine gun	7.62mm Degtyarev LMG (RPD)	
Heavy machine gun	12.7mm Degtyarev Model 38/46	Used also as anti-aircraft gun
Grenade, anti-personnel	RGD-5	
Grenade, anti-tank	RKG-3M	
Mortar	82mm, Model 1937, modernised	
	120mm M-43	
	160mm M-43	
Anti-armour weapons	82mm Recoilless Gun B-10	
	Snapper ATGW	
Armoured vehicles	BTR-40, 50, 60 and 152	

ALBANIA

Equipment basically of Russian (WW II) origin but supplemented in recent years by supplies from China.

Machine pistols	7.62mm M-40, M-41	USSR pattern
Rifles	7.62mm G-44 rifle	USSR pattern
	7.62mm SKS carbine	USSR pattern
	7.62mm AK-47 assault rifle	USSR pattern
Machine guns	7.62mm RP-46 LMG	USSR pattern
	7.62mm RPD LMC	USSR pattern
	7.62mm RPK LMG	USSR pattern
	7.62mm Maxim MMG	USSR pattern
	12.7mm DSH K-38 HMG	USSR pattern
Mortars	82mm M-37	USSR pattern
	120mm M-43	USSR pattern
	160mm M-43	USSR pattern
Anti-armour weapons	14.5mm PTRP ATk rifle	USSR pattern
	82mm RCL ATk gun T-21	Czechoslovakia
Armoured vehicles	K-63	China
	BTR-40, 50, 152	USSR

ALGERIA

Mortars	120mm M-43	USSR
	160mm M-43	USSR
Anti-armour weapon	Sagger ATGW	USSR
Anti-aircraft weapon	SA-7 SAM (Grail)	USSR
Armoured vehicles	BTR-40, 50, 60, 152	USSR
	Walid	Egypt

ANGOLA

The three-cornered war in Angola which followed the Portuguese withdrawal has brought a great many weapons across the borders and from external sources such as Cuba. It may be assumed that the official forces remaining in the country at the time of the withdrawal were equipped in much the same way as Portuguese home forces but probably with greater emphasis on such older weapons as the pre-war German 7.92mm MG13 machine gun. It is known that the Angolan 'liberation' forces had a number of Sten guns among their arms as also did the forces operating against Rhodesia. In addition, the following equipment has been reported as having been supplied to the hitherto successful MPLA forces by the USSR.

Pistol	7.62mm Tokarev	
Rifles	7.62mm AK-47	
	7.62mm AKM	
	7.62mm SKS	

Country/Category	Type	Source etc
Heavy machine gun	.5in Browning, Heavy Barrel, M2	USA
Grenade, hand defensive	HdGr 69	ARGES Accessories Ltd.
Grenade, hand offensive	HdGrO 69	ARGES Accessories Ltd.
	8cm Granatwerfer M-1	US 81mm Mortar M1
Mortars	8cm Granatwerfer M29/65: mit Gestell M23A1	US 81mm Mortar M29 with baseplate M23A1
	8cm Granatwerfer L70	UK 81mm Mortar L16 made under licence in Austria
	12cm Granatwerfer 60	Manufactured in Austria
	8.4cm PAR	Carl Gustav. Manufactured by FFV, Sweden
Anti-armour weapons	6.6cm PAR 67 (LAW)	M72. Manufactured by Raufoss
	7.4cm PAR 70	Miniman. Manufactured by FFV, Sweden
	10.6cm Panzerabwehrkanone M40	USA 106mm Recoilless Rifle M40A1
Anti-aircraft weapons	2cm FLAK 58	Oerlikon-Bührle, Switzerland
	2cm I-FLAK 65	
Armoured vehicles	Saurer 4K3/4K4 series	Steyr-Daimler Puch

BAHRAIN

Sub-machine gun	9mm Beretta M12	Pietro Beretta, Italy
Mortar	81mm UK	UK
Anti-armour weapon	120mm Mobat RCL	UK

BANGLADESH

Pistol	.38 Webley Mk 1V	The Bangladesh Army is largely equipped
	9mm Browning HP	with weapons left behind by the Pakistani Army when it withdrew
Rifles	.303 Rifle No 4	
	7.62mm L1A1	
	7.62mm G3	Heckler and Koch, Germany
Light machine gun	.303 Bren LMG	UK
Grenade, hand	No 36M	UK
Mortars	OML 2in	UK
	OML 3in	UK
Anti-armour weapon	6-pounder ATK gun	

BARBADOS

Pistols	.38 Webley Mk 1V	UK
	.38 Smith and Wesson	UK
Sub-machine gun	9mm Sterling Mk 4	UK
Rifles	.303in No 4	UK
	7.62mm L1A1	Commonwealth Small Arms Factory, Australia
Light machine gun	.303in Bren	
General purpose machine guns	7.62mm L4A3	RSAF, Enfield, UK
	7.62mm L7A1	FN, Belgium
Hand grenade	No 36M	UK
Mortar	OML 2in	UK

BELGIUM

Pistol	9mm FN Browning HP	FN
Sub-machine guns	9mm Vigneron M2	La Precision Liègeoise
	0.45in M3A1	USA
Rifles	7.62mm FN FAL	FN
	7.62mm M2 Carbine	USA
General purpose machine gun	7.62mm FN MAG	Replacing the Browning .30M 1919A4
Heavy machine gun	.5in Browning Heavy Barrel M2	USA
Grenades, hand	PRB-103, PRB-7, PRB-8	PRB
Grenade, smoke	PRB-412	PRB
Grenades, rifle	40mm Mecar	Mecar
	Anti-personnel, armour piercing, smoke and signalling	Mecar
Mortars	60mm M19	USA
	81mm M1	USA
	4.2in M30	USA
Anti-armour weapons	90mm CATI	USA Recoilless Rifle, M67
	30mm RARDEN Cannon	British weapon. Mounted on Scimitar
	Swingfire ATGW	British weapon. Mounted on Striker, CVRT
	SS 11 ATGW	Aerospatiale
	Entac ATGW	Aerospatiale
Armoured vehicles	Half-tracks	USA
	M75 APC	USA
	AMX VCI MICV	Creusot-Loire, France
	Spartan APC	Alvis/Leyland, UK

BOLIVIA

Rifles	7.62mm SG 510-4 rifle	SIG, Switzerland
	7.62mm G3 rifle	Heckler & Koch design
Armoured vehicles	M-113 APC	FMC, USA
	Commando APC	Cadillac Gage, USA

Country/Category	Type	Source etc
BRAZIL		
Sub-machine guns	.45 INA M953	Brazil. Madsen licence
	9mm Madsen M946	Madsen, Denmark
	9mm Madsen M50	Madsen, Denmark
	9mm Madsen M53	Madsen, Denmark
Rifles	SAFN 49 rifle	FN, Belgium
	7.62mm M1 rifle	USA
	7.62mm FN FAL	FN, Belgium
	7.62mm G3 Heckler & Koch	Made in Brazil under licence
Machine gun	0.5in M2 HMG	USA
Mortar	81mm M1	USA
Anti-armour weapons	106mm RCL M40	USA
	Cobra ATGW (MBB)	Made in Brazil under licence
Armoured vehicles	Half-tracks	USA
	M59 APC	FMC, USA
	M-113 APC	FMC, USA
	EE-11 Urutu APC	Engenheiros Especializados
BRUNEI		
Armoured vehicles	Saracen FV603 APC	Alvis/Leyland, UK
	AT104 ISV	GKN-Sankey, UK
BULGARIA		

Equipment generally similar to that of other Warsaw Pact forces.

Mortars	82mm M41, M43	USSR
Anti-armour weapons	82mm B10 RCL	USSR
	Sagger ATGW	USSR
	Snapper ATGW	USSR
Anti-aircraft weapon	SA-7 (Grail) SAM	USSR
Armoured vehicles	BTR-40, 60, 152	USSR
	OT-62 APC	Czechoslovakia
BURMA		
Rifles	7.62mm G3	Heckler & Koch design
	7.62mm AR-10	USA
Mortars	ML 3in	UK
	120mm	—
Anti-armour weapon	6-pounder ATK gun	UK
	17-pounder ATK gun	UK
BURUNDI		
Rifle	7.62mm FN FAL	FN, Belgium
CAMEROON		
Rifle	7.5mm MAS M49/56	France
Mortar	ML 3in	UK
Anti-armour weapon	106mm RCL M40	USA
CANADA		
Pistol	9mm FN Browning HP	Existing stocks made by John Inglis & Co
Sub-machine gun	9mm SMG C1	Canadian Arsenals, Ltd
Rifle	7.62mm FN CA1	Canadian Arsenals, Ltd
Sniping rifle	7.62mm C3	Parker Hale. UK
Light machine gun	7.62mm Rifle, automatic FN C2A1	Canadian Arsenals, Ltd
Medium machine gun	7.62mm Machine Gun C1	This is the USA .30 Browning M1919A4 converted to fire 7.62mm ammunition by Canadian Arsenals Ltd
Heavy machine gun	.5in Browning, Heavy Barrel M2	
Grenade, hand	M26 M67 with adapter M1A2	Lone Star Ordnance Plant, USA
Grenades, smoke	Grenade, Hand Smoke HC C1	Used with launcher L1A1 on Rifle C1A1
	Grenade, Hand Smoke coloured No 83 Mk 2/1 (C2A1)	Hand Chemical Industries Canadian Industries Ltd
Grenade, anti-riot	M7	USA
Light mortar	60mm M19	USA design. Made by Turnbull Elevator Co
Medium mortar	81mm Mortar C3	UK 81mm Mortar L 16A1
Heavy mortar	4.2in M-30	USA
Anti-armour weapons	66mm Rocket M72	USA
	84mm Recoilless Gun L14A1	FFV, Eskilstuna, Sweden
	Tow ATGW	Hughes, USA
	106mm Recoilless Rifle M 40A1	USA
	SS 11/Entac ATGW	Aerospatiale, France
Anti-aircraft weapon	Blowpipe	Manufactured by Short Bros & Harland, UK
Armoured vehicle	M-113 APC	FMC, USA

Country/Category	Type	Source etc
CHAD		
Rifles	7.5mm MAS M49/56	France
	7.62mm G3	Heckler and Koch design
Mortars	60mm and 81mm	—

CHILE

Changes in government have resulted in major changes in equipment policy for the Chilean Army. The current reorganization of the inventory may well result in a considerable simplification; and the following list must be treated as having no more than limited validity if indeed it is not already out of date.

Pistols	9mm FN Browning HP	FN, Belgium
	9mm P38	Carl Walther Waffenfabrik, Germany
SMG	9mm Madsen Model 1953	Denmark
Rifles	7.62mm FN FAL	Chile
	7.62mm SIG 510-4	Switzerland
	7.62mm AK-47	Limited numbers supplied by USSR
Light machine gun	7.62mm FN Heavy Barrel FAL	Chile
General purpose machine gun	7.62mm MG 42/59	Rheinmetall, Germany
Heavy machine gun	.5in Browning Heavy Barrel, M2	USA
Grenade	M26	USA
Mortars, light	60mm M19	USA
	81mm	USA
	120mm Hotchkiss-Brandt	France
Anti-armour weapons	Energa anti-tank grenade	Mecar, Belgium
	3.5in Rocket M20	USA
	106mm Recoilless Rifle M40A1	USA
Armoured vehicle	M-113 APC	FMC, USA

CHINA (People's Republic)

Pistols	7.62mm Types 51 and 54	Copy of the Russian 7.62mm Tokarev TT33
	9mm Type 59	Copy of the Russian 9mm Makarov Pistol
	7.65mm Type 64 Silenced	Chinese design and manufacture. Fires only the 7.65 × 17 rimless cartridge
Sub-machine guns	7.62mm Type 50	Copy of the Russian 7.62mm Model PPSh-41
	7.62mm Type 43	Copy of the Russian 7.62mm Model PPS-43
	7.62mm Type 64 Silenced	Chinese design and construction
	7.62mm Type 53 Carbine	Copy of Russian 7.62mm Model 1944 Carbine
Rifles	7.62mm Type 56 S.A. Carbine	Copy of the Russian 7.62mm SKS
	7.62mm Type 56 Assault Rifle	Copy of 7.62mm Russian AK-47. Late versions have permanently attached folding spike bayonet.
	7.62mm Type 56-1 Assault Rifle	Copy of the folding stock Russian 7.62mm AK-47
	7.62mm Type 68 Rifle	Chinese design combining features from the Type 56 SA Carbine and the Type 56 Assault Rifle
Light machine guns	7.62mm Type 53	Copy of Russian 7.62mm DPM
	7.62mm Type 56	Copy of Russian 7.62mm RPD
	7.62mm Type 58	Copy of Russian 7.62mm RP-46, the Coy machine gun
	7.62mm Type 67	Chinese designed. Replacing Type 53 and Type 58 MGs
Medium machine gun	7.62mm Type 57	Copy of Russian 7.62mm SGM
Heavy machine gun	12.7mm Type 54	Copy of Russian 12.7mm Model 38/46
Grenades	RG-42 Anti-personnel	USSR
	F1 Anti-personnel	USSR
	RGD-5 Anti-personnel	USSR
	RPG-6 Anti-tank	USSR
	RKG-3 Anti-tank	USSR
	RDG-2 Smoke	USSR
Mortar, light	60mm Type 31	Copy of the USA Mortar 60mm M2
Mortars, medium	82mm Type 53	Copy of the Russian 82mm M1937 (new version)
Mortars, heavy	120mm Type 53	Copy of the Russian 120mm M1943
	160mm Type	Copy of the Russian 160mm M1943
Anti-armour weapons	40mm Type 56	Copy of the Russian RPG-2
	40mm Type 69	Copy of the Russian RPG-7V
	57mm Type 36	Copy of US M18
	75mm Recoilless Gun Type 52	Copy of the USA M20 75mm RCL Gun
	75mm Recoilless Gun Type 56	An improvement on the Type 52
	90mm Anti-Tank Rocket Type 51	A copy of the USA 3.5in RL M20
	82mm Recoilless Gun Type 65	A copy of the 82mm Russian B 10 RCL
Armoured vehicles	Types 55, 56, K-63 APC	Made in China
	BTR-50 APC	USSR

CHINA (Taiwan)

Pistols	9mm Browning HP	Supplied by John Inglis, Toronto during World War II
	.45in Colt 1911A1	Supplied by USA before the Nationalists left the mainland

Country/Category	Type	Source etc
Sub-machine guns	.45in Thompson M1928	Supplied by USA during World War II
	.45in Thompson M1921	Made locally
	.45 SMG M3 and M3A1	Supplied by USA at the end of World War II
	.45 SMG Type 36	Copy of the USA M3A1
	9mm SMG Type 37	Copy of the USA M3A1 in 9mm
Rifles	.30 Rifle M1	Supplied by USA during and after World War II
	.30 Carbine M1	Supplied by USA during and after World War II
	7.62mm Rifle M14	Supplied by USA and now manufactured
	5.56mm Rifle M16	c5000 supplied by USA
Machine guns	7.92mm Type 24	German '08 Maxim (Obsolete)
	7.92mm Type 26	Czech Zb 26 (Obsolete)
	7.92mm Type 30	Czech Zb 30 (Obsolete)
	7.92mm Bren	Manufactured by John Inglis of Toronto and supplied during World War II
	.30 Browning M1919A4	Supplied by USA before leaving the mainland, and on arrival
	7.62mm M60 GPMG	Originally supplied by USA. Now manufactured on USA machinery
	.5 Browning Heavy Barrel M2	USA
Grenades	M57	USA
	M26	USA
Mortars	60mm M2	USA
	81mm M19	Supplied by USA and now manufactured
Anti-armour weapons	3.5in Rocket Launcher M20	Originally supplied by USA. Subsequently locally manufactured
	90mm Recoilless Rifle M67	USA
	106mm Recoilless Rifle M40A1	USA
Armoured vehicles	Half-tracks	USA
	M-113 APC	FMC, USA

COLOMBIA

Sub-machine guns	Madsen M46, M50, M53	Madsen, Denmark
Rifles	SAFN 49	FN, Belgium
	7.62mm G3	Heckler & Koch design
Mortar	105mm	—
Armoured vehicles	Half-tracks	USA

CONGO (People's Republic)
Equipment largely of Russian or Chinese origin

Mortars	82mm M41, M43	USSR
Anti-armour weapon	57mm M18 RCL	US pattern
Armoured vehicle	BTR-152	USSR

COSTA RICA

Sub-machine gun	9mm 38/49 Model 4	Pietro Beretta, Italy

CUBA
Equipment generally has much in common with that of Warsaw Pact forces, but includes some Western weapons

Sub-machine gun	9mm M23 and M25	Czechoslovakia
Rifles	7.62mm FN FAL	FN Belgium
	7.62mm AK	USSR
Machine gun	7.62mm FN MAG	FN Belgium
Mortars	81mm M1	USA
	82mm M41, M43	USSR
Anti-armour weapons	57mm RCL M18, 18A1	USA
	Snapper ATGW	USSR
Anti-aircraft weapons	12.7mm DShK 38	USSR
	14.5mm KPV	USSR
Armoured vehicles	Half-tracks	USA
	BTR-40,60 APC	USSR

CYPRUS
Present situation unclear. The following notes refer to the situation prior to the Turkish invasion.

Rifle	7.62mm M1	US pattern
Mortar	82mm M41, M43	USSR
Anti-armour weapons	57mm RCL M18, 18A1	USA
	106mm RCL M40AI	USA
Armoured vehicles	BTR-50 APC	USSR
	M60 APC	Yugoslavia

CZECHOSLOVAKIA

Pistols	7.62mm Vzor 52	Now used only by reserve formations
	7.65mm Vzor 61 (Skorpion)	
Sub-machine guns	7.62mm Model 24	Not used by front line troops
	7.62mm Model 26	
Rifle	7.62mm Vzor 58 Assault Rifle	
Light machine gun	7.62mm Vzor 52/57 LMG	

Country/Category	Type	Source etc
General purpose machine gun	7.62mm Vzor 59	
Heavy machine gun	12.7mm Degtyarev Model 38/46	
Grenades	RG-4 Anti-personnel grenade	
	RG-34 Fragmenting Grenade	Largely replaced by the RG-4
Mortars	81mm M1948	
	81mm M1952	
	120mm	USSR
Anti-armour weapons	RPG-7V	USSR Design. Czechoslovak Manufacture
	82mm M59 Recoilless Gun	Czech design and manufacture
	82mm M59 A Recoilless Gun	Czechoslovak manufacture
	Snapper ATGW	USSR design
	Swatter ATGW	Czech manufacture
	Sagger ATGW	USSR design
Anti-aircraft weapons	SA-7	USSR design
	12.7mm AA HMG M-53	This is a four barrelled gun on a single axled trailer
	14.5mm KPV	USSR 4-barrelled trailer mount
	23mm ZU-23	USSR
	30mm AA Gun M-53	Twin barrelled towed gun
Armoured vehicles	OT-810, OT-62, 64 APC	Czech manufacture
	BTR-40 APC	USSR
	BMP-1 MICV	USSR

DAHOMEY

Rifle	7.5mm MAS 49/56	France
Mortars	60mm and 81mm	Probably French

DENMARK

Pistols	9mm Model 40(S)	Swedish Model 40 Lahti. Limited numbers
	9mm Model 46	9mm FN Browning HP
	9mm Model 49	9mm SIG P 210-2
Sub-machine gun	9mm M49 Hovea	Designed by Husqvana in Sweden
Rifles	7.62mm G M50	USA Garand M1 converted by Beretta
	7.62mm G M66	German G3 rifle made by Heckler and Koch
Machine gun GPMG	7.62mm MG62	German MG42/59 made by Rheinmetall at Düsseldorf. This was followed by the Mg 1
Machine gun SFMG	.30 M52-1	USA M1919A4
Machine gun HMG	.5in Browning Heavy Barrel M2	USA
Grenade, hand	Handgranat M54	Ammunitionsarsenalet
Grenade, anti-tank	0.6kg gevaergranat H M49	Energa grenade, made by Mecar
Grenades, smoke	Rodhandbombe M32	Ammunitionsarsenalet
	Rodhandgranat (fosfor) M57	Phosphorus grenade made by AB Linde Maskiner, Lindesberg, Sweden
Mortars, light	51mm Mortar M/45 Fa	British 2in mortar
	60mm Mortar M/51 Fa	USA 60mm mortar M2
Mortar, medium	81mm Mortar M/57 Fa	Vabenarsenalet
Mortar, heavy	120mm Mortar M/50 Fa	Hotchkiss-Brandt design. Made by Vabenarsenalet
Anti-armour weapons	75mm RCL Rifle M20	USA origin
	84mm RCL M65	Carl Gustaf M2 supplied by FFV
	89mm RL M51	USA 3.5in RL M20, M20B1, M20A1B1
	106mm RCL M56	USA M40A1 RCL gun
	Cobra ATGW	MBB, W. Germany
	TOW ATGW	Hughes, USA
Anti-aircraft weapon	Redeye (Hamlet)	General Dynamics, USA
Armoured vehicle	M-113 APC	FMC, USA

DOMINICAN REPUBLIC

Pistols	.45 Colt M1911 A1	USA
	9mm FN Browning HP	Belgium
	.38 Smith & Wesson revolver	USA
Carbine	.30 Cristobal M2	San Cristobal Arsenal
Rifle	7.62mm G3	Heckler & Koch design
	7.62mm FN FAL	FN, Belgium
Machine gun	.30 Browning MMG	USA
Armoured vehicles	Half-tracks	USA

DUBAI

Sub-machine gun	9mm Sterling Mk 4	Sterling Armament Co. UK
Rifles	7.62mm FN FAL	FN, Belgium
	7.62mm G3	Heckler and Koch design
Machine gun GPMG	7.62mm FN MAG	FN, Belgium
Machine gun, heavy	20mm Hispano-Oerlikon	Oerlikon-Bührle, Switzerland
Grenade hand	36M	UK
Mortar	L2A1	UK
Anti-armour weapons	81mm L16A1	UK
	84mm RCL	FFV, Eskilstuna, Sweden

Country/Category	Type	Source etc
ECUADOR		
Rifle	7.62mm FN FAL	FN, Belgium
Machine gun	7.62mm FN MAG	FN, Belgium
Armoured vehicles	AMX-VCI MICV	Creusot-Loire, France
	M-113 APC	FMC, USA
EGYPT (ARAB REPUBLIC)		
Pistol	9mm Beretta Model 51	Made by Pietro Beretta, Italy
Sub-machine gun	9mm Port Said	Copy of Carl Gustaf Model 45. Used only by L of C troops
Rifles	7.62mm SKS	Russian SL Carbine
	7.62mm AK-47	Russian Assault Rifle
	7.62mm AKM	Lightened version of the AK-47
	7.62mm Rashid Carbine	Static Troops only
	7.92mm Hakim Rifle	Static Troops only
Machine guns	7.62mm RPD	USSR
	7.62mm SG-43	USSR
	7.62mm SGM	USSR
	12.7mm Degtyarev 38/46	USSR
Mortars	81mm M37M	USSR
	120mm M43	USSR
Anti-armour weapons	RPG-2	USSR Replaced almost entirely by RPG-7
	RPG-7V	USSR
	107mm B-11 RCL Gun	USSR
	Snapper ATGW	USSR
	Swatter ATGW	USSR
	Sagger ATGW	USSR
Anti-aircraft weapons	12.7mm HMG	
	14.5 KPV	On twin mount ZU-2 and Quadruple ZU-4
	23mm Cannon	On quadruple mount ZSU-23-4
	SA-7. (Grail)	
	ZSU-23-4 AA vehicle	USSR
Armoured vehicles	Walid APC	Egyptian
	OT-62, 64 APC	Czechoslovakia
	BTR-40, 50, 60 APC	USSR
	BMP-1 MICV	USSR
EL SALVADOR		
Rifle	7.62mm G3	Heckler & Koch design
ETHIOPIA		
Rifle	7.62mm Type 56 assault rifle	China (P.R.)
	7.62mm M1	US pattern
Machine gun	0.5 M2 HMG	USA
Mortar	4.2in M2A1	USA
Armoured vehicles	M59 APC	FMC, USA
	M-113 APC	FMC, USA
	Commando APC	Cadillac Gage, USA
FINLAND		
Pistols	9mm Pistol M35 Lahti	Valtion Kivaaritehdas (State Rifle Factory)
	7.65mm Pistol M23 Parabellum	Luger Pistol Model '08. Few left
Rifles	7.62mm M39 Ukko Pekka	Cadet forces only
	7.62mm M60 Assault Rifle	Valmet Oy. Reserve units only
	7.62mm M62 Assault Rifle	Valmet Oy, Paakonttori, Punanotkonkatu 2, SF-00130 Helsinki 13
Sub-machine gun	9mm SMG M44	Tikkakoski Oy, SF-41161 Tikkakoski, Finland
Machine gun, light	7.62mm M62	Fires 7.62mm × 39. Made by Valmet Oy
Machine gun, medium	7.62mm M32-33	Maxim
Mortars	81mm Mortar M38	Tampella. Also Soviet 82mm M-37 mortars
	120mm Mortar M40	Tampella. Also Soviet 120mm M38 or M43 mortars
	160mm Heavy Mortar	Tampella
Anti-armour weapons	Rocket Launcher M55	PI Vammaskosken tehdas
	Rocket Launcher M58-61	Valmet Oy and Oy Tampella Ab
	Rocket Launcher RPG-7	USSR
	SS-11 ATGW	Aerospatiale, France
	Vigilant ATGW	BAC, UK
Anti-aircraft weapon	23mm ZU-23	USSR
Armoured vehicle	BTR-50	USSR
FRANCE		
Pistols	9mm PA Mle 50	GIAT
	9mm PAP Mle F1	MAB

Country/Category	Type	Source etc
Sub-machine gun	9mm P-M Mle 49	MAT 49
Rifles	7.5mm FSA Mle 49/56	DTAT
	7.5mm FR F1	Sniping rifle
Machine gun, GPMG	7.5mm AA Mle 52	DTAT
Machine gun, light	5in Browning HB, M2	USA
Machine gun, heavy	Defensive, Mle 37/46	DTAT
Grenades, hand	Offensive, Mle 1937	DTAT
	Offensive/Defensive	Losfield Industries
rifle	65mm STRIM	Luchaire SA
	47mm Mle 1960 Smoke	Luchaire SA
Mortars	60mm light mortar	Hotchkiss-Brandt
	81mm mortars MO-81-61C and -61L	Hotchkiss-Brandt
	120mm light mortar Mle 1960	Hotchkiss-Brandt
Anti-armour weapons	LRAC de 89mm Mle F1	Luchaire SA
	SS11 B1 ATGW	Aerospatiale
	Entac ATGW	Aerospatiale
	Milan ATGW	Euromissile
Anti-aircraft weapons	20mm Gun M621	APC weapons. DTAT
	20mm gun M693 (Mle F1)	
Armoured vehicles	AMX-VCI MICV	Creusot-Loire
	AMX-10P MICV	GIAT
	VXB-170 APC (Gendarmerie)	Berliet
	M3 APC	Panhard

GABON

Sub-machine gun	9mm Beretta Model 12	Pietro Beretta, Italy

GAMBIA

Pistol	.38 Webley Mk 4	Webley and Scott
Rifles	7.62mm L1A1	Commonwealth Small Arms Factory, Australia
	.303 No 4	
LMG	7.62mm Bren	Royal Small Arms Factory, UK
Sub-machine gun	9mm Sterling Mk 4	Sterling Armament Co, UK

GERMANY (Federal Republic)

Pistols	9mm Pistole P1	Carl Walther
	9mm PP/PPK	Carl Walther
Sub-machine gun	9mm Uzi	IMI, Israel
Rifles	7.62mm G3	Heckler and Koch
	7.62mm G3 SG1	Sniping rifle
Machine gun	7.62mm MG3	Rheinmetall, Polygonal barrel from Heckler and Koch
Grenades, hand	DT11B1	Israeli Military Industries
	DM21	Raufoss, Norway
	DM41	Fabrica Militar de Braco Portugal
	DM51	Diehl
	DM19	Buck
	DM24	Buck
	DM24A1	
Mortars	120mm MRS-120-2	Soltam Ltd. Israel
	120mm Brandt Mortar	Used by Territorial Army only
	120mm Tampella Light Mortar	Soltam, Israel
	120mm AM 50 Brandt Mortar	Hotchkiss-Brandt, France
Anti-armour weapons	PZF 44	Diehl, Metallwerk
	PZB 84-1 and PZB 84-A1	Diehl under licence from FFV Eskilstuna (Carl Gustaf)
	Cobra 2000	Messerschmidt-Bolkow-Blohm
	TOW ATGW	Hughes Aircraft Co, USA
	Milan ATGW	Euromissile
Anti-aircraft weapons	20mm Maschinenkanone MK 20 DM1 and MK 20-DM1A1	Rheinmetall under licence from Hispano-Suiza. Vehicle mounted
	20mm Maschinenkanone MK 20 Rh 202	Rheinmetall. Vehicle mounted
	30mm Maschinenkanone HS 831	Rheinmetall. Vehicle mounted
	Redeye SAM	General Dynamics, USA
Armoured vehicles	SPZ 12-3 APC	Henschel and Hanomag
	M-113 APC	FMC, USA
	Marder MICV	Rheinstahl Transporttechnik

GERMANY (Democratic Republic)

Pistol	9mm Pistole M	Copy of the Russian Makarov Pistol (PM) using the 9mm × 18 pistol cartridge
Rifles	7.62mm Karabiner-S	Copy of the Russian Simonov SL Carbine SKS. Uses the 7.62mm × 39 cartridge
	7.62mm MPiK	Copy of the Russian AK-47 Assault Rifle
	7.62mm MPiKS	Copy of the Russian AK-47 with folding stock
	7.62mm MPi KM	Copy of the Russian AKM Assault Rifle
	7.62mm MPiKMS	Copy of the Russian AKMS with folding stock
	5.6mm KKMPi69	Training rifle 22in LR

Country/Category	Type	Source etc
Machine gun, light	7.62mm 1MG-K	Copy of the Russian RPK LMG
Machine gun, medium	7.62mm PK	Copy of the Russian PK. Uses the 7.62mm × 54R cartridge
	7.62mm PKB	Copy of the Russian PKB
	7.62mm PKS	Copy of the Russian PKS. Tripod mounted
Machine gun, heavy	12.7mm Degtyarev M38/46	Anti-personnel. Russian pattern
Grenade, hand	RGD-5	Anti-personnel. Russian pattern
Grenades, anti-tank	RKG-3	—
	RKG-3M	—
	RKG-3T	—
Grenade, smoke	S-32	East German design
Mortars	S-53	East German design
	81mm M37M	Copy of the Russian Modernised M37 81mm
	120mm	Copy of the Russian M1943
Anti-armour weapons	RPG-7V	German production of the Russian weapon
	RPG-7D	German production of the Russian weapon
	73mm SPG-9	German production of the Russian weapon
	Snapper ATGW	USSR
	Swatter ATGW	USSR
	Sagger ATGW	USSR
Anti-aircraft weapons	SA-7	USSR
	14.5mm KPV HMG	USSR
	23mm Cannon ZU-23	USSR
	ZSU-23-4	USSR
Armoured vehicles	BTR-40, 50, 60, 152	USSR
	BMP-1	USSR

GHANA

Rifle	.303 No 4	Enfield manufacture, UK
	7.62mm FN FAL	FN manufacture
Sub-machine gun	9mm Sterling Mark 4 SMG	Sterling Armament Co, UK
Light machine gun	.303 Bren	Enfield manufacture, UK
Grenade, anti-riot	Schermuly	Schermuly Ltd, UK
Mortars	OML 2in	UK production
	OML 3in	
	81mm Mortar	Soltam, Israel
	120mm Mortar	Soltam, Israel
Anti-tank weapons	84mm RCL	FFV, Sweden

GREECE

Sub-machine gun	.45 SMG	USA
Rifle	7.62mm M1	USA
Machine gun	.30 Browning MMG	USA
Mortars	60mm M2	USA
	81mm M1	USA
	4.2in M2 and M30	USA
Anti-armour weapons	57mm M18/18A1 RCL	USA
	88mm M20 RCL	USA
	106mm M40 RCL	USA
	TOW ATGW	USA
	Milan ATGW	Euromissile
Anti-aircraft weapon	Redeye SAM	USA
Armoured vehicles	AMX-10P MICV	GIAT, France
	Half-tracks	USA
	M59, M-113 APC	FMC, USA
	Mowag Roland APC	Mowag, Switzerland

GUATEMALA

Pistols	.45 M1911A1	USA
	9mm Star	Star Bonifacio Echeverria SA, Spain
Sub-machine gun	.45 M3A1 SMG	USA
Rifles	.30 Carbine M1	USA
	.30 Rifle M1	USA
Machine gun, light	.30 Browning M1918M2	USA
Machine gun, medium	.30 M1919-A1	USA
Grenade	M26	USA
Mortars	60mm M2	USA
	81mm M1	USA
Anti-tank weapon	3.5in Rocket Launcher M20	USA
Armoured vehicles	Half-tracks	USA
	M-113 APC	FMC, USA

GUINEA

Armoured vehicles	BTR-40, 152 APC	USSR

GUINEA-BISSAU

No definite information. Equipment is almost certainly a mixture of arms left with locally-recruited members of the Portuguese forces and Warsaw Pact weapons supplied to the now ruling independence party before the Portuguese withdrawal.

Country/Category	Type	Source etc
GUYANA		
Pistols	Pistol, Walther Model PP Cal .22 LR	Carl Walther, Germany
	Pistol, Walther Model PPK	Carl Walther, Germany
	Pistol Automatic 9mm	USA
	Smith & Wesson Model 39	
Rifles	7.62mm L1A1	Royal Small Arms Factory, UK
	7.62mm G3	Heckler and Koch design
Light machine gun	7.62mm Bren L4A3	Royal Small Arms Factory, UK
General purpose MG	7.62mm L7A2	Royal Small Arms Factory, UK
Mortar	81mm UK	UK
Armoured vehicle	Shorland APC	Short Bros and Harland, UK
HAITI		
Pistols	.45in Colt M1911A1	USA
	.38in Colt	USA
Sub-machine guns	.45in Thompson	USA
	9mm Uzi	IMI, Haifa, Israel
Rifles	.30in M1	USA
	7.62mm G3	Heckler and Koch design
Machine gun, medium	.30 Browning M1919A4	USA
Machine gun, heavy	.5 Browning Heavy Barrel M2	USA
Mortars	60mm Mortar M2	USA
	81mm Mortar M1	USA
Anti-armour weapon	57mm M18/M18A1 RCL	USA
Armoured vehicle	M-113 APC	FMC, USA
HONDURAS		
Mortar	120mm	—
Anti-armour weapon	57mm M18/M18A1 RCL	USA
HONG KONG		
Armoured vehicle	Saracen APC	Alvis/Leyland, UK
HUNGARY		
Pistol	7.62mm M48	Copy of Russian Tokarev TT-33
	7.65mm M48	Copy of German Walther PP
Sub-machine gun	7.62mm M-48 SMG	Copy of Russian PPSh-41. Used only by local militia
	7.62mm AMD	Shortened version of the Hungarian AKM rifle
Rifle	7.62mm AK-47 Assault Rifle	Copy of Russian AK-47
	7.62mm AKM Assault Rifle	Copy of Russian AKM
	7.62mm M48 Sniping Rifle	Copy of the Russian Mosin-Nagant M1891/30in 7.62mm × 54 R. Probably relegated to militia forces
Machine gun, light	7.62mm RPK	Copy of the Russian weapon. 7.62mm × 39
Machine guns, medium	7.62mm PK	Similar to the Russian PK, using the
	7.62mm PKB	7.62mm × 54 R cartridge
	7.62mm PKS	Similar to the Russian PKS and tripod mounted
Machine gun, heavy	12.7mm Degtyarev 38/46	
Grenades	Offensive Hand Grenade M42	Hungary
	Anti-tank. RKG-3, 3M and 3T	USSR
Mortars	81mm M37M	Copy of the modernised Russian M37 Mortar
	120mm M43	Copy of the Russian M43
Anti-armour weapons	RPG-7V	USSR
	RPG-7D	USSR
	73mm SPG-9	USSR
	107mm B-11 RCL	USSR
	Snapper ATGW	USSR
	Swatter ATGW	USSR
	Sagger ATGW	USSR
Anti-aircraft weapons	SA-7	USSR
	14.5mm KPV	USSR
	23mm Cannon ZU-23	USSR
Armoured vehicles	OT-62, 64 APC	Czechoslovakia
	BTR-40, 50, 60, 152	USSR
INDIA		
Pistol	9mm Browning HP	
SMG	9mm Sterling Mk 4	Manufactured in India
Rifles	7.62mm IA SL	Ishapore made FN design. Some supplied from UK
	.303 No 4	Used for grenade launching
Machine gun, light	7.62mm L4A4	Bren
Machine gun, medium	7.62mm MAG 58	Purchased from FN. Some supplied from UK during war with China
Grenade, hand	36M	UK origin
Grenade, rifle	36M with discharger plate	Discharged from No 4 Rifle with grenade discharger cup. UK origin

Country/Category	Type	Source etc
Grenade, anti-tank	No 73	UK origin
Grenade, smoke	No 77	UK origin
Mortars	OML 2in	UK
	OML 81mm M16A1	UK
Anti-armour weapons	3.5in Rocket Launcher M20	USA design. Supplied from UK manufacture
	57mm M18 RCL	USA design and supply
	106mm M40A1 RCL	USA design and supply
	6-pounder ATK gun	UK
	SS-11 ATGW	Some French-built (Aerospatiale). Some only assembled in India. Now produced in India (Bharat Dynamics)
	Harpon ATGW	Licence built (Aerospatiale) by Bharat Dynamics
Anti-aircraft weapon	SA-7 SAM	USSR
Armoured vehicles	OT-62, 64 APC	Czechoslavakia
	BTR-50, 152 APC	USSR

INDONESIA

Pistol	9mm Pindad	Manufactured at the Pindad Ordnance Factory. Copy of the 9mm FN Browning
Sub-machine guns	9mm P.M. Model V111	Produced by Bandung arsenal
	9mm Model 12 SMG	Beretta Model 12 made under licence
Rifles	7.62mm BM-59	Produced under licence from Beretta
	5.56mm AR-15	Purchased from Colt in limited quantity
Machine guns, light	.30 Browning Automatic Rifle M1918 M2	USA
	.30 Madsen LMG	Manufactured locally
	.303 Bren	Left behind by British Forces in 1945
Machine guns, medium	7.62mm DPM	USSR
	7.62mm SGM	USSR
Machine gun, heavy	12.7mm D.Sh. K.	Early Russian model
Mortars	60mm M2	USA
	3in	UK
	120mm M43	USSR
Anti-armour weapons	3.5in Rocket Launcher M20	USA
	106mm RCL Gun M40	USA
	Entac ATGW	Aerospatiale, France
Armoured vehicles	AMX VCI MICV	Creusot-Loire, France
	BTR-40, 152 APC	USSR
	Saracen APC	Alvis/Leyland, UK

IRAN

Pistol	.45in Colt M1911A1	
Rifles	7.62mm G3	Produced under licence from Heckler and Koch, Germany
	.30 M1	Now relegated to static units
Sub-machine guns	9mm Uzi	Designed and produced in Israel
	.45 M3A1	Relegated to reserve formations
Machine gun, light	7.62mm MG1A1 (bipod)	Produced under licence from Rheinmetall Germany
Machine guns, medium	7.62mm MG1A1 (tripod)	
	.30 Browning M1918A4	Being replaced by MG1A1
	7.92mm Model 30	This was produced in Iran. It is the Czech Model 30 and is now found only with static units
Machine gun, heavy	.5in Browning Heavy Barrel M2	USA
Mortars	60mm M19	USA
	81mm	USA
	4.2in M30	USA
	120mm	Soltam, Israel
Anti-armour weapons	RPG-7V	USSR
	3.5in RL M20	USA
	57mm RCL M18	USA
	75mm RCL M20	USA
	106mm M40A1C	USA
	SS 11 ATGW	Aerospatiale, France
	Entac ATGW	Aerospatiale
	TOW ATGW	Manufactured by Hughes Aircraft, USA
Anti-aircraft weapons	ZU-23	USSR
	SA-7	USSR
Armoured vehicles	BTR-40, 50, 60, 152	USSR
	M-113	FMC, USA

IRAQ

Pistol	7.62mm TT-33	USSR
Sub-machine gun	7.62mm PPS-43	Static units only. Russian wartime SMG
Rifle	7.62mm AK-47	USSR
Machine gun, light	7.62mm RPD	USSR
Machine gun, medium	7.62mm SGM	USSR
Machine gun, heavy	12.7mm Degtyarev 38/46	USSR
Grenades	RGD-5 Anti-personnel	USSR probably used only for training
	RPG-43 Anti-tank	USSR probably used only for training
	RPG-6 Anti-tank	USSR
	RKG-3, 3M, 3T Anti-tank	USSR
Mortars	81mm M37M	USSR
	120mm M43	USSR

Country/Category	Type	Source etc
Anti-armour weapons	RPG-7	USSR
	107mm B-11 RCL	USSR
	Swatter ATGW	USSR
	Sagger ATGW	USSR
Anti-aircraft weapons	SA-7	USSR
	12.7mm Degtyarev HMG	USSR
	14.5mm KPV	USSR
	23mm Cannon	USSR (towed)
Armoured vehicles	M3 APC	Panhard, France
	BTR-40, 152 APC	USSR
	BMP-1 MICV	USSR

IRELAND (EIRE)

Pistol	9mm FN Browning HP	FN, Belgium
Sub-machine gun	9mm M45 SMG	FFV, Sweden
Rifle	7.62mm FN FAL	FN, Belgium
Machine gun, light	7.62mm FN MAG (Bipod)	FN
Machine gun, medium	7.62mm FN MAG (Tripod)	FN
Grenades, hand	HdGr 69	ARGES Accessories Co. Austria
rifle	Gr69	ARGES
A.Tk.	Energa	Mecar, Belgium
Mortars	60mm	Hotchkiss-Brandt, France
	81mm	Swedish origin
	120mm	Swedish origin
Anti-armour weapons	84mm RCL Gun, Carl Gustaf M2	FFV, Sweden
	90mm RCL Gun	FFV, Sweden
Armoured vehicles	M3 APC	Panhard, France
	Timoney APC	In production, 1976

ISRAEL

Pistol	9mm Beretta Model 51	Pietro Beretta, Italy
Sub-machine gun	9mm Uzi	Israeli Military Industries
Rifles	7.62mm FN FAL	FN, Belgium
	5.56mm GALIL	Israeli Military Industries
	5.56mm M16	Supplied by USA after October war
	7.62 AK	By capture from UAR
Machine gun, light	7.62mm FN FAL Heavy Barrel	FN, Belgium
Machine gun, GPMG	7.62mm FN MAG	FN
Machine gun, heavy	.5in Browning Heavy Barrel M2	USA supply
Grenades, hand	Defensive M26	Copy of USA grenade. Produced by IMI
	Offensive No.14	Israeli design. Produced by IMI
	Smoke No.5	Israeli design. Produced by IMI
	Coloured Smoke No.5	Israeli design. Produced by IMI
Mortars	52mm light mortar	Israeli design. Produced by IMI
	81mm medium mortar	Produced by Soltam, Tampella design
	120mm heavy mortar	Produced by Soltam, Tampella design
Anti-armour weapons	84mm Carl Gustav RCL	FFV, Sweden
	106mm RCL M40A1	IMI
	Dragon ATGW	Supplied by USA during October War
	TOW ATGW	Supplied by USA during October War
	SS-10	Supplied by Nord-Aviation (now Aerospatiale), France. Probably few, if any, remaining
Anti-aircraft weapon	Redeye SAM	General Dynamics Corp., USA
Armoured vehicles	OT-62 APC	Czechoslovakia
	BTR-50, 60, 152 APC	USSR
	Walid APC	Egypt
	Half-tracks	USA
	M-113 APC	FMC, USA

Note that some of these vehicles have been captured during the Arab-Israeli wars.

ITALY

Pistols	9mm Beretta M51	Pietro Beretta SpA
	9mm (Short) Beretta M34	Beretta
Sub-machine guns	9mm M.A.B. 38/49 Model 4 and 5	Beretta
	9mm M12	Beretta
	9mm M57	L. Franchi
Rifles	7.62mm BM59 Mark Ital	Beretta
	7.62mm BM59 Mark Ital Paratrooper	Beretta
	7.62 BM59 Mark Ital Alpini	Beretta
	7.62mm BM59 Mark II	Beretta
	7.62mm BM59 Mark E	Beretta
	5.56mm AR70	Not in general use. Beretta
	5.56mm AR70 Mod SC70/.223	Employed only by specialised units. Beretta
	5.56mm AR70 Mod SC70/.223 short version	Employed only by specialised units. Beretta
Machine guns, light	7.62mm MG42/59 (Bipod mounted)	Made by Beretta Armi Roma, and Whitehead-Motofides at Livorno under licence from Rheinmetall, Dusseldorf
	.30 Browning M1919A4	USA
	7.62mm M73	USA

Country/Category	Type	Source etc
Machine gun, medium	7.62mm MG42/59 (Tripod mounted)	
Machine guns, heavy	.5 Browning Heavy Barrel M2	USA
	.5 M85	From USA
Grenade, hand	S.R.C.M. Model 35	La Precisa SpA
Grenade, rifle	Model Falcone	Ital-Italjet
Grenade, (A.Tk)	Energa	Mecar, Belgium
	Super-Energa M2	SNIA Viscosa SpA
Grenade, (illuminating)	Model 59	Mortini, SpA
Mortars	81mm Model 62	OTO Melara SpA
	120mm Model 63	Hotchkiss-Brandt production. France
Anti-armour weapons	3.5in Rocket Launcher M20	USA
	75mm RCL Model 20	USA
	106mm RCL Model 40A2	USA
	Cobra	Sigme Spa
	Mosquito ATGW	Contraves SpA. Obsolescent
	SSII B1 ATGW	Aerospatiale, France
	TOW ATGW	Hughes Aircraft, USA
Anti-aircraft weapon	.5in Browning on quadruple mount M55	USA
Armoured vehicles	AMX-VCI MICV	Creusot-Loire, France
	Half-tracks	USA
	M-113 APC	Licence-built by OTO-Melara

IVORY COAST

Rifles	7.5mm MAS 49/56	France
	7.62mm G3	Heckler & Koch design
Mortars	81mm, 120mm	Hotchkiss Brandt, France

JAMAICA

Pistol	9mm Browning No 2 Mk 1	FN (England)
Sub-machine gun	9mm Sterling Mk 4	Sterling, UK
Rifles	7.62mm L1A1	Australia
	7.62mm L2A1 Heavy Barrel	Australia
Machine gun	7.62mm L8A1 GPMG	RSAF, UK
.Mortar	81mm	Probably UK

JAPAN

Pistol	.45 M1911A1	USA
	.38 Special New Nambu Revolver M60	Issued for special duties only. Manufactured by Shin Chuo Kogyo
Sub-machine gun	.45 M3A1	USA
	9mm SCK SMG	Shin Chuo Kogyo
Rifle	7.62mm Type 64	Howa Machinery Co. Ltd.
Machine gun, GPMG	7.62mm Model 62	Nittoku Metal Industry
Machine gun, heavy	.5in Browning Heavy Barrel M2	USA
Grenades, HE	M26, M61	USA
Grenades, smoke	WP M15	USA
Grenades, riot control	Riot CS1 ABC-M25A2	USA
Mortars	60mm M19	USA
	81mm	USA
Anti-armour weapons	3.5in RL M20	USA
	90mm-RCL M67	USA
	106mm RCL M40A1	USA
	Type 64 ATM (KAM-3D)	Kawasaki Heavy Industries Ltd
Armoured vehicles	Half-tracks	USA
	SU60 APC	Mitsubishi Heavy Industries
	Type 73 MICV	Mitsubishi Heavy Indsutries

JORDAN

Rifles	7.62mm FN FAL	FN, Belgium
	7.62mm G3	Heckler & Koch design
Machine gun	0.5 M2 HMG	USA
Anti-armour weapons	106mm M40 RCL	USA
	TOW ATGW	Hughes Aircraft, USA
	Dragon ATGW	McDonnell Douglas, USA
Anti-aircraft weapon	Redeye SAM	General Dynamics, USA
Armoured vehicle	Saracen APC	Alvis/Leyland, UK

KENYA

Rifle	7.62mm FN FAL	FN, Belgium
	7.62mm G3	Heckler & Koch design
Mortars	81mm	UK
	120mm	Hotchkiss Brandt, France
Anti-armour weapon	84mm Carl Gustav	Sweden
Armoured vehicle	M3 APC	Panhard, France

KHMER REPUBLIC (CAMBODIA)

Following the takeover of the country by Khmer Rouge forces little information concerning the structure and equipment of the armed forces has become available. The following data relate to the period preceding the takeover: this equipment is probably still in service but may have been augmented by supplies from Vietnam.

Country/Category	Type	Source etc
Rifle	7.62mm FN FAL	FN, Belgium
Mortars	82mm M41, M43	USSR
	81mm M1	USA
Anti-armour weapon	106mm M40 RCL	USA
Armoured vehicles	BTR-152 APC	USSR pattern
	M-113 APC	FMC, USA

KOREA (North)

Pistols	7.62mm TT-33	Copy of the Russian Tokarev M-1933
	7.65mm Type 64	Copy of the Browning Model 1900, Made in North Korea. Fires the 7.65mm × 17SR (.32ACP) cartridge
	7.65mm Type 64 Silenced	Issued for assassination purposes
Sub-machine gun	7.62mm Type 49	Copy of Russian PPSh-41. 7.62mm × 25 cartridge
Rifles	7.62mm Type 63 Carbine	Copy of the Russian SKS Carbine using the 7.62mm × 39 cartridge
	7.62mm Type 58 Assault Rifle	Copy of the Russian Ak-47
	7.62mm Type 68 Assault Rifle	Copy of the Russian AKM. Solid stock and folding stock versions. Folding stock is perforated for lightness
	7.62mm M1891/30	Russian Mosin-Nagent sniping rifle. Uses the long 7.62mm × 54 R cartridge
Machine guns, light	7.62mm Type 64	Russian RP-46. Fires the 7.62mm × 54 R cartridge
	7.62mm RPD	Russian LMG. Fires the 7.62mm × 39 cartridge
Machine guns, medium	7.62mm PK, PKB, PKS	Russian General Purpose Machine Gun. Fires the 7.62mm × 54 R cartridge
	7.62mm SGM	Russian MMG being replaced by PK series
Machine gun, heavy	12.7mm Degtyarev M38/46	Russian HMG
Grenades, hand	F1 Anti-personnel	USSR*
	RG-42 Anti-personnel	USSR
	RGD-5 Anti-personnel	USSR
	RKG-3, 3M, and 3T A.Tk.	USSR
Mortars	82mm M37M	USSR
	120mm M43	USSR
Anti-armour weapons	RPG-2	USSR
	RPG-7V	USSR
	82mm SPG-82	Used only by People's Militia
	75mm RCL Gun Type 52	Chinese copy of the USA M20 RCL gun
	82mm B-10 RCL Gun	USSR
Anti-aircraft weapons	12.7mm Degtyarev HMG	USSR. May be Chinese copy known as Type 54 HMG
	SA-7 SAM	USSR
Armoured vehicles	BTR-40, 60, 152 APC	USSR
		*All the grenades in use in North Korea may have been supplied by China

KOREA (South)

Pistol	.45 Colt 1911A1	USA
Sub-machine gun	.45 M3A1	USA
Rifles	.30 M1 Carbine	USA
	.30 M1 Rifle	USA
	5.56mm M16A1	Production from new factory at Pusan set up by Colt Military Industries
Machine guns	7.62mm M60 GPMG	USA
	.30 Browning M1919A4	USA
Machine gun, heavy	.5 Browning, Heavy Barrel M2	USA
Grenade	M26	USA
Mortars	60mm M2	USA
	81mm M1	USA
	4.2in M30	USA
Anti-armour weapons	3.5in RL M20	USA
	75mm RCL Gun M20	USA
	106mm RCL Gun M40A1	USA
Anti-aircraft weapons	.5in Browning, Heavy Barrel M2	USA
Armoured vehicle	M-113 APC	FMC, USA

KUWAIT

Rifle	7.62mm FN FAL	FN, Belgium
Machine gun	7.62mm FN MAG	FN, Belgium
Anti-armour weapons	SS 11 ATGW	Aerospatiale, France
	TOW ATGW	Hughes, USA
	Vigilant ATGW	BAC, UK
Armoured vehicles	Saracen APC	Alvis/Leyland UK
	M-113 APC	FMC, USA

Country/Category	Type	Source etc

LAOS
Situation unclear since the communist takeover in late 1975.

Mortars	4.2in M2A1	USA
	107mm M38	USSR, ex Pathet Lao
Anti-armour weapon	57mm M18/M18A1 RCL	USA
Armoured vehicles	M-113 APC	FMC, USA
	Commando APC	Cadillac Gage, USA
	BTR-40 APC	USSR, ex Pathet Lao

LEBANON
The following notes relate to the situation prior to the outbreak of civil war and the subsequent Syrian intervention. As will be seen, most of the weapons originate in Western Europe or the USA. Since the outbreak of civil war, however it is likely that the Palestine Liberation forces have supplied or imported various weapons of East European origin. It is known, for example, that they use the 7.62mm Czech Vz 58 assault rifle and Russian M43 MG. They also had some Egyptian Walid and Russian BTR-152 APC.

Pistols	9mm FN	FN, Belgium
	9mm Walther P38	Carl Walther, W. Germany
	9mm Manurhin P1	Manurhin, France
	9mm Colt Commander	USA
Sub-machine guns	9mm MAT 49	France
	9mm Sterling	UK
Rifles	5.56mm FN CAL	FN, Belgium
	5.56mm M16A1	USA
	7.5mm M49, M49/56	France
	7.62mm FN FAL	FN, Belgium
Machine guns	7.7mm Bren (.303) LMG	UK
	7.5mm M1924/29 LMG	France
	7.5mm MAS 52 GPMG	France
	7.5mm MAS 52 Heavy Barrel	France
	7.62mm Browning (.30) MMG	USA
	7.92mm BESA	UK
	7.62mm FN MAG	FN, Belgium
	12.7mm (.50) M2 HMG	USA
Mortars	60mm M27/31	France
	60mm HB light mortar	Hotchkiss-Brandt, France
	81mm HB light mortar	Hotchkiss-Brandt, France
	81mm M27/31	France
	120mm M1950	France
	120mm M1965	France
Anti-armour weapons	83mm RL	Belgium
	88mm RL	Spain
	40mm RPG	USSR
	106mm M40 RCL	USA
	SS 11 ATGW	Aerospatiale, France
	Entac ATGW	Aerospatiale, France
	TOW ATGW	Hughes, USA
Anti-aircraft weapons	20mm and 30mm Oerlikon	Oerlikon-Bührle, Switzerland
	(types and mountings unknown)	
	20mm M55	Yugoslavia
	23mm ZU-23	USSR
Armoured vehicles	Half-tracks	USA
	M59, M-113 APC	FMC, USA
	Commando	Cadillac Gage, USA

LIBERIA

Pistols	.45 Colt 1911A1	Springfield Armoury, USA
	.38 Smith & Wesson	
Rifles	.30M1 Carbine	Springfield Armoury, USA
	.30M1 Rifle	Springfield Armoury, USA
Machine gun, light	.30 Browning M1918M2 (BAR)	Springfield Armoury, USA
Machine gun, medium	.30 Browning M1919A4	Rock Island Arsenal
Machine gun, heavy	.5 Browning Heavy Barrel M2	Springfield Armoury, USA
Grenade hand	M26	
Mortar	60mm M31	Frankford Arsenal, USA
	81mm	Frankford Arsenal, USA
	4.2in M30	Frankford Arsenal, USA
Anti-armour weapons	3.5in Rocket Launcher M20A1	Springfield Armoury, USA
	106mm RCL Gun M40A2	Watervliet Arsenal, USA

LIBYA

Sub-machine guns	9mm Beretta Model 12	Pietro Beretta, Italy
	9mm L34A1	UK
Rifle	7.62mm FN FAL	FN, Belgium
Machine gun	7.62mm FN MAG	FN, Belgium
Anti-armour weapon	Vigilant ATGW	BAC, UK
Anti-aircraft weapon	23mm ZU-23	USSR
Armoured vehicles	OT62, 64 APC	Czechoslovakia
	BTR-40, 50, 60 APC	USSR
	BMP-1 MICV	USSR
	Saracen APC	Alvis/Leyland, UK

Country/Category	Type	Source etc
LUXEMBOURG		
Rifles	SAFN 49	FN, Belgium
	7.62mm FN FAL	FN, Belgium
Mortar	81mm M1	USA
Anti-armour weapons	106mm M20 RCL	USA
	TOW ATGW	Hughes, USA
MADAGASCAR (Malagasy Republic)		
Rifle	7.5mm MAS 49/56	France
MALAWI		
Pistol	9mm FN Browning HP	FN, Belgium
Sub-machine gun	9mm Sterling Mark 4	Sterling Armament Co., UK
Rifles	7.62mm FN FAL	Made by FN
	7.62mm G3	Heckler & Koch design
Machine gun	7.62mm L7A1	Made by Royal Small Arms Factory, UK
Grenades, hand	No. 36M	UK
	No. 80WP	UK
	40mm MECAR A.Tk.	Mecar, Belgium
Mortar	81mm L16A1	UK
Anti-armour weapon	3.5in Rocket Launcher M20	UK
MALAYSIA		
Pistol	9mm FN Browning HP	FN, Belgium
Sub-machine gun	9mm Sterling	Sterling Armament Co, UK
Rifles	7.62mm L1A1	Standard Infantry Rifle, UK
	7.62mm G3	Heckler & Koch design
	5.56mm HK33	Heckler & Koch, W. Germany
	5.56mm AR70	Pietro Beretta, Italy
	5.56mm M16	Colt's Industries, USA
Machine gun, light	7.62mm Bren	Royal Small Arms Factory, UK
Machine gun, general purpose	7.62mm L7A1	Royal Small Arms Factory, UK
Grenade	No. 36M	UK
Mortars	2in OML	UK
	3in OML	UK
Anti-armour weapons	3.5in RL M20	UK manufacture
Armoured vehicles	M3 APC	Panhard, France
	M-113 APC	FMC, USA
MALI		
Mortar	81mm and 120mm	Probably USSR
Armoured vehicle	BTR-40 APC	USSR
MAURITANIA		
Mortars	60mm, 80mm, 120mm	Probably French
Anti-armour weapons	RCL 57mm, 75mm, 106mm	Probably US
MEXICO		
Pistol	.45 Obregon	Made in Mexico
	.45 Colt M1911A1	USA
Rifle	.30 M1 Carbine	USA
Machine gun	.30.6 RM2	Mendoza, Mexico
Armoured vehicles	Half-tracks	USA
	HWK-11	Rheinstahl, Germany
MONGOLIA		
Anti-armour weapon	Snapper ATGW	USSR
Armoured vehicles	BTR-60, 152 APC	USSR
MOROCCO		
Pistol	9mm Model 50	GIAT France
Sub-machine gun	9mm MAB 38/49	Pietro Beretta, Italy
Rifle	9mm MAT 49	Tulle Arsenal in France
	.30 Carbine	Pietro Beretta
	7.5mm MAS 49/56	French. Supplied by GIAT
	7.62mm AK-47	USSR
	7.62mm G3	Heckler & Koch design
Machine guns, light	7.5mm M24/29 Chatellerault	France
	7.62mm RPD	USSR
Machine gun, GPMG	7.5mm AA52	France
Machine gun, heavy	.5 Browning Heavy Barrel M2	USA
Mortar	60mm M2	USA
	81mm ECIA	Esperanza y Cia, Spain
	82mm M37	USSR
	81mm	USA
	82mm M37	USSR
	81mm	USA
	120mm M43	USSR

Country/Category	Type	Source etc
Anti-armour weapons	RPG-2	USSR
	RPG-7V	USSR
	3.5in Rocket Launcher M20	USA
	75mm RCL Gun M20	USA
	Entac ATGW	Aerospatiale, France
Armoured vehicles	Half-tracks	USA
	OT-64APC	Czechoslovakia

MOZAMBIQUE

Rifle	7.62mm FN FAL	FN, Belgium
Mortar	82mm	USSR
Anti-armour weapon	75mm RCL	US pattern
Anti-aircraft weapons	14.5mm KPV	USSR
	SA-7 SAM	USSR

NEPAL

The Nepalese Army is organised and equipped on the same basis as the Indian Army.

NETHERLANDS

Pistol	9mm FN Browning HP	FN, Herstal, Belgium
Sub-machine gun	9mm Uzi SMG	Israeli Military Industries, Israel
Rifles	7.62mm FN FAL	FN, Herstal, Belgium
	7.62mm G3	Heckler & Koch, Germany
Machine gun, GPMG	7.62mm FN MAG	FN, Herstal, Belgium
Machine gun, heavy	.5in Browning Heavy Barrel M2	USA
Grenades, hand	Fragmentation Grenade No. 1	
	Fragmentation Grenade No. 2	Copy of USA Mk 2
	Offensive Hand Grenade No. 13 C1	
	Smoke Hand Grenade Nos. 7, 8, 9, 10, and 11	
	Phosphorus Grenade Nos. 12 and 16	
	Phosphorus Grenade No. 80 Mk 1	UK
Grenade, hand rifle	Rifle Grenade HEAT No. 4	Copy of Mecar Energa Grenade
Mortars	81mm M1	USA
	4.2in M30	USA
	120mm Rifled	Hotchkiss-Brandt, France
Anti-armour weapons	66mm M72 HEAT RL	Raufoss, Norway
Anti-armour weapons, medium	84mm RCL Gun M2 (Carl Gustaf)	FFV Eskilstuna, Sweden
	106mm RCL Gun M40	USA
	TOW ATGW	Hughes Aircraft Co, USA
Anti-aircraft weapons	.5in Browning M2 on quadruple mounting M55 (towed)	USA
Armoured vehicles	AMX-VCI MICV	Creusot-Loire, France
	YP-408 APC	DAF
	UR-416 APC	Rheinstahl, Germany
	M-113 APC	FMC, USA
	AT104 1SV (Police)	GKN Sankey, UK

NEW ZEALAND

Pistol	9mm Pistol Automatic L9A1	FN HP Browning. Supplied by UK
Rifle	7.62mm SL Rifle L1A1	Commonwealth Small Arms Factory Australia
Machine gun	5.56mm M16A1	Colts' Industries, USA
Machine guns, light	7.62mm FN Automatic Rifle L2A1	Heavy Barrelled FAL by FN, Belgium
	7.62mm L4A4	Bren gun. Royal Small Arms Factory, UK
General purpose	7.62mm L7A1 and L7A2	Royal Small Arms Factory, UK
Grenades, hand	M26, M61, M67	USA
	40mm series	USA
Grenades, anti-tank	M96 Energa and Super Energa	Mecar, SA, Belgium
Grenade launcher	M79	USA
	M203	USA
Mortars	2in OML	UK
	81mm OML L16A1	UK
Anti-armour weapons	66mm M72 Rocket	USA
	106mm RCL Gun M40A1	USA
Armoured vehicle	M-113 APC	FMC, USA

NICARAGUA

Rifle	7.62mm AR-10	USA

NIGER

Rifle	7.5mm MAS 49/56	France
Mortars	60mm and 81mm	France or USA
Anti-armour weapons	57mm M18 RCL	USA
	75mm M20 RCL	USA

Country/Category	Type	Source etc

NIGERIA

During the civil war in Nigeria considerable quantitites of arms other than those used by regular formations of the Nigerian Army were imported from various sources. Notable among these weapons were Sten guns and Czech SMGs of various types and the Zb 37 MMG. Although many of these weapons may still be in service they have not been included in the list below, which relates to those weapons believed to have been acquired for the regular Nigerian forces in the ordinary course of military procurement.

Country/Category	Type	Source etc
Pistol	9mm Beretta Model 51	Pietro Beretta, Italy
Sub-machine guns	9mm Beretta Model 12	Pietro Beretta, Italy
	9mm Sterling Mk IV	Sterling Armament Co., UK
Rifles	7.62mm G3	Heckler & Koch design
	7.62mm BM59	Possibly. This rifle was to have been made under Beretta licence in Nigeria but the civil war intervened
Machine guns	No definite information. See note above	
Mortars	3in mortar	UK
	81mm Mortar	UK
Armoured vehicle	Saracen APC	Alvis/Leyland, UK

NORWAY

Country/Category	Type	Source etc
Pistols	9mm M38	German P I. Manufactured in Norway under licence from Carl Walther, Germany
	.45 M1912, 1914	Versions of Colt M1911 made in Norway
Sub-machine gun	Maskin 9mm M40	German MP40. Wartime production
Rifle	7.62mm Gevaer, Automatisk AG3	German G3 Rifle, manufactured by Kongsberg Vapenfabrikk, Norway
Machine gun, light	Gevaer, Maskin, 7.62mm MG3	German MG3, manufactured by Rheinmetall, fired off the bipod
Machine gun, medium	Mitralose, 7.62mm MG3	German MG3, manufactured by Rheinmetall, fired off tripod
Machine gun, heavy	12.7mm M2	Heavy Barrelled Browning M2. USA made
Machine gun, cannon	20mm NM45	German MK 20 DM5 made by Rheinmetall
Grenades, hand	Granet, Hand, Splint, Mk 2	Fragmentation Grenade M6A4C made by Raufoss Ammunisjonsfabrikk, Norway
	Granat, Hand, Offensiv, M100	Raufoss Ammunisjonsfabrikk, Norway
	Granat, Hand, RoK, HC M8	USA smoke grenade
	Granat, Hand, CS, M7A3	USA tear grenade
	Granat, Gevaer, HEAT, Energa	Mecar, Belgium
	Granat, Gevaer, HEAT, M31	USA A.Tk grenade
	Granat, Gevaer, RoK, M19	USA smoke grenade
	Granat, Gevaer, RoK, M22	USA smoke grenade
Mortars	Bombekaster, 81mm, NM95	UK L16A1
	Bombekaster, 107mm, M30	USA 4.2in M30
	Bombekaster, 107mm M30F1	USA 4.2in with heavy baseplate and wheeled carriage. Made by Kongsberg Vapenfabrikk, Norway
Anti-armour weapons	Rakettkaster, PV 66mm, M72	M72 manufactured by Raufoss
	Rakettkaster, PV 88mm M20B1A1, M20A1B1	USA 3.5in RL M20
	Kanon, Rekylfri, 57mm, M18	USA 57mm RCL Gun M18
	Kanon, Rekylfri, 75mm, M20	USA 75mm RCL Gun M20
	Kanon, Rekylfri, 84mm, M2	84mm Carl Gustaf M2 made by FFV
		USA 106mm RCL Gun M40
	Kanon, Rekylfri, 106mm, M40A1, M40A1C	Eskilstuna, Sweden
	Rakett, Tradstyrt, SS-11 (ATGW)	Aerospatiale, France
	Rakett, Tradstyrt, TOW (ATGW)	Hughes Aircraft, USA
Anti-aircraft weapon	20mm Rh202	Rheinmetall gun in Norwegian (Kongsberg) mounting
Armoured vehicle	M-113 APC	FMC, USA

OMAN

Country/Category	Type	Source etc
Pistol	9mm FN Browning HP	UK
Sub-machine gun	9mm Sterling Mk 4	Sterling Armament Co., UK
Rifle	7.62mm FN FAL	FN, Herstal, Belgium
Machine gun	7.62mm FN MAG	FN, Herstal, Belgium
Grenade	M 36M	UK
Mortar, light	60mm Light Mortar	Hotchkiss-Brandt
Mortar, medium	81mm L16A1	UK
Mortar, heavy	4.2in M30	USA
Anti-armour weapon	TOW ATGW	Hughes Aircraft, USA
Armoured vehicle	Commando APC	Cadillac Gage, USA

PAKISTAN

Country/Category	Type	Source etc
Pistol	9mm P38	Carl Walther, Germany
Sub-machine gun	9mm STEN Mk 5	UK
Rifles	.303 No. 1 and No. 4	Royal Small Arms Factory, UK
	.30 Rifle M1C Garand	USA
	.30 Rifle M1C (Sniping)	USA
	7.62mm Rifle G3	Heckler and Koch design made under licence in Pakistan
	7.62mm AK-47	China
Machine gun	.30 Browning M1918M2 (BAR)	USA

Country/Category	Type	Source etc
Machine guns, light	.30 Browning M1919A6	USA
	.303 Bren LMG Mks 2 and 3	UK
	7.62mm RPD	China
Machine gun, medium	7.62mm MG1A3	Rheinmetall design made in Pakistan
Machine gun, heavy	.5 Browning Heavy Barrel, M2	USA
Grenades	No. 36M	UK
	M26	USA
Mortars	2in Mk 8/1	UK
	3in Mk 2 and Mk 4	UK
	81mm with Mount M4	USA
Anti-armour weapons	3.5in Rocket Launcher M20	USA
	83mm Blindicide Rocket Launcher	Mecar, Belgium
	106mm RCL Gun M40A with ground mount M79	USA
	Cobra 2000 ATGW	Originally by Messerschmitt-Bolkow-Blohm GmbH, Germany. Now made under licence in Pakistan
	6-pounder ATk gun	UK
	17-pounder ATk gun	UK
Armoured vehicle	M-113 APC	FMC, USA

PANAMA

Pistols	9mm FN Browning HP	FN, Herstal, Belgium
	.45 Colt M1911A1	USA
	Smith & Wesson .38 Special Revolver	USA
	Colt .38 Special Revolver	USA
Sub-machine guns	9mm Uzi SMG	Israeli Military Industries
	.45 Thompson SMG	USA
Rifles	7mm Mauser-bolt action	
	7.62mm FN FAL	FN, Herstal, Belgium
	.30 Carbine and M2	USA
	.30 Rifle, M1 Garand	USA
	5.56mm M16	Colt's Industries, USA
Machine gun, light	7.62mm FN MAG on bipod	FN, Belgium
Machine guns, medium	7.62mm FN MAG on tripod	FN, Belgium
	.30 Browning M1919A4 on tripod	USA
Grenades	Local manufacture	
Mortars	60mm Soltam	Israel
	60mm M38	USA
Anti-armour weapon, light	3.5in RL M20	USA

PAPUA NEW GUINEA

Rifle	7.62mm LIAl Short	Lithgow, Australia

PARAGUAY

Sub-machine gun	9mm Madsen M46, 50, 53	Madsen, Denmark
Rifle	7.62mm FN FAL	FN, Belgium

PERU

Rifles	7.62mm FN FAL	FN, Belgium
	7.62mm G3	Heckler & Koch design
	7.62mm AK-47 Assault Rifle	USSR
Machine gun	7.62mm FN MAG	FN, Belgium
Mortar	120mm	
Anti-armour weapon	Cobra ATGW	MBB, Germany
Anti-aircraft weapon	SA-7 SAM	USSR
Armoured vehicles	UR-416 APC	Rheinstahl, Germany
	Mowag Roland APC	Mowag, Switzerland
	M-113 APC	FMC, USA
	Commando APC	Cadillac Gage, USA

PHILIPPINES

Pistol	.45 Colt M1911A1	Colt, USA
Rifles	7.62mm G3	Heckler & Koch design, probably Asian manufacture
	5.56mm AR-15 (M16)	Colt, USA. Also made under licence in the Philippines
Mortar	81mm M1	USA
Anti-armour weapons	4.2in M2A1	USA
	75mm M20 RCL	USA
	106mm M40 RCL	USA
Armoured vehicles	Half-tracks	USA
	M-113 APC	FMC, USA

Country/Category	Type	Source etc
POLAND		
Pistol	9mm Machine Pistol Wz 63	Polish designed and manufactured. Uses 9mm x 18 cartridge
	9mm Pistol M64	Polish designed and manufactured. Uses 9mm x 18 cartridge
	9mm Pistol M65 (PM)	Russian designed, Polish manufactured Makarov pistol
Rifle	7.62mm PMK Assault rifle	Polish made AK47. Found only with reserve units
	7.62mm PMK-DGN60	PMK with cone shaped muzzle to take LON-1 grenade launcher of 20mm OD (Also known as Kbk AK)
	7.62mm PMKM	Polish made copy of the AKM. Has compensator and does not fire grenades All the above Polish rifles take the 7.62mm x 39 cartridge
	7.62mm Dragunov (SVD)	Copy of Russian sniping rifle. Uses the 7.62mm x 54R cartridge
Machine guns, light	7.62mm RPD	Supporting troops only. Russian gun
	7.62mm RPK	Copy of Russian gun Both of these weapons use the 7.62mm × 39 intermediate cartridge
Machine guns, GPMG	7.62mm PK, PKB, PKS and PKT	Russian gun. Uses the 7.62mm × 54R round
Machine gun, heavy	12.7mm Degtyarev 38/46	Russian origin
Grenade, hand	RGD-5 Anti-personnel	Copy of Russian grenade
Grenade, A.Tk	RKG-3, 3M and 3T	Copy of Russian hand grenade
Grenade, smoke	RDG-2	Copy of Russian hand grenade
Grenades, rifle	F1/N60	Anti-personnel rifle grenade of Polish origin
	PGN-60	Anti-tank rifle grenade of Polish origin
Mortar, medium	82mm M37M	Copy of standard Russian mortar
Mortar, heavy	120mm M43	Copy of standard Russian mortar
	160mm M-160	Copy of standard Russian mortar
Anti-armour weapons	RPG-7V	Copy of standard Russian weapon
	82mm B-10 RCL Gun	Airborne units only
	73mm SPG-9 RCL Gun	Copy of standard Russian weapon
	Swatter ATGW	Copy of standard Russian weapon
	Sagger ATGW	Copy of standard Russian weapon
	Snapper ATGW	No longer in service with first line units. May be found in reserve and training formations
Anti-aircraft weapons	SA-7	Russian design. Manufactured in Poland
	12.7mm Degtyarev HMG	Twin and quadruple mountings
	14.5 KPV HMG	Twin (ZPU-2) and quadruple (ZPU-4) mountings
	23mm Cannon (Towed)	
Armoured vehicles	OT-62, 64 APC	Czechoslovakia
	BTR-40, 50, 60, 152 APC	USSR
	BMP-1 MICV	USSR
PORTUGAL		
Pistols	7.65mm M/908	Training units only
	7.65mm M/915	Training units only
	9mm P1	Standard German Army Pistol. Made by Carl Walther, Germany
Sub-machine guns	9mm Model 48 FBP	Fabrica Militar de Braco de Prata
	9mm Model 63	Fabrica Militar de Braco de Prata
Rifle	7.62mm G3	Manufactured, by FBP, under licence from Heckler and Koch, Germany
Machine gun, light	7.62mm HK21	Heckler & Koch, Germany
Machine gun, GPMG	7.62mm MG42/59	Rheinmetall, Germany
Grenades	Offensive M55	Made by FBP
	Defensive M60	
Mortars	60mm FBP	Portuguese design and construction
	81mm FBP	Portuguese design and construction
Anti-armour weapons	3.5in Rocket Launcher M20	USA origin
	106mm RCL	USA
Armoured vehicles	1-ton PIG	Humber, UK
	Half-tracks	USA
	Commando APC	Cadillac Gage, USA
QATAR		
Rifle	7.62mm G3	Heckler & Koch design. Probably Middle East manufacture
Machine gun	7.62mm FN MAG	FN Belgium
Mortar	81mm mortar	UK
Armoured vehicle	Saracen APC	Alvis/Leyland, UK
RAS AL KHAIMAH		
Rifle	7.62mm FN FAL	FN, Belgium
Mortar	81mm mortar	UK

Country/Category	Type	Source etc

RHODESIA

Irregular 'liberation' forces operating on the borders of Rhodesia are armed with a variety of weapons. Many of these are of Russian pattern but they also include the ubiquitous Sten. The data below relate to the Rhodesian Army: they include some captured items; but the list is fairly certainly incomplete both in this respect and with respect to more conventionally acquired weapons.

Country/Category	Type	Source etc
Rifle	7.62mm FN FAL	FN design, probably made in South Africa
Machine guns	7.62mm FN MAG	FN, Belgium
	Madsen GPMG	Obsolete Danish. Captured
	12.7mm DShK HMG	USSR. Captured
Anti-aircraft weapon	23mm ZPU-4	USSR. Captured

ROMANIA

Country/Category	Type	Source etc
Pistols	7.62mm TT33	Copy of the Russian Tokarev Pistol
	9mm Makarov	USSR
Sub-machine gun	9mm Orita M41	Romanian design and manufacture. Used by rear echelons only
Rifles	7.62mm Ak-47	Reserve units
	7.62mm AKM	Manufactured in USSR for Romania. Has distinctive wooden pistol fore grip
Machine guns, light	7.62mm RPD	Reserve units
	7.62mm RPK	First line units
Machine guns, medium	7.62mm SGM	Reservice units
	7.62mm PK, PKB, PKS, PKT	First line units
Machine gun, heavy	12.7mm Degtyarev 38/46	USSR
Grenades, hand	RGD-5 Defensive	USSR
	RKG-3 Anti-tank	USSR
	RDG-2 Smoke	USSR
Mortar, medium	82mm M37M	USSR
Mortar, heavy	120mm M43	USSR
Anti-armour weapons	RPG-7V	USSR
	73mm SPG-9	USSR
	Snapper ATGW	USSR
	Swatter ATGW	USSR
	Sagger ATGW	USSR
Anti-aircraft weapons	SA-7 SAM	USSR
	12.7 Degtyarev HMG	USSR
	14.5 KPV HMG	USSR
	23mm Zu 23 Cannon (Towed)	USSR
Armoured vehicles	TAB-70 APC	Romanian version of BTR-60
	OT-62, 810 APC	Czechoslovakia
	BTR-50, 60, 152 APC	USSR

RWANDA

Country/Category	Type	Source etc
Rifle	7.5mm MAS 49/56	France
Mortar	81mm mortar	probably France

SAUDI ARABIA

Country/Category	Type	Source etc
Sub-machine guns	9mm Ingram MAC	USA
	9mm MP69	Steyr, Austria
	9mm Beretta Model 12	Pietro Beretta, Italy
Rifle	7.62mm G3	Heckler & Koch design, locally manufactured under licence
Mortar	3in mortar	UK
Anti-armour weapons	75mm M20 RCL	USA
	SS11 ATGW	Aerospatiale, France
	Vigilant ATGW	BAC, UK
Armoured vehicles	AMX-10P MICV	GIAT, France
	M3 APC	Panhard, France
	Commando APC	Cadillac Gage, USA

SENEGAL

Country/Category	Type	Source etc
Rifle	7.5mm MAS 49/56	France
Mortar	81mm mortar	probably France
Armoured vehicle	VXB-170 APC	Berliet, France

SHARJAH

Country/Category	Type	Source etc
Rifle	7.62mm G3	Heckler & Koch design probably Middle East manufacture

SIERRA LEONE

Country/Category	Type	Source etc
Machine gun	7.62mm FN MAG	FN, Belgium
Mortars	60mm, 81mm	

SINGAPORE

Country/Category	Type	Source etc
Pistol	9mm Browning HP	FN, Belgium
Sub-machine gun	9mm Sterling	Sterling Armament Co, UK

Country/Category	Type	Source etc
Rifles	5.56mm M16	Produced by Chartered Industries of Singapore with assistance from Colt's Industries, USA
	7.62mm L1A1	Commonwealth Small Arms Factory, Australia
	.303 Rifle No.5	Static units only – UK origin
Machine guns	7.62mm L7A1	Royal Small Arms Factory, UK
	.303 Bren	Reserve units
Mortars	60mm, 81mm and 120mm	All mortars produced by Chartered Industries of Singapore under licence from Tampella, Finland
	106mm M40 RL	USA
Anti-armour weapons	3.5in RL	UK supply
	89mm Mecar RL	Mecar, Belgium
	84mm Carl Gustaf M2	FFV, Sweden
	106mm M40 RCL	USA
Anti-aircraft weapons	20mm Oerlikon	
Armoured vehicle	Commando APC	Cadillac Gage, USA

SOMALIA

Forces generally equipped with Russian weapons and equipment but few details are available.

Anti-aircraft weapon	14.5mm KPV HMG	USSR
Armoured vehicles	BTR-40, 50, 152 APC	USSR
	M-113 APC	USA

SOUTH AFRICA

South Africa is now almost completely self-sufficient in the manufacture of infantry weapons. Complex equipment required in small quantity is purchased overseas.

Rifle	7.62mm FN FAL	Made in South Africa
Machine gun	7.62mm FN MAG	FN, Belgium
Anti-armour weapons	ENTAC ATGW	Aerospatiale, France
	17-pounder ATk Gun	UK
Anti-aircraft weapon	20mm Cannon 204GK	Oerlikon design. Source not known
Armoured vehicles	Saracen APC	Alvis/Leyland, UK
	Commando APC	Cadillac Gage, USA

SPAIN

Pistol	9mm Super Star	Bonifacio Echeverria
Sub-machine guns	9mm Star Z-45	Bonifacio Echeverria.
	9mm Star Z-62	Bonifacio Echeverria. Mainly superseded by Z-70-B
	9mm Star Z-70-B	Bonifacio Echeverria
Rifles	7.62mm CETME Fusil Asalto	E.N., Santa Barbara, manufacture
	7.62mm Mauser	E.N., Santa Barbara, manufacture
Machine guns	7.62mm MG42/59	Made at Oriedo
	7.62mm MG1A3 and 3S	E.N., Santa Barbara
	7.62mm MF1	DTAT, France
	7.62mm Browning M1919A4E1	USA
	0.5in M2 Browning	USA
Grenades, hand	POII and III	Plasticas Oramil SA
	E.A. M5	Explosivos Alaveses
Grenades, rifle	GL1 and GL11	Explosivos Alaveses
	60mm AML 1961	DTAT, France
Mortars	60mm ECIA	Esperanza Y Cia
	81mm ECIA	Esperanza Y Cia
	120mm ECIA	Esperanza Y Cia
	60mm AML 1961	DTAT, France
Anti-armour weapons	88.9mm Model 65 Lanzagranadas	Copy of USA 3.5in RL M20 made by Instalaza SA
	Canon sin Retroceso 106mm	Copy of USA RCL Gun 106mm M40. Made by E.N. de Santa Barbara
	Cobra 2000 ATGW	MBB, Germany
	Milan ATGW	Euromissile
Anti-aircraft	.5 Browning HB M2	From USA
	20mm Oerlikon La/5TG (towed)	Oerlikon, Switzerland
Armoured vehicles	Half-tracks	USA
	M113 APC	FMC, USA
	M3 APC	Panhard, France
	LVTP-7 AAV	FMC, USA

SRI LANKA

Armoured vehicle	BTR/152 APC	USSR

SUDAN

Mortar	120mm	
Armoured vehicles	Saracen APC	Alvis/Leyland UK
	Commando APC	Cadillac Gage, USA
	OT-64 APC	Czechoslovakia
	BTR-40, 50, 152 APC	USSR

Country/Category	Type	Source etc
SWEDEN		
Pistol	9mm Lahti	Husqvarna Vapenfabrik
Sub-machine gun	9mm M45	Carl Gustaf, Eskilstuna
Rifles	6.5mm AG42	Ljungman rifle, now in reserve units only
	7.62mm AK-4	Carl Gustaf, Eskilstuna
	7.62mm G3	Heckler & Koch design made under licence
Machine guns	6.5mm Kulspruta 58	(MAG), FN, Belgium, early manufacture
	7.62mm Kulspruta 58	(MAG), FN, Belgium, subsequent manufacture
Grenades, hand	M54	Ammunitionarsenalet, Denmark
ATk	Energa	Mecar, Belgium
smoke	M57	AB Lind Maskiner
Mortars	80mm M29	
	120mm	
Anti-armour weapons	74mm Miniman	FFV, Eskilstuna
	84mm Carl Gustaf M2	FFV, Eskilstuna
	84mm Carl Gustaf M2-550	FFV, Eskilstuna
	SS-10 ATGW	Aerospatiale, France
	Bantam ATGW	AB Bofors
Anti-aircraft weapons	20mm cannon	
	RB-69 SAM	(Redeye), General Dynamics USA
	RBS-70 SAM	AB Bofors
Armoured vehicle	Pbv 302 APC	AB Hagglunds and Soner
SWITZERLAND		
Pistols	7.65mm Pistol 06/29	This Luger pistol was manufactured by the Swiss Ordnance works, and is now used only by static troops
	9mm Pistol 49	Designed and produced by SIG
Sub-machine gun	9mm Model 43/44	Almost completely withdrawn from service
Rifles	7.5mm Zf Kar 55	Sniping rifle
	7.5mm Sturmgewehr Model 1957	Used by almost all trooops. Designed and produced by SIG
Machine gun, light	7.5mm MG51 on bipod	Waffenfabrik, Berne. This differs from the German MG42 in having locking lugs in place of rollers
Machine gun, medium	7.5mm MG51 on tripod	As above
Grenade, hand	Model HG43	Munitionsfabrik, Thun
Grenade, rifle	Model GWG58 HEAT HE and smoke	Munitionsfabrik, Thun
Mortars	81mm Mw 33	Munitionsfabrik, Thun
	81mm Mw 72	Munitionsfabrik, Thun
	120mm Mw 64	Munitionsfabrik, Thun
		Also mounted in an APC
Anti-tank weapons	RAK Rohr 50 83mm	Rocket launchers. Copy of the Mecar Blindicide by Waffenfabrik Berne
	RAK Rohr 58 83mm	
	Bantam ATGW	Bofors, Sweden
	Mosquito ATGW	Contraves Italiana, SpA, Italy
Anti-aircraft weapon	20mm Type 10 La/5TG	Machine Tool Works, Oerlikon Bührle
Armoured vehicle	M-113 APC	FMC, USA
SYRIA		
Sub-machine gun	9mm M23/M25 SMG	Czechoslovakia
Rifles	7.62mm AK-47	USSR
	7.62mm AKM	USSR
Machine gun	12.7mm DShK 38/46 HMG	USSR
Mortars	82mm M41, M43	USSR
	120mm	USSR
	160mm M43 and M160	USSR
Anti-armour weapons	82mm SPG82 RL	USSR
	40mm RPG7, 7D, 7V RL	USSR
	Sagger ATGW	USSR
	Snapper ATGW	USSR
	Swatter ATGW	USSR
Anti-aircraft weapon	SA-7 SAM	USSR
Armoured vehicles	BMP-1 MICV	USSR
	BTR-40, 50, 60, 152 APC	USSR
	OT-64 APC	Czechoslovakia
TANZANIA		
Rifle	7.62mm G3	Heckler & Koch design. Probably Middle East manufacture
Machine gun	7.62mm FN MAG	FN, Belgium
Mortars	82mm Type 53	China
	120mm Type 53	China
Armoured vehicles	BTR-40, 152 APC	USSR
THAILAND		
Sub-machine guns	9mm M46, M50, M53	Madsen, Denmark
Rifles	7.62mm G3	Heckler & Koch design. Made in Thailand

Country/Category	Type	Source etc
	5.56mm HK33	Heckler & Koch design. Made in Thailand
	7.62mm M1 Rifle	USA
	5.56mm M16 Rifle	Colt, USA
Machine gun	0.5in Browning M2	USA
Mortar	81mm M1	USA
Anti-armour weapons	57mm M18/18A1 RCL	USA
	75mm M20 RCL	USA
	106mm M40 RCL	USA
Armoured vehicles	Half-Tracks	USA
	Saracen APC	Alvis/Leyland, UK
	LVTP-7 AAV	FMC, USA

TOGO

Rifle	7.62mm G3	Heckler & Koch design

TONGA

Pistol	0.38in Smith & Wesson	US origin, probably via UK
Sub-machine gun	9mm Sten	UK
Rifle	.303in Lee Enfield	UK
Machine guns	.303in Bren LMG	UK
	.303in Vickers MMG	UK

TRANSKEI

Rifle	7.62mm L1A1	UK pattern. Possibly made in South Africa

TRINIDAD AND TOBAGO

Mortar	81mm M1	USA

TUNISIA

Sub-machine guns	9mm 38/49 Model 4	Pietro Beretta, Italy
	9mm Sterling Mk IV	Sterling, UK

TURKEY

Pistol	7.62mm MKE	Makin ve Kimya Endustrisi
	9mm MKE	
	.45 Colt 1911A1	USA
Sub-machine gun	.45 M3A1	USA
Rifle	7.62mm G3	Heckler & Koch design, made under licence
Machine gun, light	.30 Browning M1919A6	USA
Machine gun, medium	7.62mm MG3	Rheinmetall, Germany
Machine gun, heavy	.5in Browning HB M2	USA
Mortar	81mm Soltam	Soltam, Israel
	120mm Soltam	Soltam, Israel
Anti-armour weapons	3.5in RL M20	USA
	106mm RCL Gun M40	USA
	Cobra 2000 ATG	Messerschmitt-Bolkow-Blohm, Germany. Made under licence in Turkey
	SS-11 ATGW	Nord-Aviation – now Aerospatiale, France
	TOW ATGW	Hughes Aircraft, USA
Anti-aircraft	.5in Browning HB M2	USA
Armoured vehicles	Half-tracks	USA
	M59, M113 APC	FMC, USA
	Commando APC	Cadillac Gage, USA

UGANDA

Rifle	7.62mm G3	Heckler & Koch design. Probably Middle East manufacture
Machine gun	7.62mm FN MAG	FN, Belgium
Mortar	82mm Type 53	China
	160mm	Possibly China
Anti-armour weapon	Sagger ATGW	USSR
Anti-aircraft weapon	23mm ZU-23 cannon	Probably USSR
Armoured vehicles	Saracen APC	Alvis/Leyland, UK
	OT-64 APC	Czechoslovakia
	BTR-40, 152 APC	USSR

UNION OF SOVIET SOCIALIST REPUBLICS

Pistol	9mm Makarov (PM)	Uses 9mm × 18 cartridge
	9mm Stechkin Machine Pistol	Uses 9mm × 18 cartridge Used only by Border Guards
Rifles	7.62mm Simonov	7.62mm × 39 cartridge Used only for ceremonial
	7.62mm AK-47 Assault Rifle	7.62mm × 39 cartridge used by reserve units
	7.62mm AKM Assault Rifle	7.62mm × 39 cartridge. Standard rifle
	7.62mm Dragunov Rifle (SVD)	7.62mm × 54R cartridge. Sniping rifle

Country/Category	Type	Source etc
Machine guns, light	7.62mm RPK/RPKS	7.62mm × 39 cartridge. RPKS has folding butt
Machine guns, GPMG	7.62mm PK, PKB, PKS, PKT	7.62mm × 54R cartridge
Machine guns, HMG	12.7mm Degtyarev 38/46	
Grenades	RGD-5 Anti-Personnel	
	RKG-3, 3M, and 3T Anti-tank	
	Smoke, hand. RDG-2	
Mortars	82mm M37 (m)	Modernised version
	107mm M107	
	120mm M43	
	160mm M160	
	240mm M240	
Anti-armour weapons	40mm RPG-7V	
	40mm RPG-7D	Folding version for airborne use
	73mm SPG-9 Recoilless Gun	Rocket assisted round
	Swatter ATGW	Mounted on BRDM
	Sagger ATGW	Can be man portable, BRDM mounted or on BMP
Anti-aircraft weapons	12.7mm Degtyarev 38/46	Can be twin or quadruple mounting
	14.5mm KPV HMG	Can be twin or quadruple mounting
	23mm Cannon	Can be twin or quadruple mounting on trailer or SP mount
	SA-7 SAM (Grail)	
Armoured vehicles	BMP-1 MICV	
	BTR-40, 50, 60, 152 APC	
	AT-P Artillery tractor	
	GT-T/M-1970 APC	

UNITED ARAB EMIRATES

Separate entries appear for Abu Dhabi, Dubai, Ras Al Khaimah and Sharjah. No significant details of the armament of the Union Defence Force have been ascertained, but it is a mobile force of some 3,000 men using Scorpion light tanks, Ferret scout cars and Land Rovers and equipped with the British 81mm mortar; so it may be assumed that the other armament is consistent with this.

UNITED KINGDOM

Pistol	9mm Pistol Automatic L9A1	Pistol FN Browning HP
	7.65mm Pistol Automatic Walther Type PP	Carl Walther, Germany
	XL47E1	For special duties only
	Pistol Pyrotechnic 1in No 1 Mk 5	
	Pistol Pyrotechnic 1½in No 4 Mk 1/1	
Sub-machine gun	9mm L2A3	
	9mm L34A1	Silenced version
	.22in No 8 Mk 1	Training
	.22in Conversion set L12A1. Hecker & Koch	Converts 7.62mm L1A1 to .22 LR. From Heckler & Koch, Germany
Rifle	7.62mm L1A1	Standard British rifle. Based on FN FAL
	7.62mm L39A1	Converted No 4 .303 rifle for competition shooting
	7.62mm L42A1	Converted No 4 .303 rifle for sniping
Discharger	Discharger Grenade L1A1	For smoke and anti-riot grenades
	Riot gun 1½in XL48E1	
Machine guns	7.62mm L7A1	GPMG. Basically FN MAG
	7.62mm L7A2	GPMG. Modified L7A1
	7.62mm L8	Tank MG. Coaxial
	7.62mm L20	Helicopter MG
	7.62mm L37	Tank MG. Cupola mounted. Dismountable
	.300in L3A3	Browning M1919A4. (Fixed)
	.300in L3A4	Browning M1919A4. (Flexible)
	7.62mm L4A2	Bren. Now obsolescent
	7.62mm L4A4	Bren. Current gun
	7.62mm L4A6	Bren. Now obsolescent
	7.62mm L43A1	Bren. Ranging machine gun for Scorpion
	.5in L40A1	.5 Browning HB M2. This is a spotting MG – the only one employed by Infantry
Grenades, hand	No 36M Anti-personnel	
	L2A1 Anti-personnel	
Grenades, smoke	L2A2 Anti-personnel	
	No 80 WP Smoke	
	No 83 Coloured Smoke	
	No 91 Tear Gas	
	L1 Anti-riot	
	L12 Anti-riot	
	L13 Anti-riot	Replacing L1 and L2 Grenades
Grenade, rifle	M406	USA
Mortars	OML 2in	
	OML 81mm L16A1	
Anti-armour weapons	Rocket, 66mm HEAT L1A1	Obtained from Raufoss, Norway
	Gun, 84mm Inf L14A1	Obtained from FFV, Sweden
	Gun, 120mm RCL	
	Cannon 30mm RARDEN L21E4	
	Vigilant ATGW	British Aircraft Corporation
	Swingfire ATGW	British Aircraft Corporation
Anti-aircraft weapons	Blowpipe	Short Bros & Harland Ltd
Armoured vehicles	1-ton PIG APC	Humber/GKN Sankey
	FV432 APC	GKN Sankey
	Spartan APC	Alvis/British Leyland
	Saracen APC	Alvis/British Leyland

Country/Category	Type	Source etc
UNITED STATES OF AMERICA		
Pistol	.45 Colt 1911A1	Colt's Industries
Sub-machine gun	.45 M3A1	Issued as on vehicle material with most combat vehicles
Rifle	5.56mm XM177E2	The Colt Commando – a cut down M16 Rifle
	7.62mm M14A1	Replaces the M14 which replaced the BAR
	5.56mm M16A1	Standard Infantry Rifle. Manufactured by Colt Industries
	7.62mm M21	Sniping Rifle (Modified M14)
Machine gun	7.62mm M60	Maremont Corporation
	.50 Browning Heavy Barrel, M2	On M3 mount
Grenade launchers	40mm Grenade Launcher M79	
	40mm Grenade Launcher M203	Slung beneath the barrel of the M16 Rifle
Grenades, hand	Fragmentation. M67, M33 delay M61, M26A1 Fragmentation Impact M68, M59 M57, M26A2 Offensive. Mk 3A2 Illuminating Mk 1 Smoke AN-M8	
	Grenades, 40mm	The complete list of these grenades is given in the section on US Grenades
Mortars	60mm Mortar, M19 81mm Mortar 4.2in Mortar M30	
Anti-armour weapons	66mm HEAT Rocket M72A1	
	90mm Recoilless Rifle, M67	Will be replaced entirely by Dragon
	M47 Medium Anti-armour Weapon. Dragon	McDonnell Douglas
	106mm Recoilless Rifle, M40A1 with spotting MG5	Mounted on standard carrier M151A1C ¼ ton truck
	TOW ATGW	Hughes Aircraft Corporation
Anti-aircraft weapons	.5 Browning HB, M2	Used on vehicles and with multiple mount
	Vulcan Air Defence System	GEC. Vehicle-mounted
	20mm Gun, Automatic, M139	Made in USA. Vehicle-mounted
	Redeye Guided Missile System	General Dynamics, Corp.
Armoured vehicles	M-113 APC	FMC
	Commando APC	Cadillac Gage, USA
	LVTP-7 AAV	FMC
UPPER VOLTA		
Rifles	7.5mm MAS 49/56	France
	7.62mm G3	Heckler & Koch design
Mortar	81mm mortar	Probably France
Anti-armour weapon	75mm RCL	
URUGUAY		
Armoured vehicles	Half-tracks	USA
	M-113 APC	FMC, USA
VENEZUELA		
Pistol	9mm FN Browning HP	Supplied by FN, Belgium
Rifle	7.62mm Fusil Automatico Liviano	FN FAL.
Sub-machine guns	9mm Uzi	FN, Belgium
	9mm Beretta	Pietro Beretta, Italy
Machine gun	7.62mm MAG	FN, Belgium
Grenades, hand	PRB-103	P.R.B., Belgium
	PRB-7 (Offensive)	P.R.B., Belgium
	PRB-8 (Defensive)	P.R.B., Belgium
Grenade, rifle	65mm A.Tk	Manufactured and supplied by FN under STRIM licence
Mortars	60mm Brandt	Hotchkiss-Brandt, France
	81mm Brandt	
	120mm Brandt	
Anti-armour weapon	106mm Recoilless Gun M40A1	USA
Armoured vehicles	Half-tracks	USA
	AMX-VCI MICV	Creusot-Loire, France
VIETNAM		
Pistols	7.62mm TT-3	Supplied by Russia. 7.62mm x 25 Cartridge
	7.62mm Type 68	Modified TT-33 which it has largely replaced
Sub-machine guns	7.62mm K-50M	Extensively modified People's Republic of China Type 50 SMG. 7.62mm x 25 cartridge
	7.62mm MAT 49 Modified	The French 9mm MAT 49 modified to take a long 7.62mm barrel
Rifles	7.62mm PRC Type 50	Chinese copy of the Soviet PPSh-41 SMG
	7.62mm SKS	Russian carbine
	7.62mm AK-47	Russian Assault Rifle
	7.62mm Type 56	Chinese copy of the AK-47 assault rifle

Country/Category	Type	Source etc
Machine guns, light	7.62mm TUL-1	LMG produced from the 7.62mm Type 56 Rifle. The concept is based on the Soviet RPK LMG
	7.62mm PRC Type 67 LMG	This is a PRC gun of native design, using the long Soviet 7.62 x 54R Cartridge
	7.62mm DPM	Russian LMG of wartime origin
	7.62mm Type 53	Chinese copy of the DPM using the 7.62mm x 54R
	7.62mm RPD	Russian LMG
Machine guns, medium	7.62mm SG-43	Russian MMG firing the 7.62mm x 54R round
	7.62mm SGM	Modified SG-43
Machine gun, heavy	12.7mm Degtyarev HMG	USSR
Grenades, hand	AP.F1	These Russian type grenades were supplied by PRC. In addition a large number of improvised and locally made grenades are employed.
	AP.RG-42	
	AP.RGD-5	
	A.Tk.RKG-3	
Mortars	82mm M37M	USSR and China
	120mm M43	USSR
Anti-armour weapons	RPG-2	China
	RPG-7V	USSR
	82mm B-10 RCL Gun	USSR
	75mm Type 52 RCL Gun	Chinese copy of the USA 75mm M20 RCL Gun
	75mm Type 56 RCL Gun	Chinese copy of the USA 75mm M20 RCL Gun with improvements
	107mm B-11 RCL Gun	USSR
Anti-aircraft weapons	12.7mm HMG	USSR
	14.5 KPV HMG	USSR
	SA-7 (Grail)	USSR
Armoured vehicles	K-63 APC	China
	BTR-40, 50, 60 APC	USSR

SOUTH VIETNAM

The following weapons were in service with South Vietnamese forces in the closing stages of the Vietnamese War. Many of them will now have found their way into the hands of the victors but until the stable shape of the Vietnamese Army is clearer it may be helpful to keep the two lists separate.

Pistol	.45 Colt M1911A1	USA
Sub-machine gun	.45 M3A1	USA
Rifles	.30 M1 Carbine	USA
	.30 M1 Rifle	USA
	5.56mm M16 and M16A1	USA supply. Re-built at the Saigon Arsenal
Machine guns, light	.30 Browning M1918M2	USA
	.30 Browning M1919A4	USA
	.30 Browning M1919A6	USA
Machine gun, medium	7.62mm M60	USA
Machine gun, heavy	.5in Browning HB M2	USA
Machine gun, grenades	M26 series	USA
	M67 Fragmentation	USA
	Illuminating Mk 1	USA
	Smoke. AN-M8	USA
	40mm Series	USA
Grenade launcher	M79 and M203	USA
Mortars	60mm M2, M19	USA
	81mm M1, M29	USA
Anti-armour weapons	3.5in RL M20	USA
	57mm RCL Gun M18	USA
	90mm RCL Gun, M67	USA
	106mm RCL Gun M40A1	USA
	TOW ATGW	Hughes Aircraft, USA
Anti-aircraft weapons	.50 Browning HB M2	USA
Armoured vehicles	M59, M-113 APC	FMC, USA
	Commando APC	Cadillac Gage, USA

YEMEN: ARAB REPUBLIC (North)

Sub-machine gun	9mm 38/49 Model 4	Pietro Beretta, Italy
Mortars	3in mortar	UK
	81mm mortar	UK
	120mm mortar	
Anti-armour weapons	75mm M20 RCL	USA
	Vigilant ATGW (UK)	Reported
Armoured vehicles	Walid APC	Egypt
	BTR-40 APC	USSR

YEMEN: PEOPLE'S DEMOCRATIC REPUBLIC (South)

Rifle	7.62mm AK-47	USSR
Mortar	120mm	USSR
Anti-aircraft weapon	SA-7 (Grail) SAM	USSR
Armoured vehicle	BTR-40 APC	USSR

Country/Category	Type	Source etc
YUGOSLAVIA		
Pistols	7.62mm M57	Yugoslav copy of Soviet Tokarev TT-33
	9mm M65	Yugoslav copy of the Tokarev TT-33 but chambered for the 9mm x 19 Parabellum cartridge
Sub-machine guns	7.62mm M49/57	Yugoslav copy of the Soviet PPSh-41. Static troops only
	7.62mm M56	Support troops
Rifles	7.62mm M59/66	Copy of the SKS with permanent grenade launcher
	7.62mm M64	Yugoslav copy of the AK-47, with a longer barrel, and built in grenade launcher sight
	7.62mm M70	Yugoslav copy of the AK-47, with added grenade launcher sight. Formerly called M64A
	7.62mm M70A	Yugoslav copy of the AK-47 with folding stock. Has grenade launcher sight. Formerly called M64B
Machine guns	7.92mm M53	Yugoslav manufactured copy of the German MG42
	7.62mm M65A	Fixed heavy barrel version of the M70 rifle
	7.62mm M65B	As M65A but with a quick change barrel
Grenade, rifle	M60	Fragmentation, HEAT, Smoke & Illuminating
Mortars	50mm M8	Copy of British 2in mortar
	60mm M57	Copy of US M2 mortar
	81mm M31	Yugoslav design
	81mm M68	Yugoslav design
	120mm UBM 52	Yugoslav design
Anti-armour weapons	44mm M57 A Tk Launcher	
	75mm M20 RCL Gun	USA
	82mm M60 RCL Gun	
	105 M65	
	Sagger ATGW	USSR
	Snapper ATGW	USSR
Anti-aircraft weapons	12.7mm Degtyarev 38/46 HMG	Russian. Obtained at end of WWII
	20mm AA cannon M1955	Triple mounting. Made in Yugoslavia
	SA-7 SAM	USSR
Armoured vehicles	M60 APC	Made in Yugoslavia
	BTR-152 APC	USSR
	Half-tracks	USA
	M980 MICV	Made in Yugoslavia
ZAIRE		
Rifle	SAFN 49	FN, Belgium
Mortar	4.2in M2A1	USA
Anti-armour weapons	57mm M18/M18A, RCL	USA
	75mm M20 RCL	USA
ZAMBIA		
Rifle	7.62mm G3	Heckler & Koch design probably Middle Eastern manufacture

INDEX

INDEX

Printed in Great Britain by Redwood Burn Limited Trowbridge & Esher

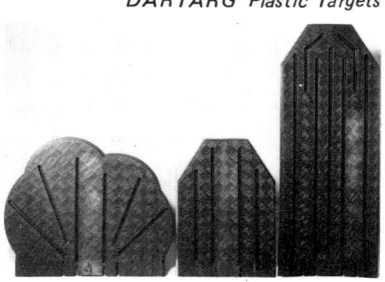